D0234722

The **Rough Gui**

France

written and researched by

David Abram, Andrew Benson, Ruth Blackmore, Brian Catlos, Jan Dodd, Marc Dubin, S. E. Kramer, James McConnachie, Roger Norum, Neville Walker and Greg Ward

NEW YORK • LONDON • DELHI

www.roughguides.com

Contents

Front section 1–24

Basics 25–96

Guide 97–1274

Contexts 1275–1346

Language 1347–1364

Advertiser 1365–1380

Small print & Index 1381–1400

▲ Azay-le-Rideau, Provence

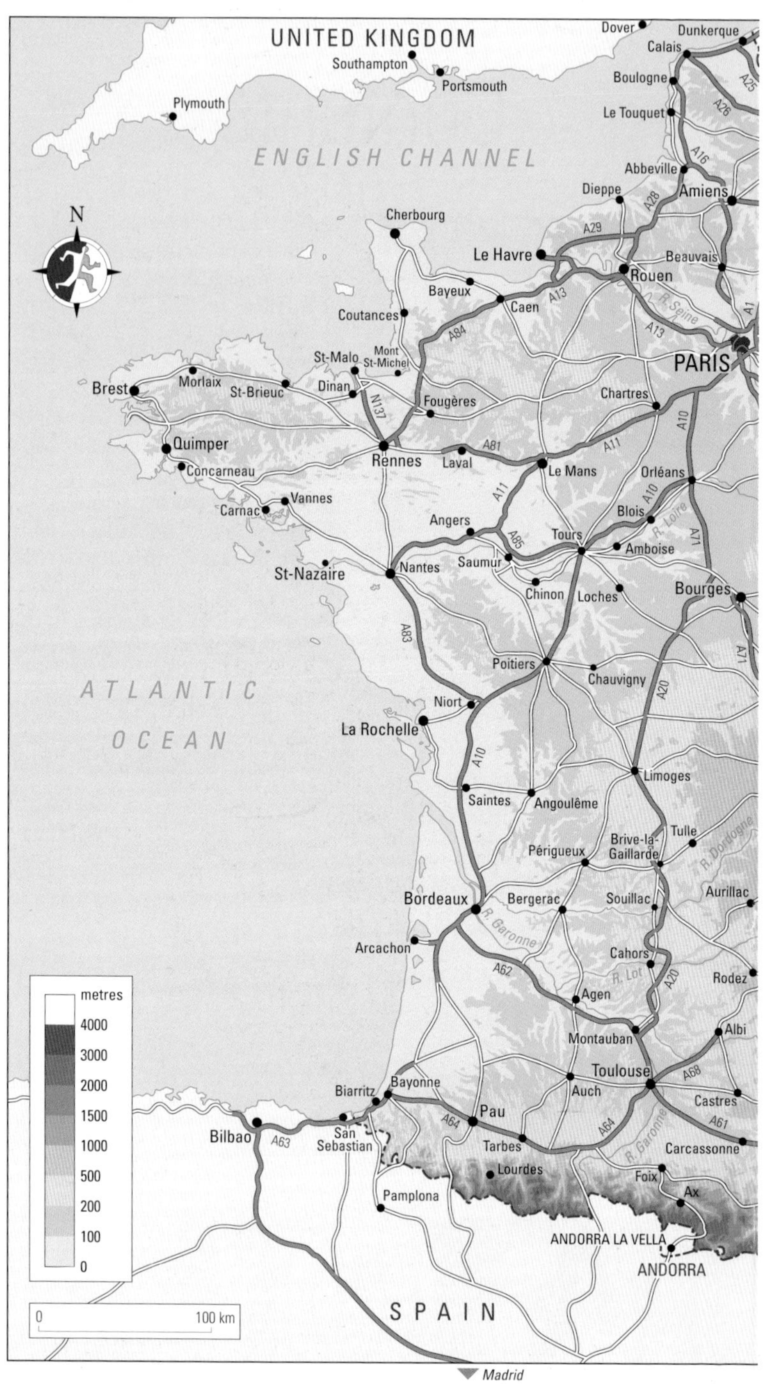
UNITED KINGDOM
Dover
Dunkerque
Calais
Southampton
Portsmouth
Plymouth
Boulogne
Le Touquet
ENGLISH CHANNEL
Abbeville
Dieppe
Amiens
N
Cherbourg
Le Havre
Beauvais
Rouen
Bayeux
Caen
R. Seine
Coutances
PARIS
St-Malo
Mont St-Michel
Brest
Morlaix
St-Brieuc
Dinan
Fougères
Chartres
Quimper
Rennes
Laval
Le Mans
Concarneau
Orléans
Vannes
Carnac
Blois
Angers
Tours
R. Loire
Amboise
Saumur
St-Nazaire
Nantes
Chinon
Loches
Bourges
Poitiers
Chauvigny
ATLANTIC
OCEAN
Niort
La Rochelle
Limoges
Saintes
Angoulême
Tulle
Brive-la-Gaillarde
Périgueux
R. Dordogne
Bordeaux
Bergerac
Souillac
Aurillac
R. Garonne
Arcachon
Cahors
R. Lot
Rodez
Agen
metres
4000
3000
2000
1500
1000
500
200
100
0
Albi
Montauban
Toulouse
Bayonne
Biarritz
Auch
Castres
Pau
Bilbao
San Sebastian
Tarbes
Carcassonne
Lourdes
Foix
Ax
Pamplona
ANDORRA LA VELLA
ANDORRA
0
100 km
SPAIN
Madrid
A1
A10
A11
A13
A16
A20
A25
A26
A28
A29
A61
A62
A63
A64
A68
A71
A81
A83
A84
A85
N137

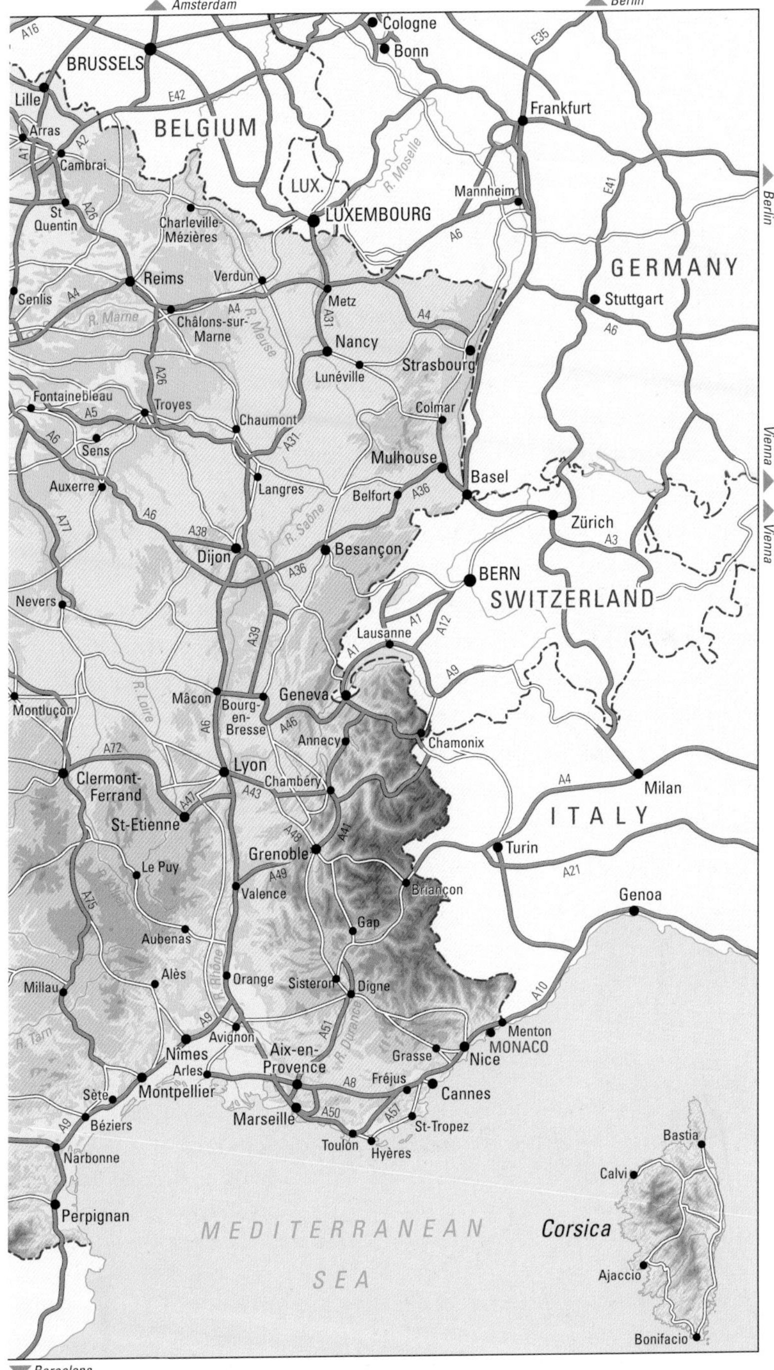
Amsterdam
Berlin
Cologne
Bonn
BRUSSELS
Lille
Arras
Cambrai
BELGIUM
LUX.
LUXEMBOURG
Frankfurt
Mannheim
R. Moselle
St Quentin
Charleville-Mézières
GERMANY
Stuttgart
Reims
Verdun
Metz
Senlis
R. Marne
Châlons-sur-Marne
R. Meuse
Nancy
Strasbourg
Lunéville
Fontainebleau
Troyes
Chaumont
Colmar
Sens
Mulhouse
Basel
Auxerre
Langres
Belfort
Zürich
R. Saône
Dijon
Besançon
BERN
SWITZERLAND
Nevers
Lausanne
Montluçon
R. Loire
Mâcon
Bourg-en-Bresse
Geneva
Annecy
Chamonix
Clermont-Ferrand
Lyon
Chambéry
Milan
St-Etienne
ITALY
Grenoble
Turin
Le Puy
Valence
Briançon
Genoa
Gap
Aubenas
R. Rhône
Alès
Orange
Sisteron
Digne
Millau
R. Tarn
Avignon
R. Durance
Menton
MONACO
Nîmes
Aix-en-Provence
Grasse
Nice
Arles
Fréjus
Cannes
Sète
Montpellier
Marseille
St-Tropez
Béziers
Toulon
Hyères
Bastia
Narbonne
Calvi
Perpignan
MEDITERRANEAN SEA
Corsica
Ajaccio
Bonifacio
Vienna
Barcelona
A16
E42
A2
A1
A26
E35
E41
A6
A4
A31
A5
A36
A38
A77
A39
A12
A9
A3
A46
A72
A47
A43
A48
A41
A49
A21
A75
A10
A51
A8
A50
A57

Introduction to

France

The sheer physical diversity of France would be hard to exhaust in a lifetime of visits. Landscapes range from the fretted coasts of Brittany and the limestone hills of Provence to the canyons of the Pyrenees and the half-moon bays of Corsica, and from the lushly wooded valleys of the Dordogne and the gentle fields of the Loire valley to the glaciated peaks of the Alps. Each region looks and feels different, has its own style of architecture, its own characteristic food and often its own dialect. Though the French word *pays* is the term for a whole country, people frequently refer to their own region as *mon pays* – my country – and this strong sense of regional identity has persisted despite centuries of centralizing governments, from Louis XIV to de Gaulle.

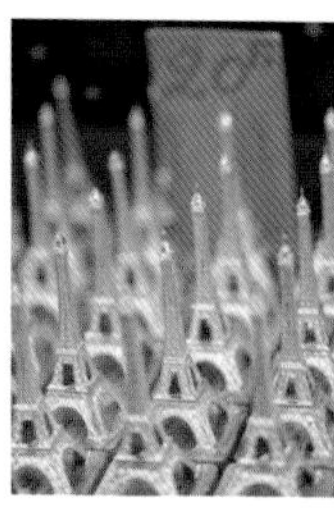

Industrialization came relatively late to France, and for all the millions of French people that live in cities, the idea persists that theirs is a rural country. The importance of the land reverberates throughout French culture, manifesting itself in areas as diverse as regional pride in local cuisine and the state's fierce defence of Europe's agricultural subsidies. Perhaps the most striking feature of the French **countryside** is the sense of space. There are huge tracts of woodland and undeveloped land without a house in sight, and, away from the main urban centres, hundreds of towns and villages have changed only slowly and organically over the years, their old houses and streets intact, as much a part of the natural landscape as the rivers, hills and fields.

Despite this image of pastoral tranquillity, France's history is notable for its extraordinary vigour. For more than a thousand years the country has

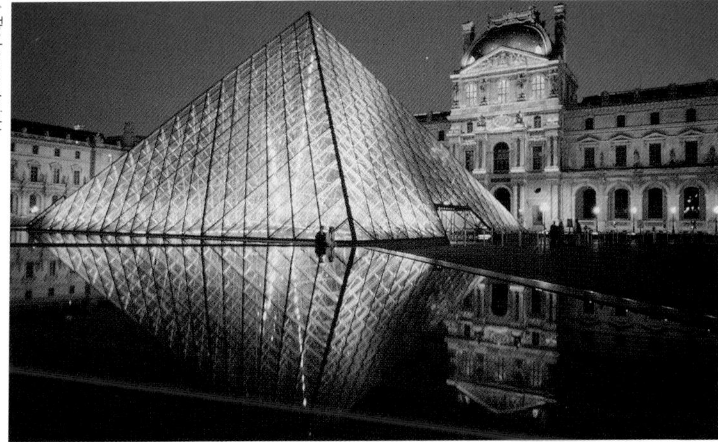

▲ The Louvre at night

been in the vanguard of European development, and the accumulation of wealth and experience is evident everywhere in the astonishing variety of **things to see**, from the Dordogne's prehistoric cave-paintings and the Roman monuments of the south, to the Gothic cathedrals of the north, the châteaux of the Loire, and the cutting-edge architecture of the *grands projets* in Paris. This legacy of history and culture – **la patrimoine** – is so widely dispersed across the land that even the briefest of stays will leave the visitor with a powerful sense of France's past.

The importance of these traditions is felt deeply by the French state, which fights to preserve and develop its national **culture** perhaps harder than any other country in the world, and private companies, who also strive to maintain French traditions in arenas as diverse as *haute couture*, pottery and, of course, food. The fruits of these efforts are evident in the subsidized **arts**, notably the film industry, and in the lavishly endowed and innovative **museums and galleries**. From colonial history to fishing techniques, aeroplane design to textiles, and migrant shepherds to manicure, these collections can be found across the nation, but, inevitably, first place must go to the fabulous displays of fine art in Paris, a city which has nurtured more than its share of the finest creative artists of the last century and a half, both French – Monet and Matisse for example – and foreign, such as Picasso and Van Gogh.

There are all kinds of pegs on which to hang a holiday in France: a city, a region, a river, a mountain range, gastronomy, cathedrals, châteaux. All that open space means there's endless scope for outdoor activities – from walking, canoeing and

Even the briefest of stays will leave the visitor with a powerful sense of France's past

Fact file

- With a land area of 547,000 square kilometres, France is the **second largest country** in Europe; its population of around 60 million is less only than its European neighbours, Germany and the UK.
- Now in its Fifth Republic, France has a long **secular republican tradition** dating back to the Revolution of 1789. Yet around 85 percent of the population is officially Roman Catholic, and there's a substantial Muslim minority of around 5–10 percent.
- **The Government** consists of a directly elected president – Jacques Chirac, since 1995 – and a two-house parliament. As a nuclear power and G8-member, and with a permanent seat on the **United Nations Security Council**, France retains a strong international profile.
- **Annual GDP** per capita is around $25,000, making France one of the world's richer countries, but unemployment is a persistent problem, at around nine percent. Taxes are high, at around 45 percent of GDP, but so is social spending, at almost 30 percent.
- France remains by far the **most popular tourist destination** in the world, with almost 80 million visitors each year.

cycling to skiing and sailing – but if you need more urban stimuli – clubs, shops, fashion, movies, music – then the great cities provide them in abundance.

Where to go

Travelling around France is easy. Restaurants and hotels proliferate, many of them relatively inexpensive when compared with other developed Western European countries. Train services are admirably efficient, as is the road network – especially the (toll-paying) autoroutes – and cyclists are much admired and encouraged. **Information** is highly organized and available from tourist offices across the country, as well as from specialist organizations for walkers, cyclists, campers and so on.

As for specific destinations, **Paris**, of course, is the outstanding cultural

▼ Market, Charolle

centre, with its stunning buildings and atmospheric backstreets, its art, trendy nightlife and ethnic diversity, though the great **provincial cities** – Lyon, Bordeaux, Toulouse, Marseille – all now vie with the capital and each other for prestige in the arts, ascendancy in sport and innovation in attracting visitors.

For most people, however, it's the unique characters of the **regions** – and not least their cuisines – that will define a trip. Few holidaymakers stay long in the largely flat, industrial **north**, but there are some fine cathedrals and energetic cities to leaven the mix. The picture is similar in **Alsace-Lorraine** where Germanic influences are strong, notably in the food; to the south, the

▲ 2CV outside farmhouse, Corsica

Food and drink

The power and influence of French culture is evident anywhere that people read, wear clothes, vote or go to the cinema, but nowhere is the country's contribution greater than in culinary affairs. In France, a picnic could be a simple crusty baguette with cheese, washed down by an inexpensive red wine, or a gourmet feast of cold meats and prepared salads, as available from practically any charcuterie; either way it's likely to be as good as you'll find anywhere in the world. The same is true of eating out, whether that means a perfect steak-*frites* at a railway-station brasserie, a lovingly prepared set menu in a provincial restaurant, featuring the homeliest of regional specialities, or the most exquisite refinements of a Parisian chef.

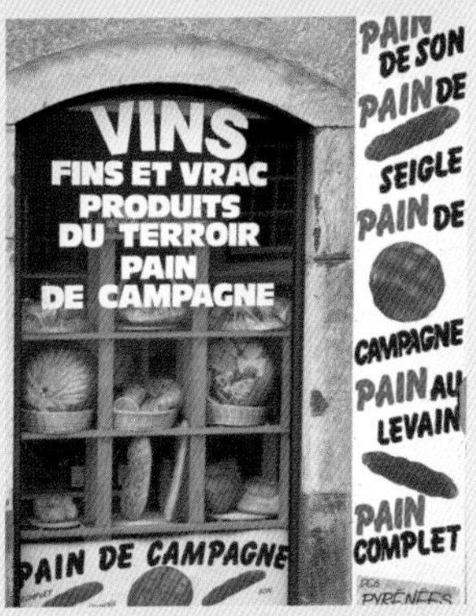

There's an endless variety of cheeses, cakes and pastries to match, as well as wines – and not just those from the renowned vineyards of Bordeaux, Burgundy and Champagne. Whether choosing a good local vintage or pondering some obscure regional speciality, never be afraid to ask advice – most French people are true enthusiasts, ever ready to convert the uninitiated.

wooded mountains of the **Jura** provide scope for outdoor pursuits. On the northern Atlantic coast, **Normandy** has a rich heritage of cathedrals, castles, battlefields and beaches – and, with its cream-based sauces, an equally rich cuisine. To the west, **Brittany** is more renowned for its Celtic links, beautiful coastline, prehistoric sites and seafood, while the **Loire** valley, extending inland towards Paris, is famed for soft, fertile countryside and a marvellous parade of châteaux. Further east, the green valleys of **Burgundy** shelter a wealth of Romanesque churches, and the wines and food are among the finest in France. More Romanesque churches follow the pilgrim routes through rural **Poitou-Charentes** and down the Atlantic coast to **Bordeaux**, where the wines rival those of Burgundy. Inland from Bordeaux, visitors flock to the gorges, prehistoric sites and picturesque fortified villages of the **Dordogne** and neighbouring **Limousin**, drawn too by the truffles and duck and goose dishes of Périgord cuisine. To the south, the great mountain chain of the **Pyrenees** rears up along the Spanish border, running from the Basque country on the Atlantic to the Catalan lands of Roussillon on the Mediterranean; there's fine walking and skiing to be had, as well as beaches at either end. Further along the Mediterranean coast, **Languedoc** offers dramatic

▼ Monet's house and garden, Giverny

▲ Le Corbusier's Chapelle de Notre-Dame-du-Haut, Ronchamp

landscapes, medieval towns and Cathar castles, as well as more beaches, while the **Massif Central**, in the centre of the country, is undeveloped and little visited, but beautiful nonetheless, with its rivers, forests and the wild volcanic uplands of the **Auvergne**. The **Alps**, of course, are prime skiing territory, but a network of signposted paths makes walking a great way to explore too. Stretching down from the mountains to the Mediterranean is **Provence**, which, as generations of travellers have discovered, seems to have everything: Roman ruins, picturesque villages, vineyards and lavender fields – and legions of visitors. Its cuisine is similarly diverse, encompassing fruit, olives, herbs, seafood, lamb and an unusual emphasis on vegetables. Along the Provençal coast, the beaches, towns and chic resorts of the **Côte d'Azur** form a giant smile extending from the vibrantly down-at-heel city of **Marseille** to the super-rich Riviera hotspots of Nice and Monaco. For truly fabulous

▲ Statue, Versailles

The people

According to the clichés, the French are stylish, romantic and passionate. They also have a reputation for rudeness – and yet they are courteous with each other to the point of formality. It's common for someone entering a shop to wish customers and shopkeeper alike a general "good morning", and foreigners on business quickly learn the importance of shaking hands, asking the right questions and maintaining respectful eye contact. At the same time, if they want something, many French people can be direct in ways that are disconcerting for Anglo-Saxons. To foreigners stumbling over the language, never mind the cultural gap, this can seem like rudeness; it isn't. It's fairer to say that the French are proud. Opinions tend to be held and argued strongly – it's not for nothing that so many revolutions have shaken the political landscape. Culture, too, is a source of great pride, and artists, writers and thinkers are held in high esteem even beyond elite circles. And French people everywhere are proud of their locality. Whether it's for a village shop-front, a civic floral display or another landmark building for the French state, no effort is too great.

▼ Camargue

beaches, however, head for the rugged island of **Corsica**, birthplace of Napoleon and home to an Italian-leaning culture and cooking and some fascinating Neolithic sculptures.

When to go

The single most important factor in deciding when to visit France is tourism itself. As most French people take their holidays in their own country, it's as well to avoid the main **French holiday periods** – mid-July to the end of August. It's at this time that almost the entire country closes down, except for the tourist industry itself. You can easily walk a kilometre and more in Paris, for example, in search of an open boulangerie, and the city seems deserted by all except fellow tourists. Prices in the resorts rise to take full advantage and often you can't find a room for love nor money, and not even a space in the campsites on the Côte d'Azur. The seaside is the worst, but the mountains and popular regions like the Dordogne are not far behind. Easter, too, is a bad time for Paris: half of Europe's schoolchildren seem to descend on the city. For the same reasons, ski buffs should keep in mind the February school ski break. And no one who values life, limb, and

▲ Montmartre art stall

sanity should ever be caught on the roads during the last weekend of July or August, and least of all on the weekend of August 15.

The unique characters of the regions – and not least their cuisines – will define a trip

Generally speaking, **climate** needn't be a major consideration in planning when to go. If you're a skier, of course, you wouldn't choose the mountains between May and November; and if you want a beach holiday, you wouldn't head for the seaside out of summer – except for the Mediterranean coast, which is at its most attractive in spring. **Northern France**, like nearby Britain, is wet and unpredictable. **Paris** has a marginally better climate than New York, rarely reaching the extremes of heat and cold of that city, but only **south of the Loire** does the weather become significantly warmer. **West coast** weather, even in the south, is tempered by the proximity of the Atlantic, subject to violent storms and close thundery days even in summer. The **centre** and **east**, as you leave the coasts behind, have a more continental climate, with colder winters and hotter summers. The most reliable weather is along and behind the **Mediterranean** coastline and on **Corsica**, where winter is short and summer long and hot.

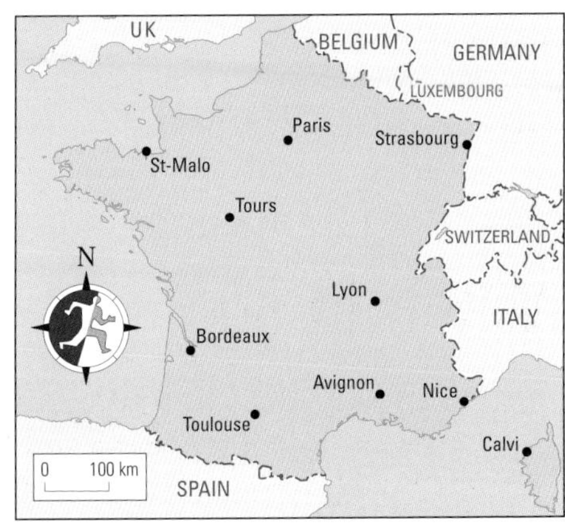

Average daily maximum temperatures

For a recorded weather forecast you can phone the main forecasting line on ⓣ08.92.68.08.08, or check online at ⓦwww.meteo.fr. Temperatures below are given in degrees Celsius.

	Jan	Feb	Mar	Apr	May	June	July	Aug	Sept	Oct	Nov	Dec
Paris	7.5	7	10.2	15.7	16.6	23.4	25	25.6	21	16.5	11.7	7.8
Strasbourg	5.5	5.3	9.3	13.7	15.8	23	24	26.3	21	14.9	7.6	4.7
St-Malo	9	8.6	11	17	16	22.7	25	24	21.2	16.5	12	9.3
Tours	7.8	6.8	10.3	16	16.4	23.6	25.8	24.5	21	16.2	11.2	7
Lyon	7.4	6.7	10.8	15.8	17.3	25.6	27.6	27.6	23.5	16.5	10.4	7.8
Bordeaux	10	9.4	12.2	19.5	18	23.7	27	25.7	24	19.7	15.4	11
Toulouse	12.4	11.5	12.5	17.6	20	26.5	28.4	28	26	21	15.8	13.5
Avignon	12	12	14	18.5	20.8	26.6	28	28.4	25.2	22.2	16.8	14
Nice	12	12	14	18.5	20.8	26.6	28	28.4	25.2	22.2	16.8	14
Calvi	13	14	16	18	21	25	27	28	26	22	117	14

33 things not to miss

It's not possible to see everything that France has to offer in one trip – and we don't suggest you try. What follows is a selective and subjective taste of the country's highlights: great places to stay, outstanding beaches, spectacular hikes and exquisite crafts. They're arranged in five colour-coded categories, so you can browse through to find the very best things to see, do, buy and experience. All highlights have a page reference to take you straight into the guide, where you can find out more.

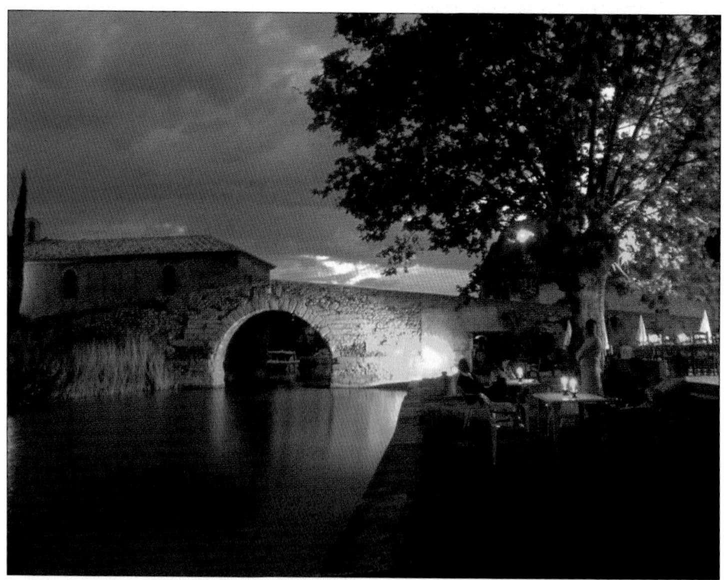

01 Canal du Midi Page **900** • A calm, watery avenue, stretching from beyond Toulouse to the Mediterranean. Cycling, walking or drifting along its tree-shaded course is the most atmospheric way of savouring France's southwest.

02 Carnac Page **505** • Archeologically, Brittany is one of the richest regions in the world and the alignments at Carnac rival Stonehenge.

03 Cheese Page **65** • For serious cheese-lovers, France is paradise. As de Gaulle once commented "You can unite the French only through fear. You cannot simply bring together a country that has over 265 kinds of cheese."

04 Bastille Day Page **75** • July 14 sees national celebrations commemorating the beginning of the French Revolution, with fireworks and parties across the whole country.

05 Tour de France Page **80** • The most famous bike race in the world takes place along a gruelling route which changes annually and is watched by millions across France and the world.

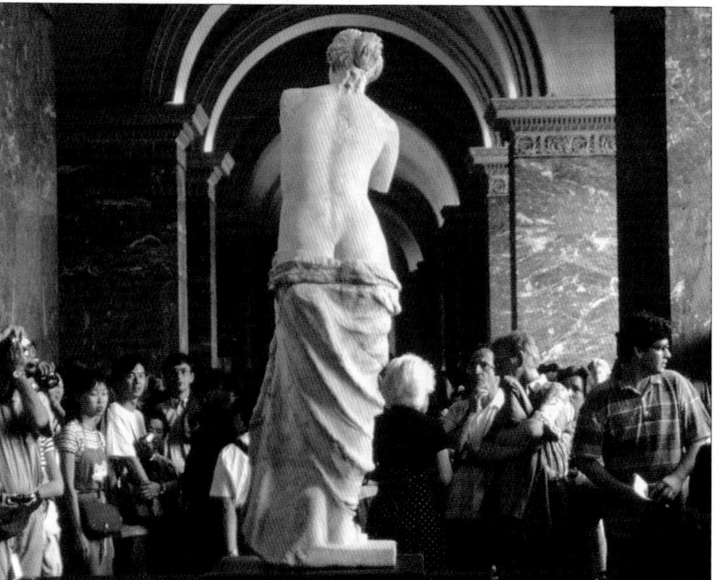

06 The Louvre Page **131** • The palace of the Louvre cuts a grand Classical swathe through the centre of Paris and houses what is nothing less than the gold standard of France's artistic tradition.

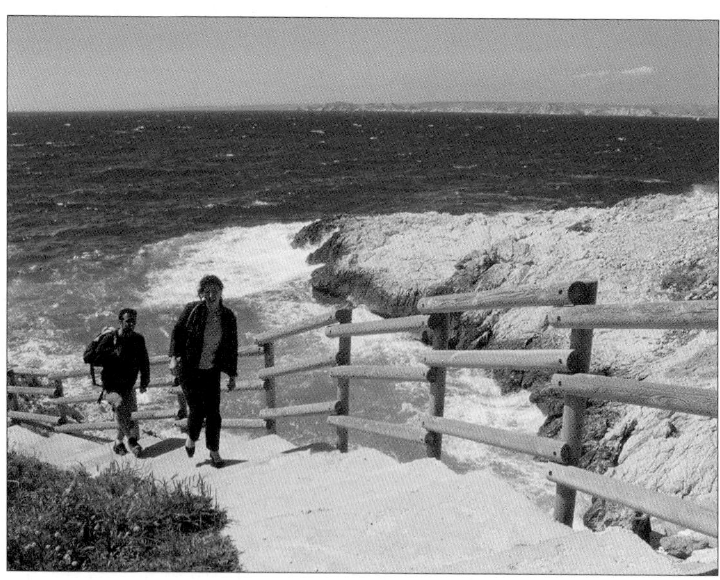

07 Les Calanques Page **1146** • The limestone cliffs on the stretch of coast between Marseille and Cassis make for excellent hikes leading down to picturesque and isolated coves in which to go swimming.

08 Wine Page **67** • French wines are unrivalled in the world for their range, sophistication, diversity and status.

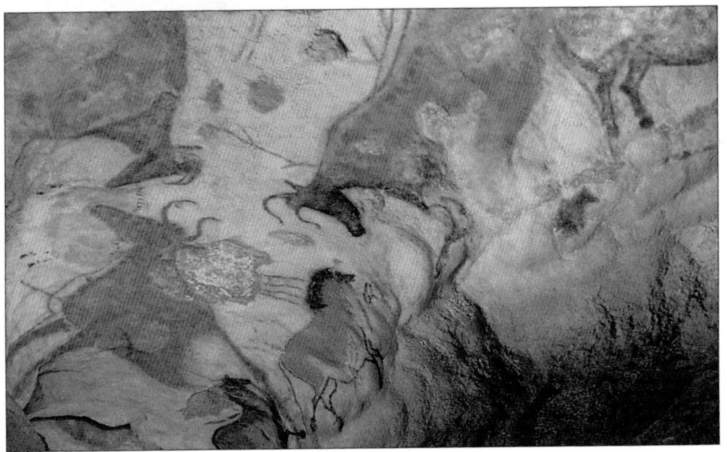

09 Prehistoric cave art Page **735** • Skilful depictions of prehistoric life can be seen in several places around France, though perhaps the most famous are the paintings at Lascaux in the Dordogne.

10 Mont St-Michel Page **424** • Second only to the Eiffel Tower as France's best-loved landmark, the *merveille* of Mont St-Michel is a magnificent spectacle.

11 Les Gorges du Verdon Page **1113** • The most exceptional geographical feature in Provence, the Gorges are Europe's answer to the Grand Canyon, offering stunning views and a range of hikes.

12 Winter sports in the Alps Page **1016** • The French Alps are home to many prestigious ski resorts, offering a wide range of winter sports options.

13 Avignon Page **1070** • Great city of the popes, and once one of France's artistic centres, Avignon can get very crowded, but it's worth braving for its spectacular monuments and museums, countless places to eat and drink, and its annual summer festival.

14 Bayeux Tapestry Page **415** • Stunningly detailed depiction of the events of 1066 which precipitated nearly eight centuries of Anglo-French conflict.

15 The GR20 Page **1236** • Corsica's most demanding long-distance footpath winds some 170km through stunning scenery, though you have to be in good physical shape to complete all sixteen stages.

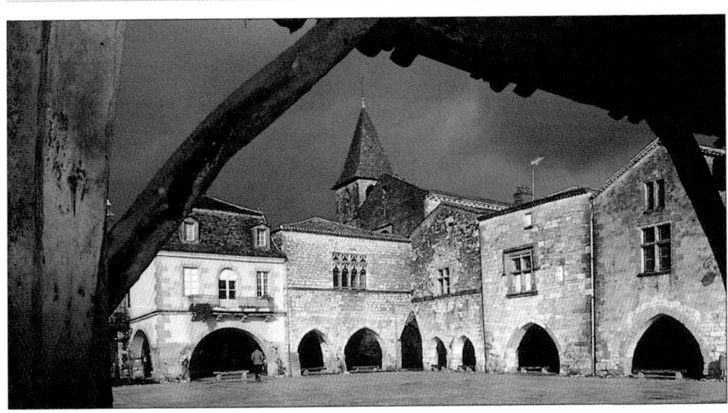

16 Bastide towns Page **726** • Monpazier is one of the fortified towns – *bastides* – built in the Dordogne during the turbulent medieval period when there was almost constant conflict between the French and English.

17 Gorges de l'Ardèche Page **973** • The fantastic gorges begin at the Pont d'Arc and cut their way through the limestone cliffs before emptying into the Rhône valley.

18 Champagne tasting at Épernay Page **295** • Pérignon might be the most famous, but there are plenty of other bubblies to try in the atmospheric cellars of Épernay's maisons.

19 The Issenheim altarpiece Page **350** • The village of Colmar might be excessively twee, but it's still worth a visit for Grünewald's amazing altarpiece, one of the most spectacular works of art in the country.

20 Amiens cathedral Page **258** • The biggest Gothic building in France, this cathedral has an unusual uniformity of style and an evening light show which gives a vivid idea of how the west front would have looked when coloured.

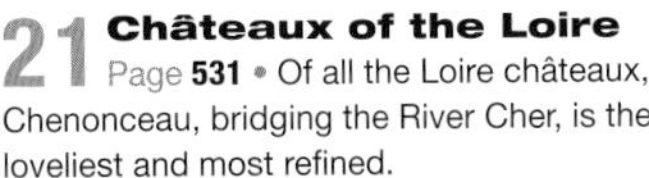

21 Châteaux of the Loire Page **531** • Of all the Loire châteaux, Chenonceau, bridging the River Cher, is the loveliest and most refined.

22 Bordeaux Page **690** • Stylish and lively Bordeaux became the principal English stronghold in France for three hundred years, and is still known for the red wines – claret – which the English popularized.

23 Strasbourg cathedral Page **333** • Visible throughout Strasbourg is the magnificent filigree spire of the pink sandstone cathedral, dominating not just the city but much of Alsace.

24 **Beaches** Pages **85** & **1229** • France's coasts have many beautiful beaches with some of the best being found on Corsica, including the plage de Saleccia, with its soft white shell sand, turquoise water and not a building or road in sight.

25 **Medieval Provençal villages** Page **1100** • Provence's hilltop villages attract visitors by the score. Gordes is one of the most famous, but less-known Saignon and Entrecasteaux are equally beautiful.

26 **Fontenay Abbey** Page **607** • One of the most complete monastic complexes anywhere, this, the only Burgundian monastery to survive intact, has an impressive setting in a beautiful stream-filled valley.

27 Cafés Page **64** • People-watching while taking your time over a coffee and a croissant is a quintessential French experience.

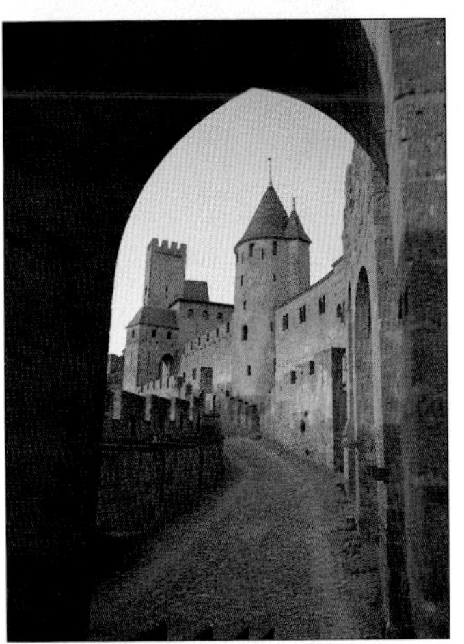

28 Carcassonne Page **898** • So strong is the atmosphere in this medieval fortress town, that it manages to resist even relentless commercialization and summer's throngs of visitors.

29 Le Canigou Page **861** • Catalonia's most sacred mountain is home to the venerated monastery of St-Martin, centre of a dramatic midsummer torchlight procession.

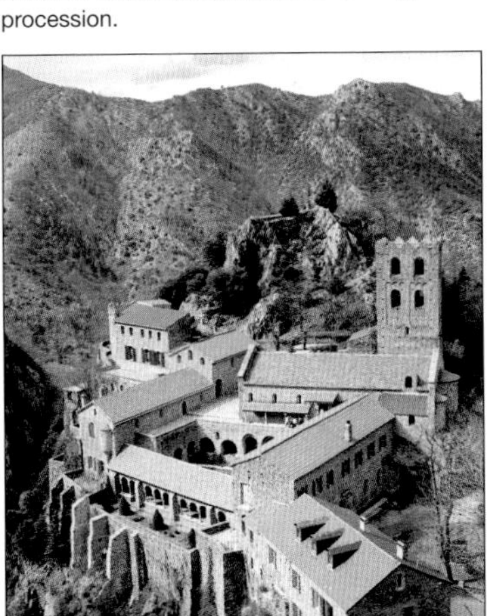

30 War memorials Pages **278** & **411** • World Wars I and II left permanent scars on the French countryside, while the dead are remembered in moving cemeteries.

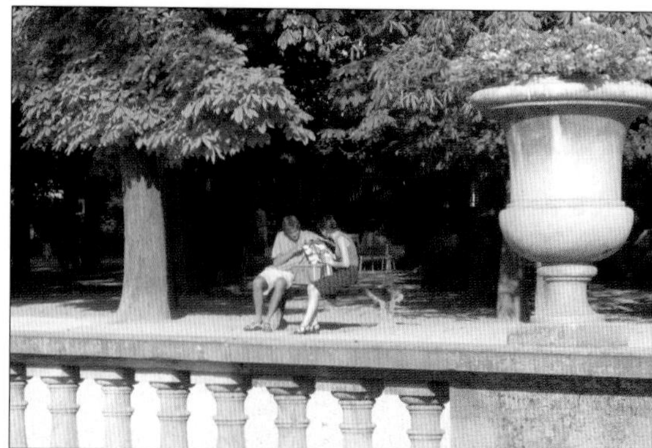

31 Jardin du Luxembourg
Page **158** • Paris's most beautiful park is the ideal spot for relaxing after all that sightseeing.

32 Annecy
Page **1001** • One of the prettiest towns in the Alps, Annecy has a picture-postcard quality which even the tourist crowds can't mar.

33 Outdoor activities
Page **83** • From surfing off Biarritz and skiing in Val d'Isère to hiking in the Pyrenees and canoeing in the Loire, France has energetic pursuits to suit everyone.

Basics

Basics

Getting there

The quickest way of reaching France from most parts of the United Kingdom and Ireland is by air. From southeast England, however, the Channel Tunnel rail link provides a viable alternative, making the journey from London to Paris in just three hours. The Tunnel is the most flexible option if you want to take your car to France, though the cross-Channel ferries are often cheaper. It's also worth bearing in mind that if you live west of London, or are heading to Brittany or to southwest France, the ferry services to Roscoff, St-Malo, Cherbourg, Caen and Le Havre can save a lot of driving time. From the US and Canada a number of airlines fly direct to Paris, from where you can pick up onward connections. You can also fly direct to Paris from Australia or New Zealand, but in general the cheapest airfares are via Asia.

Airfares generally depend on the **season**, with the highest being from around early June to the end of August, when the weather is best; fares drop during the "shoulder" seasons – roughly September to October and April to May – and are at their cheapest during the low season, November to March (excluding Christmas and New Year when prices are hiked up and seats are at a premium) and if you book well in advance. Note also that flying at weekends can be more expensive; price ranges quoted below assume midweek travel.

You can often cut costs by going through a **specialist flight agent** – either a consolidator, who buys up blocks of tickets from the airlines and sells them at a discount, or a **discount agent**, who in addition to dealing with discounted flights may also offer special student and youth fares and a range of other travel-related services such as travel insurance, rail passes, car rentals, tours and the like. Some agents specialize in **charter flights**, which may be cheaper than anything available on a scheduled flight, but departure dates are fixed and withdrawal penalties are high. You may even find it cheaper to pick up a bargain **package deal** from one of the tour operators listed below and then find your own accommodation independently. A further possibility are **courier flights**, although you'll need a flexible schedule, and preferably be travelling alone with very little luggage. In return for shepherding a parcel through customs, you can expect to get a deeply discounted ticket. You'll probably also be restricted in the duration of your stay.

If France is only one stop on a longer journey, you might want to consider buying a **Round-the-World** (RTW) ticket. Some travel agents can sell you an "off-the-shelf" RTW ticket that will have you touching down in about half a dozen cities (Paris is on many itineraries); others will have to assemble one for you, which can be tailored to your needs but is apt to be more expensive. The most comprehensive and flexible deals are offered by the three big airline alliances: Sky Team (Ⓦwww.skyteam.com), oneworld (Ⓦwww.oneworld.com) and Star Alliance (Ⓦwww.staralliance.com). Prices are based either on the overall mileage or, in the case of oneworld, on the number of continents you visit; contact member airlines for further details.

It's also worth noting that a **Eurailpass** (see p.49) may be useful if you're visiting France as part of a longer European trip, since the pass covers train travel from any part of Europe to France, and vice versa.

Booking flights online

Many airlines and discount travel websites offer you the opportunity to book your tickets, hotels and holiday packages **online**, cutting out the costs of agents and middlemen. These are worth investigating, as long as you don't mind the inflexibility of non-refundable, non-changeable deals. There are some bargains to be had on auction sites too, if you're prepared to bid keenly. Almost all airlines have their own websites, offering flight tickets that can be just as cheap *and* may be more flexible.

Online booking agents and general travel sites

Ⓦ **www.cheapflights.co.uk** (in UK & Ireland), Ⓦ **www.cheapflights.com** (in US), Ⓦ **www.cheapflights.ca** (in Canada), Ⓦ **www.cheapflights.com.au** (in Australia). Flight deals, travel agents, plus links to other travel sites.
Ⓦ **www.cheaptickets.com** Discount flight specialists (US only). Also at Ⓣ1-888/922-8849.
Ⓦ **www.ebookers.com** Efficient, easy to use flight finder, with competitive fares.
Ⓦ **www.etn.nl/discount** A portal for consolidator and discount agent Web links, maintained by the non-profit European Travel Network.
Ⓦ **www.expedia.co.uk** (in UK), Ⓦ **www.expedia.com** (in US), Ⓦ **www.expedia.ca** (in Canada). Discount airfares, all-airline search engine and daily deals.
Ⓦ **www.flyaow.com** "Airlines of the Web" – online air-travel info and reservations.
Ⓦ **www.gaytravel.com** US gay travel agent, offering accommodation, cruises, tours and more. Also at Ⓣ1-800/GAY-TRAVEL.
Ⓦ **www.geocities.com/thavery2000** An extensive list of airline websites and US toll-free numbers.
Ⓦ **www.hotwire.com** Bookings from the US only. Last-minute savings of up to forty percent on regular published fares. Travellers must be at least 18 and there are no refunds, transfers or changes allowed. Log-in required.
Ⓦ **www.lastminute.com** (in UK), Ⓦ **www.lastminute.com.au** (in Australia), Ⓦ **www.lastminute.co.nz** (in New Zealand), Ⓦ **www.site59.com** (in US). Good last-minute holiday package and flight-only deals.
Ⓦ **www.opodo.co.uk** Popular and reliable source of low UK airfares. Owned by, and run in conjunction with, nine major European airlines.
Ⓦ **www.orbitz.com** Comprehensive web travel source, with the usual flight, car hire and hotel deals but also great follow-up customer service.
Ⓦ **www.priceline.co.uk** (in UK), Ⓦ **www.priceline.com** (in US) Name-your-own-price website that has deals at around forty percent off standard fares.
Ⓦ **www.skyauction.com** Bookings from the US only. Auctions tickets and travel packages to destinations worldwide.
Ⓦ **www.travelocity.co.uk** (in UK), Ⓦ **www.travelocity.com** (in US), Ⓦ **www.travelocity.ca** (in Canada), Ⓦ **www.zuji.com.au** (in Australia). Destination guides, hot fares and great deals for car rental, accommodation and lodging.
Ⓦ **www.travelshop.com.au** Australian site offering discounted flights, packages, insurance, and online bookings. Also on Ⓣ1800/108 108.
Ⓦ **travel.yahoo.com** Incorporates some Rough Guides material in its coverage of destination countries and cities across the world, with information about places to eat and sleep.
Ⓦ **www.travelzoo.com** Great resource for news on the latest airline sales, cruise discounts and hotel deals. Links bring you directly to the carrier's site.

From the UK and Ireland

The choices available to people travelling from the UK and Ireland to France are vast, ranging from coaches and cut-price airlines to tailor-made tour packages. How you decide to go will depend on your budget, time and whether you want to take your own transport.

By plane

With the rapid increase in the number of no-frills services between the UK, Ireland and France, **flying** is becoming an ever cheaper and more attractive option, particularly if you're leaving from or heading to one of the regional airports. To find the best deals you should shop around, ideally at least a month before you plan to leave.

Travelling with pets from the UK

If you wish to take your dog (or cat) to France, the **Pet Travel Scheme (PETS)** enables you to avoid putting it in quarantine when re-entering the UK as long as certain conditions are met. Current regulations are available on the Department for Environment, Food and Rural Affairs (DEFRA) website Ⓦwww.defra.gov.uk/animalh/quarantine/index.htm or through the PETS Helpline (Ⓣ0870/241 1710).

The cheapest fares are most likely to be with one of the **low-cost airlines**, the largest of which are bmibaby, easyJet, flyBE and Ryanair. New routes are opening all the time (and some closing), but in general bmibaby flies from Cardiff, Manchester, Nottingham East Midlands and Teeside airports to Paris Charles-de-Gaulle (Paris CDG), Bordeaux, Toulouse and Nice; easyJet from Belfast, Bristol, Gatwick, Liverpool, Luton, Newcastle and Stansted to Paris CDG, Lyon, Nice, Marseille and Toulouse; flyBE from Birmingham, Bristol and Southampton to Bergerac, Bordeaux, La Rochelle, Perpignan and Toulouse; and Ryanair from Stansted, Glasgow Prestwick, Dublin and Shannon to fifteen destinations including Paris Beauvais, Disneyland, Bergerac, Carcassonne, Dinard, Montpellier and Nîmes. Fares also fluctuate, but at the time of writing, easyJet is offering a one-way ticket from Luton to Paris for as little as £7, while Ryanair has one-way fares at £21 from Stansted to Perpignan; airport taxes and other surcharges are extra. Tickets work on a quota system, so you'll need to book well ahead and travel off-peak to snap up such bargains. While they can be purchased by phone, tickets are slightly cheaper online.

It's always worth checking out the **traditional carriers**, such Air France, British Airways, bmi and Aer Lingus. The cheapest tickets usually require you to stay over a Saturday night and don't allow any amendments. Again, the further ahead you book the better, but low-season return fares to Paris start at around £70 from London, £110 from Edinburgh and €200 from Dublin; to Nice you'll pay upwards of £110, £160 and €300 respectively.

Air France, or one of its partners, offers the widest regional coverage. It flies to Paris CDG several times daily from Heathrow and regional airports such as Birmingham, Dublin, Manchester, Southampton and Glasgow. It also operates flights from Heathrow and other UK airports direct to French regional airports such as Bordeaux, Lyon, Nantes, Nice and Strasbourg. Flights to Corsica – into Ajaccio, Bastia or Calvi – involve a change in Paris. **British Airways** has several flights a day to Paris CDG from Gatwick and Heathrow and at least one daily from Birmingham, Manchester, Aberdeen, Edinburgh and Glasgow. BA also operates flights from London to Bordeaux, Lyon, Marseille, Montpellier, Nantes, Nice, Toulon and Toulouse. In Northern Ireland, British Airways flies directly from Belfast City Airport to Paris CDG on weekdays. **Bmi** flies to Paris CDG at least three times daily from Heathrow, and at least once daily from Leeds-Bradford; also twice daily to Nice from Heathrow and daily to Toulouse from Manchester. In Ireland, **Aer Lingus** offers direct flights from Dublin and Cork to Paris CDG, and from Dublin to Lyon, Nice and Toulouse.

A good place to look for **discount fares** is the travel sections of papers such as the *Independent* and the *Daily Telegraph* (Saturday editions), the *Observer*, *Sunday Times* and *Independent on Sunday*, where agents advertise special deals. In London, check the back pages of the listings magazine *Time Out*, the *Evening Standard* or the free travel mag *TNT*, found outside main-line train stations. Independent travel specialists such as STA Travel do deals for students and anyone under 26, or can simply sell a scheduled ticket at a discount price.

Airlines

Aer Lingus UK ⓣ0845/084 4444, Republic of Ireland ⓣ0818/365 000, ⓦwww.aerlingus.com.
Air France UK ⓣ0845/359 1000, Republic of Ireland ⓣ01/605 0383, ⓦwww.airfrance.com.
bmi (formerly British Midland) UK ⓣ0870/607 0555, ⓦwww.flybmi.com.
bmibaby UK ⓣ0870/264 2229, Republic of Ireland ⓣ01/435 0011, ⓦwww.bmibaby.com.
Brit Air ⓦwww.britair.com. Reservations through Air France.
British Airways UK ⓣ0870/850 9850, Republic of Ireland ⓣ1800/626 747, ⓦwww.ba.com.
easyJet UK ⓣ0871/750 0100, ⓦwww.easyjet.com.
flyBE (formerly British European) UK ⓣ0870/889 0908, Republic of Ireland ⓣ1890/925 532, ⓦwww.flybe.com.
Jet2 UK ⓣ0870/737 8282, ⓦwww.jet2.com.
Régional UK ⓣ0845/359 1000, Republic of Ireland ⓣ01/605 0383, ⓦwww.regional.com.
Ryanair UK ⓣ0871/246 0000, Republic of Ireland ⓣ0818/303 030, ⓦwww.ryanair.com.
Thomsonfly.com UK ⓣ0870/1900 737, ⓦwww.thomsonfly.com.

Travel agents

Aran Travel First Choice Republic of Ireland ⓣ091/562 595, ⓦwww.firstchoicetravel.ie. Good-value flights worldwide.

Bridge the World UK ⓣ0870/443 2399, ⓦwww.bridgetheworld.com. Specialists in long-haul travel, with good-value flight deals, Round-the-World tickets and tailor-made packages, all aimed at the backpacker market.

Co-op Travel Care UK ⓣ0870/112 0085, ⓦwww.travelcareonline.com. Flights and holidays around the world from the UK's largest independent travel agent. Non-partisan and informed advice.

ebookers UK ⓣ0870/010 7000, ⓦwww.ebookers.com, Republic of Ireland ⓣ01/241 5689, ⓦwww.ebookers.ie. Low fares on an extensive selection of scheduled flights and package deals.

Flights4Less UK ⓣ0871/222 3423, ⓦwww.flights4less.co.uk. Good discount airfares. Part of ⓦLastminute.com.

Go Holidays Republic of Ireland ⓣ01/874 4126, ⓦwww.goholidays.ie. City breaks and package tours.

Joe Walsh Tours Republic of Ireland ⓣ01/676 0991, ⓦwww.joewalshtours.ie. Long-established general budget fares and holidays agent. Also pilgrimages to Lourdes.

Lee Travel Republic of Ireland ⓣ021/427 7111, ⓦwww.leetravel.ie. Flights and holidays worldwide.

McCarthy's Travel Republic of Ireland ⓣ021/427 0127, ⓦwww.mccarthystravel.ie. Established Irish travel agent now part of the Worldchoice chain of travel shops. Featuring flights, short breaks, pilgrimages and group holidays.

Neenan Travel Republic of Ireland ⓣ01/607 9900, ⓦwww.neenantrav.ie. Specialists in European city breaks.

North South Travel UK ⓣ01245/608 291, ⓦwww.northsouthtravel.co.uk. Friendly, competitive travel agency, offering discounted fares worldwide. Profits are used to support projects in the developing world, especially the promotion of sustainable tourism.

Rosetta Travel UK ⓣ028/9064 4996, ⓦwww.rosettatravel.com. Flight and holiday agent, specializing in deals direct from Belfast.

STA Travel UK ⓣ0870/1600 599, ⓦwww.statravel.co.uk. Worldwide specialists in low-cost flights, overland and holiday deals. Good discounts for students and under-26s.

Top Deck UK ⓣ020/7244 8000, ⓦwww.topdecktravel.co.uk. Long-established agent dealing in discount flights and tours.

Trailfinders UK ⓣ020/7938 3939, ⓦwww.trailfinders.com, Republic of Ireland ⓣ01/677 7888, ⓦwww.trailfinders.ie. One of the best-informed and most efficient agents for independent travellers.

Travel Bag UK ⓣ0870/890 1456, ⓦwww.travelbag.co.uk. Discount deals worldwide.

Travel Care UK ⓣ0870/112 0085, ⓦwww.travelcare.co.uk. Flights, holiday deals and city breaks.

USIT Northern Ireland ⓣ028/9032 7111, ⓦwww.usitnow.com, Republic of Ireland ⓣ0818/200 020, ⓦwww.usit.ie. Specialists in student, youth and independent travel – flights, trains, study tours, TEFL, visas and more.

World Travel Centre Republic of Ireland ⓣ01/416 7007, ⓦwww.worldtravel.ie. Excellent fares to Europe and worldwide.

By train

Eurostar operates high-speed passenger trains daily from Waterloo International to the continent via the **Channel Tunnel**; most but not all services stop at Ashford in Kent (40min from London). Services depart roughly every hour (from around 6am to 7.30pm) for Paris Gare du Nord (2hr 40min), a few of which stop at Calais (1hr 20min) and Lille (1hr 40min), where you can connect with TGV trains heading south to Bordeaux, Lyon and Nice. In addition, Eurostar runs direct trains from London to Disneyland Paris (daily; 2hr 40min), to Avignon (mid-July to mid-Sept daily Mon–Sat; mid-Sept to mid-July daily Mon–Fri; 6hr), and a special twice-weekly ski service to Moutiers, Aime-la-Plagne and Bourg-St-Maurice in the French Alps (Dec–March; around 8hr); skis are carried free.

Standard "Leisure" **fares** from London to Paris start at £59 (£55 to Lille and £109 to Avignon) for a non-refundable, non-exchangeable return purchased up to fourteen days before departure and including a Saturday night away. The next option is the changeable "Leisure Flexi" ticket (from £119/£115/£169 respectively), which again must include a Saturday night. All these deals have limited availability, so it pays to plan ahead; tickets go on sale three months before the date of travel. Otherwise, you're looking at £298/£250/£330 for a fully refundable "Business" ticket with no restrictions. Return "Leisure" fares to Disneyland Paris start at £99 for adults (£50 for children aged 4–11) and those on the Eurostar ski train at £99 (£84 for children).

There is plentiful **parking** at Ashford station, just off the M20, at £9 per day; at Waterloo, Eurostar passengers pay £18 for 24 hours' parking. You can get **through-ticketing** from stations around Britain – including the tube journey across London to Waterloo – from Eurostar, many travel agents and mainline stations. Inter-Rail, Eurail and Eurodomino **rail passes** (see p.49 for more) give discounts on Eurostar trains. For information about **taking your bike** on Eurostar, see p.58.

Rail contacts

Eurostar UK ⓣ0870/160 6600, ⓦwww.eurostar.com.
Iarnród Éireann Republic of Ireland ⓣ01/703 1885, ⓦwww.irishrail.ie.
International Rail UK ⓣ0870/751 5000, ⓦwww.international-rail.com.
Northern Ireland Railways ⓣ028/9089 9411, ⓦwww.nirailways.co.uk. Also sells Inter-Rail passes.
Rail Europe ⓣ0870/584 8848, ⓦwww.raileurope.co.uk.
Trainseurope ⓣ0900/195 0101 (60p/min, refundable against a booking), ⓦwww.trainseurope.co.uk.

By ferry

Though slower than travelling by plane or via the Channel Tunnel, the ferries and catamaran plying between Dover and Calais offer the most frequent services to France **from the UK** and are particularly convenient if you live in southeast England. Even if your starting point is west of London, it may still be worth heading to one of the south-coast ports and catching a ferry to Brittany or Normandy, though given stiff competition from the Channel Tunnel some routes have been cut. If you're coming from the north of England or Scotland, you could consider the overnight crossings from Hull and Rosyth to Zeebrugge (Belgium) operated by P&O Ferries and Superfast Ferries respectively. Heading to southwest France, there's also the option of taking a ferry to Santander (with Brittany Ferries) or Bilbao (P&O Ferries) in northern Spain. From **Ireland**, putting the car on the ferry from Cork or Rosslare (near Wexford) to Cherbourg or to Roscoff in Brittany cuts out the drive across Britain to the Channel.

Ferry **prices** are seasonal and, for motorists, depend on the size of your vehicle, but they have been coming down recently in the face of fierce competition from the low-cost airlines and the new breed of high-speed ferries. Return fares are now available for as little as £50 (if you book online) for a car and five passengers with SpeedFerries on the Dover–Boulogne route, while companies offering the Dover-Calais route charge in the region of £100 return; fares from Ireland (Cork to Roscoff) start at around €450. You can either contact the ferry companies direct to reserve space for your car – essential in peak season – or get a travel agent to do it for you. Most ferry companies also offer fares for foot passengers, from £30 one way; accompanying bicycles can usually be carried free in low season, though there may be a small charge during peak periods.

In general the further you book ahead, the cheaper the fare and it's well worth playing around with dates and times to find the best deals: midweek, midday sailings are usually cheapest. An easy way to compare prices is via Ferry Savers (ⓣ0870/990 8492, ⓦwww.ferrysavers.com) and EuroDrive (ⓣ0870/442 9807, ⓦwww.eurodrive.co.uk), both of which offer cut-price fares; the latter only caters to people taking their cars across the Channel.

Ferry contacts

Brittany Ferries UK ⓣ08703/665 333, ⓦwww.brittanyferries.co.uk, Republic of Ireland ⓣ021/4277 801, ⓦwww.brittanyferries.ie. Poole to Cherbourg; Portsmouth to Caen, Cherbourg and St Malo; Plymouth to Roscoff, Cherbourg, St Malo and Santander (March–Nov/Dec); Cork to Roscoff (March–Oct only).
Condor Ferries UK ⓣ0845/345 2000, ⓦwww.condorferries.co.uk. Portsmouth to Cherbourg (May–Sept); Poole to Cherbourg and St-Malo (both May–Sept) and Weymouth to St-Malo via the Channel Islands.
Hoverspeed UK ⓣ0870/240 8070, ⓦwww.hoverspeed.co.uk. Twenty-four daily departures. Dover to Calais and Newhaven to Dieppe.
Irish Ferries UK ⓣ08705/171 717, Northern Ireland ⓣ00 353 818/ 300 400, Republic of Ireland ⓣ0818/300 400, ⓦwww.irishferries.com. Rosslare to Cherbourg and Roscoff (March–Sept).

Norfolkline UK ⓣ0870/870 1020, ⓦwww.norfolkline.com. Dover to Dunkerque.
P&O Ferries UK ⓣ0870/600 0600 or 01304/864 003, ⓦwww.poferries.com. Dover to Calais and Portsmouth to Bilbao. At the time of writing it seemed likely that P&O would stop operating services from Portsmouth to Cherbourg and Le Havre in 2005
Sea France ⓣ08705/711 711, ⓦwww.seafrance.com. Dover to Calais.
SpeedFerries ⓣ01304/203 000, ⓦwww.speedferries.com. Dover to Boulogne.
Superfast Ferries UK ⓣ0870/234 0870, ⓦwww.superfast.com. Rosyth near Edinburgh to Zeebrugge (Belgium).
Transmanche Ferries ⓣ0800/917 1201, ⓦwww.transmancheferries.com. Newhaven to Dieppe.

Via the Channel Tunnel

The simplest way of taking your car across to France is to load it on one of the drive-on drive-off shuttle trains operated by **Eurotunnel** (ⓣ0870/840 0046, ⓦwww.eurotunnel.com) through the Channel Tunnel. The service runs continuously between Folkestone and Coquelles, near Calais, with up to four departures per hour (only 1 per hour midnight–6am) and takes 35min (45min for some night departures). It is possible to turn up and buy your ticket at the toll booths (exit the M20 at junction 11a), though at busy times booking is advisable; if you have a booking, you must arrive at least 30min before departure. Inside the carriages, you can get out of your car to stretch your legs; there are toilets but no shops or refreshments. Note that Eurotunnel is not allowed to transport cars fitted with LPG or CNG tanks.

The good news is that **fares** have, at long last, begun to drop in order to compete with the cross-channel ferries. In 2004 the company introduced special summer-season fares for as little as £100 return. In general, the amount you pay depends on the time of year, time of day and length of stay, how long in advance you book and how flexible you need your ticket to be. If you book two weeks in advance and travel midweek you could get a 'long-stay' (over five days) round-trip fare for just under £300 per vehicle; a fully flexible and refundable 'standard' fare purchased on the spot can be as much as £323. Bicycles are carried on a specially adapted carriage that makes the crossing twice a day – it costs £61 return for a bike plus rider if you are staying more than five days, £32 if it's just a short break.

If you don't want to drive too far when you've reached France, you can take advantage of SNCF's **motorail** service, which can be booked through Rail Europe's Motorail department (ⓣ0870/241 5415, ⓦwww.raileurope.co.uk), putting your car on the train in Calais for Avignon, Nice, Brive, Narbonne and Toulouse. The service is operational only between May and mid-September and this is an expensive option: Calais–Nice, for example, costs at least £850 return for a car and two adults travelling midweek, rising to over £1000 during peak periods.

By bus

Eurolines, a network of European bus companies, offers services from London Victoria to most major French cities, crossing the Channel by ferry or Eurotunnel depending on the time of day. Prices are lower than for the same journey by train, with standard adult return fares starting at around £50 for Paris, £40 for Lille and £90 each for Lyon, Bordeaux and Toulouse; there are discounts for return journeys booked a month in advance. Regional return fares from the rest of England and from Wales are available, as are student and youth discounts. Eurolines also offers a pass for Europe-wide travel, for fifteen, thirty or sixty days. Prices range from £135 for an adult fifteen-day pass in the low season (£113 for under-26s and over-60s) to £299 for a peak-season sixty-day pass (£229 for under-26s and over-60s). Eurolines also has special Channelink fares combining bus and cross-Channel ferry transport.

Also worth investigating is **Busabout**, a hop-on, hop-off bus network operating throughout Europe in summer (April–Oct). Buses depart every two to three days on cross-continental circuits covering some 50 cities in western and central Europe, with a link from London to Paris and through tickets from elsewhere in Britain and Ireland. From Paris, the French circuit takes you south to Nice and Avignon, along the Spanish side of the Pyrenees, and then back north via Bordeaux and Tours – either on a Day Stop (where the bus continues, but you can get off and stay if you like) or a Night Stop (where the bus terminates, and you must get off), or a Bonus Stop (sites of historical interest or natural beauty, where you can take a quick look around but then get back on the bus to the next destination). There are Unlimited Passes ranging from two weeks to six months, plus a variety of Flexi Passes and add-on connections to destinations in Greece and Morocco. No bikes or surf-boards allowed.

Bus contacts

Busabout UK ⓣ020/7950 1661, ⓦwww.busabout.com.
Eurolines UK ⓣ0870/580 8808, ⓦwww.eurolines.co.uk, Republic of Ireland ⓣ01/836 6111, ⓦwww.eurolines.ie. In the UK, tickets can be purchased direct from Eurolines, from National Express (ⓣ0870/580 8080, ⓦwww.nationalexpress.com) and from Eurolines agents nationwide.

Package tours and specialist operators

Any travel agent will be able to provide details of the many operators running **package tours** to France, which can be exceptional bargains. Some deals are straightforward travel-plus-hotel affairs, while others offer tandem touring, air-and-rail packages and stays in country cottages. If your trip is geared around specific interests – like cycling or self-catering in the countryside – packages can work out much cheaper than the same arrangements made on arrival. Packages can also be a good idea if you're on a tight schedule – particularly for city breaks, as these deals often include free transfers to your hotel and guided tours or theatre tickets as well as flights and accommodation, leaving you more time to enjoy your holiday. In addition to the **specialist tour operators** listed below, bear in mind that most of the ferry companies (see p.31) also offer their own travel and accommodation deals. You'll also find operators listed on the Holiday France website (ⓦwww.holidayfrance.org.uk), run by the Association of British Tour Operators to France, and through the French Holiday Store site (ⓦwww.fr-holidaystore.co.uk).

Tour operators

Alabaster & Clarke UK ⓣ01730/893 344, ⓦwww.winetours.co.uk. Treat yourself to a Champagne weekend, a gourmet tour of Provence or a walk through the vineyards with Britain's biggest wine-tour specialist.
Alan Rogers UK ⓣ0870/405 4055, ⓦwww.alanrogers.com. Independent campsite specialist, with details of inspected sites available online or in their annual guides.
Belle France UK ⓣ01797/223 777, ⓦwww.bellefrance.co.uk. Walking, cycling and boating holidays throughout France.
Bridge Travel UK ⓣ0870/1917 270, ⓦwww.bridgetravel.co.uk. Good for short breaks to Paris as well as go-as-you-please tours and accommodation-only packages.
Canvas Holidays UK ⓣ01383/629 000, ⓦwww.canvas.co.uk. Offers tailor-made caravan and camping holidays.
Club Med UK ⓣ0700/2582 932, ⓦwww.clubmed.co.uk. Child-friendly holidays in purpose-built complexes with excellent facilities. Mostly in the Alps, but also Corsica and elsewhere.
Corsican Places UK ⓣ08701/605 744, ⓦwww.corsica.co.uk. Experienced, knowledgeable Corsica specialists, offering tailor-made stays as well as packages, in period properties, hotels and luxury villas.
Cycling for Softies UK ⓣ0161/2488 282, ⓦwww.cycling-for-softies.co.uk. An easy-going cycle holiday operator to rural France. Although luggage transfer is not included in the deals, this can be arranged for an additional fee.
Eurocamp UK ⓣ08703/667 558, ⓦwww.eurocamp.co.uk. Self-drive, go-as-you-please holidays with tent or mobile home.
Explore UK ⓣ01252/760 000, ⓦwww.explore.co.uk. Small-group activity holidays, including hiking in Provence and the Alps and rambling round Languedoc.
France Afloat UK ⓣ0870/011 0538, ⓦwww.franceafloat.com. French canal and river cruising specialist, covering Brittany, the Canal du Midi and Paris, and the northeast.
French Affair UK ⓣ020/7381 8519, ⓦwww.frenchaffair.com. Offers a wide range of self-catering accommodation in Corsica and southern France. Fly-drive deals also available.
French Country Cruises UK ⓣ01572/821 330, ⓦwww.andrewbrocktravel.co.uk. Comprehensive range of self-drive boating holidays throughout France in association with Locaboat.
French Life UK ⓣ0870/197 6675, ⓦwww.frenchlife.co.uk. Big independent tour operator with a good range of self-catering properties from country

cottages to villas with pools and seaside apartments. Can also arrange camping holidays.

Go Holidays Republic of Ireland ⓣ01/874 4126, ⓦwww.goholidays.ie. French holiday specialists offering city breaks, fly-drive packages and summer-season charter flights from Shannon airport to a number of French cities.

Headwater UK ⓣ01606/720 099, ⓦwww.headwater.com. Upmarket activity holidays (walking, cycling, cross-country skiing and canoeing) off the beaten track throughout rural France.

Inntravel UK ⓣ01653/617 788, ⓦwww.inntravel.co.uk. Full range of activity holidays, including riding, walking and cycling, as well as travel and accommodation-only packages from this well-established specialist tour operator.

Keycamp Holidays UK ⓣ0870/700 0123, ⓦwww.keycamp.com. Caravan and camping holidays, including transport to France.

Martin Randall Travel UK ⓣ020/8742 3355, ⓦwww.martinrandall.com. Small-group cultural tours, often timed specifically to coincide with special events such as music or opera festivals. Expert lecturers on art, archeology, history or music give specialist insight, and accommodation is always comfortable.

Sherpa Expeditions UK ⓣ020/8577 2717, ⓦwww.sherpa-walking-holidays.co.uk. Self-guided inn-to-inn walks and cycle trips, or escorted group treks, such as a 15-day hike across Corsica.

Simply Travel UK ⓣ020/8541 2280, ⓦwww.simply-travel.com. Upmarket tour company offering skiing in the French Alps and hand-picked villas, hotels and seaside apartments in Corsica, with excellent child-care facilities.

Thomas Cook UK ⓣ0870/750 5711, ⓦwww.thomascook.co.uk. Long-established one-stop travel agency for package holidays, city breaks or flights, with bureau de change issuing Thomas Cook branded travellers' cheques, plus travel insurance and car rental.

Travelscene Ltd UK ⓣ0870/7779 987, ⓦwww.travelscene.co.uk. City breaks, tailormade holidays and accommodation packages, travelling by air, Eurostar or self-drive.

VFB Holidays UK ⓣ01242/240 340, ⓦwww.vfbholidays.co.uk. Good-value self-catering, ferry and fly-drive holidays, plus river cruises and city breaks.

Voyages Ilena UK ⓣ020/7924 4440, ⓦwww.voyagesilena.co.uk. Specializing in self-catering villas in Corsica and Provence, this knowledgeable agency can also arrange accommodation in attractive hotels as well as flights, fly-drives and tailor-made holidays.

Wildlife Worldwide UK ⓣ020/8667 9158, ⓦwww.wildlifeworldwide.com. Fly-drive trips to the French Pyrenees for wildlife enthusiasts.

Winetrails UK t01306/712 111, ⓦwww.winetrails.co.uk. Walking, cycling and gourmet holidays in the main French wine regions.

From the US and Canada

Most major airlines operate **scheduled flights** to Paris from the US and Canada. **Air France** has the most frequent service, with good onward regional connections, but their fares tend to be on the expensive side. Other airlines offering non-stop services to Paris from a variety of US cities include **American Airlines** from New York, Chicago, Dallas and Miami; **Continental** from Newark and Houston; **Delta** from Atlanta, Cincinnati and New York; **Northwest** from Detroit; and **United** from Chicago, San Francisco and Washington DC. **Air Canada** offers non-stop services to Paris from Montréal and Toronto. Another option is to take one of the other **European carriers**, such as British Airways, bmi, Iberia or Lufthansa, from the US or Canada to their home base and then continue on to Paris or a regional French airport.

Thanks to such intense competition, transatlantic **fares** to France are very reasonable. A typical return fare for a midweek flight to Paris costs around $800 from Houston, $700 from Los Angeles and $600 from New York. From Canada, prices to Paris are in the region of CAN$1000 from Montréal and Toronto, and CAN$1400 from Vancouver.

Air passes and discounts on further flights within Europe vary from one airline to another, but the basic rule is that they must be booked at the same time as the main ticket. The airline alliances Sky Team, oneworld and Star Alliance all offer European air passes priced according to the distance travelled (see p.27 for contact details). With oneworld's "Visit Europe" pass, for example, you have to buy a minimum of two flights within Europe costing between $70/CAN$93 and $280/CAN$370 depending on the distance, not including taxes and other surcharges.

If you have a specific French destination in mind outside Paris and you're in a hurry – and are prepared to pay extra – it's possible to be ticketed straight through to any of more than a dozen **regional airports**. Most of these entail changing planes in Paris, but check to make sure there's no inconvenient transfer between Charles de Gaulle and Orly.

Hundreds of **tour operators** specialize in travel to France, and many can put together very flexible deals, sometimes amounting to no more than a flight plus car or train pass and accommodation. If you're planning to travel in moderate or luxurious style, and especially if your trip is geared around special interests, such packages can work out cheaper than the same arrangements made on arrival.

Of greater interest are the numerous **package tours**, such as walking or cycling trips, boat trips along canals and any number of theme tours based around history, art, wine and so on. Just a few of the possibilities are listed below, and a travel agent will be able to recommend others.

Airlines

Air Canada ⓣ1-888/247-2262, ⓦwww.aircanada.ca.
Air France US ⓣ1-800/237-2747, Canada ⓣ1-800/667-2747, ⓦwww.airfrance.com.
Air Transat Canada ⓣ1-800/587-2672, ⓦwww.airtransat.com.
American Airlines ⓣ1-800/433-7300, ⓦwww.aa.com.
British Airways ⓣ1-800/AIRWAYS, ⓦwww.ba.com.
Continental Airlines ⓣ1-800/231-0856, ⓦwww.continental.com.
Delta ⓣ1-800/241-4141, ⓦwww.delta.com.
Iberia ⓣ1-800/772-4642, ⓦwww.iberia.com.
Lufthansa US ⓣ1-800/645-3880, Canada ⓣ1-800/563-5954, ⓦwww.lufthansa.com.
Northwest Airlines ⓣ1-800/447-4747, ⓦwww.nwa.com.
United Airlines ⓣ1-800/538-2929, ⓦwww.united.com.
US Airways ⓣ1-800/622-1015, ⓦwww.usair.com.

Courier flights

Air Courier Association ⓣ1-800/282-1202, ⓦwww.aircourier.org. Courier flight broker. Membership (US$35 for a year) also entitles you to twenty percent discount on travel insurance and name-your-own-price non-courier flights.
International Association of Air Travel Couriers ⓣ308/632-3273, ⓦwww.courier.org. Courier flight broker. One year's membership costs US$45 in the US or Canada (US$50 elsewhere).

Travel agents

Air Brokers International US ⓣ1-800/883-3273, ⓦwww.airbrokers.com. Consolidator and specialist in Round-the-World tickets.
Airtech US ⓣ212/219-7000, ⓦwww.airtech.com. Standby seat broker; also deals in consolidator fares.
Airtreks.com US ⓣ1-877/AIRTREKS, ⓦwww.airtreks.com. Round-the-World specialist. The website features an interactive database that lets you build and price your own itinerary.
Educational Travel Center USⓣ1-800/747-5551 or 608/256-5551, ⓦwww.edtrav.com. Low-cost fares, student/youth discount offers, and Eurail passes, car rental and tours.
Flightcentre US ⓣ1-866/WORLD-51, ⓦwww.flightcentre.us, Canada ⓣ1-888/WORLD-55, ⓦwww.flightcentre.ca. Rock-bottom fares worldwide.
STA Travel US ⓣ1-800/329-9537, Canada ⓣ1-888/427-5639, ⓦwww.statravel.com. Worldwide specialists in independent travel; also student IDs, travel insurance, car rental, rail passes, and more.
Student Flights US ⓣ1-800/255-8000 or 480/951-1177, ⓦwww.isecard.com/studentflights. Student/youth fares, plus student IDs and European rail and bus passes.
TFI Tours US ⓣ1-800/745-8000 or 212/736-1140, ⓦwww.lowestairprice.com. Well-established consolidator with a wide variety of global fares.
Travel Avenue US ⓣ1-800/333-3335, ⓦwww.travelavenue.com. Full-service travel agent that offers discounts in the form of rebates.
Travel Cuts US ⓣ1-800/592-CUTS, Canada ⓣ1-888/246-9762, ⓦwww.travelcuts.com. Popular, long-established student-travel organization, with worldwide offers.
Travelers Advantage US ⓣ1-877/259-2691, ⓦwww.travelersadvantage.com. Discount travel club, with cash-back deals and discounted car rental. Membership required ($1 for 3 months' trial).
Travelosophy US ⓣ1-800/332-2687, ⓦwww.itravelosophy.com. Good range of discounted and student fares worldwide.
Worldtek Travel US ⓣ1-800/243-1723, ⓦwww.worldtek.com. Discount travel agency.

Tour operators

Abercrombie & Kent ⓣ1-800/323-7308 or 630/954-2944, ⓦwww.abercrombiekent.com. Classy canal trips, walking tours and tailor-made holidays all over France.

Above the Clouds ⓣ1-800/233-4499 or 802/482-4848, ⓦwww.aboveclouds.com. Mont Blanc climbing expeditions and hiking in the Drôme valley.

Adventure Center ⓣ1-800/228-8747 or 510/654-1879, ⓦwww.adventure-center.com. "Soft adventure" specialists offering hiking and cycling tours in mainland France and Corsica.

Adventures Abroad ⓣ1-800/665-3998, ⓦwww.adventures-abroad.com. Adventure specialists, including a 14-day Mont Blanc circuit.

Adventures on Skis/Adventure Sport Holidays ⓣ1-800/628-9655 or 413/568-2855, ⓦwww.advonskis.com. Mostly ski packages, but also van-escorted cycling tours.

AESU Travel ⓣ1-800/638-AESU or 410/366-5494, ⓦwww.aesu.com. Discount airfares and student/low-budget travel including escorted tours and independent city-stays for 18- to 35-year-olds.

Backroads ⓣ1-800/GO-ACTIVE or 510/527-1555, ⓦwww.backroads.com. Cycling and hiking tours designed for the young at heart, with the emphasis on going at your own pace. Accommodation ranges from campsites to luxury hotels. Also family-friendly options and singles trips.

The Barge Lady ⓣ1-800/880-0071, ⓦwww.bargelady.com. Well-established agency with luxury barging holidays from Alsace to the Canal du Midi and the Camargue.

BCT Scenic Walking ⓣ1-800/473-1210 or 760/944-4599, ⓦwww.bctwalk.com. Walking holidays in Normandy, Brittany, Alsace and Provence.

Butterfield & Robinson ⓣ1-800-678-1147, ⓦwww.butterfield.com. Good range of upmarket biking (including the Tour de France route), walking and multi-activity trips, including family options.

CBT Tours ⓣ1-800/736-2453 or 773/871-5510, ⓦwww.cbttours.com. Biking holidays in southern France and from Paris to Frankfurt, as well as tailor-made tours.

Classic Journeys ⓣ1-800/200-3887 or 858/454-5004, ⓦwww.classicjourneys.com. Cultural walking tours along the Loire and Dordogne valleys, amongst other destinations. Also offer a Provence cooking and walking option.

Contiki ⓣ1-888/CONTIKI, ⓦwww.contiki.com. 18- to 35-year-olds-only tour operator. Choose between a 12-day "Best of France" tour or one of their Europe-wide itineraries.

Cosmos ⓣ1-800/276-1241, ⓦwww.cosmosvacations.com. Planned vacation packages with an independent focus. They include a 15-day Grand Tour of France and various "European sampler" tours.

Cross-Culture ⓣ1-800/491-1148 or 413/256-6303, ⓦwww.crosscultureinc.com. Small-group cultural tours from the highlights of Paris and the Loire to Painters of Provence and hiking in the Alps and Pyrenees.

EC Tours ⓣ1-800/388-0877, ⓦwww.ectours.com. Paris tours and individually planned tours of regions such as Normandy, the Loire and the French Riviera.

Euro-Bike & Walking Tours ⓣ1-800/321-6060, ⓦwww.eurobike.com. Good range of bike and walking tours all over France for family groups or solo travellers.

Europe Through the Back Door ⓣ425/771-8303, ⓦwww.ricksteves.com. Off-the-beaten path, small-group trips with budget travel guru Rick Steves and his enthusiastic guides. Tours include Paris, a romp through the villages of France and Provence and the south.

France Vacations ⓣ1-800/332 5332, ⓦwww.francevacations.net. Broad range of air/hotel and fly-drive packages as well as tailored itineraries throughout France.

The French Experience ⓣ1-800/283 7262, ⓦwww.frenchexperience.com. Flexible escorted and self-drive tours, châteaux, apartment and cottage rentals, cruises, culture tours and airfare arrangements.

Globus ⓣ1-866/755-8581, ⓦwww.globusjourneys.com. Planned vacation packages, from a week in Paris to nine days exploring Provence.

Holidaze Ski Tours ⓣ1-800/526-2827 or 732/280-1120, ⓦwww.holidaze.com. Ski specialist with one-week packages to the French Alps departing from New York.

Insight International Tours ⓣ1-800/582-8380, ⓦwww.inusa.insightvacations.com. Upmarket coach tours of France or as combined with other European destinations.

Maupintour ⓣ1-800/255-4266, ⓦwww.maupintour.com. Luxury city breaks in Paris and Nice, plus escorted tours, independent packages and canal and river cruises.

Mountain Travel Sobek ⓣ1-888/MTSOBEK or 510/527-8100, ⓦwww.mtsobek.com. Hiking in Provence, the Pyrenees, Corsica and around the Mont Blanc circuit.

Rail Europe ⓣ1-877/EUROVAC, ⓦwww.raileurope.com. Rail passes and advice, plus good air-fares, bookings for hotels and rental cars, and flexible, multi-centre vacation packages.

REI Adventures ⓣ1-800/622-2236, ⓦwww.rei.com/adventures. Cycling and hiking in Provence, the Loire and the Dordogne amongst other destinations.

Trek Holidays Canada ⓣ1-800/661-7265, ⓦwww.trekholidays.com. Agent for a vast array of adventure companies, with hiking and cycling options in France.

Viator Ⓦwww.viator.com. Bookings for local tours and sightseeing trips in a broad range of destinations around France.
Viking River Cruises Ⓣ1-877/668-4546. Cruise the French waterways from Honfleur in Normandy along the Seine to Paris and down the Saone-Rhone valley from Chalon-sur-Saône to Avignon.
Wilderness Travel Ⓣ1-800/368-2794, Ⓦwww.wildernesstravel.com. Hiking specialists, with tours to the Corsica, Provence, the Alps and a 7-day jaunt around the castles and caves of the Dordogne.
World Expeditions Canada Ⓣ613/241-2700 or 514/844-6364, Ⓦwww.worldexpeditions.com. Self-guided and escorted cycling and walking holidays.
Worldwide Quest Adventures Ⓣ1-800/387-1483, Ⓦwww.worldwidequest.com. Adventure specialist offering a challenging fifteen-day ascent of Mont Blanc.

From Australia and New Zealand

Many people travelling to France from Australia and New Zealand will choose to travel via London although there are **scheduled flights** to Paris from Sydney, Melbourne, Brisbane, Perth and Auckland. Most airlines can add a Paris leg (or a flight to any other major French city) to an Australia/New Zealand–Europe ticket. Flights via Asia or the Middle East, with a transfer or overnight stop in the airlines' home ports, are generally the cheapest option; those routed through the US tend to be slightly pricier. The cheapest return **fares** start at around AUS$2000 from Sydney, Perth and Darwin and NZ$2000 from Auckland.

Alternatively, the **discount agents** listed below may offer better deals, and have the latest information on limited special offers. Some of them can also help with visas, travel insurance and tours.

If you intend to do a fair amount of travelling within Europe, it's worth considering an **air pass**. These vary with the airline, but the basic rule is that they must be pre-booked with the main ticket. The airline alliances Sky Team, oneworld and Star Alliance each offer a European pass priced according to the distance travelled (see p.27 for contact details). With oneworld's "Visit Europe" pass, for example, you have to buy a minimum of two flights within Europe, costing between roughly AUS$100/NZ$110 and AUS$390/NZ$430 depending on the distance; taxes and other surcharges are extra.

Finally, if you prefer to have everything organized for you, and especially if your visit is going to be geared around special interests, such as walking, cycling, art or wine, you may want to consider one of the **package tours** offered by the operators below. Many can put together very flexible deals, sometimes amounting to no more than a flight plus car or train pass and accommodation. They may work out cheaper than the same arrangements made on arrival in France and can help you make the most of time if you're on a tight schedule.

Airlines

Air France Australia Ⓣ02/1300/361 400, New Zealand Ⓣ09/308 3352, Ⓦwww.airfrance.com.
Air New Zealand Australia Ⓣ13 24 76, Ⓦwww.airnz.com.au, New Zealand Ⓣ0800/737 000, Ⓦwww.airnz.co.nz.
Air Tahiti Nui Australia Ⓣ02/9244 2899, New Zealand Ⓣ09/308 3360, Ⓦwww.airtahitinui-usa.com.
American Airlines Australia Ⓣ1300/130 757, New Zealand Ⓣ0800/887 997, Ⓦwww.aa.com.
Austrian Airlines Australia Ⓣ1800/642 438 or 02/9251 6155, New Zealand Ⓣ09/522 5948, Ⓦwww.aua.com.
British Airways Australia Ⓣ1300/767 177, New Zealand Ⓣ0800/274 847 or 09/356 8690, Ⓦwww.britishairways.com.
Cathay Pacific Australia Ⓣ13 17 47, New Zealand Ⓣ0508/800 454 or 09/379 0861, Ⓦwww.cathaypacific.com.
Emirates Australia Ⓣ1300/303 777 or 02/9290 9700, New Zealand Ⓣ09/377 6004, Ⓦwww.emirates.com.
Garuda Indonesia Australia Ⓣ1300/365 330 or 02/9334 9944, New Zealand Ⓣ09/366 1862, Ⓦwww.garuda-indonesia.com.
Gulf Air Australia Ⓣ02/9244 2199, New Zealand Ⓣ09/308 3366, Ⓦwww.gulfairco.com.
JAL (Japan Airlines) Australia Ⓣ02/9272 1111, New Zealand Ⓣ09/379 9906, Ⓦwww.jal.com.
KLM Australia Ⓣ1300/303 747, New Zealand Ⓣ09/309 1782, Ⓦwww.klm.com.
Korean Air Australia Ⓣ02/9262 6000, New Zealand Ⓣ09/914 2000, Ⓦwww.koreanair.com.au.
Lufthansa Australia Ⓣ1300/655 727, New Zealand Ⓣ0800/945 220, Ⓦwww.lufthansa.com.
Malaysia Airlines Australia Ⓣ13 26 27, New Zealand Ⓣ0800/777 747, Ⓦwww.malaysia-airlines.com.

Philippine Airlines Australia ⓣ02/9279 2020, New Zealand ⓣ09/379 8522, ⓦwww.philippineairlines.com.
Qantas Australia ⓣ13 13 13, New Zealand ⓣ0800/808 767 or 09/357 8900, ⓦwww.qantas.com.
Royal Jordanian Australia ⓣ02/9244 2701, New Zealand ⓣ03/365 3910, ⓦwww.rja.com.jo.
Singapore Airlines Australia ⓣ13 10 11, New Zealand ⓣ0800/808 909, ⓦwww.singaporeair.com.
Thai Airways Australia ⓣ1300/651 960, New Zealand ⓣ09/377 3886, ⓦwww.thaiair.com.
United Airlines Australia ⓣ13 17 77, ⓦwww.united.com.

Courier flights

Jupiter Air Oceania ⓣ02/9317 2230, ⓦwww.jupiterair.com.au. Courier company operating flights for around half the normal fare to Europe from Sydney to London via Japan only.

Travel agents

Flight Centre Australia ⓣ13 31 33, ⓦwww.flightcentre.com.au, New Zealand ⓣ0800 243 544 or 09/358 4310, ⓦwww.flightcentre.co.nz. Rock-bottom fares worldwide.
Holiday Shoppe New Zealand ⓣ0800/808 040, ⓦwww.holidayshoppe.co.nz. Great deals on flights, hotels and holidays.
OTC Australia ⓣ1300/855 118, ⓦwww.otctravel.com.au. Deals on flights, hotels and holidays.
STA Travel Australia ⓣ1300/733 035, New Zealand t0508/782 872, ⓦwww.statravel.com. Worldwide specialists in low-cost flights, overlands and holiday deals. Good discounts for students and under-26s.
Student Uni Travel Australia ⓣ02/9232 8444, ⓦwww.sut.com.au, New Zealand ⓣ09/379 4224, ⓦwww.sut.co.nz. Great deals for students.
Trailfinders Australia ⓣ02/9247 7666, ⓦwww.trailfinders.com.au. One of the best-informed and most efficient agents for independent travellers.
travel.com.au and **travel.co.nz** Australia ⓣ51300/130 482 or 02/9249 5444, ⓦwww.travel.com.au, New Zealand ⓣ0800/468 332, ⓦwww.travel.co.nz. Comprehensive online travel company, with discounted fares.

Specialist agents

Abercrombie & Kent Australia ⓣ1300/851 800, New Zealand ⓣ0800/441 638, ⓦwww.abercrombiekent.com.au. Classy canal trips, walking tours and tailor-made holidays all over France.
Adventure World Australia ⓣ02/8913 0755, ⓦwww.adventureworld.com.au, New Zealand ⓣ09/524 5118, ⓦwww.adventureworld.co.nz. Agents for Headwater, which specialises in independent and guided walking and cycling holidays, among an array of adventure travel companies.
Australians Studying Abroad (ASA) Australia ⓣ1800/645 755 or 03/9509 1955, ⓦwww.asatravinfo.com.au. All-inclusive three-week lecture tours exploring the cultural landscapes of France and 20-day tours of the Riviera, Provence and the Dordogne.
Contiki Australia ⓣ02/9511 2200, New Zealand ⓣ09/309 8824, ⓦwww.contiki.com. Frenetic tours for 18- to 35-year-old party animals.
Destinations Adventure New Zealand ⓣ09/416 1150, ⓦwww.destinations-adventure.co.nz. Agent for Sherpa Expeditions escorted and self-guided walking and cycling holidays in France.
France Unlimited Australia ⓣ03/9531 8787. All French travel arrangements, including châteaux stays, Alpine hiking and cycling tours.
French Travel Connection Australia ⓣ02/9966 1177, ⓦwww.frenchtravel.com.au. Everything to do with travel to and around France, including accommodation, canal boats, walking tours, train travel, cookery classes, car rental and more.
Martin Randall Travel Australia ⓣ1300/559 595, ⓦwww.martinrandall.com. British company running small-group tours, often timed specifically to coincide with the likes of music or opera festivals. Expert lecturers on art, archeology, history or music give specialist insight, and accommodation is always comfortable.
Passport Travel Australia ⓣ03/9867 3888, ⓦwww.travelcentre.com.au. Small-group walking and cycling holidays.
Peregrine Adventures Australia ⓣ03/9663 8611, ⓦwww.peregrine.net.au. Agent for a multitude of adventure companies, taking small groups on guided and independent walking and cycling holidays through various French regions. In New Zealand, contact Adventure Travel Company ⓣ09/379 9755.
Silke's Travel Australia ⓣ1800/807 860, or 02/8347 2000, ⓦwww.silkes.com.au. Gay and lesbian specialist travel agent.
Snow Bookings Only Australia ⓣ1800/623 266, ⓦwww.snowbookingsonly.com.au. Ski and snowboarding packages in the French Alps.
Travel Notions Australia ⓣ02/9552 3355, ⓦwww.unitednotions.com.au/travelnotions. France specialists, and agents for leisurely "Cycling for Softies" tours.

Travelplan Australia ⓣ1300/130 754 or 02/9958 1888, ⓦwww.travelplan.com.au. Skiing in the major French resorts.
Viatour ⓦwww.viator.com. Bookings for local tours and sightseeing trips in a broad range of destinations around France.

Walkabout Gourmet Adventures Australia ⓣ03/5159 6556, ⓦwww.walkaboutgourmet.com. Classy food, wine and walking tours, including 14 days through the Auvergne, Dordogne and Loire, two weeks in Corsica and seven days exploring Pagnol's Provence.

Red tape and visas

Citizens of European Union (EU) countries can travel freely in France, while those from Australia, Canada, New Zealand and the United States, among other countries, do not need a visa for a stay of up to ninety days. However, the situation can change and it's advisable to check with your nearest French embassy or consulate before departure.

All **non-EU citizens** who wish to remain longer than ninety days must apply to the local *mairie* or town hall for a **residence permit** (a *titre de séjour*, also known as a *carte de séjour*), for which you will have to show proof of – among other things – a regular income or sufficient funds to support yourself, evidence of medical insurance and the appropriate visa (if required). For further information about visa regulations consult the Ministry of Foreign Affairs website: ⓦwww.diplomatie.gouv.fr.

French embassies and consulates

Australia Embassy: 6 Perth Ave, Yarralumla ACT 2600 ⓣ02/6216 0100, ⓦwww.ambafrance-au.org. Consulate: St Martins Tower, 31 Market St, Sydney, NSW 2000 ⓣ02/9261 5779, ⓦwww.consulfrance-sydney.org.
Britain Embassy: 58 Knightsbridge, London SW1X 7JT ⓣ020/7073 1000, ⓦwww.ambafrance-uk.org. Consulates: 21 Cromwell Rd, London SW7 2EN ⓣ020/7073 1200, ⓦwww.consulfrance-londres.org; 11 Randolph Crescent, Edinburgh, EH3 7TT ⓣ0131/225 3377, ⓦwww.consulfrance-edimbourg.org.
Canada Embassy: 42 Promenade Sussex, Ottawa, ON K1M 2C9 ⓣ613/789 1795, ⓦwww.ambafrance-ca.org. Consulates: 777 Main St, Suite 800, Moncton, NB E1C 1E9 ⓣ506/857 4191, ⓦwww.consulfrance-moncton.org; 1 place Ville-Marie, Bureau 2601, Montreal, QC H3B 4S3 ⓣ514/878 4385, ⓦwww.consulfrance-montreal.org; 25 rue St-Louis, Québec, QC G1R 3Y8 ⓣ418/694 2294, ⓦwww.consulfrance-quebec.org; 130 Bloor St West, Suite 400, Toronto, ON M5S 1N5 ⓣ416/925 8041, ⓦwww.consulfrance-toronto.org; 1130 West Pender St, Suite 1100, Vancouver, BC V6E 4A4 ⓣ604/681 4345, ⓦwww.consulfrance-vancouver.org.
Ireland 36 Ailesbury Rd, Ballsbridge, Dublin 4 ⓣ01/277 5000, ⓦwww.ambafrance.ie.org.
New Zealand 34–42 Manners St, PO Box 11–343, Wellington ⓣ04/384 2555, ⓦwww.ambafrance-nz.org.
USA Embassy: 4101 Reservoir Rd NW, Washington DC 20007 ⓣ202/944 6000, ⓦwww.ambafrance-us.org. Consulates: Prominence in Buckhead, Suite 1840, 3475 Piedmont Rd NE, Atlanta, GA 30305 ⓣ404/495 1660, ⓦwww.consulfrance-atlanta.org; Park Square Building, Suite 750, 31 St James Ave, Boston, MA 02116 ⓣ617/542 7374, ⓦwww.consulfrance-boston.org; Michigan Plaza, Suite 3700, 205 North Michigan Ave, Chicago IL 60601 ⓣ312/327 5200, ⓦwww.consulfrance-chicago.org; 777 Post Oak Blvd, Suite 600, Houston, TX 77056 ⓣ713/572 2799, ⓦwww.consulfrance-houston.org; 10990 Wilshire Blvd, Suite 300, Los Angeles, CA 90024 ⓣ310/235 3200, ⓦwww.consulfrance-losangeles.org; 1 Biscayne Tower, Suite 1710, 2 South Biscayne Blvd, Miami, FL 33131 ⓣ305/372 9799, ⓦwww.consulfrance-miami.org; 1340 Poydras St, Suite 1710, New Orleans, LA 70112 ⓣ504/523 5772,

ⓦwww.consulfrance-nouvelleorleans.org; 934 Fifth Ave, New York, NY 10021 ⓣ212/606 3689, ⓦwww.consulfrance-newyork.org; 540 Bush St, San Francisco, CA 94108 ⓣ415/397 4330, ⓦwww.consulfrance-sanfrancisco.org; 4101 Reservoir Rd NW, Washington DC 20007 ⓣ202/944 6195, ⓦwww.consulfrance-washington.org.

Information, websites and maps

The French Government Tourist Office (Maison de la France, ⓦwww.franceguide.com) increasingly refers you to their website for information, though they still produce a useful practical guide for young travellers to France, and dispense items including maps and the Logis de France book (see "Accommodation"). For more detailed information, such as hotels, campsites, activities and festivals, in a specific location, it's best to contact the relevant regional or departmental tourist offices; contact details can be found online at ⓦwww.fncrt.com and ⓦwww.fncdt.net respectively.

Tourist offices

In France itself you'll find a tourist office – usually an **Office du Tourisme** (OT) but sometimes a **Syndicat d'Initiative** (SI) – in practically every town and many villages (addresses, contact details and opening hours are detailed in the Guide). For the practical purposes of visitors, there's little difference between them: SIs have wider responsibilities for encouraging business, while Offices du Tourisme deal exclusively with tourism; sometimes they share premises and call themselves an OTSI. In small villages where there's no OT or SI, the *mairie* (town hall) will offer a similar service.

All these offices provide specific local information, including hotel and restaurant listings, leisure activities, car and bike rental, bus times, laundries and countless other things; many can also book accommodation for you. If asked, most offices will provide a town plan (for which you may be charged a nominal fee), and will have maps and local walking guides on sale. In mountain regions they display daily meteorological information and often share premises with the local hiking and climbing organizations. In the big cities you can usually pick up free What's On guides.

French government tourist offices abroad

Australia Level 20, 25 Bligh St, Sydney, NSW 2000 ⓣ02/9231 5244, ⓔinfo.au@franceguide.com.
Britain 178 Piccadilly, London, W1J 9AL ⓣ09068/244 123, 60p/min, ⓔinfo.uk@franceguide.com.
Canada 1981 Ave McGill College, Suite 490, Montréal, QC H3A 2W9 ⓣ514/876 9881, ⓔcanada@franceguide.com.
Ireland ⓣ1560/235 235, €0.95/min, ⓔinfo.ie@franceguide.com. Info by phone and email only.
New Zealand Contact the office in Australia.
USA 9454 Wilshire Blvd, Suite 715, Beverly Hills, CA 90212 ⓣ310/271 6665, ⓔinfo.losangeles@franceguide.com; 1 Biscayne Tower, Suite 1750, 2 South Biscayne Building, Miami, FL 33131 ⓣ305/373 8177, ⓔinfo.miami@franceguide.com; 205 North Michigan Ave, Suite 3770, Chicago, IL 60601 ⓣ410/286 8310, ⓔinfo.chicago@franceguide.com; 444 Madison Ave, New York, NY 10022 ⓣ410/286 8310, ⓔinfo.us@franceguide.com.
Contact details of French tourist offices in **other countries** can be found on the Maison de la France website: ⓦwww.franceguide.com.

Websites

Information about practically every aspect of travel and French culture can now be accessed **online**, though not always in English. Many government agencies, including local tourist offices, now have their own websites, and hotels and restaurants are also coming to realize the importance of an online presence. Web or email addresses are given where available throughout the Guide, while a selection of the more useful and well-established general sites are detailed below.

Travel advice

For up-to-the-minute advice on travelling to and in France consult the following government websites:

Australian Department of Foreign Affairs ⓦwww.dfat.gov.au.
British Foreign & Commonwealth Office ⓦwww.fco.gov.uk.
Canadian Department of Foreign Affairs ⓦwww.dfait-maeci.gc.ca.
Irish Department of Foreign Affairs ⓦwww.irlgov.ie/iveagh.
New Zealand Ministry of Foreign Affairs ⓦwww.mft.govt.nz.
US State Department ⓦtravel.state.gov.

Tourism and recreation sites

FNOTSI ⓦwww.tourisme.fr. Searchable database run by the national association of tourist offices. Town listings have practical and cultural information, details of local tourist offices and links to local websites.
France Holiday Store ⓦwww.fr-holidaystore.co.uk. A useful site for planning with tour operators – everything from cycling to skiing, fly-drive and city breaks, as well as self-catering accommodation.
Maison de la France ⓦwww.franceguide.com. The official site of the French Government Tourist Office, with news, information on local festivals and useful links.
Michelin ⓦwww.viamichelin.com. This sight's excellent route-planner includes driving times, distances and motorway tolls. You also get access to interactive maps and to hotel and restaurant listings.
Monum ⓦwww.monum.fr. Good starting point for information on 200 national monuments and museums across France, including news on special events.

News and information sites

France 2 ⓦwww.france2.fr. The latest news, weather and road conditions from the France 2 TV channel. Also provides an online translation service to/from various European languages.
Governments on the WWW ⓦwww.gksoft.com/govt/en/fr.html. English-language portal site listing all French government websites, including embassies, departmental and regional authorities, political parties and state media.
Le Monde ⓦwww.lemonde.fr. The online version of one of France's most reputable daily newspapers. Includes national and international news, culture and sports – all in French.
Radio France ⓦwww.radio-france.fr. National and international news coverage, current affairs, as well as music and culture. French language only.
Service-Public ⓦwww.servicepublic.fr. Multilingual portal sight for the French civil service, containing news, information and masses of useful links.

Arts and culture sites

Bibliothèque Pompidou ⓦwww.bpi.fr. Good links to media and a very comprehensive list of arts and humanities sites for France. French language only.
La Danse ⓦwww.ladanse.com. Bilingual site with comprehensive information on French and international dance including news, links and a database of artists and companies.
Festivalissimo ⓦwww.festivalissimo.com. This is the single best site for information (in French and English) on festivals. You can search by date, theme or location.
IRMA (Informations et Ressources pour les Musiques Actuelles) ⓦwww.irma.asso.fr. The French music industry's promotional organization provides information and links to groups representing every genre and style.
Ministry of Culture ⓦwww.culture.fr. Information (in French) on cultural events and a comprehensive list of links to organizations related to the whole gamut of artistic media.
Revue Spectacle ⓦwww.revue-spectacle.com. Monthly arts review (in French) set up by a group of newspapers and radio stations in co-operation with the Ministry of Culture. Covers theatre, dance and mime events.
Via France ⓦwww.viafrance.com. Bilingual events database (including concerts, theatre, festivals, markets and sports) organized by category and region.

Maps

In addition to the **maps** in this guide and the various free town plans and regional maps you'll be offered along the way, the one extra map you might want is a good, up-to-date road map of France. The best for country-wide coverage are the 1:100,000 maps of France produced by Michelin (Ⓦwww.viamichelin.fr) or the Institut Géographique National (IGN; Ⓦwww.ign.fr). Both companies also issue good regional maps either as individual sheets or in one large spiral-bound "*atlas routier*"; Michelin's version is available in English as the *France Tourist & Motoring Atlas*.

If walking or cycling, it's worth investing in the more detailed IGN maps. The Carte de Randonnée series (1:25,000) is specifically designed for walkers, while the Carte de Promenade (1:100,000) is good for cyclists.

In the UK and Ireland

Blackwell's Map Centre 50 Broad St, Oxford OX1 3BQ Ⓣ01865/793 550, Ⓦmaps.blackwell.co.uk. Branches in Bristol, Cambridge, Cardiff, Leeds, Liverpool, Newcastle, Reading and Sheffield.
The Map Shop 30a Belvoir St, Leicester LE1 6QH Ⓣ0116/247 1400, Ⓦwww.mapshopleicester.co.uk.
National Map Centre 22–24 Caxton St, London SW1H 0QU Ⓣ020/7222 2466, Ⓦwww.mapsnmc.co.uk.
National Map Centre Ireland 34 Aungier St, Dublin Ⓣ01/476 0471, Ⓦwww.mapcentre.ie.
Stanfords 12–14 Long Acre, London WC2E 9LP Ⓣ020/7836 1321, Ⓦwww.stanfords.co.uk. Also at 39 Spring Gardens, Manchester Ⓣ0161/831 0250, and 29 Corn St, Bristol Ⓣ0117/929 9966.
The Travel Bookshop 13–15 Blenheim Crescent, London W11 2EE Ⓣ020/7229 5260, Ⓦwww.thetravelbookshop.co.uk.
Traveller 55 Grey St, Newcastle-upon-Tyne NE1 6EF Ⓣ0191/261 5622, Ⓦwww.newtraveller.com.

In the US and Canada

110 North Latitude US Ⓣ336/369-4171, Ⓦwww.110nlatitude.com.
Book Passage 51 Tamal Vista Blvd, Corte Madera, CA 94925 and in the historic San Francisco Ferry Building Ⓣ1-800/999-7909 or Ⓣ415/927-0960, Ⓦwww.bookpassage.com.
Distant Lands 56 S Raymond Ave, Pasadena, CA 91105 Ⓣ1-800/310-3220, Ⓦwww.distantlands.com.
Globe Corner Bookstore 28 Church St, Cambridge, MA 02138 Ⓣ1-800/358-6013, Ⓦwww.globercorner.com.
Longitude Books 115 W 30th St #1206, New York, NY 10001 Ⓣ1-800/342-2164, Ⓦwww.longitudebooks.com.
Map Town 400 5 Ave SW #100, Calgary, AB, T2P 0L6 Ⓣ1-877/921-6277 or Ⓣ403/266-2241, Ⓦwww.maptown.com.
Travel Bug Bookstore 3065 W Broadway, Vancouver, BC, V6K 2G9 Ⓣ604/737-1122, Ⓦwww.travelbugbooks.ca.
World of Maps 1235 Wellington St, Ottawa, ON, K1Y 3A3 Ⓣ1-800/214-8524 or Ⓣ613/724-6776, Ⓦwww.worldofmaps.com.

In Australia and New Zealand

Map Centre Ⓦwww.mapcentre.co.nz.
Mapland 372 Little Bourke St, Melbourne Ⓣ03/9670 4383, Ⓦwww.mapland.com.au.
Map Shop 6–10 Peel St, Adelaide Ⓣ08/8231 2033, Ⓦwww.mapshop.net.au.
Map World 371 Pitt St, Sydney Ⓣ02/9261 3601, Ⓦwww.mapworld.net.au. Also at 900 Hay St, Perth Ⓣ08/9322 5733, Jolimont Centre, Canberra Ⓣ02/6230 4097 and 1981 Logan Road, Brisbane Ⓣ07/3349 6633. In New Zealand: 173 Gloucester St, Christchurch Ⓣ0800/627 967, Ⓦwww.mapworld.co.nz.

Insurance

Even though EU citizens are entitled to health care privileges in France, you'd do well to take out an insurance policy before travelling to cover against theft, loss, illness or injury. Before paying for a new policy, however, it's worth checking whether you are already covered: some all-risks home insurance policies may cover your possessions when overseas, and many private medical schemes include cover when abroad. In Canada, provincial health plans usually provide partial cover for medical mishaps overseas, while holders of official student/teacher/youth cards in Canada and the US are entitled to meagre accident coverage and hospital in-patient benefits. Students will often find that their student health coverage extends during the vacations and for one term beyond the date of last enrolment.

After checking out the possibilities above, you might want to contact a specialist travel insurance company, or consider the travel insurance deal we offer (see box). A typical **travel insurance policy** usually provides cover for the loss of baggage, tickets and – up to a certain limit – cash or cheques, as well as cancellation or curtailment of your journey. Most of them exclude so-called dangerous sports unless an extra premium is paid. In France this can mean skiing, whitewater rafting, rock-climbing and potholing, and the policy should cover mountain rescue services, helicopter ambulances and the like. Many policies can be chopped and changed to exclude coverage you don't need – for example, sickness and accident benefits can often be excluded or included at will.

If you do take medical coverage, ascertain whether benefits will be paid as treatment proceeds or only after you return home, and if there is a 24-hour medical emergency number. When securing baggage cover, make sure that the per-article limit – typically under £500/$750 and sometimes as little as £250/$400 – will cover your most valuable possession. If you need to make a claim, you should keep receipts for medicines and medical treatment, and in the event you have anything stolen, you must obtain an official statement from the police (called a *constat de vol*).

Rough Guides travel insurance

Rough Guides Ltd offers a low-cost **travel insurance** policy, especially customized for our statistically low-risk readers by a leading British broker, provided by the American International Group (AIG) and registered with the British regulatory body, GISC (the General Insurance Standards Council). There are five main Rough Guides insurance plans: **No Frills** for the bare minimum for secure travel; **Essential**, which provides decent all-round cover; **Premier** for comprehensive cover with a wide range of benefits; **Extended Stay** for cover lasting four months to a year; and **Annual Multi-Trip**, a cost-effective way of getting Premier cover if you travel more than once a year. Premier, Annual Multi-Trip and Extended Stay policies can be supplemented by a "Hazardous Pursuits Extension" if you plan to indulge in sports considered dangerous, such as scuba-diving or trekking. For a policy quote, call the Rough Guide Insurance Line: toll-free in the UK ⓣ0800/015 0906 or ⓣ+44 1392 314665 from elsewhere. Alternatively, get an online quote at ⓦwww.roughguides.com/insurance

Health

Visitors to France have little to worry about as far as health is concerned. No vaccinations are required, there are no nasty diseases to be wary of and tap-water is safe to drink. The worst that's likely to happen to you is a case of sunburn or an upset stomach from eating too much rich food. If you do need treatment, however, you should be in good hands: the French healthcare system is rated one of the best in the world.

Under the French health system, all services, including doctor's consultations, prescribed medicines, hospital stays and ambulance call-outs, incur a charge which you have to pay upfront. EU citizens are entitled to a refund (usually between 70 and 100 percent) of medical and dental expenses, providing the doctor is government registered (*un médecin conventionné*) and provided you have the correct documentation (form E111, available from social security offices and, in Britain, from main post offices). This can still leave a hefty shortfall, however, especially after a stay in hospital, so you might want to take out some additional insurance. All non-EU visitors should ensure they have adequate medical insurance cover.

For minor complaints go to a **pharmacie**, signalled by an illuminated green cross. You'll find at least one in every small town and even some villages. They keep normal shop hours (roughly 9am–noon & 3–6pm), though some stay open late and in larger towns at least one (known as the *pharmacie de garde*) is open 24 hours according to a rota; details are displayed in all pharmacy windows.

For anything more serious you can get the name of a **doctor** from a pharmacy, local police station, tourist office or your hotel. Alternatively, look under "Médecins" in the Yellow Pages of the phone directory. The consultation fee is in the region of €20 to €25. You'll be given a *Feuille de Soins* (Statement of Treatment) for later insurance claims. Any prescriptions will be fulfilled by the pharmacy and must be paid for; little price stickers (*vignettes*) from each medicine will be stuck on the *Feuille de Soins*.

In serious **emergencies** you will always be admitted to the nearest general hospital (*centre hospitalier*). Phone numbers and addresses of hospitals in all the main cities are given in the Guide. The national number for calling an ambulance is ⓣ15.

Costs, money and banks

France is not an expensive place to visit, at least compared to other northern European countries, largely because of the relatively low cost of accommodation and eating out. When and where you go, however, will make a difference: in prime tourist spots hotel prices can go up by a third during July and August, while places like Paris and the Côte d'Azur are always more expensive than the other regions.

For a reasonably comfortable existence, including a hotel room for two, a light restaurant lunch and a proper restaurant dinner, plus moving around, café stops and museum visits, you need to allow around €100 a day per person. By counting the pennies, staying at youth hostels (around €12–13 bed and breakfast) or camping (from around €10 for two people), and being strong-willed about extra cups of coffee and doses of culture, you could manage on €50 a day – or even less if you're surviving on street snacks and market food.

For two or more people, **hotel accommodation** may be cheaper and is nearly always better value than hostels, which are generally only worth it if you're by yourself and want to meet other travellers. A sensible average estimate for a double room in a standard two-star hotel would be around €45, though perfectly adequate but simple doubles can be had from €30 (in Paris, the equivalent would be around €80 and €40 respectively). Single rooms are sometimes available, beginning from around €25 in the cheapest hotels; elsewhere you'll have to take the cheapest double. Breakfast at hotels is normally an extra €5 upwards, for coffee, croissant and/or bread and orange juice, though smarter places now run to yoghurts, fruit and cereals and may even offer a buffet. A coffee and croissant in a café, on the other hand, will set you back around €4–5.

As for other **food**, there are large numbers of reasonable restaurants with two- or three-course menus for between €12 and €20; a good tip is to eat your main meal at lunchtime (*midi*), when the menu is nearly always cheaper. Picnic fare, obviously, is much less costly, especially when you buy in the markets and cheap supermarket chains, and takeaway baguette sandwiches from cafés are not extortionate. **Wine** and **beer** are both very cheap in supermarkets; buying wine from the barrel at village co-op cellars will give you the best value for money. The mark-up on wine in restaurants is high, though many places serve inexpensive but perfectly decent house-wine by the carafe. Drinks in **cafés** and **bars** are what really make a hole in your pocket: black coffee, wine and draught lager are the cheapest drinks to order, while a glass of tap water is free.

Transport will inevitably be a large item of expenditure if you move around a lot. It's worth investigating the various train passes and discount tickets available, although French trains are good value in any case – two sample one-way fares are Paris to Toulouse by TGV, €80, and Paris to Nice, €100. Buses are cheaper, though prices vary enormously from one operator to another. Bicycles generally cost between €10 and €15 per day to rent. Petrol prices have been rising steadily and at the time of writing were around €1.10 a litre for unleaded (*sans plomb*), €1.20 a litre for four-star (*super*) and €0.85 a litre for diesel (*gazole* or *gasoil*); you'll find prices lowest at out-of-town hypermarkets. Most *autoroutes* have tolls: rates vary, but to give you an idea, travelling only by motorway from Calais to Montpellier would cost you roughly €64.

Admission charges to museums and monuments can also eat into your budget, though many state-owned museums have one day of the week when they're free or half-price. Reductions are often available for those over 60 and under 18 (for which you'll need your passport as proof of age) and for students under 26 (see below), while many are free for children under 12, and almost always for kids under 4. Several towns and regions offer multi-entry tickets covering a number of sights (detailed in the Guide).

Youth and student discounts

Once obtained, various official and quasi-official youth/student ID cards soon pay for themselves in savings. Full-time students are eligible for the **International Student ID Card** (ISIC, Ⓦwww.isiccard.com), which entitles the bearer to special air, rail and bus fares, and discounts at museums, theatres and other attractions. For Americans, there's also a health benefit, providing up to $3000 in emergency medical coverage and $100 a day for 60 days in hospital, plus a 24-hour hotline to call in the event of a medical, legal or financial emergency. The card costs $22 in the USA; CAN$16 in Canada; AUS$18 in Australia; NZ$20 in New Zealand; £7 in the UK; and €13 in the Republic of Ireland.

You only have to be 26 or younger to qualify for the **International Youth Travel Card**, which costs US$22/£7 and carries the same benefits. Teachers qualify for the

International Teacher Card, offering similar discounts and costing US$22, CAN$16, AUS$18 and NZ$20, UK£7 and €13. All these cards are available in the US from STA, Travel CUTS and, in Canada, Hostelling International; in Australia and New Zealand from STA or Campus Travel; in the UK from STA; and in Ireland from USIT or STA.

Several other travel organizations and accommodation groups also sell their own cards, good for various discounts. A university photo ID might open some doors, but they're not as universally recognized as ISIC cards. However, the latter are often not accepted as valid proof of age, for example in bars or liquor stores.

Currency and the exchange rate

In 2002, France was one of twelve European Union countries to change over to a single currency, the **euro**. The euro is divided into 100 cents (often still referred to as *centimes*). There are seven notes – in denominations of 5, 10, 20, 50, 100, 200 and 500 euros – and eight different coins – 1, 2, 5, 10, 20 and 50 cents, and 1 and 2 euros. Euro coins feature a common EU design on one face, but different country-specific designs on the other. No matter what the design, all euro coins and notes can be used in any of the twelve member states (Austria, Belgium, Finland, France, Germany, Greece, Ireland, Italy, Luxembourg, Portugal, Spain and The Netherlands, but not the UK, Denmark or Sweden).

At the time of writing, the exchange rate hovered around €1.50 to the pound, €0.80 to the US dollar, €0.60 to the Canadian dollar, €0.60 to the Australian dollar, and €0.50 to the New Zealand dollar. For up-to-date exchange rates, consult the Currency Converter website ⓦwww.oanda.com.

Credit and debit cards

By far the easiest way to access money in France is to use your **credit** or **debit card** to withdraw cash from an ATM (known as a *distributeur* or *point argent*); most machines give instructions in a variety of European languages. You'll need a 4-digit personal identification number (PIN) to use your cards in France. Note that there is often a transaction fee, so it's more efficient to take out a sizeable sum each time rather than making lots of small withdrawals.

Credit and debit cards are also widely accepted in shops, hotels and restaurants, although some smaller establishments don't accept cards, or only for sums above a certain threshold. Visa – called Carte Bleue in France – is almost universally recognized, followed by MasterCard (also known as EuroCard). American Express ranks a bit lower. Be aware that whereas many foreign cards work by means of a magnetic strip, French cards are equipped with a chip and require the user to provide a PIN when making a purchase. If you're asked to tap in a PIN or are told that your card has been rejected, it's worth explaining that yours is a *carte à piste* and not a *carte à puce*.

A compromise between travellers' cheques and plastic is **Visa TravelMoney**, a disposable pre-paid debit card with a PIN which works in all ATMs that take Visa cards. You load up your account with funds before leaving home, and when they run out, you simply throw the card away. You can buy up to nine cards to access the same funds – useful for couples or families travelling together – and it's a good idea to buy at least one extra as a back-up in case of loss or theft. If you need assistance, there is also a local 24-hour toll-free number: ⓣ08.00.90.11.79. The card is available in most countries from branches of Travelex and AAA. For more information, check the Visa TravelMoney website at ⓦusa.visa.com/personal/cards/visa_travel_money.html.

To cancel **lost** or **stolen cards**, call the following 24-hour numbers: American Express ⓣ01.47.77.72.00; Diners' Club ⓣ08.10.31.41.59; MasterCard ⓣ01.45.67.84.84; Visa ⓣ08.00.90.11.79.

Travellers' cheques

Travellers' cheques are obviously safer than cash and also provide a useful backup to credit cards. Major brands such as Visa, Thomas Cook and American Express can be changed at most banks; Visa, American Express and Citicorp cheques can also be exchanged at major post offices. You should have no problems changing travellers' cheques denominated in major currencies, though euro cheques have certain advantages: they can often be used as cash, and you should get the face value of the cheques when you change them, so commission is only paid on purchase.

The usual fee for buying cheques is one or two percent, though this may be waived if you purchase the cheques through a bank where you have an account. It pays to get a selection of denominations. Make sure to keep the purchase agreement and a record of the cheque serial numbers safe and separate from the cheques themselves. In the event that cheques are lost or stolen, the issuing company will expect you to report the loss immediately; most companies claim to replace lost or stolen cheques within 24 hours.

Wiring money

Having **money wired** from home using one of the companies listed opposite is never convenient or cheap, and should be considered a last resort. It's also possible to have money wired directly from a bank in your home country, although this is somewhat less reliable because it involves two separate institutions. If you go this route, your home bank will need the address of the branch bank where you want to pick up the money and the address and telex number of its head office, which will act as the clearing house; money wired this way normally takes two working days to arrive, and costs around £25/$40/CAN$54/AUS$52/NZ$59 per transaction.

Money-wiring companies

Travelers Express/Moneygram
US ⓣ1-800/444-3010, Canada ⓣ1-800/933-3278, UK, Ireland and New Zealand ⓣ00800/6663 9472, Australia ⓣ0011800/6663 9472, ⓦwww.moneygram.com.
Western Union US and Canada ⓣ1-800/CALL-CASH, UK ⓣ0800/833 833, Republic of Ireland ⓣ66/947 5603, Australia ⓣ1800/501 500, New Zealand ⓣ0800/005 253, ⓦwww.westernunion.com

Banks and exchange

Core **banking hours** are Monday to Friday 9am to noon and 2 to 4.30pm. Some branches, especially those in rural areas, close on Monday, while those in big cities may remain open at midday and may also open on Saturday morning. All are closed on Sunday and public holidays.

Banks will have a notice outside if they offer **currency exchange**. Rates and commission vary from bank to bank, so it's worth shopping around; some banks change travellers' cheques for 'free' (and then make up for it by offering a poor exchange rate), while others levy up to three percent commission, with a minimum charge which can go as high as €8, or may simply charge a flat rate whatever the amount.

There are **money-exchange counters** (*bureaux de change*) at French airports, major train stations and usually one or two in town centres as well. You'll occasionally also find them in tourist offices. These services are handy when the banks are closed though don't always offer the best exchange rates.

Getting around

With the most extensive train network in western Europe, France is a great country in which to travel by rail. The nationally owned French train company, SNCF (Société Nationale des Chemins de Fer), runs fast, efficient trains between the main towns. Buses cover the rural areas, but services can be rather sporadic, with departures often at awkward times. If you really want to get off the beaten track, by far the best option is to have your own transport.

Flying within France has the obvious advantage of speed, but is only recommended for those short on time and long on cash. Aside from Corsica, which can also be reached by air, France's islands are serviced only by **ferries**, some of which are seasonal and not all of which are equipped to carry vehicles.

For independent transport, by **car, motorbike** or **bicycle**, you'll need to be aware of a number of French road rules and peculiarities. **Hitching** is also an option, but is not easy and is not recommended for people travelling alone. The extensive network of inland waterways in France makes **boating** a very pleasant way of exploring the country. **Long-distance walking** is also extremely popular; for further information on walking, canoeing and other similar activities, see "Sports and Outdoor Pursuits".

Approximate journey times and frequencies of the main train, bus, plane and ferry services can be found in the "Travel Details" at the end of each chapter.

By train

SNCF has pioneered one of the most efficient, comfortable and user-friendly railway systems in the world. Its staff are generally courteous and helpful, and its trains – for the most part, fast, clean and reliable – continue, in spite of the closure of some rural lines, to serve a vast part of the country. For national **train information**, you can either phone (Ⓣ36.35; €0.34 per minute) or check on the SNCF website (Ⓦwww.sncf.com). Regional **timetables** and leaflets covering particular lines are available free at stations. "Autocar" (often abbreviated to "car") at the top of a column means it's an SNCF bus service, on which rail tickets and passes are valid.

Pride and joy of the French rail system is the high-speed TGV (*train à grande vitesse*), capable of speeds over 300kph, and its offspring Eurostar. The continually expanding TGV network has its main hub at Paris, from where a main line heads north to Lille, and two other trunk routes head south: one down the east side of the country to Marseille and the Mediterranean, the other west to Tours, Bordeaux and the Spanish frontier. Spur lines service Brittany and Normandy, the Alps, Pyrenees and Jura. The only difference between TGV and other train fares is that a reservation charge is included in the ticket price (seat reservations are obligatory) and you have to pay a supplement on certain peak-hour trains (*période de pointe*), generally on Friday and Sunday evenings, Monday mornings and public holidays.

Tickets for all SNCF trains can be bought online through Ⓦwww.sncf.com, which has an English-language option, and at any train station (*gare SNCF*). It's easiest to use the counter service, though if there are language problems or long queues the touch-screen computerized system available in most stations gives instructions in English and is a good way to check various fares and times. All tickets – but not passes – must be validated in the orange machines located beside the entrance to the platforms, and it's an offence not to follow the instruction *Compostez votre billet* (validate your ticket).

There's a range of reductions on standard **fares** (*période normale* or *période blanche*, normal or white period) if you travel off-peak (*période bleue* or blue period). A leaflet showing the blue and white periods is available at train stations. Any two people travelling together or a small group of up to nine people – whether a married couple, friends, family, whatever – are entitled to a 25 percent discount on return tickets on TGVs, subject to availability, or on other trains if they start their journey during a blue period (this fare is known as a Découverte à Deux); the same reduction applies to a group of up to four people travelling with a child under 12 (Découverte Enfant Plus), to under-26-year-olds (Découverte 12–25), over-60s (Découverte Senior), and for anyone who books a return journey of at least 200km in distance, including a Saturday night away (Découverte Séjour). In certain cases, tickets bought at least two weeks in advance and those bought over the Internet are also cheaper. On night trains an extra €15 or so will buy you a couchette – well worth it if you're making a long haul and don't want to waste a day recovering from a sleepless night.

Aside from the regular lines there are a number of special **tourist trains**, usually not part of the SNCF system or covered by normal rail passes, though some offer a discount to rail pass holders. Two of the most popular are the spectacular Train Jaune which winds its way up through the Pyrenees (see p.862), and the ATM train, which heads up into the hinterland of Narbonne.

Rail passes

There's a huge array of **rail passes** available, covering various regions of Europe as well as individual countries. Some have to be bought before leaving home while others can only be bought in the country itself. SNCF also offers its own passes, most of which can be bought in advance either direct or through **Rail Europe**, the umbrella company for all national and international rail purchases. Its comprehensive website (Ⓦwww.raileurope.com) is the most useful source of information on which rail passes are available, and also gives all current prices.

Eurail passes

A **Eurailpass**, which is not available to European residents and must be purchased before arrival in Europe, is not likely to pay for itself if you're planning to stick to France alone. The pass allows unlimited free first-class train travel in France and 16 other countries, and is available in increments of 15 days ($588/CAN$806/NZ$1032/AUS$90), 21 days ($762/CAN$1044/NZ$1337/AUS$1173), 1 month ($946/CAN$1297/NZ$1660/AUS$1456), 2 months ($1338/CAN$1834/NZ$2348/AUS$2059) and 3 months ($1654/CAN$2266/NZ$2902/AUS$2545). If you're under 26, you can save around a third off these prices with a **Eurailpass Youth**, which is valid for second-class travel or, if you're travelling with 1 to 5 other companions, a joint **Eurailpass Saver**, both of which are available in the same increments as the Eurailpass. You stand a better chance of getting your money's worth out of a **Eurailpass Flexi**, which is good for 10 ($694/CAN$951/NZ$1218/AUS$1068) or 15 ($914/CAN$1253/NZ$1604/AUS$1407) days' first-class travel within a 2-month period. This, too, comes in under-26/second-class (**Eurailpass Youth Flexi**) and group (**Eurailpass Saver Flexi**) versions.

In addition, a scaled-down version of the Eurailpass Flexi, the **Eurail Selectpass**, allows travel in your choice of 3, 4 or 5 of the 18 countries covered (they must be adjoining, by either rail or ship) for any 5 days, 6 days, 8 days, 10 days or 15 days (5-country option only) within a 2-month period. The pass costs between $356 and $794 (CA$488–1088/NZ$625–1393/AUS$548–1222). In this plan, Belgium, the Netherlands and Luxembourg are counted as one "country." Like the Eurailpass, the Selectpass is also available in youth and saver (group) options.

Details of prices for all these passes can be found on Ⓦwww.eurail.com. Passes can also be purchased online or from one of the agents listed below.

Inter-Rail passes

Inter-Rail passes are only available to European residents, and you will be asked to provide proof of residency before being allowed to purchase one. They come in over-26 and (cheaper) under-26 versions, and cover 28 European countries grouped

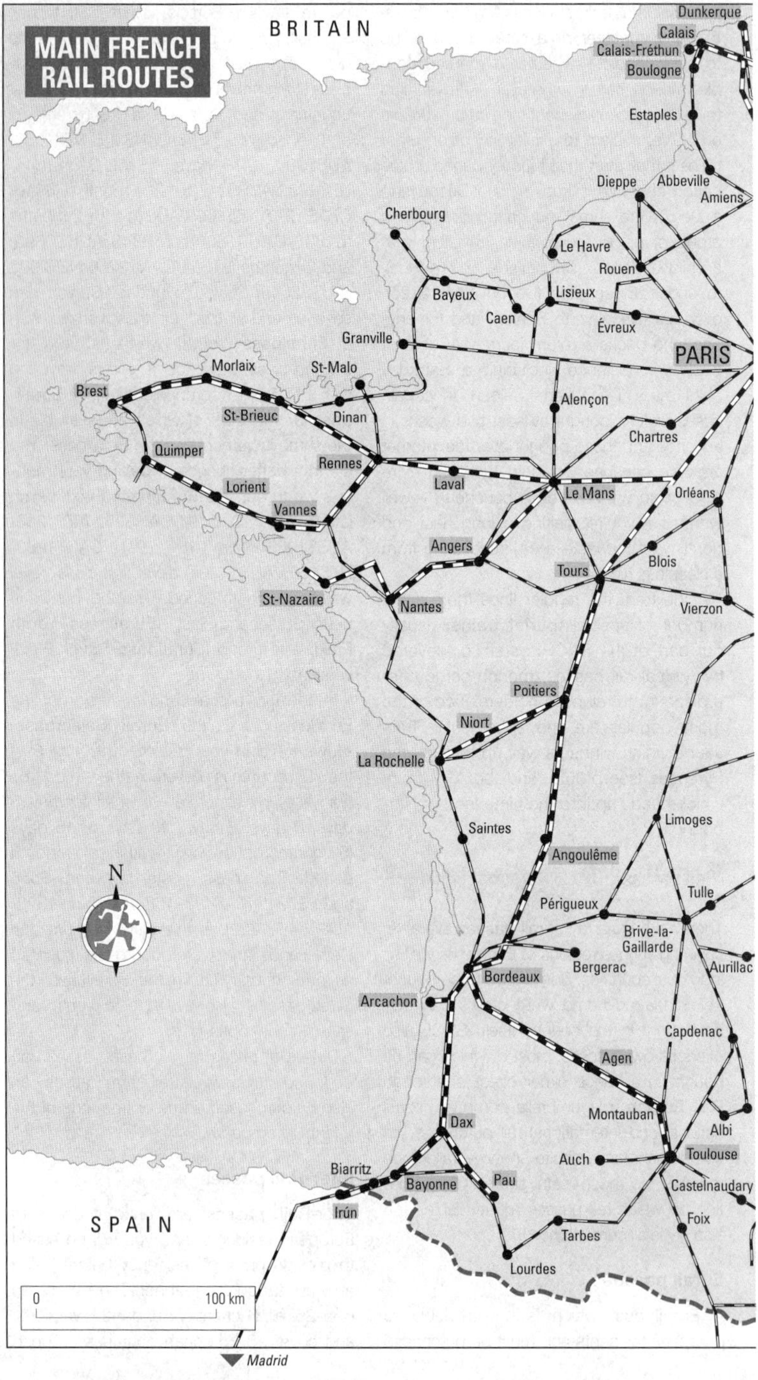

MAIN FRENCH RAIL ROUTES

BRITAIN
Dunkerque
Calais
Calais-Fréthun
Boulogne
Estaples
Dieppe
Abbeville
Amiens
Cherbourg
Le Havre
Rouen
Bayeux
Lisieux
Caen
Évreux
Granville
PARIS
Morlaix
St-Malo
Brest
St-Brieuc
Dinan
Alençon
Chartres
Quimper
Rennes
Laval
Lorient
Le Mans
Orléans
Vannes
Angers
Blois
Tours
St-Nazaire
Nantes
Vierzon
Poitiers
Niort
La Rochelle
Limoges
Saintes
Angoulême
Tulle
Périgueux
Brive-la-Gaillarde
Bergerac
Aurillac
Bordeaux
Arcachon
Capdenac
Agen
Montauban
Albi
Dax
Auch
Toulouse
Biarritz
Bayonne
Pau
Castelnaudary
Irún
Foix
SPAIN
Tarbes
Lourdes
0
100 km
Madrid

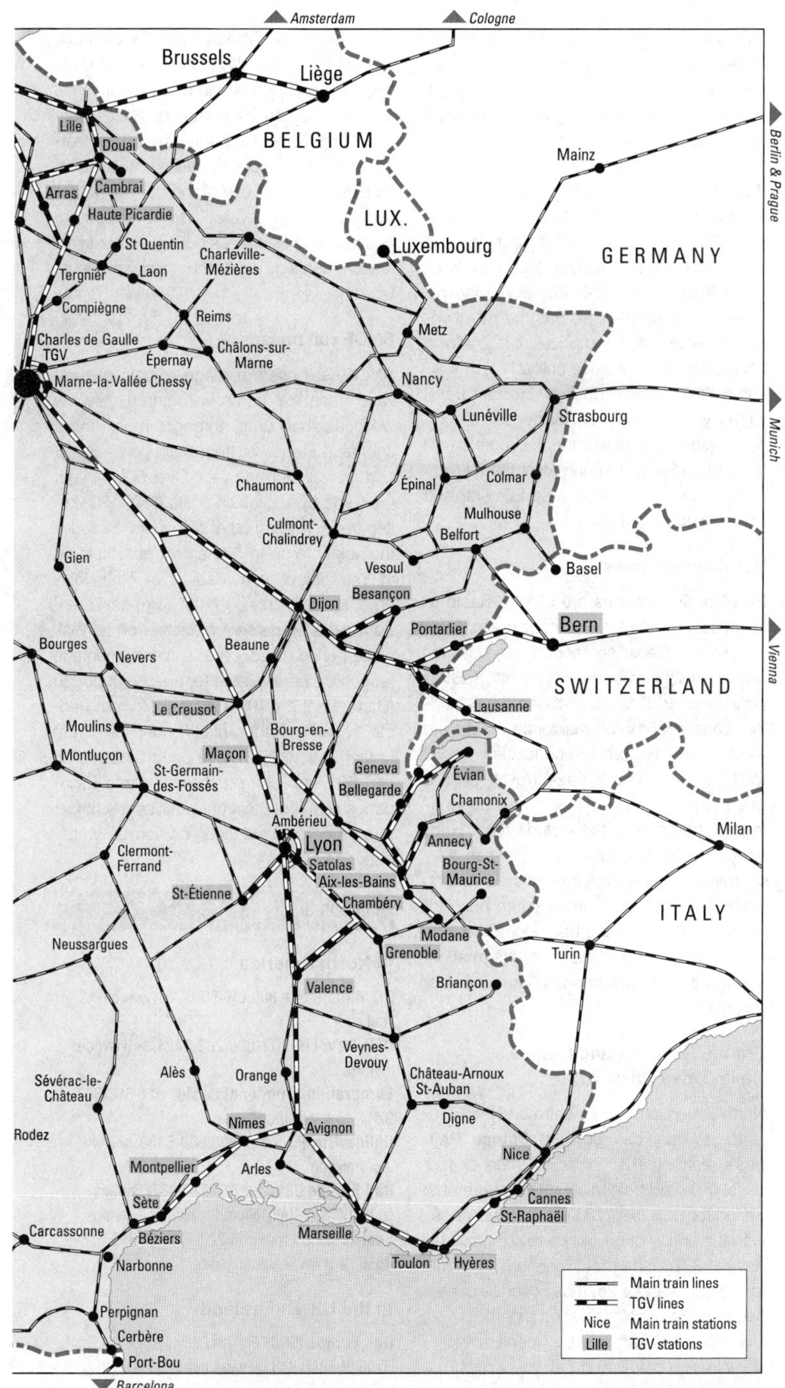
Amsterdam
Cologne
Brussels
Liège
BELGIUM
LUX.
Luxembourg
GERMANY
Mainz
Berlin & Prague
Lille
Douai
Arras
Cambrai
Haute Picardie
St Quentin
Tergnier
Laon
Charleville-Mézières
Compiègne
Reims
Charles de Gaulle TGV
Épernay
Châlons-sur-Marne
Marne-la-Vallée Chessy
Metz
Nancy
Lunéville
Strasbourg
Munich
Chaumont
Épinal
Colmar
Mulhouse
Culmont-Chalindrey
Belfort
Basel
Gien
Vesoul
Besançon
Dijon
Pontarlier
Bern
Vienna
Bourges
Nevers
Beaune
SWITZERLAND
Le Creusot
Lausanne
Moulins
Bourg-en-Bresse
Montluçon
Maçon
Geneva
Évian
St-Germain-des-Fossés
Bellegarde
Chamonix
Ambérieu
Lyon
Annecy
Milan
Clermont-Ferrand
Satolas
Bourg-St-Maurice
Aix-les-Bains
St-Étienne
Chambéry
ITALY
Neussargues
Modane
Grenoble
Turin
Valence
Briançon
Veynes-Devouy
Sévérac-le-Château
Alès
Orange
Château-Arnoux St-Auban
Rodez
Digne
Nîmes
Avignon
Nice
Montpellier
Arles
Cannes
Sète
St-Raphaël
Carcassonne
Marseille
Béziers
Toulon
Hyères
Narbonne
Main train lines
TGV lines
Nice Main train stations
Lille TGV stations
Perpignan
Cerbère
Port-Bou
Barcelona

together in zones, of which France is in Zone E along with Belgium, the Netherlands and Luxembourg.

The following prices are given first for travellers under the age of 26, then for those older than 26. Passes are available for 16 days for travel within one zone (£159/£223 or €240/€340), for 22 days in two zones (£215/£303 or €325/€460) and for one month covering all zones (£295/£415 or €445/€630). The Inter-Rail website (ⓦwww.raileurope.co.uk/inter-rail) has the most up-to-date information and prices; it also allows UK residents to purchase online.

Inter-Rail passes do not include travel within your country of residence, though pass holders are eligible for discounts on rail fares to and from the border of the relevant zone as well as reductions on Eurostar and cross-Channel ferries.

EuroDomino pass

EuroDomino passes are only available to European residents who have been living in Europe at least six months. The passes provide unlimited travel in one of 28 European and North African countries, excluding your country of residence. They are available for first and second class travel for between 3 and 8 days' travel within a one-month period; prices vary depending on the country, but include most high-speed train supplements. You can buy as many separate country passes as you want. There's a discounted youth price for those under 26, and a half-price child (age 4–11) fare. For up-to-date fare information, see the ⓦwww.raileurope.co.uk/railpasses/eurodomino.htm.

France Railpass and France Rail'n'Drive Pass

North Americans and Australian/New Zealand travellers can buy the **France Railpass**, entitling the holder to three or four days' unlimited train travel over a one-month period for US$252/218 (first-/second-class), with the option of buying up to six additional days at $32/28 per day. There are discounts for travellers under 26, those over 60 and for two or more people travelling together.

North American visitors considering a combination of rail and car travel might be interested in the **France Rail'n'Drive pass**, valid for two to five days' unlimited first-class rail travel and two or more days' car rental over the course of a month. Prices vary according to the number of travel days, category of car, number of adults and so forth. Various packages combining car hire with a rail pass are also available to travellers from Australia and New Zealand; for further information, contact one of the specialist agents listed below.

SNCF rail passes

SNCF itself offers a range of train passes, which can be purchased online (ⓦwww.voyages-sncf.com), through most travel agents in France or from main *gares SNCF* and are valid for one year. Over-60s can get the Carte Senior, which costs €50 for unlimited travel. Among other discounts, it entitles the holder to up to 50 percent off tickets on TGVs, subject to availability, or other journeys starting during "blue" (off-peak) periods and a 25 percent reduction on normal, white-period fares. The same percentage reductions are available for anyone under 26 (Carte 12–25; €49) and for up to four people travelling with a child under 12 (Carte Enfant Plus; €65). Those aged between 26 and 59 years can purchase a Carte Escapades (€99), but this only entitles the holder to a 25 percent reduction on normal, white-period fares.

Rail contacts

In North America

CIT Rail US ⓣ1-800/CIT-TOUR, ⓦwww.cit-rail.com.
DER Travel US ⓣ1-800/283-2424, ⓦwww.der.com/rail.
Europrail International Canada ⓣ1-888/667-9734, ⓦwww.europrail.net.
Online Travel US ⓣ1-800/660-5300, ⓦwww.eurorail.com.
Rail Europe US ⓣ1-877/257-2887, Canada ⓣ1-800/361-RAIL, ⓦwww.raileurope.com/us.
ScanTours US ⓣ1-800/223-7226 or 310/636-4656, ⓦwww.scantours.com.

In the UK and Ireland

Rail Europe (SNCF French Railways) UK ⓣ0870/5848 848, ⓦwww.raileurope.co.uk.

In Australia

CIT World Travel Australia ⓣ02/9267 1255 or 03/9650 5510, ⓦwww.cittravel.com.au.
Rail Plus Australia ⓣ1300/555 003 or 03/9642 8644, ⓦwww.railplus.com.au.
Trailfinders Australia ⓣ02/9247 7666 or ⓣ03/9600 3022, ⓦwww.trailfinder.com.au.

By bus

The most convenient **bus services** are those run as an extension of rail links by SNCF, which join SNCF stations and serve areas not accessible by rail. In addition to SNCF buses, private, municipal and departmental buses can be useful for local and some cross-country journeys, though if you want to see much outside the main towns be prepared for early starts and careful planning – the timetable is often constructed to suit working, market and school hours. All buses are, generally speaking, cheaper and slower than trains.

Larger towns usually have a *gare routière* (bus station), often next to the *gare SNCF*. However, the private bus companies don't always work together and you'll frequently find them leaving from an array of different points (the local tourist office should be able to help locate them).

By air

With the possible exception of Corsica, you're not likely to need to fly to get around France, though if you've come from North America, Australia or New Zealand you may be able to get a good deal on add-on **flights** (see p.34 & p.37). Air France operates the most routes within the country, although competition is hotting up, with easyJet running a few cut-price flights out of Paris to regional centres and with the addition of a number of small, independent airlines. You may also be able to pick up an internal flight on some of the foreign airlines (such as Lufthansa) whose routes include intermediate stops within France.

By ferry

The majority of France's coastal islands, which are concentrated around Brittany and the Côte d'Azur, can only be reached by **ferry**. Small local companies run routes whose timetables and prices vary according to season. Some routes have a reduced schedule or cease to operate completely in winter months, while in high season booking ahead is recommended on all but the most frequent services. Information on these local companies is listed in the Guide. SNCM and Corsica Ferries offer services to Corsica (see p.1216).

By car

Driving in France can be a real pleasure. The network of autoroutes is magnificent and often provides huge, sweeping views of countryside. Congestion, because of the size and shape of the country, is rarely a problem. This is equally true of the older main roads, or *routes nationales* (marked RN116 or just N116, for example, on signs and maps), and the smaller *routes départementales* (marked with a D). Do not shun these latter: you can often travel for kilometres across country, seeing few other cars, on a road as broad and well maintained as a major road.

Of course, there are times when it's wiser not to drive: most obviously in big urban agglomerations, around major seaside resorts in high season and at peak holiday migrations such as the beginning and end of the month-long August holiday and the notoriously congested weekends nearest July 14 and August 15. Cost of fuel can also be a discouraging factor.

In addition, there's a charge for the use of the **autoroutes** themselves, payable in cash or by credit card at the frequent tollgates (*péages*). For an idea of the costs involved, the tolls from Paris to Nice or Bordeaux is around €60 and €45 respectively, while the journey from Calais to Paris or Reims costs roughly €16.

Although *autoroutes* are expensive, they are the only realistic way of covering large distances in a single day. If you have more time, the best way to avoid them is to follow the alternative routes (known as *itinéraire bis*, or just *bis*) signposted with special green "Bison Futé" road signs across the country.

All the major car manufacturers have garages and service stations in France, which can help if you run into mechanical difficulties. You can find them listed in the Yellow Pages of the phone book under "Garages d'automobiles"; for **breakdowns**, look under "Dépannages". If you have an accident or break-in, you should contact the local police – keeping a copy of their report – in order to make an insurance claim. Within Europe, most car **insurance** policies cover taking your car to France; check with your insurer while planning your trip. However, you're advised to take out extra cover for motoring assistance in case your car breaks down; contact the motoring organizations listed opposite for a quote.

Note that **petrol stations** in rural areas tend to be few and far between, and those that do exist usually open only during normal shop hours – don't count on being able to buy petrol at night and on Sunday. Some stations are equipped with 24-hr pumps, but these only work with French bank cards.

Rules of the road

US, Canadian, Australian, New Zealand and all EU **driving licences** are valid in France, though an International Driver's Licence makes life easier. The minimum driving age is 18 and you must hold a full (not a provisional) licence. Drivers are required to carry their licence with them when driving, and you should also have the insurance papers with you in the car. If the vehicle is rented, its registration document (*carte grise*) must also be carried.

Since the French drive on the right, drivers of right-hand drive British cars must adjust their **headlights** to dip to the right. This is most easily done by sticking on black glare deflectors, which can be bought at most motor accessory shops and at the Channel ferry ports or the Eurostar terminal. It is more complicated if your car is fitted with modern High-Intensity Discharge (HID) or halogen-type lights; check with your dealer about how to adjust these well in advance.

By law all non-French cars must display their **national identification letters** ("GB" etc), either on the new Euro-style number plates or by means of a sticker. It is also a legal requirement that cars not fitted with flashing **warning lights** must carry a red warning triangle (and it's highly recommended to carry one in any case, since lights can fail or you might break down on a blind corner). You are also strongly advised to carry a spare set of bulbs, a fire extinguisher and a first-aid kit. **Seat belts** are compulsory and children under 10 years are not allowed to sit in the front of the car. It is illegal to use a hand-held **mobile phone** while driving.

The law of *priorité à droite* – **giving way** to traffic coming from your right, even when it is coming from a minor road – is being phased out as it's a major cause of accidents. However, it still applies on some roads in built-up areas and the occasional roundabout, so it pays to be vigilant at junctions. A sign showing a yellow diamond on a white background indicates that you have right of way, while the same sign with a diagonal black slash across it warns you that vehicles emerging from the right have priority. Stop signs mean you must stop completely; *Cédez le passage* means "Give way".

Unless otherwise indicated **speed limits** are: 130kph (80mph) on *autoroutes*; 110kph (68mph) on dual carriageways; 90kph (55mph) on other roads; and 50kph (31mph) in towns. In wet weather, and for drivers with less than two years' experience, these limits are 110kph (68mph), 100kph (62mph) and 80kph (50mph) respectively, while the town limit remains constant. The police are cracking down hard on speeding in a bid

Road information

For up-to-the-minute **information** regarding traffic jams and road works on *autoroutes* throughout France, ring ⓣ08.92.68.10.77 (€0.34/min; French only) or consult the bilingual website ⓦwww.autoroutes.fr. Traffic information for other roads can be obtained from the Bison Futé recorded information service (ⓣ08.26.02.20.22; €0.15/min) or their website ⓦwww.bison-fute.equipement.gouv.fr; both services are in French only.

to reduce the shockingly high accident rate in France. Radars are being installed along main roads and there are stiff penalties for **driving violations**, which can mean fines of up to €9000 and a suspended licence. The standard fine for exceeding the speed limit by 20kph (12mph), for example, is €90; above 40kph (25mph) you will not only be fined but will also have to go to court. The **alcohol limit** is 0.05 percent (50 mg per litre of blood) and random breath tests are increasingly common.

Car rental

Car rental in France costs upwards of €70 a day and €250 for a week, but can be cheaper if arranged before you leave home or online. You'll find the big firms represented at airports and in most major towns and cities; addresses are detailed throughout the Guide. Renting from airports normally includes a surcharge. Local firms can be cheaper but most don't offer one-way rentals and you need to check the small print carefully.

The **cost** of car rental includes the basic legally necessary car insurance. Under the standard contract you are liable for an excess (*franchise*) of around €500 (for the smallest car) for any damage to the vehicle – most firms accept a valid credit card rather than cash. You should return the car with a full tank of fuel or face paying an exorbitant fuel charge.

North Americans and Australians in particular should be forewarned that it's difficult to arrange the rental of a car with automatic transmission; if you can't drive a manual you should try to book an automatic well in advance, possibly before you leave home, and be prepared to pay a much higher price for it.

Most **rental companies** will only deal with people over 25 unless an extra insurance premium, typically around €20–23 per day, is paid (but you still must be over 21 and have driven for at least one year). OTU Voyages (ⓣ08.20.81.78.17, €0.12/min, ⓦwww.otu.fr), the student travel agency, can arrange car rental for young drivers, with prices beginning at €110 for a weekend.

Car rental agencies

In Britain

Avis ⓣ0870/606 0100, ⓦwww.avis.co.uk.
Budget ⓣ01442/276 266, ⓦwww.budget.co.uk.
Europcar ⓣ0870/607 5000, ⓦwww.europcar.co.uk.
Hertz ⓣ0870/844 8844, ⓦwww.hertz.co.uk.
Holiday Autos ⓣ0870/400 0099, ⓦwww.holidayautos.co.uk.
National ⓣ0870/536 5365, ⓦwww.nationalcar.co.uk.
Suncars ⓣ0870/500 5566, ⓦwww.suncars.com.
Thrifty ⓣ01494/751 600, ⓦwww.thrifty.co.uk.

In North America

Alamo US ⓣ1-800/462-5266, ⓦwww.alamo.com. **Auto Europe** US and Canada ⓣ1-888/223-5555, ⓦwww.autoeurope.com.
Avis US ⓣ1-800/230-4898, Canada ⓣ1-800/272-5871, ⓦwww.avis.com.
Budget US ⓣ1-800/527-0700, Canada ⓣ1-800/472-3325, ⓦwww.budget.com.
Dollar US ⓣ1-800/800-3665, ⓦwww.dollar.com.
Europcar US & Canada ⓣ1-877/940 6900, ⓦwww.europcar.com.
Europe by Car US ⓣ1-800/223-1516, ⓦwww.europebycar.com.

Buy-back leasing schemes

If you are not resident in an EU country and will be touring France for between 17 days and six months, it's worth investigating the special **buy-back leasing schemes** operated by Peugeot ("Peugeot Open Europe") and Renault ("Renault Eurodrive"). Under these deals, you purchase a new car tax-free and the manufacturer guarantees to buy it back from you for an agreed price at the end of the period. In general, the difference between the purchase and repurchase price works out considerably less per day than the equivalent cost of car hire. Further details are available from Peugeot and Renault dealers and online at ⓦwww.peugeot-openeruope.com and ⓦwww.eurodrive.renault.com.

Hertz US ⓣ1-800/654-3131, Canada ⓣ1-800/263-0600, ⓦwww.hertz.com.
National ⓣ1-800/962-7070, ⓦwww.nationalcar.com.
Thrifty US and Canada ⓣ1-800/847-4389, ⓦwww.thrifty.com.

In Ireland

Argus Republic of Ireland ⓣ01/490 4444, ⓦwww.argus-rentacar.com.
Avis Northern Ireland ⓣ028/9024 0404, Republic of Ireland ⓣ021/428 1111, ⓦwww.avis.ie.
Budget Republic of Ireland ⓣ09/0662 7711, ⓦwww.budget.ie.
Cosmo Thrifty Northern Ireland ⓣ028/9445 2565, ⓦwww.thrifty.co.uk.
Europcar Northern Ireland ⓣ028/9442 3444, Republic of Ireland ⓣ01/614 2888, ⓦwww.europcar.ie.
Hertz Republic of Ireland ⓣ01/676 7476, ⓦwww.hertz.ie.
Holiday Autos Republic of Ireland ⓣ01/872 9366, ⓦwww.holidayautos.ie.
SIXT Republic of Ireland ⓣ1850/206 088, ⓦwww.irishcarrentals.ie.
Suncars Republic of Ireland ⓣ1850/201-416, ⓦwww.suncars.ie.
Thrifty Republic of Ireland ⓣ1800/515 800, ⓦwww.thrifty.ie.

In Australia

Avis ⓣ13 63 33 or 02/9353 9000, ⓦwww.avis.com.au.
Budget ⓣ1300/362 848, ⓦwww.budget.com.au.
Europcar ⓣ1300/131 390, ⓦwww.deltaeuropcar.com.au.
Hertz ⓣ13 30 39, or 03/9698 2555, ⓦwww.hertz.com.au.
Holiday Autos ⓣ1300/554 432, ⓦwww.holidayautos.com.au.
National ⓣ13 10 45, ⓦwww.nationalcar.com.au.
Thrifty ⓣ1300/367 227, ⓦwww.thrifty.com.au.

In New Zealand

Apex ⓣ0800/93 95 97 or 03/379 6897, ⓦwww.apexrentals.co.nz.
Avis ⓣ09/526 2847 or 0800/655 111, ⓦwww.avis.co.nz.
Budget ⓣ09/976 2222 or 0800/652-227, ⓦwww.budget.co.nz.
Hertz ⓣ0800/654 321, ⓦwww.hertz.co.nz.
Holiday Autos ⓣ0800/144 040, ⓦwww.holidayautos.co.nz.
National ⓣ0800/800 115 or 03/366-5574, ⓦwww.nationalcar.co.nz.
Thrifty ⓣ09/309 0111, ⓦwww.thrifty.co.nz.

Motoring organizations

In the UK and Ireland

AA UK ⓣ0870/600 0371, ⓦwww.theaa.com.
AA Ireland ⓣ01/617 9999, ⓦwww.aaireland.ie.
RAC UK ⓣ0800/550 055, ⓦwww.rac.co.uk.

In North America

AAA ⓣ1-800/AAA-HELP, ⓦwww.aaa.com.
CAA ⓣ613/247-0117, ⓦwww.caa.ca.

In Australia and New Zealand

AAA Australia ⓣ02/6247 7311, ⓦwww.aaa.asn.au.
New Zealand AA New Zealand ⓣ0800/500 444, ⓦwww.nzaa.co.nz.

By scooter and motorbike

Scooters are relatively easy to find and, though they're not built for long-distance travel, are ideal for pottering around local areas. Places that rent out bicycles often also rent out scooters; you can expect to pay in the region of €40 a day for a 50cc machine, less for longer periods. No licence is needed for bikes of 50cc and under, but for anything larger you'll need a valid **motorbike** licence. Rental prices for a motorbike are around €55 a day for a 125cc bike; expect to leave a hefty deposit by cash or credit card too – over €1000 is the norm – which you may lose in the event of damage or theft. Remember take along your passport or some other form of photographic identity. **Crash helmets** are compulsory on all bikes, whatever the size, and the **headlight** must be switched on at all times. You are recommended to carry a first-aid kit and a set of spare bulbs.

By hitching

If you're intent on **hitching**, you'll have to rely almost exclusively on car drivers, as lorries very rarely give lifts. Even so, it won't be easy. Looking as clean and respectable as possible makes a very big difference, as conversations with French drivers soon make clear. Experience suggests that hitching the less-frequented D-roads is much quicker, while in country areas a rucksack and hiking gear will help procure a lift from sympathetic drivers.

Autoroutes are a special case. Hitching on the *autoroute* itself is illegal, but you can make excellent time going from one service station to another. Alternatively, tollgates (péages) are the second best (and legal) option, but ordinary approach roads can be disastrous. Look out for the free *autoroute* maps showing all the service stations, tollgates, exits, etc.

For major long-distance rides, and for a greater sense of safety, you might consider using the **national hitching organization**, Allostop, 30 rue Pierre-Sémard, 75009 Paris (Ⓣ01.53.20.42.42, Ⓦwww.allostop.net). The cost comprises a registration fee (from €4.50 for a journey under 201km up to a maximum of €10 if more than 500km, or you can buy a €36 membership card which is good for eight trips over two years), plus a fixed contribution per passenger depending on the distance covered; €5 for up to 200km, €16 for 500km and so forth.

By bicycle

Bicycles (*vélos*) have high status in France, where cyclists are given respect both on the roads and as customers at restaurants and hotels. In addition, local authorities are actively promoting cycling, not only with city cycle lanes, but comprehensive networks linking rural areas (frequently utilizing disused railways). Most towns have well-stocked **repair shops**, where parts are normally cheaper than in Britain or the US. However, if you're using a foreign-made bike with non-standard metric wheels, it's a good idea to carry spare tyres.

The **train** network runs various schemes for cyclists, all of them covered by the free leaflet *Train et Vélo*, available from most stations. Trains marked with a bicycle in the timetable and a number of TGVs (listed in the above booklet) allow you to take a bike free either in the dedicated bike racks or in the luggage van as long as there's space; in the latter case, it's a good idea to reserve a slot several days in advance during busy periods, though this will cost you €10. Otherwise, you can take your dismantled bike, packed in a carrier, on TGVs and other trains with sufficiently large luggage racks. Another option is

A cycling vocabulary

to adjust	*régler*	inner tube	*la chambre à air*
axle	*l'axe*	loose	*déserré*
ball-bearing	*le roulement à billes*	to lower	*baisser*
battery	*la pile*	mudguard	*le garde-boue*
bent	*tordu*	panier	*le panier*
bicycle	*le vélo*	pedal	*le pédale*
bottom bracket	*le logement du pédalier*	pump	*la pompe*
brake cable	*le cable*	puncture	*la crevaison*
brakes	*les freins*	rack	*le porte-bagages*
broken	*cassé*	to raise	*remonter*
bulb	*l'ampoule*	to repair	*réparer*
chain	*la chaîne*	saddle	*la selle*
cotter pin	*la clavette*	to screw	*visser/serrer*
to deflate	*dégonfler*	spanner	*la clef*
derailleur	*le dérailleur*	spoke	*le rayon*
frame	*le cadre*	to straighten	*redresser*
gears	*les vitesses*	stuck	*coincé*
grease	*la graisse*	tight	*serré*
handlebars	*le guidon*	toe clips	*les cale-pieds*
to inflate	*gonfler*	tyre	*le pneu*
		wheel	*la roue*

to send your bike parcelled up as registered luggage for a fee of €39; delivery should take two days, bearing in mind that the service doesn't operate at weekends. **Eurostar** allows you to take your bicycle as part of your baggage allowance provided it's dismantled and packed in a bag no more than 120cm by 90cm (phone ⓣ08702/649 899 for further details). However, they encourage people to send their bikes unaccompanied with Eurostar's registered baggage service, Esprit Europe (ⓣ08705/850 850, ⓦwww.espriteurope.co.uk) for £20 one way, with a guaranteed arrival time of 24 hours; you can register your bike, which does not need to be dismantled, up to 24 hours before departure. **Ferries** usually take bikes free (though you may need to register it), as do **airlines** such as British Airways and Air France, while some no-frills airlines charge – remember to check when making your booking.

Bikes – usually mountain bikes (*vélos tout terrain* or VTT) – are often available to **rent** from campsites and hostels, as well as from specialist cycle shops and some tourist offices at around €15 per day. The bikes are often not insured, however, and you will be presented with the bill for its replacement if it's stolen or damaged; check your travel insurance policy for cover.

As for **maps**, a minimum requirement is the IGN 1:100,000 series (see p.42) – the smallest scale that carries contours. The UK's national cyclists' association, the CTC (ⓣ0870/873 0060, ⓦwww.ctc.org.uk), can suggest routes and supply advice for members (£30.50 a year or £49.25 for a family of four, and £11 for under 26 years). They run a particularly good insurance scheme. Companies offering specialist bike touring holidays are listed on pp.33, 35 & 38.

By boat

With over 7000km of navigable rivers and canals, **boating** can be one of the best and most relaxed ways of exploring France. Except on parts of the Moselle, there's no charge for use of the waterways, and you can travel without a permit for up to six months in a year. For information on maximum dimensions, documentation, regulations and so forth, contact Voies Navigables de France (VNF), 175 rue Ludovic-Boutleux, 62408 Béthune (ⓣ03.21.63.24.24, ⓦwww.vnf.fr), which has information (some of it in English) on boating throughout France, and details of firms that rent out boats. British companies organizing boating holidays include Hoseasons (ⓣ01502/502 588, ⓦwww.hoseasons.co.uk) and Crown Blue Line (ⓣ01603/630 513, ⓦwww.crownblueline.com), while the France-based Locaboat (ⓣ03.86.91.72.72, ⓦwww.locaboat.com) specialize in *pénichettes*, scaled down replicas of commercial barges. Expect to pay between €800 and €2000 per week, depending on the season and level of comfort, for a 4–6 person boat. Details of North American and Australian firms offering boating holidays can be found on p.35 and p.38. For a full list of rental firms operating in France contact the Fédération des Industries Nautiques, Port de Javel Haut, 75015 Paris (ⓣ01.44.37.04.00, ⓦwww.france-nautic.com).

The principal **areas** for boating are Brittany, Burgundy, Picardy-Flanders, Alsace and Champagne. Brittany's canals join up with the Loire, but this is only navigable as far as Angers. Other waterways permit numerous permutations, including joining up via the Rhône and Saône with the Canal du Midi in Languedoc and then northwestwards to Bordeaux and the Atlantic. The eighteenth-century Canal de Bourgogne and 300-year-old Canal du Midi are fascinating examples of early canal engineering. The latter, together with its continuation the Canal du Sète à Rhône, passes within easy reach of several interesting areas.

The through-journey from the **Channel to the Mediterranean** requires some planning. The Canal de Bourgogne has an inordinate number of locks, while other waterways demand considerable skill and experience – the Rhône and Saône rivers, for example, have tricky currents. The most direct route is from Le Havre to just beyond Paris, then south either on Canal du Loing et de Briare or Canal du Nivernais to the Canal Latéral à la Loire, which you follow as far as Digoin in southern Burgundy, where it crosses the River Loire and meets the Canal du Centre. You follow the latter as far as Châlon, where you continue south on the Saône and Rhône until you reach the Mediterranean at Port St-Louis in the Camargue.

Accommodation

At most times of the year, you can turn up in any French town and find a room, or a place in a campsite. Booking a couple of nights in advance can be reassuring, however, as it saves you the effort of trudging round and ensures that you know what you'll be paying; many hoteliers, campsite managers and hostel managers speak at least a little English. In most places, you'll be able to get a simple double for €30 or so, though expect to pay around €45 for a reasonable level of comfort. Paris is more expensive, however, with equivalent rates of roughly €40 and €80. We've detailed a selection of hotels throughout the Guide, and given a price range for each (see box overleaf); as a general rule the areas around train stations have the highest density of cheap hotels.

Problems may arise between mid-July and the end of August, when the French take their own vacations en masse. During this period, hotel and hostel accommodation can be hard to come by, particularly in the coastal resorts, and you may find yourself falling back on local tourist offices for help. In addition, big cities can be difficult throughout the year: we've given a greater range of possibilities for them in the Guide and very detailed accommodation listings for Paris, the worst case of all.

Some tourist offices offer a **booking service**, although they can't guarantee rooms at a particular price, and all can provide lists of hotels, hostels, campsites and bed-and-breakfast possibilities. With **campsites**, you can be more relaxed about finding an empty space, unless you're touring with a caravan or camper van or looking for a place on the Côte d'Azur.

Hotels

Most French hotels are **graded** from zero to five stars. The price more or less corresponds to the number of stars, though the system is a little haphazard, having more to do with ratios of bathrooms-per-guest and so forth than genuine quality, and some unclassified and single-star hotels can actually be very good. What you get for your money varies enormously between establishments. For under €30, there won't be much soundproofing and the showers (*douches*) and toilets (WC or *toilettes*) may be communal (*dans le palier*). However, you should have your own washbasin (*lavabo*), often partitioned off from the rest of the room in an area referred to as a *cabinet de toilette*. The shared showers down the hall are usually included in the price but very occasionally you'll be charged a couple of euro per shower, in which case it might be worth upgrading to an en-suite room. Over €30 should get you a room with its own bath or shower though not necessarily a toilet, and, though the decor may not be anything to write home about, comfortable furniture. For around €45 you should expect a proper, separate bathroom (*salle de bain*) and TV, while at over €70, you'll find something approaching luxury. Hotels with one star or above have a telephone in the rooms, though some phones can only receive calls. **Single rooms** – if the hotel has any – are only marginally cheaper than doubles, so sharing always slashes costs, especially since most hotels willingly provide rooms with **extra beds** for three or more people at good discounts.

Big cities have a good variety of cheap establishments; in small towns or villages where the choice is limited, you may not be so lucky. Swanky resorts, particularly those on the Côte d'Azur, have very high July and August prices, but are still less expensive than Paris, which is far more expensive than the rest of the country. If you're staying more than three days in a hotel it's often possible to negotiate a lower price, particularly out of season.

Accommodation price categories

All the hotels and guesthouses listed in this book have been price-coded according to the following scale. The prices quoted are for the cheapest available double room in high season, although remember that many of the cheap places will also have more expensive rooms with en-suite facilities. In the case of a hostel, we give the price of a dormitory bed.

❶ Under €30	❹ €55–70	❼ €100–125
❷ €30–40	❺ €70–85	❽ €125–150
❸ €40–55	❻ €85–100	❾ Over €150

Breakfast, which is not normally included, will add between €5 and €15 per person to a bill, sometimes more – though there is no obligation to take it. The cost of eating **dinner** in a hotel's restaurant can be a more important factor to bear in mind when deciding where to stay. It's actually illegal for hotels to insist on your taking half-board (*demi-pension*), though you'll come across some that do, especially during the summer peak. This is not always such a bad thing, however, since the food may be excellent and you can sometimes get a real bargain.

Note that many family-run hotels close for two or three weeks a year in low season. In smaller towns and villages they may also close for one or two nights a week, usually Sunday or Monday. Details are given where relevant in the Guide, but dates change from year to year and some places may decide to close for a few days in low season if they have no bookings. The best precaution is to phone ahead to be sure.

A very useful option, especially if you're driving and if you're looking for somewhere late at night, are the **chain hotels** located at motorway exits and on the outskirts of major towns. They may be soulless, but you can count on a decent and reliable standard. Among the cheapest (from around €26 for a three-person room with communal toilets and showers) and biggest is the one-star Formule 1 chain (Ⓣ08.92.68.56.85, €0.34 per min; Ⓦwww.hotelformule1.com). Other budget chains include B&B (Ⓣ08.92.78.29.29, €0.34 per min; Ⓦwww.hotel-bb.com) and the slightly more comfortable Première Classe (Ⓣ01.64.62.46.00, Ⓦwww.premiereclasse.fr) and Etap Hôtel (Ⓣ08.92.68.89.00, €0.34 per min; Ⓦwww.etaphotel.com). More upmarket but still affordable chains are Ibis (Ⓣ08.92.68.66.86, €0.34 per min; Ⓦwww.ibishotel.com) and Campanile (Ⓣ01.64.62.46.00, Ⓦwww.campanile.fr), where en-suite rooms with satellite TV and direct-dial phones cost from around €40–50.

Aside from the chains, there are a number of well-respected **hotel federations** in France. The biggest and most useful of these is **Logis de France** (88 av d'Italie, 75013 Paris; Ⓣ01.45.84.83.84, Ⓦwww.logis-de-france.fr), an association of over 3500 hotels nationwide. They produce a free annual guide, which you can obtain from your nearest French tourist office (see p.40), from Logis de France itself or from member hotels. Two other, more upmarket federations worth mentioning are Châteaux & Hôtels de France (30 rue des Jeûneurs, 75002 Paris; Ⓣ01.72.72.92.02, Ⓦwww.chateauxhotels.com) and the Relais du Silence (17 rue d'Ouessant, 75015 Paris; Ⓣ01.44.49.90.00, Ⓦwww.silencehotel.com).

Over thirty cities in France participate in the "Bon Weekend en Villes" programme, whereby you get two nights for the price of one at participating hotels. In most cases the offer is restricted to the winter period (Nov–March). Further details are available from tourist offices or online at Ⓦwww.bon-weekend-en-villes.com.

Bed and breakfast and self-catering

In country areas, in addition to standard hotels, you will come across *chambres d'hôtes*, **bed-and-breakfast accommodation** in someone's house, château or farm. Though the quality varies widely, on the whole standards have improved dramatically in recent years and the best can offer more character and greater value for money than an equivalently priced hotel. If you're lucky, the owners may also provide traditional home-cooking and a great insight into French life. In general, prices range between €30 and €70 for two people including breakfast; payment is almost always expected in cash. Some offer meals on request (*tables d'hôtes*), usually evenings only.

If you're planning to stay a week or more in any one place it might be worth considering renting **self-catering accommodation**. This will generally consist of self-contained country cottages known as *gîtes* or *gîtes ruraux*. Many *gîtes* are in converted barns or farm outbuildings, though some can be quite grand. "Gîtes Panda" are *gîtes* located in a national park or other protected area and are run on environmentally friendly lines.

You can get lists of both *gîtes* and *chambres d'hôtes* from the government-funded agency **Gîtes de France**, 59 rue St-Lazare, Paris 75439 (Ⓣ01.49.70.75.75, Ⓦwww.gites-de-france.fr), which every year publishes a number of national guides, such as *Nouveaux Gîtes Ruraux*, listing new addresses, *Chambres et Tables d'Hôtes* and *Chambres d'Hôtes de Charme* (all around €20), and more comprehensive departmental guides which include photos (around €10 to €20). All these guides are available online or from the Paris headquarters and departmental offices of Gîtes de France, as well as from local bookstores and tourist offices. Tourist offices will also have lists of places in their area which are not affiliated to Gîtes de France.

You'll also find self-catering accommodation, mostly foreign-owned, advertised on the Internet: Ⓦwww.frenchconnections.co.uk, Ⓦwww.cheznous.com and Ⓦwww.bvdirect.co.uk are well-established sites; or try one of the agents listed in the Travel Shop section of the Maison de la France website, Ⓦwww.franceguide.com). British visitors should look at the classified ads in the Sunday newspapers (the *Observer* and *Sunday Times*, mainly). Another option is to contact one of the holiday firms that market accommodation/travel packages (see pp.33, 35 and 38 for a brief selection of these).

Youth hostels, foyers and student accommodation

At between €8 and €15 per night for a dormitory bed, sometimes with breakfast thrown in, **youth hostels** – *auberges de jeunesse* – are invaluable for single travellers on a budget. Some now offer rooms, occasionally en-suite, but they don't necessarily work out cheaper than hotels – particularly if you've had to pay a taxi fare to reach them, for example. However, many allow you to cut costs by eating in their cheap canteens, while in a few you can prepare your own meals in the communal kitchens. Many hostels are also beautifully sited.

Slightly confusingly, there are three rival French **hostelling associations**: the main two being the Fédération Unie des Auberges de Jeunesse (FUAJ), or the much smaller Ligue Française pour les Auberges de Jeunesse (LFAJ); see below for contact details. There are now also several independent hostels, particularly in Paris, where dorm beds cost €15–20 with breakfast thrown in, though these tend to be party places with an emphasis on good times rather than sleep.

Normally, to stay at FUAJ or LFAJ hostels you must show a current Hostelling International (HI) **membership card**. It's usually cheaper and easier to join before you leave home, provided your national Youth Hostel association (see below) is a full member of HI. Alternatively, you can purchase an HI card in certain French hostels for €15.25 (€10.70 for those under 26 years), or buy individual "welcome stamps" at a rate of €2.90 per night; after six nights you are entitled to the HI card.

A few large towns provide hostel accommodation in Foyers des Jeunes Travailleurs, **residential hostels** for young workers and students, where you can usually get a private room for upwards of €10. On the whole they are more luxurious than youth hostels and normally have a good cafeteria or canteen.

During July & August, there's also the possibility of staying in **student accommodation** in university towns and cities at prices similar to hostels. Contact CROUS, 39 av Georges-Bernanos, 75231 Paris

(ⓣ01.40.51.55.55, ⓦwww.crous-paris.fr) for further information.

Youth hostel associations

In France

Fédération Unie des Auberges de Jeunesse (FUAJ) 27 rue Pajol, 75018 Paris ⓣ01.44.89.87.27, ⓦwww.fuaj.org.
Ligue Française pour les Auberges de Jeunesse (LFAJ) 67 rue Vergniaud Bat K, 75013 Paris ⓣ01.44.16.78.78, ⓦwww.auberges-de-jeunesse.com.
Union des Centres de Recontres Internationales de France (UCRIF) 27 rue de Turbigo BP 6407, 75064 Paris ⓣ01.40.26.57.64, ⓦwww.ucrif.asso.fr.

In England and Wales

Youth Hostel Association (YHA) ⓣ0870/770 8868, ⓦwww.yha.org.uk and ⓦwww.iyhf.org. Annual membership £13.50; under-18s £6.70; lifetime £195 (or five annual payments of £41).

In Scotland

Scottish Youth Hostel Association ⓣ0870/155 3255, ⓦwww.syha.org.uk. Annual membership £6, for under-18s £2.50.

In Ireland

Irish Youth Hostel Association ⓣ01/830 4555, ⓦwww.irelandyha.org. Annual membership €25; under-18s €10.50; family €50; lifetime €75.

In Northern Ireland

Hostelling International Northern Ireland ⓣ028/9032 4733, ⓦwww.hini.org.uk. Adult membership £13; under-18s £6; family £25; lifetime £75.

In the US

Hostelling International-American Youth Hostels ⓣ301/495-1240, ⓦwww.hiayh.org. Annual membership for adults (18–55) is $28, for seniors (55 or over) is $18, and for under-18s and groups of ten or more, is free. Life memberships are $250.

In Canada

Hostelling International Canada ⓣ1-800/663 5777 or 613/237 7884, ⓦwww.hihostels.ca. Rather than sell the traditional 1- or 2-year memberships, the association now sells one Individual Adult membership with a 16- to 28-month term. The length of the term depends on when the membership is sold, but a member can receive up to 28 months of membership for just CAN$35+tax. Membership is free for under-18s and you can become a lifetime member for CAN$175.

In Australia

Australia Youth Hostels Association ⓣ02/9261 1111, ⓦwww.yha.com.au. Adult membership rate AUS$52 (under-18s, AUS$19) for the first twelve months and then AUS$37 each year after.

In New Zealand

Youth Hostelling Association New Zealand ⓣ0800/278 299 or 03/379 9970, ⓦwww.yha.co.nz. Adult membership NZ$40 for one year, NZ$60 for two and NZ$80 for three; under-18s free; lifetime NZ$300.

Gîtes d'étape and refuges

In the countryside, another hostel-style alternative exists: **gîtes d'étape**. Aimed primarily at hikers and long-distance bikers, *gîtes d'étape* are often run by the local village or municipality and are less formal than hostels. They provide bunk beds and primitive kitchen and washing facilities from around €10 per person, and are marked on the large-scale IGN walkers' maps and listed in the individual GR Topo-guides (see p.83). In addition, mountain areas are well supplied with **refuge huts**, mostly run by the **Club Alpin Français** (CAF; 24 av de Laumière, 75019 Paris ⓣ01.53.72.87.00, ⓦwww.clubalpin.com) and generally only open in summer. These huts are staffed in hiking season and offer dorm accommodation and meals; they are the only available shelter once you are above the villages. Costs are from between €10 and €15 for the night, half-price if you're a member of a climbing organization affiliated to FCAF. Meals – invariably four courses – cost around €12, which is good value when you consider that in some cases supplies have to be brought up by mule or helicopter.

More **information** can be found in the guides *Gîtes d'Étapes et de Séjours* (€10), published by Gîtes de France (see p.61), and *Refuges et Chalets de Club Alpin Français*, available free from CAF.

Camping

Practically every village and town in France has at least one **campsite** to cater for the thousands of people who spend their holiday under canvas. Most sites open from sometime in April to September or October. The vast majority are graded into four **categories**, from one to four stars, by the local authority. One- and two-star sites are very basic, with toilets and showers (not necessarily with hot water) but little else, and standards of cleanliness are not always brilliant. At the other extreme, four-star sites are far more spacious, have hot-water showers and electrical hook-ups. Most will have a swimming pool, sometimes heated, washing machines, a shop and sports facilities, and will provide refreshments or meals in high season. At three-star sites you can expect a selection of these facilities and less spacious plots. A further designation, **Camping Qualité** (ⓦwww.campingqualite.com), has been introduced to indicate those campsites with particularly high standards of hygiene, service and privacy, while the **Clef Verte** (ⓦwww.laclefverte.org) label is awarded to sites run along environmentally friendly lines.

Though **charging systems** vary, most places charge per site and per person, usually including a car, while others apply a global figure. As a rough guide a family of four with a tent and car should expect to pay from €10 per day at a one-star site, rising to €30 or more at a four-star. In peak season and if you plan to spend a week or more at a site, it's wise to book ahead, and note that many of the big sites now have caravans and even chalet bungalows for rent.

For those who really like to get away from it, **camping à la ferme** – on somebody's farm – is a good, simple option. Lists of sites are available at local tourist offices.

If you're planning to do a lot of camping, an **international camping carnet** is a good investment. The carnet gives discounts at member sites and serves as useful identification. Many campsites will take it instead of making you surrender your passport during your stay, and it covers you for third-party insurance when camping. In the **US and Canada**, the carnet is available from home motoring organizations, or from Family Campers and RVers (FCRV; ⓣ1-800/245-9755 or 716/668-6242, ⓦwww.fcrv.org). FCRV annual membership costs US$25, and the carnet an additional US$10. In the **UK and Ireland**, the carnet costs £4.50/€10, and is available to members of the AA or the RAC (see above), or for members only from either of the following: the Camping and Caravanning Club (ⓣ024/7669 4995, ⓦwww.campingandcaravanningclub.co.uk; annual membership £27.50 plus £5 joining fee), the CTC (ⓣ0870/873 0061, ⓦwww.ctc.org.uk, membership £30.50) or the foreign touring arm of the same company, the Carefree Travel Service (ⓣ024/7642 2024), which provides the international camping carnet free if you take out insurance with them; they also book ferry crossings and inspect camping sites in Europe.

The Fédération Française de Camping et de Caravaning (78 rue de Rivoli, 75004 Paris ⓣ01.42.72.84.08, ⓦwww.ffcc.fr) publishes an annual guide (€16) covering 11,000 campsites, details of which can also be found online on the excellent Camping France website ⓦwww.campingfrance.com. If you'd rather have everything organised for you, a number of companies specialize in **camping holidays**, including Canvas Holidays, Keycamp, Eurocamp and Alan Rogers (see pp.33–34 for details).

Lastly, a word of **caution**: never camp rough (*camping sauvage*, as the French call it) on anyone's land without first asking permission. If the dogs don't get you, the guns might – farmers have been known to shoot first, and ask later. On the other hand, a politely phrased request for permission will as often as not get positive results. Camping on public land is not officially permitted, but is widely practised by the French, and if you're discreet you're not likely to have problems. On beaches, it's best to camp out only where other people are doing so.

Eating and drinking

France is famous for producing some of the most sublime food in the world, whether you're talking about the rarefied delicacies of haute cuisine or the robust, no-nonsense fare served up at country inns. Nevertheless, French cuisine has taken a bit of a knocking in recent years. The wonderful ingredients are still there, as every town and village market testifies, but those little family restaurants serving classic dishes that celebrate the region's produce – and where the bill is less than €15 – are increasingly hard to find. The processed, boil-in-the-bag and ready-to-microwave productions of the global food industry, all so inimical to the basic culinary arts of France, are making serious inroads. That's not to say you can't eat extremely well in France, but be prepared for disappointments at run-of-the-mill establishments, and don't be taken in by restaurants which claim to "gastronomique". In all too many cases this simply means they charge inflated prices for very average but fancy-sounding food. Don't be afraid to ask locals for their recommendations; this will usually elicit strong views and sound advice.

In the rarefied world of **haute cuisine**, where the top chefs are national celebrities, a battle has long been raging between traditionalists, determined to preserve the purity of French cuisine, and those who experiment with different flavours from around the world to create novel combinations. At this level, French food is still brilliant – in both camps – and the good news is that prices are continuing to come down. Many gourmet palaces offer weekday lunchtime menus where you can sample culinary genius for under €40.

France is also a great place for **foreign cuisine**, in particular North African, Caribbean (known as Antillais) and Asiatic. Moroccan, Thai or Vietnamese restaurants are not necessarily cheap options but they are usually good value for money.

On the whole, **vegetarians** can expect a somewhat lean time in France. Most cities now have at least one specifically vegetarian restaurant, but elsewhere your best bet will probably be a crêperie or pizzeria. Failing that you may have to fall back on an omelette or a plate of vegetables (often tinned) in an ordinary restaurant. Sometimes restaurants are willing to replace a meat dish on the fixed-price menu (*menu fixe*); at other times you'll have to pick your way through the *carte*. Remember the phrase *Je suis végétarien(ne); est-ce qu'il y a quelques plats sans viande?* ("I'm a vegetarian; are there any non-meat dishes?"). **Vegans**, however, should probably forget all about eating in restaurants and stick to self-catering. See the food glossary on p.1354 for other useful vocabulary.

Breakfast and snacks

A croissant or *pain au chocolat* (a chocolate-filled, light pastry) in a café or bar, with tea, hot chocolate or coffee, is generally the most economical way to eat **breakfast**, costing around €4 to €5. If there are no croissants left, it's perfectly acceptable to go and buy your own at the nearest baker or pâtisserie. The standard hotel breakfast comprises bread and/or pastries, jam and a jug of coffee or tea, and orange juice if you're lucky, from around €5 or €6. More expensive places might offer a buffet comprising cereals, fruit, yoghurt and the works.

At **lunchtime**, and sometimes in the evening, you'll find places offering a *plat du jour* (daily special) at between €8 and €12, or *formules*, limited menus typically offering a main dish and either a starter or a dessert for a set price. *Croques-monsieur* or *croques-madame* (variations on the toasted cheese-and-ham sandwich) are on sale at cafés, brasseries and many street stands, along with *frites* (potato fries), crêpes, galettes (wholewheat pancakes), *gauffres* (waffles), *glaces* (ice creams) and all kinds of fresh-filled baguettes (these very filling sandwiches usually cost between €3 and €5 to take away). For variety, in main towns and cities you can find Tunisian snacks like *brik à l'œuf* (a fried pastry with an egg inside), *merguez* (spicy North African sausage), Greek *souvlaki* (kebabs) and Middle Eastern *falafel* (deep-fried chickpea balls in flat bread with salad). Wine bars are good for regional sausages and cheese, usually served with brown bread (*pain de campagne*).

Crêpes, or pancakes with fillings, served up at ubiquitous crêperies, are popular lunchtime food. The savoury buckwheat variety (*galettes*) provide the main course; sweet, white-flour crêpes are dessert. They can be very tasty, but are generally poor value in comparison with a restaurant meal; you need at least three, normally at over €5 each (€3 for the sweet variety), to feel full. **Pizzerias**, usually *au feu du bois* (baked in wood-fire ovens), are also very common. They are somewhat better value than crêperies, but quality and quantity vary greatly.

For **picnics**, the local outdoor market or supermarket will provide you with almost everything you need from tomatoes and avocados to cheese and pâté. Cooked meat, prepared snacks, ready-made dishes and assorted salads can be bought at charcuteries (delicatessens), which you'll find even in most small villages, and at supermarket cold-food counters. You purchase by weight, or you can ask for *une tranche* (a slice), *une barquette* (a carton) or *une part* (a portion) as appropriate.

Salons de thé, which open from mid-morning to late evening, serve brunches, salads, quiches, and the like, as well as gateaux, ice cream and a wide selection of teas. They tend to be a good deal pricier than cafés or brasseries – you're paying for the posh surroundings – and are generally more popular with women than men. For **cakes** and **pastries** to take away, you'll find mouthwatering arrays at every pâtisserie.

Meals

There's no difference between restaurants (or *auberges* or *relais* as they sometimes call themselves) and brasseries in terms of quality or price range. The distinction is that **brasseries**, which resemble cafés, serve quicker meals at most hours of the day, while **restaurants** tend to stick to the

Cheese

Charles de Gaulle famously commented that "You can unite the French only through fear. You cannot simply bring together a country that has over 265 kinds of cheese". For serious **cheese**-lovers, France is the ultimate paradise. Other countries may produce individual cheeses which are as good as, or even better than, the best of the French, but no country offers a range that comes anywhere near them in terms of sheer inventiveness. In fact, there are officially over 300 types of French cheese, and the way they are made are jealously guarded secrets. Many cheese-makers have successfully protected their products by gaining the right to label their produce **AOC** (*appellation d'origine contrôlée*), covered by laws similar to those for wines, which – among other things – controls the amount of cheese that a particular area can produce. As a result, the subtle differences between French local cheeses have not been overwhelmed by the industrialized uniformity that has plagued other countries.

The best, or most traditional, restaurants offer a well-stocked *plateau de fromages* (cheeseboard), kept at room temperature and served with bread, but not butter. Apart from the ubiquitous Brie, Camembert and numerous varieties of goat's cheese (*chèvre*), there will usually be one or two local cheeses on offer – these are the ones to go for. If you want to buy cheese, local markets are always the best bet, while in larger towns you'll generally find a *fromagerie*, a shop with perhaps 200 varieties or more to choose from. We've indicated the best regional cheeses throughout the Guide.

traditional meal times of noon to 2pm, and 7pm to 9pm or 9.30pm, sometimes later in larger towns and during the summer months. In touristy areas in high season, and for all the more upmarket places, it's wise to make reservations – easily done on the same day. In small towns it may be impossible to get anything other than a bar sandwich after 9.30pm or so; in major cities, a few town-centre brasseries may serve until 11pm or midnight if you're lucky.

When hunting for places to eat, avoid places that are half empty at peak time, use your nose and regard long menus with suspicion. Don't forget that **hotel restaurants** are open to non-residents, and can be very good value. In many small towns and villages, you'll find these are the only restaurants, but in country areas keep an eye out for **fermes auberges**, farm restaurants where the majority of ingredients are produced on the farm itself. These are often the best places to sample really traditional local cuisine at very reasonable prices; a four-course meal for between €15 and €30 is the norm, including an aperitif and wine, but reservations are a must.

Prices, and what you get for them, are posted outside. Normally there's a choice between one or more *menus fixes* – with a set number of courses and a limited choice, or sometimes no choice on the cheapest menu – and choosing individual dishes from the *carte* (menu). **Menus fixes** (often referred to simply as *menus*) are normally the cheapest option. At the bottom end of the price range, they revolve around standard dishes such as steak and chips (*steak frites*), chicken and chips (*poulet frites*) and the like. But further up the scale they can be much the best-value way of sampling regional specialities, sometimes running to five or more courses. Going **à la carte** offers greater choice and, in the better restaurants, unlimited access to the chef's inventiveness – though you'll pay for the privilege.

The standard order of courses is the appetizer or starter (*un entrée*), followed by a main course (*un plat* or *un plat principal*), salad, cheese and finally dessert. If you're splashing out, you might also have a fish course between the starter and the main dish. You'll always be offered a coffee to finish off the meal; it is very rarely included in the price of a *menu*.

In the vast majority of restaurants a **service charge** of fifteen percent is included in prices listed on the menu – in which case it should say *service compris* (*s.c.*) or *prix net*. Very occasionally you'll see *service non compris* (*s.n.c.*) or *servis en sus*, which means that it's up to you whether you leave a tip or not. **Wine** (*vin*) or a **drink** (*boisson*) is sometimes included in the cost of a *menu fixe*. Otherwise, the cheapest option will be the house wine, which is served in a jug (*pichet*) or a carafe; you'll be asked if you want *un quart* (0.25 litre), *un demi* (0.5 litre) or *un litre* (1 litre). As for choosing a bottle of wine, if you're worried about the cost ask for *vin ordinaire* or the *vin de table*.

In the Guide the lowest price menu, or sometimes the range of menus, is given. Note that the evening menus – and often those served at weekends – are in general more expensive than the standard weekday lunchtime menu. Where average à la carte prices are given it assumes you'll have three courses and half a bottle of wine.

The French are extremely well disposed towards **children** in restaurants. Not only do they offer reduced-price children's menus (albeit usually just salad, steak and chips and ice cream) but also create an atmosphere – even in otherwise fairly snooty establishments – that positively welcomes kids; some even provide games and toys.

One final note is that you should always call the waiter or waitress *Monsieur* or *Madame* (*Mademoiselle* if a young woman), never *Garçon*.

Drinking

Wherever you can eat you can invariably drink, and vice versa. **Drinking** is done at a leisurely pace whether it's a prelude to food (*apéritif*) or a sequel (*digestif*), and café-bars are the standard places to do it. By law the full price list, including service charges, must be clearly displayed. You normally pay when you leave, and it's perfectly acceptable to sit for hours over just one cup of coffee, though in this case a small tip will be appreciated.

Wine (*vin*) is drunk at just about every meal or social occasion. Red is *rouge*, white *blanc* and rosé *rosé*. *Vin de table* or *vin ordinaire* –

Wines

French **wines** are unrivalled in the world for their range, sophistication, diversity and status. With the exception of the northwest of the country and the mountains, wine is produced just about everywhere. The great **wine-producing regions** are Champagne, Bordeaux and Burgundy, closely followed by the Loire and Rhône valleys. Alsace also has some great wines, and there are some beautiful ones to be had in the lesser wine regions of Bergerac, Languedoc, Roussillon, Provence and Savoie.

The **quality** of the local *vins de pays*, though very variable, is still exceptional for the price. Quality wines are denoted by the **appellation d'origine contrôlée** (AOC) label, which strictly controls the amount of wine that a particular area, whether several hundred square kilometres or just two, may produce. Within each appellation there's enormous diversity generated by the different types of soil, the lie of the land, the type of grape grown – there are over sixty varieties – the ability of the wine to age, and the individual skills of the producer.

It's an extremely complex business and it's not difficult to feel intimidated by the seemingly innate expertise of all French people. Many individual wines and appellations are mentioned in the text, but trusting your own taste is the best test. Knowing the grape types that you particularly like (or dislike), whether you like wines very fruity, dry, light or heavy, is all useful when discussing your choice with a waiter, producer or wine merchant. The more interest you show, the more helpful advice you're likely to receive. The only thing the French cannot tolerate is people ordering Coke or the like to accompany a gourmet meal.

We've detailed the main wine-growing regions – and their produce – throughout the Guide.

table wine – is generally drinkable and always cheap, although it may be disguised and priced-up as the house wine, or *cuvée*. The price of AOC (*appellation d'origine contrôlée*, see box) wines starts at around €4, and that's the vineyard price. You can buy a very decent bottle in a shop for €6, while €10 and over will get you something worth savouring. By the time restaurants have added their considerable mark-up, wine can constitute an alarming proportion of the bill.

The basic **wine terms** are: *brut*, very dry; *sec*, dry; *demi-sec*, sweet; *doux*, very sweet; *mousseux*, sparkling; *méthode champenoise*, mature and sparkling. There are grape varieties as well, but the complexities of the subject take up volumes. A glass of wine is simply *un verre de rouge*, *rosé* or *blanc*. A glass of wine in a bar will typically cost around €3 to €6.

The best way of **buying wine** is directly from the producers (*vignerons*), either at vineyards, at Maisons or Syndicats du Vin (representing a group of wine-producers), or at Coopératifs Vinicoles (producers' co-ops). At all these places you can usually sample the wines first. It's best to make clear at the start how much you want to buy (particularly if it's only one or two bottles) and you'll not be popular if you drink several glasses and then fail to buy at least one bottle. The most economical option is to buy *en vrac*, which you can also do at some wine shops (*caves*), filling an easily obtainable plastic five- or ten-litre container (usually sold on the premises) straight from the barrel. In cities, supermarkets are the best places to buy your wine, often at very competitive prices.

Familiar light Belgian and German brands, plus French brands from Alsace, account for most of the **beer** you'll find. Draught beer (*à la pression*) – usually Kronenbourg – is the cheapest drink you can have next to coffee and wine; *un pression* or *un demi* (0.33 litre) will cost around €3. For a wider choice of draught and bottled beer you need to go to the special beer-drinking establishments such as the English- and Irish-style pubs found in larger towns and cities. A small bottle at one of these places can set you back double what you'd pay in an ordinary café-bar. In supermarkets, however, bottled or canned beer is exceptionally cheap.

Strong alcohol, such as spirits (*eaux-de-vie*, such as cognac and armagnac) and liqueurs, is consumed at any time of day, though in far smaller quantities these days thanks to the clampdown on drink-driving. *Pastis* – the generic name of aniseed drinks such as Pernod and Ricard and a favourite throughout the Languedoc – is served diluted with water and ice (*glace* or *glaçons*). It's very refreshing and not expensive. Among less familiar names, try Poire William (pear brandy), or Marc (a spirit distilled from grape pulp). Measures are generous, but they don't come cheap: the same applies for imported spirits like whisky (*Scotch*). Two drinks designed to stimulate the appetite – *un apéritif* – are Pineau (cognac and grape juice) and Kir (white wine with a dash of Cassis – blackcurrant liquor – or with champagne instead of wine for a Kir Royal). Cognac, armagnac and Chartreuse are among the many aids to digestion – *un digestif* – to relax over after a meal. **Cocktails** are served at most late-night bars, discos and clubs, as well as upmarket hotel bars and at every seaside promenade café; they usually cost at least €5.

On the **soft drink** front, you can buy cartons of unsweetened fruit juice in supermarkets, although in the cafés the bottled (sweetened) nectars such as apricot (*jus d'abricot*) and blackcurrant (*cassis*) still hold sway. Fresh orange or lemon juice (*orange/citron pressé*) is a much more refreshing choice on a hot day – the juice is served in the bottom of a long ice-filled glass, with a jug of water and a sugar bowl to sweeten it to your taste. Other soft drinks to try are syrups (*sirops*) of mint, grenadine or other flavours mixed with water. The standard fizzy drinks of lemonade (*limonade*), Coke (*coca*) and so forth are all available. There's no shortage of bottled **mineral water** (*eau minérale*) and spring water (*eau de source*) – either sparkling (*gazeuse*) or still (*plate*) – either, from the big brand names to the most obscure spa product. But there's not much wrong with the **tap water** (*l'eau de robinet*) which will always be brought free to your table if you ask for it. The only time you shouldn't drink the tap water, is if the tap is labelled *eau non potable*.

Coffee is invariably espresso – small, black and very strong. *Un café* or *un express* is the regular; *un crème* is with milk; *un grand café* or *un grand crème* are large versions. In the morning you could also ask for *un café au lait* – espresso in a large cup or bowl topped up with hot milk. *Un déca* is decaffeinated, now widely available. Ordinary **tea** (*thé*) – Lipton's nine times out of ten – is normally served black (*nature*) or with a slice of lemon (*limon*); to have milk with it, ask for *un peu de lait frais* (some fresh milk). *Chocolat chaud* – **hot chocolate** – unlike tea, lives up to the high standards of French food and drink and can be had in any café. After meals, **herb teas** (*infusions* or *tisanes*), offered by most restaurants, can be soothing. The more common ones are *verveine* (verbena), *tilleul* (lime blossom), *menthe* (mint) and *camomille* (camomile).

Communication

With France's efficient communications systems you should have no problem staying in touch with people at home. There are post offices everywhere, Internet access is becoming more widely available and, should you need to make a phone call, you can use cheap pre-paid cards and dial direct or access home-country operators. Mobile phone coverage is pretty good, too.

French **newspapers** (not to mention **radio** and **television**) will be of less interest if you're not a reader (or speaker) of French. There are some local English-language magazines, but you'll probably find yourself reaching for an international edition of a British or American newspaper or an international news magazine to keep up with current events. These are available in major cities and tourist centres.

Mail

French **post offices**, known as La Poste and identified by bright yellow-and-blue signs, are generally open from around 8.30am to 6pm or 7pm Monday to Friday, and 8.30am to noon on Saturday. However, these hours aren't set in stone: smaller branches tend to keep shorter hours and may close for an hour or so at lunch, while in Paris the main post office is open 24 hours.

You can receive letters using the **poste restante** system available at the central post office in every town. They should be addressed (preferably with the surname first and in capitals) "Poste Restante, Poste Centrale, Town x, Post Code". You'll need your passport to collect your mail and there'll be a charge of €0.50 per item. Items are usually only kept for fifteen days.

For sending letters, remember that you can buy **stamps** (*timbres*) with less queuing from *tabacs* and newsagents. Standard letters (20g or less) and postcards within France and to other European Union countries cost €0.50, or €0.90 to North America, Australia and New Zealand. Inside larger post offices is a row of yellow-coloured *guichet automatiques* – automatic stamp machines with instructions available in English where you can weigh letters and packages and buy the appropriate stamps; sticky labels and tape are also dispensed. For further information on postal rates, among other things, log on to the post office web site Ⓦwww.laposte.fr.

You can also change money at post offices and send faxes, while most larger offices also offer Internet access and photocopying. To post your letter on the street, look for the bright yellow **postboxes**.

Telephones

You can make domestic and international **phone calls** from any telephone box (*cabine*) and can also receive calls – look for the number in the top right-hand corner of the information panel. The vast majority of public phones require a **phone card** (*télécarte*), available from post offices, *tabacs*, newsagents and railway stations, and come in 50 and 120 units (€7.40 and €14.75 respectively). You can also use **credit cards** in many call boxes. Coin-operated phones have almost completely disappeared except in cafés and bars; they take coins of 10, 20 and 50 cents and €1.

France Telecom's (Ⓦwww.francetelecom.fr) **rates** and charging structures are not only horribly complicated but change frequently – fortunately, in the downward direction on the whole. At the time of writing, peak-rate calls within France from public phones are charged at €0.30 for the first minute and €0.15 per minute thereafter; international calls cost €0.26 per minute to the UK, USA and Canada, and €0.55 to Australia and New Zealand. Off-peak rates (roughly 50 percent cheaper) apply on weekdays between 7pm and 8am and all day Saturday, Sunday and national holidays. Note that when using a hotel phone, they usually add a significant mark-up to the above rates.

For **calls within France** – local or long-distance – simply dial all ten digits of the number. Numbers beginning with ⓣ08.00 up to ⓣ08.05 are free-dial numbers; those beginning ⓣ08.10 and ⓣ08.11 are charged as a local call; anything else beginning ⓣ08 is premium-rated (typically €0.34 per minute). Note that none of these ⓣ08 numbers can be accessed from abroad. Calls to mobile phones (numbers starting with ⓣ06) are also charged at premium rates.

One of the most convenient ways of **phoning abroad** from France is using a **telephone charge card** from your phone company back home, though check first whether France is covered. Using a PIN number, you can make calls from most hotel, public and private phones that will be charged to your home phone account or a credit card. Since most major charge cards are free to obtain, it's certainly worth getting one at least for emergencies, but bear in mind that rates aren't necessarily cheaper than calling from a public phone.

Another option is one of the pre-paid **phone cards** (*cartes à codes*) on sale at *tabacs*, newsagents and post offices which you can use with any public or private telephone. The €15 "L'Astuce Internationale" marketed by Tiscali (ⓣ08.00.76.80.00, ⓦwww.prepaye.tiscali.fr), for example, gives you roughly three and a half hours to the UK, USA or Canada.

To avoid payment altogether, you can, of course, make a reverse-charge or **collect call** – known in French as *téléphoner en PCV* – by contacting the international operator (see below).

Calling home from France

Note that the initial zero is omitted from the area code when dialling any of the countries below from France.

UK dial ⓣ00 + 44 + area code + number.

Republic of Ireland dial ⓣ00 + 353 + area code + number.

USA and Canada dial ⓣ00 + 1 + area code + number.

Australia dial ⓣ00 + 61 + area code + number.

New Zealand dial ⓣ00 + 64 + area code + number.

Useful telephone numbers

Directory enquiries ⓣ12 (free for up to two requests per call).

International operator ⓣ31.23.

Time ⓣ36.99.

Weather ⓣ08.92.68.02 + the two-digit number of the *département* (€0.46 per minute).

Mobile phones

If you want to use your **mobile phone**, contact your phone provider to check whether it will work in France and what the call charges are – they tend to be pretty exorbitant, and remember you're likely to be charged extra for incoming calls. If you want to retrieve messages while you're away, you'll have to ask your provider for a new access code, as your home one is unlikely to work abroad. French mobile phones operate on the European GSM standard, so **US cellphones** won't work in France unless you've got a tri-band phone.

If you are going to be in France for any length of time and will be making and receiving a lot of local calls, you could investigate buying a French SIM card (which will give you a local phone number) and pre-paid recharge cards (*mobicartes*). You can buy a SIM card from any of the big mobile providers (France Télécom's Orange, SFR and Boygues Telecom), all of which have high-street outlets.

Email

One of the best (and cheapest) ways to keep in touch while travelling is to sign

Calling France from abroad

To make a phone call **to France from abroad**, dial the International Direct Dial (IDD) code for your country followed by the **French country code** (33), then the local number minus the initial "0".

up for a free **Internet email address** that can be accessed from anywhere, for example Yahoo! (Ⓦmail.yahoo.com) or Hotmail (Ⓦwww.hotmail.com). Once you've set up an account, you'll be able to pick up and send mail from any Internet café, hotel or hostel etc with Internet access (*point internet*). Most larger post offices also have Internet terminals, which are operated with a prepaid card (€7 for the first hour, €4 for each subsequent hour), as do some tourist offices. By way of comparison, rates in cybercafés vary from around €4 to €10 per hour.

If you're bringing your own laptop, note that French phone sockets take a non-standard plug. In the majority of cases, you'll find the unit also takes an RJ-11 plug, but you may need an adaptor. These are available locally in big supermarkets and specialist phone shops. The website Ⓦwww.kropla.com is a useful source of information about getting connected while abroad.

The media

English-language newspapers, such as the *European*, *Washington Post*, *New York Times* and the *International Herald Tribune*, are on sale on the day of publication in the main cities and the day after elsewhere. Of the **French daily papers**, *Le Monde* (Ⓦwww.lemonde.fr) is the most intellectual; it's widely respected, and somewhat austere, even though it now carries such frivolities as colour photos. *Libération* (Ⓦwww.liberation.com), founded by Jean-Paul Sartre in the 1960s, is moderately left-wing, pro-European, independent and more colloquial, with good, if specific, coverage. Rigorous left-wing criticism of the French government comes from *L'Humanité* (Ⓦwww.humanite.presse.fr), the Communist Party paper, though it's struggling to survive. The other nationals are all firmly right-wing in their politics: *Le Figaro* (Ⓦwww.lefigaro.fr) is the most respected. The top-selling tabloid, predictably more readable and a good source of news, is *Aujourd'hui* (published in Paris as *Le Parisien*) followed by *France Soir* (Ⓦwww.francesoir.fr), while *L'Équipe* (Ⓦwww.lequipe.fr) is dedicated to sports coverage and *Paris-Turf* (Ⓦww.paris-turf.com) focuses on horse-racing. The widest circulations are enjoyed by the **regional dailies**, of which the most important is the Rennes-based *Ouest-France* (Ⓦwww.ouest-france.fr). For visitors, these are mainly of interest for their listings.

Weeklies of the *Newsweek/Time* model include the wide-ranging and socialist-inclined *Le Nouvel Observateur* (Ⓦwww.nouvelobs.com), its right-wing counterpoint *L'Express* (Ⓦwww.lexpress.fr) and the centrist with bite, *Marianne* (Ⓦwww.marianne-en-ligne.fr). Comprising mainly translated articles, *Courier International* (Ⓦwww.courrierinternational.com) offers an overview of what's being discussed in media around the globe. The best investigative journalism is to be found in the weekly satirical paper *Le Canard Enchainé*, while *Charlie Hebdo* is roughly equivalent to the UK's *Private Eye*.

Monthlies include the young and trendy *Nova* (Ⓦwww.novaplanet.com), which has excellent listings of cultural events. There are, of course, the French versions of *Vogue*, *Elle* and *Marie-Claire*, and the relentlessly urban *Biba*, for women's fashion and lifestyle.

Moral censorship of the press is rare. On the newsstands you'll find pornography of every shade alongside knitting patterns and DIY. You'll also find French **comics** (*bandes dessinées*), many of them aimed at the adult market, with wild and wonderful illustrations; they're considered to be quite an art form and whole museums are devoted to them.

TV and radio

French TV has six channels: three public (France 2, France 3 and Arte/France 5); one subscription (Canal Plus – with some unencrypted programmes); and two commercial open broadcasts (TF1 and M6). Of these, TF1 and France 2 are the most popular channels, showing a broad mix of programmes. In addition there are any number of cable and satellite channels, which include CNN, BBC World and BBC Prime, Eurosport, MTV, Planète, which specializes in documentaries, Ciné Première, and Canal Jimmy (*Friends* and the like in French). The main French-run music channel is MCM.

Arte/France 5 (also known as La Cinquième) is a joint Franco-German cultural venture that transmits simultaneously in French and German: offerings include highbrow programmes, daily documentaries, art criticism, serious French and German movies and complete operas. During the day (7am–7pm), France 5 uses the frequency to broadcast educational programmes. **Canal Plus** is the main movie channel, with repeats of foreign films usually shown at least once in the original language. **France 3** is strong on regional news and more heavyweight movies, including a fair number undubbed foreign films. The main French **news broadcasts** are at 8pm on France 2 and TF1.

If you've got a **radio**, you can tune into various English-language broadcasts. BBC (@www.bbc.co.uk/worldservice), Radio Canada (@www.rcinet.ca), and Voice of America (@www.voa.gov) list all the world service frequencies around the globe. In the Paris region, you can listen to the **news in English** on Radio France International (RFI, @www.rfi.fr) at 7am, 2.30pm and 4.30pm on 738 kHz.

Public holidays and festivals

France celebrates twelve public holidays (jours fériés), when most shops and businesses (though not necessarily restaurants), and some museums, are closed. May is a particularly busy month for holidays: as well as May Day and VE Day, Ascension Day normally falls then, as sometimes does Pentecost (Whitsun). In addition to public holidays there are myriad festivals held throughout the country. These are one of the joys of French life and it's often worth arranging a trip around one if it's of particular interest.

Opening hours

Basic **hours of business** are Monday to Saturday 9am to noon and 2pm to 6.30pm. In big cities shops and other businesses stay open throughout the day, and in July and August most tourist offices and museums are open without interruption. In rural areas and throughout southern France places tend to close for at least a couple of hours at lunchtime. Small food shops may not reopen till halfway through the afternoon, closing around 7.30pm or 8pm, just before the evening meal.

The standard **closing day** is Sunday, though some food shops and newsagents are open in the morning. Some shops and businesses, particularly in rural areas, also close on a Monday.

Museums tend to open from 9am or 10am to noon and from 2pm or 3pm to 5pm or 6pm, though in the big cities some stay open all day and opening hours tend to be longer in summer. Museum closing days are usually Monday or Tuesday, sometimes both. **Churches** and cathedrals are generally open from around 8am to dusk, but may close at lunchtime and are reserved for worshippers during services (times of which will be posted on the door). Country churches are increasingly kept locked; there will usually be a note on the door telling you where to get the key, usually from the priest's house (*presbytère*) or someone else living nearby.

For information on banking hours, see p.47.

Festivals

It's hard to beat the experience of arriving in a small French village, expecting no more

Major French festivals

Below are just some of the major festivals taking place in France each year. You'll find a reasonably comprehensive database of French festivals at ⓦwww.festivalissimo.com.

Aix-en-Provence Festival International d'Art Lyrique (classical music; July; ⓦwww.festival-aix.com); Danse à Aix (late July/early Aug; ⓦwww.aix-en-provence.com/danse-a-aix).

Alès Cratère/Surfaces (street theatre; early July; ⓦwww.lecratere.fr).

Amiens Festival des Cathédrales de Picardie (baroque and Renaissance music; Sept–Oct; ⓦwww.festivaldescathedrales.com).

Angoulême Musiques Metisses (Afro-Caribbean and Latin American music; late May; ⓦwww.musiques-metisses.com).

Annecy Les Noctibules (street theatre; late July).

Arles Les Suds à Arles (world music; mid-July; ⓦwww.suds-arles.com).

Aurillac Festival International de Théâtre de Rue (street theatre; Aug; ⓦwww.aurillac.net).

Avignon Festival d'Avignon (contemporary dance and theatre; July; ⓦwww.festival-avignon.com).

Bastia Les Musicales (sacred and world music; Oct; ⓦwww.musicales-de-bastia.com).

Beaune Festival International d'Opéra Baroque (early July to early Aug; ⓦwww.festivalbeaune.com).

Belfort Eurockéennes (early July; ⓦwww.eurockeennes.fr).

Biarritz Surf Festival (mid-July; ⓦwww.biarritzsurffestival.com).

Bordeaux Fête le Vin (late June in even-numbered years; ⓦwww.bordeaux-fete-le-vin.com).

Cannes Festival de Cannes (international film festival; May; ⓦwww.festival-cannes.com).

Chalon-sur-Saône Chalon dans la Rue (street theatre; third week July; ⓦwww.chalondanslarue.com).

Charleville-Mézières Festival Mondial des Théâtres de Marionnettes (triennial festival of puppet theatre; late Sept; 2006; ⓦwww.marionnette.com).

Colmar Festival International de Colmar (music festival; July; ⓦwww.festival-colmar.com).

Gannat (near Vichy) Les Cultures du Monde (late July; ⓦwww.gannat.com).

Grenoble Festival du Théâtre Européen (contemporary theatre; late June; ⓦscant.neptune.fr).

Juan-les-Pins Jazz à Juan (mid-July).

La Rochelle Festival International du Film (late June to early July; ⓦwww.festival-larochelle.org); Francofolies (contemporary French music; mid-July; ⓦwww.francofolies.fr).

La Roque d'Anthéron Festival International de Piano (mid-July to mid-Aug; ⓦwww.festival-piano.com).

Les Saintes-Maries-de-la-Mer Fête de Ste Sarah (Romany festival; May 24–25); Festival d'Abrivado (bull-running; Nov 11).

Limoges Les Francophonies en Limousin (contemporary theatre; end Sept to mid-Oct; ⓦwww.lesfrancophonies.com).

Lorient Festival Interceltique (Celtic folk festival; early Aug; ⓦwww.festival-interceltique.com).

Lyon Les Nuits de Fourvière (performance arts; early-June to early-Aug;

Ⓦwww.nuitsdefourviere.fr); Bienniale de la Dance (Sept 2006; Ⓦwww.biennale-de-lyon.org).

Marciac Jazz in Marciac (early Aug; Ⓦwww.jazzinmarciac.com).

Menton Fête du Citron (parades, concerts, fireworks; two weeks following Mardi Gras; Ⓦwww.feteducitron.com); Festival de Musique de Chambre (chamber music; Aug).

Mont-de-Marsan Arte Flamenco (Flamenco music; early July).

Montpellier Montpellier Danse (late June to early-July; Ⓦwww.montpellierdanse.com); Festival International Cinéma Méditerranéen (late Oct to early Nov; Ⓦwww.cinemed.tm.fr).

Mulhouse Festival du Jazz (mid to late Aug; Ⓦwww.jazz-mulhouse.org).

Nancy Jazz Pulsations (Oct; Ⓦwww.nancyjazzpulsations.com).

Nice Carnival (Jan/Feb; Ⓦwww.nicecarnaval.com); Jazz Festival (July; Ⓦwww.nicejazzfest.com).

Nîmes La Féria de Nîmes (bullfights; Pentecost).

Orange Chorégies d'Orange (opera; July–Aug; Ⓦwww.choregies.asso.fr).

Orcival Procession of Notre-Dame d'Orcival (Ascension Day).

Paris Festival de St-Denis (music festival; May–June; Ⓦwww.festival-saint-denis.fr); Festival Django Reinhardt (jazz; June; Ⓦdjango.samois.free.fr); La Marche des Fièrtés, Lesbienne, Gai, Bi & Trans (Gay Pride march; late June; Ⓦwww.inter-lgbt.org); Rock en Seine (late Aug; Ⓦwww.rockenseine.com); Jazz à la Villette (Sept); Festival d'Automne (theatre, concerts, dance, films & exhibitions; mid-Sept to mid-Dec; Ⓦwww.festival-automne.com); Biennial des Anitquaires (antiques fair; Sept 2006); Foire International d'Art Contemporain (Oct).

Périgueux Mimos (international mime festival; early Aug; Ⓦwww.ville-perigueux.fr/mimos).

Perpignan Visa pour l'Image (international photojournalism; late Aug to mid-Sept; Ⓦwww.visapourlimage.com).

Prades Festival Pablo Casals (chamber music; late July to mid-Aug; Ⓦwww.prades-festival-casals.com).

Puy-en-Velay Fête Renaissance du Roi de l'Oiseau (historical pageants, fireworks etc; mid-Sept; Ⓦwww.roideloiseau.com).

Quimper Semaines Musicales (classical, jazz and folk music; Aug; Ⓦwww.semaines-musicales-quimper.org).

Reims Flâneries Musicales d'Été (open-air concerts; early July to early Aug).

Rennes Les Tombées de la Nuit (concerts, cinema and performance arts; early July; Ⓦwww.lestdnuit.com); Rencontres Transmusicales (contemporary music; early Dec; Ⓦwww.lestrans.com).

St-Malo La Route du Rock (mid-Aug; Ⓦwww.laroutedurock.com).

Saintes Académies Musicales de Saintes (classical music; July; Ⓦwww.festival-saintes.org).

Sotteville-lès-Rouen Viva Cité (street theatre; late June).

Strasbourg Festival de Musique de Strasbourg (classical music; June; Ⓦwww.festival-strasbourg.com); Musica (contemporary music; Sept–Oct; Ⓦwww.festival-musica.org); Jazz d'Or (Nov; Ⓦwww.jazzdoor.com).

Uzès Uzès Danse (contemporary dance; June; Ⓦwww.uzesdanse.fr).

Vaison-la-Romaine Vaison Danse (contemporary dance; mid-July; Ⓦwww.vaison-festival.com).

Vienne Jazz à Vienne (late June to mid-July; Ⓦwww.jazzavienne.com).

Public holidays

January 1 New Year's Day
Easter Sunday
Easter Monday
Ascension Day (forty days after Easter)
Pentecost or **Whitsun** (seventh Sunday after Easter)
May 1 Labour Day
May 8 Victory in Europe (VE) Day 1945
July 14 Bastille Day
August 15 Assumption of the Virgin Mary
November 1 All Saints' Day
November 11 Armistice Day 1918
December 25 Christmas Day

than a bed for the night, to discover the streets decked out with flags and streamers, a band playing in the square and the entire population out celebrating the feast of their patron saint. As well as nationwide celebrations such as the Fête de la Musique (June 21, the summer solstice), Bastille Day (July 14) and the Assumption of the Virgin Mary (August 15), there are any number of **festivals** – both traditional and of more recent origin – held in towns and villages throughout France.

Catholicism is deeply ingrained in the culture of French rural areas, and as a result religious feast days still bring people out in all their finery, ready to indulge once Mass has been said. Most of these occasions, along with the celebrations around wine and food production, are very genuine affairs. Other festivals, based for example on historical events, folklore or literature, are often obviously money-spinners and shows for municipal prestige – though they can still be tremendous fun.

One folk festival that is definitely worth attending is the **Inter-Celtic event** held at Lorient in Brittany every August. Another annual event with deep historical roots is the great gypsy gathering at **Les Stes-Maries-de-la-Mer** in the Camargue. Though exploited for every last *centime*, it's a unique and exhilarating spectacle to be part of.

Bonfires are lit and fireworks set off for **Bastille Day**, for the **Fête de St-Jean** on 24 June, three days after the summer solstice, and for the **Assumption of the Virgin Mary** on August 15. **Mardi Gras** – the last blow-out before Lent – is far less of an occasion than in other Catholic countries, although towns on the Côte d'Azur, such as Menton, put on a show at great expense and in questionable taste. Of more recent origin, on June 21 all sorts of musical events are held throughout France, but particularly in Paris, to celebrate the **Fête de la Musique**. Another nationwide cultural blow-out is the **Journées du Patrimoine** on the third weekend in September, a great opportunity to visit private art collections and historic buildings not normally open to the public.

Music, theatre and dance

The best contemporary popular music in France is distinctly un-French, combining sounds from West, Central and North Africa, the Caribbean and Latin America. However, the old chanson tradition is undergoing something of a revival, rap has taken strides, and just being French seems to give many of today's DJs the ability to influence electronic music worldwide, while jazz and classical music continues to thrive. In theatre, the French have developed their own heavyweight brand of intellectual drama in which directors (not playwrights) dominate. France has a growing reputation for innovative dance, with several excellent regional companies, while dance festivals also attract the best international talent.

Music

Standard **French rock** largely deserves its lack-lustre reputation. Sixties rocker Johnny Halliday is still France's biggest music star; Patrick Bruel, idol of love-lorn adolescents, appeals equally across the generations; and Seventies disco music, epitomized by Claude François, remains depressingly popular. This said, half of all albums bought in France are recorded by British and American bands, and the dominance of Anglo-Saxon music on the radio prompted a law in 1996 insisting that radio stations' output must be at least forty percent French.

However, France is in the forefront of the **World Music** (*musique du monde*) scene. Algerian raï flourishes, with singers like Khaled and Cheb Mami enjoying megastar status. Daddy Yod from Guadeloupe sings ragga; Angélique Kidjo, from Benin, is a brilliant vocalist as is the Senegalese singer – and international star – Youssou N'Dour. The "ethnically French" have produced their own rewarding hybrids, best exemplified in the Pogue-like chaos of Les Négresses Vertes, who also attract an international following. Manu Chao, a former member of Mano Negra, one of France's best "alternative" rock bands until their demise in 1995, combines Latin American, rap, reggae and rock to create his own distinctive style.

To read about the role of cinema in French culture, see Contexts, p.1322.

Other names to look out for are the Parisian-based Orchestre National de Barbès, with a distinctly African flavour, and Zebda, a Maghrebi influenced band from Toulouse.

Since the 1980's the culture of the marginalized immigrant suburbs has found musical expression in **rap** and **hip-hop** and France is now the second biggest producer of rap music after the US. The 1991 emergence of MC Solaar, a young Senegalese-born Parisian-schooled hip-hopper, helped bring Francophone rap to the national and international stage. His platinum-selling album *Prose Combat* further fueled the explosion of emerging talent in the mid 1990s, which ran the gamut from laid-back hip-hoppy R&B to the explicit social protest lyrics of hardcore gangsta rap. The latter's most ardent practitioners are the controversial group Supréme NTM, whose name translates, roughly, as "engage in sexual behavior with your mum". On the whole, French rap lyrics are less overtly violent than their Anglophone counterparts, though still hit hard at the French establishment on issues ranging from European colonialism to racial profiling by the police.

Other groups, such as IAM, Alliance Ethnik, Assassins and Busta Flex have also received international acclaim, and French and American rap musicians frequently collaborate on bilingual productions. In addition to the groups mentioned above, check out Booba, Mafia K-1 Fry, Corneille and Kool Shen (of NTM fame) for a good sampling of the diversity of current French rap. You don't have to speak street French to appreciate the beats.

Electronic music has long been a French obsession, with the world-famous Jean Michel Jarre at the fore. With such a tradition, it's not surprising that house and techno are hugely popular in France. DJs to look out for are the well-known Laurent Garnier, Antoine Clamaran and Chris the French Kiss (aka Bob Sinclair), all based in Paris. The techno twosome Daft Punk; renowned throughout clubland for their thumping mix of house, funk, techno and hip-hop, radically revised France's naff disco image of yore and gained an international following in the process. Another best-selling duo, Air, creates a mellower sound; their dreamy *Moon Safari* album, a very Gallic kind of chill-out music released in 1998, remains highly influential to this day, and their latest release, 2004's *Talkie Walkie*, proved the duo has yet to run out of inspiration.

But the French are probably right not to abandon **chansons**, the tradition of ultra-sophisticated, smoky songs epitomized by Edith Piaf and developed by Charles Trenet, Georges Brassens and the Belgian Jacques Brel in the Fifties and Sixties, and reaching their sly, sexy best with the legendary Serge Gainsbourg, who died in 1991. Today, the indefatigable Charles Aznavour and younger singer-composers like Jean-Louis Murat, Arlette Denis and Dominique A continue the tradition, while Juliette, Vincent Delerm and Benjamin Biolay – a young singer-songwriter hailed as the new Serge Gainsbourg – have added a postmodern flavour. As an indication that chansons are undergoing something of a revival, in 2002 the Québécoise Isabelle Boulay made it to number two in the French album charts with a medley of Piaf, Brel and Aznavour songs entitled *Au Moment d'Être à Vous*, and even Patrick Bruel entered the fray, with his surprising but very successful *Entre-Deux*, a reprise of 1920s and 1930s favourites. Then, in 2004 veteran actor and crooner Michel Sardou returned to the genre with his hit album *Du Plaisir*.

Jazz has long enjoyed an appreciative audience in France: Charlie Parker, Dizzy Gillespie, Bud Powell and Miles Davis were being listened to in the Fifties, when elsewhere in Europe their names were known only to a tiny coterie of fans. Gypsy guitarist Django Reinhardt and his partner, violinist Stéphane Grappelli, whose work represents the distinctive and undisputed French contribution to the jazz canon, had much to do with the music's popularity. But it was also greatly enhanced by the presence of many front-rank black American musicians, for whom Paris was a haven of freedom and culture after the racial prejudice and philistinism of the States. Among them were the soprano sax player Sidney Bechet, who set up in legendary partnership with French clarinettist Claude Luter, and Bud Powell, whose turbulent exile partly inspired the tenor man played by Dexter Gordon (himself a veteran of the Montana club) in the film *Round Midnight*. In Paris you can listen to a different band every night for weeks, from traditional through bebop and free jazz, to highly contemporary experimental. And there are many excellent festivals, particularly in the south (see box, p.73).

If your taste is for **classical music** and its development, you're also in for a treat. Paris has two opera houses and in the provinces there are no fewer than thirteen companies, of which Strasbourg and Toulouse are said to be the best, while Monaco's opera house is renowned for drawing the top international stars. Furthermore, there are nearly thirty permanent orchestras in France. The Orchestre de Paris has an excellent reputation. The places to check out for concerts are the Maisons de la Culture (in all the larger cities), churches (where chamber music is as much performed as sacred music, often without charge), and festivals – of which there are hundreds, the most famous being at Aix in July.

Contemporary and experimental computer-based work flourishes: leading exponents are Paul Mefano and Pierre Boulez, founder of the IRCAM centre in Paris and himself one of the first pupils of Olivier Messiaen, the grand old man of modern French music who died in 1992.

Theatre

The earlier **theatre** generation of **Genet**, **Anouilh** and **Camus**, joined by **Beckett** and **Ionesco**, hasn't really had successors.

Buying tickets

FNAC shops in all big towns and Virgin Megastores in the main cities have copious listings of what's on and are the best booking agencies for gigs, ballet or theatre. Booking details for festivals are given in the Guide.

In the 1950s, **Roger Planchon** set up a company in a suburb of Lyon, determined to play to working-class audiences. It became the Théâtre National Populaire, the number-two state theatre after the Comédie Française, and now does the classics with all due decorum. Bourgeois farces, postwar classics, Shakespeare, Racine and Cyrano de Bergerac make up the staple fare in most theatres.

Nevertheless, certain directors in France do extraordinary things with the medium. Classic texts are shuffled to produce theatrical moments where spectacular and dazzling sensation takes precedence over speech. Their shows are overwhelming: huge casts, vast sets – sometimes in real buildings never before used for theatre – exotic lighting effects and original music scores. They are a unique experience, even if you haven't understood a word.

Directors' names to look out for are **Peter Brook** (the English director who has been in Paris for decades and is based at the Bouffes du Nord theatre), **Stéphanie Loik** and **Ariane Mnouchkine**, whose Théâtre du Soleil based at La Cartoucherie in Paris's Bois de Vincennes, is one of Europe's most celebrated theatre companies. Indeed, La Cartoucherie has become something of a centre for cutting-edge theatre. It's also home to the Théâtre de la Tempête under Philippe Adrien, the Théâtre de l'Aquarium under the young director Julie Brochen and the Théâtre de l'Epée de Bois amongst others. Keep an eye out, too, for the off-beat productions by the versatile actor-writer-directors **Jérôme Deschamps** and **Macha Makeïeff**, currently based at the Théâtre de Nîme, and their Deschiens et Compagnie troupe.

As for contemporary **playwrights**, Yasmina Reza is probably the best known outside France thanks to her play *Art* (1994), about a group of friends who fall out over a modern "painting" – in fact a blank canvas – which received the prestigious Tony Award for the best play on New York's Broadway. In 2000 she followed this with *Life x 3*, exploring the shifting grounds of relationships from three different angles. Other up-and-coming writers with a growing international reputation include Lionel Spycher and Claudine Galea.

At a less sophisticated level, **café-théâtre**, literally a revue, monologue or mini-play performed in a place where you can drink and sometimes eat, is to be found in most major towns. The humour, featuring a lot of wordplay, and allusions to current fads, phobias and politicians means that it's often not that accessible to non-French speakers.

Street theatre is also flourishing. In summer you'll find performers out in force in all the major tourists resorts and it's well worth taking in one of the many **festivals**. The most noteworthy include those held in Chalon-sur-Saône (July), Aurillac (Aug) and Sotteville-lès-Rouen near Rouen (June). As regards more "traditional" theatre, the Festival d'Avignon (July) is by far the most important and exciting event, while the Festival d'Automne in Paris (mid-Sept to mid-Dec) is gaining a solid reputation.

For details of **Paris theatres**, see Chapter One. In other cities, the theatres are often part of the Maisons de la Culture or Centres d'Animation Culturelle; local tourist offices usually have schedules and tickets are not expensive.

Dance and mime

There has been a veritable explosion in **contemporary dance** in France over the last two decades. A pivotal event was in 1989, when the Gallotta-choreographed film *Rei-Dom* opened up a whole new range of possibilities, while the opening of the Centre National de la Danse in Pantin, near Paris, in 2004 confirmed the French dance scene as among the most exciting and innovative in the world.

Humour, everyday actions and obsessions, social problems and the darker shades of life find expression in the myriad current dance forms. Indeed, many of the traits of modern epic theatre are shared with dance, including a love of spectacle and an ability to cross international frontiers; Philippe Decouflé, Angelin Preljocaj and the duo José Montalvo and Dominique Hervieu continually wow audiences at home and abroad with their elaborate productions. Another trend has seen choreographers such as Mathilde Monnier and Christian Bourigault exploring the traditional image of dancers and their sexual identity, while Marco Berrettini and Michel Schweizer, among others, have taken inspiration from tele-reality shows such as *Star Acadamy*. As an antidote to such resolute modernity, works by Jean-Claude Gallotta continue to celebrate the timeless power and beauty of the human form.

Apart from the new Centre National de la Danse, with its eleven studios and multimedia resource centre, Paris is also home to La Cartoucherie in the Bois de Vincennes, where the exciting Californian choreographer Carolyn Carlson is now based. A number of regional companies also stand out – including Gallotta's troupe from Grenoble, Régine Chopinot's from La Rochelle and the Compagnie Montalvo-Hervieu based in Créteil – and the towns of Avignon, Uzès, Dijon, Lille and Toulouse all have a vibrant contemporary dance scene.

There are any number of contemporary dance festivals in France. The major event is Lyon's Biennale de la Danse (next held in September 2006) in which groups at the cutting edge combine dance with all manner of contemporary art forms. Other noteworthy dates in the dance calendar are the festivals held at Avignon, Montpellier and Uzès; see the box on p.73 for details.

For **classical ballet**, one of the most renowned companies is the Ballet de l'Opéra National de Paris at the Opéra-Garnier and the Opéra-Bastille, whose dance director is Brigitte Lefèvre. Outside the capital, the Ballet du Théâtre du Capitole in Toulouse, Bordeaux's Ballet de l'Opéra National and the Ballet National de Marseille are also highly regarded. In recent years a number of companies, such as the Ballet de l'Opéra National du Rhin, based in Mulhouse, and the Ballet de l'Opéra National de Lyon, have broadened their repertoire to include more contemporary works.

Though French **mime** has evolved since the incomparable Marcel Marceau, his influence, and that of his contemporaries Etienne Decroux and Jacques Lecoq, is still felt through the famous schools they each founded in Paris. Not that there's any shortage of creativity among the huge diversity of artists you'll encounter on the streets and at festivals such as Périgueux's excellent Mimos (early Aug).

Combining elements of dance, mime, music and theatre (particularly street theatre), French **circus arts** have undergone a tremendous revival over recent years. France now boasts a national centre for circus arts and dozens of schools, the most famous of which is the Centre National des Arts du Cirque at Châlons-en-Champagne, east of Paris, as well as an astonishing diversity of troupes. While you still find "classic" circus troupes, where technical skills are paramount, modern performers are more likely to stress artistic expression and present an "acrobatic theatre", in other words a unified dramatic event rather than a series of virtuoso performances. Cirque Plume, for example, often includes poetry in its presentations. Other names to watch out for include the trapeze artists Les Arts Sauts, acrobats Que-Cir-Que and the clowns of Les Nouveaux Nez. In Zingaro's magnificent "equestrian theatre" horses are transformed into dancers, and the Théâtre du Centaure, based in Marseille, combines theatre and circus riding to create a unique art form inspired by the half-horse half-man of Greek mythology; in 2002 the "centaurs" performed an adaptation of Shakespeare's *Macbeth*. The two main events showcasing traditional circus are the Festival Mondial du Cirque de Demain (Jan) in Paris and the Festival International du Cirque de Monte-Carlo (Jan). Contemporary circus arts are on display at the Festival Circa in Auch (last week in Oct; ⓦwww.circa.fr.st), Furies at Chalons-en-Champagne (June; ⓦwww.festival-furies.com) and the Festival International de Théâtre de Rue in Aurillac (mid-Aug; ⓦwww.aurillac.net).

Sports and outdoor pursuits

France has a wide range of sports on offer, both for the spectator and the participant. It's not difficult to get tickets to domestic and international football and rugby matches, while the biggest event of all, the Tour de France, is free. And if you're interested in expending some energy yourself, there's a whole host of activities and adventure holidays available.

Spectator sports

More than any of the cultural jamborees, it's **sporting** events that really excite the French – particularly cycling, football, rugby and tennis. In the south, bullfighting and the Basque game of pelota are also popular. At the local, everyday level, the rather less gripping game of *boules* is the sport of choice, played in every town and village.

Cycling

The sport the French are truly mad about is **cycling**. It was, after all, in Paris's Palais Royale gardens in 1791 that the precursor of the modern bicycle, the *célerifière*, was presented, and seventy years later the Parisian father-and-son team of Pierre and Ernest Michaux constructed the *vélocipede* (hence the modern French term *vélo* for bicycle), the first really efficient bicycle. The French can also legitimately claim the sport of cycle racing as their own, with the first event, a 1200-metre sprint, held in Paris's Parc St-Cloud in 1868 – sadly for national pride, however, the first champion was an Englishman.

That most French of sporting events, and the world's premier cycling race, the **Tour de France** (held in July), celebrated its centenary in 2003. Covering around 3500 kilometres, the course of the three-week event changes every year but some truly arduous mountain stages and some time trials are always part of the action, and sometimes foreign countries are included in the itinerary (Britain and Ireland, among others, have hosted stages). An aggregate of each rider's times is made daily, the overall leader wearing the coveted yellow jersey (*maillot jaune*). Huge crowds turn out to cheer on the cyclists at the finishing line of the ultimate stage on the Champs-Élysées when the French president himself presents the jersey to the overall winner – however, the crowds have been waiting for a French cyclist to win the Tour since Bernard Hinault's victory in 1985.

Over recent years the event has been rocked by drug scandals, beginning in 1998 when evidence of systematic doping within the cycling teams came to light. These scandals have cast a shadow over

Sporting calendar

Le Mans 24-hour motorcycle rally (mid-April); 24-hour car rally (mid-June); ⓦwww.lemans.org.

Monaco Formula 1 Grand Prix (May; ⓦwww.monaco-formula1.com).

Monte Carlo Car rally (Jan; ⓦwww.acm.mc).

Nevers French Formula 1 Grand Prix (July; ⓦwww.magnyf1.com).

Paris Six Nations rugby tournament (Feb–April; ⓦwww.6-nations-rugby.com); Marathon (April; ⓦwww.parismarathon.com); Roland Garros International Tennis Championship (last week May to first week June; ⓦwww.rolandgarros.com); Grand Prix de l'Arc de Triomphe (horse-race; Oct; ⓦwww.france-galop.com).

Tour de France (cycle race; July; ⓦwww.letour.fr).

the American rider Lance Armstrong's monumental achievement of not only fighting to overcome cancer but then going on to win every race since 1999 and, in 2004, becoming the first man to have won 6 consecutive races.

Other classic long-distance bike races include the **Paris–Roubaix**, instigated in 1896, which is reputed to be the most exacting one-day race in the world, parts of it over cobblestones; the **Paris–Brussels** held since 1893; and the rugged seven-day **Paris–Nice** event, covering over 1100km. The **Grand Prix des Nations**, which takes place in September in the Seine-Maritime département, is the world's foremost time trial; the Palais Omnisport de Bercy in Paris (see p.208) holds other time trials and cycling events.

Football

In France, as in most countries, **football** is the number-one team sport. Football fever reached a pitch in the late 1990s, when the French team won the World Cup for the first time in 1998 in front of their home crowd and in 2000 became the first side ever to add a European Championships title to the world crown. Perhaps inevitably, the team has found it hard to live up to expectations since then, despite boasting some of the world's top players.

Up until 1998, most of France's football successes had taken place off the pitch through innovators such as **Jules Rimet**, who created the World Cup in 1930, and **Henri Delauney**, who conceived the European Championships thirty years later. It was not until 1984, when **Michel Platini**'s cavalier side lifted the European Championships cup, that the French were able to translate their influence in the corridors of power onto the pitch.

It was only fitting, therefore, that Platini was chosen as president of his country's bid to host the **World Cup** for the second time in 1998. Having won the right to stage it, the French went on to clinch the tournament, though the final against Brazil, the pre-tournament favourites and defending champions, proved an anti-climax. However, the result was all that mattered to the French, and a million people piled onto the streets of Paris for the biggest street party since the end of World War II.

The impact of the victory extended beyond the world of football. Of the 32 sides that made it to the finals, France's was the most diverse ethnically, with half of the squad's 22 players of foreign extraction, including their star player **Zinedine Zidane**, affectionately known as Zizou. For the first time, the national team really reflected the racial diversity of modern French society. Before the tournament Jean-Marie Le Pen's right-wing Front National party had called for a ban on players of foreign extraction playing for France, but the heroics of Zidane, Marcel Desailly and Lillian Thuram, among others caused him to backtrack sharply. Furthermore, the French president, **Jacques Chirac**, chose his Bastille Day conference, two days after the French triumph, as a political platform to denounce the Front National's policies of racial discrimination and to praise France's "tricolour and multicolour" World Cup win.

Buoyed by their success, France stormed through the 2000 European Championships in style, and set their sights on the 2002 World Cup, hosted jointly by South Korea and Japan. They were widely tipped as favourites, and certainly expected to make it to the finals. But it was not to be. France were not only eliminated in the first round, but didn't even score a single goal. They performed slightly better in the 2004 European Championships, but were unexpectedly eliminated by Greece, the eventual winner, in the quarter finals.

The reasons for such a sudden change in fortunes have been the subject of endless debate in the French media. Some attribute it to arrogance or, at least, overconfidence in the wake of the 1998 World Cup win. Others cite the fact that so many of the international squad – snapped up by Europe's richest clubs in the aftermath of the 1998 World Cup – now play their club football outside France, mainly in England, Italy and Spain.

The drain of talent out of France and the disappointing performance of the national team does not seem to have harmed the **domestic game**, however. Average attendances are on the rise, almost all clubs now have sound financial backing, and the biggest clubs, such as **Monaco**, **Marseille** and **Paris St-Germain** (PSG), have all done well in European competitions in recent years. More importantly, the infrastructure of French football has never been in better shape. The main club grounds underwent major reconstruction for the 1998 World Cup – some for the first time in sixty years – and Paris now boasts the magnificent **Stade de France**. In addition, the French football federation has invested heavily in a national football institute for outstanding young players, based in Clairefontaine, near Paris, which is the envy of the footballing world.

Rugby

Although confined mainly to the southwest of the country, **rugby** enjoys a passionate following throughout France. The French have a rich rugby heritage and are renowned throughout the world for the flair with which they play the game. Their high-risk strategies make the national team a fascinating side to watch, capable of the sublime – when everything clicks – and the abject, but rarely anything in between. French rugby's greatest moment to date came in the semi-finals of the **1999 World Cup**, when they stunned the world by trouncing favourites New Zealand with an exhilarating display of attacking rugby. Rather predictably, however, they blew cold in the final, putting up feeble resistance against an Australian side that never had to rouse itself out of second gear. In 2003 France made it as far as the semi-final, only to be thrashed by an England team on route to the podium.

More international fare is provided by the **Six Nations tournament** – the other five nations being England, Wales, Scotland, Ireland and Italy – which takes place every year between February and April. Matches are played alternately at home and away. Over the past few years, France has consistently challenged for the title, and in 1997 and 1998 it achieved the considerable feat of winning back-to-back **Grand Slams** – "Grand Slam" being the term used to describe a clean sweep of victories over the other nations. France team again clinched Grand Slams in 2002 and 2004, in the latter reversing their World Cup defeat with a nail-biting victory over England.

Domestically, the French clubs have ridden out rugby's occasionally fraught transition from amateur to professional status and look to be in good shape. Though France has lost some of its stars to predatory English clubs, unlike in football the majority of the national side still plays at home. Sides to watch for are **Toulouse, Perpignan** and **Brive** (past winners of the Europe-wide Heineken Cup), **Agen**, and the Basque teams of **Bayonne** and **Biarritz**, which still retain their reputation as keepers of the game's soul.

Pelota

In the Basque country (and also in the nearby Landes), the main draw for crowds is the national ball game of **pelota**, a lethally (sometimes literally) fast variety of team handball or raquetball played in a walled court with a ball of solid wood. The most popular form today is played with bare hands in a two-walled court called a fronton. In other varieties wooden bats are used or wicker slings strapped to the players' arms.

Bullfighting

In and around the Camargue, the number-one sport is bullfighting, though this is usually the *course camarguaise*, involving variations on the theme of removing cockades from the base of the bull's horns. It's generally the "fighters", rather than the bulls, who get hurt. Further west, particularly in the Landes département, you'll come across the similar *courses landaises*, where men perform acrobats with the by no means docile local cows.

Spanish bullfights, known as **corridas**, do take place – and draw capacity crowds – in southern France. The major events of the year are the Féria de Nîmes at Pentecost (Whitsun) and the Easter *féria* at Arles.

Boules

In every town or village square, particularly in the south, you'll see *berret*-clad men playing **boules** or its variant **pétanque** (in which contestants must keep both feet on the ground when throwing). The game is similar to British bowls but the terrain is always rough (never grass) and the area much smaller. The metal balls (*boules*) are usually thrown from a distance of about six to ten metres, the aim being to place them as close as possible to the wooden jack (*cochonnet*). Although more women are taking up *boules*, at competition level it remains very male-dominated: there are café or village teams and endless championships. There's even talk – not all of it in jest – of getting *boules* recognized as an Olympic sport.

Outdoor pursuits

In addition to the old standbys – walking, cycling and skiing – France provides a fantastically wide range of outdoor activities. Most have a national federation (see box), which can provide information on local clubs.

Walking and climbing

Long-distance **walkers** are well served in France by a network of some 60,000km of long-distance marked footpaths, known as *sentiers de grande randonnée* or, more commonly, simply as **GRs**. They're fully signposted and equipped with campsites, refuges and hostels (*gîtes d'étapes*) along the way. Some are real marathons, like the GR5 from the coast of Holland to Nice, the trans-Pyrenean GR10 or the Grande Traversée des Alpes (the GTA). The Chemin de St-Jacques – GR65 – follows the ancient pilgrim route from Le Puy in the Auvergne to the Spanish border above St-Jean-Pied-de-Port and on to the shrine of Santiago de Compostela, while GR3 traces the Loire from source to sea. There are also thousands of shorter *sentiers de promenade et de randonnée*, the **PRs**, as well as nature walks and many other local footpaths.

Each GR and many PRs are described in a **Topo-guide** (available outside France in good travel bookshops) which gives a detailed account of the route, including maps, campsites, refuges, sources of provisions, etc. In France, the guides are available from bookshops and some tourist offices, or direct from the principal French walkers' association, the Fédération Française de la Randonnée Pédestre (see overleaf for details). In addition, many tourist offices can provide guides to their local footpaths.

In mountain areas there are associations of professional mountain guides, often located in the tourist office, who organize walking and climbing (escalade) expeditions for all levels of experience.

For recommendations on walking maps, see p.42; guidebooks to look out for are listed on p.1345.

Cycling

Cyclists have around 50,000km of marked cycle paths (*pistes cyclables*) in France. Many towns and cities have established cycle lanes, while in the countryside there are an increasing number of specially designated mountain-bike tracks. Aquitaine, in southwest France, is particularly well-provided for: there are extensive routes through the Landes forest and south to the Spanish border. IGN's 1:100,000 maps are aimed at cyclists (see p.42). The Fédération Française de Cyclisme (see box, overleaf) produces a guide to mountain-biking sites, and tourist offices can provide details of local cycle ways.

For more details on cycling in France see p.80.

Skiing and snowboarding

One activity that millions of visitors come to France to practise rather than watch is **skiing and snowboarding**. And whether downhill, cross-country or mountaineering, it's also enthusiastically pursued by the French. It can be an expensive sport to practise independently, however, and the best deals are often to be had from package operators (see p.33, p.35 and p.38). These can be arranged in France or before you leave (most travel agents sell all-in packages). Though it's possible to ski from early November through to the end of April at high altitudes, peak season is February and March.

The best skiing and boarding is generally to be had in the **Alps**. The higher the

National Sports Federations

A full list of sports federations is available on the **Ministry of Sports** website Ⓦwww.jeunesse-sports.gouv.fr. Below are a few for the more popular activities.

Canoeing

Fédération Française de Canoë-Kayak 87 quai de la Marne, BP 58, 94344 Joinville-le-Pont Ⓣ01.45.11.08.50, Ⓦwww.ffck.org.

Caving

Fédération Française de Spéléologie 28 rue Delandine, 69002 Lyon Ⓣ04.72.56.09.63, Ⓦwww.ffspeleo.fr.

Cycling

Fédération Française de Cyclisme 5 rue de Rome, 93561 Rosny-sous-Bois, Ⓣ01.49.35.69.00, Ⓦwww.ffc.fr.

Fédération Française de Cyclotourisme 12 rue Louis-Bertrand, 94207 Ivry-sur-Seine Ⓣ01.56.20.88.88, Ⓦwww.ffct.org.

Diving

Fédération Française d'Etudes et de Sports Sous-Marins 24 quai de Rive-Neuve, 13007 Marseille Ⓣ04.91.33.99.31, Ⓦwww.ffessm.fr.

Golf

Fédération Française de Golf 68 rue Anatole-France, 92300 Levallois-Perret Ⓣ01.41.49.77.00, Ⓦwww.ffg.org.

Mountaineering, rock climbing & canyoning

Fédération Française de la Montagne et de l'Escalade 8–10 quai de la Marne, 75019 Paris Ⓣ01.40.18.75.50, Ⓦwww.ffme.fr.

Riding

Comité National de Tourisme Équestre 59 bd MacDonald, 75019 Paris Ⓣ01.53.26.15.50, Ⓦwww.tourisme-equestre.fr.

Fédération Française d'Equitation 81-83 ave Edouard-Vaillant, 92517 Boulogne-Billancourt Ⓣ01.58.17.58.17, Ⓦwww.ffe.com

Skiing

Fédération Française de Ski 50 rue des Marquisats, BP 2451, 74011 Annecy Ⓣ04.50.51.40.34, Ⓦwww.ffs.fr.

Snowboarding

Association Française de Snowboard Route du Parc-du-Souvenir, 06500 Menton Ⓣ04.92.41.80.00, Ⓦwww.afs-fr.com.

Surfing

Fédération Française de Surf 30 impasse de la Digue-Nord, BP 28, 40150 Hossegor Ⓣ05.58.43.55.88, Ⓦwww.surfingfrance.com.

Walking

Fédération Française de Randonnée Pédestre 14 rue Riquet, 75019 Paris Ⓣ01.44.89.93.90, Ⓦwww.ffrp.asso.fr.

Windsurfing

Fédération Française de Voile 17 rue Henri-Bocquillon, 75015 Paris Ⓣ01.40.60.37.00, Ⓦwww.ffvoile.org.

resort the longer the season, and the fewer the anxieties you'll have about there being enough snow. Resorts such as Tignes, Les Deux-Alpes or Val Thorens, are almost all modern, with the very latest in lift technology. They're terrific for full-time skiing, but they lack the cachet, charm or the nightlife of the older, lower resorts such as Megève and Courchevel. The foothills of the Alps in Provence have the same mix of old and new on a smaller scale. The clientele are Riviera residents and prices are not cheap, though at least you can nip down to the coast when you're bored with snow. The **Pyrenees** are a friendlier range of mountains, less developed (though that can be a drawback if you want to get in as many different runs as possible per day) and warmer, which means a shorter season and less reliable snow.

Cross-country skiing (*ski de fond*) is being promoted hard, especially in the smaller ranges of the Jura and Massif Central. It's easier on the joints, but don't be fooled into thinking it's any less athletic a sport. For the really experienced and fit, though, it can be a good means of transport, using snow-bound GR routes to discover villages still relatively uncommercialized. Several independent operators organize ski-mountaineering courses in the French mountains (see p.33, p.35 and p.38).

Water sports

France's extensive coasts have also been well developed for recreational activities, and this is especially true in the south. Although in summer you can **swim** just about anywhere from Normandy to the Mediterranean, the Côte d'Azur and Corsica are justly reputed as the best for beaches. In the towns and resorts of the Mediterranean coast, you'll find every conceivable sort of beachside activity, including **boating**, **sea-fishing** and **diving**. If you don't mind high prices and crowds, the too-blue waters and sandy coves are unbeatable. The western Mediterranean coast is much windier, and **windsurfers** delight in the calm of the broad salt-water inlets (*étangs*) which typify the area. The best conditions for **surfing**, however, are to be found along the rougher Atlantic coast, where Biarritz is something of a Mecca for the sport, hosting a lively international championship each July. North up the coast from Biarritz, Anglet, Hossegor and Lacanau are also excellent surf spots and regularly host international competitions. The Atlantic coast is good for **sailing** too, particularly around Brittany, while the waters around Corsica are popular for diving and **snorkelling**.

Most towns have a **swimming pool** (*piscine*), though outdoor pools tend to open only in the height of summer. You may be requested to wear a bathing cap, so come prepared. You can also swim at many river beaches (usually signposted) and in the real and artificial lakes which pepper France. Many lakes have **leisure centres** (*bases de plein airs* or *centres de loisirs*) at which you can rent pedaloes, windsurfers and dinghies, as well as larger boats and jet-skis (on the bigger reservoirs).

Canoeing is hugely popular in France, and in summer practically every navigable stretch of river has outfits renting boats and organizing excursions. The rivers of the southwest (the Dordogne, Vézère, Lot and Tarn), in particular, offer tremendous variety. For the more adventurous, there are plenty of opportunities for **rafting** and **canyoning** in the gorges and ravines of the Pyrenees, the Alps and the Massif Central.

Opportunities for **canal-boating** have increased as canals and rivers have been opened to navigation; see p.58 for information about renting boats. Popular routes include the canals linking the River Marne to the Rhine, which pass through the Champagne region; the Canal de Bourgogne, through Burgundy; the waterways crisscrossing Brittany; and the combination of canals and rivers cutting across from Bordeaux on the Atlantic coast to the Mediterranean. Note that, while no licence is required for canal-boating, the skipper will need some recognized form of certificate for navigating the main rivers.

Another relatively placid inland activity is **fishing** on permitted lakes and rivers. Brittany is one of the biggest areas for carp fishing. Salmon and trout can be caught in several rivers in Brittany and Normandy, and in the River Loire, but by far the most varied – and scenic – salmon rivers are those of the western Pyrenees. The rivers Lot, Tarn and Garonne, in the southwest, and the Saône are well stocked with bass. Local tourist offices and fishing shops will assist you in obtaining a licence.

Sea-fishing in the Mediterranean or off the Atlantic coast offers grey mullet, bass, mackerel, bream or sardines as well as lobster, crayfish and scallops. Night-fishing expeditions are becoming increasingly popular.

Golf

France has over 500 **golf** courses, of which several are ranked among the world's best. Up there at the top is the challenging – and absolutely immaculate – **Les Bordes** course (Ⓦwww.lesbordes.com), near Orléans, which boasts Europe's largest putting green and excellent practice facilities. Other first-class courses include **Kempferhof** (Ⓦwww.golf-kempferhof.com), outside Strasbourg; **Royal Park Evian** (Ⓦwww.royalparcevian.com), near Geneva and home to the Evian Masters women's tournament; and **Spérone** (Ⓦwww.sperone.net) in Corsica. This last is a very technical course made even more demanding by strong winds, but boasting superb views – on a clear day you can see Sardinia. You'll find plenty of scenic courses as well in Provence and all along the Côte d'Azur, where the **Monte-Carlo Golf Club** (Ⓣ04.93.41.09.11) stands out for its setting perched 800m up on the slopes of Mont Agel.

Down in the southwest, **Pau Golf Club** (Ⓣ05.59.13.18.56, Ⓔpau.golf.club@wanadoo.fr) was the first course to be opened in continental Europe, in 1856, followed three decades later by **Biarritz Le Phare** (Ⓦwww.golf-biarritz.com); both are still excellent and challenging courses. Also near Biarritz, the **Chiberta Golf Club** (Ⓣ05.59.52.51.10) is a traditional links alternating between pine forest and seashore which rates as one of the top ten in France. In fact, the whole area stretching north along the coast from Biarritz to Bordeaux is a golfer's paradise.

Green fees are usually in the range of €40 to €60. Alternatively, you can buy a "Golf Pass" which allows entry to several courses in a particular region at reduced rates. Contact the Fédération Française de Golf (see box on p.84) or the departmental tourist office for further details.

Other activities

In addition to cycling, walking and canoeing, **horse-riding** is another excellent way to explore the French countryside. Practically every town has an equestrian centre (*centre équestre*) where you can ride with a guide or unaccompanied, although the most famous and romantic region for riding is the flat and windswept Camargue at the Rhône Delta. **Mule-** and **donkey-trekking** are also increasingly popular, particularly along the trails of the Pyrenees and Alps.

Hang-gliding and **paragliding** (a cross between parachuting and hang-gliding) offer a completely different perspective; the best areas for these are the Hautes-Alpes of Provence, the Pyrenees and Corsica. **Caving** is popular in the limestone caverns of southwest France and along the Spanish border. You'll need to make an arrangement through a local club, which usually organize beginner courses as well as half- or full-day outings.

Crime and personal safety

While violent crime involving tourists is rare in France, petty theft is endemic in all the big cities, along the Côte d'Azur, on beaches and at major tourist sights. In Paris, be especially wary of pickpockets at train stations and on the metro and RER lines; RER line B, serving Charles de Gaulle airport and Gare du Nord, and subway line number 1 are particularly notorious. Cars with foreign number-plates face a high risk of break-ins; vehicles are rarely stolen, but car radios and luggage – even if locked out of sight – make tempting targets. Motorbike thieves operate in big cities and along the Mediterranean coast, often stealing from cars at traffic lights or in jams; don't leave valuables on the seats and keep car windows shut and doors locked at all times.

It obviously makes sense to take the normal **precautions**: don't flash wads of notes or travellers' cheques around; carry your bag or wallet securely and be especially careful in crowds; never leave cameras and other valuables lying around; and park your car overnight in a monitored parking, garage or within sight of a police station. It's wise to keep a separate record of cheque and credit card numbers and the phone numbers for cancelling them (see p.46). Finally, make sure you have a good insurance policy (see p.43).

There are two main types of **police** in France – the Police Nationale and the Gendarmerie Nationale. The former deals with all crime, parking and traffic affairs within large and mid-sized towns, where you'll find them in the Commissariat de Police. The Gendarmerie Nationale covers the rural areas. The police have the right to stop you at any time to ask for your ID and can also search you and your car without a warrant; if it happens to you, it's not worth being difficult.

Emergency numbers

Police ⓣ17.

Medical emergencies/ambulance ⓣ15.

Fire brigade/paramedics ⓣ18.

Rape crisis (SOS Viol) ⓣ08.00.05.95.95.

All emergency numbers are toll-free.

In the Alps or Pyrenees, you may come across specialized mountaineering sections of the police force. These are unfailingly helpful, friendly and approachable, providing rescue services and guidance.

If you need to **report a theft**, go to the local Gendarmerie or Commissariat de Police (addresses are given in the Guide for the major cities), where they will fill out a *constat de vol*. The first thing they'll ask for is your passport, and vehicle documents if relevant. Although the police are not always as co-operative as they might be, it's their duty to assist you if you've lost your passport or all your money.

If you have an **accident** while driving, you must fill in and sign a *constat d'accident* (declaration form) or, if another car is also involved, a *constat aimable* (jointly agreed declaration); these forms should be provided with the car's insurance documents. For minor **driving offences** such as speeding, the police can impose on-the-spot fines. For anything more serious, you could lose your licence (see p.54 for more).

Pedestrians should take great care when crossing roads. Although the authorities are trying to improve matters, French drivers pay little heed to pedestrian/zebra crossings. Never step out onto a crossing assuming that drivers will stop. Also be wary at traffic lights: check cars are not still speeding towards you even when the green man is showing.

Drug use is just as prevalent in France as anywhere else in Europe – and just as risky.

People caught smuggling or possessing drugs, even just a few grams of marijuana, are liable to find themselves in jail. Should you be **arrested** on any charge, you have the right to contact your consulate (addresses are given on p.39), though don't expect much sympathy.

Though the self-proclaimed home of "liberté, egalité, fraternité", France has an unfortunate reputation for **racism** and **anti-Semitism**. The majority of racist incidents are focused against the Arab community and occur largely, but by no means exclusively, within the cities. As a result, particularly Arab, but also black and Asian visitors may encounter an unwelcome degree of curiosity or suspicion from shopkeepers, hoteliers and the like. It is not unknown for hotels to claim they are fully booked, for example, and the police are far more likely to stop Arab and black people and demand to see their ID. In the worst cases, you might be unlucky enough to experience outright hostility.

If you suffer a **racial assault**, contact the police, your consulate or one of the local anti-racism organizations (though they may not have English-speakers): SOS Racism (Ⓦwww.sos-racisme.org) and Mouvement contre le Racisme et pour l'Amitié entre les Peuples (MRAP; Ⓦwww.mrap.solidarites.net) have offices in most regions of France.

Alternatively, you could contact the **English-speaking helpline** SOS Help (Ⓣ01.46.21.46.46, daily 3–11pm; Ⓦwww.soshelpline.org). The service is manned by trained volunteers who not only provide a confidential listening service, but also offer practical information for foreigners facing problems in France.

Some readers might be concerned by **Corsica**'s reputation for nationalist-separatist violence, but the reality is that the sporadic arson attacks, bombings and shootings rarely, if ever, affect tourists. Corsican paramilitary groups either target each other or symbols of state power such as police, government buildings and post offices. It therefore pays to be vigilant in town centres and around public buildings.

Living and working in France

Specialists aside, most non-EU citizens who manage to survive for long periods of time in France do it on luck, brazenness and willingness to live in pretty basic conditions. In the cities and larger towns, bar work, club work, teaching English, translating or working as an au pair are some of the ways people scrape by; in the countryside, the options come down to seasonal fruit- or grape-picking, teaching English, busking or DIY oddjobbing. Remember that unemployment is high. The current rate stands at almost ten percent and is on the rise.

EU citizens are free to work in France on the same basis as a French citizen. This means you no longer have to apply for a residence or work permit except in very rare cases – contact your nearest French consulate for further information. **Non-EU citizens**, however, will need both a work permit (*autorisation de travail*) and a residence permit (see p.39); again, contact your nearest French consulate or, if already in France, your local *mairie* or *préfecture* to check what rules apply in your particular situation.

France has a **minimum wage** (known as the SMIC – *Salaire Minimum Interprofessional de Croissance*), indexed to the cost of living. Employers, however, are likely to pay lower wages to temporary foreign workers who don't have easy legal resources and make them work longer hours. By law, however, all EU citizens are entitled to exactly the same pay, conditions and trade union rights as French nationals.

If you're looking for something secure, it's important to **plan well in advance**. A good starting point is to get hold of one of the books on working abroad published by Vacation Work (9 Park End St, Oxford OX1 1HJ; ⓣ01865/241 978, ⓦwww.vacationwork.co.uk). In France, check out the "Offres d'Emploi" (Job Offers) in *Le Monde*, *Le Figaro* and the *International Herald Tribune*; and try the youth information agency CIDJ (Centre d'Information et de Documentation Jeunesse; ⓦwww.cidj.com), 101 quai Branly, 17015 Paris, or CIJ (Centre d'Information Jeunesse) offices in other main cities, which sometimes have information about temporary jobs for foreigners and produce all sorts of useful information about working in France. The national employment agency, ANPE (Agence Nationale pour l'Emploi; ⓦwww.anpe.fr), with offices all over France, advertises temporary jobs in all fields and, in theory, offers a whole range of services to job-seekers open to all EU citizens, but is not renowned for its helpfulness to foreigners. Non-EU citizens will have to show a work permit to apply for any of their jobs.

In **Paris**, it's worth looking out for the free English-language magazine FUSAC, published every two weeks, which carries ads for employment and housing among other things; it's also available direct from FUSAC, 26 rue Bénard, 75014 Paris (ⓦwww.fusac.fr/english).

Teaching English

Finding a job **teaching English** is also best done in advance. Late summer is usually the best time. You don't need fluent French to get a post, but a degree and a TEFL (Teaching English as a Foreign Language) or similar qualification are normally required. The annual *EL Gazette Guide to English Lanuage Teaching Around the World* gives a thorough breakdown of TEFL courses available and provides all sorts of practical information, including lists of schools; some of their listings are also available on EFLweb (ⓦwww.eflweb.com). The guide is produced by EL Gazette Ltd, Unit 3 Constantine Court, 6 Fairclough St, London E1 1PW (ⓣ020/7481 6700, ⓦwww.elgazette.com), who also publish the monthly *EL Gazette* which is filled with job advertisements. Other useful resources are *Teaching English Abroad* published by Vacation Work (see above) and the TEFL website ⓦwww.tefl.com, with its database of English-teaching vacancies. If you apply for jobs from home, most schools will fix up the necessary papers for you.

It's just feasible to find a teaching job when you're in France, but you may have to accept semi-official status and no job security. You'll find more choice and better pay outside Paris and the main tourist centres; look under "Enseignement: Langues" in the local yellow pages for addresses of schools, or ask in the local Chambre de Commerce et d'Industrie (Chamber of Commerce). Offering private lessons (via university noticeboards or classified ads, for example), you'll have lots of competition, but it's always worth a try.

Au pair work

Au pair work is usually arranged through an agency, who should sort out any necessary paperwork; you'll find agencies listed in *The Au Pair & Nanny's Guide to Working Abroad* published by Vacation Work (see above) and on the International Au Pair Association (IAPA) website ⓦwww.iapa.org. *The Lady* (ⓦwww.lady.co.uk), published in Britain, is *the* magazine for classified adverts for au pairs.

Terms and conditions are never very generous, but should include board, lodging and pocket money. Prospective employers are required by law to provide a written job description, so there is protection on both sides. Even so, it's wise to have an escape route (such as a ticket home) in case you find the conditions intolerable and your employers insufferable.

Other work opportunities

The American/Irish/British **bars and restaurants** in the main cities and resorts sometimes have vacancies. You'll need to speak French, look smart and be prepared to work very long hours. Some people find jobs **selling magazines** on the street and **leafleting** by asking people already doing it for the agency address.

Temporary jobs in the **travel industry** revolve around courier work – supervising and working on bus tours or summer campsites. You'll need good French (and another European language will help) and should preferably write to tour operators in early spring. Getting work as a courier on a campsite is slightly easier. It usually involves putting up tents at the beginning of the season, taking them down again at the end and general maintenance and troubleshooting work in the months between; Canvas Holidays (see p.33) is often worth approaching. Travel magazines such as the reliable *Wanderlust* have a Job Shop section which often advertises job opportunities with tour companies.

An offbeat possibility if you want to discover rural life is being a **working guest** on an organic farm. The period can be anything from a week to a couple of months and the work may involve cheese-making, market gardening, beekeeping, wine-producing and building. For details of the scheme and a list of addresses in France, contact World-Wide Opportunities on Organic Farms (WWOOF; Ⓦwww.wwoof.org/home.asp), with branches in Britain, the US, Canada, Australia and New Zealand, among other places.

Study and work programmes in France

It's relatively easy to be a **student** in France. Foreigners pay no more than French nationals to enrol for a course, and the only problem then is to support yourself, though you'll be eligible for subsidized accommodation, meals and all the student reductions. In general, French **universities** are fairly informal, but there are strict entry requirements, including an exam in French, for undergraduate degrees, but not for postgraduate courses. For full details and prospectuses, contact the Cultural Service of any French embassy or consulate (see p.39). Embassies and consulates can also provide details of **language courses** at French universities and colleges, which are often combined with lectures on French "civilization" and usually very costly. You'll find ads for lesser language courses advertised all over the place.

It's also worth noting that if you're a full-time **non-EU student** in France, you can get a non-EU work permit for the following summer so long as your visa is still valid.

Further useful resources are the website Ⓦwww.studyabroad.com, with listings and links to study and work programmes worldwide, and the publication *International Jobs: Where They Are, How to Get Them* (published by HarperCollins, Ⓦwww.harpercollins.com). Alternatively, contact the organisations listed below.

Contacts in the UK and Ireland

British Council Ⓣ020/7930 8466, Ⓦwww.britishcouncil.org. The Council's Central Management of Direct Teaching (Ⓣ020/7389 4931) recruits TEFL teachers for posts worldwide, and its Central Bureau for International Education and Training (Ⓣ020/7389 4004, Ⓦwww.centralbureau.org.uk) enables those who already work as educators to find out about teacher development programmes abroad.

BTCV (British Trust for Conservation Volunteers) Ⓣ01302/572 244, Ⓦwww.btcv.org.uk. One of the largest environmental charities in Britain, with branches across the country, also offers a number of working holidays in France (as a paying volunteer); comprehensive brochure available.

Council on International Educational Exchange (CIEE) Ⓣ020/7478 2000, Ⓦwww.councilexchanges.org.uk. International study and work programmes for students and recent graduates.

Erasmus EU-run student exchange programme enabling students at participating EU universities to study in another European member country. Mobility grants available from three months to a full academic year. Anyone interested should contact their university's international relations office, or check the Erasmus website Ⓦeuropa.eu.int /comm/education/programmes/socrates /erasmus/erasmus_en.

Field Studies Council Overseas Ⓣ01743/852 150 or Ⓣ0845/852 150, Ⓦwww.fscoverseas.org.uk. Respected educational charity with over 20 years' experience of organizing specialized holidays with study tours visits worldwide. Group size is generally limited to 10–15 people. *Overseas Experiences* brochure available.

International House Ⓣ020/7518 6999, Ⓦwww.ihlondon.com. Head office for reputable English-teaching organization which offers TEFL training leading to the award of a Certificate in English Language Teaching to Adults (CELTA), and recruits for teaching positions in Britain and abroad.

Contacts in the US and Canada

AFS Intercultural Programs 10016 ⓣ1-800/727-2437 or 212/299 9000, ⓦusa.afs.org. Runs summer experiential programs aimed at fostering international understanding for teenagers and adults.
American Institute for Foreign Study ⓣ1-800/727-2437, ⓦwww.aifs.com. Language study and cultural immersion for the summer or school year, as well as au pair and Camp America programs.
Association for International Practical Training ⓣ1-800/994-2443 or 410/997-2200, ⓦwww.aipt.org. Summer internships for students who have completed at least two years of college in science, agriculture, engineering or architecture.
Bernan Associates ⓣ1-800/274-4888, ⓦwww.bernan.com. Distributes UNESCO's encyclopedic *Study Abroad*.
Council on International Educational Exchange (CIEE) ⓣ1-800/2COUNCIL, ⓦwww.ciee.org. A non-profit organization with summer, semester and academic-year programs in France among other countries. It also runs volunteer projects in France and publishes *Work, Study, Travel Abroad and Volunteer! The Comprehensive Guide to Voluntary Service in the US and Abroad.*
Experiment in International Living ⓣ1-800/345-2929 or 802/257-7751, ⓦwww.usexperiment.org. Summer program for high-school students.
Volunteers for Peace ⓣ802/259-2759, ⓦwww.vfp.org. Non-profit organization with links to a huge international network of "workcamps", two- to four-week programs that bring volunteers together from many countries to carry out needed community projects. Most workcamps are in summer, with registration in April–May. Annual membership including directory costs $20.
World Learning ⓣ1-800/257-7751, ⓦwww.worldlearning.org. World Learning's School for International Training (ⓣ1-800/257-7751, ⓦwww.sit.edu) runs accredited college semesters in France, comprising language and cultural studies.

Contacts in Australia and New Zealand

Australians Studying Abroad ⓣ03/9509 1955 or ⓣ1800/645 755, ⓦwww.asatravinfo.com.au. Study tours focusing on art and culture; AUS$500 deposit.

Travellers with disabilities

The French authorities have been making a concerted effort to improve facilities for disabled travellers. Though haphazard parking habits and stepped village streets remain serious obstacles for anyone with mobility problems, ramps or other forms of access are gradually being added to hotels, museums and other public buildings. All but the oldest hotels are required to adapt at least one room to be wheelchair accessible and a number of theatres now display the text for the deaf and hard-of-hearing during certain performances.

For **getting to France**, Eurotunnel offers the simplest option for travellers from the UK, since you can remain in your car. Alternatively, Eurostar trains have a limited number of wheelchair spaces in first-class for the price of the regular second-class fare; it's wise to reserve well in advance, when you might also like to enquire about the special assistance which Eurostar offers. If you're flying, it's worth noting that, while airlines are required to offer access to travellers with mobility problems, the level of service provided by some discount airlines may be fairly basic. All cross-Channel ferries have lifts for getting to and from the car deck, but moving between the different passenger decks may be more difficult.

Within France, most train stations now make provision for travellers with mobility problems. Spaces for wheelchairs are available in first-class carriages of all high-speed **TGVs** for the price of the regular second-class fare; note that these must be booked in advance. For other trains, a wheelchair symbol in the timetable indicates services offering special on-board facilities, though it's best to doublecheck when booking. SNCF also produces a free guide, *Le Mémento du Voyageur Handicapé*, detailing all its services, which is available from all main stations.

Drivers of **taxis** are legally obliged to help passengers in and out of the vehicle and to carry guide dogs. Specially adapted taxi services are available in some towns: contact the local tourist office for further information, or one of the organizations listed below. The big **car rental** agencies such as Hertz and Europcar provide automatic cars and cars with hand controls, but only in certain locations and you'll need to reserve well in advance.

As for finding suitable **accommodation**, guides produced by Logis de France (see p.60) and Gîtes de France (see p.61) indicate places with specially adapted rooms, though it's advisable to doublecheck when booking that the facilities meet to your needs.

Up-to-date **information** about accessibility, special programmes and discounts is best obtained before you leave home from the organizations listed below. The specialist British publisher, Smooth Ride Guides (Ⓣ01279 777966), recently issued a France guide detailing accessible accommodation, transport, attractions and other tourist facilities. French readers might also want to get hold of the *Handitourisme* guide, published by Petit Futé (Ⓦwww.petitfute.com), and *Guide Rousseau* (Ⓦwww.guide-rousseau.com), both of which cover similar ground and are available from major bookstores such as FNAC and Virgin, or direct from the publishers. Some tourist offices also have information, though it's not always completely reliable.

Contacts for travellers with disabilities

In France

Association des Paralysés de France (APF) 17 bd Auguste-Blanqui, 75013 Paris Ⓣ01.40.78.69.00, Ⓦwww.apf.asso.fr. National association which can answer general enquiries and put you in touch with their departmental offices.

Fédération Française Handisport 42 rue Louis-Lumière, 75020 Paris Ⓣ01.40.31.45.00, Ⓦwww.handisport.org. Amongst other things, this federation provides information on sports and leisure facilities for people with disabilities.

In the UK and Ireland

Access Travel 6 The Hillock, Astley, Lancashire M29 7GW Ⓣ01942/888 844, Ⓦwww.access-travel.co.uk. Tour operator that can arrange flights, transfer and accommodation. This is a small business, personally checking out places before recommendation. They can guarantee accommodation standards in France, among other European countries.

Holiday Care 2nd floor, Imperial Building, Victoria Rd, Horley, Surrey RH6 7PZ Ⓣ0845/124 9971 or 0208/760 0072, Ⓦwww.holidaycare.org.uk. Provides free lists of accessible accommodation and information on financial help for holidays.

Irish Wheelchair Association Blackheath Drive, Clontarf, Dublin 3 Ⓣ01/818 6400, Ⓦwww.iwa.ie. Useful information provided about travelling abroad with a wheelchair.

Tripscope Alexandra House, Albany Rd, Brentford, Middlesex TW8 0NE Ⓣ0845/7585 641, Ⓦwww.tripscope.org.uk. This registered charity provides a national telephone information service offering free advice on transport for those with a mobility problem.

In the US and Canada

Access-Able Ⓦwww.access-able.com. Online resource for travellers with disabilities.

Directions Unlimited 123 Green Lane, Bedford Hills, NY 10507 Ⓣ1-800/533-5343 or 914/241-1700. Travel agency specializing in bookings for people with disabilities.

Mobility International USA 451 Broadway, Eugene, OR 97401 Ⓣ541/343-1284, Ⓦwww.miusa.org. Information and referral services, access guides, tours and exchange programmes.

Society for the Advancement of Travelers with Handicaps 347 5th Ave, New York, NY 10016 Ⓣ212/447-7284, Ⓦwww.sath.org. Non-profit educational organization that has actively represented travellers with disabilities since 1976. Annual membership $45; $30 for students and seniors.

Wheels Up! Ⓣ1-888/389-4335, Ⓦwww.wheelsup.com. Provides discounted airfare, tour and cruise prices for disabled travellers, also publishes a free monthly newsletter and has a comprehensive website.

In Australia and New Zealand

Australian Council for Rehabilitation of the Disabled PO Box 60, Curtin ACT 2605 ⓣ 02/6282 4333 (also TTY), ⓦ www.acrod.org.au. Provides lists of travel agencies and tour operators for people with disabilities.

Disabled Persons Assembly 4/173–175 Victoria St, Wellington, New Zealand ⓣ 04/801 9100 (also TTY), ⓦ www.dpa.org.nz. Resource centre with lists of travel agencies and tour operators for people with disabilities.

Senior travellers

Senior travellers are well catered for in France. Most museums and other tourist sites give discounts to the over-60s (usually the same as the student reduction) while SNCF offers special deals on train tickets (see p.48 and p.52); some proof of age will be required. In addition, older visitors – who are likely to be more flexible on dates – will be able to take advantage of some of the many off-season travel and hotel bargains. These are particularly interesting in southern France, with its long summers and mild winters.

Contacts for senior travellers

In the UK

Saga Holidays ⓣ 0800/096 0078 or ⓣ 01303 771190, ⓦ www.saga.co.uk. The country's biggest and most established specialist in tours and holidays aimed at older people.

In the US and Canada

American Association of Retired Persons ⓣ 1-800/304-4222, ⓦ www.aarp.org. Can provide discounts on accommodation and vehicle rental. Membership open to US and Canadian residents aged 50 or over for an annual fee of US $12.50.

Elderhostel ⓣ 1/877-426-8056, ⓦ www.elderhostel.org. Runs an extensive worldwide network of educational and activity programs, cruises and homestays for people over 60 (companions may be younger). Programs generally last a week or more and costs are in line with those of commercial tours.

Saga Holidays ⓣ 1-800/343-0273, ⓦ www.sagaholidays.com. Specializes in worldwide cruise travel for seniors.

Vantage Deluxe World Travel ⓣ 1-800/322-6677, ⓦ www.vantagetravel.com. Specializes in worldwide group travel for seniors.

Travelling with children

France is an excellent country in which to travel with kids. They're generally welcome everywhere and young children and babies in particular will be fussed over. There are masses of family-oriented theme parks and no end of leisure activities geared towards children, while most public parks contain children's play areas.

Children under 4 years travel free on **trains** and **buses**, while those between 4 and 12 are pay half-fare. Museums and suchlike are generally free to under 12s and half-price up to the age of 18.

Hotels charge by the room, with a small supplement for an additional bed or cot, and family-run places will usually babysit or offer a listening service while you eat or go out. Some youth **hostels** are now starting to offer family-rooms. Though they tend to be of the steak-and-chips and ice cream variety, most **restaurants** provide children's menus. You'll have no difficulty finding disposable **nappies/diapers** (*couches à jeter*), but nearly all **baby foods** have added sugar and salt, and French milk powders are very rich indeed.

Local tourist offices will have details of specific **activities** for children, which might include anything from farm visits, nature walks or treasure hunts to paintball and forest rope-ways for older children. In summer most seaside resorts organize "clubs" for children on the beach, while bigger campsites put on extensive programmes of activities and entertainments.

One thing to be aware of – not that you can do much about it – is the difficulty of negotiating a child's buggy over **cobbled streets** in the medieval town centres. And lawns in parks are often out of bounds, so sprawling on the grass with toddlers and napping babies is usually not an option; look out for signs saying *pelouse interdite*.

Contacts for travellers with children

In the UK

Club Med ⓣ0700/2582 932, ⓦ**www.clubmed.co.uk.** Specializes in purpose-built holiday resorts, with kids' club, entertainment and sports facilities on site.

Mark Warner Holidays ⓣ0870/770 4222, ⓦ**www.markwarner.co.uk.** Travel agency with lots to offer families, including children's entertainment clubs and childcare included with most family holidays.

In the US

Rascals in Paradise ⓣ415/921-7000, ⓦ**www.rascalsinparadise.com.** Can arrange scheduled and customized itineraries built around activities for kids.

Travel with Your Children ⓣ1-888/822-4388 or 212/477 5524 Publishes a regular newsletter, *Family Travel Times* (ⓦwww.familytraveltimes.com), as well as a series of books on travel with children including *Great Adventure Vacations With Your Kids.*

Gay and lesbian travellers

France is more liberal on homosexuality than most other European countries. The legal age of consent is 16 and the controversial mayor of Bègles, near Bordeaux, created quite a furor by conducting the country's first gay marriage in 2004. Gay communities thrive especially in Paris and many southern towns such as Toulouse and Nice. Lesbian life is rather less upfront, although Toulouse has a particularly lively lesbian community. Addresses of local gay and/or lesbian establishments are listed in the Guide, and you'll find contact details of national groups and publications below.

In general, the French consider sexuality to be a private matter and homophobic assaults are very rare. Nevertheless, **gays** tend to keep a low profile outside specific gay venues, parades and the prime gay areas of Paris and the coastal resorts. **Lesbians** tend to be even more discreet.

In **Corsica** attitudes remain much more conservative than on the mainland. Women can get away with holding hands and walking with arms around each other, but gay men can expect hostile comments if they do the same. At the same time, Corsica has long been a popular destination for discreet gay couples and no one is likely to raise much more than an eyebrow when checking in to a hotel.

The advent of **AIDS** (SIDA in French) had a big impact in France, which has one of the highest rates of infection in Europe. The Pasteur Institute in Paris is at the forefront of research into the virus, though its gay patients have complained of being treated like cattle. A group of gay doctors and the association AIDES (Association pour l'Entraide et l'Information sur le SIDA), however, have consistently provided sympathetic counselling and treatment, and the gay press has done a great deal to disseminate the facts about AIDS and to provide hope and encouragement. Lesbian organizations fight alongside gays on the general issue of anti-homosexuality, while also lobbying for women's rights.

A useful **guidebook**, though in French only, is *Le dykeGuide*, published annually and available at FNAC stores and other major booksellers or direct from the publisher: Atprod, dykeGuide, BP 145, 94208 Ivry Cedex, Ⓦwww.dykeplanet.com. The English-language *Spartacus International Gay Guide* (published by Bruno Gmünder Verlag; Ⓦwww.spartacusworld.com) has an extensive section on France and contains some info for lesbians.

Têtu (Ⓦwww.tetu.com) is a highly rated gay/lesbian **magazine** with events listings and contact addresses; you can buy it in bookshops or through their website, which is also an excellent source of information. Other useful **websites** include Gay Friendly France (Ⓦus.franceguide.com) maintained by Maison de la France in the US, and the French-language sites Gay.com (Ⓦwww.intl-fr.gay.com) and DykeplaNET (Ⓦwww.dykeplanet.com).

Contacts for gay and lesbian travellers

For details on **organizations in France** see the Listings sections for individual cities.

In the UK

Dream Waves Holidays Ⓣ0870/042 2475, Ⓦ**www.gayholidaysdirect.com**. Specializes in exclusively gay holidays, including skiing trips and summer sun packages.

Madison Travel Ⓣ01273/202 532, Ⓦ**www.madisontravel.co.uk**. Established travel agents specializing in packages to gay- and lesbian-friendly mainstream destinations.

Respect Holidays Ⓣ0870/770 0169, Ⓦ**www.respect-holidays.co.uk**. Offers exclusively gay packages to all popular European resorts.

Ⓦ**www.gaytravel.co.uk** Online gay and lesbian travel agent, offering good deals on all types of holiday. Also lists gay- and lesbian-friendly hotels around the world.

Also check out **adverts** in the free weekly papers *Boyz* and *Pink Paper*, available in gay venues.

In the US and Canada

Damron Ⓣ1-800/462-6654 or 415/255-0404, Ⓦ**www.damron.com**. Publisher of the *Men's Travel Guide*, a pocket-sized yearbook full of listings of hotels, bars, clubs and resources for gay men; the *Women's Traveler*, which provides similar listings for lesbians; *Damron Accommodation Guides*, which provides detailed listings of over 1000 accommodations for gays and lesbians worldwide; and *Damron City Guide*, with a chapter on Paris. All titles are offered at a discount on the website.

gaytravel.com Ⓣ1-800/GAY-TRAVEL, Ⓦ**www.gaytravel.com**. The premier site for trip planning, bookings and general information about international gay and lesbian travel.

International Gay & Lesbian Travel Association Ⓣ1-800/448-8550 or 954/776-2626, Ⓦ**www.iglta.org**. Trade group that can provide a list of gay- and lesbian-owned or -friendly travel agents, accommodation and other travel businesses.

In Australia and New Zealand

Gay and Lesbian Tourism Australia Ⓦ**www.galta.com.au**. Directory and links for gay and lesbian travel worldwide.

Parkside Travel Ⓣ08/8274 1222, Ⓔ**parkside@herveyworld.com.au**. Gay travel agent associated with local branch of Hervey World Travel; all aspects of gay and lesbian travel worldwide.

Silke's Travel Ⓣ1800/807 860 or 02/8347 2000, Ⓦ**www.silkes.com.au**. Long-established gay and lesbian specialist, with the emphasis on women's travel.

Tearaway Travel Ⓣ1800/664 440 or 03/9510 6644, Ⓦ**www.tearaway.com**. Gay-specific business dealing with international and domestic travel.

Directory

Cameras and film Film is not particularly cheap in France, so stock up before travelling. If you're bringing a video camera, make sure any tapes you purchase in France will be compatible.
Contraceptives Condoms (**préservatifs** or **capotes**) are available in supermarkets and pharmacies, as well as from many clubs and street dispensers. Note that the Pill (**la pillule**) is only available on prescription.
Electricity This is almost always 220V, using plugs with two round pins. If you need a transformer, it's best to buy one before leaving home, though you can find them in big department stores in France.
Laundry Laundries are common in French towns – just ask in your hotel or the tourist office, or look in the phone book under "Laveries automatiques" or "Laveries en libre-service". They are often unattended, so come armed with small change. Machines are graded in different wash sizes, costing in the region of €4 to €5 for 7kg. Most hotels forbid doing laundry in your room, though you should get away with just one or two items.
Left luggage Out of fear of terrorist attacks, the vast majority of left-luggage facilities at train and bus stations and the like have been closed down.
Smoking Smoking is forbidden (*fumer interdit*) in public places such as museums, châteaux and on public transport. Restaurants are required to provide non-smoking areas, though few bother.
Time France is in the Central European Time Zone (GMT+1). This means it is one hour ahead of the UK, six hours ahead of Eastern Standard Time and nine hours ahead of Pacific Standard Time. Between March and October France is eight hours behind eastern Australia and ten hours behind New Zealand; from October to March it is ten hours behind southeastern Australia and twelve hours behind New Zealand. Daylight Saving Time (GMT+2) in France lasts from the last Sunday of March to the last Sunday of October.
Tipping Since restaurant prices almost always include a service charge, you only need to leave an additional cash tip if you feel you have received service out of the ordinary. It's customary to tip porters, tour guides, taxi drivers and hairdressers between one and two euros.
Toilets Ask for "les toilettes" or look for signs to the WC (pronounced "vay say"); when enquiring about hotel facilities, don't confuse *lavabo*, which means washbasin, with lavatory. Standards of cleanliness in public toilets are often poor and many tend not to have toilet paper. Toilets in railway stations and department stores are usually okay; most have an attendant and charge a small sum. You'll occasionally come across automated toilet booths in town centres; note that children under 10 aren't allowed in them on their own.

Guide

Guide

1

Paris and around

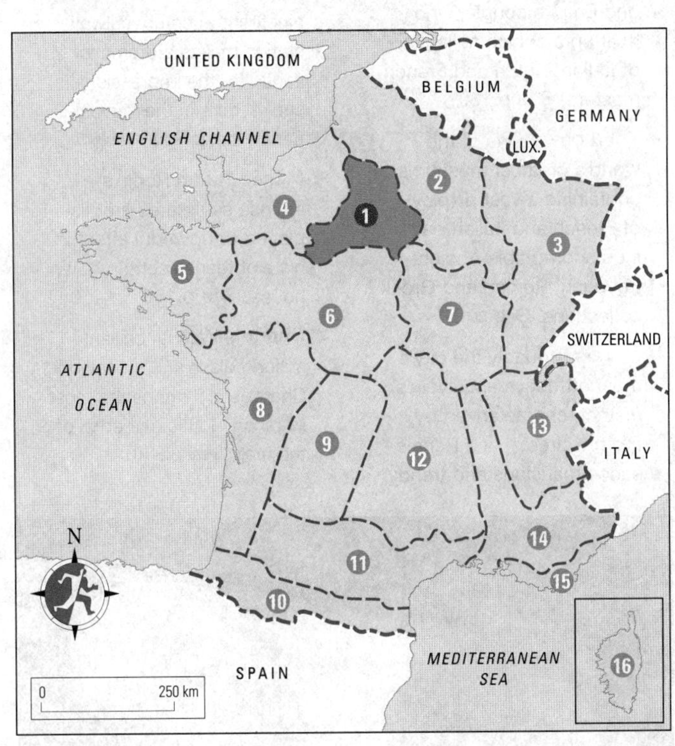

CHAPTER 1

Highlights

✱ **Sainte Chapelle** The stunning stained-glass windows of the Sainte Chapelle rank among the finest achievements of French High Gothic. See p.124

✱ **Musée Jacquemart-André** One-time sumptuous residence of a wealthy Second Empire couple, who built up a choice collection of Italian, Dutch and French masters. See p.130

✱ **The Louvre** One of the world's greatest museums containing a vast display of French and Italian paintings and notable Ancient Egyptian, Roman and Greek collections. See p.131

✱ **Marais** Arguably the city's most attractive and liveliest district, characterized by narrow streets, fine Renaissance mansions and trendy bars. See p.141

✱ **Jardin du Luxembourg** The haunt of old men playing boules, kids riding donkeys, students reading textbooks and couples kissing, these gardens capture Paris at its gentlest. See p.158

✱ **Musée d'Orsay** A nineteenth-century railway station makes a dramatic venue for the Impressionists, shown here at their revolutionary best. See p.158

✱ **Musée Rodin** Rodin's intense sculptures are displayed to powerful effect in his eighteenth-century town house. See p.166

✱ **Chartres** With its brilliant stained glass and stonework, Chartres is perhaps the most inspiring Gothic cathedral of them all. See p.230

△ Paris Metro sign

Paris and around

Long considered the paragon of style, **PARIS** is perhaps the most glamorous city in Europe. It is at once deeply traditional – a village-like metropolis whose inhabitants continue to be notorious for their hauteur – and famously cosmopolitan. The city's reputation as a magnet for writers, artists and dissidents lives on, and it remains at the forefront of Western intellectual, artistic and literary life. At the same time the cultural contributions of its large immigrant populations, particularly from Algeria and West and Central Africa, have sparked unprecedented social transformation in the past few decades. While such contradictions and contrasts may be the reality of any city, they are the makings of Paris: consider the tiny lanes and alleyways of the Quartier Latin or Montmartre against the monumental vistas from the Louvre to La Défense; the multiplicity of markets and old-fashioned pedestrian arcades against the giant underground commercial complexes of Montparnasse, the Louvre and Les Halles; or the obsession with refashioning old buildings and creating ground-breaking architecture against the old ladies who still iron sheets by hand in the laundries of Auteil.

The most tangible and immediate pleasures of Paris are to be found in its street life and along the banks and bridges of the River Seine. Few cities can compete with the cafés, bars and restaurants that line every street and boulevard, and the city's compactness makes it possible to experience the individual feel of the different *quartiers*. You can move easily, even on foot, from the calm, almost small-town atmosphere of **Montmartre** and parts of the **Quartier Latin** to the busy commercial centres of the **Bourse** and **Opéra-Garnier** or the aristocratic mansions of the **Marais**.

The city's lack of open space is redeemed by unexpected havens like the **Mosque**, **Arènes de Lutèce** and the **Place des Vosges**, and courtyards of grand houses like the **Hôtel de Sully**. The gravelled paths and formal beauty of the **Tuileries** create the backdrop for the ultimate Parisian Sunday promenade, while the islands and quaysides of the Left and Right Banks of the **River Seine** make for a wonderful wander as do the Quartier Latin's two splendid parks, the **Luxembourg** and the **Jardin des Plantes**.

Paris's architectural spirit resides in the elegant streets and boulevards begun in the nineteenth century under Baron Haussman. The mansion blocks that line them are at once grand and perfectly human in scale, a triumph in city planning proved by the fact that so many remain residential to this day. Rising above these harmonious buildings are the more arrogant monuments that define the French capital. For centuries, an imposing Classical style prevailed with great set-pieces such as the **Louvre**, **Panthéon** and **Arc de Triomphe**, but the last hundred years or so has seen the architectural mould repeatedly

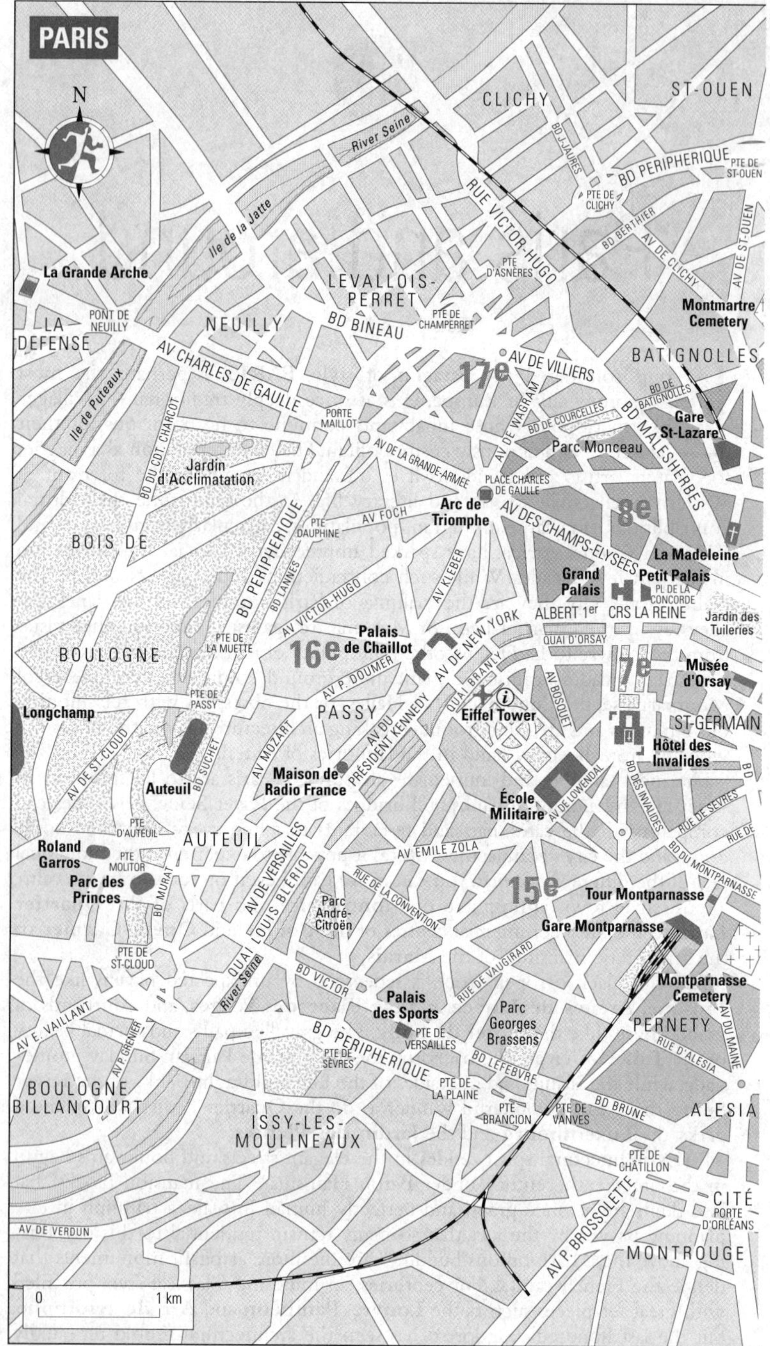
PARIS
CLICHY
ST-OUEN
River Seine
BD PERIPHERIQUE
PTE DE ST-OUEN
PTE DE CLICHY
BD J.-JAURES
RUE VICTOR-HUGO
BD BERTHIER
AV DE CLICHY
AV DE ST-OUEN
Ile de la Jatte
La Grande Arche
LEVALLOIS-PERRET
PTE D'ASNIERES
Montmartre Cemetery
PONT DE NEUILLY
LA DEFENSE
NEUILLY
BD BINEAU
PTE DE CHAMPERRET
BATIGNOLLES
AV CHARLES DE GAULLE
17e
AV DE VILLIERS
Ile de Puteaux
PORTE MAILLOT
AV DE WAGRAM
BD DE COURCELLES
BD DE BATIGNOLLES
BD MALESHERBES
Gare St-Lazare
Parc Monceau
BD DU CDT. CHARCOT
Jardin d'Acclimatation
AV DE LA GRANDE-ARMEE
PLACE CHARLES DE GAULLE
Arc de Triomphe
8e
PTE DAUPHINE
AV FOCH
AV DES CHAMPS-ELYSEES
BOIS DE
BD PERIPHERIQUE
La Madeleine
BD LANNES
AV KLEBER
Grand Palais
Petit Palais
PL DE LA CONCORDE
AV VICTOR-HUGO
ALBERT 1er
CRS LA REINE
Jardin des Tuileries
PTE DE LA MUETTE
Palais de Chaillot
AV DE NEW YORK
QUAI D'ORSAY
BOULOGNE
16e
AV P. DOUMER
QUAI BRANLY
AV BOSQUET
7e
Musée d'Orsay
PTE DE PASSY
Longchamp
PASSY
Eiffel Tower
ST-GERMAIN
AV DU PRÉSIDENT KENNEDY
AV MOZART
Hôtel des Invalides
AV DE ST-CLOUD
BD SUCHET
Auteuil
Maison de Radio France
École Militaire
AV DE LOWENDAL
BD DES INVALIDES
RUE DE SEVRES
PTE D'AUTEUIL
AUTEUIL
AV DE VERSAILLES
AV EMILE ZOLA
Roland Garros
PTE MOLITOR
BD DU MONTPARNASSE
Parc des Princes
BD MURAT
LOUIS BLERIOT
RUE DE LA CONVENTION
15e
Tour Montparnasse
Parc André-Citroën
Gare Montparnasse
PTE DE ST-CLOUD
QUAI
River Seine
BD VICTOR
RUE DE VAUGIRARD
Montparnasse Cemetery
AV E. VAILLANT
Palais des Sports
Parc Georges Brassens
PERNETY
AV DU MAINE
AV P. GRENIER
PTE DE VERSAILLES
BD PERIPHERIQUE
PTE DE SEVRES
BD LEFEBVRE
RUE D'ALESIA
BOULOGNE BILLANCOURT
PTE DE LA PLAINE
PTE BRANCION
PTE DE VANVES
BD BRUNE
ALESIA
ISSY-LES-MOULINEAUX
PTE DE CHÂTILLON
CITÉ
PORTE D'ORLÉANS
AV DE VERDUN
AV P. BROSSOLETTE
MONTROUGE
0
1 km

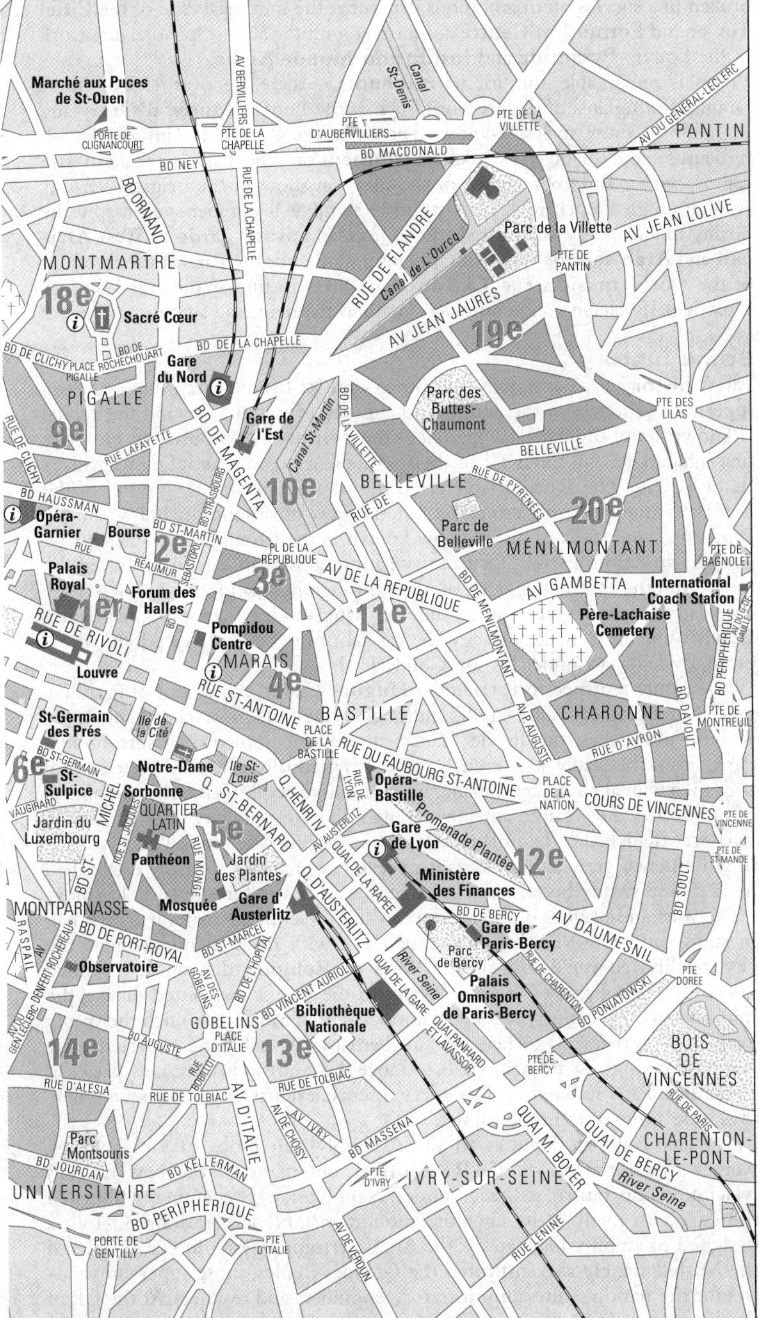
Marché aux Puces
de St-Ouen
PORTE DE
CLIGNANCOURT
AV BERVILLIERS
PTE DE LA
CHAPELLE
Canal
St-Denis
PTE
D'AUBERVILLIERS
PTE DE LA
VILLETTE
AV DU GENERAL-LECLERC
PANTIN
BD MACDONALD
BD NEY
BD ORNANO
RUE DE LA CHAPELLE
Parc de la Villette
AV JEAN LOLIVE
RUE DE FLANDRE
Canal de L'Ourcq
PTE DE
PANTIN
MONTMARTRE
18e
Sacré Cœur
AV JEAN JAURES
19e
BD DE LA CHAPELLE
BD DE CLICHY
PLACE
PIGALLE
BD DE
ROCHECHOUART
Gare
du Nord
PIGALLE
Parc des
Buttes-
Chaumont
PTE DES
LILAS
9e
RUE DE CLICHY
RUE LAFAYETTE
BD DE MAGENTA
Gare de
l'Est
Canal St-Martin
BD DE LA VILLETTE
BELLEVILLE
BELLEVILLE
RUE DE PYRENÉES
10e
20e
BD HAUSSMAN
Opéra-
Garnier
Bourse
BD ST-MARTIN
BD STRASBOURG
RUE DE
Parc de
Belleville
2e
MÉNILMONTANT
PTE DE
BAGNOLET
RUE
REAUMUR
SEBASTOPOL
PL DE LA
RÉPUBLIQUE
Palais
Royal
3e
AV DE LA REPUBLIQUE
BD DE MENILMONTANT
AV GAMBETTA
International
Coach Station
Forum des
Halles
1er
11e
Père-Lachaise
Cemetery
RUE DE RIVOLI
Pompidou
Centre
BD PERIPHERIQUE
AV DU DE GAULLE
MARAIS
Louvre
4e
RUE ST-ANTOINE
BASTILLE
AV P. AUGUSTE
CHARONNE
BD DAVOUT
PTE DE
MONTREUIL
St-Germain
des Prés
Ile de
la Cité
PLACE
DE LA
BASTILLE
RUE D'AVRON
6e
BD ST-GERMAIN
St-
Sulpice
Notre-Dame
Ile St-
Louis
RUE DU FAUBOURG ST-ANTOINE
RUE DE LYON
Opéra-
Bastille
PLACE
DE LA
NATION
COURS DE VINCENNES
PTE DE
VINCENNE
Sorbonne
Q. ST-BERNARD
Q. HENRI IV
VAUGIRARD
MICHEL
QUARTIER
LATIN
5e
Promenade Plantée
Jardin du
Luxembourg
RUE ST JACQUES
RUE MONGE
AV AUSTERLITZ
QUAI DE LA RAPEE
Gare
de Lyon
PTE DE
ST-MANDE
Panthéon
Jardin
des Plantes
12e
BD ST-
Ministère
des Finances
BD SOULT
Q. D'AUSTERLITZ
MONTPARNASSE
Mosquée
Gare d'
Austerlitz
BD DE BERCY
Gare de
Paris-Bercy
AV DAUMESNIL
RASPAIL
AV
DENFERT ROCHEREAU
BD DE PORT-ROYAL
BD ST-MARCEL
BD DE L'HOPITAL
Parc
de Bercy
RUE DE CHARENTON
Observatoire
River Seine
Palais
Omnisport
de Paris-Bercy
PTE
DOREE
AV DES
GOBELINS
BD VINCENT AURIOL
QUAI DE LA GARE
BD PONIATOWSKI
AV DU
GEN LECLERC
GOBELINS
Bibliothèque
Nationale
BOIS
DE
VINCENNES
BD AUGUSTE
PLACE
D'ITALIE
QUAI PANHARD
ET LAVASSOR
14e
13e
PTE DE
BERCY
RUE DE LYON
RUE
BOBILLOT
RUE DE TOLBIAC
RUE D'ALESIA
RUE DE TOLBIAC
AV D'ITALIE
QUAI M. BOYER
RUE DE PARIS
AV IVRY
AV DE CHOISY
Parc
Montsouris
BD MASSENA
QUAI DE BERCY
CHARENTON-
LE-PONT
BD JOURDAN
BD KELLERMAN
PTE
D'IVRY
IVRY-SUR-SEINE
River Seine
UNIVERSITAIRE
BD PERIPHERIQUE
PORTE DE
GENTILLY
PTE
D'ITALIE
AV DE VERDUN
RUE LENINE

broken in a succession of ambitious structures, the industrial chic of the **Eiffel Tower** and **Pompidou Centre** contrasting with the almost spiritual glasswork of the Louvre **Pyramide** and **Institut du Monde Arabe**.

Paris is remarkable, too, for its **museums** – there are over 150 of them, ranging from giants of the art world such as the Louvre, **Musée d'Orsay** and Pompidou Centre to lesser-known gems like the Picasso, Rodin and Jewish museums – and the diversity of **entertainment** on offer. Paris is a real **cinema** capital, with a large percentage of the films on show in the original version. And although French rock is notoriously awful, it is compensated for by the quality of current Parisian **music**, from **jazz** and **avant-garde** to **West African** and **Arab sounds** – the vibrant cultural mix putting Paris at the forefront of the **world music** scene. **Classical concerts** in fine architectural settings – particularly chapels and churches – are also frequent, and sometimes free.

Some history

Paris's **history** has conspired to create a sense of being apart from, and even superior to, the rest of the country. To this day, everything beyond the capital is known quite ordinarily as *province* – the provinces. Appropriately, the city's first inhabitants, the **Parisii**, had their settlement on an island: Lutetia, today's Île de la Cité. The **Romans** preferred the more familiar hilly ground of the Left Bank, and their city, also called Lutetia, grew up around the hill where the Panthéon stands today. This hill, now known as the Montagne Ste-Geneviève, gets its name from Paris's fifth-century patron saint, who legendarily saved the town from the marauding army of Attila through her exemplary holiness. Fifty years later **Geneviève** converted the Merovingian king Clovis to Christianity. Clovis went on to make the city the capital of his Frankish kingdom, which promptly fell apart under his son Childéric II.

Power only returned to Paris under **Hugues Capet**, the Count of Paris. He was elected king of France in 987, although at the time his territory amounted to little more than the Île de France, the region immediately surrounding Paris. From this shaky start French monarchs gradually extended their control over their feudal rivals, centralizing administrative, legal, financial and political power as they did so, until anyone seeking influence, publicity or credibility, in whatever field, had to be in Paris – which is still the case today. The city's cultural influence grew alongside its **university**, which was formally established in 1215 and swiftly became the great European centre for scholastic learning.

The wars and plagues of the fourteenth and fifteenth centuries left Paris half in ruins and more than half abandoned, but with royal encouragement, the city steadily recovered. During the **Wars of Religion** the capital remained staunchly Catholic, but Parisians' loyalty to the throne was tested during the mid-seventeenth-century rebellions known as the Frondes, in which the young Louis XIV was forced to flee the city. Perhaps this traumatic experience lay behind the king's decision, in 1670, to move the court to his vast new palace at **Versailles**. Paris suffered in the court's absence, even as grand Baroque buildings were thrown up in the capital.

Parisians, both as deputies to the Assembly and mobs of sans-culottes, were at the forefront of the **Revolution**, but many of the new citizens welcomed the return to order under Napoléon I. The emperor adorned the city with many of its signature monuments, Neoclassical almost-follies designed to amplify his majesty: the Arc de Triomphe, Arc du Carrousel and the Madeleine. He also instituted the Grandes Écoles, those super-universities for the nation's elite administrators, engineers and teachers. At the fall of the Empire, in 1814, Paris was saved from destruction by the arch-diplomat

Talleyrand, who delivered the city to the Russians with hardly a shot fired. Nationalists grumbled that the occupation continued well into the Restoration regime, as the city once again became the playground of the rich of Europe, the ultimate tourist destination.

The greatest shocks to the fabric of the city came under Napoléon III. He finally completed the Louvre, rebuilding much of the facade in the process, but it was his Prefect of the Seine, **Baron Haussmann**, who truly transformed the city, smashing through the slums to create wide boulevards that could be easily controlled by rifle-toting troops – not that it succeeded in preventing the **1871 Commune**, the most determined insurrection since 1789. In the process of slum clearance, Haussmann created the uniquely Parisian aesthetic that survives today, of long geometrical boulevards lined with rows of grey bourgeois residences. It was down these boulevards that **Nazi troops** paraded in June 1940, followed – after a relatively uneventful war for many, if not all, Parisians – by the Allies, led by General Leclerc, in August 1944.

Although riotous street protests are still a feature of modern Parisian life – most famously in **May 1968**, when students burst onto the streets of the Latin Quarter – the traditional barricade-builders have long since been booted into the suburban factory-land or depressing satellite towns, alongside the under-served populations of immigrants and their descendants. Many Parisians see the economic and cultural integration of these communities as the greatest challenge facing the contemporary city, and there's a strong undercurrent of **racism** in Paris, as throughout France.

Even as the city continues to expand outward, offices are steadily elbowing out apartments in the centre, even in this most village-like of cities. **Housing** remains a problem – trying to find an apartment in Paris is a notoriously difficult affair – and yet the decaying parts of the city, especially in the east and north, are gradually being rebuilt, and grand-scale new developments such as La Défense and the Paris Rive Gauche area attest to the vitality of the city's commercial life.

The interests of business and the bourgeoisie – not to mention those of the mayor's family and friends – flourished under the rule of **Jacques Chirac**, Paris's mayor from 1977 to 1995, and his successor Jean Tiberi, but in March 2001, a socialist politician called Bertrand Delanoë took over. It was the first time that the Left had controlled Paris since the 1871 Commune, and the first time that the city had had an openly gay mayor – not that many Parisians seem to think it matters. Delanoë has promised to restore life to Paris by taking on the traffic problem, creating new green spaces and fighting the "museumification" of the city. To date, however, the most visible projects have been more populist and superficial: "Paris Plage" sees a swathe of the Seine's quais converted into a beach every summer, while the "Nuit Blanche" keeps Parisians up all night with city-wide art and cultural events.

Arrival

Many British travellers to Paris arrive by Eurostar at the central **Gare du Nord train station**, while more far-flung visitors are likely to land at one of Paris's two main airports: Charles de Gaulle and Orly. Trains from other parts of France or continental Europe draw in at one of the six central mainline stations. Almost all the **buses** coming into Paris – whether international or domestic – arrive at the main *gare routière* at 28 av du Général-de-Gaulle,

Bagnolet, at the eastern edge of the city; métro Gallieni (line 3) links it to the centre. If you're **driving** in yourself, don't try to go straight across the city to your destination. Use the ring road – the *boulevard périphérique* – to get around to the nearest porte: it's much quicker, except at rush hour, and far easier to navigate, albeit pretty terrifying.

Disneyland Paris is linked by bus to both Charles de Gaulle and Orly airports: for details of these services, plus train links from the centre to the purpose-built Marne-la-Vallée-Chessy TGV, see p.225.

By air

The two main Paris airports that deal with international flights are **Roissy-Charles de Gaulle** and **Orly**, both well connected to the centre. Detailed information in English can be found online at Ⓦwww.adp.fr.

Roissy-Charles de Gaulle Airport

Roissy-Charles de Gaulle Airport (24hr information in English Ⓣ01.48.62.22.80), usually referred to as Charles de Gaulle and abbreviated to CDG or Paris CDG, is 23km northeast of the city. The airport has two main **terminals**, CDG 1 and CDG 2. A third terminal, CDG-T3, handles various low-cost airlines, including easyJet. Make sure you know which terminal your flight is departing from when it's time to leave Paris, so you take the correct bus or get off at the right train station. A **TGV station** links the airport (CDG 2) with Bordeaux, Brussels, Lille, Lyon, Nantes, Marseille and Rennes, among other places.

There are various ways of getting to the centre of Paris: least expensive and probably quickest is the suburban train line **RER B**, sometimes called Roissyrail, which runs at least every fifteen minutes from 5am until midnight; the journey time is thirty minutes and tickets cost €7.75 one-way. From CDG 1 you have to get the shuttle bus (*navette*; it's coded green) to the RER station. From CDG 2 and CDG-T3 it's simplest to take the pedestrian walkway, though the station is also served by a blue-coded shuttle bus. The RER train stops at Gare du Nord, Châtelet-Les Halles, St-Michel and Denfert-Rochereau, at all of which you can transfer to the ordinary métro system – your ticket is valid through to any métro station in central Paris.

An alternative to the RER is the **Roissybus** which connects all three terminals with the Opéra-Garnier (corner of rues Auber and Scribe; RER Auber/métro Opéra); it runs every 15–20 minutes from 5.45am to 11pm, costs €8.20 one-way and takes around 45–60 minutes. Air France also operates two bus services (information in English Ⓣ01.41.56.89.00, Ⓦwww.cars-airfrance.com). The green-coded line 2 (€10 one way, €17 return) leaves from CDG 1 and CDG 2 every fifteen minutes from 5.45am to 11pm stopping at Porte Maillot, on the northwest edge of the city, on its way to 1 avenue Carnot, immediately outside Charles-de-Gaulle-Étoile RER/métro. The yellow-coded line 4 (€11.50 one way, €19.55 return) departs from both CDG 1 and CDG 2 every thirty minutes from 7am to 9.30pm, stopping at 20bis boulevard Diderot, next to the Gare de Lyon, before terminating at rue du Commandant Mouchotte, beside the Gare Montparnasse; journey times vary from 40–60 minutes.

Taxis into central Paris from CDG cost around €38, plus a small luggage supplement (€0.90 per piece of luggage), and should take between fifty minutes and one hour. You might also consider the door-to-door **minibus service**, Blue Vans (€14.50 per head if there are two or more people, €22 for a single person; no extra charge for luggage; 6am–7.30pm). Bookings must be made at least 48 hours in advance on ⓣ01.30.11.13.00 or online at ⓦwww.bluvan.fr. Note that if your flight gets in after midnight your only means of transport is a taxi.

Orly Airport

Orly Airport (information in English daily 6am–11.30pm ⓣ01.49.75.15.15), 14km south of Paris, has **two terminals**, Orly Sud and Orly Ouest, linked by shuttle bus but easily walkable; Ouest (West) is used for domestic flights while Sud (South) handles international flights. One of the easiest ways into the centre is the Orlyval, a fast **train shuttle** link to RER line B station Antony, followed by métro connection stops at Denfert-Rochereau, St-Michel and Châtelet-Les Halles; it runs every four to eight minutes Monday to Saturday from 6.30am to 11pm, from 7am Sundays and holidays (€8.80 one-way; 30min to Châtelet). Alternatively, a **shuttle bus** takes you to the Pont de Rungis-Aéroport d'Orly RER station, where you can pick up RER line C trains, sometimes called Orlyrail to the Gare d'Austerlitz, St-Michel-Notre-Dame and Les Invalides (€5.25 one-way; total journey around 50min); this service runs every 15–30 minutes from 5am to 11.30pm. Leaving Paris, the train runs from Gare d'Austerlitz from 5.50am to 10.50pm.

Two fast **bus services** are also worth considering: the Orlybus which runs to Denfert-Rochereau RER/métro station in the 14e (every 15–20min 6am–11.30pm; €5.70 one-way; around 30min); and the Jetbus which runs to métro Villejuif-Louis-Aragon, in the southeast of the city (métro line 7) every fifteen minutes between 6.20am and 10.50pm (€5.15; 15min). Finally, an **Air France bus** (information in English ⓣ01.41.56.89.00, ⓦwww.cars-airfrance.com) runs to the Invalides Air France Terminal on rue Esnault Peletrie, close to Les Invalides itself, via Montparnasse (stopping at Porte d'Orléans and Duroc if requested in advance) every fifteen minutes from 6am to 11.30pm (€7.50 one-way, €12.75 return; about 35min). Leaving Paris, the bus can be caught from the Invalides Air France Terminal and from Montparnasse on rue du Commandant-René-Mouchotte in front of the *Méridien Hotel*. **Taxis** take about 35 minutes to reach the centre of Paris and cost around €35.

By train

Paris has six mainline train stations. **Eurostar** (ⓣ08.92.35.35.39, ⓦwww.eurostar.com) terminates at the busy **Gare du Nord**, rue Dunkerque, in the northeast of the city. Coming off the train, turn left for the métro and the RER, and right for taxis (expect to pay around €10–15 to central Paris). Just short of the taxi exit, head down the escalators for left luggage (*consignes*) and the various car rental desks. You can get a shower in the public toilets at the bottom of the métro escalators. Two bureaux de change (neither offer a good deal) allow you to change money at the station, or you can use your card in one of the ATM cash machines. Left luggage and all other services are open roughly 6am to 11pm. The Gare du Nord is also the arrival point for trains from Calais and other north-European countries.

Nearby, the **Gare de l'Est** (place du 11-Novembre-1918, 10e) serves eastern France and central and eastern Europe. The Gare St-Lazare (place du Havre, 8e), serving the Normandy coast and Dieppe, is the most central, close to the Madeleine and the Opéra-Garnier. Still on the Right Bank but towards the southeast corner is the **Gare de Lyon** (place Louis-Armand, 12e), for trains to Italy and Switzerland and TGV lines to southeast France. South of the river, **Gare Montparnasse** (bd de Vaugirard, 15e) is the terminus for Chartres,

Brittany, the Atlantic coast and TGV lines to Tours and southwest France. **Gare d'Austerlitz** (bd de l'Hôpital, 13e) serves the Loire Valley and the Dordogne. The **motorail station**, Gare de Paris-Bercy, is down the tracks from the Gare de Lyon on boulevard de Bercy, 12e.

All the stations are equipped with cafés, restaurants, tabacs, banks, left-luggage facilities and bureaux de change, and all are connected to the métro system; Gare du Nord and Gare de Lyon have **tourist offices** which book same-day accommodation (see below and p.116). For **information** on national train services and reservations phone Ⓣ08.92.35.35.35 (if you dial extension 2 you should get through to an English-speaking operator) or consult the website Ⓦwww.sncf-voyages.com. For information on suburban lines call Ⓣ08.90.36.10.10. You can buy tickets at any SNCF station, online, or from travel agents.

Orientation

Finding your way around Paris is remarkably easy. The city proper, excluding its suburbs (*banlieues*), is relatively small and very **walkable**. It's divided into twenty arrondissements, or districts, which radiate out from the centre; we've marked these on the map on p.102 and have included them as an integral part of addresses throughout the chapter – note that they are abbreviated as 1er (premier = first), 2e (deuxième = second), 3e, 4e and so on. The arrondissements are strictly confined within the 78-square-kilometre limits of the ring road, the *boulevard périphérique*, built over the nineteenth-century city defences.

The Seine flows roughly east to west, cutting the city in two. In the middle of the Seine lie two islands, the **Île de la Cité** – where Notre-Dame sits at the historic heart of the capital – and the **Île St-Louis**. North of the river is the Right Bank, or *rive droite*, the banking, media and commercial quarter contained within the grands boulevards. Here you'll find the **Louvre**, flanking the river at the very centre of the city; the tacky shopping quarter of **Les Halles**; the aristocratic and fashionable **Marais**; and, further to the east, the trendy **Bastille** quarter. West of the Louvre, the 8e has the **Champs-Élysées**, **Arc de Triomphe** and the most expensive shops. South of the river on the Left Bank, or *rive gauche*, is the studenty **quartier Latin**; elegant, international **St-Germain**; and, to the west, the expensive septième (7e), with the **Eiffel Tower**, Invalides, the parliament and embassies. The outer arrondissements were mostly incorporated into the city in the nineteenth century. Generally speaking, those to the east accommodated the poor and working class, while those to the west were, and still are, the addresses for the aristocracy and new rich.

Information

Branches of the Paris **tourist office** (Ⓣ08.92.68.30.00, Ⓦwww.paris-touristoffice.com) can be found all over the city. The largest office, Opéra-Grands Magasins (Mon–Sat 9am–6.30pm; RER Auber/métro Opéra or Chaussée d'Antin), and those at the two stations – Gare de Lyon, 20 Bd Boulevard Diderot (Mon–Sat 8am–6pm; Gare de Lyon) and Gare du Nord, 18 rue de Dunkerque (daily 8am–6pm; RER/métro Gare du Nord) – can help you find last-minute accommodation. Two further branch offices are located at the Eiffel Tower (May–Sept 11am–6.40pm; RER Champ-de-Mars/Tour

The museum pass and reductions

If you're planning to visit a great many museums in a short time, it's worth buying the Carte Musées et Monuments pass (€18 one-day, €36 three-day, €54 five-day). Available from the tourist office, RER/métro stations and museums, they're valid for seventy museums and monuments (though not special exhibitions) in and around Paris, and allow you to bypass ticket queues (though not the security checkpoints). Students and under-26s, as well as those over 60, can usually take advantage of reduced-price entry – bring your passport as proof of age, or an International Studenty Identity Card (Ⓦwww.isiccard.com). Children under 12 go free at all state-run monuments, while the majority of museums offer free admisison to under-18s. Some museums have free or half-price admission on Sunday; many are closed on Monday or Tuesday.

Eiffel, métro Bir-Hakeim) and in Montmartre, 21 place du Tertre (daily 7am–7pm; métro Abbesses). The branch under the Carrousel du Louvre, 99 rue de Rivoli (daily 10am–7pm; métro Palais Royal/Musée du Louvre) shares space with the tourist office for the Île-de-France, the region around Paris.

Alternative sources of information are the **Hôtel de Ville information office** – Bureau d'Accueil – at 29 rue de Rivoli, 4e (Mon–Sat 9am–6pm; Ⓣ08.20.00.75.75, Ⓦwww.paris.fr; M° Hôtel-de-Ville). For what's-on information it's worth buying one of Paris's weekly listings magazines from a newsagent or kiosk. The glossiest is *Zurban* (Ⓦwww.zurban.com), though the inexpensive *Pariscope* has a comprehensive section on films and a handy English-language endpage put together by *Time Out*. For more detail, French-speakers can scour the trendy monthly magazine, *Nova*, while the English -language free monthly, *Paris Voice* (Ⓦwww.parisvoice.com), has useful listings and classified ads. In addition, a free weekly listings newspaper called *A nous Paris* comes out every Monday and is available from métro stations.

City transport

While walking is undoubtedly the best way to discover Paris, the city's integrated **public transport system** of bus, métro and trains – the RATP (Régie Autonome des Transports Parisiens) – is cheap, fast and meticulously signposted. Free métro and bus maps of varying sizes and detail are available at most stations, bus terminals and the tourist office: the largest and most useful is the *Grand Plan de Paris numéro 2*, which overlays the métro, RER and bus routes on a map of the city so you can see exactly how transport lines and streets match up. If you just want a handy pocket-sized métro/bus map ask for the *Petit Plan de Paris* or the smaller *Paris Plan de Poche*.

The métro and RER

The **métro**, combined with the **RER** (Réseau Express Régional) suburban express lines, is the simplest way of getting around. The métro runs from 5.30am to 12.30am, RER trains from 5am to 12.30am. Stations (abbreviated: M° Concorde, RER Luxembourg, etc) are evenly spaced and you'll rarely find yourself more than 500m from one in the centre, though the interchanges can involve a lot of legwork, including many stairs. In addition to the free maps available (see above), every station has a big plan of

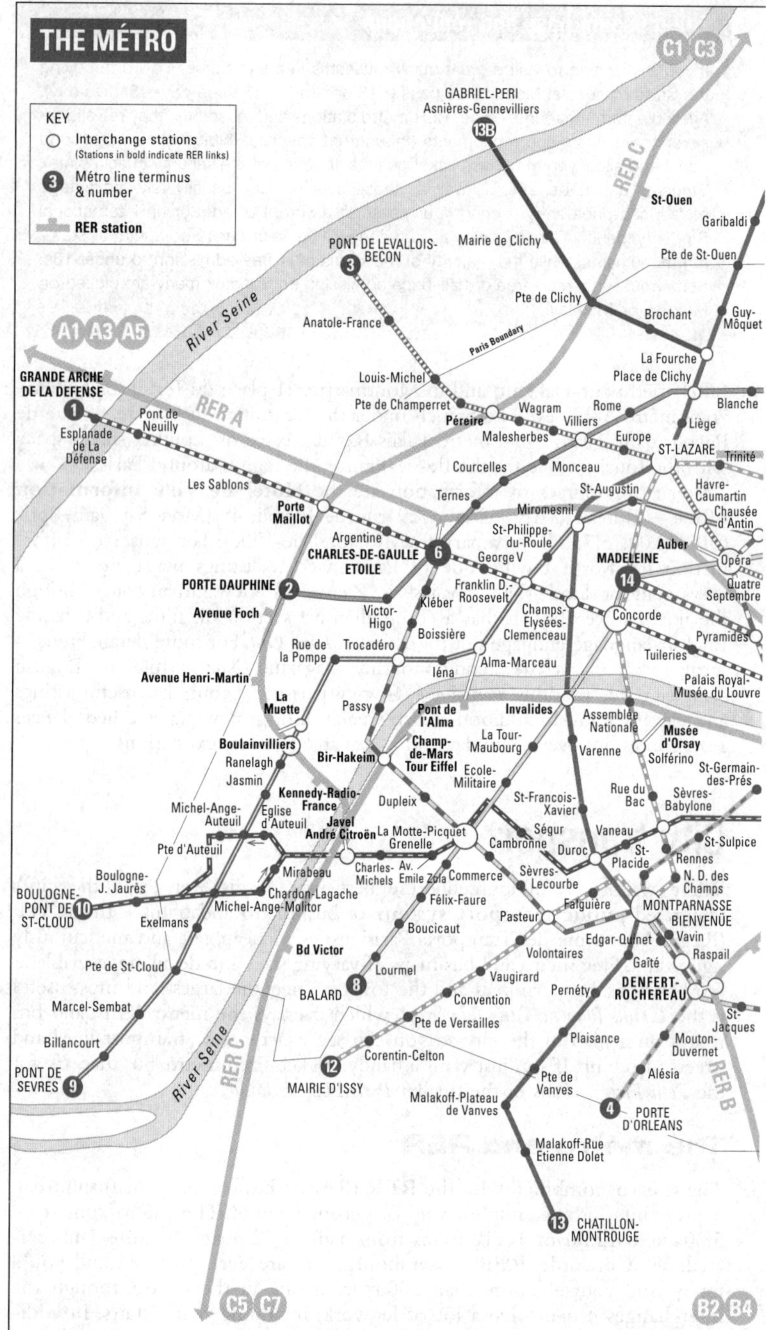
THE MÉTRO
KEY
Interchange stations
(Stations in bold indicate RER links)
Métro line terminus & number
RER station
River Seine
RER A
RER B
RER C
Paris Boundary
GRANDE ARCHE DE LA DEFENSE
PONT DE LEVALLOIS-BECON
GABRIEL-PERI Asnières-Gennevilliers
PORTE DAUPHINE
CHARLES-DE-GAULLE ETOILE
ST-LAZARE
MADELEINE
MONTPARNASSE BIENVENÜE
DENFERT-ROCHEREAU
PORTE D'ORLEANS
CHATILLON-MONTROUGE
MAIRIE D'ISSY
BALARD
BOULOGNE-PONT DE ST-CLOUD
PONT DE SEVRES

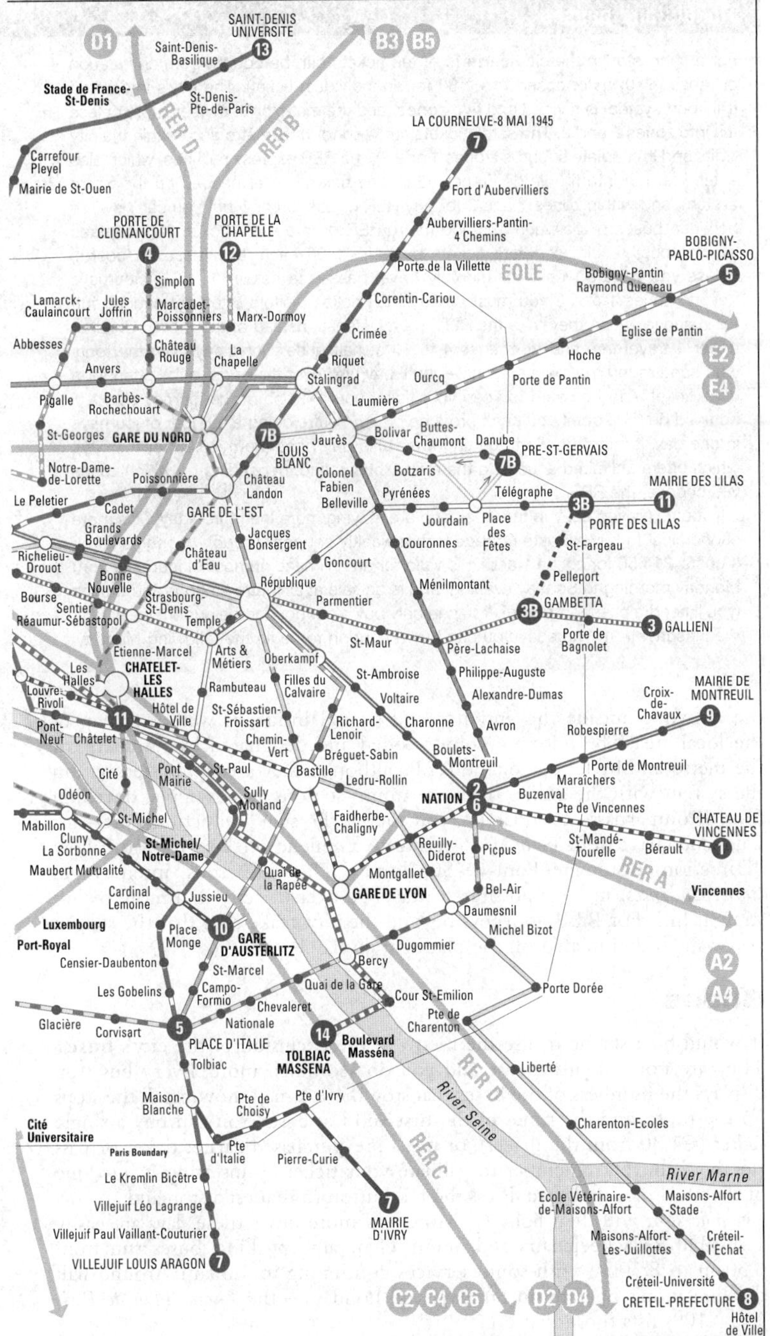

SAINT-DENIS UNIVERSITE
13
D1
B3 B5
Saint-Denis-Basilique
Stade de France-St-Denis
St-Denis-Pte-de-Paris
RER D
RER B
Carrefour Pleyel
Mairie de St-Ouen
LA COURNEUVE-8 MAI 1945
7
Fort d'Aubervilliers
Aubervilliers-Pantin-4 Chemins
PORTE DE CLIGNANCOURT
4
PORTE DE LA CHAPELLE
12
BOBIGNY-PABLO-PICASSO
5
Porte de la Villette
EOLE
Bobigny-Pantin Raymond Queneau
Simplon
Corentin-Cariou
Lamarck-Caulaincourt
Jules Joffrin
Marcadet-Poissonniers
Marx-Dormoy
Crimée
Eglise de Pantin
Abbesses
Château Rouge
La Chapelle
Hoche
E2
Riquet
Anvers
Stalingrad
Ourcq
Porte de Pantin
E4
Pigalle
Barbès-Rochechouart
Laumière
St-Georges
GARE DU NORD
7B
Jaurès
Bolivar
Buttes-Chaumont
Danube
PRE-ST-GERVAIS
LOUIS BLANC
Notre-Dame-de-Lorette
Poissonnière
Château Landon
Colonel Fabien
Botzaris
7B
Le Peletier
Cadet
GARE DE L'EST
Belleville
Pyrénées
Télégraphe
3B
MAIRIE DES LILAS
11
Jourdain
Place des Fêtes
PORTE DES LILAS
Grands Boulevards
Jacques Bonsergent
Couronnes
St-Fargeau
Richelieu-Drouot
Château d'Eau
Goncourt
Pelleport
Bonne Nouvelle
Strasbourg-St-Denis
République
Ménilmontant
Bourse
Sentier
Parmentier
3B
GAMBETTA
3
GALLIENI
Réaumur-Sébastopol
Temple
Porte de Bagnolet
Etienne-Marcel
Arts & Métiers
St-Maur
Père-Lachaise
Les Halles
CHATELET-LES HALLES
Oberkampf
St-Ambroise
Philippe-Auguste
Louvre-Rivoli
Rambuteau
Filles du Calvaire
Voltaire
Alexandre-Dumas
MAIRIE DE MONTREUIL
11
Hôtel de Ville
St-Sébastien-Froissart
Croix-de-Chavaux
9
Pont-Neuf
Châtelet
Richard-Lenoir
Charonne
Avron
Robespierre
Chemin-Vert
Bréguet-Sabin
Boulets-Montreuil
Porte de Montreuil
Cité
Pont Marie
St-Paul
Bastille
Ledru-Rollin
Maraîchers
Odéon
Sully Morland
NATION
2
6
Buzenval
Pte de Vincennes
Mabillon
St-Michel
Faidherbe-Chaligny
CHATEAU DE VINCENNES
Cluny La Sorbonne
St-Michel/Notre-Dame
Reuilly-Diderot
Picpus
St-Mandé-Tourelle
Bérault
1
Maubert Mutualité
Quai de la Rapée
Montgallet
RER A
GARE DE LYON
Bel-Air
Vincennes
Cardinal Lemoine
Jussieu
Daumesnil
Luxembourg
Place Monge
10
GARE D'AUSTERLITZ
Michel Bizot
Port-Royal
Dugommier
A2
Censier-Daubenton
St-Marcel
Bercy
Les Gobelins
Campo-Formio
Quai de la Gare
Porte Dorée
A4
Chevaleret
Cour St-Emilion
Glacière
Corvisart
5
Nationale
14
Pte de Charenton
PLACE D'ITALIE
Boulevard Masséna
TOLBIAC MASSENA
Tolbiac
RER D
Liberté
River Seine
Maison-Blanche
Pte de Choisy
Pte d'Ivry
Cité Universitaire
Paris Boundary
Pte d'Italie
Pierre-Curie
RER C
Charenton-Ecoles
River Marne
Le Kremlin Bicêtre
Ecole Vétérinaire-de-Maisons-Alfort
Maisons-Alfort-Stade
Villejuif Léo Lagrange
7
MAIRIE D'IVRY
Villejuif Paul Vaillant-Couturier
Maisons-Alfort-Les-Juillottes
Créteil-l'Echat
VILLEJUIF LOUIS ARAGON
7
Créteil-Université
C2 C4 C6
D2 D4
CRETEIL-PREFECTURE
8
Hôtel de Ville

Tickets and passes

For a short stay in the city, **carnets** of ten tickets can be bought from any station or tabac (€10, as opposed to €1.30 for an individual ticket). The city's integrated transport system is divided into **five zones**, and the metro system itself more or less fits into zones 1 and 2. The same tickets are valid for bus, métro and, within the city limits and immediate suburbs (zones 1 and 2), the RER express rail lines, which also extend far out into the Île de France. Only one ticket is ever needed on the métro system, and within zones 1 and 2 for any RER or bus journey, but you can't switch between buses or between bus and métro/RER on the same ticket. **Night buses** (Noctambus) require separate tickets costing €2.60 each (buy these on board), unless you have a weekly or monthly travel pass (see below). For RER journeys beyond zones 1 and 2 you must buy an RER ticket; visitors often get caught out, for instance, when they take the RER to La Défense instead of the métro. Children under 4 travel free and from ages 4 to 10 at half price. Don't buy from the touts who hang round the main stations – you'll pay well over the odds, quite often for a used ticket – and be sure to keep your ticket until the end of the journey as you'll be fined on the spot if you can't produce one. If you're doing a number of journeys in one day, it might be worth getting a **mobilis day pass** (from €5.20 for the city), which offers unlimited access to the métro, buses and, depending on which zones you choose, the RER.

If you've arrived early in the week and are staying more than three days, it's more economical to buy a **Carte Orange** with a weekly coupon (*coupon hebdomadaire*). It costs €14.50 for zones 1 and 2, is valid for an unlimited number of journeys from Monday morning to Sunday evening, and is on sale at all métro stations and tabacs (you'll need a passport photo). You can only buy a coupon for the current week until Wednesday; from Thursday you can buy a coupon to begin the following Monday.

the network outside the entrance and several inside, as well as a map of the local area. The lines are colour-coded and designated by numbers for the métro and by letters for the RER, although they are signposted within the system with the names of the terminus stations: for example, travelling from Montparnasse to Châtelet, you follow the sign "Direction Porte-de-Clignancourt"; from Gare d'Austerlitz to Grenelle on line 10 you follow "Direction Boulogne–Pont-de-St-Cloud". The numerous interchanges (*correspondances*) make it possible to travel all over the city in a more or less straight line. For RER journeys beyond the city, make sure that the station you want is illuminated on the platform display board.

Buses

It would be a shame to use the métro to the exclusion of the city's **buses**. They are not difficult to use and you do see much more. Every bus stop displays the numbers of the buses that stop there, a map showing all the stops on the route, and the times of the first and last buses. You can buy a single ticket (€1.30 from the driver), or use a pre-purchased carnet ticket or pass (see box, above); remember to validate your ticket by inserting it into one of the machines on board. Press the red button to request a stop and an *arrêt demandé* sign will then light up. More and more buses these days are easily accessible for wheelchairs and prams. Generally speaking, buses run from 6.30am to 8.30pm with some services continuing to 1.30am. Around half the lines don't operate on Sundays and holidays – the *Grand Plan de Paris* (see p.109) lists those that do.

There's also a monthly coupon (*mensuel*) for €48.60 for zones 1 and 2. You need to write your Carte Orange number on the coupon.

Other possibilities are the **Paris Visites**, one-, two-, three- and five-day visitors' passes at €8.35, €13.70, €18.25 and €26.65 for Paris and close suburbs, or €16.75, €26.65, €37.35 and €45.70 to include the airports, Versailles and Disneyland Paris (make sure you buy this one when you arrive at Roissy-Charles de Gaulle or Orly to get maximum value). A half-price child's version is also available. You can buy them from métro and RER stations, tourist offices and online at ⓦwww.parisvisite.tm.fr. If you're going to Paris by **Eurostar**, you could save yourself time by buying the passes at Waterloo International once you've checked in. They're available at the information point and at the souvenir shop underneath the escalator that heads up to platform entrances 21A/22A; you can also get the Carte Musées et Monuments (see box, p.109) and Disneyland tickets here, too. Paris Visites passes can begin on any day; they also allow you discounts at certain monuments and museums. Both the Carte Orange and the Paris Visites entitle you to unlimited travel (in the zones you have chosen) on bus, métro, RER, SNCF and the Montmartre funicular. On the métro you put the Carte Orange coupon through the turnstile slot (make sure to retrieve it afterwards); on a bus you show the whole carte to the driver as you board – don't put it into the punching machine.

The **RATP** also runs numerous excursions, some to quite far-flung places, which are far less expensive than those offered by commercial operators. Details are available from the RATP's Bureau de Tourisme, place de la Madeleine, 1ᵉ (ⓣ01.40.06.71.45; M° Madeleine). For 24-hour recorded information in English on all RATP services call ⓣ08.92.68.41.14 (premium rate) or visit online at ⓦwww.ratp.fr.

From mid-April to mid-September, a special orange-and-white **Balabus service** (not to be confused with Batobus, see p.115) passes all the major tourist sights between the Grande Arche de la Défense and Gare de Lyon. These buses run on Sundays and holidays every fifteen to twenty minutes from 12.30pm to 8pm. Bus stops are marked "Balabus", and you'll need one to three bus tickets, depending on the length of your journey: check the information at the bus stop or ask the driver. The Paris Visite, Mobilis and Carte Orange passes are all valid too. Night buses (Noctambus) run on eighteen routes every hour, with extra services at weekends, from 1am to 5.30am between place du Châtelet, west of the Hôtel de Ville, and the suburbs. Routes are shown on the *Grand Plan de Paris* (see p.109).

Taxis

Taxi charges are fairly reasonable: between €6.50 and €12 for a central daytime journey, though considerably more if you call one out. Before you get into the taxi you can tell which of the **three rates** is operating from the three small indicator lights on its roof: "A" (passenger side; white) indicates the daytime rate (7am–7pm) for Paris within the *boulevard périphérique* (around €0.60 per km); "B" (orange) is the rate for Paris at night, on Sunday and on public holidays, and for the suburbs during the day (around €1 per km); "C" (blue) is the night rate for the suburbs (€1.25 per km). In addition there's a minimum charge of €5, a time charge of €26 an hour for when the car is stationary, an extra charge of €0.75 if you're picked up from a mainline train station, and a €0.90 charge for each piece of luggage carried. **Tipping** is not mandatory, but ten percent will be expected. Taxi drivers do not have to take more than three passengers (they don't like people sitting in the front); if a fourth passenger is accepted, an extra charge of €2.50 will be added.

Waiting at a **taxi rank** (*arrêt taxi* – there are around 470 of them) is usually more effective than hailing one from the street. The large white light signals the taxi is free; the orange light means it's in use. You can also call a taxi out directly: phone numbers are shown at the taxi ranks, or try Taxis Bleus (Ⓣ08.91.70.10.10, Ⓦwww.taxis-bleus.com), Alpha Taxis (Ⓣ01.45.85.85.85) or Artaxi (Ⓣ01.42.03.50.50). Taxis can however be rather thin on the ground at lunchtime and any time after 7pm.

Disabled travellers

If you're disabled, **taxis** are obliged by law to carry you and to help you into the vehicle – also to carry your guide dog if you are blind or visually impaired. Specially adapted taxis are available on Ⓣ01.41.83.15.15, and for transport to

Boat trips, balloons and heli-rides

There are plenty of less conventional (and more expensive) ways to see Paris than by public transport. Specialist sightseeing trips range from the faithful old Bateaux-Mouches to more exotic helicopter and balloon rides.

Bateaux-Mouches **boat trips** start from the Embarcadère du Pont de l'Alma on the Right Bank in the 8e (reservations and information Ⓣ01.42.25.96.10; M° Alma-Marceau). The rides last one hour, cost €7 (€4 for children and over-65s) and take you past the major Seine-side sights, such as Notre Dame and the Louvre. Departures are at 10.15am, 11am, 11.30am, 12.15pm, 1pm, 1.45pm and every half-hour from 2.30pm to 8pm, then every twenty minutes from 8pm to 10pm; winter departures are fewer. The night-time cruises use lights to illuminate the streetscapes that are so bright they almost blind passers-by – much more fun on-board than off – and at all times a narration in six languages blares out. The outrageously priced lunch and dinner trips, for which "correct" dress is mandatory, are probably best avoided. Bateaux-Mouches has many competitors, all much of a muchness and detailed in Pariscope under "Croisières" in the "Visites et Promenades" section.

A more unusual way of seeing less visited sights are the **canal boat trips** run by Canauxrama (reservations Ⓣ01.42.39.15.00) between the Port de l'Arsenal, opposite 50 bd de la Bastille, 12e (M° Bastille), and the Bassin de la Villette, 13 quai de la Loire, 19e (M° Jaurès), on the Canal St-Martin. Departing daily at 9.45am and 2.45pm from the Bassin de la Villette and at 9.45am and 2.30pm from the Bastille, the ride lasts nearly three hours and costs E14. A more stylish vessel for exploring the canal is the **catamaran** of Paris-Canal, which runs three-hour trips between the Musée d'Orsay, quai Anatole-France, 7e (M° Musée d'Orsay), and the Parc de la Villette (La Folie des Visites du Parc centre; M° Porte-de -Pantin); boats operate in both directions daily from the end of March to mid -November, leaving the museum at 9.30am, and the park at 2.30pm (reservations on Ⓣ01.42.40.96.97; €16, children €9).

A **helicopter tour** above Paris's sights is somewhat prohibitively priced, but if you simply must have an aerial view, then a quick loop around the city is possible. Book online with French Adventures (Ⓦwww.frenchadventures.com) or phone them on Ⓣ01.40.01.03.97). A 45-minute trip will set you back €220 for each passenger – a minimum of five passengers is required.

Even classier are the **balloon trips** organized by France Montgolfières, 16 passage de la Main d'Or, 75011 Paris (Ⓣ01.47.00.66.44, Ⓦwww.franceballoons.com); a trip over the Île de France costs from €175 per person.

and from the airports on ⓣ01.41.29.01.29, but they need to be notified the day before and can be contacted weekdays 9am–noon & 2–6.30pm. For travel on the **buses, métro** or **RER**, the RATP offers accompanied journeys for disabled people not in wheelchairs (Les compagnons du voyage), which is available daily from 6.30am until 8pm and costs €25 an hour. You have to book on ⓣ01.45.19.15.00 (Mon–Fri 6am–7pm, Sat & Sun 9am–6pm) at least a day in advance. Blind and visually impaired passengers can request a free companion from the volunteer organization Auxiliaires des Aveugles (ⓣ01.43.06.39.68). A **Braille métro map** costing €3.10 and a separate bus map are obtainable from L'Association Valentin Haûy (AVH), 5 rue Duroc, 7e (ⓣ01.44.49.27.27, ⓦwww.avh.asso.fr).

An increasing number of RER stations are readily accessible to **wheelchair** users – you can find a list at ⓦwww.citefutee.com by clicking on the wheelchair symbol. The new métro line 14 is also geared up for wheelchair users, and a number of bus lines have specially designed lower floors for wheelchair users; these are indicated on the *Grand Plan de Paris* (see p.109). A useful **publication**, *Access in Paris* by Gordon Couch and Ben Roberts, published in Britain by Quiller Press, is available for £6.95, though bear in mind that it was published in 1993, so some of the information will be out of date.

Driving and parking

Travelling around by **car** – in the daytime at least – is hardly worth it because of the difficulty of finding parking spaces. You're better off finding a motel-style place on the edge of the city and using public transport. But if you're determined to use the **pay-and-display** parking system you must first buy a Paris Carte (€10) from a *tabac*, then look for the blue "P" signs alongside grey parking meters. Introduce the card into the meter – costs range from €1 to €3 an hour for a maximum of two hours. Covered car parks cost up to €2.50 per hour. Whatever you do, don't park in a bus lane or the Axe Rouge **express routes** (marked with a red square). Should you be towed away, you'll find your car in the pound (*fourrière*) belonging to that particular arrondissement – check with the local *mairie* for the address.

In the event of a **breakdown**, call SOS Dépannage (ⓣ01.47.07.99.99) for round-the-clock assistance. Alternatively, ask the police.

See p.217 for details of car rental.

Boats

There remains one final mode of transport, **Batobus** (ⓦwww.batobus.com), which operates from April to October, stopping at eight points along the Seine in the following order: Port de la Bourdonnais (M° Eiffel Tower/Trocadéro), quai de Solférino (M° Assemblée Nationale), quai Malaquais (M° St-Germain-des-Prés), quai de Montebello (M° Notre-Dame), quai St Bernard (Jardin des Plantes), quai de l'Hôtel de Ville (M° Hôtel-de-Ville/Centre-Pompidou), quai du Louvre (M° Musée du Louvre) and Port des Champs Élysées (Champs Élysées). Boats run every twenty-five minutes from 10am to 9pm from June to September and from 10am to 7pm in April, May and October. The total journey time is around thirty minutes, and tickets cost €7.5 for a single journey or €11 for a day pass.

Accommodation

Not surprisingly, Paris **hotels** are the most expensive in France and the rooms on offer can be surprisingly small, though compared with other European capitals prices are not exorbitant and there's a wide range of places to choose from. Paris's smaller two-star hotels often charge between about €55 and €85 (❹–❺) for a double room, though for something with a bit of style you'll probably have to pay upwards of €85 (❻), and €100 or more (❼–❾) in swankier areas. However, it's possible to find a double room with a shower, in a decent central location, for €40–45 (❸), and bargains exist in the 11^{e} near the Bastille and on the edge of the Marais, as well as in the 17^{e} or 20^{e}, where you could get a small room with just a washbasin for less than €35 (❶–❷).

If you want to secure a really good room it's worth booking a month or more in advance, as even the nicer hotels often leave their pokiest rooms at the back for last-minute reservations, and the best places will sell out well in advance in all but the coldest months. If you're stuck, the **tourist offices** at the Gare du Nord, Gare de Lyon and Opéra-Grands Magasins (see p.108) will endeavour to find you a room: all book accommodation for that day only, and you have to turn up in person (€3–8 commission for a hotel room depending on how many stars it has, €1.20 for a hostel). The student travel agency OTU Voyages, at 119 rue St-Martin, opposite the Pompidou Centre, 4^{e} (Mon–Fri 9.30am–6.30pm, Sat 10am–5pm; ⓣ01.40.29.12.22, ⓦwww.otu.fr; M° Châtelet-Les Halles) and at 39 av Georges Bernanos, 5^{e} (same hours; ⓣ01.46.33.19.98; M° Port Royal) can find inexpensive rooms for a fee of €12.

Our hotel recommendations are divided by arrondissement (see map on pp.102–103). Prices are divided into nine categories: where there are only very few rooms in a hotel in the lower price categories, we show the complete price range on offer. Hostels and campsites are listed separately on pp.121–123.

1er hotels

Agora 7 rue de la Cossonnerie ⓣ01.42.33.46.02, ⓦwww.123france.com/hotel-agora; M° Châtelet-Les Halles; see map, pp.142–143. Somewhat overpriced for a two-star, but well located on a pedestrianized street right in the heart of Les Halles. The thirty en-suite rooms are all different, many with antique furnishings and floral wallpaper. ❻

Brighton 218 rue de Rivoli ⓣ01.47.03.61.61, ⓔhotel.brighton@wanadoo.fr; M° Tuileries; see map, pp.128–129. A smart hotel, with pleasant, airy rooms. Its main asset, however, are the magnificent views of the Tuileries from the front-facing rooms – the best are the ones with a balcony right at the top. ❼–❾

Henri IV 25 place Dauphine ⓣ01.43.54.44.53; M° Pont-Neuf/Cité; see map, pp.156–157. An ancient and well-known bargain in a beautiful location. The better rooms have been recently renovated and have en-suite bathrooms, but most come with nothing more luxurious than a cabinet de toilette and are very run down. Essential to book well in advance. No credit cards. ❶

Hôtel du Lion d'Or 5 rue de la Sourdière, 1er ⓣ01.42.60.79.04, ⓦwww.hotelduliondor.com; M° Tuileries; see map, pp.128–129. A friendly and very central hotel, with twenty en-suite rooms – simple but clean and recently renovated. You can check your email in the attached cyber-café. ❹

2e hotels

De Noailles 9 rue Michodière ⓣ01.47.42.92.90, ⓦwww.hoteldenoailles.com; M° Opéra/4-Septembre; see map, pp.128–129. Although part of an international chain, the Noailles hasn't lost its own identity and offers contemporary styling with traditional pleasures of garden and terrasse. ❾

Tiquetonne 6 rue Tiquetonne ⓣ01.42.36.94.58; M° Étienne-Marcel; see map, pp.142–143. On a pedestrian street, close to the red-light stretch of St-Denis, an old-fashioned budget hotel, dating back to the 1920s and looking as though it's changed little since. Its 47 rooms are well-maintained and clean, though, and nearly all are en suite. Closed Aug & Christmas week. ❸

Vivienne 40 rue Vivienne ⓣ01.42.33.13.26, ⓔparis@hotel-vivienne.com; M° Grands-Boulevards; see map, pp.128–129. Ideally located for the Opéra Garnier and Grands Boulevards, this is a very welcoming, good-value hotel, with clean, pleasant rooms; the cheapest come with shower only. ❸–❼

3e hotels

See map, pp.142–143.

Du Cantal 7 rue des Vertus ⓣ01.42.77.65.52, ⓦhcantal.online.fr; M° Arts-et-Métiers. Located near the Picasso Museum on a quiet, pedestrianized street, this small hotel with only fourteen rooms represents extremely good value for the area. Rooms are attractively, if simply, decorated, with some period features, such as exposed beams. There's also a small family suite on the top floor. Both breakfast and dinner are available in the café-bar downstairs. Midnight curfew. ❸

Pavillon de la Reine 28 place des Vosges ⓣ01.40.29.19.19, ⓦwww.pavillon-de-la-reine.com; M° Bastille. A perfect honeymoon or romantic-weekend hotel in a beautiful ivy-covered mansion secreted away off the Place des Vosges. Rooms are sumptuously decorated with rich fabrics, antique furnishings and four-poster beds and come with all the modern comforts of a four-star hotel. Doubles from €335. ❾

Picard 26 rue de Picardie ⓣ01.48.87.53.82, ⓦwww.france-hotel-guide.com/h75003picard2.htm; M° Temple/République. A clean and comfortable hotel on the edge of the Marais run by friendly people. ❹

4e hotels

See map, pp.142–143.

Caron de Beaumarchais 12 rue Vieille-du-Temple ⓣ01.42.72.34.12, ⓔhotel.carondebeaumarchais@wanadoo.fr; M° Hôtel de Ville. A gem of a hotel with only nineteen rooms, named after the eighteenth-century French playwright who lived just up the road. Everything in the hotel – down to the original engravings and Louis XVI-style furniture in the rooms, not to mention the piano-forte in the foyer – evokes the refined tastes of high-society pre-Revolutionary Paris. Rooms overlooking the courtyard are small but cosy, while those on the street are a little more spacious, some with balcony. Book well in advance. ❼

Grand Hôtel Jeanne d'Arc 3 rue de Jarente ⓣ01.48.87.62.11, ⓦwww.hoteljeannedarc.com; M° St-Paul. An attractive old stone Marais building, just off place du Marché Sainte-Catherine. The rooms are a decent size, with nice individual touches, plus cable TV. Booking essential. ❺

Grand Hôtel Malher 5 rue Malher ⓣ01.42.72.60.92, ⓕ01.42.72.25.37; M° St-Paul. A welcoming, family-run hotel, right in the heart of the Marais. Rooms are light and well decorated, with gleaming-white bathrooms. Breakfast is served in an atmospheric seventeenth-century vaulted wine cellar. ❼

Grand Hôtel du Loiret 8 rue des Mauvais Garçons ⓣ01.48.87.77.00, ⓔhoteloiret@aol.com; M° Hôtel-de-Ville. A simple but good-value hotel. The two triples on the top floor have excellent views of the Sacré-Coeur. Cheaper rooms have washbasin only, but all have TV and telephone. ❸

De Lutèce 65 rue St-Louis-en-l'Île ⓣ01.43.26.23.52, ⓔlutece@hotel-ile-saintlouis.com; M° Pont-Marie. Small but exquisite rooms on the most desirable island in France. ❾

St-Louis Marais 1 rue Charles-V ⓣ01.48.87.87.04, ⓦwww.hotelsaintlouismarais.com; M° Sully-Morland. Formerly part of the seventeenth-century Célestins Convent, this comfortable hotel offers tastefully furnished, cosy rooms. ❼

Du Septième Art 20 rue St-Paul ⓣ01.44.54.85.00, ⓔhotel7art@wanadoo.fr; M° St-Paul/Sully-Morland. A pleasant, comfortable hotel decorated with posters and photos from old movies, with a similarly themed bar downstairs. ❺

5e hotels

See map, pp.150–151.

Agora St-Germain 42 rue des Bernardins ⓣ01.46.34.13.00, ⓦwww.agorasaintgermain.com; M° Maubert-Mutualité. Very pleasant hotel, with all the comfort you'd expect for the price, though rear-facing rooms aren't such good value. ❽

Le Central 6 rue Descartes ⓣ01.46.33.57.93; M° Maubert-Mutualité/Cardinal-Lemoine. Plain but decent rooms in a typically Parisian house above a café-restaurant on the Montagne Ste-Geneviève. ❸

Du Commerce 14 rue de la Montagne-Ste-Geneviève ⓣ01.43.54.89.69, ⓦwww.commerce-paris-hotel.com; M° Maubert-Mutualité. Professionally run budget hotel in the heart of the Quartier Latin, with newly redecorated rooms. ❸

Esmeralda 4 rue St-Julien-le-Pauvre ⓣ01.43.54.19.20, ⓕ01.40.51.00.68; M° St-Michel/Maubert-Mutualité. Nestling in an ancient house on square Viviani, this discreet, old-fashioned hotel has cosy rooms, some with superb views of Notre-Dame. A trio of singles come with washbasin only for €35. ❻

Des Grandes Écoles 75 rue du Cardinal-Lemoine ⓣ01.43.26.79.23, ⓦwww.hotel-grandes-ecoles

.com; M° Cardinal-Lemoine. Comfortable, pretty hotel in the heart of the Quartier Latin, enclosing a beautiful courtyard garden. ❼

Marignan 13 rue du Sommerard ⓣ01.43.54.63.81, ⓦwww.hotel-marignan.com; M° Maubert-Mutualité. One of the best bargains in town, with a free breakfast thrown in. Totally sympathetic to the needs of rucksack-toting foreigners, with free laundry and ironing facilities, plus a room to eat your own food in – plates, fridge and microwave provided – and rooms for up to five people. ❹

Médicis 214 rue St-Jacques ⓣ01.43.54.14.66; RER Luxembourg. Basic, tatty old hotel, but the low prices make it very popular with hard-up backpackers, and the owners are charming. ❷

De la Sorbonne 6 rue Victor-Cousin ⓣ01.43.54.58.08, ⓦwww.hotelsorbonne.com; RER Luxembourg/M° Cluny-La Sorbonne. Housed in an attractive old building close to the Luxembourg gardens, this is a quiet, comfortable hotel. ❺

Des Trois Collèges 16 rue Cujas ⓣ01.43.54.67.30, ⓦwww.3colleges.com; RER Luxembourg/M° Cluny-La Sorbonne. Light, airy rooms and young, helpful staff in this classy modernized hotel. ❻

6e hotels

See map, pp.156–157.

De l'Angleterre 44 rue Jacob ⓣ01.42.60.34.72, ⓔanglotel@wanadoo.fr; M° St-Germain-des-Prés. Classy and elegant hotel, in a building that once housed the British Embassy and, later, Ernest Hemingway, although in those days he only paid three francs a night. ❽

Hôtel Delhy's 22 rue de l'Hirondelle ⓣ01.43.26.58.25, ⓕ01.43.26.51.06; M° St-Michel. An old house in a tiny street. Nothing special, but spotlessly maintained and in a very central location just off place St-Michel. ❺

Du Globe 15 rue des Quatre-Vents ⓣ01.43.26.35.50, ⓕ01.46.33.62.69; M° Odéon. Welcoming hotel in a tall, narrow, seventeenth-century building decked out with four-posters, stone walls, roof beams and the like. ❻

Ferrandi St-Germain 92 rue du Cherche-Midi ⓣ01.42.22.97.40, ⓔhotel.ferrandi@wanadoo.fr; M° Vaneau/St-Placide. Genteel, independent hotel with an old-fashioned feel, hidden away in a charming residential corner of St-Germain. Rooms are fairly pricey, but they're sunny, homely and fairly large by Parisian standards. ❽

Grand Hôtel des Balcons 3 rue Casimir-Delavigne ⓣ01.46.34.78.50, ⓦwww.balcons.com; M° Odéon. An attractive and comfortable hotel with a few Art Deco motifs in the modern rooms. Lovely location near the Odéon and Luxembourg gardens. ❼

Des Marronniers 21 rue Jacob ⓣ01.43.25.30.60, ⓦwww.paris-hotel-marroniers.com; M° St-Germain-des-Prés. Relatively pricey, but a romantic place nonetheless, with small rooms swathed in expensive fabrics. The dining room gives onto a courtyard garden. ❾

De Nesle 7 rue de Nesle ⓣ01.43.54.62.41, ⓦwww.hoteldenesle.com; M° St-Michel. Friendly, offbeat hotel with themed rooms decorated with cartoon murals that you'll either love or hate. ❺

Récamier 3bis place St-Sulpice ⓣ01.43.26.04.89, ⓕ01.46.33.27.73; M° St-Sulpice/St-Germain-des-Prés. Comfortable, old-fashioned and solidly bourgeois hotel in a great situation on the corner of the square. ❼

Relais Christine 3 rue Christine ⓣ01.40.51.60.80, ⓦwww.relais-christine.com; M° Odéon/St-Michel. This elegant and luxurious hotel is perfect for a treat. The sixteenth-century building is set around a hidden courtyard, creating an unusually intimate atmosphere. Standard rooms are fairly small for the price – over €300 – so it's worth paying the small premium for a *supérieure*. Two particularly sought-after rooms give onto a hidden garden behind. ❾

St-André-des-Arts 66 rue St-André-des-Arts ⓣ01.43.26.96.16, ⓔhsaintand@wanadoo.fr; M° Odéon/St-Germain-des-Prés. Friendly, family-run hotel in the heart of St-Germain. Rooms are pleasantly decorated and preserves some features of the seventeenth-century building. The best rooms are the ones on the front, with big floor-to-ceiling windows, and the adorable suite under the roof. ❺

7e hotels

See map, pp.160–161, except where indicated.

Bersoly's St-Germain 28 rue de Lille ⓣ01.42.60.73.79, ⓦwww.bersolyshotel.com; M° Rue-du-Bac; see map pp.156–157. Small but exquisite rooms, each named after an artist. Impeccable service, and a good location near the shopping areas of St-Germain. ❼

Du Champs-de-Mars 7 rue du Champs-de-Mars ⓣ01.45.51.52.30, ⓦwww.hotel-du-champ-de-mars.com; M° École-Militaire. Spotless, prettily decorated rooms in a friendly hotel just off the rue Cler market.

Du Palais Bourbon 49 rue de Bourgogne ⓣ01.44.11.30.70, ⓦwww.hotel-palais-bourbon.com; M° Varenne. A handsome, substantial old building in a sunny street by the Musée Rodin, with spacious and light rooms. Family rooms available, as well as one tiny but inexpensive double and some good-value singles. The immediate area is a bit dead in terms of cafés and restaurants, but it's classy and very quiet. ❼

Grand Hôtel Lévèque 29 rue Cler ⓣ01.47.05.49.15, ⓦwww.hotel-leveque.com; M° École-Militaire/La Tour-Maubourg. Located smack in the middle of the posh rue Cler market, this is a large but decent place, run by a friendly family. Book a month ahead for one of the two brighter rooms on the rue Cler. ❻

D'Orsay 93 rue de Lille ⓣ01.47.05.85.54, ⓔhotel.orsay@esprit-de-france.com M° Solférino/RER Musée-d'Orsay. A professional and stylish three-star with large rooms by Parisian standards. ❽

Le Pavillon 54 rue St-Dominique ⓣ01.45.51.42.87, ⓔpatrickpavillon@aol.com; M° Invalides/La Tour-Maubourg. A tiny former convent set back from the tempting shops of the rue St-Dominique. Rooms are small and simple, but good value in this area. ❻

Saint Dominique 62 rue Saint-Dominique ⓣ01.47.05.51.44, ⓦwww.saintdominique.com; M° Invalides/La Tour-Maubourg. Welcoming hotel in a classy quarter close to the Eiffel Tower with prettily wallpapered rooms arranged around a bright courtyard. ❼

De la Tulipe 33 rue Malar ⓣ01.45.51.67.21, ⓦwww.paris-hotel-tulipe.com; M° Invalides/La Tour-Maubourg. Attractive, cottage-like place with a patio for summer breakfast and drinks. As with all hotels in this area, you pay for the location. ❼

8e hotels

See map, pp.128–129.

Le Bristol 112 rue du Faubourg St-Honoré ⓣ01.53.43.43.00, ⓦwww.lebristolparis.com; M° Miromesnil. Paris's most luxurious and spacious hotel manages to remain discreet and warm. Features include Gobelins tapestries, private roof gardens with some of the rooms and a large colonnaded interior garden, as well as the expected swimming pool, health club and gourmet restaurant. Doubles from €580. ❾

Des Champs-Élysées 2 rue Artois ⓣ01.43.59.11.42, ⓕ01.45.61.00.61; M° St-Philippe-du-Roule. A welcoming, family-run hotel. Rooms are decorated in warm colours and all come with shower or bath, plus TV, minibar, hairdryer and safe. Breakfast is served in a converted stone cellar. ❻

De L'Élysée 12 rue des Saussaies ⓣ01.42.65.29.25, ⓕ01.42.65.64.28; M° Miromesnil. A classic luxury hotel, done out with chandeliers, faux marble, swirly drapes and antique furnishings, some rooms with four-poster beds. ❽

9e hotels

Chopin 46 passage Jouffroy; entrance on bd Montmartre, near rue du Faubourg-Montmartre ⓣ01.47.70.58.10, ⓕ01.42.47.00.70; M° Grands-Boulevards. Splendid period building hidden away at the end of an elegant passage, with quiet and pleasantly furnished rooms, though the cheaper ones are on the small side and a little dark. ❺

Langlois/des Croisés 63 rue St-Lazare ⓣ01.48.74.78.24, ⓔhotel-des-croises@wanadoo.fr; M° Trinité. Superbly genteel hotel that's hardly changed in half a century, with a beautiful old lift and unusually large rooms. ❻

Perfect Hotel 39 Rue Rodier ⓣ01.42.81.18.86, ⓕ01.42.85.01.38; M° Anvers. Popular hotel on a lively street populated with restaurants. Simple, clean rooms – some very good value, with shared bathroom facilities – and a warm welcome. ❸

10e hotels

Gilden-Magenta 35 rue Yves Toudic ⓣ01.42.40.17.72, ⓦwww.multi-micro.com/hotel.gilden.magenta; M° République/Jacques-Bonsergent. A friendly hotel, with fresh, colourful decor; rooms 61 and 62, up in the attic, are the best and have views of the Canal St Martin. Breakfast is served in a pleasant patio area. ❹

Jarry 6 rue de Jarry ⓣ01.47.70.70.38, ⓕ01.42.46.34.45; M° Gare-de-l'Est/Château-d'Eau. Simple, welcoming hotel in a lively immigrant quarter. Distinctly fresher than the cheap dives on the same street. ❶

Moderne du Temple 3 rue d'Aix ⓣ01.42.08.09.04, ⓦhmt.chez.tiscali.fr; M° République/Goncourt. A bargain hotel in a quiet street, run by Czechs. The forty rooms are very simple but clean, some en suite. ❷

11e hotels

See map, pp.142–143.

Beaumarchais 3 rue Oberkampf ⓣ01.43.38.16.16, ⓦwww.hotelbeaumarchais.com; M° Filles-du-Calvaire/Oberkampf. Fashionable, gay-friendly hotel with personal service and colourful Fifties-inspired decor; all rooms are en suite with air conditioning, individual safes and cable TV. ❻

Mary's 15 rue de Malte ⓣ01.47.00.81.70, ⓦwww.maryshotel.com; M° République/Oberkampf. Comfortable and clean hotel on the edge of the Marais, with courteous staff. The cheaper rooms are good value for money though en-suite rooms suffer from money-saving gadgets such as hand-held showers and non-direct phones. ❸

Méridional 36 bd Richard-Lenoir ⓣ01.48.05.75.00, ⓕ01.43.57.42.85; M° Bréguet-Sabin. A welcoming three-star handy for the Marais and Bastille areas. Rooms are well-equipped and attractively furnished in light oak and pastel colours. ❽

De Nevers 53 rue de Malte ⓣ01.47.00.56.18, ⓦwww.hoteldenevers.com; M° République/Oberkampf. Three smoky-grey cats patrol the entrance to this friendly one-star. Rooms are small and basic, but well kept. When it's working, a rickety 1930s lift rumbles its way between the floors. ❷

Hôtel Verlain 97 rue Saint Maur ⓣ01.43.57.44.88, ⓦwww.verlain.co.il; M° Rue St-Maur. A three-star with neat, clean, and cheerful rooms – some with balconies – in a lively neighbourhood, close to the trendy bars of Oberkampf. ❼

12e hotels

De la Porte Dorée 273 av Daumesnil; ⓣ01.43.07.56.97.04, ⓦwww.paris-hotels-paris.com; M° Porte-Dorée. A charming two-star, renovated with great care and taste by an American-French family. Traditional features such as ceiling mouldings, fireplaces and the elegant main staircase have been retained and many of the furnishings in the rooms are antique. Modern touches include Internet point, satellite TV and hairdryers in all the rooms. It's not in the most happening of areas, but the Bastille is only seven mintues away by metro or a pleasant twenty-minute walk along the Promenade Plantée. ❹

Des Pyrénées 204 rue du Faubourg-St-Antoine; ⓣ01.43.72.07.46, ⓕ01.43.72.98.45; M° Faidherbe-Chaligny. A good-value hotel with thirty comfortable and spacious, if a little old-fashioned, rooms; those on the road are lighter and double-glazed. ❹

13e hotels

Résidence Les Gobelins 9 rue des Gobelins ⓣ01.47.07.26.90, ⓦwww.hotelgobelins.com; M° Les Gobelins. A delightful establishment that's well known, so book far in advance. ❺

Tolbiac 122 rue de Tolbiac ⓣ01.44.24.25.54, ⓦwww.hotel-tolbiac.com; M° Tolbiac. Situated on a noisy junction, but all rooms are very pleasant, with private or shared showers. In July and Aug you can rent small studios by the week. ❷

Le Vert-Galant 41 rue Croulebarbe; ⓣ01.44.08.83.50, ⓕ01.44.08.83.69; M° Les Gobelins. Pleasant hotel in a quiet, verdant backwater, above a renowned Basque restaurant, the *Auberge Etchegorry* (see p.193). Cosy rooms, some with kitchenette. ❻

14e hotels

Celtic 15 rue d'Odessa ⓣ01.43.20.93.53, ⓕ01.43.20.66.07; M° Montparnasse-Bienvenüe/Edgar-Quinet. Attractively old-fashioned but well-maintained hotel almost in the shadow of the Tour Montparnasse, with a few inexpensive rooms with shared bathroom facilities. ❸–❹

Istria 29 rue Campagne-Première ⓣ01.43.20.91.82, ⓔhotel.istria@wanadoo.fr; M° Raspail. Beautifully decorated hotel with legendary artistic associations: Duchamp, Man Ray, Aragon, Mayakovsky and Rilke all stayed here. ❼

De la Loire 39bis rue du Moulin-Vert ⓣ01.45.40.66.88, ⓕ01.45.40.89.07; M° Alésia/Plaisance. Attractive hotel on a very quiet street, with breakfast served in a little garden. ❹

15e hotels

Printemps 31 rue du Commerce ⓣ01.45.79.83.36, ⓔhotel.printemps.15e@yahoo.fr; M° La Motte-Picquet-Grenelle. This place offers a friendly welcome and rooms that are sparsely furnished but clean. Popular with backpackers. ❷

Wallace 89 rue Fondary ⓣ01.45.78.83.30, ⓦwww.escapade-paris.com; M° Émile-Zola. Unpretentious, charming hotel with a pretty garden in the courtyard. ❼

16e hotels

Hameau de Passy 48 rue Passy ⓣ01.42.88.47.55, ⓦwww.hameaudepassy.com; M° Muette/Passy. An utterly peaceful modern hotel, tucked away in a villa. Rooms are on the small side, but are pleasantly decorated in hues of green and look out onto a pretty tree-lined patio. Faultless service is assured by a charming, polyglot staff. ❼

Keppler 12 rue Keppler ⓣ01.47.20.65.05, ⓔhotel.keppler@wanadoo.fr; M° George-V/Kléber; see map, pp.128–129. Located in a quiet street, just a stone's throw away from the Champs Elysées, this place is good value for the area. Rooms are a little small, but spotless and quite comfortable. ❺

Hotel Pergolèse 3 rue Pergolèse, 16e ⓣ01.53.64.04.04, ⓦwww.hotelpergolese.com. Classy four-star boutique hotel in a tall, slender building on a quiet side-street near the Arc de

Triomphe. The decor is all contemporary – wood floors, cool colours, chic styling – but without chilliness: sofas and friendly service add a cosy touch. Rooms on six floors are comfortable and well-appointed, with great designer bathrooms. Double-glazing throughout, so street noise isn't a problem. No-smoking floor. Plenty of special deals bring prices well down below advertised rates. ❾

17e hotels

Des Batignolles 26–28 rue des Batignolles ⓣ01.43.87.70.40, ⓦwww.batignolles.com; M° Rome/Place-de-Clichy. Quiet and reasonably priced hotel, in a neighbourhood that prides itself on its village character. ❹
Eldorado 18 rue des Dames ⓣ01.45.22.35.21, ⓔeldoradohotel@wanadoo.fr; M° Rome/Place-de-Clichy. A funky, trendy and reasonably priced place to stay. ❹
Savoy 21 rue des Dames ⓣ01.42.93.13.47; M° Place-de-Clichy/Rome. Typical unmodernized Paris cheapie, with a choice of rooms with shared bathrooms or private showers. ❷

18e hotels

André Gill 4 rue André-Gill ⓣ01.42.62.48.48, ⓔblounis@aol.com; M° Pigalle/Abbesses. Quiet rooms in a great location on the slopes of Montmartre, in a dead-end alley off rue des Martyrs. No-smoking. ❺
Bonséjour 11 rue Burq ⓣ01.42.54.22.53, ⓕ01.42.54.25.92; M° Abbesses. Set in a marvellous location on a quiet untouristy street on the slopes of Montmartre, this hotel is run by friendly owners, and the rooms, which are basic but clean and spacious, are Montmartre's best deal. Ask for the corner rooms 23, 33, 43 or 53, which have a balcony. ❷
Le Bouquet de Montmartre 1 rue Durantin ⓣ01.46.06.87.54, ⓕ01.46.06.09.09; M° Jules-Joffrin. The decor is overwhelmingly chintzy, but the rooms are comfortable and good value, and the location on the corner of lively place des Abbesses, directly underneath the Butte, is excellent. ❹
Du Commerce 34 rue des Trois-Frères ⓣ01.42.64.81.69; M° Abbesses/Anvers. Grotty but cheerily run and very inexpensive hotel; for the hardened traveller only. ❶
Ermitage 24 rue Lamarck; ⓣ01.42.64.79.22; M° Lamarck-Caulaincourt/Château-Rouge. Discreet hotel characterfully decorated in deep colours. Only a stone's throw from Sacré-Coeur; approach via M° Anvers and the funicular to avoid the steep climb. ❻

19e hotels

Ibis Paris La Villette 31–35 quai de L'Oise ⓣ01.40.38.04.04, ⓦwww.ibishotel.com; M° Corentin Cariou/Ourcq. Situated right on the canal facing the Parc de la Villette, this good-value modern chain hotel is handy for exploring the park or attending concerts at the Cité de la Musique. It's also convenient if you're bringing your own car, as it's easily reached from the *boulevard périphérique* exiting at the Porte de la Villette, with free parking included. ❹
Rhin et Danube 3 place Rhin-et-Danube ⓣ01.42.45.10.13; M° Danube. Studio apartments with small kitchenettes, located near the entrance to the Parc de la Villette on the airy heights of Belleville. ❹

20e hotels

Ermitage 42bis rue de l'Ermitage ⓣ01.46.36.23.44, ⓕ01.46.36.89.13; M° Jourdain. A clean and decent budget hotel, close to the leafy rue des Pyrénées with its provincial feel. ❸
Pyrénées-Gambetta 12 av du Père-Lachaise ⓣ01.47.97.76.57, ⓦwww.hotelparisgambetta.com; M° Gambetta. On a quiet street, a very pleasant hotel, perfect for visiting the Père-Lachaise cemetery. All rooms have cable TV. ❺
Tamaris 14 rue des Maraîchers ⓣ01.43.72.85.48, ⓦwww.hotel-tamaris.fr; M° Porte-de-Vincennes. An old-fashioned, simply furnished, but clean and quiet hotel, run by pleasant people. Located in a rather dull area, but only four metro stops from the Bastille and close to the terminus of #26 bus route from Gare du Nord. ❷

Hostels, student accommodation and campsites

There are numerous places in Paris offering **hostel** accommodation. The two main hostel groups, charging around €20 for a dorm bed, are the **Fédération Unie des Auberges de Jeunesse** (FUAJ; ⓦwww.fuaj.fr), for which you need Hostelling International (HI) membership (available on the spot, no age limit), and **UCRIF** (Union des Centres de Rencontres Internationaux de France; ⓦwww.ucrif.asso.fr); there's no age limit and reservations are not always possible. We've detailed only the most central of the UCRIF hostels, but a full list is available on their website, or you can contact their main office at 27 rue de Turbigo, 2e (Mon–Fri 10am–6pm; ⓣ01.40.26.57.64; M° Étienne-Marcel). A smaller group is the **MIJE** (Maison Internationale de la Jeunesse et des Étudiants; ⓦwww.mije.com), which runs three hostels in historic buildings in the Marais district, with dorms beds from €27. There's also a handful of privately run hostels, most of which cost around €15–20, depending on season.

Single and double rooms, where available, generally cost five or ten euros extra. Most hostels impose a stay limit, which can be negotiable, depending on the season, and bear in mind, too, that some places have a curfew – usually around 11pm – though you may be given a key or entry code.

Student accommodation is let out during the summer vacation. Rooms are spartan, part of large modern university complexes, often complete with self-service kitchen facilities and shared bathrooms. Space tends to fill up quickly with international students, school groups and young travellers, so it's best to make plans well in advance. Expect to pay €15–30 per night for a room. The organization to contact for information and reservations is CROUS, Académie de Paris, 39 av Georges-Bernanos, 5e (Mon–Fri 1–4.30pm; ⓣ01.40.51.55.55, ⓦwww.crous.fr; M° Port-Royal).

The cheapest accommodation option of all is camping. There are three **campsites** on the outskirts of Paris, which, although pleasant enough, are a bit of a pain to get to on public transport.

Hostels

D'Artagnan 80 rue Vitruve, 20e ⓣ01.40.32.34.56; M° Porte-de-Bagnolet. A colourful, funky, modern HI hostel, with a fun atmosphere and lots of facilities including a small cinema, restaurant and bar, and a local swimming pool nearby. Located on the eastern edge of the city near Charonne, which has some good bars. Very popular so try to get here early – reservations by fax or from other HI hostels only. Beds cost €20.50 a night.

Auberge Internationale des Jeunes 10 rue Trousseau, 11e ⓣ01.47.00.62.00, ⓦwww.aijparis.com; M° Bastille/Ledru-Rollin. Despite the official-sounding name, a laid-back (but very noisy) independent hostel in a great location five minutes' walk from the Bastille. Clean and professionally run with 24hr reception, generous breakfast (included in price) and free luggage storage. Rooms for 2, 3 and 4. €13 Nov–Feb, €14 March–Oct.

BVJ Paris Quartier Latin 44 rue des Bernardins, 5e ⓣ01.43.29.34.80, ⓦwww.bvjhotel.com; M° Maubert-Mutualité; see map, pp.150–151. Typically institutional UCRIF hostel, but spick and span and in a good location. Dorm beds (€26), plus single or double rooms (€35/28 per person).

Centre International de Paris/Louvre 20 rue Jean-Jacques-Rousseau, 1er ⓣ01.53.00.90.90, ⓕ01.53.00.90.91; M° Louvre/Châtelet-Les Halles; see map, pp.128–129. A clean, modern and efficiently run independent hostel for 18- to 35-year-olds. Bookings can be made up to ten days prior to your stay. Accommodation ranges from single rooms to dorms sleeping eight. From €18.30 per person.

Le Fauconnier 11 rue du Fauconnier, 4e ⓣ01.42.74.23.45, ⓕ01.40.27.81.64; M° St-Paul/Pont-Marie; see map, pp.142–143. MIJE hostel in a superbly renovated seventeenth-century building with a courtyard. Dorms (€27 per person) sleep three to eight, and there are some single (€42) and double rooms too (€32), with en-suite showers. Breakfast included.

Le Fourcy 6 rue de Fourcy, 4e ⓣ01.42.74.23.45; M° St-Paul; see map, pp.142–143. Another MIJE hostel (same prices as Le Fauconnier, above) housed in a beautiful mansion, this one has a small garden and an inexpensive restaurant. Dorms and some doubles and triples.

Jules Ferry 8 bd Jules-Ferry, 11e ⓣ01.43.57.55.60, ⓕ01.43.14.82.09; M° République. Fairly central HI hostel, in a lively area at the foot of the Belleville hill. Show up early in the morning and you should get a place; if they're full they will help you find a bed elsewhere. Beds in dorms of four to six cost €19.50, doubles €20. Breakfast included.

Maison Internationale des Jeunes 4 rue Titon, 11e ⓣ01.43.71.99.21, ⓕ01.43.71.78.58, ⓔmij.cp@wanadoo.fr; M° Faidherbe-Chaligny. A clean, well-run establishment located between Bastille and Nation, geared to 18- to 30-year-olds for stays of between three and five days. Doors are open from 6am till 2am. Rooms range from doubles to dorms sleeping eight. €22.50 per person including shower, breakfast and sheets. Reservations should be made in advance and a fifty percent deposit is required.

Maubuisson 12 rue des Barres, 4e ☎01.42.74.23.45; M° Pont-Marie/Hôtel-de-Ville. A MIJE hostel in a magnificent medieval building on a quiet street. Shared use of the restaurant at Le Fourcy (see above). Dorms only, sleeping four (€27 per person). Breakfast included.

Three Ducks Hostel 6 place Étienne-Pernet, 15e ☎01.48.42.04.05, Ⓦwww.3ducks.fr; M° Commerce/Félix-Faure. A private youth hostel with no age limit. In high season, beds cost €22 in dorm rooms (sleeping from four to ten people), and double rooms cost €26 per person; there are discounts in winter. Kitchen facilities as well as a bar with the cheapest beer in town. Essential to book ahead between May and Oct: send the price of the first night or leave a credit card number online. Lockout noon–4pm, curfew at 2am.

Le Village Hostel 20 rue d'Orsel, 18e ☎01.42.64.22.02, Ⓦwww.villagehostel.fr; M° Anvers. Attractive, brand-new hostel with a relatively old-fashioned feel, and good facilities such as phones in the rooms. There's a view of the Sacré-Coeur from the terrace. Dorms cost €21.50, triples and twins are €23 and €25 respectively, though there are small discounts in winter, and prices include breakfast.

Woodstock Hostel 48 rue Rodier, 9e ☎01.48.78.87.76, Ⓦwww.woodstock.fr; M° Anvers/St-Georges. Another reliable hostel in the Three Ducks stable, with its own bar, and set in a great location on a pretty street not far from Montmartre. Dorms cost €20, twin rooms €25; prices include breakfast and drop €5 in winter (Oct–March). Lockout 11am–3pm, curfew at 2am.

Young and Happy Hostel 80 rue Mouffetard, 5e ☎01.47.07.47.07, Ⓦwww.youngandhappy.fr; M° Monge/Censier-Daubenton; see map, pp.150–151. Noisy, basic and studenty independent hostel in a lively, if a tad touristy, position. Dorms, with shower, sleep four (€22 per person), and there are a few doubles (€25 per person). Lockout 11am–3pm, curfew at 2am.

Campsites

Camping du Bois de Boulogne Allée du Bord-de-l'Eau, 16e ☎01.45.24.30.00, Ⓦwww.abccamping.com/boulogne.htm; M° Porte-Maillot then bus #244 to Moulins Camping (bus runs 6am–9pm). Much the most central campsite, with space for 436 tents, next to the River Seine in the Bois de Boulogne, and usually booked up in summer. The ground is pebbly, but the site is well equipped and has a useful information office. Prices start at €11 for a tent with two people; and there are also bungalows for four to six people starting at €49 per night. An extra shuttle bus runs every morning from April to October between the campsite and M° Porte-Maillot.

Camping la Colline Route de Lagny, Torcy ☎01.60.05.42.32, Ⓦwww.camping-de-la-colline.com; RER line A4 to Torcy, then phone from the station and they will come and collect you or take bus #421 to stop Le Clos. Pleasant wooded lakeside site to the east of the city near Disneyland (minibus shuttle to Disneyland costs €12.50 return), offering rental of anything from luxury tents to bungalows; erecting your own tent costs €15 per night for two people.

Camping du Parc-Étang St-Quentin-en-Yvelines Montigny-le-Bretonneux ☎01.30.58.56.20; RER line C St-Quentin-en-Yvelines. Adequately equipped large campsite in a leisure complex southwest of Paris. Open March–Oct; costs €14 for two people and a tent.

The City

There are any number of ways of exploring Paris – you certainly don't have to start with the Louvre or Notre-Dame – and our account is structured in chunks of territory that share a common identity even though they don't always correspond exactly with the boundaries of the twenty arrondissements (see p.108). We start with the **Île de la Cité**, then move to the **Right Bank** and the **Voie Triomphale**, the city's greatest vista. This leads from the **Louvre** right out to the northwest perimeter, from where we move east to the **Marais** and the **Bastille**. We continue with the inner arrondissements on the **Left Bank**, followed by the southern arrondissements, the rich **Beaux Quartiers** to the west, and beyond them, outside the city, the modern business district of **La Défense**, then **Montmartre** and the northern arrondissements and, finally, the east of the city, from the old villages of **Belleville** and **Ménilmontant**, including the Père-Lachaise cemetery, out to Vincennes.

Île de la Cité

The **Île de la Cité** is where Paris began. The earliest settlements were built here, followed by the small Gallic town of Lutetia, overrun by Julius Caesar's troops in 52 BC. A natural defensive site commanding a major east–west river trade route, it was an obvious candidate for a bright future. The Romans garrisoned it and laid out one of their standard military town plans. While they never attached any great political importance to the settlement, they endowed it with an administrative centre that became the stronghold of the Merovingian kings in 508, then of the counts of Paris who in 987 became kings of France.

The Frankish kings built themselves a splendid palace at the western tip of the island, of which the **Sainte Chapelle** and **Conciergerie** survive today. At the other end of the island, they erected their most famous monument, the great cathedral of **Notre-Dame**. By the early thirteenth century this tiny island had become the bustling heart of the capital, accommodating twelve parishes, not to mention numerous chapels and convents. It's hard to imagine this today: virtually the whole medieval city was erased by heavy-handed nineteenth-century demolition and much of it replaced by four vast edifices largely given over to housing the law. The warren of narrow streets around the cathedral was swept away and replaced with a huge expanse of paving, allowing an uncluttered view of Notre-Dame's facade.

Pont-Neuf and the quais, Sainte-Chapelle and the Conciergerie

One of the most popular approaches to the island is via the graceful, twelve-arched **Pont-Neuf**, which despite its name is Paris's oldest surviving bridge, built in 1607 by Henri IV. It was the first in the city to be built of stone, hence it's name "new". The bridge became a popular spot with street entertainers and actors, who played to the crowds teeming around the stalls and booths installed in the bridge's bays, these days occupied by stone seats. Henri is commemorated with an equestrian statue halfway across, and also lends his nickname to the **square du Vert-Galant**, enclosed within the triangular stern of the island and reached via steps leading down behind the statue. "Vert-Galant", meaning a "green" or "lusty gentleman", is a reference to Henri's legendary amorous exploits, and he would no doubt have approved of this tranquil, tree-lined garden, a popular haunt of lovers. The prime spot to occupy is the knoll dotted with trees at the extreme point of the island.

Back on Pont-Neuf, opposite the square du Vert-Galant, red-bricked seventeenth-century houses flank the entrance to **place Dauphine**, one of the city's most secluded squares. Traffic noise recedes and is likely to be replaced by nothing more intrusive than the gentle tap of boules being played in the shade of the chestnuts. The further end is blocked by the huge facade of the **Palais de Justice**, which swallowed up the palace that was home to the French kings until Étienne Marcel's bloody revolt in 1358 frightened them off to the greater security of the Louvre.

The only part of the older complex that remains in its entirety is the stunning **Sainte-Chapelle** (daily April–Sept 9.30am–6.30pm; Oct–March 10am–5pm; €5.50, combined admission to the Conciergerie €8; M° Cité), its slender

Gothic spire soaring above the Palais de Justice buildings. It was built by Louis IX between 1242 and 1248 to house a collection of holy relics, including Christ's crown of thorns and a fragment of the True Cross, bought at extortionate rates from the bankrupt empire of Byzantium. Though much restored, the chapel remains one of the finest achievements of French High Gothic. Its most radical feature is its seeming fragility – created by reducing the structural masonry to a minimum to make way for a huge expanse of exquisite stained glass. The impression inside is of being enclosed within the wings of a myriad brilliant butterflies.

Nearby is the **Conciergerie** (same hours as Sainte-Chapelle; €6.10, combined ticket with Ste-Chapelle €8; M° Cité), Paris's oldest prison, where Marie-Antoinette and, in their turn, the leading figures of the Revolution – were incarcerated before execution. The entrance around the corner from Ste-Chapelle, on quai de l'Horloge, is flanked by two fine medieval towers – the one on the right was known as the Bonbec tower, so named because prisoners incarcerated here were tortured and reduced to a *bonbec* ("babbler"). Inside are several splendidly vaulted late-Gothic halls, vestiges of the old Capetian kings' palace. The most impressive is the Salle des Gens d'armes, originally the canteen and recreation room of the royal household staff. The far end, separated off by an iron grille, was reserved during the French Revolution for prisoners who couldn't afford to bribe a guard for their own cell and were known as the *pailleux* because all they had to sleep on was hay (*paille*).

Beyond, a number of rooms and prisoners' cells have been reconstructed to show what they might have been like at the time of the Revolution. Among them is the innocent-sounding *salle de toilette*, the room where the condemned had their hair cropped and shirt collars ripped in preparation for the guillotine. You can also see a mock-up of Marie-Antoinette's cell, in which the condemned queen's crucifix hangs forlornly against peeling fleur-de-lys wallpaper.

Back outside the Conciergerie, on the corner of boulevard du Palais, you'll see the **Tour de l'Horloge**, built around 1350, and so called because it displayed Paris's first public clock. The original was replaced in 1585 and survives to this day – an ornate affair flanked with classical figures representing Law and Justice. East from here, along the north side of the island, you come to **place Lépine**, named after the police boss who gave Paris's cops their white truncheons and whistles. The police headquarters, better known as the Quai des Orfèvres to readers of Georges Simenon's Maigret novels, stands on one side of the square, while the other side is enlivened by an exuberant **flower market**, held daily and augmented by a chirruping bird market on Sundays.

Cathédrale de Notre-Dame

One of the masterpieces of the Gothic age, the **Cathédrale de Notre-Dame** (Mon–Fri & Sun 8am–7pm, Sat 8am–12.30pm & 2–7pm; free; M° St-Michel/Cité) rears up from the Île de la Cité's southeast corner like a ship moored by huge flying buttresses. It was among the first of the great Gothic cathedrals built in northern France and one of the most ambitious, its nave reaching an uprecedented 33m.

Built on the site of the old Merovingian cathedral of Saint-Étienne, Notre-Dame was begun in 1160 under the auspices of Bishop de Sully and completed around 1345. In the seventeenth and eighteenth centuries it fell into decline, suffering its worst depredations during the French Revolution when the frieze of Old Testament kings on the facade was damaged by enthusiasts who mistook them for the kings of France. It was only in the 1820s that the cathedral was at last given a much-needed restoration, a task entrusted to the great architect-restorer, Viollet-le-Duc, who carried out a thorough – some would say too thorough – renovation, including remaking most of the statuary on the facade (the originals can be seen in the Musée National du Moyen-Age, see p.152) – and adding the steeple and baleful-looking gargoyles, which you can see close up if you brave the ascent of the towers (April–Sept Mon–Thurs 9am–7.30pm, Fri–Sun 9am–9pm; Oct–March 10am–5pm; €5.50). Queues for the towers often start before they open, so it pays to get here early or to come in the evening when it's often quieter. The same goes for visiting the cathedral itself.

The cathedral's **facade** is one of its most impressive exterior features; the Romanesque influence is still visible, not least in its solid H-shape, but the overriding impression is one of lightness and grace, created in part by the delicate filigree work of the central rose window and gallery above. There are some magnificent **carvings over the portals**; perhaps the most arresting is the scene over the central portal, showing the *Day of Judgement*: the lower frieze is a whirl of movement as the dead are summoned from their graves, while above Christ presides, sending those on his right to heaven and those on the left to grisly torments in hell – those condemned include a fair number of what look like bishops and kings, suggesting that the craftsmen of the day were not without freedom to criticize the authorities. The left portal shows Mary being crowned by Christ, with scenes of her life in the lower friezes, while the right portal depicts the Virgin enthroned above the life of Christ, the episodes of which are masterfully put together, making the most of the limited space.

The interior

Inside Notre-Dame, the immediately striking feature is the dramatic contrast between the darkness of the nave and the light falling on the first great clustered pillars of the choir, emphasizing the sacred nature of the sanctuary. It's the end walls of the transepts that admit all this light, nearly two-thirds glass, including two magnificent rose windows coloured in imperial purple. These, the vaulting and the soaring shafts reaching to the springs of the vaults, are all definite Gothic elements, while there remains a strong sense of Romanesque in the stout round pillars of the nave and the general sense of four-squareness. The **trésor** (daily 9.30am–6pm; €2.50) contains mostly ornate nineteenth-century monstrances and chalices and isn't really worth the entry fee. Free guided tours (1hr–1hr 30min) take place in French every weekday at noon and on Saturday at 2pm, and in English on Wednesday at noon; the gathering point is the welcome desk near the entrance. There are free organ concerts every Sunday, around 4 or 5pm, plus four Masses on Sunday morning and one at 6.30pm.

The kilomètre zéro and crypte archéologique

On the pavement by the west door of the cathedral is a spot known as **kilomètre zéro**, the symbolic heart of France, from which all main road distances in the country are calculated. At the far end of the *place* is the entrance to the atmospheric **crypte archéologique** (Tues–Sun 10am–6pm; €3.30), a large excavated area under the square revealing remains of the original cathedral, as well as remnants of the streets and houses that once clustered around Notre-Dame: most are medieval, but some date as far back as Gallo-Roman times and include parts of a Roman hypocaust (heating system).

Le Mémorial de la Déportation

At the eastern tip of the island is the symbolic tomb of the 200,000 French who died in Nazi concentration camps during World War II – Resistance fighters, Jews and forced labourers among them. The stark and moving **Mémorial de la Déportation** (daily 10am–noon & 2–5pm; free) is scarcely visible above ground; stairs hardly shoulder-wide descend into a space like a prison yard and then into the crypt, off which is a long, narrow, stifling corridor, its wall covered in thousands of points of light representing the dead. Floor and ceiling are black, and it ends in a black, raw hole, with a single naked bulb hanging in the middle. Above the exit are the words "Forgive. Do not forget."

The Voie Triomphale

The **Voie Triomphale**, or Triumphal Way, is the name often used to describe the grand nine-kilometre axis that extends from the Louvre at the heart of the city to the Grande Arche de la Défense in the west. Offering impressive vistas all along its length, it incorporates some of the city's most famous landmarks – the **Tuileries** gardens, **Place de la Concorde**, the **Champs-Élysées** avenue and the **Arc de Triomphe**. The whole ensemble is so regular and geometrical it looks as though it was laid out by a single town planner rather than by successive kings, emperors and presidents, all keen to add their stamp and promote French power and prestige.

The Arc de Triomphe

The best view of the Voie Triomphale is from the top of the **Arc de Triomphe** (daily: April–Sept 10am–11pm; Oct–March 10am–10.30pm; €7; M° Charles-de-Gaulle-Étoile), towering above the traffic in the middle of **place Charles-de-Gaulle**, better known as l'Étoile ("star") on account of the twelve avenues radiating out from it. Access is via underground stairs from the north corner of the Champs-Élysées. The arch was started by Napoleon as a homage to the armies of France and himself, but it wasn't actually finished until 1836 by Louis Philippe, who dedicated it to the French army in general. The names of 660 generals and numerous French battles are engraved on the inside of the arch, and reliefs adorn the exterior: the best is François Rude's extraordinarily dramatic *Marseillaise*, in which an Amazon-type figure personifying the Revolution charges forward with a sword, her face contorted in a fierce rallying cry. A quiet reminder of the less glorious side of war is the **tomb of the unknown soldier** placed beneath the arch and marked by an eternal flame that is stoked up every evening at 6.30pm by war veterans. If you're up for climbing the 280 steps to the top you'll be amply rewarded by the panoramic views; the best time to come is towards dusk on a sunny day when the marble of the Grande Arche de la Défense sparkles in the setting sun and the Louvre is bathed in warm light.

The Champs-Élysées

Tree-lined and broad, the celebrated **avenue des Champs-Élysées** sweeps down from the Arc de Triomphe towards the place de la Concorde. Seen from a distance it's an impressive sight, but close up can be a little disappointing, with its constant stream of traffic and fast-food outlets, airline offices and chain stores. Over the last few years, however, it's begun shedding its tacky image and regained something of its former cachet as a chic address: Louis Vuitton and other designer outlets have moved in, once dowdy shops such as the Publicis

drugstore and the Renault car showroom have undergone stylish makeovers and acquired cool bar-restaurants, while new, fashionable cafés and restaurants in the streets around have injected fresh buzz and glamour. Just off the avenue, **rue Francois 1er** and **avenue Montaigne**, part of the "*triangle d'or*" (golden triangle), are home to the most exclusive names in fashion: Dior, Prada, Chanel and many others.

The Champs-Élysées began life as a leafy promenade, an extension of the Tuileries gardens. It was transformed into a fashionable thoroughfare during the Second Empire when members of the *haute bourgeoisie* built themselves splendid mansions along its length and high society would come to stroll and frequent the cafés and theatres. Most of the mansions subsequently gave way to office blocks and the *beau monde* moved elsewhere, but remnants of the avenue's glitzy heyday live on at the *Lido* cabaret, *Fouquet's* café-restaurant, the perfumier Guerlain's shop and the former *Claridges* hotel, now a swanky shopping arcade.

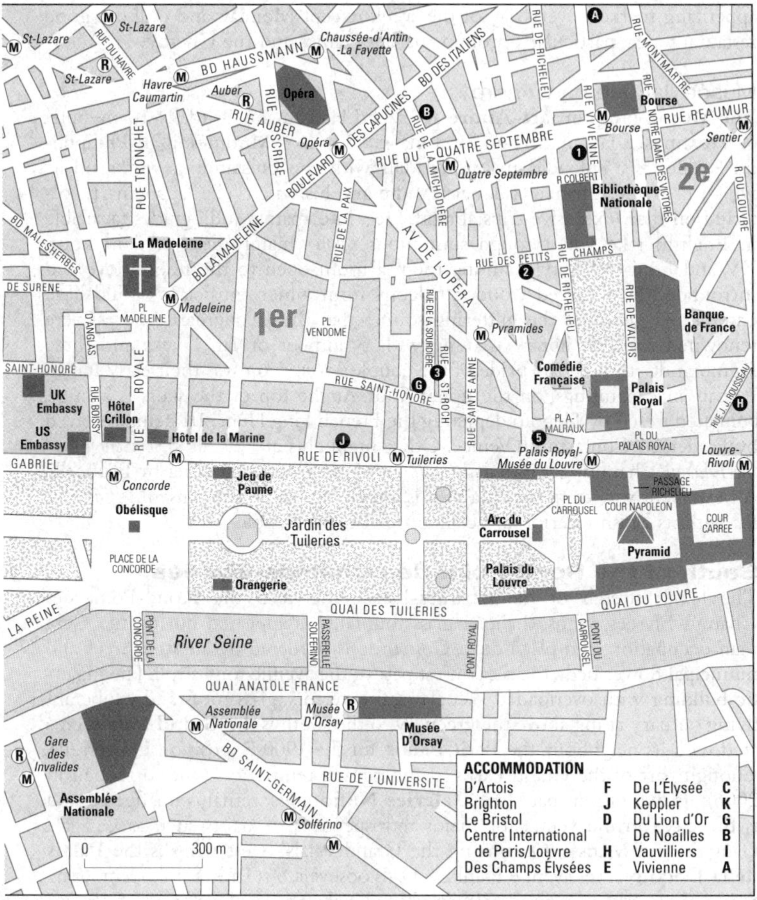

ACCOMMODATION

D'Artois	F	De L'Élysée	C
Brighton	J	Keppler	K
Le Bristol	D	Du Lion d'Or	G
Centre International de Paris/Louvre	H	De Noailles	B
		Vauvilliers	I
Des Champs Élysées	E	Vivienne	A

The Champs-Élysées is a popular rallying point at times of national crisis as well as celebration: crowds thronged here to greet Général de Gaulle as he walked down the avenue just after the Liberation in May 1944 and many turned out to support him again in 1968 in the wake of the student riots, while thousands congregated in 1998 to party all night after France won the World Cup. It's also the scene of annual processions on November 11 and Bastille Day, and the Tour de France ends here in July with a final flourish.

North of the Champs-Élysées

Just north of the Champs-Élysées are a number of *hôtels particuliers* housing select museums, the best of which is the **Musée Jacquemart-André** with its magnificent art collection. North of here is the small and formal **Parc Monceau**, surrounded by grand residences. **Rue de Lévis** (a few blocks up rue Berger from M° Monceau) has one of the city's most strident, colourful and appetizing markets every day of the week except Monday, and is also a good restaurant area, particularly around rue des Dames and rue Cheroy.

Musée Jacquemart-André

The **Musée Jacquemart-André** at 158 bd Haussmann, 8e (daily 10am–6pm; Ⓦwww.musee-jacquemart-andre.com; €8.50; M° Miromesnil/St-Philippe-du-Roule) is a splendid mansion laden with the outstanding works of art which its owners, banker Édouard André and his wife Nélie Jacquemart, collected on their extensive trips abroad. Free, informative audioguides (available in English) take you through sumptuous *salons*, mainly decorated in Louis XV and Louis XVI style, among them a room open to the floor above and surrounded by a carved wooden balcony from which musicians would have entertained guests at the glittering soirées that the Jacquemart-Andrés were renowned for. The library is hung with a number of Van Dycks and three Rembrandts, though the pride of the couple's collection was their early Italian Renaissance paintings, on the upper floor. At the top of the stairs is a huge, animated fresco by Tiepolo depicting the French king Henri III being received by Frederigo Contarini in Venice. Other highlights are Ucello's *St George and the Dragon*, a haunting *Virgin and Child* by Mantegna, and another by Botticelli. An excellent way to finish off a visit is a reviving halt at the museum's *salon de thé* with its lavish interior and ceiling frescoes by Tiepolo.

South of the Rond-Point des Champs-Élysées

The lower stretch of the Champs-Élysées between the Rond-Point des Champs-Élysées, whose Lalique glass fountains disappeared during the German occupation, and place de la Concorde is bordered by chestnut trees and municipal flower beds, the pleasantest part of the avenue for a stroll. The gigantic building with overloaded Neoclassical exteriors, glass roofs and exuberant flying statuary rising above the greenery to the south is the **Grand Palais**, created with its neighbour, the **Petit Palais**, for the 1900 Exposition Universelle. Though part of the Grand Palais is undergoing renovation (due to reopen in 2006), its exhibition space, the **Galeries Nationales**, remains unaffected and is the city's prime venue for major retrospectives of artists such as Chagall, Gauguin and Matisse. Occupying the Grand Palais's west wing is the **Palais de la Découverte**, avenue Franklin-D.-Roosevelt, 8e (Tues–Sat 9.30am–6pm, Sun & hols 10am–7pm; €6.50, combined ticket with planetarium €10; M° Champs-Élysées-Clemenceau/Franklin-D.-Roosevelt), a science museum with plenty of interactive exhibits, some very good temporary exhibitions and an excellent planetarium.

The Petit Palais houses the **Musée des Beaux-Arts** (currently closed for renovation; due to reopen in autumn 2005), which offers the odd Impressionist gem, among them Monet's *Sunset at Lavacourt*; lots of Art Nouveau furniture and jewellery; and vast canvases recording Paris street battles during the 1830 and 1848 revolutions. On the other side of the avenue, to the north of place Clemenceau, combat police guard the high walls round the presidential **Palais de l'Élysée** and the line of ministries and embassies ending with the US in prime position on the corner of place de la Concorde. On Thursdays and at weekends you can see a different manifestation of the self-images of states in the **postage-stamp market** at the corner of avenues Gabriel and Marigny.

Place de la Concorde and the Tuileries

At the lower end of the Champs is the vast **place de la Concorde** where crazed traffic makes crossing over to the middle a death-defying task. As it happens, some 1300 people did die here between 1793 and 1795, beneath the Revolutionary guillotine – Louis XVI, Marie-Antoinette, Danton and Robespierre among them. The centrepiece of the square is a stunning gold-tipped **obelisk** from the temple of Luxor, offered as a favour-currying gesture by the viceroy of Egypt in 1829. From here there are sweeping vistas in all directions – the Champs-Élysées looks particularly impressive and you can admire the alignment of the Assemblée Nationale, in the south, with the church of the Madeleine – sporting an identical Neoclassical facade – to the north (see p.137).

The symmetry continues beyond place de la Concorde in the formal layout of the **Tuileries gardens**, the formal French garden *par excellence*. It dates back to the 1570s, when Catherine de Médicis had the site cleared of the medieval warren of tilemakers (*tuileries*) to make way for a palace and grounds. One hundred years later, Louis XIV commissioned Le Nôtre to redesign them and the results are largely what you see today: straight avenues, formal flowerbeds and splendid vistas.

Shady tree-lined paths flank the grand central alley, and ornamental ponds frame both ends. The much-sought-after chairs strewn around the ponds are a good spot from which to admire the landscaped surroundings and contemplate the superb statues executed by the likes of Coustou and Coysevox, many of them now replaced by copies, the originals transferred to the Louvre.

The two buildings flanking the garden at the Concorde end are the Orangerie, by the river, and the **Jeu de Paume**, by rue de Rivoli (M° Concorde), an ex-royal tennis court and the place where French Impressionist paintings were displayed before being transferred to the Musée d'Orsay. In a subsequent renovation, huge windows were cut into its classical temple walls, allowing light to flood in. At the time of writing, it was due to be turned into a major exhibition space for photography, video and film, kicking off with a homage to fashion photographer Guy Bourdin.

Opposite the Jeu de Paume, the **Orangerie**, a private art collection including eight of Monet's giant waterlily paintings and works by Renoir, Matisse, Cézanne, Utrillo and Modigliani, is currently closed for renovation. The aim of the project is to convert many of the existing exterior walls to glass, in line with Monet's request that as much natural light as possible reach his masterpieces. However, an unexpected glitch has delayed completion till 2005 at least. Architects are having to decide what to do about a stretch of sixteenth-century wall stumbled upon by the workmen as they dug an underground extension; embarrassingly, the French culture ministry overseeing the project hadn't realized it was there, despite its presence being amply documented.

The Louvre

The palace of the **Louvre** cuts a grand Classical swathe right through the centre of the city, its stately ranks of carved pilasters, arches and pediments stretching west along the right bank of the Seine from the Île de la Cité towards the Voie Triomphale. Inside, the giant collection of the Louvre museum acts as nothing less than the gold standard of France's artistic tradition.

Before becoming a museum during the French Revolution, the Louvre was for centuries the home of the French court, and almost every French ruler with a taste for grandeur built on the site, right down to President Mitterand. The original fortress was begun by Philippe-Auguste in 1200 to store his scrolls, jewels and swords, while he himself lived on the Île de la Cité. Charles V was the first French king to make the castle his residence, but not until

François I in the mid-sixteenth century were the beginnings of the palace laid and the fortress demolished. François' daughter-in-law, Catherine de Médicis, added the **Palais des Tuileries** some 500m to the west, and fifty years later Henri IV joined the two together with a long extension along the bank of the Seine. Louis XIV completed the square plan of the Cour Carré, but it wasn't until Napoléon III completed the Richelieu wing and remodelled all the facades of the Cour Napoléon in the 1860s that the Louvre and Tuileries palaces were finally united. It didn't last long – the Tuileries was razed during the Paris Commune of 1871 and the Louvre now opens out onto the lovely gardens (see p.131) that bear its name.

For all its many transformations, the palace remained a surprisingly harmonious building, with a grandeur, symmetry, and Frenchness entirely suited to this most historic of Parisian edifices. Then came the controversial **Pyramide**, designed by I.M. Pei and opened in 1989, which erupted from the centre of the Cour Napoléon like a visitor from another architectural planet. As part of the same late 1980s makeover, Mitterrand also managed to persuade the Finance Ministry to move out of the northern Richelieu wing, which then had its two main courtyards dramatically roofed over in glass. A public passageway, the **passage Richelieu**, linking the Cour Napoléon with rue de Rivoli, offers a better view of the sculptures in these courtyards than you get from inside the museum.

Napoléon's pink marble **Arc du Carrousel**, just east of place du Carrousel, which originally formed a gateway for the former Tuileries Palace, has always looked a bit out of place (though it sits precisely on the Voie Triomphale axis); now it's definitively and forlornly upstaged by the Pyramide.

Quite separate from the Louvre proper, but still within the palace, are three museums under the aegis of the **Union Centrale des Arts Décoratifs**, dedicated to fashion and textiles, decorative arts and advertising. The entrance to the **Musée de la Mode et du Textile**, the **Musée des Arts Décoratifs** and the **Musée de la Publicité** can be found at 107 rue de Rivoli.

The Musée du Louvre

It's easy to be put off by tales of long queues outside the Pyramide, miles of foot-wearying corridors or paparazzi-style jostles in front of the *Mona Lisa*, but there are ways around such hassles – you can use a back entrance, stop at one of the cafés or make for a less well-known section – and ultimately, the draw of the mighty collections of the **Musée du Louvre** is irresistible.

Access and opening hours

The Pyramide is the main **entrance** to the Musée du Louvre, although the often lengthy lines can be avoided by using one of the alternative entrances: at the Porte des Lions, just east of the Pont Royal; at the Arc du Carrousel; at 99 rue de Rivoli; or directly from the métro station Palais Royal-Musée du Louvre (line 1 platform). If you've already got a ticket or a museum pass (see p.109) you can also enter from the passage Richelieu.

The permanent collection is open every day except Tuesday. **Opening hours** are 9am to 6pm from Thursday to Sunday, and 9am to 9.45pm on Mondays and Wednesdays. Parts of the museum are closed one day a week on a rotating basis, so if you're interested in a particular section it's worth checking the schedule on the museum notice boards or online at ⓦwww.louvre.fr, though the most popular rooms are always open.

The usual **entry fee** is €8.50 but after 3pm and on Sunday this is reduced to €5. Under-18s get in free at all times, and on the first Sunday of each month admission is free for everyone else, unless it's a public holiday. For a small surcharge, tickets can be bought in advance through Ticketnet (Ⓣ01.46.91.57.57, Ⓦwww.ticketnet.fr) or from FNAC (Ⓣ01.41.57.32.28, Ⓦlouvre.francebillet .com; see p.212 for branches). Your ticket allows you to leave and re-enter as many times as you like throughout the day, handy if the crowds get too much or you just need to get some fresh air.

Orientation

The museum is divided into **three main wings**, Denon (south), Richelieu (north) and Sully (east, around the giant quadrangle of the Cour Carré). These wings are further subdivided into seven sections: **Antiquities** (Oriental, Egyptian and Classical); **Sculpture**; **Painting**; the **Medieval Louvre**; and **Objets d'art**. Some sections spread across two wings, or two floors of the same wing.

From the Hall Napoléon, under the Pyramide, stairs lead south into the **Denon wing**, which is by far the most popular area of the museum, with the must-see Italian masterpieces of the Grande Galerie, the famous nineteenth-century French large-scale paintings and the *Mona Lisa*, all on the first floor. Denon also houses Classical and Italian sculpture on the two lower floors.

Serious lovers of French art will head north to the **Richelieu wing**, for the French sculpture collection in the glazed-over courtyards; the grand chronology of French painting, which begins on the second floor; and the superb *objets d'art* collection on the first floor, which includes everything French that's not painting or sculpture – furniture, tapestries, crystal, jewels. Richelieu also houses Middle-Eastern antiquities and Islamic art (ground and lower ground floors), and northern European painting (second floor).

Rather fewer visitors begin with the **Sully wing**, although it's here that the story begins, with the foundations of Philippe-Auguste's twelfth-century fortress on the lower ground floor. The floors above mostly continue chronologies begun on other wings, with antiquities from Greece and the Levant (ground floor), and the seventeenth- and eighteenth-century periods from the *objets d'art* (first floor) and French painting (second floor) sections. The complete Pharaonic Egypt collection is here too.

The **Pavillon des Sessions** (nearest entrance Porte des Lions) currently houses works of art from Africa, Asia, Oceania and the Americas, though the collection is due to move to the new museum at quai Branly (see p.163) in 2005.

With all that in mind, it's well worth picking up a **floor plan** from the information booth in the Hall Napoléon, or at one of the alternative entrances. This makes sense of it all by colour-coding the museum's seven main sections. A few of the best-known masterpieces are highlighted on the plan, and the whole system is surprisingly painless once you get to grips with it. The plan's only drawback is that it depicts the Louvre as a gallery rather than a palace, and doesn't spotlight the magnificently decorated suites and rooms that give such a strong identity to certain sections of the museum.

You can always step outside for a break, but three moderately expensive **cafés** are enticing and open all day: *Café Richelieu* (first floor, Richelieu) is elegant and relatively quiet; *Café Denon* (lower ground floor, Denon) is cosily romantic; and *Café Mollien* (first floor, Denon) has a summer terrace and some inexpensive snacks. The various cafés and restaurants under the Pyramide are mostly noisy and overpriced.

Antiquities

Oriental Antiquities covers the sculptures, stone-carved writings, pottery and other relics of the ancient Middle and Near East, including the Mesopotamian,

Sumerian, Babylonian, Assyrian and Phoenician civilizations, plus the art of ancient Persia. The highlight of this section is the boldly sculpted stonework, much of it in relief. Watch out for the statues and busts depicting the young Sumerian prince Gudea, and the black, two-metre-high Code of Hammurabi, which dates from around 1800 BC. Standing erect like a warning finger, a series of royal precepts (the "code") is crowned with a stern depiction of the king meeting the sun god Shamash, dispenser of justice. The Cour Khorsabad, adjacent, is dominated by two giant, Assyrian winged bulls that once acted as guardians to the palace of Sargon II, from which many treasures were brought to the Louvre by the French archeologist Paul-Emilie Botta, in the mid nineteenth century. The utterly refined **Arts of Islam** collection is next door. **Egyptian Antiquities** contains jewellery, domestic objects, sandals, sarcophagi and dozens of examples of the delicate naturalism of Egyptian decorative technique, such as the wall tiles depicting a piebald calf galloping through fields of papyrus, and a duck taking off from a marsh. Among the major exhibits are the Great Sphinx, carved from a single block of pink granite, the polychrome Seated Scribe statue, the striking, life-size, wooden statue of Chancellor Nakhti, a bust of Amenophis IV and a low-relief sculpture of Sethi I and the goddess Hathor.

The collection of **Greek and Roman Antiquities**, mostly statues, is one of the finest in the world. The biggest crowd-pullers in the museum, after the *Mona Lisa*, are here: the *Winged Victory of Samothrace*, at the top of Denon's great staircase, and the *Venus de Milo*. Venus is surrounded by hordes of antecedent Aphrodites, from the graceful marble head known as the "Kaufmann Head" and the delightful Venus of Arles – both early copies of the work of the great sculptor Praxiteles – to the strange *Dame d'Auxerre*. In the Roman section a sterner style takes over, but there are some very attractive mosaics from Asia Minor and luminous frescoes from Pompeii and Herculaneum.

Sculpture

The **French Sculpture** section is arranged on the lowest two levels of the Richelieu wing, with the more monumental pieces housed in two grand, glass-roofed courtyards: the four triumphal *Marly Horses* grace the Cour Marly, while Cour Puget has Puget's dynamic *Milon de Crotone* as its centrepiece. The surrounding rooms trace the development of sculpture in France from painful Romanesque Crucifixions through to the lofty public works of David d'Angers. The startlingly realistic Gothic pieces – notably the Burgundian *Tomb of Philippe Pot*, complete with hooded mourners – and the experimental Mannerist works are particularly rewarding, but towards the end of the course you may find yourself crying out for an end to all those gracefully perfect nudes and grandiose busts of noblemen. You'll have to leave the Louvre for Rodin, but an alternative antidote lies in the smaller, more intense **Italian and northern European** sections, on the lower two floors of Denon, where you'll find such bold masterpieces as two of Michelangelo's writhing *Slaves*, Duccio's virtuoso *Virgin and Child Surrounded by Angels*, and some severely Gothic Virgins from Flanders and Germany.

Objets d'Art

The vast **objets d'art** section presents the finest tapestries, ceramics, jewellery and furniture commissioned by France's most wealthy and influential patrons, beginning with an exquisite little equestrian sculpture of Charlemagne and continuing through eighty-one relentlessly superb rooms through to a salon decorated in the style of Louis-Philippe, the last king of France. Walking through the entire chronology is an enlightening experience, giving a powerful sense of the evolution of aesthetic taste at its most refined and opulent. The exception is the Middle Ages section, of a more pious nature, which includes carved ivories and Limoges enamels. Towards the end, the circuit passes through the breathtaking apartments of Napoléon III's Minister of State, full of plush upholstery, immense chandeliers, gilded putti and caryatids, and dramatic ceiling frescoes in true Second Empire style.

Painting

The largest section by far is **Painting**. The main **French collection** begins on the second floor of the Richelieu wing, and continues right round the Cour Carré, which comprises the Sully wing. It traces the development of French painting from its beginnings as far as Corot, whose airy landscapes anticipate the Impressionists. Surprisingly few works predate the Renaissance, and the preliminary Richelieu section is chiefly of interest for the portraits of French kings, from the Sienese-style *Portrait of John the Good* to Jean Clouet's *François I*. As you turn the corner into Sully, look out for the strange Mannerist atmosphere of the two Schools of Fontainebleau, and the luminous, Caravaggiesque paintings of Georges de la Tour and the Le Nain brothers. It's not until Poussin breaks onto the scene that an obviously French style emerges, and you'll need a healthy appetite for Classical grandeur in the next suite of rooms, with large-scale works by the likes of Lorrain, Le Brun and Rigaud. The more intimate paintings of Watteau come as a relief, followed by Chardin's intense still lifes and the inspired Rococo sketches by Fragonard known as the *Figures of Fantasy*. From the southern wing of Sully to the end of this section, the chilly wind of Neoclassicism blows through the paintings of Gros, Gérard, Prud'hon, David and Ingres, contrasting with the more sentimental style that begins with Greuze and continues into the Romanticism of Géricault and Delacroix. The final set of rooms takes in Milet, Corot and the Barbizon school of painting.

The nineteenth century is most dramatically represented in the second area of the Louvre devoted to painting, on the first floor of the Denon wing. A pair of giant rooms is dedicated to Nationalism and Romanticism respectively, featuring some of France's best-known works including such gigantic, epic canvases as David's *Coronation of Napoleon in Notre Dame*, Géricault's *The Raft of the Medusa*, and Delacroix's *Liberty Leading the People*, the icon of nineteenth-century revolution.

Denon also houses the frankly staggering **Italian collection**. The high-ceilinged Salon Carré – which has been used to exhibit paintings since the first "salon" of the Royal Academy in 1725 – displays the so-called Primitives, with works by Giotto, Cimabue and Fra Angelico, as well as one of Uccello's bizarrely theoretical panels of the *Battle of San Romano*. To the west of the Salon, the famous Grande Galerie stretches into the distance, parading all the great names of the Italian Renaissance – Mantegna, Filippo Lippi, da Vinci, Raphael, Coreggio, Titian. The playfully troubled Mannerists kick in about halfway along, but the second half of the Galerie dwindles in quality and representativeness as it moves towards the eighteenth century. At the time of writing, Da Vinci's *Mona Lisa* was hung in the room beyond the gallery's westernmost end, though it's expected to move to the Salle des États at some point in 2005. If you want to catch *La Jioconde* – as she's known to the French – without a swarm of snap-happy admirers for company, go first or last thing in the day. At the far end of Denon, the relatively small but worthwhile **Spanish** collection has some notable Goya portraits. For the time being, Paolo Veronese's huge *Marriage at Cana* stands just beyond the Salle des États, on the courtyard side of the Denon wing, between the two nineteenth-century French rooms.

The western end of Richelieu's second floor is given over to a more selective collection of **German**, **Flemish** and **Dutch** paintings, with a brilliant set of works by Rubens, and twelve Rembrandts, including some powerful self-portraits. Interspersed throughout the painting section are rooms dedicated to the Louvre's impressive collection of **Prints and Drawings**, including prized sketches and preliminary drawings by Ingres and Rubens and some attributed to Leonardo. Because of their susceptibility to the light, however, they are exhibited in rotation.

Union Centrale des Arts Décoratifs

The other museums housed in the Louvre palace, under an umbrella organization with the snappy title of **Union Centrale des Arts Décoratifs** (entrance at 107 rue de Rivoli; Ⓦwww.ucad.fr) are often unjustly overlooked, yet their exhibitions can be among the city's most innovative.

The **Musée de la Mode et du Textile** (Tues–Fri 11am–6pm, Sat & Sun 10am–6pm; €6 combined ticket with the Musée des Arts Décoratifs and the Musée de la Publicité) holds high-quality temporary exhibitions – they rotate items from the large permanent collection – aimed at demonstrating the most brilliant and cutting-edge of Paris fashions from all eras. Recent exhibitions have included Jackie Kennedy's famous 1960s dresses, displayed alongside photos of the First Lady wearing them, and a look at the work of the couturier.

On the top floor, the **Musée de la Publicité** (same hours and ticket) shows off its collection of advertising posters through cleverly themed, temporary exhibitions. The space is appropriately trendy – half exposed brickwork and steel panelling, and half crumbling Louvre finery – and there's a bar as well as a dozen computers at which you can freely access the archive.

Until the modern collections reopen, which is expected to be in early 2006, the restrained, traditional **Musée des Arts Décoratifs** (same hours and ticket), seems something of the odd man out, though its eclectic collection of art and superbly crafted furnishing fits the Union Centrale's "design" theme. The work may seem humble in comparison with the Louvre's airy *objets d'art* section next door, but most were made to be lived with or actually used, and the museum is a less daunting prospect as a result. At the time of writing, only the medieval and Renaissance rooms were open, showing off curiously shaped and beautifully carved chairs, dressers and tables, religious paintings, Venetian glass, some wonderful tapestries and a room entirely decorated and furnished as a late-medieval bedroom. The contemporary collections will display works by French, Italian and Japanese designers, including some great examples of the work of Philippe Starck.

The Opéra district

In the narrow streets of the 1er and 2e arrondissements, between the Louvre and **boulevards Haussmann**, **Montmartre**, **Poissonnière** and **Bonne-Nouvelle**, the grandiose financial, cultural and political institutions are surrounded by well-established **commerce** – the rag trade, media, sex and well-heeled shopping. In contrast to the hulks of the Bourse, Banque de France and the Bibliothèque Nationale, and the monumental style of the **Madeleine**, **Opéra** and the **Palais Royal**, are the secretive **passages** – glass-roofed shopping arcades built in the mid-nineteenth century. After years of decay, many have now been renovated and are beginning to regain something of their original splendour, gradually attracting new shops and custom.

The passages

Among the most attractive of the *passages* is the **Galerie Vivienne**, between rue Vivienne and rue des Petits-Champs, with its flamboyant decor of Grecian and marine motifs providing an elegant backdrop for smart shops including a secondhand bookshop complete with its original fittings. But the best stylistically are the three-storey **passage du Grand-Cerf**, between rue St-Denis and rue Dussoubs, and **Galerie Véro-Dodat**, between rue Croix-des-Petits-Champs and rue Jean-Jacques Rousseau, named after the two pork butchers who set it up in 1824. This last is the most homogeneous and aristocratic *passage*, with painted ceilings and faux marble columns. There are some lovely old shops here such as Monsieur Capia at no. 26, full of antique dolls and miscellaneous curios. North of rue St-Marc, the several arcades making up the **passage des Panoramas** are somewhat tatty, though retain much character: there's an old brasserie with carved wood panelling, a printshop with its original 1867 fittings, as well as bric-a-brac shops, and stamp and secondhand postcard dealers. In **passage Jouffroy**, across boulevard Montmartre, a Monsieur Segas sells unusual walking canes and theatrical antiques opposite a shop with exquisite dolls' house furniture, while Paul Vulin spreads his secondhand books further down along the passageway, and Ciné-Doc appeals to cinephiles with its collection of old film posters.

The Madeleine and the Opéra-Garnier

Set back from the boulevard des Capucines and crowning the avenue de l'Opéra is the dazzling **Opéra-Garnier**, which was constructed from 1860 to 1875 in the scheme of Napoléon III's new vision of Paris. The building's architect, Charles Garnier, whose golden bust by Carpeaux can be seen on the rue Auber side of his edifice, pulled out all the stops to provide a suitably grand space in which Second-Empire high society could parade and be seen. The facade is a fabulous extravaganza of white, pink and green marble, colonnades, rearing horses, winged angels and niches holding gleaming gold busts of composers. You can see round the equally sumptuous **interior** (daily 10am–5pm; €6), including the plush auditorium – rehearsals permitting – the colourful ceiling of which is the work of Chagall, depicting scenes from well-known operas and ballets. The visit includes the **Bibliothèque-Musée de l'Opéra**, dedicated to the artists connected with the Opéra throughout its history, and containing model sets, dreadful nineteenth-century paintings and rather better temporary exhibitions on operatic themes.

West of the Opéra, occupying nearly the whole of the place de la Madeleine, the imperious-looking **église de la Madeleine** is the parish church of the cream of Parisian high society. Modelled on a Greek classical temple, it's surrounded by 52 Corinthian columns and fronted by a huge pediment depicting the *Last Judgement*. Originally intended as a monument to Napoleon's army, it narrowly escaped being turned into a railway station before finally being consecrated to Mary Magdalene in 1845. Inside, Charles Marochetti's wonderfully theatrical sculpture *Mary Magdalene Ascending to Heaven* draws your eye to the high altar. In the half-dome above, Ziegler's fresco *The History of Christianity* commemorates the concordat signed between the church and the state after the Revolution and depicts all the major figures in Christendom, with Napoleon centre-stage, naturally.

If the Madeleine caters to spiritual needs, the rest of the square is given over to nourishment of quite a different kind, for this is where Paris's top gourmet food stores Fauchon and Hédiard are located. Their remarkable displays are a feast for the eyes, and both have *salons de thé* where you can sample some of their epicurean treats. On the east side of the Madeleine church is one of the city's oldest **flower markets** dating back to 1832, open every day except

Monday, while nearby, some rather fine Art Nouveau public toilets are definitely worth inspecting.

Place Vendôme

A short walk east of the Madeleine along ancient rue St-Honoré, a preserve of top fashion designers and art galleries, lies **place Vendôme**, one of the city's most impressive set pieces. Built by Versailles architect Hardouin-Mansart, it's a pleasingly symmetrical, eight-sided *place*, enclosed by a harmonious ensemble of elegant mansions, graced with Corinthian pilasters, mascarons and steeply pitched roofs. Once the grand residences of tax collectors and financiers, they now house such luxury establishments as the *Ritz* hotel, Cartier, Bulgari and other top-flight jewellers, lending the square a decidedly exclusive air. No. 12, now occupied by Chaumet jewellers, is where Chopin died in 1849.

Somewhat out of proportion with the rest of the square, the centrepiece is a towering triumphal **column**, surmounted by a statue of Napoleon dressed as Caesar, raised in 1806 to celebrate the Battle of Austerlitz – bronze reliefs of scenes of the battle, cast from 1200 recycled Austro-Russian cannons, spiral their way up the column.

Palais Royal

At the eastern end of rue St-Honoré stands the **Palais Royal**, built for Cardinal Richelieu in 1624, though little now remains of the original. The current building houses various governmental bodies and the **Comédie Française**, longstanding venue for the classics of French theatre. Hidden away behind lie sedate gardens lined with stately three-storey houses built over arcades housing mainly upmarket antique and designer shops. Past residents included Cocteau and Colette. It's an attractive and peaceful oasis, with avenues of limes, fountains and flowerbeds, popular on weekends with newlyweds who come here to be photographed, though surprisingly unfrequented at other times. You'd hardly guess that for a time this was a site of gambling dens, brothels and funfair attractions until the Grands Boulevards took up the baton in the 1830s. Folly, some might say, has returned in the form of Daniel Buren's black-and-white striped pillars, rather like sticks of Brighton rock, all of varying heights, dotted about the main courtyard in front of the palace. Installed in 1986 after the space was cleared of cars, they're a rather disconcerting sight, but are certainly popular with children and rollerbladers who treat them as an adventure playground and obstacle course respectively. The gardens are a handy shortcut from the rue de Rivoli to the **Bibliothèque National** (Tues–Sat 10am–7pm, Sun noon–7pm) on the north side; you can enter free of charge and peer into the atmospheric reading rooms or pay to see the various temporary exhibitions.

Les Halles to Beaubourg

Les Halles was the city's main food market for over eight hundred years until it was moved out to the suburbs in 1969, despite widespread opposition, and replaced by a large underground shopping and leisure complex, known as the Forum des Halles, and an RER/metro interchange. Unsightly, rundown, even unsavoury in parts, the complex has never endeared itself to the city inhabitants. Paris's mayor, Bertrand Delanoë, however, is hoping to reverse the mistakes of his predecessors and has recently announced an exciting new project to revamp the site by 2012, when Paris hopes to host the Olympic

Games. Four plans are currently being considered, the most inspiring of which is Jean Nouvel's proposal to create a hanging garden 27 metres high, affording wonderful views over the city. The final project will be settled on by the end of 2004 and work is due to start in 2007.

The Forum des Halles

The **Forum des Halles** centre stretches underground from the Bourse du Commerce rotunda to rue Pierre-Lescot and is spread over four levels. The overground section comprises aquarium-like arcades of shops, arranged around a sunken patio, and landscaped gardens. The shops are mostly devoted to high-street fashion and there's also a large FNAC bookshop and the Forum des Créateurs, an outlet for young fashion designers. It's not all commerce, however: there's scope for various diversions including swimming, billiards and movie-going.

After the air conditioning and artificial light, you can seek relief outside in the water cascading down the perfect Renaissance proportions of the **Fontaine des Innocents**, or in the high Gothic and Renaissance church of **St-Eustache**, where a woman preached the abolition of marriage from the pulpit during the Commune.

There are always hundreds of people around the Forum filling in time, hustling or just loafing about. Pickpocketing is pretty routine; the law plus canine arm is often in evidence, and at night the atmosphere can be quite tense, although the labyrinth of tiny streets southeastwards to **place du Châtelet** teems with jazz bars, nightclubs and restaurants, and is far more crowded at 2am than 2pm.

To the north something of the old Les Halles market atmosphere lingers on in pedestrianized **rue Montorgueil** and its extension rue des Petits Carreaux. This is a bustling thoroughfare, where grocery stalls, butchers and patisseries of longstanding (one, Stohrer's, has been here since 1730) ply their trade alongside newer arrivals. A number of hip fashion boutiques have also moved into the area, especially on rues Tiquetonne and Étienne Marcel. On the riverfront due south, the **Samaritaine department store** (Mon–Sat 9.30am–7pm, Thurs till 9pm) recalls the days when art rather than marketing psychology determined the decoration of a store. Built in 1903 in the Art Nouveau style, its gold, green and glass exteriors, interior ceramic tiles and wrought-iron staircases and balconies have all been restored, though best of all are the excellent views of the Seine and Paris skyline from the restaurant and top-floor café.

Centre Georges Pompidou

The **Centre Georges Pompidou** (aka Beaubourg; Ⓦwww.centrepompidou.fr; M° Rambuteau/Hôtel-de-Ville), housing the Musée Nationale d'Art Moderne, is one of the twentieth century's most radical buildings and its opening in 1977 gave rise to some violent reactions. Since then, however, it has won over critics and public alike, and has become one of the city's most recognizable landmarks. Architects Renzo Piano and Richard Rogers freed up maximum gallery space inside by placing all infrastructure outside: utility pipes and escalator tubes, all brightly colour-coded according to their function, climb around the exterior in crazy snakes-and-ladder fashion. The transparent escalator on the front of the building, giving access to the modern art museum, affords superb views over the city. Aside from the museum there are two cinemas, performance spaces and the BPI or **Bibliothèque Publique d'Information** (Mon–Fri noon–10pm, Sat & Sun 11am–10pm; free), which has an impressive collection of 2500 periodicals including international press, 10,000 CDs and 2200 documentary films.

On the northern edge of the centre, down some steps off the sloping piazza, in a small separate one-level building, is the **Atelier Brancusi** (daily except Tues 2–6pm; combined ticket with the Musée National d'Art Moderne). When he died in 1956, the sculptor Constantin Brancusi bequeathed the contents of his 15ᵉ arrondissement studio to the state: the condition was that it had to be reconstructed exactly as it was found. The artist had become obsessed with the spatial relationship of the sculptures in his studio, going so far as to supplant a sold work with a plaster copy, and the four interlinked rooms of the studio faithfully adhere to his arrangements. Studios one and two are crowded with fluid sculptures of highly polished brass and marble, his trademark abstract bird and column shapes, stylized busts and poised objects that look as though they want to take off into space. Unfortunately the rooms are behind glass, creating a feeling of sterility and distance. Perhaps the most satisfying rooms are studios three and four, his private quarters, where you really get an idea of how the artist lived and worked.

Musée National d'Art Moderne

The superb **Musée National d'Art Moderne** (daily except Tues 11am–9pm; €7) presides over the fourth and fifth floors of the Centre Pompidou, with the fifth floor covering 1905 to 1960, and the fourth 1960 to the present day. Thanks to an astute acquisitions policy and some generous gifts, the collection is a near-complete visual essay on the history of twentieth-century art and is so large that only a fraction of the 50,000 works are on display at any one time (they're frequently rotated). The collection on floor five kicks off in a blaze of colour with the Fauvists – Braque, Derain, Vlaminck and Matisse, among others. A fine example of the movement's desire to create form rather than imitate nature is Braque's L'Estaque (1906; room 2), in which colour becomes a way of composing and structuring a picture, with trees and sky broken down into blocks of vibrant reds and greens.

Room 3 is devoted to the early Cubist experiments of Picasso and Braque. One of the highlights here is Picasso's portrait of his lover Fernande (*Femme assise dans un fauteuil*; 1910), in which different angles of the figure are shown all at once, giving rise to complex patterns and creating the effect of movement.

Room 7 is devoted to the nihilistic Dada movement; art students cluster round leading Dadaist Marcel Duchamp's notorious *Fontaine* (1917), a urinal elevated to the rank of "art" simply by being taken out of its ordinary context and put on display.

Room 10 contains a particularly rich collection of Kandinskys. You can follow the artist's experiments with abstract art through his series Impressions, Improvisations and Compositions. Fellow abstract-art pioneers Robert and Sonia Delaunay are represented in room 12 by a number of their characteristically colourful paintings.

Surrealism dominates in later rooms, with works by Magritte, Dalí and Ernst. Typical of the movement's exploration of the darker recesses of the mind is Ernst's disturbing *Ubu Imperator* (1923; room 20), depicting a figure that is part man, part Tower of Pisa and part spinning top, apparently symbolizing the perversion of male authority.

Shying away from the figurative, American abstract expressionists Jackson Pollock and Mark Rothko make an appearance in room 34. In Pollock's splattery *No 26A, Black and white* (1948), the two colours seem to struggle for domination; the dark bands of colour in Rothko's large canvas No. 14 (*Browns over Dark*), in contrast, draw the viewer in.

Matisse's later experiments with form and colour are on show in room 41.

His cut-out gouache technique is perfected in his masterpiece *La Tristesse du Roi* (1952), a meditation on old age and memory.

The collection continues on the fourth floor with Pop Art. Easily recognizable is Andy Warhol's piece *Ten Lizes* (1963), which features the actress Elizabeth Taylor sporting a Mona Lisa-like smile. In room 3 Yves Klein prefigures performance art with his Grande anthropophagie bleue; *Hommage a Tennessee Williams* (1960), one in a series of "body prints" in which the artist turned female models into human paintbrushes, covering them in paint to create his artworks. Displays of more recent works are subject to change, but established artists you're likely to come across include Claes Oldenburg, Christian Boltanski and Daniel Buren. Christian Boltanski is known for his large mise-en-scène installations, often containing veiled allusions to the Holocaust. Daniel Buren's works are easy to spot: they all bear his trademark stripes, exactly 8.7cm in width. Up-and-coming names you might come across are Pierre Huyghe, who uses video to explore the relationships between reality and fiction, history and memory, often taking film clips as his source material; and Annette Messager, whose large-scale installations use everyday objects to create unsettling works, often challenging perceptions of women.

Quartier Beaubourg and the Hôtel de Ville

The *quartier* around the Centre Pompidou, known as **Beaubourg**, is home to more contemporary art. Jean Tinguely and Niki de St-Phalle created the colourful moving sculptures and fountains in the pool in front of Église St-Merry on **place Igor Stravinsky**. This squirting waterworks pays homage to Stravinsky – each fountain corresponds to one of his compositions (*The Firebird*, *The Rite of Spring*, etc) – and shows scant respect for passers-by. On the west side of the square is the entrance to **IRCAM**, a research centre for contemporary music founded by the composer Pierre Boulez and an occasional venue for concerts; much of it is underground, with an overground extension by Renzo Piano. To the north are numerous commercial art galleries, occupying the attractive old *hôtels particuliers* on pedestrianized rue Quincampoix – make sure you take a detour down the delightful *passage* Molière about halfway down the street on the right.

Heading back towards the river along rue Renard will bring you to the **Hôtel de Ville**, the seat of the city's government. It's a mansion of gargantuan proportions in florid neo-Renaissance style, modelled pretty much on the previous building burned down in the Commune. Those opposed to the establishments of kings and emperors created their alternative municipal governments on this spot in 1789, 1848 and 1870. But with the defeat of the Commune in 1871, the conservatives concluded that the Parisian municipal authority had to go if order was to be maintained and the working class kept in their place. Thereafter Paris was ruled directly by the ministry of the interior until eventually in 1977 the city was allowed to run its own affairs again and Jacques Chirac was elected mayor. In front of the Hotel de Ville, the huge square – a notorious guillotine site in the French Revolution – becomes the location of a popular ice-skating rink from December to February; it's free and is particularly magical at night – it's open till midnight at weekends. You can hire skates for around €5.

The Marais, the Île St-Louis and the Bastille

Jack Kerouac translated **rue des Francs-Bourgeois**, the Marais' main east–west axis along with rue Rivoli/rue St-Antoine, as "street of the outspoken middle classes", though the original owners of the mansions lining its length

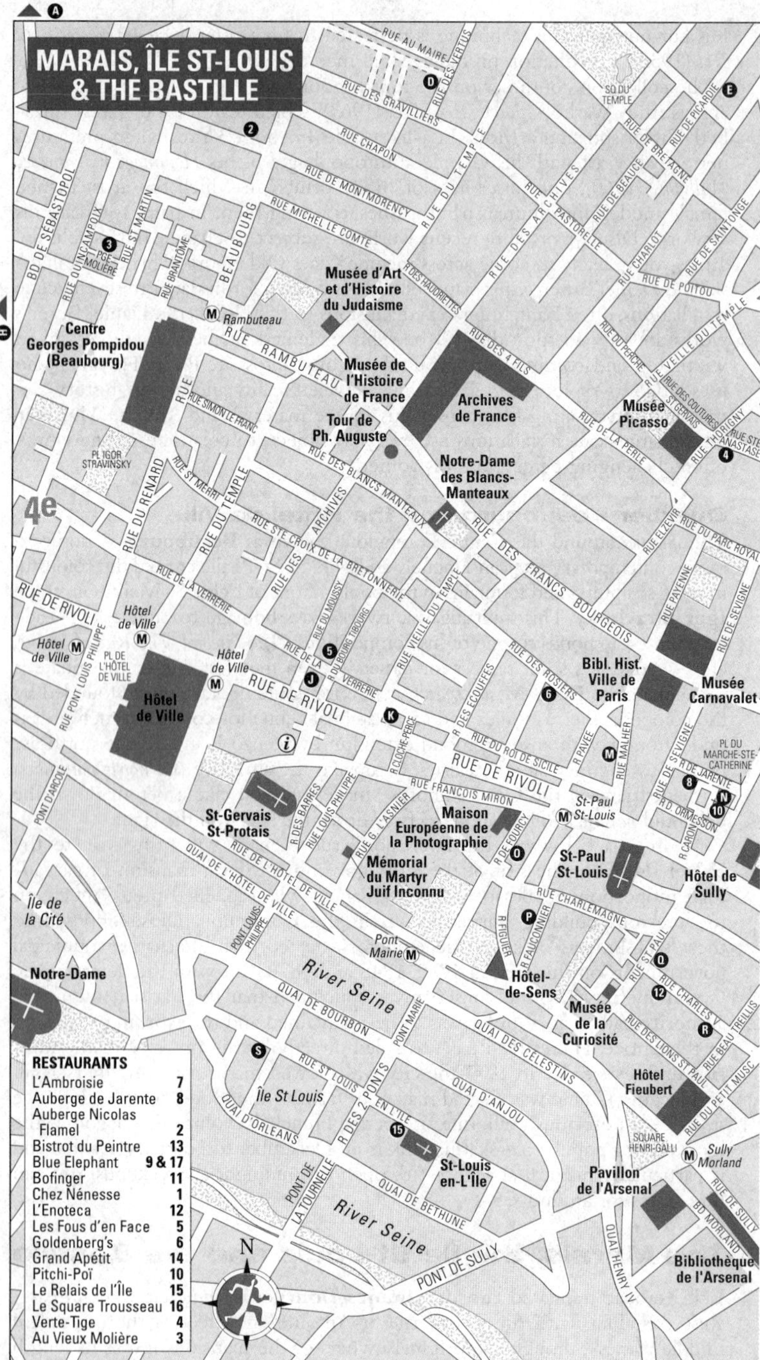
MARAIS, ÎLE ST-LOUIS
& THE BASTILLE
A
H
RESTAURANTS
L'Ambroisie 7
Auberge de Jarente 8
Auberge Nicolas Flamel 2
Bistrot du Peintre 13
Blue Elephant 9 & 17
Bofinger 11
Chez Nénesse 1
L'Enoteca 12
Les Fous d'en Face 5
Goldenberg's 6
Grand Apétit 14
Pitchi-Poï 10
Le Relais de l'Île 15
Le Square Trousseau 16
Verte-Tige 4
Au Vieux Molière 3
Centre Georges Pompidou (Beaubourg)
Rambuteau
Musée d'Art et d'Histoire du Judaisme
Musée de l'Histoire de France
Archives de France
Tour de Ph. Auguste
Notre-Dame des Blancs-Manteaux
Musée Picasso
PL IGOR STRAVINSKY
4e
Hôtel de Ville
PL DE L'HÔTEL DE VILLE
Bibl. Hist. Ville de Paris
Musée Carnavalet
PL DU MARCHE-STE-CATHERINE
St-Gervais St-Protais
Maison Européenne de la Photographie
Mémorial du Martyr Juif Inconnu
St-Paul St-Louis
Hôtel de Sully
Île de la Cité
Notre-Dame
Pont Marie
River Seine
Hôtel-de-Sens
Musée de la Curiosité
Île St Louis
St-Louis en-L'Île
Hôtel Fieubert
SQUARE HENRI-GALLI
Sully Morland
Pavillon de l'Arsenal
Bibliothèque de l'Arsenal
SQ DU TEMPLE
RUE AU MAIRE
RUE DES VERTUS
RUE DES GRAVILLIERS
RUE CHAPON
RUE DE MONTMORENCY
RUE MICHEL LE COMTE
RUE DU TEMPLE
RUE DES ARCHIVES
RUE PASTORELLE
RUE DE BRETAGNE
RUE DE PICARDIE
RUE DE BEAUCE
RUE CHARLOT
RUE DE SAINTONGE
RUE DE POITOU
BD DE SÉBASTOPOL
RUE QUINCAMPOIX
PGE MOLIÈRE
RUE ST MARTIN
RUE BRANTÔME
BEAUBOURG
RUE RAMBUTEAU
RUE DES HAUDRIETTES
RUE DES 4 FILS
RUE DU PERCHE
RUE VEILLE DU TEMPLE
RUE DES COUTURES ST GERVAIS
RUE THORIGNY
RUE STE ANASTASE
RUE DE LA PERLE
RUE SIMON LE FRANC
RUE ST MERRI
RUE DU RENARD
RUE DES BLANCS MANTEAUX
RUE STE CROIX DE LA BRETONNERIE
RUE DES FRANCS BOURGEOIS
RUE ELZEVIR
RUE DU PARC ROYAL
RUE PAYENNE
RUE DE SEVIGNE
RUE DE LA VERRERIE
RUE DE RIVOLI
RUE DU MOUSSY
RUE DU BOURG TIBOURG
RUE VIEILLE DU TEMPLE
RUE DES ROSIERS
R DES ECOUFFES
RUE PONT LOUIS PHILIPPE
R CLOCHE-PERCE
RUE DU ROI DE SICILE
R PAVEE
RUE MALHER
R DE JARENTE
R D. ORMESSON
R CARON
RUE FRANCOIS MIRON
St-Paul
St-Louis
PONT D'ARCOLE
R DES BARRES
RUE LOUIS PHILIPPE
RUE G. L'ASNIER
R DE FOURCY
QUAI DE L'HÔTEL DE VILLE
RUE DE L'HÔTEL DE VILLE
RUE CHARLEMAGNE
R FIGUIER
R FAUCONNIER
RUE ST PAUL
RUE CHARLES V
RUE DES LIONS ST PAUL
RUE BEAUTREILLIS
RUE DU PETIT MUSC
PONT LOUIS-PHILIPPE
QUAI DE BOURBON
PONT MARIE
QUAI DES CELESTINS
RUE ST LOUIS EN L'ÎLE
R DES 2 PONTS
QUAI D'ANJOU
QUAI D'ORLEANS
PONT DE LA TOURNELLE
QUAI DE BETHUNE
PONT DE SULLY
QUAI HENRY IV
BD MORLAND
RUE DE SULLY
N

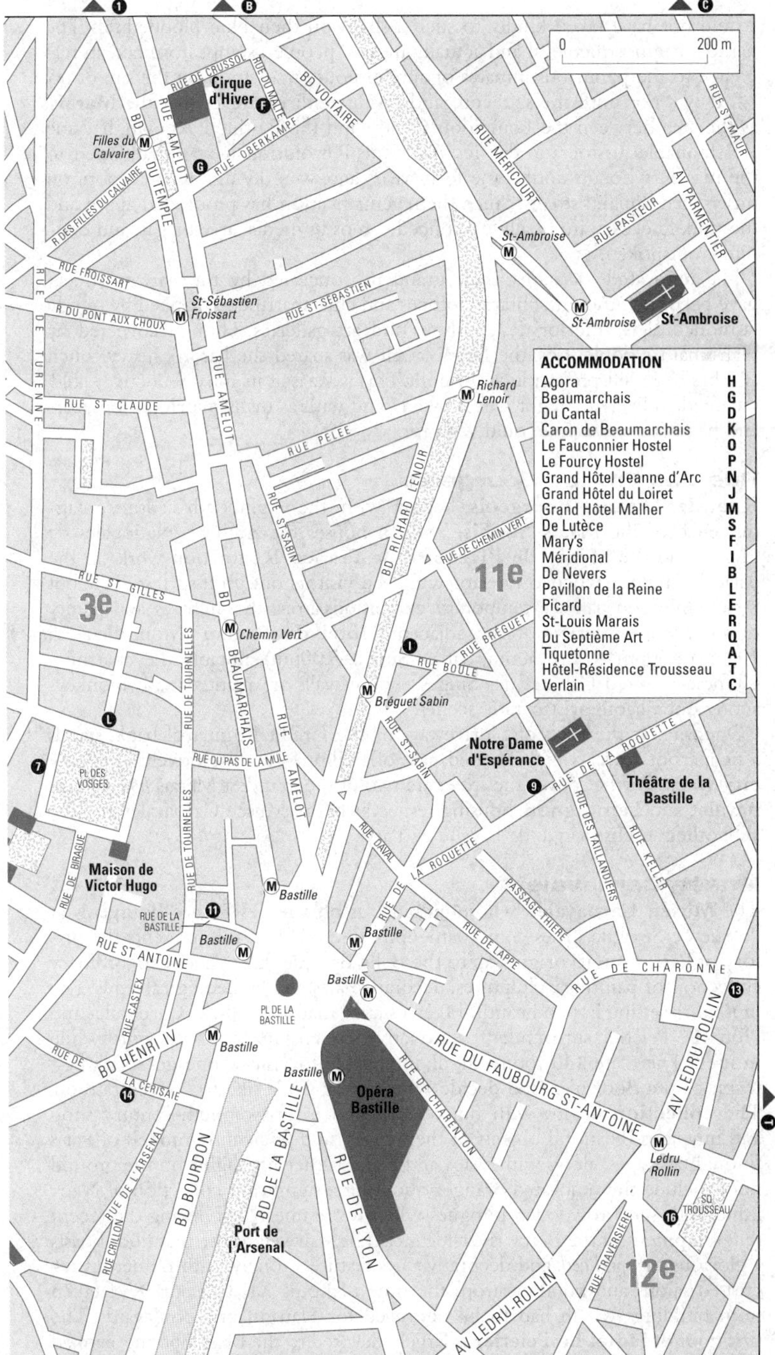

0 200 m
ACCOMMODATION
Agora H
Beaumarchais G
Du Cantal D
Caron de Beaumarchais K
Le Fauconnier Hostel O
Le Fourcy Hostel P
Grand Hôtel Jeanne d'Arc N
Grand Hôtel du Loiret J
Grand Hôtel Malher M
De Lutèce S
Mary's F
Méridional I
De Nevers B
Pavillon de la Reine L
Picard E
St-Louis Marais R
Du Septième Art Q
Tiquetonne A
Hôtel-Résidence Trousseau T
Verlain C
Cirque d'Hiver
St-Ambroise
Notre Dame d'Espérance
Théâtre de la Bastille
Maison de Victor Hugo
Opéra Bastille
Port de l'Arsenal
PL DES VOSGES
PL DE LA BASTILLE
SQ. TROUSSEAU
3e
11e
12e
Filles du Calvaire
St-Sébastien Froissart
Richard Lenoir
Chemin Vert
Bréguet Sabin
Bastille
Ledru Rollin
RUE DE CRUSSOL
RUE DU MALTE
BD VOLTAIRE
RUE OBERKAMPF
RUE AMELOT
BD DU TEMPLE
R DES FILLES DU CALVAIRE
RUE MERICOURT
RUE ST-MAUR
AV PARMENTIER
RUE PASTEUR
RUE FROISSART
R DU PONT AUX CHOUX
RUE ST-SEBASTIEN
RUE DE TURENNE
RUE ST CLAUDE
RUE PELEE
RUE ST-SABIN
BD RICHARD LENOIR
RUE DE CHEMIN VERT
RUE ST GILLES
BD BEAUMARCHAIS
RUE DE TOURNELLES
RUE BREGUET
RUE BOULE
RUE DU PAS DE LA MULE
RUE DE LA ROQUETTE
RUE DES TAILLANDIERS
RUE KELLER
RUE DAVAL
PASSAGE THIERE
RUE DE LAPPE
RUE DE CHARONNE
RUE DE BIRAGUE
RUE DE LA BASTILLE
RUE ST ANTOINE
RUE CASTEX
BD HENRI IV
RUE DE LA CERISAIE
RUE DE L'ARSENAL
RUE CRILLON
BD BOURDON
BD DE LA BASTILLE
RUE DE LYON
RUE DE CHARENTON
RUE DU FAUBOURG ST-ANTOINE
AV LEDRU ROLLIN
AV LEDRU-ROLLIN
RUE TRAVERSIERE

would not have taken kindly to such a slight on their blue-bloodedness. The name's origin is medieval and actually means "people exempt from tax" in reference to the penurious inmates of an almshouse that stood on the site of no. 34. It was not until the sixteenth and seventeenth centuries that the **Marais**, as the area between the Pompidou Centre and the Bastille is known, became a fashionable aristocratic district. After the Revolution it was abandoned to the masses, who, up until some forty years ago, were living ten to a room on unserviced, squalid streets. Since then, gentrification has proceeded apace and the middle classes are finally ensconced – mostly media, arty or gay, and definitely outspoken.

The renovated mansions, their grandeur concealed by the narrow streets, have become museums, libraries, offices and chic apartments, flanked by trendy fashion outlets, interior design shops and art galleries. Though cornered by Haussmann's boulevards, the Marais itself was spared the baron's heavy touch and has been left pretty much unspoilt. This is Paris at its most seductive – old, secluded, as lively by night as it is by day, and with as many alluring shops, bars and places to eat as you could wish for.

Rue des Francs-Bourgeois

Rue des Francs-Bourgeois begins with the eighteenth-century magnificence of the **Palais Soubise**, which houses the Archives Nationales de France and the **Musée de l'Histoire de France**. Restoration work on the palace's fabulous Rococo interior will keep visitors out until spring 2005, but meanwhile you can see temporary exhibitions from the archives and plenty of sumptuous interiors at the adjacent **Hôtel de Rohan** (Mon, Wed–Fri 10am–12.30pm & 2–5.30pm, Sat & Sun 2–5.30pm), notably the charming Chinese-inspired Cabinet des Singes, whose walls are painted with monkeys acting out various aristocratic scenes.

Opposite, at the back of a driveway for the Crédit Municipal bank, stands a pepperpot tower which formed part of Philippe-Auguste's twelfth-century **city walls**. Further down the street are two of the grandest Marais *hôtels*, **Carnavalet** and **Lamoignon**, housing respectively the Musée Carnavalet and the Bibliothèque Historique de la Ville de Paris.

Musée Carnavalet

The **Musée Carnavalet**, whose entrance is off rue des Francs-Bourgeois at 23 rue de Sévigné (Tues–Sun 10am–6pm; free; M° St-Paul), presents the history of Paris from its origins up to the Belle Époque through an extraordinary collection of paintings, sculptures, decorative arts and archeological finds. The museum's setting in two beautiful Renaissance mansions, Hôtel Carnavalet and Hôtel Le Peletier, surrounded by attractive gardens, makes a visit worthwhile in itself. There are 140 rooms in all, impossible to visit in one go, so it's best to pick up a floor plan and decide which areas you'd like to concentrate on. The **collection** begins with nineteenth- and early twentieth-century shop and inn signs (beautiful objects in themselves) and fascinating models of Paris through the ages, along with maps and plans. Other highlights on the ground floor include the renovated orangery housing a significant collection of Neolithic finds such as wooden pirogues which were unearthed during the recent redevelopment of the Bercy riverside area. The stairwell to the first floor boasts a glorious *trompe-l'oeil*; and decorative arts feature strongly, with numerous recreated salons and boudoirs from the time of Louis XII to Louis XVI taken from buildings which had to be destroyed for Haussmann's boulevards. The first floor of **Hôtel Le Peletier** is largely devoted to the Belle Époque, evoked through numerous paintings of the period and some wonderful Art Nouveau interiors, most stunning of which is a jewellery shop designed by Alphonse Mucha reassembled in its entirety. Nearby is a section on literary life at the beginning of the twentieth century, including a reconstruction of Proust's cork-lined bedroom. The second floor has rooms full of mementos of the **French Revolution**: models of the Bastille, original *Declarations of the Rights of Man and the Citizen*, tricolors and liberty caps, sculpted allegories of Reason, crockery with Revolutionary slogans, models of the guillotine and execution orders to make you shed a tear for the royalists as well.

Musée Picasso

To the north of the rue des Francs-Bourgeois, at 5 rue de Thorigny, is the **Musée Picasso** (daily except Tues 9.30am–6pm; €5.50; free first Sun of the month; M° Filles du Calvaire/St-Paul), housed in the magnificent seventeenth-century Hôtel Salé. It's the largest collection of Picassos anywhere, representing almost all the major periods of the artist's life from 1905 onwards. Many of the works were owned by Picasso and on his death in 1973 were seized by the state in lieu of taxes owed. The result is an unedited body of work that provides a sense of the artist's development and an insight into the person behind the myth. In addition, the collection includes paintings Picasso bought or was given by contemporaries such as Matisse and Cézanne; his African masks and sculptures; and photographs of him in his studio taken by Brassaï.

The **exhibition** unfolds chronologically, starting with the artist's blue period, his experiments with Cubism and Surrealism, and moves on to his larger-scale works on themes of war and peace and his later preoccupations with love and death, reflected in his Minotaur and bullfighting paintings. Perhaps some of the most striking works on display are Picasso's more personal ones – those of his children, wives and lovers – such as *Olga pensive* (1923), in which his first wife is shown lost in thought, the deep blue of her dress reflecting her mood. The breakdown of their marriage was probably behind the Surrealist-influenced *Femme dans le Fauteuil Rouge*: the violent clash of colours and the woman's grotesquely deformed body tell of acute distress. Two portraits of later lovers Dora Maar and Marie-Thérèse (both painted in 1937), exhibited side by side, show how the two women inspired Picasso in very different ways: they strike the same pose, but Dora Maar is painted with strong lines and vibrant colours, suggesting a passionate, vivacious personality, while Marie-Thérèse's muted colours and soft contours convey serenity and peace.

The museum also holds a substantial number of Picasso's **engravings**, **ceramics** and **sculpture**, reflecting the remarkable ease with which the artist moved from one medium to another. Some of the most arresting sculptures are those he created from recycled household objects, such as the endearing *La Chèvre* (Goat), whose stomach is made from a basket, and *Tête de Taureau*, an ingenious pairing of a bicycle seat and handlebars.

The Jewish quarter

One block south of the rue des Francs-Bourgeois, the area around narrow **rue des Rosiers** has traditionally been the **Jewish quarter** of the city, and remains so, despite incursions by trendy clothes shops. It has a distinctly Mediterranean flavour, testimony to the influence of the North African Sephardim, who replenished Paris's Jewish population, depleted when its Ashkenazim were rounded up by the Nazis and the French police and transported to the concentration camps. This was the fate that befell some of the inhabitants who once lived in the Hôtel de St-Aignan, at 71 rue de Temple, now fittingly home to the **Musée d'Art et d'Histoire du Judaisme** (Mon–Fri 11am–6pm, Sun 10am–6pm; €6.10; M° Rambuteau). The museum is a combination of the collections of the now closed Musée d'Art Juif in Montmartre, Isaac Strauss, conductor of the Paris Opera orchestra, and the Dreyfus archives, a gift to the museum from his grandchildren. Free audioguides in English are well worth picking up if you want to get the most out of your visit. The museum traces the culture, history and artistic endeavours of the Jewish people from the Middle Ages to the present day. The focus is on the history of Jews in France, but there are also many artefacts from the rest of Europe and North Africa. Some of the most notable exhibits are a Gothic-style hannukkah lamp, one of the very few French Jewish artefacts to survive from the period before the expulsion of the Jews from France in 1394; an Italian gilded circumcision chair from the seventeenth century; and a completely intact late-nineteenth-century Austrian *Sukkah*, a brightly painted wooden hut built as a temporary dwelling for the celebration of the Harvest. Other artefacts include Moroccan wedding garments, highly decorated marriage contracts from eighteenth-century Modena and gorgeous, almost whimsical, spice containers. One room, appropriately enough, is devoted to the Dreyfus affair, documented with letters, postcards and press clippings; you can read Émile Zola's famous letter "*J'accuse*" and the letters that Dreyfus sent to his wife from Devil's Island in which he talks of *épouvantable* ("terrible") suffering and loneliness. There's also a significant collection of paintings and sculpture by Jewish artists who came to live in Paris at the beginning of the twentieth century. Though it may seem an odd omission, there's nothing about the Holocaust. The only reference is an installation by contemporary artist Christian Boltanski: one of the exterior walls of a small courtyard is covered with black-bordered death announcements printed with the names of the Jewish artisans who once lived in the building, a number of whom were deported. Its very understatement has a powerful impact and is perhaps all that's needed to evoke recent Jewish history.

Place des Vosges

At the eastern end of rue des Francs-Bourgeois is a masterpiece of aristocratic urban planning, the **place des Vosges**, a vast square of stone and brick symmetry built for the majesty of Henri IV and Louis XIII, whose statue is hidden by trees in the middle of the grass and gravel gardens. Expensive high-heels tap through the arcades, pausing at art, antique and fashion shops, and people lunch al fresco at the restaurants while buskers play classical music. In the garden, toddlers, octogenarians, workers and schoolchildren on lunch breaks sit or play in the only green space of any size in the locality.

Through all the vicissitudes of history, the square has never lost its cachet as a smart address. Among the many celebrities who made their homes here was Victor Hugo: his house, at no. 6, where he wrote much of *Les Misérables*, is now a museum, the **Maison de Victor Hugo** (Tues–Sun 10am–6pm; closed hols; free; M° Chemin-Vert/Bastille); a whole room is devoted to posters of the various stage adaptations of his most famous novel. Hugo was extraordinarily multi-talented: as well as writing, he drew – many of his ink drawings are exhibited – and designed his own furniture; he even put together the extraordinary Chinese-style dining room on display here. That apart, the usual portraits, manuscripts and memorabilia shed sparse light on the man and his work, particularly if you don't read French.

From the southwest corner of the square, a door leads through to the formal château garden, orangerie and exquisite Renaissance facade of the **Hôtel de Sully**. The garden makes for a peaceful rest-stop, or you can pass through the building, nodding at the sphinxes on the stairs, as a pleasing short cut to rue St-Antoine. Temporary photographic exhibitions, usually with social, historical or anthropological themes, are mounted in the *hôtel* by the **Patrimoine Photographique** (Tues–Sun 10am–6.30pm; €4), or you can browse in the bookshop with its extensive collection of books on Paris, some in English (Tues–Sun 10am–7pm).

South of rue de Rivoli

The southern section of the Marais, **south of rue St-Antoine**, harbours some of Paris's most atmospheric streets: the crooked steps and lanterns of rue Cloche-Perce, the tottering timbered houses of rue François-Miron, the medieval buildings behind St-Gervais–St-Protais and the scent of roses from nearby gardens on rue des Barres. Between rues Fourcy and François-Miron, the Hôtel Hénault de Cantoube, with its two-storey crypt, has become the **Maison Européenne de la Photographie** (Wed–Sun 11am–7.45pm; €5, free Wed after 5pm; M° St-Paul/Pont-Marie), hosting excellent exhibitions of contemporary photography, with a stylish café designed by architect Nestor Perkal; the entrance is at 4 rue du Fourcy. Shift eastwards to the next tangle of streets and you'll find the modern, chi-chi flats of the "Village St-Paul" and its expensive clusters of antique shops. Amid further antiques on **rue St-Paul** itself is the **Musée de la Curiosité et de la Magie** at no. 11 (Wed, Sat & Sun 2–7pm; €7; M° St-Paul/Sully-Morland), dedicated to the art of illusion, with a magician regularly performing seemingly impossible sleights of hand.

Further east again, at 21 bd Morland, the **Pavillon de l'Arsenal** (Tues–Sat 10.30am–6.30pm, Sun 11am–7pm; free; M° Sully-Morland) presents current architectural projects to the public and shows how past and present developments have evolved as part and parcel of Parisian history. To this end they have a permanent exhibition of photographs, plans and models, including a model of the whole city linked to a touch-screen choice of 30,000 images.

The Île St-Louis

Often considered the most romantic part of Paris, the peaceful **Île St-Louis** is prime strolling territory. Unlike its larger neighbour, the Île de la Cité, the Île St-Louis has no heavyweight sights, just mellow-stone seventeenth-century houses on single-lane streets, tree-lined *quais*, a school, church, restaurants, cafés, interesting little shops, and the best sorbets in the world at *Berthillon*, 31 rue St-Louis-en-l'Île (see p.185). Unsurprisingly, the island is one of the most coveted of the city's addresses (Baron Guy de Rothschild has a house here). A popular approach to bring you right to *Berthillon* is to cross Pont Louis-Philippe, just east of the Hôtel de Ville; you're then positioned to join the throngs strolling with their ice creams down rue St-Louis-en-l'Île for a spot of window-shopping. Alternatively, you can find seclusion on the **southern quais** or climb over the low gate on the right of the garden across boulevard Henri-IV to reach the best sunbathing spot in Paris. The island is particularly atmospheric in the evening, and an arm-in-arm wander along the *quais* is a must in any lovers' itinerary.

The Bastille

The landmark column topped with the gilded "Spirit of Liberty" on **place de la Bastille** was erected not to commemorate the surrender in 1789 of the prison – whose only visible remains have been transported to square Henri-Galli at the end of boulevard Henri-IV – but the July Revolution of 1830 that replaced the autocratic Charles X with the "Citizen King" Louis-Philippe.

When Louis-Philippe fled in the more significant 1848 Revolution, his throne was burnt beside the column and a new inscription added. Four months later, the workers again took to the streets. All of eastern Paris was barricaded, with the fiercest fighting on rue du Faubourg-St-Antoine, until the rebellion was quelled with the usual massacres and deportation of survivors. However, it is the events of July 14, 1789, symbol of the end of feudalism in Europe, that France celebrates every year on Bastille Day.

The Bicentennial in 1989 was marked by the inauguration of the **Opéra-Bastille** (see p.201), Mitterrand's pet project and subject of the most virulent sequence of rows and resignations. Filling almost the entire block between rues de Lyon, Charenton and Moreau, it has shifted the focus of place de la Bastille, so that the column is no longer the pivotal point; in fact, it's easy to miss it altogether when dazzled by the night-time glare of lights emanating from this "hippopotamus in a bathtub", as one critic dubbed the Opéra.

The building's construction destroyed no small amount of low-rent housing, but, as with most speculative developments, the pace of change is uneven, and cobblers and ironmongers still survive alongside cocktail haunts and sushi bars, making the **quartier de la Bastille** a simultaneously gritty and trendy quarter. **Place and rue d'Aligre**, east of square Trousseau, still have their raucous daily market and, on **rue de Lappe**, *Balajo* is one remnant of a very Parisian tradition: the *bals musettes*, or music halls of 1930s *gai Paris*, frequented between the wars by Piaf, Jean Gabin and Rita Hayworth. It was founded by one Jo de France, who introduced glitter and spectacle into what were then seedy gangster dives, and brought Parisians from the other side of the city to the rue de Lappe lowlife. Now the street is full of fun, cool bars, full to bursting at the weekends. Hip bars and cafés have also sprung up in the surrounding streets, especially on rue de **Charonne**, also home to fashion boutiques and whacky interior designers, while alternative, hippy outfits cluster on **rues Keller** and **de la Roquette.**

Just south of here you can find quiet havens from the mania of the Bastille traffic in the courtyards of **rue du Faubourg-St-Antoine**. Since the fifteenth century, this has been the principal artisan and working-class *quartier* of Paris, the cradle of revolutions and mother of street-fighters. From its beginnings the principal trade associated with it has been **furniture-making**, and the maze of interconnecting yards and *passages* are still full of the workshops of the related trades: marquetry, stainers, polishers and inlayers.

Quartier Latin

South of the river, the **Rive Gauche** (Left Bank) has long maintained an "alternative" identity, opposed to the formal, businesslike ambience of the Right Bank – as much left wing as left bank. These days, this image is mostly kept up by the student population, which first settled on the high ground of the Montagne Ste-Geneviève in the twelfth century, on the ruins of the Roman city of Lutetia. It was either the learned Latin of the scholars or the conversation of the Romans themselves that caused the area to be dubbed the **Quartier Latin**.

The pivotal point of this "Latin quarter" is **place St-Michel**, where the tree-lined **boulevard St-Michel** begins. The *boul' Mich* has lost its radical penniless chic to hard commercial values these days, though the universities on all sides at least maintain the area's student traditions. The cafés and shops are jammed with people, mainly young and – in summer – largely foreign.

Around St-Séverin

The touristy scrum is at its ugliest around **rue de la Huchette**, just east of the place St-Michel. The Théâtre de la Huchette still shows Ionesco's *La Cantatrice Chauve* (*The Bald Prima Donna*) almost fifty years on, but it's a last bastion of the area's postwar heyday, and is now hemmed in by cheap bars and indifferent Greek restaurants. Connecting rue de la Huchette to the riverside is **rue du Chat-qui-Pêche**, a narrow slice of medieval Paris as it was before Haussman got to work.

At the end of rue de la Huchette, **rue St-Jacques** is aligned on the main street of Roman Paris, and was in medieval times the road up which millions of pilgrims trudged at the start of their long march to Santiago de Compostela in Spain. One block south of rue de la Huchette, and west of rue St-Jacques, is the mainly fifteenth-century church of **St-Séverin**, whose entrance is on rue des Prêtres St-Séverin (Mon–Sat 11am–7.15pm, Sun 9am–8.30pm; M° St-Michel/Cluny-La Sorbonne). It's one of the city's most elegant churches, with splendidly virtuoso chiselwork in the pillars of the Flamboyant choir, as well as stained glass by the modern French painter Jean Bazaine.

East of rue St-Jacques, and back towards the river, **square Viviani** – a welcome patch of grass and trees – provides the most flattering of all views of Notre-Dame. The mutilated and disfigured church is **St-Julien-le-Pauvre** (daily 9.30am–12.30pm & 3–6.30pm; M° St-Michel/Maubert Mutualité). The same age as Notre-Dame, it used to be the venue for university assemblies until rumbustious students tore it apart in 1524. Across rue Lagrange from the square, rue de la Bûcherie is the home of the American-run English-language bookshop **Shakespeare and Co** (see p.212), haunted by the shades of James Joyce and other expatriate literati – though the original site of the shop, under Sylvia Beach, publisher of *Ulysses*, was on rue de l'Odéon.

The river bank and Institut du Monde Arabe

A short walk from square Viviani on the river bank, you'll find books, postcards, prints and assorted goods on sale from the **bouquinistes**, who display their wares in green padlocked boxes hooked onto the parapet of the **riverside quais**. It's a pleasant walk upstream to the **Pont de Sully** – which leads across to the Île St-Louis and offers a dramatic view of the apse and steeple of Notre-Dame – and the beginning of a sunny riverside garden dotted with interesting though worn pieces of modern sculpture.

Opposite the Pont de Sully, you can't miss the bold glass and aluminium mass of the **Institut du Monde Arabe** (Tues–Sun 10am–6pm; Ⓦwww.imarabe.org; €4; M° Jussieu/Cardinal-Lemoine), a cultural centre built to further understanding of the Arab world. Designed by Paris's architect of the moment, Jean Nouvel, its broad southern facade comprises thousands of tiny shutters which modulate the light levels inside while simultaneously mimicking a *moucharabiyah*, or traditional Arab latticework balcony. Originally designed to be light-sensitive, they now simply open and shut on the hour every hour to show off the effect. Inside, a sleek **museum** winds down from the seventh floor as it traces the evolution of art in the Islamic world, with precious glass, rugs, ceramics, illuminated manuscripts, woodcarving, metalwork and scientific instruments. On other levels there's a library and multimedia centre for scholars, an auditorium for films and concerts, and a specialist bookshop with a very good selection of CDs from the Arab world. The café-restaurant on the ninth floor has a great view over the Seine.

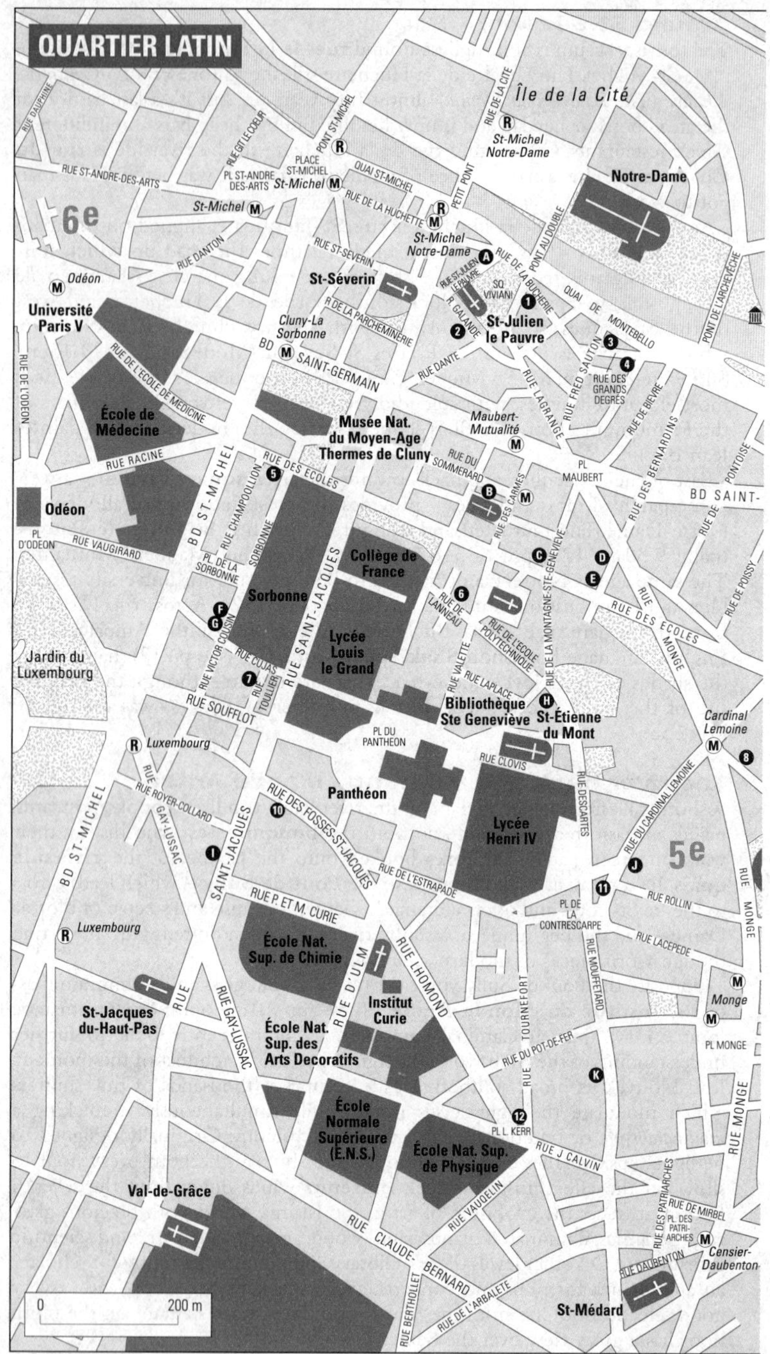
QUARTIER LATIN
Île de la Cité
Notre-Dame
St-Michel Notre-Dame
St-Michel
Odéon
6e
5e
St-Séverin
St-Julien le Pauvre
Cluny-La Sorbonne
Université Paris V
École de Médecine
Musée Nat. du Moyen-Age Thermes de Cluny
Maubert-Mutualité
Odéon
Collège de France
Sorbonne
Lycée Louis le Grand
Jardin du Luxembourg
Bibliothèque Ste Geneviève
St-Étienne du Mont
Cardinal Lemoine
Luxembourg
Panthéon
Lycée Henri IV
École Nat. Sup. de Chimie
Institut Curie
St-Jacques du-Haut-Pas
École Nat. Sup. des Arts Decoratifs
Monge
École Normale Supérieure (E.N.S.)
École Nat. Sup. de Physique
Val-de-Grâce
Censier-Daubenton
St-Médard
0
200 m

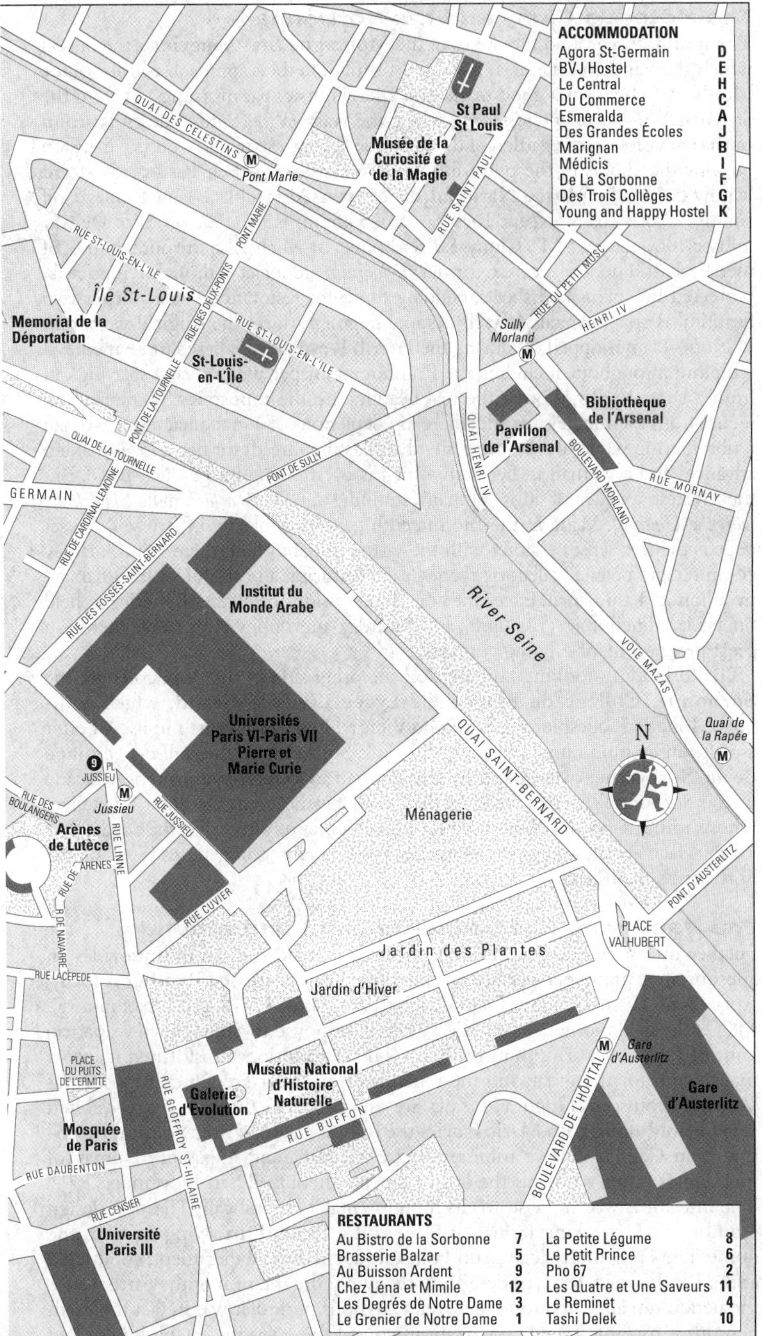
ACCOMMODATION
Agora St-Germain D
BVJ Hostel E
Le Central H
Du Commerce C
Esmeralda A
Des Grandes Écoles J
Marignan B
Médicis I
De La Sorbonne F
Des Trois Collèges G
Young and Happy Hostel K
RESTAURANTS
Au Bistro de la Sorbonne 7
Brasserie Balzar 5
Au Buisson Ardent 9
Chez Léna et Mimile 12
Les Degrés de Notre Dame 3
Le Grenier de Notre Dame 1
La Petite Légume 8
Le Petit Prince 6
Pho 67 2
Les Quatre et Une Saveurs 11
Le Reminet 4
Tashi Delek 10
QUAI DES CELESTINS
Pont Marie
PONT MARIE
St Paul
St Louis
Musée de la Curiosité et de la Magie
RUE SAINT PAUL
RUE ST-LOUIS-EN-L'ILE
Île St-Louis
RUE DES DEUX-PONTS
Memorial de la Déportation
St-Louis-en-L'Île
RUE DU PETIT MUSC
HENRI IV
Sully Morland
Bibliothèque de l'Arsenal
Pavillon de l'Arsenal
QUAI HENRI IV
BOULEVARD MORLAND
RUE MORNAY
PONT DE LA TOURNELLE
QUAI DE LA TOURNELLE
PONT DE SULLY
GERMAIN
RUE DE CARDINAL LEMOINE
RUE DES FOSSES-SAINT-BERNARD
Institut du Monde Arabe
River Seine
VOIE MAZAS
Universités Paris VI-Paris VII Pierre et Marie Curie
Quai de la Rapée
N
9
PL JUSSIEU
Jussieu
RUE DES BOULANGERS
RUE JUSSIEU
QUAI SAINT-BERNARD
Ménagerie
Arènes de Lutèce
RUE LINNE
ARENES
RUE DE
R DE NAVARRE
RUE CUVIER
PONT D'AUSTERLITZ
PLACE VALHUBERT
Jardin des Plantes
RUE LACEPEDE
Jardin d'Hiver
Gare d'Austerlitz
PLACE DU PUITS DE L'ERMITE
Muséum National d'Histoire Naturelle
Galerie d'Evolution
RUE GEOFFROY ST-HILAIRE
RUE BUFFON
BOULEVARD DE L'HÔPITAL
Mosquée de Paris
RUE DAUBENTON
RUE CENSIER
Université Paris III

The Hôtel de Cluny and the Sorbonne

The nearby area around the slopes of the **Montagne Ste-Geneviève**, the hill on which the Panthéon stands, is good for a stroll. The best approach is from **place Maubert** (which has a good market on Tues, Thurs & Sat mornings) or from the St-Michel/St-Germain crossroads, where the walls of the third-century **Roman baths** are visible in the garden of the Hôtel de Cluny, a sixteenth-century mansion built by the abbots of the powerful Cluny monastery as their Paris pied-à-terre. It now houses the **Musée National du Moyen-Âge**, 6 place Paul-Painlevé, off rue des Écoles (daily except Tues 9.15am–5.45pm; €5.50, €4 on Sun; Ⓦwww.musee-moyenage.fr; M° Cluny-La Sorbonne/St-Michel), a treasure house of medieval art. The vaults of the former *frigidarium* are intact – though temporarily protected by corrugated sheets, pending funds for restoration – and shelter two beautiful Roman capitals, as well as some fragments from the original west front of Notre-Dame, lopped off during the French Revolution. There's more medieval sculpture throughout, including the Flamboyant chapel, with its vault splaying out from a central pillar, though the real beauties are the **tapestries**. Conjuring up scenes from the medieval world, there are depictions of a grape harvest, a woman embroidering while her servant patiently holds the threads for her, a lover making advances and a woman in her bath which is overflowing into a duck pond. But the greatest wonder of all is the truly stunning *La Dame à la Licorne* (*The Lady with the Unicorn*). Made in the late fifteenth century, probably in Brussels, the set depicts the five senses – along with the virtue in controlling them – in six richly coloured and detailed allegoric scenes, each featuring a beautiful woman flanked by a lion and a unicorn. Excellent hour-long sessions of medieval music are held on Friday lunchtimes (12.30pm) and Saturday afternoons (4pm), and there is a great programme of evening concerts.

The forbidding-looking buildings on the other side of rue des Écoles are the **Sorbonne**, **Collège de France** and **Lycée Louis-le-Grand**, which numbers Molière, Robespierre, Sartre and Victor Hugo among its pupils. A better aspect can be found if you head up rue de la Sorbonne to the traffic-free **place de la Sorbonne**, overlooked by the dramatic Counter-Reformation facade of the Sorbonne's chapel, built in the 1640s by the great Cardinal Richelieu, whose tomb it houses. With its lime trees, fountains and cafés, the square is a lovely place to sit, and you can watch the students going in and out of the Sorbonne's main gate.

The Panthéon, St-Étienne-du-Mont and around

Further up the Montagne Ste-Geneviève, the broad rue Soufflot provides an appropriately grand perspective on the domed and porticoed **Panthéon** (daily: April–Sept 10am–6.30pm; Oct–March 10am–6pm; €7; RER Luxembourg/M° Cardinal-Lemoine), Louis XV's grateful response to Ste Geneviève, patron saint of Paris, for curing him of illness. The Revolution transformed it into a mausoleum for the great, and the remains of giants of French culture such as Voltaire, Rousseau, Hugo and Zola are entombed in the vast, barrel-vaulted crypt below, along with Marie Curie (the only woman), writer, political adventurer and Gaullist culture minister André Malraux, and Alexandre Dumas, of musketeers fame, who was the last to be "panthéonized", in November 2002. The interior is worth a visit for its monumental, bombastically Classical design – and to see a working model of **Foucault's Pendulum** swinging from the dome. The French physicist Léon Foucault devised the experiment, conducted at the Panthéon in 1851, to demonstrate vividly the rotation of the earth: while the pendulum appeared to rotate over a 24-hour period, it was in fact the earth beneath it turning. The demonstration wowed the scientific establishment and the public alike, with huge crowds turning up to watch the ground move beneath their feet.

The remains of two seventeenth-century literary giants, Pascal and Racine, lie close at hand in the church of **St-Étienne-du-Mont**, immediately behind the Panthéon on the corner of rue Clovis. The church's garbled facade conceals a stunning and highly unexpected interior. The sudden transition from Flamboyant Gothic choir to sixteenth-century nave is made smooth by a bizarre narrow catwalk which runs right round the interior, twisting down the pillars of the crossing in two spiral staircases before arching across the width of the church in the broad span of the rood screen. This last feature is highly unusual in itself, as most others in France have fallen victim to Protestant iconoclasts, reformers or revolutionaries. Exceptionally tall windows at the triforium level fill the church with light, and there is also some good seventeenth-century glass in the cloister. Further down rue Clovis, a huge piece of Philippe-Auguste's twelfth-century **city walls** emerges from among the houses.

There's not much point in going further south on rue St-Jacques: the area is dull and lifeless once you are over the Gay-Lussac intersection, though you might like to take a look at the resplendent seventeenth-century Baroque church of **Val-de-Grâce** on place Alphonse-Laveran (Wed, Thurs, Sat & Sun noon–5pm; €5; closed Aug; RER Port-Royal), with its pedimented front and ornate cupola copied from St Peter's in Rome, or visit the big **market** and several brasseries around the corner on **boulevard de Port-Royal**.

Place Maubert to the rue Mouffetard

North of St-Étienne-du-Mont, the villagey **rue de la Montagne-Ste-Geneviève** descends towards place Maubert, passing the pleasant cafés and restaurants around rue de l'École-Polytechnique. Heading uphill, rue Descartes runs into the tiny and attractive **place de la Contrescarpe**, once an arty hangout where Hemingway wrote – in the café *La Chope* – and Georges Brassens sang, now a rowdy and dog-eared student hangout. The ancient **rue Mouffetard** begins here, a cobbled lane winding downhill to the church of **St-Médard**, once a country parish beside the now-covered river Bièvre. Most of the upper half of the street is given over to rather touristy eating places; the bottom half, however, with its sumptuous fruit and vegetable stalls – among lots of clothes and shoe shops and cafés – still maintains an authentic neighbourhood air.

The Paris mosque and Jardin des Plantes

A little further east, across rue Monge, are some of the city's most agreeable surprises. Just past Place du Puits de l'Ermite stand the crenellated walls of the **Paris mosque** (daily except Fri & Muslim hols 9am–noon & 2–6pm; Ⓦwww.mosquee-de-paris.org; €3). You can walk in the sunken garden and patios with their polychrome tiles and carved ceilings, but not the prayer room. There's also a lovely, gardened **tearoom** (see p.186), open to all, and an atmospheric **hamam** (see p.209).

Behind the mosque is the **Jardin des Plantes** (daily: summer 7.30am–8pm; winter 8am–dusk; free; M° Austerlitz/Jussieu/Monge), founded as a medicinal herb garden in 1626 and gradually evolved as Paris's botanical gardens, with shady avenues of trees, lawns to sprawl on, museums and a zoo. The wonderful hothouses were undergoing a major renovation at the time of writing, due to be completed by late 2005. The gardens are a pleasant space to while away the middle of a day. By the rue Cuvier exit is a fine cedar of Lebanon planted in 1734, raised from a seed sent over from the Oxford Botanical Gardens, and a slice of an American sequoia more than 2000 years old. In the nearby physics labs, Henri Becquerel discovered radioactivity in 1896, and two years later the Curies discovered radium.

Magnificent, varied floral beds make a fine approach to the collection of buildings which form the **Muséum National d'Histoire Naturelle** (Ⓦwww.mnhn.fr). Musty museums of palaeontology, anatomy, mineralogy, entomology and palaeobotany should be sidestepped in favour of the **Grand Galerie de l'Évolution** (daily except Tues 10am–6pm, Thurs till 8pm; €7), housed in a dramatically restored nineteenth-century glass-domed building; the entrance is off rue Buffon. You'll be wowed by the sheer scale of the interior, where the story of evolution and the relations between human beings and nature is told using stuffed animals that look real, a combination of clever lighting effects, ambient music and birdsong, videos and touch-screen databases.

Real animals can be seen in the small **menagerie** across the park to the northeast near rue Cuvier (April–Sept Mon–Sat 9am–6pm, Sun 9am–6.30pm; winter daily 9am–5pm; €6). Founded here just after the Revolution, it is France's oldest zoo – and looks it. The old-fashioned iron cages of the big cats' *fauverie*, the stinky vivarium and the unkempt, glazed-in primate house are frankly depressing, though these animals are at least spared the fate of their predecessors during the starvation months of the 1870 Prussian siege. Most of the zoo is pleasantly park-like, however, and given over to some marvellous species of deer, antelope, goats, buffaloes and other beasts that seem happy enough in their outdoor enclosures. The **Microzoo** allows you to inspect headlice and other minuscule wonders.

A short distance away to the northwest, with entrances in rue de Navarre, rue des Arènes and through a passage on rue Monge, is the **Arènes de Lutèce**, an unexpected backwater hidden from the street, and, along with the Roman baths (see p.152), Paris's only Roman remains. Once an amphitheatre for ten thousand, a few ghostly rows of stone seats now look down on old men playing boules in the sand, and benches, gardens and a kids' playground stand behind.

St-Germain

The northern half of the 6e arrondissement, asymmetrically centred on **place St-Germain-des-Prés**, is one of the most attractive, lively and wealthy square kilometres in the city. The most dramatic approach is to cross the river from the Louvre by the footbridge, the **Pont des Arts**, from where there's a classic upstream view of the Île de la Cité, with barges moored at the quai de Conti, and the Tour St-Jacques and Hôtel de Ville breaking the skyline of the Right Bank. The dome and pediment at the end of the bridge belong to the **Institut de France**, seat of the Académie Française, an august body of writers and scholars whose mission is to safeguard the purity of the French language. This is the most grandiose bit of the Left Bank riverfront: to the left is the **Hôtel des Monnaies**, redesigned as the Mint in the late eighteenth century; to the right is the **Beaux-Arts**, the School of Fine Art, whose students throng the *quais* on sunny days, sketchpads on knees. More students can be found relaxing in the **Jardin du Luxembourg**, bordering the Quartier Latin towards the southern end of the *sixième*, which is one of the largest and loveliest green spaces in the city.

The riverside

The riverside chunk of the 6e arrondissement is cut lengthwise by **rue St-André-des-Arts** and **rue Jacob**. It's an area full of bookshops, commercial art galleries, antique shops, cafés and restaurants, and if you poke your nose into the courtyards and side streets, you'll find foliage, fountains and peaceful enclaves removed from the bustle of the city. The houses are four to six storeys high, seventeenth- and eighteenth-century, some noble, some bulging and skew, all painted in infinite gradations of grey, pearl and off-white. Broadly speaking, the further west you go the posher the houses get.

Historical associations are legion: Picasso painted *Guernica* in rue des Grands-Augustins; Molière started his career in rue Mazarine; Robespierre et al split ideological hairs at the *Café Procope* in rue de l'Ancienne-Comédie. In rue Visconti, Racine died, Delacroix painted, and Balzac's printing business went bust. In the parallel rue des Beaux-Arts, Oscar Wilde died, Corot and Ampère (father of amps) lived, and the crazy poet Gérard de Nerval went walking with a lobster on a lead.

If you're looking for lunch, you'll find numerous places on **place and rue St-André-des-Arts**, and along **rue de Buci**, up towards boulevard St-Germain, which preserves a strong flavour of its origins as a market street, with food shops, delis and lots of cafés and brasseries. Before you get to rue de Buci, there is an intriguing little passage on the left, **Cour du Commerce St André**, where Marat had a printing press and Dr Guillotin perfected his notorious machine by lopping off sheep's heads in the loft next door. A couple of smaller courtyards open off it, revealing another stretch of Philippe-Auguste's twelfth-century city wall.

An alternative corner for midday food or quiet is around rue de l'Abbaye and rue du Furstemberg. Halfway down rue du Furstemburg at no. 6, opposite a tiny square, is Delacroix's old studio. The studio backs onto a secret garden and is now the **Musée Delacroix** (daily except Tues 9.30am–5pm; €5), with a small collection of the artist's personal belongings as well as minor exhibitions of his work. This is also the beginning of some very upmarket shopping territory, in rue Jacob, rue de Seine and rue Bonaparte in particular.

St-Germain-des-Prés to St-Sulpice

Place St-Germain-des-Prés, the hub of the *quartier*, is only a stone's throw away from the Musée Delacroix, with the *Deux Magots* café (see p.187) on the corner of the square, *Flore* (see p.187) adjacent and *Lipp* (see p.188)across the boulevard St-Germain. All three are renowned for the number of philosophico-politico-literary backsides that have shined – and continue to shine – their seats, along with plenty of celebrity-hunters. The tower opposite the *Deux Magots* belongs to the church of **St-Germain**, all that remains of an enormous Benedictine monastery. The interior is its best aspect, with the transformation from Romanesque to early Gothic visible under the heavy greens and golds of nineteenth-century paintwork. The last chapel on the south side contains the tomb of the philosopher René Descartes.

South of boulevard St-Germain, the streets round St-Sulpice are calm and classy. **Rue Mabillon** is pretty, with a row of old houses set back below the level of the modern street. On the left are the **halles St-Germain**, on the site of a fifteenth-century market. Rue St-Sulpice leads through to the front of the enormous church of **St-Sulpice** (daily 7.30am–7.30pm), an austerely classical church, erected either side of 1700, with a Doric colonnade surmounted by an Ionic, and Corinthian pilasters in the towers; uncut masonry blocks still protrude from the south tower, awaiting the sculptor's chisel. For many, however, the main attraction of **place St-Sulpice** is Yves Saint Laurent Rive Gauche, and the sunny *Café de la Mairie*, with its outside tables on the square. All is expensive elegance in these parts, but if you're heading east towards boulevard St-Michel, the glitzy shops quickly fade into the worthy bookshops and inexpensive restaurants around the École de Médecine.

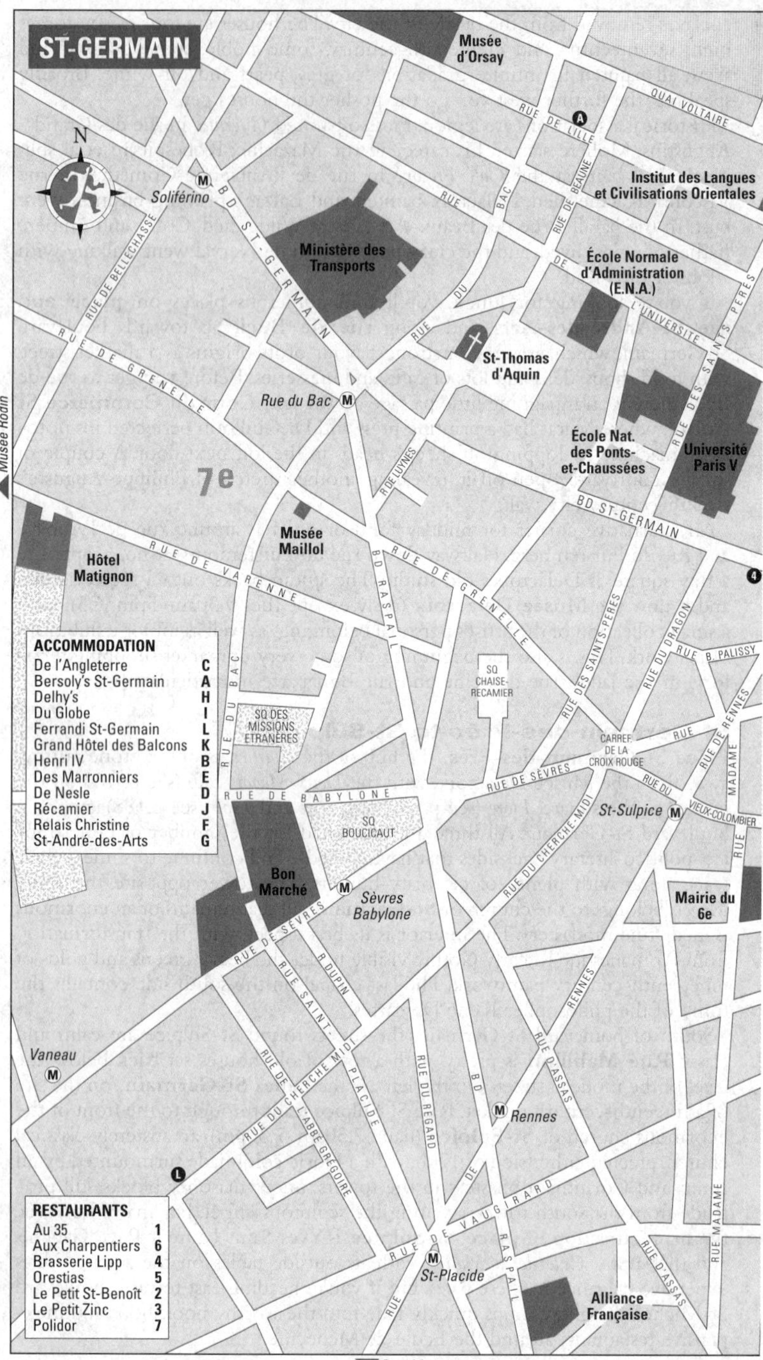
ST-GERMAIN
Musée d'Orsay
QUAI VOLTAIRE
RUE DE LILLE
Institut des Langues et Civilisations Orientales
RUE DE BEAUNE
RUE DU BAC
Solférino
BD ST-GERMAIN
Ministère des Transports
RUE DE BELLECHASSE
RUE DE GRENELLE
École Normale d'Administration (E.N.A.)
RUE DE L'UNIVERSITÉ
RUE DES SAINTS PÈRES
St-Thomas d'Aquin
Rue du Bac
École Nat. des Ponts-et-Chaussées
Université Paris V
Musée Rodin
7e
R. DE LUYNES
BD ST-GERMAIN
Musée Maillol
Hôtel Matignon
RUE DE VARENNE
BD RASPAIL
RUE DE GRENELLE
SQ CHAISE-RECAMIER
RUE DES SAINTS-PÈRES
RUE DU DRAGON
RUE B. PALISSY
RUE DE RENNES
ACCOMMODATION
De l'Angleterre C
Bersoly's St-Germain A
Delhy's H
Du Globe I
Ferrandi St-Germain L
Grand Hôtel des Balcons K
Henri IV B
Des Marronniers E
De Nesle D
Récamier J
Relais Christine F
St-André-des-Arts G
RUE DU BAC
SQ DES MISSIONS ETRANÈRES
CARREF. DE LA CROIX ROUGE
RUE DE SÈVRES
MADAME
RUE DE BABYLONE
SQ BOUCICAUT
RUE DU VIEUX-COLOMBIER
St-Sulpice
RUE DU CHERCHE-MIDI
Bon Marché
Sèvres Babylone
Mairie du 6e
RUE DE SÈVRES
R. DUPIN
RUE SAINT-PLACIDE
RENNES
Vaneau
RUE DU CHERCHE MIDI
RUE DU REGARD
RUE D'ASSAS
RUE DE L'ABBÉ GRÉGOIRE
BD
Rennes
RUE DE VAUGIRARD
RUE MADAME
RESTAURANTS
Au 35 1
Aux Charpentiers 6
Brasserie Lipp 4
Orestias 5
Le Petit St-Benoît 2
Le Petit Zinc 3
Polidor 7
St-Placide
RASPAIL
RUE D'ASSAS
Alliance Française
Gare Montparnasse

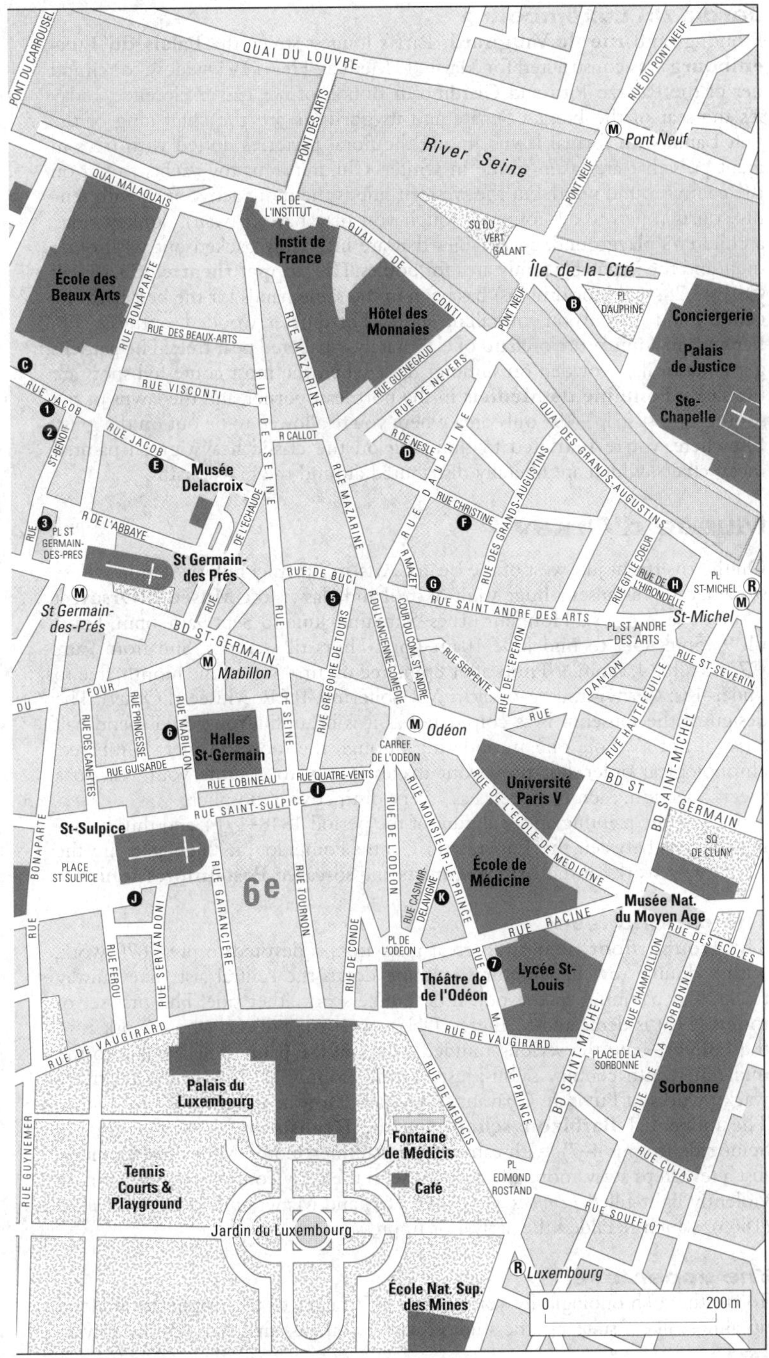
QUAI DU LOUVRE
PONT DU CARROUSEL
PONT DES ARTS
RUE DU PONT NEUF
Pont Neuf
River Seine
QUAI MALAQUAIS
PL DE L'INSTITUT
SQ DU VERT GALANT
PONT NEUF
Île de la Cité
Instit de France
QUAI DE CONTI
École des Beaux Arts
Hôtel des Monnaies
PL DAUPHINE
Conciergerie
Palais de Justice
Ste-Chapelle
RUE BONAPARTE
RUE DES BEAUX-ARTS
RUE VISCONTI
RUE MAZARINE
RUE DE SEINE
RUE GUENEGAUD
RUE DE NEVERS
RUE DAUPHINE
QUAI DES GRANDS-AUGUSTINS
RUE JACOB
ST-BENOIT
R CALLOT
R DE NESLE
Musée Delacroix
RUE CHRISTINE
RUE DES GRANDS-AUGUSTINS
R DE L'ABBAYE
DE L'ECHAUDE
PL ST GERMAIN-DES-PRES
St Germain-des Prés
R MAZET
RUE GIT LE COEUR
RUE DE L'HIRONDELLE
PL ST-MICHEL
St Germain-des-Prés
RUE DE BUCI
RUE SAINT ANDRE DES ARTS
St-Michel
PL ST ANDRE DES ARTS
BD ST-GERMAIN
Mabillon
RUE GREGOIRE DE TOURS
R DE L'ANCIENNE-COMEDIE
COUR DU COM. ST ANDRE
RUE SERPENTE
RUE DE L'EPERON
DANTON
RUE ST-SEVERIN
RUE DU FOUR
RUE PRINCESSE
RUE MABILLON
Halles St-Germain
Odéon
RUE HAUTEFEUILLE
BD SAINT-MICHEL
RUE DES CANETTES
RUE GUISARDE
RUE LOBINEAU
CARREF. DE L'ODEON
RUE QUATRE-VENTS
Université Paris V
BD ST GERMAIN
RUE SAINT-SULPICE
St-Sulpice
RUE DE L'ECOLE DE MEDICINE
RUE MONSIEUR-LE-PRINCE
SQ DE CLUNY
PLACE ST SULPICE
6e
RUE GARANCIERE
RUE TOURNON
RUE DE L'ODEON
École de Médicine
RUE CASIMIR-DELAVIGNE
Musée Nat. du Moyen Age
RUE RACINE
RUE DES ECOLES
RUE SERVANDONI
RUE FEROU
RUE DE CONDE
PL DE L'ODEON
Théâtre de de l'Odéon
Lycée St-Louis
RUE CHAMPOLLION
RUE DE LA SORBONNE
RUE DE VAUGIRARD
LE PRINCE
BD SAINT-MICHEL
PLACE DE LA SORBONNE
Palais du Luxembourg
RUE DE MEDICIS
Sorbonne
RUE GUYNEMER
Fontaine de Médicis
Tennis Courts & Playground
Café
PL EDMOND ROSTAND
RUE CUJAS
RUE SOUFFLOT
Jardin du Luxembourg
Luxembourg
École Nat. Sup. des Mines
0
200 m

Jardin du Luxembourg

Fronting onto **rue de Vaugirard**, Paris's longest street, the **Palais du Luxembourg** was constructed for Marie de Médicis, Henri IV's widow, to remind her of the Palazzo Pitti and Giardino di Boboli of her native Florence. Today it's the seat of the French Senate and its **gardens** are the chief lung of the Left Bank, with formal lawns among the floral parterres dotted with trees in giant pots that are taken inside in winter. Children rent toy yachts to sail on the central round pond, but the western side is the more active area, with tennis courts (open to all-comers, though you may have to wait), donkey rides, a children's playground, chess tables that are invariably packed out with older men, and the inevitable sandy area for boules. The **puppet theatre** (€3.90; call Ⓣ01.43.26.46.47 for timings) has been in the same hands for the best part of a century, and still puts on enthralling shows. The quieter, wooded southeast corner ends in a miniature orchard of elaborately espaliered pear trees. The gardens get fantastically crowded on summer days, when the most contested spots are the shady **Fontaine de Médicis** in the northeast corner, and the lawns of the southernmost strip – the only area where you're allowed to lie out on the grass. Elsewhere, you're restricted to slumping on the classic heavy, green-painted metal chairs, which are liberally distributed around the gravel paths.

Musée d'Orsay

On the riverfront just west of the Beaux-Arts, in a former railway station whose stone facade disguises a huge vault of steel and glass, is the **Musée-d'Orsay**, at 1 rue de la Légion d'Honneur (Tues–Sun: mid-June to Sept 9am–6pm, Thurs till 9.45pm; Oct to mid-June 10am–6pm, Thurs till 9.15pm, Sun from 9am; €7, €5 after 4.15pm & Thurs after 8pm, free on first Sun of the month, free to under-18s; Ⓦwww.musee-orsay.fr; M° Solférino/RER Musée-d'Orsay). The design of the museum is as considered as it is beautiful. You could spend half a day, if not a whole one, meandering through the rooms in their numbered, chronological order, but the layout makes it easy to confine your visit to a specific section, each of which has a very distinctive atmosphere.

Housing the painting and sculpture of the period 1848–1914, and thus bridging the gap between the Louvre and Centre Pompidou, its highlights are the electrifying works of the **Impressionists** and so-called **Post-Impressionists**.

The ground level

The **ground floor**, under the great glass arch, is devoted to pre-1870 work, with a double row of sculptures running down the central aisle like railway tracks, and paintings in the odd little bunkers on either side. The first set of rooms (1–3) is dedicated to Ingres, Delacroix – the bulk of whose work is in the Louvre – and the serious-minded works of the painters acceptable to the mid-nineteenth century salons; just beyond (rooms 11–13) are the relatively wacky works of Puvis de Chavannes, Gustave Moreau and the younger Degas. The influential **Barbizon school** and the **Realists** are showcased on the Seine side (rooms 4–7), with canvases by Daumier, Corot, Millet and Courbet. Just a few steps away, room 14 explodes with the early controversies of Monet's violently light-filled *Femmes au Jardin* (1867) and Manet's provocative *Olympia* (1863), which heralded the arrival of Impressionism.

The upper level

To continue chronologically you have to go straight to the **upper level**, done up almost like a suite of attic studios, where you pass first through the private collection donated by Moreau-Nélaton (room 29). An assiduous collector and art historian, his collection contains some of the most famous **Impressionist** images: Monet's *Poppies*, as well as Manet's *Déjeuner sur l'Herbe*, which sent the critics into apoplexies of rage and disgust when it appeared in 1863, and was refused for that year's Salon. From this point on, you'll have to fight off a persistent sense of familiarity or recognition – Degas' *L'Absinthe*, Renoir's *Bal du Moulin de la Galette*, Monet's *Femme a l'Ombrelle* – in order to appreciate Impressionism's vibrant, experimental vigour. There's a host of small-scale landscapes and outdoor scenes by Renoir, Sisley, Pissarro and Monet, paintings which owed much of their brilliance to the novel practice of setting up easels in the open to capture the light. Less typical works include Degas' ballet-dancers, which demonstrate his principal interest in movement and line as opposed to the more common Impressionist concern with light, and *Le Berceau* (1872), by Berthe Morisot, the first woman to join the early Impressionists. More heavyweight masterpieces can be found in rooms 34 and 39, devoted to **Monet** and **Renoir** in their middle and late periods – the development of Monet's obsession with light is shown with five of his Rouen cathedral series, each painted in different light conditions. Room 35 is full of the fervid colours and disturbing rhythms of **Van Gogh**, while **Cézanne**, another step removed from the preoccupations of the mainstream Impressionists, is wonderfully represented in room 36: one of the canvases most revealing of his art is *Pommes et Oranges* (1895–1900), in which the background abandons perspective while the fruit has an extraordinary solidity.

Passing the **café** – with a summer terrace and a wonderful view of Montmartre through the giant railway clock – you arrive at a dimly lit, melancholy chamber (40) devoted to **pastels** by Redon, Manet, Mondrian and others. The next and final suite of rooms on this level is given over to the various offspring of Impressionism, and has an edgier, more modern feel, with a much greater emphasis on psychology. It begins with Rousseau's dreamlike *La Charmeuse de Serpent* (1907) and continues past **Gauguin**'s ambivalent Tahitian paintings to **Pointillist** works by Seurat (the famous *Cirque*), Signac and others, ending with **Toulouse-Lautrec** at his caricaturial nightclubbing best.

The middle level

Don't miss the covetable little Kaganovitch collection (rooms 49 & 50) on your way down to the **middle level**, where the flow of the painting section continues with Vuillard and Bonnard (rooms 71 & 72), tucked away behind Pompon's irresistible sculpture of a polar bear, on the rue de Lille side of the railway chamber. On the far side, overlooking the Seine, you can see a less familiar side of late nineteenth-century painting in rooms 55 and 58, with epic, naturalist works such as Detaille's stirring *Le Rêve* (1888) and Cormon's *Caïn* (1880), as well as a troubling handful of **Symbolist** paintings from artists as diverse as Munch, Klimt and Odilon Redon (rooms 59 & 60). On the parallel sculpture terraces, nineteenth-century marbles on the Seine side face early twentieth-century pieces across the divide, while the **Rodin terrace** bridging the two puts almost everything else to shame. It's a pity, but few visitors will have energy left for the half-dozen rooms of superb Art Nouveau furniture and *objets*, or the sumptuous reception room (51) of the station hotel.

The Trocadéro, Eiffel Tower and the septième

As examples of landmark architecture, the **Palais de Tokyo** and **Palais de Chaillot** are hard to love. These twin white elephants have long given the

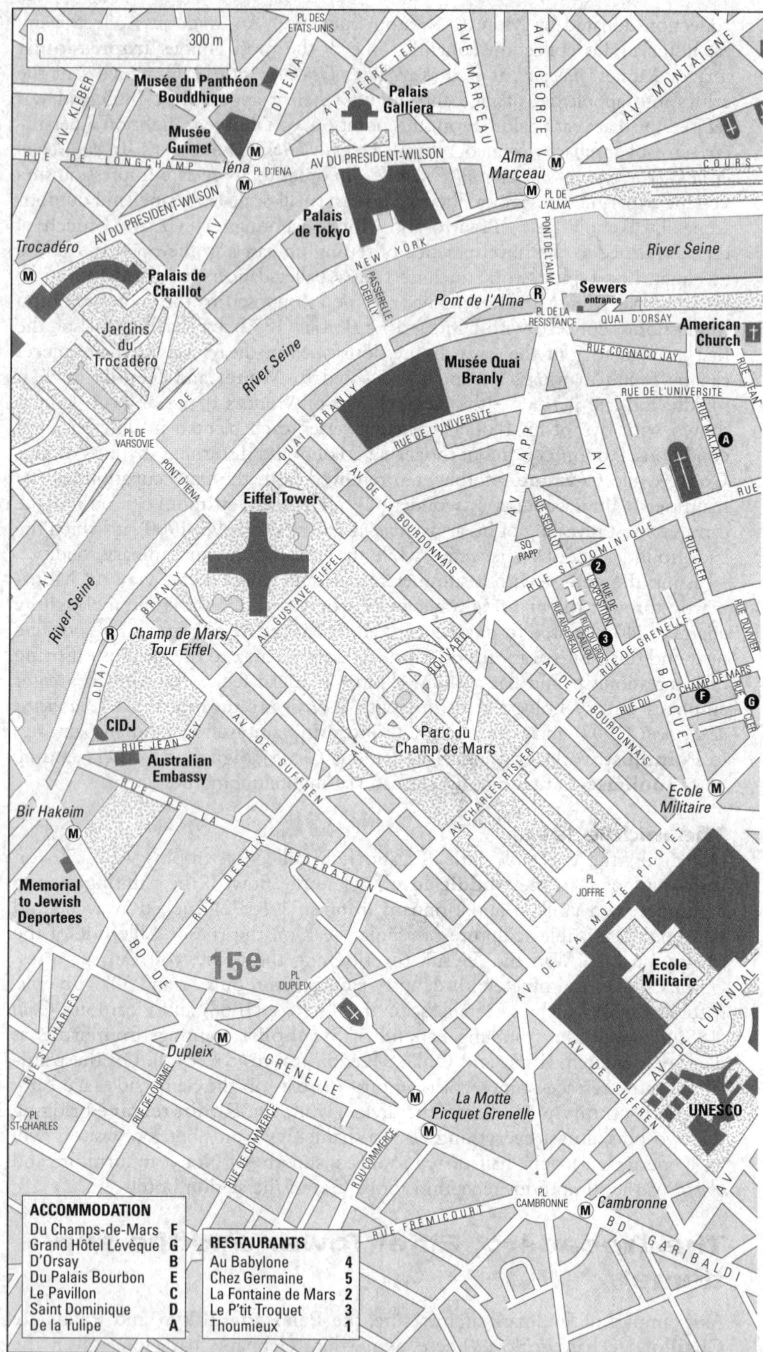
0 300 m
Musée du Panthéon Bouddhique
Palais Galliera
Musée Guimet
Iéna
Alma Marceau
Palais de Tokyo
Trocadéro
Palais de Chaillot
River Seine
Sewers entrance
Pont de l'Alma
American Church
Jardins du Trocadéro
Musée Quai Branly
Eiffel Tower
Champ de Mars/ Tour Eiffel
Parc du Champ de Mars
CIDJ
Australian Embassy
Bir Hakeim
Ecole Militaire
Memorial to Jewish Deportees
15e
Dupleix
La Motte Picquet Grenelle
UNESCO
Cambronne
ACCOMMODATION
Du Champs-de-Mars F
Grand Hôtel Lévèque G
D'Orsay B
Du Palais Bourbon E
Le Pavillon C
Saint Dominique D
De la Tulipe A
RESTAURANTS
Au Babylone 4
Chez Germaine 5
La Fontaine de Mars 2
Le P'tit Troquet 3
Thoumieux 1

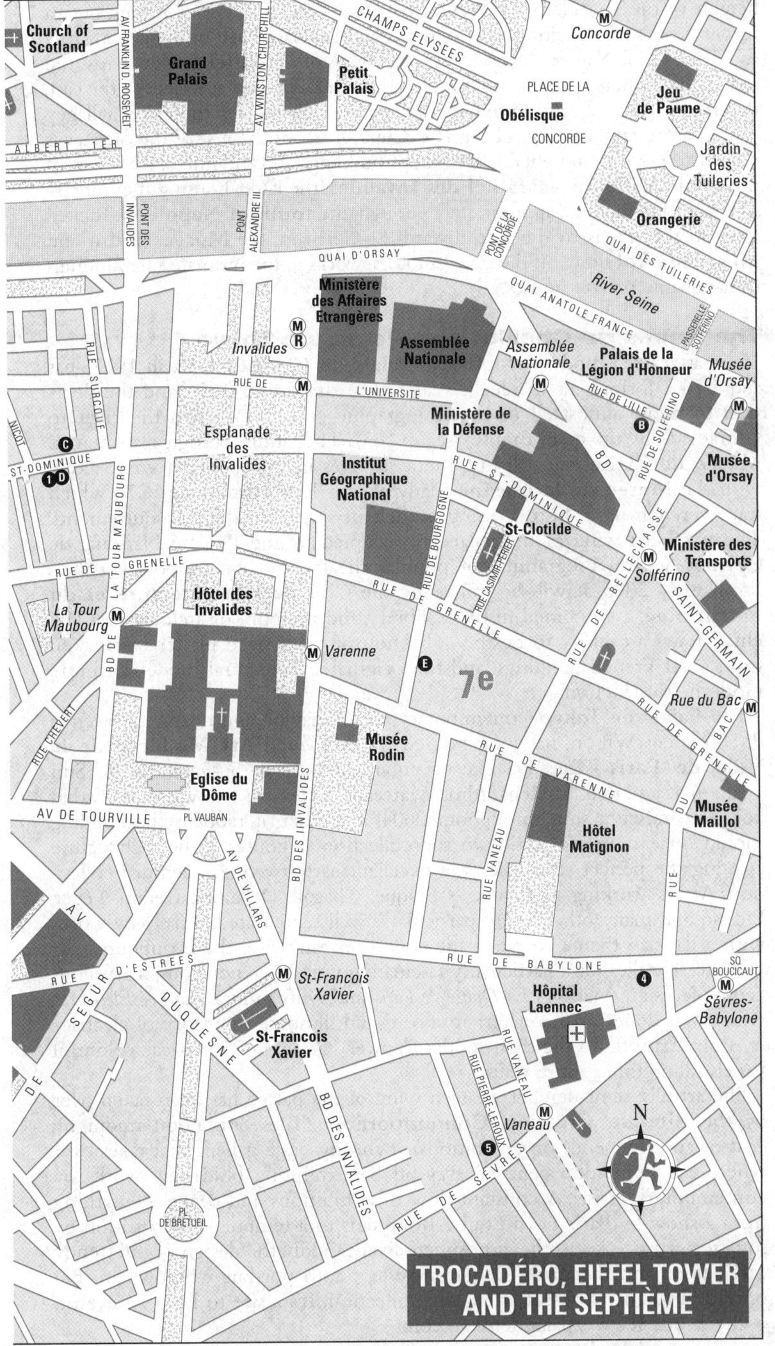
Church of Scotland
Grand Palais
Petit Palais
CHAMPS ELYSEES
Concorde
PLACE DE LA CONCORDE
Obélisque
Jeu de Paume
Jardin des Tuileries
Orangerie
AV FRANKLIN D. ROOSEVELT
AV WINSTON CHURCHILL
ALBERT 1ER
PONT DES INVALIDES
PONT ALEXANDRE III
PONT DE LA CONCORDE
QUAI D'ORSAY
QUAI DES TUILERIES
River Seine
QUAI ANATOLE FRANCE
PASSERELLE SOLFERINO
Ministère des Affaires Etrangères
Assemblée Nationale
Invalides
Assemblée Nationale
Palais de la Légion d'Honneur
Musée d'Orsay
RUE DE L'UNIVERSITE
RUE DE LILLE
RUE SURCOUF
NICOT
ST-DOMINIQUE
Esplanade des Invalides
Ministère de la Défense
Institut Géographique National
RUE ST-DOMINIQUE
BD ST-GERMAIN
RUE DE SOLFERINO
Musée d'Orsay
BD LA TOUR MAUBOURG
RUE DE BOURGOGNE
St-Clotilde
RUE CASIMIR-PERIER
RUE DE BELLECHASSE
Ministère des Transports
Solférino
RUE DE GRENELLE
Hôtel des Invalides
La Tour Maubourg
Varenne
7e
Rue du Bac
RUE DE GRENELLE
RUE CHEVERT
Musée Rodin
RUE DE VARENNE
RUE DU BAC
Musée Maillol
Eglise du Dôme
AV DE TOURVILLE
PL VAUBAN
BD DES INVALIDES
AV DE VILLARS
RUE VANEAU
Hôtel Matignon
AV DE SEGUR
RUE D'ESTREES
DUQUESNE
St-Francois Xavier
St-Francois Xavier
RUE DE BABYLONE
SQ BOUCICAUT
Hôpital Laennec
Sévres-Babylone
RUE VANEAU
RUE PIERRE-LEROUX
Vaneau
BD DES INVALIDES
RUE DE SEVRES
PL DE BRETUEIL
N
TROCADÉRO, EIFFEL TOWER AND THE SEPTIÈME

heights of the Trocadéro, on the north bank of the river, a forlorn air, but in recent years some exciting new musems and galleries have brought both palaces back to life. You can always enjoy the views of the **Eiffel Tower**, across the river, which offers the most impressive vista of all. The area at its feet to the east, the **septième** (7e) arrondissement, is worth exploring for the classy, villagey shops and restaurants around the **rue Cler**. Much of the rest of the quarter is dominated by monumental government buildings and the military edifices of the **École Militaire** and **Hôtel des Invalides**, the latter housing the impressive war museum and, appropriately enough, the **tomb of Napoleon**. Tucked away in the streets to the east, towards St-Germain, the **Musée Rodin** and **Musée Maillol** show off the two sculptors' works in the intimate surroundings of handsome private houses.

The Palais de Chaillot and Palais de Tokyo

The bastardized modernist-Classical **Palais de Chaillot**, built in 1937, has acquired a forlorn air in recent years, since the fire of 1996 and the decision to move almost all of its ethnographic collection across the river to Chirac's folly on quai Branly (see p.163). The anthropologically themed **Musée de l'Homme** still just about survives in the southern wing, along with the **Musée de la Marine** (daily except Tues 10am–6pm; €7), which traces French naval history using models of ships and their accoutrements. The northern wing of the palace is occupied by the Théâtre National de Chaillot, with a programme of popular theatre and contemporary dance. From early 2005, it will be joined by the **Cité de l'Architecture et du Patrimoine**, a combined institute, library and museum of architecture. The chief draws are likely to be the collection of giant-sized plaster casts taken from great French buildings, and the original architectural models of more modern constructions.

The **Palais de Tokyo**, contemporary with Chaillot, and nearby on avenue du Président-Wilson, has long housed the **Musée d'Art Moderne de la Ville de Paris** (Tues–Fri except public hols 10am–5.45pm, Sat & Sun 10am–6.45pm; free; M° Iéna/Alma-Marceau). Extensive renovation work has kept the museum shut throughout 2004, but when it reopens the building should once more do justice to the collection it houses – the architecture creating the perfect setting for the excellent early twentieth-century collection. Artists working in France – Braque, Chagall, Delaunay, Derain, Léger, Picasso and many others – are particularly well represented, usually by works with a Parisian theme, so while the collection can't rival the Beaubourg's for prestige, it makes for a particularly fascinating visit. The enormous, marvellous centrepieces are Matisse's *La Danse de Paris*; and Dufy's mural, *La Fée Électricité*, which was done for the electricity board and illustrates the story of electricity from Aristotle to the then-modern power station, in 250 lyrical, colourful panels filling three entire walls.

The artfully semi-derelict western wing of the palace has been taken over by the **Site de Création Contemporaine** (Tues–Sun noon–midnight; cost of entry depends on exhibitions), a cutting-edge gallery that takes over where the Pompidou centre leaves off by exhibiting bold new works by contemporary artists. A constant flow of exhibitions and events – anything from a show by Paris-born Louise Bourgeois to a temporary occupation by squatter-artists – keeps the atmosphere lively. Oddly the design of the trendy café's floor and the giant, Benetton-style, photo-portrait windows are the only permanent works of art in the collection. It's a site to keep an eye on – check out Ⓦwww.palaisdetokyo.com.

Just beyond the Palais de Tokyo, in place de l'Alma, a replica of the flame from the Statue of Liberty – given to France in 1987 as a symbol of Franco-American relations – has been adopted by mourners from all over the world as a memorial to **Princess Diana**, following her fatal car crash in the adjacent underpass. You can still see the odd bunch of flowers, or graffiti messages along the lines of "Mexico love you Diana".

The Eiffel Tower

It's hard to believe that the **Eiffel Tower**, the quintessential symbol both of Paris and of the brilliance of industrial engineering, was designed to be a temporary structure. Late-nineteenth-century Europe had a decadent taste for such giant-scale, colonialist-capitalist extravaganzas, but the 1889 Exposition – for which it was built – was particularly ambitious, and when completed the tower was the tallest building in the world, at 300m. Reactions were violent. Outraged critics protested "in the name of menaced French art and history" against this "useless and monstrous" tower. "Is Paris", they asked, "going to be associated with the grotesque, mercantile imaginings of a constructor of machines?"

Curiously, Paris's most famous landmark was only saved from demolition by the sudden need for "wireless telegraphy" aerials, in the first decade of the twentieth century. The tower's role in telecommunications – its only function apart from tourism – has become increasingly important, and the original crown is now masked by an efflorescence of antennae. Over the last century, the tower has needed few structural adjustments, but it has seen some surprising cosmetic changes: the original deep-red paint-scheme has been covered up with a sobre, dusty-chocolate brown since the late 1960s – at least Paris is spared the canary yellow that covered the tower for some of the 1890s. In the 1980s the tower was given a new system of illumination from within its superstructure, and for the millennium celebrations, a fireworks spectacular transformed it into a gargantuan space rocket, seemingly about to take off. A giant searchlight, added at the same time, still sweeps the skies from the top of the tower, making it look like some monstrous urban lighthouse, and after dusk thousands of effervescent lights fizz maniacally all over the structure for the first ten minutes of every hour – an effect well worth seeing from a distant vantage point.

Going up (daily: mid-June to Aug 9am–midnight; Sept to mid-June 9.30am–11pm) costs €10.40 for the top, €7.30 for the second level (or €3.50 by the stairs) and €4 for the first level. Note that access to the upward-bound lifts stops ninety minutes before closing time, and to the stairs at 6.30pm from September to mid-June. Paris looks surreally microscopic from the top, and the views are almost better from the second level, especially on hazier days, but there's something irresistible about taking the lift all the way.

Stretching back from the legs of the Eiffel Tower, the long rectangular gardens of the **Champs de Mars** lead to the eighteenth-century buildings of the **École Militaire**, originally founded in 1751 by Louis XV for the training of aristocratic army officers, and attended by Napoléon, among other fledgling leaders. The surrounding *quartier* may be expensive and sought after as an address, but it's mostly uninspiring to visit.

The riverside

A short distance upstream of the Eiffel Tower, on quai Branly, works are ongoing on a new museum to be called the **Musée du Quai Branly** (Ⓦwww.quaibranly.fr), which is expected to open in 2006. One of President Chirac's

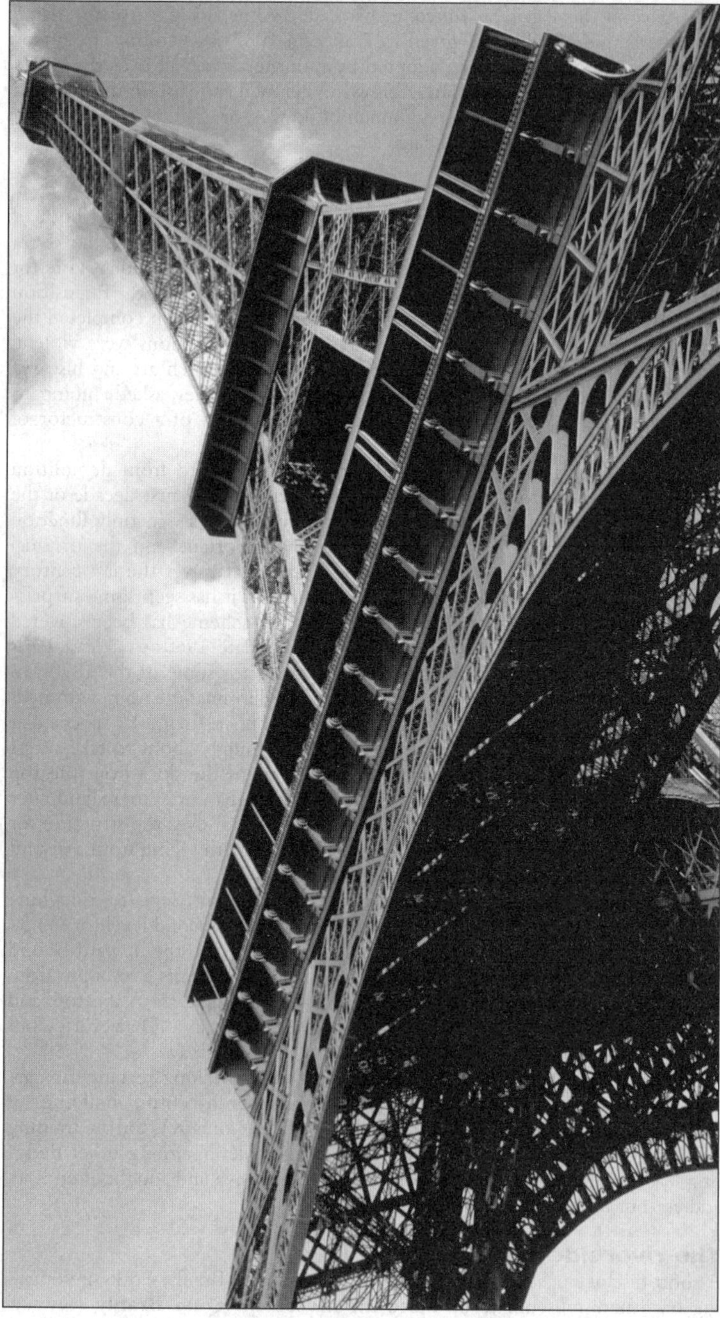

△ Eiffel tower

pet projects, it will bring together the Musée des Arts d'Afrique et d'Océanie and the ethnography department from the Musée de l'Homme on a theme of what is sometimes called Primitive Art. Architect Jean Nouvel's design is for a curving, futuristic edifice on stilts with a garden behind a giant glass curtain – just like his Cartier Fondation, in the 14e (see p.168).

Just beyond, opposite the Pont d'Alma on the northeast side of the busy junction of Place de la Résistance, is the entrance to the **sewers**, or *les égouts* (Mon–Wed, Sat & Sun: May–Sept 11am–5pm; Oct–April 11am–4pm; €3.80). Once you're underground it's dark, damp and noisy from the gushing water, though the main exhibition, which runs along a gantry walk poised above a main sewer, turns the history of the city's water supply and waste management into a surprisingly fascinating topic. Children, however, may be disappointed to find that it's not all that smelly.

A little further upstream still, the **American Church** on quai d'Orsay, together with the American College nearby at 31 av Bosquet, is a nodal point in the well-organized life of Paris's large American community. The notice-board is usually plastered with job and accommodation offers and demands. Immediately to the south lies a chi chi, villagey wedge of early nineteenth-century streets. This tiny neighbourhood, between rue St-Dominique and rue de Grenelle, is full of appealingly bijou shops, hotels and restaurants, with the lively market street of **rue Cler** at the centre of it all.

Les Invalides

The **Esplanade des Invalides**, striking due south from **Pont Alexandre III**, is a more attractive vista than the one from the Palais de Chaillot to the École Militaire. The resplendently gilded dome and heavy facade of the **Hôtel des Invalides**, built as a home for soldiers on the orders of Louis XIV, looms at the further end of the Esplanade. Under the dome are two churches, one for the soldiers, the other intended as a mausoleum for the king but now containing the mortal remains of Napoleon.

Les Invalides today houses the vast **Musée de l'Armée** (April–June daily except the first Mon of every month 10am–6pm; July–Sept daily 10am–6pm; Oct–March daily except the first Mon of every month 10am–5pm; €7 ticket also valid for the Église du Dôme and Musée des Plans-Reliefs), an enormous national war museum whose most interesting wing, reached via the south entrance beside the Église du Dôme, is devoted to Général de Gaulle and World War II. The battles, the resistance and the slow liberation are documented through imaginatively displayed war memorabilia combined with stirring reels of contemporary footage, most of which have an English-language option. Oddly, one leaves with the distinct impression that de Gaulle was personally responsible for the liberation of France. By comparison, the vast collection of armour, uniforms, weapons and Napoleonic relics that makes up the main part of the musuem, in the two wings on either side of the front court, is really for tin soldier fanatics or military history buffs only. Up under the roof of the east wing, the super-scale models of French ports and fortified cities in the **Musée des Plans-Reliefs** (same hours and ticket as Musée de l'Armée above), are crying out for a few miniature armies. Essentially giant three-dimensional maps, they were created to plan defences or plot potential artillery positions. With the eerie green glow of their landscapes only just illuminating the long, tunnel-like attic, the effect is rather chilling.

Both of the Invalides churches are cold and dreary inside. The **Église du Dôme** (same hours and ticket as Musée de l'Armée above; mid-June to mid-Sept open till 7pm), in particular, is a supreme example of the architectural pomposity of Louis XIV's day, with Corinthian columns and pilasters, and grandiose frescoes in abundance. **Napoleon** himself, or rather his ashes, lie in a hole in the floor in a cold, smooth sarcophagus of red porphyry, installed there on December 14, 1840. Freshly returned from St Helena, his remains were carried through the streets from the newly completed Arc de Triomphe to the Invalides. As many as half a million people came out to watch the emperor's last journey, and Victor Hugo commented that "it felt as if the whole of Paris had been poured to one side of the city, like liquid in a vase which has been tilted". Curiously, in 2002 a French historian asked for the ashes to be exhumed for DNA testing, claiming that Napoleon's remains had been swapped for those of his *maître d'hôtel* on St.Helena, one Jean-Baptiste Cipriani. There's some reason for suspicion, as the last round of tests – on a lock of the emperor's hair – suggested he had died of arsenic poisoning, not cancer, as the British claimed.

Musée Rodin and Musée Maillol

Immediately east of Les Invalides is the **Musée Rodin**, on the corner of rue de Varenne (Tues–Sun: April–Sept 9.30am–5.45pm, garden closes 6.45pm; Oct–March 9.30am–4.45pm, garden closes 5pm; €5, garden only €1; M° Varenne), elegantly presented in a beautiful eighteenth-century mansion which the sculptor leased from the state in return for the gift of all his work at his death. Major projects like *The Burghers of Calais*, *The Thinker*, *The Gate of Hell* and *Ugolini and Son* are exhibited in the garden – the latter forming the centrepiece of the ornamental pond. Indoors, which is usually very crowded, are well-loved works like *The Kiss* and *The Hand of God*. There's something particularly fascinating about works such as *Romeo and Juliet* and *The Centaur*, which seem only half-created and not totally liberated from the raw block of stone.

The rest of rue de Varenne and the parallel rue de Grenelle, is full of aristocratic mansions, including the **Hôtel Matignon**, the prime minister's residence. At 61 rue de Grenelle, a handsome eighteenth-century house has been turned into the **Musée Maillol** (daily except Tues 11am–6pm; €7; M° Rue-du-Bac), overstuffed with Aristide Maillol's endlessly buxom sculpted female nudes, copies of which can be seen to better effect in the Louvre's Jardin du Carrousel. His paintings follow a similar theme, and there are also minor works by contemporaries like Matisse, Dufy, Bonnard, Picasso, Degas, Gauguin and Kandinsky.

From here, **rue du Bac** leads south to rue de Sèvres, cutting across **rue de Babylone**, another of the *quartier*'s livelier streets, with the crazy, rich man's folly, **La Pagode**, at no. 57bis. The building was brought over from Japan at the turn of the century and long used as an arts cinema; it has been recently renovated, with a café in the Japanese garden inside.

Montparnasse and southern Paris

Montparnasse divides the lands of the well-heeled opinion-formers and powerbrokers of St-Germain and the 7e from the amorphous populations of the three southern arrondissements which have been subjected to large-scale developments, most notably along the riverfronts both east and west. Lively areas such as **rue du Commerce** in the 15e, **Pernety** in the 14e and the **Buttes-aux-Cailles** in the 13e are well worth a foray, and there are three great parks, **André Citroën**, **Georges-Brassens** and **Montsouris**.

Like other Left Bank *quartiers*, Montparnasse still trades on its association with the wild characters of the inter-war artistic and literary boom. Many were *habitués* of the cafés *Select*, *Coupole*, *Dôme*, *Rotonde* and *Closerie des Lilas*, all still going strong on **boulevard du Montparnasse**. Another major subcommunity in the *quartier* in the early years of the century consisted of outlawed Russian revolutionaries. There were so many that the Tsarist police ran a special Paris section to keep tabs on them. Trotsky lived in rue de la Gaîté near the cemetery – a fascinating street of old theatres and cafés – and Lenin lodged a little further south.

Around Montparnasse station

Most of the life of the quarter is concentrated between the junction with boulevard Raspail, where Rodin's *Balzac* broods over the traffic, and at the station end of boulevard du Montparnasse, where the colossal **Tour du Montparnasse** has become one of the city's principal, if unloved, landmarks. Although central Paris is more distant, the view from the top is better than the one from the Eiffel Tower in that it includes the Eiffel Tower, and it costs less to ascend (daily: April–Sept 9.30am–11pm; Oct–March Mon–Thurs & Sun 9.30am–10pm, Fri & Sat 9.30am–10.30pm; €8.20). Alternatively, you could sit down for an expensive drink in the 56th-storey bar, from where you get a tremendous view westwards.

One block northwest of the tower, on rue Antoine-Bourdelle, a garden of sculptures invites you into the **Musée Bourdelle** (Tues–Sun 10am–6pm; free), which has been built around the sculptor's atmospheric old studio. As Rodin's pupil and Giacometti's teacher, Bourdelle's bronze and stone works move from a naturalistic style – as in the wonderful series of Beethoven busts – towards a more geometric, Modernist style, seen in his best-known, monumental sculptures.

Montparnasse station was once the great arrival and departure point for travellers heading across the Atlantic, a connection commemorated in the extraordinary **Jardin Atlantique**, a sizeable park that the city planners have actually suspended on top of the train tracks. Hemmed in by cliff-like, high-rise apartment blocks, the park is a wonderful example of French design. There's a field of Atlantic-coast grasses, wave-like undulations in the lawns, a giant sun-dial and thermometer – which broke in the heatwave of 2003 when it exceeded its maximum – and a grid through which you can look down on the platforms below.

Montparnasse cemetery, the catacombs and the Observatoire

Just south of boulevard Edgar-Quinet (which has a good street market and cafés full of traders) is the main entrance to the **Montparnasse cemetery** (mid-March to Oct Mon–Fri 8am–6pm, Sat 8.30am–6pm, Sun 9am–6pm; Nov–March closes at 5.30pm), a gloomy city of the dead, with ranks of miniature temples, dreary and bizarre, and plenty of illustrious names, from Baudelaire to Beckett and Gainsbourg to Saint-Saëns. The joint grave of Jean-Paul Sartre and Simone de Beauvoir lies immediately right of the main entrance. In the southwest corner is an old windmill, one of the seventeenth-century taverns frequented by the carousing, versifying students who caused the district to be named after Mount Parnassus, the legendary home of the muses of poetry and song, and of Bacchus's drunken revels.

If you're determined to spend your time among the dear departed, you can also get down into the **catacombs** (Tues–Sun 10am–4pm; €5) in nearby **place Denfert-Rochereau**, formerly place d'Enfer (Hell Square) – though they are to be shut for structural works of an uncertain duration at some point during 2005. The catacombs are abandoned quarries stacked with millions of bones cleared from overstocked charnel houses and cemeteries between 1785 and 1871. Lining the passageway, the long thigh bones are stacked end-on, forming a wall to keep in the smaller bones, which can just be seen heaped higgledy-piggledy behind. These high femoral walls are further inset with skulls and plaques carrying macabre quotations such as "happy is he who always has the hour of his death in front of his eyes, and readies himself every day to die". Older children often love the whole experience, but there are a good couple of kilometres to walk, and it can quickly become claustrophobic in the extreme, and cold.

Rue Schoelcher and boulevard Raspail, on the east side of the cemetery, have some interesting examples of twentieth-century architecture, from Art Nouveau to contemporary facades of glass in the **Cartier Foundation** at 259 bd Raspail (Tues–Sun noon–8pm; €6.50). Built in 1994 by Jean Nouvel, architect of the Institut du Monde Arabe (see p.149), this presents all kinds of contemporary art – installations, videos, multimedia – in temporary exhibitions. About 500m to the northeast, on avenue de l'Observatoire, the classical **Observatoire de Paris** sat on France's zero meridian line from the 1660s, when it was constructed, until 1884. After that date, they reluctantly agreed that 0° longitude should pass through a small village in Normandy that happens to be due south of Greenwich. The Paris meridian line is visible in the garden behind on boulevard Arago.

The 15e arrondissement

The western edge of the 15e arrondissement fronts the Seine from the **Porte de Javel** to the Eiffel Tower. From Pont Mirabeau northwards, the river bank is marred by a sort of mini-Défense development of half-cocked futuristic towers with pretentious galactic names, rising out of a litter-blown pedestrian platform some 10m above street level. Far pleasanter riverside strolling is to be had on the narrow midstream island, the **Allée des Cygnes**, which you can reach from the Pont de Grenelle. A scaled-down version of the **Statue of Liberty** stands at the downstream end. South of Pont Mirabeau, between rue Balard and the river, is the city's newest park, the hyper-designed **Parc André-Citroën** (M° Balard), so named because the site used to be the Citroën motor works. Its best features are the glasshouses full of exotic-smelling shrubs, the fountain display, which on a hot day tempts park-goers to run through, and the tethered **balloon** (fine days only 9am–5pm; Mon–Fri €10, Sat & Sun €12), which offers eye-wateringly spectacular views.

It was in the **rue du Commerce**, running down the middle of the arrondissement from M° La Motte Piquet-Grenelle, that George Orwell worked as a dishwasher, an experience described in his *Down and Out in Paris and London*. These days it's a lively, old-fashioned high street full of small shops and peeling, shuttered houses. Towards the end of the street is place du Commerce, with a bandstand in the middle, a model of old-fashioned petit-bourgeois respectability.

The other park in the 15e, the **Parc Georges-Brassens**, lies in the southeast corner (M° Convention/Porte-de-Vanves). It's a delight, with a garden of scented herbs and shrubs (best in late spring) designed principally for blind and visually impaired visitors, puppets and rocks and merry-go-rounds for kids, a mountain stream with pine and birch trees, beehives and a tiny terraced vineyard. The corrugated pyramid with a helter-skelter-like spiral is the Silvia-Montfort theatre.

On the west side of the park, in a secluded garden in passage Dantzig, off rue Dantzig, stands an unusual polygonal building known as **La Ruche**. Home to

Fernand Léger, Modigliani, Chagall, Soutine and many other artists at the start of the century, it's still used by creative types. In the sheds of the old horse market between the park and rue Brançion, a **book market** is held every Saturday and Sunday morning.

The 14e below Montparnasse

The joky quasi-Classical Ricardo Bofill apartment complex around place de Catalogne gives way to a walkway along the old rue Vercingétorix and to the changing but still cosy atmosphere, long lived in by artists, of **Pernety**. Wandering around Cité Bauer, rue des Thermopyles and rue Didot reveals adorable houses, secluded courtyards and quiet mews, and on the corner of rue du Moulin Vert and rue Hippolyte-Maindron you'll find Giacometti's old ramshackle studio and home.

Rue d'Alésia, the main east–west route through the 14e, is best known for its good-value clothes shops, many selling discounted couturier creations. There are more artistic associations south of rue d'Alésia near the junction with avenue Réné-Coty: Dalí, Lurcat, Miller and Durrell lived in the tiny cobbled street of **Villa Seurat** off rue de la Tombe-Issoire; Lenin and his wife, Krupskaya, lodged across the street at 4 rue Marie-Rose; Le Corbusier built the studio at 53 av Reille, close to the secretive and verdant square du Montsouris which links with rue Nansouty; and Georges Braque's home was in the cul-de-sac now named after him off this street.

All these characters would have taken strolls in **Parc Montsouris** (RER Cité-Universitaire). Along with a lake and waterfall, its more surprising features include a meteorological office, a marker of the old meridian line, near boulevard Jourdan, and, by the southwest entrance, a kiosk run by the French Astronomy Association. The strange array of buildings across the boulevard from the park form the **Cité Universitaire**, home to several thousand students from over one hundred different countries.

The 13e arrondissement

The 13e is one of the most disparate areas of the city, with its eastern edge in the throes of mammoth development. **Place d'Italie**, with the ornate *mairie* and vast new Gaumont cinema, is the hub, with each of the major roads radiating out into very different *quartiers*.

Avenue des Gobelins, leading north, has the **Gobelins tapestry workshops** at no. 42, which have operated here for some four hundred years. Tapestries are still being made by the same painfully slow methods, but are now based on cartoons by contemporary painters (guided visits in French Tues–Thurs 2pm & 2.45pm; €8; M° Gobelins). Almost all of the dozen or so works completed each year are destined for French government offices, though an on-site museum is planned to open in 2005. Hidden away just to the north, visible from rue des Gobelins or the courtyard at 4 rue Gustave-Geffroy, is an exquisite fairytale octagonal tower and gateway, all that remains of the **Château de la Reine Blanche**, where the young Charles VI of France supposedly went mad after a riotous party.

Between boulevard Auguste-Blanqui and rue Bobillot is the Butte-aux-Cailles – named either after the quails who used to live on this hill or possibly just because of a local Monsieur Cailles. **Rue de la Butte-aux-Cailles** and its side streets have the fabric of pre-1960s Paris and still a spattering of trendy little bars, restaurants and shops. Over to the east, amongst all the 1960s high-rise, is what is known as the **Chinese quarter** of Paris. Avenues de Choisy and d'Ivry are full of Vietnamese, Chinese, Thai, Cambodian and Laotian restaurants and food shops, as is **Les Olympiades**, an extraordinary semi-derelict pedestrian area seemingly suspended between giant tower blocks.

Following rue Tolbiac or boulevard Vincent-Auriol to the river, you reach a vast building site which, French economy permitting, is to become an entirely new district called **Paris Rive Gauche**, stretching from the Gare d'Austerlitz to the *périphérique*. Its star attraction, which Mitterrand managed to inaugurate though not open just before his death, is the **Bibliothèque Nationale de France**. Accessible from its northern and southern corners (M° Quai-de-la-Gare or Bibliothèque François Mitterand), it has four enormous towers – intended to look like open books – framing a huge platform surrounding a sunken pine copse with glass walls that allow light to filter through to the underground library spaces. Architect Dominique Perrault's design attracted widespread derision after shutters had to be added to the towers to protect the books and manuscripts from sunlight. There are occasional small-scale exhibitions, and the reading rooms on the "haut-jardin" level are open to everyone over 16 (Tues–Sat 10am–8pm, Sun noon–7pm; €3 for a day pass; Ⓦwww.bnf.fr); the garden level is reserved for accredited researchers only.

The Beaux Quartiers and Bois de Boulogne

The **Beaux Quartiers** are the 16^e^ and 17^e^ arrondissements. The 16e is aristocratic and rich; and the 17e – or at least the southern part of it – middle-class and rich, both embodying the cautious values of the nineteenth-century manufacturing and trading classes. The northern half of the 16e, towards place Victor-Hugo and place de l'Étoile, is leafy and distinctly metropolitan in feel. The southern part, around the old villages of **Auteuil** and **Passy**, has an almost provincial character and is full of pleasant surprises for the walker. There are several interesting pieces of early twentieth-century architecture in the district, especially those by Hector Guimard (designer of the swirly green Art Nouveau métro stations) and by Le Corbusier and Mallet-Stevens, architects of the first Cubist buildings. Also in the area is the **Musée Marmottan** with its wonderful collection of late Monets, and, further to the northwest across the Seine, the Manhattan-style business district of **La Défense** and its enormous architectural marvel, the **Grande Arche**.

Auteuil

A good place to start an architectural exploration is the **Église-d'Auteuil** métro station, with several Guimard buildings in the vicinity: at 34 rue Boileau, 8 av de la Villa-de-la-Réunion, 41 rue Chardon-Lagache, 142 av de Versailles and 39 bd Exelmans. From the métro exit, **rue d'Auteuil**, with its lingering village high-street air, leads to **place Lorrain**, which has a Saturday market. There are more Guimard houses at the further end of rue La Fontaine, which begins here: no. 14, the "Castel Béranger" (1898), with its flower motifs and sinuous, curling lines, is perhaps the best in the city. On rue Poussin, just off the square, is the entrance to **Villa Montmorency**, a typical 16e *villa*, a sort of private village of leafy lanes and English-style gardens. Gide and the Goncourt brothers of *Prix Goncourt* fame lived in this one.

Behind it is rue du Dr-Blanche where, in a cul-de-sac on the right, are **Le Corbusier**'s first private houses (1923), looked after by the Fondation Le Corbusier. You can visit one of the houses, the **Villa Roche** (Tues–Fri 10am–12.30pm & 1.30–5/6pm; Mon 1.30–6pm; closed Aug; €2.40). Built in strictly Cubist style, very plain, with windows in bands, the only extravagance is the raising of one wing on piers and a curved frontage. The houses look commonplace enough now from the outside, but were a big contrast to anything that had gone before, and once you're inside, the spatial play still seems groundbreaking. Further along rue du Dr-Blanche, the tiny **rue Mallet-Stevens** was built entirely by Mallet-Stevens, also in Cubist style.

After taking a left at the northern end of rue du Dr-Blanche, then right on boulevard Beauséjour, use the shortcut immediately opposite rue du Ranelagh across the disused *Petite Ceinture* train line to reach avenue Raphaël, from where it's a pleasant walk along the shady trees of pretty green-lawned Jardin du Ranelagh to the **Musée Marmottan**, 2 rue Louis-Boilly (Tues–Sun 10am–6pm; €6.50; M° Muette), which showcases Impressionist works. Among its collection of Monet paintings, bequeathed by the artist's son, is the canvas entitled *Impression, Soleil Levant* (Impression, Sunrise), an 1872 rendering of a misty sunrise over Le Havre, whose title the critics usurped to give the Impressionist movement its name. There's a dazzling collection of canvases from Monet's last years at Giverny, including several *Nymphéas* (Water Lilies), *Le Pont Japonais*, *L'Allée des Rosiers* and *La Saule Pleureur*, where rich colours are laid on in thick, excited whorls and lines. To all intents and purposes, these are abstractions, much more "advanced" than the work of, say, Renoir, Monet's exact contemporary, some of whose paintings are also on display.

Passy

Passy, too, offers scope for a good meandering walk. From La Muette métro, head east along the old high street, **rue de Passy**, past an eye-catching parade of boutiques, until you reach **place de Passy** and the crowded but leisurely terrace of *Le Paris Passy* café. From the square, stroll southeast along cobbled, pedestrianized **rue de l'Annonciation**, a pleasant mixture of down-to-earth and well-heeled which gives more of the flavour of old Passy. You may not want your Bechstein repaired or your furniture lacquered, but as you approach the end of the street, past several food shops with delectable displays, there'll be no holding back the salivary glands. When you hit rue Raynouard, cross the road and veer to your right, where at no. 47 you'll discover a delightful, summery little house with pale-green shutters and a decorative iron entrance porch, tucked away down some steps amongst a tree-filled garden. Balzac moved here in the 1840s to outrun his creditors. In fact the deceptively tiny house extends down the hillside for three storeys, which made it easy for Balzac to slip out of the back door and into town unnoticed. The **Maison de Balzac** (Tues–Sun 10am–6pm; free) preserves the novelist's study, his writing desk and monogrammed cafetiere – fuelled by coffee, Balzac would write for sixteen hours at a stretch for weeks on end. He wrote some of his best-known works here, including *La Cousine Bette* and *Le Cousin Pons*.

Behind the house, and reached via some steps descending from rue Raynouard, **rue Berton** is a cobbled path with gas lights still in place, blocked off by the heavy security of the Turkish embassy. The building, an eighteenth-century château half hidden by greenery and screened by a high wall and guards, was once a clinic where the pioneering Dr Blanche tried to treat the mad Maupassant and Gérard de Nerval, amongst others. You can get a better view of the building by heading down avenue de Lamballe and then left into avenue du Général Mangin to cobbled **rue d'Ankara**. It's a short walk from here down to the river which is crossed at this point by the **Pont Bir Hakeim**, a bridge famously featured in *Last Tango in Paris*. You're well placed now to cross the bridge and head north along the water to the Eiffel Tower about 500m along.

Bois de Boulogne

The **Bois de Boulogne**, running all down the west side of the 16^e^, is supposedly modelled on London's Hyde Park, though it's a very French interpretation. It offers all sorts of facilities: the **Jardin d'Acclimatation**, with lots of attractions for kids (see p.210); the **Parc de Bagatelle** (M° Port-de-Neuilly, then bus #43, or M° Porte-Maillot, then bus #244), which features beautiful displays of tulips, hyacinths and daffodils in the first half of April, irises in May, water lilies and roses at the end of June; a riding school; **bike rental** (you'll need your passport) at the entrance to the Jardin d'Acclimatation; **boating** on the Lac Inférieur; and **race courses** at Longchamp and Auteuil. The best, and wildest, part for walking is towards the southwest corner.

When it was opened to the public in the eighteenth century, people said of it *Les mariages du bois de Boulogne ne se font pas devant Monsieur le Curé* ("Unions cemented in the Bois de Boulogne do not take place in the presence of a priest"). Despite a more obvious police presence, the park is not a safe place for an evening stroll, as the sex trade practised within is accompanied by a fair amount of crime, rendering it somewhat seedy and potentially dangerous.

If you have any interest in the beautiful and highly specialized skills, techniques and artefacts developed in the centuries that preceded industrialization and mass production, you should visit the fascinating **Musée National des Arts et Traditions Populaires**, 6 av du Mahatma Gandhi, Bois de Boulogne (daily except Tues 9.30am–5pm; €4; M° Les Sablons/Porte-Maillot), beside the main entrance to the Jardin d'Acclimatation. Boat-building, shepherding, farming, weaving, blacksmithing, pottery, stone-cutting, games and clairvoyance are all beautifully illustrated and displayed.

La Défense

La Défense (M°/RER Grande-Arche-de-la-Défense) has been elevated to one of the top places of pilgrimage for visitors to Paris by the **Grande Arche**, an astounding 112-metre hollow cube clad in white marble, standing 6km out from the Arc de Triomphe at the far end of the Voie Triomphale, from which it stands at a slight angle. Suspended within its hollow – which could enclose Notre-Dame with ease – are open lift shafts and a "cloud" canopy. You can take a lift up to the roof (daily 10am–7pm; €7) and, on a clear day, scan to the Louvre and beyond, though the view from the bottom of the arch is nearly as good.

Between the Grande Arche and the river is the **business complex** of La Défense, a perfect monument to late-twentieth-century capitalism. There is no formal pattern to the arrangements of towers. Token apartment blocks, offices of ELF, Gan, Total, banks and other businesses compete for size and dazzle of surface. Bizarre **artworks** bring some light relief, like **Joan Mirò**'s giant wobbly creatures despairing at their misfit status beneath the biting edges and curveless heights of the buildings and **Alexander Calder**'s red-iron offering, a *stabile* rather than a mobile. A statue commemorating the defence of Paris in 1870 (after which the district is named) perches on a concrete plinth in front of a coloured plastic waterfall and fountain pool, while nearer the river disembodied people clutch each other round endlessly repeated concrete flower beds. You'll find details of all the sculptures in the **Art Défense** exhibition space beside the waterfall. To the left of the Grand Arche as you face it is the **Dôme-Imax**, a 180° projection cinema (temporarily closed for renovation), and the enormous Quatre-Temps shopping centre. A good way to approach the Grande Arche, see the sculptures and watch the main attraction loom is to get out of the métro a stop before at Esplanade-de-la-Défense.

Montmartre and northern Paris

Montmartre lies in the middle of the largely petit-bourgeois and working-class 18e arrondissement, respectable round the slopes of the Butte, distinctly less so towards the **Gare du Nord** and **Gare de l'Est**, where depressing slums crowd along the train tracks. The Butte itself has a relaxed, sunny, countrified air; **Pigalle**, at the foot of the hill, is full of sex shops and peep-shows, interspersed with tired-looking women in shop doorways. On its northern edge lies the extensive **St-Ouen flea market**.

Place des Abbesses and up to the Butte

In spite of being one of the city's chief tourist attractions, the **Butte Montmartre** manages to retain the quiet, almost secretive, air of its rural origins. The most popular access route is via the rue de Steinkerque and the steps below the Sacré-Coeur (the funicular railway from place Suzanne-Valadon is covered by the Carte Orange, see box, p.112). For a quieter approach, go up via place des Abbesses or rue Lepic.

Place des Abbesses is postcard-pretty, with one of the few complete surviving Guimard métro entrances. To the east, at the Chapelle des Auxiliatrices in rue Yvonne-Le-Tac, Ignatius Loyola founded the Jesuit movement in 1534. It's also supposed to be the place where St Denis, the first bishop of Paris, had his head chopped off by the Romans around 250 AD. He is said to have carried it until he dropped, where the cathedral of St-Denis now stands north of the city.

Continuing from place des Abbesses to the top of the Butte, two quiet and attractive routes are up rue de la Vieuville and the stairs in rue Drevet to the minuscule **place du Calvaire**, with a lovely view back over the city, or up rue Tholozé, then right below the **Moulin de la Galette** – the last survivor of Montmartre's forty-odd windmills, immortalized by Renoir – into rue des Norvins.

Artistic associations abound hereabouts. Zola, Berlioz, Turgenev, Seurat, Degas and Van Gogh lived in the area. Picasso, Braque and Juan Gris invented Cubism in an old piano factory in place Émile-Goudeau, known as the **Bateau-Lavoir**, still serving as artists' studios, though the original building burnt down years ago. And Toulouse-Lautrec's inspiration, the **Moulin Rouge**, survives also, albeit a mere shadow of its former self, on the corner of boulevard de Clichy and place Blanche (see p.199).

The **Musée de Montmartre**, at 12 rue Cortot (Tues–Sun 11am–6pm; €4.50), just over the brow of the hill, tries to recapture something of the feel of those pioneering days, but it's a bit of a disappointment, except for the occasional temporary exhibition. The house itself, rented at various times by Renoir, Dufy, Suzanne Valadon and her alcoholic son Utrillo, is worth visiting for the view over the neat terraces of the tiny **Montmartre vineyard** and the north side of the Butte. The entrance to the vineyard is on the steep rue de Saules.

Place du Tertre and Sacré-Coeur

The **place du Tertre** is the heart of Montmartre, photogenic but totally bogus, jammed with tourists, overpriced restaurants and "artists" knocking up garish paintings practically with their eyes shut. Between place du Tertre and the Sacré-Coeur, the old church of **St-Pierre** is all that remains of the Benedictine abbey that occupied the Butte Montmartre from the twelfth century on. Though much altered, it still retains its Romanesque and early

Gothic feel. In it are four ancient columns, two by the door, two in the choir, leftovers from a Roman shrine that stood on the hill – *mons mercurii* (Mercury's Hill), the Romans called it. Crowning the Butte is the **Sacré-Cœur** (daily 6am–10.30pm), a romantic and graceful pastiche, whose white pimply domes are an essential part of the Paris skyline. The best thing about it is the view from the **tower** (daily 9am–6.30pm; €5), almost as high as the Eiffel Tower and showing the layout of the whole city. Construction was started in the 1870s on the initiative of the Catholic Church to atone for the "crimes" of the Commune. **Square Willette**, the space at the foot of the monumental staircase, is named after the local artist who turned out on inauguration day to shout "Long live the devil!"

Montmartre cemetery

West of the Butte, near the beginning of rue Caulaincourt in place Clichy, lies the **Montmartre cemetery** (mid-March to Oct Mon–Fri 8am–6pm, Sat 8.30am–6pm, Sun 9am–6pm; Nov to mid-March closes 5.30pm; free). Ramshackle and peeling, on a tiny courtyard full of plants, it epitomizes the kind-hearted, instinctively arty, sepia-tinged Paris that every romantic visitor secretly cherishes. The cemetery is tucked down below street level in the hollow of an old quarry with its entrance on avenue Rachel under rue Caulaincourt. A tangle of trees and funereal pomposity, it holds the graves of Zola, Stendhal, Berlioz, Degas, Feydeau, Offenbach and Truffaut, among others.

St-Ouen flea market

Officially open Saturday to Monday 9am to 7pm – unofficially, from 5am – the **puces de St-Ouen** (M° Porte-de-Clignancourt) claims to be the largest flea market in the world, the name "flea" deriving from the state of the secondhand mattresses, clothes and other junk sold here when the market first operated outside the city walls. Nowadays it's predominantly a proper – and expensive – antiques market (mainly furniture, but including old café-bar counters, telephones, traffic lights, posters, jukeboxes and petrol pumps), with what is left of the rag-and-bone element confined to the further reaches of rues Fabre and Lécuyer.

Pigalle

From place Clichy in the west to Barbès-Rochechouart in the east, the hill of Montmartre is underlined by the sleazy **boulevards of Clichy and Rochechouart**, the centre of the roadway often occupied by bumper-cars and other funfair sideshows. At the Barbès end of boulevard Rochechouart, where the métro clatters by on iron trestles, the crowds teem round the Tati department stores, the city's cheapest, while the pavements are lined with West and North African street vendors offering fabrics, watches and trinkets. At the place Clichy end, tour buses from all over Europe feed their contents into massive hotels. In the middle, between place Blanche and place Pigalle, sex shows, sex shops, tiny bars where hostesses lurk in complicated tackle, and street prostitutes (both male and female) coexist with one of Paris's most elegant private *villas* on avenue Frochot. In the adjacent streets are the city's best specialist music shops.

Perfectly placed amongst all the sex shops and shows is the **Musée de l'Erotisme** (daily 10am–2am; €7), which explores different cultures' approaches to sex. The ground floor and first floor are dedicated to sacred and ethnographic art, displaying proud phalluses and well-practised positions from Asia, Africa and pre-Colombian Latin America, plus a few more satirical European pieces. The rest of the floors upstairs are devoted to temporary exhibitions.

The Goutte d'Or

Along the north side of boulevard de la Chapelle, between boulevard Barbès and the Gare du Nord rail lines, stretches the poetically named quarter of the **Goutte d'Or** ("Drop of Gold"), a name that derives from the medieval vineyard that occupied this site. It has gradually become an immigrant ghetto since World War I, when large numbers of North Africans were first imported to replenish the ranks of Frenchmen dying in the trenches. It's currently in the throes of redevelopment, but old men still talk for hours over tea in the numerous tiny cafés, restaurants serve Tunisian delicacies for next to nothing, tiny shops sell snazzy cloth and jewellery and Raï music resonates from the upper balconies. Much of rue de la Goutte d'Or itself is new, but remains, with its tributary lanes, distinctly North African and poor. On Wednesday and Saturday the **boulevard de la Chapelle market** attracts large crowds.

Canal St-Martin and La Villette

The **Bassin de la Villette** and the **canals** at the northeastern gate of the city were for generations the centre of a densely populated working-class district. Most of the jobs were in the La Villette abattoirs and meat market or the related industries that spread around the waterways. The amusements were skating or swimming, betting on cockfights or eating at the numerous restaurants famed for their fresh meat. The abattoirs and meat market are gone, having been replaced by the huge complex of La Villette, a postmodernist park of science and technology.

The whole Villette complex stands at the junction of the **Ourcq** and **St-Denis canals**. The first was built by Napoleon to bring fresh water into the city; the second is an extension of the Canal St-Martin built as a short cut to the great western loop of the Seine around Paris. The canals have undergone extensive renovation recently, and the derelict sections of the *quais* are being made more appealing to cyclists, rollerbladers and pedestrians.

Canal St-Martin and place de Stalingrad

The **Canal St-Martin** runs underground at the Bastille to surface again in boulevard Jules-Ferry by rue du Faubourg-du-Temple. The canal still has a slightly industrial feel, especially along its upper stretch. The lower part is more attractive, with plane trees, cobbled *quais* and elegant, high-arched footbridges. In the last decade or so the area has been colonized by the new arty and media intelligentsia, and the bars, cafés and boutiques fronting the canal and in the surrounding streets have an alternative, bohemian feel. The area is particularly lively on Sunday afternoons when the *quais* are closed to traffic, and pedestrians, cyclists and rollerbladers take over the streets, and students hang out along the canal's edge, nursing beers or softly strumming guitars. Inevitably, having acquired a certain cachet, the district has attracted property developers, and bland apartment blocks have elbowed in among the traditional, solid, mid-nineteenth-century residences. One of these older buildings is the **Hôtel du Nord** of Marcel Carné's film, at 102 quai de Jemappes, now a popular bar.

The canal disappears underground again further north at **place de Stalingrad**. To one side of the square stands the beautifully restored Rotonde de la Villette, one of Ledoux's tollhouses in Louis XVI's tax wall, where taxes were levied on all goods coming into the city – a major bone of contention in the lead-up to the 1789 Revolution.

Beyond the square is the renovated **Bassin de la Villette** dock, popular for Sunday strolls, fishing and canoeing. Recobbled, and with its dockside buildings converted into offices for canal boat trips, and a cinema (the MK2) with an attached waterfront brasserie, the Bassin has lost all vestiges of its former status as France's premier port. At rue de Crimée a unique hydraulic bridge marks the end of the dock and the beginning of the Canal de l'Ourcq. If you keep to the south bank on quai de la Marne, you can cross directly into the Parc de la Villette.

The Parc de la Villette

The **Parc de la Villette** (daily 6am–1am; free; Ⓦwww.villette.com) music, art and science complex, between avenues Corentin-Cariou and Jean-Jaurès, has so many disparate and disconnected elements, and such a clash of architectural styles, that it's hard to know where to start. To help you get your bearings, there's an **information centre** at the entrance by M° Porte-de-Pantin, to the south; all the different films and exhibitions are detailed in *Pariscope.*

The main attraction has to be the enormous **Cité des Sciences et de l'Industrie** (Tues–Sat 10am–6pm, Sun 10am–7pm; €7.50; Ⓦwww.cite-sciences.fr; M° Porte-de-la-Villette). This high-tech museum devoted to science and all its applications is built into the concrete hulk of the abandoned abattoirs on the north side of the Canal de l'Ourcq. Four times the size of the Pompidou Centre, it's a colossal place; its giant glass walls hang beneath a dark-blue lattice of steel, with white rod walkways accelerating out towards the Géode (see below) across a moat. Inside are crow's-nests and cantilevered platforms, bridges and suspended walkways, the different levels linked by lifts and escalators around a huge central space open to the full 40-metre height of the roof. The permanent exhibition, called **Explora**, covers different subjects ranging from robotics, language and behaviour to energy, ecology and medicine. As the name suggests, the emphasis is on exploring, encouraged through interactive computers, videos, holograms, animated models and games. In *Expressions et comportements* you can intervene in stories acted out on videos, changing the behaviour of the characters to engineer a different outcome. Hydroponic plants grow for real in a green bridge across the central space. Elsewhere, you can steer robots through mazes, make music by your own movements, experiment with motion in an "inertia carousel", watch computer-guided puppet shows and see holograms of different periods' visions of the universe.

When all this interrogation and stimulation becomes too much, you can relax in cafés within Explora, before joining the queue for the **planetarium** (€2.50). Back on the ground floor there's the **Louis-Lumière Cinema**, which shows 3-D films (included in Cité des Sciences et de l'Industrie ticket), and the **Cité des Enfants** for children and teenagers (see p.210), as well as a whole programme of excellent **temporary exhibitions**. Below ground is the multimedia library, the **médiathèque** (Tues–Sun noon–6.30pm, till 7.45 on Wed; free), **restaurants** and an **aquarium** (free).

In front of the complex floats the **Géode** (hourly shows Tues–Sat 10.30am–9pm, Sun 10.30am–7pm; €8.75), a bubble of reflecting steel that looks as though it's been dropped from an intergalactic boules game into a pool of water. Inside is a screen for Omnimax 180° films, not noted for their plots, but a great visual experience. There's also the **Cinaxe**, between the Cité and the Canal St-Denis (screenings every 15min Tues–Sun 11am–5pm; €5.40, or

€4.80 with Explora ticket), combining 70mm film shot at thirty frames a second with seats that move. Beside the Géode is a real 1957 French **submarine**, the **Argonaute** (Tues–Fri 10.30am–5.30pm, Sat & Sun 11am–6pm; €3), and towards the bridge over the Canal de l'Ourcq, a **dragon slide**. South of the canal are bizarrely landscaped **themed gardens** of "mirrors", "mists", "winds and dunes" and "islands", and over to the east is the **Zénith** inflatable rock music venue. To the south, the largest of the old **market halls** – an iron-frame structure designed by Baltard, the engineer of the vanished Les Halles pavilions – is now a vast and brilliant exhibition space, the **Grande Salle**.

South of the Grande Salle stands the **Cité de la Musique**, in two complexes to either side of the Porte-de-Pantin entrance. To the west is the national music academy; while to the east are a concert hall, the very chic *Café de la Musique*, a music and dance information centre and the excellent **Musée de la Musique** (Tues–Sat noon–6pm, Sun 10am–6pm; €6.50), presenting the history of music from the end of the Renaissance to the present day, both visually – a collection of 4500 instruments – and aurally, with headsets and interactive displays. The buildings' abstract designs are meant to evoke their function; the academy's windows are arranged in sequence like musical notation and the wavy roof, according to its architect Christian de Portzamparc, is like Gregorian chant, but could equally suggest the movement of a dancer or a conductor's baton.

Belleville, Ménilmontant and Père-Lachaise

Traditionally working class, with a history of radical and revolutionary activity, the gritty **eastern districts** of Paris, particularly the old villages of **Belleville** and **Ménilmontant**, are nowadays some of the most diverse and vibrant parts of the city, home to sizeable ethnic populations, as well as students and impoverished artists, attracted by the low rents. The main visitor attraction in the area is the **Père-Lachaise cemetery**, final resting place of many well-known artists and writers. Visiting the modern **Parc de Belleville** and the fairytale-like **Parc des Buttes-Chaumont** will reveal the area's other main asset – wonderful views of the city below.

Parc des Buttes-Chaumont

At the northern end of the Belleville heights, a short walk from La Villette, is the **parc des Buttes-Chaumont** (M° Buttes-Chaumont/Botzaris), constructed by Haussmann in the 1860s to camouflage what until then had been a desolate warren of disused quarries and miserable shacks. Out of this rather unlikely setting a wonderfully romantic park was created – there'a a grotto with a cascade and artificial stalactites, and a picturesque lake from which a huge rock rises up topped with a delicate Corinthian temple. From the temple you get fine views of Sacré-Coeur and beyond. The park stays open all night and, equally rarely for Paris, you're not cautioned off the grass.

Belleville and Ménilmontant

The route from Buttes-Chaumont to Père-Lachaise will take you through the one-time villages of **Belleville** and **Ménilmontant**. Many of the old village lanes disappeared in the tower-block mania of the 1960s and 1970s, but others have now been opened up, and many of the newest buildings are imaginative infill, following the height and curves of their older neighbours. Dozens of cobbled and gardened *villas* remain intact: east of Buttes-Chaumont towards place Rhin-et-Danube, between rue Boyer (with a 1920s

Soviet-style building at no. 25) and rue des Pyrénées just north of Père-Lachaise, and out to the east by Porte de Bagnolet, up the very picturesque steps from place Octave-Chanute.

The first main street you cross coming down from Buttes-Chaumont, **rue de Belleville**, is the Chinatown of Paris. Vietnamese and Chinese shops and restaurants have proliferated over the years, adding considerable visual and gastronomic cheer to the area. African and oriental fruits, spices, music and fabrics can be bought at the **boulevard de Belleville market** on Tuesdays and Fridays. On the steps of no. 72 rue de Belleville, Édith Piaf was abandoned when just a few hours old, and there's a small **museum** dedicated to her at 5 rue Créspin-du-Gast (Mon–Thurs 1–6pm; closed Sept; by appointment on ⓣ01.43.55.52.72; donation; M° Ménilmontant/St-Maur). Rue Ramponneau, just southeast of the crossroads with boulevard de Belleville and now entirely rebuilt, was where the last Communard on the last barricade held out alone for a final fifteen minutes.

You get fantastic views down onto the city centre from the higher reaches of Belleville and Ménilmontant: the best place to watch the sun set is the **Parc de Belleville** (M° Couronnes/Pyrénées), which descends in a series of terraces and waterfalls from rue Piat. And from **rue de Ménilmontant**, by rues de l'Ermitage and Boyer, you can look straight down to the Pompidou Centre. Over the past few years, large numbers of students and artists have moved into rue de Ménilmontant and its extension **rue Oberkampf** – the latter in particular has undergone quite a transformation as a result, with an explosion of trend-setting bars and cafés jostling for space alongside the ethnic bakeries, cheap goods stores and grocers.

Père-Lachaise cemetery

Père-Lachaise cemetery (Mon–Fri 8am–5.30pm, Sat 8.30am–5.30pm, Sun 9am–5.30pm; M° Gambetta/Père-Lachaise/Alexandre-Dumas/Phillipe-Auguste), final resting place of numerous notables, is an atmospheric, eerily beautiful haven, with little cobbled footpaths, terraced slopes and magnificent old trees which spread their branches over the tombs as though shading them from the outside world. The cemetery was opened in 1804, after an urgent stop had been put to further burials in the overflowing city cemeteries and churchyards, and to be interred in Père-Lachaise quickly became the ultimate symbol of riches and success. A free **map** of the cemetery is available at all the entrances or you can buy a more detailed one for €2 at nearby newsagents and florists.

Swarms of admirers flock to the now-sanitized tomb of ex-Doors lead singer Jim Morrison (division 6), cleansed of all its graffiti and watched over by a security guard. Colette's tomb (division 4), close to the main Ménilmontant entrance, is very plain though always covered in flowers. The same is true of the tombs of Sarah Bernhardt (division 44) and the great chanteuse Édith Piaf (division 97). Marcel Proust lies in his family's simple, black-marble tomb (division 85). Corot (division 24) and Balzac (division 48) both have superb busts, Balzac looking particularly satisfied with his life. Géricault reclines on cushions of stone (division 12), paint palette in hand; Chopin (division 11) has a willowy muse weeping for his loss. One of the most impressive of the individual tombs and covered in lipstick kisses is that of Oscar Wilde (division 89), adorned with a strange pharaonic winged messenger (sadly robbed almost immediately of its prominent penis by a scandalized cemetery employee, who, so the story goes, used it as a paperweight), sculpted by Jacob Epstein, and inscribed with a grim verse from *The Ballad of Reading Gaol*. Nearby, in division 96, is the grave of

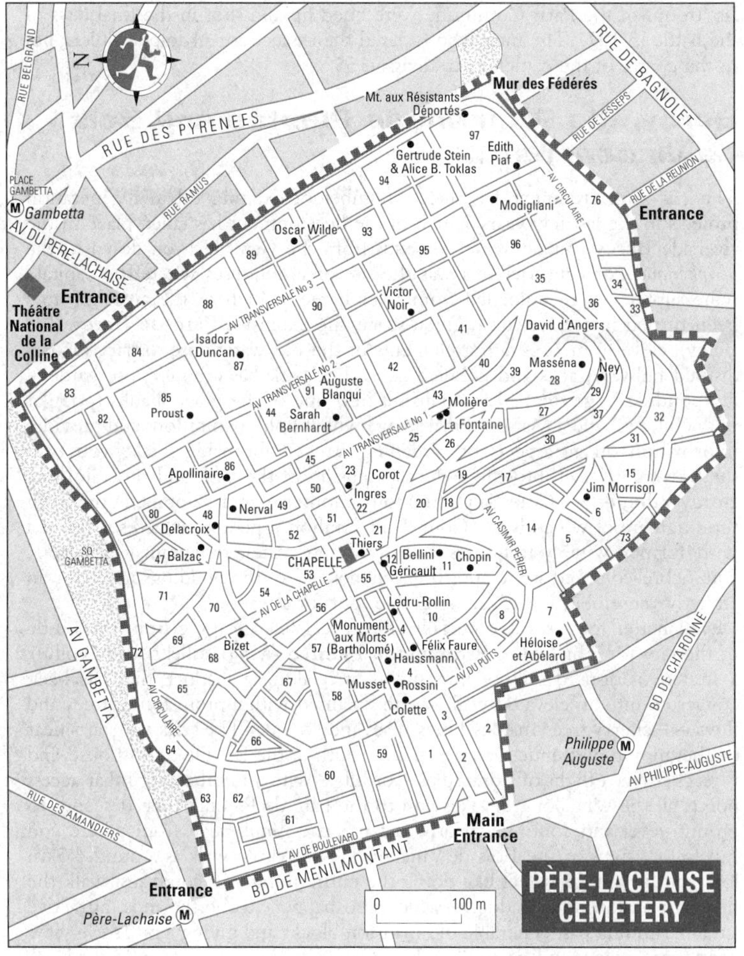

Modigliani and his lover Jeanne Herbuterne, who killed herself in crazed grief a few days after the artist died in agony from meningitis. Some non-celebrities also attract attention: in division 92, nineteenth-century journalist Victor Noir – shot for daring to criticize a relative of Napoléon III – lies flat on his back, fully clothed, a prominent part of his anatomy worn shiny by infertile women hoping to increase their chances of conceiving.

Changing a sunny outing to Père-Lachaise into a much more sombre experience are the memorials in division 97 to those who died in the Nazi concentration camps, to executed Resistance fighters and to those who were never accounted for in the genocide of the last World War. The sculptures are relentless in their images of inhumanity, of people forced to collaborate in their own degradation and death. Another sober monument, and a place of pilgrimage for the French Left, is the *Mur des Fedérés* (division 76), the wall where the last troops of the Paris Commune were lined up and shot in the final days of the battle in 1871. The man who ordered their execution, Adolphe Thiers, lies in the centre of the cemetery in division 55.

Bercy, the Promenade Plantée and Bois de Vincennes

The 12e arrondissement has seen a number of exciting urban regeneration projects in the last few years. Much of the development has taken place in the riverside **Bercy** *quartier*, which extends from the Gare de Lyon down to the *périphérique*. For centuries this was the site of warehouses where the capital's wine supplies were unloaded from river barges. Much of the area has now been turned into a welcome green space, the extensive **Parc de Bercy** (M° Bercy), cleverly incorporating elements of the old warehouse district such as disused railway tracks and cobbled lanes. The park has arbours, rose gardens, lily ponds, a huge stepped fountain set into one of the grassy banks (popular with children) and a Maison du Jardinage which holds exhibitions and provides information on all aspects of gardening. Arched footbridges take you over the busy rue Kessel into the eastern extension of the park and the adjoining **Bercy Village** (M° Cour Saint-Émilion), another new development, the main thoroughfare of which is the Cour Saint Émilion, a pedestrianized street lined with former wine warehouses converted into cafés, restaurants and shops. The ochre-coloured stone and the homogeneity of the buildings make for an attractive ensemble and it's an agreeable spot for a wander.

Even better for a stroll, especially if you feel like escaping from the bustle of the city for a bit, is the **Promenade Plantée** (M° Bastille/Ledru-Rollin), a stretch of disused railway line, much of it along a viaduct, that has been converted into an elevated walkway and planted with a profusion of trees and flowers – cherry trees, maples, limes, roses and lavender. The walkway starts near the beginning of avenue Daumesnil, just south of the Bastille opera house, and is reached via a flight of stone steps – or lifts – with a number of similar access points all the way along. It takes you to the Parc de Reuilly, then descends to ground level and continues nearly as far as the *périphérique*, from where you can follow signs to the Bois de Vincennes. The whole walk is around 4.5km long, but if you don't feel like doing the entire thing you could just walk the first part – along the viaduct – which also happens to be the most attractive stretch, running past venerable old mansion blocks and giving a bird's eye view of the area below and of small architectural details not seen from street level. What's more, the arches of the viaduct itself have been ingeniously converted into spaces for artisans' *ateliers* and craftshops, collectively known as the **Viaduc des Arts**. There are 51 of them, including furniture restorers, interior designers, cabinet makers and fashion and jewellery boutiques; a full list and map is available from no. 23 avenue Daumesnil.

The Bois de Vincennes

The **Bois de Vincennes** is the city's only extensive green space besides the Bois de Boulogne. You can spend an afternoon boating on Lac Daumesnil (by the zoo) or rent a bike from the same place and feed the ducks on Lac des Minimes on the other side of the wood (bus #112 from Vincennes métro). As far as real woods go, the forest itself opens out once you're east of avenue de St-Maurice. To the north is the **Parc Floral** (daily: summer 9.30am–8pm; winter 9.30am–dusk; €1.50; bus #112 or short walk from M° Château-de-Vincennes), arguably the best garden in Paris. Flowers are always in bloom in the

Jardin des Quatres Saisons; you can picnic beneath pines, then wander through concentrations of camellias, cacti, ferns, irises and bonsai trees. Abutting the Parc Floral is the **Cartoucherie de Vincennes**, an old ammunitions factory, now home to four theatre companies, including the radical Théâtre du Soleil.

On the northern edge of the *bois*, the **Château de Vincennes** (daily 10am–5/6pm; choice of two guided visits, €4 or €5.50; M° Château-de-Vincennes), royal medieval residence, then state prison, porcelain factory, weapons dump and military training school, is still undergoing restoration work started by Napoléon III. The best of the tours available is that to the flamboyant Gothic **Chapelle Royale**, completed in the mid-sixteenth century and decorated with superb Renaissance stained-glass windows around the choir.

Eating and drinking

Eating and drinking are among the chief delights of Paris, as they are in France as a whole. Many restaurants remain defiantly traditional, offering the classic *cuisine bourgeoise* based on well-sauced meat dishes, but you can find a tremendous variety of foods, from Senegalese to Vietnamese, and from eastern European to North African. Regional French cuisines, notably from the southwest, are always popular, as is inventive, contemporary French gastronomy. There is a huge diversity of places to eat: luxurious **restaurants** beautifully decked with crystal and white linen; noisy, elbow-to-elbow bench-and-trestle-table joints; splendid **brasseries** and artfully distressed **cafés**. Drinking venues

△ Café scene

Student restaurants

Students of any age – with an ISIC card – are eligible to apply for meal tickets for the university restaurants under the direction of CROUS de Paris. A list of addresses, which includes cafeterias and restaurants, is available from their website ⓦwww.crous-paris.fr. The tickets, which cost €4.50, have to be obtained from the particular restaurant of your choice (opening hours generally 11.30am–2pm & 6–8pm). Not all serve both midday and evening meals, and most are closed on the weekend and only operate during term time; the chief exception is Bullier, 39 av Georges-Bernanos, 5e (M° Port-Royal), which is open every day, including during vacations. Though the food is not wonderful, it's certainly filling, and you can't complain about the price.

The most conveniently located student restaurants are all in the 5e and 6e arrondissements: *Assas*, 92 rue d'Assas, 6e (RER Port-Royal/M° Notre-Dame-des-Champs; Mon–Fri lunch only); *Bullier*, 39 av Georges-Bernanos, 5e (M° Port-Royal); *Censier*, 31 rue Geoffroy-Saint-Hilaire, 5e (M° Censier-Daubenton; Mon–Fri lunch only); *Châtelet*, 10 rue Jean-Calvin, 5e (M° Censier-Daubenton; closed Sat & Sun); *Cuvier-Jussieu*, 8bis rue Cuvier, 5e (M° Jussieu; Mon–Fri lunch only); *Mabillon*, 3 rue Mabillon, 6e (M° Mabillon); *Mazet*, rue André Mazet, 6e (M° Odéon; lunch only).

range from the many **cafés** that move seamlessly from coffees to cocktails as evening approaches, to the tiny, dedicated **wine bars** offering little-known vintages from every region of France. Then there are cavernous **beer cellars**, designer **bars** with DJ *soirées* at weekends, and the ubiquitous Irish/British/Canadian **pubs**. You can take coffee and cakes in a chintzy **salon de thé**, in a bookshop or gallery, or even in the courtyard of a mosque. **Gay** establishments proliferate in the Marais and around the Bastille *quartier* (see "Gay and lesbian Paris").

Quality varies and it goes without saying that restaurants in the tourist hotspots are usually best avoided, but elsewhere you'll be spoilt for choice. You may not find so many of the old-fashioned inexpensive neighbourhood cafés and bistros around these days, but it's still easy to eat on a modest budget. Many places offer a fixed-price menu of two or three courses, called a menu, or sometimes a *formule* at lunchtime, and these often represent the least expensive way to eat. You can find lots of choice for as little as €10–15 at lunchtime. In the evening, expect to pay €15–20 at the lower end, though typical prices are in the €20–30 range. Above that you should be getting some gourmet satisfaction.

The big boulevard cafés and brasseries are always more expensive than those a little further removed, and addresses in the smarter or more touristy arrondissements set prices soaring. A snack or drink on the Champs-Élysées, place St-Germain-des-Prés or rue de Rivoli, for instance, will be double or triple the price of one in Belleville, Batignolles or the southern 14e. Many bars have happy hours, but prices can double after 10pm, and any clearly trendy, glitzy or stylish place is bound to be expensive.

The different **eating** and **drinking establishments** are listed here by arrondissement. They are divided into restaurants, including brasseries and bistros, and bars and cafés, a term used to incorporate anywhere you might go for a drink or a lighter meal – cafés, ice-cream parlours and *salons de thé*. You'll also find boxes listing vegetarian (not Paris's strongest suit; see opposite), ethnic (see p.191) and late-night (see p.194) possibilities. Restaurant **opening times** are typically noon–2/2.30pm and 7.30–10.30/11pm; exceptions to this are noted in the text. Where possible, we have marked restaurants listed on the maps.

Paris for vegetarians

The chances of finding vegetarian main dishes on the menus of traditional French restaurants are not good, though these days some of the newer, more innovative restaurants will often have one or two vegetarian dishes on offer. It's also possible to put together a meal from vegetarian starters, omelettes and salads. Your other option of course is to go for a Middle Eastern or Indian restaurant or head for one of the city's handful of proper **vegetarian restaurants** – they do however tend to be based on a healthy diet principle rather than *haute cuisine*, but at least you get a choice. All the establishments listed below are reviewed in the pages that follow. Each restaurant is listed under the relevant *arrondissement*.

Au Grain de Folie 24 rue de la Vieuville, 18e.
Grand Appétit 9 rue de la Cerisaie, 4e.
Le Grenier de Notre Dame 18 rue de la Bûcherie, 5e.
La Petite Légume 36 rue Boulangers, 5e.
Les Quatre et Une Saveurs 72 rue du Cardinal-Lemoine, 5e.
La Victoire Suprême du Coeur 41 rue des Bourdonnais, 1er.

1er arrondissement

Bars and cafés

Angelina 226 rue de Rivoli; M° Tuileries. A long-established gilded cage where the well-coiffed come to sip the best hot chocolate in town – served in a large jug with whipped cream on the side. Patisseries and savouries are of the same high quality. Mon–Fri 9.15am–7pm, Sat & Sun 9.15am–7.30pm; closed Tues in July & Aug.

Aux Bons Crus 7 rue des Petits-Champs; M° Palais-Royal. A relaxed, workaday place that has been serving good wines and cheese, sausage and ham for nearly a century. A carafe costs from €5, a plate of cold meats from €10. Mon 9am–4pm, Tues–Sat 9am–11pm; closed Sun.

Le Rubis 10 rue du Marché-St-Honoré; M° Pyramides. One of the oldest wine bars in Paris, known for its excellent wines – mostly from the Beaujolais and Loire regions – and home-made *rillettes* (a kind of pork pâté). Very small and very crowded. Glasses of wine from €2.50 and *plats du jour* around €9. Mon–Fri 7.30am–10pm, Sat 9am–3pm; closed mid-Aug.

Le Sous-Bock 49 rue St-Honoré; M° Châtelet-Les Halles. Hundreds of beers – bottled and on tap – and whiskies to sample, plus simple, inexpensive food. Mussels a speciality (from €9). Frequented by night owls. Prices go up after 7pm. Mon–Sat 11am–5am, Sun 3pm–5am.

Taverne Henri IV 13 place du Pont-Neuf, Île de la Cité; M° Pont-Neuf. An old-style wine bar that's probably changed little since Yves Montand used to come here with Simone Signoret. It's especially buzzy at lunchtime when lawyers from the nearby Palais de Justice drop in for generous plates of meats and cheeses (for around €11) and *tartines* (with a choice of cheeses, hams, pâté and saucisson). Mon–Fri 11.30am–3.30pm & 6–9pm, Sat noon–4pm; closed Sun & Aug.

Restaurants

Le Dauphin 167 rue St-Honoré ⓣ01.42.60.40.11; M° Palais-Royal/Musée-du-Louvre; see map, pp.128–129. This old bistro with its original Art Deco stained glass serves up inventive southwestern dishes. Specialities are the *parilladas*, such as the meaty *parillada du boucher* made up of steak, duck, chicken breast and sausage; veggies are catered for too with the *parillada de la terre* (tomatoes, courgette, aubergine, fennel, peppers and endives). Lunchtime *menu* (except Sun) €23, evening €34. Daily noon–2.30pm & 7.30–10.30pm.

Foujita 41 rue St-Roch ⓣ01.42.61.42.93; M° Tuileries/Pyramides; see map, pp.128–129. One of the city's best Japanese restaurants, as proven by the number of Japanese eating here. Prices are reasonable too, especially the €10 lunchtime *menu* of soup, sushi, rice and tea. It's best to get here early to be sure of a table. Closed Sun & mid-Aug.

Au Pied de Cochon 6 rue Coquillière ⓣ01.40.13.77.00; M° Châtelet-Les Halles. A Les Halles institution, this is the place to go for extravagant middle-of-the-night pork chops, oysters and of course pigs' trotters. Carte around €45. Daily 24hr.

La Robe et le Palais 13 rue des Lavandières St-Opportune ⓣ01.45.08.07.41; M° Châtelet. A

small, busy *restaurant à vins* serving traditional cuisine and an excellent selection of wines. Typical main courses include sea bream, *boudin noir* (black pudding), *andouillette* (tripe sausage), and steak. The two-course lunch *menu* is good value at €14.30, and large meat or cheese platters for around €10 are also available. Mon–Sat noon–2.30 & 7–11pm.
À la Tour de Montlhéry (Chez Denise) 5 rue des Prouvaires ☎01.42.36.21.82; M° Louvre-Rivoli/Châtelet. An old-style all-night Les Halles bistro serving substantial food; always crowded and smoky. *Plats* from €15. Open 24hr Mon–Fri. Closed mid-July to mid-Aug.
La Victoire Suprème du Coeur 41 rue des Bourdonnais ☎01.40.41.93.95; M° Louvre-Rivoli/Châtelet. An excellent vegetarian restaurant offering a range of salads, as well as more unusual dishes such as mushroom roast with blackberry sauce. Two courses at lunch cost as little as €10.80, €14 for dinner. Mon–Sat noon–2.30pm & 6.40–10pm.

2e arrondissement

Bars and cafés

L'Arbre à Cannelle 57 passage des Panoramas; M° Rue-Montmartre. Tucked away in an attractive *passage*, this *salon de thé* with its exquisite wood panelling, frescoes and painted ceilings makes an excellent spot to treat yourself to salads and tarts both savoury and sweet. Mon–Sat till 6pm.
Le Café 62 rue Tiquetonne; M° Les Halles/Étienne-Marcel. A hip, buzzing café, full of old travel posters, yellowing maps and African sculptures. *Plats du jour* €8. Mon–Sat 10am–2am.
Juveniles 47 rue de Richelieu; M° Palais-Royal. A very popular tiny wine bar run by a Scot. Wine from €13 a bottle; reasonably priced snacks and *plats du jour*, too. Mon–Sat noon–11pm.
Kitty O'Shea's 10 rue des Capucines; M° Opéra. A favourite haunt of Irish expats with excellent Guinness and Smithwicks. The *John Jameson* restaurant upstairs (noon–2.30pm & 7.30–10.30pm) serves high-quality, pricey, Gaelic food, including seafood flown in from Galway. Daily noon–1.30am.

Restaurants

Chez Dilan 13 rue Mandar ☎01.42.21.14.88; M° Les Halles/Sentier. An excellent-value Kurdish restaurant, offering beautiful starters, stuffed aubergines (*babaqunuc*), fish with yoghurt and courgettes (*kanarya*). Set menu for €18. Closed Sun.
Higuma 32bis rue Sainte Anne ☎01.47.03.38.59; M° Pyramides. An authentic Japanese canteen with cheap, filling ramen dishes and a variety of set menus starting at €10. Daily 11.30am–10pm.
Vaudeville 29 rue Vivienne ☎01.40.20.04.62; M° Bourse. There's often a queue to get a table at this lively, late-night brasserie, attractively decorated with marble and mosaics. Dishes include grilled cod with truffle sauce and *belle tête de veau*. À la carte from €30; lunchtime *formule* €22.90. Last orders at 1am. Daily noon–3pm & 7pm–2am.

3e arrondissement

Bars and cafés

L'Apparemment Café 18 rue des Coutures-St-Gervais; M° St-Sébastien-Froissart. Chic but cosy café resembling a series of comfortable sitting rooms, with quiet corners and deep sofas. Recommended are the *salades composées* – which in this case you compose yourself by ticking off your chosen ingredients and handing your order to the waiter. Popular Sunday brunch until 4pm for €15. Mon–Fri noon–2am, Sat 4pm–2am, Sun 12.30pm–midnight.
The Quiet Man 5 rue des Haudriettes; M° Rambuteau or Hotel-de-Ville. A very small Irish bar with great atmosphere and Celtic music (Irish, Breton, Quebecquois and so on) from Tues to Sun. Daily 5pm–2am.

Restaurants

See map, pp.142–143.
Auberge Nicolas Flamel 51 rue de Montmorency ☎01.42.71.77.78; M° Rambuteau. No stranger to Harry Potter fans, Nicolas Flamel was an alchemist who lived in this building in the early 1400s. One of the oldest houses in Paris, it's now a popular restaurant conjuring up classic French bistro fare from fresh ingredients; the slow-cooked lamb is not to missed. Lunchtime formule €12, dinner à la carte around €35. Closed Sat lunch and all day Sun.
Chez Nénesse 17 rue Saintonge ☎01.42.78.46.49; M° Arts-et-Métiers. Steak in bilberry sauce, figs stuffed with cream of almonds, and home-made chips on Thursday lunchtimes are some of the unique delights at this friendly, old-style restaurant. À la carte around €30. Mon–Fri noon–2pm & 8–10.30pm; closed Aug.
Verte-Tige 13 rue Ste-Anastase ☎01.42.77.22.15; M° St-Sébastien-Froissart. Near the Musée Picasso, an excellent vegetarian restaurant, serving appetizing Middle East-influenced dishes, many suitable for vegans. Their set menu at €18 is particularly good value, and there's a good choice of wine and beer. Tues–Sat noon–2.30pm & 7.30–10.30pm, Sun 12.30–4pm. Closed Aug.

Au Vieux Molière Passage Molière, 157 rue Saint-Martin ⓣ01.42.78.37.87, ⓦwww.vieuxmoliere.com; M° Étienne-Marcel/Rambuteau/RER Châtelet. Tucked away down a characterful *passage*, this is an atmospheric restaurant, with French chansons playing softly in the background and outdoor seating in summer. The menu changes daily, but typical dishes are garlic-roasted chicken and mullet in saffron sauce. Lunchtime *formule* €15.24, evening à la carte from €40. Closed Sun lunch & Mon.

4e arrondissement

Bars and cafés

L'As du Fallafel 34 rue des Rosiers ⓣ01.48.87.63.60; M° St-Paul. The best falafel shop in the Jewish quarter. Falafels to take away cost only €5, or pay a bit more and sit in the buzzy little dining room. Noon–midnight; closed Fri eve & Sat.

Bar de Jarente 5 rue de Jarente; M° St-Paul. Off the pretty place du Marché Ste-Catherine, a tiny old-fashioned café-bar, which remains nonchalantly indifferent to the shifting trends around it. Closed Sun & Mon.

Berthillon 31 rue St-Louis-en-l'Île; M° Pont-Marie. Long queues for these excellent ice creams and sorbets with a big choice of fruity flavours – like rhubarb – that you've probably never tasted before. Also available at other island sites listed on the door. Wed–Sun 10am–8pm.

Café Beaubourg 43 rue St-Merri; M° Rambuteau/Hôtel-de-Ville. A seat under the expansive, not to say expensive (€5 for a *café crème*), awnings of this stylish café is one of the best places for people-watching on the Pompidou Centre's piazza. Mon–Thurs & Sun 8am–1am, Sat 8am–2am.

L'Ébouillanté 6 rue des Barres; M° Hôtel-de-Ville. A two-floor café with outdoor seating on a picturesque, cobbled street behind the church of St-Gervais. An extensive choice of drinks, from home-made hot chocolate to iced fruit cocktails. Savoury dishes include soup of the day and Tunisian crêpes, or indulge in their excellent chocolate cakes and *tartes*. Tues–Sun noon–10pm, till 9pm in winter.

Le Loir dans la Théière 3 rue des Rosiers; M° Saint-Paul. A characterful, laid-back *salon de thé* where you can sink into a battered sofa and feast on enormous portions of home-made cakes and vegetarian quiches. Mon–Fri 11am–7pm, Sat & Sun 10am–7pm.

Le Petit Fer à Cheval 30 rue Vieille-du-Temple; M° St-Paul. A very attractive small bistro/bar with original *fin-de-siècle* decor, including a marble-topped bar in the shape of a horseshoe (*fer à cheval*). It's a popular drinking spot, with agreeable wine, or you can snack on sandwiches or something more substantial in the little back room furnished with old wooden metro seats. Mon–Fri 9am–2am, Sat & Sun 11am–2am; food noon–midnight.

Le Petit Marcel 63 rue Rambuteau; M° Rambuteau. Speckled tabletops, mirrors and Art Nouveau tiles, cracked and faded ceiling and about eight square metres of drinking space. Friendly bar staff and "local" atmosphere. Mon–Sat till 2am.

Le Rouge Gorge 8 rue St-Paul; M° St-Paul. Friendly wine bar with bare stone walls and jazz or classical music playing in the background. Devoted to exploring a wide range of wines: one week it might be Corsica, the next Spain or the Loire, and the theme is taken up in the frequently changing menu. For three courses at lunchtime count on paying €23 and at dinner €30. Mon–Sat 11am–11.30pm. Closed last fortnight in Aug.

Restaurants

See map, pp.142–143.

L'Ambroisie 9 place des Vosges ⓣ01.42.78.51.45; M° Chemin-Vert/St-Paul. Scoring 19 out of 20 in the gourmet's bible *Gault et Millau* and run by celebrity chef Bernard Pacaud, *L'Ambroisie* offers exquisite food in a magnificent dining room hung with tapestries. It will put a serious dent in your budget however, with a meal costing upwards of €200. You'll need to book well in advance or else turn up and hope they have a last-minute cancellation. Closed Sun, Mon & Aug.

Auberge de Jarente 7 rue Jarente ⓣ01.42.77.49.35; M° St-Paul. A warm and hospitable Basque restaurant, serving first-class food. Dishes include cassoulet, hare stew, *magret de canard* and *piperade* – the Basque omelette. Menus from €20. Closed Sun, Mon & Aug.

Bofinger 7 rue de la Bastille ⓣ01.42.72.87.82; M° Bastille. A popular *fin-de-siècle* brasserie with its splendid original decor perfectly preserved. Specialities are sauerkraut and seafood. You'll get a better chance of sitting in the main dining room under the splendid glass coupole if you ask for a smoking rather than a non-smoking table. Three courses plus wine around €45. Daily noon–3pm & 7–midnight.

L'Enoteca 25 rue Charles V ⓣ01.42.78.91.44; M° St-Paul. A fashionable Italian *bistro à vins* in an old Marais building. If you take your Italian wine seriously then this is the place to come: the list runs to 22 pages and features over 400 varieties, with an ever-changing selection available by the glass. Food doesn't take a back seat either:

choose from an array of antipasti laid out enticingly in the middle of the room, fresh pasta or more substantial dishes such as *courgettes farcis à la viande de veau.* Two-course lunchtime menu for €12 including a glass of wine. Daily; closed one week in Aug.

Les Fous d'en Face 3 rue du Bourg-Tibourg ⓣ01.48.87.03.75; M° Hôtel-de-Ville. Delightful little restaurant and wine bar serving wonderful marinated salmon and scallops. Midday menu €17.50, otherwise reckon on €30 upwards. Tues–Sat 11.30am–3pm & 7pm–midnight. Closed Aug & Feb.

Georges Centre Georges Pompidou ⓣ01.44.78.47.99; M° Rambuteau/Hôtel-de-Ville. On the top-floor of the Pompidou Centre, this trendy minimalist restaurant with outdoor terrace commands stunning views over Paris and makes a stylish place for lunch or dinner. The French-Asian fusion cuisine is passable, though somewhat overpriced, but then that's not really why you come. Daily except Tues noon–midnight.

Goldenberg's 7 rue des Rosiers ⓣ01.48.87.20.16; M° St-Paul. Dating back to the 1920s, this is the best-known Jewish restaurant in the capital, serving up fine borscht, blinis, zakouski and apfel strudel. Occasional live music, often violin and guitar playing jazz favourites, lends atmosphere. Daily changing *plat du jour* €13, *carte* around €35. Daily until 1am.

Grand Appétit 9 rue de la Cerisaie; M° Bastille. Inexpensive vegetarian and vegan dishes, such as soups and vegetable sushi, served by dedicated eco-veggies at the back of an unassuming *épicerie.* Mon–Thurs noon–7pm, Fri noon–2pm.

Pitchi-Poï 7 rue Caron, cnr place du Marché-Ste-Catherine ⓣ01.42.77.46.15, ⓦwww.pitchipoi.com; M° St-Paul. A warm and homely restaurant with outdoor seating on one of the Marais' most attractive squares. The cuisine revolves around central European/Jewish dishes such as tchoulent and salmon coulibiac. Don't leave without sampling one of the Polish flavoured vodkas – the honey one goes down a treat. €21.50 lunch and dinner menu, kids' menu €12. Daily noon–2.30pm & 7.30–11pm.

Le Relais de l'Île 37 rue St-Louis-en-l'Île ⓣ01.46.34.72.34; M° Pont-Marie. A cosy, candle-lit restaurant serving decent food, with mains such as rabbit in prune sauce or chicken with lemon and honey (around €45 a head for three courses with wine). It's the convivial atmosphere though that makes this place special: the friendly service, the pianist tinkling away on the piano and the chef occasionally popping out from the kitchen to join in. Closed Tues.

5e arrondissement

Bars and cafés

Café de la Mosquée 39 rue Geoffroy-St-Hilaire; M° Monge. You can drink mint tea and eat sweet cakes beside a fountain and assorted fig trees in the courtyard of this Paris mosque – a delightful haven of calm. Meals are served in the adjoining restaurant for around €15 and up. Daily 9am–11pm.

La Fourmi Ailée 8 rue du Fouarre; M° Maubert-Mutualité. Simple, light fare in this former feminist bookshop which has been transformed into a *salon de thé.* A high ceiling painted with a lovely mural and a book-filled wall contribute to the unusual atmosphere. From noon to 3pm it's restaurant service only – count on around €10–15 for a plat. Daily noon–7pm.

Le Piano Vache 8 rue Laplace; M° Cardinal-Lemoine. Venerable bar crammed with students drinking at little tables, with cool music and a laid-back atmosphere. Mon–Fri noon–2am, Sat & Sun 9pm–2am.

Les Pipos 2 rue de l'École-Polytechnique; M° Maubert-Mutualité/Cardinal-Lemoine. Old, wooden bar, serving wines from €2.50 a glass along with simple plates of charcuterie, cheese and the like. Mon–Sat 8am–1am; closed two weeks in Aug.

Le Violon Dingue 46 rue de la Montagne-Ste-Geneviève; M° Maubert-Mutualité. A long, dark student pub that's also popular with young travellers; noisy and friendly. English-speaking bar staff and cheap drinks. The cellar bar stays open until 4.30am on busy nights. Daily 6pm–2.30am; happy hour 8–10pm.

Restaurants

See map, pp.150–151.

Au Bistro de la Sorbonne 4 rue Toullier ⓣ01.43.54.41.49; RER Luxembourg. Traditional French and delicious North African food – tagines, couscous – served at reasonable prices to a crowd of locals and students. Attractively bright, muralled interior. Lunch menus from €12, evening menu at €16 or choose à la carte. Closed Sun.

Brasserie Balzar 49 rue des Écoles ⓣ01.43.54.13.67; M° Maubert-Mutualité. Truly classic high-ceilinged brasserie long frequented by the literary intelligentsia of the Quartier Latin, though it's more international earlier on. À la carte around €30. Daily 8am–11.30pm.

Au Buisson Ardent 25 rue Jussieu ⓣ01.43.54.93.02; M° Jussieu. Copious helpings of inventive, first-class cooking served in a cosy dining room. Lunch menu €15, evenings €29. Reservations recommended. Closed Sat lunch & Sun, and Aug.

Chez Léna et Mimile 32 rue Tournefort ☎01.47.07.72.47; M° Censier-Daubenton. The broad, south-facing terrasse, perched above a shady little square, is the main attraction, but the food is good – a mixture of solid cuisine bourgeoise with a few Spanish inflections. The single €35 menu, with wine and coffee included, is excellent; at lunch, count on €21 for two courses. Closed Sun and Mon & Sat lunch.

Les Degrés de Notre Dame 10 rue des Grands Degrés ☎01.55.42.88.88; M° Maubet-Mutualité. Reliable, inexpensive and substantial French food served in a friendly, faintly rustic dining room. Good-value lunch menu. Closed Sun.

Le Grenier de Notre Dame 18 rue de la Bûcherie ☎01.43.29.98.29; M° Maubert-Mutualité/St-Michel. A real hit-and-miss place, but useful to know about. Some people love the menu of unreconstructed veggie classics, others find it dull. At around €20 for a meal, the prices aren't low. Mon–Fri noon–2.30pm & 7–11pm, Sat & Sun noon–11pm.

Le Petit Prince 12 rue Lanneau ☎01.43.54.77.26. Classic French food with occasionally inventive combinations that can be hit and miss. Welcoming, cheerily camp ambience. Menus at €16 & €23. Mon–Thurs & Sun 7.30pm–midnight, Fri & Sat 7.30pm–12.30am.

La Petite Légume 36 rue Boulangers ☎01.40.46.06.85; M° Jussieu. A health-food grocery that doubles as a vegetarian restaurant and tea room, serving homely, organic *plats* for €8–12, along with organic Loire wines. Closed Sun.

Pho 67 59 rue Galande ☎01.45.25.56.69; M° Maubet-Mutualité. Authentic Vietnamese with dishes for around €6. Try the famous pho soup, in this case made with tender French steak.

Les Quatre et Une Saveurs 72 rue du Cardinal-Lemoine ☎01.43.26.88.80; M° Cardinal-Lemoine. Inventive, high-class, organic vegetarian food. *Plats* around €14, with a menu at €25. Closed Fri eve.

Le Reminet 3 rue des Grands Degrés ☎01.44.07.04.24; M° Maubert-Mutualité. This artful little bistro-restaurant shows its class through small touches: snowy-white tablecloths and fancy chandeliers; and carefully considered and imaginative sauces. Gastronomic menu at €50, but you can get away with two courses à la carte for about half that. Closed Tues & Wed.

Tashi Delek 4 rue des Fossés-St-Jacques ☎01.43.26.55.55; RER Luxembourg. Elegantly styled Tibetan restaurant serving Himalayan regional dishes ranging from watery but delicious broths to the addictive, ravioli-like *momok*. You can eat handsomely for around €15, and there's an €18 menu with wine. Closed Sun & two weeks in Aug.

6e arrondissement

Bars and cafés

Le 10 10 rue de l'Odéon; M° Odéon. Small dark bar with old posters, a jukebox and a lot of chatting-up among the studenty and international clientele. Daily 6pm–2am.

L'Assignat 7 rue Guénégaud; M° Pont-Neuf. Zinc counter, bar stools, bar football and young regulars from the nearby art school in an untouristy café close to quai des Augustins. Homely *plats du jour* around €7. Mon–Sat 7.30am–8.30pm, food noon–3pm; closed three weeks in July.

Chez Georges 11 rue des Canettes; M° Mabillon. Deeply old-fashioned, tobacco-stained wine bar with its old shop-front still in place, though sadly old Georges himself is not. Young and beery in the evenings. Tues–Sat noon–2am; closed Aug.

La Closerie des Lilas 171 bd du Montparnasse; M° Port-Royal. The smartest, artiest, classiest Montparnasse café, with excellent cocktails for around €12 and a resident pianist. The tables are name-plated after celebrated former habitués (Verlaine, Mallarmé, Lenin, Modigliani, Léger, Strindberg). Very expensive restaurant, but brasserie main courses can be had for under €20. Daily noon–1.30am.

Cosi 54 rue de Seine; M° St-Germain-des-Prés. Fantastic sandwiches (€5–8) made on home-made focaccia bread, using wonderful Italian deli ingredients. You can eat in, with a glass of wine, and the opera-loving owner has a different opera on the CD player each day. Daily noon–midnight.

Les Deux Magots 170 bd St-Germain; M° St-Germain-des-Prés. Right on the corner of place St-Germain-des-Prés, this expensive café is the victim of its own reputation as the historic hangout of Left Bank intellectuals, but it's great for people-watching. It's worth arriving early for the breakfasts. Daily 7.30am–1am.

Le Flore 172 bd St-Germain; M° St-Germain-des-Prés. The great rival and immediate neighbour of Les Deux Magots, with a very similar clientele. Sartre, De Beauvoir, Camus and Marcel Carné used to hang out here. Best enjoyed during a late-afternoon coffee or after-dinner drink, preferably in the insiders' haunt – upstairs. Daily 7am–1.30am.

Fubar 5 rue St-Sulpice; M° Odéon. Small beer and cocktail bar that manages to be trendy and welcoming at the same time. Offers a good, varied playlist, and a cosy upstairs room with comfy arm-chairs. Packed out on Tuesdays (student night) and at weekends. Daily 5pm–2am.

La Mezzanine de l'Alcazar 62 rue Mazarine; M° Odéon. Both decor and clientele are *très design* at this über-cool cocktail bar, set on a terrace level overlooking Conran's Alcazar restaurant. Expensive (€10 for a drink) but exquisite – again, much like the clientele. Most nights start off relaxed and finish with feverish dancing, the harder core moving on to *Le Wagg* club (see p.201). DJs Wed–Sat. Daily 7pm–2am.

La Palette 43 rue de Seine; M° Odéon. Once-famous Beaux-Arts student hangout, now frequented by art dealers and their customers. The decor is superb, including, of course, a large selection of colourful, used palettes. Mon–Sat 8am–2am.

Le Procope 13 rue de l'Ancienne-Comédie ☎01.40.46.79.00; M° Odéon. Opened in 1686 as the first establishment to serve coffee in Paris, it's still a great place to enjoy a cup and bask in the knowledge that over the years, Voltaire, Benjamin Franklin, Rousseau, Marat and Robespierre, among others, have done the very same thing. Diners can enjoy a decent but slightly overpriced evening menu. Daily noon–1am.

La Taverne de Nesle 32 rue Dauphine; M° Odéon. Full of young, local night-birds fuelled up by happy hour (6–11pm) cocktails. DJs at weekends. Daily 6pm till around 4am.

Restaurants

See map, pp.156–157.

Au 35 35 rue Jacob; M° St-Germain-des-Prés. Intimate St-Germain bistro with all the trimmings – yellowing walls, old mirrors, Art Deco lamps, a spiral staircase in one corner and film and fashion posters on the walls. The menu is more innovative, with beautifully cooked French dishes rubbing shoulders with some exquisite Moroccan classics, such as a lamb *pastilla* with honey and spices. Expect to pay €30, without wine. Daily noon–2.30pm & 7.30–11pm.

Aux Charpentiers 10 rue Mabillon ☎01.43.26.30.05; M° Mabillon. A bright, friendly, old-fashioned place that once belonged to the Compagnons des Charpentiers (Carpenters' Guild) – hence the decor of model roof-trees and tie beams. Traditional *plats du jour* are their forte – tripe sausage, calf's head and the like. Lunch menu at €19, evenings €25. Daily until 11.30pm; closed hols.

Brasserie Lipp 151 bd St-Germain; M° St -Germain-des-Prés. One of the most celebrated of all the classic Paris brasseries, the haunt of the very successful and very famous, with a wonderful 1900s wood-and-glass interior. Decent *plats du jour*, including the famous sauerkraut, for under €20, but the full menu is expensive. No reservations, so be prepared to wait. Daily noon–1am.

Orestias 4 rue Grégoire-de-Tours ☎01.43.54.62.01; M° Odéon. Large helpings of honest, inexpensive Greek and French food, with a budget menu at €8, and an all-Greek menu at €14. Closed Sun.

Le Petit St-Benoît 4 rue St-Benoît ☎01.42.60.27.92; M° St-Germain-des-Prés. A simple, genuine and very appealing local serving solid fare in a brown-stained, aproned atmosphere. Three good, traditional courses for under €20. Closed Sun.

Le Petit Zinc 11 rue St-Benoit ☎01.42.61.20.60; M° St-Germain-des-Prés. Excellent traditional dishes, especially seafood, in stunning Art-Nouveau-style premises (actually built thirty years ago). Not cheap – menu €32, lavish seafood platter €82 for two. Daily noon–midnight.

Polidor 41 rue Monsieur-le-Prince ☎01.43.26.95.34; M° Odéon. A traditional bistro, open since 1845, whose visitors' book, they say, boasts more of history's big names than all the glittering palaces put together. Packed with noisy regulars until late in the evening, when the menu costs €18. Bargain lunch menu for €9. Mon–Sat noon–2.30pm & 7pm–12.30am, Sun noon–2.30pm & 7–11.30pm.

7e arrondissement

Bars and cafés

Café du Museé d'Orsay 1 rue Bellechasse; RER Musée-d'Orsay/M° Solférino. Superb views through the giant clockface dominating the museum's rooftop café, which serves snacks and drinks. Tues–Sun 11am–5pm.

Le Poch'tron 25 rue de Bellechasse; M° Solférino. With a fine selection of snacks and wines by the glass, this is an excellent place to revive yourself after visiting the museums in the arrondissement. Also serves lunch and dinner; main dishes at around €12. Mon–Fri 9am–10.30pm.

Restaurants

See map, pp.160–161.

Au Babylone 13 rue de Babylone ☎01.45.48.72.13; M° Sèvres-Babylone. Lots of old-fashioned charm and culinary basics like rôti de veau and steak, plus wine on the €18.50 menu. Mon–Sat lunch only; closed Aug.

Chez Germaine 30 rue Pierre-Leroux ☎01.42.73.28.34; M° Duroc/Vaneau. A simple and tiny restaurant, with an excellent-value, inexpensive menu. Closed Sat eve, Sun & Aug.

La Fontaine de Mars 19 rue St-Dominique ☎01.47.05.46.44; M° Ecole-Militaire/La Tour-Maubourg. This well-mannered local restaurant is almost entirely decked out in genteel pinks – tablecloths, napkins, gingham café-curtains. The service is attentive, and the traditional cuisine reliably good, with some real hits among the blackboard specials – think perfectly cooked *tartare de bœuf* or a zingy *filet de St-Pierre* with basil. Menu at €23.

Le P'tit Troquet 28 rue de l'Exposition ⓣ01.47.05.80.39; M° École Militaire. Tiny, discreet restaurant done out like an elegant antiques shop, serving delicate and classy traditional cuisine to the diplomats and politicians of the quartier. Lunch menu at €19, evenings at €27. Closed Mon lunch & Sun.

Thoumieux 79 rue St-Dominique ⓣ01.47.05.49.75; M° La Tour-Maubourg. Cavernous, be-mirrored traditional brasserie, popular with a smart local clientele for reliable classics. Menu at €33. Daily noon–3.30pm & 6.30pm–midnight.

8e arrondissement

Bars and cafés

Le Fouquet's 99 av des Champs-Élysées; M° George-V. Dating from 1899, *Le Fouquet's* brasserie is such a well-established watering hole for the rich and famous, that it's now been classified as a Monument Historique. You can either have a drink on the terrace and watch the world go by on the Champs-Elysées or eat in the restaurant inside with its lovely decor of dark-wood and deep-red velvet. The restaurant (last order 11.30pm) isn't quite as pricey as you might expect, with meals around €35, though there's little on the wine list for under €30. Daily till 1.30am.

Musée Jacquemart-André 158 bd Haussmann ⓣ01.45.62.11.59; M° St-Philippe-du-Roule/Miromesnil. Part of the Musée Jacquemart-André but with independent access, this is the most sumptuously appointed *salon de thé* in the city. Admire the ceiling frescoes by Tiepolo while savouring fine pastries or salads. Daily 11.30am–5.30pm.

Restaurants

See map, pp.128–129.

Alain Ducasse at the Plaza-Athénée Hotel Plaza-Athénée, 25 av Montaigne; M° Alma-Marceau ⓣ01.53.67.65.00. Reckoned to be one of Paris's, not to say the world's, top haute cuisine temples, run by star chef Alain Ducasse, whose sublime dishes are likely to revive even the most jaded palate. The decor is Louis XV with a modern gloss and the service – as you'd expect – is impeccable. Mon–Fri 1–2.30pm & 8–10.30pm.

Dragons Élysées 11 rue de Berri ⓣ01.42.89.85.10; M° George-V. The Chinese-Thai cuisine encompasses dim sum, curried seafood and baked mussels, but the overriding attraction is the extraordinary decor: beneath a floor of glass tiles water runs from pool to pool inhabited by exotic fish. Midweek lunchtime menu €14, otherwise count on around €35 a head. Daily 11am–3pm & 7–11pm.

Rue Balzac 3–5 rue Balzac ⓣ01.53.89.90.91; M° Charles-de-Gaulle. This ultra-stylish restaurant is the enterprise of singer Johnny Hallyday and chef Michel Rostang. The low lighting and subdued reds and yellows of the decor provide an atmospheric backdrop to classy cuisine, available in small or large servings ("petit modèle" and "grand modèle"); most people find the former filling enough. Three courses with wine comes to around €60. M° George V. Daily noon–2pm & 7.30–11pm.

Spoon, Food and Wine 14 rue de Marignan ⓣ01.40.76.34.44; M° Franklin-D.-Roosevelt. An innovative world-food bistro headed up by star chef Alain Ducasse. The chic, minimalist decor and inventive cuisine, marrying unusual flavours and ingredients, attract a fashionable crowd. Count on around €50 a head. Closed Sat, Sun & mid-July to mid-Aug.

Taillevent 15 rue Lamennais ⓣ01.44.95.15.01; M° Charles-de-Gaulle. One of Paris's finest gourmet restaurants. The Provencal-influenced cuisine and wine list are exceptional, the decor classy and refined. Reckon on an average of €150 a head, excluding wine, and book well in advance. Mon–Fri 12.30–2.30pm & 7.30–11.30pm.

Yvan 1bis rue J-Mermoz ⓣ01.43.59.18.40; M° Franklin-D.-Roosevelt. An elegant restaurant with deep-red plush decor. The excellent cuisine pays homage to the owner's Belgian roots, featuring offerings such as cod and endives in Hoegarden beer sauce. Set lunch €29, set dinner €37. Closed Sat lunch & Sun.

9e arrondissement

Bars and cafés

Le Dépanneur 27 rue Fontaine; M° Pigalle. Relaxed all-night bar with a fashionable pre- and post-club crowd. Daily 11am–7am.

Restaurants

Chartier 7 rue du Faubourg-Montmartre ⓣ01.47.70.86.29, ⓦwww.bouillon-chartier.com; M° Montmartre. Dark-stained woodwork, brass hat-racks, mirrors, waiters in long aprons – the original decor of an early twentieth-century soup kitchen. Though crowded and rushed, it's worth a visit, and the food's not bad at all. Three courses for €15, and a bottle of wine from €6. Daily 11.30am–3pm & 6–10pm.

Aux Deux-Théâtres 18 rue Blanche, cnr rue Pigalle ⓣ01.45.26.41.43; M° Trinité. Classic luvvie hangout serving a wonderful menu at €31 – everything included from apéritif to coffee. The long, plush dining room is decorated with actors' photos. Daily noon–2.30pm & 7pm–12.30am.
Le Grand Café Capucines 4 bd des Capucines; M° Opéra. A popular post-cinema or -opera spot, with over-the-top belle époque decor and excellent seafood. Count on around €45 a head for three courses, not including wine. Open 24hr.
Le Relais Savoyard 13 rue Rodier, cnr rue Agent-Bailly ⓣ01.45.26.17.48; M° Notre-Dame-de-Lorette/Anvers/Cadet. Generous helpings of hearty Savoyard cuisine in a little dining room at the back of a local bar. Two courses for €16, three for €23. Closed Sun, Mon lunch & 2 weeks in Aug.

10e arrondissement

Bars and cafés

L'Atmosphère 49 rue Lucien-Sampaix; M° Gare-de-l'Est. Lively bar with food next to the canal St-Martin. Tables on the towpath on sunny days, and live music at weekends. Tues–Fri 11am–2am, Sat 3pm–4am, Sun 3pm–8pm.
Chez Prune 36 rue Beaurepaire ⓣ01.42.41.30.47; M° Jacques-Bonsergent. One of the most popular hangouts in the 10e, this is a very friendly and laid-back café-restaurant with pleasant outdoor seating overlooking the canal. Creative *assiettes* (around €8) guaranteed to tempt both meat-eaters and vegetarians, and a romantic place to sip a glass of wine or indulge in a dessert. Mon–Sat 7.30am–1.45am, Sun 10am–1.45am.
Le Réveil du Dixième 35 rue du Château-d'Eau ⓣ01.42.41.77.59; M° Château-d'Eau. A welcoming, unpretentious market bar serving inexpensive but decent glasses of wine to a local clientele, along with regional plats (around €10), snacks and salads. Mon–Sat 7.15am–9pm.
Café Tribal cour des Petites-Écuries; M° Château-d'Eau. The fashionable, young and left-leaning denizens of the 10e flock to this noisy, vibrant haunt for chatter, music and late-night drinks. Free couscous served Fri and Sat evenings, and moules frites on Wed and Thurs. Daily noon–2am.

Restaurants

Flo 7 cour des Petites-Écuries ⓣ01.47.70.13.59; M° Château-d'Eau. Dark, extremely handsome old-time brasserie where you eat elbow to elbow at long tables, served with panache by waiters in ankle-length aprons. Excellent food and atmosphere. Good-value menus from around €23. Daily 11am–1am.
Julien 16 rue du Faubourg-St-Denis ⓣ01.47.70.12.06; M° Strasbourg-St-Denis. Part of the same enterprise as Flo (above), with an even more splendid decor. Same good traditional French cuisine at the same prices, and it's just as crowded. Daily until 1am.
Pooja 91 passage Brady ⓣ01.48.24.00.83; M° Strasbourg-St-Denis/Château-d'Eau. Not quite London, let alone Bombay, but friendly and located in a glazed passage that is lined with Indian restaurants, all offering good if rather similar fare. Lunch *formules* for under €10; evening menu for €20. Daily noon–3pm & 6–11pm; closed Mon lunchtime.
Terminus Nord 23 rue de Dunkerque ⓣ01.42.85.05.15; M° Gare-du-Nord. Another magnificent 1920s brasserie in the prestigious Flo family (same hours and prices; see opposite). The location right opposite the Gare du Nord draws a less local clientele, but it's a fine introduction – or farewell – to old-style Paris dining if you've just come off the Eurostar.

11e arrondissement

Bars and cafés

Bar des Ferrailleurs 18 rue de Lappe; M° Bastille. Dark and stylishly sinister bar, with rusting metal decor, an eccentric owner and fun wig-wearing staff. Relaxed, friendly crowd. Daily 5pm–2am.
Boca Chica 58 rue de Charonne ⓣ01. 43.57.93.13; M° Ledru-Rollin. Popular tapas bar/bodega with colourful arty decor, heaving by night and restful in the day. Tapas around €5, plats from €9. Happy hour 4–7pm when beer and sangria are half price. Daily 8am–2am.
Café Charbon 109 rue Oberkampf; M° St-Maur/Parmentier. A very successful and attractive resuscitation of a *fin-de-siècle* café, packed in the evenings with a young and trendy clientele, quieter during the day and ideal for a leisurely breakfast or an aperitif in the early evening. Beer €2.30; full-blown meals (€20) also available noon–2.30 & 8–11pm. Daily 9am–2am.
Cithéa 112 rue Oberkampf ⓣ01.40 21 70 95; M° Parmentier. Next door to *Café Charbon*, a bar and venue for Afro funk, funk reggae, world beat, jazz fusion, etc on Fri & Sat nights. Cocktails €7. No admission charge for the music. Daily 5pm–5.30am.
Café de l'Industrie 16 rue St-Sabin; M° Bastille. Rugs on the floor around solid old wooden tables, miscellaneous objects – from stuffed crocodiles to atmospheric black-and-white photos – on the walls, and a young, unpretentious crowd enjoying

Ethnic restaurants of Paris

Our selection of Paris's ethnic restaurants only scratches the surface of what's available. North African places can be found just about everywhere, as can Indo–Chinese restaurants, with notable concentrations around avenue de la Porte-de-Choisy in the 13e and in the Belleville Chinatown. Indian restaurants abound in and around the passage Brady in the 10e. The Greeks, bunched together in rue de la Huchette, rue Xavier-Privas and along rue Mouffetard, all in the 5e, are for the most part disappointing and overpriced. Each restaurant is listed under the relevant *arrondissement*.

African and North African

Chez Omar 47 Rue de Bretagne, 11e.

L'Homme Bleu 57 rue Jean-Pierre-Timbaud, 11e.

La Mansouria 11 rue Faidherbe-Chaligny, 11e.

Le Mono 40 rue Véron, 18e.

N'Zadette M'Foua 152 rue du Château, 14e.

Waly Fay 6 rue Godefroy-Cavaignac, 11e.

Greek

Orestias 4 rue Grégoire-de-Tours, 6e.

Indian

Pooja 91 passage Brady, 10e.

Indo-Chinese

Le Bambou 70 rue Baudricourt; 13e.

Blue Elephant 43–45 rue de la Roquette, 11e.

Dragons Élysées 11 rue de Berri, 8e.

Lao Siam 49 rue de Belleville, 20e.

Lao-Thai 128 rue de Tolbiac; 13e.

Pho 67 59 rue Galande, 5e.

Pho-Dong-Huong 14 rue Louis-Bonnet, 20e.

Phuong Hoang Terrasse des Olympiades, 52 rue du Javelot, 13e.

Italian

L'Enoteca 25 rue Charles V, 4e.

Japanese

Foujita 41 rue St-Roch, 1er.

Higuma 32bis rue Sainte Anne 2e.

Jewish

Goldenberg's 7 rue des Rosiers, 4e.

Pitchi-Poï 7 rue Caron, 4e.

Kurdish

Dilan 13 rue Mandar, 2e.

Lebanese

Aux Saveurs du Liban 11 rue Eugène-Jumin, 19e.

Tibetan

Tashi Delek 4 rue des Fossés-St-Jacques, 5e.

the comfortable absence of minimalism. One of the best Bastille cafés, packed out every evening. *Plats du jour* around €12. Daily 10–2am.
Iguana 15 rue de la Roquette, cnr rue Daval; M° Bastille. A place to be seen in. Decor of trellises, colonial fans and a brushed bronze bar. The clientele studies recherché art reviews, and the coffee is excellent. Daily 10am–2am.
Jacques-Mélac 42 rue Léon-Frot; M° Charonne. Some way off the beaten track (between Père-Lachaise and place Léon-Blum) but a highly respected and very popular *bistro à vins*, whose patron even makes his own wine – the solitary vine winds round the front of the shop. The food (*plats* around €11), wines and atmosphere are great; no bookings. Tues–Sat 9am–10.30pm; closed Aug.
SanZSanS 49 rue du Faubourg-St-Antoine; M° Bastille. Bar, club and restaurant all rolled into one, *SanZSanS* features a Gothic decor of red velvet, oil paintings and chandeliers. Drinks are reasonably priced and its lunchtime *plat du jour* is particularly good value at €9. DJ every evening playing house, rap or funk. Tues–Sat 9am–6am, Mon 9am–2am, Sun 11am–2am.

Restaurants

Les Amognes 243 rue du Faubourg-St-Antoine ☎01.43.72.73.05; M° Faidherbe-Chaligny. Old stone walls and exposed beams form the backdrop to this intimate little bistro. The menu revolves around game and vegetables in season and puts a creative spin on traditional dishes. Booking essential. Menu at €34, otherwise around €50. Closed Sat & Mon lunch, Sun & most of Aug.
Astier 44 rue Jean-Pierre-Timbaud ☎01.43.57.16.35; M° Parmentier. Very successful and popular restaurant with unstuffy atmosphere, and food renowned for its freshness and refinement. Outstanding selection of perfectly ripe cheeses and excellent wine list. Essential to book; lunch is often less crowded (€21 *menu*) and just as enjoyable. Evening menu €25. Closed Sat & Sun, Aug & fortnight in May & at Christmas.
Bistrot du Peintre 116 av Ledru-Rollin ☎01.47.00.34.39; M° Faidherbe-Chaligny; see map, pp.142–143. A traditional neighbourhood bistro, where small tables are jammed together beneath faded Art Nouveau frescoes and wood panelling. The emphasis is on hearty cuisine, with dishes such as beef tartare and *confit de canard* for around €13. Mon–Sat 7am–2am, Sun 10am–8pm.
Blue Elephant 43–45 rue de la Roquette; ☎01.47.00.42.00; M° Bastille/Richard-Lenoir; see map, pp.142–143. Superb Thai restaurant, with a tropical forest decor. Reckon on around €45 a head. Booking essential. Daily noon–2pm & 7pm–midnight; closed Sat lunchtime.
Chez Omar 47 rue de Bretagne; M° Arts-et-Métiers. Very popular North African restaurant in a nice old brasserie set with mirrors, attracting a young crowd. €20–25 a head. Does not accept credit cards; no bookings. Closed Sun lunch.
L'Homme Bleu 57 rue Jean-Pierre-Timbaud; M° Parmentier. A very pleasant Berber restaurant, popular with students. Count on €25 a head. Mon–Sat 5pm–2am.
La Mansouria 11 rue Faidherbe-Chaligny ☎01.43.71.00.16; M° Faidherbe-Chaligny. An excellent, elegant Moroccan restaurant, serving superb couscous and tagines. Expect to pay between €30 and €40 a head. Closed Mon & Tues lunchtime & two weeks in Aug.
Waly Fay 6 rue Godefroy-Cavaignac, ☎01.40.24.17.79; M° Charonne. A moderately priced West African restaurant with a cosy, stylish atmosphere, the dim lighting, rattan and old, faded photographs creating an intimate, faintly colonial ambience. Smart, young black and white Parisians come here to dine on perfumed, richly spiced stews and other West African delicacies. Mon–Sat noon–2pm & 7.30–11pm; closed last 2 weeks of Aug.

12e arrondissement

Bars and cafés

Le Baron Rouge 1 rue Théophile-Roussel, cnr place d'Aligre market; M° Ledru-Rollin. Locals and shoppers repair to this traditional *bar à vins* for a light lunch or aperitif after visiting the place d'Aligre market. If it's crowded inside, join the locals on the pavement lunching on saucisson or mussels washed down with a glass of wine. Tues–Sat 10am–2pm & 5–9.30pm, Sun 10am–2pm.
Le Viaduc Café 43 av Daumesnil; M° Gare-de-Lyon. A stylish restaurant-bar in one of the Viaduc des Arts' converted railway arches, with seating outside in nice weather. Ideal for lunch (€16) or drinks after perusing the galleries or walking the Promenade Plantée. The three-course (€22) Sunday jazz brunch from noon to 4pm is especially popular. *Plats* around €15. Daily 8am–4am (food served till 3am).

Restaurants

L'Ébauchoir 43–45 rue de Cîteaux ☎01.43.42.49.31; M° Faidherbe-Chaligny. Good bistro fare in a relaxed and convivial atmosphere. A little out of the way, but worth the detour. Midday menu for €12; carte €25 upwards. Best to book for the evening. Closed Sun.

Le Square Trousseau 1 rue Antoine Vollon ☎01.43.43.06.00; M° Ledru-Rollin; see map, pp.142–143. Just round the corner from the Place d'Aligre market, a handsome belle époque brasserie patronized by a chic, but relaxed crowd. The regularly changing menu features excellent traditional cuisine. Lunch *menu* for €20, evening is à la carte – reckon on €35. Booking recommended in the evening. Tues–Sat noon–2pm & 7.30–midnight; closed in Aug.

13e arrondissement

Bars and cafés

La Folie en Tête 33 rue Butte-aux-Cailles; M° Place-d'Italie/Corvisart. Alternative-spirited bar with friendly Saturday-night World music dance sessions. Cheap drinks and snacks in the daytime. A very warm and laid-back address. Mon–Sat 5pm–2am.

Le Merle Moqueur 11 rue Butte-aux-Cailles; M° Place-d'Italie/Corvisart. Tiny, slightly ramshackle bar serving up trendy music and home-made flavoured rums to young Parisians. Daily 5pm–2am.

Restaurants

Auberge Etchegorry 41 rue Croulebarbe ☎01.44.08.83.51; M° Gobelins. A former *guinguette* (dance hall) on the banks of the Bièvre, this Basque restaurant has an old-fashioned atmosphere of relaxed conviviality, and the food's good too. Menus around €20. Closed Sun & Mon.

L'Avant Goût 37 rue Bobillot ☎01.45.81.14.06; M° Place d'Italie. Small neighbourhood restaurant with a big reputation for excitingly good modern French cuisine, and wines to match. Cool contemporary decor and presentation. The lunch menu is one of the city's best deals, and you can eat superbly for just over €30 in the evenings. Tues–Sat noon–2.30pm & 7.30–11pm; closed 3 weeks in Aug.

Le Bambou 70 rue Baudricourt ☎01.45.70.91.75; M° Tolbiac. Tiny bistro crammed with punters, French and Vietnamese alike, tucking into sublimely fresh-tasting Vietnamese food, including giant, strongly flavoured pho soups. Closed Mon.

Chez Gladines 30 rue des Cinq-Diamants ☎01.45.80.70.10; M° Corvisart. This tiny corner bistro is always welcoming. Excellent wines and hearty Basque and southwest dishes; the mashed/fried potato is a must and goes best with *magret de canard*. Less than €20 for a (very) full meal. Daily 9am–1am.

Lao-Thai 128 rue de Tolbiac ☎01.44.24.28.10; M° Tolbiac. Big glass-fronted place on a busy interchange, serving fine Thai and Laotian food. Midday menu at €7.95, otherwise €21.50 for two. Daily except Wed.

Phuong Hoang Terrasse des Olympiades, 52 rue du Javelot ☎01.45.84.75.07; M° Tolbiac (take the escalator up from rue Tolbiac). Large, well-known restaurant serving Vietnamese, Thai and Singaporean specialities on a variety of menus from €8 and up. The food is reliably good, and the surroundings, up on the Terrasse, are extraordinary. Daily until 11pm.

Le Temps des Cerises 18–20 rue Butte-aux-Cailles ☎01.45.89.69.48; M° Place-d'Italie/Corvisart. Welcoming restaurant – it's run as a workers' co-op – with elbow-to-elbow seating and a different daily choice of imaginative dishes. Lunch menu at €10 and evening menus at €13.50 and €22. Mon–Fri noon–2pm & 7.30–11.45pm, Sat 7.30pm–midnight.

14e arrondissement

Bars and cafés

L'Entrepôt 7–9 rue Francis-de-Pressensé; M° Pernety. Arty cinema with a spacious, relaxed café and outside seating in the courtyard. Plats for €12–15. Mon–Sat noon–2am.

Mustang Café 84 bd du Montparnasse; M° Montparnasse-Bienvenüe. Young international crowd and happy atmosphere. A good place to finish up the evening after nightclubbing in St-Germain. Tex-Mex food, cocktails and beers. Daily 10am–5am.

Restaurants

Aquarius 40 rue de Gergovie ☎01.45.41.36.88; M° Pernety/Plaisance. Hearty vegetarian restaurant serving wholesome if not spectacular meals to a friendly, noisy crowd, with main courses for around €10. Closed Sun and three weeks in Aug/Sept.

La Coupole 102 bd du Montparnasse ☎01.43.20.14.20; M° Vavin. The largest and perhaps most famous and enduring arty-chic Parisian hangout for dining, dancing and debate. Lunch menus at €16.50 and €29, evening menu at €30.50, with a €21.50 menu served after 10.30pm. The downstairs club gets going from around 9.30pm. Daily 8.30am–1am.

N'Zadette M'Foua 152 rue du Château ☎01.43.22.00.16; M° Pernety. A small and cheery Congolese restaurant serving tasty dishes such as *maboké* (meat or fish baked in banana leaves). Menu at €14. Tues–Sun 7pm–2am.

Au Rendez-Vous des Camionneurs 34 rue des Plantes ☎01.45.40.43.36; M° Alésia. No lorry drivers any more, but you'll get a warm welcome and a really good meal with a small pichet of wine

Late-night Paris

It's not at all unusual for bars and brasseries in Paris to stay open after midnight; the list below is of cafés and bars that remain open after 2am, and restaurants that are open beyond midnight. Note that the three Drugstores, at 133 av des Champs-Élysées and 1 av Matignon in the 8e, and 149 bd St-Germain in the 6e, stay open till 2am, with bars, restaurants, shops and *tabacs*. Each restaurant is listed under the relevant *arrondissement*.

Bars and cafés

Cithéa 112 rue Oberkampf, 11e. Daily 5pm–5.30am.
Le Dépanneur 27 rue Fontaine, 9e. All-nighter.
Fourmi Café 74 rue des Martyrs, 18e. Mon–Thurs & Sun till 2am, Fri & Sat till 4am.
Au Général Lafayette 52 rue Lafayette, 9e. Daily till 4am.
Le Grand Café Capucines 4 bd des Capucines, 9e. All-nighter.
Le Procope 13 rue de l'Ancienne-Comédie, 6e. Daily till 1am.
Le Sous-Bock 49 rue St-Honoré, 1er. Daily till 5am.
La Taverne de Nesle 32 rue Dauphine, 6e. Mon–Thurs & Sun till 4am, Fri & Sat till 5am.
Le Viaduc Café 43 av Daumesnil, 12e. Daily 8am–4am (food served till 3am).

Restaurants

Chez Gladines 30 rue des Cinq-Diamants, 13e. Daily till 1am.
La Coupole 102 bd du Montparnasse, 14e. Daily till 1am.
Flo 7 cours des Petites-Écuries, 10e. Daily till 1.30am.
Goldenberg's 7 rue des Rosiers, 4e. Daily till 1am.
L'Homme Bleu 57 rue Jean-Pierre-Timbaud, 11e. Mon–Sat 5pm–2am.
Julien 16 rue du Faubourg-St-Denis, 10e. Daily till 1am.
Brasserie Lipp 151 bd St-Germain, 6e. Daily till 1am.
N'Zadette M'Foua 152 rue due Château, 14e. Daily till 2am.
Au Pied de Cochon 6 rue Coquillière, 1er. All-nighter.
Polidor 41 rue Monsieur-le-Prince, 6e. Mon–Sat till 12.30am.
Terminus Nord 23 rue de Dunkerque, 10e. Daily till 1am.
À la Tour de Montlhéry (Chez Denise) 5 rue des Prouvaires, 1e. Open 24hr Mon–Fri.

Vaudeville 29 rue Vivienne, 2e. Daily till 2am.
Au Virage Lepic 61 rue Lepic, 18e. Daily except Tues till 2am.

for around €25, and there's a good basic menu at €13.50. Wise to book. Closed Sun.

15e arrondissement

Bars and cafés

Au Roi du Café 59 rue Lecourbe; M° Volontaires/Sèvres-Lecourbe. Traditional café with a decor that didn't change much during the twentieth century and a pleasant terrace, albeit on a busy road. Daily 7am–2am.

Restaurants

Le Bistrot d'André 232 rue St-Charles ☎01.45.57.89.14; M° Balard. A reminder of the old Citroën works before the Parc André-Citroën was created, with pictures and models of the classic French car. Homely dishes and great puds. Midday menu €12.50, otherwise around €25. Closed Sun.

Le Café du Commerce 51 rue du Commerce ☎01.45.75.03.27; M° Émile-Zola. Atmospheric two-storey restaurant with tables ranged around four sides of a central courtyard. Serves trustworthy French classics, including an excellent *andouillette*. Inexpensive lunch menus, evening meals around €25. Daily noon–midnight.

16e arrondissement

Bars and cafés

La Gare 19 Chaussée de la Muette ☎01.42.15.15.31; M° Muette.This renovated train station is now an elegant restaurant with pleasant terrace serving, among other things, a superb and very popular €26 lunch menu. Daily noon–3pm & 7pm–midnight (bar until 2am).

17e arrondissement

Bars and cafés

Chamignon 64 rue des Batignolles; M° Rome/Place-de-Clichy. A local boulangerie on one side and an old café on the other where you can sit and snack on quiche, sandwiches and pastries. Tables on the street in the summer. Daily except Wed till 8pm.

Restaurants

Le Morosophe 83 rue Legendre ☎01.53.06.82.82; M° Brochant. Relaxed contemporary bistro serving unpretentious but well-cooked seasonal dishes. Lunchtime menu at €12, evenings at €25. Closed Sun.

18e arrondissement

Bars and cafés

Le Bar du Relais 12 rue Ravignan; M° Abbesses. A quaint building in a beautiful spot just under the Butte, with tables out just below the little square where Picasso's Beateau-Lavoir studio used to be. Restaurant on one side, café-bar on the other. Daily 8am–2am.

La Fourmi Café 74 rue des Martyrs; M° Pigalle/Abbesses. Trendy, high-ceilinged café-bar full of beautiful and voluble Parisians drinking coffee by day and cocktails at night. Mon–Thurs 8am–2am, Fri & Sat 8am–4am, Sun 10am–2am.

Café Burq 6 rue Burq, 18e; M° Pigalle/Abbesses. This buzzy bar-restaurant is typical of the Abbesses scene, attracting an amiable crowd of twenty-somethings. One half of the room is a pleasant, informal restaurant that's decent but unexceptional; the other half is dominated by the well-stocked bar, noisy with music and chatter. Good wines by the glass. Tues–Sun 8pm–midnight; closed Aug.

Au Rendez-vous des Amis 23 rue Gabrielle; M° Abbesses. Halfway up the Butte, this small, ramshackle, smoky and community-spirited hangout is a magnet for Montmartre locals, especially the young, artsy and alternative-leaning. Daily 8.30am–2am.

Le Sancerre 35 rue des Abbesses; M° Abbesses. A fashionable hangout for the young and trendy of all nationalities under the southern slope of Montmartre. The food can be disappointing. Daily 7am–2am.

Restaurants

L'Assiette 78 rue Labat ☎01.42.59.06.63; M° Château-Rouge. A bit out of the way, but a very friendly place, serving delicious southwestern food as well as the occasional Ukrainian speciality on the blackboard. Good-value €15 menu. Closed Wed eve, Sat lunch & all day Sun.

Au Grain de Folie 24 rue La Vieuville ☎01.42.58.15.57; M° Abbesses. Tiny, simple and colourfully dilapidated vegetarian place with a short, wholesome and inexpensive menu. Mon–Sat 12.30–2.30pm & 7–10.30pm, Sun 12.30–10.30pm.

Le Mono 40 rue Véron ☎01.46.06.99.20; M° Abbesses. Welcoming, family-run Togolese restaurant. The delicious mains are mostly grilled fish or meats served with sour-sweet, slightly hot sauces and rice or cassava meal on the side. Great atmosphere, with soukous on the stereo and Togolese carvings on the walls. Closed Wed.

Le Restaurant 32 rue Véron ☎01.42.23.06.22; M° Abbesses. Trendy but welcoming corner restaurant giving some contemporary twists to classic French ingredients. Count on €20 and up. Daily 12.30–3pm & 7.30pm–11.30pm.

Au Virage Lepic 61 rue Lepic ☎01.42.52.46.79; M° Blanche/Abbesses. Simple but good-quality meaty fare served in a small and friendly bistro. Actors' and actresses' photos adorn the walls, pink gingham shades are draped over the lights, and camp pop classics play softly in the background. Intimate, smoky, international and very enjoyable. Two-course menu at €16. Daily except Tues 7pm–2am.

19e arrondissement

Bars and cafés

Café de la Musique 213 av Jean-Jaures; M° Porte-de Pantin. Part of the Cité de la Musique, this café, with a popular terrace just inside the La Villette complex, was designed by the Cité architect Portzamparc and exudes sophistication, discretion and comfort, but be prepared to pay over the odds for a coffee. Daily till 2am.

Le Rendez-vous des Quais 10 quai de la Seine; M° Jaurès/Stalingrad. Attached to the MK2 art-house cinema, the outside tables of this café/brasserie sit right on the banks of the Bassin de la Villette providing a relaxing spot for refreshment before or after the canal cruises which depart opposite. Daily 11.30am–12.30am.

Restaurant

Aux Saveurs du Liban 11 rue Eugène-Jumin; M° Porte-de-Pantin. Excellent, very cheap,

Gourmet restaurants of Paris

It's worth budgeting for at least one meal in one of Paris's truly spectacular **restaurants**. Top rated is *Alain Ducasse at the Plaza Athénée* hotel, considered one of the best restaurants in Europe (see p.189). The first-ever chef to have been awarded six Michelin stars (shared between two restaurants), Alain Ducasse swept like a tidal wave through the world of French cuisine in the early 1990s and hasn't looked back. Other greats include *L'Ambroisie*, on place des Vosges (see p.185); the splendid Art Nouveau restaurant *Lucas Carton*, 9 place de la Madeleine, 8e (Ⓣ01.42.65.22.90, Ⓦwww.lucascarton.com), directed by chef Alain Senderens; and *Taillevent* (see p.189) where Alain Solivérès is introducing some Mediterranean touches to the menus. Prices at most of these restaurants are often cheaper if you go at midday during the week, and some offer a set lunch menu for around €60. Over on the Left Bank, *Hélène Darroze*, 4 rue d'Assas, 6e (Ⓣ01.42.22.00.11) breaks the mould not just by virtue of being run by a woman, but by offering exciting, bold combinations at relatively low prices. At *Le Jules Verne*, up on the top floor of the Eiffel Tower (Ⓣ01.45.55.61.44), the surprise is that the cooking matches the view – even if the decor is rather 1980s. In general, prices begin at about €100, but the top menus can soar above €200, and there's no limit on the amount you can pay for the finest wines.

Recently, some of the star chefs have made their fine cuisine more accessible to a wider range of customers by opening up less expensive, more casual, but still high-quality establishments. In addition to presiding over the *Plaza Athénée*, for example, Alain Ducasse also runs the cutting-edge bistro *Spoon, Food & Wine* (see p.189), while Hélène Darroze has her relatively relaxed *Salon d'Hélène* on the ground floor.

authentic Lebanese food at this tiny restaurant in a lively local street not far from the Parc de la Villette. €7.50 lunchtime *formule*; between €12 and €20 for dinner. Mon–Sat 11.30am–4pm & 7–11pm.

20e arrondissement

Bars and cafés

Le Baratin 3 rue Jouye-Rouve; Mº Pyrénées. Friendly, unpretentious *bistro à vins* in a run-down area with a good mix of people. Fine selection of lesser-known wines and whiskies. Midday menu €12, à la carte for around €20 in the evening. Tues–Fri noon–midnight, Sat 6pm–midnight. Closed first week of Jan & 3 weeks in Aug.

La Flèche d'Or 102bis rue de Bagnolet, cnr rue des Pyrénées Ⓦwww.flechedor.com; Mº Alexandre-Dumas. A large, lively café attracting the biker, arty, punkish Parisian young. The decor is très destroy – ie railway sleepers and a sawn-off bus front hanging from the ceiling – and the building itself is the old Bagnolet station on the petite ceinture railway that encircled the city until around thirty years ago. It's a nightly venue for live world music, pop, punk, ska, fusion and chanson, and the reasonably priced food (available 8pm–1am) also has a multicultural slant. Mon–Fri 6pm–2am, Sat & Sun 10am–2am.

Restaurants

Les Allobroges 71 rue des Grands-Champs Ⓣ01.43.73.40.00; Mº Maraîchers. A charming neighbourhood restaurant, serving traditional French cuisine to consistently high standards. The *menu* at €15 is excellent value, though the wines are a bit pricey. Booking essential. Closed Sat–Mon.

Lao Siam 49 rue de Belleville Ⓣ01.40.40.09.68; Mº Belleville. The surroundings are nothing special, but the excellent Thai and Lao food, popular with locals, makes up for it. Reckon on €15 upwards. Best to book in advance. Mon–Fri noon–3pm & 6–11.30pm, Sat & Sun noon–11.30pm.

Pho-Dong-Huong 14 rue Louis-Bonnet Ⓣ01.43.57.18.88; Mº Belleville. Spotlessly clean Vietnamese restaurant, where all dishes are around €7. Spicy soups, crispy pancakes, but slow service. Daily except Tues noon–11pm.

Le Zéphyr 1 rue Jourdain Ⓣ01.46.36.65.81; Mº Jourdain. A trendy but relaxed 1930s-style bistro with a lunch menu for €12.50; à la carte €30. Daily 8am–2am, except Sat lunch and all day Sun.

Music and nightlife

The strength of the Paris **music scene** is its diversity – a reputation gained mainly from its absorption of immigrant and exile populations. The city has no rivals in Europe for the variety of **world music** to be discovered: Algerian, West and Central African, Caribbean and Latin American sounds are represented in force. You'll have to look out for individual gigs in one of the listings magazines (see p.109), as most venues don't specialize but instead pursue eclectic programmes that might feature Congolese hip-hop acts cheek-by-jowl with home-grown pop-rock bands. For the authentic Parisian experience try to find a **chanson** night – chanson has long been associated with the city through wartime cabaret artists such as Edith Piaf, Maurice Chevalier and Charles Trenet, and 1960s poet-musicians ranging from Georges Brassens to Serge Gainsbourg. **Jazz** fans are in for a treat, with all styles from New Orleans to current experimental to be heard, although in most clubs admission and drinks prices are a real drawback.

Nightlife recommendations for **clubs** are listed separately from live venues, though bear in mind that many clubs also showcase live acts on certain nights, and many concert venues hold DJ-led sessions after hours. Most clubs play *électro*, which covers anything from house-funk to techno, though you'll also find some interesting Latin and African flavours, and rock music is once more on the up. Places that cater for a primarily **gay or lesbian** clientele are listed in the "Gay and lesbian Paris" section. Bear in mind that some clubs operate very snooty door policies.

Classical music, as you might expect in this Neoclassical city, is alive and well and takes up twice the space of "jazz-pop-folk-rock" in the listings magazines. The **Paris Opéra**, with its two homes – the Opéra-Garnier and Opéra-Bastille – puts on a fine selection of opera and ballet. The need for advance reservations (except sometimes for the concerts held in churches) rather than the price is the major inhibiting factor here. If you're interested in the **contemporary** scene of Systems composition and the like, check out the Cité de la Musique auditorium at La Villette. On June 21 the **Fête de la Musique** sees live bands and free concerts of every kind of music throughout the city.

Information and tickets

See p.109 for **listings magazines**. The best places to get **tickets** for concerts, whether rock, jazz, chansons or classical, are: FNAC Forum des Halles, 1–5 rue Pierre-Lescot, 1er (Ⓣ01.40.41.40.00, Ⓦwww.fnac.fr; M° Chatelet-Les Halles); the FNAC Musique branches (see p.215); or Virgin Megastore (see p.215).

Music venues

Most of the **music venues** listed below are also clubs, and some fall into many categories – the boundaries between world music and jazz, in particular, can be blurred. A few places have live music all week, but the majority host bands on just a couple of nights, usually Thursday to Saturday. **Admission prices** depend on who's playing, but you can expect to pay around €7–15 entry.

Rock and world music venues

Le Bataclan 50 bd Voltaire, 11e ⓣ01.43.14.35.35; M° Oberkampf. Classic ex-music-hall venue with one of the best and most eclectic line-ups of any venue, covering anything from international and local dance and rock musicians – Francis Cabrel, Chemical Brothers, Khaled, Moby – to opera, comedy and techno nights.

Café de la Danse 5 passage Louis-Philippe, 11e ⓣ01.47.00.57.59; M° Bastille. Rock, pop, world and folk music played in an intimate and attractive space. Open nights of concerts only.

La Cigale, 120 bd de Rochechouart, 18e ⓣ01.49.25.89.99, ⓦwww.lacigale.fr; M° Pigalle. An eclectic programming policy in an old -fashioned converted theatre, long a fixture on the Pigalle scene.

Le Divan du Monde 75 rue des Martyrs, 18e ⓣ01.40.05.06.99, ⓦwww.divandumonde.com; M° Pigalle. A youthful venue in a café whose regulars once included Toulouse-Lautrec. One of the city's most eclectic, exciting programmes, ranging from techno to Congolese rumba, with dancing till dawn on weekend nights.

Élysée Montmartre 72 bd de Rochechouart, 18e ⓣ01.55.07.06.00, ⓦwww.elyseemontmartre.com; M° Anvers. A historic Montmartre nightspot with a wonderful, vast, arched-roof dance floor. Pulls in some big-name acts, and every other Saturday there's an unforgettably cheesy party night called Le Bal, with live acts and DJs playing all those 1980s French pop tunes you never sang along to, but everyone around you clearly did. Frequent gigs midweek.

La Flèche d'Or 102bis rue de Bagnolet 20e ⓣ01.43.72.42.44, ⓦwww.flechedor.com; M° Porte-de-Bagnolet. Friendly alternative venue set in a converted train station. Most nights from around 9pm there's a cutting-edge programme of inexpensive electro, dub, world music concerts and club nights, while political and arty events take place in the daytime, and there's a bal salsa from 5pm on Sunday afternoons.

La Guinguette Pirate quai François Mauriac, 13e ⓣ01.43.49.68.68, ⓦwww.guinguettepirate.com; M° Quai-de-la-Gare. Beautiful Chinese barge, moored alongside the quay in front of the Bibliothéque Nationale, hosting relaxed but upbeat world music nights from Tuesday to Sunday. Moored adjacent, *Péniche Alternat* (ⓦwww.alternat.org) and *Batofar* (see p.200) are excellent alternatives.

House of Live 124 rue de la Boétie, 8e ⓣ01.42.25.13.28, ⓦwww.houseoflive.com. Large bar-restaurant venue with an excellent live concert programme. Features mostly up-and-coming French acts in a rock/pop/soul idiom, though Gloria Gaynor, John McEnroe and Alanis Morisette have also graced the stage (not at the same time). Entry is free, and all gigs are followed by after-show clubbing until around 5am.

Maison des Cultures du Monde 101 bd Raspail, 6e ⓣ01.45.44.72.30, ⓦwww.mcm.asso.fr; M° Rennes. All the arts from all over the world, for once not dominated by Europeans. Runs its own world music label, Inedit, and holds a festival of world theatre and music in March.

Le Nouveau Casino 109 rue Oberkampf, 11e ⓣ01.43.57.57.40, ⓦwww.nouveaucasino.net. A sample month might include Swedish indie, electro trip-pop and Belgian pop-chanson, with a metal-hybrid Battle of the Bands to lighten things up a bit. Turns into a club later on.

Olympia 28 bd des Capucines, 9e ⓣ08.92.68.33.68, ⓦwww.olympiahall.com; M° Madeleine/Opéra. A recently renovated old-style music hall hosting well-known international rock and pop acts, with a good programme of domestic stars as well.

Trabendo Parc de la Villette, 19e ⓣ01.49.25.81.75, ⓦwww.trabendo.fr; M° Porte-de-Pantin. Despite its moderate size, this place attracts some big French and international names, in the world, jazz and rock fields. Open nights of concerts only.

Zenith Parc de la Villette, 211 av Jean-Jaurès, 20e ⓣ01.42.08.60.00, ⓦwww.le-zenith.com/paris; M° Porte-de-Pantin. Seating for 6000 people in a giant tent designed exclusively for rock and pop concerts. Large, but more appealing than the stadium venues. Acts include anything from Cher to Coldplay.

Jazz venues

Le Baiser Salé 58 rue des Lombards, 1er ⓣ01.42.33.37.71; M° Châtelet. A bar downstairs and a small, crowded upstairs room with live music every night from 10pm – usually jazz, rhythm & blues, Latino-rock, reggae or Brazilian. Admission €8–16. Mon–Sat 8am–5am.

Le Bilboquet 13 rue St-Benoît, 6e ⓣ01.45.48.81.84; M° St-Germain. A smart, comfortable bar-restaurant with traditional live jazz every night from local and international stars. The music starts at 9.30pm, and food is served until 1am. Admission €18. Mon–Sat 9pm–dawn.

Caveau de la Huchette 5 rue de la Huchette, 5e ⓣ01.43.26.65.05, ⓦwww.caveaudelahuchette.fr; M° St-Michel. One of the city's oldest jazz clubs dating back to the mid-1940s. Both Lionel Hampton and Sidney Bechet played here. Live jazz, usually trad and big band, to dance to on a floor surrounded by tiers of benches. Popular with students. Admission Mon–Thurs & Sun €10.50; Fri & Sat €13; drinks from €4.50. Daily 9.30pm–2am.

Instants Chavirés 7 rue Richard-Lenoir, Montreuil ⓣ01.42.87.25.91, ⓦwww.instantschavires.com; M° Robespierre. Avant-garde jazz joint on the eastern edge of the city where musicians go to hear each other play. Admission €11. Tues–Sat 8pm–1am; concerts at 9pm.

New Morning 7–9 rue des Petites-Écuries, 10e ⓣ01.45.23.51.41, ⓦwww.newmorning.com; M° Château-d'Eau. The decor's somewhat spartan, a bit like an underground garage, but this is the place where the big international names in jazz come to play. It's often standing room only unless you get here early. Admission €16.50–20. Usually Mon–Sat 8pm–1.30am (concerts start around 9pm).

Le Petit Journal 71 bd St-Michel, 5e ⓣ01.43.26.28.59; RER Luxembourg. A small, smoky bar-restaurant with good, mainly French, traditional and mainstream sounds. Admission €15.24; €31–40 including meal. Mon–Sat 9pm–2am; closed Aug.

Le Petit Journal Montparnasse 13 rue du Commandant-Mouchotte, 14e ⓣ01.43.21.56.70, ⓦwww.petitjournal-montparnasse.com; M° Montparnasse. Under the Hôtel Montparnasse, and sister establishment to the above, with bigger visiting names, both French and international. Admission, including first drink, around €20. Mon–Sat 8.30pm–2am; music from 10pm. Closed mid-July to mid-Aug.

Le Petit Opportun 15 rue des Lavandières-Ste-Opportune, 1er ⓣ01.42.36.01.36; M° Châtelet-Les Halles. The first set starts at 10.30pm. Arrive early to get a seat for the live music in the dungeon-like cellar where the acoustics play strange tricks and you can't always see the musicians. Fairly eclectic policy and a crowd of genuine connoisseurs. Admission €13–16. Tues–Sat 9pm–dawn; closed Aug.

Le Sunside/Le Sunset 60 rue des Lombards, 1er ⓣ01.40.26.46.60; M° Châtelet-Les Halles. Two clubs in one: *Le Sunside* on the ground floor features mostly traditional jazz, whereas the downstairs *Sunset* is a venue for electric and fusion jazz. The *Sunside* concert usually starts at 9pm and the *Sunset* at 10pm, so you can sample a bit of both. Admission €8–25. Mon–Sat 9.30pm–2.30am.

Utopia 79 rue de l'Ouest, 14e ⓣ01.43.22.79.66; M° Pernety. Mon–Sat 10pm–dawn; closed Aug. No genius here, but good French blues singers interspersed with jazz and blues tapes, with a mainly young and studenty audience. Generally very pleasant atmosphere. Admission free; drinks from €8.

Chanson venues

Casino de Paris 16 rue de Clichy, 9e ⓣ01.49.95.99.99, ⓦwww.casinodeparis.fr;

Cabaret

Paris's **cabaret clubs** are still high-kicking along, but if you're looking for an atmosphere of sexy, bohemian exuberance you're better off in the gay bars of the Marais (see p.203), and if it's titillation you're after try the sex clubs of Pigalle. That said, the cabaret shows listed below provide a certain glitzy good time, and the dancers are superbly professional. Audiences are mostly groups of international tourists, paying top dollar.

Crazy Horse 12 av George V, 8e ⓣ01.47.23.32.32, ⓦwww.lecrazyhorseparis.com; M° George V. At the sexier end of the scene, with lots of provocative "dancing". Two shows daily at 8.30pm and 11pm. €90 including two drinks, or €49 standing at the bar.

Le Lido 116bis av des Champs-Élysées, 8e ⓣ01.40.76.56.10, ⓦwww.lido.fr; M° George V. The most spectacular show, with expensive lighting and sound effects, and lots of professional glitz. Two shows daily at 9.30pm and 11.30pm (€80, or €60 on Sun & Mon). Dinner and show option begins at 7pm (€140–200, depending on menu).

Le Moulin Rouge 82 bd de Clichy, 18e ⓣ01.53.09.82.82, ⓦwww.moulinrouge.fr; M° Blanche. The traditional Paris show, with the serried ranks of the sixty Doriss Girls' frilly knickers as the highlight. Shows at 9pm (€95) and 11pm (Thurs–Sun only; €85), or with dinner included at 7pm (€135–165, depending on menu). Book up to two months in advance at weekends.

M° Trinité. This decaying, once-plush casino in one of the seediest streets in Paris is a venue for all

Le Lapin Agile 22 rue des Saules, 18e ⓣ01.46.06.85.87, ⓦwww.au-lapin-agile.com; M° Lamarck-Caulaincourt. Old haunt of Apollinaire, Utrillo and other Montmartre artists, some of whose pictures adorn the walls, still offering cabaret, poetry and chanson. Admission €24 including first drink; subsequent drinks €7.

Au Limonaire 18 Cité Bergère, 9e ⓣ01.45.23.33.33; M° Grands Boulevards. Tiny backstreet venue, perfect for Parisian chanson nights showcasing young singers and zany music/poetry/performance acts. Dinner beforehand – traditional, inexpensive, and fairly good – guarantees a seat for the show at 10pm – otherwise you'll be crammed up against the bar, if you can get in at all.

Le Locandiera 145 rue Oberkampf, 11e ⓣ01.56.98.12.18; M° Ménilmontant. Friendly Italian bar-restaurant with a vaulted basement featuring frequent chanson acts – both in the classic French manner, or with pop, world and jazz inflections. Free.

Clubs

The **clubs** listed below are recommended as dance venues, although a few also put on live music gigs. It's worth remembering that most of the places listed under "Music venues" also function as clubs, and many gay and lesbian venues attract mixed crowds, often from the trendy end of the nightlife spectrum. Things rarely kick off before 1am. You'll have to keep your ear to the ground to find the very latest must-go *soirée* – check out the listings in *Zurban* magazine (see p.109), or try simply asking around in likely-looking bars or music shops. Most entry prices include one free drink, and vary according to when you turn up – usually anything from €10–12 on weekdays to €15-20 on Friday and Saturday after midnight; exceptions are noted below. Given the difficulty of finding a taxi after hours (see p.114), many Parisian clubbers just keep going until the metro starts running at around 5.30am.

Les Bains 7 rue du Bourg-l'Abbé, 3e ⓣ01.48.87.01.80; M° Étienne-Marcel. This is as posey as they come, set in an old Turkish bathhouse with a chill-out area in the old plunge pool. The music is mostly house, hip-hop and garage. Fussy bouncers and expensive drinks. Daily midnight–dawn.

Batofar quai François Mauriac, 13e ⓣ01.56.29.10.00, ⓦwww.batofar.net; M° Quai-de-la-Gare/Bibliothèque-Tolbiac. An old lighthouse boat moored at the foot of the Bibliothèque Nationale. Brilliant line-up of DJs from all over the world spinning techno for the most part. Your best bet for a not-too-expensive club night out. Admission under €12. Daily 9pm–3am.

Chapelle des Lombards 19 rue de Lappe, 11e ⓣ01.43.57.24.24; M° Bastille. This erstwhile bal musette still plays the occasional waltz and tango, but for the most part the music is Afro-Latin: R&B, n'dambolo, zouk, dance hall and the rest. It's renown as a pick-up joint means unabashed advances. Tues–Sun from 11.30pm.

La Coupole 100 boulevard du Montparnasse, 14e ⓣ01.43.20.14.20; M° Vavin. La Coupole's formula survived most of the twentieth century – gorgeous, historic brasserie upstairs, cool nightclub downstairs – though the music has changed. Fabulous live salsa nights on Tues, otherwise mainstream house at weekends. Tues–Sat 11.30pm–3am.

Folies Pigalle 11 place Pigalle, 9e ⓣ01.48.78.25.26; M° Pigalle. Famed for its sleazy past, and only slightly less sleazy present, transsexual clientele and all, the Folies is a landmark on the club scene for its house nights and "after" events early on Saturday and Sunday mornings, as well as for the Sunday afternoon gay tea dance, BBB. Tues–Sun midnight–dawn or beyond.

La Java 105 rue du Faubourg-du-Temple, 10e ⓣ01.42.02.20.52; M° Belleville. Fast-moving salsa-tropical club, with regular live bands and a seriously good-time vibe. Admission €10. Thurs 10pm–2am, Fri & Sat 11pm–5am.

La Locomotive 90 bd de Clichy, 18e ⓣ08.36.69.69.28, ⓦwww.laloco.com; M° Blanche. High-tech monster club with three dance floors, all playing variations on house. Tues–Sun 11pm–dawn.

Le Queen 102 Champs-Élysées, 8e ⓣ01.53.89.08.89, ⓦwww.queen.fr; M° George-V. Legendary club whose success has far transcended its gay origins, though still only the best-dressed women get past the door. Not half as fashionable as it once was, with fairly mainstream house Thursday to Saturday. The more interesting nights are Sunday and Monday (gay disco), and Wednesday (R&B and hip-hop). Daily midnight–dawn.

Rex Club 5 bd Poissonnière, 2e ⓣ01.42.36.28.83; M° Grands-Boulevards. The clubbers' club: spacious and serious about its music, which is strictly electronic, notably techno. Attracts big-name DJs such as Laurent Garnier. Admission €10–15. Thurs–Sat 11.30pm–6am; closed Aug.

WAGG 62 rue Mazarine, 6e ⓣ01.55.42.22.00; M° Odéon. Adjoining Terence Conran's flashy Alcazar restaurant and bar, the *WAGG* continues the UK theme with the Seventies-themed "Carwash" nights on Fridays (free before midnight, €15 after) and UK house on Saturdays (€12). Fri & Sat midnight–6am.

Classical music

Paris is a stimulating environment for **classical music**, both established and contemporary. The former is well represented in performances within churches – sometimes free or very cheap – and in an enormous choice of commercially promoted concerts held every day of the week. Contemporary and experimental computer-based work also flourishes.

Concert venues

Some of the city's most dynamic and eclectic programming is to be found at the **Cité de la Musique** at La Villette (ⓦwww.cite-musique.fr; M° Porte-de-Pantin). Ancient music, contemporary works, jazz, chansons and music from all over the world can be heard at the complex's two major concert venues: the **Conservatoire** (the national music academy) at 209 av Jean-Jaurès, 19e (ⓣ01.40.40.46.46); and the **Salle des Concerts** at 221 av Jean-Jaurès, 19e (ⓣ01.44.84.44.84).

These apart, the top **auditoriums** are: Salle Gaveau, 45 rue de la Boëtie, 8e (ⓣ01.49.53.05.07; M° Miromesnil); Théâtre des Champs-Élysées, 15 av Montaigne, 8e (ⓣ01.49.52.50.50, ⓦwww.theatrechampselysees.fr; M° Alma-Marceau); the Théâtre Musical de Paris (ⓦwww.chatelet-theatre.com; M° Châtelet) and the Salle Pleyel, 252 rue du Faubourg-St-Honoré, 8e (ⓣ08.25.00.02.52; M° Concorde), currently undergoing renovation and due to reopen sometime in 2004. **Tickets** are best bought at the box offices, though for big names you may find overnight queues, and a large number of seats are always booked by subscribers. The price range is very reasonable.

Churches and **museums** are also good places to hear classical music. The Église St-Séverin, 1 rue des Prètres st-Séverin, 5e (ⓣ01.48.24.16.97; M° St-Michel); the Église St-Julien le Pauvre, 23 quai de Montebello, 5e (ⓣ01.42.26.00.00; M° St-Michel); and the Sainte Chapelle, 4 bd du Palais, 1er (ⓣ01.42.77.65.65; M° Cité), all host regular concerts. The Musée du Louvre (ⓦwww.louvre.com) and the Musée d'Orsay (ⓦwww.musee-orsay.fr) both host chamber music recitals in their auditoriums, while from time to time the Musée National du Moyen-Âge holds recitals of medieval music. Sometimes classical concerts take place for free at **Radio France**, 166 av du Président-Kennedy, 16e (ⓣ01.56.40.15.16, ⓦradio-france.fr; M° Passy).

Opera

Since its opening in 1989 the **Opéra-Bastille** has weathered some stormy times. Its first performance – the six-hour-long *Les Troyens* by Berlioz – cast something of a shadow on the project's proclaimed commitment to popularizing its art, and for some years the opera house was plagued by high-profile rows and resignations. Things at last seem to be settling down, however, and there's been a period of stability under its current director James Conlon. While the building's facade hasn't weathered particularly well – it's started to crumble in places and unsightly netting holds bits of it in place – the auditorium is well designed and has fine acoustics. Most performances are packed out, so it's best to book ahead. Tickets (€9–130) can be bought Monday to Saturday 9am to 7pm on ⓣ08.36.69.78.68 at least four weeks in advance, on the Internet (ⓦwww.opera-de-paris.fr) from three months to three days in advance, or at the ticket office (Mon–Sat 11am–6.30pm) within two weeks of the performance – the number of tickets available by this stage however is limited and for popular performances people start queuing at 9am, if not earlier. The cheapest seats are available to personal callers only; unfilled seats are sold at a discount to students five minutes before the curtain goes up. For programme details, phone the above number, or have a look at their website.

The Opéra-Bastille enjoys a friendly rivalry with the **Théâtre du Châtelet**, 1 place du Châtelet, 1er (ⓣ01.40.28.28.40; M° Châtelet), which also puts on large-scale productions. Operas are still staged at the old **Opéra-Garnier**, place de l'Opéra, 9e (ⓣ08.92.89.90.90, ⓦwww.opera-de-paris.fr; M° Opéra), though these days it hosts mostly ballets; the procedure for getting tickets for the latter is the same as for the Opéra Bastille above. Smaller, more daring classical and modern operas are performed at the **Opéra-Comique**, Salle Favart, 5 rue Favart, 2e (ⓣ01.42.44.45.46; M° Richelieu-Drouot).

Contemporary music

Pierre Boulez' post-serialist experiments received massive public funding for many years in the form of a vast laboratory of acoustics and "digital signal processing" – a complex known as **IRCAM** – housed underneath the Pompidou Centre. Boulez' Ensemble Intercontemporain is now based in the Cité de la Musique, but IRCAM (ⓦwww.ircam.fr) occasionally has concerts.

Other Paris-based practitioners of contemporary and experimental music include Laurent Bayle, Jean-Claude Eloy, Pascal Dusapin and Luc Ferrarie, who can occasionally be heard at the Cité de la Musique.

Festivals

Festivals are plentiful in all the diverse fields that come under the far too general term of "classical". The **Festival d'Art Sacré** consists mainly of concerts and recitals of early sacred music (end of Nov to mid-Dec); concerts feature in the general arts **Festival d'Automne** (mid-Sept to end Dec; ⓦwww.festival-automne.com); and a summer **festival of chamber music** is held at the Château de Sceaux to the south of the city (mid-July to third week in Sept).

For details of these and more, pick up the current year's **festival schedule** from one of the tourist offices or from the Hôtel de Ville, 29 rue du Rivoli, 4e (M° Hôtel-de-Ville). During January the Hôtel de Ville sponsors a week of two concert tickets for the price of one.

Gay and lesbian Paris

Paris is one of Europe's major centres for **gay men**, with numerous bars, clubs, restaurants, saunas and shops catering for a gay clientele. Its focal point is the **Marais**, whose central street, rue Ste-Croix-de-la-Bretonnerie, has visibly gay commerces at almost every other address. **Lesbians** have many fewer dedicated addresses, but there are a handful of women-only places. The high spot of the calendar is the annual **Marche des Fiertés LGBT**, or gay pride march, which normally takes place on the last Saturday in June.

Information and contacts

The gay and lesbian community is well catered for by the media, the best source of information being *Têtu* (Ⓦwww.tetu.com), France's main gay monthly magazine – the name means "headstrong". The pull-out section, *Agenda*, is full of contact details, addresses and reviews. Alternatively, you can pick up the free Parisian gay news magazine, *Illico*.

Centre Gai et Lesbien de Paris 3 rue Keller, 11e Ⓣ01.43.57.21.47 Ⓦwww.cglparis.org; M° Ledru-Rollin/Bastille. Paris's main information centre is the first port of call for information, contacts and addresses. Legal and psychological advice is available on request. Mon–Sat 4–8pm.

Inter-LGBT 127 rue Amelot, 11e Ⓣ01.53.01.47.01, Ⓦwww.inter-lgbt.org; M° St-Sébastien-Froissart. Actively fights for gay rights and organizes the annual pride march.

Maison des Femmes 163 rue de Charenton, 12e Ⓣ01.43.43.41.13, Ⓦmaisondesfemmes.free.fr; M° Reuilly-Diderot. The main women's centre in Paris and home to a number of lesbian groups which organize workshops and hold frequent meetings. Mon–Wed 9am–7pm, Thurs & Fri 9am–5pm.

Les Mots à la Bouche 6 rue Ste-Croix-de-la-Bretonnerie, 4e Ⓣ01.42.78.88.30, Ⓦwww.motsbouche.com; M° Hôtel-de-Ville. The main gay and lesbian bookshop, with exhibition space and meeting rooms; a selection of literature in English, too. Lots of free listings maps and club flyers to pick up, and one of the helpful assistants usually speaks English. Mon–Sat 11am–11pm, Sun 2–8pm.

SOS Homophobie Ⓣ01.48.06.42.41, Ⓦwww.sos-homophobie.org. First-stop helpline for victims of homophobia open Mon–Fri 8–10pm.

Bars and clubs

In terms of nightlife, Paris is one of the world's great cities to be gay. The Marais area, especially, has a wide range of **gay venues** – the selection given below only scratches the surface – and although lesbians do not enjoy a wide selection of women-only places, they are welcome in some of the predominantly male clubs. The reputation of wild hedonism in gay clubs has spread outside the gay community and attracted heterosexuals in search of a good time. Consequently, heterosexuals are welcome in some gay establishments if in gay company – some gay clubs have all but abandoned a gay policy (the legendary gay club *Le Queen* – see p.200 – is gay-only on weekends) – whilst many of the more mainstream clubs have started doing gay nights. For a complete rundown, consult *Têtu* magazine's Agenda section.

Banana Café 13 rue de la Ferronnerie, 1er Ⓣ01.42.33.35.31; M° Châtelet. Seriously hedonistic club-bar, packing in the punters with up-tempo clubby tunes. Daily 6pm–5am.

Boobsbourg 26 rue de Montmorency, 3e Ⓣ01.42.74.04.82; M° Rambuteau. Fashionable but relaxed mainly-lesbian bar, with good food, classy decor and a chic young clientele. Tues–Sun 5pm–2am.

Le Central 33 rue Vieille-du-Temple, 4e Ⓣ01.48.87.99.33; M° Hôtel-de-Ville. The oldest gay local in the Marais. Small, friendly and always crowded with tourists and locals. Mon–Thurs 4pm–2am, Fri–Sun 2pm–2am.

Le Cox 15 rue des Archives, 3e Ⓣ01.42.72.08.00; M° Hôtel-de-Ville. Muscly, body-beautiful clientele up for a seriously good time. A good pre-club place, with DJs on weekend nights. Daily 1pm–2am.

Le Duplex 25 rue Michel-le-Comte, 3e Ⓣ01.42.72.80.86; M° Rambuteau. Popular with trendy media types for its relatively sophisticated atmosphere, but still relaxed and friendly. Sun–Thurs 8pm–2am, Fri & Sat 8pm–4am.

Le Mixer 23 rue Ste-Croix-de-la-Bretonnerie, 4e Ⓣ01.48.87.55.44; M° Hôtel-de-Ville. Popular gay, lesbian and straight-friendly bar with a friendly atmosphere. The small dancefloor is overlooked by a DJ on a giddy plinth, and there's a cosy mezzanine level. Futuristic Beaubourg-meets-Blade Runner decor. Daily 5pm–2am.

Open Café 17 rue des Archives, 4e Ⓣ01.48.87.80.25; M° Hôtel-de-Ville. The first gay bar/café to have tables out on the pavement.

Hugely popular as a "look-at-me" pre-club venue, but more relaxed during the day. Daily 11am–2am.

Le Pulp 25 bd Poissonnière, 2e ⓣ01.40.26.01.93; M° Montmartre. Paris's lesbian club par excellence, playing music from techno to Madonna. So cool that it pulls in a DJ-led, straight crowd on midweek nights. Thurs–Sun from midnight.

Redlight 34 rue du Départ, 15e ⓣ01.42.79.94.53; M° Montparnasse-Bienvenüe. Gay flavour of the moment for its huge weekend club nights, which begin well after midnight and end around 10am, or noon on Sundays. Expect to hear a lot of house.

Les Scandaleuses 8 rue des Ecouffes, 4e ⓣ01.48.87.39.26; M° Hôtel-de-Ville. Trendy and high-profile lesbian bar in the Marais – men are welcome if accompanied. Lively atmosphere guaranteed, with DJs at weekends. Daily 6pm–5am.

Le Tango 13 rue au-Maire, 3e ⓣ01.42.72.17.78; M° Arts-et-Métiers. Classic gay and lesbian venue with relaxed, straight-friendly nights from 10.30pm on Fridays and Saturdays, in which the music runs the gamut from traditional French *musette* to hardcore. Tea dances Sun 6–11pm.

Film, theatre and dance

Cinema addicts will do well in Paris, with a choice of around three hundred films showing in any one week. The city's plethora of little arts cinemas screen unrivalled programmes of classic and contemporary films, and you can find mainstream movies at almost any time of the day or night. **Theatre**, on the other hand, is less accessible to non-French-speakers, especially the cabaret and comics of the *café-théâtres*. However, there is stimulation in the cult of the director – Paris is home to Peter Brook, Ariane Mnouchkine and other exiles, as well as French talent, whose dazzling productions are highly visual. Suburban theatres rival the city proper for bold experimental theatre. Also, transcending language barriers, there are exciting developments in **dance**, much of it incorporating **mime**. Traditional **circus** has a seasonal home at the Cirque d'Hiver Bouglione (see p.212); more cutting-edge troupes are programmed at the Parc de la Villette, and there's an international festival every January.

The main **festivals** include the Festival de Films des Femmes (end March/beginning of April); the Festival Exit (March), featuring international contemporary dance, performance and theatre at Créteil's Maison des Arts; Paris Quartier d'Été (July), with music, theatre and cinema events around the city; the Festival d'Automne (Sept–Dec), with traditional and experimental theatrical, musical, dance and multimedia productions from all over the world; and the Festival du Cinéma en Plein Air (mid-July to end Aug) at Parc de la Villette, showing free films in the park.

Information and tickets

The most comprehensive **film listings** are given in the inexpensive weeklies *Zurban* (ⓦwww.zurban.com) and *Pariscope*. In *Pariscope*, watch out for the smaller Reprises section, where you'll usually find a number of British or American classics listed, though often enough these turn out to be one-off screenings at an unlikely hour of the afternoon. You rarely need to book in advance; programmes (*séances*) often start around midday and continue through to the early hours. The average price is around €8, but many smaller cinemas have lower rates on Monday or Wednesday and for earlier *séances*, and student reductions are available from Monday to Thursday. Almost all of the huge selection of foreign films will be shown at some cinemas in the original language – *version originale* or *v.o.* in the listings. Dubbed films will be listed as *v.f.* and English versions of co-productions as *version anglaise* or *v.a.*

Stage productions are detailed in *Pariscope* and *L'Officiel des Spectacles* with brief résumés or reviews. Ticket prices are often around €15–20, though you may pay less in smaller venues, and more for many commercial and major state productions (most closed Sun & Mon). Half-price previews are advertised in *Pariscope* and *L'Officiel des Spectacles*, and there are weekday student discounts. Prices are high for epic productions by top directors which may even carry over several days; these always need booking in advance. Tickets can be bought directly from the theatres, from FNAC shops and Virgin Megastores (see p.215), or at the **ticket kiosks** on place de la Madeleine, 8e, opposite no. 15, and on the parvis of the Gare du Montparnasse, 15e (Tues–Sat 12.30–7.45pm, Sun 12.30–3.45pm). They sell half-price same-day tickets and charge a small commission, but be prepared to queue. Tickets for **café-théâtres** average around €12, and it's best to book in advance for Friday and Saturday performances, directly from the venues.

Film

Even though many of the smaller movie houses in obscure corners of the city have closed in recent years, and the big chains, UGC and Gaumont, keep opening new multi-screen cinemas, you still have an unbeatable choice of non-mainstream **films** in Paris, covering every place and period. You can go and see Senegalese, Taiwanese, Brazilian or Finnish films, for example, that would never be shown in Britain or the US or watch your way through the entire careers of individual directors in the mini-festivals held at many of the independents.

The Quartier Latin, around the Sorbonne, has a particularly high concentration of arts cinemas showing an almost incredible repertoire of classic films, while the area around the Gare Montparnasse is chock-full with big-screen movie-houses offering the latest glossy releases. For the biggest screen of all, check-out the Gaumont cinema on Place de l'Italie. The **Festival de Films de Femmes**, held in the last week in March, is organized by the Maison des Arts in Créteil (Ⓣ01.49.80.38.98, Ⓦwww.filmsdefemmes.com; M° Créteil-Préfecture).

Classic venues

L'Arlequin 76 rue des Rennes, 6e, M° St-Suplice. The Quartier Latin's best cinephile's palace, offering special screenings of classics every Sunday at 11pm followed by debates in the café opposite.

Cinemathèque Française Palais de Chaillot, 7 av Albert-de-Mun, 16e (M° Iéna/Trocadéro); 42 bd Bonne-Nouvelle, 10e (M° Bonne-Nouvelle). At the time of writing, the two branches of the cinemathèque were still showing the great classics of French cinema, waiting for a definitive date for the big move to the new museum of cinema complex at 51 rue de Bercy, still under construction – see Ⓦwww.51ruedebercy.com for updates, or just check the listings magazines.

L'Entrepôt 7–9 rue Francis-de-Pressensé, 14e Ⓦwww.lentrepot.fr; M° Pernety. One of the best alternative Paris cinemas, which has been keeping ciné-addicts happy for years with its three screens dedicated to the obscure, the subversive and the brilliant, as well as its bookshop and bar-restaurant.

Forum des Images 2 Grande Galerie, Porte St-Eustache, Forum des Halles, 1er Ⓦwww.forumdesimages.net; RER Châtelet-Les Halles. This venue screens several films or videos daily, but also has a large library of newsreel footage, film clips, adverts, documentaries, etc – all connected with Paris – that you can access yourself from a computer terminal. You can make your choice via a Paris place name, an actor, a director, a date, and so on; there are instructions in English at the desk, and a friendly librarian to help you out. €5.50 for two hours research, plus any films shown that day. Tues–Sun 1–9pm, Thurs till 10pm.

Grand Action and Action Écoles 5 & 23 rue des Écoles, 5e, M° Cardinal-Lemoine/Maubert-Mutualité; Action Christine, 4 rue Christine, 6e;

Mº Odéon/St-Michel. The Action chain specializes in new prints of ancient classics and screens contemporary films from different countries.

Le Grand Rex 1 bd Poissonnière, 2e, Mº Bonne-Nouvelle. Just as outrageous as La Pagode (see below), but in the kitsch line, with a Metropolis-style tower blazing its neon name, 2750 seats and a ceiling of stars and Moorish city skyline. Foreign films are always dubbed.

Max Linder Panorama 24 bd Poissonnière, 9e, Mº Bonne-Nouvelle. Opposite Le Grand Rex, and with almost as big a screen, this cinema always shows films in the original and has state-of-the-art sound and Art Deco decor.

MK2 Quai de la Seine 14 quai de la Seine, 19e, Mº Jaurès/Stalingrad. Part of the MK2 chain but distinctive in style – covered in famous cinematic quotes and on the banks of the Bassin de la Villette – and with a varied art-house repertoire.

La Pagode 57bis rue de Babylone, 7e, Mº François-Xavier. The most beautiful of the city's cinemas, transplanted from Japan at the turn of the last century to be a rich Parisienne's party place. The wall panels of the Grande Salle auditorium are embroidered in silk; golden dragons and elephants hold up the candelabra; and a battle between Japanese and Chinese warriors rages on the ceiling. Financial problems have made its future uncertain but at the time of writing it was due to keep going; check Pariscope for details.

Reflet Medicis II and III, Quartier Latin and Le Champo 3 rue Champollion, 9 rue Champollion and 51 rue des Écoles, 5e, Mº Cluny-La-Sorbonne/Odéon. A cluster of inventive little cinemas, tirelessly offering up rare screenings and classics, including frequent retrospective cycles covering great directors, both French and international (always in *v.o.*). The small, all-black cinema café Le Reflet, on the other side of the street, is a little-known cult classic in itself.

Le Studio 28 10 rue de Tholozé, 18e, Mº Blanche/Abbesses. In its early days, after one of the first showings of Buñuel's *L'Age d'Or*, this was done over by extreme right-wing Catholics who destroyed the screen and the paintings by Dalí and Ernst in the foyer. The cinema still hosts avant-garde premieres, followed occasionally by discussions with the director, as well as regular festivals.

UGC Ciné-Cité Les Halles 7 place de la Rotonde, Forum des Halles, 1er, Mº Châtelet-Les Halles. A nightmare to find – on the bottom level of the Forum des Halles complex, on the Porte Rambuteau side – but worth perservering for the frequent screenings of art house and *v.o.* films, for once on large screens backed by up-to-date sound. Expect to queue for tickets.

Theatre

Bourgeois farces, postwar classics, Shakespeare, Racine and Molière are all staged with the same range of talent or lack of it that you'd find in London or New York. What is rare are home-grown, socially concerned and realist dramas, though touring foreign companies make up for that. Exciting contemporary work is provided by the superstar breed of directors such as Peter Brook, Ariane Mnouchkine and Patrice Chéreau; spectacular and dazzling sensation tends to take precedence over speech in their productions, which feature huge casts, extraordinary sets and overwhelming sound and light effects – an experience, even if you haven't understood a word.

Bouffes du Nord 37bis bd de la Chapelle, 10e ⓣ01.46.07.34.50, ⓦwww.bouffesdunord.com; Mº La Chapelle. Peter Brook's permanent base in Paris; the occasional concert is also performed.

Cartoucherie route du Champ-de-Manoeuvre, 12e, Mº Château-de-Vincennes. Home to several interesting theatre companies including workers' co-op, Théâtre du Soleil, set up by Ariane Mnouchkine (ⓣ01.43.74.24.08, ⓦwww.theatre-du-soleil.fr).

Comédie Française 2 rue de Richelieu, 1er ⓣ01.44.58.15.15, ⓦwww.comedie-francaise.fr; Mº Palais-Royal. The national theatre, staging mainly Racine, Molière and other classics, but also some contemporary work.

MC93 1 bd Lénine, Bobigny ⓣ01.41.60.72.72, ⓦwww.mc93.com; Mº Pablo-Picasso. MC93 stages highly challenging productions and often invites in foreign directors.

Odéon Théâtre de l'Europe 1 place Paul-Claudel, 6e ⓣ01.44.41.36.36, ⓦwww.theatre-odeon.fr; Mº Odéon. Contemporary plays and foreign-language productions in the theatre that became an open parliament during May 1968.

Opéra Comique place Boïeldieu, rue Favart, 2e ⓣ01.42.44.45.46; Mº Richelieu-Drouot. Director Jérôme Savary's diverse and exciting programme blends all forms of stage arts: modern and classical opera, musicals, comedy, dance and pop music.

Théâtre National de Chaillot Palais de Chaillot, place du Trocadéro, 16e ⓣ01.53.65.30.00, ⓦwww.theatre-chaillot.fr; M° Trocadéro. Puts on an exciting programme of contemporary dance and theatre and regularly hosts foreign productions.

Théâtre National de la Colline 15 rue Malte-Brun, 20e ⓣ01.44.62.52.52, ⓦwww.colline.fr; M° Gambetta. Puts on works by both well-known directors and less well-established innovators.

Café-théâtre

Café-théâtre, with its word-play and allusions to current fads, phobias and politicians, can be incomprehensible even to a fluent French-speaker. Puerile, dirty jokes are also its stock in trade. But the atmosphere can be fun, and every so often an original talent will appear.

The Marais has a high concentration of **venues**: you could try the tiny Blancs-Manteaux, 15 rue des Blancs-Manteaux, 4e (ⓣ01.48.87.15.84; M° Hôtel-de-Ville/Rambuteau); or the *Café de la Gare*, 41 rue du Temple, 4e (ⓣ01.42.78.52.51; M° Hôtel-de-Ville/Rambuteau), which has a reputation for novelty.

Dance and mime

The Paris dance companies are easily rivalled by dance troupes in La Rochelle, Marseille, Grenoble, Angers and Montpellier, but there are a number of choreographers either based in Paris or who regularly tour here that are worth looking out for, especially Maguy Marin, Karine Saporta and François Verret. Some of the most innovative French dance companies combine different media and genres to create dazzling, unclassifiable spectacles. The Compagnie Montalvo-Hervieu for example, based in Créteil, just outside Paris, puts on hugely entertaining shows combining every dance genre going, from ballet to hip-hop, all set against a background of giant video screens with which the dancers interact, and accompanied by a soundtrack ranging from Vivaldi to Fat Boy Slim.

Though the famous **mime** schools of Marcel Marceau and Lecoq still turn out excellent artists, pure mime hardly exists except on the streets; the Pompidou Centre's piazza is one of the best place to catch performances. Plenty of space and critical attention is also given to **tap**, **tango**, **folk** and **jazz dancing**, and to visiting traditional dance troupes from all over the world. As for **ballet**, the principal stage is at the old opera house, the Opéra-Garnier; other major productions are put on at the Théâtre de la Ville and the Théâtre Musical de Paris. Many of the theatres listed above under "Theatre" also host dance productions.

Centre Mandapa 6 rue Wurtz, 13e ⓣ01.45.89.01.60; M° Glacière. Dedicated to traditional dance from around the world and also gives lessons in classical Indian dance.

Centre Pompidou rue Beaubourg, 4e ⓣ01.44.78.13.15; M° Rambuteau/RER Châtelet-Les Halles. The Grande Salle in the basement is used for dance performances by visiting companies.

Maison des Arts de Créteil place Salvador-Allende, Créteil ⓣ01.45.13.19.19, ⓦwww.maccreteil.com; M° Créteil-Préfecture. A lively suburban dance and theatre venue, hosting the acclaimed Festival Exit (see p.204) and home of the innovative dance troupe Compagnie Montalvo-Hervieu.

Opéra-Garnier place de l'Opéra, 9e ⓣ08.36.69.78.68, ⓦwww.opera-de-paris.fr; M° Opéra. Main home of the Ballet de l'Opéra National de Paris.

Théâtre des Abbesses 31 rue des Abbesses, 18e ⓣ01.42.74.22.77; M° Abbesses. Sister company to the Théâtre de la Ville, with slightly more offbeat and daring performances.

Théâtre Musical de Paris place du Châtelet, 4e ⓣ01.40.28.28.40, ⓦwww.chatelet-theatre.com; M° Châtelet. A major ballet venue where, in 1910, Diaghilev put on the first season of Russian ballet. Though mainly used for classical concerts and opera, it also hosts top-notch visiting ballet companies like the Mariinsky.

Théâtre de la Ville 2 place du Châtelet, 4e ⓣ01.42.74.22.77, ⓦwww.theatredelaville-paris.com; M° Châtelet. The height of success for contemporary dance productions is to end up here. Works by Karine Saporta, Maguy Marin and Pina Bausch are regularly featured, along with modern theatre classics, comedy and concerts.

Sports and activities

When it's cold and wet and you've had your fill of café vistas and peering at museums, monuments and the dripping panes of shop-fronts, don't despair or retreat back to your hotel. As well as movies, Paris offers a whole host of pleasant ways to pass the time indoors – **skating**, **swimming**, **hamams** – or outdoors, with all the **popular sports** to watch or participate in.

Information

L'Officiel des Spectacles has the best listings of **sports facilities** (under "Activités sportives"). Information on municipal facilities is available from the town hall, the Mairie de Paris (information ⓣ08.20.00.75.75), which gives away a weighty free book, *Le Guide du Sport à Paris* (ask for it at tourist offices or town halls). For details of current **sporting events**, try the daily sports paper *L'Équipe*. A major venue for all sports, including athletics, cycling, show jumping, ice hockey, ballroom dancing, judo and motorcross, is the Palais Omnisport Paris-Bercy (POPB), 8 bd Bercy, 12e (ⓣ01.40.02.60.60, ⓦwww.bercy.fr; M° Bercy).

Spectator sports

Cycling The biggest event of the French sporting year is the grand finale of the Tour de France on the Champs-Élysées in late July. Huge crowds turn out to cheer on the cyclists at the finishing line of the ultimate stage in the gruelling three-week 3500-odd-kilometre event, and the French president presents the yellow jersey (*maillot jaune*) to the overall winner. Races commencing in Paris include the Paris–Roubaix, instigated in 1896, which is reputed to be the most exacting one-day race in the world, and the rugged six-day Paris–Nice event, covering over 1100km. The Palais Omnisport (see above) holds other bike races and cycling events. For more information on the Tour de France and other cycling events, see Basics.

Football and rugby The Parc des Princes, 24 rue du Commandant-Guilbaud, 16e (ⓣ01.42.30.03.60, ⓦwww.bercy.fr; M° Porte-de-St-Cloud), is the capital's main stadium for domestic rugby union and football events: it's the home ground for the first-division football team Paris-St-Germain (PSG) plus the rugby team Le Racing. The Stade de France, on rue Francis de Pressensé in St-Denis (ⓣ01.55.93.00.00, ⓦwww.stadefrance.fr; RER Stade-de-France-St-Denis), is the venue for international football matches and rugby's Six Nations' Cup and other international matches.

Horse-racing The biggest races are the Prix de la République and the Grand Prix de l'Arc de Triomphe on the first and last Sun in Oct at Auteuil and Longchamp, both in the Bois de Boulogne. Trotting races, with the jockeys in chariots, run from Aug to Sept on the Route de la Ferme in the Bois de Vincennes. L'Humanité and Paris-Turf carry details of all races; admission charges are under €5. If you want to place a bet, any bar or café with the letters "PMU" will take your money on a three-horse bet, known as *le tiercé*.

Running The Paris Marathon is held in April over a route from place de la Concorde to Vincennes. Up-to-date information is available online at ⓦwww.parismarathon.com.

Tennis The French Open takes place in the last week of May and first week of June at Roland-Garros, 2 av Gordon-Bennett, 16e (ⓣ01.47.43.48.00, ⓦwww.frenchopen.org; M° Porte-d'Auteuil). A few tickets are sold each day, but only for unseeded matches. Smaller tournaments, including November's Paris Open, take place throughout the year.

Activities

Boules The classic French game involving balls, boules (or pétanque), is best performed (if you have your own set or are prepared to make some new French friends) or watched at the Arènes de

Lutèce (p.154) and the Bois de Vincennes (p.180). On balmy summer evenings it's a common sight in the city's parks and gardens.

Cycling Since 1996 the Mairie de Paris has made great efforts to introduce dedicated cycle lanes in Paris, which now add up to some 300km. You can pick up a free leaflet, *Paris à Vélo*, outlining the routes, from town halls, the tourist office, or bike rental outlets (see p.216). If you prefer cycling in a more natural environment, the Bois de Boulogne and the Bois de Vincennes have extensive bike tracks. On Sundays cycling and rollerblading (see below) by the Seine is popular, when its central quais are closed to cars between 9am and 5pm; the quais along the Canal St-Martin are closed to cars from 10am to 6pm on Sundays. Excellent day and night bicycle tours (€ 22–30) are offered by Paris à Vélo C'est Sympa/Vélo Bastille, 22 rue Alphonse Baudin, 11e (Ⓣ01.48.87.60.01, Ⓦwww.parisvelosympa.com; M° Bastille), and Fat Tire Bike Tours, 24 rue Edgar Faure, 15e (Ⓣ01.56.58.10.54, Ⓦwww.FatTireBikeToursParis.com; M° Dupleix). For bike rental, see Listings, p.216.

Hamams The most atmospheric hamam or Turkish baths is the Hamam de la Mosquée, 39 rue Geoffroy-St-Hilaire, 5e (Ⓣ01.43.31.38.20; Turkish bath €15, massage extra; M° Censier-Daubenton), with its vaulted cooling-off room and marble-lined steam chamber; times may change, so check first, but generally women on Mon & Wed–Sat 10am–9pm, men Tues 2–9pm & Sun 10am–9pm. For a more upmarket, Parisian version of a hamam, head for Les Bains du Marais, 31–33 rue des Blancs Manteaux, 4e (Ⓣ01.44.61.02.02, Ⓦwww.lesbainsdumarais.com; sauna and steam room €30, massage €30 extra; M° Rambuteau); there are mixed sessions on Wednesday evenings (7–11pm), Saturdays (10–8pm) and Sundays (11am–11pm) for which you have to bring a partner and a swimsuit.

Ice skating From Dec to March a small rink is set up in the place Hôtel de Ville (daily 9am–10pm; M° Hôtel de Ville); skating is free and skates are available for rental.

In-line skating Rollerblading has become so popular in Paris that it takes over the streets most Friday nights from 9.45pm, when expert skaters – up to 15,000 on fine evenings – meet on the esplanade of the Gare Montparnasse in the 14e (M° Montparnasse) for a three-hour circuit of the city; check out Ⓦwww.pari-roller.com for details. Three good places to find more information and rent rollerblades (around €7 for a half day) are: Vertical Line, 4 rue de la Bastille 4e (Ⓣ01.42.74.70.00, Ⓦwww.vertical-line.com; M° Bastille); Nomades, 37 blvd Bourdon, 4e (Ⓣ01.44.54.07.44, Ⓦwww.nomadeshop.com; M° Bastille); and Bike 'N Roller, 38 rue Fabert, 7e (Mon–Sat 10am–7.30pm, Sun 10am–7pm; Ⓣ01.45.50.38.27, Ⓦwww.bikenroller.fr; M° Invalides); all hold their own roller events. The main outdoor in-line skating and skateboarding arena is the concourse of the Palais de Chaillot (M° Trocadéro). Les Halles (around the Fontaine des Innocents), the Pompidou Centre piazza and place du Palais-Royal are also very popular, as well as the central quais of the Seine on Sundays (see above).

Swimming L'Officiel des Spectacles lists all the municipal pools (€2.40), of which the best are the unchlorinated student hangout Jean Taris, 16 rue de Thouin, 5e (M° Cardinal-Lemoine); the 1930s-style, also studenty Piscine de Pointoise, 18 rue de Pointoise, 5e (M° Maubert-Mutualité); the Art Deco Butte aux Cailles, 5 place Verlaine, 13e (M° Place-d'Italie); and the 50-metre-long Piscine Susanne Berlioux/Les Halles, 10 place de la Rotonde, niveau 3, Porte du Jour, Forum des Halles, 1er (RER Châtelet-Les Halles). For something more spectacular, Aquaboulevard, 4 rue Louis Armand (Ⓣ01.40.60.10.00; M° Balard/Porte de Versailles), provides an array of pools, wave machines, jacuzzis and waterslides; for the €20 all-day ticket (€10 for children aged 3–11) you can use all the other fitness and sports facilities as well.

Tennis One of the nicest places to play tennis is on one of the six asphalt courts at the Jardins du Luxembourg (daily 8am–9pm; €6 per hour; M° Notre-Dame-des-Champs). Unless you possess a Carte Paris Sports and have access to French minitel system (3615 Paris, code RTEN), you'll just have to book on the spot and wait – usually no more than an hour.

Kids' Paris

For most **kids** the biggest attraction for miles around is **Disneyland Paris** (see p.224), though within the city there are plenty of other, far less expensive and more educational possibilities for keeping them entertained. Wednesday afternoons, when primary school children have free time, and Saturdays are the big times for children's activities and entertainments; Wednesdays continue to be child-centred even during the school holidays. The tours around the **sewers** and the **catacombs** will delight some children; while smaller ones can enjoy performances of **Guignol** (the equivalent of Punch and Judy) in the city's parks. Many of the **museums** and **amusements** already detailed will appeal, particularly the Musée de la Curiosité (see p.147); and the best treat for children of every age from three upwards is the **Cité des Sciences** (see p.176) in the Parc de la Villette. A number of museums have special children's activities on Wednesdays and Saturdays, details of which are carried in the free booklet *Objectif Musée*, available from the museums. The Musée du Moyen-Age, Musée d'Art Moderne de la Ville de Paris, Carnavalet, the Louvre, the Institut du Monde Arabe and the Musée d'Orsay have regular or special programmes but they will of course be conducted in French. Otherwise, the most useful **sources of information** for current shows, exhibitions and events are the special sections in the listings magazines ("Enfants" in *Pariscope*, and "Jeunes" in *L'Officiel des Spectacles*) and the Kiosque Paris-Jeunes at the Direction Jeunesse et Sports, 25 bd Bourdon, 4e (Mon–Fri noon–7pm; ⓣ01.42.76.22.60; M° Bastille), and at the CIDJ, 101 quai Branley, 15e (Mon–Fri 9.30am–6pm, Sat 9.30am–1pm; ⓣ01.44.49.12.00; M° Bir-Hakeim). The tourist office also publishes a free booklet in French, *Paris-Ile-de-France Avec Des Yeux Enfants*, with lots of ideas and contacts.

Cité des Enfants

The **Cité des Enfants** (for kids aged 3–12) is a totally engaging special section of the Cité des Sciences et de l'Industrie – detailed on p.176 – in the Parc de la Villette (Tues–Sat 10am–6pm, Sun 10am–7pm; adults and children over 3 €5, children under 3 free; children must be accompanied by at least one adult; M° Porte-de-la-Villette). The kids can touch, smell and feel things, play about with water, construct buildings on a miniature construction site, experiment with sound and light, manipulate robots, put together their own television news and race their own shadows. It's beautifully organized and managed, and if you haven't got a child it's worth borrowing one to get in here. Sessions run for an hour and a half (Tues, Thurs & Fri 11.30am, 1.30pm & 3.30pm; Wed, Sat, Sun & public hols 10.30am, 12.30pm, 2.30pm & 4.30pm).

The rest of the museum is also pretty good for kids, particularly the planetarium, the various film shows, the *Argonaute* submarine and the frequent temporary exhibitions designed for the young. And in the park, there's lots of green space, a dragon slide and seven themed gardens featuring mirrors, trampolines, water jets and spooky music.

Jardin d'Acclimatation

The **Jardin d'Acclimatation**, in the Bois de Boulogne by Porte des Sablons (daily: June–Sept 10am–7pm; Oct–May 10am–6pm; adults and children €2.50, under-3s free; ⓦwww.jardindacclimatation.fr); M° Les Sablons/Porte-Maillot) is a children's paradise: a cross between a funfair, zoo and amusement park. Temptations range from bumper cars, go-karts, pony and camel rides to sea lions, birds, bears and monkeys; plus there's a magical mini-canal ride (*la rivière enchantée*), distorting mirrors, scaled-down farm buildings and a puppet theatre. Rides cost extra however – around €2.50. The best way to get to the park is via the *petit train* (€5 return, including entrance fee) which leaves every fifteen minutes from behind the *L'Orée du Bois* restaurant near Porte Maillot metro station. On Wednesdays, weekends and during school holidays there are often extra special attractions, such as Astérix and friends explaining life in their **Gaulish village**, or Babar and the world of the elephants in the **Musée en Herbe**. The **Théâtre du Jardin pour l'Enfance et la Jeunesse** puts on musicals and ballets.

Outside the garden, in the Bois de Boulogne, older children can amuse themselves with **minigolf** and **bowling**, or **boating** on the Lac Inférieur. By the entrance to the garden there's **bike rental** for roaming the wood's cycle trails (bring your passport or photo ID along).

Parc Floral

Fun and games are always to be had at the **Parc Floral**, in the Bois de Vincennes, route de la Pyramide (daily: April–Sept 9.30am–8pm; Oct–March 9.30am–5/6pm; €3, children aged 7–17 €1.50 plus supplements for some activities, under-6s free; Ⓦwww.parcfloraldeparis.com; M° Château-de -Vincennes, then a seven-minute walk past the Château de Vincennes, or bus #112). The excellent playground has slides, swings, ping-pong, pedal carts, minigolf modelled on Paris monuments (from 2pm), an electric car circuit and a little train touring all the gardens (April–Oct daily 1pm–5pm; €1). Tickets for the activities are sold at the playground between 2pm and 5.30pm weekdays and until 7pm on weekends; activities stop fifteen minutes afterwards. Note that many of these activities are available from March/April to August only and on Wednesdays and weekends only in September and October. On Wednesdays at 2.30pm (May–Sept) there are free performances by clowns, puppets and magicians. Also in the park is a children's theatre, the **Théâtre Astral**, which has mime, clowns or other not-too-verbal shows for small children aged 3 to 8 (Wed 3pm, Sun & public hols 4.30pm & during school hols Mon–Fri 3pm; Ⓣ01.43.71.31.10). There's also a series of pavilions with child-friendly educational exhibitions (free entry) which look at nature in Paris; the best is the **butterfly garden** (mid-May to mid-Oct Mon–Fri 1.30–5.15pm, Sat & Sun 1.30–6pm).

Parc Zoologique

The top Paris **zoo** is in the Bois de Vincennes at 53 av de St-Maurice, 12e (daily 9am–5pm; adults €8, children over 4 €5, under-4s free; M° Porte-Dorée). It was one of the first zoos in the world to get rid of cages and use landscaping to simulate a more natural environment.

Jardin des Enfants aux Halles

Right in the centre of town, just west of the Forum, the **Jardin des Enfants aux Halles**, is great if you want to lose your charges for the odd hour (Tues, Thurs & Fri 9am–noon & 2–6pm, Sat & Wed 10am–6pm, Sun & holidays 1–6pm; Nov–March till 4pm; closed Mon & during bad weather; €0.40 for a one-hour slot; M°/RER Châtelet-Les Halles; 7–11-year olds only except Sat am). You may have to reserve a place an hour or so in advance for this small but cleverly designed space filled with a whole series of fantasy landscapes. On Wednesday, animators organize adventure games; and at all times the children are supervised by professional child-carers, who speak several languages, including English. On Saturdays (10am–2pm), adults too can go in and play while they take charge of their under-7-year-olds.

Funfairs and the circus

The Tuileries gardens normally have a **funfair** in July, and there's usually a **merry-go-round** at the Forum des Halles and beneath Tour St-Jacques at

Châtelet, with carousels for smaller children on place de la République and at the Rond-Point des Champs-Élysées, by avenue Matignon; the going rate for a ride is €1.60. The Cirque d'Hiver Bouglione, 110 rue Amelot, 11e (M° Filles-du-Calvaire; details in *Pariscope* and *L'Officiel des Spectacles*) is open from October to January, or you can spend an entire day at the **circus** courtesy of the Cirque de Paris in the Parc des Chanteraines, 115 bd Charles-de-Gaulle, Villeneuve-La Garenne (Oct–June Wed, Sun & school hols 10am–5pm; €41, under-12s €29, including a meal; book in advance on ⓣ01.47.99.40.40; RER Gennevilliers/St-Denis); lessons in juggling, tightrope-walking, clowning and make-up are followed by lunch in the ring then by the show. You can, if you prefer, just attend the show at 3pm (from €7).

Shopping

Even if you don't plan – or can't afford – to buy, browsing Paris's **shops and markets** is one of the chief delights of the city. Flair for style and design is as evident here as it is in other aspects of the city's life. Parisians' epicurean tendencies and fierce attachment to their small local traders has kept alive a wonderful variety of speciality shops, despite the pressures to concentrate consumption in gargantuan underground and multistorey complexes. Among specific areas, the square kilometre around **place St-Germain-des-Prés** is hard to beat, packed with books, antiques, gorgeous garments, artworks and playthings. But in every *quartier* you'll find enticing displays of all manner of consumables.

Bookshops

Books are not cheap in France – foreign books least of all – but don't let that stop you from browsing. The best areas are in the studenty Quartier Latin and along the Seine where rows of **bouquinistes**' stalls are perched on the parapets of the *quais*. Here we've listed a few specialists and favourites.

Abbey Bookshop 29 rue de la Parcheminerie, 5e, M° St-Michel. A Canadian bookshop round the corner from Shakespeare & Co (see below), with lots of secondhand British and North American fiction; good social science sections; knowledgeable and helpful staff – and free coffee. Mon–Sat 10am–7pm.

Artcurial 9 av Matignon, 8e, M° Franklin-D.-Roosevelt. The best art bookshop in Paris. Tues–Sun 10am–7.15pm; closed two weeks in Aug.

FNAC 74 av des Champs-Élysées, 8e; M° George-V; Forum des Halles, niveau 2, Porte Pierre-Lescot, 1er; M°/RER Châtelet-Les Halles; 136 rue de Rennes, 6e; M° Montparnasse; ⓦwww.fnac.com. Not the most congenial of bookshops, but it's the biggest and covers everything. Mon–Sat 10am–7.30pm; the Champs-Élysées branch is open till midnight daily.

Gibert Jeune 10 place St-Michel, 5e, M° St-Michel. The biggest of the Quartier Latin student/academic bookshops. The shop at no. 10 has the chief English selection, and you can find any other subject covered at the other branches on the *place*. An institution.

Parallèles 47 rue St-Honoré 1er, M° Châtelet-Les Halles. An alternative bookshop, with everything from anarchism to New Age. Good for info on current events and gigs. Mon–Sat 10am–7pm.

Shakespeare & Co 37 rue de la Bûcherie, 5e, M° Maubert-Mutualité. A cosy, famous literary haunt, staffed by American wannabe Hemingways, with the biggest selection of secondhand English books in town. Also poetry readings and the like. Daily noon–midnight.

Village Voice 6 rue Princesse, 6e, M° Mabillon. Welcoming recreation of a neighbourhood bookstore, with a good selection of contemporary titles, and a decent list of British and American classics. Mon 2–8pm, Tues–Sat 10am–8pm, Sun 2–7pm.

W.H. Smith 248 rue de Rivoli, 1er, M° Concorde. Paris outlet of the British chain. Wide range of new books and newspapers. Mon–Sat 9.30am–7pm.

Clothes

The 2002 retirement of Yves Saint-Laurent – Paris's greatest designer and the inventor of prêt-à-porter – marked the end of an era in which Paris's historic couture industry has steadily become little more than a publicity machine for the luxury-goods brands that actually own the big names. Despite having pioneered the process, Saint-Laurent ended his career disillusioned by the big-business realities of branded perfumes and handbags, by the loss of the client-couturier relationship and the theatrical excess of the younger generation. Yet the shows go on with the old French names at the head of them, even if the names of the designers are more international.

The good news is that these days no one has to pay hand-stitched couture prices in order to get inside Paris fashions, and even if designer labels are beyond budget, there's nothing to prevent you trying on fabulously expensive creations in rue du Faubourg-St-Honoré, avenue François-1er and avenue Victor-Hugo – apart from the intimidating air of the assistants and the awe-some chill of the marble portals. The simplest way to shop is to make for one of the classier **department stores** – Galeries Lafayette, Au Printemps and Au Bon Marché all have excellent selections. For one-offs and window-shopping check out the **younger designers** in the Marais, around place des Victoires, and around place des Abbesses, just below Montmartre. St-Germain, in the vicinity of the St-Sulpice metro stop, is a good compromise area, with designer-led chains rubbing shoulders with more affordable labels. For smart clothes without the fancy names the best areas are rue St-Placide and rue St-Dominique in the 6e and 7e. The **sales** take place in January and July, with reductions of up to forty percent on designer clothes. Ends of lines and old stock of the couturiers are sold year round in **discount shops** concentrated in rue d'Alésia in the 14e and rue St-Placide in the 6e. For **shoes**, take a wander down rue Meslay in the 3e.

Designer fashion

The addresses below are those of the main or most conveniently located shops for designer clothes. For a more complete list, including branch boutiques and web-sites, get online at ⓦwww.modeaparis.com.

Agnès B 6 rue du Jour, 1er, M° Châtelet-Les Halles; 6 & 10 rue du Vieux Colombier, 6e; M° St-Sulpice.

Azzedine Alaïa 7 rue de Moussy, 4e, M° Hôtel-de-Ville.

Chanel 31 rue Cambon, 1er, M° Madeleine.

Christian Lacroix 73 rue du Faubourg-St-Honoré, 8e, M° Concorde.

Gianni Versace 62 rue du Faubourg-St-Honoré, 8e, M° Concorde.

Giorgio Armani 6 place Vendôme, 1er, M° Opéra.

Inès de la Fressange 14 av Montaigne, 8e, M° Alma-Marceau.

Issey Miyake 3 place des Vosges, 4e, M° St-Paul.

Jean-Paul Gaultier 30 rue du Faubourg St-Antoine, 12e, M° Bastille.

Jil Sander 52 av Montaigne, 8e, M° Franklin-D.-Roosevelt.

Junko Shimada 54 rue Étienne-Marcel, 2e, M° Châtelet-Les Halles.

Kenzo 3 place des Victoires, 1er, M° Bourse.

Sonia Rykiel 175 bd St-Germain, 6e, M° St-Germain-des-Prés.

Thierry Mugler 49 av Montaigne, 8e, M° Alma-Marceau.

YSL Rive Gauche 6 place St-Sulpice, 6e, M° St-Sulpice/Mabillon.

Department stores

Au Bon Marché 38 rue de Sèvres, 7e, ⓦwww.lebonmarché.fr; M° Sèvres-Babylone. Paris's oldest department store, founded in 1852. Prices are lower on average than at the slightly more chic Galeries Lafayette and Printemps. Excellent kids' department and a legendary food hall. Mon–Wed & Fri 9.30am–7pm, Thurs 10am–9pm, Sat 9.30am–8pm.

Galeries Lafayette 40 bd Haussmann, 9^{e}, ⓦwww.galerieslafayette.com; M° Havre-Caumartin. The store's forte is, above all, high fashion. Three floors are given over to the latest creations by leading designers for women, while an adjoining three-storey store is devoted to men's fashion. Then there's a huge *parfumerie* and a host of big names in men and women's accessories – all under a superb 1900 dome. It's also worth checking out Lafayette Maison, the huge and impressive new home store just up the road at 35 bd Haussmann. Mon–Sat 9.30am–7.30pm, Thurs till 9pm.

Au Printemps 64 bd Haussmann 9e, M° Havre-Caumartin. Books, records, a *parfumerie* even bigger than that of rival Galeries Lafayette and excellent fashion for women (less so for men). Mon, Wed, Fri & Sat 9.35am–7pm, Thurs till 10pm.

La Samaritaine 75 rue de Rivoli, 1er, M° Louvre-Rivoli/Châtelet. This venerable belle époque building has been taken over by the luxury goods group LVMH and has undergone something of an upmarket makeover. What haven't changed however are the superb views of Paris from the restaurant and top-floor café. Mon–Fri 9.30am–7pm, Thurs till 9pm, Sat till 8pm.

Food and drink

You can, of course, find sumptuous food stores all over Paris: the listings below are for the **specialist places**, palaces of gluttony many of them, with prices to match. Economical food shopping is invariably best done at the **street markets** or **supermarkets**, though save your bread buying at least for the local boulangerie. The least expensive supermarket chain is Ed ("l'épicier"). Food markets are detailed at the end of this section.

Le Baron Rouge 1 rue Théophile-Roussel, 12e, M° Ledru-Rollin. A good selection of dependable lower-range French wines; €2 for a small tasting glass. Very drinkable Merlot at €2.50 a litre, if you bring your own containers. Tues–Fri 10am–2pm & 5–9.30pm, Sat 10am–9.30pm, Sun 10.30am–1pm.

Barthélémy 51 rue de Grenelle, 7e, M° Bac. Purveyors of cheeses to the rich and powerful. Tues–Sat 8am–1pm & 4–7.15pm; closed Aug.

Caves Michel Renaud 12 place de la Nation, 12e, M° Nation. Established in 1870, this wine shop purveys superb-value French and Spanish wines, champagnes and Armagnac. 9.30am–1pm & 2–8.30pm; closed Sun pm and Mon am.

Comptoir du Saumon 60 rue François-Miron, 4e, M° St-Paul. This place specializes in salmon, but also sells eels, trout and all things fishy, as well as having a delightful little restaurant in which to taste the fare. Mon–Sat 10am–10pm.

Debauve and Gallais 30 rue des Sts-Pères, 7e, M° St-Germain-des-Prés/Sèvres-Babylone. A beautiful, ancient shop specializing in chocolate and elaborate sweets. Mon–Sat 9am–7pm; closed Aug.

Fauchon 26 place de la Madeleine, 8e, M° Madeleine. An amazing range of groceries and wine, all at exorbitant prices; there's a self-service counter for patisseries and *plats du jour*, and a *traiteur* which stays open until 8.30pm. Mon–Sat 9.40am–7pm.

Goldenberg's 7 rue des Rosiers, 4e, M° St-Paul. Superlative Jewish deli and restaurant, specializing in charcuterie. Daily 9am–midnight.

Hédiard 21 place de la Madeleine, 8e, M° Madeleine. The aristocrat's grocer since 1850. Several other branches throughout the city. Mon–Sat 8am–10pm.

La Maison de l'Escargot 79 rue Fondary, 15e, M° Dupleix. As the name suggests, this place specializes in snails: they even sauce them and re-shell them while you wait. Tues–Sat 9.30am–7pm; closed Aug.

Mariage Frères 30 rue du Bourg-Tibourg, 4e, M° Hôtel-de-Ville. Hundreds of teas, neatly packed in tins, line the floor-to-ceiling shelves of this 100-year-old emporium. There's a *salon de thé* in the back with exquisite pastries (daily noon–7pm). Daily 10.30am–7.30pm.

Poilâne 8 rue du Cherche-Midi, 6e, M° Sèvres-Babylone. The source of the famous "Pain Poilâne" – a bread baked using traditional methods (albeit ramped up on an industrial scale) as conceived by the late, legendary Monsieur Poilâne himself. A few croissants and pastries available too. Mon–Sat 7.15am–8.15pm.

Rendez-Vous de la Nature 96 rue Mouffetard, 5e, Mº Cardinal-Lemoine. One of the city's most comprehensive health-food stores, with everything from fresh organic produce to herbal teas. Tues–Sat 9.30am–7.30pm, Sun 9.30am–1pm.

Music

New **cassettes and CDs** are not particularly cheap in Paris, but there are plenty of secondhand bargains, and you may come across selections that are novel enough to tempt you. Like the live music scene, there are albums of Brazilian, Caribbean, Antillais, African and Arab sounds that would be specialist rarities in London or the States, and there's every kind of jazz.

Camara 45 rue Marcadet, 18e, Mº Marcadet-Poissonnière. The best selection of West African and Congolese music on CD, cassette and video in town. Daily 10am–8pm.

Crocodisc 40–42 rue des Écoles, 5e, Ⓦwww.crocodisc.com; Mº Maubert-Mutualité. Folk, Oriental, Afro-Antillais, raï, funk, reggae, salsa, hip-hop, soul, country. New and secondhand, at some of the best prices in town. Tues–Sat 11am–7pm.

Crocojazz 64 rue de la Montagne-Ste-Geneviève, 5e, Mº Maubert-Mutualité. Mainly new imports of jazz and blues from all eras. Tues–Sat 11am–1pm & 2–7pm.

Dream Store 4 place St-Michel, 6e, Mº St-Michel. Good discounts on new classical CDs in particular but also some jazz and French chanson. Mon–Sat 9.30am–7.30pm.

FNAC Musique 4 place de la Bastille, 12e, Mº Bastille. Extremely stylish shop in black, grey and chrome, with computerized catalogues, books, every variety of music and a concert booking agency. Mon–Sat 10am–8pm.

Paul Beuscher 15–29 bd Beaumarchais, 4e, Mº Bastille. A music department store that's been going strong for over 100 years, selling instruments, scores, books and recording equipment. Mon–Fri 9.45am–12.30pm & 2–7pm, Sat 9.45am–7pm.

Virgin Megastore 52–60 av des Champs-Élysées, 8e, Mº Franklin-D.-Roosevelt (Mon–Sat 10am–midnight, Sun noon–midnight) and 99 rue de Rivoli, 1er; Mº Palais-Royal (Wed–Sat 10am–10pm, Sun & Mon 10am–8pm). The biggest and trendiest of all Paris's music shops. Concert booking agency and expensive Internet connection.

Sport and outdoor activities

Le Ciel Est à Tout le Monde 10 rue Gay-Lussac, 5e, RER Luxembourg. The best kite shop in Europe. It also sells frisbees, boomerangs, etc, plus books and traditional toys. Mon–Sat 10am–7pm; closed Mon in Aug.

Nomades 37 bd Bourdon, 4e, Mº Bastille. The place to buy and rent rollerblades and equipment, with its own bar out back where you can find out about the scene. See also "In-line skating", p.209. Mon–Fri 11am–7pm, Sat & Sun 10am–7pm.

Au Vieux Campeur 48 rue des Écoles, 5e, Mº Maubert-Mutualité. This giant outdoor activities group has colonized an entire couple of blocks immediately north of rue des Écoles and east of rue St-Jacques with over a dozen well-stocked shops – there's even a small climbing wall. You'll be directed to the right branch for maps, guides, boots, climbing, hiking, camping and ski gear, tents, sleeping bags and so on. Mon–Wed & Fri 11am–7.30pm, Thurs 11am–9pm, Sat 10am–7.30pm.

Markets

Paris's **markets**, like its shops, are grand spectacles. Mouthwatering arrays of **food** from half the countries of the globe, captivating in colour, shape and smell, assail the senses in even the drabbest parts of town. A full list is available online at Ⓦwww.paris.fr/fr/marches. Though the food is perhaps the best offering of the Paris markets, there are also street markets dedicated to **secondhand goods** (the flea markets, or *marchés aux puces*), **clothes** and **textiles**, **flowers**, **birds**, **books** and **stamps**. Though all have semi-official opening and closing hours, many begin business in advance and drag on till dusk. Food markets usually start between 7am and 8am and tail off around 1pm, though a few stalls may carry on into the afternoon and evening. The covered markets have specific opening hours, which are detailed below.

Flea markets

Porte de Montreuil 20e, Mº Porte-de-Montreuil. The most junkyard-like of them all, and the best for secondhand clothes – cheapest on Mon when leftovers from the weekend are sold off. Also good for old furniture and household goods. Sat, Sun & Mon 7am–5pm.

St-Ouen/Porte de Clignancourt 18e, Mº Porte-de-Clignancourt. The biggest and most touristy flea market, with stalls selling new and secondhand clothes, shoes, records, books and junk of all sorts, as well as lots of expensive antique shops and trendy bric-à-brac specialists. Mon, Sat & Sun 7.30am–7pm.

Food markets

Belleville bd de Belleville, 20e, Mº Belleville/Ménilmontant. Tues & Fri.

Buci rue de Buci & rue de Seine, 6e, Mº Mabillon. More a collection of shops than a transient market, but good nonetheless. Tues–Sun.

Convention rue de la Convention, 15e, Mº Convention. Tues, Thurs & Sun.

Dejean place du Château-Rouge, 18e, Mº Château-Rouge. Afro-Caribbean heaven. Tues–Sun.

Enfants-Rouges 39 rue de Bretagne, 3e, Mº Filles-du-Calvaire. Tues–Sat 8am–1pm & 4–7pm, Sun 9am–1pm.

Maubert place Maubert, 5e, Mº Maubert-Mutualité. Tues, Thurs & Sat.

Monge place Monge, 5e, Mº Monge. Wed, Fri & Sun.

Montorgueil rue Montorgueil & rue Montmartre, 1er, Mº Châtelet-Les Halles/Sentier. Tues–Sat 8am–1pm & 4pm–7pm, Sun 9am–1pm.

Place d'Aligre 12e, Mº Ledru-Rollin. Tues–Sun until 1pm.

Port-Royal bd Port-Royal, nr Val-de-Grâce, 5e, RER Port-Royal. Tues, Thurs & Sat.

Porte-St-Martin rue du Château-d'Eau, 10e, Mº Château-d'Eau. Tues–Sat 8am–1pm & 4–7.30pm, Sun 8am–1pm.

Raspail bd Raspail, between rue du Cherche-Midi & rue de Rennes, 6e, Mº Rennes. Tues & Fri. Organic on Sun.

Richard Lenoir bd Richard Lenoir, 11e, Mº Bastille/Richard Lenoir. Thurs & Sun.

Rue Cler 7e, Mº École-Militaire. Mostly permanent shops, with a few stalls. Tues–Sat.

Rue de Lévis 17e, Mº Villiers. Tues–Sun.

Saint-Germain rue Mabillon, 6e, Mº Mabillon. Tues–Sat 8.30am–1pm & 4–7.30pm, Sun 8.30am–1pm.

Saxe-Breteuil ave de Saxe, 7e, Mº Ségur. Thurs & Sat.

Secrétan av Secrétan/rue Riquet, 19e, Mº Bolivar. Tues–Sat 8am–1pm & 4–7.30pm, Sun 8am–1pm.

Tang Frères 48 av d'Ivry, 13e, Mº Porte-d'Ivry. More a supermarket yard than a market; a vast emporium of all things oriental.Tues–Sun 9am–7.30pm.

Ternes rue Lemercier, 17e, Mº Ternes. Tues–Sat 8am–1pm & 4–7.30pm, Sun 8am–1pm.

Listings

Airlines Aer Lingus ⓣ01.70.20.00.72; Air Canada ⓣ08.25.88.08.81; Air France ⓣ08.20.82.08.20; British Airways ⓣ08.25.82.54.00; Bmibaby ⓣ08.90.71.00.81; Delta ⓣ08.00.30.13.01; easyJet ⓣ08.25.08.25.08; Qantas ⓣ08.20.82.05.00; Ryanair ⓣ08.92.55.56.66.

Banks and exchange Money-exchange bureaux and automatic exchange machines can be found at all airports and mainline train stations, along with ATM points. Beware of exchange bureaux, which may advertise the selling rather than buying rate, and add on hefty commission fees. On the whole, you're better off in a bank, or by just using credit and debit cards in many cash machines.

Bike rental Charges start from about €13 a day; you'll need to show a picture ID, and you'll also be asked to pay a deposit of €250 or more, and/or leave a passport or credit card. If you want a bike for Sunday, when all of Paris takes to the quais, you'll need to book in advance. Try Paris-Vélo, 2 rue du Fer-à-Moulin, 5e (ⓣ01.43.37.59.22, ⓦwww.paris-velo-rent-a-bike.fr; Mº Censier-Daubenton), for 21-speed and mountain bikes; Paris à Vélo C'est Sympa, Vélo Bastille, 37 bd Bourdon, 4e (ⓣ01.48.87.60.01, ⓦwww.parisvelosympa.com; Mº Bastille), who also offer commendable bicycle tours; Bike N'Roller, 38 rue Fabert, 7e (ⓣ01.45.50.38.27, ⓦwww.bikenroller.fr; Mº

Invalides), which also rents out rollerblades; Fat Tire Bike Tours, 24 rue Edgar Faure, 5e (Ⓣ01.56.58.10.54, Ⓦwww.fattirebiketoursparis.com; M° Dupleix), offering a wide range of bikes, including tandems, childrens' bikes and bikes with child seats; they also run highly-rated bike tours. In addition, RATP, the transport authority, has a bike rental office at 1 passage Mondétour, opposite 120 de la rue Rambuteau, 1e (daily 9am–7pm; Ⓣ08.10.44.15.34, Ⓦwww.rouelibre.fr; M° Les Halles), as well as a few Cyclobus mobile bike-rental vans parked at the Hôtel de Ville (Sun only), Parc de la Villette, Porte d'Auteuil and Château de Vincennes.

Buses For national and international buses, including Eurolines (Ⓣ08.36.69.52.52), you can get information and tickets at the main terminus, 28 av du Général-de-Gaulle, Bagnolet (M° Gallieni).

Car rental The big international car rental companies have offices at the airports, at the Gare du Nord – down the stairs near the Eurostar platform and taxis gate – and at various points around the city. Two reliable local firms are Buchard, 99 bd Auguste-Blanqui Ⓣ01.45.88.28.38; and Locabest Ⓣ01.48.31.77.05, Ⓦwww.locabest.fr, with offices at 3 rue Abel (M° Gare-de-Lyon) and at 104 bd Magenta, 10e (M° Gare-du-Nord).

Dental treatment A useful (private) emergency service is SOS Dentaire, 87 bd Port-Royal, 5e Ⓣ01.43.37.51.00; M° Port-Royal.

Embassies/Consulates Australia, 4 rue Jean-Rey, 15e Ⓣ01.40.59.33.00, Ⓦwww.austgov.fr; M° Bir-Hakeim; M° Concorde; Canada, 35 av Montaigne, 8e Ⓣ01.44.43.29.00, Ⓦwww.amb-canada.fr; M° Franklin-D.-Roosevelt; Germany, 13–15 av Franklin D. Roosevelt, 8e Ⓣ01.53.83.45.00, Ⓦwww.amb-allemagne.fr; Ireland, 4 rue Rude, 16e Ⓣ01.44.17.67.00; M° Charles-de-Gaulle-Étoile; New Zealand, 7ter rue Léonardo-de-Vinci, 16e Ⓣ01.45.01.43.43; M° Victor-Hugo; UK, 35 rue du Faubourg-St-Honoré, 8e Ⓣ01.44.51.31.00, Ⓦwww.amb-grandebretagne.fr; US, rue St-Florentin, 1er Ⓣ01.43.12.22.22, Ⓦwww.amb-usa.fr; M° Concorde.

Emergencies Call the SAMU ambulance service on Ⓣ15 (operators can put you through to an English-speaker) or the private association SOS-Médecins on Ⓣ01.47.07.77.77 for 24hr medical help.

Festivals There are free concerts and street performers all over Paris for the Fête de la Musique which coincides with the summer solstice (June 21; Ⓦwww.fetedelamusique.culture.fr). Gay Pride follows swiftly afterwards, on the last Saturday of June. July 14 (Bastille Day) is celebrated with official pomp in parades of tanks down the Champs-Élysées, firework displays and concerts. For a month from this date, the quais are transformed into a beach along the Seine as part of the Paris Plage scheme. The Tour de France finishes along the Champs-Élysées on the third or fourth Sunday of July. In early October, the Nuit Blanche ("sleepless night") persuades Parisians to stay up all night for an energetic programme of arts events and parties all over the city. See "Basics" for other music and religious festivals.

Hospitals English-speaking hospitals include the Hertford British Hospital, 3 rue Barbès, Levallois-Perret (Ⓣ01.46.39.22.22; M° Anatole-France) and the American Hospital 63 bd Victor-Hugo, Neuilly-sur-Seine (Ⓣ01.46.41.25.25; M° Porte-Maillot then bus #82 to terminus).

Internet Internet access is everywhere in Paris – if it's not in your hotel it'll be in a café nearby, and there are lots of *points internet* around the city. Most post offices offer online access, too.

Language schools French lessons are available from the Alliance Française, 101 bd Raspail, 6e Ⓣ01.45.44.38.28, Ⓦwww.alliancefr.org, and numerous other establishments. A full list is obtainable from embassy cultural sections.

Laundries Self-service places have multiplied in Paris over the last few years, and you'll probably find one near where you're staying. They generally cost €3.50 for a small load, or €7 for the bigger machines and open from 7am to between 7pm and 9pm.

Left luggage Lockers are available at all train stations.

Libraries The American Library in Paris, 10 rue du Général-Camou, 7e (Tues–Sat 10am–7pm; (Ⓣ01.53.59.12.61; M° École-Militaire), has American papers and a vast range of books; to use the library you'll need to get a day pass (€11). Interesting French collections include the BPI (Bibliothèque Publique d'Information), Pompidou Centre, 3e (Mon & Wed–Fri noon–10pm, Sat, Sun & public hols 11am–10pm; closed Tues & May 1; free; M° Rambuteau), with a vast collection, including all the foreign press, videos and a language lab; Bibliothèque Forney at the Hôtel de Sens, 1 rue du Figuier in the 4e (Mon–Fri 1.30–8.30pm, Sat 10am–8.30pm; M° Pont-Marie) specializes in decorative and applied arts; and the Bibliothèque Historique de la Ville de Paris, in the Hôtel Lamoignon, a sixteenth-century mansion housing centuries of texts and picture books on the city at 24 rue Pavée, 4e (Mon–Sat 9.30am–6pm; M° St-Paul).

Lost property Bureau des Objets Trouvés, 36 rue des Morillons, 15e (Ⓣ08.21.00.25.25; M° Convention; Mon & Wed 8.30am–5pm, Thurs 8.30am–8pm, Fri 8.30am–5.30pm);

lost property on metro/RER and bus services ⓣ01.40.30.52.00. If you lose your passport, report it to a police station and then your embassy.
Pharmacies 24hr service at Dhery, 84 av des Champs-Élysées, 8e ⓣ01.45.62.02.41; Mº George-V. There's a nearby British pharmacy, SNC, at 62 av des Champs-Élysées, 8e ⓣ01.43.59.22.52. When closed, each pharmacy should post the address of the nearest open one.
Police ⓣ17 (ⓣ112 if you're ringing from a mobile) for emergencies. To report a theft, go to the commissariat de police of the arrondissement in which the theft took place.
Post office Main office at 52 rue du Louvre 1e; Mº Châtelet-Les-Halles. Open daily 24hr for letters, poste restante, faxes, telegrams and phone calls; currency exchange Mon–Fri 8am–7pm, Sat 8am–noon. Other offices are usually open Mon–Fri 8am–7pm, Sat 8am–noon.
Telephones Public phones accept phonecards (*télécartes*), sold at *tabacs*, and sometimes credit cards – rarely coins. To call within Paris you need to dial the ⓣ01 code.
Travel agencies OTU Voyages, 119 rue St-Martin, 4e, opposite the Pompidou Centre (ⓣ08.20.81.78.17, ⓦwww.otu.fr) is good for student and discount travel, as is Voyages Wasteels, 11 rue Dupuytren, 6e (ⓣ08.25.88.70.70, ⓦwww.wasteels.fr).

Around Paris

The region around the capital – the **Île de France** – and the borders of the neighbouring provinces are studded with large-scale **châteaux**. Many were royal or noble retreats for hunting and other leisured pursuits, some – like **Versailles** – were for more serious state show. However, they are all undoubtedly impressive, especially **Vaux-le-Vicomte** for its homogeneity and **Chantilly** for its masterpiece-studded art collection. If you have even the slightest curiosity about church buildings, make sure you visit the **cathedral of Chartres**, which more than fulfils expectations. Closer in, on the edge of Paris itself, **St-Denis** boasts a cathedral second only to Notre-Dame – a visit which can be combined with a wander back into the centre of Paris along the banks of the St-Denis canal. Other **waterside walks** include **Chatou** and the Marne-side towns, with their memories of carousing, carefree painters and musicians in the early 1900s, when these places were open countryside or small villages. **Auvers-Sur-Oise** has a museum that transports you back to Impressionist days and landscapes, as well as laying claim to Van Gogh's final inspiration and resting-place. Whether the various suburban museums deserve your attention will depend on your degree of interest in the subjects they represent – china at **Sèvres**, French prehistory at **St-Germain-en-Laye**, Napoleon at **Malmaison** or horses at **Chantilly**. The biggest pull for kids is without question **Disneyland Paris**, out beyond the bizarre satellite town of **Marne-la-Vallée**, but they might also like the air and space museum at **Le Bourget**.

All of the attractions listed in this section are easily accessible by the region's public transport links of train, RER, métro and bus. We have arranged the accounts geographically, moving in a clockwise direction around Paris from St-Denis in the north to Malmaison in the west.

St-Denis

ST-DENIS, 10km north of the centre of Paris and accessible by métro (Mº St-Denis-Basilique), has long been the bastion of the Red suburbs and the stronghold of the Communist Party, and one of the most heavily industrialized communities in France. Recession has, however, taken a heavy toll in the form of closed factories and unemployment. The centre of St-Denis retains traces of small-town origins, but the area immediately abutting its cathedral has been transformed into an astonishing fortress-like housing and shopping complex. A thrice-weekly **market** (Tues, Fri & Sun mornings) takes place in the square by the Hôtel de Ville and the covered *halles*, at the end of rue Dupont, which leads off the square. It's an exuberant, multi-ethnic affair where the swathes of cheap fabrics on the market stalls, and the quantity of butcher's offal in the covered section – ears, feet and tails – shows this is not wealthy territory.

The town's chief claim to fame, though, is its magnificent cathedral, close by the St-Denis-Basilique métro station, the burial place of the kings of France. Begun by Abbot Suger, friend and adviser to kings, in the first half of the twelfth century, the **Basilique St-Denis** (April–Sept Mon–Sat 10am–6.15pm, Sun noon–6.15pm; Oct–March Mon–Sat 10am–5.15pm, Sun noon–5pm; tombs €5.50, closed during services) is generally regarded as the birthplace of the Gothic style in European architecture. The west front was the first ever to have a rose window, but it is in the choir that you best see the clear emergence of the new style: the slimness and lightness that comes with the use of the pointed arch, the ribbed vault and the long shafts of half-column rising from pillar to roof. It's a remarkably well-lit church thanks to the clerestory being almost one hundred percent glass – another first for St-Denis – and the transept windows being so big that they occupy their entire end walls.

Legend holds that the first church here was founded by a mid-third -century Parisian bishop, later known as St-Denis. The story goes that after he was beheaded for his beliefs at Montmartre (Mount of the Martyr), he picked up his head and walked all the way to St-Denis, thereby establishing the abbey. It's not that far – just over five kilometres – though as a friend of Edward Gibbon's once remarked, "the distance is nothing, it's the first step that counts". The abbey maintained royal connections by holding the coronation of Pepin the Short, in 754, and appointing the king as its abbot during much of the Carolingian era. It was with Hugh Capet, in 996, that it became the burial place of the French monarchs, and since then all but three French kings have been enterred here. Their very fine **tombs** and effigies are distributed about the transepts and ambulatory.

Among the most interesting are the enormous Renaissance memorial to François I on the right just beyond the entrance, and the tombs of Louis XII, Henri II and Catherine de Médicis on the left side of the church. To the right of the ambulatory steps you can see the stocky little general Bertrand du Guesclin, who gave the English the runaround after the death of the Black Prince, and on the level above him – invariably graced by bouquets of flowers – the undistinguished statues of Louis XVI and Marie-Antoinette. Around the corner on the far side of the ambulatory is Clovis himself, king of the Franks way back in 500, a canny little German who wiped out Roman Gaul and turned it into France, with Paris for a capital.

Most visitors to St-Denis, however, come for a match or concert at the **Stade de France**. At least €430 million was spent on the construction of this high-tech stadium, whose cosmic elliptic structure is best appreciated at night when lit up. If there isn't an event on, you can visit its grounds, facilities and small **museum** (daily 10am–6pm; €6).

To **walk back to Paris**, follow rue de la République from the Hôtel de Ville to the church of St-Denis-de-l'Estrée, then go down the left side of the church until you reach the canal bridge. If you turn left, you can walk practically all the way along the towpath (parts of the canalside are being rehabilitated and may necessitate a slight detour) – between an hour-and-a-half and two hours – to Porte de la Villette. There are stretches where it looks as if you're probably not supposed to be there, but pay no attention and keep going. You pass peeling *villas* with unkempt gardens, patches of

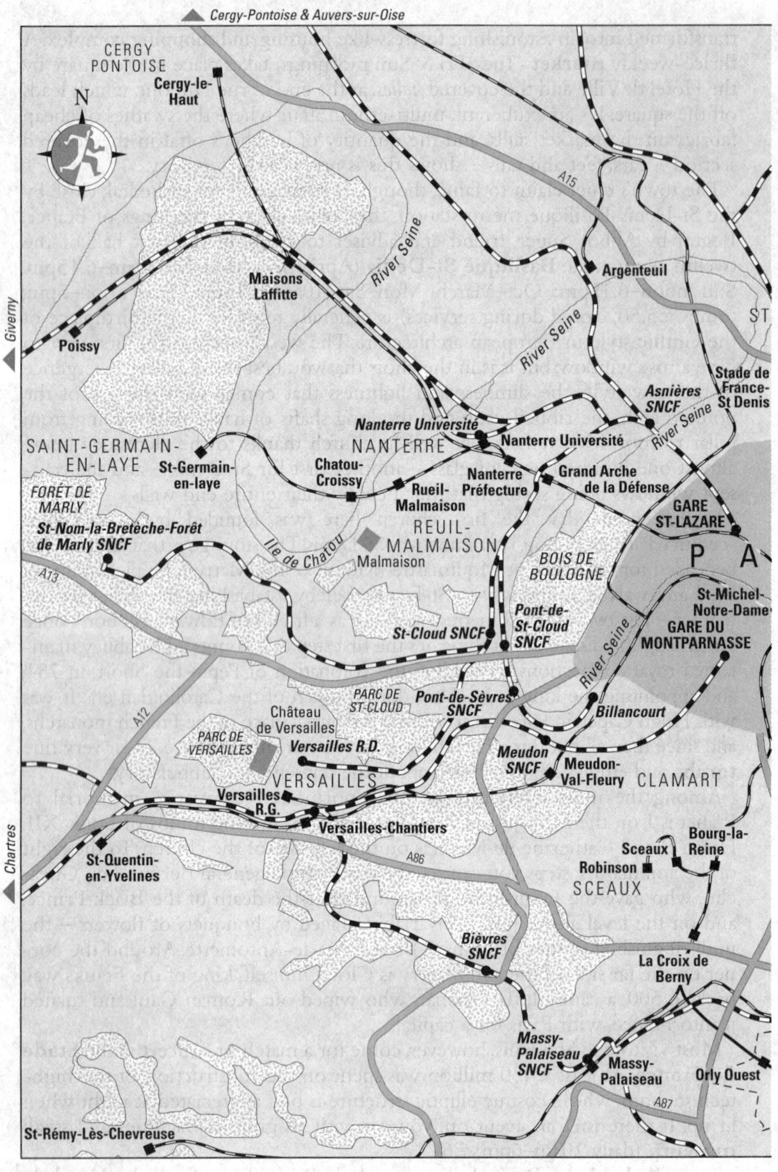

greenery, sand and gravel docks, and waste ground where larks rise above rusting bedsteads and doorless fridges. Decaying tenements and improvised shacks give way to lock-keepers' cottages with roses and vegetable gardens, then derelict factories and huge sheds where trundling gantries load bundles of steel rods onto Belgian barges.

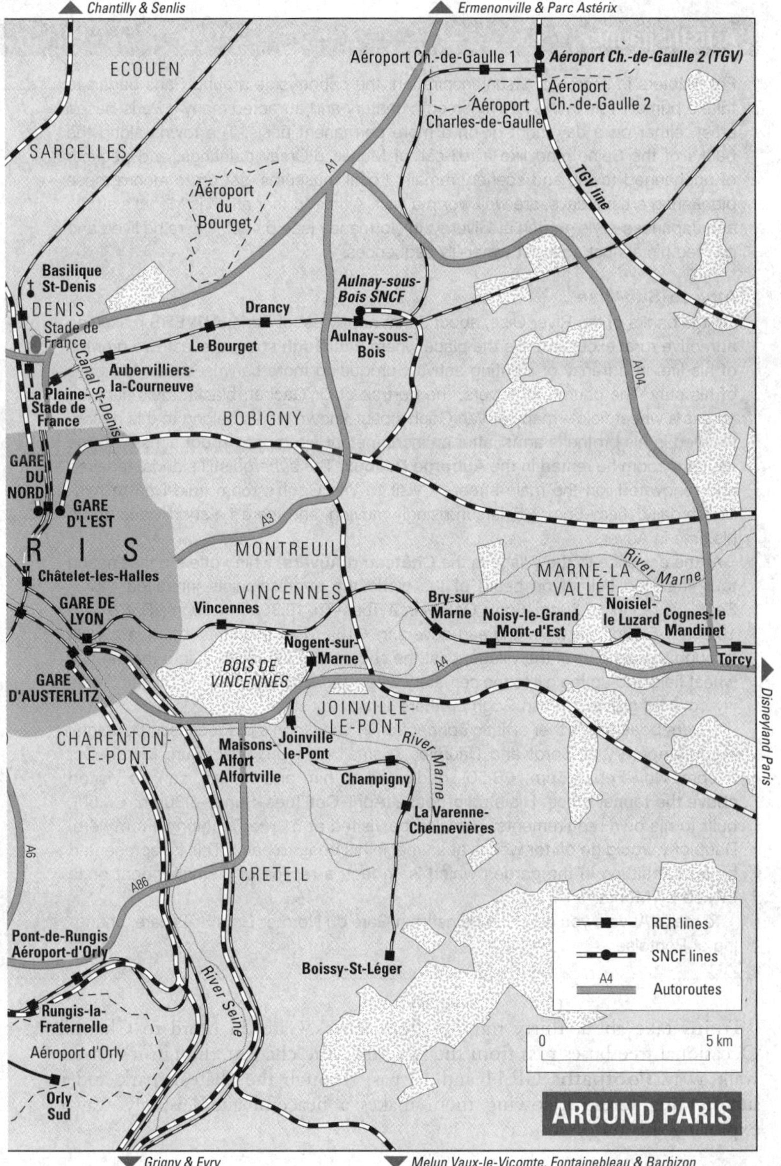

Chantilly

CHANTILLY, a small town 40km north of Paris, is associated mainly with horses. Some 3000 thoroughbreds prance the forest rides of a morning, and two of the season's classiest flat races, the Jockey Club and the Prix de Diane, are held here. The old château stables are given over to a horse museum.

Artistic haunts

For painters in search of visual inspiration, the countryside around Paris began to take a primary role in the late nineteenth century and attracted many a Paris-based artist, either on a day jaunt or on a more permanent basis. The towns along the banks of the Seine read like a roll-call of Musée d'Orsay paintings, and pockets of unchanged towns and scenery remain. Local museums, set up to record these pioneering artistic days, are well worth a visit. A little further afield is Monet's studio and Japanese-style garden at Giverny, in Normandy (see p.400), where he lived and painted his almost abstract water-lily sequences.

Auvers-Sur-Oise

On the banks of the River Oise, about 35km northwest of Paris, **AUVERS** makes an attractive rural excursion. It's the place where **Van Gogh** spent the last two months of his life, in a frenzy of painting activity, producing more canvases than the days of his stay. The church at Auvers, the portrait of Dr Gachet, black crows flapping across a wheat field – many of Van Gogh's best-known works belong to this period. He died in his brother's arms, after an incompetent attempt to shoot himself, in the tiny attic room he rented in the **Auberge Ravoux**. The *auberge* still stands, repaired and renovated, on the main street. A visit to Van Gogh's room (mid-Dec to mid-March daily 10am–6pm; €5) is surprisingly moving, and there's a short video about his time in Auvers.

At the entrance to the village is the **Château d'Auvers**, which offers a fascinating tour (infra-red helmet on head) of the world the Impressionists inhabited (April–Sept Tues–Sun 10.30am–6pm; Oct–March Tues–Fri 10.30am–4.30pm, Sat & Sun 10.30am–5.30pm; ⓦwww.chateau-auvers.fr; €10). Most evocative of all is a walk through the old part of the village, past the church and the red lane into the famous wheat field and up the hill to the cemetery where, against the far left wall in a humble ivy-covered grave, the Van Gogh brothers lie side by side.

Auvers boasts a further artistic connection in Van Gogh's predecessor, Daubigny – contemporary of Corot and Daumier. A small museum (Wed–Sun: March–Oct 2–6pm, Nov–Feb 2–5pm; €3.50), dedicated to him and his art, can be visited above the tourist office. His studio-house (April–Oct Tues–Sun 2–6.30pm; €4.50), built to his own requirements, can also be visited at 61 rue Daubigny. From here, Daubigny would go off for weeks at a time, in his boat, to paint. This is represented by a boat sitting in the garden which is, in fact, a replica of a smaller boat once owned by Monet.

To reach Auvers you can take trains from Gare du Nord or Gare St-Lazare, changing at Pontoise.

Trains take about thirty minutes from Paris's Gare du Nord to Chantilly. Occasional free buses pass from the station to the château, though it's an easy walk away. **Footpaths** GR11 and 12 pass through the château park and its surrounding forest: following them makes a peaceful and leisurely way of exploring this bit of country.

The château and the Musée Vivant du Cheval

The Chantilly estate used to belong to two of the most powerful clans in France: first to the Montmorencys, then, through marriage, to the Condés. The present **Château** (March–Oct daily except Tues 10am–6pm; Nov–Feb Mon & Wed–Fri 10.30am–12.45pm & 2–5pm, Sat & Sun 10.30am–5pm; €7; park open daily same hours, €3.50) was built in the late nineteenth century on the ruins of the so-called Grand Château built for the Grand Condé, who helped Louis XIV smash Spanish power in the mid-seventeenth century. It's

Chatou

A long narrow island in the Seine, the **Île de Chatou** was once a rustic spot to which Parisians came on the newly opened train line in the mid-nineteenth century to row on the river, and to dine and flirt at the *guinguettes*. A favourite haunt of many artists was the **Maison Fournaise**, just below the Pont de Chatou road bridge, which is now once again a restaurant (closed Sun evening in winter; ☎01.30.71.41.91; menu €25), with a small museum of memorabilia (Wed–Sun 10am–6pm; €4). One of **Renoir**'s best-known canvases, *Le Déjeuner des Canotiers*, shows his friends lunching on the balcony, which is still shaded by a magnificent riverside plane tree. As well as many Impressionists, Vlaminck, Derain, other Fauves, and Matisse, were also *habitués*.

Access to the island is from the Rueil-Malmaison RER stop. Take the exit av Albert-1er, go left out of the station and right along the dual carriageway onto the bridge – a ten-minute walk. Bizarrely, the island hosts a twice-yearly **ham and antiques fair** (March & Sept), which is fun to check out.

Barbizon

The landscape and country-living around **BARBIZON**, southeast of Paris, inspired painters such as **Rousseau** and **Millet** to set up camp here, initiating an artistic movement known as the Barbizon group. More painters followed, as well as writers and musicians, all attracted by the lifestyle and community. The **Auberge du Père Ganne**, on the main road, became the place to stay, not unrelated to the fact that the generous owner accepted the artists' decorations of his inn and furniture as payment. Now home to a museum (Mon & Wed–Fri 10am–12.30pm & 2–5.30pm; €4.50), the inn still contains the original painted furniture as well as many Barbizon paintings.

Meudon

The tranquil suburb of **MEUDON**, to the southwest of Paris, was where **Rodin** spent the last years of his life. In 1895, he acquired the **Villa des Brillants** at 19 av Rodin (May–Oct Fri–Sun 1–6pm; €2; RER line C to Meudon-Val Fleury, then a fifteen-minute walk along avenues Barbusse and Rodin), and installed his studio in the first room you encounter as you enter through the veranda. It was in this room that he used to dine with his companion, Rose Beuret, on summer evenings, and here that he married her, after fifty years together, just a fortnight before her death in February 1917. His own death followed in November, and they are buried together on the terrace below the house, beneath a version of *The Thinker*. The classical facade behind them masks an enormous pavilion containing plaster casts of many of his most famous works.

a beautiful structure, graceful and romantic, surrounded by water and looking out over a formal arrangement of pools and pathways designed by Le Nôtre, Louis XIV's gardener.

The entrance is across a moat, past two realistic bronzes of hunting hounds. The visitable parts are mainly made up of an enormous collection of **paintings and drawings** owned by the Institut de France (see p.154). Stipulated to remain as organized by Henri d'Orléans (the donor of the château), the arrangement is haphazard by modern standards, but immensely satisfying to eclectic appetites. Some highlights can be found in the Rotunda of the picture gallery – Piero di Cosimo's *Simonetta Vespucci* and Raphael's *Madone de Lorette* – and in the so-called Sanctuary, with Raphael's *Three Graces* displayed alongside Filippo Lippi's *Esther et Assuerius* and forty miniatures from a fifteenth-century Book of Hours attributed to the great French Renaissance artist Jean Fouquet. Pass through the Galerie de Psyche with its series of sepia stained glass illustrating Apuleius' *Golden Ass*, to the room known as the Tribune, where Italian art, including Botticelli's *Autumn*, takes up two walls, and Ingres and Delacroix have a wall each.

A free guided tour will take you round the apartments of the sixteenth-century wing known as the **Petit Château**. The first port of call is the well-stocked **library**, where a facsimile of the museum's single greatest treasure is on display, *Les Très Riches Heures du Duc de Berry*, the most celebrated of all the Books of Hours. The illuminated pages illustrating the months of the year with representative scenes from contemporary (early 1400s) rural life – like harvesting and ploughing, sheep-shearing and pruning – are richly coloured and drawn with a delicate naturalism. The remaining half-dozen rooms on the tour mostly show off superb furnishings, with exquisite *boisieries* panelling the walls of the Monkey Gallery, wittily painted with allegorical stories in a pseudo-Chinese style. A grand parade of canvases in the long gallery depicts the many battles won by the Grand Condé.

Five minutes' walk back towards town along the château drive, the colossal stable block has been transformed into a horse museum, the **Musée Vivant du Cheval** (Mon & Wed–Fri 10.30am–5.30pm, Sat & Sun 10.30am–6pm; May & June also open Tues 10.30–5.30pm; €8, or €14 combined ticket with château and park; Ⓦwww.musee-vivant-du-cheval.fr). The building was erected at the beginning of the eighteenth century by the incumbent Condé prince, who believed he would be reincarnated as a horse and wished to provide fitting accommodation for 240 of his future relatives. In the vast main hall, horses of different breeds from around the world are stalled, with a central ring for **demonstrations** (April–Oct 11.30am, 3.30pm & 5.15pm; Nov–March weekends 11.30am, 3.30pm & 5.15pm, weekdays 3.30pm only).

Disneyland Paris

Children will love **Disneyland Paris**, 32km east of the capital – there are no two ways about it, and some of the high-speed rides will thrill even the most jaded adult. The park takes its inspiration from (Disney) films as much as funfair rides, and the results are sometimes clever and high-tech, sometimes enjoyably old-fashioned with a bit of added branding. Commercialism is shrilly insistent, however – it would be hard to find sponsors less magical than Esso, McDonalds and Nestlé – and prices for food and drink are inflated. Bad weather can take the Florida shine off the outing, too, but it does have one advantage: on a wet and windy off-season weekday (Mon & Thurs are the best) you can get round every ride you want. Otherwise, lines for the big rides are common, though you can reduce the wait at the most popular attractions by reserving a time in advance on the spot, the so-called Fastpass scheme.

The complex is divided into three areas: **Disneyland Park**, the original Magic Kingdom, with most of the big rides; **Walt Disney Studios Park**, a more technology-based attempt to recreate the world of cartoon film-making, with fake sets and virtual reality rides; and **Disney Village**, where you can eat overpriced, mostly American-style food. A clutch of Disney hotels allow you to sleep locally if you're planning on making more than a day of it.

Disneyland Park

Since the opening of Space Mountain, **Disneyland Park** has provided a variety of good thrill rides, though the majority of attractions remain relatively sedate. The **Magic Kingdom** is divided into four "lands" radiating out from **Main Street USA**. **Fantasyland** appeals to the youngest kids, with Sleeping

Beauty's Castle, Peter Pan's Flight, the Mad Hatter's Teacups and Alice's Curious Labyrinth among its attractions. **Adventureland** has the most outlandish sets and two of the best rides – Pirates of the Caribbean and Indiana Jones and the Temple of Peril: Backwards. **Frontierland** has the *Psycho*-inspired but insipid Phantom Manor and the hair-raising roller coaster Big Thunder Mountain, modelled on a runaway mine train. In **Discoveryland** there's a high-tech 3-D experience called "Honey, I Shrunk The Audience", a 360-degree Parisian exposé in Le Visionarium, the Nautilus submarine of *20,000 Leagues Under the Sea* and the startling Space Mountain. The grand **parade** of floats representing all the top box-office Disney movies sallies down Main Street USA at 4pm every day (a good time to try for the more popular rides). Night-time Electrical Parades and **firework displays** take place several times a week.

Walt Disney Studios Park

Other than the "Rock 'N' Roller Coaster Starring Aerosmith", a terrifyingly fast, corkscrew-looping, Metal-playing white-knuckler, the new **Walt Disney Studios Park** lacks the bigger, scarier rides offered by its older neighbour. In some ways it's a more satisfying affair, focusing on what Disney was and is still renowned for – animation. Cartoonists can be visited "at work", there are mock film and TV sets where you can be part of the audience, and the special effects and stunt shows are impressive in their way, although probably not as impressive as just going to the cinema. The virtual-reality ride Armageddon is genuinely thrilling – your space-station is bombarded by meteors – and the tram tour's passage through the collapsing Catastrophe Canyon is good fun. A few minutes' walk away, you can book a two-hour football coaching session for 7- to 14-year-olds at the high-tech **Manchester United Soccer School**.

Practicalities

To reach Disneyland from Paris, take RER line A to Marne-la-Vallée Chessy/Disneyland (about 40 min; €6). If you're coming from Charles de Gaulle airport, you can take the TGV straight to the park in ten minutes (14 trains daily from roughly 9am–9pm; €13.80). From both CDG or Orly airports, shuttle buses run to individual hotels (times and frequencies change seasonally, but roughly every 20–30min 8.30am–7.45pm; €14, children aged 3-11 €11.50; Ⓦwww.vea.fr). Marne-la-Vallée Chessy also has its own TGV train station, linked to Lille, Lyon and London (see p.30 for details of the direct Eurostar from London Waterloo and Ashford in Kent). If you're **driving**, follow the A4 east from Paris for 32km (Exit 13 for Ranch Davy Crockett and Exit 14 for the park and the hotels); from Calais follow the A26 changing to the A1, the A104 and finally the A4.

Admission charges for the one-day "passport" are €40 for an adult or €30 for a child (aged 3–11). The passport allows entry to either the Disneyland Park or Walt Disney Studios Park, not both, though if you opt for the Studios you can visit the Disneyland Park for the last three hours of opening. Three-day passes are also available. **Opening hours** vary depending on the season and whether it's a weekend, and should be checked when you buy your ticket (which can be done online at Ⓦwww.disneylandparis.com) but they are roughly: April to October daily 9am to 11pm; November to March daily 10am to 8pm. You can buy admission passes and train tickets in Paris at all RER line A and B stations and in major métro stations. Disney's six heavily themed **hotels** are a mixed bag, and only worth staying in as part of a multi-day package; these are mostly pricey, even at the bottom-of-the-range *Hotel Santa Fé*, and you may think it more worthwhile to fly to Florida. The least expensive alternative if you have a car is the park's *Davey Crockett Ranch*, a fifteen-minute drive away, with self-catering log cabins (sleeping four to six) from €55 to €130. To really economize, you could camp at the nearby *Camping du Parc de la Colline*, Route de Lagny, 77200 Torcy (ⓣ01.30.58.56.20), which is open all year and offers minibus shuttles to the park.

Vaux-le-Vicomte

Of all the great mansions within reach of a day's outing from Paris, the classical **Château of Vaux-le-Vicomte** (end March to mid-Nov daily 10am–6pm; ⓦwww.vaux-le-vicomte.com; €12), 46km southeast of Paris, is the most architecturally harmonious, the most aesthetically pleasing and the most human in scale.

To get there, take a train from Gare de Lyon (or RER line D from Châtelet) to Melun (40min), then a bus (weekends only; €1), or else taxi (approximately €15–18) for the seven-kilometre ride to the château.

The château

Louis XIV's finance superintendent, Nicholas Fouquet, had the **château** built at colossal expense, using the top designers of the day – architect Le Vau, painter Le Brun and landscape gardener Le Nôtre. The result was magnificence and precision in perfect proportion, and a bill that could only be paid by someone who occasionally confused the state's accounts with his own. The house-warming party, to which the king was invited, was more extravagant than any royal event – a comparison which other finance ministers ensured that Louis took to heart. Within three weeks Fouquet was jailed for life on trumped-up charges, and the design team carted off to build the king's own gaudy piece of one-upmanship at Versailles.

Seen from the entrance, the château is a rather austere grey pile surrounded by an artificial moat, and it's only when you go through to the south side – where clipped box and yew, fountains and statuary stand in formal gardens – that you can look back and appreciate the very harmonious and very French qualities of the building: the combination of steep, tall roof and central dome with classical pediment and pilasters.

As to the interior, the main artistic interest lies in the work of Le Brun, who was responsible for the two fine **tapestries** in the entrance, made in the local workshops set up by Fouquet specifically to adorn his house (and subsequently removed by Louis XIV to become the famous Gobelins works in Paris), as well as numerous **painted ceilings**, notably in Fouquet's Bedroom, the Salon des Muses, *Sleep* in the Cabinet des Jeux, and the so-called King's Bedroom, whose decor is the first example of the style that became known as "Louis Quatorze".

Other points of interest are the **kitchens**, which have not been altered since construction, and a room displaying letters in the hand of Fouquet, Louis XIV and other notables. One, dated November 1794 (mid-Revolution), addresses the incumbent Duc de Choiseul-Praslin as *tu*. "Citizen," it says, "you've got a week to hand over one hundred thousand pounds …", and signs off with "Cheers and brotherhood". You can imagine the shock to the aristocratic system.

Every fine Saturday evening from May to mid-October, between 8pm and midnight (€15 entrance), the **state rooms** and gardens are illuminated with two thousand candles, as they probably were on the occasion of Fouquet's fateful party. The **fountains** and other waterworks can be seen in action on

Museums around Paris

The assortment of **museums** in the general vicinity of Paris are of specialist interest: **ceramics** at Sèvres, **prehistory** at St-Germain-en-Laye and **aviation** at Le Bourget. All are excellent and shouldn't be missed if any of the subjects arouse interest.

Musée de l'Air et d'Espace

A short hop up the A1 motorway from St-Denis, is **LE BOURGET** airport. The French were always pioneering aviators, and Le Bourget is intimately connected with their earliest exploits. Lindbergh landed here after his epic first flight across the Atlantic, and until the development of Orly in the 1950s, this was Paris's principal airport.

The **museum** (Tues–Sun: April–Sept 10am–6pm; Oct–March 10am–5pm; ⓦwww.mae.org; €7) occupies the old airport buildings, and consists of five adjacent hangars and the Grande Galerie, taking you from the earliest attempts to fly through to the latest spacecraft. The Montgolfier brothers are first with their invention of the hot-air balloon. The room dedicated to them shows society going balloon-crazy before real aeroplane madness begins in the **Grande Galerie** with the first contraption to fly 1km, the first cross-Channel flight and the first aerobatics. The Grande Galerie also showcases World War I planes, while highlights of World War II are on display with the first Concorde prototype in the Hall Concorde. **Hangars C and D** cover 1945 to the present day. France's high-tech achievements are represented here by the super-sophisticated best-selling Mirage fighters and two Ariane space-launchers, Ariane I and the latest, Ariane V (both parked on the tarmac outside). **Hangar E** contains light and sporty aircraft and **Hangar F**, nearest to the entrance, is devoted to **space**, with rockets, satellites, space capsules, and the like. Some are mock-ups, some the real thing. Among the latter are a Lunar Roving Vehicle, the Soyuz craft in which a French astronaut flew and France's own first successful space rocket.

To get there, take RER line B from Gare du Nord to Gare du Bourget, then bus #152 to Le Bourget/Musée de l'Air. Alternatively, take bus #350 from Gare du Nord, Gare de l'Est and Porte de la Chapelle, or #152 from Porte de la Villette.

Musée National de la Céramique

The **Musée National de la Céramique** (daily except Tues 10am–5pm; €5) in **SÈVRES** is within easy reach of Paris: take the métro to the Pont-de-Sèvres terminus; cross the bridge and spaghetti junction and the museum is the massive building facing the river bank on your right. If you're interested in ceramics there's much to savour here – not just French pottery and china, but Islamic, Chinese, Italian, German, Dutch and English. There is also, inevitably, a comprehensive collection of Sèvres ware, as the stuff is made right here. Close by, overlooking the river, the **Parc de St-Cloud** is good for fresh air and has a geometrical sequence of pools and fountains delineating a route down to the river and across to the city.

Musée des Antiquités Nationales

ST-GERMAIN is a pleasant town, but the **Musée des Antiquités Nationales** (daily except Tues 9am–5.15pm; ⓦwww.musee-antiquitesnationales.fr; €4, Sun €2.60) is the main attraction. It's housed opposite St-Germain-en-Laye RER station in a renovated château, which was one of the main residences of the French court before Versailles was built.

The extensive Stone Age section includes mock-ups of several cave drawings and carvings, and a beautiful collection of decorative objects, tools and so forth. All ages of prehistory are covered with Celts, Romans and Franks: there's a great section on the battle of Alésia when Vercingétorix found himself besieged by the Romans. A model of Caesar's double fortifications that ringed the hilltop of Alésia shows how the Romans managed to win.

Outside the château, a **terrace** – Le Nôtre again – stretches for more than 2km above the Seine, with a view over the whole of Paris.

the second and last Saturdays of each month between April and October, from 3pm until 6pm. In the stables, the **Musée des Équipages** comprises a collection of horse-drawn vehicles, including those used by Charles X fleeing Paris and the Duc de Rohan retreating from Moscow.

Fontainebleau

From the Gare de Lyon it's just a fifty-minute train ride to **FONTAINEBLEAU**, famous for its vast, rambling **Château** (daily except Tues: June–Sept 9.30am–6pm; Oct–May 9.30am–5pm; €5.50, Ⓦwww.musee-chateau-fontainebleau.fr). The connecting buses #A and #B from Fontainebleau-Avon station take you to the château gates in fifteen minutes.

The château owes its existence to its situation in the middle of a magnificent forest, which made it the perfect base for royal hunting expeditions. A lodge was built here as early as the twelfth century, but it only began its transformation into a luxurious palace during the sixteenth on the initiative of François I, who imported a colony of Italian artists – most notably Rosso il Fiorentino and Niccolò dell'Abate – to carry out the decoration. They were responsible for the celebrated **Galerie François-1er** – which had a seminal influence on the subsequent development of French aristocratic art and design – the Salle de Bal, the Salon Louis XIII and the Salle du Conseil with its eighteenth-century decoration. The palace continued to enjoy royal favour well into the nineteenth century; Napoleon spent huge amounts of money on it, as did Louis-Philippe.

You can take various guided tours (all €3), of which the most interesting takes you round the Petits Appartements, which were fitted out for Napoleon and his first wife Josephine, and preserve their original decor. Of more recherché interest are the tours of the Musée Chinois, created for Eugénie, the wife of Napoléon III, and the Musée Napoléon Ier, which mostly attracts those nostalgic for the First Empire. For details of tour times, ring ⓣ01.60.71.50.70.

The **gardens** are equally luscious, but if you want to escape to the relative wilds, the surrounding **forest** of Fontainebleau is full of walking and cycling trails, all marked on Michelin map #196 (*Environs de Paris*).

Versailles

The **Palace of Versailles** (Tues–Sun: May–Sept 9am–6pm; Oct–April 9am–5pm; closed public hols; €7.50, Ⓦwww.chateauversailles.fr) is rightly one of the most visited monuments in France. Apart from a few areas you can visit on your own, most of the palace can only be viewed on one of the (excellent) guided tours (€4.50–8 extra), whose various itineraries can be booked in the morning at entrance D. Long queues are common, though by hiring an audioguide (€4 from entrance C) you avoid the queues and have access to more rooms. Don't set out to see all the palace in one day – it's not possible.

To **get there**, take the RER line C5 to Versailles-Rive Gauche (40min), turn right out of the station and immediately left to approach the palace.

The palace

The **palace** was inspired by the young Louis XIV's envy of his finance minister's château at Vaux-le-Vicomte (see p.226), which he was determined to outdo. He recruited the design team of Vaux-le-Vicomte architect Le Vau, painter Le Brun and gardener Le Nôtre and ordered something a hundred times the size. Versailles is the apotheosis of French regal indulgence and, even if its extravagant decor and the blatant self-propaganda of the Sun King are not to your liking, it will certainly leave an impression.

Construction began in 1664 and lasted virtually until Louis XIV's death in 1715. Second only to God, and the head of an immensely powerful state, Louis XIV was an institution rather than a private individual. His risings and sittings, comings and goings, were minutely regulated and rigidly encased in ceremony, attendance at which was an honour much sought after by courtiers. Versailles was the headquarters of every arm of the state. More than 20,000 people – nobles, administrative staff, merchants, soldiers and servants – lived in the palace in a state of unhygienic squalor, according to contemporary accounts.

Following Louis XIV's death, the château was abandoned for a few years before being reoccupied by Louis XV in 1722. It remained the residence of the royal family until the Revolution of 1789, when the furniture was sold and the pictures dispatched to the Louvre. Thereafter Versailles fell into ruin until Louis-Philippe established his giant museum of French Glory here – it still exists, though most is mothballed. In 1871, during the Paris Commune, the château became the seat of the nationalist government, and the French parliament continued to meet in Louis XV's opera building until 1879. Restoration only began in earnest between the two world wars, and today the château's management is eagerly buying back the original furnishings every time they come up for auction. Curiously, it has chosen to restore the château as it appeared in the last days of the monarchy.

Of the rooms you can visit without a guide, the most stunning is the dazzling **Galerie des Glaces** – or Hall of Mirrors – where the Treaty of Versailles was signed to end World War I. Restoration works are expected to continue until 2008, but at least half the gallery will be visible at any one time; it's best viewed at the end of the day, when the crowds have departed and sunlight fills it from the west. Overdoses of gilding await you in the **grands appartements**, the state apartments of the king and queen, and the royal **chapel**, a grand structure that ranks among France's finest Baroque creations.

The park and Grand and Petit Trianons

You could spend the whole day just exploring the **park** at Versailles (daily 7/8am–dusk; €3), along with its lesser outcrops of royal mania: the Italianate **Grand Trianon**, designed by Hardouin-Mansart in 1687 as a "country retreat" for Louis XIV; and the more modest Greek **Petit Trianon**, built by Gabriel in the 1760s for Louis XV's mistress, Mme de Pompadour (daily noon–5/6pm; combined ticket for both Trianons €5). More charming than either of these is **Le Hameau de la Reine**, a play village and farm built in 1783 for Marie-Antoinette to indulge the fashionable Rousseau-inspired fantasy of returning to the natural life. It's quintessentially picturesque, but you can't get inside and parts of the surrounding area are still off-limits since works finished on returning the elaborate "English" gardens to their original design. At weekends in summer, the various Louis XIV **fountains** are switched on, to the accompaniment of Baroque music (April–Sept Sat & Sun 11am–noon & 3.30–5pm, with the finale at the Bassin de Neptune at 5.20pm; €6 including park admission).

Distances in the park are considerable. If you can't manage them on foot, a *petit train* shuttles between the terrace in front of the château and the Trianons (€3.50). There are **bikes** for hire at the Grille de la Reine, Porte St-Antoine and by the Grande Canal. **Boats** are for hire on the Grande Canal, within the Park.

Near the park entrance at the end of boulevard de la Reine is the **Hôtel Palais Trianon**, where the final negotiations for the Treaty of Versailles took place in 1919; the hotel has a wonderfully posh **tearoom**. The style of the *Trianon* is very much that of the town in general. The dominant population is aristocratic, with the pre-revolutionary titles disdainful of those dating merely from Napoleon. On Bastille Day, local conservatives like to show their colours, donning black ribbons and ties to mourn the passing of the *ancien régime*.

Chartres

About 80km southwest of Paris, **CHARTRES** is a modest but charming market town whose existence is almost entirely overshadowed by its extraordinary **cathedral** (daily: Jan–April & Nov–Dec 8.30am–7.30pm; May–Oct 8am–8pm; free). Built between 1194 and 1260, it was one of the quickest ever constructed and, as a result, preserves a uniquely harmonious design. The astounding size of the cathedral is entirely due to the presence of the Sancta Camisia – supposed to have been the robe Mary wore when she gave birth to Jesus. After an earlier Romanesque structure burnt down in 1194, the relic was discovered three days later, miraculously unharmed. It was a sign that the Virgin wanted her church lavishly rebuilt – at least, so said the canny medieval fundraisers. In the medieval heyday of the pilgrimage to Santiago de Compostela, hordes of pilgrims on their way south to Spain would stop here to venerate the relic – the sloping floor evident today allowed for it to be washed down more easily. The Sancta Camisia still exists, though after many years on open display it was recently rolled up and put into storage. It may yet be restored to the cathedral.

The geometry of Chartres is unique in being almost unaltered since its consecration, and virtually all of the magnificent **stained glass** is original thirteenth-century work. But if a group of medieval pilgrims suddenly found themselves here they would be deeply dismayed. The paint and gilt work that once brought the portal sculptures to life has vanished, while the walls have lost the whitewash that reflected the vivid colours of the stained-glass windows. Worse still, the high altar has been brought down into the body of the church, among the hoi polloi, and chairs usually cover up the thirteenth-century **labyrinth** on the floor of the nave. The cathedral's **stonework**, however, is still captivating, particularly the **choir screen**, which curves around the ambulatory. Outside, hosts of sculpted figures stand like guardians at each **entrance portal**. Like the south tower and spire which abuts it, the mid-twelfth century **Royal Portal** actually survives from the earlier Romanesque church. You have to pay extra to visit the crypt and treasury, though these are relatively unimpressive. Crowds permitting, it's worth climbing the **north tower** for its bird's-eye view of the sculptures and structure of the cathedral (Mon–Sat 9am–12.30pm & 2–4.30pm, Sun 2–4.30pm; May–Aug open until 5.30pm; €4). There are **gardens** at the back from where you can contemplate the innovative flying buttresses.

In the former episcopal palace immediately behind the cathedral, the **Musée des Beaux Arts** (May–Oct Mon & Wed–Sat 10am–noon & 2–6pm, Sun 2–6pm; Nov–April Mon & Wed–Sat 10am–noon & 2–5pm, Sun 2–6pm; €2.45), has some beautiful tapestries, a room full of works by Maurice de Vlaminck, and an excellent *Sainte Lucie* by Zurbaran. Behind the museum, rue Chantault leads past old town houses to the River Eure and Pont du Massacre. You can follow the river upstream, passing ancient wash-houses. A left turn at the end of rue de la Tannerie, then third right, will bring you to the **Maison Picassiette**, at 22 rue du Repos (April–Oct Mon & Wed–Sat 10am–noon & 2–6pm, Sun 2–6pm; €2.40). This house was entirely decorated with mosaics by a local road-mender and later cemetery-caretaker, Raymond Isidore, creating a strange yet moving folly – "I took the things that other people threw away", as he put it. Back at the end of rue de la Tannerie, the bridge over the river brings you back to the medieval town, where you can wander about spotting little details such as the sixteenth-century carved salmon that decorates a house at the eastern end of place de la Poissonnerie. A large food **market** takes place on place Billard and rue des Changes on Saturday morning, and there's a flower market on place du Cygne (Tues, Thurs & Sat).

At the edge of the old town, at the junction of boulevard de la Résistance and rue Collin-d'Arleville, stands a memorial to **Jean Moulin**, Prefect of Chartres until 1942. In 1940, he refused to sign a document claiming that Senegalese soldiers in the French army were responsible for Nazi atrocities. He later became de Gaulle's number-one man on the ground, coordinating the Resistance, but died at the hands of Klaus Barbie in 1943, on his way to a concentration camp in Germany.

Practicalities

Trains run from Paris's Gare du Montparnasse at least every hour on weekdays (1hr). From the **gare SNCF**, it's less than ten minutes' walk to the cathedral and **tourist office** (April–Sept Mon–Sat 9am–7pm, Sun 9.30am–5.30pm; Oct–March Mon–Sat 10am–6pm, Sun 10am–1pm & 2.30–4.30pm; ⓣ02.37.18.26.26). The latter can supply free maps and help with accommodation.

For a snack, the friendly *Café Serpente* is usefully located at 2 Cloître-Notre-Dame, opposite the south side of the cathedral. For a proper **restaurant** meal, try *Le Pichet*, 19 rue de Cheval Blanc, almost under the northwest spire (ⓣ02.37.21.08.35; closed Mon, Wed, Tues evening & Sun evening), or the slightly upmarket *L'Estocade*, 1 rue de la Porte Guillaume (ⓣ02.37.34.27.17; closed Mon & Nov–April), which has a lovely situation down by the River Eure.

Malmaison

The **Château of Malmaison** (April–Oct Mon & Wed–Fri 10am–5.45pm, Sat & Sun 10am–6.15pm; Nov–March Mon & Wed–Fri 10am–12.30pm & 1.30–5.15pm, Sat & Sun 10am–noon & 1.30–5.45pm; combined ticket with Bois-Préau museum €4.50), set in the beautiful grounds of the **Bois-Préau**, about 15km west of central Paris, is a relatively small and surprisingly enjoyable place to visit.

It was the home of the Empress Josephine, and – during the 1800–1804 Consulate – of Napoleon, too. According to his secretary, "it was the only place next to the battlefield where he was truly himself." After their divorce, Josephine stayed on here, building up her superb rose garden and occasionally receiving visits from the emperor until her death in 1814.

Tours of the château include the private and official apartments, some with original furnishings, as well as Josephine's clothes, china, glass and personal possessions. There are other Napoleonic bits in the **Bois-Préau museum** (closed for renovation at the time of writing).

To get to Malmaison take the métro to Grande-Arche-de-la-Défense, then bus #258 to Malmaison-Château. Alternatively, if you'd like a walk, take the RER to Rueil-Malmaison and follow the GR11 footpath for about two kilometres from the Pont de Chatou along the left bank of the Seine and into the château park.

Travel details

Trains

Gare de'Austerlitz to: Tours (hourly; 2hr 30min).
Gare de l'Est to: Metz (10 daily; 2hr 50min); Nancy (12 daily; 2hr 50min–3hr 20min); Reims (15 daily; 1hr 40min–2hr 20min); Strasbourg (11 daily; 4hr).
Gare de Lyon to: Avignon (13 daily; 2hr 40min–3hr 30min); Besançon (8 daily; 2hr 30min–3hr); Dijon (hourly; 1hr 40min); Grenoble (13 daily; 2hr 50min–3hr 50min); Lyon (hourly; 2hr–2hr 30min); Marseille (hourly; 3hr 10min); Nice (7 daily; 5hr 30min–6hr 30min).
Gare Montparnasse to: Bayonne (6 daily; 4hr 45min–6hr 30min); Bordeaux (at least hourly; 3hr–3hr 30min); Brest (8 daily; 4hr 20min–5hr 20min); Nantes (11 daily; 2hr); Pau (7 daily; 5hr 15min–7hr 20min); Poitiers (14 daily; 1hr 40min); Rennes (at least hourly; 2hr 15min); Toulouse (10 daily; 5hr–6hr 30min); Tours (hourly; 1hr–1hr 30min).
Gare du Nord to: Amiens (at least hourly; 1hr 45min); Arras (roughly every 2hr; 50min); Boulogne (at least hourly; 2hr 10min); Lille (hourly; 1hr).
Gare St-Lazare to: Caen (hourly; 1hr 50min–2hr 30min); Cherbourg (roughly every 2hr; 3hr–3hr 30min); Dieppe (2 daily; 2hr 15min); Le Havre (every 2–3hr; 2hr–2hr 30min); Rouen (hourly; 1hr 15min).

2

The north

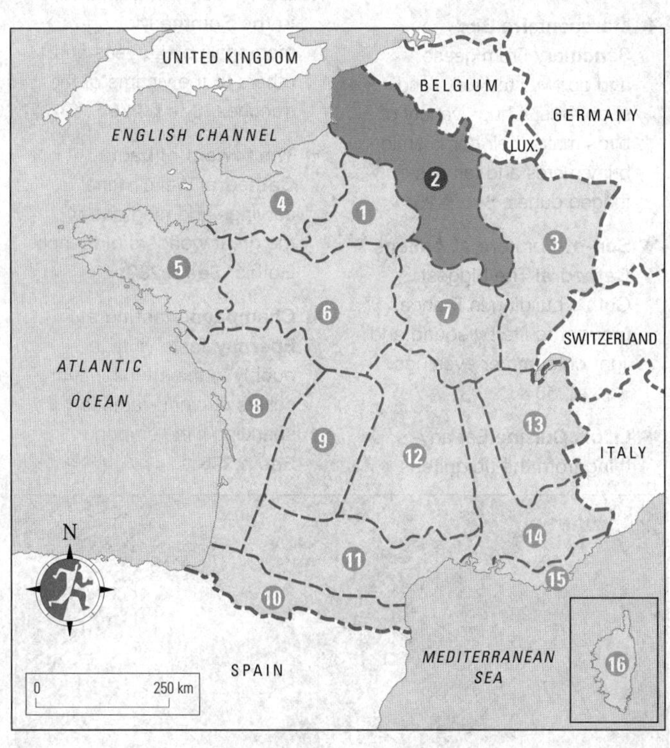
UNITED KINGDOM
BELGIUM
GERMANY
LUX.
ENGLISH CHANNEL
ATLANTIC OCEAN
SWITZERLAND
ITALY
SPAIN
MEDITERRANEAN SEA
N
0
250 km
1
2
3
4
5
6
7
8
9
10
11
12
13
14
15
16

CHAPTER 2 Highlights

* **Dunes along the Channel** Drive along the rolling, windswept shore of the Côte d'Opale, passing through scenic villages and keeping your eyes on the white cliffs of Dover, just a short swim away. See p.247
* **Marquenterre Bird Sanctuary** From geese and godwits to storks and spoonbills, a huge variety of birds make their home amid briny meres and tamarisk-fringed dunes. See p.254
* **Son-et-Lumière at Amiens Cathedral** The biggest Gothic building in France, brought to life by sound and light on summer evenings. See p.258
* **Lillois Cuisine** Eat anything from the ubiquitous *moules-frites*, washed down with micro-brewed beer, to fried *escargots* with onions roasted in lavender oil in the historic centre of Lille, the cultural capital of northern France. See p.267
* **World War I monuments in the Somme** Moving memorials by Lutyens and others to the victims of the trenches. See p.279
* **The towers of Laon Cathedral** Weird stone carvings adorning one of the great wonders of French Gothic. See p.282
* **Champagne tasting at Épernay** Taste vintage bubbly in the atmospheric cellars of world-famous sparkling wine emporia. See p.296

△ Wall of Names at Thiepval Memorial

2

The north

When conjuring up exotic holiday locations, you're unlikely to light upon the **north** of France. Even among the French, the most enthusiastic tourists of their own country, it has few adherents. Largely flat Artois and Flanders include the most heavily industrialized parts of the country, these days hit by post-industrial depression, while across the wheat fields of the more sparsely populated regions of Picardy and Champagne a few drops of rain are all that is required for total gloom to descend. Coming from Britain it's likely, however, that you'll arrive and leave France via this region, and there are good reasons to stop within easy reach of Calais and the Channel Tunnel, even at **Boulogne**, by far the most appealing of the northern Channel ports. Just inland the delightful village of **Cassel** is a rare example of a Flemish hill settlement, while **St-Omer** and **Montreuil-sur-Mer** are also strong contenders in terms of charm and interest.

Northern France has been on the path of various invaders into the country, from northern Europe as well as from Britain, and the events that have taken place in Flanders, Artois and Picardy have shaped French history. The bloodiest battles were those of World War I, above all the **Battle of the Somme**, which took place north of Amiens, and **Vimy Ridge**, near Arras, where the trenches have been preserved in perpetuity.

On a more cheerful note, **Picardy** boasts some of France's finest cathedrals, including those at **Amiens**, **Beauvais** and **Laon**. Further south, the wineries, vineyards and world-famous produce of the **Champagne** region are the main draw, for which the best bases are **Épernay** and **Reims**, the latter with another fine cathedral. Other attractions include the bird sanctuary of **Marquenterre**; the wooded wilderness of the **Ardennes**; industrial archeology in the coalfields around **Douai**, where Zola's *Germinal* was set; the great medieval castle of **Coucy-le-Château**; and the battle sites of the Middle Ages – **Agincourt** and **Crécy** – familiar names in the long history of Anglo-French rivalry.

In city centres from **Lille** to **Troyes**, you'll find your fill of food, culture and entertainment in the company of locals similarly intent on having a good time. And in addition to the more obvious pleasures of the Champagne region, there's the possibility of finding relatively lucrative employment during the harvest season towards the end of September.

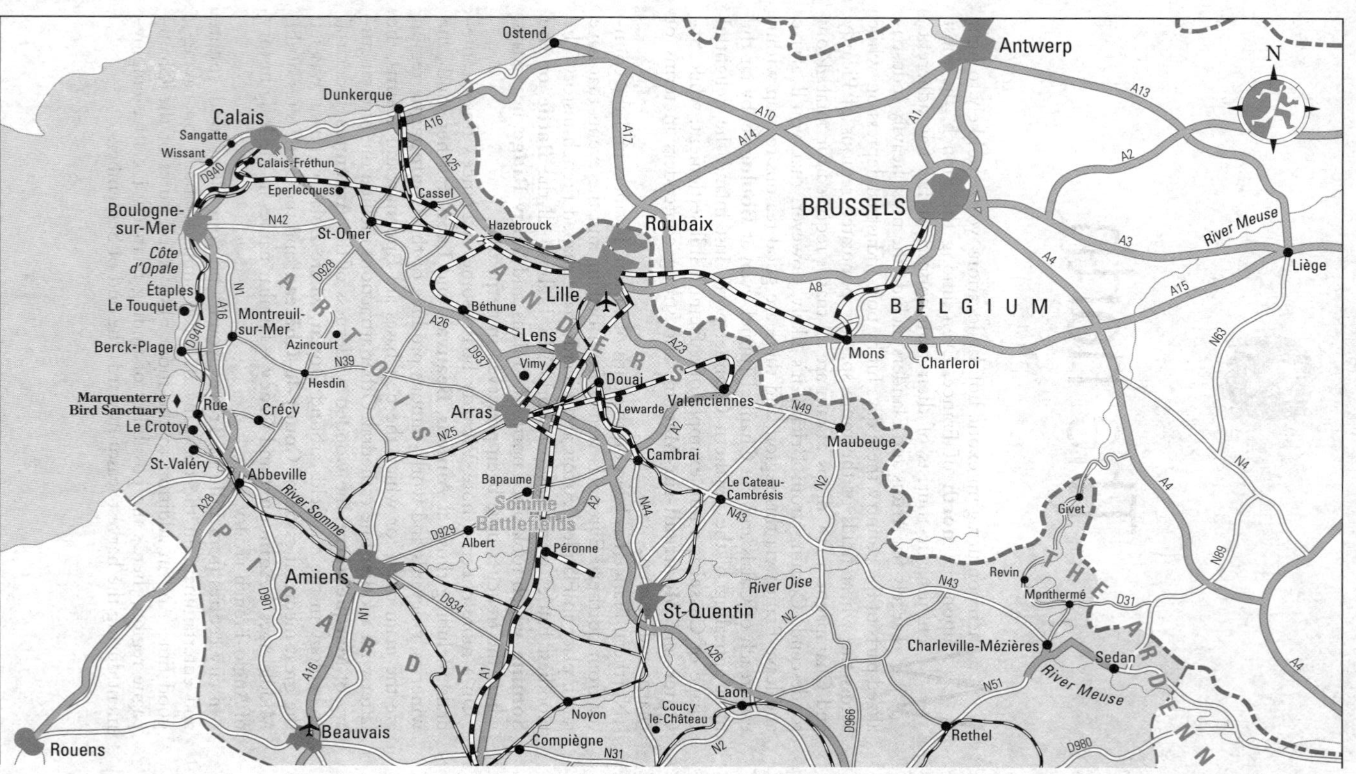
Ostend
Antwerp
Dunkerque
Calais
Sangatte
Wissant
Calais-Fréthun
Eperlecques
Cassel
Boulogne-sur-Mer
St-Omer
Hazebrouck
Roubaix
BRUSSELS
River Meuse
Liège
Côte d'Opale
Étaples
Le Touquet
Montreuil-sur-Mer
Azincourt
Berck-Plage
Béthune
Lille
Lens
BELGIUM
Mons
Charleroi
Vimy
Hesdin
Douai
Marquenterre Bird Sanctuary
Rue
Crécy
Le Crotoy
Arras
Lewarde
Valenciennes
Maubeuge
St-Valéry
Abbeville
Cambrai
Bapaume
Le Cateau-Cambrésis
Somme Battlefields
Albert
Péronne
Givet
Revin
Monthermé
Amiens
River Somme
River Oise
St-Quentin
Charleville-Mézières
Sedan
River Meuse
Laon
Coucy le-Château
Noyon
Rethel
Beauvais
Compiègne
Rouens
FLANDERS
ARTOIS
PICARDY
THE ARDENN
A1
A2
A3
A4
A8
A10
A13
A14
A15
A16
A17
A23
A25
A26
A28
N1
N2
N4
N25
N31
N39
N42
N43
N44
N49
N51
N63
N89
D31
D901
D928
D929
D934
D937
D940
D966
D980
N

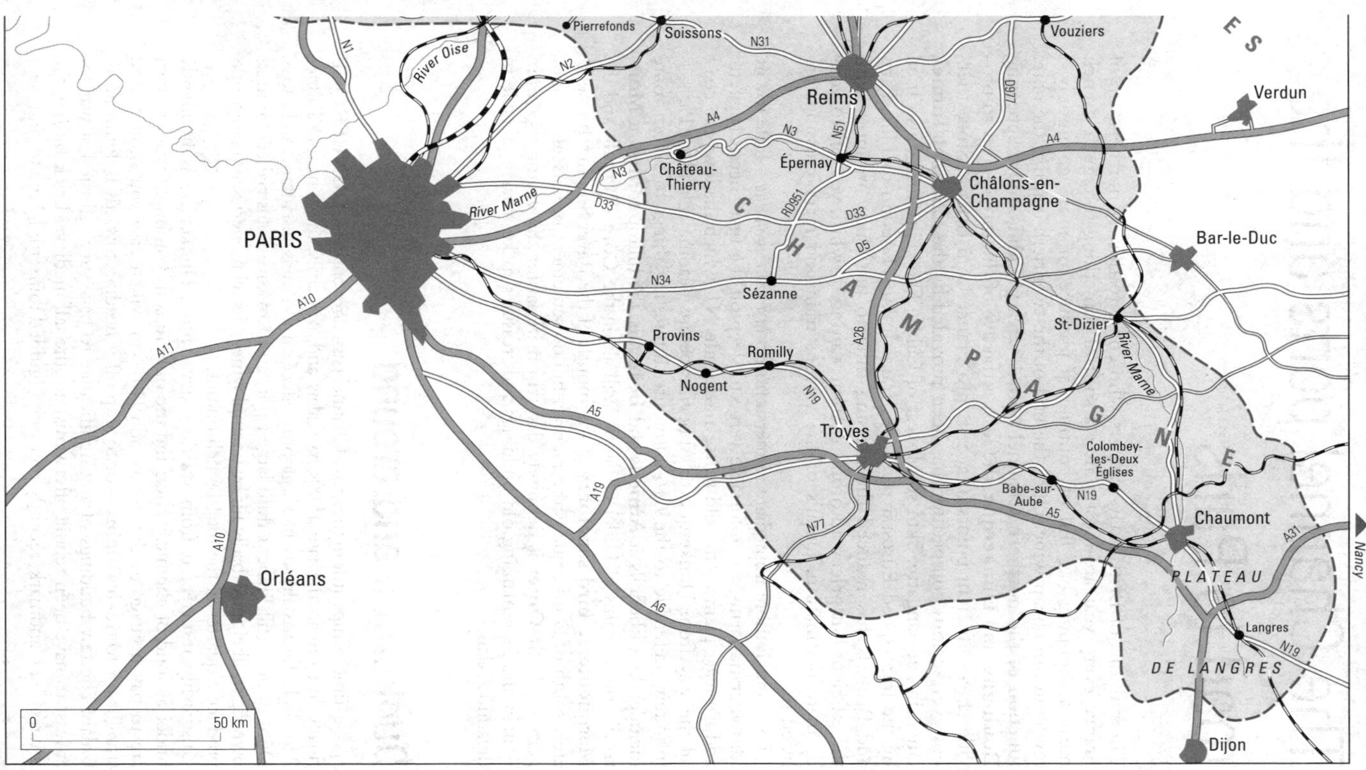

Pierrefonds
Soissons
N31
Vouziers
E S
N1
River Oise
N2
Reims
Verdun
A4
D977
A4
N3
N51
Épernay
Château-Thierry
N3
Châlons-en-Champagne
PARIS
River Marne
D33
RD951
D33
CHAMPAGNE
Bar-le-Duc
D5
N34
Sézanne
A10
St-Dizier
A26
Provins
Romilly
River Marne
A11
Nogent
N19
A5
Troyes
Colombey-les-Deux Églises
Babe-sur-Aube
N19
A19
A5
N77
Chaumont
A31
Nancy
A10
Orléans
PLATEAU DE LANGRES
A6
Langres
N19
0
50 km
Dijon

The Channel ports and the road to Paris

The millions of British day-trippers who come to this far northern tip of France every year are mostly after a sniff of something foreign: a French meal, a shopping bag full of continental produce, or more commonly a few crates of cheap wine. Until the end of the twentieth century the chief function of the northern Channel ports – dreary **Calais**, more appealing **Boulogne**, and **Dunkerque**, the least attractive of the three – was to provide cheap, efficient points of access into France from Britain. Since then, however, serious competition has been provided by the **Channel Tunnel**, emerging at Sangatte, 5km southwest of Calais. The "Chunnel", also used by the high-speed Eurostar passenger trains linking London to Lille, Paris and Brussels, has reduced the crossing time to just thirty minutes, with the efficient but pricey autoroute system waiting to whisk you off to your ultimate destination. Details of the various train and ferry crossings are listed in.

For a much more immediate immersion into *la France profonde* – little towns, idiosyncratic farms, a comfortable verge to sleep off the first cheese, baguette and *vin rouge* picnic – the old **route nationale N1**, which shadows the coast all the way from Dunkerque to Abbeville before heading inland to Paris, is infinitely preferable to the A16 autoroute. Interesting things to see en route include: the cathedrals at **Amiens** and **Beauvais**, the hilltop fortress at **Montreuil**, the remains of Hitler's Atlantic Wall along the **Côte d'Opale** and the **Marquenterre bird sanctuary** at the mouth of the River Somme. Immediately south of Dunkerque is the Flemish hilltop settlement of **Cassel**, a minor gem, while **St-Omer** is definitely day-trip material for the visitor over from Britain and its remaining old buildings and treasures make it far preferable to dreadful Calais.

Dunkerque and around

A one-time competitor in the cross-Channel passenger business, **DUNKERQUE** finally lost out in the late 1990s to Calais and, primarily, the Channel Tunnel. Although this has already had a gloomy effect on its hotels, restaurants and shops, Dunkerque is still France's third largest port and a massive industrial centre in its own right, albeit now badly hit by unemployment; its oil refineries and steelworks produce a quarter of the total French output.

Unstylishly resurrected from wartime devastation, Dunkerque is frequently under a cloud of chemical smog and the only reasons you might want to visit are to pay homage to the events of 1940 – in which case you should head straight for **Malo-les-Bains** – or to stop off if heading towards Belgium from Calais. The few buildings of any significance to have survived the last war (or at least to have been rebuilt afterwards) are the tall medieval brick **belfry**, the town's chief landmark, recently renovated (guided tours: mid-June to mid-Sept

Dunkerque 1940

The evacuation of 350,000 Allied troops from the beaches of **Dunkerque** from May 27 to June 4, 1940, has become a heroic wartime legend. However, this legend conveniently conceals the fact that the Allies, through their own incompetence, almost lost their entire armed forces in the first few weeks of the war.

The German army had taken just ten days to reach the English Channel and could very easily have cut off the Allied armies. Unable to believe the ease with which he had overcome a numerically superior enemy, however, Hitler ordered his generals to halt their lightning advance, giving Allied forces trapped in the Pas-de-Calais enough time to organize **Operation Dynamo**, the largest wartime evacuation ever undertaken. Initially it was hoped that around 10,000 men would be saved, but thanks to low-lying cloud and the assistance of over 1750 vessels – among them pleasure cruisers, fishing boats and river ferries – 140,000 French and over 200,000 British soldiers were successfully shipped back to England.

In France, the ratio of British to French evacuees caused bitter resentment, since Churchill had promised that the two sides would go *bras dessus, bras dessous* ("arm in arm"). Meanwhile, the British media played up the "remarkable discipline" of the troops as they waited to embark, the "victory" of the RAF over the Luftwaffe and the "disintegration" of the French army all around. In fact, there was widespread indiscipline in the early stages as men fought for places on board; the battle for the skies was evenly matched; and the French fought long and hard to cover the whole operation, some 150,000 of them remaining behind to become prisoners of war. In addition, the Allies lost seven destroyers and 177 fighter planes and were forced to abandon over 60,000 vehicles. After 1940 Dunkerque remained occupied by Germans until the bitter end of the war – it was the last French town to be liberated in 1945.

Mon–Sat 10am, 11am & hourly 2–5pm; July & Aug also Sun and hols 11am, 2pm & 3pm; €2.50); the nearby fifteenth-century **church of St-Éloi**; and, a few blocks north of the church on place Charles Valentin, the early twentieth century **Hôtel de Ville**, a Flemish fancy to rival that of Calais. Dunkerque does have a couple of museums that can help pass the time if you do end up here. **The Musée des Beaux-Arts** (daily except Tues 10am–12.15pm & 1.45–6pm; €3.05, first Sun of the month free), on place du Général-de-Gaulle near the post office, three blocks along rue du Président Poincaré from the belfry, has a minor collection of seventeenth- and eighteenth-century French, Dutch and Flemish paintings, with bits of natural history and a display on the May 1940 evacuations. The Musée d'Art Contemporain is billed to reopen in the second half of 2005 (check with the tourist office), but its **sculpture park** remains open (daily: July & Aug 9am–8pm; Sept–June 9.30am–5.30pm; free), beside the canal on avenue des Bains. More interesting, especially for children, is the **Musée Portuaire** (daily except Tues: July & Aug 10am–6pm; Sept–June 10am–12.45pm & 1.30–6pm; €4) at 9 quai de la Citadelle on the Bassin du Commerce, which illustrates the history of Dunkerque from its beginnings as a fishing hamlet, using models of boats and tools of the various trades associated with the port.

Practicalities

From Dunkerque's **gare SNCF** – where buses also stop – it's a short walk to the **tourist office** (July & Aug Mon–Sat 9am–6.30pm, Sun 10am–noon & 2–6pm; Sept–June Mon–Fri 9am–12.30pm & 1.30–6.30pm, Sat 9am–6.30pm,

Sun 10am–noon & 2–4pm; ⓣ03.28.26.27.27, ⓦwww.ot-dunkerque.fr) housed in the belfry itself. If you're looking to rent a **car**, there's an Avis at the station (ⓣ03.28.66.67.95).

A reasonable **accommodation** option by the station on 22/27 place de la Gare is the comfortable two-star *Le Select* (ⓣ03.28.66.64.47, ⓦwww.leselect-hotel.fr.st; ❷). More salubrious hotels away from the station include the *Borel*, a modern three-star with well-set-up rooms overlooking the fishing boats of the Bassin du Commerce at 6 rue Hermitte (ⓣ03.28.66.51.80, ⓔborel@hotelborel.fr; ❹) and the equally well-equipped but more old-fashioned *Europ'Hôtel*, close by at 13 rue Leughenaer (ⓣ03.28.66.29.07, ⓦwww.europ-hotel.com; ❺). There's also a seafront **HI hostel** on place Paul Asseman, 2km east of the centre, practically at Malo-les-Bains (ⓣ03.28.63.36.34, ⓕ03.28.63.24.54; take blue bus #3 to Piscine, direction "Malo-les-Bains"; €12.20 including breakfast, plus €2.80 for sheets).

There are more enjoyable **eating** options in Malo-les-Bains, but if you're staying in Dunkerque, try *La Sirène*, 65 rue de l'Amiral-Ronarc'h, near the belfry, for good seafood (menus from €20; ⓣ03.28.59.03.29; closed Sat & Sun); or *The Famous Tormore Pub* at 11 place Charles-Valentin near the town hall, which is better than its name suggests – it's a brasserie-cum-grill serving Flemish dishes and popular with locals (€15 or so à la carte, €12 lunch menu, ⓣ03.28.63.15.95). At 6 quai de la Citadelle, *Le Corsaire* has menus from €23, as well as a view over the port and the *Duchesse Anne*, a 1901 German ship given to France as part of the war reparations in 1946.

Regional food and drink

Champagne's cuisine is dominated by the famous **sparkling wine**, large quantities of which are sloshed in sauces or over sorbets. Otherwise the province's cooking is known for little apart from its **cheeses** – sharp-tasting, creamy white *Chaource* and orange skinned *Langres* – and Champagne's main contribution to French food, the **andouillette**, for which Troyes is famed. Translated euphemistically into English as "chitterling sausage", it is in actual fact an intestine crammed full of more intestines, all chopped up. An acquired taste (and texture), it's better than it sounds – look out for the notation AAAAA, a seal of approval awarded by the Association of Amateurs of the Authentic Andouillette. The **Ardennes** is another area that really lacks a distinctive repertoire (*à l'ardennaise* just means flavoured with juniper berries); game looms large on all menus, **pâté d'Ardennes** being the main famous dish. **French Flanders**, however, has one of France's richest regional cuisines. Especially on the coast the **seafood** – oysters, shrimps and scallops – and **fish** – above all sole and turbot – are outstanding, while in Lille **moules-frites** are appreciated every bit as much as in neighbouring Belgium. Here, too, **beer** is the favourite drink, with pale and brown Pelforth the local brew. Traditional **estaminets** or brasseries also serve a range of dishes cooked in beer, most famously the **carbonades à la flamande**, a kind of beef stew; rabbit, chicken, game and fish may also be prepared *à la bière*. Other pot-cooked dishes include the **hochepot** (a meaty broth), **waterzooi** (chicken in a creamy sauce) and **potjevlesch** (various white meats in a rich sauce). In addition to the *boulette d'Avesnes*, the Flemish cheese par excellence is the strong-flavoured **maroilles**, used to make **flamiche**, a kind of open tart of cheese pastry, also made with leeks (*aux poireaux*). For the sweet toothed, *crêpes à la cassonade* (pancakes with muscovado sugar) are often on menus, but **waffles** (*gaufres*) are the local speciality and come in two basic varieties: the thick honeycomb type served with sugar or cream, or the wafer-like biscuit filled with jam or syrup. Charles de Gaulle, who was from Lille, was apparently particularly fond of the latter sort.

Malo-les-Bains

MALO-LES-BAINS is Dunkerque's better half. Still not really a tourist destination, it's a pleasant enough nineteenth-century seaside suburb on the east side of town (buses #3 & #9), from whose vast sandy beach the Allied troops embarked in 1940 (see box, p.239). Digue des Alliés is the dirtier end of an extensive beachfront promenade lined with cafés and restaurants; at the cleaner end, Digue des Mers, the beach can almost seem pleasant when the sun comes out – as long as you avert your eyes from the industrial inferno to the west. However, the suburb actually reveals its *fin-de-siècle* charm away from the seafront, a few parallel blocks inland along avenue Faidherbe and its continuation avenue Kléber, with place Turenne sandwiched in between; around here you'll find some excellent patisseries, boulangeries and charcuteries.

A beachfront **campsite**, *La Licorne*, is at 1005 boulevard de l'Europe (Ⓣ03.28.69.26.68, Ⓔcampingdelalicorne@wanadoo.fr). Other **places to stay** include the *Hirondelle*, 46/48 av Faidherbe (Ⓣ03.28.63.17.65, Ⓦwww.hotelhirondelle.com; ❹), a modern two-star in a great position; and the unassuming, less expensive *Au Bon Coin*, 49 av Kléber (Ⓣ03.28.69.12.63, Ⓕ03.28.69.64.03; ❸), whose cosy bar is good for a drink. Both have well-regarded **restaurants** specializing in seafood: menus cost from around €14 at both. Also on avenue Kléber are a few more exotic eateries, including a Vietnamese and a North African restaurant. Two popular beachfront brasseries, again focusing on seafood, are *L'Iguane*, 15 Digue des Alliés (towards Dunkerque), a down-to-earth establishment offering generous servings at €7.50 a *plat*, and the stylish but more expensive *Le Pavois*, at 175 Digue de Mer (menu €17).

Cassel

Barely 30km southeast of Dunkerque and just off the A25 autoroute towards Lille, is the tiny hilltop town of **CASSEL**. Hills are rare in Flanders, and consequently Cassel was much fought over from Roman times onwards. Marshal Foch spent "some of the most distressing hours" of his life here during World War I, and it was up to the top of Cassel's hill that the "Grand Old Duke of York" marched his 10,000 men in 1793, though, as hinted at in the nursery rhyme, he failed to take the town.

There's no public transport from Cassel's train station (a regular service on the Dunkerque-Lille line), a full 3km west of town, so your own transport would come in handy. Once there, however, your efforts will be rewarded with the very Flemish **Grand' Place**, lined with some magnificent mansions, from which narrow cobbled streets fan out to the ramparts. The town's useful **tourist office** is on the square (June–Aug Mon–Fri 9am–noon & 1.30–6pm, Sat 9am–noon & 2–6pm, Sun 2–6pm; Sept–June Mon–Fri 8.30am–noon & 1.30–5.30pm, Sat 9am–noon; Ⓣ03.28.40.52.55, Ⓦwww.ot-cassel.fr); they have a list of bed-and-breakfast *gîtes* and other **places to stay** in or near Cassel. From the public gardens in the upper town, with the inevitable statue of hero Foch, you have an unrivalled view over Flanders, with Belgium just 10km away. Here among the trees is eighteenth-century **Kasteel Meulen**, the last of Cassel's wooden **windmills** (April–Sept daily 10am–12.30pm & 2–6pm; Oct–March Sat, Sun & school holidays; free), which once numbered 29 across the town, pounding out flour and linseed oil for educational purposes.

Of the several places to **eat** on the Grand' Place *La Taverne Flamande*, at no. 35 (closed Tues evening & Wed; from €16) specializes in Flemish cuisine, while *Le*

Sauvage, no. 38 (☎03.28.42.40.88), is more for classic French food at similar prices. Up near the windmill at 8 rue St Nicolas, *'T Kasteel Hof* (☎03.28.40.59.29; menu €15) oozes local ambience and has a variety of beers to go with the typical cuisine, including a delicious *carbonade*; its popularity makes bookings advisable at weekends. Cassel is home to an annual international artisanal **beer festival** for a weekend at the end of September (☎03.28.42.45.35 or check with the tourist office for details).

Calais and around

CALAIS is less than 40km from Dover – the Channel's shortest crossing – and is by far the busiest French passenger port, though the new ferry service to Boulogne-sur-Mer (see p.248) promises to give it a run for its money. The port (and its accompanying petrochemical works) dominates the town; in fact, there's not much else here. In the last war the British destroyed it to prevent it being used as a base for a German invasion, but the French still refer to it as "the most English town in France", an influence that began after the battle of Crécy in 1346, when Edward III seized it for use as a beachhead in the Hundred Years War. It remained in English hands for over two hundred years until 1558, when its loss caused Mary Tudor famously to say: "When I am dead and opened, you shall find Calais lying in my heart." The association has been

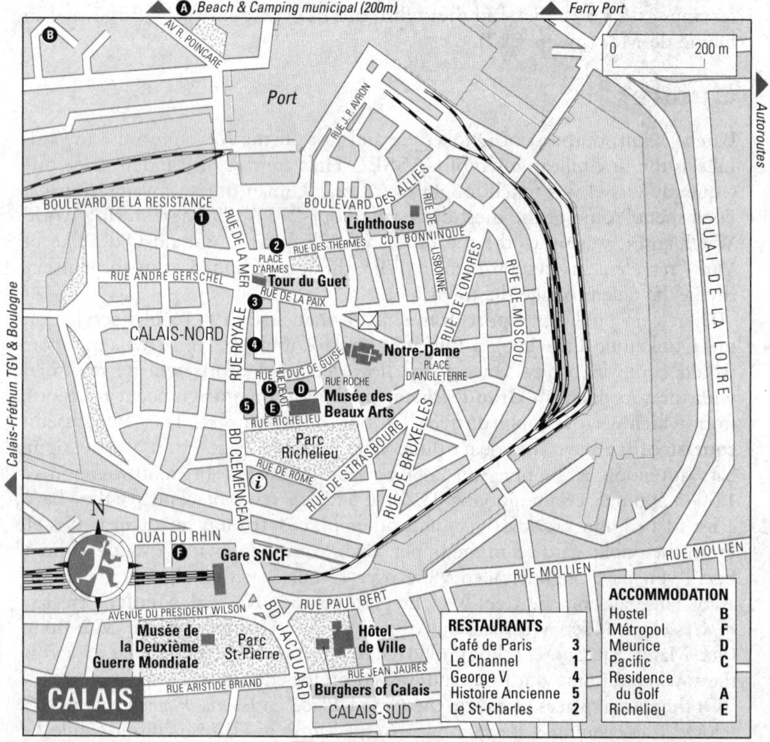

maintained by various Brits across the centuries: Lady Emma Hamilton, Lord Nelson's mistress; Oscar Wilde; Nottingham lacemakers who set up business in the early nineteenth century; and, nowadays, nine million British travellers per year, plus another million-odd day-trippers.

Arrival, information and accommodation

There's a free if infrequent daytime **bus** service from the Ferry Terminal to place d'Armes and the central **Calais-Ville train station**, in front of which is a de facto bus station, with departures for Dunkerque, Boulogne and the out-of-city hypermarkets. To get to the outlying **gare TGV** ("Calais-Fréthun" is actually much further from Calais than the name suggests) for Eurostar trains to London and Paris, either take a bus (free on demonstration of a SNCF ticket) or one of the regular trains to Boulogne, checking first that it stops there (most do). If you're driving and intent on skipping Calais in favour of Paris, which would be understandable, take a left out of the ferry terminal – the new autoroute bypass begins almost immediately, leading to both the A26 and the original N1. If you plan to rent a **car**, you could try Avis (ⓣ03.21.34.66.50) and Budget (ⓣ03.21.96.42.20), both located in place d'Armes and at the ferry terminal; a cheaper option, also at the ferry terminal, is National/Citer (ⓣ03.21.34.58.45). For details of ferry crossings, see Basics.

If, for some reason, you decide to stay in Calais, plenty of **accommodation** is available, though it can be tricky finding a room late in the day in high season, and it's wise to book ahead. The **tourist office** at 12 bd Clemenceau, the continuation of rue Royale (June–Aug Mon–Sat 9am–7pm, Sun 10am–1pm, Sept–June Mon–Sat 10am–1pm & 2–6.30pm; ⓣ03.21.96.62.40, ⓦwww.ot-calais.fr) has a free accommodation booking service as well as a list of *gîtes* in the region.

Hotels

Métropol 43 quai du Rhin ⓣ03.21.97.54.00, ⓦwww.metropolhotel.com. Situated on the canal between the tourist office and town hall, this is a comfortable, modern but nondescript hotel with small rooms right next to the train station. ❸

Meurice 5 rue Edmond-Roche ⓣ03.21.34.57.03, ⓦwww.hotel-meurice.fr. Comfortable three-star with a grand entrance, luxurious high beds and antique furniture in a quiet street behind the Musée des Beaux-Arts. ❺

Pacific 40 rue Duc de Guise ⓣ03.21.34.50.24, ⓦwww.cofrase.com/hotel/pacific. Tidy, clean, and, crucially, cheap rooms with friendly staff in the centre of town. ❷

Richelieu 17 rue Richelieu ⓣ03.21.34.61.60, ⓕ03.21.85.89.28. Overlooking the park of the same name, this hotel has light and airy rooms, all equipped with shower, TV and toilet. ❸

Résidence du Golf 74 Digue G. Berthe ⓣ03.21.96.88.99, ⓦwww.lodgingfrance.com/calais/residencedugolf. Neat, bright motel-style rooms, each with a kitchenette and a view of the water, in a hotel opposite the beach and not far from the centre of town. ❹

Hostel and campsite

Hostel av du Maréchal-de-Lattre-de-Tassigny ⓣ03.21.34.70.20, ⓔadjcalais@wanadoo.fr. Modern hostel located right at the seaward end of rue Royale, just one block from the beach. Double rooms, breakfast included. €14.50 with card, €16 without.

Camping municipal 26 av Raymond Poincaré ⓣ03.21.97.89.79. A large exposed site close to the beach, open all year.

The Town

Calais divides in two with **Calais-Nord**, the old town rebuilt after the war with the drab place d'Armes and rue Royale as its focus, separated by canals from the sprawling "new town" or **Calais-Sud**, centred around the Hôtel de Ville and the main shopping streets, boulevards Lafayette and Jacquard – the latter named after the inventor of looms, who mechanized Calais' lacemaking industry.

Shopping

Place d'Armes and **rue Royale** are the main shopping arteries in Calais-Nord, with a string of boutiques selling mainly clothes and chocolate; try La Maison du Fromage et des Vins (closed Mon & Tues but open Sun morning) for a good selection of cheeses and wine. Generally, however, the streets of Calais-Sud – particularly boulevards Jacquard and Lafayette – are a better bet. More colourful still are the markets around place d'Armes (Wed & Sat) and boulevard Lafayette (Thurs & Sat). For truly epic cross-the-border shopping it's best to head to the **hypermarkets**, or *grandes surfaces*, a few kilometres out of town. The best of these is the **Auchan** complex on the Boulogne road, the old N1 (Mon–Sat 9am–9pm; bus #5, giving change in sterling if you wish); this is closely followed by **Carrefour/Mi-Voix**, on the east side of town, on av Georges-Guynemer (daily 9am–9pm; bus #4). **Cité Europe**, a vast shopping complex by the Channel Tunnel terminal and just off the A16 in the direction of Boulogne (bus #7), offers you another large Carrefour (Mon–Fri 9am–10pm, Sat 8.30am–10pm) as well as high-street clothes shops and food shops (Mon–Thurs & Sat 10am–8pm, Fri 10am–9pm) all under one roof.

Calais-Nord's charms, such as they are, soon wear thin. The grim **Tour du Guet**, on place d'Armes, is the only medieval building in the quarter to have survived wartime bombardment. From the Tour, rue de la Paix leads to the **church of Notre-Dame**, where Charles de Gaulle married local girl Yvonne Vendroux in 1921. Rather spuriously dubbed the only English Perpendicular church on the continent, it's not a particularly good example of the style, especially in its present state of dereliction. Frill-fanciers can enjoy the unusual lacemaking exhibition, along with a small but interesting collection of sixteenth- to twentieth-century art, including paintings by Picasso and Dubuffet, and a Rodin sculpture, in the **Musée des Beaux-Arts et de la Dentelle** on rue Richelieu (Mon & Wed–Fri 10am–noon & 2–5.30pm, Sat 10am–noon & 2–6.30pm, Sun 2–6.30pm; €5, free Wed), which runs alongside the Parc Richelieu, at the other end of rue Royale from the place d'Armes. Continue in the other direction on rue Royal and you'll come to the city's underwhelming **beach**, where the waters are nevertheless swimmable, and from which on a fine day the English shore is visible, or take rue des Thermes to visit the 51-metre **lighthouse**, with 271 steps to a panoramic view at place Henri Barbusse (June–Sept daily 10am–noon & 2–5.30pm; Oct–May Wed 2–5.30pm; €2.50).

Calais-Sud is scarcely more exciting. Just over the canal bridge, the town's landmark, the **Hôtel de Ville**, raises its belfry over 60m into the sky; this Flemish extravaganza was finished in 1926, and miraculously survived World War II. Somewhat dwarfed by the building, Rodin's famous bronze, the **Burghers of Calais**, records for ever the self-sacrifice of local dignitaries, who offered their lives to assuage the blood lust of the victor at Crécy, Edward III – only to be spared at the last minute by the intervention of Queen Philippa, Edward's wife. For a record of Calais' wartime travails you can consult the fascinating **Musée de la Deuxième Guerre Mondiale** (May–Aug daily 10am–6pm; mid-Feb to April & Sept to mid-Nov daily except Tues 11am–5pm; €6), installed in a former German Blockhaus in the Parc St-Pierre across the street, with exhibits of uniforms, weapons and models from World War II and a small section devoted to World War I.

Eating and drinking

Calais is full of mediocre **eateries**, catering for its day-tripper trade – place d'Armes is full of such examples – and there are plenty of self-service and fast-food outlets near the beach. **Drinking** establishments are mainly of the Gaelic theme-pub variety and are in abundance on rue Royale and its continuation, rue de la Mer. *Le Troubadour* on quai du Rhin is a popular hangout for local music-heads, with lots of long hair around the games tables by day and bands by night.

Café de Paris 72 rue Royale. Signalled by its tacky Eiffel tower outside, and the closest France gets to an American diner, this brasserie is popular with locals and tourists alike for its cheap fare; *plats du jour* from €9.30, menu at €12.50.
Le Channel 3 bd de la Résistance ⓣ03.21.34.42.30. Generous menus – ranging from €18 to €60 – and stylish decor. Beautifully prepared but safely unadventurous food, with a wide range of delicious desserts, and views over the yacht basin. Closed Sun eve & Tues. Booking recommended.
George V 36 rue Royale ⓣ03.21.97.68.00, ⓦwww.georgev-calais.com. Traditional brasserie-restaurant with immaculate white tablecloths and a classic menu (€22–44) or half menu (€17). Closed Sat & Sun lunch. Also smart en-suite rooms (❺).
Histoire Ancienne 20 rue Royale ⓣ03.21.34.11.20. Greek-run brasserie with a charming interior, particularly its old bar; the good, mainly French menu includes the occasional Greek dish plus salads that will delight vegetarians. Menus from €11 for early lunch and dinner; otherwise from €17.50.
Le St-Charles 47 place d'Armes ⓣ03.21.96.02.96. By far the best option on the place d'Armes, and consequently often crowded. Menus consist of traditional French and Italian dishes and start from €10. Closed Tues and Sun eve.

Around Calais

Understandably, most tourists travel non-stop through the **Pas-de-Calais** – Calais' hinterland – en route to warmer climes and more varied scenery. However, if you're on a short break from across the Channel, it's worth making the effort to venture inland to the likes of **St-Omer** and its surrounding World War II museums.

St-Omer

Away from the ports, the landscape becomes more rural and the roads straighter and quieter. The first stop inland for many visitors to France is **ST-OMER**, a quiet, unassuming and attractive little town, 43km southeast of Calais. It displays flights of Flemish magnificence, especially in the Hôtel de Ville and some of the recently restored mansions on rue Gambetta. The Gothic **Basilique Notre-Dame** (daily March–Sept 8.30am–6pm, Oct–Feb 8.30am–5pm) contains some fine statues. The fascinating and recently renovated **Musée de l'Hôtel Sandelin** at 14 rue Carnot (Wed–Sun 10am–noon & 2–6pm; €6.50) is worth a stop. The decor and artwork of each room is representative of a certain period and country, with some fine furniture, sculpture, and remarkable French, Dutch, and Flemish paintings, all meticulously laid out. In the Flemish room you'll find a Breugel, while in the next room are two works by his son. The museum also contains some of the finest decorative art in France, including a glorious piece of medieval goldsmithing known as the *Pied de Croix de St-Bertin*.

Aside from visiting the pleasant **public gardens** to the west of town, you can explore the nearby **marais**, a network of Flemish waterways cut between plots of land on reclaimed marshes east of town along the river. Boat trips, or *bateaux-promenade*, run by Isnor Location (ⓣ03.21.39.15.15, ⓦwww.isnor.fr) leave from the church in nearby Clairmarais (July & Aug daily 11am & hourly 2–5pm; Sept–June Sat & Sun hourly 2–5pm; €6.20); round trips take about an hour, and include a commentary in French on the flora and fauna of the marshes. Longer trips also feature a ride down the unique vertical boat-lift at Arques. For further information, including times, plus details of kayak and canoe rental, contact the tourist office (see below).

To get to the centre of town from the exuberant 1903 **gare SNCF**, cross over the canal and walk ten minutes down rue F.-Ringot, past the post office and into rue Carnot. The **tourist office** is in the western end of town near the park on rue Lion d'Or (Easter–Sept Mon–Sat 9am–6pm, Sun 10am–1pm; Oct–Easter Mon–Sat 9am–12.30pm & 2–6pm; ⓣ03.21.98.08.51, ⓦwww.tourisme-saintomer.com). For **accommodation**, try the pretty, old *Hôtel St-Louis* at 25 rue d'Arras (ⓣ03.21.38.35.21, ⓦwww.hotel-saintlouis.com; ❸; restaurant *Le Flaubert* from €16); the *Bretagne*, 2 place du Vainquai, near the train station (ⓣ03.21.38.25.78, ⓦwww.hotellebretagne.com; ❹; restaurant *Le Vainquai* from €18), or the *Au Vivier*, 22 rue Louis-Martel, on a small pedestrian street near the town hall (ⓣ03.21.95.76.00, ⓔlevivier@wanadoo.fr; ❸; closed beginning of Jan), whose restaurant specializes in fish (closed Sun, menus from €16). The closest **campsite** is *Le Clair Marais* on rue du Romelaër near the Forêt de Clairmarais, 4.5km east of St-Omer (ⓣ03.21.38.34.80, ⓕ03.21.98.37.05; April–Oct), although there's no transport out there. For places to **eat** other than the hotels, try the *Auberge du Bachelin*, 12 bd de Strasbourg, on the north side of the town centre (menus from €13; ⓣ03.21.38.42.77; closed Mon, dinners on Fri & Sat night only – reserve), or establishments around place Maréchal-Foch: *Les Trois Caves*, at no. 18 has the best reputation (menu €24; ⓣ03.21.39.72.52; closed Wed & Mon lunch).

The Blockhaus at Eperlecques

In the Forêt d'Eperlecques, 12km north of St-Omer off the D300 (several trains daily from Calais to Watten station, on the eastern edge of the forest, about 4km and a twenty-minute walk from the site; no buses), you can visit the largest ever **Blockhaus**, or concrete bunker, built in 1943–44 by the Germans – or rather by 6000 of their half-starved prisoners of war (daily: March 2.15–6pm; April & Oct 10am–noon & 2.15–6pm; May–Sept 10am–7pm; Nov 2.15–5pm); €7 or dual ticket with La Coupole, see below, €13). It was designed to launch V2 rockets against London, but fortunately the RAF and French Resistance prevented it ever being ready for use by bombing it during construction – unfortunately killing many of the Allied prisoners at the same time. As well as the impressively if depressingly large Blockhaus, you will also see remnants of many weapons that attacked, or were built with the purpose of attacking, London, including a 45-metre ramp for launching V1s.

La Coupole

Of all the World War II converted bunker museums **La Coupole** (daily: Jan–June & Sept–Dec 9am–6pm; Jul–Aug 10am–7pm; closed for two weeks over Christmas and New Year; ⓦwww.lacoupole.com; €9), 5km southwest of St-Omer, is the most modern and stimulating. As you walk around the site of an intended V2 rocket launch pad, you can listen on multilingual infra-red headphones to a discussion of the occupation of northern France by the Nazis, the use of prisoners as slave labour, and the technology and ethics of the first liquid-fuelled rocket – advanced by Hitler and taken at the end of the war by the Soviets, the French and the Americans and developed in the space race. Visits last two-and-a-half hours: films, models and photographs, all with accompanying text in four different languages, help to develop each theme. Getting there by car is easy: it's just off the D928 (A26 junctions 3 & 4), but there are only a few buses running from St-Omer train station (ring La Coupole or St-Omer tourist office for times).

The Côte d'Opale

The **Côte d'Opale** is the stretch of Channel coast between Calais and the mouth of the River Somme, characterized by huge, wild and windswept sandy beaches more attractive than anything to be found in any of the port cities. In the northern part, as far as Boulogne, the beaches are fringed, as on the English side of the Channel, by white chalk cliffs. Here, between the prominent headlands of **Cap Blanc-Nez** and **Cap Gris-Nez**, the D940 coast road winds high above the sea, allowing you to appreciate the "opal" in the name – the sea and sky merging in an opalescent, oyster-grey continuum. The southern part of the coast is flatter, and the beach, uninterrupted for 40km, is backed by a landscape of pine-anchored dunes and brackish tarns, punctuated every few hundred metres by solid German pillboxes now toppled on their noses by the shifting sand foundations. An organization called **Eden 62** publishes ten free leaflets detailing walks around the area, which you can get hold of by either writing to them or telephoning (Ⓣ03.21.32.13.74, Ⓔcommunication@eden62.fr). They also offer six guided nature walks per month.

South from Calais: the Channel Tunnel and Wissant

Right on the southern outskirts of Calais, **BLÉRIOT-PLAGE** was thus named to commemorate Louis Blériot's epic first cross-Channel flight in 1909. Six kilometres further along the foreshore of well-conserved dunes, by the dreary village of **SANGATTE**, formerly the site of the highly controversial refugee camp, the Channel Tunnel comes ashore; the actual terminal is 5km to the east outside the village of **FRÉTHUN**. Thereafter, the D940 winds up onto the grassy windswept heights of Cap Blanc-Nez, topped by an obelisk commemorating the Dover Patrol who kept the Channel free from U-boats during World War I. Just off the D940, opposite the turn-off to the Cap Blanc-Nez obelisk, is the **Musée du Transmanche** (April–June & Sept Tues–Sun 2–6pm; July & Aug daily 10am–6pm; €3.80), which offers an overall history of Channel Tunnel exploits; the museum is housed in the basement of *Le Thomé du Gamond*, a rather pricey restaurant with panoramic views (open all year from noon; menus from €15). From here, 130m above sea level, you can spot the Channel craft plying the water to the north, while to the south you look down on **WISSANT** and its enormous beach between the capes from which Julius Caesar set sail in 55 BC for a first look at Britain.

Before arriving in Wissant, you pass through the small beachside town of **ESCALLES**, where you can stay at the clean, modern, and appropriately named *Escale* (Ⓣ03.21.85.25.00, Ⓦwww.hotel-lescale.com; ❸; restaurant from €14). Modern Wissant remains a small and quietly attractive place, popular out of season with windsurfers and weekending Britons. The **tourist office** (May–Sept Mon–Sat 9am–noon & 2–6pm, Sun 10am–1pm & 3–6pm; Oct–April Mon–Sat 9am–noon & 2–6pm, Ⓣ03.21.82.48.00, Ⓦwww.ville-wissant.fr) is on place de la Mairie. The **hotels** here are expensive, which is not surprising given their proximity to the sea. First and foremost among the good places to stay is the old, red-timbered *Hôtel de la Plage*, 1 place Edouard Houssen (Ⓣ03.21.35.91.87, Ⓕ03.21.85.48.10; ❸; good restaurant from €14), whose rooms are arranged around a wide courtyard. The two-star *Bellevue*, 10 Rue P.Crampel, is an alternative, and less expensive than some of the one stars in town (Ⓣ03.21.35.91.07, Ⓔhbellevue@wanadoo.fr; ❸). Wissant also has a **campsite**, *La Source* (Ⓣ03.21.35.92.46; closed mid-Nov to March). The best place to **eat** in town is *À l'Amiral Benbow*, 7 rue Gambetta, where you can feast on oysters and *filet mignon* in the meticulously decorated rooms of an old house (menus from €25; ☎03.21.35.90.07, reserve; closed Jan & Mon–Fri in off-season).

To Cap Gris-Nez and the Blockhaus at Audinghen

The GR du Littoral footpath passes through Wissant and continues up to Cap **Gris-Nez**, just 28km from the English coast. To get to the cape by road, take the turn-off 1km outside **AUDINGHEN**, from where it's a three-kilometre walk, drive or cycle.

Just after the Cap Gris-Nez turn-off beside the D940 is one of the many massive concrete bunkers, or *Blockhäuser*, which stud the length of the Côte d'Opale, and which were part of the German World War II defences known as the Atlantic Wall. The Blockhaus has been converted by a private owner, a military enthusiast, into an overpriced and uninformative **museum** (daily: June–Sept 9am–7pm; Oct–May 9am–noon & 2–6pm; closed Dec & Jan; €5.50), with a disturbing number of Nazi uniforms on display. Its main attraction is the bunker's gun which could shoot a distance of 42 kilometres (the British coast is 30km away), but those with a real interest in the subject should visit the Blockhaus at Eperlecques (see p.246).

The remainder of the drive along the D940 towards Boulogne-Sur-Mer is lined with beautiful and undeveloped dunes with frequent turn-offs for **walking paths** to the shore, each of which is tempting on a nice day.

Boulogne-sur-Mer

BOULOGNE-SUR-MER is quite different from Dunkerque and Calais – recommendation in itself. Though its seashore is as industrial and unattractive

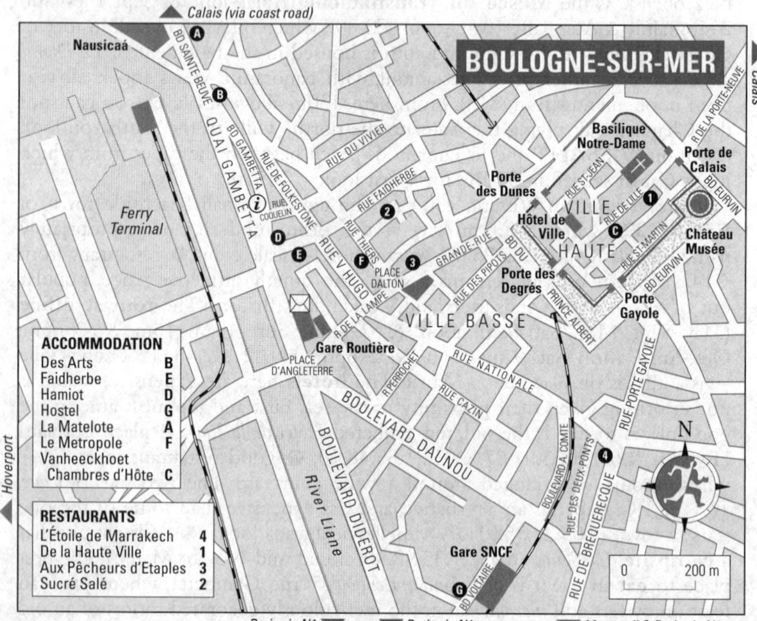

as its neighbours' (it claims to be the largest fishing base in Europe), away from the port the town is much more welcoming. Moreover, the arrival of a new high-speed, low-cost (vehicle only) ferry service has brought new waves of British tourists to the area, and away from Calais, livening up the area's restaurants and shops. Rising above the drab lower town is an attractive medieval quarter, the **ville haute**, contained within the old town walls and dominated by a grand, domed cathedral that apes St Paul's in London. Amid the newer shopping streets of the *ville basse* are some of the best food shops in the whole region, along with a large array of fish restaurants. As long as you keep in mind that Boulogne is first and foremost a port city, you'll find that it has some virtues and might actually tempt you to stay.

Arrival, information and accommodation

It is only a fifteen-minute walk across the river from the **ferry terminal** into town, though currently the service is not open to foot passengers; there is no bus service. The centre is a ten-minute walk from the **gare SNCF** (Boulogne-Ville), down boulevard Voltaire then right along boulevard Diderot.

Shopping

There is some good shopping to be had in and around Boulogne: in the centre you can sample some tasty local food specialities, while the hypermarkets outside of town provide the chance to stock up on a vast range of cheap goods. For general retail opportunities, head for the Centre Commercial Liane on the corner of boulevards Diderot and Daunou, a downmarket **shopping mall** on two levels – lots of neon, milling teenagers, food stalls, a supermarket and a cheap cafeteria. If you want to hit the serious hypermarkets, catch bus #20 for the Leclerc or bus #8 for the monstrous Auchan complex, 8km along the N42 towards St-Omer – certainly the most convenient place for large-scale food and wine shopping. More fastidious foodies should stay in town and head for the Grande-Rue and streets leading off it, but be aware that most are closed all day Monday. For charcuterie, locals' favourite Bourgeois is at 1 Grande-Rue; for chocolates and other goodies, head for Timmerman at no 40. Check out the fabulous fish displays at Aux Pêcheurs d'Étaples, at no 31; you can also sample the seafood at the brasserie tucked behind (see p.251). A shop definitely not to be missed is Philippe Olivier's famous fromagerie, just around the corner at 43 rue Thiers, which has a selection of over two hundred cheeses – in various states of maturation. To go with it you'll find a great choice of wines at Les Vins de France, 10 rue Nationale, but for buying wine in bulk try Le Chais at 49 rue des Deux-Ponts, in the Bréquerecque district by the train station. You'll find everything in the consumer line – clothing and household goods – around Grande-Rue and rues Thiers, Faidherbe and Nationale. Boulogne's only traditional department store is Nouvelles Galeries at 57 rue Thiers, a street where you'll also find plenty of fashion boutiques for both sexes, all ages and every style; for men's clothes, try Prestige at 41 rue Nationale. A wide selection of hats is on sale at Monteil, on the corner of rues Faidherbe and Hugo; you can choose from over 600 handbags at Maroquinerie Florence, on rue Faidherbe between rues Thiers and Victor-Hugo; and Divine, further up rue Faidherbe, sells exquisite French lingerie. From place Lorraine and place Charpentier, rue Faidherbe heads uphill, but downmarket, with lots of bargain shops, hi-fi and electronics. At Leclercq, 15 Grande-Rue, you'll find beautiful homeware, including glass, cutlery and plates; opposite, at no 14, is Boulogne's best bookshop, Le Furet du Nord, with a wide selection of maps and an excellent *papeterie* downstairs. Last but not least, don't miss the Wednesday and Saturday morning markets on place Dalton.

The **tourist office** (July & Aug Mon–Sat 9am–7pm, Sun 10am–12.30pm & 2.30–5pm; Sept–June Mon–Sat 9am–12.30pm & 1.30–6.30pm, Sun 10.15am–1pm; ⓣ03.21.10.88.10, ⓦwww.tourisme-boulognesurmer.com), at 24 quai Gambetta, can advise on availability of rooms – which, in summer, get taken early. There's plenty of inexpensive **accommodation** in Boulogne, plus a couple of upmarket places around the centre.

Hotels

Des Arts 102–112 quai Gambetta ⓣ03.21.31.53.31, ⓕ03.21.33.69.05. Very reasonable hotel right opposite the port; rooms are clean and light, and some have a balcony. No lift, long climb. ❶

Faidherbe 12 rue Faidherbe ⓣ03.21.31.60.93, ⓕ03.21.87.01.14. Great value two-star near the water and shops, with elegant rooms and friendly proprietors. ❸

Hamiot 1 rue Faidherbe at corner with bd Gambetta ⓣ03.21.31.44.20, ⓕ03.21.83.71.56. Harbourside hotel over a popular bistro (see opposite). The recently renovated rooms have bath and double-glazing. ❹

La Matelote 70 bd Ste-Beuve ⓣ03.21.30.33.33, ⓦwww.la-matelote.com. Very smart rooms in a row of converted town houses along from the famed restaurant; minibar, a/c, cable TV and tasteful decor in all rooms. ❻

Le Metropole 51 rue Thiers ⓣ03.21.31.54.30, ⓔhotel.metropole@wanadoo.fr. A plush three-star with spacious rooms in the middle of a fashionable street; central but not noisy. ❺

Vanheeckhoet Chambres d'Hôte 24–26 rue de Lille ⓣ03.21.80.41.50, ⓔPVanheeckhoet@aol.com. A pleasant B&B in the centre of the old town; the owner's son owns the restaurant next door which specializes in freshly caught fish. ❷

Hostel and campsite

Hostel (HI) place Rouget-de-l'Îsle ⓣ03.21.99.15.30, ⓔboulogne-sur-mer@fuaj.org, opposite the *gare SNCF* in the middle of a housing estate. Friendly hostel with rooms for three to four people at €15.50 per person, breakfast included; en-suite double rooms cost €20, €2.90 extra for non-members.

Camping municipal *Les Sapins*, at La Capelle-lès-Boulogne, near the Auchan centre on the N42 ⓣ03.21.83.16.61. Closed mid-Sept to mid-April.

The Town

Boulogne's number one attraction – and one of the most visited in northern France – is the Centre National de la Mer, or **Nausicaá**, on boulevard Sainte-Beuve (daily: July & Aug 9.30am–8pm; Sept–June 9.30am–6.30pm, closed for 3 weeks in Jan; ⓦwww.nausicaa.fr; €9.50–12.50, depending on time of year; combined ticket with the Château Musée), though in May and June all of the floors are crawling with French and British school groups, and you may find it best to stay away altogether.

With ultraviolet lighting and New Age music creating a suitably weird ambience, you wander from tank to tank while hammerhead sharks circle overhead, a shoal of tuna lurks in a diamond-shaped aquarium, and giant conger eels conceal themselves in rusty pipes – definitely not for ichthyophobes. Compared with the startling colours of the tropical fish and the clownish antics of the sea lions at feeding time, some of the educational stuff (in French and English throughout – one in five visitors is British) is rather dull. Although little over a decade old, it's all beginning to look a bit tired and dated, though the 3D film show goes some way to alleviating the boredom. Environmental issues are addressed, perhaps too timidly for some tastes, even though the centre works on marine conservation projects together with UNESCO. But, as you'd expect in France, the sea as a source of food seems to be given more importance – witness the chic *Bistrot de la Mer* where you can sample suitably fresh fish and wine, the latter probably a necessity for those adults who have lost their children several times in the labyrinthine five-storey layout.

The quiet cobbled streets of the **ville haute**, southeast of Nausicaá and uphill, make a pleasant respite from the noise and drabness of the *ville basse*.

The most impressive sight here are the **medieval walls** themselves, which are decked out with rosebeds, gravel paths and benches for picnicking, and provide impressive views of the city below. Within the square walls, the domed **Basilique Notre-Dame** (summer 9am–noon & 2–6pm; winter 10am–noon 2–5pm) is an odd building – raised in the nineteenth century by the town's vicar without any architectural knowledge or advice – yet it seems to work. In the vast and labyrinthine **crypt** (Tues–Sun 2–5pm; €2) you can see frescoed remains of the Romanesque building and relics of a Roman temple to Diana. In the main part of the church sits a bizarre white statue of the Virgin and Child on a boat-chariot, drawn here on its own wheels from Lourdes over the course of six years during a pilgrimage in the 1940s.

Nearby, the **Château Musée** (July & Aug Mon & Wed–Sat 10am–5pm, Sun 10am–5.30pm; Sept–June Mon & Wed–Sat 10am–12.30pm & 2–5pm, Sun 10am–12.30pm & 2–5pm; closed 3 weeks in Jan; €3.50; combined ticket with Nausicaá) contains Egyptian funerary objects donated by a local-born Egyptologist, an unusual set of Eskimo masks and a sizeable collection of Greek pots. A short walk down the main tourist street, **rue de Lille**, will bring you to the **Hôtel de Ville**, whose twelfth-century belfry is the most ancient monument in the old town, but is only accessible by arranging a guided tour with the tourist office.

Three kilometres north of Boulogne on the N1 stands the **Colonne de la Grande Armée** where, in 1803, Napoleon is said to have changed his mind about invading Britain and turned his troops east towards Austria. The column was originally topped by a bronze figure of Napoleon symbolically clad in Roman garb – though his head, equally symbolically, was shot off by the British navy during World War II. It's now displayed in the Château Musée (see above).

Eating and drinking

As you might expect from a large fishing port, Boulogne is a good spot to **eat** fresh fish and seafood. With dozens of possibilities for eating around place Dalton and the *ville haute* bear in mind the day-tripper trade and be selective. If you're just after a **drink**, there is a concentration of bars in place Godefroy de Bouillon, opposite the Hôtel de Ville, and a raft of lively bars in place Dalton, with *Au Bureau* and the *Welsh Pub* the most popular.

L'Étoile de Marrakech 228 rue Nationale. A friendly and well-regarded Moroccan restaurant; olives, bread and spicy sausage come as complimentary starters, and the servings of couscous (from €11) are incredibly generous. Closed Wed.

Bar Hamiot 1 rue Faidherbe. Under the hotel of the same name, this brasserie remains as popular as ever with locals and tourists alike, offering a large range of dishes from €7 omelettes and €10–16 fish dishes to €14–19 menus.

De la Haute Ville 60 rue de Lille ⓣ03.21.80.54.10. Just one of the many lining the rue de Lille in the *ville haute*, this restaurant is especially appealing for its terrace garden in the back. Menus from €12.

La Matelote 80 bd Ste-Beuve ⓣ03.21.30.17.97. The smartest restaurant in town, located opposite Nausicaá, featuring a *dégustation* menu at €60. If you'd rather not spend that much, you could go for the €30 menu or à la carte fish from €19. Loving care is taken over the food and service, but it's not especially creative and rather snooty. Closed Sun eve.

Aux Pêcheurs d'Etaples 31 Grande-Rue. The freshest fish and seafood cooked expertly in a modern restaurant hidden behind the *poissonnerie* front. Menus at €15 upwards.

Sucré Salé 13 rue Monsigny. Petite and modern café, *salon de thé* and patisserie; its speciality is gourmet salads, making it a good choice for vegetarians, though it's worth dropping by just for one of the delicious, meticulously decorated pastries. Light, airy and sparse, with a wonderful range of teas and coffees. Mon–Sat 8am–8pm, Sun am takeaway only.

South to Amiens

South of Boulogne the coast is as wild and magnificent as the Côte d'Opale but without your own transport it's hard to get down to the beach: a band of unstable dunes forces the D940 coast road and the Calais–Paris railway to keep a few kilometres inland. With the exception of **Étaples**, the seaside towns are artificial resorts of twentieth-century creation – only of interest in that they provide access to the beach. The beach, however, really is worth getting to, and its eerie beauty is best experienced by walking the coastal GR path or any one of the several marked trails that the local tourist offices promote, or by visiting the **Marquenterre bird sanctuary**. For car-drivers, the D119 between Boulogne and just north of Dannes is closer to the water with turn-offs directly into the dunes.

The quickest route south is the **A16** Boulogne to **Abbeville** motorway, which continues all the way to Paris. More interesting, if you have time and want to take in the battlefield of **Agincourt**, would be a winding cross-country route exploring some of the English-looking side valleys on the north side of the River Canche – such as the Crequoise, Planquette and Ternoise – whose farms and hamlets have been largely bypassed by the onward march of French modernity. For more detailed information on the whole region consult Ⓦwww.somme-tourisme.com.

Le Touquet and Étaples

Situated among dunes and wind-flattened tamarisks and pines, **LE TOUQUET** (officially called Le Touquet-Paris-Plage) is a kind of French Hollywood on the Channel coast, with ambitious villas freed from the discipline of architectural fashion hidden away behind its trees. Now dully suburban, the town was the height of fashion in the 1920s and 1930s and for a spell after World War II, ranking alongside places on the Côte d'Azur.

To get to Le Touquet, take the train from Boulogne to Étaples, from where a local bus covers the last 4km; alternatively, you can take a **bus** (Mon–Sat only) directly from Boulogne (Ⓣ03.21.83.88.52 in Boulogne or Ⓣ03.21.05.09.43 in Le Touquet for times) from outside the ANPE office on boulevard Daunou; the bus heads on down the coast through Le Touquet to Berck-sur-Mer. Le Touquet's **tourist office** is in the Palais de l'Europe on place de l'Hermitage (Mon–Sat 9am–7pm, Sun 10am–7pm; Ⓣ03.21.06.72.00, Ⓦwww.letouquet.com), and can furnish you with a free map of the town.

If you're looking for somewhere reasonable to **stay**, try the hostel *Riva Bella*, 12 rue Léon-Garet (Ⓣ03.21.05.08.22, Ⓦwww.rivabella-touquet.com; €15–23), or the two-star *Armide*, 56 rue Léon-Garet (Ⓣ03.21.05.21.76, Ⓕ03.21.05.97.77; half-board ❸). There's also a **campsite**, the *Stoneham* (Ⓣ03.21.05.16.55, Ⓕ03.21.05.06.48; closed late Nov to early Feb), on avenue François-Godin, 1km from the centre and 1km from the beach. If you fancy splashing out, you have the choice of several luxurious hotels, including the palatial *Le Manoir* on avenue du Golf (Ⓣ03.21.06.28.28, Ⓦwww.opengolfclub.com/mnh; ❽) and *Le Westminster*, 5 av du Verger (Ⓣ03.21.05.48.48, Ⓦwww.opengolfclub.com/wes; ❽). Places to **eat** are also generally expensive in Le Touquet. For a treat, visit *Le Café des Arts*, 80 rue de Paris (menus from €30; Ⓣ03.21.05.21.55; closed Tues & Wed), or for more traditional cuisine try the *Auberge de la Dune aux Loups* on the avenue of the same name (menus €18 & €25; Ⓣ03.21.05.42.54; closed Wed), where you can eat their speciality fish on the terrace. Less expensive than these is *Les Sports*, 22 rue St-Jean, a classic brasserie with a menu at €15.

An affordable treat worth indulging in – especially if you've got kids – is Le Touquet's **Aqualud** swimming complex right on the beach (July–Aug €14.50, Sept–June €11.50), which boasts three giant water slides and a series of indoor and outdoor themed pools; there's also the vast **Bagatelle** amusement park, 10km south of Le Touquet on the D940 (April to mid-Sept daily 10am–7pm; €19).

On the other side of the River Canche is the much more workaday **ÉTAPLES**, a picturesque fishing port whose charm lies in its unassuming air. Between April and September **boat trips** departing from the port can be booked via the **tourist office** (Mon–Fri 9am–noon & 2–6pm, Sat 10am–noon & 3–6pm; ⓣ03.21.09.56.94), at Le Clos St-Victor, boulevard Bigot Descelers. You can choose between a fifty-minute sea jaunt (€7) and a more rigorous twelve-hour fishing stint with experienced fishermen (€50). Étaples also boasts a good seafood **restaurant**, *Aux Pêcheurs d'Etaples*, situated upstairs from the bustling and well-stocked **fish market** on quai de la Canche (from €13; ⓣ03.21.94.06.90).

Montreuil-sur-Mer

Once a port, **MONTREUIL-SUR-MER** is now stranded 13km inland from the *mer*, owing to the silting up of the River Canche. Perched on a sharp little hilltop above the river and surrounded by ancient walls, it's an immediately appealing place. Quite compact, it's easily walkable, with its hilltop ramparts offering amazing views. Laurence Sterne spent a night here on his *Sentimental Journey*, and it was the scene of much of the action in Victor Hugo's *Les Misérables*, perhaps best evoked by the steep cobbled street of pavée St-Firmin, first left after the Porte de Boulogne, a short climb from the *gare SNCF*.

Two heavily damaged Gothic churches grace the main square: the **church of St-Saulve** and a tiny wood-panelled **chapelle** tucked into the side of the red-brick hospital, now a three-star hotel (see below). To the south there are numerous cobbled lanes to wander down, all lined with half-timbered artisan houses. In the northwestern corner of the walls lies Vauban's **Citadelle** (March to mid-Dec daily 10am–noon & 2–6pm; €2.50) – ruined, overgrown and, after dark, pretty atmospheric, with subterranean gun emplacements and a fourteenth-century tower that records the coats of arms of the French noblemen killed at Agincourt. A path following the top of the walls provides views out across the Canche estuary.

The **tourist office** is by the citadel at 21 rue Carnot (April–Sept Mon–Sat 9.30am–12.30pm & 2–6pm, Sun 10am–12.30pm & 2.30–5pm; Oct–March Mon–Sat 9.30am–12.30pm & 2–5.30pm, Sun 10am–12.30pm; ⓣ03.21.06.04.27). For a real **accommodation** treat, there's the classy and expensive *Château de Montreuil* (ⓣ03.21.81.53.04, ⓦwww.chateaudemontreuil.com; ❾; closed mid-Dec to Jan), which overlooks the citadel and is popular with the English. It contains a top-class restaurant (closed Thurs lunch & Mon out of season), whose lunchtime menu is good value at €38. For delightful food and accommodation at more manageable prices, there's no beating *Le Darnétal*, in place Darnétal (ⓣ03.21.06.04.87, ⓕ03.21.86.64.67; ❷; closed Mon eve, Tues & first two weeks in July; restaurant from €16). Another good bet is the *Clos des Capucins* on the wide place de Gaulle, the shopping centre of the town (ⓣ03.21.06.08.65, ⓔclos-des-capucins@wanadoo.fr; ❸; menu from €15). The former Hôtel Dieu on the main square now houses a large upmarket hotel, the *Hermitage* (ⓣ03.21.06.74.74, ⓦwww.hermitage-montreuil.com; ❺), with friendly and accommodating service and spacious if corporate-style rooms. There's also an **HI hostel** (☎03.21.06.10.83; closed Nov–Feb; €7.70, plus extra for sheets and breakfast), housed in one of the citadel's outbuildings and giving access to the place long after the gates have been closed to the public; reception is only open from 2 pm to 6pm – make sure you arrive on time. There's also a **campsite**, *La Fontaine des Clercs*, (☎03.21.06.07.28, ℗03.21.86.15.10; open all year) below the walls, by the Canche on rue d'Église.

In the second half of August, Montreuil puts on a surprisingly lively mini-arts festival of opera, theatre and dance, *Les Malins Plaisirs*, while between September and June the theatre/cinema *Passerelles* (☎03.21.81.57.78) on place St-Walloy puts on plays and dances, and shows old movies, with a special festival in May.

The Agincourt and Crécy battlefields

Agincourt and Crécy, two of the bloodiest Anglo-French battles of the Middle Ages, took place near the attractive little town of **HESDIN** on the River Canche (a town that will be familiar to Simenon fans from the TV series *Inspector Maigret*). Getting to either site is really only feasible with your own transport.

Twenty kilometres southwest of Hesdin, at the **Battle of Crécy**, Edward III inflicted the first of his many defeats of the French in 1346. This was the first appearance on the continent of the new English weapon, the six-foot longbow, and the first use in European history of gunpowder. There's not a lot to see today: just the **Moulin Édouard III** (now a watchtower), 1km northeast of the little town of **CRÉCY-EN-PONTHIEU** on the D111 to Wadicourt, site of the windmill from which Edward watched the hurly-burly of battle. Further south, on the D56 to Fontaine, the battered **croix de Bohème** marks the place where King John of Bohemia – fighting for the French – died, having insisted on leading his men into the fight in spite of his blindness.

Ten thousand more died in the heaviest defeat ever of France's feudal knighthood at the **Battle of Agincourt** on October 25, 1415. Forced by muddy conditions to fight on foot in their heavy armour, the French, though more than three times as strong in number, were sitting ducks to the lighter, mobile English archers. The rout took place near present-day **AZINCOURT**, about 12km northeast of Hesdin off the D928, and a **museum** in the village, the Centre Historique Médiéval Azincourt (April–June & Sept–Oct daily 10am–6pm; July–Aug daily 9am–7pm; Nov–March Wed–Mon 10am–5pm; €6.50) includes a short film about the battle. On the battle site itself notice boards are placed at strategic points to indicate the sequence of fighting. Just east of the village, by the crossroads of the D104 and the road to Maisoncelle, a cross marks the position of the original grave pits.

The Marquenterre bird sanctuary

Even if you know nothing about birds, the **Parc ornithologique du Marquenterre** (daily: April–Sept 9.30am–7pm; Oct–March 10am–6pm; Ⓦwww.marcanterra.fr; €9.60), situated off the D940 between the estuaries of the rivers Canche and Somme, 30km south of Étaples, will be a revelation. In terms of landscape, it's beautiful and strange: all dunes, tamarisks and pine forest, full of salty meres and ponds thick with water plants. This is "new" land, formed by the erosion of the Normandy coast and the silting of the Somme estuary, where thousands of cattle are grazed today to give their meat the much-prized flavour of the "salt meadows".

One of only two bird sanctuaries in the whole of France, Marquenterre is a reserve in an area not known for valuing the fowl that pass through each year – though protected inside the park's tiny boundaries, almost all species are prey to local hunters, and between September and January the sound of gunshot is not uncommon.

It's useful to rent binoculars (€3.50) unless you carry your own; otherwise you can rely on the guides posted at some of the observation huts, who set up portable telescopes and will tell you about the nesting birds. Once inside, there's a choice of three itineraries – two longer, more interesting walks (2–3hr) and a shorter one (roughly 1hr 30min). The routes take you from resting area to resting area from where you can train your field glasses on dozens of species – ducks, geese, oyster-catchers, terns, egrets, redshanks, greenshanks, spoonbills, herons, storks, godwits – some of them residents, most taking a breather from their epic migratory flights. In April and May they head north, returning from the end of August to October, while in early summer the young nesting chicks can be seen learning to find food under the sharp eyes of their mothers. Keen natural historians might also want to drop into the **Maison de l'Oiseau** on the other side of the bay, between St-Valéry-sur-Somme (see below) and Cayeux-sur-Mer, which has a display of stuffed birds, as well as live demonstrations with birds of prey (daily: March–Oct 11am–6pm, Nov–Feb 11am–5pm; Ⓦwww.maisondeloiseau.com; €6.20).

The nearest town of any size is **RUE**, 5km east of Marquenterre, one of a number of attractive former fishing villages in the area now stranded inland by the silting up of the Somme. It's worth a halt for the splendid Gothic vaulting and facade of the **Chapelle du St-Esprit** (April–Oct daily 9.30am–5.30pm). The best place to **eat** is the *Lion d'Or* on rue Barrière (menus €13–29; Ⓣ03.22.25.74.18, Ⓕ03.22.25.66.63; closed Mon and Sun eve); it also has simple **rooms** (❸). Only 7km to the south, near the tiny hamlet of **FAVIÈRES**, you'll find one of the area's finest restaurants, the *Clé des Champs* on place des Frères Caudron (menus €13–37; Ⓣ03.22.27.88.00); excellent country cooking is served in a beautiful white farmhouse, its walls decorated with plates and copper pans.

The Somme estuary

After Rue, the D940 meanders through yet more dry fishing hamlets, whose crouching cottages are reminders of their former poverty. Some, like **LE CROTOY**, have enough sea still to attract the yachties, and are enjoying the inevitable holiday- and second-home boom. Le Crotoy's south-facing beach has attracted numerous writers and painters over the years: Jules Verne wrote *Twenty Thousand Leagues under the Sea* here, and Colette, Toulouse-Lautrec and Seurat were also frequent visitors. For **accommodation**, try the seaside *Hotel Les Tourelles*, 2–4 rue Pierre Guerlain (Ⓣ03.22.27.16.33, Ⓦwww.lestourelles.com; ❹); or, for bed and breakfast in town, the *Les Abris-Côtiers* (Ⓣ03.22.27.0945, Ⓦwww.abris-cotiers.com; ❸) or *La Villa Marine*, 14 rue du Phare (Ⓣ03.22.37.84.56, Ⓦwww.villamarine.com; ❹).

At the mouth of the bay lies **ST-VALÉRY-SUR-SOMME**, accessible in summer by a **steam train** (Easter–June & Sept to mid-Oct Wed, Sat & Sun; July & Aug daily; Ⓦwww.chemin-fer-baie-somme.asso.fr; €7–14) from Le Crotoy and Noyelles, and by two buses a day from Noyelles. This is the place from which William, Duke of Normandy, set sail to conquer England in 1066. With its walled and gated medieval citadel still intact and its brightly painted quays, free of modern development, looking out over mudflats and tilting boats, St-Valéry really is the jewel of the coast. Apart from the **Écomusée**

Picarvie at 5 quai du Romerel (April–Sept Mon & Wed–Sun 2–6.30pm; July & Aug also open Tues; €5) with its interesting collection of tools and artefacts relating to vanished trades and ways of life, there's little to do but enjoy the quiet. People walk and dig for shellfish, but you have to be extremely careful about the tide. When it's high it reaches up to the quays, but withdraws 14km at low tide, creating a dangerous current; equally, it returns very suddenly, cutting off the unwary.

The town's **tourist office** (Jun–Aug daily 9.30am–noon & 2.30–6pm; Sept–May Tues–Sun 9.30am–noon & 2.30–5pm; ⓣ03.22.60.93.50) is situated on the quayside. There are two very attractive **hotels**, both with deservedly popular restaurants: the modest three-star *Hôtel du Port et des Bains* (ⓣ03.22.60.80.09; ⓦwww.hotelhpb.fr; ❹; restaurant from €15), right on the quayside after the tourist office as you drive in from Rue; and the grander two-star *Relais Guillaume de Normandie* (ⓣ03.22.60.82.36, ⓦwww.guillaumedenormandy.com; ❸; restaurant from €16) on the waterside promenade at the foot of the old town. Rue de la Ferté is lined with **seafood restaurants**; of these, *Les Pilotes* at no. 62 has over thirty different ways of serving mussels, with most options under €10.

About 9km to the east of St-Valéry, and 2km from the station in Noyelles-sur-Mer (served by the steam train) lies the hamlet of **NOLETTE**. This is home to one of the most unusual war graves in France: a **Chinese cemetery**, where 887 members of the Chinese Labour Corps are buried. Employed by the British army in World War I, most of them died of disease. Their neat headstones, sharing two or three rather perfunctory epitaphs, along with two lion statues donated by the Chinese, lie in a field just outside the village.

Abbeville

ABBEVILLE lies about halfway from Calais to Paris and makes a convenient stop-off on the N1. Until hit by a German air raid in May 1940, it was a very beautiful town. Nowadays, all that remain of its former glories are a superbly ornate Flemish-style **gare SNCF**; a **belfry**, reputedly the oldest in France; and the Gothic **church of St-Vulfran**, which was on a par with the cathedrals at Amiens and Beauvais. Restoration work on the church, which was badly scarred during the war, only finished in 1993. The western facade still bears superficial scars but the interior pillars have been replaced with exact copies and the keystones painted with their original colours. Also worth a visit is the eighteenth-century **Château de Bagatelle**, 2km south of town – not to be confused with the nearby amusement park of the same name – set in ten hectares of parkland (guided visits July & Aug daily except Tues 2–6pm; €8). When the château is closed you can sometimes visit the **gardens** (mid-May to mid-July & Sept to mid-Oct Mon–Fri 2–4.30pm; mid-July to Aug daily except Tues 2–6pm; €4), famed for their elaborate topiaries and rare species of tree.

The **tourist office** is at 1 place de l'Amiral-Courbet (ⓣ03.22.24.27.92). It provides a free booking service and organizes guided visits to the church of St-Vulfran. For those who want to **stay** in style, two suites in the château are used for bed-and-breakfast accommodation (ⓣ06.08.05.96.83, ⓦwww.chateaudebagatelle.com; ❹). Otherwise, Abbeville has a chain **hotel** at every price level, but few establishments with individual charm. The most comfortable and central of the chains is the *Mercure Hôtel de France*, in place du Pilori in the town centre (ⓣ03.22.24.00.42, ⓕ03.22.24.26.15; ❺; menus from €16), while a very cheap local option is the neat but basic *Le Liberty*, 5 rue St-Catherine (ⓣ/ⓕ03.22.24.21.71; ❶). If you just want a **meal** then *L'Escale en Picardie*, at 15 rue des Teinturiers (menus from €20;

☎03.22.24.21.51) is highly commendable, and specializes in fresh fish with crisp white wines, while the pizzeria *Le Céladon*, 30 place du Grand Marché, is pastel plush and full of locals, with pasta from under €7.

Amiens and the route south

Were it not for its renowned cathedral, few travellers would stop at **AMIENS**. Badly scarred during both world wars, and with heavy traffic pounding along the ring road built over its old city walls, it's not an immediately likeable place. Yet there's more to the town than first meets the eye. **St-Leu**, the medieval quarter north of the cathedral with its network of canals, has been renovated; the town's university makes its presence felt; and within a few minutes' walk from the train station the *hortillonnages* (see overleaf) transport you into a peaceful rural landscape.

Arrival, information and accommodation

The main **gare SNCF** (Amiens-Nord) and **gare routière** are both situated on the rectangular place A.-Fiquet. Connected to the train station is a

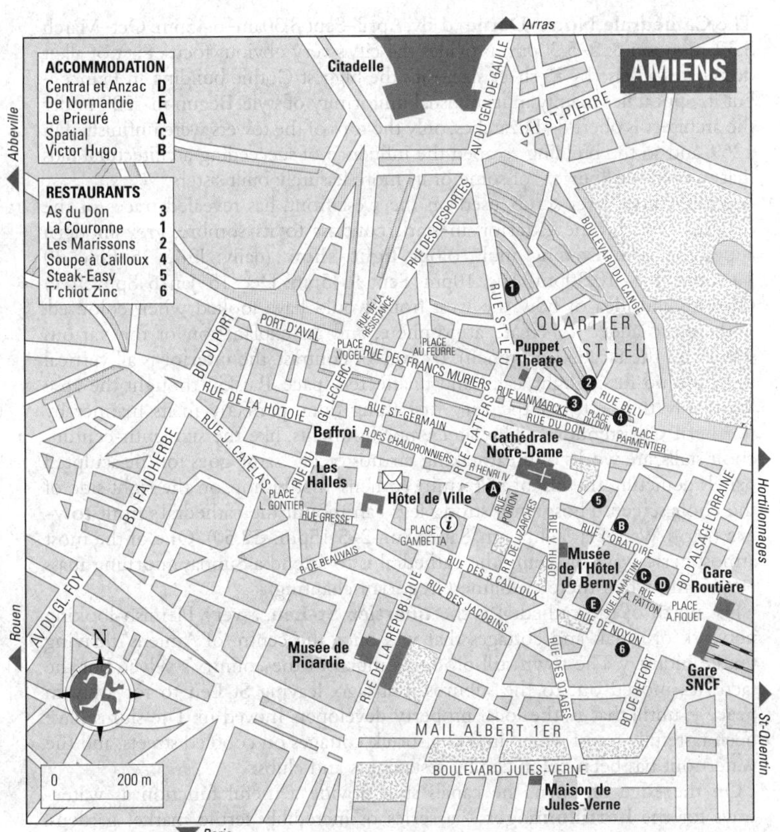

two-storey shopping complex, Amiens 2, that can be useful for its supermarket and public toilets. The **tourist office** is south of the cathedral, just off place Gambetta at 6bis rue Dusevel (April–Sept Mon–Sat 9.30am–7pm, Sun 10am–noon & 2–5pm; Oct–March Mon–Sat 9.30am–6pm, Sun 10am–noon & 2–5pm; ⓣ03.22.71.60.50, ⓦwww.amiens.com/tourisme).

Amiens is overrun with two-star **hotels** in various degrees of disrepair, but all with similar prices, which tend to fill up fairly fast. The best of these is the fully renovated *Victor Hugo*, 2 rue de l'Oratoire, just a block from the cathedral, whose ten rooms resemble those of an attractive country bed and breakfast (ⓣ03.22.91.57.91, ⓕ03.22.92.74.02; ❷). Also near the cathedral is the slightly more upmarket *Le Prieuré*, 17 rue Porion (ⓣ03.22.92.27.67, ⓕ03.22.92.46.16; ❸). If the *Victor Hugo* is full, try one of the two hotels next door to each other on rue Alexandre-Fatton, one of the streets opposite the station: at no. 17 the *Central et Anzac* (ⓣ03.22.91.34.08, ⓦwww.hoteletcentralanzac.com; ❷) is both less expensive and more comfortable than its neighbour, the *Spatial*, at no. 15 (ⓣ03.22.91.53.23, ⓦwww.hotelspatial.com; ❷). Another option just around the corner on rue Lamartine is the *Hôtel de Normandie* (ⓣ03.22.91.74.99, ⓦwww.hotelnormandie-80.com; ❷).

The City

The **Cathédrale Notre-Dame** (daily: April–Sept 8.30am–6.45pm; Oct–March 8.30am–noon & 2–5.30pm) provides the city's very obvious focus. First of all, it dominates all else by its sheer size – it's the biggest Gothic building in France – but its appeal lies mainly in its unusual uniformity of style. Begun in 1220 under the architect Robert de Luzarches, only the tops of the towers were unfinished in 1269, and so the building escaped the influence of succeeding architectural fads that marred the "purity" of some of its more leisurely built sisters.

A miraculous laser scrub, used on the west front, has revealed traces of the original polychrome exterior, in stark contrast to its sombre, grey modern appearance. An evening multicolour **light show** (daily: June 15–June 30 10.45pm, July 10.30pm, Aug 10pm, Sept 9.45pm, Dec 15–Jan 6 8pm; free) gives a vivid idea of how the west front would have looked when coloured, with music added to create atmosphere, and an explanation of the various statues on the facade (in French). By way of contrast, the interior is all vertical lines and no fuss: a light, calm and unaffected space. Ruskin thought the apse "not only the best, but the very first thing done perfectly in its manner by northern Christendom". The later embellishments, like the sixteenth-century choir stalls, are works of breathtaking virtuosity. The same goes for the sculpted panels depicting the life of St Firmin, Amiens' first bishop, on the right side of the choir screen. Those with strong legs can mount the cathedral's front **towers** (Mon, Wed–Fri 3–4.30pm, Sat & Sun 2–5.15pm; €2.50). One of the most atmospheric ways of seeing the cathedral is to attend a Sunday morning mass (10.15am), when there's sublime Gregorian chanting.

Just north of the cathedral is the **quartier St-Leu**, a very Flemish-looking network of canals and cottages that was once the centre of Amiens' thriving textile industry. The town still produces much of the country's velvet, but the factories moved out to the suburbs long ago, leaving St-Leu to rot away in peace – until, that is, the local property developers moved in. The slums have been tastefully transformed into neat brick cottages on cobbled streets, and the waterfront has been colonized by restaurants and clubs.

On the edge of town, the canals still provide a useful function as waterways for the **hortillonnages** – a series of incredibly fertile market gardens, reclaimed from the marshes created by the very slow-flowing Somme. Farmers travel about them in black, high-prowed punts and a few still take their produce into the city by boat for the Saturday morning **market**, the *marché sur l'eau*, on the river bank of place Parmentier. The best way to see the *hortillonnages* is from the water: the Association des Hortillonnages provides inexpensive **boat tours** from its office at 54 boulevard de Beauvillé (April–Oct daily 2–6pm, ticket office open from 1.30pm – best to arrive early; €5). They also provide free maps so that you can wander some of the footpaths around the water gardens on foot.

If you're interested in Picardy culture, you might take a look at Amiens' two regional museums. Five minutes' walk down rue de la République, south of central place Gambetta, an opulent nineteenth-century mansion houses the splendidly laid out **Musée de Picardie** (Tues–Sun 10am–12.30pm & 2–6pm; €4), whose star exhibits are the Puvis de Chavannes paintings on the main stairwell, the room created by Sol LeWitt, and a collection of rare sixteenth-century paintings on wood donated to the cathedral by a local literary society. Close by the cathedral, in the seventeenth-century **Musée de l'Hôtel de Berny** (May–Sept Thurs–Sun 2–6pm; Oct–April Sun 10am–12.30pm & 2–6pm; €1.50) is an annexe to the main museum, with *objets d'art* and local history collections, including a portrait of Choderlos de Laclos, author of *Les Liaisons Dangereuses*, who was born in Amiens in 1741. A third museum, at 2 rue Dubois, was once the **house of Jules Verne** (Mon–Fri 9am–noon & 2–6pm, Sat 2–6pm; €3) – the author spent most of his life in Amiens, and died here. Although a historic and attractive building, with a romantic turret, the museum, which focuses on Verne's life, is really worth the trip for fans only.

Just to the west of the city, at Tirancourt off the N1 to Abbeville, a large museum-cum-park, **Samara** (from Samarobriva, the Roman name for Amiens), recreates the life of prehistoric man in northern Europe with reconstructions of dwellings and displays illustrating the way of life, trades and so on (mid-March to April & Sept to mid-Nov Mon–Fri 9.30am–5.30pm, Sat & Sun 9.30am–6.30pm; May Mon–Fri 9.30am–5.30pm, Sat & Sun 10am–7.30pm; June Mon–Fri 9.30am–5.30pm, Sat & Sun 9.30am–7.30pm; July & Aug daily 10am–7.30pm; Ⓦwww.samara.fr; €9).

Eating, drinking and entertainment

By far the most attractive area to **eat** is around **St-Leu**, where many of the restaurants have outdoor seating overlooking a canal. Two favourite places are in the pretty, cobbled place du Don directly below the cathedral, with room to sit outside in good weather. The *Soupe à Cailloux* serves delicious cuisine, including regional dishes, for a reasonable price (weekday lunch menu at €11, other times from €15; Ⓣ03.22.91.92.70; closed Mon in winter), and is consequently very popular. The equally attractive *As du Don*, across the square, does a *formule* for €18 and has a heated terrace, while just over the canal by the pont de la Dodane is Amiens' best gourmet restaurant, *Les Marissons* (menus from €40, *carte* from around €50, €20 for lunch; Ⓣ03.22.92.96.66; closed Sat lunch & Sun). Also try *La Couronne* at 64 rue St Leu (€22–30; Ⓣ03.22.91.88.57; closed Sat lunch & Sun dinner), where delicious food at reasonable prices is served in pleasantly sober surroundings. Bars and pubs abound in the area.

For eating in the **upper town**, the handsome *T'chiot Zinc* (menu at €14, *plats* for €8; closed Mon lunch & Sun), conveniently located at 18 rue Noyon, opposite the station, serves traditional country fare. A total contrast is the hip Tex-Mex *Steak-Easy* at 18 rue Metz-l'Évêque, with an aeroplane hanging from the ceiling and guacamole, spare ribs and other un-Gallic fare on the menu (around €14 for a meal; ⓣ03.22.91.48.38; closed Sun).

For one week in late March Amiens bursts into life for its annual international **jazz festival**; on the third weekend in June, the local costumes come out for the **Fête d'Amiens**, which is the best time of year to visit the *hortillonnages*. Traditional Picardy **marionette** (*cabotans*) performances take place (July & Aug Tues–Sun; Sept–June Wed & Sun) at the Théâtre de Chés Cabotans d'Amiens, 31 rue Édouard David: contact Théâtre d'Animation Picard (ⓣ03.22.22.30.90, ⓦwww.ches-cabotans-damiens.com) for reservations – tickets are around €10. To purchase or take a look at hand-made marionettes, visit the workshop of Jean-Pierre Facquier at 67 rue du Don.

Beauvais

As you head south from Amiens towards Paris, the countryside becomes broad and flat – agricultural, though not rustic. **BEAUVAIS**, 60km south of Amiens, seems to fit into this landscape. Rebuilt, like Amiens, after the last world war, it's a drab, neutral place redeemed only by its radiating Gothic cathedral, the **Cathédrale St-Pierre** (daily: May–Oct 9am–12.15pm & 2–6.15pm, Nov–April 9am–12.15pm & 2–5.30pm), which rises above the town, its roof, unadorned by towers or a spire, seeming squat for all its height. It's a building that perhaps more than any other in northern France demonstrates the religious materialism of the Middle Ages – its main intention to be taller and larger than its rivals. The choir, completed in 1272, was once 5m higher than that of Amiens, though only briefly, as it collapsed in 1284. Its replacement, only completed three centuries later, was raised by the sale of indulgences – a right granted to the local bishops by Pope Leo X. This, too, fell within a few years, and, the authorities having overreached themselves financially, the church remained unfinished, forlorn and mutilated. In some respects the cathedral has succeeded in its original ambitious aim – at over 155m high, the interior vaults are undeniably impressive, giving the cathedral an impression of a larger scale than at Amiens. The building's real beauty however lies in its glass, its sculpted doorways and the remnants of the so-called Basse-Oeuvre, a ninth-century Carolingian church incorporated into the structure. It also contains a couple of remarkable clocks: one, a 12m-high **astronomical clock** built in 1865, above which on the hour 68 figures mimic scenes from the Last Judgement; the other, a **medieval clock** that's been working for seven hundred years.

The church is the town's only remarkable sight – stopping through Beauvais you'll probably want to give the rest of the town no more than a passing look. However, if you're stuck here for the night the church of **St-Étienne**, a few blocks to the south of the cathedral on rue de Malherbe, houses yet more spectacular Renaissance stained-glass windows. There's also the **Galerie Nationale de Tapisserie** behind the cathedral (April–Sept daily 9.30am–12.30pm & 2–6pm; Oct–March daily 10am–12.30pm & 2–5pm; €4.60), a museum of the tapestry for which Beauvais was once renowned, and the **Musée Départemental** (daily except Tues: July–Sept 10am–6pm, Oct–June 10am–noon & 2–6pm; €2), devoted to painting, local history and archeology, in the sharp, black-towered building opposite. The rousing statue in the central square is of local heroine Jeanne Hachette, a fighter and inspiration in the defence of the town in 1472 against Charles the Bold, Duke of Burgundy.

Beauvais is just over an hour by train from Paris, and the **gare SNCF** is a short walk from the centre of town – take avenue de la République, then turn right up rue de Malherbe. **Paris-Beauvais airport**, used by no-frills airlines based in northern Europe and the British Isles, is just outside the town, but there is no public transport into Beauvais; a bus meets flights and takes you to the Porte Maillot in Paris for €10 one way (in the opposite direction buses leave 2hr 45min before departures and tickets can be bought at the Paris-Beauvais Airport Shop, 1 bd Pershing, Paris; Ⓦwww.aeroportbeauvais.com). Opposite the Galerie Nationale de la Tapisserie, at 1 rue Beauregard, the **tourist office** (Mon 10am–1pm & 2–6pm, Tues–Sat 9.30am–7pm, Sun 10am–5pm; Ⓣ03.44.15.30.30) can provide exhaustive information. If you want to **stay**, two choices at rock-bottom prices are the *Hôtel le Commerce*, 11 rue Chambiges (Ⓣ03.44.15.34.34, Ⓕ03.44.15.34.33; ❶), and *Hôtel L'Irlandais*, 19 rue Gambetta, over a popular Irish **pub** (Ⓣ03.44.35.14.97; ❶). Slightly plusher are the newly renovated *Hôtel du Palais*, within sight of the cathedral, 9 rue St-Nicolas (Ⓣ03.44.45.12.58, Ⓕ03.44.15.06.34; ❸); and *The Cygne*, 24 rue Carnot (Ⓣ03.44.48.68.40, Ⓦwww.hotelducygne-beauvais.com; ❷). There's a *camping municipal* (Ⓣ03.44.02.00.22; closed mid-Sept to mid-May) just out of town on the Paris road.

For fine **food** on the square, call in at *Le Marignan*, 1 rue de Malherbe (Ⓣ03.44.48.15.15), which has menus from €12 in the brasserie downstairs, and from €20 in the very good restaurant upstairs. Less expensive is the charming *L'Auberge de la Meule*, 8 rue du 27 Juin, which specializes in cheese-based dishes including fondues and cheesy salads, with *plats* at around €10.

The Flemish cities and world war battlefields

From the Middle Ages until the late twentieth century great Flemish cities like **Lille**, **Roubaix**, **Douai** and **Cambrai** flourished, mainly thanks to their thriving textiles industries which used locally grown flax and imported wool. The other dominating – though now all but extinct – presence in this part of northern France was the **coalfields** and related industries, which, at their peak in the nineteenth century, formed a continuous stretch from Béthune in the west to Valenciennes in the east. At **Lewarde** you can visit one of the pits, while in the region's big industrial cities you can see what the masters built with their profits: noble town houses, magnificent city halls, ornate churches and some of the country's finest art collections. Lille is now a major trans-European communications hub and, despite visible problems of post-industrial urban decay, has transformed itself into a city with a thriving centre and a genuine tourist attraction.

On a more sombre note, Picardy, Artois and Flanders are littered with the monuments, battlefields and cemeteries of the two world wars, and nowhere as intensely as the region northeast of Amiens, between **Albert** and the appealing market town of **Arras** with its pair of handsome squares. It was here, among the fields and villages of the Somme, that the main battle lines of World War I were drawn. They can be visited most spectacularly at **Vimy Ridge**, just off the A26 north of Arras, where the trenches have been left in situ. Lesser sites, often more poignant, are dotted over the countryside around Albert and along the **Circuit de Souvenir**.

Lille

LILLE (Rijsel in Flemish), northern France's largest city by far, surprises many visitors with its impressive architecture, the winding streets of its tastefully restored old quarter (Vieux Lille), a plethora of excellent restaurants, and a bustling nightlife scene. It boasts some vibrant and obviously prosperous commercial areas, modern residential squares, a large university, a brand-new métro system, and a very serious attitude to culture, reflected in a busy music and arts scene and some great museums. At the same time, the city spreads far into the countryside in every direction, a mass of suburbs and largely abandoned factories and for the French it remains the very symbol of the country's heavy industry and working-class politics. Lille is facing up to many of the tough issues of contemporary France: some of the worst poverty and racial conflict in the country, a crime rate similar to that in Paris and Marseille, and a certain regionalism – Lillois sprinkle their speech with a French-Flemish patois ("Ch'ti") and to some extent assert a Flemish identity. But Lille managed to scrub its streets, sights and monuments until they were squeaky clean for its stint as the European Capital of Culture in 2004, making itself worthy of its incredible location – it takes less than an hour to Paris and Brussels by train, and just an hour and forty minutes to London by Eurostar. While in the past Lille was unfamiliar as tourist destination, today it is a deservedly popular place to spend a weekend.

Arrival, information and accommodation

The central Grand' Place is just a few minutes' walk from **Gare Lille-Flandres** (originally Paris's Gare du Nord, but brought here brick by brick in 1865), served by regional trains plus the hourly shuttle service to Paris, one hour away. TGV and Eurostar services from London, Brussels and further afield stop at the modern **Lille-Europe** station, five minutes' walk farther out from the centre, or one stop on the métro – check which station your train uses. Despite being the fifth-largest city in France, Lille's centre is small enough to walk round and, unless you choose to visit the modern art museum at Villeneuve-d'Ascq, or to travel to Roubaix for La Piscine, you won't even need to use the city's efficient **métro** system (tickets €1.15 per trip). A shuttle bus service (Ⓣ03.20.90.79.79; €4.60 one way) whisks you to Euralille in the city centre in twenty minutes from **Lesquin airport**.

The **tourist office** in place Rihour (Mon–Sat 9.30am–6.30pm, Sun & public hols 10am–noon & 2–5pm; Ⓣ03.59.57.94.00, Ⓦwww.lilletourisme.com), ten minutes' walk from the station along rue Faidherbe and through place du Théâtre and the Grand' Place, has a free hotel booking service. **Hotels** are expensive in Lille, with prices on par with Paris rather than with the other cities in the region. The two-stars are expensive, while the one-stars huddled around the train station are truly dismal, though there are enough of them to guarantee that you'll find a room.

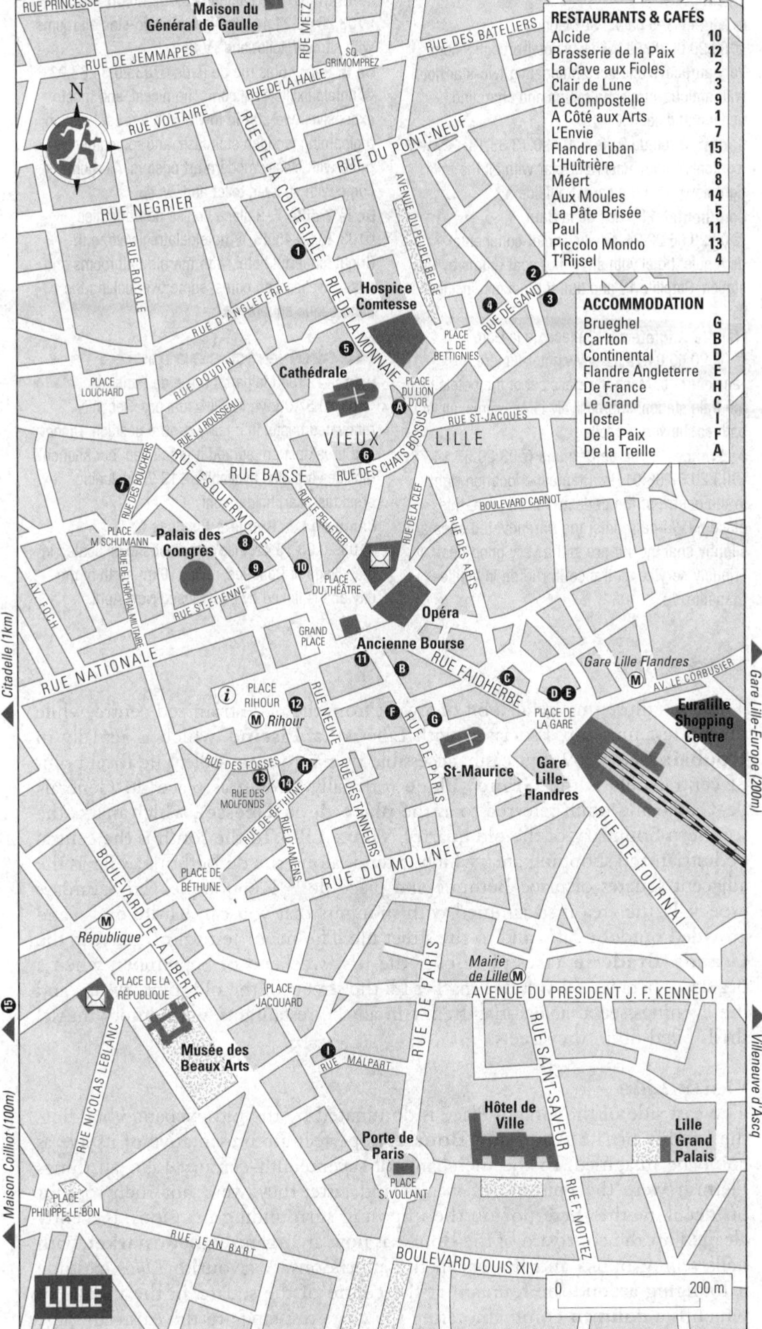
RESTAURANTS & CAFÉS
Alcide 10
Brasserie de la Paix 12
La Cave aux Fioles 2
Clair de Lune 3
Le Compostelle 9
A Côté aux Arts 1
L'Envie 7
Flandre Liban 15
L'Huîtrière 6
Méert 8
Aux Moules 14
La Pâte Brisée 5
Paul 11
Piccolo Mondo 13
T'Rijsel 4
ACCOMMODATION
Brueghel G
Carlton B
Continental D
Flandre Angleterre E
De France H
Le Grand C
Hostel I
De la Paix F
De la Treille A
Maison du Général de Gaulle
RUE PRINCESSE
RUE DE JEMMAPES
RUE METZ
SQ. GRIMOMPREZ
RUE DES BATELIERS
RUE DE LA HALLE
RUE VOLTAIRE
RUE DE LA COLLEGIALE
RUE DU PONT-NEUF
AVENUE DU PEUPLE BELGE
RUE NEGRIER
RUE ROYALE
RUE D'ANGLETERRE
Hospice Comtesse
RUE DE LA MONNAIE
RUE DE GAND
PLACE L. DE BETTIGNIES
Cathédrale
PLACE LOUCHARD
RUE DOUDIN
RUE J.J. ROUSSEAU
PLACE DU LION D'OR
RUE ST-JACQUES
VIEUX LILLE
RUE DES BOUCHERS
RUE ESQUERMOISE
RUE BASSE
RUE DES CHATS BOSSUS
RUE LE PELLETIER
RUE DE LA CLEF
BOULEVARD CARNOT
RUE DES ARTS
PLACE M SCHUMANN
Palais des Congrès
RUE DE L'HÔPITAL MILITAIRE
PLACE DU THÉÂTRE
RUE ST-ETIENNE
AV. FOCH
Opéra
GRAND PLACE
Ancienne Bourse
RUE NATIONALE
RUE FAIDHERBE
Gare Lille Flandres
AV. LE CORBUSIER
PLACE RIHOUR
Rihour
RUE NEUVE
PLACE DE LA GARE
Euralille Shopping Centre
RUE DE PARIS
St-Maurice
Gare Lille-Flandres
RUE DES FOSSES
RUE DES MOLFONDS
RUE DE BÉTHUNE
RUE DES TANNEURS
RUE D'AMIENS
RUE DE TOURNAI
RUE DU MOLINEL
PLACE DE BÉTHUNE
BOULEVARD DE LA LIBERTÉ
République
Mairie de Lille
AVENUE DU PRESIDENT J. F. KENNEDY
PLACE DE LA RÉPUBLIQUE
PLACE JACQUARD
RUE SAINT-SAVEUR
Musée des Beaux Arts
RUE MALPART
RUE NICOLAS LEBLANC
Hôtel de Ville
Porte de Paris
Lille Grand Palais
PLACE S. VOLLANT
RUE F. MOTTEZ
PLACE PHILIPPE-LE-BON
RUE JEAN BART
BOULEVARD LOUIS XIV
0
200 m
LILLE
Citadelle (1km)
Maison Coilliot (100m)
Musée d'Histoire Naturelle (50m)
Gare Lille-Europe (200m)
Villeneuve d'Ascq

Hotels

Brueghel 3–5 parvis St-Maurice ⓣ03.20.06.06.69, ⓦwww.hotel-brueghel.com. Very attractive and accommodating two-star hotel with antique-furnished rooms and charming, understated service. ❺

Carlton 3 rue de Paris ⓣ03.20.13.33.13, ⓦwww.carltonlille.com. Posh four-star with all the frills, right down to a red carpet outside. ❾

Continental 11 place de la Gare ⓣ03.20.06.22.24, ⓦwww.hotel-continental.fr. A quiet hotel with small but neat rooms by the station. Satellite TV and buffet breakfast included. ❹

Flandre Angleterre 13 place de la Gare ⓣ03.20.06.04.12, ⓦwww.hotel-flandre-angleterre.fr. Much the classiest of the hotels near the train station: impressively large rooms, all with bath or shower and toilet. ❹

De France 10 rue de Béthune ⓣ03.20.57.14.78, ⓕ03.20.57.06.01. In a fantastic location right in the centre of the pedestrianized area, this place has large rooms; the unrenovated ones are slightly shabby, but are still a very good deal. Friendly service, entrance in rue de la Vieille-Comédie. ❷

Le Grand 51 rue Faidherbe ⓣ03.20.06.31.57, ⓕ03.20.06.24.44. Comfortable two-star, all rooms with shower, toilet and TV. ❹

De la Paix 46bis rue de Paris ⓣ03.20.54.63.93, ⓔhotelpaixlille@aol.com. The nicest, and most expensive, two-star in town, with a great location, a gleaming wooden staircase, and rooms decorated with classy modern art posters. All rooms come with shower, toilet and TV. ❺

De la Treille 7–9 place Louise de Bettignies ⓣ03.20.55.45.46, ⓔhoteldelatreille@free.fr. Bright, cheerful hotel, with marble bathrooms and pastel-walled bedrooms, some overlooking the picturesque square. ❻

Hostel and campsite

Hostel 12 rue Malpart, off rue de Paris ⓣ03.20.57.08.94, ⓔlille@fuaj.org. Recently renovated hostel in a fairly central position. Dinner and breakfast are served if requested, but kitchen facilities are also available. €13.25 including breakfast; cardholders only.

Camping Les Ramiers Bondues ⓣ & ⓕ03.20.23.13.42. Lille's nearest site is located in the village of Bondues, about 10km north of the city and is linked by bus. Closed Nov–April.

The City

The city's museums are all a bit of a walk from the pedestrianized centre, while the hottest museum associated with Lille is **La Piscine**, which is actually in **Roubaix** (see p.269) but easily accessible by métro from Lille. The focal point of central Lille is the **Grand' Place** (officially known as place du Général-de-Gaulle and often referred to as the **place de la Déesse**), which marks the southern boundary of the old quarter, **Vieux Lille**. To the south is the central pedestrianized shopping area, which extends along rue de Béthune as far as the adjacent squares of place Béthune and place de la République. On Saturdays especially, the area is so jammed with shoppers that you can hardly move, and crowded outdoor cafés add to the street life. The major festival of the year, the **Grande Braderie**, takes place over the first weekend of September, when a big street parade and vast flea market fill the streets of the old town by day, and the evenings see a *moules-frites* frenzy in all the restaurants, with empty mussel shells piled up in the streets.

Vieux Lille

The east side of the Grand' Place is dominated by the old exchange building, the lavishly ornate **Ancienne Bourse**, as perfect a representative of its age as could be imagined. To the merchants of seventeenth-century Lille, all things Flemish were the epitome of wealth and taste; they were not men to stint on detail, neither here nor on the imposing surrounding mansions. Recently cleaned up, the courtyard of the Bourse is now an organized **flea market**, with stalls selling books and flowers in the afternoons. A favourite *Lillois* pastime is lounging around the fountain at the centre of the square, in the middle of which is a **column** commemorating the city's resistance to the Austrian siege of 1792, topped by *La Déesse* (the goddess), modelled on the wife of the mayor at the time – hence the square's alternative moniker.

In the adjacent **place du Théâtre**, you can see how Flemish Renaissance architecture became assimilated and Frenchified in grand flights of Baroque extravagance. The superlative example of this style is the so-called **Opéra**, recently renovated and now back in business (ⓣ03.28.38.40.40, ⓦwww.opera-lille.fr; closed July–Aug). It was built at the turn of the twentieth century by Louis Cordonnier, who also designed the extravagant **belfry** of the neighbouring Nouvelle Bourse – now the regional Chamber of Commerce – a small part of which is given over to the city's most central post office.

From the north side of these two squares, the smart shopping streets, rues Esquermoise and Lepelletier, lead towards the heart of old Lille, a warren of red-brick terraces on cobbled lanes and passages. It's an area of great character and charm, successfully reclaimed and reintegrated into the mainstream of the city's life, having been for years a dilapidated North African ghetto. To experience the atmosphere of Vieux Lille, head up towards rue d'Angleterre, rue du Pont-Neuf and the Porte de Gand, rue de la Monnaie and place Lion-d'Or. Places to eat and drink are everywhere, interspersed with chic boutiques.

Vieux Lille's main sight is the **Hospice Comtesse** on rue de la Monnaie. Twelfth-century in origin – though much reconstructed in the eighteenth century – it served as a hospital until as recently as 1945 and its medicinal garden, a riot of poppies and verbena, is a delight. The old ward, the Salle des Malades, often used for concerts, and the chapel can be visited (Mon 2–6pm, Wed–Sun 10am–12.30pm 2–6pm; €2.30).

Charles de Gaulle was born in this part of the town, at 9 rue Princesse, in 1890. His house is now a **museum** which normally exhibits, amongst de Gaulle's effects, the bullet-riddled Citroën in which he was driving when the OAS attempted to assassinate him in 1962 (see Contexts), though was closed for renovations at the time of writing – it is scheduled to reopen in June 2005 (ⓣ03.28.38.12.05). Another must for military buffs is the **citadelle** that overlooks the old town to the northwest, constructed in familiar star-shaped fashion by Vauban in the seventeenth century. Still in military hands, it can be visited on Sundays between May and August only by guided tour (€7; tours depart from the citadelle's Porte Royale at 3pm). To get there, go along rue de la Barre from Vieux Lille.

Amid all the city's secular pomp, Lille's ecclesiastical architecture used to seem rather subdued. However, the facade of the cathedral, **Notre-Dame-de-la-Treille**, just off rue de la Monnaie, breaks this mould. The body of the cathedral is a fairly homogeneous, but not unattractive, neo-Gothic construction begun in 1854, but the new facade, completed in 1999, is completely different – a translucent marble front supported by steel wires, best appreciated from inside, or at night when lit up from within. More traditional, but also impressive, is the **church of St-Maurice**, close to the station off place de la Gare, a classic red-brick Flemish Hallekerke, with the characteristic five aisles of the style.

South of the Grand' Place

Just south of the Grand' Place is **place Rihour**, a largely modern square flanked by brasseries and the remains of an old palace that now houses the tourist office, hidden behind an ugly war monument of gigantic proportions. Close by, the busiest shopping street, rue de Béthune, leads into place de Béthune, home to some excellent cafés, and beyond to the **Musée des Beaux-Arts** on place de la République (Mon 2–6pm, Wed–Sun 10am–6pm,

Fri till 7pm; €4.60). The late-1990s redesign is rather disappointing – too sleek and spacious to give any coherence to the collection – but the museum does contain some important works. Flemish painters form the core of the collection, from "primitives" like Dirck Bouts, through the northern Renaissance to Ruisdael, de Hooch and the seventeenth-century schools. Other works include Goya's interpretation of youth and old age, *Les Jeunes et Les Vieilles*, and a scattering of the nineteenth-century French greats including Renoir, Monet and Rodin. Watch out for the temporary exhibitions, which cost more but can be worthwhile.

A few hundred metres to the south of the museum, near the green avenue Jean-Baptiste Lebas, is the **Musée d'Histoire Naturelle**, 19 rue de Bruxelles (Mon–Fri 9am–noon & 2–5pm, free; Sun 10am–5pm, €2.30, more during times of special exhibitions). It's a small museum, a manageable size for children, with a lovely collection of dinosaur bones, fossils, and an impressive array of beautifully stuffed birds, including a dodo.

West of the Musée des Beaux-Arts, on rue de Fleurus, lies **Maison Coilliot**, a ceramics shop and one of the few houses built by Hector Guimard, who made his name designing the Art Nouveau entrances to the Paris métro. Built at the height of the Art Nouveau movement, it's as striking today as it obviously was to the conservative burghers of Lille (there are no other such buildings in the city), but it also displays the somewhat muddled eclecticism of the style, coming over as half brick-faced mansion, half timber-framed cottage. East of the museum, near the triumphal arch of Porte de Paris, is the city's ugly but serviceable **Hôtel de Ville**, executed in a bizarre Flemish Art Deco style, with an extremely tall belfry.

Around the stations: Euralille

Thanks to Eurostar and the international extension of the TGV network, Lille has become the transport hub of northern Europe, a position it is trying to exploit to turn itself into an international business centre, with the appropriate space-age facilities. Hence, **Euralille**, the burgeoning complex of buildings behind the old *gare SNCF*. One definite success is the new Lille-Europe station: composed of lots of props and struts and glass and sunscreens, it's lean, elegant and functional, a fitting setting for the magnificent TGV and Eurostar trains that use it. Some of the buildings in the complex are, however, less successful – for example, the boot-shaped tower treading on the roof of the new station, or the enormous shopping centre opposite with galvanized walkways, marbled malls and relentless muzak.

Villeneuve d'Ascq: the Musée d'Art Moderne

The suburb ofVilleneuve-d'Ascq is a mark of Lille's cultural ambition: acres of parkland, an old windmill or two, and a whole series of mini-lakes form the setting for the **Musée d'Art Moderne** (daily except Tues 10am–6pm; €6.50), which houses an unusually good, if small, collection in its uninviting red-brick buildings. It's 8km from the city but accessible by public transport – to get there take the métro to Pont-de-Bois, then bus #41.

The ground floor is generally given over to exhibitions of varying quality by contemporary French artists, while the permanent collection, on the first floor, contains canvases by Picasso, Braque, Modigliani, Miró and a whole room devoted to Fernand Léger and Georges Rouault. On the top floor, a small room – easy to miss but worth the search – contains graphics by many of the above. Meanwhile, outside on the grass, Giacometti and Calder provide some playful picnic backdrops.

Eating

A Flemish flavour and a taste for mussels (*moules*) characterize the city's traditional cuisine, with the main area for **cafés**, **brasseries** and **restaurants** around **place Rihour** and along rue de Béthune. But Lille is also gaining a reputation for gastronomic excellence, and for something more exotic **Rue Royale** has a selection of fairly pricey but generally very good options, ranging from Cambodian or Japanese to French with a twist. The best general area for cheap restaurants is the student quarter along the rues Solférino and Masséna, while Vieux Lille in general is definitely fashionable, in particular the **rue de Gand** where cuisines as varied as Brazilian, Senegalese, Italian and Moroccan vie for your attention alongside temples to *cordon bleu* and even a traditional Flemish tavern.

Alcide 5 rue Débris St-Etienne ⓣ03.20.12.06.95. A *Lillois* institution, an upmarket brasserie tucked down a narrow alleyway near the Grand' Place. Reliable, hearty fare (*flamiche*, fish, *crêpes à la cassonade*) and homemade ice creams served in a wood-panelled dining room. Menus from €20, half-menu €15. Open daily, closed mid-July to mid-Aug.

Brasserie de la Paix 25 pl Rihour. Sumptuous brasserie, unrelated to its namesake hotel, specializing in mussels and seafood. Lunch menus at €15, dinner from €23. Closed Sun.

La Cave aux Fioles 39 rue de Gand ⓣ03.20.55.18.43. The jazz-related decor is backed by the music and mellow ambience. Food ranges from classics and Flemish specials to more adventurous fare. Menus at €29 or *plats* for €13.

Clair de Lune 50 rue de Gand ⓣ03.20.51.46.55. Call ahead or arrive early to get into this popular local restaurant that pays special attention to its creative French dishes and thoughtful wine list. Friendly service and relaxed ambience, menus from €14, *carte* from €11. Closed Sat lunch but open for Sun brunch 11am–4pm.

Le Compostelle 4 rue St-Etienne ⓣ03.28.38.08.30. In a much renovated Renaissance palace this airy restaurant with indoor trees offers refined versions of traditional French specialities, including vegetarian options. Reasonably priced menu at €26.50 (for two courses), €31.50 (for three), or a lunch menu at €17 which varies each week.

A Côté aux Arts 5 place du Concert. Friendly little brasserie serving dishes such as *andouillette*, stuffed pig's trotters, and *magret* of duck with fresh figs (€13–20 for main course).

L'Envie 34 rue des Bouchers ⓣ03.20.15.29.39. Classically delicious French food served in creative ways in a small restaurant on a quiet street, but just steps away from the trendy bars on rue Royale. À la carte only, from €15.

Flandre Liban 125 rue des Postes. Excellent, friendly Lebanese restaurant in a mainly North African and Middle Eastern quarter. Go for the mezze menu at €15.

L'Huîtrière 3 rue des Chats-Bossus ⓣ03.20.55.43.41. A wonderful shop with an expensive, chandelier-hung restaurant at the back – acclaimed as Lille's best – specializing in fish and oysters at €25–35 a dish; there's a staggering €118 menu, and a €43 one for lunch. Closed Sun eve, hols & late July to late Aug.

Méert 25–27 rue Esquermoise. Lille's most famous (and expensive) *salon de thé* specializes in *gaufres* as well as excellent cakes and teas. Closed Mon morning. *Méert* also runs the restaurant at La Piscine in Roubaix (see p.271).

Aux Moules 34 rue de Béthune ⓣ03.20.12.90.92. The best place to eat mussels; it's been serving them since 1930 in its Art Deco-style interior. Nothing costs much over €10, including the other brasserie fare, and it's all excellent value. Daily noon–midnight.

La Pâte Brisée 63–65 rue de la Monnaie. Delicious quiches and tarts in a bright, modern decor. *Formules* at €8, 11, 13 & 17.

Paul place du Théâtre, cnr rue Faidherbe ⓣ03.20.78.20.78. *Paul* is an institution in Lille; though it's now becoming a bit of a chain, it started here with the boulangerie, patisserie and *salon de thé* all under one roof. Daily 7am–7.30pm.

Piccolo Mondo 2 rue des Molfonds, off rue de Béthune. Erratic service but Lille's best pizza place. Also serves fresh pasta and offers several vegetarian alternatives.

T'Rijsel 25 rue de Gand. Traditional Flemish *estaminet*, open evening only, serving the whole gamut of regional dishes and over 40 beers. *Plats* from €9. Closed Sun & Mon.

△ Troyes houses

Drinking and nightlife

The **cafés** around the Grand' Place and place Rihour are always buzzing with life. Rue de Paris has lots of tacky, loud, crushed **bars** raging at all hours, while up near the cathedral rue Basse and place Louise-de-Bettignies have some trendier spots. West of place de la Republique, bars are thick on the ground in rues Solférino and Masséna, and attract a young crowd, while student bars, both trendy and friendly, fill up along the base of Rue Royale. For **gay bars**, of which there are several, try either *Mum's Bar* at 4 rue Doudin or *Yo* at 11 place Louchard, both west of the cathedral. Art and music events are always worth checking up on – there's a particularly lively **jazz** scene. Pick up a copy of the free weekly listings magazine, *Sortir*, from the tourist office, or look in the local paper, *La Voix du Nord*.

Bateau Ivre 41 rue Lepelletier. Loud music ranging from house to soul in a pleasant street in the old quarter. Mainly young crowd. Sun–Fri 3pm–3am, Sat 11am–3am.

Café aux Arts 1 place du Concert. Good old-fashioned café with wicker chairs on its terrace, in an unbeatable vantage point over the market.

Club le 30 30 rue de Paris ⓣ03.20.30.15.54. One of Lille's many jazz venues, this one probably attracts the best artists. Open every evening except Mon.

L'Imaginaire place Louise-de-Bettignies, next door to the *Hôtel Treille*. Arty young bar with paintings adorning the walls. Mon–Sat 10pm–2am.

La Part des Anges 50 rue de la Monnaie. Trendy wine bar with an enviable cellar, serving simple meals and snacks to accompany the wine.

La Pirogue 16 rue J.J. Rousseau. Antilles-themed bar with reasonably priced cocktails, especially popular with local students.

Le Smiley 2 rue Royale. Funky cocktail bar in basement open every evening except Sunday; Internet café on ground floor.

Les Trois Brasseurs 22 place de la Gare. Dark, smoke-stained dining stalls surround copper cauldrons in this genuine brasserie that brews its own beer. Food is also served but it's the beer that's the main attraction.

Listings

Banks All the banks have big branches on rue Nationale, and you can guarantee to find one open until 4pm on Saturday.

Books Le Furet du Nord, 11 place Général-de-Gaulle, is a huge, seven-storey bookshop (it claims to be Europe's biggest) with a wide selection of books in English.

Car rental is mostly from the two train stations, ADA Gare Europe ⓣ03.20.55.18.18; Avis Gare Flandres ⓣ03.20.06.35.55, Gare Europe ⓣ03.20.51.12.31; Hertz Gare Flandres ⓣ03.28.36.28.70, Gare Europe ⓣ03.28.36.25.90.

Cinema Lille's two main cinemas, Le Majestic and UGC, are along the rue de Béthune; UGC at no. 40 shows blockbusters with usually at least one film in English, Le Majestic at nos. 54–56 is more arty and sometimes runs festivals. Le Métropole at 26 rue des Ponts-de-Comines normally shows original-language versions.

Doctors SOS Médecins ⓣ03.20.29.91.91.

Internet Le Smiley, 2 rue Royale (Mon–Sat 11am–2am); Cyber Office 20 place des Reignaux (open daily till late).

Laundry There are several outlets of Lavotec, the most central being at 72 rue Pierre-LeGrand, 57 rue des Postes and 137 rue Solférino, open daily 6am–9pm.

Markets The loud and colourful Wazemmes flea market, selling food and clothes, spills around place de la Nouvelle Aventure, to the west of central Lille. Main day Sun but also open Tues and Thurs (7am–2pm). A smaller food market takes place in vieux Lille on place du Concert (Wed, Fri & Sun 7am–2pm).

Post office 8 place de la République (ⓣ03.28.36.10.20) and 13–15 rue Nationale (ⓣ03.28.38.18.40); both Mon–Fri 8am–6.30pm, Sat 8.30am–12.30pm.

Taxi Gare ⓣ03.20.06.64.00; Taxi Union ⓣ03.20.06.06.06.

Roubaix

Just 15km northeast of Lille, right up against the Belgian border, **ROUBAIX** is another great Flemish city whose erstwhile wealth was founded on the wool industry. Nowadays it's best known in France as the origin of mail-order clothes, and as the destination of the gruelling 250-kilometre Paris-Roubaix cycle race, held in mid-April. In the nineteenth century, however, the Industrial Revolution turned Roubaix into one of France's most prosperous cities. The population multiplied fifteen-fold between 1800 and World War I, and the city's prosperity was reflected in great textiles mills, Art Nouveau houses, parks, hospitals, a sophisticated social welfare system and a flamboyant Hôtel de Ville whose architect was also responsible for Gare d'Orsay in Paris. Coincidentally, the main attraction of present-day Roubaix is a disused Art Deco swimming pool, converted into an outstanding museum of fine art and industry by the same architect responsible for the conversion of the Paris station into the Musée d'Orsay. Another worthwhile museum is housed in a working textile factory, and a couple of manufacturer outlets in town offer a chance to snap up bargain-priced clothing.

Arrival, information and accommodation

The best way to get to Roubaix is via the **métro** from Lille, which takes twenty minutes and stops at Roubaix Gare/Jean Lebas, Grand' Place and Eurotélépor, the last of which, immediately to the east of Grand' Place, is also the terminus of the tramway from Lille's Eurostar station. The tram has the sightseeing advantage of being overground, though the journey takes ten minutes extra (fares are the same, €1.15 one way). The **gare SNCF** is at the western end of avenue Jean-Baptiste Lebas, a five-minute walk along which leads to the central Grand'Place. The **tourist office** is another couple of minutes' walk to the southeast, at 10 rue de la Tuilerie (Mon 10am–7pm, Tues–Fri 9am–noon & 1–6pm, Sat 9am–noon; Ⓣ03.20.65.31.90, Ⓦwww.roubaixtourisme.com).

You're really better off staying in Lille, but there are plenty of chain **hotels** in Roubaix including the renovated *Grand Hôtel Mercure*, a nineteenth-century palace with comfortable, stylish rooms and a beautiful brasserie, at 22 av J-B Lebas (Ⓣ03.20.73.40.00, Ⓔh1250@accor-hotels.com; ❺; brasserie menus from €18); the standard but decent two-star *Campanile*, 36 rue de la Communauté Urbaine (Ⓣ03.20.70.19.20, Ⓕ03.20.27.43.25; ❸); and the *Ibis*, another chain hotel, reliable if nothing else, at 37 bd du Général Leclerc (Ⓣ03.20.45.00.00, Ⓔh1017@accor-hotels.com; ❸). Ask at the tourist office for details of *chambres d'hôtes*.

The Town

Modern Roubaix is not a beautiful place, partly owing to severe world war bombardment, but also the result of decades of industrial decline. The **Grand'Place** has a desolate feel, not helped by the bombastic opulence of the Hôtel de Ville, built in 1911. But the city has been earnestly trying to overcome its difficulties in recent years, and nowhere is this more manifest than in **La Piscine**, or the **Musée d'Art et d'Industrie** (Tues–Thurs 11am–6pm, Fri 11am–8pm, Sat & Sun 1–6pm; €3 for the permanent collection, plus €3 for temporary exhibitions; or €5 joint ticket), one of most original art museums in the country, halfway between the *gare SNCF* and the Grand'Place at 23 rue de l'Espérance. This fascinating, partly interactive museum opened its doors in 2001, after years of work to convert one of France's most beautiful swimming pools and water cure complexes. Originally built in the early 1930s by local architect Albert Baert, contemporary architect Paul Philippon retained various aspects of the baths – part of the pool, the shower-cubicles, the changing-rooms and the bathhouses – and used each part of the complex to display a splendid collection of mostly nineteenth- and early twentieth-century sculpture and painting, plus haute couture clothing, textiles and a collection of photographs of the swimming pool in its heyday. A fine set of sculptures is reflected in the water, and don't miss the water-filter machinery in the museum's excellent shop. Interesting temporary exhibitions are staged throughout the year.

A short way to the southeast of central Roubaix, at 25 rue de la Prudence, is the massive **La Manufacture des Flandres**, a working tapestry factory, where you'll find the **Musée du Jacquard** (Tues–Sun 1.30–5pm; €5). One-hour guided tours take you round an interesting collection of looms and other machinery, plus tapestries from the Middle Ages to the present day, and end up in a boutique selling the factory's wares.

Although the choice and range are nothing like as good as at Troyes (see p.298), there are some good deals to be had on designer-label clothing in Roubaix, with prices at up to fifty percent off normal shop prices. Two major **factory outlets** are worth investigating: L'Usine (Mon–Sat 10am–7pm), at 228 av Alfred Motte, a short distance away from the centre; and McArthur Glen (same opening hours), at 44 Mail de Lannoy, right in the centre – Cacharel, Bruce Field, Adidas and Reebok are just a few names which may entice you.

Eating and drinking

There are plenty of **restaurants** in Roubaix, many serving regional specialities. One of the best is in the Piscine museum itself – a gastronomic restaurant and *salon du thé* run by *Méert*, the famous Lillois patisserie (☎03.20.57.07.44; open daily except Mon for lunch, Fri only for dinner). Another establishment of high repute is the *Auberge de Beaumont*, 143 rue de Beaumont (menus from €23; ☎03.20.75.43.28; closed Wed lunch, Sun & Mon eve), with appealingly rustic decor, while *Chez Charly*, 127 ave J-B Lebas is an excellent place for lunch (menus €17–29; ☎03.20.70.78.58; closed eves and all day Sun), serving classic food in a cosy wood-panelled dining room. For couscous and other North African fare head for *Les Hammadites*, 45 rue du Chemin de Fer, or for a **drink** there's *La Grande Brasserie de l'Impératrice Eugénie* at 22 place de la Liberté.

Douai and around

Right at the heart of mining country, 40km south of Lille, and badly damaged in both world wars, **DOUAI** is a surprisingly attractive and lively town, its handsome streets of eighteenth-century houses cut through by both the River Scarpe and a canal. Once a haven for English Catholics fleeing Protestant oppression in Tudor England, Douai later became the seat of Flemish local government under Louis XIV, an aristocratic past evoked in the novels of Balzac.

Centre of activity is the **place d'Armes**, where life focuses around a fountain, while rue de la Mairie, leading west, is overlooked by the massive Gothic belfry of the **Hôtel de Ville**, popularized by Victor Hugo and renowned for its carillon of 62 bells – the largest single collection in Europe. It rings every fifteen minutes, and there are hour-long concerts every Saturday at 10.45am, on public holidays at 11am, and in summer on Monday at 9pm (hourly guided tours: July & Aug daily 10–11am & 2–5pm; Sept–June Mon–Sat 2–5pm, Sun 10am, 11am, 3pm & 5pm; €3.50).

One block north of the town hall, on **rue Bellegambe**, is an outrageous Art Nouveau facade fronting a very ordinary haberdashery store. At the end of the street, rising above the old town, are the Baroque dome and tower of the **church of St-Pierre**, an immense, mainly eighteenth-century church with – among other treasures – a spectacular carved Baroque organ case. East of the place d'Armes, Douai's oldest church, the twelfth-century **church of Notre-Dame**, suffered badly in the last war but has been refreshingly modernized inside. Beyond the church is the better of the town's two surviving medieval gateways, the **Porte Valenciennes**, now the centre of a triumphal roundabout. With the exception of the 1970s extension to the old Flemish Parliament building, the riverfront west of the town hall is pleasant to wander along. Between the river and the canal to the west, on rue de Chartreux, the **Ancienne Chartreuse** has been converted into a wonderful **museum** (Mon & Wed–Sat 10am–noon & 2–5pm, Sun 10am–noon & 3–6pm; €3), with a fine collection of paintings by Flemish, Dutch and French masters, including Van Dyck, Jordaens, Rubens and Douai's own Jean Bellegambe. The adjacent chapel, magnificently converted in 2001, shows off to full effect an array of sculptures including a poignant *Enfant prodige* by Rodin.

The **gare SNCF** is a five-minute walk from the centre – from the station head left down avenue Maréchal Leclerc, then right onto the place d'Armes. The **tourist office** (April–Sept Mon–Sat 10am–1pm & 2–7pm, Sun 3–6pm; Oct–March Mon–Sat 10am–12.30pm & 2–6.30pm; Ⓣ03.27.88.26.79, Ⓦwww.ville-douai.fr) is housed within the fifteenth-century Hôtel du Dauphin on the square. For **accommodation** there's the central but shabby *Hôtel au Grand Balcon*, on 26 place Carnot (Ⓣ03.27.88.91.07; ❷), or the better *Le Cerf*, 46 rue St-Jacques (Ⓣ03.27.88.79.60, Ⓕ03.27.98.05.74; ❹). A far classier option is *La Terrasse*, a swanky four-star in the narrow terrasse St-Pierre (Ⓣ03.27.88.70.04, Ⓕ03.27.88.36.05; ❹), to one side of the church of St-Pierre; its restaurant is well regarded, with menus from €25.

Just northeast of the place d'Armes is the post office, from where buses leave for Lewarde (Line #1 orange).

Lewarde

A visit to the colliery at **LEWARDE**, 7km east of Douai, is a must for admirers of Zola's *Germinal*, perhaps the most electrifying "naturalistic" novel ever written. The bus from Douai heads east across the flat and featureless beet fields, down a road lined with poor brick dwellings that recall the company-owned housing of *Germinal*, intersected by streets named after Pablo Neruda, Jean-Jacques Rousseau, Georges Brassens and other luminaries of the French and international Left. This is the traditional heart of France's coal-mining country, always dispiriting and now depressed by closures and recession. Even the distinctive landmarks of slag heaps and winding gear are fast disappearing in the face of demolition and landscaping.

The bus puts you down at the main square, leaving a fifteen-minute walk down the D132 towards Erchin to get to the colliery. **The Centre Historique Minier** (2hr guided tours: March–Oct daily 9am–5.30pm; Nov–Feb Mon–Sat 1–5pm, Sun 10am–5pm; March–Oct €10.60, Nov–Feb €9.40) is on the left in the old Fosse Delloye, sited, like so many pits, amid woods and fields. Visits are guided by retired miners, many of whom are not French, but Polish, Italian or North African – Polish labour was introduced in the 1920s, other nationalities successively after World War II.

The main part of the tour – in addition to film shows and visits to the surface installations of winding gear, machine shops, cages, sorting areas and the rest – is the exploration of the pit-bottom roadways and faces, equipped to show the evolution of mining from the earliest times to today. These French pits were extremely deep and hot, with steeply inclined narrow seams that forced the miners to work on slopes of 55 degrees and more, just as Étienne and the Maheu family do in Zola's story. Accidents were a regular occurrence in the old days: the northern French pits had a particularly bad record in the last years of the nineteenth century. The worst mining disaster occurred at Courrières in 1906, when 1100 men were killed. Incredibly, despite the fact that the owners made little effort to search for survivors, thirteen men suddenly emerged after twenty days of wandering in the gas-filled tunnels without food, water or light. The first person they met thought that they were ghosts and fainted in fright. More incredible still, a fourteenth man surfaced alone after another four days.

Cambrai and around

Despite the tank battle of November 1917 (see box below) and the fact that the heavily defended Hindenburg Line ran through the town centre for most of World War I, **CAMBRAI** has kept enough of its character to repay a passing visit, though it is less attractive than either Douai, its sister town 27km to the north, or Arras to the northwest.

The huge, cobbled main square, **place Aristide-Briand**, is dominated by the Neoclassical Hôtel de Ville, and still suggests the town's former wealth, which was based on the textile and agricultural industries. Unlike most places, Cambrai's chief ecclesiastical treasure is not its cathedral – the medieval one was dismantled after the Revolution – but the **church of St-Géry**, off rue St-Aubert west of the main square, worth a visit for a celebrated *Mise au Tombeau* by Rubens. The appealingly presented **Musée de Cambrai** (Wed–Sun 10am–noon & 2–6pm; €3, free first weekend of every month) on rue de l'Épée, a short way south of the town square, is also worth a visit. Paintings by Velázquez, Utrillo and Ingres feature prominently alongside works by various Flemish old masters, plus great twentieth-century artists like Zadkine and Van Dongen. Don't turn down the audio-guided tour and don't leave out the archeological display in the basement, where you can see some fascinating exhibits including elegant statues rescued

Cambrai 1917

At dawn on November 20, 1917, the first full-scale **tank battle** in history began at Cambrai, when over 400 British tanks poured over the Hindenburg Line. In just 24 hours, the Royal Tank Corps and British Third Army made an advance that was further than any undertaken by either side since the trenches had first been dug in 1914. A fortnight later, however, casualties on both sides had reached 50,000, and the armies were back where they'd started.

Although in some respects the tanks were ahead of their time, they still relied on cavalry and plodding infantry as their back-up and runners for their lines of communication. And, before they even reached the "green fields beyond", most of them had broken down. World War I tanks were primitive machines, operated by a crew of eight who endured almost intolerable conditions – with no ventilation system, the temperature inside could rise to 48°C. The steering alone required three men, each on separate gearboxes, communicating by hand signals through the din of the tank's internal noise. Maximum speed (6kph) dropped to almost 1kph over rough terrain, and refuelling was necessary every 55km. Consequently, of the 179 tanks lost in the battle at Cambrai, very few were destroyed by the enemy; the majority broke down and were abandoned by their crews.

from the decimated cathedral. Look out for the *gourde eucharistique de Concevreux*, an amazingly well-preserved sixth-century bronze hipflask.

Cambrai's **tourist office** is housed in the Maison Espagnole on the corner of avenue de la Victoire, at 48 rue de Noyon (Mon–Fri 10am–12.15pm & 2–5pm, Sat 10am–noon & 2–5pm, Sun 2–5pm only; ⓣ03.27.78.36.15, ⓦwww.cambraiofficedetourisme.com). Central **accommodation** includes *Le Mouton Blanc*, 33 rue d'Alsace-Lorraine (ⓣ03.27.81.30.16, ⓕ03.27.81.83.54; ④), which is a convenient and moderately priced hotel close to the station, with a posh **restaurant** inside (from €18; closed Sun eve & Mon, plus the evenings of public hols & Aug 1–15). Alternatively, there is a small, family-oriented **hostel**, *L'Étape*, 1.5 km southeast of the centre of town on Sentier de l'Eglise (ⓣ03.27.37.80.80; ⓔeducrotois@l-etape.asso.fr; €11.70). The nearest **campsite** is *Les Colombes* at Aubencheul-au-Bac (mid-March to mid-Oct; ⓣ03.27.89.25.90), 10km away off the N43 to Douai. Crêperie *La Sarrazine* opposite the tourist office at 1 place St-Sépulcre is the best bet for an economical meal.

Le Cateau-Cambrésis

Twenty-two kilometres east of Cambrai along an old Roman road, the small town of **LE CATEAU-CAMBRÉSIS** is the birthplace of Henri Matisse (1869–1954), and as a gift to his home town, the artist bequeathed it a collection of his works. Some of them are displayed in the **Musée Matisse** (daily except Tues: June–Sept 10am–6pm; Oct–May 10am–noon & 2–6pm; €4.50, free 1st Sun of month), housed in Palais Fénelon in the centre of town. Although no major works are displayed, this is the third-largest Matisse collection in France, and the paintings here are no less attractive and interesting than the better-known ones exhibited elsewhere. The collection includes several studies for the chapel in Vence, plus a whole series of his characteristically simple pen-and-ink sketches. Also worth looking at is the work of local Cubist Auguste Herbin, particularly his psychedelic upright piano. For somewhere to **stay** and eat there's the simple but comfortable *Hostellerie du Marché* on rue Landrecies (ⓣ03.27.84.09.32, ⓔhostellerie-du-marche@wanadoo.fr; ②; menus €14 & €20).

Arras, Albert and the Somme battlefields

Around **Arras**, 35km northwest of Cambrai, and **Albert**, 40km to the southwest of Cambrai, some of the fiercest and most futile battles of World War I took place. The beautiful town of Arras, easily accessible from Paris and Lille by TGV is the best base for exploring the battlefields. Nearby, to the north, at the moving **Vimy Ridge** Canadians fell in their thousands, while at Notre-Dame de Lorette, the French suffered the same fate; the battlefields and cemeteries of the Somme lie to the south, around **Albert** and **Péronne**, home to a fascinating museum devoted to explaining and remembering the war.

Arras

ARRAS, with its fine old centre, is one of the prettiest towns in northern France. It was renowned for its tapestries in the Middle Ages, giving its name to the hangings behind which Shakespeare's Polonius was killed by Hamlet. Subsequently the town fell under Spanish control, and many of its citizens today claim that Spanish blood runs in their veins. Only in 1640 was Arras returned to the kingdom of France, with the help of Cyrano de Bergerac. During World War I, the British used it as a base, digging tunnels under the town to try to surprise the Germans to the northeast.

Although destroyed by the Germans in World War I, the town bears few obvious battle scars. Reconstruction here, particularly after the last war, has been careful and stylish, and two grand arcaded Flemish-and Dutch-style squares in the centre – **Grand' Place** and the smaller **place des Héros** – preserve their historic, harmonious character. On every side are restored seventeenth- and eighteenth-century mansions and, on place des Héros, there's a grandly ornate **Hôtel de Ville**, its entrance hall housing a permanent photographic display documenting the wartime destruction of the town and sheltering a set of *géants* (festival giants) awaiting the city's next fête.

Also inside the town hall is the entrance to the **belfry** viewing platform, 150m high – to which a lift fortunately takes you up almost all the way (€2.30) – and **les souterrains** (or *les boves*) – cold, dark passageways and spacious vaults tunnelled since the Middle Ages, and completed by the British during World War I, beneath the centre of the city (frequent bilingual guided tours – ask for times in the tourist office; €4.40). Once down, you're escorted around an impressive area and given an interesting survey of local history. The rooms – many of which have fine, tiled floors and lovely pillars and stairways – were used as a British barracks and hospital. Pictures from this period are on display, as is a bilingual newspaper published for the soldiers. In the spring, some of the rooms are converted into an underground garden.

Next to its enormous cathedral is Arras's other main sight, the **Benedictine Abbaye St-Vaast**, a grey-stone classical building – still pockmarked by world-war shrapnel – erected in the eighteenth century by Cardinal Rohen. The abbey now houses the **Musée des Beaux-Arts**, with its entrance at 22 rue Paul-Donnier (Wed & Fri–Mon 9.30am–noon & 2–5.30pm, Thurs 9.30am–5.30pm; €4), which contains a motley collection of paintings, including a couple of Jordaens and Brueghels, fragments of sculpture and local porcelain. Only one of the tapestries or *arras* that made the town famous in medieval times survived the world-war bombardments. Figuring among the highlights are a pair of delicately sculpted thirteenth-century angels, the *Anges de Saudemont*, and a room on the first floor filled with vivid seventeenth-century paintings by Philippe de Champaigne and his contemporaries, including his own *Présentation de la Vierge au Temple*.

Nearby, on the small dark rue Maximillien Robespierre, opposite a ghostly mask and costume shop, is the **Maison Robespierre**, home between 1787 and 1789 to the revolutionary leader before his hands were stained with blood, and now a small museum (May–Sept Tues–Fri 2–5.30pm, Sat-Sun 2.30–6.30pm; Oct–April Tues & Thurs 2–5.30pm, Sat–Sun 3.30–6.30pm; free).

Thirty minutes away by foot on the mournful western edge of town, along boulevard Général de Gaulle from the Vauban barracks (which although a citadel was monikered "*la belle inutile*" because it served no purpose in protecting the city, even on construction in 1668) is a **war cemetery** and memorial by the British architect Sir Edwin Lutyens. It's a movingly elegiac, classical colonnade of ivy-covered brick and stone, commemorating 35,928 missing soldiers, the endless columns of their names inscribed on the walls. Around the back of the barracks, alongside an overgrown moat, is the **Mémorial des Fusillés**, a stark wall accessed via the avenue of the same name; its plaques commemorate two hundred Resistance fighters shot by firing squad in World War II – many of them of Polish descent, nearly all of them miners, and most of them Communists.

Practicalities

From the **gare SNCF** it's a ten-minute walk up rue Gambetta then rue Désiré Delansorne, to the **tourist office**, located in the Hôtel de Ville on place des Héros (May–Sept Mon 10am–6pm, Tues–Sat 9am–6.30pm, Sun 10am–1pm & 2.30–6.30pm; Oct–April Mon 10am–noon & 2–6pm, Tues–Sat 9am–noon & 2–6pm, Sun 10am–12.30pm & 3–6.30pm; ⓣ03.21.51.26.95, ⓦwww.ot-arras.fr); the tourist office is worth consulting for details of transport and tours of local battlefields (see "Vimy Ridge and around" below). To reach the Vimy memorial, you can also rent a car from Hertz, bd Carnot (ⓣ03.21.23.11.14), or Euroto, 15 av Paul-Michonneau (ⓣ03.21.55.05.05).

There are two good, inexpensive **hotels** on the beautiful squares in the centre: the *Diamant*, 5 place des Héros (ⓣ03.21.71.23.23, ⓦwww.arras-hotel-diamant.com; ❸), a comfortable, reliable two-star; and *Hôtel des Trois Luppars*, 47 Grand' Place (ⓣ03.21.60.02.03, ⓕ03.21.24.24.80; ❸), a friendly family-run place with modern facilities in a characterful old building. For a more luxurious night, go to the *Univers*, a beautiful former monastery round a courtyard in place de la Croix-Rouge, near the Abbaye St-Vaast (ⓣ03.21.71.34.01, ⓔhoteluniversarras@wanadoo.fr; ❹; restaurant €20–42). Near the train station there are hotels in nearly every price range, including the inexpensive and shabby one-star *Le Passe Temps* (ⓣ03.21.50.04.04, ⓕ03.21.50.33.78; ❶); and the top-of-the-range *Hotel d'Angleterre* (ⓣ03.21.51.51.16, ⓔhotelangleterre@pilortec.fr; ❻). The newly modernized **hostel** is extremely well positioned at 59 Grand' Place (ⓣ03.21.22.70.02, ⓕ03.21.07.46.15; closed Dec–Jan; €11.70, cardholders only). The municipal **campsite** at 166 rue du Temple (ⓣ03.21.71.55.06; closed Feb–March) lies 1km out of town on the Bapaume road.

Restaurants worth trying include *La Rapière*, 44 Grand' Place, with excellent regional food and menus from €14.50; and, for a splurge, the gourmet *La Faisanderie*, across the square at no. 45 (from €23; ⓣ03.21.48.20.76). In between the two squares, at 11 rue de la Taillerie, is a fun little wine bar and restaurant, *Espace Grand Crus*, which for around €12.50 serves with each main a glass of appropriate wine (ⓣ03.21.51.44.78; open Mon–Fri lunch, Fri & Sat dinner). Pizzerias abound: try *Le Petit Théâtre* at 7 rue Petits-Viéziers or *Le Palerme* at 50 Grand' Place. Nearer the station at 26 bd de Strasbourg is an attractive, old-fashioned brasserie, *La Coupole*, where you'll find locals and Brits eating oysters and other fresh seafood, as well as traditional brasserie dishes (€29 menu, closed Sat lunch).

There's a good *fromagerie*, Jean-Claude Leclercq, at 39 place des Héros (closed Mon). Saturdays are the best day for food and wine, when the squares are taken up with a morning **market**, and Resto Cave, an extensive sixteenth-century wine cellar run by the delightfully large and quirky proprietor of the *Trois Luppars*, is open for the sale of fine wines (10am–1pm & 3–8pm).

Vimy Ridge and around

Eight kilometres north of Arras on the D49, **Vimy Ridge**, or Hill 145, was the scene of some of the worst trench warfare of World War I: almost two full years of battle, culminating in its capture by the Canadian Corps in April 1917. It's a vast site, given in perpetuity to the Canadian people out of respect for their sacrifices, and the churned land has been preserved, in part, as it was during the conflict. You really need your own transport to get there as the nearest bus stop is 45 minutes' walk away (for details contact the tourist office in Arras, see above). But it is well worth the journey – of all the battlefields, it is perhaps easiest here to gain an impression of the lay of the land, and of how it may actually have felt to be part of a World War I battle.

There's an **information centre** (☎03.21.50.68.68, daily 10am–6pm) supervised by friendly, bilingual Canadian students, who run free guided tours (daily 10am–5.30pm; call to book, or check in at the office near the trenches upon arrival). Tours are run either of the subway, the Canadian term for the series of interlinking **underground tunnels** used as secret passageways and to hoard ammunition and equipment, or of the cemeteries and battlefields.

Near the information centre, long worms of neat, sanitized **trenches** meander over the now grassy ground, still heavily pitted by shell bursts beneath the planted pines. Grenades and shrapnel are still found here, although pedestrians are warned not to stray from the directed paths on to the grassy areas. Filled in by topsoil and grass, some of the craters have become smaller over time, but the ground remains sufficiently damaged and uneven, almost a hundred years later, to relay the impact of these battles. Beneath the ground lie some 11,000 bodies still unaccounted for and countless rounds of unexploded ammunition.

On the brow of the ridge to the north of the trenches, overlooking the slag-heap-dotted plain of Artois, a great white **monument** towers like a giant funerary stele, rent down the middle by elemental force, with allegorical figures half-emerging from the stone towards the top. It is inscribed with the names of 11,285 Canadians and Newfoundlanders whose bodies were never found, only a small proportion of the 60,000 Canadians who died during the war. It must have been an unenviable task to design a fitting memorial to such slaughter, but this one, aided by its setting, succeeds with great drama. Undergoing renovation work, the monument is currently closed, with reopening scheduled for autumn 2006. Nearby is a subdued but informative **museum** (same hours as the information centre; free), which illustrates the well-planned Canadian attack and and its importance for the Canadians – this was the first time that they were recognized as being separate from "British Forces".

Back from the ridge lies a memorial to the Moroccan Division who also fought at Vimy, and in the woods behind, on the headstones of another exquisitely maintained **cemetery**, you can read the names of half the counties of rural England.

La Targette, Neuville-St-Vaast and Notre-Dame de Lorette

At the crossroads (D937/D49) of **LA TARGETTE**, 8km north from the centre of Arras and accessible from there by bus, the **Musée de la Targette** (daily 9am–8pm; €3) contains an interesting collection of World War I and II *objets de guerre*. It's the private collection of one David Bardiaux, assembled with passion and meticulous attention to detail under the inspiration of tales told by his grandfather, a veteran of Verdun. Its interest lies in the absolute precision with which the thirty-odd mannequins of British, French, Canadian and German soldiers are dressed and equipped, down to their sweet and tobacco tins and such rarities as a 1915 British-issue cap with earflaps, very comfortable for the troops but withdrawn because the top brass thought it made their men look like yokels. All the exhibits have been under fire; some belonged to known individuals and are complete with stitched-up tears of old wounds.

More **cemeteries** lie a little to the south of La Targette, nominally at **NEUVILLE-ST-VAAST**, though the village is actually 1km away to the east. There's a small British cemetery, a huge French one, and an equally large and moving German cemetery, containing the remains of 44,833 Germans, four to a cross or singly under a Star of David. In the village itself a Polish **memorial** –

among the Poles that died in action here was the sculptor Henri Gaudier-Brzeska, in 1915 – and a Czech **cemetery** face each other across the main street.

On a bleak hill a few kilometres to the northwest of Vimy Ridge (and 5km north of Neuville-St-Vaast) is the church of **Notre-Dame de Lorette**, scene of a costly French offensive in May 1915. The original church was blasted to bits during the war and rebuilt in grim neo-Byzantine style in the 1920s, grey and dour on the outside but rich and bejewelled inside. It now stands at the centre of a vast graveyard with over 20,000 crosses laid out in pairs, back to back, each one separated by a cluster of roses. There are 20,000 more buried in the ossuary, and there's the small **Musée Vivant 1914–1918** (daily 9am–8pm; €3) behind the church, displaying photographs, uniforms and other military paraphernalia. You can reach Notre-Dame de Lorette by bus from Arras, direction "Lens".

Albert and around

The church at **ALBERT**, 40km south of Arras and 30km northeast of Amiens – now, with the rest of the town, completely rebuilt – was one of the minor landmarks of World War I. Its tall tower was hit by German bombing early on in the campaign, leaving the statue of the Madonna on top leaning at a precarious angle. The British, entrenched over three years in the region, came to know it as the "Leaning Virgin". Army superstition had it that when she fell the war would end, a myth inspiring frequent hopeful pot shots by disgruntled troops. Before embarking on a visit of the region's battle sites and war cemeteries, otherwise known as the Circuit de Souvenir (see below), you might want to stop in at the **Musée "Somme 1916"** (daily: Feb–March & Oct–Nov 10am–3.45pm, April–Oct 10am–5.45pm; €4), an underground museum which has reenactments of fifteen different scenes from life in the trenches of the Somme in 1916. The mannequins look slightly too jolly and eager but it does go some way to bringing the props to life. The museum's final section recreates the actual battle scene, complete with flashing lights and the sound of exploding shells. Enthusiastically portrayed, some may find this a little tasteless, though to others it may in part succeed in explaining how soldiers, forced to live in these conditions for long periods, returned home with shell-shock.

As you arrive (trains from Amiens or Arras), the town's new tower, capped now by an equally improbably posed statue, is the first thing that catches your eye. The **tourist office** is close by on rue Gambetta (April–Sept Mon–Sat 10am–noon & 2–6.30pm, Sun 9.30am–noon; Oct–March Mon–Sat 10am–noon & 3–5pm; ⓣ03.22.75.16.42). Of the town's hotels, *La Paix*, a friendly establishment with a decent restaurant, at 43 rue Victor-Hugo (ⓣ03.22.75.01.64, ⓕ03.22.75.44.17; ❸; menus from €14) is the only one that can be recommended.

The Circuit de Souvenir

Was it for this the clay grew tall?
O what made fatuous sunbeams toil
To break earth's sleep at all?

Wilfred Owen, *Futility*

The **Circuit de Souvenir** conducts you from graveyard to mine crater, trench to memorial. There's not a lot to see; certainly no evidence of the shocking atrocities and scenes of destruction that happened here fewer than a hundred years ago. Neither do you get much sense of movement or even of battle tactics. But you will find that, no matter what the level of your interest in the Great War, you have in fact embarked on a sort of pilgrimage, in which each successive step becomes more harrowing and oppressive.

The Battle of the Somme

On July 1, 1916, the British and French launched the **Battle of the Somme** to relieve pressure on the French army defending Verdun. The front ran roughly northwest–southeast, 6km east of Albert across the valley of the Ancre and over the almost treeless high ground north of the Somme – huge hedgeless wheat fields now. These windy open hills had no intrinsic value, nor was there any long-term strategic objective – the region around Albert was chosen simply because it was where the two Allied armies met.

There were 57,000 British casualties on the first day alone, approximately 20,000 of them dead, making it the costliest defeat the British army has ever suffered. Sir Douglas Haig is the usual scapegoat for the Somme, yet he was only following the military thinking of the day, which is where the real problem lay. As A.J.P. Taylor put it, "Defence was mechanized: attack was not." Machine guns were efficient, barbed wire effective, and, most important of all, the rail lines could move defensive reserves far faster than the attacking army could march. The often ineffective heavy bombardment that presaged an advance was favoured by both sides but only made matters worse, since the shells forewarned the enemy of an offensive and churned the trenches into a giant muddy quagmire.

Despite the bloody disaster of the first day, the battle wore on until bad weather in November made further attacks impossible. The cost of this futile struggle was 415,000 British, 195,000 French and around 600,000 German casualties.

The **cemeteries** are the most moving aspect of the region – beautiful, the grass perfectly mown, an individual bed of flowers at the foot of every gravestone. And there are tens of thousands of gravestones, all identical, with a man's name, if it's known (nearly half the British dead have never been found), and his rank and regiment. In the lanes between Albert and Bapaume you'll see the cemeteries everywhere: at the angle of copses, halfway across a wheat field, in the middle of a bluebell wood, terrible in their simple beauty.

Lying on minor roads, the circuit can be explored by either car or bicycle. Both **Albert** to the west and **Peronne** to the southeast make good starting points, the tourist offices and museums in either town able to provide you with a free **map** of the circuit. Once en route, sights of interest are marked along the road by arrows and poppy symbols, with Commonwealth graves also indicated in English. It would be impossible to see all of the 400 British and Commonwealth cemeteries in the area, though getting off the beaten track to visit one or two small ones can be rewarding. What follows is necessarily just a selected handful of some of the better-known sites.

If you start from Albert the first town you'll reach is **BEAUMONT-HAMEL** (7km north), where the 51st Highland Division walked abreast to their deaths with their pipes playing. Here, on the hilltop where most of them died, a series of trenches, now grassed over and eroding, is preserved, commemorating where German faced Canadian just a few paces apart. Just across the river, towards the village of **THIEPVAL**, the 5000 Ulstermen who died in the Battle of the Somme are commemorated by the incongruously Celtic **Ulster Memorial**, a replica of Helen's Tower at Clandeboyne near Belfast (information bureau open Mon–Sat 11am–5pm; closed Dec & Jan). Probably the most famous of Edwin Lutyens' many memorials is south of Thiepval: the colossal **Memorial to the Missing**, in memory of the 73,357 British troops whose bodies were never recovered at the Somme.

Five kilometres east at **POZIÈRES**, on the Albert–Bapaume road is perhaps the oddest memorial. Here, *Le Tommy* café has a World War I permanent exhibition (daily 9.30am–6pm; free) in its back garden, consisting mainly of a reconstructed section of trench and "equipped" with genuine battlefield relics, all accompanied by a recorded loop of patriotic British war songs. It's a bit amateurish, but worth a look if you're passing through. The French owner of the café had first collected objects from the battlefield as a boy to sell for pocket money. Farmers apparently still turn up several tonnes of shells every year – not really surprising when you think the British alone fired one-and-a-half million shells in the last week of June 1916.

Delville Wood, known as "**Devil's Wood**", lies another 5km to the east at **LONGUEVAL**. Here, thousands of South Africans lost their lives, and a memorial to the dead from both world wars has been erected, as well as a small **museum** (Tues–Sun April–Oct 10am–5.45pm, Nov & March 10am–3.45pm) relating not just the battle in France but also the longest march of the war, undertaken thousands of kilometres away, when South African troops walked 800km to drive the Germans out of East Africa (now Tanzania).

The most informative of all the World War I museums in the surrounding *départements* is at **PÉRONNE**, on the River Somme some 25km east of Albert – the **Historial de la Grande Guerre** (May–Sept daily 10am–6pm; mid-Jan to April & Oct to mid-Dec Tues–Sun 10am–5.30pm; €7). All kinds of exhibits – such as newsreel and film footage, newspapers, posters, commemorative plates, Otto Dix drawings and artificial limbs – combine with displays of hardware to provide a broad, modern view of the whole catastrophe. It also provides an excellent history of the complex political and cultural tensions that led to war, something that is lacking in most of the other sights. There's a **TGV** station about 15km away from Péronne – the **Gare Haute Picardie** – which is thirty minutes from the Eurostar stop at Lille-Europe; for a taxi to or from the station, call Mouret (Ⓣ03.22.84.15.83) or Fouque (Ⓣ03.22.84.52.49).

There's not much else to keep you in Péronne, although it's pleasant enough. The **tourist office** is on rue Louis XI, opposite the museum (June–Aug Mon–Sat 9am–noon & 2–6.30pm, Sun 10am–noon & 3–6pm; Sept–May closed Sun; Ⓣ03.22.84.42.38). If you want to stay the night, you could try the old-fashioned *Hostellerie des Remparts*, on the opposite side of the main square at 23 rue Beaubois (Ⓣ03.22.84.01.22, Ⓕ03.22.84.38.96; ❸; restaurant from €16), or the modern *Campanile* (Ⓣ03.22.84.22.22, Ⓕ03.22.84.16.86; ❸), part of a chain, just out of town on the N17 to Roye and Paris.

To the southwest of the main circuit near **VILLERS-BRETONNEUX**, 18km southwest of Albert near the River Somme, stands another fine Lutyens memorial. As at Vimy, the landscaping of the **Australian Memorial** here is dramatic – for the full effect, climb up to the viewing platform of the stark white central tower. The monument was one of the last to be inaugurated, in July 1938, when the prospects for peace were again looking bleak.

Aisne and Oise

To the southeast of the Somme, away from the coast and the main Paris through-routes, the often rainwashed and dull province of Picardy becomes considerably more inviting. Particularly in the *départements* of **Aisne** and **Oise**, where the region merges with neighbouring Champagne, there are some real attractions amid the lush wooded hills. **Laon**, **Soissons** and **Noyon** all centre around handsome Gothic cathedrals, while at **Compiègne**, Napoleon Bonaparte and Napoléon III enjoyed the luxury of a magnificent château and embellished it to their hearts' content. The most rewarding place to stay is off the beaten track in the tiny fortified town of **Coucy-le-Château-Auffrique**, in the forest and on a hill between Soissons and Laon.

Transport is good, too, with a network of bus connections from Amiens and good train and bus links with Paris.

St-Quentin and around

A pleasant and prosperous industrial centre, **ST-QUENTIN** is a convenient place to pause on the way south, but makes no great demands on your time.

The central **place de l'Hôtel de Ville** is now completely closed to traffic. Its north side is dominated by a particularly good-looking, arcaded, late-Gothic **Hôtel de Ville**, whose bells ring protracted, syncopated changes every quarter-hour. To the east, rue St-André leads to the town's skyscrapingly massive Gothic **basilique**. Inside, its main virtue is its sheer size. In fact, it's a miracle that it is still standing at all, since the retreating Germans mined all 300 pillars in 1918 and were only prevented from setting the explosives off by lack of time – you can still see the marks left by the mines. Another curiosity is the maze in the paving of the nave, designed for penitents to figure out on their knees.

Of much greater interest is the **Musée Antoine-Lécuyer** on rue Lécuyer, at the end of rue Raspail (Mon & Wed–Fri 10am–noon & 2–5pm, Sat 10am–noon & 2–6pm, Sun 2–6pm; closed Tues & public hols; €2.50, Wed free), which contains a big collection of pastel portraits of the leading politicians, nobles, artists and socialites of eighteenth-century France by locally born Maurice-Quentin de Latour. The portraits evince subtleties of character, perhaps even with greater success than most photographs. The town's other interesting collection, the largest in Europe and said to be one of the largest in the world, is of a vast array of butterflies, housed in the **Musée d'Entomologie**, at 14 rue de la Sellerie, just off the main square (Mon & Wed–Sat 2–6pm, Sun 3–6pm; €2.50).

To get to the centre of town from the **gare SNCF**, follow rue Général-Leclerc over the Somme, and up rue d'Isle. The **tourist office** is at 27 rue Victor Basch, just off the main square (Mon–Fri 8am–12.30pm & 1.30–6pm, Sat 9am–noon & 2–6pm, Sun 2.30–5.30pm; ⓣ03.23.67.05.00). For super-cheap **accommodation**, try the very basic *Hôtel du Départ*, place du Monument-aux-Morts (ⓣ03.23.62.31.69; ❶), just to the right as you come out of the station, or one of two cleaner, decent hotels off the main square in the centre of town: *Le Florence*, 42 rue Zola (ⓣ03.23.64.22.22, ⓔaccuil@hotel-le-florence.fr; ❶), or the *Hôtel de la Paix*, 3 place du 8-Octobre (ⓣ03.23.62.77.62, ⓔhoteldelapaix@worldonline.fr; ❸), on the road between the train station and the town centre. The municipal **campsite** and **hostel** are next door to each other by the river on boulevard Jean-Bouin 2km from the station – take any bus to the Basilica then bus #4 to the *piscine municipale* (ⓣ03.23.62.68.66; closed Dec; hostel €7.20 including sheets, HI card not required).

Laon

Looking out over the plains of Champagne and Picardy from the spine of a high narrow ridge, girt still by its gated medieval walls, **LAON** (pronounced "Lon"), 36km southeast of St-Quentin, is one of the highlights of the region. Dominating the town, and visible for miles around, are the five great towers of one of the earliest and finest Gothic cathedrals in the country. Of all the cathedral towns in the Aisne, Laon is the one to head for.

Arrival, information and accommodation

Arriving by train or road, you'll find yourself in the disappointingly shabby and characterless lower town, or **ville basse**. To get to the upper town – **ville haute** – without your own transport, you can make the stiff climb up the steps at the end of avenue Carnot, or take the **Poma 2000** (Mon–Sat 7am–8pm every 3–6 min, irregularly on Sun 2.30–6pm in summer only; one-day return ticket €1), a fully automated, diminutive, rubber-tyred, overland métro, Laon's pride and joy. You board next to the train station and get out by the town hall (Terminus "Hôtel de Ville") on place Général-Leclerc; from there a left turn down rue Sérurier brings you nose to nose with the cathedral.

The **tourist office** (daily 10am–1pm & 2–6pm; ⓣ03.23.20.28.62, ⓦwww.ville-laon.fr) is right by the western end of the cathedral, housed within the impressive Gothic Hôtel-Dieu, built in 1209; ask for information about local *gîtes* and guesthouses. If you need **accommodation** in the *ville basse* (if you arrive too late to take the Poma), try *Hôtel Welcome* (ⓣ03.23.23.06.11, ⓔhotel-welcome.laon@wanadoo.fr; ❶), at 2 av Carnot, straight in front of the *gare SNCF*. Otherwise, in the *ville haute*, *Hôtel de la Paix*, 52 rue St-Jean (ⓣ03.23.79.06.34; ❶; restaurant from €11, closed Sat & Sun), is inexpensive, though you'd do better at the charming and characterful old *Les Chevaliers*, at 3–5 rue Sérurier, near the Poma stop (ⓣ03.23.27.17.50, ⓔhotelchevaliers@aol.com; ❸). Laon's smartest accommodation is at the three-star *Hôtel de la Bannière de France*, 11 rue Franklin Roosevelt (ⓣ03.23.23.21.44, ⓦwww.hoteldelabannieredefrance.com; ❹; decent traditional restaurant from €20). *La Chênaie* (ⓣ03.23.20.25.56; Jan–Sept), Laon's **campsite**, is on allée de la Chênaie, on the northwest side of town.

The Town

Laon really only has one attraction, its magnificent **Cathédrale Notre-Dame** (daily 9am–6.30pm; guided tours from tourist office: July & Aug daily 3pm; Sept–June Sat, Sun & public hols 3pm). Built in the second half of the twelfth century, the cathedral was a trendsetter in its day, elements of its design – the gabled porches, the imposing towers and the gallery of arcades above the west front – being repeated at Chartres, Reims and Notre-Dame in Paris. When wrapped in thick mist, the towers seem other-worldly. The creatures craning from the uppermost ledges, looking like reckless mountain goats borrowed from a medieval bestiary, are reputed to have been carved in memory of the valiant horned steers who lugged the cathedral's masonry up from the plains below. Inside, the effects are no less dramatic – the high white nave is lit by the dense ruby, sapphire and emerald tones of the stained glass, which at close range reveals the appealing scratchy, smoky quality of medieval glass.

Crowding in the cathedral's lee is a web of quiet, grey, eighteenth-century streets. One – rue Pourier – leads past the post office and onto the thirteenth-century Porte d'Ardon, which looks out over the southern part of the *ville basse*. A left turn at the post office along rue Ermant leads to the little twelfth-century octagonal **Chapelle des Templiers** – the Knights Templar – set in a secluded garden. Next door is the **Musée de Laon**, 32 rue Georges-Ermant (June–Sept Tues–Sun 11am–6pm; Oct–May Tues–Sun 2–6pm; €3.20), which contains a pitifully displayed collection of classical antiquities, albeit with some fine Grecian ceramics among them, and a jumble of furniture and paintings, including an acclaimed seventeenth-century work, *Le Concert*, by local lad Mathieu Le Nain. The rest of the *ville haute*, which rambles along the ridge to the west of the cathedral into the Le Bourg quarter around the early Gothic church of St-Martin, is enjoyable to wander round, with grand views from the **ramparts**.

Eating, drinking and entertainment

Along pedestrianized Rue Châtelaine, in the *ville haute*, is an excellent selection of wine shops, boulangeries and fromageries for assembling picnics. Simple **snacks** and basic meals can be had at the *Brasserie du Parvis*, which overlooks the west front of the cathedral (*plats* around €10); at *Crêperie L'Agora*, an inexpensive Breton place near the cathedral at 16 rue des Cordeliers (open until 1am; closed Sat lunch & Mon; menu €7.50); at *La Bonne Heure*, specializing in quiche-like *tourtinettes* (€6 each) at 53 rue Châtelaine; or at the lively *Brasserie les Chenizelles*, at no. 1 on rue du Bourg, the continuation of rue Châtelaine (menus from €13.50). Proper **restaurants** in Laon tend to be expensive: *La Petite Auberge*, the gourmets' favourite, at 45 bd Pierre-Brossolette in the *ville basse* near the station, falls into this category, serving traditional French cuisine using the freshest ingredients (menus from €23; ⓣ03.23.23.02.38, booking recommended; closed Sat lunch, Sun and Mon eve). They also own the bistro next door, which is slightly less pricey.

There's usually something going on at the **Maison des Arts de Laon** (MAL), headquartered in a theatre on the place Aubry to the north of the cathedral – including a concentration of events during the Fêtes Médiévales de Laon held in late May. October sees a series of big-name classical concerts during the Festival de Laon, either in the cathedral or MAL venues (details from the tourist office), while for a week in June Laon plays host to hundreds of antique cars, which come and follow a circuit of the city and surrounding region (ⓣ03.23.79.83.58 for details). *Le Welcome*, next door to MAL arts complex on the place, is an Irish-style **bar** and a good place for a drink.

Coucy-le-Château and the Forêt St-Gobain

About 30km west of Laon, and just over 15km north of Soissons, in hilly countryside on the far side of the forest of St-Gobain, lie the straggling ruins of one of the greatest castles of the Middle Ages, **Coucy-le-Château** (daily: May–Aug 10am–12.30pm & 2–6.30pm; April & Sept 10am–12.30pm & 2–6pm; Oct–March Mon–Fri 10am–12.30pm & 2–5pm; €4.60). The castle's walls still stand, and encircle the attractive village of **COUCY-LE-CHÂTEAU-AUFFRIQUE**. In the past this was a seat of great power, the influence of its lords, the Sires de Coucy, rivalling and often even exceeding that of the king – "King I am not, neither Prince, Duke nor Count. I am the Sire of Coucy" was Enguerrand III's proud boast. The retreating Germans capped the destruction of World War I battles by blowing up the castle's keep as they left in 1917, but enough remains, crowning a wooded spur, to be extremely evocative.

Enter the village through one of three original gates, squeezed between powerful, round flanking towers – there's a footpath all around the outside which is open even when the castle is closed. A small museum, the **Tour de Coucy**

Musée Panorama (daily: May–Sept 2.30–6.30pm; Oct–April 2.30–6pm; free), in the tower at the **Porte de Soissons** on the south side of the walled part of town, has a display of photographs showing how it looked pre-1917, which can be compared with today's remains from the vantage point of the roof.

Bicycles can be rented from the **tourist office**, in the central square (May–Aug Mon–Sat 9.30am–12.30pm & 2–6pm, Sun 2–6pm; Sept–April Mon–Sat 10am–12.30pm & 2–6pm; ⊕03.23.52.44.55), just north of the Porte de Soissons. Staying the night here, especially if you have children, is something special – for **accommodation**, try the *Hôtel Le Belle Vue* within the walls (⊕03.23.52.69.70, ⓔhotel.restaurant.belle.vue@wanadoo.fr; ❷; closed last week Dec); its restaurant specializes in Picardy cuisine (menus from €20), and serves special "medieval" meals (€17) on certain summer nights, when medieval re-enactments are held across the city (details from the tourist office in Laon).

It's hard to get to Coucy-le-Château without a car, though several Laon–Soissons trains stop at **ANIZY-PINON** – which cuts the distance by about half – and there is an infrequent bus on to Soissons. If you continue into the nearby **Forêt St-Gobain**, a pleasant cycle ride, it's worth including **ST-GOBAIN**, 13km north of Coucy, in your itinerary. Some original eighteenth-century glassworks – the firm is now a vast conglomerate – hide behind a classical facade, pretending it's nothing so vulgar as a factory (visits by appointment only, ⊕03.23.52.84.75).

Soissons

Half an hour by train, or 30km down the N2, southwest of Laon, **SOISSONS** can lay claim to a long and highly strategic history. Before the Romans arrived it was already a town, and in 486 AD it was here that the last Roman ruler, Syagrius, suffered a decisive defeat at the hands of Clovis the Frank, making Soissons one of the first real centres of the Frankish kingdom. Napoleon, too, considered it a crucial military base, a judgement borne out in the twentieth century by extensive war damage.

The town boasts the fine, if little-sung, **Cathédrale Notre-Dame** – thirteenth century for the most part with majestic glass and vaulting – at the west end of the main square, place F.-Marquigny. More impressive still is the ruined **Abbaye de St-Jean-des-Vignes**, to the south of the cathedral down rue Panleu and then right down rue St Jean. The facade of the tremendous Gothic abbey church rises sheer and grand, impervious to the now empty space behind it. The rest of the complex, save for remnants of a **cloister** and **refectory** (Mon–Sat 9am–12.30pm & 1.30–6pm, Sun 10am–12.30pm & 1.30pm–7pm; free), was dismantled in 1804. Near the *abbaye* is the impressive eighteenth-century **Hôtel de Ville** with its grand stone gate.

Practicalities

Soissons is relatively compact. From the **gare SNCF** (with good services to Laon and Paris) the main square is a fifteen-minute walk away along avenue du Général-de-Gaulle, which becomes rue St-Martin. The **gare routière** is closer to the centre by the river on Le Mail: infrequent buses leave for Compiègne and Laon. The **tourist office** is on place F.-Marquigny behind the cathedral (mid-June to mid-Sept Mon–Sat 9.30am–6.30pm, Sun 9.30am–12.30pm & 2–6pm; mid-Sept to mid-June Mon–Sat 9.30am–12.30pm & 2–6.30pm, Sun 9.30am–12.30pm & 2–6pm; ⊕03.23.53.17.37).

The town is more of a place to stop through than to **stay**, but if you're keen to explore the nearby forest or are just stuck, try the reasonably priced *Terminus* by the station at 56 avenue General de Gaulle (☎03.23.53.33.59; ❷; closed Sun & Aug), or the **campsite** (☎03.23.74.52.69), 1km from the station on avenue du Mail. An excellent place for *galettes* is *La Galetière* (closed Mon) at 1 rue du Beffroi by the cathedral, and there's a good Tunisian **restaurant**, the *Sidi Bou*, at 4 rue de la Bannière down towards the river.

Compiègne and around

Thirty-eight kilometres west of Soissons lies **COMPIÈGNE**, whose reputation as a tourist centre rests on the presence of a vast royal palace, built at the edge of the Forêt de Compiègne in order that generations of French kings could play at "being peasants", in Louis XIV's words. Although the town itself is a bit of a one-horse place with a bland, Sunday-afternoon feel, it's worth a visit for the opulent palace interiors, and the car and Second Empire museums.

Arrival, information and accommodation

The **gares routière** and **SNCF** are adjacent to each other, just a few minutes' walk away from the centre of town: cross the wide River Oise and go up rue Solférino to place de l'Hôtel-de-Ville. The **tourist office** (Easter–Sept Mon–Sat 9.15am–12.15pm & 1.45–6.15pm, Sun 10am–1pm & 2.30–5pm; Oct–Easter Mon 1.45–5.15pm, Tue–Sat 9.15am–12.15pm & 1.45–5.15pm; ☎03.44.40.01.00) takes up part of the ornate Hôtel de Ville. It offers free hotel bookings, and will provide you with a plan of the town, on which is conveniently marked an exhaustive visitors' route, including the forest paths (see p.286).

As for **accommodation**, there are cheap rooms at the *Hôtel St-Antoine*, 17 rue de Paris (☎03.44.23.22.27; ❶), concealed above a Chinese restaurant. A little more expensive but much more comfortable is the *Hôtel Vega*, 4 rue du Général-Leclerc (☎03.44.23.32.17; ❷), while *Hôtel de Flandre*, at 16 quai de la République (☎03.44.83.24.40, ⓕ03.44.90.02.75; ❶-❸), with some good-value, simple top-floor rooms with hall showers, and *Hôtel du Nord*, 1 place de la Gare (☎03.44.83.22.30, ⓕ03.44.86.82.27; ❸), are both large hotels near the train station overlooking the river.

The Town

Compiègne itself is plain disappointing, though that shouldn't come as a surprise, as a platoon of German soldiers burnt it down in 1942 to provide their commander with evidence of a subjugated community. Fortunately, however, they spared the town's star attraction, the oversized and opulent **Palais National**, with its extensive gardens which make an excellent picnicking ground. The seventeenth- and eighteenth-century Palais stands two blocks east of the Hôtel de Ville (see overleaf) on rue des Minimes, and for all its pompous excess, inspires a certain fascination, particularly its interior which can only be visited on a guided tour (daily except Tues: March–Oct 10am–5.15pm; Nov–Feb 10am–3.45pm; €4.50; €5.50 for combined ticket with the Musée de la Voiture, see overleaf). The lavishness of Marie-Antoinette's rooms, the sheer, vulgar sumptuousness of the First and Second Empire and the evidence of the unseemly haste with which Napoleon I moved in, scarcely a dozen years after the Revolution, are impressive. The palace also houses the **Musée** du **Second Empire** and the **Musée de la Voiture** (same hours as Palais National; €4; €5.50 combined ticket), the latter containing a wonderful array of antique bicycles, tricycles and fancy aristocratic carriages, as well as the world's first steam coach. The **Théâtre Impérial**, planned (but never finished) by Napoléon III, was finally completed in 1991 at a cost of some thirty million francs. Originally designed with just two seats for Napoléon and his wife, it now seats 900 and is regularly used for concerts.

If you don't want to take the guided tour, a visit to the palace gardens or **petit parc** (daily: summer 7.30am–8pm; winter 8am–6.30pm) is a pleasant alternative. Much of the formal French-style gardens were replaced with a *jardin à l'Angleterre* during the first Empire, which explains the long, lightly landscaped avenue which extends far into the Forêt de Compiègne (see below) on the edge of town.

The centre of town is much less picturesque, though several half-timbered buildings remain on the pedestrianized rue Napoléon and rue des Lombards, south of the main place de l'Hôtel-de-Ville. The most striking building, as so often in these parts, is the **Hôtel de Ville** – Louis XII Gothic – its ebullient nineteenth-century statuary including the image of Joan of Arc, who was captured in this town by the Burgundians before being handed to the English.

By the side of the town hall is the **Musée des Figurines** (Tues–Sat 9am–noon & 2–6pm, Sun 2–6pm; closes at 5pm in winter; €2), which features reputedly the world's largest collection of wafer-thin military figurines in mock-up battles from ancient Greece to World War II. Also of specialist interest is the **Musée Vivenel**, on rue d'Austerlitz (same hours and price), which has one of the best collections of Greek vases around, especially a series illustrating the Panathenaic Games from Italy – a welcome dose of classical restraint and good taste compared with the palace. There's also a section on the flora and fauna of the Forêt de Compiègne, which includes a wild boar the size of an armoured car.

Eating and drinking

Compiègne lacks a very wide variety of good places to **eat**, but one restaurant that guarantees a good meal at a reasonable price is *Le Bouchon*, 4 rue Austerlitz, a wine bar with a sense of humour and an excellent chef (lunch menu €10.50, dinner menus from €19, ⓣ03.44.20.02.03). Other places worth noting are *Le Cordelier*, 1 rue des Cordeliers (lunch €9.50, dinner from €14.50, ⓣ03.44.40.23.38; closed Sun) and *Le Bistrot de Flandre*, 2 rue d'Amiens, next to the hotel of the same name. Next to the *Hôtel des Beaux Arts*, at 35 cours Guynemer, is one of Compiègne's best restaurants, the *Bistrot des Arts*; it serves traditional bistro food with a twist, accompanied by excellent wines, for around €25 a head (ⓣ03.44.20.10.10; closed at weekend lunchtimes). On Saturdays, there's a big all-day **market** in the square by place de l'Hôtel-de-Ville.

Into the forest: the Clairière de l'Armistice

Very ancient, and cut by a succession of hills, streams and valleys, the **Forêt de Compiègne**, with the GR12 running through it, is a grand rambling country for walkers or cyclists. East of Compiègne, some 6km into the forest and not far from the banks of the Aisne, is a green and sandy clearing guarded by cypress trees, known as the **Clairière de l'Armistice**. Here, in what was then a rail siding for rail-mounted artillery, World War I was brought to an end on November 11, 1918. A plaque commemorates the deed: "Here the criminal pride of the German empire was brought low, vanquished by the free peoples whom it had sought to enslave." To avenge this humiliation, Hitler had the French sign their capitulation on June 22, 1940, on the same spot, in the very same rail carriage. The original car was taken immediately to Berlin, then destroyed by fire in the last days of the war. Its replacement, housed in a small **museum** (daily except Tues: April–Sept 9am–noon & 1.30–6.30pm; Oct–March 9am–noon & 2–5.30pm; €2), is similar, and the objects inside are the originals.

VIEUX-MOULIN and **ST-JEAN-AUX-BOIS** are a couple of picturesque villages worth heading for right in the heart of the forest, the latter retaining part of its twelfth-century fortifications; while 13km southeast of Compiègne at **PIERREFONDS** there's a classic medieval **château** (March to mid-May & mid-Sept to Oct Mon–Sat 10am–12.30pm & 2–6pm, Sun 10am–6pm; mid-May to mid-Sept daily 9.30am–6pm; Nov–Feb Mon–Sat 10am–12.30pm & 2–5pm, Sun 10am–5.30pm; €6.10), built in the twelfth century, and heavily restored since, to make it into a model castle – a fantastic fairy-tale affair of turrets, towers and moat. The inside displays a varied range of medieval artefacts.

Noyon

Further up the Oise, and a possible day-trip from Compiègne, is **NOYON**, another of Picardy's cathedral towns. Its quiet provinciality belies a long, illustrious history, first as a Roman prefecture, then as seat of a bishopric from 531. Here, in 768, Charlemagne was crowned king of Neustria, largest of the Frankish kingdoms; in 987, Hugues Capet was crowned king of France; and John Calvin was born here in 1509.

Rowing along the Oise on his *Inland Journey* of 1876, Robert Louis Stevenson stopped briefly at Noyon, which he described as "a stack of brown roofs at the best, where I believe people live very respectably in a quiet way". It's still like that, though the **cathedral**, to which Stevenson warmed, is impressive, at least in passing. Spacious and a little stark, it successfully blends Romanesque and Gothic, and is flanked by the ruins of thirteenth-century cloisters and a strange, exquisitely shaped Renaissance library that contains a ninth-century illuminated Bible (only open to the public on the two days of the year, normally the third weekend of September, known as *journées du patrimoine*). On the south side of the cathedral, the old episcopal palace now houses the **Musée du Noyonnais** (Tues–Sun 10am–noon & 2–6pm; Nov–March closes 5pm; €2.50, including admission to Musée Calvin), a small, well-presented collection of local archeological finds and cathedral treasure. Close by, signs direct you to the **Musée Calvin** (daily except Tues 10am–noon & 2–6pm; Nov–March closes 5pm; same ticket as Musée du Noyonnais), ostensibly on the site of the reformer's birthplace. The respectable citizens of Noyon were never among their local boy's adherents and tore down the original long before its tourist potential was appreciated.

There's a **tourist office** in the town hall (Mon–Fri 9am–noon & 2–6.15pm, closed Mon morning; in summer also open Sat & Sun 10am–noon; ⓣ03.44.44.21.88, ⓦwww.noyon.com/tourisme). If you intend to **stay**, your best option is *Le St Eloi*, at 81 bd Carnot (ⓣ03.44.44.01.49, ⓦwww.hotelsainteloi.fr; ❸; restaurant €26), just off the roundabout between the train station and the cathedral. The nearest **campsite**, *La Montagne* (ⓣ03.44.76.98.29, ⓕ03.44.76.98.29; open April–Sept), is 5km out of town along the N32 to Compiègne. Local buses leave from outside the *gare SNCF*. Big days in Noyon are Saturday morning, when a colourful **market** spills out across place de l'Hôtel-de-Ville, and the first Tuesday of the month, when a livestock market takes over virtually the entire town centre.

Champagne and the Ardennes

The bubbly stuff is the reason most people visit **Champagne**. The cultivation of vines was already well established in Roman times, when Reims was the capital of the Roman province of Belgae (Belgium), and by the seventeenth century still wines from the region had gained a considerable reputation. Contrary to popular myth, however, it was not Dom Pérignon, cellar master of the Abbaye de Hautvillers near Épernay, who then "invented" champagne. He was probably responsible for the innovation of mixing grapes from different vineyards, but the wine's well-known tendency to re-ferment within the bottle was not controllable until eighteenth-century glass-moulding techniques (developed in Britain) produced sufficiently strong vessels to contain the natural effervescence.

Away from the vineyards with their serried ranks of vines, the region's rolling plains are an uninspiring sight, growing more wheat and cabbages per hectare than any other region of France, though it seems to bring the villages no great benefit. Some places look so run-down it looks like the shutters would fall off if you popped a paper bag, and few are not much more than hamlets, with grocery vans doing the rounds once a week, and not a boulangerie in sight.

At least the official capital of Champagne, the cathedral city of **Reims**, is worth a visit in its own right, and has a reasonably full cultural calendar. Some of the most extravagant champagne houses are found here, the *caves* beneath them certainly worth a visit for their vaulted ceilings and kilometres of bottles. **Épernay**, a smaller town surrounded by vineyards, is the scenic heart of the region. The champagne *maisons* here are not hidden among city streets but set aside on their own avenue, enabling visitors to float from one house to another like so many bubbles. Across the plains, neither **Châlons-en-Champagne** nor the smaller further-flung towns like **Chaumont** or **Langres**, dotted along the Marne towards its source, are much of an incentive to break your journey. The only real attraction in the rest of the region is the town of **Troyes**, some way off to the southwest. Smaller than Reims, although visitors won't find much in the way of sparkling wine here, it's a great place to stop through for an afternoon to purchase inexpensive clothing or to stroll through the cobbled streets to admire the city's ancient timbered houses.

Reims

Laid flat by the bombs of World War I, **REIMS** (pronounced like a nasal "Rance", and traditionally spelled Rheims in English) may give the first impression of being a large industrial centre with little to redeem it. Despite appearances however, the city centre is a walkable size, while lurking beneath its dull streets lie its real treasure – kilometre upon kilometre of bottles of fermenting champagne. Moreover, beyond its status as champagne capital of the world, Reims possesses one of the most impressive Gothic cathedrals in France – formerly the coronation church of dynasties of French monarchs going back to Clovis, first king of the Franks – whose 1500th anniversary celebrations in 1996 provoked fierce controversy between Catholics and secularists.

Arrival, information and accommodation

The cathedral is less than ten minutes' walk from the **gare SNCF** and **gare routière**. The **tourist office** (Easter to mid-Oct Mon–Sat 9am–7pm, Sun 10am–6pm; mid-Oct to Easter Mon–Sat 9am–6pm, Sun 10am–5pm; ⓣ03.26.77.45.00, ⓦwww.tourisme.fr/reims) is located next door to the cathedral in a picturesque ruin. Reliable **Internet access** is available at *Clique et*

Champagne: the facts

Nowhere else in France, let alone the rest of the world, are you allowed to make a drink called **champagne**, though many people do all the same, calling it "champan", "shampanskoye" and all manner of variants. You can blend grape juice harvested from chalk-soil vineyards, double-ferment it, store the result for years at the requisite constant temperature and high humidity in sweating underground *caves*, turn and tilt the bottles little by little to clear the sediment, add some vintage liqueur, and finally produce a bubbling golden (or pink) liquid; but in accordance with national and international trade law you cannot call it "champagne", although you may refer to the "*méthode champenoise*". It's perhaps an outrageous monopoly guarded to keep the region's sparkling wines in the luxury class, although the locals will tell you the difference comes from the squid fossils in the chalk, the lie of the land and its critical climate, the evolution of the grapes, the regulated pruning methods and the legally enforced quantity of juice pressed.

Three authorized **grape varieties** are used in champagne: Chardonnay, the only white grape, growing best on the Côte des Blancs and contributing a light and elegant element; Pinot Noir, grown mainly on the Montagne de Reims slopes, giving body and long life; and Pinot Meunier, cultivated primarily in the Marne valley, adding flowery aromas.

The **vineyards** are owned either by *maisons*, who produce the *grande marque* champagne, or by small cultivators called *vignerons*, who sell the grapes to the *maisons*. The *vignerons* also make their own champagne and will happily offer you a glass and sell you a bottle at two-thirds the price of a grande marque (ask at any tourist office in the Champagne region for a list of addresses). The difference between the two comes down to capital. The *maisons* can afford to blend grapes from anything up to sixty different vineyards and to tie up their investment while their champagne matures for several years longer than the legal minimum (one year for non-vintage, three years vintage). So the wine they produce is undoubtedly superior – and not a lot cheaper here than in a good discount off-licence/liquor store in Britain or the US.

If you could visit the head offices of Cartier or Dior, the atmosphere would probably be similar to that in the champagne *maisons* whose palaces are divided between Épernay and Reims. Visits to the handful of *maisons* that organize regular **guided tours** are not free, and some require appointments, but don't be put off – their staff all speak English and a generous *dégustation* is nearly always thrown in. Their audiovisuals and (cold) cellar tours are on the whole very informative, and do more than merely plug brand names. Local tourist offices can provide full lists of addresses and times of visits.

If you want to work on the **harvest**, contact any of the smaller *maisons* direct; the Agence Nationale pour l'Emploi, Cour de la Gare, Épernay (ⓣ03.26.54.88.29), or 40 rue de Talleyrand, Reims (ⓣ03.26.89.52.60); or try the **hostel** in Verzy, 22km from Reims, at 16 rue du Bassin (ⓣ03.26.97.90.10), where casual workers are often recruited and work is advertised.

Museum pass

If you're planning to visit more than one of Reims' museums, it's well worth picking up a €3 **museum pass** from the tourist office, which gives entry to the Musée des Beaux-Arts, Musée St-Remi, Ancien Collège des Jésuites and the Musée de la Reddition. Alternatively €12 will buy you, in addition to the museum pass, a one-day bus pass, a visit and *dégustation* at one of the champagne houses, and a some *biscuits roses de Reims*, pink champagne biscuits traditionally dunked in a glass of bubbly.

Croque, a cybercafé serving snacks throughout the day, located in a shopping gallery at 27 rue de Vesle (Mon–Sat 10am–12.30am, Sun 2–9pm).

Rooms are at city sizes and prices in Reims, which is to say, smaller and more costly than anywhere in the surrounding region, but they are fairly easy to come by. Bear in mind too that Reims is an easy day-trip from Épernay or Paris, so it may not be necessary to stay at all.

Hotels

Au Bon Accueil 31 rue de Thillois ⓣ03.26.88.55.74, ⓕ03.26.05.12.38. A small if rather dilapidated hotel in an excellent central location with some of the cheapest single rates in town. Hall showers cost €1.50, though rooms with proper facilities are also available. ❶

Boyer Les Crayères 64 bd Henry-Vasnier ⓣ03.26.82.80.80, ⓔcrayeres@relaischateaux.fr. Ideal for a very special occasion, this refined hotel, a member of Relais & Châteaux, with one of the region's most sophisticated restaurants (see p.294), has a beautiful garden, luxurious rooms and impeccable service. ❾

De la Cathédrale 20 rue Libergier ⓣ03.26.47.28.46, ⓕ03.26.88.65.81. Old-fashioned but comfortable two-star near, as the name suggests, the cathedral. ❸

Crystal 86 place Drouet-d'Erlon ⓣ03.26.88.44.44, ⓔhotelcrystal@wanadoo.fr. Small rooms, pleasant service and a small courtyard which blocks out much of noise from the lively street below. ❸

Gambetta 13 rue Gambetta ⓣ03.26.47.22.00, ⓕ03.26.47.22.43. Neat, well-designed, modern rooms, all with shower and toilet above an excellent restaurant, *Le Vonelly*. ❸

Grand Hôtel Continental 93 place Drouet-d'Erlon ⓣ03.26.40.39.35, ⓦwww.grandhotelcontinental.com. Well-situated hotel, with quiet rooms, all with bathroom and TV. ❹

Grand Hôtel Europe 29 rue Buirette ⓣ03.26.47.39.39, ⓦwww.hotels-exclusive.com/france. Formerly the *New Hôtel Europe*, this is a quiet fin-de-siècle four-storey three-star. ❺

Univers 41 bd Foch ⓣ03.26.88.68.08, ⓔhotel-univers@ebc.net. Handsomely located on the tree-lined Hautes Promenades, this smart neo-Art Deco style establishment, with double-glazing, is the best mid-range hotel in the city. ❺

Hostel

Centre International de Séjour 1 chaussée Bocquaine, Parc Léo Lagrange ⓣ03.26.40.52.60, ⓦwww.cis-reims.com. A large, well-run HI hostel with single (€28 with shower, €18 without) or double rooms (€16 per person with bath, €12 without). Either take bus H to "Pont de Gaulle", or it's a fifteen-minute walk from the station on the other side of the canal: cross over the big roundabout in front of the station, turn right down bd du Général-Leclerc to Pont de Vesle; chaussée Bocquaine is the first left after the bridge. Bike rental available.

The City

The old centre of Reims stretches from the **cathedral** and its adjacent episcopal palace north to place de la République's triumphal Roman arch, the **Porte de Mars**, punctuated by the grand squares of place Royale, place du Forum and place de l'Hôtel-de-Ville. Over to the south, about fifteen minutes' walk from the cathedral, is the other historical focus of the town, the **Abbaye St-Remi**, and nearby the Jesuits' College. To the east of here are most of the **champagne maisons** and, further east still, a museum of cars.

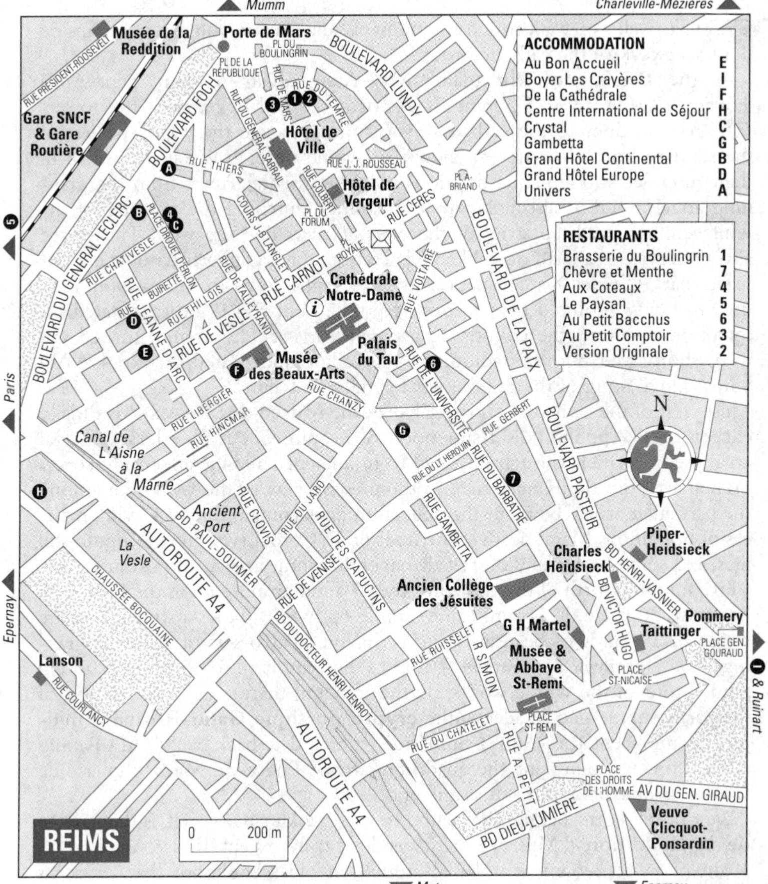

The cathedral and around

The thirteenth-century **Cathédrale Notre-Dame** (daily 7.30am–7.30pm) features prominently in French history: in 1429 Joan of Arc succeeded in getting the Dauphin crowned here as Charles VII – an act of immense significance when France was more or less wiped off the map by the English and their allies. In all, 26 kings of France were crowned in the Gothic glory of this edifice.

The lure of the cathedral's interior is the kaleidoscopic patterns in the stained glass, with fantastic Marc **Chagall** designs in the east chapel and champagne processes glorified in the south transept. But the greatest appeal is outside: an inexplicable joke runs around the restored but still badly mutilated statuary on the west front – the giggling angels who seem to be responsible for disseminating the prank are a delight. Not all the figures on the cathedral's west front are originals – some have been removed to spare them further erosion and are now at the former bishop's palace, the Palais du Tau. The **towers** of the cathedral are open to the public (April to Sept daily 10–11am & 2–5pm, Sept–Mar Sat & Sun 10–11am & 2–5pm; €4.60, or combined ticket with the Palais du Tau

€7.50); as well as a walk round the transepts and chevet, you get to see inside the framework of the cathedral roof.

At the **Palais du Tau** (daily: May–Aug 9.30am–6.30pm; Sept–April 9.30am–12.30pm & 2–5.30pm; €6.10, or combined ticket with the towers €7.50), next door to the cathedral, you can appreciate the expressiveness of the statuary from close up – a view that would never have been possible in their intended monumental positions on the cathedral. Apart from the grinning angels, there is also a superb Eve, shiftily clutching the monster of sin, while embroidered tapestries of the *Song of Songs* line the walls. The palace also preserves, in a state of unlikely veneration, the paraphernalia of the arch-reactionary Charles X's coronation in 1824, right down to the dauphin's hat box. In being anointed here in purple pomp, Louis XVI's brother stated his intention to return the country to the *ancien régime*. His attempt turned out to be short-lived, but the tradition he was calling upon dated back to 496 AD when Clovis, king of the Franks, was baptized in Reims.

Just west of the cathedral on rue Chanzy, the **Musée des Beaux-Arts** (daily except Tues & public hols 10am–noon & 2–6pm; €3) is the city's principal art museum, which, though ill suited to its ancient building, effectively covers French art from the Renaissance to the present. Few of the works are among the particular artists' best, but the collection does contain one of David's replicas of his famous Marat death scene, a set of 27 Corots, two great Gauguin still lifes, and some beautifully observed sixteenth-century German portraits.

Five minutes north of the cathedral, there's another museum in the **Hôtel de Vergeur**, 36 place du Forum (Tues–Sun 2–6pm; €3.90). It's a stuffed treasure house of all kinds of beautiful objects, including two sets of Dürer engravings – an *Apocalypse* and *Passion of Christ* – but you have to go through a long guided tour of the whole works. By the museum there's access to sections of the partly submerged arcades of the **crypto portique Gallo-Romain** (mid-June to mid-Sept Tues–Sun 2–5pm; free), which date back to 200 AD. Reims' other Roman monument, the quadruple-arched **Porte de Mars**, on place de la République, belongs to the same era.

West of the Porte, behind the station in rue Franklin-Roosevelt, is the **Musée de la Reddition** ("Museum of Surrender"; daily except Tues & public hols 10am–noon & 2–6pm; €3), based around an old schoolroom that served as Eisenhower's HQ from February 1945. In the early hours of May 7, 1945, General Jodl agreed to the unconditional surrender of the German army here, thus ending World War II in Europe. The room has been left exactly as it was (minus the ashtrays and carpet), with the Allies' battle maps on the walls. The visit includes a good documentary film and numerous photographs and press cuttings.

The Abbaye St-Remi, Jesuits' College and surrounding museums

Most of the early French kings were buried in Reims' oldest building, the eleventh-century **Basilique St-Remi**, fifteen minutes' walk from the cathedral on rue Simon (Mon–Wed, Fri & Sun 8am–dusk, Thurs & Sat 9am–dusk; closed during services; music & light show July–Sept Sat 9.30pm; free), part of a former Benedictine abbey named after the 22-year-old bishop who baptized Clovis and 3000 of his warriors. An immensely spacious building, with aisles wide enough to drive a bus along, it preserves its Romanesque transept walls and ambulatory chapels, some of them with modern stained glass that works beautifully. The spectacular abbey buildings alongside the church house the **Musée St-Remi** (Mon–Fri 2–6.30pm, Sat & Sun 2–7pm; €1.50), the city's archeological and historical museum, whose eclectic collection includes some fine tapestries on St Remi's life, plus sixteenth-century weapons and armour. Its twelfth- to thirteenth-century chapter house has been listed as a UNESCO World Heritage site.

The **Ancien Collège des Jésuites** (guided tours: daily 10am, 11am, 2.15pm, 3.30pm & 4.45pm, Tues afternoon hours only, Sat & Sun morning hours only; €3), a short walk north on rue du Grand-Cerf, was founded in Reims in 1606, and the building completed in 1678. Guided tours in French take you round the refectory, kitchens and, highlight of the visit, the beautifully ornate carved wooden fittings of the library. The books on the shelves are false and remain from the filming of *La Reine Margot* for which they were made.

If you have even a passing interest in old cars you should make for the **Centre de l'Automobile**, 84 av Georges-Clemenceau (daily except Tues 10am–noon & 2–6pm; €6), fifteen minutes' walk southeast of the cathedral. All the vehicles are part of the private collection of Philippe Charbonneaux, designer of a number of the postwar classics on display. In addition to the full-scale cars, there's an impressive selection of models, antique toys and period posters.

Champagne tasting

Tours of the Reims champagne houses and *caves* range from the Disney-esque to the extremely technical. A tour at an appointment-only house does not necessarily guarantee personal attention – central houses such as Pommery and Veuve Cliquot often host quite large groups. Those in the southern part of town near the Abbaye St-Remi tend to have the most impressive cellars – some have been carved in cathedral-esque formations from the **Gallo-Roman** quarries used to build the city, long before champagne was invented.

Non-appointment houses

G. H. Martel & Co 17 rue des Créneaux near the Basilique St-Remi ⓣ03.26.82.70.67, ⓦwww.champagnemartel.com. At €4.50, this is the best value tour, with a *dégustation* of three champagnes including a vintage and a rosé. Though the cellars are average, in the *caves* there is a display of the old tools used for each step of the process, and the tour can be truly informative as you're likely to have a small group. Open daily year-round (10am–7pm), this is a good option when most other houses are closed (over lunch or after 5pm).

Mumm 34 rue du Champ-de-Mars ⓣ03.26.49.59.70, ⓦwww.mumm.com. Known by its red-slashed Cordon Rouge label, Mumm's un-French-sounding name is the legacy of its founders, affluent German wine-makers from the Rhine Valley who established the business in 1827. The tour is fairly informal – you can wander freely about its cellar museum and throw questions at the approachable guides – though you pick up the basics from a corny pre-tour video. It all ends with a generous glass of either Cordon Rouge, the populist choice; the sweeter Cordon Vert; or their Extra Dry. March–Oct daily 9–11am & 2–5pm; Nov–Feb by appointment only, Mon–Fri same hours, Sat & Sun afternoons only; tour takes 45min; €5.

Piper-Heidsieck 51 bd Henry-Vasnier ⓣ03.26.84.43.44, ⓔvisit@piper-heidsiek.com. At 20mins, and complete with animated characters, this is something of a Mickey Mouse tour. Although founded in 1785, Piper is better known in the New World than the Old, having been the champagne of the American movie industry since first appearing – with Laurel and Hardy – in the 1934 classic *Sons of the Desert*. The only folk who'll get anything out of the tour – which ends up at a gallery of celebrity snaps – are confirmed film buffs and lovers of tackiness: the antique *caves* are toured in a five-seater shuttle resembling a ghost train; out of the darkness and timed to a cliché-ridden narration loom giant fibreglass grapes and life-size lumpy figures positioned as cellar masters. You emerge to a much-needed drink. March–Nov daily 9–11.45am & 2–5.15pm; Dec–Feb closed Tues & Wed; €7 for one tasting, €12.50 for three.

Taittinger 9 place St-Niçaise ⓣ03.26.85.84.33, ⓦwww.tattinger.com. Similar to Mumm's tour, with information on the making of champagne and a stroll through the ancient cellars, some of which have doodles and carvings added by more recent workers, while there are also statues of St Vincent and St Jean, patron saints respectively of *vignerons* and cellar hands. Mon–Fri 9.30am–noon & 2–4.30pm, Sat & Sun 9–11am & 2–5pm; Dec–Feb Mon–Fri only; tour takes 1hr; €6.50.

Appointment-only houses

These houses prefer that you call or email a week in advance, but in **summer** you may often be able to walk right in, or at least just show up in the morning and reserve something for the afternoon. More upmarket hotels can make reservations, and some will offer discounts for tours as well. This is not a comprehensive list of all the *maisons* in the city, but includes the most visitor-friendly places. If the marque that's always on your table isn't listed here, it's worth looking the house up and calling – there's a good chance they'll be able to show you around.

Lanson 66 rue de Courlancy ⓣ03.26.78.50.50, ⓔvisites@lanson.fr. It's worth the trip across the river to tour the factory of the champagne of Tesco, Waitrose and the Queen of England. Small and in-depth, the tours here actually bring you into the factory, and demonstrate the mechanized day-to-day process of champagne making. On most days you'll be able to see the machines degorging the bottles, as well as labelling and filling them in preparation for the second fermentation. A refreshing change from those houses that just talk about the process and show their cellars. Mon–Fri only, closed Aug; €5.

Pommery 5 place du Général-Gouraud ⓣ03.26.61.62.55, ⓔdomaine@pommery.fr. The creator of the cute one-eighth size "Pop" bottles has excavated Roman quarries for its cellars – it claims to have been the first *maison* to do so. The tour descends a 116-step stairway into the cellars, which are a showcase for contemporary art and often a greater focus than the champagne itself. Tours 1hr–1hr30 mins; €7.50.

Ruinart 4 rue des Crayères ⓣ03.26.77.51.51, ⓦwww.ruinart.com. The fanciest of the champagne houses, in a swanky mansion. Reserved and upmarket, the tours are nonetheless informative. €8–20, depending on number of tastings.

Veuve Clicquot-Ponsardin 1 place des Droits-de-l'Homme ⓣ03.26.89.54.41, ⓦwww.veuve-cliquot.fr. In 1805 the prematurely widowed Mme Clicquot not only took over her husband's business – *veuve* means "widow" in French – but also later bequeathed it to her business manager rather than to her children, a radical break with tradition. She also took great interest not only in the business of champagne but in its fabrication, inventing the first riddling table that many houses still use to settle sediment from the second fermentation in the bottles' necks. In keeping with its innovative past, the *maison* is one of the least pompous, and its *caves* some of the most spectacular, sited in ancient Gallo-Roman quarries, with high vaulted ceilings. April–Oct Mon–Sat 10am–6pm, Nov–March Mon–Fri 10am–6pm, €7.

Eating and drinking

Place Drouet-d'Erlon, a wide pedestrianized boulevard lined with **bars** and **restaurants**, is where you'll find most of the city's nightlife, such as it is. For self-catering, there's a big Wednesday and Saturday **market** in place du Boulingrin (6am–1pm).

Boyer Les Crayeres 64 bd Henry-Vasnier ⓣ03.26.82.80.80. Reputed to be one of France's finest gastronomic restaurants – with prices and style to match – Boyer is set in a restored eighteenth-century château and equipped with a helipad. Closed Mon & Tues lunch. Menus from €140.

Brasserie du Boulingrin 48 rue de Mars ⓣ03.26.40.96.22. Charming and good value 1925 brasserie famed for its seafood platters and *fondant au chocolat* (chocolate cake with runny filling). Weekday menus at €16 & €23, including wine. Open until midnight, closed Sun.

Chèvre et Menthe 63 rue de Barbâtre. A homely, inexpensive establishment with a range of gourmet salads from €5.50; recommended for vegetarians. Daily *carte* dishes (some contain meat) might include moussaka (€7) as well as more traditional choices, plus the eponymous goat's cheese and fresh mint quiche. Closed Sun eve & Mon.

Aux Coteaux 86–88 place Drouet D'Erlon ⓣ03.26.47.38.84. The best of the many restaurants on this popular street, with a wide range of pizzas and salads from under €8. Closed Sun.

Le Paysan 16 rue de Fismes ⓣ03.26.40.25.51. Serves genuine peasant dishes, copious and delicious, in suitably rustic surroundings with genuinely warm service. It's some way northwest of the station: follow rue de Courcelles, and rue de Fismes will be on your left. Menus under €16 during the week. Closed Sat lunch & Sun eve.

Au Petit Bacchus 11 rue de l'Université. Reasonably priced traditional cooking in an interior of sparse brick floor with bare tables. Around €19. Closed Sun & Mon.

Au Petit Comptoir 17 rue de Mars ☎03.26.40.58.58. Close to the Marché du Boulingrin, with traditional and inventive dishes from €15 and a menu at €26, served in beautiful surroundings – a subtle grey decor with white leather chairs. Champagne by the glass. Closed Sat & Mon lunch & all day Sun.

Version Originale 25 bis rue du Temple ☎03.26.02.69.32. Creative, fresh menus with flavours from all over the world in a small restaurant with tasteful but informal decor. A great deal at lunchtime with menus at €14.50 and €17, à la carte only for dinner with mains from €14. Closed Sun.

Nightlife and entertainment

For **drinking** into the early hours there are plenty of large terrace cafés on place Drouet-d'Erlon, including the chain *Café Leffe*, at no. 85, which has a wide selection of beers, and *Le Gaulois*, at nos. 2–4, with excellent cocktails and ice creams. One of the trendiest nightspots in town is *L'Apostrophe* at no. 59, for tapas, cocktails, special music nights and a designer decor. Closer to the classy restaurants near the Hôtel de Ville is *Le Mâles*, 12 rue de Mars, a gay-friendly bar that serves tapas in the winter and has a DJ on the weekends (daily from 4pm, from noon on Sun). If you want to **dance**, try *Le Curtayn Club* at 7 bd Général-Leclerc (daily 10pm–4am, ☎03.26.49.09.02) or *Le Diam's* at 15 rue Lesage (Thurs–Sun 11pm till very late, ☎03.26.88.33.83). *Azimuth Productions* (☎03.26.04.56.38) puts on a rock festival, Octob'Rock, every October. The *Opéra Cinema*, 3 rue T.-Dubois (☎03.26.47.29.36), shows undubbed films. From July 1 to mid-August, over a hundred classical concerts – many of them free – take place as part of **Les Flâneries Musicales d'Été**; pick up a leaflet at the tourist office.

Épernay

ÉPERNAY is 26km south of Reims and a more attractive place to stay, beautifully situated below rolling, vine-covered hills, with opulent tree-lined streets. It's a small town but contains some of the most famous champagne *maisons* as well as several smaller houses. Épernay also makes an excellent base for exploring the surrounding villages and vineyards.

Arrival, information and accommodation

Épernay's **gare SNCF** is a five-minute walk north of place de la République, down rue Jean Moët. The **gare routière** is on the corner of rues Dr-Verron and Dr-Rousseau one block northeast from place de la République. The information-packed **tourist office** is at 7 av de Champagne (Easter to mid-Oct Mon–Sat 9.30am–12.30pm & 1.30–7pm, Sun 11am–4pm; mid-Oct to Easter Mon–Sat 9.30am–12.30pm & 1.30–5.30pm; ☎03.26.53.33.00). If you feel like roaming around the vineyards (*vignobles*), you could rent a **mountain bike (VTT)** from Royer Cycles, place Hugues-Plomb (Tues–Sat 9am–noon & 2–7pm; ☎03.26.55.29.61), not far from place de la République at the other end of rue Général-Leclerc.

The best of the cheap **hotels** in Épernay is the excellent one-star *St-Pierre*, 1 rue Jeanne-d'Arc (☎03.26.54.40.80, ℱ03.26.57.88.68; ❶), in a quiet street away from the centre. *Le Chapon Fin*, 2 place Mendès-France (☎03.26.55.40.03; ❷), is also inexpensive and is closer to train station, but on a loud street above a restaurant can be noisy. More comfortable rooms are to be had at the excellent-value *Les Berceaux*, at 13 rue des Berceaux (Ⓣ03.26.55.28.84, Ⓔles.berceaux@wanadoo.fr; ❺), which also has one of the best restaurants in town; or failing that the Best Western-run *Hôtel de Champagne*, 30 rue E.-Mercier (Ⓣ03.26.53.10.60, Ⓕ03.26.51.94.63; ❺). Classiest of all is the elegant *Clos Raymi*, 3 rue Joseph de Venoge (Ⓣ03.26.51.00.58, Ⓦwww.closraymi-hotel.com; ❼), in a beautiful red-brick house once belonging to the Chandon family. For even more luxurious accommodation out of town, see "Eating and drinking". At the opposite end of the scale, the local **campsite** is 2km to the north on route de Cumières in the Parc des Sports, on the south bank of the Marne (Ⓣ03.26.55.32.14; closed Oct–May).

The Town

The first place to head for in Épernay is the appropriately named **avenue de Champagne**, running east from the central place de la République. Dubbed "the most drinkable street in the world" by champagne-lover Winston Churchill, it's worth a stroll for its impressive eighteenth- and nineteenth-century mansions and champagne *maisons*.

The largest, and probably the most famous *maison* of all, though neither the most beautiful nor necessarily the most interesting to tour, is **Moët et Chandon**, 18 av de Champagne (April to mid-Nov daily 9.30–11.30am & 2–4.30pm; mid-Nov to March Mon–Fri 9.30–11.30am & 2–4.30pm; €7.50 including *dégustation* of the brut Impérial; free for drivers), one of the keystones of the LVMH (Louis Vuitton, Moët and Hennessy) empire which owns Mercier, Veuve Clicquot, Krug and Ruinart, and a variety of other concerns, including Dior perfumes. In the champagne world Moët is known for its cut-throat business practices – having bought both Pommery and Lanson in good faith, the company quickly sold the names while keeping the vineyards associated with them. The house is also the creator of the iconic **Dom Perignon** label, with bottles aged for at least six years and priced from just over €100 a bottle. The tour is rather generic, beginning with a mawkish video, followed by a walk through the cellars, which are adorned with mementos of Napoleon (a good friend of the original M. Moët), and concluding with a tasting of their truly excellent champagne.

Just next door at no. 26 is **Perrier Jouët** (Mon–Fri 9–11.15am & 2–4.15pm; tour with tasting of the cuvée Belle Epoque €9, call or email in advance for more expensive vineyard tours Ⓣ03.26.53.38.10, Ⓦwww.perrier-jouet.com). Another upmarket brand, its Belle Epoque bottles are recognizable by the flowers painted on the exterior. The *maison* is beautiful, full of Art Nouveau furniture, paintings, and stained glass to match its bottles, while the tour here is much more personalized than at Moët et Chandon. At the other end of the scale, **Esterlin**, just across the street at 25 av de Champagne (daily 10am–noon & 2–5pm; free), will sit you down with a glass of free champagne in front of a ten-minute video, no questions asked.

Further up the street, **Mercier**, at 70 av de Champagne, runs a fairly rewarding tour around its cellars in an electric train (Mon–Fri 9.30–11.30am & 2–4.30pm, Sat & Sun 9.30–11.30am & 2–5pm; Dec–Feb closed Tues & Wed; €6, including *dégustation*). Nowadays Mercier is known as the lower-end champagne of French supermarkets, showing that M. Mercier was successful in his goal: he founded the house, aged 20, in 1858 with a plan to make champagne more accessible to the French people. In 1889 he carted a giant barrel that held 200,000 bottles' worth to the Paris Exposition, with the help of 24 oxen – only to be upstaged by the Eiffel Tower. The barrel is on display in the lobby – you can drop in to see it without taking the tour.

Castellane, by the station at 57 rue de Verdun (April–Oct daily 10am–noon & 2–6pm; €6.50 including *dégustation*), provides Épernay with its chief landmark: a tower looking like a kind of Neoclassical signal box. As well as the inevitable cellars, the visit shows off the working assembly lines that fill the champagne bottles, and the huge vats that hold the grape juice prior to fermentation. After the tour you can wander the little museum freely and climb the tower, which reveals a great view of the surrounding vineyards.

Épernay has a few other *grandes maisons* that can be visited by appointment, but perhaps more worthwhile are the many smaller houses. Since these houses have fewer employees it's best to call or email well in advance. Two which offer tours with *dégustation*, as well as visits to their vineyards, are located on rue Chaude-Ruelle, west of avenue de Champagne, with views over the town: **Leclerc-Briant** is at no. 67 (Ⓣ03.26.54.45.33, Ⓦwww.leclercbriant.com) For €6 they give a tour of their presshouse, museum and cellars, as well as a tasting of three vintages and a souvenir champagne glass. **Janisson-Baradon** is across the street at no. 65 (Ⓣ03.26.54.45.85, Ⓔinfo@champagne-janisson.com), and offers personalized tours and tastings for €5.

Eating and drinking

Restaurants in Épernay are not generally cheap, but good food is assured at *Au Bacchus Gourmet*, 21 rue Gambetta (*plats* from €16; Ⓣ03.26.51.11.44), a real treat with creative, gastronomic and surprisingly reasonably priced cuisine, and at the superb value *Les Berceaux*, 13 rue des Berceaux (menus from €28; Ⓣ03.26.55.28.84; closed Sun eve & Mon), which also has a wine bar. Several cheaper, culturally varied places are also on rue Gambetta, between the gare and place de la République: call in advance to squeeze into *La Cave à Champagne* at no. 16 (Ⓣ03.26.55.50.70; from €15), or stop in for inexpensive Italian at *Le Rimini* across the street at no. 17. For a major blowout, head 5km north on the N2051 to Champillon and the *Royal Champagne* (surprise *dégustation* menu at €95, weekday lunchtime menus from €25, and evening menus from €50; Ⓣ03.26.52.87.11), which also has luxurious rooms (❾) with vineyard views.

Around Épernay

The villages in the appealing vineyards of the Montagne de Reims, Côte des Blancs and Vallée de la Marne which surround Épernay promote a range of curiosities: the world's largest champagne bottle and cork in **Mardeuil**; the world's largest champagne glass and an artisan chocolate producer in **Pierry**; a snail farm in **Olizy-Violaine**; a museum of marriage in **Oger**; and a traditional *vigneron*'s house and early twentieth-century school room at **Oeuilly**. Many of the villages have conserved their sleepy old stone charm: **VERTUS**, 16km south of Épernay, is particularly pretty, and so too is **HAUTVILLERS**, 6km north of town, where you can see the abbey of Dom Pérignon fame (though it is unfortunately closed to the public). But the best reason for taking yourself out into the countryside is simply to view the vines and taste lesser known but often delicious champagnes, such as those made by Charlier & Fils, in an attractive *maison* surrounded by flowers at 4 rue des Pervenches, **MONTIGNY-SOUS-CHATILLON**, 15km west of Épernay (Ⓣ03.26.58.35.18, Ⓦwww.champagne-charlier.com). Full details of things to do around Épernay are available from the tourist office, along with lists of all the champagne producers, plus contacts for tours by horse-drawn carriage or hot-air balloon. Although there are regular local buses from Épernay's *gare routière*, various champagne excursions by minibus are touted at the tourist office and are a far more convenient way of seeing the area. The best of these (in French and English), lasting three hours and costing €20, is run by a local wine-grower from the Domi Moreau house in **MANCY** (ⓣ03.26.59.45.85, ⓔchampagne-domi.moreau@wanadoo.fr).

Troyes

TROYES was the ancient capital of the Champagne region, but lying an hour from the vineyards of Épernay and Reims to the north it is better known for its shopping outlets and museums than for its sparkling wines. Though Troyes is a sizeable city with plenty of noise and traffic, it is easy to find charm in its medieval half-timbered houses that lean into the streets and the cathedrals and churches that seem to materialize around every corner. The town is also the best place around to try the regional speciality, *andouillette* (see p.240).

Arrival, information and accommodation

The **gare SNCF** and **gare routière** are side by side off boulevard Carnot (part of the ring road). Not all buses use the main station, though, and if you're heading for the outlet stores or the countryside it's best to check first with the **tourist office** near the station at 16 bd Carnot (Mon–Sat 9am–12.30pm & 2–6.30pm; ⓣ03.25.82.62.70, ⓦwww.tourisme-troyes.com); or the town centre branch on rue Mignard facing the église St-Jean (Apr–May & mid-Sept to Oct Mon–Sat 9am–12.30pm & 2–6.50pm, Sun 10am–noon and 2–5pm; July to mid-Sept daily 10am–7pm; Nov–March Tues–Sat 9am–12.30pm & 2–6.30pm, Sun 10am–1pm; ⓣ03.25.73.36.88). For information concerning the Aube

Clothes shopping

Today the clothes industry still accounts for more than half Troyes' employment, and buying clothes from **factory outlets** is one of the town's chief attractions: designer-label clothes can be bought at two-thirds or less of the normal shop price. **Espace Belgrand** in rue Belgrand, off bd du 14-Juillet, has quite a range (Mon 2–7pm, Tues–Fri 10am–7pm, Sat 9am–7pm); rues Émile-Zola and des Bas Trévois are also worth a wander. Or better still you can go out to the manufacturers on the outskirts, where gigantic warehouse stores defy any preconceived notions about petite French boutiques. Dozens of factory shops sell clothes, shoes and leather goods designed for everyone, from Nike to Laura Ashley, Boss to Kenzo, and Yves St-Laurent to Jean-Paul Gaultier. The best array is in the four giant sheds of **Marques Avenue**, 114 bd de Dijon, St-Julien-les-Villas a couple of kilometres south of the city on the N71 to Dijon (Mon 2–7pm, Tues–Fri 10am–7pm, Sat 9.30am–7pm, some Sundays, extended hours during sale periods; ⓦwww.marquesavenue.com); there's also a special "shed" for household goods a few blocks towards town including luxury glass- and chinaware. At Pont-Ste-Marie, a short way to the northeast of Troyes along the D960 to Nancy, are **Marques City**, on rue Marc-Verdier (ⓦwww.marquescity.com), and **McArthur Glen**, on rue Danton (ⓦwww.mcarthurglen.fr), both with the same hours as Espace Belgrand. Buses for the outlets on the outskirts of town depart from the bus stops by Marché les Halles (ask at the tourist offices for details).

département, of which Troyes is the capital, consult Ⓦwww.aube-champagne.com or visit the Aube tourist office on place de la Libération (Mon–Fri 9.30am–12.30pm & 1.30–6pm). If you want to **rent a car** try ADA at 2, rue Voltaire near the station (Ⓣ03.25.73.41.68).

Places to stay around the station are plentiful, though for not much more you can find **accommodation** right in the centre of the old town. Outside term-time there may be room in the city's *foyers* for longer stays – the tourist office has details, along with information about *chambres d'hôtes* and places to stay in the wine villages around Troyes.

Hotels

Champs des Oiseaux/La Maison de Rhodes 20 rue Linard Gonthier Ⓣ03.25.80.58.50, Ⓦwww.champdesoiseaux.com. Two Renaissance houses near the cathedral transformed into a fine four-star boutique hotel with contemporary interior decor and a medieval touch. Tea and delicious cakes are served to non-guests in the patio or sitting-room. ❻–❽

Les Comptes de Champagne 56 rue de la Monnaie Ⓣ03.25.73.11.70. Central and charming two-star in a twelfth-century house with slanted floors. Friendly proprietors and covered parking. ❷

Grand Hôtel/Patiotel 4 av Mal-Joffre Ⓣ03.25.79.90.90, Ⓦwww.grand-hotel-troyes.com. Right opposite the station, a big three-star hotel with swimming pool and garden; "Patiotel" rooms are less grand (only two-star) and accordingly cheaper. ❸–❹

Le Relais St-Jean 51 rue Paillot-de-Montabert Ⓣ03.25.73.89.90, Ⓦwww.relais-st-jean.com. Posh hotel in a half-timbered building on a narrow street right in the centre. ❺

Royal 22 bd Carnot Ⓣ03.25.73.19.99, Ⓦwww.royal-hotel-troyes-com. Decent, pleasantly restored hotel behind a stern facade near the station; spacious bathrooms and a copious breakfast. ❹

Splendid 44 bd Carnot Ⓣ03.25.73.08.52, Ⓕ03.25.73.41.04. The best of the cheap places near the station; rooms have shower and TV. ❷

Du Théâtre 35 rue Jules-Lebocey Ⓣ03.25.73.18.47, Ⓕ03.25.73.85.73. In a quiet location virtually opposite the Théâtre Madeleine; friendly management and a good-value, old-fashioned brasserie downstairs. ❷

Hostel and campsite

HI hostel chemin Ste-Scholastique, Rosières Ⓣ03.25.82.00.65, Ⓦwww.fuaj.org/aj/troyes. Decent hostel located in a former fourteenth-century priory, 5.5km out of town on the Dijon road; take bus #8 direction "Rosières", stop "Liberté". Opposite the sign saying "Vielaines", a path leads down to the priory. Open year round; HI card required. Beds in 5–6-person dorms €8.80, breakfast and bedding extra.

Camping municipal 7 rue Roger-Salengro, Pont Ste-Marie Ⓣ/Ⓕ03.25.81.02.64. Attractive grassy campsite, situated 5km out on the N60 to Châlons, on the left, with good facilities including washing machines and children's play area. Minimum two-night reservation, closed mid-Oct to March.

The Town

The central part of Troyes between the station and the cathedral is scattered with marvellous churches, of which four stand out. Leading the way, and the

Museum pass

For €12 you can buy a **pass** to visit all of the city's museums, well worth the fee if you plan to visit the **Musée d'Art Moderne** (usually €5), **La Maison de l'Outil et de la Pensée Ouverte** (usually €6.50) and one other. The pass also includes a *dégustation* of two champagnes from a local shop, an hour's free parking, 30min of Internet use, and discount vouchers for the factory outlets. It's only valid for one visit to each establishment, but can be used over the course of a year. Buy it from the tourist office or in any of the city's museums. It's worth noting as well that all the museums are **free** for those under 18 and for students under 26.

first you come to, on rue de Vauluisant, is the sumptuous, high-naved church of **St-Pantaléon** (daily 10am–noon & 2–5pm; July & Aug till 6pm), almost a museum of sculpture. A short walk to the north is Troyes' oldest remaining church, twelfth-century **Ste-Madeleine**, on the road of the same name (same hours as St-Pantaléon). It was considerably remodelled in the sixteenth century, when the delicate stonework rood screen (*jubé*) – used to keep the priest separate from the congregation – was added; it's one of the few left in France. A short way to the southeast, between rues Émile-Zola and Champeaux and opposite the municipal tourist office, is the church of **St-Jean-au-Marché**. It's historically important as the church where Henry V of England married Catherine of France after being recognized as heir to the French throne in the 1420 Treaty of Troyes, known to the French as the "shameful treaty". Between it and the cathedral is the elegant Gothic **Basilique St-Urbain**, on place Vernier (same hours as St-Pantaléon), its exterior dramatizing the Day of Judgement.

Across the Canal de la Haute Seine lies the city's most outstanding museum, the **Musée d'Art Moderne** (Tues–Sun 11am–6pm; €5, or part of the museum pass, see box p.299), magnificently housed in the old bishops' palace next to the cathedral on place St-Pierre. The museum displays part of an extraordinary private collection, particularly rich in Fauvist paintings by the likes of Vlaminck and Derain (including the famous paintings of Hyde Park and Big Ben) – along with other first-class works by Degas, Courbet, Gauguin, Bonnard, Braque, Modigliani, Rodin, Robert Delaunay and Ernst. One room is given over to a beautiful collection of African masks and other carvings. Belonging to Pierre and Denise Lévy, the collection is not just impressive for its breadth, but for its impeccable taste and its depth, with several rooms devoted entirely to a single artist.

This is the ancient **quartier de la Cité**, an area with many of the city's oldest buildings, which all huddle around the **Cathédrale St-Pierre-et-St-Paul** (daily: July to mid-Sept 10am–7pm; mid-Sept to June 9am–noon & 2–5pm), whose pale Gothic nave is stroked with reflections from the wonderful stained-glass windows. On the other side of the cathedral from the Musée d'Art Moderne, at 1 rue Chrestien-de-Troyes, the once glorious **Abbaye St-Loup** houses the **Musée des Beaux-Arts** (daily except Tues 10am–noon & 2–6pm; €4 or part of museum pass scheme, see box p.299), seemingly endless galleries of mostly French paintings, including a couple by Watteau, an impressive collection of medieval sculpture, and some dismally displayed natural history and archeological exhibits. Down rue de la Cité, but with its entrance round the corner on quai des Comtes de Champagne, is the "**apothicairerie**", a richly decorated sixteenth-century pharmacy (Mon, Wed, Sat & Sun 10am–noon & 2–6pm; €4.60 or part of museum pass scheme, see box p.299) occupying one corner of the majestic eighteenth-century **Hôtel-Dieu-le-Comte**; rows of painted wooden "simple" boxes dating from the eighteenth century adorn its shelves.

Despite being raked by numerous fires since the Middle Ages, Troyes has retained many of its timber-framed buildings: to see them wander around the streets and alleyways of the old town, off the pedestrianized rue Champeaux, and around the maze of streets south of the main shopping thoroughfare, rue Émile-Zola. Indeed, the most famous fire, in 1524, led to a massive rebuilding scheme that resulted in Troyes' wealth of Renaissance palaces. An outstanding example, just to the east of the church of St Pantaléon, is the beautiful sixteenth-century Hôtel de Mauroy, 7 rue de la Trinité, once an orphanage, then a textile factory, but now occupied by the **Maison de l'Outil et de la Pensée Ouverte** (Mon 1–6pm, Tues–Sun 10am–6pm; €6.50 or part of the museum pass scheme, see box p.299). Troyes' most original tourist attraction by far, this surprisingly fascinating museum of tools, with exhibits from the seventeenth, eighteenth and nineteenth centuries, provides a window into the world of workers who used them and the people who crafted them. State-of-the-art techniques somehow transform shoals of hammers and spanners, flocks of axes and chisels, and myriad implements used by coopers, wheelwrights and tile-makers into jewel-like treasures.

Nearby, along rue Brunneval, lined with another row of wooden houses in varying states of repair, is Troyes' **synagogue**, inaugurated in the 1980s in memory of the Jewish scholar Rachi (1040–1105). He was a member of the small Jewish community which flourished for a time during the eleventh and twelfth centuries under the protection of the counts of Champagne. His commentaries on both the Old Testament and the Talmud are still important to academics today: the Rachi University Institute opposite is devoted to studying his work.

As tourist pamphlets are at pains to point out, the ring of boulevards round the town is shaped like a champagne cork. In fact it also looks a bit like a sock – a shape that's just as suitable, since hosiery ("bonneterie") and woollens have been Troyes' most important industry since the late Middle Ages. In the seventeenth century Louis XIII decreed that charitable houses had to be self-supporting and the orphanage of the Hôpital de la Trinité (the Hôtel de Mauroy) set its charges to knitting stockings. Some of the old machines and products used for creating garments can be seen in the sixteenth-century palace, the **Hôtel de Vauluisant**, part of which houses the **Musée de la Bonneterie** (4 rue de Vauluisant; June–Sept daily except Tues 10am–1pm & 2–6pm; Oct–May Wed–Sun 10am–noon & 2–6pm; €3 or part of the museum pass scheme, see box p.299); well restored and visually appealing, it sets an example for all crafts museums with its respect for traditions and lack of sentimentality. The palace also houses the **Musée Historique de Troyes et de la Champagne Méridionale** (same hours and ticket), which contains some fascinating and original religious paintings on wooden shutters. The exteriors are painted in black and white *trompe l'oeil*, but when thrown open (as they would be on holidays) reveal beautifully coloured paintings beneath. An impressively steep tower staircase leads to a cellar with a small exhibit of ceramic floor tiles.

Eating, drinking and entertainment

Central Troyes is packed with places to **eat**, mostly economical but unexciting. Along rue Champeaux there are several crêperies, and the themed restaurant *Le Gaulois* at no. 12 (☎03.25.43.90.27), where skewers of meat are grilled and served with bowls of sauces for €13. A great place to try the regional speciality of *andouillette* (see box on "Regional food and drink", p.240), along with delicious homestyle cooking, is the classic *Bistroquet* on place Langevin (menus from €16.50; ☎03.25.73.65.65; closed Sun eve). *La Marinière*, 3 rue de la Trinité behind the Musée d'Outil, has an oceanic theme and specializes in fish for those who'd prefer something lighter (☎03.25.73.77.29, closed Sun, from €11). Troyes' top restaurant is the gastronomic but reasonably priced *Le Valentino*, 11 cour de la Rencontre (menus €20 for lunch, from €29 for dinner; ☎03.25.73.14.14, reservations essential; closed Mon & Sat lunch, Sun dinner & for 3 weeks in Aug & Sept), whose inventive chef combines different flavours from all over the world.

Le Tricasse is a perennially popular **bar**, with tables and the occasional live band, at 2 rue Charbonnet, on the corner with narrow rue Paillot-de-Montabert, down which you'll find a few more bars, including the tiny and consistently packed-out *Bar des Bougnets des Pouilles*. Self-caterers should head for the Marché les Halles, a daily (except Sun) covered **market** on the corner of rue Général-de-Gaulle and rue de la République, close to the Hôtel de Ville. Vegetarians and the health-conscious will think they're in heaven at Coopérative Hermès, 39 rue Général-Saussier, an excellent healthfood store.

From late June to mid-September the city organizes a series of free **Ville en Lumière** concerts in outdoor venues around town – pick up a schedule at the tourist office.

The Plateau de Langres

The Seine, Marne, Aube and several other lesser rivers rise in the **Plateau de Langres** between Troyes and Dijon, with main routes from the former to the Burgundian capital skirting this area. To the east, the N19 (which the train follows) takes in **Chaumont** and **Langres**, two towns that could briefly slow your progress if you're in no hurry, and the childhood home village of General de Gaulle, **Colombey-Les-Deux-Églises**.

Chaumont

Situated on a steep ridge between the Marne and Suize valleys, **CHAUMONT** (Chaumont-en-Bassigny to give its full name), 93km east of Troyes, is best approached by train, which enables you to cross the town's stupendous mid-nineteenth-century viaduct.

The main ancient building to look at is the **Basilique St-Jean-Baptiste**. Built with the same dour, grey stone of most Champagne churches, it has, nevertheless, a wonderful Renaissance addition to the Gothic transept of balconies and turreted stairway. The decoration includes a fifteenth-century polychrome *Mise en Tombeau* with muddy tears but expressive faces, and an *Arbre de Jessé* of the early sixteenth-century Troyes school, in which all the characters are sitting in the tree, dressed in the style of the day.

You shouldn't leave without taking a look at **Les Silos**, 7–9 av Foch, near the *gare SNCF* (Tues, Thurs & Fri 2–7pm, Wed & Sat 10am–6pm; free), a 1930s agricultural co-op transformed into a graphic arts centre and médiathèque. As well as hosting temporary exhibitions, it's the main venue for Chaumont's international **poster festival** (Festival de l'Affiche), held every year from mid-May to mid-June. As for the rest of the old town, there's not much to do except admire the strange, bulging towers of the houses, through which the shapes of wide spiral staircases are visible.

The **tourist office** is on place de la Gare (Mon–Sat 9.30am–12.30pm, Sun 10am–noon & 2–5pm; ⓣ03.25.03.80.80). If you decide to stay, try *Le Terminus Reine*, on place Général Charles de Gaulle (ⓣ03.25.03.66.66, ⓕ03.25.03.28.95; ④), an old-fashioned hotel with great charm; its restaurant, *La Chaufferie*, is the best place to eat. For a cheap room, there's a small **hostel** at 1 rue Carcassonne (ⓣ03.25.03.22.77; bus #2 from the *gare SNCF* to La Suize; €10–12 including breakfast).

Colombey-Les-Deux-Églises

Twenty-seven kilometres northwest of Chaumont, on the N19 to Troyes, is **COLOMBEY-LES-DEUX ÉGLISES**, the village where Gaullist leaders come to pay homage at the grave of **General de Gaulle**. De Gaulle's family home, **La Boisserie**, is open to the public (Feb–Nov daily except Tues 10am–noon & 2–5.30pm; €4), but the most impressive memorial is the pink granite **Cross of Lorraine**, symbol of the French Resistance movement, standing over 40m high on a hill just west of the village, signposted off the N19.

The best place to **stay** here is the rather corporate *Les Dhuits*, which has a restaurant, on the main road (Ⓣ03.25.01.50.10, Ⓕ03.25.01.56.22; ❸; menu around €18). The restaurant at the *Auberge de la Montagne*, 17 rue de la Montagne (Ⓣ03.25.01.51.69; rooms ❸), is superior, however, with unusual dishes like turbot in a vanilla sauce.

Langres

LANGRES, 35km south of Chaumont and just as spectacularly situated above the Marne, suffered far less war damage and retains its encirclement of gateways, towers and ramparts. Walking this circuit, which gives views east to the hills of Alsace and southwest across the Plateau de Langres, is the best thing to do if you're just stopping for an hour or so. Don't miss the **St-Ferjeux tower** with its beautiful metal sculpture *Air and Dreams*. Wandering inside the walls is also rewarding – Renaissance houses and narrow streets give the feel of a place time has left behind, swathed in the mists of south Champagne. Langres was home to the eighteenth-century Enlightenment philosopher Diderot for the first sixteen years of his life, and people like to make the point that, if he were to return to Langres today, he'd have no trouble finding his way around.

The **Hôtel du Breuil de St-Germain**, one of the best of the town's sixteenth-century mansions at 2 rue Chambrûlard, is unfortunately closed for renovations but its museum collection can be visited in the **Musée d'Art et Histoire** on place du Centenaire, near the cathedral (daily: April–Oct 10am–noon & 2–6pm; Nov–March 10am–noon & 2–5pm; free). Head to level 1 of the new wing for the section devoted to Diderot, with his encyclopedias and various other first editions of his works, plus a portrait by Van Loos. Of the museum's own collection, the first part is devoted mainly to local archeology, with a rich Gallo-Roman section, but the highlight is the superbly restored Romanesque **chapel of St Didier**, incorporated into the old wing of the museum and containing a fourteenth-century painted ivory *Annunciation*. Sets of dining knives, a craft for which this area was famous for several centuries, are also on display along with other decorative arts. Local *faïence* – glazed terracotta – is featured, though these nicely crafted pieces are upstaged by the sixteenth-century tiles from Rouen in one of the nave chapels of the **Cathédrale St-Mammès**. This grey-stone edifice has not been improved by the eighteenth-century addition of a new facade, but there's an amusing sixteenth-century relief of the Raising of Lazarus, in which the apostles watch, totally blasé, while the locals look like kids at a good horror movie.

Practicalities

The **tourist office** is just inside the town's main gate, the **Porte des Moulins**, on place Bel'Air (May–Sept Mon–Sat 9am–noon & 1.30–6.30pm, Sun 10am–noon & 2–6pm; April & Oct Mon–Sat 9am–noon & 1.30–6pm; Nov–March Mon–Sat 9am–noon & 1.30–5.30pm; Ⓣ03.25.87.67.67, Ⓦwww.tourisme-langres.com), on the other side of town from the **gare SNCF** (infrequent connections to Troyes and Dijon); they can give you a useful map of the main sights in town, and also have information on the four lakes in the surrounding region. The bus timetable from the train station to the Porte des Moulins is loosely based on the train timetable; however, the last **bus** leaves at 7pm Monday to Friday, 4pm on Saturday and there's no connection on Sunday.

For **accommodation**, there's a **hostel** close by the Porte des Moulins on place Bel'Air (ⓣ03.25.87.09.69, ⓕ03.25.87.76.74; book ahead for Sat & Sun as the reception closes at weekends; €12 single room, €8 per person in double room; breakfast and bedding extra), and the reasonable *Auberge Jeanne d'Arc*, 26 rue Gambetta (ⓣ03.25.86.87.88, ⓦwww.aubergejeannedarc.com; ❷), in the centre of town. More comfortable rooms can be had at the characterful *Cheval Blanc*, in a converted church at 4 rue de l'Estrés (ⓣ03.25.87.07.00, ⓦwww.hotel-langres.com; ❹); or in the seventeenth-century, though rather less elegant, *Grand Hôtel de l'Europe*, 23–25 rue Diderot (ⓣ03.25.87.10.88, ⓕ03.25.87.60.65; ❸). For good but expensive **food**, try *Restaurant Diderot* at the *Cheval Blanc* (closed Tues eve & Wed lunch). Better value is to be had at the *Lion d'Or* (ⓣ03.25.87.03.30), a restaurant and hotel just outside the town on the route de Vesoul with views of the surrounding lakes. Langres has its own excellent bright-orange cheese which you can buy at the Friday **market** on place Jenson.

The Ardennes

To the northeast of Reims, the scenery of the **Ardennes** region along the Meuse valley knocks spots off any landscape in Champagne. Most of the hills lie over the border in Belgium, but there's enough of interest on the French side to make it well worth exploring.

In war after war, the people of the Ardennes have been engaged in protracted last-ditch battles down the valley of the Meuse, which, once lost, gave invading armies a clear path to Paris. The rugged, hilly terrain and deep forests (frightening even to Julius Caesar's legionnaires) gave some advantage to World War II's Resistance fighters when the Ardennes was annexed to Germany, but even peacetime living has never been easy. The land is unsuitable for crops, and the slateworks and ironworks, which were the main source of employment during the nineteenth century, were closed in the 1980s. The only major investment in the region has been a nuclear power station in the loop of the Meuse at Chooz, to which locals responded by etching "Nuke the Élysée!" high on a half-cut cliff of slate just downstream.

Tourism, the main growth industry, is developing apace – there are walking and boating possibilities, plus good train and bus connections – though the eerie isolated atmosphere of this region remains.

Charleville-Mézières

The twin towns of **CHARLEVILLE** and **MÉZIÈRES** provide a good starting point for exploring the northern part of the region, which spreads across the meandering Meuse before the valley closes in and the forests take over. Of the two, Charleville is the one to head for.

The **place Ducale**, in the centre of Charleville, was the result of the seventeenth-century local duke's envy of the contemporary place des Vosges in Paris. Despite the posh setting, the shops in the arcades remain very down-to-earth – *poissonnières* amongst them – and the cafés charge reasonable prices to sit outside: a very good position on Tuesdays, Thursdays and Saturdays, when the **market** is held here.

From 31 place Ducale you can reach the complex of old and new buildings that house the **Musée de l'Ardenne** (Tues–Sun 10am–noon & 2–6pm; €4 combined ticket with Musée Arthur Rimbaud, see below), which covers the different economic activities of the region over the ages through local paintings, prehistoric artefacts, legends, puppetry, weapons and coins. You need to keep up a good pace to get round all the rooms, but it's fun and informative.

The most famous person to emerge from the town was Arthur Rimbaud (1854–91), who ran away from Charleville four times before he was 17, so desperate was he to escape from its quiet provincialism. He is honoured in the **Musée Arthur Rimbaud**, housed in a very grand stone windmill – a contemporary of the place Ducale – on quai Arthur-Rimbaud, two blocks north of the main square (Tues–Sun 10am–noon & 2–6pm; €4 combined ticket with Musée de l'Ardenne, see above). It contains a host of pictures of him and people he hung out with, including his lover Verlaine, as well as facsimiles of his writings and related documents. A few steps down the quayside is the spot where he composed his most famous poem, *Le Bateau Ivre*. After penning poetry in Paris, journeying to the Far East and trading in Ethiopia and Yemen, Rimbaud died in a Marseille hospital. His body was brought back to his home town – probably the last place he would have wanted to be buried – and true Rimbaud fanatics can visit his **tomb** in the cemetery west of the place Ducale at the end of avenue Charles Boutet.

Charleville is also a major international **puppetry centre** (its school is justly famous), and every three years it hosts one of the largest puppet festivals in the world, the **Festival Mondial des Théâtres de Marionnettes** (details can be found at Ⓦwww.marionnette.com). As many as 150 professional troupes – some from as far away as Mali and Burma – put on something like fifty shows a day on the streets and in every available space in town. Tickets are cheap, and there are shows for adults as well as the usual stuff aimed at kids. If you miss the festival you can still catch one of the puppet performances in the summer months every year (Ⓣ03.24.33.72.50 for booking and information, tickets around €12), or if you're passing by the **Institut de la Marionnette** between 10am and 9pm, you can see one of the automated episodes of the *Four Sons of Aymon* enacted on the facade's clock every hour, or all twelve scenes on Saturday at 9.15am.

Practicalities

From the **gare SNCF**, place Ducale is a five-minute ride away on bus #1, #3 or #5; the **gare routière** is a couple of blocks northeast of the square, between rues du Daga and Noël. The **regional tourist office** for the Ardennes is at 22 place Ducale (July & Aug Mon–Sat 9am–7pm, Sun 10am–7pm; Sept–June Mon–Sat 9am–12.30pm & 1.30–7pm, Sun 2–7pm; Ⓣ03.24.56.06.08), with Charleville-Mézières' **tourist office** at no. 4 (June–Aug Mon–Fri 9.30am–noon & 1.30–7pm, Sat & Sun 9.30am–noon & 1.30–6pm; Sept–May Mon–Sat 9.30am–noon & 1.30–6pm; Ⓣ03.24.55.69.90, Ⓔcharl.mez@wanadoo.fr).

Three fairly central **hotels** that are worth trying are the *Hôtel de Paris*, 24 av G.-Corneau (Ⓣ03.24.33.34.38, Ⓦwww.hoteldeparis08.fr; ❷); the *Central*, 23 av du Maréchal Leclerc (Ⓣ03.24.33.33.69, Ⓕ03.24.59.38.25; ❸); and *Le Relais du Square*, 3 place de la Gare (Ⓣ03.24.33.38.76, Ⓕ03.24.33.56.66; ❸; closed Sat & Sun), a smart two-star hotel in a tree-filled square near the station. The town **campsite**, *Camping du Mont Olympe* (Ⓣ03.24.33.23.60, Ⓔcamping-charlevill emezieres@wanadoo.fr; open May–mid-Oct) is north of place Ducale, over the river and left along rue des Paquis. There are plenty of places to **eat and drink** in Charleville. For something a bit special, *La Côte à l'Os*, at 11 cours

Aristide-Briand (☎03.24.59.20.16), specializes in *fruits de mer* and local cuisine, in which juniper-flavoured game is the star; daily chalkboard menus cost from €13.50. *La Cigogne*, at 40 rue Dubois-Crancé (☎03.24.33.25.39; closed Sun eve, Mon & first week Aug), also serves good regional dishes, with menus again from €13.50. At 33 rue du Moulin, *La Clef des Champs* (☎03.24.56.17.50) offers menus from €15 and is known for family cooking.

North of Charleville

George Sand wrote of the stretch of the Meuse that winds through the Ardennes that "its high wooded cliffs, strangely solid and compact, are like some inexorable destiny that encloses, pushes and twists the river without permitting it a single whim or any escape". What all the tourist literature emphasises, however, are the legends of medieval struggles between Good and Evil whose characters have given names to some of the curious rocks and crests. The grandest of these, where the schist formations have taken the most peculiar turns, is the **Roc de la Tour**, also known as the **Devil's Castle**, up a path off the D31, 3.5km out of **MONTHERMÉ**, a slate-roofed little town with nothing of great interest except a twelfth-century church with late medieval frescoes.

The journey through this frontier country should ideally be done on foot or skis, or **by boat**. The alternatives for the latter are good old *bateau-mouche*-type cruises (RDTA; April–June & Sept–Oct weekends only; July & Aug Tues–Sun; ☎03.24.33.77.77, Ⓦwww.rdta.fr), which depart from the Vieux Moulin (Musée Rimbaud) in Charleville-Mézières and the quai des Paquis in Monthermé, or live-in pleasure boats – not wildly expensive if you can split the cost four or six ways. These are rented out, with bikes on board, by Ardennes Plaisance in Charleville-Mézières, 76 rue des Forges-St-Charles (☎03.24.56.47.61), and Ardennes Nautisme in **SEDAN**, 16 rue du Château (☎03.24.27.05.15, Ⓦwww.ardennes-nautisme.com), the next town downstream from Charleville. The latter moor their boats just east of Dom-Le-Mesnil on the D764 at the junction of the Meuse and the Canal des Ardennes. The regional tourist office at Charleville (see p.305) can provide information on hiking, canoeing, biking or riding. For **public transport** from Charleville, trains follow the Meuse into Belgium, and a few buses run up to Monthermé and **LES HAUTES-RIVIÈRES**, the latter on the River Semoy.

The **GR12** is a good walking route, circling the **Lac des Vieilles Forges**, 17km northwest of Charleville, then meeting the Meuse at Bogny and crossing over to Hautes-Rivières in the even more sinuous **Semoy Valley**. There are plenty of other tracks, too, though beware of chasse (hunting) signs – French hunters tend to hack through the undergrowth with their safety catches off and are notoriously trigger-happy. Wild boar are the main quarry being hunted – they are nowhere near as dangerous as their pursuers, and would seem to be more intelligent, too, rooting about near the crosses of the Resistance memorial near **REVIN**, while hunters stalk the forest at a respectful distance. A good place to stay, overlooking the river at Revin, is the *Hôtel François-1er*, 46 quai Camille-Desmoulins (☎03.24.40.15.88, Ⓕ03.24.40.32.93; ❸), which rents out bikes and canoes, and gives good advice on walks.

The abundance of wild boar is partly explained when you rummage around on the forest floor yourself and discover, between the trees to either side of the river, an astonishing variety of mushrooms, and, in late summer, wild strawberries and bilberries. For a quaint insight into life in the forest, stop in at the **Musée de la Forêt**, situated right on the edge of the Ardennes, 2km north of

RENWEZ on the D40 (☎03.24.54.82.66, March–May & mid-Sept to mid-Nov daily 9am–noon & 2–5pm; June to mid-Sept daily 9am–7pm; mid-Nov to Feb Mon–Fri 9am–noon & 2–5pm; €8). All manner of wood-cutting, gathering and transporting is enacted by wooden dummies along with displays of utensils and flora and fauna of the forest; it's also a tranquil spot for a picnic.

Travel details

Trains

Amiens to: Arras (10 daily; 40–50min); Compiègne (5 daily; 1hr 20min); Laon (6 daily; 1hr 40min); Lille (frequent; 1hr 20min); Paris (hourly; 1hr 20min); St-Quentin (5 daily; 1hr).
Arras to: Albert (10 daily; 25min); Douai (very frequent; 15–30min); Paris (frequent; 50min); Lille (several daily; 1hr).
Beauvais to: Paris (hourly; 1hr 10min).
Boulogne-Ville to: Amiens (8 daily; 1hr 15min); Arras (4 daily; 2hr–2hr 30min); Calais-Ville (very frequent; 30min); Étaples-Le Touquet (hourly; 20min); Montreuil-sur-Mer (7 daily; 30–40min); Paris (8 daily; 2hr 40min; very frequent connections to Calais for TGV; 2hr 10min).
Calais-Ville to: Boulogne-Ville (very frequent; 30min); Étaples-Le Touquet (9 daily; 1hr); Lille via the Calais-Fréthun Eurostar station (3 daily; 30min, otherwise frequent; 1hr–1hr 50min); Paris (TGV 6 daily; 1hr 30min).
Compiègne to: Paris (frequent; 40–50min).
Dunkerque to: Arras (10 daily; 1hr 20min); Calais-Ville (frequent; 1hr–1hr 15min via Hazebrouck); Paris (TGV frequent; 2hr 20min via Arras).
Laon to: Paris (8 daily; 1hr 40min–2hr); Reims (10 daily; 40min); Soissons (1 hourly; 30min).
Lille to: Arras (TGV frequent; 40 min; otherwise very frequent; 40min–1hr); Brussels (TGV 6 daily; 40min); Cambrai (frequent, mostly via Douai; 1hr); Douai (very frequent; 20–30min); London (Eurostar 6 daily; 1hr 40min); Lyon (TGV 7 daily; 3hr–3hr 30min; or 4hr via Paris); Marseille (TGV several daily; 4hr 50min–6hr, sometimes via Lyon); Paris (TGV 1 hourly; 1hr); St-Quentin (hourly; 1hr 30min–2hr, often via Douai).
Reims to: Charleville-Mézières (almost hourly; 50min); Épernay (frequent; 30min); Paris (frequent; 1hr 30min–2hr).
St-Quentin to: Compiègne (frequent; 30–50min); Paris (8 daily; 1hr 15min–1hr 45min).
Troyes to: Chaumont (hourly; 50min); Langres (6 daily; 1hr 15min); Paris (frequent; 1hr 30min).

Buses

Amiens to: Abbeville (2 daily; 1hr 30min); Albert (4 daily; 40min); Arras (2 daily; 2hr); Beauvais (4 daily; 1hr 15min).
Boulogne to: Calais (4 daily; 1hr); Le Touquet (4 daily; 1hr).
Calais to: Boulogne (4 daily; 1hr); Le Touquet (4 daily; 2hr).
Dunkerque to: Calais (2–9 daily; 30min).
Reims to: Troyes (1–3 daily; 2hr 30min).

Ferries

See "Basics".

3

Alsace, Lorraine and the Jura mountains

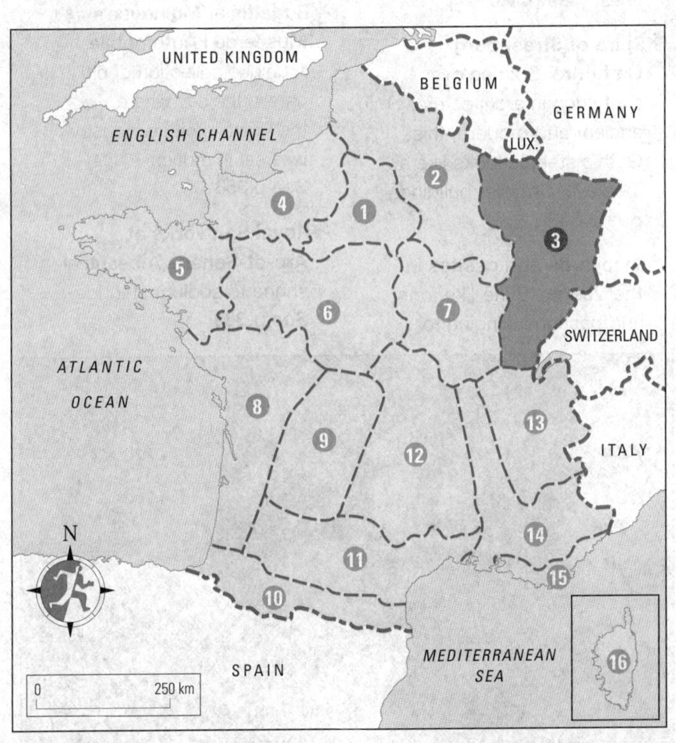

CHAPTER 3

Highlights

✱ **Chagall windows, Metz Cathedral** Moses & Co captured in glorious technicolour glass. See p.316

✱ **Place Stanislas, Nancy** The height of eighteenth-century elegance makes this city square one of the world's finest. See p.326

✱ **Spire of Strasbourg Cathedral** Soaring over a city rich in architecture, ancient and modern, this Gothic steeple looks like a medieval Chrysler building. See p.333

✱ **Vineyards and castles in the Vosges** Eyrie-like forts and bastions clinging to craggy peaks along the Alsatian Wine Route. See p.343

✱ **The Issenheim Altarpiece, Colmar** Luridly expressive, this Renaissance masterpiece alone makes picturesque Colmar worth a visit. See p.350

✱ **Bugattis at Mulhouse's Musée de l'Automobile** A unique collection of old cars in the city where the French voiture industry was set in motion. See p.353

✱ **Royal Saltworks at Arc-et-Senans** A beautiful shrine to sodium chloride. See p.363

△ Hunawihr

3

Alsace, Lorraine and the Jura mountains

France's eastern frontier provinces, **Alsace** and **Lorraine**, plus lesser-known **Franche-Comté** where the Jura mountains lie, have had a complex and tumultuous history. For a thousand years they were a battleground, disputed through the Middle Ages by independent dukes and bishops whose allegiance was endlessly contested by the kings of France and the princes of the Holy Roman Empire, and were the scene, in the twentieth century, of some of the worst fighting of both world wars.

The democratically minded burghers of **Alsace** had already created a plethora of well-heeled, semi-autonomous towns for themselves centuries before their seventeenth-century incorporation into the French state. Sharing the Germans' taste for Hansel-and-Gretel-type decoration, they adorned their buildings with all manner of frills and fancies – oriel windows, carved timberwork and Toytown gables – and with Teutonic orderliness they still maintain them, festooned with flowers and in pristine condition. Not that you should ever call an Alsatian German. Many people converse in Elsässisch, a Germanic dialect, but their neighbours across the Rhine have behaved in a decidedly unneighbourly fashion twice in the last 130 years, annexing them, along with much of Lorraine, from 1870 to 1918, and again from 1940 to 1944 under Hitler's Third Reich. Locals remain fiercely and proudly Alsatian, European and French – in that order.

The combination of influences makes for a culture and atmosphere as distinctive as any in France. It's seen at its most vivid in the numerous little wine towns that punctuate the **Route du Vin** along the eastern margin of the wet and woody Vosges mountains; at quaint **Colmar**; and in the great cathedral city of **Strasbourg**, now one of the capitals of the European Union. But the province is not just a photogenic setting for coach tours: it's also a densely populated industrial powerhouse, making cars, textiles, machine tools and telephones, as well as half the beer in France.

By comparison, **Lorraine**, a large region taking in the northern border shared with Luxembourg, Germany and Belgium, is rather colourless, although it has suffered much the same vicissitudes as Alsace. However, the elegant eighteenth-century town of **Nancy**, the cathedral city and provincial capital **Metz**, and the depressing but unforgettable World War I battlefields near **Verdun** are well worth visiting.

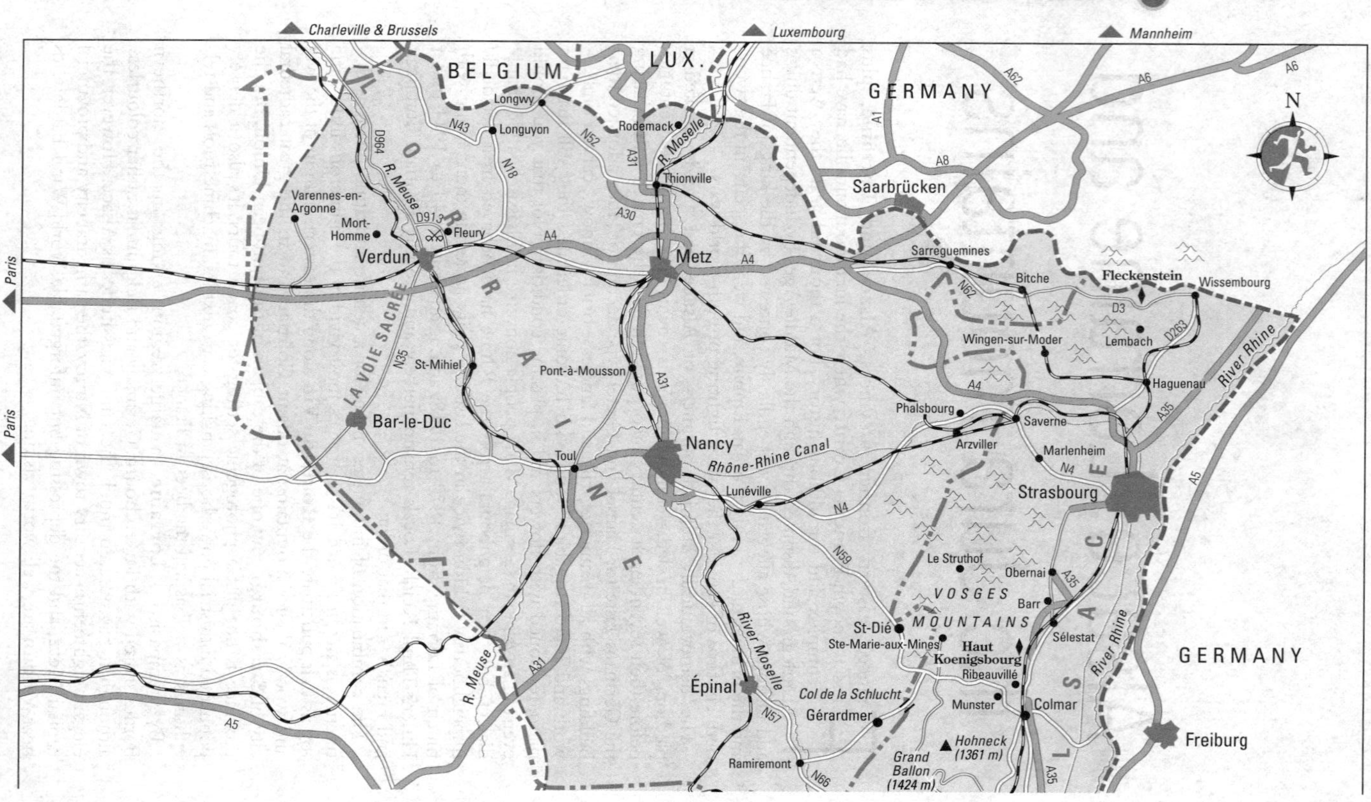
Charleville & Brussels
Luxembourg
Mannheim
BELGIUM
LUX.
GERMANY
N
Longwy
Longuyon
Rodemack
R. Moselle
Thionville
Saarbrücken
Varennes-en-Argonne
Mort-Homme
R. Meuse
Fleury
Verdun
Metz
Sarreguemines
Bitche
Fleckenstein
Wissembourg
Lembach
Wingen-sur-Moder
Haguenau
River Rhine
LA VOIE SACRÉE
St-Mihiel
Pont-à-Mousson
Phalsbourg
Saverne
Arzviller
Marlenheim
Bar-le-Duc
Toul
Nancy
Rhône-Rhine Canal
Lunéville
Strasbourg
LORRAINE
ALSACE
Le Struthof
Obernai
VOSGES
Barr
MOUNTAINS
Sélestat
St-Dié
Ste-Marie-aux-Mines
Haut Koenigsbourg
Ribeauvillé
River Moselle
Épinal
Col de la Schlucht
Munster
Colmar
Gérardmer
Hohneck (1361 m)
Grand Ballon (1424 m)
Ramiremont
R. Meuse
Freiburg
GERMANY
Paris
Paris
A1
A4
A5
A6
A8
A30
A31
A35
A62
D3
D263
D913
D964
N4
N18
N35
N43
N52
N57
N59
N62
N66

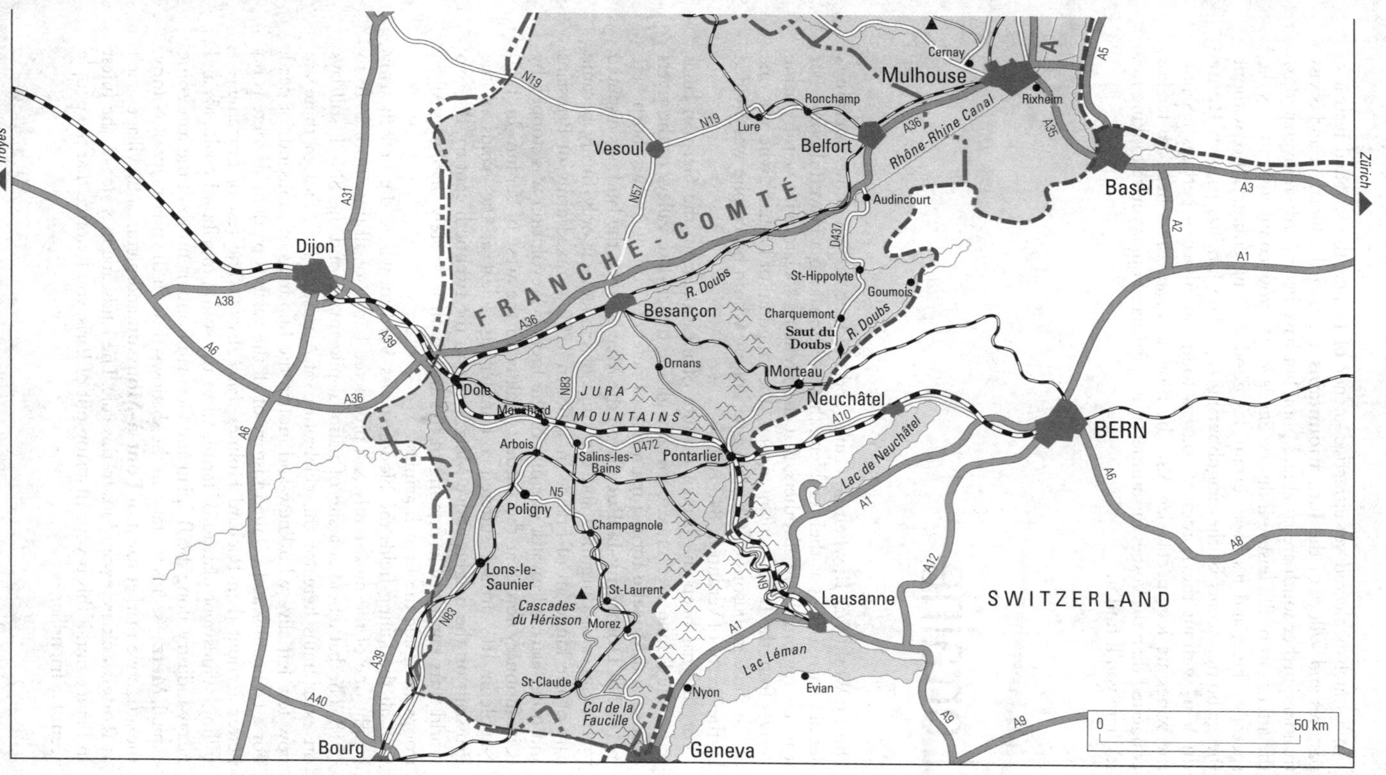

Troyes
Zürich
Mulhouse
Cernay
Rixheim
Basel
A5
A35
A3
A2
A1
A36
Rhône-Rhine Canal
Ronchamp
Lure
N19
Belfort
Vesoul
N57
Audincourt
D437
FRANCHE-COMTÉ
Dijon
A31
A38
A6
A39
A36
R. Doubs
Besançon
St-Hippolyte
Goumois
Charquemont
Saut du Doubs
Ornans
Morteau
Neuchâtel
A10
Dole
JURA MOUNTAINS
N83
Arbois
Salins-les-Bains
D472
Pontarlier
Lac de Neuchâtel
BERN
A6
A8
Poligny
N5
Champagnole
Lons-le-Saunier
St-Laurent
Cascades du Hérisson
Morez
N9
Lausanne
A12
SWITZERLAND
A1
Lac Léman
Nyon
Evian
St-Claude
Col de la Faucille
A40
Bourg
Geneva
A9
0
50 km

In a much neglected yet attractive corner of France, the wooded plateaux, pastures and valleys of the **Jura mountains** abutting the German and Swiss frontiers further south are rural and poor, but have been partly rejuvenated by the attentions of the leisure industry. *Ski de fond* – cross-country skiing – is the speciality here, and it's ideal terrain. It's good walking country, too, without the grinding ascents of the neighbouring Alps. The Jura has its own **Route du Vin**, without the hordes of tourists found in Alsace – perhaps because the wines are less spectacular. Also the mountains and lakes here are far less congested than the Vosges in summer; if it's peace and quiet you're looking for, it's here you'll find it.

Lorraine

During World War II, when de Gaulle and the Free French chose **Lorraine**'s double-barred cross as their emblem, they were making a powerful point. For it is this region, above all others, that the French associate with war. Its name derives from the Latin, *Lotharii regnum*, "the kingdom of Lothar", who was one of the three grandsons of Charlemagne, among whom his empire was divided by the Treaty of Verdun in 843 AD.

Lorraine has been the principal route of invasion from the German lands across the Rhine ever since, even though the trench-like valleys of the rivers **Meuse** and **Moselle** form a main line of defence. Joan of Arc was born here in 1412, at **Domrémy-la-Pucelle** on the Meuse, when the land was disputed by the dukes of Burgundy and the kings of France – it only finally became part of the kingdom of France in 1766. In 1792 a mixed army of Prussians and other alarmed royalist enemies of the French Revolution was stopped by Revolutionary forces at the battle of Valmy to the west of Verdun. In 1870 Napoléon III's armies suffered a humiliating defeat at the hands of the Prussians on the heights above Metz. Then, in the twentieth century, the two world wars saw terrible fighting in the area, both ultimately involving Allied troops alongside the French armies.

Of all the killing fields the bloodiest was **Verdun**, where the French army fought one of the most costly and protracted battles of all time from 1916 to 1918. The battlefield is a site of national pilgrimage, and the SNCF still lays on extra trains here for the celebration of Armistice Day, though there are now few left alive who knew and mourn the hundreds of thousands of dead. For a fascinating and detailed history of all the various battlefields there is no better account than Richard Holmes' *Fatal Avenue*. The rest of Lorraine – a rolling, windswept plateau of farmland to the south, moribund coalfields and heavy industry along the Belgian and German frontiers north of the handsome capital, **Metz** – seems to stand in the shadows, though the smart city of **Nancy**, the attractive market town of **Pont-à-Mousson** and picturesque villages such as **Rodemack** are exceptions to this rule. The landscape may not be the finest in France but, if this is your first stop out of Paris, you'll notice that the people seem far friendlier.

Metz and around

METZ (pronounced "Mess"), the capital of Lorraine, lies on the east bank of the River Moselle, close to the Autoroute de l'Est, linking Paris and Strasbourg, and the main Strasbourg to Brussels train line. Its origins go back at least to Roman times, when, as now, it stood astride major trade routes. On the death of Charlemagne it became the capital of Lothar's portion of his empire, managing to maintain its prosperity in spite of the dynastic wars that followed. By the Middle Ages it had sufficient wealth and strength to proclaim itself an independent republic, which it remained until its absorption into France in 1552.

A frontier town caught between warring influences, Metz has endured more than its share of historical hand-changing. In 1870, when Napoléon III's defeated armies were forced to surrender to Kaiser Wilhelm I, it was ceded to Germany. It recovered its liberty at the end of World War I in 1918, only to be re-annexed by Hitler in 1940 before being liberated again by Allied troops in 1944.

Although its only really important sight is the magnificent **cathedral**, Metz is not at all the dour place you might expect from its northern geography and industrial background – indeed it deserves its self-styled title of *Ville jardin* or Garden City, with impeccable flower-beds, the warm hues of mustard-yellow stone buildings and the waters of the Moselle all making for an appealing cityscape. The university founded here in the 1970s is at least partly responsible for its liveliness.

Arrival, information and accommodation

The huge granite **gare SNCF** stands opposite the **post office** at the end of rue Gambetta. The **gare routière** is east of the train station and on the other side of the railway tracks on avenue de l'Amphithéâtre. The **tourist office** (July & Aug Mon–Sat 9am–9pm, Sun 10am–1pm & 3–5pm; Sept–June Mon–Sat 9am–7pm, Sun 10am–1pm & 3–5pm; ⓣ03.87.55.53.76, ⓕ03.87.36.59.43, ⓦwww.ot-metz.fr) is located by the side of the Hôtel de Ville on place d'Armes in the old town. Almost any bus from the station will take you there.

There's a good range of hotels and budget **accommodation** in Metz, including an HI hostel, foyer (the tourist office has information about other foyers available in summer) and campsite, as well as the odd ritzy establishment. The several reasonable hotels in front of the train station tend to fill up fast in season.

Hotels

De la Cathédrale 25 place de Chambre ⓣ03.87.75.00.02, ⓕ03.87.75.40.75. Charming hotel with original beams and stained-glass windows in a wonderful location opposite the cathedral. ❺

Du Centre 14 rue Dupont-des-Loges ⓣ03.87.36.06.93, ⓕ03.87.75.60.66. A well-established, comfortably modernized hotel between rue des Clercs and place St-Louis. ❸

Grand-Hôtel de Metz 3 rue des Clercs ⓣ03.87.36.16.33, ⓕ03.87.60.40.38. An ancient, characterful establishment, near the cathedral in the heart of the old town, with friendly staff. ❸

Lafayette 24 rue des Clercs ⓣ03.87.75.21.09. Cheap and cheerful place on the busy shopping street leading from place de la République to the cathedral. ❷

Métropole 5 place du Général-de-Gaulle ⓣ03.87.66.26.22, ⓕ03.87.66.29.91. Not a particularly welcoming place but fine for a stopover, located directly in front of the station. ❷

Moderne 1 rue Lafayette ⓣ03.87.66.57.33, ⓕ03.87.55.98.59. Functional and friendly hotel, just a short distance to the left as you come out of the station. ❸

Du Théâtre 3 rue du Pont-St-Marcel, Île Chambière ⓣ03.87.31.10.10, ⓕ03.87.30.04.66, ⓦwww.port-saint-marcel.com. Smart hotel in an exquisite location on the island in the Moselle below the cathedral. Facilities include a swimming pool. ❼

Hostels and campsite

Camping municipal allée de Metz-Plage, Île Chambière ⓣ03.87.68.26.48, ⓕ03.87.38.03.39. Quiet, grassy campsite right next door to *Metz Plage* (see below). Open May–Sept.

Carrefour 6 rue Marchant ⓣ03.87.75.07.26, ⓔascarrefour@wanadoo.fr. Friendly and conveniently located HI hostel (membership compulsory), with double rooms and dorms, close to place d'Armes and the cathedral. You may want to take your own sheets, as the ones provided here are of disposable paper, but comfortable enough. Internet access available.

Metz Plage 1 allée de Metz-Plage, Île Chambière ⓣ03.87.30.44.02, ⓕ03.87.33.19.80. Clean, friendly hostel on the island by the bridge at the further end of rue Belle-Isle which crosses the end of rue du Pont-St-Marcel. Bus #3 or #11 (stop "Pontiffroy") from the *gare SNCF*. €12.30 including breakfast.

The City

Metz in effect is two towns: the original French quarters, gathered round the cathedral, and the Ville allemande, undertaken as part of a once-and-for-all process of Germanification after the Prussian occupation in 1870. The latter, unmistakably Teutonic in style, has considerable elegance and grandeur. The gare SNCF sets the tone, a vast and splendid granite structure of 1870 in Rhenish Romanesque, which looks like a bizarre cross between a Scottish laird's hunting lodge and a dungeon. Its gigantic dimensions reflect the Germans' long-term strategic intention to use it as the fulcrum of their military transport system in subsequent wars against the French. It's matched in style by the post office opposite as well as by some imposing bourgeois apartment buildings in the surrounding streets. The whole quarter was meant to serve as a model of superior town planning, in contrast to the squalid Latin hugger-mugger of the old French neighbourhoods, which begin five minutes' walk to the north in place de la République.

The place de la République is a main parking area, bounded on the east side by shops and cafés, with army barracks to the south and the formal gardens of the **Esplanade**, overlooking the Moselle, to the west. To the right, as you look down the esplanade from the square, is the handsome classical **Palais de Justice** in the city's characteristic yellow stone. To the left, a gravel drive leads past the old arsenal, now converted into a prestigious concert hall by the postmodernist architect Ricardo Bofill. It continues to the **church of St-Pierre-aux-Nonnains**, not much to look at but claiming to be one of the oldest churches in France, with elements from the fourth century. Nearby is another historic church: the octagonal thirteenth-century **Chapelle des Templiers**.

From the north side of place de la République, **rue des Clercs** cuts through the attractive, bustling and largely pedestrianized heart of the old city, where most of the shops are located. Past the **place St-Jacques**, with its numerous outdoor cafés, you come to the eighteenth-century **place d'Armes**, where the lofty Gothic **Cathedral of St-Étienne** towers above the pedimented and colonnaded classical facade of the Hôtel de Ville. It boasts the third tallest nave in France – after Beauvais and Amiens cathedrals – but its best feature is without doubt the stained glass, both medieval and modern, including windows by Chagall in the north transept and ambulatory.

From the cathedral, a short walk up rue des Jardins brings you to the city's main museum complex, the **Musées de la Cour d'Or**, 2 rue du Haut-Poirier (Mon & Wed–Fri 9am–5pm, Sat & Sun 10am–5pm; €4.60, free Sun 11am–1pm, Wed 10am–1pm), a treasurehouse of Gallo-Roman sculpture, but equally strong on mock-ups of vernacular architecture from the medieval and Renaissance periods. The art museum is less impressive, although it includes works by Corot and Delacroix. When the complex was extended in the 1930s, the remains of Roman baths were discovered, and they are now one of the most interesting things about the museums.

For the city's most compelling townscape, as well as the most dramatic view of the cathedral, you have only to go down to the river bank and cross to the tiny **Île de la Comédie**, dominated by its classical eighteenth-century square and theatre (the oldest in France) and a rather striking Protestant church erected under the German occupation. An older and equally beautiful square is the **place St-Louis** with its Gothic arcades some ten minutes' walk to the east of the cathedral along rue En-Fournirue. On the way, wander up into the Italianate streets climbing the **hill of Ste-Croix** to your left, the legacy of the Lombard bankers who came to run the city's finances in the thirteenth century. It's worth continuing east from the place des Paraiges, at the end of rue En-Fournirue, down the rue des Allemands to have a look at the **Porte des Allemands** – a massive, fortified double gate that once barred the eastern entrances to the medieval city.

After a long day, you'll have no trouble finding a pleasant café or bar to relax in. **Rue des Jardins** has some interesting shops – clothes, records and antiques – and at night, the cathedral and other significant buildings are lit up, making for a pleasant late stroll.

Eating and drinking

Eating is easy in Metz, with lots of cafés on place St-Jacques that are popular with locals and tourists and some excellent restaurants in the old city. For night-time **drinking**, you'll find plenty of bars, clubs and music venues.

Restaurants

Café de l'Abreuvoir 8 rue de l'Abreuvoir, near place St-Louis. Cosy, noisy and fashionable place, with a very French atmosphere and simple, good wine-bar fare (*andouillette* and *quiche lorraine* at around €9 per plat).

La Fleur de Lys 5 rue des Piques ☎03.87.36.64.51. Charming restaurant between the cathedral and the river offering traditional French food, with excellent service. Menus change regularly and cost from €18.50. Closed Sat lunch & Sun.

Du Pont-St-Marcel 1 rue du Pont-St-Marcel, Île Chambière ☎03.87.30.12.29. A seventeenth-century establishment on the island, distinctive for its excellent regional cuisine and staff dressed in regional costume. Menus at €18 and €28, including eel and suckling-pig, and wines from the French Moselle. Closed Sun eve & Mon.

Le Relais des Tanneurs 2bis rue des Tanneurs, off the end of rue En-Fournirue ☎03.87.75.49.09. Unpretentious restaurant, serving traditional French dishes. Lots of specialities, including mussels, scallops and *ris de veau*, menus €12–25, *carte* around €20, *plats du jour* €9–14. Closed Sun & Aug 1–15.

Des Roches 29 rue des Roches ☎03.87.74.06.51. Wonderfully located by the river, this old-fashioned inn serves up traditional fare (*plats* from €14), including fish selected from a tank. Closed Sun & Mon eves.

À la Ville de Lyon 7 rue Piques ☎03.87.36.07.01. Located just below the cathedral, this restaurant specializes in the best traditional cooking. The atmosphere is quite formal and jeans are frowned upon. From €32. Closed Mon, Sun eve & Aug.

Cafés and bars

Comédie Café quai Vautris, just across the Pont-Des-Roches from the theatre. Studenty bar/café with games, jukebox and TV. Open daily to 2am.

Café Jehanne d'Arc place Jeanne-d'Arc. Situated a fifteen-minute walk northeast of place d'Armes, this place features medieval beams and frescoes, and occasional music. There are free jazz concerts in the square every Thursday evening in summer. Open until 2 or 3am.

Café Mathis 72 rue En-Fournirue. A minute old-time place spilling over into the garden of the former chapel of St-Genest in summertime, opposite a house where Rabelais once lived. Closed Sun.

Les Trinitaires 10–12 rue des Trinitaires, north of place Ste-Croix, opposite *Café Jehanne d'Arc*. The place to go for serious jazz, rock, folk and chanson, enhanced by the Gothic cellars. Live music at 9pm. Closed Sun & Mon.

Le Tunnel 27 place du Quarteau at the south end of place St-Louis. Loud rock music with your drink. Till 12.30am during the week and 2.30/3.30am weekends.

Amnéville and the Coteaux de la Moselle

Most people heading north from Metz whiz along the A31 motorway towards Luxembourg and Belgium to avoid numbingly dull towns like Thionville. But that means missing out on the attractions in the Bois de Coulange near **Amnéville**, including a spa and a collection of motorbikes; while a scenic alternative to the *autoroute* heads along quiet country roads that snake along the green slopes – or *coteaux* – of the Moselle valley, where the medieval village of **Rodemack** is one of the region's hidden gems. The Amnéville complex can be reached from Metz by a combination of local train, several times a day, to Hagondange, and shuttle bus (*navette*), more frequent at weekends. Bus services along the Moselle valley from Thionville are infrequent to say the least; your own transport is the best way to explore.

Amnéville

Hardly anyone comes to **AMNÉVILLE** to visit the town itself. A former industrial centre it offers little in the way of attractions. However, just 3km south of the town in the Coulange forest are a host of things to see and visit, in a leisure park complex, including **Termapolis** (Mon–Wed 10am–10pm, Thurs 9am–10pm, Fri & Sat 10am–midnight, Sun 9am–8pm; closed Sept, Christmas and New Year; €9 for two hours), where you can soak away pains or just relax in a series of pools fed by a ferruginous spring; kitsch decor adorns the saunas, hammams and rest areas. There's also a zoo, an aquarium and all kinds of other curiosities, plus a multiplex cinema. For more information about all tourist attractions contact the tourist office (ⓣ03.87.70.10.40, ⓦwww.amneville.com).

Of all the attractions in the complex, the top of most people's list, though, is the **Musée de la Moto et du Vélo** (May–Sept daily 9am–7pm, until 10pm on Fri; Oct–April Tues, Thurs & Fri 2–6pm, Wed, Sat & Sun 9am–noon & 2–6pm; €5). Monsieur Chapleur started collecting bikes and motorbikes in the 1930s when he was a mechanic at Citroën, and the museum has over 200 models of different origins on display, all overhauled and in working order. And they are beauties – works of art in copper, brass, chrome and steel, with some of the bicycles dating back to 1865, and the motorbikes being mostly from 1900 to 1940. One unique object to look out for is the 1906 René Gillet 4.5hp belt-driven tandem.

If you need a **place to stay**, the *Hôtel Orion* (ⓣ03.87.70.20.20, ⓔaccueilhotel@wanadoo.fr; ❺) in the leisure park itself, is modern and comfortable. The best place **to eat** is the *Forêt*, also located in the leisure park (ⓣ03.87.70.34.34), which has traditional menus from €23.

The Coteaux de la Moselle

From Thionville, 15km north of Amnéville, the N53 strikes north towards Luxembourg. Some 8km along it the scenic D57 meanders in a northeasterly direction towards Mondorf-les-Bains and the German/Luxembourg border, following the verdant contours of the **Coteaux del la Moselle**, or Moselle valley slopes. Of a number of picturesque villages along the way that defy Lorraine's dismal reputation, the one that stands out is **RODEMACK**, revelling in the nickname of the "*Carcassonne lorraine*" since its well-preserved fortifications resemble those of the famous southern city. Some 18km from Thionville, it's a charmingly sleepy place, made up of well-preserved medieval houses and gigantic timber **barns**, topped by a stern **fortress** and guarded on one side by a magnificent gate with two barbican towers, the **Porte de Sierck**. Along one flank of the ancient walls a traditional **herb garden** has been restored to its former glory. For guided visits of the town and fortress ask at the **tourist office** on the main place des Baillis (daily 10am–noon & 2–5.30pm; ⓣ03.82.51.25.50). The best of the town's **restaurants** is *La Petite Carcassonne* at 12 place de la Porte de Sierck, next to the village café, where you have a choice of three delicious menus starting from €21.

Pont-à-Mousson

Often overlooked, the quiet little town of **PONT-À-MOUSSON** lies south of Metz, exactly halfway between the city and Lorraine's former capital, Nancy – and a regular stop for all but the fastest trains between the two. There has been a bridge across the Moselle here since the Middle Ages but the present one was built after heavy bombardment during both world wars. The town survived relatively unscathed, despite the importance of the St-Gobain iron foundry – the name Pont-à-Mousson is familiar throughout France as just about every manhole cover in the country is made there. For a bird's-eye introduction to the town and fine views of its hilly surroundings it's worth making your way to the **Butte de Mousson**, where castle ruins top a steep knoll a few kilometres southeast of the town centre, reached via the D910 road.

Pont-à-Mousson is the headquarters of the **Parc naturel régional de Lorraine**, home to some of the region's best hiking territory, but the main reason to visit is to see the imposing eighteenth-century **Abbaye des Prémontrés** (daily 10am–5.30pm; €5), a former Premonstratensian abbey on the river bank now used for concerts and temporary art exhibitions. Primarily of architectural interest, its top attractions are three staircases in the convent buildings, one square, one spiral and one oval-shaped. Across the river, the town is centred on the elegant **place Duroc**, a rough triangle of arcaded houses, mostly dating from the sixteenth to eighteenth centuries. Particularly outstanding is the **Maison des Sept Péchés Capitaux**, also known as the "Château d'Amour", adorned with caryatid-like figures representing the seven deadly sins. In the rue St-Laurent, an elegant street boasting a number of fine Renaissance facades, the **Eglise St-Laurent** houses a sixteenth-century polychrome Flemish altarpiece and a lifelike statue of Christ by Ligier Richier, famous for his St-Mihiel Entombment (see p.324). Work by the town's printers and engravers, dating from times when the town hosted the Jesuit University of Lorraine, and some unique lacquered papier-mâché objects are the mainstay at the **Musée régional** (May–Sept Mon & Wed–Sat 2–6pm, Sun 10am–1pm & 2–6pm; Oct–April Wed–Mon 2–5pm; €4.60), 13 rue Magot de Rogeville, just off the main square.

The **tourist office** is at 52 place Duroc (July & Aug Mon–Fri 9am–noon & 2–6pm, Sat 9am–noon & 2–4pm; Sept–June Mon–Fri 9am–noon & 2–5pm, Sat 9am–noon; ⓣ03.83.81.06.90). For **accommodation**, you're better off in Metz or Nancy but you can always try the *Hôtel Bagatelle* at 74 rue Gambetta (ⓣ03.83.81.03.64, ⓕ03.83.81.12.63; ④) which offers views of the abbey. Decent **meals** (lunch menu at €13) can be had at the *Fourneau d'Alain*, on the upper floor of 64 place Duroc.

Verdun and the battlefield

At Verdun even the pretence of rationality failed. The slaughter was so hideous that even a trench system could not survive ... In the town, tourists inspect the memorials. One monument shows French soldiers forming a human wall of comradeship against the enemy. In another, France is personified as a medieval knight; resting on a sword, he dominates a steep flight of steps built into the old ramparts. There is another view of reality. Near the railway station, Rodin's statue shows a winged Victory as neither calm nor triumphant, but demented by rage and horror. Her legs are tangled in a dead soldier and she shrieks for survival.

Donald Horne, *The Great Museum*

The small country town of **VERDUN** lies in a bend of the River Meuse, 68km west of Metz. Of no great interest in itself, what makes it remarkable is its association with the ghastly battle that took place on the bleak uplands to the north between 1916 and 1918.

Long a frontier town, in the aftermath of German victory in the 1870–71 war Verdun and its environs became the most heavily fortified military region in France, the linch-pin of its northeastern defences. For this reason, and in order to break the stalemate of trench warfare, the German General Erich von Falkenhayn chose it as the target for an offensive that, in 1916, was the most devastating ever launched in the annals of war. His intention was "to bleed the French army to death and strike a devastating blow at the morale of the French people". He advanced to within 5km of the town, but never succeeded in taking it. Gradually the French clawed back the lost ground, but final victory came only in the last months of the war in 1918 and then only with the aid of US troops under the command of General Pershing.

Hundreds of thousands of men died in the battle, both French and German, to say nothing of the numbers scarred for life by their experiences. But it was particularly devastating for the French: the battle was fought on their native soil against the enemy who had humiliated them so badly in 1870, and it decimated the country's young male population. Most of the names inscribed on the thousands of sad memorials that stand in every village, hamlet and town of France belong to men who died at Verdun. It was also the battle that made the reputation of Philippe Pétain, the general who organized the defence of Verdun. Without it, it is arguable whether he would have become head of the collaborationist Vichy regime in 1940.

The Town

Given the pounding it received in World War I and the bomb damage of World War II, Verdun is not as grim as you might expect. The liveliest part lies between the river and the steep little hill dominated by the cathedral, along rues St-Paul and Mazel. The **Rodin memorial** (see quote above) stands beside a handsome eighteenth-century gateway at the northern end of rue St-Paul, where it joins avenue Garibaldi. Nearby, and as striking as the Rodin memorial, is a simple engraving listing all the years between 450 and 1916 that Verdun has been involved in bloody conflict. Another fine gate, the fourteenth-century **Porte Chaussée**, guards the river-crossing in the middle of town. Beyond it, further along rue Mazel, a flight of steps climbs up to the **Monument de la Victoire**, where a helmeted warrior leans on his sword in commemoration of the 1916 battle, while in the crypt below a roll is kept of all the soldiers, French and American, who took part. Beyond the monument, on rue de la Belle Vierge, lies the **Musée de la Princerie** (April–Oct daily except Tues 9.30am–noon & 2–6pm; €3), a small museum housed in a sixteenth-century town house exhibiting ceramics, furniture and paintings from Verdun's ancient and religious history. The rue de la Belle Vierge leads round to the **Cathedral of Notre-Dame**, whose outward characteristics are Gothic. Ironically, its earlier Romanesque origins were only uncovered by shell damage in 1916. The superbly sober crypt was subsequently dug out, revealing some of the original carved capitals; the new replacements show scenes from the World War I fighting. The rather beautiful **bishop's palace** behind it has been converted into a **Centre Mondial de la Paix et des Droits de l'Homme** (Feb–May & Sept 16 to Dec 20 daily except Mon 9.30am–noon & 2–6pm; June to Sept 15 daily 9.30am–7pm; €5.50), hosting exhibitions and conferences about peacekeeping and human rights.

Rue du Rû, the continuation of rue Mazel, takes you to the underground galleries of the **Citadelle** (daily 9am–12.30pm & 1.30–6pm; €6), used as shelter and hospital for thousands of soldiers during the battle. The Unknown Soldier, whose remains now lie under the Arc de Triomphe in Paris, was chosen from among the dead who lie here.

Practicalities

The **gare SNCF** and the **bus station** are both on avenue Garibaldi. The **tourist office** (May–Sept Mon–Sat 8.30am–6.30pm, Sun 9am–5pm; Oct–April Mon–Sat 9am–noon & 2–5.30pm, Sun 10am–1pm; ⓣ03.29.86.14.18, ⓦwww.verdun-tourisme.com) lies just across the River Meuse from the Porte Chaussée opposite the end of the bridge. Staff at the tourist office run daily four-hour minibus **tours of the battlefield** (in French only: 2pm May–Sept; €25.50) – not exactly cheap, but the guides are interesting and the experience is not one that you're likely to repeat. Call ahead to try and arrange an English-speaking guide if your French is not up to it.

As for **accommodation**, there's much more to choose from in Metz or Nancy. However, if you do need to spend the night in Verdun, head for the very friendly *Hôtel St-Paul*, 12 place St-Paul (ⓣ & ⓕ03.29.86.02.16; ❸; closed Dec 7–Jan 7), close to the Rodin memorial. Decent and inexpensive alternatives are *Hôtel Montaulbain*, 4 rue de la Vieille-Prison (ⓣ03.29.86.00.47; ❷), and the *Auberge de Jeunesse* (ⓣ03.29.86.28.28, ⓕ03.29.86.28.82; ❶; closed Jan), located between the cathedral and Centre Mondial, with a fantastic view over the town and its surroundings.

You shouldn't have trouble finding somewhere to **eat**: there are plenty of brasseries and crêperies along the river, and *Hôtel St-Paul* (see above) has a good traditional restaurant with menus from €15. For **drinking**, *L'Estaminet*, on rue des Rouyers, has a great selection of beers and a pleasant terrace open from 2pm to 3am.

The battlefield

The **Battle of Verdun** opened on the morning of February 21, 1916, with a German artillery barrage that lasted ten hours and expended two million shells. It concentrated on the forts of Vaux and Douaumont, which the French had built after the 1870 Franco-Prussian War. By the time the main battle ended ten months later, nine villages had been pounded to nothing. Not even their sites are detectable in aerial photos of the time. The heavy artillery

The Maginot Line

Like the Séré de Rivières forts constructed along the line of the rivers Meuse and Moselle after the 1870–71 war, the **Maginot Line** was designed to keep the Germans out. Constructed between 1930 and 1940, it was the brainchild of the French Minister of War (1929–31), André Maginot. Spanning the entire length of the French–German border – plus a section of the French-Belgian border – it comprised a complete system of defence in depth. There were advance posts equipped with anti-tank weapons and machine guns. There were fortified police stations close to the frontier. But the main line consisted of a continuous chain of underground strongpoints linked by anti-tank obstacles and equipped with state-of-the-art machinery. It was of course hugely expensive and, when put to the test in 1940, proved to be worse than useless: the Germans simply violated Belgian neutrality and drove round the other end of the Line.

One of the largest forts, the **Fort de Fermont**, situated about 50km north of Verdun near the small town of Longuyon, is open to the public (guided visits June–Aug Mon–Fri 3pm, Sat & Sun 2pm & 3.30pm; April, May & Sept weekends only 2pm & 3.30pm; ⓣ03.82.39.21.21; €5; times are susceptible to change so check in advance. Armed with nine fire points, it was served by 6km of underground tunnels and a garrison of 600. The entrance is hidden in woodland and nothing shows above ground but the scarcely noticeable cupolas of the gun turrets. Below, the tunnels are equipped with power plants, electric trains, monorails, elevators and all the other technological paraphernalia necessary to support such a lunatic enterprise. The place has the feel of a nuclear bunker.

Getting there without your own transport is not easy. There are trains to Longuyon from Metz and Verdun (change at Conflans), but you'll have to hitch or walk the last 5km to the fort. Over in the Alsace region, 15km north of Haguenau, the **Four à Chaux** fortress, dating from 1930, at Lembach has been restored, and now houses a museum of World War II (guided tours daily: mid-March to June & Sept to mid-Nov 10am, 2pm, 3pm & 4pm; July & Aug 10am, 11am, and hourly 2–5pm; ⓣ03.88.94.48.62; €4.50).

shells ploughed the ground to a depth of 8m and, although much of it is now reforested, there are parts even today that steadfastly refuse anchorage to any but the coarsest vegetation.

The most visited part of the battlefield extends along the hills north of Verdun, but the fighting also spread well to the west of the Meuse, to the hills of Mort-Homme and Hill 304, to Vauquois and the Argonne, and south along the Meuse to St-Mihiel, where the Germans held an important salient until dislodged by US forces in 1918.

The only really effective way to explore the area is with your own transport. The main sights are reached via two minor roads that snake through the battlefields, forming a crossroads northeast of Verdun: the D913 and D112. The former branches left from the main N3 to Metz, 5km east of Verdun; the latter leaves the same N3 opposite the Cimetière du Faubourg-Pavé on the eastern outskirts of Verdun and is soon enclosed by appropriately gloomy conifer plantations. If you take the D112, on the right you pass a **monument** to André Maginot, who was himself wounded in the battle and under whose later stewardship at the Ministry of War the famous Maginot Line (see box above) was built.

Shortly afterwards a sign points out a forest ride to the **Fort de Souville**, the furthest point of the German advance in 1916. The site is not on the main tourist beat, and is a very moving, if rather frightening, twenty-minute walk over ground absolutely shattered by artillery fire, with pools of black water standing in the now grassy shell-holes. The fort itself lies half-hidden among the scrub, the armoured gun turrets still lowering in their pits, the tunnels to their control rooms dank and dangerous with collapse. A little way beyond the fort, where the D112 intersects the D913, a stone lion marks the precise spot at which the German advance was checked. To the left the D913 continues to Fleury, 1km from the crossroads, and on to Douaumont, before curling back round to the D964.

Fleury and the Fort de Vaux

The horrifying story of the battle is graphically documented at **FLEURY**, in the **Musée-Memorial de Fleury** (daily: Feb & Mar 9am–noon & 2–5pm; April to mid-Sept 9am–6pm; mid-Sept to mid-Nov 9am–noon & 2–6pm; mid-Nov to December 20 9am–noon & 2–5pm; €5), which is included in the Verdun tourist office's guided tour. Contemporary newsreels and photos present the stark truth; and in the well of the museum, a section of the shell-torn terrain that was once the village of Fleury has been reconstructed as the battle left it.

Another major monument is the **Fort de Vaux**, 4km east of Fleury (Feb to Dec 23 daily 9am–5pm; €3), where, after six days' hand-to-hand combat in the confined, gas-filled tunnels, the French garrison, reduced to drinking their own urine, were left with no alternative but surrender. On the exterior wall of the fort a plaque commemorates the last messenger pigeon sent to the command post in Verdun vainly asking for reinforcements. Having safely delivered its message, the pigeon expired as a result of flying through the gas-filled air above the battlefield. It was posthumously awarded the Légion d'Honneur.

Douaumont

The principal memorial to the carnage stands in the middle of the battlefield a short distance along the D913 beyond Fleury. It is the **Ossuaire de Douaumont** (daily: March & Oct 9am–noon & 2–5.30pm; April 9am–6pm; May–Aug 9am–6.30pm; Sept 9am–noon & 2–6pm; Nov 9am–noon & 2–5pm; €3.50), a vast and surreal structure with the stark simplicity of a Romanesque crypt or a Carolingian sarcophagus, from which rises a central tower shaped like a projectile aimed at the heavens. Its vaults contain the bones of thousands upon thousands of unidentified soldiers, French and German, some of them visible through windows set in the base of the building. When the battle ended in 1918, the ground was covered in fragments of corpses; 120,000 French bodies were identified, perhaps a third of the total killed.

Across the road, a **cemetery** contains the graves of 15,000 men who died more or less whole – Christians commemorated by rows of identical crosses, Muslims of the French colonial regiments by gravestones aligned in the direction of Mecca. Nearby, a wall commemorates the Jewish dead, beneath a treeless ridge-top on whose tortured, pitted ground around the remains of the Fort de Thiaumont some of them must have died.

The **Fort de Douaumont** (daily: Feb, March & Oct–Dec 10am–1pm & 2–5pm; April–June & Sept 10am–6pm; July & Aug 10am–7pm; closed Jan; €3.50) is 900m down the road from the cemetery. Completed in 1912 and commanding the highest point of land, it was the strongest of the 38 forts built to defend Verdun. But, in one of those inexplicable aberrations of military top brass, the armament of these forts was greatly reduced in 1915 – when the Germans attacked in 1916, twenty men were enough to overrun the garrison of 57 French territorials. The fort is on three levels, two of them underground, and

St-Mihiel and the Voie Sacrée

In an attempt to cut Verdun off as early as 1914, the Germans captured the town of **St-Mihiel** on the River Meuse to the south, which gave them control of the main supply route into Verdun. The only route left open to the French – and that far from safe – was the N35, winding north from Bar-le-Duc over the open hills and wheat fields. In memory of all those who kept the supplies going, the road is called **La Voie Sacrée** (The Sacred Way) and marked with milestones capped with the helmet of the *poilu* (the slang term for the French infantryman). In St-Mihiel itself, the **Eglise St-Michel** contains the **Sépulcre** or *Entombment of Christ*, by local sculptor **Ligier Richier** – a set of thirteen stone figures, carved in the mid-16th century and regarded as one of the masterpieces of the French Renaissance. Just beyond the town to the east, on the Butte de Montsec, is a memorial to the Americans who died here in 1918 and a US cemetery at **Thiancourt** on the main road.

its claustrophobic, dungeon-like galleries are hung with stalactites. The Germans, who held it for eight months, had 3000 men housed in its cramped quarters with no toilets, continuously under siege, its ventilation ducts blocked for protection against gas, infested with fleas and lice and plagued by rats that attacked the sleeping and the dead indiscriminately. In one night, when their ammunition exploded, 1300 men died in the blast. When the French retook the fort, it was with Moroccan troops in the vanguard. General Mangin, revered by officialdom as the heroic victor of the battle, was known to his troops as "the butcher" for his practice of shoving colonial troops into the front line as cannon fodder.

Furthest from Verdun, well signposted from the D913, is the so-called **Tranchée des Baïonnettes** (Trench of the Bayonets), where, according to legend, two entire infantry platoons are thought to have been buried alive in an upright position with fixed bayonets during a German bombardment on June 11, 1916. A concrete memorial has been built around the area. Though not particularly interesting to look at, it still makes for a very moving experience. Sadly, the bayonets have been stolen.

Nancy

NANCY, on the River Meurthe, was not occupied by the Prussians after 1870, and its centre, largely unaffected by the undistinguished modern sprawl that blights the valley sides, remains a model of eighteenth-century Classicism. For this, it has the last of the independent dukes of Lorraine to thank, the dethroned King of Poland and father-in-law of Louis XV, Stanislas Leszczynski. During the twenty-odd years of his office in the mid-eighteenth century, he ordered some of the most successful urban renewal of the period in all France.

Arrival, information and accommodation

The part of Nancy you're likely to want to see extends to no more than a ten- or fifteen-minute walk either side of **rue Stanislas**, the main axis and shopping street connecting the **gare SNCF** and the principal **place Stanislas**. The **tourist office**, on the south side of place Stanislas in the Hôtel de Ville (April–Oct Mon–Sat 9am–7pm, Sun & hols 10am–5pm; Nov–March Mon–Sat 9am–6pm, Sun 10am–1pm; ☎03.83.35.22.41,

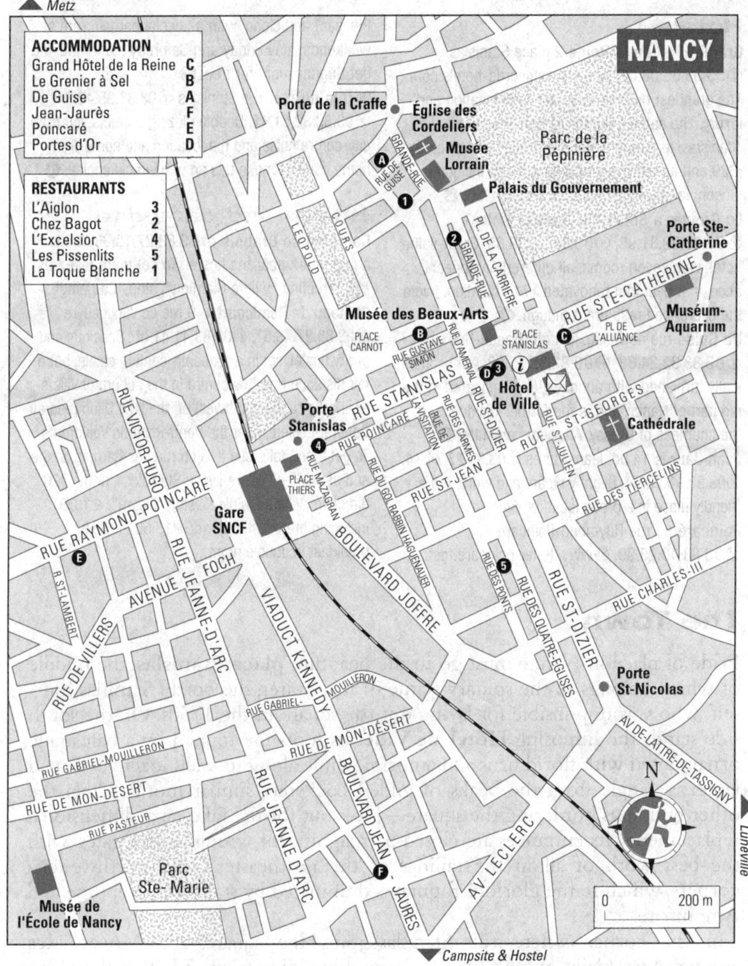

ⓦwww.ot-nancy.fr), is well stocked with information about both the city and region, and organizes the *petit train touristique*, a frequent 45-minute **guided tour** of the town (May–Sept; €6; departure from place de la Carrière), as well as several other themed visits of the town. Regional **buses** depart from rue de l'Île de Corse and boulevard d'Austrasie, both on the eastern side of town. **Internet** access is available at the excellent e-café, 11 rue des Quatre-Eglises.

Reasonable **accommodation** is not hard to find in Nancy. There are plenty of hotels visible from the station, and signs directing you to most of the others – all are within ten to fifteen minutes' walk of the station. For somewhere special out of town, try the *Château d'Adoménil* near Lunéville, 37km southeast by the A33 *autoroute* (ⓣ03.83.74.04.81, ⓦwww.relaischateaux.fr/adomenil; ❾; closed Sun out of season); it has seven beautifully furnished rooms overlooking water, orchards and a home farm, and its small restaurant is highly rated (cheapest menu €40; *carte* upwards of €70).

Hotels

Grand Hôtel de la Reine 2 place Stanislas ⓣ03.83.35.03.01, ⓦwww.concorde-hotels.com. The grandest hotel in town, for both location and luxury. The same goes for its chic restaurant, *Le Stanislas*, featuring a succulent business lunch at €29 and an extravagant dinner menu including pigeon, lamb and all kinds of fish at €55. ❽

Le Grenier à Sel 28 rue Gustave Simon ⓣ03.83.32.31.98, ⓕ03.83.35.32.88. Great-value hotel, with seven rooms, all different in appearance, in a beautiful renovated 1714 building. Avoid the overpriced restaurant though. ❹

De Guise rue de Guise, just off Grande-Rue ⓣ03.83.32.24.68, ⓕ03.83.35.75.63. Atmospherically furnished with antiques, this is located in the old part of Nancy, and is the former residence of the countess of Bressy. All rooms en suite. ❹

Jean-Jaurès 14 bd Jean-Jaurès ⓣ03.83.27.74.14, ⓕ03.83.90.20.94. Slightly weary and worn, but a friendly place in a pretty location. ❸

Poincaré 81 rue Raymond-Poincaré ⓣ03.83.40.25.99, ⓦwww.hotel-poincare.fr.st. Pleasant and clean, with a special bargain rate at weekends: stay Friday and Saturday night, and you get Sunday night for free. ❷

Portes d'Or 21 rue Stanislas ⓣ03.83.35.42.34, ⓕ03.83.32.51.41. Double glazing protects you from city-centre noise and the location and home-from-home comfort make this an unbeatable choice. ❸

Hostel and campsite

Camping de Brabois ⓣ03.83.27.18.28. Set in a large park near the hostel. To get there take bus #26 direction "Villers Clairlieu", stop "Camping".

Château de Rémicourt 149 rue de Vandoeuvre ⓣ03.83.27.73.67, ⓕ03.83.41.41.35. Spacious and pretty hostel, set in a sixteenth-century castle, but a fair distance from the centre in the suburb of Villers-lès-Nancy to the southwest off the N74 Dijon road/av Général-Leclerc, near the Rond-Point du Vélodrome. To get there, take bus #16 on rue des Carmes, to the end of the line "Villers-Lycée Stanislas", or the #26 direction "Villers Clairlieu", stop "Fiacre". €13.50 including breakfast in dorm; €15.50 including breakfast in double room.

The Town

Pride of place in Nancy must go to the beautiful **place Stanislas**, the middle of which belongs to the solitary statue of its inspirer, the portly Stanislas himself, who was responsible for laying out the square in the 1750s. On the south side stands the imposing **Hôtel de Ville**, its roof-line topped by a balustrade ornamented with florid urns and amorini, while along its walls lozenge-shaped lanterns dangle from the beaks of gilded cockerels; similar motifs adorn the other buildings bordering the square – look out for the fake, two-dimensional replacements. Its entrances are closed by magnificent wrought-iron gates, with the best work of all in the railings of the northeastern and northwestern corners, which frame glorious fountains dominated by statues of Neptune and Amphitrite.

In the corner where rue Stanislas joins the square, the **Musée des Beaux-Arts** (daily except Tues 10.30am–6pm; €4.60, or €5.40 if there's an exhibition; €6.10 combined ticket with Musée de l'École de Nancy – see opposite) has an excellent presentation of French nineteenth- and twentieth-century art on the ground floor, with a good selection of paintings by Émile Friant and Nancy's own Victor Prouvé, as well as a Manet, a Matisse and a Picasso. The rest of the collection upstairs, encompassing Italian, German, northern European and the rest of French painting, is less interesting. Time is better spent in the basement, where works from Nancy's glass company, Daum, are beautifully lit in black rooms. The layout of the basement follows the shape of fortifications dating from the fifteenth century through to Vauban's seventeenth-century alterations, which were found during the 1990s renovation. For a glimpse of Daum's contemporary creations you can visit their shop, also on place Stanislas. A short walk east of the square is the excellent **Muséum-Aquarium de Nancy**, at 34 rue Ste-Catherine (daily 10am–noon & 2–6pm; €3). Upstairs is a colossal collection of stuffed animals and birds, while downstairs is a startling aquarium of exotic fish whose colours surpass even the daring of Matisse.

On its north side, place Stanislas opens into the long, tree-lined **place de la Carrière**, a handsome eighteenth-century transformation of what was originally a jousting ground. Its far end is closed by the classical colonnades of the **Palais du Gouvernement**, former residence of the governor of Lorraine. Behind it, housed in the fifteenth-century Palais Ducal and entered through a handsome doorway surmounted by an equestrian statue of one of the dukes, is the **Musée Lorrain**, 64 Grande-Rue (daily except Tues: 10am–12.30pm & 2–6pm; closed public hols; €3.10, €4.60 combined ticket with the Musée des Cordeliers). Dedicated to the history and traditions of Lorraine, it contains, among other treasures, a room full of superb etchings by the Nancy-born seventeenth-century artist, Jacques Callot, whose concern with social issues, evident in series such as *The Miseries of War* and *Les Gueux* (or *The Beggars*), presaged much nineteenth- and twentieth-century art. Next door, in the Église des Cordeliers et Chapelle Ducale, is the **Musée des Cordeliers** (same hours as Musée Lorrain; €3.10, €4.60 combined ticket with the Musée Lorrain), where rural life in the region in days gone by is illustrated. On the other side of the Palais du Gouvernement, you can play crazy golf, admire the deer or just collapse with exhaustion on the green grass of the **Parc de la Pépinière**, a sort of cross between a formal French garden and an English park – there's also a free zoo. At the end of Grande-Rue is the medieval city gate, **Porte de la Craffe**.

A half-hour walk southwest of the train station, the **Musée de l'École de Nancy**, 36 rue Sergent-Blandan (Wed–Sun 10.30am–6pm; €4.60, free first Sun of month 10am–1.30pm), is housed in a 1909 villa built for the Corbin family, founders of the Magasins Réunis chain of department stores. Even if you're not into Art Nouveau, this collection is exciting. Although not all of it belonged to the Corbins, the museum is arranged as if it were a private house. The furniture is outstanding – all swirling curvilinear forms – and the standards of workmanship are superlative, with a fair sprinkling of Gallé's work on display, too. The beautiful **gardens** are worth exploring – they're planted with irises, magnolias, saxifrages and all kinds of other plants that inspired the School of Nancy's creations (see box below).

Eating and drinking

There are plenty of places to **eat** and **drink** in Nancy, led by the excellent restaurant in the *Grand Hôtel de la Reine*. Good streets for restaurants include Grande-Rue, rue Maréchaux and rue des Ponts. Place Stanislas is perfect for a coffee, day or night, with several cafés that make good vantage points to watch Nancy go by: *Grand Café du Commerce*, *Jean Lamour* and, restored to its original

Nouveau Nancy

A traditional handicraft and metalworking town, at the turn of the twentieth century Nancy became a centre of Art Nouveau to rival Paris. The practitioners of **Art Nouveau** in Nancy attempted to marry the artistic styles of orientalism and Baroque with the industrial advances of the day, and their style became known as the "**L'École de Nancy**" ("**School of Nancy**"). The most illustrious exponents of the school were the manufacturer of glass and ceramics, Émile Gallé, and the glass manufacturer Daum. But the town's moment of glory was short-lived, and all that now remains are a handful of buildings and the Musée de l'École de Nancy, housed in a fin-de-siècle villa. For a post-museum coffee in the same kind of atmosphere, try the Art Nouveau café-restaurant of the former hotel *L'Excelsior*, opposite the train station, built in 1910 and preserved virtually intact to this day. The Nancy tourist office distributes a free leaflet, *École de Nancy – Itinéraire Art Nouveau*, which details several itineraries around Nancy's Art Nouveau heritage.

splendour, the sumptuous *Grand Café Foy*, to name but three. It's a good place to start an evening, or you could dine at the sumptuous *Le Stanislas* restaurant in Nancy's most exclusive hotel – later on you can continue along the Grande-Rue and its offshoots, where you will certainly find a late-night bar. A good website to consult is ⓦwww.nancybynight.com.

Restaurants

L'Aiglon 5 rue Stanislas, near the square ⓣ03.83.32.21.43. An interesting and well-prepared meal is around €16–18, including wine and coffee. For more sophisticated traditional and local cuisine, with dishes like *choucroute*, *tourte lorraine*, *baeckeoffe*, and *poule-au-pot*, there's the *menu terroir* at €15.

Chez Bagot 45 Grande-Rue ⓣ03.83.37.42.43. Fresh fish dishes cooked to Breton recipes served up in an appropriately decorated restaurant. Menus from €12.50. Closed Mon & Tues lunch.

L'Excelsior 50 rue Henri-Poincaré, cnr rue Mazagran in front of the train station ⓣ03.83.35.24.57. A *fin-de-siècle* Art Nouveau brasserie, frequented by everyone who aspires to be anyone in Nancy. Now part of the Flo brasserie chain but managing to retain its superb interior and good food (menus at €20 and €27). It's also the best daytime stop for coffee.

Les Pissenlits 25 rue des Ponts ⓣ03.83.37.43.97. Real old-fashioned bistro fare on a menu at €15, in an attractive atmosphere. Awarded the *Bib Gourmand* by Michelin for well-prepared meals at moderate prices. Closed Sun & Mon.

La Toque Blanche 1 rue Mgr-Trouillet, just off place St-Epvre ⓣ03.83.30.17.20. One of the finest gourmet restaurants in Nancy. The €21 menu is a bargain; à la carte costs €60 and more. Closed Sun eve & Mon.

Cafés and bars

L'Arquebuse 13 rue Héré. In the winter months you can sample sushi from 6–10pm. Later on, all year round, jazz and salsa bring the chic leather and wood surroundings to life. Closed Sun & Mon.

Le Blitz 76 rue St-Julien. One of several lively bars along this street, with danceable music and a trendy clientele, open till late.

BpM 90 Grande-Rue. Popular with young Nancy boys this techno bar is the nearest the town gets to a gay bar. Only really gets going at weekends. Open till late.

O Circo 25 rue St-Julien. Cuban and other world music, sometimes live, are the attractions here along with an immodest statue.

Pinocchio place St-Epvre. Features stylish wooden interior furnishings and a terrace facing the church St-Epvre; good for drinks at all hours. Open Mon–Sat 8am–2am.

La Place place Stanislas. Extravagant decor and varied music attracts a mixed crowd of drinkers, boppers and general revellers. Open Mon–Sat 8am–2am.

Réservoir Café 13 rue Callot. Leather armchairs and mellow music add to the cosiness of this fashionable café-bar known for its stiff cocktails. Open 4pm–2am, closed Sun.

Théâtre le Vertigo 29 rue de la Visitation. Post-modern gargoyles contribute to its interesting theatrical atmosphere. Bands and other performances regularly. Mon–Sat until 2am; open till 5am if there's a show.

Alsace

There's no denying **Alsace**'s attractiveness, with its old stone and half-timbered towns set amid the thickly wooded hills of the Vosges, but it's a quaintness that in many places has become a commodity. **Strasbourg**, the Alsatian capital and, along with Brussels, one of the "capitals" of the European Union, mostly escapes the tweeness of some of the smaller towns of the foothills. **Saverne** and **Wissembourg**, to the north, also avoid the worst of the tourist-brochure image, and give access to some spectacular ruined castles in the **northern Vosges**.

South of Strasbourg, along the **Route du Vin**, there are countless picturesque medieval villages and yet more ruined castles which suffer to varying degrees from the attention of the tour buses. A very different, horribly sobering experience is the concentration camp of **Le Struthof**, hidden away in the Vosges forest. **Colmar** is almost excessively twee, yet still worth a visit for Grünewald's amazing Issenheim altarpiece, one of the most spectacular works of art in the country. By contrast, **Mulhouse** is thoroughly industrial but boasts some wonderful museums devoted to subjects as varied as cars, trains, electricity and printed fabrics.

Every town has a **tourist office** (Ⓦwww.tourisme-alsace.com), in smaller places usually housed in the *mairie* or Hôtel de Ville. Special tourist maps cost around €0.50, but free maps containing a reasonable amount of information are always available.

The food and wine of Alsace

The cuisine of Alsace is quite distinct from that of other regions of France and clearly shows its German origins, albeit tempered by Gallic refinement. The classic dish is *choucroute*, the aromatic pickled cabbage known in German as **sauerkraut**. The secret here is the inclusion of juniper berries in the pickling stage and the addition of goose grease or lard. Traditionally it's served with large helpings of smoked pork, ham and a variety of sausages but some restaurants offer a succulent variant replacing the meat with fish (*choucroute aux poissons*), usually salmon and monkfish. The qualification *à l'alsacienne* after the name of a dish means "with *choucroute*". **Foie gras**, both duck and goose, is another prized delicacy and locals swear theirs is better than the stuff from the southwest.

Strasbourg **sausages** and boiled **potatoes** are another common ingredient in Alsatian cooking. One of the best culinary incarnations of the spud is the three-meat hotpot, **baeckoffe**, which consists of pork, mutton and beef marinated in wine and cooked between layers of potato for a couple of hours in a baker's oven. **Onions**, too, are a favourite dish, either in the form of an onion tart, made with a béchamel sauce, or *flammeküche* (*tarte flambée* in French), made with a mixture of onion, cream and pieces of chopped smoked pork breast baked on a base of thin pizza-like pastry. **Noodles** are also a common feature, and don't miss the chance to sample a *matelote* (a stew of river fish cooked in Riesling) or Vosges trout cooked *au bleu* (briefly boiled in Riesling with a dash of vinegar).

Like the Germans, Alsatians are fond of their **pastries**. The dessert fruit tarts made with rhubarb (topped with meringue) or wild blueberries, apple or red cherries, red *quetsch* or yellow *mirabelle* plums – *tartes alsaciennes* – are delicious. Cake-lovers should try *kugelhopf*, a moulded dome-shaped cake with a hollow in the middle, made with raisins and almonds, and *birewecks*, made with dried fruit marinated in Kirsch.

All of these delights can be washed down with the region's outstanding **white wines**, renowned for their dry, clean-tasting fruitiness and compatibility with any kind of food. The best-known of them are the tart Rieslings, flowery Gewürztraminers, refreshing Sylvaners and the three Pinots (blanc, gris and noir – dry white, fruity white and dark rosé, respectively), named after the type of grape from which they are made. There are, incidentally, a few reds – light in colour and bouquet – from Ottrott, Marlenheim and Cleebourg.

Alsace also shares the German predilection for **beer** – look out for the flavoursome Christmas and March brews – and has long been the heartland of French hop-growing. Look out, too, for the clear fruit **brandies**, sold in elegant bottles, especially *kirsch*, made from cherries, and *quetsch* and *mirabelle* distilled from the two varieties of plum also used in tarts. They round off a hearty Alsatian feast perfectly, often trickled over mouthwatering sorbets made with the same fruit.

Strasbourg

STRASBOURG owes both its name – "the City of the Roads" in German – and its wealth to its position on the west bank of the Rhine, long one of the great natural transport arteries of Europe. Self-styled "*le Carrefour de l'Europe*" ("Europe's Crossroads"), it certainly lies at the very heart of western Europe, closer to Frankfurt, Zurich and even Milan than to Paris. The city's medieval commercial pre-eminence was damaged by too close an involvement in the religious struggles of the sixteenth and seventeenth centuries, but recovered with the absorption into France in 1681. Along with the rest of Alsace, Strasbourg was annexed by Germany from 1871 to the end of World War I and again from 1940 to 1944.

Today old animosities have been submerged in the togetherness of the European Union, with Strasbourg the seat of the Council of Europe, the European Court of Human Rights and the European Parliament. Prosperous, beautiful and easy to get around, with an orderliness that is Germanic rather than Latin, the city is big enough – with a population of over a quarter of a million people – to have a metropolitan air without being overwhelming. It has one of the loveliest cathedrals in France and one of the oldest and most active universities: this is the one city in eastern France that is definitely worth a detour.

Arrival and information

The **gare SNCF** lies on the west side of the city centre, barely fifteen minutes' walk from the cathedral along rue du Maire-Kuss and rue du 22-Novembre. The **airport shuttle bus** (*navette*), departing every twenty minutes (5.30am–11pm), drops off at Baggersee, from where you can catch the very convenient and futuristic tram into central Strasbourg (€4.90 combined ticket).

The main **tourist office** is at 17 place de la Cathédrale (daily 9am–7pm; ⓣ03.88.52.28.28, ⓦwww.strasbourg.com), with the regional office for the Bas-Rhin *département* (northern Alsace) nearby at 9 rue du Dôme (Mon–Fri 9am–noon & 1.30–5pm; ⓣ03.88.15.45.85/88, ⓔalsace-tourisme@sdv.fr). There's also a tourist office just in front of the train station (Mon–Sat 9am–7pm, Sun 9am–6pm), in the new underground shopping complex, and one at the airport (daily 8.30am–12.30pm & 1.15–5pm). It may be worth investing in a **Strasbourg Pass** (€10.60), entitling you to free entrances and discounts: one museum entrance and one half-price, a boat-tour, a full-day bike hire and the cathedral tower and clock.

Much of the city centre is now pedestrian-only, but several car parks around Strasbourg cater for those who are **driving** into town. At Parking Rotonde, to the north, and at Parking Étoile to the south, a €2.30 fee gives you unlimited parking and tram tickets for the journey into the town centre; further south, Parking Baggersee is free and has easy access to the tram, which takes you to the town centre in fifteen minutes. Strasbourg is also France's most bicycle-friendly city, and 300km of **bicycle** lanes and particularly cheap bicycle rental (see "Listings", p.339) making cycling a tempting option.

Accommodation

When looking for a place to **stay**, bear in mind that once a month (except August, and twice in October) the European Parliament is in session for the best part of a week, bringing hundreds of MEPs and their numerous entourages into town, putting all the city's facilities under pressure, especially hotel

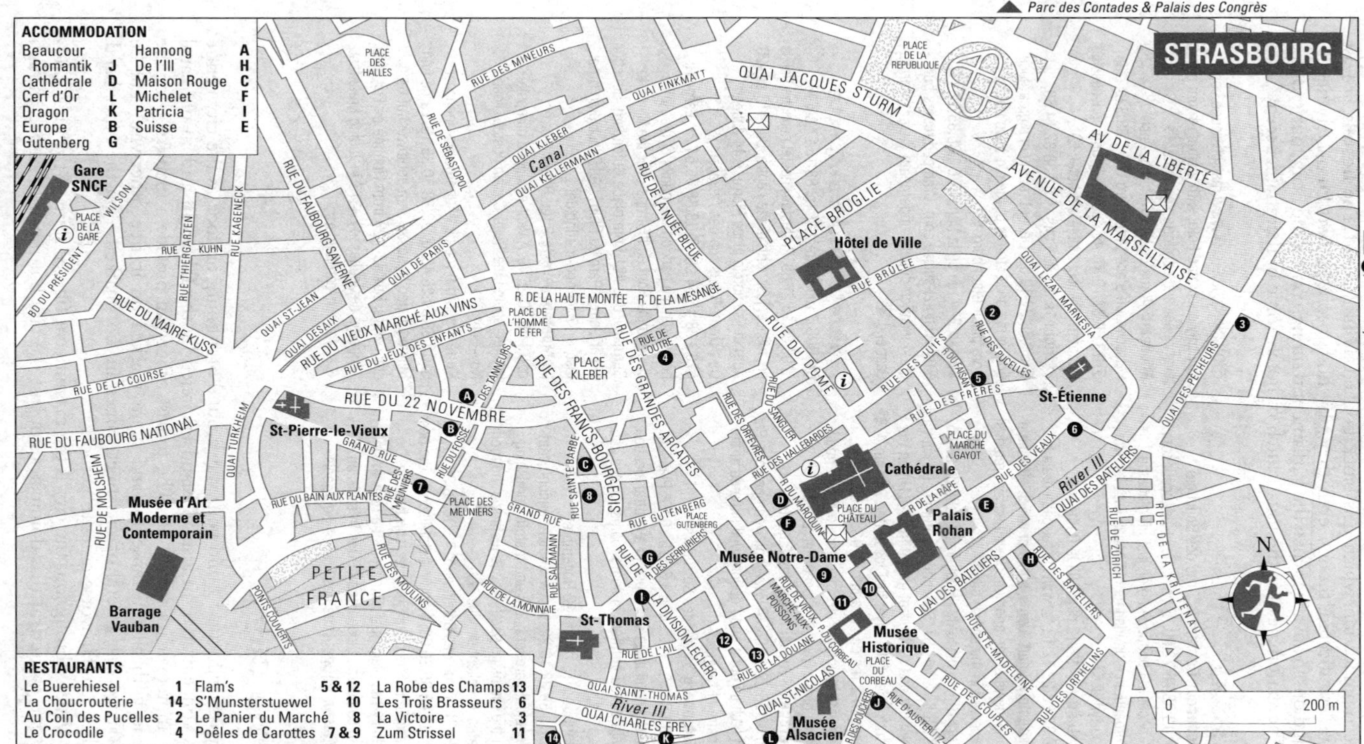
STRASBOURG
Parc des Contades & Palais des Congrès
1, University & Botanical Gardens
ACCOMMODATION
Beaucour Romantik J
Cathédrale D
Cerf d'Or L
Dragon K
Europe B
Gutenberg G
Hannong A
De l'Ill H
Maison Rouge C
Michelet F
Patricia I
Suisse E
RESTAURANTS
Le Buerehiesel 1
La Choucrouterie 14
Au Coin des Pucelles 2
Le Crocodile 4
Flam's 5 & 12
S'Munsterstuewel 10
Le Panier du Marché 8
Poêles de Carottes 7 & 9
La Robe des Champs 13
Les Trois Brasseurs 6
La Victoire 3
Zum Strissel 11
Gare SNCF
Place de la Gare
Hôtel de Ville
Cathédrale
Palais Rohan
St-Étienne
Musée Notre-Dame
Musée Historique
Musée Alsacien
St-Thomas
St-Pierre-le-Vieux
Musée d'Art Moderne et Contemporain
Barrage Vauban
Petite France
Place Kleber
Place Broglie
Place de la République
Place des Halles
Place Gutenberg
Place du Château
Place du Corbeau
Place du Marché Gayot
Place des Meuniers
Place de l'Homme de Fer
Quai Jacques Sturm
Av de la Liberté
Avenue de la Marseillaise
Rue du 22 Novembre
Rue des Francs-Bourgeois
Rue des Grandes Arcades
Rue du Dôme
Rue du Faubourg National
Rue du Faubourg Saverne
Rue du Vieux Marché aux Vins
Rue de la Division Leclerc
Quai des Bateliers
Rue de la Krutenau
Rue de Zurich
River Ill
Canal
N
0
200 m

accommodation which gets block booked months ahead. The **hostels**, at least, are less affected, though even they play host to one or two Euro-Deputies. To find out in advance when the Parliament is sitting, contact the main tourist office. The station area has the usual clutch of hotels, some of them rather seedy.

Hotels

Beaucour Romantik 5 rue des Bouchers ⓣ03.88.76.72.00, ⓦwww.hotel-beaucour.com. Very central boutique hotel, just off place du Corbeau, in a handsome old house with its own courtyard. ❻

Cathédrale 12-13 place de la Cathédrale ⓣ03.88.22.12.12, ⓦwww.hotel-cathedrale.fr. Extremely smart rooms, some of which offer stunning views of the eponymous cathedral; breakfast is served in the stylish bar. ❻

Cerf d'Or 6 place de l'Hôpital ⓣ03.88.36.20.05, ⓕ03.88.36.68.67. Sixteenth-century hotel with its own bar and restaurant (menu from €18) on the south side of the River Ill. Closed Dec 24–Jan 4. ❺

Dragon 2 rue de l'Écarlate ⓣ03.88.35.79.80, ⓦwww.dragon.fr. Fully modernized luxury hotel south of the River Ill. Closed Dec 23–27. ❺

Europe 38 rue du Fossé des Tanneurs ⓣ03.88.32.17.88, ⓦwww.hotel-europe.com. Part of a chain but a good option, well situated in the centre of town. ❺

Gutenberg 31 rue des Serruriers ⓣ03.88.32.17.15, ⓕ03.88.75.76.67. Pleasant, quirky hotel in an old house in a central location, with period furniture in some rooms. Closed Jan 1–13. ❹

Hannong 15 rue du 22 Novembre ⓣ03.88.32.16.22, ⓦwww.hotel-hannong.com. Beautiful parquet floors and tasteful furnishing in the rooms go some way to justifying the room rates. Excellent service. ❼

De l'Ill 8 rue des Bateliers ⓣ03.88.36.20.01, ⓕ03.88.35.30.03, ⓦwww.hotel-ill.com. The best bargain in Strasbourg; a quiet, comfortable, family-run place just 50m from the river, in sight of the cathedral. Closed end of Dec to mid-Jan. ❸

Maison Rouge 4 rue des Francs-Bourgeois ⓣ03.88.32.08.60, ⓦwww.maison-rouge.com. Lavishly decorated hotel with a sitting-room on every floor and comfortable rooms. ❽

Michelet 48 rue du Vieux-Marché-aux-Poissons, off place Gutenberg ⓣ03.88.32.47.38, ⓕ03.88.32.79.87. An outwardly unprepossessing but perfectly acceptable old hotel. ❷

Patricia 1a rue du Puits ⓣ03.88.32.14.60, ⓕ03.88.32.19.08. Decent rooms in a great location in the back streets of the old town not far from place Gutenberg. ❸

Suisse 2–4 rue de la Râpe ⓣ03.88.35.22.11, ⓦwww.hotel-suisse.com. Cramped rooms but great location directly underneath the cathedral's east end. ❺

Hostels and campsite

CIARUS 7 rue Finkmatt ⓣ03.88.15.27.88/90, ⓕ03.88.15.27.89. Protestant hostel near the Palais de Justice, just north of the centre. Bus #10 or #20 from the station to place Pierre. €44 double.

Des Deux Rives rue des Cavaliers ⓣ03.88.45.54.20, ⓕ03.88.45.54.21. Large HI hostel set in a park on the banks of the Rhine close to the Pont de l'Europe over the Rhine to Germany. Bus #21 from place Gutenberg, direction "Kehl", stop "Parc du Rhin". €15 including breakfast, €17 for non-cardholders.

La Montagne-Verte 2 rue Robert-Forrer ⓣ03.88.30.25.46. A well-equipped campsite, located behind the *René-Cassin* hostel. Closed Nov–Feb.

René-Cassin 9 rue de l'Auberge-de-Jeunesse ⓣ03.88.30.26.46, ⓕ03.88.30.35.16. Large and fully equipped HI hostel 3km southwest of the city centre. Bus #3, #23 from Homme de Fer, stop "Auberge de Jeunesse". €13 including breakfast, €15 for non-cardholders.

The City

It isn't difficult to find your way around Strasbourg on foot, as the city centre is concentrated on a small island encircled by the **River Ill** and an old canal – moreover it's totally flat. The tourist office can provide a map (€1 for the one with all the museums and sights marked on it; free otherwise), but be warned that several of the street names are not marked – on the other hand, there are far worse cities to get lost in.

Visible throughout the city is the magnificent filigree spire of the pink sandstone **cathedral** that dominates not just the city but much of Alsace, though its silhouette at the time of writing was deformed by scaffolding likely to be in place for some time, owing to urgent restoration work. To the immediate south of this building are the best of the museums, to the north, unappealing **place Kléber** at the heart of the commercial district, and, to the west, more intimate **place Gutenberg**, nominally the main square. About a fifteen-minute walk west on the tip of the island is picturesque **La Petite France**, where timber-framed houses and gently flowing canals hark back to the city's medieval trades of tanning and dyeing.

Place Gutenberg and the cathedral

Right at the heart of medieval Strasbourg, **place Gutenberg**, with its steep-pitched roofs and brightly painted facades, was named after the printer and pioneer of moveable type, whose statue occupies the middle of the square; he lived in the city in the early fifteenth century. On the west side stands the sixteenth-century **Hôtel de Commerce**, where the writer Arthur Young watched the destruction of the magistrates' records during the Revolution; excellent art exhibitions are often held on the ground floor. And on the corner of rue du Vieux-Marché-aux-Poissons, the sculptor Hans-Jean Arp was born.

From wherever you are in the city centre, the one landmark you can see is the **Cathédrale de Notre-Dame** (daily 7–11.30am & 12.40–7pm; closed during services), soaring out of the close huddle of medieval houses at its feet, with a single spire of such delicate, flaky lightness that it seems the work of confectioners rather than masons. It's worth slogging up the 332 steps to the spire's **viewing platform** (daily: March & Oct 9am–5.30pm; April–June & Sept 9am–6.30pm; July & Aug 8.30am–7pm; Nov–Feb 9am–4.30pm; €3) for the superb view of the old town, and, in the distance, the Vosges to the west and the Black Forest to the east.

The **interior**, too, is magnificent, the high nave a model of proportion and enhanced by a glorious sequence of stained-glass windows. The finest are those in the south aisle next to the door, depicting the life of Christ and the Creation, but all are beautiful, including, in the apse, the modern glass designed in 1956 by Max Ingrand to commemorate the first European institutions in the city. On the left of the nave, the cathedral's organ perches precariously above one of the arches, like a giant gilded eagle, while further down on the same side is the late fifteenth-century pulpit, a masterpiece of intricacy in stone by the aptly named Hans Hammer.

In the south transept are the cathedral's two most popular sights. One is the slender triple-tiered central column known as the **Pilier des Anges**, decorated with some of the most graceful and expressive statuary of the thirteenth century. The other is the huge and enormously complicated **astrological clock** built by Schwilgué of Strasbourg in 1842: a favourite with the tour-group operators, whose customers roll up in droves to witness the clock's crowning performance of the day, striking the hour of noon, which it does with unerring accuracy, at 12.30pm – that being 12 o'clock "Strasbourg time" as the city lies well east of the Greenwich meridian (tickets can be bought from the postcard stand 9am–11.30am, then at the cash desk at the south door 11.50am–12.20pm; €0.80, children free). Death strikes the chimes; the apostles parade in front of Christ, who occupies the highest storey of the clock and gives each one his blessing.

Strasbourg's museums

Most of Strasbourg's **museums** are to be found to the south of the cathedral (the main exception being the Musée d'Art Moderne et Contemporain), between the tree-lined place du Château and the river. Check with the tourist office for museum passes/discounts if you're planning to visit them all.

Right next to the cathedral, place du Château is enclosed to the east and south by the Lycée Fustel and the imposing **Palais Rohan**, both eighteenth-century buildings, the latter designed for the immensely powerful Rohan family, who, for several generations in a row, cornered the market in cardinals' hats. There are three museums in the Palais Rohan itself (Mon & Wed–Sun 10am–6pm; closed public hols; €6 for all three): the **Musée des Arts Décoratifs**, **Musée des Beaux-Arts**, with a decent collection of European paintings from Giotto to the nineteenth century, and the rather specialist **Musée Archéologique**. Of the three collections, the Arts Décoratifs stands out with its eighteenth-century *faïence* tiles crafted in the city by Paul Hannong. The rooms of the palace are vast, opulent and ostentatious but not especially interesting.

Next door, in the mansion lived in by the cathedral architects, the excellent **Musée de l'Oeuvre Notre-Dame** (Tues–Sun 10am–6pm; €3) houses the original sculptures from the cathedral exterior, damaged in the Revolution and replaced today by copies; both sets are worth seeing. Other treasures here include glass from the city's original Romanesque cathedral; the eleventh-century Wissembourg Christ, said to be the oldest representation of a human figure in stained glass; and the architect's original parchment drawings for the statuary, done in fascinating detail down to the expressions on each figure's face.

The **Musée Historique** (closed for lengthy renovation at time of writing; reopening due in 2005) is at 3 place de la Grande Boucherie, near the especially picturesque place du Marché-aux-Cochons-de-Lait, and is mainly concerned with the city's past. On the other side of the river, in a typically Alsatian house on quai St-Nicolas across the Pont du Corbeau, is the charming **Musée Alsacien**, 23 quai St-Nicholas (Mon & Wed–Sat noon–6pm, Sun 10am–6pm; €4), which contains painted furniture and other local artefacts.

The latest addition to Strasbourg's museums is the **Musée d'Art Moderne et Contemporain** (Tues, Wed & Fri–Sun 11am–7pm; Thurs noon–10pm; €5), 1 place Hans-Jean Arp, housed in a mega-budget, purpose-built, glass-fronted building overlooking the river and Vauban's dam (see opposite). It's a light and airy space and its collection is well presented, making up for its shortcomings by acknowledging the importance of some lesser-known artists. The ground floor confronts the themes, challenges and roots of modern European art from the late nineteenth century through to the 1950s, by way of the Impressionists, Symbolists, a good section on Surrealism, with plenty of folkloric, mystical paintings by Brauner, and of course a room devoted to the voluptuous curves sculpted by Strasbourg's own Arp. The chronology continues upstairs with conceptual art and Arte Povera, and finishes up with stripy creations by Daniel Buren and video art by Bill Viola. The temporary exhibitions – devoted to the likes of Kandinsky and Picasso – have been reliably good.

La Petite France and the rest of the old city

On the south side of the Pont du Corbeau, the medieval **Impasse du Corbeau** still looks much as it must have done in the fourteenth century. Downstream, the **quai des Bateliers** was part of the old business quarter, and the streets leading off it – rue Ste-Madeleine, rue de la Krutenau and rue de

Zurich – are still worth a wander. Two bridges upstream, the Pont St-Thomas leads to the **church of St-Thomas** (Jan & Feb Sat & Sun 2–5pm; March & Nov–Dec daily 10am–noon & 2–5pm; April–Oct daily 10am–noon & 2–6pm; closed Sun morning for services; ☎03.88.32.14.46), with a Romanesque facade and Gothic towers. Since 1549 it has been the city's principal Protestant church. Strasbourg was a bastion of the Reformation, and one of its leaders, Martin Bucer, preached in this church. The amazing piece of sculpture behind the altar is Jean-Baptiste Pigalle's **tomb of the Maréchal de Saxe**, a very capable French military commander active against the Duke of Cumberland in the campaigns of the War of the Austrian Succession in the middle of the eighteenth century.

From here, it's a short walk upstream to the **Pont St-Martin**, which marks the beginning of the district known as **La Petite France**, where the city's millers, tanners and fishermen used to live. At the far end of a series of canals are the so-called **Ponts Couverts** (they are in fact no longer covered), built as part of the fourteenth-century city fortifications and still punctuated by watchtowers. Just beyond is a **dam** built by Vauban (daily 9am–7.30pm; mid-March to mid-Oct till 8pm; free) to protect the city from waterborne assault. The whole area is picture-postcard pretty, with winding streets – most notably rue du Bain-aux-Plantes – bordered by sixteenth- and seventeenth-century houses adorned with flowers and elaborately carved woodwork.

The area east of the cathedral is good for a stroll, too, where rue des Frères leads to place St-Étienne. **Place du Marché-Gayot**, off rue des Frères behind the cathedral, is very lively, almost southern in feel, with a row of trendy studenty cafés on the north side and a mixed bunch of eateries opposite. From the north side of the cathedral, rue du Dôme leads to the eighteenth-century **place Broglie**, with the Hôtel de Ville, the bijou Opera House and some imposing eighteenth-century mansions. It was at 4 place Broglie in 1792 that Rouget de l'Isle first sang what later became known as the Marseillaise for the mayor of Strasbourg, who had challenged him to compose a rousing song for the troops of the army of the Rhine.

The Alsatian language

Travelling through the province, it's easy to mistake the language being spoken in the shops and streets for German. In fact, it is **Elsässisch**, or Alsatian, a High German dialect, known to philologists as Alemannic. To confuse matters further, there are two versions, High and Low Alemannic, as well as an obscure Frankish dialect spoken in the Wissembourg region and a Romance one called *Welche* from the valleys around Orbey. You'll hear a different version spoken in almost every town.

In many ways, it's a miracle that the language has survived, since Alsatian was actively discouraged under both French and German rule. During the French Revolution, the language was suppressed in favour of French for nationalistic reasons, only to be ousted by German when the Prussians annexed the region in 1870. On its return to French rule, all things Germanic were disdained, and many Alsatians began to speak French once more ... until the Nazi occupation brought in laws that made the speaking of French and even the wearing of berets imprisonable offences.

Nowadays, most daily transactions are conducted in French, and Elsässisch has still not made it onto the school curriculum. Yet it remains a living language, with a rich medieval literary legacy, and is still spoken by young and old throughout Alsace – especially in rural areas – and even parts of Lorraine. A renaissance of regional identity has meant that Elsässisch is also beginning to reappear on signs and to be spoken at official level too.

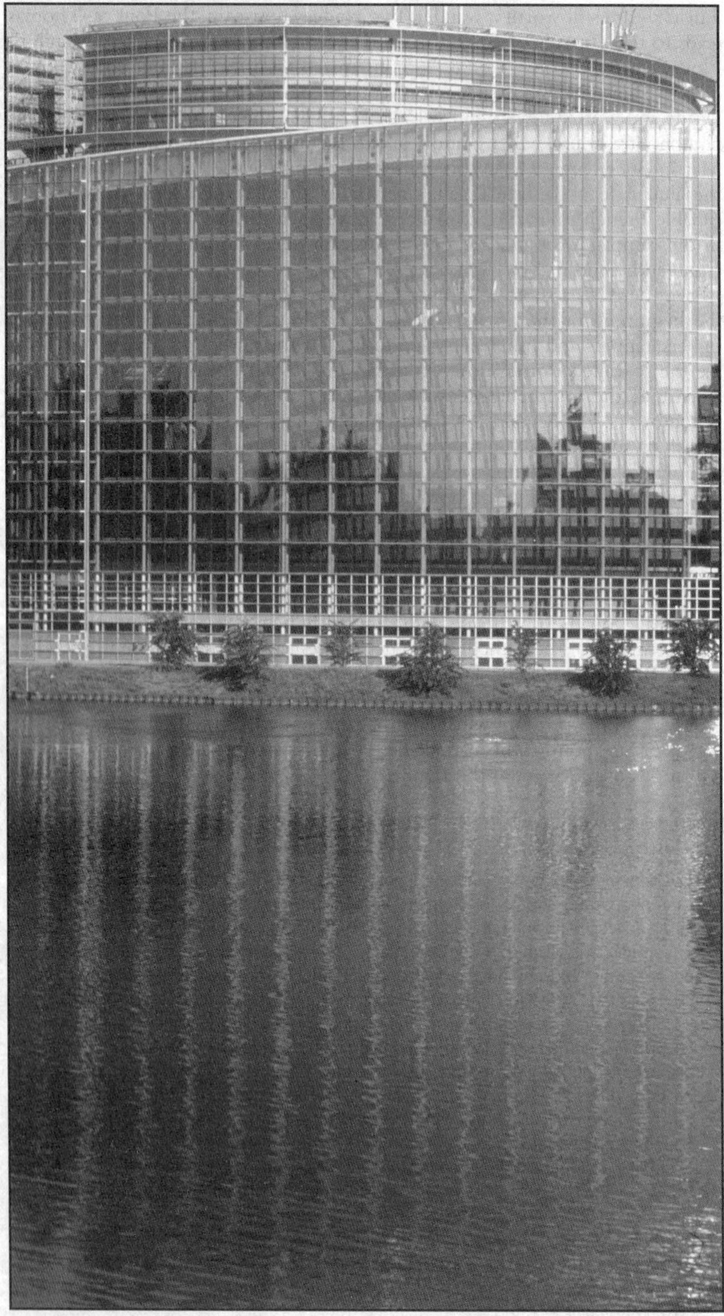

△ The European Parliament, Strasbourg

The German quarter (Neustadt) and the European institutions

Across the canal from place Broglie, **place de la République** is surrounded by vast German neo-Gothic edifices erected during the post-1870 Imperial Prussian occupation, one example being the main **post office** on avenue de la Liberté. At the centre of the square is a war memorial showing a mother holding two dead sons in her arms, neither of which, unusually for such monuments, wears a military uniform. This testifies to the horrific family divisions faced by Alsatian families, whose members often found themselves fighting on opposing sides in World War II. At the other end of avenue de la Liberté, across the confluence of the Ill and Aar, is the city's **university**, where Goethe studied. Adjacent, at the beginning of boulevard de la Victoire, are the splendidly Teutonic municipal baths, the **Grand Établissement Municipal de Bains**, where you can take a sauna or Turkish bath (€10.20) or just swim (consult the complicated opening hours on the board outside).

From in front of the university, the wide, straight alleé de la Robertsau, flanked by confident *fin-de-siècle* bourgeois residences and beautiful early-twentieth century buildings including some Jugenstil masterpieces, leads to the headquarters of the three major European institutions: the bunker-like **Palais de l'Europe**, 1970s-built home of the 44-member Council of Europe; the glass and steel curvilinear **European Parliament building**, opened in 1999; and Richard Rogers' 1995 contribution for the **European Court of Human Rights**, with its curving glass entrance and silver towers rising to a boat-like superstructure overlooking a sweep of canal. To visit the European Parliament (☎03.88.17.20.07; free) or the European Court of Human Rights and the Council of Europe (☎03.90.21.49.40; free) you have to book.

Opposite the Palais, the **Orangerie** is Strasbourg's best bit of greenery, and hosts a variety of exhibitions and free concerts. Here the *cigognes* (storks), to be seen perching on many buildings in the town, have their main nesting site. There's also a zoo with small animals, such as monkeys, and exotic birds including flamingos apparently fed pink sausage-colouring to enhance the vivid hue of their plumage.

Eating and drinking

For the classic Strasbourg **eating** experience, you have to go to a **winstub**, loosely translated as a "wine bar", a cosy establishment with bare beams, panels and benches, and a noisy, convivial atmosphere. In the classic version there is a special table, a "Stamtisch", set aside for the *patron's* buddies and regulars. The food revolves around the Alsatian classics: *choucroute*, *tarte à l'oignon*, knuckle of pork with horseradish and ham *en croûte*, all accompanied by local wines (or beer, especially in a *bierstub*), though the more sophisticated ones offer interesting variations on these themes. Place du Marché-Gayot ("PMG") near the cathedral is one of the best spots for **cafés**, most open until late, while there is a good selection of less touristy **restaurants** in rue du Faubourg Saverne. The city and rest of the region have more than their fair share of **Michelin stars**; to splash out on a special occasion book ahead for a gastronomic experience to remember at either of the two star-bearers listed below. For some variety you could also tap into Strasbourg's astonishing array of eateries representing **foreign cuisines**, including excellent Italian and Chinese, plus Japanese, Jewish, Afghan and Thai.

Restaurants

Le Buerehiesel 4 parc de l'Orangerie ⓣ03.88.45.56.65, ⓦwww.buerehiesel.com. With three Michelin stars, this outstanding restaurant, delightfully housed in a farmhouse in the Parc de l'Orangerie, is the ideal place for an extravagant bout of self-pampering. Menus €50–130.

La Choucrouterie 20 rue St-Louis, by the church of St-Louis, just across Pont St-Thomas ⓣ03.88.36.07.28. *Choucroute* specialist with menus starting at €18.30, *plats* from about €11. Cabaret acts. Closed Sun & first two weeks Aug.

Au Coin des Pucelles 12 rue des Pucelles ⓣ03.88.35.35.14. Reasonably priced *winstub* popular with theatre-goers as it's open late, serving traditional fare with an original twist and reliable wines. Closed Tues and Sun.

Le Crocodile 10 rue de l'Outre ⓣ03.88.32.13.02, ⓦwww.au-crocodile.com. The chef at this slightly starchy institution, boasting a couple of Michelin stars, invents startlingly original menus using local produce such as game, foie gras and plums. Menus €55–115.

Flam's 1 rue de l'Epine, and another at cnr of rues des Frères & du Faisan ⓣ03.88.75.77.44 or 03.88.36.36.90). *Tarte flambée* (pizza-like speciality) restaurant, very popular with locals. A good place to sample the local speciality with the €11 all-you-can-eat *tarte flambée* menu (includes dessert). Meals from €5.

S'Munsterstuewel 8 place du Marché-aux-Cochons-de-Lait ⓣ03.88.32.17.63, ⓔmunsterstuewel@wanadoo.fr. A very special *winstub* on one of the city's most attractive squares and serving both traditional and more unusual dishes till late, with excellent wines to match. Closed Sun & Mon. Meals around €40.

Le Panier du Marché 15 rue Sainte Barbe ⓣ03.88.32.04.07. Stylish gourmet restaurant with young clientele and a fixed menu (€25 without drinks), using seasonal ingredients to compose meals of outstanding quality. Closed Sat & Sun.

Poêles de Carottes 2 place des Meuniers ⓣ03.88.32.33.23. Good vegetarian restaurant in picturesque Petite France. Lunch €9, dinner €17. Closed Sun.

La Robe des Champs 4 rue de l'Écurie ⓣ03.88.22.36.82. Potato-fanciers will enjoy the variety of things they can do – inexpensively – with the spud here. Menu €6–20. Closed lunchtimes Sat & Sun, last week in July & first week in Aug.

Les Trois Brasseurs 22 rue des Veaux. Wonderful *winstub*, which brews its own beer: the enormous copper brewing equipment is part of the decor. *Tarte flambée* from €4.60. Other Alsatian specialities available. Happy hour 5–7pm.

La Victoire 24 quai des Pêcheurs ⓣ03.88.35.39.35. A popular inn, worth experiencing for its lively student ambience rather than the food. Menu from €15, plats €6.75. Closed Sat eve, Sun & first three weeks in Aug.

Zum Strissel 5 place de la Grande-Boucherie ⓣ03.88.32.14.73. Traditional *winstub* with a faithful clientele and famous for its rhubarb tart, with menus at €10–21 (€7 for the *plat du jour*). Closed Sun, Mon & one week in Feb & July.

Cafés and bars

Académie de la Bière 17 rue Adolphe-Seyboth, near the church of St-Pierre. Strasbourg's most famous *bierstub*. Open daily till 4am.

Les Aviateurs 12 rue des Sœurs. *Les Aviat'*, as it's known locally, is regularly packed with Strasbourg's fashionable intelligentsia sipping cocktails or draught Guinness until 4am.

Café Brant place Sebastian-Brant. Atmospheric café close to the University. Outdoor tables make it perfect for summer meals.

Le Divan 6 impasse de l'Ecrevisse, off Place Broglie. Trendy music bar with mellow decor, open in evening until late; gay nights on Wed, closed Sun & Mon.

Montmartre 6 rue du Vieux-Marché-aux-Poissons. Shiny Parisian-style café near the cathedral.

La Salamandre 3 rue Paul-Janet ⓣ03.88.25.79.42. A popular bar-disco (free entrance) famous for its rock concerts (tickets €8–20) and theme nights (€3–5).

Tapas Café 16 rue du Bain-Finkwiller, south of Petit France, across the Pont des Moulins and next to the fire-station. Cool Spanish bar, with wonderful, affordable tapas and refreshing sangria.

Troc' Café 8 rue du Faubourg de Saverne ⓣ03.88.23.23.29. Easy-going café often hosting concerts or theme nights. Also does a good brunch. Closed Sun.

Entertainment

Strasbourg usually has lots going on, above all musically. Pick up free monthly **magazine** *Spectacles à Strasbourg et alentours* (ⓦwww.spectaclespublications.com), with entertainment info and practical listings and, in summer months, the free *Saison d'Été* **listings leaflet**, both available from the tourist offices. If you're here during university term-time, you might want to check the notice boards at the university as well. **Free concerts** are held regularly in the Parc des Contades and Parc de l'Orangerie, which also boasts a bowling alley. The best of the annual festivals starts with classical music in mid-June, followed by jazz in July, and "contemporary classical" music from mid-September to early October. In addition, there's **Les Nuits de Strasbourg**, a firework, light and music display at the Ponts Couverts during July and August, and an impressive illumination of the Cathedral facade every summer evening. At the Christkindelsmärik or **Marché de Noël** (late Nov to Dec 24), an increasingly commercial event dating back over 400 years, central Strasbourg is taken over by wooden stalls selling mulled wine, crafts of varying quality and spicy Christmas cookies known as *bredele*.

Listings

Ambulance (SAMU) ⓣ15.

Bike rental Bicycles can be rented from 4 rue du Maire Kuss, Parking Ste-Aurélie, place du Château and Impasse de la Grande Écluse (near the Ponts Couverts) for €5 a day.

Boat trips Strasbourg Fluvial (ⓣ03.88.84.13.13, ⓦwww.strasbourg.port.fr) runs cruises on the Ill year round. Cruises depart from the landing stage in front of the Palais Rohan (daily: April–Nov every 30min 9.30am–9pm; Dec–March four departures 10.30am–4pm). The itinerary includes Petite-France, the Vauban dam and the Palais de l'Europe. Evening cruises depart at 9.30pm and 10pm May to September only. The trip costs €6.80, half price for students and children (€7.20 for evening cruises) and lasts 1hr 10min.

Books FNAC, 22 place Kléber, for huge selection of books, records and concert tickets; Librairie Internationale Kléber, 1 rue des Francs-Bourgeois, sells new books, some in English; La Librocase, 2 quai des Pêcheurs, sells secondhand books; Quai des Brumes, 120 Grand' Rue, has a very good range; Bookworm, 4 rue de Pâques, is a small English bookshop with new and used books and greetings cards.

Buses Eurolines has an office at 5 rue des Frères ⓣ03.88.22.73.74. Some out-of-town buses leave from place des Halles.

Car rental Europcar, airport ⓣ03.88.68.95.55; 15 place de la Gare ⓣ03.88.15.55.66; Avis, Galérie Marchande, place de la Gare ⓣ03.88.32.30.44; Hertz, airport ⓣ03.88.64.69.50; 6 bd de Metz by the gare SNCF ⓣ03.88.32.57.62.

Cinemas Le Star, 27 rue du Jeu-des-Enfants (ⓣ03.88.22.73.20) and Le Star St Exupéry, 18 rue du 22 novembre (ⓣ03.88.22.28.79); L'Odyssée, 3 rue des Francs-Bourgeois (ⓣ03.88.75.10.47), a sumptuous restored cinema with red velvet seats, shows a combination of classic and contemporary films, many in v.o.

Internet Midi minuit, 5 place du Corbeau (Mon–Wed 7am–7pm, Thurs–Sat 7am–10pm, Sun 8am–7pm; access for a minimum of 30min; €0.15 per minute).

Markets The city's biggest fruit and vegetable market takes place every Tues and Sat morning on bd de la Marne; mostly organic local produce, including foie gras and honey, is sold on the small square next to the forecourt of the Palais des Rohan every Sat morning; the Marché aux Puces (Wed & Sat) is on rue du Vieil-Hôpital (near the cathedral).

Post office 5 av de la Marseillaise and place de la Cathédrale.

Taxis Novotaxi ⓣ03.88.75.19.19; Taxis 13 ⓣ03.88.36.13.13.

The northern Vosges

The **northern Vosges** begin at the Saverne gap northwest of Strasbourg and run up to the German border, where they continue as the Pfälzerwald. They don't reach the same heights as the southern Vosges, nor do they boast particularly photogenic villages or famous vineyards but, as a result, they're spared the mass tourism of the southern range. Much of the region comes under the auspices of the Parc Régional des Vosges du Nord, and there are numerous hiking possibilities, as well as a couple of attractive towns – **Saverne** and **Wissembourg** – built in the characteristic red sandstone of the area.

Transport here is erratic, as elsewhere in Alsace, though not hopeless. SNCF buses wind their way through the villages and apple orchards around Hagenau, and the Strasbourg–Sarreguemines and Hagenau–Bitche train lines cut across the range. Saverne and Wissembourg are also linked to Strasbourg by rail. Even so, the ideal way to explore the region is with your own transport – hilly but rewarding work, if it's a bike.

Saverne and around

SAVERNE, seat of the exiled Catholic prince-bishops of Strasbourg during the Reformation, commands the only easy route across the Vosges into Alsace, at a point where the hills are pinched to a narrow waist. It's a small and friendly town, not as pretty as some of its neighbours, but possessing the region's characteristic steep-pitched roofs and window boxes full of geraniums. It's also the best launch pad from which to explore the northern Vosges.

The town has a couple of sights worth visiting, not least the vast red sandstone **Château des Rohan**, on place de Gaulle, built in rather austere classical style by one of the Rohans who was prince-bishop at the time, and now housing the **Musée Rohan** (March–June & Sept–Nov daily except Tues 2–5pm; July & Aug daily except Tues 10am–noon & 2–6pm; Dec–March Sun only 2–5pm; €2.50) and hostel. A feature of the museum is the collection of local Resistance journalist Louise Weiss. The River Zorn and the Marne–Rhine canal both weave their way through the town, the latter framing the château's formal gardens in a graceful right-angle bend. Alongside the château, the **church of Notre-Dame-de-la-Nativité** contains another finely carved pulpit by Hans Hammer. Horticultural distraction can be found in the town's famed rose garden, **La Roseraie** (June–Sept daily 9am–7pm; ☎03.88.71.83.33; €2.30), to the west of the centre by the river, which boasts over four hundred varieties; and the **botanical gardens** 3km out of town off the N4 Metz–Nancy road (May, June & first two weeks Sept Mon–Fri 9am–5pm, Sun 2–6pm; July & Aug Mon–Fri 9am–5pm, Sat & Sun 2–7pm; €2.50).

There are several relatively easy **walks** around Saverne (the tourist office can give details), the most popular being the one to the ruined **Château du Haut-Barr** (2hr return). Follow rue du Haut-Barr southeast along the canal past the leafy suburban villas until you reach the woods, where a signboard indicates the various walks possible. Take the path marked "Haut-Barr" through woods of chestnut, beech and larch, and you'll see the castle standing dramatically on a narrow sandstone ridge, with fearsome drops on both sides and views across the wooded hills and eastward over the plain towards Strasbourg. Approaching by road you'll pass the reconstruction of a late eighteenth-century **relay tower** that was part of the optical telegraph link between Paris and Strasbourg until the middle of the nineteenth century; an audiovisual presentation inside explains the pioneering system invented by Claude Chappe in 1794 (July & Aug Tues–Sun noon–6pm; €1.50).

If you're driving, you can easily get to the several beautiful small towns and villages around Saverne, in particular Bouxwiller, Neuwiller, Pfaffenhoffen and Ingwiller, from where an alternative road to Bitche leads through the densely wooded heart of the northern Vosges. A focus to your explorations could be the **Château of Lichtenburg** (March & Nov Mon–Sat 1–4pm, Sun 10am–7pm; April, May, Sept & Oct Mon 1.30–6pm, Tues–Sat 10am–noon & 1.30–4pm, Sun & hols 10am–7pm; June–Aug Mon 1.30–6pm,

Tues–Sat 10am–6pm, Sun & hols 10am–7pm; €2.50), dating back to the thirteenth century and much restored, situated just a short way outside Ingwiller.

Practicalities

The **tourist office** is at 37 Grand' Rue (Mon–Sat 9am–12.30pm & 2–7pm; May–Oct also open Sun 10am–12.30pm & 2–5pm; ⓣ03.88.91.80.47, ⓕ03.88.71.02.90); they can provide a map of walks in the area published by the Saverne Centre de Randonnées Pedestres (part of the Club Vosgien).

For **accommodation** in town, try the *Europe*, at 7 rue de la Gare (ⓣ03.88.71.12.07, ⓕ3.88.71.11.43; ❹), with bright, modern rooms. The *Hotel/Restaurant Chez Jean*, 3 rue de la Gare (ⓣ03.88.91.10.19, ⓦwww.chez-jean.com; ❺), has a restaurant with good Alsatian food (menus €17–45). A less expensive option is the *National*, 2 Grand' Rue (ⓣ03.88.91.14.54; ❹), and cheaper still is the friendly **HI hostel** in the Château Rohan, on place de Gaulle (ⓣ03.88.91.14.84, ⓕ03.88.71.15.97; reception open 8–10am & 5–10pm; cardholders only). There's also a **campsite** about 1km from town below the Château du Haut-Barr, on rue du Père Liebermann (ⓣ03.88.91.35.65; closed Oct–March). As for **food**, gourmets will appreciate the *Taverne Katz* on the main street, 80 Grand' Rue (ⓣ03.88.71.16.56; closed Tues eve & Wed; menu €15–25): not only is it a beautiful old house with an ornately carved facade and plush decor within, but the food is excellent, traditional cuisine, with very good *baeckoffe* and divine sorbets. Also worth a visit is *Restaurant Staeffele*, 1 rue Poincaré (ⓣ03.88.91.63.94; closed Wed, Thurs lunch & Sun eve; menus €35–50), for impeccably prepared Alsatian fare in stylish surroundings. More modest, and with a local ambience, is the *Restaurant de la Marne*, 5 rue du Griffon (ⓣ03.88.91.19.18; closed Mon), overlooking the Marne–Rhine canal in the centre of town, serving good copious salads amongst their varied menu. There's also a restaurant specializing in foie gras at the Château du Haut-Barr (see opposite: ⓣ03.88.91.17.61; closed all day Mon and Thurs dinner; menus €18–40).

Wissembourg

WISSEMBOURG, 60km north of Strasbourg and right on the German border, is a small town of cobbled and higgledy-piggledy prettiness, largely given over to moneyed German weekenders. The townspeople have a curious linguistic anomaly; they speak an ancient dialect derived from Frankish, unlike their fellow Alsatians whose language is closer to modern German.

At the end of rue Nationale, the town's main commercial street, stands the imposing Gothic **church of St-Paul-et-St-Pierre**, with a Romanesque belfry and some fine twelfth- and thirteenth-century stained glass, once attached to the town's abbey. Beneath the apse, the meandering River Lauter flows under the Pont du Sel beside the town's most striking secular building and first hospital, the **Maison du Sel** (1450), in a part of town dubbed **la Petite Venise** (Little Venice). A few minutes' walk away, on the northern edge of town, another fine old building, with beautifully carved woodwork round its windows, contains the town's folk museum, the **Musée Westercamp**, 3 rue du Musée (Mon, Wed & Thurs 2–6pm, Fri & Sat 9am–noon & 2–6pm, Sun & hols 10am–noon & 2–6pm; closed Jan & Feb; €2.50). Along the southern edge of town, following the riverbank from the Tour des Husgenossen in the western corner, a long section of the **medieval walls** survives intact, built – like the houses – in the local red sandstone.

The Poles of Wissembourg

Stanislas Leszczynski, born in the Polish-Ukrainian city of Lemberg (now Lviv) in 1677, lasted just five years as the elected king of Poland before being forced into exile by the Russian tsar Peter the Great. For the next twenty-odd years he lived on a French pension in Wissembourg, along with a motley entourage of Polish expats. After fifteen years of relatively humdrum existence in the town's Ancien Hôpital south of the main church, Stanislas' luck changed when he managed, against all odds, to get his daughter, Marie, betrothed to the 15-year-old king of France, Louis XV. Marie was not quite so fortunate: married by proxy in Strasbourg Cathedral, and having never even set eyes on the groom, she subsequently had a total of ten children, only to be ultimately rejected by Louis, who preferred hunting and the company of his two more powerful mistresses, Madame de Pompadour and Madame du Barry. Bolstered by his daughter's marriage, Stanislas had another brief spell on the Polish throne from 1733 to 1736, but eventually gave it up in favour of the comfortable dukedom of Barr and Lorraine. He lived out his final years in true aristocratic style in the capital, Nancy, which he transformed into one of France's most beautiful towns.

Practicalities

Wissembourg's **tourist office** is at 9 place de la République (May–Sept Mon–Sat 9am–12.30pm & 2–6pm, Sun 2–5.30pm; Oct–April Mon–Sat 9am–noon & 2–5.30pm; ⓣ03.88.94.10.11, ⓦwww.ot-wissembourg.fr). From the **gare SNCF** the "Office du Tourisme" signs are for cars – if you're on foot the quickest route is to turn left out of the station and walk to the roundabout, where you'll see signs of café life. Turn right and you're in town.

For **accommodation**, the most attractive hotel is the *Hôtel du Cygne*, 3 rue du Sel, next to the town hall on the central place de la République (ⓣ03.88.94.00.16, ⓕ03.88.54.38.28; ❸; closed two weeks in Feb & two weeks in July; restaurant €20–54). Otherwise, try the *Hôtel-Restaurant au Moulin de la Walk*, 2 rue de la Walk, by the hospital just outside the old town (ⓣ03.88.94.06.44, ⓕ03.88.54.38.03; ❹; closed Sun eve, Mon, Jan 8–30 & June 15–30), which has a very good but rather pricey restaurant, with the cheapest menu at €30 – easy-listening music included. Friendly and less expensive is the *Hôtel de la Gare*, opposite the train station (ⓣ03.88.94.13.67, ⓕ03.88.94.06.88; ❸), whose restaurant is also cheaper (closed Sun; menu at €14–27). In the main street, the hotel-restaurant *L'Escargot*, 40 rue Nationale (ⓣ03.88.94.90.29, ⓕ03.88.94.90.29; ❸; menu at €11.50–23; closed Sun), is less expensive still and its restaurant serves traditional Alsatian cuisine.

In addition to the hotel restaurants above there are a couple of reasonable **places to eat** on the main rue Nationale, including *Au Petit Dominicain*, 36 rue Nationale (ⓣ03.88.94.90.87; closed Mon and Tues; menu at €9–20), which serves traditional Alsatian food. A much fancier establishment, with a chef who serves his own inventive variations on the traditional regional cuisine, is *À l'Ange*, 2 rue de la République (ⓣ03.88.94.12.11; closed Tues eve, Wed & last two weeks in Feb), in a beautiful old house by the stream next to place du Marché-aux-Choux (the cheapest menu is the lunchtime €28, otherwise you're looking at twice that). For simple *tartes flambées*, *Au Saumon*, behind the Maison du Sel (ⓣ03.88.94.17.60), has a delightful garden and outdoor oven (from €6). *La Mirabelle*, 3 rue Générale Leclerc (ⓣ03.88.54.82.14) is an agreeable outdoor café for summer meals, also from €6.

The Route des Châteaux

Scattered among the wooded hills to the west of Wissembourg are a host of ruined castles that once stood guard over the frontier with Germany, and the winding D3 and its smaller tributaries, which cross the now untenanted frontier, take you close to most of them. The ruins of the **Château du Fleckenstein** (daily: mid-March to April & Nov 1–15 10am–5pm; May–Oct 10am–6pm; €2.60 in the summer and at weekends, otherwise €2), 7km north of Lembach (see below), are perhaps the most spectacular, rising above the forest on a narrow sandstone outcrop, just a stone's throw from the German border. Six kilometres further on at Obersteinbach, the **Maison des Châteaux-Forts**, at 42 rue Principal (March–Oct Wed 2–5pm, Sat & Sun 3–6pm; €2), is an information centre, with displays and maps on the other castles in the area. A rather more modern fortress, just outside Lembach, is the **Four à Chaux**, part of the Maginot Line (guided tours: mid-March to June & Sept to mid-Nov 10am, 2pm & 3pm; July & Aug 10am, 11am & hourly 2–5pm; ⓣ03.88.94.48.62; €4).

An agreeable base for exploring this area is the village of **LEMBACH**, where the homely and unpretentious *Hôtel au Heimbach*, 15 rue de Wissembourg (ⓣ03.88.94.43.46, ⓕ03.88.94.20.85; ❸), is a pleasant **place to stay**. Directly opposite, the *Auberge du Cheval Blanc* (ⓣ03.88.94.41.86, ⓕ03.88.94.20.74; closed Mon & Tues Feb & July; menu at €30–75) serves exquisite but expensive cuisine.

The southern Vosges

The **southern Vosges** cover a much greater area than the northern range, stretching as far south as Belfort in Franche-Comté. The major tourist attractions are along the **Route du Vin**, which follows the foot of the mountains along the western edge of the wide flat valley of the Rhine; every turn in the road reveals yet another exquisitely preserved medieval village. Many of these, such as **Colmar**, the main centre for the route, suffer from an overdose of visitors, so to escape from the crowds, you need to head for the hills proper, along the **Route des Crêtes**, which traces the central ridge of the Vosges to the west.

The Route du Vin

Alsace is a region both blessed and cursed by tourism, and no more so than along the so-called **Route du Vin**, which stretches from Marlenheim, west of Strasbourg, to Thann, near Mulhouse. Although, when left to its own devices, Alsace stays on the right side of Disneyland, under the impact of tourism and out of the desire to make money, it comes painfully close to caricaturing itself. That said the winegrowers themselves certainly do not rely on tourists to earn a living, most of the wine being sold to restaurants and merchants or exported to major markets such as Switzerland, Japan and Britain.

Set against the "blue line of the Vosges", the route winds north–south through endless terraced vineyards which produce the region's famous white wines. Opportunities for tasting the local produce are plentiful, with free *dégustations* along the roadside and in the *caveaux* of most villages (though you're expected to buy at least a couple of bottles), and also at the region's countless wine festivals – mostly coinciding with the October harvest. For a closer look at the vines themselves you can follow various *sentiers vinicoles* (vineyard paths); Strasbourg and local tourist offices have details. In the midst of this sea of vines are dozens of typically picturesque Alsatian villages, outdoing each other to have the biggest display of window-box geraniums and dominated from the nearby craggy heights by an extraordinary number of ancient ruined castles, testimony to the province's turbulent past.

The Route du Vin is deceptively hilly work on a bike, but **getting around** is definitely easier with your own transport. Otherwise you're dependent either on the train, which narrowly misses some of the best villages, or the region's so-so bus service. In summer and autumn there's a **food or wine festival** each weekend in a different town or village, with wine tastings, *tarte flambée* and other local delicacies, arts and crafts and, if you're unlucky, traditional Alsatian music.

Obernai and around

Picturesque little **OBERNAI**, on the D422, is the first place most people head for when travelling south along the route from Strasbourg. Miraculously unscathed during the last two world wars, Obernai has retained almost its entire **rampart system**, including no fewer than fifteen towers, as well as street after street of carefully maintained medieval houses. Not surprisingly, it also gets more than its fair share of visitors, though this shouldn't put you off as the town is just about big enough to absorb the crowds – though try to come on a weekday in the summer. The **tourist office**, on place du Beffroi (May–Oct Mon–Sat 9.30am–12.30pm & 2–7pm, Sun 9am–12.30pm & 2–5.30pm; Nov–April Mon–Sat 9am–noon & 2–5pm; ⓣ03.88.95.64.13), has lots of useful information about wine and easy-to-follow routes for exploring the region. The only reasonably priced **hotels** are the *Maison du Vin*, 1 rue de la Paille (ⓣ03.88.95.46.82, ⓕ03.88.95.54.00; ❸), whose pretty rooms are above a wine shop; and *La Diligence*, 23 place de la Mairie (ⓣ03.88.95.55.69, ⓕ03.88.95.42.46; ❸), with a charming and reasonably priced *salon de thé* serving *petits plats* all day. *La Halle au Blé* café is a good place for a hot chocolate after a hard day's hiking in the Vosges.

ROSHEIM, 7km north of Obernai and up in the hills a little to the west of the D422, is relatively off the beaten track. Its two main sights are the Romanesque **church of St-Pierre-et-St-Paul**, whose roof is peppered with comical sculptured figures contemporary with the building, and the twelfth-century **Heidenhüs**, at 24 rue de la Principale, thought to be the oldest building in Alsace. The simple, clean, friendly family-run *Hôtel Alpina*, 39 rue du Lion (ⓣ03.88.50.49.30, ⓕ03.88.49.25.75; ❸), with an attractive terrace and breakfast room, is a great place to stay. **ROSENWILLER**, a couple of kilometres up the hill among the vineyards, has a prettily sited and atmospherically overgrown **Jewish cemetery** at the edge of the woods, testimony to Alsace's once numerous Jewish community.

From Rosheim's *gare SNCF*, 1.5km northeast of the village, a **steam train** runs up the valley on Sundays and holidays to **OTTROTT**, which produces one of the few red wines of Alsace. An elegantly restored and modernized village house at 11 rue des Châteaux has been transformed into a rather luxurious **hotel**, the *Hostellerie des Châteaux* (ⓣ03.88.48.14.14, ⓕ03.88.95.95.20; ❽), with a sauna, swimming pool and overpriced restaurant. Just out of town is the Aquarium d'Ottrot, **Les Naïades** (daily 9.30am–6.30pm; €7), with sharks, crocodiles and thousands of fish from all over the world: follow the signs.

Ottrott brings you within hiking distance – 6km – of **Mont Ste-Odile** (763m), whose summit is surrounded by a mysterious Celtic wall, originally built in the seventh century BC. The wall is almost 10km in length and in parts reaches a height of 3.5m. St Odilia herself is buried in the small **chapel** on top of the hill, a pilgrimage site even today. According to tradition, she was cast out by her father at birth on account of her blindness, but miraculously regained her sight during childhood and returned to found the convent on Mont Ste-Odile, where she cured thousands of cases of blindness and leprosy. Accommodation is available here at *Le Mont Ste-Odile* (ⓣ03.88.95.80.53, ⓕ03.88.95.82.96; ❸; bookings advisable).

Barr

For some reason, **BARR**, west of the main road, is overlooked by mass tourism. Every bit as charming as Obernai, it's easy to while away a couple of hours wandering its twisting cobbled streets, at their busiest during the mid-July **wine festival** and on Sundays when the vintners come to ply their wines. The town has just one specific sight, **La Folie Marco**, at 30 rue du Docteur-Sultzer (July–Sept daily except Tues 10am–noon & 2–6pm; June & Oct Sat & Sun 10am–noon & 2–6pm; ⓣ03.88.08.94.72; €3), an unusually large eighteenth-century house on the outskirts of town along the road to Obernai, which has displays of period French and Alsatian furniture. There are regular *dégustations* in the garden cellar, and a festival of dance and waltz at the end of May. There's also a **restaurant** serving Alsatian specialities (menus €17–24, *tarte flambée* €7). Some interesting walks begin behind the Hôtel de Ville, including one to Mont Ste-Odile (14km; 3–4 hours).

The nearest **gare SNCF** is in the neighbouring village of Gertwiller, 1km to the east. The nicest **place to stay** in Barr is the superb *Hôtel Le Manoir*, 11 rue St-Marc (ⓣ03.88.08.03.40, ⓕ03.88.08.53.71; ❹), on the edge of town, with light, spacious rooms and a splendid buffet breakfast. Alternatively, there are two **campsites**: the *Camping St-Martin*, at rue de l'Ill, near the Catholic church (ⓣ03.88.08.00.45; June to mid-Oct), and *Camping Municipal Ste-Odile "Wepfermatt"*, 3km out of town at 137 rue de la Vallée (ⓣ03.88.08.02.38; May–Oct). St-Pierre, 3km south of Barr, also has a campsite – the *Beau Séjour* (ⓣ03.88.08.52.24 or 03.88.08.90.79; mid-May to Sept). For a really good *tarte flambée* in a **restaurant** with great atmosphere, try *Les Caveau des Tanneurs*, 32 rue Neuve (ⓣ03.88.08.91.50; *tarte flambée* from €6; Wed–Sun dinner only): the *munster* (a pungent kind of cheese) with cumin seeds is particularly good. *Winstub S'Barrer Stubbel*, 5 place de l'Hôtel de Ville (ⓣ03.88.08.57.44), also serves good local specialities at reasonable prices.

Le Struthof concentration camp

Deep in the forests and hills of the Vosges, over 20km west of Barr, **Le Struthof-Natzwiller** (daily: March–June 10am–noon & 2–4.30pm; July & Aug 10am–5pm; Sept–Dec 10am–noon & 2–4.30pm; closed Jan & Feb; ⓣ03.88.97.04.49; €1.52) was the only Nazi concentration camp to be built on French soil (though at the time, of course, it was part of the Greater German Reich). The site is almost perversely beautiful, its stepped terraces cut into steep hillside, giving fantastic views across the Bruche valley. Set up shortly after Hitler's occupation of Alsace-Lorraine in 1940, it is thought that over 10,000 people died here. When the Allies liberated the camp on November 23, 1944, they found it empty – the remaining prisoners having already been transported to Dachau.

The barbed wire and watchtowers are as they were, though only two of the prisoners' barracks remain, one of which is now a **museum** of the deportations. Captions are in French only, but the pictures suffice to tell the story. An

Alsace and Hitler's Reich

When **Hitler** conquered France in 1940, he not only occupied Alsace, but also incorporated it into the German state, making it subject to German laws and outlawing all manifestations of French and Alsatian culture. Worst of all, he conscripted 140,000 young Alsatian men, citizens of France, into the German armies, on pain of reprisals against their families if they attempted to escape. They are known as the "**malgré-nous**": soldiers against their will.

Most of the *malgré-nous* were sent to the Russian front, where, as one survivor related, they were used as human minesweepers, sent into attack first across the Russian minefields. Forty thousand died and forty thousand have never been accounted for. Some deserted, and were hidden by their families, and others mutilated themselves. Many were taken prisoner and ended up in the Soviet Gulag, in the notorious camp at Tambov, in particular, northeast of Odessa, where they either died or were eventually repatriated in broken health. Having experienced the fascist Legion of French Volunteers against Bolshevism, the Russians were understandably not very sympathetic to Frenchmen fighting in German uniform, and dragged their feet over sending them back. The last *malgré-nous* to be released came home in 1955, after ten years in a Siberian camp.

Yet the most bitter experience for these soldiers was finding themselves, after so much suffering, treated as traitors by their fellow Frenchmen. A friend, recounting her father's experience as a *malgré-nous*, said: "The Germans took our children as if they were their own and after all that we were treated by France as the bloody Germans of the east."

For nearly sixty years the **veterans' association** has fought for recognition of these unwilling soldiers of the Reich and for compensation in the form of pensions and invalidity benefits. And still the painful ambiguity endures. Thirteen Alsatian *malgré-nous* fought with the infamous Waffen SS Das Reich division, which was responsible, on its march to join battle with the Allies in Normandy in 1944, for the terrible massacres in Tulle and Oradour-sur-Glane (see p.749). Put on trial in the 1950s, they were granted amnesty for domestic political reasons. But the request in 1996 for a war veteran's pension by one of these old soldiers caused outrage amongst the survivors of Oradour.

arson attack on the museum by neo-Nazis in 1976 only served to underline the need for such displays. At the foot of the camp is the crematorium with its ovens still intact. A couple of kilometres down the road to the west, towards Schirmeck, the Germans built a gas chamber – proof that Le Struthof was a fully integrated part of the Nazi killing machine. To the east, the two main granite quarries worked by the internees still survive, clearly signposted from the main road.

Sélestat

Back on the Route du Vin, **SÉLESTAT**, midway between Strasbourg and Colmar, is a delightful, relatively cosmopolitan old town, which makes a good base for exploring the central and most popular section of the route. The choice of reasonable accommodation is better than average, and the town itself contains a couple of interesting churches and a great museum for bibliophiles.

The oldest and finest of the two churches is the **church of Ste-Foy**. Built by the monks of Conques, it has been much restored since but its clean, austerely Romanesque lines have not been entirely wiped out. Close by, to the north, the much larger Gothic **church of St-Georges** sports spectacularly multicoloured roof tiles and some very fine stained glass. For a brief period in the late fifteenth and early sixteenth centuries, Sélestat was the intellectual centre of Alsace, due mainly to its Latin School, which attracted a group of Humanists led by Beatus Rhenanus, whose personal library was one of the most impressive collections of its time. At the **Bibliothèque Humaniste**, founded in the fifteenth century and housed in the town's former corn exchange just by St-Georges (July & Aug Mon & Wed–Fri 9am–noon & 2–6pm, Sat 9am–noon & 2–5pm, Sun 2–5pm; Sept–June Mon & Wed–Fri 9am–noon & 2–6pm, Sat 9am–noon; €3.60), Rhenanus' collection is now on display along with some unusual and very rare books and manuscripts from as far back as the seventh century. A highlight for many is the 1507 manuscript *Cosmographiae Introductio*, the first document ever to use the word "America".

Sélestat is comparatively well served transport-wise, with frequent train connections to Strasbourg and Colmar, as well as a branch line that heads north to Strasbourg via Molsheim; the **gare SNCF** is west of the town centre down avenue de la Liberté. For a **place to stay**, there's none better than the comfortable, friendly *Auberge des Alliés*, 39 rue des Chevaliers, in the middle of town (ⓣ03.88.92.09.34, ⓕ03.88.92.12.88; ❹; closed Sun eve & Mon); its restaurant is good value and worth a look for its splendid tiled stove (menus €18–40). A funky modern alternative is the *Vaillant* on place de la République (ⓣ03.88.92.09.46; ❹; restaurant €17–37). There's a **campsite**, *Les Cigognes* (ⓣ03.88.92.03.98; May to mid-Oct), south of the centre behind Vauban's remaining ramparts. Further information is available from the **tourist office** by the ring road on boulevard du Général-Leclerc (May–Sept Mon–Fri 9am–12.30pm & 1.30–7pm, Sat 9am–noon & 2–5pm, Sun 9am–3pm; Oct–April Mon–Fri 8.30am–noon & 1.30–6pm, Sat 9am–noon & 2–5pm; ⓣ03.88.58.87.20, ⓕ03.88.92.88.63).

Castles around Sélestat

Within easy range of Sélestat is a whole host of **ruined castles**. Seven kilometres north, and accessible by train, the village of **DAMBACH-LA-VILLE**, with its walls and three fortified gates all intact, is one of the highlights of the route. A thirty-minute climb west of the village is the formidable **Castle of Bernstein**. In the Middle Ages, Alsace was culturally more German than French, and this is a typically German mountain keep: tall and narrow with few openings and little use for everyday living. Around it are residential buildings enclosed within an outer wall, the masonry cut into protruding knobs giving it a curious pimpled texture. You can also go on a mini-train **tour** of the town and vineyards (July & Aug Mon, Thurs & Sat 5pm; €5), leaving from the main town square. Dambach has an inexpensive *Camping Municipal* (ⓣ03.88.92.48.60; mid-May to mid-Oct), 1km east on the D210, and a small but most attractive and inexpensive restaurant, *À la Couronne*, 13 place du Marché (ⓣ03.88.92.40.85; closed Thurs, Feb 12–March 1 & Nov 15–30; menus €11–23).

Just 3km northwest of Sélestat is **SCHIRWILLER**, another attractive village, from where you can climb a steep, marked path to the **Castle of Ortenbourg**. Like Bernstein, it has a lofty refuge-tower with courtyards outside, very well preserved and protected by a rock-cut ditch. A few hundred metres southwest of here is **Ramstein Castle**, built in 1293 to protect the besiegers of Ortenbourg.

The best cluster of castles, however, is southwest of Sélestat. Four kilometres away, **KINTZHEIM** boasts a small but wonderful ruined castle built around a cylindrical refuge-tower. Today it's an aviary, the **Volerie des Aigles**, for birds of prey, with magnificent displays of aerial prowess by eagles and vultures (April–Nov; ⓣ03.88.92.84.33 for details of afternoon demonstrations; €7). If watching Barbary apes at play in the Vosgian jungle takes your fancy, you can do just that a couple of kilometres further west at the **Montagne des Singes** (daily: April & Oct–Nov 10am–noon & 1–5pm; May, June & Sept 10am–noon & 1–6pm; July & Aug no lunchtime closure; ⓣ03.88.92.11.09, ⓦwww.montagnedessinges.com; €7.50, children €4.50). Also on the way to Kintzheim from Sélestat is the rather tacky bird-based amusement park, the **Parc des Cigognes et Loisirs** aka "**Cigoland**" (April–Sept daily 10am–7pm; March, Oct & Nov Wed, Sat & Sun 10am–7pm; ⓣ03.88.92.05.94, ⓦwww.cigoland.com; €9, children €7.50).

Another 5km on from Kintzheim, the ruins of **Oudenbourg Castle**, its sizeable hall preserved among the trees, is dwarfed by the massive **Haut-Koenigsbourg** (daily: Mar & Oct 9.45am–5pm; Apr, May & Sept 9.30am–5.30pm; June, July & Aug 9.30am–6.30pm; Nov–Feb 9.45am–noon & 1–5pm; ⓣ03.88.82.50.60, ⓔhaut-koenigsbourg@monum.fr; €7, free for children and on first Sun of month Oct–Mar), one of the biggest, most visited castles in Alsace, and – astride its 757-metre bluff – by far the highest. Ruined after an assault in 1633, it was heavily restored in the early years of the twentieth century for Kaiser Wilhelm II. It's easy to criticize some of the detail of the restoration, but it's an enjoyable experience and a remarkably convincing re-creation of a castle-palace of the period. There are guided tours, but it's best explored on your own, taking in the fantastic views. There's a winding road down to Bergheim from here (see below), if you'd rather not retrace your tracks to Sélestat.

Ribeauvillé and around

RIBEAUVILLÉ is the largest town between Sélestat and Colmar – not as pretty as some of its immediate neighbours, but right at the foot of the mountains and well placed for exploring the many castles and villages that surround it. If you wish to **stay**, you could try the fancy but friendly little *Hôtel de la Tour*, in a converted winery at 1 rue de la Mairie (ⓣ03.89.73.72.73, ⓕ03.89.73.38.74; ❹; closed Jan to mid-March), with a Turkish bath and a *winstub*. Two local **campsites** are *Camping des Trois Châteaux* (ⓣ03.89.73.20.00; July & Aug), to the north of Ribeauvillé, and the much plusher *Pierre-de-Courbertin* site (ⓣ03.89.73.66.71; March–Nov) to the south.

In the vicinity of the town are the romantic ruins of a trio of fortresses built by the counts of Ribeaupierre: **St-Ulrich**, an hour's haul up a marked path; just north of it the smaller **Girsberg**, balanced on a pinnacle which somehow provides room for a bailey, two towers and other buildings; and, further on, the ruins of the **Château du Haut-Ribeaupierre**. In varying states of decay, all three fortresses are open to the public, free of charge, but the keep at Haut-Ribeaupierre is inaccessible for safety reasons.

BERGHEIM, 3.5km northeast of Ribeauvillé, retains a good part of its old fortifications, with three towers still surviving – despite being one of the most beautiful Alsatian villages, it rarely attracts the attentions of the tour groups. Also within easy walking range of Ribeauvillé, this time to the south, the village of **HUNAWIHR** is another beguiling hamlet, with a fourteenth-century walled church standing out amid the green vines. Hunawihr is at the forefront of the Alsatian ecological movement aimed at protecting the stork – the *cigogne* – of the region, and there's a **reserve** for them plus otters and other fishing mammals to the east of the village, the **Centre de Réintroduction des Cigognes et des Loutres** (April–May & Sept to mid-Nov daily

10am–noon & 2–6pm; June–Aug daily 10am–6pm; call to check show times, ⓣ03.89.73.72.62; €7.50).

Lastly, nearer to the hub of Colmar are a couple of very busy tourist targets, which are best visited midweek or out of season. A couple of kilometres south of Hunawihr, the walled village of **RIQUEWIHR** is exceptionally well preserved, with plenty of medieval houses and a château containing a **postal museum**, the Musée d'Histoire des PTT d'Alsace (April to mid-Nov daily except Tues 10am–noon & 2–6pm; €3); consequently it suffers more visitors per annum than any other village along the route. **KAYSERSBERG**, still further southwest, boasts a fortified **bridge** and a handsome sixteenth-century wooden altarpiece in the main **church**. But the town's principal renown is as the birthplace of Nobel Peace Prize winner Albert Schweitzer, who spent most of his extremely active, and not always peaceful, life at the leprosy hospital he founded at Lambaréné in French Equatorial Africa, now Gabon. During World War I he was interned by the French authorities as an "enemy alien", but nowadays he's suitably honoured with the **Centre Culturel Albert Schweitzer**, 126 rue du Général-de-Gaulle (Easter & May–Oct daily 9am–noon & 2–6pm; €1).

Two kilometres from Kaysersberg in the village of **KIENTZHEIM** (see also box on p.352), the very comfortable *Hostellerie de l'Abbaye d'Alspach*, 2–4 rue Foch (ⓣ03.89.47.16.00, ⓕ03.89.78.29.73; ❹; closed mid-Jan to mid-March), in a former abbey, makes a good base for visiting Colmar, 10km away. If staying, be sure to try some of the homemade wine.

Colmar

The old centre of **COLMAR**, a fifty-minute train ride south of Strasbourg, is typically and whimsically Alsatian, with crooked houses, half-timbered and painted, on crooked lanes – all extremely pretty, and very touristy. The modern city, however, has sprawled unattractively on both sides of the train tracks. Colmar's attractions don't stop at its buildings; it is also the proud possessor of one of the last and most extraordinary of all Gothic paintings – the altarpiece for St Anthony's monastery at Issenheim, painted by Mathias Grünewald.

Arrival, information and accommodation

From the **gare SNCF** it's a ten-minute walk down avenue de la République to the **tourist office** on place d'Unterlinden (April–June, Sept & Oct Mon–Sat 9am–6pm, Sun 10am–2pm; July & Aug Mon–Sat 9am–7pm, Sun 9.30am–2pm; Nov–March Mon–Sat 9am–noon & 2–6pm, Sun 10am–2pm; ⓣ03.89.20.68.92, ⓦwww.ot-colmar.fr). Besides selling Club Vosgien hiking maps and a booklet of day walks in the hills behind the town, they'll also give you details of the **buses** to the towns and villages of the Route du Vin, which leave from outside the *gare SNCF*. **Bikes** can be rented from La Cyclothéque, 31 route d'Ingersheim (Mon 2–6.30pm, Tues–Sat 8am–noon & 2–6.30pm; ⓣ03.89.79.14.18), Cycles Geiswiller, 6 bd du Champ de Mars (Tues–Fri 8.30am–noon & 2–6.30pm, Sat 8.30–noon & 2–6pm; ⓣ03.89.41.30.59), and Cycles Mayer, 6 rue du Pont-Rouge (Tues–Sat 8.30am–noon & 2–6.30pm; ⓣ03.89.79.12.47).

Accommodation is not as overpriced as you might expect, with a number of reasonable hotels very close to the *gare SNCF*. Try the quiet and comfortable *Hôtel Colbert*, 2 rue des Trois-Épis, parallel to av de la République (ⓣ03.89.41.31.05, ⓕ03.89.23.66.75; ❷), or *La Chaumière*, 74 av de la République (ⓣ03.89.41.08.99; ❸). For more luxury, there's the *Grand Hôtel Bristol*,

7 place de la Gare, directly opposite the station exit (ⓣ03.89.23.59.59, ⓦwww.grand-hotel-bristol.fr; ❻), a relic of the grand old prewar days of tourism, now comfortably refurbished and part of a chain. The **HI hostel**, *Auberge de Jeunesse Mittelhardt*, is at 2 rue Pasteur (ⓣ03.89.80.57.39, ⓕ03.89.80.76.16); take bus #4 from the station or rue d'Unterlinden, stop "Lycée Technique" – it gets very busy in summer with lots of teenagers. The nearest **campsite**, *Camping Colmar-Horbourg-Wihr*, is 2km from the centre of town on Route de Neuf-Brisach (ⓣ03.89.41.15.94; closed Jan & Feb); take bus #1 from the station, direction "Wihr", stop "Plage de l'Ill". You could also ask at the tourist office for a list of recommended *chambres d'hôtes* and *fermes-auberges* (farms with guest rooms) in and near the city.

The Town

The *pièce de résistance* of the unmissable **Musée d'Unterlinden**, housed in a former Dominican convent at 1 rue d'Unterlinden (April–Oct daily 9am–6pm; Nov–March daily except Tues 10.30am–4.30pm; closed public hols; €7; ⓦwww.musee-unterlinden.com) is the **Issenheim altarpiece**. Originally designed as a single piece, on the front was the Crucifixion, almost luridly expressive: a tortured Christ with stretched ribcage and outsize hands turned upwards, fingers splayed in pain, flanked by his pale, fainting mother and saints John and Mary Magdalene. Then it unfolded, relative to its function on feast days, Sundays and weekdays, to reveal an Annunciation, Resurrection, Virgin and Child, and finally a sculpted panel depicting saints Anthony, Augustine and Jerome. Completed in 1515, the painting is affected by Renaissance innovations in light and perspective while still rooted in the medieval spirit, and visitors are invariably struck by the "modern" appearance of some details. Also worth a look is the collection of modern paintings in the basement, which includes works by Picasso, Léger and Vasarely.

A short walk into the old town, the **Dominican church** on rue des Serruriers (April–Dec daily 10am–1pm & 3–6pm; €1.50) has some fine glass and, above all, a radiantly beautiful altarpiece known as *The Virgin in a Bower of Roses*, painted in 1473 by Martin Schongauer, who is also represented in the Musée d'Unterlinden. At the other end of rue des Serruriers you come to the **Collégiale St-Martin** on a café-lined square. Known locally as "the cathedral", it's worth a quick peek for its stonework and stained glass, as is the sixteenth-century **Maison Pfister**, on the south side of the church, for its painted panels. Frédéric Auguste Bartholdi, the nineteenth-century sculptor responsible for New York's Statue of Liberty, was born at 30 rue des Marchands. This has been turned into the **Musée Bartholdi** (March–Dec daily except Tues 10am–noon & 2–6pm; closed public hols; €4), containing Bartholdi's personal effects, plus the original designs for the statue, along with sundry Colmarabilia.

Rue des Marchands continues south to the Ancienne Douane or **Koïfhus**, its gaily painted roof tiles loudly proclaiming the city's medieval prosperity. This is the heart of Colmar's old town, a short step away from the archly picturesque quarter down the Grand' Rue, cut through by the River Lauch and known as **La Petite Venise** (Little Venice). The dolly-mixture colours of the old fishing cottages on quai de la Poissonnerie are even more touristy than Strasbourg's Petite France. Twice as tall, but similarly over-restored, are the black-and-white half-timbered tanners' houses on **quai des Tanneurs**, which leads off from the Koïfhus, with open verandas on the top floor originally designed for drying hides.

There are two other museums to see if you take a stroll through the old town: the **Musée Animé du Jouet et des Petits Trains**, 40 rue Vauban (July

& Aug daily 10am–6pm; Sept–June daily except Tues 10am–noon & 2–6pm; €4), whose collection of toys and toy trains is fun for children; and, for a truly rainy day, the unexciting **Museum d'Histoire Naturelle**, 11 rue Turenne (March–Dec Mon & Wed–Sat 10am–noon & 2–6pm, Sun 2–6pm; €4).

Eating and drinking

Restaurants in Colmar are generally overpriced, particularly Alsatian ones. However, *Winstub Brenner*, 1 rue de Turenne (Ⓣ03.89.41.42.43; closed Tues eve and Wed, second fortnight Jan, third week June & third week Nov; main course from €10), serves delicious, generous meals and has a lovely terrace by Little Venice. A fun establishment for both food and atmosphere is *S'Parisser Stewwele*, 4 place Jeanne-d'Arc (Ⓣ03.89.24.53.15; closed Tues, second half of Feb, third week June & third week Nov; main course €11–15, or from €27 à la carte), while a good place for regional food is *Le Petit Gourmand* on quai de la Poissonnerie, in Little Venice (Ⓣ03.89.41.09.32; closed Mon & Tues eve; menus from €21). Otherwise, you could amass a sumptuous picnic from the town's patisseries, charcuteries and fruit and veg **markets** (every Thursday around the Koïfhus; every Saturday on place St-Joseph).

Munster and the Route des Crêtes

MUNSTER owes its existence and its name to a band of Irish monks who founded a monastery here in the seventh century, some 19km west of Colmar up the narrowing valley of the River Fecht, overlooked by Le Petit Ballon (1267m) and Le Hohneck (1362m), among the highest peaks of the Vosges. Its name today is particularly associated with a rich, creamy and exceedingly smelly cheese, the crowning glory of many an Alsatian meal. Although of no special interest in itself, the town makes a peaceful and verdant base either for exploring further into the mountain range, much of which lies within the Parc Régional des Ballons des Vosges, or for visiting Colmar and other places along the Route du Vin. The town also holds a reputed **jazz festival** in early May each year (Ⓔjazzalsace@aol.com).

Munster is accessible by **train** from Colmar. The **tourist office**, 1 rue du Couvnet (July & Aug Mon–Sat 9.30am–12.30pm & 1.30–6.30pm; Sept–June Mon–Fri 9.30am–12.30pm & 2–6pm, Sat 10am–noon & 2–6pm; Ⓣ03.89.77.31.80), has lots of information about hiking in the Munster valley and the *parc régional*. However, the Maison du Parc, 1 cour de l'Abbaye (May–Sept Tues–Sun 9am–noon & 2–6pm; Oct–April Mon–Fri 10am–noon & 2–6pm, Ⓣ03.89.77.90.20), is the best place to get information about the park.

If you want to **stay**, you could try the large, modern *Hôtel Verte-Vallée*, 10 rue Alfred-Hartmann (Ⓣ03.89.77.15.15, Ⓦwww.alsanet.com/verte-vallee; ❻), in the depths of the wooded valley, which, with its squeaky-clean atmosphere and pastel colours, makes a perfect haven for a day or two. It has a good restaurant specializing in traditional French dishes, with a terrace overlooking the stream (closed most of Jan; menu €18–52, *carte* from €33). Less well appointed but blessed with stupendous views are two hotels perched high on the north side of the valley in the hamlet of **HOHRODBERG**: *Hôtel Panorama*, 3 route du Linge (Ⓣ03.89.77.36.53, Ⓔhotel.panorama@libertysurf.fr; ❸), and, with rather awful 1960s decor but a billiard-table, *Hôtel Roess* (Ⓣ03.89.77.36.00, Ⓕ03.89.77.01.95; ❷), 100m higher up. Both have restaurants. Munster's **campsite**, *Camping municipal du Parc de la Fecht*, is on the route de Gunsbach (Ⓣ03.89.77.31.08; May to mid-Sept).

Hiking in the southern Vosges

There's no shortage of waymarked paths in the **southern Vosges**. Six **GRs** cross the Vosges and are a good way to see the less-frequented castles.

GR7: Ballon d'Alsace to Remiremont.
GR53: Wissembourg to Belfort (part of the route coincides with GR5).
GR59: Ballon d'Alsace to Besançon.
GR531: Wissembourg to the Ballon d'Alsace.
GR532: Soultz-sous-Forêts to Belfort.
GR533: Sarrebourg to Belfort, along the west flank of the Vosges.

There are five treks of between five and eleven days' duration described in *Les Grandes Traversées des Vosges*, published by the Office Départemental du Tourisme du Bas-Rhin, 9 rue du Dôme, 67000 Strasbourg (ⓣ03.88.15.45.80), with details of accommodation, access and so on. Another useful contact for information is the Association Départmentale du Tourisme du Haut-Rhin, 1 rue Schlumberger, 68006 Colmar /(ⓣ03.89.20.10.62/68, ⓦwww.tourisme68.asso.fr).

Organized walks, involving guides or luggage transport or both, are arranged by tourist offices and a handful of companies, the most reliable of which is Horizons d'Alsace, 7 Grand' Rue, Kientzheim (ⓣ03.89.78.35.20, ⓦwww.horizons-alsace.com). Three- to six-night walks, with emphasis on wine-tasting and gourmet cuisine, cost on average €400–500 per person, meals included.

Belfort in Franche-Comté is another good place to base a hiking trip in the southern Vosges. The Ballon d'Alsace, in the centre of the Parc Régional des Ballons des Vosges, is the meeting point of the GR5, GR7 and GR59, and a discovery trail has been marked out around the summit. A number of PR trails (rambles) begin from here. The Malsaucy lake along the GR5 trail is another popular hiking area. Contact the Belfort tourist office (see p.356) for maps and information.

The Route des Crêtes

Above Munster the main road west to Gérardmer crosses the mountains by the principal pass, the Col de la Schlucht, where it intersects the so-called Route des Crêtes, built for strategic purposes during World War I. It's a spectacular trail, traversing thick forest and open pasture, where the herds of cows that produce the Munster cheese graze in summer; in winter it becomes one long cross-country ski route. Starting in **CERNAY**, 15km west of Mulhouse, it follows the main ridge of the Vosges, including the highest peak of the range, the Grand Ballon (1424m), north as far as **STE-MARIE-AUX-MINES**, 20km west of Sélestat, once at the heart of a silver-mining district. From Munster it's also accessible by a twisting minor road through Hohrodberg, which takes you past beautiful glacial lakes, the Lac Blanc and the Lac Noir, as well as the eerie World War I battlefield of Linge, where the French and German trenches, once separated literally by a few metres, are still clearly visible.

Mulhouse and around

Thirty-five kilometres south of Colmar, **MULHOUSE** is a large sprawling industrial city. It was Swiss until 1798 when, at the peak of its prosperity (based on printed cotton fabrics and allied trades), it voted to become part of France. Even now many people who live here work in Basle in Switzerland. It's also the home city of Alfred Dreyfus, the unfortunate Jewish army officer who was wrongly convicted of espionage in 1894 (see "Contexts", p.1289). Not having much of an old town, it is no city for strollers, but there are a handful of outstanding – and rather unusual – museums in the town and its vicinity that delve into the region's manufacturing past: wallpaper, firemen, trains, automobiles and fabrics are all given their platform. There's also a **jazz festival** in August, which is a good time to be out partying in this town, with concerts in the museums, the schools and the streets, as well as in the cafés and bars.

Close to the *gare SNCF*, just along the canal to the right, is the excellent **Musée de l'Impression sur Étoffes**, 14 rue Jean-Jacques Henner (Oct–April daily 10am–noon & 2–6pm; May–Sept Tues–Sun 10am–noon & 2–6pm printing demonstration on Wed, Fri & Sun at 3pm; €6). It contains a vast collection of the most beautiful fabrics imaginable: eighteenth-century Indian and Persian imports that revolutionized the European ready-to-wear market in their time; silks from Turkestan; batiks from Java; Senegalese materials; some superb kimonos from Japan; and a unique display of scarves from France, Britain and the USA. Also in the centre, the Hôtel de Ville on place de la Réunion contains a beautifully presented history of Mulhouse and its region in the **Musée Historique** (daily except Tues: July & Aug 10am–noon & 2–6.30pm; Sept–June 10am–noon & 2–6pm; free until renovation work is complete) which exhibits seventeenth- and eighteenth-century furnishings. A section devoted to local archeological finds is closed until further notice.

Out of the centre of Mulhouse, near the northwestern suburb of **DORNACH**, in the direction of the A36 autoroute, is the **Musée Français du Chemin de Fer**, 2 rue Alfred-de-Glehn (closed for renovation until 2005); take bus #17 from Porte-Jeune Place to stop "Musée du Chemin de Fer". Railway rolling stock on display includes Napoléon III's aide-de-camp's drawing room, decorated by Viollet-le-Duc in 1856, and a luxuriously appointed 1926 diner from the Golden Arrow. There are cranes, stations, signals and related artefacts, but the stars of the show are the big locomotive engines with brightly painted boilers, gleaming wheels and pistons, and tangles of brass and copper piping – real works of art. In the same complex is the **Musée des Sapeurs-Pompiers** (daily 10am–5/6pm; €8), its antique fire engines and other memorabilia the personal collection of a retired local fireman. A third museum, **Electropolis – Musée de l'Énergie Électrique**, 55 rue du Pâturage (Tues–Sun 10am–6pm; €7.50), is devoted to the production and uses of electricity.

A couple of kilometres north of the city centre, the **Musée National de l'Automobile**, 192 av de Colmar (daily 10am–5/6pm, Jan closed weekday mornings; €10; bus #1, #4 or #17 from Porte-Jeune Schuman or Porte-Jeune Place to stop "Musée Auto"), has a collection of over six hundred cars, originally the private collection of local business sharks, the Schlumpf brothers. The vehicles range from the industry's earliest attempts, like the extraordinary wooden-wheeled Jacquot steam "car" of 1878, to 1968 Porsche racing vehicles and contemporary factory prototypes. The largest group is that of locally made Bugatti models: dozens of glorious racing cars, coupés and limousines, the pride of them being the two Bugatti Royales, out of only seven that were constructed – one of them Ettore Bugatti's own, with bodywork designed by his son.

Practicalities

Place de la Réunion, nominally the centre of town, is five minutes' walk north of the **gare SNCF**. The **tourist office** underneath the Muséee Historique in the Hôtel de Ville (July, Aug & Dec daily 10am–7pm, rest of year Mon–Sat

10am–6pm, Sun and public holidays 10am–noon & 2–6pm; ⓣ03.89.66.93.13, ⓦwww.tourisme-mulhouse.com). As for **accommodation**, rooms are generally overpriced in Mulhouse, but the following hotels are comfortable and affordable: *St-Bernard*, 3 rue des Fleurs (ⓣ03.89.45.82.32, ⓕ03.39.45.26.32; ❸), with Internet access in the "library" in the foyer; *De Paris*, 5 passage de l'Hôtel-de-Ville (ⓣ03.89.45.21.41, ⓕ03.89.36.08.31; ❶); *Schoenberg*, 14 rue Schoenberg, behind the station (ⓣ03.89.44.19.41, ⓕ03.89.44.49.80; ❸); and *Central*, 15–17 passage Central (ⓣ03.89.46.18.84, ⓕ03.89.56.31.66, ❸). For something more luxurious there's the stylish *Hôtel du Parc* (ⓣ03.89.66.12.22, ⓦwww.hotelduparc-mulhouse.com ❽), with spacious rooms, some overlooking a shady garden, at 26 rue de la Sinne. The **HI hostel** is at 37 rue de l'Illberg (ⓣ03.89.42.63.28, ⓕ03.89.59.74.95; bus #1 or #2, stop "Salle des Sports"; closed Dec 25 to Jan 1), and also has facilities for camping. Otherwise there's another pleasant **campsite**, *Camping de l'Ill*, on rue Pierre-de-Coubertin, near the suburb of Dornach, 4km from the city centre on the banks of the River Ill (ⓣ03.89.06.20.66; closed Oct–March); take bus #7 from place Porte-Jeune.

As at Colmar and Strasbourg, Mulhouse's Alsatian **restaurants** are none too cheap and can be busy, but there are plenty of them. One of the best, in a pleasantly tranquil street off the Place de la Réunion where tables are put outside weather permitting, is the *Winstub Henriette* at 9 rue Henriette, with all the usual dishes for €10–18. The *Crêperie Crampous Mad*, 14 impasse des Tondeurs (ⓣ03.89.45.79.43; closed Sun; menu €8–17), is a good standby, while superb seafood is served at *Le Bistrot à Huîtres*, 2 rue Moenschberg (ⓣ03.89.64.01.60; closed Sun & Mon; menus from €23). You can drown your sorrows at *Gambrinus*, 5 rue des Franciscains, north of place de la Réunion (ⓣ03.89.66.18.65; closed Sun & Mon menu €7–25), which boasts over thirty **beers** on tap and offers simple dishes to help keep you sober.

At the beginning of August you can see some of the vintage cars from the Musée de l'Automobile in gear as part of a **Grande Parade**, and in late August, Mulhouse hosts the region's hottest **jazz festival** (festival dates and information: ⓣ03.89.45.63.95, ⓦwww.alsacom.com/jazz-a-mulhouse). To find out what's going on throughout the year, get hold of a copy of *Spectacles*, the free regional **listings** monthly, or *L'Echo Mulhousien*, also free but focused on events in the city; the tourist office stocks both.

Rixheim and Ungersheim

In the village of **RIXHEIM**, 6km east of Mulhouse, the **Musée du Papier-Peint**, 28 rue Zuber (June–Sept Mon–Fri 9am–noon & 2–6pm, Sat, Sun & hols 10am–noon & 2–6pm; Oct–May daily except Tues 10am–noon & 2–6pm; €6; train to Rixheim or bus #10 from Mulhouse, direction "Commanderie", stop "Centre Europe") is housed in the splendid former headquarters of the Teutonic Knights, a branch of the medieval crusaders. A wallpaper museum may not be everyone's idea of a fun afternoon out, but this space contains a stunning cornucopia of antique painted wallpaper including a series of luxuriant panoramas and impressive antique machinery. The thematic temporary exhibitions are often excellent, and there are frequent demonstrations of printing the stuff (June–Sept Tues, Thurs & Sat at 3.30pm).

Just past Pulversheim, 10km northwest of Mulhouse off the D430 at **UNGERSHEIM**, the **Écomusée d'Alsace** (daily: March–June & Sept 10am–6pm; July & Aug 9.30am–7pm; Oct–Feb 10am–5pm; ⓣ03.89.74.44.74, ⓦwww.ecomusee-alsace.com; €12.50–15, children €7–9.50, depending on time of year) is an open-air museum presenting regional traditions and customs. It's plenty of fun for adults and kids, with over fifty traditional Alsatian buildings spanning the centuries, as well as on-site craft workers doing their various things. It's a vast complex and from April to October you can also visit the nearby potassium mine that ceased production in the 1990s but is run as a tourist attraction by the former miners. You can even stay there, at the *Loges* (❹), in comfortable well-equipped rooms. A regional bus runs frequent services Monday to Saturday from Mulhouse's *gare SNCF*, direction "Guebwiller" (€7 one way).

Franche-Comté and the Jura mountains

The **Jura mountains** – gentle in the west, precipitous in the east, with wide, high forested plateaux in between – cover most of the old county of **Franche-Comté**, once part of the realms of the Grand Dukes of Burgundy, but properly French only since the late seventeenth century. Within its four *départements* – the Territoire de Belfort, the Haute-Saône, the Doubs and, largest of all, the Jura – the towns, especially the capital **Besançon**, are beautiful and tranquil, with the River Doubs flowing through, and the villages, such as **Baume-les-Messieurs** and **Château Chalon**, are some of the prettiest in France. Otherwise, what there is to see is countryside – hundreds of square kilometres of woodland, lake and pasture that are hard to reach without a car – but are best explored once you're there on foot or by bicycle. There are several GR **footpaths** in the area, including the marathon GR5 from the Netherlands to the Mediterranean, and the GR9, which snakes its way through the Parc Régional du Haut-Jura. One of the best things about this part of France in summer is that it sees a lot fewer visitors than its neighbouring regions.

Belfort and around

Nestled in the gap between the southern reaches of the Vosges and the northern outliers of the Jura mountains – the one natural chink in France's eastern geological armour and the obvious route for invaders – **BELFORT** is assured of a place in French hearts for its deeds of military daring. Its name is particularly linked with the 1870 Prussian War, when its long resistance to siege spared it the humiliating annexation to Germany suffered by much of neighbouring Alsace-Lorraine. The commanding officer at the time, Colonel Denfert-Rochereau (the "Lion of Belfort"), earned himself the honour of numerous street names as well as that of a Parisian square and métro station. These days it's an interesting town with a mixed population.

Finding your way around Belfort is easy enough. The town is sliced in two by the River Savoureuse: the **new town** to the west is the commercial hub; to the east lies the quieter **old town**, laid out below the massive red **château**. Built by the ubiquitous fortress-architect Vauban on the site of a medieval fort, it now houses the **Musée d'Art et d'Histoire** (May–Sept daily 10am–7pm; Oct–April daily except Tues 10am–noon & 2–5pm; ⓣ03.84.54.25.51/52; €2.90, or €3.20 including entry to the viewing platform at the lion – see below), containing works by Dürer, Doré and Rodin. The other collections include military objects from Belfort's centuries of conflicts, and artefacts from the Bronze and Iron ages found in the funeral cave at Cravanche in 1876. Vauban is also responsible for the fortifications surrounding Belfort, which created a five-sided old town whose street plan is still largely unchanged. Belfort's other museum, the **Donation Maurice Jardot** (daily except Tues 10am–6pm; €4), is a ten-minute walk away from the tourist office down rue de Mulhouse, at no. 8, and will be of interest to fans of Cubism. Jardot was an associate of Daniel-Henry Kahnweiler, one of the great twentieth-century art dealers: his collection, left to the town of Belfort on his death in 1997, contains 110 works of art, including some by Braque, Léger and Picasso.

The most famous and photographed phenomenon in town is the eleven-metre-high red sandstone **lion** carved out of the rock-face that you pass on the way up to the castle, Bartholdi's monument to commemorate the 1870 siege. From the **viewing platform** at the front paw of the lion (April & Oct daily 8am–noon & 2–6pm; May & June daily 8am–noon & 2–7pm; July–Sept daily 8am–7pm; Nov–March Mon–Fri 10am–noon & 2–5pm, weekends & hols 8am–noon & 2–5pm; €1, or €3.20, combined ticket to the Musée d'Art et d'Histoire), you get some stunning views over the town and surrounding countryside.

Belfort is also a good base for exploring the northeastern corner of the **River Doubs**. After that, it's either follow the *autoroute* directly to Besançon, or take your time and lose yourself in the hills and forests and pretty towns and villages along the scenic route.

Practicalities

The **gare SNCF** and departure point for local **buses** are at the end of Faubourg-de-France, the main pedestrianized shopping drag in the new town. The **tourist office** (mid-June to mid-Sept Mon–Sat 9am–7pm; mid-Sept to mid-June Mon–Sat 9am–12.30pm & 1.45–6pm; ⓣ03.84.55.90.90, ⓔotbtb@essor-info.fr) is at 2bis rue Clemenceau, a ten-minute walk from the station down Faubourg de France as far as the river, then left along quai Charles-Vallet until you reach rue Clemenceau; the castle houses a tourist information annexe during the summer (July & Aug daily 10am–12.30pm & 2–6.30pm).

There is an excellent choice of **hotels**: the *Au Relais d'Alsace*, 5 av de la Laurencie (ⓣ03.84.22.15.55, ⓕ03.84.28.70.48; ❸), is where out-of-town musicians stay when they perform in Belfort, and the staff will be happy to advise you about what's happening in the region. Other options include the *Hôtel Vauban*, 4 rue du Magasin (ⓣ03.84.21.59.37, ⓕ03.84.21.41.67; ❹), where the owners are also artists, and, for a bit more grandeur, the *Grand Hôtel du Tonneau d'Or*, 1 rue Reiset (ⓣ03.84.58.57.56, ⓕ03.84.58.57.50; ❼). Belfort's **hostel**, *Résidence Madrid*, is 1km west of the railway line at 6 rue de Madrid (ⓣ03.84.21.39.16, ⓕ03.84.28.58.95), and its campsite, *Camping International de l'Etang des Forges*, is on rue du Général Béthouart, north of the old town (ⓣ03.84.22.54.92; ⓦwww.campings-belfort.com; May to mid-Oct).

Inexpensive places to **eat** and cafés can be found in the place d'Armes and place de la République, in between antique shops and old-fashioned grocery stores such as Épicerie de Lion, on rue de la Porte de France. *Aux*

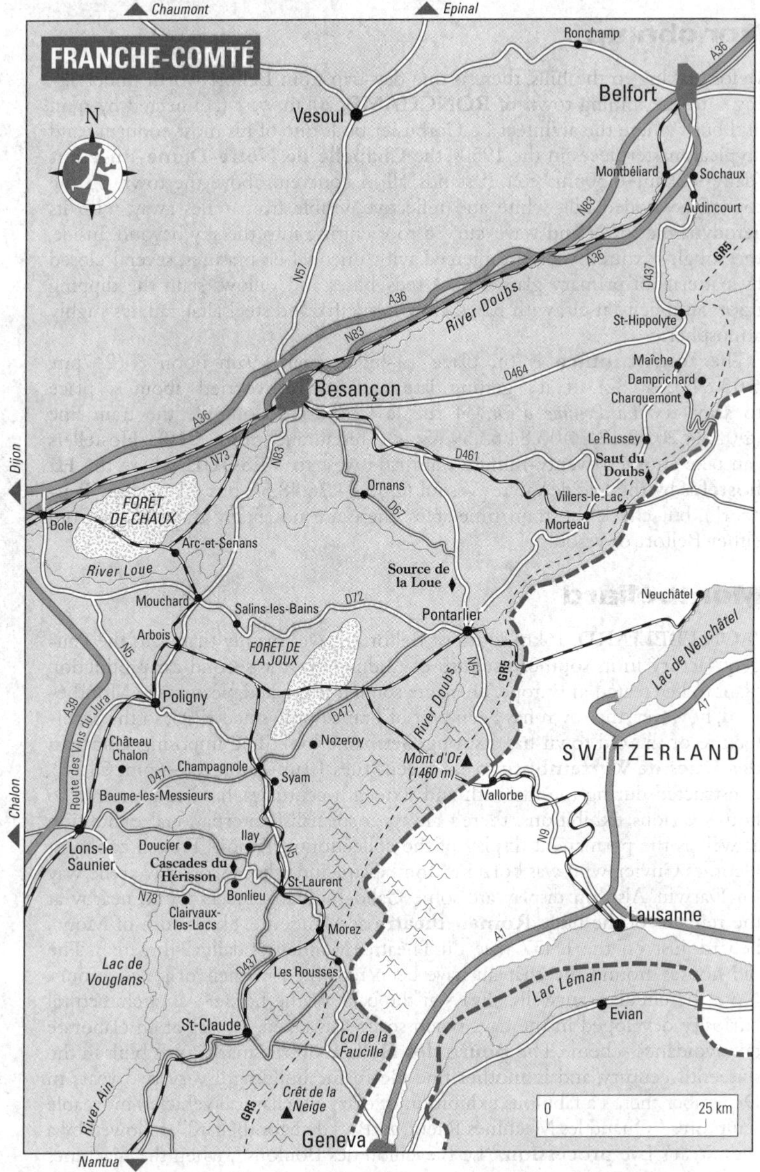

Crêpes d'Antan, 13 rue du Quai, has delicious crêpes, starting from €5. *Bistrot Boeuf-Carottes*, 14 rue Lecourbe (☎03.84.21.15.40; closed Sun eve & Mon), is another good place to eat, with menus from €17. *Café Théâtre*, behind the theatre on place Corbis, has outdoor tables by the river and is a pleasant place for a coffee, while *La Poudrière*, place de l'Arsenal (closed late July & Aug), is the best place for **live music**.

Ronchamp

Before taking to the hills, there is one day-trip from Belfort worth undertaking – to the mining town of **RONCHAMP**, 20km west (connected by train and bus), where the architect Le Corbusier built one of his most enduring and atypical masterpieces in the 1950s, the **Chapelle de Notre-Dame-du-Haut** (daily 9.30am–6.30pm; €2). It stands, all in concrete, above the town on the top of a wooded hill, white and reflective, visible from miles away, with its aerodynamic tower and wave-curved roof cutting into the sky beyond. Inside, the rough-textured walls are pierced with unequal embrasures, several closed by patterns of primary glass, whose reds, blues and yellows stain the dipping floor. Simplicity itself, with pared-down crucifix and steel altar rail, it's highly atmospheric.

The **tourist office** is on place 14-Juillet (daily 9am–noon & 2–7pm; ⓣ03.84.63.50.82). If it's getting late and you're worried about a place to **stay**, try *La Pomme d'Or*, 34 rue le Corbusier, alongside the train line (ⓣ03.84.20.62.12, ⓕ03.84.63.59.45; ❸; restaurant from €10). Hostellers can take another twenty-minute train ride west to **VESOUL**, where the **HI hostel** is by the Lac de Vaivre–Vesoul (ⓣ03.84.76.48.55; bus #1 to stop "Peugeot"), but check the train timetables: there are not many trains to or from either Belfort or Vesoul.

Montbéliard

MONTBÉLIARD, 16km south of Belfort, thrives mainly thanks to the Peugeot factory in its southern suburb of Audincourt, the second car production plant to be created in Europe. There are some unexpected pleasures in Montbéliard, however: the town has been part of France only since 1793, so the architecture of the old town has a strong Germanic look. The imposing **Château des Ducs de Wurtemburg** (daily except Tues 10am–noon & 2–6pm; €1.50), constructed during the fifteenth and sixteenth centuries, has been restored to house various exhibitions: there's always a specialist international exhibition as well as the permanent display of the collection of famous French zoologist Georges Cuvier, who was born in Montbéliard and whose work paved the way for Darwin. Also on display are some Gallo-Roman objects found nearby at the remains of the huge **Roman theatre** at Mandeure, 8km south of Montbéliard, just off the D437 (rue du Théâtre, Mandeure; daily 24hr; free). The old houses around the château have been repainted in their original colours. Note the circular stairwells, always at the back of the house – an architectural curiosity developed in the days when space was taxed, as part of an elaborate tax-avoidance scheme. The **Bourg des Halles** covered market was built in the sixteenth century, and is another fine Germanic building. Every two years in December there's a fabulous exhibition of crazy mechanical vehicles/moveable sculptures, "Quand les Machines Rient: au Pays de Montbéliard", followed by a New Year's Eve **procession**, "Le Réveillon des Boulons", when the machines and their creators fill the streets. An outdoor Christmas **market**, "Lumières de Noël", is held annually around the St-Martin church, and there's also a three-kilometre labyrinth at the **Parc du Près-la-Rose**.

The **tourist office** is at 1 rue Henri Mouhot (mid-June to mid-Sept Mon–Fri 9am–noon & 1.30–7pm, Sat 9am–noon & 1.30–6pm, Sun 10am–noon & 2–4pm; mid-Sept to mid-June Mon–Fri 9am–noon & 1.30–6pm, Sat 9am–noon & 1.30–6pm; ⓣ03.81.94.45.60, ⓦwww.montbeliard.com). For local events, which may influence whether you stay in Montbéliard or

Cross-country skiing and mountain biking in the Jura

The nature of the Jura's terrain – its high plateaux guaranteeing winter snow but without excessively steep gradients – has made it France's most popular destination for **cross-country skiing**, or *ski du fond*. The goal of any superfit *fondeur* is the 210-kilometre Grande Traversée du Jura (GTJ), which roughly follows the long-distance GR5 footpath across the high plateau from Villers-le-Lac to Hauteville-Lompnes.

The same gentle topography and established infrastructure which enable cross-country skiing have made this region an ideal high-summer venue for **mountain biking**, with hundreds of waymarked cross-country skiing pistes used out of season as trails for adventuresome mountain bikers. The 300-kilometre **GTJ–VTT**, starting near Montbéliard, has become the greatest long-distance challenge in the area. Many people cycle on the roads in the area; there aren't that many cars, so if you can handle the hills, go for it.

Cycling in the Doubs region is flatter and very scenic, with proper cycling paths. The 65-kilometre **Tour des Lacs** takes in some caves and waterfalls. There are 21 routes listed in the *Guide de Cyclotourisme du Doubs* (€8), published by ADED, 7 av de la Gare d'Eau, 25031 Besançon, and also available from the tourist offices in the Doubs.

The headquarters of the departmental tourist board, the **Comité Departemental du Tourisme de Jura**, 8 rue Louis-Rousseau, Lons-le-Saunier, in the south of the region (ⓣ03.84.87.08.88), can supply plenty of information, maps and literature – in English – on outdoor leisure opportunities of all kinds in the Jura.

Belfort, as both have some good music and art festivals, get the free cultural magazine *Atmosphere*, or *Montbéliard Magazine*, available in tourist offices. For **accommodation**, the choice is better in Belfort, but you could try the *Hôtel de la Balance*, 40 rue de Belfort (ⓣ03.81.96.77.41, ⓔhotelbalance@wanadoo.fr; ❹), in the old town, which also has a restaurant with menus from €13. There are plenty of outdoor cafés in the old town area: *Café de la Paix*, 12 rue des Febvres, near Les Halles, is a great place to relax.

The Doubs Valley

The River Doubs runs a course like a series of hairpins, doubling back on itself repeatedly, with its most dramatic change of course at **AUDINCOURT**, a southern suburb of Montbéliard and the place where Peugeots are made. Audincourt's chief sight is the modern **church of Sacré-Coeur**, which has windows and a tapestry by Fernand Léger. Just north of Audincourt, **SOCHAUX**, another Montbéliard suburb, is home to the **Musée Peugeot** (daily 10am–6pm; ⓦwww.peugeot.com/musee; €7), which displays the products of over a century of automotive manufacturing, from the Bey of Tunis's one-off quadricycle to contemporary rally winners and concept cars.

From Audincourt, southwards and upstream, the D437 follows the valley of the Doubs, winding and climbing steadily between steep, wooded banks to the bridging point at **ST-HIPPOLYTE**, where you'll find the riverside *Hôtel Bellevue* (ⓣ03.81.96.51.53, ⓕ03.81.96.52.40; ❸) and a **campsite** (May–Sept). Seven kilometres west along the D39, the *Auberge de Moricemaison*, in Valoreille (ⓣ03.81.64.01.72; ❶), offers rustic simplicity and wholesome evening meals from €14.

A less congested scenic route from Besançon follows the D464 south of the river, but without a car you'd have to hitch all this – manageable but slow. Beyond St-Hippolyte the road climbs onto a wide plateau at an altitude of around 850m, with grassy cattle pastures encompassed by fir-clad ridges and dotted with broad-roofed farms and barns. Once up here, cycling is easy enough. Alternatively, it's a lovely but long hike of well over 50km along the **GR5 footpath** from St-Hippolyte across the plateau and up the Doubs valley to the plunging waterfall of the **Saut du Doubs** outside Villers-le-Lac – the beginning of the **GTJ** marathon cross-country ski piste. To reach the fall, it's a four-kilometre walk from the last houses above the north end of the lake in **VILLERS** along a track through the woods.

By road, Villers is 47km south of St-Hippolyte along the D437, which turns east at **MORTEAU**, a village with nothing more than a much-altered, thirteenth-century priory church to recommend it. The D437 is part of the Route du Comté, so if you like cheese, it's worth the detour. There is **accommodation** up on the plateau at the welcoming *Hôtel des Montagnards* (ⓣ03.81.67.08.86, ⓕ03.81.67.14.57; ❸; closed Sun out of season).

Besançon and around

The capital of Franche-Comté, **BESANÇON** is an ancient and attractive grey-stone town at the northern edge of the Jura mountains, enclosed in a loop of the River Doubs, whose lugubrious meanders define the layout of the old town. The tongue of land it sits on has been protected since Roman times, when it lay on a major trading route; the indefatigable Vauban added the still-extant fortifications and a citadel to guard the natural breach in the river. Once a major centre of French clock-making, Besançon was also the birthplace of artificial silk – or rayon – in 1890. It counts among its native sons both the pioneering Lumière brothers and epic novelist Victor Hugo.

The **River Doubs** rises on the high plateau 100km to the south of here, making a diversion far to the northeast of the town, gathering tributaries and broadening as it briefly crosses the Swiss border before entering Besançon. A lazy journey upstream to **Pontarlier** can make a rewarding excursion over a couple of days. From Pontarlier a direct return north to Besançon can be made by following the **River Loue**'s steep descent through its heavily wooded valley past the pretty mill town of **Ornans**.

Arrival, information and accommodation

The **gare SNCF** is at the end of avenue Maréchal-Foch, while the **gare routière** is at 9 rue Proudhon off rue de la République; buses for Pontarlier and Ornans leave from here. The best way to reach the town centre from the train station is to take the underground passage (next to the monument in front of the station) and cut across the park down to the *quais* – the old town is on the other side of the river. The **tourist office** is upstream on the right bank by the Pont de la République on place de la Première Armée-Française (April–May Mon 10am–6.30pm, Tues–Sat 9.30am–7pm; June–Sept Mon 10am–6.30pm, Tues–Sat 9.30am–7pm, Sun 10am–noon & 3–5pm; Oct–March Mon 10am–6pm, Tues–Sat 9am–6pm; ⓣ03.81.80.92.55, ⓦwww.besancon.com). On the other side of the Pont de la République from the tourist office is the departure point for the **bateaux-mouches** (daily April–Oct; €8), which tour round the outer limits of the town centre.

Hotels include the comfortable and friendly family-run *Granvelle*, 13 rue Lecourbe, close to the citadel (ⓣ03.81.81.33.92, ⓕ03.81.81.31.77; ❸); the central *Regina*, 91 Grande-Rue (ⓣ03.81.81.50.22, ⓕ03.81.81.60.20; ❸); the *Hôtel de Paris*, 33 rue des Granges (ⓣ03.81.81.36.56, ⓕ03.81.61.94.90; ❹), with free parking for guests; and the *Hôtel du Nord*, at 8–10 rue de Moncey in the centre (ⓣ03.81.81.34.56, ⓕ03.81.81.85.96; ❸). For something more upmarket, the *Castan*, 6 square Castan (ⓣ03.81.65.02.00, ⓦwww.hotelcastan.fr; ❼) is housed in a beautiful seventeenth-century town house and offers supreme comfort. Besançon's **hostel**, *Les Oiseaux*, is a couple of kilometres northeast of the train station at 48 rue des Cras (ⓣ03.81.40.32.00, ⓕ03.81.40.32.01; bus #7, stop "Les Oiseaux"; €21 single, €30 double). The *Centre International de Séjour* at 19 rue Martin-du-Gard, 4km northwest of the centre (ⓣ03.81.50.07.54, ⓦwww.cis-besancon.com; bus #8, stop "L'Épitaphe"; €9–21 without breakfast), fulfils the same function. Alternatively, there's the *Foyer de la Cassotte*, 18 rue de la Cassotte (ⓣ03.81.80.90.01; €13.50 including breakfast), for 16- to 25-year-olds. **Camping** is at Plage de Chalezeule, 5km out on the Belfort road (ⓣ03.81.88.04.26; April–Oct; bus #1 towards Palente).

The Town

Once you're in the old town, getting around is simple, and some of the most interesting things to see are outdoors and free – such as the beautiful bluish stone walls of most buildings, and the signs of Roman life that still remain. Rue de la République leads from the river to the central **place du 8-Septembre** and the sixteenth-century **Hôtel de Ville**. The principal street, **Grande-Rue**, cuts across the square along the line of an old Roman road. At its northwestern end – the livelier part of town with shops and cafés – is the place de la Révolution and the excellent **Musée des Beaux-Arts** (daily except Tues 9.30am–noon & 2–6pm; €3.20), with some good nineteenth- and twentieth-century works, two magnificent Bonnards and a wonderful clock collection. Midway down Grande-Rue, the fine sixteenth-century **Palais Granvelle** (Wed–Sun 1–7pm; €3, free Sat) contains an interactive museum paying homage to the town's history of clock-making, the Musée du Temps. Continuing up the street, you pass place Victor-Hugo (he was born at no. 140) and arrive at the **Porte Noire**, a second-century Roman triumphal arch spanning the street and partially embedded in the adjoining houses. Beside it, in the shady little **square Archéologique A.-Castan**, are the remains of a *nymphaeum*, a small reservoir of water fed by an aqueduct. Beyond the arch is the pompous eighteenth-century **Cathédrale St-Jean** (closed Tues) which houses the nineteenth-century **Horloge Astronomique** (hourly guided visits in French: April–Sept daily except Tues 9.50–11.50am & 2.50–5.50pm; rest of year Mon & Thurs–Sun same hours; closed Jan; €2.50), detailing over a hundred terrestrial and celestial positions and containing some 30,000 parts.

The spectacular **Citadelle** (daily: July & Aug 9am–7pm; April–June and Sept to mid-Nov 9am–6pm; rest of year 10am–5pm; €6.10) is a steep fifteen-minute climb from the cathedral, and has a crow's-nest view of the town and the noose-like bend in the river that contains it. It houses many worthwhile museums (times as above): for animal lovers there's the **Musée d'Histoire Naturelle** (with aquarium, insectarium and zoo); the **Musée Comtois**, with pottery, furniture and a good collection of nineteenth-century marionettes, as well as some marvellous old farming implements; the **Espace Vauban**, devoted to the military architect; and – best of all – the **Musée de la Résistance et de la Déportation**, a superb aid to understanding postwar France's political consciousness (English audio commentary available). The first rooms document the rise of Nazism and French Fascism through photographs and exhibits, including a bar of soap stamped RIF – "Pure Jew Fat". In the section on the Vichy government, there's a telegram of encouragement sent by Marshal Pétain to the French troops of the "legion of volunteers against Bolshevism", who were fighting alongside the Germans on the eastern front. Finally, as counterbalance, much is made of General Leclerc's vow at Koufra in the Libyan desert, whose capture in January 1941 was the first, entirely French, victory of the war – "We will not stop until the French flag flies once more over Metz and Strasbourg" – a vow which he kept when he entered the latter city at the head of a division in November 1944.

Eating, drinking and entertainment

There are plenty of lively and inexpensive **restaurants**, **cafés** and **bars** by the Doubs near place Battant, particularly along the little streets running parallel to the river. *Brasserie du Commerce*, 31 rue des Granges, has rather grand decor and ambience, and *Brasserie du Palais Granvelle*, in a lovely shady park next door to the Palais Granvelle, is the best place for breakfast and coffee. For a substantial **meal** try the century-old *Restaurant au Petit Polonais*, 81 rue des Granges (⑦03.81.81.23.67; closed Sat eve & Sun; menus from €12), which serves regional food; or *Le Poker d'As*, 14 square St-Amour (⑦03.81.81.42.49; closed Sun eve & Mon; menus from €21), a touch old-fashioned but one hundred percent reliable. For lunch, there's the superb *Le Café-Café*, 5bis rue Luc Breton (⑦03.81.81.15.24; Mon–Sat lunch only; *plats* from €10); or the trendy *La Femme du Boulanger*, 6 rue Morand (⑦03.81.82.86.93; Mon–Sat 7.30am–8pm, Sun 9am–7pm) where fresh salads cost around €11.

The two biggest **cultural events** of the year in Besançon are **Jazz en Franche-Comté**, which takes place in June and July, and an international young conductors' competition in the first two weeks of September.

Pontarlier and around

Sixty kilometres southeast of Besançon lies **PONTARLIER**, one of the bigger Jura towns, and not very interesting in itself except as a transit point and recreational base. If you need **accommodation** here, try the *Hôtel de Morteau*, 26 rue Jeanne-d'Arc, near the river (⑦03.81.39.14.83, ⑥03.81.39.75.07; ③), which has an excellent restaurant (menus from €12). There's also an **HI hostel** at 2 rue Jouffroy, near the station (⑦ & ⑥03.81.39.06.57); a *gîte* – the *Chalet-Refuge du Larmont* (⑦03.81.46.61.07); plus a municipal **campsite** in rue de Toulombief. For places to **eat**, try the rue de Besançon, which is full of cafés and brasseries, or, for a fuller meal, the *Brasserie de la Poste*, 55 rue de la République. Good-quality **mountain bikes** can be rented from Vélos Pernet, 23 rue de la République (⑦03.81.46.48.00), for €15 per day; and cross-country **ski gear** can be found at Sports et Neige, along the street at no. 4 (⑦03.81.39.04.69). The **tourist office**, 14 bis rue de la Gare (Mon–Sat 9am–noon & 2–6pm; June–Sept also Sun 10.30am–noon & 5.30–7pm; ⑦03.81.46.48.33, ⑥03.81.46.83.32), has some good hiking maps.

Just south of town, past a divinely aromatic chocolate factory, a steep road to the left ascends for 11km to **Le Grand Taureau**, whose 1328-metre summit is just a short walk from the road's end and offers a view over the whole Jura Massif and across Switzerland to the Alps. A couple of kilometres further south of Pontarlier, the **Château de Joux** (French guided tours daily: Jan–June & Sept–Oct 10am, 11.30am, 2pm & 3.30pm; July & Aug every 30min 9am–4.30pm; closed Nov & Dec; €5) stands over the defile known as La Cluse et Mijoux, the ancient Franco-Swiss frontier. It was originally constructed in the eleventh century, and Vauban had a hand in remodelling and modernizing it, but most of what you see today is less than a century old. The fort's history and impressive appearance are of more interest than its collection of military uniforms.

Moving on, there are **trains** and **buses** to Besançon, the TGV to Dijon and Paris, and local buses to the six-kilometre-long **Lac de St-Point**, where you can pick up the GR5 again to make the ascent of **Mont d'Or** (1460m) overlooking Lake Geneva and the Alps, and to **Mouthe**, where the River Doubs emerges from an underground cavern.

Ornans and the Valley of the Loue

Some 17km north of Pontarlier, the D67 splits west off the N57 and plunges precipitously into the **Valley of the Loue**. A couple of kilometres above the village of Ouhans lies the source of the river, issuing from an enormous rock beneath a tiered cliff, in winter entirely fringed with icicles. From this point you can continue on foot along the **GR595 footpath** down the valley bounded by densely wooded limestone cliffs, a descent no less dramatic by road, passing through a string of pretty villages.

Roughly halfway between Pontarlier and Besançon, **ORNANS** is the prettiest of all, an archetypal Franche-Comté town that has become the touristic focal point of the valley. The Loue here is an abrupt trench with the river washing the foundations of ancient balconied houses. The town is easily appreciated from the numerous footbridges spanning the river. Pierre Vernier, inventor of the eponymous gauge, and the painter Gustave Courbet were both born here: the latter's house is now the **Musée de la Maison Natale de Gustave Courbet** (daily 10am–noon & 2–6pm; Nov–March closed Tues; July & Aug 10am–6pm; €3, €6 during summer exhibitions), displaying some of his drawings, sculpture and locally painted scenes. The **tourist office** is at 7 rue Pierre Vernier (April–June, Sept, Oct & school hols Mon–Sat 9.30am–noon & 2–6pm; July & Aug Mon–Sat 9am–7pm, Sun 10am–noon & 3–6pm; Nov–March Mon–Fri 10am–noon & 3–5pm; ⓣ & ⓕ03.81.62.21.50). There's **accommodation** in the form of the riverside *Hôtel Le Progrès*, 11 rue Jacques Gervais (ⓣ03.81.62.16.79, ⓕ03.81.62.19.10; ❸), and the pricier but better-placed *De la Cascade* (ⓣ03.81.60.95.30, ⓕ03.81.60.94.55; ❹), in the centre of **MOUTHIER**, further down the D67. There are **campsites** and *gîtes d'étapes* in Ornans, Vuillifans and Mouthier.

Arc-et-Senans and Salins-les-Bains

At the southeastern edge of the Forêt de Chaux, some 35km south of Besançon, is the unfinished eighteenth-century "salt city" of the **Saline Royale d'Arc-et-Senans** (guided tours in French and English April–June, Sept & Oct 9am–noon & 2–6pm; July & Aug 9am–7pm; Nov–March 10am–noon & 2–5pm; €7; ⓣ03.81.54.45.45), commissioned by royal decree in 1773 to replace the ageing works at Salins-les-Bains. The complex, dreamed up by the avant-garde architect Claude-Nicolas Ledoux, was to have become a model utopian city. His grandiose project reflected the pseudo-egalitarian social concerns of the pre-Revolutionary era: the settlement was to have radiated along the primary axes of a clock-face from a nucleus housing the administrative offices, distillation plants, public baths and other municipal utilities.

Sadly, the socio-aesthetic ideals could not overcome the works' functional deficiencies: the pipeworks linking the new plant with Salins deteriorated rapidly and only half of the central arc was ever completed. Moreover it was effectively a labour camp, with the workers' movements severely restricted and children exploited in the process. Salt production continued until the end of the nineteenth century, but all that remains today is the impressively restored semicircle of eleven buildings, a monumental epitaph to Ledoux's unconsummated vision. The beautiful complex now houses two museums, usually with exhibitions about architecture.

SALINS-LES-BAINS, 15km southeast of Arc-et-Senans, is worth a further detour (back along the tree-lined country road that leads to the entrance to the Saline Royale). Confined at the bottom of a narrow valley piercing the flank of the Jura's central plateau, the recuperative spa town of Salins has been producing salt for around a thousand years. The Chalon family moved in on the town in the thirteenth century and the wealth they accrued from the control and sale of the "white gold" essential for the preservation of food enabled them to become among the most influential of the Comté's medieval overlords. This prominence, as well as the town's key position on the route to Switzerland, accounts for the two lofty forts overlooking the town, which are good walking destinations. The **Salines de Salins**, or brine-wells (one-hour guided tours daily: Feb–Easter & mid-Sept to Nov 10.30am, 2.30pm & 4pm; Easter to mid-Sept hourly 9–11am & 2.30–5.30pm; closed Jan & Dec; €4.20), are inevitably the town's main attraction.

The **tourist office** is on place des Salines (daily 9am–noon & 2–6pm; Nov–Easter closed Sun; ⓣ03.84.73.01.34). Having styled itself as a spa town since the 1840s (and still doing so), Salins has some distinguished **hotels** that once accommodated the fashionably ailing gentry. The *Grand Hôtel des Bains*, in place des Alliés (ⓣ03.84.37.90.50, ⓕ03.84.37.96.80; ❹), offers comfortable accommodation. Alternatively, try the old-fashioned *Hôtel des Deux Forts*, in place du Vigneron (ⓣ03.84.73.70.40; ❸), or the *Bon Accueil*, on 50 rue de la Liberté, north of the central square (ⓣ03.84.37.94.31; ❷), which is slightly less expensive, and has a café/restaurant with menus from €10. There's a **campsite** (ⓣ03.84.37.92.70; April–Sept) on avenue Général-de-Gaulle.

Dole and the Forêt de Chaux

Halfway between Besançon and Dijon, on the edge of the flat and fertile valley of the Saône, **DOLE** is a quiet and provincial town. The medieval capital of the Comté region until Louis XI ordered its destruction in 1479, it's a place to stay overnight, or rest, and attractive enough in a subdued way. Grey-stone houses with barred ground-floor windows stand on narrow streets around the vast, stolid **collegiate of Notre-Dame**, with its lofty belfry (July & Aug guided visits roughly three times a week; check with the tourist office for the days and times; €4) – worth climbing for the view. Inside the church, there are beautiful windows and a wonderful Rococo organ. The Rhône–Rhine canal washes the feet of the town, and along its bank below the church runs the narrow rue Pasteur, birthplace of the French biologist and chemist **Louis Pasteur**. The son of a tanner, he is best known for discovering the rabies virus (and its cure), and is commemorated in the process of "pasteurization", another of his discoveries. His house, like those of his father's workmates, backs onto a pretty waterside walkway leading to an island. The house is now a **museum** (April–June, Sept & Oct Mon–Sat 10am–noon & 2–6pm, Sun 2–6pm; July & Aug Mon–Sat 10am–6pm, Sun 2–6pm; Nov–March Sat 10am–noon & 2–5pm, Sun 2–5pm; €3).

The **gare routière** is next to the **train station**, a ten-minute walk northeast of the Collegiate Notre-Dame down avenue A. Briand. Whatever happens in

Dole happens between the Grande-Rue – the street leading to the main bridge over the Doubs – and place Grévy; **the tourist office** is on the northern side of the square at no. 6 (June Mon–Fri 9am–6pm, Sat 9am–noon & 2–6pm; July & Aug Mon–Fri 8.30am–6.30pm, Sat 9am–noon & 2–6pm; Sept–May Mon 2–6pm, Tues–Fri 9am–noon & 2–6pm, Sat 9am–noon; ⓣ03.84.72.11.22), and cafés on the other. At the top of Grande-Rue is the delightful place aux Fleurs, with its fountain and amusing bronze sculpture of *Les Trois Commères* ("The Three Gossips"). There are some reasonable **hotels** in Dole, including *Le Grand Cerf*, 6 rue Arney, near place Grévy (ⓣ03.84.72.11.68; ❷). For more comfort and prices to match, try *La Chaumière*, across the river on avenue Maréchal-Juin (ⓣ03.84.70.72.40, ⓕ03.84.79.25.60; ❺). The cheapest rooms, as usual, are at the **HI hostel**, St-Jean, place Jean XXIII (ⓣ03.84.82.36.74, ⓕ03.84.79.17.69, ⓔlestjean@wanadoo.fr); take bus #1, direction "Mesnils-Poiset", stop "Les Paters". The local **campsite**, *Camping du Pasquier*, is down by the river (ⓣ03.84.72.02.61; mid-March to mid-Oct). For **food**, there are various pizzerias and crêperies – such as the canal-side *La Demi-Lune*, 39 rue Pasteur (closed Mon out of season) – and *Le Bec Fin*, 67 rue Pasteur (ⓣ03.84.82.43.43), for the gourmands (menus from €17.50).

The Forêt de Chaux

To the east of Dole lie the 200 square kilometres of the ancient **Forêt de Chaux**, France's third-largest forest and site of some of the country's earliest industrial endeavours. Set in a clearing in the southern central part of the forest are the ancient settlements of **La Vieille-Loye** and **Turot**, since early Christian times centres of charcoal burning – once essential in the production of metals – and, until recently, glass manufacture, at one time producing up to one million bottles a year.

Access to the forest – which makes an agreeable alternative to the main roads to Salins-les-Bains or Besançon – is easiest from the N5/N72 Salins road to the south and west. In this part of the forest you'll find many waymarked walking trails wending their way beneath the overhead canopy of oak, chestnut and beech.

Lons-le-Saunier to Arbois

At the base of the central plateau's west-facing rim, set picturesquely astride rivers and in the midst of fertile soils, are a number of towns that have supported centuries of agriculture, and have recently accommodated the small, specialist industries so typical of the Jura. The spa town and departmental capital of **Lons-le-Saunier** is a tranquil place, with fireworks on July 14, and on July 31 for St-Désiré, and outdoor music concerts throughout the summer. North of the town a string of vineyards traces the plateau's edge to just beyond Arbois, the Jura's wine-making capital. This is the eighty-kilometre **Route des Vins du Jura**, where the region's distinctive wines – such as the sherry-like *vin jaune* – are cultivated and manufactured from a variety of vines.

Between Lons and Arbois, a scenic detour can be made into the hills to visit the ancient, time-locked villages of **Baume-les-Messieurs** and **Château Chalon**. And at **Poligny** more wines and the long-refined flavour of Comté cheese, produced in the Jura since the thirteenth century, are available for sampling at the Maison du Comté.

Lons-le-Saunier

Once the site of a Neolithic settlement, **LONS-LE-SAUNIER** was all but destroyed by a fire in the early seventeenth century. Most buildings today date from this era, and a wander around some of the older examples is an agreeable way to fill half a day.

The central **place de la Liberté**, a ten-minute walk north of the train station, is a good place to start. Should you happen to be in the square on the hour, the **theatre clock** at the eastern end will chime a familiar half-dozen notes from *La Marseillaise* to honour Lons' most famous son, Rouget de Lisle, the anthem's composer. Just north of the square is the attractive, colonnaded thoroughfare of **rue du Commerce**, where some of Lons' oldest buildings line the street in which de Lisle was born. Continuing north through the place de la Comédie and past the ancient **salt well**, Le Puits Salé, you arrive at the **Musée Municipal d'Archéologie**, 25 rue Richebourg (Mon & Wed–Fri 10am–noon & 2–6pm, Sat & Sun 2–5pm; €2). It presents some absorbing prehistoric displays, including a touching Neolithic family scene circa 4000 BC, a dug-out canoe found locally and a life-size replica of a 210-million-year-old plateosaurus, France's oldest-known dinosaur. The museum, which also mounts various temporary exhibitions, is housed in the old Bel cheese factory, whose enduringly popular *La Vache Qui Rit* ("Laughing cow") cheese spread is now produced in larger premises near the station. Returning south along rue Richebourg to avenue Jean-Moulin, you come to the inevitable **statue** of Rouget de Lisle, designed by Frédéric Bartholdi, the sculptor who went on to refine de Lisle's stirring pose on a much grander scale in the Statue of Liberty. A left turn here leads to the pleasant **Parc Edouard Guenon**, where you'll find the **Salines**, or mineral baths (℡03.84.24.20.34 for admission details), with their ornate *fin-de-siècle* exterior, lavishly equipped with a sauna, Turkish bath and jacuzzi: the saline immersions not only soothe the usual aches and pains, but are also renowned for their ability to cure juvenile bed-wetting.

Practicalities

Lons' **tourist office** is in the same building as its theatre (Mon–Fri 8am–noon & 2–6pm, Sat 8am–noon & 2–5pm; ℡03.84.24.65.01). For information about the Jura region, the **Comité Départemental du Tourisme** is at 8 rue Louis Rousseau (Mon–Fri: April–Nov 8.30am–12.30pm & 2–6pm; Dec–March 8.30am–6pm; ℡03.84.87.08.88). Two good **hotels** are the smart *Terminus*, 37 av Aristide-Briand, by the train station (℡03.84.24.41.83, ⓕ03.84.24.68.07; ❸), and the cosy *Nouvel Hôtel*, 50 rue Lecourbe (℡03.84.47.20.67, ⓕ03.84.43.27.49; ❸), just west of place de la Liberté. There's a **campsite**, *Camping de la Marjorie* (℡03.84.24.26.94; April to mid-Oct), on the northeast edge of town. For a truly inspired **meal** in a charming setting, pay a visit to the *Bistrot des Marronniers*, 22 rue de Vallière, west off rue St-Désiré (closed Sun; menu from €11). For a coffee or drink, head for the *Grand Café de Strasbourg*, next to the theatre and boasting a beautiful interior.

Baume-les-Messieurs and Château Chalon

Twenty kilometres east of Lons is the tiny village of **BAUME-LES-MESSIEURS**, tucked in a cliff-bound valley festooned with foliage on all but the steepest faces. From Lons, the quickest – as well as most interesting – way to get there is to take the D471 Champagnole road and turn down the narrow and steep lanes descending into the valley from the north; the **Belvédère des**

Roches de Baume, signposted off the D471, gives stunning views of the village and the verdant Seille valley out as far as the Château Chalon and beyond if the weather is up to it.

In the village, the main attraction is the **abbey** (daily 10am–noon & 2–6pm; hourly guided tours: first two weeks June 10am–noon & 2–6pm; mid-June to mid-Sept 10am–6pm; €2.30). Monks were active in the area in the fourth century, and it's thought that the Irish St Columba was here in the sixth century, along with other monks, before leaving for Cluny. In spite of visitors clacking over the ancient stone floors, an atmosphere of monastic tranquillity still pervades the place. Consecrated in 909 by Benedictines, it was disbanded by the newly formed Republic in 1792, and today the interior and its twelfth-century **church**, in whose crypt rest three members of the once-dominant Chalon family, remain open to the public. **Accommodation** is available at the abbey at the *Gothique Café* (☎03.84.44.64.47; ❹), whose three beautiful rooms make you feel like you're back in the Middle Ages; the café itself serves lovely meals using local produce (menus from €15).

Two kilometres south of the village, at the very end of the valley, are the **Grottes de Baume** (several 40min guided tours daily: April–June & Sept 10am–noon & 2–5.30pm; July & Aug 9am–6pm; €5), one of the many limestone stalactite cave systems throughout the region. If you're particularly energetic you can ascend the stairway cut into the rock on the valley's eastern face; exposed in places and best avoided if conditions are wet, it leads to the clifftop and the Belvédère des Roches de Baume viewpoint described above. Otherwise opt for a meal at the *Restaurant des Grottes* (☎03.84.44.61.59; €15–25; mid-April to Sept lunchtimes only), not far from the caves and near the beautiful, fern-draped **waterfall**, with a stunning view back down the valley.

As you head north out of Baume, you'll see the limestone cliffs recede as the valley opens out, revealing miles of vineyards that yield the distinctive yellow wine of Château Chalon, produced from the Sauvignon grape. The fortified hilltop village of **CHÂTEAU CHALON** overlooks the vines and was built around a castle (not open to the public) of the once-influential family who give the village its name. A short wander will lead you past promising baskets of Chalon (expect to pay around €25 a bottle) to the fortified **church**, dating from the eleventh century and possessing some impressive stained glass and early examples of vaulting. An archway outside by the porch leads to the **Belvédère de la Rochette**, looking out across the valley back towards Baume. The views from the village are indescribably beautiful.

Poligny and Arbois

Back on the Route des Vins du Jura, the attractive medieval town of **POLIGNY**, at the southern end of the Culée de Vaux valley, is noteworthy for its well-preserved, early Romanesque buildings, including the **church of St-Hippolyte**, which features the characteristic, bell-like tower seen all over Franche-Comté. But the town's principal attraction is the hallowed **Maison du Comté** (July & Aug daily 1hr guided tours at 10am, 11am, 2pm, 3.30pm & 4.30pm; ☎03.84.37.23.51; €2) on avenue de la Résistance, which leads south from the central place des Deportés, an old fromagerie that now forms the headquarters of the Comité Interprofessional du Gruyère du Comté. Displays show the process of cheese-making, from extracting milk to producing the finished article, alongside audiovisual presentations exalting the industry. Gruyère officers, an institution of tax collectors founded by Charlemagne, once collected the 60-centimetre-wide *meules* of cheese as payment – each the product of 500 litres of milk; now, with over 800 years' experience of production, Comté cheese has earned the distinguished *Appellation d'Origine Contrôlée* (AOC) label more commonly reserved for vintage wines.

The attractive medieval houses and other sites of interest in Poligny are indicated on the blue *Walking Through the Old Town* leaflet available from the friendly **tourist office** on rue Victor-Hugo (July & Aug Mon–Fri 9am–12.30pm & 1.30–6.30pm, Sat 9am–12.30pm & 2–6pm, Sun 9am–12.30pm; Sept–June Mon–Fri 9am–12.30pm & 2–6pm, Sat 9am–noon & 2–5pm; ⓣ03.84.37.24.21).

Arbois

There's no mistaking that **ARBOIS**, 10km to the north, is the capital of this region's viticulture. Glittering wine emporia line the central place de la Liberté, entreating you to sample the unusual local wines, of which the sweet *vin de paille* is rarest – so called because its grapes are dried on beds of straw, giving the wine a strong aftertaste equal to that of the better-known Château Chalon. Chocolatier M. Hirsinger has developed chocolates to eat with wines, especially the Jura's own *vin jaune*, a wine flavoured with walnuts. A visit to the Hirsinger chocolate shop on place de la Liberté is a must, especially for the delicious ice cream.

Louis Pasteur lived in Arbois after his family moved from Dole, and his boyhood home, the **Maison de Louis Pasteur** on avenue Pasteur, is open to the public (hourly guided visits daily: April, May & Oct 2.15–5.15pm; June–Sept 9.45am–11.45am & every 30min 2.15–6.15pm; €5). The **tourist office** is at 10 rue de l'Hôtel de Ville (July & Aug Mon–Sat 9am–12.30pm & 2–6.30pm, Sun 10am–noon & 2–5pm; Sept–June Mon 3–6pm, Tues–Sat 9am–noon & 2–6pm; ⓣ03.84.66.55.50); in the basement of the same building is the **Musée de la Vigne et du Vin** (July & Aug daily 10am–12.30pm & 2–6pm; March–June, Sept & Oct daily except Tues 10am–noon & 2–6pm; Nov–Feb daily except Tues 2–6pm; €3.20), which details the development and production of wine in the Jura.

If you're **staying** overnight in town, try the decent *Les Messageries* (ⓣ03.84.66.15.45, ⓕ03.84.37.41.09; ❹), up from the Maison Pasteur. There's a **campsite**, *Camping Municipal Les Vignes*, on avenue Général-Leclerc (ⓣ03.84.66.14.12, ⓕ03.84.66.25.50; April–Sept), 1km east of the centre. For a meal, head to *La Balance*, at 47 rue de Courcelles (ⓣ03.84.37.45.00) where an array of interesting menus (€16–24) have been concocted to complement the local wines; or *Au Jardin Venitien*, a good pizzeria at 1 rue Mercière (ⓣ03.84.37.49.22; pizzas from €6).

The Central Plateau and the Jura mountains

On the broad upland plateau, the Jura landscape unrolls, stretches and rises in increasingly abrupt steps to the mountains bordering the Swiss frontier. With its lakes and pine forests, small farming communities and – at the higher altitudes – huge ski resorts enveloping tiny villages, semi-deserted in summer, this is the most beautiful area of the Jura and, as you might expect – despite trains linking **Champagnole**, **Morez** and **St-Claude** with Arbois and Pontarlier – best appreciated with your own transport.

Champagnole and the Forêt de la Joux

Situated at a major crossroads on the plateau, **CHAMPAGNOLE**, an industrial town largely rebuilt after a major fire in 1798, holds little intrinsic interest for the passing visitor, with the exception of an **archeological museum**, 26 rue Baronne-Delfort (May & June Wed 2–6pm, July & Aug daily except Tues 2–6pm; €2), above the tourist office, which displays an interesting array of Gallic and Roman artefacts found in the vicinity. However, the town does serve as a useful base for exploring the surrounding countryside, in particular the Forêt de la Joux, to the northeast.

For central **accommodation**, try the *Hôtel de la Londaine*, 31 rue du Général-Leclerc (ⓣ03.84.52.06.69; ❶), or, for old-style grandeur, the *Grand Hôtel Ripotot*, 54 rue Maréchal-Foch (ⓣ03.84.52.15.45, ⓕ03.84.52.09.11; ❹), which is definitely the nicest hotel in town. The campsite, *Camping de Boyse*, is on rue Georges-Vallery (ⓣ03.84.52.00.32; June to mid-Sept). The tourist office is in an annexe of the *Mairie* at 26 rue Baronne-Delfort (Mon–Fri 9am–noon & 2–6pm, Sat 9am–noon & 2–5pm; ⓣ03.84.52.43.67), and provides lots of information about exploring the surrounding forests and lakes, including hiking and mountain-biking kits for €5 each.

A couple of kilometres north of the source, spread over a small hill surrounded by pastures, is the old walled village of **NOZEROY**, ancestral home of the Chalon family, who dominated regional politics in feudal times. The town preserves much of its medieval charm today, with the **Porte de l'Horloge** – once part of the town's fortifications – framing the beginning of the Grande-Rue. This thoroughfare, lined with many ancient houses, ends at the place des Annonciades and the ruins of the thirteenth-century **castle**.

Forêt de la Joux

North of Nozeroy, on the other side of the D471 Champagnole–Pontarlier road, the **Forêt de la Joux** is considered one of the most beautiful of France's native pine forests. It's crisscrossed by a net of narrow fire roads, but if you don't have a car, you can use the Gare de la Joux, in the heart of the forest on the Champagnole–Pontarlier train line, from where you can explore further on foot or by bicycle. There are many well-marked walking trails through the forest: the most popular area is the **Sapins de la Glacière**. The **Route des Sapins** is the approved tourist drive, signposted for 50km from the D471 to the village of Levier, passing lookouts and the 45-metre-high **Sapin Président** (a 200-year-old fir tree) along the way. But the less regimented can just as easily enjoy getting mildly disorientated by following any number of lesser, unmarked roads and discovering the wonder of the forest for themselves.

The Lake District

South of Champagnole, the flattened plateau, unable to shed the Haut Jura's winter run-off, collects the meltwaters in a series of natural and not-so-natural lakes, known as the **Région des Lacs**, loosely strung along the valley of the River Ain. Where the ground begins to crumple upward to the eastern summits, gorges and waterfalls highlight each successive step, and lookouts survey the tiny villages, each with its characteristic domed belfry beaten from metal or composed from a mosaic of tiles and slates. Some of the lakes charge parking fees during the day, but after 6pm, when the crowds and swimming supervisors go home, the lakes are deserted and peaceful – perfect for an evening picnic watching the sun set.

Clairvaux-les-Lacs and the Cascades du Hérisson

The region's main resort town is **CLAIRVAUX-LES-LACS**. It's here that the northern tip of the serpentine **Lac de Vouglans**, dammed 25km downstream, reverts to the River Ain that feeds it. The **Grand Lac**, just south of town, is the focus of summer resort activity, with a beach area and watersports facilities. It's calm and scenic, in spite of all the camping activity going on around it. The **Office du Tourisme du Pays des Lacs**, 36 Grande-Rue (Mon–Sat 9am–noon & 2–6pm; July & Aug also Sun 10am–noon; ⓣ03.84.25.27.47, ⓕ03.84.25.23.00), is the place to find information about the region and outdoor activities such as boat and bike rental. For hiking, the *63 Circuits de Petite Randonnée* (€7 from the tourist office) has maps and descriptions of the circuits.

Simple, reasonably priced **accommodation** can be found on the Grand Lac, at the *Chaumière du Lac* (ⓣ03.84.25.81.52, ⓕ03.83.25.24.54; ❸; closed Oct–March) and the *Bellevue* (ⓣ03.84.25.82.37; ❸; closed Oct–May) – the latter offering a view worthy of its name.

Surrounded by hills, **Lac de Chalain**, 16km north of Clairvaux and near the village of Doucier, has a much more impressive setting. It's also a very popular spot for **camping**, hence the prices can be high, especially in mid-summer. There are five campsites in town: jointly run *Fayolan* and *Le Grand Lac*, both on the lake (ⓣ03.84.25.26.19; May to mid-Sept); *La Ferme du Villaret*, on a farm, route des Moirans (ⓣ03.84.25.26.03; July & Aug); *La Grisière et Europe Vacances*, near the lake with mobile homes for hire (ⓣ03.84.25.80.48; May–Sept); and *Les Tilleuls*, 6 chemin des Tilleuls (ⓣ03.84.25.81.45; May–Sept), also with mobile homes for hire.

By far the most interesting sight around here – and one of the Jura's best-known natural spectacles – is the **Cascades du Hérisson**, a septet of waterfalls descending nearly 300m in just 3km. Well-marked from either end of the gorge, the easiest walk, accessible by road via Val-Dessous southeast of Doucier, leads to the best-known and prettiest of the falls, the **Éventail**. A ten-minute stroll from the car park leads to the cascade, which spreads out in ever-widening tiers, giving it the fan-like appearance after which it is named. Continuing upstream, you'll shake off most casual spectators and pass through the woods of wild oak and springtime daffodils to the dramatic **Grand Saut**, with its clear drop of sixty metres; the pathway passes behind the waterfall – an alarmingly windy spot to shower in. A steep climb leads to smaller *sauts* feeding the odd swimming-hole, past a drinks kiosk – at the intersection of another path which leads south to the village of Bonlieu – to the uppermost Saut Girard, 3km up from the Éventail and close to the village of **ILAY**. There's a choice of restaurants in Ilay, but only one **hotel**, the *Auberge du Hérisson*, 5 rue des Lacs (ⓣ03.84.25.58.18, ⓕ03.84.25.51.11; ❸; closed Nov–Jan; restaurant from €12); they'll also be able to provide some tourist information.

A short drive up the N78 east of Ilay leads to a lookout atop **Pic de l'Aigle**: at nearly 1000m high, this is one of the best spots from which to view the Jura's topography. On fine days, the views extend as far as Mont Blanc to the east, and west to the plain of the Saône.

The Haut Jura

As you climb from the plateau through the pine forests to the scrawny higher pastures, the temperatures dip and the landscape takes a bleaker turn towards the summits of the **Haut Jura**. The main roads struggle up the valleys towards the Swiss border, but less demanding routes run along the mountains' narrow folds linking Pontarlier to **Morez** and **St-Claude**; when they're not passing through woodland or low cloud, these can provide memorable motoring. While the main towns in the area are valley-bound and claustrophobic, the resort towns tend to be expensive or rather soulless out of season, but most people come up here for the views across Lac Léman (Lake Geneva) in Switzerland towards the perennial snowscapes of the Alps.

Up to Morez and Les Rousses

The main trans-Jura route into Switzerland is the N5, which begins its ascent to the frontier around **ST-LAURENT-EN-GRANDVAUX**, which is great for cross-country skiing but unmemorable apart from the picturesque **Lac de l'Abbaye**, 4km south of town on the D437. Also on the Arbois–St-Claude train line is **MOREZ**, 12km southeast, a town squeezed along the narrow valley floor and noted for the manufacture of watches and spectacles. Its **tourist office** is in the central place Jaurès (mid-July to mid-Aug Mon–Sat 9am–noon & 2–6pm, Sun 10am–noon; rest of year Mon 2–6pm, Tues–Fri 9am–noon & 2–6pm, Sat 10am–noon; ⓣ03.84.33.08.73), along with the **gare routière**, from where buses depart for La Cure on the Franco-Swiss border. Once on the Swiss side, you can catch trains down to Nyon on Lac Léman and to Geneva itself.

A couple of kilometres before the frontier, **LES ROUSSES** exists purely for skiing – downhill and especially cross-country – but just before it a lane leads down to a very attractive **HI hostel** in an old, red-shuttered farmhouse by a stream, 2km away at Bief-de-la-Chaille (ⓣ03.84.60.02.80, ⓕ03.84.60.09.67; closed mid-April to mid-May & Oct to mid-Dec); from here you can see the eerie spheres of the satellite-tracking station on the summit of La Dôle (1677m), the Jura's highest peak, just over the Swiss border. The **GR9 footpath** passes through here, beginning a magnificent hiking section all along the crest of the ridge to the Col de la Faucille and beyond.

There are plenty of **hotels** in Les Rousses itself: the *Hôtel de France*, 323 rue Pasteur (ⓣ03.84.60.01.45, ⓕ03.84.60.04.63; ❹), is the town's best, but less extravagant lodgings can be found at the *Du Gai Pinson*, 1465 route Blanche (ⓣ03.84.60.02.15; ❸), or *Le Village*, 344 rue Pasteur (ⓣ03.84.34.12.75; ❸). For a meal, try the **restaurant** at the *Hôtel-Restaurant Les Gentianes* (menus from €13), or the *Restaurant Les P'Losses* (from €16), in the winter-sports centre on the Geneva road southwest of town. There are also plenty of cafés and pizzerias.

St-Claude

From Morez, the train line leaves the N5 and heads along the Gorges de la Bienne to the industrial town of **ST-CLAUDE** to the southwest, hemmed in by even higher mountains than those around Morez. It's famous for pipes (the smoking kind) and diamonds and other cut stones, with a museum, the **Musée des Pipiers, Diamantaires et Lapidaires** (Jan–April & Oct Mon–Sat 2–6pm; May, June & Sept daily 9.30am–noon & 2–6.30pm; July & Aug daily 9.30am–6.30pm; closed Nov & Dec; €4), dedicated to the makers of all three, opposite the fortified cathedral of St-Pierre on rue du Marché. The **tourist office**, 19 rue du Marché (July & Aug Mon–Fri 8.30am–7pm, Sat 9am–noon & 2–6pm, Sun 10am–1pm; Sept–June Mon–Fri 8.30am–noon & 2–6.30pm, Sat 9am–noon & 2–6pm; ⓣ03.84.45.34.24), distributes a free leaflet in English, *The City's Discovery Tour*, which gives a florid description of a two-hour walk around town.

Should you wish to **stay** here, try the *Hôtel de la Poste*, on rue Reybert (ⓣ03.84.45.52.34; ❷), opposite the tourist office. Plusher accommodation can be found at the *Jura Hôtel*, 40 av de la Gare (ⓣ03.84.45.24.04, ⓕ03.84.45.58.10; ❸), or *Le Joly* (ⓣ03.84.45.12.36; ❸) in Le Martinet, 3km southeast of town on the Col de la Faucille road, right next to a **campsite**. Wholesome, inexpensive food is served at the **restaurant** of *Hôtel St-Hubert* on the place St-Hubert and at *Brasserie le Lacuzon*, at 5 rue Victor-Hugo.

What gives purpose to the rest of the onward route from either St-Claude or Les Rousses are the superb views from the crest of the great fir-clad ridge that overlooks Lac Léman to the east. The N5 crosses the ridge at the **Col de la Faucille** (1323m). If it's clear, the view is unbelievably dramatic from the Col or the GR footpath; the whole range of the western Alps stretches out before you, dominated by Mont Blanc, with the steely cusp of Lac Léman at your feet. There's an even better view from the top of nearby **Mont Rond** (1534m), accessible by chair lift. Of course, if it's not clear, the journey will have been in vain, but if you're carrying on south of Geneva, 30km away, it's downhill all the way – with the thought of some revitalizing bars of Swiss chocolate at the day's end.

Travel details

Trains

Belfort to: Besançon (10 daily; 1hr–1hr 15min); Dole (5 daily; 1hr 30min); Montbéliard (hourly; 20min), Paris-Est (2 daily; 5hr); Ronchamp (12 daily; 5 min).
Besançon to: Bourg-en-Bresse (4–5 daily; 2hr 30min); Dijon (10 daily; 1hr); Dole (10 daily; 30min); Lons (several daily; 1hr–1hr 30min); Morez (4 daily; 2hr 10min–2hr 30min); Morteau (4 daily; 1hr–1hr 45min); Paris-Lyon (up to 6 daily; 2hr 30min); St-Claude (4 daily; 2hr 30min–3hr); St-Laurent (4 daily; 1hr 40min–2hr).
Dole to: Dijon (10 daily; 30min); Paris-Lyon (10 daily; 4hr); Pontarlier (3 daily; 1hr 20min).
Metz to: Amnéville (hourly, 20min); Hagondange (for Termapolis) (4 hourly; 15min); Longuyon (2 daily; 1hr 30min); Mulhouse (7 daily; 2hr 30min); Nancy (hourly; 1hr); Paris-Est (4 daily; 3hr); Strasbourg (every 2hr; 1hr 30min).
Mulhouse to: Belfort (up to 5 daily; 30–45 min); Colmar (every 30min; 20min).
Nancy to: Paris-Est (hourly; 2hr 40min–3hr); Pont-à-Mousson (hourly; 20min); Saverne (3 daily; 1hr); Strasbourg (every 2hr; 1hr 20 min).
St-Claude to: Bourg (4–5 daily; 1hr 40min–2hr), connecting with TGV to Paris; Champagnole (5 daily; 1hr).
Strasbourg to: Barr (9 daily; 55min); Basel (hourly; 1hr 30min–2hr); Besançon (8 daily; 2hr 15min); Colmar (hourly; 50min); Dambach (9 daily; 1hr); Dole (10 daily; 3hr 30min); Kehl (Germany) (hourly; 10min); Molsheim (frequent; 20min); Mulhouse (hourly; 1hr 20min); Obernai (9 daily; 40min); Paris-Est via Nancy (every 2hr; 4hr–4hr 30min); Rosheim (9 daily; 25min); Sarreguemines (6 daily; 1hr 20min); St-Dié (3 daily; 1hr 50min); Sélestat (hourly; 20min); Wissembourg (up to 5 daily; 1hr).
Verdun to: Metz (4 daily; 1hr–1hr 15min); Nancy (2 daily; 1hr 40min); Paris-Est (up to 5 daily; 3hr).

Buses

Belfort to: Ronchamp (1 daily; 45min).
Besançon to: Ornans (4 daily; 30min); Pontarlier (4 daily; 1hr).
Colmar to: Mulhouse (at least 1 hourly; 1hr); Sélestat (hourly; 1hr).
Haguenau to: Neuwiller (4 daily; 1hr 10min); Pfaffenhoffen (4 daily; 30min); Saverne (4 daily; 1hr 40min).
Lons-le-Saunier to: Dole (5 daily; 1hr).
Morez to: St-Claude (3 weekly; 1hr).
St-Claude to: Lyon (daily; 3hr 40min).
Saverne to: Molsheim (2 daily; 1hr).
Sélestat to: St-Dié (5–6 daily; 1hr 10min).
Verdun to: Metz (5 daily Mon–Sat; 2hr).

Normandy

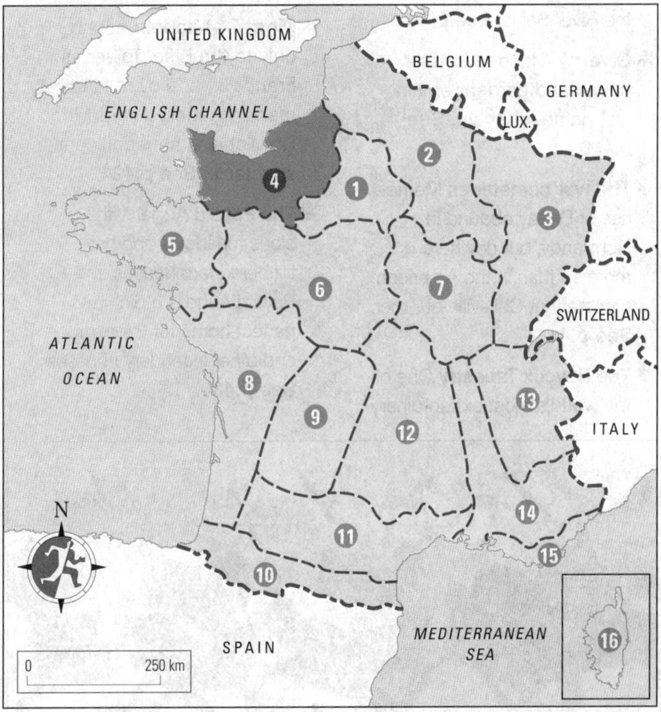

UNITED KINGDOM
BELGIUM
GERMANY
LUX.
ENGLISH CHANNEL
SWITZERLAND
ATLANTIC
OCEAN
ITALY
SPAIN
MEDITERRANEAN
SEA
N
0 250 km
1 2 3 4 5 6 7 8 9 10 11 12 13 14 15 16

CHAPTER 4

Highlights

✱ **Rouen** This fine old medieval city would still seem familiar to Joan of Arc, whose life came to a tragic end in its main square. **See p.391**

✱ **Château Gaillard** Richard the Lionheart's sturdy fortress commands superb views of the River Seine. **See p.400**

✱ **Giverny** Claude Monet's house and garden remain just as he left them. **See p.400**

✱ **The war cemeteries** Memories of D-Day abound in Normandy, but nowhere more so than in the American cemetery at Colleville-sur-mer. **See p.411**

✱ **The Bayeux Tapestry** One of the world's most extraordinary historical documents, embroidering the saga of William the Conqueror in every colourful detail. **See p.415**

✱ **Barfleur** This beautiful ancient port makes a great last-night stop for ferry passengers returning to England. **See p.420**

✱ **Mont St-Michel** Second only to the Eiffel Tower as France's best-loved landmark, the merveille of Mont St-Michel is a magnificent spectacle. **See p.424**

✱ **The Pays d'Auge** With luscious meadows and half-timbered farmhouses, the Pays d'Auge is a picture-perfect home for Camembert and other legendary cheeses. **See p.430**

△ The Bayeux Tapestry, Normandy

4

Normandy

Though now firmly incorporated into the French mainstream, the seaboard province of **Normandy** has a history of prosperous independence as one of the crucial powers of medieval Europe. Colonized by Scandinavian Vikings (or Norsemen) from the ninth century onwards, it in turn began to colonize during the eleventh and twelfth centuries, with military expeditions conquering not only England but as far afield as Sicily and areas of the Near East. Later, as part of France, it was instrumental in the settlement of Canada.

Normandy has always had large ports: **Rouen**, on the Seine, is the nearest navigable point to Paris, while **Dieppe**, **Le Havre** and **Cherbourg** have important transatlantic trade. Inland, it is overwhelmingly agricultural – a fertile belt of tranquil pastureland, where the chief interest for most visitors will be the groaning restaurant tables of regions such as the **Pays d'Auge**. Much of the seaside is a little overdeveloped; the last French emperor created, in the second half of the nineteenth century, a "Norman Riviera" around **Trouville** and **Deauville**, and an air of pretension still hangs about their elegant promenades. But more ancient harbours such as **Honfleur** and **Barfleur** remain visually irresistible, and there are numerous seaside villages with few crowds or affectations. The banks of the Seine, too, hold several delightful little communities.

Normandy also boasts extraordinary Romanesque and Gothic architectural treasures, although only the much-restored capital, Rouen, retains a complete medieval centre. Elsewhere, the attractions are more often single buildings than entire towns. Most famous of all is the spectacular *merveille* on the island of **Mont St-Michel**, but there are also the monasteries at **Jumièges** and **Caen**; the cathedrals of **Bayeux** and **Coutances**; and Richard the Lionheart's castle above the Seine at **Les Andelys**. In addition, **Bayeux** has its vivid and astonishing tapestry, while among more recent creations are Monet's garden at **Giverny** and, at Le Havre, a fabulous collection of paintings by Dufy, Boudin, as well as other Impressionists. Furthermore, Normandy's vernacular architecture makes it well worth exploring inland – the back roads through the countryside are lined with splendid centuries-old half-timbered manor houses. It's remarkable how much has survived or been restored since the Allied landings in 1944 and the subsequent **Battle of Normandy**, which has its own legacy in a series of war museums, memorials and cemeteries.

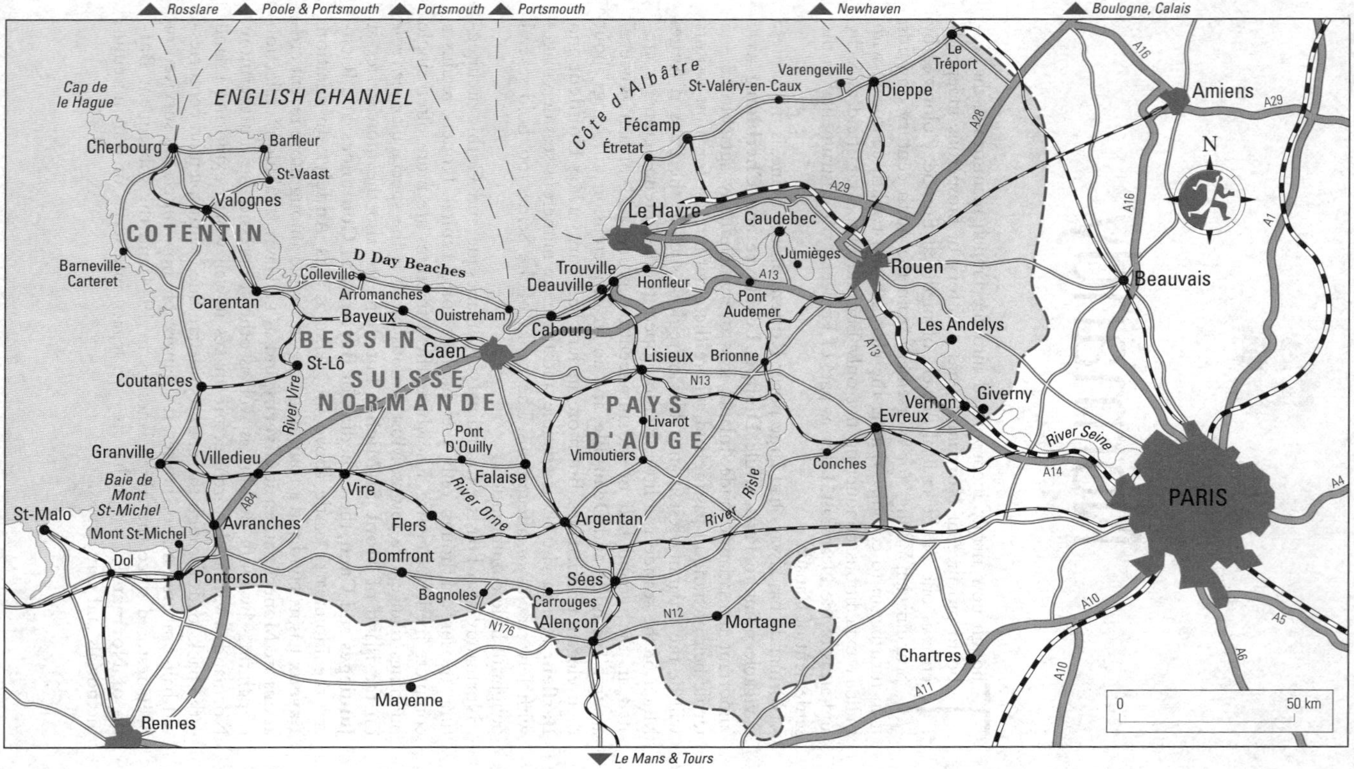

Rosslare
Poole & Portsmouth
Portsmouth
Portsmouth
Newhaven
Boulogne, Calais
ENGLISH CHANNEL
Cap de le Hague
Côte d'Albâtre
Cherbourg
Barfleur
St-Vaast
Valognes
COTENTIN
Barneville-Carteret
Carentan
D Day Beaches
Colleville
Arromanches
Bayeux
Ouistreham
BESSIN
Caen
St-Lô
Coutances
River Vire
SUISSE NORMANDE
Granville
Villedieu
Baie de Mont St-Michel
St-Malo
Mont St-Michel
Dol
Avranches
Pontorson
Rennes
A84
Vire
Flers
River Orne
Falaise
Pont D'Ouilly
Domfront
Bagnoles
Carrouges
Alençon
N176
Mayenne
Le Mans & Tours
Sées
Argentan
Vimoutiers
Livarot
PAYS D'AUGE
Lisieux
N13
Brionne
River Risle
Mortagne
N12
Trouville
Deauville
Cabourg
Honfleur
Pont Audemer
A13
Le Havre
Étretat
Fécamp
St-Valéry-en-Caux
Varengeville
Dieppe
Le Tréport
A28
A29
Caudebec
Jumièges
Rouen
Les Andelys
Vernon
Giverny
Evreux
Conches
River Seine
A14
Chartres
A11
A10
PARIS
A4
A5
A6
Beauvais
A16
Amiens
A1
N
0
50 km

The food of Normandy

The **food of Normandy** owes its most distinctive characteristic – its gut-bursting, heart-pounding richness – to the lush orchards and dairy herds of its agricultural heartland, and most especially the area southeast of Caen known as the Pays d'Auge. Menus abound in **meat** such as veal (*veau*) cooked in *vallée d'Auge* style, which consists largely of the profligate addition of cream and butter. Many dishes also feature orchard fruit, either in its natural state or in successively more alcoholic forms – either as apple or pear cider, or perhaps further distilled to produce brandies.

Normans have a great propensity for blood and guts. In addition to gamier meat and fowl such as rabbit and duck (a speciality in Rouen, where the birds are strangled to ensure that all their blood gets into the sauce), they enjoy such intestinal preparations as *andouilles*, the sausages known in English as chitterlings, and tripes, stewed for hours *à la mode de Caen*. A full blowout at a country restaurant in one of the small towns of inland Normandy – places like Conches, Vire and the Suisse Normande – will also traditionally entail one or two pauses between courses for the *trou normand*: a glass of the apple brandy Calvados while you catch your breath before struggling on with the feast.

Normandy's long coastline ensures that it is also a wonderful region for **seafood**. Many of the larger ports and resorts have long waterfront lines of restaurants competing for attention, each with its *"copieuse" assiette de fruits de mer*. **Honfleur** is probably the most enjoyable of these, but **Dieppe**, **Étretat**, and **Cherbourg** also spring to mind as offering endless eating opportunities. The menus tend to be much the same as those on offer in Brittany, if perhaps slightly more expensive.

The most famous products of Normandy's meadow-munching cows are, of course, their **cheeses**. The tradition of cheese-making in the Pays d'Auge is thought to have started in the monasteries during the Dark Ages. By the eleventh century the local products were already well defined; in 1236, the Roman de la Rose referred to Angelot cheese, identified with a small coin depicting a young angel killing a dragon. The principal modern varieties began to emerge in the seventeenth century – Pont l'Evêque, which is square with a washed crust, soft but not runny, and Livarot, which is round, thick and firm, and has a stronger flavour. Although Marie Herel is generally credited with having invented Camembert in the 1790s, a smaller and stodgier version of that cheese had already existed for some time. A priest fleeing the Revolution seems to have stayed in Mme Herel's farmhouse at Camembert, and suggested modifications in her cheese-making in line with the techniques he'd seen employed to manufacture Brie de Meaux – a slower process, gentler on the curd and with more thorough drainage. The rich full cheese thus created was an instant success in the market at Vimoutiers, and the development of the railways (and the invention of the chipboard cheesebox in 1880) helped to give it a worldwide popularity.

To the French, at least, the essence of Normandy is its produce. This is the land of Camembert and Calvados, cider and seafood, and a butter- and cream-based cuisine with a proud disdain for most things *nouvelle*. Economically, however, the richness of the dairy pastures has been Normandy's downfall in recent years. EU milk quotas have liquidated many small farms, and stringent sanitary regulations have forced many small-scale traditional cheese factories to close. Parts of inland Normandy are now among the most depressed in the whole country, and in the forested areas to the south, where life has never been easy, things have not improved.

Seine Maritime

The *département* of Seine Maritime comprises three very distinct sections: Normandy's dramatic **northern coastline**, home not only to major ports like Dieppe and Le Havre but also to such delightful resorts as **Étretat**; the meandering course of the **River Seine**, where unchanged villages stand both up- and downstream of the provincial capital of Rouen; and the flat chalky **Caux plateau**, which makes for pleasant cycling country but there's little of note to detain visitors.

Dieppe in particular offers a much more appealing introduction to France than its counterparts further north in Picardy, and with the impressive white cliffs of the aptly named **Côte d'Albâtre** (Alabaster Coast) stretching away to either side it could easily serve as the base for a long stay. The most direct route to Rouen from here is simply to head due south, but it's well worth tracing the shore all the way west to **Le Havre**, and then following the Seine inland.

Driving along the D982 along the northern bank of the Seine, you'll often find your course paralleled by mighty tankers and container ships out on the water. Potential stops en route include the medieval abbeys of **Jumièges** and **St-Wandrille**, but **Rouen** itself is the prime destination, its association with the execution of Joan of Arc merely the most compelling episode in its fascinating and still conspicuous history. Further upstream, Monet's wonderful house and garden at **Giverny** and the redoubtable English frontier stronghold of Château Gaillard at **Les Andelys** also justify taking a slow route into Paris.

Dieppe

Crowded between high cliff headlands, **DIEPPE** is an enjoyably small-scale port that used to be more of a resort. During the nineteenth century, Parisians came here by train to take the sea air, promenading along the front while the English colony indulged in the peculiar pastime of swimming. These days, it's not a place many travellers go out of their way to visit, but it's one of the nicer ferry ports in northern France, and you're unlikely to regret spending an afternoon or evening here before or after a Channel crossing. With kids in tow, the aquariums of the **Cité de la Mer** are the obvious attraction; otherwise, you could settle for admiring the cliffs and the castle as you stroll the extravagant seafront lawns. Meanwhile, the business of the port goes on as ever, with Dieppe's commercial docks unloading half the bananas of the Antilles and forty percent of all shellfish destined to slither down French throats. The markets sell fish right off the boats, displayed with the usual Gallic flair, and the sole, scallops and turbot available in profusion at the restaurants may well tempt you to stay.

Arrival and information

Dieppe's **tourist office** is on the pont Ango, which separates the ferry harbour from the pleasure port (May, June & Sept Mon–Sat 9am–1pm & 2–7pm, Sun 10am–1pm & 3–6pm; July & Aug Mon–Sat 9am–1pm & 2–8pm, Sun 10am–1pm & 3–6pm; Oct–April Mon–Sat 9am–noon & 2–6pm; ☎02.32.14.40.60,

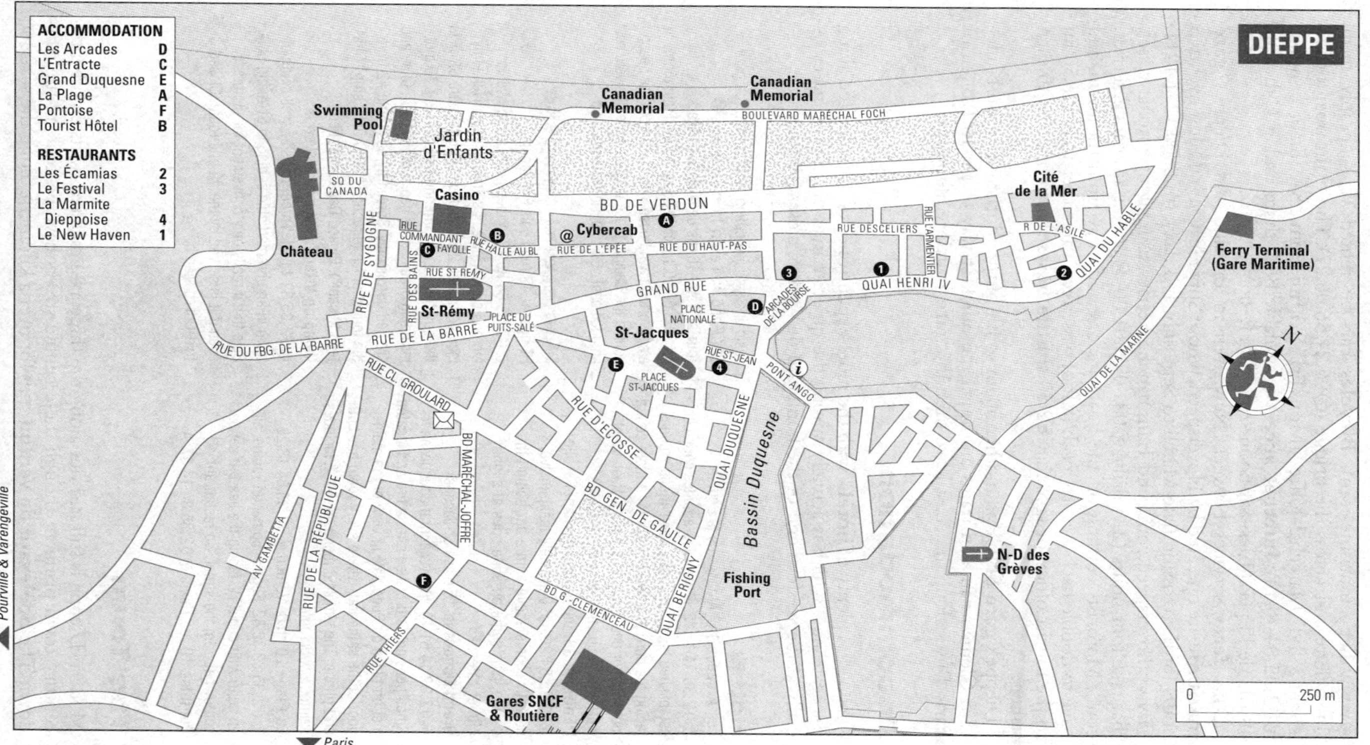
DIEPPE
ACCOMMODATION
Les Arcades D
L'Entracte C
Grand Duquesne E
La Plage A
Pontoise F
Tourist Hôtel B
RESTAURANTS
Les Écamias 2
Le Festival 3
La Marmite Dieppoise 4
Le New Haven 1
Swimming Pool
Jardin d'Enfants
Canadian Memorial
Canadian Memorial
BOULEVARD MARÉCHAL FOCH
Cité de la Mer
Ferry Terminal (Gare Maritime)
Château
SQ DU CANADA
Casino
BD DE VERDUN
Cybercab
RUE COMMANDANT FAYOLLE
RUE HALLE AU BL
RUE DE L'ÉPÉE
RUE DU HAUT-PAS
RUE DESCELIERS
RUE L'ARMENTIER
R DE L'ASILE
QUAI DU HABLE
QUAI HENRI IV
RUE ST RÉMY
RUE DES BAINS
RUE DE SYGOGNE
St-Rémy
PLACE DU PUITS-SALÉ
GRAND RUE
PLACE NATIONALE
ARCADES DE LA BOURSE
St-Jacques
RUE DE LA BARRE
RUE DU FBG. DE LA BARRE
RUE ST-JEAN
PONT ANGO
PLACE ST-JACQUES
RUE CL. GROULARD
RUE D'ECOSSE
BD MARÉCHAL-JOFFRE
QUAI DUQUESNE
Bassin Duquesne
QUAI DE LA MARNE
BD GEN. DE GAULLE
AV GAMBETTA
RUE DE LA RÉPUBLIQUE
BD G.-CLEMENCEAU
QUAI BERIGNY
Fishing Port
N-D des Grèves
RUE THIERS
Gares SNCF & Routière
Pourville & Varengeville
Paris
N
0 250 m

ⓦwww.dieppetourisme.com). **Bicycles** can be rented very cheaply from Buscyclette, just across the bridge (ⓣ06.24.56.06.27). The main **post office** is at 2 bd Maréchal-Joffre (Mon–Fri 8.30am–6pm, Sat 8.30am–noon; ⓣ02.35.04.70.14); **Internet access** is available both there, and at Cybercab, 48 rue de l'Epée (Tues–Sat noon–7pm, Sun 2–6pm).

Daily **ferry** services between Newhaven in England and Dieppe's **gare maritime** are operated by Hoverspeed, whose SuperSeaCats take just over two hours for the crossing (late March to Sept only, 1–3 daily; ⓣ00800.1211.1211, ⓦwww.hoverspeed.com), and Transmanche Ferries, using conventional vessels that take four hours (2–3 daily; ⓣ08.00.65.01.00, ⓦwww.transmancheferries.com). Motorists coming off the boats are directed away from the town, and have to double back west to reach it; foot passengers can either walk the 500m to the tourist office, or take the €2.50 **shuttle buses** that connect with each sailing.

Dieppe's **gare SNCF** is another 500m south of the tourist office, on boulevard Clemenceau, and trains are much the quickest way to get to Rouen or Paris. Buses along the coast leave from the **gare routière** alongside.

Accommodation

Dieppe has plenty of **hotels**, with the more expensive ones concentrated along the seafront – which is actually among the quietest areas of town – and especially at the western end of the boulevard de Verdun, closest to the castle.

Hotels

Les Arcades 1–3 Arcades de la Bourse ⓣ02.35.84.14.12, ⓦwww.les-arcades.com. Long-established hotel, under the eponymous arcades facing the port; you couldn't ask for a more central location, nor one closer to the ferry. Restaurant with good-value menus from €16. ❹

L'Entracte 39 rue du Commandant Fayolle ⓣ02.35.84.26.45. Extremely inexpensive, no-frills rooms above a little bar behind the casino, plus some en-suite ones at slightly higher rates. ❶

Grand Duquesne 15 place St-Jacques ⓣ02.32.14.61.10, ⓦwww.augrandduquesne.fr. Small pension, refurbished after a fire and located just off place du Puits Salé in view of the main door of the cathedral, where every room has bath and phone. The simplest menu, at €12, includes salmon *choucroute*. ❸

La Plage 20 bd de Verdun ⓣ02.35.84.18.28, ⓕ02.35.82.36.82. Slightly upmarket rooms, all en suite with cable TV, facing the sea but set back somewhat from the street. No restaurant. ❸

Pontoise 10 rue Thiers ⓣ02.35.84.14.57. A basic, inexpensive option, not far from the *gare SNCF* and well away from the beach. ❷

Tourist Hôtel 16 rue de la Halle au Blé ⓣ02.35.06.10.10, ⓕ02.35.84.15.87. Plain rooms in a converted town house, one block from the beach behind the Casino; those with en-suite showers cost an additional €12.50. No restaurant. ❶

Hostel and campsite

HI hostel 48 rue Louis Fromager ⓣ02.35.84.85.73, ⓔdieppe@fuaj.org. Welcoming and comfortable, if somewhat inconveniently located hostel, 2km southwest of the *gare SNCF* in the quartier Janval, offering beds for €7.70 (not including breakfast or bed linen) in two-, four- and six-bed dorms only. Served by bus route #2 from the tourist office (direction "Val Druel", stop "Château Michel"). Closed Dec to mid-Feb.

Camping Vitamin chemin des Vertus ⓣ02.35.82.11.11. Three-star site, well south of town in an unremarkable setting in St-Aubin-sur-Scie that's really only convenient for motorists, even if it is served by the #2 bus route. Closed mid-Oct to March.

The Town

Modern Dieppe is still laid out along the three axes dictated by its eighteenth-century town planners, though these central streets have become a little run-down. The **boulevard de Verdun** runs for over a kilometre along the seafront, from the fifteenth-century castle in the west to the port entrance, and passes the Casino, along with the grandest and oldest hotels. A short way inland, parallel to the seafront, is the **rue de la Barre** and its pedestrianized continuation, the Grande Rue. Along the harbour's edge, an extension of the **Grande Rue**, **quai Henry IV** has a colourful backdrop of cafés, brasseries and restaurants.

The **place du Puits Salé**, at the centre of the old town, is dominated by the huge, restored **Café des Tribunaux**, built as an inn towards the end of the seventeenth century. Two hundred years later, it was favoured by painters and writers such as Renoir, Monet, Sickert, Whistler and Pissarro. For English visitors, its most evocative association is with the exiled and unhappy Oscar Wilde, who drank here regularly. It's now a cavernous café, the haunt of college students and open until after midnight.

As for monuments, the obvious place to start is the medieval **castle** overlooking the seafront from the west, home of the **Musée de Dieppe** and two showpiece collections (June–Sept daily 10am–noon & 2–6pm; Oct–May Mon & Wed–Sat 10am–noon & 2–5pm, Sun 10am–noon & 2–5pm; €2.50). The first collection is a group of carved ivories – virtuoso pieces of sawing, filing and chipping of the plundered riches of Africa, shipped back to the town by early Dieppe "explorers". The other permanent exhibition is made up of a hundred or so prints by the co-founder of Cubism, Georges Braque, who went to school in Le Havre, spent summers in Dieppe and is buried just west of the town at Varengeville-sur-Mer. Other galleries upstairs hold paintings of local scenes by the likes of Pissaro, Renoir, Dufy, Sickert and Boudin, while a separate much newer wing of the castle stages temporary exhibitions.

An exit from the western side of the castle takes you out onto a path up to the **cliffs**. On the other side, a flight of steps leads down to the **square du Canada**, originally named in commemoration of the role played by Dieppe sailors in the colonization of Canada. Now a small plaque is dedicated to the Canadian soldiers who died in the suicidal 1942 raid on Dieppe, justified later as a trial run for the 1944 Normandy landings.

Cité de la Mer

On the eastern end of town just back from the harbour, the **Cité de la Mer**, at 37 rue de l'Asile-Thomas, sets out simultaneously to entertain children and to serve as a centre for scientific research, and succeeds in both without being all that interesting for the casual adult visitor (daily 10am–noon & 2–6pm; €4.30). Kids are certain to enjoy learning the principles of navigation by operating radio-controlled boats (€1 for 3min). Thereafter, the museum traces the history of sea-going vessels, featuring a Viking *drakkar* under construction, following methods depicted in the Bayeux Tapestry. Next comes a very detailed geological exhibition covering the formation of the local cliffs, in which you learn how to convert shingle into sandpaper. Visits culminate with large **aquariums** filled with the marine life of the Channel: flat fish with bulbous eyes and twisted faces, retiring octopuses, battling lobsters and hermaphrodite scallops (the white part is male, the orange, female). A lack of sentimentality means that jars of fish soup, whose exact provenance is not made explicit, are on sale at the exit.

Eating and drinking

The most promising area to look for **restaurants** in Dieppe is along the quai Henri IV, which makes a lovely place to stroll and compare menus of a summer's evening. The beach itself holds no formal restaurants, but it does have a couple of open-air cafés selling mussels, salads and so on, and plenty of crêpe stands. As well as the daily spectacle of the fish on sale in the **fishing port**, there's an all-day open-air **market** in the place Nationale and Grande Rue on Saturday. The largest of several hypermarkets in the area is Auchan (Mon–Sat 8.30am–10pm), out of town at the Centre Commercial du Belvédère on the route de Rouen (RN 27), and reached by free courtesy buses from the tourist office.

Les Écamias 129 quai Henri IV ☎02.35.84.67.67. Small, friendly, traditional restaurant, at the quieter, seaward end of the main quay, where the €12 option includes *moules marinières*. Another worthwhile pick is the skate with capers. Closed Mon.

Le Festival 11 quai Henri IV ☎02.35.40.24.29. Quick-fire brasserie at the busiest end of the quayside, delivering fishy goods at top speed without skimping on quality. *Moules frites* is a mere €7, while the €18 menu includes half a crab, and the €23 one half a lobster. There's also *fruits de mer* by the boatload, served in blue china ships.

La Marmite Dieppoise 8 rue St-Jean ☎02.35.84.24.26. Rustic, busy little restaurant, between St-Jacques church and the arcades de la Bourse. Lunch menus from €17, dinners at €25, €30 or €38, with the two latter featuring *marmite Dieppoise* (seafood pot, with shellfish and white fish). Closed Sun evening and Mon, plus Thurs evening out of season.

Le New Haven 53 quai Henri IV ☎02.35.84.89.72. Reliable seafood specialist on the quayside that serves good menus from €15. The €19 *menu de la Jetée* is fine if you hanker after fish livers and squid, while €18 buys you a *choucroute de la mer*. Closed Tues evening, plus all Wed in winter.

The Côte d'Albâtre

As the shoreline of the Côte d'Albâtre is eroding at a ferocious rate, it's conceivable that the small resorts here, tucked in among the cliffs at the ends of a succession of valleys, may not last more than another century or so. For the moment, however, they are quietly prospering, with casinos, sports centres and yacht marinas ensuring a modest but steady summer trade. To the east of Dieppe **Le Tréport** is pleasant enough, but the obvious direction to head is west, where you can take your pick of **St-Valéry**, **Fécamp** and the best of the bunch, **Étretat**.

Le Tréport

Thirty kilometres east of Dieppe, on the border with Picardy, **LE TRÉPORT** is a seaside resort that has clearly seen better days. It was already something of a bathing station when the railways arrived in 1873 and promoted this as "the prettiest beach in Europe, just three hours from Paris". It remained the capital's favoured resort until the 1950s – and is still served by around five trains daily – but it can't ever have been that pretty, and these days its charms are definitely fading.

Le Tréport divides into three sections: the flat wedge-shaped **seafront** area, bounded on one side by the Channel, on another by the harbour at the mouth of the river Bresle, and on the third by imposing 100-metre-high white chalk cliffs; the **old town**, higher up the slopes on safer ground; and the **modern town** further inland. Only the parts closest to the shore are of any interest to visitors. The seafront itself is entirely taken up by a hideous pink-and-orange concrete apartment block, with one or two snack bars but no other sign of life, facing the Casino and a drab grey shingle beach. The more sheltered harbourside quai Francois-1er around the corner holds most of the action, lined with restaurants, souvenir shops and cafés. The assorted stone jetties and wooden piers around the harbour make an enjoyable stroll, watching the comings and goings of the fishing boats.

Climbing up from the *quai*, you come to the heavily nautical **Église St-Jacques**, built in the fifteenth century to replace an eleventh-century original that crumbled into the sea, along with the cliff on which it stood. Nearby, next to the fortified former town hall that is now the local library, successive flights of steps, 365 of them in all, climb to the top of the cliffs.

Practicalities

Trains and **buses** arrive in Le Tréport on the far side of the harbour, a short walk from the main *quai*. Turning left as you hit the main drag will bring you to the **tourist office**, on quai Sadi-Carnot (April–June & Sept daily 9am–12.30pm & 2–6.30pm; July & Aug daily 9am–1pm & 2–7pm; Oct–March Mon–Sat 9am–noon & 2–6pm; ⓣ02.35.86.05.69). Of the **hotels**, the best in terms of a sea view and good-quality food is the *Riche Lieu* at 50 quai Francois-1er (ⓣ02.35.86.26.55; ❷), which has modernized rooms with showers and a wide range of menus starting at €15 for a "bistro" meal. The *Matelote*, 34 quai Francois-1er (ⓣ02.35.86.01.13), is a quayside seafood **restaurant** with a high gourmet reputation.

Varengeville

If the museum in Dieppe (see p.381) awakened your interest in Georges Braque, you may be interested in visiting his grave in the clifftop church some way further up the coast of **VARENGEVILLE**, 8km west of Dieppe (25min ride on bus #311 or #312, afternoon only). Braque's marble **tomb** is topped by a sadly decaying mosaic of a white dove in flight. More impressive is his vivid blue Tree of Jesse stained-glass window inside the church, through which the sun rises in summer.

Also in Varengeville, 300m south of the D75, is the **Manoir d'Ango**, the "summer palace" of sixteenth-century Dieppe's leading shipbuilder (mid-March to mid-Nov daily 10am–12.30pm & 2–6.30pm; €5). Jean Ango outfitted such major expeditions as Verrazzano's, which "discovered" the site of New York in 1524, and made himself rich from pillaging treasure ships out on the Spanish Main. His former home consists of a rectangular ensemble of fine brick buildings arranged around a central courtyard. The intricate patterning of red bricks, shaped flint slabs, stone blocks and supporting timbers is at its finest in the remarkable central dovecote, topped by a dome that rises to an elegant point, which is aflutter with pigeons.

Back along the road towards Dieppe from the church, the house at the **Bois des Moutiers**, built for Guillaume Mallet from 1898 onwards and un-French in almost every respect, was one of architect Edwin Lutyens' first commissions. Lutyens, then aged just 29, was at the start of a career that was to culminate during the 1920s when he laid out most of the city of New Delhi. The real reason to visit, however, is to enjoy the magnificent **gardens**, designed by Mallet in conjunction with Gertrude Jekyll, which are at their most spectacular in the second half of May (mid-March to mid-Nov daily 10am–noon & 2–6pm; €7 during May & June, otherwise €5). Enthusiastic guides lead you through the highly innovative engineering of the house and grounds, full of quirks and games. The colours of the Burne-Jones tapestry hanging in the stairwell were copied from Renaissance cloth in William Morris's studio; the rhododendrons were chosen from similar samples.

Outside, paths lead through vistas based on paintings by Poussin, Lorrain and other seventeenth-century artists.

Varengeville holds one single, very lovely **accommodation** option, the *Hôtel de la Terrasse*, atop the cliffs on route de Vastérival west of town (ⓣ02.35.85.12.54; ❸; closed mid-Oct to mid-March). Fishy menus in its panoramic dining room cost from €15.

St-Valéry-en-Caux

The first sizeable community west of Dieppe is **ST-VALÉRY-EN-CAUX**, a rebuilt town that is the clearest reminder of the fighting – and massive destruction – of the Allied retreat of 1940. A monument on the western cliffs pays tribute to the French cavalry division who faced Rommel's tanks on horseback, brandishing their sabres with hopeless heroism, while beside the ruins of a German artillery emplacement on the opposite cliffs another commemorates a Scottish division, rounded up while fighting their way back to Le Havre and the boats home.

Much the most attractive house to survive in St-Valéry, the Renaissance Maison Henri-IV on the quai d'Aval, serves as the **tourist office** (May to mid-Sept daily 10am–1pm & 3–7pm; mid-Sept to April daily 10am–12.30pm & 2.30–6.30pm; ⓣ02.35.97.00.63, ⓦwww.ville.saint-valery-en-caux.fr). *The Terrasses*, 22 rue le Perrey (ⓣ02.35.97.11.22; ❹; closed Christmas & Jan), is the only **hotel-restaurant** actually facing the sea – en-suite rooms cost almost double those without shower or bath – but several others surround the main market square. In high season the 149 comfortable if characterless rooms of the *Relais Mercure*, 500m back from the seafront at 14 av Clémenceau (ⓣ02.35.57.88.00; ❺), can be a godsend. There are also two **campsites**: the large four-star *D'Etennemare* (ⓣ02.35.97.15.79), set back from the sea southwest of the harbour and open year round, and the two-star *Falaise d'Amont* (ⓣ02.35.97.05.07; closed mid-Oct to mid-March), on the eastern cliffs. The *Restaurant du Port*, overlooking the harbour at 18 quai d'Amont (ⓣ02.35.97.08.93; closed Sun evening & Mon in low season), serves a delicious €19 seafood menu.

Fécamp

FÉCAMP, just over halfway from Dieppe to Le Havre, is a serious fishing port with an attractive seafront promenade. One compelling reason to pay a brief visit is to see the **Benedictine Distillery** on rue Alexandre-le-Grand, in the narrow strip of streets running parallel to the port towards the town centre. Tours lasting an hour and a half (daily: Feb, March & Oct–Dec 10–11.15am & 2–5pm; April to mid-July & Sept 10am–noon & 2–5.30pm; mid-July to Aug 10am–6.30pm; closed Jan; €5) start with a small **museum**, set firmly in the Middle Ages with props of manuscripts, locks, testaments, lamps and religious paintings beneath a nightmarish mock-Gothic roof. The first whiff of Benedictine – a sweet herby liqueur often combined with brandy – comes in the grim rust-and-grey-coloured Salle des Abbés, and at this point the script abruptly changes – from mysterious monks to PR for an exclusive product. The boxes of ingredients are a rare treat for the nose (take it easy with the myrrh), and there's further theatricality in the old distillery where boxes of herbs are flung with gusto into copper vats and alembics, though commercial production has long since moved to an out-of-town site. Finally you're offered a *dégustation* in their bar across the road – neat, in a cocktail, or on crêpes; make sure you hold onto your ticket to qualify.

If your aesthetic sensibilities need soothing after this, head for the soaring medieval nave and Renaissance carved screens of the **church of the Trinité**, up in the town centre, or the modern **Musée des Terres-Neuvas et de la Pêche**, on the seafront at 27 bd Albert 1er (July & Aug daily 10am–7pm; Sept–June daily except Tues 10am–noon & 2–5.30pm; €3). Spreading across two floors, with lots of miniature model boats and amateur paintings, it focuses on the long tradition whereby the fishermen of Fécamp decamp en masse each year to catch cod in the cold, foggy waters off Newfoundland. Sailing vessels continued to make the trek from the sixteenth century right up until 1931; today vast refrigerated container ships have taken their place.

Practicalties

Fécamp's main **tourist office** is opposite the distillery at 113 rue Alexandre-le-Grand (July & Aug daily 10am–6pm; Sept–June Mon–Sat 9am–12.15pm & 1.45–6pm; ⓣ02.35.28.51.01, ⓦwww.fecamptourisme.com). **Hotels**, which tend to be set back away from the sea on odd side streets, should be booked in advance. Two of the best are the appealing *Du Commerce*, in the old town at 26–28 place Bigot (ⓣ02.35.28.19.28, ⓦwww.hotel-lecommerce.com; ❸), and the good-value *De la Mer*, on the seafront at 89 bd Albert 1er (ⓣ02.35.28.24.64; ❸), which is nicer inside than it looks from the outside. There's also a superb **campsite**, the *Camping de Renneville* (ⓣ02.35.28.20.97; closed Jan & Feb), a short walk out of town on the western cliffs.

Among good-value fish **restaurants** are *La Marée*, 75 quai Bérigny (ⓣ02.35.29.39.15; Sept–June closed Sun evening, Mon, & Tues evening), which is attached to a fish shop and offers dinner menus from €23, and the friendly little *Marine*, 23 quai de la Vicomté (ⓣ02.35.28.15.94), that's open daily for good-value €11 lunches and serves a great *choucroute de la mer*.

Étretat

ÉTRETAT, another 20km west towards Le Havre, is a very different kettle of fish to Fécamp. Here the alabaster cliffs are at their most spectacular – their arches, tunnels and the solitary "needle" will doubtless be familiar from tourist brochures – and the town itself has grown up simply as a pleasure resort. There isn't even a port of any kind: the seafront consists of a sweeping unbroken curve of concrete above a shingle beach.

Thanks partly to its superb setting, and the lovely architectural ensemble that surrounds its central **place Foch**, Étretat is a very pretty little place. The old wooden market *halles* still dominate the main square, the ground floor now converted into souvenir shops, but the beams of the balcony and roof are bare and ancient. As soon as you step onto the beach you'll see the cliff formations to either side. To the west, on the **Falaise d'Aval**, a straightforward if precarious walk leads up the crumbling side of the cliff, with lush lawns and pastures to the inland side and German fortifications on the shore side extending to the point where the turf abruptly stops, occasionally ripped by the latest fall of cliff. From the windswept top you can see further rock formations and possibly even glimpse Le Havre, but the views back to the village sheltered in the valley, and the **Falaise d'Amont** on its eastern side – which Maupassant compared to an elephant dipping its trunk into the ocean – are what stick in the memory. The cliff itself presents an idyllic rural scene, with a gentle footpath winding up the green hillside to the little chapel of Notre-Dame.

Practicalties

Étretat's **tourist office** is alongside the main road through the centre of town, on place M.-Guillard (mid-June to mid-Sept daily 10am–7pm; mid-Sept to mid-June Mon–Sat 10am–noon & 2–6pm; ⓣ02.35.27.05.21, ⓦwww.etretat.net). Four **hotels** crowd onto the corners of place Foch, all significantly cheaper than the grand sea-view places. Most picturesque is the *Hôtel la Résidence*, 4 bd René-Coty (ⓣ02.35.27.02.87; ❸), a dramatic half-timbered old mansion that has beautiful wooden carvings decorating its every nook and cranny – the quality of rooms however is variable, and few are as elegant as the facade. More dependable is the *Hôtel des Falaises*, opposite at 1 bd René-Coty (ⓣ02.35.27.02.77; ❷) – in fact from its modernized rooms you get a better view of the *Résidence* than if you're actually staying there. *L'Escale*, on place Foch itself (ⓣ02.35.27.03.69; ❸), has simple but pleasant rooms, and a snack restaurant downstairs specializing in *moules frites* and crêpes. The grand, modern *Dormy House*, perched above town on the coastal route du Havre to the west (ⓣ02.35.27.07.88, ⓦwww.dormy-house.com; ❸), offers comfortable rooms with superlative views, and a good restaurant. **Campers** will find the *Camping municipal* (ⓣ02.35.27.07.67; closed mid-Oct to late March) 1km out on rue Guy-de-Maupassant.

The top **restaurant** in town is the *Galion*, distinct from the adjoining *Résidence* at 4 bd René-Coty (ⓣ02.35.29.48.74; closed Tues evening, Wed & mid-Dec to mid-Jan), where the €20 menu makes a definitive introduction to all that's best in Norman cuisine.

Le Havre

Most ferry passengers head straight out of the port of **LE HAVRE** as quickly as the traffic will allow to escape a city that guidebooks tend to dismiss as dismal, disastrous and gargantuan. While it's not the most picturesque or tranquil place in Normandy, however, it's not the soulless urban sprawl the warnings suggest, even if the port – the largest in France after Marseille – does take up half the Seine estuary, extending way beyond the town; the authorities are trying to promote its parks and gardens, listed in a glossy leaflet. The city was originally built on the orders of François I in 1517 to replace the ancient ports of Harfleur and Honfleur, then silting up, and its name was soon changed from the mouth-challenging Franciscopolis to Le Havre – "The Harbour". It became the principal trading post of France's northern coast, prospering especially during the American War of Independence and thereafter, importing cotton, sugar and tobacco. In the years before the outbreak of war in 1939, it was the European home of the great luxury liners such as the *Normandie*, *Île de France* and *France*.

Le Havre suffered heavier damage than any other port in Europe during World War II. Following its near-total destruction, it was rebuilt to the specifications of a single architect, **Auguste Perret**, between 1946 and 1964, making it a rare entity, and one visibly circumscribed by constraints of time and money. The sheer sense of space can be exhilarating, as the showpiece monuments have a dramatic and winning self-confidence, and the few surviving churches and other relics of the old city have been sensitively integrated into the whole. While the skyline has been kept deliberately low, the endless mundane residential blocks, thrown up as economically and swiftly as possible after the war, do eventually become dispiriting. Nonetheless, with the sea visible at the end of almost every street and open public space and expanses of water at every turn,

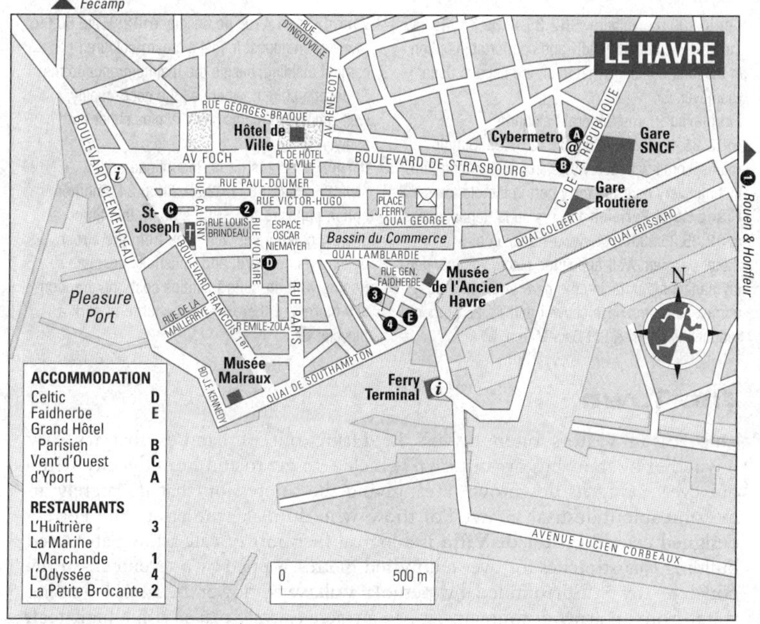

even those visitors who ultimately fail to agree with Perret's famous dictum that "concrete is beautiful" should enjoy a stroll around his city.

Arrival and information

Three daily P&O **ferries** sail from Portsmouth to the **Terminal de Grande Bretagne**, not far from the train and bus stations in the Bassin de la Citadelle (☎08.03.01.30.13).The terminal, which has a tourist information kiosk in summer, is connected by shuttle buses with the **gare SNCF** (☎02.35.98.50.50), 1.5km east of the Hôtel de Ville on cours de la République, and the **gare routière** alongside, the base for local and long distance buses.

Le Havre's rather inconspicuous and not very central **tourist office** is on the main seafront drag, at 186 bd Clémenceau (May–Sept Mon–Sat 9am–7pm, Sun 10am–12.30pm & 2.30–6pm; Oct–April Mon–Sat 9am–6.30pm, Sun 10am–1pm; ☎02.32.74.04.04, Ⓦwww.lehavretourisme.com) The **post office** at 62 rue Jules Siegfried (Mon–Fri 8am–7pm, Sat 8am–noon; ☎02.32.92.59.00) offers **Internet** access, as does Cybermetro, facing the *gare SNCF* at 15 cours de la République (daily 9am–midnight; ☎02.32.73.04.28).

Accommodation

Le Havre holds two main concentrations of **hotels**: one group faces the *gare SNCF*, while most of the rest lie within walking distance of the ferry terminal. The nearest **campsite** is the surprisingly attractive four-star *Forêt de Montgeon* (☎02.35.46.48.84, Ⓔchlorophile@wanadoo.fr; closed Jan–April), north of the town centre in a 700-acre forest; take bus #1 from the Hôtel de Ville or *gare SNCF*, direction "Jacques-Monod".

Celtic 106 rue Voltaire ⓣ02.35.42.39.77, ⓦwww.hotel-celtic.com. Friendly and comfortable option, in the long buildings that flank the Espace Oscar Niemeyer. ❷
Faidherbe 21 rue Général-Faidherbe ⓣ02.35.42.20.27, ⓕ02.35.42.57.03. Simple rooms, some with sea views, in a welcoming family hotel very near the ferry port in the old town. ❶
Grand Hôtel Parisien 1 cours de la République ⓣ02.35.25.23.83, ⓦwww.i-france.com/hotel-parisien. Well-appointed place, with congenial management, facing the *gare SNCF* on a busy corner. All rooms have shower and TV. 25 percent reductions on Fri & Sat Dec–March. ❸
Vent d'Ouest 4 rue de Caligny ⓣ02.35.42.50.69, ⓦwww.ventdouest.fr. Plain, cream-coloured cement building, beside the main entrance to the St-Joseph church, where all the good-quality, well-renovated rooms have TV plus either bath or shower. ❺
d'Yport 27 cours de la République ⓣ02.35.25.21.08, ⓕ02.35.24.06.34. Another option opposite the SNCF station, this time slightly quieter, set well back from the street beyond a courtyard, and unusually hospitable. Rooms with en-suite facilities cost only fractionally more, but there's a €3 charge to park a bicycle. ❷

The Town

One reason visitors often dismiss Le Havre out of hand is that it's easy – whether by train, bus or your own vehicle – to get to and from the city without ever seeing its downtown area, giving the impression that it's merely an interminable industrial sprawl. For those who do make the effort, the Perret-designed central **Hôtel de Ville** is a logical first port of call, a low flat-roofed building that stretches for over a hundred metres, topped by a seventeen-storey concrete tower. Surrounded by pergola walkways, flower beds and flowing water from an array of fountains, it's an attractive, lively place with a high-tech feel, and is often the venue for imaginative civic-minded exhibitions.

Perret's other major creation, clearly visible southwest of the town hall, is the **church of St-Joseph**. Instead of the traditional elongated cross shape, the church is built on a cross of which all four arms are equally short. From the outside it's a plain mass of speckled concrete, the main doors thrown open to hint at dark interior spaces within resembling an underground car park. In fact, when you get inside it all makes sense: the altar is right in the centre, with the hundred-metre bell tower rising directly above it. Very simple patterns of stained glass, all around the church and right the way up the tower, create a bright interplay of coloured light, focusing on the altar.

Le Havre's boldest specimen of modern architecture is even newer – the cultural centre known as the **Volcano** (or less reverentially as the "yoghurt pot"), standing at the end of the Bassin du Commerce, and dominating the Espace Oscar Niemeyer. The Volcano, designed by the Brazilian architect after which the *espace* is named, is a slightly asymmetrical, smooth, gleaming white cone, cut off abruptly just above the level of the surrounding buildings, so that its curving planes are undisturbed by doors or windows; the entrance is concealed beneath a white walkway in the open plaza below.

The **Bassin du Commerce**, which stretches away from the complex, is of minimal commercial significance. Kayaks and rowing boats can be rented to explore its regular contours, and a couple of larger boats are moored permanently to serve as clubs or restaurants – it's all disconcertingly quiet, serving mainly as an appropriate stretch of water for the graceful white footbridge of the Passarelle du Commerce to cross.

Overlooking the harbour entrance, the modern **Musée Malraux** (Mon & Wed–Fri 11am–6pm, Sat & Sun 11am–7pm; €3.80) ranks among the best-designed art galleries in France, using natural light to its full advantage to display an enjoyable assortment of nineteenth- and twentieth-century French paintings. Its principal highlights are over two hundred canvases by Eugène

Boudin, including greyish landscapes produced all along the Norman coastline, with views of Trouville, Honfleur and Étretat, as well as an entire wall of miniature cows and a lovely set of works by Raoul Dufy (1877–1953), which make Le Havre seem positively radiant, whatever the weather outside.

If you have the time to spare, you might like to see what old Le Havre looked like in the prewar days when Jean-Paul Sartre wrote *La Nausée* here. He taught philosophy for five years during the 1930s in a local school, and his almost transcendent disgust with the place cannot obscure the fascination he felt in exploring the seedy dockside quarter of St-François, in those spare moments when he wasn't visiting Simone de Beauvoir in Rouen. Little survives of the city Sartre knew, but pictures and bits gathered from the rubble are on display in one of the very few buildings that escaped World War II intact, the **Musée de l'Ancien Havre** at 1 rue Jérôme-Bellarmato, just south of the Bassin du Commerce (Wed–Sun 10am–noon & 2–6pm; €1.50).

The once-great port of **Harfleur** is now no more than a suburb of Le Havre, 6km upstream from the centre. While no longer sufficiently distinctive to be worth visiting, it earned an undying place in history as the landing place of Henry V's English army in 1415, en route to victory at Agincourt. Laid under siege, Harfleur surrendered in late September, following a final English onslaught spurred on – according to Shakespeare – by Henry's cry of "Once more unto the breach, dear friends …"

Eating

Few of the **restaurants** in Le Havre are worth making a fuss about. There are, however, lots of bars, cafés and brasseries around the *gare SNCF*, and all sorts of crêperies and ethnic alternatives – North African, South American, Caribbean – in the back streets of the St-François district around quai Michel Fere. If you're shopping for food to take home, you could try the central **market**, just west of place Gambetta and ideal for fresh produce, or two Auchan **hypermarkets** (both open Mon–Sat 8.30am–10pm): the larger, at the Mont Gaillard Centre Commercial, is reached by following cours de la République beyond the *gare SNCF*, through the tunnel; the other, at Montivilliers, is signposted off the Tancarville road.

L'Huîtrière 12 quai Michel Féré ⓣ02.35.21.24.16. Seafood specialists in the historic St-François quarter. Even the simplest €14 *assiette* includes clams, shrimps and langoustines; the two-person €115 *Abondance* has to be seen to be believed. They also have another branch in Étretat.

La Marine Marchande 27 bd Mouchez ⓣ02.35.25.11.77. Budget eaters congregate five minutes' walk east of the *gare SNCF* to enjoy a fine all-you-can-eat spread of French starters, which with a main course, dessert and wine costs just €10. Closed Sat lunch & Sun.

L'Odyssée 41 rue Général-Faidherbe ⓣ02.35.21.31.42. First-rate seafood restaurant close to the ferry terminal in the old town, serving a reliable €20 weekday lunch menu and a changing, more adventurous €25 dinner option. Closed Sat lunch, Sun evening, Mon & mid-July to mid-Aug.

La Petite Brocante 75 rue Louis Brindeau ⓣ02.35.21.42.20. Lively central bistro, where the set menus are a little pricey at €22 and up, but there's always a good-value *plat du jour*, as often as not fresh fish. Closed Sun & first three weeks in Aug.

Along the Seine to Rouen

Until relatively recently, no bridges crossed the Seine any lower than Rouen, which made the river an all but impassable barrier for motorists heading between Upper and Lower Normandy. Since 1995, however, the enormous **Pont de Normandie** has spanned the rivermouth, enabling motorists to zip across from Le Havre to Honfleur (for a hefty €5 toll), while further inland, the immense **Tancarville** suspension bridge and the magnificent **Pont de Brotonne**, just upstream from Caudebec, offer alternative routes across the river. If Rouen is your destination from Le Havre, however, it makes much more sense to stick to the north bank of the river. A succession of quiet roads follow the Seine's every loop, leading through sleepy towns such as **Caudebec-en-Caux** and past intriguing ruins like the abbey of **Jumièges**.

Caudebec-en-Caux

The first town of any size on the right bank of the Seine is **CAUDEBEC-EN-CAUX**. Most traces of its long past were destroyed by fire in the last war, after which it was rebuilt. The damage – and previous local history – is recorded in the thirteenth-century **Maison des Templiers**, one of the few buildings to be spared (Easter–May & Oct Sat & Sun 2.30–6.30pm; June–Sept Tues–Fri 3–6pm, Sat & Sun 2.30–6.30pm; €3). A **market** has been held every Saturday since 1390 in the main square.

Caudebec's **tourist office** is slightly south of the centre, in place Charles de Gaulle (April–Nov daily 10am–12.45pm & 2.15–7pm; Dec–March Mon–Sat 3–6pm, Sun 10am–noon & 3–6pm; ⓣ02.32.70.46.32, ⓦwww.caudebec-en-caux.com). Two indistinguishable *logis de France* face the river side by side from quai Guilbaud, with similar room rates: the *Normotel La Marine* at no. 18 (ⓣ02.35.96.20.11; ❸; closed Jan), and the slightly cheaper *Normandie* at no. 19 (ⓣ02.35.96.25.11; ❸; closed Feb). There's also a riverside **campsite** to the north, the *Barre Y Va* (ⓣ02.35.96.26.38; closed Oct–March).

Abbaye de St-Wandrille

Just beyond the Pont de Brotonne as you continue towards Rouen, the medieval abbey in **ST-WANDRILLE** was founded – so legend has it – by a seventh-century count who, with his wife, renounced all earthly pleasures on the day of their wedding. The abbey's buildings make an attractive if curious architectural ensemble: part ruin, part restoration and, in the case of the main buildings, part transplant – a fifteenth-century barn brought in a few years ago from another Norman village miles away.

St-Wandrille remains an active monastery, home to fifty Benedictine monks who in addition to their spiritual duties turn their hands to money-making tasks that range from candle-making to running a reprographic studio; they also show visitors around the abbey on **guided tours** (Tues–Sat 3.30pm, Sun 11.30am & 3.30pm; €3; ⓦwww.st-wandrille.com). You can wander through the grounds for no charge in summer (July & Aug Tues–Sun 10.45am–12.30pm & 3–5pm), and you can also listen to the monks' **Gregorian chanting** in their new church (Mon–Sat 9.45am & 5.30pm, Sun 10am & 5pm).

There's a crêperie opposite the abbey, and, a few doors along in the place de l'Église, the more upmarket *Deux Coronnes* **restaurant** (ⓣ02.35.96.11.44; closed Sun evening & Mon), a seventeenth-century inn – half-timbered, naturally – serving delicious menus starting at €22.50.

Abbaye de Jumièges

In the next loop of the Seine, 12km on from St-Wandrille, comes the highlight of the Seine valley: the majestic **abbey** in **JUMIÈGES** (daily: mid-April to mid-Sept 9.30am–7pm; mid-Sept to mid-April 9.30am–1pm & 2.30–5.30pm; €4.60), said to have been founded by St Philibert in 654 AD, just five years after St-Wandrille. A haunting ruin, the abbey was burned by marauding Vikings in 841, rebuilt a century later, then destroyed again – as a deliberate act – during the Revolution. Its main surviving outline, as far as it can still be discerned, dates from the eleventh century – William the Conqueror himself attended its re-consecration in 1067. The twin towers, 52m high, are still standing, as is one arch of the roofless nave, while a one-sided yew tree stands in the centre of what were once the cloisters. A superb **restaurant** faces the abbey from 17 place de la Mairie: the *Auberge des Ruines* (☎02.35.37.24.05; closed Sun evening & Mon, plus all evenings except Fri & Sat Nov–Feb).

Rouen

ROUEN, the capital of Upper Normandy, is one of France's most ancient and historic cities. Standing on the site of Roman Rotomagus, the lowest point on the river then capable of being bridged, it was laid out by the Viking Rollo shortly after he became Duke of Normandy in 911. Captured by the English in 1419, it was the stage in 1431 for the trial and execution of Joan of Arc, and returned to French control in 1449.

Over the centuries, Rouen has suffered repeated devastation; there were 45 major fires in the first half of the thirteenth century alone. It has had to be almost entirely rebuilt during the last sixty years, and now you could spend a whole day wandering around the city without realizing that the Seine ran through its centre. Wartime bombs destroyed all its bridges, the area between the cathedral and the *quais*, and much of the industrial quarter. The riverside area has never been adequately restored, and what you might expect to be the most beautiful part of the city is in fact something of an abomination.

Enormous sums have, however, been lavished on an upmarket restoration job on the streets a few hundred metres north of the river, which turned the centre into the closest approximation to a medieval city that modern imaginations could come up with. The suggestion that for historical authenticity the houses should be painted in bright, clashing colours was not deemed appropriate, but so far as it goes, the whole of this inner core can be very seductive, and its churches are impressive by any standards.

Outside the renovated quarters, things are rather different. The city spreads deep into the loop of the Seine, with its docks and industrial infrastructure stretching endlessly away to the south, and it's increasingly expanding up into the hills to the north as well, while the river bank is lined with a fume-filled, multi-laned motorway. As the nearest point that large container ships can get to Paris, even in decline this remains the fourth largest port in the country.

Arrival and information

Rouen's **airport** is at **Boos**, 9km southeast of town (☎02.35.79.41.00). Shuttle buses connect with each arrival and departure, running to the main *gare SNCF* via the Palais de Justice. Avis (☎02.35.70.95.12), Budget (☎02.32.81.95.00), and Hertz (☎02.35.98.16.57) offer **car rental** both in the terminal and in town.

The main *gare SNCF*, Gare Rive Droite, stands at the north end of rue Jeanne-d'Arc; it's connected to the centre by a multibillion-franc **métro** system, completed in 1998. From the train station (M° Gare Rue Verte), the métro

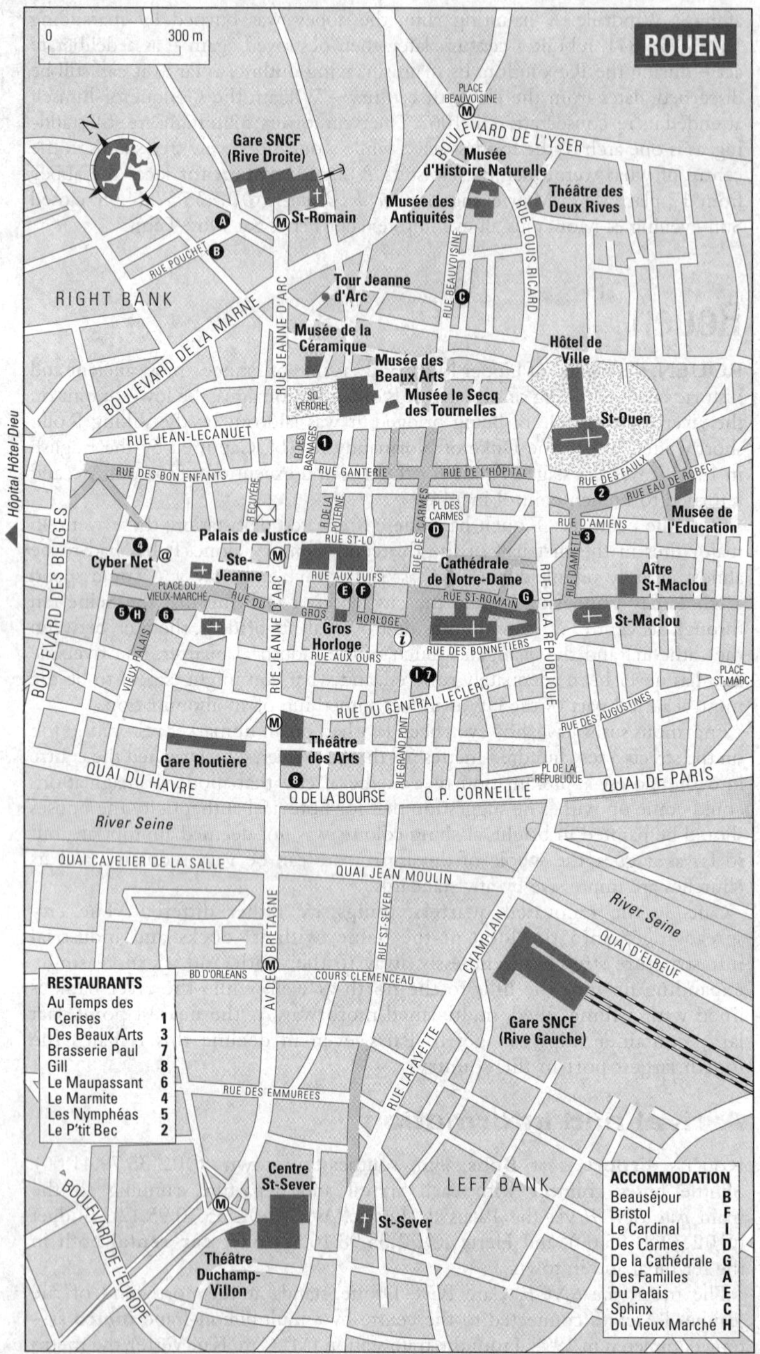
ROUEN
0 300 m
RIGHT BANK
LEFT BANK
Gare SNCF (Rive Droite)
St-Romain
PLACE BEAUVOISINE
BOULEVARD DE L'YSER
Musée d'Histoire Naturelle
Musée des Antiquités
Théâtre des Deux Rives
RUE BEAUVOISINE
RUE LOUIS RICARD
RUE POUCHET
Tour Jeanne d'Arc
BOULEVARD DE LA MARNE
RUE JEANNE D'ARC
Musée de la Céramique
Musée des Beaux Arts
SQ. VERDREL
Musée le Secq des Tournelles
Hôtel de Ville
St-Ouen
RUE JEAN-LECANUET
R. DES BASNAGES
RUE GANTERIE
RUE DE L'HÔPITAL
RUE DES BON ENFANTS
RUE DES FAULX
RUE EAU DE ROBEC
Musée de l'Education
Hôpital Hôtel-Dieu
BOULEVARD DES BELGES
R. ECUYÈRE
R. DE LA POTERNE
PL DES CARMES
RUE DES CARMES
RUE D'AMIENS
RUE DAMIETTE
Palais de Justice
RUE ST-LO
Cyber Net
Ste-Jeanne
Cathédrale de Notre-Dame
Aître St-Maclou
PLACE DU VIEUX-MARCHÉ
RUE AUX JUIFS
RUE DU GROS HORLOGE
RUE ST-ROMAIN
RUE DE LA RÉPUBLIQUE
St-Maclou
Gros Horloge
RUE AUX OURS
RUE DES BONNETIERS
VIEUX PALAIS
PLACE ST-MARC
RUE DU GENERAL LECLERC
RUE DES AUGUSTINES
RUE GRAND PONT
Théâtre des Arts
Gare Routière
PL DE LA RÉPUBLIQUE
QUAI DU HAVRE
Q DE LA BOURSE
Q P. CORNEILLE
QUAI DE PARIS
River Seine
QUAI CAVELIER DE LA SALLE
QUAI JEAN MOULIN
River Seine
QUAI D'ELBEUF
AV DE BRETAGNE
RUE ST-SEVER
CHAMPLAIN
BD D'ORLEANS
COURS CLEMENCEAU
Gare SNCF (Rive Gauche)
RUE LAFAYETTE
RUE DES EMMUREES
Centre St-Sever
St-Sever
BOULEVARD DE L'EUROPE
Théâtre Duchamp-Villon
RESTAURANTS
Au Temps des Cerises 1
Des Beaux Arts 3
Brasserie Paul 7
Gill 8
Le Maupassant 6
Le Marmite 4
Les Nymphéas 5
Le P'tit Bec 2
ACCOMMODATION
Beauséjour B
Bristol F
Le Cardinal I
Des Carmes D
De la Cathédrale G
Des Familles A
Du Palais E
Sphinx C
Du Vieux Marché H

follows the line of the rue Jeanne-d'Arc, making two stops before it resurfaces to cross the river by bridge. Individual journeys cost €1.20 and a book of tickets is €10. All **buses** except #2A from the *gare SNCF* run down rue Jeanne-d'Arc to the centre, which takes five minutes. From the fifth stop, the "Théâtre des Arts" by the river, the **gare routière** is one block west in rue des Charettes, tucked away behind the riverfront buildings (ⓣ02.35.52.92.00).

Rouen's **tourist office** stands opposite the cathedral at 25 place de la Cathédrale (May–Sept Mon–Sat 9am–7pm, Sun 9.30am–12.30pm & 2–6pm; Oct–April Mon–Sat 9am–6pm, Sun and hols 10am–1pm; ⓣ02.32.08.32.40, ⓦwww.rouen.fr). It serves as the starting point for two-hour **walking tours** of the city, departing daily at 2.30pm, as well as one on Saturdays at 5pm that covers the Jewish quarter; both cost €6. For more sedate visitors, a motorized "**petit train**" makes a forty-minute-loop tour from the tourist office at regular intervals (April–Oct daily 10am, 11am, 2pm, 3pm, 4pm & 5pm; €4.90).

You can rent **bicycles** from Rouen Cycles, 45 rue St-Éloi (Tues–Sat 8.30am–noon & 2–7pm; ⓣ02.35.71.34.30). The **post office** is at 45 rue Jeanne-d'Arc, in the centre of town (Mon–Fri 8am–7pm, Sat 8am–noon; ⓣ02.35.15.66.73). For **Internet** access, head to the café-style *Cyber Net*, 59 place du Vieux-Marché (daily 10am–11pm).

Accommodation

With over three thousand **hotel** rooms in town, there should be no difficulty in finding appropriate accommodation in Rouen, even at the busiest times, and most of those listed below remain open all year. Few of the hotels have restaurants, chiefly because there's so wide a choice of places to eat all over town.

Hotels

Beauséjour 9 rue Pouchet ⓣ02.35.71.93.47, ⓔbeausejour@lerapporteur.fr. Good-value place near the main station (turn right as you come out), though once you're past the attractive orange facade, and the nice garden courtyard, the rooms themselves are on the plain side, even if they do all have TV, phone and en-suite facilities. Closed second half of July. ❸

Bristol 45 rue aux Juifs ⓣ02.35.71.54.21, ⓕ02.35.52.06.33. Clean, pretty little nine-room hotel, above its own small brasserie in a half-timbered house overlooking the Palais de Justice. All rooms are en suite, and have TV. ❷

Le Cardinal 1 place de la Cathédrale ⓣ02.35.70.24.42, ⓦwww.hotels-rouen.com. Very good value hotel in a stunning location facing the cathedral; the rooms have excellent en-suite facilities, and ample buffet breakfasts are served for €6.80. ❹

Des Carmes 33 place des Carmes ⓣ02.35.71.92.31, ⓦwww.villederouen.fr/hotels. Twelve-room hotel in a beautifully decorated nineteenth-century house on a quiet central square, a short walk north from the cathedral. "Normandy" breakfasts for €6. ❸

De la Cathédrale 12 rue St-Romain ⓣ02.35.71.57.95, ⓔhcarm@mcom.fr. One of Rouen's most attractive and conveniently located hotels, in a quiet pedestrianized street alongside the cathedral, though the plain rooms themselves don't live up to the appealing facade and quaint old flower-filled courtyard. Buffet breakfasts €7.50. ❹

Des Familles 4 rue Pouchet ⓣ02.35.71.88.51, ⓦwww.hoteldesfamilles.com. Very friendly and characterful place, set back beyond a small gravel yard and a short walk to the right as you come out from the *gare Rive Droite*. ❹

Du Palais 12 rue du Tambour ⓣ02.35.71.41.40. Very inexpensive central hotel, tucked away just north of the Gros-Horloge, offering stylish though not fancy en-suite rooms at unbeatable prices. ❷

Sphinx 130 rue Beauvoisine ⓣ02.35.71.35.86. Very basic, even grim, accommodation, near the Musée des Antiquités, but this may be the only hotel left in Normandy where you can get a room, albeit without shower or bath, for €20. ❶

Du Vieux Marché 15 rue de la Pie ⓣ02.35.71.00.88, ⓦwww.hotelduvieuxmarche.com. Very modern place, set around a venerable old courtyard, just a toss of a match from the place du Vieux-Marché. A high standard of comfort has quickly made this the most popular upmarket hotel in town. ⑦

Campsites

Camping de l'Aubette 23 Vert Buisson in St-Léger du Bourg-Denis ⊕02.35.08.47.69. Basic site in a more rural, but much less accessible setting than the *Camping municipal*, 4km east of town on bus route #8.

Camping municipal rue Jules-Ferry in Déville-lès-Rouen ⊕02.35.74.07.59. Surprisingly small site, 4km northwest of town, that's geared towards caravans rather than tents; bus #2.

The Town

Rouen has traditionally spent a bigger slice of its budget on monuments than any other provincial town, which maddens many a Rouennais. As a tourist, however, your one complaint may be the lack of time to visit them all.

The place du Vieux-Marché to the cathedral

The obvious place to start sightseeing is the **place du Vieux-Marché**, where a small plaque and a huge cross (nearly 20m high) mark the spot on which Joan of Arc (see box, p.396) was burnt to death on May 30, 1431. A new memorial **church** to the saint has been built in the square (Mon–Sat 10am–12.30pm & 2–6pm, Sun 2–6pm): it's a wacky, spiky-looking thing, incorporating some sixteenth-century stained glass and said to represent either an upturned boat or the flames that consumed Joan. Indisputably an architectural triumph, it forms part of an ensemble that manages to incorporate in similar style a covered food market. The theme of the church's fish-shaped windows is continued in the scaly tiles that adorn its roof, which is elongated to form a walkway across the square. The outline of its vanished predecessor's foundations is visible on the adjacent lawns, which also mark the precise spot of Joan's martyrdom. The square itself is surrounded by fine old brown-and-white half-timbered houses, many of those on the south side now serving as restaurants. The private **Musée Jeanne d'Arc**, tucked in among them in an ancient cellar in the back of a gift shop, draws large crowds to its collection of tawdry waxworks and facsimile manuscripts (Tues–Sun: May to mid-Sept 9.30am–7pm; mid-Sept to April 10am–noon & 2–6.30pm; €4).

From place du Vieux-Marché, **rue du Gros-Horloge** leads east towards the cathedral. Just across the intersection with rue Jeanne-d'Arc you come to the **Gros Horloge** itself. A colourful one-handed clock, it used to be on the adjacent Gothic **belfry** until it was moved down by popular demand in 1529, so that people could see it better.

Despite the addition of all sorts of different towers, spires and vertical extensions, the **Cathédrale de Notre-Dame** (Mon 2–6pm, Tues–Sun 8am–6pm) remains at heart the Gothic masterpiece that was built in the twelfth and thirteenth centuries. The west facade of the cathedral, intricately sculpted like the rest of the exterior, was Monet's subject for over thirty studies of changing light, which now hang in the Musée d'Orsay in Paris. Monet might not recognize it now, however – in the last few years, it's been scrubbed a gleaming white, free from the centuries of accreted dirt he so carefully recorded. Inside, the carvings of the misericords in the choir provide a study of fifteenth-century life – in secular scenes of work and habits along with the usual mythical beasts. The **ambulatory** and **crypt** – closed on Sundays and during services – hold the assorted tombs of various recumbent royalty, stretching back as far as Duke Rollo, who died "enfeebled by toil" in 933 AD, and the actual heart of Richard the Lionheart.

△ Statue of St Peter, Rouen Cathedral

Joan of Arc

When the 17-year-old peasant girl known to history as **Joan of Arc** (Jeanne d'Arc in French) arrived at the French court early in 1429, the Hundred Years War had already dragged on for over ninety years. Most of northern France was in the grip of an Anglo-Burgundian alliance, but Joan, who since 1425 had been hearing voices, was certain that she could save the country, and came to present her case to the as-yet-uncrowned Dauphin. Partly through recognizing him despite a simple disguise he wore to fool her at their first meeting, she convinced him of her divine guidance; and after a remarkable three-week examination by a tribunal of the French *parlement*, she went on to secure command of the armies of France. In a whirlwind **campaign**, which culminated in the raising of the siege of Orléans on May 8, 1429, she broke the English hold on the Loire Valley. She then escorted the Dauphin deep into enemy territory so that, in accordance with ancient tradition, he could be crowned King Charles VII of France in the cathedral at Reims, on July 17.

Within a year of her greatest triumph, Joan was **captured** by the Burgundian army at Compiègne in May 1430, and held to ransom. Chivalry dictated that any offer of payment from the vacillating Charles must be accepted, but in the absence of such an offer Joan was handed over to the English for 10,000 ducats. On Christmas Day 1430, she was imprisoned in the château of Philippe-Auguste at Rouen.

Charged with heresy, on account of her "false and diabolical" visions and refusal not to wear men's clothing, Joan was put on trial for her life on February 21, 1431. For three months, a changing panel of 131 assessors – only eight of whom were English-born – heard the evidence against her. Condemned, inevitably, to death, Joan recanted on the scaffold in St-Ouen cemetery on May 24, and her sentence was commuted to life imprisonment. The presiding judge, Bishop Pierre Cauchon of Beauvais, reassured disappointed English representatives that "we will get her yet". The next Sunday, Joan was tricked into breaking her vow and putting on male clothing, and taken to the archbishop's chapel in rue St-Romain to be condemned to death for the second time. On May 30, 1431, she was burned at the stake in the place du Vieux-Marché; her ashes, together with her unburned heart, were thrown into the Seine.

Joan passed into legend, until the discovery and publication of the full transcript of her trial in the 1840s. The forbearance and devout humility she displayed throughout her ordeal added to her status as France's greatest religious heroine. She was canonized as recently as 1920, and soon afterwards became the country's patron saint.

St-Ouen and around

The **church of St-Ouen**, next to the Hôtel de Ville (which itself occupies buildings that were once part of the abbey), is larger than the cathedral and has far less decoration, so from the outside there's nothing to diminish the instant impact of its vast Gothic proportions and the purity of its lines. Inside, it holds some stunning fourteenth-century stained glass, though much was destroyed during the Revolution (mid-March to Oct daily except Tues 10am–12.30pm & 2–6pm; mid-Jan to mid-March & Nov to mid-Dec Wed, Sat & Sun 10am–12.30pm & 2–4.30pm; closed mid-Dec to mid-Jan). The world that produced it – and, nearer the end of the era, the light and grace of the **church of St-Maclou** not far to the south – was one of mass death from the plague: thus the **Aître St-Maclou** immediately to the east, a cemetery for the victims, was an integral part of the St-Maclou complex (daily 8am–8pm; entrance between 184 & 186 rue Martainville; free). It's now the tranquil garden courtyard of the Fine Arts school, but if you examine the one open lower storey of the surrounding buildings you'll discover the original deathly decorations and a mummified cat. In the square outside are several good antique bookshops, and a few art shops

The **rue Eau de Robec**, which runs east from rue Damiette just south of St-Ouen, was described by one of Flaubert's characters in an earlier age as a "degraded little Venice". It's now a textbook example of how Rouen has been restored. Where once a shallow stream flowed beneath the raised doorsteps of venerable half-timbered houses, a thin trickle now makes its way along a stylized cement bed crossed by concrete walkways. In a fine old mansion at no. 185, the **Musée National de l'Éducation** (Mon & Wed–Fri 10am–12.30pm & 1.30–6pm, Sat & Sun 2–6pm; €3) tells the story of the last five centuries of schooling in France, with photos, paintings, ancient textbooks and a mocked-up schoolroom. Unless you read French well, however, it's unlikely to hold your interest, and you're better off heading north past the Hôtel de Ville to the **Musée des Antiquités**, which occupies a seventeenth-century convent on rue Beauvoisine (Mon & Wed–Sat 10am–12.15pm & 1.30–5.30pm, Sun 2–6pm; €3): its tapestries and Medieval collection are particularly good.

The Musée des Beaux-Arts and around

Rouen's imposing **Musée des Beaux-Arts** commands the square Verdrel from just east of the central rue Jeanne d'Arc (daily except Tues 10am–6pm; €3). Even this grand edifice is not quite large enough to display some of its medieval tapestries, which trail inelegantly along the floor, but the collection as a whole is consistently absorbing. Unexpected highlights include dazzling Russian icons from the sixteenth century onwards, and an entertaining three-dimensional eighteenth-century Nativity from Naples. Many of the biggest names among the painters – Caravaggio (the centrepiece *Flagellation of Christ*), Velázquez, Rubens – tend to be represented by a single minor work, but there are several Modiglianis and a couple of Monets: *Rouen Cathedral* (1894), and the *Vue Générale de Rouen*. The central sculpture court, roofed over but very light, is dominated by a wonderful three-part mural of the course of the Seine from Paris to Le Havre, prepared by Raoul Dufy in 1937 for the Palais de Chaillot in Paris.

Rouen's history as a centre for *faïencerie*, or earthenware pottery, is recorded in the **Musée de la Céramique**, facing the Beaux-Arts from the north (daily except Tues 10am–1pm & 2–6pm; €2.30). A series of beautiful rooms, some of which incorporate sixteenth-century wood panelling rescued from a demolished nunnery of St-Amand, display specimens from the 1600s onwards. Assorted tiles and plates reflect the eighteenth-century craze for *chinoiserie*, although the genuine Chinese and Japanese pieces nearby possess a sophistication contemporary French craftsmen could only dream of emulating. The mood changes abruptly in the Revolutionary era, as witnessed by plates bearing slogans from both sides of the political fence.

Behind the Beaux-Arts, housed in the old and barely altered church of St-Laurent on rue Jacques-Villon, the **Musée Le Secq des Tournelles** (daily except Tues 10am–1pm & 2–6pm; €2.30) consists of a brilliant collection of wrought-iron objects of all dates and descriptions, among them nutcrackers and door knockers, spiral staircases that lead nowhere and hideous implements of torture.

The Tour Jeanne d'Arc

The pencil-thin **Tour Jeanne d'Arc** (April–Sept Mon & Wed–Sat 10am–12.30pm & 2–6pm, Sun 2–6.30pm; Oct–March Mon & Wed–Sat 10am–12.30pm & 2–5pm, Sun 2–5.30pm; €1.50), a short way southeast of the *gare SNCF*, is all that remains of the castle of Philippe-Auguste, built in 1205 and scene of the imprisonment and trial of Joan of Arc. It served as the castle's keep and entrance-way, and was itself fully surrounded by a moat. It was not however Joan's actual prison – that was the Tour de la Pucelle, demolished in 1809 – while the trial took place first of all in the castle's St-Romain chapel, and then later in its great central hall, both of which were destroyed in 1590. The tall, sharp-pointed tower was bought by public subscription in 1860, and restored to its present state. After seeing a small collection of Joan-related memorabilia, you can climb a steep spiral staircase to the very top, but you can't see out over the city, let alone step outside into the open air.

Eating and drinking

Unlike the hotels, which sometimes have cheaper weekend rates, Rouen's upmarket **restaurants** tend to charge more over weekends, when families eat out. The greatest concentration of restaurants is in place du Vieux-Marché, where there's a daily **food market**, while the area just north is full of Tunisian **takeaways**, **crêperies** and so forth. Some of Rouen's most agreeable **bars** are in the maze of streets between rue Thiers and place du Vieux-Marché. Incoming sailors used to head straight for this area of the city, and the small bars are still there even if the sailors aren't.

Restaurants

Au Temps des Cerises 4–6 rue des Basnages ☎02.35.89.98.00. If you've come to Normandy for the cheeses, this is the place to get them. Turkey breast in Camembert, goats cheese crêpes, and above all fondues of every description. Lunch menus from €11, dinners from €15. Trendy if slightly overstyled. Closed Mon lunch, Sat lunch & Sun.

Des Beaux Arts 34 rue Damiette ☎02.35.70.17.15. Very good-value Algerian cuisine, on a pretty pedestrianized street north of St-Maclou church: couscous from €8 or tajine from €11, with all kinds of sausages and assorted meats. Closed Mon.

Brasserie Paul 1 place de la Cathédrale ☎02.35.71.86.07. The definitive address for Rouen's definitive bistro, an attractive neo-Belle Époque place with seating both indoors and on a terrace in full view of the cathedral. Daily lunch specials, such as the goats' cheese and smoked duck salad that was Simone de Beauvoir's regular favourite in the 1930s, cost around €10.

Gill 9 quai de la Bourse ☎02.35.71.16.14. Absolutely classic French restaurant with specialities such as lobster grilled with asparagus and pigeon baked in puff pastry. Weekday lunches start at just under €30, while the cheapest dinner menu will set you back €35. Closed Sun & Mon June–Sept, otherwise Sun evening, all Mon, & Tues lunch.

Le Marmite 3 rue de Florence ☎02.35.71.75.55. Romantic little place just west of the place du Vieux-Marché, offering beautiful, elegantly presented gourmet dishes on well-priced menus at €22, €32 (featuring delicious hot oysters) and €48. Closed Sun evening & Mon.

Le Maupassant 39 place du Vieux-Marché ☎02.35.07.56.90. Currently the most popular of the Vieux-Marché's many restaurants, with a streetside terrace in front of the St-Jeanne church and an indoor dining room as well. It serves an excellent €17 menu until 10.30pm nightly, featuring beautifully cooked duck's breast and great chocolate desserts.

Les Nymphéas 7–9 rue de la Pie ☎02.35.89.26.69. Situated beyond a half-timbered courtyard just west of place du Vieux-Marché, this is the chic-est restaurant in Rouen, if a little over the top for most tastes. Set menus from €28 to €40; try the scallop salad or the beef with truffles. Closed Sun evening, all Mon, & Tues lunch, plus first fortnight of Sept.

Le P'tit Bec 182 rue Eau de Robec ☎02.35.07.63.33. Friendly brasserie-cum-tearoom that's Rouen's most popular lunch spot, with two simple menus at €11 and €13.50, holding such joys as salmon tagliatelle and chocolate fondants, plus plenty of vegetarian options. It also serves afternoon tea. Closed in the evenings except Fri & Sat; closed all day Sun.

Bars and music venues

Le Bateau Ivre 17 rue des Sapins. Low-key but atmospheric hangout which puts on a mostly rock-oriented programme of music and performance, with an open-mike night on Thurs attracting lovers of traditional French chansons. Tues & Wed 10pm–2am, Thurs–Sat 10pm–4am. Closed Sun, Mon & all Aug.

Big Ben Pub 95 rue du Gros-Horloge. Right under the big clock – hence the name – this always-packed bar is strictly speaking entered from a side street, at 30 rue des Vergetiers. Usually as crowded inside as is the street outside. Karaoke at weekends. Tues–Sat noon–2am.

Le Café Curieux 3 rue des Fossés Louis VIII. Incredibly loud and hectic bar, where Rouen's beautiful mingle to a techno and drum 'n' bass soundtrack. Tues & Fri 7pm–4am, Wed, Thurs & Sat 7pm–2am.

Exo 7 13 place des Chartreux. Traditionally the centre of Rouen's heavy-rock scene, a long way south of the centre, the *Exo 7* (pronounced "Exocet") is these days becoming a bit more eclectic, with the odd techno dance night as well. Fri & Sat 11pm–5am.

La Luna 26 rue St-Étienne-des-Tonneliers. Glamorous late-night club that specializes in all things South American, with steamy salsa dancing most nights. Tues–Sat 7pm–4am.

La Taverne St-Amant 11 rue St-Amant. Popular bar with draught Guinness and bistro meals, off rue de la République above the cathedral. Closed Sun & first three weeks of Aug.

Le Traxx 4 bd Ferdinand-de-Lesseps. Rouen's top gay club offers a regular diet of house and techno to a flamboyant clientele that loves to go wild on a special occasion. Wed–Sat 10pm–4am.

XXL 25–27 rue de la Savonnerie ☎02.35.88.84.00. Gay (male) bar that's a premier clubbing rendezvous and stays open all night Sat to serve breakfast on Sun. Closed Mon.

Entertainment

As you would expect in a conurbation of 400,000, there's always plenty going on in Rouen, from classical concerts in churches to alternative events in community and commercial centres. The city holds several **theatres**, which mainly work to winter seasons. The most highbrow and big-spectacle is the **Théâtre des Arts**, 7 rue de Dr-Rambert (☎02.35.71.41.36), which puts on opera, ballet and concerts. The more adventurous repertory company of the **Théâtre des Deux Rives** (☎02.35.70.22.82), based opposite the Antiquités museum at the top end of rue Louis-Ricard, presents work by playwrights such as Beaumarchais, Shakespeare, Beckett and Gorky.

Major **concerts** often take place in the **Théâtre Duchamp-Villon** in the St-Sever complex (☎02.32.18.28.10). Also south of the river, but a long way further out, are the **Théâtre Charles Dullin**, allée des Arcades, Grand Quévilly (☎02.35.69.51.18), and the **Théâtre Maxime-Gorki**, rue François-Mitterrand, Petit Quévilly (☎02.35.03.29.78), which specializes in contemporary and traditional music from around Europe. There are two multi-screen **cinemas** just north of the river, and another in the St-Sever complex.

Upstream from Rouen

Upstream from Rouen towards Paris, high cliffs on the north bank of the Seine imitate the coast, looking down on waves of green and scattered river islands. By the time you reach **Les Andelys**, 25km southeast of Rouen, you're within 100km of the capital, meaning that accommodation and eating prices tend to be geared towards affluent weekend and day-trippers. Large country estates abound in this agreeable countryside, and public transport is minimal. However, infrequent buses run from Rouen to Les Andelys, and trains from Rouen call at **Vernon**, just across the river from one of Normandy's most visited tourist attractions, the village of **Giverny**.

Les Andelys

The most dramatic sight anywhere along the Seine has to be Richard the Lionheart's **Château Gaillard**, perched high above **LES ANDELYS**. Constructed in a position of impregnable power, it looked down over any movement on the river at the frontier of the English king's domains. Built in less than a year (1196–97), the castle might have survived intact had Henri IV not ordered its destruction in 1603. As it is, the dominant outline remains. Visits to the château are permitted between mid-March and mid-November only (Mon & Thurs–Sun 10am–noon & 2–6pm, Wed 2–6pm; €3). On foot, you can make the steep climb up via a path that leads off rue Richard Coeur-de-Lion in Petit Andely. The only route for motorists is extraordinarily convoluted, following a long-winded one-way system that starts opposite the church in Grand Andely.

The **tourist office** for Les Andelys is in Petit Andely, at 24 rue Philippe-Auguste (April–Sept Mon–Fri 9.30am–12.30pm & 2.30–6pm, Sat 9.30am–12.30pm & 2.30–5.30pm, Sun 10am–noon & 2–5pm; Oct to mid-Dec & mid-Feb to March Mon–Fri 2–5.30pm, Sat 9.30am–12.30pm & 2.30–5.30pm, Sun 10am–noon & 2–5pm; ⓣ02.32.54.41.93). One of the nicest **hotels**, on the banks of the Seine, is the eighteenth-century *Chaîne d'Or*, opposite the thirteenth-century church of St-Sauveur at 27 rue Grande (ⓣ02.32.54.00.31; ❺; closed Jan, Sun evening & Mon, restaurant also closed Tues lunch). There's also a lovely riverside **campsite**, far below the château, the *Île des Trois Rois* (ⓣ02.32.54.23.79; closed Nov–March).

Giverny

Roughly 15km south of the ancient fortifications of Les Andelys, on the north bank of the river, you come to **Monet's house and gardens** – complete with water-lily pond – at **GIVERNY** (April–Oct Tues–Sun 10am–6pm; last ticket sold 5.30pm, no advance sales; house and gardens €5.50, gardens only €4). Monet lived here from 1883 till his death in 1926, and the gardens that he laid out were considered by many of his friends to be his masterpiece. In fact art lovers who make the pilgrimage here tend to be outnumbered by garden enthusiasts. None of Monet's original paintings is on display – most are in the Orangerie and Musée d'Orsay in Paris – whereas the gardens are still lovingly tended in all their glory.

You enter the house through the huge studio, built in 1915, where Monet painted the last and largest of his canvases depicting water lilies (in French, *nymphéas*). It now serves as a well-stocked book and gift shop. A gravel footpath leads to the actual house, a long two-storey structure facing down to the river. Monet's bedroom is bedecked with family photos and paintings by friends and family, while his salon holds further washed-out reproductions. All other main rooms are crammed floor-to-ceiling with his collection of Japanese prints, especially works by Hokusai and Hiroshige. Most of the original furnishings are gone, but you do get a real sense of how the dining room used to be, with all its walls and fittings painted a glorious bright yellow; Monet designed his own yellow crockery to harmonize with the surroundings. By contrast, the stairs and upstairs rooms are a pale blue.

Colourful flower gardens, with trellised walkways and shady bowers, stretch down from the house. At the bottom, a dank underpass beneath the road leads to the *jardin d'eau*, focused around the narrow **water-lily pond**. Footpaths around the perimeter, as well of course as arching Japanese footbridges, offer differing views of the water lilies themselves, cherished by gardeners in rowing boats. May and June, when the rhododendrons flower around the pond, and the wisteria that winds over the Japanese bridge is in bloom, are the best times to visit. Whenever you come, however, you'll have to contend with camera-happy crowds jostling to capture their own impressions of the water lilies.

A few minutes' walk up Giverny's village street, the **Musée d'Art Américain** is an unattractive edifice that hides a spacious and well-lit gallery devoted to American artists resident in France between 1865 and 1915 (April–Oct Tues–Sun 10am–6pm; €5.50). Some took their admiration of Monet to a point that now seems embarrassing, painting many of the same scenes, but there are some interesting works by John Singer Sargent, Winslow Homer and, especially, Mary Cassatt.

Giverny's one **hotel**, the *Musardière*, stands not far beyond Monet's house at 123 rue Claude-Monet (☎02.32.21.03.18; ❸); dinner menus in its restaurant start at €22. The nearest inexpensive accommodation is the *Hôtel d'Évreux*, 11 place d'Évreux (☎02.32.21.16.12; ❷), in the heart of **VERNON**, across the river, a fine seventeenth-century town house offering good food and comfortable accommodation. Connecting buses from Vernon's **gare SNCF** run to the gardens in Giverny.

Basse Normandie

As you head west along the coast of Basse Normandie from Le Havre, a succession of somewhat smug and exclusive resorts – of which only **Honfleur** is especially memorable – is followed first by the beaches where the Allied armies landed in 1944, and then by the wilder, and in places deserted, shore around the **Cotentin Peninsula**. There are two absolutely unmissable sights along this stretch – the glorious island abbey of **Mont St-Michel** and the **Bayeux Tapestry**.

The Norman Riviera

The only section of the Norman coast to have serious delusions of grandeur is the stretch that lies immediately west of the mouth of the Seine. The **Pont de Normandie** across the river estuary from Le Havre has made such places as **Trouville** and **Deauville** too hectic for comfort, though only **Honfleur** could be said to have had all that much to lose.

Honfleur

HONFLEUR, the best preserved of the old ports of Normandy and the first you come to on the eastern Calvados coast, is a near-perfect seaside town that lacks only a beach. It used to have one, but with the accumulation of silt from the Seine the sea has steadily withdrawn, leaving the eighteenth-century waterfront houses of **boulevard Charles-V** stranded and a little surreal. The ancient port, however, still functions – the channel to the beautiful Vieux

Bassin is kept open by regular dredging – and though only pleasure craft now use the moorings in the harbour basin, fishing boats tie up alongside the pier nearby, and you can usually buy fish either directly from the boats or from stands on the pier, still by right run by fishermen's wives.

Honfleur is highly picturesque, and has moved significantly upmarket since the opening of the Pont de Normandie. Despite now being just a few minutes' drive from Le Havre, the old port still feels not so very different to the fishing village that appealed so greatly to artists in the second half of the nineteenth century.

Arrival and information

Honfleur's **gare routière**, just to the east of the Vieux Bassin, is served by over a dozen direct daily **buses** from Caen (#20), and up to eight express services from Le Havre (Bus Verts; ⓣ08.01.21.42.14, ⓦwww.busverts14.fr). The nearest **train station** is at Pont l'Évêque, connected to Honfleur by the Lisieux bus (#50) – a twenty-minute ride.

The **tourist office** adjoins the glass-fronted Mediathèque on quai Le Paulmier, between the Vieux Bassin and the *gare routière* (Easter to mid-July & Sept Mon–Sat 10am–12.30pm & 2–6.30pm, Sun 10am–5pm; mid-July to Aug Mon–Sat 10am–7pm, Sun 10am–5pm; Oct–Easter Mon–Sat 10am–noon & 2–5.30pm; ⓣ02.31.89.23.30, ⓦwww.ot-honfleur.fr). Ask about their summer programme of **guided tours** of the town, which range from two-hour walkabouts to full-day excursions including meals.

Accommodation

If finding budget **accommodation** is one of your main priorities, it probably makes sense for you not to stay in Honfleur at all, and simply to visit for the day. Especially on summer weekends, so many visitors turn up that even the most ordinary hotel can get away with charging rates well above the average for Normandy. No hotels overlook the harbour itself. The two-star **Camping du Phare** (ⓣ02.31.89.10.26; closed Oct–March), is on place Jean-de-Vienne at the western end of boulevard Charles-V.

Belvédère 36 route Emile Renouf ⓣ02.31.89.08.13, ⓕ02.31.89.51.40. Peaceful, traditional hotel, with garden and terrace, roughly ten minutes' walk east of (and up from) the harbour. All rooms are en suite; some are in a cottage in the grounds, and there's a good restaurant. Closed Jan. ❹

Cascades 17 place Thiers ⓣ02.31.89.05.83, ⓕ02.31.89.32.13. Large hotel-restaurant open onto both place Thiers and the cobbled rue de la Ville behind. Slightly noisy rooms upstairs, and a good-value if not all that exciting restaurant with outdoor seating; menus climb from €13 towards the expensive *fruits de mer*. Closed Mon evening, all Tues out of season, and mid-Nov to Jan. ❷

Loges 18 rue Brûlée ⓣ02.31.89.38.26, ⓦwww.hoteldesloges.com. Smart, bright hotel on a quiet side street just 100m inland from Ste-Catherine church, decked out with flowers and offering a high standard of accommodation. ❻

Motel Monet Charrière du Puits ⓣ02.31.89.00.90, ⓦwww.motelmonet.fr. Not quite a motel as such, but this place is in a very quiet location ten minutes' walk from the centre and offers modern rooms arranged around a courtyard – so parking is easy. ❹

Tilbury 30 place Hamelin ⓣ02.31.98.83.33, ⓕ02.31.89.85.06. Absolutely central, a stone's throw from the Lieutenance. Well-equipped and comfortable rooms, all with bath, above a crêperie. ❹

The Town

Visitors to Honfleur inevitably gravitate towards the old centre, around the **Vieux Bassin**. At the *bassin*, slate-fronted houses, each of them one or two storeys higher than seems possible, harmonize – despite their tottering and ill-matched forms – into a backdrop that is only excelled by the **Lieutenance** at the harbour entrance. The latter was the dwelling of the king's lieutenant, and has been the gateway to the inner town at least since 1608, when Samuel Champlain sailed from Honfleur to found Québec. The **church of St-Étienne** nearby is now the **Musée de la Marine**, which combines a collection of model ships with several rooms of antique Norman furnishings (April–June & Sept Tues–Sun 10am–noon & 2–6pm; July & Aug daily 10am–1pm & 2–6.30pm; Oct to mid-Nov & mid-Feb to March Tues–Fri 2–5.30pm, Sat & Sun 10am–noon & 2–5.30pm; closed mid-Nov to mid-Feb; €2.50). Just behind it, two seventeenth-century **salt stores**, used to contain the precious commodity during the days of the much-hated *gabelle* or salt tax, now serve as the **Musée du Vieux Honfleur** (same hours; €2.50), filled with everyday artefacts from old Honfleur.

The town's artistic past – and its present concentration of galleries and painters – owes most to Eugène Boudin, forerunner of Impressionism. He was born and worked in the town, trained the 18-year-old Monet and was joined for various periods by Pissarro, Renoir and Cézanne. Boudin was among the founders of what's now the **Musée Eugène Boudin**, west of the port on place Erik-Satie, and left 53 works to it after his death in 1898 (mid-Feb to mid-March & Oct–Dec Mon & Wed–Fri 2.30–5pm, Sat & Sun 10am–noon & 2.30–5pm; mid-March to Sept daily except Tues 10am–noon & 2–6pm; €5.10). His pastel seascapes and sunsets in particular are quite appealing here in context, and they're accompanied by changing temporary exhibitions and a few ethnographic displays.

Admission to the museum also gives you access to the detached belfry of the **church of Ste-Catherine** (daily 9am–6pm). Both church and belfry are built almost entirely of wood – supposedly owing to economic restraints after the Hundred Years War. The church itself makes a change from the usual Norman stone constructions, and has the added peculiarity of being divided into twin naves, with one balcony running around both. From **rue de l'Homme-de-Bois** behind you can see yacht masts through the houses overlooking the *bassin* and, in the distance, the huge industrial panorama of Le Havre's docks.

Just down the hill from the Musée Boudin, at 67 bd Charles-V, is **Les Maisons Satie** (daily except Tues: May–Sept 10am–7pm; Oct–Dec and late Feb to April 11am–6pm; closed Jan to late Feb; €5), the red-timbered house of Erik Satie. From the outside it looks unchanged since the composer was born there in 1866. Step inside, however, and you'll find yourself in Normandy's most unusual and enjoyable museum. As befits a close associate of the Surrealists, Satie is commemorated by all sorts of weird interactive surprises. It would be a shame to give too many of them away here; suffice it to say that you're immediately confronted by a giant pear, bouncing into the air on huge wings to the strains of his best-known piano piece, *Gymnopédies*. You also get to see a filmed reconstruction of *Parade*, a ballet on which Satie collaborated with Picasso, Stravinsky and Cocteau, which created a furore in Paris in 1917.

Eating

With its abundance of day-trippers and hotel guests, Honfleur supports an astonishing number of **restaurants**, most specializing in seafood. Surprisingly few face onto the harbour itself; the narrow buildings around the edge seem to be better suited to being snack bars, crêperies, cafés and ice-cream parlours.

L'Absinthe 10 quai de la Quarantaine ☎02.31.89.39.00. Imaginative restaurant housed in an eighteenth-century mansion just around the corner from the *bassin*. Such dishes as scallop *carpaccio* or foie gras in ginger nestle on menus that range from €28 up to a seven-course €61 extravaganza. Closed mid-Nov to mid-Dec.

Au P'tit Mareyeur 4 rue Haute ☎02.31.98.84.23. Conveniently close to the centre, but all the seating is indoors so there are no views. Very good fish dishes – try the red crab soup with garlic – plus plenty of creamy *pays d'Auge* sauces and superb desserts. The main menu, at €20, includes skate marinated in coriander; for a €7 supplement you can enjoy lobster salad and chips. Closed Mon, Tues & all Jan.

La Fleur de Sel 17 rue Haute ☎02.31.89.01.92. Elegant, formal option, with indoor seating only, offering gourmet menus at €22, €29 and €39 that are strong on meat and fish. Closed Tues & Wed.

La Tortue 36 rue de l'Homme de Bois ☎02.31.98.87.91. A welcoming place near the Musée Boudin, where €17 buys a great-value five-course meal, and there's even a €13 vegetarian menu, consisting of apple soup, a couple of salads, vegetables and dessert. Closed Tues, plus mid-Jan to mid-Feb.

Le Vieux Honfleur 13 quai St-Étienne ☎02.31.89.15.31. The best of the restaurants around the harbour itself, with spacious alfresco dining – in shade at lunchtime – on its pedestrianized eastern side. Very simple menus, but the seafood is good, as befits prices starting at €28. The only other set menu, at €48, offers lobster or turbot, with no meat other than foie gras. Closed Jan.

Trouville and Deauville

Heading west along the corniche from Honfleur, green fields and fruit trees lull the land's edge, and cliffs rise from sandy beaches all the way to Trouville, 15km away. The resorts aren't exactly cheap but they're relatively undeveloped, and if you want to stop along the coast this is the place to do it. The next stretch, from Trouville to Cabourg, is what you might call the Riviera of Normandy with Trouville as "Nice" and Deauville as "Cannes", within a stone's throw of each other.

TROUVILLE retains some semblance of a real town, with a constant population and industries other than tourism. But it is still a resort, with a tangle of busy pedestrian streets just back from the beach that are alive with restaurants and hotels. It's been a chic destination ever since Napoléon III started bringing his court here every summer in the 1860s. One of his dukes, looking across the river, saw, instead of marshlands, money – and lots of it, in the form of a racetrack. His vision materialized, and villas appeared between the racetrack and the sea to become **DEAUVILLE**, which likes to style itself the "21st *arrondissement*" of Paris. Now you can lose money on the horses, cross five streets and lose more in the casino, then lose yourself across 200m of sports and "cure" facilities and private swimming huts before reaching the *planches*, 500m of boardwalk, beyond which rows of primary-coloured parasols obscure the view of the sea.

Practicalities

Trouville and Deauville share their **gare SNCF** and **gare routière**, in between the two just south of the marina. Each day, seven of the hourly buses from Caen continue along the coast to Honfleur. Visits to the **tourist office** on place de la Mairie in Deauville (May & June Mon, Tues & Thurs 9am–12.30pm & 2–6.30pm, Wed 10am–12.30pm & 2–6.30pm, Fri & Sat 9am–6.30pm, Sun 10am–1pm & 2–5pm; July to mid-Sept Mon–Sat 9am–7pm, Sun 10am–1pm & 3–6pm; mid-Sept to April Mon, Tues & Thurs–Sat 9am–12.30pm & 2–6.30pm, Wed 10am–12.30pm & 2–6.30pm, Sun 10am–1pm & 2–5pm; ☎02.31.14.40.00, Ⓦwww.deauville.org), or the one at 32 quai F. Moureaux in Trouville (April–June, Sept & Oct Mon–Sat 9.30am–noon & 2–6.30pm, Sun 10am–1pm; July & Aug Mon–Sat 9.30am–7pm, Sun 10am–4pm; Nov–March

Mon–Sat 9.30am–noon & 1.30–6pm, Sun 10am–1pm; ⓣ02.31.14.60.70, ⓦwww.trouvillesurmer.org), are repaid with the usual lavish brochures.

As you might imagine, **hotels** tend to be either luxurious or overpriced. The *Hôtel des Sports*, 27 rue Gambetta (ⓣ02.31.88.22.67; ❹; closed Sun in winter), behind Deauville's fish market, is among the least expensive, while *Le Trouville*, 1 rue Thiers (ⓣ02.31.98.45.48; ❸; closed Jan), is Trouville's closest equivalent. If you fancy staying right on the seafront, it's hard to beat the *Flaubert*, rue Gustave-Flaubert (ⓣ02.31.88.37.23, ⓦwww.flaubert.fr; ❺), a grand faux-timbered mansion at the start of Trouville's boardwalk, which is home to the recommended *Le Vivier* restaurant. Trouville also has a **campsite**, *Le Chant des Oiseaux* (ⓣ02.31.88.06.42; closed mid-Nov to March).

A good place to eat in Deauville is *Chez Miocque* at 81 rue Eugène-Colas (ⓣ02.31.88.09.52), a top-quality Parisian-style bistro with prices (around €40) that are high but not outrageous. Trouville has some good fish restaurants including *Les Vapeurs*, opposite the attractive old half-timbered fish market at 160 bd F. Moureaux (ⓣ02.31.88.15.24), and *La Petite Auberge*, 7 rue Carnot (ⓣ02.31.88.11.07; closed Tues all year, plus Wed in winter), though both get very crowded at weekends.

Deauville's **American Film Festival**, held in the first week of September, is the antithesis of Cannes, with public admission to a wide selection of previews.

Houlgate

A hundred years ago, **HOULGATE**, 15km west of Deauville, was every bit as glamorous and sophisticated a destination as its neighbours. What makes it different today is that it has barely changed since then. Its long straight beach remains lined with a stately procession of Victorian villas, while the town's handful of commercial enterprises are confined to the narrow parallel street, the **rue des Bains**, fifty metres inland. As a result, Houlgate is the most relaxed of the local resorts, ideal if you're looking for a peaceful family break where the only stress is deciding whether to paddle or play mini-golf.

The **tourist office** is well back from the sea on boulevard des Belges (daily 10am–12.30pm & 2–6.30pm; mid-Sept to mid-June closed Sun; ⓣ02.31.24.34.79, ⓦwww.ville-houlgate.fr). The *Hostellerie Normande*, just off the rue des Bains at 11 rue E.-Deschanel (ⓣ02.31.24.85.50; ❹; closed Oct–March, plus Mon evening & Tues in low season), is a pretty little **hotel** covered with ivy and creeping flowers, with a €10 lunch menu on which you can follow fish soup with a plate of *moules frites*. Above the Vaches Noires ("Black Cows") cliffs on the corniche road east of town, *La Ferme Auberge des Aulnettes* (ⓣ02.31.28.00.28; ❸; closed Tues eve, plus Wed in low season, and mid-Nov to mid-Feb), is a lovely country house set in pleasant gardens, with a good restaurant (at least one meal a day compulsory) and room to sit outside in the evening. The best **campsite** in the area, the four-star *Les Falaises* (ⓣ02.31.24.81.09, ⓔcamping.lesfalaises@voila.fr; closed Nov–March), is close at hand.

Dives and Cabourg

DIVES, the port from which William the Conqueror sailed for Hastings, is another 3km west from Houlgate, though like Honfleur it's now pushed well back from the sea. A lively Saturday **market** focuses around the ancient oak *halles*, whose steep tiled roof must be five times the height of its walls; on market days, it's crammed with mouthwatering delicacies and Norman specialities.

Dives is also home to a large, inexpensive *Etap* **hotel**, on voie nouvelle de Port-Guillaume (Ⓣ08.92.68.08.54; ❸).

At the much newer town of **CABOURG**, across the mouth of the Dives river, the *fin-de-siècle* streets of the town centre fan out in perfect symmetry from what must be the straightest promenade in France, with semi-circular avenues linking them together. The resort, contemporary with Deauville, seems to be stuck in the nineteenth century – immobilized by memories of Proust, perhaps, who wrote for a while in the **Grand Hôtel**, one of an outrageous ensemble of buildings around the **Jardins du Casino**. The **tourist office** in the Jardins du Casino has full details on hotels (July & Aug daily 9.30am–7pm; Sept–June Mon–Sat 9.30am–12.30pm & 2–6pm, Sun 10am–noon & 2–4pm; Ⓣ02.31.91.20.00, Ⓦwww.cabourg.net). A pleasant place to **stay** and eat is *L'Oie qui Fume*, a *logis de France* at 18 av de la Brèche-Buhot (Ⓣ02.31.91.27.79; ❺ including breakfast; closed Jan to mid-Feb, plus Mon eve, Tues & Wed in low season), 100m back from the sea on a quiet road half a dozen streets west of the centre; its €22 menu features goose (*oie*) as either starter or main course.

Caen

CAEN, capital and largest city of Basse Normandie, may well not be a place where you'll want to spend much time: in the months of fighting in 1944, it was devastated. Nonetheless, the city that nine hundred years ago

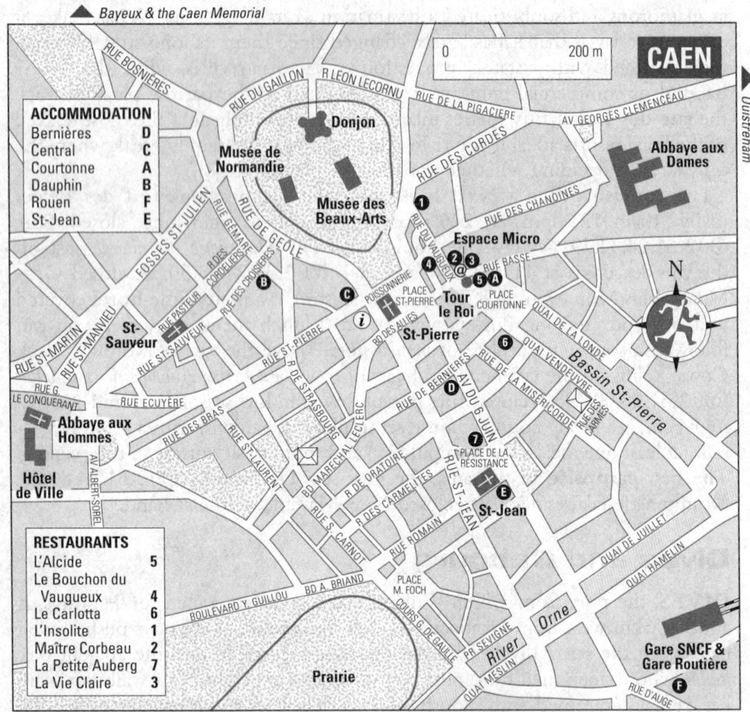

was the favoured residence of William the Conqueror remains – in parts – impressive.

Its central feature is a ring of ramparts that no longer have a castle to protect, and, though there are the scattered spires and buttresses of two abbeys and eight old churches, roads and roundabouts fill the wide spaces where prewar houses stood. Approaches are along thunderous dual carriageways through industrial suburbs, now prospering once more following an influx of high-tech newcomers.

Arrival and information

Caen's small, modern **airport**, just outside **Carpiquet** 7km west (ⓣ02.31.71.20.10), is served by **buses** (€1) connecting with all services, taking 25 minutes to run to and from the Tour-le-Roi stop in place Courtonne. Avis (ⓣ02.31.84.73.80), National (ⓣ02.31.52.22.22) and Rent A Car (ⓣ02.31.84.10.10) provide **car rental** both in the terminal and in town.

The **gare SNCF** (ⓣ08.36.35.35.35) is a rather dull kilometre's walk south of the town centre across the river, with the **gare routière** alongside. An extensive network of local **buses** and **trams** is run by TWISTO (ⓣ02.31.15.55.55, ⓦwww.twisto.fr), which has ticket and information centres at 15 rue de Geôle (just north of the tourist office), and on boulevard Maréchal-Leclerc. The main tram route, inaugurated in 2002, connects the southern and northern suburbs, running through the heart of the city from the *gare SNCF* up Avenue de 6-Juin to the university and beyond.

Caen's **tourist office** is on place St-Pierre across from the church of St-Pierre (Apr–June & Sept Mon–Sat 9.30am–6.30pm, Sun 10am–1pm; July & Aug Mon–Sat 9am–7pm, Sun 10am–1pm & 2–5pm; Oct–March Mon–Sat 9.30am–1pm & 2–6pm, Sun 10am–1pm; ⓣ02.31.27.14.14, ⓦwww.caen.fr/tourisme). You can go **online** at *Espace Micro*, on place Courtonne at 1 rue Basse (Mon–Thurs 10am–11pm, Fri & Sat 10am–1am, Sun 10am–1pm & 3–9pm; ⓣ02.31.53.68.68), or the main **post office** on place Gambetta (Mon–Fri 8am–7pm, Sat 8am–noon; ⓣ02.31.39.35.78).

Accommodation

Caen has a great number of **hotels**, though, as ever in the bomb-damaged cities of Normandy, few could be called attractive. They're not particularly concentrated in any one area either, though you'll find clusters just west of the castle and tourist office – a convenient location for motorists heading to or from the ferry – as well as around the pleasure port, and a handful facing the *gare SNCF*. With plenty of dedicated restaurants in town, few hotels other than those specifically mentioned below bother to provide food.

Hotels

Bernières 50 rue de Bernières ⓣ02.31.86.01.26, ⓦwww.hotelbernieres.com. Bright, central and very good value hotel, offering appealing en-suite rooms above a brasserie halfway between the churches of St-Pierre and St-Jean. ❸

Central 23 place J.-Letellier ⓣ02.31.86.18.52, ⓦwww.centralhotel-caen.com. By Caen standards a budget hotel, and though noisy it's very central and has good views of the château from the higher rooms, all of which are en suite. ❸

Courtonne place Courtonne ⓣ02.31.93.47.83, ⓕ02.31.93.50.50. Very welcoming modernized hotel, overlooking the pleasure port, that's so narrow it's easy to miss. All rooms have bath or shower, phone and TV. ❸

Dauphin 29 rue Gémare ⓣ02.31.86.22.26, ⓔdauphin.caen@wanadoo.fr. Upmarket central Best Western hotel, tucked away behind the tourist office. Part of it was a priory during the eighteenth century, not that you'd ever guess; the rooms are comfortable without being exciting in any way. Grand restaurant, with an €18 weekday menu;

weekend menus €28, €43 and €50. Closed Sat, & mid-July to early Aug. ❺

Rouen 8 place de la Gare ⓣ02.31.34.06.03, ⓕ02.31.34.05.16. Reasonably smart budget option, furthest to the right (west) in the parade that faces you as you exit the *gare SNCF*, and offering rooms with and without en-suite facilities. ❸

St-Jean 20 rue des Martyrs ⓣ02.31.86.23.35, ⓕ02.31.86.74.15. Simple but well-equipped rooms – all have shower or bath – facing St-Jean church across from *La Petite Auberge* (see p.410). ❷

Hostel and campsite

HI hostel Foyer Robert-Remé, 68 bis rue E.-Restout, Grâce-de-Dieu ⓣ02.31.52.19.96. Lively and welcoming hostel, albeit situated in an otherwise sleepy area about 500m southwest of the *gare SNCF*. Beds in both four-bed dorms or two-bed private rooms cost €10 per person. Take bus #17 from the town centre or *gare SNCF*, direction "Grace de Dieu", stop "Lycée Fresnil". Closed Oct–May.

Camping OMJ route de Louvigny ⓣ02.31.72.60.92. Two-star municipal campsite near the hostel, beside the River Orne (bus #13, direction "Louvigny", stop "Camping"). Closed Oct to mid-May.

The Town

A virtue has been made of the necessity of clearing away the rubble of Caen's medieval houses, which formerly pressed up against its ancient **château ramparts**. The resulting open green space means that those walls are now fully visible for the first time in centuries. In turn, walking the circuit of the ramparts gives a good overview of the city, with a particularly fine prospect of the reconstructed fourteenth-century facade of the nearby **church of St-Pierre**. Some magnificent Renaissance stonework has survived intact at the church's east end.

Within the castle walls, it's possible to visit the former **Exchequer** – which dates from shortly after the Norman conquest of England, and was the scene of a banquet thrown by Richard the Lionheart en route to the Crusades – and inspect a garden that has been replanted with the herbs and medicinal plants that were cultivated here during the Middle Ages. Also inside the precinct, though not in original structures, are two museums. Most visitors will prefer the **Musée des Beaux-Arts** (daily except Tues 9.30am–6pm; €4, free on Sun), which traces a potted history of European art from Renaissance Italy through such Dutch masters as Brueghel the Younger up to grand portraits from eighteenth-century France in the upstairs galleries. Downstairs brings things up to date with some powerful twentieth-century art, though there are few big-name works. The other museum, the **Musée de Normandie** (daily except Tues 9.30am–6pm; €1.60, free on Sun), provides a cursory overview of Norman history, ranging from archeological finds like stone tools from the region's megalithic period and glass jewellery from Gallo-Roman Rouen up to the impact of the Industrial Revolution.

The **Abbaye aux Hommes**, at the west end of rue St-Pierre, was founded by William the Conqueror and designed to hold his tomb within the huge, austere Romanesque **church of St-Étienne** (daily 8.15am–noon & 2–7.30pm, free; 1hr 15min guided tours leave adjacent Hôtel de Ville daily 9.30am, 11am, 2.30pm & 4pm, €2, free on Sun). However, his burial here, in 1087, was hopelessly undignified. The funeral procession first caught fire and was then held to ransom, as various factions squabbled over his rotting corpse for any spoils they could grab. A further interruption came when a man halted the service to object that the grave had been constructed without compensation on the site of his family house, and the assembled nobles had to pay him off before William could be laid to rest. During the Revolution the tomb was again ransacked, and it now holds a solitary thighbone rescued from the river. Still, the building itself is a wonderful

Romanesque monument. Adjoining the church are the abbey buildings, designed during the eighteenth century and now housing the Hôtel de Ville.

At the other end of the town centre, at the end of rue des Chanoines, is the **Abbaye aux Dames**, commissioned by William's wife Matilda in the hope of saving her soul after committing the godless sin of marrying her cousin. Her monument – the **church of La Trinité** – is even more starkly impressive than her husband's, with a gloomy pillared crypt, wonderful stained glass behind the altar and odd sculptural details like the fish curled up in the holy-water stoup. The convent buildings today house the regional council but are open to the public (daily 2–5.30pm; guided tours 2.30pm & 4pm; free).

Most of the centre of Caen is taken up with busy new shopping developments and pedestrian precincts, where the cafés are distinguished by names such as Fast Food Glamour Vault. Outlets of the big Parisian stores – and of the aristocrats' grocers, Hédiard, in the cours des Halles – are here, along with good local rivals. The main city **market** takes place on Friday, spreading along both sides of Fosse St-Julien, and there's also a Sunday market in place Courtonne. The **pleasure port**, at the end of the canal which links Caen to the sea, is where most life goes on, at least in summer.

The Caen Memorial

Just north of Caen, at the end of avenue Marshal-Montgomery in the Folie Couvrechef area, the **Caen Memorial** – "a museum for peace" – stands on a plateau named after General Eisenhower (daily: mid-Jan to mid-Feb & Nov–Dec 9am–6pm; mid-Feb to mid-July, Sept & Oct 9am–7pm; mid-July to Aug 9am–8pm; closed first half of Jan; last admission 75min before closing; ⓣ02.31.06.06.44, ⓦwww.memorial-caen.fr; €16.50–18 depending on time of year), on a clifftop beneath which the Germans had their HQ in June and July 1944. Funds and material for it came from the US, Britain, Canada, Germany, Poland, Czechoslovakia, the USSR and France. The museum is a typically French high-tech, novel-architecture conception, with excellent displays divided into several distinct sections; allow two hours at the very least for a visit. The first section deals with the rise of fascism in Germany, another with resistance and collaboration in France, while a third charts all the major battles of World War II. Most of the captions, though not always the written exhibits themselves, are translated into English. Further areas examine the course of the Cold War, and the prospects for global peace, with the former German bunkers below housing the Nobel Peace Prize Winners' Gallery. Portraits and short essays commemorate each recipient in turn, placing their achievements in context. There's also a good-value self-service restaurant upstairs. The memorial is on bus routes #17 (Mon–Sat) and #S (Sun) from the "Tour le Roi" stop in the centre of town.

Eating

Caen's town centre offers two major areas for **eating**: with cosmopolitan restaurants in the pedestrianized **quartier Vaugueux** and more traditional French restaurants on the streets off **rue de Geôle**, near the western ramparts, particularly rue des Croisiers and rue Gémare.

L'Alcide 1 place Courtonne ⓣ02.31.44.18.06. Conspicuous but unexceptional-looking bistro-style place that turns out to be surprisingly good, serving classic rich French dishes cooked with great attention to detail. Menus from €13.80 up to €21.90. Closed Sat.

Le Bouchon du Vaugueux 12 rue du Graindorge ⓣ02.31.44.26.26. Intimate little brasserie in the

Vaugueux quarter, offering daily lunch specials for €7–10, good-value salads for €8, and dinner menus from €15.20. Closed Mon eve, Sun, and first three weeks of Aug.

Le Carlotta 16 quai Vendeuvre ⊕02.31.44.26.26. Smart, busy, fashionable Paris-style brasserie beside the pleasure port, which serves good Norman cooking both à la carte and on menus from €20. Closed Sun.

L'Insolite 16 rue du Vaugueux ⊕02.31.43.87.87. Attractive half-timbered restaurant with terrace and indoor seating in the Vaugueux district. The main emphasis is on seafood, with a €22 menu that features a trio of steamed fish, and a knockout €45 *Prestige* menu. Closed Sun eve, plus Mon in low season.

Maître Corbeau 8 rue Bouquet ⊕02.31.93.93.00. Fondue is the speciality in this eccentric little place, and they won't let you forget it, festooning the whole place with cheesy iconography. A typical fondue costs around €13, while set menus start from €15. Closed Sat lunch, Sun, Mon lunch & all Aug.

La Petite Auberge 17 rue des Équipes-d'Urgence ⊕02.31.86.43.30. Plain and simple restaurant, with a nice view of the St-Jean church. Very good value Norman specialities, served on an €11 menu (daily except Sat) that doesn't force you to eat tripe, or a wide-ranging €17 one. Closed Sun, Mon & first three weeks of Aug.

La Vie Claire 4 rue Basse ⊕02.31.93.66.72. Vegetarian restaurant, attached to a pricey health-food shop, that serves pasta and salad specials – and also some fish – for €5–8. Open Tues–Sat for lunch only.

The D-Day beaches

Despite the best efforts of Steven Spielberg, it's all but impossible now to picture the scene at dawn on **D-Day**, June 6, 1944, when Allied troops landed along the Norman coast between the mouth of the Orne and Les Dunes de Varneville on the Cotentin Peninsula. For the most part, these are innocuous beaches backed by gentle dunes, and yet this foothold in Europe was won at the cost of 100,000 soldiers' lives. That the invasion happened here and not nearer to Germany, was partly a result of the failed Canadian raid on Dieppe in 1942. The ensuing **Battle of Normandy** killed thousands of civilians and reduced nearly six hundred towns and villages to rubble but, within a week of its eventual conclusion, Paris was liberated.

The **beaches** are still often referred to by their wartime code names: from east to west, Sword, Juno, Gold, Omaha and Utah. Substantial traces of the fighting are rare, the most remarkable being the remains of the astounding **Mulberry Harbour** at **Arromanches**, 10km northeast of Bayeux. Further west, at **Pointe du Hoc** on Omaha Beach, the cliff heights are still deeply pitted with German bunkers and shell holes, while the church at **Ste-Mère-Église**, from which the US paratrooper who became entangled in the steeple dangled during heavy fighting throughout *The Longest Day*, still stands, and now has a model parachute permanently fastened to the roof. Note that **Utah Beach**, the westernmost of the Invasion Beaches, is on the Cotentin Peninsula, and covered on p.421 onwards.

Just about every coastal town has its **war museum**. These tend as a rule to shy away from the unbearable reality of war in favour of *Boy's Own*-style heroics, but the wealth of incidental human detail can nonetheless be overpowering. Veterans and their descendants apart, visitors these days come to this stretch of coast for its **seaside**: sand and seafood (the best oysters are at Courseulles), plenty of campsites and no Deauville chic.

Bus Verts (⊕08.10.21.42.14, ⓦwww.busverts14.fr) run all along this coast. From Bayeux, bus #75 goes to Arromanches, Courseulles, and Ouistreham, and bus #70 to the pointe du Hoc, the US cemetery at Colleville-sur-mer, and Port-en-Bessin. From Caen, bus #30 runs inland to Isigny via Bayeux, express bus #1 to Ouistreham, and express bus #3 to Courseulles. On weekends in June, and daily in July and August, Bus Verts' special **D-Day Line** departs daily from Caen's *gare routière*

The war cemeteries

The **World War II** cemeteries that dot the Norman countryside are filled with foreigners – most of the French dead are buried in the churchyards of their home towns. After the war, some felt that the soldiers should remain buried in the original makeshift graves that were dug where they fell. Instead, commissions gathered the remains into purpose-built cemeteries devoted to the separate warring nations.

The **British** and **Commonwealth** cemeteries are magnificently maintained, and open in every sense. They tend not to be screened off with hedges or walls, or to be forbidding expanses of manicured lawn, but are instead intimate, punctuated with bright flowers. The family of each soldier was invited to suggest an inscription for his tomb, making each grave very personal, and yet part of a common attempt to bring meaning to the carnage. Some epitaphs are questioning – "One day we will understand"; some are accepting – "Our lad at rest"; some matter-of-fact, simply giving the home address; some patriotic, quoting the "corner of a foreign field that is forever England". And interspersed among them all is the chilling refrain of the anonymous "A soldier ... known unto God". Thus the cemetery at **Ryes**, where so many of the graves bear the date of D-Day, and so many of the victims are under 20, remains immediate and accessible – each grave clearly contains a unique individual. Even the monumental sculpture is subdued, a very British sort of fumbling for the decent thing to say. The understatement of the memorial at **Bayeux**, with its painfully contrived Latin epigram commemorating the return as liberators of "those whom William conquered", conveys an entirely appropriate humility and deep sadness.

An even more eloquent testimony to the futility of war is afforded by the **German** cemeteries, filled with soldiers who served a cause so despicable as to render any talk of "nobility" or "sacrifice" simply obscene. What such cemeteries might have been like had the Nazis won doesn't bear contemplation. As it is, they are sombre places, inconspicuous to minimize the bitterness they still arouse. At **Orglandes** ten thousand are buried, three to each of the plain headstones set in the long flat lawn, almost hidden behind an anonymous wall. There are no noble slogans and the plain entrance is without a dedicatory monument. At the superb site of **Mont d'Huisnes** near Mont St-Michel, the circular mausoleum holds another ten thousand, filed away in cold concrete tiers. Though no attempt is made to defend the indefensible, there's still an overpowering sense of sorrow – that there is nothing to be said in such a place bitterly underlines the sheer waste and stupidity.

The largest **American** cemetery, at **Colleville-sur-mer** near the Pointe du Hoc, may already be familiar from the opening sequences of *Saving Private Ryan*. Here, by contrast, neat rows of crosses cover the tranquil clifftop lawns, with no individual epitaphs, just gold lettering for a few exceptional warriors. At one end, a muscular giant dominates a huge array of battlefield plans and diagrams, covered with surging arrows and pincer movements.

and place Courtonne at 9.30am, calls at Courseulles, and stops at Arromanches, the German gun emplacements at Longues-sur-mer, the US cemetery and the Pointe du Hoc, before returning to Caen around 6pm (€17 flat fare).

In addition, the Caen Memorial (see p.409) organizes expensive bilingual **guided tours** of the beaches, with four hours on the road and a visit to the Memorial at your own pace (April–Sept daily 9am & 2pm; Oct–Dec & mid-Jan to March daily 1pm; no tours first half of Jan; €67.50).

Ouistreham and around

The small community of **OUISTREHAM**, on the coast 15km north of Caen and connected to it by a fast dual carriageway, gives the impression that it can

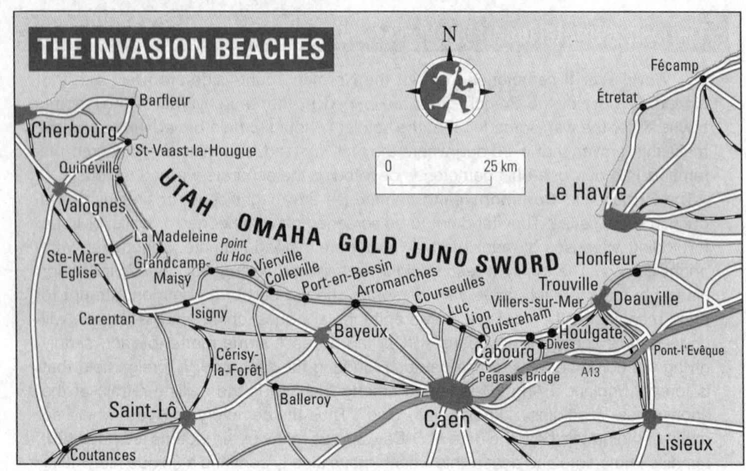

barely believe its luck at having become a major ferry port. Since Brittany Ferries started their service here in 1986, the easternmost of the D-Day resorts has developed an extensive array of reasonable hotels and restaurants.

Several cafés and brasseries in the place Courbonne, immediately outside the *gare maritime*, are eager to liberate passengers from their spare change, while *Le Channel*, just around the corner at 79 av Michel-Cabieu (ⓣ02.31.96.51.69; ❶), is the best value for both **eating and sleeping**: menus start with the €8.50 *menu pêcheur*, while the many higher priced options increase in splendour; guest rooms are in a separate building across the street. The smart *Le Normandie et le Chalut*, a few doors down at 71 av Michel-Cabieu (ⓣ02.31.97.19.57, ⓦwww.lenormandie.com; ❹; closed mid-Dec to mid-Jan, plus Sun evening & Mon Nov–March), has pleasant, quiet rooms; its Normand menu at €15 features a lethal triple plate of tripe, *andouille* and *boudin noir*, while the €32 option makes an excellent last-night blowout.

Pegasus Bridge

Roughly 5km south of Ouistreham, the main road towards Caen passes close by the site now known as **Pegasus Bridge**. On the night before D-Day, the twin bridges here that cross the Caen canal and the River Orne were a crucial Allied objective, and were the target of a daring but successful glider assault just after midnight. The original bridge was replaced in 1994, but is now the focus of the **Mémorial Pegasus** immediately to the east (daily: May–Sept 9.30am–6.30pm; Oct to mid-Nov & Feb–April 10am–1pm & 2–5pm; closed mid-Dec to Jan; €5). This vaguely glider-shaped museum holds the expected array of helmets, goggles, medals and other memorabilia, most captioned in English, as well as various model bridges used in planning the attack.

Arromanches

At **ARROMANCHES**, 10km northeast of Bayeux, an artificial **Mulberry harbour**, "Port Winston", protected the landings of 2,500,000 men and 500,000 vehicles during the invasion. Two of these prefab concrete constructions were built in Britain, while "doodlebugs" blitzed overhead; they were then submerged in rivers away from the prying eyes of German aircraft, and finally towed across the Channel at 6kph as the invasion began. The seafront **Musée du Débarquement**, in Arromanches' main square (Feb & Nov–Dec daily 10am–12.30pm & 1.30–5pm; March & Oct Mon–Sat 9.30am–12.30pm & 1.30–5.30pm, Sun 10am–12.30pm & 1.30–5.30pm; April Mon–Sat 9am–12.30pm & 1.30–6pm, Sun 10am–12.30pm & 1.30–6pm; May Mon–Sat 9am–7pm, Sun 10am–7pm; June–Aug daily 9am–7pm; Sept Mon–Sat 9am–6pm, Sun 10am–6pm; closed Jan; €6; Ⓦwww.normandy1944.com), recounts the whole story by means of models, machinery and movies. A huge picture window runs the length of the museum, enabling you to look straight out to where the bulky remains of the harbour, whose sheer scale is impossible to appreciate at this distance, make a strange intrusion on the beach and shallow sea bed (the other one, slightly further west on Omaha Beach, was destroyed by a ferocious storm within a few weeks). There are war memorials throughout Arromanches, with Jesus and Mary high up on the cliffs above the invasion site and helicopter trips available to overlook the area.

Nonetheless, Arromanches somehow manages to be quite a cheerful place to stay, with a lively pedestrian street of **bars** and **brasseries**, and a long expanse of sand where you can rent windsurfing boards. *La Marine* at 2 quai Canada (Ⓣ02.31.22.34.19, Ⓔhotel.de.la.marine@wanadoo.fr; ❹; closed mid-Nov to mid-Feb), is a slightly expensive **hotel**, with an excellent sea-view restaurant serving fishy menus from €16. Across the main square stands the *Arromanches*, 2 rue du Colonel René Michel (Ⓣ02.31.22.36.26; ❹; closed Jan to mid-Feb, Tues, & Wed in winter), whose restaurant has menus from €13.80 up to €28, and nearby at 5 place du 6-Juin is the cheaper *Normandie* (Ⓣ02.31.22.34.32; ❷). The spacious three-star municipal **campsite** is 200m back from the seafront (Ⓣ02.31.22.36.78; closed Sept–March).

Bayeux and around

BAYEUX, with its perfectly preserved medieval ensemble, magnificent cathedral and world-famous tapestry, is 23km west of Caen – a mere twenty-minute train ride. It's a smaller and much more intimate city, and, despite the large crowds of summer tourists, a far more enjoyable place to visit.

Arrival, information and accommodation

Bayeux's **tourist office** stands in the centre of town, on the arched pont St-Jean (April, May, Sept & Oct daily 9.30am–12.30pm & 2–6pm; June–Aug Mon–Sat 9am–7pm, Sun 9am–1pm & 2–6pm; Nov–March Mon–Sat 9.30am–12.30pm & 2–5.30pm; Ⓣ02.31.51.28.28, Ⓦwww.bayeux-tourism.com). The **gare SNCF** is fifteen minutes' walk away to the south, just outside the ring road, while the **gare routière** is on the north side of place St-Patrice. For information on local **buses**, contact Bus Verts du Calvados (Ⓣ08.10.21.42.14, Ⓦwww.busverts14.fr), whose services stop at both the *gare SNCF* and the *gare routière*. Travellers without cars who plan to visit the landing beaches and/or the war cemeteries are better advised to join a **minibus trip** (half day €35, full day €75); ask at the tourist office for details.

As one of Normandy's most important tourist destinations, Bayeux is well equipped with **accommodation**. On the whole, however, the hotels are more expensive than usual. There's a large three-star **campsite** on boulevard d'Eindhoven (Ⓣ02.31.92.08.43; closed Oct–April), on the northern ring road (RN13) near the river.

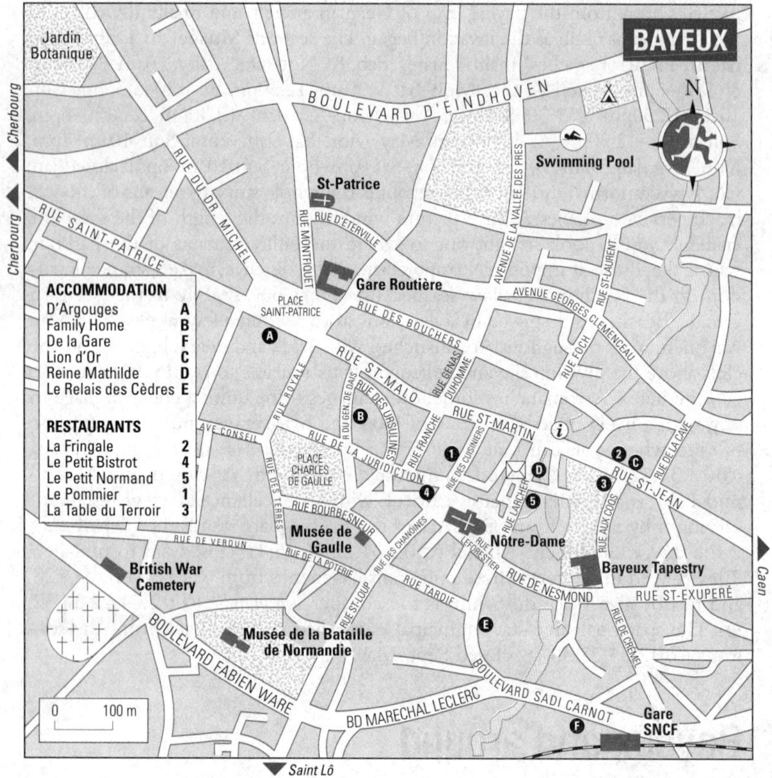

D'Argouges 21 rue St-Patrice ⓣ02.31.92.88.86, ⓔdargouges@aol.com. Quiet, central and very stylish eighteenth-century building, behind an imposing courtyard off place St-Patrice. Several rooms are very grand, with magnificent exposed wooden beams, and the rates are very reasonable for what you get. ❸

Family Home 39 rue Général-de-Dais ⓣ02.31.92.15.22, ⓕ02.31.92.55.72. Central seventeenth-century building which describes itself as both guesthouse and youth hostel. Its prices are a little over the odds – hostel accommodation works out €16 each for members, €18 for non-members, while private doubles are €28 – and it's a bit self-consciously jolly, but people return again and again. Rates include breakfast. Communal dinners, served at 7.30pm nightly, cost €9.15 per person, or you can dine privately for €12. They also rent bikes and run D-Day tours. ❶

De la Gare 26 place de la Gare ⓣ02.31.92.10.70, ⓕ02.31.51.95.99. Old but perfectly adequate basic hotel, with a simple brasserie, beside the station, on the ring road fifteen minutes' walk from the cathedral. Tours of D-Day beaches arranged. ❶

Lion d'Or 71 rue St-Jean ⓣ02.31.92.06.90, ⓔlion.d-or.bayeux@wanadoo.fr. Grand old coaching inn set back behind a courtyard, just beyond the pedestrianized section of the rue St-Jean. The rooms themselves are brighter and newer than the exterior might lead you to expect. Closed mid-Dec to late Jan. Menus from €23. ❺

Reine Mathilde 23 rue Larcher ⓣ02.31.92.08.13, ⓕ02.31.92.09.93. Simple but well-equipped rooms – all have showers and TV – backing onto the canal. The nice open-air brasserie downstairs serves dinner between May and Sept, and lunch all year round (€9.50 menu). Closed Jan. ❸

Le Relais des Cèdres 1 bd Sadi-Carnot ⓣ02.31.21.98.07. Pretty guesthouse, not far from the station but within sight of the cathedral. The three rooms are fine, and good value, although the atmosphere is not all that welcoming. ❸

The Town

Housed in an impressive eighteenth-century seminary on rue de Nesmond, the **Bayeux Tapestry** – also known to the French as the Tapisserie de la Reine Mathilde – is a seventy-metre strip of embroidered linen that recounts the story of the Norman conquest of England (daily: mid-March to April & Sept–Oct 9am–6.30pm; May–Aug 9am–7pm; Nov to mid-March 9.30am–12.30pm & 2–6pm; last admission 45min before closing; €7.40). Although created over nine centuries ago, the brilliance of its coloured wools has barely faded, and the tale is enlivened throughout with parallel scenes of medieval life, popular fables and mythical beasts; the skill of its draughtsmanship, and the sheer vigour and detail, are stunning. The work is thought to have been carried out by monks or nuns in England, commissioned by Bishop Odo, William's half-brother, in time for the inauguration of Bayeux cathedral in 1077.

Visits are well planned and highly atmospheric, if somewhat exhausting. First comes a slide show, projected onto billowing sheets of canvas; you then pass along a photographic replica of the tapestry, with enlargements and detailed commentaries. After an optional film show, you finally approach the real thing, to find that it has a strong three-dimensional presence you might not expect from all the flat reproductions. The tapestry looks – and reads – like a modern comic strip. Harold is every inch the villain, with his dastardly little moustache and shifty eyes. He looks extremely self-satisfied as he breaks his oath to accept William as king of England and seizes the throne for himself, but his come-uppance swiftly follows, as William, the noble hero, crosses the Channel and defeats the English armies at Hastings.

The **Cathédrale Notre-Dame** (daily: July–Sept 8.30am–7pm; Oct–June 8.30am–6pm) was the first home of the tapestry and is just a short walk away from its latest resting-place. Despite such eighteenth-century vandalism as the monstrous fungoid baldachin that flanks the pulpit, the original Romanesque plan of the building is still intact, although only the crypt and towers date from the original work of 1077. The crypt is a beauty, its columns graced with frescoes of angels playing trumpets and bagpipes, looking exhausted by their performance for eternity.

Set behind massive guns, next to the ring road on the southwest side of town, Bayeux's **Musée de la Bataille de Normandie** (daily: May to mid-Sept 9.30am–6.30pm; mid-Sept to April 10am–12.30pm & 2–6pm; €5.50) is one of the old school of war museums, with its emphasis firmly on hardware rather than humans. By way of contrast, the understated and touching **British War Cemetery** stands immediately across the road (see box, p.411).

Although the **Musée-Mémorial Général de Gaulle**, at 10 rue de Bourbesneur near place de Gaulle (mid-March to mid-Nov daily 9.30am–12.30pm & 2–6.30pm; €3.50), is aimed squarely at French devotees of the great man, it does make an interesting detour for foreign visitors. The sheer obsessiveness of the displays, which focus on the three separate day-trips De Gaulle made to Bayeux during the course of his long life, somehow illuminates the extent to which he came to epitomize the very essence of a certain kind of Frenchness, which seems scarcely removed from self-parody.

Eating

Some of Bayeux's hotels have good dining rooms, while most **restaurants** are in the rue St-Jean leading east from the river; on Sundays most places are shut.

La Fringale 43 rue St-Jean ☎02.31.21.34.40. The nicest of the many pavement restaurants along the pedestrian rue St-Jean, offering good-value lunch menus from €9, and also generous salads and snacks, as well as more formal fishy dinners. Closed mid-Dec to Jan, plus Wed in low season.

Le Petit Bistrot 2 rue Bienvenue ☎02.31.51.85.40. Tiny old place opposite the cathedral, where the menus (€18 and €30.50) feature duck and fish. Closed Sun, plus Mon in low season.

Le Petit Normand 35 rue Larcher ☎02.31.22.88.66. Sixteenth-century house by the cathedral, offering good traditional cooking, with seafood specialities and local cider. Lunch menus from €9.50, dinner from €17.50. Closed Jan, plus Thurs Oct–April.

Le Pommier 40 rue des Cuisiniers ☎02.31.21.52.10. Ever-expanding traditional restaurant near the cathedral, with a tiny terrace. Meat- and dairy-rich Norman cuisine on menus from €10 (lunch only) to the €25.50 "D-Day Menu", plus an €13.50 vegetarian option. Closed Tues & Wed, plus all Feb.

La Table du Terroir 42 rue St-Jean ☎02.31.92.05.53. A charming rendezvous for carnivores serving the freshest possible meat at stylishly decorated wooden tables, on a well-judged quartet of menus, from €14 to €26 – plus an €11 lunch menu. Closed Sun evening & Mon all year; open Fri & Sat eve only in low season.

Cerisy and Balleroy

Heading southwest from Bayeux towards St-Lô, you pass close to the remarkable Romanesque **Abbaye de Cerisy-la-Forêt** (Easter to mid-Nov Tues–Sun 9am–6.30pm, free; guided tours Easter–Sept Tues–Sun 10.30am–12.30pm & 2.30–6.30pm, Oct to mid-Nov Sat & Sun 10.30am–noon & 2–6pm, €3), halfway along the D572 and 5km to the north of it. Its triple tiers of windows and arches and the delicate workmanship of its nave and choir are testimony to the breathtaking skills of medieval Norman masons.

No less notable is the **Château de Balleroy** (mid-March to June & Sept to mid-Oct daily except Tues 9am–noon & 2–6pm; July & Aug daily 10am–6pm; €7; Ⓦwww.chareau-balleroy.com), 3km southeast of the same junction, where you switch to an era when architects ruled over craftsmen. The main street of the village leads straight to the brick-and-stone château, a masterpiece of the celebrated seventeenth-century architect, François Mansart, and standing like a faultlessly reasoned and dogmatic argument for the power of its owners and their class. It belongs to the family of the late American press magnate Malcolm Forbes, owner of *Forbes* magazine and pal of Nixon, Ford and Nancy Reagan. His is the enlarged colour photograph sharing the stairwell with Dutch still lifes, and he left his mark on most other aspects of the house, too – only the salon remains in its original state of glory, with brilliant portraits of the (then) royal family by Mignard. Admission also includes a **hot-air balloon museum**, which was one of Mr Forbes' hobbies.

The Cotentin Peninsula

Hard against the frontier with Brittany, and cut off from the rest of Normandy by difficult marshy terrain, the **Cotentin Peninsula** has traditionally been seen as something of a backwater, far removed from the French mainstream. It nonetheless makes a surprisingly rewarding goal for travellers, and one that by sea at least is very easily accessible. Regular ferries from both England and Ireland dock at the peninsula's major port, **Cherbourg**, a city turned resolutely seaward. Nearby are a plethora of attractive little villages, such as **Barfleur** and **St-Vaast**, nestled amid the hills to the east, and the handsome landscapes of heather-clad cliffs and stone-wall-divided patchwork fields to be found in La Hague to the west.

For many visitors the Cotentin's long western flank, with its flat beaches, serves primarily as a prelude to **Mont St-Michel**, with hill towns such as **Coutances** and **Avranches** cherishing architectural and historical relics associated with the abbey. Halfway down, however, the walled port of **Granville**, an extremely popular destination with French holiday-makers, is a sort of small-scale mirror-image of Brittany's St-Malo.

Cherbourg

If you are arriving from Britain or Ireland, **CHERBOURG** may well be your port of arrival. Many people head straight out and on, yet the town offers a busy network of pedestrian streets lined with appealing stone facades, the labyrinth of alleyways known as *boëls*, some lively bars, and an impressive maritime museum in a converted Art Deco station. In addition there are some extremely appealing destinations a short distance to either side, not least the varied landscapes of

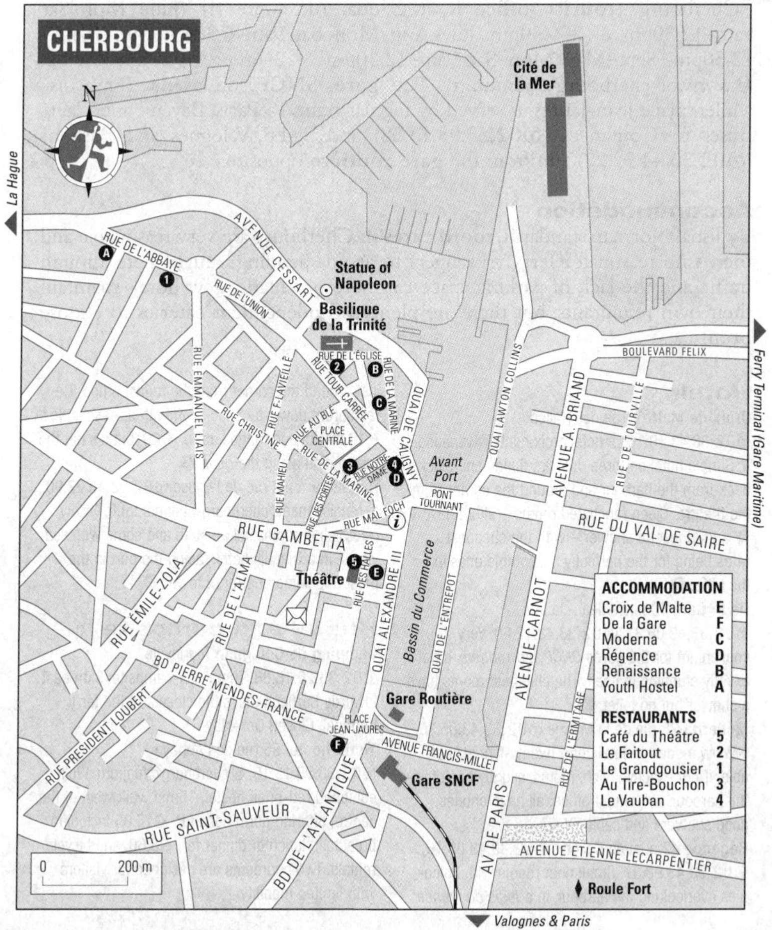

La Hague. Napoleon inaugurated the transformation of what had been a rather poor, but perfectly situated, natural harbour into a major transatlantic port, by means of massive artificial breakwaters. An equestrian statue commemorates his boast that in Cherbourg he would "recreate the wonders of Egypt"; although there are as yet no pyramids nearer than the Louvre, he succeeded in providing the city with one of the biggest fortified harbours in the world.

Arrival and information

Several cross-Channel ferry companies still sail into Cherbourg's **gare maritime**, just east of the town centre (daily 5.30am–11.30pm; ⓣ02.33.44.20.13). Services from **Portsmouth**, including the Superstar Express catamaran, which takes a mere 2hr 45min for the crossing, are operated by P&O (5–6 daily; ⓣ08.03.01.30.13, ⓦwww.poferries.com), and from **Poole** by Brittany Ferries (1–2 daily; 4hr 15min; ⓣ08.03.82.88.28, ⓦwww.brittany-ferries.com). Irish Ferries also sail to Cherbourg, from Rosslare (2–4 weekly; ⓣ02.33.23.44.44, ⓦwww.irishferries.com). Regular €1 shuttle buses connect the terminal with the tourist office and *gare SNCF*.

Cherbourg's **tourist office** is at 2 quai Alexandre III (June Mon–Sat 9am–12.30pm & 2–6.30pm; July–Aug Mon–Sat 9am–6.30pm, Sun 10am–12.30pm; Sept–May Mon–Sat 9am–12.30pm & 2–6pm; ⓣ02.33.93.52.02, ⓦwww.ot-cherbourg-cotentin.fr). The **gare SNCF**, on avenue François-Miller/place Jean-Jaurès, is served by regular trains to Paris, Bayeux and Caen. Buses to Coutances (ⓣ02.33.98.13.38) and St-Lô, Valognes and Barfleur (ⓣ02.33.44.32.22) run from the **gare routière** opposite.

Accommodation

By usual Norman standards, **room rates** in Cherbourg are very reasonable and there's no reason for ferry passengers to avoid spending a night here, though traffic and the lack of parking space can be problematic. Few hotels maintain their own restaurants, but there are plenty of independent eateries to choose from.

Hotels

Croix de Malte 7 rue des Halles ⓣ02.33.43.19.16, ⓔhotel.croix.malte@wanadoo.fr. Simple hotel on three upstairs floors, one block back from the harbour and around the corner from the theatre. Clean renovated rooms – all 24 have TV and at least a shower – with the cheapest rates being for the perfectly acceptable ones in the attic. ❷

De la Gare 10 place Jean-Jaurès ⓣ02.33.43.06.81, ⓕ02.33.43.12.20. Very convenient for the *gares SNCF* and *routière*, if not exactly stunning in itself. The cheapest rooms have a shower but no toilet. ❸

Moderna 28 rue de la Marine ⓣ02.33.43.05.30, ⓦwww.moderna-hotel.com. Twenty-five acceptable, if not exactly lavish, rooms, slightly back from the harbour and tourist office; all have phones, good showers and cable TV. ❸

Régence 42 quai de Caligny ⓣ02.33.43.05.16, ⓕ02.33.43.98.37. Small neat rooms with balconies overlooking the harbour, in a *logis de France* just around the corner from the tourist office. The restaurant downstairs kicks off with a reasonable €16 menu, and ranges up to €29, but it's not the best option along the *quai*. ❹

Renaissance 4 rue de l'Église ⓣ02.33.43.23.90, ⓔrenaissance@cherbourg-channel.tm.fr. Nicely refurbished rooms, all en suite and some with sea views, in a friendly hotel, facing the port in the most appealing quarter of town. ❸

Hostel and campsite

Camping de Collignon Tourlaville ⓣ02.33.20.16.88. Three-star campsite, 3km east towards Barfleur, that's the closest to the ferry terminal. Closed Oct–May.

Youth hostel 55 rue de l'Abbaye ⓣ02.33.78.15.15, ⓔcherbourg@fuaj.org. Well-equipped red-brick hostel, 15min walk west of the centre, offering dorm beds for €16.05 including breakfast, lunch or dinner for €8.60, and bicycle rentals. Two bedrooms are designed for visitors with limited mobility.

The Town

Cherbourg's best, and newest, attraction is **La Cité de la Mer** (June to mid-Sept daily 9.30am–7pm, mid–Sept to Dec & late Jan to May daily 10am–6pm; closed 3 wks in Jan; May–Sept €13, Oct–April €11.50; Ⓦ www.citedelamer.com). The museum combines often quite technical displays, explained in both French and English, on every aspect of the sea – myths and legends, environmental issues including climatic change, economic activities and, above all, exploration of the seabed – with aquariums and a visitable nuclear submarine. You enter through the grand former Transatlantic ferry terminal, a fabulously restored Art Deco treasure, housing the ticket offices, a cafeteria, an excellent restaurant unsurprisingly specializing in seafood, a mediatheque and temporary exhibits. Frequently interactive displays in a new building behind tell the story of underwater exploration in history and fiction, moving swiftly via Jules Verne and H.P. Lovecraft to Jacques Cousteau, pictured with his diving saucer "shaped like a giant lentil" in 1959. Separate fish tanks hold giant crabs, sharks, eels, jellyfish, seahorses, and large (though sadly not giant) squid, while at different levels you can peer into a vast cylindrical aquarium where shoals of vivid fish offer a colourful spectacle – all with an educational emphasis on aspects such as how marine creatures move and survive.

The overarching idea is to show how human submarine technology was inspired by the wonders of nature, preparing the visitor for the main attraction: in a dry dock alongside stands the dark cigar-shaped hulk of *Le Redoutable*, France's first ballistic missile submarine. Armed with an audio-commentary you can scramble through its labyrinth of tube-like corridors and control rooms, though as the miniature nuclear power station that once powered it has been removed, there's a cavernous empty space at its heart. The cramped crew quarters will feel very familiar if you've just shared a cabin on an overnight ferry crossing, while the plush carpeting and moulded chairs in the living room are remarkably reminiscent of Elvis's Graceland.

Otherwise, if you're waiting for a boat, the best way of filling time is to settle into a café or restaurant or do some last-minute shopping. Try the excellent Thursday **market**, held on and off rue des Halles, near the majestic theatre with its Belle Epoque facade, or the tempting array of small shops and boutiques clustered round the Place Centrale – including a place to buy the city's most famous product, the genuine **Cherbourg umbrella**, at 30 rue des Portes.

As for walking off lunch, the only area in the centre that really encourages a ramble is over by the **Basilique de la Trinité**, worth a quick look inside for its English alabaster decorations dating from the Hundred Years War, and the former town **beach**, now grassed over to form the "Plage Verte". Over to the south, you could alternatively climb up to **Roule Fort** for an impressive view of the whole port. The fort itself contains a **Musée de la Libération** (May–Sept Tues–Sat 10am–noon & 2–6pm, Sun & Mon 2–6pm; Oct–April Wed–Sun 2–6pm; €3), with the usual dry maps and diagrams but plenty of contemporary newsreel – much of it, for once, in English – commemorating the period in 1944 when Cherbourg was briefly the busiest port in the world.

Eating

Restaurants in Cherbourg divide readily into the glass-fronted seafood places along the quai de Caligny, each with its "copious" *assiette de fruits de mer*, and the more varied, more adventurous and less expensive little places tucked away in the pedestrianized streets and alleyways of the old town. This is also where you'll find some animated **bars**, especially along rue de l'Union.

Café du Théâtre 8 place de Gaulle ☎02.33.43.01.49. Attractive setup adjoining the theatre, with a café behind plate-glass windows on the ground floor and a full-scale brasserie upstairs, arranged on three sides of the central opening. The varied menus, from €12.50, hold more than just seafood; the €18 one features snails, for example. Closed Sun.

Le Faitout 25 rue Tour-Carrée. Shopping-district restaurant that offers traditional French cuisine at very reasonable prices; a bowl of mussels can be had for less than €7, and there's a daily special for €10. Most dishes are à la carte, at around €9–11, but there's also an €18 menu. Closed Sun, & Mon lunchtime.

Le Grandgousier 21 rue de l'Abbaye ☎02.33.53.19.43. Formal, definitive French fish restaurant, well worth the walk to its unprepossessing location at the west end of town. Menus start at €17, but this is a place to expect to spend a lot and dine well. Closed Sat lunch and Sun evening, plus Mon lunch in low season.

Au Tire-Bouchon 17 rue Notre-Dame. Reliable bistro with a terrace serving a dish of the day for only €8, with menus ranging from €10 to €13. Specialities include oysters and skate with butter and capers, and the wines are carefully chosen.

Le Vauban 22 quai de Caligny. Arguably the best fish restaurant in Cherbourg, with monkfish, langoustines and John Dory all exquisitely prepared with a wine list to match, polite service and understated decor. Save room for the fabulous chocolate *vulcano*. Menus at €20, €28 and €35.

Around the Cotentin

Once you get away from the industrial harbour city of Cherbourg, the largely rural Cotentin Peninsula is geographically an area of transition. Little ports such as **Barfleur** on the indented northern headland presage the rocky Breton coast, while inland the meadows resemble the farmlands of the Bocage and the Bessin. **La Hague** is a little explored gem – many people are put off by its associations with a nuclear reprocessing plant – where all manner of activities, from sailing and diving to riding and rambling, can be practised. In any case, the temptation to race south towards Mont St-Michel is likely to be thwarted by slow traffic on the peninsula's narrow roads, though the Cherbourg–St-Lô route is now mostly four-lane, so you might as well stop off in your pick of the towns and resorts that line its western shore, such as **Coutances**, **Granville** and **Avranches**.

Barfleur

The pleasant little harbour village of **BARFLEUR**, 25km east of Cherbourg, was seven centuries ago the biggest port in Normandy. The population has since dwindled from nine thousand to six hundred, and fortunes have diminished alongside – most recently through the invasion of a strain of plankton that poisoned all the mussels. It's now a surprisingly low-key place, where the sweeping crescent of the grey granite quayside sees little tourist activity. Near the town, about a thirty-minute walk away, the **Gatteville lighthouse** is the second tallest in France (daily: April–Sept 10am–noon & 2–7pm; Oct to mid-Nov & Feb–March 10am–noon & 2–4pm; €2). It guards the rocks on which William, son and heir of Henry I of England, was drowned in 1120, together with three hundred of his nobles.

Barfleur has a fine selection of **hotels**. *Le Conquérant* stands a short distance back from the sea at 16–18 rue St-Thomas-à-Becket (☎02.33.54.00.82; ❹; closed mid-Nov to mid-March); its nicest rooms face onto a lovely garden, and there's a summer-only crêperie. *Le Moderne* is tucked away south of the main road at 1 place de Gaulle (☎02.33.23.12.44; ❸; closed Jan to mid-Feb); some of the rooms are very inexpensive, while the restaurant is superb, with the €24 menu featuring a fish-shaped *feuilleton* (pastry) of seafood. The house speciality is oysters, stuffed or raw.

St-Vaast

Pretty **ST-VAAST-LA-HOUGUE**, 11km south of Barfleur, is more of a resort, with lots of tiny Channel-crossing yachts moored in the bay where Edward III landed on his way to Crécy and a string of fortifications from Vauban's time. The *Hôtel de France et des Fuchsias*, just back from the sea at 18 rue du Maréchal-Foch (Ⓣ02.33.54.42.26, Ⓦwww.france-fuchsias.com; ❸; closed Jan–Feb, plus Mon Sept–June, & Sun pm & Tues lunch Nov–Dec & March), with its splendid gardens and excellent restaurant, is an ideal stopover for ferry passengers – in fact both it and the annexe at the end of the garden are packed throughout the season with British visitors.

Utah Beach

The westernmost of the main Invasion Beaches, **Utah Beach** stretches for approximately thirty kilometres south from St-Vaast. From 6.30am onwards on D-Day, 23,000 men and 1700 vehicles landed here. A minor coast road, the D241, traces the edge of the dunes and enables visitors to follow the course of the fighting, though in truth there's precious little to see these days. Ships that were deliberately sunk to create artificial breakwaters are still visible at low tide, while markers along the seafront commemorate individual fallen heroes.

Two museums now tell the story: the Musée de la Liberté in **QUINÉVILLE** (daily: June–Sept 9.30am–7.30pm; mid-March to May & Oct to mid-Nov 10am–6pm; closed Dec to mid-March; €5), which focuses on everyday life for the people of Normandy under Nazi occupation, and the much more comprehensive **Musée du Débarquement d'Utah-Beach** in **STE-MARIE-DU-MONT** (Ⓦwww.utah-beach.org; May–Sept daily 9.30am–7pm; April & Oct daily 10am–12.30pm & 2–6pm; Nov–March Sat, Sun & hols 10am–12.30pm & 2–5.30pm; €4.50), which explains the operations in exhaustive detail, with huge sea-view windows to lend immediacy to the copious models, maps, films and diagrams.

La Hague

If you go west from Cherbourg to **La Hague**, the northern tip of the peninsula, you'll find wild and isolated countryside where you can lean into the wind, watch waves smashing against rocks in secluded inlets or sunbathe amid a spring profusion of wild flowers, while a whole range of activities are on offer, The area's main tourist office, at 45 rue Jallot in Beaumont-Hague, can supply the details (June Mon–Sat 9am–12.30pm & 2–6.30pm; July–Aug Mon–Sat 9am–6.30pm, Sun 10am–12.30pm; Sept–May Mon–Sat 9am–12.30pm & 2–6pm; Ⓣ02.33.52.74.94, Ⓦwww.lahague.org). The main road, the D901, continues a couple of kilometres beyond the infamous nuclear reprocessing plant near Herqueville to **GOURY**, where the fields finally roll down to a craggy pebble coastline. Almost the only building here, the *Auberge de Goury* (Ⓣ02.33.52.77.01; closed Mon), is a really excellent restaurant, facing the octagonal lifeboat station and looking out towards a slate-grey lighthouse. It specializes in charcoal-grilled fish and meat, with a wide-ranging cheeseboard that includes the extraordinary voluptueuse, and is very popular at lunchtimes.

Other attractions on the cape include some of the highest cliffs in Europe at the Nez de Jobourg, just 5km south of Goury and reachable by the Sentier des Douaniers, a well marked ramblers' path that hugs the coast for 43km between Urville-Nacqueville, on the north coast, to the dunes at Biville, in the far south of the region. Crêperies, bars and little restaurants dot the headland, as do *gîtes-rurales* (information also from the tourist office), many in the area's handsome, immaculately kept stone cottages, with their slate roofs and pretty gardens. An austere but superbly restored fifteenth-century farmhouse, *Le Tourp* (Ⓣ02.33.01.84.60, Ⓦwww.letourp.com), near **OMONVILLE-LA-ROGUE** on the north coast, not only hosts photography and other art exhibitions but also houses a gastronomic restaurant – the €25 menu is unbeatable value – and has extremely attractive rooms (❹).

Art and poetry fans might like to visit the houses where Jean-François Millet and Jacques Prévert were born and died respectively. The painter of poster-favourite *Les Glaneuses* was born at Hameau Gruchy (daily April & May 2–6pm; June–Sept 11am–6pm; €4), at **GRÉVILLE-HAGUE**, where temporary exhibitions are held, while the great twentieth-century writers' workshop and garden at the home he retired to in the 1970s can be visited at Le Val, **OMONVILLE-LA-PETITE** (same opening hours and fee as the Millet house). Two other interests, star-gazing and botany, are catered for at the Ludiver planetarium at the village of **TONNEVILLE**, in the east of the promontory (July & Aug daily 10am–7pm; Sept–June Mon–Fri 9am–1pm & 2–5.30pm, Sat, Sun & public holidays 2–6pm; €3.50; Ⓦwww.ludiver.com), and at the tropical-looking garden at the Château de Vauville, in the especially picturesque village of **VAUVILLE** to the west (May, June & Sept Tues & Fri–Sun 2–6pm; July & Aug daily 2–6pm; €6; Ⓦwww.ludiver.com); it is famed for its huge palm-grove, a sure sign of the area's mild microclimate.

South of La Hague a great curve of sand – some of it military training ground – takes the land's edge to **Flamanville** and another nuclear installation. But the next two sweeps of beach down to **Carteret**, with sand dunes like mini-mountain ranges, are probably the best beaches in Normandy: there are no resorts, no hotels and just two campsites – at **Le Rozel** (*Le Ranch*; Ⓣ02.33.10.07.10, Ⓦwww.campingleranch.fr; closed Nov–March) and **Surtainville** (*Les Mielles*; Ⓣ02.33.04.31.04).

Coutances

The old hill town of **COUTANCES**, 65km south of Cherbourg, confined by its site to just one main street, has on its summit a landmark for all the surrounding countryside, the **Cathédrale de Notre-Dame**. Essentially Gothic, it is still very Norman in its unconventional blending of architectural traditions, and the octagonal lantern crowning the crossing in the nave is nothing short of divinely inspired. The *son et lumière* on Sunday evenings and throughout the summer is for once a true complement to the light stone building. Also illuminated on summer nights (and left open) are the formal fountained **public gardens**.

Coutances' **gare SNCF**, about 1.5km southeast of the town centre (at the bottom of the hill), also serves as the stop for **buses** heading north and south. The local **tourist office** is housed behind the Hôtel de Ville in place Georges-Léclerc (July & Aug Mon–Sat 10am–1pm & 1.30–7pm, Sun 1.30–7pm; Sept–June Mon–Sat 10am–12.30pm & 2–6pm; Ⓣ02.33.19.08.10). The cream-coloured *Hôtel de Normandie*, behind and below the cathedral at 2 place de Gaulle (Ⓣ02.33.45.01.40; ❸; closed Sun eve & Fri Sept to mid-May), has the usual assortment of rooms, and a restaurant with menus that range from the good-value €9 option (not Sun) to an excellent €15 spread. A better alternative for motorists is the *Relais du Viaduc* (Ⓣ02.33.45.02.68; ❷; closed first fortnight of July & second fortnight of Dec, plus Fri evening & Sat in low season), at the junction of the D7 and D971, south of town, which serves fine food. The excellent year-round municipal **campsite**, *Les Vignettes* (Ⓣ02.33.45.43.13), halfway up the hill west of town, stands next to a large, comfortable chain hotel, the *Cositel* (ⓣ02.33.19.15.00; ❹).

Granville

From Coutances, the D971 runs down to the coast at **GRANVILLE**, the Norman equivalent of Brittany's St-Malo, with a history of piracy and the severe citadel of the **haute ville** guarding the approaches to the bay of Mont St-Michel. Thanks in part to the long beach that stretches away north of town, and disappears almost completely at low tide, it's the most lively town and most popular resort in the area. However, it simply doesn't match the appeal of its Breton rival, because of its nightmarish traffic and hordes of tourists milling around in summer in the vain hope of finding some way of amusing themselves.

The great difference between Granville and St-Malo is that in Granville the fortified citadel contains little of interest, just three or four long, narrow, parallel streets of forbidding grey-granite eighteenth-century houses, although the views up and down the coast, across to Mont St-Michel and out to the Îles Chausey, whose granite was quarried for the Mont St-Michel buildings, are dramatic. In pride of place at the inland end of the haute ville is the **Musée d'Art Moderne Richard Anacréon** (daily except Tues 2–6pm; €2.50), housing art accumulated by a Parisian bookseller from 1940 onwards. Filled with sketches and autographs from the likes of Jean Cocteau and André Derain, it's not all that compelling, but the gallery itself is impressive, and hosts interesting temporary exhibitions.

The **tourist office** is below the citadel at 4 cours Jonville (daily 9am–noon & 2–6.30pm; ⓣ02.33.91.30.03, ⓦwww.ville-granville.fr). Trains between Paris and Cherbourg arrive well to the east at the **gare SNCF** on avenue Maréchal-Leclerc, which also serves as the **gare routière**. **Ferries** run from Granville to the Channel Islands and the Îles Chausey. With so many visitors in summer, it's well worth booking **accommodation** in advance, most of it concentrated in the new town, either beneath the walls on the seaward side, or near the station. The *Michelet*, 5 rue Jules-Michelet (ⓣ02.33.50.06.55; ❸), is well equipped but characterless; the *Des Bains*, closer to the tourist office at 19 rue G-Clemenceau, (ⓣ02.33.50.17.31; ❸; closed Jan & Feb, restaurant closed Mon & Tues out of season), has a reasonable restaurant. An option nearer the station is the *Terminus* at 5 place de la Gare (ⓣ02.33.50.02.05; ❷). The modern, oceanfront *Centre Régional de Nautisme* (ⓣ02.33.91.22.62; closed Sat & Sun Nov–Feb; €14.50 per person), a kilometre south of the station in the town centre, serves as Granville's **hostel**.

Where Granville really does excel is in its waterfront **restaurants**, hard below the citadel walls, though be warned that the views here are of a gritty commercial port rather than a delightful harbour. The best are the *Restaurant du Port*, 19 rue du Port (ⓣ02.33.50.00.55; closed Sun pm, plus Mon in low season), with its mouthwatering assortment of very fishy menus, and the *Phare*, nearby at no. 11 (ⓣ02.33.50.12.94; closed Tues eve & Wed Sept–June), which has the standard mussels and *panaché de poissons* on its €15 menu, and a superb *assiette des fruits de mer* on the €26 one. Up in the old town, *L'Échauguette*, 24 rue St-Jean (ⓣ02.33.50.51.87; closed Tues, plus Wed in low season), serves good crêpes and simple meals, cooked over an open fire.

St-Jean-Le-Thomas and Gênets

South of Granville the crowded towns and small resorts all compete for views and proximity to Mont St-Michel. **ST-JEAN-LE-THOMAS** is the first point from which you can walk at low tide across the bay to the abbey, although it's not a walk to take on a drunken – or any other – impulse. The tide, as they like to tell you, comes up faster than galloping horses. A special phone line (ⓣ02.33.50.02.67) gives advice on timing, or you can join a **guided walk** from the beach at **GÊNETS** with Chemins de la Baie (most days mid-April to Oct, depending on tides; ⓣ02.33.89.80.88; €5.50–8).

Avranches

AVRANCHES is the nearest large town to Mont St-Michel, and it has always had close connections with the abbey. The Mont's original church was founded by a bishop of Avranches, spurred on by the Archangel Michael, who supposedly became so impatient with the lack of progress that he prodded a hole in the bishop's skull – still to be seen in Avranches' **St-Gervais basilica**. Robert of Torigny, a subsequent abbot of St-Michel, played host in the town on several occasions to Henry II of England, the most memorable being when Henry was obliged, barefoot and bareheaded, to do public penance for the murder of Thomas Becket, on May 22, 1172. The arena for this act of contrition was Avranches cathedral, designed, most inexpertly, by de Torigny himself: the cathedral swiftly "crumbled and fell for want of proper support", and all that marks the site today is a fenced-off platform – the *plate-forme*. A more vivid evocation of the area's medieval splendours comes from the illuminated manuscripts from the Mont, on display in the town **museum** (April & May daily except Tues 9.30am–noon & 2–6pm; June–Sept daily 9.30am–noon & 2–6pm; €2.30).

The **gare SNCF** is far below the town centre. In high summer, one bus per day runs to Mont St-Michel from the **tourist office** on place Général-de-Gaulle (July & Aug daily 9am–8pm; Sept–June Mon–Fri 10am–noon & 2–6pm, Sat 10am–noon & 2–5pm; ⓣ02.33.58.00.22, ⓦwww.ville-avranches.fr). The nicest **hotel** has to be the gloriously old-fashioned *Croix d'Or*, near the Patton monument at 83 rue de la Constitution (ⓣ02.33.58.04.88; ❹; closed Jan), which boasts beautiful hydrangea-filled gardens and absolutely the best **restaurant** in town. Reasonable alternatives include *Le Jardin des Plantes*, across town at 10 place Carnot (ⓣ02.33.58.03.68; ❹), where the restaurant is more basic but still good value.

Mont St-Michel

The island of **MONT ST-MICHEL** was once known as the "Mount in Peril from the Sea", as many pilgrims in medieval times drowned or were sucked under by quicksand while trying to cross the bay to the eighty-metre-high rocky outcrop. The Archangel Michael was its vigorous protector, the most militant spirit of the Church Militant, with a marked tendency to leap from rock to rock in titanic struggles against Paganism and Evil. The abbey dates back to the eighth century, when the archangel supposedly appeared to a bishop of Avranches, Aubert, who duly founded a monastery on the island poking out of the Baie du Mont St-Michel. Since the eleventh century – when work on the sturdy church at the peak commenced – new buildings have been grafted onto the island to produce a fortified hotch-potch of Romanesque and Gothic buildings clambering to the pinnacle of the graceful church, forming probably the most recognizable silhouette in France after the Eiffel Tower.

Although it was such a prominent religious community, there were never more than forty monks resident on the Mont up to the time of the Revolution, when it was converted into a prison. In 1966, exactly a thousand years

Visiting Mont St-Michel

Access to the island of Mont St-Michel is free and unrestricted, although there's a €4 fee to park on either the causeway or the sands below it (which are submerged by the tides). If you're visiting by car in summer, you might prefer to park on the mainland well short of the Mont, both to enjoy the walk across the causeway and to avoid the dense traffic jams.

Between May and September, the **abbey** is open daily from 9am to 7pm, with last admission at 6pm; from October to April, it's open daily from 9.30am until 6pm, last admission at 5pm. It's closed on Jan 1, May 1, and Dec 25. Paying the standard €7 **admission fee** – ages 18–25 €4.50, under-18s free – entitles you to wander the generally accessible areas, and to join an expert-led **guided tour** in the language of your choice (tickets may be purchased at various tourist offices in the region at the lower price of €5.50). Tours last 45 minutes between mid-June and mid-Sept, and a full hour the rest of the year; the daily schedule for each language is displayed at the entrance. There are also a number of more detailed two-hour tours, in French only, which take you both higher and deeper (July & Aug daily 10.30am, 11.30am, 2pm & 3pm; Sept–June Sat & Sun 10.30am & 2pm; €4 extra).

In July and August only, the Mont also stays open **after hours**, both in the early evening when visitors are free to stroll in the gardens (Mon–Sat 7–9pm; free with paid admission for any other time of day), and at night, when the abbey itself reopens for musical and video installations (Mon–Sat 9pm–midnight, last admission 11pm; €9, ages 13–24 €6.50).

after Duke Richard the First originally brought the order to the Mont, the Benedictines were invited to return; today, a dozen nuns and monks from the Monastic Fraternity of Jerusalem maintain a presence.

For many years now, the Mont has no longer, strictly speaking, been an island – the causeway (*digue*) that leads to it is never submerged, and is continuing to silt up to either side. Major works are due to begin in 2005 that will replace the causeway with a bridge; trams or buses will ferry visitors across from landscaped car parks on the mainland. That should not only make tourist numbers easier to control, but also enable the sea to wash away much of the accumulated silt, but the optimistic completion date is currently 2009.

The abbey

The **abbey**, an architectural ensemble that incorporates the high-spired archangel-topped church and the magnificent Gothic buildings known since 1228 as the **Merveille** ("The Marvel") – incorporating the entire north face, with the cloister, Knights' Hall, Refectory, Guest Hall and cellars – is visible from all around the bay, but it becomes if anything more awe-inspiring the closer you approach. In Maupassant's words:

I reached the huge pile of rocks which bears the little city dominated by the great church. Climbing the steep narrow street, I entered the most wonderful Gothic dwelling ever made for God on this earth, a building as vast as a town, full of low rooms under oppressive ceilings and lofty galleries supported by frail pillars. I entered that gigantic granite jewel, which is as delicate as a piece of lacework, thronged with towers and slender belfries which thrust into the blue sky of day and the black sky of night their strange heads bristling with chimeras, devils, fantastic beasts and monstrous flowers, and which are linked together by carved arches of intricate design.

The Mont's rock comes to a sharp point just below what is now the transept of the **church**, a building where the transition from Romanesque to Gothic is only too evident in the vaulting of the nave. In order to lay out the church's ground plan in the traditional shape of the cross, supporting crypts had to be built up from the surrounding hillside, and in all construction work the Chausey granite has had to be sculpted to match the exact contours of the hill. Space was always limited, and yet the building has grown through the centuries, with an architectural ingenuity that constantly surprises in its geometry – witness the shock of emerging into the light of the cloisters from the sombre Great Hall.

Not surprisingly, the building of the monastery was no smooth progression: the original church, choir, nave and tower all had to be replaced after collapsing. The style of decoration has varied, too, along with the architecture. That you now walk through halls of plain grey stone is a reflection of modern taste. In the Middle Ages, the walls of public areas such as the refectory would have been festooned with tapestries and frescoes, while the original coloured tiles of the cloisters have long since been stripped away to reveal bare walls.

To get a clearer sense of the abbey's historical development, be sure to take a look at the intriguing scale models in the reception area, which depict it during four different epochs.

The rest of the island

The base of Mont St-Michel rests on a primeval slime of sand and mud. Just above that, you pass through the heavily fortified **Porte du Roi** onto the narrow **Grande Rue**, climbing steadily around the base of the rock and lined with medieval gabled houses and a jumble of overpriced postcard and souvenir shops, maintaining the ancient tradition of prising pilgrims from their money. A plaque near the main staircase records that Jacques Cartier was presented to King François I here on May 8, 1532, and charged with exploring the shores of Canada.

The rather dry **Musée Maritime** offers an insight into the island's ties with the sea, while the Archangel Michael manages in just fifteen minutes to lead visitors on a voyage through space and time in the **Archéoscope**, with the full majestic panoply of multimedia mumbo jumbo. Further along the Grande Rue and up the steps towards the abbey church, next door to the eleventh-century **church of St-Pierre**, the absurd **Musée Grévin** contains such edifying specimens as a wax model of a woman drowning in a sea of mud. All open February to mid-November daily 9am–6pm; €15 for all, or €7 each one.

Large crowds gather each day at the **North Tower**, to watch the tide sweep in across the bay. Seagulls wheel away in alarm, and those foolish enough to be wandering too late on the sands have to sprint to safety.

Practicalities

Mont St-Michel has its own **tourist office,** in the lowest gateway (mid-June to mid-Sept Mon–Sat 9am–7pm, Sun 9am–noon & 2–6pm; mid-Sept to mid-June; Mon, Tues & Thurs–Sat 9am–noon & 2–6pm; ⓣ02.33.60.14.30). Regular **buses** connect it with the SNCF stations at Pontorson (see below), Rennes and St-Malo.

The island holds a surprising number of **hotels** and **restaurants**, albeit nothing like enough to cope with the sheer number of visitors. Most are predictably expensive, though virtually all seem to keep a few cheaper rooms. The most famous hotel, *La Mère Poulard* (ⓣ02.33.89.68.68, ⓦwww.mere-poulard.com; ❻), uses the time-honoured legend of its fluffy omelettes, as enjoyed by Leon Trotsky and Margaret Thatcher (not simultaneously), to justify extortionate charges. Higher up the Mont, however, prices fall to more realistic levels. The cheapest option is the *Du Guesclin* (ⓣ02.33.60.14.10; ❹), where all the rooms have TV, but both the *Croix Blanche* (ⓣ02.33.60.14.04; ❻; closed mid-Nov to Jan) and the *Mouton Blanc* (ⓣ02.33.60.14.08; ❺; closed Jan) have higher standards. Sadly, restaurants on the Mont are consistently worse than almost anywhere in France; it's impossible to make any confident recommendations other than eat elsewhere.

In addition, the main approach road to the island, the D976, is lined shortly before the causeway by around a dozen large and virtually indistinguishable hotels and motels, each with its own brasserie or restaurant. Typical among these are the *Motel Vert* (ⓣ02.33.60.09.33, ⓦwww.le-mont-saint-michel.com; ❷; closed mid-Nov to mid-Feb), the *Hôtel Formule Verte* (ⓣ02.33.60.14.13, ⓦwww.le-mont-saint-michel.com; ❷; closed mid-Nov to mid-Feb) and the *Hôtel de la Digue* (ⓣ02.33.60.14.02, ⓦwww.ladigue.fr; ❹; closed mid-Nov to mid-March). The three-star, 350-pitch *Camping du Mont-St-Michel* (ⓣ02.33.60.22.10; ⓦwww.le-mont-saint-michel.com; closed mid-Nov to mid-Feb) is also on the mainland just short of the causeway.

Many visitors to Mont St-Michel find themselves lodging at **PONTORSON**, 6km inland, which has the nearest **gare SNCF**, connected to the Mont by a bus service (€5 return). The **hotels** here are not especially interesting, but both the *Montgomery*, in a fine old ivy-covered mansion at 13 rue du Couesnon (ⓣ02.33.60.00.09, ⓦwww.hotel-montgomery.fr; ❹; closed two weeks in Feb), and the *Bretagne*, 59 rue du Couesnon (ⓣ02.33.60.10.55, ⓔdebretagne@destination-bretagne.com; ❹; closed Mon & Jan), have distinguished restaurants.

Inland Normandy

It's hard to pin down specific highlights in **inland Normandy**. The pleasures lie in the feel of particular landscapes – the lush meadows and orchards, the classic half-timbered houses and farm buildings, and the rivers and forests of the Norman countryside. **Gastronomy** is, of course, another major motivation for coming here. The cheeses, creams, apple and pear brandies and ciders for which the region is famous are at their best in the **Pays d'Auge**, south of Lisieux, and the **Vire Valley** to the west. The **Suisse Normande** is canoeing and rock-climbing country, and there are endless good walks in the stretch along the southern border of the province designated as the **Parc Naturel Régional de Normandie-Maine**. Of the towns, **Conches** is the most charming, **Falaise** has William the Conqueror as a constant fall-back attraction, and **Lisieux** has its religious significance.

South of the Seine

Heading south from the Seine you can follow the River Risle from the estuary just east of Honfleur, or the Eure and its tributaries from upstream of Rouen. Between the two stretches the long featureless **Neubourg Plain**. The lowest major crossing point over the Risle is at **PONT-AUDEMER**, where medieval houses lean out at alarming angles over the crisscrossing roads, rivers and canals. From here, perfect cycling roads lined with timbered farmhouses follow the river south.

Le Bec-Hellouin

The size and tranquillity of the **Abbaye de Bec-Hellouin**, upstream from Pont-Audemer just before Brionne, give a monastic feel to the whole Risle valley. Bells echo across the water and white-robed monks go soberly about their business. From the eleventh century onwards, the abbey was one of the most important centres of intellectual learning in the Christian world; the philosopher Anselm was abbot here before becoming Archbishop of Canterbury in 1093. Owing to the Revolution, most of the monastery buildings are recent – the monks only returned in 1948 – but there are some survivors and appealing clusters of stone ruins, including the fifteenth-century **bell tower of St-Nicholas** and the cloister. Recent archbishops of Canterbury have maintained tradition by coming here on retreat. Visitors are welcome to wander through the grounds for no charge, though you can also join regular **guided tours** (June–Sept Mon & Wed–Fri 10.30am, 3pm, 4pm & 5pm, Sat 10.30am, 3pm & 4pm, Sun & hols noon, 3pm & 4pm; Oct–May Mon & Wed–Sat 10.30am, 3pm & 4pm, Sun & hols noon, 3pm & 4pm; €4; Ⓦ www.abbayedubec.com).

The rather twee adjacent town of **BEC-HELLOUIN** holds a distinctly unascetic **restaurant**, the wonderful *Auberge de l'Abbaye* (Ⓣ 02.32.44.86.02; ❺; closed Mon eve, all day Tues in winter & all Jan), which also has half a dozen expensive rooms. *Restaurant de la Tour* on place Guillaume-le-Conquérant nearby (Ⓣ 02.32.44.86.15; closed Dec, plus Tues evening & Wed in low season) is a more affordable place to eat, with some outdoor tables.

Brionne and Beaumont-le-Roger

BRIONNE, on the Rouen–Lisieux rail line, is a small town with large regional markets on Thursday and Sunday. The fish hall is on the left bank, the rest by the church on the right bank. Above them both, with panoramic views, is an excellent example of a Norman **donjon** (keep). If you decide to stay, try the lovely old half-timbered **Auberge du Vieux Donjon**, 19 rue Soie (Ⓣ 02.32.44.80.62; ❸; closed Mon & Sun eve in low season & last fortnight in Oct), which has a good restaurant.

The River Charentonne joins the Risle near Serquigny. The town is also the meeting point of rail lines and main roads and the banks are clogged with fuming industrial conglomerations. But 7km upstream, at **BEAUMONT-LE-ROGER**, you are back in pastoral tranquillity. The ruins of a thirteenth-century **priory church** slowly crumble to the ground, the slow restoration of one or two arches unable to keep pace. In the village, little happens beyond the hammering of the church bell next door to the abbey by a nodding musketeer.

The next riverside village, **LA FERRIÈRE-SUR-RISLE**, has an especially beautiful **church**, with some interesting sculpture, and a fourteenth-century covered **market hall**. Paddocks and meadows lead down to the river and a small and inviting **hotel**, the *Vieux-Marché* (Ⓣ02.32.30.25.93; ❷; closed mid-Sept to mid-Oct).

Conches-en-Ouche

Fourteen kilometres east of La Ferrière across the wild and open woodland of the **Forêt de Conches**, standing above the River Rouloir on an abrupt and narrow spur, is **CONCHES-EN-OUCHE**, many a Norman's favourite heartland town. At the highest point, in the middle of a row of medieval houses, is the **church of Ste-Foy**, its windows a stunning sequence of Renaissance stained glass. Behind are the gardens of the **Hôtel de Ville**, where a robust, if anatomically odd, stone boar gazes proudly out over a spectacular view. Next to that, you can scramble up the slippery steps of the ruined twelfth-century **castle**. Conches is given a certain edge over other towns with equal lists of historic relics by the pieces of modern sculpture that seem to lie around every other corner.

The town's **tourist office**, close to the castle, 200m south of the church in place Aristide-Briand (Tues–Sat 10am–12.30pm & 2–6pm, Sun 10am–noon; Ⓣ02.32.30.76.42, Ⓦwww.conches-en-ouche.fr), rents out mountain bikes. The best **accommodation** option is *Le Cygne*, a *logis de France* at 2 rue Paul Guilbaud at the north end of town (Ⓣ02.32.30.20.60; ❸; closed Sun eve & Mon). There's also a two-star municipal **campsite**, *La Forêt* (Ⓣ02.32.30.22.49; closed Oct–March), while on Thursday the whole town is taken up by a **market**.

Évreux

If you're heading south to Conches from Rouen, you follow first the River Eure, and then its tributary the Iton, passing through **ÉVREUX**, capital of the Eure *département*. It's hardly an exciting place, but an afternoon's wander in the vicinity of the **cathedral** – a minor classic with its flamboyant exterior decoration and original fourteenth-century windows – and the **ramparts** alongside the Iton river bank is pleasant. The old *Biche*, at 9 rue St-Joséphine on place St-Taurin at the edge of town (Ⓣ02.32.38.66.00; ❸; closed Sun in July & Aug, Sun eve Sept–June), is a strange but splendid Belle Époque **hotel**, with a lurid pink interior, a triangular dining room and even some triangular bedrooms. In its **restaurant**, €24 will buy you a magnificent meal of oysters braised in cider and a garlicky seafood *pot au feu*, to the musical accompaniment of an unlikely assortment of funk and disco classics.

Lisieux and the Pays d'Auge

The rolling hills and green twisting valleys of the **Pays d'Auge** stretch south of the cathedral town of **Lisieux** and are scattered with magnificent half-timbered manor houses. The pastures here are the lushest in the province, their produce the world-famous cheeses of Camembert, Livarot and Pont L'Évêque. And beside them are hectares of orchards, yielding the best of Norman ciders, both apple and pear (*poiré*), as well as Calvados apple brandy.

Lisieux

LISIEUX, 35 minutes by train from Caen, is the main town of the Pays d'Auge, and a good place to get to know its cheeses and ciders is at the large street

market on Wednesday and Saturday. Most people, however, come to Lisieux as a place of pilgrimage based around the cult of St Thérèse, the most popular French spiritual figure of the last hundred years. Passivity, self-effacement and a self-denial that verged on masochism were her trademarks, and she is honoured by the gaudy and gigantic **Basilique de Ste-Thérèse**, completed in 1954 on a slope to the southwest of the town centre. The huge modern mosaics that decorate the nave are undeniably impressive, but the overall impression is of a quasi-medieval hagiography. The faithful can ride on a white, flag-bedecked fairground train around the holiest sites, which include the infinitely restrained and sober **Cathédrale St-Pierre**.

Lisieux's **tourist office**, 11 rue d'Alençon, is the best place to gather information on the rural areas further inland (mid-June to Sept Mon–Sat 8.30am–6.30pm, Sun 10am–12.30pm & 2–5pm; Oct to mid-June Mon–Sat 8.30am–noon & 1.30–6pm; ⓣ02.31.48.18.10, ⓦwww.ville-lisieux.fr). The quantity of pilgrims means the town is full of good-value **hotels**, such as *De la Terrasse*, near the basilica at 25 av Ste-Thérèse (ⓣ02.31.62.17.65; ❸; closed Jan & Mon in winter), and the inexpensive *Des Arts*, backing onto the bishop's gardens at 26 rue Condorcet (ⓣ02.31.62.00.02; ❷). There's also a large two-star **campsite**, *de la Vallée* (ⓣ02.31.62.00.40; closed Oct to mid-April), but campers would probably be better off somewhere more rural, such as Livarot or Orbec. If Thérèse isn't your prime motivation, Saturday is the best day to visit, for the large **street market** stacked with Pays d'Auge cheeses.

Into the Pays d'Auge

Though the tourist authorities responsible for the Pays d'Auge have laid out a **Route du Fromage** and a **Route du Cidre**, you won't be missing out if you don't follow these itineraries. For really good solid Norman cooking this is the perfect area to look out for *fermes auberges*, working farms which welcome paying visitors to share their meals. Local tourist offices can provide copious lists of these and of local producers from whom you can buy your cheese and booze.

Beuvron-en-Auge

By far the prettiest of the Pays d'Auge villages is **BEUVRON-EN-AUGE**, 7km north of the N13 halfway between Lisieux and Caen. It consists of an oval central square, ringed by a glorious ensemble of multicoloured half-timbered houses, including the yellow and brown sixteenth-century **Vieux Manoir**. The very centre of the square is taken up by the *Pavé d'Auge* **restaurant** (ⓣ02.31.79.26.71; closed Mon May–Aug), where menus featuring chicken and *andouille* in cider or salmon start at €24.

Orbec and Livarot

The larger town of **ORBEC**, 19km southeast of Lisieux, also epitomizes the simple pleasures of the region. Along the rue Grande, you'll see several houses in which the gaps between the timbers are filled with intricate patterns of coloured tiles and bricks. Debussy composed *Jardin sous la Pluie* in one of these, and the oldest and prettiest of the lot – a tanner's house dating back to 1568, and once again called the **Vieux Manoir** – holds a museum of local history. On the whole, though, it's more fun just to walk down behind the church to the river, and its watermill and paddocks.

The centre of the cheese country is the old town of **LIVAROT**, with the appealing **hotel** and restaurant *Du Vivier* (ⓣ02.31.32.04.10; ❸) in its heart.

Set in a grand house near the River Vie on its western outskirts, the **Musée du Fromage** illustrates the history and manufacture of Livarot's eponymous cheese, and doles out free samples (March Tues–Sat 2–5pm; April & Sept–Oct Mon–Sat 10am–noon & 2–6pm, Sun 2–6pm; May–Aug daily 10am–noon & 2–6pm; €3).

Vimoutiers and Camembert

VIMOUTIERS, due south of Livarot, contains yet another **cheese museum**, at 10 av Général-de-Gaulle (May–Oct Mon 2–6pm, Tues–Sat 9am–noon & 2–6pm, Sun 10am–noon & 2.30–6.30pm; March, April, Nov & Dec Mon 2–6pm, Tues–Fri 9am–noon & 2–6pm, Sat 9am–noon; €3). This one specializes in labels – the cheeses underneath are mostly polystyrene.

A statue in the town's main square honours Marie Harel, who, at the nearby village of **CAMEMBERT**, developed the original cheese early in the nineteenth century, promoting it with a skilful campaign that included sending free samples to Napoleon. Marie is confronted across the main street by what might be called the statue of the Unknown Cow.

Vimoutiers is the venue of a **market** on Monday afternoons. Its **tourist office**, in the cheese museum (same hours; ⓣ02.33.39.30.29), has piles of information on local cheese-related attractions. Of its **hotels**, the central *Soleil d'Or*, 15 place Mackau (ⓣ02.33.39.07.15; ❷; closed mid-Feb to mid-March), has a reasonable €13 menu and a better €18 one.

A short way south of Vimoutiers, en route to Camembert, the beautifully sited lake known as the **Escale du Vitou** offers everything you need for windsurfing, swimming and horse-riding, as well as its own comfortable, rural **hotel**, *L' Escale du Vitou* (ⓣ02.33.39.12.04; ❷). There's also a clean and very cheap year-round **campsite** nearby, the two-star *La Campière*, 9 rue du 8-Mai (ⓣ02.33.39.18.86).

Camembert itself, 3km southeast of Vimoutiers, is tiny, hilly and very rural, home to far more cows than humans. On one side of its little central square, the largest local cheese producers, La Ferme Président, run their own **cheese museum** (May daily 10am–12.30pm & 2–6pm; June–Aug 10am–12.30pm & 2–7pm; €3), where the forty-minute tour adds little to anything you may have learned in Vimoutiers. On the other side, the rival Le Relais du Camembert is a British-run cheese and souvenir stall with another ramshackle free cheese museum, open to no fixed hours, that has long been engaged in a bitter and much-publicized feud with the village *mairie* alongside.

Falaise

William the Conqueror, or William the Bastard as he is more commonly known over here, was born in **FALAISE**, 40km southwest of Lisieux. His mother, Arlette, a laundrywoman, was spotted by his father, Duke Robert of Normandy, at the washing place below the château. She was a shrewd woman, scorning secrecy in her eventual assignation by riding publicly through the main entrance to meet him. During her pregnancy, she is said to have dreamed of bearing a mighty tree that cast its shade over Normandy and England.

Falaise's **castle** keep, firmly planted on the massive rocks of the cliff (*falaise*) that gave the town its name, and towering over the **Fontaine d'Arlette** down by the river, is one of the most evocative historic sights imaginable. Nonetheless, it was so heavily damaged during the war that it took over fifty years to reopen for regular visits (April–June & Sept daily 10am–6pm; July & Aug daily 10am–7pm; Oct–March Mon & Thurs–Sun 10am–6pm;

English-language tours daily 11.30am, with another at 3.30pm in July & Aug; €6). Huge resources have been lavished on restoring the central **donjon**, reminiscent of the Tower of London with its cream-coloured Caen stone. A guiding principle was to avoid any possible confusion as to what is original and authentic, and what is new. Rest assured you'll be in no doubt whatever. Steel slabs, concrete blocks, glass floors and tent-like canvas awnings have been slapped down atop the bare ruins, and metal staircases even squeezed into the wall cavities. The raw structure of the keep, down to its very foundations, lies exposed to view, while the newly created rooms are used for changing exhibitions that focus on the castle's fascinating past.

The town too was devastated in the war. The struggle to close the "Falaise Gap" in August 1944 was the climax of the Battle of Normandy, as the Allied armies sought to encircle the Germans and cut off their retreat. By the time the Canadians entered the town on August 17, they could no longer tell where the roads had been and had to bulldoze a new four-metre strip straight through the middle.

Practicalities

The **tourist office** can be found on the boulevard de la Libération (May, June & first half of Sept Mon 10am–12.30pm & 1.30–6.30pm, Tues–Sat 9.30am–12.30pm & 1.30–6.30pm, Sun 10.30am–12.30pm; July & Aug Mon–Sat 9.30am–6.30pm, Sun 10.30am–12.30pm & 3–5.30pm; mid-Sept to April Mon 1.30–6.30pm, Tues–Sat 9.30am–12.30pm & 1.30–6.30pm; ⓣ02.31.90.17.26, ⓦwww.otsifalaise.com). Most of the **hotels** stand along the main, noisy Caen–Argentan road. *The Poste*, near the tourist office at 38 rue Georges-Clémenceau (ⓣ02.31.90.13.14, ⓔhotel.delaposte@wanadoo.fr; ❸; restaurant closed Sun eve & Mon), serves good food on menus from €15, while rooms and meals at the *De la Place*, 1 place St-Gervais (ⓣ02.31.40.19.00; ❷; closed Sun eve & Wed), are significantly cheaper. The three-star **campsite**, *Camping du Château* (ⓣ02.31.90.16.55; closed Oct to mid-April), next to Arlette's fountain and the municipal swimming pool, is in a much better location.

The Suisse Normande

The area known as the **Suisse Normande** lies roughly 25km south of Caen, along the gorge of the River Orne, between Thury-Harcourt and Putanges. While the name is a little far-fetched – there are certainly no mountains – it is quite distinctive, with cliffs and crags and wooded hills at every turn. There are plenty of opportunities for outdoor pursuits: you can race along the Orne in canoes and kayaks, cruise more sedately on pedaloes or a bizarre species of inflatable rubber tractor, or dangle on ropes from the sheer rock-faces high above. For mere walkers the Orne can be frustrating: footpaths along the river are few and far between, and often entirely overgrown.

The Suisse Normande is usually approached from Caen or Falaise and contrasts dramatically with the prairie-like expanse of wheat fields en route. On wheels, the best access is via the D235 from Caen (signed to Falaise then right through Ifs). Bus Verts #34 will take you to **Thury-Harcourt** or **Clécy** on its way to Flers, and there are occasional special summer train excursions from Caen.

Thury-Harcourt and Clécy

At **THURY-HARCOURT**, the **tourist office** on place St-Sauveur (May–Sept Mon–Sat 10am–12.30pm & 2.30–6.30pm, Sun 10am–12.30pm;

Oct–April Mon–Fri 10am–12.30pm & 2.30–5pm, Sat 10am–12.30pm; ⓣ02.31.79.70.45, ⓦwww.suisse-normande.com) can suggest walks, rides and *gîtes d'étape* throughout the Suisse Normande. **Hotels** are for the most part overpriced, but there is an attractive four-star **campsite**, the *Vallée du Traspy* (ⓣ02.31.79.61.80; closed mid-Sept to mid-April).

CLÉCY, 10km to the south, is a slightly better bet for finding a room, although visitors outnumber residents in peak season. The **hotel** facing the church in the village centre, *Au Site Normand*, 1 rue des Châtelets (ⓣ02.31.69.71.05; ❸; closed Nov–Feb), consists of an old-fashioned and good-value dining room in the main timber-framed building, and a cluster of newer units around the back. The river is a kilometre away, down the hill. En route, in the Parc des Loisirs, is a **Musée du Chemin de Fer Miniature** (March–Easter Sun 2–5.30pm; Easter–June & Sept daily 10am–noon & 2–6pm; July & Aug daily 10am–noon & 2–6.30pm; Oct–Nov Sun 2–5pm; €4), featuring a gigantic model railway certain to appeal to children. Set in spacious grounds on the far bank of the river, the *Moulin du Vey* (ⓣ02.31.69.71.08, ⓦwww.moulinduvey.com; ❺; closed Dec & Jan) is a luxury **hotel** that takes its name from the restored watermill right by the bridge, which is itself, confusingly, now a restaurant. The western riverbank continues in a brief splurge of restaurants, takeaways and snack bars as far as the two-star municipal **campsite** (ⓣ02.31.69.70.36; closed Oct–March).

Pont d'Ouilly

If you're planning on walking, or cycling, a good central spot in which to base yourself is **PONT D'OUILLY**, at the point where the main road from Vire to Falaise crosses the river. It's a small town, with a few basic shops, an old covered market hall and a promenade (with bar) slightly upstream alongside the weir. Continuing upstream a pleasant walk leads for 3.5km alongside the river to the pretty little village of Le Mesnil Villement.

As well as a **campsite** overlooking the river (ⓣ02.31.69.46.12; closed Oct–Easter), Pont d'Ouilly offers an attractive **hotel**, the *Du Commerce* (ⓣ02.31.69.80.16; ❸; closed Sun eve & Mon Oct–May), the quintessential French village hotel, with a friendly welcome and attentive service. Its **restaurant** is very popular with local families, serving superb, definitive Norman cooking, with plenty of creamy *Pays d'Auge* sauces, on menus that start at €11. About a kilometre north, the more upmarket *Auberge St-Christophe* (ⓣ02.31.69.81.23; ❸; closed Sun evening, Mon & mid-Feb to mid-March) stands, covered with ivy and geraniums, in a beautiful setting on the right bank of the Orne.

A short distance south of Pont-d'Ouilly is the **Roche d'Oëtre**, a high rock with a tremendous view into the deep and totally wooded gorge of the Rouvre, a tributary of the Orne. The river widens soon afterwards into the **Lac du Rabodanges**, formed by the many-arched Rabodanges Dam.

Southern Normandy

As an alternative to following the more northerly routes across Normandy, motorists heading west from Paris towards Brittany may prefer to cut directly across the province by following the line of the N12 through **Alençon** and then heading northwest on the N176. Much of the terrain along Normandy's southern border is taken up by the dense woodlands of the **Forêt d'Écouves** and the **Forêt des Andaines**, so there's plenty of good walking to be had, while the hill towns of **Carrouges** and **Domfront** make great stopovers.

Alençon and around

ALENÇON, a fair-sized and busy town, is known for its traditional – and now pretty much defunct – lacemaking industry. The **Musée des Beaux-Arts et de la Dentelle** (July & Aug daily 10am–noon & 2–6pm; Sept–June daily except Mon 10am–noon & 2–6pm; €2.80) is housed in a former Jesuit school and has all the best trappings of a modern museum. The highly informative history of lacemaking upstairs, with examples of numerous different techniques, can, however, be tedious for anyone not already riveted by the subject. It also contains an unexpected collection of gruesome Cambodian artefacts like spears and lances, tiger skulls and elephants' feet, gathered by a "militant socialist" French governor at the turn of the century. The paintings in the adjoining Beaux-Arts section are nondescript, except for a few works by Courbet and Géricault. The **Château des Ducs**, the old town castle close by the museum, looks impressive but doesn't encourage visitors: it's now a prison, and people in Alençon have nightmarish memories of its use by the Gestapo during the war. Wandering around the town might also take you to St Thérèse's birthplace on rue St-Blaise, just in front of the *gare routière*.

The **tourist office** is housed in the fifteenth-century Maison d'Ozé on place La Magdelaine (July & Aug Mon–Sat 9.30am–7pm, Sun 10am–12.30pm & 3–5.30pm; Sept–June Mon–Sat 9.30am–noon & 2–6.30pm; ⓣ02.33.80.66.33, ⓦwww.paysdalencontourisme.com). The **gare routière** and the **gare SNCF** are both northeast of the centre, in an area that holds Alençon's prime concentration of **hotels**. The two *logis*, *L'Industrie*, 22 place Général-de-Gaulle (ⓣ02.33.27.19.30; ❷; closed Fri eve & Sat), and the *Grand Hôtel de la Gare*, 50 av Wilson (ⓣ02.33.29.03.93; ❸; restaurant closed Sat & Sun), are decent and have fixed-price menus for about €11. Alençon has good shops and **cafés** in a few pedestrianized streets at the heart of its abysmal one-way traffic system. A good place to sample the thriving local **bar scene** is the half-timbered *Café des Sept Colonnes* at 2 rue du Château.

The **Forêt d'Écouves**, north of Alençon and inaccessible by public transport, is a dense mixture of spruce, pine, oak and beech, unfortunately a favoured spot of the military – and, in autumn, deer hunters, too. You can usually ramble along the cool paths, happening on wild mushrooms and even the odd wild boar.

Carrouges

An alternative base to Alençon, at the western end of the Forêt d'Écouves, is the hill town of **CARROUGES**, with its fine old-style **château** set in spacious grounds at the foot of the hill (daily: April to mid-June & Sept 10am–noon & 2–6pm; mid-June to Aug 9.30am–noon & 2–6.30pm; Oct–March 10am–noon & 2–5pm; €6). Its two highlights are a superb restored brick staircase and a room in which hang portraits of fourteen successive generations of the Le Veneur family, an extraordinary illustration of the processes of heredity. The town also offers two appealing, very similar and almost adjacent small **hotels**: the *Hôtel du Nord* (ⓣ02.33.27.20.14; ❷; closed mid-Dec to mid-Jan, plus Fri Sept–June), with a restaurant serving substantial local cuisine on menus that start at €10, and the tiny *St-Pierre* (Ⓣ02.33.27.20.02; ❷), whose rooms all have showers, and where the restaurant has menus starting at €8.

Bagnoles-de-l'Orne

West of Carrouges, the spa town of **BAGNOLES-DE-L'ORNE** is quite unlike anywhere else in this part of the world, attracting the moneyed sick and convalescent from all over France to its thermal baths. The layout is formal and spacious, centring on a lake with gardens, from where horse-drawn *calèches* take the clients to an enormous casino. With so many visitors to keep entertained, and spending money, there are also innumerable cultural events of a restrained and stressless nature.

Whether you'd actually want to spend time in Bagnoles depends on your disposable income as well as your health. Furthermore, the town as a whole operates to a season that lasts roughly from early April to the end of October; arrive in winter, and you may find everything shut. The numerous hotels are expensive and sedate places, in which it's possible to be too late for dinner at seven o'clock and locked out altogether at nine, and the three-star **campsite**, *De la Vée* (Ⓣ02.33.37.87.45; closed Nov–March), south of town, is rather forlorn.

The **tourist office** on place du Marché (April–Oct Mon–Sat 9am–1pm & 2–6.30pm, Sun 10am–12.30pm & 2.30–6.30pm; Nov–March Mon–Fri 10am–noon & 2–6pm; Ⓣ02.33.37.85.66, Ⓦwww.bagnoles-de-lorne.com) will give details on accommodation in Bagnoles and its less exclusive sister town of **TESSE-MADELEINE**. Despite its ugly would-be-Deco exterior, the *Cetlos*, on rue des Casinos (Ⓣ02.33.38.44.44, Ⓔcetlos@wanadoo.fr; ❹), is the best of the hotels, bedecked with balconies and terraces overlooking the lake. Cheaper alternatives near the central roundabout in Bagnoles include the *Albert 1er* at 7 av Dr-Poulain (Ⓣ02.33.37.80.97; ❸; closed Nov–Feb), which has excellent menus from €14, and the *Grand Veneur* at 6 place République (Ⓣ02.33.37.86.79; ❸; closed Nov–March).

Domfront

The road through the forest from Bagnoles, the D335 and then the D908, climbs above the lush woodlands and progressively narrows to a hog's back before entering **DOMFRONT**. Less happens here than at Bagnoles, but it has the edge on countryside.

A public park, near the long-abandoned former train station, leads up to some redoubtable castle ruins perched on an isolated rock. Eleanor of Aquitaine was born in this **castle** in October 1162, and Thomas à Becket came to stay for Christmas 1166, saying Mass in the **Notre-Dame-sur-l'Eau** church down by the river, which has sadly been ruined by vandals. The views from the flower-filled gardens that surround the mangled keep are spectacular, including a very graphic panorama of the ascent you've made to get up. A slender footbridge connects the castle with the narrow little village itself, which boasts an abundance of half-timbered houses. Near its sweet little central square, the modern **St Julien church**, constructed out of concrete segments during the 1920s, is bursting with exciting mosaics.

On summer afternoons (July & Aug Mon–Sat 3pm), free **guided tours** (in French) of old Domfront leave from the **tourist office**, facing the castle entrance at 12 place de la Roirie (Mon–Sat 10am–noon & 2.30–6.30pm; Ⓣ02.33.38.53.97, Ⓦwww.domfront.com). Domfront's **hotels**, clustered together at the foot of the hill below the old town, make useful and very pleasant stopovers. Two *logis de France* stand side by side: the *Relais St-Michel*, rue du Mont St-Michel (Ⓣ02.33.38.64.99; ❸; closed Fri) has widely varied menus from around €15, while the *Hôtel de France*, 7 rue du Mont St-Michel (Ⓣ02.33.38.51.44, Ⓦwww.region-normande.com/hoteldefrance; ❸) is a little cheaper, and has a nice bar and garden. Campers should note that the two-star local **campsite**, *Du Champs Passais* (Ⓣ02.33.37.37.66; closed mid-Oct to mid-April), is exceptionally small.

The Bocage

The region that centres on **St-Lô**, just south of the Cotentin, is known as the **Bocage**, from a word that refers to a type of cultivated countryside common in the west of France, where fields are cut by tight hedgerows rooted into walls of earth well over a metre high. An effective form of smallhold farming – at least in pre-industrial days – it also proved to be a perfect system of anti-tank barricades. When the Allied troops tried to advance through the region in 1944, it was almost impenetrable – certainly bearing no resemblance to the East Anglian plains where they had trained. The war here was hand-to-hand slaughter, and the destruction of villages was often wholesale.

St-Lô

The city of **ST-LÔ**, 60km south of Cherbourg and 36km southwest of Bayeux, is still known as the "Capital of the Ruins". Memorial sites are everywhere and what is new speaks as tellingly of the destruction as the ruins that have been preserved. In the main square, the gate of the old prison commemorates Resistance members executed by the Nazis, people deported east to the concentration camps and soldiers killed in action. When the bombardment of St-Lô was at its fiercest, the Germans refused to take any measures to protect the prisoners and the gate was all that survived. Samuel Beckett was here during and after the battle, working for the Irish Red Cross as interpreter, driver and provision-seeker – for such things as rat poison for the maternity hospitals. He said he took away with him a "time-honoured conception of humanity in ruins".

All the trees in the city are the same height, all planted to replace the battle's mutilated stumps. But the most visible – and brilliant – reconstruction is the **Cathédrale de Notre-Dame**. Its main body, with a strange southward-veering nave, has been conventionally repaired and rebuilt. But the shattered west front and the base of the collapsed north tower have been joined by a startling sheer wall of icy green stone that makes no attempt to mask the destruction.

By way of contrast to such memories, a lighthouse-like 1950s folly spirals to nowhere on the main square. Should you feel the urge to climb its staircase, make your way into the new and even more pointless labyrinth of glass at its feet, and pay the €1.50 admission fee. More compelling, around behind the Mairie, is the **Musée des Beaux-Arts** (daily except Tues 10am–noon & 2–6pm; €2), which is full of treasures: a Boudin sunset; a Lurçat tapestry of his dog, *Nadir and the Pirates*; works by Corot, van Loo, Moreau; a Léger watercolour; a fine series of unfaded sixteenth-century Flemish tapestries on the lives of two peasants; and sad bombardment relics of the town.

St-Lô's **tourist office** adjoins the "lighthouse" on the main square (mid-June to mid-Sept Mon–Sat 9am–6pm; mid-Sept to mid-June Mon 2–6pm, Tues–Fri

9.30am–12.30pm & 2–6pm, Sat 9.30am–1pm & 2–6pm; ⓣ02.33.77.60.35, ⓦwww.mairie-saint-lo.fr). Most of the **hotels**, restaurants and bars are across the river, near the **gare SNCF**. Overlooking the river from the brow of a ridge beside the station, the upmarket *logis Hôtel des Voyageurs*, 5–7 av Briovère (ⓣ02.33.05.08.63; ❺), is home to the *Tocqueville* **restaurant**, which serves a delicious trout soufflé on its €17 menu. If you'd rather be up in town, try *La Crémaillère*, 10 rue de la Chancellerie (ⓣ02.33.57.14.68; ❷; closed Fri evening & Sat).

The Vire Valley

Once St-Lô was taken in the Battle of Normandy, the armies speedily moved on southwestwards for their next confrontation. The **Vire Valley**, trailing south from St-Lô, saw little action – and its towns and villages seem to have been rarely touched by any historic or cultural mainstream. The motivation in coming to this landscape of rolling hills and occasional gorges is essentially to consume the region's cider, its Calvados (much of it bootleg), its fruit pastries, and its sausages made from pigs' intestines.

From St-Lô to Tessy

The best section of the valley is south of St-Lô through the Roches de Ham to Tessy-sur-Vire. The **Roches de Ham** are a pair of sheer rocky promontories high above the river. Though these are promoted as "viewing tables", the pleasure lies as much in the walk up, through lanes lined with blackberries, hazelnuts and rich orchards. Downstream from the Roches, and a good place to stop for the night, is **LA CHAPELLE-SUR-VIRE**. Its church, towering majestically above the river, has been an object of pilgrimage since the twelfth century. According to legend, in the Middle Ages a shepherd tending his flock noticed a lamb rooted to the spot; after digging he unearthed a statue of the Virgin Mary, since revered as a miraculous relic. Next to the bridge on the lower road is the *Auberge de la Chapelle* (ⓣ02.33.56.32.83; ❷), a good but rather expensive **restaurant** with a few cheap rooms. At **TESSY-SUR-VIRE**, 5km on, there's little to see other than the river itself, though the town has a luxurious campsite, along with a couple of hotels and a Wednesday market.

Vire

VIRE itself is worth visiting specifically for the **food**; in fact the one problem is what to do when you're not eating. The town is best known for its dreaded *andouille* sausages, but you can gorge yourself instead on salmon or trout fresh from the river, accompanied by local *poiré*. Choosing a **hotel**, it makes sense to go for one with a good dining room. At the central *Hôtel de France*, 4 rue d'Aignaux (ⓣ02.31.68.00.35; ❸), the €20 *menu du terroir* is packed with local specialities, including *andouillettes*, but always *tripes a là mode de Caen* instead. The *Hôtel des Voyageurs*, at the bottom of avenue de la Gare (ⓣ02.31.68.01.16; ❷), serves sumptuous buffets of hors d'oeuvres and desserts; you can sample both for €13.

Villedieu-les-Poêles

VILLEDIEU-LES-POÊLES – literally "City of God the Frying Pans" – is a lively though touristy place, 28km west of Vire. Copper souvenirs and kitchen utensils gleam from its rows of shops, and the tourist office has lists of dozens of local *ateliers* for more direct purchases, plus details of the copperwork museum.

All of this can seem a bit obsessive, though there is more authentic interest at the **Fonderie de Cloches** at 13 rue du Pont-Chignon, one of the twelve remaining bell foundries in Europe. Work here is only part-time as demand is limited, but it's open to visits all year round, and you may find the forge lit (July & Aug daily 9am–6pm; June & Sept Mon–Sat 9am–noon & 2–5.30pm, Sun 9.30am–noon & 2–5.30pm; Oct–May Tues–Sat 9am–noon & 2–5.30pm; €4). Expert craftsmen will show you the moulds, composed of an unpleasant-looking combination of clay, goat's hair and horse manure.

The local **tourist office** is on place des Costils (July & Aug daily 9am–6pm; Sept–June Tues–Sat 10am–noon & 2–6pm; ⓣ02.33.61.05.69, ⓔot.villedieu-les-poeles@wanadoo.fr). If you're charmed into staying, the welcoming *logis Hôtel St-Pierre et St-Michel*, 12 place de la République (ⓣ02.33.61.00.11, ⓦwww.st-pierre-hotel.com; ❸; closed Jan, plus Fri in low season), houses the stylish *Le Sourdin* restaurant, where the €20 menu features fine local ham, and the €32 menu is seriously gastronomic. There's also a three-star **campsite** by the river, *Jean-Louis Bougord* (ⓣ02.33.61.02.44; closed Oct–Easter).

Travel details

Trains

Through services to Paris connect with all ferries at Dieppe, Le Havre and Cherbourg: if you're doing this journey, it's easiest to buy a combined rail–ferry–rail ticket at your point of departure.

Alençon to: Caen (8 daily; 1hr 20min) via Sées (13min) and Argentan (30min); Tours (3 daily; 2hr 10min) via Le Mans (1hr).

Caen to: Cherbourg (10 daily; 1hr 15min) via Bayeux (20min) and Valognes (1hr); Lisieux (hourly; 30min); Le Mans (7 daily; 2hr) via Argentan (45min) and Alençon (1hr 15min); Paris-St-Lazare (at least hourly; 2hr 10min); Rennes (4 daily; 3hr) via Bayeux (20min), St-Lô (50min), Coutances (1hr 15min) and Pontorson (2hr); Rouen (6 daily; 2hr); Tours (3 daily; 3hr).

Cherbourg to: Paris (10 daily; 3hr) via Valognes (15min) and Caen (1hr 15min).

Dieppe to: Paris-St-Lazare (14 daily; 2hr 10min) via Rouen (14 daily; 50min).

Granville to: Coutances (7 daily; 30min).

Le Havre to: Paris (12 daily; 2hr 15min); Rouen (12 daily; 1hr).

Rouen to: Caen (9 daily; 2hr); Paris-St-Lazare (24 daily; 1hr 15min); Vernon (20 daily; 30min).

St-Lô to: Caen (4 daily; 50min) via Bayeux (30min); Rennes (4 daily; 2hr 10min) via Coutances (20min) and Pontorson (1hr 15min).

Trouville-Deauville to: Lisieux (6 daily in winter, much more frequently in summer; 20min); Paris (6 daily in winter, much more frequently in summer; 2hr).

Buses

Alençon to: Bagnoles (3 daily; 1hr); Bellême (1–2 daily; 1hr); Évreux (1 daily; 2hr) via L'Aigle (1hr 40min); Mortagne (1–3 daily; 1hr); Vimoutiers (1–3 daily; 1hr 30min) via Sées (30min).

Bayeux to: Arromanches (4 daily; 25min); Ouistreham (4 daily; 1hr 15min).

Caen to: Arromanches (1 daily; 1hr 10min); Bayeux (4 daily; 50min); Clécy (3–5 daily; 50min); Falaise (5–6 daily; 50min); Le Havre Honfleur (14 daily; 1hr 30min) via Cabourg (40min), Houlgate (55min) and Deauville (1hr 5min), of which 4 continue to Le Havre (2hr 30min); (2 daily bus #80 express services; 1hr 25min) via Honfleur (1hr); Ouistreham (20 daily; 30min); Pont L'Évêque (1–3 daily; 45min); Thury-Harcourt (3–5 daily; 40min).

Cherbourg to: St-Lô (2–3 daily; 1hr 30min); St-Vaast (2 daily; 1hr) via Barfleur (45min).

Dieppe to: Fécamp (4 daily; 2hr 20min); Le Havre (2 daily; 3hr 50min) via St-Valéry, Fécamp and Étretat; Le Tréport (3 daily; 30min); Paris (5 daily; 2hr 15min); St-Valéry (5 daily; 1hr).

Le Havre to: Caen (2 daily express services; 1hr 25min); Étretat (7 daily; 50min); Fécamp (7 daily; 1hr 30min); Honfleur (6 daily; 30min).

Mont St-Michel to: Rennes (6 daily; 1hr 20min); St-Malo (4 daily; 1hr 30min).

Rouen to: Dieppe (4 daily; 1hr 45min); Fécamp (2 daily; 2hr 30min); Le Havre (hourly; 2hr 45min) via Jumièges and Caudebec; Lisieux (2 daily; 2hr 30min); Le Tréport (2 daily; 2hr 30min).

St-Lô to: Bayeux (8 daily; 30min); Cherbourg (6 daily; 1hr 30min); Coutances (5 daily; 30min).

Ferries

Caen (Ouistreham) to: Portsmouth (2–3 daily; 4–6hr), with Brittany Ferries (Ⓣ08.25.82.88.28, Ⓦwww.brittany-ferries.com).
Cherbourg to: Poole (1–2 daily; 4hr 15min), with Brittany Ferries (see above); Portsmouth (5–6 daily; 2hr 45min to 4hr 45min), with P&O Ⓣ08.03.01.30.13, Ⓦwww.poferries.com); Rosslare (2–4 weekly; 17hr), with Irish Continental (Ⓣ02.33.23.44.44, Ⓦwww.irishferries.com).
Dieppe to: Newhaven with Hoverspeed (late March to Sept only, 1–3 daily; 2hr 15min; Ⓣ00800.1211.1211, Ⓦwww.hoverspeed.com) and Transmanche Ferries (2–3 daily; 4hr; Ⓣ08.00.65.01.00, Ⓦwww.transmancheferries.com).
Le Havre to: Portsmouth (3 daily; 5hr 30min) with P&O (see above).

5

Brittany

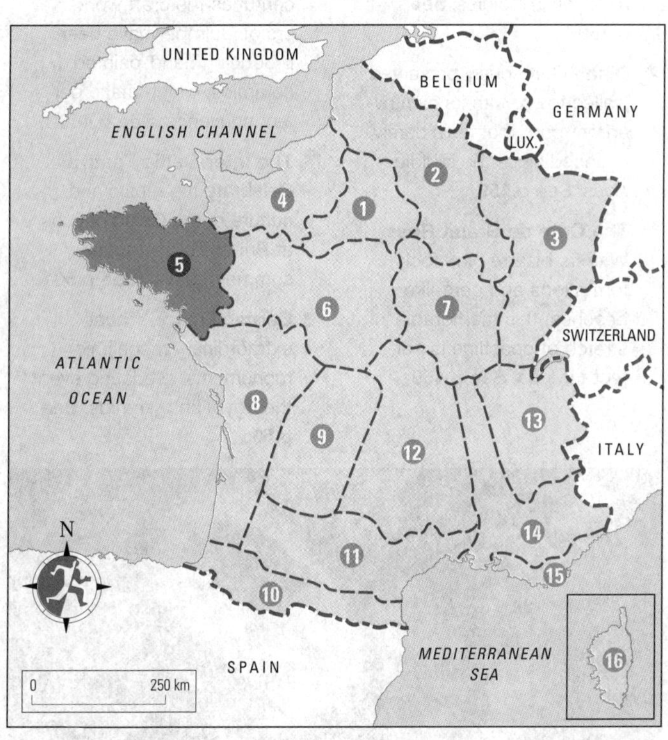
UNITED KINGDOM
BELGIUM
GERMANY
LUX.
ENGLISH CHANNEL
SWITZERLAND
ATLANTIC
OCEAN
ITALY
N
SPAIN
MEDITERRANEAN
SEA
0
250 km
1
2
3
4
5
6
7
8
9
10
11
12
13
14
15
16

CHAPTER 5

Highlights

* **Île de Sein** Misty and mysterious island, barely rising from the Atlantic, that makes a great day trip from western Finistère. **See p.487**
* **Cancale** If you love oysters, the stalls and restaurants in Cancale's little harbour will have you in raptures. **See p.459**
* **Dinan** Gorgeously preserved walled town, with its own riverfront port, that feels barely changed since the Middle Ages. **See p.459**
* **The Côte de Granit Rose** With its bizarre pink rock formations and gem-like beaches, this memorable stretch of coastline is perfect for kids. **See p.459**
* **Hôtel de la Baie des Trés-passés** Brittany holds no more romantic destination than this land's-end hotel, facing its own colossal beach in splendid isolation. **See p.469**
* **Faïence de Quimper** For centuries the craft workers of Quimper have been producing hand-painted ceramics, which make perfect souvenirs. **See p.488**
* **The Inter-Celtic Festival** Celebrate the music and culture of the Celtic nations at Brittany's best-loved summer festival. **See p.501**
* **Carnac** France's most extraordinary megalithic monuments, predating even the Egyptian pyramids. **See p.505**

△ Cancale oysters

5

Brittany

No one area – and certainly no one city or town – in **Brittany** encapsulates the character of the province; that lies in its people and in its geographical unity. For generations Bretons risked their lives fishing and trading on the violent seas and struggled with the arid soil of the interior. This toughness and resilience is tinged with **Celtic** culture: mystical, musical, sometimes morbid and defeatist, sometimes vital and inspired.

Though archeologically Brittany is one of the richest regions in the world – the alignments at **Carnac** rival Stonehenge – its first appearance in recorded history is as the quasi-mythical "Little Britain" of Arthurian legend. In the days when to travel by sea was safer and easier than by land, it was intimately connected with "Great Britain" across the water. Settlements such as St-Malo, St-Pol and Quimper were founded by Welsh and Irish missionary "saints" whose names are not to be found in any official breviary. Brittany remained **independent** until the sixteenth century, its last ruler, Duchess Anne, only managing to protect the province's autonomy through marriage to two consecutive French monarchs. After her death, in 1532, François I took her daughter and lands, and sealed the **union with France** with an act supposedly enshsining certain privileges. These included a veto over taxes by the local *parlement* and the people's right to be tried, or conscripted to fight, only in their province. The successive violations of this treaty by Paris, and subsequent revolts, form the core of Breton history since the Middle Ages.

As their language has been steadily eradicated, and the interior of the province severely depopulated, many Bretons continue to treat France as a separate country. Few, however, actively support Breton nationalism (which it's a criminal offence to advocate) much beyond putting *Breizh* (Breton for "Brittany") stickers on their cars. But there have been many successes in reviving the language, and the economic resurgence of the last three decades, helped partly by summer tourism, has largely been due to local initiatives, like Brittany Ferries re-establishing an old trading link, carrying produce and passengers across to Britain and Ireland. At the same time a Celtic artistic identity has consciously been revived, and local festivals – above all August's **Inter-Celtic Festival** at Lorient – celebrate traditional Breton music, poetry and dance, with fellow Celts treated as comrades.

If you're looking for traditional Breton fun, and you can't make the Lorient festival (or the smaller *Quinzaine Celtique* at Nantes in June/July), look out for gatherings organized by **Celtic folklore groups** – *Circles* or *Bagadou*. You may also be interested by the **pardons**, pilgrimage festivals commemorating local saints, which guidebooks (and tourist offices) tend to promote as exciting

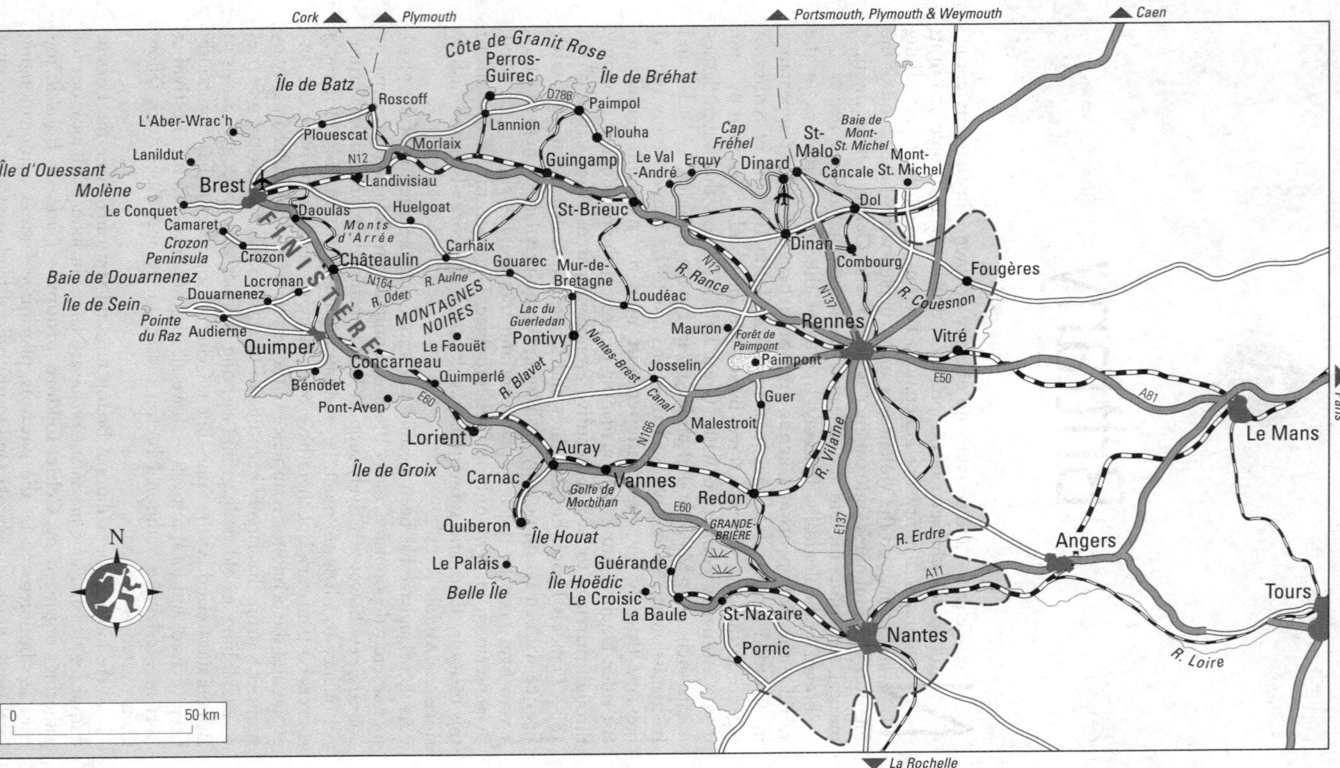
Cork
Plymouth
Portsmouth, Plymouth & Weymouth
Caen
Paris
La Rochelle
Côte de Granit Rose
Perros-Guirec
Île de Batz
Île de Bréhat
Roscoff
D786
Paimpol
L'Aber-Wrac'h
Plouescat
Lannion
Plouha
Lanildut
Morlaix
N12
Guingamp
Le Val-André
Erquy
Cap Fréhel
Dinard
St-Malo
Baie de Mont-St. Michel
Cancale
Mont-St. Michel
Île d'Ouessant
Molène
Brest
Landivisiau
St-Brieuc
Dol
Le Conquet
Daoulas
Huelgoat
Camaret
Monts d'Arrée
Crozon Peninsula
Crozon
FINISTÈRE
Carhaix
Dinan
Combourg
Châteaulin
Gouarec
Mur-de-Bretagne
N12
R. Rance
Fougères
Baie de Douarnenez
Locronan
N164
R. Aulne
N137
Douarnenez
R. Odet
MONTAGNES NOIRES
Loudéac
R. Couesnon
Île de Sein
Lac du Guerledan
Pointe du Raz
Audierne
Pontivy
Rennes
Mauron
Forêt de Paimpont
Vitré
Quimper
Le Faouët
Nantes-Brest
Paimpont
Concarneau
Josselin
E50
Quimperlé
R. Blavet
Canal
Bénodet
Guer
A81
Pont-Aven
E60
Malestroit
Lorient
N166
R. Vilaine
Le Mans
Auray
Île de Groix
Carnac
Vannes
Golfe de Morbihan
Redon
E60
E137
Quiberon
Île Houat
GRANDE-BRIÈRE
R. Erdre
Angers
N
Guérande
Le Palais
A11
Île Hoëdic
Belle Île
Le Croisic
Tours
La Baule
St-Nazaire
Nantes
Pornic
R. Loire
0
50 km

spectacles. In truth, unlike most French festivals, these are not phoney affairs kept alive for tourists, but deeply serious and rather gloomy religious occasions.

For most visitors, however, it is the Breton **coast** that is the dominant feature. Apart from the Côte d'Azur, this is the most popular summer resort area in France, for both French and foreign tourists. Its attractions are obvious: warm white-sand beaches, towering cliffs, rock formations and offshore islands and islets, and everywhere the stone dolmen and menhir monuments of a prehistoric past. The most frequented areas are the **Côte d'Émeraude** around **St-Malo**; the **Côte de Granit Rose** in the north; the **Crozon peninsula** in far western **Finistère** (Land's End); the family resorts such as **Bénodet** just to the south; and the **Morbihan coast** below **Vannes**. Accommodation and campsites here are plentiful, if pushed to their limits from mid-June to the end of August, and for all the crowds there are resorts as enticing as any in the country. Be aware, though, that out of season, many of the coastal resorts close down completely.

Food in Brittany

Brittany's proudest addition to the great cuisines of the world has to be the **crêpe** and its savoury equivalent the **galette**; crêperies throughout the region attempt to pass them off as satisfying meals, serving them with every imaginable filling. However, few people can plan their holidays specifically around eating pancakes, and gourmets are far more likely to be enticed to Brittany by its magnificent array of **seafood**. Restaurants in resorts such as St-Malo and Quiberon jostle for the attention of fish connoisseurs, while some smaller towns – like Cancale, which specializes in oysters (*huîtres*), and Erquy, with its scallops (*coquilles St-Jacques*) – depend wholly on one specific mollusc for their livelihood.

Although they can't quite claim to be uniquely Breton, two appetizers feature on every self-respecting menu. These are **moules marinières**, giant bowls of succulent orange mussels steamed open in a combination of white wine, shallots and parsley (and perhaps enriched by the addition of cream or *crème fraîche* to become *moules à la crème*), and **soupe de poissons** (fish soup), traditionally served with a little pot of the garlicky mayonnaise known as *rouille* (coloured by the addition of pulverized sweet red pepper), a mound of grated *gruyère*, and a bowl of croutons. Jars of freshly made *soupe de poissons* – or even crab or lobster – are always on sale in seaside *poissonneries*, and make an ideal way to take a taste of France home with you. Paying a bit more in a restaurant – typically on menus costing €25 or more – brings you into the realm of the **assiette de fruits de mer**, a mountainous heap of langoustines, crabs, oysters, mussels, clams, whelks and cockles, most of them raw and all delicious. **Main courses** tend to be plainer than in Normandy, for example, with fresh local fish being prepared with relatively simple sauces. Skate served with capers, or salmon baked with a mustard or cheese sauce, are typical dishes, while even the **cotriade**, a stew containing sole, turbot or bass, as well as shellfish, is distinctly less rich than its Mediterranean equivalent, the *bouillabaisse*. Brittany is also better than much of France in maintaining its respect for fresh green **vegetables**, thanks to the extensive local production of peas, cauliflowers, artichokes and the like. Only with the **desserts** can things get a little heavy; **for Breton**, considered a great delicacy, is a baked concoction of sponge and custard dotted with chopped plums, while *îles flottantes* are soft meringue icebergs adrift in a sea of *crème anglaise*, a light egg custard.

Strictly speaking, no **wine** is produced in Brittany itself. However, along the lower Loire valley, the *département* of Loire-Atlantique, centred on Nantes, is still generally regarded as "belonging" to Brittany – and is treated as such in this chapter. Vineyards here are responsible for the dry white Muscadet – which is what normally goes into *moules marinières* – and the even drier Gros-Plant.

Whenever you come, don't leave Brittany without visiting one of its scores of **islands** – such as the **Île de Bréhat**, the **Île de Sein**, or **Belle Île** – or taking in cities like **Quimper** or **Morlaix**, testimony to the riches of the medieval duchy. Allow time, too, to leave the coast and explore the interior, particularly the western country around the **Monts d'Arrée**, even if the price you pay for the solitude is sketchy transport and a shortage of hotels and campsites.

Eastern Brittany and the north coast

All roads in Brittany curl eventually inland to **Rennes**, the capital, which lies a short way northeast of the legendary **Forêt de Paimpont**, the location of the Arthurian tales. East of Rennes, the heavily fortified citadels of **Fougères** and **Vitré** protected the eastern approaches to medieval Brittany, which was obliged vigorously to defend its independence against incursors. Along the north coast, west of Normandy's Mont St-Michel, stand some of Brittany's finest old towns. One of the most spectacular introductions to the province is that which greets ferry passengers from Portsmouth: the **River Rance**, guarded by magnificently preserved **St-Malo** on its estuary, and beautiful medieval **Dinan** 20km upstream. Further west stretches a varied coastline that culminates in one of the most seductive of the islands, the **Île de Bréhat**, and the colourful chaos of the **Côte de Granit Rose**.

Rennes and around

For a city that has been the capital and power centre of Brittany since the 1532 union with France, **RENNES** is – outwardly at least – uncharacteristic of the province, with its Neoclassical layout and pompous major buildings. What potential it had to be a picturesque tourist spot was destroyed in 1720, when a drunken carpenter managed to set light to virtually the whole city. Only the area known as **Les Lices**, at the junction of the canalized Ille and the River Vilaine, was undamaged. The remodelling of the rest of the city was handed over to Parisian architects, not in deference to the capital but in an attempt to rival it. The result, on the north side of the river at any rate, is something of a patchwork quilt, consisting of grand eighteenth-century public squares interspersed with intimate little alleys of half-timbered houses. It's quite a pleasant city to stroll around for half a day, but it lacks a cohesive personality.

Arrival, information and accommodation

Rennes' **gare SNCF** (Ⓣ08.36.35.35.35) is south of the Vilaine, twenty minutes' walk from the tourist office and a little more from the medieval quarter.

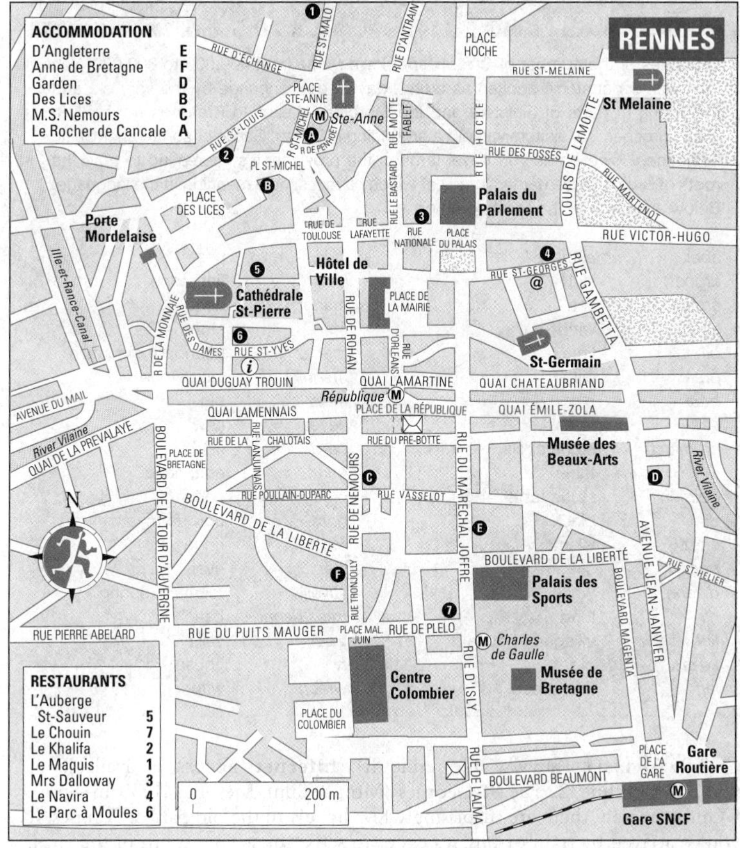

The **gare routière** stands alongside on boulevard Solferino, but most local buses start and finish by the canal in the heart of town, on or near place de la République. Rennes is a busy junction, with direct services to St-Malo (TIV; ⓣ02.99.79.23.44), Dinan and Dinard (Armor Express; ⓣ02.99.50.64.17), and Nantes (Société Transports Tourisme de l'Ouest; ⓣ02.40.20.45.20). Les Courriers Bretons (ⓣ02.99.30.87.80; ⓦwww.lescourriersbretons.fr) run regular services to **Mont St-Michel** (€22 return) from the *gare routière*, timed to connect with arriving TGVs from Paris.

Rennes has a fast, efficient and ultra-clean new **Métro** system (VAL) (Mon–Sat 5–0.45am, Sun 7.15–0.45am); the most useful stops for tourists are at the *gare SNCF*, the place de la République and the place Ste-Anne. Any one-way journey costs €1, or you can ride all day for €3, and all week for €9.20. Alternatively, the town council provides **free bikes** for visitors –up to seven hours on receipt of a €80 deposit – from a kiosk on the quai Duguay-Trouin in the central place de la République (daily 9am–7pm; ⓣ02.96.79.63.72).

The **tourist office** stands in a disused church, the Chapelle St-Yves, just north of the river at 11 rue St-Yves (April–Sept Mon–Sat 9am–7pm, Sun 11am–6pm; Oct–March Mon–Sat 9am–6pm, Sun 11am–6pm;

A Breton glossary

Estimates of the number of **Breton-speakers** range from 400,000 to 800,000. You may well encounter it spoken as a first, day-to-day language by the very old and the young in parts of Finistère and the Morbihan. Learning Breton is not really a viable prospect for visitors without a grounding in Welsh, Gaelic or some other Celtic language. However, as you travel through the province, it's interesting to note the roots of Breton place names, many of which have a simple meaning in the language. Below are some of the most common:

aber	estuary	*lann*	heath
argoat	land	*lech*	flat stone
armor	sea	*mario*	dead
avel	wind	*men*	stone
bihan	little	*menez*	(rounded) mountain
bran	hill	*menhir*	long stone
braz	big	*meur*	big
coat	forest	*nevez*	new
cromlech	stone circle	*parc*	field
dol	table	*penn*	end, head
dolmen	stone table	*plou*	parish
du	black	*pors*	port, farmyard
enez	island	*roc'h*	ridge
goaz	stream	*ster*	river
gwenn	white	*stivel*	fountain, spring
hir	long	*traez henn*	beach
ker	village or house	*trou*	valley
kozh	old	*ty*	house
lan	holy place	*wrach*	witch

ⓣ02.99.67.11.11, ⓦwww.ville-rennes.fr). **Internet access** is available at Cybernet Online, 22 rue St-Georges (Mon 2–8pm, Tues–Fri 10.30am–8pm).

Unfortunately, there are surprisingly few **hotels** in the old part of Rennes. If you've arrived by train or bus, it's easier to settle for staying south of the river, near the *gares SNCF* and *routière*. Contact the tourist office if you plan to spend the weekend here; under the **Bon Week-end scheme**, you can get two nights' accommodation for the price of one.

Hotels

D'Angleterre 19 rue du Maréchal-Joffre ⓣ02.99.79.38.61, ⓕ02.99.79.43.85. Unexceptional, but cheap and scrupulously maintained hotel a short way south of the river. ❸

Anne de Bretagne 12 rue de Tronjolly ⓣ02.99.31.49.49, ⓕ02.99.30.53.48. Although housed in a nondescript modern building in an equally mundane neighbourhood, inside this hotel is quiet, bright and understatedly trendy, with spacious, smart rooms and shiny new bathrooms. ❻

Garden 3 rue Duhamel ⓣ02.99.65.45.06, ⓕ02.99.65.02.62. Comfortable, nicely decorated and very personal *logis de France*, north of the *gare SNCF* not far from the river, with a pleasant little garden café. ❹

Des Lices 7 place des Lices ⓣ02.99.79.14.81, ⓦwww.hotel-des-lices.com. Forty-five rooms, all with TV, in a very comfortable and friendly modern hotel on the edge of the prettiest part of old Rennes, handy for the place des Lices car park. ❹

M.S. Nemours 5 rue de Nemours ⓣ02.99.78.26.26, ⓦwww.hotelnemours.com. Idiosyncratic nautical-themed hotel south of the river, where all the en-suite rooms are spick and span, and "Commandant Chappey" and his crew say "welcome aboard". ❸

Le Rocher de Cancale 10 rue St-Michel ⓣ02.99.79.20.83. Beautifully restored four-room hotel with modern facilities on a lively pedestrian street, between place Ste-Anne and place

St-Michel, in the heart of medieval Rennes. The restaurant, closed at weekends, has lunch menus from €9, dinners from €14; the €20 exclusively fish menu is excellent. ❸

Hostel and campsite

Centre International de Séjour 10–12 Canal St-Martin ⓣ02.99.33.22.33, ⓔrennes@fuaj.org. Welcoming, attractively positioned HI hostel, 3km north of the centre beside the Canal d'Ille et Rance. Charging €13.55 per person per night for a dorm bed, or €34 for a private double, it has a cafeteria and a laundry, and operates a midnight curfew; membership of a hostelling association is compulsory. Buses #20 and #22 run weekdays only from the *gare SNCF*, direction "St-Gregoire", stop "Coëtlogon"; at weekends catch bus #18. Open all year.

Camping Municipal des Gayeulles, rue de Professeur-Maurice-Audin ⓣ02.99.36.91.22. An appealingly verdant site 1km east of central Rennes; take bus #3. Closed Nov–March.

The City

Rennes' surviving **medieval quarter**, bordered by the canal to the west and the river to the south, radiates from **Porte Mordelaise**, the old ceremonial entrance to the city. Just to the northeast of the *porte*, the **place des Lices** is dominated by two usually empty market halls but comes alive every Saturday for one of France's largest **street markets**. The place was originally the venue for jousting tournaments, and it was on this spot in 1337 that the hitherto unknown Bertrand du Guesclin, then aged 17, fought and defeated several older opponents. This set him on his career as a soldier, during which he was to save Rennes when it was under siege by the English. However, after the Bretons were defeated at Auray in 1364, he fought for the French, and twice invaded Brittany.

The one central building to escape the 1720 fire was the **Palais du Parlement** (Mon–Sat 9am–7pm, Sun 11am–6pm; €6.10; guided visits at given times on given days - consult the tourist office) on rue Hoche downtown. Ironically, however, the Palais was all but ruined by a major conflagration in 1994, thought to have been sparked by a stray flare set off during a demonstration by Breton fishermen. Since then, the entire structure has been rebuilt and restored, including the opulent interior, and is once more topped by an impressive array of gleaming gilded statues.

If you head south from the Palais, you'll soon reach the **River Vilaine**, which flows through the centre of Rennes, narrowly confined into a steep-sided channel. The south bank of the river is every bit as busy, if not busier, than the north, with a former university building at 20 quai Émile-Zola housing the **Musée des Beaux-Arts** (daily except Tues 10am–noon & 2–6pm; €4). Unfortunately many of its finest artworks – which include drawings by Leonardo da Vinci, Botticelli, Fra Lippo Lippi and Dürer – are not usually on public display. Instead you'll find a number of indifferent Impressionist views of Normandy by the likes of Boudin and Sisley, interspersed with the occasional treasure such as Pieter Boel's startlingly contemporary-looking seventeenth-century animal studies, and Pierre-Paul Rubens' *Tiger Hunt*, enlivened by the occasional lion.

Heading south away from the river, **rue Vasselot** has its own array of half-timbered old houses, while the **Centre Colombier**, just west of the *gare SNCF*, is Rennes at its most modern – a mall packed with shops of all kinds, plus cafés and snack bars, and featuring an amazing crystal model of itself in its main entrance hall. Immediately to its east, in a shiny, purpose-built structure near the Charles de Gaulle metro station, the relocated **Musée de Bretagne** (ⓦwww.musee-bretagne.fr), covering the history and culture of Brittany, is due to open in November 2005.

Eating and drinking

Most of Rennes' more interesting bars and **restaurants** are to be found in the streets just south of the **place Ste-Anne**, towards the place des Lices. Rues St-Michel and Penhoët, each with a fine assemblage of ancient wooden buildings, are the epicentre at the moment. Ethnic alternatives are concentrated along **rue St-Malo** just to the north, and also on **rue St-Georges** near the place du Palais. Rue Vasselot is the nearest equivalent south of the river, though if you're just looking for a quick snack, don't forget the various outlets in the Centre Colombier.

One of the city's favourite **bars** is the *Barantic* at 4 rue St-Michel, which puts on occasional live music for a mixed crowd of Breton nationalists and boisterous students; if you don't like the look of it, or it's too full, there are half a dozen similar alternatives within spitting distance. Live **jazz** gigs take place twice weekly at *Déjazey Jazz Club*, 54 rue St-Malo (☎02.99.38.70.72; closed Sun).

L'Auberge St-Sauveur 6 rue St-Sauveur ☎02.99.79.32.56. Classy, romantic restaurant, in a medieval house near the cathedral, with meaty dinner menus between €18 and €50, and lighter lunches for €12. Closed for lunch on Sat & Mon, & all day Sun.

Le Chouin 12 rue d'Isly ☎02.99.30.87.86. A fine fish restaurant, a little north of the Centre Colombier towards the river. A set lunch costs €13, while both the €16 and €21 dinner menus include nine oysters to start. Closed Sun evening & Mon, plus first two weeks of Aug.

Le Khalifa 20 haut de la place des Lices ☎02.99.30.87.30. Assorted Moroccan dishes, served outside or in an atmospheric dining room. Couscous and *brochettes* €10 and up, tagine €11.50, as well as various set menus. Closed Mon.

Le Maquis 13 rue St-Malo ☎02.99.63.83.06. Lively, friendly African restaurant, north of Ste-Anne church, serving Senegalese marinated chicken and fish dishes for around €9, plus Cameroonian beef stew. Tues–Sun for dinner only, until late.

Mrs Dalloway 5 rue Nationale ☎02.99.79.27.27. Eccentric English tearooms in the heart of the city, serving teacakes, boiled eggs and pies, plus salads and savoury tarts. Open Tues–Sat noon–6pm, closed late July to late Aug.

Le Navira 39 rue St-Georges ☎02.99.38.88.90. Simple, friendly French restaurant with outdoor seating on a busy semi-pedestrian alley east of the Palais du Parlement, offering good-value lunch (€15) and dinner (€20) menus. Closed Sun.

Le Parc à Moules 8 rue Georges-Dottin ☎02.99.31.44.28. On a small street north from the river, near the tourist office, this place has mussels cooked in 32 different delicious ways for €8 at lunch, with *frites* €2.50 extra, or from €9 to €15 later on, plus more expensive fishy dishes. Closed Sun lunch & Tues.

Festivals and theatre

Rennes is seen at its best in the first ten days of July, when the **Festival des Tombées de la Nuit** takes over the whole city to celebrate Breton culture with music, theatre, film, mime and poetry (information from the tourist office). In the first week of December, the **Transmusicales** rock festival attracts big-name acts from all over France and the world at large, though still with a Breton emphasis (☎02.99.31.12.10). The **Théâtre National de Bretagne**, 1 rue St-Helier (☎02.99.31.12.31), puts on varied events throughout the year, except in August. All year round, in a different auditorium on the same premises, *Club Ubu* (☎02.99.31.12.00) puts on large-scale gigs.

The Forêt de Paimpont

Thirty kilometres west of Rennes, the **Forêt de Paimpont**, known also by its ancient name of Brocéliande, is – according to song and legend – the forest of the wizard Merlin. Medieval Breton minstrels, like their Welsh counterparts, set the tales of King Arthur and the Holy Grail both in Grande Bretagne and here in Petite Bretagne. For all the magic of these shared legends, however, and a succession of likely sites, few people come out here.

Roaming around for a day is easy, with **MAURON**, reachable by bus from Rennes, making a good place to start. From the hamlet of Folle Pensée, just south of Mauron, it's a circuitous but enjoyable twenty-minute walk to La **Fontaine de Barenton** – Merlin's spring. The path leads off from the end of the road at Folle Pensée, turning to the right, running through pines and gorse to a junction of forest tracks: here, take the track straight ahead for about 100m, where an unobvious path to the left goes into the woods and turns back north to the spring – walled, and filled by the most delicious water imaginable. After drinking, stroke the great stone slab beside the spring to call up a storm, roaring lions and a horseman in black armour. Here Merlin first set eyes on Vivianne, who bound him willingly in a prison of air.

The Fountain of Eternal Youth is hidden nearby and accessible only to the pure in heart. Another forest walk, more scenic but without a goal, is the **Val sans Retour** (the Valley of No Return), off the GR37 from Tréhorenteuc to La Guette. The path to follow leads out from the D141 just south of Tréhorenteuc to a steep valley from which exits are barred by thickets of gorse and giant furze on the rocks above; at one point it skirts an overgrown table of rock, the **Rocher des Faux Amants** (Rock of the False Lovers), from which the seductress Morgane le Fay supposedly enticed unwary boys.

Practicalities

The **bus** from Rennes to Guer runs twice a day past the southern edge of the forest, stopping at Forges-les-Paimpont, while another bus runs around the north corner to Mauron – again twice a day. Information on the forest can be picked up from the **tourist office** next to the lakeside abbey in the little market village of **PAIMPONT** (March–May Tues–Sun 10am–noon & 2–5pm; June–Sept daily 10am–noon & 2–6pm; ⓣ02.99.07.84.23). Paimpont is the most obvious and enjoyable base for exploring the forest: it's right at the centre of the woods, backs onto a marshy lake whose shores are thick with wild mushrooms (*cèpes*), and has some excellent **accommodation**. At the *Relais de Brocéliande* in town (ⓣ02.99.07.84.94; ⓦwww.le-relais-de-broceliande.fr; ❸), a real flower-bedecked delight, you can fill up for €23.50, or much more, in the restaurant under the gaze of stuffed animal heads. There's also a two-star municipal **campsite** on the edge of the village (ⓣ02.97.07.89.16; closed Oct–April). Other accommodation in the forest includes a *gîte d'étape*-cum-*chambre d'hôte* in tiny Trudeau on the D40 (ⓣ02.99.07.81.40; dorm beds €8.80, B&B ❸) and a lovely **hostel**, at Le Choucan-en-Brocéliande, a couple of kilometres out on the Concoret road (ⓣ02.97.22.76.75; dorm beds €7.90; closed mid-Sept to end May).

The frontier towns

If you're entering Brittany by road from Normandy, Maine or Le Mans, you're likely to pass through or close to **Fougères, Vitré and Dol-de-Bretagne**, all of which were, at one time or another, heavily fortified strategic sites.

Fougères and its forest

The topography of **FOUGÈRES**, which lies on the main Caen–Rennes road, is impossible to grasp from a map; streets that look a few metres long turn out to be precipitous plunges down the escarpments of its split-levelled site, and lanes collapse into flights of steps. The dominant feature is the town's robust **château**, built well below the level of the main part of town, on a low spit of land that separates, and is towered over by, two mighty rock faces. Its massive and seemingly impregnable bulk is protected by great curtain walls growing out of the rock, and encircled by a hacked-out moat full of weirs and waterfalls – none of which prevented its repeated capture by such medieval adventurers as du Guesclin.

The best approach to the castle is from place des Arbres beside St-Léonard's church off the main street of the old fortified town. Footpaths, ramps and stairways drop down through successive tiers of formal public gardens, offering magnificent views of the ramparts and towers along the way, to reach the water meadows of the River Nançon, which you cross beside a little cluster of medieval houses still standing on the river bank. Sadly, however, the interior of the château fails to live up to its compelling exterior; instead the hourly **château tours** place a rather deadening emphasis on the local shoe industry (daily: April to mid-June & last two weeks of Sept 9.30am–noon & 2–6pm; mid-June to mid-Sept 9am–7pm; Oct–March 10am–noon & 2–5pm; closed Jan; €3.55).

The **Forêt de Fougères**, a short way out on the D177 towards Vire (served by the twice daily buses to Vire), is one of the most enjoyable in the province. The beech woods are spacious and light, with various megaliths and trails of old stones scattered in among the chestnut and spruce. It's quite a contrast to their normal bleak and windswept haunts to see dolmens sporting themselves in such verdant surroundings.

Fougères' **tourist office**, at 1 place Aristide-Briand, provides copious information on all aspects of the town and local countryside (July & Aug Mon–Sat 9am–7pm, Sun 2–4pm; Sept–June Mon–Sat 9.30am–12.30pm & 2–6pm, Sun 1.30–5.30pm; Ⓣ02.99.94.12.20, Ⓦwww.ot-fougeres.fr). The *Hôtel des Voyageurs*, nearby at 10 place Gambetta (Ⓣ02.99.99.08.20, Ⓦwww.hotel-voyageurs-fougeres.com; ❸; closed second fortnight of Aug) is a particularly nice **place to stay**, with a separate but excellent **restaurant** downstairs (closed Sat lunch & Sun dinner). There are no hotels in the immediate vicinity of the château, but the squares on all sides are crammed with an abundance of appealing **bars** and **crêperies**. At *Le Medieval* (Ⓣ02.99.94.92.59), which has lots of outdoor seating beside the moat, you can snack on *moules-frites* or crêpes, or get a full dinner from €13.50.

Vitré

VITRÉ, just north of the Le Mans–Rennes motorway, rivals Dinan as the best-preserved medieval town in Brittany. While its walls are not quite complete, the thickets of medieval stone cottages that lie outside them have hardly changed. The towers of the **castle**, which dominates the western end of the ramparts, have pointed slate-grey roofs in best fairy-tale fashion, looking like freshly sharpened pencils, but sadly the municipal offices and **museum** of shells, birds, bugs and local history inside are not exactly thrilling (April–June & Sept daily 10am–noon & 2–5.30pm; July & Aug daily 10am–6pm; Oct–March Mon, Sat & Sun 2–5.30pm, Wed–Fri 10am–noon & 2–5.30pm; €4).

Vitré is a market town rather than an industrial centre, with its principal **market** held on Mondays in the square in front of **Notre-Dame church**. The old city is full of twisting streets of half-timbered houses, a good proportion of which are bars – **rue Beaudrairie** in particular has a fine selection.

Vitré's **gare SNCF** is a little way south of the centre, where the ramparts have disappeared and the town blends into its newer sectors. Just across the square from the station you'll find the **tourist office** (July & Aug daily 9am–7pm; Sept–June Mon–Fri 9.30am–noon & 1.30–5.30pm, Sat 10am–noon; ⓣ02.99.75.04.46, ⓦwww.ot-vitre.fr), and most of the **hotels** too. The *Petit-Billot*, 5bis place du Général-Leclerc (ⓣ02.99.75.02.10, ⓦwww.petit-billot.com; ❸), is good value, while rooms on the higher floors of the *Hôtel du Château*, 5 rue Rallon (ⓣ02.99.74.58.59; ❸; closed Sun out of season), on a quiet road just below the castle, have views of the ramparts. Of the town's **restaurants**, *Le St-Yves*, immediately below the castle at 1 place St-Yves (ⓣ02.99.74.68.76; closed Mon), serves menus from €9 to €29 (the €13.50 one should suit most requirements), and *La Soupe aux Choux*, at the top of rue de la Baudrairie at 32 rue Notre-Dame (ⓣ02.99.75.10.86; closed Sun in low season), prepares simple but classic French food.

Dol-de-Bretagne and around

During the Middle Ages, **DOL-DE-BRETAGNE**, 30km west of Mont St-Michel, was an important bishopric. It no longer has a bishop, though its huge granite **cathedral** endures, with its strange, squat, tiled towers. The ambitious new **CathédralOscope** (April–Oct daily 10am–7pm; rest of the year consult tourist office; €7.50), in the cathedral square, sets out to explain the construction and significance of medieval cathedrals in general, but for all its high-tech presentation and flair, non-French-speakers may well find it rather heavy going. Also in the square, the more traditional **Musée Historique de Dol** (Easter–Sept daily 2–6pm; €2) holds two rooms of astonishing wooden bits and pieces rescued in assorted states of decay from churches, often equally rotten, all over Brittany.

Dol still has a few streets packed with venerable buildings, most notably its central axis, the pretty **Grande-Rue**, where one Romanesque edifice dates back as far as the eleventh century, alongside an assortment of 500-year-old half-timbered houses that look down on the bustle of shoppers below.

All approaches to Dol from the bay are guarded by the former island of **Mont Dol**, now eight rather marshy kilometres in from the sea. This abrupt granite outcrop, looking mountainous beyond its size on such a flat plain, was the legendary site of a battle between the Archangel Michael and the Devil. Various fancifully named indentations in the rock, such as the "Devil's Claw", testify to the savagery of their encounter, which as usual the Devil lost. The site has been occupied since prehistoric times – flint implements have been unearthed alongside the bones of mammoths, sabre-toothed tigers and even rhinoceroses. Later on, it appears to have been used for worship by the druids, before becoming, like Mont St-Michel, an island monastery, all traces of which have long vanished. A plaque proclaims that visiting the small chapel on top earns a papal indulgence. The climb is pleasant too, a steep footpath winding up among the chestnuts and beeches to a solitary bar.

There's not a great deal to keep casual visitors in Dol for very long. However, the **tourist office**, at 3 Grande-Rue (July & Aug daily 10am–7.30pm; Sept–June Mon 2–6pm, Tues–Sat 10am–12.30pm & 2–6pm; ⓣ02.99.48.15.37, ⓦwww.pays-de-dol.com), can direct you eastwards to a reasonable **hotel**, the *Bretagne*, next to the market at 17 place Chateaubriand (ⓣ02.99.48.02.03; ❶; closed Oct), where rooms at the back look out across a vestige of ramparts towards Mont Dol; menus vary from €14 to €27. The best **campsite** in the area is the luxurious *Castel-Camping des Ormes* (ⓣ02.99.73.53.00, ⓦwww.lesormes.com; closed mid-Sept to April), set around a lake 6km south towards Combourg on the N795, which offers horse-riding, golf and even cricket.

A couple of nice **fish restaurants** stand opposite each other in the ancient houses on rue Ceinte, as it winds its way from Grande-Rue to the Cathedral: *Le Porche au Pain* at no. 1, and *La Grabotais* at no. 4 (Ⓣ02.99.48.19.89; closed Mon).

St-Malo and around

Walled and built with the same grey granite stone as Mont St-Michel, **ST-MALO** was originally in the Middle Ages a fortified island at the mouth of the Rance, controlling not only the estuary but the open sea beyond. The promontory fort of Alet, south of the modern centre in what's now the St-Servan district, commanded approaches to the Rance even before the Romans, but modern St-Malo traces its origins to a monastic settlement founded by saints Aaron and Brendan early in the sixth century. In later centuries it became notorious as the home of a fierce breed of pirate-mariners, who were never quite under anybody's control but their own; for four years from 1590, St-Malo even declared itself to be an independent republic. The *corsaires* of St-Malo not only forced English ships passing up the Channel to pay tribute, but also brought wealth from further afield. **Jacques Cartier**, who colonized Canada, lived in and sailed from St-Malo, as did the first colonists to settle the Falklands – hence the islands' Argentine name, Las Malvinas, from the French *Malouins*.

Now inseparably attached to the mainland, St-Malo is the most visited place in Brittany, thanks more to its superb old **citadelle** than to the ferry terminal that's tucked into the harbour behind. From outside the walls, the dignified ensemble of the old city might seem stern and forbidding, but passing through into the streets within the walls brings you into a busy, lively and very characterful town, packed with hotels, restaurants, bars and shops. Though the summer crowds can be oppressive, a stroll atop the ramparts should restore your equilibrium, and the presence of vast, clean beaches right on the city's doorstep is a big bonus if you're travelling with kids in tow. Having to spend a night here before or after a ferry crossing is a positive pleasure – so long as you take the trouble to reserve accommodation in advance.

Arrival and information

Though almost all St-Malo buses, whether local or long-distance, coincide also with trains at the **gare SNCF** – 2km out from the citadelle on place Hermine, and convenient neither for the old town nor the ferry – the **gare routière** is officially an expanse of concrete right next to the tourist office. The two main local bus companies both have ticket offices here: the Compagnie de Transport d'Ille et Vilaine (TIV; Ⓣ02.99.40.82.67), which runs services to Dinard, Dinan, Cancale, Combourg and Rennes, and Les Courriers Bretons (Ⓣ02.99.19.70.70, Ⓦwww.lescourriersbretons.fr), which goes to Cancale, Mont St-Michel, Dol, Rennes and Fougères, and also runs **day-trips to Mont St-Michel** (April–June, Sept & Oct Tues–Thurs & Sat; July & Aug Tues–Sat, €18.40).

St-Malo is always busy with **boats**. Summer ferries from Portsmouth, Weymouth (via Guernsey) and Poole arrive at the **Terminal Ferry du Naye** (Ⓣ02.99.40.64.41), a few hundred metres' walk from the old town. Between April and early November, regular passenger **ferries to Dinard** operate from the **quai Dinan**, in front of the port (Compagnie Corsaire; Ⓣ08.25.16.80.35, Ⓦwww.compagniecorsaire.com; €3.70 single, €5.90

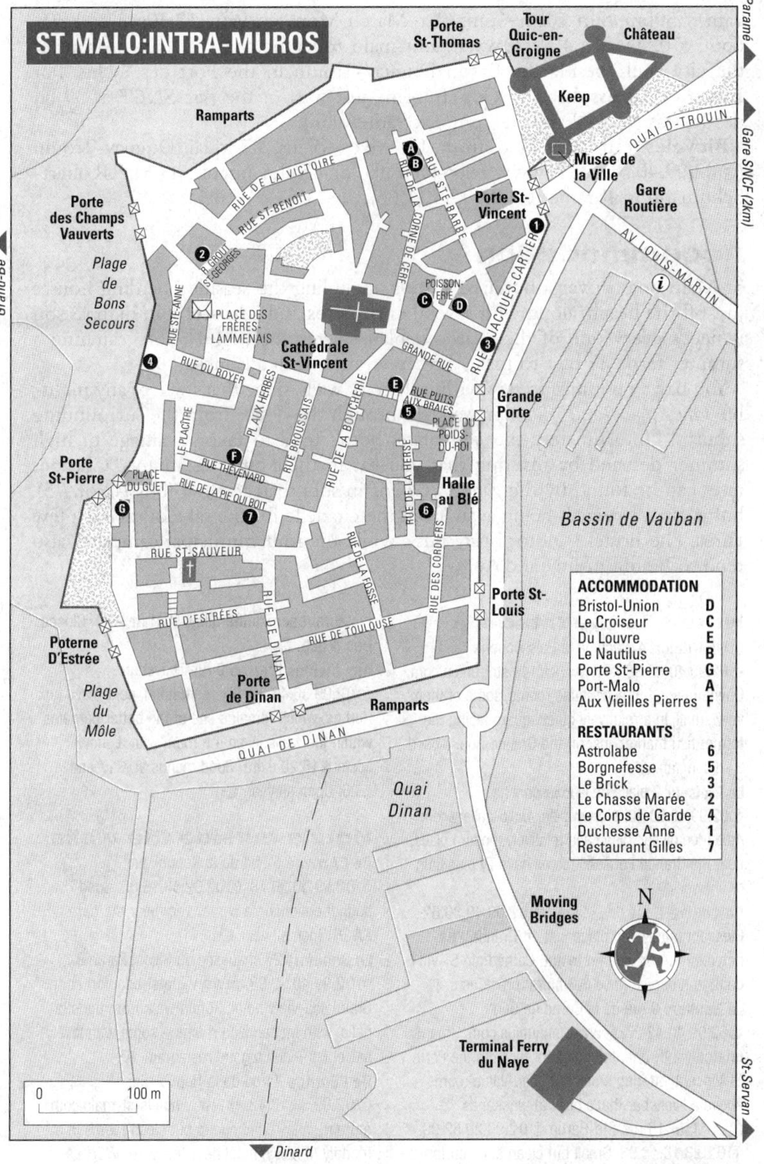

return, bikes €4.50 each way); the trip across the estuary takes an all-too-short ten minutes. Ask at the tourist office for details of excursions up the river to Dinan, day-trips to and from Granville in Normandy, and cruises along the Brittany coast.

St-Malo's helpful **tourist office** (April–June & Sept Mon–Sat 9am–12.30pm & 1.30–6.30pm, Sun 10am–12.30pm & 2.30–6pm; July & Aug Mon–Sat

9am–7.30pm, Sun 10am–6pm; Oct–March Mon–Sat 9am–12.30pm & 1.30–6pm; ⓣ02.99.56.64.48, ⓦwww.saint-malo-tourisme.com) is right in front of the city walls, beside the Bassin Duguay-Trouin in the Port des Yachts. For **Internet access**, head to Cop' Imprim, just west of the *gare SNCF* at 39 bd des Talards (Mon–Fri 9am–7pm, Sat 9am–noon).

Bicycles can be rented from Les Velos Bleus, 47 quai Duguay-Trouin (ⓣ02.99.40.31.63, ⓦwww.velos-bleus.fr), or Cycles Nicole, 11 rue Robert-Schumann in Paramé (ⓣ02.99.56.11.06).

Accommodation

St-Malo boasts over a hundred **hotels**, including the seaside boarding houses just off the beach, along with several **campsites** and a **hostel** – in high season it needs every one of them. If you plan to stay the night before catching a summer ferry, it's best to make a reservation well in advance.

You pay a premium to stay within the city walls, since that's where any night-life takes place, and it's a fair walk in through the docks from the surrounding suburbs. Unfortunately, the *intra-muros* hotels tend to take advantage of high summer demand by insisting that you eat in their own restaurants. Cheaper rates can be found by the *gare SNCF*, or in suburban Paramé (bus #2 or #5), but it's hardly worth being away from the citadelle for the sake of saving a few euros. The hostel is notoriously busy, while the four municipal campsites also tend to be full in July and August.

Hotels in the citadelle

Bristol-Union 4 place de la Poissonnerie ⓣ02.99.40.83.36, ⓦwww.hotel-bristol-union.com. Unenthralling but acceptable rooms, some of them very small, in a relatively quiet square facing the former fish market, just off the Grande Rue. Closed 3 wks in Jan. ❸

Le Croiseur 2 place de la Poissonnerie ⓣ02.99.40.80.40, ⓦwww.saint-malo-gallery.com/hotel-lecroiseur. Clean and relatively modern place, near the Grande Porte. All rooms have TV plus bath or shower. ❷

Du Louvre 2 rue des Marins ⓣ02.99.40.86.62. Pleasant family-run place just off Grande Rue, between the Grande Porte and Cathédrale St-Vincent, that serves good €7 buffet breakfasts. ❺

Le Nautilus 9 rue de la Corne de Cerf ⓣ02.99.40.42.27, ⓦwww.lenautilus.com. Smartly refitted youth-oriented hotel not far from the Porte St-Vincent, offering small but good-value rooms above a lively bar that's busy at weekends. ❹

Port-Malo 15 rue Ste-Barbe ⓣ02.99.20.52.99, ⓕ02.23.18.48.93. Small but clean and comfortable en-suite rooms – above a nice old-fashioned bar, so go for the higher floors – with friendly and helpful management. No restaurant. ❷

Porte St-Pierre 2 place du Guet ⓣ02.99.40.91.27, ⓕ02.99.56.09.94. Comfortable *logis de France*, peeping out to sea over the walls of the citadelle, near the small Porte St-Pierre. Dinner menus, in the separate restaurant across the alley, start at €24. Closed Dec & Jan. ❹

Aux Vieilles Pierres 9 rue Thévenard ⓣ02.99.56.46.80. Six-room hotel, near place aux Herbes, which remains one of the better bargains within the walls, even if a room with a shower costs €15.20 extra. Good menus at €17 and €26. Open all year. ❸

Hotels outside the walls

De l'Arrivée 52 bd de la République ⓣ02.99.56.30.78, ⓕ02.99.56.16.05. Good budget option, on a corner very near the *gare SNCF*. Open all year. ❷

Le Beaufort 25 chaussée du Sillon, Paramé ⓣ02.99.40.99.99, ⓦwww.hotel-beaufort.com. Grand sea-view hotel, 30min walk from the citadelle, with modernized rooms – some with lovely balconies – and a good restaurant. ❺

De l'Europe 44 bd de la République ⓣ02.99.56.13.42, ⓦwww.hotels-st-malo.com/europe. Year-round cheap but clean rooms in a friendly (if noisy) hotel near the *gare SNCF*. ❶

La Rance 15 quai Sébastopol, St-Servan ⓣ02.99.81.78.63, ⓔhotel-la-rance@wanadoo.fr. Small, tasteful option in sight of the Tour Solidor, with eleven spacious rooms. ❹

Hostel and campsites

Centre Patrick Varangot 37 av du Père-Umbricht, Paramé ⓣ02.99.40.29.80,

ⓦwww.centrevarangot.com. Dominated as a rule by lively young travellers, this is one of France's busiest hostels, 2km northeast of the *gare SNCF* in the suburb of Paramé, not far from the beach. Dorm bed €11.40, private doubles €30.40; hostelling association membership required. Rates include breakfast, and there's also a cut-price cafeteria, as well as kitchen facilities and tennis courts. No curfew, open all year.

La Cité d'Aleth St-Servan ⓣ02.99.81.60.91. The nearest campsite to the citadelle, overlooking the city from within the wartime German stronghold on the headland to the southwest. Reachable in summer on bus #1 from the *gare SNCF* and the *gare routière*. Open all year.

Les Ilôts av de la Guimorais, Rothéneuf ⓣ02.99.56.98.72. Green little site, located five minutes' walk from either of two crescent beaches, 5km east of the citadelle. Closed mid-Sept to April.

Le Nicet av de la Varde, Rothéneuf ⓣ02.99.40.26.32. Right on the coast, just beyond the headland that marks the eastern limit of Paramé. Closed mid-Sept to late June.

Les Nielles av John Kennedy, Paramé ⓣ02.99.40.26.35. On Paramé's smaller beach, the plage du Minhic, just a short walk from the town's facilities. Closed Sept to late June.

The Town

The **citadelle** of St-Malo, very much the prime destination for visitors, was for many years joined to the mainland only by a long causeway, before the original line of the coast was hidden forever by the construction of the harbour basin. Although its streets of restored seventeenth- and eighteenth-century houses can be crowded to the point of absurdity in summer, away from the more popular thoroughfares random exploration is fun.

Owing to the limitations of space, **buildings** within the walls tend to be higher-rise than you might expect. Ancient as they look, they are almost entirely reconstructed; following the two-week bombardment that forced the German surrender in 1944, eighty percent of the city had to be lovingly and precisely rebuilt, stone by stone. Beneath grey skies, the narrow lanes can appear sombre, even grim, but in high summer or at sunset they become light and almost unreal. In any case, you can always surface on the **ramparts** – first erected in the fourteenth century – to enjoy wonderful, all-round views.

Besides the prominent **Grande Porte**, the main gate of the citadelle is the **Porte St-Vincent**. To the right is the town's **castle**, which houses the **Musée de la Ville** (April–Sept daily 10am–12.30pm & 2–6pm; Oct–March Tues–Sun 10am–noon & 2–6pm; €4.80). The museum is something of a hymn of praise to the "prodigious prosperity" enjoyed by St-Malo during its days of piracy, colonialism and slave trading. Climbing the 169 steps of the castle keep, you pass a fascinating mixture of maps, diagrams and exhibits – chilling handbills from the Nazi occupation, accounts of the "infernal machine" used by the English to blow up the port in 1693, and savage four-pronged *chausse-trappes* (a kind of early version of barbed wire), thrown by pirates onto the decks of ships being boarded to immobilize their crews.

You can pass under the ramparts at several points to reach the open shore, where a huge **beach** stretches away east beyond the rather featureless resort-suburb of **Paramé**. When the tide is low, it's safe to walk out to the small island of **Grand-Bé** – the walk is so popular that sometimes you even need to queue to get onto the short causeway. Solemn warnings are posted of the dangers of attempting to return from the island when the tide has risen too far – if you're caught there, there you have to stay. The island's "sight" is the tomb of the nineteenth-century writer-politician **Chateaubriand** (1768–1848), who was described by Marx as "the most classic incarnation of French *vanité* … the false profundity, Byzantine exaggeration, emotional coquetry … a never -before-seen mishmash of lies".

The **St-Servan** district, within walking distance along the corniche south of the citadelle, was the city's original settlement, converted to Christianity by St Malou (or Maclou) in the sixth century; later, in the twelfth century, the townspeople moved to the impregnable island now called St-Malo. St-Servan curves round several small inlets and beaches to face the river. It's dominated by the distinctive **Tour Solidor**, which consists of three linked towers built in 1382, and in cross-section looks just like an ace of clubs. Originally known in Breton as the *Steir Dor*, or "gate of the river", it now holds a **museum** of Cape Horn clipper ships, open for ninety-minute guided visits (April–Sept daily 10am–noon & 2–6pm; Oct–March Tues–Sun 10am–noon & 2–6pm; €4.80). Most of the great European explorers of the Pacific are covered, from Magellan onwards, but naturally the emphasis is on French heroes such as Bougainville, who was responsible for spreading the brightly coloured bougainvillea plant around the globe. Tours culminate with a superb view from the topmost ramparts.

If you follow the main road due south from St-Servan, ignoring signs for the Barrage de la Rance – or take bus #5 from the *gare SNCF* – you'll come to the **Grand Aquarium**, on a roundabout high above town (daily: April–June & Sept 10am–7pm; July 9.30am–8pm; Aug 9.30am–10pm; Oct–March 10am–6.30pm – note that these hours are variable; €13, under-18s €9.50; ⓣ02.99.21.19.07; ⓦwww.aquarium-st-malo.com). The postmodern aquarium itself can be a bit bewildering at first, but once you get the hang of it it's an entertaining place where you can either learn interesting facts about slimy monsters of the deep or simply pull faces back at them. Its eight distinct fish tanks include one shaped so that visitors stand in the hole in the middle as myriad fish whirl around them. St-Malo actually has another aquarium, logically enough named the **Petit Aquarium**, set into the walls of the old city, but this one is far superior.

For last-minute **shopping**, St-Malo's citadelle contains a few specialists, but buying in any quantity is best done in the Carrefour **hypermarket**, near the aquarium on the southern outskirts of town. There are **markets** in both St-Malo (*intra-muros*) and St-Servan on Tuesdays and Fridays, and in Paramé on Wednesdays and Saturdays.

Eating

Intra-muros St-Malo boasts even more **restaurants** than hotels, with a long crescent lining the inside of the ramparts between the Porte St-Vincent and the Grande Porte. Prices are probably higher than anywhere else in Brittany, however, especially on the open café terraces – the demand is inflated by day-trippers and ferry passengers having last-night blowouts. Bear in mind that most of the crêperies also serve *moules* and similar quasi-snacks. All the restaurants listed below are in the citadelle.

Astrolabe 8 rue des Cordiers ⓣ02.99.40.36.82. Quality cuisine, not far south of the Grande Porte. A full weekday lunch costs €19; at other times, plot your way through an intricate selection of *menus* to get some sensational grilled langoustines and a *gratin du Granny-Smith* dessert for €30 or so. Serves until late. Closed all day Mon & Tues lunchtime.

Borgnefesse 10 rue du Puits aux Braies ⓣ02.99.40.05.05. Heavily pirate-themed dining room with good solid French cooking, where you can have a two-course meal for €15.80 or a three-course one for €19.80. Closed for lunch on Sat & dinner on Sun, plus all day Mon.

Le Brick 5 rue Jacques-Cartier ⓣ02.99.40.18.88. Perhaps the best of the many seafood restaurants set into the walls near the Grande Porte, with a €14.50 menu that offers fish soup or "big size winkles" followed by skate, and more lavish options up to €33. Closed Mon off season.

Le Chasse Marée 4 rue Grout de St-Georges Ⓣ02.99.40.85.10. Nautical decor and haute cuisine, round the corner from the post office, with a few tables on the quiet street and more upstairs. There's a €15 menu, served until 9pm, with oysters and red mullet, and a €24 one featuring scallop or duck salad to start, and a mixed fish grill or fish couscous. Closed Sun in low season, plus all Feb.

Le Corps de Garde 3 montée Notre Dame Ⓣ02.99.40.91.46. The only restaurant right up on St-Malo's ramparts is unfortunately an ordinary crêperie, serving standard €5-or-so crêpes. The views from the terrace are sensational, though, looking out over the beach to the myriad little islets.

Duchesse Anne 5–7 place Guy-la-Chambre Ⓣ02.99.40.85.33. Situated next to the Porte St-Vincent, St-Malo's best-known upmarket restaurant continues to keep up its reputation – and its prices. The only set menu is a €65 lobster option; you might manage to get a lunch for under €16, but dinner will be over twice that. Whole baked fish is the main speciality. Closed Wed & Mon lunch, plus Sun evening in low season, and all Dec & Jan.

Restaurant Gilles 2 rue de la Pie-qui-Boit Ⓣ02.99.40.97.25. Bright, modern, good-value restaurant, just off the central pedestrian axis. The basic €15 menu is fine; alternatively €21 brings you oysters or duck pâté and a rabbit *cuissot* with cider. Closed Wed.

The Pointe du Grouin and Cancale

Along the coast east of St-Malo is the **Pointe du Grouin**, a perilous and windy height, which offers spectacular views of the pinnacle of Mont St-Michel and the bird sanctuary of the **Îles des Landes** to the east. Just south of the *pointe*, and less than 15km from St-Malo across the peninsula, **CANCALE** is renowned for its oysters. In the old church of **St-Méen** at the top of the hill, the town's obsession is documented with meticulous precision by the small **Musée des Arts et Traditions Populaires** (June & Sept Thurs–Sun 2.30–6.30pm; July & Aug Mon 2.30–6.30pm, Tues–Sun 10am–noon & 2.30–6.30pm; groups at other times by appointment Ⓣ02.99.89.71.26; €2.30). Cancale oysters were found in the camps of Julius Caesar, taken daily to Versailles for Louis XIV and even accompanied Napoléon on the march to Moscow.

From the rue des Parcs next to the jetty of the port, you can see at low tide the *parcs* where the oysters are grown. The rocks of the cliff behind are streaked and shiny like mother-of-pearl; underfoot the beach is littered with countless generations of empty shells. The port area is very pretty and very smart, with a long line of upmarket glass-fronted hotels and restaurants. Cancale's **hotels** mostly insist that you eat in if you want to stay; among the best value are *La Houle*, with its nice balconies overlooking the middle of the port at 18 quai Gambetta (Ⓣ02.99.89.62.38; ❷), and *Le Phare* (Ⓣ02.99.89.60.24; ❸; closed Thurs in low season) and the *Émeraude* (Ⓣ02.99.89.61.76; ❸), both set above their own restaurants, at nos. 6 and 7 respectively on quai Thomas. Budget travellers can head instead for the **hostel** 2km north of town at Port Picain (Ⓣ02.99.89.62.62, Ⓔcancale@fuaj.org; closed Jan), where a dorm bed costs €9 for the night. *Au Pied de Cheval*, 10 quai Gambetta (Ⓣ02.99.89.76.95), is an informal place to sample a few oysters, with great baskets of them spread across its wooden quayside tables. A dozen raw oysters on a bed of seaweed can cost just €4.

Dinan

The wonderful citadel of **DINAN** has preserved almost intact its three-kilometre encirclement of protective masonry, with street upon colourful street of late medieval houses within. Like St-Malo, just 25km to the north, it's best seen when arriving by boat up the River Rance, which allows you to appreciate its castle and fortifications to their best advantage. Behind the houses on the left bank quay where the boats tie up, a steep and cobbled street with fields and bramble thickets on either side climbs up to the thirteenth-century ramparts, partly hidden by trees.

Arrival, information and accommodation

Both the Art Deco **gare SNCF** and the **gare routière** (⊕02.96.39.21.05) are in the rather gloomy modern quarter, on place du 11-Novembre, ten minutes' walk west of the walled town. The **tourist office** can be found at the southwest corner of the place du Guesclin, at 9 rue du Chateau (mid-June to Sept Mon–Sat 9am–7pm, Sun 10am–12.30pm & 2.30–6pm; Oct to mid-June Mon–Sat 9am –12.30pm & 2–6pm; ⊕02.96.87.69.76, Ⓦwww.dinan-tourisme.com). **Internet access** is available at @rospace, in the heart of the walled town at 9 rue de la Chaux (Tues–Sat 10am–12.30pm & 2–7pm).

Between mid-April and late September, **boats** along the Rance sail between the port downstream and Dinard and St-Malo. The trip takes just over two and a half hours, with the exact schedule varying according to the tides (adults €18, under-13s €11). It's only possible to do a day return by boat (adults €24, under-13s €14.50) if you start from St-Malo or Dinard. For details, contact Compagnie Corsaire (Dinan ⊕08.25.16.81.20; Dinard ⊕08.25.16.81.30; St-Malo ⊕08.25.16.80.35, Ⓦwww.compagniecorsaire.com).

Dinan has a surprising shortage of the kind of welcoming mid-range hotel -restaurant **accommodation** that characterizes so many a Breton town, so if that's what you're looking for you might do best to visit only as a day-trip. There are, however, plenty of budget options around including a hostel, and a couple of boutique hotels if you're after something a little classier.

Hotels and B&Bs

D'Avaugour 1 place du Champ ⊕02.96.39.07.49, Ⓦwww.avaugourhotel.com. Smart, elegant hotel, entered from the main square but backing onto the ramparts, with very tastefully renovated rooms and lovely gardens. ❽

Bed & Breakfast 55 rue de Coëtquen ⊕02.96.85.23.49, Ⓕ02.96.87.51.44. Very friendly English-run B&B just southwest of the city walls, with a couple of en-suite double bedrooms. Closed Dec. ❹

Harlequin 8 rue du quai Talard ⊕02.96.39.68.68, Ⓕ02.96.39.10.16. Distinguished old building in a lovely setting just across the Rance in the port, offering pleasant en-suite rooms and serving "selfish French cooking" on its gorgeous riverside terrace for €19 and up. ❸

Logis de Jerzual 25–27 rue du Petit Fort ⊕02.96.85.46.54, Ⓔsry.logis@9online.fr. *Chambres d'hôte* on the exquisite little lane that leads from the port, halfway up to the Porte du Jerzual. Garden terrace looking down on the street. Inaccessible by car, so very quiet. ❹

De l'Océan 9 place du 11-Novembre ⊕02.96.39.21.51, Ⓕ02.96.87.05.27. Extremely convenient and well-run (if rather basic) hotel, outside the walls opposite the *gare SNCF*. ❶

De la Porte St-Malo 35 rue St-Malo ⊕02.96.39.19.76, Ⓦwww.hotelportemalo.com. Very comfortable rooms in a tasteful small hotel just outside the walls, beyond the Porte St-Malo. ❸

Du Théâtre 2 rue Ste-Claire ⊕02.96.39.06.91. Seven very simple rooms above a bar, right by the Théâtre des Jacobins, and under the same management as the nearby *Le Cantorbery* (see opposite). ❶

Hostel and campsite

HI hostel Moulin de Méen, Vallée de la Fontaine-des-Eaux ⊕02.96.39.10.83, Ⓔdinan@fuaj.org. Attractive, rural hostel, set in green fields below the town centre. Unfortunately it's not on any bus route: to walk there, follow the quay downstream from the port on the town side. Dorm bed €8.50, and camping is permitted in the grounds. Closed Jan.

Camping Municipal 103 rue Châteaubriand ⊕02.96.39.11.96, Ⓕ02.96.87.08.40. Just outside the western ramparts. Closed late Sept to late May.

The Town

For all its slightly unreal perfection, Dinan is not excessively overrun with tourists. There are no great museums; the monument is the town itself, and time is best spent wandering from crêperie to café, admiring overhanging houses along the way. Unfortunately, you can only walk along one small stretch of the **ramparts**, from the Jardin Anglais behind St Sauveur church to a point just short of Tour Sillon overlooking the river. You can get a good general overview from the **Tour de l'Horloge**, dating from the end of the fifteenth century (daily: April & May 2–6pm; June–Sept 10am–7pm; €2.60).

As you might guess from its blending of two separate towers, the fourteenth-century **keep** that once protected the town's southern approach was built by Estienne Le Tour, architect of St-Malo's Tour Solidor. It's now known as the **Château de Duchesse Anne**, and houses a small **local history museum** in the ancient Tour Coëtquen (daily June–Sept 10am–6.30pm; Feb–May & Oct–Dec 1.30–5.30pm; closed Jan; €4). On the lower floor, a group of stone fifteenth-century notables look for all the world like a medieval time capsule, about to de-petrify at any moment.

St Sauveur church, very much the town's focus, is a real mixture of ages, with a Romanesque porch and an eighteenth-century steeple. Even its nine Gothic chapels feature five different patterns of vaulting in no symmetrical order, and the most complex pair, in the centre, would make any spider proud. A cenotaph contains the heart of Bertrand du Guesclin, the fourteenth-century Breton warrior (and later Constable of France), who fought and won a single combat with the English knight Thomas of Canterbury, in what is now place du Guesclin, to settle the outcome of the siege of Dinan in 1364. Relics of his life and battles are scattered all over Brittany and Normandy; in death, he spread himself between four separate burial places for four different parts of his body (the French kings restricted themselves to three burial sites). North of the church, rue du Jerzual leads down to the gate of the same name and on down (as rue du Petit-Fort) to the lovely **port du Dinan**. Here the river is sufficiently narrow to be spanned by a small but majestic old stone bridge, and artisans' shops and restaurants line the quay.

On the third weekend of July, every other (even-numbered) year, the **Fête des Remparts** is celebrated with medieval-style jousting, banquets, fairs and processions, culminating in an immense fireworks display. There's a **market** every Thursday in the places du Champ and du Guesclin (the original medieval fairground).

Eating and drinking

All sorts of specialist **restaurants**, including several ethnic alternatives, are tucked away in the old streets of Dinan. Stroll of an evening through the town and down to the port, and you'll pass at least twenty places. For **bars**, explore the series of tiny parallel alleyways between place des Merciers and rue de Marchix. Along rue de la Cordonnerie, the busiest of the lot, the various hang-outs define themselves by their taste in music: *À la Truye qui File* at no. 14 is a sort of contemporary folky Breton dive, while *Morgan's Tavern*, next door at no. 12, is considerably more raucous.

Le Cantorbery 6 rue Ste-Claire ⓣ02.96.39.02.52. Reasonable food served in an old stone house with rafters, a spiral staircase and a real wood fire on which fish and meat are grilled. Set lunch menu at €15, while traditional dinner menus start with a good €22 option. Closed Sun evening & Mon out of season.

Chez La Mère Pourcel 3 place des Merciers ⓣ02.96.39.03.80. Beautiful half-timbered fifteenth-century house in the central square. Lunch menus can be pretty minimal, but the dinners, from €28 up to €62, are gourmet class, featuring for example exquisite *agneau pré-salé* from Mont St-Michel. Closed Sun evening and Mon in low season.

Crêperie Ahna 7 rue de la Poissonerie. Smart central crêperie with no outdoor seating, but popular with lunching locals. Savoury pancakes cost €4.20–8, and they also serve potato blinis and grilled meats. Closed Sun in low season.

Crêperie Connetable 1 rue de l'Apport. Magnificent old house, opposite the *Mère Pourcel* beside the place des Merciers, with crêpes for around €5 and snacks. The perfect spot for people-watching.

La Fleur du Sel 7 rue Ste-Claire ⓣ02.96.85.15.14. Cheerful, attractive fish restaurant daring to serve out of the ordinary dishes alongside the classics. Menus from €19 to €30, plus lunch at €13.

Le Myrian 3 rue du Port ⓣ02.96.87.93.36. Attractive and inexpensive pizzeria in a waterfront cottage down by the port, serving €6–12 pizzas, plus assorted salads and wine by the carafe, on its shady terrace.

Le Relais des Corsaires 7 rue du Quai, port du Dinan ⓣ02.96.39.40.17. Attractive waterfront restaurant split between a formal dining room and the less expensive all-hours "grill", the *Petit Corsaire*. Both serve much the same wide range of traditional French cuisine. In low season closed Sun evening & Wed.

The north coast from Dinard to Lannion

The coast that stretches from the resort town of **Dinard** to Finistère at the far western end of Brittany is divided into two distinct regions, either side of the bay of **St-Brieuc**. Between Dinard and St-Brieuc are the exposed green headlands of the **Côte d'Émeraude**, while beyond St-Brieuc, along the **Côte de Goëlo**, the shore becomes more extravagantly indented, with a succession of secluded little bays and an increasing proliferation of huge pink granite boulders, seen at their best on the **Côte de Granit Rose** near Perros-Guirec.

Dinard

The former fishing village of **DINARD** sprawls around the western approaches to the Rance estuary, just across from St-Malo but a good twenty minutes away by road. While it might not feel out of place on the Côte d'Azur, with its casino, spacious villas and social calendar of regattas and ballet, here in Brittany it's a little incongruous. Its nineteenth-century metamorphosis was largely thanks to the tastes of the affluent English and Americans, though these days age rather than nationality seems to be the common factor uniting most of its summer influx of tourists. Although Dinard is a hilly town, undulating over a succession of pretty little coastal inlets, it attracts great numbers of older visitors; as a result, prices tend to be high, and pleasures sedate.

Central Dinard faces north to the open sea, across the curving bay that holds the attractive **plage de l'Écluse**. As so often, the buildings that line the waterfront are – with the exception of the casino in the middle – venerable Victorian villas rather than hotels or shops, and so the beach itself has a low-key atmosphere, despite the summer crowds. An unexpected statue of **Alfred Hitchcock** dominates its main access point. Standing on a giant egg, with a ferocious-looking bird perched on each shoulder, he was placed here to commemorate the town's annual festival of English-language films.

Enjoyable **coastal footpaths** lead off in either direction from the principal beach, enlivened by notice boards holding reproductions of paintings produced at points along the way. It may well come as a surprise to see that Pablo Picasso's *Deux Femmes Courants sur la Plage* and *Baigneuses sur la Plage*, both of which look quintessentially Mediterranean with their blue skies and golden sands, were in fact painted here in Dinard during his annual summer visits throughout the 1920s. The path that heads east leads up to the Pointe du Moulinet for views over to St-Malo, and then as the **Promenade du Clair de Lune** continues past the tiny and now-exclusive port, and down to the estuary beach, the plage du Prieuré.

Practicalities

Dinard's small **airport** is 4km southeast of the town centre, off the D168 near **Pleurtuit**. TIV **bus** #56, timed to connect with the Ryanair flights, runs via Dinard proper to St-Malo's *gare SNCF* and Porte St-Vincent for a €3.50 flat fare. Many visitors simply come over for the day on one of the regular Émeraude Lines **boats** from St-Malo; tickets can be bought in Dinard at 27 av George-V, above the pleasure port. A couple of hundred metres west is the **tourist office**, in the centre at 2 bd Féart (Easter–June & Sept Mon–Sat 9am–12.15pm & 2–7pm; July & Aug daily 9.30am–7.30pm; Oct–Easter Mon–Sat 9am–12.15pm & 2–6pm; ⓣ02.99.46.94.12, ⓦwww.ville-dinard.fr).

Dinard tends to be an expensive place to stay, but it does have a wide selection of **hotels** to choose from, many of which can be found at ⓦwww.dinard-hotel-plus.com. Options include two nice places near the pleasure port: the *Hôtel-Restaurant Printania*, 5 av George-V (ⓣ02.99.46.13.07, ⓔprintania.dinard@wanadoo.fr; ❹; closed mid-Nov to mid-March), on a quiet street as it drops down to the port with a magnificent terrace restaurant looking towards St-Malo; and the *Hôtel-Restaurant de la Vallée*, 6 av George-V (ⓣ02.99.46.94.00, ⓦwww.hoteldelavallee.com; ❺; closed mid-Nov to mid-Dec), though unfortunately it faces the wrong way for views of St-Malo, its most basic rooms looking straight onto a bare cliff. The best local **campsite** is the municipal *Port Blanc*, also near the plage du Port-Blanc, on rue du Sergent-Boulanger (ⓣ02.99.46.10.74; closed Oct–March).

The Côte d'Émeraude

To the west of the Rance, beyond Dinard, begins the green of the **Côte d'Émeraude**. Though composed mainly of developed family resorts, it also offers wonderful camping, at its best around the heather-backed beaches near **Cap Fréhel**, a high, warm expanse of heath and cliffs with views extending on good days as far as Jersey and the Île de Bréhat – camping is, however, forbidden within 5km of the headland itself. The **Fort la Latte**, to the east, is used regularly as a film set. Its tower, containing a cannonball factory, is accessible only over two drawbridges (guided tours: April–Sept daily 10am–12.30pm & 2.30–6.30pm; Oct–March Sat, Sun & hols only 2.30–5.30pm; €4) and offers good views.

The nearest places to stay are the ideal, isolated **campsite** at Pléherel, the *Camping du Pont L'Étang* (ⓣ02.96.41.40.45; closed Oct–April), and a basic summer-only **hostel** on the D16 just outside Plévenon en route towards the Cap – full address Kérivet-en-Frehel, La Ville Hardrieux (ⓣ02.96.41.48.98; €8 dorm bed; closed Oct to mid-March) – which also rents out bicycles.

Erquy

Further round the headland, the perfect crescent of beach at **ERQUY** curves through more than 180 degrees. At low tide, the sea disappears way beyond the harbour entrance, leaving gentle ripples of paddling sand. Equipped with suitable boots, you can walk right across its mouth, from the grassy wooded headland on the left side over to the picturesque little lighthouse at the end of the jetty on the right.

Erquy's **tourist office** on the boulevard de la Mer (July & Aug Mon–Sat 9.30am–1pm & 2–7pm, Sun 10am–12.30pm & 3.30–6.30pm; Sept–June daily 9.30am–noon & 2–6pm; ⓣ02.96.72.30.12, ⓦwww.erquy-tourisme.com) co-ordinates information for the surrounding area. The *Hôtel Beauséjour*, 21 rue de la Corniche (ⓣ02.96.72.30.39, ⓔhotel.beausejour@wanadoo.fr; ❸; closed Sun evening & Mon in winter), has a good view of the bay, and excellent fish dinners from €15, while the more upmarket **restaurant** *l'Escurial* (ⓣ02.96.72.31.56; closed Sun evening & Mon) by the seafront serves a five-course menu for €40 that consists entirely of **scallops**, the town's speciality. There are several **campsites** on the promontory (dotted with tiny coves) that leads to the Cap d'Erquy north of town, including the three-star *St-Pabu* (ⓣ02.96.72.24.65; closed mid-Oct to March) right beside the sea.

Le Val-André

The huge beach in the broader bay of **LE VAL-ANDRÉ** to the west is of finer sand, and the endless pedestrian promenade that stretches along the seafront feels oddly Victorian, consisting solely of huge old houses undisturbed by shops or bars. However, Le Val-André is definitely more of a town than Erquy, and rue A.-Charner, running parallel to the sea one street back, is busy with holiday-makers in summer.

The helpful **tourist office** (April–Sept Mon–Sat 9am–1pm & 2–7pm, Sun 10am–12.30pm & 4–6pm; Oct–March Mon–Sat 10am–12.30pm & 4–6pm) is located in the modern casino at the very centre of the waterfront. Of its hotels, the tastefully refurbished *Hôtel de la Mer*, 63 rue A-Charner (ⓣ02.96.72.20.44; ❸; closed mid-Nov to mid-Dec & all Jan), has a restaurant which uses a fine Muscadet to transport *moules marinières* onto a hitherto undreamed-of plane. However, with the success of the business, many guests find themselves having to sleep in the characterless *Nuit et Jour* motel, run by the same management (❷).

St-Brieuc

The major city on the Côte d'Émeraude, **ST-BRIEUC** is far too busy being the industrial centre of northern Brittany to concern itself with entertaining tourists. It's an odd-looking city, with two very deep wooded valleys spanned by viaducts at its core, and it's almost impossible to bypass. The streets are hectic, with the town centre cut in two by a virtual motorway and unrelieved by any public parks. Motorists and cyclists, unfortunately, have little choice but to plough straight through rather than attempting to negotiate the backroads and steep hills around. Apart from the sturdy-looking **cathedral of St Stephen**, the fine views of the valley from **Tertre Aubé** and a handful of half-timbered houses in the streets around place au Lin, there's nothing to keep you here.

Trains between Paris, Dol and Brest stop at the **gare SNCF**, around 1km south of the centre of St-Brieuc, and regular **buses** run to the nearby resorts. If you decide to use the city as a base, the best place to **stay** is the central *Champ-de-Mars*, 13 rue du Général-Leclerc (ⓣ02.96.33.60.99, ⓔhoteldemars@wanadoo.fr; ❸), which offers mussels or fish soup for €9.50 in the old-fashioned, green-painted brasserie downstairs. St-Brieuc also has a **hostel**, two kilometres out, in the magnificent fifteenth-century Manoir de la Ville-Guyomard (ⓣ02.96.78.70.70, ⓔsaint-brieuc@fuaj.org; €13.25), on bus route #1 from the station. Some of the nicest **eating** options in town are in the old quarter, behind the cathedral. The traditional French cooking at *Le Madure*, 14 rue Quinquaine (ⓣ02.96.61.21.07; closed Sat lunch, Sun & Mon), is served à la carte, with steaks around €15 and salads half that; the fondues at *Le Chaudron*, 19 rue Fardel (ⓣ02.96.33.01.72; closed Sun), start at €13 per person.

The Côte de Goëlo

Moving northwest towards Paimpol along the **Côte de Goëlo**, the shoreline becomes wilder and harsher and the seaside towns tend to be crammed into narrow rocky inlets or set well back in river estuaries. **BINIC** is a narrow port surrounded by meadows, with a thin strip of beach and the decent (if relatively pricey) *Hôtel Benhuyc*, 1 quai Jean-Bart (ⓣ02.96.73.39.00, ⓦwww.benhuyc.com; ❸; closed Jan). A little further on at the sedate family resort of **ST-QUAY-PORTRIEUX**, the *Gerbot d'Avoine* (ⓣ02.96.70.40.09, ⓦwww.gerbotdavoine.com; ❸; closed Jan) beside the beach is the best place to stay, despite the hideous decor of its rooms.

After St-Quay, the coastal road shifts inland, through **PLOUHA**, the traditional boundary between French-speaking and Breton-speaking Brittany. A worthwhile diversion is the village of **KERMARIA-AN-ISQUIT**, signposted off the D21 from Plouha, with the extraordinary medieval frescoes of a *Danse Macabre* in its thirteenth-century **chapel** (daily 9am–noon & 2–6pm; donation). They show Ankou, who is death or death's assistant, leading representatives of every social class in a Dance of Death. An encounter between three living nobles out hunting and three philosophical corpses is also depicted, and there's a statue of the infant Jesus refusing milk from Mary's proffered breast.

Paimpol and around

Back on the coast, **PAIMPOL** is an attractive town with a tangle of cobbled alleyways and fine grey-granite houses, but has lost something in its transition from working fishing port to pleasure harbour. It was once the centre of a cod and whaling fleet, which sailed to Iceland each February after being sent off with a ceremony marked by a famous *pardon*. From then until September the town would be empty of its young men. The whole area was commemorated in Pierre Loti's book, *Pêcheur d'Islande*; the author, and his heroine, lived in the **place du Martray** in the centre of town.

Thanks to naval shipyards and the like, the open sea is not visible from Paimpol; a maze of waterways leads to its two separate **harbours**. Both are usually filled with the high masts of yachts, but are still also used by the fishing vessels that keep a fish market and a plethora of *poissonneries* busy. This is doubtless a very pleasant place to arrive by boat, threading through the rocks, but from close quarters the tiny port area is a little disappointing, very much rebuilt and quite plain. Even so, it's always lively in summer.

A couple of kilometres short of town, in a superbly romantic setting, the D786 passes the substantial ruins of the **Abbaye de Beauport** (mid-June to mid-Sept daily 10am–7pm, with regular 90-minute guided tours; mid-Sept to mid-June daily 10am–noon & 2–5pm; €4.50, €5 during temporary exhibitions; ⓦwww.abbaye-beauport.com), established in 1202 by Count Alain de Goëlo. Its stone walls are covered with wild flowers and ivy, the central cloisters are engulfed by a huge tree, and birds fly everywhere. The Norman Gothic chapterhouse is the most noteworthy building to survive, but wandering through and over the roofless halls you may spot architectural relics from all periods of its history. Footpaths lead down through the salt meadows, where the monks raised their sheep, to the sea, offering the same superb views of the hilltop abbey that must have been appreciated by generations of arriving pilgrims. In summer, the abbey reopens for **late-night** visits, with imaginative lighting effects and concerts (June–Sept; €8-12).

Possible places to **stay** in Paimpol include the luxurious *Repaire de Kerroc'h*, overlooking the small-boat harbour from 29 quai Morand (Ⓣ02.96.20.50.13, Ⓔkerroch@libertysurf.com; ❹), which serves gourmet meals from €25 up to €40; the very hospitable *Hôtel Berthelot* at 1 rue du Port (Ⓣ02.96.20.88.66; ❷); and the plainer *Hôtel Origano*, just back from the front at 7bis rue du Quai (Ⓣ02.96.22.05.49; ❸; closed mid-Nov to Easter). As for **restaurants**, *La Cotriade*, on the far side of the harbour on the quai Armand-Dayot (Ⓣ02.96.20.81.08; closed Wed evening & Thurs), is the best bet for authentic fish dishes, with a simple €16 menu that features a *véritable Cassoulet Paimpolais*.

The Île de Bréhat

Two kilometres off the coast at Pointe de l'Arcouest, 6km northwest of Paimpol, the **ÎLE DE BRÉHAT** – in reality two islands joined by a tiny bridge – gives the appearance of spanning great latitudes. On its north side are windswept meadows of hemlock and yarrow, sloping down to chaotic erosions of rock; on the south, you're in the midst of palm trees, mimosa and eucalyptus. All around is a multitude of little islets – some accessible at low tide, others *propriété privée*, most just pink-orange rocks. All in all, it is one of the most beautiful places in Brittany, renowned as a sanctuary not

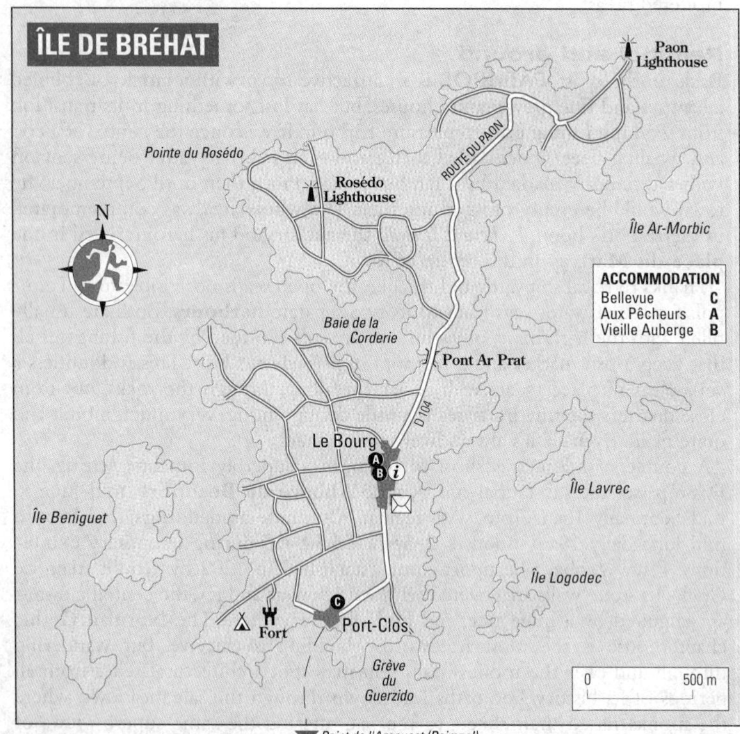

only for rare species of wild flowers, but also for birds of all kinds. Individual private gardens are also meticulously tended, so you can always anticipate a magnificent display of colour, in summer, for example, from the erupting blue acanthus.

As you might expect, a high proportion of the homes on this island paradise now belong to summer-only visitors from Paris and beyond, and young Bréhatins leave in ever-increasing numbers for lack of a place of their own, let alone a job. In winter the remaining three hundred or so natives have the place to themselves, without even a *gendarme*; the summer sees two police officers imported from the mainland, along with upwards of three thousand temporary residents and a hundred times as many day-trippers.

All boats to Bréhat (see below) arrive at the small harbour of **PORT-CLOS**, though depending on the tide passengers may have to walk several hundred metres before setting foot on terra firma. No **cars** are permitted on the island, so many visitors rent **bikes** at the port, for €11 per day. However, it's easy enough to explore the whole place on foot; walking from one end to the other takes less than an hour.

Each batch of new arrivals heads first to Bréhat's village, **LE BOURG**, five hundred metres up from the port. As well as a handful of hotels, restaurants and bars, it also holds a limited array of shops, a post office, a bank, and an ATM, and hosts a small **market** most days. In high season, the attractive central square tends to be packed fit to burst, with exasperated holiday-home owners pushing their little hand-wagons through the throngs of day-trippers.

Continue a short distance north of Le Bourg, however, and you'll soon cross over the slender **Pont ar Prat bridge** to the northern island, where the crowds thin out, and countless little coves offer opportunities to sprawl on the tough grass or clamber across the rugged boulders. Though the coastal footpath around this northern half offers the most attractive walking on the island, the best **beaches** line the southern shores, with the **Grève du Guerzido** at its southeastern corner, being the pick of the crop.

Practicalities

Bréhat is connected regularly by **ferry** from the Pointe de l'Arcouest, 6km northwest of Paimpol, and served by summer buses from the *gare SNCF* there. Roughly speaking, sailings, with Les Vedettes de Bréhat (Ⓣ02.96.55.79.50, Ⓦwww.vedettesdebrehat.com), are half-hourly in July & Aug, hourly between April and June and in September, and every two hours otherwise, with the first boat out to Bréhat at 8.30am in summer, and the last boat back at 7.45pm. The return trip costs €7.50 (bikes, €8 extra, are only allowed outside peak crossing times). The same company also operates boats in summer from Erquy, Dahouët, Binic and St-Quay-Portrieux.

Bréhat's **tourist office** is in the main square in Le Bourg (April–June & Sept Mon–Sat 10am–1pm & 2.30–6pm; July & Aug daily 10am–6pm). All three of its **hotels** tend to be booked through the summer, and close for at least part of the winter. Both the *Bellevue* in Port-Clos (Ⓣ02.96.20.00.05, Ⓦwww.hotel-bellevue-brehat.com; ❺; closed mid-Nov to mid-Feb), and the *Vieille Auberge*, on your left as you enter Le Bourg (Ⓣ02.96.20.00.24; ❻; closed Dec to Easter), insist on *demi-pension* in high season. The smaller *Aux Pêcheurs* (Ⓣ02.96.20.00.14; ❸; closed Nov–March), on the main square in Le Bourg, has a nice little garden terrace. There's also a wonderful **campsite** in the woods high above the sea west of the port (Ⓣ02.96.20.00.36; closed Oct–April).

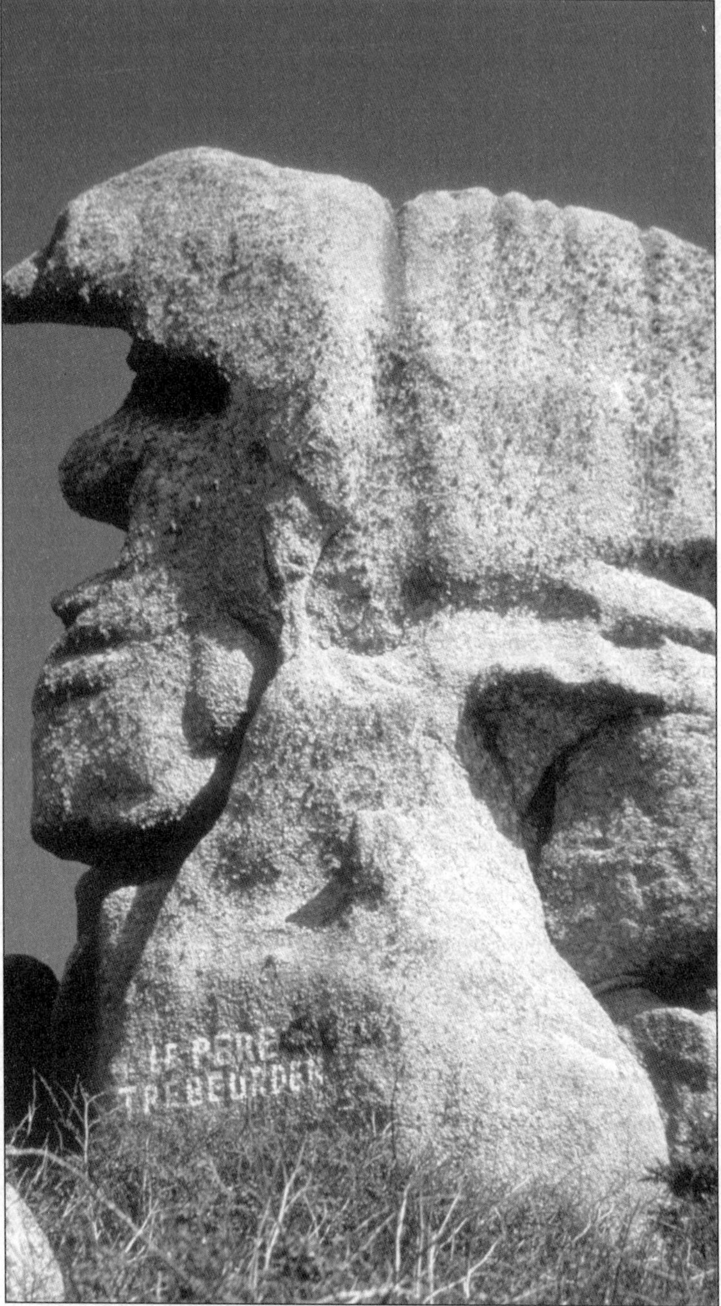

△ Côte de Granit Rose

The Côte de Granit Rose

The entire northernmost stretch of the Breton coast, from Bréhat to **Trégastel**, has loosely come to be known as the **Côte de Granit Rose**. There are indeed great granite boulders scattered in the sea around the island of Bréhat, and at the various headlands to the west, but the most memorable stretch of coast lies around **Perros-Guirec**, where the pink granite rocks are eroded into fantastic shapes.

Tréguier

The D786 turns west from Paimpol, passing over a green *ria* on the bridge outside Lézardrieux before arriving at **TRÉGUIER**, one of the very few hill-towns in Brittany. Its central feature is the **Cathédrale de St-Tugdual**, which contains the tomb of St Yves, a native of the town who died in 1303 and – for his incorruptibility – became the patron saint of lawyers. Attempts to bribe him continue to this day; his tomb is surrounded by marble plaques and an inferno of candles invoking his aid.

The *Hôtel-Restaurant d'Estuaire* on the waterfront (Ⓣ02.96.92.30.25; ❷) is a very basic place to **stay** – though the sea views are great – with reasonable menus from €14. Up in town at 2 rue Renan, *La Poissonnerie du Trégor* (Ⓣ02.96.92.30.27) is an excellent fish **restaurant** that's no more expensive. During the **market** each Wednesday, clothes are spread out in the square by the cathedral, with food and fresh fish down by the port.

Château de la Roche-Jagu

About 10km inland from Tréguier, on a heavily wooded slope above the Trieux river, stands the fifteenth-century **Château de la Roche-Jagu** (daily: Easter–June & Sept–Oct 10.30am–12.30pm & 2–6pm; July & Aug 10am–7pm; park access free, château €4, or more during special exhibitions). It's a gorgeous building – a harmonious combination of fortress and home – and plays host to lavish annual exhibitions, usually on some sort of Celtic theme. The rooms within are bare, but if you climb to the top, you can admire the beautiful woodwork of the restored eaves, and walk the two long indoor galleries, offering tremendous views over the river.

Perros-Guirec and Ploumanac'h

PERROS-GUIREC is the most popular resort along this coast, though not perhaps the most exciting, consisting largely of a network of tree-lined avenues of suburban villas. It does stand, however, at one end of the long **Sentier des Douaniers** pathway, which winds round the clifftops to the tiny resort of **PLOUMANAC'H** past an astonishing succession of deformed and water-sculpted rocks. Birds wheel overhead towards the offshore bird sanctuary of **Sept-Îles**, and battered boats shelter in the narrow inlets or bob uncontrollably out on the waves. There are patches and brief causeways of grass, clumps of purple heather and yellow gorse. Occasionally the rocks have crumbled into a sort of granite grit to make up a tiny beach; one boulder is strapped down by bands of ivy that prevent it rolling into the sea.

Perros-Guirec's extremely efficient **tourist office** is at 21 place de l'Hôtel-de-Ville (July & Aug Mon–Sat 9am–7.30pm, Sun 10am–12.30pm & 4–7pm; Sept–June Mon–Sat 9am–12.30pm & 2–6.30pm; Ⓦwww.perros-guirec.com). **Hotels** in Perros-Guirec itself include the old-fashioned *Les Violettes*, 19 rue du Calvaire (Ⓣ02.96.23.21.33; ❶), which has a seriously cheap restaurant, and two places with sea views: the *Gulf Stream*, high on the hillside at 26 rue des

Sept-Îles (Ⓣ02.96.23.21.86; ❷; closed Jan), and the *Bon Accueil*, 11 rue de Landerval (Ⓣ02.96.23.25.77; ❸), which has a gourmet restaurant. Ploumanac'h offers the *St-Guirec et de la Plage* (Ⓣ02.96.91.40.89, Ⓦwww.hotelsaint-guirec.com; ❺ half-board; closed mid-Nov to mid-Feb, and most of March), which has some lovely sea-view rooms at bargain rates, and serves simple but good food to all guests in a separate dining room. The *Hôtel du Parc*, on the main square nearby (Ⓣ02.96.91.40.80; ❸; closed mid-Nov to mid-Dec & Jan), has more reasonably priced rooms, and serves good seafood menus from €14. The nicest place to **camp** is the four-star *Le Ranolien* (Ⓣ02.96.91.43.58, Ⓔleranolien@wanadoo.fr; closed late Sept to March), backing onto the Sentier des Douaniers near a little beach about halfway round, but directly accessible on the other side by road.

Trégastel and Trébeurden

Of the smaller villages further round the coast to the west, **TRÉGASTEL**, with a couple of campsites, including the *Tourony* by the beach (Ⓣ02.96.23.86.61; closed Oct–Easter), and **TRÉBEURDEN**, with the seafront *Le Toëno* hostel, 60 route de la Corniche (Ⓣ02.96.23.52.22; €9.10 without sheets or breakfast; closed mid-Nov to Feb), are functional stopovers. Trégastel has managed to squeeze in an **aquarium** under a massive pile of boulders, and has a couple of huge lumps of pink granite slap in the middle of its fine beach.

The strangest sight along this coast, however, outdoing anything the erosions can manage, is just south of Trégastel on the **route de Calvaire**, where an old stone saint halfway up a high calvary raises his arm to bless or harangue the gleaming white discs and puffball dome of **the Pleumier-Bodou Telecommunications Centre**. A new pink granite "dolmen" commemorates its opening by De Gaulle in 1962, when it was the first receiving station to pick up signals from the American Telstar satellite. The centre is no longer operational, and has been re-modelled as a **Musée de Télécommunications** that's also known as Cosmopolis (Feb daily except Sat 2–6pm; March & Oct–Dec during school holidays or by appointment only; April & Sept Mon–Fri 11am–6pm, Sat & Sun 2–6pm; May & June daily 11am–6pm; July & Aug daily 11am–7pm; €7; Ⓦwww.leradome.com). Inside the **Radôme**, the golf-ball itself, frequent spectacular *son-et-lumière* shows explain the history of the whole ensemble, and there's also a smaller **planetarium** alongside. One final incongruous note is struck by the reconstructed **Gaulish village** nearby (same hours; additional donation €3), which is designed to raise money for a French charity working in Africa, and thus incorporates some traditional huts from Togo.

The Bay of Lannion

Despite being set significantly back from the sea on the estuary of the River Léguer, **Lannion** gives its name to the next bay west along the Breton coast – and it's the bay rather than the town that is most likely to impress visitors. One enormous beach stretches from **St-Michel-en-Grève**, which is little more than a bend in the road, as far as **Locquirec**; at low tide you can walk hundreds of metres out on the sands.

Lannion

LANNION, set amid plummeting hills and stairways, is a historic city with streets of medieval housing and a couple of interesting old churches – but it's also a centre for a burgeoning and extremely high-tech telecommunications industry, and one of modern Brittany's real success stories. Hence its rather self -satisfied nickname, *ville heureuse* or "happy town". In addition to admiring the half-timbered houses around the **place de Général-Leclerc** and along **rue des Chapeliers**, it's well worth climbing from the town up the 142 granite steps which lead to the twelfth-century Templar **Église de Brélévenez**. This church was remodelled three hundred years later to incorporate a granite bell tower, and the views from its terrace are quite stupendous.

Lannion's **tourist office** at 2 quai d'Aiguillon (July & Aug Mon–Sat 9am–7pm, Sun 10am–1pm; Sept–June Mon–Sat 9.30am–12.30pm & 2–6pm; ⓣ02.96.46.41.00, ⓦwww.ot-lannion.fr) can advise on the many *chambres d'hôte* possibilities in the vicinity. The best-value accommodation options are bed-and-breakfast places such as the extremely charming *Manoir de Crec'h Gouliffern* (ⓣ02.96.47.26.17; ❹), a converted farmhouse with a fantastic garden at Servel, Beg-Léguer, a short way west of the town centre. There's also a year-round hostel, *Les Korrigans*, conveniently positioned very near the station and the town centre at 6 rue du 73e-Territorial (ⓣ02.96.37.91.28, ⓔlannion@fuaj.org; €13.45), which has its own lively bar and restaurant.

Locquirec

LOCQUIREC, across the bay from Lannion, manages to have beaches on both sides without ever quite being thin enough to be a real peninsula. Around the main port, smart houses stand in sloping gardens, looking very southern English with their whitewashed stone panels, grey slate roofs and jutting turreted windows. On the last Sunday in July, Locquirec holds a combined *pardon de St Jacques* and Festival of the Sea.

Locquirec veers dangerously close to being over-twee, and none of its **hotels** is all that cheap – although the *Grand Hôtel des Bains*, 15 rue de l'Église (ⓣ02.98.67.41.02, ⓔhotel-des-bains@wanadoo.fr; ❾ half-board; closed Jan) has so gorgeous a setting that perhaps it doesn't matter; there is also an excellent restaurant with menus starting at €34. The *Sables-Blancs*, 15 rue des Sables-Blancs (ⓣ02.98.67.42.07; ❸; closed Jan & Feb), offers sea views at considerably lower prices, while the municipal **campsite**, the *Toul ar Goue*, 1km south along the corniche (ⓣ02.98.67.40.85; closed mid-Sept to mid-April), is beautifully positioned, too.

The Cairn du Barnenez

At the mouth of the Morlaix estuary, 6km north of Plouézoch, the prehistoric stone **Cairn du Barnenez** surveys the waters from the summit of a hill (May–Aug daily 10am–6.30pm; Sept–April Tues–Sun 10am–12.30pm & 2–5.30pm; €4). As on the island of Gavrinis in the Morbihan, its ancient masonry has been laid bare by recent excavations, and provides a stunning sense of the architectural prowess of the megalith builders. Radiocarbon testing has shown the work here to date back to around 4500 BC, which makes this one of the oldest large-scale monuments in the world.

The ensemble consists of two distinct stepped pyramids. Each rises in successive tiers, built of large flat stones chinked with pebbles; the second was added onto the side of the first, and the two are encircled by a series of terraces and ramps. The whole thing measures roughly 70m long by 15–25m wide and 6m high. Both pyramids were long buried under the same eighty-metre-long earthen mound. While the actual cairns are completely exposed to view, most of the passages and chambers that lie within them are sealed off. The two minor corridors that are open simply cut through the edifice from one side to the other, and were exposed by quarrying activities around thirty years ago; visitors are not permitted to pass through. Local tradition has it that one tunnel runs right through this "home of the fairies", and continues out deep under the sea.

Finistère

It's hard to resist the appeal of the **Finistère coast**, with its ocean-fronting cliffs and headlands. Summer crowds may detract from the best parts of the **Crozon peninsula** and the **Pointe de Raz**, but there are many kilometres of coast where you can enjoy near solitude. If you have transport, explore the semi-wilderness of the **northern stretches** beyond Brest and the little fishing village of **Le Conquet**, or take a ferry trip to the misty offshore islands of **Ouessant**, **Molène** and **Sein**. From the top of **Ménez-Hom** you can admire the anarchic limits of western France, while the cities of **Morlaix** and **Quimper** display modern Breton life as well as ancient splendours, and the **parish closes** south of Morlaix reveal much about the beliefs of the past.

Léon

Memories of the days when Brittany was "Petite Bretagne", as opposed to "Grande Bretagne" across the water, linger in the names of Finistère's two main areas, **Léon** (once Lyonesse), the northern peninsula, and its southern neighbour Cornouaille (Cornwall). Both feature prominently in Arthurian legend. In the north of Léon, the ragged **coastline** is the prime attraction, indented with a succession of estuaries or **abers**, each of which shelters its own tiny harbour: heading west from either the thriving historic town of **Morlaix** or the appealing little Channel port of **Roscoff**, there are possible stopping places all the way to **Le Conquet**. From Le Conquet, you can reach the islands of **Ouessant** and **Molène** across a treacherous stretch of ocean. Inland, by contrast, the ornate medieval village churches known as **parish closes** hold some of Brittany's finest religious architecture.

Morlaix

MORLAIX, one of the great old Breton ports, thrived on trade with England in between wars during the "Golden Period" of the late Middle Ages. Built up the slopes of a steep valley with sober stone houses, the town was originally protected by an eleventh-century castle and a circuit of walls. Little is left of either, but the old centre remains in part medieval with its cobbled streets and half-timbered houses. The present grandeur comes from the pink-granite **viaduct** carrying trains from Paris to Brest way above the town centre. Coming by road from the north, the opening view is of shiny yacht masts paralleling the pillars of the viaduct.

On her way from Roscoff to Paris, Mary Queen of Scots passed through Morlaix in 1548 and stayed at the **Jacobin convent** that fronts place des Jacobins. She was at the time just 5 years old, and a contemporary account records that the crush to catch a glimpse of the infant was so great that the inner town's "gates were thrown off their hinges and the chains from all the bridges were broken down". The **Musée des Jacobins** (April, May & Sept Wed–Sun 1.30–6pm; July & Aug daily 11am–6.30pm; Oct–March & June Wed–Sat 1.30–6pm; €4.10) in the convent church contains a reasonably entertaining assortment of Roman wine jars, bits that have fallen off medieval churches, cannon and kitchen utensils, and a few modern paintings.

Unfortunately, bits of the museum itself have also started falling off, so most of the displays are out of bounds until 2007 at least. By way of compensation, with the same ticket you can go on a guided tour of the **Maison à Pondalez**, at 9 Grand-Rue. This fabulously restored sixteenth-century house takes its name from the Breton word for the sculpted wooden internal gallery that dominates the ground floor. The impressive staircase leads to a series of rooms displaying local enamel- and silverware, but not much in the way of original furnishing, and you can see a couple of totem-like staircase stems rescued from elsewhere in the town.

The nearby **church of St Mathieu**, off rue de Paris, contains a sombre and curious statue of the Madonna and Child; Mary's breast was apparently lopped off by a prudish former priest, to leave the babe suckling at nothing. The whole statue opens down the middle to reveal a separate figure of God the Father, clutching a crucifix.

Anne, Duchess of Brittany and Queen of France, visited Morlaix in 1506. She is reputed to have stayed at the **Maison de la Reine Anne** (May & June Mon–Sat 10am–noon & 2–6pm; July & Aug Mon–Sat 10am–6pm; Sept Mon–Sat 10am–noon & 2–5pm; €1.60), 33 rue du Mur, which, although much restored, does indeed date from the sixteenth century like the Maison à Pondalez. Look out for the intricate external carvings, and the lantern roof and splendid Renaissance staircase inside; each of the house's storeys overhangs the square below by a few more centimetres.

Practicalities

The **tourist office** in Morlaix is in a solitary but central one-storey building, almost under the viaduct in place des Otages (mid-June to mid-Sept Mon & Sat 10am–12.30pm & 2–6pm, Tues–Fri 10am–12.30pm & 1.30–7pm, Sun 10.30am–12.30pm; mid-Sept to mid-June Tues–Sat 10am–noon & 2–6pm; ⓣ02.98.62.14.94). All **buses** conveniently depart from place Cornic, right under the viaduct, but the **gare SNCF** is on rue Armand-Rousseau, high above the town at the western end of the viaduct. To reach it on foot, you have to climb the steep steps of Venelle de la Roche.

On the whole, Morlaix's **hotels** are fairly uninspiring, but worth a try is the *De l'Europe*, 1 rue d'Aiguillon (ⓣ02.98.62.11.99, ⓦwww.hotel-europe-com.fr; ❹), an eccentric old place, but very central, with modern and well-equipped rooms and a superb restaurant downstairs. Less expensive options include *Hôtel de la Gare*, 25 place St-Martin close to the *gare SNCF* (ⓣ02.98.88.03.29; ❷), with reasonable-value en-suite rooms above an American-themed bar, the *Green Wood Café*; and *Le Roy d'Ys*, 8 place des Jacobins (ⓣ02.98.63.30.55; ❶; closed Nov), a small hotel across the square from the town museum.

The best hunting ground for **restaurants** in Morlaix is to be found between St-Melaine church and place des Jacobins. Alternatives include *La Marée Bleue*, 3 rampe Ste-Mélaine (ⓣ02.98.63.24.21; closed Sun evening & Mon Sept–June), a well-respected seafood restaurant a minute's walk up from the tourist office – the €14 menu is a bit limited, but €28.50 ensures you a superb *assiette de fruits de mer*, and €36.50 buys a five-course feast – and the *Brocéliande*, 5 rue des Bouchers (ⓣ02.98.88.73.78; closed Tues & Nov; menu €19), in the southeast of town, which offers elegant evening-only dining in a *fin-de-siècle* atmosphere.

The parish closes

Morlaix makes an excellent base for visiting the countryside towards Brest, where **parish closes**, or *enclos paroissiaux* (walled churchyards incorporating cemetery, calvary and ossuary), celebrate the distinctive character of Breton Catholicism – closer to the Celtic past than to Rome – in elaborately sculpted scenes. Stone calvaries are covered in detailed scenes of the Crucifixion above a crowd of saints, gospel stories and legends; in richer parishes, a high stone arch leads into the churchyard, adjoining an equally majestic ossuary, where bones would be taken when the tiny cemeteries filled up. Most of the parish closes date from the two centuries either side of the union with France in 1532, Brittany's wealthiest period.

The most famous *enclos* are in three neighbouring parishes off the N12 between Morlaix and Landivisiau, on a clearly signposted route that's served by an SNCF bus. At **ST-THÉGONNEC**, the entire east wall of the church, currently being restored after a disastrous fire in 1998, is a carved and painted retable, with saints in niches and a hundred scenes depicted, while the pulpit and the painted oak entombment in the crypt beneath the ossuary are acknowledged masterpieces. At **LAMPAUL-GUIMILIAU**, the painted wooden baptistry, the dragons on the beams and the suitably wicked faces of the robbers on the calvary are the key components. Poor Katel Gollet (Katherine the Damned) is depicted as being tormented in hell at **GUIMILIAU** – for the crime of hedonism rather than manslaughter. In the legend she danced all her suitors to death until the reaper-figure Ankou stepped in to whirl her to eternal damnation. Further on at **LA ROCHE** (15km or so on towards Brest), where the ruined castle above the Elhorn estuary is said to have been her home, it is Ankou who appears on the ossuary with the inscription "I kill you all". A five-kilometre detour southeast of La Roche brings further variations at **LA MARTYRE** (where Ankou clutches his disembodied head) and its adjoining parish **PLOUDIRY**, the sculpting of its ossuary affirming the equality of social classes – in the eyes of Ankou.

In St-Thégonnec the *Auberge de St-Thégonnec*, 6 place de la Mairie (ⓣ02.98.79.61.18, ⓦwww.aubergesaintthegonnec.com; ❻; closed Sun evening & Mon, mid-Sept to mid-June), has a superb **restaurant**, while the *Moulin de Kerlaviou*, 2km west of St-Thégonnec (ⓣ02.98.79.60.57; ❸), is a ravishing farmhouse **B&B** in an almost absurdly pastoral riverside setting.

Roscoff and around

The opening of the deep-water port at **ROSCOFF** in 1973 was part of a general attempt to revitalize the Breton economy. The ferry services to Plymouth and to Cork aim not just to bring tourists, but also to revive the traditional trading links between the Celtic nations of Brittany, Ireland and southwest England. In fact, Roscoff had already long been a significant port. It was here that Mary Queen of Scots landed in 1548 on her way to Paris to be engaged to François, the son and heir of Henri II of France. And it was here that Bonnie Prince Charlie, the Young Pretender, landed in 1746 after his defeat at Culloden.

Roscoff itself, nonetheless, remains a small resort, where almost all activity is confined to **rue Gambetta** and to the old port – the rest of the roads are residential back streets full of retirement homes and institutions. One factor in preserving its old character is that both the ferry port and the *gare SNCF* are some way from the centre.

The town's sixteenth-century church, **Notre-Dame-de-Croas-Batz**, at the far end of rue Gambetta, is embellished with an ornate Renaissance belfry, complete with sculpted ships and a protruding stone cannon. From the side, rows of bells can be seen hanging in galleries, one above the other like a wedding cake created by Walt Disney. Some way beyond is the grand **Thalassotherapy Institute** of Rock Roum, while a kilometre further on is Roscoff's best **beach**, at Laber, surrounded by expensive hotels and apartments.

The old **harbour** is livelier, mixing an economy based on fishing with relatively low-key pleasure trips to the **Île de Batz**. The island looks almost walkable; a narrow pier stretches over 300m towards it before abruptly plunging into deep rocky waters. The Pointe de Bloscon and the fishermen's white chapel, the **Chapelle Ste-Barbe**, make a good vantage point, particularly when the tide is in.

In 1828, Henri Ollivier took **onions** to England from Roscoff, thereby founding a trade which flourished until the 1930s. The story of the "Johnnies" – that classic French image of men in black berets with strings of onions hanging over the handlebars of their bicycles – is told in the new **Musée des Johnnies** at 48 rue Brizeux, next to the *gare SNCF* (late June to mid-Sept daily except Tues 3–7pm; mid-Sept to Dec Sat & Sun only 2-6pm; €4).

Practicalities

Boats run by Brittany Ferries (ⓣ08.03.82.88.28, ⓦwww.brittany-ferries.com) from Plymouth (6hr) and Cork (19hr), and those run by Irish Ferries (ⓣ02.98.61.17.17, ⓦwww.irishferries.com) from Rosslare (21hr) dock at the Port de Bloscon, to the east (and just out of sight) of Roscoff. In summer, a direct **bus** service to Morlaix, Quimper and Benodet leaves from the ferry terminal coinciding with arrivals (Mon, Thurs & Sat 7am; Wed, Fri & Sun 3.30pm; CAT; ⓣ02.98.90.88.89). From the **gare SNCF**, a few hundred metres south of the town proper, a restricted rail service runs to Morlaix.

The **tourist office** is at 46 rue Gambetta in town (April–June & Sept Mon–Sat 9am–noon & 2–6pm; July & Aug Mon–Sat 9am–12.30pm & 1.30–7pm, Sun 10am–12.30pm; Oct–March Mon–Fri 10am–noon & 2–5pm, Sat 10am–noon; ⓦwww.roscoff-tourisme.com).

For a small town, Roscoff is well equipped with **hotels**, which are accustomed to late-night arrivals from the ferries. Good options in the old town include the *Hôtel-Restaurant des Arcades*, 15 rue Amiral-Réveillère (ⓣ02.98.69.70.45; ❸; closed Oct–Easter; menus from €9.50), housed in a sixteenth-century building with superb views; the family-run *Du Centre*, 5 rue Gambetta (ⓣ02.98.61.24.25; ❺; closed mid-Dec to Jan), looking out on the port, above the café-bar *Chez Janie*; and *Les Chardons Bleus*, 4 rue Amiral-Réveillère (ⓣ02.98.69.72.03, ⓕ02.98.61.27.86; ❹; closed Feb), a very friendly and helpful hotel with a good restaurant (closed Thurs Sept–June, plus Sun in winter). An outstanding newcomer at 19 place Lacaze-Duthiers, near Notre-Dame-de-Croas-Batz, is the gorgeously decorated *Hotel Le Temps de Vivre* (ⓣ02.98.19.33.19, ⓦwww.letempsdevivre.net; ❽), which has some luxuriously spacious rooms with interior-design bathrooms and wonderful sea views; rates are 25 percent lower for much of the winter. Nearer the ferry terminal is the *Hôtel-Restaurant le Bellevue*, rue Jeanne d'Arc (ⓣ02.98.61.23.38, ⓕ02.98.61.11.80; ❹; closed mid-Nov to mid-March, except Christmas and New Year), which has a lively bar, pleasant rooms and fine views from the dining room. Lower down the price range, there's an **HI hostel** on the Île de Batz and two **campsites**: *Camping municipal de Perharidy*, 2km west of town (ⓣ02.98.69.70.86, ⓔcamping-perharidy@wanadoo.fr; closed Oct–March), just off the route de Santec, and the roomier *Manoir de Kérestat*, 2km south towards St-Pol, which only holds 22 sites (ⓣ02.98.69.71.92; closed late Aug to early July). Hotels often have very decent dining rooms, though it's not easy to get a meal much after 9pm. Away from the hotels, the unanimously acclaimed favourite is the brasserie-style *Le Surcouf* at 14 rue Amiral-Réveillère, a smart, stylish place where the delicious menus – at €9.50 and €14.50 – are unbeatable value.

St-Pol-de-Léon

The main road south from Roscoff passes by fields of the famous Breton artichokes before arriving after 6km at **ST-POL-DE-LÉON**. It's not an exciting place but – assuming you've got your own transport – its two churches at least merit a pause. The **cathédrale**, in the main town square, was rebuilt towards the end of the thirteenth century along the lines of Coutances – a quiet classic of unified Norman architecture. The remains of St Pol are inside, alongside a large bell, rung over the heads of pilgrims during his *pardon* on March 12 in the unlikely hope of curing headaches and ear diseases. Just downhill is the original **Kreisker Chapel**, with access to the top of its sharp-pointed soaring granite belfry (now coated in yellow moss).

The Île de Batz

The long, narrow **ÎLE DE BATZ** (pronounced "Ba") mirrors Roscoff across the water, separated from it by a sea channel that's barely 200m wide at low tide but perhaps five times that when the tide is high. Appearances from the mainland are somewhat deceptive: the island's old town, home to a thousand or so farmers and fishermen, fills much of its southern shoreline, but those parts of Batz not visible from Roscoff are much wilder and more windswept. With no cars permitted, and some great expanses of sandy beach, it makes a wonderfully quiet retreat for families in particular, whether you're camping or staying in one of its two old-fashioned little hotels.

Ferries from Roscoff arrive at the quayside of the old town. There's a nice small beach along the edge of the harbour, though the sea withdraws so far at low tide that the port turns into a morass of slimy seaweed. You may well spot the island's best beach from the boat – it's the white-sand **Grève Blanche** towards its eastern end. Walking in that direction also brings you to the hostel (see below), and the 44-metre lighthouse that stands on the island's peak, all of 23m above sea level (second half of June daily except Wed 2–5pm; July to mid-Sept daily 1–5.30pm; €1.70).

An association of three different companies jointly operate fifteen-minute **ferry** services to the Île de Batz from Roscoff's long pier. Between late June and mid-September, the service is pretty much non-stop between 8am and 8pm daily, while at other times of year there are eight to ten trips daily between 8.30am and 7pm. The return fare is €6.50, with a €5 charge for bikes.

The island's nicest **hotel**, at the centre of the harbour, is the *Grand Hôtel Morvan* (Ⓣ02.98.61.78.06; ❹; closed Dec to mid-Feb), which serves good meals on its large seafront terraces. There's a **hostel** in a beautiful setting by the beach at the evocatively named Creach ar Bolloc'h (Ⓣ02.98.61.77.69; closed Oct–Easter; €12.10).

The abers

The coast west of Roscoff is among the most dramatic in Brittany, a jagged series of **abers** – deep, narrow estuaries – that hold a succession of small, isolated resorts. It's a little on the bracing side, especially if you're making use of the numerous **campsites**, but that just has to be counted as part of the appeal. In summer, at least, the temperatures are mild enough, and things get progressively more sheltered as you move around towards Le Conquet and Brest.

Around the abers

If you're dependent on public transport, bear in mind that the only stop on the Roscoff–Brest bus before it turns inland is **PLOUESCAT**. It's not quite on the sea itself, but there are campsites nearby on each of three adjacent beaches; of the **hotels**, best value is the *Roc'h-Ar-Mor*, right on the beach at Porsmeur (Ⓣ02.98.69.63.01, Ⓔroch.ar.mor@wanadoo.fr; ❶; closed Oct–March).

BRIGNOGAN-PLAGE, on the next *aber*, has a small natural harbour, once the lair of wreckers, with beaches and weather-beaten rocks to either side, as well as its own menhir. The two high-season **campsites** are the central municipal site at Kéravezan, the *Côte des Legendes* (Ⓣ02.98.83.41.65; closed Nov–March) and the *Du Phare*, east of town (Ⓣ02.98.83.45.06; closed Oct–April), while the *Castel Regis* **hotel** (Ⓣ02.98.83.40.22, Ⓦwww.castelregis.com; ❾ half-board; closed Oct–March), is expensive but beautifully sited among the rocks, right at the headland. There are also schools of sailing and riding.

The *aber* between Plouguerneau and **L'ABER-WRAC'H** has a stepping-stone crossing just upstream from the bridge at Llanellis, built in Gallo-Roman times, and its long cut stones still cross the three channels of water (access off the D28 signposted "Rascoll", and continue past farm buildings to the right to "Pont du Diable"). L'Aber-Wrac'h itself is a promising place to spend a little time. It's an attractive, modest-sized resort, within easy reach of a whole range of sandy beaches and a couple of worthwhile excursions. Beyond the town's little strip of bars and restaurants, the Baie des Anges stretches away towards the Atlantic, with the only sound the cry of seagulls feasting on the oyster beds. At the start of the bay, the irresistible *Hôtel la Baie des Anges*, 350 route des Anges (Ⓣ02.98.04.90.04, Ⓦwww.baie-des-anges.com; ❼; closed Jan & Feb), makes a peaceful and exceptionally comfortable place to **stay**. The best local **restaurant**, *Le Brennig* (Ⓣ02.98.04.81.12; closed Tues, and Feb & Oct), is back at the other end of town.

At the small harbour of **PORTSALL**, 5km along the coast from the far side of the next *aber*, l'Aber-Benoît, the **Espace Amoco Cadiz** commemorates a defining moment in local history (daily 9.30am–1pm & 2.30–7pm; free): on March 17, 1978, the sinking of the *Amoco Cadiz* supertanker resulted in an oil spill that devastated 350km of the Breton coastline, and threatened to ruin the local economy. Displays and films document not only the immense task of cleaning up the mess, but also the long legal battle to obtain compensation from the "multinational monster" responsible.

Five kilometres west of Portsall is **TRÉMAZAN**, whose ruined castle was the point of arrival in Brittany for Tristan and Iseult. From here a beautiful corniche road leads further along the coast. Odd little chapels dot the route, and the views of sea and rocks are unhindered before turning inland just before Le Conquet.

Le Conquet

LE CONQUET, at the far western tip of Brittany 24km beyond Brest, is a wonderful place, scarcely developed, with a long beach of clean white sand, protected from the winds by the narrow spit of the Kermorvan peninsula. It's very much a working fishing village, with grey-stone houses leading down to the stone jetties of a cramped harbour. It occasionally floods, causing great amusement to locals who watch the waves wash over cars left there by tourists taking the ferry out to Ouessant and Molène. A good walk 5km south brings you to the lighthouse at **Pointe St-Mathieu**, looking out to the islands from its site among the ruins of a Benedictine abbey. A small exhibition explains the abbey's history, including the legend that it holds the skull of St Matthew, brought here from Ethiopia by local seafarers (April–Sept daily 2.30–6.30pm; Oct–March Wed, Sat & Sun 2–6pm; €1.50).

The *Relais du Vieux Port*, quai Drellac (⊕02.98.89.15.91; ❷; closed Jan), offers a handful of attractive but inexpensive **rooms** right by the jetty in Le Conquet, and has a simple crêperie downstairs. Nearby, the larger *Pointe Ste Barbe* (⊕02.98.89.00.26; ❹–❻; closed Mon out of season & mid-Nov to mid-Dec), offers amazing sea views to guests in its more expensive rooms, and has a great restaurant, where menus start at €17. There's also a well-equipped **campsite** close to the sands of the Kermorvan peninsula, *Le Théven* (⊕02.98.89.06.90; closed Oct–March).

The Îles d'Ouessant and de Molène

The **Île d'Ouessant** ("Ushant" to the English) lies 30km northwest of Le Conquet, and its lighthouse at **Creac'h** (said to be the strongest in the world) is regarded as the entrance to the English Channel. The island is the last in a chain of smaller islands and half-submerged granite rocks. Most are uninhabited, or like Beniguet the preserve only of rabbits, but the **Île de Molène**, midway, has a village and can be visited. Both Molène and Ouessant are served by at least one ferry each day from Le Conquet and Brest; however, it's not practicable to visit more than one in a single day.

Île d'Ouessant

You arrive on the **Île d'Ouessant** at the modern **harbour** in the ominous-sounding Baie du Stiff. There's a scattering of houses here and dotted around

Getting to Ouessant and Molène

Penn Ar Bed (⊕02.98.80.80.80, Ⓦwww.pennarbed.fr) sail to **Ouessant** and **Molène** all year, with up to five daily departures from **Le Conquet** (first sailing at 8am daily in July & Aug; €26 to Ouessant return, under-17s €15.50; €23 to Molène return, under-17s €14), and one or two daily from Brest, always including one at 8.30am, which is the only one that stops at Molène (€30 to Ouessant return, under-17s €18; €27 to Molène return, under-17s €16). They also run from **Camaret** to **Ouessant** at 8.45am on Wednesday from May until early July, and on Monday to Saturday at 8.45am from early July until the end of August (€26.80 return, under-17s €16.10). Only on Wednesdays between early July and the start of September is it possible to sail from Camaret to **Molène**, at 8.45am (€22.80 return, under-17s €13.70).

Finist'Mer (Ⓦwww.finist-mer.fr) operate high-speed ferries to **Ouessant** in summer only. From **Camaret**, they offer a daily departure from mid-June until early July, and again from late August until mid-September, at 8.45am, while from early July until late August the boat leaves daily at 9.30am (⊕02.98.27.88.44; €26 return, under-17s €15). From **Le Conquet**, they offer three or four departures daily between June and September, with the first one being at 8.45am from early July until late August, and 9.30am otherwise (⊕02.98.89.16.61; €25 return, under-17s €14). Between early July and late August, they also sail to Ouessant from **Lanildut**, 25km northwest of Brest, as the first departure from Le Conquet calls in there at 9.15am (⊕08.00.50.03.88; €26 return, under-17s €15).

In addition, you can **fly** to Ouessant with **Finist'Air** (⊕02.98.84.64.87, Ⓦwww.finistair.fr). The fifteen-minute flights leave Brest's Guipavas airport daily at 8.30am and 4.45pm, with an adult one-way fare of €60.98, or €35.07 for under-13s. Groups of three or more adults go for €50.31 each.

the island, but the single town – with the only hotels and restaurants – is 4km away at **LAMPAUL**. Everybody from the boat heads there, either by the bus that meets each ferry or on bicycles rented from one of the many waiting entrepreneurs – a good idea, as the island is a bit too big to explore on foot.

Lampaul hasn't got a lot to it. The best beaches are sprawled around its bay, and, in case you should forget the perils of the sea, the town cemetery's **war memorial** lists all the ships in which townsfolk were lost, alongside graves of unknown sailors washed ashore and a chapel of wax "*proëlla* crosses" symbolizing the many islanders who never returned.

At nearby **NIOU**, the **Maison du Niou** (April Tues–Sun 2–6.30pm; May to mid-July & Sept daily 10.30am–6.30pm; mid-July to Aug daily 10.30am–6.30pm & 9–11pm; Oct–March Tues–Sun 2–4pm; €4) is actually two houses, one of which is a museum of island history, and the other a reconstruction of a traditional island house, complete with two massive "box beds", one for the parents and the other for the children. Officially, it forms half of the **Eco-Musée d'Ouessant**, in combination with the **Creac'h lighthouse** (same hours), which stands 1km northwest of Niou. This contains a small museum about lighthouses, and makes a good point from which to set out along the barren and exposed rocks of the north coast. Particularly in September and other times of migration, this stretch of coast is a remarkable spot for birdwatching. The star-shaped formations of crumbling walls that you'll see are not extra-terrestrial relics, but built so that the sheep – peculiarly tame here – can shelter from the strong winds.

Lampaul boasts several accommodation options. The adjacent **hotels** *Océan* (ⓣ02.98.48.80.03; ❸) and *Fromveur* (ⓣ02.98.48.81.30; ❸) both offer reasonable renovated rooms. The *Roch Ar Mor*, just down the street (ⓣ02.98.48.80.19, ⓔroch.armor@wanadoo.fr; ❸; closed Jan–March), makes a marginally more attractive alternative. There is also a small **campsite**, the *Penn ar Bed* (ⓣ02.98.48.84.65; closed Oct–April), and a little **hostel**, *La Croix Rouge* (ⓣ02.98.48.84.53; €13.35). All the hotel **restaurants** serve menus for under €20, but if you just come for a day, it's a good idea to buy a picnic before you set out – the Lampaul shops have limited and rather pricey supplies.

Île de Molène

The **Île de Molène** is quite well populated for a sparse strip of sand. Its inhabitants make their money from seaweed collecting and drying – and to an extent from crabbing and from crayfish, which they gather on foot, canoe or even tractor at low tide. The tides here are more than usually dramatic, halving or doubling the island's territory at a stroke – it's not called "the bald isle" for nothing. Few people do more than look at Molène as an afternoon's excursion from Le Conquet, but it's possible to stay too. There are **rooms** – very chilly in winter – at *Kastell An Doal* (ⓣ02.98.07.39.11; ❼ half-board; closed Jan), one of the old buildings by the port.

Brest

Set in a magnificent natural harbour, known as the Rade de Brest, the city of **BREST** is doubly sheltered from ocean storms by the bulk of Léon to the north and by the Crozon peninsula to the south. It has always played an important role in war, and in trade whenever peace allowed. Today it is the base of the French Atlantic Fleet with a dry dock that can accommodate ships of up to 500,000 tonnes; as a ship repair centre, Brest ranks sixth in the world.

During World War II, Brest was continually bombed to prevent the Germans from using it as a submarine base. When the Americans liberated it on September 18, 1944 after a six-week siege, they found the town devastated beyond recognition. The architecture of the postwar town is raw and bleak and though there have been attempts to green the city, it has proved too windswept to respond.

Arrival, information and accommodation

The **gare SNCF** and **gare routière** (ⓣ02.98.44.46.73) are side-by-side in place du 19ème-RI at the bottom of avenue Clémenceau. Bus services include those to Plouescat and Roscoff (Les Cars du Kreisker; ⓣ02.98.69.00.93); to the Crozon peninsula via Landévennec (ⓣ02.98.27.02.02); and to Le Conquet (Sarl St Mathieu Transports; ⓣ02.98.98.12.02).

Brest's **airport** (ⓣ02.98.32.01.00), 9km northeast of the centre at **Guipavas**, is seeing much more tourist traffic these days, though no local buses coincide with flights. A **taxi** into central Brest should cost little more than €12. At the airport you'll find **car rental** desks for all the major chains.

As well as the sailings to Ouessant, detailed on p.478, in summer from two to four **boats** per day make the 25-minute crossing from Brest's Port de Commerce to **Le Fret** on the Crozon peninsula (Société Azenor; June–Sept; ⓣ02.98.41.46.23, ⓦwww.azenor.com; €14 return, under-17s €10). Sailings are met at the port in Le Fret by buses for Crozon (15min), Morgat (30min) and Camaret (40min). Société Azenor and other operators also run excursions around the harbour and the Rade de Brest (1hr 30min), typically costing €13.50.

Brest's **tourist office** on avenue Clémenceau faces place de la Liberté (July & Aug Mon–Sat 9.30am–7pm, Sun 2–4pm; Sept–June Mon–Sat 10am–12.30pm & 2–6pm; ⓣ02.98.44.24.96).

The vast majority of Brest's **hotels** remain open throughout the year; only a few however bother to maintain their own restaurants. Several lie within easy walking distance of the stations, in the vicinity of the central place de la Liberté. The year-round **hostel** is on rue de Kerbriant, Port de Plaisance du Moulin-Blanc (ⓣ02.98.41.90.41, ⓔbrest.aj.cis@wanadoo.fr; €12.10 including breakfast), 3km east of the *gares SNCF* and *routière* in a wooded setting near Océanopolis, on bus route #7 – beware the limited Sunday service however.

Hotels

Astoria 9 rue Traverse ⓣ02.98.80.19.10, ⓕ02.98.80.52.41. Peaceful central hotel with a cheerful ambience and decor, not far up from the port. Closed 3 wks Dec–Jan. ❶

Comoedia 21 rue d'Aguillon ⓣ02.98.46.54.82. Simple but very cheap rooms in a quiet street just up from the port – none of them en suite – with an equally no-frills restaurant downstairs. ❶

De la Gare 4 bd Gambetta ⓣ02.98.44.47.01, ⓕ02.98.43.34.07. En-suite rooms opposite the stations; you can pay a little extra for an uninterrupted view of the Rade de Brest from the upper storeys. ❸

Mercure Continental square de la Tour d'Auvergne ⓣ02.98.80.50.40, ⓕ02.98.43.17.47. Grand, recently refurbished luxury hotel not far from the tourist office, with helpful staff and spotlessly clean rooms, several of them with fine Art Deco features. ❺

Pasteur 29 rue Louis-Pasteur ⓣ02.98.46.08.73, ⓕ02.98.43.46.80. Clean, good-value hotel, offering plain en-suite rooms above a bar near the St-Louis church. ❷

The Town

For the casual tourist, Brest has little to offer, and few relics of the past remain. The fifteenth-century **castle** looks impressive on its headland and offers a superb panorama of the city, but inside it's not especially interesting. Three of its towers house part of the collection of the **Musée National de la Marine** (Feb, March & mid-Sept to mid-Dec daily except Tues 10am–noon & 2–6pm; April to mid-Sept daily 10am–6.30pm; €4.60, €3 from the tourist office). The fourteenth-century **Tour Tanguy** on the opposite bank of the River Penfeld, with its conical slate roof, serves as a history museum of Brest before 1939 (June–Sept daily 10am–noon & 2–7pm; Oct–May Wed & Thurs 2–5pm, Sat & Sun 2–6pm; free).

Brest's most up-to-the-minute attraction is **Océanopolis**, a couple of kilometres east of the city centre beside the Port de Plaisance du Moulin-Blanc (April to mid-July daily 9am–6pm; mid-July to Aug daily 9am–7pm; Sept–March Tues–Sat 10am–5pm, plus Sun in school holidays 10am–6pm; Ⓦwww.oceanopolis.com; €14.50, under-18s €10). This futuristic complex currently consists of three distinct aquariums and a 3-D cinema. The aquarium in the main white dome, known as the Temperate Pavilion, focuses on the Breton littoral and Finistère's fishing industry, holding all kinds of fish, seals, molluscs, seaweed and sea anemones. The emphasis is very much on the edible, with the displays on the life-cycle of a scallop, for example, culminating in a detailed recipe. That's complemented by a Tropical Pavilion, with a tankful of ferocious-looking sharks plus a myriad of rainbow-hued smaller fish that populate a highly convincing coral reef, and a Polar Pavilion, complete with polar bears and penguins. Everything's very high-tech, and perhaps a little too earnest for some visitors' tastes, but it's quite possible to spend an entertaining day on site – especially if you take the assorted restaurants, snack bars and gift stores into consideration.

Eating

As well as a concentration of low-priced places near the stations, Brest offers a wide assortment of **restaurants**. Rue Jean-Jaurès, climbing east from the place de la Liberté, holds plenty of bistros and bars, while just to the north, place Guérin is the centre of the student-dominated quartier St-Martin.

L'Amour de Pomme de Terre 23 rue des Halles Ⓣ02.98.43.48.51. The name says it all. This central restaurant specializes not merely in potatoes, but in one single kind of potato – the "samba". Dishes range from simple baked spuds to far more eccentric offerings, typically costing around €20. There are also some tasty Breton stews. Open daily until late.

La Maison de l'Océan 2 quai de la Douane Ⓣ02.98.80.44.84. Blue-hued fish restaurant down by the port, open daily for lunch and dinner, and serving wonderful assortments of seafood from €15.

Ma Petite Folie plage du Moulin-Blanc Ⓣ02.98.42.44.42. Converted fishing boat, moored in the pleasure port, which serves a wonderfully fishy €18 set menu and also offers a wide range of à la carte dishes and daily specials. Closed Sun & two weeks in mid-Aug.

Le Ruffé 1 rue Yves-Collet Ⓣ02.98.46.07.70. An attractive place between the *gare SNCF* and the tourist office, open late, that prides itself on good, traditional French seafood dishes, served on menus costing €14 and upwards. Closed Sun.

The Crozon peninsula

The **Crozon peninsula**, a craggy outcrop of land shaped like a long-robed giant, arms outstretched to defend bay and roadstead, is the central feature of Finistère's torn chaos of estuaries and promontories. Much the easiest way for cyclists and travellers relying on public transport to reach the peninsula from Brest is via the **ferries** to Le Fret (see opposite).

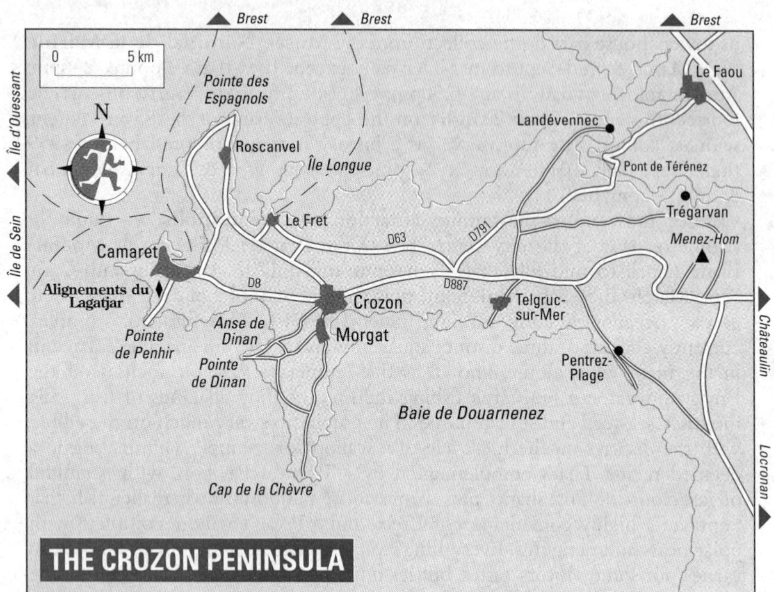

Motorists heading for Crozon have to follow a circuitous route skirting this complex coast through **PLOUGASTEL-DAOULAS** – famed for its **strawberries**, *les fraises de Plougastel*. At the church here, the calvary shows more torment for Katel Gollet (Katherine the Damned), in this case being raped by devils, but with a more sympathetic sculpting of Katel herself than at Guimiliau. To taste the strawberries, either wrapped in or preceded by delicious crêpes, head for the **Pointe de l'Armorique**, the extreme tip of the Presqu'île de Plougastel-Daoulas; nestling amid a flourishing garden and with wonderful views of the *rade* towards Brest, *An Ty Coz* is open every day for lunch and dinner.

As you approach the Crozon peninsula, it's well worth making a slight detour to climb the hill of **Menez-Hom**, "at the giant's feet", for a fabulous view of the land and water alternating out to the ocean. Getting down to the coastal headlands themselves can be a bit of a disappointment after this vision: those extremities that don't house military installations tend to be too crowded. But it is the cliffs that tourists head for here, and some of the **beaches**, like **La Palue** on the southern arm, are almost deserted.

Daoulas and Le Faou

Ten kilometres beyond Plougastel-Daoulas, the **abbey** at **DAOULAS** holds Brittany's only Romanesque cloister. It now stands beautiful and isolated at the edge of cool monastery gardens, since its surrounding buildings were destroyed during the Revolution. Since 1984 it has been used as a cultural centre for Finistère, which stages ambitious historical exhibitions lasting for around six months at a time (daily: May–June & Oct–Nov 10am–6pm; July–Aug 10am –7pm; Ⓦwww.abbaye-daoulas.com; €6).

From Daoulas the motorway and railway cut down to Châteaulin and Quimper. For Crozon, you'll need to veer west at **LE FAOU**, a tiny medieval port, still boasting a few sixteenth-century gabled houses and set on its own individual estuary. From beside the pretty little village church – whose porch holds some intriguing carved apostles – a sheltered corniche follows the river to the sea, where there are sailing and windsurfing facilities.

Le Faou holds two good and very similar **hotels**, both *logis de France* with top-class restaurants – the *Relais de la Place* (ⓣ02.98.81.91.19; ❸; closed mid-Sept to mid-Jan), and the Best Western *Hôtel de Beauvoir* (ⓣ02.98.81.90.31, ⓦwww.hotel-beauvoir.com; ❺; closed mid-Nov to Dec & Mon Sept–June). The one snag is that they're not in the most attractive part of town – near the river – but a few hundred metres south in the newer and much noisier main square.

Landévennec

Nine kilometres west of Le Faou, by way of a beautiful shoreline road, the **Pont de Térénez** spans the Aulne – outlet for the Nantes–Brest canal – to the Crozon peninsula. Doubling back to the right as soon as you cross the bridge brings you after a further 5km to **LANDÉVENNEC**, where archeologists are uncovering the outline of what may be Brittany's oldest abbey (May, June & last 2 weeks of Sept daily except Sat 2–6pm; July to mid-Sept daily 10am–7pm; Oct–April Sun 2–6pm; ⓦabbaye-landevennec.cef.fr; €4). Nothing survives above ground of the original thatched hut, constructed in a forest clearing by St Gwennolé around 485 AD. After the abbey had been pillaged by raiding Normans in 913 AD, however, it was rebuilt in stone. Those foundations can now be seen, together with displays on monastic history and facsimile manuscripts. There's a small but attractive **hotel** in the heart of Landévennec, *Le St-Patrick* (ⓣ02.98.27.70.83; ❷; closed mid-Oct to mid-March).

Crozon and Morgat

The first town on the peninsula proper, **CROZON**, is not much more than a one-way traffic system to distribute tourists among the various resorts – though it does keep a market running most of the week. **MORGAT**, just down the hill, is a more realistic and enticing base. It has a long crescent beach that ends in a pine slope, and a well-sheltered harbour full of pleasure boats raced down from England and Ireland. The main attractions are **boat trips** around the various headlands, such as the **Cap de la Chèvre** (which is a good clifftop walk if you'd rather make your own way). The most popular is the 45-minute tour of the **Grottes**, multicoloured caves in the cliffs, accessible only by sea but with steep "chimneys" up to the clifftops. Organized by two rival companies on the quay, the trips run every quarter of an hour in high season; they often leave full, however, so it's worth booking a few hours in advance (daily May–Sept; ⓣ02.98.27.10.71 or ⓣ02.98.26.20.10; €9).

The **tourist office** for the whole peninsula is in the *gare routière* at Crozon (mid-June to mid-Sept Mon–Sat 9.15am–12.30pm & 1.30–7pm, Sun 10am–12.30pm; mid-Sept to mid-June Mon–Fri 10am–12.30pm & 2.30–5.30pm, Sat 10am–noon; ⓣ02.98.26.17.18, ⓦwww.menez-hom.com). Morgat has its own little summer-only information office in its main square (June & Sept Mon–Sat 10am–noon & 2–6.30pm; July & Aug Mon–Sat 10am–12.30pm & 2–7.30pm, Sun 4–7pm; ⓣ02.98.27.29.49).

All the **hotels** in Morgat are quite expensive. Appealing options include the *Grand Hôtel de la Mer*, an imposing 1930s structure set at the eastern end of the beach (ⓣ02.98.27.02.09; ❸; closed Nov–March), and the quieter *Julia*, 400 metres from the beach at 43 rue de Tréflez (ⓣ02.98.27.05.89; ❸; closed

Nov–Feb). With over 800 pitches available, **campers** are spoilt for choice: the best sites are the three-stars at *Plage de Goulien* (Ⓣ02.98.27.17.10, Ⓔcamping.goulien@presquile-crozon.com; closed late Sept to May) and *Les Pins*, towards the pointe de Dinan (Ⓣ02.98.27.21.95, Ⓔcamping.lespins@presquile-crozon.com; closed Nov to March). The best place to eat in Morgat is *Assiette et Marée*, at 52 boulevard de la Plage, where the interior and terrace chairs are done out in a sunny yellow and you can have a very decent seafood platter for just under €20. One of the best **restaurants** on the peninsula is in Crozon itself: *Le Mutin gourmand*, at 1 rue Graveran, offers a wide range of menus from €16 to €49, featuring such delicacies as mackerel and tomato tart and strawberry gratin with almond cream.

Camaret

CAMARET is another sheltered port, at the very tip of the peninsula. Its most distinguishing feature is the pink-orange **Château de Vauban**, standing four-square at the end of the long jetty that runs back parallel to the main town waterfront. Walled, moated, and accessible via a little gatehouse reached by means of a drawbridge, it was built in 1689 to guard the approaches to Brest; these days it guards no more than a motley assortment of decaying half-submerged fishing boats, abandoned to rot beside the jetty. There are two beaches nearby – a small one to the north and another, larger and more attractive, in the low-lying (and rather marshy) Anse de Dinan. In summer Penn Ar Bed (Ⓣ02.98.80.80.80, Ⓦwww.pennarbed.fr) operates an irregular **ferry** service from Camaret to the islands of Ouessant and Sein, while Finist'Mer sails to Ouessant only (Ⓣ02.98.27.88.44, Ⓦwww.finist-mer.fr); the fare is around €26 return.

Camaret has its own little **tourist office** at 15 quai Kleber (July & Aug Mon–Sat 9am–7pm, Sun 10am–1pm; Sept to June Mon 2.15–6pm, Tues–Sat 9.15am–noon & 2–6pm; Ⓣ02.98.27.93.60). A little walk away from the centre, around the port towards the protective jetty, the quai du Styvel contains a row of excellent **hotels**. Both the *Vauban* (Ⓣ02.98.27.91.36; ❷; closed Dec & Jan) and *Du Styvel* (Ⓣ02.98.27.92.74; ❸; closed Jan) are exceptionally hospitable, with rooms that look right out across the bay, but only the *Styvel* has a restaurant. There are also various **campsites**, such as the four-star *Le Grand Large* (Ⓣ02.98.27.91.41, Ⓦwww.campinglegrandlarge.com; closed Oct–March) and the two-star municipal *Lannic* (Ⓣ02.98.27.91.31; closed Oct–Easter). Back along the quayside in the centre of town, *La Voilerie*, 7 quai Toudouze (Ⓣ02.98.27.99.55), is an excellent fish **restaurant**, with a €25 menu, while further along at no. 22, *Chez Philippe*, specializing in mussels at around €8, has menus between €9 and €20. Halfway between the two, amid a row of busy bars offering a variety of French and foreign beers, sometimes on tap, is *Côté Mer*, another restaurant with a solid reputation and an appetizing menu at €24.

South towards Quimper

Moving south of the Crozon peninsula, you soon enter the ancient kingdom of **Cornouaille**. The most direct route to the region's principal city, **Quimper**, leaves the sea behind and heads due south, passing close to the unchanged medieval village of **Locronan**. However, if you can spare the time, it's worth following the supremely isolated coastline instead around the Baie de

Douarnenez to the **Pointe du Raz**, the western tip of Finistère. With a few exceptions – most notably its "land's end" capes – this stretch of coast has kept out of the tourist mainstream, and nowhere does that hold more true than on the remarkable, remote **Île de Sein**.

Locronan

LOCRONAN, a short way from the sea on the minor road that leads down from the Crozon peninsula, is a prime example of a Breton town that has remained frozen in its ancient form by more recent economic decline. From 1469 through to the seventeenth century, it was a successful centre for woven linen, supplying sails to the French, English and Spanish navies. It was first rivalled by Vitré and Rennes, before suffering the "agony and ruin" so graphically described in its small **museum** (Mon–Sat 10am–1pm & 2–6pm; €3). As a result, the rich medieval houses of the town centre have never been superseded or surrounded by modern development. Film directors love its authenticity, even if Roman Polanski, filming *Tess*, deemed it necessary to change all the porches, put new windows on the Renaissance houses, and bury the main square in mud to make it all look a bit more English.

Today Locronan is once more prosperous, with its main source of income the tourists who buy wooden statues carved by local artisans, pottery brought up from the Midi, and leather jackets of less specified provenance. This commercialization should not, however, put you off making at least a passing visit, for the town itself is genuinely remarkable, centred around the focal **Église St-Ronan**. Be sure to take the time to walk down the hill of the **rue Moal**, where the lovely little stone chapel of Nôtre-Dame de Bonne Nouvelle holds some surprising modern stained glass, and a wooden statue of a depressed-looking Jesus.

Simply to park on the outskirts of Locronan costs €2.50, though at least your ticket remains valid for a full year. The **tourist office** (Mon–Sat 10am–1pm & 2–6pm; ⓣ02.98.91.70.14) adjoins a local history museum. The one **hotel**, *Du Prieuré*, on the edge of town at 11 rue du Prieuré (ⓣ02.98.91.70.89, ⓦwww.hotel-le-prieure.com; ❹; closed mid-Nov to mid-March) is not particularly attractive, but offers well-equipped rooms and posseses a good restaurant.

Douarnenez

Sufficient quantities of tuna, sardines and assorted crustaceans are still landed at the port of **DOUARNENEZ**, in the superbly sheltered Baie de Douarnenez, south of the Crozon peninsula, to keep the largest fish canneries in Europe busy. However, the catch has been declining ever since 1923, when eight hundred fishing boats brought in 100 million sardines during the six-month season. Over the last twenty years or so, Douarnenez has therefore set out – at phenomenal expense, the subject of considerable local controversy – to redefine itself as a living museum of all matters maritime.

Since 1993, **Port-Rhû**, on the west side of town, has been designated as the **Port-Musée**, with its entire waterfront taken up with fishing and other vessels gathered from throughout northern Europe. Its centrepiece, the **Musée du Bateau** in the place de l'Enfer (April to mid-June & mid-Sept to early Nov Tues–Sun 10am–12.30pm & 2–6pm; mid-June to mid-Sept daily 10am–7pm; €2 entry to quayside, €6.20 with boats visit), doubles as a working boatyard, where visitors can watch or join in the construction of seagoing vessels, using techniques from all over the world and from all different periods. When the museum first opened, it was possible to roam in and out of all the boats in the port itself. Sadly, however, although you can still admire them from the quayside all year, for no charge, only three remain accessible, during only those hours (and months) when the museum is open.

Of the three separate harbour areas in Douarnenez, the most appealing is the rough-and-ready **port de Rosmeur**, on the east side, which is nominally the fishing port used by the smaller local craft. Its quayside – far from totally commercialized, but holding a reasonable number of cafés and restaurants – curves between a pristine wooded promontory to the right and the fish canneries to the left, which continue around the north of the headland. The various **beaches** around town look pretty enough, but are dangerous for swimming.

The **tourist office** in Douarnenez is at 2 rue du Dr-Mével (Mon–Sat 9am–noon & 2–5/7pm; ⓣ02.98.92.13.35, ⓦwww.douarnenez-tourisme.com), a short walk up from the Port-Musée. Among good-value **hotels** are *Le Bretagne*, nearby at 23 rue Duguay-Trouin (ⓣ02.98.92.30.44; ❷), and the more upmarket *De France*, also nearby, on the main street at 4 rue Jean Jaurès (ⓣ02.98.92.00.02, ⓔhotel.de.france.dz@wanadoo.fr; ❹), which is home to the high-quality *Le Doyen* restaurant. Close by on the bay, there's a two-star **campsite**, *Croas Men* (ⓣ02.98.74.00.18, ⓦwww.croas-men.com; closed mid-Oct to March), at Tréboul/Les Sables Blancs. One of the best central seafood **restaurants** is *Le Bigorneau Amoureux* (ⓣ02.98.92.35.55; closed Tues), which has a terrace overlooking the plage des Dames.

The Baie des Trépassés and the Pointe du Raz

The **Baie des Trépassés** (Bay of the Dead), 30km west of Douarnenez, gets its grim name from the shipwrecked bodies that used to be washed up there, and is a possible site of the lost city of Ys (see p.488). However, it's a very attractive spot of green meadows, too exposed to support trees, which end abruptly – on the low cliffs to either side, a huge expanse of flat sand (in fact little else at low tide), and crashing waves that thrash surfers and windsurfers to within an inch of their lives. Beyond the waves, you can usually make out the white-painted houses along the harbour on the Île de Sein, while the various uninhabited rocks in between hold a veritable forest of lighthouses.

In total, less than half a dozen scattered buildings intrude upon the emptiness, including two **hotels**, both with tremendous views. Right in the middle is the pink *Hôtel de la Baie des Trépassés* (ⓣ02.98.70.61.34, ⓔhoteldelabaie@aol.com; ❸; closed mid-Nov to Jan), which has menus of wonderfully fresh seafood from €15. The larger *Relais de la Pointe du Van*, run by the same management, is slightly higher up, to the right (ⓣ02.98.70.62.79, ⓔpointeduvan@free.fr; ❸; closed Oct–March).

The **Pointe du Raz** – the Land's End of both Finistère and France – has recently been designated as a "Grande Site National", and with its former military installations now thankfully cleared away it makes a dramatic spectacle. You can walk out to the plummeting fissures of the *pointe*, filling and draining with a deafening surf-roar, and beyond, high above on precarious paths.

Audierne

Though on the whole the exposed southwestern extremities of Brittany are not areas you'd immediately associate with a classic summer sun-and-sand holiday, **AUDIERNE**, 25km west of Douarnenez on the Baie d'Audierne, is an exception. An active fishing port, specializing in prawns and crayfish, it spreads along the northern shore of the Goyen estuary a short way back from the sea. At the inland end of town, a new **aquarium** holds tankfuls of mostly local fish, captioned as ever with the stress on gastronomy – "the flesh is firm and much enjoyed" – and captive cormorants and gulls put on regular aerobatic displays (April–Sept daily 10am–7pm, €10.50, under-15s €7.50; Oct–March daily during school holidays 2-5pm, €6, under-15s €4; Ⓦwww.aquarium.fr. From the town centre, the road continues just over 1km to the long, curving and surprisingly sheltered **beach** of Ste-Evette.

Audierne's **tourist office** is on the main square in the heart of town, at 8 rue Victor-Hugo (July & Aug Mon–Sat 9am–7pm; Sept–June Mon–Sat 9.30am–noon & 2–6pm; Ⓣ02.98.70.12.20, Ⓦwww.audierne-tourisme.com). On the seaward side of the road, in a superb position right at Ste-Evette beach, stands the **hotel** *Au Roi Gradlon*, 3 bd Manu-Brusq (Ⓣ02.98.70.04.51, Ⓦwww.auroigradlon.com; ❸; closed mid-Dec to Jan). Its unusual design means that its high-quality street-level dining room is in fact on the top storey, with several further floors, concealed from the road, dropping down below it to the beach.

The Île de Sein

Of all the Breton islands, the tiny **Île de Sein**, just 8km off the end of the Pointe du Raz, has to be the most extraordinary. Its very grip on existence seems so tenuous that it's hard to believe anyone could truly survive here; nowhere does it rise more than six metres above the surrounding ocean, and for much of its 2.5-kilometre length it's barely broader than the breakwater wall of bricks that serves as its central spine.

In fact, the island has been inhabited since prehistoric times, and it was reputed to have been the very last refuge of the druids in Brittany. It also became famous during World War II, when its entire male population answered Général de Gaulle's call to join him in exile in England. Today, over three hundred islanders continue to make their living from the sea, gathering rainwater and seaweed, and fishing for scallops, lobster and crayfish.

Setting off to reach the island on a misty morning feels as though you're sailing off the edge of the world. There are no cars here, and even bicycles are not permitted. Depending on the tide, boats pull in at one or other of the two adjoining harbours that constitute Sein's one tightknit village, in front of which a little beach appears at low tide. The village also holds a **museum** of local history (June & Sept daily 10am–noon & 2–4pm, July & Aug daily 10am–noon & 2–6pm; €2.50), packed with black-and-white photos and press clippings, and displaying a long list of shipwrecks from 1476 onwards. The basic activity for visitors, however, is to take a bracing walk.

The principal departure point for **boats** to Sein is Ste-Evette beach, just outside **Audierne**. The crossing takes around an hour, with services operated by Vedette-Biniou (daily: second half of June & first half of Sept 10am; early July 10am & 1.30pm; mid-July to Aug 10am, 1.30pm & 5pm; Ⓣ02.98.70.21.15; Ⓦwww.vedette-biniou.fr.st; adults €24 return, under-16s €13.50), and Penn Ar Bed (daily: July & Aug 9am, 11.30am & 4.50pm; Sept–June 9.30am; Ⓣ02.98.70.70.70, Ⓦwww.pennarbed.fr; adults €22.50 return, under-16s €13.50). On Sundays in July and August, Penn Ar Bed also runs trips to Sein from **Brest** (departs 8am; adults €30 return, under-16s €18) via **Camaret** (8.45am; adults €26.80 return, under-16s €16.10).

Sein is hardly bursting with facilities, but it does hold two **hotels**: the *Trois Dauphins*, looking out over the beach from the middle of the port (Ⓣ02.98.70.92.09; ❷; closed Mon), and the *Hôtel-Restaurant d'Armen* (Ⓣ02.98.70.90.77, Ⓦwww.hotel.armen.free.fr; ❸), the very last building you come to as you walk west out of town – all its rooms face the sea as there's ocean on both sides, and it serves good food.

Quimper

QUIMPER, capital of the ancient diocese, kingdom and later duchy of Cornouaille, is the oldest Breton city. According to legend, the first bishop of Quimper, St Corentin, came with the first Bretons across the Channel some time between the fourth and seventh centuries to the place they named Little Britain. He lived by eating a regenerating and immortal fish all his life, and was made bishop by one King Gradlon, whose life he later saved when the sea-bed city of **Ys** was destroyed. According to one version, Gradlon built Ys in the Baie de Douarnenez, protected from the water by gates and locks to which only he and his daughter had keys. However, St Corentin suspected her of evil doings, and was proven right: at the urging of the Devil, the princess unlocked the gates, the city flooded and Gradlon escaped only by obeying Corentin and throwing his daughter into the sea. Back on dry land and in need of a new capital, Gradlon founded Quimper. Ys remains on the sea floor – it will rise again when Paris ("*Par-Ys*", "equal to Ys") sinks – and, according to tradition, on feast days sailors can still hear church bells and hymns under the water.

A relaxed kind of place, modern Quimper is still active enough to have the bars – and the atmosphere – to make it worth going out café-crawling. "The charming little place" known to Flaubert takes at most half an hour to cross on foot. The town's name comes from "kemper", denoting the junction of the two rivers, the Steir and the Odet, around which cram the cobbled streets (now mainly pedestrianized) of the **medieval quarter**, dominated by the cathedral nearby. As the Odet curves from east to southwest it's crossed by numerous low, flat bridges, bedecked with geraniums and chrysanthemums in the autumn. You can stroll along the boulevards on both banks of the river, where several ultramodern edifices blend in a surprisingly harmonious way with their ancient – and attractive – surroundings. Overlooking all are the wooded slopes of **Mont Frugy**. There's no great pressure in Quimper to rush around monuments or museums, and the most enjoyable option may be to take a boat and drift down "the prettiest river in France" to the open sea at Bénodet.

Arrival, information and accommodation

The **gare SNCF** (Ⓣ02.98.98.31.26) and **gare routière** (Ⓣ02.98.90.88.89) are next to each other on avenue de la Gare, some way east of the town centre. Local **buses** #1 and #6 connect with both, but all pass through place de la Résistance near the tourist office. If you want to use public transport to get to the coast anywhere nearby, the bus is your only option. The most useful local operator is the Compagnie Amoricaine de Transport or CAT, 10 rue Jules Verne; (Ⓣ02.98.95.02.36), which runs services to **Bénodet**, leaving from the *gare routière* or place de la Résistance; to **Audierne** and Pointe du Raz, from the *gare routière* or place de Locronan; and to **Concarneau** and **Quimperlé** from the *gare routière*.

Between June and September you can **sail** from Quimper down the Odet to Bénodet, which takes about 1hr 15min, on Vedettes de l'Odet (Bénodet Ⓣ02.98.57.00.58, Quimper Ⓣ02.98.52.98.41, Ⓦwww.vedettes-odet.com;

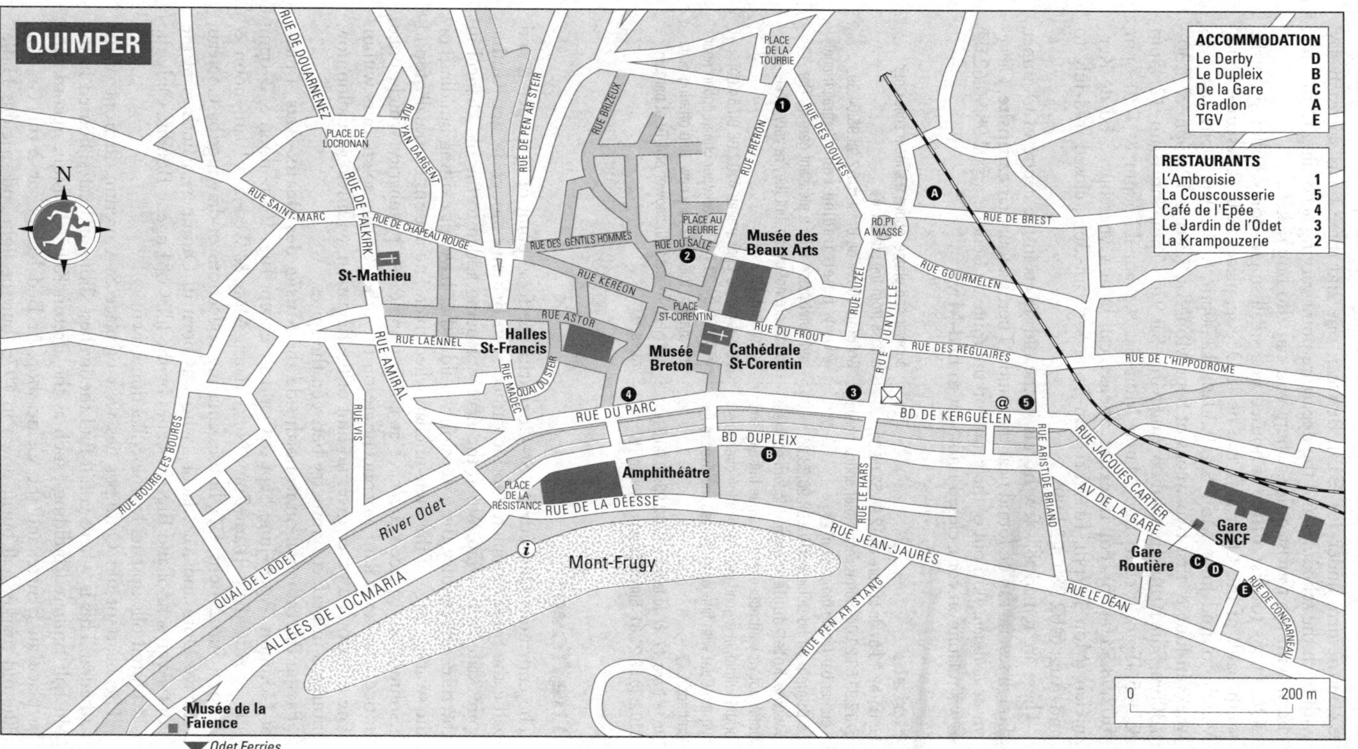
QUIMPER
ACCOMMODATION
Le Derby D
Le Dupleix B
De la Gare C
Gradlon A
TGV E
RESTAURANTS
L'Ambroisie 1
La Couscousserie 5
Café de l'Epée 4
Le Jardin de l'Odet 3
La Krampouzerie 2
0
200 m
N
Musée des Beaux Arts
Cathédrale St-Corentin
Musée Breton
Amphithéâtre
Mont-Frugy
Halles St-Francis
St-Mathieu
Gare SNCF
Gare Routière
River Odet
Musée de la Faïence
Odet Ferries
PLACE DE LA TOURBIE
RUE DES DOUVES
RUE FRERON
RUE DE BREST
RD.PT A MASSÉ
RUE GOURMELEN
RUE DES RÉGUAIRES
RUE DE L'HIPPODROME
RUE LUZEL
RUE JUNVILLE
BD DE KERGUÉLEN
RUE ARISTIDE BRIAND
RUE JACQUES CARTIER
AV DE LA GARE
RUE LE DÉAN
RUE DE CONCARNEAU
RUE JEAN-JAURES
RUE PEN AR STANG
RUE LE HARS
BD DUPLEIX
RUE DU FROUT
PLACE AU BEURRE
RUE DU SALLE
PLACE ST-CORENTIN
RUE KEREON
RUE ASTOR
RUE BRIZEUX
RUE DES GENTILS HOMMES
RUE DE PEN AR STEIR
RUE DU PARC
RUE DE LA DÉESSE
PLACE DE LA RÉSISTANCE
QUAI DU STEIR
RUE MADEC
RUE LAENNEL
RUE AMIRAL
RUE VIS
RUE YAN DARGENT
RUE DE CHAPEAU ROUGE
RUE DE FALKIRK
PLACE DE LOCRONAN
RUE DE DOUARNENEZ
RUE SAINT-MARC
RUE BOURG LES BOURGS
QUAI DE L'ODET
ALLÉES DE LOCMARIA

€21.50 return, under-13s €13). Between one and three boats sail each day, with both the schedules and the departure point varying according to the tide; check with the tourist office, where you can also buy tickets.

Quimper's **tourist office** is housed in a small single-storey building on the south bank of the Odet at 7 rue de la Déesse, place de la Résistance (mid-March to mid-June Mon–Sat 9.30am–12.30pm & 1.30–6.30pm; last two weeks in June & first two weeks of Sept Mon–Sat 9.30am–12.30pm & 1.30–6.30pm, Sun 10am–1pm; July & Aug Mon–Sat 9am–7pm, Sun 10am–12.45pm & 3–5.45pm; Oct to mid-March Mon–Sat 9.30am–12.30pm & 1.30–6pm; ⓣ02.98.53.04.05). For **Internet access**, call in at Cybercopy, 3 bd de Kerguélen (Mon 1–7pm, Tues–Fri 9am–7pm, Sat 9am–3pm, closed mid-July to mid-Aug; ⓣ02.98.64.33.99).

There are remarkably few **hotels** in the old streets in the centre of Quimper, though several can be found near the station. There's a four-star **campsite**, *Orangerie de Lannion*, 4km out of the centre on the route de Bénodet (ⓣ02.98.90.62.02; ⓦwww.lanniron.com; closed mid-Sept to mid-May).

Hotels

Le Derby 13 av de la Gare ⓣ02.98.52.06.91, ⓕ02.98.53.39.04. Surprisingly quiet option above a corner bar facing the station. ❶

Le Dupleix 34 bd Dupleix ⓣ02.98.90.53.35, ⓦwww.hotel-dupleix.com. Modern concrete hotel, not very attractive from outside but airy and bright within, in a good central location overlooking the Odet with fine views across the river to the cathedral. ❺

De la Gare 17 av de la Gare ⓣ02.98.90.00.81, ⓕ02.98.53.21.81. Simple rooms, all with TV, shower and phone, above a simple snack bar across from the station. ❷

Gradlon 30 rue du Brest ⓣ02.98.95.04.39, ⓦwww.hotel-gradlon.com. Central, friendly and quiet place, with a pleasant garden. The rooms are not cheap, but they're very nicely decorated. ❺

TGV 4 rue de Concarneau ⓣ02.98.90.54.00, ⓕ02.98.94.23.74. Yet another cheap option near the station, this time very new, and offering plain but clean rooms with shower and TV at bargain rates. ❷

The Town

The enormous **Cathédrale St-Corentin**, the focal point of Quimper, is said to be the most complete Gothic cathedral in Brittany, though its neo-Gothic spires date from 1856. When the nave was being added to the old chancel in the fifteenth century, the extension would either have hit existing buildings or the swampy edge of the then-unchannelled river. The masons eventually found a solution and placed the nave at a slight angle – a peculiarity which, once noticed, makes it hard to concentrate on the other Gothic splendours within. The exterior, however, gives no hint of the deviation, with King Gradlon now mounted in perfect symmetry between the spires.

Facing the cathedral on its north side, the **Musée des Beaux-Arts**, 4 place St-Corentin (April–June, Sept & Oct daily except Tues 10am–noon & 2–6pm; July & Aug daily 10am–7pm; Nov–March Mon & Wed–Sat 10am–noon & 2–6pm, Sun 2–6pm; €4), houses amazing collections of drawings by Cocteau, Gustave Doré and Max Jacob (who was born in Quimper), paintings of the Pont-Aven school and Breton scenes by the likes of Eugène Boudin. Only the old Dutch oils upstairs let the collection down.

The heart of old Quimper lies west of place St-Corentin, in front of the cathedral. This is where you'll find the liveliest shops and cafés, housed in the old half-timbered buildings, such as the Breton Keltia-Musique record shop in place au Beurre, and the Celtic shop, Ar Bed Keltiek, at 2 rue Gradlon. The old market hall burnt down in 1976, but the light and spacious **Halles**

St-Francis in rue Astor, built to replace it, are quite a delight, not just for the food but for the view past the upturned boat rafters through the roof to the cathedral's twin spires.

South of the covered market, on the opposite bank of the Odet at 14 rue Jean-Baptiste-Bosquet, is the excellent **Musée de la Faïence Jules Verlinque** (mid-April to mid-Oct Mon–Sat 10am–6pm; €4). The museum tells the story of Quimper's long association with **faïence** – tin-glazed earthenware – which has been made in and around the town since 1690, and demonstrates that little has changed in the Breton pottery business since some unknown artisan hit on the idea of painting ceramic ware with naive "folk" designs. That was in around 1875, when the coming of the railways brought the first influx of tourists, and a consequent demand for souvenirs. Highlights of the collection include pieces commemorating such events as the Great War, the first automobile accident and the death of Zola, but there are also some fascinating specimens produced by fine artists in the 1920s.

As you walk through the town, it's impossible to ignore faïence – you're invited to look and to buy on every corner. On weekdays, it's also possible to visit the major *atelier* **H.-B. Henriot**, in the allées de Locmaria just behind the museum (March–June & Sept Mon–Fri 9am–11.15am & 1.30–4.15pm; July & Aug Mon–Fri 9am–11.15am & 1.30–4.45pm; Oct–Feb tours only Mon–Thurs 11am & 3.45pm; ⓣ02.98.90.09.36, ⓦwww.hb-henriot.com; €3). H.-B. Henriot maintain two bright, modern **gift shops** alongside; the prices, even for the seconds, are similar to those on offer everywhere else, but the selection is superb.

Eating and drinking

Although the pedestrian streets west of the cathedral are unexpectedly short on places to eat, there are quite a few **restaurants** further east on the north side of the river, en route towards the *gare SNCF*. Rue Aristide-Briand here also contains a lively Celtic **bar**, the *Ceili* at no 4. For crêperies, the place au Beurre, a short walk northwest of the cathedral, is a good bet.

L'Ambroisie 49 rue Élie-Fréron ⓣ02.98.95.00.02. Upmarket French restaurant a short climb north from the cathedral, featuring lots of fine seafood and meat dishes on menus from €20. Closed Mon.

La Couscousserie 1 bd de Kerguélen ⓣ02.98.95.46.50. Plush, enjoyable Middle Eastern restaurant by the river, serving couscous platters at €12–22, and *tagines* at around €15, in two Arabian Nights-themed rooms decked out with hookahs and the like.

Café de l'Epée 14 rue du Parc ⓣ02.98.95.28.97. Stunning Art-Nouveau brasserie serving seafood platters with style, along with Breton specialities such as *cotriade* and a range of beef carpaccios and salads for warmer weather.

Le Jardin de l'Odet 39 bd de Kerguélen ⓣ02.98.95.76.76. Charmingly understated Art-Deco restaurant, facing the river close to the cathedral and with a nice garden, serving top-value menus at €19, €27 and €35. Specialities include crab, and boned rabbit cooked in red wine. Closed Sun, plus Tues evening in winter.

La Krampouzerie 9 rue du Sallé ⓣ02.98.95.13.08. One of the best of Quimper's many crêperies, with some outdoor seating on the place au Beurre. Most crêpes cost around €3, though you can get a wholewheat *galette* with scallops for €6.40, or with seaweed for €4.60. Closed Sun, & Mon in winter.

Entertainment

Quimper's **Festival de Cornouaille** started in 1923 and has gone from strength to strength since. This great jamboree of Breton music, costumes, theatre and dance is held in the week before the fourth Sunday in July, attracting guest performers from the other Celtic countries and a scattering of other, sometimes highly unusual, ethnic-cultural ensembles. The whole thing culminates in an incredible Sunday parade through the town. The official programme does not appear until July, but you can get provisional details in advance from the tourist office or at Ⓦwww.festival-cornouaille.com. Accommodation is at a premium in Quimper while the festival is on.

Not so widely known are the **Semaines Musicales** (Ⓦwww.semaines-musicales-quimper.org), which breathe life into the rather stuffy nineteenth-century theatre on boulevard Dupleix during the first three weeks of August. The music is predominantly classical and tends to favour French composers such as Berlioz, Debussy, Bizet and Poulenc.

South from Quimper

More tourists flock to Finistère's southern coast than to any other part of the region, with the busiest segment of all in summer centring on the family-friendly resort of **Bénodet**. The beaches between here and **La Forêt-Fouesnant** to the east rank among the finest in Brittany. A little further along the coast, the walled, sea-circled town of **Concarneau** makes a perfect day-trip destination, though a prettier place to spend a night or two would be the flowery village of **Pont-Aven**, immortalized by Paul Gauguin, slightly further to the east still.

Bénodet and around

Once out of its city channel, the Odet takes on the shape of most Breton inlets, spreading out to lake proportions then turning narrow corners between gorges. The family resort of **BÉNODET** at the mouth of the river (reachable by boat from Quimper) has a long, sheltered beach on the ocean side, with amusements for children and beachside nurseries. Among the nicest hotels in Bénodet are the *Hôtel-Restaurant Le Minaret*, an odd-looking building in a superb seafront position on the corniche de l'Estuaire (Ⓣ02.98.57.03.13, Ⓕ02.98.57.11.07; ❸; closed mid-Oct to March), and the *Bains de Mer*, 11 rue du Kerguelen (Ⓣ02.98.57.03.41; Ⓔbainsdemer@portdebenodet.com; ❸; closed mid-Nov to Feb). Bénodet also has several large **campsites** – if anything, rather too many of them – such as the enormous four-star *Du Letty*, southeast of the village by plage du Letty on rue du Canvez (Ⓣ02.98.57.04.69, Ⓦwww.campingduletty.com; closed early Sept to mid-June). An excellent **restaurant** is *Le Safran* at 10 avenue de l'Odet, where the €19, €23 and €29 menus are all thoroughly satisfactory, but should a splurge be in the offing plump for the €54 lobster menu. You'll also find a sprinkling of decent crêperies across town.

The coast that continues east of Bénodet is rocky and repeatedly cut by deep valleys. Not so much a town as a loose conglomeration of villages, **FOUESNANT**, 9km along, is coming to rival its neighbour as a prime destination for family holidays. While Fouesnant itself is renowned for its cider-makers, and holds a pretty little Romanesque church, most local tourist amenities are gathered in its sister community of **LA FORÊT-FOUESNANT**, 3km further east. Clustered along the waterfront at the foot of a hill so steep that caravans are banned from even approaching, it holds an assortment of attractive hotels such as the *Hôtel de l'Esperance*, place de l'Église (Ⓣ02.98.56.96.58; ❷; closed Oct–March), and the pricier *Aux Cerisiers*, 3 rue des Cerisiers (Ⓣ02.98.56.97.24, Ⓦwww.auxcerisiers.com; ❸; closed mid-Dec to mid-Jan).

Concarneau

The first sizeable town you come to east of Bénodet is **CONCARNEAU**, where the third most important fishing port in France does a reasonable job of passing itself off as a holiday resort. Its greatest asset is its **Ville Close**, the small and very well-fortified old city located a few metres offshore on an irregular rocky island in the bay, connected to the mainland by a narrow bridge. This can get too crowded for comfort in high summer, but otherwise it's a real delight. Like those of the citadelle at Le Palais on Belle-Île, its ramparts were completed by Vauban in the seventeenth century. The island itself, however, had been inhabited for at least a thousand years before that, and is first recorded as the site of a priory founded by King Gradlon of Quimper.

Concarneau boasts that it is a *ville fleurie*, and the flowers are most in evidence inside the walls, where climbing roses and clematis swarm all over the various gift shops, restaurants and crêperies. Walk the central pedestrianized street to the far end, and you can pass through a gateway to the shoreline to watch the fishing boats go by. In summer, however, the best views of all come from the promenade on top of the **ramparts**, though as there's no railing it's perilous for children (daily: May, June & Sept 10am–6pm; July & Aug 10am–9pm; €0.80).

The **Musée de la Pêche**, immediately inside the Ville Close (daily: mid-June to mid-Sept 9.30am–8pm; mid-Sept to mid-June 10am–noon & 2–6pm; €6), provides an insight into the traditional life Concarneau shared with so many other Breton ports, illuminating the history and practice of catching whales, tuna (with dragnets the size of central Paris), herring and sardines.

Practicalities

There's no rail service to Concarneau, but SNCF **buses** connect the town with Quimper and Rosporden. The **tourist office** (May & June Mon–Sat 9am–noon & 2–7pm, Sun 9.30am–12.30pm; July & Aug daily 9am–8pm; Sept–April Mon–Sat 9am–noon & 2–6pm; Ⓣ02.98.97.01.44) is on the quai d'Aiguillon, not far from the long-distance bus stop.

The Ville Close is almost completely devoid of **hotels**, so most of those that Concarneau has to offer skulk in the back streets of the mainland, and tend to be full most of the time. Decent options include the bright, modernized *Hôtel de France et d'Europe*, 9 av de la Gare (Ⓣ02.98.97.00.64, Ⓕ02.98.50.76.66; ❸; closed Sat mid-Nov to mid-March), near the main bus stop, and the *Hôtel-Restaurant les Océanides*, 3 rue du Lin (Ⓣ02.98.97.08.61, Ⓕ02.98.97.09.13; ❷; closed Sun evening in May & June, all Sun Oct–April), a *logis de France*, a couple of streets up from the sea above the fishing port, with a highly recommended and far from expensive restaurant – some of the fancier rooms are in the nominally distinct *Petites Océanides* across the street (❸). Opposite the entrance to the Ville Close on place de l'Hôtel de Ville, you'll find the spruce, pastel-orange *Des Halles* (Ⓣ02.98.97.11.41, Ⓕ02.98.50.58.54; ❸; closed Sun evening in low season), offering well-equipped rooms at reasonable rates.

Probably the best bet of all is the **hostel** (Ⓣ02.98.97.03.47, Ⓔconcarneau .aj.cis@wanadoo.fr; €9.40; open all year), for once very near the city centre and with the added bonus of magnificent ocean views. It's just around the tip of the headland on the quai de la Croix, with a good crêperie opposite and a windsurfing shop nearby. There are also some lovely **campsites** a little further on, close to the Sables-Blancs beach; the spacious *Prés Verts* spreads through verdant fields at Kernous Plage at the far end (Ⓣ02.98.97.09.74; closed late Sept to April).

For an atmospheric meal in Concarneau, choose from any of the **restaurants** along the main street that runs through the Ville Close, or explore the lanes that lead off it. There are, however, plenty of cheaper places back in town. Worth a try on the mainland are *Chez Armande*, 15 av du Dr-Nicholas (menus from €18, ⓣ02.98.97.00.76; closed Wed all year, plus Tues in winter), an excellent seafood restaurant not far south of the market; *Le Bélem*, place Jean-Jaurès (ⓣ02.98.97.02.78; closed Wed), a pretty little indoor restaurant, next to the market, serving mussels for €9 and good seafood menus from €16; and *L'Escale*, 19 quai Carnot (ⓣ02.98.97.03.31; closed Sun), a waterfront restaurant on the main road in town that's a favourite with local fishermen, offering lunch menus for around €9. In the heart of the Ville Close is *Le Pennti*, 8 place St-Guénolé, with menus from €8 at lunchtime and €10 in the evening, one of several good-value **crêperies** in that part of town, with a ravishing courtyard at the back.

Pont-Aven and around

PONT-AVEN, 14km east of Concarneau and just inland from the tip of the Aven estuary, is a small port packed with art galleries – and tourists. This was where Gauguin came to paint in the 1880s before he left for Tahiti. Though Gauguin inspired the **Pont-Aven School** of fellow artists, including Émile Bernard, for all the local hype the town has no permanent collection of his work. The **Musée Municipal** (daily: mid-Feb to mid-June & mid-Sept to Dec 10am–12.30pm & 2–6pm; mid-June to mid-Sept 10am–7pm; €4) in the *mairie* holds changing exhibitions of the school and other artists active during the same period, but you can't count on paintings by the man himself.

Gauguin aside, Pont-Aven is pleasant in its own right. Just upstream of the little granite bridge at the heart of town, the **promenade Xavier-Grall** criss-crosses the tiny river itself on landscaped walkways, offering glimpses of the backs of venerable mansions, dripping with ivy, and a little "chaos" of rocks in the stream itself. A longer walk – allow an hour – leads into the romantically named **Bois d'Amour**, wooded gardens which have long provided inspiration to painters, poets and musicians.

Pont-Aven's **tourist office**, 5 place de l'Hôtel de Ville (April–June & Sept–Oct daily 9.15am–12.30pm & 2–7pm; July & Aug daily 9.30am–7.30pm; Nov–March Mon–Sat 10am–12.30pm & 2–6pm; ⓣ02.98.06.04.70), sells an excellent English-language booklet on the town for €0.50, which includes route maps of local walks. Much the best of the town's three relatively expensive **hotels** is the central *Hôtel des Ajoncs d'Or*, 1 place de l'Hôtel de Ville (ⓣ02.98.06.02.06; ❸; closed Jan), where gourmet menus start at €15. The nicest of the local **campsites** is *Le Spinnaker* (ⓣ02.98.06.01.77; closed Oct–April), set in a large wooded park.

Quimperlé

The final town of any size in this stretch of Finistère, before you enter Morbihan, **QUIMPERLÉ** straddles a hill and two rivers, the Isole and the Elle, cut by a sequence of bridges. It's an atmospheric place, particularly in the medieval muddle of streets around **Ste-Croix church**. This was copied in plan from schema brought back by crusaders of the Church of the Holy Sepulchre in Jerusalem and is notable for its original Romanesque apse. There are some good **bars** nearby and, on Fridays, a **market** on the square higher up on the hill.

Reasonable **rooms** can be had at *Le Brizeux*, 7 quai Brizeux (ⓣ02.98.96.19.25; ❶), and *Le Kervidanou*, in the village of Mellac 5km northwest (ⓣ02.98.39.18.00;

③). The nicest **campsite** in the vicinity is the two-star, British-owned *Bois des Ecureuils* (ⓣ02.98.71.70.98, ⓦwww.bois-des-ecureuils.fr; closed mid-Sept to mid-May), 15km northeast in the verdant countryside at Guilligomarch, north of Arzano.

Inland Brittany: the Nantes–Brest Canal

The **Nantes–Brest canal** is a meandering chain of waterways from Finistère to the Loire, interweaving rivers with stretches of canal built at Napoleon's instigation to bypass the belligerent English fleets off the coast. Finally completed in 1836, it came into its own at the end of the nineteenth century as a coal, slate and fertilizer route. The building of the dam **at Lac Guerlédan** in the 1920s chopped the canal in two, leaving a whole section unnavigable by barge. Road transport had by then already superseded water haulage, but modern tourism has breathed life back into the canal.

En route the canal passes through riverside towns, such as **Josselin** and **Malestroit**, that long predate its construction; commercial ports and junctions – **Pontivy**, most notably – that developed in the nineteenth century because of it; the old port of **Redon**, a patchwork of water, where the canal crosses the River Vilaine; and a sequence of scenic splendours, including the string of lakes around the **Barrage de Guerlédan**, near Mur-de-Bretagne. As a focus for exploring **inland Brittany**, whether by barge, bike, foot, or all three, the canal is ideal. Not every stretch is accessible, but there are detours to be made away from it, such as into the wild and desolate **Monts d'Arrée** to the north of the canal in Finistère.

The Finistère stretch

As late as the 1920s, steamers would make their way across the Rade de Brest and down the Aulne River to **Châteaulin**, the first real town on the canal route. If you're walking the canal seriously, **Pont-Coblant** and **Pleyben** are just 10km further away on the map, but be warned that the meanders make it a several-hour hike. Pick your side of the water, too: there are no bridges between Châteaulin and Pont-Coblant.

Châteaulin

CHÂTEAULIN is a quiet place, where the main reason to stay is the canal itself – or river, as it is here. Most bars sell permits for local salmon and trout **fishing** (as do fishing shops, some of which rent out tackle). You should have little difficulty finding a room at the **hotel** *Le Christmas*, 33 Grande-Rue (ⓣ02.98.86.01.24; ④), which serves excellent food. Within a couple of minutes' walk upstream from the statue to Jean Moulin – the Resistance leader who was *sous-préfet* here from 1930 to 1933 – and the town centre, you'll find yourself on towpaths full of rabbits and squirrels and overhung by trees full of birds.

Carhaix

CARHAIX, a further 25km east of Châteaulin, is a road junction that dates back to the Romans. It has cafés and shops to replenish supplies, but other than in mid-July, when it hosts the massive three-day **rock festival** des Vieilles Charrues, there's little reason to visit. The most interesting building in town is the granite Renaissance **Maison de Sénéchal** on rue Brisieux, which houses the **tourist office** (July & Aug Mon–Sat 9am–12.30pm & 1.30–7pm, Sun 10am–1pm; Sept–June Mon–Sat 10am–noon & 2–6pm; ⓣ02.98.93.04.42).

Huelgoat and its forest

HUELGOAT, next to its own small **lake** half way between Morlaix and Carhaix on the minor road D769, makes a pleasant overnight stop. Spreading north and east from the village is the **Forêt de Huelgoat**, a landscape of trees, giant boulders and waterfalls tangled together in primeval chaos. Various paths lead into the depths of the woods, allowing for long walks amid spectacularly wild scenery.

The *Hôtel du Lac*, beside the lake at 12 rue du Général-de-Gaulle (ⓣ02.98.99.71.14; ❸; closed mid-Nov to mid-Jan), offers well-refurbished rooms and good food. Also beside the lake, on the road towards Brest, the two-star *Camping du Lac* (ⓣ02.98.99.78.80; closed mid-Sept to mid-June) comes complete with swimming pool.

Le Faouët, St-Fiacre and Kernascléden

Thirty kilometres south of Carhaix on the D769, the secluded town of **LE FAOUËT** is served by neither buses nor trains but is distinguished mainly by its large old **market hall**. Above a floor of mud and straw, still used by local traders, rises an intricate latticework of ancient wood, propped on granite pillars and topped by a little clock tower.

The church at **ST-FIACRE**, just over 2km south, is notable for its rood screen, brightly polychromed and carved as intricately as lace. The original purpose of a rood screen was to separate the chancel from the congregation, but the decorations of this 1480 masterpiece go rather further than that. They depict scenes from the Old and New Testaments as well as a dramatic series on the wages of sin. Drunkenness is demonstrated by a man somehow vomiting a fox; theft by a peasant stealing apples; and so on.

At the ornate and gargoyle-coated church at **KERNASCLÉDEN**, 15km southeast of Le Faouët along the D782, the focus turns from carving to frescoes. The themes, however, contemporary with St-Fiacre, are equally gruesome. On the damp-infested wall of a side chapel, horned devils stoke the fires beneath a vast cauldron filled with the souls of the damned, and you may be able to discern the outlines of a Dance of Death, a faded cousin to that at Kermaria.

The central stretch: Gouarec to Redon

Although the canal is limited to canoeists between Carhaix and Pontivy, it's worth some effort to follow on land, particularly for the scenery from **Gouarec** to **Mur-de-Bretagne**. At the centre is the trailing **Lac de Guerlédan**, created by the construction of a dam near Mur, and backed, to the south, by the enticing **Forêt de Quénécan**. Approaching by road, the canal path is most easily joined at Gouarec, covered by the five daily buses between Carhaix and Loudéac.

Gouarec

At **GOUAREC**, the River Blavet and the canal meet in a confusing swirl of water that shoots off, edged by footpaths, in the most unlikely directions. The old schist houses of the town are barely disturbed by traffic or development, nor are there great numbers of tourists. For a comfortable overnight stop, the *Hôtel du Blavet* (Ⓣ02.96.24.90.03, Ⓔlouis.le.loir@wanadoo.fr; ❷), is in an ideal waterside position. Don't be put off by its extravagant menus – they have affordable meals as well. There's also a well-positioned two-star municipal **campsite**, the *Tost Aven* (Ⓣ02.96.24.85.42; closed Nov–Easter), next to the canal and away from the main road.

Quénécan Forest

For the 15km between Gouarec and Mur-de-Bretagne, the N164 skirts the edge of **Quénécan Forest**, within which is a series of artificial lakes created when the **Barrage de Guerlédan** was completed in 1928. It's a beautiful stretch of river, peaceful enough despite the summer influx of campers and caravans.

The best places to stay are just off the road, past the villages of **ST-GELVEN** and Caurel. At the former, the ravishing *Les Jardins de l'Abbaye* (Ⓣ02.96.24.95.77; ❸; closed Tues evening & Wed in low season) is an absolutely irresistible, inexpensive **hotel-restaurant**, nestling beside the water at the end of an impressive avenue of ancient trees, and housed in the intact outbuildings of a twelfth-century Cistercian abbey. Porthole-like windows pierce the thick slate walls of its six cosy guest rooms, to look out across extensive riverfront grounds to the dramatic wooded slopes beyond.

From just before **CAUREL**, the brief loop of the D111 leads to tiny sandy beaches. At the spot known, justifiably, as **BEAU RIVAGE** (beautiful bank), a lavish holiday complex features the *Nautic International* campsite (Ⓣ02.96.28.57.94; closed Oct to mid-May), and the *Hôtel Beau Rivage* (Ⓣ02.96.28.52.15; ❸; closed Mon evening & Tues in low season), plus a restaurant, a snack bar and a 140-seat glass-topped cruise boat.

Pontivy

Today you can again take **barges** all the way to the Loire from **PONTIVY**, the central junction of the Nantes–Brest canal, where the course of the canal breaks off once more from the Blavet. When the waterway opened, the small medieval centre of the town was expanded, redesigned and given broad avenues to fit its new role. It was even briefly renamed Napoléonville, in honour of the man responsible for its new prosperity.

These days, Pontivy is a bright market town, its twisting old streets contrasting with the stately riverside promenades. At its northern end, occupying a commanding hillside site, is the **Château de Rohan**, built by the lord of Josselin in the fifteenth century (June–Sept Mon–Sat 9am–noon & 2–6pm; Oct–May Wed–Sat 10am–noon & 2–6pm; €4.10, or €1.30 when there is no exhibition). Used in summer for low-key cultural events and temporary exhibitions, the castle still belongs to the Josselin family, who are slowly restoring it. At the moment, one impressive facade, complete with deep moat and two forbidding towers, looks out over the river – behind that, the structure rather peters out.

Pontivy's **tourist office** is just below the castle, on place de Gaulle (Mon–Sat 10am–noon & 2–6pm; Ⓣ02.97.25.04.10). Among local hotels are the low-priced *Porhoët*, nearby at 41 rue du Général-de-Gaulle (Ⓣ02.97.25.34.88, Ⓔporhoet@destination-bretagne.com; ❶), and the grander *De l'Europe*, 12 rue François-Mitterand (Ⓣ02.97.25.11.14; ❸), which has a good restaurant. In addition, the local **hostel**, 2km from the *gare SNCF* on the Île des Récollets (Ⓣ02.97.25.58.27; €9.30), is in good condition and serves cheap meals, but may be closed at weekends out of season.

Josselin

About 30km further along the canal from Pontivy, you come to the three Rapunzel towers embedded in a vast sheet of stone of the **château** in **JOSSELIN**. The Rohan family used to own a third of Brittany, but the present duke contents himself with the position of local mayor. The pompous apartments of his residence are not very interesting, even if they do contain the table on which the Edict of Nantes was signed in 1598. But the duchess's collection of dolls, housed in the **Musée des Poupées**, behind the castle, is something special (château and doll museum open April & May Wed, Sat, Sun & hols 2–6pm; June & Sept daily 2–6pm; July & Aug daily 10am–6pm; each €6.30, combined ticket €11).

The town is full of medieval splendours, from the gargoyles of the **basilica**, Notre-Dame-du-Roncier, to the castle **ramparts**, and the half-timbered houses in between. **Notre-Dame-du-Roncier** is built on the spot where, in the ninth century, a peasant supposedly found a statue of the Virgin under a bramble bush. The statue was burnt during the Revolution, but an important *pardon* is held each year on September 8.

Josselin's **tourist office** is in a superb old house on the place de la Congrégation, up in town next to the castle entrance (April–June, Sept & Oct Mon–Fri 10am–noon & 2–6pm, Sat & Sun 2–6pm; July & Aug daily 10am–6pm; Nov–March Mon–Fri 10am–noon & 2–6pm; Ⓣ02.97.22.36.43). Just across from the basilica, the *Hôtel de France*, 6 place Notre Dame (Ⓣ02.97.22.23.06; ❸; closed Jan, plus Sun evening & Mon between Oct and March), is an ivy-covered *logis* which is amazingly quiet considering its central location; it also has a decent crêperie. The nearest good campsite is the three-star *Bas de la Lande* (Ⓣ02.97.22.22.20, Ⓔcampingbassedelalande@wanadoo.fr; closed Nov–March), half an hour's walk from the castle, south of the river and west of town.

Guéhenno and Lizio

One of the largest and best Breton calvaries is at **GUÉHENNO**, south of Josselin on the D123. Sculpted in 1550, the figures include the cock that crowed after Peter's denials, Mary Magdalene with the shroud and a recumbent Christ in the crypt. Its appeal is enhanced by the naivety of its amateur restoration. After damage caused by Revolutionary soldiers in 1794 – who amused themselves by playing boules with the heads of the statues – all the sculptors approached for the work demanded exorbitant fees, so the parish priest and his assistant decided to undertake the task themselves.

Over to the east, off the D151, **LIZIO** has set itself up as a centre for arts and crafts, with ceramic and weaving workshops its speciality. One venerable old cottage also houses an **Insectarium** (April–Sept daily 10am–12.30pm & 1.30–6.30pm; Oct–March Wed & Sat 10am–12.30pm & 1.30–6.30pm, Sun 1.30–6.30pm; €5.50), holding creepy-crawlies that include hairy spiders, giant millipedes, praying mantises and stick insects in amazing colours.

Malestroit and around

Though not a lot happens in the thousand-year-old town of **MALESTROIT**, 25km southeast of Josselin, it's full of unexpected and enjoyable corners. As you come into the main square, the **place du Bouffay** in front of the church, the houses are covered with unlikely carvings – an anxious bagpipe-playing hare looking over its shoulder at a dragon's head on one beam, an oblivious sow in a blue buckled belt threading her distaff on another. The **church** itself is decorated with drunkards and acrobats outside, torturing demons and erupting towers within. Beside the grey canal, the matching grey slate tiles on the turreted rooftops bulge and dip, while on its central island, overgrown houses stand next to the stern walls of an old mill.

Two kilometres west of Malestroit (there is no bus connection), the village of **ST-MARCEL** hosts a **Musée de la Résistance Bretonne** (April to mid-June daily 10am–noon & 2–6pm; mid-June to mid-Sept daily 10am–7pm; mid-Sept to March daily except Tues 10am–noon & 2–6pm; €4). The museum stands on the site of a June 1944 battle in which the Breton *maquis* (guerrilla Resistance fighters), joined by Free French forces parachuted in from England, successfully diverted the local German troops from the main Normandy invasion movements.

If you arrive in Malestroit by barge (this is a good stretch to travel), you'll moor very near the town centre. The local **tourist office** stands at the edge of the main square at 17 place du Bouffay (mid-June to mid-Sept Mon–Sat 9am–7pm, Sun 10am–3pm; mid-Sept to mid-June Mon–Sat 9.30am–12.30pm & 2.30–6.30pm; ⓣ02.97.75.14.57, ⓦwww.malestroit.com). Sadly, Malestroit no longer has a hotel, but there's a two-star **campsite**, *La Daufresne* (ⓣ02.97.75.13.33; closed mid-Sept to April), down below the bridge in the Impasse d'Abattoir next to the swimming pool.

Rochefort-en-Terre

ROCHEFORT-EN-TERRE, commanding a high eminence 17km south of Malestroit, may be a prettified and polished version of its neighbour, but it ranks nonetheless among the most delightful villages in Brittany. Every available stone surface, from the window ledges to the picturesque wishing well, is festooned with colourful geraniums, a tradition that originated with the painter Alfred Klots, who was born in France to a wealthy American family in 1875, and bought Rochefort's ruined **château** in 1907. Perched on the town's highest point, the castle is now open for guided tours (April & May daily 10am–noon & 2–6.30pm; June & Sept daily 10am–noon & 2–7pm; July & Aug daily 10am–7pm; Oct Mon–Fri 12–6pm, Sat & Sun 10am–noon & 2–6pm; €4), though not until you go through its dramatic gateway do you find out that in fact that gateway is all that survives of the original fifteenth-century structure.

Rochefort's modern **tourist office**, in the central place des Halles (June & Sept Mon–Fri 10am–12.30pm & 2.30–6pm, Sat & Sun 2–6pm; July & Aug Mon–Fri 10am–12.30pm & 2–6.30pm, Sat & Sun 2–6.30pm; Oct–May Mon–Fri 10am–noon & 2.30–5pm, Sat 2–5pm; ⓣ02.97.43.33.57), displays a list of expensive *chambres d'hôte* in the neighbourhood, and operates the three-star municipal **campsite**, *Le Moulin Neuf*, in the chemin de Bogeais (ⓣ02.97.43.37.52; closed mid-Sept to Easter). The one **hotel** stands alongside the tourist office: *Le Pélican* (ⓣ02.97.43.38.48; ❸; closed mid-Jan to mid-Feb) offers reasonable rooms and good food, with dinner menus starting at around €15.

Redon

Thirty-four kilometres east of Malestroit, at the junction not only of the rivers Oust and Vilaine and the canal, but also of the train lines to Rennes, Vannes and Nantes, and of six major roads, **REDON** is not easy to avoid. And you shouldn't try to, either. A wonderful grouping of water and locks, it's a town with history, charm and life.

Until World War I, Redon was the seaport for Rennes. Its industrial docks – or what remains of them – are therefore on the Vilaine, while the canal, even in the very centre of town, is almost totally rural, its towpaths shaded avenues. Shipowners' houses from the seventeenth and eighteenth centuries can be seen along quai Jean-Bart by the *bassin* and quai Duguay-Truin next to the river. A rusted wrought-iron workbridge, equipped with a gantry, still crosses the river, but the main users of the port now are cruise ships heading down the Vilaine to La Roche-Bernard.

Redon was once also a religious centre, its first abbey founded in 832 by St Conwoion. The most prominent church today is **St-Sauveur**. Its unique four-storeyed Romanesque belfry is squat, almost obscured by later roofs and the high choir, and best seen from the adjacent cloisters; the Gothic tower was entirely separated from the main building by a fire. In the crypt, you'll find the tomb of the judge who tried the legendary Bluebeard – Joan of Arc's friend, Gilles de Rais.

Redon's **gare SNCF** is five minutes' walk west from the **tourist office** in the place de la République (July & Aug Mon–Sat 9am–7pm, Sun 10am–1pm & 4–6pm; Sept–June Mon–Sat 9am–noon & 2–6pm; ⓣ02.99.71.06.04, ⓦwww.redon.fr), north across the railway tracks from the town centre. Most of the **hotels** are concentrated in town and near the *gare SNCF* rather than in the port area. The off-white *Hôtel de France* looks down on the canal from 30 rue Duguesclin (ⓣ02.99.71.06.11, ⓔlefrance@worldonline.fr; ❷); its en-suite rooms offer a considerable degree of comfort for the price. Nearer the station, the *Hôtel Chandouineau*, 1 rue Thiers (ⓣ02.99.71.02.04; ❺), is a luxurious establishment with just seven bedrooms, where the restaurant serves gourmet menus from €20.

The southern coast

Brittany's **southern coast** takes in the province's – and indeed mainland Europe's – most famous prehistoric site, the alignments of **Carnac**, with the associated megaliths of the beautiful, island-studded **Golfe de Morbihan**. The beaches are not as spectacular as in Finistère, but there are more safe places to swim and the water is warmer. Of the cities, **Lorient** has Brittany's most compelling **festival** and **Vannes** has one of the liveliest medieval town centres. Further east, **La Baule** does a good impression of a Breton St-Tropez, and you can escape to the islands of **Belle-Île**, **Hoëdic** and **Houat**. Inevitably it's popular, and in summer you can be hard pressed to find a room, but if you're prepared to make reservations, or you're camping, there shouldn't be much problem.

Lorient and around

LORIENT, Brittany's fourth largest city, lies on an immense natural harbour protected from the ocean by the Île de Groix and strategically located at the junction of the rivers Scorff, Ter and Blavet. A functional, rather depressing port today, it was once a key base for French colonialism, and was founded in the mid-seventeenth century for trading operations by the Compagnie des Indes, an equivalent of the Dutch and English East India Companies. Apart from the name, little else remains to suggest the plundered wealth that once arrived here. During the last war, Lorient was a major target for the Allies, but the Germans held out until the very end, and by the time they surrendered in May 1945 the city was almost completely destroyed. The only substantial remains were the U-boat pens, which have subsequently been expanded by the French for their nuclear submarines.

Across the estuary in **Port-Louis** is the **Musée de la Compagnie des Indes**, a pretty dismal temple to imperialism (Jan–March, Oct & Nov daily except Tues 2–6pm; April & May daily except Tues 10am–6.30pm; June–Sept daily 10am–6.30pm; closed Dec; €5). Time would be more enjoyably spent on a boat trip, either up the estuary towards **Hennebont** or out to the **Île de Groix**. This eight-kilometre-long steep-sided rock is a somewhat smaller version of Belle-Île, and holds some gorgeous beaches to encourage day-trippers.

Lorient's **tourist office**, beside the pleasure port on the quai de Rohan (July & Aug Mon–Sat 9am–7pm, Sun 10am–1pm; Sept–June Mon–Fri 9am–12.30pm & 1.30–5pm, Sat 10am–12.30pm; Ⓣ02.97.21.07.84, Ⓦwww.lorient-tourisme.com), can provide full details on local boat trips and organizes some excursions itself. Unless you arrive during the festival (see box, below), there's a huge choice of **hotels**. Among reasonable, fairly central options are two on rue Lazare-Carnot as it curves away south of the tourist office: the *Victor Hugo Hôtel* at no. 36 (Ⓣ02.97.21.16.24; ❸), which offers an action-packed €16 menu; and the *Hôtel d'Arvor*, at no. 104 (Ⓣ02.97.21.07.55; ❶), also with a good-value restaurant. There's an **HI hostel**, next to the River Ter at 41 rue Victor-Schoelcher, 3km out on bus line C from the *gare SNCF* (Ⓣ02.97.37.11.65,

The Inter-Celtic Festival

The overriding reason people come to Lorient is for the **Inter-Celtic Festival**, held for ten days from the first Friday to the second Sunday in August. The biggest Celtic event in Brittany, or anywhere else for that matter, attracts representatives from all seven Celtic "countries" (Asturias and Galicia in Spain, Cornwall, Wales, Scotland, Ireland and Brittany). In a popular celebration of cultural solidarity, well over a quarter of a million people attend over a hundred different shows, five languages mingle, and Scotch and Guinness flow with French and Spanish wines and ciders. There is a certain competitive element, with championships in various categories, but the feeling of mutual enthusiasm and conviviality is paramount. Most of the **activities** – music, dance and literature – take place around the central place Jules-Ferry, and this is where most people end up sleeping, too, as accommodation is pushed to the limit.

For **schedules** of the festival, and further details of temporary accommodation, contact the Office du Tourisme de Pays de Lorient, 2 rue Paul-Bert, 56100 Lorient (Ⓣ02.97.21.24.29, Ⓦwww.festival-interceltique.com), bearing in mind that the festival programme is not finalized before May. For certain specific events, you'll need to reserve tickets well in advance.

Ⓔlorient@fuaj.org; €9.60). Good central **restaurants** include *Yesterday's*, 1 cours de la Bôve (Ⓣ02.97.84.85.07), a brasserie near the town hall that serves an excellent €15 menu, and *Le Café Leffe* (Ⓣ02.97.21.21.30; closed Jan), in the same building as the tourist office, facing the port.

St-Cado

Twelve kilometres east of Port-Louis, a large bridge spans the broad estuary of the Etel river. A short detour north of the village of Belz on the eastern shore brings you to the delightful islet of **ST-CADO**, a speck on the water dotted with perhaps twenty white-painted houses.

From the mainland, you walk across a spindly little bridge to reach the island itself. Its main feature is a twelfth-century chapel that stands on the site of a Romanesque predecessor built by St Cado around the sixth century. Cado, who was a prince of "Glamorgant", returned in due course to his native Wales and was martyred, but Welsh pilgrims still make their way to this pretty little spot. As Cado is a patron saint of the deaf, it's said that hearing problems can be cured by lying on his stone "bed" inside the chapel. A little fountain behind the chapel only emerges from the sea at low tide.

The Presqu'île de Quiberon

The **Presqu'île de Quiberon**, south of Carnac, is well worth visiting on its own merits; **Quiberon** is quite a lively port, and you can get boats out to the islands or walk the shores of this narrow peninsula. The ocean-facing shore, known as the **Côte Sauvage**, is a wild and highly unswimmable stretch, where the stormy seas look like flashing scenes of snowy mountain tops. The sheltered eastern side has safe and calm sandy beaches, and plenty of campsites.

Quiberon

Much of the peninsula has become built up over the years, but it still holds only one true town, **QUIBERON**, at its southern tip. Its most active area, **Port-Maria**, is home to the **gare maritime** for the islands of Belle-Île, Houat and Hoëdic, and also holds a fishing harbour that was once famous for its sardines. Stretching away to the east is a long curve of fine sandy beach, lined for several hundred yards with bars, cafes and restaurants. At its centre is a busy little park and miniature golf course, but few of the streets further back hold anything of great interest. The exception is the little hill that leads down to the port from the **gare SNCF**, where browsing around is rewarded with some surprisingly good clothes and antique shops.

Arrival and information

In July and August, the special Tire Bouchon train links Quiberon's *gare SNCF*, which is a short way above the town proper, with Auray. Bus #1 (TIM; Ⓣ02.97.01.22.10) runs right to the *gare maritime* from Vannes, via Auray and Carnac.

The **tourist office** at 14 rue de Verdun (July & Aug Mon–Sat 9am–7.30pm, Sun 9.30am–12.30pm & 2.30–7pm; Sept–June Mon–Sat 9am–12.30pm & 2–6pm; Ⓣ02.97.50.45.12, Ⓦwww.quiberon.com), downhill from the *gare SNCF*, has a 24hr computer terminal outside showing which hotels are full, hour by hour.

Accommodation

For most of the year, it's hard to get a **room** in Quiberon. In July and August, the whole peninsula is packed, while in winter it's so quiet that virtually all its facilities closed down. The nicest area in which to stay is along the seafront in **Port-Maria**, where several good hotel-restaurants face the Belle-Île ferry terminal. The local **hostel**, the spartan *Filets Bleus*, inland at 45 rue du Roc'h-Priol (Ⓣ02.97.50.15.54; €7.85; closed Oct–March), 1.5km southeast of the *gare SNCF*, also provides space for camping.

Hôtel-Restaurant Bellevue rue de Tiviec Ⓣ02.97.50.16.28, Ⓦwww.bellevuequiberon.com. Quiet *logis de France*, set slightly back from the sea near the Casino, 500m east of the port, with its own pool and a good restaurant. Closed Oct–March. ❹

Hôtel-Restaurant Au Bon Accueil 6 quai de Houat Ⓣ02.97.50.07.92, Ⓕ02.97.50.28.62. Basic but inexpensive seafront hotel rooms in Port-Maria. A friendly dining room, with something of the atmosphere and decor of a village bar, serves good fish soup and seafood specialities. Closed Jan. ❸

Le Neptune 4 quai de Houat Ⓣ02.97.50.09.62, Ⓕ02.97.50.41.44. Very close to *Au Bon Accueil*, and significantly more luxurious. All the rooms enjoy sea views – some have private balconies – and there are the usual seafood menus from €16 to €28. Closed Jan, & Mon in low season. ❹

L'Océan 7 quai de l'Océan Ⓣ02.97.50.07.58, Ⓕ02.97.50.27.81. Attractive little hotel in the port, with multi-coloured pastel shutters; no restaurant, but reasonably priced rooms. Closed Oct–March. ❸

Eating and drinking

The most appealing area in which to browse the menus is along the waterfront in Port-Maria, where a line of seafood **restaurants** compete to attract the ferry passengers. Hotel owners are very insistent on persuading guests to pay for half-board but there are plenty of alternatives to choose from if you do manage to escape their clutches. For **cafés**, those by the long bathing beach are the most enjoyable, along with the old-fashioned *Café du Marché* next to the PTT.

La Chaumine 36 place de Manémeur Ⓣ02.97.50.17.67. Set by the main square of Manémeur – technically a separate village, though it's not too far to walk around the headland west of the port – this lovely little fish restaurant serves menus from €13 to €45, with a €22.50 option featuring salmon braised in champagne. Closed Sun pm & Mon.

Le Corsaire 24 quai de Belle-Île Ⓣ02.97.50.15.05. Large waterfront restaurant, facing the ferry terminal and serving fine seafood spreads on a sprawling terrace for €13 and upwards.

De la Criée 11 quai de l'Océan Ⓣ02.97.30.53.09. Superb, inexpensive local fish restaurant, serving changing specialities every day. The €14 menu includes baked mackerel, and fish smoked on the premises, while €14.50 buys a great seafood couscous. Closed Jan, Sun evening & Mon in low season.

Belle-Île

The island of **BELLE-ÎLE**, 45 minutes by ferry from Quiberon, has its own Côte Sauvage on its Atlantic coast, while the landward side is fertile, cultivated ground, interrupted by deep estuaries with tiny ports. To appreciate the island's contrasts, some form of transport is advisable – you can **rent bikes** at the port and main town of **LE PALAIS**, and if you're in a small car the ferry fare is relatively low.

The island once belonged to the monks of Redon, then to the ambitious Nicolas Fouquet, Louis XIV's minister, and later to the English, who in 1761 swapped it for Menorca in an unrepeatable bargain deal. Docking at Le Palais, the abrupt star-shaped fortifications of the **citadelle** are the first thing you see (daily: April–June, Sept & Oct 9.30am–6pm; July & Aug 9am–7pm;

Nov–March 9.30am–noon & 2–5pm; €6.10). Built along stylish and ordered lines by the great fortress-builder, Vauban, it is startling in size – filled with doorways leading to mysterious cellars and underground passages, endless sequences of rooms, dungeons and deserted cells. It only ceased being a prison in 1961, having numbered a succession of state enemies and revolutionaries among its inmates, including Ben Bella of Algeria. Less involuntarily, painters such as Monet and Matisse, the writers Flaubert and Proust and the actress Sarah Bernhardt all spent time on the island. And presumably Alexandre Dumas, too, as Porthos's death, in *The Three Musketeers*, takes place here. A **museum** documents the island's history, in fiction as much as in fact.

As for exploring the island, it's far too large to walk round, but a coastal footpath does run on bare soil for the length of the **Côte Sauvage**. Near the west end you'll find the **Grotte de l'Apothicairerie**, so called because it was once full of cormorants' nests, arranged like the jars on a pharmacist's shelves. Inland, on the D25 back towards Le Palais, you pass the two **menhirs**, Jean and Jeanne, said to be lovers petrified as punishment for wanting to meet before their marriage. Another larger menhir used to lie near these two; it was broken up to help construct the road that separates them.

Belle-Île's second town, **SAUZON**, is a beautiful little village arrayed along one side of a long estuary, 6km west of Le Palais. If you're staying any length of time, and you've got transport, it's probably a better place to base yourself.

Practicalities

Throughout the year, the Societé Morbihannaise et Nantaise de Navigation (ⓣ08.20.05.60.00, or, if you're calling from outside France, ⓣ02.97.35.02.00, ⓦwww.smn-navigation.fr) sends at least five **ferries** daily from **Port-Maria**, on the Quiberon peninsula, to **Le Palais**. The crossing normally takes 45 minutes, though between May and September a high-speed vessel makes three daily crossings in just 20 minutes. The standard adult return fare is around €25, rising to nearly €30 for the high-speed trip; under-25s pay about €15 to €17, depending on the time of year. Small cars can be taken on the slower crossings for around €120 return; bikes are also allowed.

Between June and mid-September, the same company sends two or three boats daily direct to **Sauzon** from **Port-Maria**, which takes 25 minutes. The same passenger fares apply, but no cars or bikes can be carried. From mid-July until the end of August, the fast *Locmaria 56* makes one daily return trip to **Sauzon** from **Lorient** (approximate fares: adults €30 return, under-25s €21, under-13s €15).

The island's **tourist office** is next to the **gare maritime** in Le Palais (mid-March to mid-Oct Mon–Sat 9am–6pm, Sun 10am–12.30pm & 5–6.45pm; mid-Oct to mid-March Mon–Sat 9am–6pm, Sun 10am–12.30pm; ⓣ02.97.31.81.93, ⓦwww.belle-ile.com).

Accommodation in Le Palais includes the simple *Frégate*, above a nice little bar on the quayside (ⓣ02.97.31.54.16; ❶; closed mid-Nov to March), and a couple of more expensive options: the *Vauban*, 1 rue des Remparts (ⓣ02.97.31.45.42, ⓦwww.hotelvauban.com; ❺; closed Nov–March), and the *Hôtel-Restaurant de Bretagne* on quai Macé (ⓣ02.97.31.80.14; ❺–❻), both of which have excellent sea-view **restaurants**. There are also three **campsites**, including the three-star *Camping de l'Océan* (ⓣ02.97.31.83.86, ⓦwww.camping-ocean-belle-ile.com; closed mid-Oct to March), and a **hostel** (ⓣ02.97.31.81.33, ⓔbelle-ile@fuaj.org; €9.60; closed Oct), which despite holding almost a hundred beds is always wildly oversubscribed; it's located a short way out of town along the clifftops from the Citadelle at Haute-Boulogne.

Sauzon has one good hotel in a magnificent setting, the *Du Phare* (Ⓣ02.97.31.60.36; ❸; closed Oct–March), where guests must eat its delicious fish dinners, and two two-star **campsites**, *Pen Prad* (Ⓣ02.97.31.64.82, Ⓔmariedesauzon@wanadoo.fr; closed Oct–March) and *La Source* (Ⓣ02.97.31.60.95; closed Oct–March).

Houat and Hoëdic

The islands of **Houat** and **Hoëdic** can also be reached by ferry from Quiberon-Port-Maria with the Societé Morbihannaise et Nantaise de Navigation (1–6 sailings daily depending on the season; Ⓣ08.20.05.60.00, or, from outside France, Ⓣ02.97.35.02.00, Ⓦwww.smn-navigation.fr; around €23 return). The crossing to Houat takes forty minutes, to Hoëdic another 25. Alternatively, Vedettes Ar'moor sail to both islands from **Le Croisic** and nearby **La Turballe** daily in summer (July & Aug only, departs Le Croisic 7.45am, La Turballe 8.15am; Ⓣ02.97.62.94.43; approximately €23 return). Navix (Ⓣ02.97.46.60.00, Ⓦwww.navix.fr; €25 return) run day-trips to Houat only on most days in July and August, leaving **Vannes** at 7.30 and 8.45am, **La Trinité** at 8 and 11am, and **Port-Navalo** at 8.45am and other times during the day. Finally, Compagnie des Iles (Ⓣ08.25.16.41.00, Ⓦwww.compagniedesiles.com; €25 return) run similar trips from Vannes, Port-Navalo and Locmariaquer from March to September; times vary.

You can't take your car to these two very much smaller versions of Belle-Île, and both have a feeling of being left behind by the passing centuries, although the younger fishermen of Houat have revived the island's fortunes by establishing a successful fishing co-operative. Houat in particular has excellent **beaches** – as ever on its sheltered (eastern) side – that fill up with campers in the summer even though camping is not strictly legal. Hoëdic on the other hand has a large municipal **campsite**, overlooking the port (Ⓣ02.97.30.63.32; closed Sept–June). There are a couple of small **hotels** on Houat – *L'Ezenn* (Ⓣ02.97.30.69.73; ❸) and the pricier *Hôtel-Restaurant des Îles* (Ⓣ02.97.30.68.02; ❸; closed Dec & Jan) – and one on Hoëdic, *Les Cardinaux* (Ⓣ02.97.52.37.27, Ⓔlescardinaux@aol.com; ❸; closed Sun pm & Mon in winter).

Carnac and around

The **alignments** at **CARNAC** – rows of 2000 or so menhirs, or standing stones, stretching for over 4km to the north of the village – constitute the most important prehistoric site in Europe, long predating Knossos, the Pyramids, Stonehenge or the great Egyptian temples of the same name at Karnak. Mercifully, they now stand a few kilometres in from the sea, meaning you can combine a reasonably tranquil visit to the stones with a stay in the popular, modern seaside resort, pretty hectic by Brittany's mild standards.

The alignments

The **megaliths** of Carnac make up three distinct major alignments, running roughly in the same northeast–southwest direction, but each with a slightly separate orientation. These are the **Alignements de Menec**, "the place of stones" or "place of remembrance", with 1169 stones in eleven rows; the **Alignements de Kermario**, "the place of the dead", with 1029 stones in ten rows; and the **Alignements de Kerlescan**, "the place of burning", with

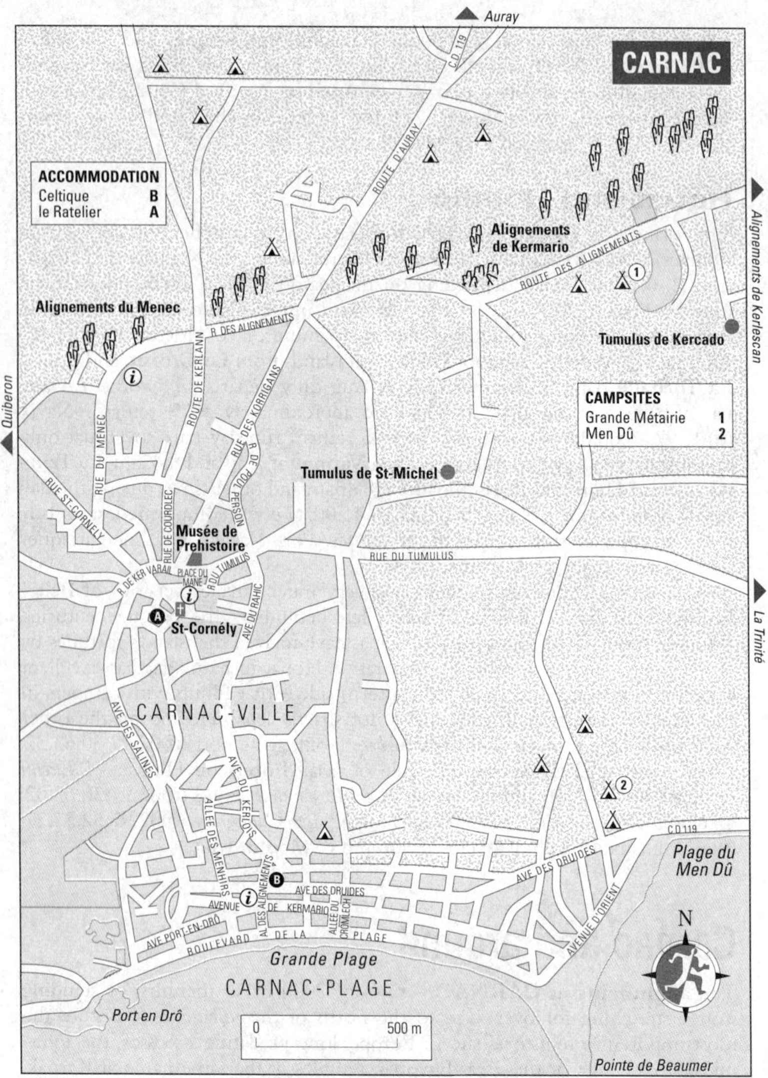

555 stones in thirteen lines. All three are sited parallel to the sea alongside the **Route des Alignements**, 1km or so to the north of Carnac-Ville.

Thanks to increasing numbers of visitors, however, the principal alignments have been fenced off, and you're not free to wander at will among them. The area is being allowed to re-vegetate, but there's no predicting how long that will take, and access may well still be restricted when it's complete. A temporary **visitor centre** near the Alignements de Menec (daily: May & June 9am–7pm; July & Aug 9am–8pm; Sept–April 10am–5.15pm; ⓣ02.97.52.89.99) sells books and maps of the site; a larger facility is due to be constructed somewhere on the site in the near future. The stones themselves are clearly visible but protected by fences, though thanks to their destruction and displacement by generations of meddling humans, and several millennia of Breton winters, many look like no more than stumps in the heather. It has become hard to see any real consistency in the size or the shape of individual stones, or enough regularity in the lines to pinpoint their direction.

There are several distinct types of megalithic monuments. **Menhirs**, or "standing stones", range in size from mere stumps to five-metre-high blocks; some stand alone, others in circles known as **cromlechs**, or in approximate lines. In addition there are **dolmens**, groups of standing stones roofed with further stones laid across the top, which are generally assumed to be burial chambers. And there are **tumuli** – most notably the **Tumulus de St-Michel**, near the town centre, a vast artificial mound containing rudimentary graves. You can scramble through subterranean passages and tunnels beneath the mound to view little stone cairns and piles of charred bones; the tunnels are, however, not authentic, being the recent creation of archeologists.

Carnac's **Musée de Préhistoire**, at 10 place de la Chapelle in town (mid-June to mid-Sept Mon–Fri 10am–6.30pm, Sat & Sun 10am–noon & 2–6.30pm; mid-Sept to mid-June daily except Wed am 10am–noon & 1.30–6pm; €5), is a disappointingly dry museum of archeology that's likely to leave anyone whose command of French is less than perfect almost completely in the dark as to what all the fuss is about. It traces the history of the area from earliest times, starting with 450,000-year-old chipping tools and leading by way of the Neanderthals to the megalith builders and beyond. As well as authentic physical relics, it holds reproductions and casts of the carvings at Locmariaquer, a scale model of the Alignements de Menec and diagrams of how the stones may have been moved into place.

The Town

Carnac itself, divided between the original **Carnac-Ville** and the seaside resort of **Carnac-Plage**, is extremely popular and swarming with holiday-makers in July and August. For most of these, the alignments are, if anything, only a sideshow. But, as a holiday centre, Carnac has a special charm, especially in late spring and early autumn when it is less crowded – and cheaper. The town and seafront remain well wooded, and the tree-lined avenues and gardens are a delight, the climate being mild enough for evergreen oak and Mediterranean mimosa to grow alongside native stone pine and cypress.

The town's five **beaches** extend for nearly 3km in total. The two most attractive beaches, usually counted as one of the five, are **plages Men Dû** and **Beaumer**, which lie to the east towards La Trinité beyond Pointe Churchill.

Practicalities

Buses to Auray, Quiberon and Vannes stop near the tourist office on avenue des Druides, and on rue St-Cornély in Carnac-Ville. In July and August, when the Tire Bouchon **rail** link runs between Auray and Quiberon, trains call at Plouharnel, 4km northwest of Carnac. Carnac's main **tourist office** is slightly back from the main beach at 74 av des Druides (July & Aug Mon–Sat 9am–7pm, Sun 3–7pm; Sept–June Mon–Sat 9am–noon & 2–6pm; Ⓣ02.97.52.13.52, Ⓦwww.ot-carnac.fr). An annexe in the place de l'Église in town is open in summer (April–Sept Tues–Sat 9.30am–12.30 & 2–6pm). **Bicycles** can be rented from

The Megaliths of Brittany

Megalithic sites can be found all around the Mediterranean, notably in Malta and Sardinia, and along the Atlantic seaboard from Spain to Scandinavia. Among the most significant are Newgrange in Ireland, Stonehenge in England, and the Ring of Brodgar in the Orkneys. However, the megalith-building culture did not necessarily originate in the Mediterranean and spread to the "barbarian" outposts of Europe. In fact, the tumuli, alignments and single standing stones of Brittany are of pre-eminent importance.

Archeological evidence suggests that late **Stone Age settlements** existed along the Breton coast by around 6000 BC. Soon afterwards, the culture responsible either evolved to become the megalith builders, or was displaced by megalith-building newcomers. Dated at 5700 BC, the tumulus of Kercado at Carnac appears to be the earliest stone construction in Europe.

Each megalithic centre had its own distinct styles and traditions. Brittany has relatively few stone circles, and a greater proportion of free-standing stones; fewer burials, and more evidence of ritual fires; different styles of carving; and, uniquely, the sheer complexity of the Carnac alignments. Little is known of the people who erected the megaliths. Only rarely have skeletons been found in the graves, but what few there have been seem to indicate a short, dark, hairy race with a life expectancy of no more than the mid-thirties. What is certain is that the civilization was a long-lasting one; the earliest and the latest constructions at Carnac are over five thousand years apart.

As for the actual **purpose** of the megaliths, the most fashionable theory these days sees them as part of a vast system of astronomical measurement, record-keeping, and prediction. In Brittany, the argument goes, the now fallen Grand Menhir of Locmariaquer served as a "universal lunar foresight", its alignments with eight other sites corresponding to the eight extreme points of the rising and setting of the moon during its 18.61-year cycle. The Golfe de Morbihan made an ideal location for such a marking stone, set on a lagoon surrounded by low peninsulas. Once the need for the Grand Menhir was decided upon, it would have taken hundreds of years of

several local campsites, or from Le Randonneur, 20 av des Druides, Carnac-Plage (☎02.97.52.02.55). The *Grande Métairie* site (see below) also arranges horseback tours. There's a **market** in Carnac Ville on Wednesday and Sunday mornings.

Hotels in Carnac are at a premium in July and August, when you can expect higher prices and intense pressure to take half-board (*demi-pension*). Carnac-Ville is marginally cheaper than Carnac-Plage, although the distinction is blurred where the two merge. In **Carnac-Ville**, the old stone, ivy-clad *Le Ratelier*, 4 Chemin de Douët (☎02.97.52.05.04; ❸; closed Oct–March), has menus from €17. In **Carnac-Plage** an excellent option is the *Celtique*, 82 av des Druides (☎02.97.52.73.27, Ⓦwww.hotel-celtique.com; ❼–❽). As befits such a family-oriented place, Carnac holds as many as nineteen **campsites**. Among the best are the two-star *Men Dû* (☎02.97.52.04.23; closed Oct–Easter) near the sea, inland from the plage du Men Dû, and the more expensive four-star *Grande Métairie* (☎02.97.52.24.01; closed mid-Sept to March), near the Kercado tumulus. Most of the **restaurants** worth recommending are in hotels, including those listed above.

Locmariaquer

With its complex patterning, the stone of the roof on Gavrinis (see p.513) has been identified as part of the same piece as the dolmen known as the **Table** careful observation of the moon to fix the exact spot for it. It's thought that this was done by lighting fires on the top of high poles at trial points on the crucial nights every nine years. The alignments of Carnac are thus explained as the graph paper on which the lunar movements were plotted.

However, this has been hotly disputed. Controversy rages as to whether the Grand Menhir ever stood at all, or, even if it did, whether it fell or was broken up before the eight supposedly associated sites came into being; moreover, sceptics say, these measurements ignore the fact that the sea level in southern Brittany 6600 years ago was 10m lower than it is today.

In any case, the stones at Carnac have been so greatly eroded that perhaps it's little more than wishful thinking to imagine that their original size, shape and orientation can be accurately determined. They have been knocked down by farmers seeking to cultivate the land; quarried for use in making roads; removed by landowners angry at the trespass of tourists and scientists; and shifted and re-erected by nineteenth-century pseudo-scientists.

An alternative approach places greater emphasis on sociological factors. This argues that the stones date from the period of transition when humankind was changing from a predatory role to a productive one, and that they can only have been put in place by the co-ordinated efforts of a large and stable **community**. It's possible that the megaliths were erected by Neolithic settlers, who generation by generation advanced across Europe from the east bringing advances in agriculture. As they came into conflict with existing Stone Age groups, they may have set up menhirs as territorial markers.

It also makes sense to imagine setting up a menhir as serving a valuable social purpose, both as an achievement in its own right and as a celebration of some other event. The annual or occasional setting-up of a new stone is easier to envisage than the vast effort required to erect them all at once – in which case the fact that they were arranged in lines, mounds and circles might have been of peripheral importance.

des Marchands at **LOCMARIAQUER**, 12km east of Carnac. Locmariaquer also has the **Grand Menhir Brisé**, supposedly the crucial central point of the megalithic observatory of Carnac. Before being floored by an earthquake in 1722, it was by far the largest known menhir – 22m high and weighing more than a full jumbo jet at 347 tonnes. It now lies on the ground in four pieces, with a possible fifth missing, close to the Table des Marchands (daily: mid-Jan to March & Oct to mid-Dec 2–5pm; April & May 10am–1pm & 2–6pm; June–Sept 10am–7pm; July & Aug €5, Sept–June €4).

Locmariaquer boasts a couple of reasonable small **hotels**, both with good restaurants: *L'Escale* (Ⓣ02.97.57.32.51; ❸; closed Oct–March), is right on the waterfront, with a great view from its terrace, while the *Lautram* is set slightly back from the sea, facing the church (Ⓣ02.97.57.31.32; ❸; closed March & Oct–Dec). **Campsites** include the excellent *La Ferme Fleurie* (Ⓣ02.97.57.34.06; closed Dec & Jan), 1km towards Kerinis, and the *Lann Brick* (Ⓣ02.97.57.32.79; closed Oct–April), 1.5km further on, nearer the beach. Both are two-stars.

Auray

Some people find **AURAY**, with its over-restored ancient quarter, slightly dull – but it's a lot less crowded than Vannes, a lot cheaper than Quiberon town and usefully placed for exploring Carnac, the Quiberon peninsula and the Gulf of Morbihan.

The centre of the town today is the **place de la République**, with its eighteenth-century Hôtel de Ville. In a neighbouring square, linked to the place de la République by rue du Lait, is the seventeenth-century **church of St Gildas**, with its fine Renaissance porch. A covered market adjoins the Hôtel de Ville, but on Mondays an open-air **market** fills the surrounding streets with colour – and stops all traffic for a considerable radius.

However, Auray's showpiece is undoubtedly the ancient quarter of **St-Goustan**, with its delightful fifteenth- and sixteenth-century houses. The bend in the River Loch, an early defended site, was a natural setting for a town – and, with its easy access to the gulf, it soon became one of the busiest ports of Brittany. Today, as you look at it from the Promenade du Loch on the opposite bank, with the small seventeenth-century stone bridge still spanning the river, it's not difficult to imagine it in its heyday. In 1776, Benjamin Franklin landed here on his way to seek the help of Louis XVI in the American War of Independence.

The **gare SNCF** is twenty minutes' walk from the centre; **buses** run from the station through the centre of Auray and on to Carnac and Quiberon. Auray's **tourist office** is up in town at 20 rue du Lait, very near the Hôtel de Ville on place de la République (mid-June to mid-Sept Mon–Fri 9.30am–7pm, Sun 9am–noon; mid-Sept to mid-June Mon–Fri 9.30am–noon & 2–6pm, Sat 9.30am–noon; ⓣ02.97.24.09.75, ⓦwww.auray-tourisme.com). A small annexe is maintained in July and August at the train station. The most appealing place to **stay** would be by the port in the St-Goustan quarter, but in the absence of waterfront hotels the best option is *Le Branhoc*, about 300m from the waterfront at 5 route du Bono (ⓣ02.97.56.41.55, ⓔle.branhoc@wanadoo.fr; ❸; closed mid-Dec to mid-Feb), which offers clean, well-equipped rooms and a reasonable restaurant. Up in town, *Le Cadoudal*, 9 place Notre-Dame (ⓣ02.97.24.14.65; ❷), is a cheaper, more basic alternative.

Vannes

Thanks to its position at the head of the Golfe de Morbihan, **VANNES**, 20km east of Auray, is southern Brittany's major tourist town. Modern Vannes is such a large and thriving community that the small size of the old walled town at its core, **Vieux Vannes**, may well come as a surprise. Its focal point, the old gateway of the **Porte St-Vincent**, commands a busy little square at the northern end of the long canalized port that provides access to the gulf itself. Once inside the ramparts, the old centre of chaotic streets – crammed around the cathedral, and enclosed by gardens and a tiny stream – is largely pedestrianized, in refreshing contrast to the somewhat insane road system beyond.

Arrival, information and accommodation

Vannes' **gare SNCF** is 25 minutes' walk north of the town centre. Buses to Auray, Carnac, Quiberon and other destinations leave from the **gare routière** alongside. The **tourist office** is at 1 rue Thiers (July & Aug Mon–Sat 9am–7pm, Sun 10am–6pm; Sept–June Mon–Sat 9.30am–12.30pm & 2–6pm; ⓣ02.97.47.24.34, ⓦwww.tourisme-vannes.com), near place Gambetta. **Internet access** is available at Futur I-Media, 14 rue de la Boucherie.

In peak season, Vannes can get claustrophobic, but it offers a better choice of **hotels** than anywhere else around the gulf. The town also has a **hostel**, 4km

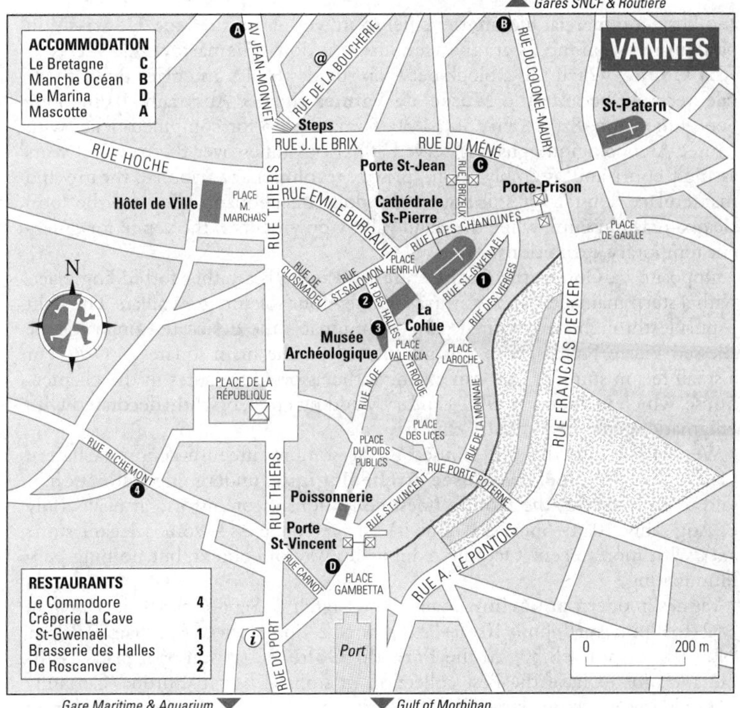

southeast of the town centre in Séné (Ⓣ02.97.66.94.25, Ⓔsene@wanadoo.fr; dorm bed €10.60; closed July & Aug), on bus route #4 from place de la République. The nearest **campsite** is the three-star *Camping Conleau* at the far end of avenue du Maréchal-Juin, beyond the aquarium, and alongside the gulf (Ⓣ02.97.63.13.88; closed Oct–March).

Hotels

Le Bretagne 36 rue du Méné Ⓣ02.97.47.20.21. Reasonable hotel situated just outside the walls, around the corner from the Porte-Prison. The rooms aren't fancy, but all have showers or bath plus TV. ❷

Manche Océan 31 rue du Colonel Maury Ⓣ02.97.47.26.46, Ⓕ02.97.47.30.86. Ordinary but perfectly acceptable rooms between the station and the walled town, used mainly by tour groups. Small-scale buffet breakfasts. ❺

Le Marina 4 place Gambetta Ⓣ02.97.47.22.81, Ⓕ02.97.47.00.34. Fourteen pleasantly refurbished rooms – and a downstairs bar – right by the port, with sea views. ❸

Mascotte av Jean-Monnet Ⓣ02.97.47.59.60, Ⓕ02.97.47.07.54. Functional upscale hotel a short walk northwest of the walled town, with 65 en-suite rooms and an adequate restaurant. ❺

The Town

The new town centre of Vannes is **place de la République** – the focus was shifted outside the medieval city in the nineteenth-century craze for urbanization. The grandest of the public buildings here, guarded by a pair of sleek and dignified bronze lions, is the **Hôtel de Ville** at the top of rue Thiers. By day, however, the streets of the old city, with their overhanging, witch-hatted houses and busy commercial life, are the chief source of pleasure. **Place Henri-IV** in particular is stunning, as are the views from it down the narrow side streets.

La Cohue, which fills a block between rue des Halles and place du Cathédrale, recently became the **Musée de Vannes** (July & Aug daily 10am–6pm; Sept–June Mon–Sat 2–6pm, Sun 1.30–6pm; €4, €5 for combined ticket with Musée Archéologique), having served at various times over the past 750 years as high court and assembly room, prison, revolutionary tribunal, theatre and marketplace. Upstairs it still houses the dull collection of what was the local Beaux-Arts museum, while the main gallery downstairs is the venue for different temporary exhibitions.

Opposite La Cohue, the **Cathédrale St-Pierre** is a rather forbidding place, with a stern main altar almost imprisoned by four solemn grey pillars. The light – purple through new stained glass – illuminates the desiccated finger of the Blessed Pierre Rogue, who was guillotined on the main square in 1796. For a small fee, in summer you can examine the assorted treasures in the chapter-house, which include a twelfth-century wedding chest, brightly decorated with enigmatic scenes of romantic chivalry.

West of the cathedral and housed in the sombre fifteenth-century Château Gaillard on rue Noé, the **Musée Archéologique**, undergoing restoration, is said to have one of the world's finest collections of prehistoric artefacts (July & Aug daily 10am–6pm; €3). But it's all pretty lifeless – some elegant stone axes with more recent Oceanic exhibits by way of context, but nothing very illuminating.

Vannes' modern **aquarium** (daily: Feb–March & Sept–Oct 10am–12.30pm & 2–6.30pm; April–June 10am–12.30pm & 2–7pm; July & Aug 9am-7.30pm; Nov-Jan 2-6pm; €8.50), in the **Parc du Golfe**, 500m south of place Gambetta, claims to have the best collection of tropical fish in Europe. Certainly it holds some pretty extraordinary specimens, including four-eyed fish from Venezuela that can see simultaneously above and below the water, and are also divided into four sexes for good measure; cave fish from Mexico that by contrast have no eyes at all; and *arowana* from Guyana, which jump two metres out of the water to catch birds. A Nile crocodile found in the Paris sewers in 1984 shares its tank with a group of piranhas.

Eating, drinking and entertainment

Dining out in old Vannes can be an expensive experience, whether you eat in the intimate little restaurants along the rue des Halles, or down by the port. If you're just looking for a snack, try the area outside the walls in the northeast, extending from the Porte-Prison towards the *gare SNCF*. The leading venue for **live music** is the *John R. O'Flaherty*, at 22 rue Hoche (☎02.97.42.40.11; closed Sun), which has traditional Irish music on Fridays, while there's a **gay** bar, *Le Bateau Ivre*, at 12 place Cabello in the St-Patern district (☎02.97.68.19.14). At the end of July, the open-air concerts of the **Vannes Jazz Festival** take place in the Théâtre de Verdure.

Brasserie des Halles 9 rue des Halles ☎02.97.54.08.34. Inexpensive brasserie, which manages to squeeze a few tables out onto the pavement. A bowl of mussels costs €9, a seafood *choucroute* €12, and there's a wide range of mainly fishy dishes at similar prices. Open daily.

Le Commodore 3 rue Pasteur ☎02.97.46.42.62. Unassuming marine-themed local restaurant, tucked away around the back of the post office, which offers plenty of fishy treats on menus that start at €10 at lunchtime, and from around €12 in the evening. Closed Sun.

Crêperie La Cave St-Gwenaël 23 rue St-Gwenaël ☎02.97.47.47.94. Atmospheric, good-value crêperie in the cellar of a lovely old house, facing the cathedral. Closed Sun, Mon lunchtime & all Jan.

Restaurant de Roscanvec 17 rue des Halles ☎02.97.47.15.96. Superb formal gourmet restaurant, in a lovely half-timbered house in the old town. Lunch at €17 is a bargain, while even the cheapest dinner menu, at €23, features unusual dishes such as a starter of pumpkin and chestnut mousse, beautifully prepared and presented. Closed Sun in summer, Sun evening & all Mon Sept–June.

The Golfe de Morbihan

It comes as rather a surprise to discover that Vannes is on the sea. Its harbour is a channelled inlet of the ragged-edged **Golfe de Morbihan** – *mor bihan* means "little sea" in Breton – which lets in the tides through a narrow gap between the peninsulas of **Rhuys** and **Locmariaquer**. By popular tradition the **islands** scattered around this enclosure used to number the days of the year, though for centuries the waters have been rising and there are now fewer than one for each week. Of these, thirty are owned by film stars and the like, while two – the **Île aux Moines** and **Île d'Arz** – have regular populations and ferry services and end up extremely crowded in summer. The rest are the best, and a **boat tour** around them, or at least a trip out to **Gavrinis** near the mouth of the gulf, is a compelling attraction. As the boats thread their way through the baffling muddle of channels, you lose track of what is island and what is

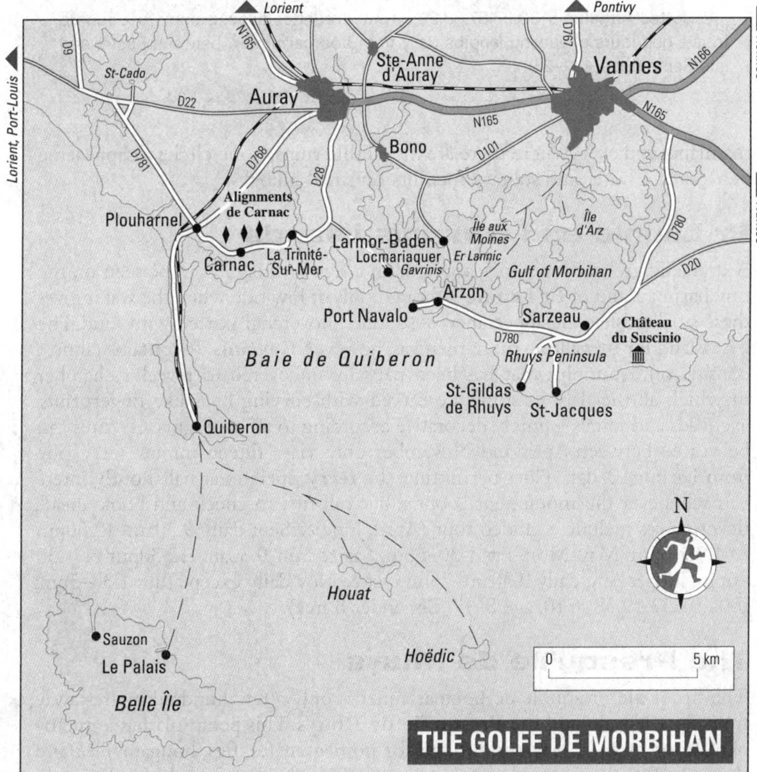

Gulf tours

In season, dozens of boats leave on **gulf tours** each day from Vannes, Port Navalo, La Trinité, Locmariaquer, Auray, Bono and Larmor-Baden. These are among the options:

Navix ⓣ02.97.46.60.00, ⓦwww.navix.fr. Up to six deluxe half-day (€19) and full-day (€26.50) tours around the gulf from both **Vannes** and **Port Navalo** every day between April and September, most of which offer the option of stopping off on the Île aux Moines and/or the Île d'Arz. You can have lunch or dinner on the Île d'Arz for an all-inclusive price of €43. There's a slightly smaller selection of tours from **Locmariaquer** between April and September, and from **Auray**, **Le Bono**, and **La Trinité** in July and August.

Compagnie des Îles ⓣ02.97.46.18.19, ⓦwww.compagniedesiles.com. At least three gulf tours daily from **Vannes** between April and October (€19–26.50), plus slightly more limited schedules from **Port Navalo** (April–Sept; €13.50–26.50); Locmariaquer (April–Oct €12–26.50); and Port Haliguen in **Quiberon** (April–Sept; €21.50–24.50).

Izenah Croisières ⓣ02.97.57.23.24 or 02.97.26.31.45, ⓦwww.izenah-croisieres.com. One to three gulf tours daily in summer (€12–20) and a year-round ferry service, with departures every half-hour, to the Île aux Moines (€3.50 return), from **Port Blanc** at Baden.

Vedettes L'Aiglon ⓣ02.97.57.39.15. Extensive itinerary of gulf tours from **Locmariaquer** (mid-June to mid-Sept; €11–23).

Vedettes Angelus ⓣ02.97.57.30.29, ⓦwww.vedettes-angelus.com. Also run up to five gulf tours of varying lengths daily from **Locmariaquer**, between Easter and late September (€11–23).

mainland; and everywhere there are megalithic ruins, stone circles disappearing beneath the water and solitary menhirs on small hillocks.

Er Lannic and Gavrinis islands

A dramatic group of menhirs, arranged in a figure of eight, can be seen on the tiny barren island of **Er Lannic** – though only at low tide when the water gives these smaller islets the appearance of stranded hovercraft skirted with mud. The best island for megalithic monuments is, however, **Gavrinis**. It contains (almost consists of) a tumulus that has been partially uncovered to reveal a chamber in which all the slabs of stone are carved with curving lines like fingerprints, axeheads and spirals – purely decorative according to archeologists. Gavrinis can be visited between April and November only, via a fifteen-minute ferry ride from Larmor-Baden. Tides permitting, the **ferry** operates at half-hourly intervals whenever the monument is open, but call first to check and book ahead; ticket prices include a guided tour (April, June & Sept daily 9.30am–12.30pm & 1.30–6pm; May Mon–Fri 1.30–6pm, Sat & Sun 9.30am–12.30pm & 1.30–6pm; July & Aug daily 9.30am–7pm; Oct & Nov daily except Tues 1.30–5pm; ⓣ02.97.57.19.38; €10, age 8–17 €4, under 8 free).

The Presqu'île de Rhuys

The tip of the Presqu'île de Locmariaquer is only a few hundred metres away from Port Navalo and the **Presqu'île de Rhuys**. This peninsula has a microclimate of its own – warm enough for pomegranates, figs, bougainvillea and the only Breton vineyards. Oysters are cultivated on the muddy gulf shores, but the currents of the gulf make this no place for swimming. The ocean beaches are the ones to head for: east from St-Gildas-de-Rhuys is the most enticing and least crowded stretch, with glittering gold- and silver-coloured rocks. For details on the whole peninsula, call in at the **information centre** just off the main road as you come into Sarzeau (daily: mid-June to mid-Sept 9am–8pm; mid-Sept to mid-June Mon–Sat 9am–noon & 1.30–6pm, Sun 2–6pm; Ⓣ02.97.26.45.26, Ⓦwww.rhuys.com).

Near **SARZEAU**, the impressive fourteenth-century **Château de Suscinio** is a completely moated castle that was once a hunting lodge of the dukes of Brittany, set in marshland at the edge of a tiny village and holding a sagging but still vivid mosaic floor. You can take a precarious stroll around its high ramparts (April & May daily 10am–noon & 2–7pm; June–Sept daily 10am–7pm; Oct–March daily except Tues 10am–noon & 2–5pm; €5). At the beautifully positioned little *Hôtel Bar du Port* in **ST-JACQUES**, 6km south, (Ⓣ02.97.41.93.51; ④), all seven rooms have balconies that look out across the port to the gulf.

Closer to the tip of the peninsula, clearly visible north of the main road, stands the **Tumulus de Thumiac**, from the top of which Julius Caesar is said to have watched the sea battle in which the Romans defeated the Veneti. Further on, **PORT NAVALO** has little more character than larger **ARZON** which precedes it, but there's a cute little beach tucked into the headland. Vedettes Thalassa (Ⓣ02.97.53.70.25) runs ferries to the islands and across the gulf from the jetty nearby.

South to the Loire

When you cross the **Vilaine** on the way south, you're not only leaving the Morbihan *département* but also technically leaving Brittany itself. The roads veer firmly east and west – to Nantes or **La Baule**, avoiding the marshes of the **Grande-Brière**. For centuries these 20,000 acres of peat bog have been deemed to be the common property of all who lived in them. The scattered population, the *Brièrois*, still make their living by fishing for eels in the streams, gathering reeds and – on the nine days permitted each year – cutting the peat. Tourism has arrived only recently, and is resented. The touted attraction is renting a punt to get yourself lost for a few hours with your pole tangled in the rushes.

Guérande

On the edge of the marshes of the Grande-Brière, just before you come to the sea, stands the tiny, gorgeous walled town of **GUÉRANDE**. It gave its name to this peninsula, and derived its fortune from controlling the salt pans that form a chequerboard across the surrounding inlets. This "white country" is composed of bizarre-looking *oeillets*, each 70 to 80 square metres in extent, in which sea water has been collected and evaporated since Roman times.

Guérande today is still entirely enclosed by its stout fifteenth-century ramparts. Although you can't walk along them, a spacious promenade leads right the way around the outside, passing four fortified gateways; for half its length the broad old moat remains filled with water. The main entrance, the **Porte St-Michel** on the east side of town, now holds a small **museum** of local history (daily: April–Sept 10am–12.30pm & 2.30–7pm; Oct 10am–noon & 2–6pm; €3).

Guérande's **tourist office** is just outside the Porte St-Michel at 1 place du Marché au Bois (July & Aug Mon–Sat 9.30am–7pm, Sun 10am–1pm; Sept–June Mon–Sat 9.30am–12.30pm & 1.30–6pm; ⓣ02.40.24.96.71, ⓦwww.ot-guerande.fr). Tucked out of sight behind the market, the pretty *Roc-Maria*, 1 rue des Halles (ⓣ02.40.24.90.51; ❸; closed Tues in low season), offers cosy **rooms** above a crêperie in a fifteenth-century town house. To the north, opposite the Porte Vannetoise and the most impressive stretch of ramparts, the *Hôtel des Voyageurs*, 1 place du 8 Mai 1945 (ⓣ02.40.24.90.13; ❸; closed Sun evening & Mon in low season), is a *logis* serving good menus from €17.

La Baule

There is something very surreal about emerging from the Brière to the coast at **LA BAULE** – an imposing, moneyed landscape where the dunes are no longer bonded together with scrub and pines, but with massive apartment buildings and luxury hotels. Sited on the long stretch of dunes that links the former island of Le Croisic to the mainland, it owes its existence to a storm in 1779 that engulfed the old town of Escoublac in silt from the Loire, and thereby created a wonderful crescent of sandy beach.

Neither La Baule's permanence nor its affluence seems in any doubt these days. It's a resort that very firmly imagines itself in the south of France: around the crab-shaped bay, bronzed nymphettes and would-be Clint Eastwoods ride across the sands into the sunset against a backdrop of cruising lifeguards, horse-dung removers and fantastically priced cocktails. It can be fun if you feel like a break from the more subdued Breton attractions – and the beach is undeniably impressive. It's not a place to enjoy strolling around in search of hidden charms; the back streets have an oddly rural feel, but hold nothing of any interest.

La Baule has two **gare SNCF**s, the barely used La-Baule-les-Pins, and the main La-Baule-Escoublac near the tourist office on place Rhin-et-Danube, where the TGVs from Paris arrive. The **gare routière** is at 4 place de la Victoire (ⓣ02.40.11.53.00). Full details on staying in La Baule can be had from the **tourist office**, away from the seafront at 8 place de la Victoire (mid-May to mid-Sept daily 9am–8pm; mid-Sept to mid-May Mon–Sat 9am–12.30pm & 1.45–6pm, Sun 10am–1pm & 2.30–5pm; ⓣ02.40.24.34.44, ⓦwww.labaule.tm.fr).

Few of the **hotels** are cheap, particularly in high season, and in low season more than half are closed. Low-priced options near the main *gare SNCF* include the *Marini*, 22 av Clémenceau (ⓣ02.40.60.23.29; ❸), while the *Mascotte*, 26 av Marie-Louise (ⓣ02.40.60.26.55, ⓦwww.la-mascotte.fr; ❹), is a quieter and classier option less than 100m back from the beach. The finest of the many local **campsites**, 2km from the sea, is the four-star *La Roseraie*, 20 av Sohier (ⓣ02.40.60.46.66, ⓦwww.laroseraie.com; closed Oct–March).

Le Croisic

The small port of **LE CROISIC**, sheltering from the ocean around the corner of the headland, is a more attractive place to stay than La Baule. These days it's basically a pleasure port, but fishing boats do still sail from its harbour, near the very slender mouth of the bay, and there's a modern **fish market** near the long Tréhic jetty, where you can watch the day's catch being auctioned. The hills on either side of the harbour, Mont Lenigo and Mont Esprit, are not natural; they were formed from the ballast left by the ships of the salt trade. If you're staying, choose between the **hotels** *Les Nids*, 15 rue Pasteur (ⓣ02.40.23.00.63, ⓦwww.hotellesnids.com; ❹; closed Oct–March), or the purple and white *Estacade*, near the end of the port at 4 quai de Lénigo (ⓣ02.40.23.03.77,

Ⓦwww.estacade.com; ❸), where the €15 menu includes *soupe de poissons* and fish of the day.

Close by, all around the rocky sea coast known as the **Grande Côte**, are a range of **campsites**, including the *Océan* (Ⓣ02.40.23.07.69; closed Oct–March). For equally good beaches and a chance of cheaper hotel accommodation, you could go east past La Baule to **PORNICHET** (though preferably keeping away from the plush marina) or to the tiny **ST-MARC**, where in 1953 Jacques Tati filmed *Monsieur Hulot's Holiday*.

St-Nazaire

The best sandy coves in the region are to be found on the western outskirts of **ST-NAZAIRE**, linked by wooded paths and almost deserted. But it's a gloomy city, bombed to extinction in World War II, and with shipyards, in more or less continuous operation since constructing Julius Caesar's fleet, now closing. The one reason you might want to stay is the relative ease of finding inexpensive **hotel** space – so elusive in this area in summer. Modern, well-equipped options include the *Touraine*, 4 av de la République (Ⓣ02.40.22.47.56, Ⓔhoteltouraine@free.fr; ❶), and the *Korali*, opposite the station on place de la Gare (Ⓣ02.40.01.89.89; ❸). Even if St-Nazaire is a familiarly depressing town in total industrial decline, it has one inspiring piece of engineering – the **Pont St-Nazaire**, a great elongated S-curved suspension bridge over the mouth of the Loire. Driving across it incurs a heavy toll, but bikes go over for free.

Nantes

NANTES, the former capital of Brittany, is no longer officially part of the province: it was transferred to the Pays de la Loire in 1962 when the modern administrative regions were established. Nonetheless, such bureaucracy is not taken too seriously in a city whose history is so intimately bound up with Breton fortunes. A considerable medieval centre, it later achieved great wealth from colonial expeditions, the slave trade and shipbuilding – activities in turn surpassed by more recent industrial growth. Although much of the former provincial character of the city has been lost, thanks to such recent accretions as the tower blocks masking the Loire and motorways tearing past the city, it remains to its inhabitants an integral part of Brittany.

Arrival, information and accommodation

Nantes' **gare SNCF**, a little way east of the centre, is served by a dozen TGVs daily from Paris (just 2hrs away). It has two exits; for most facilities (tramway, buses, hotels) use Accès Nord. There are two main **bus** stations. The one just south of the centre on allée Baco, near place Ricordeau, is used by buses heading south and southwest, while the one where the cours des 50 Ôtages meets rue de l'Hôtel de Ville serves routes that stay north of the river. Modern rubber-wheeled **trams** run along the old riverfront, past the *gare SNCF* and the two bus stations. Flat-fare tickets, at €1.50, are valid for one hour, rather than just a single journey, though one-day tickets are also available for €3.50.

Nantes' **tourist office** has a new purpose-built location on the cours Olivier Clisson (Mon–Sat 10am–6pm; Ⓣ02.40.20.60.00, Ⓦwww.nantes-tourisme.com); it provides free book-size guides to local hotels and restaurants, and runs various guided tours of the city. They also sell the **Nantes City Card**, available

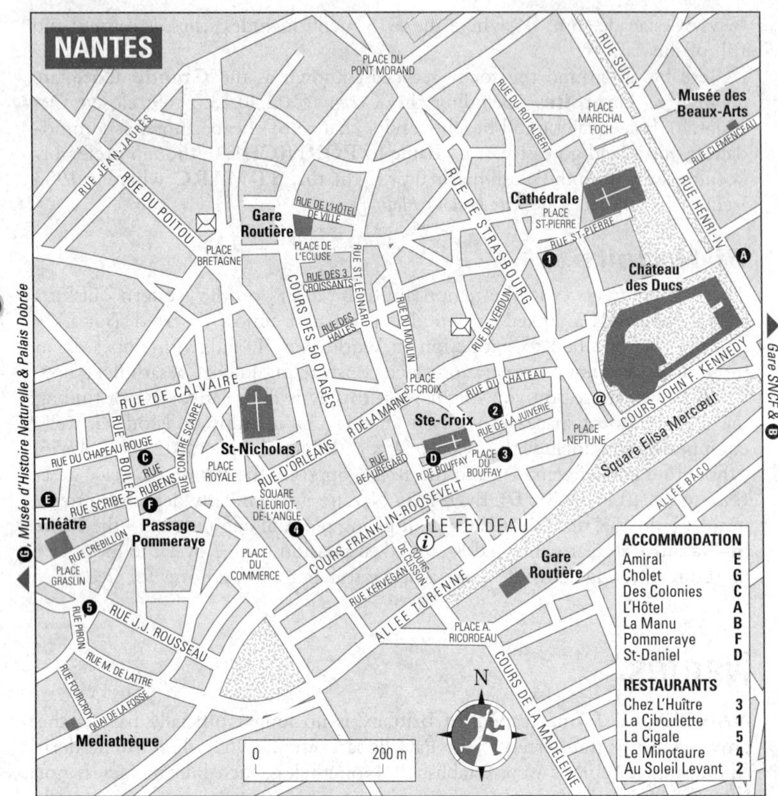

in 1-day (€14), 2-day (€24) and 3-day (€30) versions, which grants unrestricted use of local transport, including river cruises, and free admission to a wide range of museums. Cyber City, 14 rue de Strasbourg, offers **Internet access** (daily noon–midnight; ⓣ02.40.89.57.92; €4 per hr). Two weekly information publications, *PIL* and *Nantes Poche*, both sold for €0.45, are sometimes available free at the tourist office and at hotels.

Although it holds plenty of **hotels** to suit all budgets, Nantes is one of those cities where you won't necessarily stumble upon a suitable place just by walking or driving around at whim. Instead, there are two main concentrations: one, as ever, in the immediate vicinity of the *gare SNCF*, and the other in the narrow streets around the place Greslin. The **hostel**, *La Manu*, in a postmodern former tobacco factory at 2 place de la Manu (ⓣ02.40.29.29.20, ⓔnanteslamanu@fuaj.org; €11.85 per night), is a few hundred metres east of the *gare SNCF*, and accessible by taking tramway #1 towards Malachère and getting off at "Manufacture".

Hotels

Amiral 26bis rue Scribe ⓣ02.40.69.20.21, ⓦwww.hotel-nantes.fr. Well-maintained little hotel on lively pedestrianized street just north of place Graslin, perfect for young night owls. All rooms have TV, bath and double-glazing. Mon–Fri ❹, Sat & Sun ❷

Cholet 10 rue Gresset ⓣ02.40.73.31.04, ⓔhotelcholet@wanadoo.fr. Quiet, friendly option very close to place Graslin, where the assortment of rooms all have en-suite facilities. Rates drop at weekends. ❸

Des Colonies 5 rue du Chapeau Rouge ⓣ02.40.48.79.76, ⓦwww.hoteldescolonies.fr. Spruce, good-value hotel a couple of blocks up from place Graslin, within walking distance of everything. The lobby doubles as an art gallery, and one floor is reserved for non-smokers. Discounts on weekends. No restaurant. ❸

L'Hôtel 6 rue Henri-IV ⓣ02.40.29.30.31. An insouciant name for one of the city's finest options, a grand modern edifice facing the château that offers all mod cons, plus an €8 buffet breakfast. Parking costs €6. ❹

Pommeraye 2 rue Boileau ⓣ02.40.48.78.79, ⓦwww.hotel-pommeraye.com. Extremely good value modern boutique hotel with large, designer-decor rooms, beautiful bathrooms and free parking; good buffet breakfast. ❹

St-Daniel 4 rue du Bouffay ⓣ02.40.47.41.25. These simple but pleasant and well-lit rooms, on a cobbled street just off the place du Bouffay in the very heart of the old city, are much in demand in summer. Paying €3 extra secures an en-suite shower, while another €3 gets you a TV. ❶

The City

The Loire, the source of Nantes' riches, has dwindled from the centre. As recently as the 1930s, the river crossed the city in seven separate channels, but German labour as part of reparations for World War I filled in five. What are still called "islands" in the centre are now surrounded and isolated, not by water, but by hectic dual carriageways. These are not easy to cross, but they do at least mean that Nantes is separated into a series of discernible districts: the older **medieval city** is concentrated around the cathedral, with the château prominent in its southeast corner, while the elegant **nineteenth-century town** lies to the west, across the cours des 50-Otages.

The old town

Though no longer on the waterfront, and subjected to a certain amount of damage over the centuries, the **Château des Ducs** still preserves the form in which it was built by two of the last rulers of independent Brittany, François II, and his daughter Duchess Anne, born here in 1477. The list of famous people who have been guests or prisoners, defenders or belligerents, of the castle is impressive. It includes Gilles de Rais (Bluebeard), publicly executed in 1440; Machiavelli, in 1498; John Knox as a galley-slave from 1547–49; and Bonnie Prince Charlie preparing for Culloden in 1745. The most significant act in the castle was the signing of the **Edict of Nantes** in 1598 by Henri IV. The edict ended the Wars of Religion by granting a certain degree of toleration to the Protestants, but had far more crucial consequences when it was revoked, by Louis XIV, in 1685.

The stout **ramparts** of the château remain pretty much intact, and most of the encircling moat is filled with water, surrounded by well-tended lawns which make a popular spot for lunchtime picnics. Within the walls stand a rather incongruous pot-pourri of buildings added in differing styles over the years. Until recently, these housed a number of museums, but all are currently closed while their contents are rationalized into one much larger mega-museum, not due to open before 2006 at the very earliest. For the moment, **visits** consist of a brief walk into the courtyard and up onto the walls (daily 10am–6pm; guided tours in July & Aug only daily at 2.30pm & 4pm; free), though the former museums host temporary exhibitions from time to time.

In 1800 the Spaniards Tower, the castle's arsenal, exploded, shattering the stained glass of the **Cathédrale de St-Pierre-et-St-Paul** over 200m away. This was just one of many disasters that have befallen the church. It was used as a barn during the Revolution, bombed during World War II, and damaged by a fire in 1971, just when things seemed in order again. Restored and finally reopened, its soaring height and lightness are emphasized by its clean white stone. It contains the tomb of François II and his wife Margaret – with somewhat grating symbols of Power, Strength and Justice for him and Fidelity, Prudence and Temperance for her.

Nantes' **Musée des Beaux-Arts**, east of the cathedral on rue Clemenceau, has a respectable collection of paintings displayed in excellent modern galleries, and plays host to a high standard of temporary exhibitions (Mon, Wed, Thurs & Sat 10am–6pm, Fri 10am–8pm, Sun 11am–6pm; €3). Not all its Renaissance and contemporary works are on display at any one time, but you should be able to take in canvases ranging from a gorgeous *David Triumphant* by Delaunay to Chagall's *Le Cheval Rouge* and Monet's *Nymphéas*.

The nineteenth-century town

The financier Graslin took charge of the development of the western part of the city in the 1780s, when Nantes' prosperity was at a high due to the sugar and slave trades. **Place Royale**, with its distinctive fountain, was first laid out in the closing years of the eighteenth century, and has been rebuilt since it was bombed in 1943; the 1780s also produced the nearby **place Graslin**, named after its creator, with the elaborately styled **Grand Théâtre**, whose Corinthian portico contrasts with the 1895 Art Nouveau of not-to-be-missed *La Cigale* brasserie (see opposite) on the corner.

West of the place Royale on rue Crebillon, a spectacular nineteenth-century multi-level shopping centre mentioned by Flaubert, the **Passage Pommeraye**, drops down three flights of stairs towards the place du Commerce. The attention to detail lavished upon it is on a scale undreamt of in modern malls, giving a glimpse of early consumerism; each of the gas lamps that light the central area is held by an individually crafted marble cherub.

Rue Voltaire runs west of the place Graslin, leading to the **Musée d'Histoire Naturelle** at no. 12 (Tues–Sat 10am–noon & 2–5pm, Sun 2–5pm; €3.10). This holds an eccentric assortment of oddities, including tatty stuffed specimens of virtually every bird and animal imaginable, plus rhinoceros toenails, a coelecanth, an aepyornis egg and an Egyptian mummy. There's even a complete tanned human skin, taken in 1793 from the body of a soldier whose dying wish was to be made into a drum, while a small vivarium shelters living snakes and reptiles. Further along is Viollet-le-Duc's **Palais Dobrée** (Tues–Fri 9.45am–5.30pm, Sat & Sun 2.30–5.30pm; €3), a nineteenth-century mansion given over to two museums, one of which claims to feature Duchess Anne's heart in a box.

Eating

Unlike hotels, **restaurants** fill the winding lanes of the old city and it shouldn't take long to come up with something if you wander the pedestrian streets in the centre. Nantes is big enough to have all sorts of ethnic alternatives as well, with Algerian, Italian, Chinese, Vietnamese and Indian places in addition to those listed here.

Au Soleil Levant 12 rue de la Juiverie ⓣ02.40.35.68.65. One of several Asian options along a little pedestrian street, with seating indoors and out, this Japanese restaurant serves good-quality sushi, sashimi, *maki* rolls and noodles in all sorts of combinations, with full dinners €15–20, and lunch menus as cheap as €9. Closed Mon lunch.

Chez L'Huître 5 rue des Petites-Écuries ⓣ02.51.82.02.02. Much as the name suggests, this lovely little restaurant specializes in oysters, priced from €5–12 per half-dozen, but you can also get smoked fish, *soupe de poissons* and other simple dishes. Open until late, closed Sun lunch.

La Ciboulette 9 rue St-Pierre ⓣ02.40.47.88.71. Simple neighbourhood restaurant, tucked away on a side street very close to the cathedral, and serving imaginative dinner menus at €15 and €22, plus bargain lunch specials at €8 for a four-course meal. Closed Sun.

La Cigale 4 place Graslin ⓣ02.51.84.94.94. Justly famous brasserie, offering impeccably concocted meals in sumptuous Art Nouveau surroundings, with seating either at terrace tables or in the tile-adorned dining room. Fish and oysters are specialities, with seafood platters from €29 up to €85. The €15.20 and €24.80 menus are served until midnight. The €8 breakfast will doubtless outdo that on offer at your hotel while weekend brunches at €15 are an event.

Le Minotaure 5 square Fleuriot-de-l'Angle (ⓣ02.40.20.35.20). The slogan "enter and you'll be astonished" may overstate things, but this place has something for everyone: all-you-can-eat *moules-frites* for €11, steak for €13, a good fishy menu for €19, plus plenty of lighter options. Open daily from noon until late, with outdoor seating on the square.

Travel details

Trains

Brest to: Le Mans (1 daily; 3hr 40min); Morlaix (14 daily; 35min); Paris-Montparnasse (10 daily; 4hr 20min); Quimper (6 daily; 1hr 15min); Rennes (10 daily; 2hr 15min).

Guingamp to: Paimpol (June–Sept only, 4–5 daily; 45min).

Quimper to: Bordeaux (1 daily; 6hr 30min); Lorient (10 daily; 40min); Nantes (5 daily; 2hr 30min); Redon (10 daily; 1hr 40min); Vannes (10 daily; 1hr 10min).

Rennes to: Brest (10 daily; 2hr 15min); Caen (4 daily; 3hr); Dol (4 daily; 35min); Morlaix (10 daily; 1hr 40min); Nantes (5 daily; 1hr 40min); Paris-Montparnasse (8 daily; 2hr 10min); Pontorson (4 daily; 50min); Quimper (8 daily; 2hr 30min); St-Brieuc (10 daily; 50min); Vannes (4 daily; 1hr).

Roscoff to: Morlaix (2–3 daily; 30min).

St-Brieuc to: Guingamp (June–Sept only, 1–4 daily; 15min); Lannion (June–Sept only, 1–4 daily; 1hr).

St-Malo to: Caen (8 daily; 3hr 30min); Dinan (8 daily; 1hr); Dol (12 daily; 20min); Rennes (12 daily; 1hr; connections for Paris on TGV).

Buses

Brest to: Le Conquet (4 daily; 30min); Camaret (2–5 daily; 2hr); Quimper (6 daily; 1hr 30min); Roscoff (5 daily; 1hr 30min).

Quimper to: Audierne (7 daily; 50min); Benodet (8 daily; 30min); Camaret (5 daily; 1hr 20min); Crozon (5 daily; 1hr 10min); Concarneau (6 daily; 30min); Locronan (5 daily; 25min); Pointe du Raz (3 daily; 1hr 30min).

Rennes to: Dinan (6 daily; 1hr 20min); Dinard (8 daily; 1hr 40min); Fougères (7 daily; 1hr); Mont St-Michel (6 daily; 1hr 20min); Vannes (8 daily; 2hr).

Roscoff to: Benodet (1 daily; 2hr 30min); Morlaix (3–6 daily; 50min); Quimper (1 daily; 2hr).

St-Brieuc to: Guingamp (2 daily; 50min); Lannion (2 daily; 1hr 40min); St-Cast, via Lamballe, Le Val-André, Erquy & Cap Fréhel (6 daily; 2hr); Paimpol (8 daily; 1hr 20min); Vannes (4 daily; 2hr).

St-Malo to: Cancale (4 daily; 45min); Combourg (2 daily; 1hr); Dinan (4 daily; 45min); Dinard (8 daily; 30min); Fougères (3 daily; 2hr 15min); Mont St-Michel (4 daily; 1hr 30min); Pontorson (3 daily; 1hr 15min); Rennes (4 daily; 1hr); St-Cast (3 daily; 1hr).

Vannes to: Auray (4 daily; 45min); Carnac (4 daily; 1hr 15min); Josselin (6 daily; 1hr 15min); Malestroit (4 daily; 45min); Quiberon (4 daily; 1hr 45min); Rennes (8 daily; 2hr).

Ferries

St-Malo: Brittany Ferries (ⓣ02.99.40.64.01, ⓦwww.brittanyferries.co.uk) to Portsmouth (1 daily mid-March to mid-Nov, otherwise less frequently; 9hr). Regular ferries to Dinard (10min) in season, operated by Émeraude Lines (ⓣ02.23.18.15.15, ⓦwww.emeraudelines.com), which also sail to Dinan up the River Rance, and along the Brittany coast to Cap Fréhel and Île Cézembre (May–Sept). They also go to Jersey, to Guernsey (April–Oct), and Sark (April–Sept), and to the Îles Chausey in Normandy. Condor Ferries (ⓣ02.99.20.03.00, ⓦwww.condorferries.co.uk) runs services to Weymouth (via Guernsey; late March to Sept, 1 daily, 4hr 30min–8hr 30min), Poole (late May to Oct, 2 daily; 4hr 30min), Jersey (4 daily April–Sept, 2 daily Oct, 1 daily second half of March and first half of Nov), Guernsey (2 daily April–Oct, 1 daily second half of March and first half of Nov) and Sark (daily April–Oct).

Roscoff: Brittany Ferries to Plymouth (6hr) & Cork (13–17hr).

For details of ferries to Ouessant & Molène, see p.478; to Bréhat, see p.467; to Batz, see p.476; to Sein, see p.487; to Belle-Île, see p.503; and for tours of the Gulf of Morbihan see p.514.

The Loire

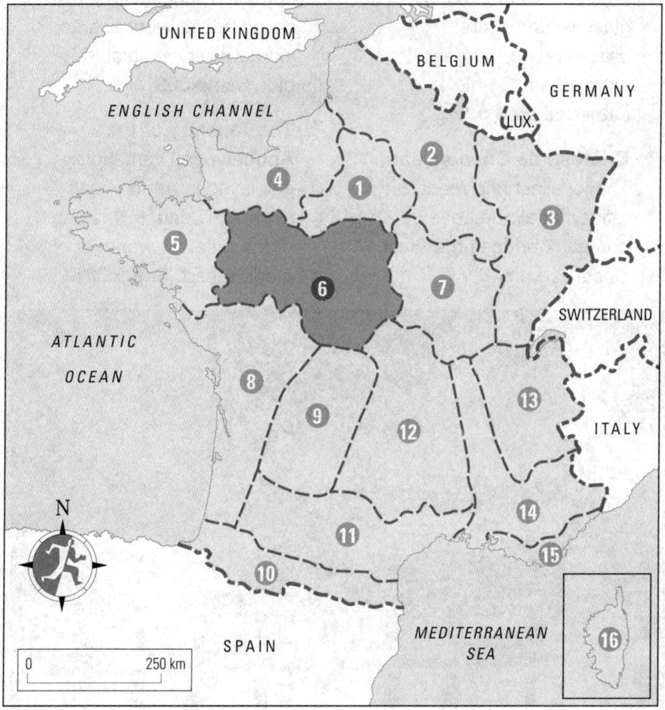

UNITED KINGDOM
BELGIUM
GERMANY
LUX.
ENGLISH CHANNEL
SWITZERLAND
ATLANTIC
OCEAN
ITALY
N
SPAIN
MEDITERRANEAN
SEA
0
250 km
1
2
3
4
5
6
7
8
9
10
11
12
13
14
15
16

CHAPTER 6 Highlights

* **Smaller châteaux** You can have a lesser-known château such as La Bussière or Beauregard almost to yourself. See pp.540 & 557

* **Stained glass at Bourges cathedral** Some of France's finest stained-glass windows are preserved in Bourges' extravagant Gothic cathedral. See p.543

* **Château de Chenonceau** The loveliest and most refined of all the Loire châteaux bridges the River Cher. See p.546

* **Château de Chambord** With this little Renaissance "hunting lodge", François I planned to outshine the kings of Europe. See p.558

* **The gardens at Villandry** These superb gardens are home to allegorical Renaissance hedge-work and an extraordinary vegetable plot. See p.569

* **The Tapestry of the Apocalypse** Dramatically displayed in Angers' half-ruined château, this is one of the greatest works of medieval art. See p.581

△ Chenonceau

6

The Loire

When the **Loire** reaches its halfway point and finally turns west towards the Atlantic, locals say that it ceases to be a mere *rivière*, it becomes a *fleuve* – which is something altogether grander. In this proudest stretch, from the hills of Sancerre to the city of Angers, it flows past an extraordinary parade of castles, palaces and fine mansions. In fact, the Loire Valley is so densely populated with these *châteaux* that when it came to choosing which should be awarded the title of World Heritage Site, UNESCO just bestowed the label on the entire valley. The roll call can be intimidating for the visitor, but if you pick your châteaux carefully, rid yourself of a sense of duty to guided tours and spend days on riverbanks with supplies of local cheese, fruit and wines, the Loire can be the most beguiling of all French regions.

The region's heartland **Touraine**, long known as "the garden of France", has the best wines, the tastiest goat's cheese, the most regal history and, it's argued, the purest French accent in the land. It also has one of the finest château in **Chenonceau** and by far the most developed tourist industry to match. But Touraine also takes in three of the Loire's pleasantest tributaries: the **Cher**, **Indre** and **Vienne**, each of which can be explored at a slower, more intimate pace. If you have just a week to spare for the region, then these are the parts to concentrate on. The attractive towns of **Blois** and **Amboise**, each with their own exceptional châteaux, make good bases for visiting the area upstream of Tours. Numerous grand châteaux dot the wooded country immediately south and east of Blois, including **Chambord**, the grandest of them all, while the wild and watery region of the **Sologne** stretches away further to the south-east. Downstream of Tours, around handsome **Saumur**, fascinating troglodyte dwellings have been carved out of the rock-faces.

As well as the many châteaux, the region has a few unexpected sights, most compelling of which are the gardens at **Villandry**, outside Tours; the abbey at **Fontevraud**; and the apocalyptic tapestry sequence in **Angers**, capital of the ancient wine-producing county of **Anjou**. Of the three main cities, **Tours** and

Museum pass

The handy **Passeport Val de Loire** "la clef des temps" (€25, free to under-18s) allows you to visit ten national monuments in the Loire Valley over the course of a year. You can purchase it at any participating site, including the châteaux at Angers, Azay-le-Rideau, Chambord and Chaumont, the Cloître de la Psalette at Tours cathedral, and the Abbaye de Fontevraud.

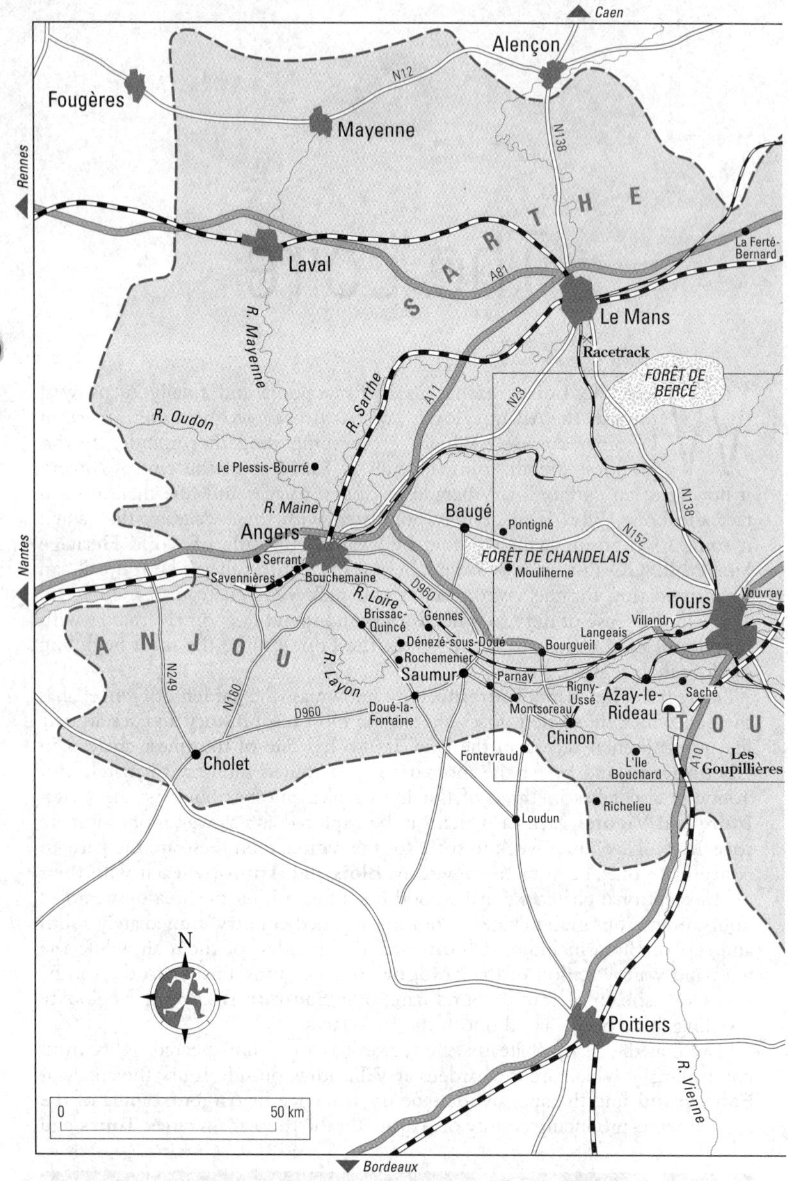

Angers provide the best urban bases, though **Orléans** has its own charm. Each city has its distinctive cathedral, though none is as impressive as the hybrid Romanesque-Gothic cathedral of busy, modern **Le Mans**, located some way north of the Loire valley in the topographically uninspiring *département* of **Sarthe**, or the stunningly glazed Gothic fantasy of medieval **Bourges**, which lies well south of the Loire, in the marshy farmland of the **Berry**.

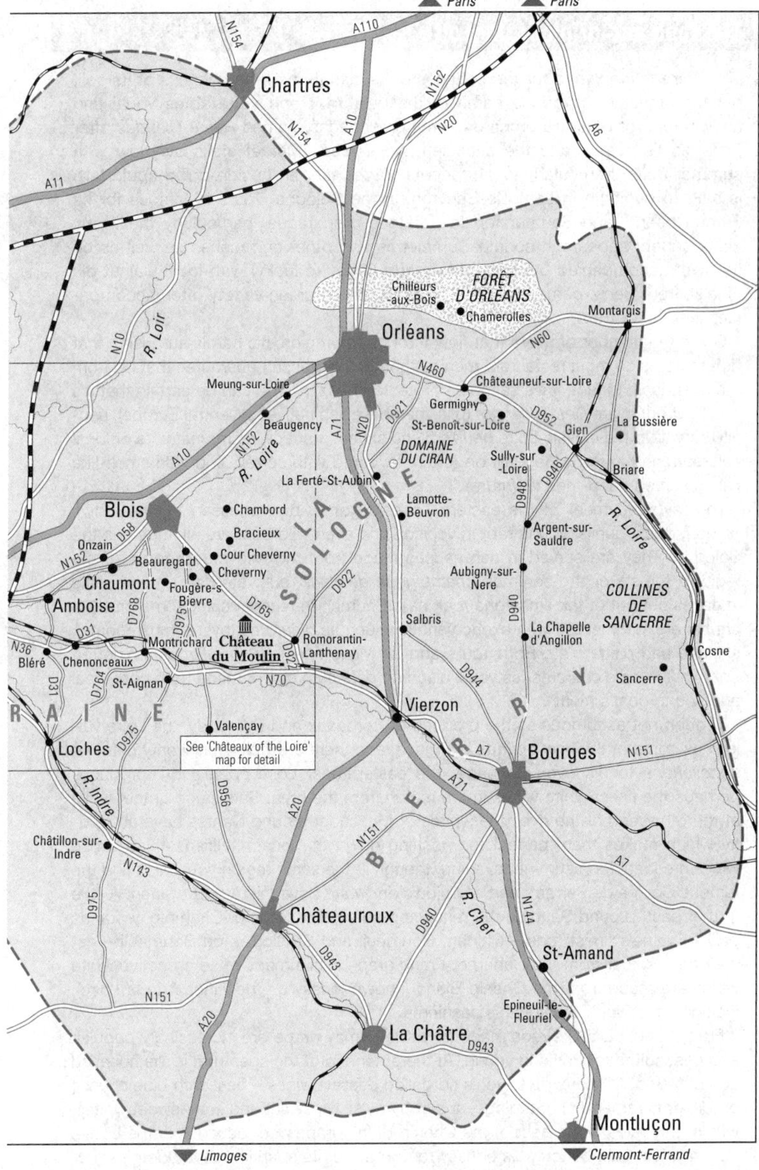

The Loire itself is often called the last wild river in France, mostly because unpredictable currents and shallow water brought an end to commercial river traffic as soon as the railways arrived, and the many quays remain largely forgotten, except by the occasional tour boat. The river's wildness also takes shape in dramatic floods, but for most of the year it meanders gently past its shifting sandbanks, shaded by reeds and willows, and punctuated by long,

The food and drink of the Loire

The **Loire** is renowned for the softness of its climate and the richness of its soil, qualities that help produce some of the best **fruit** and **vegetables** you'll find anywhere. From Anjou's orchards come greengages, named *Reine Claudes* after François I's queen, and the succulent Anjou pear. Market stalls overflow with summer fruits, particularly local apricots. *Tarte tatin*, an upside-down apple tart, is said to originate in Lamotte-Beuvron, in the Sologne. Tours is famous for its French beans, and Saumur for its potatoes. Asparagus, particularly the fleshy white variety appears in soufflés, omelettes and other egg dishes as well as on its own, accompanied by vinaigrette made (if you're lucky) with local walnut oil. Finally, from Berry, comes the humble lentil, whose green variety often accompanies salmon or trout.

Given the number of rivers that flow through the region, it's hardly surprising that **fish** features on most restaurant menus, though this doesn't guarantee that it's from the river itself. In fact, if it's salmon – protected by law – you can be certain that it's not. Favourites are *filet de sandre* (pike-perch – a fish native to Central Europe), usually served in the classic Loire *beurre blanc* sauce; stuffed bream; *matelote* of local eels softened in red wine; salmon (often flavoured with sorrel); and little smelt-like fishes served deep-fried (*la friture*).

The favoured meat of the eastern Loire is **game**, and pheasant, guinea fowl, pigeon, duck, quails, young rabbit, venison and even wild boar are all hunted in the Sologne. They are served in rich sauces made from the wild **mushrooms** of the region's forests or the common *champignon de Paris*, cultivated on a huge scale in caves cut out of the limestone rock near Saumur. In recent years, some producers have experimented with exotic varieties such as *pleurotes* (oyster mushrooms), shiitake and *pieds bleu*. Both Tours and Le Mans specialize in *rillettes*, or potted pork; in Touraine charcuteries you'll also find *pâté au biquion*, made from pork, veal and young goat's meat.

Though not as famous as the produce of Bordeaux and Burgundy, the Loire valley has some of the finest **wines** in France, and there are well over twenty different *appellations* to discover. Sancerre, the easternmost Loire *appellation*, produces perhaps the finest white wines in the region from the great Sauvignon grape, while at the other end of the river, the whites of Muscadet around Nantes have an acidity which makes them perfect for washing down the local shellfish. Anjou's rosé wines are ideal for a summer evening, though in the same region you'll also find the famous Coulée de Serrant, part of Anjou's dry white Savennières *appellation*. A little further east, around Saumur, the renowned soft red of Saumur-Champigny stands out. Touraine's finest reds – Chinon, Bourgeuil and St-Nicolas de Bourgeuil – get their ruby colour from the Cabernet Franc grape, while many of its attractive white wines are made from the Chenin Blanc (known locally as the Pineau de la Loire), including the highly fashionable Jasnières.

Fruity, Beaujolais-like reds made from the gamay grape are increasingly popular, and best suited for drinking young. At the other end of the spectrum is the honeyed complexity of Côteaux du Layon's so-called dessert wines – best with blue cheese or foie gras rather than pudding – and Vouvray's still, sweet and semi-sweet whites, which only release the best of the Chenin Blanc grape after decades in the bottle. Vouvray, just east of Tours, is equally renowned for its sparkling *méthode champenoise* wines, a rival to Montlouis, across the river, and the full, fruity sparkling Saumur – a good example of which is a serious match for most Champagnes.

Touraine makes something of a cult of its **goat's cheese**, and a local *chèvre fermier* (farm-produced goat's cheese) can be a revelation. Four named cheeses are found on most boards, and each can be recognized by its distinctive shape: Ste-Maure is a long cylinder with a piece of straw running through the middle; Pouligny-St-Pierre and Valençay are pyramid-shaped; and Selles-sur-Cher is flat and round.

sandy islands beloved by birds. The dangers of collapsing sandbanks and strong currents mean that swimmers should confine themselves to one of the many tributaries, though it's possible to rent a kayak in many places.

In general, this is a prime tourism region, where rental cars and bus tours are the norm. Yet train lines run along the river towards Nantes and Brittany and up through Tours to Paris, and most sites are accessible by public transport. If you're exploring on your own, however, it's a good idea to rent some means of **transport**, at least for occasional forays, because bus schedules can be skeletal and mostly geared to commuters and schoolchildren, and trains too limiting. Renting a bike is a good option: this is wonderful and easy cycling country, best of all on the flood banks, or *levées*, of the river itself, and on the quiet country backroads.

Orléans and around

ORLÉANS is the northernmost city on the Loire, sitting at the apex of a huge arc in the river as it switches direction and starts to flow southwest. Its proximity to Paris, just over 100km away, has always shaped this ancient city. Goods and passengers sailing up the Loire would disembark at Orléans for the journey to the capital, and it became an important port. The city's glory may have faded in the late nineteenth century along with the fortunes of the river, but recent years have seen an economic renaissance. High-speed train and motorway links to the capital and a rash of cosmetics factories set up in the suburbs have brought new jobs and prosperity. The ancient riverside quays are being re-developed and ultra-modern trams have been introduced – a perfect foil to the handsome eighteenth- and nineteenth-century streets of the old centre.

Despite a rich early history of being a centre of revolt against Julius Caesar in 52 BC (for which it was burnt to the ground), besieged by Attila the Hun in the mid-fifth century, and elevated to the position of temporary capital of the Frankish kingdom in 498, it's **Joan of Arc**'s deliverance of the city in May 1429 that the town feels bound to commemorate. This was the turning point in the Hundred Years War (1339–1453), when Paris had been captured by the English and Orléans, as the key city in central France, was under siege. Joan, a 17-year-old peasant girl in men's clothing, had talked her way into meeting Charles, the heir to the French throne, and persuaded him to reconquer his kingdom. Her role in the week-long battle that lifted the siege was probably slighter than is usually claimed, but her standard and sheer conviction certainly inspired the troops to victory. Less than three years later she was captured in battle, tried as a heretic, and burnt at the stake. Today, the Maid of Orléans is honoured everywhere, in museums, in civic statues and most memorably, in the stained glass of the vast Neogothic cathedral. One of the best times to visit is the evening before and the day of May 8 (**Joan of Arc Day**), when the city is filled with parades, fireworks and a medieval fair.

Arrival, information and accommodation

The **gare SNCF** leads straight into the modern shopping centre on place d'Arc, which fronts onto a huge swathe of busy roads; the old town centre lies on the far side of the traffic. The main **tourist office**, 6 rue Albert-1er (Tues 10am–1pm & 2–6pm, Wed–Sat 9.30am–1pm & 2–6pm; ⓣ02.38.24.05.05, ⓦwww.ville-orleans.fr), is just across the road which runs alongside the shopping centre. For online information on the region around the city, visit Ⓦwww.tourismloiret.com. The **gare routière**, on rue Marcel-Proust, is just north from the tourist office.

Accommodation in Orléans is mostly uninspiring, but a few inexpensive central hotels stand out from the rest, and there are plenty of fall-back choices near the station.

Hotels

Le Brin de Zinc 62 rue Ste-Catherine Ⓣ02.38.53.88.77. Half a dozen pleasant, well-maintained rooms in an old building above a popular and very central restaurant. ❷

Des Cèdres 17 rue Maréchal Foch Ⓣ02.38.62.22.92, Ⓦwww.hoteldescedres.com. Welcoming, newly renovated three-star with a garden in a peaceful quarter of town. The interconnecting rooms are useful for families. ❹

Charles Sanglier 8 rue Charles-Sanglier Ⓣ02.38.53.38.50, Ⓕ02.38.81.24.07. Very central, so tends to get booked up. The modern building is unprepossessing, and the rooms are small, but it's well maintained and comfortable. ❷

Jackotel 18 Cloître-St-Aignan Ⓣ02.38.54.48.48, Ⓕ02.38.77.17.59. Unrivalled location overlooking the church of St-Aignan across a shaded square, but the decor is anonymous 1980s-style. ❸

Marguerite 14 place du Vieux-Marché Ⓣ02.38.53.74.32, Ⓔhotel.marguerite@wanadoo.fr. Central, friendly and well run. The large, immaculate rooms are painted in cheery modern colours. ❸

De Paris 29 Faubourg-Bannier Ⓣ02.38.53.39.58. Old-fashioned but clean rooms above a very ordinary bar, near the train station. Extremely friendly and helpful management. ❶

Du Sauvage 71 rue de Boulogne Ⓣ02.38.62.42.39, Ⓕ02.38.77.17.59. Traditional and distinctly faded hotel in the quiet area behind the cathedral. The old, timbered rooms are let down by ugly modern furnishings. ❷

Hostel and campsite

Hostel 1 bd de la Motte Sanguin Ⓣ02.38.53.60.06, Ⓔasse.crjs@libertysurf.fr. Clean if institutional-feeling hostel just south of the eastern foot of rue de Bourgogne, in a park by the river. Ten minutes' walk from the cathedral, or take bus #4 or #8 from the bus and train stations, stop at "Pont Bourgogne". Reception Mon–Sat 8am–9pm, Sun 9–11am & 5–7pm.

Camping Gaston Marchand chemin de la Roche, St-Jean-de-la-Ruelle Ⓣ02.38.88.39.39. The municipal campsite, and the closest to Orléans, 3km away out on the Blois road, beside the Loire; bus #26, stop "Petite Espère". Closed mid-Oct to March.

The City

St Joan turns up all over town. In pride of place in the large, central **place du Martroi**, a mostly pedestrianized square at the end of rue de la République, rises a bulky mid-nineteenth-century likeness of her on horseback. Just beyond place du Martroi, the grand nineteenth-century boulevard of rue Jeanne d'Arc marches arrow-straight up to the doors of the **Cathédrale Ste-Croix** (daily 9.15am–noon & 2.15–5pm), where Joan celebrated her victory over the English – although the uniformly Gothic structure actually dates from well after her death. Huguenot iconoclasts destroyed the transepts in 1568, and in 1601 Henri IV inaugurated a rebuilding programme which lasted until the nineteenth century. The lofty towers of the west front, which culminate in a delicate stone pallisade, were only completed at the time of the revolution. Inside, skeletal columns of stone extend in a single vertical sweep from the cathedral floor to the vault. Joan's canonization in 1920 is marked by a garish monumental altar next to the north transept, supported by two jagged and golden leopards that represent the English. In the nave, the late-nineteenth-century stained-glass windows tell the story of her life, starting from the north transept. In a series of cartoon-like images, *L'Anglois Perfide*, or perfidious Albion, gets a rough ride, while the role of the Burgundians in her capture and the French clergy in her trial is rather brushed over. Across place d'Étape from the cathedral, outside the red-brick Renaissance **Hôtel Groslot**, the old

Which châteaux?

Choosing which Loire châteaux to visit can be a bewildering business, and trying to pack in the maximum can quickly blunt your sensibilities. The most famous sites usually justify the crowds they draw, but it's often wise to time your visit for lunchtime, or first and last thing. Visiting one of the lower-key sites, particularly if you have the place practically to yourself, is something special.

Of the most famous, **Azay-le-Rideau** (see p.571) and **Chenonceau** (see p.546) both belong exclusively to the Renaissance period, and their settings in the middle of moat and river respectively are very beautiful, rivalled only by the wonderful Renaissance gardens of **Villandry** (see p.569). **Blois** (see p.553), with its four wings representing four distinct eras, is extremely impressive, as is the monstrously huge **Chambord** (see p.558), the triumph of François I's Renaissance. At **Valençay** (see p.550), the interior of the Renaissance château is Napoleonic, while **Cheverny** (see p.556) is the prime example of seventeenth-century magnificence.

Many châteaux that started life as serious military defences were turned into luxurious residences by their regal or ducal owners: good examples are **Brissac** (see p.586), **Chaumont** (see p.556), with its nineteenth-century stables, and **Ussé** (see p.572), the most fairy-tale of them all. **Le Plessis-Bourré** (see p.586) is a fine example of late fifteenth-century elegant residence and strong defences combined, while **Sully** (see p.536) projects the power of its most famous owner, the Duc de Sully. Other feudal fortresses have preserved their medieval feel, among them the ruined **Chinon** (see p.616), **Langeais** (see p.571), beautifully furnished in fifteenth-century style, **Meung-sur-Loire** (see p.534), with its dungeons, **Fougères-sur-Bièvre** (see p.557), whose towers and staircases you can explore on your own, and **Amboise** (see p.567), which rears above the Loire like a cliff. For an evocation of medieval times, the citadel of **Loches** (see p.550) is hard to beat.

Other châteaux are more compelling for their contents than for their architecture: **Beauregard** (see p.557) is most famous for its portrait gallery while **La Bussière** (see p.540) for its obsessive nineteenth-century decoration, entirely dedicated to freshwater fishing, and **La Ferté-St-Aubin** is a living aristocratic home. At **Saumur** (see p.576), a museum on horses rivals the attraction of the castle itself, while at **Angers** (see p.581) the stark, largely ruined medieval castle houses the tapestry of the Apocalypse, the greatest work of art in the Loire valley.

Entry prices are pretty steep, particularly for the châteaux that have remained in private hands – and there are a surprising number of French aristocrats still living the fine life in the region. There is no consistency in concessions offered, and children rarely go free. If you're over 65, under 25, a student or still at school, check for any reductions and make sure you've got proof of age or a student card with you.

Hôtel de Ville, Joan appears again, in pensive mood, her skirt now shredded by World War II bullets.

You're spared the Maid in the cavernous **Musée des Beaux-Arts**, opposite the Hôtel Groslot (Tues & Thurs–Sat 10am–12.15pm & 1.30–6pm, Wed 10am–12.15pm & 1.30–8pm; Sun 2–6pm, €3), where the highlights of the main French collection on the first floor include Claude Deruet's *Four Elements*, the Le Nain brothers' dream-like and compelling *Bacchus Discovering Ariane on Naxos* (c.1635), and the exquisite collection of eighteenth-century pastel portraits in room 8. The suite of rooms on the mezzanine level leads from nineteenth-century Neoclassicism through Romanticism and on to a large chamber devoted to the early Realists, dominated by Antigna's taut, melodramatic *The Fire*. Foreign art, mainly Flemish and Italian sixteenth- and seventeenth-century works, is banished to the second floor – look out for Coreggio's renowned *Holy Family* (1522) and Velazquez's *St Thomas*. Twentieth-century art lurks in

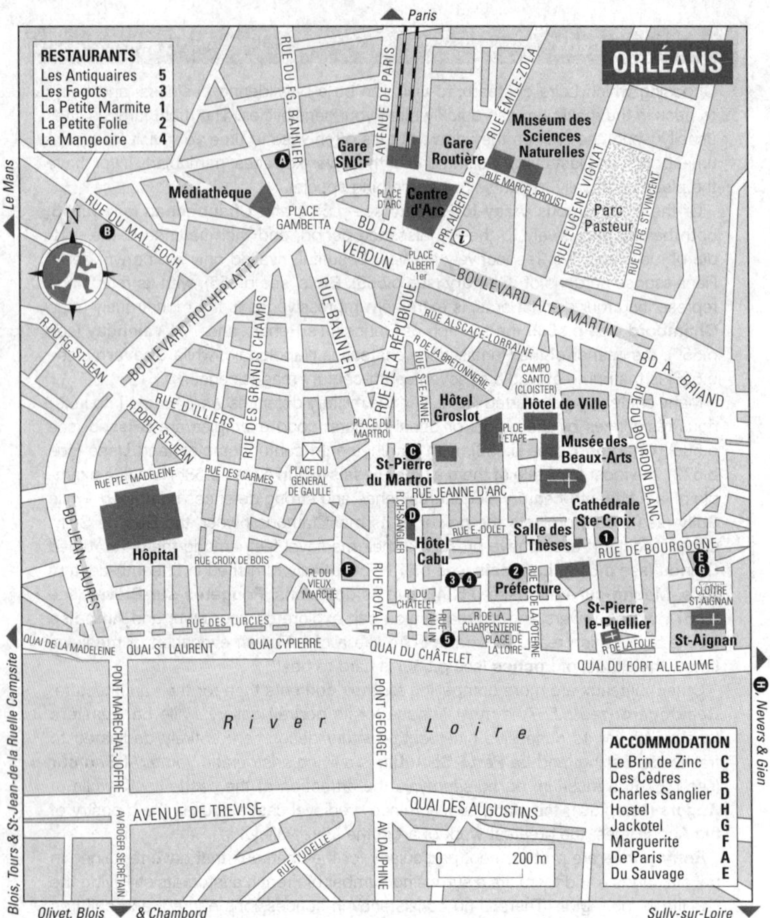

the basement, where the big names include Picasso and Gauguin; a small inner chamber has a number of African-influenced sculptures by Henri Gaudier-Brzeska (1891–1915), who was born just outside Orléans at St-Jean-de-Braye.

If you follow rue Jeanne-d'Arc east from the cathedral and turn left down rue Charles-Sanglier, you'll find the ornate **Hôtel Cabu** (May, June & Sept Tues–Sun 1.30–6pm; July & Aug Tues–Sat 10am–noon & 1.30–6pm Sun 1.30–6pm; Oct–April Wed, Sat & Sun 1.30–6pm; same ticket as Musée des Beaux-Arts), whose three tiers faithfully follow the three main classical orders in strict Renaissance style. Inside, a small historical and archeological museum houses the extraordinary **Treasure of Neuvy-en-Sullias**, a collection of bronze animals and figurines found near Orléans in 1861. The cache was probably buried in the second half of the third century AD either to protect it from Germanic invaders or to stop it being melted down for coinage at a time of rampant inflation, and possibly represents the last flourishing of Celtic religion at the end of the Gallo-Roman period. The floors above house various medieval oddities and Joan-related pieces, as well as exhibits on the history of Orléans. The entrance is on square Abbé-Desnoyers.

At the end of rue Jeanne-d'Arc, on place Général-de-Gaulle, is the semi-timbered **Maison de Jeanne d'Arc** (May–Oct Tues–Sun 10am–12.15pm & 1.30–6pm; €2), a 1960s reconstruction of the house where Joan stayed. Its contents are fun, most of all for children, with good models and displays of the breaking of the Orléans siege. Despite the consistency in artists' renderings of the saint, it seems the pageboy haircut and demure little face are part of the myth – there is no contemporary portrait of her, save for a clerk's doodle in the margin of her trial proceedings, kept in the National Archives in Paris.

The riverfront and around

If you head back east, and down towards the river, you'll find the scattered vestiges of the old city. **Rue de Bourgogne** was the Gallo-Roman main street, and now lined with lively bars and restaurants. The **Salles des Thèses** is all that remains of the medieval university of Orléans where the hardline Reformation theologian Calvin studied Roman law. A short distance further west on rue de Bourgogne, the circular Greek revival-style **Protestant chapel** dates from the 1830s.

To the south, the attractive narrow streets of the old industrial area slope gently down towards the river. Once semi-derelict, it is now the focus of a campaign to make the riverfront once more the focus of the city. On the new **place de la Loire**, which slopes down to the river from a nine-screen cinema complex, the flagstones are inset with a pattern that's supposed to suggest waves. At least two of the quarter's churches are on the list of precious monuments: the remains of **St-Aignan** and its well-preserved eleventh-century crypt; and the Romanesque **St-Pierre-le-Puellier**, an old university church now used for concerts and exhibitions. St-Aignan was destroyed during the English siege, rebuilt by the Dauphin and extended into one of the greatest churches in France by Louis XII, but more sieges of the city during the Wars of Religion took their toll, leaving just the choir and transepts standing. If you're not visiting during the summer months, visits to the **crypt** (July & Aug daily 2–6pm), which was built in the early eleventh century to house the relics of St-Aignan, can be arranged through the tourist office.

Eating and drinking

Rue de Bourgogne is the main street for **restaurants** and **nightlife**. You can choose from among French, Spanish, North African, Middle Eastern, Indian and Asian cuisines, all of which can be sampled at very reasonable prices. For buying your own provisions there are the covered **market halls** on place du Châtelet, near the river.

Restaurants

Les Antiquaires 2 & 4 rue au Lin ⓣ02.38.53.52.35. Run by a renowned chef, this is Orléans' best restaurant and must be booked in advance. Lobster consommé, wild turbot with girolle mushrooms and pike-perch steak are some of its delights. Menus at €42 and €52, plus an excellent €38 menu (not available Sat eve or Sun) which includes selected wines. Closed Sun evening & Mon.

Le Brin de Zinc 62 rue Ste-Catherine. Bustling bistro just off Place du Martroi in hotel of the same name. The outside tables are packed with a noisy crowd tucking into huge cocottes of mussels (€10–12) and giant desserts.

Les Fagots 32 rue du Poirier ⓣ02.38.62.22.79. Wonderfully convivial place that looks like it has been crammed into someone's grandmother's kitchen. Traditional main courses and grilled meats around €12–14. Closed Sun & Mon.

La Mangeoire 28 rue du Poirier ⓣ02.38.68.15.38. A hidden-away secret: homely, brightly lit bistro packed full of locals enjoying straightforward pasta, salads and French standards, with starters at €5 and mains at a little over €10. Closed Sun.

La Petite Folie 223 rue de Bourgogne ⓣ02.38.53.39.87. Youthful, designer bar-restaurant serving fresh, light and exciting food – you might have asparagus flan, chicken with *sauce Canadienne*, then strawberry soup with wine – all for around €20. Closed Sun.

La Petite Marmite 178 rue de Bourgogne ⓣ02.38.54.23.83. The most highly regarded restaurant on this busy street combines a stylish but homely feel with excellent regional cuisine. The basic €18 *menu du terroir* features local products such as Jargeau *andouille* and guinea-fowl from the Sologne.

Bars and nightlife

L'Arrozoir 224 rue de Bourgogne. One of the classier venues on the rue de Bourgogne strip, with restaurant service at lunchtime and from 6 till 10.30pm and a busy but laid-back bar carrying through till 3am on weekend nights. Closed Mon & Sun.

Le Ka place du Châtelet. The busiest and most central club in town, if not the coolest. Open daily 10.30pm–5am, but only gets going late.

Paxton's Head 264–266 rue de Bourgogne. English pub with a club in the cellars that's popular with a trendy, twenty-something crowd, with occasional live music. Tues–Sat 3pm–3am.

Listings

Bike rental Try Kit Loisirs, 1720 rue Marcel Belot (ⓣ02.38.63.44.34) in Olivet, a suburb in the south of Orléans (take tram #A to the Victor Hugo stop).

Car rental Avis, 13 rue Sansonnières ⓣ02.38.62.27.04; Budget, 5 rue Sansonnières ⓣ02.38.54.54.30; Europcar, 81 rue A.-Dessaux ⓣ02.38.73.00.40.

Cinemas Le Select, 45 rue Jeanne-d'Arc (ⓣ08.92.68.69.25), often shows good art-house movies in the original language; the nine-screen cinema on place de la Loire, Cinema Multiplex Pathé, 45 rue des Halles (ⓣ08.92.68.69.25), shows some Hollywood blockbusters in English.

Festivals Fête de Jeanne d'Arc is a series of period-costume parades held on April 29, May 1 and May 7–8, with the big set-pieces occurring in front of the cathedral on the night of the 7th and morning of the 8th May. The Festival de Jazz d'Orléans is held right through June, culminating in concerts held in the Campo Santo (ⓦwww.ville-orleans.fr/orleansjazz). Every September in odd years, the Loire Festival takes place, with five days of concerts and shows beside the Châtelet quay.

Internet Access available at 256 rue de Bourgogne, and 32 rue du Colombier, just north of Place du Martroi.

Medical assistance Centre Hospitalier, 1 rue Porte-Madeleine ⓣ02.38.51.44.44; emergencies ⓣ15.

Police 63 rue du Faubourg-St-Jean ⓣ02.38.24.30.00; emergencies ⓣ17.

Taxis Taxi Radio d'Orléans ⓣ02.38.53.11.11.

Château de Meung

Little streams known as *les mauves* flow between the houses in the village of **MEUNG-SUR-LOIRE**, 14km southwest of Orléans on the Blois rail line. During the summer months they leave slimy green high-water marks, but the sound of water is always pleasant, and Meung is an agreeable place to spend an afternoon, having accumulated a number of literary associations over the centuries.

More than seven hundred years ago one Jean de Meun added 18,000 lines to the already 4000-line-long *Roman de la Rose*, written half a century earlier in 1225 by Guillaume de Lorris, from the town of the same name in the nearby Forêt d'Orléans. Inspired by the philosophical spirit of the times, de Meun transformed de Lorris's exquisite, allegorical poem into a finely argued disquisition on the nature of love, and the resulting *roman* inspired generations of European writers, Chaucer among them. Most recently, the town featured in the works of Georges Simenon – his fictional hero, Maigret, takes his holidays here.

Looming at the western edge of the old town centre, the **Château de Meung** (March–Oct daily 10–noon & 2–6pm; Nov–Feb Sat & Sun 2–6pm; €6.50) remained in the hands of the bishops of Orléans from its construction in the twelfth century right up to the Revolution, since when it's passed through seven or eight private hands. The exterior of the château on the side facing the old drawbridge looks grimly defensive, retaining its thirteenth-century pepper-pot towers, while the side facing the park presents a much warmer facade, its eighteenth-century windows framed by salmon-pink stucco. You can explore the older part on your own, even climbing up under the roof, but most of this pleasantly shambolic section of the building was remodelled in the nineteenth century, and little sense of the building's history remains. A guided tour takes you through the more impressive eighteenth-century wing, where the bishops entertained their guests in relative comfort, and then down into the **cellars** where criminals condemned by the Episcopal courts were imprisoned. The most famous of the detainees was the poet François Villon – murderer, thief and originator of the much-quoted line *Où sont les neiges d'antan?* ("Where are the snows of yesteryear?"). His writings indicate that he was imprisoned in the bottom of a well, outside the main body of the château, and the guide will show you an appalling chamber sunk into the ground of the gardens. Villon was imprisoned at the château between May and October 1461, which seems a short time until you actually look down into the dank hole.

For a spirit-restoring **lunch**, head for the *Café du Commerce* (closed Mon), on the adjacent place de l'Église, which has decent *plats du jour* at around €8.

Beaugency

Six kilometres southwest of Meung along the Loire, **BEAUGENCY** is a pretty little town, which, in contrast to its innocuous appearance today, played its part in the conniving games of early medieval politics. In 1152 the marriage of Louis VII of France and Eleanor of Aquitaine was annulled by the Council of Beaugency in the church of Notre-Dame, allowing Eleanor to marry Henry Plantagenet, the future Henry II of England. Her huge land holdings in southwest France thus passed to the English crown – which already controlled Normandy, Maine, Anjou and Touraine – and the struggles between the French and English kings over their claims to these territories, and to the French throne itself, lasted for centuries.

Liberated by the indefatigable Joan of Arc on her way to Orléans in 1429, Beaugency was a constant battleground in the Hundred Years War due to its strategic significance as the only Loire bridge-crossing at that time between Orléans and Blois. Remarkably, the 26-arch **bridge** still stands and gives an excellent view of the once heavily fortified medieval heart of the town, which clusters tightly around a handful of central squares. **Place St-Firmin**, with its statue of Joan, is overlooked by a tower of a church destroyed during the Revolution, while **place Dunois** is bordered by the massive eleventh-century **Tour de César**, formerly part of the rather plain, fifteenth-century **Château Dunois**, which is closed to visitors for major structural works. The square is completed by the rather severe Romanesque **abbey church of Notre-Dame**, the venue for the council's fateful matrimonial decision in 1152. Shady Place du Docteur-Hyvernaud, two blocks north of place Dunois, is dominated by the elaborate sixteenth-century facade of the **Hôtel de Ville**. Inside, the main council chamber is graced by eight fine **embroidered wall hangings** from the era of Louis XIII, but you'll have to ask at the tourist office (on the same square) to be allowed inside to have a look. One set illustrates the four continents as perceived in the seventeenth century, with the rest dramatizing pagan rites such as gathering mistletoe and sacrificing animals.

Practicalities

A small **tourist office** (May–Sept 10am–12.30pm & 2.30–6.30pm, Sun 10am–noon; Oct–April Mon–Sat 9.30–noon & 2.30–6pm; ⓣ02.38.44.54.42, ⓔtourisme.beaugency@wanadoo.fr) can be found on place Docteur-Hyvernaud. Two rather lovely **hotels** make the most of Beaugency's atmosphere of genteel charm: the *Hôtel de l'Abbaye*, 2 quai de l'Abbaye (ⓣ02.38.44.67.35, ⓕ02.38.44.87.92; ❺–❼) is set in a beautiful seventeenth-century abbey with painted ceilings and beds on raised platforms; while the small, delightful *Hôtel de la Sologne*, 6 place St-Firmin (ⓣ02.38.44.50.27, ⓦwww.hoteldelasologne.com; ❸; closed Dec 20–Jan 15) has some rooms with views of the Tour de César. The *Hôtel des Vieux Fossés*, 4 rue des Vieux-Fossés (ⓣ02.38.44.51.65, ⓔchpouradier@wanadoo.fr; ❶–❷) is central and inexpensive. There's also an **HI hostel** in the suburb of Vernon at 152 rte de Châteaudun, 2km north off the main Orléans–Blois road from the east side of town (ⓣ02.38.44.61.31; ring to check seasonal opening hours), and a riverside **campsite** (ⓣ02.38.44.50.39; closed Oct–Easter), on the opposite bank from town.

Le Relais du Château, 8 rue du Pont (ⓣ02.38.44.55.10; closed Wed & Thurs lunch), is a decent, traditional **restaurant** with inexpensive menus; alternatively, *Le P'tit Bateau*, 54 rue du Pont (ⓣ02.38.44.56.38; closed Sun eve, and Mon), has a pleasant terrace and slightly more elevated gastronomic ambitions, with menus of €20 upwards.

Château de Chamerolles

Situated approximately 30km northeast of Orléans towards Pithiviers, **Chamerolles** is a sixteenth-century château (Feb, March & Oct–Dec daily except Tues 10am–noon & 2–5pm; April–June & Sept daily except Tues 10am–6pm; July & Aug daily 10am–6pm; €5), whose pristine condition is devoid of the well-worn patina you may have come to expect. Its history is unusually sedate, having passed peacefully through various private hands to the local government of the Loiret region, in 1987. The principal attraction is the **Promenade des Parfums** in the south wing, which traces the use of scents from the sixteenth century to the present day. With its "press-and-smell" buttons and reconstructed "toilets" it's great fun, not least for its revelations about European lavatorial habits over the last four hundred years. Behind the château is a reconstruction of the Renaissance gardens laid out by the château's first lord, one Lancelot du Lac. To **get there** using public transport, take a bus from Orléans to Chielleurs-aux-Boix, from where you'll have to walk the last 3km.

Château de la Ferté-St-Aubin and around

The **Château de la Ferté-St-Aubin** lies 20km south of Orléans (mid-Feb to mid-Nov daily 10am–7pm; €7, children aged 4–15 €4.50; ⓦwww.chateau-ferte-st-aubin.com). The late-sixteenth and early seventeenth-century building presents an enticing combination of salmon-coloured brick, creamy limestone and dark roof slates, while the interior is a real nineteenth-century home – and you are invited to treat it as such. You can wander freely into almost every room, playing billiards or the piano, picking up the old telephone, sitting on the worn armchairs or washing your hands in a porcelain sink; only the rather fancier grand salon, with its *boiseries* painted with views of the château and its antique furnishings, is cordoned off. Roughly every hour there are demonstrations down in the kitchens of how to make Madeleine cakes – the sweet spongy biscuit that so inspired Proust – while at the rear of the château, also enclosed by the moat, there's a fort with sponge balls supplied for storming it, little cabins with models acting out fairy tales, and a play farm. Older children and adults can explore the reconstructed 1930s station building adjacent, with its original *Compagnie des Wagons Lits* (Orient Express) carriages pulled up outside.

The **gare SNCF** is roughly 200m southwest of the main square, with around nine trains arriving daily from Orléans and continuing south to Vierzon and Bourges. For **eating**, an inexpensive option is the *Auberge Solognote*, at 50 rue des Poulies (closed Tues evening & Wed), behind the covered market on La Ferté's main square.

Six kilometres east of La Ferté-St-Aubin, halfway between Ménestreau-en-Villette and Marcilly-en-Villette, just off the D108, is the little hamlet of **CIRAN**, where you can explore the 300 hectares of the **Domaine de Ciran** (daily 10am–sunset; €5). Its working farm is a typical Sologne setup where the principal activities are deer breeding, keeping goats and making *chèvre*, but the main reason to come is to explore the forested parts of the *domaine*, where you may well catch a glimpse of wild deer, as well as herons and geese around the ponds and sometimes even coypus. It's also possible to come across wild boar, so be careful, though they are not very threatening unless they're with their babies. The 6km signed walk – for which waterproof footwear is advisable – gives a good taste of the different landscapes of the region.

East to the Burgundy border

Upstream from Orléans, single-lane roads – ideal for cycling – run along the top of the flood embankments of the Loire. To the north is the rambling **Forêt d'Orléans**, crisscrossed with roads. Beyond it, a bland, treeless wheat plain stretches to Paris, and the immediate countryside to the south is likewise drab: sticking to the Loire itself is the best advice.

Along the river are plenty of lesser-known attractions, most notably the **abbey at St-Benoît**, the **château at Sully-sur-Loire**, the small town of **Gien**, the **aqueduct at Briare** and the hilltop town of **Sancerre**, right on the Burgundy border, which makes some of the best dry whites in France. If you're out on or in the river, or even camping on the bank, be aware that the Loire's placid flow along these reaches is deceptive; it can swell within 24 hours and has been known to break its banks.

Germigny-des-Prés and St-Benoît-sur-Loire

An afternoon's bike ride or a short drive east out of Orléans, passing through **CHÂTEAUNEUF-SUR-LOIRE** (whose château has very pleasant gardens of rhododendrons and magnolias and a small museum of traditional Loire shipping), brings you to **GERMIGNY-DES-PRÈS**. The small, plain **church** here (daily: April–Oct 8.30am–7pm; Nov–March 8.30am–5pm) incorporates at its east end one of the few surviving buildings from the Carolingian Renaissance, a tiny, perfectly formed church in the shape of a Greek cross. It was built in 806 as a private oratory for Theodulf, who was one of Charlemagne's counsellors as well as bishop of Orléans and abbot of St-Benoît. The chapel's horseshoe arches suggest the Arabic form, but in fact reflect Theodulf's Visigothic origins, while the chapel itself is a typically Carolingian design, rationally planned and Classical in temper. The oratory's sheer antiquity is spoiled by too-perfect restoration work, but the unique gold and silver mosaic on the dome of the eastern chapel preserves all its rare beauty. Covered by distemper, it was only discovered by accident in the middle of last century when children were found playing with coloured glass cubes in the church.

A few kilometres further south along the D60, **ST-BENOÎT-SUR-LOIRE** offers a more impressive edifice, the Romanesque **Abbaye de Fleury** (daily 6.30am–10pm; Ⓦwww.abbaye-fleury.com). In around 672, monks from Fleury returned home from a daring expedition to Monte Cassino in Lombard-occupied Italy with the remains of St-Benoît (St Benedict), the sixth-century founder of the reforming Benedictine order. The presence of the relics secured a prestigious future for the abbey, and over the course of the next 1100 years, its abbots included many familiar names from French and Loire history, including the Cardinal of Guise murdered in the château at Blois and the great Cardinal Richelieu, who received the title of abbot as a political reward in 1621. For all its importance, the abbey stagnated as often as it flourished, and its population had dwindled to ten monks at the time of the Revolution, after which it was abandoned and dismantled. But the church itself survived, and Benedictine monks returned in 1944. The community now numbers forty brothers, who still observe the original Rule – poverty, chastity and obedience – and can be heard singing Gregorian chant at the daily midday mass (11am on Sun).

Built in warm, cream-coloured stone between 1020 and 1218, the church dates from the abbey's greatest epoch. The oldest part, the porch tower, illustrates St John's vision of the New Jerusalem in Revelation – foursquare, with twelve foundations and three open gates on each side. The fantastically sculpted capitals of the heavy pillars are alive with acanthus leaves, birds and exotic animals. Three of them depict scenes from the Apocalypse, while another shows Mary's flight into Egypt. Inside, the choir is split into two levels: above, a marble mosaic of Roman origin covers the chancel floor; below, in the ancient crypt, the relics of St-Benoît lie buried at the very root of the church's forest of columns and arches. You can leave by the north door, where an unfinished Romanesque frieze, discovered only in 1996, shows the progress of sculpture from blind block of stone to finished work.

Sully-sur-Loire

SULLY-SUR-LOIRE lies on the south bank of the Loire, 7km east of St-Benoît and accessible by bus from Orléans. The grand **château** here is pure fantasy (daily: April–Sept 10am–6pm; Oct–March 10am–noon & 2–5pm; closed Jan; €5; guided visits only), despite savage wartime bombing that twice destroyed the nearby Loire bridge and caused incidental damage to the château itself. From the outside, rising massively out of its gigantic moat, the château has all the picture-book requirements of pointed towers, machicolations and drawbridge. Whether sunlit or floodlit, it's a real treat. The interior is slowly being refurnished by its owners – the department of the Loiret – but it's still quite bare, though the Great Hall is adorned with a beautiful series of sixteenth-century tapestries, and the rebuilt Louis XV wing has rooms decorated in seventeenth-century style.

The castle originally belonged to one of Charles VII's favourites, Georges de la Trémoïlle, who infuriated Joan of Arc by encouraging the Dauphin to devote himself to idle hunting in the forests around Sully, and by pursuing a pacifying, diplomatic solution to the wars. After Joan's failure to liberate Paris in 1430, de la Trémoïlle virtually imprisoned her in the castle. She escaped, but was captured less than two months later at the disastrous battle of Compiègne. The castle changed hands in 1602, this time being snapped up by Henri IV's minister, the Duke of Sully, who added the moat and park, and pushed out the river bank to protect his glorious creation from the vagaries of the Loire. After Henri's death, the arrogant minister was forced into retirement, which he spent writing in his castle. In the eighteenth century young Voltaire, exiled from Paris for libellous political verse, also spent time at the château, sharpening his wit in the company of enlightened thinkers with whom the Duke of Sully of the time liked to surround himself. Sully's **International Music Festival** (Ⓦwww.festival-sully.com) runs right through June, featuring classical concerts held in a huge marquee in the grounds of the château.

The **train station**, on the Bourges–Etampes line, is ten minutes' walk from the centre of the village, where the **tourist office** can be found on place de Gaulle (June–Sept Mon–Sat 9.15am–12.15pm & 2–6pm, Sun 10.30am–1pm; Oct–May Mon & Thurs 2–6pm, Tues, Wed, Fri & Sat 10am–noon & 2–6pm; Ⓣ02.38.36.23.70). **Bikes** are a good way to explore and can be rented from Cycles et Motocycles Venon on rue du Marechal Foch (Ⓣ02.38.36.24.78).

Two decent **hotels** stand around the central marketplace: the *Hostellerie du Grand Sully*, 10 bd du Champ-de-Foire (Ⓣ02.38.36.27.56, Ⓕ02.38.36.44.54; ❸; closed Sun eve & Mon) is a reliable choice with a swish restaurant (menus from €25); while the large, rambling *Le Pont de Sologne*, 21 rue Porte de Sologne (Ⓣ02.38.36.26.34, Ⓕ02.38.36.37.86; ❷–❸), has a choice of attractive, newly refurbished rooms or inexpensive tatty ones. The municipal **campsite** (Ⓣ02.38.36.23.93; closed Nov–April) has a great riverside location, practically in the grounds of the château. For **eating** out, *Côtes et Jardin*, 8 rue du Grand Sully (Ⓣ02.38.36.35.89; closed Tues eve, Wed & last 2 weeks in Sept), on the château side of the village, is a distinctly classy affair, with an exceptionally good-value lunchtime menu for €12.

Gien and around

The town of **GIEN** is pretty enough, having been restored to its late fifteenth-century quaintness after extensive wartime bombing, and the sixteenth-century stone **bridge** spanning the river gives excellent views as you approach from the south. Looking downstream, the great cooling towers of the nuclear power station at Dampierre-en-Burly, can be seen emitting streaming clouds of water vapour. The fifteenth-century **Château** in the town centre – where the young Louis XIV and his mother Anne of Austria hid during the revolts against taxation known as the *Frondes* (see p.1283) – has been turned over to the **Musée International de la Chasse et de la Nature** (June–Sept daily 9am–6pm; Oct–May Mon & Wed–Sat 9am–noon & 2–6pm; closed Jan; €5.60), with the numerous exhibits venerating *la chasse* – hunting horns, tapestries, exquisite watercolours of horseback hunts, guns and falconers' gear – rather outweighing *la nature*. The château itself is modest, but unusual in its brick construction, a pattern of dark red interrupted by geometric inlays of grey; the interior is similarly striking, with its warm combination of brick and timber. Though the exhibits here are dominated by depictions of royal and aristocratic hunting as a sport, it's worth remembering that one of the significant consequences of the French Revolution for rural people was the right to hunt; a right jealously guarded today, particularly in the nearby Sologne.

Gien has also long been known in France for its fine china, and a large factory employs over two hundred people today. You can buy the ordinary tableware, some of it attractive enough, in the **factory shop** on place de la Victoire, 1km west of the château and bridge, and the hand-worked, arty stuff either in the shops all over town, or direct from the **Musée de la Faïencerie**, immediately adjacent to the shop (Mon–Sat 9am–noon & 2–6pm, Sun 10am–noon & 2–6pm; €3.50), which displays the more extravagant ceramic knick-knacks produced over the last 180-odd years, ranging from exquisitely worked vases to some monstrously pretentious *objets d'art*. A video shows current fabrication techniques, which you can sometimes see for real in the **factory** (by appointment only; closed July, Aug & Dec; ⓣ02.38.67.00.05).

Practicalities

Gien's **tourist office** is on place Jean-Jaurès, between the château and the river (June & Sept Mon–Sat 9.30am–12.30pm & 2–6.30pm; July & Aug Mon–Sat 9.30am–6.30pm, Sun 10am–noon; Oct–May Mon–Sat 9.30am–noon & 2–6pm; ⓣ02.38.67.25.28). **Bus** #3, which runs between Briare and Orléans, stops at place Leclerc, at the north end of the bridge. For **accommodation**, *La Poularde*, 13 Quai de Nice (ⓣ02.38.67.36.05; ⓕ02.38.38.18.78; ❸), on the way out of town on the road to Briare, has some lovely rooms looking out onto the river, and an excellent restaurant (menus €17–50). If they're full, try the rather ugly, modern *Sanotel* (ⓣ02.38.67.61.46, ⓕ02.38.67.13.01; ❷–❸), which is redeemed by its location on the south bank of the river and its views, though the inexpensive rooms face away from the river. Adjacent is the **campsite** (ⓣ02.38.67.12.50, ⓦwww.camping-gien.com), which has a swimming pool. For an alternative to the **restaurant** at *La Poularde*, make for the small strip of decent places on quai Lenoir, by the bridge; *Le Regency*, at no. 12 (ⓣ02.38.67.04.96; closed Sun evening, Wed & first two weeks in July), is a good choice, with carefully prepared fish dishes.

La Bussière

Twelve kilometres northeast of Gien is another château dedicated to catching your own dinner – this time by fishing. The so-called **Château des Pêcheurs** at **LA BUSSIÈRE** is moored like a ship on its enormous, six-hectare fishpond, connected to a formal arrangement on its mainland of gardens and huge outbuildings (April–June & Sept to mid-Nov Mon & Wed–Sat 10am–noon & 2–6pm; July & Aug daily 10am–6pm; €7). Initially a fortress, the château was turned into a luxurious residence at the end of the sixteenth century, but only the gateway and one pepper-pot tower are recognizably medieval. Guided tours are available, but you're free to wander around, soaking up the genteel atmosphere evoked by the handsome, largely nineteenth-century furnishings and the eccentrically huge collection of freshwater fishing memorabilia bequeathed by Count Henri de Chasseval, whose widow lives in an apartment in one of the outbuildings. Paintings, models, stuffed fish, engravings, flies and rods are scattered throughout the house, while a huge coelacanth (a giant prehistoric relic discovered in the Comoros islands) lurks in a formaldehyde tank in the basement, next to the well-preserved kitchens and laundry.

Briare

The small town of **BRIARE**, 10km southeast of Gien on the Orléans–Nevers road and the Paris–Nevers rail line, centres on its Belle Époque iron aqueduct, the **Pont Canal**, linking the Canal de Briare to the north with the Canal Lateral à la Loire, which runs south to the Saône. The design of the Pont Canal came from the workshops of Gustav Eiffel (of Tower fame), but parts of the canal scheme date back to the early seventeenth century, when internal waterways linking the Mediterranean, Atlantic and Channel coasts were devised. Poised high above the Loire, you can walk along the aqueduct's extraordinary 625-metre span, with its wrought-iron crested lamps and railings, hopefully without a *bâteau-mouche* spoiling the effect.

On the opposite side of town from the canal, at the northern end, the tiny **Maison des Deux Marines** (daily: March–May & June–Sept 10am–12.30pm & 2–6.30pm; Oct to mid-Nov 2–6pm; €4.50) is dedicated to the rival boatmen who plied the Loire and the Canal Lateral. Just across the street, the modest **Musée de la Mosaïque et des Emaux** (daily: Feb–May & June–Sept 10–6.30pm; Oct–Dec 2–6pm; €4), has a small collection of reproduction and contemporary mosaics made using locally manufactured tiles – Briare's wares adorn sites as prestigious and varied as the mosque at Medina and Paris's RER stations.

The **tourist office**, 1 place Charles-de-Gaulle (Mon–Sat 10am–noon & 2–6pm, Sun 2–6pm; ⓣ02.38.31.24.51), can provide details of canal boats and canoe rental as well as maps of footpaths, towpaths and the locks (the one at Chatillon-sur-Loire, 4km upstream, is particularly appealing). For **accommodation**, the modern *Hôtel le Canal* at 19 rue du Pont-Canal (ⓣ02.38.31.24.24, ⓔauberge-du-pont-canal@wanadoo.fr; ❷–❸) is right next to the bridge.

Sancerre and around

Huddled at the top of a steep, round hill with the vineyards below, **SANCERRE** could almost be in Tuscany. The village trades heavily on its famous wines – there are endless *caves* offering tastings – rather than any particular sights or attractions, but it's certainly picturesque and the rolling hills of the Sancerrois, to the northwest, make an attractive venue for walks and cycle rides.

Wine outlets in the village itself tend to belong to the most famous names, with mark-ups to match, but the informative *Aronde Sancerroise*, at 4 rue de la Tour, just off the central Nouvelle Place (ⓣ02.48.78.05.72, ⓦwww.sancerre.net/aronde) offers excellent, free tastings as well as tours of local vineyards. Alternatively, the **tourist office**, on Nouvelle Place (daily: June–Sept 10am–6pm; Oct–May 10am–12.30pm & 2.30–5.30pm; ⓣ02.48.54.08.21, ⓦwww.sancerre.net/otsi) can supply a list of over three hundred **vignerons** in the immediate area. Most are small-scale, traditional winemakers and welcome visitors on at least six days of the week. The Daumy family, based in Crézancy-en-Sancerre (ⓣ02.48.79.05.75), has been making excellent organic wines for three generations, including the wonderful but much less commonly made red Sancerre. For a more unusual buy than the well-known white Sancerre, it's well worth exploring the neighbouring areas of Menetou-Salon and Pouilly-Fumé. Well suited to the wines is the local *crottin de Chavignol*, a goat's cheese named after the neighbouring village in which it's made; signs in Chavignol direct you to **fromageries** open to visitors.

The stretch of the Loire upstream of Sancerre is particularly lovely, and **kayaks** are available to rent (April–Oct 7.30am–9pm; ⓣ02.48.78.00.34) from a shop at the campsite in **ST-SATUR**, the town at the foot of the hill below Sancerre. The owner, Yvan Thibaudat, is something of a naturalist, and his guided kayak expeditions (€14 for a half day) are fascinating, even if you don't speak French.

The choice of **hotels** in Sancerre is surprisingly poor, but two utterly charming *chambres d'hôtes* more than make up for it: *Le Logis du*

Grillon, 3 rue du Chantre (ⓣ02.48.78.09.45; ❸); and *La Belle Epoque*, rue St-André (ⓣ02.48.78.00.04; ❸). The two-star *St-Martin*, rue St-Martin (ⓣ02.48.54.21.11; ❸), is comfortable and well run, but you're better off down by the river in St-Satur, at the antique-furnished *Hôtel de la Loire*, 2 Quai de la Loire (ⓣ02.48.78.22.22, ⓦwww.hotel-de-la-loire.com; ❺) or the welcoming *Auberge de St-Thibault*, 37 rue J. Combes (ⓣ02.48.78.04.10; ❶), a block away from the river, which has five simple and exceptional value rooms. An excellent **campsite** (ⓣ02.48.54.04.67; closed Oct–April) is found a little further along the quay, beyond the kayak shop. There are also two fine **restaurants** in Sancerre: *La Pomme d'Or*, 1 rue de la Panneterie (ⓣ02.48.54.13.30; closed Tues & Wed eve); and the more formal *La Tour*, 31 place de la Halle (ⓣ02.48.54.00.81), both with reasonably priced as well as more showy menus. The *Auberge Joseph Mellot*, Nouvelle Place (ⓣ02.48.54.20.53; closed Sun, Tues eve & all Wed) serves good, simple meals that are designed to complement its own top-notch wines.

Bourges

BOURGES, the chief town of the rather bland region of Berry, is some way from the Loire valley proper but linked to it historically. The miserable Dauphin (later Charles VII), mockingly dubbed "King of Bourges" by the English, retreated to the city after Henry V's victory at Agincourt had put all of northern France under English control. The presence of one of the finest Gothic cathedrals in France, rising gloriously out of the unpretentious and handsome medieval quarter, provides reason enough for making a detour, but the city also offers an impressive mansion belonging to the Dauphin's financial advisor, Jacques Coeur.

Bourges's **festival** programme is also impressive. Les Printemps de Bourges (ⓦwww.printemps-bourges.com) features hundreds of contemporary music acts from rock to rap, and lasts for one week during the French Easter holidays. More esoteric are the Festival Synthèse, an electronic and acoustic music bash during the first week of June, and Un Été à Bourges (late June to late Sept), a line-up of free, outdoor performances of anything from local organ music to Chinese jazz. Atmospheric ambient lighting transforms the streets of the old town every evening in July and August (and from Thursday to Saturday in May, June and September). Sadly, the citizens of Bourges aren't called "Bourgeois" but instead, "Berruyer".

Arrival, information and accommodation

The **gare routière** is west of the city beyond boulevard Juranville on rue du Prado, while the **gare SNCF** lies 1km to the north of the centre, on avenue Pierre Sémard. The **tourist office**, which faces the south facade of the cathedral, is at 21 rue Victor-Hugo (April–Sept Mon–Sat 9am–7pm, Sun 10am–7pm; Oct–March Mon–Sat 9am–6pm, Sun 2–5pm; ⓣ02.48.23.02.60, ⓦwww.bourgestourisme.com). The main street, **rue Moyenne**, runs north from rue Victor-Hugo, with the old medieval quarter falling away to the east, below the cathedral.

Accommodation in Bourges mostly fails to make the best of the old city, the only attractive options being two three-star hotels and a superb bed-and-breakfast.

Hotels and chambres d'hôtes

D'Angleterre place des Quatre-Piliers ⓣ02.48.24.68.51, ⓦwww.bestwestern.fr/hoteldangleterre. The atmosphere is an odd mixture of old-fashioned, slightly shabby charm and the professional three-star standards of the Best Western conglomerate, to which it belongs. The inexpensive rooms are very small for the price, however, while the more expensive ones aren't all that special. ❺–❻

Les Bonnets Rouges 3 rue de la Thaumassière ⓣ02.48.65.79.92, ⓦbonnets-rouges.bourges.net. Five beautifully furnished and *chambres d'hôtes* in a striking seventeenth-century house with views of the cathedral from the rooftop rooms. ❹

De Bourbon bd de la République ⓣ02.48.70.70.00, ⓔh1888@accor-hotels.com. Between the town centre and the railway station, this is a luxurious hotel converted from a seventeenth-century abbey, though inside it's standard luxury hotel-chain fare. ❻

Le Central 6 rue du Docteur Témoin ⓣ02.48.24.10.25. Tiny, inexpensive and deeply old-fashioned rooms above a friendly bar just off rue Moyenne. ❶

Le Christina 5 rue de la Halle ⓣ02.48.70.56.50, ⓦwww.le-christina.com. The six-storey modern exterior is uninspiring, but inside you'll find a friendly, professionally run hotel with seventy cheerfully decorated rooms. Good value and close to the old centre. ❸

Hostel and campsite

HI hostel 22 rue Henri-Sellier ⓣ02.48.24.58.09, ⓔbourges@fuaj.org. Hostel located a short way southwest of the centre, overlooking the River Auron. Bus #1 to "Val d'Auron", stop "Condé"; or a 10min walk from the cathedral or *gare routière*. Open mid-Jan to mid-Dec daily 8am–noon & 5–10pm. HI membership required.

Camping municipal 26 bd de l'Industrie ⓣ02.48.20.16.85. Decent-sized site located south of the HI hostel. Bus #6 from place Cujas, stop "Joffre", or a 10min walk from the *gare routière*. Closed mid-Nov to mid-March.

The City

The centre of **Bourges** sits on a hill rising from the marshes of the River Yèvre, in the shadow of its main attraction, the magnificent early Gothic cathedral. Having seen the cathedral, many people move straight on, but the rest of the city is worth at least a couple of hours of wandering, with a number of ancient *hôtels* and burghers' houses displaying the wealth of a place that was built to rival the ruling provincial city of Dijon.

The cathedral

The exterior of the twelfth-century **Cathédrale St-Étienne** (daily: April–Sept 8.30am–7.15pm; Oct–March 9am–5.45pm) is characterized by the delicate, almost skeletal appearance of flying buttresses supporting an entire nave that has no transepts to break up its bulk. A much-vaunted example of Gothic architecture, it's modelled on Notre-Dame in Paris but incorporates improvements on the latter's design, such as the astonishing height of the inner aisles.

The **tympanum** above the main door of the west portal could engross you for hours with its tableau of the Last Judgement, featuring carved, naked figures with bodies full of movement and faces alive with expression. Thirteenth-century imagination has been given full rein in the depiction of the devils, complete with snakes' tails and winged bottoms and faces appearing from below the waist, symbolic of the soul in the service of sinful appetites.

The interior's best feature is the twelfth- to thirteenth-century **stained glass**. There are geometric designs in the main body of the cathedral, but the most glorious windows, with astonishing deep colours, are around the choir, all created between 1215 and 1225. You can follow the stories of the Prodigal Son, the Rich Man and Lazarus, the life of Mary, Joseph in Egypt, the Good Samaritan, Christ's Crucifixion, the Last Judgement and the Apocalypse – binoculars come in handy for picking up the exquisite detail. On either side of the central absidal chapel, polychrome figures kneel in prayer; these are **Jean de Berry**, the great artistic patron of late fourteenth-century Bourges, and his wife. The painted decoration of the **astronomical clock** in the nave celebrates the wedding of Charles VII, who married Marie d'Anjou here on April 22, 1422.

On the northwest side of the nave aisle is the door to the **Tour de Beurre** (daily: May & June 9.30am–12.15pm & 2–6pm; July & Aug 9.30am–6.15pm; Sept–April 9.30am–12.15pm & 2–5.15pm; tours roughly every 1hr; €5.50, or €8.50 with Palais de Jacques-Cœur), which you can climb unsupervised for fantastic views over the old city, the marshes and the countryside beyond. The same ticket allows you to join a guided tour of the **crypt**, where you can see the puggish alabaster statue of Jean de Berry. Along with the *pleurants* that can be seen in the Musée du Berry (see opposite), the statue of the duke is one of the few parts of his original, elaborate tomb to have survived the demolition of the Sainte-Chapelle in 1757; a small bear, symbol of strength, lies asleep at his feet. Alongside are fragments of the cathedral's original rood screen, which survived the Protestant siege of 1562 but not the modernizers of the mid-eighteenth century, while a wonderful polychrome *Entombment* from the 1530s adorns the dark centre of the crypt. The same ticket allows you to climb unsupervised to the top of the north **tower**, rebuilt in flamboyant style after the original collapsed in 1506.

Next to the cathedral in place E.-Dolet, the **Musée des Meilleurs Ouvriers de France** (Tues–Sat 10am–noon & 2–6pm, Sun 2–6pm; free) displays show-off pieces by French artisans. The theme changes each year, and recent features have included glassblowing, woodwork and pastry-making.

The rest of the city

Bourges's museums may be modest, but they are housed in some beautiful medieval buildings, the finest of which are all within a stone's throw of the north end of rue Moyenne. Rue Bourbonnoux, parallel to rue Moyenne to the east of the cathedral, is worth a wander for the early Renaissance **Hôtel Lallemant**, richly decorated in an Italianate style. It houses the **Musée des Arts Décoratifs** (Tues–Sat 10am–noon & 2–6pm, Sun 2–6pm; free), a diverting enough museum of paintings, tapestries, furniture and *objets d'art*, including works by the Berrichon artist Jean Boucher (1575–1633). The coffered ceiling of the oratory is carved with alchemical symbols. Halfway along the street, you can take a narrow passage up to the remains of the Gallo-Roman town **ramparts**, lined with old houses and trees. On rue Edouard Branly, you'll find the fifteenth-century **Hôtel des Échevins**, home to the **Musée de Maurice Estève** (Mon & Wed–Sat 10am–noon & 2–6pm, Sun 2–6pm; free), dedicated to the highly coloured, mostly abstract paintings and tapestries by the locally born artist, who died in 2001.

The continuation of rue Edouard Branly, **rue Jacques-Coeur**, was the site of the head office, stock exchange, dealing rooms, bank safes and home of Charles VII's finance minister, Jacques Coeur (1400–56), a medieval shipping magnate, moneylender and arms dealer who dominates Bourges as Joan of Arc does Orléans – Charles VII just doesn't get a look-in. The **Palais de Jacques-Coeur** (daily: July & Aug 9am–7pm; Sept–June hours vary but generally 9am–noon & 2–5pm; guided tours every 45min in season beginning at 9.30am; €6.10) is one of the most remarkable examples of fifteenth-century domestic architecture in France. The visit starts with the fake windows on the entrance front from which two realistically sculpted half-figures look down. There are hardly any furnishings, but much of the decoration of the house's stonework recalls the man who had it built, including a pair of bas-reliefs on the courtyard tower that may represent Jacques and his wife, and numerous hearts and scallop shells inside that playfully allude to his name – *cœur* means "heart" in French, and scallop shells are known in France as *coquilles St-Jacques*, as they are the traditional symbol of St James. On the first floor, a wonderful bas-relief of a *galleasse*, with its oars and sails spread, symbolizes Jacques' trading empire. The house is unusually modern for its time, with latrines, a steamroom, and a rationally planned design that predates the symmetries of French Renaissance architecture. A reconstruction of the tomb of Jean de Berry dominates one of the rooms on the upper floor.

Steps lead down beside the palace to rue des Arènes, where the sixteenth-century **Hôtel Cujas** houses the **Musée du Berry** (Mon & Wed–Sat 10am–noon & 2–6pm, Sun 2–6pm; free), which has an interesting collection of local artefacts, most notably ten of the forty *pleurants* that survived the breaking up of Jean de Berry's tomb; Rodin considered these weeping statues so beautiful that he paid 6000 francs for one, shortly before his death. Etruscan bronzes and Roman funerary monuments bear witness to Bourges's ancient history, while an exhibition on the theme of traditional rural life occupies the first floor. Close by is the pleasant **place Notre-Dame**, with its church clearly showing the shift from Gothic to Renaissance.

Eating and drinking

Bourges's main centre for **eating** is along rue Bourbonnoux, which runs between place Gordaine and the cathedral – place Gordaine itself is attractively medieval but mostly good only for pizzas. *D'Antan Sancerrois*, at no. 50 rue Bourbonnoux (☎02.48.65.96.26; closed Sun & Mon lunch), features excellent local goodies (à la carte mains around €12); while the classier *Bourbonnoux*, at no. 44 (☎02.48.24.14.76; closed Sat lunch, Fri & Sun eve out of season) has some ambitious regional menus (€12–30); and *La Crêperie des Remparts* (☎02.48.24.55.44; closed Sun & Mon lunch) has a better-than-usual range of crêpes, *galettes* and salads. Nearby, *Le Louis XI*, 11 rue Porte Jaune (☎02.48.70.92.14; closed Sun), serves impeccable steaks and chargrilled meats in a small, informal dining room (menus €9–23). For a complete change, the friendly *Margouillat*, at 53 rue Édouard Vaillant, beyond place Gordaine (☎02.48.24.08.13; closed Sun and Sat & Mon lunch) offers delicious, reasonably priced food from Réunion such as giant prawns or pork and beans served with hot dips, plus delicious tropical desserts and cocktails.

Those with a sweet tooth should head for the excellent **pâtisserie** *Aux Trois Flûtes*, on the corner of rues Joyeuse and Bourbonnoux; for chocolates and the local sweet speciality of *fourrées au praliné* try the imposing Maison Forestines, on place Cujas. Good **drinking** venues include *Pub Murrayfield*, 11 rue Jean Girard (Mon–Sat 2pm–2am, Sun 4pm–2am), just off place Gordaine; on warm nights, make for place Cujas, where you'll find the café-bars *Beau Bar* and *Le Cujas*.

The Cher and upper Indre

Of all the Loire's many tributaries, the slow-moving **Cher** and **Indre** are closest to the heart of the region, watering a host of châteaux as they flow northwest from the little-visited region to the south. Twenty kilometres southeast of Tours, spanning the Cher, the **Château de Chenonceau** is perhaps the best of all the Loire châteaux for its architecture, site, contents and atmosphere. Further upstream, **Montrichard** and **St-Aignan** make quieter diversions from the endless stream of castle tours. To the south is the châteaux of **Valençay**, with its exquisite Empire interiors. A short drive west of here, on the River Indre itself, **Loches** possesses the most magnificent medieval citadel in the region.

Château de Chenonceau

Unlike the Loire, the gentle River Cher flows so slowly and passively between the exquisite arches of the **Château de Chenonceau** (daily: mid-March to mid-Sept 9am–7pm; last 2 weeks Sept 9am–6.30pm; first 2 weeks Oct & first 2 weeks 9am–6pm; last 2 weeks Oct & last 2 weeks Feb 9am–5.30pm; first 2 weeks Nov &first 2 weeks Feb 9am–5pm; mid-Nov to Jan 9am–4.30pm; €8; Ⓦwww.chenonceau.com) that you're almost always assured of a perfect reflection. The château is not visible from the road so you have to pay before even getting a peek at the residence. While the tree-lined path to the front door is dramatic, for a more intimate approach, head through the gardens laid out under Diane de Poitiers.

The building of Chenonceau was always controlled by women. Katherine Briçonnet – whose husband Thomas Bohier bought the site on the proceeds of embezzling from his master, François I – hired the first architects in 1515 and had them begin building on the foundations of an old mill that stood on the granite bed of the Cher. The château's most characteristic feature, the set of arches spanning the River Cher, was begun later in the century by Diane de Poitiers (mistress of Henri II) and completed by the indomitable Catherine de Médicis (wife of Henri II), after she had evicted Diane and forced her to hand over the château in return for Chaumont (see p.556). Mary, Queen of Scots, child bride of François II, also spent time here until her husband's early death. Then, after a long period of disuse, one Madame Dupin brought eighteenth-century life to this gorgeous residence, along with her guests Voltaire, Montesquieu and Rousseau, whom she hired as tutor to her son. Restoration back to the sixteenth-century designs was completed by another woman, Madame Pelouze, in the late nineteenth century. It's now a profitable business, owned and run by the Menier chocolate family firm.

During summer the place teems with people, and it can become uncomfortably crowded, especially mid-morning and mid-afternoon. Visits are unguided – a relief, for there's an endless array of arresting tapestries, paintings, ceilings, floors and furniture on show. It's worth seeking out the numerous portraits of the château's female owners. On the ground floor the François I room features two contrasting images of the goddess Diana, one is in fact a portrait of Diane de Poitiers by Primaticcio while the other represents a relatively aristocratic Gabrielle d'Estrées. In the same room is Zurbaran's superb *Archimedes*, and elsewhere you'll find works by or attributed to Veronese, Tintoretto, Coreggio, Murillo and Rubens, among others; Madame Dupin's winsome portrait hangs in the Louis XIV room. The tiled floors throughout, many original, are particularly lovely, and there are some unique decorative details, such as the seventeenth century window-frame in the César de Vendôme room, supported by two carved caryatids, and the moving ceiling in the bedroom of Louise de Lorraine, which mourns her murdered husband Henri III in black paint picked out with painted tears and the couple's intertwined initials. The vaulted kitchens, poised above the water in the foundations, are well worth a look as well.

The section of the château that spans the Cher is relatively empty. The seemingly incongruous chequerboard flooring of the elegant long gallery is in fact true to the Renaissance design, though potted plants have replaced the classical statues which Louis XIV carried off to Versailles. Catherine de Médicis used to

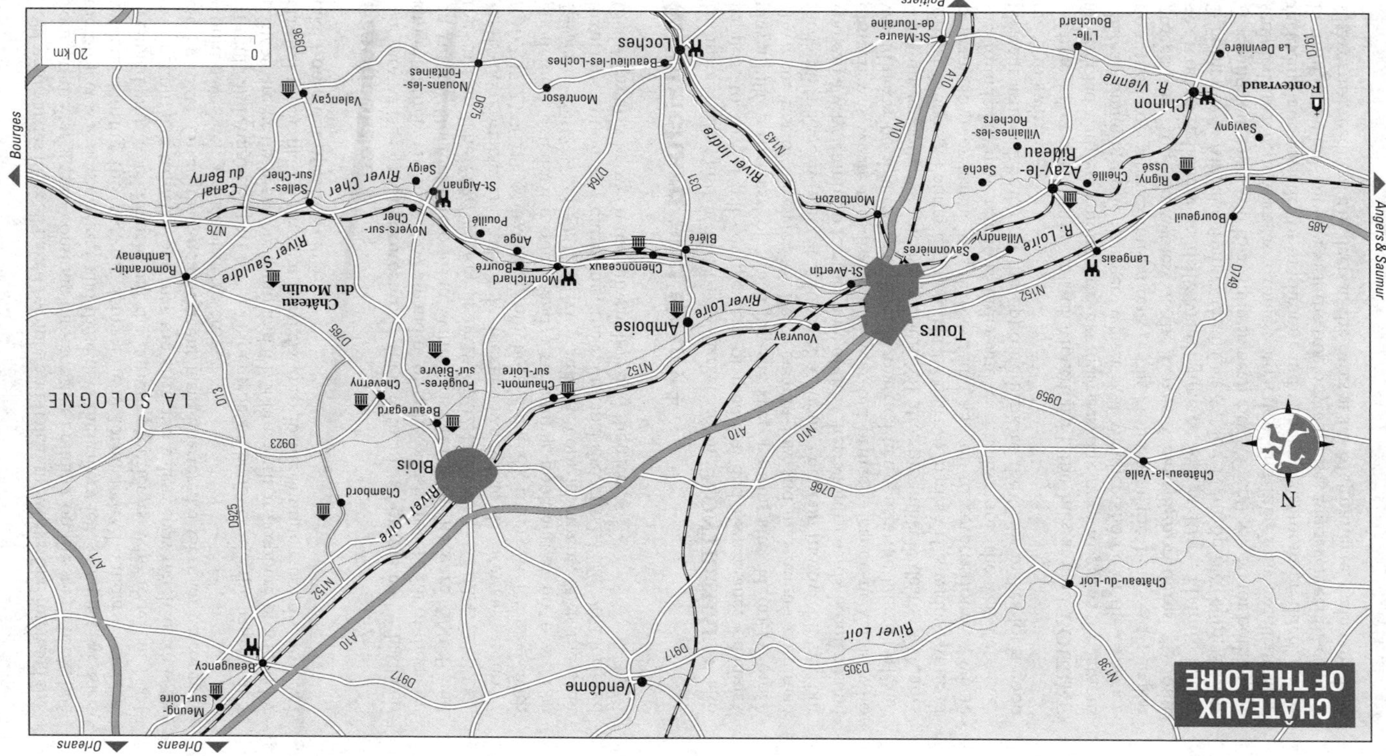
CHÂTEAUX OF THE LOIRE
Orleans
Orleans
Bourges
Poitiers
Angers & Saumur
LA SOLOGNE
0 20 km
N
Meung-sur-Loire
Beaugency
Vendôme
Chambord
Blois
River Loire
Beauregard
Cheverny
Fougères-sur-Bièvre
Château du Moulin
Romorantin-Lanthenay
River Sauldre
Canal du Berry
Selles-sur-Cher
River Cher
Valençay
Noyers-sur-Cher
Seigy
St-Aignan
Pouillé
Ange
Bourré
Montrichard
Chaumont-sur-Loire
Amboise
Chenonceaux
Bléré
Nouans-les-Fontaines
Montrésor
Beaulieu-les-Loches
Loches
River Indre
Montbazon
St-Maure-de-Touraine
Vouvray
St-Avertin
Tours
Savonnières
Villandry
R. Loire
Saché
Villaines-les-Rochers
Azay-le-Rideau
Langeais
Cheillé
Rigny-Ussé
Chinon
R. Vienne
L'Ile-Bouchard
Savigny
La Devinière
Fontevraud
Bourgeuil
Château-la-Valle
Château-du-Loir
River Loir
A10
A71
A85
N10
N76
N138
N143
N152
D13
D31
D305
D675
D749
D761
D764
D765
D766
D917
D923
D925
D936
D959

hold wild parties here, all naked nymphs and Italian fireworks. She intended the door on the far side to continue into another building on the south bank, but the project was never begun, and these days the gallery leads to quiet, wooded gardens. During the war, the Cher briefly formed the boundary between occupied and "free" France, and the current proprietors, who rode out Nazi occupation, like to make out that the château's gallery was much used as an escape route. Given that their adjacent farm quartered a German garrison, it would have been a risky place to cross.

In July and August, as part of the "Nocturne à Chenonceau", the gardens and château are lit up between 10pm and 11.30pm, with atmosphere provided by classical music played through speakers. Also in the summer months, you can take **boats** out onto the Cher.

Practicalities

The tiny village of **Chenonceaux** – spelt with an "x" on the end – has been almost entirely taken over by a handful of rather swish **hotels**. All of them are on rue du Docteur-Bretonneau, within easy reach of the **gare SNCF** and the château. The *Hôtel du Roy* at no. 9 (Ⓣ02.47.23.90.17, Ⓕ02.47.23.89.81; ❸) is comfortable and relatively inexpensive; while *La Roseraie*, at no. 7 (Ⓣ02.47.23.90.09, Ⓦwww.charminghotel.com; ❸), is very welcoming, with good food, extensive grounds and a swimming pool; and at no. 6, *Le Bon Laboureur* (Ⓣ02.47.23.90.02, Ⓦwww.amboise.com/laboureur; ❹) is the most luxurious option. For **camping**, the municipal site (Ⓣ02.47.23.90.13; closed Oct–March) is between the railway line and the river.

Montrichard and Bourré

In many ways just a laid-back market town, **MONTRICHARD** also happens to have a full complement of medieval and Renaissance buildings, plus a hilltop **fortress**, of which just the keep remains after Henri IV broke down the rest of the defences. Between mid-July and mid-August costumed medieval spectacles (daily at 2.30pm & 4.30pm) entertain mostly children, but you can always climb up for the view of the Cher. Montrichard's Romanesque **church** was where the disabled 12-year-old princess, Jeanne de Valois, who would never be able to have children, married her cousin the Duc d'Orléans, who subsequently became King Louis XII after the unlikely death of Charles VIII at Amboise. Politics dictated that he marry Charles VIII's widow, Anne of Brittany, so poor Jeanne was divorced and sent off to govern Bourges, where she founded a new religious order and eventually took the veil herself. A pleasant artificial beach on the opposite bank of the Cher makes for a good place to **swim**.

Three kilometres to the east of Montrichard, the hills around **BOURRÉ** are riddled with enormous, cave-like quarries, dug deep to get at the famous château-building stone that gets whiter as it weathers. Some of the caves are now used to cultivate mushrooms – big business in the Loire – a peculiar process that you can witness at the **Caves Champignonnières**, 40 route des Roches (guided visits daily March–June & Sept at 10am, 11am & hourly 2–5pm; July & Aug also 1pm & 6pm; Oct & Nov 11am, 3pm & 4pm; €5.50). A second tour takes you to a "subterranean city" (€5.50, €9.50 for both tours) sculpted in recent years as a tourist attraction, and there's an excellent shop including rare varieties of mushroom and various mushroom products. At the bottom of the hill, you can visit the troglodyte houses and seventeenth-century silkworm-breeding farm deep in the caves at **La Magnanerie**, 4 chemin de la

Croix-Bardin (April–Aug guided tours Mon & Wed–Sun at 11am, 3pm, 4pm & 5pm, Oct & Nov Mon & Thurs–Sun 3–5pm; €5.50).

Practicalities

Montrichard's **tourist office** is in the Maison Ave Maria (ⓣ02.54.32.05.10, ⓦwww.montrichard-fr.com), an ancient house with saints and beasties sculpted down its beams, on rue du Pont. The only enticing hotel is *La Tête Noir*, 24 rue de Tours (ⓣ02.54.32.05.55, ⓕ02.54.32.78.37; ❸), with its terrace on the river, but the *Hôtel de la Gare*, beside the station (ⓣ02.54.32.04.36; ❷) is inexpensive and decent enough. The atmospheric *Manoir de la Salle du Roc*, 69 route de Vierzon (ⓣ02.54.32.73.54, ⓕ02.54.32.47.90; ❺), offers grand *chambres d'hôtes* set in an ancient manor house above the main road leading west from Bourré. There's also a **campsite**, *L'Étourneau* (ⓣ02.54.32.10.16; closed mid-Sept to May), right in town, on the banks of the Cher. Decent meals can be had at *Les Tuffeaux*, a brasserie on Montrichard's main square, place Bartélémy Gilbert.

St-Aignan

ST-AIGNAN, 15km southeast of Montrichard, is a small town comprising a cluster of houses below a huge Romanesque collegiate church and sixteenth-century private château. The lofty **Collégiale de St-Aignan** (Mon–Sat 9am–7pm, Sun 1–7pm) features some fine capitals carved in the twelfth century, though many more are nineteenth-century recreations. The crypt is renowned for its remarkably preserved, brightly coloured twelfth- and thirteenth-century frescoes, some of which show the beginnings of naturalistic Gothic tendencies. A flight of 144 steps climbs from the *collégiale* to a grand gravelled terrace of the **château**, enclosed on one side by the L-shape of the Renaissance *logis*, and on the other by the remnants of the eleventh-century fortress. Private ownership means it's closed to visitors, but you're free to stroll around – the far corner of the terrace leads through to a great **view** of the river, and you can continue down some steep steps to the river. You can ask at the tourist office for details of **boat trips** on the Cher, or rent out windsurfers, canoes and sail boats at the lake a couple of kilometres upstream, in **SEIGY**. The Maison du Vin, on place Wilson, is open for tastings and sales of Côteaux du Cher wines (July & Aug).

One of the region's biggest tourist attractions is the excellent **Zoo Parc Beauval** (daily: mid-March to Oct 9am–dusk; Nov to mid-March 10am–dusk; €15, children aged 3–10 years €13; ⓦwww.zoobeauval.com), 2km to the south of town on the D675. The space given to the animals is ample, and it's part of the European programme for breeding threatened species in captivity. Sumptuous flower beds give way to little streams and lakes where islands provide natural enclosures for some of the monkeys. Two hothouses with tropical flowers and greenery are home to an extraordinary collection of birds as well as a large group of chimpanzees and two families of orang-utans.

Practicalities

The **tourist office**, 60 rue Constant Ragot (June–Sept Mon–Sat 9.30am–12.30pm & 2–6.30pm, Sun 10am–noon & 3–6pm; Oct–May Mon–Sat 10am–12.30pm & 2–6pm; ⓣ02.54.75.22.85) is just off the car park-like place President Wilson, in the upper part of town. The only two **hotels** are both alongside the river, on either side of the bridge: *Hôtel du Moulin*, 7 rue Novilliers (ⓣ02.54.75.15.54; ❶; closed Sun), is fairly basic but friendly; while *Le*

Grand Hôtel St-Aignan, 7–9 quai J.-J.-Delorme (Ⓣ02.54.75.18.04, Ⓔgrand.hotel.st.aignan@wanadoo.fr; ❸; Nov–March closed Sun evening) is a hushed, well-furnished affair, with a good restaurant (menus €15–33). St-Aignan has an excellent **campsite** on the bank of the river near Seigy, the *Camping des Cochards* (Ⓣ02.54.75.15.59; closed mid-Oct to March). For an alternative to the hotel **restaurants**, the extremely welcoming *L'Amarena*, place de la Paix (Ⓣ02.54.75.47.98, closed Mon lunch), serves inexpensive Italian food on an attractive square.

Château de Valençay

There is nothing medieval about the fittings and furnishings of the **Château de Valençay**, 20km southeast of St-Aignan on the main Blois–Châteauroux road (daily: April–June, Sept & Oct 9.30am–6pm; July & Aug 9.30am–7.30pm; €8.50), for all its huge pepper-pot towers and turreted, decorated keep. This refined castle was originally built to show off the wealth of a sixteenth-century financier, but the lasting impression of a visit today is the imperial legacy of its greatest owner, the Prince de Talleyrand.

One of the great political operators and survivors, Talleyrand owes his greatest fame to his post as Napoleon's foreign minister. A bishop before the Revolution, with a reputation for having the most desirable mistresses, he proposed the nationalization of church property, renounced his bishopric, escaped to America during the Terror, backed Napoléon and continued to serve the state under the restored Bourbons. One of his tasks for the emperor was keeping Ferdinand VII of Spain entertained for six years here after the king had been forced to abdicate in favour of Napoleon's brother Joseph. The Treaty of Valençay, signed in the château in 1813, put an end to Ferdinand's forced guest status, giving him back his throne. The interior consequently is largely First Empire: elaborately embroidered chairs, Chinese vases, ornate inlays to all the tables, faux-Egyptian details, finicky clocks and chandeliers. A single discordant note is struck by the leg-brace and shoe displayed in a glass cabinet along with Talleyrand's uniforms – the statesman's deformed foot was concealed in every painting of the man, including the one displayed in the portrait gallery that runs the length of the graceful Neoclassical wing.

The château **park** (same hours as above) keeps a collection of unhappy-looking camels, zebras, llamas and goats, and there's a small, imaginative maze for which you'll need to understand some French in order to work out the riddling passwords that open the various doors – or ask for the answers at the ticket office. In the village, about 100m from the château gates, a **car museum** (daily: April–June, Sept & Oct 10.30am–12.30pm & 2–6pm, July & Aug 10.30am–12.30pm & 1.30–7.30pm; €4) houses an excellent collection of sixty-odd mostly prewar cars.

Loches and around

LOCHES, 42km southeast of Tours, is the obvious place to head for in the Indre valley. Its walled **citadel** is by far the most impressive of the Loire valley fortresses, with its unbreached ramparts and the Renaissance houses below still partly enclosed by the outer wall of the medieval town. Tours is only an hour away by bus, but Loches makes for a quiet, relatively untouristy base for exploring the Cher valley, or the much lesser-known country south, up the Indre.

The **old town** is announced by the Tour St-Antoine belfry, close to the handsome place du Marché, linking rue St-Antoine with Grande Rue. Two fifteenth-century gates to the old town still stand: the **Porte des Cordeliers**, by the river at the end of Grande Rue, and the **Porte Picois** to the west, at the end of rue St-Antoine. Rue du Château, lined with Renaissance buildings, leads to the twelfth-century towers of **Porte Royale**, the main entrance to the citadel.

The citadel

Behind the Porte Royale, the **Musée Lansyer** occupies the house of local nineteenth-century landscape painter Lansyer, done up in period style (Jan & Oct–March Mon–Sat 10am–1pm & 2–5pm; April–Sept daily 10am–12.30pm & 2–6.30pm; €4.30). Straight ahead is the Romanesque church, the **Collégiale de St-Ours**, with its distinctively odd roofline – the nave bays are capped by two octagonal stone pyramids, sandwiched between two more conventional spires. The porch has some entertaining twelfth-century monster carvings, and the stoup, or basin for holy water, is a Gallo-Roman altar.

The northern end of the citadel is taken up by the **Logis Royal**, or Royal Lodgings, of Charles VII and his three successors (daily: Jan–March & Oct–Dec 9.30am–5pm; April–Sept 9am–7pm; €5, €7 including *donjon*). It has two distinct halves, similar at first glance, but separated by a century in which the medieval need for defence began to give way to a more courtly, luxurious lifestyle. The first section was built in the late fourteenth century as a kind of pleasure palace for the Dauphin Charles and his official mistress, Agnès Sorel, who as the owner of the manor at Beauté-sur-Marne, as well as Loches, adopted the title of "La dame de Beauté" (The Lady of Beauty). A copy of Charles's portrait by Fouquet can be seen in the antechamber to the Grande Salle, where the Dauphin met the second woman of importance in his life between June 3 and June 5, 1429 – Joan of Arc, who came here victorious from Orléans to give the defeatist Dauphin another pep talk about coronations. Agnès was buried at the adjacent collégiale de St-Ours, but her shining white tomb now lies in the late-fifteenth-century section of the *logis*, a recumbent figure tenderly watched over by angels.

From the Logis Royal, cobbled streets overlooked by handsome townhouses wind through to the far end of the elevated citadel, where the **donjon** (same hours as Logis Royal; €5, €7 including Logis Royal) begun by Foulques Nerra, the eleventh-century count of Anjou, stands in grim ruin. Vertiginous gantry stairways climb up through the empty shell of the massive keep to its very top, but the main interest lies in the dungeons and lesser towers. The Tour Ronde was built under Louis XI to provide a platform for artillery and also served as a prison for his adviser, Cardinal Balue, who was kept locked up in a wooden cage in one of the upper rooms, perhaps the extraordinary graffiti chamber on the second floor, which is decorated with an enigmatic series of deeply-carved, soldier-like figures that may date from the thirteenth century. From the courtyard, steps lead down into the bowels of the Martelet, which became the home of a more famous prisoner: Ludovico "Il Moro" Sforza, duke of Milan, patron of Leonardo da Vinci and captive of Louis XII. In the four years he was imprisoned here, he found time to decorate his cave-like cell with ruddy wall-paintings, still faintly visible. The dungeons peter out into quarried-out galleries which produced the stone for the keep.

Practicalities

From Tours, trains and buses alike arrive at the **gare SNCF** on the east side of the Indre, just up from place de la Marne, where the **tourist office** is housed in a little wooden chalet (July & Aug daily 9.30am–7pm; Sept–June Mon–Sat

9am–12.30pm & 1.30–5.30pm, Sun 10am–1pm & 2–5pm; ⓣ02.47.91.82.82, ⓦwww.lochesentouraine.com).

If you decide to **stay**, the *Hôtel George Sand*, 37 rue Quintefol (ⓣ02.47.59.39.74, ⓔgsandhotel@compuserve.com; ❺), just below the eastern ramparts, has its best rooms at the back, looking onto the river; its restaurant is usually very good, and worth it for the dining terrace overlooking the Indre. The *Hôtel Tour Ste-Antoine*, 2 rue des Moulins (ⓣ02.47.59.01.06, ⓕ02.47.59.13.80; ❷), is large and central, but the old-fashioned *Hôtel de France*, 6 rue Picois, near the Porte Picois (ⓣ02.47.59.00.32, ⓕ02.47.59.28.66; ❸), is more pleasant, with an excellent and inexpensive restaurant. The municipal **campsite** *La Citadelle* (ⓣ02.47.59.05.91; closed mid-Oct to mid-March) is between two branches of the Indre by the swimming pool and stadium, looking up at the east side of the citadel.

For a drink or a simple **meal**, either of the café-brasseries on the central place du Blé makes a good choice. The best option of all is to stock up at the superb **market**, held in the winding streets just above the château gate on Wednesday and Saturday mornings.

Beaulieu-les-Loches

Just across the Indre from Loches is the village of **BEAULIEU-LES-LOCHES** – a little-known place, thoroughly medieval in appearance, with its parish church built into the spectacular ruins of an abbey contemporary with Loches' *donjon*. Its other church, St-Pierre, holds the bones of Foulques Nerra, the eleventh-century count of Anjou responsible for Loches's grisly *donjon*. Next to the ruined abbey, there's a charming low-budget **hotel**, the *Hôtel de Beaulieu*, 3 rue Foulques-Nerra (ⓣ02.47.91.60.80; ❷), with a little bistro next door.

Blois and around

The château at **BLOIS**, the handsome former seat of the dukes of Orléans, is one of the most stately and historic of them all. Its great facade rises above the modern town like an Italianate cliff, with the dramatic esplanade and courtyard behind and the rooms within steeped in, sometimes bloody, history. The town itself is unexceptional but makes a good base for getting out into the countryside, with several stretches of woodland within striking distance including the **Forêt de Blois** to the west of the town on the north bank of the Loire, and the **Parc de Chambord** and **Forêt de Boulogne**, further upstream. To the south and east, the forested, watery, game-rich area known as the **Sologne** lies between the Loire and Cher, stretching beyond Orléans almost as far as Gien. And if you haven't yet tired of **châteaux**, some of the grandest of all, as well as some of the most intimate, are within cycling distance.

Arrival, information and accommodation

Blois is easy to get around: avenue Jean-Laigret is the main street leading south from the **gare SNCF** to place Victor-Hugo and the château, and past it to the town centre. The **gare routière** is directly in front of the *gare SNCF*, with **buses** leaving up to three times a day for Cheverny and Chambord. The **tourist office**, 23 place du Château, the château esplanade (May–Sept Tues–Sat 9am–7pm, Mon & Sun 10am–7pm; Oct–April Mon 10am–12.30pm & 2–6pm; Tues–Sat 9am–12.30pm & 2–6pm, ⓣ02.54.90.41.41, ⓦwww.loiredeschateaux.com), organizes hotel rooms for a small fee and has information on day coach tours of Chambord and Cheverny. It also sells the **Pass de Blois** (€16.50), which includes entry to the château and son-et-lumière, as well as the Maison de Magie and other attractions. Regional information is available online at Ⓦwww.chambordcountry.com. **Bikes** can be rented from Cycles Leblond, 44 Levée des Tuileries (Ⓣ02.54.74.30.13), or Amstercycles, 7 rue du Dr Desfray (summer only; Ⓣ02.54.56.07.73).

There are decent **hotels** to be found in Blois, but nothing outstanding.

Hotels

Hôtel du Bellay 12 rue des Minimes Ⓣ02.54.78.23.62, Ⓦhoteldubellay.free.fr. Comfortable budget option with twelve well-worn but clean little rooms, much cheered up by floral wallpaper, pictures of local sights and the odd wooden beam. Good location at the top of the hill, above the town centre. ❶

Hôtel de France et de Guise Ⓣ02.54.78.00.53, Ⓔhoteldefranceetguise@free.fr. Grand old hotel on a busy road just below the château. Formerly the Guise's townhouse, though modernization largely hides the evidence. Some rooms have balconies with views of the château's loggia. ❸

Mercure 28 quai St-Jean Ⓣ02.54.56.66.66, Ⓦwww.mercure.com. No character whatsoever, but it certainly offers *tout confort* – all mod cons, including a pool. Overlooks the river to the east of the town centre. ❼

Le Monarch 61 rue Porte Chartraine Ⓣ02.54.78.02.35, Ⓔlemonarque@free.fr. Professional and energetically managed hotel with rooms cheerfully renovated in a modern style. Usefully located at the top end of town. ❸

St-Jacques 7 rue Ducoux Ⓣ02.54.78.04.15, Ⓕ02.54.78.33.05. Plain and institutional, but also inexpensive, well maintained and near the train station. ❷

Le Savoie 6 rue du Ducoux Ⓣ02.54.74.32.21, Ⓔhotel.le.savoie@wanadoo.fr. Unexceptional but nonetheless likable hotel near the train station, with pretty little rooms. Run by a friendly young couple. ❸

À la Ville de Tours 2 place de la Grève Ⓣ02.54.78.07.86, Ⓕ02.54.56.87.33. Small family hotel set in a quiet quarter of town, with eight rooms. Restaurant below serves homely cuisine. ❷

Hostel and campsite

HI hostel 18 rue de l'Hôtel-Pasquier Ⓣ02.54.78.27.21, Ⓔblois@fuaj.org. Five kilometres downstream from Blois, between the Forêt de Blois and the river. Bus #4 runs on average every 45min, so you'll probably need wheels. Closed mid-Nov to Feb.

Camping des Châteaux Lac de Loire Vineuil Ⓣ08.00.30.04.10 the south bank of the river, 3km from the town centre. Bus #57 (stop "Mairie Vineuil") only runs three times daily, but the campsite offers bike rental.

The château

The six great kings of the sixteenth century all spent time at the **Château de Blois** (daily: April–June, Sept & Oct 9am–6pm; July & Aug 9am–7pm; Nov–March 9am–12.30pm & 2–5.30pm; €6.50), and the ones who didn't build here left their mark on its history instead. From the plateau-like esplanade in front of the château, you step into the courtyard, where the extraordinary clash of architectural styles has only been slightly muted by time. The relatively plain stone of the Gothic Salle des États, the manorial assembly hall, juts forward in the near right-hand corner, while immediately to the left, the graceful lines and inspired Italianate stonework of François I's Renaissance north wing is interrupted by a superb spiral staircase. Ahead, the grandly Classical west wing was built in the 1630s by François Mansart for Gaston d'Orléans, the brother of Louis XIII. Turning to the south side you return 140-odd years to Louis XII's St-Calais chapel, which contrasts with the more exuberant brickwork of his Flamboyant Gothic east wing.

The signposts point you straight ahead and up Mansart's breathtaking staircase, which leads you round to the **François I wing**. The garish decor dates from Félix Duban's mid-nineteenth-century efforts to turn an empty barn of a château into a showcase for sixteenth-century decorative motifs. One of the largest rooms is given over to paintings of the notorious murder of the Duke of Guise and his brother, the Cardinal of Lorraine, by Henri III. As leaders of the radical Catholic League, the Guises were responsible for the summary execution of Huguenots at Amboise. The king had summoned the States-General to a meeting in the Grande Salle, only to find that an overwhelming majority supported the Duke, along with the stringing up of Protestants, and aristocratic rather than royal power. Henri had the duke summoned to his bedroom in the palace, where he was ambushed and hacked to death, and the cardinal was murdered in prison the next day. Their deaths were avenged a year later when a monk assassinated the king himself.

The château was also home to Henri III's mother and manipulator, Catherine de Médicis, who died here a few days after the murders in 1589. The most famous of her suite of rooms is the study, where, according to Alexandre Dumas' novel, *La Reine Margot*, she kept poison hidden in secret caches in the skirting boards and behind some of the 237 narrow carved wooden panels; they now contain small Renaissance *objets d'art*. In the nineteenth century, revolutionaries were tried in the Grande Salle for conspiring to assassinate Napoléon III, a year before the Paris Commune of 1870. You can return to the courtyard via the vast space of the Salle des États, where the arches, pillars and fireplaces are another riot of nineteenth-century colour.

The Louis XII wing houses an undistinguished **Musée des Beaux-Arts**, with portraits from the gallery at Beauregard and a tapestry collection. If you're still not flagging, you can head back across the courtyard to the ground floor of the François I wing, where an **archeological museum** displays original stonework from the staircase and dormer windows, as well as carved details rescued from other châteaux.

French-speakers may want to take the two-hour guided **visite insolite** (July & Aug daily at 3pm; €7), which explores parts of the château you won't normally see, such as the roof and cellars. You can usually just turn up at the gate for the **son et lumière** (mid-April to mid-Sept daily; €9.50, or €11.50 including château entrance), which takes place in the courtyard at dusk on summer evenings. The usual melodramatic historical narrative, backed by a light show and strident classical music, is presented in English on Wednesdays.

The rest of the town

Just below the château on rue St-Laumen, the **church of St Nicholas** (daily 9am–6.30pm) once belonged to an abbey, and the choir is a handsome example of the humble Benedictine treatment of the Romanesque style. Children are unlikely to be convinced by the rather shoddy optical illusions housed in the cavernous **Maison de la Magie**, facing the château on the far side of the esplanade (daily: April–June & Sept 10am–12.30pm & 2–6pm; July & Aug 10am–6.30pm; €7.50); the afternoon magic shows are in mime, so at least there's no need to understand French. More instructive is the **Musée d'Histoire Naturelle**, rue Anne de Bretagne (daily except Mon 2–6pm; €2.50), with some good dioramas showing the different environments of the region, and the birds and animals that live in them.

At the top of town, the superb **Musée de l'Objet**, 6 rue Franciade (March–June & Sept–Nov Sat & Sun 1.30–6.30pm; July & Aug daily except Mon 1.30–6.30pm; €4), celebrates modern sculptures created from found objects rather than traditional materials. A forest of hammers hanging from the staircase ceiling gradually morphs into handbags, and the two long, spacious galleries are filled with similarly witty or alarming artworks, including some by major figures in modern art.

At the east end of town, on the handsome **place St-Louis**, look out for the half-timbered and sculpted **Maison des Acrobates**. The Gothic **cathédrale St-Louis** (daily 7.30am–6pm), at the west end of the square, leans against a weighty bell tower whose lowest storey is twelfth-century. The interior is fairly bare, but the most interesting feature is the modern **stained-glass windows**, completed in 2003 by the Dutch artist Jan Dibbets. Leading off place St-Louis, rue du Palais traverses above the town centre, passing the long stairs at the head of rue Denis Papin and leading into rue St-Honoré. At no. 8, the elaborate **Hôtel Alluye**, the private house of the royal treasurer Florimond Robertet, is a rare survival of Blois' golden years under Louis XII.

Eating and drinking

Most of Blois' traditional **restaurants** can be found on or around rue Saint Lubin, between the château and the river. *La Garbure*, 36 rue St-Lubin (ⓣ02.54.74.32.89; closed Thurs & Sat lunch, & all day Wed), serves specialities from the Périgord and Gascogne regions for around €15, but it's rather touristy. Next door, across the side-street that both use for a few outside tables, the similarly priced *Le Castelet* (ⓣ02.54.74.66.09; closed Wed & Sun) specializes in homely Loire cuisine, using regional produce. A little further along the same street, *Les Banquettes Rouges*, 16 rue des Trois Marchands (ⓣ02.54.78.74.92; closed Sun & Mon), serves modern French, Mediterranean-influenced food, with menus at €18.50 and €24.50. The best gastronomic experience in town is unquestionably *Au Rendez-Vous des Pêcheurs*, 27 rue Foix (ⓣ02.54.74.67.48; closed Sun & Mon lunch, and 3 weeks in Aug), with elaborate fish dishes on the eight-course, €64 *menu découverte*, though there is also a *menu* at €24.

The small square at the end of rue Vauvert, on the east side of town, has a number of crêperies and pizzerias with tables set out under the trees. Immediately below, rue de la Foulérie is the best place for ethnic food – Portuguese, Moroccan and Indian – and for late-night **bars** as well. *Le Loch Ness*, a Beamish-serving "pub" nearby at 7 rue des Juifs, is perennially popular.

Around Blois

On the south bank of the river, within a twenty-kilometre radius south and east of Blois, is a cluster of impressive and easily visited **châteaux**. By car you could call at all of them in a couple of days, but they also make ideal cycling or walking targets if you arm yourself with a map and strike out along minor roads and woodland rides. A new 300-kilometre-long network of tranquil cycle routes and dedicated cycle paths takes advantage of the mostly flat forest alleys and wooded back roads. Bikes can be rented in Blois and many of the smaller towns in this chapter, while tourist offices and some hotels stock a free map of the cycle network, *Le Pays des Châteaux à Vélo*.

Chaumont has frequent daily trains from Blois (make for Onzain, on the north side of the river, then cross the bridge), but otherwise **public transport** in the area is very poor, with even the main routes served by only a couple of commuter buses a day. Note, however, that the local bus company TLC (ⓣ02.54.58.55.55, ⓦwww.tlcinfo.net) runs **coach trips** to Chambord and Cheverny, with morning and lunchtime departures from Blois' *gare SNCF* (mid-May to Aug; €10). Check exact times when you buy your ticket – from the tourist office. Staff may also be able to find places on a chartered taxi or minibus tour.

Château de Chaumont

Catherine de Médicis forced Diane de Poitiers to hand over Chenonceau in return for the **Château de Chaumont** (daily: April & late Sept 10.30am–5.30pm; May to mid-Sept 9.30am–6.30pm; Oct–March 10am–5pm; €6.10; grounds open daily 9.30am–dusk; free), 20km downstream from Blois. Diane got a bad deal, but this is still one of the lovelier châteaux.

The original fortress was destroyed by Louis XI in the mid-fifteenth century in revenge for the part its owner, Pierre d'Amboise, played in the "League of Public Weal", an alliance of powerful nobles against the ever-increasing power of the monarch. But Pierre found his way back into the king's favour, and with his son Charles I, built much of the quintessentially medieval castle that stands today. Proto-Renaissance design is more obvious in the courtyard, which today forms three sides of a square, the fourth side having been demolished in 1739 to improve views over the river, which are spectacular. Inside, the heavy nineteenth-century decor of the ground floor rooms dates from the ownership of the Broglie family, but a few rooms on the first floor have been remodelled in the Renaissance style. The large council chamber is particularly fine, with seventeenth-century majolica tiles on the floor and its walls adorned with wonderfully busy sixteenth-century tapestries showing the gods of each of the seven planets known at the time.

The Broglie family also transformed the 21-hectare landscaped **park** into the fashionable English style and built the remarkable Belle Époque **stables**, with their porcelain troughs and elegant electric lamps for the benefit of the horses at a time before the château itself was wired – let alone the rest of the country. A corner of the château grounds now plays host to an annual **Festival des Jardins** (June to mid-Oct 9.30am–8.30pm; €8), which shows off the extravagant efforts of contemporary garden designers.

On weekends in summer, you can secure the best view of the château from the deck of a traditional Loire boat. Contact the Association Millière Raboton (Ⓣ06.88.76.57.14, Ⓦwww.milliere-raboton.net), whose **boat trips** (€12–15) leave from the quay immediately below the château, and last roughly an hour and a half. Best for wildlife are the regular dawn excursions.

Château de Cheverny

Fifteen kilometres southeast of Blois, the **Château de Cheverny** (daily: April–June & Sept 9.15am–6.15pm; July & Aug 9.15am–6.45pm; Oct–March 9.45am–5pm; Ⓦwww.chateau-cheverny.fr; €6.10) is the perfect example of a seventeenth-century château. Built between 1604 and 1634 and never altered, it presents an immaculate picture of symmetry, harmony and the aristocratic good life – descendants of the first owners still own, live in and go hunting from Cheverny today. Its stone, from Bourré on the River Cher, lightens with age, and the château gleams like a great white brick in its acres of rolling parkland. The interior decoration has only been added to, never destroyed, and the extravagant display of paintings, furniture, tapestries and armour against the gilded, sculpted and carved walls and ceilings is extremely impressive. The most precious objects are hard to pick out from the sumptuous whole, but some highlights are the painted wall panels in the dining room telling stories from *Don Quixote*; the vibrant, unfaded colours of the Gobelin tapestry in the arms room; and the three rare family portraits by François I's court painter, François Clouet, in the gallery.

You can explore the elegant **grounds** on foot, or take a sedate tour by golf-buggy and boat (April to mid-Nov; €10.80 including château entry). The **kennels** near the main entrance are certainly worth a look: a hundred lithe

Tintin in the Loire

Cheverny's architecture, minus the outermost towers, was used by Hergé as a model for Marlinspike Hall (Moulinsart in French), the ancestral home of Tintin's nautical friend Captain Haddock. The connection is milked dry in the slick exhibition, **Les Secrets de Moulinsart**, housed in the outbuilding next to the main gate (daily 9.30am–6.45pm; €10.50 including château entry, children aged 7–14 years e6.20), which retells various stories of the Belgian fictional hero in rooms dressed up in the style of the cartoon, enlivened by audiovisual effects and film clips.

hunting hounds mill and loll about while they wait for the next stag; feeding time (5pm) is something to be seen. Cheverny's hunt culls (or kills, depending on your point of view) around thirty animals a year, a figure set by the National Forestry Office.

Near Cheverny you can **stay** at the elegant, rustic and good-value *Hôtel des Trois Marchands* (ⓣ02.54.79.96.44, ⓦwww.hoteldes3marchands.com; ❸; closed March), in **COUR-CHEVERNY**, Cheverny's larger neighbour; the hotel's **restaurant** is rather smart, or there's the inexpensive bar and grill next door.

Château de Fougères

The proudly defensive **Château de Fougères** (mid-May to mid-Sept daily 9.30am–noon & 2–6pm; mid-Sept to mid-May daily except Tues 10am–noon & 2–4.30pm; €4.60) provides a good contrast to Cheverny. It lies in the village of **FOUGÈRES-SUR-BIÈVRE**, 10km southwest of Cheverny, and was built in 1470 by Louis XI's chancellor, who was clearly sceptical about long-term peace. It is a veritable fortress, turned tightly in on its internal courtyard, and you can scurry freely about the many corridors, rooms and spiral staircases, even clambering under the roof and strolling along the guard's walk. There are rarely other visitors to interfere with the medieval fantasy, though various exhibits along the way explain medieval building techniques. You'll need fairly good French to appreciate the explanations.

Château de Beauregard

An easy cycle ride from Blois, the little-visited **Château de Beauregard**, 7km south of Blois on the D956 to Contres (8 Feb to March & Oct–Dec daily except Wed 9.30–noon & 2–5pm; April–June & Sept daily 9.30am–noon & 2–6.30pm; July & Aug daily 9.30am–6.30pm; €6.50), lies amid the Forêt de Russy. It was – like Chambord – one of François I's hunting lodges, but its transformation in the sixteenth century involved beautification rather than aggrandizement. It was added to in the seventeenth century and the result is sober and serene, very much at ease in its manicured geometric park.

The highlight of the château is a richly decorated, long **portrait gallery**, whose floor of Delft tiling depicts an army on the march. The walls are entirely panelled with 327 portraits of kings, queens and great nobles, including European celebrities such as Francis Drake, Anne Boleyn and Charles V of Spain. All of France's kings are represented from Philippe VI (1328–50), who precipitated the Hundred Years War, to Louis XIII (1610–43), who occupied the throne when the gallery was created. Kings, nobles and executed wives alike are given equal billing – except for Louis XIII, whose portrait is exactly nine times the size of any other. It's worth strolling down through the grounds to the sunken **Jardin des Portraits**, a Renaissance-influenced creation by contemporary landscaper Gilles Clément, who was responsible for Paris's futuristic Parc André Citroën. It could be better tended, but the garden's formal arrangement – by colour of flower and foliage – is fascinating.

Château de Chambord

The **Château de Chambord**, François I's little "hunting lodge", is the largest and most popular of the Loire châteaux (daily: April–Sept 9am–5.45pm; Oct–March 9am–4.45pm; €7) and one of the most extravagant commissions of its age. Its patron's principal object – to outshine the Holy Roman Emperor Charles V – would, he claimed, leave him renowned as "one of the greatest builders in the universe".

Before you even get close, the sheer gargantuan scale of the place is awe-inspiring: there are over 440 rooms and 85 staircases, and a petrified forest of 365 chimneys runs wild on the roof. In architectural terms, the mixture of styles is as outrageous as the size. The Italian architect Domenico de Cortona was chosen to design the château in 1519 in an effort to establish prestigious Italian Renaissance art forms in France, though the labour was supplied by French masons. The château's plan (attributed by some to da Vinci) is pure Renaissance: rational, symmetrical and totally designed to express a single idea – the central power of its owner. Four hallways run crossways through the central keep, at the heart of which the Great Staircase rises up in two unconnected spirals before opening out into the great lantern tower, which draws together the confusion on the roof like a great crown.

The cold, draughty size of the château made it unpopular as an actual residence – François I himself stayed there for less than forty days in total – and Chambord's role in history is slight. A number of rooms on the first floor were fitted out by Louis XIV and his son, the Comte de Chambord, and as reconstructed today they feel like separate apartments within the unmanageable whole. You can explore them freely, along with the adjacent eighteenth-century apartments, where the château was made habitable by lowering ceilings, building small fireplaces within the larger ones, and cladding the walls with the fashionable wooden panelling known as *boiseries*. The second floor houses a rambling **Museum of Hunting** where, among the endless guns and glorificatory paintings, are two superb seventeenth-century tapestry cycles: one depicts Diana, goddess of the hunt; another, based on cartoons by Lebrun, tells the story of Meleager, the heroic huntsman from Ovid's *Metamorphoses*. Children love playing on the double spiral staircase that leads up to the airy rooftop, where you can get a good feel for the contrasting and occasionally discordant architectural styles.

The summer events and festivals calendar is a busy one, with evening lighting displays, guided nature walks and cycle rides in the forest, costumed tours for children and a twice-daily dressage display, among other attractions.

The **Parc de Chambord** around the château is an enormous walled game reserve – the largest in Europe. Wild boars roam freely, though red deer are the beasts you're most likely to spot. You can explore on foot or by bike or boat – both rentable from the jetty where the Cosson passes alongside the main facade of the château.

Accommodation in the village of **CHAMBORD** itself can be found opposite the château (and beside the cafeterias and postcard stalls) at the *Hôtel du Grand St-Michel* (ⓣ02.54.20.31.31, ⓕ02.54.20.36.40; ❹). Taking in the sight of Chambord after the crowds have left is very satisfying, but the hotel is distinctly scruffy. In **BRACIEUX**, a small village just beyond the southern wall of the Parc de Chambord, 8km from the château, the *Hôtel de la Bonnheure*,

9bis rue R.-Masson (Ⓣ02.54.46.41.57, Ⓕ02.54.46.05.90; ❸) has various rooms and apartments set around floral gardens. Bracieux also has a **campsite** (Ⓣ02.54.46.41.84; closed mid-Oct to mid-April) with a summer-only pool, and a top-flight **restaurant**, *Le Relais de Bracieux* (Ⓣ02.54.46.41.22; €38–120; closed Tues & Wed).

The Sologne

Stretching southeast of Blois, **the Sologne** is one of those traditionally rural regions of France that help keep alive the national self-image. Depending on the weather and the season, it can be one of the most dismal areas in central France: damp, flat, featureless and foggy. But at other times its forests, lakes, ponds and marshes have a quiet magic – in summer, for example, when the heather is in bloom and the ponds are full of water lilies, or in early autumn when you can go hunting for mushrooms. Wild boar and deer roam here, not to mention the ducks, geese, quails and pheasants, who far outnumber the small human population. The Sologne remains the refuge of the French aristocracy, along with the descendants of rich industrialists who bought land and built châteaux here in the latter part of the nineteenth century. Hunting is the thing, not tourism, and much of the region is out-of-bounds or simply physically impenetrable.

Two *grandes randonnées* lead through the Sologne, both variants of the main GR3 along the Loire. The northern **GR3C** runs through Chambord and east mostly along forest roads to Thoury and La Ferté-St-Cyr, where it rejoins the southern branch, the **GR31**, which has taken a more attractive route through Bracieux and along footpaths through the southern part of the Forêt de Chambord. There are numerous other well-signposted paths, and tourist offices in most of Sologne's towns and villages can provide maps and details of bike rental or horse riding, as well as accommodation details. If you're exploring the Sologne during the hunting season (Oct 1–March 1), don't stray from the marked paths: there are endless stories of people being accidentally shot.

Romorantin-Lanthenay

ROMORANTIN-LANTHENAY, 67km due south of Orléans, is the biggest town in the Sologne and best visited in the last weekend in October for the **Journées Gastronomiques**, a major food festival when every restaurant and hundreds of street stalls tempt you with traditional and novel dishes centred on game, wild mushrooms, apples and pumpkins. The rest of the year the only sight of interest is the **Musée de Sologne**, in the old mills in the centre

La Fête Étrange

There is much dispute as to where the magical party in **Alain Fournier's novel** *Le Grand Meaulnes* was set, despite the fact that it was clearly an imaginary mixture of many places. Fournier was born in La Chapelle d'Angillon, 24km south of Argent-sur-Sauldre on the D940. He spent much of his childhood in the château there, but went to school in Épineuil-le-Fleurial (the Ste-Agathe of the novel) well beyond the Sologne and Bourges, some 25km south of St-Armand-Montrond (turn right off the Montluçon road from Bourges to cross the Cher at Meaulne). Albicoco's film of the book was shot around Épineuil, where the elementary school described in the book now houses a small museum. But the "domain with no name" where the *fête étrange* takes place is certainly in the Sologne: "In the whole of the Sologne," he wrote, "it would have been hard to find a more desolate spot."

of Romorantin (April–Nov Mon & Wed–Sat 10am–noon & 2–6pm, Sun 2–6pm; €4.50), which presents the history, ecology and traditions of the area.

Five kilometres outside Romorantin, on the road to Salbris, the huge, child-friendly Aliotis **aquarium** (daily: mid-Feb to March 1.30–5.30pm; April–June 10am–6pm; July & Aug 10am–7.30pm; Sept 10.30–6pm; €9) has displays of local fish like pike-perch and catfish, as well as exotic species such as large sharks and turtles, and a tank containing around a thousand piranhas.

For information on walking routes in the Sologne, as well as bike rental, contact the **tourist office** on place de la Paix (Mon 10am–12.15pm & 2–6.30pm, Tues–Sat 8.45am–12.15pm & 1.30–6pm; July & Aug also Sun 10am–noon; ⓣ02.54.76.43.89). If you fancy a splurge, head for *Grand Hôtel du Lion d'Or*, 69 rue G.-Clemenceau (ⓣ02.54.94.15.15, ⓦwww.hotel-liondor.fr; ❽), an old manor house, with a fabulous courtyard garden, sixteen well-appointed **rooms** and a stellar **restaurant** (meals over €75). Inexpensive regional specialities can be had at the friendly *Le Colombie*, 18 place du Vieux-Marché (ⓣ02.54.76.12.76; closed Mon, Sat lunch & Sun eve).

Château du Moulin

Built almost entirely of brick, surrounded by water, and standing in romantic isolation at the end of a long avenue of oak trees, the **château du Moulin** (April–Sept daily except Wed 10am–12.30pm & 2–6.30pm; €6.50) is the quintessential Sologne château. It lies just outside the village of Lassay-sur-Croisne, 10km west of Romorantin-Lanthenay, and is still occupied by its elderly owner, Mme de Marchéville, whose family bought it off the du Moulins in 1901. The original builder, Philippe du Moulin, earned the right to set himself up as a nobleman with a fortified château after saving Charles VIII's life at the 1495 Battle of Fornova. The château's brickwork is striking, curving smoothly around the various towers, the pink tint offset by an inlaid lozenge pattern in dark grey and the window frames of white tufa stone. Guided visits of the **interior**, on which you're shown half a dozen beautifully furnished rooms in the main keep section, take place roughly every half hour.

Tours and around

Straddling a spit of land between the rivers Loire and Cher, the ancient cathedral city of **TOURS** has an air of quiet confidence. Chief town of the Loire valley, Tours has long had a reputation as a staid, bourgeois place, the home of lawyers and administrators rather than, say, artists or factory workers. However, the city's proximity to Paris – less than an hour away on the high-speed TGV line – has always tempered its nature, ensuring that Tours is indefinably more switched on than other French provincial cities, and in recent years an influx of smart commuters has perceptibly modified its conservative feel.

There are scores of bustling bars and cafés, an active if limited nightlife, and some fine restaurants – among the best in the region. It has a prettified and animated **old quarter**, some unusual **museums** – of wine, crafts, stained glass and an above-average Beaux-Arts museum – and a great many fine buildings, not least of which is **St Gatien cathedral**. And if you don't have your own transport, it's the obvious Touraine base, with both bus and train connections to some of the most notable châteaux – **Villandry**, **Langeais**, **Azay-le-Rideau** and **Amboise**.

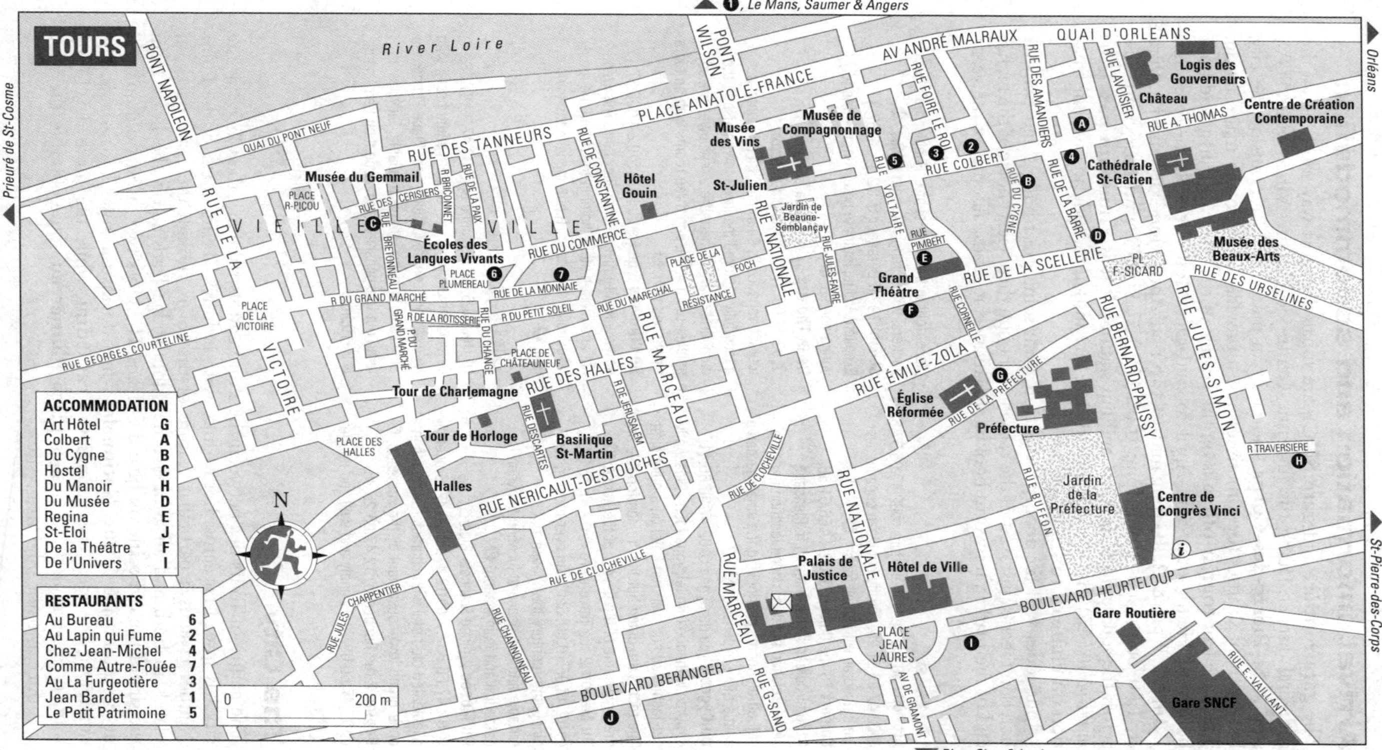
TOURS
1, Le Mans, Saumer & Angers
Orléans
St-Pierre-des-Corps
River Cher & Loches
Prieuré de St-Cosme
River Loire
ACCOMMODATION
Art Hôtel G
Colbert A
Du Cygne B
Hostel C
Du Manoir H
Du Musée D
Regina E
St-Eloi J
De la Théâtre F
De l'Univers I
RESTAURANTS
Au Bureau 6
Au Lapin qui Fume 2
Chez Jean-Michel 4
Comme Autre-Fouée 7
Au La Furgeotière 3
Jean Bardet 1
Le Petit Patrimoine 5
0
200 m
N
Logis des Gouverneurs
Château
Centre de Création Contemporaine
Cathédrale St-Gatien
Musée des Beaux-Arts
Musée de Compagnonnage
Musée des Vins
St-Julien
Hôtel Gouin
Musée du Gemmail
Écoles des Langues Vivants
Grand Théâtre
Église Réformée
Préfecture
Jardin de la Préfecture
Centre de Congrès Vinci
Tour de Charlemagne
Tour de Horloge
Basilique St-Martin
Halles
Palais de Justice
Hôtel de Ville
Gare Routière
Gare SNCF
Jardin de Beaune-Semblançay
VIEILLE VILLE
PONT NAPOLEON
PONT WILSON
QUAI D'ORLEANS
AV ANDRÉ MALRAUX
PLACE ANATOLE-FRANCE
QUAI DU PONT NEUF
RUE DES TANNEURS
RUE DE LA VICTOIRE
RUE LAVOISIER
RUE A. THOMAS
RUE DES AMANDIERS
RUE FOIRE LE ROI
RUE COLBERT
RUE DU CYGNE
RUE DE LA BARRE
RUE VOLTAIRE
RUE PIMBERT
RUE DE LA SCELLERIE
PL F.-SICARD
RUE DES URSELINES
RUE JULES-SIMON
R TRAVERSIERE
RUE BERNARD-PALISSY
RUE DE CONSTANTINE
RUE DU COMMERCE
RUE NATIONALE
RUE JULES-FAVRE
PLACE DE LA RÉSISTANCE
FOCH
RUE DU MARECHAL
RUE MARCEAU
RUE CORNEILLE
RUE ÉMILE-ZOLA
RUE DE LA PREFECTURE
RUE BUFFON
PLACE R-PICOU
RUE DES CERISIERS
R BRICONNET
RUE DE LA PAIX
RUE BRETONNEAU
PLACE PLUMEREAU
RUE DE LA MONNAIE
R DU GRAND MARCHÉ
P. DU GRAND MARCHÉ
R DE LA ROTISSERIE
RUE DU CHANGE
R DU PETIT SOLEIL
PLACE DE CHÂTEAUNEUF
PLACE DE LA VICTOIRE
RUE GEORGES COURTELINE
RUE DES HALLES
R DE JERUSALEM
RUE DESCARTES
PLACE DES HALLES
RUE NERICAULT-DESTOUCHES
RUE DE CLOCHEVILLE
RUE CHANNOINEAU
RUE JULES CHARPENTIER
BOULEVARD BERANGER
RUE G-SAND
AV DE GRAMONT
PLACE JEAN JAURES
BOULEVARD HEURTELOUP
RUE E.-VAILLANT

Arrival, information and accommodation

The **gare routière** and **gare SNCF** are situated a short way southeast of the cathedral district, facing the futuristic Centre de Congrès Vinci. Most TGVs stop at **St-Pierre-des-Corps** station, in an industrial estate outside the city, but frequent shuttles (or sometimes buses) provide a link to the main station. The excellent **tourist office** is on the corner of rue Bernard Palissy and busy boulevard Heurteloup (mid-April to mid-Oct Mon–Sat 8.30am–7pm, Sun 10am–12.30pm & 2.30–5pm; mid-Oct to mid-April Mon–Sat 9am–12.30pm & 1.30–6pm, Sun 10am–1pm; ⓣ02.47.70.37.37, ⓦwww.ligeris.com), just across the square from the train and bus stations. It sells a **museum pass** (*carte multi-visites*; €7) that lets you into the five city museums, and can give information on **château tours**.

Tours does well for **accommodation**, with some great budget and two-star hotels in the area just west of the cathedral, though there's less choice at the higher end of the market. It's worth booking in advance at almost all times of the year.

Hotels

Art Hôtel 40 rue de la Préfecture ⓣ02.47.05.67.53, ⓕ02.47.05.21.88. Scruffy but clean cheapie near the cathedral, with small rooms. ❶

Colbert 78 rue Colbert ⓣ02.47.66.61.56, ⓔhotel-colbert@club-internet.fr. Pleasant, well-furnished hotel in a good location near the cathedral. Rooms overlooking the small garden are a little more expensive. ❸

Du Cygne 6 rue du Cygne ⓣ02.47.66.66.41, ⓦperso.wanadoo.fr/hotelcygne.tours. Pleasantly old-fashioned and well-run hotel on a quiet street. The rooms are dated but they're comfortable and preserve some of the flavour of the house. ❹

Du Manoir 2 rue Traversière ⓣ02.47.05.37.37, ⓕ02.47.05.16.00. Set in an over-modernized nineteenth-century townhouse, but friendly, comfortable and in a peaceful location between the cathedral and train station. ❸

Du Musée 2 place François-Sicard ⓣ02.47.66.63.81, ⓕ02.47.20.10.42. Gracefully dilapidated old hotel with characterful rooms in a once-grand townhouse right by the cathedral. ❷

Regina 2 rue Pimbert ⓣ02.47.05.25.36, ⓕ02.47.66.08.72. Friendly and well-run budget place right in the town centre. Popular with backpackers, with a range of room prices. ❶

St-Éloi 79 bd Béranger ⓣ02.47.37.67.34. Excellent-value, intimate hotel run by a friendly young couple. ❶

De la Théâtre 57 rue de la Scellerie ⓣ02.47.05.31.29, ⓔhoteldutheatre.tours@wanadoo.fr. Charming, friendly hotel set in a tastefully restored medieval townhouse in the cathedral quarter. There are a few lower-priced, smaller rooms (❷), and three rooms with an extra single bed (❹). ❸

De l'Univers 5 bd Heurteloup ⓣ02.47.05.37.12, ⓦwww.hotel-univers-loirevalley.com. The grandest and most historic hotel in town, and the most luxuriously expensive. Right opposite the town hall. ❽

Hostel

HI Hostel 5 rue Bretonneau ⓣ02.47.37.81.58, ⓔtours@fuaj.org. Large, modern youth hostel with an excellent central location near Place Plumereau. Singles or twin-bed rooms available. Bicycles are hired out inexpensively, too. Reception 8am–noon & 6–10pm.

The City

The centre of Tours lies between the Loire and its tributary, the Cher, but the city has spread far across both banks, with industrial Tours north of the Loire. Neither river is a particular feature of the town, though there are parks on islands in both and an attractive new footbridge leads across the Loire from the site of the old castle on quai d'Orléans. The city's two distinct old quarters lie on either side of **rue Nationale**, which forms the town's main axis. The quieter of the areas lies around the **cathedral**, while the more developed, touristy zone around picturesque **place Plumereau**, some 600m to the west, was once a major pilgrimage site.

Château tours

It's possible to visit most of the more-visited châteaux by public transport, but if you're short of time it's worth considering a minibus trip. A number of companies run **excursions** from Tours, and on most schedules you'll find the following châteaux: Amboise, Azay-le-Rideau, Blois, Chambord, Chenonceau, Cheverny, Clos Lucé (in Amboise), Fougères-sur-Bièvre, Langeais, Ussé and Villandry. **Ticket** prices are usually around €16 for a morning trip, taking in one or two châteaux, and €37–45 for a full-day tour; prices do not usually include entrance fees or lunch.

Ask at tourist offices or contact the following Touraine-based **agencies** directly: Acco Dispo ⓣ06.82.00.64.51, ⓦwww.accodispo-tours.com; Saint-Eloi Excursions ⓣ02.47.37.08.04, ⓦwww.saint-eloi.com; Services Touristiques de Touraine ⓣ02.47.05.46.09; and Touraine Excursions ⓣ06.07.39.13.31, ⓦwww.tourevasion.com. Most pick up from the tourist office in Tours or from your hotel.

The cathedral quarter

The great west towers of the **Cathédrale St-Gatien**, standing on the square of the same name, are visible all over the city. Their surfaces crawl with decorated stone in the Flamboyant Gothic style, and even the Renaissance belfries that cap them share the same spirit of refined exuberance. Inside, the style moves back in time with the more sobre High Gothic east end – built in the thirteenth-century – and its glorious stained-glass windows. Just beyond the south transept stands the tomb of the sons of Charles VIII and Anne de Bretagne. After their deaths, and the accidental death of their father, the Valois line proper came to an end, and Anne was obliged by law to marry Charles's cousin, Louis XII.

A door in the north aisle leads to the **Cloître de la Psalette** (Mon–Sat 9.30am–12.30pm & 2–6pm; Sun 2–6pm; Oct–March closes 5pm; €2.30), which has an unfinished air, with the great foot of a flying buttress planted in the southeast corner and the missing south arcade – lost when a road was driven through in 1802 by the same progressive, anticlerical prefect who destroyed the basilica of St-Martin. The area behind the cathedral and museum, to the east, is good for a short stroll. There's a fine view of the spidery buttresses supporting the cathedral's painfully thin-walled apse from **place Grégoire de Tours**. Overlooking the square is the oldest wing of the **archbishop's palace**, whose end wall is a mongrel of Romanesque and eighteenth-century work, with an early sixteenth-century projecting balcony once used by clerics to address their flock.

Just south of the cathedral, the **Musée des Beaux-Arts** (daily except Tues 9am–12.45pm & 2–6pm; free) is housed in the former archbishop's palace. Other than Mantegna's intense, unmissable *Agony in the Garden* (1457–9), in the basement, there are few celebrity works in the large collection. Even Rembrandt's much-advertised *Flight into Egypt* is a small oil study rather than a full-scale work. But the stately, loosely chronological progression of palatial seventeenth- and eighteenth-century rooms, each furnished and decorated to match the era of the paintings it displays, is extremely attractive. Local gems include Boulanger's portrait of Balzac, and engravings of *The Five Senses* by the locally born Abraham Bosse, which have been interpreted as full-size canvases in the handsome Louis XIII room.

On the other side of the cathedral, between rue Albert-Thomas and the river, just two towers remain of the ancient royal **château** of Tours. You can get inside when an exhibition is being held but there's nothing much left of the interior. In the fifteenth-century **Logis des Gouverneurs** alongside (mid-March to mid-Dec Wed & Sat 2–6pm; free), across the remnants of the city's Gallo-Roman wall, there's an exhibition of historical artefacts called "Vivre à Tours" (Life in Tours) that gives a good sense of how the city has developed over the centuries.

The old quarter

To the west, the pulse of the city quickens as you approach **place Plumereau** – or place Plum' as it's known locally. The square's tightly clustered, ancient houses have been carefully restored as the city's showpiece, transforming what was once a slum into a vibrant and wealthy quarter. On sunny days, the square is packed almost end to end with café tables, and students and families drink and dine out until late in the evening. One of the less brash places on the square is the *Café du Vieux Mûrier*, so named for the large **mulberry tree** outside, a reminder of the days when Tours' silkworms used to feed on mulberries planted in their thousands in and around the city.

To escape the maelstrom, slip down **rue Briçonnet** into a miniature maze of quiet, ancient streets. Opposite an oddly Venetian-looking, fourteenth-century house, at 41 rue Briçonnet, a passageway leads past a palm tree and an ancient outdoor staircase to the quiet and insulated **Jardin de St-Pierre-le-Puellier**, laid out around the dug-out ruins of a conventual church. Further down rue Briçonnet, at no. 16, just before the heavily modernized riverfront, is the Gothic **Maison de Tristan**.

Off rue Briconnet, at 7 rue du Mûrier, the **Musée du Gemmail** (April to mid-Oct Tues–Sun 10am–noon & 2–6.30pm; mid-Oct to March Sat & Sun 10am–noon & 2–6pm; €4.60) is dedicated to an obscure, locally invented modern art form that uses fragments of backlit stained glass as a medium. Although some of the works are signed by such luminaries as Dufy, Modigliani and Picasso – who was particularly enamoured of the technique – the actual execution is by professional technicians working from a design.

To the south lay the pilgrim city once known as **Martinopolis** after St Martin, the ex-soldier who became bishop of Tours in the fourth century and went on to be a key figure in the spread of Christianity through France. Among Catholics he is usually remembered for giving half his cloak to a beggar, an image repeated on capitals and in stained-glass windows all over the region. The Romanesque **basilica** stretched along rue des Halles from rue des Trois-Pavées-Ronds almost to place de Châteauneuf: the outline is traced out in the street, but only the north tower, the Tour de Charlemagne, and the western clock tower survived the iconoclastic Huguenot riots of 1562, along with the **Cloître de St-Martin**, behind rue Rapin, where you can see a single Renaissance gallery. The new **Basilique de St-Martin**, on rue Descartes, is a late nineteenth-century neo-Byzantine affair built to honour the relics of St Martin, rediscovered in 1860. They are now housed in the crypt, watched over by hundreds of votive prayers carved into the walls. St Martin's day, 11 November, is still celebrated. A short distance away, down rue des Halles, lies the huge, modern **Halles**, or covered market – an excellent place to browse for a picnic in the morning.

Around rue Nationale

At the head of **rue Nationale**, Tours' main street, statues of Descartes and Rabelais overlook the scruffy walkways that run along the bank of the Loire. A short walk back from the river and you come to the Benedictine **church of St Julien**, whose old monastic buildings are home to two museums. The dry-as-dust **Musée des Vins**, 16 rue Nationale (daily except Tues 9am–noon & 2–6pm; €2.50), is only worth visiting for its location in the barn-like twelfth-century cellars of the abbey, though if your French is up to it, there's a comprehensive display on the history, mythology and production of wine. Behind the museum, a Gallo-Roman winepress from Cheillé sits in the former cloisters of the church. The **Musée de Compagnonnage**, at 8 rue Nationale (mid-June to mid-Sept daily 9am–noon & 2–6pm; mid-Sept to mid-June closed Tues; €4) is housed in the eleventh-century guesthouse and sixteenth-century monks' dormitory. It honours the peculiarly French cult of the artisan, displaying the "masterpieces" that craftsmen had to create in order to join their guild (*compagnonnage*) as a master craftsman. The skills are unquestionable, but many of these showpieces are breathtakingly vulgar, displaying arts as diverse as cake-making, carpentry, clog-making and cooperage.

A few steps west of rue Nationale, the **Hôtel Gouin**, 25 rue du Commerce, has a Renaissance facade to stop you in your tracks, but the **museum** inside (daily: April–Sept 9.30am–12.30pm & 1.15–6.30pm; Oct–March 9.30am–12.30pm & 2–5.30pm; €3.50) is a dull collection of archeological oddities and the remnants of a private scientific laboratory from Chenonceau – more rich man's toys than cutting-edge research tools.

At the southern end of rue Nationale, the huge, traffic-ridden place Jean-Jaurès is the site of the grandiose Hôtel de Ville and Palais de Justice. To the west of place Jean-Jaurès, a giant **flower market** takes over boulevard Béranger on Wednesdays and Saturdays, lasting from 8am into the early evening.

St-Cosme

In May, when the roses are in full bloom, the **Prieuré de St-Cosme**, 3km east of the centre (daily: April–Sept 9am–7pm; Oct–March 9.30am–12.30pm & 2–5pm; €3.80), is one of the loveliest sights in Touraine even if it is hemmed in by suburbs and barred off from the nearby Loire by a trunk road. Once an island priory, now a semi-ruin, it was here that Pierre de Ronsard – arguably France's greatest poet – lived as prior from 1565 until his death, in 1585. Vestiges of many monastic buildings survive, but the most affecting sight is the lovingly tended garden of roses, which has some 2000 rose bushes, and 250 varieties – including the tightly rounded, pink rose called "Pierre de Ronsard". To get there by public transport, take **bus** #7 from immediately outside the Palais de Justice, on place Jean-Jaurès, towards La Riche-Petit Plessis, getting off at the La Pléiade stop.

Eating

The streets around Place Plumereau, especially rue du Grand Marché, are overrun with cafés, bars and **bistros**, and if you're looking for pizza, pasta or steak frites, and don't mind paying a little extra for the bustling atmosphere and an outside table, this is the area to head for. On the cathedral side of rue Nationale, rue Colbert is lined with much less touristy bars and ethnic eateries, as well as a few good restaurants serving regional cuisine. For a drink or a **snack**, make for the pleasant café-patisserie *Aux Délices de Michel Colombe*, 1 place François-Sicard, near the cathedral, or *Scarlett*, a relaxed tearoom at 70 rue Colbert.

Au Bureau place Plumereau. One of a number of places serving pizzas and simple dishes on the square, but worth recommending for its decent *plats du jour*, late-night service and outside tables.

Au Lapin qui Fume 90 rue Colbert ⓣ02.47.66.95.49. Relaxed but elegant miniature restaurant serving a good menu that's half Loire and half south of France. Lots of *lapin* (rabbit) – as a terrine, as a fricassée with rosemary, as a confit leg – but it's not obligatory. Menus around the €20 mark.

Chez Jean-Michel 123 rue Colbert ⓣ02.47.20.80.20. Intimate wine bar and restaurant that manages to be elegant and relaxed at the same time. Serves good regional dishes to go along with the excellent local wines. Evening menus upwards of €20, with good-value lunchtime choices from €10. Closed Sat & Sun.

Comme Autre-Fouée 11 rue de la Monnaie ⓣ02.47.05.94.78. Something of a gimmick, in that the food is a revival of the archaic *fouace* (or *fouée*) breads praised by Rabelais, served hot and heavily garnished with local titbits. Good fun and inexpensive. Closed Sat eve, Sun & Mon.

Au La Furgeotière 19 place Foire-le-Roi ⓣ02.47.66.94.75. Enthusiastic little restaurant with outside tables on historic place Foire-le-Roi. Inside it's quasi-medieval, while the food is traditional French. Menus upwards of €20. Closed Tues & Wed.

Jean Bardet 57 rue Groison ⓣ02.47.41.41.11, ⓦwww.jeanbardet.com. Tours' top restaurant, on the north side of the Loire. Extremely sophisticated, healthy food with rare herbs and old varieties of vegetables straight from the hotel's renowned vegetable garden. Menus at €60 and €104, plus a wonderful all-vegetable menu at €69.

Le Petit Patrimoine 58 rue Colbert ⓣ02.47.66.05.81. Romantic little place serving rich, lovingly prepared Loire dishes and good Loire wines. Menus €12.50–26.

Drinking and nightlife

Packed with tables and chairs, Place Plumereau is *the* place to start the evening with an open-air apéritif and to finish it with a coffee. Giant Irish **pubs**, pizzerias and branded ice cream parlours are slowly making inroads into the area, but there are plenty of less commercial places to be found in the streets around, with some good **café-bars** on rue du Commerce. In the cathedral quarter, the bars on rue Colbert are mostly strip-lit local affairs, but the *Académie de la Bière*, just up from the cathedral at 43 rue Lavoisier, is a lively, student-friendly place, though dead when school's out.

Even in summer, when local students are away, the **nightclubs** just off place Plumereau fill up with backpackers, locals and language students, though things don't usually get going until past midnight. Try *Les 3 Orfèvres*, 6 rue des Orfèvres; *VIP Club*, 22 rue de la Monnaie; and *L'Excalibur*, in a vaulted cellar at 35 rue Briçonnet. For details of **classical music** concerts, ask at the tourist office which provides a free monthly magazine of exhibitions, concerts and events in Touraine, *Détours et des nuits*.

Listings

Airport Aéroport Tours Val de Loire ⓣ02.47.49.37.00, ⓦwww.tours-aeroport.com. Daily flights to London Stansted on Ryanair, plus two weekly flights to Lyon on Airlinair. Ryanair's telephone number in France is ⓣ0892.555.666 (Mon–Fri 8am–6pm; €0.34 per minute).

Bike rental Amster Cycles, 5 rue du Rempart, immediately east of the train station (ⓣ02.47.61.22.23), or Vélomania, 109 rue Colbert (ⓣ02.47.05.10.11).

Car rental Avis, gare de Tours ⓣ02.47.20.53.27; Budget, 2 place de la Gare ⓣ02.47.46.22.21; Europcar, 76 rue Bernard-Palissy ⓣ08.25.82.50.45; Hertz, 57 rue Marcel Tribut ⓣ02.47.75.50.00. All offer pickup/drop at Tours airport.

Cinema Les Studios, 2 rue des Urselines (ⓣ02.47.20.27.00), shows arty, obscure and old favourites in their original language.

Emergencies Ambulance (ⓣ15); Hôpital Bretonneau, 2 bd Tonnelé ⓣ02.47.47.47.47; late-night pharmacy, phone police for address.

Internet Alliance Micro, 32bis rue Briçonnet and 7ter rue de la Monnaie (Mon–Sat 9.30am–7pm), is good value. Otherwise try L'Alexandra, 106 rue du Commerce (daily 3pm–1am or 2am); and Top Communication, 68–70 rue du Grand Marché (daily 10am–10pm).

Laundries In the old quarter: 20 rue Bretonneau, 45 rue Georges-Courteline and 17 place du Grand Marché. Just west of the train station: 88 rue Michelet.

Police Commisariat Générale 70–72 rue Marceau ⓣ02.47.60.70.69.

Taxis Groupement Taxis Radio Tours ⓣ02.47.20.30.40; Taxis Radio Ville de Tours ⓣ02.47.05.20.90.

Amboise

Twenty kilometres upstream of Tours, **AMBOISE** is a prim little riverside town trading on long-gone splendours, notably its impressive but disappointingly empty **château** and Leonardo da Vinci's peaceful residence of **Clos-Lucé**, with its exhibition of the great man's inventions. Amboise draws a busy tourist trade that may detract from the quieter pleasures of strolling around town, but makes it a good destination for children. In July and August, **son et lumière** shows are held around 10pm at the château (Wed & Sat; adults €13, kids €7; Ⓦwww.renaissance-amboise.com), with Leonardo images projected on the walls and costumed actors prancing about to loud Renaissance-style music. The one concession to modern art in Amboise is a twentieth-century **fountain** by Max Ernst of a turtle topped by a teddy bear figure, standing in front of the spot where the **market** takes place every Saturday and Sunday morning by the riverside.

Château d'Amboise

Rising above the river are the remains of the **château** (daily: Feb to mid-March 9am–noon & 1.30–5.30pm; last two weeks March, Sept & Oct 9am–6pm; April–June 9am–6.30pm; July & Aug 9am–7pm; first two weeks Nov 9am–5.30pm; mid-Nov to Jan 9am–noon & 2–4.45pm; €7.50; Ⓦwww.chateau-amboise.com), once five times its present size, but much reduced by wars and lack of finance. It was in the late fifteenth century, following his marriage to Anne of Brittany at Langeais that Charles VIII decided to turn the old castle of his childhood days into an extravagant palace, adding the flamboyant Gothic wing that overlooks the river and the **chapelle de St-Hubert**, which perches incongruously atop a buttress of the defensive walls. But not long after the work was completed, he managed to hit his head, fatally, on a door lintel. He left the kingdom to his cousin, Louis XII, who spent most of his time at Blois but built a new wing at Amboise (at right angles to the main body) to house his nearest male relative, the young François d'Angoulême, thereby keeping him within easy reach. When the young heir acceded to the throne as François I he didn't forget his childhood home. He embellished it with classical stonework (visible on the east facade of the Louis XII wing), invited Leonardo da Vinci to work in Amboise under his protection, and eventually died in the château's collegiate church.

Henri II continued to add to the château, but it was during the reign of his sickly son, François II, that it achieved notoriety. The Tumult of Amboise was one of the first skirmishes in the Wars of Religion. Persecuted by the young king's powerful advisors, the Guise brothers, Huguenot conspirators set out for Amboise in 1560 to "rescue" their king and establish a more tolerant monarchy under their tutelage. But they were ambushed by royal troops in woods outside the town, rounded up and summarily tried in the Salle des Conseils. Some were drowned in the Loire below the château, some were beheaded in the grounds, and others were hung from the château's balconies.

After such a history, the interior of the château is a letdown, though there's a fairly atmospheric progression of large rooms hung with tapestries. The last French king, Louis-Philippe, also stayed in the château, hence the abrupt switch from the solid Gothic furnishings of the ground floor to the 1830s post-First Empire style of the first-floor apartments. The **Tour des Minimes**, the original fifteenth-century entrance, is architecturally the most exciting part of the castle. With its massive internal ramp, it was designed for the maximum number of fully armoured men on horseback to get in and out as quickly as possible. These days it leads down to the pleasant gardens which in turn lead to the exit.

Clos-Lucé

Following his campaigns in Lombardy, François I decided that the best way to bring back the ideas of the Italian Renaissance was to import one of the finest exponents of the new arts. In 1516, **Leonardo da Vinci** ventured across the Alps in response to the royal invitation, carrying with him the Mona Lisa among other paintings. For three years before his death in 1519, he made his home at the **Clos-Lucé**, at the end of rue Victor-Hugo (daily: Jan 10am–5pm; Feb, March, Nov & Dec 9am–6pm; April–June, Sept & Oct 9am–7pm; July & Aug 9am–8pm; €9.50; Ⓦwww.vinci-closluce.com). Leonardo seems to have enjoyed a semi-retirement at Amboise, devoting himself to inventions of varying brilliance and impracticability, and enjoying conversations with his royal patron. The house – an attractive brick mansion with Italianate details added by Charles VIII – is now a museum to Leonardo, and if you can ignore the persistently piped Renaissance music it's interesting to browse through the forty models of his mechanical inventions. From the suspension bridge to the paddle-wheel boat and turbine, they are all meticulously constructed according to Leonardo's plans and sketches.

Beyond the town centre

If you take the main road south out of Amboise and turn right just before the junction with the D31, you'll come to an unlikely-looking eighteenth-century **pagoda**, once part of the enormous but now demolished château of Chanteloup. You can climb to the top for fabulous views and also explore the grounds of the surrounding park (April Mon–Fri 10am–noon & 2–6pm, Sat & Sun 10–6pm; May & Sept daily 10am–6.30pm; June daily 10am–7pm; July & Aug daily 9.30am–7pm; Oct to mid-Nov Sat & Sun 10am–5pm; €6.30). Just south of town on the D751 to Chenonceaux, near the pagoda, the park **Mini-Châteaux** (daily: April to mid-July & last two weeks of Aug 10am–7pm; mid-July to mid-Aug 10am–8pm; Sept 10.30am–7pm; Oct to mid-Nov 10.30am–6pm; €12, kids €8; Ⓦwww.mini-chateaux.com) houses more than forty surprisingly good scale models of the chief Loire châteaux.

At Lussault, 5km west towards Tours, the mammoth **Aquarium du Val de Loire** (daily: Feb, March & Sept–Dec 10.30am–6pm; April to mid-July 10am–7pm; mid-July to mid-Aug 9.30am–10pm; €12, kids €8, Ⓦwww.aquariumduvaldeloire.com) boasts 10,000 fish, along with turtles, alligators and a tunnel through a large shark tank.

Practicalities

Information on Amboise and its environs, including the vineyards of the Touraine-Amboise *appellation*, is available at the **tourist office** on quai du Général-de-Gaulle, on the riverfront (April–June & Sept Mon–Sat 10am–1pm & 2–6pm, Sun 10am–1pm & 3–6pm; July & Aug Mon–Sat 9am–7pm, Sun 10am–6pm; Oct–March Mon–Sat 10am–1pm & 2–6.30pm, Sun 10am–1pm; Ⓣ02.47.57.09.28, Ⓦwww.amboise-valdeloire.com). **Bikes** can be rented from Cycles Richard, 2 rue Nazelles, near the station (Ⓣ02.47.57.01.79), or Locacycle, on rue Jean-Jacques Rousseau (April–Oct; Ⓣ02.47.57.00.28). **Canoes** are available from the Club de Canoë-Kayak, at the Base de l'Île d'Or (Ⓣ02.47.23.26.52, Ⓦwww.loire-aventure.com), which also runs guided trips.

There's a wide choice of good **hotels**, beginning with the backpacker-oriented *Café des Arts*, place Michel Debré (Ⓣ02.47.57.25.04; ❷), and the characterless but inexpensive *Chaptal*, 13 rue Chaptal (Ⓣ02.47.57.14.46; ❷). More comfortable are the *Belle Vue*, 12 quai Charles-Guinot (Ⓣ02.47.57.02.26, Ⓕ02.47.30.51.23; ❸; closed mid-Nov to mid-March), a long-established three-star with comfortable, old-fashioned bedrooms; and the smartly kept but homely *Le Blason*, 11 place Richelieu (Ⓣ02.47.23.22.41, Ⓦwww.leblason.fr; ❸). For a thoroughly romantic stay, make for the *Vieux Manoir*, 13 rue Rabelais (Ⓣ02.47.30.41.27, Ⓦwww.le-vieux-manoir.com; ❼–❽), lovingly run by an American couple. *Le Choiseul*, 36 quai Charles-Guinot (Ⓣ02.47.30.45.45, Ⓦwww.le-choiseul.com; ❾) offers serious elegance, set in an eighteenth-century riverside mansion almost below the château. A good **campsite** sits on the island across from the castle, the Île d'Or (Ⓣ02.47.57.23.37), alongside the **hostel**, the *Centre Charles Péguy* (Ⓣ02.47.30.69.90; reception Mon–Fri 3–8pm or reserve in advance), next door.

For a real blow-out **meal**, make for Pascal Bouvier's Michelin-starred dining room at the hotel *Le Choiseul* (Ⓣ02.47.30.45.45; menus at €46 & €80). The most enticing choice for ordinary mortals is *L'Épicerie*, 46 place M. Debré (Ⓣ02.47.57.08.94; menus €11–35; closed Mon & Tues), which serves good and fairly refined country cuisine. On the Île d'Or just next to the bridge, *Le Saint Vincent*, 7 rue Commire (Ⓣ02.47.30.49.49; menus €18–35), has good views of the château from the dining room, and serves traditional French dishes. For something a little more lively, *Chez Hippeau*, 1 rue François I (Ⓣ02.47.57.26.30; menus €10–30), is a bustling brasserie next to the Hôtel de Ville.

Château de Villandry

Even if gardens aren't your thing, those at the **Château de Villandry** (château daily: Feb & early Nov 9am–5pm, March 9am–5.30pm, April–June, Sept & Oct 9am–6pm, July & Aug 9am–6.30pm; gardens daily: Feb & early Nov 9am–5.30pm, March 9am–6pm, April, May, early June & late Sept 9am–7pm, mid-June to mid-Sept 9am–7.30pm, Oct 9am–6.30pm; mid-Nov to Jan 9am–5pm; €7.50 château and gardens, €5 gardens only, Ⓦwww.chateauvillandry.com) are definitely worth a visit. Thirteen kilometres west of Tours along the Cher – a superb cycle trip – this recreated Renaissance garden is as much symbolical as ornamental or practical. At the topmost level and in the elevated Classical spirit is a large, formal water garden. Next down, beside the château itself, is the ornamental garden, which features geometrical arrangements of box hedges symbolizing different kinds of love: tender, passionate, fickle and tragic. But the highlight, spread out across 12,500 square metres, is the potager, or Renaissance kitchen garden, at the lowest level. Carrots, cabbages and aubergines are arranged into intricate patterns, while rose bowers and miniature box hedges form a kind of frame. Even in winter, there is almost always something to see, as the entire area is replanted twice a year. At the far end of the garden, overlooked by the squat tower of the village church, beautiful vine-shaded paths give onto the medieval herb garden and the maze.

The elegant **château** was erected in the 1530s by one of François I's royal financiers, Jean le Breton, though the keep – from which there's a fine view of the gardens – dates back to a twelfth-century feudal castle. Le Breton's Renaissance structure is arranged around three sides of a *cour d'honneur*, the fourth wing having been demolished in the eighteenth century.

In summer you can take a minibus directly from Tours to Villandry; the service leaves morning and afternoon from the tourist office and costs €17 return.

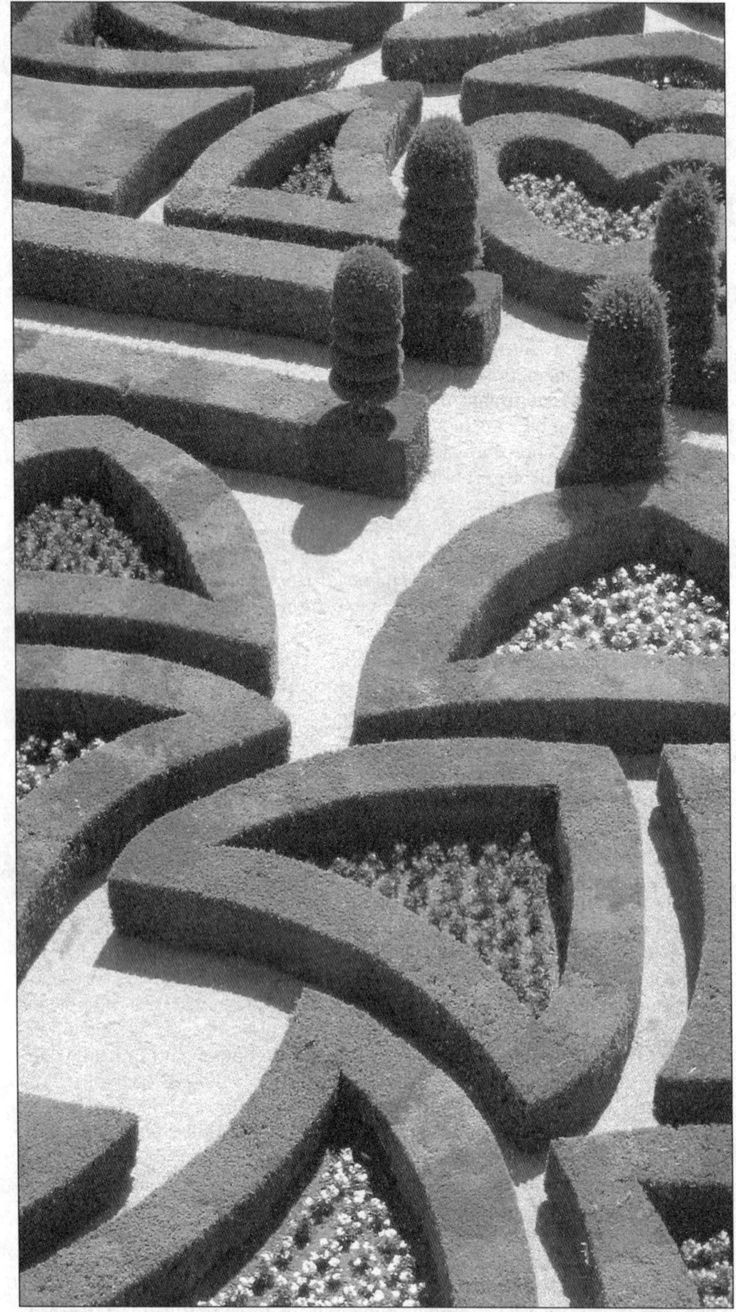

△ Garden of Love, Villandry

Just past the château, 1km down the D121 towards Druye, there's an upmarket farmhouse **restaurant**, the *Domaine de la Giraudière* (T02.47.50.08.60; closed mid-Nov to mid-March; expect to pay around €20–25 for a full meal), which throngs with families enjoying meals in the courtyard on summer evenings.

Château de Langeais

Twenty-three kilometres west of Tours, the small riverside town of **LANGEAIS** huddles in the shadow of its forbidding **château** (daily: April to mid-July, Sept & Oct 9.30am–6.30pm; mid-July to Aug 9.30am–8pm; Nov–March 10am–5.30pm; €6.50), which was built to stop any incursions up the Loire by the Bretons. This threat ended with the marriage of Charles VIII and Duchess Anne of Brittany in 1491, which was celebrated in the castle, and a diptych of the couple portrays them looking less than joyous at their union – Anne had little choice in giving up her independence. The event is also recreated in waxworks in the chapel.

Few châteaux have such a good collection of furnishings, and the ones here are mostly fifteenth century, to match the building. There are fascinating tapestries, some rare paintings, cots and beds, a number of *chaires*, or seigneurial chairs, and in the huge marriage chamber, the gilded and bejewelled wedding coffer of Charles and Anne, carved with a miniature scene of the Annunciation and figures of the apostles, the wise and foolish virgins depicted on the lid.

Langeais has a pleasant **hotel**, the *Errard-Hosten*, 2 rue Gambetta (T02.47.96.82.12, Wwww.errard.com; 3), with a good but expensive **restaurant**. The *Anne de Bretagne*, 27 rue Anne de Bretagne (T02.47.96.08.52; 3), offers some exceptional *chambres d'hôtes* in a restored early nineteenth-century home.

Azay-le-Rideau and around

Even without its **château** (daily: April–June & Sept 9.30am–6pm; July & Aug 9.30am–7pm; Oct–March 10am–12.30pm & 2–5.30pm; €6.10), the quiet village of **AZAY-LE-RIDEAU** would bask in its serene setting, complete with an old mill by the bridge and curious, doll-like Carolingian statues embedded in the facade of the church of St Symphorien. On its little island in the Indre, the château is one of the loveliest in the Loire: perfect turreted early Renaissance, pure in style right down to the blood-red paint of its window frames. Visiting the interior, furnished in mostly period style, doesn't add much to the experience, but the grand staircase is worth seeing, and it's fun to look out through the mullioned windows across the moat and park and imagine yourself the *seigneur*. In summer, the château's grounds are the setting for a restrained and rather lovely **son et lumière** (mid-May to June & Sept Fri & Sat at 9.30pm; July daily at 10.30pm; Aug daily at 10pm; €9 or €12 with château).

Practicalities

Azay's **tourist office** sits just off the main rue Nationale, on place de l'Europe (May, June & Sept Mon–Sat 9am–1pm & 2–6pm, Sun 10am–1pm & 2–5pm; July & Aug Mon–Sat 9am–7pm, Sun 10am–6pm; Oct–April Mon–Sat 9am–1pm & 2–6pm; T02.47.45.44.40, Wwww.ot-paysazaylerideau.com). The **bus stop** is on the main road, immediately beside it, but the **gare SNCF** is awkwardly situated a fifteen-minute walk west of the centre, along ave Riché – trains from Tours call at Azay-le-Rideau on their way to Chinon roughly every two hours (some services are replaced by SNCF buses). You can rent **bikes** from Cycles Leprovost, 13 rue Carnot

(Ⓣ02.47.45.40.94), and in summer **canoes** can be hired from beside the bridge on the road out towards Chinon.

Azay-le-Rideau has some of the best **accommodation** in the area, with a few pleasant hotels dotted on or around the main square. The plain but acceptable *Les Trois Lys*, 2 rue du Château (Ⓣ02. 47.45.20.36; ❷), is the only budget option. You're better off at the attractive *Hôtel de Biencourt*, 7 rue Balzac (Ⓣ02.47.45.20.75, Ⓔbiencourt@infonie.fr; ❹; closed mid-Nov to Feb), or the posh and very traditional *Le Grand Monarque*, 3 place de la République (Ⓣ02.47.45.40.08, Ⓦwww.legrandmonarque.com; ❺–❾). The best options are both *chambres d'hôtes*: the welcoming *Manoir de la Rémonière*, 1km from Azay on the opposite side of the Indre, on the road to Saché (Ⓣ02.47.45.24.88; ❻–❼) was once the château's fifteenth-century hunting lodge; while the two rooms offered by *M et Mme Sarrazin*, 9 chemin des Caves Mecquelines (Ⓣ02.47.45.31.25, Ⓔsrrazin.alaincathy@wanadoo.fr; ❸) are both in troglodyte chambers hollowed out of the rock. Upstream from the château is a large **campsite**, the *Camping du Sabot* (Ⓣ02.47.45.42.72; closed Nov–March), signposted off the D84 to Saché.

For **restaurants**, *La Ridelloise*, 24 rue Nationale (Ⓣ02.47.45.46.53; menus €11–23) has a family atmosphere and inexpensive but decent cooking. In summer, *L'Aigle d'Or*, 10 av Adélaïde Riché (Ⓣ02.47.45.24.58; closed Wed & Sun evening), serves elegant cuisine in its delightful garden, with menus from €25–56. At *Les Grottes*, 23 ter rue Pineau (Ⓣ02.47.45.21.04; menus from €16), you can eat good regional specialities in a troglodyte cave carved out of the rock.

Château d'Ussé

Fourteen kilometres west of Azay-le-Rideau, as the Indre approaches its confluence with the Loire, is the **Château d'Ussé** in **RIGNY-USSÉ** (daily: mid-Feb to March & Oct to mid-Nov 10am–noon & 2–5pm; April–Sept 9.30am–6.30pm; €9.80). With its shimmering white towers and terraced gardens, this is the ultimate fairy-tale château – so much so that it's supposed to have inspired Charles Perrault's classic retelling of the Sleeping Beauty myth. The exterior is a beautiful, late fifteenth-century vision of white turrets and machicolations largely built by Antoine de Bueil, comte de Sancerre, who married the illegitimate daughter of Charles VII and Agnès Sorel. The inner courtyard was once closed by a fourth wing, demolished in the seventeenth century to improve the picturesque view. Going inside for the **guided tour** isn't half as compelling as you'd expect, but the **gardens**, designed by Le Nôtre, are pleasant to wander, and children may enjoy climbing the tall **round tower** whose theatrical attic rooms are populated by dressed-up dummies illustrating the story of Sleeping Beauty. The loveliest feature of all is the Renaissance **chapel** in the grounds, shaded by ancient cedars.

Les Goupillières

As the D84 backroad passes out of Azay-le-Rideau, heading east, it's overshadowed on the left by low, creamy cliffs riddled with **caves** used as storehouses, wine *caves* and even homes. These are the modern-day remnants of the region's fascinating troglodyte (cave-dwelling) traditions, which can be explored at the fascinating complex of **Les Goupillières**, 3km from Azay-le-Rideau (April–Nov Mon–Fri 10am–7pm, Sat & Sun 2–7pm; €4). The "troglodyte valley" is actually a paddock-like area depressed below the level of the surrounding farmland, its outer edges burrowed away to create cave-farmhouses, cave-barns, cave-grain-silos and even a cave-rabbit-hutch. The whole "village" was hacked out of the soft tufa rock by hand, over hundreds of years. It was gradually abandoned around a hundred years ago, but has been rediscovered and re-excavated by a knowledgeable local family, who now run the guided tours with infectious enthusiasm.

Chinon and around

CHINON lies on the north bank of the Vienne, 12km from its confluence with the Loire, and is surrounded by some of the best vineyards in the Loire valley. The spectacular line of towers and ramparts on the high ridge to the east of the town look as if they must enclose one of the best of this region's châteaux, but all is ruined within, and the town's dedication to tourism detracts from its charm.

Arrival, information and accommodation

The **gare SNCF** lies to the east of the town, from where rue du Dr-P.-Labussière and rue du 11-Novembre lead to the **gare routière** on place Jeanne-d'Arc, where Joan is sculptured in mid-battle charge. Keep heading west, either along the riverbank or across place Mirabeau into rue Rabelais, and you'll soon reach the old quarter. The **tourist office** is on place d'Hofheim, on the central rue Jean-Jacques Rousseau (May–Sept daily 10am–7pm; Oct–April Mon–Sat 10am–noon & 2–6pm; ⓣ02.47.93.17.85, ⓦwww.chinon.com), and can provide addresses of local vineyards where you can taste Chinon's famous red wine.

Hotels in Chinon charge a little more than elsewhere; for something inexpensive, book well in advance at the tiny *Hôtel de la Treille*, 4 place Jeanne d'Arc (ⓣ02.47.93.07.71; ❷). The *Diderot*, in a venerable townhouse east of the church of St Mexme at 7 rue Diderot (ⓣ02.47.93.18.87, ⓦwww.hoteldiderot.com; ❸–❹), has some grand old rooms as well as the brighter modern ones in the annexe, while the historic, immaculate *Hôtel de France*, 47–49 place du Général de Gaulle (ⓣ02.47.93.33.91, ⓔelmachinon@aol.com; ❹) overlooks the leafy main square – Best Western welcomes you on the doormat but five hundred years of hotel history still manage to cut through the corporate sheen. The *Agnès Sorel*, 4 quai Pasteur (ⓣ02.47.93.04.37, ⓦwww.agnes-sorel.com; ❸) has some attractive rooms with balconies overlooking the river; it also rents **bikes** to all-comers. The **campsite**, *Camping de l'Île Auger* (ⓣ02.47.93.08.35; mid-March to mid-Oct), overlooks the old town and château from the south bank of the Vienne; turn right from the bridge along quai Danton. Just beside the campsite, Confluence Chinon Canoë-Kayak (ⓣ06.84.94.74.69) hires out **canoes** and kayaks, and runs half-day and full-day guided trips in summer.

The Town

A fortress of one kind or another existed at Chinon from the Stone Age until the time of Louis XIV, the age of the most recent of its ruins. It was a favourite residence of Henry Plantagenet, who held title to it long before he inherited the throne of England. He added a new castle to the first medieval fortress on the site, built by his ancestor Foulques Nerra, and died here, crying vengeance on his son Richard, who had treacherously allied himself with the French king Philippe Auguste. Henry's youngest son, John, with no English inheritance, stayed in Chinon off and on but after a year's siege in 1204–05, Philippe

Auguste finally took the castle and put an end to the Plantagenet rule over Touraine and Anjou.

Over two hundred years later, Chinon was one of the few places where the Dauphin Charles, later the VII, could safely stay while Henry V of England held Paris and the title to the French throne. Charles's situation changed with the arrival here in 1429 of Joan of Arc from Domrémy in Lorraine, who was able to talk her way into meeting him. The usual story – as depicted in a tapestry on display on the site – is that as Joan entered the great hall, the Dauphin remained hidden anonymously among the assembled nobles, as a test, but that Joan picked him out straight away. Joan herself told a different story, claiming that an angel had appeared before the court, bearing a crown. Either way, it is clear that she begged him to allow her to rally his army against the English. To the horror of the courtiers, Charles said yes.

Today, all that remains in the **château** (daily: April–Sept 9am–7pm; Oct–March 9.30am–5pm; €6) of the scene of this encounter, the Grande Salle, is a wall and first-floor fireplace. More interesting is the Tour Coudray, over to the west, covered with intricate thirteenth-century graffiti carved by imprisoned and doomed Templar knights, and the Tour de l'Horloge, on the east side by the main gate, which houses an eccentric little museum of Joan-related odds and ends.

Below, the medieval streets with their half-timbered and sculpted townhouses are pleasant enough to wander, or you could duck into one of the town's low-key museums – but avoid the tacky wine- and barrel-making museum. The **Musée des Amis du Vieux Chinon**, 44 rue Haute St-Maurice (hours vary – usually July & Aug 2–6pm; €2.30), has some diverting oddments of sculpture, pottery and paintings related to the town's history. The **Maison de la Rivière**, on the riverbank at 12 Quai Pasteur (Easter–Sept Tues–Fri 10am–12.30pm & 2–5.30pm, Sat & Sun 2–5.30pm; free), displays models of the many kinds of Loire river vessels, and on weekend afternoons in summer you can take a short river trip on a traditional *fûtreau* or *toue* (€6); staff also lead regular guided nature walks. Though it's better with a good meal, if you want to try a glass of Chinon you could visit the **Caves Peinctes**, off rue Voltaire, a deep cellar carved out of the rock where a fancy local winegrowers' guild runs **tastings** (July to mid-Sept daily except Mon 11am, 3pm, 4.30pm & 6pm; €3). The name of the *cave* supposedly derives from Rabelais, the author of the sixteenth-century satirical romps *Gargantua* and *Pantagruel*. Rabelais was born locally at the manor farm of **La Devinière**, 6km southwest of town, where there's a good but rather dry museum.

The troglodyte saint

A rewarding excursion out of Chinon starts along the road that leads east through town from rue Jean-Jacques-Rousseau, passing the Romanesque church of **St-Mexme** and then continuing along the cliffs past numerous **troglodyte dwellings**, some of which are still inhabited. After a kilometre or so the path runs out at the **Chapelle Ste-Radegonde**, a rock-cut church which is part of a complex of cave dwellings in which St Radegonde lived with her followers. The sixth-century German princess renounced the world and her husband – probably not a great sacrifice, since he eventually murdered her brother – in order to devote her life to God. The chapel's guardian has lived in the troglodyte house next door for nearly thirty years and often takes visitors into the chapel and caves behind – check with the tourist office in advance, or ask politely.

On the first weekend in August there is a reconstruction of a medieval market, and a **flea market** comes to town every third Sunday of the month. The two last weekends of July bring a touristy medieval fair to the château's grounds, with costumed reconstructions of battles.

Eating and drinking

Many of the **restaurants** in Chinon's medieval quarter feature overpriced "Gargantuan" menus with little connection to local cuisine, but the "Assiettes Rabelaisiennes" served at *La Maison Rouge*, 38 rue Voltaire, do in fact feature regional specialities; lunch menus begin at €12, and inexpensive Chinon wines are available by the glass and carafe. You'll find a good meal at *Les Années 30*, 78 rue Voltaire (Ⓣ02.47.93.37.18; menus from around €23), but the most enticing option is the old-fashioned hotel-restaurant *La Treille*, 4 place Jeanne d'Arc (Ⓣ02.47.93.07.71; closed Thurs eve & Wed), where the cooking is thoughtful and traditional, with excellent set menus at €20 and €30.

Richelieu

RICHELIEU, 24km south of Chinon, is a small, provincial town that would be resolutely ordinary if it hadn't been for the efforts of the eponymous Cardinal who, in the 1630s, decided to create a sumptuous new town with a palace to match. Sadly, his giant château has been destroyed, but the perfectly symmetrical **Grande Rue**, lined with 28 noble townhouses and bracketed by two handsome squares, survives. Number 15 houses the little **Musée du Chat** (daily 2–5pm; €4), and even if you're not interested in modern cartoon-caricatures of Richelieu's fourteen cats (which apparently went everywhere with him), it's well worth visiting for the chance to look round the almost untouched interior. The southern square, place du Grand Marché, is framed on either side by a huge covered market and a Baroque church. Just beyond, you can enter the 480-hectare **park** of the former château (daily: April–Oct 10am–7pm; Nov–March 9am–5pm; €2); in summer, you can hire **boats** (April–Oct; €2.30/hr) and splash about on the remnants of the canal.

You'll need your own transport to get to Richelieu. The **tourist office**, 6 Grande Rue (April–Oct Mon–Sat 9am–12.30pm & 2–5.30pm; Nov–March Mon, Tues & Thurs–Sat 9am–12.30pm & 2–5.30pm; Ⓣ02.47.58.13.62, Ⓦwww.cc-pays-de-richelieu.fr), can provide lots of information on the many local **chambres d'hôtes**, most appealing among which are the beautifully preserved *Maison Louis Barbier*, 15 Grande Rue (Ⓣ02.47.58.19.23; ❺), and the elegant *La Maison*, 6 rue Henri Proust (Ⓣ02.47.58.29.40, Ⓦwww.lamaisondemichele.com; ❻), a beautifully decorated early nineteenth-century house. Alternatively, there's the long-standing, traditional town **hotel**, *Le Puits Doré*, 24 place du Grand Marché (Ⓣ02.47.58.16.02, Ⓔkiengat@wanadoo.fr; ❸), where the **restaurant** serves honest bourgeois fare.

Saumur and around

Of all the Loire's comfortable towns, **SAUMUR** is perhaps the most elegantly bourgeois, with its graceful château lording it over the handsome townhouses spread out below on both banks of the river and on the large island midstream. The town's 250-year association with the military, as home to the French Cavalry Academy and its successor, the Armoured Corps Academy, has only further elevated its pretensions. Even the local sparkling wines are renowned for their charm.

The stretch of the Loire from Chinon to Angers, which passes through Saumur, is particularly lovely, with the bizarre added draw of **troglodyte dwellings** carved out of the cliffs. The land on the south bank, under grapes and sunflowers, gradually rises away from the river, with long-inactive windmills still standing. Across the water cows graze in wooded pastures. For **transport** you can either take the train or one of three buses to get to Angers: #5 along the south bank, #11 crossing halfway, or #10 inland via Beaufort-en-Vallée, to the north.

Arrival, information and accommodation

Saumur spreads along both banks of the Loire and over the small Île d'Offard in the middle of the river too. Arriving at the **gare SNCF**, you'll find yourself on the north bank: turn right onto avenue David-d'Angers and either take bus #A to the centre or cross the bridge to the island on foot. From the island the old **Pont Cessart** leads across to the main part of the town on the south bank, where you'll find the **gare routière**, a couple of blocks west of the bridge on place St-Nicolas, and the **tourist office**, next to the bridge on place de la Bilange (mid-May to mid-Oct Mon–Sat 9.15am–7pm, Sun 10.30am–12.30pm & 2.30–5.30pm; mid-Oct to mid-May Mon–Sat 9.15am–12.30pm & 2–6pm, Sun 10am–noon; ⓣ02.41.40.20.60, ⓦwww.saumur-tourisme.com). The **old quarter**, around St-Pierre and the castle, lies immediately behind the Hôtel de Ville, on the riverbank 100m east of the bridge.

Accommodation in Saumur is mostly upmarket and overpriced, but there are a number of very attractive hotels.

Hotels

Anne d'Anjou 32 quai Mayaud ⓣ02.41.67.30.30, ⓦwww.hotel-anneanjou.com. Comfortable hotel, with excellent service and a wide range of attractively decorated rooms in an eighteenth-century listed building. ❺–❾

La Bouère-Salée rue Grange-Couronne ⓣ02.41.67.38.85, ⓦwww.ifrance.com/labouere. Delightful bed and breakfast in a handsome nineteenth-century townhouse, though it's two blocks north of the train station, on the far side of the river from the historic centre. ❸

Cristal Hôtel 10–12 place de la République ⓣ02.41.51.09.54, ⓦwww.cristal-hotel.fr. One of the nicest hotels in town, with river or château views from most rooms and very friendly proprietors. Offers bike rental and Internet access. ❸

De Londres ⓣ02.41.51.23.98, ⓦwww.lelondres.com. Comfortable old town-centre hotel spotlessly done up in Mediterranean colours. ❸

St-Pierre 3 rue Haute-St-Pierre ⓣ02.41.50.33.00, ⓦwww.saintpierresaumur.com. Aims at a hushed, prestigious atmosphere with its ancient beams and stone spiral staircase, but the rooms are a little fussy and overpriced. ❻

Le Volney 1 rue Volney ⓣ02.41.51.25.41, ⓦwww.le-volney.com. Simple hotel with friendly management on the south side of town. Newly redecorated throughout, with inexpensive but cosy little rooms under the roof. ❷

Hostel and campsite

Hostel rue de Verden, Île d'Offard ⓣ02.41.40.30.00, ⓕ02.41.67.37.81. Large hostel at the east end of the island with laundry facilities, swimming-pool access and views of the château. Reception 9am–noon & 2–7pm. Boat and bike rental available. Closed Nov–Feb.

Camping municipal rue de Verden, Île d'Offard ⓣ02.41.40.30.00, ⓕ02.41.67.37.81. Situated next door to the hostel. You can even swim in the Loire from the north side of the island – though check locally first, as it is potentially dangerous.

The Town

Set high above town, Saumur's airy, gleaming white fantasy of a **château** (daily except Tues: April–Oct 10am–1pm & 2–6pm; Nov–March 10am–12.30pm &

2–5pm; €2), may seem oddly familiar, but then its famous depiction in *Les Très Riches Heures du Duc de Berry*, the most celebrated of all the medieval illuminated prayer books, is reproduced all over the region. It was largely built in the latter half of the fourteenth century by Louis I, duc d'Anjou, who wanted to compete with his brothers Jean de Berry and Charles V. The threat of marauding bands of English soldiers made the masons work flat out – they weren't even allowed to stop for feast days. The château's serenely impregnable image took a knock in April 2001, when a huge chunk of the star-shaped outer fortifications collapsed down the hill towards the river. In the aftermath, the alarmed authorities decided to embark on a major renovation programme, which is likely to last into 2007. Until works are complete, large parts of the interior will remain closed to visitors, including the formerly excellent Musée des Arts Décoratifs and Musée du Cheval.

Down by the public gardens south of the château, Saumur's oldest church, **Notre-Dame de Nantilly** (9am–6pm), houses a large tapestry collection in its Romanesque nave. The original Gothic **church of St Pierre**, in the centre of the old town (9am–noon & 2–5pm), hides behind a Counter-Reformation facade built as part of the church's efforts to overawe its persistently Protestant population – Louise de Bourbon, abbess of Fontevraud, called the town a "second Geneva", horrified at the thought that Saumur might become a similarly radical Calvinist power-base. Meanwhile, the theological college at **Notre-Dame des Ardilliers**, down by the river on the eastern edge of town (daily 8am–noon & 2–6.30pm) is dominated by the tremendous dome of its classical rotunda, rebuilt after bombing in June 1940.

For relief from military and ecclesiastical history, try a glass of the famous Saumur *méthode champenoise* wines at the **Maison du Vin** on quai Lucien Gautier (April–Sept Mon 2–7pm, Tues–Sat 9.30am–1pm & 2–7pm, Sun 9.30am–1pm; mid-Feb to March and Oct to mid-Jan Tues–Sat 10am–1pm & 2–6.30pm; Ⓦwww.interloire.com), which can also provide addresses of wine-growers and *caves* that you can visit. Alternatively, make for the Caves Coopératives at St-Cyr-en-Bourg (Ⓣ02.41.53.06.08), a short train hop south of Saumur and near the station, where there are kilometres of cellars.

Beyond the town centre

Saumur's cavalry traditions are displayed most proudly at the **École Nationale d'Équitation**, in St-Hilaire-St-Florent, a suburb to the east of the centre; take bus #B from the town centre. The Riding School (April–Sept Tues–Sat 9.30–11am & 2–4pm; €7 for morning visits, €5 afternoons) provides guided tours in which you can watch training sessions (mornings only) and view the stables. Displays of dressage and anachronistic battle manoeuvres by the crack-shot Cadre Noir, the former cavalry trainers, are regular events (programme details from the tourist office or online at Ⓦwww.cadrenoir.tm.fr). The history of the tank – traditionally considered as cavalry not infantry – is covered in the separate **Musée des Blindés**, at 1043 rue Fricotelle, to the southeast of the centre (daily: May–Sept 9.30am–6.30pm; Oct–April 10am–5pm; €5.50).

The main activity in St-Hilaire-St-Florent, especially along the main stretch of the riverside road, along rue Ackerman and rue Leopold Palustre, is making **sparkling wine**. You can visit the impressive rock-carved cellars of any of Ackerman-Laurance, Bouvet-Ladubay, Langlois-Château, Gratien & Meyer, Louis de Grenelle and Veuve Amiot. Choosing between them is a matter of personal taste, and possibly a question of opening hours, though most are open all day every day throughout the warmer months (generally 10am–6pm, though most close for a couple of hours at lunchtime out of season).

Eating and drinking

There are several inexpensive **eating places** around place St-Pierre, best of which must be the bustling *Auberge St-Pierre*, 6 place St-Pierre (☎02.41.51.26.25; May–Sept closed Tues lunch & Mon, Oct–April closed Mon & Sun), which has evening menus from €14.50 up to €25. Opposite, at no. 1, *Les Forges de St-Pierre* (☎02.41.38.21.79; closed Tues evening & Sun) specializes in grilled meat. Over the bridge, on the Ile d'Offard, the ancient *Auberge Reine de Sicile*, 71 rue Waldeck-Rousseau (☎02.41.67.30.48; closed Mon, Sat lunch & Sun eve, and the last 3 weeks in Aug), serves delicious traditional cuisine, with fish dishes grilled in front of you in the old chimney-place. For a special treat, head up to the château, where *Les Délices du Château* (☎02.41.67.65.60 Oct–April closed Sun & Tues eve, & Mon) serves the most *haute* cuisine in town, with similarly elevated prices. The best place to enjoy the wonderful local sparkling wines is at an outside table on place St-Pierre.

Troglodyte dwellings

The "falun" or soft shellstone found in the Loire valley lends itself to **troglodyte dwellings** – homes carved out of rocky outcrops, of which there are more in this area (between Saumur and Angers) than anywhere else in France. It's reckoned that in the twelfth century half the local population lived in homes carved out of the rock. Today, some of the rock dwellings have surprising uses, along with the more predictable "Troglo" bars and restaurants.

Away from the Loire cliffs on the plains to the south, troglodyte villages were built by digging holes like large craters and then carving out the walls. The best example is at **ROCHEMENIER**, northwest of Doué-la-Fontaine and about 20km west of Saumur, where an underground village housed a small farming community with its own underground chapel (daily: April–Nov 9.30am–7pm; €4), and was only abandoned in the 1930s. The visit includes a typical troglodyte dwelling, along with a museum of domestic items, including wine and oil presses. Just 3km north, at **DÉNEZÉ-SOUS-DOUÉ**, there are underground carvings thought to have been sculpted by a secret sixteenth-century sect of libertarians. The cartoon-style figures mock religion, morality, the state and the ruling class, with scenes of sex, strange deformities and perverted Christian imagery (Tues–Sun: April & May 2–6pm; June–Aug 10am–7pm; Sept 10am–6pm; €4).

East of Saumur, the sunny microclimate and rocky soil provides the ideal conditions for making red wine, which is produced locally under the renowned *appellation* of Saumur-Champigny. You can visit numerous wine-growers' caves in the pretty villages around **PARNAY**. Set well back from the Loire's floodplain in the shelter of the tufa escarpment, the sandy stone walls of its ancient houses are hardly distinguishable from the surrounding natural rock. Just beyond, in **LE VAL-HULIN**, are the last producers of the once common Saumurois dried whole apples, known as *pommes tapées* – each apple, after drying, is given a little expert tap to check its readiness for bottling. At the **Troglo des Pommes Tapées** (July & Aug daily 2.30–6pm, Sept–June Sat & Sun 2.30–6pm; €4.60), you're taken through the apple drying and tapping process, before rounding off the visit with a tasting. **TURQUANT**, a few hundred metres beyond Le-Val-Hulin, is the starting point for a **sentier d'interprétation**, a two-hour circular walk around the village following signposts describing the local flora and fauna set up by the regional Parc Naturel.

The **château de Brézé**, 10km southeast of Saumur (Feb to mid-April & Oct–Dec Tues–Fri 2–6pm, Sat & Sun 10am–6pm; mid-April to Sept daily

10am–6.30pm; tunnels €7.10, château and tunnels €11), is outwardly a typically noble sixteenth-century château built in creamy-white tufa. The interior decor is very refined, but what goes on underground is the main point of the visit. Just over a kilometre of tunnels were hacked out of the soft rock beneath the château in the medieval era. A guide will take you on a tour round the many chambers, staircases, storerooms and passages.

The Abbaye de Fontevraud

At the heart of the stunning Romanesque complex of the **abbaye de Fontevraud**, 13km southeast of Saumur on bus #16 (4–6 daily; 30min), are the tombs of the Plantagenet royal family, eerily lifelike works of funereal art that powerfully evoke the historical bonds between England and France (daily: June–Sept 9am–6.30pm; Oct–May 10am–5.30pm; €6.10). A religious community was established in around 1100 as both a nunnery and a monastery with an abbess in charge – an unconventional move, even if the post was filled solely by queens and princesses. The remaining buildings date from the twelfth century and are immense, built as they were to house and separate not only the nuns and monks but also the sick, lepers and repentant prostitutes. There were originally five separate institutions, of which three still stand in graceful Romanesque solidity. Used as a prison from the Revolution until 1963, its most famous inmate was the writer Jean Genet.

The **abbey church** is an awe-inspiring space, not least for the four tombstone effigies: Henry II, his wife Eleanor of Aquitaine, who died here, their son Richard the Lionheart and daughter-in-law Isabelle of Angoulême, King John's queen. Carved as they were at the time of their deaths, the figures are eerily lifelike. The strange domed roof, the great cream-coloured columns of the choir and the graceful capitals of the nave add to the atmosphere. Elsewhere in the complex you can explore the magnificent **cloisters**, the **chapterhouse**, decorated with sixteenth-century murals, and the vast **refectory**. All the cooking for the religious community, which would have numbered several hundred, was done in the – now perfectly restored – Romanesque **kitchen**, an octagonal building as extraordinary from the outside (with its 21 spiky chimneys) as it is from within.

The abbey is now the **Centre Culturel de l'Ouest** (CCO), the cultural centre for western France, and one of Europe's most important centres of medieval archeology, and is used for a great many activities, from concerts to lectures, art exhibitions and theatre. Programme details are available at the abbey (Ⓣ02.41.51.73.52, Ⓦwww.abbaye-fontevraud.com) or from the Saumur tourist office.

Candes St-Martin and Montsoreau

The ancient village of **CANDES-ST-MARTIN**, on the Loire 5km north of Fontevraud, gets part of its name from the great local saint, Martin, who died here in around 400 while trying to settle a dispute between squabbling monks. This is a beautiful corner of the region, the village set under a rocky bluff overlooking the confluence of the Loire and Vienne. The principal sight is the airy collégiale, notably its elaborately sculpted porch. The oldest part of the church, though heavily restored, is the chapelle St-Martin, on the left of the choir, where you can trace the life of the saint in nineteenth-century stained-glass windows.

The fifteenth-century **château de Montsoreau**, 1km downstream (Feb–April & Oct to mid-Nov 2–6pm; May–Sept daily 10am–7pm; €7.50), is one of the most photogenic châteaux of them all, its north side rising cliff-like almost straight out of the river. The interior has been turned into an elaborately presented museum dedicated to the river trade and the history of the castle, and there's a panoramic view from the open-air battlements.

Right beside the Candes-St-Martin's church in a venerable building is an excellent, relaxed local **restaurant**, the *Auberge de la Route d'Or* (Ⓣ02.47.95.81.10; closed Tues & Wed). In Monstoreau, the welcoming and well-run *Hôtel le Bussy*, 4 rue Jehanne d'Arc (Ⓣ02.41.38.11.11, Ⓕ02.41.38.18.10; ❹), is a tranquil place to spend the night.

Angers and around

ANGERS, capital of the ancient county of Anjou, stands majestically on the banks of the Maine, which feeds the Loire just south of the city with the waters of the Mayenne, Sarthe and Loir rivers. Long known as "Black Angers" from the gloomy-coloured slate and stone quarried here since the ninth century, it is actually a very pretty, friendly town, with a lively atmosphere. The overriding reason for coming here is to see its two stunning **tapestry** series, the fourteenth-century *Apocalypse* and the twentieth-century *Chant du Monde*.

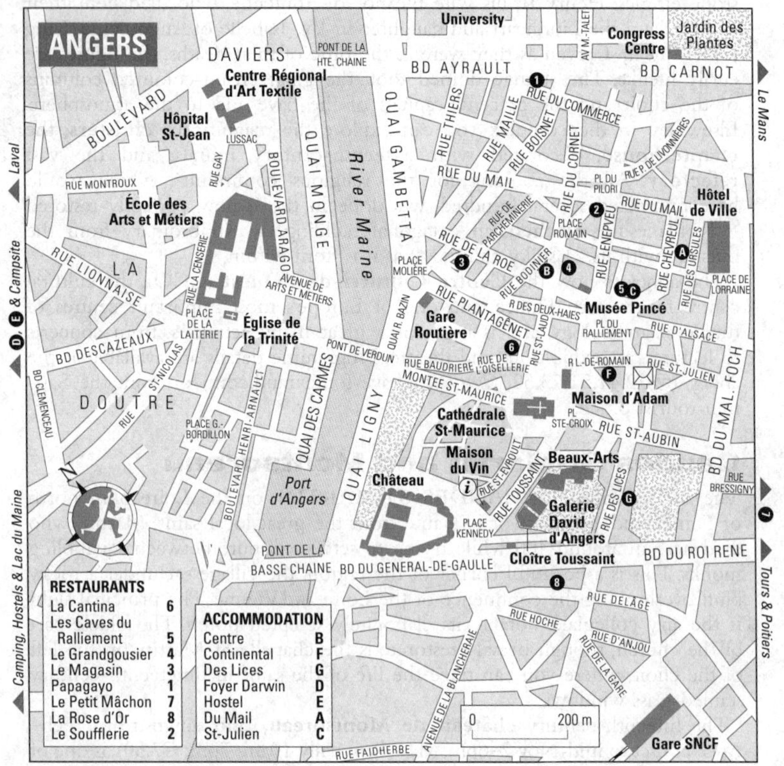

Arrival, information and accommodation

The **gare SNCF** is south of the centre, about a ten-minute walk from the château. Bus #6 (#25 on Sun) makes the journey to the tourist office and château, while buses #1 and #16 will take you to central place du Raillement; a flat-rate **bus** ticket, which you can buy on board, costs €1. The **gare routière** is down by the river, just past the Pont de Verdun on place Molière. The main **tourist office** is on place Kennedy, facing the château (May–Sept Mon–Sat 9am–7pm, Sun 10am–6pm; Oct–April Mon 2–6pm, Tues–Sat 9am–6pm, Sun 10am–1pm; ⓣ02.41.23.50.00, ⓦwww.angers-tourisme.com); it sells a €12 **museum pass**, which allows access to the tapestries as well as the city's museums and galleries.

There's a wide range of **accommodation** on offer, and finding a room shouldn't present too many problems, though it's still wise to book ahead in summer.

Hotels

Centre 12 rue St-Laud ⓣ02.41.87.45.07. Battered but cheerful rooms above a central bar on a pedestrianized street. Noisy nightime chatter from the street is a drawback in front-facing rooms. ❶

Continental 12–14 rue Louis de Romain ⓣ02.41.86.94.94, ⓔle.continental@wanadoo.fr. Well-equipped and well-run hotel with good service and bright, super-pastel decor. Nice location on a quiet street just off place Ralliement. Gets busy during the week with a business crowd. ❸

Des Lices 25 rue des Lices ⓣ02.41.87.44.10. A real bargain in a balustraded townhouse on a distinctly posh, town-centre street. Closed August 1–15. ❷

Du Mail 8 rue des Ursules ⓣ02.41.25.05.25, ⓔhotedumailangers@yahoo.fr. Old-fashioned and extremely attractive two-star, with a courtyard, pleasant rooms and a great location in a quiet corner of the centre. Parking available. ❸

St-Julien 9 place du Ralliement ⓣ02.41.88.41.62, ⓦwww.destination-anjou.com/saintjulien. Large hotel right in the centre of the city, offering a good spread of modernized rooms. Some of the pretty little ones under the roof have views over town. ❸

Hostels and campsite

Centre d'Accueil du Lac de Maine 49 av du Lac de Maine ⓣ02.41.22.32.10, ⓦwww.lacdemaine.fr. Rather swish hostel-style accommodation, complete with extensive sports facilities, a 20min ride southwest of the town; bus #6 (bus #11 from 7.30pm–midnight, bus #26 on Sun) either from the train station or bd Général-de-Gaulle. Single rooms €29, twins €38. You can rent canoes at the Base Nautique in the complex. There's also a campsite here (ⓣ02.41.73.05.03, ⓕ02.41.73.02.20; closed mid-Oct to late March), agreeably situated next to the lake.

Foyer Darwin 3 rue Darwin ⓣ02.41.22.61.20, ⓔcontact@foyerdarwin.com. Inexpensive hostel twenty minutes' walk west of la Doutre, near the Belle-Beille campus; take bus #6 or #8.

The City

Your lasting impression of Angers will be of the **château**, an impressive, sturdy fortress by the river, its moat now filled with striking formal flower arrangements and softened by trees. From here, it's just a fifteen-minute stroll east to the **cathedral** and its entourage of several smaller churches and museums.

Across the pont Verdun from the château is the suburb of **La Doutre**, where the **Hôpital St-Jean** houses the modern response to the castle's Apocalypse tapestry, *Le Chant du Monde*. Further out in the suburbs are a rash of interesting museums, easily reached by bus, exalting everything from early aeroplanes to Cointreau and communication methods.

The château and Apocalypse tapestry

The **Château d'Angers** (daily: May–Aug 9.30am–6.30pm; Sept–April 10am–5.30pm; €6.10) is a formidable early medieval fortress whose sense of impregnability is accentuated by the darkness of the western Anjou schist with which it is built. The mighty kilometre-long curtain wall is reinforced by seventeen circular towers, their brooding stones offset by decorative bands of pale tufa. Inside are a few miscellaneous remains of the counts' royal lodgings and chapels, but the chief focus is the astonishing **Tapestry of the Apocalypse**. Woven between 1373 and 1382 for Louis I of Anjou, it was originally 140m long, of which 100m now survives. From the start, it was treated as a masterpiece, and only brought out to decorate the cathedral of Angers on major festival days. The sheer grandeur of the conception is overwhelming, but the tapestry's reputation rests as much on its superb detail and stunning colours, preserved today by the very low light levels in the long viewing hall. These reds and greens and golds were once even more vivid – as you can see if you buy the handy English-language booklet (€5.50), which uses photographs of the tapestry's unfaded reverse side – astonishingly, this is a perfectly finished mirror-image of the front. If you plan to follow the apocalypse story right through, the booklet comes in handy but a Bible would be even better. In brief: the Day of Judgement is signalled by the breaking of the seven seals – note the four horsemen – and the seven angels blowing their trumpets. As the battle of Armageddon rages, Satan appears first as a seven-headed red dragon, then as the seven-headed lion-like Beast. The holy forces break the seven vials of plagues, whereupon the Whore of Babylon appears mounted on the Beast. She is challenged by the Word of God, seen riding a galloping horse, who chases the hordes of Satan into the lake of fire, allowing the establishment of the heavenly Jerusalem.

Those feeling in need of a drink can head straight out of the castle and into the **Maison du Vin de l'Anjou**, 5bis place Kennedy (May–Sept Tues–Sat 9am–1pm & 3–6.30pm, Sun 9am–1pm; Oct–April Tues–Sat 9.30am–1pm & 3–6.30pm), where the helpful staff will offer you wine to taste before you buy, and can provide lists of wine-growers to visit.

The cathedral and around

The most dramatic approach to the **cathédrale St-Maurice** is via the quayside, from where a long flight of steps leads straight up to the mid-twelfth-century portal – which shows another version of the apocalypse. Built in the 1150s and 1160s, the cathedral exemplifies the Plantagenet style – in fact, it's probably the earliest example in France of this influential architectural development The three aisle-less bays of the nave span a distance of over 16m, the dome-like Plantagenet or Angevin vaulting creating structural strength as well as a faintly Byzantine feel. The fifteenth-century rose windows in the transepts are particularly impressive.

In front of the cathedral, on place Ste-Croix, is the town's favourite carpentry detail, the unlikely genitals of one of the carved characters on the medieval **Maison d'Adam**. Heading north from place Ste-Croix, you pass **place du Ralliement**, hub of modern Angers and site of the nineteenth-century **Théâtre Municipal**. From here, proceed into rue Lenepveu, where a Renaissance mansion (at no. 32) houses the **Musée Pincé** (mid-June to mid-Sept daily 9am–6.30pm; mid-Sept to mid-June daily except Mon 10am–noon & 2–6pm; €3). It's a mixed bag of antiquities – mostly ceramics from Greece, China and Japan, with a few Japanese caricatures of actors – but the staircase is handsome, as is the carved stone roof on the first floor.

Arguably the greatest stoneworks in Angers, however, are the creations of the famous local sculptor David d'Angers (1788–1856), whose Calvary adorns the cathedral. His great civic commissions can be seen all over France, but these large-scale marbles and bronzes are almost all copies of the smaller plaster of Paris works created by the artist himself. It's mostly these plaster originals that are exhibited in the **Galerie David d'Angers**, 37bis rue Toussaint (mid-June to mid-Sept daily 9am–6.30pm; mid-Sept to mid-June Tues–Sun 10am–noon & 2–6pm; €4), set impressively in the glazed-over nave of a ruined thirteenth-century church, the **Église Toussaint**.

The **Musée des Beaux-Arts**, at 10 rue du Musée (mid-June to mid-Sept daily 10am–7pm; mid-Sept to mid-June Tues–Sun 1–6pm; €4), is housed in the **Logis Barrault**, a proudly decorated mansion built by a wealthy late-fifteenth-century mayor. Years of extensive restoration have cleaned up – and in some places entirely remade – the flamboyant Gothic stone carving. Eighteenth- and nineteenth-century paintings dominate the collection, with works by Watteau, Chardin and Fragonard, as well as Ingres' operatic *Paolo et Francesca* – the same subject depicted by Rodin in *The Kiss* – and a small collection devoted to Boucher's *Génie des Arts*.

La Doutre

The district facing the château across the Maine is known as **La Doutre** (literally, "the other side"), and still has a few mansions and houses dating from the medieval period, despite redevelopment over the years.

In the north of the area, a short way from the Pont de la Haute-Chaine (about 20 minutes' walk from the château), the **Hôpital St-Jean**, at 4 bd Arago, was built by Henry Plantagenet in 1174 as a hospital for the poor, a function it continued to fulfil until 1854. Today it houses the **Musée Jean Lurçat et de la Tapisserie Contemporaine** (mid-June to mid-Sept daily 9.30am–6.30pm; mid-Sept to mid-June daily except Mon 10am–noon & 2–6pm; €4), which contains the city's great twentieth-century tapestry, **Le Chant du Monde**. The tapestry sequence was designed by Jean Lurçat in 1957 in response to the Apocalypse tapestry, though he died nine years later before its completion (the artist's own commentary is available in English). It hangs in a vast vaulted space, the original ward for the sick, or Salle des Malades. The first four tapestries deal with *La Grande Menace*, the threat of nuclear war: first the bomb itself; then *Hiroshima Man*, flayed and burnt with the broken symbols of belief dropping from him; then the collective massacre of the *Great Charnel House*; and the last dying rose falling with the post-Holocaust ash through black space – the *End of Everything*. From then on, the tapestries celebrate the joys of life: *Man in Glory in Peace*; *Water and Fire*; *Champagne* – "that blissful ejaculation", according to Lurçat; *Conquest of Space*; *Poetry*; and *Sacred Ornaments*. Subject matter and treatment are intense, and the setting helps: it's a huge echoey space, with rows of columns supporting soaring Angevin vaulting. The Romanesque cloisters at the back, with their graceful double columns, are also worth a peek.

There are more modern tapestries in the building adjoining the Salle des Malades, where the collection is built up around the donation by Lurçat's widow of several of his paintings, ceramics and tapestries, along with the highly tactile but more muted abstract tapestries of Thomas Gleb, who died in Angers in 1991. With four local *ateliers*, Angers is a leading centre for contemporary tapestry, and the neighbouring **Centre Régional d'Art Textile**, 3 bd Daviers (Mon–Fri 10am–noon & 2–4pm), can put you in touch with local artists and let you know where to find private exhibitions.

South of the Hôpital St-Jean, on La Doutre's central square, place de la Laiterie, the ancient buildings of the **Abbaye de Ronceray** are now occupied by one of France's elite *grandes écoles*, the École des Arts et Métiers, which trains the leading students of aerospace technology, among others. The abbey church is used to mount art exhibitions, worth visiting just to see the Romanesque galleries of the old abbey and admire their beautiful murals. When there's no exhibition, you can only visit as part of the tourist office's weekly tour of La Doutre. Inside the adjacent twelfth-century **church of the Trinity**, on the square, an exquisite Renaissance wooden spiral staircase fails to mask a great piece of medieval bodging used to fit the wall of the church around a part of the abbey that juts into it.

Suburban museums

For something completely different, you could go on a guided tour around the **Distillerie Cointreau**, just off the ring road between Angers and St-Barthelemy d'Anjou (closed Jan; call ⓣ02.41.31.50.50 for guided tours in English; €5.50; take bus #7 from bd Maréchal Foch), where the famous orange liqueur has been distilled since the mid-nineteenth century. You'll learn a lot about the Cointreau brothers and how marvellous the drink is, a little bit about distilling techniques, and nothing, of course, about the recipe. You get a little sip of a cocktail at the end, but the highlight is definitely the rows of gleaming copper stills.

The **Musée de l'Ardoise** (July to mid-Sept daily except Mon 2–6pm; mid-Feb to June & mid-Sept to Nov Sun 2–6pm; €5.40) is rather lost in the industrial satellite village of **TRELAZE**, 2km southeast of the centre. It's not a museum as such, rather a demonstration of traditional slate-mining techniques by former miners, on the site of an open-cast slate mine. Just watching a sexagenarian split a giant block of shist into millimetre-perfect, size-graded slates using a big wooden hammer and a pair of outsize clogs is fairly astounding, even if you don't get the commentary.

Eating

The streets around place du Ralliement and place Romain have a wide variety of **cafés** and **restaurants**, many of them very inexpensive.

La Cantina 9 rue de l'Oisellerie ⓣ02.41.87.36.34. Relaxed café-bistro serving southwestern dishes such as *magret de canard* (duck steak). Good value for lunch, with straightforward fish and meat *plats* and salads for around €15. Closed Sun lunch, Tues eve, & Mon.

Les Caves du Ralliement 9 place du Ralliement ⓣ02.41.88.47.77. Busy brasserie underneath the posh and well-regarded *Provence Caffè*. Good for inexpensive *moules-* or *steak-frites* at lunchtime, and oysters or eels with a glass of wine in the evening, sitting at an outside table on the square. Closed Mon evening.

Le Grandgousier 7 rue St-Laud ⓣ02.41.87.81.47. Serves traditional regional dishes complemented by local wines, which are included in the price of the €24 menu. Closed Sun.

Le Magasin 48 rue de la Parcheminerie ⓣ02.41.81.05.89. Trendy restaurant serving good modern Mediterranean food to a bright young crowd in a 70s-retro dining room. Expect to pay around €20 without wine. Open until midnight; closed Sun.

Papagayo 44 bd Ayrault ⓣ02.41.87.03.35. Friendly bar-bistro near the university campus, with a great atmosphere during term-time and a conservatory room for summer. Serves decent, fairly inexpensive traditional French food. Closed Sun & Mon eve.

Le Petit Mâchon 43 rue Bressigny ⓣ02.41.86.01.13. Low-priced local wines to go with inexpensive *andouillettes* and other regional delicacies. Closed Sat lunch & Sun.

La Rose d'Or 21 rue Delâge ⓣ02.41.88.38.38. Old-fashioned restaurant with ambitions. The entrecôte comes in a Bourgueil sauce from the chef's own vineyard. Menus in the €20–30 range. Closed Sun evening & Mon.

Le Soufflerie 8 place Pilori ⓣ02.41.87.45.32. Popular café specializing in soufflés, both large and savoury (at around €9) and small and sweet (around €6). Closed Sun, Mon & first half Aug.

Drinking and nightlife

Late-opening **bars** congregate around rue St-Laud: *Bar du Centre*, below *Hôtel Centre* is full of young Angevins, and there's a cluster of popular Irish-type places at the bottom end of the road, around place Romain. Just beyond the square, *Safari*, 23 rue du Mail (closed Mon), is a trendy bar with DJs playing funk and hip-hop at weekends. Two small, laid-back places can be found on rue de la Parcheminerie: *Au Jacare*, at 46bis, plays electro and jazz; while two doors down, *Ti Bazar* does good snacks (oysters in winter) in the early evening, then gets loud and busy towards midnight. Over in **La Doutre**, the *Sun Café*, 3bis bd Henri Arnauld, is one of the nicer student bars – though don't bother coming during the summer vacation – while *La Descente de la Marine*, at 28 quai des Carmes, is an old-time bar with a strong nautical flavour, attracting lots of students and young people who come down for an outdoor, early evening *apéro* on the quay. Later on, *Le V.I.P. Café*, 5 rue Montaubon (closed Sun), is a friendly, relatively upmarket venue, with DJ nights alternating with gigs. Among the full-on **clubs**, *Le Mid'Star*, 25 quai Félix Faure, is the biggest and best-known clubbing venue.

Listings

Bike rental A desk in the tourist office rents bikes and mountain bikes.
Boat rental Numerous companies rent out canoes and run guided kayak trips on the five rivers in the vicinity of Angers. Try: Anjou Loisirs, Base de Loisirs à Notre-Dame du Marillais, St-Florent-le-Veil (on the Èvre; ⓣ02.41.70.56.78); and Canoe Kayak Club d'Angers, 75 av du lac de Maine (on the Maine and Lac de Maine; ⓣ02.41.72.07.04, ⓦwww.ckca.fr.st). The tourist office has details of more sedate trips on sightseeing boats.
Car rental ADA, place de la Gare ⓣ02.41.20.06.66; Autop, 30 rue Denis-Papin ⓣ02.41.88.54.44; Europcar Inter-Rent, 3 av Turpinde Crissé ⓣ02.41.87.87.10; Hertz, 14 rue Denis-Papin ⓣ02.41.88.15.16, National/Citer ⓣ02.41.86.89.89.
Emergencies Ambulance ⓣ15; Centre Hospitalier, 4 rue Larrey (ⓣ02.41.35.36.37); for late-night pharmacies, phone the police on ⓣ02.41.47.75.22.
Festivals At the end of May, the Tour de Scènes festival brings rock and world music acts to the city centre for four days of concerts. The Festival Angers l'Eté features jazz and world music gigs in the atmospheric Cloître Toussaint, the cloisters behind the Galerie David d'Angers, on Tuesday and Thursday evenings throughout July and August; book through the tourist office. In early September, the festival Les Accroche Cœurs brings a host of theatrical companies, musicians and street-performers for three days of surreal entertainment.
Internet You can get online at 8 rue Plantagenet, near Les Halles; 37 rue Bressigny, near bd Foch; 25 rue de la Roë, just east of place de la République; and 55 rue Beaurepaire, in La Doutre.
Laundries 9 place Hérault; 17 rue Marceau; 15 rue Plantagenet; 5 place de la Visitation.
Market There are a number of markets Tues–Sat throughout the city including a flower market on place Leclerc on Sat – Anjou is a major flower-growing region – and an organic produce market on rue Saint-Laud on Sat.
Police Commissariat, 15 rue Dupetit-Thouars ⓣ02.41.66.86.35.
Taxis Allo Anjou Taxi ⓣ02.41.87.65.00; Accueil Taxi Angevin ⓣ02.41.36.25.20.

Around Angers

Lazing around the Loire and its tributaries between visits to vineyards can fill a good summer week around Angers, as long as you have your own transport, and you can easily reach a couple more châteaux in these parts: **Brissac-Quincé**, 20km south of the town (also bus #9), and **Le Plessis-Bourré** near Ecuillé (impossible to get to by public transport), 17km to the north. For a more accessible glimpse of a real monster of a mansion, head for the

Château de Serrant, just outside St-Georges-sur-Loire, on bus route #18 from Angers.

Château de Brissac

The giant **Château de Brissac** at **BRISSAC-QUINCÉ** (guided tours only: April–June & mid-Sept to Oct daily except Tues 10am–noon & 2.15–5.15pm; July & Aug daily 10am–5.45pm; €8, Ⓦwww.brissac.net) has been owned since 1502 by the same line of dukes. It boasts of its status as the tallest in France, but it's by no means the most handsome, looking like an ugly duckling frozen halfway through its transformation into a swan. On the main west front, two round towers survive from an earlier, fifteenth-century fortress, with the château's ill-proportioned seventeenth-century facade awkwardly wedged in between them. Under the original rebuilding plan, the old fortified towers were to be pulled down, but the death of Duke Charles II in 1621 brought the project to a standstill. The interior is a riot of opulent taste, with some beautiful ceilings and tapestries, and lots of priceless furnishings; the guided tours supplies various family anecdotes. The château has had a **vineyard** since 1515, with its own label, and a wine tasting, with opportunity to buy, of course, concludes the tour.

Château du Plessis-Bourré

Five years' work at the end of the fifteenth century produced the fortress of **Le Plessis-Bourré** (guided tours only: mid-Feb to end March, Oct & Nov daily except Wed 2–6pm; April–June & Sept Mon, Tues & Fri–Sun 10am–noon & 2–6pm, Thurs 2–6pm; July & Aug daily 10am–6pm; closed Jan & Dec; €8, Ⓦwww.plessis-bourre.com), 17km north of Angers, between the Sarthe and Mayenne rivers. Despite the vast, full moat, spanned by an arched bridge with a still-functioning drawbridge, it was built as a luxurious residence rather than a defensive castle. The treasurer of France at the time, Jean Bourré, received important visitors here, among them Louis XI and Charles VIII.

The first three rooms on the ground floor are a surprise, beautifully decorated and furnished in the Louis XVI, XV and Régence styles respectively, but things revert to type in the Gothic Salle du Parlement. The highlight of the tour comes in the Salle des Gardes, just above, where the original, deeply coffered ceiling stems from Bourré's fashionable interest in alchemy. Every inch is painted with allegorical scenes: sixteen panels depict alchemical symbols such as the phoenix, the pregnant siren and the donkey singing Mass, while eight cartoon-like paintings come with morals attached – look out for "Chicheface", the hungry wolf that only eats faithful women, whose victim is supposed to be Jean Bourré's wife.

Château de Serrant

At the **Château de Serrant**, 15km west of Angers beside the N23 near **ST-GEORGES-SUR-LOIRE**, the combination of dark-brown schist and creamy tufa give a rather pleasant biscuit-cake effect to the outside (April–June & Sept to mid-Nov Wed–Sun guided tours leave hourly 10am–1pm & every 30min 2.15–4.15pm, plus 5.15pm; July & Aug daily guided tours leave regularly 10am–5.30pm; mid-Nov to Dec Sat & Sun guided tours at 10.30am, 11.30am, 2.30pm & 3.30pm; €9). But with its heavy slate bell-shaped cupolas pressing down on massive towers, the exterior is grandiose and imposing rather than graceful. The building was begun in the sixteenth century and added to, discreetly for the most part, up until the eighteenth century. In 1755 it belonged to an Irishman, Francis Walsh, to whom Louis XV had given the title Count of Serrant as a reward for Walsh's help against the old enemy, the English – Walsh had provided the ship for Bonnie Prince Charlie to return to Scotland for the 1745 uprising. The Walsh family married into the ancient La Trémoille clan, whose descendants – via a Belgian offshoot – still own the château. The massive rooms of the interior are packed with all the trappings of old wealth. Much of the decor dates from the late nineteenth and early twentieth centuries, but it's tastefully – expensively – done, and you are also shown the Renaissance staircase, the sombre private chapel designed by Mansart, a bedroom prepared for Napoleon (who only stopped here for a couple of hours), and the attractive vaulted kitchens.

Le Mans and around

LE MANS, the historic capital of the Maine region, is taken over by car fanatics in the middle of June for the famous 24-hour race, but during the rest of the year it's a fascinating and unusually peaceful place to visit. As a large, industrial and traditionally left wing city, its atmosphere could hardly be more different from the bourgeois Loire valley proper, 80km to the south, but it shares a good deal of history: Le Mans was the favourite home of the Plantagenet family, the counts of Anjou, Touraine and Maine. The old quarter, in the shadow of the magnificent cathedral, is unusually well preserved, while outside town you can visit the serene Cistercian abbey of Epau and, of course, the racetrack.

Arrival, information and accommodation

The hub of Le Mans today is **place de la République**, beneath which, in the underground shopping centre, is the city **bus terminal**; bus #16 runs between here and the **gare SNCF** via avenue Général-Leclerc, where the **gare routière** is located. From place de la République, rue Bolton leads east into rue de l'Étoile, where you'll find the **tourist office** (Mon–Fri 9am–6pm, Sat 9am–noon & 2–6pm, Sun 10am–noon; ⓣ02.43.28.17.22, ⓦwww.ville-lemans.fr). **Bikes** can be rented from Top Team, on place St-Pierre in the old town.

Unless your visit coincides with one of the big racing events during April, June or September, you should be able to find **accommodation** easily without having to book, though there's nothing in the old town.

Hotels

Chantecler 50 rue de la Pelouse ⓣ02.43.14.40.00, ⓕ02.43.77.16.28. Quiet, professionally run hotel, offering well-fitted-out rooms and parking. ❹

Levasseur 5–7 bd René Levasseur ⓣ02.43.39.61.61, ⓕ02.43.39.61.65. Well-located just off place de la République, if rambling and functional in feel. Closed Aug. ❸

De Rennes 43 bd de la Gare ⓣ02.43.24.86.40, ⓕ02.43.87.02.95. Simple, inexpensive hotel right next to the station done up in bright colours and cheery pastels, and spotlessly kept. ❷

Select 13 rue du Père-Mersenne, off av du Général-Leclerc ⓣ02.43.24.17.74. Small and basic hotel, with little sinks behind screens and grubby floral wallpaper, but the price is right. ❶

Hostel

Le Flore 23 rue Maupertuis ⓣ02.43.81.27.55. A clean and modern HI hostel, quite close to the centre. Take av du Général-de-Gaulle from place de la République, continue along av Bollée; rue Maupertuis is the third on the left.

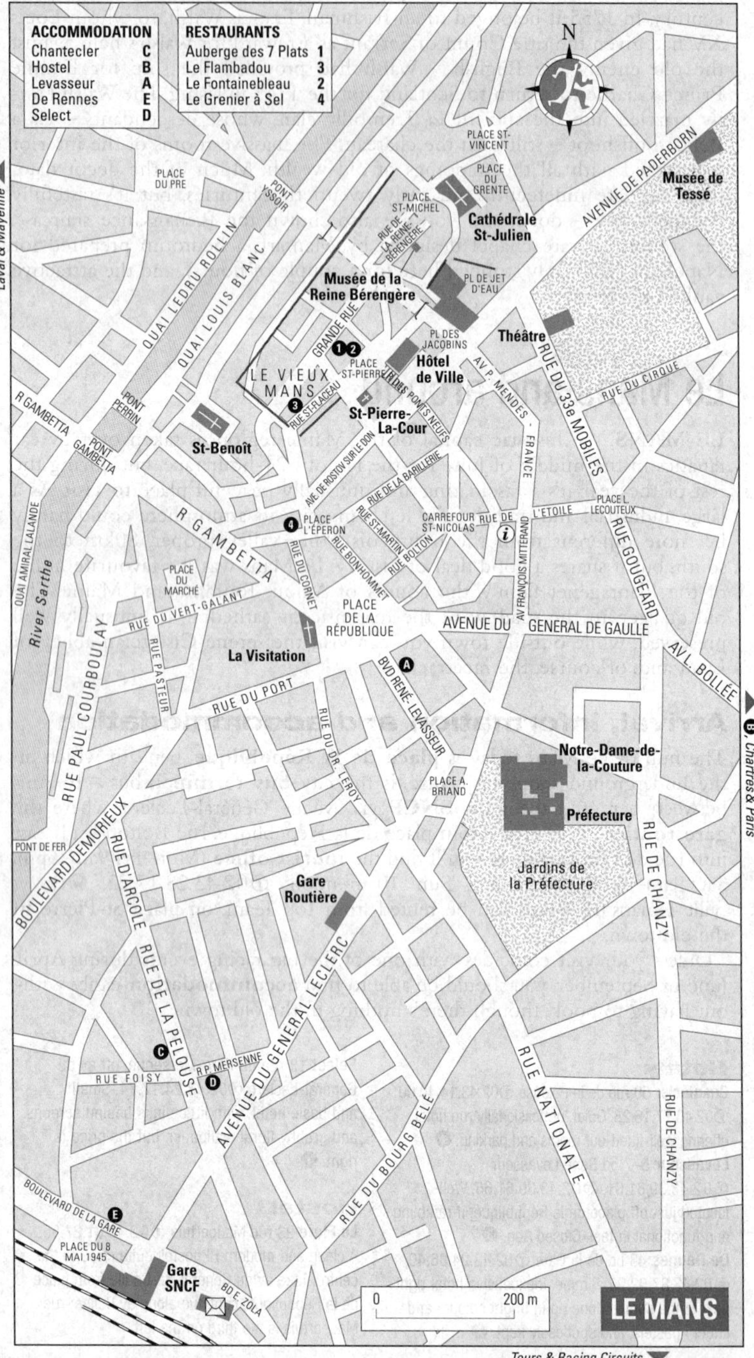
ACCOMMODATION
Chantecler C
Hostel B
Levasseur A
De Rennes E
Select D
RESTAURANTS
Auberge des 7 Plats 1
Le Flambadou 3
Le Fontainebleau 2
Le Grenier à Sel 4
Laval & Mayenne
B, Chartres & Paris
Tours & Racing Circuits
Musée de Tessé
Cathédrale St-Julien
Musée de la Reine Bérengère
Théâtre
Hôtel de Ville
LE VIEUX MANS
St-Pierre-La-Cour
St-Benoît
La Visitation
Notre-Dame-de-la-Couture
Préfecture
Jardins de la Préfecture
Gare Routière
Gare SNCF
River Sarthe
PLACE DE LA RÉPUBLIQUE
AVENUE DU GENERAL DE GAULLE
AVENUE DE PADERBORN
RUE DU 33e MOBILES
RUE NATIONALE
AVENUE DU GENERAL LECLERC
QUAI LEDRU ROLLIN
QUAI LOUIS BLANC
R GAMBETTA
BOULEVARD DEMORIEUX
RUE PAUL COURBOULAY
RUE DE LA PELOUSE
RUE DU BOURG BELÉ
RUE DE CHANZY
BVD RENÉ-LEVASSEUR
0 200 m
LE MANS

The City

The complicated web of the **old town** lies on a hill above the River Sarthe to the north of the central place de la République. Its medieval streets, a hotch-potch of intricate Renaissance stonework, medieval half-timbering, sculpted pillars and beams and grand classical facades, are still encircled by the original third- and fourth-century **Gallo-Roman walls**, supposedly the best-preserved in Europe and running for several hundred metres. Steep, walled steps lead up from the river, and longer flights descend on the southern side of the enclosure, using old Gallo-Roman entrances. If intrigued, you can see pictures, maps and plans of Vieux Mans, plus examples of the city's ancient arts and crafts, in the rather dull **Musée de la Reine Bérengère** (Tues–Sun: May–Sept 10am–12.30pm & 2–6.30pm; Oct–April 2–6pm; €2.80 or €5.20 with Musée de Tessé), housed in a beautiful fifteenth-century construction on rue de la Reine-Bérengère. The **Maison des Deux-Amis**, opposite, gets its name for the carving of two men (the "two friends") supporting a coat of arms between the doors of numbers 18 and 20. Heading away from the cathedral, you enter the equally ancient **Grande Rue**.

The high ground of the old town has been sacred since ancient times, as testified by a strangely human, pink-tinted menhir now propped up against the southwest corner of the immense, hybrid **Cathédrale St-Julien**, which crowns the hilltop. The nave of the cathedral was only just completed when Geoffroi Plantagenet, the count of Maine and Anjou, married Matilda, daughter of Henry I of England, in 1129, thus founding the English dynastic line. Inside, for all the power and measured beauty of this Romanesque structure, it's impossible not to be drawn towards the vertiginous High Gothic choir, filled with coloured light filtering through the stained-glass windows. At the easternmost end of the choir, the vault of the chapelle de la Vierge is painted with angels singing, dancing and playing medieval musical instruments.

In the 1850s a road was tunnelled under the quarter – a slum at the time – helping to preserve its self-contained unity. On the north side of the quarter, the road tunnel comes out by an impressive **monument to Wilbur Wright** – who tested an early flying machine in Le Mans – which points you into place des Jacobins, the vantage point for St-Julien's double-tiered flying buttresses and apse. From here, you can walk northeast alongside the park to the **Musée de Tessé**, on avenue de Paderborn (July & Aug daily except Mon 10.30am–12.30pm & 2–6.30pm; Sept–June Tues–Sat 9am–noon & 2–6pm, Sun 10am–noon & 2–6pm; €4 or €5.20 with Musée de la Reine Bérengère), where the highlight is an exquisite enamel portrait of Geoffroi Le Bel, originally part of his tomb in the cathedral. Otherwise it's a mixed bag of paintings, furnishings and sculptures, while in the basement there's a full-scale reconstruction of the ancient Egyptian tomb of Queen Nefertari.

The modern centre of Le Mans is **place de la République**, bordered by a mixture of Belle Époque buildings and more modern office blocks, and the Baroque bulk of the **church of the Visitation**, built in 1730, with a balustrade inside designed by one of the sisters of the order.

Eating and drinking

In the centre of town, the **cafés** and **brasseries** on place de la République stay open till late, while on nearby place l'Éperon there's a very good, if expensive, **restaurant**, *Le Grenier à Sel* (Ⓣ02.43.23.26.30; closed Sat lunch

& Sun; menus from €21). The most atmospheric restaurants, however, are located in the old town. The *Auberge des 7 Plats*, 79 Grande-Rue (closed Sun & Mon), does a good range of good-value *plats* and menus. For a special occasion make for the rustically styled *Le Flambadou*, 14bis rue St-Flaceau (Ⓣ02.43.24.88.38; closed Sun), which offers a very meaty menu from Périgord and the Landes from around €30. Nearby on place St-Pierre, *Le Fontainebleau* (Ⓣ02.43.14.25.74; closed Tues) has pleasant outside seating facing the Hôtel de Ville and serves moderately priced classic French cuisine. There's a daily **market** in the covered halls on place du Marché, plus a bric-a-brac market on Wednesday, Friday (when there's also food) and Sunday mornings on place du Jet-d'Eau, below the cathedral on the new town side.

The racetrack and car museum

The first big race at Le Mans was in 1906, and two years later aviator **Wilbur Wright** took off along what is now the fastest stretch of the racetrack, remaining in the air for a record-breaking one hour and 31.5 minutes. 1923 saw the first 24-hour car race, run on the present 13.6-kilometre circuit, with average speeds of 92kph (57mph) – these days, the drivers average around 210kph (130mph). The Sarthe circuit, on which the world-renowned **24 Heures du Mans** car race takes place each year, stretches south from the outskirts of the city, along ordinary roads. The simplest way to get a taste of the track is just to take the main road south of the city towards Tours, a stretch of ordinary highway which follows the infamous **Mulsanne straight** for 5.7km – a distance that saw race cars reach speeds of up to 375kph (230mph), until two chicanes were introduced in 1989. Entrance to the actual 24 Heures race, in mid-June, costs from around €30 to €60, depending on the level of access. Tickets can be bought direct from the organisers at Ⓦwww.lemans.org, but be sure to book well in advance.

At other times of year, you can watch practice sessions, or there's the Le Mans Classic in September. Alternatively, visit the **Musée de l'Automobile** (daily: March–May & Oct–Dec 10am–6pm; June–Sept 10am–7pm; €6), on the edge of the Bugatti circuit – the dedicated track section of the main Sarthe circuit. It parades some 150 vehicles, ranging from the humble 2CV to classic Lotus and Porsche race cars.

The Abbaye de L'Epau

If car racing holds no romance, there's another outing from Le Mans of a much quieter nature, to the Cistercian **Abbaye de l'Epau** (daily 9.30–noon & 2–5.30pm; opening hours may vary in summer to accommodate exhibitions; Ⓣ02.43.84.22.29; €2.30), 4km out of town off the Chartres–Paris road (bus #14 from place de la République in Le Mans, stop "Pologne", then five-minute walk). The abbey was founded in 1229 by Queen Berengaria, consort of Richard the Lionheart, and it stands in a rural setting on the outskirts of the Bois de Changé more or less unaltered since its fifteenth-century restoration after a fire. The visit includes the dormitory, with the remains of a fourteenth-century fresco, the abbey church and the scriptorium, or writing room. The church contains the recumbent figure of Queen Berengaria over her tomb.

Travel details

Trains

Angers to: Le Mans (frequent; 40min–1hr 20min); Nantes (frequent; 45min); Paris (frequent; 1hr 40min); Saumur (frequent; 20–30min); Tours (frequent; 1hr–1hr 30min).
Bourges to: Nevers (8–12 daily; 50min); Orléans (9 daily; 1hr–1hr 40min); Tours (12 daily; 1hr 40min).
Le Mans to: Angers (frequent, 40min–1hr 20min); Nantes (frequent, 55min–1hr 45min); Paris (frequent; 1hr); Rennes (frequent; 2hr); Saumur (3 daily; 2hr); Tours (frequent; 1hr).
Orléans to: Beaugency (frequent; 20min); Blois (frequent; 40min); La Ferté-St-Aubin (frequent; 15–25min); Meung-sur-Loire (frequent; 15min); Paris (at least hourly; 1hr); Romorantin-Lanthenay (change at Salbris; 7 daily; 1hr 30min); Tours (frequent; 1hr–1hr 30min).
Tours to: Amboise (frequent; 20min); Azay-le-Rideau (7 daily; 30min); Blois (frequent; 40min); Chenonceaux (6 daily; 35min); Chinon (7 daily; 45min); Langeais (8 daily; 25min); Le Mans (7 daily; 1hr); Montrichard (10 daily; 30min); Orléans (frequent; 1hr–1hr 30min); Paris (hourly; 2hr 30min, TGVs via St-Pierre-des-Corps 1hr); Saumur (frequent; 45min).

Buses

Angers to: Brissac-Quincé (5–7 daily; 30min).
Blois to: Chambord (1–3 daily; 45min); Cour-Cheverny (3 daily; 35min); Romorantin-Lanthenay (3 daily; 1hr); St-Aignan (2–3 daily; 1hr 10min); Valençay (3 daily; 1hr 30min).
Bourges to: Sancerre (1–3 daily; 1hr 15min).
Orléans to: Beaugency (4–6 daily; 45min); Chartres (9 daily; 1hr 10min–1hr 45min); Germigny-des-Près (3 daily; 1hr); Gien (3 daily; 1hr 50min); Meung-sur-Loire (8 daily; 35min); St-Benoît-sur-Loire (3 daily; 1hr); Sully-sur-Loire (2–3 daily; 45min–1hr 20min).
Saumur to: Fontevraud (4–6 daily; 35min).
Tours to: Amboise (7 daily; 50min); Azay-le-Rideau (2 daily; 50min); Chinon (2 daily; 1hr 10min); Loches (12 daily; 40min); Richelieu (1–4 daily; 1hr 50min).

7

Burgundy

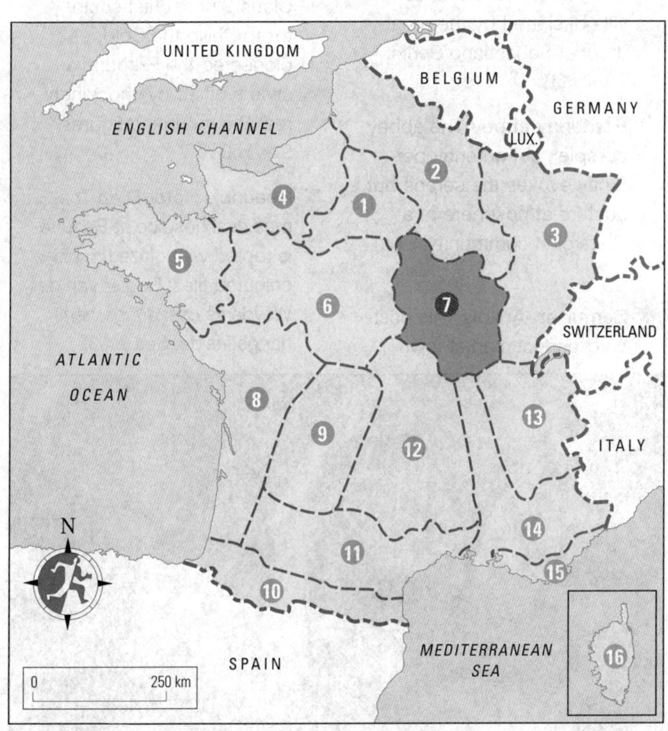

UNITED KINGDOM
BELGIUM
GERMANY
LUX.
ENGLISH CHANNEL
SWITZERLAND
ATLANTIC
OCEAN
ITALY
N
SPAIN
MEDITERRANEAN
SEA
0
250 km
1
2
3
4
5
6
7
8
9
10
11
12
13
14
15
16

CHAPTER 7 Highlights

* **à la Bourguignonne** Burgundy's richest sauces are based on the region's full-flavoured red wines; snails, on the other hand, get stewed in dry white Chablis. See p.597

* **Château d'Ancy-le-Franc** A textbook Renaissance villa designed by the great theorist Sebastiano Serlio. See p.605

* **Fontenay abbey** The abbey complex at Fontenay perfectly evokes the serene but austere atmosphere of a Cistercian community. See p.607

* **Semur-en-Auxois** This postcard-perfect market town perches above the lovely river Armançon. See p.609

* **Vézelay** The abbey of La Madeleine here is a testament to the splendour of the Romanesque period. See p.612

* **Sluteresque sculpture** Claus Sluter, chief sculptor to Philip the Bold, pioneered the Burgundian style typified by shockingly realistic mourning figures. See p.630

* **Beaune's Hôtel-Dieu** The medieval hospice at Beaune is roofed with glazed, multicoloured tiles; Rogier van der Weyden's *Last Judgement* hangs inside. See p.633

△ Tonnerre tomb

7

Burgundy

Peaceful, rural **Burgundy** is one of the most prosperous regions in modern France, but for centuries its powerful dukes remained independent of the French crown. During the Hundred Years War, they even sided with the English, selling them the captured Joan of Arc. By the fifteenth century their power extended over all of Franche-Comté, Alsace and Lorraine, Belgium, Holland, Picardy and Flanders, and their state was the best organized and richest in Europe, its revenues equalled only by Venice. It finally fell to the French kings only when Duke Charles le Téméraire (the Bold) was killed besieging Nancy in 1477.

There's evidence everywhere of this former wealth and power, both secular and religious: in the dukes' capital of **Dijon**, in the great abbeys of **Vézelay** and **Fontenay**, in the ruins of the monastery of **Cluny** (whose abbots' influence was second only to the pope's), and in the châteaux of **Tanlay** and **Ancy**.

Because of its monastic foundations, Burgundy became – along with Poitou and Provence – one of the great church-building areas in the Middle Ages. Practically every village has its Romanesque church, especially in the country around Cluny and Paray-le-Monial. It's hard not to believe that this had something to do with its illustrious Roman past, so visible in the substantial Roman remains at **Autun**. And the history goes back further: **Bibracte**, on the atmospheric hill of Mont-Beuvray, was an important Gallic capital, and **Alésia** was the scene of Julius Caesar's epic victory over the Gauls in 52 BC. In more modern times the rustic backwater of **Le Creusot** became a powerhouse of the Industrial Revolution, with the manufacture of railway engines, artillery pieces and nuclear boilers, using the ample forests and iron-ore deposits to fuel the forges.

For voluptuaries, **wine** is, of course, the region's most obvious attraction, and devotees head straight for the great **vineyards**, whose produce has played the key role in the local economy since Louis XIV's doctor prescribed wine as a palliative for the royal dyspepsia. If you lack the funds to indulge your taste for expensive drink, go in September or October when the *vignerons* are recruiting harvesters.

Between bouts of gastronomic indulgence, you can engage in some moderate activity: for **walkers** there's a wide range of hikes, from the gentle to the relatively demanding, in the **Parc Régional du Morvan** and the **Côte d'Or**. There are also several long-distance canal paths, which make great **bike** trips. As for the waterways themselves, aficionados rate most highly the **Canal de Bourgogne** and the **Canal du Nivernais**, both of which can be cruised by rented barge; contact the Comité Régional du Tourisme de Bourgogne, BP 1602, 21035 Dijon (Ⓣ03.80.28.02.80, Ⓦwww.burgundy-tourism.com/fleuve).

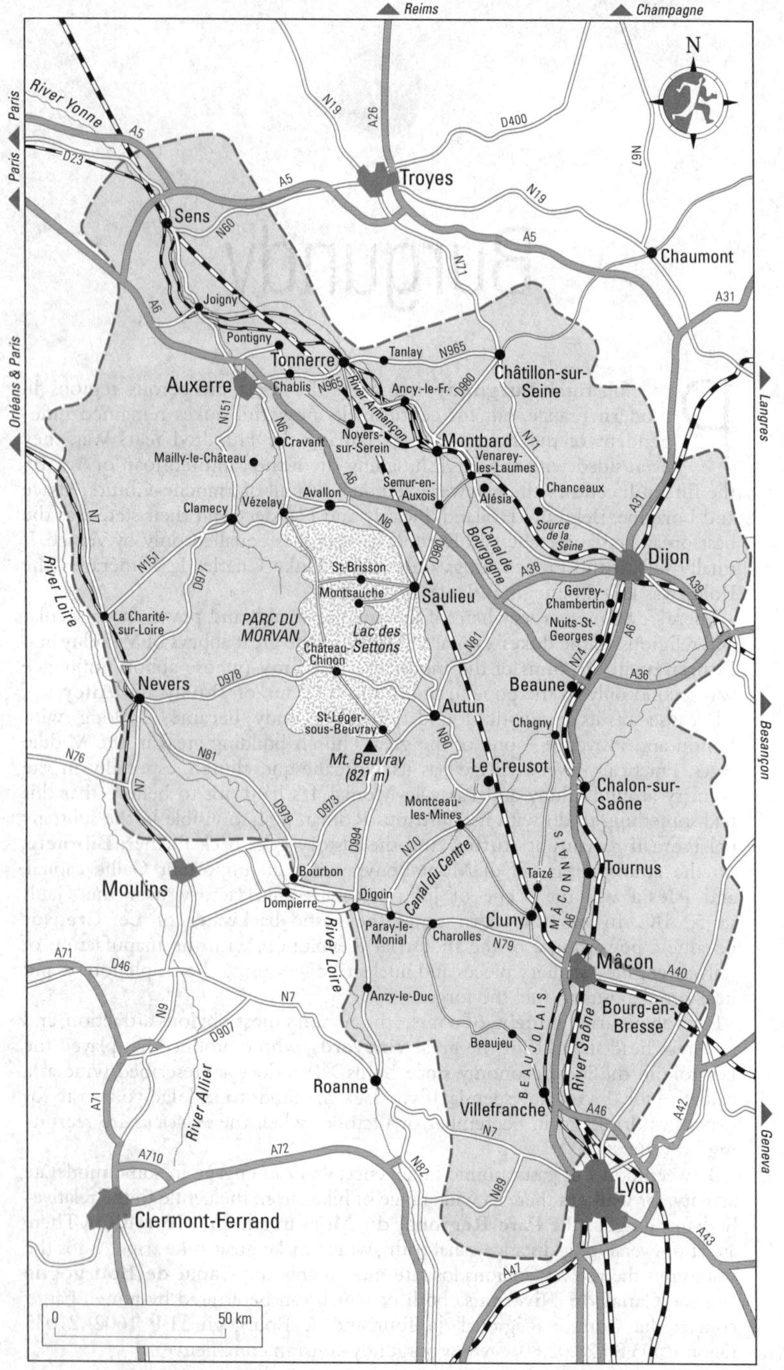
Reims
Champagne
N
Paris
Paris
Orléans & Paris
Langres
Besançon
Geneva
River Yonne
A5
D23
N19
A26
D400
N67
Troyes
A5
N19
A5
Sens
N60
N71
Chaumont
A31
A6
Joigny
Pontigny
Tonnerre
Tanlay
N965
Châtillon-sur-Seine
Auxerre
Chablis
N965
River Armançon
D980
Ancy.-le-Fr.
N151
N6
Cravant
Noyers-sur-Serein
Montbard
N71
Mailly-le-Château
Venarey-les-Laumes
Semur-en-Auxois
Alésia
Chanceaux
Source de la Seine
A31
Avallon
A6
Clamecy
Vézelay
N6
Canal de Bourgogne
N7
D980
Dijon
A38
A39
N151
D977
River Loire
St-Brisson
Montsauche
Saulieu
Gevrey-Chambertin
La Charité-sur-Loire
PARC DU MORVAN
Lac des Settons
Nuits-St-Georges
Château-Chinon
N81
A6
N74
A36
Nevers
D978
Beaune
Autun
St-Léger-sous-Beuvray
Mt. Beuvray (821 m)
N80
Chagny
N76
N81
Le Creusot
N7
D979
D973
Chalon-sur-Saône
Montceau-les-Mines
D994
N70
Canal du Centre
MÂCONNAIS
Moulins
Bourbon
Taizé
Tournus
Dompierre
Digoin
Paray-le-Monial
Charolles
Cluny
A6
River Loire
N79
A71
D46
Mâcon
A40
N9
N7
Anzy-le-Duc
BEAUJOLAIS
Bourg-en-Bresse
D907
Beaujeu
River Saône
Roanne
A71
River Allier
Villefranche
A46
A42
N7
A710
A72
N82
N89
Lyon
Clermont-Ferrand
A43
A47
0
50 km

The food of Burgundy

The **cuisine** of Burgundy is known for its richness, due in large part to two factors: the region's heavy red wines and its possession of one of the world's finest breeds of beef cattle, the Charollais. The **wines** are used in the preparation of the sauces which earn a dish the designation of *à la bourguignonne*. Essentially, this means cooked in a red wine sauce to which baby onions, mushrooms and *lardons* (pieces of bacon) are added. The classic Burgundy dishes cooked in this manner are *bœuf bourguignon* and *coq au vin*. Another term which frequently appears on menus is *meurette*, also a red wine sauce but made without mushrooms and flambéed with a touch of marc brandy. It's used with eggs, fish and poultry as well as red meat.

Snails (*escargots*) are hard to avoid in Burgundy, and the local style of cooking them involves stewing for several hours in the white wine of Chablis with shallots, carrots and onions, then stuffing them with a butter of garlic and parsley and finishing them off in the oven. **Other specialities** include the parsley-flavoured ham (*jambon persillé*); hams from the Morvan hills cooked in a cream *saupiquet* sauce; calf's head (*tête de veau*, or *sansiot*); a *pauchouse* of river fish (that is, poached in white wine with onions, butter, garlic and *lardons*); a *poussin* from Bresse; a saddle of hare (*rable de lièvre à la Piron*); and a *potée bourguignonne*, or soup of vegetables cooked in the juices of long-simmered bacon and pork bits.

Like other regions of France, Burgundy produces a variety of **cheeses**. The best-known are the creamy white Chaource, the soft St-Florentin from the Yonne valley, the orange-skinned Époisses and the delicious goat's cheeses from the Morvan. And then there is *gougère*, a kind of cheesecake, best eaten warm with a glass of Chablis.

The road to Dijon

The old **road to Dijon**, the Nationale 6, runs from Paris down to the Côte d'Azur, the route taken by the National Guardsmen of Marseille when they marched on Paris singing the *Marseillaise* in 1792. It enters the province of Burgundy just south of Fontainebleau, near where the River Yonne joins the Seine, and follows the Yonne valley through the historic towns of **Sens**, **Joigny** and **Auxerre**. Scattered in a broad corridor to the west and east of the road, in the valleys of the Yonne's tributaries, the Armançon, Serein, Cure and Cousin rivers, is a fascinating collection of abbeys, châteaux, towns, villages and other sites as ancient as the history of France. It makes for a route far more interesting, albeit slower, than speeding around the bland curves of its modern replacement, the **Autoroute du Soleil** (A6), entrance to which requires a modest toll payment.

Sens

The name of **SENS**, the northernmost town in Burgundy, commemorates the Senones, the Gallic tribe whose shaggy troops all but captured Rome in 390 BC; they were only thwarted by the Capitoline geese cackling and waking the garrison. Its heyday as a major ecclesiastical centre was in the twelfth and thirteenth centuries, but it lost its pre-eminence in the ensuing centuries largely through damage caused by the Hundred Years War and the Wars of Religion. Nowadays, it is a quiet and unexciting place on the banks of the River Yonne, although the cathedral, its treasury and the adjacent museum make a stop worthwhile.

The Town

Contained within a ring of tree-lined boulevards where the city walls once stood, the town's ancient centre is still dominated by the **Cathédrale St-Étienne** (daily except Sun morning: April–Oct 7.30am–7pm; Nov–March 8am–6pm) close to the intersection of Grande-Rue and rue de la République, which, together with their prolongations, neatly quarter the town centre. Begun around 1130, it was the first of the great French Gothic cathedrals, and having been built without flying buttresses – these were added later for stability – its profile is relatively wide and squat. The architect who completed it, William of Sens, went on to rebuild the choir of Canterbury Cathedral in England – the link being Thomas Becket, who had previously spent several years in exile around Sens. The story of Thomas's murder is told in the twelfth-century windows in the north aisle of the choir, just part of the cathedral's outstanding collection of stained glass. Facing each other at either end of the transepts, the fine rose windows depict the Last Judgement and Paradise. The **treasury**, which can be entered either from the cathedral or the museum (see below for times), is also uncommonly rich, containing Islamic, Byzantine and French vestments – including those belonging to Thomas Becket – jewels and embroideries.

Next door is the thirteenth-century **Palais Synodal**, with its roof of Burgundian glazed tiles restored by the nineteenth-century "purist" Viollet-le-Duc, as were those of so many other buildings in this region. Its vaulted halls, originally designed to accommodate the ecclesiastical courts, now house the excellent **Musée de Sens** (July & Aug daily 10am–6pm; June & Sept daily 10am–noon & 2–6pm; Oct–May Tues–Fri 2–6pm, Wed, Sat & Sun 10am–noon & 2–6pm; €2.60), which makes use of all available space to display a prize collection of artifacts found in the region, including statuary from the cathedral and Gallo-Roman mosaics. Prize exhibits include the Villethierry treasure, which consists of 867 items of bronze jewellery in a jar, and is thought to be a jeweller's hoard; a collection of bone combs; and the facade of Sens' second-century public baths. The vaults of the building – partly constituting the remains of a Gallo-Roman building, including baths heated through the pavement – have also been incorporated into the museum, along with displays of Gallo-Roman metalwork, jewellery and textile crafts, many of which were discovered when the basement was excavated. Bilingual guided tours of the cathedral, treasury and museum are led in French and English, afternoons from June until the end of August (€4).

Facing the cathedral across place de la République are fine wood and iron *halles*, where a **market** is held on Monday, Friday and Saturday mornings. The square stands right in the centre of town and is intersected by the two main streets, **rue de la République** and **Grande-Rue**, lined with old houses now converted into shops, and mainly reserved for pedestrians. There are three particularly finely carved and timbered houses on the corner of rue Jean-Cousin one block south of the square: the **Maison d'Abraham** and the **Maison du Pilier**, with **Maison Jean Cousin** on rue du Général-Alix.

Practicalities

From the **gare SNCF**, Grande-Rue crosses over the two broad arms of the River Yonne and leads straight to the place de la République and the cathedral, about fifteen minutes' walk. The **tourist office** is a booth on place Jean-Jaurès (July & Aug Mon–Sat 9am–12.30pm & 1.30–7pm, Sun 10am–12.30pm & 2–5.30pm; Sept–June Mon–Fri 9am–noon & 1.30–6.15pm, Sat 9am–noon & 1.30–5.15pm; Ⓣ03.86.65.19.49, Ⓦwww.office-de-tourisme-sens.com), just north of the Hôtel de Ville, where rue de la République becomes rue Leclerc.

For **places to stay**, try the simple *Esplanade*, 2 bd du Mail (Ⓣ03.86.83.14.70, Ⓕ03.86.83.14.71; ❷; closed Sun & Aug), above a bar at the east end of place Jean-Jaurès, or the nearby *Croix-Blanche*, 9 rue Victor-Guichard (Ⓣ03.86.64.00.02; ❷), offering slightly dingier but acceptable rooms. Close to the cathedral, and a cut above the others, is the recently restored old-time-feel *Hôtel de Paris et de la Poste*, 97 rue de la République (Ⓣ03.86.65.17.43, Ⓦwww.hotel-paris-poste.com; ❹), with an excellent restaurant specializing in traditional country cuisine (menus €20–30). The local **campsite**, *Entre-deux-Vannes*, is on avenue de Sénigallia (Ⓣ03.86.65.64.71; closed Nov–March), just out of town.

For **eating**, you'll find pizza, Mexican and French food on place de la République, which is also the place for a coffee or drink. There's a good crêperie, *Au P'tit Creux*, 3 rue de Brennus, almost on the doorstep of the cathedral, while excellent seafood can be had at *Le Soleil Levant*, 51 rue Emile-Zola (Ⓣ03.86.65.71.82; closed Sun & Wed eve & Aug; menus €11.50–27).

Joigny

As you travel from Sens towards Auxerre, the next place of any size on the Yonne is the modest town of **JOIGNY**, its elegant old houses ranged up the slope above the river. The first fort was constructed here at the end of the tenth century, with houses built beneath it, though much of the original settlement was destroyed by a fire in 1530. The town is not worth a prolonged visit, but makes a pleasant rest stop, particularly on market days (Wed & Sat). Buildings worthy of attention are the **Château des Gondi**, built by Cardinal Gondi in the sixteenth century and wilfully Classical, and the remains of the twelfth-century **ramparts** on Chemin de la Guimbard. The **église St-Jean** is a hybrid of styles, with Gothic piers and arches rising to an Italianate clerestory level, above which the elaborate vault was added in 1596. A few half-timbered houses that somehow escaped the 1530 fire can be seen on **rue Montant-au-Palais**, the street leading up to the church of St-Jean, including the best-known **Maison du Pilori**, combining Gothic and Renaissance styles, with some carvings strangely reminiscent of crocodile heads. On place Jean de Joigny, the main beam supporting the **Maison de l'Arbre de Jessé** illustrates Christ's family tree, with worn, tendril-like branches adorned with figures from the Old Testament.

The helpful **tourist office** is at 4 quai Ragobert (July & Aug Mon–Sat 9am–12.30pm & 2–7pm, Sun 10am–1pm; Sept–June Mon 2–5/6pm, Tues–Sat 9am–noon & 2–5/6pm; Ⓣ03.86.62.11.05, Ⓦwww.tourisme-joigny.fr.fm), by the **gare routière**. There are no hotels in the old town, but the simple, adequate *L'Escargot de Sab*, 1 av Roger-Varrey (Ⓣ03.86.62.10.38; ❶), is just back from the river, at the southeast corner of town, and the *Relais Paris-Nice*, Rond Point de la Résistance (Ⓣ03.86.62.06.72, Ⓕ03.86.62.56.99; ❷; closed Sun evening & Mon) is on the south side of the river, near the train station. The nicest place, both to stay and eat, is 6km west of town, along the D182 towards St-Julien-du-Sault – *Le P'tit Claridge*, in Thèmes (Ⓣ03.86.63.10.92, Ⓕ03.86.63.01.34; ❸; closed Jan & Feb), with rooms full of charm and a restaurant offering a very good-value menu (closed Sun evening, Mon, Jan & Feb).

An interesting side trip from Joigny, located about 45 minutes away by car, is the village of **ST-SAUVEUR-EN-PUISAYE**, the birthplace, in 1873, of Colette. The **Musée Colette** is in the château (April–Sept daily except Tues 10am–6pm; Oct–March Sat & Sun 2–6pm; €4.30) and includes a reconstruction of her apartment in Paris, as well as personal items and original manuscripts.

Auxerre and around

A pretty old town of narrow lanes and unexpected open squares, **AUXERRE** stands on a hill a further 15km up the Yonne from Joigny. It looks its best from Pont Paul-Bert and the riverside **quais**, where houseboats and barges moor, its churches soaring dramatically and harmoniously above the surrounding rooftops. The most interesting of the churches is the disused abbey church of **St Germain**, now a museum (daily except Tues: June–Sept 10am–6.30pm; Oct–May 10am–noon & 2–6pm; €4.20), at the opposite end of rue Cauchois from the cathedral. Partial demolition has left its belfry detached from the body of the building, but what gives it special interest is the **crypt**, one of the few surviving examples of Carolingian architecture, with its plain barrel vaults still resting on their thousand-year-old oak beams. Deep inside, the faded ochre frescoes of St Stephen (St Étienne) are among the most ancient in France, dating back to around 850 AD.

The **cathedral** itself (daily except Sun morning: April–Oct 7.30am–7pm; Nov–March 7.30am–5.30pm) still remains unfinished, despite the fact that its construction was drawn out over more than three centuries from 1215 to 1560: the southernmost of the two west front towers has never been completed. Compensation for this lies in the richly detailed sculpture of the porches and in the glorious colours of the original thirteenth-century glass that still fills the windows of the choir, despite the savagery of the Wars of Religion and the Revolution. There has been a church on the site since about 400 AD, though nothing visible survives earlier than the eleventh-century **crypt** (€2.50). Among its frescoes is a unique depiction of a warrior Christ mounted on a white charger, accompanied by four mounted angels.

From in front of the cathedral, rue Fourier leads to place du Marché and off left to the Hôtel de Ville and the old city gateway known as the **Tour de l'Horloge**, with its fifteenth-century coloured clock face. The whole quarter, from place Surugue through rue Joubert and down to the river, is full of attractive old houses. Of somewhat specialist interest, the **Musée Leblanc-Duvernoy**, in an eighteenth-century *hôtel* at 9 rue Egleny, contains a collection of faïence and china of local provenance, furniture and tapestries (daily except Tues 2–6pm; €2, or same ticket as St Germain).

If you're finding the narrow streets a bit confining, then take a stroll to the **Clos de Chaînette**, off to the northeast, the only vineyard in Auxerre to be spared in the phylloxera beetle disaster which decimated France's vines in the nineteenth century.

Practicalities

Arriving by train at the **gare SNCF** in rue Paul-Doumer, you'll find yourself across the river from the town: follow signs for the *centreville*, crossing Pont Paul-Bert. The **tourist office** is by the bridge at 2 quai de la République (mid-June to mid-Sept Mon–Fri 9am–1pm & 2–7pm, Sun 9.30am–1pm & 3–6.30pm; mid-Sept to mid-June Mon–Sat 9.30am–12.30pm & 2–6pm, Sun 10am–1pm; ⓣ03.86.52.06.19, ⓦwww.ot-auxerre.fr), with an annexe in place des Cordeliers in summer. The **gare routière** lies in place des Migraines off the *boulevard périphérique*. There's a **market** in place de l'Arquebuse (Tues & Fri morning), and another on the *périphérique* at the end of rue du Temple (Wed morning).

For central **accommodation**, try the simple and inexpensive *Hôtel de la Renommée*, 27 rue d'Egleny (ⓣ03.86.52.03.53, ⓕ03.86.51.47.83; ❶; closed Sun & three weeks in Aug), whose restaurant has lunch menus from €10; or the comfortable and friendly *Hôtel le Seignelay*, 2 rue du Pont (ⓣ03.86.52.03.48, ⓦwww.leseignelay.com; ❸; closed Feb), with a good little restaurant in its courtyard. Down by the river, the elegant *Maxime*, 2 quai de la Marine (ⓣ03.86.52.14.19, ⓔhotel-maxime@ipoint.fr; ❺; closed mid-Dec to Jan), has an excellent €33 menu in its restaurant. Just outside the old town centre, the *Hôtel Normandie*, 41 bd Vauban (ⓣ03.86.52.57.80, ⓦwww.hotelnormandie.fr; ❹), is a fairly luxurious chain hotel with lots of amenities, including 24hr sauna and billiards. For **hostel**-style accommodation (€13 for a bare-bones, shared-bath single including breakfast), there's a *foyer* at 16 bd Vaulabelle (ⓣ03.86.52.45.38), at the back of the courtyard of the Peugeot and Citroën garage, on the southern side of the ring road. There's also a pleasant municipal **campsite**, south at 8 rte de Vaux (ⓣ03.86.52.11.15; closed Oct–March), next to the riverside football ground.

For somewhere to **eat**, try *Le Bistrot du Palais*, 69 rue de Paris (ⓣ03.86.51.47.02; closed Mon, Sun & Aug), a lively place with a changing menu from €10. *Le Saint Pélerin*, 56 rue St-Pélerin, near the Pont Paul-Bert (ⓣ03.86.52.77.05; closed Sun, Mon & three weeks in Aug), has an excellent traditional menu at €22, while *Le Quai*, in the very pretty place St-Nicholas, beside the river, does pizzas and *plats du jour* at lunchtime for around €12. Top of the range in culinary terms, is the imaginative *Le Jardin Gourmand*, 56 bd Vauban (ⓣ03.86.51.53.52; closed Tues & Wed), where the least expensive menu comes in at €40 (though they admittedly give you a lot of food for your money). Should you tire of continental cuisine, *Le Royal D'Auxerre*, 47 bl Vouban (ⓣ03.86.42.96.30), serves well-priced pan-Asian dishes.

Around Auxerre

On or close to the D965 and the Paris–Dijon train route in the open, rolling country east of Auxerre lie several minor attractions, ranging from Greek treasures to Cistercian abbeys and Renaissance châteaux. The valley of the aptly named Serein River is the location of the villages of **Pontigny**, of monastic origin, **Chablis**, famed for its excellent vineyards, and the time-locked **Noyers-sur-Serein**; while to the south, a string of villages along the **upper valley of the Yonne** provides a glimpse of a gentler, more intimate countryside.

Pontigny

The ravages of time – in particular the 1789 Revolution – have destroyed most of the great monastic buildings of the Cistercian order of monks, whose rigorous insistence on simplicity and manual labour under their most influential twelfth-century leader, St Bernard, was a revolutionary response to the worldliness and luxury of the Benedictine abbots of Cluny. The only places in Burgundy where you can get an idea of how Cistercian ideas translated into bricks and mortar are at Pontigny and Fontenay.

PONTIGNY lies 18km northeast of Auxerre, and its beautifully preserved twelfth-century **abbey church** stands on the edge of the village, where its functional mass rises from the meadows. There's no tower, no stained glass and no statuary to distract from its austere, harmonious lines, though the effect is marred by the seventeenth-century choir that occupies much of the nave. Built through the 1100s, it spans the transition between the old Romanesque and the new Gothic, and was much copied in the country round about – in Chablis, for example.

Three Englishmen played a major role in the abbey's early history, all of them archbishops of Canterbury: Thomas Becket took refuge from Henry II in the abbey in 1164, Stephen Langton similarly hid here during an argument over his eligibility for the primacy from 1207 to 1213, and Edmund Rich retired here in 1240 after unsuccessfully trying to stand up to Henry III. The abbey was also the origin of a tourist attraction with which a nearby village is more often associated: the famous **Chablis wine**. It was the monks of Pontigny who originally developed and refined the variety, and the village and its unassuming neighbouring hamlets are better places to sample the wine than in the expensive bars of Chablis itself.

There's a simple **hotel-restaurant** in Pontigny: the *Relais de Pontigny* on the N77 (Ⓣ03.86.47.96.74; ❶), but, with more cash, it's better to go for the comfortable *Relais St-Vincent*, 14 Grande-Rue in nearby **LIGNY-LE-CHATEL**, 4km along the D91 (Ⓣ03.86.47.53.38, Ⓔrelais.saint.vincent@libertysurf.fr; ❸; restaurant from €12.50). Ligny also has a **campsite** by the Serein off the D8 Auxerre road (mid-May to Sept).

Chablis

Sixteen kilometres to the south of Pontigny on winding, rural D965, the pretty red-roofed village of **CHABLIS** is the home of the region's famous light dry white wines. It lies in the valley of the River Serein between the wide and mainly treeless upland wheat fields typical of this corner of Burgundy. While wandering around the village you could take a look at the side door of the **church of St-Martin**, decorated with ancient horseshoes and other bits of rustic ironwork left as *ex votos* by visiting pilgrims. Legend has it that Joan of Arc was one of them.

The **tourist office** (Maison de la Vigne et du Vin) is just over the Serein bridge at 3 rue du Maréchal de Lattre de Tassigny (April–Nov daily 10am–12.30pm & 1.30–6pm; Dec–March Sun 10am–1pm; Ⓣ03.86.42.80.80, Ⓦwww.chablis.net). If you need to **stay** the night, try the nearby *Relais de la Belle Etoile*, 4 rue des Moulins (Ⓣ03.86.18.96.08, Ⓕ03.86.42.81.21, Ⓔberger-and-belleetoile@wanadoo.fr; ❸; closed Sun evening, Mon in winter & Jan), a charming bed & breakfast-style hotel. A slightly more luxurious, if predictable, choice is the *Hostellerie des Clos*, rue Jules-Rathier (Ⓣ03.86.42.10.63, Ⓕ03.86.42.17.11, Ⓦwww.hostellerie-des-clos.fr; ❹), complete with a pricey restaurant. There's also an attractive **campsite**, the *Camping de Chablis* (Ⓣ03.86.42.44.39; June–Sept), beside the river just outside the village. For **food**, *Le Vieux Moulin*, 18 rue des Moulins (Ⓣ03.86.42.47.30), is good, with menus ranging from €16 to €39. Alternatively, *Bistro des Grand Clus*, 8 rue Jules-Rathier, serves spartan but very affordable menus starting at €9.50, including your choice of wine.

Chablis: the wine

The neatly staked **Chablis** vineyards, originally planted by the monks of Pontigny (see p.601), cover the sunny, well-drained, stony slopes on both sides of the valley. The grape is the *chardonnay*, which is to white wine what the *pinot noir* is to red: raw material of all the greatest Burgundies. To taste the wines, avoid Chablis itself: the town milks its product for all it's worth. Overpriced wine bars and stuffy restaurants abound, meaning you don't get the opportunity to taste the cheaper varieties, and there's haughty disapproval if you hope to spend less than €15 a bottle. You'd be better off heading for the co-operative, **La Chablisienne**, 8 bd Pasteur (Mon–Sat 8am–noon & 2–6pm, Sun 9.30am–noon & 2–6pm; ⓣ03.86.42.89.89, ⓦwww.chablisienne.com), which offers maximum variety in a casual environment – better still, drink in one of the other villages like Pontigny or Maligny. If you want to buy a good wine, go for one with an *appellation*; the seven distinguished *grands crus*, from the northern slopes of the valley, are the best, with the *premiers crus*, made from more widely planted grapes, next in line.

Noyers-sur-Serein

Twenty-three kilometres to the southeast of Chablis – there's no choice but to hitch if you don't have your own transport – you come to the beautiful little town of **NOYERS-SUR-SEREIN**, sealed from the modern world in a medieval time warp. Its half-timbered and arcaded houses, ornamented with rustic carvings – particularly those on place de la Petite-Étape-aux-Vins and round place de l'Hôtel-de-Ville – are corralled inside a loop of the river and the town walls, and pleasant hours can be passed wandering the path between the river and the irregular walls, with their robust towers. The Serein here is as pretty as in Chablis, but Noyers, being remarkably free of commercialism, has more charm.

The town's main sight is the **Musée de Noyers** (June–Sept daily except Tues 11am–6.30pm; Oct–Dec & Feb–May Sat & Sun only 2.30–6.30pm; €4), comprising the remarkable collection of art historian Jacques Yankel. The Naive painters had no formal training and were often workers lacking academic education (one, Augustine Lesage, worked as a miner for sixty years before he started painting). Some star exhibits include Gérard Lattier's morbid comic-strip-style work, the excellent collages of Louis Quilici and dreamy early twentieth century paintings of Jacques Lagrange. If you're in shape, you might want to attempt the hike up to the **Chateau Vieux** after visiting the museum; the ruins of the twelfth century castle are in the midst of a slow restoration, but the site offers a beautiful panorama over the town. To reach the dilapidated castle, turn right just before the town entrance archway.

The best place to **stay** is the creeper-covered seventeenth-century *Hôtel de la Vieille Tour* in place du Grenier-à-Sel in the town centre (ⓣ03.86.82.87.69, ⓕ03.86.82.66.04; ❸). The Dutch-owned establishment offers ten beautifully furnished rooms rife with personality and views across the gardens to the river; it's also the best place to eat (excellent *table d'hôte* meal for €15), though reservations are essential for dinner. At the entrance to the village the *Porte Peinte* restaurant (ⓣ03.86.82.81.07, closed in winter) has a single menu at €18; they frequently offer live piano music in the evenings.

The valley of the Yonne

If you're travelling south from Auxerre and want a break from the main roads, head along the D163, a twisting minor road which follows the course of the

River Yonne through a score of peaceful rural villages. Several have places both to stay and eat, making for a much more restful overnight stop than the towns.

VAUX and **ESCOLIVES-STE-CAMILLE**, the first villages you come to, both have attractive Romanesque churches. **VINCELOTTES** and **IRANCY**, on the opposite bank of the river, are flower-decked and picturesque: Irancy produces the only red wine in this area, much loved by Louis XIV, while Vincelottes was the port for shipping it.

A nice place to stay hereabouts is *Le Castel*, a *chambre d'hôte* on place de l'Église in **MAILLY-LE-CHÂTEAU**, a further 10km along the river (Ⓣ03.86.81.43.06, Ⓕ03.86.81.49.26, Ⓦwww.lecastelmailly.com; ❹), which offers an excellent *table d'hôte* for €30, including wine. The main part of the village is on high ground above the river, but there's also a lovely riverside quarter, with ancient houses huddling under cliffs.

Half a dozen kilometres further upstream, more cliffs (the **Rochers du Saussois**) flank the east bank of the river. About 50m high, they are a series of broken rock walls, ideal for rock climbing – which is indeed what they are used for, with routes of all sorts of different grades. From here south to Clamecy, the river is at its most attractive, becoming more and more of a mountain stream.

The Canal de Bourgogne

From Migennes near Joigny on the N6, the River Armançon, in tandem with the **Canal de Bourgogne**, branches off to the north of the River Yonne. Along or close to its valley are several places of real interest: the Renaissance châteaux of **Ancy-le-Franc** and **Tanlay**, **Fontenay abbey**, and the site of Julius Caesar's victory over the Gauls at **Alésia**. Just east of the Canal, perched above the River Armançon as it flows through a miniature gorge, is the exquisitely picturesque town of **Semur-en-Auxois**.

Further east the Canal encompasses the upper reaches of the River Seine: at **Châtillon-sur-Seine** is the famous Celtic Treasure of Vix, and you can trace the river south as far as its source.

Tonnerre and around

On the Paris–Sens–Dijon TGV train route, **TONNERRE** is a useful, though not that inspiring, starting point for exploring this corner of the region. A rundown little town that has clearly not enjoyed the same prosperity as its neighbour Chablis, it has as its principal sight the vast and well-conserved medieval hospital, the **Hôtel-Dieu** (hourly guided tours: June–Sept daily except Tues 10.30am–12.30pm & 1.30–6.30pm; April, May & Oct Sat & Sun only 1–6pm; €3.80), right on the main road in the middle of town. The late thirteenth-century building is dominated by the staggering curve of a huge boat's-keel roof in pale oak, but it's otherwise mostly empty, apart from occasional exhibitions. A gnomon line traced on the floor allowed the calculation of astronomic time, but the real draw lurks in the small chapel at the far end, where there's an expressive and realistic *Entombment of Christ* in the Burgundian style pioneered by Claus Sluter.

A couple of blocks from the hospital, the **Hôtel d'Uzès** saw the birth of Tonnerre's quirkiest claim to fame, an eighteenth-century gentleman with the fittingly excessive moniker Charles-Geneviève-Louis-Auguste-André-Timothé Déon de Beaumont (b.1728). He tickled his contemporaries' prurience by going about his important diplomatic missions for King Louis XV dressed in women's clothes. His act was so convincing that while he was in London bookmakers took bets on his real sex. Oddly enough, he was also a fearsome swordsman, though history does not relate what he wore to fight in. When he died, the results of the autopsy were eagerly awaited by the gossip columnists of the day.

A pleasant stroll up to the top end of town takes you to the **Fosse Dionne**, a curious blue-green pool encircled by an eighteenth-century *lavoir*, or washing place. A number of legends are attached to the spring (the name derives from Divona, Celtic goddess of water), one of which holds that it was the lair of a ferocious serpent slain by a local saint – a tale which may refer to the draining of the malarial marshes. The alarming hole at the bottom is popularly supposed to lead to hell, and divers have penetrated 360m along a narrow underwater passageway with no end in sight. Further exploration is now banned as three divers have died in exploration attempts.

The **tourist office** is at 12 rue François Mitterrand (April–Oct Mon–Sat 9am–12.30pm & 2–6.30pm, Sun 10am–12pm & 2–5pm; Nov–March closed Sun; ⓣ03.86.55.14.48, ⓦwww.tonnerre.fr). The least expensive **accommodation** is at the *Hôtel du Centre*, 65 rue de l'Hôpital (ⓣ03.86.55.10.56, ⓕ03.86.51.10.63; ❷), an old-fashioned provincial hotel with a reasonable little **restaurant** (menus from €12). For real luxury, try *L'Abbaye Saint Michel*, montée St-Michel (ⓣ03.86.55.05.99, ⓕ03.86.55.00.10; ❽), which sits spectacularly atop the town in an orchard of green serenity. Overlooking the spring, the woody *Ferme de la Fosse* Dionne, 11 rue de la Fosse Dionne (ⓣ03.86.54.82.62, ⓦwww.fermefossedionne.com; ❸), offers spotless *chambres d'hôtes*, breakfast included. The local **campsite**, *La Cascade* (ⓣ03.86.55.15.44; closed Oct–mid-April), is between the River Armançon and the Canal de Bourgogne. *Ankara*, a popular local hangout on rue de l'Hôpital in the centre, has decent kebabs for €3.50.

The châteaux of Ancy-le-Franc and Tanlay

Close to Tonnerre are two of the finest, though least-known and least-visited, châteaux in France: Ancy-le-Franc and Tanlay. The former has the edge for architectural purity, the latter for romantic appeal. There's no longer any public transport from Tonnerre, but if you turn up at the *gare SNCF* 24 hours in advance you can **book a taxi** for the same price per kilometre as for a train journey of equivalent length.

The **Château d'Ancy-le-Franc**, 25km from Tonnerre, was built in the mid-sixteenth century for the brother-in-law of the notorious Diane de Poitiers, mistress of Henri II (guided tours daily except Mon: April–Oct hourly at 10.30am, 11.30am & 2–4pm; June–Aug also 5pm; €6; ⓦwww.chateau-ancy.com). More Italian than French, with its textbook classical countenance, it is the only accepted work of the Italian Sebastiano Serlio, one of the most important architectural theorists of the Renaissance, who was brought to France in 1540 by François I to work on his palace at Fontainebleau. The exterior is rather austere and forbidding, but the inner courtyard is an utterly refined embodiment of the principles of classical architecture. Some of the apartments are sumptuous, decorated by the Italian artists Primaticcio and Niccolò dell'Abbate, who also worked at Fontainebleau. The most impressive rooms are La Chambre des Arts, with medallions by Primaticcio, and La Galerie des Sacrifices, with monumental battle scenes in monochrome by Abbate. Ancy has just one small **hotel**, the modernized *Hostellerie du Centre*, 34 Grande-Rue (ⓣ03.86.75.15.11, ⓦwww.diaphora.com/hostellerieducentre; ❸; good restaurant from €15), which has a tiny indoor heated swimming pool. The brasserie at *Bar du Chateau*, 12 Place Clermont Tonnerre, serves a *plat du jour* for €10.

The **Château de Tanlay** (guided tours daily except Tues: April to mid-Nov hourly 9.30–11.30am, every 45min 2.15–5.15pm; €7), 8km from Tonnerre, is by contrast much more French and full of *fantaisie*. It's only slightly later in date, about 1559, but those extra few years were enough for the purer Italian influences visible in Ancy to have become Frenchified. It also feels much more feudal, the village crouching humbly at its gate and its approach road – a long straight tree-lined avenue – like a private drive, tying down the land on either side, proclaiming ownership.

Encircling the château are water-filled moats, and a wooded hill provides an effective backdrop. Standing guard over the entrance to the first grassy courtyard is the grand lodge, and it's here that you enter the château proper across a stone drawbridge. Domed and lanterned turrets terminate the wings of the *cour d'honneur*, urns line the ridge of the roof, from whose slates project carved and pedimented dormers. The white stone and round medieval towers, leftovers from the original fortress, add to the irregularity and charm. Inside, the most remarkable, if overpowering, room is the Grande Galerie, entirely covered by monochrome *trompe-l'œil* frescoes. For a bite to **eat**, *Le Bonheur Gourmand*, just next to the Château entrance, has ample menus from €15.

Châtillon-sur-Seine

For those interested in pre-Roman France, there is one compelling reason for going to **CHÂTILLON-SUR-SEINE**: the so-called **Treasure of Vix**. Housed in the town's **museum** in the Maison Philandrier, 7 rue du Bourg, close to the centre (July & Aug daily 10am–6pm; Sept–June daily except Tues 9.30am–noon & 2–5pm; €4.80), it consists of the finds from the sixth-century BC tomb of a Celtic princess buried in a four-wheeled chariot at **Vix**, 6km northwest of Châtillon. In addition to pieces of the chariot, the finds include staggeringly beautiful jewellery, Greek vases and Etruscan bowls. But the best object on show is a gloriously simple gold tiara, actually found on the princess's head, and the largest bronze vase (*krater*) of Greek origin known from antiquity. It stands an incredible 1.64m high on triple tripod legs, and around its rim is a superbly modelled high-relief frieze depicting naked hoplites and horse-drawn chariots, with Gorgons' heads for handles. How these magnificent objects found their way to such a remote place is a mystery. One explanation lies in the fact that the village ofVix is the highest navigable point on the Seine, and it's thought that the Celtic chieftains who controlled it received such gifts, possibly from traders in Cornish tin shipped south from Britain via here on its way to the Adriatic, or perhaps to the bronze workers of Bibracte, the capital of the Aedui.

The town of Châtillon has a few other points of interest. On the rocky bluff overlooking the steep-pitched roofs of the old quarter are the ruins of a **castle** and the early Romanesque **church of St Vorles**. At its foot in a luxuriantly verdant spot, a **spring** swells out of the rock to join the infant Seine.

The **tourist office** is off place Marmont (April–Oct Mon–Sat 9am–noon & 2–6pm, Sun 10am–noon; Nov–March Mon–Sat 9am–noon & 2–6pm; Ⓣ03.80.91.13.19). If you decide to **stay**, try the *Sylvia*, 9 av de la Gare (Ⓣ03.80.91.02.44, Ⓔsylviahotel@aol.com; ❸), which stands in attractive grounds and has small rooms with moderate amounts of rustic charm. There is also the more central three-star *Hôtel de la Côte d'Or*, 2 rue Charles-Ronot (Ⓣ03.80.91.13.29, Ⓕ03.80.91.29.15; ❹; closed mid-Nov to Jan), which has a good **restaurant** (from €15). Otherwise, kick back a pint of Belgian draught and scoff down a baguette (€3) along the banks of the Seine at *Pub le Splendide*, just at the bridge.

Fontenay Abbey

Six kilometres east of the small industrial town of Montbard, and accessible from the GR213 footpath, is the privately owned **Abbey of Fontenay** (daily: April–June & Sept to mid-Nov tours hourly 10am–noon & 2–5pm; July & Aug tours hourly 10am–noon & every half-hour 2–5pm; mid-Nov to March 10am–noon & 2–5pm, though no tours; €8.50). Founded in 1118, it's the only Burgundian monastery to survive intact, despite conversion to a paper mill in the early nineteenth century. It was restored in the early 1900s to its original form and is one of the most complete monastic complexes anywhere, comprising caretaker's lodge, guesthouse and chapel, dormitory, hospital, prison, bakery, kennels, dovecote and abbot's house, as well as a church, cloister, chapterhouse and even a forge.

On top of all this, the abbey's physical setting, at the head of a quiet stream-filled valley enclosed by woods of pine, fir, sycamore and beech, is superb. There's a bucolic calm about the place, particularly in the graceful cloister, and in these surroundings the spartan simplicity of Cistercian life seems utterly attractive. Hardly a scrap of decoration softens the church: even the carving on the capitals is reduced to the barest-bones outline of an acanthus leaf – the motherly statue of the Virgin arrived after St Bernard's death. There's no direct lighting in the nave, just an other-worldly glow from the square-ended apse. The effect is beautiful but daunting, the perfect structural embodiment of St Bernard's ascetic principles.

Alésia and around

One train stop south of Montbard (or 3hr on the GR213) brings you to the dull little industrial town of **VENAREY-LES-LAUMES**. It was here, or rather behind and above the town, on the flat-topped hill of Mont Auxois, that the Gauls, united for once under the leadership of Vercingétorix, made their last stand against the military might of Rome at the **Battle of Alésia** in 52 BC. Julius Caesar himself commanded the Roman army, surrounding the hilltop town with a huge double ditch and earthworks and starving the Gauls out, bloodily defeating any and all attempts at escape. Vercingétorix surrendered to save his people, was imprisoned in Rome for six years until Caesar's formal triumph and then strangled. The battle was a great turning point in the fortunes of the region. Thereafter, Gaul remained under Roman rule for four hundred years.

The **site** of Alésia, treeless and exposed, is back along the ridge 3km from the modern village of **ALISE-STE-REINE**, which overlooks Venarey from the top of Mont Auxois. Little more than the extensive layout can be seen today, and the interest of the area lies in imagined atmosphere rather than in anything concrete. The visitor centre at the battlefield is primarily a gift shop and a means of collecting the €3 entrance fee to the site. Time is better spent at the small archaeological **museum** (March–Nov daily 10am–12.30pm & 2–6pm, July & Aug 9am–12.30pm & 2–7pm; €3) in Alise-Ste-Reine, home to a plethora of artefacts found in the Gallic town of Alésia along with Caesar's earthworks (the line of them still clearly visible in aerial photographs). On the first weekend of September the martyrdom of St Reine is celebrated in a **costume procession** through the village, a custom that goes back to the year 866. St Reine was a young Christian girl who was put to death in 263 for refusing to marry the proconsul of the Gauls, Olibrius. The year of her martyrdom is held to mark the advent of Christianity in Alésia.

Directly above Alise-Ste-Reine, steps climb up to a great bronze **statue of Vercingétorix**. Erected by Napoléon III, whose influence popularized the rediscovery of France's pre-Roman roots, the statue represents Vercingétorix as a romantic Celt, half virginal Christ, half long-haired 1970s matinee idol. On the plinth is inscribed a quotation from Vercingétorix's address to the Gauls as imagined by Julius Caesar: "United and forming a single nation inspired by a single ideal, Gaul can defy the world." Napoléon signs his dedication, "Emperor of the French", inspired by a vain desire to gain legitimacy by linking his own name to that of a "legendary" Celt.

Practicalities

There's a **tourist office** in Venarey at place de Bingerbrûck (April–Sept Mon–Sat 9.30am–12.30pm & 2–7pm, Sun 10am–noon; Oct–March Mon–Sat 10am–noon & 3–6pm, Sun 10am–noon; ⓣ03.80.96.89.13), which can direct you to local **accommodation**. The most attractive local hotel is three kilometres away up in Alise-Ste-Reine, where the *Hotel-Restaurant Alésia* on rue du Miroir (ⓣ03.80.96.19.67; ❶) is a welcoming, family-run hotel with a simple restaurant; all rooms have shared baths. A little further up the street, *L'Auberge du Cheval Blanc* (ⓣ03.80.96.01.55) serves excellent regional cuisine, with menus from €26 (choose from rabbit or *foie gras de canard*); closed Mon and Tues. In Venarey, *L'Orient Express*, a popular pizza-and-kebab locale by the *gare*, serves great, inexpensive food.

The Château de Bussy-Rabutin

Eight kilometres east of Alésia, on the D954, stands the handsome **Château de Bussy-Rabutin** (guided tours daily except Mon: mid-May to mid-Sept 9.15am–noon & 2–6pm; mid-Sept to mid-May 9.15am–noon & 2–5pm; €5.50), built for Roger de Rabutin, member of the Academy in the reign of Louis XIV and a notorious womanizer. The scurrilous tales of life at the royal court told in his book *Histoires Amoureuses des Gaules* earned him a spell in the Bastille, followed by years of exile in this château, which contains some interesting portraits of great characters of the time, including the famous female beauties of the age, each underlined by an acerbic little comment such as: "The most beautiful woman of her day, less renowned for her beauty than the uses she put it to".

The source of the Seine

You'll need your own car to get to the **source of the Seine**, which lies some 15km southeast of Alésia, or be prepared to hitch to the hamlet of **COURCEAU**. From there, by road, take the D103 through the upland hamlet of St-Germain, all crumbling stone farms and barns; or, better still, because rides are unlikely, pick up the GR2 at the bridge in Courceau for a two-hour walk.

The Seine, no more than a trickle here, rises in a tight little vale of beech woods. The spring is now covered by an artificial grotto complete with a languid nymph, Sequana, spirit of the Seine. In Celtic times it was a place of worship, as is clear from the numerous votive offerings discovered there, including a neat bronze of Sequana standing in a bird-shaped boat, now in the Dijon archaeological museum. If you're here alone, it's a good place for rustic reverie, but if your arrival coincides with a coachload of Parisian day-trippers (the site belongs to the city of Paris), you'd be wise to retreat downstream. There's a

campsite at **CHANCEAUX**, 5km away on the N71 (mid-April to Sept).

Semur-en-Auxois

Thirteen kilometres west of Alésia, the small fortress town of **SEMUR-EN-AUXOIS** sits on a rocky bluff, an extraordinarily beautiful little place of cobbled lanes, medieval gateways and ancient gardens cascading down to the River Armançon. All roads here lead to place Notre-Dame, a handsome square dominated by the large thirteenth-century **church of Notre-Dame**, another Viollet-le-Duc restoration, characterized by its huge entrance porch and the narrowness of its nave. The best view is from the east in place de l'Ancienne-Comédie, past the finely sculpted north transept door (depicting the Life of Doubting Thomas), with a couple of Burgundy snails, symbol of the region's culinary traditions, carved on the flanking columns. Inside, the windows of the second chapel on the left commemorate American soldiers of World War I – Semur was the general headquarters of the 78th division, and the battlefields were not far away. In the same chapel a masterly Sluteresque polychrome *Entombment* dates from the fifteenth century, as do some fine windows, dedicated by the butchers' and drapers' guilds and illustrating their trades.

Down the street in front of the church and off to the left you come to the four sturdy towers of Semur's once powerful **castle**, all that is left after the body of the fortress was dismantled in 1602 because of its utility to enemies of the French crown. You can explore the winding streets around the castle – there's scarcely a street in town without some building of note – and continue down to the delightful stretch of river between the Pont des Minimes and the Pont Joly, from where there's a dramatic view of town. At the otherwise not very interesting town **museum** on rue J.-J.-Collenot (mid-June to mid-Sept Sat–Mon 2–6pm, Wed–Fri 10am–noon & 2–6pm; Oct–March Mon & Wed–Fri 2–5pm; April to mid-June Tues–Sun 2–6pm; €3.15), ask to see the **library**, which has a fantastic collection of illuminated manuscripts and early printed books.

Cheese connoisseurs might like to take a twelve-kilometre hop **further** west on the Avallon road to **ÉPOISSES**, not just for its village and château (July & Aug daily except Tues 10am–noon & 3–6pm; €4.80), but for its distinctive soft orange-skinned cheeses washed in *marc de Bourgogne*.

Practicalities

Semur's **tourist office** is on the small place Gaveau (mid-June to mid-Sept Mon–Sat 9am–7pm, Sun 10am–noon & 3–6pm; mid-Sept to mid-June Mon 2–5pm, Tues–Sat 9am–noon & 2–5pm; ⓣ03.80.97.05.96), at the junction of rues de l'Ancienne-Comédie, de la Liberté and Buffon, where the medieval Porte Sauvigny and Porte Guillier combine to form a single long, covered gateway. Cyber Kfé, nearby next to the hotel *Le Commerce*, has **Internet** access (Mon–Wed & Fri 7.30am–8pm, Thurs 7.30am–10pm; €4 per hour).

The least expensive **hotel rooms** in town are at *Le Commerce*, 19 rue de la Liberté (ⓣ03.80.96.64.40; ❷), 100m from the tourist office, and the *Hôtel des Gourmets*, inside the medieval city proper at 4 rue de Varenne (ⓣ03.80.97.09.41, ⓦwww.hotellesgourmets.fr.st; ❷); both have somewhat rustic rooms decked out in wood and a pleasant garden for meals; closed Mon & Tues. The latter has a good, reasonably priced **restaurant** (closed Mon, Tues & Dec). Though somewhat less stylish, the *Hôtel des Cymaises*, tucked away off a winding backstreet at 7 rue du Renaudot (ⓣ03.80.97.21.44, ⓦwww.proveis.com/lescymaises; ❸; closed Nov & Feb) provides well-furnished rooms in a grand old mansion house. The local **campsite** is at Lac-de-Pont, 3km south of town.

Decent *plats du jour* and grills can be had at *Le Saint-Vernier*, 13 rue Févret, but for something special, it's well worth wandering down to the river and the Pont des Minimes, where the *Restaurant Les Minimes* (ⓣ03.80.97.26.86; closed Sun eve & Mon; menus at €15 and €26) serves refined meals in a warm and familial atmosphere. In the heart of the old town, the patisserie-**chocolaterie** at 14 rue Buffon (closed Mon) specializes in local *semurettes*, addictive little nuggets of chocolate made without butter.

The Morvan to the Loire

The **Morvan** region lies smack in the middle of Burgundy between the valleys of the Loire and the Saône, stretching roughly from **Clamecy**, **Vézelay** and **Avallon** in the north to **Autun** and **Le Creusot** in the south. It's a land of wooded hills, close and rounded rather than mountainous, although they rise to 900m above Autun. With poor soil and pastures only good for a few cattle, villages and farms are few and far between. In the old days, wood was the main business – supplying firewood and charcoal to Paris – and large tracts of hillside are now covered in coniferous plantations. But the region's chief export has been its escaping young, helping it earn a reputation as one of the poorest and most backward regions in the country, with few resources to trade on and little inspiration for outside investment.

In fine weather it's a lush and verdant home to all manner of foliage, flora and wild animals; in foul weather it's damp, muddy, lonely and rather depressing. The creation of a **parc naturel régional** in 1970 did something to promote the area as a place for outdoor activities and refuge from commuterdom, but more than anything it was the election of François Mitterrand, local politician and mayor of **Château-Chinon** for years, as president of the Republic that rescued the Morvan from oblivion. In addition to lending it some of the glamour of his office, he took concrete steps to beef up the local economy. Plentiful local information can be found **online** at ⓦwww.morvan.com.

West of the Morvan, the landscape softens as it descends towards the River Loire and the fine medieval town of **Nevers**, on Burgundy's western border.

Avallon

Approaching **AVALLON** along the N6 from the north, you wouldn't give the place a second look. But the southern aspect is altogether more promising, as the town stands high on a ridge above the wooded valley of the River Cousin, looking out over the hilly, sparsely populated country of the Morvan regional park. Once a staging post on the Romans' *Via Agrippa* from Lyon to Boulogne, it's a small and ancient town of stone facades and comatose cobbled streets, bisected north-south by the narrow **Grande-Rue-Aristide-Briand**. Under the straddling arch of the fifteenth-century **Tour de l'Horloge**, the spire of which dominates the town, this street brings you to the pilgrim **church of St Lazare**, on whose battered Romanesque facade you can still decipher the graceful carvings of signs of the zodiac, labours of the months and the old musicians of the Apocalypse. Almost opposite, in a fifteenth-century house, is the tourist office, with the municipal **museum** (May–Oct daily except Tues 2–6pm; €3) behind it; exhibits include a room of modern silverware, designed by local boy Jean Despres, and a second-century mosaic from a Gallo-Roman villa. There is also the **Musée du Costume** at 6 rue Belgrand (April–Nov daily 10.30am–12.30pm & 1.30–5.30pm; €4), just off Grande-Rue, with a collection of regional dress. Continuing from St-Lazare down the street, now called rue Bocquillot, brings you to the lime-shaded **Promenade de la Petite Porte**, with precipitous views across the plunging valley of the Cousin. You can walk from here around the outside of the **walls**. From the **Parc des Chaumes**, on the east side of town, there's a great view back to the old quarter, snug within its walls, with garden terraces descending on the slope beneath. You can't miss the **statue of Vauban**, standing guard over the place Vauban – the great military architect was born in the Morvan in 1633.

The lovely **Square Hourdaille**, located just outside of town as you head south, is a peaceful garden of shrubbery and a few statues; if the weather cooperates, you also have some splendid views of the Vallée du Cousin below.

Practicalities

The **tourist office** is at 4 rue Bocquillot (May, June & Sept daily 10am–noon & 2–6pm; July & Aug daily 10am–7pm; Oct–April Mon–Sat 10am–noon & 2–6pm; ⓣ03.86.34.14.19, ⓦwww.avallonnais-tourisme.com), between the clock tower and the church. **Bikes** can be hired from Touvélo, rue de Paris (ⓣ03.86.34.28.11).

For inexpensive **accommodation**, head for the *Hôtel du Parc*, opposite the train station at 3 place de la Gare (ⓣ03.86.34.17.00; ❶), clean and friendly, with an equally bargain-priced restaurant and locals' café. More comfortable and modern is the *Dak' Hôtel*, 119 rue de Lyon, 1km from the town centre (ⓣ03.86.31.63.20, ⓕ03.86.34.25.28, ⓔdakhotel@voila.fr; ❹), while the most expensive option is the charming ***Hostellerie de la Poste***, 13 place Vauban (ⓣ03.86.34.16.16, ⓦwww.hostelleriedelaposte.com; ❻), a former coaching inn with twelve sumptuous, stylish rooms and some more expensive suites, plus a restaurant serving an overwhelming choice of desserts (menus from €35, entrées from €10) and a flower-strewn courtyard. Another nice little choice is the *Hôtel du Rocher* (ⓣ03.86.34.19.03; ❶), 11 rue des Iles Labaume, situated alongside the water as you leave town heading south; they offer modest but tidy rooms, some with terrace. For a special **meal**, the *Relais des Gourmets*, 45–47 rue de Paris (ⓣ03.86.34.18.90) has menus from €18, but if you can afford it, go for the €69 menu, served with appropriate wines.

If you have a car, take the scenic, wooded road that runs alongside the river Cousin towards Vézelay. After 5km, you'll find the swish, efficient *Moulin de Ruats* (ⓣ03.86.34.97.00, ⓦwww.hostellerie-moulin-ruats.fr; ❺; closed mid-Jan to mid-Feb), with an exceptional restaurant (menu from €25; evenings only). A kilometre or two further along, just short of Pontaubert, where the back road joins the main road to Vézelay, the lovely, creeper-covered *Moulin des Templiers* (ⓣ03.86.34.10.80, ⓦwww.hotel-moulin-des-templiers.com; ❸; closed Nov to mid-March) provides a more romantic atmosphere smack alongside the bank of the Cousin; they serve guests a *table d'hôte* for €15.

The attractive *Camping Municipal de Sous-Roche* (ⓣ03.86.34.10.39; March–

Oct), and the *Ferme-Auberge des Chatelaines* (☎03.86.34.16.37; closed Thurs–Sun mid-Oct to April), are a couple of kilometres out of town on the route de Corbigny/Us.

Vézelay

The coach buses winding their way like ants up the steep incline to **VÉZELAY** should not deter you from visiting this picturesque hilltop hamlet, surrounded by ramparts and home to one of the seminal buildings of the Romanesque period, the abbey church of **La Madeleine** (daily sunrise–sunset; closed Sun 11am for Mass).

Saved from collapse by Viollet-le-Duc in 1840, the church's restored west front begins with the colossal narthex, added to the nave around 1150 to accommodate the swelling numbers of pilgrims attracted by the presence of bones alleged to be Mary Magdalene's. **Inside**, your eye is first drawn to the superlative sculptures of the central doorway, on whose tympanum a Pentecostal Christ is shown swathed in exquisitely figured drapery that takes on a mesmerizing decorative life of its own while still managing to suggest the limbs beneath in bas-relief. From Christ's outstretched hands, the message of the Gospel shoots out to the apostles in the form of beams of fire, while the frieze below depicts the converted and the pagan peoples – among those featured are giants, pygmies (one mounting his horse with a ladder), a man with breasts and huge ears, and dog-headed heathens. Better preserved are the charmingly small-scale medallions of the zodiac signs and labours of the months in the outermost arch.

From this great doorway you look down the long body of the church, vaulted by arches of alternating black and white stone, to a **choir** of pure early Gothic (completed in 1215), with a delicacy in sharp contrast to the more measured Romanesque nave. Its arches and arcades are edged with fretted mouldings, and the supporting pillars are crowned with 99 finely cut capitals, depicting scenes from the Bible, classical mythology, allegories and morality stories. One of the more impenetrable is "The Mystic Mill" at the end of the fourth bay on the right, showing Moses pouring grain (Old Testament Law) through a mill (Christ), the flour (New Testament) being gathered by St Paul. The compound also houses the **Musée de l'Oeuvre de la Madeleine**, where you can peruse some of the statues and stone fragments discarded during the church's restoration (daily Jul & Aug; April–Oct Sat, Sun & holidays; €3).

St Bernard preached the Second Crusade at Vézelay in 1146. Because the church was too small, he preached in the open, down the hill to the north, where a **commemorative cross** marks the spot. Richard the Lionheart and Philippe-Auguste, king of France, also made their rendezvous here before setting off on the Third Crusade in 1190. But by the mid-thirteenth century the abbey was in decline, the final blow coming in 1279 when rumours spread that Mary Magdalene's bones were false relics. The monastery's surviving buildings were pillaged by Protestants in the sixteenth-century Wars of Religion, and the whole establishment was finally dismantled during the Revolution. Today, a significant Franciscan community has been re-established.

Before moving on, be sure to take a look at the beautiful Gothic **church** in the village of **ST-PÈRE**, a half-hour walk from the abbey at the southern foot of the hill. The village is also home to one of the greatest restaurants in the land, *Marc Meneau* (☎03.86.33.33.33; menus from €85), and its luxury hotel

(Ⓣ03.86.33.39.10, Ⓦwww.marc-meneau-esperance.com; ❺).

Practicalities

Most visitors arrive by car or coach, but **cycling** is a pleasant way of covering the 20km from Avallon to Vézelay, despite the final ascent. Otherwise those without transport are reduced to taking a **taxi** (Ⓣ03.86.32.31.88; €15–20) from the train station at Sermizelles, 10km from Vézelay on the Auxerre–Avallon line (Mon–Sat 5–7 daily). Vézelay's small **tourist office** (daily 10am–1pm & 2–6pm; Nov to mid-June closed Thurs; Ⓣ03.86.33.23.69, Ⓦwww.vezelaytourisme.com) is on the right of rue St-Pierre as you go up towards the abbey; ask for a brochure listing the numerous summer concerts and art exhibitions.

For **accommodation**, you'll need to book far in advance at weekends and in high season. There are only two hotels in the old town: *La Terrasse* (Ⓣ03.86.33.25.50; ❷; closed March & Tues except July & Aug) has seven good-value rooms, and the location right outside the church is excellent; at the other end of the scale, and just 50m down from the church at rue Bonnette, *Le Pontot* (Ⓣ03.86.33.24.40, Ⓕ03.86.33.30.05; ❻–❾) must have one of the most beautiful situations in Burgundy, with its terrace enclosed by ancient stone walls, and the rooms are high quality. Just opposite, *Au Porc Épic* (Ⓣ03.86.33.32.16, Ⓦwww.le-porc-epic.com; ❸) offers comfortable *chambres d'hôtes*.

Most of the town hotels cluster round busy place Champ-du-Foire, at the foot of town: *Le Compostelle* (Ⓣ03.86.33.28.63, Ⓕ03.86.33.34.34; ❸) is a good choice. If you can find someone to let you in, it's well worth trying the eccentric *Maison St-Bernard* (Ⓣ03.86.32.36.12; ❶) or its sister *Centre Ste-Madeleine* (Ⓣ03.86.33.22.14; ❶), two pilgrim's **hostels** at the foot of rue des Écoles, in a quiet part of town. The inexpensive youth hostel is about 1km along the route de l'Étang (Ⓣ03.86.33.24.18; closed mid-Oct to April except for large pre-reserved groups); it also offers camping space (also closed mid-Oct to April). Alternatively, the farming village of **BRÈVES**, right beside the Yonne, midway between Vézelay and Clamecy has a beautiful little **campsite** (closed mid-Sept to mid-June).

Vézelay's **restaurants** are mostly rather touristy and overpriced, and at lunchtime you're better off with a picnic, but *Le Bougainville*, on Rue St-Étienne just before it becomes rue St-Pierre (Ⓣ03.86.33.27.57; closed Tues, Wed & Nov–Feb), serves good regional cuisine in a genteel dining room.

Clamecy

In sharp contrast to its rustic neighbours, **CLAMECY**, 23km to the west of Vézelay on the banks of the River Yonne, has a distinctly industrial feel as the centre of the Morvan's logging trade from the sixteenth century to the completion of the Canal du Nivernais in 1834. Individual woodcutting gangs working in the hills floated their logs down the Yonne and its tributaries as far as Clamecy, where they were made up into great rafts for shipment on to Paris. This contact with the capital – and cradle of new egalitarian political ideas – led to the early spread of revolutionary thoughts among the workers and peasantry of the Morvan, who staged a number of violent insurrections even before 1789. The history of the logging trade is documented in the **museum** on rue de la Mirandole (daily 10am–noon & 2–6pm; Nov–Easter closed Sun; €3).

There's nothing special to see in town, apart from the many fifteenth- to eighteenth-century buildings in the centre, but it does have an interesting history and a bizarre connection with Bethlehem. In 1168 William IV, crusading Count of Nevers, died in Palestine, bequeathing one of his properties in Clamecy to the bishopric of Bethlehem, to serve as a sanctuary in the case of Palestine falling into the hands of the infidel. When the Latin Kingdom of Jerusalem fell, the first bishop arrived to claim his legacy, and from 1225 until the Revolution fifty bishops of Bethlehem succeeded each other in Clamecy, honouring the little town with the title of bishopric. A curious little **chapel** by the bridge, built in 1927 in reinforced concrete, commemorates the connection.

The **tourist office** is on rue du Grand-Marché (April–Sept Mon–Sat 9am–12.30pm & 2–7pm, Sun 10am–1pm; Oct–March Mon, Tues & Thurs–Sat 9am–12.30pm & 2–5pm; Ⓣ03.86.27.02.51). For places to **stay**, try the lovely, old-fashioned *Hostellerie de la Poste*, on place Émile-Zola not far from the bridge (Ⓣ03.86.27.01.55, Ⓕ03.86.27.05.99, Ⓦwww.hostelleriedelaposte.fr; ❸; restaurant from €18), or the good-value *Auberge de la Chapelle*, 5 place Bethléem (Ⓣ03.86.27.11.55, Ⓕ03.86.27.06.21; ❷), with an attractive restaurant, located in a renovated thirteenth-century chapel just across the river, on the road to Auxerre. There's also a good riverside **campsite** on the edge of town on the route de Chevroches (Ⓣ03.86.27.05.97; May–Sept). If you're travelling south towards Nevers, the *Ferme-Auberge du Vieux Château*, 20km from Clamecy near the village of Oulon just off the D977, makes an ideal place to treat yourself to a little bucolic luxury in beautiful surroundings (Ⓣ03.86.68.06.77, Ⓦwww.vieuxchateau.com; ❸ w/breakfast; dinner at €17); meals are served exclusively with ingredients from the château's garden and farm.

Saulieu

SAULIEU, having suffered something of a decline with the depopulation of the Morvan, then the construction of the A6 *autoroute* that took away the traffic from the old N6, is once more a relatively thriving market town, best known for its gastronomy. Every year the town waits hungrily for its Charollais **festival**, on the third weekend of August – a super-gourmet festival featuring lots of meat and other local produce, and there's a festival of produce from the Morvan on the Ascension Day weekend.

The old town – on the west side of the N6 – is pretty enough, perfect for an after-dinner stroll. Its main sight is the twelfth-century **Basilique St-Andoche**, noted for its lovely capitals (probably carved by a disciple of Gislebertus, the master sculptor of Autun), but little else. Next door, the **Musée François-Pompon** (Wed–Sat 10am–12.30pm & 2–6pm, Sun 10.30am–noon & 2.30–5pm, Mon 10.30–noon; closed Jan & Feb; €4) is surprisingly interesting, with good local folklore displays and a large collection of the works of the local nineteenth-century animal sculptor, François Pompon.

The **tourist office** (mid-June to mid-Sept Mon–Sat 9am–12.30pm & 2–7pm, Sun 9am–12.30pm & 2–5pm; mid-Sept to Feb Tues–Sat 9am–noon & 2–5pm; March to mid-June Tues–Sat 9am–noon & 2–6pm; Ⓣ03.80.64.00.21, Ⓔsaulieu.tourisme@wanadoo.fr) is on the N6 near the hospital, in the direction of Paris – there is a Pompon statue of a bull in the little garden almost opposite. The **gare SNCF** is straight up avenue de la Gare opposite the marketplace/car park.

You may want to **stay** the night if you've been tempted by the menus and wine lists at some of the restaurants (Saulieu makes for an excellent stopping point, halfway between Paris and Lyon). A good nine or ten hotel-restaurants are ranged along the N6, which roars through town under the old walls; luckily, most have very quiet rooms that face peaceful gardens at the back. *La Borne Imperiale*, 14–16 rue d'Argentine (Ⓣ03.80.64.19.76, Ⓕ03.80.64.30.63; ❸; restaurant from €18, closed Wed evening & Thurs), has a fantastic atmosphere, a lovely terrace and rooms which all have a view of the garden. *Le Lion d'Or*, at 5 rue Courtépée (Ⓣ03.80.64.14.64; ❷; restaurant from €12, closed Sun & Dec 23–Jan 1), is a decent inexpensive option, further north along the N6. Should your trust fund mature while in Saulieu, dine at *La Côte d'Or* at 2 rue d'Argentine (Ⓣ03.80.90.53.53, Ⓦwww.bernard-loiseau.com; ❾), the beyond-luxurious restaurant-cum-inn started by the famed chef Bernard Loiseau (made even more famous after his suicide in 2003 following a long bout with depression); menus *start* at €145. There are also a couple of *gîtes d'étape* (Easter–Nov) and a **campsite** (Ⓣ03.80.64.16.19; April–Oct 20), 1km out along the Paris road. A small **cinema** next to the basilica frequently runs both foreign and French films, though non-Francophones should proceed with caution as the movies are almost always dubbed in French.

The Parc du Morvan

The **Parc Régional du Morvan** was only officially designated in 1970, when 170,000 hectares of hilly countryside were set aside in an attempt to protect the local cultural and natural heritage with a series of nature trails, animal reserves, museums and local craft shops. The Maison du Parc, its official **information centre** (April–June & Sept to mid-Nov Mon–Sat 9.30am–5pm, Sun 10am–5pm; July & Aug Mon–Fri 10am–6pm, Sat 10am–5pm, Sun 10am–1pm; mid-Nov to March Mon–Fri 8.45am–noon & 1.30–5.30pm; Ⓣ03.86.78.79.00, Ⓦwww.parcdumorvan.org), is located 13km from Saulieu in beautiful grounds – which include a small lake and a deer park – about a kilometre outside **ST-BRISSON** on the D6. There's no public transport to get you there, but if you're walking or cycling it's a good place to head for, as they have all available information on routes and facilities in the park, as well as a small **museum** (April to mid-Nov daily 10.15–6pm; €4), devoted to the region's World War II Resistance movement, which was particularly active in this hard-to-patrol forested backwater. There's also a **herbarium** of regional plants.

A map, *Saulieu Vélo Tout-Terrain en Morvan*, marks cycling and walking routes. For **walkers** the most challenging trip is the **GR13** footpath, crossing the park from Vézelay to Mont-Beuvray and taking in the major lakes, which are among the park's most developed attractions. There are also less strenuous possibilities: for example, the four-kilometre walk to Lac Chamboux, leaving Saulieu by the D26 and taking a track to the left (blue and yellow markers) after about ten minutes. For a starting point deeper into the park, there are buses to Château Chinon. **Riding** is a fairly popular way of seeing the park, and numerous *gîtes d'étape* offer pony-trekking facilities – tourist offices in the area can supply a complete list.

Every other village in the park seems to have its own **campsite** (most of which are open from April or May to Sept), and the larger ones often have a couple of simple **hotels** as well. There are several campsites and small, beachresortish hotels round the large, wooded **Lac des Settons**, which basks at the heart of the park and makes for a good break from more strenuous activities with its watersports, café-restaurants and small beach areas. The plain, modern village of **MONTSAUCHE**, 4km to the northwest of the lake, is a good bet for provisions, including camping gas, and has a municipal campsite; **MOUX**, a similar distance to the southeast, can provide the same facilities, and also has a couple of decent hotels. **Bikes** are available from most campsites in the area: for a complete list ask at any tourist office, or check online for VTT (mountain bikes) at Ⓦwww.morvan.com.

Château-Chinon

The most substantial community – approximately 2500 residents – in the park itself is the rather ugly village of **CHÂTEAU-CHINON**, nestled in contrastingly beautiful countryside dotted with evergreens, lakes and limestone deposits (bus connection to Autun). President Mitterrand was mayor here from 1959 to 1981, and the town was the home base of his political life for half a century. Thanks largely to him, it now boasts a major hosiery factory and military printing works, both of which have provided much needed employment to an isolated and often forgotten region.

Atop the town in the **Musée du Septennat** (July & Aug daily 10am–1pm & 2–7pm; May, June & Sept daily except Tues 10am–1pm & 2–6pm; Feb–April & Oct–Dec daily except Tues 10am–noon & 2–6pm; €4), you can see the extraordinary variety of gifts Mitterrand received as head of state. The museum is light and airy, purpose-built to hold a collection of some of the finest handicrafts from their many countries of origin: carpets from the Middle East, ivory from Togo, Japanese puppets, beaded spears from Burundi and bizarre gifts, like a table decorated with butterfly wings. Another of the town's attractions is the **Musée du Costume**, 4 rue du Château (same hours and ticket as Musée du Septennat), featuring a collection of over five thousand articles, the biggest collection in France, and interesting temporary exhibitions.

Mitterrand's preferred **hotel** was the *Au Vieux Morvan*, just past the main drag at 8 place Gudin (Ⓣ03.86.85.05.01, Ⓕ03.86.85.02.78; ❸; closed mid-Dec to Jan), with a nice restaurant (from €15). Cheaper is the cozy and comfortable *Lion d'Or*, 10 rue des Fossés (Ⓣ03.86.85.13.56, Ⓕ03.86.79.42.22; ❷; restaurant from €12, closed Sun evening & Mon); be sure to ask for one of the rooms with views to the hillside surrounding Château-Chinon. There's also a **campsite** here, *Le Perthuy d'Oiseau* (Ⓣ03.86.85.08.17; May–Sept).

Autun and around

With its Gothic spire rising against a backdrop of Morvan hills, **AUTUN**, even today, is scarcely bigger than the circumference of its medieval **walls**, and they in turn follow the line of earlier Roman fortifications. The emperor Augustus founded the town in about 10 BC as part of a massive and, in the long term, highly successful campaign to pacify and Romanize the brooding Celts of defeated Vercingétorix. Augustodunum, as it was called, was designed to eclipse by its splendour the memory of **Bibracte** (see p.619), the neighbouring capital of the powerful tribe of the Aedui. And it did indeed become one of the leading cities of Roman Gaul.

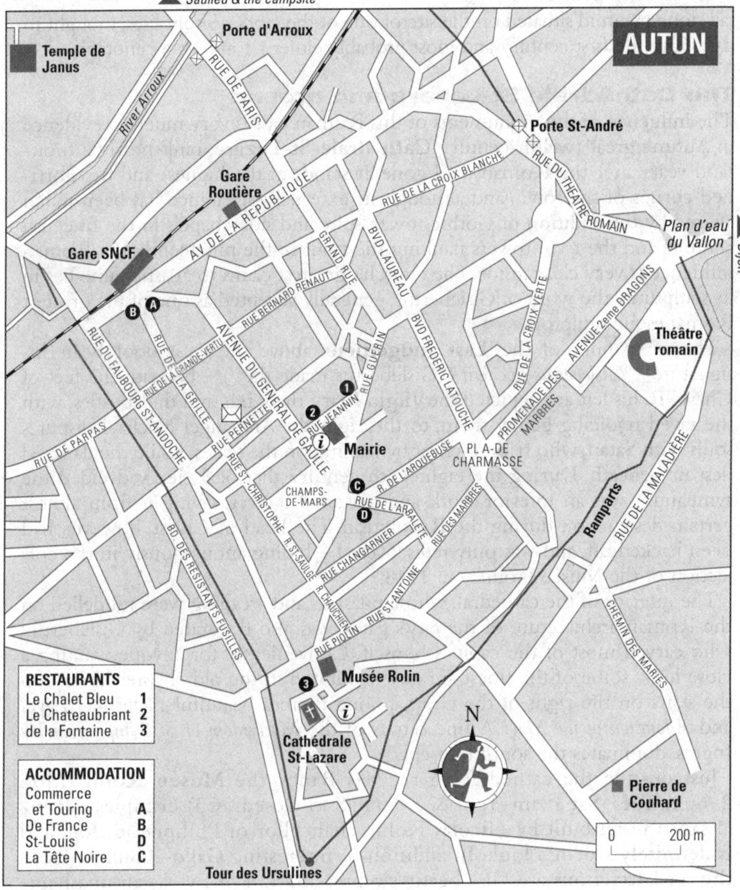

The Town

Traces of the Roman period are still much in evidence. Two of the city's four Roman gates survive: **Porte St-André**, spanning rue de la Croix-Blanche in the northeast, and **Porte d'Arroux** in Faubourg d'Arroux in the northwest. In a field just across the River Arroux stands a lofty section of brick wall known as the **Temple of Janus**, which was probably part of the sanctuary of some Gallic deity, while on the east side of the town, on avenue du 2ème-Dragon just off the Dijon road, you can see the remains of what was the largest **Roman theatre** in Gaul, with a capacity of fifteen thousand – in itself a measure of Autun's importance at that time. It's not an evocative site – the remaining seats now overlook a football pitch – but in July and August its authenticity is enhanced by the performances of a play in which six hundred locals, dressed in period costume, reconstruct the Gallo-Roman past of the town. An artificial lake below the football pitch, the **Plan d'eau du Vallon**, provides the usual watersports.

The most enigmatic of the Gallo-Roman remains in the region is the **Pierre de Couhard**, off Faubourg St-Pancrace to the southeast of the town. It's a 27-metre-tall stone pyramid situated on the site of one of the city's necropolises, thought to date from the first century, and most probably either a tomb or a cenotaph.

The Cathédrale St-Lazare and around

The influence of the monuments of this Roman past is very much in evidence in Autun's great twelfth-century **Cathédrale St-Lazare**, built nearly a thousand years after the Romans had gone. It stands in the highest and best fortified corner of the town, and although its external appearance has been much altered by the addition of Gothic tower, spire and side chapels in the fifteenth century, and the twin towers flanking the front in the nineteenth, the Roman influence is very clear inside. The church's greatest claim to artistic fame lies in its sculptures, the work of Gislebertus, generally accepted as one of the greatest Romanesque sculptors.

The tympanum of the **Last Judgement** above the west door bears his signature – *Gislebertus hoc fecit* ("Gislebertus made this") – beneath the feet of Christ. To his left are depicted the Virgin Mary, the saints and the apostles, with the saved rejoicing below them; to the right the Archangel Michael disputes souls with Satan, who tries to cheat by leaning on the scales, while the damned despair beneath. During the eighteenth century the local clergy decided the tympanum was an inferior work and plastered it over, saving it from almost certain destruction during the Revolution. The head of Christ, however, had been hacked off, and was only rediscovered – hiding anonymously in the collection of the Musée Rolin – in 1948.

The interior of the cathedral, whose pilasters and arcading were modelled on the Roman architecture of the city's gates, was also decorated by Gislebertus, who carved most of the capitals himself. Conveniently for anyone wanting a close look, some of the finest are now exhibited in the old chapter library, up the stairs on the right of the choir, among them a beautiful *Flight into Egypt* and *Adoration of the Magi*. A fine canvas of the *Martyrdom of St Symphorien*, by Ingres, dominates the south transept.

Just outside the cathedral on rue des Bancs, the **Musée Rolin** (Mon 2–6pm, Tues–Sat 10am–1pm & 3–6pm; Sun closed; €3) occupies a Renaissance hôtel built by Nicolas Rolin, chancellor of Philippe le Bon, and is definitely worth a look. In addition to interesting Gallo-Roman pieces, the star attractions are Gislebertus's representation of Eve as an unashamedly sensual nude – one of the few pieces surviving from a tympanum that didn't make it – and the Maître de Moulins' brilliantly coloured Nativity. At the highest corner of the ramparts' course, just south of the cathedral, the **Tour des Ursulines** is a last remnant of the once-powerful fortress of Rivault built by the Dukes of Burgundy in the twelfth century; the statue of the Virgin on the top was added in the mid-nineteenth century.

Practicalities

Whether you arrive at the **gare SNCF** or **gare routière** down the road, you'll find yourself on avenue de la République, bisected at right angles by avenue Charles-de-Gaulle, which in turn leads to the wide square of the Champs-de-Mars and into the old town. The main **tourist office** is at 2 av de Charles-de-Gaulle (June–Sept daily 9am–7pm, Oct–May Mon–Sat 10am–1pm & 3–6pm; Ⓣ03.85.86.80.38, Ⓦwww.autun.com), and there's an information point opposite the cathedral, at place du Terreau (June–Sept daily 9am–7pm; Apr–May & Oct–Nov Mon–Fri 9am–1pm & 3–6pm, Sat & Sun 10am–6pm; Ⓣ03.85.52.56.03). **Bikes** can be rented at the campsite and at the Plan d'eau du Vallon (Ⓣ03.85.86.95.80).

There's a good choice of **accommodation** in Autun. The inexpensive options are all on the main road opposite the station: the *Hôtel de France*, 18 av de la République (Ⓣ03.85.52.14.00, Ⓕ03.85.86.14.52; ❷) and the *Commerce et Touring*, 20 av de la République (Ⓣ03.85.52.17.90, Ⓕ03.85.52.37.63; ❷; closed Jan; reasonable restaurant from €11) are perfectly decent. For something a bit more quiet and classy, try one of the old coaching inns just off the Champs-de-Mars. Napoléon twice slept at the once-magnificent *St-Louis*, 6 rue de l'Arbalète (Ⓣ03.85.52.01.01, Ⓦwww.hotelsaintlouis.net; ❺), and though it's recently seen its illustrious four-star rating slide down to two stars, it's still quite grand: you can stay in Napoléon's room for €250. The comfortable *Hôtel de La Tête Noire* is just opposite at 3 rue de l'Arquebuse (Ⓣ03.85.86.59.99, Ⓦwww.hoteltetenoire.fr; ❷; restaurant from €15). There's also a **campsite** just across the river on the road to Saulieu, *Camping Pont d'Arroux* (Ⓣ03.85.52.10.82; closed Oct–Easter).

In addition to the hotel **restaurants**, there are a couple of brasseries on the Champs-de-Mars, but the best options are in the street behind the Hôtel de Ville: *Le Chalet Bleu*, 3 rue Jeannin (Ⓣ03.85.86.27.30; closed Mon evening, Tues & most of Feb; menus from €14.50) is innovative and distinctly classy, while *Le Chateaubriant*, 14 rue Jeannin (Ⓣ03.85.52.21.58; closed Sun evening, Mon & most of July; menu from €14) offers a more traditional menu. Next to the cathedral is the atmospheric *Restaurant de la Fontaine*, a great little place to try out *escargots* and other regional specialties (Ⓣ03.85.86.25.57; menus from €16).

Mont-Beuvray and Bibracte

The base for the climb up Mont-Beuvray to the 2000-year-old site of the Gallic capital of Bibracte is **ST-LÉGER-SOUS-BEUVRAY**, about 26km southwest of Autun and reached along the N81 and D61 through typical Morvan countryside of wooded hills and scattered farms, coarse marshy pastures and brown streams. There's a morning and an afternoon bus from Autun to St-Léger. Should you need to spend the night, St-Léger has a **hostel** with rooms for €23 (Ⓣ03.85.82.55.46) and **campsite** (May–Oct).

From St-Léger, it's the best part of a two-hour walk, or 8km by road, to **BIBRACTE** on top of the hill, at an altitude of 800m. If you want to recapture a Celtic mood, it's worth doing it on foot along the path winding up through woods of conifer and beech. The settlement of Bibracte, the lines of which you can still follow through the trees, was inhabited from 5000 BC. In 52 BC it was the scene of an assembly of all the Gallic tribes, which resulted in the election of Vercingétorix as their commander-in-chief, in one last desperate attempt to fight off Roman imperialism. Although it is two millennia since Bibracte was abandoned – probably on Roman orders – vague memories of its significance were preserved in the folk tales of the Morvan and a fair was held on the summit every May until the beginning of World War I. Close to the fortified earthwork that surrounds the site, great ceremonial stones like the **Pierre de la Wivre** are still standing. The Bibracte **Musée de la Civilisation Celtique** (July & Aug daily 10am–7pm; mid–March to June and Sept–Oct daily except Tues 10am–6pm; €5.50 museum entry, €8 with guided tour of archeological site; Ⓣ03.85.86.52.35 for bookings) is a fascinating state-of-the-art museum displaying the many Celtic coins, jugs, platters and pieces of statues unearthed from the neighbouring site.

Le Creusot

LE CREUSOT (not to be confused with Le Creuset, the northern French town of cast iron cookware fame) means one thing to French ears:

the **Schneider iron and steelworks**, maker of the first French locomotive in 1838, the first steamship in 1839, the 75mm field gun – mainstay of World War I artillery – and the ironwork of the Pont Alexandre-III and the Gare d'Austerlitz in Paris. The last Schneider died in 1960, whereupon the company was broken up, and a number of different companies now carry on the tradition: Creusot-Loire manufactures specialized steels for the French military and nuclear industry, while Alstom manufactures parts of the TGV.

The town's main attraction is the **Écomusée le Creusot-Montceau** in the Château de la Verrerie on place Schneider (June to mid-Sept Mon–Fri 10am–noon & 1–6pm, Sat & Sun 3–7pm; mid-Sept to May Mon–Fri 10am–noon & 2–6pm, Sat & Sun 2–6pm; €6). Built as a glassworks in 1786–87 – Louis XVI was a shareholder before losing his head – the château was sold to the Schneider family in 1838 and transformed into their private home and the administrative centre of their business empire. The Schneiders were paternalistic but despotic employers, providing housing, schools and health care for their workers, but expecting "gratitude and obedience" in return.

Today, the château houses a museum dedicated to the iron and steel industry, with oil paintings of various Schneiders and their forges, mock-ups of workers' quarters, examples of local glass work, giant model trains and a large coin-slot push-button model of an old metal works. The neighbouring **Salle du Jeu de Paume** traces Le Creusot's role in the development of metallurgy through models and photographs, beginning with the earliest iron forges and ending with today's nuclear industry. The peculiar cone-shaped constructions in the courtyard of the château were glass furnaces; one of them was transformed into a tiny Neoclassical theatre where plays were put on to entertain the Schneiders' wealthy and influential guests, and can be visited on regular tours.

A more recent development in town is the huge **Parc Touristique des Combes**, which boasts a narrow-gauge steam train (April–Oct; €6), a karting track, a 435-metre-long dry luge piste (April–Oct; €2.50) and an unusual panorama. From the top of the Combe des Mineurs the view takes in the modern steelworks, the gleaming white Château de la Verrerie and the terraces of old workers' houses, all set against the northeastern bulwark of the Massif Central.

Practicalities

The **tourist office** in the gatehouse of the Château de la Verrerie (Mon–Fri 9am–noon & 2–6pm, Sat & Sun 2–6pm; ⓣ03.85.55.02.46; ⓦwww.creusot.net) can arrange visits to coal mines in the vicinity, and may be able to help if you want to tour the modern ironworks. Frequent buses connect Le Creusot with the **TGV station** 6km away in Montchanin, connecting with Paris. If you need to **stay** overnight, head for *La Belle Epoque*, 9 place Schneider (ⓣ03.85.73.00.00, ⓕ03.85.73.00.10; ❸), featuring a decent restaurant and rooms decked out in peach, orange and blue pastel, or if on a budget, *Le Bodsonn*, 26 rue de l'Yser (ⓣ03.85.55.32.02, ⓕ03.85.55.63.96; ❶), a bit out of the centre but with comfy rooms. Towards the pricier side, try *Le Petite Verrerie*, 4 rue Jules Guesde (ⓣ03.85.73.97.97, ⓕ03.85.73.97.90, ⓦwww.hotelfp-lecreusot.com; ❺), featuring 43 meticulously decorated rooms and a posh restaurant (menus €26.50).

Nevers

Some sixty kilometres west of the Parc du Morvan, at the western confines of Burgundy, **NEVERS** is a small provincial city on the confluence of the rivers

Loire and Nièvre. In France it's known for its *nougatine* sweets and fine porcelain, hand-painted with a deep blue colour known as *bleue de Nevers*. Faïence, as it's called, has been a hallmark of Nevers since the seventeenth century and is now something of a growth industry, with six small artisans' workshops in town, all of which sell their wares in elegant, expensive shops called faïenceries. Parts of the **old town** date back to the twelfth century and make for a relaxed stroll away from the busier centre. The town is best viewed from the bridge over the Loire, where you can often see terns diving and swooping, like a graceful cross between a gull and a swallow. Not necessarily a destination in itself, Nevers nonetheless makes, with its open-air concert programme in summer and a few lively bars and restaurants, a useful and pleasant stopover if you're travelling in the region.

The Town

Nevers centres on **place Carnot**, close to the fifteenth-century **Palais Ducal**, former home of the dukes of Nevers, with octagonal turrets and an elegant central tower decorated with sculptures illustrating the family history of the first duke, François de Clèves, in the mid-seventeenth century. The building now houses an annexe of the law courts. Nearby, opposite the Hôtel de Ville, the **Cathédrale de St-Cyr** reveals a sort of wall display of French architectural styles from the tenth to the sixteenth centuries; it even manages to have two opposite apses, one Gothic, the other Romanesque. But more interesting and aesthetically satisfying is the late eleventh-century **church of St-Étienne**, on the east side of the town centre. Behind its plain exterior lies one of the prototype pilgrim churches, with galleries above the aisles, ambulatory and three radiating chapels around the apse.

From the station, avenue de-Gaulle leads to place Carnot, where you take a left turn for the **Parc Roger-Salengro**, which has some unexpected sculptures – look out for *Les Sangliers* (wild boar). The north side of the park edges onto the **convent of St-Gildard**, where Bernadette of Lourdes ended her days. Her embalmed body is displayed in a glass-fronted **shrine** (daily: April–Oct 7am–12.30pm & 1.30–7.30pm; Nov–March 7.30am–noon & 2–7pm) in the convent chapel and next-door you can visit a small free museum displaying some of her belongings and correspondence. A short walk away is the modern **church of Ste-Bernadette du Banlay**, built in 1966 in the bunker-like architectural style known as *fonction oblique*.

Crossing to the other side of avenue de-Gaulle, five minutes' walk from the station by place Mossé and the bridge over the Loire, you pass a section of the old town walls and the **Tour Goguin**, partly dating back to the eleventh century. If you turn in here to the right you come to the **Porte de Croux**, a cream stone tower with intact machicolations and a steep tiled roof like those of its surrounding buildings; inside, there's an **archaeology museum** displaying mainly Greek and Roman statuary, though it's undergoing an all-out restoration and not due to reopen until 2007 (until then, some of the main pieces can be viewed in the basement of the Palais Ducal). Nearby, rue du 14-Juillet has a number of **faïencerie** shops where you can see the pieces being painted by hand. To your right again you get back to the oldest quarter of town around the cathedral – rue Morlon and rue de la Cathédrale – with its dilapidated half-timbered houses, alleys and stairs descending to the river.

To the north of the ducal palace on the way out of town towards Orléans, **Porte de Paris**, a triumphal arch, straddles rue des Ardilliers. It commemorates one of Europe's major conflicts, the battle of Fontenoy, fought out between

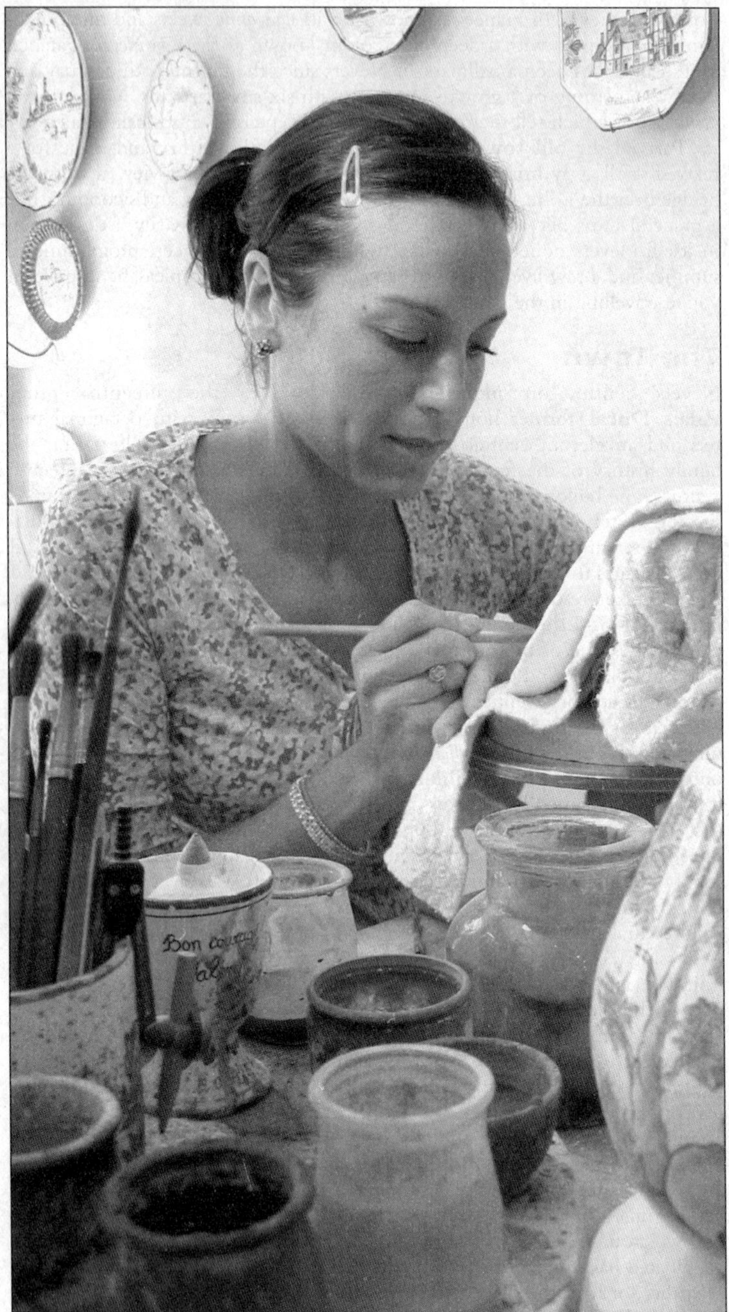

△ Faiience workshop

Charlemagne's sons in 841 AD. The stakes were Charlemagne's empire, and the outcome the division of his lands east and west of the Rhine, which formed the basis of modern France and Germany.

Practicalities

The **gare SNCF** and **gare routière** are on rue du Chemin-de-Fer. The **tourist office**, in the foyer of the Palais Ducal (Apr–Sept Mon–Sat 9am–6.30pm, Sun 10am–1pm & 3–6pm; Oct–March Mon–Sat 9am–noon & 2–6pm, Sun 10am–1pm & 3–6pm; ⓣ03.86.68.46.00, ⓦwww.nevers-tourisme.fr), provides maps and information on events in the summer music festival, and can arrange trips in the traditional wooden **boats** that used to ply the Loire – ask for Pascal Boutreue (ⓣ06.89.57.10.33), who runs two-hour excursions for around €13 a head, as well as two-day expeditions. **Bike** and **canoe** rental is available from L.O.I.R.E. 6 Quai des Mariniers (ⓣ03.86.57.69.76). **Internet** access can be found at the bakers' at 5 rue de la Pelleterie (€3.60 per hour) or at *Forum*, 50m further on (€5 per hour).

There are few **hotels** in the old centre, though the *Hotel de Cleves*, 8 rue St Didier (ⓣ03.86.61.15.87, ⓕ03.86.57.13.80; ❷), is very comfortable and well-located just off Place Carnot. Nearer the train station, the pleasant *Beauséjour*, 5 rue St-Gildard (ⓣ03.86.61.20.84, ⓕ03.86.59.15.37; ❷), is almost opposite the church of Ste Bernadette and has small rooms and a small outdoor garden for breakfast. *Hôtel Thermidor*, nearer still to the station at 14 rue Claude-Tillier (ⓣ03.86.57.15.47; ❷), is also good value and quiet. The municipal **campsite** is currently under a full reconstruction so you're best off checking with the tourist office; the next closest is at Fourchambault (ⓣ03.86.60.81.59; May–Nov), on a riverside site 4.5km from town.

Avenue de-Gaulle has a few inexpensive **restaurants** and **cafés**, such as *La Mange'oir*, 24 av de-Gaulle (closed Sat & Sun lunch, & all day Mon; menus at €10.50), and some more upmarket places too, such as the *Gambrinus*, 37 av de-Gaulle (ⓣ03.86.57.19.48; closed Mon & Sat lunch, & all day Sun; menu from €18.50), and the excellent *Aux Chœurs de Bacchus*, 25 av de-Gaulle (ⓣ03.86.36.72.70; closed Mon & Sat lunch, & all day Sun), which has a good menu at €14.50 and a wine-tasting version at €21.40. *Le Goemon*, 9 rue du 14-Juillet (closed Sun & Mon evening), is a crêperie with good salads, and live jazz on Saturday nights. *Donald's Pub*, on rue François Mitterand near the river, is a good place for a drink.

Dijon and southern Burgundy

If the much-touted image of "rural Burgundy" has conjured up an image of slightly ramshackle rustic charm in your mind, you'll have to do some adjusting when you encounter the slick prosperity of **Dijon** and the wine-producing country to the south, known as the **Côte d'Or**. It may look peacefully pastoral, but there's nothing medieval about the methods or the profits made in today's wine business. For any trace of the older traditions you have to head into the southwestern corner of the region, into the wine-producing regions of the **Mâconnais** and **Beaujolais**, and the cattle country of the **Charollais**.

Dijon

DIJON owes its origins to its strategic position in Celtic times on the tin merchants' route from Britain up the Seine and across the Alps to the Adriatic.

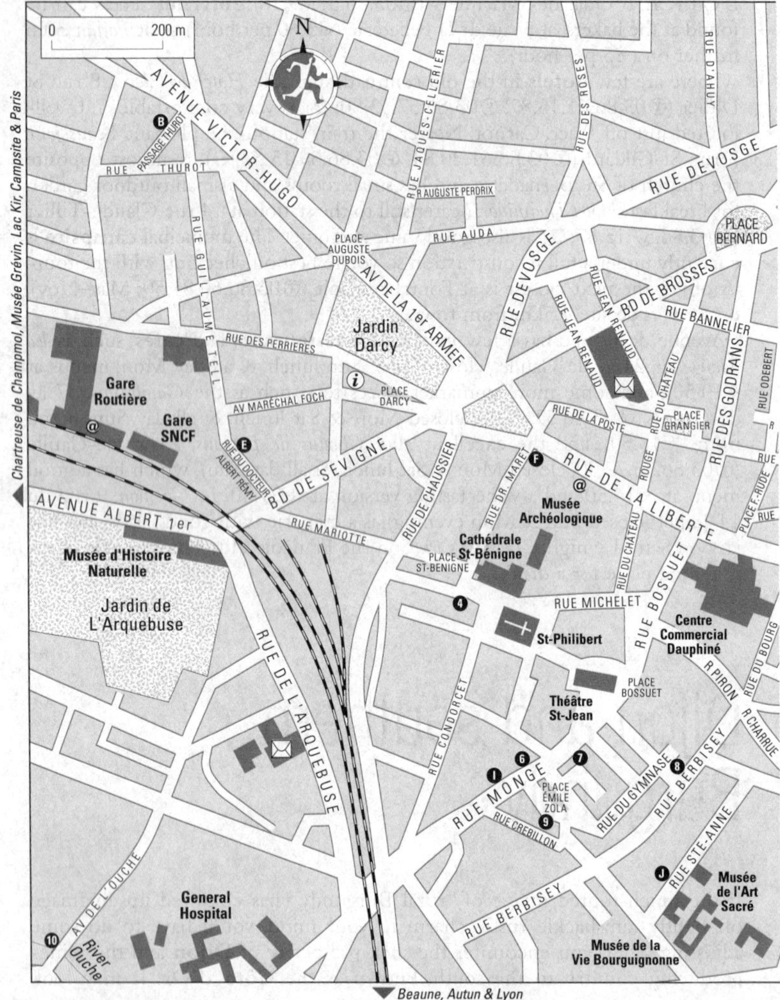

It became the capital of the dukes of Burgundy around 1000 AD, but its golden age occurred in the fourteenth and fifteenth centuries under the auspices of dukes Philippe le Hardi (the Bold), who as a boy had fought the English at Poitiers and been taken prisoner, Jean sans Peur (the Fearless), Philippe le Bon (the Good), who sold Joan of Arc to the English, and Charles le Téméraire (also the Bold). They used their tremendous wealth and power – especially their control of Flanders, the dominant manufacturing region of the age – to make Dijon one of the greatest centres of art, learning and science in Europe. It lost its capital status on incorporation into the kingdom of France in 1477, but has remained one of the country's pre-eminent provincial cities, especially since the rail and industrial booms of the mid-nineteenth century. Today, it's smart, modern and young, especially when the students are around.

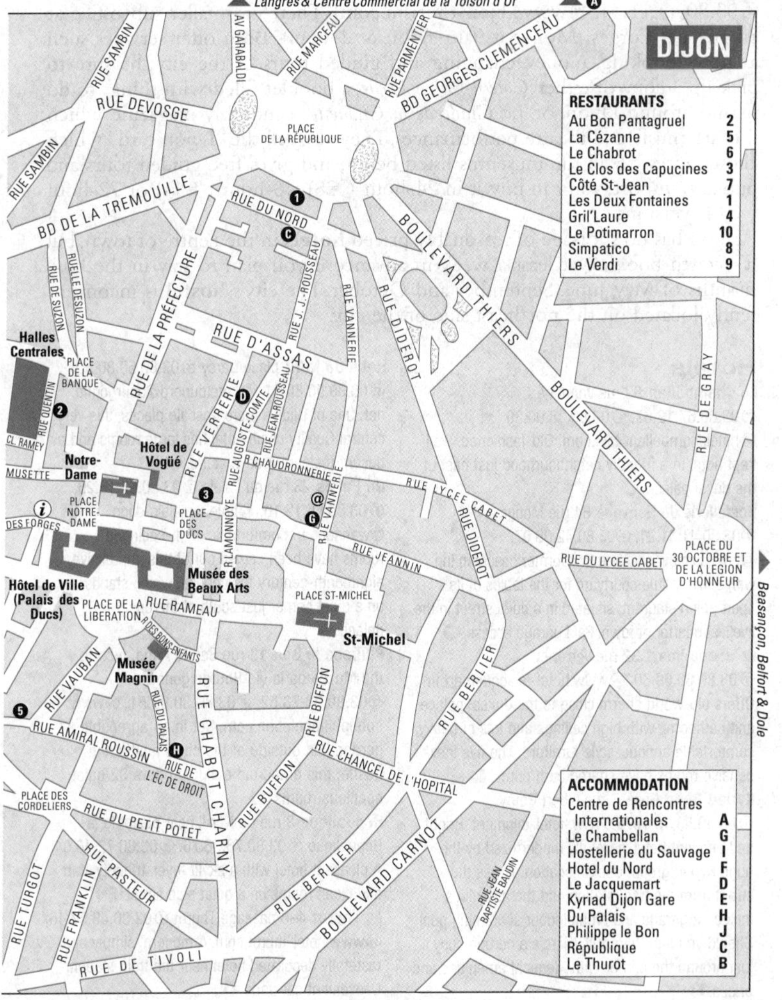

Arrival, information and accommodation

Dijon is not an enormous city and the part you'll want to see is neatly confined in the centre and eminently walkable. Whether you arrive by road or rail from either Paris and the north or Lyon and the south, you find yourself almost inevitably at the **gare SNCF** – the **gare routière** is next door, along with an **Internet** access shop, Multi-Rezo, at 21 cour de la gare routière (Mon–Sat 9am–midnight, Sun 2–10pm; €3 per hour), with an annexe at 74 rue Vannerie. EasyJet flies daily from London Stansted to Dijon **airport**; all arrivals and departures are served by a bus operated by and from the main tourist office on place Darcy.

From immediately outside the station, a five-minute walk down avenue Maréchal-Foch takes you to place Darcy, in the middle of which is the **tourist office** (daily: May to mid-Oct 9am–7pm; mid-Oct to April 10am–6pm; Ⓣ03.80.44.11.44, Ⓦwww.dijon-tourism.com). There's a smaller sub-office at 34 rue des Forges (Mon–Sat 9am–noon & 2–6pm). Both offer services such as hotel booking, money changing and guided tours of the city; be sure to pick up a copy of either *Cote d'Or en Poche*, a booklet filled with things to do in and around Dijon, or *La Guide de la Chouette*, a monthly magazine which lists art, music and theatre performances. They also sell the "Dijon card" which allows access to all the museums listed below, and gives free guided tours and public transport; you can buy it in 24-hour (€8), 48-hour (€11) or 72-hour (€14) versions.

Dijon has no shortage of reasonably priced **hotels** in the centre of town, but it's worth booking at least a week in advance if you plan to stay in the busy months of May, June, September and October. The city's **hostel** is inconveniently located on the northeast side of the city.

Hotels

Le Chambellan 92 rue Vannerie Ⓣ03.80.67.12.67, Ⓕ03.80.38.00.39, Ⓔhotelchambellan@aol.com. Old-fashioned, well-kept hotel in a friendly neighbourhood just east of the ducal palace. ❷

Hostellerie du Sauvage 64 rue Monge Ⓣ03.80.41.31.21, Ⓕ03.80.42.06.07, Ⓔhoteldusauvage@free.fr. A former coaching inn with a lovely little courtyard for the tables of its open-grill restaurant; situated in a quiet street in the liveliest quarter of town. Paid garage access. ❷

Le Jacquemart 32 rue Verreriet Ⓣ03.80.60.09.60, Ⓦwww.hotel-lejacquemart.fr. Offers old-world charm close to the dukes' palace and cathedral, with high ceilings and lots of heavy, comfortable antique-style furniture. The five inexpensive rooms have shared bathrooms. ❶–❸

Kyriad Dijon Gare 7 rue Albert Remy Ⓣ03.80.53.10.10, Ⓦwww.hotel-dijon.net. Bright and efficient hotel, carefully modernized by the huge Kyriad group. Useful location across the street from the train station and the amenities include a garage and small indoor swimming pool. Should you find them full, there's a carbon copy just around the corner with identical amenities and prices. ❹

Hotel du Nord place Darcy Ⓣ03.80.50.80.50, Ⓕ03.80.50.80.51, Ⓔhoteldunord@bourgogne.net. One of Dijon's more upscale places, this very central Quality chain hotel has large rooms and a decent restaurant downstairs. ❺

Du Palais 23 rue du Palais Ⓣ03.80.67.16.26, Ⓕ03.80.65.12.16, Ⓔhoteldupalais-dijon@wanadoo.fr. Comfortable, high-ceilinged rooms have been carved out of this impressive eighteenth-century townhouse, which stands on a quiet corner just south of the ducal palace. ❷

Philippe le Bon 18 rue Sainte Anne, next to the Musée da la vie Bourguigonne Ⓣ03.80.30.73.52, Ⓕ03.80.30.95.51, Ⓦwww.hotelphilippelebon.com. Set in an agreeable garden just outside of the city's hustle and bustle, this grand old building offers 32 quiet, spacious rooms. ❻

République 3 rue du Nord, near place de la République Ⓣ03.80.73.36.76, Ⓕ03.80.72.46.04. A pleasant hotel with a skylit foyer, friendly staff and clean rooms on a quiet side street. ❷

Le Thurot 4–6 passage Thurot Ⓣ03.80.43.57.46, Ⓦwww.hotel-thurot.com. A modern, simply and tastefully decorated hotel near the train station. Convenient car park. ❸

Hostel and campsite

Camping du Lac ⓣ03.80.43.54.72. Pleasant and popular establishment about 1km out of town off boulevard Chanoine-Kir near Lake Kir: follow the signs for Paris. Take bus #12, direction "Fontaine d'Ouche", or #18, direction "Plombières".

Centre de Rencontres Internationales 1 bd Champollion ⓣ03.80.72.95.20, ⓦwww.auberge-cri-dijon.com. Not-quite-central HI hostel in a modern complex, with well-kept dorm rooms, a self-service canteen and sports facilities next door; often teeming with adolescent school groups. Take bus #5, direction "Épirey", from place Grangier. The last bus back is at 9pm, however, so you can't really go out at night.

The City

The **rue de la Liberté** forms the spine of the town, running east from the wide, attractive **place Darcy** and the eighteenth-century triumphal arch of **Porte Guillaume**, once a city gate, past the **palace of the dukes of Burgundy** on the semicircular **place de la Libération**. From this elegant, Classical square, Rue Rameau continues directly east to place du Théâtre, from where Rue Vaillant leads on to the **church of St Michel**. Pedestrianized and lined with smart shops, mammoth department stores and elegant old houses, most places of interest are within ten minutes' walk to the north or south of this main axis.

The Palais des Ducs

The geographical focus of a visit to Dijon is inevitably the seat of its former rulers, the **Palais des Ducs**, which stands at the hub of the city. Facing the main courtyard, Mansart's serene **place de la Libération** was built towards the end of the seventeenth century (as place Royale) to show off a statue of the Sun King; these days it's something of a sun trap on a good day, and a decision to close it to traffic has caused a boom in café trade. The ducal palace itself now functions as the town hall, and its exterior has undergone so many alterations – especially in the sixteenth and seventeenth centuries when it became Burgundy's parliament – that the dukes themselves would only recognize it by the two surviving towers. The fourteenth-century **Tour de Bar** dominates the courtyard in front of the east wing, which now houses the Musée des Beaux-Arts, while the loftier, fifteenth-century **Tour Philippe-le-Bon** can be visited only on guided tours (April–Nov 10 tours daily; Dec–March Sat & Sun 6 tours daily, Wed tours at 1.30pm, 2.30pm & 3.30pm; €2.30). The scene from the top is particularly worthwhile for the unobstructed views of the glazed Burgundian tiles of the Hôtel de Vogüé and the cathedral; on a clear day the Alps loom on the horizon.

Given the dukes' possessions in the Netherlands, it's hardly surprising that the **Musée des Beaux-Arts** (daily except Tues: May–Oct 9.30am–6pm; Nov–April 10am–5pm; €3.40, Sun free) boasts a Flemish collection. Lording it among the rather dull sequence of French and Italian works on the first floor is the *Nativity* by the so-called Master of Flémalle, a shadowy figure who may have been the teacher of Rogier van der Weyden and who ranks with van Eyck as one of the first artists to break from the chilly stranglehold of International Gothic. Elsewhere, minor works by Titian and Rubens leaven an otherwise doughy mix, while one of the more interesting rooms is devoted to the intricate woodcarving of the sixteenth-century designer and architect Hugues Sambin, whose work appears throughout the old quarter of the city in the massive doors and facades of the aristocratic *hôtels*. The two upper floors house the modern and contemporary galleries (though these are often only open in the afternoons), with an intimate Vuillard canvas, some attractive works by the local early-nineteenth-century painter Félix Trutat, and a handful of rather second-rate examples of the work of Manet and Monet. This section of the museum takes you right under the roof of the palace, and has been designed on some unusual principles; the layout is bewildering, but bears fruit in an unusual, scarcely lit room where modern images of skulls provide a thought-provoking backdrop to Georges de la Tour's luminous *Boy with a Lamp*.

Visiting the museum also provides the opportunity to see the surviving portions of the original ducal palace, including the vast **kitchen** and the magnificent **Salle des Gardes**, richly appointed with panelling, tapestries and a minstrels' gallery. Here are displayed the lavish, almost decadent **tombs** from the Chartreuse de Champmol (see p.602) of Philippe le Hardi and Jean sans Peur and his wife, Marguerite de Bavière. Both follow the same pattern: painted effigies of the dead, attended by gold-plated angels holding their helmets and heraldic shields, and accompanied by a cortege of brilliantly sculpted mourners.

The Quartier Notre-Dame

Architecturally more interesting than the palace, and much more suggestive of the city's former glories, are the lavish townhouses of its rich burghers. These abound in the streets behind the palace: rue Verrerie, rue Vannerie, rue des Forges, rue Chaudronnière (look out for no. 28, **Maison des Cariatides**). Some are half-timbered, with storeys projecting over the street, others are in more formal and imposing Renaissance stone. Particularly fine are the Renaissance **Hôtel de Vogüe**, 12 rue de la Chouette, and at no. 34, the **Hôtel Chambellan** (1490), housing one of Dijon's tourist offices. From the tourist office's courtyard, you can admire the open galleries reached by a spiral staircase. At the top of the steps is a marvellous piece of stonemason's virtuosity, the vaulting of the roof springing from a basket held by the statue of a gardener. For a glimpse of what must be nearly genuine medieval character, take a look in the cobbled alleys by the **Tour St-Nicholas**, off rue Jean-Jacques-Rousseau.

Also in this quarter behind the dukes' palace, in the angle between rue de la Chouette and rue de la Préfecture, is the **church of Notre-Dame**, built in the early thirteenth century in the Burgundian Gothic style, with an unusual west front adorned with tiers of spectacularly leaning gargoyles – most were replaced in the nineteenth century. Inside, the original stained glass has survived in the five panels below the rose window in the north transept, while in the south transept there is a ninth-century wooden "black" Virgin, one of the oldest in France. Known as "Our Lady of Good Hope", she receives prayers for health and happiness written into the open book on a lecturn in front of the altar. Outside on rue de la Chouette, in the north wall of the church, is a small sculpted owl – *chouette* – polished by the hands of passers-by who for centuries have touched it for luck and which gives the street its name. High on the south tower of the west front is a Jacquemard clock, taken from Courtrai in Belgium as a present for Dijon in 1382, when Philippe le Hardi defeated the people of Ghent. Interestingly, the four familial figures that adorn the clock were each added individually by subsequent generations of Dijon.

From here rue de la Musette leads west, passing just south of the **market square** and the covered *halles*. The whole area is full of sumptuous displays of food and attractive cafés and restaurants, and always thronged with people. Opening at 6am, the market operates on Tuesday, Thursday and Friday mornings, and all day on Saturday; it spills over into the surrounding streets, with bric-a-brac in rue de Soissons on the north side and clothes in the beautiful little **place François-Rude,** named after the sculptor, and a favourite hangout, with its cafés and fountain graced by the bronze figure of a grape harvester.

South of the place de la Libération

On the south side of the place Darcy–church of St-Michel axis, and especially in the *quartier* behind place de la Libération, there's a concentration of magnificent hôtels from the seventeenth and eighteenth centuries. These were built for the most part by men who had bought themselves offices and privileges with the Parliament of Burgundy, established by Louis XI in 1477 after the death of Duke Charles le Téméraire (the Bold) as a concession designed to win the compliance of this newly acquired frontier province. One of them, 4 rue des Bons-Enfants, houses the **Musée Magnin** (daily except Mon 10am–noon & 2–6pm; €3): the building, a seventeenth-century *hôtel particulier*, complete with its original furnishings, is more interesting than the exhibition of paintings by good but lesser-known artists, which constituted the personal collection of Maurice Magnin, and which were donated to the state in 1938. Other noteworthy houses are to be found nearby in rue Vauban, some showing the marks of Hugues Sambin's influence in their decorative details (lions' heads, garlands of fruit, tendrils of ivy and his famous *chou bourguignon*, or "Burgundy cabbage"): notably, nos. 3, 12, 21 and 23. Also worth a look for its elaborate west front is the **church of St-Michel**, a ten-minute walk to the east behind place du Théâtre.

Continuing south from Musée Magnin, rue Ste-Anne, near place des Cordeliers, contains two museums. The **Musée de la Vie Bourguignonne** at no. 17 (daily except Tues: May–Sept 9am–6pm; Oct–April 9am–noon & 2–6pm; €2.80, Sun free, ticket includes the Musée d'Art Sacré), is housed in a stark, well-designed modern setting within a former convent, and is all about nineteenth-century Burgundian life, featuring costumes, furniture and domestic industries like butter-, cheese- and bread-making, along with a reconstructed kitchen. Practically next door at no. 15, the **Musée d'Art Sacré** (same hours and ticket as Musée de la Vie Bourguignonne) contains an important collection of church treasures, including a seventeenth-century statue of St Paul, the first in the world to be restored using an extraordinary technique that involves injecting the stone with resin and then solidifying the resulting compound using gamma rays. Formerly crumbling to dust, the guinea-pig saint is now completely firm.

The streets to the west – especially **rue Monge** and **rue Berbisey** – are very active at night with lots of bars and restaurants. The latter ends in a curious postmodern perspective joke: a sort of parody of a medieval housing estate. In place Bossuet at the start of rue Monge is the **Théâtre du Parvis St-Jean** (Mon–Fri 9am–noon & 2–6pm; ⓣ03.80.30.63.53), whose innovative programmes of dance, theatre and performance art are worth looking out for.

A little further to the west, the **cathedral** – the once great abbey church of St-Bénigne – is no longer of very great interest, although its garishly tiled roof and nineteenth-century spire dominate the skyline impressively enough. Its circular crypt is the original tenth-century Romanesque church. A little historical curiosity, however, is the fact that Raoul Glaber was a monk here: Glaber is famed as the historian who described the great burgeoning of Romanesque churches across France once the apocalyptic dangers of the first millennium were safely past and the earth began "clothing herself in a white garment of churches".

In a chestnut-shaded garden next to the cathedral, the **Musée Archéologique**, 5 rue du Dr-Maret (mid-May to Sept daily except Mon & Tues: 9am–6pm; Oct to mid-May 9am–12.30pm & 1.30–6pm; €2.20, Sun free), has some extremely interesting finds from the Gallo-Roman period, especially funerary bas-reliefs depicting the perennial Gallic preoccupation with food and wine, and a collection of *ex votos* from the source of the Seine, among them the little bronze of the goddess Sequana (Seine) upright in her bird-prowed boat. Also on show is Sluter's bust of Christ from the Chartreuse.

The Chartreuse de Champmol and around

One of the greatest of Dijon's artistic monuments lies some 1.5km west of the city centre along avenue Albert-1er, beyond the gare SNCF. It is the **Chartreuse de Champmol** (currently only available by guided group tour; inquire at the main tourist office), founded by Duke Philippe le Hardi in 1383 to be the burial place of his dynasty – Dijon's equivalent of the cathedral of St-Denis in Paris. To adorn it, Philippe recruited a talented team of artists, foremost among them the Dutchman Claus Sluter, pioneer of Realism in sculpture and founder of the Burgundian school. Although it was practically destroyed in the Revolution and most of the surviving works of art are in the city's museums, two of Sluter's finest – the so-called *Well of Moses*, featuring six highly realistic portrayals of Old Testament prophets, and the portal of the chapel – remain *in situ*. The site itself is now part of a psychiatric hospital. In between the station and the Chartreuse de Champmol, you can promenade about the botanical garden, the **Jardin de l'Arquebuse** (daily 7.30am–6/8pm), site of the **Natural History Museum** (Mon & Wed–Fri 9am–noon & 2–6pm, Tues, Sat & Sun 2–6pm; €2.20), with just about every stuffed bird and mammal you can think of, plus an exquisite collection of butterflies.

Eating, drinking and entertainment

Dijon has an inordinate number of **pâtisseries**, full of high-quality, tempting confectionery in which marzipan and fruit feature prominently. The more exotic places also promote the Dijon specialities: *pain d'épices*, a gingerbread made with honey and spices and eaten with butter or jam (from Mulot et Petitjean, 13 place Bossuet and other branches all over town), and *cassissines* – blackcurrant candies. **Chocolate**, best made on the premises, is another speciality – try Au Parrain Généreux, 21 rue du Bourg, southwest of the Palais. And you can hardly forget that Dijon is also the high temple of **mustard** – there's the shop of leading producer Maille at 30 rue de la Liberté, selling a range from mild to cauterizing. Finally, a couple of ideas for buying good but affordable **wine**: first and foremost, there's Nicot, 48 rue Jean-Jacques-Rousseau, where you can taste, seek advice or take courses; alternatively, try La Cave du Clos, 3 rue Jeannin, or Nicolas, 6 rue François-Rude.

There are a large number of excellent **restaurants** in town. Lively rue Berbisey, rue Monge and place Émile Zola hold the most promise for both eating and drinking options.

Restaurants

Au Bon Pantagruel Place du Marché, 20 rue Quentin ☎03.80.30.68.69. One of the more popular, lively bistros ranged round the market, with a good range of regional specialties on a menu that changes with healthy frequency. Menus at €19.50. Closed Sun.

La Cézanne 38 rue Amiral Roussin ☎03.80.58.91.92. One of a string of tiny restaurants whose tables are crammed into a narrow, atmospheric old street, with a Provençal-influenced menu (€17–46). If that doesn't suit, then there's Italian, classic French and crêpes very close to hand. Closed Mon lunch, Sun & last two weeks of Aug.

Le Chabrot 36 rue Monge ☎03.80.50.02.35. Small, friendly restaurant on the west side of Place Émile Zola with a staunchly Burgundian menu at €20.50 and a more refined offering at €30. Doubles as a wine bar-cum-cellar; the superb wine list offers lots of help for amateurs. Closed Sun & second week in Aug.

Le Clos des Capucines 3 rue Jeannin, at the end of rue Jean-Jacques-Rousseau ⓣ03.80.65.83.03. Situated in a beautiful medieval setting, this restaurant serves very good traditional, rich Burgundy cuisine (*jambon persillé*, escargots, *bœuf bourguignon*) at very reasonable prices. Menus at €12.50–29. Closed Sun & Sat lunch.

Côté St-Jean 13 rue Monge ⓣ03.80.50.11.77. Rather chic restaurant offering such delights as langoustines, duck tournedos and gratin of pears and almonds. Menus €29–39, with a good-value lunch menu at €16. Closed Wed & Sat lunch, Tues & mid-July to mid-Aug.

Les Deux Fontaines 16 place de la République ⓣ03.80.60.86.45. A short walk from the centre, in the northeast corner of the old town, but worth it for the airy, garden-like atmosphere and fresh, Mediterranean-influenced daily specials (*plats* €11–13).

Gril'Laure 8 place St-Bénigne ⓣ03.80.41.86.76. Popular with the business lunch crowd for its convenient cathedral-side location, and pizzas, pasta and grilled dishes hot out of the wood-fired oven. Menus at €16 & €23.

Le Potimarron 4 av de l'Ouche ⓣ03.80.43.38.07. A bit out of the way, but serves homemade vegetarian and macrobiotic dishes as well as organic meat and fish. Reasonably priced with menus from €13.75. Closed Sun & Mon.

Simpatico 30 rue Berbisey ⓣ03.80.30.53.53 Likeable, trendy Italian restaurant with funky decor. Lunch menus at €11.40, dinners à la carte from around €20. Closed Sun, Mon & Aug.

Le Verdi 10 place Émile Zola ⓣ03.80.30.25.88. Wildly popular lunch menu (€10), and the outdoor seating on the square gets busy in the evening too. Menu includes grills, pizza, fish and good inexpensive escargots. Dinners in the €18–25 range. Closed Sun.

Cafés, bars and nightclubs

Dijon is an important university city as well as one of France's main conference centres, so **nightspots** and cultural centres at both ends of the range are worth exploring. Place Émile Zola and rue Berbisey are good places to start a night out. The English/Irish theme pubs are predictably popular, but there are plenty of alternatives. For **information** on bands and DJs, pick up a free *Mag de la Nuit* (ⓦwww.magdelanuit.net) at the tourist office or various establishments around the city.

Le Brighton 33 rue Auguste-Comte. English pub with 200 different kinds of beer, and dancing. Daily till around 3am or later.

Le Cappuccino 132 rue Berbisey. Speciality beers in a youthful, slightly bohemian bar. Daily till around 1.30am.

Le Chez Nous just behind rue Quentin. Tucked down a tiny alleyway just off rue Quentin, a genuine community bar with a proudly alternative ethos and a genuine atmosphere. Strip lighting, mismatched old tables, exhibitions, impromptu performances and conversations. Opening times and days vary, but usually daily till around 1am.

Le Crockodil 88 rue Berbisey. Pub-cum-café characterized by distressed chic. A good place for an afternoon coffee leading into an early evening drink. Mon–Sat till 2am.

Messire Bar 3 rue Jules Mercier. Very Seventies bar, tucked away in a side street in the old town. Open till late night every night.

Le Privé Ave Garibaldi. Large, traditional disco and pick-up joint, just off place de la République. Two rooms: one mainstream Euro-house, the other more retro. Wed–Sat till 5am.

Pub Kilkenny 1 rue Auguste-Perdrix. Noisy, popular Irish bar: draught Guinness and week-night Irish bands. Daily till 3am.

Le Quentin rue Quentin. Café-bar on the southeast corner of the market square that's popular for its cheap bottles of wine, drunk early evening as an aperitif mixed with *sirop de violettes* – or any of a host of other *sirop* flavours.

Rhumerie la Jamaïque 14 place de la République. Popular with a trendy late-twenties/early-thirties crowd for its pricey cocktails and rock-opera décor; they have live bands on the weekend playing Caribbean music. Daily except Sun 3pm–3am. For something more Latin-based, traverse the square to *Salsapelpa* on rue Marceau, open daily until 2am.

Shanti 69 rue Berbisey. Great little hookah joint, decked out with divans in transcendental South Asian décor, serving delicious teas and flavoured sheesha (€7 for a tobacco pipe). Open until 2am.

L'Univers 47 rue Berbisey. Popular, central pub-bar with frequent blues, jazz and rock concerts in the cellar. Open till midnight and later.

Au Vieux Léon 52 rue Jeannin. Tiny, noisy, friendly little bar that's positively jumping with students. Decorated like an old-fashioned French café on acid.

Listings

Cinemas L'Eldorado, 21 rue Alfred de Musset (Ⓣ03.80.66.12.34; Ⓦwww.cinema-eldorado.com), is a three-screen arts cinema showing all films in original language with a concentration of foreign films. Devosge, 6 rue Devosge (Ⓣ03.80.30.74.79), shows some films in the original, and tries to deviate from the obvious classics.
Festivals The city has a good summer music season, with classical concerts throughout June in its Été Musical programme. L'Estivade, which takes place at various locations around the city between late June and mid-Aug, puts on endless music, dance and street theatre performances. The Fête de la Vigne, in the last week of Aug, is a traditional costume/folklore jamboree; while the Foire gastronomique, during the first two weeks of Nov, celebrates all things edible.
Markets From 6am Tues, Thurs (Les Halles only) & Fri mornings, and all day Sat along the four streets surrounding the covered market – rue Bannelier, rue Quentin, rue C.-Ramey and rue Odebert.
Swimming pool Oxygène-Parc Aquatique, Centre Commercial de la Toison d'Or (mid-June to Aug daily 10.30am–7.30pm, April–May & Sept–Oct Wed, Sat & Sun 10.30am–6.30pm; closed Nov–March; Ⓣ03.80.74.16.16; adults €9, kids €7.50; bus #16). Wave machine, jacuzzi and water slides.

The Côte d'Or

South of Dijon, the attractive countryside of the **Côte d'Or** is characterized by the steep scarp of the *côte*, wooded along the top and cut by steep little valleys called *combes*, where local rock climbers hone their skills (footpaths **GR7** and **GR76** run the whole length of the wine country as far south as Lyon). Spring is a good time to visit this region, when you avoid the crowds and the landscape is a dramatic symphony of browns – trees, earth and vines, along with millions of bone-coloured vine stakes wheeling past as you travel through, like crosses in a vast war cemetery.

The place names that line the N74 – Gevrey-Chambertin, Vougeot, Vosne-Romanée, Nuits-St-Georges, Pommard, Volnay, Meursault Beaune – are music to the ears of wine buffs. But apart from the busy tourist centre of **Beaune**, they turn out to be sleepy, dull though exceedingly prosperous villages, full of houses inhabited by well-heeled *vignerons*. You can make a very good living on a patch of four or five hectares, the average-sized plot, the proof being that none is ever up for sale.

There are numerous **caves** where you can taste (usually for a charge of €4.50–6) and buy the local elixir, but remember that the former is meant to be a prelude to the latter. And there's no such thing as a cheap wine here, red or white, €15–18 being the minimum price you'll pay for a bottle. The Hautes Côtes (Nuits and Beaune) – wines from the top of the slope – are cheaper, but they lack the connoisseur cachet of the big names.

Beaune

BEAUNE, the principal town of the Côte d'Or, just about manages to maintain its attractively ancient air, despite a near constant stream of tourists and rampant commercialism – this must be one of the few towns in France where most of the shops stay open at lunchtime. Narrow cobbled streets and sunny squares dotted with cafés make it a lovely spot to sample the region's wine, though you may find it cheaper and easier to use Dijon as a base for getting around in the area, as there are good connections by train and Transco buses, which service all the villages down the N74.

Beaune's town centre is a tightly clustered, rampart-enclosed *vieille ville*, and its chief attraction is the fifteenth-century hospital, the **Hôtel-Dieu** (April–Sept daily 9am–6.30pm, Oct–March 9am–1.30pm & 2–6.30pm; €5.40), on the corner of place de la Halle. Once past the turnstile you find yourself in a cobbled courtyard surrounded by a wooden gallery overhung by a massive roof patterned with diamonds of gaudy tiles – green, burnt sienna, black and yellow – and similarly multicoloured steep-pitched dormers and turrets. Inside is a vast paved hall with a glorious arched timber roof, the Grande Salle des Malades, which preserves the heavy, enclosed wooden beds used in the nineteenth century and beyond – patients were accommodated here up until 1971. Passing through two smaller, furnished wards, the kitchen and the pharmacy, you reach a dark chamber housing the splendid fifteenth-century altarpiece of the *Last Judgement* by Rogier van der Weyden. The painting was commissioned by Nicolas Rolin, who also founded the hospital in 1443 (King Louis XI commented: "It was only fair that a man who had made so many people poor during his life should create an asylum for them before his death"). A major wine auction takes place here during the annual Trois Glorieuses festival (see p.635), the prices paid setting the pattern for the season.

The private residence of the dukes of Burgundy on rue d'Enfer now contains the **Musée du Vin** (daily 9.30am–6pm; winter daily except Tues 9.30am–5pm; €5.10, same ticket allows entry to the two fine arts museums listed overleaf), with giant winepresses, a collection of traditional tools of the trade and a relief map of the vineyards that begins to make sense of it all. At the other end of rue

The wines of Burgundy

Burgundy farmers have been growing grapes since Roman times, and their rulers, the dukes, frequently put their **wines** to effective use as a tool of diplomacy. Today they have never had it so good, which is why they're reticent about the quirks of soil and climate and the tricks of pruning and spraying that make their wines so special. **Vines** are temperamental: frost on the wrong day, sun at the wrong time, too much water or poor drainage, and they won't come up with the goods. And they like a slope, which is why so many wines are called "Côte (hill) de" somewhere. Burgundy's best wines come from a narrow strip of hillside called the **Côte d'Or** that runs southwest from Dijon to Santenay, and is divided into two regions, Côte de Nuits and Côte de Beaune. With few exceptions the reds of the Côte de Nuits are considered the best: they are richer, age better and cost more. Côte de Beaune is known particularly for its whites: Meursault, Montrachet and Puligny.

The single most important factor determining the "character" of wines is the **soil**. In the Côte d'Or, the relative mixture of chalk, flint and clay varies over very short distances, making for an enormous variety of taste. Chalky soil makes a wine *virile* or *corsé*, in other words "heady" – *il y a de la mâche*, they say, "something to bite on" – while clay makes it *féminin*, more *agréable*.

These and other more extravagant judgements are made after the hallowed procedure of **tasting**: in order to do it properly, by one account, you have to "introduce a draft of wine into your mouth, swill it across the tongue, roll it around the palate, churn it around, emitting the gargling sound so beloved of tasters, which is produced by slowly inhaling air through the centre of your mouth, and finally eject it". The ejection is what has to be learnt.

For an **apéritif** in Burgundy, you should try *kir*, named after the man who was both mayor and MP for Dijon for many years after World War II – two parts dry white wine, traditionally *aligoté*, and one part *cassis* or blackcurrant liqueur. To round the evening off there are many **liqueurs** to choose from, but Burgundy is particularly famous for its marcs, of which the best are matured for years in oak casks.

d'Enfer – one of Beaune's quieter, lovelier cobbled streets – is the Burgundian Romanesque **church of Nôtre-Dame**. Inside are five very special Tournai tapestries from the fifteenth century, depicting the life of the Virgin and commissioned, once again, by the Rolin family.

There are two other museums in town: the not-very-interesting **Musée des Beaux-Arts**, in the Porte Marie de Bourgogne, and the **Musée Marey**, devoted to early movie photography, housed in the Hôtel de Ville (both April–Oct daily 2–6pm; same ticket as wine museum). On the outskirts of the town, by the A6 Beaune–Tailly–Merceuil rest area, there's an open-air park called the **Archéodrome** (Ⓣ03.80.26.87.00; Ⓦwww.archeodrome-bourgogne.com; April–June & Sept daily 10am–6pm; July & Aug daily 10am–7pm; Feb, March & Oct–Dec Wed–Sun 10am–5pm; adults €6.10, children €4.40), illustrating the history of Burgundy, with film and reconstructions of a Neolithic house, Caesar's siege of Alésia, a farm with ancient breeds of farm animals and so on.

Practicalities

Beaune's **gare SNCF** is outside the old walls to the east of town on avenue du 8-Septembre. If you arrive by bus, you're likely to be dropped at the main **gare routière** on the southwest side of town, just outside the walls at the end of rue Maufoux, a five-minute walk from the town's highlights. The slick **tourist office**, 1 rue de l'Hôtel-Dieu (mid-June to Sept Mon–Sat 9.30am–7.30pm, Sun 10am–12.30pm & 2–6pm; April to mid-June, Oct to mid-Nov Mon–Sat 9.30am–6.30pm, Sun 10am–12.30pm & 2–5pm; mid-Nov to March Mon–Sat 10am–6pm, Sun 10am–12.30 & 2–5pm; Ⓣ03.80.26.21.30, Ⓦwww.ot-beaune.fr), is opposite the Hôtel-Dieu, and the friendly, helpful staff can give you plenty of information on touring the region and tasting its wines. You can also rent **bikes** from the tourist office or, alternatively, visit *Bourgogne Randonnées* at ave de 8 Septembre by the *gare* (€3 per hour, €15 per day). For **Internet**, you'll need to head to the bibliothèque municipale at 11 place Marey (€2 per hour, though you may find there's a wait).

If you're going to **stay** in Beaune, be prepared to book well in advance and pay at least €40 a night, probably more. There are only five hotels within the town walls, though a host of them just outside. Two of the less extravagantly priced are the pleasant *Central*, right in the middle of things at 2 rue Victor-Millot (Ⓣ03.80.24.69.70, Ⓔhotel.central.beaune@wanadoo.fr; ❺), with a good restaurant; and the more secluded *Hôtel des Remparts*, at 48 rue Thiers (Ⓣ03.80.24.94.94, Ⓦwww.webstore.fr/hotel-remparts; ❹), which has some lovely wooden-beamed rooms set around a small cobbled courtyard and internet access in all the rooms. Most of Beaune's hotels are found just outside the town walls to the southeast, around rue du Faubourg Madeleine and place Madeleine; *La Cloche*, at 40 place de la Madeleine (Ⓣ03.80.24.66.33; Ⓔhotel.cloche.beaune@wanadoo.fr; ❹) is pleasant and reliable. Further out, *Hôtel Grillon*, 21 route de Seurre, (Ⓣ03.80.22.44.25, Ⓦwww.hotel-grillon.fr; ❸) is set in pleasant gardens about 1km east of town, and has a small heated swimming pool. The pretty *Les Cent Vignes* **campsite**, 10 rue Dubois (Ⓣ03.80.22.03.91; mid-March to Oct), is about 1km out of town, off rue du Faubourg-St-Nicolas (the N74 to Dijon), before the bridge over the *autoroute*; booking is advisable.

Eating out is an expensive business here, although *Le Carnot*, 18 rue Carnot (Ⓣ03.80.22.32.93), is a decent brasserie with reasonable prices and passable pizza (though just), and there are simple but excellent *plats* such as steaks and salads to be had at the *Bistrot Bourguignon*, on the *peotonal* at 8 rue Monge

(ⓣ03.80.22.23.24), as well as a good range of wines by the glass – and live jazz on Saturday nights. For something more sophisticated, try *Le Gourmandin*, 8 place Carnot (ⓣ03.80.24.07.88; ⓦwww.hotellegourmandin.com), with good menus at €22 and €38 (and two rooms at ❻), or the decidedly upscale *Bernard Morillon*, 31 rue Maufoux (ⓣ03.80.24.12.06; closed Mon & Tues lunch), where menus start at €35 and soar to €76. Just outside the town walls, *Les Tontons,* at 22 rue du Faubourg Madeleine (ⓣ03.80.24.19.64; closed Sun & Mon), is stylish and unpretentious, with menus from €18–25).

Château du Clos-de-Vougeot

If you find French wine culture fascinating, it's worth April the **Château du Clos-de-Vougeot** to see the wine-making process (April–Sept daily 9am–6.30pm; Oct–March daily 9–11.30am & 2–5.30pm; Sat closes 5pm; €3.40), 15km north of Beaune between Gévry-Chambertin and Nuits-St-Georges, where you get to see the mammoth thirteenth-century winepresses installed by the Cistercian monks to whom these vineyards belonged for nearly 700 years until the Revolution. The château today is the home of a phoney chivalrous order founded in 1934, the Confrèrie des Chevaliers du Tastevin. Chivalrous or not, the "new" monks continue the good wine work. After you've seen how it's made, you can taste it nearby at La Grand Cave à Vougeot (9am–7pm). There's a three-day wine **festival**, Les Trois Glorieuses on the third Saturday in November, starting in Vougeot and continuing in Beaune and Meursault.

The Saône valley

The **Saône valley** is prosperous and modern, nourished by the *autoroute*, tourism, industry and the wine trade. But turn your back on the river and head west and at once you enter a different Burgundy: hilly pasture and woodland, utterly rural and more populated by cattle than people. This is the hinterland – the Deep South – of Burgundy, where every village clusters under the tower of a Romanesque church, spawned by the influence of Cluny in the 1000s and 1100s. It is only when you reach the Loire and encounter the main traffic routes again that you re-enter the modern world.

It's beautiful country for **cycling**, though there are few places from which to actually rent a bike. There are, however, plenty of bus and train connections, and all these are very conveniently listed in the *Guide des Transports Régionaux* available from any railway station in Burgundy.

Chalon-sur-Saône

CHALON, a sizeable port and bustling industrial centre on a broad meander of the Saône, is generally uninteresting, though its old riverside quarter does have an easy charm, and it makes a good base for exploring the more expensive areas of the Côte d'Or. It's a thriving business centre, and trade fairs frequently take over the town, but more festive occasions are also an important part of its appeal and good reasons to stop if you're around at the right time. The pre-Lent carnival (February or March) features a parade of giant masks and a confetti battle, and there's a national festival of street artists and theatre in July.

The **old town** is just back from the river around Grande-Rue and rue du Châtelet. At the junction of these two streets stands a fifteenth-century timber-framed house, and around the quarter you'll find a number of half-timbered jettied facades. Nearby, 200m to the west on place de l'Hôtel-de-Ville, is the **Musée Denon** (daily except Tues & hols 9.30am–noon & 2–5.30pm; €3.10, free on Wed & first Sun of the month), whose most vaunted exhibit is the 18,000-year-old Volgu flint, rated one of the finest stone tools yet discovered. Apart from the usual collection of bits and pieces excavated nearby, look out for the local furniture and a painting by Vuillard.

More interesting and unusual is the **Musée Niépce**, 28 quai des Messageries (daily except Tues: July & Aug 10am–12.30pm & 1.30–6pm; Sept–June 9.30–11.45am & 2–5.45pm; €3.10, free on Wed & first Sun of the month), just downstream from Pont St-Laurent. Nicéphore Niépce, who was born in Chalon, is credited with inventing photography in 1816 – though he named it 'heliography' – and he in fact worked alongside Daguerre (innovator of the daguerrotype process). The museum possesses a fascinating range of cameras, from the first machine ever to the Apollo moon mission's equipment, plus a number of 007-type spy-camera devices, all attractively displayed under a set of glass domes. Upstairs is a library of works on photography and a space for temporary exhibitions.

The other interesting target in town is the **Maison des Vins** on Promenade Ste-Marie (Mon–Sat 9am–7pm), where you can taste and buy Côte Chalonnaise wines, chosen from the wines of 44 local villages by a choice committee of professional wine tasters.

Practicalities

The **tourist office** is located just off the pedestrian walkway at boulevard de la République (July & Aug Mon–Sat 10am–7pm, Sun 10am–12pm & 4–7pm; Sept–June Mon–Sat 9.30am–12.30pm & 1.30–6.30pm, Sun 10am–noon; ⓣ03.85.48.37.97, ⓦwww.chalon-sur-saone.net), and gives out excellent listings and a free town plan. The **gare SNCF** is just five minutes' walk away at the end of avenue Jean-Jaurès; the **bus** to Cluny (four daily) leaves from behind platform 1.

The most attractive **hotel** in town is undoubtedly the *St-Jean*, right on the riverbank at 24 quai Gambetta (ⓣ03.85.48.45.65, ⓕ03.85.93.62.69; ❸), with classical-style rooms. For something a little cheaper, there's *Aux Vendanges de Bourgogne*, 21 rue du Général-Leclerc (ⓣ03.85.48.01.90; ❷), with a crêperie downstairs, or the central, no-starred *Hôtel Saint-Pierre*, 10 place de l'Hôtel de Ville (ⓣ03.85.48.44.92; ❷; closed Sun). If you're looking for dirt-cheap without the dirt, stay at the *Residences Chalon Jeunes* at 18 ave Pierre Nugue (ⓣ03.85.46.44.90, ⓦwww.chalonjeunes.org), which has rooms for €11 a night and a cafeteria-style restaurant. *Camping de la Butte* (ⓣ03.85.48.26.86), 3km east of town in St-Marcel, is accessible on bus #5 during the summer; if you're walking, cross either Pont St-Laurent or Pont J.-Richard and head east.

Rue de Strasbourg, across Pont St-Laurent on the so-called *île aux restos*, is lined with excellent places to **eat**. The more expensive French or Burgundian restaurants are at the north end, near the bridge: *Chez Jules* at no. 11 (ⓣ03.85.48.08.34, closed Sat lunch and Sun) is one of the more refined choices and has menus from €18. Also worthwhile are *L'air du Temps* at no. 7 (ⓣ03.85.93.39.01, closed Sun & Mon), which does standard French fare with the obligatory *escargots* from €20, and *Le Bistrot* at no. 31 (ⓣ03.85.93.22.01; closed July & Aug and weekends; from €16). For authentic Italian cuisine, visit *da Nunzio* at no. 3 (ⓣ03.85.48.39.83, closed Tues and Sat lunch), which has fresh pasta menus from €15. Further down the street, you can choose from a handful of Lebanese, Chinese-Vietnamese, Indian and North African restaurants in all price ranges – not to mention local Saônois cuisine. A handful of late-night bars can be found just off rue de Strasbourg, including the *Boogie Blues Bar* in the cross-street, rue d'Uxelles. In the centre, the place for cafés is place St-Vincent, with its lovely half-timbered houses. For picnic supplies, there are food **markets** on rue aux Fèvres and place St-Vincent between 8am and noon on Friday and Sunday.

Tournus

TOURNUS is a beautiful little town on the banks of the Saône, just off the *autoroute* and N6, 27km south of Chalon and 30km north of Mâcon. Squeezed between the N6 and the river, the narrow huddled streets have the inward-looking, self-protecting feel of a Mediterranean town, belying a prosperous past when commercial traffic thronged the busy riverside quays. The quays are quiet today, and Tournus's modern prosperity is based on agriculture, light industry – domestic appliances in particular – and, increasingly, tourism, with a nice sideline in art galleries and antique shops. But the quays still make a delightful picnic spot, looking out over the broad sweep of the river and its wide flat valley.

You enter the town from the N6 through a **gateway** flanked by medieval towers – once the entrance to a monastery compound – and are confronted by the old **abbey church of St-Philibert**, one of the earliest and most influential Romanesque buildings in Burgundy. The first construction dates back to around 900 AD and the foundation of the monastic community by monks fleeing Norman raids on their home community of Noirmoutier off the Atlantic coast, although the present building dates to the first half of the eleventh century.

The facade of the church, with its powerful towers and simple decoration of Lombard arcading, has the massive qualities and clean, pared-down lines more associated with a fortress. A narrow staircase opposite the main entrance in the west front leads up to a **high chapel** that looks down into the body of the church, a vestige of the Carolingian tradition of church building which doubled as a defensive feature. The chapel's main arch is inset with two extraordinary sculptures that may represent the abbot responsible for the rebuilding (on the right, holding a hammer and giving a blessing) and possibly the sculptor himself (on the left, full-face), who may even be the "Gerlamus" of the inscription – in which case this may be one of the earliest self-portraits of the medieval period. The nave and transept below are surprisingly light and graceful for such an early church. They have suffered slightly from nineteenth-century meddling, but the three exquisitely carved arches at the far end of the choir remain unharmed, although the effect is marred by aggressively abstract 1950s stained glass. Steps in the north transept lead down to the crypt, where a well plunges down to the level of the Saône – useful in times of siege.

Beside the church, the **Musée Bourguignon** (April–Oct daily except Mon 10am–1pm & 2–5pm; €2.30) is a moderately interesting exposition of nineteenth century Burgundian life that uses carefully costumed wax dummies and nineteenth-century furniture to create various everyday tableaux. More compelling is the **Hôtel Dieu** (April–Oct daily except Tues 11am–6pm; €4.60), one of the region's many charity hospitals, and one of the best preserved – by the time Tournus decided to modernize its hospital, the historical importance of the old one was already clear. The sisters of Saint Martha, an order established in the fifteenth century to serve the hospital in Beaune, worked as ward nurses from the hospital's inception in 1674 right up until it closed in 1978, tending to patients in the ordered rows of closed oak beds, set in high-ceilinged wards to allow the noxious air to circulate. It's worth visiting for the elaborate dispensary alone, complete with a host of faïence pots and hand-blown glass jars. Another wing of the complex houses the **Musée Greuze** (same hours and ticket), centred around local painter, Jean-Baptiste Greuze, who was fashionable in the late eighteenth century for sentimental, moralistic works. The collection here does little to suggest that he deserved a longer-lived reputation, though there's an interesting self-portrait and some instructive drawings.

Practicalities

The **gare SNCF** is on avenue Gambetta, across the road from the old town and a ten-minute walk from the **tourist office**, 2 place Carnot (Tues–Sat 9am–noon & 2–6pm; ⓣ03.85.27.00.20). A second information point stands opposite the west front of the abbey church.

The nicest reasonably priced **hotel** in town is *Hôtel aux Terrasses*, 18 av du 23 Janvier (ⓣ03.85.51.01.74, ⓕ03.85.51.09.99; ❸; closed Jan; excellent restaurant from €22.50, closed Jan, Sun eve through to Tues lunch), at the southern end of the old town where the continuation of rue de la République rejoins the N6. The *Hotel Gras*, 2 rue Fénelon (ⓣ03.85.51.07.25; ❶; restaurant €13.50) has few frills but is friendly and traditional, very close to the abbey church, and serves excellent home-cooked meals. Alternatively, there are the simple *chambres d'hôtes* at the restaurant *Le Voleur de Temps*, 32 rue du Docteur Privey (ⓣ03.85.51.71.93; ❸; restaurant from €17, closed Mon); rooms are reserved for clients of the restaurant, which offers an idiosyncratic menu of West African and Asian dishes – the perfect antidote, perhaps, to an overdose of *bœuf bourguignon*. The *Hôtel-Restaurant de Saône*, quai Georges-Bardin (ⓣ03.85.51.20.65, ⓕ03.85.51.05.45; ❷), offers little character but enjoys a splendid location on the east bank of the river. **Campers** should head for *Camping Municipal en Bagatelle* (ⓣ03.85.51.16.58, ⓕ03.85.27.03.39; May–Sept), just south of the town; take avenue du 23-Janvier out of town to the N6, in the direction of Lyon.

For further **eating** possibilities outside of the hotels, there are a number of cafés and brasseries in and around place de l'Hôtel-de-Ville.

Mâcon and around

MÂCON is a lively, prosperous place on the banks of the River Saône, 58km south of Chalon and 68km north of Lyon, with excellent transport connections between the two. It's a centre for the wine trade and numerous light industries, with a surprisingly sunny southern seaside feel, thanks to its long café-lined **riverbank**. There are no great sights here, but it's worth finding the time for a riverside drink or a stroll through its pedestrian quarter. If you're visiting in late July–early August, look out for the free outdoor jazz concerts.

Lamartine, the nineteenth-century French Romantic poet (see box opposite), was born here in 1790 and his name is much in evidence. He is remembered in the handsome eighteenth-century mansion, the Hôtel Senecé in rue Sigorgne, which houses the **Musée Lamartine** (Mon–Sat 10am–noon & 2–6pm, Sun 2–6pm; €2.30), part of which is dedicated to documents and other memorabilia to do with his personal, political and poetic lives. Nearby, on the corner of place des Herbes where a summertime fruit and veg market is held, stands the town's main tourist curiosity, an elaborate wooden house built around 1500 and known as the **Maison du Bois Doré**, with a wonderful bar/café downstairs that serves cocktails until 2 or 3am. The town also has a medieval art and Gallo-Roman archeological museum, the **Musée des Ursulines**, at 5 rue des Ursulines (Tues–Sat 10am–noon & 2–6pm, Sun 2–6pm; €2.30), housed in a

Alphonse Lamartine (1790–1869)

Often referred to as the French Byron, **Alphonse Lamartine** is one of the best-known of the French Romantic poets. He was born and grew up in Milly, about 15km west of Mâcon, and published his first poetic work, *Méditations poétiques*, in 1820. In 1825 he published *Le Dernier Chant du Pélérinage d'Harold* as a tribute to Byron.

After the 1830 Revolution in Paris, he became involved in politics, being elected to the Chambre des Députés in 1833 and quickly acquiring a reputation as a powerful orator on the weighty questions of the day, like the abolition of slavery and capital punishment. His finest hour was as the leading figure in the provisional government of the Second Republic, which was proclaimed from the Hôtel de Ville in Paris on February 23, 1848. He withdrew from politics when reactionary forces, under the leadership of General Cavaignac, let the army loose on the protesting workers of Paris and Marseille in June 1848, after which he retired to St-Point, continuing to write and publish until his death in 1869.

seventeenth-century convent.

The most enjoyable way to bone up on the Mâcon, Beaujolais and Chalonnais **wines** is to head off on one of the much-signposted wine roads (Ⓦwww.bourgogne-tourisme.com), which extend north into the Maconnais, and south into the Beaujolais, sampling as you go. If you don't have a car or a bike, however, you'll have to fall back on tasting with your meal. Alternatively, the **Maison Mâconnaise des Vins**, 484 av Lattre-de-Tassigny (daily 9am–7pm), can be found where the N6 comes into town along the riverside from Chalon – a ten-minute walk from the centre of town. It's little more than an outlet for a big producer, but they will arrange tastings of four wines for around €3.

Practicalities

The **gare SNCF** (adjacent to the **gare routière**) lies on rue Bigonnet at the southern end of rue Victor-Hugo, but TGV trains leave from Mâcon-Loché station 6km out of town – you'll have to make the connection by taxi. The **tourist office**, 1 place St Pierre (March–May & Oct–Sept Mon–Sat 10am–12.30pm & 1.30–6pm; June–Sept Mon–Sat 10am–7pm, Sun 3–7pm; Nov–Feb Mon–Sat 10am–12.30 & 2–6pm; Ⓣ03.85.21.07.07, Ⓦwww.macon-tourism.com), has good maps and brochures covering the city and surrounding region.

There should be no difficulty finding a **place to stay**. Across the Pont de St-Laurent is one of the nicest and cheapest hotels, *Hôtel du Beaujolais*, at 86 place République (Ⓣ03.85.38.42.06, Ⓕ03.85.38.78.02; ❷), which has very clean, simple rooms. The *Hôtel d'Europe et d'Angleterre*, on the river at 92 quai Jean-Jaurès (Ⓣ03.85.38.27.94, Ⓦwww.hotel-europeangleterre-macon.com; ❸), has an air of former times – Queen Victoria once stayed here – and the *Grand Hôtel de Bourgogne*, on the north side of place de la Barre at 6 rue Victor-Hugo (Ⓣ03.85.38.36.57, Ⓔhotel-de-bourgogne@wanadoo.fr; ❹; restaurant from €18), though it's part of the Interhotel chain, does have some character and a lively atmosphere. For more of a budget place, try *La Promenade*, 266 quai Lamartine (Ⓣ03.85.38.10.98; ❶), which looks right onto the Saône and houses a rather fancy restaurant, *Le Florian*. There's a **campsite** 3km north out of town on the N6 (Ⓣ03.85.38.16.22; closed Nov to mid-March).

Mâcon has no shortage of good **restaurants** to choose from. For cheap eats, head for the river: the pleasant *Lamartine*, 266 quai Lamartine (closed Mon eve through to Wed lunch), is popular for both meals and drinks, while the *St Laurent*, on the other side of the river, has great views and menus from €16. *Au Rocher de Cancale*, 393 quai Jean-Jaurés (ⓣ03.85.38.07.50; closed Sun evenings & Mon), is a traditional restaurant serving excellent snails and Bresse chicken (menus €16–38), and if you're really pushing the boat out, the elegant *Pierre*, 7/9 rue Joseph Dufour (ⓣ03.85.38.14.23; closed Sun evenings, Mon & Tues afternoon, plus first three weeks in July), is well worth a splurge for a special occasion, not least for its soufflés (menus €24–68).

Brou

BROU is an uninteresting suburban village outside Bourg-en-Bresse, 32km east of Mâcon, which happens to have an early sixteenth-century **church** (daily; €5.50). If you're heading east to Geneva or the Alps, take a look, but don't lose a lift or miss a train for it. Aldous Huxley found it "a horrible little architectural nightmare", its monuments "positively and piercingly vulgar". Certainly, it was a very rich woman's expensive folly, crammed with virtuoso craftsmanship from the dying moments of the Gothic style; it was undertaken by Margaret of Austria after the death of her husband, Philibert, Duke of Savoy, as a mausoleum for the two of them and Philibert's mother. No longer a place of worship, it's interesting to see, but soulless, without a trace of vision or inspiration.

Bourg-en-Bresse

BOURG-EN-BRESSE is the place to base yourself if you want to visit Brou's church, just a short bus ride away (#5; every 30min), leaving from place Carriat. The **tourist office** (Mon–Fri 9am–noon & 2–6.30pm, Sat 10am–noon & 2–6pm; ⓣ04.74.22.49.40, ⓦwww.bourg-en-bresse.org) is in Centre Albert-Camus, 6 av Alsace-Lorraine, with an annexe by Brou church in summer. Wednesday is **market** day in place Carriat, and on the first and third Wednesdays of each month there's a livestock market as well. An attractive place to **stay** is the *Hôtel du Mail* near the station at 46 av du Mail (ⓣ04.74.21.00.26, ⓕ04.74.21.29.55; ❸; closed Dec to mid-Jan & mid-July to Aug 8). The municipal **campsite** (ⓣ04.74.45.37.21; April to mid-Oct) is on avenue des Sports, the N83 northeast of town heading for Lons-le-Saunier.

The Mâconnais, Beaujolais and Charollais

West of the valley of the Saône lies a tract of hilly country that is best known for its produce: the white wines of the **Mâconnais** are justly renowned, while the fashion for drinking the young red wine of **Beaujolais** has spread far beyond France. Further west still, the handsome white cattle that luxuriate in the green fields of the **Charollais** are an obvious sign that this is serious beef country.

In the past, however, the region was famed for its religion, and many large and powerful abbeys were established in the eleventh and twelfth centuries under the influence of the great monastery at Cluny. Few monks remain, and **Cluny** itself is largely destroyed, but Romanesque churches are almost as thick on the ground as cattle, and few are more impressive than the great basilica at

Paray-le-Monial.

The Mâconnais

The **Mâconnais** wine-producing country lies to the west of the Saône, a strip hardly 20km wide, stretching from Mâcon to Tournus. The land rises sharply into steep little hills and valleys, at its prettiest in the south, where the region's best white wines come from, around the villages of **POUILLY**, **VINZELLES**, **PRISSÉ** and **FUISSÉ**, at the last of which, should you yearn for rustic rest, the *Hôtel La Vigne Blanche* (Ⓣ03.85.35.60.50, Ⓕ03.85.35.67.13; ❸), will provide just the setting you're looking for, along with good regional cooking (menus from €11).

Directly above these villages rises the distinctive and precipitous 500-metre rock of **Solutré**, which in prehistoric times – around 20,000 BC – seems to have served as some kind of ambush site for hunters after migrating animals: the bones of 100,000 horses have been found in the soil beneath the rock, along with mammoth, bison and reindeer carcasses. The history and results of the excavations are displayed in a museum at the foot of the rock, the **Musée Départemental de Préhistoire** (April–Sept daily 10am–6pm; Feb–March & Oct–Nov daily except Tuesday 10am–noon & 2–7pm; €3.50). A steep path climbs to the top of the rock, where you get a superb view as far as Mont Blanc and the Matterhorn on a clear day, as well as looking down on the huddled roofs of **SOLUTRÉ-POUILLY**, the slopes beneath you covered with the vines of the Chardonnay grape that makes the exquisite greenish Pouilly-Fuissé wine. The area is at its most enchanting in early spring when the earth still shows its *terre-cuite* colours, punctuated by bursts of white cherry blossom and the blue drift of bonfire smoke from prunings amid the neatly staked rows of vines.

Aside from the sheer pleasure of wandering about in such reposeful landscapes – not so, however, if you're trying to tackle this very hilly country on a bike – there are some specific places to make for. One such is the sleepy hamlet of **ST-POINT**, where the poet Lamartine (see box on p.639) spent much of his life in the little medieval **Château de St-Point**, now a museum dedicated to his memory (March to mid-Nov Mon & Thurs–Sat 10am–noon & 3–6pm, Sun 3–6pm; €4.80), next to the Romanesque church where he's buried. If you continue up the road behind the château you come to an utterly rural farm where you can buy goat's cheese. There is a **campsite** by the Lac St-Point (Ⓣ03.85.50.52.31; April–Oct).

Cluny and around

The abbey of **CLUNY** is the major tourist destination of the region. The voice of its abbot once made monarchs tremble, as his power in the Christian world was second only to that of the pope. The monastery was founded in 910 in response to the corruption of the existing church, and it took only a couple of vigorous early abbots to build the power of Cluny into a veritable empire. Gradually its spiritual influence declined, and Cluny became a royal gift. Both Richelieu and Mazarin did stints in the monastery as abbot.

Now, although the reputation of the place still pulls in the tourist coaches, little remains apart from the very attractive village. The Revolution suppressed the monastery, and Hugues de Semur's vast and influential eleventh-century **church**, the largest building in Christendom until the construction of St Peter's in Rome, was dismantled in 1810. Now all you can see of the former **abbey** (daily: May–Aug 9.30am–6.30pm; Sept–April 9.30am–noon & 1.30–5pm; €6.10 combined ticket with museum) is an octagonal belfry, the south transept and, in the impressive granary, the surviving capitals from its immense columns. Access to the belfry leads through the Grand École des Ingénieurs, one of France's elite higher-education institutions, and you can often see the students in their fraternity gowns decorated with cabalistic signs. From the top of the **Tour des Fromages** (entered through the tourist office for €1.50) you can reconstruct it in your imagination. The **Musée d'Art et d'Archaeologie** (same hours and ticket as abbey), in the fifteenth-century palace of the last freely elected abbot, helps to flesh out the picture with reconstructions and fragments of sculpture, while the octagonal Romanesque belfry of the parish **church of St-Marcel** also recalls the belfries that once adorned the abbey.

There are some interesting old houses in rue Mercière/rue Lamartine and, in particular, rue de la République/rue d'Avril; nos. 25 and 6 of the latter are nearly as old as the abbey itself. At the back of the abbey is one of France's national stud farms, **Haras National** (daily 9am–7pm; free), which can also be visited.

The **tourist office** is beside the Tours des Fromages, at 6 rue Mercière (April–June & Sept 10am–12.30pm & 2.30–6.45pm; July & Aug daily 10am–7pm; Oct–March 10am–12.30pm & 2.30–5pm; ⓣ03.85.59.05.34; ⓔcluny@wanadoo.fr). **Bicycles** can be rented at the campsite, or at Ludisport, by the platform of the abandoned railway station, on the southeast edge of town. For **accommodation**, the showy *Hôtel de Bourgogne*, Place de l'Abbaye (ⓣ03.85.59.00.58, ⓦwww.hotel-cluny.com; ❺; closed Dec & Jan), has an irresistible location in what must have been the north aisle of the church, while *Le Potin Gourmand*, though a bit of a hike from the centre at 4 place du Champ de Foire (ⓣ03.85.59.02.06, ⓕ03.85.59.22.58; ❸; closed Jan & Feb) has eight beguiling rooms arranged around a rustic, gardened courtyard. The best inexpensive choice is the plain but reasonably central *Hôtel du Commerce*, 8 place du Commerce (ⓣ03.85.59.03.09, ⓕ03.85.59.00.87; ❶), though be sure to call ahead as they are given to closing early. There's a municipal **hostel**, *Cluny Séjour*, on rue Porte-de-Paris (ⓣ03.85.59.08.83; closed Dec to mid-Jan), and a municipal **campsite**, St-Vital (ⓣ03.85.59.08.34; closed mid-Sept to April), across Pont de la Levée in the direction of Tournus.

For **meals**, there's good country cooking to be had at *Le Potin Gourmand* (closed Sun evening & Mon; menus €23–30), while the *Brasserie du Nord*, right in the heart of things on the Place de l'Abbaye, serves simple classics.

Taizé

Another powerful attraction for the faithful might be the modern ecumenical community at **TAIZÉ**, 10km north of Cluny. It was founded in 1940 by the Swiss pastor Roger Schutz and centres around a restored Romanesque church and the new Church of Reconciliation. Hordes of youngsters come to take part in discussion groups and camp out. If you're seriously interested – and it's not likely to be to the taste of the merely curious – write to The Taizé Community, 71250 Taizé, France or visit the website (ⓦwww.taize.fr), which gives full details. If you're passing through, you're more than welcome to visit the popular gift shop, where the brothers sell their wares, which include glazed dishware and musical recordings and writings translated into twenty languages.

The Beaujolais

Imperceptibly, as you continue south, the Mâconnais becomes the **Beaujolais**, a larger area of terraced hills producing lighter, fruity red wines, which it is now fashionable to drink very early. The Beaujolais grape is the Gamay, which, in contrast to other parts of Burgundy, thrives here on this granite soil. Of the four *appellations* of Beaujolais, the best are the *crus*, including Morgon and Fleurie, which come from the northern part of the region between St-Amour (the northernmost *cru*), and Brouilly in the south. If you have transport, you can follow the *cru* trail south from Mâcon by turning right at Crêches-sur-Saône up the D31 to St-Amour, and then south along the D68. Beaujolais Villages, which produces the most highly regarded *nouveau*, comes from the middle of the Beaujolais region, south of the *cru* belt, while plain Beaujolais and Beaujolais Supérieur are produced in the vineyards southwest of Villefranche.

The well-marked **route de Beaujolais** winds down through the wine villages to **VILLEFRANCHE**, not far from Lyon and a good base for the route. Here, the **tourist office** at 290 rue de Thizy (July & Aug Mon–Sat 9am–12.30pm & 2–6.30pm, Sun 9am–noon; Sept–June Mon–Sat 9am–noon & 1.30–5.30pm; ⓣ04.74.07.27.40) has information about caves, visits and wine tours. There are numerous cheap **hotels**, almost all near the **gare SNCF**. Two great options are the friendly and clean *Hôtel de Bourgogne*, 91 rue Stalingrad (ⓣ04.74.65.06.42; ❶), and *Moulin a Vent*, 81 rue d'Anse just across from the *gare* (ⓣ04.74.68.36.13; ⓕ04.74.65.09.70; ❶), which has a few decent rooms looking out onto a mural of the lovely Beaujolais landscape. Rue de la Gare proffers a multitude of ethnic **restaurants**, and most of the cafés on rue Nationale are good for snacks or cheap menus, too.

Paray-le-Monial

Fifty kilometres west of Cluny, across countryside that becomes ever gentler and flatter as you approach the broad valley of the Loire, is **PARAY-LE-MONIAL**, whose major attraction is its **Basilique du Sacré-Coeur** (9am–9pm daily). Not only is it a superb building in its own right, with a marvellously satisfying arrangement of apses and chapels stacking up in sturdy symmetry to its fine octagonal belfry, it's the best place to get an idea of what the abbey of Cluny looked like, as it was built shortly afterwards in devoted imitation of the mother church.

The town itself is the archetypal country town, quiet and unpretentious, straddling the slow waters of the River Bourbince and the Canal du Centre. The only thing that disturbs its calm is the arrival of pilgrims of the Sacré-Coeur, or "Sacred Heart", a cult which originated here with Marguerite-Marie Alacoque, a local nun who received revelations advocating the worship of the sacred heart. The cult was later adopted by the entire Roman Catholic Church. The first pilgrimage took place in 1873, encouraged as a means of combating the socialist ideas espoused by the Paris Commune, and it raised the money to construct the church of the Sacré-Coeur on the hill of Montmartre in Paris. Paray is now second only to Lourdes as a pilgrim centre.

The one secular building definitely worth a look, aside from just browsing down the main street – rue de la République/rue des Deux-Ponts/rue Victor-Hugo – is the highly ornamented **Maison Jayet**, now the Hôtel de Ville on place Guignaud, built in the 1520s.

Practicalities

The **tourist office** is on avenue Jean-Paul-II (July & Aug Mon–Sat 9am–7pm & Sun 10am–7pm; Sept–June Mon–Sat 9am–noon & 1–6pm, Sun 10am–12.30pm & 2.30–5.30pm; ⓣ03.85.81.10.92). You can rent **bikes** from Cycles Kaikinger, 24 rue de la République (ⓣ03.85.88.85.15).

For **accommodation**, try the *Hostellerie des Trois Pigeons*, 2 rue Daugard, just beyond the Hôtel de Ville (ⓣ03.85.81.03.77, ⓕ03.85.81.58.59, ⓔhotel3pigeons@wanadoo.fr; ❷; closed Dec–Feb; restaurant from €13), or the slightly-less-fancy *Hôtel aux Vendanges de Bourgogne*, 5 rue Denis-Papin (ⓣ03.85.81.13.43, ⓕ03.85.88.87.59, ⓦwww.auxvendangesdebourgogne.fr; ❸; closed Nov 25–Dec 15; good-value restaurant from €14.50), on the south side of the Canal du Centre, has roomier rooms, some overlooking the pebbled courtyard. The most attractive option, however, is the pleasantly old fashioned yet well-appointed *Grand Hôtel de la Basilique*, 18 rue de la Visitation (ⓣ03.85.81.11.13, ⓦwww.hotelbasilique.com; ❸; closed Nov to April; restaurant from €11.50). A few yards further up the road, *Au Foyer de Sacré Coeur*, 14 rue de la Visitation (ⓣ03.85.81.11.01, ⓦwww.chez.com/fsc; ❷) is bang opposite the chapel that stands on the spot where Ste Marguerite had her revelations, and consequently occupied almost solely by pilgrims, who don't seem to mind the institutional, albeit friendly, atmosphere. The *Mambré* **campsite** is on route du Gué-Léger (ⓣ03.85.88.89.20; mid-March to Oct). If you want to explore the little villages throughout the Mâconnais, there's no better base than the Merle family's organic farm at Vitry-en-Charollais (ⓣ03.85.81.30.62; €40 with breakfast for two, dinner has to be booked ahead), with delicious home-cooking, about 6km southwest of Paray.

The Charollais

The **Charollais** is cattle country, taking its name from the pretty little water-enclosed market town of **CHAROLLES**, with its 32 bridges, on the main N79 road, and in turn giving its name to one of the world's most illustrious breeds of cattle: the white, curly-haired and stocky Charollais, bred for its lean meat. The fields south of Paray are full of the beasts. Throughout this landscape, scattered across the rich farmland along the River Arconce, are dozens of small villages, all with more or less remarkable Romanesque churches, offspring of Cluny in its vigorous youth.

ANZY-LE-DUC, about 15km south of Paray off the main D982 to Roanne, boasts an exquisite complex of buildings: a perfect Romanesque church with jackdaw chatter echoing off the octagonal belfry, side by side with the remains of the old priory incorporated into a sort of fortified farm looking out over the Arconce valley, the whole built in a rich, warm stone. **MONTCEAUX-L'ÉTOILE**, a little nearer to Paray, has its special charm too: a quiet, worn church with beautiful sculptures adorning the porch, standing likewise above the Arconce valley, and, a little way down the village street, a curious tower-like house where a Marquis of Vichy is said to have practised alchemy with the notorious Italian wizard, Cagliostro. There's a farm **campsite** (ⓣ03.85.25.38.66; May–Sept) on the Paray side of the village that will give you a hookup for €10 a night.

Ten kilometres to the west of Paray, the Arconce flows into the Loire just upstream from **DIGOIN**, France's chief centre of pottery manufacture. Although it's not a place you're likely to do more than pass through, the nineteenth-century **bridge** carrying the Canal du Centre over the Loire is worth a look (you can take a short trip across on a sightseeing boat for €7.60) and the riverside quays make a quiet, sunny picnic spot. If you feel you need it, there's a **tourist office** just along the canal at 8 rue Guilleminot (July to mid-Sept daily 10am–noon & 2–6pm, Sun 1.30–6.30pm, mid-Sept to June Tues–Sat 10am–noon & 1.30–4.30pm; ⓣ03.85.53.00.81); the same building also houses the self-explanatory **Musée de la Céramique**, which allows only guided visits (April–Oct Mon–Sat, mid-June to mid-Sept Mon–Sat & Sun afternoons; hour-long tours begin at 10.30am, 2.30pm (Jun–Oct) & 3pm; €3.35). The town also has two very good **hotel-restaurants**: *De la Gare*, 79 av de Gaulle (ⓣ03.85.53.03.04, ⓕ03.85.53.14.70, ⓦwww.hoteldelagare.fr; ❸; closed mid-Jan to mid-Feb; restaurant menus from €17, closed Wed except in July & Aug), and *Les Diligences*, 14 rue Nationale (ⓣ03.85.53.06.31, ⓦwww.les-diligences.com; ❸; closed mid-Nov to mid-Dec; restaurant menus from €17, closed Mon & Tues except in July & Aug), the latter offering a pleasant setting with six rooms of varying sizes, some with terrace. There's a **campsite**, *La Chevrette*, by the Loire on the Moulins road (ⓣ03.85.53.11.49, ⓦwww.lachevrette.com; March–Oct).

Travel details

Trains

Autun to: Avallon (2 daily; 1hr 45min); Chalon-sur-Saône (2 daily; 1hr 10min–1hr 50min); Le Creusot-Ville (4–6 daily; 45min); Saulieu (5–6 daily; 50min).
Auxerre to: Avallon (5–7 daily; 1hr 5min); Dijon (8–10 daily; 1hr 50min–2hr 20min); Joigny (9–11 daily; 35min); Paris (6–8 daily; 1hr 50min–2hr 30min); Sens (6–8 daily; 1hr).
Avallon to: Autun (2 daily; 1hr 45min); Auxerre (4–6 daily; 1hr 5min); Dijon (3 daily; 1hr 45min); Saulieu (4 daily; 50min–1hr).
Beaune to: Dijon (frequent; 25min); Lyon (10–12 daily; 1hr 50min–2hr 10min).
Bourg-en-Bresse to: Dijon (9 daily; 1hr 30min–2hr 10min); Lyon (frequent; 45min–1hr 30min); Mâcon (10 daily; 30–50min).
Dijon to: Auxerre (8–11 daily; 1hr 50min–2hr 20min); Beaune (frequent; 25min); Chalon-sur–Saône (frequent; 40min); Les Laumes-Alésia (8–11 daily; 30–50min); Lyon (10–15 daily; 1hr 35min–2hr 10min); Mâcon (frequent; 1hr–1hr 20min); Montbard (8–11 daily; 30min); Nevers (4–6 daily; 2hr 10min–2hr 50min); Nuits-St-Georges (frequent; 15min); Paris (frequent; 1hr 40min–3hr 15min); Tournus (10 daily; 1hr); Sens (6–9 daily; 1hr 45min–2hr 10min); Tonnerre (8–11 daily; 1hr–1hr 30min); Villefranche (frequent; 1hr 40min–2hr).
Mâcon to: Bourg-en-Bresse (10 daily; 30–50min); Dijon (frequent; 1hr–1hr 20min); Geneva (12 daily; 2hr 30min–3hr 30min); Lyon (frequent; 30min–1hr).
Nevers to: Autun (4 daily; 1hr 40min–2hr 20min); Chalon-sur-Saône (3 daily; 2hr 45min); Clermont-Ferrand (7–8 daily; 1hr 30min–2hr 10min); Le Creusot (5–7 daily; 1hr 30min); Dijon (5–7 daily; 2hr 30min); Paris (frequent; 2–3hr).
Paray-le-Monial to: Chalon-sur-Saône (4–5 daily; 1hr 40min); Le Creusot (4 daily; 40min); Dijon (2 daily; 2hr 15min); Lyon (2–3 daily; 2hr); Moulins (3–5 daily; 1hr).
Sens to: Auxerre (7–10 daily; 1hr–1hr 10min); Avallon (4–6 daily; 2hr); Dijon (9 daily; 1hr 50min–2hr 30min); Joigny (13 daily; 20min); Paris (9 daily; 1hr–1hr 30min); Tonnerre (9 daily; 1hr).
Tournus to: Chalon-sur-Saône (15 daily; 15min); Dijon (10 daily; 1hr); Macon (10 daily; 15min).

Buses

Autun to: Beaune (1 daily; 1hr 10min); Chalon-sur-Saône (2–3 daily; 1hr 30min); Château-Chinon (1–2 daily; 1hr); Le Creusot (3–5; 45min).
Avallon to: Dijon (1 daily; 2hr 30min–3hr); Montbard (3 daily; 50min); Vézelay (summer only 1 daily; 30min).
Chablis to: Auxerre (2 daily, 35min); Tonnerre (2 daily; 1hr).
Châtillon-sur-Seine to: Dijon (3 daily; 1hr 30min–2hr); Montbard (6 daily; 40min).
Cluny to: Chalon-sur-Saône (3–4 daily; 1hr 30min); Charolles (2–5 daily; 45min); Mâcon (7 daily; 45min); Paray-le-Monial (2–5 daily; 1hr); Taizé (7 daily; 15min).

Dijon to: Autun (1 daily; 2hr 30min); Avallon (3 daily; 2hr 30min); Beaune (7 daily; 1hr); Châtillon-sur-Seine (3 daily; 1hr 30min–2hr); Saulieu (3 daily; 1hr 30min).

Mâcon to: Chalon-sur-Saône (6–7 daily; 2hr 15min); Charolles (2–5 daily; 2hr); Cluny (8 daily; 45min); Paray-le-Monial (2–5 daily; 2hr 20min).

Semur-en-Auxois to: Montbard (8 daily; 1hr); Saulieu (1 daily; 35min); Venarey-les-Laumes for Alésia (1–3 daily; 20–30min).

Sens to: Joigny (1 daily; 1hr 10min); Troyes (3 daily; 1hr 45min).

Poitou-Charentes and the Atlantic coast

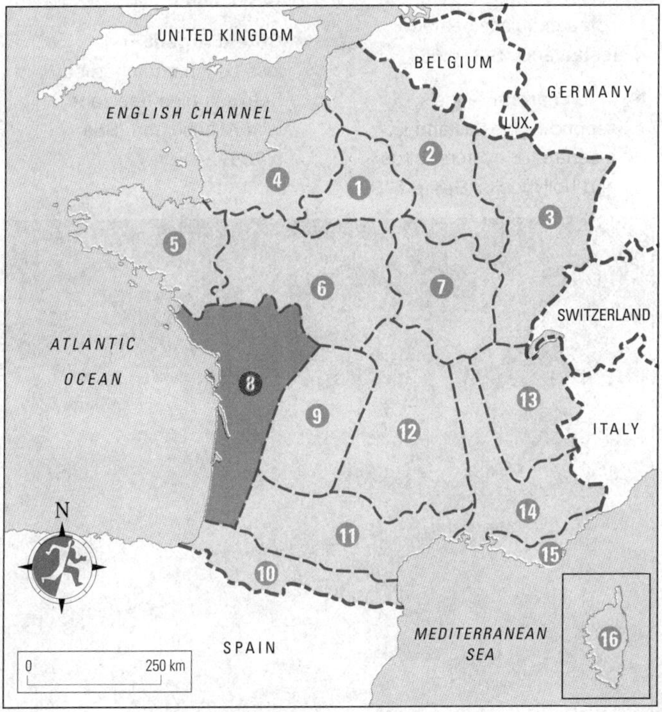

CHAPTER 8

Highlights

* **Marais Poitevin** The "green Venice", an intricate network of land and water that's perfect to explore by bike. **See p.661**
* **La Rochelle** This charming and unspoilt port town is the jewel of the west coast, with a well-preserved historic centre and some exquisite seafood restaurants. **See p.664**
* **Île d'Oléron** France's second biggest island is a centre for oysters, birds and hollyhocks. **See p.678**
* **Angoulême** Wholly underrated, this enchanting old-school town hosts an animated nightlife and rightfully lays claim to some of the best restaurants in the region. **See p.687**
* **Bordeaux** Lively, stylish city surrounded by some of the world's best vineyards. **See p.690**
* **Côte d'Argent** Endless beach stretched out between pine trees and wild Atlantic surf. **See p.708**

△ Pointe de la Coubre, near Royan

8

Poitou-Charentes and the Atlantic coast

Newsstands selling *Sud-Ouest* remind you where you are: this is not the Mediterranean, certainly, but in summer the quality of the light, the warm air, the fields of sunflowers and the shuttered siesta-silence of the farmhouses give you the first exciting promises of the south.

The coast, on the other hand, remains unmistakably Atlantic – dunes, pine forest, reclaimed marshland and misty mudflats. While it has great charm in places, particularly out of season on the islands of **Noirmoutier**, **Ré** and **Oléron**, it's a family, camper-caravanner seaside, lacking the glamour and excitement of the Côte d'Azur. The principal port in the north, **La Rochelle**, is one of the prettiest and most distinctive towns in France. The sandy beaches are beautiful everywhere, though can occasionally be disappointing, especially the northern stretches, where the water is murky and shallow for a long way out. On the dune-backed **Côte d'Argent**, south of Bordeaux, however, the sea can be outright dangerous.

Inland, the valley of the slow and green **River Charente** epitomizes blue-overalled, Gauloise-smoking, peasant France. The towpath is accessible for long stretches, on foot or mountain bike, and there are boat trips from **Saintes** and **Cognac**. The **Marais Poitevin**, too, with its groves of poplars and island fields reticulated by countless canals and ditches, is both an unusual landscape and easy-going walking or cycling country.

But perhaps the most memorable aspect of the countryside – and indeed of towns like **Poitiers** and **Angoulême** – is the presence of exquisite Romanesque churches. This region formed a significant stretch of the medieval pilgrim routes across France and from Britain and northern Europe to the shrine of St Jacques (St James, or Santiago as the Spanish know him) at Compostela in northwest Spain, and was well endowed by its followers. The finest of the churches, among the best in all of France, are to be found in the countryside around Saintes and Poitiers: informal, highly individual and so integrated with their landscape they often seem as rooted as the trees.

Lastly, of course, remember that this is a region of seafood – fresh and cheap in every market for miles inland – and, around the modern, charismatic urban centre that is **Bordeaux**, some of the world's top vineyards.

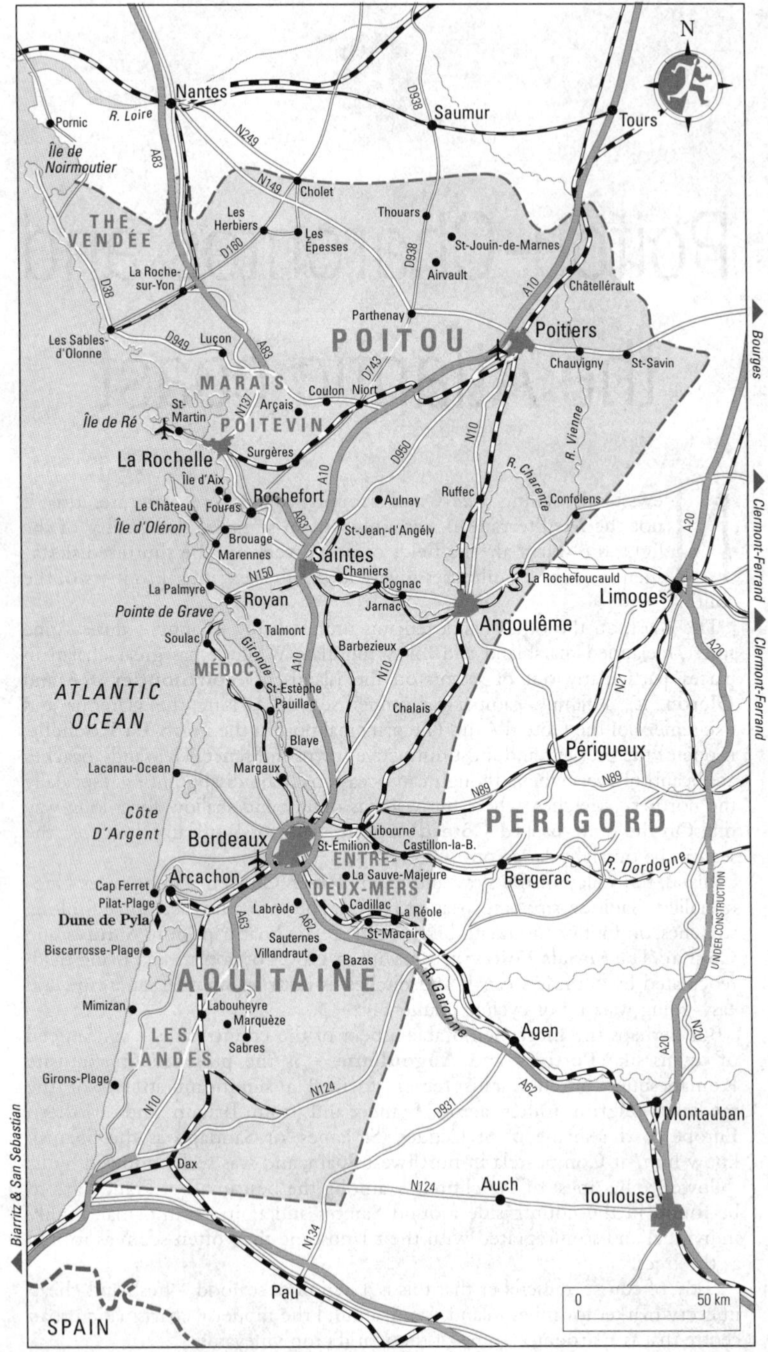

8

POITOU-CHARENTES & THE ATLANTIC COAST

Poitou

Most of the old province of **Poitou** is a huge expanse of rolling wheat fields and sunflower and maize plantations where the combines crawl and giant sprinklers shoot great arcs of white water over the fields in summertime, and villages are strung out along the valley floors. Heartland of the domains of Eleanor, Duchess of Aquitaine, whose marriage to King Henry II in 1152 brought the whole of southwest France under English control for 300 years, it is also the northern limit of the *langue d'oc*-speaking part of the country, whose Occitan dialect survives among the older generations even today.

West of **Poitiers** the open landscape of the Poitou plain gradually gives way to *bocages* – small fields enclosed by hedges and trees. The local farmers' co-operatives say that digging up woodland and creating vast windswept acreages in the name of efficiency and productivity is going out of fashion. And not just for aesthetic reasons: wind erosion has left scarcely 15cm of topsoil.

Poitiers

Heading south from Tours on the Autoroute de l'Aquitaine, you'd hardly be tempted by the cluster of towers and office blocks rising from the plain, which is all you see of **POITIERS**. But draw nearer and things look very different. Sitting on a hilltop overlooking two rivers, Poitiers is a country town with a unique charm that comes from a long and sometimes influential history – as the seat of the dukes of Aquitaine, for instance – discernible in the winding lines of the streets and the breadth of civic, domestic and ecclesiastical architectural fashions represented in its buildings. Its pedestrian precincts, restaurants and pavement cafés – and some wonderful central gardens – make for comfortable sightseeing.

Arrival, information and accommodation

It is a short taxi ride (around €5) into the centre from Poitiers-Biard **airport**, located to the west of town. The **gare SNCF** is on boulevard du Grand Cerf, part of the ring-road system that encircles the base of the hill on which Poitiers is built. There is no *gare routière*: out-of-town **buses**, run by Rapides de Poitou (Ⓣ05.49.46.27.45), leave from the train station. The **tourist office** is a fifteen-minute walk away at 45 place Charles-de-Gaulle (mid-June to mid-Sept Mon–Fri 9.30am–7.30pm, Sat & Sun 10am–6pm; mid-Sept to mid-June Mon–Sat 10am–7pm; Ⓣ05.49.41.21.24, Ⓦwww.mairie-poitiers.fr), and will supply **walkers** with a guide to the regional opportunities: the GR364 sets out from here, reaching the Vendée coast via Parthenay.

Bikes can be rented from Cyclamen, 49 rue Arsène-Orillard (Ⓣ05.49.88.13.25), **cars** from outlets near the train station on boulevard du Grand Cerf, such as National/Citer at no. 48 (Ⓣ05.49.58.51.58). There's a self-service **laundry** at 90 rue Carnot (daily 7am-8.30pm; €3 for 7 kg). If you can hear yourself think over the hoards of teens playing computer games, you'll enjoy the fast **Internet** connection at Cybercorner at 18 rue Charles Gide, just off rue Carnot (daily 10am-4am; €2 per hr). Somewhat of an anomaly outside of Paris, the art-house and independent **films** shown

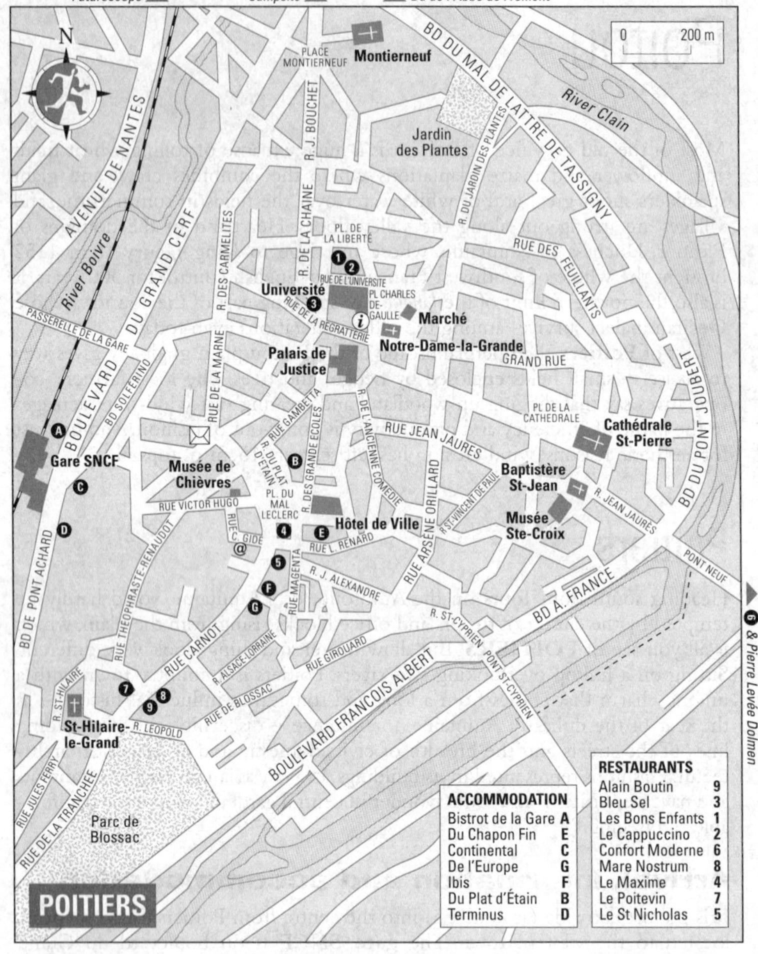

at Le Théâter, place du Maréchal Leclerc (ⓦwww.letheatre-poitiers.com), are shown in their original language with French subtitles.

There are plenty of **hotels** along boulevard du Grand Cerf by the train station, but the area is not particularly salubrious and at night streetwalkers are not uncommon; for more agreeable surroundings it's only a short uphill walk – boulevard Solférino, then to the right up the steep steps – to the town centre on place du Maréchal Leclerc.

Hotels

Bistrot de la Gare 131 bd du Grand Cerf ⓣ05.49.58.56.30. Cheapest of the station hotels, with reasonably priced though barebones rooms; it's sometimes noisy. ❷

Du Chapon Fin 11 rue Lebascles ⓣ05.49.88.02.97, ⓔhotel.chaponfin-poitiers@wanadoo.fr. Recently renovated and very central location, near the grand Hôtel de Ville; the spacious rooms all have showers. Closed mid-Dec to mid-Jan. ❸

Continental 2 bd Solférino Ⓣ05.49.37.93.93, Ⓦwww.continental-poitiers.com. Comfortable two-star opposite the train station, whose soundproofed rooms all have bath or shower and TV. ❸

Hôtel de l'Europe 39 rue Carnot Ⓣ05.49.88.12.00, Ⓦwww.hoteldeleuropepoitiers.com. Smart and very central hotel; its front courtyard is set back from the street, making it very quiet. Covered parking available. ❹

Ibis 15 rue du Petit Bonneveau Ⓣ05.49.88.30.42, Ⓦwww.ibishotel.com. One of the better deals in town, a central chain hotel with comfortable rooms. ❸

Du Plat d'Étain 7 rue du Plat d'Étain Ⓣ05.49.41.04.80, Ⓕ05.49.52.25.84. An attractive, well-run hotel in a central quiet street just off the main shopping precinct. Closed mid-Dec to early Jan. ❸

Terminus 3 bd de Pont Achard Ⓣ05.49.62.92.30, Ⓕ05.49.62.92.40. One of the better hotels around the train station, with an excellent brasserie. Rooms are very clean, modern and soundproofed. ❷

Hostel and campsite

HI hostel 17 rue de la Jeunesse Ⓣ05.49.30.09.70, Ⓕ05.49.30.09.79. Large, modern hostel next to a swimming pool, often overrun with school groups. Take bus #3 from the *gare SNCF* to "Bellejouanne", 3km away. Well signposted, it's to the right off the N10 Angoulême road.

Camping municipal rue du Porteau Ⓣ05.49.41.44.88. Grassy site with clean facilities situated 2km north of town; bus #7. Closed Oct–March.

The Town

The two poles of communal life in Poitiers are the tree-lined **place du Maréchal-Leclerc**, with its popular cafés and lively outdoor culture, and **place Charles-de-Gaulle** to the north, where a big and bustling food and clothes **market** takes place (Mon–Sat 7am–6pm, Sun 7.30am–1pm). Between the two is a warren of prosperous streets – as far along as the half-timbered medieval houses of **rue de la Chaine** – with the rue Gambetta cutting north past the old **Palais de Justice** (Mon–Fri 9am–6pm; free), with a nineteenth-century facade that hides a much older core including the magnificent thirteenth-century Gothic grand hall.

The church of Notre-Dame-la-Grande

From the Palais de Justice, you can look down upon one of the greatest and most idiosyncratic churches in France, **Notre-Dame-la-Grande** (daily 8am–7pm), begun in the twelfth-century reign of Eleanor and still undergoing a long renovation; strangely enough, pigeon droppings and pollution weren't the major concern, but rather the salt from the market stalls of fishmongers and salt merchants seeping into the ground and up into the church's facade.

The weirdest and most spectacular thing about the church is the west front. You can't call it beautiful, at least not in a conventional sense, squat and loaded as it is with detail to a degree that the modern eye could regard as fussy. And yet it's this detail which is enthralling, ranging from the domestic to the disturbingly anarchic: in the blind arch to the right of the door, a woman sits in the keystone with her hair blowing out from her head; in the frieze above, Mary places her hand familiarly on Elizabeth's pregnant belly. You see the newborn Jesus admired by a couple of daft-looking sheep and gurgling in his bathtub. Higher still are images of the apostles, and at the apex, where the eye is carried deliberately and inevitably, Christ in Majesty in an almond-shaped inset. Such elaborate sculpted facades – and domes like pine cones on turret and belfry – are the hallmarks of the Poitou brand of Romanesque. The interior, which is crudely overlaid with nineteenth-century frescoes, is not nearly as interesting.

The cathedral and around

At the eastern edge of the old town stands the **Cathédrale St-Pierre** (May–Sept Mon–Fri 8am–7.30pm; Oct–April Mon–Fri 8am–6pm), an enormous building on whose broad, pale facade pigeons roost and plants take root. Some of the stained glass dates from the twelfth century, notably the Crucifixion in the central window of the apse, in which the features of Henry II and Eleanor are supposedly discernible. The choir stalls, too, are full of characteristic medieval detail: a coquettish Mary and Child, a peasant killing a boar, the architect at work with his dividers, a baker with a basket of loaves. But it's the grand eighteenth-century organ, the Orgue Clicquot, which is the cathedral's most striking feature, often playing deafening tunes, with organized concerts in the summer.

Opposite – literally in the middle of rue Jean-Jaurès – you come upon a chunky, square edifice with the air of a second-rate Roman temple. It's actually the mid-fourth-century **Baptistère St-Jean** (April–June & Sept daily except Tues 10.30am–12.30pm & 3–6pm; July & Aug daily 10am–12.30pm & 2.30–6pm; Oct–March daily except Tues 2.30–4.30pm; €0.80), reputedly the oldest Christian building in France and, until the seventeenth century, the only place in town you could have a proper baptism. The "font" was the octagonal pool sunk into the floor. The guide argues that the water pipes uncovered in the bottom show the water could not have been more than 30–40cm deep, which casts doubt upon the popular belief that early Christian baptism was by total immersion. There are also some very ancient and faded frescoes on the walls, including one of the emperor Constantine on horseback, and a collection of Merovingian sarcophagi. Striking a postmodern note between the cathedral and baptistry is the small domed shape of **Espace Mendès-France** (Tues–Fri 9.30am–6.30pm, Sat & Sun 2–6.30pm; €4.50; Ⓦwww.maison-des-sciences.org), which presents expositions on science and technology and contains a state-of-the-art planetarium (€6).

Next to the baptistry is the town museum, the **Musée Ste-Croix**, 3bis rue Jean-Jaurès (June–Sept Mon 1.15–6pm, Tues–Fri 10am–noon & 1.15–6pm, Sat & Sun 10am–noon & 2–6pm; Oct–May Mon 1.15–5pm, Tues–Fri 10am–noon & 1.15–5pm, Sat & Sun 2–6pm; €3.50, free on Tues and 1st Sun of the month; Ⓦwww.musees-poitiers.org), featuring an interesting collection of farming implements. There's also a good Gallo-Roman section with some handsome glass, pottery and sculpture, notably a white marble Minerva of the first century. The same ticket is valid for the **Musée de Chièvres** at 9 rue V.-Hugo (same hours as Musée Ste-Croix), a rather dusty old collection of not very exciting paintings, pottery, furniture and arms.

If you still have an appetite for sightseeing, there's the **Pierre Levée dolmen**, a prehistoric stone chamber located on the eastern side of the river across the Pont Neuf, where Rabelais came with fellow students to talk, carouse and scratch his name.

Alternatively, you could take a more relaxed walk along the **riverside path** – on the right across Pont Neuf – upstream to Pont St-Cyprien. On the far bank, you'll see a characteristic feature of every French provincial town: neat, well-manured *potagers* – vegetable gardens – coming down to the water's edge with a little mud quay at the end and a moored punt.

The Parc de Blossac and St-Hilaire

Towards the southern tip of the old town, where the hump of the hill narrows to a point, the **Parc de Blossac** is a great spot to sit among the clipped limes and gravelled walks, to watch the boules and munch a baguette. Nearby is the eleventh-century **church of St-Hilaire-le-Grand** on rue du Doyenné, which unbelievably was pruned of part of its nave in the nineteenth century, though the chevet from the outside is still a fine sight; the apse has a particularly beautiful group of chapels surrounding it. Inside, there's the usual ambulatory to accommodate the many pilgrims who flocked here, one of whom perhaps caused the fire around 1100 that destroyed the original wooden roof and necessitated the improvised arrangement that makes St-Hilaire architecturally unique: eight heavy domes introduced for the reroofing had to be supported somehow, hence the forest of auxiliary columns that make three aisles either side of the nave.

Eating and drinking

Poitiers offers good opportunities for fine **food** whatever your culinary persuasions. If you know where to head, you'll find everything from cheap fast food to high-priced restaurants with so many recommendations you can't see in the windows for stickers – and there's a good range of ethnic options to try if you're bored with French cuisine. If you're really keen to make your money last, you can ask for any student/youth offers that may be available at the Centre Information Jeunesse (CIJ), 64 rue Gambetta (Ⓣ05.49.60.68.78). The students at the university in Poitiers generate lively **nightlife**, particularly in the bars along rue Carnot and on place de la Liberté, and posters announcing live music and dancing are easy to spot throughout town.

Alain Boutin 65 rue Carnot Ⓣ05.49.88.25.53. A good bet for regional dishes like *cailles au pineau* (quails cooked in a brandy liqueur), with a small, carefully chosen selection; menus from €18. Closed Sat & Mon lunch, all Sun & first half of Aug.

Bleu Sel 40 rue du Moulin à Vent. Serves a good range of salads and sandwiches at affordable prices and is popular with students. Closed Sun lunch.

Les Bons Enfants 11bis rue Cloche Perse Ⓣ05.49.41.49.82. Good value for money: serves lunchtime menu at €10.50 on weekdays, evenings at €18 and €22. Try the scrumptious house speciality of *escargots* melted in a parsley-buttered baked potato. Closed Sun & Mon.

Le Cappuccino 5 rue de l'Université Ⓣ05.49.88.27.39. One of a number of Italian restaurants in this area, with menus starting at €16.50. Closed Sun & Mon.

Confort Moderne 185 Faubourg du Pont Neuf Ⓣ05.49.46.69.61, Ⓦwww.confort-moderne.fr. Just over the Pont Neuf, this café serves French and Moroccan food, and is connected to an exhibition centre and record store. Check their website for concert listings.

Mare Nostrum 74 rue Carnot Ⓣ05.49.41.58.80. Mediterranean specialities from nearly every port of the sea, including *moussaka* and *kawage*, a baked ratatouille-style dish with aubergine and haricots verts. The *menu narguile* (€20) includes a hookah pipe after dinner to help digestion. Closed Sat and Sun lunch.

Le Maxime 4 rue St-Nicolas Ⓣ05.49.41.09.55. *Gastronomique* cuisine at its finest, these delicious dishes are served in an elegant setting, and lunches here are quite popular with the well-to-do business crowd.

Le Poitevin 76 rue Carnot Ⓣ05.49.88.35.04. Regional food at decent prices, in an exaggeratedly "rustic" interior. Menus from €18. Closed Sun.

Le St Nicolas 7 rue Carnot Ⓣ05.49.41.44.48. Actually located on a small traffic-free lane off rue Carnot, meaning you can eat outside peacefully. Traditional food served with a contemporary feel. Menus €14.80 and €18.60. Closed Wed & Sun lunch.

Around Poitiers

The area immediately surrounding Poitiers is dominated by the postmodern cinema theme park **Futuroscope**, to the north, though more traditional attractions can be found at nearby **Chauvigny** and **St-Savin**, which boast two fine Romanesque churches, with some great sculpture and frescoes. Less inspired are the small town of **Parthenay** and the larger city of **Niort**, neither of which is worth a special trip, though both make useful stopovers for provisions before heading further westward into the verdant marshes of the **Marais Poitevin**.

Futuroscope

Poitiers' best-known attraction is the giant high-tech film theme park called **Futuroscope: Le Parc Européen de l'Image**, 8km north of the city, a collection of virtual-reality rides which draw onlookers into the action on screen, with the result that you feel you're flying, being flung around, rocketing down a ski slope or catapulting through the solar system in a vertigo-inducing 3-D nightmare. It's not for young children or faint-hearted adults.

The futuristic **cinema pavilions** are set in several acres of greenery around a series of undulating lakes, and the fifteen screens take some getting around, with plenty of walking between them, so it's wise to arrive early to beat the huge queues. To see everything in the park in one day, with time off for lunch, takes about ten exhausting hours, and as well as seeing the screen entertainment, you should give yourself time to ride the oversized floating bicycles on the park's lakes. To orientate yourself, head first for **La Gyrotour** where a lift takes you to the top of the high rotating tower and you can get the full effect of the futuristic scenario.

All the films are in French, with English commentaries on headphones often available, but as these are not very effective, and as it's the visual impact that's most important anyway, it's better to do without (see box for recommended screenings). Apart from the films, there's a **laser show**, *La Symphonie des Eaux*,

Futuroscope presentations

Le Cinéma 360° Spain's contribution to Seville Expo '92 is now housed here permanently.

Le Cinéma Dynamique You literally have to hang onto your seat for this one: a fast and thrilling ride as the seats move in sync with the images on the screen, among them a journey through the traps and pits found in the short film *The Mysteries of the Lost Temple*.

Cyber Avenue To keep the computer kids busy – 72 multimedia kiosks with virtual games and video games.

Imax Solido An enormous screen, measuring 540 square metres, in conjunction with 3-D vision glasses brings you face to face with T-Rex and his prehistoric cohorts.

Le Pavillon de Communication A dizzying high-tech system of projection fires multiple images in rapid succession and attempts to tell the story of human communication.

Le Pavillon du Futuroscope Using holographic images, a robot tells the story of the universe and its atoms.

Le Pavillon de Vienne Moving seats parade before a huge wall of multiple images patchworking into a film on the region, which also tells the story of Futuroscope.

Paysages d'Europe Very slow – for a change – and good for the faint-hearted and those in need of a rest, as a boat floats serenely past images of the continent.

Le Tapis Magique Probably the most stunning presentation, with a vast screen in front of you, and another under your feet, creating the incredible feeling of flying.

a display of music, colour and effects focused on the park's dancing fountains (shows start just after sunset: April–June & early Sept to Oct Sat only; July to early Sept daily).

The Paris Montparnasse–Poitiers TGV stops at Futuroscope; there are also regular buses (#9, #16 or #17; €1.20 return) from Poitiers' Hôtel de Ville or *gare SNCF*. The park's opening hours vary according to the season (daily: Feb–June & Sept–Nov 10am–6pm; July & Aug 9am till end of laser show; ⓣ05.49.49.30.80, ⓦwww.futuroscope.fr). **Tickets** are valid for one or two days, with prices depending on season (April–Aug plus Sat in Sept–Nov: adult one-day pass €30, child aged 5–16 €22; adult two-day pass €57, child €40; Feb–April plus Sun–Fri in Sept–Nov: adult one-day pass €21, child €16; adult two-day pass €40, child €29). In the summer you can get a ticket just for the evening laser show (adult €15, child €9). To avoid queues at the park, you can purchase tickets in advance from a booth at Poitiers' *gare SNCF*. **Food** is predictably expensive inside, and a picnic lunch can cut costs substantially. There are various deals available that include admission plus a wide selection of accommodation on site, the cheapest of which costs €70 per adult in a four-bed room.

Chauvigny

Twenty-three kilometres east of Poitiers, **CHAUVIGNY** is a busy market town on the banks of the Vienne with half a dozen porcelain factories and lumber mills providing work for the area. Overlooking the bustling *ville basse*, the old town boasts five **medieval castles** whose imposing ruins stand atop a precipitous rock spur, but its pride and joy are the sculpted capitals in the Romanesque **church of St-Pierre**. If you take rue du Château, which winds up the spur from the central place de la Poste, you'll pass the ruins of the Château Baronnial, which belonged to the bishops of Poitiers, and the better-preserved Château d'Harcourt, before coming to the attractive and unusual east end of St-Pierre. A short walk away on the place du Donjon, there's an interesting **Musée d'Archéologie** (daily 2-6pm; €4.60), displaying pieces of ceramics and stoneware in a good state of preservation.

Inside, the church of St-Pierre is damp and in poor repair, but the choir capitals are a visual treat. Each one is different, evoking a terrifying, nightmarish world. Graphically illustrated monsters – bearded, moustached, winged, scaly, human-headed with manes of flame – grab hapless mortals – naked, upside-down and puny – ripping their bowels out and crunching their heads. The only escape offered is in the naively serene events of the Nativity. On the second capital on the south side of the choir, for instance, the angel Gabriel announces Christ's birth to the shepherds, their flock represented by four sheep that look like Pooh's companion Eeyore, while just around the corner the archangel Michael weighs souls in hand-held scales and a devil tries to grab one for his dinner.

Coinciding your visit with the Saturday, Tuesday (particularly the second Tuesday of each month) or Thursday **market** gives an extra dimension to a day-trip here. Held between the church of Notre-Dame and the river, it offers a mouthwatering selection of food – oysters, prawns, crayfish, cheeses galore and pâtés in aspic. The cafés are fun, too, bursting with noisy wine-flushed farmers mixing business with pleasure.

There are five **buses** a day from Poitiers to Chauvigny, which will drop you in the *ville basse*. The **tourist office** is located in the old town at 5 rue St-Pierre (June & Sept Tues–Sun 10am–12.30pm & 2–6.30pm; July & Aug daily

10am–1pm & 2–7pm; Oct–March Tues–Fri 2–6pm, Sat 9am–noon – in the winter months the tourist office moves to a small booth on the arcade in front of the *mairie*; ⓣ05.49.46.39.01, ⓦwww.chauvigny.cg86.fr). If you want to **stay** overnight, your best bet is *Le Lion d'Or*, 8 rue du Marché (ⓣ05.49.46.30.28, ⓕ05.49.47.74.28; ❸) which also has a restaurant with menus from €11. Chauvigny's municipal **campsite** is just east of the centre on rue de la Fontaine (ⓣ05.49.46.31.94; ⓕ05.49.46.40.60). To **eat**, step down into *La Bigorne*, on place du Donjon next to the church; resembling a hobbit watering-hole, it serves excellent crêpes and omelettes.

St-Savin

You need to get an early start from Poitiers if you want to make a single day-trip by public transport to see both Chauvigny and **ST-SAVIN**, which is scarcely more than a hamlet in comparison with bustling Chauvigny.

The bus sets you down beside the abbey near the modern bridge over the poplar-lined River Gartempe; walk downstream a little way to the medieval bridge for a perfect view of the **abbey church**, now listed as a UNESCO monument of universal importance. Built in the eleventh century, possibly on the site of a church founded by Charlemagne, it rises strong and severe above the gazebos, vegetable gardens and lichened tile roofs of the houses at its feet. Inside, steps descend to the narthex and from there to the floor of the nave, stretching out to the raised choir: high, narrow, barrel-vaulted and flanked by bare round columns, their capitals deeply carved with interlacing foliage. The entire vault is covered with paintings, and, though colours are few, they're full of light and grace, depicting scenes from the stories of Genesis and Exodus. Some are instantly recognizable: Noah's three-decked ark, Pharaoh's horses rearing at the engulfing waves of the Red Sea, graceful workers constructing the Tower of Babel. Attached to the abbey is a fascinating multimedia **museum** of Romanesque art history with a number of innovative exhibits (Feb–March & Oct–Dec daily 1.30–5pm; April–June & Sept Tues–Sat 10am–12.30pm & 2-6pm, Sun & Mon 2-6pm; July & Aug daily 10am-7pm; ⓦwww.pays-montmorillonnais.com).

If you do get stuck in St-Savin, you'll find **rooms** at the squeaky-clean *Hôtel de France*, 38 place République (ⓣ05.49.48.19.03, ⓦwww.hoteldefrance86.fr; ❸), which has a good restaurant serving menus from €13 (closed Sun evening & Mon except in July & Aug). There's a municipal **campsite**, too (ⓣ05.49.48.18.02; closed mid-Sept to mid-May).

Parthenay and around

Directly west of Poitiers, and served by regular SNCF buses, the attractive small town of **PARTHENAY** was once an important stop on the pilgrim routes to Compostela and is now the site of a major cattle market every Wednesday. It's not a place to make a special detour for, but it's worth a stopover if you're heading north to Brittany or west to the sea.

Parthenay has nothing very remarkable to see, though its medieval heart is quite interesting. Rue Jean-Jaurès and rue de la Saunerie cut in through the largely pedestrian shopping precinct to the Gothic **Porte de l'Horloge**, the fortified gateway to the old citadel on a steep-sided neck of land above a loop of the River Thouet.

Through the gateway, on rue de la Citadelle, the attractively simple Romanesque **church of Ste-Croix** faces the *mairie* across a small garden, which offers views over the ramparts and the **gully of St-Jacques**, with its medieval houses and vegetable plots climbing the opposite slope. Further along rue de la Citadelle is a house where Cardinal Richelieu used to visit his grandfather, and then a handsome but badly damaged Romanesque door, all that remains of the castle chapel of **Notre-Dame-de-la-Couldre**. Of the castle itself, practically nothing is left, but from the tip of the spur where it once stood you can look down on the twin-towered **gateway** and the **Pont St-Jacques**, a thirteenth-century bridge through which the nightly flocks of pilgrims poured into the town for shelter and security. To reach it, turn left under the Tour de l'Horloge and down the medieval lane known as **Vaux St-Jacques**. The lane is highly evocative of that period, with crooked half-timbered dwellings crowding up to the bridge.

Practicalities

Finding your way around Parthenay is easy. From the **gare SNCF**, avenue de Gaulle leads directly west to the central square, with the **tourist office** on the right-hand corner (Mon–Fri 8.30am–12.30pm & 2–6pm, Sat & Sun 2.30–6.30pm; ⓣ05.49.64.24.24, ⓦwww.cc-parthenay.fr). If you're after **accommodation**, you'll find the smart two-star *Hôtel du Nord*, 86 av de Gaulle, opposite the station (ⓣ05.49.94.29.11; ❸; restaurant from €12.50, closed Sat), or there is the somewhat blander *Saint Jacques*, av de 114ème RI (ⓣ04.89.88.40.05, ⓕ04.89.88.40.10; ❸). There's a **hostel** some way from the centre at 16 rue Blaise-Pascal (ⓣ05.49.95.46.89), with a central annexe at 115 bd Meilleraye: phone first and they will let you into the annexe. **Campers** have to head to the three-star site at Le Tallud (ⓣ05.49.94.39.52; open all year), part of the huge Base de Loisirs riverbank recreation area, about 3km west of Parthenay on the D949.

As for **eating**, Parthenay has the usual range of restaurants for a provincial town: Italian, Tunisian and Chinese, as well as traditional French. Best of the latter is *Le Fin Gourmet*, 28 rue Ganne (ⓣ05.49.64.04.53; closed Sun evening, Mon & Wed lunch), where high-quality cuisine combines with a jovial atmosphere, though it's a little pricey with menus from €23 to €38. Though no longer a grand hotel, *Grand Hôtel*, by the main square at 85 bd Meilleraye (ⓣ05.49.64.00.16; closed Sat evening & Sun out of season) has good inexpensive menus from €8.70.

Around Parthenay

There are three more beautiful **Romanesque churches** within easy reach of Parthenay. One – with a sculpted facade depicting a mounted knight hawking – is only a twenty-minute walk away on the Niort road, at **PARTHENAY-LE-VIEUX**. The others are at **AIRVAULT**, 20km northeast of Parthenay and easily accessible on the Parthenay–Thouars SNCF bus route, and **ST-JOUIN-DE-MARNES**, 9km northeast of Airvault (no public transport). A trip to St-Jouin can easily be combined with a visit to the sixteenth-century **Château d'Oiron**, 8.5km to the northwest. Alternatively, you could go on north to **THOUARS**, 21km from Airvault or 16km from St-Jouin, to see the abbey church of St-Laon; here there are accommodation options in the form of cheap hotels and a *Camping municipal*.

Niort

NIORT, 50km southwest of Poitiers, and connected to it by regular trains, makes a useful stopover if your goal is the Marais Poitevin. The town itself has enough of interest to fill a pleasant morning's stroll, and it's the last

place before the marshes to get a really wide choice of provisions. The most interesting part of the town is the mainly pedestrian area around **rue Victor-Hugo** and **rue St-Jean**, full of stone-fronted or half-timbered medieval houses. Coming from the *gare SNCF*, take rue de la Gare as far as avenue de Verdun, with the tourist office and main post office on the corner, then turn right into place de la Brèche. Rue Ricard leaves the square on the left; rue Victor-Hugo is its continuation, following the line of the medieval market in a gully separating the two small hills on which Niort is built. Up to the right, opposite the end of rue St-Jean, is the old **town hall**, a triangular building of the early sixteenth century with lantern, belfry and ornamental machicolations, perhaps capable of repelling drunken revellers but no match for catapult or sledgehammer.

At the end of the street is the river, the **Sèvre Niortaise**, with gardens and trees along the bank and, over the bridge, the ruins of a glove factory, the last vestige of Niort's once thriving leather industry. At the time of the Revolution, it kept more than thirty cavalry regiments in breeches. Today Niort's biggest industry is insurance: the most bourgeois town in France, so it's said, because of the prosperity brought by the large number of major insurance firms making their headquarters here. Accordingly, restaurants are usually packed at lunchtime, and well-heeled shoppers throng the pedestrianized streets, giving it a fairly lively, affluent feel.

Just downstream, opposite a riverside car park, is the **market hall** (with a café doing a good cheap lunch) and, beyond, vast and unmistakable on a slight rise, the keep of a **castle** begun by Henry II of England. Inside, a **museum** displays mainly local furniture and an extraordinary variety of costumes that were still commonly worn in the villages until the beginning of the twentieth century. At the time of writing, both castle and museum were under renovation, due to reopen in early 2005, so check with the tourist office for current hours and prices.

If you want to see the surrounding Marais area, the most pleasurable way is by bike – it's completely flat and small enough to cover pretty well in three days.

Practicalities

The **gare SNCF** is on rue Mazagran and has **bicycles** for rental – note that the station has no *consigne automatique*, charging a hefty €4.50 for each piece of left luggage. **Buses** leave from the **gare routière**, just off place de la Brèche on rue Viala. The excellent **tourist office** at 16 rue de Petit St-Jean (July–Sept Mon–Fri 9.30am–7pm, Sat 10am–5pm, Sun 10am–1pm; Oct–June Mon–Fri 9.30–6.30pm, Sat 9.30am–12.30pm & 1.30–6.30pm; ⓣ05.49.24.18.79, ⓦwww.niortourisme.com) has plenty of information about walking itineraries around the Marais, and offers a free room reservation service (ⓣ05.49.24.98.92); for more rustic accommodation in the Marais itself, contact Relais des Gîtes Ruraux, at 15 rue Thiers (ⓣ05.49.24.00.42). You can rent cars at any of the agencies that line rue de la Gare by the station, for example Avis at no. 89 (ⓣ05.49.24.36.98). **Internet** access is available at Médi@clic, 8 rue Porte St-Jean (€4 per hour)

There's the usual crop of **hotels** close to the station, far and away the best deal being the recently renovated *Ambassadeur*, 82 rue de la Gare (ⓣ05.49.24.00.38, ⓔhotel-ambassadeur2@wanadoo.fr; ❸), with quite luxurious rooms. For those on a tight budget, the *Hôtel de la Paix*, a bit closer to the station at 109 rue de la Gare, has small, clean rooms (ⓣ05.49.24.17.90; ❶). More centrally, the *St-Jean*, 21 av St-Jean-d'Angély (ⓣ05.49.79.20.76,

Ⓕ05.49.35.03.27; ❶), is another good bet for cheap, comfortable rooms, while several more upmarket hotels cluster on avenue de Paris, including *Le Paris* at no. 12 (Ⓣ05.49.24.93.78, Ⓦwww.hotelparis79.com; ❹), and the three-star *Grand Hôtel* at no. 32 (Ⓣ05.49.24.22.21, Ⓕ05.49.24.42.41; ❺), which, having shed its Best Western skin, has become more upmarket. The three-star **campsite**, *De Noron* (Ⓣ05.49.79.05.06; closed Oct–Jan), is on boulevard S.-Allende next door to the stadium; take bus #6 from place de la Brèche. **Restaurants** to head for include *L'Atelier de Mets,* on 247 av de la Rochelle (Ⓣ05.49.79.41.06; closed Sun), for traditional Marais Poitevin specialities (menus from €10), and, for lunches, *Sucrée Salée*, at 2 rue du Temple (Ⓣ05.49.24.77.16), which specializes in tarts and crumbles *à l'anglaise*; there is a €10.50 menu which includes a salad, or an €11 menu including a glass of wine. Alternatively, try *L'Atlas*, just down from the *St-Jean* hotel at 29 av St-Jean-d'Angély (Ⓣ05.49.09.09.83), which features a host of Moroccan dishes starting at €9.

The Marais Poitevin

The **Marais Poitevin** is a strange, lazy landscape of fens and meadows, shielded by poplar trees and crisscrossed by an elaborate system of canals, dykes and slow-flowing rivers. Recently declared a regional park, it is known as "La Venise Verte" – the Green Venice – and indeed, farmers in this area frequently travel through the marshes in flat-bottomed punts as their fields lack dry-land access. A tourist industry of sorts has been developing around the villages, so it's best to avoid weekends, when evidence of the transformation is all too clear.

Access to the eastern edge of the marsh is easiest at the whitewashed village of **COULON**, on the River Sèvre, just 11km from Niort by bike or occasional bus. The **tourist office** is at 18 place de l'Eglise (July & Aug Mon–Sat 10am–1pm & 2–6pm, Sun 10am–1pm; Sept–June Mon–Sat 10am–1pm & 2–5.30pm; Ⓣ05.49.35.99.29, Ⓦwww.marais-poitevin.fr), while **punts** can be rented, with or without a guide, just down the road at no. 6 (Ⓣ05.49.35.02.29 or Ⓣ06.15.55.36.55).

There are two **hotels** in the village, both likely to be full in season: the family-run *Central*, 4 rue d'Autremont (Ⓣ05.49.35.90.20, Ⓕ05.49.35.81.07; ❸; closed Sun & Mon, and mid-Jan to early Feb), and the pricey *Au Marais*, 46–48 quai Louis Tardiy (Ⓣ05.49.35.90.43, Ⓕ05.49.35.81.98; ❹; closed mid-Dec to late Jan). If you're **camping**, head for the attractively sited *Camping Venise Verte* (Ⓣ05.49.35.90.36), in a meadow about 2km downstream (a 25min walk), or the *Camping Municipal La Niquière* (Ⓣ05.49.35.81.19; closed mid-Sept to March), north of Coulon on the road to Benet. The best eating option in Coulon is the regional cuisine of *Le Central*'s characterful **restaurant**; with generous servings, a well-deserved reputation and a menu from €16.50, it's wise to book.

An excellent place from which to rent **bikes** is La Bicyclette Verte (Ⓣ05.49.35.42.56, Ⓦwww.bicyclette-verte.com; €9 per day), on rue du Coursault in the village of **ARÇAIS**, 10km west of Coulon; they also have children's bikes and tandems. If you're walking the marshes, it's best to stick to the lanes, since cross-country routes tend to end in fields surrounded by water, and you have to backtrack continually. Once you're away from the riverside road from Coulon to Arçais, there's practically no traffic, just meadows and cows. At the seaward end of the marsh – the area south of **LUÇON** – the landscape changes, becoming all straight lines and open fields of wheat and sunflowers. The villages cap low mounds that were once islands.

The Vendée

The northwest of the Poitou region falls within the rural *département* of the **Vendée**, whose main attraction is the eighty-kilometre stretch of coast between chic **Les Sables-d'Olonne** and the northernmost tip of the scenic **Île de Noirmoutier**. Inland, there is little of interest, aside from a marvellous summertime *spectacle* at **Les Épesses**.

Les Sables-d'Olonne

The area around **LES SABLES-D'OLONNE** and northwards has been heavily developed with Costa-style apartment blocks. If you're passing through, though, it's worth having a look at the surprisingly good modern art section in the **Musée de l'Abbaye Ste-Croix** on rue Verdun (mid-June to Sept Tues–Sun 10am–noon & 2.30–6.30pm; Oct to mid-June Tues–Sun 2.30–6.30pm; ⓣ02.51.32.01.16; €4.60, free first Sun of the month) and the collection of 150 classic autos and other vehicles at the **Musée d'Automobile**, 8km southeast of town on the road to Talmont (April, May, Sept & Oct daily 9.30am–noon & 2–6.30pm; June–Aug daily 9.30am–7pm; ⓦwww.musee-auto-vendee.com; €7.80). The main reason to stay, though, is the town's vast curve of clean, beautiful **beach**, which lures hordes in the summer. **Internet** is surfable at Medi-afun 85, 52 av De Gaulle just next to the train station (Tues–Sat 9.30am–noon & 2–7pm; €3 per hour).

Hotels get booked up well in advance for July and August, but you could try the friendly *Hôtel les Olonnes*, 25 rue de la Patrie (ⓣ02.51.32.04.12, ⓦwww.chez.com/olonnes; ❸), with a restaurant (closed Sun evening & Mon, plus Nov–March). *La Vague*, a few blocks from the beach at 8 rue des Escoliers (ⓣ & ⓕ02.51.32.05.29; ❷) is possibly the cheapest stay in town and open year-round. For a bit more money and comfort, try the *Arundel* (ⓣ02.51.32.03.77, ⓦwww.arundel-hotel.fr; ❻) at 8 bd Franklin Roosevelt just behind the tourist office; rooms are spacious and some have Jacuzzi baths and (partial) views of the water; prices drop by up to forty percent out of season. The municipal **campsite** (ⓣ02.51.95.10.42, ⓕ02.51.33.94.04; closed Dec–March) is on rue des Roses, 400m from the beach; and there are several more campsites in the Pironnière district, 3km south of town on the D949. For more accommodation options, ask at the **tourist office** on 1 promenade Joffre (June & Sept Mon–Sat 9am–12.15pm & 2–6.30pm, Sun 10am–12.30pm; July & Aug daily 9am–7pm; ⓣ02.51.96.85.85, ⓦwww.ot-lessablesdolonne.fr). The greatest selection of **restaurants** is on quai des Boucanniers, reached by crossing the footbridge over the port channel.

The Île de Noirmoutier

The twenty-kilometre-long **Île de Noirmoutier**, approximately 60km north of Les Sables-d'Olonne on the D38, was an early monastic settlement of the seventh century; now it has bowed to pilgrims of a different type, serving as a relatively plush tourist resort, though it has been spared the high-rise development of the adjoining coast. Although tourism is the island's main economy, it doesn't dominate everything. Salt marshes here are still worked, spring potatoes sown and fishes fished. The island can be reached in three hours by bus from Les Sables, and is connected to the shore by both bridge and the *passage de gois,* a channel across which you can drive your car when the tides are low.

The island town, **NOIRMOUTIER-EN-L'ÎLE**, is a low-key type of place but still has a twelfth-century **castle**, a **church** with a Romanesque crypt, an excellent **market** (Tues, Fri & Sun) in place de la République and most of the island's **nightlife** in the form of piano bars with longer-than-usual café hours. There are campsites dotted around the island – maps are available from the **tourist office** (July & Aug Mon–Sat 9am–7pm, Sun 10am–1pm; Sept–June Mon–Fri 9am–12.30pm & 2–6pm, Sat 9.30am–12.30pm & 2–6pm; ⓣ02.51.39.80.71, ⓦwww.ile-noirmoutier.com) on the main road from the bridge at Marmatre. **Bikes** can be rented from Vel-hop, 55 av Joseph Pineau in Noirmoutier (ⓣ02.51.39.01.34), or Charier, 23 av Joseph Pineau (ⓣ02.51.39.01.25). Among the **hotels** to try in the town are the plainish *Le Bois de la Chaise*, 23 av de la Victoire (ⓣ02.51.39.04.62, ⓕ02.51.39.11.89; ❹), the more stately *Les Capucines*, 38 av de la Victoire (ⓣ02.51.39.06.82, ⓕ02.51.39.33.10; ❹; closed Nov–Jan), which has a nice restaurant with menus from €12, or the luxuriously appointed *Fleur de Sel*, in rue des Saulniers (ⓣ02.51.39.21.59, ⓦwww.fleurdesel.fr; ❻–❾), with an excellent seafood restaurant (menus €21–34). If you're on a very tight budget, head to *Chez Bébert*, 37 av Joseph Pineau (ⓣ02.51.39.08.97; ❶), while a further option in the south of the island is the *Hôtel Goéland*, 15 route du Gois, in Barbâtre (ⓣ02.51.39.68.66; ❷; closed mid-Nov to Jan; restaurant from €11.50). Food options are pretty easy to come by, with a number of **restaurants** in the centre. Some good people-watching can be had on place St-Louis at *Le Blé Noir*, which serves excellent crêpes and *galettes* starting at €3.

As for exploring the island, the western coast, with its great curves of sand, resembles the mainland, while the northern side dips in and out of little bays with rocky promontories between. Inland, were it not for the saltwater dykes, the horizon would suggest that you were far away from the sea. The more southerly resorts, though built up, have not been the main targets for developers. In the village centres there are still the one-storey houses that you see throughout La Vendée and southern Brittany – whitewashed and ochre-tiled with decorative brickwork around the windows and S- or Z-shaped coloured bars on the shutters. During the spring, the weather is fickle – sunny one moment, stormy the next – and the heat of the summer cultivates a vicious mosquito population.

Les Épesses

Some 80km inland from Les Sables (on the N160 if you're driving), at the ruined **Château du Puy du Fou** in the village of **LES ÉPESSES**, a remarkable lakeside extravaganza takes place during the summer months (end May to early Sept Fri & Sat 10pm or 10.30pm; 1hr 45min; booking essential, ⓣ02.54.64.11.11, ⓦwww.puydufou.com; €24). It's a weird affair: the enactment of the life of a local peasant from the Middle Ages to World War II, complete with fireworks, lasers, dances on the lake and Comédie Française voice-overs. The story, summarized in a brief English text, is interesting but incidental – the massive spectacle itself is the real attraction, and all proceeds from the event go to charity.

To get to Les Épesses by public **transport**, you'll need to venture to **CHOLET** (connected by train from Nantes) and take a bus south from there; Puy du Fou itself is 2.5km from Les Épesses on the D27 to Chambretaud. The tourist office in Cholet (ⓣ02.41.49.80.05) can provide information about transport. There is one reasonably priced **hotel** in Les Épesses, *Le Lion d'Or*, 2 rue de la Libération (ⓣ & ⓕ02.51.57.30.01; ❷), and there are three more options, all with restaurants, 10km west in **LES HERBIERS**: the comfortable *Relais* (Ⓣ02.51.91.01.64, Ⓦwww.cotriade.com; ❸) and the quieter *Le Centre* (Ⓣ02.51.67.01.75, Ⓕ02.51.66.82.24; ❸), both on Grand Rue in the centre of town. Alternatively, *Chez Camille* (Ⓣ02.51.91.07.57, Ⓔchez.camille@online.fr; ❹) is a few minutes out of town on rue Monseigneur Massé, right across from the towering St-Sauveur church.

The coast around La Rochelle

The coast around **La Rochelle** – especially the **islands** – is great for young families, with miles of safe sandy beaches and shallow water. Be aware, however, that in August, unless you're camping or book in advance, accommodation is a near-insuperable problem. Out of season you can't rely on sunny weather, but that shouldn't deter you since the quiet misty seascapes and working fishing ports have a melancholy romance all their own. La Rochelle and **Royan** in the south are the best bases, and are both served by train. Away from these centres – if you're not driving – you'll have to take pot luck with the rather quirky bus routes.

La Rochelle and around

LA ROCHELLE is the most attractive and unspoilt seaside town in France. Thanks to the foresight of 1970s mayor Michel Crépeau, its historic seventeenth- to eighteenth-century centre and waterfront were plucked from the clutches of the developers and its streets freed of traffic for the delectation of pedestrians. A real shock-horror outrage at the time, the policy has become standard practice for preserving old town centres across the country – more successful than Crépeau's picturesque yellow bicycle plan, designed to relieve the traffic problem.

La Rochelle has a long history, as you would expect of such a sheltered Atlantic port. Eleanor of Aquitaine gave it a charter in 1199, which released it from its feudal obligations, and it rapidly became a port of major importance, trading in salt and wine and skilfully exploiting the Anglo-French quarrels. The Wars of Religion, however, were particularly destructive for La Rochelle. It turned Protestant and, because of its strategic importance, drew the remorseless enmity of Cardinal Richelieu, who laid siege to it in 1627. To the dismay of the townspeople, who reasoned that no one could effectively blockade seasoned mariners like themselves, he succeeded in sealing the harbour approaches with a dyke. The English dispatched the Duke of Buckingham to their aid, but he was caught napping on the Île de Ré and badly defeated. By the end of 1628 Richelieu had starved the city into submission. Out of the pre-siege population of 28,000, only 5000 survived. The walls were demolished and the city's privileges revoked.

La Rochelle later became the principal port for trade with the French colonies in the Caribbean Antilles and Canada. Indeed, many of the settlers, especially in Canada, came from this part of France.

Arrival, information and transport

Ryanair now runs daily flights here from London's Stansted airport, which accounts for the large number of Brits who visit. Several buses an hour run between the **airport** and town centre (Mon–Sat 7am–7.20pm; €1.20; 10min) Once in town, finding your way around La Rochelle is very straightforward. Arriving by train at the elaborate **gare SNCF** on boulevard Joffre, take avenue de Gaulle opposite to reach the town centre; on the left as you reach the waterfront you'll see the efficient **tourist office**, on quai du Gabut (May Mon–Sat 9am–6pm, Sun 10am–noon; June & Sept Mon–Sat 9am–7pm, Sun 11am–5pm; July & Aug Mon–Sat 9am–8pm, Sun 11am–5pm; Oct–April 9am–noon & 2–6pm, Sun 10am–noon; ⓣ05.46.41.14.68, ⓦwww.larochelle-tourisme.com), which has excellent maps and a €6.60 **museum pass** covering the Nouveau Monde, the Orbigny-Bernon and the Beaux-Arts. The office also leads morning **walking tours** of the old town (July & Aug Mon–Sat 10.30am, Sept–June Tues, Sat & Sun 10.30am; €6), and rather more fun two-hour evening tours of the city, led by a local donning medieval garb (mid-June to mid-Sept Thurs 8.30pm & 9pm; €8). In addition, the **CDIJ Youth Centre**, 14 rue des Gentilshommes (ⓣ05.46.41.16.36), has an information service for young people. Most things you'll want to see are in the area behind the waterfront; in effect, between the harbour and the place de Verdun, where the **gare routière** is situated. If you need an **Internet** connection, head to Cybersquat at 63 rue St-Nicolas (ⓣ05.46.34.53.67; Mon–Sat noon–10pm; €6 per hr).

Transport

The bus terminal for Autoplus, the town's efficient **public transport** system, is also located on place de Verdun, and there is another local bus terminal at 44 cours des Dames. Once you've stowed your luggage, you can use **bikes** to get around: there are two free municipal **bike parks**, part of the Autoplus system and heir to Michel Crépeau's original no-identity-check, no-restrictions, pick-up-and-leave scheme: one (open all year, 9am–12.30pm & 1.30–7pm), in place de Verdun by the *gare routière*, the other on quai Valin (same times, May–Sept only), near the tourist office. You get two hours of free bike time after handing over a piece of ID; after this it's a generous €1 per hour. You can also rent bikes from the *gare SNCF* and from Motive Location, opposite the Maritime Museum (ⓣ05.46.31.03.66). **Car rental** is available from Ada/Budget, 1 av de Gaulle (ⓣ05.46.41.35.53), and Rent-a-car, 29 av de Gaulle (ⓣ05.46.27.27.27). Autoplus also has a nifty **taxi system** with flat rates between any two of 46 "*bornes*" – terminal posts with a card-activated calling system, operating 24 hours. You can buy the cards and find out the inexpensive going rate at Boutique Autoplus, 5 rue de l'Aimable-Nanette, near the tourist office (Mon–Fri 9am–noon & 2–6pm, Sat 9am–noon).

La Rochelle is the area's hub for **maritime transport**, with boat tours of the town as well as services to the Île de Ré, Île d'Oléron, Île d'Aix and Fort Boyard. Companies with depart-ures from the port here include Océcars (ⓣ05.46.00.92.12), Croisières Océanes (ⓣ05.46.50.68.44, ⓦcroisieres-oceanes.ifrance.com) and Interîles (ⓣ05.46.50.51.88, ⓦwww.inter-iles.com); times and prices vary seasonally, and weather and tides may affect crossings.

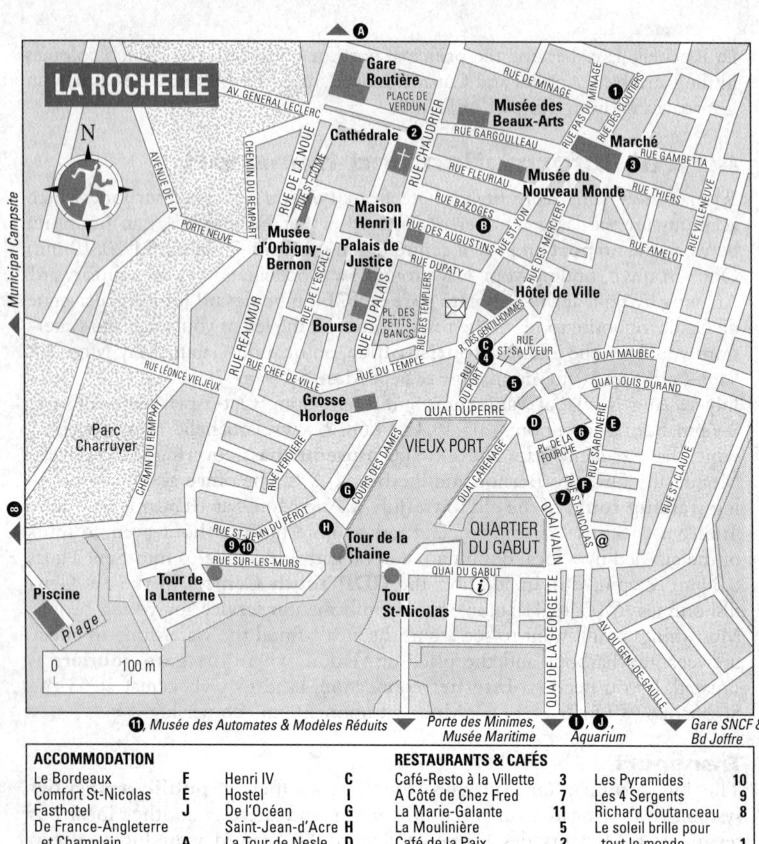

ACCOMMODATION				RESTAURANTS & CAFÉS			
Le Bordeaux	F	Henri IV	C	Café-Resto à la Villette	3	Les Pyramides	10
Comfort St-Nicolas	E	Hostel	I	A Côté de Chez Fred	7	Les 4 Sergents	9
Fasthotel	J	De l'Océan	G	La Marie-Galante	11	Richard Coutanceau	8
De France-Angleterre et Champlain	A	Saint-Jean-d'Acre	H	La Moulinière	5	Le soleil brille pour tout le monde	1
François I	B	La Tour de Nesle	D	Café de la Paix	2	La Solette	6
				Pub Lutèce	4		

Accommodation

Accommodation in La Rochelle can be a bit of a problem, so you should be sure to book in advance from May until well into autumn, even if you're camping. While there's a handful of inexpensive – though often quite noisy – hotels in the town centre, in general you can expect to pay resort prices at most establishments, especially in season. Alternatively, you might try the **self-catering apartments** that abound, particularly around Les Minimes and its Village Informatique. The tourist office has a handy board of rented accommodation and is able to reserve hotel rooms for a small fee.

Hotels

Le Bordeaux 43 rue St-Nicolas ⓣ05.46.41.31.22, ⓦwww.hotel-bordeaux-fr.com. Comfortable, friendly hotel in a characterful pedestrianized street between the train station and the port. Closed Dec. ❸

Comfort St-Nicolas 13 rue Sardinerie ⓣ05.46.41.71.55, ⓦwww.comfortstnicolas.com. A very attractive, modernized hotel in a pretty street 2min from the harbour. ❺

Fasthotel Village Informatique, Les Minimes ⓣ05.46.45.46.00, ⓦwww.3y.fr/larochelle. Small, quiet hotel made up of modern bungalows, near the port des Minimes and the beach. ❷

De France-Angleterre et Champlain 20 rue Rambaud ⓣ05.46.41.23.99, ⓦwww.bw-fa-champlain

.com. Comfortable hotel located close to the extensive parklands. The old, venerable half is *Le Champlain* and the new Great Western addition is the *France-Angleterre*; both are what you'd expect from a modern and an old-fashioned three-star. ❼

François I 15 rue Bazoges ⓣ05.46.41.28.46, ⓦwww.hotelfrancois1er.fr. Well-maintained hotel in a historic building with a walled courtyard. There's an Internet access terminal for guests, and all rooms have bath, TV and phone. Prices drop by up to 40 percent in the off season. ❺

Henri IV 31 rue des Gentilhommes ⓣ05.46.41.25.79, ⓔhenri-iv@wanadoo.fr. Just renovated, this popular hotel has sparkling rooms right in the town centre on place de la Caille, a short stroll from the harbour front. ❸

De l'Océan 36 cours des Dames ⓣ05.46.41.31.97, ⓕ05.46.41.51.12. Comfortable two-star hotel in an enviable location, with air-conditioned rooms – many with views of the port. ❷–❹

Saint-Jean-d'Acre 4 place de la Chaine ⓣ05.46.41.73.33, ⓦwww.hotel-la-rochelle.com. This modern, luxurious Inter-hôtel offers good-sized rooms with probably the city's best views of the towers and harbour. ❼

La Tour de Nesle 2 quai Louis-Durand ⓣ05.46.41.05.86, ⓕ05.46.41.95.17. A large comfortable old hotel, right in the middle of things, though the more-expensive harbour-side rooms can be noisy at times. ❸

Hostel and campsites

HI hostel av des Minimes ⓣ05.46.44.43.11, ⓕ05.46.45.41.48. A big modern hostel overlooking the marina at Port des Minimes, a 10min walk from the beach, shops and restaurants, and with a self-service restaurant and bar. Shared dorm-style rooms here cost around €13. Catch bus #10 from place de Verdun to Les Minimes, or walk from the train station, following the signs to the left.

Camping municipal de Port-Neuf on the north-west side of town ⓣ05.46.43.81.20. Well-kept and shaded campsite about 40min walk from the town centre. Take bus #6 from Grosse Horloge, direction "Port-Neuf".

Camping Le Soleil Port des Minimes ⓣ05.46.44.42.53. In a great location near the hostel and close to the beaches, this site is often crowded with raucous young holidaymakers. Take bus #10 from place Verdun to Les Minimes. Closed Sept–May.

The Town

The **Vieux Port** is very much the focus of the town, with pleasure boats moored in serried ranks in front of the two impressive towers guarding the entrance to the port. Leading north from the **Porte de la Grosse Horloge**, the **rue du Palais** runs towards the cathedral and several of the museums on rue Thiers. Between the harbour and the **Port des Minimes**, a new marina development 2km south of the town centre, there are several excellent museums for children and a large frigate (permanently moored) providing some insight into the town's seagoing past.

The Vieux Port

Dominating the inner harbour, the heavy Gothic gateway of the **Porte de la Grosse Horloge** straddles the entrance to the old town. The quays in front of it are too full of traffic to encourage loitering; for that, it's best to head out along the tree-lined cours des Dames towards the fourteenth-century **Tour de la Chaine** (mid-May to June & Sept daily 10am–12.30pm & 2–6.30pm; July & Aug daily 10am–7pm; mid-Sept to mid-May daily except Tues 10am–12.30pm & 2–5.30pm; €4.60, or €10 for entry to all three towers), so called because of the heavy chain that was slung from here across to the opposite tower, **Tour St-Nicolas**, to close the harbour at night. Today the only night-time intruders are likely to be yachties from across the Channel, whose craft far outnumber the working boats – mainly garishly painted trawlers. Beyond the tower, steps climb up to rue Sur-les-Murs, which follows the top of the old sea wall to a third tower, the **Tour de la Lanterne** or Tour des Quatre Sergents, named after four sergeants imprisoned and executed for defying the Restoration monarchy in 1822 (same times and prices as at Tour de la

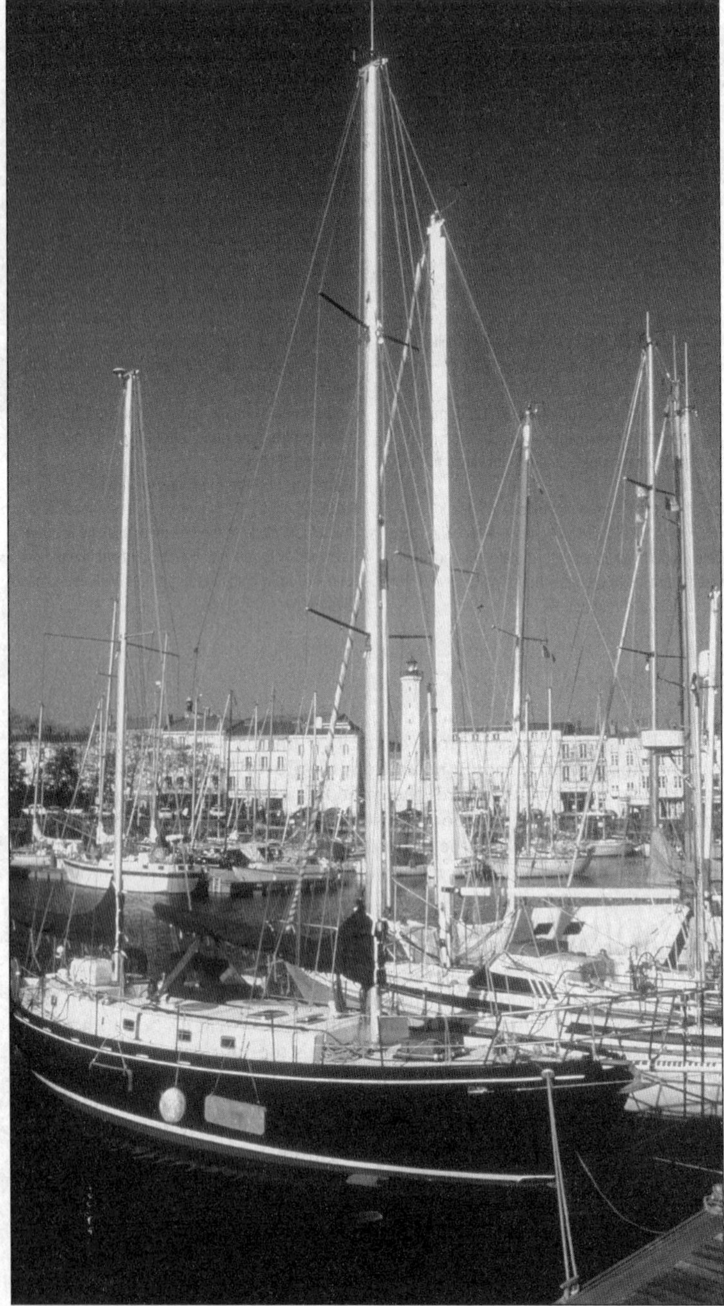

△ Vieux Port, La Rochelle

Chaine). There's a way up onto what's left of the **city walls**, planted with unkempt greenery. Beyond is the beach, backed by casino, hot-dog stands and amusement booths, along with an extensive, truly beautiful belt of park that continues up the western edge of the town centre and along the avenue du Mail behind the beach, where the first seaside village was built by the Rochelais rich.

The rue du Palais and around

The real charm of La Rochelle lies on the city's main shopping street, **rue du Palais**, leading up from the Vieux Port to place de Verdun. Lining the street are eighteenth-century houses, some grey-stone, some half-timbered, with distinctive Rochelais-style slates overlapped like fish scales, while the shop fronts are set back beneath the ground-floor arcades. Among the finest are the **Hôtel de la Bourse** – actually the Chamber of Commerce – and the **Palais de Justice** with its colonnaded facade, both on the left-hand side. A few metres further on, in **rue des Augustins**, there is another grandiose affair built for a wealthy Rochelais in 1555, the so-called **Maison Henri II**, complete with loggia, gallery and slated turrets, where the regional tourist board has its offices. Place de Verdun itself is dull and characterless, with an uninspiring, humpbacked, eighteenth-century classical **cathedral** on the corner. Its only redeeming feature is the marvellously opulent Belle Époque *Café de la Paix* (see "Eating and drinking", p. 67).

To the west of rue du Palais, especially in **rue de l'Escale**, paved with granite setts brought back from Canada as ballast in the Rochelais cargo vessels, you get the discreet residences of the eighteenth-century shipowners and chandlers, veiling their wealth with high walls and classical restraint. A rather less modest gentleman once installed himself on the corner of **rue Fromentin**: a seventeenth-century doctor who adorned his house front with the statues of famous medical men – Hippocrates, Galen and others. In rue St-Côme closer to the town walls is the **Musée d'Orbigny-Bernon** (April–Sept Mon & Wed–Sat 10am–12.30pm & 2–6pm, Sun 2.30–6pm; Oct–March Mon & Wed–Fri 9.30am–12.30pm & 1.30–5pm, Sat & Sun 2.30–6pm; €3.50, or part of the museum pass, see p.665), with an extensive section on local history, important collections of local faïence, porcelain from China and Japan and some handsome furniture.

East of rue du Palais, and starting out from place des Petits-Bancs, rue du Temple takes you up alongside the **Hôtel de Ville**, protected by a decorative but seriously fortified wall. It was begun around 1600 in the reign of Henri IV, whose initials, intertwined with those of Marie de Médici, are carved on the ground-floor gallery. It's a beautiful specimen of Frenchified Italian taste, adorned with niches and statues and coffered ceilings, all done in a stone the colour of ripe barley. And if you feel like quiet contemplation of these seemingly more gracious times, there's no better place for it than the terrace of the *Café de la Poste*, right next to the post office, in the small, traffic-free square outside. For more relaxed vernacular architecture nearly as ancient, carry on up rue des Merciers, the other main shopping area, to the cramped and noisy **market square**, close to which you'll find the **Musée du Nouveau Monde** (same opening times and price as Musée d'Orbigny-Bernon, see above; included in the museum pass, see p.665), whose entrance is in rue Fleuriau. Out of the ordinary, this museum occupies the former residence of the Fleuriau family, rich shipowners and traders who, like many of their fellow Rochelais, made fortunes out of the slave trade and Caribbean sugar, spices and coffee. There's a fine collection of prints, paintings and photos of the old West

Indian plantations; seventeenth- and eighteenth-century maps of America; photogravures of Native Americans from around 1900, with incredible names like Piopio Maksmaks Wallawalla and Lawyer Nez Percé; and an interesting display of aquatint illustrations for Marmontel's novel *Les Incas* – an amazing mixture of sentimentality and coy salaciousness. Nearby in rue Gargoulleau is the **Musée des Beaux-Arts** (opening times and prices as Musée d'Orbigny-Bernon, see previous page; included in the museum pass, see p.665), whose works are centred around a few Rochelais artists and illustrate the history of art from the primitives to the present day.

To get back towards the port from the maze of pedestrianized streets around the Hôtel de Ville, head down rue St-Sauveur, with its large gloomy church, across quai Maubec and quai Louis-Durand to **rue St-Nicolas** and adjoining **place de la Fourche** – with its huge shady tree and outdoor café – both pedestrianized and boasting several antiques dealers, second hand bookshops and a vintage clothes shop. The two streets share a Saturday flea/antiques **market**.

Towards Port des Minimes

On the east side of the old harbour behind the Tour St-Nicolas is the **quartier du Gabut**, the one-time fishermen's quarter of wooden cabins and sheds, now converted into bars, shops and eating places. Beyond it lies an extensive dock and the market and service buildings of the old fishing port. This is now the **Musée Maritime** (daily: mid-Feb to June & Sept 10am–6.30pm; July & Aug 10am–7pm; adults €7.60, under 17s €5.30; Ⓦwww.museemaritimelarochelle.fr), which includes an interesting collection of superannuated vessels as well as land-based exhibits. A further ten-minute walk brings you to the **Musée des Automates** (daily: July & Aug 9.30am–7pm; Sept–June 10am–noon & 2–6pm; adults €7.50, children €5, or joint ticket with Musée des Modèles Réduits, adults €11, children €6.50; Ⓦwww.museedesautomates.com) on rue de la Désirée, a fascinating collection of three hundred automated puppets, drawing you into an irresistible fantasy world. Some of the puppets are interesting from a historical angle; others, like one that writes the name "Pierrot", are interesting from a mechanical viewpoint. Further down the same street is the **Musée des Modèles Réduits** (same hours and ticket prices as the Automates). The prices may be a bit prohibitive for families – especially considering the whole tour takes barely half an hour – but this does combine well with a visit to the neighbouring Musée des Automates. Scale models of every variety and era are on show, starting with cars and including models of a submerged shipwreck and La Rochelle train station.

The **Port des Minimes** is a large modern marina development with mooring for thousands of yachts, about 2km south of the old harbour. Bus #10 from place Verdun will get you there, as will the more entertaining **bus de mer**, a small boat which runs from the old port to Port des Minimes, stopping off at avenue Marillac en route (April, May & Sept Sat & Sun hourly 10am–noon & 2–7pm; June hourly 9am–noon & 2–7pm; July & Aug half-hourly 9am–12.30pm & 1.30–11.30pm; Oct–March Sat & Sun hourly 10am–noon & 2–6pm; €1.50 one way), otherwise it's a thirty-minute walk along the waterfront. There are shops, restaurants, bars and apartments, and the young and gorgeous flock out here at weekends and on summer evenings to parade on the beautiful **plage des Minimes**. Right next to the beach is the spectacular **aquarium** (daily: April–June & Sept 9am–8pm, last entry 6.30pm; July & Aug 9am–11pm, last entry 9.30pm; Oct–March 10am–8pm, last entry 6.30pm; Ⓦwww.aquarium-larochelle.com; adults €12, students & under 18s €9).

Eating and drinking

For **eating**, try the rue du Port/rue St-Sauveur area just off the waterfront, or the attractive rue St-Jean-du-Pérot, which has everything from crêperies and pizzerias to expensive gourmet restaurants and several ethnic eateries including Indian and Chinese places. Particularly worth seeking out are the town's many excellent **fish restaurants**. *Ernest Le Glacier*, 15 rue du Port, and *Olivier Glacier*, 21 rue St Jean du Pérot, both serve excellent **ice cream** well into the evening.

As well as the numerous brasseries round the old harbour, popular daytime **bars** to hang out at include the dark and down-to-earth wine bar *Cave de la Guignette* at 8 rue St-Nicolas, offering great pitchers of sangria, and the *Lou-Foc*, next to the tourist office in quartier du Gabut. *Corrigans*, 20 rue des Cloutiers, near the market, serves pub grub and has an affable English-speaking owner, Barry – it also has also live music on Thursday nights.

Cafés and restaurants

Café-Resto à la Villette 4 rue de la Forme, behind the market. Tiny, authentic place popular with locals; good *plats du jour* from €7.70. Closed Sun.

A Côté de Chez Fred 30–32 rue St-Nicolas ⓣ05.46.41.65.76. A characterful corner restaurant with charming fishing and seafaring paraphernalia. A blackboard *carte* changes depending on what's in at Fred the fishmonger's next door. Fish and oyster dishes from €9; around €17 for a full meal. Booking advisable. Closed Sun.

La Marie-Galante 35 av des Minimes ⓣ05.46.44.05.54. Pretty yellow- and white-striped awnings over the outdoor seating overlooking the yacht basin at Les Minimes. Fish of the day is €10; generous menus from €14. Its three neighbours are also good value.

La Moulinière 24 rue St-Sauveur ⓣ05.46.41.18.16. Unpretentious restaurant opposite the old Protestant church, with tasty fish dishes. It's good for families, with a tank filled with tropical piscine types providing some entertainment for bored children. Menus €10.90 and €17.50. Closed Sun, and Mon evening out of season.

Café de la Paix place de Verdun. All mirrors, gilt and plush, La Rochelle's ladies of means come here to sip lemon tea and nibble daintily at sticky cakes – and there is a tempting charcuterie and seafood shop next door.

Pub Lutèce 1bis rue St-Sauveur. Reasonably priced brasserie with outdoor tables smack in the middle of all the action.

Les Pyramides 59 rue St-Jean-du-Pérot ⓣ05.46.41.75.72. Serves a mixture of expensive Egyptian and Greek food in bright, pleasant surroundings.

Les 4 Sergents 49 rue St-Jean-du-Pérot ⓣ05.46.41.35.80. Despite its smart appearance, the food here is not quite *haute cuisine*, but it's tasty nonetheless. Closed Mon lunch.

Richard Coutanceau plage de la Concurrence ⓣ05.46.41.48.19. Located on the seafront just to the west of the old harbour, this place is expensive but it's a veritable palace of gastronomic excellence, renowned for its fish and seafood and specialities. Menus €45–€92.

Le soleil brille pour tout le monde 13 rue des Cloutiers ⓣ05.46.41.11.42. Cheerful and colourful food in agreeable surroundings. The *tartes* (€7.50) are outstanding and, like almost everything else here, are made from fresh organic ingredients. Mostly vegetarian, though seafood is served. Very popular, so book or get here early. Closed Sun & Mon.

La Solette place de la Fourche ⓣ05.40.41.74.45. A pleasant little restaurant on a pretty square with *plats* from €13. Closed Sun and Jan.

Nightlife and entertainment

To find out **what's on**, pick up the thrice-weekly *Sortir* from the tourist office, with theatre, cinema and mainstream and classical music listings. For **nightlife**, head for the rue St-Nicolas: many bars line the streets, some offering **live music** and most with a lively atmosphere. An older crowd heads for rue des Templiers, where you'll find the *Piano Pub*, the *Mayflower*, the *St-James* and the *Académie de la Bière*. There is also some good jazz at *Chez Jules*

& Jim, 18 rue Rimbaut. **Nightclubs** worth checking out include *L'Oxford*, plage de la Concurrence (Ⓣ05.46.41.51.81), and *Le Triolet*, 8 rue des Carmes (Ⓣ05.46.41.03.58).

La Rochelle is also host to the major **festival** of French-language music, Les Francofolies (Ⓦwww.francofolies.fr), in mid-July, which features musicians from overseas as well as France and attracts the best part of 100,000 fans to the city.

The Île de Ré

A half-hour drive west from La Rochelle, the **Île de Ré** is a low, narrow island some 30km long, fringed by sandy beaches to the southwest and salt marshes and oyster beds to the northeast, with the interior a motley mix of small-scale vine, asparagus and wheat cultivation. All the buildings on Ré are restricted to two storeys and are required to incorporate the typical local features of whitewashed walls, curly orange tiles and green-painted shutters, which gives the island villages a southern holiday atmosphere but unfortunately also makes them look nearly identical.

Out of season the island has a slow, misty charm, and life in its little ports revolves exclusively around the cultivation of oysters and mussels. In season, though, it's extraordinarily crowded, with upwards of 400,000 visitors passing through. The crowds mainly head for the **southern** beaches; those to the north-east are covered in rocks and seaweed, and the sea is too shallow for bathing.

The island is connected to the mainland at **LA PALLICE**, a suburb of La Rochelle, by a three-kilometre-long toll bridge (€16.50 round trip per car in high season, €9 in low season). La Pallice was once a big commercial port with important shipyards, and although it still serves as a naval base, times have changed. As you drive past, you'll notice some colossal weather-stained concrete sheds, submarine pens built by the Germans to service their Atlantic U-boat fleet during World War II. Too difficult to demolish, they are still in use. As an alternative to the toll-bridge connection, Interîles, 14 cours des Dames, La Rochelle (Ⓦwww.inter-iles.com), also runs a passenger bus and boat service to Sablonceaux on Ré (€10 return), and combined trips to the Îles de Ré and Oléron.

ST-MARTIN, the island's capital, is an atmospheric north-coast fishing port with whitewashed houses clustered around the stone quays of a well-protected harbour, from where trawlers and flat-bottomed oyster boats, piled high with cage-like devices used for "growing" oysters, slip out every morning on the muddy tide.

The quayside *Café Boucquingam* recalls the military adventures of the Duke of Buckingham, who attacked the island unsuccessfully in 1627. To the east of the harbour, you can walk along the almost perfectly preserved **fortifications** – redesigned by Vauban in the late seventeenth century after Buckingham's attentions – to the citadel, long used as a prison. From 1860 until 1938, it served as departure point for the *bagnards* – prisoners sentenced to hard labour in the penal colonies of French Guiana and New Caledonia. Most were headed for swift death and oblivion; one who wasn't was Henri Charrière, aka "Papillon", who floated away from Devil's Island on a sack of coconuts after nine escape attempts and thirteen years in the colonies, and went on to write a bestseller about it.

Practicalities

Rébus runs **bus services** all over the island from La Rochelle, leaving from place Verdun via the train station every hour; crossing to **Sablonceaux** just across the bridge costs €2.80. For frequent travelling, ten-trip cards are better value: La Rochelle–Sablonceaux costs €22.10, La Rochelle–St-Martin €40.40, La Rochelle to anywhere on the island €59.30, but the timetable can be awkward if you want to tour the island.

The alternative is to **rent a bike** (approx €9 per day): from the Sablonceaux bus depot; from Cyclo-Surf Location, 14 rue Henri-Lainé (Ⓣ05.46.09.51.60), in seaside La Flotte between Sablonceaux and St-Martin; Clos Vauban, avenue Bouthillier in St-Martin; or Cycland, impasse de Sully in St-Martin or 2 route Joachim in La Couarde on the southern side of the island. Though it will cost you dearly, your only option for **Internet** on the island is Dimension IT, located in St-Martin inside the small shopping centre behind the tourist office on the quay (July–Aug daily 10.30am–1.30pm & 3–7pm; Sept–June Mon–Sat 10.30am–1.30pm & 5–10pm; €9 per hour).

Hotels are plentiful in all the island's villages, though obviously packed in July and August. Most reasonably priced are the one-star *Le Sénéchal*, 6 rue Gambetta in Ars-en-Ré, in a protected bay on the western side of the island (Ⓣ05.46.29.40.42, Ⓔhotel.le.senechal@wanadoo.fr; ❷; closed Oct–March); *L'Océan*, 172 rue St-Martin in Le-Bois-Plage (Ⓣ05.46.09.23.07, Ⓦwww.re-hotel-ocean.com; ❹; closed mid-Nov to Jan); and, in La Flotte, the *L'Hippocampe*, 16 rue du Château-des-Mauléons (Ⓣ05.46.09.60.68; ❷), and *Le Français*, 1 quai de Sénac (Ⓣ05.46.09.60.06, Ⓦwww.hotellefrancais.com; ❸; closed mid-Nov to March), with its own restaurant. For more pampering, try the very comfortable but not-quite-luxury *La Jetée* on the quayside in St-Martin (Ⓣ05.46.09.60.68, Ⓔinfo@hotel-lajetee.com; ❺).

There are even more **campsites** on the island than there are hotels, and it shouldn't be difficult finding a place, except perhaps in desirable locations near the southern beaches at the height of the summer. A few names, if you want to book ahead, are the *Camp du Soleil* in Ars-en-Ré (Ⓣ05.46.29.40.62, Ⓦwww.campdusoleil.com; closed mid-Nov to mid-March), *L'Océan*, La Passe in La Couarde (Ⓣ05.46.29.87.70; closed Oct–March) and *L'Île Blanche* in La Flotte (Ⓣ05.46.09.52.43, Ⓦwww.ileblanche.com; closed Nov–March), with an outdoor heated pool and restaurant. Online, Ⓦwww.campings-ile-de-re.com lists other options.

Good-value **food** is available on the quayside in St-Martin at *La Merine*, 31 quai de la Poitheviniere (Ⓣ05.46.09.20.39), with outdoor heated seating and seafood menus starting at €16.50. The airy *La Salicorne*, 16 rue de l'Olivette in La Couarde (Ⓣ05.46.29.82.37), has a high standard of cuisine starting at €16 for lunchtime menus, as does *Le Bistrot de Bernard*, 1 quai de la Criée, in Ars-en-Ré. Though not quite local cuisine, *Les Basques*, on the port in La Flotte, serves excellent tapas in an *assiette basque* for €10 and has a number of weighty Basque wines to complement.

Rochefort and around

ROCHEFORT dates from the seventeenth century, when it was created by Colbert, Louis XIII's navy minister, to protect the coast from English raids. It remained an important naval base until modern times with its shipyards, sail-makers, munitions factories and hospital. Built on a grid plan with regular ranks of identical houses, the town is a monument to the tidiness of the military mind, but is not without charm for all that. The central **place Colbert** is very pretty and nearby **rue Courbet** is exactly as the seventeenth century left it, complete with lime trees, and cobblestones brought from Canada as ships' ballast. There are some sights worth making a special effort for, including the Centre International de la Mer, located in the seventeenth-century royal arsenal and ropeworks.

Many of the towns along the pretty surrounding coastline are served by the Aunis-Saintonge buses (ⓣ05.46.97.52.08), though the simplest solution to travelling along this whole section of coast is to rent a car, or even to cycle. Unless you have your own transport, Rochefort is a useless base for nearby Royan or the Île d'Oléron. Bus times are inconvenient and buses to Oléron generally involve a wait at Bourcefranc.

Arrival, information and accommodation

The **gare SNCF** is located at the northern end of avenue du Président Wilson, about a fifteen-minute walk from the centre of town. The efficient **tourist office** (mid-June to mid-Sept, daily 9.30am–7pm, till 7.30pm in July & Aug; mid-Sept to mid-June Mon–Sat 9.30am–12.30pm & 2–6.30pm; ⓣ05.46.99.08.60, ⓦwww.ville-rochefort.fr) is on avenue Sadi-Carnot off rue du Dr-Pelletier, two blocks north of the **gare routière**; the staff will reserve rooms for a charge of €2.30.

Should you want to stay, you'll need to book **hotels** in advance to ensure reasonably priced accommodation. The cheapest hotel rooms in town are at the mediocre *Lafayette*, 10 rue Lafayette (ⓣ05.46.99.03.31, ⓕ05.46.79.20.76; ❷), though better options can be found at both *Le Welcome* on place de la Gare, opposite the handsome station buildings (ⓣ05.46.99.00.90; ❸), and the extremely comfortable and friendly two-star *Caravelle*, at 34 rue Jaurès, off avenue Charles-de-Gaulle (ⓣ05.46.99.02.53, ⓕ05.46.87.29.25; ❸). *La Corderie Royale*, within the seventeenth-century ropeworks on rue Audebert (ⓣ05.46.99.35.35, ⓦwww.corderieroyale-hotel.com; ❾; closed Feb 1–19), is the town's smartest place to stay. There's also a new, modern **hostel**, centrally located at 97 rue de la République (ⓣ05.46.82.10.40). The municipal **campsite** (ⓣ05.46.99.14.33; closed Dec–Feb) is a long haul if you've arrived at the *gare SNCF*: take avenue du Président-Wilson and keep going straight, until you reach the bottom of rue Toufaire, where you turn right, then left – about half an hour all the way.

The Town

If you have a taste for the bizarre, then there's one good reason for visiting Rochefort – the house of the novelist Julien Viaud (1850–1923), alias Pierre Loti. Forty years a naval officer, he wrote numerous bestselling romances with exotic oriental settings and characters. The **Maison Pierre Loti**, at 141 rue Pierre-Loti (guided tours: July to mid-Sept, daily every 30min from 10am; mid-Sept to June Mon & Wed–Sat, 10.30am, 11.30am, 2pm, 3pm & 4pm; closed Mon, Jan & public hols; €7.65; ⓣ05.46.99.16.88, reservations recommended), is part of a row of modestly proportioned grey-stone houses, outwardly a model of petit-bourgeois conformity and respectability, inside an outrageous and fantastical series of rooms decorated to exotic themes. There's a medieval banqueting hall complete with Gothic fireplace and Gobelin tapestries; a monastery refectory with windows pinched from a ruined abbey; a Damascus mosque; and a Turkish room, with kilim wall-hangings and a ceiling made from an Alhambra mould. To suit the mood of the place, Loti used to throw extravagant parties: a medieval banquet with swan's meat and hedgehog and a *fête chinoise* with the guests in costumes he had brought back from China, where he took part in the suppression of the Boxer rebellion.

Also worth a quick look is the **Centre International de la Mer** (April–Sept 9am–7pm; Oct–March 10am–6pm; €6.30) situated in the Corderie Royale, or the royal ropeworks, off rue Toufaire. At 372m, the Corderie is the longest building in France and a rare and splendid example of seventeenth-century industrial architecture, substantially restored after damage in World War II. From 1660 until the Revolution, it furnished the entire French navy with rope, and the building now houses an appropriate exhibition on ropes and rope-making, including machinery from the nineteenth century. If you don't fancy visiting the museum, it's definitely worth a wander around the extensive building and its lawns along the River Charente, whose reed-fringed banks support a garden made up of plants brought back from long-forgotten expeditions overseas. One such, financed by Michel Bégon, quartermaster of Rochefort in 1688, brought back the flower we know as the begonia. The small harbour, the **Bassin Laperouse**, next to the Corderie, is also worth a stroll.

The interesting Musée d'Art et d'Histoire, 63 av Charles-de-Gaulle, is under renovation until late 2005, but the **Musée de la Marine** (Feb & March, mid-Sept to mid-Dec daily except Mon 10am–noon & 2–6pm; April to mid-Sept daily 10am–6.30pm; €4.60; Ⓦwww.musee-marine.fr), in the seventeenth-century Hôtel de Cheusses on place de la Galissonnière, houses an excellent collection of model ships, figureheads, navigational instruments and other naval paraphernalia. Fifteen minutes south is the **Pont Transbordeur**, France's only working transporter bridge, built in 1900 – a technological wonder in its time. One other attractive small museum is the **Musée des Métiers de Mercure** at 12 rue Lessan, which displays lovingly and authentically reconstructed shop interiors from the beginning of the twentieth century (July & Aug daily 10am–8pm; Sept–June daily except Tues 10am–noon & 2–7pm; €4.60).

Eating and drinking

Strolling through Rochefort, you should have no trouble finding somewhere to **eat**, though few establishments are culinary standouts. For inexpensive meals head to rue Toufaire, where there's *Le Galion*, a self-service restaurant by the arsenal, or try the more than adequate Vietnamese/Chinese, *L'Asie*, at no. 45. Probably the best restaurant in Rochefort is *Le Tourne-Broche*, 56 av Charles-de-Gaulle (Ⓣ05.46.99.20.19; closed Sun night, Mon all day and Tues afternoons, & three weeks in Jan), specializing in *grillades* but offering fish and seafood as well; menus from €18. *Café de la Paix* makes great morning coffee and the local bar *Le Comptoir des Îles* serves good **beer**; both are on place Colbert. You can finish the evening playing billiards, snooker or pool around the corner at *Le Roller*, 48 rue de la République.

Fouras and the Île d'Aix

FOURAS, some 30km south of La Rochelle, is the main embarkation point for the tiny Île d'Aix (see below), where Napoleon spent his last days in Europe. It's an uninspiring town, redeemed only by a clutch of popular beaches and the *presqu'île*, the peninsula that extends 3km out to sea from the town centre, terminating at the ferry dock, **Pointe de la Fumée**. The peninsula is bordered by oyster beds, and off its westernmost tip at low tide can be seen the *bouchots à moules*, lines of mussel-encrusted stumps of wood. At high tide this is a popular place to fish for *crevettes* (shrimp). The finger of land is hemmed by sea-dashed fortresses, originally intended to protect the Charente, and particularly La Rochelle, against Norman attack, and later employed against the Dutch in the seventeenth century and English in the eighteenth. The seventeenth-century **Fort Vauban** (daily 9am–7pm) now houses a small, uninspiring, local maritime museum (€2), but its esplanade offers a magnificent panorama of neighbouring forts and islands. A **boat service** (€3 one way; €4 round trip) has recently begun between Fouras and Port-des-Barques, across the mouth of the Charente, from where you can take a guided bike tour (€8) to explore the lesser visited **Île Madame**; check with the tourist office for an up-to-date schedule.

Fouras's **tourist office**, which also serves the Île d'Aix, is situated in the Fort Vauban (mid-June to mid-Sept Mon–Sat 9am–12.30pm & 1.30–6.30pm, Sun 9am–noon & 3–6pm; mid-Sept to mid-June Mon–Sat 9am–noon & 2–6pm, Sun 10am–noon & 3–6pm; ⓣ05.46.84.60.69). As for places to **stay**, Fouras has a posse of overpriced **hotels**, many of which can be contacted online at ⓦwww.fouras.net, but first options should be the good-value *Roseraie*, at 2 av du Port-Nord (ⓣ05.46.84.64.89; ❹), and the comfortable *Grand Hotel des Bains*, 15 rue Général Brüncher (ⓣ05.46.84.03.44, ⓦperso.wanadoo.fr/grand.hotel.des.bains; ❸), housed in an old post office with a lovely courtyard and a snazzy restaurant (menus €11.50–34). There are also three **campsites** around the town: the *Fumée*, near the ferry port (ⓣ05.46.84.26.77; closed mid-Oct to mid-March); the *L'Espérance* off avenue Philippe-Jannet (ⓣ05.46.84.24.18; closed Oct to mid-April); and nicest off all, the three-star *Cadoret*, near to plage Nord on avenue du Cadoret (ⓣ05.46.82.19.19), with a swimming pool and miniature golf course. The best-value **food** in town is probably from *Restaurant La Jetée* at Pointe de la Fumée (ⓣ05.46.84.60.43; closed Jan & Tues out of season), which serves excellent seafood at affordable prices (menus €18.50–34).

Île d'Aix

Less frequented than the bigger islands, the crescent-shaped **Île d'Aix** (pronounced 'eel-dex') is small enough – just 2km long – to be walked around in about three hours, giving a greater sense of its island status than is felt on the Île de Ré.

The island is well defended, with a pair of forts and ramparts around its southern tip; the whole island, particularly **Fort Liédot**, served as a prison for members of the Paris Commune and later held prisoners of war in the Crimean and First World Wars. There's a **museum** (daily except Tues: April, May & Oct 9.30am–12.30pm & 2–6pm; June–Sept 9.30–6pm; Nov–March 9.30am–12.30pm & 2–5pm; €3; ⓦwww.musees-nationaux-napoleoniens.org) in the house constructed to Napoleon's orders. He lived in it for a week in 1815 while he was planning his escape to America, only to find himself en route to St Helena and exile, via Portsmouth. Extensive displays fill ten rooms with the emperor's works of art, clothing, portraits and arms. The white dromedary from which he conducted his Egyptian campaign is lodged nearby in the **Musée Africain**, with its entire collection devoted to African wildlife (daily except Wed: April, May & Oct 9.30am–12.30pm & 2–6pm; June–Sept 9.30–noon & 1pm–6pm; Nov–March daily except Tues 9.30am–12.30pm & 2–5pm; €3). Check out ⓦwww.iledaix.fr for more information about the island.

Access is by frequent ferry (half-hourly in season, according to tide schedule) from Pointe de la Fumée (ⓣ05.46.84.26.77), or with Interîles from La Rochelle (May–Sept 2–4 daily). The only **hotel** on the island is the overpriced but somewhat charming *Napoléon* on rue Gourgard (ⓣ05.46.84.66.02, ⓦwww.hotelnapoleon-aix.com; ❹), and there's also a **campsite**, the *Fort de la Rade* (ⓣ05.46.84.28.28; closed Oct–April).

Brouage and Marennes

Eighteen kilometres southwest of Rochefort, **BROUAGE** is another seventeenth-century military base, this time created by Richelieu after the siege of La Rochelle. It is surrounded by salt marshes, now reclaimed and transformed into meadows grazed by white Charollais cattle and intersected by dozens of reed-filled drainage ditches, where herons watch and yellow flag blooms. It's a strangely beautiful landscape with huge skies specked with wheeling buzzards and kestrels and, being flat as a pancake, it's good cycling and walking country. To reach the town from Rochefort, you cross the Charente on the D733 near the Pont Transbordeur (see p.675). From there, turn right to Soubise and follow the D3 to Moëze and Brouage.

The way into Brouage is through the **Porte Royale** in the north wall of the mid-seventeenth-century fortifications, which remain totally intact. Locked within its 400 square metres, the town now seems abandoned and somnolent; even the sea has retreated, and all that's left of the harbour are the partly freshwater pools, or *claires*, where oysters are fattened in the last stage of their rearing (see box, below).

Within the walls, the streets are laid out on a grid pattern, lined with low two-storey houses. On the second cross-street to the right is a **memorial** to Samuel de Champlain, the local boy who founded the French colony of Québec in 1608. In the same century, Brouage witnessed the last painful pangs of a royal romance: here, Cardinal Mazarin, successor to Richelieu, locked up his daughter, Marie Mancini, to keep her from her youthful sweetheart, Louis XIV. The politics of the time made the Infanta of Spain a more suitable consort for the King of France than his daughter – in his own judgement. Louis gave in, while Marie pined and sighed on the walls of Brouage. Returning from his marriage in St-Jean-de-Luz, Louis dodged his escort and stole away to see her. Finding her gone, he slept in her room and paced the walls in her footsteps.

Half a dozen kilometres south, on a narrow, drier spit of land, past the graceful eighteenth-century **Château de la Gataudière** with its unique interior and original furnishings (March–Nov Mon–Sat 10am–noon & 2–6.30pm, Sun 2–6.30pm; €5.40) – built by the man who introduced rubber to France – you come to the village of **MARENNES**. This is the centre of oyster production for an area that supplies over sixty percent of France's requirements. If you

Oysters

Marennes' speciality is fattening the **oysters** known as *creuses*. It's a lucrative but precarious business, extremely vulnerable to storm damage, changes of temperature or salinity in the water, the ravages of starfish and umpteen other improbable natural disasters.

Oysters begin life as minuscule larvae, which are "born" about three times a year. When a birth happens, the oystermen are alerted by a special radio service, and they all rush out to place their "collectors" – usually arrangements of roofing tiles – for the larvae to cling to. There the immature oysters remain for eight or nine months, after which they are scraped off and moved to *parcs* in the tidal waters of the sea: sometimes covered, sometimes uncovered. Their last move is to the *claires* – shallow rectangular pools where they are kept permanently covered by water less salty than normal sea water. Here they fatten up and acquire the greenish colour the market expects. With "improved" modern oysters, the whole cycle takes about two years, as opposed to four or five with the old varieties.

want to visit the oyster beds and see how the business works, you can do so here; just ask at the **tourist office** on place Chasseloup-Laubat (April & May Tues–Sun 10am–noon & 2–6pm; June–Sept daily 10am–noon & 2–6pm; Oct & Nov Tues–Sun 10am–noon & 2–5pm; ⓣ05.46.85.04.36) or out of season at the *mairie*, 6 rue Foch (ⓣ05.46.85.25.55) – visits cost around €9 for an adult, €4 for a child.

For **accommodation** in Marennes, try the inexpensive *Hôtel du Commerce* at 9 rue de la République (ⓣ05.46.85.00.09; ❶), with a restaurant where you can eat generously and well from €12. A good alternative for **eating** is *La Verte Ostréa* at the end of the pier at La Cayenne, where oysters and shellfish form the basis of every menu (from €10).

The Île d'Oléron

The **Île d'Oléron** is France's largest island after Corsica and a favourite of day-trippers and families in the summer months for its beautiful sandy beaches. It's up the road from Marennes, joined to the mainland by a bridge. Buses from Rochefort are awkward, with irritating changes at Saintes or Bourcefranc, and it's easier to go direct from Saintes on one of the several daily Citram buses that stop at all the main towns on the island; alternatively, take a guided day-trip from La Rochelle.

Flat and more wooded than the Île de Ré, Oléron has plenty of greenery, with the extensive pine-studded **Forêt des Saumonards** in the northeast of the island; here you can eyeball a dazzling panorama of the surrounding *parcs à huitres* and the mighty **Fort Boyard** stranded in the midst of the sea between Oléron and the Île d'Aix to the northeast. At the island's southern tip, the larger **Forêt de St-Trojan** creeps up the western coast along **La Grande Plage**, a popular spot but far enough from the main towns not to be too crowded. The island interior is pretty and distinctive. Waterways wind right into the land, their gleaming muddy banks overhung by round fishing nets suspended from ranks of piers. There are so many oyster *claires* that, from above, the island must look like an Afghan mirrored cushion; the stretch from Boyardville to St-Pierre – with its pines, tamarisks and woods of evergreen oak – is the most attractive.

The island's most interesting attraction is off the D126 between St-Pierre and Dolus, right in the middle of the island. The bird park of **Le Marais aux Oiseaux** (daily: April, May & Sept 10am–1pm & 2–6pm; June–Aug 10am–7pm; €4.20) was originally established as a hospital for injured birds found in the wild, but is now a breeding centre with many examples of rare or endangered species. Some 300 to 400 types of bird are given the freedom of twenty hectares of beautiful countryside, while sixty species are caged for observation alongside public walkways.

Most of the little towns on the island inevitably have been ruined by the development of hundreds of holiday homes – and it can be a real battle in the summer season to find a place to stay. There are a few places that still retain some amount of charm, however, not least of which is the main town in the south of the island, **LE CHÂTEAU**, named after the **citadel** that still stands, along with some seventeenth-century **fortifications**: the town thrives on its traditional oyster farming and boat-building, and there's a lively **market** in place de la République every morning. The chief town in the north – and most picturesque of the island's settlements – is **ST-PIERRE**, whose market square has an unusual thirteenth-century monument, **La Lanterne des Morts**. A few kilometres to the northeast, **BOYARDVILLE** has no interest except for the ranks of *bouchots* – stakes for growing mussels – along the shore. It's tempting to help yourself, but these are private property and you'll be in trouble if someone sees you. Instead, head to the major attraction around here: the superb stretch of sandy beach at **LA BRÉE-LES-BAINS**. Halfway down the west coast is the pretty fishing port of **LA COTINIÈRE**, with a daily morning fish market (except Sun), Criée aux Poissons, where the fishermen traditionally cry out their wares.

Practicalities

The main **tourist office** is on place de la République in Le Château (July–Aug Mon–Sat 9.30am–12.30pm & 2.30–6pm; Sun 10–12.30pm; Sept–June closed Sun; ⓣ05.46.47.60.51, ⓦwww.oleron.org), also the location of a couple of affordable restaurants. St-Pierre's tourist office is on place Gambetta (June–Aug Mon–Sat 9am–7pm, Sun 10am–1pm; Sept–May Tues–Sat 9.15am–12.30pm & 2–6pm; ⓣ05.46.47.11.39). **Bikes** are available in St-Pierre from Lespagnol, rue de la République, and from Lacellerie Michel, rue Foch.

Well-priced **accommodation** on the Île d'Oléron can be had at *Les Tamaris* in the port of St-Denis (ⓣ05.46.47.86.04, ⓕ05.46.75.73.08; ❷); at the modestly outfitted *Hôtel de la Petite Plage à Domino*, rue de l'Océan, St-Georges (ⓣ05.46.76.52.28; ❷); and smack on the rocky shore at *L'Albatros*, 11 bd du Dr-Pineau, St-Trojan-les-Bains (ⓣ05.46.76.00.08, ⓕ05.46.76.03.58; ❸; closed Oct–Feb), all offering restaurant service. For the cream of the crop, venture out to the *Novotel Thalassa Oléron*, Plage de Gatseau in St-Trojan-les-Bains (ⓣ05.46.76.02.46, ⓦwww.accorthalassa.com; ❺), a hotel-cum-spa offering every amenity under the sun to pacify body and mind. Detailed information on accommodation can be found at ⓦwww.hotels-oleron.com or ⓦwww.camping-oleron.com. There are **campsites** all over the island: at La Brée, where the best beaches are, there's *Pertuis d'Antioche* (ⓣ05.46.47.92.00), 150m from the beach off the D273. Further down the east coast, *Signol* at Boyardville (ⓣ05.46.47.01.22) is pleasantly sited near pine forests. If you want to stay a week or so, you could rent a **holiday apartment**, easy enough outside of July and August: ask for a list at any of the tourist offices, or contact the Agence Centrale Oléronaise (ⓣ05.46.75.32.53).

Places to **eat** abound on the island, and St-Pierre has the greatest choice of restaurants and brasseries. One place worth mentioning is in La Cotinière: at *L'Écailler*, 65 rue du Port (ⓣ05.46.47.10.31; closed Dec & Jan), you can have a slap-up, super-fresh seafood meal facing the port from €18.50.

Royan and around

Before World War II, **ROYAN**, at the mouth of the Gironde, was a fashionable resort for the bourgeoisie. It's still popular, if no longer exclusive, but the modern town has lost its elegance to the dreary rationalism of 1950s town planning: broad boulevards, car parks, shopping centres, planned greenery. Ironically, the occasion for this planners' romp was provided by Allied bombing, an attempt to dislodge a large contingent of German troops who had withdrawn into the area after the D-Day landings. But the **beaches** – the most elegant and fashionable of which is in the suburb of **Pontaillac** to the northwest – are beautiful: fine pale sand, meticulously harrowed and raked near town, and wild, pine-backed and pounded by the Atlantic to the north.

Arrival, information and accommodation

The **gare routière** and **gare SNCF** are located in cours de l'Europe. The nearby **tourist office** (mid-May to mid-June Mon–Sat 9am–12.30pm & 2–6pm, Sun 10am–12.30pm; mid-June to Aug Mon–Sat 9am–7.30pm, Sun 10am–1pm & 3–6pm; Sept to mid-May Mon–Sat 9am–12.30pm & 2–6pm; ⓣ05.46.05.04.71, ⓦwww.royan-tourisme.com) and **PTT** are close to the Rond-Point-de-la-Poste at the east end of the seafront. You can rent **bikes** from Royan Bicycles at 1 bd de la Grandière (ⓣ05.46.06.08.18); **car rental** is available from either Europcar, 13 place du Dr-Gantier (ⓣ05.46.05.20.88), or Avis, 75 av de Pontaillac (ⓣ05.46.38.48.48).

Accommodation in Royan is expensive and in short supply in season, when your best bet is to camp up the coast to the north or visit for the day from Saintes or Rochefort. See ⓦwww.hotels-royan.com for detailed information on accommodation in the town and surrounding area. One of Royan's nicest options is the *Miramar*, 173 av de Pontaillac ⓣ05.46.39.03.64, ⓕ05.46.39.23.75; ❹), at Pontaillac beach to the west of town; frequent Aunis-Saintonge buses run from the train station via place Charles-de-Gaulle. ❹. A more budget option is the acceptable *Crystal*, 1 bd Aristide-Briand (ⓣ05.46.05.00.64; ❶), quite close to the beach; so too is the *Hôtel de la Plage*, right amidst the action at 26–28 Front de Mer (ⓣ05.46.05.10.27, ⓕ05.46.38.37.79; closed Oct–Feb; ❷). There's also the more comfortable and central two-star *Les Bleuets*, 21 facade de Foncillon (ⓣ05.46.38.51.79, ⓦwww.hotel-les-bleuets.com; ❸), with sea or garden views and a heated pool. Alternatively, 3km southeast of Royan, in **St-Georges-De-Didonne**, there's an excellent little hotel, the *Colinette*, 16 av de la Grande-Plage (ⓣ05.46.05.15.75, ⓕ05.46.06.54.17; ❸; half-board only mid-June to mid-Sept), in pleasant surroundings 100m from the sea.

There are a number of **campsites** in the region and around Royan itself, including the *Clairefontaine* (ⓣ05.46.39.08.11, ⓕ05.46.38.13.79; closed Oct–May), a fairly pricey site at avenue Louise, allée des Peupliers in **Pontaillac**, and the municipal *La Triloterie* (ⓣ05.46.05.26.91, ⓕ05.46.06.20.74) off avenue d'Aquitaine – the road to Bordeaux.

The Town

One sight worth seeing in Royan is the 1950s **church of Notre-Dame**, designed by Gillet and Hébrard, in a tatty square behind the main waterfront. Though the concrete has weathered badly, the overall effect is dramatic and surprising. Tall V-sectioned columns give the outside the appearance of massive fluting, and a stepped roof-line rises dramatically to culminate in a 65-metre bell tower, like the prow of a giant vessel. The interior is even more striking: using uncompromisingly modern materials and designs, the architects have succeeded in out-Gothicking Gothic. The stained-glass panels, in each of which a different tone predominates, borrow their colours from the local seascapes – oyster, sea, mist and murk – before a sudden explosion of colour in the Christ figure above the altar.

The most attractive area in Royan is around **boulevard Garnier**, which leads southeast from Rond-Point-de-la-Poste along the beach, and once housed Parisian high society in purpose-built, Belle Époque holiday villas. Some of these have survived, including **Le Rêve**, 58 bd Garnier, where Émile Zola lived and wrote; **Kosiki**, 100 av du Parc (running parallel to bd Garnier), a nineteenth-century folly of Japanese inspiration; and **Tanagra**, 34 av du Parc, whose facade is covered in sculptures and balconies.

Various **cruises** are organized from Royan in season, including one to the **Cordouan lighthouse**, erected by Edward III's son, the Black Prince, and commanding the mouth of the Gironde River. There's a frequent thirty-minute **ferry** crossing (one way: pedestrians €3, bikes €1.50, motorbikes €9.50, cars €20.50) to the headland on the other side of the Gironde, the **Pointe de Grave**, from where a **bicycle trail** and the **GR8** head down the coast through the pines and dunes to the bay of Arcachon.

A few minutes walk from the *gare SNCF*, there is the family-oriented **Jardins du Monde**, a sort of Epcot Centre-meets-botanical garden theme park where the hyperreal exists in a number of recreated global milieus, such as Tuscan countryside or Bonsai pavilion. It is not spectacularly thrilling, but could make for a nice afternoon if you have children in tow (Ⓣ05.46.38.89.11, Ⓦwww.jardins-du-monde.com; adults €8, children €5, toddlers free).

If you're in the market for some airborne excitement, Skydive Royan (Ⓣ05.46.06.51.48, Ⓦwww.europhenix17.fr), located just outside of town on the N150, offers **parachuting** trips for around €200, though you'll need to reserve at least a week in advance and bring a doctor's note showing you're in good enough health to jump.

Eating, drinking and nightlife

As for **food**, good-value menus can be found at the huge, old-fashioned *Relais de la Mairie*, 1 rue du Chay, quite far from the centre off avenue de Pontaillac (Ⓣ05.46.39.03.15), and at *Les Filets Bleus*, near the cathedral at 14 rue Notre-Dame (Ⓣ05.46.05.74.00), which specializes in seafood dishes and gourmet salads, with *plats du jour* from €12 and menus from €20. The smart *Le Chalet*, 6 bd de la Grandière (Ⓣ05.46.05.04.90; closed Wed), serves imaginative seafood dishes reasonably cheaply and is crammed with French families on Sundays, when you'd be wise to book. Several **crêperies**, **pizzerias** and **snack bars** are situated on Front de Mer, the brassy strip leading from the tourist office to the beach and pleasure boats, with the *Crêperie de la Plage* at no. 40 recommended. The town's best-value bistro, though, is the packed-out *Le Tiki*, a Polynesian-styled joint on the beachfront right by the tourist office, which dishes out an above-average variety of *plats du jour* from €8.20 as well as fish, pizza and grills. Self-caterers can head for the large covered **market**, the Marché Central, at the end of boulevard A.-Briand, open every day (except Mon out of season) but particularly crowded and lively on Wednesday and Sunday mornings.

Nightlife has sadly all but died in Royan; though the younger set tries to make a go of it at *Ponton 10* (Ⓣ05.46.39.01.10), Voûtes du Port, a self-described *bar d'ambience*. Some of the restaurants have music, but even then not very often.

La Palmyre, Jardins du Monde and Talmont

It's worth knowing about the **zoo park** in **LA PALMYRE** (daily: April–Sept 9am–7pm; Oct–March 9am–6pm; Ⓦwww.zoo-palmyre.fr; €12), 10km northwest of Royan up the D25 coast road, especially if you're travelling with children, although its tacky advertising, with chimps dressed in human clothes, may put you off. Once you're inside, there are plenty of exotic species – from elephants and wild cats to gorillas and monkeys – housed in spacious enclosures covering fourteen hectares. To reach it, there are **buses** all day from Royan's *gare routière* and the place Charles-de-Gaulle.

An ideal bicycle or picnic excursion just over an hour's ride from Royan is to **TALMONT**, 16km up the Gironde on the GR360 – apart from a few ups and downs through the woods outside Royan, it's all level terrain. The low-crouching village clusters about the twelfth-century **church of Ste-Radegonde**, standing at the edge of a cliff above the Gironde. With gabled transepts, a squat tower and an apse simply but elegantly decorated with blind arcading – all in weathered tawny stone and pocked like a sponge – it stands magnificently against the forlorn browny-grey seascapes typical of the Gironde. The entrance is through the north transept, where the rings of carving in the arched doorway depict acrobats standing on each other's shoulders and, in the outer braid, two tug-of-war teams hauling roped lions up the arch. The inside is as unpretentiously beautiful as the exterior.

The Charente

It's hard to believe that the tranquil fertile valley of the **River Charente** was once a busy industrial waterway, bringing armaments from **Angoulême** to the naval shipyards at Rochefort. Today peaceful, low, ochre-coloured farms crown the valley slopes, with green swathes of vineyard sweeping up to the walls, and the graceful turrets of minor châteaux – properties of wealthy cognac-producers – poke up from out of the woods. The towns and villages may look old-fashioned, but the prosperous shops and classy new villas are proof that where the grape grows, money and modernity are not far behind.

The **valley** itself is easy to travel as the main road and train lines to Limoges run this way. North and south, Poitiers, Périgueux (for the Dordogne) and Bordeaux are also easily reached by train. Otherwise, for cross-country journeys, you're heavily reliant on your own transport.

Saintes and around

SAINTES was formerly much more important than its present size suggests. Today a busy market town for the surrounding region, it was capital of the old province of Saintonge and a major administrative and cultural centre in

Pineau des Charentes

Roadside signs throughout the Charente advertise **Pineau des Charentes**, a sweet liqueur that's a blending of grape juice stopped in its fermentation by adding cognac from the same vineyard. It's best drunk chilled as an apéritif; the locals also like it with oysters and love cooking with it. Favourite dishes include *moules au Pineau* (mussels cooked with tomatoes, Pineau, garlic and parsley) and *lapin à la saintongeaise* (rabbit casseroled with Pineau rosé, shallots, garlic, tomatoes, thyme and bay leaves).

Roman times. It still retains some impressive remains from that period, as well as two beautiful Romanesque pilgrim churches and an attractive centre of narrow lanes and medieval houses. It also has the doubtful distinction of being the birthplace of Dr Guillotin, whose instrument of decapitation came into its own during the Revolution.

The Town

The abbey church, the **Abbaye aux Dames** (daily: mid-April to Sept 10am–12.30pm & 2–7pm; Oct to mid-April 1–6pm; €3), is as quirky as Notre-Dame in Poitiers. It stands back from the street on rue St-Pallais, in a sandy courtyard behind the smaller Romanesque church of St-Pallais. An elaborately sculpted doorway conceals the plain, domed interior. Its rarest feature is the eleventh-century tower, by turns square, octagonal and lantern-shaped, flanked with pinnacles and capped with the Poitou pine cone.

From here rue Arc de Triomphe brings you out on the riverbank beside an imposing Roman arch – the **Arc de Germanicus** – which originally stood on the bridge until 1843, when it was demolished to make way for the modern crossing and rebuilt here. The arch was dedicated to the emperor Tiberius, his son Drusus and nephew Germanicus in 19 AD. In a stone building next door is an **archeological museum** (June–Sept Mon–Sat 10am–6pm, Sun 1.30–6pm; Oct–May Mon–Sat 10am–5pm, Sun 1.30–5pm; €1.50), with a great many more Roman bits and pieces strewn about, mostly rescued from the fifth-century city walls into which they had been incorporated. This whole area comes alive on the first Monday of every month when a sprawling **market** extends from the abbey right through here and up most of avenue Gambetta.

A footbridge crosses from the archeological museum to the covered market on the west bank of the river and place du Marché at the foot of the rather uninspiring **Cathédrale de St-Pierre**, which began life as a Romanesque church but was significantly altered in the aftermath of damage inflicted during the Wars of Religion, when Saintes was a Huguenot stronghold. Its enormous, heavily buttressed tower, capped by a hat-like dome instead of the intended spire, is the town's chief landmark. In front, the lime trees of place du Synode stretch away to the municipal buildings, while up to the right are the old quarter and the Hôtel Martineau library in the rue des Jacobins, with an exquisite central courtyard full of trees and shrubs. North of the cathedral, an early seventeenth-century mansion on rue Victor-Hugo houses the

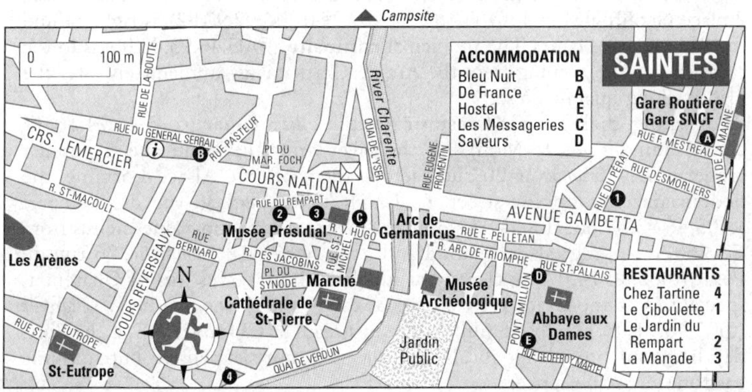

Musée Présidial (June–Sept 11am–6pm, Sun 1.30–6pm; Oct–May Tues–Sat 10am–12.30 & 1.30–5pm, Sun 1.30–5pm; €1.50), containing a collection of local pottery and some unexciting paintings.

Saintes' Roman heritage is best seen at **Les Arènes** (June–Sept daily 10am–7pm; Oct–May Mon–Sat 10am–5pm, Sun 1.30–5pm; €1), an amphitheatre whose ruins lie at the head of a leafy little valley reached by a footpath which begins by 54 cours Reverseaux. The amphitheatre was dug into the end of the valley in around 40 AD, making it one of the oldest surviving examples in France. Although most of the seats are now grassed over, it's still an evocative spot.

On the way back from the amphitheatre, it's no extra trouble to take in the eleventh-century **church of St-Eutrope** (9am–7pm; free). The upper church, which lost its nave in 1803, has some brilliant capital-carving in the old choir, best seen from the gallery. But it's the crypt – entered from the street – which is most atmospheric and primitive: here massive pillars carved with stylized vegetation support the vaulting in semi-darkness, and there's a huge old font and the third-century tomb of Saintes' first bishop, Eutropius himself.

Practicalities

Saintes' **gare SNCF** is on avenue de la Marne at the east end of the main road, avenue Gambetta. The **tourist office** is housed in grand old Villa Musso, 62 cours National (May–June & Sept Mon–Sat 9am–12.30pm & 2–6pm, Sun 10am–1pm & 2–6pm; July & Aug Mon–Sat: 9am–1pm & 2–7pm; Oct–April Mon–Sat 9.30am–12.30pm & 2.15–6pm; ⓣ05.46.74.23.82, ⓦwww.ot-saintes.fr), and organizes **boat trips** to Cognac during the summer.

One of the best **hotel** options in town is the sleek new *Saveurs* (ⓣ05.46.94.17.91; ❸), in a great location just next to the abbey at 1 place St-Palais, featuring a design-happy nouveau-French restaurant beneath (menus from €15, closed Mon). There are several hotels in the vicinity of the *gare SNCF*, the best of the bunch being the now rather tatty old *Hôtel de France* at 56 rue Frédéric Mestreau (ⓣ05.46.93.01.16, ⓕ05.46.74.37.90; ❷). More congenial and more central is *Les Messageries* in tiny rue des Messageries, off rue Victor-Hugo (ⓣ05.46.93.64.99, ⓦwww.hotel-des-messageries.com; ❸), with a laundry service available. Another agreeable place is the *Bleu Nuit* at 1 rue Pasteur, the crossroads of cours National and cours Reverseaux (ⓣ05.46.93.01.72, ⓔau-bleu-nuit@t3a.com; ❷; locked garage available); it has some character and is well insulated against the noise of the street. The **hostel**, 2 place Geoffroy Martel (ⓣ05.46.92.14.92, ⓕ05.46.92.97.82), is right behind the Abbaye aux Dames. The municipal **campsite** (ⓣ05.46.93.08.00) is to the right (if you are coming from the Arc de Germanicus) immediately after the bridge, along quai de l'Yser.

For eating, there's a good **restaurant**, the *Chez Tartine* (ⓣ05.46.74.16.38; closed Sun dinner & Mon), by the river on place Blair, and a popular crêperie, *La Manade*, at 20 rue Victor-Hugo, off rue Alsace-Lorraine, the pedestrianized shopping street. *Le Jardin du Rempart*, 36 rue du Rempart (ⓣ05.46.93.37.66; closed Tues dinner & Wed), serves top-value menus from €13.50, including salads, seafood and grills, while *Le Ciboulette*, 36 rue du Pérat (ⓣ05.46.74.07.36; closed Sat lunch & Sun), serves lots of Charentais specialities at moderate prices. Out of town, the *Restaurant de la Charente* (ⓣ05.46.91.03.17; closed Sun), 10km upstream at **CHANIERS**, is the Sunday haunt of prosperous locals and makes a more expensive but fulfilling gastronomic experience.

Around Saintes

If you have a car, you could explore several of the marvellous Romanesque churches within easy reach of Saintes. In **FENIOUX**, 29km to the north towards St-Jean-d'Angély, there's the superb church of St-Eutrope with its mighty spire, while the church at **RIOUX**, 12km to the south, is well worth visiting for its detailed facade. There's also the fine **Château of Roche-Courbon**, 18km northwest off the Rochefort road – once described as the Sleeping Beauty's castle – with some stylish interiors and gardens.

One place worth any amount of trouble to get to is the twelfth-century pilgrim **church of St-Pierre** at **AULNAY**, 37km northeast of Saintes, and sadly not served by public transport. Aulnay church's finest sculpture is on the west front, the south transept and apse, with some more fine work inside. On the building's main facade, two blind arches flank the central portal. The tympanum of the right depicts Christ in Majesty; the left, St Peter, crucified upside down with two extraordinarily lithe and graceful soldiers balancing on the arms of his cross to get a better swing at the nails in his feet. On the south side, the doorway is decorated with four bands of even more intricate carving. The apse, too, is a beauty, framed by five slender columns and lit by three perfectly arched windows, the centre one enclosed by figures wrapped in the finest twining foliage. Inside, there is more extraordinary carving: capitals depicting Delilah cutting Samson's hair, devils pulling a man's beard, human-eared elephants bearing the Latin inscription *Hic sunt elephants* – "Here are elephants" – presumably for the edification of ignorant locals.

You might also like to visit **Nuaillé-sur-Boutonne**, 9km west of Aulnay, which boasts another remarkable church; and, even nearer just down the D129 east of Aulnay, you can walk to **Salles-les-Aulnay** (20min), or **St-Mandé** (1hr), with humbler churches of the same period.

Cognac and around

Anyone who does not already know what **COGNAC** is about will quickly nose its quintessential air as they stroll about the medieval lanes of the town's riverside quarter. For here is the greatest concentration of *chais* (warehouses), where the high-quality brandy is matured, its fumes blackening the walls with tiny fungi. Cognac *is* cognac, from the tractor driver and pruning-knife wielder to the manufacturer of corks, bottles and cartons. Untouched by recession (80 percent of production is exported), it is likely to thrive as long as the world has sorrows to drown – a sunny, prosperous, respectable, self-satisfied little place.

The Town

Cognac has a number of medieval stone and half-timbered buildings in the narrow streets of the old town, of which rue Saulnier and rue de l'Isle-d'Or make atmospheric backdrops for a stroll, and picturesque **Grande-Rue** winds through the heart of the old quarter to the *chais*. On the right is all that remains of the **castle** where King François I was born in 1494.

To the left are the *chais* and offices of the **Hennessy Cognac Company** (daily: March–May & Oct–Dec 10am–5pm; June–Sept 10am–6pm; €6 for guided tour), a seventh-generation family firm and widely thought the best of the houses to visit. The first Hennessy, an officer in the Irish brigade serving with the French army, hailed from Ballymacnoy in County Cork and gave up soldiering in 1765 to set up a little business here. The visit begins with a film explaining what's what in the world of cognac. Only an *eau de vie* distilled from grapes grown in a strictly defined area can be called cognac, and this stretches from the coast at La Rochelle and Royan to Angoulême. It's all carefully graded according to soil properties – chalk essentially. The inner circle, from which the finest cognac comes – Grand Champagne and Petit Champagne (not to be confused with bubbly) – lies mainly south of the River Charente. Hennessy alone keeps 180,000 barrels in stock; the most attention-grabbing moment of the tour is a glimpse of the safeguarded barrels containing vintages from the late 1800s. All barrels are regularly checked and various *coupages* (blendings) made, of which only the best are kept – depending on the well-honed taste buds of the sober *maître du chais*.

Another important cog in the cognac mechanism is Europe's second biggest bottle-maker, the modern **St-Gobain glassworks**, which lies 2km south of town; guided tours of the works (€5) can be arranged through the tourist office (see below).

Practicalities

From the very industrial **gare SNCF**, to get to the central place François-I, go down rue Mousnier, right on rue Bayard, past the **PTT** and up rue du 14-Juillet. The square is dominated by an equestrian statue of the king rising from a bed of begonias; in fine weather the cafés here are teeming with locals. The **tourist office** is on rue du 14-Juillet at no. 16 (daily: July & Aug 9.30am–6.30pm; Sept–June 9am–12.30pm & 2–6.15pm; ⓣ05.45.82.10.71, ⓦwww.ville-cognac.fr), where you can ask about visiting the various *chais* and the St-Gobain glassworks, as well as get information on river trips.

As for **rooms**, the cheapest are at the train station, *Hotel de la Gare* (ⓣ05.45.82.04.15; ⓕ05.45.82.64.44; ❷), and at the central *Le Cheval Blanc*, 6–8 place Bayard (ⓣ05.45.82.09.55, ⓦwww.hotel-chevalblanc.fr; ❸), with a simple inexpensive restaurant downstairs. For something with a bit more comfort, try the characterful, newly-renovated *Hôtel d'Orleans*, 25 rue d'Angoulême (ⓣ05.45.82.01.26, ⓕ05.45.82.20.33; ❸), in a calm pedestrianized street in the old part of town, or *La Résidence*, 25 av Victor-Hugo (ⓣ05.45.36.62.40, ⓕ05.45.36.62.49; ❸), an attractive two-star with a clean, modern interior. Moving upmarket, a great option is *Les Pigeouns Blancs* (ⓣ05.45.82.16.36, ⓦwww.chateauxhotels.com/pigeonsblancs; ❹), an inn with an exquisite restaurant located just across the Charente in a quiet, green setting. Upstream from the bridge, the oak woods of the Parc François-I – where you can swim either in the river or in a pool – stretch along the riverbank to the Pont Chatenay and the town **campsite** (ⓣ05.45.32.13.32).

For **eating** out, the relaxed *La Bonne Goule*, 42 allée de la Corderie (from €11; ⓣ05.45.82.06.37; closed Sun evening), serves up excellent Charentais specialities at inexpensive prices, and there's a good list of local wines. Those after a fine dining experience will find it at *La Boîte-à-Sel*, 68 av Victor-Hugo (ⓣ05.45.32.07.68; closed Mon), a seasoned restaurant with an emphasis on fresh natural produce: menus start at €26, while the excellent *menu des gourmets* will set you back €38. There's also good brasserie fare to be had at the *Coq d'Or* on the central place François-Ier (ⓣ05.45.82.02.56), which has *plats* for €25.70.

Around Cognac

The area around Cognac is gentle enough for some restful walks, taking in some pretty little Charentais villages. The best is the towpath or *chemin de halage* that follows the south bank of the Charente upstream to Pont de la Trâche, then on along a track to the village of **BOURG-CHARENTE**, with an excellent **restaurant** called *La Ribaudière* (ⓣ05.45.81.30.54, ⓦwww.laribaudiere.com; closed Sun evening, Mon & Tues lunch; menus €22–50.30), where you should most definitely try their speciality, *matelote d'anguilles* – eels cooked in wine sauce. From there, you can amble to the village's interesting castle and Romanesque church; the walk takes about three hours in all. A byroad leads back to **ST-BRICE** on the other bank, past sleepy farms and acres of shoulder-high vines. From there, another lane winds 3km up the hill and over to the ruined **abbaie de La Châtre**, abandoned amid brambles and fields. Alternatively, at the hamlet of **RICHEMONT**, 5km northwest of Cognac, you can swim in the pools of the tiny River Antenne below an ancient church on a steep bluff lost in the woods.

Further afield, 18km northwest of Cognac between the villages of Migron and Authon, there's the fascinating **Écomusée du Cognac** (daily 9.30am–12.30pm & 2.30–6.30pm; free), which illustrates the history of the distillation process and the various tools involved, finishing off with a tasting of cognacs, liqueurs and cocktails; follow the D731 to St-Jean-d'Angely for 13km as far as Burie, then turn right onto the D131, 4km from Migron.

A particularly beautiful excursion – arranged through the tourist office – is a **boat trip** east, upstream through the locks to **JARNAC** (ⓦwww.jarnac-tourisme.com), where the late President Mitterrand's modest grave has become a place of pilgrimage for elderly left-wingers. Also here is the **Espace Culturel de l'Orangerie**, 10 quai de l'Orangerie (Jan–June & Sept daily except Tues 2–6pm; July & Aug daily 10am–noon & 2–6pm; ⓣ05.45.81.38.88; €3.50), which houses a permanent exhibition on the public works carried out during Mitterrand's two terms of office.

Angoulême and around

The charming cathedral city of **ANGOULÊME** used to be dominated by paper mills that employed thousands of workers and bolstered the city's prosperity. The industry collapsed in the 1980s, and today only a couple of small, specialized mills still function. Since then the economy has picked up again, especially the tourist industry, and it's now a moderately prosperous place.

In the past, however, the former capital of the Angoumois province was a much-coveted city politically, being heavily fought over during the fourteenth-century Anglo-French squabbles and again in the sixteenth century during the Wars of Religion, when it was a Protestant stronghold. After the revocation of the Edict of Nantes, a good proportion of its citizens – among them many of its skilled papermakers – emigrated to Holland, never to return.

The Town

The **old town** occupies a high steep-sided plateau overlooking a bend in the Charente, a natural fortress. It has many charms, if few notable sights. The labyrinthine streets to the north of the delightful **place Louvel** and the massive Hôtel de Ville have been largely restored and pedestrianized. It's here that the restaurants and bars are concentrated, while the eastern section, down rue Marango and rue St-Martial, has become the main commercial centre. On the southern edge of the plateau stands the **cathedral**, whose west front – like Notre-Dame at Poitiers – is a fascinating display board for some expressive and lively twelfth-century sculpture, culminating in a Risen Christ with angels and clouds about his head, framed in the usual blaze of a halo. The lively frieze beneath the tympanum to the right of the west door commemorates the recapture of Spanish Zaragoza from the Moors, showing a bishop transfixing a Moorish giant with his lance and Roland killing the Moorish king.

Next to the cathedral in the old bishop's palace, there's more art on show at the Musée des Beaux-Arts, though, sadly, it will be closed until 2006 due to ongoing renovation work. From the front of the cathedral, you can walk all around the **ramparts** encircling the plateau, with long views over the surrounding country, now largely filled with urban sprawl. There are **public gardens** below the parapet at the far end of the fortifications, and a gravelly esplanade by the *lycée* where locals gather to play boules.

Angoulême's most fascinating museum lies just below the city walls on the north side close to the River Charente: the **Centre National de la Bande Dessinée**, 121 rue de Bordeaux (July & Aug Mon–Fri 10am–7pm, Sat & Sun 2–7pm; Sept–June Tues–Fri 10am–6pm, Sat & Sun 2–6pm; €5; bus #3 or #5; Ⓦwww.cnbdi.fr), devoted entirely to comic strips. Housed in a hundred-year-old brewery, with contemporary high-rise and glass additions, the museum gets across the message that comics ("BD") – from politics to pornography – are regarded as a serious art form in France. The museum owns a collection of some four thousand original drawings, which it displays in rotating exhibitions of about three hundred at a time. They range from the earliest stories with pictures and captions, the nineteenth-century *images d'Épinal*, through the introduction of the speech bubble in the 1920s to some of the darker contemporary productions. Astérix, Peanuts, Tintin and many other characters and artists are represented. There's also a vast library, much of it in English, where you're welcome to relax on cushions and flick through the comics.

Another riverfront museum close by is the **Atelier-Musée du Papier**, 134 rue de Bordeaux (April to mid-June Mon–Fri 10am–noon & 2–6pm, Sat & Sun 3–6pm; mid-June to mid-Sept Mon–Fri 10am–noon & 2–7pm, Sat & Sun 10–11.30am & 3–6pm; Nov–March Mon–Fri 2–6pm; closed Tues year-round; €4.50), located in a disused cigarette-paper factory – a fitting tribute to the declining Charentais paper industry. While exhibits get into the history and technicalities of paper-making, art isn't forgotten, with contemporary creations on show, utilizing paper, cardboard and pulp.

Practicalities

Angoulême is easily accessible by **train** from Cognac, Limoges and Poitiers. From the **gare SNCF**, avenue Gambetta, with the **gare routière** and several cheap hotels, leads uphill to the town centre through place Pérot, a fifteen-minute walk. The main **tourist office**, 2 place St-Pierre (July & Aug Mon–Sat 9.30am–7pm, Sun 10am–noon & 2–5pm; Sept–June Mon–Fri 9am–12.30pm & 1.30–6pm, Sat 10am–noon & 2–5pm, Sun 10am–noon; Ⓣ05.45.95.16.84, Ⓦwww.angouleme.fr), is by the cathedral and can provide route details for walks in the area – *circuits pédèstres*; there's another branch office outside the *gare SNCF*. Free **Internet** access is available at Le Kaléi Espace Culture Multimédia at 1 bd Berthelot.

Both tourist offices can help with **accommodation**, although if you want to go it alone the cheapest rooms in town are at the peaceful family-run *Le Crab*, 27 rue Kléber (Ⓣ05.45.93.02.93, Ⓕ05.45.93.02.70; ❷), with a decent restaurant serving menus from €11, and at *Hôtel Gasté*, 381 rte de Bordeaux (Ⓣ05.45.91.89.98, Ⓕ05.45.25.24.67; ❷; closed first three weeks in Aug; restaurant from €12.30), a long haul from the station on the opposite side of town. But far and away the nicest place to stay is the elegant old *Hôtel du Palais*, overlooking the charming shady place Louvel in the heart of the old town (Ⓣ05.45.92.54.11, Ⓕ05.45.92.01.83; ❸; garage available). Another place worth trying, especially for its excellent regional cuisine, is the *Hôtel La Palma*, 4 rampe d'Aguesseau, on the road leading up into the old town from the station (Ⓣ05.45.95.22.89, Ⓕ05.45.94.26.66; ❷; restaurant from €13). Alternatively, there's a large **HI hostel** (Ⓣ05.45.92.45.80, Ⓕ05.45.95.90.71), with canteen, on an island in the Charente; it's a fifteen -minute walk, or take bus #7 from place du Champ-de-Mars; the 10pm curfew complicates exploring Angoulême's rocking nightlife however. The municipal **campsite** (Ⓣ05.45.92.83.22) is nearby, beyond the Pont de Bourgines.

Likely **restaurant** areas are rue de Genève, offering both traditional French and international options, and the narrow, pedestrianized rue Massillon. One of the best restaurants in the region, with superb service and a number of interesting and inventive menus, starting at €22, is *La Ruelle*, 6 rue Trois-Notre-Dames (Ⓣ05.45.95.15.19; closed all day Sun, Mon & Sat lunch, plus April 8–14 & Aug 5–18), carved out of two buildings and the alley between them. Near the excellent daily covered market of Les Halles, you'll find *Le Shéhérazade*, 6 rue Massillon (Ⓣ05.46.27.07.17), with good Algerian cuisine in a great setting, and *Le Chat Noir*, on rue du Chat, crowded with lunchers after its cheap salads and snacks. *La Marine* on rue Ludovic-Trarieux is a modern and airy oyster/wine bar, while *Chez Paul*, 1 place France Louval (Ⓣ05.45.90.04.61), is a friendly and very reasonable restaurant with a beautiful garden; the food is fantastic, with menus starting at €10.80, and it's well worth a visit.

Around Angoulême

LA ROCHEFOUCAULD, 22km east of Angoulême, is the site of a huge Renaissance **château** on the banks of the River Tardoire, which still belongs to the family that gave its name to the town a thousand years ago. The stately pile, although still lived in, opens its elaborate portals to the public (Easter–Nov daily 10am–7pm; Dec–Easter Mon–Sat 10am–7pm, Sun 2–7pm; €6.10). In August it stages a massive *son et lumière* with a brigade-sized cast. If you want to **stay**, try the lovely old *Auberge de la Carpe d'Or* at 13 Grande-Rue (Ⓣ05.45.62.02.72, Ⓕ05.45.63.01.88; ❷). There's also a municipal **campsite** on rue des Flots beneath the château.

Further east, the country becomes hillier and more wooded, with buttercup pastures grazed by liver-coloured Limousin cattle. A good way to see it is to drive up the back roads along the River Vienne to the beautiful, if now rather touristy, little town of **CONFOLENS**, about 40km northeast of La Rochefoucauld. Its ancient houses are stacked up a hillside above a broad brown sweep of the river, here crossed by a long narrow medieval bridge. The town's chief claim to fame today is the huge **International Folklore Festival**, held every year in the second week of August, when, of course, it's impossible to find anywhere to stay (festival information Ⓣ05.45.84.00.77, Ⓦwww.festivaldeconfolens.com). There is a municipal **campsite** by the tributary River Goire.

Having come this far, it's worth continuing the extra 6km to the minuscule village of **ST-GERMAIN-DE-CONFOLENS**, huddled by the riverside beneath the romantic towers of its ruined castle, where you can eat good country fare at the *Auberge de la Tour* (closed Mon except in July & Aug) for as little as €11.50.

Aquitaine

In Roman times, **Bordeaux** was capital of the province of *Aquitania Secunda*. With the marriage of Eleanor of Aquitaine and King Henry II of England in 1152, it quickly became the principal English foothold for their three-hundred-year Aquitanian adventure, and it was to their presence, and particularly their taste for its red wines – imported back to England and termed "claret" – that the region owed its first great economic boom. The second boom, which financed the building of the gracious eighteenth-century centre of Bordeaux, came with the expansion of colonial trade.

The surrounding countryside is more notable for its wines and **vineyards** than its scenery, though the hills of **Entre-Deux-Mers** and the pretty town of **St-Émilion** are worth visiting in their own right. More interesting is the vast pine-covered expanse of **Les Landes** and the huge, wild Atlantic beaches of the **Côte d'Argent** to the south, but it's not a landscape that charms. Its appeal is more in its size and uniqueness – and you definitely need your own transport to explore it.

Bordeaux

The city of **BORDEAUX** is stunning when approached from the south along the river. It's big, with a population of over half a million, and obviously rich – as it has been since the Romans set up a lively trading centre here; even today it still functions as the regional transport hub for Aquitaine. Especially attractive is the relatively small eighteenth-century centre, paid for by the expansion of colonial trade. In addition, the city's brand-new space-age tram network gives it a modern, electric feel that juxtaposes nicely with its classical architecture. With a few sights worth checking out, plenty of cheap places to sleep and eat and a fantastic nightlife, Bordeaux's atmosphere is inviting and worth sticking around for.

Arrival, information and accommodation

Bordeaux-Mérignac **airport** is 12km west of the city and is connected by half-hourly shuttles to the main tourist office (45min; €6.50). Arriving by **train**, you'll find yourself at the gare St-Jean, with its own small tourist office (May–Oct Mon–Sat 9am–noon & 1–6pm, Sun 10am–noon & 1–3pm; Nov–April Mon–Fri 9.30am–12.30pm & 2–6pm; ⓣ05.56.91.64.70), right at the heart of a somewhat insalubrious area, nearly 3km south of the city centre; buses #7 or #8 run into the centre, and the tram line C will take you close by. There's no central **gare routière**, but most regional bus services terminate on the north side of the esplanade des Quinconces.

The new billion-Euro **tram system**, opened in late 2003, has changed much of the landscape of the city: for one, traffic is now much more organized and a number of central streets have been pedestrianized, making the city more democratic. Services operate on the three lines frequently from 5am to 1am, and run throughout the city centre, extending several kilometres into Bordeaux's suburbs. You can purchase either single-ride tickets (€1.30) or carnets of ten (€9), available from the efficient machines at tram stops or at *tabacs* all over the city. Tickets are valid for up to four connections within an hour on any type of city transport (tram, bus or navette), and must be punched each time you begin a journey. Though the city is certainly walkable, some sights are a fair distance away from each other, and if you're going to be here for a few days, it pays to buy an **unlimited-use pass**, available for between one and six days. Bordeaux's efficient electric **navette buses** run daily every 10–15 minutes between place de la Victoire and place de la Quinconces, with stops in between at Gambetta, St. Pierre and St. Michel; tickets (the same ones used for the trams) can be purchased on board. For **car** drivers, there should be ample parking in the numerous underground car parks in the town centre, though it's cheaper to use the car parks next to the tram stations on the east bank of the Garonne: buy a round-trip park-and-ride ticket (€2.60), and hop on a tram into the centre.

Bordeaux's main **tourist office**, near the Grand Théâtre on 12 cours du 30-Juillet (May–June & Sept–Oct, Mon–Sat 9am–7pm, Sun 9.30am–6.30pm; July & Aug Mon–Sat 9am–7.30pm, Sun 9.30am–6.30pm; Nov–April Mon–Sat 9am–6.30pm, Sun 9.45am–4.30pm; ⓣ05.56.00.66.00, ⓦwww.bordeaux-tourisme.com), can book accommodation free of charge, and it has useful information on the city and surrounding vineyards, to which it also arranges tours (see box on p.700 for details). The tourist office for the **Gironde region** is at 21 cours de l'Intendance (ⓣ05.56.52.61.40, ⓦwww.tourisme-gironde.cg33.fr).

The area right by the station – particularly rue Charles-Domercq and cours de la Marne – is full of one- and two-star **hotels**, though this is not the most appealing area to stay, as it's neither clean nor central and is lined with sex shops and other dodgy storefronts. Better to head for the city centre, where there's a good choice, from the basic to the luxurious. Rooms are generally not difficult to come by, with the notable exception of the week of the Vinexpo trade fair (in odd-numbered years) and Fête du Vin (in even-numbered years) in June, when Bordeaux is packed to the gunnels.

Hotels

Blayais 17 rue Mautrec ⓣ05.56.48.17.87, ⓦwww.studiotel-blayais.com. Small hotel just off place de la Comédie, with functional, clean and reasonably sized rooms, all en suite and some with a kitchenette. ❸

De la Boétie 4 rue de la Boétie ⓣ05.56.81.76.68, ⓕ05.56.51.24.06. A good bargain, this cheap and central one-star hotel is on a quiet back street. Owned by the *Bristol* (see below), it shares its reception. ❶

Bristol 4 rue Bouffard ⓣ05.56.81.85.01, ⓔbristol@hotel-bordeaux.com. Comfortable, relaxed two-star hotel just south of place Gambetta; its well-equipped, en-suite rooms are decently sized and stylishly decorated. ❷

Dauphin 82 rue du Palais Gallien ⓣ05.56.52.24.62, ⓕ05.56.01.10.91. Though a little out of the action, this fabulously decorated, old-fashioned hotel is justifiably popular; its recent renovation has added parquet floors and snazzy paint jobs in nearly all the rooms. The more spacious, top-price rooms, with their huge windows and high ceilings, offer best value for money. ❷

Maison du Lierre 57 rue Huguerie ⓣ05.56.51.92.71, ⓕ05.56.79.15.16, ⓦwww.maisondulierre.com. Inexpensive hotel-restaurant with a friendly proprietor. Top-floor rooms are a long climb. ❸

Notre-Dame 36 rue Notre-Dame ⓣ05.56.52.88.24, ⓦwww.hotelnotredame.free.fr. Quiet, refined establishment offering reasonable value for money in an interesting area of old streets just north of esplanade des Quinconces. Air conditioning and generous bathrooms come as standard, though the decor is unexciting and the cheapest rooms are small for two people. ❸

De la Presse 6–8 rue Porte Dijeaux ⓣ05.56.48.53.88, ⓦwww.hoteldelapresse.com. With very friendly staff, this well-kept family-run hotel in the pedestrian heart of Bordeaux is a good find. Its light, bright rooms are well proportioned, with big beds to match, and provide three-star comforts such as minibar, air conditioning, and Internet access in the rooms. Closed one week at Christmas. ❹

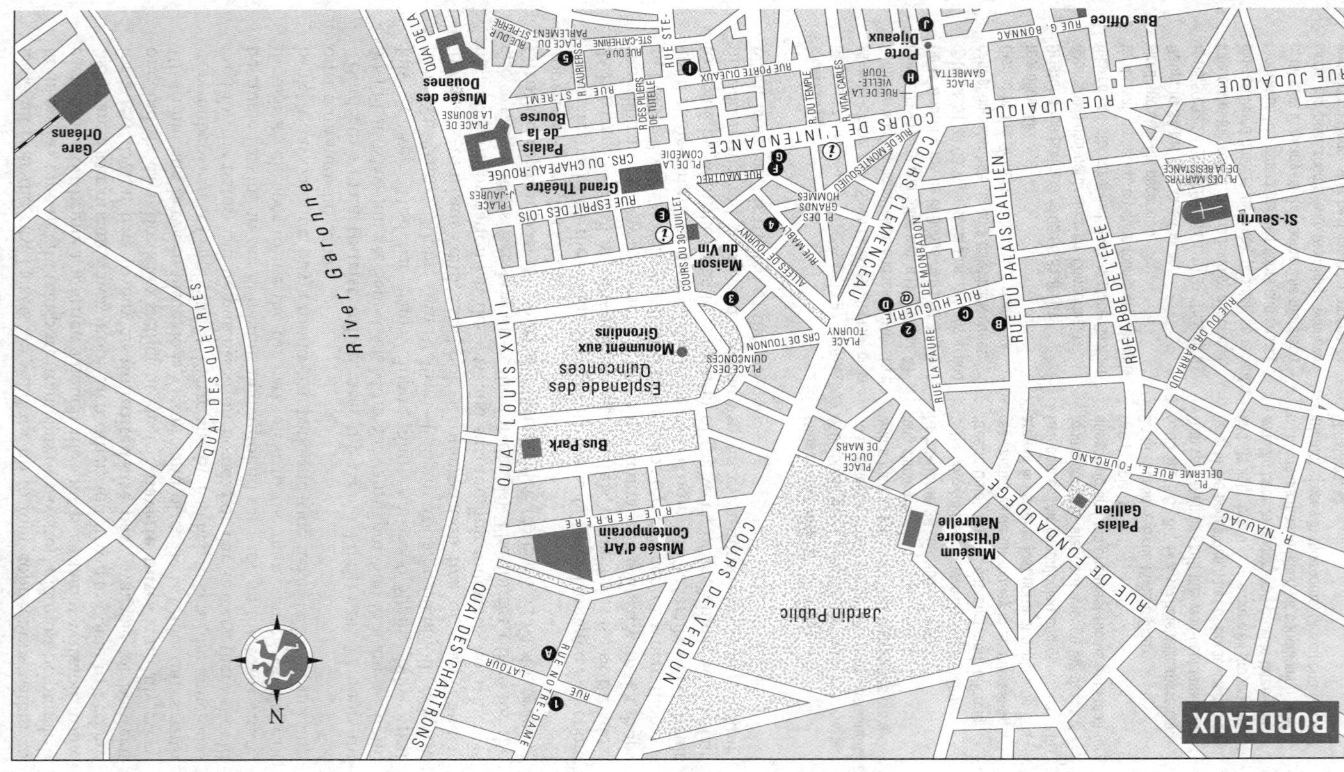
BORDEAUX
N
River Garonne
QUAI DES QUEYRIES
Gare Orléans
QUAI DES CHARTRONS
QUAI LOUIS XVIII
QUAI DE LA
Musée des Douanes
PLACE DE LA BOURSE
Palais de la Bourse
CRS. DU CHAPEAU-ROUGE
Grand Théâtre
PLACE J-JAURES
RUE ESPRIT DES LOIS
R. LAURIERS
RUE ST-REMI
PLACE DU PARLEMENT ST-PIERRE
RUE DU P. ST-PIERRE
RUE DU P. STE-CATHERINE
R DES PILIERS DE TUTELLE
RUE STE-
RUE PORTE DIJEAUX
PL DE LA COMÉDIE
COURS DE L'INTENDANCE
RUE MAUTREC
R. DU TEMPLE
R. VITAL CARLES
RUE DE LA VIELLE-TOUR
RUE DE MONTESQUIEU
PLACE GAMBETTA
Porte Dijeaux
Bus Office
RUE G. BONNAC
RUE JUDAIQUE
COURS DU 30-JUILLET
Maison du Vin
PL DES GRANDS HOMMES
RUE MABLY
ALLEES DE TOURNY
COURS CLEMENCEAU
Esplanade des Quinconces
Monument aux Girondins
PLACE DES QUINCONCES
CRS DE TOUNON
PLACE TOURNY
Bus Park
RUE FERRERE
Musée d'Art Contemporain
RUE NOTRE-DAME
RUE LATOUR
COURS DE VERDUN
Jardin Public
PLACE DU CH. DE MARS
RUE HUGUERIE
RUE LA FAURE
DE MONBADON
RUE DU PALAIS GALLIEN
RUE ABBE DE L'EPEE
St-Seurin
PL. DES MARTYRS DE LA RESISTANCE
RUE DU DR BARRAUD
Muséum d'Histoire Naturelle
RUE DE FONDAUDEGE
RUE E. FOURCAND
PL. DELERME
Palais Gallien
R. NAUJAC

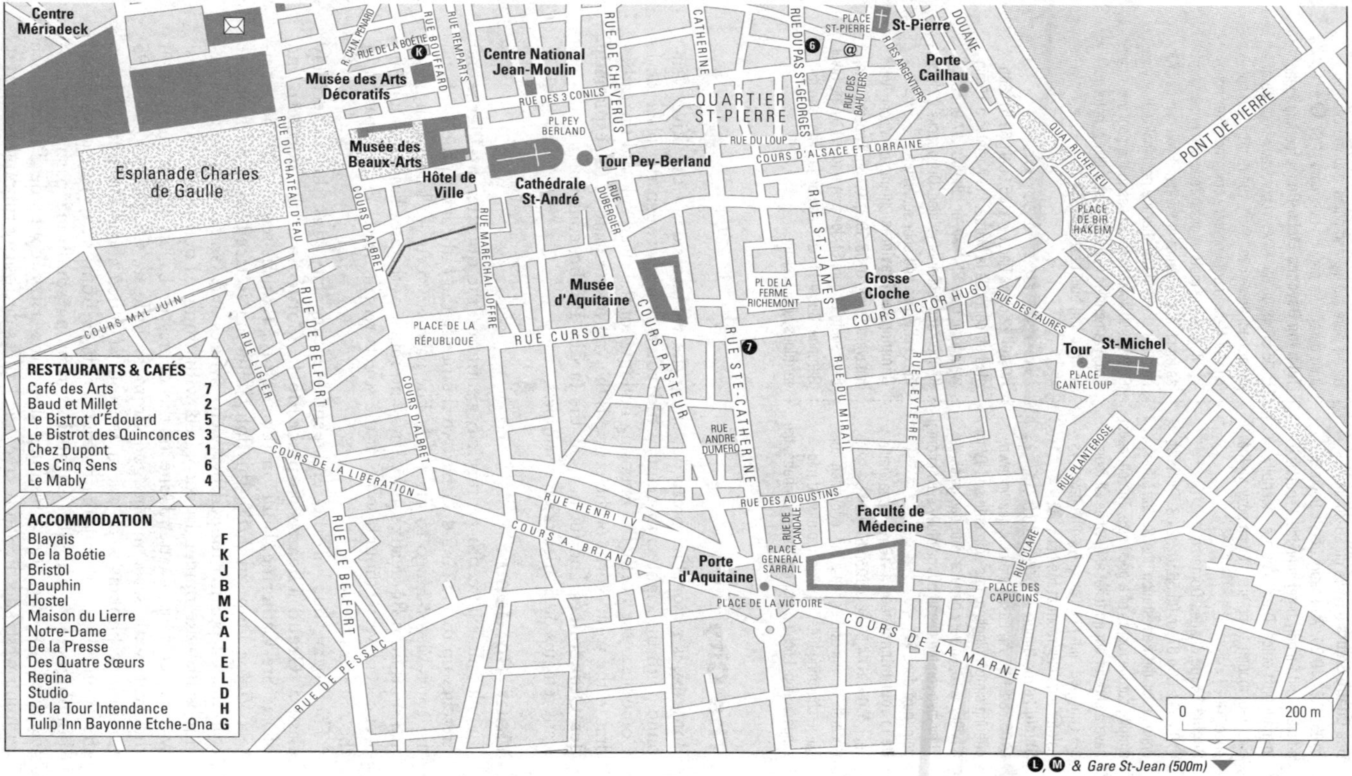

(L), (M) & Gare St-Jean (500m)

0 200 m

RESTAURANTS & CAFÉS

Café des Arts	7
Baud et Millet	2
Le Bistrot d'Édouard	5
Le Bistrot des Quinconces	3
Chez Dupont	1
Les Cinq Sens	6
Le Mably	4

ACCOMMODATION

Blayais	F
De la Boétie	K
Bristol	J
Dauphin	B
Hostel	M
Maison du Lierre	C
Notre-Dame	A
De la Presse	I
Des Quatre Sœurs	E
Regina	L
Studio	D
De la Tour Intendance	H
Tulip Inn Bayonne Etche-Ona	G

Centre Mériadeck
Esplanade Charles de Gaulle
Musée des Arts Décoratifs
Musée des Beaux-Arts
Hôtel de Ville
Centre National Jean-Moulin
Cathédrale St-André
Tour Pey-Berland
Musée d'Aquitaine
Quartier St-Pierre
St-Pierre
Porte Cailhau
Grosse Cloche
Tour St-Michel
Faculté de Médecine
Porte d'Aquitaine
Pont de Pierre
Quai Richelieu
Douane
Place de Bir Hakeim
Place St-Pierre
Place Canteloup
Place des Capucins
Place Général Sarrail
Place de la Victoire
Place de la République
Pl de la Ferme Richemont
Pl Pey Berland
Rue du Pas St-Georges
Rue des Bahutiers
R des Argentiers
Rue du Loup
Cours d'Alsace et Lorraine
Rue St-James
Rue Ste-Catherine
Catherine
Rue de Cheverus
Rue des 3 Conils
Rue Dubergier
Rue Remparts
Rue Bouffard
Rue de la Boétie
R Ch N Penard
Rue Maréchal Joffre
Cours d'Albret
Rue du Château d'Eau
Rue de Belfort
Rue Ligier
Cours Mal Juin
Cours de la Libération
Rue de Pessac
Cours Pasteur
Rue Cursol
Rue André Dumerq
Rue Henri IV
Cours A. Briand
Rue des Augustins
Rue de Candale
Rue du Mirail
Rue Leyteire
Cours Victor Hugo
Rue des Faures
Rue Planterose
Rue Clare
Cours de la Marne

Des Quatre Sœurs 6 cours du 30-Juillet ⓣ05.57.81.19.20, ⓦ4soeurs.free.fr. Popular, efficient and friendly hotel in an ideal spot next to the tourist office. The rooms are cheerfully coloured, though some are a touch boxy for the price. ❺

Regina 34 rue Charles-Domercq ⓣ05.56.91.66.07, ⓕ05.56.91.32.88. The best option near the train station, the *Regina* offers simple, spruce rooms of a good size. The cheapest have a shower but no toilet and, while all rooms are equipped with phones, only some have TVs. Ask for a quieter room at the back. ❸

Studio 26 rue Huguerie ⓣ05.56.48.00.14, ⓕ05.56.81.25.71. Easily the best deal in town, offering simple single rooms with bath and TV for a paltry €16, so very popular with backpackers. They also run the cheap but painfully slow Internet point next door. ❶

De la Tour Intendance 14–16 rue de la Vieille-Tour ⓣ05.56.44.56.56, ⓕ05.56.44.54.54. Recently having undergone a full renovation, this quiet, charming hotel emerges as a good mid-range option. Located just off place Gambetta, the rooms here are big and plush, and you can use their garage for parking overnight (€8). ❺

Tulip Inn Bayonne Etche-Ona 4 rue Martignac ⓣ05.56.48.00.88, ⓦwww.bordeaux-hotel.com. A great find, these two family-run refurbished hotels, one all classy contemporary chic, the other echoing its Basque roots in plush reds and greens, are as much in the centre of things as you can get. All mod cons and top-of-the-line personalized service. Guests will soon have access to the pool and other luxury amenities in the four-star luxury hotel currently being built next-door. ❺

Hostel and campsite

Hostel 22 cours Barbey ⓣ05.56.91.59.51. Situated off cours de la Marne, the hostel is a 10min walk from gare St-Jean, or take bus #7 or #8. Kitchen and laundry facilities. Drawbacks include the seedy area and poor security.

Camping les Gravières Chemin de Macau, Villenave-d'Ornon ⓣ05.56.87.00.36. Two-star site, 8km south of gare St-Jean, in a forest by the River Garonne. Bus #B from place de la Victoire to its terminus at Courejean.

The City

Bordeaux is reasonably spread out along the western side of the River Garonne, with the eighteenth-century **old town** lying between the place de la Comédie to the north, the imposing buildings of the riverbank and the cathedral to the west. North of the centre is the vast open square of the **esplanade des Quinconces**, and further still, the **Jardin Public**, containing some very scant remains of Bordeaux's Roman past.

Vieux Bordeaux

The elegant, eighteenth-century city centres on the **quartier St-Pierre** and stretches up to the Grand Théâtre to the north, the cathedral to the west and the cours Victor-Hugo to the south. The narrow streets are lined with grand mansions from Bordeaux's glory days, and much of the area has been done up over recent years, though some of the streets remain seedy in anticipation of the restorer's touch.

The social hub of the eighteenth-century city was the impeccably classical **Grand Théâtre** on **place de la Comédie** at the northern end of rue Ste-Catherine. Built on the site of a Roman temple by the architect Victor Louis in 1780, this lofty building is faced with an immense colonnaded portico topped by twelve Muses and Graces. Inside, the interior is likewise opulently decorated with trompe l'oeil paintings; the best way to see it is to attend one of the operas or ballets staged throughout the year, with seats in the gods from as little as €8 (ⓣ05.56.00.85.95 for info & bookings), or ask at the tourist office about the guided tours they sometimes offer. Smart streets radiate from here: the city's main shopping street, **rue Ste-Catherine**, running south and partially pedestrianized to ease the consumer flow; the ritzy cours de l'Intendance running west; and the sandy, tree-lined allées de Tourny running northwest, commemorating the Marquis Louis Aubert de Tourny – the eighteenth-century administrator who was prime mover of the city's "Golden Age" and supervised much of the rebuilding. Back in the narrow streets of the old town, the harmonious **place du Parlement** and **place St-Pierre** are both lined with typical Bordelais mansions and peppered with wrought-iron balconies and arcading, making impressive examples of town planning.

The riverfront was also given the once-over by early eighteenth-century planners, with the imposing **place de la Bourse** creating a focal point on the quayside. The impressive bulk of the old customs house of 1733 contains the **Musée des Douanes** (Tues–Sun 10am–6pm; €3), which gives a rundown on Bordeaux's port and seafaring past and retraces the history of the administration and work of French Customs. The square is balanced by the **Palais de la Bourse** (stock exchange) looking out over the quayside and the broad River Garonne. Further south along the riverbank, the fifteenth-century **Porte Cailhau** takes its name from the stones (*cailloux – cailhaux* in dialect) unloaded on the neighbouring quay to be used as ballast for boats. Crossing the river just south of here, the only testimony to a nobler past is the impressive **Pont de Pierre** – "Stone Bridge", though in fact it's mostly brick – built at Napoleon's command during the Spanish campaigns, with seventeen arches in honour of his victories. The views of the river and quays from here are memorable, particularly when floodlit at night.

Place Gambetta, the cathedral and around

Cours de l'Intendance, a street lined with chic shops, links place de la Comédie with café-lined **place Gambetta**, a pivotal square for the city's museums, shops and the cathedral. Once a majestic space conceived as an architectural whole in the time of Louis XV, place Gambetta's house fronts are arcaded at street level and decorated with rows of carved masks. In the middle of the square a valiant attempt at an English garden adds some welcome relief, belying the fact that the guillotine lopped three hundred heads off here at the time of the Revolution. In one corner stands the eighteenth-century arch of the **Porte Dijeaux**, an old city gate.

South of place Gambetta is the **Cathédrale St-André** (Mon–Sat 7.30–11.30am & 2–6/6.30pm), whose most eye-catching feature is the great upward sweep of the twin steeples over the north transept, an effect heightened by the adjacent but separate bell tower, the fifteenth-century **Tour Pey-Berland** (June–Sept daily 10am–6.30pm; Oct–May Tues–Sun 10am–noon & 2–5pm; €3.80). The interior of the cathedral, begun in the twelfth century, is not particularly interesting apart from the choir, which provides one of the few complete examples of the florid late Gothic style known as *Rayonnant*, and the north transept door and the Porte Royale to the right, which feature some fine carving.

The cream of Bordeaux's museums is to be found scattered in the streets around the cathedral. Directly behind the classical Hôtel de Ville, formerly Archbishop Rohan's palace, the **Musée des Beaux-Arts** (daily except Tues 11am–6pm; €4) has a small but worthy selection of European fine art, featuring works by Reynolds, Titian, Rubens, Matisse and Marquet (a native of the city), as well as Delacroix's superb painting of *La Grèce sur les ruines de Missolonghi*. More engaging, however, is the **Musée des Arts Décoratifs** (daily except Tues 2pm–6pm; €4), two blocks north on rue Bouffard and housed in a handsome eighteenth-century house. The extensive collection includes some beautiful, mainly French, porcelain and faïence, period furniture, glass, miniatures, Barye animal sculptures and prints of the city in its maritime heyday.

Continuing to circle clockwise round the cathedral, you'll pass the **Centre National Jean-Moulin** (Tues–Fri 11am–6pm, Sat & Sun 2–6pm; free), an interesting museum dedicated to the local Resistance, featuring a history of the occupation of Bordeaux and a harrowing permanant exhibit of Holocaust-inspired paintings by French artist J.J. Morran, before reaching the imaginatively laid-out **Musée d'Aquitaine**, on cours Pasteur (Tues–Sun 11am–6pm; €4), one of the city's best museums. A stimulating variety of objects and types of display emphasizes regional ethnography and covers the three main facets of the region's development: maritime, commercial and agricultural. Drawings and writings of the period enable you to see why eighteenth-century Bordeaux was so extolled by contemporary writers, who compared it to Paris. It's also worth taking a look at the section on the wine trade before venturing off on a vineyard tour in the region. A couple of blocks east, rue St-James is straddled by a heavy Gothic tower, the fifteenth-century **Grosse Cloche**, originally part of the medieval town hall.

North of the centre

North of the Grand Théâtre, cours du 30-Juillet leads into the bare, gravelly – and frankly unattractive – expanse of the **esplanade des Quinconces**, said to be Europe's largest municipal square. At the quayside end are two tall columns, erected in 1829 and topped by allegorical statues of Commerce and Navigation; at the opposite end of the esplanade is the **Monument aux Girondins**, a glorious *fin-de-siècle* ensemble of statues and fountains built in honour of the influential local deputies to the 1789 Revolutionary Assembly, later purged by Robespierre as moderates and counter-revolutionaries. During World War II, in a fit of anti-French spite, the occupying Germans made plans to melt the monument down, only to be foiled by the local Resistance, who got there first and, under cover of darkness, dismantled it piece by piece and hid it in a barn in the Médoc for the duration of the war.

To the northwest is the beautiful formal park, the **Jardin Public** (daily April–Oct 7am–8/9pm; Nov–March 7am–6pm; free), containing the city's botanical gardens as well as a small **natural history museum** (Mon & Wed–Fri 11am–6pm, Sat & Sun 2–6pm; €4, free 1st Sun of month). Behind it, to west and north, lies a quiet, provincial quarter of two-storey stone houses. Concealed among the narrow streets, on rue du Dr. Albert Barraud, is a large chunk of brick and stone masonry, the so-called **Palais Gallien**, in fact a third-century arena that's all that remains of *Burdigala*, Aquitaine's Roman capital. Nearby, on place Delerme, the unusual round **market hall** makes a focus for a stroll through the quarter. To the east of the gardens, closer to the river, the **Musée d'Art Contemporain** on rue Ferrère (Tues & Thurs–Sun 11am–6pm, Wed 11am–8pm; €5.50) occupies a converted nineteenth-century warehouse for colonial imports. The vast, arcaded hall provides a magnificent setting for the mostly post-1960 sculpture and installation-based work by artists such as Richard Long, Daniel Buren and Sol LeWitt. Few pieces from the permanent collection are on display at any one time, the main space being filled by temporary exhibitions, so it's hit and miss as to whether you'll like what's on offer. However, there's a superb collection of glossy art books in the library and an elegant café-restaurant on the roof (lunch only).

Further out, the **Conservatoire International de la Plaisance**, in Dock no. 2 off bd Alfred-Daney (Wed–Sun 2–6pm; €4.50), an old German submarine base, with concrete walls and roof up to 9m thick, has been converted into an unusual museum combining pleasure boats and naval history.

Eating and drinking

Bordeaux is packed with numerous **restaurants**, many of them top-notch, and due to its position close to the Atlantic coast, fresh seafood features prominently on many a Bordelais menu. The best place to look for restaurants is around place du Parlement and place St-Pierre, where you'll find something to satisfy all tastes and budgets. There are numerous sandwich bars and fast-food outlets at the south end of rue Ste-Catherine and spilling into studenty place de la Victoire. In the summer, *guinguettes* – open-air **riverside stalls** selling shrimps, king prawns and other seafood snacks – set up along the quai des Chartrons. Surprisingly, Bordeaux lacks any truly grand, people-watching **cafés**. Though *Café Regent* on place Gambetta is the place to be seen, a nicer, cheaper alternative is to be found across the square at *Café Dijeaux* beside the city gate. For **picnic fodder**, there's a marvellous, round **market** in the place des Grands-Hommes, and on rue de Montesquieu, just off the square, Jean d'Alos runs the city's best *fromagerie*, with dozens of farm-produced cheeses.

Bordeaux's student population ensures a collection of young, lively **bars**, a host of which are found on and around place de la Victoire. Several offer live music and all are packed on Thursday nights. There's also a clutch of English, Irish and antipodean **pubs** now in Bordeaux and a low-key **gay scene** concentrated at the south end of rue des Remparts.

Cafés and restaurants

Café des Arts 138 cours Victor Hugo. This café-brasserie on the corner of rue Ste-Catherine is one of the city's few old-style cafés, its unique ambience created from faded relics of the 1940s. The food is good, too, and the kitchens stay open till 1am.

Baud et Millet 19 rue Huguerie ⓣ05.56.79.05.77. The ultimate cheese-and-wine feast consumed around a few tables at the back of a wine shop where you choose your own bottle from the shelves. Portions are generous and the food rich, so one dish goes a long way. Menus from €23. Closed Sun.

Le Bistrot d'Édouard 16 place du Parlement. Undeniably touristy place, but in a great position on a lovely square, with outdoor seating in summer. There's a good-value, three-course menu (€12) offering a choice of regional dishes, as well as standard brasserie fare. If they're full, try the slightly more upmarket sister-restaurant, *L'Ombrière*, next door. Closed Sun evening Nov–Feb.

Le Bistrot des Quinconces 4 place des Quinconces ⓣ05.56.52.84.56. Lively daytime and evening bistro. In fine weather locals vie for the outdoor tables, in a great spot facing the fountains. The modern, eclectic *carte* includes main dishes from around €14.50, with a three-course weekday lunch menu at €19.

Chez Dupont 45 rue de Notre-Dame ⓣ05.56.81.49.59. Bustling, old-fashioned restaurant in the Chartrons district, with wooden floors, old posters and waiters sporting colourful waistcoats. Prices are very reasonable, with a two-course lunch for €14.50, and *plats* between €11.50 and €17.

Les Cinq Sens 26 rue du Pas St-Georges ⓣ05.56.52.84.25. Not to be missed, this respected institution is one of the high spots of Bordeaux cuisine where you can eat exquisitely cooked, imaginative food at affordable prices. Seasonal dishes include truffles, lobster and pigeon, all beautifully presented in an elegant dining room with four-star service. The €25 menu includes two glasses of wine off a list which is a veritable bible of regional vintages. Closed Sat lunch & Sun.

Le Mably 12 rue Mably ⓣ05.56.44.30.10. Informal, friendly and popular restaurant with a warm, bistro atmosphere. Choose from a variety of *formules* starting with a *plat du jour* at €11 or three-course menus from €22. The food is plentiful and of excellent quality. Closed Sun & Mon.

Bars

Bar de l'Hôtel de Ville (BHV) 4 rue de l'Hôtel-de-Ville. Friendly little gay café-bar which stages a variety of free events every other Sunday (10.30pm).

Calle Ocho 24 rue des Piliers-de-Tutelle ⓣ05.56.48.08.68. Bordeaux's best-known and liveliest salsa bar is packed out on Thursday, Friday and Saturday nights. They serve real Cuban rum and *mojitos*, and the self-inebriating barstaff frequently showers the crowds with water sprayed from the bar tap.

Connemara 18 cours d'Albret. For the homesick pining for a pint of Guinness, this is Bordeaux's liveliest Irish pub, with free concerts or some other event most nights, plus cheap bar snacks, such as fish and chips, beef and Guinness pie and apple crumble.
Dick Turpin's 72 rue du Loup. Opposite the wisteria-filled courtyard of the municipal archives, this is a pretty good rendition of an English town pub with a great atmosphere and an international clientele. There's the standard range of beers – Guinness, Bass and Newcastle Brown – in addition to well-priced bar meals, and tea and cakes in the quieter afternoons. Happy hour 5.30–8.30pm.
Le Plana 22 place de la Victoire. One of the more relaxed student hangouts around the square, though, like everywhere else, it's jumping on Thursday nights. Free live music on Sun (jazz), Mon & Tues (various).

Nightlife and entertainment

Since Bordeaux's **dance clubs** are constantly changing it's best to ask around for the latest hotspots. There are one or two discos in the city centre, such as *Paris-Pékin*, at 10 rue de la Merci (☎05.56.44.19.88), but the majority of clubs are spread out along southerly quai du Paludate, where things don't really get going until two in the morning and continue till around four or five; Sunday is generally closing day. *Dame de Shangai*, 1 quai Armand la Lande, is a favourite among the metrosexual crowd, and one of the district's longer-lived clubs is *La Plage* at no. 40, a fun disco in a tropical-beach setting, while the wonderfully Baroque *Shadow Lounge*, 5 rue Cabannac, plays house and techno.

To find out the latest **events and happenings** in and around Bordeaux, get hold of a copy of the regional newspaper *Sud-Ouest*. Alternatively there are the fortnightly listings booklet *Spectaculair 33* (€0.50), the free but less comprehensive *Bordeaux Plus* and *Clubs & Concerts*, also free, detailing the city's current favourite clubs. The tourist office issues *Bordeaux Magazine*, a free monthly in French with coverage of more highbrow cultural events around town. To buy **tickets** for city and regional events, contact the venue direct or head for the box office (☎05.56.48.26.26) in the nineteenth-century Galerie Bordelaise arcade, wedged between rue Ste-Catherine and rue des Piliers-de-Tutelle. Virgin Megastore (☎05.56.56.05.55) on place Gambetta also has a ticket outlet.

Jazz and blues fans should head south down the river to the *Comptoir du Jazz*, 59 quai de Paludate (☎05.56.49.15.55); entry is free but you're expected to buy at least one drink. Other options are the *Café des Arts* (see p.697) and the more frenetic *L'Alligator*, 3 place du Général-Sarrail (☎05.56.92.78.47), which blasts out the blues on Wednesday nights.

There's no shortage of more **contemporary music**, either. Rock is alive and kicking at *Le Barclay*, 57 cours de l'Argonne (☎05.56.31.44.66), a music-bar near place de la Victoire, and near the station at the *Rock School Barbey*, 18 cours Barbey (☎05.56.33.66.00). *Le Jimmy*, 68 rue de Madrid (☎05.56.98.20.83), meanwhile, is perhaps Bordeaux's most famous rock-bar, popular for its DJ nights and music ranging from heavy metal to techno.

Listings

Airlines Air France ☎05.56.44.05.69; Air Liberté ☎08.03.80.58.05; British Airways ☎08.02.80.29.02.
Bike rental Bord'eaux Velo Loisirs (☎05.56.44.77.31), on quai Louis-XVIII beside the Quinconces boat dock, rents out everything from bikes to rollerblades and baby-strollers (closed Mon & Thurs; open afternoons only Oct–May). Another option is Cycles Pasteur at 42 cours Pasteur (☎05.56.92.68.20).
Books and newspapers Maison de la Presse, at 61 rue Ste-Catherine and place Gambetta, sells the main English-language papers in addition to some regional guides and maps. Bordeaux's largest bookstore, Mollat, 15 rue Vital Carles, has a good selection of local guides and maps. They also

stock a few English-language titles, though there's a better choice at helpful Bradley's Bookshop, 8 cours d'Albret.

Car rental Numerous rental firms are located in and around the train station, including Avis ⓣ05.56.91.65.50; Budget ⓣ05.56.31.41.40; Europcar ⓣ05.56.31.20.30; Hertz ⓣ05.57.59.05.95; and National/Citer ⓣ05.56.92.19.62. They all have outlets at the airport as well.

Cinema You're most likely to find original-language (*version originale*, or *v.o.*) films at the wonderful art-house cinema Utopia, 5 place Camille-Jullian (ⓣ05.56.52.00.03, ⓦwww.cinemas-utopia.org), in a converted church. Other good options include Trianon-Jean Vigo, 6 rue Franklin, near place des Grands-Hommes (ⓣ05.56.44.35.17, ⓦwww.jeanvigo.com), and UGC Cinécité, 13–15 rue Georges Bonnac (ⓣ08.36.68.68.58, ⓦwww.ugc.fr). For more standard fare, there's the vast, new seventeen-screen Megarama (ⓣ08.36.69.33.17, ⓦwww.megarama.fr) across the Pont de Pierre in the old Gare d'Orléans.

Consulates UK, 353 bd du Président-Wilson ⓣ05.57.22.21.10. USA, 10 place de la Bourse ⓣ05.56.48.63.80.

Emergencies To call an ambulance, phone SAMU on ⓣ15 or ⓣ05.56.96.70.70.

Hitching Allostop, 79 cours d'Argonne ⓣ05.57.95.60.74.

Hospital Centre Hospitalier Pellegrin-Tripode, place Amélie-Raba-Léon (ⓣ05.56.79.56.79), to the west of central Bordeaux.

Internet Cyberstation, 23 cours Pasteur is a friendly and helpful cybercafé with rates from €2 per hour (before 2pm), while Artobas, 7 rue Maucoudinat just off the place St-Pierre, is more expensive but has a faster connection (Mon–Sat 11am–1am; €3 per hour). The gare St-Jean claims to have a free Wi-Fi connection, but it seems about as reliable as the wind.

Money exchange American Express, 14 cours de l'Intendance (Mon–Fri 9.30am–5.30pm), handles most travellers' cheques and foreign currencies. The main banks along cours de l'Intendance also offer exchange facilities and 24hr ATMs.

Police Commissariat Central, 23 rue François de Sourdis (ⓣ05.57.85.77.77 or ⓣ17).

The Bordeaux wine region

Touring the **vineyards** and sampling a few local wines is one of the great pleasures of the Bordeaux region. The wine-producing districts lie in a great semicircle around the city, starting with the **Médoc** in the north, then skirting east through **St-Émilion**, before finishing south of the city among the vineyards of the **Sauternes**. In between, the less prestigious districts are also worth investigating, notably those of **Blaye**, to the north of Bordeaux, and **Entre-Deux-Mers**, to the east.

There's more to the region than its wine, however. Many of the Médoc's eighteenth-century châteaux are striking buildings in their own right, while the town of Blaye is dominated by a vast fortress, and there's a far older, more ruined castle at Villandraut on the edge of the Sauternes. St-Émilion is by far the prettiest of the wine towns, and has the unexpected bonus of a cavernous underground church. For scenic views, however, you can't beat the green, gentle hills of Entre-Deux-Mers and its ruined abbey, **La Sauve-Majeur**.

All these places are relatively well served by **public transport**. There are train lines from Bordeaux running north through the Médoc to Margaux and Pauillac, and south along the Garonne valley to St-Macaire and La Réole. St-Émilion, meanwhile, lies on the Bordeaux–Sarlat line, but the station is a couple of kilometres out of town. In addition, there's a very comprehensive regional bus network, with connections from Bordeaux to most of the towns mentioned below – you can pick up a route map at the tourist office in Bordeaux (see p.691). Buses are operated by several different companies, the two largest being Sera (ⓣ05.56.70.12.12), which covers the area just east of Bordeaux, and Citram (ⓣ05.56.43.68.43), which runs to nearly everywhere

The wines of Bordeaux

With Burgundy and Champagne, the **wines of Bordeaux** form the "Holy Trinity" of French viticulture. Despite producing as many whites as reds, it is the latter – known as claret to the British – that have graced the tables of the discerning for centuries. The countryside that produces them encircles the city, enjoying near-perfect climatic conditions and soils ranging from limestone to sand and pebbles. It's the largest quality wine district in the world, turning out around 500 million bottles a year – over half the country's quality wine output and ten percent, by value, of the world's wine trade.

The Gironde estuary, fed by the Garonne and the Dordogne, determines the lie of the land. The **Médoc** lies northwest of Bordeaux between the Atlantic coast and the River Gironde, with its vines deeply rooted in poor, gravelly soil, producing good, full-bodied red wines; the region's **eight appellations** are Médoc, Haut Médoc, St-Estèphe, Pauillac, St-Julien, Moulis en Médoc, Listrac-Médoc and Margaux. Southwest of Bordeaux are the vast vineyards of **Graves**, producing the best of the region's dry white wines, along with some punchy reds, from some of the most prestigious communes in France – Pessac, Talence, Martillac and Villenave d'Ornon amongst them. They spread down to Langon and envelop the areas of **Sauternes** and **Barsac**, whose extremely sweet white dessert wines are considered among the world's best.

On the east side of the Gironde estuary and the Dordogne, the **Côtes de Blaye** feature some good-quality white table wines, mostly dry, and a smaller quantity of reds. The **Côtes de Bourg** specialize in solid whites and reds, spreading down to the renowned **St-Émilion** area. Here, there are a dozen producers who have earned the accolade of *Premiers Grands Crus Classés*, and their output is a full, rich red wine that doesn't have to be kept as long as the Médoc wines. Lesser-known neighbouring areas include the vineyards of **Pomerol**, **Lalande** and **Côtes de Francs**, all producing reds similar to St-Émilion but at more affordable prices.

Between the Garonne and the Dordogne is **Entre-Deux-Mers**, an area which yields large quantities of inexpensive, drinkable table whites, mainly from the Sauvignon grape. The less important sweet whites of **Ste-Croix du Mont** come out of the area south of **Cadillac**. Stretching along the north bank of the Garonne, the

else. **Cycling** is yet another option, as many of the towns are interconnected by well-marked, clean, blacktop footpaths that wend their way through the woods.

The Médoc

The landscape of **the Médoc**, a slice of land northwest of Bordeaux wedged between the forests bordering the Atlantic coast and the Gironde estuary, is itself rather monotonous: its gravel plains, occupying the west bank of the brown, island-spotted estuary, rarely swell into anything resembling a hill. Paradoxically, however, this poor soil is ideal for viticulture – vines root more deeply if they don't find the sustenance they need in the topsoil and, firmly rooted, they are less subject to drought and flooding. The region's eight *appellations* produce only red wines, from the grape varieties of Cabernet Sauvignon, Cabernet Franc, Merlot and, to a lesser degree, Petit Verdot. Cabernet Sauvignon gives body, bouquet, colour and maturing potential to the wine, while Merlot gives it its "animal" quality, making it rounder and softer. The D2 wine road, heading off the N15 from Bordeaux, passes through Margaux, St-Julien, Pauillac and St-Estèphe and, while the vineyards of the **Côtes de Bordeaux** feature fruity reds and a smaller number of dry and sweet whites.

The **classification** of Bordeaux wines is an extremely complex affair. Apart from the usual *appellation d'origine contrôlée* (AOC) labelling – guaranteeing origin but not quality – the wines of the Médoc châteaux are graded into five *crus*, or growths. These were established as long ago as 1855, based on the prices the wines had fetched over the previous hundred years. Four were voted the best or *Premiers Grands Crus Classés*: Margaux, Lafitte, Latour and Haut-Brion. With the exception of Château Mouton-Rothschild, which moved up a class in 1973 to become the fifth *Premier Grand Cru Classé*, there have been no official changes, so divisions between the *crus* should not be taken too seriously. Since then, additional categories have been devised, for instance *Crus Bourgeois*, which has three categories of its own. The wines of Sauternes were also classified in 1855.

If you're interested in **buying wines**, it's possible to find bargains at some of the châteaux. Advantages of buying at source include the opportunity to sample before purchasing and to receive expert advice about different vintages. In Bordeaux, the best place to go is La Vinotèque (Mon–Sat 9.15am–7.30pm), next to the tourist office. There's a growing fashion for organic methods and "green" wines, already available on many good labels.

To **visit the châteaux**, Bordeaux's efficient Maison du Vin, just across the road from the tourist office (Mon–Fri 8.30am–5.30/6pm, late May to mid-Oct also Sat 9am–4.30pm), has various pamphlets detailing those châteaux which accept visitors. In addition, each wine-producing village has its own tourist office and Maison du Vin, which can provide the same service. Since getting to any of these places except St-Émilion without your own transport is hard work, the simplest thing is to take one of the Bordeaux tourist office's own half-day **guided tours**, covering a different area each day (May–Oct daily 1.30pm; Nov–April Wed & Sat 1.30pm; €26). Generally interesting and informative, the guide translates into English the wine-maker's commentary and answers any questions. Tastings are generous, and expert tuition on how to go about it is part of the deal.

scenery might not be stunning, the many famous – albeit mostly inaccessible – châteaux are.

The problem of accommodation is much worse in the Médoc than in the rest of the wine region, but it's possible to visit the area on a day-trip from Bordeaux. Considering it's one of the most prestigious wine-growing areas in Bordeaux, it's surprisingly unwelcoming to visitors, with places to eat, and particularly affordable ones, also in short supply. There are regular bus services to Pauillac, but it's worth considering car rental (see Bordeaux "Listings", p.699).

Château Margaux and Fort Médoc

Easily the prettiest of the Bordeaux châteaux, **Château Margaux** is an eighteenth-century villa in extensive, sculpture-dotted gardens close to the west bank of the Gironde, some 20km north of Bordeaux. Its wine, a classified *Premier Grand Cru* and world-famous in the 1940s and 1950s, went through a rough patch in the two succeeding decades but improved in the 1980s after the estate was bought by a Greek family. The château (by appointment only Mon–Fri 10am–noon & 2–4pm; closed Aug and during harvest; ⓣ05.57.88.83.83, ⓦwww.chateau-margaux.com; free) is not included in any tours, and it's best to book at least two weeks in advance.

In the small village of **MARGAUX** itself, there's an unusually friendly **Maison du Vin** (daily: July & Aug 9am–7pm; Sept–June 9am–noon & 2–6pm; ⓣ05.57.88.70.82, ⓔsyndicat.margaux@wanadoo.fr) that can book accommodation and advise on visits to the *appellation*'s châteaux. At the other end of the village, the enterprising and inviting cellar La Cave d'Ulysse provides free tastings from a variety of Margaux châteaux, giving you a chance to try and buy (and ship, if you need) some very good wines. Prices range from a €5 run-of-the-mill Médoc to €2400 for a delicate, rare 1990 Petrus). Margaux has a somewhat expensive but very comfortable **hotel**, *Le Pavillon de Margaux* (ⓣ05.57.88.77.54, ⓦwww.pavillondemargaux.com; ❺), with a fine restaurant (menus from €12). Otherwise, try the *chambre d'hôte Domaine de Carrat* (ⓣ & ⓕ05.56.58.24.80; ❹; closed Christmas & New Year) at **CASTELNAU-DE-MÉDOC**, 10km to the west. Besides the hotel, you can **eat** at Margaux's *Auberge de Savoie* (ⓣ05.57.88.31.76; closed Sun), next to the Maison du Vin, with good traditional food on menus from €15.

The seventeenth-century **Fort Médoc**, off the D2 road between Margaux and St-Julien by the banks of the estuary, is a good place to tuck into a few purchases between châteaux. It was designed by the prolific military architect Vauban to defend the Gironde estuary against the British. The remains of the fort are scant but scrambleable, and in summer its Toytown aspect has a leafy charm, marred only by the view of a nuclear power station across the river to the north of Blaye. Since 1990, the annual Fort Médoc **jazz festival**, with big-name international acts, has been held here in mid-July (ⓣ05.56.58.91.30 for details).

A couple of kilometres south, **LAMARQUE** is a very pretty village, full of flowers and with a sweet church. It's a pleasant place to stop for lunch, with a very agreeable restaurant, *L'Escale* (menus from €10; closed Tues & evenings off season), down by the port. From here at least four ferries (one way: passengers €3, cycles €1.50, cars €12.20) cross the muddy Gironde daily to Blaye, another place fortified by Vauban, and an important, though less well-known, Bordeaux wine-growing centre.

Pauillac and around

PAUILLAC is the largest town in the Médoc region and central to the most important vineyards of Bordeaux: no fewer than three of the top five *Grands Crus* come from around here. It has grown rapidly in recent years and, while its little harbour and riverfront are pretty enough, they can't counteract the presence of the nuclear power plant across the Gironde.

Pauillac has a huge **Maison du Tourisme et du Vin** along the waterfront (June & mid-Sept to Oct daily 9.30am–12.30pm & 2–6.30pm; July & Aug daily 9am–7pm; mid-Sept to May Mon–Sat 9.30am–12.30pm & 2–6pm, Sun 10am–12.30pm & 3.00–6pm; ⓣ05.56.59.03.08, ⓦwww.pauillac-medoc.com). It can provide you with a list of *gîtes*, rent out **bikes** and make appointments for you to visit the surrounding châteaux (€3.80 per château). Pauillac itself is not a great **place to stay**, but should you wish to, try the *Hôtel de France et d'Angleterre*, opposite the little harbour (ⓣ05.56.59.01.20, ⓦwww.hoteldefrance-angleterre.com; ❹; closed Christmas & New Year), with a good restaurant serving menus from €18 (closed Sun & Mon off season), or the welcoming riverfront **campsite** further south on route de la Rivière (ⓣ05.56.59.10.03; closed mid-Sept to March). Campsites are rare in the Médoc: the only other alternative is the two-star *Camping Le Bled* at **BERNOS** (ⓣ05.56.59.41.33; closed mid-Sept to mid-June), 8km southwest near St-Laurent-de-Médoc, a peaceful, shady and clean option. Alternatively, there's an excellent *chambres d'hôte* about 8km northwest near the village of **CISSAC**: *Château Gugès* (Ⓣ05.56.59.58.04, Ⓦwww.chateau-guges.com; ❹), in a large eighteenth-century house attached to a vineyard on the road to Gunes.

The most famous of the **Médoc châteaux** – Château Lafite-Rothschild (Ⓣ05.56.73.18.18), Château Latour (Ⓣ05.56.73.19.80) and Château Mouton-Rothschild (Ⓣ05.56.73.21.29) – can be visited by appointment only, either direct (all have English-speaking staff) or through the Maison du Vin. Their vineyards occupy larger single tracts of land than elsewhere in the Médoc, and consequently neighbouring wines can differ markedly: a good vintage Lafite is perfumed and refined, whereas a Mouton-Rothschild is strong and dark and should be kept for at least ten years. **Château Mouton-Rothschild** and its wine **museum** (April–Oct daily 9.30–11am & 2–4pm; Nov–March closed Sat & Sun; €5, or €13 including one tasting) is the most absorbing of the big houses: as well as the viticultural stuff, you also get to see the Rothschilds' amazing collection of art treasures, all loosely connected with wine.

St-Estèphe

North of Pauillac, the wine commune of **ST-ESTÈPHE** is Médoc's largest *appellation*, consisting predominantly of *crus bourgeois* properties and growers belonging to the local *cave coopérative*, **Marquis de St-Estèphe**, on the D2 towards Pauillac (tastings July & Aug daily 9am–noon & 2–7pm; Sept–June by appointment, Ⓣ05.56.73.35.30). One of the *appellation*'s five *crus classés* is the distinctive **Château Cos d'Estournel**, with its over-the-top nineteenth-century French version of a pagoda; the *chais* (warehouses) can be visited by appointment (Ⓣ05.56.73.15.50; English spoken). The village of St-Estèphe itself is a sleepy affair dominated by its landmark, the eighteenth-century **church of St-Étienne**, with its highly decorative interior. The small, home-spun **Maison du Vin** (May & Oct Mon–Fri 10am–12.30pm & 1.30–5pm; June & Sept Mon–Sat 10am–5.30pm; July & Aug Mon–Sat 10am–7pm; Ⓣ05.56.59.30.59) is hidden in the church square.

For an elegant place to **stay**, head for *Château Pomys* (Ⓣ05.56.59.73.44, Ⓦwww.chateaupomys.com; ❹), just south of the village, a mansion set in its own park. There are also several good *chambres d'hôte* in the area, including *Clos de Puyzac* in Pez village (Ⓣ & Ⓕ05.56.59.35.28; ❷) and, further along the same road near Vertheuil-en-Médoc, the hacienda-style *Cantemerle* (Ⓣ05.56.41.96.24, Ⓦwww.bab-medoc.com; ❹), both with *tables d'hôte*.

Blaye

The green slopes north of the Garonne, the **Côtes de Bourg** and **Côtes de Blaye**, were home to wine production long before the Médoc was planted. The wine is a rather heavier, plummier red, and cheaper than anything found on the opposite side of the river, and the **Maison du Vin des Premières Côtes de Blaye** on cours Vauban (Mon–Sat 8.30am–12.15pm & 2–6pm), the main street of the pretty little town of **BLAYE**, serves up a representative selection of the local produce, with some ridiculously inexpensive wines – you can get a good bottle for around €5.

Blaye has long played a strategic role defending Bordeaux, and was fortified by Vauban in the seventeenth century. The **citadelle** deserves a wander: people still live here, and it's a strange combination of peaceful village and tourist attraction. A beautiful spot, it has grass, trees, birds and a spectacular view over the Gironde estuary. Blaye is also the last resting place of the heroic paladin **Roland**, whose body was brought here in 778 after the battle of Roncevaux. However, his mausoleum is now no more than a heap of rocks.

The riverfront **tourist office**, opposite the fort (Mon–Sat 9.30am–12.30pm & 2–6pm; ⓣ05.57.42.12.09; ⓦwww.blaye.net) is really helpful and can reserve rooms free of charge and give out details on wine tasting. If you fancy **staying** here, try the *Auberge du Porche*, 5 rue Ernest-Régnier (ⓣ05.57.42.22.69, ⓦwww.auberge-du-porche.com; ❸; closed one week in March & one week in Oct), a pleasant two-star south along the riverfront with a good-value restaurant (closed Sun evening & Mon; from €15). Alternatively, there's the more expensive *Hôtel La Citadelle* within the old fort with views over the Garonne (ⓣ05.57.42.17.10, ⓦwww.hotel-la-citadelle.com; ❺; restaurant from €28). Finally, there's a small municipal **campsite** within the citadelle (ⓣ05.57.42.00.20; closed Oct–April).

St-Émilion

ST-ÉMILION, 35km east of Bordeaux, and a short train trip, is well worth a visit. The old grey houses of this fortified medieval town straggle down the south-hanging slope of a low hill, with the green froth of the summer's vines crawling over its walls. Many of the growers still keep up the old tradition of planting roses at the ends of the rows, which in pre-pesticide days served as an early-warning system against infection, the idea being that the commonest bug, *oidium*, went for the roses first, giving three days' notice of its intentions.

The Town

The town's **belfry** belongs to the rock-hewn subterranean **Église Monolithe** beneath it, which can be visited only on a **guided tour** from the tourist office (daily 10–11.30am & 2–5pm; €5.50). The tour starts in a dark hole in someone's backyard, supposedly the cave where St Émilion lived a hermit's life in the eighth century. A rough-hewn ledge served as his bed and a carved seat as his chair, where infertile women reputedly still come to sit in the hope of getting pregnant.

Above is the half-ruined thirteenth-century **Trinity Chapel**, which was built in honour of St Émilion and converted into a cooperage during the Revolution; fragments of frescoes are still visible, including a kneeling figure who is thought to be the saint himself. On the other side of the yard, a passage tunnels beneath the belfry to the **catacombs**, where three chambers dug out of the soft limestone were used as ossuary and cemetery from the eighth to the eleventh centuries. In the innermost chamber – discovered by a neighbour enlarging his cellar some fifty years ago – an eleventh-century tombstone bears the inscription: "Aulius is buried between saints Valéry, Émilion and Avic", St Valéry being the patron saint of local wine-growers.

The ninth- and twelfth-century **church** itself is an incredible place. Simple and huge, the entire structure – barrel-vaulting, great square piers and all – has been hacked out of the rock. The impact has been somewhat diminished, however, by the installation of massive concrete supports after cracks were discovered in the bell tower above in 1990. The whole interior was painted once, but only faint traces survived the Revolution, when a gunpowder factory was installed here. These days, every June, the wine council – *La Jurade* – assembles in the church in distinctive red robes to evaluate the previous season's wine and decide whether each *viticulteur*'s produce deserves the *appellation contrôlée* rating.

Behind the tourist office, the town comes to an abrupt end with a grand view of the **moat** and old **walls**. To the right is the twelfth-century **collegiate**

church, with a handsome but badly mutilated doorway and a lovely fourteenth-century **cloister**, accessed via the tourist office (same hours; free).

You should take advantage of the produce of this well-respected wine region, whose most famous wine originates at **Château Ausone**, immediately south of St-Émilion (not open to the public). If you're interested in visiting local vineyards, ask at the tourist office, which has detailed lists of those that are open, or at the **Maison du Vin** (Mon–Sat 9.30am–12.30pm & 2–6.30pm, Sun 10am–12.30pm & 2.30–6.30pm; ⓣ05.57.55.50.55), also at the top of the hill by the belfry.

Practicalities

The super-efficient **tourist office** on place des Créneaux by the belfry (daily: July & Aug 9.30am–8pm; Sept–June 9.30am–12.30pm & 1.45–6/6.30pm; ⓣ05.57.55.28.28, ⓦwww.saint-emilion-tourisme.com) is a good source of information and organizes bilingual (French and English) vineyard tours in season (May–Sept; €9). They also have **bikes** for rent (€14 per day).

If you're short of funds or without your own transport, St-Émilion is best seen as a day-trip from Bordeaux, as there's a chronic shortage of budget **accommodation** within the town. However, the tourist office can furnish you with an extensive list of *chambres d'hôte* in the area, many of which are very reasonably priced. Within the town itself, the two-star *Auberge de la Commanderie* on rue des Cordeliers (ⓣ05.57.24.70.19, ⓕ05.57.74.44.53; ❹; closed mid-Dec to mid-Feb) offers the cheapest option. Three kilometres northwest in the village of Montagne, there's a fantastic three-star campsite, *La Barbanne* (ⓣ05.57.24.75.80; closed mid-Sept to March), with several heated swimming pools.

You should try the town's speciality while you're here: **macaroons** were devised here by the Ursuline sisters in 1620, and the one authentic place to buy them is at Blanchez, 9 rue Gaudet, where the tiny melt-in-the-mouth biscuits are baked to the original recipe. An excellent place for a **meal** is the relaxed contemporary-style bistro *L'Envers du Décor* (closed Sun Nov–April) on rue du Clocher, with *plats du jour* for €10 and local wine by the glass, which you can accompany with omelettes, cheese, salads and light snacks.

Entre-Deux-Mers

The landscape of **Entre-Deux-Mers** (literally "between two seas") – so called because it's sandwiched between the tidal waters of the Dordogne and Garonne – is the prettiest of the Bordeaux wine regions, with its gentle hills and scattered medieval villages. Its wines, including the *Premières Côtes de Bordeaux*, are mainly dry whites produced by over forty *caves coopératives*, and are regarded as good but inferior to the Médocs or super-dry Graves to the south. It's also a region which can be explored, at least in part, by public transport, should you feel like avoiding the tourist office tour.

La Sauve-Majeure

The one place you should really try to see is the ruined **Abbey** (June–Sept daily 10am–6pm; Oct–May Tues–Sun 10am–1pm & 2.30–5.30pm; €4.60) at **LA SAUVE-MAJEURE**, some 25km east of Bordeaux, an important stop for pilgrims en route to Santiago de Compostela in Spain. Once it was all forest here, the abbey's name being a corruption of the Latin *silva major* (big wood). It was founded in 1079, and the treasures of what remains are the twelfth-century Romanesque apse and apsidal chapels and the outstanding sculpted capitals in the chancel. The finest are the ones illustrating stories from the Old and New Testaments (Daniel in the lions' den, Delilah shearing Samson's hair and so on), while others show fabulous beasts and decorative motifs. There is a small **museum** at the entrance, with some excellent photos of the ruins, along with keystones from the fallen roofs. But what makes the visit so worthwhile is not just the capitals themselves, but the remote, undisturbed nature of the site.

St-Macaire and La Réole

If you're heading south through Entre-Deux-Mers, Langon is the first town of any size you come to. But **ST-MACAIRE**, across the Garonne from Langon, is far better for a rest or food stop. The village still has its original **gates** and **battlements** and a beautiful medieval church, the **Église-Prieuré**. The well-organized **tourist office**, 8 rue Canton (April–Sept Mon 9am–noon & 1–5pm, Tues–Sun 10am–1pm & 3–7pm; Oct–March Tues–Sat 10am–noon & 2–6pm; ⓣ05.56.63.32.14), doubles as a Maison du Pays, promoting regional produce, which here means honey and wine. Staff can help arrange visits to the *chais*, and in season (July & Aug daily) they organize tastings hosted by various local wine-makers. Opposite is a good **hotel**, *Les Feuilles d'Acanthe* (ⓣ05.56.62.33.75, ⓦwww.feuilles-dacanthe.fr; closed Jan; ❹) with good-sized rooms and a roof solarium and Jacuzzi; its restaurant serves the usual (regional) suspects on a menu for €18. A cheaper option, *Les Tilleuls* (ⓣ06.14.77.47.47; ❷), is located just outside the medieval city next to the Hôtel de Ville; their restaurant, *Le Médiéval*, has menus from €12. For **camping**, you'll need to head just out of town to the municipal camping site in St-Pierre d'Aurillac (ⓣ05.56.63.30.27; June–Oct only).

LA RÉOLE, on the north bank 18km further east, boasts a wealth of medieval architecture along a well-signposted walk through its narrow, hilly streets. France's oldest **town hall**, constructed for Richard the Lionheart in the twelfth century, and the well-preserved simple **Abbaye des Bénédictins** – with a fantastic view over the River Garonne and the surrounding countryside – reward a stroll through the town, although little remains of the fortified **castle**. If you have some time to kill here, you could check out the mammoth **Grand Musée**, which documents the history of the automobile with a large number of interesting examples of early military, railway and agricultural vehicles (Feb–April & Oct–Nov Wed 2–6pm, Sun 2–6.30pm; May, June & Sept Wed, Thurs & Sat 2–6pm, Sunday 2–6.30pm; July–Aug daily 10am–7pm; ⓣ05.56.61.29.25).

La Réole's **tourist office** is on place de la Libération (June–Sept Mon 2.30–6.30pm, Tues–Sat 9.30am–12.30pm & 2.30–6.30pm, Sun 9.30am–12.30pm; Oct–May closed Sun; ⓣ05.56.61.13.55, ⓔlareole@entredeuxmers.com), and it conducts tours of the sights in July and August, though only for groups of ten or more (€5). For **accommodation**, the two-star *Hôtel de l'Abbaye*, 42 rue Armand-Caduc (ⓣ05.56.61.02.64, ⓕ05.56.71.24.40; ❸), on the road up to the abbey, is a bit chaotic, but the rooms are clean and not too bad for the price. A good **restaurant** is *Aux Fontaines* on rue du Verdun (closed Sun & Wed evenings & all day Mon, also fifteen days in Feb & Nov), serving classic French cuisine, albeit with a modern touch, and several menus from €15; in the summer you can eat outside in their thatched roof terrace. A lively Saturday **market** on the esplanade des Quais along the Garonne provides good picnic provisions.

Sauternes and around

The **Sauternes** region, which extends southeast from Bordeaux for 40km along the left bank of the Garonne, is an ancient wine-making area, originally planted during the Roman occupation. The distinctive golden wine of the area is certainly sweet, but also round, full-bodied and spicy, with a long aftertaste. It's not necessarily a dessert wine, either: try it with some Roquefort cheese. Gravelly terraces with a limestone subsoil help create the delicious taste, but mostly it's due to a peculiar microclimate of morning autumn mists and afternoons of sun and heat which causes *Botrytis cinerea* fungus, or "noble rot", to flourish on the grapes, letting the sugar concentrate and introducing some intense flavours. When they're picked, they're not a pretty sight: carefully selected by hand, only the most shrivelled, rotting bunches are taken. The wines of Sauternes make up some of the most highly sought-after in the world, with bottles of Château d'Yquem, in particular, fetching thousands of euros.

SAUTERNES itself is a fairly quiet little village surrounded by vines and dominated by the **Maison du Sauternes** (Mon–Fri 9am–7pm, Sat & Sun 10am–7pm; ⓣ05.56.76.69.83) at one end of the village, with a pretty church at the other. The *maison* is a room full of treasures, the golden bottles with white and gold labels being quite beautiful objects in themselves. Although they do offer tastings, staff are unfortunately rather snooty about it, unless you obviously intend to buy.

For a luxurious place to **stay**, try the sumptuous *Relais du Château d'Arche*, on the A62 just outside of Sauternes heading north (ⓣ05.56.76.67.67, ⓦwww.chateaudarche-sauternes.com; ❼). The seventeenth-century estate was recently restored to its original lustre and has been refurbished with near-period styling and paraphernalia; rooms are large and plush and many look directly onto the vineyard. There are two good places to **eat** in Sauternes. By the church, the *Auberge Les Vignes* (ⓣ05.56.76.60.06; closed Mon evening & Feb) is a typical country restaurant with regional specialities like *grillades aux Sauternes* (meats grilled over vine clippings), a great wine list and a lunch menu at €11. The other option is the more refined *Le Saprien* (ⓣ05.56.76.60.87; closed Christmas & Feb, also Mon and for dinner Sun & Wed), opposite the tourist office, combining regional-style elements with modern eclectic additions and featuring menus from €23.

Ten kilometres south of Sauternes, the ruinous curtain walls and corner towers of a colossal moated **château** (daily: July & Aug 10am–7pm; Sept–June 2–6pm; €3.20) still dominate **VILLANDRAUT**. Purchasing a ticket to the château gets you a complimentary tasting at the town's friendly new Maison des Vins, just on the central square a block from the castle (mid-June to Aug daily 9.30am–12.30pm & 2.30pm–7pm; Sept to mid-June Mon–Sat 9.30am–12.30pm & 2.30pm–7pm). The castle itself was built by Pope Clement V, a native of the area who caused a schism by moving the papacy to Avignon in the fourteenth century. You can visit his tomb in the even smaller village of **UZESTE** en route to **BAZAS**, 15km east, which has a laid-back, southern air. Bazas' most attractive feature is the wide, arcaded place de la Cathédrale, overlooked by the grey, lichen-covered **Cathédrale St-Jean-Baptiste**, which displays a harmonious blend of Romanesque, Gothic and classical styles in its west front.

For places to **stay** in Bazas try the cheap, friendly *Hostellerie St-Sauveur*, 14 cours du Général-de-Gaulle (ⓣ05.56.25.12.18; ❸; closed early Oct), or the plush *Domaine de Fompeyre*, on the southern edge of town (ⓣ05.56.25.98.00; ⓔdomainedefompeyre@wanadoo.fr; ❺), which has a restaurant (closed Sun evening Oct–March; from €31). Other good places to **eat** are *Les Remparts*, off the central square (ⓣ05.56.25.95.24; closed Sun evening & Mon, and evenings Nov–March), for delicious local specialities and menus from €11, and the cosy *Bistrot St-Jean* nearby (lunch only Oct–May; from €12.50). Many towns around this area offer *chambres d'hotes* from around €35 upwards: enquire at Villandraut's **tourist office** (Ⓣ05.56.25.31.39), located on place de la Mairie, for more information.

The Côte d'Argent

The **Côte d'Argent** is the long stretch of coast from the mouth of the Gironde estuary to Biarritz, which – at over 200km – is the longest, straightest and sandiest in Europe. The endless beaches are backed by high sand dunes, while behind lies the largest forest in western Europe, **Les Landes**. Despite these attractions, the lack of conventional tourist sights means that outside July and August the coast gets comparatively few visitors, and away from the main resorts it's still possible to find deserted stretches of coastline.

Arcachon

On summer weekends, the Bordelais escape en masse to **ARCACHON**, the oldest resort on the Côte d'Argent and a forty-minute train ride across flat, sandy forest from Bordeaux. The beaches of white sand are magnificent but can be crowded, and its central jetties, Thiers and Eyrac, are busy with boats going off on an array of cruises.

The town itself is a sprawl of villas great and small, the most exclusive area being the **ville d'hiver** (winter town), whose wide shady streets are full of fanciful Second Empire mansions overlooking the seaside **ville d'été** (summer town). Well worth a wander, the area can be reached by following the lively pedestrianized and restaurant-filled rue de Maréchal-de-Lattre-de-Tassigny, running perpendicular to the seafront boulevard de la Plage; at the end of this mouthful of a street, a lift (daily 9am–12.45pm & 2.30–7pm) carries you up to the flower-filled, wooded **Parc Mauresque** (daily: April–Oct 7.30am–10pm; Nov–March 8am–7.30pm; free), with the *ville d'hiver* beyond it. From the park, there are fine views over the seafront.

Practicalities

A well-stocked **tourist office**, esplanade Georges-Pompidou (April–June & Sept Mon–Sat 9am–6pm, Sun 10am–1pm & 2–5pm; July & Aug daily 9am–7pm; Oct–March Mon–Fri 9am–6pm, Sat 9am–5pm; Ⓣ05.57.52.97.97; Ⓦwww.arcachon.com), can be reached by following avenue Gambetta back from seafront place Thiers. In summer, boats leave the jetties of Thiers and Eyrac on various **cruises**, including the Île aux Oiseaux (2hr; €13), and an exploration of the Arcachon basin with a look at the Dune de Pyla (2hr 30min; €15). There's also a regular boat service from here to Cap Ferret on the opposite peninsula (30min; €10 return). Discounted tickets can be purchased for all excursions at the tourist office.

You'll be hard-pushed to find an inexpensive **hotel**, but a couple of reasonable ones are the small, friendly *La Pergola*, 40 cours Lamarque-de-Plaisance (Ⓣ05.56.83.07.89, Ⓦwww.hotel-lapergola.net; ❸), and the *St-Christaud*, 8 allée de la Chapelle (Ⓣ05.56.83.38.53; ❸), further out of town. Up the hill in the *ville d'hiver*, your only option is the *Marinette*, 15 allée José-Maria-de-Hérédia (Ⓣ05.56.83.06.67, Ⓦwww.hotel-marinette.com; ❹; closed Nov to mid-March), with a few nondescript rooms, some with terrace. Alternatively, there are many **holiday apartments** to rent; ask for the booklet *Clévacances* from the tourist office. **Camping** is another option, with plenty of sites around the Arcachon basin, though only the three-star *Le Camping Club*, allée de la Galaxie (ⓣ05.56.83.24.15, ⓦwww.camping-arcachon.com), is actually within the town; set in an expanse of bird-filled woodland beyond the *ville d'hiver*, it's worth the high summer prices.

For something approximating *gastronomique* **eating**, you're best off at *Chez Yvette*, 59 bd de Général Leclerc, which offers traditional menus from €17.50. Another good option, just round the corner at 17 rue Jehenne, is *La Plancha*, serving ample tapas (from €5.50 per dish), paella and other Spanish fare (closed all day Wed and Sat & Sun lunch).

Cap Ferret and the north coast

The Atlantic coast between the Bassin d'Arcachon and the Gironde has a wild, undeveloped feel and despite its proximity to Bordeaux and Arcachon, is seldom crowded. No motorable road follows the coast for most of the way, which contributes to the relaxed nature of the place; instead a cycle path, built at the end of World War II, winds through more than 75km of pine-forested dunes from the low-key holiday village of **Cap Ferret** to the resort of Soulac in the north, from where trains run through the Médoc vineyards to Bordeaux or to the Pointe de Grave and Verdon for the ferry to Royan. Apart from the occasional surf shack or beach restaurant, the only settlement of any size is Lacanau-Ocean, 30km north of Cap Ferret, best avoided unless you're into overpriced hotels and golf courses. Cap Ferret can be reached by boat from Arcachon. There are a few places to **stay,** including the small, basic **HI hostel** at 87 av de Bordeaux (ⓣ05.56.60.64.62; July & Aug only) and the rather more plush *Hotel des Pins*, at 23 rue des Fauvettes, overlooking the ocean (ⓣ05.56.60.60.11, ⓕ05.56.60.67.41; April to mid-Nov; ❸); 10km to the north there's a **campsite** at Grand Crohot, Bremontier (ⓣ05.56.60.03.99). For more information contact the **tourist office** in Cap Ferret at 1 av du Général de Gaulle (ⓣ05.56.03.94.49, ⓦwww.lege-capferret.com).

The Dune du Pyla and Le Teich

The Côte d'Argent's chief curiosity is the **Dune du Pyla**. At over 100m it's the highest sand dune in Europe – a veritable mountain of wind-carved sand, about 12km south of Arcachon. Buses leave from the *gare SNCF* (where you can also rent bikes in summer) every hour in July and August – two to five a day at other times. From the end of the line the road continues straight on uphill for about fifteen minutes – if you're driving, it costs €2.30–3.05 to use the obligatory car park, though to save a few euros you could park closer to the station for free and make the hike up. There's the inevitable group of stands selling ice cream, *galettes* and junk, but from the top you get a superb view over the bay of Arcachon and the forest of the Landes stretching away to the south. It's a great sandy slide down to the sea (the sides are as steep as an Olympic ski-jump) and a long haul back up but well worth the effort.

At **LE TEICH**, about 14km east of Arcachon in the southeast corner of the Bassin d'Arcachon, one of the most important expanses of wetlands remaining in France has been converted into a bird sanctuary, the **Parc Ornithologique du Teich** (ⓦwww.parc-ornithologique-du-teich.com; daily: mid-April to June 10am–7pm; July & Aug 10am–8pm; Sept to mid-April 10am–6pm; €6.40), one of only two in the country. There's no **accommodation** in Le Teich beyond a couple of **campsites**, but you can easily come here on a day-trip by train from Arcachon or Bordeaux.

Les Landes

Travelling south from Bordeaux by road or rail, you pass for what seems like hours through an unremitting, flat, sandy pine forest known as **Les Landes**. Until the nineteenth century it was a vast, infertile swamp, badly drained because of the impermeable layer of grit deposited by the glaciers of the quaternary age and steadily encroached upon by the shifting sand dunes of the coast. Today it supports nearly 10,000 square kilometres of trees and since 1970 has been designated a *parc naturel régional*.

At **SABRES**, off the Bordeaux–Bayonne road 18km east of Labouheyre, you can take a restored steam train to the excellent **Écomusée de Marquèze** (Ⓦwww.parc-landes-de-gascogne.fr; trains depart every 40mins April–May & mid-Sept to Oct Mon–Sat 2–4.40, Sun 10am–4.40pm; June to mid-Sept daily 10am–5.20pm; €7.50 including entrance), set up by the park authorities to illustrate the traditional *landais* way of life, when shepherds used to clomp around the scrub on long stilts.

Travel details

Trains

Angoulême to: Bordeaux (19 daily; 1hr–1hr 30min); Limoges (4 daily; 1hr 30min–2hr); Poitiers (23 daily; 40min–1hr 10min); Royan (12 daily; 2hr).
Bordeaux to: Angoulême (20 daily; 1hr–1hr 30min); Arcachon (10–23 daily; 40–45min); Bayonne (6–12 daily; 1hr 40min–2hr 10min); Bergerac (4–8 daily; 50min–1hr 30min); Biarritz (6–12 daily; 2hr–2hr 45min); Brive (1–2 daily; 2hr 15min); La Rochelle (7–10 daily; 2hr 20min); Lourdes (4–5 daily; 2hr 30min–3hr 20min); Marseille (5–6 daily; 5–7hr); Nice (4 daily; 8–10hr); Paris-Montparnasse (3–8 daily; 3hr–3hr 30min); Périgueux (10–16 daily; 1hr–1hr 25min); Pointe de Grave (2 daily, 2hr 30min); Poitiers (3–15 daily; 1hr 45min); Saintes (7–14 daily; 1hr 10min–1hr 30min); Sarlat (3–4 daily; 2hr 30min); St-Jean-de-Luz (8–12 daily; 2hr–2hr 40min); Toulouse (10–15 daily; 2hr–2hr 40min).
La Rochelle to: Bordeaux (6 daily; 2hr 20min); Nantes (6–7 daily; 1hr 50min); Rochefort (13–19 daily; 20min); Paris-Montparnasse (12 daily; 3hr 10min); Saintes (about 4 daily; 50min–1hr).
Les Sables-d'Olonne to: Nantes (19 daily; 1hr 30min); Paris-Montparnasse (8 daily; 4hr 45min).
Poitiers to: Angoulême (17 daily; 1hr); Bayonne (8 daily; 3hr 10min–4hr 30min); Biarritz (10 daily; 4hr 30min); Bordeaux (3–15 daily; 1hr 45min); Châtellérault (15 daily; 20min); Dax (2–3 daily; 2hr 45min–3hr 40min); Hendaye (3 daily; 4–5hr); Irun (2 daily; 4hr 5min–5hr 5min); La Rochelle (12 daily; 1hr 45min); Limoges (6 daily; 2hr); Niort (4–5 daily; 45min); Paris-Austerlitz (7 daily; 2hr 50min); Paris-Montparnasse (16 daily; 1hr 45min); Surgères (frequent; 1hr 25min).
Royan to: Angoulême (3–4 daily; 2hr); Cognac (3–4 daily; 1hr); Saintes (3–4 daily; 40min).

Buses

Bordeaux to: Blaye (4–20 daily; 1hr 15min–1hr 25min); Cap Ferret (4–6 daily; 2hr); Margaux (2–8 daily; 45min–1hr); Lacanau (3–4 daily; 1hr 15min); Pauillac (2–8 daily; 1hr–1hr 20min); La Sauve-Majeure (1–4 daily; 40min).
La Rochelle to: St-Martin de Ré (6–16 daily; 1hr)
Les Sables-d'Olonne to: Luçon (4 daily; 2hr); Nantes (4 daily; 5hr 30min).
Parthenay to: Airvault (several daily; 25min); Niort (8 daily; 50min); Thouars (at least 10 daily; 1hr).
Poitiers to: Châteauroux (3 daily; 3hr); Chauvigny (3 daily; 45min); Le Blanc (3 daily; 1hr 25min); Limoges (daily; 3hr); Parthenay (6–10 daily; 1hr 30min); Ruffec (daily; 2hr 30min); St-Savin (3 daily; 1hr).
Rochefort to: Château d'Oléron (4–6 daily; 1hr); La Fumée-Île d'Aix (4 daily; 30min).
Saintes to: Rochefort (2 daily; 1hr 20min); Royan (6 daily; 1hr 20min); St-Pierre d'Oléron (2 daily; 2hr).

9

The Dordogne, Limousin and Lot

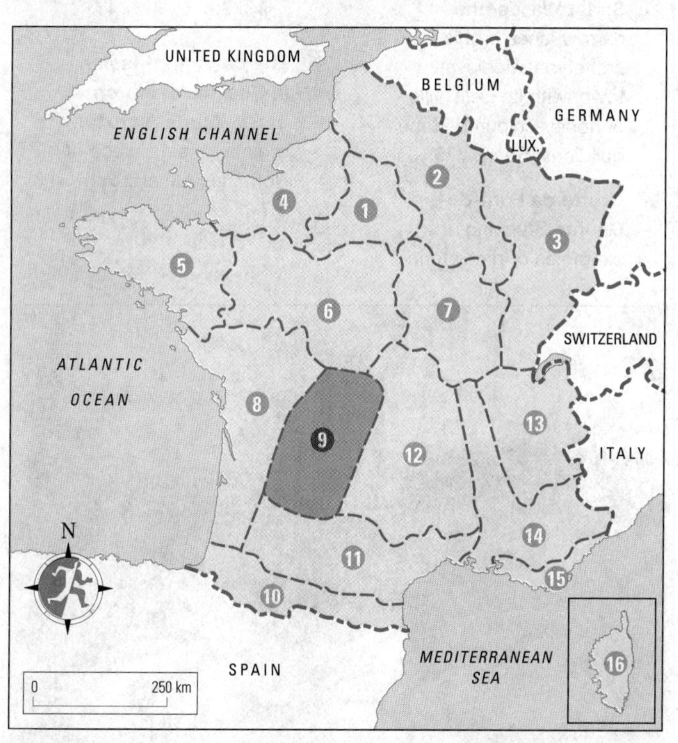

CHAPTER 9

Highlights

* **Cuisine** The Dordogne is the place to sample French country cooking at its best. See p.716
* **Monpazier** An almost perfectly preserved *bastide* (fortified town). See p.726
* **Sarlat** Wander the narrow lanes of this archetypal medieval town, with its *vielle ville* of honey-coloured stone buildings. See p.729
* **Grotte de Font-de-Gaume** Stunning examples of prehistoric cave-art, including the spectacular frieze of five bison. See p.732
* **Châteaux of Beynac and Castelnaud** Two of the region's most majestic castles eye each other across the Dordogne Valley. See p.735
* **The carving of Isaiah in Souillac's church of Ste-Marie** An extra-ordinary masterpiece of Romanesque art. See p.741

△ Cave painting, Lascaux

9

The Dordogne, Limousin and Lot

The land covered in this chapter forms a rough oval bordered to the east by the uplands of the Massif Central and to the west by the Atlantic plains. It's the area which was most in dispute between the English and the French during the Hundred Years War and which has been most in demand among English visitors and second-home buyers in more recent times.

Although it doesn't coincide exactly with either the modern French administrative boundaries or the old provinces of Périgord and Quercy, which constitute the core of the region, the land has a physical and geographical homogeneity thanks to its great rivers: the **Dordogne**, the **Lot** and the **Aveyron**, all of which drain westwards from the Massif Central into the mighty **Garonne**, which forms the southern limit covered by this chapter.

There are no great cities in the area: its charm lies in the landscapes and the dozens of harmonious small towns and villages. Some, like **Sarlat** and **Rocamadour**, are so well known that they are overrun with tourists. Others, like **Figeac**, **Villefranche-de-Rouergue**, **Gourdon**, **Montauban**, **Monflanquin** and the many *bastides* (fortified towns) that pepper the area between the Lot and Dordogne, boast no single notable sight but are perfect organic ensembles.

The landscapes are surprisingly homogenous, too. From **Limoges** in the province of Limousin in the north to Montauban in the south towards Toulouse, the country is gently hilly, full of lush hidden valleys and miles of woodland, mainly oak. **Limousin**, at the north of this area, is slightly greener and wetter, the south more open and arid. But you can travel a long way without seeing a radical shift, except in the uplands of the **Plateau de Millevaches**, where the rivers plunge into gorges and the woods are beech, chestnut and conifer plantations. The other characteristic landscape is the *causses*, the dry scrubby limestone plateaux like the **Causse de Gramat** between the Dordogne and the Lot and the **Causse de Limogne** between the Lot and Aveyron. Where the rivers have cut their way through the limestone, the valleys are walled with overhanging cliffs, riddled with fissures, underground stream-beds and caves. And in these caves – especially in the valley of the Vézère around **Les Eyzies** – are some of the most awe-inspiring **prehistoric paintings** and reliefs to be found anywhere in the world.

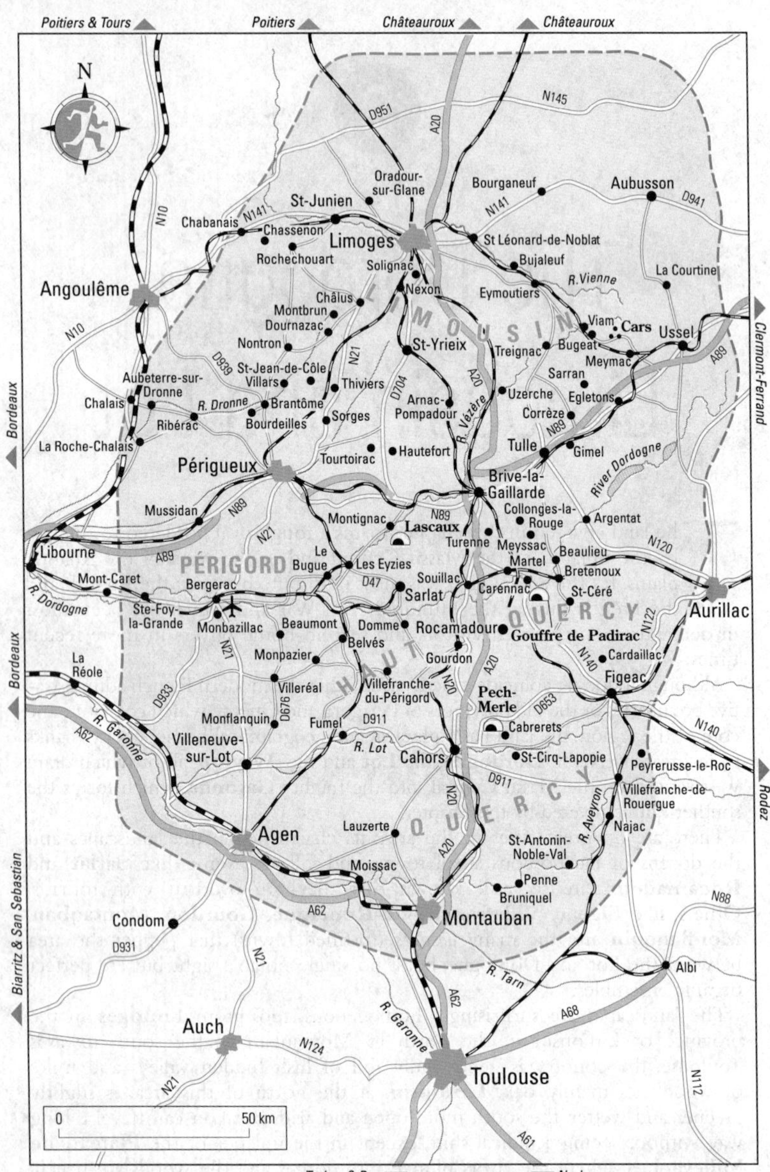

The other great artistic legacy of the area is the Romanesque sculpture, most notably adorning the churches at **Souillac** and **Beaulieu-sur-Dordogne**, but all modelled on the supreme example of the cloister of St-Pierre in **Moissac**. And the dearth of luxurious châteaux is compensated for by the numerous splendid **fortresses** of purely military design, such as **Bonaguil**, **Najac**, **Biron**, **Beynac** and **Castelnaud**.

The wartime Resistance was very active in these out-of-the-way regions, and the roadsides are dotted with tiny memorials to those killed in ambushes or shot in reprisals. There is also one monstrous monument to wartime atrocity: the ruined village of **Oradour-sur-Glane**, still as the Nazis left it after massacring the population and setting fire to the houses.

The Dordogne

To the French, the **Dordogne** is a river. To the British, it is a much looser term, covering a vast area roughly equivalent to what the French call Périgord. This starts south of Limoges and includes the Vézère and Dordogne valleys. The Dordogne is also a *département*, with fixed boundaries that pay no heed to either definition. The central part of the *département*, around Périgueux and the River Isle, is known as **Périgord Blanc**, after the light, white colour of its rock outcrops; the southeastern half around Sarlat as **Périgord Noir**, said to be darker in aspect than the Blanc because of the preponderance of oak woods. To confuse matters further, the tourist authorities have added another two colours to the Périgord patchwork: **Périgord Vert**, the far north of the *département*, so called because of the green of its woods and pastureland; and **Périgord Pourpre** in the southwest, purple because it includes the wine-growing area around Bergerac. This southern region is also known for its **bastides** – fortified towns – built during the turbulent medieval period when there was almost constant conflict between the French and English.

Périgord Vert and Périgord Blanc

The close green valleys of **Périgord Vert** are very rural, with plenty of space and few people, large tracts of woodland and uncultivated land. Less well known than the much-frequented Périgord Noir, its largely granite landscape bears a closer resemblance to the neighbouring Limousin than to the rest of the Périgord. It's partly for this reason that in 1998 the most northerly tip, together with the southwestern part of the Haute-Vienne, was designated as the **Parc Naturel Régional Périgord-Limousin** – to give it a sense of identity and draw attention to its natural assets – in an attempt to promote "green" tourism in this economically fragile and depopulated area.

Périgueux, in the centre of **Périgord Blanc**, is interesting for its domed cathedral and its Roman remains, whose existence is a reminder of how long these parts have been civilized. But it's in the countryside that the region's finest monuments lie. One of the loveliest stretches is the **valley of the Dronne**, from **Aubeterre** on the Charente border through **Brantôme** to the marvellous Renaissance château of **Puyguilhem** and the picture-postcard village of **St-Jean-de-Côle**, and on to the Limousin border, where the scenery becomes higher and less intimate. Truffle-lovers might like to take a look at **Sorges**, where there's a nature trail through truffle country and a museum to explain it all.

The food and wine of Périgord

The two great stars of Périgord cuisine are **foie gras** and **truffles** (*truffes*). Foie gras is best eaten either chilled in succulent, buttery slabs, or lightly fried and served with a fruit compote to provide contrasting sweetness and acidity. Truffle is often dished up in omelettes and the rich *périgourdin* sauces which accompany many local meat dishes, but to really appreciate the delicate earthy flavour to the full, you really need to eat truffle on its own, with just a salad and some coarse, country bread.

The other mainstay of Périgord cuisine is the grey Toulouse **goose**, whose fat is used in the cooking of everything, including the flavourful potato dish, *pommes sarladaises*. The goose fattens well: *gavé* or crammed with corn, it goes from six to ten kilos in weight in three weeks, with its liver alone weighing nearly a kilo. Though some may find the process off-putting, small local producers are very careful not to harm their birds, if for no other reason than that stress ruins the liver. Geese are also raised for their meat alone, which is cooked and preserved in its own thick yellow grease as *confits d'oie*, which you can either eat on its own or use in the preparation of other dishes, like *cassoulet*. **Duck** is used in the same way, both for foie gras and *confits*. *Magret de canard*, or duck breast fillet, is one of the favourite ways of eating duck and appears on practically every restaurant menu.

Another common goose delicacy is *cou d'oie farci* – goose neck stuffed with sausage meat, duck liver and truffles; a favourite salad throughout the region is made with warm *gésiers* or goose gizzards. Try not to be put off by fare such as this, or your palate will miss out on some delicious experiences – like *tripoux*, sheep's stomach stuffed with tripe, trotters, pork and garlic, which is really an Auvergnat dish but is quite often served in neighbouring areas like the Rouergue. Other less challenging specialities include stuffed *cèpes*, or wild mushrooms; **ballottines**, fillets of poultry stuffed, rolled and poached; the little flat discs of goat's cheese known as *cabécou* or *rocamadour*; and, for dessert there's *pastis*, a light apple tart topped with crinkled, wafer-thin pastry laced with armagnac.

The **wines** should not be scorned either. There are the fine dark, almost peppery reds from Cahors, and both reds and whites from the vineyards of Bergerac, of which the sweet, white Monbazillac is the most famous. Pécharmant is the fanciest of the reds, but there are some very drinkable Côtes de Bergerac, much like the neighbouring Bordeaux and far cheaper. The same goes for the wines of Duras, Marmande and Buzet. If you're thinking of taking a stock of wine home, you could do much worse than make some enquiries in Bergerac itself, Ste-Foy, or any of the villages in the vineyard areas.

Périgueux

PÉRIGUEUX, capital of the *département* of the Dordogne and a central base for exploring the countryside of Périgord Blanc, is a small, busy and not particularly attractive market town for a province made rich by tourism and specialized farming. Its name derives from the Petrocorii, the local Gallic tribe, but it was the Romans who transformed it into an important settlement. A few Roman remains, as well as a medieval *vieille ville*, survive to this day.

Arrival, information and accommodation

The busiest and most interesting part of Périgueux is the square formed by the river, the allées Tourny, boulevard Montaigne and cours Fénelon. At the junction of the two latter is place Francheville, a wide, open square presently being redeveloped as a shopping and cinema complex, on the east side of which you'll find the **tourist office** (June 15–Sept 15 Mon–Sat 9am–6pm,

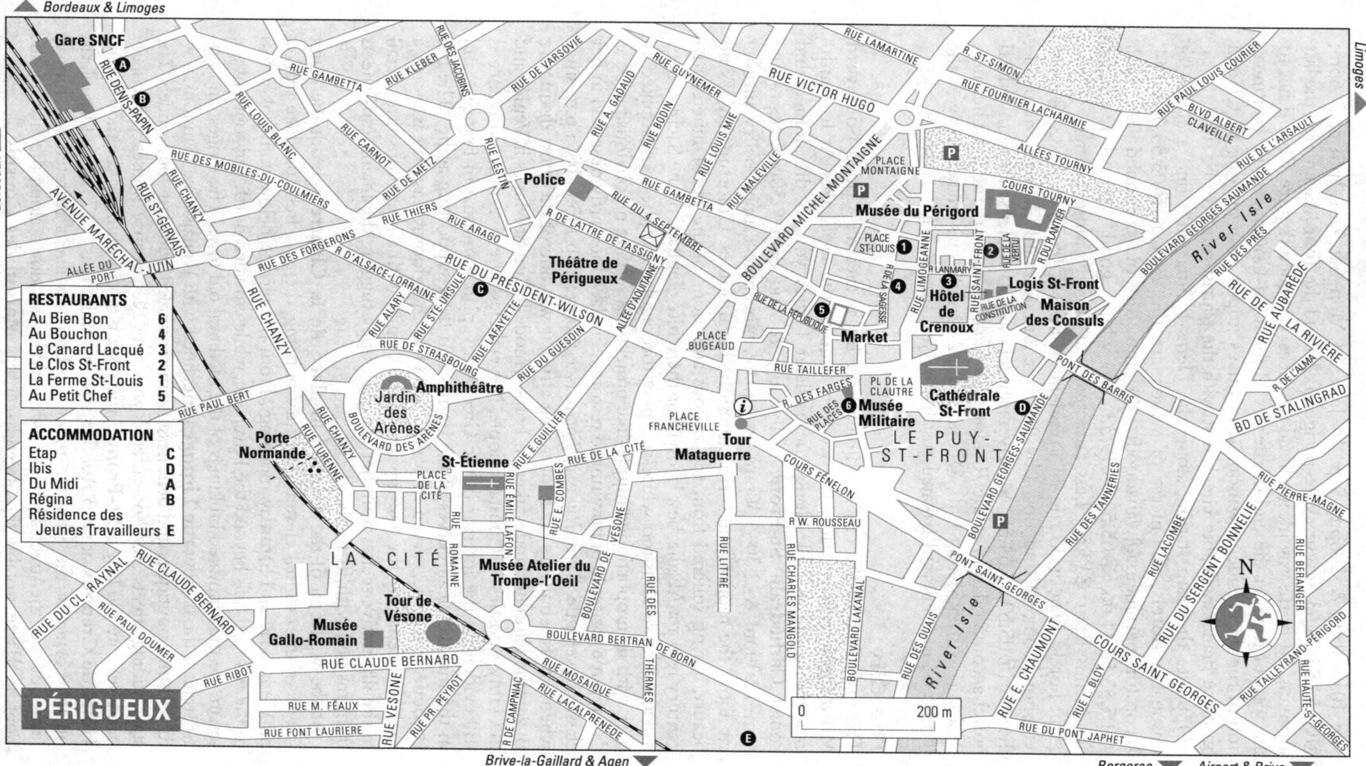
PÉRIGUEUX
RESTAURANTS
Au Bien Bon 6
Au Bouchon 4
Le Canard Lacqué 3
Le Clos St-Front 2
La Ferme St-Louis 1
Au Petit Chef 5
ACCOMMODATION
Etap C
Ibis D
Du Midi A
Régina B
Résidence des Jeunes Travailleurs E
Bordeaux & Limoges
Bordeaux
Limoges
Brive-la-Gaillard & Agen
Bergerac
Airport & Brive
Gare SNCF
Police
Théâtre de Périgueux
Musée du Périgord
Logis St-Front
Maison des Consuls
Hôtel de Crenoux
Market
Cathédrale St-Front
Musée Militaire
Tour Mataguerre
Amphithéâtre
Jardin des Arènes
Porte Normande
St-Étienne
Musée Atelier du Trompe-l'Oeil
Tour de Vésone
Musée Gallo-Romain
LE PUY-ST-FRONT
LA CITÉ
River Isle
PLACE MONTAIGNE
PLACE ST-LOUIS
PLACE BUGEAUD
PLACE FRANCHEVILLE
PL DE LA CLAUTRE
PLACE DE LA CITÉ
RUE DENIS-PAPIN
RUE GAMBETTA
RUE KLEBER
RUE DES JACOBINS
RUE DE VARSOVIE
RUE GUYNEMER
RUE VICTOR HUGO
RUE LAMARTINE
R. ST-SIMON
RUE FOURNIER LACHARMIE
RUE PAUL LOUIS COURIER
BLVD ALBERT CLAVEILLE
ALLÉES TOURNY
COURS TOURNY
RUE DE L'ARSAULT
BOULEVARD GEORGES SAUMANDE
RUE DES PRÉS
RUE AUBARÈDE
RUE DE LA RIVIÈRE
R. DE L'ALMA
BD DE STALINGRAD
RUE PIERRE-MAGNE
RUE BERANGER
RUE HAUTE-ST-GEORGES
RUE TALLEYRAND-PÉRIGORD
RUE DU SERGENT BONNELIE
RUE LACOMBE
RUE DES TANNERIES
COURS SAINT GEORGES
RUE L. BLOY
RUE E. CHAUMONT
RUE DU PONT JAPHET
PONT SAINT-GEORGES
PONT DES BARRIS
RUE DES QUAIS
BOULEVARD LAKANAL
RUE CHARLES MANGOLD
R W. ROUSSEAU
RUE LITTRE
RUE DES THERMES
COURS FÉNELON
RUE TAILLEFER
R. DES FARGES
RUE DES PLACES
RUE DE LA RÉPUBLIQUE
R DE LA SAGESSE
RUE LIMOGEANNE
R LANMARY
RUE SAINT-FRONT
RUE DE LA VERTU
R DU PLANTIER
RUE DE LA CONSTITUTION
BOULEVARD MICHEL MONTAIGNE
RUE MALEVILLE
RUE LOUIS MIE
RUE BODIN
RUE A. GADAUD
RUE GAMBETTA
RUE DU 4 SEPTEMBRE
R DE LATTRE DE TASSIGNY
ALLÉE D'AQUITAINE
RUE DU PRÉSIDENT-WILSON
RUE DU GUESDIN
RUE LAFAYETTE
RUE STE-URSULE
RUE ALARY
R D'ALSACE-LORRAINE
RUE DES FORGERONS
RUE ARAGO
RUE THIERS
RUE LESTIN
RUE DE METZ
RUE CARNOT
RUE LOUIS BLANC
RUE DES MOBILES-DU-COULMIERS
RUE CHANZY
RUE ST-GERVAIS
AVENUE MARÉCHAL-JUIN
ALLÉE DU PORT
RUE PAUL BERT
RUE DE STRASBOURG
BOULEVARD DES ARÈNES
RUE TURENNE
RUE E. GUILLIER
RUE DE LA CITÉ
RUE E. COMBES
RUE ÉMILE LAFON
RUE ROMAINE
BOULEVARD DE VÉSONE
BOULEVARD BERTRAN DE BORN
RUE MOSAIQUE
RUE LACALPRENÈDE
R DE CAMPNIAC
RUE PR. PEYROT
RUE VÉSONE
RUE CLAUDE BERNARD
RUE M. FÉAUX
RUE FONT LAURIERE
RUE RIBOT
RUE PAUL DOUMER
RUE DU CL. RAYNAL
N
0 200 m

Sun 10am–1pm & 2–6pm; Sept 16–June 14 Mon–Sat 9am–1pm & 2–6pm; ⓣ05.53.53.10.63, ⓦwww.ville-perigueux.fr) and the Tour Mataguerre, the last surviving bit of the town's medieval defences. Périgueux's **gare SNCF** lies to the west of town at the end of rue des Mobiles-du-Coulmiers, the continuation of rue du Président-Wilson. Most **buses** stop at both the *gare SNCF* and on place Francheville, but check first with the tourist office to be sure.

Opposite the train station, along rue Denis-Papin, you'll find a clutch of reasonable **hotels**, the nicest of which are the *Régina* (ⓣ05.53.08.40.44, ⓔcomfort.perigueux@wanadoo.fr; ❸) and the old-fashioned *Du Midi* (ⓣ05.53.53.41.06, ⓕ05.53.08.19.32; ❷), whose good regional restaurant has menus from €13.50. Less attractive, but slightly more central are two chain hotels: *Etap*, at 33 rue du Président-Wilson (ⓣ05.53.05.53.82, ⓦwww.etaphotel.com; ❸), and, down by the river on boulevard Georges-Saumande, the *Ibis* (ⓣ05.53.53.64.58, ⓦwww.ibishotel.com; ❸). There's also limited HI hostel accommodation at the *Résidence des Jeunes Travailleurs*, rue des Thermes-Prolongés (ⓣ05.53.06.81.40, ⓔcontact@fjt24.com) – it's tucked away at the south end of boulevard Lakanal, just before you hit the train tracks.

The City

The main hub of the city's contemporary life is the tree-shaded **boulevard Montaigne**, which marks the western edge of the *vieille ville*. At its southern end, a short walk along rue Taillefer brings you to the domed and coned **Cathédrale St-Front** (daily: July & Aug 8am–7.30pm; Sept–June 8am–12.30pm & 2.30–6.30pm), its square, pineapple-capped belfry surging far above the roofs of the surrounding medieval houses. Unfortunately, it's no beauty, having suffered from the zealous attentions of the purist nineteenth-century restorer Abadie, best known for the white elephant of the Sacré-Coeur in Paris. The result is too white, too new, too regular, and the roof is spiked all over with ill-proportioned nipple-like projections serving no obvious purpose: "a supreme example of how not to restore", Freda White tartly observed in her classic travelogue, *Three Rivers of France* (see Contexts, p.1338). It's a pity, since when it was rebuilt in 1173 following a fire, it was one of the most distinctive Byzantine churches undertaken in France, modelled on St Mark's in Venice and the Holy Apostles in Constantinople. Nevertheless, the Byzantine influence is still evident in the interior in the Greek-cross plan – unusual in France – and in the massive clean curves of the domes and their supporting arches. The big Baroque altarpiece, carved in walnut wood in the gloomy east bay, is worth a look too, depicting the Assumption of the Virgin, with a humorous little detail in the illustrative scenes from her life of a puppy tugging the infant Jesus' sheets from his bed with its teeth.

At the west end of the cathedral in **place de la Clautre** beneath the blank facade of the original eleventh-century building, there's a fresh produce market on Wednesday and Saturday mornings. From the terrace below you look across to the wooded hills beyond the River Isle, while crowded north and south of the square are the renovated buildings of the medieval old town. The longest and finest street is the narrow **rue Limogeanne**, lined with Renaissance mansions, now turned into boutiques and delicatessens, intermingled with fast-food outlets. The surrounding streets are also scattered with fine Renaissance houses: particularly handsome are the **Logis St-Front**, 7 rue de la Constitution, and the more sedate **Hôtel de Crenoux** at no. 3. Another striking building is at 17 rue de l'Éguillerie, on the corner of the attractive **place St-Louis**, where a turreted watchtower leans out over the street. There are other old houses down along the river by the Pont des Barris, notably the fifteenth-century **Maison des Consuls**.

At the northern end of rue Limogeanne, out on the broad tree-lined cours Tourny, the **Musée du Périgord** (April–Sept Mon & Wed–Fri 10.30am–5.30pm, Sat & Sun 1–6pm; Oct–March Mon & Wed–Fri 10am–5pm, Sat & Sun 1–6pm; €4; ⓦmusee-perigord.museum.com) is best known for its extensive and important prehistoric collection and some beautiful Gallo-Roman mosaics. Exhibits include a 70,000-year-old skeleton, the oldest yet found in France, and a beautiful engraving of a bison's head; however, these and many of the more fragile items on display are copies, and the museum's old-fashioned layout makes it hard to appreciate what's on offer. More lively but of less general interest is the **Musée Militaire**, near the cathedral at 32 rue des Farges (Jan–March Wed & Sat 2–6pm; April–Sept Mon–Sat 1–6pm; Oct–Dec Mon–Sat 2–6pm; €3.50), which contains some unusual exhibits, particularly relating to the French colonial wars in Vietnam.

Roman Périgueux

Roman Périgueux, known as **La Cité**, lies to the west of the town centre towards the *gare SNCF*. The most prominent vestige is the high brick **Tour de Vésone**, the last remains of a temple to the city's guardian goddess, standing in a public garden just south of the train tracks. Beside the tower, the foundations of an exceptionally well-preserved Roman villa form the basis of the new **Musée Gallo-Romain** (Feb, March & Oct–Dec Tues–Sun 10am–12.30pm & 2–5.30pm, April–June & Sept Tues–Sun 10am–6pm, July & Aug daily 10am–7pm; €5.50; ⓦwww.semitour.com). This was no humble abode: the villa, complete with under-floor heating, thermal baths and colonnaded walkways around the central garden with its cooling pond and fountains, boasted at least sixty rooms. Around the walls you can see the remains of first-century murals of river and marine life, the colours still amazingly vibrant, and here and there, graffiti of hunting scenes, gladiatorial combat and even an ostrich – no doubt the work of some bored Roman urchin.

A short hop across the train tracks, the atmospheric ruins of the city's **amphitheatre** are concealed in the Jardin des Arènes, while further Roman bits and pieces – chiefly jumbled masonry – are visible in the nearby Porte Normande off rue Turenne. These defensive works were hastily cobbled together to keep the invading Visigoths at bay in the fourth century.

The rather mutilated church in this neighbourhood – the result of Huguenot anger in 1577 – is the former cathedral, the church of **St-Étienne**, condemned to life as a traffic island in place de la Cité.

Eating

Surprisingly, there's no great abundance of good **restaurants** in Périgueux. Apart from the restaurant at the *Hôtel du Midi* (see opposite), the best general area to look is the *vieille ville*, particularly around rue Limogeanne and place St-Louis. Two popular lunch spots are the friendly *Au Petit Chef*, 5 place du Coderc (closed Sat evening & Sun; menus from €11.50) with its attractive upstairs restaurant, and the slightly smarter *Au Bien Bon*, 15 rue des Places (closed Sat lunch, Sun & Mon; menus from €14), both serving fresh and tasty dishes. In the evening, you could try *Au Bouchon*, 12 rue de la Sagesse (closed Sun & Mon), a wine bar offering daily specials from the slate boards – count on around €16–20 per head. For something slightly smarter, *La Ferme St-Louis* on place St-Louis (ⓣ05.53.53.82.77; closed Sun & Mon) serves a limited but well-priced three-course menu (€17 at lunchtime, dinner €22), while *Le Clos St-Front*, 5 rue de la Vertu (ⓣ05.53.46.78.58; closed Sun evening & Mon), offers top-quality food at surprisingly affordable prices (weekday menus from

€19, weekends from €26) and a delightful summer courtyard. If you fancy a change from strictly French fare, *Le Canard Laqué*, 2 rue Lanmary, is a good and popular Chinese place with menus from €10 (closed Sun & Mon).

Brantôme and the valley of the Dronne

Although **Brantôme** itself is very much on the tourist trail, the country to both the west and east of the town along the **River Dronne** remains largely undisturbed. It's tranquil and very beautiful, and best savoured at a gentle pace, perhaps by bike or even by canoeing along the river.

Brantôme

BRANTÔME, 27km north of Périgueux on the Angoulême road and beloved of British tourists, sits in a bend of the River Dronne, whose still, water-lilied surface mirrors the limes and weeping willows of the riverside gardens. On the north bank of the river are the church and convent buildings of the former **Benedictine abbey** that for centuries has been Brantôme's focus. Its stone facades, now masking the secular offices of the Hôtel de Ville, have that pallor and blank stare so characteristic of the self-denying institutional life – not that self-denial was a virtue associated with this monastery's most notorious abbot, Pierre de Bourdeilles, the sixteenth-century author of scurrilous tales of life at the royal court. It's worth taking a look inside the abbey church for the palm-frond vaulting of the chapterhouse and the font made from a carved and grounded pillar capital. Brantôme's best architectural feature, however, is the Limousin-style Romanesque **belfry** standing behind the church against the wooded and cave-riddled scarp that forms the backdrop to the village.

There are more pleasant views to be had wandering the nearby **gardens** and the balustraded riverbanks, while in summer you can take a leisurely **boat trip** on the river (Easter to mid-Oct; €6.50).

Three **buses** a week (Mon, Fri & Sun) connect Brantôme with the TGV in Angoulême. The **tourist office** (Feb, March & Oct–Dec daily except Tues 10am–noon & 2–5pm; April–June & Sept daily except Tues 10am–12.30pm & 2–6pm; July & Aug daily 10am–7pm; Ⓣ05.53.05.80.52) is next to the abbey church. From May to September you can rent **canoes** and a handful of **bikes** from Brantôme Canoë (Ⓣ05.53.05.77.24, Ⓔbrantome-canoe@wanadoo.fr), just over the bridge on the road to Thiviers.

The cheapest **accommodation** is to be found at the friendly *Hôtel Versaveau*, 8 place de Gaulle, at the north end of town (Ⓣ05.53.05.71.42; ❶–❷; restaurant from €10; closed three weeks in Nov & Christmas/New Year), though prettier and much more comfortable rooms are available at *Hôtel Chabrol* across the river (Ⓣ05.53.05.70.15, Ⓦwww.logis-de-france.fr; ❸; closed Feb & mid-Nov to mid-Dec), whose restaurant, *Les Frères Charbonnel*, is in the gourmet class, with its cheapest menu at €26 (closed Sun eve & Mon Oct–June). Another nice place to stay is the *Maison Fleurie*, an English-owned *chambres d'hôte* at 54 rue Gambetta (Ⓣ05.53.35.17.04, Ⓦwww.maisonfleurie.net; ❸), with a pool and quiet courtyard garden. Other good **eating** options include *Les Jardins de Brantôme*, with a lovely garden, a short walk north of town at 33 rue Pierre-de-Mareuil (closed Nov & Feb, plus Wed & lunch Thurs; menus €12–25), and *Au Fil de l'Eau*, on quai Bertin, which specializes in not too expensive fish dishes (closed mid-Oct to Easter; menus from €25) and spreads along the riverbank in fine weather. Campers should head for the well-run municipal **campsite** just east of Brantôme on the D78 Thiviers road (Ⓣ05.53.05.75.24; closed Oct–April).

Bourdeilles

BOURDEILLES, 16km down the Dronne from Brantôme by a beautiful back road, is relatively hard to reach – perhaps the most appealing way is by canoe. It's a sleepy backwater, an ancient village clustering round its **château** (Feb, March & mid-Nov to mid-Dec Mon, Wed, Thurs & Sun 10am–12.30pm & 2–5.30pm; April–June, Sept to mid-Nov & last two weeks Dec daily except Tues 10am–12.30pm & 2–6pm; July & Aug daily 10am–7pm; €5.20; Ⓦwww.semitour.com) on a rocky spur above the river. The château consists of two buildings: one a thirteenth-century fortress, the other an elegant Renaissance residence begun by the lady of the house as a piece of unsuccessful favour-currying with Catherine de Medici – unsuccessful because Catherine never came to stay and the château remained unfinished. If you climb the octagonal keep, you can look down on the town's clustered roofs, the weir and the boat-shaped mill parting the current, and along the Dronne to the corn fields and the manors hidden among the trees.

The château is now home to an exceptional collection of **furniture** and **religious statuary** bequeathed to the state by its former owners. Among the more notable pieces are some splendid Spanish dowry chests and a sixteenth-century Rhenish Entombment with life-sized statues, embodying the very image of the serious, self-satisfied medieval burgher. The *salon doré*, the room in which Catherine de Medici was supposed to sleep, has also been preserved.

Lesser mortals wanting to **stay** the night could try the appealing *Hôtel du Donjon* (Ⓣ05.53.04.82.81, Ⓦwww.hotel-ledonjon.com; ❹; menus €12–25; closed mid-Nov to mid-Dec, Jan & March), on the main street, or the more upmarket *Hostellerie Les Griffons* (Ⓣ05.53.45.45.35, Ⓦwww.griffons.fr; ❺; closed mid-Oct to Easter) in a sixteenth-century house beside the old bridge, with a restaurant serving top-notch regional cuisine (menus €22 & €38).

Ribérac

Surrounded by an intimate, hilly countryside of woods and hay meadows and drowsy hilltop villages, **RIBÉRAC**, 30km downstream from Bourdeilles, is a pleasant if unremarkable town whose greatest claim to fame is its major Friday **market**, which brings in producers and wholesalers from all around. With a couple of decent **hotels**, it makes an agreeable base from which to explore the quiet, lush Dronne landscape. A good cheap option is the *Du Commerce* at 8 rue Gambetta on the corner of the wide central place de Gaulle (Ⓣ05.53.91.28.59; ❷), with a decent restaurant from €11. More attractive and excellent value is the *De France* on the north side of the square at 3 rue Marc-Dufraisse (Ⓣ05.53.90.00.61, Ⓦwww.hoteldefranceriberac.com; ❸; closed Mon, also mid-Nov to mid-Dec & Jan), with a terrace garden and a locally renowned restaurant serving original cuisine (closed Mon, Tues lunch & Sat; menu at €23). There's also a riverside municipal **campsite** just outside Ribérac on the Angoulême road (Ⓣ05.53.90.50.08; closed 16 Sept–May).

For further ideas about *chambres d'hôtes* in the surrounding country, Ribérac's **tourist office** on place de Gaulle is the place to ask (July & Aug Mon–Sat 9am–noon & 1.30–6.30pm, Sun 10am–noon; Sept–June Mon–Sat 9am–noon & 2–5pm; Ⓣ05.53.90.03.10, Ⓦwww.riberac.fr); they can also provide information about the numerous Romanesque churches in outlying villages that could provide a focus for leisurely wandering. **Bikes** can be rented from the campsite and from Cycle Cum's, 35 rue du 26-Mars-1944 (Ⓣ05.53.90.33.23).

Aubeterre-sur-Dronne and around

Rather touristy, but very beautiful with its ancient galleried and turreted houses, **AUBETERRE-SUR-DRONNE** hangs on a steep hillside above the river some 30km downstream of Ribérac. Its principal curiosity is the cavernous **Église Monolithe** (daily: June 15–Oct 15 9.30am–12.30pm & 2–7pm; Oct 16–June 14 9.30am–12.30pm & 2–6pm; €4), carved out of the soft rock of the cliff face in the twelfth century, with its rock-hewn tombs going back to the sixth. A (blocked-off) tunnel connects with the **château** on the bluff overhead. There's also the extremely beautiful church of **St-Jacques**, with an eleventh-century facade sculpted and decorated in the richly carved Poitiers style on the street leading uphill from the square.

The **tourist office** is beside the main car park (July & Aug daily 10am–7pm; Sept–June Mon 2–6pm, Tues–Sun 10am–noon & 2–6pm; Ⓣ05.45.98.57.18, Ⓦaubeterresurdronne.free.fr), round the corner from the simple, rather faded *Hôtel de France* (Ⓣ05.45.98.50.43, Ⓦwww.hoteldefrance-aubeterre.com; ❷) on the central square. Alternatively, you'll find more comfortable **accommodation** and a fine restaurant beside the bridge just below the village at the *Hostellerie du Périgord*, beside the bridge (Ⓣ05.45.98.50.46, Ⓦwww.hostellerie-perigord.com; ❸; menus €15.50–36). There's also a **campsite** (Ⓣ05.45.98.60.17; closed 15 Sept–14 June) across the other side of the river. On weekdays a daily **bus** runs to Angoulême, while Chalais, which is on the Angoulême train line, is only 12km away.

South of Aubeterre, towards **LA ROCHE-CHALAIS**, the country gradually changes. Farmland gives way to an extensive forest of oak and sweet chestnut, bracken and broom, interspersed with sour, marshy pasture, very sparsely populated. It's ideal cycling and picnicking country. In La Roche-Chalais, the **tourist office** on the main square (May–Sept Tues–Fri 9am–noon & 2–7pm, Sat 9am–noon & 2–6pm; Oct–April Tues–Fri 9am–noon & 2–6pm, Sat 9am–noon; Ⓣ05.53.90.18.95) has information on local walking routes and farm visits. For an overnight **stay**, the *Hôtel Soleil d'Or*, across the square from the tourist office (Ⓣ05.53.90.86.71, Ⓦwww.logis-de-france.fr; ❸; restaurant from €11), has a magnificent view over the surrounding area and very comfortable rooms. There's also a nice three-star **campsite** down on the riverbank (Ⓣ05.53.91.40.65; closed Oct to mid-April).

St-Jean-de-Côle and around

Twenty kilometres northeast of Brantôme, **ST-JEAN-DE-CÔLE** ranks as one of the loveliest villages in the Dordogne. Its ancient houses huddle together in typical medieval fashion around a wide sandy square dominated by the charmingly ill-proportioned eleventh-century **church of St-Jean-Baptiste** and the rugged-looking **Château de la Marthonie** (not open to the public). The château, which dates from the twelfth century, has acquired various additions in a pleasingly organic fashion.

The **tourist office** (July & Aug Mon 9am–6pm, Tues–Fri 9am–9pm, Sat & Sun 2–7pm; Sept–June daily except Wed 2–5pm; Ⓣ05.53.62.14.15, Ⓦwww.ville-saint-jean-de-cole.fr) is also on the square, as well as a couple of **restaurants**. However, for good traditional fare you can't beat the wisteria-covered *Hôtel St-Jean* (Ⓣ05.53.52.23.20, Ⓔlesaintjean@ville-saint-jean-de-cole.fr; ❷; menus from €11, closed Sun eve & Mon) on the main road through the village; it also offers a few simple but clean and comfortable **rooms**.

Around 10km west of St-Jean, just outside the village of **VILLARS**, the **Château de Puyguilhem** (Feb, March & mid-Nov to Dec Tues–Thurs

& Sun 10am–12.30pm & 2–5.30pm; April–June & Sept to mid-Nov daily 10am–12.30pm & 2–6pm; July & Aug daily 10am–7pm; €5.20; Ⓦwww.semitour.com) sits on the edge of a valley backed by oak woods. The building you see today was erected at the beginning of the sixteenth century on the site of an earlier military fortress. With its octagonal tower, broad spiral staircase, steep roofs, magnificent fireplaces and false dormer windows, it's a perfect example of French Renaissance architecture. From the gallery at the top of the stairs you get a close-up of the roof and window decoration, as well as a view down the valley, which once was filled by an ornamental lake.

In the next valley south, the ruined Cistercian **Boschaud abbey** merits a quick visit while you're in the area. Standing on the edge of the woods and reached by a lane not much wider than a farm track, its charm lies as much in the fact that it is – for once – unfenced, unpampered and free, as in the pure, stark lines of its twelfth-century architecture.

A short distance north of Villars, local cavers discovered an extensive cave system in 1958, part of which is open to the public. While the **Grotte de Villars** (daily: April–June & Sept 10am–noon & 2–7pm; July & Aug 10am–7.30pm; Oct 2–6.30pm; €6.50; Ⓦwww.grotte-villars.com) boasts a few prehistoric paintings – notably of horses and a still unexplained scene of a man and a bison – the main reason for coming here is the impressive array of stalactites and stalagmites.

Thiviers and Sorges

If you're heading along the main N21 Périgueux–Limoges road, it's worth stopping off at the small market town of **THIVIERS**, which styles itself as the foie gras capital of the region. Its helpful **tourist office**, on the central square (July–Sept daily 9am–7pm; Oct–June Mon–Sat 10am–noon & 2–6pm; Ⓣ05.53.55.12.50, Ⓔot.thiviers@wanadoo.fr), makes the most of this with a small **museum** dedicated to the history and production of foie gras (same hours; €1.50). If you're looking for somewhere to **stay**, try the attractive *Hôtel de France et de Russie*, 51 rue du Général-Lamy (Ⓣ05.53.55.17.80, Ⓦwww.hoteldefranceetderussie.com; ③), between the tourist office and the **gare SNCF**, a couple of minutes' walk to the north.

SORGES, closer to Périgueux and strung out along the road, has less to offer aesthetically than Thiviers. However, the **tourist office** (July & Aug daily 9.30am–12.30pm & 2.30–6.30pm; Sept–June Tues–Sun 10am–noon & 2–5pm; Ⓣ05.53.46.71.43, Ⓦwww.sorges-perigord.com) contains an informative **truffle museum** (same hours; €4), and staff can also direct you to a nature trail that gives an idea of how and where truffles grow. There's a very reasonable **hotel** here, too, the *Auberge de la Truffe* on the main road (Ⓣ05.53.05.02.05, Ⓦwww.auberge-de-la-truffe.com; ③), with an excellent restaurant (menus €16–52, closed Mon lunch).

The Château de Hautefort

Forty kilometres east of Périgueux, the **Château de Hautefort** (daily: Feb, March, Oct & Nov 2–6pm April–June & Sept 10am–noon & 2–6pm; July & Aug 9.30am–7pm; €8) enjoys a majestic position at the end of a wooded spur above its feudal village. A magnificent example of good living on a grand scale, the castle has an elegance that is out of step with the usual rough stone fortresses of Périgord. The approach is across a wide esplanade flanked by formal gardens, over the moat by a drawbridge, and into a stylish Renaissance

The King of Araucania

Born near Tourtoirac in 1825, **Antoine de Thounens** went on to become a successful Périgueux lawyer, but, deciding he was destined for higher things, borrowed money and set sail for Patagonia. He found a warm welcome among the local Araucanians – who regarded him as a liberator – and declared himself Antoine-Orélie I, **King of Araucania** in 1860. The Chilean authorities had other ideas and promptly threw him out. Undaunted, Antoine gathered more funds and tried again nine years later, but to no avail. He eventually retired, returning to Tourtoirac where he died in poverty in 1878.

courtyard, opening to the south. Once the property of well-known troubadour Bertrand de Born, it passed into the hands of the Hautefort family in the seventeenth century and was extensively remodelled. In 1968 a fire gutted the castle, but it has since been meticulously restored using traditional techniques; it's all unmistakably new, but the quality of the craftsmanship is superb.

Hautefort has a very pleasant **hotel**, the *Auberge du Parc* (ⓣ05.53.50.88.98, ⓕ05.53.51.61.72; ❷; closed mid-Dec to mid-March; restaurant from €15, closed Sun eve & Wed), just beneath the castle walls. By car, the most attractive route from Périgueux is on the D5 along the River Auvézère via Cubjac and **TOURTOIRAC**, which is best known as the birthplace of Antoine de Thounens, a colourful local character who single-handedly tried to establish a colony in South America (see box above).

Périgord Pourpre

The area known as the **Périgord Pourpre** takes its name from the wine-growing region concentrated in the southwest corner of the Dordogne *département*, most famous for the sweet white wines produced around **Monbazillac**. The only town of any size is **Bergerac**, which makes a good base for visiting the Roman remains at **Montcaret** and the nearby **Château de Montaigne**, home of the famous sixteenth-century philosopher. The uplands south of Bergerac are peppered with *bastides*, medieval fortified towns (see box on p.727), such as the beautifully preserved **Monpazier**, and here also you'll find the **Château de Biron**, which dominates the countryside for miles around.

Bergerac and around

BERGERAC, "capital" of Périgord Pourpre, lies on the riverbank in the wide plain of the Dordogne. Once a flourishing port for the wine trade, it is still the main market centre for the surrounding maize, vine and tobacco farms. Devastated in the Wars of Religion, when most of its Protestant population fled overseas, Bergerac is now essentially a modern town with some interesting and attractive reminders of the past.

The **vieille ville** is a calm and pleasant area to wander through, with drinking fountains on the street corners and numerous late medieval houses. In rue de l'Ancien-Pont, the splendid seventeenth-century Maison Peyrarède houses an informative **Musée du Tabac** (March 15–Nov 15 Tues–Fri 10am–noon & 2–6pm, Sat 10am–noon & 2–5pm, Sun 2.30–6.30pm; Nov 16–March 14 Tues–Fri 10am–noon & 2–6pm, Sat 10am–noon; €3), detailing the history of the weed, with collections of pipes and tools of the trade.

Bergerac has a couple of other museums, the best of which is the small **Musée Régional du Vin et de la Batellerie** in rue des Conférences in the heart of the old town (March 15–Nov 15 Tues–Fri 10am–noon & 2–5.30pm, Sat 10am–noon, Sun 2.30–6.30pm; Nov 16–March 14 Tues–Fri 10am–noon & 2–5.30pm, Sat 10am–noon; €2), with displays on viticulture, barrel-making and the town's once-bustling river-trading past. Nearby, on the very picturesque place de la Myrpe, is a statue in honour of **Cyrano de Bergerac**, the town's most famous association, on whom a 1990 film starring Gérard Dépardieu was based. The big-nosed lead character in Edmond Rostand's play, though fictional, was inspired by the seventeenth-century philosopher of the same name, who, sadly, had nothing to do with the town.

Wine-lovers should make a beeline for the **Maison des Vins**, down by the river on quai Salvette (July & Aug daily 10am–7pm; Sept–June Tues–Sat 10am–noon & 2–6pm), which offers free tastings and sells a selection of local wines. You can also pick up the free booklet *Route des Vins de Bergerac* detailing the surrounding vineyards.

Practicalities

The **gare SNCF** is at the end of cours Alsace-Lorraine, ten minutes' walk north from the old town, while the **airport** (Ⓣ05.53.22.25.25) lies 5km southeast of Bergerac (roughly €10 by taxi). The **tourist office** is at 97 rue Neuve-d'Argenson, two minutes' walk northeast of the old town (July & Aug Mon–Sat 9.30am–7.30pm, Sun 10.30am–1pm & 2.30–7pm; Sept–June Mon–Sat 9.30am–1pm & 2–7pm; Ⓣ05.53.57.03.11, Ⓦwww.bergerac-tourisme.com). You can rent **bicycles** from Périgord Cycles at 11 place Gambetta (Ⓣ05.53.57.07.19) and Apolo at 31 bd Victor-Hugo (Ⓣ05.53.61.08.16); the latter also rents out scooters, motorbikes and **cars**, with airport pickups available. There's a vast **market** on Wednesday and Saturday mornings in the covered *halles* in the old town centre and around Notre-Dame church.

There's a decent range of **accommodation** to choose from. The best budget option is *Le Moderne*, opposite the station (Ⓣ05.53.57.19.62, Ⓕ05.53.61.80.50; ❶–❷; closed two weeks in Oct), a welcoming, well-kept place with a brasserie restaurant (closed Sun; menus from €10.50). For something more comfortable, try one of the three-star hotels on place Gambetta between the station and the old town: the *De France* (Ⓣ05.53.57.11.61, Ⓕ05.53.61.25.70; ❸), or the slightly smarter *De Bordeaux* (Ⓣ05.53.57.12.83, Ⓦwww.hotel-bordeaux-bergerac.com; ❹); both have small swimming pools, while the latter also boasts a good restaurant (closed Sat lunch & Sun eve; menus from €17). There's also a municipal **campsite**, *La Pelouse* (Ⓣ & Ⓕ05.53.57.06.67; closed Nov to mid-Feb), on the south bank of the river.

Apart from the hotel **restaurants** mentioned above, there are some good eating options around the market hall, including *La Blanche Hermine*, a cheerful crêperie (closed Sun & Mon); *La Cocotte des Halles* in the hall itself, with a choice of daily specials from around €10 on the slateboards (closed Sun & Feb); and *Le Jardin d'Epicure*, popular for its no-nonsense regional dishes (menus from €17). For something more refined, try *Poivre et Sel*, 11 rue de l'Ancien-Pont, opposite the Musée du Tabac (closed Mon Oct–April; menus from €15), or the even more upmarket *L'Imparfait*, nearby at 8 rue des Fontaines (Ⓣ05.53.57.47.92; closed mid-Nov to mid-Jan and Sun off season; menus €19–45), which specializes in fresh fish.

If you should find yourself here in July, don't miss the magnificent **food festival** called La Table de Cyrano in the week of July 14. Classical music concerts also take place throughout the month, with jazz on Wednesday evenings throughout July and August.

Château de Monbazillac

Half a dozen kilometres south of Bergerac, looking out over the gentle slopes of its long-favoured vineyards, stands the handsome Renaissance **Château de Monbazillac** (Feb, March, Nov & Dec Tues–Sun 10am–noon & 2–5pm; April daily 10am–noon & 2–6pm; May & Oct daily 10am–12.30pm & 2–6pm; June & Sept daily 10am–7pm; July & Aug daily 10am–7.30pm; €5.80), part residence and part fortress, with its corners reinforced by four sturdy towers. Inside is a moderately interesting **museum** of local traditions and crafts. Most engaging are the ground-floor grand salon, with its richly decorated ceiling and parquet floor of oak, pine and cherry wood, and the wine-related displays in the cellar. You can taste – and buy – the velvety sweet white Monbazillac **wine** here, too; it's generally consumed with desserts or chilled as an apéritif.

Ste-Foy-la-Grande and Montcaret

Driving west from Bergerac along the River Dordogne, the first place you come to of any size is the *bastide* town of **STE-FOY-LA-GRANDE**, whose narrow central streets still retain a number of ancient houses. One of these, at 102 rue de la République, now houses the **tourist office** (June & Sept Mon–Sat 9.30am–12.30pm & 2.30–6pm; July & Aug Mon–Sat 9.30am–12.30pm & 2.30–6.30pm, Sun 10am–1pm; Oct–May Mon–Sat 9.30am–12.30pm & 2.30–5.30pm; ⓣ05.57.46.03.00, ⓦwww.paysfoyen.com), which has lists of *chambres d'hôtes* and local wine-tasting sessions. Another draw is the town's mouthwatering Saturday **market**, and there's a very pleasant **place to stay**, the *Grand Hôtel*, 117 rue de la République (ⓣ05.57.46.00.08, ⓦwww.grandhotel-mce.com; ❸; restaurant from €11), just east of the tourist office.

Thirteen kilometres west from Ste-Foy lies **MONTCARET**, whose main attraction is a fourth-century **Gallo-Roman villa** (daily: April–June & Sept 9.30am–12.30pm & 2–6pm; July & Aug 9.30am–1pm & 2–6.30pm; Oct–March 10am–12.30pm & 2–4.30pm; €4.60) with superb mosaics and baths plus an adjoining museum displaying the many objects exhumed on the site. It's another 3.5km to the **Château de Montaigne** (Feb–April & Nov–Dec Wed–Sun 10am–noon & 2–5.30pm; May, June, Sept & Oct Wed–Sun 10am–noon & 2–6.30pm; July & Aug daily 10am–6.30pm; €5), where Michel de Montaigne wrote many of his chatty, digressive essays on the nature of life and humankind. All that remains of the original building is Montaigne's tower-study, its beams inscribed with his maxims; the rest of the château was rebuilt in pseudo-Renaissance style after a fire in 1885.

Monpazier and around

MONPAZIER, founded in 1284 by King Edward I of England (who was also Duke of Aquitaine), is one of the most complete of the surviving *bastides*, and still relatively free of the commercialism that suffocates a place like Domme. Picturesque and placid though it is today, the village has a hard and bitter history, being twice – in 1594 and 1637 – the centre of peasant rebellions provoked by the misery that followed the Wars of Religion. Both uprisings were brutally suppressed: the 1637 peasants' leader was broken on the wheel in the square. Sully, the Protestant general, describes a rare moment of light relief in the terrible wars, when the men of the Catholic *bastide* of Villefranche-du-Périgord planned to capture Monpazier on the same night as

Bastides

From the Occitan word *bastida*, meaning a group of buildings, **bastides** were the new towns of the thirteenth and fourteenth centuries. Although they are found all over southwest France, from the Dordogne to the foothills of the Pyrenees, there is a particularly high concentration in the area between the Dordogne and Lot rivers, which at that time formed the disputed "frontier" region between English-held Aquitaine and Capetian France.

That said, the earliest *bastides* were founded largely for **economic and political** reasons. They were a means of bringing new land into production – this was a period of rapid population growth and technological innovation – and thus extending the power of the local lord. But as tensions between the French and English forces intensified during the late thirteenth century, so the motive became increasingly **military**. The *bastides* now provided a handy way of securing the land along the frontier, and it was generally at this point that they were fortified.

As an incentive, anyone who was prepared to build, inhabit and defend the *bastide* was granted various perks and concessions in a founding **charter**. All new residents were allocated a building plot, garden and cultivable land outside the town. The charter might also offer asylum to certain types of criminal or grant exemption from military service, and would allow the election of **consuls** charged with day-to-day administration – a measure of self-government remarkable in feudal times. Taxes and judicial affairs, meanwhile, remained the preserve of the representative of the king or local lord under whose ultimate authority the *bastide* lay.

The other defining feature of a *bastide* is its **layout**. They are nearly always square or rectangular in shape, depending on the nature of the terrain, and are divided by streets at right angles to each other to produce a chequerboard pattern. The focal point is the market square, often missing its covered *halle* nowadays, but generally still surrounded by arcades, while the church is relegated to one side, or may even form part of the town walls.

The busiest *bastide* founders were **Alphonse de Poitiers** (1249–1271), on behalf of the French crown, after he became Count of Toulouse in 1249, and **King Edward** I of England (1272–1307), who wished to consolidate his hold on the northern borders of his Duchy of Aquitaine. The former chalked up a total of 57 *bastides*, including Villeneuve-sur-Lot (1251), Monflanquin (1252) and Ste-Foy-la-Grande (1255), while Edward was responsible for Beaumont (1272) and Monpazier (1284) amongst others. While many *bastides* retain no more than vestiges of their original aspect, both Monpazier and Monflanquin have survived almost entirely intact.

the men of Monpazier planned to capture Villefranche. By chance, both sides took different routes, met no resistance, looted to their hearts' content and returned home congratulating themselves on their luck and skill, only to find in the morning that things were rather different. The peace terms were that everyone should return everything to its proper place.

Monpazier follows the typical *bastide* layout, with a grid of streets built around a gem of a central square – sunny, still and slightly menacing. Deep, shady arcades pass under all the houses, which are separated from each other by a small gap to reduce fire risk; at the corners the buttresses are cut away to allow the passage of laden pack animals. There's also an ancient *lavoir* where women used to wash clothes, and a much altered church.

The well-organized **tourist office** is on the central square (Ⓣ05.53.22.68.59, Ⓦwww.pays-des-bastides.com; Jan & Dec Mon–Sat 10.30am–12.30pm & 2.30–5.30pm; Feb, March, Oct & Nov Mon–Sat 10am–12.30pm & 2.30–6pm; April–June & Sept daily 10am–12.30pm & 2–6.30pm; July & Aug daily

10am–7pm), where you'll also find simple **accommodation** at the *Hôtel de France*, 21 rue St-Jacques (ⓣ05.53.22.60.06, ⓕ05.53.22.07.27; ❷; closed Nov–March; restaurant from €17). Another attractive option is the *Hôtel de Londres* just outside the north gate (ⓣ05.53.22.60.64, ⓔcorupsis@wanadoo.fr; ❷), also with a fine restaurant (menus from €19), but when it comes to **eating**, you can't beat *La Bastide*, at 52 rue St-Jacques (ⓣ05.53.22.60.59; closed Mon & Feb; menus €13–45), for traditional atmosphere and classic, regional cooking. The best of the **campsites** in the vicinity is the luxurious *Moulin de David*, roughly 3km to the south on the road to Villeréal (ⓣ05.53.22.65.25, ⓦwww.moulin-de-david.com; closed mid-Sept to mid-May).

The Château de Biron

Eight kilometres south of Monpazier, the vast **Château de Biron** (Feb, March & mid-Nov to Dec Tues–Thurs & Sun 10am–12.30pm & 2–5.30pm; April–June & Sept to mid-Nov daily 10am–12.30pm & 2–6pm; July & Aug daily 10am–7pm; €5.20; ⓦwww.semitour.com) was begun in the eleventh century and added to piecemeal afterwards. You can take a guided tour (in French only), but better to borrow the English-language translation and wander at will around the rooms and the grassy courtyard, where there is a restored Renaissance chapel and guardhouse with tremendous views over the roofs of the feudal village below.

A single street runs through the village of **BIRON**, past a covered **market** on timber supports iron-hard with age, and out under an arched gateway, where well-manured vegetable plots interspersed with iris, lily and Iceland poppies lie under the tumbledown walls. At the bottom of the hill, another group of houses stands on a small square with a well in front of the village **church**, its Romanesque origins hidden by motley alterations. The *Auberge du Château*, back near the market hall, makes a perfect lunch spot (ⓣ05.53.63.13.33; closed Mon & mid-Dec to Jan; menus from €14.50).

Périgord Noir and the upper Dordogne

Périgord Noir encompasses the central part of the valley of the Dordogne, and the valley of the Vézère. This is the distinctive Dordogne country: deep-cut valleys enclosed by the water-smooth cliffs their rivers have eroded, with fields of maize in the alluvial bottoms and dense oak woods on the heights, interspersed with patches of not very fertile farmland. Plantations of walnut trees (cultivated for their oil), flocks of low-slung grey geese (their livers enlarged for foie gras) and prehistoric-looking stone huts called *bories* are other hallmarks of Périgord Noir, and beyond the region, along the **upper Dordogne valley** towards Argentat in the east.

In the **valley of the Vézère** the slightly overhanging cliffs have been worn away by frost action over the millennia and are riddled with caves that have been used as dwellings and sanctuaries for thousands of years. It was here in the Vézère valley that the first skeletons of **Cro-Magnon people** – the first Homo sapiens, tall and muscular with a large skull – were unearthed in 1868 by labourers digging out the Périgueux–Agen train line, and here, too, that an incredible wealth of archeological and artistic evidence of the life of late Stone Age people has since been found.

The **prehistoric cave paintings** are the absolute highlight of Périgord Noir, remarkable not only for their great age, but also for their exquisite colouring and the skill with which they are drawn. However, the international renown of the caves and their paintings, combined with the well-preserved medieval architecture of **Sarlat**, has made this one of the most heavily touristed inland areas of France, with all the concomitant problems of crowds, high prices and tack. If possible, it's worth coming out of season, but if you can't, seek accommodation away from the main centres, and always drive along the back roads – the smaller the better – even when there is a more direct route available.

Sarlat and around

SARLAT-LA-CANÉDA, capital of Périgord Noir, lies in a hollow between hills 10km or so back from the Dordogne river. You hardly notice the modern town, as it's the mainly fifteenth- and sixteenth-century houses of the *vieille ville* in mellow, honey-coloured stone that draw the attention.

The **vieille ville**, now thankfully pedestrianized, is an excellent example of medieval organic urban growth, violated only by the straight swath of the rue de la République which cuts through its middle. The west side remains relatively un-chic; the east side is where most people wander. As you approach the old town from the station, turn right down rue Lakanal which leads to the large and unexciting **Cathédrale St-Sacerdos**, mostly dating from its seventeenth-century renovation. Opposite stands the town's finest house, the

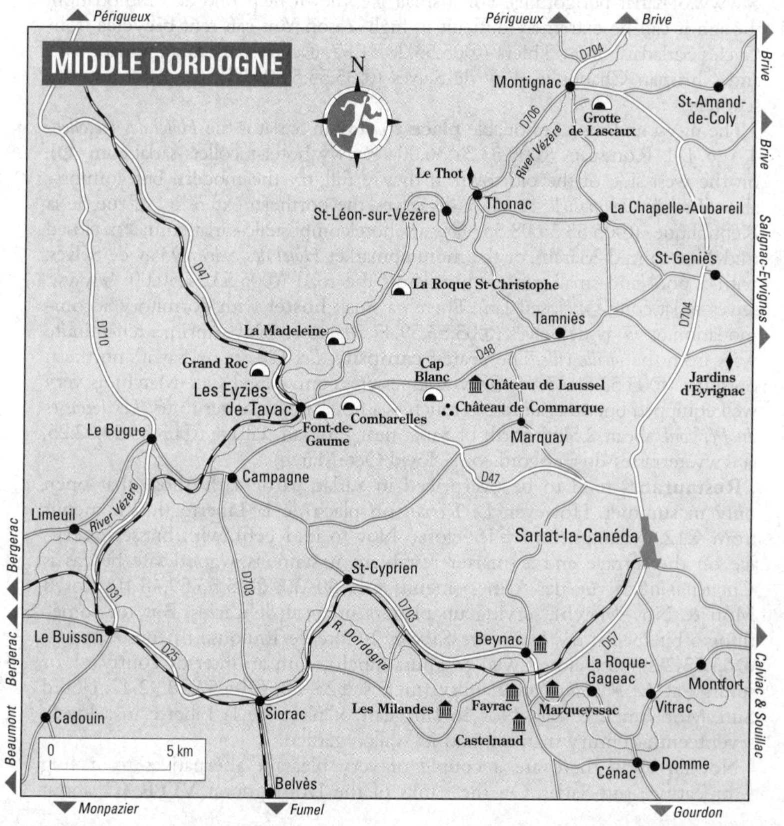

Maison de La Boétie (not open to the public) once the home of Montaigne's friend Étienne de La Boétie, with its gabled tiers of windows and characteristic steep roof stacked with heavy limestone tiles (*lauzes*).

For a better sense of the medieval town, wander through the cool, shady lanes and courtyards – **cour des Fontaines** and **cour des Chanoines** – around the back of the cathedral. On a slope directly behind the cathedral stands the curious twelfth-century coned tower, the **Lanterne des Morts**, whose exact function has escaped historians, though the most popular theory is that it was built to commemorate St Bernard, who performed various miracles when he visited the town in 1147.

There are more wonderful old houses in the streets to the north, especially **rue des Consuls**, and up the slopes to the east. Eventually, though, Sarlat's labyrinthine lanes will lead you back to the central **place de la Liberté**, where the big Saturday **market** spreads its stands bearing foie gras, truffles, walnuts and mushrooms according to the season, and where various people try to make a living from the hordes who hit Sarlat in the summer.

Practicalities

The **gare SNCF** is just over 1km south of the old town, where on rue Tourny you'll find the **tourist office** (April–Oct Mon–Sat 9am–7pm, Sun 10am–noon & 2–6pm; Nov–March Mon–Sat 9am–noon & 2–7pm; ⓣ05.53.31.45.45, ⓦwww.ot-sarlat-perigord.fr). For a small fee, they'll help find accommodation, though it can be extremely difficult in high season. You can rent **bicycles** from Cycles Sarladais, 36 av Thiers (ⓣ05.53.28.51.87, ⓔcycles.sarladais@wanadoo.fr), and Christian Chapoulie, 4 av de Selves (ⓣ05.53.59.06.11); the latter also has scooters.

The nicest and most reasonable **place to stay** in Sarlat is the *Hôtel des Récollets*, 4 rue J.-J.-Rousseau (ⓣ05.53.31.36.00, ⓦwww.hotel-recollets-sarlat.com; ❸), on the west side of the old town. If they're full, try the modern but comfortable *Hôtel de Compostelle* at 64 av de Selves, the northern extension of rue de la République (ⓣ05.53.59.08.53, ⓦwww.hotelcompostelle-sarlat.com; ❹; closed mid-Nov to mid-March), or the more upmarket *Hôtel des Selves*, 93 av de Selves, with a pool and small garden, just across the road (ⓣ05.53.31.50.00, ⓦwww.selves-sarlat.com; ❺; closed Jan). There's a small **hostel** with dormitory accommodation at 77 av de Selves (ⓣ05.53.59.47.59; closed Nov–April), a ten-minute walk from the *vieille ville*. The nearest **campsite**, *Les Périères*, on Sarlat's northern outskirts (ⓣ05.53.59.05.84, ⓦwww.lesperieres.com; closed Oct–March), is very well equipped but costs almost as much as a hotel; much better to try *Les Terrasses du Périgord*, about 2.5km north of Sarlat near Proissans village (ⓣ05.53.59.02.25, ⓦwww.terrasses-du-perigord.com; closed Oct–March).

Restaurants tend to be overpriced in Sarlat, particularly those that open only in summer. However, *Le Régent* on place de la Liberté (lunch menus from €12, evenings from €15; closed Nov to mid-Feb), with brasserie service on the terrace and a smarter restaurant upstairs, is a good safe bet, as is *Criquettamu's*, 5 rue des Armes (menus €13.50–30; ⓣ05.53.59.48.10; closed Mon & Nov–March), serving up platters of local delicacies. But for something a bit special try *Le Quatre Saisons*, 2 Côte de Toulouse (menus €18–34; ⓣ05.53.29.48.59; closed Wed & Thurs lunch), with an interior courtyard, or splurge at *Le Présidial*, rue Landry (menus €25–38; ⓣ05.53.28.92.47; closed Sun, Mon lunch & mid-Nov to Jan), east of place de la Liberté in a lovely seventeenth-century mansion and its walled garden.

Not far away there are a couple of very pleasant alternatives to staying – or eating – in Sarlat. On the banks of the Dordogne at **VITRAC**, about

7km south of Sarlat, the *Hôtel La Treille* (ⓣ05.53.28.33.19, ⓔhotel.rest.la-treille@perigord.com; ❸; closed Sun evening & Mon, also mid-Nov to Feb) has simple rooms and an excellent restaurant (menus from €15.50). Another good choice is the little hilltop hamlet of **MARQUAY** about halfway to Les Eyzies, where the *Hôtel des Bories* (ⓣ05.53.29.67.02, ⓦwww.logis-de-france.fr; ❸; closed Nov–March) offers a marvellous view, swimming pool and attached restaurant, *L'Esterel* (menus from €14), for which it's vital to book several months in advance for July and August.

Les Jardins d'Eyrignac

The *manoir* of **Eyrignac** is a very lovely seventeenth-century example of what in English would be called a country house. It lies in the hilly country to the northeast of Sarlat, about 13km by road. Its great glory is its **garden**, which is remarkable for its special effects and atmosphere (guided tours daily: April & May 10am–12.30pm & 2–7pm; June–Sept 9.30am–7pm; Oct–March 10.30am–12.30pm & 2.30pm to dusk; €8; house closed to the public). The original formal garden was the work of an eighteenth-century Italian architect, but it was later converted to an English romantic garden as the owners – still the same family – followed subsequent fashions. What you see today is the work of the last forty years, the creation of the present owner's father in a combination of Italian and French styles. There are practically no flowers: the garden consists of evergreens – mainly box, hornbeam, cypress and yew – clipped and arranged in formal patterns of alleys and parterres. A work of art in its own right, it's now classified as a national monument.

Les Eyzies

The main base for visiting many of the prehistoric painted caves of the Vézère valley is **LES EYZIES-DE-TAYAC**, an unattractive one-street village completely dedicated to tourism. But while you're here, visit the **Musée National de Préhistoire** (daily except Tues: July & Aug 9.30am–6.30pm; Sept–June 9.30am–12.30pm & 2.30–5.30pm; €4.50; ⓦwww.musee-prehistoire-eyzies.fr), at long last in its marvellous new home, which contains the country's most important collection of prehistoric artefacts and traces over 400,000 years of human habitation in the region. Look out for the oil lamp from Lascaux and the exhibits from La Madeleine, to the north of Les Eyzies, including a superb bas-relief of a bison licking its flank.

Practicalities

The **tourist office** is on Les Eyzies' one street (April–June & Sept Mon–Sat 9am–noon & 2–6pm, Sun 10am–noon & 2–5pm; July & Aug Mon–Sat 9am–7pm, Sun 10am–noon & 2–6pm; Oct–March Mon–Sat 9am–noon & 2–6pm; ⓣ05.53.06.97.05, ⓦwww.leseyzies.com). In addition to **bicycle rental**, they also offer Internet access and give out information on local *chambres d'hôtes* and *gîtes d'étape*.

Hotels are pricey and may require *demi-pension* (half-board) in high season. The cheapest is *Les Falaises*, in the main street (ⓣ05.53.06.97.35, ⓔhotel-des-falaises@wanadoo.fr; ❷; closed Dec), but a nicer choice is the slightly more expensive *La Rivière*, about 1km away on the Périgueux road (ⓣ05.53.06.97.14, ⓔla-riviere@wanadoo.fr; ❷; closed Nov–March; simple meals from €12). Moving up a notch, the ivy-covered *Hostellerie du Passeur*, by the tourist office (ⓣ05.53.06.97.13, ⓦwww.hostellerie-du-passeur.com; ❹; closed Nov–Jan; restaurant €22–45, closed Tues lunch), has small but very comfortable rooms, while just east of the centre, in a lovely spot by a mill-race, *Le Moulin de la Beune* (ⓣ05.53.06.94.33, ⓦwww.moulindelabeune.com; ❹; closed Nov–March) has well-priced rooms and an excellent restaurant (closed Tues lunch, Wed & Sat; menus €29–50). Alternatively, you could stay in **CAMPAGNE**, a pretty village 6km downstream, where you'll find big, bright rooms and regional menus at the *Hôtel du Château* (ⓣ05.53.07.23.50, ⓔhotduchateau@aol.com; ❸; closed mid-Oct to Easter; restaurant from €18). The closest **campsite** to Les Eyzies is the well-tended *La Rivière* under the same management as the hotel (see above; closed Nov–March).

When it comes to **eating**, *Café de la Mairie*, opposite the tourist office, serves no-nonsense brasserie-style food (menus from €12; closed Dec). Otherwise, try *Le Chateaubriant* (ⓣ05.53.35.06.11; closed Jan, also Wed & for dinner Sun), a bit further north along the main street, with a nice terrace and lunch menus from €11 to €25, or one of the hotels mentioned above.

Around Les Eyzies

There are more **prehistoric caves** around Les Eyzies than you could possibly hope to visit in one day. Besides, the compulsory guided tours are tiring, so it's best to select just a couple of the ones listed below.

No one ever lived in these caves, and there are various theories as to why such inaccessible spots were chosen. Most agree that they were sanctuaries and, if not actually places of worship, at least had religious significance. One suggestion is that making images of animals that were commonly hunted – like reindeer and bison – or feared – like bears and mammoths – was a kind of sympathetic magic intended to help men either catch or evade these animals. Another is that they were part of a fertility cult: sexual images of women with pendulous breasts and protuberant behinds are common. Others argue that these cave paintings served educational purposes, making parallels with Australian aborigines who used similar images to teach their young vital survival information as well as the history and mythological origins of their people. But much remains unexplained – the abstract signs that appear in so many caves, for example, and the arrows which clearly cannot be arrows, since Stone Age arrowheads looked different from these representations.

Grotte de Font-de-Gaume

Since its discovery in 1901, dozens of polychrome paintings have been found in the tunnel-like **Grotte de Font-de-Gaume** (daily except Sat: May 15–Sept 15 9.30am–5.30pm; Sept 16–May 14 9.30am–12.30pm & 2–5.30pm; €6.10; ⓣ05.53.06.86.00, ⓕ05.53.35.26.18), 1.5km along the D47 to Sarlat. Be aware that only 180 people are allowed to visit the cave each day and tickets sell out fast. You are advised to book (by phone or fax) at least a month ahead in high season and well in advance at other times. However, if you want to chance it, fifty tickets are sold on the spot each day; start queuing early.

The **cave** was first settled by Stone Age people during the last Ice Age – about 25,000 BC – when the Dordogne was the domain of roaming bison, reindeer and mammoths. The cave mouth is no more than a fissure concealed by rocks and trees above a small lush valley, while inside it's a narrow twisting passage of irregular height in which you quickly lose your bearings in the dark. The first painting you see is a frieze of bison, at about eye level: reddish-brown in colour, massive, full of movement, and very far from the primitive representations you might expect. Further on, a horse stands with one hoof slightly raised, resting, but the most miraculous of all is a **frieze** of five bison discovered in 1966 during cleaning operations. The colour, remarkably sharp and vivid, is preserved by a protective layer of calcite. Shading under the belly and down the thighs is used to give three-dimensionality with a sophistication that seems utterly modern. Another panel consists of superimposed drawings, a fairly common phenomenon in cave painting, sometimes the result of work by successive generations, but here an obviously deliberate technique. A reindeer in the foreground shares legs with a large bison behind to indicate perspective.

Stocks of **artists' materials** have also been found: kilos of prepared pigments; palettes – stones stained with ground-up earth pigments; and wooden painting sticks. Painting was clearly a specialized, perhaps professional, business, reproduced in dozens and dozens of caves located in the central Pyrenees and areas of northern Spain.

Grotte des Combarelles

The **Grotte des Combarelles** (same hours as Font-de-Gaume; €6.10; maximum six people per tour), 2km along the D47 towards Sarlat, was discovered in 1910. The innermost part of the cave is covered with **engravings** from the Magdalenian period (about 12,000 years ago). Drawn over a period of 2000 years, many are superimposed one upon another, and include horses, reindeer, mammoths and stylized human figures – among the finest are the heads of a horse and a lioness.

As with Font-de-Gaume, pre-booking is essential, especially in peak season (same phone and fax); collect tickets from Font-de-Gaume.

Abri du Cap Blanc and the Château de Commarque

Not a cave but a natural rock shelter, the **Abri du Cap Blanc** (daily: April–June, Sept & Oct 10am–noon & 2–6pm; July & Aug 10am–7pm; €5.90), lies on a steep wooded hillside about 7km east of Les Eyzies (turn left onto the D48 shortly after Les Combarelles). It contains a **sculpted frieze** of horses and bison dating from the Middle Magdalenian period, about 14,000 years ago. Of only ten surviving prehistoric sculptures in France, this is undoubtedly the best. The design is deliberate, with the sculptures polished and set off against a pockmarked background. But what makes this place extraordinary is not just the large scale, but the high relief of some of the sculptures. This was only possible in places where light reached in, which in turn brought the danger of destruction by exposure to the air. Cro-Magnon people actually lived in this shelter, and a female skeleton has been found that is some 2000 years younger than the frieze.

For a non-cave detour, continue a little further up the heavily wooded Beune valley from Cap Blanc, to the elegant sixteenth-century **Château de Laussel** (closed to the public). On the opposite side of the valley stand the romantic ruins of the **Château de Commarque** (daily: April 10am–6pm; May, June & Sept 10am–7pm; July & Aug 10am–8pm; €5.90; Ⓦwww.commarque.com). Dating from the twelfth century, it was originally a **castrum**, a fortified village made up of six separate fortresses, each belonging to a different noble family. The ruins have now been made structurally sound and it's possible once again to climb the thirty-metre-high tower for views over the surrounding countryside. The easiest way to reach the château is by a footpath starting below Cap Blanc. Cars have to approach from the south, following signs from the D47 Sarlat road.

Grotte du Grand Roc

As well as prehistoric cave paintings, you can see some truly spectacular **stalactites** and **stalagmites** in the area around Les Eyzies. Some of the best examples are off the D47 towards Périgueux, 2km north of Les Eyzies, in the

Grotte du Grand Roc (daily: Feb–June, Sept–Nov & Christmas holidays 10am–6pm; July & Aug 9.30am–7pm; €7; Ⓦwww.grandroc.com), whose entrance is high up in the cliffs that line much of the Vézère valley. There's a great view from the mouth of the cave and, inside, along some 80m of tunnel, a fantastic array of rock formations.

La Roque St-Christophe

The enormous prehistoric dwelling site, **La Roque St-Christophe** (daily: Jan, Feb, Nov & Dec 11am–5pm; March–June, Sept & Oct 10am–6pm; July & Aug 10am–7pm; €6; Ⓦwww.roque-st-christophe.com), 9km northeast of Les Eyzies along the D706 to Montignac, is made up of about one hundred **rock shelters** on five levels, hollowed out of the limestone cliffs. The whole complex is nearly a kilometre long and about 80m above ground-level, where the River Vézère once flowed. The earliest traces of occupation go back over 50,000 years. The view is pretty good, and the French guided tour instructive, but most of the finds are on display at the Musée National de Préhistoire in Les Eyzies (see p.731).

Montignac and the Lascaux caves

Some 26km up the Vézère valley, **MONTIGNAC** is the main base for visiting the Lascaux caves. It's a more attractive place than Les Eyzies, with several wooden-balconied houses leaning appealingly over the river, a good weekly **market** (Wednesday morning) and a lively annual **arts festival** in mid-July, featuring international folk groups.

The **tourist office** is on place Bertran-de-Born (April–June, Sept & Oct Mon–Sat 9am–noon & 2–6pm; July & Aug daily 9am–7pm; Nov–March Mon–Sat 10am–noon & 2–5pm; Ⓣ05.53.51.82.60, Ⓦwww.bienvenue-montignac.com). In summer, **tickets** for Lascaux II can be bought from a separate office next door.

Accommodation, as everywhere around here, can be a problem. The *Hôtel de la Grotte*, on rue du 4-Septembre (Ⓣ05.53.51.80.48, Ⓔhoteldelagrotte@wanadoo.fr; ❸; restaurant from €18), is a good, cheap option, with a pleasant garden beside a stream. If they're full, try *Le P'tit Monde*, just round the corner on the road to Sarlat (Ⓣ05.53.50.49.51, Ⓦwww.le-ptit-monde.com; ❷; closed Christmas holidays; restaurant from €15, closed Sun). Then it's a big leap up to the three-star *Soleil d'Or*, also on the main rue du 4-Septembre (Ⓣ05.53.51.80.22, Ⓦwww.le-soleil-dor.com; ❹; closed Feb), whose restaurant menus start at €21. For not much more, however, you can stay in the pretty period rooms of the ivy- and wisteria-clad *Hostellerie de la Roseraie*, across the river in quiet place d'Armes (Ⓣ05.53.50.53.92, Ⓦwww.laroseraie.fr.st; ❺; closed mid-Nov to March; restaurant from €20). And finally there's a well-tended three-star **campsite**, Le Moulin Bleufond (Ⓣ05.53.51.83.95, Ⓦwww.bleufond.com; closed mid-Oct to March), on the riverbank 500m downstream.

There are other interesting restaurant and accommodation options in the area. If you book ahead, you're in for a feast at *Le Bareil*, a farm restaurant near **LA CHAPELLE-AUBAREIL**, a few kilometres beyond the Lascaux caves (Ⓣ05.53.50.74.28; closed Mon & mid-Oct to mid-Nov), which serves traditional home cooking (Tues–Fri lunch menu at €15, evenings and weekends at €21). A particularly good spot for campers in search of luxury is the four-star *Le Paradis* site (Ⓣ05.53.50.72.64, Ⓦwww.le-paradis.com; closed Nov–March) near the exquisite riverside village of **ST-LÉON-SUR-VÉZÈRE**, some 9km south of Montignac. Further south again at **TAMNIÈS**, midway between Montignac and Sarlat, the *Hôtel Laborderie* (Ⓣ05.53.29.68.59, Ⓔhotel.laborderie@worldonline.fr; ❸; closed Nov–March) offers comfortable accommodation and good food (menus from €18). For other possibilities, ask at the tourist office in Montignac for their extensive list of B&Bs and farm campsites.

Grotte de Lascaux and Lascaux II

The **Grotte de Lascaux** was discovered in 1940 by four boys who were, according to popular myth, looking for their dog and fell into a deep cavern decorated with marvellously preserved **paintings** of animals. Executed by Cro-Magnon people 17,000 years ago, the paintings are among the finest examples of prehistoric art in existence. There are five or six identifiable styles, and subjects include the bison, mammoth and horse, plus the biggest known prehistoric drawing, of a 5.5-metre bull with astonishingly expressive head and face. In 1948, the cave was opened to the public, and over the course of the next fifteen years more than a million tourists came to Lascaux. Sadly, because of deterioration from the body heat and breath of visitors, the cave had to be closed in 1963; now you have to be content with the replica known as **Lascaux II**, 2km south of Montignac on the D704 (Feb, March & mid-Nov to Dec Tues–Sun 10am–12.30pm & 2–5.30pm; April–June & Sept daily 9.30am–6.30pm; July & Aug daily 9am–8pm; Oct to mid-Nov daily 10.30am–12.30pm & 2–6pm; €8, combined ticket with Le Thot €9; Ⓦwww.semitour.com). There are 2000 tickets on sale each day but these go fast in peak season; you can buy them in person a day or so in advance, while telephone bookings are accepted only in July and August (Ⓣ05.53.51.96.23). Note also that in winter (Oct–March) tickets are normally on sale at the site, while in summer (April–Sept) they are only available from an office beside Montignac tourist office – the system varies from year to year, however, so check in Montignac before heading up to the cave.

Opened in 1983, Lascaux II was the result of eleven years' painstaking work by twenty artists and sculptors, using the same methods and materials as the original cave painters. While the visit can't offer the excitement of a real cave, the reconstruction rarely disappoints the thousands who trek here every year. The guided tour lasts forty minutes (commentary in French or English). If you have bought the joint ticket to include entry into **Le Thot prehistoric theme park** (Feb, March & mid-Nov to Dec Tues–Sun 10am–12.30pm & 2–5.30pm; April–June & Sept daily 10am–6pm; July & Aug daily 10am–7pm; Oct to mid-Nov daily 10am–12.30pm & 2–6pm; closed Jan; €5.20 for Le Thot alone, €9 for joint ticket; Ⓦwww.semitour.com), 5km down the Vézère near **THONAC**, it's best to visit the park first for an enhanced appreciation of the cave itself, particularly if you have kids. The video showing the construction of Lascaux II is particularly interesting, and there are Disneyesque mock-ups of prehistoric scenes and live examples of some of the animals that feature in the paintings: European bison, long-horned cattle and Przewalski's horses, rare and beautiful animals from Mongolia believed to resemble the prehistoric wild horse – notice the erect mane.

St-Amand-de-Coly

Nine kilometres east of Montignac, the village of **ST-AMAND-DE-COLY** boasts a superbly beautiful fortified Romanesque church, a magical venue for concerts in the summer. Despite its bristling military architecture, the twelfth-century church manages to combine great delicacy and spirituality, with its purity of line and simple decoration most evocative in the low sun of late afternoon or early evening. Its defences left nothing to chance: the walls are 4m thick, a ditch runs all the way around, and a passage once skirted the eaves, with numerous positions for archers to rain down arrows and blind stairways to mislead attackers. Near the church, the simple *Hôtel Gardette* (ⓣ05.53.51.68.50, ⓦwww.hotel-gardette.com; ❷; restaurant from €15, closed Oct–Easter) makes it possible to stay overnight in this tiny, idyllic place.

The upper Dordogne

East of Bergerac the River Dordogne is at its most appealing, forming great loops between rich fields, wooded hills and craggy outcrops. The stretch around **Beynac** and **La Roque-Gageac** is particularly spectacular, with clifftop châteaux facing each other across the valley. The most imposing of these châteaux date from the Hundred Years War, when the river marked the frontier between French-held land to the north and English territory to the south.

Just south of the river, the **Abbaye de Cadouin** lies tucked out of harm's way in a fold of the landscape, hiding a lovely Gothic cloister. Further upstream there are marvellous examples of Romanesque sculpture in the churches at **Souillac** and **Beaulieu**, and superbly preserved medieval villages at **Martel** and **Carennac**, both much less touristy than Sarlat or the *bastide* village of **Domme**. Public transport is poor, although you can reach Souillac, Bretenoux, Beaulieu and Argentat by train or bus. Alternatively, you can paddle downstream by canoe all the way from Argentat to Beynac (see box, p.740 for details).

The Abbaye de Cadouin

Before setting off up the Dordogne, it's worth taking a detour about 6km south of **Le Buisson** to the twelfth-century Cistercian **Abbaye de Cadouin**. For eight hundred years until 1935 it drew flocks of pilgrims to wonder at a piece of cloth first mentioned by Simon de Montfort in 1214 and thought to be part of Christ's shroud. In 1935 the two bands of embroidery at either end of the cloth were shown to contain an Arabic text from around the eleventh century. Since then the main attraction has been the finely sculpted but badly damaged capitals of the flamboyant Gothic **cloister** (Feb & March daily except Tues 10am–12.30pm & 2–5.30pm; April–June & Sept to mid-Nov daily except Tues 10am–12.30pm & 2–6pm; July & Aug daily 10am–7pm; mid-Nov to Dec Mon, Wed, Thurs & Sun 10am–12.30pm & 2–5.30pm; €5.20; ⓦwww.semitour.com). Beside it stands a Romanesque **church** with a stark, bold front and wooden belfry roofed with chestnut shingles (chestnut trees abound around here – their timber was used in furniture-making and their nuts ground for flour during the formerly frequent famines). Inside the church, the nave is slightly out of alignment; this is thought to be deliberate and perhaps a vestige of pagan attachments, as the three windows are aligned so that at the winter and summer solstices the sun shines through all three in a single shaft.

You can **stay** across the road from the abbey at the *Restaurant de l'Abbaye* (ⓣ05.53.63.40.93, ⓕ05.53.63.40.28; ❷; closed Sun eve & Mon), which has five simple en-suite rooms and serves reasonably priced meals (menus from €11.50), or in the monks' dormitories themselves, now an excellent HI **youth hostel** (ⓣ05.53.73.28.78, ⓔcadouin@fuaj.org; closed mid-Dec to Jan). There's also a small municipal **campsite** on the Monpazier road (ⓣ05.53.63.46.43, ⓕ05.53.73.36.72; closed mid-Sept to mid-June).

Another possibility is to stay in the hilltop town of **BELVÈS**, some 15km further east along the D54. The *Hôtel Le Home*, on the through road at the top of the hill, provides good cheap **accommodation** and food (ⓣ05.53.29.01.65, ⓕ05.53.59.46.99; ❷; closed Sun & two weeks at Christmas; restaurant from €10). Next door is the more upmarket *Belvédère* (ⓣ05.53.31.51.41, ⓦwww.belvedere-perigord.com; ❸; closed Oct–March; restaurant €12–35, closed for lunch Mon–Wed), or there's the very comfortable *Hôtel Clément V* on rue Machotte, the main shopping street (ⓣ05.53.28.68.80, ⓦwww.clement5.com; ❸). The nearest **campsite** is the three-star *Les Nauves* (ⓣ05.53.29.12.64, ⓔcampinglesnauves@hotmail.com; closed Oct–March), 4.5km off the Monpazier road, and there's a small *camping à la ferme* called *Le Bon Accueil* (ⓣ05.53.28.16.20; closed Oct–April) 5km southeast of Belvès near St-Amand-de-Belvès.

The châteaux of Les Milandes, Fayrac and Castelnaud

The first of the string of châteaux that line the Dordogne east of Le Buisson is **Les Milandes** (daily April–June, Sept & Oct 10am–6.15pm; July & Aug 9.30am–7.30pm; €7.50; ⓦwww.milandes.com), perched high on the south bank. Built in 1489, it was the property of the de Caumont family until the

Josephine Baker and the Rainbow Tribe

Born on June 3, 1906, in the black ghetto of East St Louis, Illinois, **Josephine Baker** was one of the most remarkable women of the twentieth century. Her mother washed clothes for a living, her father a drummer who soon deserted his family, yet by the late 1920s Josephine was the most celebrated cabaret star in France, primarily due to her role in the legendary Folies Bergères show in Paris. On her first night, de Gaulle, Hemingway, Piaf and Stravinsky were among the audience, and her notoriety was further enhanced by her long line of illustrious husbands and lovers, which included the Crown Prince of Sweden and the crime novelist Georges Simenon. She also mixed with the likes of Le Corbusier and Adolf Loos, and kept a pet cheetah called Mildred, with whom she used to walk around Paris. During the war, she was active in the Resistance, for which she won the Croix de Guerre. Later on, she became involved in the civil rights movement in North America, where she insisted on playing to non-segregated audiences, a stance which got her arrested in Canada and tailed by the FBI in the US.

By far her most bizarre project was the château of **Les Milandes**, which she rented from 1936 and then bought in 1947, after her marriage to the French orchestra leader Jo Bouillon. Having equipped the place with two hotels, three restaurants, a mini-golf course, tennis court and an autobiographical wax museum, she opened the château to the general public as a model multicultural community, popularly dubbed the "village du monde". In the course of the 1950s, she adopted babies (mostly orphans) of different ethnic and religious backgrounds from around the world, and by the end of the decade, she had brought twelve children to Les Milandes, including a black Catholic Colombian and a Buddhist Korean, along with her mother, brother and sister from East St Louis.

Over 300,000 people a year visited the château in the 1950s, but the conservative local population were never very happy about Les Milandes and what Josephine dubbed her "Rainbow Tribe". In the 1960s, Baker's financial problems, divorce and two heart attacks spelled the end for the project, and despite a sit-in protest by Baker herself (by then in her sixties), the château was sold off in 1968. Josephine died of a stroke in 1975 and was given a grand state funeral at La Madeleine in Paris, mourned by thousands of her adopted countryfolk.

Revolution, but its most famous owner was the Folies Bergères star, Josephine Baker (see box, p.737), who lived here from 1936 to 1968. The stories surrounding the place are more intriguing than the château itself, which contains a motley collection of Ms Baker's effects.

Further along on the same side of the river, the **Château de Fayrac** was an English forward position in the Hundred Years War, built to watch over Beynac, on the opposite bank, where the French were holed up. All slated pepper-pot towers, it's unfortunately closed to the public, but you can visit the partially ruined **Château de Castelnaud** (daily: Feb–April & Oct to mid-Nov 10am–6pm; May, June & Sept 10am–7pm; July & Aug 9am–8pm; mid-Nov to Jan 2–5pm; €6.60; Ⓦwww.castelnaud.com), a little to the south of Fayrac and the true rival to Beynac in terms of impregnability – although it was successfully captured by the bellicose Simon de Montfort as early as 1214. The English held it for much of the Hundred Years War, and it wasn't until the Revolution that it was finally abandoned. Fairly heavily restored in the last two decades, it now houses a highly informative **museum of medieval warfare**. Its core is an extensive collection of original weaponry, including all sorts of bizarre contraptions, and a fine assortment of armour.

Beynac

Clearly visible on an impregnable cliff edge on the north bank of the river, the eye-catching village and castle of **BEYNAC-ET-CAZENAC** (generally shortened to Beynac) was built in the days when the river was the only route open to traders and invaders. By road, it's 3km to the **château** (daily: March–Sept 10am–6pm, Oct & Nov 10am–dusk, Dec–Feb noon–dusk; €7) but a steep lane leads up through the village and takes only fifteen minutes by foot. It's protected on the landward side by a double wall; elsewhere the sheer drop of almost 200m does the job. The flat terrace at the base of the keep, which was added by the English, conceals the remains of the houses where the beleaguered villagers lived; one of the houses has been partly excavated. Richard the Lionheart held the place for a time, until a gangrenous wound received while besieging the castle of Châlus, north of Périgueux ended his term of blood-letting.

Originally, to facilitate defence, the rooms inside the keep were only connected by a narrow spiral staircase – in stone, not wood as in the reconstruction, because of the danger of fire. The division of domestic space into dining rooms and so forth only came about when the advent of artillery made these old châteaux-forts militarily obsolete. From the roof there's a stupendous – and vertiginous – view upriver to the **Château de Marqueyssac**, whose beautiful seventeenth- and nineteenth-century **gardens** extend along the ridge (daily: mid-Feb to March & Oct to mid-Nov 10am–6pm; April–June & Sept 10am–7pm; July & Aug 9am–8pm; mid-Nov to mid-Feb 2–5pm; €5.20).

Beynac's best all-round **hotel** is the *Du Château*, on the main road beside the turn-off to the château (Ⓣ05.53.29.19.20, Ⓦwww.hotelduchateau-dordogne.com; ❸), with a good restaurant serving menus from €16 (closed Mon) on its riverside terrace. Next choice would be the nearby *Hostellerie Maleville* (Ⓣ05.53.29.50.06, Ⓦwww.hostellerie-maleville.com; ❸; closed Jan; restaurant from €15), which has the benefit that rooms in its annex are off the main drag, or there's the simple and old-fashioned *Hôtel Bonnet* (Ⓣ05.53.29.50.01, Ⓦwww.hotelbonnet.com; ❸; closed Nov–March; restaurant from €15) on the eastern outskirts of Beynac. There's also a riverside **campsite**, *Le Capeyrou* (Ⓣ05.53.29.54.95, Ⓔlecapeyrou@wanadoo.fr; closed mid-Sept to mid-May) a little further east again.

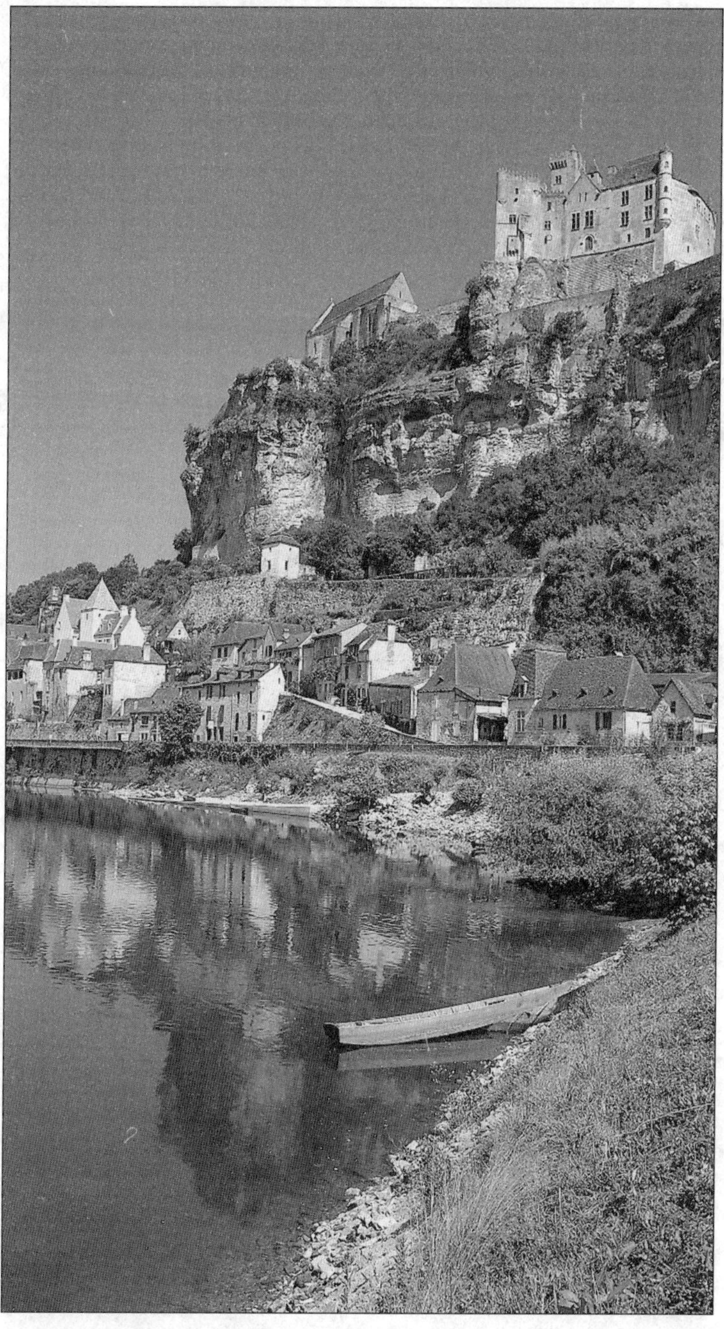

△ The Dordogne at Beynac

La Roque-Gageac

The village of **LA ROQUE-GAGEAC** is almost too perfect, its ochre-coloured houses sheltering under dramatically overhanging cliffs. Regular winner of France's prettiest village contest, it inevitably pulls in the tourist buses, and since the main road separates the village from the river, the noise and fumes of the traffic can become oppressive. The best way to escape is to slip away through the lanes and alleyways that wind up through the terraced houses. The other option is to rent a canoe and paddle over to the opposite bank, where you can picnic and enjoy a great view of the village, at its best in the burnt-orange glow of the evening sun.

Canoeing on the Dordogne and Vézère

Canoeing is hugely popular in the Dordogne, especially during the summer months when the Vézère and Dordogne rivers are shallow and slow-flowing – ideal for beginners. There are rental outlets at just about every twist in both rivers, and although it's possible to rent one-person kayaks or two-person canoes by the hour, it's best to take at least a half-day or longer, and simply cruise downstream. The company you book through will either take you to your departure point or send a minibus to pick you up from your final destination. **Prices** vary according to what's on offer; expect to pay around €18–20 per day. Most places function daily in July and August, on demand in May, June and September, and are closed the rest of the year. All companies are obliged to equip you with lifejackets (*gilets*) and teach you basic safety procedures, most importantly how to capsize and get out without drowning. You must be able to swim. Below are just a handful of the choices on offer.

River Dordogne

Cénac Périgord Loisirs Cénac ⓣ05.53.29.99.69, ⓔcpl.infos@wanadoo.fr. Based near Domme, offering a choice of distances from 12km to 25km between Calviac and Beynac.

Canoë Dordogne La Roque-Gageac ⓣ05.53.29.58.50, ⓦwww.canoe-dordogne.fr. Ideally placed to paddle downstream past Castelnaud, Beynac and Les Milandes. Choice of three distances: 7km, 14km or 21km.

Canoë Loisirs Vitrac ⓣ05.53.28.23.43, ⓦwww.perigord-insolite.net. Rental available from their bases at Vitrac and Cénac to be picked up at Castelnaud or Beynac.

Copeyre Canoë Souillac ⓣ05.65.37.33.51, ⓦwww.copeyre.com. Ten bases from Argentat to Beynac; choose your own day-trip or longer outings of up to seven days.

Safaraid Albas ⓣ05.65.30.74.47, ⓦwww.canoe-dordogne.com. Eight bases from Argentat to Beynac; choose your own route, with rental available by the hour, day, week or longer.

River Vézère

Canoës Vallée Vézère Les Eyzies ⓣ05.53.05.10.11, ⓦwww.canoesvalleevezere.com. You can choose your distance, starting at a number of locations between Montignac and Les Eyzies and downstream stopping between Les Eyzies and Trémolat.

Canoës Les 7 Rives Montignac ⓣ05.53.50.19.26, ⓔbernau@wanadoo.fr. Choice of distances downstream to Thonac, St-Léon or La Roque St-Christophe.

Les Trois Drapeaux Les Eyzies ⓣ05.53.06.91.89, ⓦwww.les3drapeaux.com. Choice of excursions between the Château de Losse, near Thonac, and Les Eyzies.

Most people just come here for the afternoon, so there's usually space if you want to **stay** the night, most pleasantly at *La Belle Étoile* (Ⓣ05.53.29.51.44, Ⓔhotel.belle-etoile@wanadoo.fr; ❸; closed Nov–March), whose restaurant serves good traditional cuisine (from €23, closed Mon & lunch Wed). Of the many **campsites** in the vicinity, *Le Lauzier* (Ⓣ05.53.29.54.59, Ⓕ05.53.29.51.66; closed mid-Sept to mid-June) is one of the closest, while *Le Beau Rivage* (Ⓣ05.53.28.32.05, Ⓦwww.camping-beau-rivage.com; closed Oct to mid-March) offers the greatest luxury; they're both east of La Roque on the D703 Sarlat road.

Domme

High on the scarp on the south bank of the river, **DOMME** is one of the best preserved of the *bastides*, although it's now wholly given over to tourism. Its attractions, in addition to its position, include three original thirteenth-century **gateways** and a section of the old **walls**. From the northern edge of the village, marked by a drop so precipitous that fortifications were deemed unnecessary, you look out over a wide sweep of river country. Beneath the village is a warren of **caves** (Feb–June & Sept to mid-Nov daily 10am–noon & 2–6pm; July & Aug daily 10am–7pm; mid-Nov to Dec Mon–Fri 10am–noon & 2–6pm; €6) in which the townspeople took refuge in times of danger. The entrance to the complex is opposite the **tourist office** (same hours as the caves; Ⓣ05.53.31.71.00, Ⓦwww.domme-tourisme.com) on the main square, though there's not a lot to see.

The smartest **hotel** in town is *L'Esplanade*, right on the cliff edge (Ⓣ05.53.28.31.41, Ⓔesplanade.domme@wanadoo.fr; ❺; closed mid-Nov to Feb), with a fine restaurant (menus €30–90); note that rooms with a view are premium-rated. A cheaper alternative is *Le Nouvel Hôtel*, at the top of the Grand'rue (Ⓣ05.53.28.38.67, Ⓦwww.domme-nouvel-hotel.com; ❸; closed Sun eve & Mon, also mid-Nov to Easter), which has several simple, reasonably priced rooms above a restaurant (menus €16–30). The closest **campsite** is the municipal site (Ⓣ05.53.28.31.91, Ⓕ05.53.31.41.32; closed mid-Sept to May) down by the river at **Cénac**.

Souillac

The first place of any size east of Sarlat is **SOUILLAC**, at the confluence of the Borrèze and Dordogne rivers and on a major road junction. Virginia Woolf stayed here in 1937, and was pleased to meet "no tourists … England seems like a chocolate box bursting with trippers afterward." There are still few tourists, since Souillac's only real point of interest is the twelfth-century **church of Ste-Marie**, just off the main road. Roofed with massive domes like the cathedrals of Périgueux and Cahors, its spacious interior creates just the atmosphere for cool reflection on a summer's day. On the inside of the west door are some of the most wonderful Romanesque sculptures, including a seething mass of beasts devouring each other. The greatest piece of craftsmanship, though, is a **bas-relief of Isaiah**, fluid and supple, thought to be by one of the artists who worked at Moissac. Next to the church, the **Musée de l'Automate** (Jan–March, Nov & Dec Wed–Sun 2.30–5.30pm; April, May & Oct Tues–Sun 10am–noon & 3–6pm; June & Sept daily 10am–noon & 3–6pm; July & Aug daily 10am–7pm; €5) contains an impressive collection of nineteenth- and twentieth-century mechanical dolls and animals, which dance, sing and perform magical tricks; look out for the irresistible laughing man.

The **tourist office** (July & Aug Mon–Sat 9.30am–12.30pm & 2–7pm, Sun 10am–noon & 3–5pm; Sept–June Mon–Sat 10am–noon & 2–6pm;

Ⓣ05.65.37.81.56, Ⓦwww.tourisme-souillac.com) is on the main boulevard Louis-Jean Malvy, next to the *Grand Hôtel* (Ⓣ05.65.32.78.30, Ⓦwww.grandhotel-souillac.com; ❸; closed Nov–March; restaurant from €14.50), all rather glitzy after its recent renovation but offering a range of comfortable rooms. There's cheaper **accommodation** at the *Auberge du Puits*, in the pretty place du Puits in the old quarter (Ⓣ05.65.37.80.32, Ⓦwww.auberge-du-puits.fr; ❶; closed Dec & Jan), with a good restaurant (menus from €15.40; closed Sat lunch, Sun eve and Mon), while Souillac's most upmarket hotel is *La Vieille Auberge* at 1 rue de la Recège, also in the old quarter (Ⓣ05.65.32.79.43, Ⓦwww.la-vieille-auberge.com; ❸; closed mid-Nov to mid-Dec; restaurant from €25, closed Sun eve, Mon and lunch Tues). There's also a large riverside **campsite**, *Les Ondines* (Ⓣ05.65.37.86.44; closed Oct–Easter). You can rent **bicycles and canoes** from Copeyre Canoë (Ⓣ05.65.32.72.61), next to the campsite, and bikes only from Carrefour du Cycle, 23 av de Gaulle (Ⓣ05.65.37.07.52).

Martel

About 15km east of Souillac and set back even further from the river, **MARTEL** is a minor medieval masterpiece, built in a pale, almost white, stone, offset by warm reddish-brown roofs, yet it suffers none of the crowds endured by the likes of Sarlat. A Turenne-administered town (see p.757), its heyday came during the thirteenth and fourteenth centuries, when the viscounts established a court of appeal here.

The main square, **place des Consuls**, is mostly taken up by the eighteenth-century **market hall**, but on every side there are reminders of the town's illustrious past, most notably in the superb Gothic **Hôtel de la Raymondie**. Begun in 1280, it served as the Turenne law courts, though it doubled as the town's refuge, hence the distinctive corner turrets. Facing the hôtel is the **Tour des Pénitents**, one of the many medieval towers which gave the town its epithet, *la ville aux sept tours* ("the town with seven towers"). The Young King Henry, son of Henry II (see box, below) died in the striking building in the southeast corner of the square, the **Maison Fabri**. One block south, rue Droite leads east to the town's main **church**, St-Maur, built in a fiercely defensive, mostly Gothic style, with a finely carved Romanesque tympanum depicting the Last Judgement above the west door.

The tale of Young King Henry

At the end of the twelfth century, Martel was the stage for one of the tragic events in the internecine conflicts of the Plantagenet family. When Henry Plantagenet (King Henry II of England) imprisoned his estranged wife Eleanor of Aquitaine, his sons took up arms against their father. The eldest son, also **Henry** (nicknamed the Young King since he was crowned while his father was still on the throne), even went so far as to plunder the viscountcy of Turenne and Quercy. Furious, Henry II immediately stopped his allowance and handed over his lands to the third son, Richard the Lionheart. Financially insecure, and with a considerable army of soldiers to feed and clothe, Young King Henry began looting the treasures of every abbey and shrine in the region. Finally, he decided to sack the shrine at Rocamadour, making off with various artefacts, including Roland's famous sword, Durandal. This last act was to be his downfall, for shortly afterwards he fled to Martel and fell ill with a fever. Guilt-ridden and afraid for his life, he confessed his crimes and asked his father for forgiveness. Henry II was busy besieging Limoges, but sent a messenger to pardon him. On the messenger's arrival in Martel, young Henry died, and Richard the Lionheart became heir to the English throne.

If you'd rather **stay** here than in Souillac, head for the *Auberge des 7 Tours* (Ⓣ05.65.37.30.16, Ⓦwww.auberge7tours.com; ❷; closed Feb school holidays; restaurant from €12, closed Sat lunch, Sun eve & Mon), or treat yourself to a spot of luxury at the *Relais Ste-Anne* (Ⓣ05.65.36.40.56, Ⓦwww.relais-sainte-anne.com; ❺; closed mid-Nov to mid-March). There's a basic municipal **campsite**, *La Callopie* (Ⓣ05.65.37.30.03, Ⓕ05.65.37.37.27; closed Oct–April), on the northern edge of town, and the more attractive riverside *Camping les Falaises* (Ⓣ05.65.37.37.78, Ⓕ05.65.32.20.40; closed Oct–April), 5km away in the village of **Gluges**, where you can also rent **canoes and bikes** from Copeyre Canoë down by the water (see box, p.740).

Carennac and Castelnau-Bretenoux

CARENNAC is without doubt one of the most beautiful villages along this part of the Dordogne river. Elevated just above the south bank of the river, 13km or so east of Martel, it's best known for its typical Quercy architecture, its Romanesque priory, where the French writer Fénelon spent the best years of his life, and for its greengages.

Carennac's feature, as so often in these parts, is the Romanesque tympanum – in the Moissac style – above the west door of its church, the **église St-Pierre**. Christ sits in majesty with the Book of Judgement in his left hand, with the apostles and adoring angels below him. Next to the church, you can gain access to the old **cloisters and chapterhouse** (Jan–March and Oct–Dec Mon–Sat 10am–noon & 2–5pm; April & May Mon–Sat 10am–noon & 2–6pm; June & Sept Mon–Sat 10am–noon & 2–6.30pm; July & Aug daily 10am–12.30pm & 2–7pm; €2), which contain an exceptionally expressive life-size Entombment of Christ.

There are two comfortable and reasonably priced **hotels** in the village, both with good **restaurants** specializing in traditional regional cuisine: the *Auberge du Vieux Quercy*, to the south of the church (Ⓣ05.65.10.96.59, Ⓦwww.vieuxquercy.com; ❹; closed mid-Nov to March), whose restaurant offers well-priced menus from €18 (closed for lunch Mon–Fri); and the more rustic *Hostellerie Fénelon* on the main street (Ⓣ05.65.10.96.46, Ⓦwww.hotel-fenelon.com; ❸; closed Jan to mid-March; restaurant from €19, closed Fri, also lunchtime Sat & Mon). There's also a **campsite**, *L'Eau Vive*, 1km east of Carennac (Ⓣ05.65.10.97.39, Ⓔinfo@dordogne-soleil.com; closed mid-Oct to April).

Another 10km further upstream, the sturdy towers and machicolated red-brown walls of the eleventh-century **Château de Castelnau-Bretenoux** (May & June daily 9.30am–12.30pm & 2–6.30pm; July & Aug daily 9.30am–7pm; Sept–April daily except Tues 10am–12.30pm & 2–5.30pm; €6.10) dominate a sharp knoll above the Dordogne. Most of it has now been restored and refurnished. Below, on the banks of the River Cère, you come to the graceful little *bastide* of **BRETENOUX**, with two sides of its cobbled and arcaded square still intact.

Beaulieu-sur-Dordogne

Beautifully situated on the banks of the Dordogne, 8km upriver from Castelnau-Bretenoux, **BEAULIEU-SUR-DORDOGNE** boasts another of the great masterpieces of Romanesque sculpture on the porch of the **church of St-Pierre** in the centre of town. This doorway is unusually deep-set, with a tympanum presided over by an oriental-looking Christ with one arm extended to welcome the chosen. All around him is a complicated pattern of angels and apostles, executed in characteristic "dancing" style, similar to that at Carennac. The dead raise the lids of their coffins hopefully, while underneath a frieze depicts monsters crunching heads. Take the opportunity also to wander north along rue de la Chapelle past some handsome sculpted facades and down to the river.

The most appealing **hotel** is the riverside *Les Charmilles*, on the northeast side of town (Ⓣ05.55.91.29.29, Ⓦwww.auberge-charmilles.com; ❸; restaurant from €17), with *Le Turenne*, in a former abbey on central place Marbot (Ⓣ05.55.91.10.16, Ⓦwww.hotel-le-turenne.com; ❸; menus €15–65), coming a close second. The welcoming HI **hostel** is at the far end of rue de la Chapelle in a magnificent half-timbered and turreted building, with surprisingly modern rooms inside (Ⓣ05.55.91.13.82, Ⓔbeaulieu@fuaj.org; closed Nov–March). There are river-bathing and canoeing possibilities and a good riverside **campsite**, *Camping des Îles*, close by (Ⓣ05.55.91.02.65, Ⓦwww.camping-des-iles.net; closed mid-Oct to mid-April).

Argentat

Further upstream, **ARGENTAT** is the last major town on the Dordogne and the last part of the river accessible by anything other than foot. Beyond Argentat, the Dordogne changes character entirely, due to the series of hydroelectric dams (*barrages*) that turn the river into a succession of grand reservoirs.

Argentat's whitewashed houses and rather sombre grey slate rooftops make a distinct change from the warm yellow stone of the rest of the Dordogne. It's easy enough to while away an hour or so sitting at one of the riverbank cafés or exploring the cobbled alleyways which slope down to the river. But there's nothing else to make you stay, except for the comfortable, reasonably priced **rooms** at *Le Sablier du Temps*, 13 rue Joseph-Vachal (Ⓣ05.55.28.94.90, Ⓦwww.logis-de-france.fr; ❸; closed Feb school holidays; restaurant from €12, closed Fri eve and Sat lunch), and at the recently renovated *Hôtel Fouillade*, 11 place Gambetta (Ⓣ05.55.28.10.17, Ⓦwww.fouillade.com; ❸; closed mid-Nov to mid-Dec). The latter has the added attraction of an excellent restaurant (from €12; closed Sun eve & Mon).

The Limousin

The **Limousin** – the country around **Limoges** – is hilly, wooded, wet and not particularly fertile: ideal pasture for the famous Limousin breed of cattle. This is herdsman's country, from where – presumably – the widespread use of the shepherd's cape known as a limousine gave its name to the big, wraparound, covered twentieth-century car.

The modern Limousin region stretches south to the Dordogne valley to include **Brive** and **Tulle**. But while these places, together with Limoges itself, are not without interest, the star of the show is the countryside – especially in the east on the **Plateau de Millevaches** round **Eymoutiers**, **Meymac** and **La Courtine**. Walkers, cyclists and other outdoor sports enthusiasts are well catered for and there are plenty of small hotels, *gîtes* and campsites to accommodate the wanderer. Although the region is remote and sparsely populated, a mountain rail line still survives, connecting Limoges and **Ussel**.

Limoges

LIMOGES is not a city that calls for a long stay, but it's worth a look for a magnificent Art Deco train station and the craft industries that made the city a household name: enamel in the Middle Ages and, since the eighteenth century, china, including some of the finest ever produced. If these appeal, then the city's unique museum collections – and its Gothic cathedral – will reward a visit. But it has to be said that the industry today seems a spent tradition, hard hit by recession and changing tastes among the rich. The local *kaolin* (china clay) mines that gave Limoges china its special quality are exhausted, and the workshops survive mainly on the tourist trade.

Arrival, information and accommodation

The town is built on high ground overlooking the River Vienne, with a small, attractive city centre enclosed by modern boulevards. The cathe-

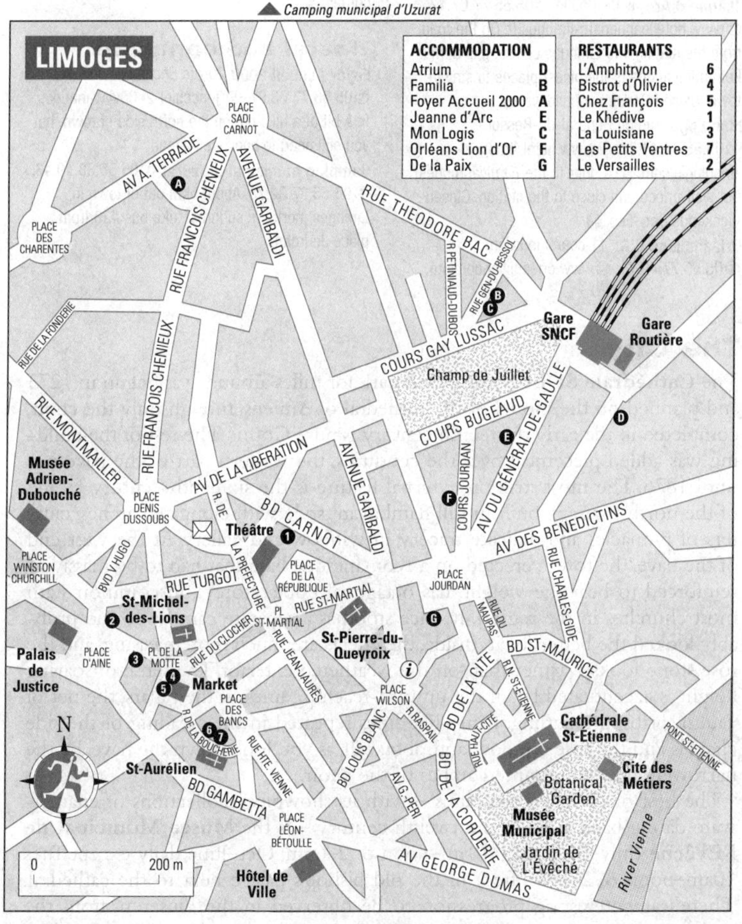

dral stands directly above the river, with the main commercial streets behind it. The magnificent **gare des Bénédictins** and neighbouring **gare routière** (Ⓣ05.55.45.10.72) lie slightly off to the northeast, connected to the chestnut-shaded place Jourdan by avenue de Gaulle. The **tourist office** is on place Wilson (April–June 14 & Sept 16–30 Mon & Sat 9am–noon & 2–7pm, Tues–Fri 9am–7pm; June 15–Sept 15 Mon–Sat 9am–7pm, Sun 10am–6pm; Oct–March Mon–Sat 9am–noon & 2–7pm; Ⓣ05.55.34.46.87, Ⓦwww.tourismelimoges.com).

Hotels

Atrium Ⓣ05.55.10.75.75, Ⓦwww.inter-hotel.com. New and functional three-star beside the station. Restaurant from €17. ❹

Familia 18 rue du Général-du-Bessol Ⓣ05.55.77.51.40, Ⓕ05.55.10.27.69. A cheap and spotless option in a quiet back street near the station. ❷

Jeanne d'Arc av de-Gaulle Ⓣ05.55.77.67.77, Ⓦwww.hoteljeannedarc-limoges.fr. On the road from the station into Limoges centre, this upmarket option is one of the nicest places to stay in town. Closed Christmas holidays. ❹

Mon Logis rue du Général-du-Bessol Ⓣ05.55.77.41.43, Ⓦwww.hotel-limoges-monlogis.com. Next door to the *Familia*; modest but well-priced and close to the station. Closed weekends Dec–Feb. ❶

Orléans Lion d'Or 11 cours Jourdan Ⓣ05.55.77.49.71, Ⓦwww.orleansliondor.com. A reliable mid-range hotel located between the station and the old town. Closed two weeks at Christmas. ❸

De la Paix place Jourdan Ⓣ05.55.34.36.00, Ⓕ05.55.32.37.06. The best value in town is to be found at this atmospheric – but very spruce – old hotel a short walk from the old centre. Though on a fairly busy square, it's tucked into its quietest corner. ❷

Hostel and campsite

Foyer Accueil 2000 20 rue Encombe-Vineuse Ⓣ05.55.77.63.97, Ⓔfjt.accuiel-2000@wanadoo.fr. A bit of a hike out on the north side of town, but you still need to book well ahead.

Camping municipal d'Uzurat Ⓣ05.55.38.49.43, Ⓕ05.55.37.32.78. About 5km out of town in Limoges' northern suburbs; take bus #20 from place Jourdan.

The City

The **Cathédrale St-Étienne**, a landmark for miles around, was begun in 1273 and planned on the model of the cathedral of Amiens, though only the choir, completed in the early thirteenth century, is pure Gothic. The rest of the building was added piecemeal over the centuries, the western part of the nave not until 1876. The most striking external feature is the sixteenth-century facade of the north transept, built in full flamboyant style with elongated arches, clusters of pinnacles and delicate tracery in window and gallery. At the west end of the nave, the tower, erected on a Romanesque base that had to be massively reinforced to bear the weight, has octagonal upper storeys, in common with most churches in the region. It once stood as a separate campanile and probably looked the better for it. Inside, the effects are much more pleasing, and the rose stone looks warmer than on the weathered exterior. The sense of soaring height is accentuated by all the upward-reaching lines of the pillars, the net of vaulting ribs, the curling, flame-like lines repeated in the arcading of the side chapels and the rose window, and, above all, as you look down the nave, by the narrower and more pointed arches of the choir.

The best of the city's museums – with its showpiece collections of enamelware dating back as far as the twelfth century – is the **Musée Municipal de l'Évêché** (July–Sept daily 10am–noon & 2–6pm; Oct–June daily except Tues 10am–noon & 2–5pm; free) in the old bishop's palace next to the cathedral. There's an interesting progression to be observed in the museum, from the simple, sober, Byzantine-influenced *champlevé* (copper filled with enamel), to the later, especially seventeenth- and eighteenth-century work that used a far greater range of colours and indulged in elaborate virtuoso portraiture. By the nineteenth century, however, the spirit and vigour had dissipated, and although there are contemporary artisans in the city using the medium, their work, too – judging from this display – is not much more successful. There's also an **exhibition** of the wartime Resistance (same hours; free) housed in an outbuilding opposite the museum's main entrance.

Outside, the well-laid-out and interesting **botanical garden** (daily sunrise to sunset; free) is an inviting prospect, descending gracefully towards the River Vienne. In the garden's northern corner an old refectory now houses the excellent **Cité des Métiers et des Arts** (Easter–May & Oct Wed, Sat & Sun 2–6pm; June–Sept daily 10.30am–1pm & 2.30–7pm; €4) displaying pieces – mostly carpentry – by France's top crafts' guild members.

Over to the west of the cathedral is the partly renovated **old quarter** of the town. Make your way through to rue de la Boucherie, for a thousand years the domain of the butchers' guild, and today featuring several good restaurants. The dark, cluttered **chapel of St-Aurélien**, with a delicate fourteenth-century cross outside, belongs to them, while one of their former shophouses makes an interesting little museum, the **Maison de la Boucherie**, at no. 36 (July–Sept daily 10am–1pm & 2.30–7pm; free). At the top of the street is the **market** in place de la Motte and, to the right, partly hidden by adjoining houses, the fourteenth- and fifteenth-century **church of St-Michel-des-Lions**, named after the two badly weathered Celtic lions guarding the south door and topped by one of the best towers and spires in the region. The inside is dark and atmospheric, with two beautiful, densely coloured fifteenth-century windows either side of the choir.

From place de la Motte, rue du Clocher leads to rue Jean-Jaurès, with the **post office** a couple of blocks up to the left. Straight across, rue St-Martial leads past place de la République – where the fourth-century crypt of the long-vanished **Abbey of St-Martial** (July–Sept daily 10am–noon & 2–7pm; free), containing the saint's massive sarcophagus, was discovered during building operations in the 1960s – to the **church of St-Pierre-du-Queyroix** under another typically Limousin belfry. The interior, partly twelfth-century (the exterior was remodelled in the sixteenth century), gains a sombre strength from the massive round pillars which still support the roof. Like the cathedral, it has a slightly pink granite glow. There's more fine stained glass here, including an eye-catching window at the end of the south aisle depicting the Dormition of the Virgin, signed by the great enamel artist Jean Pénicault in 1510.

Limoges is renowned the world over for its **porcelain**, a craft well represented in the **Musée Adrien-Dubouché** (daily except Tues: July & Aug 10am–5.45pm; Sept–June 10am–12.30pm & 2–5.45pm; €4, Ⓦwww.musee-adriendubouche.fr), west of the old quarter on place Winston-Churchill. The collection includes samples of the local product and china displays from around the world, as well as various celebrity services ordered for the likes of Napoleon Bonaparte, Charles and Di, and sundry French royals. The exhibits are well laid out, with explanatory panels describing the processes for making the different wares, and form a much more interesting display than you might expect.

Eating, drinking and festivals

Limoges has an abundance of good and not too expensive **places to eat**. For **drinks** at any time of the day, people sit out in the not very attractive place de la République; a nicer option is lively place Denis Dussoubs, a short walk further west, where you'll find fine beers on tap at the Michard micro-brewery (closed Sun). Over on the other side of town, the *Lord John* pub on avenue de-Gaulle near the train station – complete with darts – is a popular hangout, with live jazz on Thursdays (except July & Aug).

Cafés and restaurants

L'Amphitryon 26 rue de la Boucherie ⓣ05.55.33.36.39. There's no better place for a real treat of subtle and sophisticated cuisine – foie gras and a tagine of pigeon and dates, for example – than this chic restaurant opposite the St-Aurélien chapel. Their lunch menus start at €18 and at €26 for dinner. Closed Sun, Mon lunch & three weeks in Aug.

Chez François place de la Motte. For a good-value lunch and a lively atmosphere, head straight to the central market hall to join the locals round communal tables. Menus €9 & €15. Closed Sun & Aug.

Le Khédive 39 bd Carnot. A good choice for a relaxed lunch or dinner, serving salads and brasserie fare from €8. Closed Sun & Aug.

La Louisiane place d'Aine. Elegant *salon de thé* serving salads, quiches and other light lunches, with great pastries to follow. Closed Sun & Mon.

Bistrot d'Olivier place de la Motte. Next door to *Chez François* in the market hall, and a good alternative if it's full. Menus from €9. Closed Sun & Mon; also July.

Les Petits Ventres, 20 rue de la Boucherie ⓣ05.55.34.22.90. Practically next door to *L'Amphitryon*, this restaurant will delight lovers of brain, brawn, tongue and other unmentionable cuts – though they also do more everyday dishes and even a vegetarian platter. Lunch menus from €11.50, dinner from €17. Closed Sun & Mon.

Le Versailles place d'Aine. Upmarket brasserie-style restaurant that's strong on fish, with menus from €11 to €22.

Festivals

In late September, there's an interesting and important gathering of writers, dramatists and musicians from other French-speaking countries at the **Festival International des Théâtres Francophones** (ⓦwww.fest-theatres-francolesfrancophonies.com). Gourmets should make sure their visit coincides with the third Friday in October for the **Frairie des Petits Ventres**, when the entire population turns out to gorge on everything from pig's trotters to sheep's testicles in the rue de la Boucherie. Otherwise, there's **Urbaka**, a festival of street theatre held at the end of June, and the **Danse émoi** contemporary dance festival every two years in January, the next one being in 2007.

Around Limoges

There's a clutch of villages within a day's reach of Limoges. A route linking places of interest on the south bank of the Vienne, like the **châteaux** of **Rochechouart**, **Châlus**, **Montbrun** and **Nexon** are detailed in the *Route Richard-Cœur-de-Lion* leaflet (available at local tourist offices), so called because of its associations with the English king. The route also takes you near the Roman baths at **Chassenon** and **Solignac**'s abbey church, close by which the **Château de Châlucet** is now reduced to atmospheric ruins. North of the Vienne, the charred walls of **Oradour-sur-Glane** stand testimony to a World War II massacre, while east of Limoges, beyond the attractive market town of **St-Léonard-de-Noblat**, the master weavers of **Aubusson** have been producing tapestries for more than six hundred years.

Visiting all these places really requires a car, but some at least are accessible by a combination of public transport, walking and patient hitching.

Oradour-sur-Glane

Twenty-five kilometres northwest of Limoges and a few kilometres north of the N141 road to Angoulême, the village of **ORADOUR-SUR-GLANE** stands just as the soldiers of the SS left it on June 10, 1944, after killing 642 of the inhabitants in reprisal for attacks by French *maquisards*. The village has been preserved both as a shrine and a chilling reminder of human brutality.

Before entering the village, the **Centre de la Mémoire**, immediately southeast of Oradour on the Limoges road (daily: Feb & Nov–Dec 16 9am–5pm; March–May 14 & Sept 16–Oct 9am–6pm; May 15–Sept 15 9am–7pm; entry to village free, exhibition €6; Ⓦwww.oradour.org), sets the historical context and attempts to answer some of the questions. From here an underground passage leads into the village itself, where a sign admonishes *Souviens-toi* ("Remember"), and the main street leads past roofless houses gutted by fire. Telephone poles, iron bedsteads and gutters are fixed in tormented attitudes where the fire's heat left them; pre-war cars rust in the garages; cooking pots hang over empty grates; last year's grapes hang wizened on a vine whose trellis has long rotted away.

To the north of the village a dolmen-like slab on a shallow plinth covers a crypt containing relics of the dead, and the awful list of names, while to the southeast, by the stream, stands the church where the women and children – five hundred of them – were burnt to death.

The modern village of Oradour has been constructed beside the old, with a 1950s concrete church that tries to be impressive but struggles with the task of commemorating what happened here.

There are **buses** from Limoges to Oradour, or alternatively you can take the train to **ST-JUNIEN** and pick up a bus there. The *Relais de Comodoliac*, 22 av Sadi-Carnot (Ⓣ05.55.02.27.26, Ⓦwww.logis-de-france.fr; ❸), about 1km northwest of the train station, with a garden and a good restaurant (menus €14–33), makes a decent **place to stay** in St-Junien. There's also a **hostel**, 13 rue de St-Amand (Ⓣ & Ⓕ05.55.02.22.79), in an old abbey 500m further west along avenue Sadi-Carnot.

Rochechouart and Chassenon

ROCHECHOUART, a beautiful little walled town roughly 45km west of Limoges, has two claims to fame. Two hundred million years ago it was the site of impact of one of the largest **meteorites** ever to hit earth, a monster 1.5km in diameter and some 6000 million tonnes in weight. The traces of this cosmic calamity still attract the curiosity of astronomers, though the only evidence that a layman might notice is the unusual-looking breccia stone many of the region's older buildings are made of: the squashed, shattered, heat-transformed and reconstituted result of the collision. A small museum in town, the **Espace Meteorite**, 16 rue Jean Parvy (mid-June to mid-Sept & during school holidays Mon–Fri 10am–12.30pm & 1.30–6pm, Sat & Sun 2–6pm; rest of year Mon–Fri 2–6pm; Ⓣ05.55.03.02.70, Ⓦ//perso.wanadoo.fr/pierredelune; €3) attempts to uncover the history of the meteorite with artists' impressions, an interactive model and a collection of other space debris which has reached the Earth.

One building using the stone from the impact is Rochechouart's other source of pride: the handsome **château** that stands at the town's edge. It started life as a rough fortress before 1000 AD, was "modernized" in the thirteenth century (the sawn-off keep and entrance survive from this period) and civilized with Renaissance decoration and additions in the fifteenth. Until it was acquired as the *mairie* in 1832, it had belonged to the de Rochechouart family for 800 years. Today it houses not only the town hall, but also the very well-regarded and adventurous **Musée Départemental d'Art Contemporain** (daily except Tues: March–Sept 10am–12.30pm & 1.30–6pm, Oct to mid-Dec 10am–12.30pm & 2–5pm; €4.60), with an important collection of works by the Dadaist Raoul Haussman, who died in Limoges in 1949. In another room decorated with its original sixteenth-century frescoes of the Labours of Hercules, the British artist, Richard Long, has made a special installation of white stones, while in the garden Guiseppe Penone's metal sculpture grapples with a tree.

The Rochechouart **tourist office** is at 6 rue Victor-Hugo (mid-June to mid-Sept daily 10am–noon & 3–6.30pm; mid-Sept to mid-June Mon–Sat 10am–noon & 3.30–5.30pm; Ⓣ05.55.03.72.73, Ⓦwww.ville-rochechouart.fr). Should you wish to **stay**, the *Hôtel de France*, just outside the old town centre on place Octave-Marquet (Ⓣ05.55.03.77.40, Ⓦwww.logis-de-france.fr; ❶–❷), provides simple lodgings and interesting food (restaurant closed Sun evening & Mon lunch; menus from €11). There's also another recommended restaurant, the *Auberge de la Vallée de la Gorre* (Ⓣ05.55.00.01.27; closed Sun & Mon evenings, also Jan; menus €12–30), in nearby **ST-AUVENT**.

One side trip worth making if you have come this far is to the Roman baths 5km along the Chabanais road at **CHASSENON** (daily guided tours: Easter to mid-May & mid-Sept to mid-Nov 2–5.30pm; mid-May to mid-Sept 10am–noon & 2–7pm; €4.80). The site, known as Cassinomagus in Gallo-Roman times, stood at an important crossroads on the Via Agrippa, the Roman road that connected Lyon to Saintes via Clermont-Ferrand and Limoges. Only the baths survive: a grand temple and theatre were destroyed for their breccia stone. But the baths alone are ample testimony to the magnificence of the place. There are hot and cold pools with some of the original floor tiles in places, and waterproof plastering, boiler rooms and elaborate hypocaust piping systems; you can even see the marks of the shuttering used to make the vaults in some of the subterranean passages.

Châlus and Nexon

The small town of **CHÂLUS**, 35km southwest of Limoges, is dominated by the ruined **Château de Châlus-Chabrol** (not open to the public), where in 1199 Richard the Lionheart was mortally wounded by an archer shooting from the still-extant keep. Richard, son of Eleanor of Aquitaine and as much French as English, was campaigning to suppress a local rebellion against English rule. On capturing the castle, Richard – by now on his deathbed – ordered all the rebels hanged save the archer, whom he pardoned. It was a short-lived reprieve; as soon as Richard was dead, the archer was flayed alive by the captain of the English troops.

Of several other castles around Châlus, the most rewarding is the medieval **Château de Montbrun** (July & Aug daily 11am–6pm; Sept–June Sat & Sun 2pm–5pm; €8), 8km to the southwest. The château, now a private home, has been beautifully restored and furnished, though its best attribute is perhaps its fairytale lakeside location – even more spectacular when floodlit at night. It also offers luxury *chambres d'hôte* **accommodation** (Ⓣ05.55.78.65.26, Ⓔmontbrun@montbrun.com; ❺), and one of the outhouses has been converted into an equally atmospheric restaurant, *La Taverne* (closed Tues & Wed; menus from €15). Otherwise, you can stay in Châlus itself at the simple but reasonably comfortable *Auberge Richard Cœur de Lion*, 29 av Jean-Jaurès (Ⓣ & Ⓕ05.55.78.43.42; ❶–❷), with menus from €12 in its restaurant.

Eighteen kilometres east, past another early medieval fortress at Rilhac-Lastours, the village of **NEXON**, also directly accessible by bus and train from Limoges, is of more general interest, with a fine, heavily restored seventeenth-century **château** (now the *mairie*). The magnificent parkland surrounding the château was once renowned for its stud farm breeding Anglo-Arabs, but nowadays is more famous for the **festival of circus arts** held here each summer (Ⓦwww.cirquenexon.com). There are no hotels in Nexon but you can **camp** at the *Étang de la Lande* (Ⓣ05.55.58.35.44, Ⓕ05.55.58.33.50; closed Oct–May).

Châlucet and Solignac

A dozen kilometres south of Limoges in the lovely wooded valley of the Briance, the Château de Châlucet and the church of **SOLIGNAC** make the most attractive day's outing from the city. There are **trains** to Solignac-Le Vigen station, 1km away on the Limoges–Brive line, and infrequent **bus** services to Solignac itself; you'll have more choice if you take a bus to **LE VIGEN** and walk the final kilometre. Should you wish to stay the night, there's a very pleasant, comfortable **hotel** in Solignac opposite the church, *Le St-Éloi* (Ⓣ05.55.00.44.52, Ⓦwww.lesainteloi.fr; ❸; closed Jan & one week each in Sept & Nov), with a good restaurant (closed Sat lunch, Sun eve & Mon; menus from €13).

Approaching from Le Vigen you can see Solignac's Romanesque **abbey church** (daily 9am–6.30pm; free) ahead of you, with the tiled roofs of its octagonal apse and neat little brood of radiating chapels. The twelfth-century facade is plain with just a little sculpture, as the granite from which it is built is too hard to permit intricate carving. Inside it's beautiful, a flight of steps leading down into the nave with a dramatic view of the length of the church. There are no aisles, just a single space roofed with three big domes, and no ambulatory either – an absolutely plain Latin cross in design. It's a simple, sturdy church, with the same feel of plain robust Christianity as the crypt of St-Eutrope in Saintes.

The **Château de Châlucet** is a good five-kilometre walk up the valley of the Briance in the other direction – uphill quite a lot of the way along the D32 and D32a. After about 45 minutes, at the highest point of the climb, there is a dramatic view across the valley to the romantic, ruined keep of the castle, rising above the woods. It's a further kilometre down to the bridge on the Briance, where a path follows the riverbank before climbing steeply up again into the woods. Built in the twelfth century, the château was in English hands during the Hundred Years War and, in the lawless aftermath, became the lair of a notorious local brigand, Perrot le Béarnais. Dismantled in 1593 for harbouring Protestants, it has recently been acquired by the local authorities who are in the middle of major restoration works, including an archeological dig. It's still possible to visit, though you are restricted to safe areas along fenced-off paths. You can borrow an explanatory guide from the visitors' centre (daily: mid-April to mid-June & mid-Sept to Oct 10am–12.30pm & 1.30–6pm; mid-June to mid-Sept 11am–7pm) on the path up to the ruins.

St-Léonard-de-Noblat

ST-LÉONARD-DE-NOBLAT, twenty minutes by train from Limoges or 35 minutes by bus, is an appealing little market town of narrow streets and medieval houses with jutting eaves and corbelled turrets. There's a very lovely eleventh- and twelfth-century church, whose six-storey tower looks out over the rising hills and woods where the River Vienne threads its course down from the heights of the Massif Central. The interior is strong and simple, with barrel vaults on big, square piles, a high dome on an octagonal drum and domed transepts – the whole in grey granite. A couple of kilometres northwest of town on the banks of the Vienne, demonstrations of papermaking and printing are on offer at a lovingly restored fifteenth-century paper mill, the **Moulin du Got** (Wed, Thurs & Sat 2–6pm; €5; ⓦwww.moulindugot.com).

The **tourist office** on place du Champs-de-Mars (July & Aug Mon–Sat 9.30am–6.30pm, Sun 9.30am–12.30pm; Sept–June Mon–Sat 10.30am–12.30pm & 2.30–5pm; ⓣ05.55.56.25.06, ⓔotsi.stleo@wanadoo.fr) publishes route maps for local walks and will point you to *chambres d'hôte* possibilities round about. A good **place to stay** is the *Relais St-Jacques* on the boulevard encircling the old town (ⓣ05.55.56.00.25, ⓕ05.55.56.19.87; ❸; closed Sun eve & Mon Oct–May; restaurant from €15), and you can **eat** well just round the corner at *Le Gay Lussac*, 18 rue Victor-Hugo (ⓣ05.55.56.98.45; closed Sun eve, Mon & lunch Tues), which offers well-priced, imaginative menus from €11.50 at lunch on weekdays and €17 in the evening. There's a municipal **campsite**, the *Camping de Beaufort* (ⓣ05.55.56.02.79, ⓕ05.55.56.98.01; closed mid-Sept to mid-June), beside the river a couple of kilometres out of town on the D39.

Aubusson

AUBUSSON is 90km east of Limoges and served by regular buses and trains. A neat grey-stone town in the bottom of a ravine formed by the River Creuse, it's of no great interest in itself. What makes it unique is its reputation as a centre for weaving **tapestries**, second only to the Gobelins in Paris. If you're interested, you should aim for the **Musée Départemental de la Tapisserie** in avenue des Lissiers (July & Aug Mon & Wed–Sun 10am–6pm, Tues 2–6pm; Sept–June daily except Tues 9.30am–noon & 2–6pm; €4), which traces the history of Aubusson tapestries over six centuries, coming up to the modern day with works by Jean Lurçat, Pierre Baudouin and Sylvain Dubuisson. The **Maison du Tapissier** next to the tourist office (same hours as tourist office; €4) is also worth a quick look for its broad overview of weaving techniques and local history displayed in the sixteenth-century home of a master weaver.

For information about further exhibitions and workshop visits, ask at the **tourist office** in pedestrianized rue Vieille (July & Aug Mon–Sat 10am–7pm, Sun 9.30am–12.30pm & 2.30–5.30pm; Sept–June Mon–Sat 9.30am–12.30pm & 2–6pm; ⓣ05.55.66.32.12, ⓦwww.ot-aubusson.fr). The smartest **hotel** in town is the two-star *De France* at 6 rue des Déportés (ⓣ05.55.66.10.22, ⓔhotel.lefranceaubusson@wanadoo.fr; ❹), with elegant rooms and a decent restaurant (menus €16–28). There are also two good budget places in the main Grande-Rue: the *Lissier*, at no. 82 (ⓣ05.55.66.14.18, ⓕ05.55.66.33.87; ❷), with a popular and good-value restaurant (menus from €12), and the slightly cheaper *Chapitre*, above a bar at no. 53 (ⓣ05.55.66.18.54; ❷). The town's *La Croix Blanche* **campsite** (ⓣ05.55.66.18.00, ⓕ05.55.66.12.20; closed Oct–March), is by the river on the Felletin road.

The Plateau de Millevaches

Millevaches, the plateau of a thousand springs, is undulating upland country 800–900m in altitude, a sort of step on the northern edge of the Massif Central, with a wild and sparsely populated landscape and villages few and far between.

Steam trains on Millevaches

From June to September every year **steam trains** potter along the beautiful Limoges–Ussel mountain line. Trips cost in the range of €8–40 (adults) and €5–18 (children), according to the length of the journey. There are various options, including Limoges–Meymac, Limoges–Eymoutiers, Eymoutiers–Bujaleuf and Meymac–Ussel. For dates and times, consult the brochure *Train Touristiques à Vapeur en Limousin*, the website Ⓦwww.trainvapeur.com or the tourist offices in Limoges, St-Léonard-de-Noblat, Bujaleuf, Peyrat-le-Château, Eymoutiers, Bugeat, Meymac, Treignac or Ussel.

Those that do exist appear small, grey and sturdy, inured like their mainly elderly inhabitants to the buffeting of upland weather. It's a country of conifer plantations and natural woodland – of beech, birch and chestnut – interspersed with reed-fringed tarns, dam-created lakes and pasture grazed by sheep and cows, where you still find people haymaking with rake and pitchfork.

The small towns, like **Eymoutiers** and **Meymac**, have a primitive architectural beauty and an old-world charm largely untouched by modern development. It's an area to walk or cycle in, or at least savour at a gentle pace, and there's a surprisingly large number of attractive old-fashioned hotels.

Obviously, getting around by car is easiest, but there is access by public transport. **Ussel**, the largest town, is on the main road and rail link between Brive and Clermont-Ferrand, and is also connected by a cross-country line through Meymac and Eymoutiers to Limoges.

Ussel

On the southeastern edge of the plateau is **USSEL**, some 100km southeast of Limoges and 60km northeast of Tulle, where the land begins its gradual descent to the uppermost reaches of the Dordogne valley, thickly wooded and cut by deep tributary valleys. It's not a place with much to see, though the town is pleasant enough, with some attractive sixteenth- and seventeenth-century houses scattered about the central part, while a giant battered granite eagle on the place Voltaire stands as the sole reminder of a Roman settlement hereabouts.

One building worth a look is the house of the local lords, the **Maison Ducal des Ventadour**, who moved here from their draughty fortress in the hills to the south (see p.755). On the north side of place de la République, behind the church, it has a very provincial and rather amateurish Renaissance grandeur, perhaps aping their rich metropolitan cousins. Also worth a quick look is the local **Musée du Pays d'Ussel** (July & Aug daily 10am–noon & 2–7pm; free), which is dedicated to traditional crafts and trades of the region and has a surprisingly good collection of tapestries. It's located in the eighteenth-century Hôtel Bonnot de Bay on rue Michelet, on the west side of town.

The **tourist office** is nearby on the wide place Voltaire (July & Aug Mon–Sat 10am–12.30pm & 2–6.30pm; Sept–June Mon–Fri 9am–noon & 2–5pm; Ⓣ05.55.72.11.50, Ⓦwww.ot-ussel.fr), immediately southwest of the old centre, while the **gare SNCF** is to the north along av Carnot.

The most comfortable **place to stay** is the striking 1970s *Les Gravades* (Ⓣ05.55.46.06.00, Ⓕ05.55.46.06.10; ❸; closed Christmas holidays; restaurant from €15), a couple of kilometres east of Ussel on the N89 and set in its own grounds. Alternatively, try the less impressive *Grand Hôtel de la Gare*, beside the train station (Ⓣ05.55.72.25.98, Ⓕ05.55.96.25.63; ❸; closed Christmas & Sun off season), with a good restaurant from €17.50. There's a municipal **campsite**, the *Camping du Ponty* (Ⓣ05.55.72.30.05, Ⓕ05.55.72.95.19; closed Oct–May), just off the road to Tulle. Your best bet for **food** is the *Flamboyant*, which spreads its tables out on place de la République in fine weather (closed Sun eve & Mon, plus three weeks in Oct; menus from €13).

Meymac and around

Pepper-pot turrets and steep slate roofs adorn the ancient grey houses of **MEYMAC**, 17km west of Ussel. The village is packed tightly around its Romanesque church, whose porch is flanked by striking pink capitals. Adjoining it are the remains of the original Benedictine **abbey**, whose foundation a thousand years ago brought the town into being. Part of the abbey now houses the innovative **Centre National d'Art Contemporain** (daily except Mon: July & Aug 10am–1pm & 2–7pm; Sept–June 2–6pm; closed three weeks at Christmas; €4), featuring changing exhibitions of young, local artists as well as big-name retrospectives. It's also worth popping into the adjacent **Musée de la Fondation Marius Vazeilles** (May–Oct daily except Tues 10am–noon & 2.30–6.30pm; €2.30) to learn about the history and traditions of the plateau.

Grande-Rue, the main street, ends in steps that climb past the round **bell tower**, the town's landmark, to the lime-shaded square in front of the town hall. The **tourist office** (June 15–Sept 15 Mon–Sat 10am–12.30pm & 2–6.30pm, Sun 10am–12.30pm; Sept 16–June 14 Mon–Fri 10am–noon & 2–4.30pm; Ⓣ05.55.95.18.43, Ⓔofficetourisme.meymac@wanadoo.fr) is opposite the other side of a pretty fountain, and has plenty of information on hiking amongst other things.

There's a reasonable two-star **hotel** on the main road, the *Limousin*, 76 av Limousine (Ⓣ05.55.46.12.11, Ⓦwww.logis-de-france.fr; ❸; closed Sat off season & Sun eve all year; restaurant from €13.50), but better to book ahead for one of the four rooms at *Chez Françoise*, up the hill from the tourist office (Ⓣ05.55.95.10.63, Ⓕ05.55.95.40.22; ❸; closed Jan). They also run a well-respected **restaurant** serving local specialities (closed Sun eve & Mon; menus €15–50) and a wonderful, old-fashioned cheese and wine shop. Finally, there's a municipal **campsite**, *Camping de la Garenne* (Ⓣ05.55.95.22.80, Ⓕ05.55.95.19.99; closed Sept 16–May 14), close at hand on the Sornac road.

One of the most touted sights in the area is the remains of a second-century **temple** and, a short walk through the woods, a **Gallo-Roman villa** at **CARS**, about 20km northwest of Meymac. Although there's nothing very spectacular to see, the very presence of Roman influence in such a remote location on the very edge of the Massif Central is interesting. If you want to **stay**, the simple, old-fashioned *Hôtel des Touristes* is just a few kilometres away in the village of **PÉROLS-SUR-VÉZÈRE** (Ⓣ05.55.95.51.71, Ⓔhotel-des-touristes@wanadoo.fr; ❷; closed mid-Dec to mid-Jan), serving up tasty home-cooking from €10.50. A few kilometres further west, just outside **BUGEAT**, there's also a well-run riverside **campsite**, the *Camping des 3 Ponts* (Ⓣ & Ⓕ05.55.95.50.03; closed Oct–April).

Five kilometres northwest of Bugeat, the hamlet of **VIAM** perches prettily on the shores of an artificial lake, its houses clustered around an exquisite and proportionately minute, lopsided church. There's a municipal **campsite** down by the lake (Ⓣ05.55.95.52.05, Ⓔviam.mairie@correze.net; closed Oct to mid-June), but the nearest **hotel** is 15km southwest, just outside **TREIGNAC**, where the *Du Lac* (Ⓣ05.55.98.00.44; ❸; closed Sun eve & Mon; also closed mid-Jan to mid-Feb) offers bright, modern rooms overlooking a lake, and a well-rated **restaurant** (closed Mon & lunch Tues; menus from €10).

Egletons and around

Some 20km southwest of Meymac, the ancient market town of **EGLETONS** flourished during medieval times under the powerful dukes of Ventadour, whose château is now a magnificent ruin about 6km southeast of Egletons near the hamlet of Moustier. It stands on the very tip of a high narrow spur way above the river valleys converging at its feet, with a lone tower rising above the trees. Built in the twelfth century, the **Château de Ventadour** was abandoned in around 1600 in favour of a more comfortable house in Ussel. The celebrated troubadour Bernard de Ventadour was born here, child of a castle servant. The ruins are now undergoing lengthy restoration work to make them safe; you can get quite close but the site itself is fenced off.

By way of contrast, the area's other main sight is the **Musée du Président Jacques Chirac** (Jan & Feb Sat & Sun 10am–12.30pm & 1.30–6pm; March–June & Sept–Dec Tues–Sun 10am–12.30pm & 1.30–6pm; July & Aug daily 10am–12.30pm & 1.30–6pm; €4; Ⓦwww.museepresidentjchirac.fr) at **SARRAN**, in the depths of the country around 10km west of Egletons. This quirky, ultra-modern museum is a showcase of the gifts given to the president during state visits and other official duties. Look out for the natty cowboy boots (from then US President Bill Clinton), the stuffed coelacanth (a gift from the Comoros Islands for the man who has everything) and the delightful South African chess set in which the pieces are caricatures of Mandela, de Klerk, Archbishop Tutu and other famous personalities.

Egletons has a clutch of **hotels**, of which the smartest is the *Ibis* on the main road 1.5km east of town (Ⓣ05.55.93.25.16, Ⓦwww.ibishotel.com; ❸; restaurant from €16). A simpler option is the *Borie* in the centre of town on avenue Charles-de-Gaulle (Ⓣ05.55.93.12.00, Ⓦwww.hotelrestaurantborie.com; ❷; restaurant from €11, closed Sun eve). When it comes to **eating**, try *Le Jardin de Ventadour*, immediately north of the centre on place du Marchadial, which serves a range of imaginative dishes (closed Sun eve & Mon; menus €19–36).

Eymoutiers

EYMOUTIERS, in the north of the Plateau de Millevaches, 45km southeast of Limoges, is another upland town of tall, narrow stone houses crowding round a much-altered Romanesque **church**. Not interesting enough for a prolonged stay, it nonetheless makes another agreeable stopover, especially for campers, as it has a simple but magnificently sited municipal **campsite**, the *Château St-Pierre* (Ⓣ05.55.69.27.81, Ⓕ05.55.69.14.24; closed Oct–May), on a hill 2km southeast of town off the Treignac–Tulle road. If you prefer a **hotel**, you'll find simple rooms and excellent food at *Le Ranch des Lacs* (Ⓣ05.55.69.15.66, Ⓦwww.le-ranch-des-lacs.com; ❷; menus €12–32) about 7km northeast of Eymoutier, signposted off the Bujaleuf road.

Brive-la-Gaillarde and around

BRIVE-LA-GAILLARDE is a major rail junction and the nearest thing to an industrial centre for miles around, but it makes an agreeable base for exploring the Corrèze *département* and its beautiful villages, as well as the upper reaches of the Vézère and Dordogne rivers.

Though it has no commanding sights, Brive-la-Gaillarde does have a few distractions. Right in the middle of town is the much-restored **church of St-Martin**, originally Romanesque in style, though only the transept, apse and a few comically carved capitals survive from that era. St Martin himself, a Spanish aristocrat, arrived in pagan Brive in 407 AD on the feast of Saturnus, smashed various idols and was promptly stoned to death by the outraged onlookers.

Numerous streets fan out from the surrounding square, place du Général-de-Gaulle, with a number of turreted and towered houses, some dating back to the thirteenth century. The most impressive is the sixteenth-century **Hôtel de Labenche** on boulevard Jules-Ferry, now housing the town's archeological finds as well as a collection of seventeenth-century tapestries in the **Musée Labenche** (daily except Tues: April–Oct 10am–6.30pm; Nov–March 1.30–6pm; €4.50). There's also the **Centre National d'Etudes Edmond Michelet** at 4 rue Champanatier (Mon–Sat 10am–noon & 2–6pm; free), based in the former house of this minister of de Gaulle, and one of the town's leading *résistants*, with exhibitions portraying the occupation and Resistance through photographs, posters and objects of the time.

From the **gare SNCF**, it's a ten-minute walk north along avenue Jean-Jaurès to the boulevard ringing the old town. A right turn here brings you to place de Lattre-de-Tassigny, with the **post office** nearby. The **tourist office** is north of the ring road on place 14-Juillet (April–June & Sept Mon–Sat 9am–12.30pm & 1.30–6.30pm; July & Aug Mon–Sat 9am–7pm, Sun 10am–1pm; Oct–March Mon–Sat 9am–noon & 2–6pm; ⓣ05.55.24.08.80, ⓦwww.brive-tourisme.com), where you'll also find a large car park and the modern market hall.

There are numerous cheap **hotels** around the station, of which the *Andréa*, just down the hill at 39 av Jean-Jaurès (ⓣ05.55.74.11.84, ⓕ05.55.17.25.73; ❷) is the nicest, with its cheerful rooms, friendly welcome and a decent restaurant serving mainly Italian cuisine (menus from €16.50). For something smarter, try *Le Chapon Fin*, on place de Lattre-de-Tassigny (ⓣ05.55.74.23.40, ⓦwww.chaponfin-brive.com; ❸; good restaurant from €16), or *Le Collonges* (ⓣ05.55.74.09.58, ⓔlecollonges@wanadoo.fr; ❸) on nearby place Winston-Churchill. Alternatively, there's the very grand *La Truffe Noir*, 22 bd Anatole-France (ⓣ05.55.92.45.00, ⓦwww.la-truffe-noire.com; ❻), with a restaurant to match (menus from €26). There's also a decent **HI hostel** a short walk east of town at 56 av Maréchal-Bugeaud (ⓣ05.55.24.34.00, ⓔbrive@fuaj.org; closed Dec 15–Jan 15), 25 minutes by foot from the *gare SNCF*, and a **campsite**, *Les Îles* (ⓣ05.55.24.34.74, ⓔcampingmunicipalbrive@wanadoo.fr), across the river.

For alternative **places to eat**, try *Le Corrèze* at 3 rue de Corrèze for its good-value regional cooking (closed Sun; menus from €8.50), or the slightly smarter *Viviers St-Martin*, at 4 rue Traversière (closed two weeks each in March & Oct; menus from €10), tucked down an alley near St-Martin; both places offer a wide range of menus. Though it doesn't look much from the outside, *Le Boulevard* at 8 bd Jules-Ferry hides a cosy dining room where locals come for dishes such as duck breast with mustard (closed Sun eve & Mon; menus from €10).

Uzerche and Arnac-Pompadour

A half-hour train ride north of Brive along the course of the bubbling River Vézère, the town of **UZERCHE** is impressively located above a loop in the river's course. It's worth a passing visit as the town has several fine old buildings. The **tourist office** (June 15–Sept 15 daily 10am–12.30pm & 2.30–7pm; school holidays Mon–Fri 10am–noon & 2–5pm, Sat 10am–noon; rest of year Mon–Fri 10am–noon; Ⓣ05.55.73.15.71, Ⓦwww.uzerche.fr), behind the main church, provides a suggested walking route, but the place is so small you can easily find your own way around. If you need a **place to stay**, the *Ambroise*, down by the river is a good option (Ⓣ05.55.73.28.60, Ⓕ05.55.98.45.73; ❷; restaurant from €13, closed Sun eve, Mon & lunch Tues). There's also a three-star municipal **campsite** (Ⓣ & Ⓕ05.55.73.12.75; closed Oct–April) at the Minoterie leisure centre, 2km south along the river, from where you can rent **canoes** and **bikes** (Ⓣ05.55.73.02.84, Ⓦwww.vezerepassion.com).

Roughly 20km west of Uzerche (40min by train, on a different line, from Brive), is **ARNAC-POMPADOUR**. It's a town dominated by its grey, turreted château, presented in 1745 by Louis XV to his mistress, Madame de Pompadour, though she never actually visited it. Set in the green countryside of southern Limousin – reminiscent of parts of Ireland – the **château** is home to one of France's best-known **stud farms** (*haras*), created by Louis XV in 1761, where Anglo-Arabs were first bred. Only the château gardens are open to the public (daily: July–Sept 10am–5.30pm; Oct–June 10am–noon & 2–4.30/5pm depending on the weather; €3), but it's more interesting to visit the *dépôt des étalons* where the stallions are kept (daily: July–Sept 10am–5pm; Oct–June 2.30–4.30/5pm; €6), across the square from the château; the stables are occasionally closed for special events, so phone ahead (Ⓣ05.55.98.51.10) to be on the safe side. The mares live in the Jumenterie de la Rivière (daily: mid-Feb to June 2–5pm; July–Sept 3–5pm; €6), 4km away near the village of Beyssac. In spring the fields around are full of mares and foals, the best being kept for breeding, the rest sold worldwide as two-year-olds. From March to October there are frequent race meetings on the magnificent track in front of the château, plus events and open days, the biggest of which is the **Fête du Cheval** on August 15; there's even a special day for donkeys on July 14.

The **gare SNCF** is 500m southeast of the old town along the main D7 Vigeois road. There's a reasonable **place to stay** and **eat**, the *Hôtel du Parc* (Ⓣ05.55.73.30.54, Ⓦwww.logis-de-france.fr; ❸; closed Christmas to mid-Jan; restaurant from €11), behind the château. Or you could try the modern *Auberge de la Mandrie*, 4km west on the D7, with chalet rooms around a pool (Ⓣ05.55.73.37.14, Ⓦwww.la-mandrie.com; ❸; closed Jan; restaurant from €14, closed Sun eve).

Turenne

TURENNE, just 16km south of Brive, is one of two very picturesque villages close to the town. Capital of the viscountcy of Turenne, whose most illustrious seigneur was Henri de la Tour d'Auvergne – the "Grand Turenne", whom Napoleon rated the finest tactician of modern times – the village today would still seem familiar to him. The same mellow stone houses crowd in the lee of the sharp bluff on whose summit sprout the towers of the castle, one forming part of someone's house. The other, known as **La Tour de César**, can be visited (April–June, Sept & Oct daily 10am–noon & 2–6pm; July & Aug daily 10am–7pm; Nov–March Sun 2–5pm; €3.20; Ⓦwww.chateau-turenne.com), and it's worth climbing for vertiginous views away over the ridges and valleys to the mountains of Cantal.

Collonges-la-Rouge

COLLONGES-LA-ROUGE, 7km east of Turenne, is the epitome of rustic charm with its red sandstone houses, pepper-pot towers and pink-candled chestnut trees, although you need to time your visit carefully, as the village is now very much on the tourist bus circuit. Though small-scale, there's a grandeur about the place, as if the resident Turenne administrators were aping, within their means, the grandiloquence of their superiors. On the main square a twelfth-century **church** testifies to the imbecility of shedding blood over religious differences: here, side by side, Protestant and Catholic conducted their services simultaneously. Outside, the covered **market hall** still retains its old-fashioned baker's oven.

If you want to **stay** somewhere nearby, it's best to head downhill a few minutes to **MEYSSAC**, a town built in the same red sandstone, though less grandly, to the very pleasant *Relais du Quercy* (Ⓣ05.55.25.40.31, Ⓦwww.logis-de-france.fr; ❸; closed three weeks in Nov; restaurant from €12), or the **campsite**, *Moulin de la Valanne* (Ⓣ05.55.25.41.59, Ⓕ05.55.84.07.28; closed Oct–April).

On weekdays it's possible to get to Collonges by **bus** from Brive, and with an early start you can see the town and return by the late-afternoon service. The prettiest route on foot from Turenne is along the back lanes through meadow and walnut orchards via **SAILLAC** (3hr), whose Romanesque church sports an elaborately carved tympanum upheld by a column of spiralling animal motifs.

Tulle

Seen from a distance, **TULLE**, 29km east of Brive, is a strange, unattractive-looking place. Strung out along the bottom of the narrow and deep valley of the Corrèze, it looks grey, run down and industrial. But once you get down to the riverside and the area around the cathedral, it reveals itself to be full of fascinating winding lanes and stairways bordered by very handsome houses – many as old as the fourteenth century – with an imposing **Hôtel de Ville** at the end of rue du Trech, the main commercial street. If not worth a prolonged stay, Tulle certainly makes an interesting stopover.

The **Cathédrale Notre-Dame**, whose construction was drawn out from the Romanesque to Gothic periods, stands on the riverside quays in place Émile-Zola. The cloister beside it has a small **museum** (April–Sept Mon, Tues, Thurs, Fri & Sun 9am–noon & 2–6pm, Wed & Sat 2–6pm; Oct–March Mon, Tues, Thurs, Fri & Sun 9am–noon & 2–5pm; Wed & Sat 2–5pm; €2.35), containing a mishmash of exhibits ranging from archeology to accordions, with a large contingent of firearms, along with lace, once one of the town's major industries. Around the block, at 2 quai Edmond-Perrier, is a collection of documents to do with the Resistance at the **Musée Départemental de la Résistance et de la Déportation** (Mon–Fri 9am–noon & 2–6pm; free), particularly the terrible reprisals wreaked by the Germans when they recaptured the town from the Resistance on June 8, 1944, and hanged 99 people.

The **tourist office** is opposite the cathedral at 2 place Émile-Zola (July & Aug Mon–Fri 9.30am–7pm, Sat 9.30am–6pm, Sun 10.30am–12.30pm; Sept–June Mon–Sat 9am–noon & 2–6pm; Ⓣ05.55.26.59.61, Ⓔoffice-de-tourisme-de-tulle@wanadoo.fr), while the **bus** and **train stations** are side by side on the southwest edge of the town on avenue Winston-Churchill. The **market** takes place on Wednesday and Saturday mornings by the cathedral.

By far the nicest budget **hotel** is *Le Bon Accueil*, 10 rue du Canton (Ⓣ & Ⓕ05.55.26.70.57; ❷; closed two weeks at Christmas; restaurant from €12.50), in an old beamed house with stone mullion windows, across the river from the cathedral. Other places to stay include *Hôtel de la Gare* (Ⓣ05.55.20.04.04,

Ⓕ05.55.20.15.87; ❸; closed two weeks in Sept; restaurant from €11), by the train station, and the more upmarket *La Toque Blanche* at 29 rue Jean-Jaurès (Ⓣ05.55.26.75.41, Ⓦwww.hotel-latoqueblanche.com; ❸), overlooking the very unattractive municipal offices, but only five minutes from the cathedral. The **restaurant** at *La Toque Blanche* is renowned, with an affordable menu at €22 (closed Sun eve & Mon), while brasserie fare is on offer at the contemporary and very popular *La Taverne du Sommelier*, beside the theatre on the quai de la République (*formules* and menus from €8.50 to €29). There's a municipal **campsite** by the river on the Ussel side of town (Ⓣ & Ⓕ05.55.26.75.97; closed Oct–April).

Gimel

If you're travelling by car, you might consider staying in one of the villages in the hilly wooded country northeast of Tulle. **GIMEL-LES-CASCADES**, in particular, is very beautiful and, out of season at least, very quiet. It is a minute hamlet, about 10km away and clinging to the edge of a steep valley beside a spectacular **waterfall**, which has sadly been turned into a paying "sight" (March–June, Sept & Oct Mon, Tues & Thurs–Sun 10am–6pm, Wed 11am–6pm; July & Aug daily 10am–7pm; €4). There's also a superb twelfth-century **reliquary**, known as the Chasse de St-Étienne, in the treasury of the local church.

The attractive *Hostellerie de la Vallée* (Ⓣ05.55.21.40.60, Ⓦwww.logis-de-france.fr; ❸; closed one week each in Dec & Jan) in the village has a few simple rooms and a good restaurant from €19. There's also a good three-star **campsite** (Ⓣ05.55.21.26.65, Ⓕ05.55.26.82.61; closed Oct–May) northeast of Gimel by a small but beautiful lake, the Étang de Ruffaud.

The Lot

The core of this section is formed by the old provinces of **Haut Quercy** and **Quercy**: the land between the Dordogne and the Lot and between the Lot and the Garonne, Aveyron and Tarn. We have extended it slightly eastwards to include the gorges of the River **Aveyron** and Villefranche-de-Rouergue on the edge of the province of Rouergue.

The area is hotter, drier, less well known and, with few exceptions, less crowded than the Dordogne, though no less interesting. The cave paintings at **Pech-Merle** are on a par with those at Les Eyzies. **Najac**, **Penne** and **Peyrerusse** have ruined castles to rival those of the Dordogne. Towns like **Figeac** and **Villefranche-de-Rouergue** are without equal, as are villages like **St-Antonin-Noble-Val**, and stretches of country like that below **Gourdon**, around **Les Arques** where Osip Zadkine had his studio, and the **Célé Valley**.

Again, without transport, many places are out of reach. Some consolation, however, is the existence of the Brive–Toulouse train line that makes Figeac, Villefranche-de-Rouergue and Najac accessible, while **Agen**, **Moissac** and **Montauban** are on the Bordeaux–Toulouse line.

Rocamadour and around

Half-way up a cliff in the deep and abrupt canyon of the Alzou stream, the spectacular setting of **ROCAMADOUR** is hard to beat; the town itself must have been beautiful once, too, but for centuries it has been inundated by religious pilgrims and, latterly, more secular-minded tourists. The constant stream has turned the place into something of a nightmare in high season, with every house displaying mountains of unbelievable junk. The reason for its popularity since medieval times is the supposed miraculous ability of the cathedral's Black Madonna. Nowadays, pilgrims are outnumbered by tourists, who come here to wonder at the sheer audacity of its location, built almost vertically into its rocky backdrop.

Legend has it that the history of Rocamadour began with the arrival of **Zacchaeus**, husband of St Veronica, who fled to France to escape religious persecution and lived out his last years here as a hermit. When in 1166 a perfectly preserved body was found in a grave high up on the rock, it was declared to be Zacchaeus, known in France as **St Amadour**. Rocamadour soon became a major pilgrimage site and a staging post on the road to Santiago de Compostela in Spain. St Bernard, numerous kings of England and France and thousands of others crawled up the chapel steps on their knees to pay their respects and seek cures for their illnesses. Young King Henry, son of Henry II of England (see box, p.742), was the first to plunder the shrine, but he was easily outclassed by the Huguenots, who tried in vain to burn the saint's corpse and finally resigned themselves simply to hacking it to bits. What you see today, therefore, is not the real thing but a nineteenth-century reconstruction, carried out in the hope of reviving the flagging pilgrimage.

The area's other main sight is the **Gouffre de Padirac**, with its vast underground river system, which lies across open country to the northeast of Rocamadour. Further east again, the town of **St-Céré** is an attractive spot, best known for its museum dedicated to the twentieth-century artist Jean Lurçat.

The Town

Rocamadour is easy enough to find your way around. There's just one street, rue de la Couronnerie, strung out between two medieval gateways. Above it, the steep hillside supports no fewer than seven churches. There's a lift dug into the rock-face (€3 return), but it's far better to climb the 223 steps of the Via Sancta, up which the devout drag themselves on their knees to the smoke-blackened and votive-packed **Chapelle Notre-Dame** where the miracle-working twelfth-century Black Madonna resides. The tiny, macabre statue of walnut wood is appropriately lit in the mysterious half-light of her protective black cage, but the rest of the chapel is unremarkable. High up in the rock above the entrance to the chapel is a sword, supposedly Roland's legendary blade, Durandal (see box, p.742).

There's no relief for the non-religious in the neighbouring **Musée d'Art Sacré** (June 15–Sept 15 daily 10am–7pm; Sept 16–Oct & April–June 14 10am–noon & 1.30–6pm, closed two days – which vary – per week; ⓣ05.65.33.23.23; €4.70), which contains sacred art treasures, reliquaries and various historical documents. It's dedicated to the French composer Francis Poulenc (1899–1963) since he was one of the modern pilgrims to receive miraculous inspiration from the shrine, though in his case the results were musical rather than medical.

You can climb still further to the ancient **ramparts** (daily 9am–7pm; €2.60) above Rocamadour in **L'Hospitalet**, reachable either via a winding shady path, La Calvarie, past the Stations of the Cross, or along a more direct path; both routes offer stunning views across the valley.

There are two different **wildlife centres** worth visiting in L'Hospitalet: the **Rocher des Aigles** (April–June & Sept Mon–Sat 1–5pm, Sun 1–6pm; July & Aug daily 1–6pm; Oct to mid-Nov Mon–Sat 2–4pm, Sun 2–5pm; €6.50, Ⓦwww.rocherdesaigles.com), a breeding centre for birds of prey – don't miss the demonstrations of the birds in flight; and the **Forêt des Singes**, off the D673 (April–June & first two weeks Sept daily 10am–noon & 1–6pm; July & Aug daily 9.30am–6.30pm; 16–30 Sept & Oct to mid-Nov Mon–Sat 1–5pm, Sun 10am–noon & 1–5pm; €7; Ⓦwww.la-foret-des-singes.com), where more than a hundred Barbary apes roam the plateau in relative freedom.

Practicalities

Getting to Rocamadour without your own transport is awkward, unless you're prepared to walk or take a taxi the 4km from the Rocamadour-Padirac **gare SNCF** on the Brive–Capdenac line. If you arrive by car, you'll have to park in L'Hospitalet, on the hilltop above Rocamadour (which has the best view of the town), or else in the car park several hundred metres below the town. There are two **tourist offices**: the main one in l'Hospitalet (April Mon–Fri & Sun 10am–noon & 2–6pm, Sat 2–6pm; May to mid-July & first two weeks Sept daily 10am–12.30pm & 2–6.30pm; mid-July to Aug daily 10am–7.30pm; mid-Sept to mid-Nov Mon–Fri 10am–noon & 2–6pm, Sat & Sun 2–5.30pm; mid-Nov to March Mon–Fri 10am–noon & 2–5.30pm; Ⓣ05.65.33.22.00, Ⓦwww.rocamadour.com), and a second next to the Hôtel de Ville (daily: April to mid-July & first two weeks Sept 10am–12.30pm & 1.30–6pm; mid-July to Aug 9.30am–7.30pm; mid-Sept to mid-Nov 10am–noon & 2–5.30pm; mid-Nov to March 2–5pm), on the main street.

Rocamadour's **hotels** are not too expensive but they're completely booked out in the summer and closed for the winter months. If you ring ahead, you might get in at the *Lion d'Or*, on rue de la Couronnerie (Ⓣ05.65.33.62.04, Ⓦwww.liondor-rocamadour.com; ❷; closed Nov–March; restaurant from €11.50), or *Le Terminus des Pèlerins*, at the bottom of the Via Sancta (Ⓣ05.65.33.62.14, Ⓦwww.terminus-des-pelerins.com; ❸; closed Nov–March; restaurant from €13). For a night of luxury, try the *Beau Site*, also on rue de la Couronnerie (Ⓣ05.65.33.63.08, Ⓦwww.bw-beausite.com; ❹; closed mid-Nov to early Feb), which also has an excellent restaurant, the *Jehan de Valon* (menus €16–49). Up in L'Hospitalet, the modern *Comp'Hostel* (Ⓣ05.65.33.73.50, Ⓕ05.65.10.68.21; ❸; closed mid-Oct to March) is about the best on offer, with clean, functional rooms. They also run the neighbouring **campsite**, *Le Relais du Campeur* (Ⓣ05.65.33.63.28; closed Oct–March).

Gouffre de Padirac

The **Gouffre de Padirac** (daily guided tours: April to mid-July, Sept & Oct 9am–noon & 2–5pm; last two weeks July 9am–6pm; Aug 8.30am–6.30pm; €8; Ⓦwww.gouffre-de-padirac.com) is about 20km east of Rocamadour on the other side of the main Brive–Figeac road. An enormous limestone sinkhole, about 100m deep and over 100m wide, it contains some spectacular formations of stalactites and waterfalls created by the accumulation of lime, and beautiful underground lakes, but is very, very popular – so much so that it's best avoided at weekends and other peak periods, or you'll wait an age for tickets. Visits are partly on foot, partly by boat, and the guided tours last an hour and a half. In wet weather you'll need a waterproof jacket. If you have no car, the nearest **gare SNCF** is Rocamadour-Padirac, more than 10km to the west; the only alternative is walking or hitching.

St-Céré

East of Padirac and about 9km from Bretenoux on the River Bave, a minor tributary of the Dordogne, you come to the medieval town of **ST-CÉRÉ**, dominated by the brooding ruins of the **Château de St-Laurent-les-Tours** and full of ancient houses crowding around place du Mercadial. The two powerful keeps of St-Laurent, partially rebuilt, date from the twelfth and fifteenth centuries and were part of a fortress belonging to the Turennes. During World War II, the artist Jean Lurçat operated a secret Resistance radio post here; after the war he turned it into a studio, and it's now a marvellous **museum** of his work, mainly huge tapestries but also sketches, paintings and pottery (July 14–Sept daily 9.30am–noon & 2.30–6.30pm; also open two weeks at Easter; ⓣ05.65.38.28.21; €2.50). At over 200m altitude, the site is spectacular, with stunning views all around.

St-Céré has one very pleasant and reasonable **place to stay**: the *Hôtel Victor-Hugo*, 7 av des Maquis, by the river (ⓣ05.65.38.16.15, ⓦwww.hotel-victor-hugo.fr; ❸; closed two weeks in March & three weeks in Oct; restaurant from €14, closed Sun eve and Mon). Otherwise, there's *Le Soulhol* riverside **campsite** (ⓣ05.65.38.12.37, ⓕ05.65.10.61.75; closed Oct–April) nearby.

Bikes can be rented from Peugeot Cycles, 45 rue Faidherbe (ⓣ05.65.38.03.23) – one of the best trips you could do is to the extremely pretty little village of **AUTOIRE**, in a tight side valley about 10km to the west of St-Céré. Much hillier but glorious country lies to the east along the road to Aurillac via Sousceyrac and Laroquebrou.

Gourdon and around

GOURDON lies between Sarlat and Cahors, conveniently served by the Brive–Toulouse train line, and makes a quiet, pleasant base for visiting some of the major places in this part of the Dordogne and Lot. It's 17km south of the River Dordogne and pretty much at the eastern limit of the luxuriant woods and valleys of Périgord, which give way quite suddenly, at the line of the N20, to the arid limestone landscape of the **Causse de Gramat**.

In the Middle Ages, Gourdon was an important place, deriving wealth and influence from the presence of four monasteries. It was besieged and captured in 1189 by Richard the Lionheart, who promptly murdered its feudal lords. Legend has it that the archer who fired the fatal shot at Richard during the siege of Châlus was the last surviving member of this family. But more than anything it was the devastation of the Wars of Religion that dispatched the place into centuries of oblivion.

Gourdon is a beautiful town, its medieval centre of yellow-stone houses attached like a swarm of bees to a prominent hilltop, neatly ringed by modern boulevards containing all the shops. From whichever direction you approach, all roads lead to place de la Libération in front of the fortified **gateway** over rue du Majou, the narrow main street of the old town. It's lined all the way up with splendid stone houses, some, like the **Maison d'Anglars** at no. 17, dating as far back as the thirteenth century. At its upper end, rue du Majou leads into a lovely square in front of the massive but not particularly interesting fourteenth-century **church of St-Pierre**, where in summer there's a farmers' market on Thursday mornings. The handsome **Hôtel de Ville** stands on one side of the square, and in place des Marronniers, behind the church, is the family home of the Cavaignacs, who supplied the nation with numerous prominent public figures in the eighteenth and nineteenth centuries, including the notoriously brutal general who put down the Paris workers' attempts to defend the Second Republic in June 1848. From the square, steps climb to the top of the hill, where the castle once stood and from where there is a superb view over the Dordogne valley and surroundings.

A couple of kilometres along the Sarlat Road in the direction of Cougnac from Gourdon, is a very interesting cave, the **Grottes de Cougnac**, discovered in 1949 (April–June & Sept daily 10–11.30am & 2.30–5pm; July & Aug daily 10am–6pm; Oct Mon–Sat 2–6pm; €5.80). It has beautiful rock formations as well as some fine prehistoric paintings rather similar to those at Pech-Merle.

Practicalities

Gourdon's **train station** is located roughly 1km northeast of the town centre; from the station, walk south on avenue de la Gare, then turn right on to avenue Gambetta to reach the boulevard encircling the old town. Turn left here to find rue du Majou and the **tourist office** at no. 24 (Jan, Feb, Nov & Dec Mon–Sat 10am–noon & 2–5pm; March–June, Sept & Oct Mon–Sat 10am–noon & 2–6pm; July & Aug Mon–Sat 10am–7pm, Sun 10am–noon; ⓣ05.65.27.52.50, ⓦwww.quercy-tourisme.com/gourdon), which has lists of B&B options in the area. **Bikes** can be rented from Nature Évasion, 73 av Cavignac (ⓣ05.65.37.65.17), out on the west side of town.

For an overnight **stay**, the *Hôtel de la Promenade*, on the northwestern side of the ring road at 48 bd Galiot-de-Genouillac (ⓣ05.65.41.41.44, ⓦwww.lapromenadegourdon.fr; ❷), is a cheerful place with immaculate rooms and a decent restaurant (closed Sun; menus from €11.10). On the opposite side of town, near the post office, is the agreeable *Bissonnier*, 51 bd des Martyrs (ⓣ05.65.41.02.48, ⓦwww.hotelbissonnier.com; ❹), with a restaurant serving international fare such as vegetable curry as well as the more classic snails with garlic (closed Mon; menu from €12.50). There's a well-equipped municipal campsite, *Écoute s'il Pleut* (ⓣ05.65.41.06.19, ⓕ05.65.41.09.88; closed Oct–May), 1km north on the Sarlat road.

In addition to the hotels above, you'll find cafés and **restaurants** scattered along the main boulevard – the Tour-de-Ville – which encircles the old town.

Les Arques

Twenty-five kilometres southwest of Gourdon on the Fumel road, you come to a pretty but not remarkable *bastide* called **Cazals**. A left turn here takes you along the bottom of the valley of the Masse and up its left flank to the exquisite hamlet of **LES ARQUES**. This is quiet, remote, small-scale farming country, emptied of people by the slaughter of rustic sons in World War I and by migration to the towns in search of jobs and money.

Les Arques' main claim to fame is the Russian Cubist/Expressionist sculptor Osip Zadkine, who bought the old house by the church here in 1934. Some of his sculptures adorn the space outside the church as well as its lovely interior, and there's also a **museum** with a number of his other works (daily: April–Sept 10am–1pm & 2–7pm; Oct–March 2–5pm; €2.50).

The other reason to come here is the old village school, now transformed into a most unusual **restaurant**, *La Récréation* (☎05.65.22.88.08; April–Sept daily except Wed & Thurs, Oct–Dec open Fri eve to Sun lunch), where you get a copious and delicious meal to eat beneath the chestnut trees of the school yard for €16 at midday in July and August, or otherwise for €26. On a summer night, with the swifts flying overhead, it's idyllic.

On the other side of the valley and well signposted, the tiny Romanesque **chapel of St-André-des-Arques** has some very lovely fifteenth-century frescoes discovered by Zadkine; get the key from the museum in Les Arques (see p.763).

Cahors and around

CAHORS, on the River Lot, was the capital of the old province of Quercy. In its time, it has been a Gallic settlement; a Roman town; a briefly held Moorish possession; a town under English rule; a bastion of Catholicism in the Wars of Religion, sacked in consequence by Henri IV; a university town for four hundred years; and birthplace of the politician Léon Gambetta (1838–82), after whom so many French streets and squares are named. Modern Cahors is a sunny southern backwater, with two interesting sights in its **cathedral** and the remarkable **Pont Valentré**.

While you're in the Cahors area, don't miss out on the local **wine**, heady and black but dry to the taste and not at all plummy like the Gironde wines from Blaye and Bourg, which use the same Malbec grape.

The Town

Small and easily walkable, the town squats on a peninsula formed by a tight loop in the River Lot, and is protected on the northern side by a rank of fourteenth-century **fortifications**, with the **Barbacane de St-Jean** making a breach in the walls.

Right in the middle of the town is the **cathedral** which, consecrated in 1119, is the oldest and simplest in plan of the Périgord-style churches. The exterior is not exciting: a heavy square tower dominates the plain west front, whose best feature is the elaborately decorated portal in the street on the north side, where a Christ in Majesty dominates the tympanum, surrounded by angels and apostles, while cherubim fly out of the clouds to relieve him of his halo. Side panels show scenes from the life of St Stephen. The outer ring of figures over the portal shows a line of naked figures being stabbed in the behind and hacked with axes.

Inside, the cathedral is much like St-Front at Périgueux, with a nave lacking aisles and transepts, roofed with two big domes; in the first are fourteenth-century frescoes of the stoning of St Stephen. The Gothic choir and apse are extensively but crudely painted, while to their right a door opens into a delicate **cloister** (July–Sept Tues–Sat 10am–12.30pm & 2–6.30pm; Oct–June enquire at tourist office; €2) in the flamboyant style, still retaining some intricate, though damaged, carving. On the northwest corner pillar the Virgin is portrayed as a graceful girl with broad brow and ringlets to her waist. In the cloister's northeast corner St Gaubert's chapel holds the Holy Coif, a cloth said to have covered Christ's head in the tomb, which according to legend was brought back from the Holy Land in the twelfth century by Bishop Géraud de Cardaillac.

The area between the cathedral and the river is filled by a warren of narrow lanes and alleys, most of them handsomely restored during the last

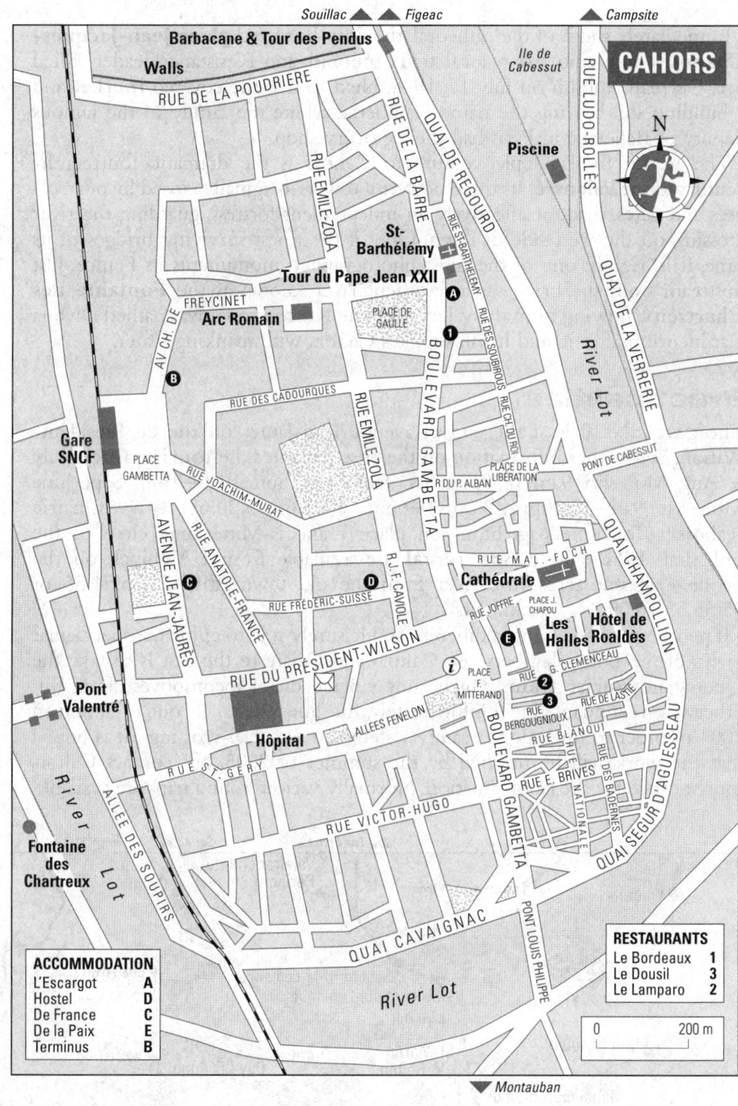

ten years. Many of the houses, turreted and built of flat, thin, southern brick, date from the fourteenth and fifteenth centuries. Rue Nationale, rue Bergougnioux and rue de Lastié are particularly interesting, along with rue du Château-du-Roi and its extension, rue des Soubirous, to the north. It's worth taking a look at the impressive **Hôtel d'Issale** in rue Bergougnioux and the **Hôtel de Roaldès** in place Henri-IV; also of interest are the **Hôpital Grossia** in rue des Soubirous and the **Palais Duèze**, further north opposite the church of St-Barthélémy, built for the brothers of Pope John XXII in the fourteenth century.

Immediately south of the cathedral, the lime-bordered **place Jean-Jacques-Chapou** commemorates a local trade unionist and Resistance leader, killed in a German ambush on July 17, 1944. Next to it is the covered **market** and a building still bearing the name Gambetta, where the family of the famous deputy of Belleville in Paris had their grocery shop.

The reason most people venture to Cahors is the dramatic fourteenth-century **Pont Valentré**. Its three powerful towers, originally closed by portcullises and gates, made it effectively an independent fortress, guarding the river crossing on the west side of town. One of the finest surviving bridges of its time, it is, rightly, one of the most photographed monuments in France. Just upstream from the bridge is a resurgent river known as the **Fontaine des Chartreux**, flowing from the valley side. The Roman town was named Divona Carducorum after it, and it still supplies Cahors with drinking water.

Practicalities

The **gare SNCF** is at the end of avenue Jean-Jaurès off rue du Président-Wilson. For further information on the area, make for the **tourist office** (July & Aug Mon–Fri 9am–6.30pm, Sat 9am–6pm, Sun 10am–1pm; Sept–June Mon–Sat 9am–12.30pm & 1.30–6pm; ⓣ05.65.53.20.65, ⓦwww.mairie-cahors.fr/Tourisme/page.html) on place François-Mitterrand, close to the cathedral. **Bike** and **canoe rental** are available from L'Archipel, on the Île de Cabessut across the river from the old town (ⓣ06.23.35.51.56 or 05.55.53.16.09; ⓦwww.knoe.fr).

If pedalling is too taxing, a different and leisurely way to enjoy the spectacular views of the Lot valley between Cahors and Cajarc to the east is to take the Quercyrail **tourist train**, which runs vintage diesel locomotives along this otherwise redundant line. Unfortunately, the line was taken out of action in 2004 in order to upgrade the safety systems on the level-crossings. It is hoped that the work will be finished by the summer of 2005, but contact Cahors tourist office for the latest situation. Normally, various round trips are available,

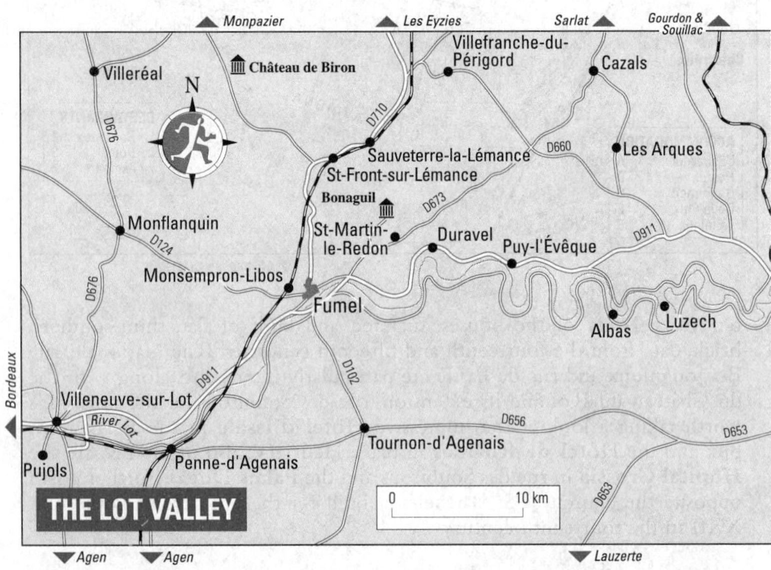

including a boat trip at Cajarc, a walk along the towpath hewn into the rock at St-Cirq-Lapopie, and a visit to the château of Cénevières.

The cheapest **hotel** in Cahors is the simple *De la Paix*, place de la Halle, near the cathedral (Ⓣ05.65.35.03.40, Ⓕ05.65.35.40.88; ❷–❸), though *L'Escargot*, at the north end of boulevard Gambetta (Ⓣ05.65.35.07.66, Ⓕ05.65.53.92.38; ❸), offers more atmosphere. Near the station, the *De France*, 252 av Jean-Jaurès (Ⓣ05.65.35.16.76, Ⓦwww.hoteldefrance-cahors.fr; ❸; closed three weeks over Christmas), is another decent option, or you could splurge out on the lovely creeper-covered *Terminus*, 5 av Charles de Freycinet (Ⓣ05.65.53.32.00, Ⓦwww.balandre.com; ❹), boasting the famous *Le Balandre* restaurant (July to mid-Sept closed for lunch Sun & Mon; rest of year closed all day Sun & Mon; menus €40–90, brasserie menu at €16). There's also a **HI hostel** near the tourist office at 20 rue Frédéric-Suisse (Ⓣ05.65.35.64.71, Ⓔfjt46@club-internet.fr), and an expensive **campsite** (Ⓣ05.65.30.06.30, Ⓦwww.cabessut.com; closed Oct–March) across Pont de Cabessut.

In addition to the hotel **restaurants** mentioned above, there's a lively brasserie, *Le Bordeaux*, at the top end of boulevard Gambetta (with menus from €13) while *Le Lamparo*, on the south side of the market square, is equally popular for its varied menus (from €15; closed Sun) and generous portions. *Le Dousil*, a wine bar just round the corner on rue Nationale (closed Sun & Mon), is a great place to sample the local reds – and it dishes up good food, too: salads, open-sandwiches and cheese and charcuterie platters from around €9.

St-Cirq-Lapopie

If you have your own transport you could easily make a side trip from Cahors to the cliff-edge village of **ST-CIRQ-LAPOPIE**, 30km to the east, perched high above the south bank of the Lot. The village was saved from ruin when poet André Breton came to live here in the early twentieth century, and though it's now an irresistible draw for the tour buses with its cobbled lanes, half-timbered houses and gardens, it's still worth the trouble, especially if early or late in the day.

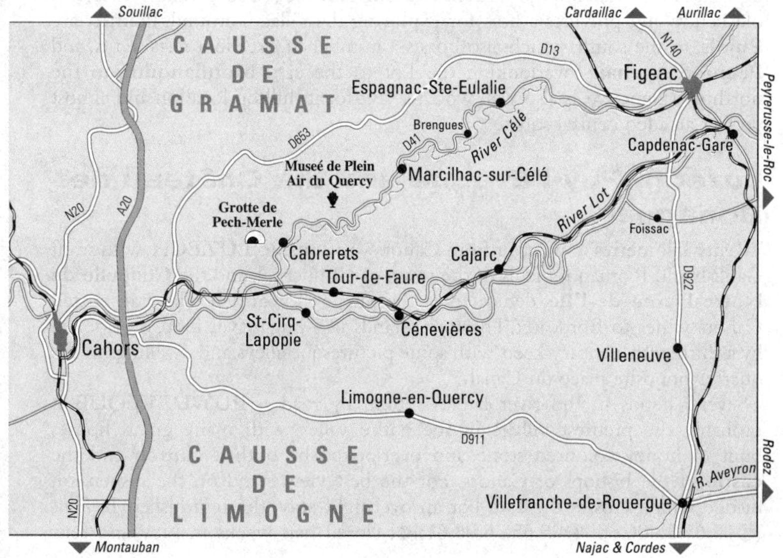

Public transport in the form of an SNCF bus will get you from Cahors to Gare-St-Cirq in the valley bottom at Tour-de-Faure, from where there's no alternative but to leg it up the steep hill for the final two kilometres. For **accommodation**, there's the simple and very pretty *Auberge du Sombral* on the central square (Ⓣ05.65.31.26.08, Ⓕ05.65.30.26.37; ❸; closed mid-Nov to March) and *La Pélissaria* (Ⓣ05.65.31.25.14, Ⓦperso.wanadoo.fr/hoteldelapelissaria; ❺; closed Oct 15–April 15), in a sixteenth-century house perched on the cliff at the eastern entrance to St-Cirq. There's also a very comfortable *gîte d'étape* in the village centre (Ⓣ & Ⓕ05.65.31.21.51; closed Nov 15–March 14), and two well-run **campsites**: *Camping de la Plage* (Ⓣ05.65.30.29.51, Ⓦwww.campingplage.com; open all year), down by the river with swimming and canoeing possibilities, and *La Truffière* (Ⓣ05.65.30.20.22, Ⓦwww.camping-truffiere.com; closed Oct–March), 3km to the southeast over the rim of the valley. When it comes to **restaurants**, you can eat very well at *L'Oustal* (Ⓣ05.65.31.20.17; closed Mon & mid-Nov to mid-March; menus from €13), tucked into a corner of rue de la Pélissaria just south of the church. At the top of the village, with views from its terrace over jumbled roofs, *Lou Bolat* serves a varied menu of crêpes, salads and regional dishes (closed mid-Nov to mid-Feb; menus from €12).

Downstream from Cahors

West of Cahors the vine-cloaked banks of the Lot are dotted with small and ancient villages. The first of these, **Luzech** and the dramatic **Puy-l'Évêque**, are served by an SNCF bus that threads along the valley from Cahors via Fumel to Monsempron-Libos, on the Agen–Périgueux train line. You'll need your own transport, however, to reach the splendid **Château de Bonaguil**, in the hills northwest of Puy-l'Évêque, worth the effort for its elaborate fortifications and spectacular position. From here on the Lot valley starts to get ugly and industrial, though **Villeneuve-sur-Lot** hides a surprisingly attractive old centre and provides a base for exploring the villages around. Prettiest are **Pujols**, to the south, which also boasts a number of excellent restaurants, and **Penne-d'Agenais**, overlooking the Lot to the east. **Monflanquin**, to the north ofVilleneuve, is also well worth a visit for its hilltop location and almost perfect arcaded central square.

Luzech, Puy-l'Évêque and the Château de Bonaguil

Twenty kilometres downriver from Cahors you come to **LUZECH**, with scant Gaulish and Roman remains of the town of L'Impernal, and the **Chapelle de Notre-Dame-de-l'Île**, dedicated to the medieval boatmen who transported Cahors wines to Bordeaux. The town stands in a huge river loop, overlooked by a thirteenth-century keep, with some picturesque alleys and dwellings in the quarter opposite place du Canal.

Several bends in the river later – 15km by road – **PUY-L'ÉVÊQUE** is probably the prettiest village in the entire valley, with many grand houses built in honey-coloured stone and overlooked by both a **church** and the **castle** of the bishops of Cahors. For the best view, stand on the suspension bridge which crosses the Lot. For an overnight **stay**, the refurbished *Bellevue* (Ⓣ05.65.36.06.60, Ⓕ05.65.36.06.61; ❹; closed two weeks in Nov and four weeks in Jan/Feb), perched on the cliff edge, has stylish rooms and a good restaurant (from €30, or €12.50 in the brasserie). For something cheaper, at the bottom of the town, the *Henry* has cheap and decent rooms (Ⓣ05.65.21.32.24, Ⓕ05.65.30.85.18; ❷), or there's a well-tended **campsite**, *Camping Les Vignes* (Ⓣ05.65.30.81.72, Ⓦwww.campinglesvignes.com; closed Oct–March), 3km south by the river.

With your own transport, follow the Lot as far as Duravel and then cut across country via the picturesque hamlet of St-Martin-le-Redon to reach the **Château de Bonaguil** (daily: Feb & March 11am–1pm & 2.30–5.30pm; April & May 10.30am–1pm & 2.30–5.30pm; June–Aug 10am–6pm; Sept 10.30am–1pm & 2.30–5pm; Oct, Nov & Christmas hols 11am–1pm & 2.30–5pm; €4.50) some 15km later. It's spectacularly perched at the end of a wooden spur commanding two valleys, about 8km northeast of Fumel. Dating largely from the fifteenth and sixteenth centuries with a double ring of walls, five huge towers and a narrow boat-shaped keep designed to resist artillery, it was the last of a dying breed, completed just when military architects were abandoning such elaborate fortifications.

Villeneuve-sur-Lot and around

VILLENEUVE-SUR-LOT, 75km west and downstream from Cahors, is a pleasant, workaday sort of town but otherwise does not have a great deal to commend it: there are no very interesting sights, though the handful of attractive timbered houses in the old town go some way to compensate. If you're reliant on public transport note that there's no train station in Villeneuve itself, but SNCF runs regular bus services to Agen, which is on the Bordeaux–Toulouse line.

The town's most striking landmark is the red-brick tower of the **church of Ste-Catherine**, completed as late as 1937 in typically dramatic neo-Byzantine style, but rather unusually built on a north–south axis; inside, the church retains some attractive stained glass from the previous fourteenth-century building. In the streets around the main square, **place La Fayette**, a couple of towers alone survive from the fortifications of this originally *bastide* town, and to the south the main avenue, rue des Cieutats, crosses thirteenth-century **Pont des Cieutat**, resembling the Pont Valentré in Cahors but devoid of its towers.

The **tourist office**, 47 rue de Paris (July & Aug Mon–Sat 9am–12.30pm & 2–7pm, Sun 10am–1pm; Sept–June Mon–Sat 9am–noon & 2–6pm; Ⓣ05.53.36.17.30, Ⓦwww.ville-villeneuve-sur-lot.fr), lies just within the town's northern gate. The best place to look for **accommodation** is around the former train station, five minutes' walk south of centre, where the friendly *La Résidence*, 17 av Lazare-Carnot (Ⓣ05.53.40.17.03, Ⓔhotel.laresidence@wanadoo.fr; ❶; closed 15 days in Nov), offers unbeatable value for money. If it's full, try nearby *Le Terminus* (Ⓣ05.53.70.94.36, Ⓔcarrerea@wanadoo.fr; ❷; restaurant from €10.50, closed Sun), or, if you'd rather be closer to the centre, *Les Platanes*, 40 bd de la Marine (Ⓣ05.53.40.11.40, Ⓔhotel.des.platanes.villeneuve.sur.lot@wanadoo.fr; ❷; restaurant from €13), north along boulevard de la République from the tourist office. For campers, there's the *Camping du Rooy*, signed off the Agen road 1.5km south of the centre (Ⓣ05.53.70.24.18; closed Oct–April 14).

When it comes to **eating**, *Chez Câline* in rue Notre-Dame (closed Tues eve & Sun; menus from €14), near the Pont des Cieutat, is a pretty little place offering traditional cuisine, or you could try *L'Entracte* at 30 bd de la Marine (closed Wed; menus from €12.50), where you can sit out under the plane trees.

The nearby *La Galerie*, 38 bd de la Marine (ⓣ05.53.71.52.12; closed Mon eve & Tues), is the place to go for a bit more luxury and classic cuisine; lunchtime menus start at €13 and at €15 for dinner. Alternatively, head south to Pujols (see below).

Pujols and Penne-d'Agenais

Three kilometres south of Villeneuve the tiny hilltop village of **PUJOLS** makes a popular excursion, partly to see the faded Romanesque frescoes in the **church of Ste-Foy** and partly for the views over the surrounding country. But the main reason locals come here is for the quality of its **restaurants**. Top of the list is the excellent but expensive *La Toque Blanche* (ⓣ05.53.49.00.30, ⓦwww.la-toque-blanche.com; closed Sun eve, Mon & lunch Tues; menus €24–78), just south of Pujols with views back to the village. The panorama is even better, however, from their less formal outlet, *Lou Calel*, overlooking the Lot valley in Pujols itself, where you can sample some beautifully cooked traditional but light menus (ⓣ05.53.70.46.14; closed Tues eve, Wed & lunch Thurs; menus from €15).

Another side trip could be to the beautiful but touristy old fortress town of **PENNE-D'AGENAIS**, 8km upstream on a steep hill also on the south bank of the Lot, with remains of a thirteenth-century castle teetering on a cliff edge. The **tourist office**, in rue du 14-Juillet just inside the old town gate (June–Sept Mon–Sat 9am–1pm & 2–7pm, Sun 3–7pm; Oct–May Mon–Sat 9am–12.30pm & 2–6pm, Sun 2–6pm; ⓣ05.53.41.37.80, ⓔoffice-tourisme.canton-penne@wanadoo.fr), can supply comprehensive lists of B&Bs and *gîtes* in the area. There's a good municipal **campsite** (ⓣ05.53.36.25.25 or ⓣ05.53.41.30.97, ⓕ05.53.36.25.29; open mid-June to Aug) beside the Ferrié leisure lake just south of Penne, down near the **gare SNCF** on the Agen–Paris line, and another more basic site across the river in St-Sylvestre (ⓣ05.53.41.22.23; closed Oct to mid-May). If you're looking for somewhere to **eat**, try *Le Bombecul*, beside the church, which serves large salads and daily specials with a north African flavour (ⓣ05.53.71.11.76; salads €8, menu €16; open daily in July & Aug, call ahead to check the rest of the year).

Monflanquin

Some 30km north of Villeneuve-sur-Lot, pretty **MONFLANQUIN**, founded by Alphonse de Poitiers in 1256, is another perfectly preserved *bastide* (see p.727), less touristy than Monpazier and even more impressively positioned on the top of a hill that rises sharply from the surrounding country. It conforms to the regular pattern of right-angled streets leading from a central square to the four town gates. The square – **place des Arcades** – with its distinctly Gothic houses, derives a special charm from being on a slope and tree-shaded. On the square's north side you'll find the high-tech **Musée des Bastides** (July & Aug daily 10am–7pm; Sept–June Mon–Sat 10am–noon & 2–6pm, Sun 3–6pm; €1), full of information about the life and history of *bastides*.

Located beneath the museum is the **tourist office** (same hours as the Musée des Bastides; ⓣ05.53.36.40.19, ⓦwww.cc-monflanquinois.fr), which can furnish you with lists of *chambres d'hôtes*. The best hotel in Monflanquin is the modern and slightly soulless *Monform*, just west of town (ⓣ05.53.49.85.85, ⓦwww.logis-de-france.fr; ❸; closed Feb; restaurant menus from €12.50), which doubles as a health centre with heated pool, sauna and gym. **Campers** are better served by the four-star *Camping des Bastides* (ⓣ05.53.40.83.09, ⓦwww.campingdesbastides.com), 10km east of

Monflanquin, near the village of Salles. If you're looking for somewhere to eat, try one of the **cafés** and **restaurants** on place des Arcades: both the *Bistrot du Prince Noir* (open daily July & Aug; Sept–June closed Tues & Wed; lunch menus from €12, evenings from €23) and *La Mercerie* (closed mid-Nov to mid-Jan; July & Aug closed Tues; Sept–June closed Mon–Wed and lunch Sat; menus from €13) serve good quality local fare as well as more unusual dishes.

Figeac and around

FIGEAC lies on the River Célé, 71km east of Cahors and some 8km north of the Lot. It's a beautiful town with an unspoilt medieval centre not too encumbered by tourism. Like many other provincial towns hereabouts, it owes its beginnings to the foundation of an abbey in the early days of Christianity in France, one which quickly became wealthy because of its position on the pilgrim routes to both Rocamadour and Compostela. In the Middle Ages it became a centre of tanning, which partly accounts for the many houses whose top floors have *solelhos*, or open-sided wooden galleries used for drying skins and other produce. Again, as so often, it was the Wars of Religion that pushed it into eclipse, for Figeac threw in its lot with the nearby Protestant stronghold of Montauban and suffered the same punishing reprisals by the victorious royalists in 1662.

Roads and train line both funnel you automatically into the town centre, where the **Hôtel de la Monnaie** surveys place Vival. It's a splendid building whose origins go back to the thirteenth century, when the city's mint was located in this district. The building now houses the tourist office, as well as a none-too-exciting **museum** of old coins and archeological bits and pieces found in the surrounding area (same hours as tourist office – see below; €2). In the streets radiating off to the north of the square – Caviale, République, Gambetta and their cross-streets – there's a delightful range of houses of the medieval and classical periods, both stone and half-timbered with brick noggings, adorned with carvings and colonnettes, ogees, and interesting bits of ironwork. At the end of these streets are the two small squares of **place Carnot** and **place Champollion**, both of great charm. The former is the site of the old *halles*, under whose awning cafés now spreads their tables.

Jean-François Champollion, who cracked Egyptian hieroglyphics by deciphering the triple text of the Rosetta Stone, was born in a house at 4 impasse Champollion, off the square, and the building now houses a **museum** dedicated to his life and work. At the time of writing, the museum was being extended to include coverage of the history of the languages and scripts of the lower Mediterranean basin. It is expected to reopen in 2006, but contact the tourist office for the latest situation. At the end of impasse Champollion, a larger-than-life reproduction of the Rosetta Stone forms the floor of the tiny **place des Écritures**, above which is a little garden planted with tufts of papyrus.

On the other side of place Champollion, rue Boutaric leads up to the cedar-shaded **church of Notre-Dame-du-Puy**, from where you get views over the roofs of the town. More interesting is the **church of St-Sauveur** off place des Herbes near the tourist office, with its lovely Gothic chapterhouse decorated with heavily gilded but dramatically realistic seventeenth-century carved wood panels illustrating the life of Christ.

Practicalities

The **gare SNCF** is a few minutes' walk to the south of place Vival across the river at the end of rue de la Gare and avenue des Poilus. SNCF **buses** leave from the train station, and others from the **gare routière** on avenue Maréchal-Joffre, a few minutes' walk west of place Vival. You'll find the **tourist office** in the Hôtel de la Monnaie on place Vival (May, June & Sept Mon–Sat 10am–12.30pm & 2.30–6pm, Sun 10am–1pm; July & Aug daily 10am–7.30pm; Oct–April Mon–Sat 10am–noon & 2.30–6pm; ⓣ05.65.34.06.25, ⓦwww.quercy.net/figeac).

The nicest **place to stay** is the *Hôtel des Bains*, 1 rue du Griffoul (ⓣ05.65.34.10.89, ⓦwww.hoteldesbains.fr; ❷–❸; closed mid-Dec to mid-Jan), in a lovely riverside location just across from the old town. For something smarter, there's the *Pont d'Or*, beside the bridge at 2 av Jean-Jaurès (ⓣ05.65.50.95.00, ⓦwww.hotelpontdor.com; ❹; restaurant from €12.50), and one block further back, the *Hostellerie de l'Europe* at 51 allée Victor-Hugo (ⓣ05.65.34.10.16, ⓦwww.logis-de-france.fr; ❸), which is better than it looks from the outside. If you'd rather be more central, the *Champollion*, on place Champollion (ⓣ05.65.34.04.37, ⓕ05.65.34.61.69; ❸), offers a few functional but cheery rooms above a popular café. The tourist office can recommend *chambres d'hôtes*, and there's a well-equipped **campsite**, *Les Rives du Célé* (ⓣ05.65.34.59.00, ⓦwww.domainedesurgie.com; closed Oct–March), by the river just east of town, with a restaurant, shop and swimming pool, by the sports ground, where you can also rent **bikes** and **canoes**.

Figeac boasts some excellent **restaurants**. Honest home cooking is the order of the day at *À l'Escargot*, behind the *Pont d'Or* hotel at 2 av Jean-Jaurès (menus from €14; closed Thurs & Jan), while the more upmarket *La Table de Marinette*, next to the *Hostellerie de l'Europe*, has a well-deserved reputation for its traditional Quercy dishes (ⓣ05.65.50.06.07; menus €14–39; mid-Oct to May closed Fri & Sat, also closed Jan & Nov). Also worth trying is the elegant *La Cuisine du Marché*, 15 rue Clermont, just north of St-Sauveur church, which offers a limited range of well-prepared local dishes in menus that range from €18 to €35 (ⓣ05.65.50.18.55; closed Sun). For a lighter meal, head for the bars, cafés and crêperies around place Carnot and place Champollion.

Cardaillac

Home of one of the great families of Quercy in the Middle Ages, the old part of the village of **CARDAILLAC**, about 10km to the north of Figeac off the N140, is gathered on the tip of a steep ridge above wild wooded valleys, an organic pile of houses, primitive machinery and crumbling fortifications of such antiquity you wonder how they're still there. The village has created what they call a **musée éclaté**, consisting of a tour (in French only) of several old houses and giving an insight into the lifestyle and practices of yore, like bread-making, drying chestnuts and preparing prunes (daily except Sat: July 1–13 & Aug 26–Sept 15 3pm; July 14–Aug 25 3pm & 4.30pm; Sept 16–June by appointment on ⓣ05.65.40.10.63 or ⓣ05.65.40.15.65; donation expected). An additional plus point is the minute but delightful, simple **hotel** *Chez Marcel*, on the through road (ⓣ05.65.40.11.16, ⓕ05.65.40.49.08; ❶; closed Sun–Thurs Jan–March, also closed two weeks in Feb & two weeks in Oct), with a first-rate **restaurant** offering such delights as a *gigot* of lamb from the *causse* and the regional offal speciality, *tripoux* (menus from €13; closed Sun eve & Mon, from Jan–March also closed Sun lunch & for dinner Tues–Thurs).

Foissac and Peyrerusse-le-Roc

Coming out of Figeac on the road to Villefranche-de-Rouerge, keep an eye out on the right for one of the **aiguilles**, or stone needles, that used to ring Figeac. They are 8m high and date from the 1100s; no one knows whether they were milestones, boundary markers for the abbey, or something completely different.

Some 20km further south, and west of the road to Villeneuve, is the village of **FOISSAC**, which has given its name to a local **cave** (April, May & Oct daily except Sat 2–6pm; June & Sept daily 10–11.30am & 2–6pm; July & Aug daily 10am–6pm; €6.80; Ⓦwww.grotte-de-foissac.com). In addition to a variety of weird and wonderful formations, you'll see an unusual prehistoric **potter's workshop** dating from about 4000 BC.

To the east of Foissac, about 20km by a beautiful lane across the *causse*, you happen upon one of the most remarkable old villages in this corner of France, **PEYRERUSSE-LE-ROC**. The "modern" village sits astride a ridge above a narrow wooded valley: a tiny huddle of long-eaved, half-timbered houses gathered round a seventeenth-century church. On the slopes below, hidden in the steep woods, lie the remains of a medieval stronghold, abandoned around 1700, that once stood guard over the silver-rich country round about, and which has only recently begun to be excavated. A cobbled mule path leads to the gate towers and on into the woods, where the stones of a Gothic church, synagogue and hospital stand roofless beneath an unscalable pinnacle of rock crowned by twin towers. A path crosses the stream and climbs along the overgrown bank to an ancient packhorse bridge and ruined mill. From here you can scramble back up the valley side to a bridge of rock where a vertiginous ladder gives access to the towers. The site is gradually being tidied up and some of the buildings restored, but for the moment at least, it remains a moving and atmospheric place.

The valley of the Célé

For the last stretch of its course from Figeac to Conduché, where it joins the Lot, the **River Célé** flows through a luxuriant canyon-like valley cut into the limestone uplands of the Causse de Gramat. A twisting minor road follows the river here: a silent backwater of a place, hot in summer, frequented mainly by canoeists (with any number of opportunities to rent craft). The **GR651** follows the same route, sometimes close to the river, sometimes on the edge of the *causse* on the north bank.

Espagnac-Ste-Eulalie and Marcilhac-sur-Célé

Travelling downstream from Figeac, two villages in particular are worth a stop. The first is **ESPAGNAC-STE-EULALIE**, about 18km west of Figeac. It's a tiny and beautiful hamlet reached across an old stone bridge on the south bank of the river, under the limestone outcrops of the *causse*. An eye-catching octagonal lantern crowns the belfry of the **church** (guided visits: daily 10.30am, 4pm & 5.30pm by appointment, call Mme Bonzani on Ⓣ05.65.40.06.17; €2), and under a weathered tower next door, an ancient gateway now houses a *gîte d'étape* (Ⓣ05.65.11.42.66; closed early Nov to Feb). There are two quiet riverside **campsites** in the next hamlet, **Brengues**: *Le Moulin Vieux* (Ⓣ05.65.40.00.41, Ⓕ05.65.40.05.65; closed Oct–March), and the smaller municipal site (Ⓣ05.65.40.06.82, Ⓕ05.65.40.05.71; closed Oct–May).

The second village of real interest is **MARCILHAC-SUR-CÉLÉ**, 9km downstream of Brengues, whose partially ruined **abbey** (April & May Wed–Sat

10am–noon & 2–5pm; June & Sept Tues–Sun 10am–noon & 2–6pm; July & Aug Tues–Sat 10am–12.30pm & 2–6.30pm, Sun 2–7.30pm; €3), with its gaping walls and broken columns, conjures a strongly romantic atmosphere. Very early and rather primitive ninth-century Carolingian sculpture decorates the lintel, and there are some handsome Romanesque capitals in the chapterhouse. In the damp interior are frescoes from around 1500 and old coats of arms of the local nobility, testimony to Marcilhac's once mighty power, when even Rocamadour was under its sway. During World War II, it was the scene of one of the *maquis'* first theatrical gestures of turning the tables on the occupier: on November 11, 1943 – Armistice Day – Jean-Jacques Chapou's group (see p.766) briefly occupied the village and laid a wreath at the war memorial.

It's worth timing your visit to **eat** at the attractive *Restaurant des Touristes* on the main street (Ⓣ05.65.40.65.61, reservations required; closed Nov–Easter), where you'll feast on hearty home cooking for around €17. There's a *gîte d'étape* in the abbey (Ⓣ05.65.40.61.43, Ⓔsecretariat.mairie-de-marcilhac@wanadoo.fr; closed Oct–March), as well as the *Pré de Monsieur* **campsite** just outside the village (Ⓣ & Ⓕ05.65.40.77.88; closed Nov–March).

Musée de Plein Air du Quercy

Set back from the north side of the River Célé, about 13km from Marcilhac, near **CUZALS**, the **Musée de Plein Air du Quercy** (daily except Sat: April, May, Sept & Oct 2–6pm; June 9.30am–6.30pm; July & Aug 10am–7pm; July & Aug €8, otherwise €6; Ⓦwww.museeduquercy.com) is one of the better open-air museums, and was set up in the 1980s to preserve the distinctive rural architecture of France. Reconstructions that range from a half-timbered eighteenth-century farmhouse to a garage from the 1920s are scattered around the site, which is centred around a twentieth-century château burnt down by the Nazis in the last war. It's best on Sundays in summer (June–Aug), when many traditional activities like milling, haymaking and blacksmithing are demonstrated. The information is dished out with an appealing blend of humour and didactics, and the whole place is less blatantly commercial than many other écomusées. And you don't have to take it all in at once – tickets are valid for eight days.

Grotte de Pech-Merle

Discovered in 1922, the **Grotte de Pech-Merle** (mid-Jan to March and Nov to mid-Dec by group reservation only; April–Oct daily 9.30am–noon & 1.30–5pm; Ⓣ05.65.31.27.05, Ⓦwww.pechmerle.com; 15 June–15 Sept €7, rest of year €6) is less accessible than the caves at Les Eyzies but still attracts sufficient visitors to warrant restricting numbers to 700 per day; it's advisable to book at least three or four days ahead in July and August. The cave is well hidden on the scrubby hillsides above Cabrerets, which lies 15km from Marcilhac and 4km from Conduché.

The cave itself is far more beautiful than those at Padirac or Les Eyzies, with galleries full of the most spectacular stalactites and stalagmites – structures tiered like wedding cakes, hanging like curtains, or shaped like whale baffles, discs or cave pearls. On the downside, the cave is wired for electric light and the guides make sure you're processed through in the scheduled time.

The first **drawings** you come to are in the so-called Chapelle des Mammouths, executed on a white calcite panel that looks as if it's been specially prepared for the purpose. There are horses, bison – charging head down with tiny rumps and arched tails – and tusked, whiskery mammoths. You then pass into a vast chamber where the glorious horse panel is visible on a lower level;

it's a remarkable example of the way in which the artist used the contour and relief of the rock to do the work, producing an utterly convincing mammoth by just two strokes of black. The cave ceiling is covered with finger marks, preserved in the soft clay. You pass the skeleton of a cave hyena that has been lying there for 20,000 years – wild animals used these caves for shelter and sometimes, unable to find their way out, starved to death in them. And finally, the most spine-tingling experience at Pech-Merle: the footprints of an adolescent preserved in a muddy pool.

The admission charge includes an excellent film and **museum**, where prehistory is illustrated by colourful and intelligible charts, a selection of objects (rather than the usual 10,000 flints), skulls and beautiful slides displayed in wall panels.

There's a *gîte d'étape* (Ⓣ05.65.31.27.04, Ⓕ05.65.30.25.46; closed Nov–Easter) and a **campsite**, *Le Cantal* (Ⓣ05.65.31.26.61, Ⓕ05.65.31.20.47; closed Nov–March), close by at **CABRERETS**. This tiny place also has a pair of two-star **hotels**: the *Auberge de la Sagne*, 1km outside the village on the road to Peche-Merle (Ⓣ05.65.31.26.62, Ⓦwww.logis-de-france.fr; ❸; closed 15 Sept–15 May), which has a pool and a good restaurant (evening only; menus €15 & €21); and the riverside *Les Grottes* (Ⓣ05.65.31.27.02, Ⓦwww.hoteldesgrottes.com; ❷; closed Nov–Easter), also with a decent restaurant attached (menus from €14.50).

The valley of the Aveyron

Thirty-seven kilometres south of Figeac, **Villefranche-de-Rouerge** lies on a bend in the River Aveyron, clustered around its perfectly preserved, arcaded market square. From Villefranche the Aveyron flows south through increasingly deep, thickly wooded valleys, past the hilltop village of **Najac** and then turns abruptly west as it enters the **Gorges de l'Aveyron**. The most impressive stretch of this defile begins not far east of **St-Antonin-de-Noble-Val**, an ancient village caught between soaring limestone cliffs, and continues downstream to the villages of **Penne** and **Bruniquel**, perched beside their crumbling castles. Bruniquel marks the end of the gorges, as you suddenly break out into flat alluvial plains where the Aveyron joins the great rivers of the Tarn and Garonne.

Villefranche-de-Rouergue

No medieval junketing, not a craft shop in sight, **VILLEFRANCHE-DE-ROUERGUE** must be as close as you can get to what a French provincial town used to be like, the sort of place where the old folk are as likely to speak Occitan as French. It's a small town, lying on a bend in the Aveyron, 35km due south of Figeac and 61km east of Cahors across the **Causse de Limogne**. Built as a *bastide* by Alphonse de Poitiers in 1252 as part of the royal policy of extending control over the recalcitrant lands of the south, the town became rich on copper from the surrounding mines and its privilege of minting coins. From the fifteenth to the eighteenth centuries, its wealthy men built the magnificent houses that grace the cobbled streets to this day.

Rue du Sergent-Bories and rue de la République, the main commercial street, are both very attractive, but they are no preparation for **place Notre-Dame**, the loveliest *bastide* central square in the region. It's built on a slope, so the uphill houses are much higher than the downhill, and you enter at the corners underneath the buildings. All the houses are arcaded at ground-floor level, providing for a **market** (Thurs morning) where local merchants and farmers spread out their weekly produce – the quintessential Villefranche experience. The houses are unusually tall and some are very elaborately decorated, notably the so-called **Maison du Président Raynal** on the lower side at the top of rue de la République.

The east side of the square is dominated by the **church of Notre-Dame** with its colossal porch and bell tower, nearly 60m high. The interior has some fine late fifteenth-century stained glass, carved choir stalls and misericords.

On the boulevard that forms the northern limit of the old town, the seventeenth-century **Chapelle des Pénitents-Noirs** (July–Sept daily 10am–noon & 2–6pm; €3.50) boasts a splendidly Baroque painted ceiling and an enormous gilded retable. Another ecclesiastical building worth the slight detour is the **Chartreuse St-Sauveur** (same hours; €3.50), about 1km out of town on the Gaillac road. It was completed in the space of ten years from 1450, giving it a singular architectural harmony, and has a very beautiful cloister and choir stalls by the same master as Notre-Dame in Villefranche, which, by contrast, took nearly 300 years to complete.

Aside from the pleasing details of many of the houses you notice as you explore the side streets, the town reserves one other most unexpected surprise. The **Médiathèque**, on rue Sénéchal (Ⓣ05.65.45.59.45), includes an amazing collection of jazz records, books, papers, recordings and documents belonging to the late Hugues Panassié, famous French jazz critic and one of the founders of the Hot Club de France. Much of the material is unrecorded or unobtainable elsewhere and is open to perusal by members. CD selections are on sale both here and at the tourist office.

Practicalities

The **gare SNCF** is located a couple of minutes' walk south across the Aveyron from the old town. For information about buses, contact the **tourist office** just north of the river on promenade du Guiraudet (May–June & Sept Mon–Fri 9am–noon & 2–7pm, Sat 9am–noon & 2–6pm; July & Aug also open Sun 10am–12.30pm; Oct–April Mon–Fri 9am–noon & 2–6pm, Sat 9am–noon; Ⓣ05.65.45.13.18, Ⓦwww.villefranche.com), beside the bridge.

For those who want to stay overnight, there are two pleasant **hotels**: *L'Univers*, 2 place de la République at the end of the bridge opposite the tourist office (Ⓣ05.65.45.15.63, Ⓦwww.logis-de-france.com; ❸), with a good traditional restaurant (from €15); and the more modest *Bellevue*, 3 av du Ségala (Ⓣ05.65.45.23.17, Ⓕ05.65.45.11.19; ❶; closed school hols in Feb & Nov, also Sun & Mon), also with a decent restaurant (menus €10–43), a little further out of town on the Rodez road. In a rather unpromising location, 3km out on the Figeac road, *Le Relais de Farrou* (Ⓣ05.65.45.18.11, Ⓦwww.villefranche.com/relais_farrou; ❸–❹; restaurant from €15) offers more luxurious surroundings and good food. For cheaper accommodation, there's an excellent *Foyer de Jeunes Travailleurs* **HI hostel** (Ⓣ05.65.45.09.68, Ⓕ05.65.45.82.82), next to the *gare SNCF*. There's also a *gîte d'étape* by the river at La Gasse (Ⓣ05.65.45.10.80; closed Nov–April), 3km out of town on the D269 back road to La Bastide-L'Évêque, at the start of GR62b, plus a **campsite**, the *Camping du Rouergue* (Ⓣ05.65.45.16.24, Ⓦwww.villefranche.com/rouerge; closed mid-Oct to mid-April), 1.5km to the south on the D47 to Monteil.

For **eating**, next to the covered market is a welcoming workers' diner, *Restaurant de la Halle*, where you can eat a substantial meal for €9.50

(☎05.65.45.07.74) at communal tables. Or try the *Globe*, a bustling modern brasserie across the river from the tourist office, where main dishes start at around €8–10.

Najac

NAJAC occupies an extraordinary site on a conical hill isolated in a wide bend in the deep valley of the Aveyron, 25km south of Villefranche-de-Rouergue and on the Aurillac–Toulouse train line. Its photogenic castle, which graces many a travel poster, sits right on the peak of the hill, while the half-timbered and stone-tiled village houses tail out in a single street along the narrow back of the spur that joins the hill to the valley side. It's all very attractive and consequently touristy, with the inevitable resident knick-knack shops and craftspeople.

The **château** (April, May & Sept daily 10am–12.30pm & 3–5.30pm; June daily 10am–12.30pm & 3–6.30pm; July & Aug daily 10am–1pm & 3–7pm; Oct Sun 10am–12.30pm & 3–5.30pm; last entry 30min before closing; €3.75) is a model of medieval defensive architecture and was endlessly fought over because of its commanding and impregnable position in a region once rich in silver and copper mines. You can clearly see all the devices for restricting an attacker once he was inside the castle: the covered passages and stairs within the thickness of the walls, the multistorey positions for archers and, of course, the most magnificent all-round view from the top of the keep. In one of the chambers of the keep you can see the stone portraits of St Louis, king of France, his brother Alphonse de Poitiers and Jeanne, the daughter of the count of Toulouse, whose marriage to Alphonse was arranged in 1229 to end the Cathar wars by bringing the domains of Count Raymond and his allies under royal control. It was Alphonse who "modernized" the castle and made the place we see today. Signatures of the masons who worked on it are clearly visible on many stones.

Below the rather dull central square stretches the **faubourg**, a sort of elongated square bordered by houses raised on pillars as in the central square of a *bastide*, which reduces to a narrow waist of a street overlooked by more ancient houses and leading past a fountain to the castle gate. At the foot of the castle, in the centre of what was the medieval village, stands the very solid-looking **church of St-Jean**, which the villagers of Najac were forced by the Inquisition to build at their own expense in 1258 as a punishment for their conversion to Catharism. In addition to a collection of reliquaries and an extraordinary iron cage for holding candles, the church has one architectural oddity: its windows are solid panels of stone from which the lights have been cut out in trefoil form. Below the church, by a derelict farm, a surviving stretch of **Roman road** leads downhill to where a thirteenth-century bridge spans the Aveyron.

The **tourist office** is on the faubourg (April–June & Sept Mon–Sat 9am–noon & 2.30–6pm; July & Aug Mon–Sat 8am–noon & 2.30–6.30pm, Sun 10am–noon; Oct–March Mon–Fri 9am–noon & 2.30–6pm, Sat 9am–noon; ☎05.65.29.72.05). At the eastern entrance to the faubourg the modern village balances on the shoulder of the spur round an open square where you'll find a very comfortable **hotel**, *L'Oustal del Barry* (☎05.65.29.74.32, Ⓦwww.oustaldelbarry.com; ❹–❺; closed mid-Nov to mid-March), whose restaurant is renowned for its subtle and inventive cuisine (closed Mon & lunchtime Tues except 15 June–15 Sept; menus €18–48). Below Najac is a **campsite**, *Le Païsserou* (☎05.65.29.73.96, or ☎ 04.73.34.75.53 off season, Ⓔsogeval@wanadoo.fr; closed Oct–April), with a *gîte d'étape* (same contact details; open all year).

St-Antonin-Noble-Val

One of the finest and most substantial towns in the valley is **ST-ANTONIN-NOBLE-VAL**, 30km southwest of Najac. It sits on the bank of the Aveyron beneath the beetling cliffs of the Roc d'Anglars, and has endured all the vicissitudes of the old towns of the southwest: it went Cathar, then Protestant and each time was walloped by the alien power of the kings from the north. Yet, in spite of all this, it recovered its prosperity, manufacturing cloth and leather goods, endowed by its wealthy merchants with a marvellous heritage of medieval houses in all the streets leading out from the lovely **place de la Halle**.

There's a café most conveniently and picturesquely placed next to the ancient *halle*, with a view of the town's finest building, the **Maison des Consuls**, whose origins go back to 1120. It now houses the town museum, **Musée du Vieux St-Antonin** (July & Aug daily except Tues 10am–1pm & 3–6pm; Sept–June apply to the tourist office; €2.50), with collections of objects to do with the former life of the place, as well as a section on local prehistoric sites.

The **tourist office** is in the "new" town hall next to the church (July & Aug daily 9.30am–12.30pm & 2–6.30pm; Sept–June Mon–Sat 2–5.30pm; Ⓣ05.63.30.63.47, Ⓦwww.saint-antonin-noble-val.com), and will supply information about B&Bs, canoeing on the Aveyron and walks in the region. By the bridge, as you cross from the Montauban road, there's a simple and attractive **hotel** immediately on the left, *Les Thermes*, with a terrace overlooking the water (Ⓣ05.63.25.06.00, Ⓦwww.nobleval.com; ❷) and a good traditional restaurant (closed Jan, also Tues & Wed Sept–June; menus €10–29). There are four local **campsites**, of which the riverside *Camping d'Anglars* is the closest, 1km upstream on the D115 (Ⓣ05.63.30.69.76, Ⓕ05.63.30.67.61; closed Oct to mid-April).

Penne and Bruniquel

Twenty kilometres downstream of St-Antonin you come to the beautiful ridge-top village of **PENNE**, once a Cathar stronghold, with its ruined castle impossibly perched on an airy crag. Everything is old and leaning and bulging, but holding together nonetheless, with a harmony that would be impossible to create purposely.

BRUNIQUEL, a few kilometres further on, is another hilltop village clustered round its **castle** (April & Oct Sun 10am–12.30pm & 2–6pm, May, June & Sept daily same hours; July & Aug daily 10am–7pm; €2.50, or €3.50 including guided visit). You can also visit a handsome house in the village, the aristocratic **Maison des Comtes de Payrol** (March & Oct Sat & Sun 10am–6pm; April–Sept daily 10am–6pm; €3). If you want to **stay**, Marc de Badouin runs a good *chambres d'hôte* to the right of the church (Ⓣ05.63.67.26.16, Ⓔrandodo@wanadoo.fr; ❸; meals from €17); he's also a keen mountain-biker and can advise on local trails and footpaths. There's also a small two-star **campsite**, *Le Payssel* (Ⓣ05.63.67.25.95; closed Oct–April), about 700m south on the D964 to Albi.

Montauban and around

MONTAUBAN today is a prosperous middle-sized provincial city, capital of the largely agricultural *département* of Tarn-et-Garonne. It lies on the banks of the River Tarn, 53km from Toulouse, close to its junction with the Aveyron and their joint confluence with the Garonne, where the wide alluvial plain of the three rivers stretches boringly for miles around. But this is where the lines of communication run, and Montauban lies, conveniently, on the southwest Bordeaux–Toulouse autoroute and train line.

The city's **history** goes back to 1144, when the count of Toulouse decided to create a *bastide* here as a bulwark against English and French royal power. In fact, it's generally regarded as the first *bastide*, the model for those rationally laid-out medieval new towns, and that plan is still clearly evident in the beautiful town centre.

Montauban has enjoyed various periods of great prosperity, as one can guess from the proliferation of fine town houses. The first followed the suppression of the Cathar heresy and the final submission of the counts of Toulouse in 1229, and was greatly enhanced by the building of the Pont-Vieux in 1335, making it the best crossing-point on the Tarn for miles around. The Hundred Years War did its share of damage, as did Montauban's opting for the Protestant cause in the Wars of Religion, but by the time of the Revolution it had become once more one of the richest cities in the southwest, particularly successful in the manufacture of cloth.

Arrival, information and accommodation

At Montauban's centre lies the exquisite **place Nationale**, with the cathedral ten minutes' walk to the south on the unattractive **place Roosevelt** (where, if driving, you'll find the most convenient parking). From here, rue de l'Hôtel-de-Ville leads directly to the Pont-Vieux and across the river to avenue de Mayenne, at the end of which is the **gare SNCF**. There's no central *gare routière*, so you'll need to ask for bus information at the **tourist office**, on the northern corner of boulevard Midi-Pyrénées by the hideous market hall on place Prax-Paris (July & Aug Mon–Sat 9.30am–12.30pm & 2–6.30pm, Sun 10am–noon; Sept–June Mon–Sat 9.30am–12.30pm & 2–6.30pm; Ⓣ05.63.63.60.60, Ⓔofficetourisme@montauban.com).

Montauban has a surprisingly poor choice of **hotels**. Despite its recent renovation, the attractive *Du Commerce*, 9 place Roosevelt (Ⓣ05.63.66.31.32, Ⓦhotel.du-commerce.com; ❸), still offers the cheapest accommodation in the town centre, whereas the *Mercure*, opposite at 12 rue Notre-Dame (Ⓣ05.63.63.17.23, Ⓦwww.mercure.com; ❻; restaurant from €14), is getting into the luxury bracket – though some rooms are decidedly small. For a mid-range hotel, your best option is the *D'Orsay*, 31 rue Roger-Salengro, outside the train station (Ⓣ05.63.66.06.66, Ⓔcuisinedalain@wanadoo.fr; ❸; closed Sun & during Christmas hols); it doesn't look much, but the rooms are comfortable enough and it has an excellent restaurant (closed Sun & for lunch on Mon & Sat; menus €22–52).

The Town

Montauban couldn't be easier to find your way around. The greatest delight is simply to wander the streets of the city centre, with their lovely pink brick houses; the town is only a ten- or fifteen-minute stroll from end to end. The visitable part is the small kernel of central streets based on the original *bastide*, and is enclosed within an inner ring of boulevards between boulevard Midi-Pyrénées on the east and the river on the west. The finest point of all is the **place Nationale**, rebuilt after a fire in the seventeenth century and surrounded on all sides by exquisite double-vaulted arcades with the octagonal belfry of St-Jacques showing above the western rooftops. It's the hub of the city's social life and the first place to head for coffee, drinks or food.

The adjacent **place du Coq** on rue de la République is also pretty, and if you follow the street down it brings you out by the **church of St-Jacques** (first built in the thirteenth century on the pilgrim route to Compostela) and the end of the **Pont-Vieux** with a wide view of the river. At the near end of the bridge, the former bishop's residence is a massive half-palace, half-fortress, begun by the Black Prince in 1363 but never finished because the English lost control of the town. It's now the **Musée Ingres** (Easter to June & first two weeks Sept Tues–Sat 10am–noon & 2–6pm, Sun 2–6pm; July & Aug daily 10am–6pm; mid-Sept to Easter Tues–Sun 10am–noon & 2–6pm; €4.50), so called because it houses drawings and paintings that artist Jean-Auguste-Dominique Ingres, a native of Montauban, left to the city on his death. It's a collection the city is very proud of, though his supremely realistic, luminous portraits won't be to everyone's taste. The museum also contains a substantial collection of works by another native, Émile-Antoine Bourdelle, the ubiquitous monumental sculptor and a student of Rodin, alongside a hotch-potch of other exhibits, from Gallo-Roman mosaics to fifteenth- and sixteenth-century European fine art.

The **Cathédrale Notre-Dame**, ten minutes' walk up rue de l'Hôtel-de-Ville, is a cold fish: an austere and unsympathetic building erected just before 1700 as part of the triumphalist campaign to reassert the glories of the Catholic faith after the cruel defeat and repression of the Protestants. But it's a bit of an architectural rarity in France, where there are few cathedrals built in the classical style.

Eating and drinking

In addition to the hotel restaurants mentioned above, the simplest way of finding a **place to eat** is to go to the place Nationale, where you'll find *Le Couvert des Drapiers* under the arcades at no. 27 (closed for dinner Mon–Wed), serving good-value lunchtime *plats du jour* at around €8, and the equally popular *Brasserie des Arts* at no. 4 (closed Sun; menus from €15). The *Bistrot du Faubourg* at 111 faubourg Lacapelle, east of the cathedral (closed Sat eve & Sun; menus from €11.30), is a nicely old-fashioned place offering excellent value for money. Last but not least, the *Ventadour*, 23 quai Villebourbon (Ⓣ05.63.63.34.58; closed Sun, Mon & lunch Sat; lunch menus from €18.50, dinner from €24), magnificently sited in an old house on the west bank near the Pont-Vieux, is the place to go for a splurge.

The most atmospheric place for a **drink** is *Le Flamand* at 8 rue de la République (closed Sun), with a wide range of beers on tap, or you could try *Le Maracana*, the liveliest option on place Nationale, which hosts live music on summer weekends. Another good possibility is *Le Santa Maria*, north of the Musée Ingres on quai Montmurat (closed Sun & Mon), with a terrace overlooking the Tarn; they also serve tapas and more substantial Tex-Mex meals.

Lauzerte

As you head north from Montauban towards Cahors, leaving the wide flat valleys of the Tarn and Garonne behind you, the land rises gradually to gently undulating country, green and woody, cut obliquely by parallel valleys running down to meet the Garonne and planted with vines and sunflowers, maize, and apple and plum orchards. It's a very soft landscape, and villages are small and widely scattered. The pace of life seems about equal with that of a turning sunflower.

Should you find yourself taking this route, then the place to make a halt is **LAUZERTE**, one of Raymond of Toulouse's *bastides* and once of great military importance as it commanded the road to Cahors – the route down which the pilgrims of St-Jacques came pouring every spring, as they still do today (or at least the hardy who follow the GR65 on foot). The town is short on sights, but there are some old houses, a pretty arcaded central square and a good Baroque altarpiece in the church, as well as views of the countryside round about.

There's a very pleasant **hotel** at the entrance to the village for those who want to stay: *Le Quercy* (Ⓣ05.63.94.66.36; ❷–❸; closed Sun eve & Mon), which also serves superb food, with lunch menus from €10 and dinner from €24.50. If they're full, try *Le Luzerta*, at the bottom of the hill (Ⓣ05.63.94.64.43, Ⓦwww.hotel-quercy.com; ❷), which has several modern bungalows around a swimming pool and a decent restaurant (Nov to mid-April closed Sun eve & Tues; menus from €17). There's a **campsite** nearby, *Le Melvin* (Ⓣ & Ⓕ05.63.94.75.60; open all year), and a *gîte d'étape* in the village for walkers on the GR65 (Ⓣ05.63.94.61.94, Ⓕ05.63.94.61.93; open March–Oct).

Moissac

There's nothing very memorable about the modern town of **MOISSAC**, 30km northwest of Montauban, largely because of the terrible damage done by the flood of March 1930, when the Tarn, swollen by a sudden thaw in the Massif Central, burst its banks, destroying 617 houses and killing 120 people.

Luckily, the one thing that makes Moissac a household name in the history of art survived: the cloister and porch of the **abbey church of St-Pierre**, a masterpiece of Romanesque sculpture and the model for hundreds of churches and buildings elsewhere. Indeed, the fact that it has survived countless wars, including siege and sack by Simon de Montfort senior in 1212 during the crusade against the Cathars, is something of a miracle. During the Revolution it was used as a gunpowder factory and billet for soldiers, who damaged many of the sculptures. In the 1830s it only escaped demolition to make way for the Bordeaux–Toulouse train line by a whisker.

Legend has it that Clovis the Frank first founded a monastery here, though it seems more probable that its origins belong a hundred years or so later in the seventh century, which saw the foundation of so many monasteries throughout Aquitaine. The first Romanesque church on the site was consecrated in 1063 and enlarged in the following century. The famous south **porch**, with its magnificent tympanum and curious wavy door jambs and pillars, dates from this second phase of building. It depicts Christ in Majesty, right hand raised in benediction, the Book of Life in his hand, surrounded by the evangelists and the elders of the Apocalypse as described by St John in the Book of Revelation. It's a display whose influence, assimilated with varying degrees of success, can be seen in the work of artists who decorated the porches of countless churches across the south of France. There's more fine carving in the capitals inside the porch, and the interior of the church, which was remodelled in the fifteenth century, is interesting too, especially for some of the wood and stone statuary it contains.

The adjoining **cloister** (same hours as tourist office – see below; €5) is entered through the tourist office, and if you want to experience the silent contemplation for which it was originally built, get there first thing in the morning. The cloister surrounds a garden shaded by a majestic cedar, and its pantile roof is supported by 76 alternating single and double marble columns.

Each column supports a single inverted wedge-shaped block of stone, on which are carved with extraordinary delicacy all manner of animals and plant motifs, as well as scenes from Bible stories and the lives of the saints. An inscription on the middle pillar on the west side explains that the cloister was made in the time of Abbot Ansquitil in the year of Our Lord 1100.

Practicalities

The **tourist office** (April–June & Sept Mon–Fri 9am–noon & 2–6pm, Sat & Sun 10am–noon & 2–6pm; July & Aug daily 9am–7pm; Oct–March Mon–Fri 10am–noon & 2–5pm, Sat & Sun 2–5pm; ⓣ05.63.04.01.85, ⓦwww.moissac.fr) is next to the cloister, with the **gare SNCF** further west along avenue Pierre-Chabrié. There's a weekend **market** in place des Récollets at the end of rue de la République, which leads away from the abbey, a marvel of colour and temptation.

The *Moulin de Moissac* (ⓣ05.63.32.88.88, ⓦwww.lemoulindemoissac.com; ❸; restaurant from €20), occupying a former mill on the riverfront, rates as the top **hotel** in town; the building is large and not particularly attractive, but the interior has been beautifully refurbished. Between the river and the abbey church, *Le Chapon Fin* on place des Récollets (ⓣ05.63.04.04.22, ⓦwww.lechaponfin-moissac.com; ❹; restaurant from €25) also makes a pleasant place to stay. Alternatively, try the nicely old-fashioned *Le Luxembourg*, 2 av Pierre-Chabrié (ⓣ05.63.04.00.27, ⓦwww.hotelluxembourg82.com; ❸), with a well-rated traditional restaurant (closed Sun eve; menus €12–25). For **campers**, there's a shady site across the river on a little island, the *Île du Bidounet* (ⓣ05.63.32.52.52, ⓔcamping.bidounet@wanadoo.fr; closed Oct–March), and a *gîte d'étape* at 5 sente du Calvaire (ⓣ05.63.04.62.21, ⓔaccueil.cafmoissac@wanadoo.fr) for walkers only on the hill above town. The nicest **place to eat** is the magnolia-shaded *Auberge du Cloître* (closed Mon & evenings on Wed & Sun; lunch menus from €12.40, dinner from €20), beside the tourist office.

Agen

AGEN, capital of the Lot-et-Garonne *département*, is a more pleasant town than it first appears. It was quartered by modern boulevards in the nineteenth century in its own version of a Haussmann clean-up, and it's down these roads that you're funnelled into the town, with the result that you see nothing of interest.

The town lies on the broad, powerful River Garonne halfway between Bordeaux and Toulouse, and lived through the Middle Ages racked by war with England and internecine strife between Catholics and Protestants. But it was able to extract some advantage from disputes as it seesawed between the English and French, gaining more and more privileges of independence as the price of its loyalty – a tradition that it maintained during and after the Revolution by being staunchly republican (the churches still bear the legend: *Liberté, Fraternité, Égalité*).

Its pre-Revolutionary wealth derived from the manufacture of various kinds of cloth and its thriving port on the Garonne, which in those days was alive with river traffic. But the Industrial Revolution put paid to all of that. Agen's prosperity now is based on agriculture – in particular, its famous prunes and plums, said to have been brought back from Syria during the Crusades.

The interesting part of Agen centres on **place Goya**, where boulevard de la République, leading to the river, crosses boulevard du Président-Carnot.

On the south side of boulevard de la République, the main shopping area is around place Wilson, rue Garonne and the partly arcaded place des Laitiers. A left turn at the end of rue Garonne brings you to the wide place du Dr-Esquirol and an exuberant *fin-de-siècle* municipal **theatre**; opposite this is the **Musée Municipal des Beaux-Arts** (daily except Tues 10am–6pm; €3.60), magnificently housed in four adjacent sixteenth- and seventeeth-century mansions. The collections include a rich variety of archeological finds, Roman and medieval, furniture and paintings – among the latter some Goyas and a Tintoretto rediscovered in the museum basement during an inventory in 1997. Not far from the museum, in place du Bourg at the end of rue des Droits-de-l'Homme, the cute little thirteenth-century **church of Notre-Dame** is also worth a look.

South of the theatre, rue Beauville, with heavily restored but beautiful medieval houses, leads to rue Richard-Cœur-de-Lion and the **Église des Jacobins**. The barn-like interior of this big, brick Dominican church of the thirteenth century, is divided by a single centre row of pillars, very like its counterpart in Toulouse; the deconsecrated church is now an annex of the Musée des Beaux-Arts and hosts temporary exhibitions. Beyond lie the river and the public gardens of **Le Gravier**, where a **market** is held every Saturday morning; there's a footbridge across the Garonne, from where you can see a canal bridge dating from 1839 further downstream.

Opposite place Wilson on the north side of boulevard de la République, the arcaded rue Cornières leads through to the **Cathédrale St-Caprais**, somewhat misshapen but with a finely proportioned Romanesque apse and radiating chapels still surviving. There's a piece of the original fortifications still showing in rue des Augustins close by – the **Tour du Chapelet** – dating from around 1100. Again nearby, in rue du Puits-du-Saumon, is one of the finest houses in town, the fourteenth-century **Maison du Sénéchal**, with an elaborate open loggia on the first floor.

Practicalities

From the central place Goya, boulevard du Président-Carnot leads to the **gares SNCF** and **routière**. The **tourist office** is at 107 bd Carnot (July & Aug Mon–Sat 9am–7pm, Sun 9.30am–12.30pm; Sept–June Mon–Sat 9am–12.30pm & 2–6.30pm; ⓣ05.53.47.36.09, ⓦwww.ot-agen.org).

There are several reasonable **hotel** options in Agen. Near the tourist office, the *Ibis*, 16 rue Camille-Desmoulins (ⓣ05.53.47.43.43, ⓦwww.ibishotel.com; ❸), doesn't look much but is comfortable and welcoming. Also very central is the simple *Des Ambans*, 59 rue des Ambans (ⓣ05.53.66.28.60, ⓕ05.53.87.94.01; ❶), near place Goya. At the east end of boulevard de la République, close to the river, the attractive *Des Îles*, 25 rue Baudin (ⓣ05.53.47.11.33, ⓕ05.53.66.19.25; ❷), is less convenient but has light, airy rooms. For four-star luxury and buckets of atmosphere, head for the *Château des Jacobins*, in an elegant nineteenth-century town house beside the Jacobins church (ⓣ05.53.47.03.31, ⓦwww.chateau-des-jacobins.com; ❻).

The best **places to eat** well at reasonable prices are *Les Mignardises*, 40 rue Camille-Desmoulins (closed Sun lunch & Mon), popular for its good-value menus (from €10.80), and the convivial *L'Atelier*, 14 rue du Jeu-de-Paume (ⓣ05.53.87.89.22; closed Sat & Sun; from €16). For a bit of a splurge, there's the *Mariottat*, 25 rue Louis-Vivent to the south of the Jacobins church, which concentrates on top-quality local produce (ⓣ05.53.77.99.77; closed Sun eve, Mon & lunch Sat; menus €22–55).

Travel details

Trains

Agen to: Belvès (1–6 daily; 1hr); Bordeaux (hourly; 1hr 10min–1hr 50min); Le Buisson (1–6 daily; 1hr 10min–1hr 40min); Les Eyzies (1–6 daily; 1hr 40min); Moissac (1–5 daily; 25min); Monsempron-Libos (6–7 daily; 40min); Montauban (every 1–2 hours; 40–50min); Périgueux (1–6 daily; 2hr–2hr 20min); Toulouse (every 1–2 hours; 40min–1hr 20min).

Bergerac to: Bordeaux (5–7 daily; 1hr 10min–1hr 30min); Montcaret (1–3 daily; 30–40min); St-Émilion (1–3 daily; 55min); Ste-Foy-la-Grande (7–9 daily; 20min); Sarlat (3–5 daily; 1hr–1hr 30min).

Brive to: Bordeaux (1–3 daily; 2hr 15min–2hr 30min); Cahors (6–8 daily; 1hr–1hr 10min); Clermont-Ferrand (2–4 daily; 3hr 40min); Figeac (5–6 daily; 1hr 15min–1hr 30min); Gourdon (6–8 daily; 40min); Limoges (10–15 daily; 1hr–1hr 15min); Montauban (6–8 daily; 1hr 45min–2hr); Paris-Austerlitz (9–14 daily; 4hr–4hr 45min); Périgueux (4–5 daily; 50min–1hr); Rocamadour-Padirac (5–6 daily; 40–50min); Souillac (6–8 daily; 25min); Toulouse (6–10 daily; 2hr–2hr 30min); Uzerche (6–8 daily; 30–45min); Villefranche-de-Rouergue (2 daily; 2hr–2hr 20min).

Cahors to: Brive (4–5 daily; 1hr–1hr 10min); Montauban (5–7 daily; 45min); Toulouse (6–8 daily; 1hr–1hr 20min).

Figeac to: Brive (5–6 daily; 1hr 30min–2hr); Najac (5–6 daily; 1hr); Rodez (4–6 daily; 1hr–1hr 20min); Toulouse (4–5 daily; 2hr 30min); Villefranche-de-Rouergue (6 daily; 40min).

Limoges to: Angoulême (2–3 daily; 2hr); Bordeaux (5–7 daily; 2hr 30min); Brive (10–15 daily; 1hr–1hr 15min); Eymoutiers (4–5 daily; 40–50min); Meymac (3–4 daily; 1hr 40min); Nexon (4–6 daily; 15min); Paris-Austerlitz (10–14 daily; 3hr–3hr 30min); Périgueux (8–15 daily; 1hr–1hr 20min); Poitiers (3–5 daily; 2hr); Pompadour (1–2 daily; 1hr 10min); St-Junien (3–5 daily; 40min); St-Léonard (4–5 daily; 20min); Solignac-Le Vigen (1–3 daily; 10min); Thiviers (8–15 daily; 40–50min); Ussel (3–4 daily; 1hr 35min–2hr).

Montauban to: Agen (hourly; 40–50min); Bordeaux (hourly; 1hr 30min–2hr); Moissac (3–6 daily; 20min); Toulouse (1–2 hourly; 25–35min).

Périgueux to: Agen (3–5 daily; 2hr–2hr 20min); Belvès (3–5 daily; 1hr–1hr 20min); Bordeaux (8–13 daily; 1hr–1hr 40min); Brive (3–5 daily; 50min–1hr); Le Buisson (2–6 daily; 50min); Les Eyzies (2–6 daily; 30min); Limoges (10–13 daily; 1hr–1hr 30min); Monsempron-Libos (3–5 daily; 1hr 30min).

Sarlat to: Bergerac (4–6 daily; 1hr–1hr 30min); Bordeaux (3–4 daily; 2hr 15min); Le Buisson (4–6 daily; 30–40min); Ste-Foy-la-Grande (4–6 daily; 1hr 20min–1hr 50min).

Buses

Agen to: Auch (7–10 daily; 1hr 30min); Condom (2 daily; 45min); Mont-de-Marsan (daily except Sat; 2hr 30min); Villeneuve-sur-Lot (5–13 daily; 45min).

Argentat to: Beaulieu-sur-Dordogne (July & Aug Mon–Sat 2 daily; 1hr 20min–2hr); Tulle (1–5 daily; 40–50min).

Bergerac to: Marmande (Mon–Sat 1 daily; 2hr); Villeneuve-sur-Lot (Mon–Fri 1–2 daily; 1hr 15min).

Brive to: Argentat (Mon–Sat 2–3 daily; 1hr 40min); Arnac-Pompadour (Mon–Sat 1 daily; 2hr); Collonges-la-Rouge (Mon–Sat 1–4 daily; 20–50min); Meyssac (Mon–Sat 1–4 daily; 30min–1hr); Tulle (Mon–Sat 1–6 daily; 40–50min); Turenne (Mon–Sat 2–4 daily; 20–40min); Uzerche (Mon–Sat 2 daily; 1hr 10min–1hr 30min); Vayrac (Mon–Sat 1–3 daily; 1hr).

Cahors to: Cajarc (2–6 daily; 1hr); Figeac (2–6 daily; 1hr 45min); Fumel (5–6 daily; 1hr 10min); Luzech (3–9 daily; 20min); Montauban (Mon–Fri 1 daily; 1hr 20min); Monsempron-Libos (5–6 daily; 1hr 20min); Puy-l'Évêque (3–8 daily; 45min); Rodez (Mon–Fri 1 daily; 2hr 40min).

Limoges to: Aubusson (Mon–Sat 2–4 daily; 1hr 40min); Châlus (Mon–Sat 1–2 daily; 1hr); Nexon (Mon–Sat 2–3 daily; 50min); Oradour-sur-Glane (3–7 daily; 30–40min); St-Junien (Mon–Fri 1 daily; 1hr); St-Léonard (3–4 daily; 35min); Solignac (Mon–Sat 1 daily; 30min); Le Vigen (Mon–Sat 2–3 daily; 20–30min).

Périgueux to: Angoulême (Mon, Fri & Sun 1 daily; 1hr 45min); Bergerac (Mon–Fri 3–5 daily; 1hr–1hr 30min); Brantôme (Mon, Fri & Sun 1 daily; 40min); Montignac (school term Mon–Fri 1–2 daily; 1hr); Ribérac (Mon–Fri 3–5 daily; 1hr); Sarlat (school term Mon–Fri 1–2 daily; 1hr 30min).

Ribérac to: Angoulême via Mareuil (Mon & Fri 1 daily; 1hr 30min).

10

The Pyrenees

CHAPTER 10

Highlights

* **Pelota** Aka *jai alai*, the Basque region's favourite sport is the fastest ball game in the world. Catch it in St-Jean-de-Luz. See p.797

* **Lourdes** Religion at its most fervent and most crass. Since an apparition of the Virgin Mary was sighted in 1858, the town has been transformed into a supermarket of the soul. See p.815

* **The Cirque de Gavarnie** A breathtaking panorama of jagged peaks in the western Pyrenees, best enjoyed off-peak when the crowds subside. See p.827

* **Niaux and the prehistoric caves** The upper Ariège valley is home to a constellation of prehistoric caves whose intriguing 10,000-plus-year-old paintings mirror the consciousness of our distant human ancestors. See p.838

* **Cathar castles** The crumbling castles of the upper Aude hark back to southwest Languedoc's era of independence. See p.848

* **Pic du Canigou** Catalonia's most sacred mountain is home to the venerated monastery of St-Martin, centre of a dramatic midsummer torchlight procession. See p.861

* **Petit Train Jaune** Travel up the winding valley of Roussillon's Têt valley in a restored narrow-gauge train. See p.862

△ The Ariège valley

10

The Pyrenees

Basque-speaking, wet and green in the west; craggy, snowy, Gascon-influenced in the middle; dry, Mediterranean and Catalan-speaking in the east – the **Pyrenees** are physically beautiful, culturally varied and considerably less developed than the Alps. The whole range is marvellous walkers' country, especially the central region around the **Parc National des Pyrénées**, with its 3000-metre peaks, streams, forests, flowers and wildlife. If you're a committed **hiker**, it's possible to traverse these mountains, from the Atlantic to the Mediterranean, along the **GR10** or the higher, more difficult **Haute Randonnée Pyrénéenne** (HRP). There are numerous local alpine resorts as well – **Cauterets**, **Luz-St-Sauveur**, **Barèges**, **Ax-les-Thermes** – with shorter hikes to suit all temperaments and abilities, as well as **skiing** opportunities in winter.

As for the more conventional of the tourist attractions, the **Côte Basque** is lovely but very popular, suffering from seaside sprawl and a surfeit of campsites. **St-Jean-de-Luz** is arguably the prettiest of the resorts, while once-elitist **Biarritz** is now enjoying a renaissance. **Bayonne**, which lies 6km inland, is an attractive, if heavily touristed town, with an excellent museum of Basque culture. The foothill towns are on the whole rather dull, although **Pau** merits at least a day or two, while **Lourdes** is such a monster of kitsch that it just has to be seen. The coast of Catalan-speaking **Roussillon** in the east, anchored by busy **Perpignan**, has beaches every bit as popular as those of the Côte Basque, nestled into the compact coves of its rocky coast, while its interior consists of craggy terrain split by spectacular canyons, sprouting a crop of fine Romanesque abbeys – of which **St-Martin-de-Canigou** and **Serrabonne** are the most dramatic – and a landscape bathed in Mediterranean heat and light. Finally, the sun-drenched foothills just to the north are home to the famous **Cathar castles**, striking testament to the once-independent and ever-rebellious inhabitants of southwestern Languedoc.

Hiking in the Pyrenees

If you're planning on doing even very basic **hiking** or other outdoor activities – canoeing, riding, cycling, paragliding – in the Pyrenees, a good contact point for **ideas**, **information** and **publications** (in French) is Randonnées Pyrénéennes, 4 rue Maye-Lane, 65420 Ibos, near Tarbes (☎05.62.90.09.90; information centre ☎05.62.90.09.92).

In addition, there are plenty of walkers' **guidebooks** to the area in both French and English (see p.1345). The most detailed **maps** are the French IGN 1:25,000 "TOP 25" series; #1547OT, #1647ET, #1647OT, #1748ET and #1748OT cover the Parc National des Pyrénées. Less demanding walkers can

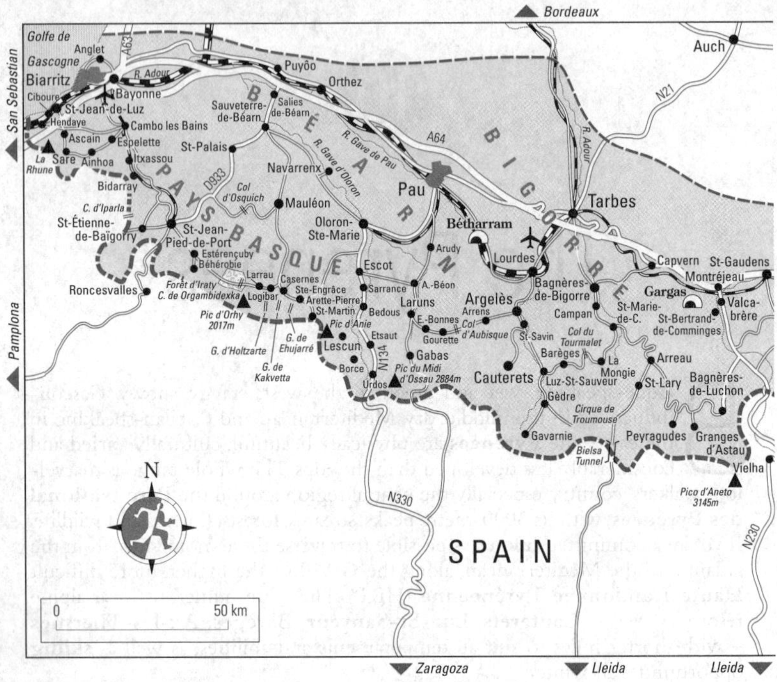

make do with Rando Éditions' *Cartes de Randonnées*, which covers the range at 1:50,000 in eleven sheets numbered from west to east, or the excellent and widely-available Topoguide series, which contains details of walks of varying length and difficulty for each *département*.

The **walking season** usually lasts from mid-June until late September; earlier in the year, few staffed refuges function, and you'll find snow even on parts of the GR10. Whatever you intend, bear in mind that these are big mountains and should be treated with respect: to tackle any of the main walks **preparation** is crucial. Before taking to the hills, check weather forecasts – usually posted at the local tourist office – and be sure you're properly equipped with water, food, maps, bivvy bag, emergency signalling, whistle and knife, as well as warm, water- and windproof clothing and suitable boots – not to mention ice axe and crampons if you're going anywhere near permanent snow, which you shouldn't be doing unless you have experience in high-altitude mountaineering. Above all, don't take any chances: mountain conditions can change very quickly, and sunny, warm weather in the valley doesn't necessarily mean it will be the same higher up, three hours later. If you don't have any mountain-walking experience, it's probably best not to undertake anything more than a well-frequented path unless you're accompanied by someone who does.

One kilometre in twelve minutes (5kph) is a fairly average **walking pace** for level ground; if you're going uphill, allow an hour for every 500m in elevation gained. If you're out of condition it'll take longer. Work yourself in gently, otherwise you could easily ruin your holiday: if you overdo it on your first day, you'll be plagued by blisters and aching muscles on the second. The best rule of thumb is: if in doubt, don't do it.

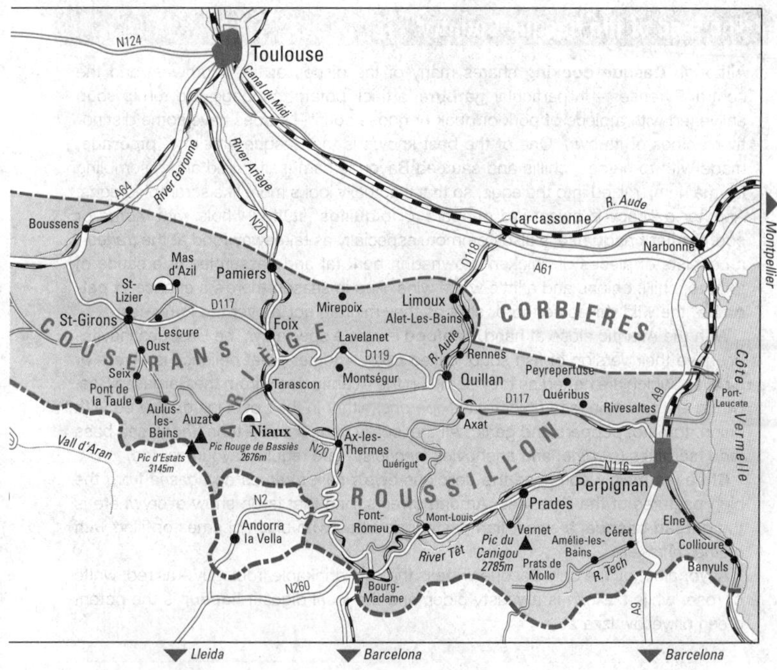

The Pays Basque

The three **Basque provinces** – Labourd (Lapurdi), Basse Navarre (Behe Nafarroa) and Soule (Zuberoa) – share with their Spanish neighbours a common language – Euskera – and a strong sense of separate identity. The language is widely spoken, and Basques refer to their country as a land in itself, Euskalherri, or, across the border in Spain, Euskadi. You see bilingual French/Euskera signage throughout the region (sometimes only the latter), so in this section we have given the Euskera for all locations in brackets after the French. Unlike their Spanish counterparts, few French Basques favour an independent state or secession from France, though a Basque *département* has been mooted (see below). For decades the French authorities turned a blind eye to the Spanish Basque terrorist organization ETA, which used the region as a safe haven and organizational base. In recent years, however, as France has extradited suspected terrorists, incidents of violence and vandalism associated with nationalists have increased, notably around Bayonne and Pau. Such events, however, are so exceptional as to be of no concern for visitors.

Administratively, the three French Basque provinces were organized together with Béarn in the single *département* of Basses-Pyrénées, now Pyrénées-Atlantiques, at the time of the 1789 Revolution, when the Basques' thousand-year-old *fors* (rights) were abolished. It was a move designed to curtail their nationalism, but ironically has probably been responsible for preserving their unity. Of late there have been proposals for the creation of a Pays-Basque

The food of the Basque Country

Although **Basque cooking** shares many of the dishes of the southwest and the central Pyrenees – in particular **garbure**, a thick potato, cabbage and turnip soup enlivened with a piece of pork or duck or goose confit – it does have some distinctive recipes of its own. One of the best known is the Basque omelette, **pipérade**, made with tomatoes, chillis and sautéed Bayonne ham (salt-cured and resembling Parma ham), mixed into the eggs, so that it actually looks more like scrambled eggs. Another delicacy is sweet red peppers, or **piquillos**, stuffed whole with *morue* or cod**. Poulet basquaise** is also common, especially as takeaway food at the *traiteur*: it consists of pieces of chicken browned in pork fat and casseroled in a sauce of tomato, chilli, onions and a little white wine. And in season there's a chance of **palombe**, the wild doves netted or shot as they migrate north over the Pyrenees.

With the Atlantic close at hand, **seafood** is also a speciality. The Basques inevitably have their version of fish soup, called *ttoro*. Another great delicacy is **elvers** or *piballes*, which are netted as they come up the Atlantic rivers from the Sargasso Sea. **Squid** are common, served here as *txiperons*, either in their own ink or stewed with onion, tomato, peppers and garlic. All the locally caught fish – tuna (*thon*), sea bass (*bor*), sardines (*sardine*) and anchovies (*anchois*) – are regular favourites, too.

Cheeses mainly comprise the delicious ewe's-milk *tommes* and *gasna* from the high pastures of the Pyrenees. Among sweets, one that is on show everywhere is the **gâteau basque**, a sweet flan pastry garnished with black cherries or filled with *crême pâtissière*.

As for alcohol, the only Basque **wine** is the very drinkable Irouléguy – as red, white or rosé, while *txakolín* is a yeasty cider, and the local digestif **liqueur** is the potent green or yellow Izzara.

département, hived off from the Pyrénées-Atlantiques, with its capital at Bayonne.

Apart from the language and the traditional broad beret, the most obvious manifestations of Basque national identity are the ubiquitous *trinquets* or *frontons*, the huge concrete courts in which the national game of **pelota** is played. Pairs of players wallop a hard leather-covered ball, either with their bare hands or a long basket-work extension of the hand called a *chistera* (in the variation known as *jai alai*), against a high wall blocking one end of the court. It's extraordinarily dangerous – the ball travels at speeds of up to 200kph – and knockouts and worse are not uncommon. Trials of strength (*force Basque*), rather like Scottish Highland Games, are also popular, and include tugs-of-war, lifting heavy weights, turning massive carts and sawing giant tree trunks.

The Côte Basque

Barely 30km long, the **Basque coast** is easily accessible by air, bus and train, and reasonably priced hotel accommodation is not that difficult to find – though space should be reserved a month in advance during summer. **Bayonne**, slightly inland, is the cultural focus and only town with some life apart from tourism. **Biarritz**, the most prestigious and varied resort, is flanked by magnificent beaches but can be a rather noisy place to stay in high season. Families will probably prefer **St-Jean-de-Luz** to the south – an attractive and more manageable town in any case – or **Anglet** just to the north, with more fine beaches which attract surfers from near and far.

Bayonne (Baïona)

BAYONNE stands back some 6km from the Atlantic, a position that until recently protected it from any real exploitation by tourism. It bestrides the confluence of the River Adour, which rises to the east in the region of the Pic du Midi de Bigorre, and the much smaller Nive, whose source is the Basque Pyrenees above St-Jean-Pied-de-Port. Although purists dispute whether it's truly a Basque rather than a Gascon city, it is the effective economic and political capital of the Pays Basque. To the lay person, at least, there seems no doubt about its Basque flavour, with its tall timber-frame houses and woodwork painted in the peculiarly Basque tones of green and red. Here, too, Basques in flight from Franco's Spain came without hesitation to seek refuge amongst their own. For many years the Petit Bayonne quarter on the right bank of the Nive was a hotbed of violent Basque nationalism, until the French government clamped down on such dangerous tendencies.

The city's origins go back to Roman times, since when its Latin name of Lapurdum, corrupted to Labourd (Lapurdi), has been extended to cover the

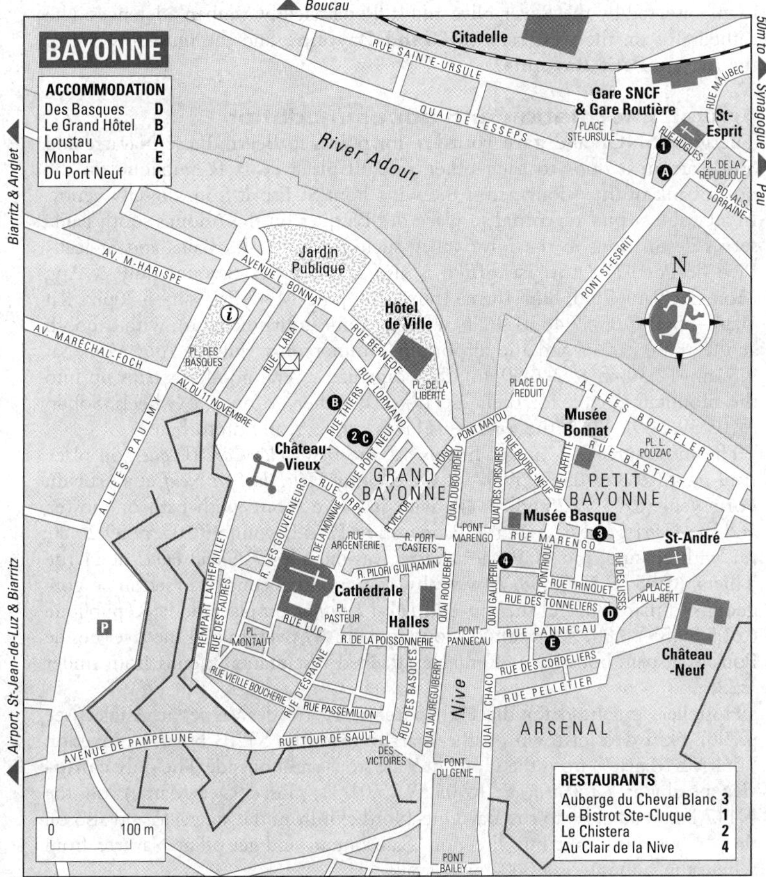

whole of this westernmost of the three Basque provinces. For three centuries until 1453 and the end of the Hundred Years War, it enjoyed prosperity and security under English domination, and this wealth was consolidated when, in the sixteenth century, Sephardic Jews fleeing the Spanish Inquisition arrived, bringing their chocolate-manufacturing trade with them. The city reached the peak of its commercial success in the eighteenth century, when it was also a centre of the armaments industry (it gave its name to the bayonet). Later, its prestige suffered a blow in the 1789 Revolution when the anti-regionalist, centralizing Paris government subsumed the three Basque provinces under a single *département*, with its capital at Pau. More recently, economic activity has been based on the processing of by-products from the natural gas field at Lacq near Pau, although this has recently been through some hard times, leaving Bayonne with a higher-than-national-average level of unemployment.

These issues don't immediately impinge on the visitor, however, and first impressions are likely to be favourable. It's a small-scale, easily manageable city, and, as the hub of all major road and rail routes from the north and east, it's worth considering as a base for a seaside sojourn. Although there are no great sights in Bayonne, it's a pleasure to walk the narrow streets of the old town, bisected by the River Nive and still encircled by Vauban's defences. The cathedral is on the west bank in **Grand Bayonne**, and the museums east of the river in **Petit Bayonne**.

Arrival, information and accommodation

The **gare SNCF** and **gare routière** for points in Béarn, Basse Navarre and Soule are next door to each other, just off place de la République on the north bank of the Adour, across the wide Pont St-Esprit from the city centre. In addition, a **bus terminal** in place des Basques on the Adour's south bank, serves destinations in the Nive valley, such as Cambo-les-Bains and St-Jean-Pied-de-Port. The **tourist office** is also in place des Basques (July & Aug Mon–Sat 9am–7pm, Sun 10am–1pm; Sept–June Mon–Fri 9am–6.30pm, Sat 10am–6pm; ⓣ05.59.46.01.46, ⓦwww.bayonne-tourisme.com), with a booth at the train station and the airport in summer only (July & Aug Mon–Sat 9.30am–12.30pm & 2–6.30pm); they organize several good bus trips up into the mountains – ask for their list. If you'd rather go on two wheels, Sobilo (ⓣ05.59.24.94.47) at the *gares* rents bikes, mopeds, and motorbikes.

The most agreeable budget **hotels** are the basic *Hôtel des Basques*, on place Paul-Bert (ⓣ & ⓕ05.59.59.08.02; ❶), the tiny *Hôtel du Port Neuf*, at 44 rue du Port-Neuf (ⓣ05.59.25.65.83; ❷), with just five rooms with bath or shower, and the *Hôtel Monbar*, at 24 rue Pannecau in Petit Bayonne (ⓣ05.59.59.26.80; ❷), with en-suite rooms. Pricier alternatives include *Le Grand Hôtel*, at 21 rue Thiers (ⓣ05.59.55.08.08, ⓦwww.bw-legrandhotel.com; ❹), set in a gorgeous old mansion, and the top-end *Hôtel Loustau*, on place de la République (ⓣ05.59.55.08.08, ⓦwww.hotel-loustau.com; ❻), overlooking the river beside Pont St-Esprit; both have affordable attached restaurants (menus from under €22).

Hostellers can head for the **HI hostel** at 19 rte des Vignes in Anglet (see p.796), 6km west of town on the Biarritz road; the STAB bus #4 (direction "Biarritz Mairie") from the Hôtel de Ville stops right outside. The only **campsite** nearby is *La Chêneraie* (ⓣ05.59.55.01.31; closed Oct–March), off the N117 Pau road close to the Bayonne-Nord exit from the *autoroute*, and also on the #4 bus route; take bus direction "Sainsontan" and get off at Navarre, from where the campsite is a 500-metre walk.

Grand Bayonne

In Grand Bayonne, just up the avenue from the tourist office, stands the town's fourteenth-century **castle** (closed to the public). The oldest part, the Chateau-Vieux, is a genuine example of no-nonsense late-medieval fortification – a contrast to the fairy-tale fakery of nineteenth-century Romantics like Viollet-le-Duc (for example, the Château d'Abbadie near Hendaye). A plaque on the east wall lists some of the more famous who were willing or unwilling guest, including the Black Prince, King Pedro the Cruel of Castile, and the notorious mercenary Betrand de Guescelin, among many others.

Just around the corner on the magnolia-shaded place Pasteur, the **Cathédrale Ste-Marie** (Mon–Sat 7.30am–noon & 3–7pm, Sun 3.30–6.30pm), with its twin towers and steeple rising with airy grace above the houses, is best seen from across the broad expanse of its own **cloister** (daily 9am–12.30pm & 2–6/7pm) on its south side. Up close, the yellowish stone reveals bad weathering, with most of the decorative detail lost. Inside, its most impressive features are the height of the nave and some sixteenth-century glass, set off by the prevailing gloom. Like other southern Gothic cathedrals of the period (around 1260), it was based on more famous northern models, in this case Soissons and Reims.

The smartest streets in town are those around the cathedral: **rue d'Espagne**, the old commercial centre, heading south, and **rue de la Monnaie**, leading into rue Port-Neuf, with its aromatic pâtisseries and *confiseries*, running north. Southwest of the cathedral, along **rue des Faures** and the streets above the old walls, there is a distinctly Spanish feel, with washing strung at the windows and strains of music drifting from dark interiors.

Petit Bayonne, the north bank and La Barre

Below the cathedral, the riverside **quays** of the Nive are the city's most picturesque focus, with sixteenth-century arcaded houses on the Petit Bayonne side, one of which contains the excellent Basque ethnographic museum, the **Musée Basque** (May–Oct Tues–Sun 10am–6.30pm; Nov–April Tues–Sun 10am–12.30pm & 2–6pm; €5.50, €9 with Musée Bonnat). Its exhibits illustrate Basque life through the centuries, and include reconstructed farm buildings, house interiors, implements, tools and *makhilas* – innocent-looking carved, wooden walking sticks with a concealed steel spear tip at one end, used by pilgrims and shepherds for self-protection if need be. There's also a section on Basque seagoing activities (Columbus's skipper was a Basque), and rooms on pelota – its history and stars – and famous Basques.

The city's second museum, the **Musée Bonnat**, close by at 5 rue Jacques-Lafitte (Wed–Sun 10am–12.30pm & 2–6pm; €5.50, €9 with Musée Basque), with an annex at 9 rue Fredéric-Bastiat, provides an unexpected treasury of art. Thirteenth- and fourteenth-century Italian painting is well represented, as are most periods before Impressionism. Highlights include Goya's *Self-Portrait* and *Portrait of Don Francisco de Borja*, Rubens' powerful *Apollo and Daphne* and *The Triumph of Venus*, plus works by Murrillo, El Greco and Ingrès. A whole gallery is devoted to high-society portraits by Léon Bonnat (1833–1922), whose personal collection formed the original core of the museum. There are also frequent temporary exhibits of the work of prominent artists, well worth catching.

Apart from savouring the wide river skies, there is little to draw you to the northern bank of the Adour. The **church of St-Esprit**, opposite the station, is all that remains of a hostel that once ministered to the sore feet and other ailments of the Santiago pilgrims – it's worth a peek inside for an interesting wood sculpture of *The Flight into Egypt*. Just behind the station is Vauban's massive **citadelle**; built in 1680 to defend the town against Spanish attack, it actually saw little action until the Napoleonic wars, when its garrison resisted a siege by Wellington for four months in 1813. Don't miss the beautiful **Jardin Botanique** inside the castle walls, with its huge collection of plants labelled in French, Basque and Latin (mid-April to mid-Oct daily 9am–noon & 2–6pm; free).

If you have a car, it's worth making an evening trip northwest through the industrial suburb of **Boucau** and out to the breakwater, **La Barre**, that protects the mouth of the Adour. It's a pleasant place to sit and watch the leaden-hued Atlantic rollers come in; if you're tempted to swim off the beautiful white beach that stretches from here to Bordeaux, remember that there are lethal currents close inshore, so be extremely careful.

Eating, drinking and entertainment

The best area for **eating** and **drinking** is along the right bank of the Nive and in the back streets to either side of the river, especially along rue Pannecau, rue des Cordeliers and rue des Tonneliers in Petit Bayonne. Two of the best **restaurants** in this part of town are the *Auberge du Cheval Blanc*, 68 rue Bourgneuf (☎05.59.59.01.33; closed Sun eve & Mon except Aug; weekday lunch menus €18–70; booking essential), a durable gourmets' mecca specializing in decadent desserts; and *Au Clair de la Nive*, 28 quai Galuperie (closed Mon lunch & Sun; menu €13, à la carte €18–29), with a riverside terrace, serving tasty cuisine, such as roast anchovies and steamed cod in pepper sauce. In Grand Bayonne, *Le Chistera*, 42 rue Port-Neuf (closed Mon–Wed eve except July & Aug; menu €13, à la carte €15.50–19), is the best option, dishing up hearty Bayonnais specialities based on fish, pork and tripe, best ordered off the daily-specials board. The one culinary bright spot across the Adour is *Le Bistrot Ste-Cluque*, 9 rue Hugues (☎05.59.55.82.43; menu at €9–13, à la carte around €15; bookings essential; closed Mon), which is perennially packed for its excellent-value French cuisine and is also a popular gay hangout.

For **bar** snacks, head to *Bar du Marché*, 39 rue des Basques in Grand Bayonne (closed Sun), which begins serving food and drink at 5am to a mix of market sellers and bar-flies on their way home to bed, continuing with good-value *plats de jour* at lunchtime. Nearby is *Bodega Ibaia*, 49 quai Jauréguiberry (closed Sun & Mon Sept–June), a lively, well-loved bar, with *plats de jour* for under €9 at lunchtime. If you fancy an afternoon drink, try *Chocolats Cazenave*, 19 rue du Port-Neuf, which serves hot cups of cocoa, and also sells every conceivable chocolate goodie to take home.

As far as **festivals** go, Bayonne's biggest bash of the year is the Fêtes Traditionelles, which starts on the first Wednesday in August and consists of five days and nights of continuous boozing and entertainment. This finishes with a *corrida* (bullfight) on the following Sunday. Following the festival there are three or four more days of bullfighting beginning on August 15. A well-established jazz festival takes place in mid-July, and every October there is a Franco-Spanish theatre festival.

Biarritz (Miarritze)

A few minutes by rail or road from Bayonne, **BIARRITZ** was, until forty years ago, the Monte Carlo of the Atlantic coast, transformed by Napoléon III in the mid-nineteenth century into a playground for monarchs, aristos and glitterati. With the rise of the Côte d'Azur during the 1960s, however, the place went into seemingly terminal decline. It's only during the last decade that the city has been rediscovered by Parisian yuppies and the international surfing fraternity, who together fuel a respectable nightlife.

Arrival, information and accommodation

The **gare SNCF** is 3km southeast of the centre at the end of avenue Foch/avenue Kennedy in the *quartier* known as La Négresse (STAB bus #2 or #9 from square d'Ixelles). The **tourist office** is on square d'Ixelles (daily: July & Aug 8am–8pm; Sept–June Mon–Sat 10am–6pm, Sun 10am–5pm; ⓣ05.59.22.37.10, ⓦwww.biarritz.fr), in the vicinity of the casino. You can rent bikes and scooters at Sobilo (ⓣ05.59.24.94.47) at 24 rue Peyroloubilh.

Accommodation is heavily booked in July and August, but is less expensive than you might expect. *Hôtel Palym* at 7 rue du Port-Vieux (ⓣ05.59.24.16.56, ⓦwww.le-palmarium.com; ❸), with a variety of old-fashioned rooms and a ground-floor bar-restaurant, is a stone's throw from the Grand Plage and a solid choice. Nearby is the equally welcoming but more expensive *Le Petit Hotel*, 11 rue Gardères (ⓣ05.59.24.87.00, ⓦwww.petithotel-biarritz.com; ❺). Better value and quieter than both is the *Belle Époque Hôtel Atalaye*, 6 rue des Goélands (ⓣ05.59.24.06.76, ⓦwww.hotelatalaye.com; ❸), off of rue Mazargran, a short walk west of the post office. Finally, those looking for a little more luxury should head for the small but well-appointed *Maison Garnier* (ⓣ05.59.01.60.70, ⓦwww.hotel-biarritz.com; ❻) set in a refurbished bourgeouis home at no. 29 on the main rue Gambetta.

The nearest **HI hostel** (ⓣ05.59.41.76.07, ⓔaubergejeune.biarrtiz@wanadoo.fr) is 2km southwest of the centre on the shore of Lac Mouriscot, just walkable from the *gare SNCF*; otherwise take bus #2 from the centre, stop "Bois de Boulogne". **Campers** should try *Biarritz-Camping*, at 28 route d'Harcet, the inland continuation of avenue de la Plage (ⓣ05.59.23.00.12, ⓦwww.biarritz-camping.fr; closed late-Sept to mid-May), behind Plage de la Milady to the south of town.

The Town

The focus of Biarritz is the **Casino Municipal**, just behind the Grande Plage, now restored to its 1930s grandeur. Inland, the town forms a surprisingly amorphous and workaday sprawl, with the sole point of interest being the **Musée Asiatica**, 1 rue Guy-Petit (Mon–Fri 10.30am–7pm, Sat & Sun 2pm–8pm; €7.20), exhibiting the collection of Indian and Tibetan art specialist Michel Postel.

Between here and the Plage du Port-Vieux are the only streets and squares conducive to relaxed strolling. At the far west end of **place Clemenceau**, one of several central squares, you can nibble a cake or sip a lemon tea at *Miremont's Salon de Thé* – a frightfully superior place epitomizing old-money Biarritz. To the west, the faded old-time hotels ringing the **place Attalaye**, high above the port, are worth a glance for their elegant facades, as is the characterful if touristy **rue du Port-Vieux** just below, leading down to its namesake beach (see below).

The **shore**, however, is undeniably beautiful. White breakers crash on sandy strands, where beautiful people bronze their limbs cheek by jowl with suburban families and surf bums, against a backdrop of casinos and ocean-liner hotels, ornate churches, Gothic follies and modern apartment blocks. The **beaches** – served by STAB buses #4 and #9 from Biarritz centre – extend northwards from Plage de la Milady through Plage Marbella, Côte des Basques, Plage du Port-Vieux, Grande Plage and Plage Miramar to the Pointe St-Martin. Most of the action takes place between the Plage du Port-Vieux and the Plage Miramar, overlooked by the huge **Hôtel du Palais** (formerly the Villa Eugénie), built by Napoléon III in the mid-nineteenth century for his wife, whom he met and courted in Biarritz.

Just beside the **Plage du Port-Vieux**, the most sheltered and intimate of the beaches, a rocky promontory sticks out into the sea, ending in the **Rocher de la Vierge**, an offshore rock topped by a white statue of the Virgin, and linked to the mainland by an Eiffel-built iron catwalk. Around it are scattered other rocky islets where the swell heaves and combs. On the bluff above the Virgin stands the **Musée de la Mer** (daily: July & Aug 9.30am–midnight; May weekends, June & Sept 9.30am–7pm; Oct–May 9.30am–12.30pm & 2–6pm; €7.20), which contains interesting displays on the fishing industry and the region's birds, and an aquarium of North Atlantic fish as well as the obligatory seal tank.

Just below is the picturesque **Port des Pêcheurs** harbour, most easily approached by a switchback pedestrian lane. The fishermen have now gone, replaced by pleasure boats, but there's a scuba outfitter here and a clutch of pricey seafood restaurants. To the northeast lies the **Grande Plage**, an immaculate sweep of sand once dubbed the "Plage des Fous" after the 1850s practice of taking mental patients to bathe here as a primitive form of thalassotherapy.

Eating, drinking and nightlife

There are some reasonable places to **eat** near the market *halles*, 200m southwest of place Clemenceau, and it's easy to eat well for a price, away from the touristy snack bars on rue du Port-Vieux. Two of the best options around the market are *Le St Amour*, at 26 rue Gambetta, a Lyonnais-style bistro with a sausage-strong lunch menu at €16 (closed Sun & Mon), and *Bistrot des Halles* (ⓣ05.59.24.21.22), at 1 rue du Centre, which serves generously portioned, tasty fish dishes (menu €16, lunch only; closed Sun eve & Mon). *Le Close Basque* at 12 rue Louis–Bathrou is a favourite local bistrot (ⓣ05.59.24.24.96; menu €24; closed Sun lunch & Mon & intermittently), whereas the finest dining can be enjoyed at *Villa Eugénie* in the *Hotel Palais* at 1 av de l'Imperatrice (ⓣ05.59.41.64.00; closed part Feb), although this comes at a price (from €50). *Le Surfing*, behind Plage de Côte des Basques and festooned with antique boards, serves decent grills and *frites*, while clubbers repair to *Le Morgan*, at 4 rue du Helder off place Clemenceau, open 7pm until dawn, though the cheaper menus are only available until 10pm.

More formal **nightlife** in the town centre includes *Cayo Coco*, a Cuban theme bar at 5 rue Jaulerry offering free salsa dance lessons, a slightly naff *Irish Pub* at 10 rue Victor-Hugo downhill from the *halles*, and *Ventilo Caffe* on rue du Port-Vieux, the favourite haunt of Parisian thirtysomethings. Whether you've slept the night before or not, the best start to the day is at *Salon de Thé L'Orangerie* at 1 rue Gambetta, serving all sorts of hot drinks and a great variety of breakfasts.

Anglet (Angelu)

Immediately north of Biarritz, **ANGLET** sprawls up the coast from the Pointe St-Martin to the mouth of the Adour. There's nothing to see except for two superb beaches – the **Chambre d'Amour**, so named for two lovers trapped in their trysting place by the tide, and the **Sables d'Or**, much favoured by the surfers and with boards for rent. Here, too, the swimming is very dangerous, so do heed the warning signs.

You can catch a #6 or #9 bus here from the central stops in Biarritz, or walk the distance in about thirty minutes, along avenue de l'Impératrice, avenue MacCroskey, then second left down to the seaside boulevard des Plages. Anglet has a **HI hostel** at 19 rte des Vignes (Ⓣ05.59.58.70.00, Ⓔanglet@fuaj.org; closed mid-Nov to Feb; STAB bus #4, direction "Bayonne-Sainsontan" from Biarritz). There's also a **campsite**, *Camping de Parme*, on Route de l'Aviation (Ⓣ05.59.23.03.00) in the Brindos neighbourhood. For **eating and drinking**, the most notable seaside establishments are the *Havana Café* at Chambre d'Amour, a permanently crowded bar that serves *plats du jour* at lunch for under €8, and the nearby *Café Bleu*, more of a proper restaurant with a menu for €15 (closed Wed Sept–June). Inland, choose between long-running *Udala* at 165 av de l'Adour, for traditional Basque seafood (menu €15, à la carte €22), and the popular *La Fleur de Sel*, 5 av de la Forêt (closed Sun eve & Wed; weekday lunch menu €14, otherwise €25), in the Chiberta pine forest, serving more *nouvelle* dishes. For high rollers, the *Château de Brindos* on 1 allée du Château (Ⓣ05.59.23.17.68), home to one of the region's most celebrated chef's, is the place to head (from €45).

St-Jean-de-Luz (Donibane Lohitzun)

With its fine sandy bay and magnificent old quarter speckled with half-timbered mansions, **ST-JEAN-DE-LUZ** remains the most attractive resort on the Basque coast, despite being fairly overrun in peak season. As the only natural harbour between Arcachon and Spain, it has been a major port for centuries, with whaling and cod fishing the traditional preoccupations of its fleets. Even now, St-Jean remains one of the busiest fishing ports in France, and the principal one for landing anchovy and tuna.

Arrival, information and accommodation

St-Jean's **gare SNCF** is on the southern edge of the town centre, 500m from the beach. The somewhat harried **tourist office** is close by on place Maréchal-Foch, behind the Hôtel de Ville (Apr–May & Sept Mon–Sat 9am–12.30pm & 2–7pm, Sun 10am–1pm; July & Aug Mon–Sat 9am–7.30pm, Sun 10am–1pm & 3–7pm; Oct–March Mon–Sat 9am–12.30pm & 1.30–6.30pm, Sun 10am–1pm; Ⓣ05.59.26.03.16, Ⓦwww.saint-jean-de-luz.com). On Friday and Tuesday there's a **market** in the adjacent boulevard Victor-Hugo. **Bikes** can be rented at Luz Evasion on place Maurice-Ravel and ADO on avenue Labrouche, as well as at the *gare SNCF*. **Pelota** matches take place throughout the summer in both St-Jean and nearby Ciboure; ask in the tourist office for details.

Opposite the train station, on and around avenue Verdun, are a few inexpensive (for St-Jean) if uninspiringly located **hotels**, among them the en-suite, well-kept *Hôtel de Paris*, 1 bd du Comandant-Passicot, on the corner of av Labrouche (Ⓣ05.59.85.20.20, Ⓔhoteldeparis@aol.com; ❷). Slightly more expensive are the *Hotel Bolivar*, near the beach at 18 rue Sopite (Ⓣ05.59.26.02.00, Ⓕ05.59.26.38.28; ❸), and the *Ohartzia* (Ⓣ05.59.26.00.06, Ⓔhotel.ohartzia@wanadoo.fr; ❹), just inland from the beach at 28 rue Garat, with a huge garden where breakfast is served. A better-value choice overlooking the Grande Plage, the *Hôtel de la Plage* (Ⓣ05.59.51.03.44, Ⓦwww.hoteldelaplage.com; ❹; closed mid-Nov to mid-Feb & part March & April), has its own (paying) car park and ground-floor brasserie. Finally, if you want to splurge, the stately *Hotel du Parc Victoria* (Ⓣ05.59.26.04.53, Ⓔparcvictoria@relaischateaux.com; ❾; closed mid-Nov to mid-March) offers four-star luxury and excellent service. There are numerous **campsites**, all grouped in the so-called *zone des campings* to the left of the N10 between St-Jean and Guéthary.

The Town

The wealth and vigour of St-Jean's seafaring past is evident in the town, most notably in the surviving seventeenth- and eighteenth-century houses of the merchants and shipowners. One of the finest, adjacent to the Hôtel de Ville on the plane-tree-studded place Louis XIV, is the turreted **Maison Louis XIV** (guided tours: June & Sept Mon–Sat 10.30am–noon & 2.30–5.30pm; July & Aug Mon–Sat 10.30am–12.30 & 2.30–6.30pm; €4.50), built for the shipowning Lohobiague family in 1643, but taking its name from the fact that the young King Louis stayed here for a month in 1660 during the preparations for his marriage to Maria Teresa, Infanta of Castile. She lodged in the equally impressive pink Italianate villa known as the **Maison de l'Infante** (mid-June to mid-Oct 11am–12.30pm & 2.30–6.30pm; €3), overlooking the harbour on the quay of the same name, which also houses the **Musée Grévin** waxworks museum (April–Oct Mon–Sat 10am–noon & 2–6/6.30pm; €5.60). The corner house on rue Mazarin, nearby, was the Duke of Wellington's HQ during the 1813–14 winter campaign against Marshal Soult.

In the history of St-Jean-de-Luz, the wedding of King Louis and Maria Teresa was a major event. The couple were married in the **church of St-Jean-Baptiste** on pedestrianized **rue Gambetta**, the main shopping street today, though the door through which they left the church has been walled up ever since. The extravagance of the event defies belief. Cardinal Mazarin alone presented the queen with twelve thousand pounds of pearls and diamonds, a gold dinner service and a pair of sumptuous carriages drawn by teams of six horses – all paid for by money made in the service of France. Plain and fortress-like on the outside, this is the largest French Basque church inside, with a barn-like nave roofed in wood and lined on three sides with tiers of dark oak galleries. These are a distinctive feature of Basque churches, and were reserved for the men, while the women sat at ground level in the nave. Equally Basque is the elaborate gilded retable of tiered angels, saints and prophets behind the altar. The walled-up door through which Louis and his bride passed is on the right of the main entrance. Hanging from the ceiling is an ex voto model of the Empress Eugénie's paddle-steamer, the *Eagle*, which narrowly escaped being wrecked on the rocks outside St-Jean in 1867.

Ciboure (Ziburu), the docks and Urrugne (Urruña)

On the other side of the harbour, **CIBOURE** seems a continuation of St-Jean but is in fact a separate community, terminating in the little fortress of Socoa, today home to a sailing club. Its streets are even prettier (and emptier) than its neighbour's, especially opposite the end of the bridge from St-Jean, the waterfront **quai Maurice-Ravel** (the composer was born at no. 12) and the parallel **rue Pocolette** behind. Wide-fronted, half-timbered, gaily painted and sometimes balconied, the houses epitomize the local Labourdian Basque style. The octagonal tower protruding above the houses belongs to the sixteenth-century **church of St-Vincent**, where you'll find more characteristic Basque galleries and a Baroque altarpiece; the entrance is in rue Pocolette through a paved courtyard with gravestones embedded in it.

From the Pont Charles de Gaulle linking St-Jean and Ciboure, the **fish dock** sticks out into the harbour, stacked with nets and blackened lobster traps, with grubby blue-painted tuna boats tied up alongside. Upstream, smaller boats lie keeled over on the tidal mudflats of the little River Nivelle against a backdrop of green fields and the emerald flanks of **La Rhune** (900m); to ascend the peak, catch a bus from the *gare SNCF* to Col de St-Ignace and Sare (2–3 buses daily).

Also worth considering is a visit to the **Château d'Urtubie** (guided tours April–Oct 11am & 2–6pm; €5.50) at **URRUGNE**, just outside Ciboure, 3km southwest of St-Jean-de-Luz, which has belonged to the same family since its construction as a fortified château in 1341. It was enlarged and gentrified during the sixteenth and eighteenth centuries, and provided hospitality for the French King Louis XI, as well as for Soult and later Wellington during the Napoleonic Wars. If you fancy following in their footsteps, it's also a very upmarket **hotel** (Ⓣ05.59.54.31.15, Ⓦwww.chateaudurtubie.fr; ❺–❽), with a restaurant offering dinner, including wine and a visit of the château, for €40.

Eating and drinking

There's ample scope in St-Jean for good-value **eating**, especially for seafood. The *Buvette de la Halle* (lunch only, closed Mon off season), on the corner of the market hall on boulevard Victor-Hugo, serves abundant meals of impeccably fresh crab, oysters and sardines, plus *pipérade*, drink and dessert for around €25. Leading off place Louis-XIV – with its cafés, sidewalk artists and **free summertime concerts** in the bandstand (Tues–Sun 10pm) – rue de la République also has numerous restaurants, among them the cheap and cheerful *La Ruelle* (closed Mon), at no. 19, with seafood menus from €18, and *L'Alcalde* at no. 22, serving mixed platters and seafood specials (€17). Another well-reputed establishment featuring regional cuisine, *La Taverne Basque*, is at no. 5 (à la carte from €20). For something more elegant, head to *Le Rosewood* in the *Grand Hotel*, which features ocean-side dining and *gastronomique* menus from €30. Follow up your meal with the traditional local sweets, *macarons*, *mouchous* or *kanougas*.

Hendaye (Hendaïa) and the Spanish frontier

HENDAYE, 16km south of St-Jean-de-Luz, is the last town in France before the Spanish frontier. Neither the town itself, **Hendaye-Ville**, nor the seaside quarter, **Hendaye-Plage**, is of any great interest, though the latter has a fine, safe beach and modern tourist amenities.

The town, served by both the Paris–Bordeaux–Irún and Toulouse–Irún train lines, lies on the estuary of the River Bidassoa, which forms the border with Spain at this point. Just upstream, a tiny wooded island known as the **Île des Faisans** was once used as a meeting place for the monarchs of the two countries. François I, taken prisoner at the battle of Pavia in 1525, was ransomed here. In 1659 it was the scene of the signature of the Treaty of the Pyrenees and in the following year of the marriage contract between Louis XIV and Maria Teresa, when the painter Velázquez, responsible for the decor of the negotiations chamber, caught a cold resulting in his death. Another interesting encounter was the meeting between Hitler and Franco at Hendaye station on October 23, 1940, when Hitler refused to commit himself to supporting Franco's colonial claims on Morocco, resulting in Franco's refusal to join the ranks of the Axis. In typical Spanish style Franco had arrived late, keeping the furious Führer waiting.

The main sight in the town itself is the **Château d'Abbadie**, home of the nineteenth-century Dublin-born explorer Antoine d'Abbadie, on the headland overlooking Hendaye Plage, just off the Route de la Corniche (guided visits in afternoon: Feb–May & Oct to mid-Dec Mon–Fri guided 10am–11am & no guide 2–5pm; June to Sept Mon–Fri guided 10am–6pm & no guide 12.30–2pm, no guide Sat 10am–1pm & 2–6pm & Sun 2–6pm; €6.40). After expeditions in Ethiopia and Egypt, d'Abbadie had the neo-Gothic château built between 1860 and 1870; the architect was Viollet-le-Duc, whose Romantic ideal of the Middle Ages resulted in a bizarre Franco-Hibernian folly, with Arabian boudoirs, Ethiopian frescoes and inscriptions over the doors and lintels inside in Irish, Basque, Arabic and Ethiopian. It's also filled with objects collected by d'Abbadie on his travels. He became president of the Académie des Sciences in 1891, to which he donated the château on his death in 1897.

Hendaye's **tourist office** is at 12 rue des Aubépines in Hendaye-Plage (Apr–June & Sept–Oct Mon–Sat 9am–12.30pm & 2–6pm, July & Aug Mon–Sat 9am–7pm, Sun 10.30am–1pm; Nov–March Mon–Sat 9am–12.30pm & 2–5pm; ⓣ05.59.20.00.34, ⓦwww.hendaye.com). **Hotel** prices are cheaper in Hendaye-Ville, where accommodation clusters around the *gare SNCF*, but Hendaye-Plage is more pleasant. Worth a try is the *Hôtel de la Gare*, 1 rue des Déportés (ⓣ05.59.20.81.90, ⓕ05.59.48.18.28; ❸), in a converted mansion behind the east end of boulevard de la Mer, with a pool and garden. The **campsites** are mainly grouped around Hendaye-Plage; *Le Moulin,* off the D658 (between the N10 and coastal D912), is one of the cheaper options.

Around Hendaye: up the coast and inland

The best thing about Hendaye is in fact getting there, for the stretch of **coast** from St-Jean south has remained miraculously unspoilt, especially in the region of the **Pointe Ste-Anne** promontory, accessible from the **Chemin Piéton Littoral** footpath, which runs parallel to the coastal D912 "Corniche Basque" road. It's equally accessible from the beach at Hendaye-Plage.

Inland, both trans-Pyrenean walking routes – the **GR10** and **HRP** – officially begin their course in Hendaye-Plage at the former casino on the front. The first, two-hour stage is dull and gives no sense of the glories that lie ahead. Go along boulevard Général-Leclerc, through the town on rue des Citronniers, under the rail line, then 50m east on the N10 before following the waymarks to the right towards the A63 *autoroute*. A cattle track passes underneath and continues to the tiny hilltop village of **BIRIATOU** (Biriatu), where the walking starts to get interesting. If you're not concerned about the romance of starting at the very beginning, splash out on a taxi and start at Biriatou. A short steep section leads to a Basque **church** with a collection of weather-worn Celtic-type tombstones, next door to the pretty *Auberge Hirribarren*, a temporary haven for many escaping Allied soldiers during World War II. From here the main footpaths and a number of local variations rise rapidly above the coast to semi-isolation, where only the buzzing power lines (soon left behind) and the occasional walker or jogger disturb the peace.

Inland: Labourd (Lapurdi) and Basse Navarre (Behe Nafarroa)

If you don't have your own transport, the simplest forays into the soft, seductive landscapes of the Basque hinterland are along the **St-Jean-de-Luz–Sare bus route** or the **Bayonne–St-Jean-Pied-de-Port train line**. Both give a representative sample of the area's main characteristics.

La Rhune (Larrun), Ascain (Azkaine), Sare (Sara) and Ainhoa

The 900-metre cone of **La Rhune**, straddling the frontier with Spain, is the last skyward thrust of the Pyrenees before they decline into the Atlantic. As the landmark of Labourd, in spite of its unsightly TV mast, and duly equipped with a rack-and-pinion rail service, it is predictably popular as a vantage point, offering fine vistas way up the Basque coast and east to the rising Pyrenees. Two or three **buses** a day (July & Aug Mon–Sat; Sept–June Mon–Fri), run by Le Basque Bondissant, ply the thirty-minute route from the *gare SNCF* in St-Jean-de-Luz, stopping at Ascain, Col de St-Ignace and Sare.

ASCAIN, where Pierre Loti wrote his romantic novel *Ramuntcho*, is like so many Labourdan villages – pretty as a picture and in danger of caricaturing itself, with its galleried church, *fronton* and half-timbered houses. Loti's house is now one of several **hotel-restaurants** in town, the *De la Rhune* (Ⓣ05.59.54.00.04, Ⓔaspirot@club-intenet.fr; ❹) with a garden at the back.

To shake off this sweetness you could walk up La Rhune from here in about two and a half hours, or take the **little tourist train** from **Col de St-Ignace** (daily: July–Aug about every 35min from 9am; late-March & Oct Tues, Wed & Fri–Sun 10am–3pm; April–June & Sept 9am–3pm, according to demand and weather conditions; book on Ⓣ05.59.54.20.26, Ⓦwww.rhune.com; return €11). The ascent takes thirty minutes, but you need to allow up to two hours for the round trip. Be warned: it's massively popular in high season, with long waits and two snack bars near the base station taking advantage of a captive clientele.

With or without the bus, it's worth going on to **SARE**, another perfectly proportioned Basque hilltop village ringed by satellite hamlets. You can either walk on the **GR10** from the intermediate station below the summit of La Rhune in about an hour and a quarter or follow the 3km of road from St-Ignace in rather less time. If you plan to continue further east, you can make an overnight stop at one of the village's **hotels**: the *Pikassaria*, 1km southwest in Lehenbiscay hamlet (Ⓣ05.59.54.21.51, Ⓕ05.59.54.27.40; ❸), or the three-star *Arraya* on the village square (Ⓣ05.59.54.20.46, Ⓦwww.arraya.com; ❹), a former hospice on the Santiago pilgrimage route. Alternatively, try the **campsites** just south of the village: *La Petite Rhune* (Ⓣ05.59.54.23.97; closed Oct–May) or *Telletchea* (Ⓣ05.59.54.20.12; closed Oct–May).

Instead of going back to St-Jean-de-Luz from Sare, an easy three-to-four-hour stint on the GR10 takes you on to **AINHOA** to link up with the valley of the Nive (see below). Another gem of a village, once patronized by the Duke of Windsor and busy in season, it consists of little more than a single street lined with substantial, mainly seventeenth-century houses, whose lintel plaques offer mini-genealogies as well as foundation dates. Take a look at the bulky towered **church** with its extravagant Baroque altarpiece of prophets and apostles in niches, framed by Corinthian columns. For **accommodation**, try the comfortable *Hôtel Oppoca* (Ⓣ05.59.29.90.72, Ⓕ05.59.29.81.03; ❸) with a good restaurant (four menus €16–28). **Campers** should head for *Camping Harazpy* near the village centre (Ⓣ05.59.29.89.38; closed Oct to mid-June).

The valley of the Nive

The valley of the **River Nive** is the only public-transport artery southeast into the Basque interior, with four or five trains a day making the riverside journey from Bayonne to St-Jean-Pied-de-Port in about an hour. The luminous green landscape on the approach to the mountains is scattered with villages untouched by speculative development, and remains as peaceful and harmonious as in the lowlands.

Cambo-les-Bains (Kambo)

The first major stop is **CAMBO-LES-BAINS**, an old spa town whose favourable microclimate made it an ideal centre for the treatment of tuberculosis in the nineteenth century; the locals like to claim that camellias flower a month earlier here than elsewhere in the region. It's an attractive town, green and open, but suffers from the usual genteel stuffiness of spas. The "new" town, with its ornate houses and hotels, radiates out from the baths over the heights above the River Nive, while the old quarter, typically Basque with its whitewashed houses and galleried church, lies beside the river.

The main thing to see here is the **Villa Arnaga**, 1.5km northwest of town on the Bayonne road (guided visits: April, May, June & Sept 10am–12.30pm & 2.30–7pm; March Sun 2.30–6.30pm; July & Aug 10am–7pm; Oct Sat 2.30–6.30pm; €4.70), built for Edmond Rostand, author of *Cyrano de Bergerac*, who came here to cure his pleurisy in 1903. This larger-than-life Basque house overlooks an almost surreal formal garden with discs and rectangles of water and segments of grass punctuated by blobs, cubes and cones of box, lined by limes and blue cedars, with a distant view of green hills. Inside, it's very kitsch, with a minstrels' gallery, fake pilasters, allegorical frescoes, chandeliers, numerous portraits and various memorabilia.

The **tourist office** is in the Parc St-Joseph in the upper town centre (mid-July to Aug Mon–Fri 8.30am–6.30pm, Sat 8.30am–noon & 2–5.30pm, Sun 10am–12.30pm; Sept to mid-July Mon–Fri 8.30am–12.30pm & 2–6.30pm, Sat 8.30am–noon & 2–5.30pm; Ⓣ05.59.29.70.25, Ⓔcambo.les.bains.tourisme@wanadoo.fr). For an overnight **stay**, try the *Auberge de Tante Ursule* in the old quarter by the pelota court (Ⓣ05.59.29.78.23, Ⓔchez.tante.ursule@wanadoo.fr; ❶), with an excellent **restaurant** offering menus from €15–35. The nearest year-round **campsite** is *Ur-Hégia* on route des Sept-Chênes (Ⓣ05.59.29.72.03), also in Bas Cambo; *Camping Bixta Eder* is on the other side of town along avenue d'Espagne (Ⓣ05.59.29.94.23; closed mid-Oct to March). Henri Breuillé (Ⓣ05.59.29.73.10) on place de l'Église rents mountain bikes.

Espelette (Ezpeleta) and Itxassou (Itsasu)

Buses cover the 5km southwest from Cambo to **ESPELETTE**, a somewhat traffic-plagued village of wide-eaved houses, with a **church** notable for its heavy square tower, painted ceiling and disc-shaped gravestones. The village's principal source of renown is its large red **pimentos**, much used in Basque cuisine, and its **pottok** sales. *Pottoks* are a small stocky Basque breed of pony, once favoured for work in British coal mines but now reared mainly for meat and riding – herds of them are a common sight on the upland pastures. The annual sales take place on the last Tuesday and Wednesday in January; the pimento jamboree takes place on the last Sunday in October. There's a very good **hotel-restaurant** in the village, too, the *Euzkadi* on the through road at the northeast edge of the village (Ⓣ05.59.93.91.88, Ⓔhotel.euzkadi@wanadoo.fr; ❸; restaurant closed Mon), with quiet rear rooms, a pool, tennis courts and three menus (€15.50–26) featuring Basque country cooking.

About the same distance from Cambo-les-Bains, next stop up the train line (though only one train a day stops here), is the delightful village of **ITXASSOU**, quieter than most of the others in the area, and surrounded by green wooded hills. Nearby, the River Nive cuts through a narrow looping defile by the so-called **Pas de Roland** – hardly more than a roadside boulder with a hole in it, supposedly struck by the hooves of the great knight's horse. Somewhat more arresting is the little seventeenth-century **church of St-Fructueux**, about 1km out on the minor D349 road to the Pas de Roland, its white-plastered walls set in a lush green bowl; inside, its typical wooden galleries are worth a quick look. Itxassou is a great base for a gentle recharge of the batteries, with about a half-dozen **hotel-restaurants** scattered locally. These include the very central *Hôtel du Fronton* (Ⓣ05.59.29.75.10, Ⓦwww.hotelrestaurantfronton.com; ❷; closed Jan to mid-Feb & part Nov), with its affiliated *Restaurant Bonnet*; and the remoter *Hôtel du Chêne* (Ⓣ05.59.29.75.01, Ⓕ05.59.29.27.39; ❸; closed Jan–Feb, part March, June & Oct) and *Hôtel-Restaurant La Place* (Ⓣ05.59.29.75.14, Ⓔetchecoco@aol.com; ❷), both a few hundred metres along the road to the Pas de Roland and Laxia hamlet.

Bidarray (Bidarrai) and St-Étienne-de-Baïgorry (Baigorri)

The GR10 from Ainhoa, as well as the train line (station Pont-Noblia), both call at **BIDARRAY**, which at first glance seems restricted to a few houses clustered around its medieval bridge. Further investigation, however, reveals the upper village, scattered appealingly on a ridge with superb views. On the way into the village on the GR10 is a **gîte d'étape**, *Auñamendi* (Ⓣ05.59.37.71.34, Ⓦwww.aunamendi.com; ❶), while the central place de l'Église is flanked by the *Hôtel Restaurant Barberaenea* (Ⓣ05.59.37.74.86, Ⓦwww.hotel-barberaenea.fr; ❷), where it's worth enduring leisurely service for the tasty five-course €22 *menu du terroir* served under the plane trees. Another good option down in the riverbank quarter, the welcoming *Hôtel-Restaurant du Pont d'Enfer* (Ⓣ05.59.37.70.88, Ⓦwww.hotel-restaurant-du-pont-enfer.com; ❸; closed Nov–Easter), also known as *Chez Anny* after the owner, has good-sized rooms and a restaurant serving on a river-view terrace in summer – among several menus, the €20 one is best value. A short walk east, equidistant from upper and riverside quarters, lies the *Camping Errekaldia* (Ⓣ05.59.37.72.36).

Bidarray is the preferred starting point for the classic **ridge walk** of the Basque country, the section of the GR10 running roughly south along the **Crête d'Iparla**, and then descending east to **ST-ÉTIENNE-DE-BAÏGORRY**. It's seven hours one way, and should only be attempted in settled conditions – when bad weather closes in, you won't get its famous views and close-range sightings of vultures, and you'll be at risk from lightning strikes or falling from the mist-shrouded brink, both of which kill hikers here regularly. Consult current SNCF schedules before setting out so that you coincide with one of the afternoon **rail-buses** that run the eight kilometres between St-Étienne and the train station of Ossès-St-Martin-d'Arrossa, one stop above Pont-Noblia.

Like most other Basque villages, St-Étienne is divided into quite distinct quarters, more like separate hamlets than a unified village. A prosperous, sleek place, its business is still predominantly agriculture rather than tourism, with the Pays Basque's only vineyards scattered all around, producing a good, strong wine named Irouléguy (Irulegi) after the village 5km east; a local shop, on the road north to St-Jean, offers **dégustation**. There's little to see here, other than a seventeenth-century **church** with a sumptuous Baroque retable and a picturesque medieval bridge posing against a backdrop of romantic castle (now a hotel, see below) and distant hills.

The **tourist office** is opposite the church (May & June Mon–Sat 9am–12.30pm & 2–6.30pm, Sun 10am–12.30pm; July & Aug Mon–Sat

9am–7pm, Sun 10am–4pm; Sept–April Mon–Sat 9am–12.30pm & 2–6.30pm; ⓣ05.59.37.47.28). For budget **accommodation**, there's only the *Gîte d'étape Mendy* (ⓣ05.59.37.42.39, ⓔjcmendy@aol.com; ❶), with camping space, in the northerly Lespars quarter. More expensive but worthwhile, the tranquil *Hôtel-Restaurant Maechenea*, 4km north in the hamlet of Urdos (ⓣ05.59.37.41.68, ⓔhotel-manechenea@wanadoo.fr; ❸; closed mid-Nov to March; menu from €14.50), is set on the bank of a stream. If money is no object, head to the *Château d'Etchauz*, a *chambre d'hôte set* in a sixteenth-century fairy tale castle (ⓣ05.59.37.48.58, ⓔetchauz@wanadoo.fr; ❼).

St-Jean-Pied-de-Port (Donibane Garazi)

The old capital of Basse Navarre, **ST-JEAN-PIED-DE-PORT** lies in a circle of hills at the foot of the Roncevaux pass into Spain. It owes its name to its position "at the foot of the *port*" – a Pyrenean word for "pass". Only part of France since the Treaty of the Pyrenees in 1659, it was an important centre for the pilgrimage to Santiago de Compostela in the Middle Ages. The routes from Paris, Vézelay and Le Puy converged just northeast of here at Ostabat, and it was the pilgrims' last port of call before struggling over the pass to the Spanish monastery of Roncesvalles (Roncevaux in French), where Roland, a general of Charlemagne celebrated in medieval romance, sounded his horn for aid in vain.

The town lies on the River Nive, enclosed by walls of pinky-red sandstone. Above it rises a wooded hill crowned by the Richelieu-Vauban **fortress**, while to the east a further defensive system guards the road to Spain. The pleasant but unremarkable modern town spreads down across the main road onto lower ground.

The old town consists of a single cobbled street, **rue de la Citadelle**, running downhill from the fifteenth-century **Porte St-Jacques** – so named because it was the gate by which the pilgrims entered the town, St Jacques being the French name for Santiago – to the **Porte d'Espagne**, commanding the bridge over the Nive, with a view of balconied houses overlooking the stream. Many of the painted houses bear inscriptions on their lintels from the sixteenth, seventeenth and eighteenth centuries. A fourteenth-century plain red church, **Notre-Dame-du-Bout-du-Pont**, stands beside the Porte d'Espagne and, opposite, a short street leads through the **Porte de Navarre** to place de-Gaulle and the modern road. Just to the north, beyond the dusky-pink Hôtel de Ville, is the *fronton* where a bare-handed **pelota match** – the most macho kind – is held every Monday at 5pm.

The **tourist office** is at 14 place de-Gaulle (July & Aug Mon–Sat 9am–7pm, Sun 10am–12.30pm; Sept–June Mon–Sat 9am–noon & 2–6pm;

The Chanson de Roland

Roland, with his sword Durandal, is the hero of the medieval **Chanson de Roland**. But he was also a historical character, warden of the Breton marches, who in 778 accompanied the Emperor Charlemagne on a campaign to support the Muslim ruler of Zaragoza against the Emir of Córdoba. The mission was a fiasco, and on the way home the Franks sacked the Navarrese capital of Pamplona. In revenge, the Basques ambushed and decimated Charlemagne's rearguard, commanded by Roland, as it withdrew through the gorges above Roncevaux. The chanson has it that infidel Saracens were the dastardly foe, but this was propaganda dreamed up five hundred years later during the Crusades, in order to demonize the Muslim foe.

ⓣ05.59.37.03.57, ⓦwww.terre-basque.com), with the **gare SNCF** a ten-minute walk away at the end of avenue Renaud, on the northern edge of the centre. Cycles Garazi at 32bis ave du Jaï Alaï rents everything from bikes up to 600cc motorcycles. The least expensive **hotels** are the relatively quiet *Les Remparts*, 16 place Floquet (ⓣ05.59.37.13.79, ⓦwww.touradour.com/hotel-remparts.htm; ❷; closed Nov & Dec), just before you cross the Nive coming into town on the Bayonne road, and the *Itzalpea*, 5 place du Trinquet (ⓣ05.59.37.03.66, ⓔitzalpea@wanadoo.fr; ❷–❺), whose restaurant offers a wide choice of menus (average €35–45). More comfortable are the *Ramuntcho*, just inside the city walls at 1 rue de France (ⓣ05.59.37.03.91, ⓕ05.59.37.35.17; ❸; closed Wed), with a good and reasonably priced restaurant (from €11.70), and the posh *Central* on place de-Gaulle (ⓣ05.59.37.00.22, ⓕ05.59.37.27.79; ❸; closed mid-Dec to March; restaurant €18–41), with some river-view rooms and free parking. There are also several budget options for hikers, among them the tiny, helpful *Gîte d'Étape Etchegoin* at 9 rte d'Uhart, on the Bayonne road (ⓣ05.59.37.12.08), while the municipal **campsite**, the *Plaza Berri* (ⓣ05.59.37.11.19, ⓕ05.59.37.99.78; closed mid-Nov to mid-April), is on the south bank of the Nive, beside the *fronton*. A new addition is the *hostal L'Esprit du Chemin*, 40 rue de la Citadelle (ⓣ05.59.37.24.68, ⓦwww.espritduchemin.org), offering sound advice to walkers and Santiago pilgrims and bargain accommodation (❶) and meals (dinner €9).

Independent **restaurants** are apt to be slapdash and aimed at the day-tripper trade. Two exceptions are *Arbillaga* at 8 rue de l'Église just inside the walls (menus at €13–39; closed Tues eve, also Wed low season), and *Restaurant-Cidrerie* at 3bis rue de la Citadelle (ⓣ05.59.37.09.18; closed Wed low season), just inside the Porte Notre-Dame and serving abundant portions of country cooking.

Estérençuby, Béhérobie and the source of the Nive

From St-Jean, the D301 follows the deepening valley of the Nive to the southeast, past small red- and green-shuttered farms and attractive villages, while the GR10 stays well northeast of the river, first on paved lanes and then on track or trail along Handiamendi ridge. Both routes converge at **ESTÉRENÇUBY** (Esterenzubi), 8km from St-Jean and an attractive spot, well supplied with **accommodation**. A good option is the *Auberge Carricaburu* (ⓣ05.59.37.09.77; ❶), with a streamside restaurant (€12–25) and the lively village bar.

Beyond Estérençuby the valley-floor road continues alongside the Nive, now no more than a mountain stream, tumbling down between steep green slopes, covered in hay and bracken. In late June and early July, you'll see entire families scything the meadows and turning the sweet-smelling hay with rakes. After 2km you'll pass another worthy establishment, the *Hôtel Artzaïn Etchea* (ⓣ05.59.37.11.55, ⓦwww.artzain-etchea.com; ❷; closed Feb), a modern, well-run place with a popular restaurant (menus from €18).

Some 4km from Estérençuby the road reaches tiny **BÉHÉROBIE** before climbing up to the border and fizzling out. Here, the *Hôtel de la Source de la Nive* (ⓣ05.59.37.10.57, ⓕ05.59.37.39.06; ❷; closed Jan and Tues out of season, usually booked out in Oct for the wood-pigeon shooting season), beside the stream, is a marvellous place for a quiet stay, with a restaurant serving game-dominated menus (€12–27). Just before the bridge at Béhérobie, a lane leads to the left, signposted to the *Source de la Nive*. With a car, you can drive the

400m to the end of the asphalt, then continue on foot along the dirt track going left, not the one going over the bridge. After fifteen minutes, you'll reach the springs, where water percolates a thousand metres down through the karstic hillside to well up as surging rapids. Hidden in dense beech woods, it's a magic spot in any weather, with a faint mist often rising from the surface of the water.

Haute Soule

East of the Nive valley, you enter largely uninhabited country, known as the **Haute Soule**, threaded only by the GR10 and a couple of minor roads. The border between Basse Navarre and Soule skims the western edge of the **Forêt d'Iraty**, one of Europe's largest surviving beech woods, a popular summer retreat and winter cross-country skiing area. There are no shops or proper hotels until you reach **Larrau**, the only real village in these mountains, though the scattered hamlet of **Ste-Engrâce** in the east of the district has some facilities. There's even a downhill ski resort, westernmost in the Pyrenees, at **Arette-la-Pierre-St-Martin**, technically just over the border in Béarn but included here for convenience.

The Haute Soule is a land of open skies, where griffon vultures turn on the thermals high above countless flocks of sheep (their occasional corpses providing sustenance for the vultures), with three vast gorges to explore. Although the overall distance from the Nive valley to the Béarn is not very great, the slowness of the roads (there's no public transport) and the GR10 – it's a day-and-a-half minimum from Estérençuby to Larrau – and the grandeur of the scenery seem to magnify it. Carrying a tent would give you the greatest flexibility: no one objects if you pitch it discreetly, though to be on the safe side you can always ask the nearest shepherd. For the latest on **weather information** in the western Pyrenees, call ⓣ08.36.68.02.64.

The GR65 from St-Jean

The mountains south of St-Jean towards the Spanish border are sheep country, and if you're interested in getting an idea of what the old pastoral life was like, this is a good place to do it. For walkers, the last French leg of the **GR65** pilgrim route starts from St-Jean and follows the line of the old Roman road across to Roncesvalles in Spanish Navarra, an easy day's walk.

Follow the Route de St-Michel out of St-Jean, soon adopting the D428; the typical yellow waymarks of the Chemin St-Jacques show the way. Though the climb is initially dull, on a tarmac lane, there are attractive farmhouses to look at, with immensely broad roofs, one side short, the other long enough to cover space for stalls and tools; it's all very quiet and rural, with long views out across the valleys. After a couple of hours you reach the tiny hamlet of **HONTO**, which for late starters in particular offers excellent *chambres d'hôte* (as well as cheaper dorm beds) and hearty evening meals at Ferme Ithurburia (ⓣ05.59.37.11.17; ❹; year round). Beyond Honto, the grade sharpens, but there's only one brief path shortcut from the D428 before you finally leave the latter for a proper trail at Pic Urdanarré (1240m), some four hours along and just before the frontier.

The Forêt d'Iraty (Irati)

To drive to the **Forêt d'Iraty**, follow the D301 east out of the Nive valley from the junction near the *Hôtel Artzaïn Etchea* (see p.805), where the forest is signposted. The road is very steep, narrow and full of tight hairpins and ambling livestock – it's best avoided at night or in misty conditions – but as you climb higher up the steep spurs and round the heads of labyrinthine gullies, ever more spectacular views open beneath you. You can see way back over the valley of the Nive, St-Jean and the hills beyond. Stands of beech fill the gullies, shadowing the lighter grass whose green is so intense it seems almost theatrical – an effect produced, apparently, by the juxtaposition of outcrops of rock whose purplish hue brings out the cadmium yellow in the grass.

Along the cols and ridges stand ranks of shooting butts, from which the well-heeled urban bourgeoisie open fire every October on the millions of migrating *palombes*, as wood pigeons are called here, heading north over the western Pyrenees from Spain. Many other bird species can be seen too; among them honey buzzards, black kites, red kites, cranes and storks. Herds of healthy-looking horses and ponies, masses of sheep and big sleek caramel cows with bells at their throats on wooden collars marked with their owners' names, wander across the road. There are superb places to camp, with views west to the orange and crimson striations of the sunset and the revolving beacon of the Biarritz lighthouse visible in the dark.

Once past the north flank of **Occabé** (1456m), you're in Soule, and from here the road loops down to meet the D18 on the **plateau d'Iraty**, with its small lake, clutch of snack bars and flat ground to camp on. A minor road leads south to Ochagavia in Spain via the *Chalet Pedro* (1km), the best restaurant in the area, where the GR10 emerges from its descent of flat-topped Occabé (75min up from here), with its Iron Age **stone circle** and views across the forest and south to the Sierra de Abodi. Continuing east from the plateau, the D18 road enters the densest part of the forest, climbing past another small lake and a **campsite** half hidden in the magnificent beeches, to a collection of nine wooden chalets and a *gîte d'étape* at the **Col de Bargagiak**. An **information** office at the col (open all year; ⓣ05.59.28.51.29) takes bookings for the chalets

Transhumance in the Pyrenees

Like other shepherds in south European or Mediterranean climes, the Basques are forced to take their flocks to the high **mountain pastures** in summer in search of better grazing. They live out on the bare slopes in stone-hut sheepfolds called *cayolars*, with a couple of dogs, milking the ewes twice a day and making cheese, the *fromage de brébis*, whose soft and hard versions are a speciality throughout the pastoral Pyrenees. Most of the pastures today are accessible by car, at least at the gentler Basque end of the Pyrenees, so the shepherd's life is not as harsh and isolated as it used to be – though there are still areas in the higher mountains accessible only by mule or pony. A measure of the pre-eminence of sheep in the Basque economy is the Basque word for "rich", *aberats*, the literal meaning of which is "he who owns large flocks".

Much of the grazing is owned in common by various *communes*, who have over the centuries made elaborate agreements to ensure a fair share of the best pasture and avoid disputes. One of the oldest of these **faceries**, as they are called, concluded by the inhabitants of Spanish Roncal and French Barétous in 1326, is still in force and renewed each July 13 at the frontier **Col de la Pierre-St-Martin** on symbolic payment of three white heifers.

and the *gîte d'étape*; across the car park is a small shop and inexpensive restaurant. From here you descend slightly to the nearby **Col d'Orgambidexka**, which is one of the prime viewing fields for the autumn bird migrations. As you emerge into the open beyond Bargagiak, the ground drops sharply away on the left into the **Valleé de Larrau**, 600m lower. To the right, the brilliant grassy swards of the **Pic d'Orhy** (2017m; allow 5hr return hike) culminate in swirling strata of rock below the summit, barring the way to Spain. And ahead, for the first breath-stopping time, you can see the serrated horizon of peaks that dominate the **Cirque de Lescun**, a harbinger of the central Pyrenees.

Larrau (Larrañe) to Arette-la-Pierre-St-Martin

The first thing you notice coming into **LARRAU** from the west is how different the architecture is. In contrast to the gaily painted facades and tiled roofs of Labourd and Basse Navarre, the houses here are grey and stuccoed, with steep-pitched slate roofs to shed heavy snow. And, although it's the biggest place since St-Jean, it is nonetheless very small and quiet – almost dead out of season. There are two friendly **hotels**: the simple, old-fashioned *Hôtel Despouey* (Ⓣ05.59.28.60.82; ❷; closed mid-Nov to mid-Feb), with the local shop on the ground floor, and the fancier *Hôtel-Restaurant Etchémaïté* (Ⓣ05.59.28.61.45, Ⓦwww.hotel-etchemaite.fr; ❸; closed late Jan), with a superb restaurant serving such treats as guinea-fowl roulade with braised bacon and cabbage (closed Sun eve & Mon low season; menus €15–32; reservations advisable).

There's one **campsite** in Larrau, the *Ixtila* (Ⓣ05.59.28.63.09; closed mid-Nov to mid-March), and a *gîte d'étape* – with restaurant – 3km away at **LOGIBAR** (Ⓣ05.59.28.61.14; closed Dec–Feb), close to the mouth of the **Gorges d'Holzarte**. This gorge is one of several in the region, cutting deep into northern slopes of the ridge that forms the frontier with Spain. A short track leads from Logibar across the turbulent and freezing stream to a car park, from where a steep, usually very busy path, a variant of the GR10, climbs through the beech woods to the junction of the Holzarte gorge with the Olhadybia (Olhadubi) in about 45 minutes. Slung across the mouth of the latter is a spectacular Himalayan-style **suspension bridge**, the *passerelle*, which bounces and swings dizzily as you walk out over the 180-metre drop. You can continue along the **GR10** to Ste-Engrâce in seven hours, or down to the beginning of the Gorges de Kakuetta in about six: it is definitely worth the walk – in June and July, the open spaces are full of flowers (columbines, cranesbills, orchids and vetches), and, if you're lucky, you might see the beautiful, long-stemmed *bimbette des Pyrénées*.

The Gorges de Kakuetta and Gorges d'Ehujarré

Ten kilometres by road east of Larrau, you reach the **Gorges de Kakuetta** (mid-March to mid-Nov daily 8am–nightfall; €4) by turning right off the D26 and up onto the D113. About 3km along the latter, the minuscule hamlet of **CASERNES** offers a food shop opposite the *mairie*, and an attractive riverside **campsite**, the *Ibarra* (Ⓣ05.59.28.73.59; closed Nov–March).

Kakuetta gorge is truly dramatic and, outside peak season, not crowded at all. It pays to be well shod – the path is precarious and very slippery in places – and you'll be glad of the handrail. The walls of the gorge are up to 300m high and scarcely more than 5m apart in spots, and jungle-thick with luxuriant vegetation that thrives on the hothouse atmosphere, including a range of ferns that you wouldn't expect to see outside a houseplant nursery. Myriad seepages and waterfalls fill the air with a fine spray, refracting and filtering what sunlight gets in; the path continues for about an hour (2km) with a small cave at the end and just before it a full-blown waterfall spewing out of a hole in the rock.

There's a third, scarcely visited gorge, the **Gorges d'Ehujarré**, a short distance east at Senta, the easternmost of the three hamlets that comprise Ste-Engrâce (see below). It's a straightforward walk up – the route has been used for centuries for moving sheep up to the pastures of Pic Lakhoura – but is about a five-hour round trip.

Ste-Engrâce and Arette-la-Pierre-St-Martin

Le bout du monde – "the end of the earth" – is what they used to call the tiny settlement of **STE-ENGRÂCE**, locked in its cul-de-sac valley beneath the Spanish frontier at the easternmost extremity of the Basque country. And, although a road runs through it to Arette-la-Pierre-St-Martin, the place remains beautifully remote and peaceful. Life is not so idyllic for the locals – there's no work and the young won't stay – but for an outsider not caught in the rural poverty trap, it has great charm.

Ste-Engrâce's hallmark is the eleventh-century Romanesque **church** in the hamlet of **SENTA**, which features in all the coffee-table books on the Pyrenees. It stands just as it should, with its heavily buttressed walls, belfry and penthouse roof, a sharply defined and angular assertion of humanity against the often mist-shrouded bulwarks of the mountains behind. Very simple inside, it has some good carved column capitals, and the graveyard is full of traditional disc-shaped headstones. There's a **gîte d'étape** opposite the church, the *Auberge Elichalt* (ⓣ05.59.28.61.63), with a few *chambres d'hôte* (❸), a back garden to pitch a tent and a café-bar that serves light meals.

The road up to the ski resort of **ARETTE-LA-PIERRE-ST-MARTIN** gives fabulous views of the valley of Ste-Engrâce, through magnificent forests of pine and beech, though if the cloud is down, which it often is, you'll be lucky to see much at all. At a little col with a three-way junction, you're already in the ancient county of Béarn, and can glimpse the descent east into the Vallée d'Aspe. The upper, right-hand turning leads into Arette, an ugly ski resort with eighteen pistes, and the excellent *Refuge-Gîte d'Étape Jeandel* or *Hourticq* (ⓣ05.59.66.14.46; June–Sept or by arrangement), mostly serving trekkers on the GR10, with enthusiastic management and meals (May to mid-Oct). The skiing here is better than you'd imagine at the modest altitude (2153m top point), owing to moist Atlantic exposure and some quite long runs for beginners and intermediates. There are also two nordic skiing areas nearby.

The Central Pyrenees

The **Central Pyrenees** area, immediately east of the Pays Basque, is home to the range's highest mountain peaks and is the most spectacular part of the region, with the southernmost section, by the border, protected within the **Parc National des Pyrénées Occidentales**. Getting here is simple enough, at least as far as the foothill towns, by train on the

The Parc National des Pyrénées Occidentales

The **Parc National des Pyrénées Occidentales** was created in 1967 to protect at least part of the high Pyrenees from the development engendered by modern tourism – ski resorts, roads, mountain-top restaurants, car parks and other amenities. It runs for more than 100km along the Spanish border: from Pic de Laraille (2147m), south of Lescun, in the west, to beyond Pic de la Munia (3133m), east of Gavarnie. Varying in altitude between 1070m and 3298m at the Pic de Vignemale, south of Cauterets, the park takes in the spectacular cirques of Gavarnie and Troumouse, as well as over two hundred lakes, more than a dozen valleys and about 400km of marked walking routes.

Through the **banning of hunting** – apart from the traditional mountain peasants' pursuit of poaching or *braconnage* – and all dogs, the park has also provided sanctuary for many rare and endangered species of birds and mammals. Among them are chamois, marmots, genets, griffon vultures, golden eagles, eagle owls and capercaillies, to say nothing of the rich and varied flora. The most celebrated animal – and the most depleted by hunting – is the Pyrenean **brown bear**, whose prewar numbers ran to as many as two hundred, but now amount to barely half a dozen individuals. Although largely herbivorous, bears will take sheep or cows when given the opportunity, and the mountain shepherds are their remorseless enemies. To appease them, the park pays prompt and generous compensation for any losses, but this is not always enough to overcome the atavistic fear of the bear – there's a farmers' lobby to cancel the programme and at least one animal has been illegally shot since the program began. Park authorities have been criticized for not doing enough to protect the bears – an accusation which angers the hard-pressed rangers, who complain that distant armchair ecologists have no conception of what it's like trying to reconcile legitimate local economic needs with the protection of wild species and unsullied landscapes, to say nothing of coping with the litter, wear and tear on footpaths, illicit camping and other problems caused by visitors.

The **GR10** runs through the entire park on its 700-kilometre journey from coast to coast, starting at Argelès-sur-Mer on the Mediterranean and ending up at Hendaye-Plage on the Atlantic shore; the tougher trail of the **Haute Randonnée Pyrénéenne** (HRP) also finishes its course in Hendaye-Plage and runs roughly parallel to the GR10, but takes in much more rugged, alpine terrain. Hikers following either route are strongly advised to wear appropriate clothing, carry detailed maps and equipment and heed the words of warning on p.788. Though the Pyrenees have a modest maximum altitude by world-mountain standards, their climate can be as extreme as ranges twice their height – in short, this is not the place for a casual stroll.

There are **Maisons du Parc** (park information centres) in Etsaut, Cauterets, Luz-St-Sauveur, Gavarnie, Gabas and Arrens-Marsous, giving information about the park's wildlife and vegetation, lists of accommodation options and the best walks to do. There are over a dozen wardened refuges and plenty of hotels, campsites and *gîtes* throughout the park, listed in the text of this chapter or highlighted on the map on p.819. Backcountry camping (*camping sauvage)* is technically forbidden in many areas; if in doubt inquire at local tourist offices. For an update on weather conditions in the *département* of Hautes-Pyrénées, telephone ⓣ08.36.68.02.65.

Bayonne–Toulouse line. But travelling uphill and around once there can be very slow. The few buses – and most other traffic – keep mainly to the north-south valleys, which is frustrating when you want to switch from one valley system to the next without having to come all the way out of the mountains each time. The **GR10** provides a good lateral link if you're ready to walk all the way, and it's possible to hitch up the valleys and across the main passes at **Col d'Aubisque** and **Col du Tourmalet**, though you'll find you often get left on the top by drivers who come up for the view and go back the same way.

Highlights – apart from the lakes, torrents, forests and 3000-metre peaks around **Cauterets** – are the cirques of **Lescun**, **Gavarnie** and **Troumouse**, each with its distinctive character. And for less hearty interests, there's many a flower-starred mountain meadow accessible by car, especially near **Barèges** and **Bagnères-de-Luchon**, in which to picnic. The only real urban centres are **Pau**, a probable entry point to the area, dull **Tarbes** and the tacky pilgrimage target of **Lourdes**. Great monuments of the bricks-and-mortar kind – with the exception of the fortified churches at **Luz-St-Sauveur**, **St-Savin** and **St-Bertrand-de-Comminges** – are equally scarce.

Pau and around

From humble beginnings as a crossing on the Gave de Pau ("Gave" roughly translates as valley) for flocks en route to and from the mountains, **PAU** became the capital of the ancient viscountcy of Béarn in 1464, and of the French part of the kingdom of Navarre in 1512. In 1567 its sovereign, Henri d'Albret, married the sister of the king of France, Marguerite d'Angoulême, friend and protector of artists and intellectuals and herself the author of a celebrated Boccaccio-like tale (the *Heptameron*), who transformed the town into a centre of the arts and nonconformist thinking.

Their daughter was Jeanne d'Albret, an ardent Protestant, whose zeal offended her own subjects as well as attracting the wrath of the Catholic king of France, Charles X, thus embroiling Béarn in the Wars of Religion – whose resolution, albeit only temporary, had to await the accession to the French throne of her own son, Henri IV, in 1589. An adroit politician, he renounced his faith to facilitate this transition, quipping that "Paris is worth a Mass" and then appeasing the regional sensibilities of his Béarnais subjects by announcing that he was giving France to Béarn rather than Béarn to France. He did not incorporate Béarn into the French state; that was left to his son and successor, Louis XIII, in 1620. As Pau's most famous son, Henri acquired a suitably colourful reputation. He was baptized in traditional Béarnais style with the local Jurançon wine, and his infant lips were rubbed with garlic. In his adult life he was known as the *vert-galant* for his prowess as a lover. He also gave France one of its more famous recipes, *poulet au pot* – chicken stuffed and boiled with vegetables: he is reputed to have said that he did not want anyone in his realm to be so poor as not to be able to afford a *poulet* in the *pot* once a week.

The least-expected thing about Pau is its English connection, which dates from the arrival of Wellington and his troops after the defeat of Marshal Soult at Orthez in 1814. Seduced by its climate and persuaded of its curative powers by the Scottish doctor Alexander Taylor, the English flocked to Pau throughout the nineteenth century, bringing along their peculiar cultural obsessions – fox-hunting, horse-racing, polo, croquet, cricket, golf (the first eighteen-hole course in continental Europe in 1860 and the first in the world to admit women), tearooms and parks. When the rail line arrived here in 1866, the French came, too: writers and artists like Victor Hugo, Stendhal and Lamartine, as well as the socialites. The first French rugby club opened here in 1902, after which the sport spread throughout the southwest. During the 1950s, natural gas was discovered at nearby Lacq, bringing new jobs and subsidiary industries, as well as massive production of sulphur-dioxide-based pollution, now reduced by filtration but still substantial. In addition, there's a well-respected university, founded in 1972, whose eight thousand or so students give the town a youthful buzz.

Pau lies within easy reach of numerous small, picturesque villages in **northwest Béarn**, as well as the GR65 footpath that runs some 60km down to the Spanish border.

Arrival and information

Pau's **airport** (ⓣ05.59.33.33.00, ⓦwww.pau.aeroport.fr), is overshadowed by those nearby at Tarbes-Lourdes and Biarritz, though Ryan Air offers service from Stansted (London). Regular *navettes* run to the city centre (€5 one-way), as well as to Lourdes and Tarbes (€64), and a taxi to town will cost about €20. The town lies on the A64 *autoroute Pyrénéenne* and on the main east–west rail route, with connections to Bayonne and Biarritz to the west, and Lourdes, Tarbes and Toulouse to the east, as well as to Bordeaux and Paris. The **gare SNCF** is on the southern edge of the city centre by the riverside: SNCF **buses** leave from here, and private buses from various kerbside terminals in rue Gachet, off place Clemenceau. Buses run south down the Vallée d'Ossau and to Oloron-Ste-Marie, with onward connections to the Vallée d'Aspe.

A **free funicular** carries you up from the train station to the boulevard des Pyrénées, opposite place Royale, at the far end of which is the **tourist office** (July & Aug daily 9am–6pm; Sept–June Mon–Sat 9am–6pm, Sun 9.30am–1pm; ⓣ05.59.27.27.08, ⓦwww.pau.fr). For information on walking and climbing, try the local CAF (Club Alpin Français; see Basics, p.62) on 5 rue René Fournets (call Rappin Didier Mon–Fri eve only; ⓣ05.59.30.50.37), or Librairie des Pyrénées, 14 rue St-Louis, which stocks a wide range of books on the mountains. There is a central **Internet café**, CyberSeventys, at 7 rue Léon-Duran.

Accommodation

For a friendly, clean and quiet budget **hotel**, try either the *Hôtel le Matisse*, 17 rue Mathieu-Lalanne, opposite the Musée des Beaux-Arts (ⓣ05.59.27.73.80; ❷), or *Pomme d'Or* at 11 rue Maréchal-Foch (ⓣ05.59.11.23.23, ⓕ05.59.11.23.24; ❷). The best deal for your money is the *Central*, 15 rue Léon-Daran (ⓣ05.59.27.33.28, ⓦwww.hotelcentralpau.com; ❸), which is warm, stylishly decorated and even boasts wireless Internet connections in many rooms. If booked, head for the two-star, en-suite comfort available at the *Postillon* at 10 Cours Camou behind place de Verdun (ⓣ05.59.72.83.00, ⓦwww.hotel-le-postillon.fr; ❸), arrayed around its own courtyard.

There is a **hostel** at 30 rue Michel-Hounau (ⓣ05.59.11.05.05, ⓦwww.ldjpau.org), and a pair of **campsites**; the *Base de Plein Air* at Gelos (ⓣ05.59.06.57.37; closed Oct–May), just over the river from the train station, has better amenities and is more convenient than the municipal one on boulevard du Cami-Salié, off avenue Sallenave towards the *autoroute*, on the northern edge of town (ⓣ05.59.02.30.49; closed mid-Sept to May).

The Town

Pau has no must-see sights or museums, enabling you to enjoy its relaxed and friendly elegance without any sense of guilt. The parts to wander are the streets behind the **boulevard des Pyrénées**, especially the western end, which stretches along the rim of the scarp above the Gave de Pau, from the castle to the Palais de Beaumont, now a convention centre, in the English-style

Parc Beaumont. On a (rare) clear day, the view from the boulevard is out of this world, encompassing a hundred-kilometre sweep of the highest Pyrenean peaks, with the distinctive Pic du Midi d'Ossau slap in front of you.

In the narrow streets around the castle and down in the gully of the chemin du Hédas are numerous cafés, restaurants, bars and boutiques, with the main **market** in the *halles* just northeast on place de la République each Saturday morning. The **Château** itself (one-hour guided tours daily: April to mid-June & mid-Sept to Oct 9.30–11.45am & 2–5pm; mid-June to mid-Sept 9.30am–12.15pm & 1.30–5.45pm; Nov–March 9.30–11.45am & 2–4.15pm; €4.50) is very much a landmark building. Not much remains of its original appearance beyond the brick keep built by Gaston Fébus in 1370. The handsome Renaissance windows and other details on the inner courtyard were added by Henri d'Albret. Louis-Philippe renovated it in the nineteenth century after it had stood empty for two hundred years, and Napoléon III and Eugénie titivated it further to make it suitable for weekend house parties. The visitable apartments are essentially theirs, with some fine tapestries and bits of Henri-IV memorabilia, like the turtle shell that allegedly served him for a cradle.

A short distance northeast of the château, the mildly interesting **Musée Bernadotte**, 6 rue Tran (Tues–Sun 10am–noon & 2–6pm; €2), is the birthplace of the man who, having served as one of Napoléon's commanders, went on to become Charles XIV of Sweden. As well as fine pieces of traditional Béarnais furniture, the house contains some valuable works of art collected over his lifetime. Pau's other museum, the **Musée des Beaux-Arts** in rue Mathieu-Lalanne (daily except Tues 10am–noon & 2–6pm; €2), has an eclectic collection of little-known works from various European schools spanning the fourteenth to twentieth centuries; the only really world-class items are Rubens' *The Last Judgement* and Degas' *The Cotton Exchange*, a slice of finely observed Belle Époque New Orleans life.

Eating and drinking

Of the **restaurants** around the château, *La Brochetterie*, 16 rue Henri-IV, is the best, serving good grills and fish in a pleasant, family atmosphere with menus from €15, and a lunch special for €11, while *O'Gascon*, at 13 rue du Château, is the most popular – the €23 menu is splendid (closed Wed lunch & Tues). Alternatively, try *Chez Maman*, a decent crêperie/*cidrerie* opposite the castle at 6 rue du Château, or *L'Entracte* (closed Mon eve in winter & Sun), opposite the municipal theatre in rue St-Louis, which offers a range of original salads and other vegetarian dishes. For a splurge, visit *La Table d'Hôte*, 1 Chemin du Hédas (closed Sun), with gourmet menus at €18 and €22.70; or, near the station, *Au Fin Gourmet*, 24 av Gaston-Lacoste (closed Sun eve & Mon), with several game-oriented menus from €15. Lastly, one of the best deals in Pau is the popular brasserie, *Le Berry*, at the south end of rue Gachet. Service is efficient and goes late (seating till 11pm), and the habitual queue is worth enduring for the outstanding *magret de canard* or their well-reputed Chateaubriand steaks (a la carte meals €20 and up).

Around Pau

One excursion worth making from Pau, particularly for families with children, is to the **Grottes de Bétharram** (guided tours: late-March to late-Oct daily 9am–noon & 1.30–5.30pm; Jan to late-March Mon–Fri 2.30–4pm; €9.50) at St-Pé-de-Bigorre, just off the D938/937 between Pau and Lourdes, 14km from the latter. Part of the eighty-minute tour around its spectacular stalactites and stalagmites takes place in a barge on an underground lake; the remaining kilometre is by miniature railway.

Orthez

Thirty kilometres northwest of Pau, **ORTHEZ** was the original capital of Béarn, its wealth due in large part to its beautiful and still-surviving thirteenth-century **fortified bridge**, which controlled the most important commercial route across the Gave de Pau for English and Flemish textiles, Aragonese wool, olive oil and wine. It was also a major centre on the pilgrim routes to Compostela; the modern route, the **GR65**, crosses the river just 8km east of Orthez at Argagnon, and you can follow it 60km south to the Spanish frontier. The town also serves as a gateway to the hinterland of the Pays Basque: SNCF **buses** run from Puyôo, 12km west, to Salies-de-Béarn, Sauveterre and Mauléon.

The **tourist office** (July & Aug Mon–Sat 9am–12.30pm & 2–7pm, Sun 9.30am–12.30pm; Sept–June Mon–Sat 9am–noon & 2–6pm; ⓣ05.59.69.02.75, ⓔtourisme.orthez@wanadoo.fr) occupies the sixteenth-century Maison Jeanne d'Albret on rue du Bourg-Vieux, which also hosts a **Musée Jean d'Albret** on the second floor (Mon–Sat 10am–noon & 2–6pm; €2.30), tracing the history of local Protestantism. Other fine old houses can be found in the town centre, especially along **rue Moncade**, the continuation of rue du Bourg-Vieux, where the five-sided Tour Moncade is all that remains of Orthez's castle. The **church of St-Pierre**, close to the tourist office, still has some interesting Gothic sculptures, though it was badly damaged when the town was sacked by Jeanne d'Albret's Protestant general Montgomery in 1569. Should you need to **stay** overnight, your best option is the historic, en-suite *Hôtel Restaurant Au Temps de la Reine Jeanne*, opposite the tourist office at 44 rue du Bourg-Vieux (ⓣ05.59.67.00.76, ⓕ05.59.69.09.63; ❸; closed late-Feb & Sun Oct–Apr), with a traditional-fare restaurant (menus €15–34). The municipal **campsite**, *Camping de la Source* is on Boulevard Charles de Gaulle (ⓣ05.59.69.04.81, ⓔtourisme.orthez@wanado.fr; closed mid-Sept to March).

Salies-de-Béarn and around

Fifteen kilometres west from Orthez (TPR bus from Pau), **SALIES-DE-BÉARN** is a typical Béarnais village of winding lanes and flower-decked houses with brightly painted woodwork. The River Saleys, hardly more than a stream, runs through the middle of it, separating the old village from the nineteenth-century development that sprang up to exploit the powerful saline spring for which it has long been famous. You can try the **curative waters** yourself at the wonderful old Les Thermes (ⓦwww.thermes-de-salies.com), in place Jardin Public from €7.60.

Overall, Salies is a charming, if unremarkable place, good for an overnight stop. If staying, head for the economical and comfortable *Au Petit Béarn* (ⓣ05.59.38.17.42, ⓕ05.59.65.01.75; ❶; closed Fri & Sun eves Oct–May) on rue Bellecave. A better value option is the surprisingly luxurious *Helios* (ⓣ05.59.38.37.59, ⓔgolf.salies@wanadoo.fr; ❶), though it's on the outskirts of town. There's also a municipal **campsite** (ⓣ05.59.38.53.30, ⓔcamping-du-gave@wanadoo.fr; closed mid-Oct to March). Cyclotourisme by the village's outdoor recreation grounds rents bikes. The **tourist office** is on rue des Bains (mid-June to mid-Sept Mon–Sat 9.30am–12.30pm & 2–6.30pm, Sun 9.30am–12.30pm; mid-Sept to mid-June Mon–Sat 9.30am–noon & 2–6pm; ⓣ05.59.38.00.33, ⓦwww.bearn-gaves.com).

Heading south, the D933 winds over hilly farming country to **SAUVET-**

ERRE-DE-BÉARN, another pretty country town beautifully sited on a scarp high above the Gave d'Oloron. From the terrace by the thirteenth-century **church of St-André** you look down over the river and the remains of another fortified bridge, while at the end of the terrace a ruined castle dominates the steep slope. For **accommodation**, there's the rustic *Auberge du Saumon Hostellerie du Château* in rue Léon-Bérard (Ⓣ05.59.38.53.20, ❶; closed mid-Jan to mid-Feb), and a municipal **campsite** by the medieval bridge (Ⓣ05.59.38.53.30; closed Oct–May). The *Auberge* serves hearty *terroir* menus for €15–25.

Just across the river, the D936 bears southeast along the flat valley bottom to **NAVARRENX**, 20km away on the Pau–Mauléon bus route, a sleepy, old-fashioned market town built as a *bastide* in 1316 and still surrounded by its medieval **walls**; you enter by the fortified **Porte St-Antoine**. The *Hôtel du Commerce* by here makes an agreeable place to stay (Ⓣ05.59.66.50.16, Ⓦwww.hotel-commerce.fr; ❸; closed Jan; excellent restaurant from €18–30), whereas hikers might head for the municipal *gite* (Ⓣ05.59.66.50.78, Ⓕ05.59.66.11.01, closed Jan to mid-March). There's also a municipal **campsite** in allée des Marronniers (Ⓣ05.59.66.10.00, Ⓕ05.59.66.11.01; closed mid-Sept to March).

Lourdes

LOURDES, about 30km southeast of Pau, has just one function. Over seven million Catholic pilgrims arrive here each year, and the town is totally given over to looking after and exploiting them. Lourdes was hardly more than a village before 1858, when Bernadette Soubirous, the 14-year-old daughter of an ex-miller, had the first of eighteen visions of the Virgin Mary in the so-called Grotte de Massabielle by the Gave de Pau. Since then, Lourdes has grown a great deal, and is now one of the biggest attractions in this part of France, many of its visitors hoping for a miraculous cure for conventionally intractable ailments.

The first large-scale **pilgrimage** took place in 1873, organized by a fundamentalist Catholic movement called the *Assomptionistes*, whose avowed purpose was to stem the advancing tide of republicanism and rationalism. They took over the management of Lourdes, shoving aside the local priest who had wanted to organize the pilgrimages himself. Adroit propagandists and agitators, they sought to promote their cause by publishing a cheap mass-circulation paper called *La Croix*, aimed at the poor and uneducated, and by organizing these massive pilgrimages.

Practically every shop is given over to the sale of indescribable religious kitsch: Bernadette in every shape and size, adorning barometers, thermometers, plastic tree trunks, key rings, empty bottles that you can fill with holy Lourdes water, bellows, candles, sweets and illuminated plastic grottoes. There's even a waxworks museum, the **Musée Grévin**, at 87 rue de la Grotte (daily: Easter to mid-July & late-Aug to mid-Nov Mon–Sat 9–11.40am & 1.30–6.30pm; Sun 10–11.40am & 1.30–6.30pm; mid-July to late-Aug also 8.30–10pm; €5.70), with over a hundred life-size figures illustrating the lives of Bernadette and Christ. Clustered around the miraculous grotto are the churches of the Domaine de la Grotte, an annexe to the town proper that sprang up last century. The first to be built was an underground crypt in 1866, followed by the Flamboyant **Basilique du Rosaire et de l'Immaculée Concep-**

△ Lourdes

tion (1871–1883), and then in 1958 by the massive subterranean **Basilique St-Pie-X**, which claims to be able to house 20,000 people at a time. The **Grotte de Massabielle** itself, where Bernadette had her visions, is the focus of the pilgrimages – a moisture-blackened overhang by the riverside with a marble statue of the Virgin in waxwork white and baby blue.

Musée Pyrénéen

Lourdes' only secular attraction is its **castle**, poised on a rocky bluff guarding the approaches to the valleys and passes of the central Pyrenees. Briefly an English stronghold in the late fourteenth century, it later became a state prison. Inside, it houses the surprisingly excellent **Musée Pyrénéen** (1hr guided visits daily: April to mid-July & mid-Aug to Sept 9am–noon & 1.30–6.30pm; mid-July to mid-Aug 9am–6.30pm; Oct–March 9am–noon & 2–5/6pm; last tour 1hr before closing; €5). Its collections include Pyrenean fauna, all sorts of fascinating pastoral and farming gear, and an interesting section on the history of Pyrenean mountaineering. In the rock garden outside are some beautiful models of various Pyrenean styles of house, as well as of the churches of St-Bertrand-de-Comminges and Luz-St-Sauveur. Walking up the nearby Pic du Jer affords stunning views of the town.

Practicalities

At the time of writing, those coming into the Tarbes-Lourdes **airport** must take a taxi into town (approx. €22 to the city centre), pending the end of long-term negotiations for a new shuttle bus contract. Lourdes' **gare SNCF** is on the northeast edge of the town centre, at the end of avenue de la Gare; the **gare routière** is in the central place Capdevieille, and the not terribly helpful **tourist office** is in place Peyramale (Easter–June & Sept to mid-Oct Mon–Sat 9am–7pm, Sun 10am–6pm; July & Aug Mon–Sat 9am–7pm, Sun 10am–6pm; mid-Oct to Easter Mon–Sat 9am–noon & 2–6pm; ⓣ05.62.42.77.40, ⓦwww.lourdes-infotourisme.com).

Lourdes has more **hotels** than any city in France outside Paris. A good, comfortable hotel choice, opposite the food halles, some 300m south of place Peyramale, is the two-star *Hôtel d'Albret* (ⓣ05.62.94.75.00, ⓔalbret.taverne.lourdes@libertysurf.fr; ❷; closed mid-Nov to mid-March), with the *Taverne de Bigorre* on the ground floor offering a range of menus (€18 gets you three hearty courses). At the other end of the scale, the luxurious *Grand Hôtel de la Grotte* at 66 rue de la Grotte (ⓣ05.62.94.58.87, ⓦwww.hotel-grotte.com; ❺; closed mid-Oct to mid-March) offers nineteenth-century style and luxury in an unbeatable location. Otherwise there is a plethora of accommodation possibilities in the small central streets around the castle. The nearest **campsite** is the *Poste*, 26 rue de Langelle, just south of the *gare SNCF* (ⓣ05.62.94.40.35; closed mid-Oct to March).

Tarbes

Twenty minutes away by train to the north, **TARBES** is a relatively dull town dominated by its history as a military base, but useful for visiting Lourdes or launching into the mountains to the south. The airport midway between Tarbes and Lourdes gets busy in winter with charter ski flights. The town's only real highlight is the Napoleonic stud farm, **Les Haras**, entered from chemin de Mauhourat (guided visits by appointment only: Mon–Fri

10am–noon & 2–5pm; last tour 1hr before closing; ⓣ05.62.56.30.80; €5.50), best known for the *cheval Tarbais*, bred from English and Moorish stock as a cavalry horse. You can watch them drilling during July and August at 3.15pm. World War I buffs may also want to visit the house, at 2 rue de la Victoire, where **Maréchal Foch**, supreme Allied commander in World War I, was born (guided tours Mon & Thurs–Sun: June–Sept 9am–noon & 2–6.30pm; Oct–May 9am–noon & 2–5pm; €4.60), containing a dull repository of family and personal mementos.

The **gare SNCF** is on avenue Maréchal Joffre, north of the centre, and the **gare routière** on the other side of town on place au Bois, off rue Larrey. The **tourist office** is near the central place de Verdun, at 3 cours Gambetta (Mon–Sat 9am–12.30pm & 2–7pm; ⓣ05.62.51.30.31, ⓦwww.tarbes.com). Tarbes has some reasonable **hotels** in the vicinity of the station, although the best of the cheapies is *Hôtel Isard*, 70 av Maréchal Joffre (ⓣ05.62.93.06.69, ⓕ05.62.93.99.55; ❶). A solid step up is *Henry IV*, no. 7 in central av Bertrand Barère (ⓣ05.62. 34.01.68, ⓕ05.62.93.71.32; ❹–❻). There's also a **HI hostel** at 88 av Alsace-Lorraine (ⓣ05.62.38.91.20, ⓔaj.tarbes@wanadoo.fr). Down the street from the *Henry IV* at no. 66, *Le Petit Gourmand* is a great place for local specialities (menu €18 and up; closed Sat lunch).

The valleys of the Aspe and Ossau

The parallel north–south valleys of the **Aspe** and **Ossau** are the central Pyrenees at their most *sauvage*, and the region in which the Pyrenean brown bear most tenaciously resists extinction. About six survive on the slopes of the valleys, in the **Cirque de Lescun** and in the adjoining parts of Spain.

Tourism is less developed here, especially in the Aspe valley, because unreliable snow conditions have precluded ski-resort construction – but what tourism has failed to do, a major road-building scheme threatens to achieve (see box, p.820). To see the best of the region you should get out your map and walk perpendicular to the line of the valleys, using the handful of refuges or camping in permitted areas along the way.

Oloron-Ste-Marie

The valley of the Aspe begins at the grey town of **OLORON-STE-MARIE**, around 45km west of Lourdes and only 32km southwest of Pau, where the mountain streams of the Aspe and Ossau meet. It's served by train from Pau as well as by CITRAM buses, with five to seven daily SNCF buses continuing down the valley to Urdos, most of these continuing as far as Canfranc in Spain. The town's claim to fame is as the centre of the manufacture of the famous woollen pancake-shaped *beret basque*, once the standard headgear for all French men but now seldom seen. There is little here to detain the visitor. The **Cathédrale Ste-Marie** boasts an unusually beautiful Romanesque portal in Pyrenean marble. In the upper arch, the elders of the Apocalypse play violins and rebecs, while in the second arch scenes from medieval life – a cooper, the slaying of a wild boar, fishing for salmon – are represented. The gallant knight on horseback over the outer column on the right is Gaston IV, Count of Béarn, who commissioned the portal on his return from the first Crusade at the beginning of the twelfth century, hence the reference to Saracens in chains among the sculptures. The magnificent studded doors were a present from Henri IV. Inside, well away from the main

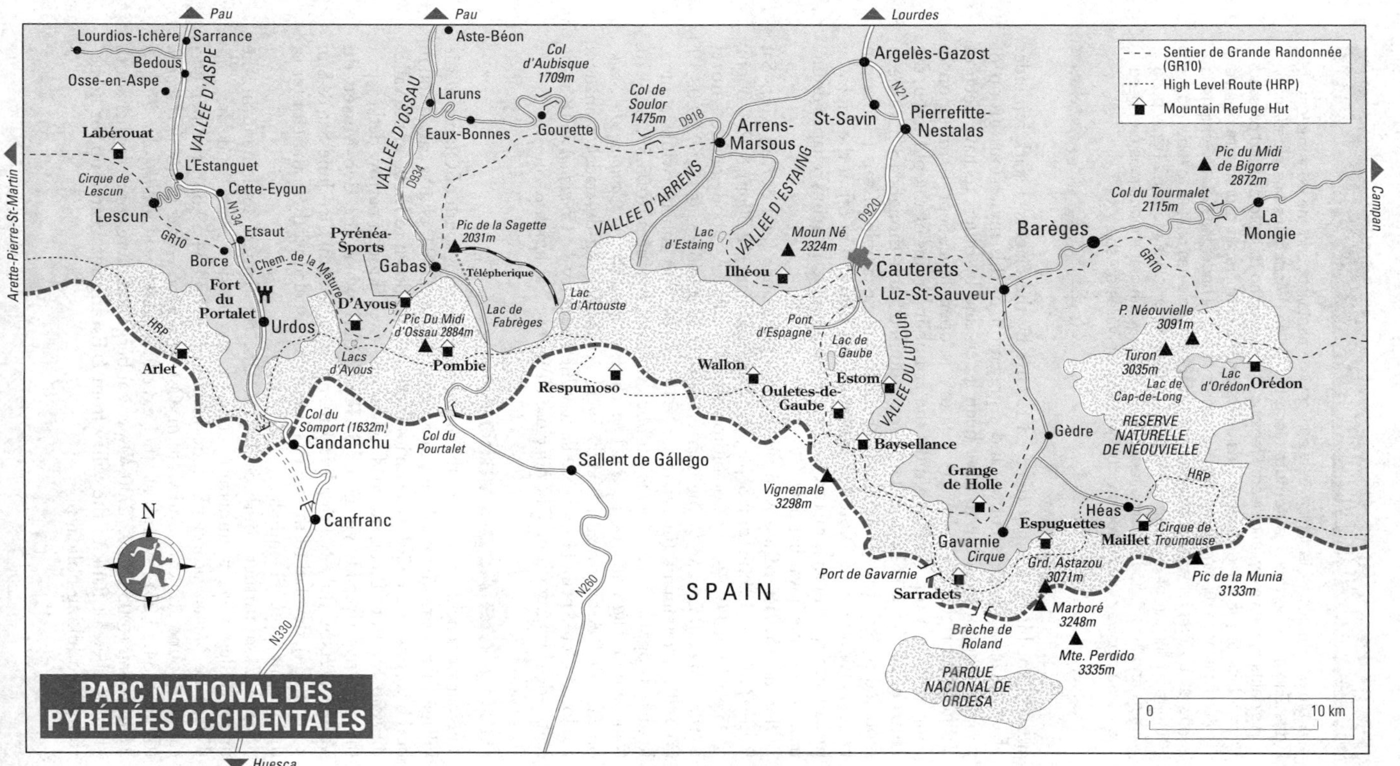

PARC NATIONAL DES PYRÉNÉES OCCIDENTALES
Sentier de Grande Randonnée (GR10)
High Level Route (HRP)
Mountain Refuge Hut
Pau
Pau
Lourdes
Campan
Huesca
Arette-Pierre-St-Martin
Lourdios-Ichère
Sarrance
Bedous
Osse-en-Aspe
VALLEE D'ASPE
Labérouat
Cirque de Lescun
Lescun
L'Estanguet
Cette-Eygun
N134
Etsaut
GR10
Borce
Fort du Portalet
Urdos
Chem. de la Mâture
HRP
Arlet
Col du Somport (1632m)
Candanchu
Canfranc
N330
N
Aste-Béon
Laruns
Eaux-Bonnes
VALLEE D'OSSAU
D934
Col d'Aubisque 1709m
Gourette
Pyrénéa-Sports
Gabas
D'Ayous
Lacs d'Ayous
Pic de la Sagette 2031m
Télépherique
Pic Du Midi d'Ossau 2884m
Pombie
Lac de Fabrèges
Col du Pourtalet
Lac d'Artouste
Respumoso
Sallent de Gállego
N260
Col de Soulor 1475m
D918
Arrens-Marsous
VALLEE D'ARRENS
VALLEE D'ESTAING
Lac d'Estaing
Ilhéou
Moun Né 2324m
Argelès-Gazost
St-Savin
N21
Pierrefitte-Nestalas
D920
Cauterets
Luz-St-Sauveur
Pont d'Espagne
Lac de Gaube
Wallon
Ouletes-de-Gaube
Estom
VALLEE DU LUTOUR
Baysellance
Vignemale 3298m
SPAIN
Barèges
GR10
Col du Tourmalet 2115m
Pic du Midi de Bigorre 2872m
La Mongie
P. Néouvielle 3091m
Turon 3035m
Lac de Cap-de-Long
Lac d'Orédon
Orédon
RESERVE NATURELLE DE NÉOUVIELLE
Gèdre
HRP
Grange de Holle
Héas
Gavarnie
Cirque
Espuguettes
Maillet
Cirque de Troumouse
Port de Gavarnie
Sarradets
Grd. Astazou 3071m
Marboré 3248m
Brèche de Roland
Mte. Perdido 3335m
Pic de la Munia 3133m
PARQUE NACIONAL DE ORDESA
0
10 km

The Zaragoza–Bordeaux autoroute

A bitter controversy is raging between environmentalists and the constructors of the Zaragoza–Bordeaux **autoroute** along the Vallée d'Aspe. This has pitted many residents of the valley (and nearby regions of Spain), who claim to be hard pressed from lack of livelihood, against ecologists from elsewhere, in a protracted battle which has been running since 1990. The hi-tech tunnel under the Col du Somport is now an accomplished fact and the focus of the struggle has shifted to lobbying for the rehabilitation of the long-abandoned trans-frontier railway to carry high-speed trains and freight, and the simultaneous limiting in width of the monstrous proposed six-lane highway which would virtually flatten the Vallée d'Aspe.

area of worship, is a stoup reserved for use by the Cagots, a stark reminder of centuries-long persecution and segregation of this mysterious group of people, thought by some to have been lepers and by others to have been of Visigothic origin. The church's treasury is open June–Sept 10am–noon & 3–6pm (€3). A top the hill amidst the crumbling ruins of the old town, the **church of Ste-Croix** is notable for a domed vault thought to have been modeled in Spanish Muslim style. A much finer example of this feature can be seen 10km east of Oloron at **Hospital-St-Blais**, 5km off of the highway to Sauveterre, where a picture perfect Romanesque pilgrims' chapel dominates a tiny medieval hamlet.

Oloron's **tourist office** is in place de la Résistance (July & Aug Mon–Sat 9am–7pm, Sun 10am–1pm; Sept–June Mon–Sat 9am–12.30pm & 2–6.30pm; Ⓣ05.59.39.98.00, Ⓦwww.ot-oloron-ste-marie.fr). A good budget **hotel** is the *Hôtel Bristol* at 9 rue Carréot (Ⓣ05.59.39.43.78, Ⓕ05.59.39.08.19; ❷) with a restaurant (menus from €18; closed Sun lunch), while a more luxurious option is the *Alysson* on boulevard des Pyrénées (Ⓣ05.59.39.70.70, Ⓔalysson;notel@wanadoo.fr; ❺). The closest **campsite** is *Camping du Stade*, on the D919 Arrette road (Ⓣ05.59.39.11.26, Ⓔcamping-du-stade@wanadoo.fr; closed Oct–April). For an excellent-value **meal** try *Le Chaudron* at 18 av de Lattre-de-Tassigny (from €17.50; closed Tues eve, Sat lunch & Sun).

Along the Aspe valley

The narrow enclosed world of the valley proper begins south of Oloron at the village of **Escot**, where a beautiful side route, the D294, climbs east through beech woods to the **Col de Marie-Blanque** and down to Bielle in the Vallée d'Ossau. South of Escot, the road follows the river through narrow defiles, past the attractive riverside village of **SARRANCE**, where the **Eco-Musée du Vallée d'Aspe** (July–Sept daily 10am–noon & 2–7pm; Oct–June Sat & Sun 2–6pm; €4), devoted to the valley's history, is installed partly in the cloister of the ancient monastic church.

Some 7km further south is **BEDOUS**, the largest settlement in the upper valley, with a miniature château, an arcaded *mairie* and the *Gîte d'étape Le Mandragot*, on place de l'Église (Ⓣ05.59.34.59.33). Further *gîtes* can be found 1.5km southwest in Osse-en-Aspe – *Les Amis de Chaneü* (Ⓣ05.59.34.73.23) – and at the excellent *Auberge Cavalière-des Ecuyers Montagnards* (Ⓣ05.59.34.72.30, Ⓦwww.auberge-cavaliere.com), further south 1km up the east flank of the valley from **L'Estanguet**, geared up for horse-riding and hiking holidays.

Lescun

Six steep kilometres southwest of the N134 from L'Estanguet, the ancient grey-stone houses of **LESCUN** huddle tightly together on the north slopes of a huge and magnificent green cirque. The floor of the cirque and the lower slopes, dimpled with vales and hollows, have been gently and harmoniously shaped by generations of farming, while to the west it's overlooked by the great grey molars of **Le Billare** and **Le Petit Billare**, beyond whose shoulders bristle further leaning teeth of rock and the storm-lashed bulk of the **Pic d'Anie** (2504m). Below the village in the hollow of the cirque, the grassy *Camping Le Lauzart* (Ⓣ05.59.34.51.77; closed Oct–April) must be one of the best sites anywhere, with an uninterrupted view of the peaks and no sound to disturb beyond the chiming of cowbells. If you're on foot, be sure to take provisions with you – it's some way from the village and the only food shop. Lescun itself has a lovely old **hotel**, the *Pic d'Anie* (Ⓣ05.59.34.71.54, Ⓕ05.59.34.53.22; ❷; closed mid-Sept to March), with a decent restaurant and a *gîte d'étape* opposite (same number).

The obvious **walk** in the area is along the GR10 in the direction of Arette-Pierre-St-Martin. From Lescun, the path keeps close to the road as far as the *Refuge de Labérouat* (Ⓣ05.59.34.50.43 & Ⓣ05.59.30.53.33; Jan to mid-Sept) – around a two-hour walk – then crosses meadows before entering beech forest beneath the organ-pipe crags of **Les Orgues de Camplong**, with fantastic views of the pine-stippled ridges of the Billares. It emerges above the tree line in a long, flower-strewn, hanging valley by the primitive **Cabane d'Ardinet**, reaching the shepherds' hut at **Cap de la Baigt** (1700m) in a further ninety minutes. From there you can either continue on the GR towards Arette-Pierre-St-Martin, or swing south for the Col des Anies and the Pic d'Anie itself – a good two-and-a-half to three hours to the summit.

Cette-Eygun south to the border

A couple of kilometres beyond the turnoff for Lescun at L'Estanguet, **Cette-Eygun** offers a *bar-gîte*, *La Goutte d'Eau* (Ⓣ05.59.34.78.83), occupying the disused train station between the road and the river, and run by the CSAVA (Coordination pour la Sauvegarde de la Vallée d'Aspe), the most vocal opponents of the road-building project in the valley. If you're desperate they can provide accommodation of dubious quality in an old train carriage parked on the tracks, camping space on the banks of the river and food if you're lucky at negotiable prices.

Past Cette-Eygun, the road curls southeast to **ETSAUT**, where there's a **Maison du Parc** (Ⓣ05.59.34.88.30) in the old *gare SNCF*, which has information on walks and accommodation in the Parc National des Pyrénées Occidentales, a **gîte d'étape**, *La Maison de l'Ours* (Ⓣ05.59.34.88.98, Ⓕ05.59.34.87.50), a **hotel**, *Des Pyrénées* (Ⓣ05.59.34.88.62, Ⓕ05.59.34.86.96; ❶; closed mid-Dec to early-Jan), and a food shop. **BORCE**, a more attractive medieval village 1km away on the west flank of the valley, is home to another, communally run *gîte d'étape* (Ⓣ05.59.34.86.40) in the centre, and a campsite on the outskirts. Further upstream at one of the narrowest points of the Aspe squats the menacing **Fort du Portalet** (now privately owned), which served as a prison for 1930s socialist premier Léon Blum under Pétain's Vichy government, and then for Pétain himself after the liberation of France. Just before the fort, at the Pont de Cebers, the GR10 threads east along the **Chemin de la Mâture**, an eighteenth-century mule path hacked out of the precipitous rock slabs that form the sides of a dizzy ravine, facilitating the transport of tree trunks felled for use as ships' masts. The GR10 reaches the **Lacs d'Ayous refuge** opposite the Pic du Midi d'Ossau in about five hours.

Less than 2km south of the fort, **URDOS** is the last village on the French side of the frontier, and has arguably the best hotel-restaurant in the valley: the *Hôtel des Voyageurs* (Ⓣ05.59.34.88.05, Ⓕ05.59.34.86.74; closed mid-Oct to mid-March; ❷) – with an annexe across the road known as the *Hôtel Somport* – which serves a wonderful, four-course set meal (€18). From here, you can continue through the new tunnel under the **Col de Somport** and on to Canfranc in Spain, the terminus for trains from Jaca.

Along the Ossau valley

The **Ossau valley** is notable mainly for its distinctive **Pic du Midi** and some beautiful lakes set in rugged country. Given that at the time of writing the *département* was in the midst of reorganizing its public transport, check ahead with the relevant tourist offices to confirm bus service into the valley. Beware that several services operate only during certain periods, either July and August, or the winter ski season.

Pau to Laruns

Between Pau and Laruns, there are only a couple places worth stopping. First is **ARUDY**, for its **Maison d'Ossau** (July & Aug 10am–noon & 3–6pm; rest of year Mon 10am–noon, Tues, Thurs & Sat 2.30–5pm, Sun 3–6pm; €2.50), which offers a comprehensive account of the prehistoric Pyrenees and an exhibition of the flora and fauna of the *parc national*. And 2km upvalley from here, **ASTE-BÉON** is home to **La Falaise aux Vautours** (May & Sept daily 2.30–6.30pm; June–Aug daily 10am–1pm & 2–7pm; rest of year school vacations only Mon–Fri 10am–noon & 2.30–5.30pm, Sat & Sun 2.30–5.30pm; €6), a vulture-watching installation where the creatures are observed nesting naturally.

At **LARUNS**, enclosed in the valley bottom by steep wooded heights, you'll find some fine old farms towards the river in the quarter known as Le Pon. For six days in early July the town comes alive with a festival celebrating traditional Béarnaise transhumance in which the flocks are driven high up into the mountains for summer pasturing. The **tourist office** is in the main place de la Mairie (Mon–Sat 9am–noon & 2–6pm, Sun 9am–noon; Ⓣ05.59.05.31.41, Ⓔossau.tourisme@wanadoo.fr). If you **stay** the night, try the central *Hôtel D'Ossau* (Ⓣ05.59.05.30.14, Ⓕ05.59.05.47.00; ❷) or the characterful *Hôtel de France*, at the eastern end of town opposite the disused gare (Ⓣ05.59.05.33.71, Ⓕ05.59.05.43.83; ❶; closed first two weeks of June & Dec). There's also the 28-bunk *Chalet-Refuge L'Embaradère* (Ⓣ05.59.05.41.88; cheap meals offered), more or less opposite the *Hôtel de France*, while the nearest **campsites** are *Ayguebere* (Ⓣ05.59.05.38.55) and *Pont Lauguère* (Ⓣ05.59.05.35.99), both in Le Pon quarter and open all year. For **food**, *L'Arrégalet*, 37 rue du Bourguet (closed Mon lunch), is strong on local recipes.

Gabas

The road to **GABAS**, 13km south, winds steeply into the upper reaches of the Gave d'Ossau valley. On days when there's no bus, you should get a lift without much difficulty from other walkers or employees of the Parc National des Pyrénées Occidentales, especially early in the morning. Primarily a base for climbers and walkers, there's nothing to it beyond a minuscule chapel, a **Maison du Parc** (mid-June to mid-Sept daily 10am–1pm & 2–7pm; Ⓣ05.59.05.32.13), which has useful walking information, and a fair amount of **accommodation**. Of this, the best value is the CAF **refuge** (Ⓣ05.59.05.33.14;

closed part Jan, part March, May & Nov to late-Dec) at the top of the hamlet, and *Hôtel Chez Vignau* at the north entrance to town (Ⓣ05.59.05.34.06, Ⓕ05.59.05.46.12; ❶; closed 2 weeks in Nov). The latter also has the best **restaurant**, with delicacies such as frogs' legs and prune pie (menus from €9).

Pic du Midi d'Ossau

The **Pic du Midi**, with its rocky twin-peaked summit (2884m), is a classic Pyrenean landmark, visible for kilometres around. From Gabas, it's a steep 4.5-kilometre climb on a road up a wooded ravine (or take the daily Sarl Canonge bus) to the artificial **Lac de Bious-Artigues**, so named because it flooded the *artigue* – a Pyrenean word for "mountain pasture" – that formerly existed beside the infant *gave*. Just below the dam, where the bus stops, are the stony terraces of *Camping Bious-Oumettes* (Ⓣ05.59.05.38.76; closed mid-Sept to mid-June), which also has a small shop (roughly the same season). Beside the lake are the *Refuge Pyrénéa Sports* (Ⓣ05.59.27.23.11; daily mid-June to mid-Sept, weekends spring/autumn), and a good snack bar, the *Cantine de Bious*. The area within immediate reach of the road gets very crowded in summer and the refuges are likely to be full at weekends, so it's worth phoning ahead.

A round trip of the peak, excluding the summit, takes about seven hours. It can be broken by a **stay** at the CAF *Refuge de Pombie* (Ⓣ05.59.05.71.81, Ⓔg.serandour@worldonline.fr; open June–Sept, weekends May & Oct), below the vast southern walls of the mountain. From the lake, follow the GR10 up the left bank of the *gave* and past the turning to the Lacs d'Ayous (see below). Cross the Pont de Bious and continue upstream across an expanse of flat meadow until you come to a signpost indicating "Pombie Par Peyreget" to the left. There follows a steepish zigzagging climb to the timber line and a long traverse right to the junction with the HRP path (1hr from *Pyrénéa Sports*). Keep left, with the ground falling away on your right. At the **Lac de Peyreget**, you can either follow the HRP steeply left towards the **Col de Peyreget**, or alternatively keep right – due south – to the gentler **Col d'Iou**. From the latter, traverse leftwards, following the contour to the **Col de Soum**, where you turn due northwards towards the *Refuge de Pombie* (about 4hr). The path continues north, then west back to *Pyrénéa Sports* (about 3hr) via the **Col de Suzon** – where the standard ascent of the *pic* begins – the Col de Moundelhs and the Col Long de Magnabaigt.

There's a path south off the mountain from the Col du Soum, and another – part of the HRP – from the *Refuge de Pombie*. The latter leads due east down the valley of the Pombie stream, through meadows full of daffodils, orchids, violets and fritillaries in June, when you might also catch a glimpse of lizards. At the **Cabane de Puchéoux**, a shepherds' hut, cross to the left bank of the stream and carry on down to the next bridge. A non-HRP path continues on the left bank past the Cabane d'Arrégatiou and comes out at the southern end of the **Lac de Fabrèges**. The right-hand HRP crosses the bridge and descends through woods to the **Gave de Brousset** at Caillou de Soques (about 2hr from Pombie), where you meet the Col du Pourtalet road (which leads to the Spanish frontier) and can hitch back to Gabas.

The Lacs d'Ayous

Starting again from the *Refuge Pyrénéa Sports*, the walk up to the **Lacs d'Ayous** is another classic, in some ways more impressive than circling the Pic du Midi d'Ossau itself, especially if you spend the night by the lakes to get the quintessential dawn view of the peak silhouetted against the rising sun and reflected in the slaty waters of Lac Gentau.

It's a steady but manageable climb south, then west from *Pyrénéa Sports*, which will take around two hours in all. Instead of crossing the Pont de Bious, which you'll reach after 30 minutes, turn up the GR10 to the right – a sign says "Lacs d'Ayous 1hr 30min" – through woods of pine and beech, with ever-widening views of the valley scattered with herds of horses and cows and flocks of sheep. In early summer the meadows are full of orchids and the stream banks thick with azalea-like alpenrose. Near the top, you reach three small lakes, the third and largest of which is **Lac Gentau**, whose reddish shallows are full of minnows that turn into the trout so sought after by numerous fishermen. On its banks there's an expanse of flat, soft meadow for camping, while above it stands the *Refuge d'Ayous* at 1960m (Ⓣ05.59.05.37.00; closed mid-Sept to mid-June). Over the Col d'Ayous behind it, the GR10 continues west to the Chemin de la Mâture and the Aspe valley (see p.818).

Lac d'Artouste

Some 7km out of Gabas, the Pourtalet road passes the dammed **Lac de Fabrèges**, whence a *télépherique* swings up to the **Pic de la Sagette** (2031m) to connect with a **miniature rail line** that runs 10km southeast through the mountains to the **Lac d'Artouste**. Built in the 1920s to service a hydro-electric project which raised the lake level 25m, it was later converted for tourist purposes. Weather permitting, the train starts operating in early June and keeps going until late September. It's a beautiful trip, lasting about four hours, including time to walk down to the lake and back. Round-trip fares are €17 (June & Sept 10am–3pm, July & Aug 9am–5pm; contact the OT in Laruns for further information); walkers may be able to negotiate one-ways, but allow a half-hour for the *télépherique* (first departure 8.30–9.30am). Don't forget to take warm clothes, too, as you'll be at an altitude of over 2000m. In **winter** the same *télépherique* gives access to the small beginner-to-intermediate downhill **ski centre** on the northeast side of the Col de la Sagette.

The Col d'Aubisque and the road to the Gave de Pau

The only way of reaching the Gave de Pau by road without going back towards Pau is via the minor D918 over the **Col d'Aubisque**, a grassy, rounded ridge 17km east of (and nearly 1000m above) Laruns. There's a café on the top, served by a single CITRAM bus from Laruns (July to mid-Sept). If you attempt to hitch on east, it's best to get a ride the 18km to attractive **Arrens-Marsous**, where you'll find uninspiring accommodation and restaurants, among which *La Maison Camélat*, a *gîte d'étape* in a fine, rambling old house just off the central place (Ⓣ05.62.97.40.94, Ⓕ05.62.97.43.01), is the best option (private rooms ❺). Between Laruns and the col, there are two resorts: the old Second Empire **spa** of Eaux-Bonnes, and the ugly **ski centre** of Gourette, which offers some thirty intermediate to advanced runs off Pic de Ger (2613m).

The col is a favourite place for slaughtering migrating wood pigeons in autumn, as the numerous shooting butts along the ridge bear witness. The Tour de France also usually passes this way, making the pass an irresistible challenge to any French cyclist worth his salt. You see swarms of them toiling up from the west, making it a matter of pride to find the breath for a cheery "Bonjour".

The Gave de Pau and around

From its namesake city, the **Gave de Pau** forges southeast towards the mountains, veering sharply south at Lourdes and shortly fraying into several tributaries: the **Gave d'Azun** (flowing down from Arrens), the **Gave de Cauterets**, the **Gave de Gavarnie** (draining its cirque) and the **Gave de Bastan**, dropping from the Col du Tourmalet. All four of these valleys, and the holiday bases in them, are served by SNCF buses from Lourdes. **Cauterets**, 30km due south of Lourdes, and **Gavarnie**, a further 20km southeast, are busy, established resorts on the edge of the Parc National des Pyrénées Occidentales, but the country they give access to is so spectacular that you should tolerate their congestion en route to the hills. If you want a smaller, more manageable base that's enjoyable in its own right, then **Barèges**, up a side valley from the spa resort of **Luz-St-Sauveur**, is a much better bet. As ever, if you pick your season right or even the time of day, you can still enjoy the most popular sites in relative solitude. At Gavarnie, for instance, few people stay the night, so it's quiet in the early morning and evening, and the **Cirque de Troumouse**, which is just as impressive in its way (though much harder to get to without a car), has very few visitors. By contrast, the spa of **Bagnères-de-Bigorre**, just east of the gave within striking distance of Lourdes, is fairly dull, merely a gateway to the Vallée de Campan.

St-Savin

Between Lourdes and Cauterets, some 3km southeast of the dull, congested town of Argelès-Gazost, pleasant, sleepy **ST-SAVIN** merits a stop for its twelfth-century **abbey-church**, with later fortifications and a fine Romanesque doorway. The interior offers an interesting stoup, and an amusing organ cabinet carved with grotesque faces – supposedly those of damned souls – that were designed to grimace as the music played. For a fee of €2 you can view the **treasury**, installed in the vaulted former chapterhouse. The collection is home to a particularly interesting piece, a twelfth-century "black Madonna" which tradition holds was carried back from Syria by Crusaders and which is certified as a national heritage item. Also worth a visit is the little hilltop chapel of **Nôtre-Dame-de-Piétat** (erratic hours; free), 1km south of the village, which has an elaborately painted ceiling, where birds perch on floral motifs covering every available space.

Cauterets and around

Thirty kilometres south of Lourdes, **CAUTERETS** is a pleasant if unexciting little town that owes its fame and its rather elegant Neoclassical architecture to its waters, still much in demand for the treatment of rheumatism and ear, nose and throat complaints. In modern times, it has also become one of the main Pyrenean ski and mountaineering centres.

Its origins as a spa began with Count Raymond de Bigorre's grant of land to the monks of St-Savin in 945 AD. In the seventeenth century, Marguerite d'Angoulême came to take the waters and wrote her *Heptameron* here. The eighteenth and nineteenth centuries were its heyday, especially the latter with its Romantic worship of mountains. Hugo visited, as did Chateaubriand, Baudelaire, Debussy, Edward VII and many other celebrities.

The modern town is so small that there's no difficulty in finding your way around. Most of it is still squeezed between the steep wooded heights that close the mouth of the Gave de Cauterets valley. Next door to the **gare routière** on the north edge of the centre, where SNCF coaches stop, the **Maison du Parc** (daily 9.30am–noon & 3.30–7pm; ⓣ05.62.92.52.56; free) has a small museum of flora and fauna, and free film shows on Wednesday and Saturday in season (5.30pm). In the centre, three minutes' walk from here, you'll find the **tourist office** in place Maréchal Foch (daily: July & Aug 9am–12.30pm & 1.30–7pm; Sept–June 9am–12.30pm & 2–6.30pm; ⓣ05.62.92.50.50, ⓦwww.cauterets.com); adjacent stands the Bureaux des Guides (mid-June to mid-Sept daily 10.30am–12.30pm & 4.30–7.30pm; ⓣ05.62.92.62.02), which organizes walks and other activities.

Inexpensive **hotels** include *Le Bigorre*, 15 rue de Belfort (ⓣ05.62.92.52.81, ⓦwww.bigorrehotel.com; ❶; closed Nov to early-May), and *Le Centre et Poste*, 11 rue de Belfort (ⓣ05.62.92.52.69, ⓔcentre.pos@voila.fr; ❷, closed part April & late-Sept to mid-Nov). For something a little more upmarket, try the *César*, 3 rue César (ⓣ05.62.92.52.57, ⓔcharles.fontan@wanadoo.fr; ❷; closed part April & late-Sept to mid-Nov), or the atmospheric *Lion d'Or* nearby (ⓣ05.62.92.52.87, ⓔhotel.lion.dor@wanadoo.fr; ❷; closed Oct to mid-Dec). There are also a couple of *gîtes* – *Le Beau Soleil*, at 25 rue Maréchal-Joffre (ⓣ05.62.92.53.52, ⓔgite.beau.soleil@wanadoo.fr) and *Le Pas de l'Ours*, 21 rue de la Raillère (ⓣ05.62.92.58.07, ⓦwww.lepasdelours.com), which also runs a hotel (❸). Several well-equipped **campsites** sit along the road north out of town, one of the quietest being *Les Bergeronnettes* (ⓣ05.62.92.50.69; closed Oct–May), across the river on the right.

As most hotels require half-board, independent **restaurants** are thin on the ground: the *Giovanni Pizzeria* at 5 rue de la Raillère and *Casa Bodega Manolo* nearby at no. 11 are pretty much it. However, *La Brulerie du Gave*, at no. 7 on pedestrianized avenue de l'Esplanade, by the river, is an excellent spot for English breakfasts, crêpes, coffee, tea and juice.

Hikes around Cauterets

Most classic excursions around Cauterets begin up the Val de Jéret at the **Pont d'Espagne**, where the Gave de Gaube and Gave du Marcadau hurtle together in a boiling spume of spray, before rushing down to Cauterets over a series of spectacular waterfalls. In season there are six daily *navettes* from the town centre to the giant visitor centre and car park here; purists can walk there along an attractive, streamside section of the GR10, which doubles as a *parc national* path. This starts from the disused satellite spa of **La Raillère**, 3km south of Cauterets, and takes two hours uphill through the forest (90min down).

From Pont d'Espagne, you can proceed southwest up the **Marcadau valley** along a branch of the GR10 to the *Refuge Wallon* (ⓣ05.62.85.93.43; open mid-May to Oct; about 5hr round trip), or due south up into the alpine valley of the Gave de Gaube, with the lovely little **Lac de Gaube** backed by the snowy wall and glaciers of **Vignemale** (3298m). There's even a *télésiège* (€6 return) to save you the first part of the ascent from Pont d'Espagne. Beyond the lake, the path continues to the *Refuge Ouletes-de-Gaube* below the north face of Vignemale (ⓣ06.64.45.41.46; open Mar–Sept; about 3hr from Pont d'Espagne), from where you can return to La Raillère via one of two routes. The HRP from *Refuge Ouletes* goes over a high pass to the *Refuge de Bayssellance* (ⓣ04.93.24.95.05; open May–Sept; weekends April & Oct weather permitting) and then loops broadly around to the *Refuge d'Estom* (ⓣ05.62.92.74.86; open June–Sept) in the beautiful and quieter **Lutour valley**; alternatively you can omit Bayssellance and head straight to Estom over the lower Col d'Arrailé. Even with a bus ride at the start and using this lower route, you should allow eight hours for the walking day; if you take in the high country around *Bayssellance*, it's best to schedule an overnight at *Oulettes* or *Estom*.

A less-frequented walk from Cauterets is to the **Lac d'Ilhéou** along the **GR10** (about 3hr). To avoid the initial steep climb you can take the *Téléphérique* du Lys (€5 one way, €7.50 return; July to early Sept) to the **gare intermédiaire de Cambasque**, crossing the stream there and continuing up the right bank to the **Cabane de Courbet**, where you follow a track, first on the left bank, then on the right. After a short distance, the GR10 leaves the track and climbs up the slope to the left, steadily gaining height to cross a chute of boulders beside the long white thread of the **Cascade d'Ilhéou** waterfall. Over the rim of the chute, you come to a small lake, with the *Refuge d'Ilhéou* (Ⓣ05.62.92.75.07; open June–Sept) in sight ahead on the shore – it's very pretty in June, with snow still on the surrounding peaks and ice floes drifting on its still surface.

Luz-St-Sauveur and the road south

The only road approach to Gavarnie and Troumouse, best known of the Pyrenean cirques, is through **LUZ-ST-SAUVEUR**, on the GR10 and a daily SNCF bus route from Lourdes. Like Cauterets, it was a nineteenth-century spa, patronized by Napoléon III and Eugénie, and the left-bank St-Saveur quarter owes its elegant Neoclassical facades to this period. The principal sight, at the top of Luz's medieval, right-bank quarter, is the **church of St-André**. Built in the late twelfth century and fortified in the fourteenth by the Knights of St John, it's a classic of its kind, with a crenellated outer wall and two stout towers. The north entrance, beneath one of the towers, sports a handsome portal surmounted by a Christ in Majesty carved in fine-grained local stone. The lanes radiating down from the church are crammed with **market stalls** every Monday.

The **tourist office** (mid-April to mid-June & mid-Sept to mid-Dec Mon–Sat 9am–noon & 2–6.30pm; mid-Dec to mid-April daily 8.30am–7pm; mid-June to mid-Sept daily 9am–7.30pm; Ⓣ05.62.92.30.30, Ⓦwww.luz.org), edges the central place du Huit-Mai, by the crossroads for Gavarnie or Barèges. Two worthwhile central **hotels** are the quiet and atmospheric *Les Templiers* (Ⓣ05.62.92.81.52; ❷; closed May & Oct), opposite the church, and *Les Cimes* (Ⓣ05.62.92.83.03; ❶), 70m downhill on the same lane. There's also a **campsite** and **gîte d'étape**, *Les Cascades* (Ⓣ05.62.92.94.14), uphill from the church, and *Camping Le Toy*, near the tourist office (Ⓣ05.62.92.86.85; closed May & Oct–Dec). **Restaurants** are generally indifferent, catering to French day-trippers, though *Chez Christine* (closed May, Oct & Nov), near the post office, serves decent pizzas and salads.

Twelve kilometres south is tiny **GÈDRE**, where a further 2km past another side road veers off for the Cirque de Troumouse, there is a comfortable **hotel**, *La Brèche de Roland* (Ⓣ05.62.92.48.54, Ⓦwww.gavarnie.com/hotel-la-breche; ❸; closed mid-Nov to Apr), with a reasonable restaurant – plus a pair of highly rated **gîtes d'étape** nearby: *Le Saugué* (Ⓣ05.62.92.48.73; closed Nov–April), with camping space, and *L'Escapade* (Ⓣ05.69.92.49.37; closed April, May, Oct & Nov).

The Cirque de Gavarnie

South of Luz-St-Sauveur, and a further 8km up the ravine from Gèdre, **GAVARNIE** is connected with Luz by two daily **bus** services (July & Aug only; otherwise a taxi from Luz-St-Saveur costs about €13), though you can walk it on the higher variant of the GR10 from Cauterets in two days. If you drive up a parking fee of €4 is charged during July and August, otherwise there is plenty of free parking around the shops and hotels. Once poor and depopulated, Gavarnie has found the attractions of mass tourism, much of it the excursion trade from Lourdes, too seductive to resist, and is now an unpleasant mess of pricey accommodation, souvenir shops and mediocre snack bars. During high season, the main street stinks, too, from the droppings of the dozens of mules, donkeys and horses used to ferry visitors up into the cirque. Like other overly popular sites, the key is to try to visit in shoulder season and before 9am or after 7pm, to avoid the bus-borne hordes. However, the **cirque** itself – Victor Hugo called it "Nature's Colosseum" – is magnificent, a natural amphitheatre scoured out by a glacier. Nearly 1700m high, it consists of three sheer bands of rock discoloured by the striations of seepage and waterfalls, and separated by sloping ledges covered with snow. To the east, it's dominated by the jagged peaks of **Astazou** and **Marboré**, both over 3000m. In the middle, a corniced ridge sweeps round to Le Taillon, hidden behind the Pic des Sarradets, which stands slightly forward of the rim of the cirque, obscuring the **Brèche de Roland**, a curious vertical slash, 100m deep and about 60m wide, said to have been hewn from the ridge by Roland's sword, Durandal. In winter, there's good **skiing** for beginners and intermediates at the nearby, nineteen-run resort of **Gavarnie-Gèdre**, with great views of the cirque from the top point of 2400m.

Practicalities

For those with a **tent**, there's the stunningly located *Camping La Bergerie* (Ⓣ05.62.92.48.41; closed Nov to mid-May) on the true right bank of the *gave*, on the cirque side of the village. The facilities leave a great deal to be desired, but the site is away from the crowds and has a view right into the cirque. The other campsite, *Le Pain de Sucre* (Ⓣ & Ⓕ05.62.92.47.55; closed Oct–Christmas & Easter–May), is on the Luz side of the village.

As for **hotels**, inexpensive options include *Le Taillon* (Ⓣ05.65.92.48.20, Ⓦwww.letaillon.com; ❷; closed Nov to mid-Dec) and the small *Hôtel Compostelle* by the church (Ⓣ05.62.92.49.43, Ⓦwww.compostellehotel.com; ❷; closed Oct to late-Dec), whose management offers guided walks. Otherwise, the best bets are the CAF refuge, *Les Granges de Holle*, on the Port de Gavarnie road (Ⓣ05.62.92.48.77; closed Nov to mid-Dec), which also does meals, and the high-standard **gîte d'étape** *Le Gypaëte* (Ⓣ05.62.92.40.61), just below *Les Voyageurs*. The only surviving independent **restaurant** of note is *Le P'tit Toy*, beyond the *Compostelle*, with two appetizing menus below €20.

For **weather information and snow conditions**, ask the CRS mountain rescue unit opposite *La Bergerie* (or ring Ⓣ08.36.68.02.65); for general **tourist information**, ask at the Maison du Parc (Mon–Sat 9.30am–noon & 1.30–6.30pm; Ⓣ05.62.92.49.10) as you come into the village.

The cirque and around

It's an easy one-hour walk from Gavarnie to the cirque, using either the main or the west-bank trails beside the *gave* draining from it. Luckily, the scale of it is sufficient to dwarf the tourists, but for a bit of serenity it's still best to use the west-bank path, or go up before 10am or after 5pm, when the grandeur and silence are almost alarming. The track ends at the *Hôtel du Cirque et de la Cascade*, once a famous meeting place for mountaineers and now a popular snack bar in summer. To get to the foot of the cirque walls, you have to clamber over slopes of frozen snow. Take care not to stand too close, especially in the afternoon, because of falling stones. To the left, the **Grande Cascade**, at 423m the highest waterfall in Europe, wavers and plumets down the rock faces – a fine sight in the morning, when it appeas to pour right out of the eye of the sun. Scaling the cliffs is obviously a matter for climbers, but the relatively intrepid can get a powerful impression of the majesty of the place – and a superb vantage point for photography – by climbing the first stage of the **HRP path** towards the **Refuge Sarradets** (aka *Refuge la Brèche de Roland*); the path begins in the right-hand corner of the cirque as you face it, at the edge of the first band of rock. The first, very exposed 100m or so are a little nerve-racking if you're not used to heights, but in dry weather it is perfectly safe.

If you don't want to retrace your steps, an enjoyable and not too demanding walk back to Gavarnie is via the path from the *Hôtel du Cirque* up the east flank of the Gavarnie valley to the **Refuge des Espuguettes** (☎05.62.92.40.63; daily June–Sept, weekends Easter, May, Oct; 2hr). It's a beautiful path, cut into rocky, pine-shaded slopes; at the top, you emerge into open meadows tilting up to the refuge. The climb is well worth the effort for the views of the cirque and the Brèche de Roland. The committed may want to go from here on to **Piméné**, the bare peak above you. It's a couple of easy, if tedious, hours' climbing, but the view is fantastic: the Cirque d'Estaubé, Monte Perdido and away into Spain. To return to Gavarnie, turn right at the signposted trail fork below the refuge (allow 90min total).

La Brèche de Roland

La Brèche de Roland is *the* walk to do in Gavarnie. It's high, and involves crossing a glacier, which means being properly equipped with ice axe and crampons. It is, however, extremely popular in summer, so there's a good chance of being able to team up with someone more experienced.

There are three approaches to the *brèche*, all converging on the **Refuge des Sarradets/Brèche de Roland** (☎06.83.38.13.24; open May–Sept, weekends in Oct); or contact Lionel Marquis (☎05.59.71.45.98) for reservations at the refuge, which are always necessary in high season. The easiest route is up the road to the Port de Gavarnie/Col de Boucharo, where a clear path climbs under the north face of Le Taillon to join the footpath coming directly from Gavarnie (1hr). The latter path starts beside the church, climbs steadily up the valley of Pouey Aspé, then zigzags steeply up to join the Port de Gavarnie path (2hr 45min). From the junction of these two paths, it's less than an hour to the refuge. The third and trickiest route (4hr 30min–5hr from Gavarnie to the hut) is via the **Échelle des Sarradets** section of the HRP path (see above). The *brèche* is about forty minutes above the refuge, with the glacier crossing occupying the final moments.

The Cirque de Troumouse

A vast, wild place, much bigger than Gavarnie and, in bad weather, rather intimidating, the **Cirque de Troumouse** lies up a desolate valley, whose only habitations are the handful of farmsteads and pilgrimage chapel that make up the hamlet of **HÉAS** – one of the loneliest outposts in France before the road in was constructed. In Héas, two establishments offer **camping** space, **rooms** (❶) and simple **meals**: *La Chaumière* (☎05.62.92.48.66, closed Nov–April) and *Auberge de la Munia* (☎05.62.92.48.39). As you reach the head of the valley there is a **tollgate** (9am–5pm; €3 per car), after which the road climbs in tight hairpins up treeless slopes 4km to the *Auberge du Maillet* (☎05.62.92.48.97; ❷; closed mid-Oct to May), by the side of a small tarn. After this the road climbs again, even more steeply over 3km, beneath bare shining crags, to a car park. Nearby, a prominent statue of the Virgin Mary crowns a grassy knoll, enclosed by the wide sweeping walls of the cirque and enough pasture to feed thousands of cows and sheep. The moorland turf is channelled with streams and cut into dingles and hummocks, where gentians and saxifrage, sedums and houseleeks grow among the rock crevices. Beneath the eastern walls of the cirque are scattered a half-dozen blue glacial lakelets, the **Lacs des Aires**. A *parc national* path does the circuit from Héas (no toll for walkers, 4hr).

The Vallée de Bastan

Luz-St-Sauveur marks the start of the eighteen-kilometre climb east along the D918 through the **Vallée de Bastan**, culminating in the **Col du Tourmalet**, one of the major torments of the Tour de France and the fulcrum of a giant **skiing** *domaine*. North of the pass rises the landmark **Pic du Midi de Bigorre** (2872m), with its observatory and funicular.

The only major village in between is **BARÈGES**, 7km along, linked with Lourdes by the SNCF bus to Luz. An attractive, one-street town, Barèges has been a popular spa since 1677, when it was visited by Madame de Maintenon with her infant charge, the seven-year-old Duc de Maine, son of Louis XIV. A military hospital opened here in 1744, as its waters became renowned for the treatment of gunshot wounds, and a low-key army connection endures – a mountain warfare training centre and an R&R facility stand across from each other. But today it's primarily a skiing, mountaineering and paragliding centre, and by far the most congenial resort around the Gave de Pau.

The central **tourist office** (July & Aug Mon–Sat 9am–12.30pm & 2–7pm, Sun 10am–noon & 4–6pm; Sept–June shorter afternoon hours; Ⓣ05.62.92.16.00, Ⓦwww.bareges.com) can supply accommodation lists and ski-lift plans. The through road is lined with a half-dozen gracefully ageing **hotels**, all fairly similar in standards, opening season (May–Oct) and price (typically ❷–❸). More interesting, perhaps, are two high-quality **gîtes d'étape**, open year-round except April and October: *L'Hospitalet* (Ⓣ05.62.92.68.08, Ⓕ05.62.92.66.15), at the southern edge of town, somewhat institutional owing to its past as a military hospital, and the welcoming, Anglo-French *L'Oasis*, right behind the spa (Ⓣ05.62.92.69.47, Ⓦwww.gite-oasis.com); both offer evening meals and reasonable half-board rates. Another possibility is the small, English-run inn *Les Sorbiers* on the main street (Ⓣ05.62.92.68.95, Ⓦwww.borderlinehols.com; ❷; closed Oct to mid-Dec & April to mid-May), which mainly handles one-week, pre-booked holidays, but accepts walk-ins and offers vegetarian meals on request.

The Col du Tourmalet and the Pic du Midi de Bigorre

Just out of Barèges and passing the peak of La Laquette, the D918 begins climbing in earnest over denuded slopes to the **Col du Tourmalet**, at 2115m the highest road pass in the French Pyrenees. Even in summer it's apt to be a desolate, windy spot, flanked by a sporadically functioning café, and a rough-hewn, nude statue of the Unknown Cyclist, commemorating the first passage of the Tour through here in 1910. By the statue, a dirt road meanders off in the direction of the **Pic du Midi**, though the public can no longer use this to drive up to the observatory at the top, but must visit either on foot or by **téléphérique** (June–Sept daily 9.30am–4.30pm; €20 or June–Sept €23, including admission to museum) from La Mongie. The venerable observatory, continuously staffed since opening in 1880 and still a serious research facility,

Skiing and hiking around Barèges

With its links to the adjacent resort of **LA MONGIE** over 10km east on the far side of the Col du Tourmalet, Barèges claims to offer access to the largest **skiing** area in the Pyrenees, including 32 downhill *pistes* totalling 53km (1850–2400m) and 31km of cross-country trails running through the wooded Lienz plateau (1350–1700m). The beginners' runs finishing in Barèges itself are much too low (1250m) to retain natural snow, so beginners and intermediates usually have to start from the areas of Tournaboup or Tourmalet a few kilometres east. New chair lifts were installed in autumn 2000, and runs regraded to make the resort more competitive, but La Mongie over the hill, despite its hideous purpose-built development, offers higher, longer pistes. For more information see Ⓦwww.bareges-tourmalet.com or contact the tourist office in Barèges.

The **GR10** passes through Barège on its way southeast into the lake-filled **Néouvielle Massif**, part of France's oldest (1935) natural reserve, and highly recommended as a hiking area. A manic, eight-hour walking day would take you to either the *Chalet-Refuge d'Orédon* (Ⓣ05.62.39.61.69; closed mid-Sept to mid-June), which serves superb meals, or the *Chalet-Hôtel de l'Oule* (Ⓣ05.62.98.48.62; closed mid-Sept to mid-Dec & mid-April to June).

long resisted commercialization but has now bowed to the inevitable with an on-site **astronomical museum.**

From the col the road descends past La Mongie, continuing through lovely woods of spruce, pine and beech, down into the gentle green Vallée de Campan. If travelling between November and June, check road conditions before setting out from Barèges – the pass is usually snow-bound for these months.

Bagnères-de-Bigorre and the Vallée de Campan

BAGNÈRES-DE-BIGORRE, nearly equidistant from Tarbes and Lourdes, is yet another pleasant Pyrenean spa town trying with mixed success to refurbish its somewhat faded image. It's not a place to make a special stop, though it is served by frequent SNCF buses from Tarbes, which call at the disused **gare SNCF** on avenue de Belgique, 400m north of the town centre. The **tourist office** is at 3 allée Tournefort (July & Aug daily 9am–12.30pm & 2–7pm, Sept–Oct Mon–Sat 9am–noon & 2–6pm; Nov–June 9.30am–noon & 2–6pm; Ⓣ05.62.95.50.71), close to the leafy allées des Coustous, the main drag, lined with pavement sidewalk **cafés**.

Hotels facing the spa tend to be overpriced. The quietest area is just north of the *halles*, itself 200m northwest of the tourist office, on rue de l'Horloge, where you'll find the old-fashioned *Hôtel l'Horloge* at no. 3bis (Ⓣ05.62.91.00.20; ❷; closed Dec–Feb), and the similar *Hôtel d'Albret* at no. 26 (Ⓣ05.62.95.00.90, Ⓕ05.62.91.19.13; ❶; closed Nov–Jan). The more luxurious options tend to have a distinctly therapeutic air, among which *La Residence* west of the town center in the Vallon de Salut (Ⓣ05.62.91.19.19, Ⓕ05.62.95.29.88; ❹) is the best deal. **Restaurants** aren't Bagnères' strong point: try *Le Bigourdan* (closed Mon) at 14 rue Victor-Hugo, corner rue de l'Horloge, with a great variety of menus (from €9.50 at lunch, €23 for dinner), or next door at no. 12, the *Crêperie d' l'Horloge* for a range of *plats du jour* for under €12, plus of course crêpes to eat in or take away.

The Vallée de Campan

From Bagnères, regular daily summer buses serve the meadowy **Vallée de Campan**, upstream from town, whose architecture is quite distinct from the valleys to the west. Farm roofs are still slate, but house and barn are built in line as one building, with the balconied living quarters always to the right as you face the sun. The valley's "capital" is **CAMPAN**, with its interesting sixteenth-century covered market, old houses and another curious-looking fortified church with a presumed Cagot door in the west wall. **STE-MARIE-DE-CAMPAN**, 6km further along, has less character as a village but better **accommodation** and **eating** choices in its *Hôtel les Deux Cols* (Ⓣ05.62.91.85.60, Ⓕ05.62.91.85.31; ❶) and the *Gîte L'Ardoiserie* (Ⓣ05.62.91.88.88), both offering half-board. If you are planning on driving on towards the Pic du Midi, be warned that the pass, the Col du Tourmalet, is normallly open only from June until the snows (November).

The Comminges

Stretching from **Bagnères-de-Luchon** (or just Luchon) almost as far as Toulouse, the **Comminges** is an ancient feudal county that encompasses the upper valley of the River Garonne. It also boasts one of the finest buildings in the Pyrenees, the magnificent cathedral of **St-Bertrand-de-Comminges**, the product of three distinct periods of architecture. The mountainous southern part is what you will want to see, and access is via the unprepossessing little town of **Montréjeau**, from where there are daily bus and train services to Luchon.

Valcabrère

The village of **VALCABRÈRE** lies a short way south of Montréjeau on the main Bayonne–Toulouse rail line. It can be reached by SNCF bus (direction "Luchon") to the hamlet of Labroquère, by the Garonne, and then a 1km stroll across the river. It's a little place of rough stone barns and open lofts for drying hay, with an exquisite Romanesque church, **St-Just** (April, May & Oct daily 9am–noon & 2–6pm; June–Sept daily 9am–7pm; Nov–March Sat & Sun 2–5pm; €2), whose square tower rises above a cemetery full of cypress trees. The north portal is girded by four elegant full-length sculptures and the apse contains a shrine to the relics of St-Pasteur and St-Suplice, which pilgrims could mount by means of the now off-limits stone staircase. Both interior and exterior are full of recycled masonry from the old Roman settlement of **Lugdunum Convenarum**, whose remains are visible at the crossroads just beyond the village. Founded by Pompey in 72 BC, this was a town of some 60,000 inhabitants in its prime, making it one of the most important in Roman Aquitaine. Josephus, the Jewish historian, says it was the place of exile of Herod Antipas and his wife Herodias, who had John the Baptist beheaded. Destroyed by Vandals in the fifth century and again by Burgundians in the sixth century, it remained deserted until Bishop Bertrand, the future saint, appeared toward the end of the eleventh century. A number of building foundations have now been excavated, including a fifth-century basilica (free entry).

St-Bertrand-de-Comminges and around

Further south is **ST-BERTRAND-DE-COMMINGES**, whose grey fortress-like **Cathedral** (Jan–Mar & Nov–Dec Mon–Sat 10am–noon &

2–5pm, Sun 2–5pm; April & Oct Mon–Sat 10am–noon & 2–6pm, Sun 2–6pm; May–Sept Mon–Sat 9am–7pm, Sun 2–7pm; admission to cloister and choir €4) commands the plain from the knoll ahead, the austere white-veined facade and heavily buttressed nave totally subduing the clutch of fifteenth- and sixteenth-century houses huddled at its feet. To the right of the west door a Romanesque cloister with engaging carved capitals looks out across a green valley to hills, where a local *maquis* unit had its lair during the war. In the aisleless interior, the small area at the west end reserved for the laity has a superbly carved sixteenth-century oak organ, pulpit and spiral stair, although the church's great attraction is the central choir, built by *toulousain* craftsmen and installed in 1535. The elaborately carved stalls – 66 in all – are a feast of virtuosity, mingling piety, irony and malicious satire, each one the work of a different craftsman. In the misericords and partitions separating them, the ingenuity and humour of their creators is best seen; each of the gangways dividing the misericords has a representation of a cardinal sin on top of the end partition. By the middle gangway on the south side, for example, Envy is represented by two monks, faces contorted with hate, fighting over the abbot's baton of office, pushing against each other foot to foot in a furious tug-of-war. The armrest on the left of the rood-screen entrance depicts the abbot birching a monk, while the bishop's throne has a particularly lovely back panel in marquetry, depicting St Bertrand himself and St John. In the ambulatory a fifteenth-century shrine depicts scenes from St Bertrand's life, with the church and village visible in the background of the top right panel.

During peak season cars are not allowed in the village itself, but a minibus operates a shuttle service from the car park at the base of the hill. In July and August the cathedral and St-Just in Valcabrère (see p.832), both with marvellous acoustics, host the musical **Festival du Comminges**; more details from the **tourist office** on the cathedral square (Feb–March & Nov–Dec Tues–Sun 10am–5pm; April–June & Sept–Oct daily 10am –6pm; July–Aug 10am–7pm; ⓣ05.61.95.44.44, ⓔolivetains@wanadoo.fr; or for specific enquiries about the festival ⓣ05.61.88.32.00 in summer, ⓣ05.61.95.81.25 the rest of the year). **Staying** overnight is an attractive proposition, at least outside peak season. Opposite the cathedral, the *Hôtel du Comminges* (ⓣ05.61.88.31.43, ⓕ05.61.94.98.22; ❷; closed Nov–March) makes for a fine, old-fashioned overnight and has a reasonable restaurant (closed Oct–March). Otherwise the more modern *Hôtel L'Oppidum* (ⓣ05.61.88.33.50, ⓕ05.61.95.94.04; ❸; closed mid-Nov to mid-Dec & Wed out of season), north of the cathedral on rue de la Poste, has variable but engaging en-suite rooms, with an excellent ground-floor restaurant (menu €16.80), which doubles as a *salon de thé*. The nearest **campsite** – shady and well laid out – is *Es Pibous* (ⓣ05.61.94.98.20), north of the road to St-Just.

The Grottes de Gargas

About 6km from St-Bertrand in the direction of Mazères-de-Neste, the **Grottes de Gargas** (45-minute guided tours daily: July & Aug 9.30am–noon & 2–6pm; rest of year by prior arrangement, but reservations always necessary ⓣ05.62.39.72.39, ⓔcontact@gargas.org; last tour 45min before stated closing time; €6) are renowned for their 231 prehistoric painted hand-prints. Outlined in black, red, yellow or white, they mostly seem deformed – perhaps the result of leprosy, frostbite or ritual mutilation, though no one really knows why. There are representations of large animals as well.

Bagnères-de-Luchon

There's none of the usual spa-town fustiness about **BAGNÈRES-DE-LUCHON**, long one of the focuses of Pyrenean exploration. The main street, **allée d'Étigny**, lined with cafés and snack bars, has a distinctly metropolitan elegance and bustle. There is not, however, much to see, apart from the slightly moth-eaten **Musée du Pays de Luchon** (daily 9am–noon & 2–6pm; €1.60) attached to the tourist office, which has an extraordinarily eclectic collection of archeological finds, old skis, art and natural history displays on the Pyrenees, and the nineteenth-century **baths** (guided tours Tues & Thurs 2pm; €5; bathing daily 4–8pm; €12) at the end of allée d'Étigny in the **Parc des Quinconces**. The area around the town is also home to dozens of twelfth-century Romanesque churches, many with rich mural decoration – counterparts to the famous chapels of Spain's Boí Valley on the southern slopes. The most accessible of these is at **St-Aventin**, 5km west of Bagnères. The exterior has a fine carved portal and the walls are set with recycled Roman funerary stones. A key can be borrowed from the *mairie* (Mon–Fri 9am–noon & 2–5pm) in exchange for a piece of ID.

That said, Luchon is best seen as a comfortable base for exploring the surrounding mountains in summer, and for **skiing** at the nearby centres of Superbagnères and Peyragudes in winter. Because of the peculiar local topography, the valley here is one of the major French centres for **para-gliding** and **light aviation** as well.

Practicalities

The **gare SNCF**, which is also the **gare routière**, is in avenue de Toulouse across the River One in the northern part of the town. The **tourist office** is at 18 allée d'Étigny (daily: mid-Dec to Oct 9am–7pm; Nov 9am–noon & 2–6pm; ⓣ05.61.79.21.21, ⓦwww.luchon.com), and can give details about local skiing. Adjacent to the tourist office are the premises of the Bureau des Guides who organize walks and climbs. Luchon Mountain Bike (ⓣ05.61.79.88.56) and Cycles Demiguel (ⓣ05.61.79.12.87), both on avenue Maréchal Foch, and Sun Park (ⓣ05.61.79.81.41) on rue de Superbagnères, all **rent bikes**.

You're best off forsaking the obvious **accommodation** on allée d'Étigny for better value in the quieter side streets. Possibilities include *Hôtel des Deux Nations* to the west at 5 rue Victor-Hugo (ⓣ05.61.79.01.71, ⓦwww.hotel-des2nations.com; ❷), a well-kept, popular, en-suite one-star with a busy downstairs restaurant; *Hôtel Céleste*, to the east at 32 rue Lamartine (ⓣ05.61.94.74.84, ⓔhotel.celeste@wanadoo.fr; ❶), a bit well-worn but friendly; or, also east of the main street, the more pricey *Hôtel la Petite Auberge*, 15 rue Lamartine (ⓣ05.61.79.02.88, ⓕ05.61.79.30.03; ❶), in a Belle Époque mansion, with ample parking and a decent restaurant. However, perhaps the most appealing option is the romantically sited *Hôtel Le Jardin des Cascades*, above the church in **Montauban-de-Luchon**, 2km east (ⓣ05.61.79.83.09, ⓕ05.61.79.79.16; ❸; closed Oct–March), with just a half-dozen peaceful, wood-decor rooms in a lovely spot backed by a wild, hilly garden nurtured by the falls of the name. There's no *gîte* or hostel in town, but there are ten **campsites** in the vicinity; least cramped, and with the best amenities, is *Camping La Lanette* (ⓣ05.61.79.00.38, ⓦwww.camping-la-lanette.com; open mid-Dec to Oct), 1.5km east over the Pique (down rue Lamartine) near Montauban-de-Luchon.

As with lodging, the best **eating-out** prospects are some distance away from the allée d'Etigny. Most central is *Le Clos du Silène*, 19 cours des

Quinconces (closed Tues low season & mid-Nov to mid-Dec), a welcoming spot with sumptuous interior salons and a garden, offering menus from €15. Alternatively, the shaded terrace restaurant at *Le Jardin des Cascades* (directions and phone same as hotel on opposite page) serves creative gourmet food, and offers sweeping views west and good service; there are cheaper lunch menus, but reckon normally on €32 per person, and mandatory reservations. Just out of town, try *L'Auberge de Castel-Vielh*, 2.5km south on the D125 (April–Oct daily; Nov–March weekends only; menus from €18), in a converted country house, serving excellent game and regional dishes, including snails and trout.

Hiking and skiing around Luchon

There are several classic hikes south and southwest of Luchon, though with one exception there's no public transport to the various trailheads. The exception is to **Granges d'Astau**, jump-off point for the **Lac d'Oô**, 14km southwest of Luchon, and served by three daily shuttle buses (July–Sept). Here, you'll find the *Auberge d'Astau* (ⓣ05.61.79.35.63; ❷; closed mid-Oct to March), which also functions as a *gîte d'étape* and restaurant. From the car park here a busy section of the GR10 climbs an hour to the dammed lake, where *Refuge Chez Tintin* (ⓣ05.61.79.12.29, ⓦwww.hebergementsdefrance.com/lac-oo; closed Nov–April; meals €14) perches beyond the west end of the dam. The onward path leads to the *Refuge d'Espingo* just below the Col d'Espingo, exactly an hour above Oô. The hut here (ⓣ05.61.79.20.01; staffed late May to early Oct) overlooks the beautiful, undammed **Lac d'Espingo**, and the frontier ridge; most day-trippers stop here, as beyond lies serious high-mountain country. If the shuttle's not available, you can also get to the lakes by taking the *téléphérique* from Luchon up to Superbagnères (see below), then continuing west to the *Refuge d'Espingo* (5hr total).

Another possible walking route from Luchon is to follow the Pique valley south 11km, partly on the D125, to the derelict Hospice de France (1385m), originally founded by the Knights of St John, from where a signposted path climbs a steep, narrow valley to the **Boums du Port** (2hr 15min), four small lakes beside the highest of which is the small but welcoming *Refuge de Vénasque* (ⓣ05.61.79.26.46; closed mid-Sept to mid-June), which serves unusually good meals. Suitably fortified, you can tackle the short, sharp path-climb (prone to avalanches in spring) to the notch on the frontier ridge known as the **Port de Venasque** (3hr from Hospice de France), with superb views of the **Maladeta massif** and the **Pico d'Aneto**, the highest summit of the Pyrenees (3404m).

Luchon has two downhill **ski resorts** within striking distance. The low-altitude **Superbagnères** (ⓦwww.luchon.com), right above the town and accessible by *téléphérique* (ski pass only in winter; €23.70), otherwise April daily 1.30–5pm; May to mid-June & Sept to mid-Oct Sat & Sun 1.30–5pm; mid-June to Aug daily 9.45am–12.15pm & 1.30–6pm; €8 return, €5 one way), has 24 pistes ranging from expert to intermediate served by chair-lifts and T-bars and 4km of (free) cross-country trails, while the higher, better designed **Peyragudes** (ⓦwww.peyragudes.com; €26.50 ski pass), 15km by road west, has 43 runs with lifts reaching 2400m, along with 14km of Nordic trails.

The Eastern Pyrenees

The dominant climatic influence of the **Eastern Pyrenees** is the Mediterranean. The climate is hotter and drier here, and the landscape more arid. Mediterranean plants like the cistus, broom and thyme make their appearance, and the lower slopes of the hills are planted with vines. The way of life is laid-back and outdoor-oriented. The proximity of Spain is evident, too, and much of the region is Catalan, definitively incorporated into France only in 1659. As with the rest of the Pyrenees, the countryside is spectacular, and densely networked with well-organized hiking trails. The historical sights, with the exception of the prehistoric caves at **Niaux** and the Cathar castles of **Montségur**, are most richly concentrated in the east towards the coast, in the foothills which separated what is essentially French Catalonia, comprising Roussillon and La Cerdagne (Rosilló and La Cerdanya) from the lowlands of Languedoc.

Along the River Ariège

The first clear herald of the approaching Mediterranean, whether you're coming from the western Pyrenees or heading south from the major transport hub of Toulouse, is the **Valley of the Ariège**, thorny scrub and white eroded limestone cliffs beginning to make their appearance from **Tarascon** onwards. Transport is no problem as long as you stick to the valley, but for side trips – into the **Couserans** and to **Montségur** – you really need a car.

Foix and around

Administrative centre of the *département* of Ariège, **FOIX** lies 82km south of Toulouse on the main Paris–Barcelona train line and the N20 road to Ax-les-Thermes and the Spanish border. It's an agreeable country town of narrow alleys and half-timbered houses, with an attractive old quarter squeezed between the rivers Ariège and Arget, filled with houses from the sixteenth and seventeenth centuries.

Dominating all are the three distinctive hilltop towers of the **Château des Comtes de Foix**, which contains the rather dull **Musée d'Ariège** (July & Aug daily 9.30am–6.30pm; May, June & Sept daily 9.45am–noon & 2–6pm; Oct–April Wed–Sun 10.30am–noon & 2–5.30pm; €4) – though the views are worth the climb. Determined opponents of the territorial ambitions of the Capetian kings of France and stout defenders of Catharism, the counts of Foix drew upon themselves the wrath of Simon de Montfort senior, who four times laid unsuccessful siege to the castle, though he did capture the town in 1211. Their resistance was finally broken in 1229 when Roger-Bernard, the count of the time, was obliged to accept the feudal dominance of the French king. Foix's age of glory came in 1290 when its counts married into the house of Béarn. Although they transferred their court to Orthez in the fourteenth century, this was the beginning of a powerful Pyrenean mini-state, whose influence lasted three centuries and came to include the kingdom of Navarre, leading finally to the throne of France with the accession of Henri III of Béarn and Navarre as Henri IV of France in 1589.

The **gares SNCF and routière** are together on avenue de la Gare, off the N20 on the right bank of the Ariège; except on Sundays, there's a daily **bus** service east via Lavelanet to Quillan and four buses a day west to St-Girons.

The **tourist office** is at 45 cours Gabriel-Fauré (July & Aug Mon–Sat 9am–7pm, Sun 10am–noon & 2–6pm; Sept–June Mon–Sat 9am–noon & 2–6pm; ⓣ05.61.65.12.12, ⓦwww.ot-foix.fr).

Most **accommodation** is found in the old town, on the west bank of the Ariège, though little of it is inspiring. The quietest and most comfortable option is the three-star *Hôtel Lons*, on 6 place Duthil, near the Pont Vieux (ⓣ05.61.65.52.44, ⓔhotel-lons-foix@wanadoo.fr; ❸; closed late-Dec to early Jan). The slightly cheaper *La Barbacane*, 1 av de Lerida (ⓣ05.61.65.50.44, ⓕ04.61.02.74.33; ❷–❹) is impressive looking but suffers from traffic noise, while the *Auberge Léo Lagrange* (ⓣ05.61.65.09.04, ⓔleogagrange-foix@wanadoo.fr; ❶) at 16 rue Noël Peyrevidal offers hostel-style accommodation. The municipal **campsite**, *Lac de Labarre* (ⓣ05.61.65.11.58; closed Nov–April), is on the N20 towards Toulouse.

One of the nicest places to **eat** in the old town is *Les 4 Saisons*, at 11 rue de la Faurie (menus from €13.50–16), while a pricier, but worthwhile option is *Le Sainte-Marthe* (ⓣ05.61.02.87.87; closed Wed off-season, Tues & part-Feb), at 21 rue Peyrevidal, which has a range of specialties, including a *cassoulet*, which is the restaurant's pride (menus €33–44).

Labouiche and Mas d'Azil

Six kilometres northwest of Foix, the **underground river** at **Labouiche** (July & Aug Mon–Sat 9.30am–5.30pm, Sun 10–11.45am & 2–5.15pm; June & Sept Mon–Sat 10–11.15am & 12–5.15pm, Sun 10–11.45am & 2–5.15pm; April, May, Oct & Nov Mon–Sat 2–5.15pm, Sun 10–11.45am & 2–5.15pm, usually a 15min wait; €7.50) is the longest navigable subterranean river in Europe. The visit consists of a barge trip lasting one and a quarter hours, along 1km of the river, 60m underground, to admire its stalactites and stalagmites.

Twenty-five kilometres west of Foix, the **Mas d'Azil** was one of the first prehistoric caves to yield evidence of human habitation, but its most impressive feature is a magnificent 500-metre natural tunnel, scoured by the River Arize, which now carries the main road (the D119) from here towards Pamiers. Without your own transport it's not easy to get to as it lies 12km north of the Foix to St-Girons bus route: get off at Vic after La-Bastide-de-Sérou and take the D15. It's a pretty road, but without a lift it'll take a good two hours on foot. Failing that, four Semvat buses a day run from Toulouse.

Secondary caves leading off the river cavern are the focus of historical interest; they were inhabited in prehistoric times for more than 20,000 years and used as a refuge by Cathars and Protestants in more recent times. As usual, the most important galleries are sealed off, though this hasn't stopped damage from road pollution, and those caves you can visit are interesting mainly for their sheer size (March, Oct & Nov Sun 2–6pm; April–May Mon–Fri 2–6pm, Sun 10am–noon & 2–6pm; June & Sept daily 10am–noon & 2–6pm; July & Aug daily 10am–6pm; €6.10, including museum entry).

A few tools, animal bones and other objects found during excavation remain on view in glass cases in the caves, but the best pieces are now on display in the attractive, sleepy village of **LE MAS-D'AZIL**, 1km to the north, in the **Musée de la Préhistoire** (same hours and ticket as the cave). Among other engraved tools and weapons, the museum's most outstanding exhibit is the beautiful carved antler known as *le faon aux oiseaux*, perhaps used as a spear-thrower. The best **hotel** in the hamlet is the *Hôtel Gardelt* (ⓣ05.61.69.90.05, ⓕ04.61.69.70.27; ❷; closed mid-Nov to mid-March) and there's a municipal **campsite** (ⓣ05.61.69.71.37; closed mid-Sept to mid-June) a twenty-minute walk away. The best place to eat is *Le Jardin de Cadettou* (closed Sat lunch time, Sun eve & Mon; ⓣ05.61.69.95.23), a homely restaurant with excellent menus of regional cuisine from €20; they also rent rooms (❸). More luxurious accommodation can be found at the renovated eighteenth-century *Château Rhodes* (ⓣ05.61.03.24.50, ⓦwww.chateaurhodes.com; ❸–❾) just outside La-Bastide-de-Sérou.

Tarascon and around

TARASCON-SUR-ARIÈGE lies 16km south of Foix, where the N20 crosses the Ariège (a bypass diverts the worst of the traffic). Once a centre for the local iron-mining industry – there's still an aluminium plant in operation – it's a hot and unexciting little town enclosed by high wooded ridges. However, it is useful as a base for the Vicdessos valley and the prehistoric cave of Niaux.

The **cafés** on the east bank of the river, dominated by the clock tower, are pleasant, sunny places to sit. Apart from that, it's worth taking a stroll up the narrow **rue de Barri** to the wide square by the church, a pleasant expanse with just one arcaded side and a single wooden house still standing, to the **Porte d'Espagne**, the only surviving piece of the town walls.

The **gare SNCF** is a few minutes' walk from the N20 bridge. The **tourist office** is west of the bridge on avenue des Pyrénées in the smart Centre Multimédia François Mitterrand (July & Aug daily 9am–7pm; Sept–June Mon–Sat 9am–6pm; ⓣ05.61.05.94.94, ⓔpays.de.tarascon@wanadoo.fr). The best **accommodation** option is the eighteenth-century manor house, *Domaine Fournie* (ⓣ05.61.05.54.52, ⓔContact@domaine-fournie.com; ❸), set within impressive grounds 1km from the town centre on route Saurat. In town, the most attractive hotel is the *Confort* on the riverside quai Armand-Sylvestre (ⓣ&ⓕ05.61.05.61.90; ❸), with some rooms facing a courtyard. There's a **campsite**, *Pré Lombard* (ⓣ05.61.05.61.94), on the left bank of the river, ten minutes' walk upstream from the bridge.

Niaux and the prehistoric caves

Just south of Tarascon, by the aluminium plant, the D8 cuts up right into the green valley of the Vicdessos past the riverside remains of a Catalan ironworks. The hamlet of **NIAUX** lies in the valley bottom, 5km further on. The tiny settlement has an interesting **Musée Pyrénéen** (daily: July & Aug 9am–8pm; Sept–June 10am–noon & 2–6pm; €6), with an unrivalled collection of tools, furnishings, old photos and odds and ends illustrating the vanished traditions of peasant Ariège.

But the real reason people descend on the little hamlet is for the **Grotte de Niaux**, a huge cave complex under an enormous rock overhang high on the south flank of the valley (guided tours: July & Aug daily 9.15am–5.30pm, English tours at 9.30am & 1pm; Sept daily 10am–5.30pm, English at 1pm; Oct–June Tues–Sun, tours at 11am, 2.30pm & 4pm; €9; reservations mandatory on ⓣ05.61.05.88.37, ⓦwww.sesta.org;). There are about 4km of galleries in all, with paintings of the Magdalenian period (circa 11,000 BC) widely scattered throughout, although the twenty people allowed in the cave at any one time are led through just a fraction of the complex. The paintings you can see are in a vast chamber, a slippery 800-metre walk from the entrance of the cave along a subterranean riverbed. No colour is used to depict the subjects – horses, ibex, stags and bison – just a dark outline and shading to give body to the drawings, which have been executed with a "crayon" made of bison fat and manganese oxide. They are an extraordinary mix of bold impressionistic strokes and delicate attention to detail: the nostrils, pupils and the tendons on the inner thighs of the bison are all drawn in. Reserve as far ahead as possible – this is deservedly the Pyrenees' most popular cave.

The village of **ALLIAT**, right across the valley from Niaux, is home to **La Grotte de la Vache** (July & Aug daily 10am–6pm; Easter–June & Sept Mon & Wed–Sun 2.30–4.15pm; other times by arrangement – ring ⓣ05.61.05.95.06; €7), a relatively rare example of an inhabited cave where you can observe hearths, bones, tools and other remnants *in situ*. If you want to stay locally, there's a well-equipped but somewhat expensive **campsite**, *Les Grottes* (ⓣ05.61.05.88.21; closed mid-Sept to May), in the village.

Although it can't compete with visiting the caves themselves, the **Parc Pyrénéen de l'Art Préhistorique** (April–May & Sept–Oct Tues–Fri 10am–6pm, Sat & Sun 10am–7pm; June–Aug Mon–Fri 10am–6pm, Sat & Sun 10am–7pm; €9), a few kilometres west of Tarascon on the road to Banat, provides a remarkable overview of cave art. A highlight is the "Grand Atelier", a compelling multimedia exploration including recreations of Niaux's inaccessible Clastres system, with its enigmatic footprints, and the famous "Salon Noir" as it would have looked to its creators 10,000 years ago. The surrounding landscaped park, complete with Magdalenian flower meadow, footprints stream and hunting panorama, continues the prehistoric theme.

Into the Couserans

From Niaux, the road continues along the valley bottom, beneath the romantically pinnacled ruins of the Château of Miglos (unrestricted access), to Vicdessos and Auzat, the latter with an unsightly aluminium works. From Vicdessos, a really stunning route – the D18 – climbs the **valley of the Suc,** tunnelling through trees, past abandoned barns and occasional cottages in lush meadows, by waterfalls and streams, to the pass at the **Port de Lers** (1517m). On the far side, herds of grey cows graze the alpine meadows down to the Étang de Lers. Then the road climbs again to another col overlooking the head of the valley of the little **River Garbet**. Below, the steep slopes are luxuriant with beech, while directly south you look into a high-walled crenellated cirque formed by the **Pic Rouge de Bassiès** and the **Pic des Trois Comtes** above the **Étang de Garbet**, where the heights are underlined by wedges of snow lying beneath the sheerest faces. This is the beginning of the **Pays de Couserans**, one of the poorest, least developed and most depopulated regions of the Pyrenees. Its villages, **Aulus-les-Bains** in particular, were once renowned for their bear-trainers, who, driven by poverty, toured the lowland towns with their performing beasts.

Aulus-les-Bains

Once in the Garbet valley, the road drops quickly west to **AULUS-LES-BAINS**, a remote village lying among moist and fragrant meadows ringed by dramatic peaks. Like other spa towns, Aulus enjoyed its moment of glory and fell again into rustic somnolence, from which it is trying to resurrect itself once more. This is country for walking and enjoying the landscapes: there's nothing else, and, remote though it feels, it's not inaccessible – there are one to three daily buses (Mon–Sat) to St-Girons. The classic walk here involves heading south to the **Étang de Guzet** and then east to the **Cascade d'Ars** on a bit of the GR10, then returning to Aulus via the stream draining from it (round trip about 5hr).

For summer bike rental and information on other activities, consult the **tourist office** in the allée des Thermes (daily: July & Aug 10am–1pm &

2–7pm; Sept–June 10am–noon & 2–6pm; ⓣ05.61.96.01.79, ⓔtourisme@haut-couserans.com). Among the places to **stay**, try the beautiful, turreted *Les Oussaillès* (ⓣ05.61.96.03.68, ⓔjcharrue@free.fr; ❷; closed mid-Oct to mid-Dec), with a restaurant serving a hearty, four-course *menu de jour* for under €20 and English-speaking staff, or the cheaper *Hôtel de France* (ⓣ05.61.96.00.90, ⓕ05.61.96.03.29; ❶; closed Nov) which has comfortable rooms and an excellent and affordable restaurant (from €11), both near the spa. There's also a **gîte d'étape** 150m downhill from the church, *La Presbytère* (ⓣ05.61.96.02.21, ⓔhel-aulus@hotmail.com), and year-round **camping** at *Le Couledous* (ⓣ05.61.96.02.26), 500m west along the river.

St-Girons

With numerous SNCF buses a day from Boussens, on the main Tarbes–Toulouse rail line, and ordinary bus connections on to Aulus, Ustou, Massat and Sentein, **ST-GIRONS** may be your first taste of this out-of-the-way region. Apart from its long association with cigarette-paper manufacture, the most striking thing about St-Girons is its central pavements, made of a local reddish-pink marble with finely chiselled gutters to take the rainwater from down-pipes. And although there are no other memorable sights, it's far from a unpleasant town, with a **folklore festival** in mid-July and a **theatre festival** in early August.

The simplest point for orientation is the **Pont-Vieux**, just below picturesque rapids on the River Salat. The bridge points you into the old commercial centre of the town on the right bank, with some marvellously old-fashioned shops, their fronts and fittings unchanged for generations. To the right, past the tiny cathedral, is the typically provincial **place des Poilus**, its cachet largely due to the faded elegance of the *Grand Hôtel de France* and the equally old-fashioned *Hôtel de l'Union*, where you can still stay. The latter's ground-floor café is a splendid balconied period piece facing the riverside **Champ de Mars**, a wide gravelled *allée* of plane trees, which provides the site for a big general market on the second and fourth Mondays of every month, and for a regular produce market every Saturday morning.

Buses arrive at place des Capots on the left bank of the river. The well-stocked **tourist office** is inside the Maison de Couserans (July & Aug Mon–Sat 9am–7pm, Sun 10am–1pm; Sept–June Mon–Sat 9am–noon & 2–6pm; ⓣ05.61.96.26.60, ⓦwww.ville-st-girons.fr), on the right bank, in place Alphonse-Sentein. If you want to **stay**, the modern, two-star *La Clairière*, at the edge of town on the road to Seix (ⓣ05.61.66.66.66, ⓕ05.34.14.30.30; ❷–❺) has a pool and the best restaurant in town (gourmet fare from €14). More central and cheaper is the *Hôtel de Union* (ⓣ05.61.66.09.12, ⓕ05.61.04.81.73; ❶–❸), on allée Champs de Mars. There's also a **campsite** at the *Centre de Loisirs du Parc de Palétès* (ⓣ05.61.66.06.79), 2km out along avenue des Évadés, with an excellent affiliated terrace hotel-restaurant, *La Table de l'Ours* (ⓣ05.61.66.10.31; ❷).

St-Lizier

ST-LIZIER, a five-minute ride by bus from the old *gare SNCF* on the St-Gaudens road, totally outclasses St-Girons in the tourism stakes. It sits on a hilltop, and is full of history; it's walled, arcaded, cobbled, cathedraled, half-timbered, pretty, and lifeless outside of summer.

Architecturally the most interesting building in town is the **Cathédrale de St-Lizier** (daily 10am–3pm; free), with its distinctive octagonal tower posing photogenically against the mountains to the south. Inside are some twelfth-century frescoes faded almost to invisibility, and a fine Romanesque cloister, also twelfth century, with an array of unique, sculpted column capitals. A second cathedral, **Nôtre-Dame-de-Sède**, within the grounds of the bishop's palace, is closed indefinitely for renovation, though the palace is also home to the **Musée Départmentale de l'Ariège** on the first floor (Apr–May & Oct Tues–Fri & Sun 2–6pm; June daily 10am–noon & 2–6pm; July & Aug daily 10am–7pm; €4), which contains a permanent ethnographic collection devoted to the Vallée du Bethmale, not really worth the admission fee. It is, however, worth walking up to the palace anyway, for views over St-Lizier, and continuing on round the old **ramparts** (same hours; free).

The helpful **tourist office** is located by the lower cathedral (July & Aug Mon–Sat 9am–7pm, Sun 10am–1pm; Sept–June Mon–Sat 9am–noon & 2–6pm; ⓣ05.61.96.77.77, ⓔsaintlizier@wanadoo.fr). There are some excellent **accommodation** options in town as well. The *Hôtel de la Tour* (ⓣ05.61.66.38.02, ⓔHoteldelaTour@Hotel-Restaurant.net; ❷), in a remodelled old building down by the River Salat on rue du Pont, is home to an affordable gourmet restaurant overlooking the rapids; you can eat superbly for just €20, or resort to the more economical weekday lunch menu. For all hotels, you'll need to book ahead during the town's **international music festival** (information on ⓣ05.61.66.67.89).

Ax-les-Thermes

Twenty kilometres southeast of Tarascon, on the banks of the Ariège, the spa town of **AX-LES-THERMES** is completely walled in by mountains and its principal value is as a base for exploring the surrounding peaks and as a staging post on the way to Andorra or on down the N20 to Font-Romeu and, ultimately, Perpignan and the Mediterranean.

The town itself is small and agreeable enough, but there's little to see once you've wandered a couple of streets in the quarter to the right of the N20, which forms the main street, avenue Delcassé. Rue de l'École and rue de la Boucarie retain a few medieval buildings, and above place du Breilh, the **church of St-Vincent** is of architectural interest for its Romanesque tower. Just across the road you can dangle your feet for free in the **Bassin des Ladres**, a pool of hot sulphurous water which is all that remains of the hospital founded in 1260 by St Louis for soldiers wounded in the Crusades.

The **gare SNCF** is off avenue Delcassé on the northwest side of town. The useful **tourist office** (July & Aug daily 9am–1pm & 2–7pm; Sept–June 9am–noon & 2–6pm; ⓣ05.61.64.60.60, ⓦwww.vallees-ax.com) is halfway through town on the northside of the main road, and has hiking information and lists of walks. A nice place to **stay** is the *L'Auzeraie* (ⓣ05.61.64.20.70, ⓔauzeriae@free.fr; ❷). *Le France* at no. 10 on the main avenue Delcassé (ⓣ05.61.64.20.30, ⓔhotel.france.az@wanadoo.fr; closed Jan & Dec; ❸), offers a few more amenities and has a gastronomique restaurant (menus €12–30). There's also a **campsite**, *Le Malazéou* (ⓣ05.61.64.09.14), on the riverbank just before the *gare SNCF* as you come into town from Tarascon. The most atmospheric places to eat are the old *Grand Café*, next to *Hôtel Les Pyrénées*, and *Brasserie Le Club*, on place Roussel, which has live jazz.

Lavelanet and around

LAVELANET is a nondescript but not unattractive little town on the banks of the River Touyre, 20km from Foix to the west and 35km from Quillan to the east. However, it has little to offer beyond its bus connections – which include a route north to **Mirepoix** – and the easiest access to the famous Cathar castle of **Montségur**, 12km to the south. If you get stuck there, head for the very clean and modern municipal **campsite** (closed Oct–March), from which you can just see Montségur nudging over the brow of the intervening ridges. There's a **tourist office** (July & Aug Mon–Sat 9am–noon & 2–7pm, Sun 9am–noon; Sept–June Mon–Sat 9am–noon & 2–7pm; ⓣ05.61.01.22.20, ⓔlavelanet.tourisme@wanadoo.fr), and a couple of restaurants off the main square.

Montségur

The village of **MONTSÉGUR** is strung out in terraced lines at the foot of its castle rock. Silent and depopulated now, the place comes to life only with the influx of tourists, most of them day-trippers. It's worth having a glance at the one-room **museum** (daily: Feb & Nov 2–4.30pm; March, April & Oct 2–5pm; May & Sept 10.30am–12.30pm & 2–7pm; June–Aug 10am–12.30pm & 2–7.30pm; closed Dec; free), with its collection of bits and pieces from the castle, before going up to the ruin itself.

A footpath from the top of the village shortens the way up to the saddle of the hill and the Prats des Cramats, the field where the Cathar martyrs were burnt. From here it's a steep half-hour climb to the **Château** (daily: Feb 10.30am–4pm; March 10am–5pm; April & Sept–Oct 9.30am–6pm; May–Aug 9am–7.30pm; Nov 10am–5.30pm; Dec 10.30am–4.30pm; €3.50), of which all that remain are the stout and now truncated curtain walls and keep. The space within is terribly cramped, and one can easily imagine the sufferings of the besieged. A somewhat precarious stairway leads to the top of the walls, from where you look out over kilometres of forested hills and snowy peaks, giving a sense of solitude and airy isolation that is in itself highly evocative.

In summer there's a **tourist office** in the village (July–Sept daily 10am–1pm & 2–6pm; ⓣ05.61.03.03.03, ⓦwww.citaenet.com/montsegur); at other times

The fall of Montségur

In the early years of the thirteenth century, Montségur's castle was reconstructed by a local feudal lord as a strongpoint for the **Cathars** (see p.848) under attack by the Crusade. In 1232 it became the capital of the banned Cathar Church, with a population of some five hundred people, bishops and clergy as well as ordinary believers on the run from the persecution of the Inquisition, under the protection of a garrison commanded by Pierre-Roger de Mirepoix.

Provoked by a raid on Avignonet in May 1242, in which several Inquisitors were killed, the forces of the Catholic Church and the king of France laid siege to the castle in the spring of 1243. By March 1244, Pierre-Roger, despairing of relief, agreed to terms with them. At the end of a fortnight's truce, the 225 Cathars who still refused to recant were burnt on a communal pyre on March 16.

Four men who had made good their escape recovered the Cathar "treasure", which had been hidden in a cave for safekeeping since the preceding Christmas, and vanished. Two of them later reappeared in Lombardy, where it seems probable these funds were used to support the refugee Cathar community established there. But numerous legends have grown up, especially in German writings, identifying this "treasure" with the Holy Grail, and the Cathars themselves with the Knights of the Round Table.

From Montségur to the Têt

From Montségur, you can take a dramatic four-hour **walk** over the Montagne de la Frau (1950m) to Comus, just off the road between Ax-les-Thermes and Quillan in the Têt valley. At the hairpin turn on the highway to the south of the village, take a small road south along the Lasset River. After about 1km, the GR7B branches off to the east, crossing the stream and heading across a ridge to the north of the Montagne de la Frau. The trail eventually descends to the farm of Pelail (signposted as Liam), just above the Hers river. Turning south, the trail continues up the Hers valley, following the D5 from Bélesta into the deep sunless ravine known as the **Gorges de la Frau**. When the highway ends, the path continues up the deep gully thickly wooded with beech, ash, wild cherry and fir, climbing until it reaches an old tarmac road which crosses the river by a farm. Here, turn east again, and you'll come to Comus after about 3km.

you'll have to go to the one in Lavelanet. There are a handful of **accommodation** options, the nicest of them being the old-fashioned *Hôtel Couquet* (ⓣ05.61.01.10.28; ❶), a rambling country pension fronted by pollarded lime trees and with a café and restaurant on the first floor (menus from €12). The more expensive *Hôtel Costes* (ⓣ05.61.01.10.24, ⓦwww.logis-de-france.fr; ❷; menus from €15) also has a *gîte d'étape*. A more homey option is the B&B *L'Oustal* at 46 Rue Du Village (ⓣ05.61.02.80.70, ⓔserge.goma@wanadoo.fr; ❹), which also offers an abundant table.

Mirepoix

Heading north from Lavelanet in the direction of Carcassonne, it's definitely worth taking a look at **MIREPOIX**, a late thirteenth-century bastide built around one of the loveliest surviving arcaded market squares in the country. The square is bordered by houses dating from between the thirteenth and the fifteenth centuries, and a relatively harmonious modern *halle* on one side, but its highlight is the medieval Maison des Consuls (council house), whose arcaded rafters are carved with hundreds of unique portrayals of animals, monsters, and caricatures of medieval social groups and professions, as well as ethnic groups from across the world.

There's a **tourist office** in the main square (Mon–Sat 9am–noon & 2–6pm; ⓣ05.61.68.83.76, ⓦwww.ot-mirepoix.fr). If you're feeling extravagant, **stay** on the main square in the *Maison des Consuls* (ⓣ05.61.68.81.81, ⓔpyrene@afatvoyages.fr; ❹–❻); otherwise head for the *Hôtel Le Commerce*, on the boulevard encircling the old town near the church (ⓣ05.61.68.10.29, ⓦwww.logis-de-france.com; ❸; closed Jan, part Nov & Sat Sept–June). There's a municipal **campsite** on the Limoux road (ⓣ05.61.01.55.44; closed mid-Sept to mid-June). The best **restaurant** is the *Porte d'Aval* (ⓣ05.61.68.19.19; closed Mon) on cours Maréchal de Mirepoix, which specializes in regional dishes from €15. Unfortunately, the only bus link from Mirepoix is to Pamiers – to get to Carcassonne without transport, you'll have to hitch.

Along the Aude

South of Carcassonne, the road and the rail line both climb steadily up the twisting valley of the **River Aude**, between scrubby hills and vineyards and ever deeper and more forested ravines to **Quillan**. From there, the road squeezes through the **Gorges de l'Aude** in a sunless bottom before emerging once again towards the river's headwaters above Les Angles on the east side of the Carlit Massif in the high Pyrenees. It's a magnificent drive, and quite hitchable, being one of the main routes to Andorra, though buses do make the run through to **Quérigut** three times a week.

Limoux

The first stop on the D118 road, 24km south of Carcassonne, **LIMOUX** is served several times daily by both the SNCF and the private Cars Teissier buses. It stands astride the Aude, which for much of the year is a powerful grey flood of snowmelt. Life revolves around the pretty **place de la République**

in the heart of the old town, with its Friday market, and the nineteenth-century **promenade du Tivoli**, in effect a bypass road. Known in the past for its woollens and the tanning of hides brought down from the mountains, the town's claim to fame today is the production of its excellent sparkling wine, Blanquette de Limoux, much cheaper than champagne.

The **tourist office**, on promenade du Tivoli (July & Aug daily 9–7pm; Sept–June Mon–Fri 9–noon & 2–6pm, Sat & Sun 10am–noon & 2–5pm; ⓣ04.68.31.11.82, ⓔlimoux@fnotsi.net), shares a building with the **Musée Petiet** (same hours; €3), displaying a collection of local nineteenth-century paintings. The top two **hotel** choices are the splendid and stately *Modern & Pigeon* in place Général Leclerc (ⓣ04.68.31.00.25, ⓔhotelmodernepigeon@wanadoo.fr; ❹;

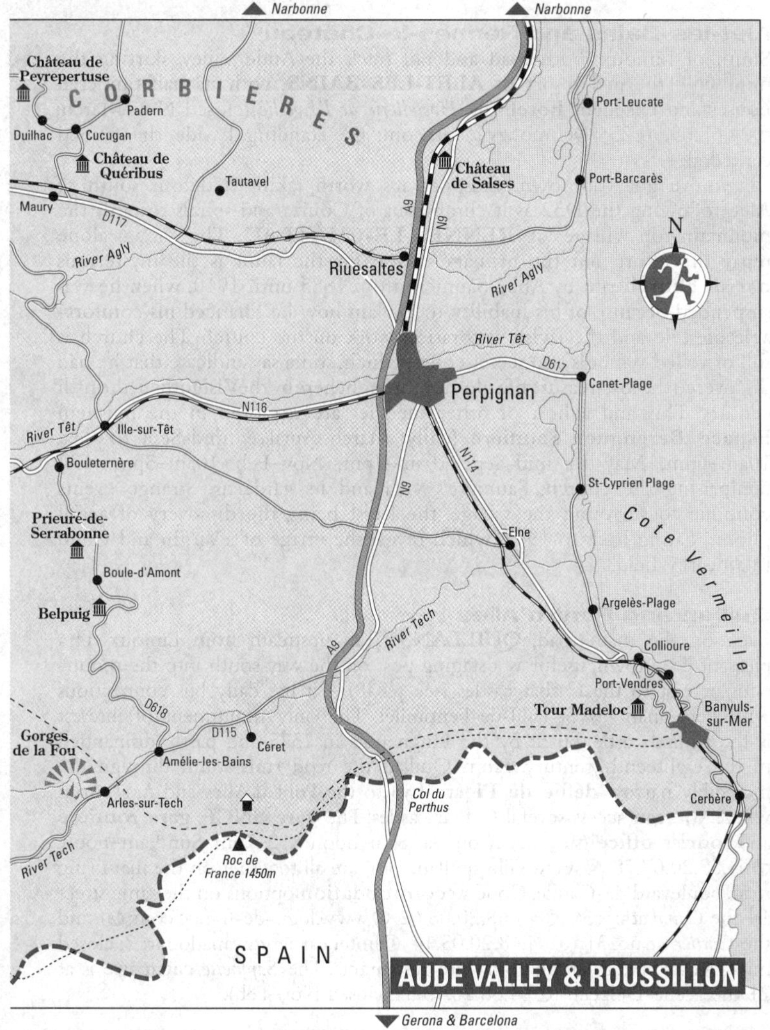

closed Wed), and the humbler *Des Arcades*, south of the church at 96 rue St-Martin (ⓣ04.68.31.02.57, ⓦwww.logis-de-france.fr; ❷; closed mid-Dec to mid-Jan & Wed); both are comfortable and have television in the rooms and garage parking. The municipal **campsite** (ⓣ04.68.31.13.63; closed Oct to mid-May) is on the east bank of the river, south of the old bridge.

For an unusual and colourful place to **eat**, try the *Maison de la Blanquette*, at 46bis promenade du Tivoli, which sells local wines and serves excellent food (closed Wed; from €12.25; ⓣ04.68.31.01.63); otherwise there are plenty of cafés and brasseries on the main square, or head to one of the hotels above – the hearty menus at the *Modern & Pigeon* (closed Sun noon & Mon) start at €27. If you're interested in sampling or buying any **wine**, the best place to go is the co-operative, Aimery-Sieur d'Arques, in avenue du Mauzac (daily 9am–noon & 2.30–7pm).

Alet-les-Bains and Rennes-le-Château

South of Limoux, both road and rail track the Aude valley, skirting the minuscule thermal resort of **ALET-LES-BAINS**, with its half-timbered houses and excellent **hotel**, the *Hostellerie de l'Évêché* (closed Nov–March; ⓣ04.68.69.90.25, ⓔclimouzy@aol..com; ❸), standing beside the ruined cathedral.

If you've got your own transport, it's worth taking a detour south of Alet, following the D52 as it climbs out of Couiza and spirals towards the mountain-top village of **RENNES-LE-CHÂTEAU**. The views alone repay the effort, but the primary reason for the jaunt is the mysterious **parish church** run by Abbé Saunière from 1885 until 1910, when he was suspended because of his inability to explain how he financed his comfortable lifestyle and the lavish restoration work on the church. The church is full of veiled symbols and secret codes, which, some say, indicate that he had discovered the lost treasure of Solomon, brought here by the Visigoths in the fifth century. This and a host of other theories are explored in the musuem **Espace Bérenguer Saunière** (daily: March–April & mid-Sept to Oct, 10am–6pm, May to mid-Sept 10am–7pm, Nov–Feb 10am–5pm; €4) comprising the church, Saunière's villa and its garderns. Strange events continue to surround the village, the latest being the discovery of aerial photos, dating back to 1967, which reveal the image of a Virgin and Child in a nearby field.

Quillan and Pont d'Aliès

Back on the main road, **QUILLAN**, 27km upstream from Limoux, is a pleasant little town, useful as a staging post on the way south into the mountains or east to the Cathar castles (see p.848) – it has daily bus connections with Perpignan via St-Paul-de-Fenouillet. The only monument of interest is the ruined castle, burnt by the Huguenots in 1575 and partly dismantled in the eighteenth century. From Quillan the road runs south through the incredibly narrow **défilé de Pierre-Lys** to the Pont d'Aliès and Axat, from where you can access several Cathar castles. The **gare SNCF**, **gare routière** and **tourist office** (summer Mon–Sat 8am–noon & 2–7pm, Sun 9am–noon; ⓣ04.68.20.07.78, ⓦwww.ville-quillan.com) are all together on the main ring road, boulevard de-Gaulle. Good **accommodation** options on the same street are the *Canal* at no. 36 (ⓣ04.68.20.08.62, ⓦwww.logis-de-france.com; ❷), and the *Cartier*, at no. 31 (ⓣ04.68.20.05.14, ⓔhotel.cartier@wanadoo.fr; 2; closed mid-Dec to mid-March), both with restaurants. The *Sapinette* **campsite** is at 21 rue René-Delpech (ⓣ04.68.20.13.52; closed Nov–Feb).

There's another campsite by the river at **Pont d'Aliès** (Ⓣ04.68.20.53.27), a further 11km along the D117 by the junction for Axat and the Gorges de l'Aude (see below). At this junction you'll also find the Maison des Pyrénées Cathares for local **information** (July & Aug daily 8am–7pm; Sept–June Mon–Fri 8am–noon & 2–6pm; Ⓣ04.68.20.59.61).

The valley of the Rebenty and Gorges de l'Aude

From Pont d'Aliès a beautiful route runs west up the **valley of the Rebenty** on the tiny D107 through woods of beech, fir and oak, with a magnificent early summer display of orchids and other Pyrenean flowers. It's a marvellous cycling route, too, except for the agony of the climb out of the valley. The road continues to Ax-les-Thermes over the Col du Pradel, or you can escape onto the Plateau de Sault at **ESPEZEL**, some 20km west of **AXAT**. Axat itself hardly merits a visit were it not for the fact that it is the terminus of the Train du Pays Cathare et du Fenoiullèdes which gives access to the castle of Puilaurens and points east, and the last town of any size before entering the rocky canyons to the south. The narrowest and deepest stretch of the scenic **Gorges de l'Aude** is the eighteen or so kilometres between Axat and Usson. If you want to admire the scenery, don't drive: the road is much too dangerous to allow your eyes to wander. Towards the end is a magnificent cave to investigate, the **Grotte de l'Aguzou**. It's expensive to visit, but as near the real thing as you can get without being a caver – you spend the entire day underground, accoutred like a professional. Visits must be arranged a week in advance and there's a minimum of four people (contact Philippe Moreno, Ⓣ04.68.20.45.38, Ⓔgrotte.aguzou@wanadoo.fr; or the Quillan tourist office – see above; €30–60). Camping *sauvage* is allowed by the river.

On to Quérigut

Upstream, the road divides just after Usson-les-Bains. On a shaggy bluff between the arms of the fork, dwarfed in turn by the heights either side, stand the forlorn ruins of the Château d'Usson, allegedly the hiding place of the "Cathar treasure" during the siege of Montségur (see box, p.842). Passing its foot, a road winds up through the attractive grey tiers of houses at **MIJANÉS** – where there's a good hotel, the *Relais de Pailhères* (Ⓣ04.68.20.46.97; ❷; restaurant from €18) – to the pass at the **Col de Pailhères**, which is at its loveliest in June when a cornice of snow still lines the crests above the small round lake.

From Mijanès another road branches up the valley to **QUÉRIGUT** passing through the village of **Le Pla**, which is served infrequently by bus. Quérigut stands at the head of a slope of neglected terraces, guarded by the ruin of its **castle**, last refuge of the Cathars who held out for eleven years after the fall of Montségur. You'll find accommodation either at the village **campsite** or the *Hôtel du Donezan* (Ⓣ04.68.20.42.40, Ⓕ04.68.20.47.06; ❷). Above, the forest begins: kilometres of beech and pine, interspersed with lush meadows, stretching to the windy plateau above Font-Romeu. This is the **Donezan** region, beautiful but the poorest, most neglected and depopulated corner of Ariège. Travellers with their own transport or good shoes may continue south skirting the eastern slopes of the Capcir to arrive at Mont-Louis, 25km or so to the south.

The Cathar castles

Romantic and ruined, the medieval fortresses which pepper the hills to the west and north of Perpignan have come to be known as the **Cathar castles**, though in fact many of the castles in question were built after the Cathars' demise. The **Cathars** were a sect strong in this part of France, who were proscribed as heretics by Pope Innocent III. With papal blessing and the connivance of the French kings, hungry northern nobles descended on the area in a series of Albigensian crusades, beginning in 1208 and led for many years by the notoriously cruel Simon de Montfort. The name of the sect derives from the Greek word for "clean, pure", *katharos*, as they abhorred the materialism and worldly power of the established Church, proclaiming the simple and humble Christianity of the Sermon on the Mount. Although their **adherents** probably never accounted for more than ten percent of the population, there were many members of the nobility and the influential classes among them, which alarmed the powers that be.

Cathars who were caught were burnt in communal conflagrations, 100 or 200 at a time. Their lands were laid waste or seized by the northern nobles, de Montfort himself grabbing the properties of the count of Toulouse. The effect of this brutality was to unite both the Cathars and their Catholic neighbours in southern solidarity against the barbarous north. Though military defeat became irreversible with the capitulation of Toulouse in 1229 and the fall of the castle of Montségur (see box, p.842) in 1244, it took the informers and torturers of the Holy Inquisition another seventy years to root out Cathars completely.

The best of the castles are in the arid, herb-scented hills of the **Corbières** which separate the eastern Pyrenees from the Aude Valley to the north. **Walking** is undoubtedly the most direct way to experience them, and there are numerous paths, of which the **GR36**, crossing from Carcassonne to St-Paul-de-Fenouillet, and the Sentier Cathare, crossing east to west from Port La-Nouvelle to Foix, are the most exciting. The Sentier Cathare is divided into twelve stages with *gîtes d'étape*, described in *Sentier Cathare Topoguide* (Rando Editions), available in local bookstores.

Without transport or walking boots, the best way to tackle them is from the south, as the most spectacular ones are close to the **Quillan–Perpignan** road. This route is served by bus, but a better option is the narrow-gauge **Train du Pays Cathare et du Fenouillèdes** (Ⓣ & Ⓕ04.68.59.96.18) which runs from Rivesaltes to Axat, stopping at the main towns along the way. The service runs on weekends in April, May, June & Sept and Tues–Sun in July & Aug (adult fare varies from €8–13). With your own transport, it becomes possible to explore the wilder back roads and utterly ruinous castles like Durfort and Termes, and to cross the cols where orchids and cowslips shudder in the spring winds and the views southward all end in the snowy Pyrenean bulk of Canigou.

Intersite Card

If you're planning on visiting several of the Cathar-related and other medieval sites of the Aude Valley, you might consider purchasing an **Intersite Card**, available for €4 at any of the 16 participating monuments. The card entitles families to discounts of 12–37 percent (often with free entry for one child) for the walls of Carcassonne, Lastours, Saissac, Caunes-Minervois, St-Hilaire, Lagrasse, Fontfroide, Puilaurens, Peyrepetuse, Queribus, and other sites.

Puilaurens

The eastern most of the Cathar castles of the Fenouillèdes can be accessed by road from Quillan or rail from Axat, or as the penultimate stop for the westbound Train du Pays Cathare et du Fenouillèdes. The hamlet of Lapradelle 5km east of Axat is the jumping off point for the dramatically sited **Château de Puilaurens** (Feb, March & early-Nov Sat, Sun & hols 10am–5pm; April–June & Sept daily 10am–6pm; July & Aug daily 9am–8pm; Dec–Jan Christmas hols daily 10am–5pm; €3.50). You can either drive up or there's a shorter and fairly gentle path from the hamlet of **PUILAURENS**. The castle is perched on top of a high, wooded hill at 700m, its fine crenellated walls built around the very top of the rock outcrops. Although the site of a castle from the tenth century, it seems most likely that it was fortified to something like its present extent in the early thirteenth century, when it passed from the king of France to the count of Roussillon, and then to the king of Aragon. It sheltered many Cathars up to 1256, when Chabert de Barbera, the region's *de facto* ruler, was captured and forced to hand over his strongholds here and at Quéribus further east, to secure his release. The castle remained strategically important, being close to the Spanish border, until 1659, when France annexed Roussillon and the frontier was pushed away to the south. The view from the battlements, which you can climb up to at one point, is quite breathtaking.

Five kilometres south of the village is the *Hostellerie du Grand Duc* in **GINCLA** (ⓣ04.68.20.55.02, ⓦwww.host-du-grand-duc.com; ❹; closed in winter), and a *gîte* (ⓣ04.68.20.59.39) nearby at Col de Tuilla.

Quéribus, Cucugnan and Duilhac

The **Château de Quéribus** (Jan Sat, Sun & school hols 10am–5pm; Feb daily 10am–5.30pm; March, Nov & Dec daily 10am–6pm; April–June & Sept daily 10am–8pm; July & Aug daily 10am–9pm; Oct daily 10am–7.30pm; €4), 30km further east towards Perpignan, stands on the ridge above the vine-ringed village of Cucugnan (see below) which marked the French-Spanish border until the seventeenth century. It is spectacularly situated, balanced on a pillar of rock above a sheer cliff, whose crevices nourish a variety of beautiful wild flowers, and lies just a few kilometres north of the main Quillan–Perpignan road – with a good chance of a lift up to the castle.

Because of the extreme, cramped topography of the rock, the space within the walls is stepped in terraces, dominated by the polygonal keep and accessible by a single stairway. Inside, at the heart of the keep, is the remarkable **chapel** of St-Louis-de-Quéribus, surprisingly high and wide when you consider the keep's tortured position, and supported by a single pillar. The stairs to the roof are broken, but from the window halfway up there are fantastic views to Canigou and Perpignan, with other castles and watchtowers of the Spanish Marches dotting the peaks and ridges. To the northwest you're within easy eyeshot of Peyrepertuse.

The history of Quéribus is similar to that of Puilaurens, though the fortifications visible today are thirteenth century. It was the last stronghold of Cathar resistance, holding out until 1255, eleven years after the fall of Montségur. Never reduced by siege, its role as a sanctuary for the Cathars ended with the capture of the luckless Chabert.

Entry to Quéribus also includes the **Théâtre Achille Mir** (same hours) in the small village of **CUCUGNAN**, in the valley to the north of the château. Through an imaginative slide-show the theatre retells the story of the Curé de Cucugnan, hero of Alphonse Daudet's book *Lettres de Mon Moulin*; locals claim he's based on their own nineteenth-century abbot Ruffié. The village also has a rare statue of a pregnant Virgin Mary in its pretty little church. There's **accommodation** at the *Auberge du Vigneron*, opposite the theatre (Ⓣ04.68.45.03.00, Ⓔauberge.vigneron@ataraxie.fr; ❷; restaurant closed Sun eve & Mon), while the *Auberge de Cucugnan* (Ⓣ04.68.45.40.84, Ⓕ04.68.45.01.52; ❸; closed Jan & Feb), near the church, has a restaurant known for its hearty servings of game (from €16 including wine; closed on Wed Sept–June). The nearest other rooms are in **DUILHAC**, about 4km away below Peyrepertuse (see below), at the *Auberge du Vieux Moulin* (Ⓣ04.68.45.02.17; ❷; closed late Dec to early Feb; restaurant from €12). There's also an *alimentation* in the village, selling bread, open even on Sunday morning.

Peyrepertuse

If you only have time to visit one of the Cathar castles, then your best bet is the **Château de Peyrepertuse** (Feb, March & early-Nov Sat, Sun & hols 10am–5pm; April–June & Sept daily 10am–6pm; July & Aug daily 9am–8pm; Dec–Jan Christmas hols daily 10am–5pm; €3.50), not only for its unbeatable site and stunning views, but also because the complex is unusually well preserved. The access road starts in Duilhac (see above) or, alternatively, you can walk up from Rouffiac village, on the north side, by the GR36; in summer it's a tough, hot climb that takes the best part of an hour. But either way the effort is rewarded, for Peyrepertuse is one of the most awe-inspiring castles anywhere in Europe, clinging to the crest of a long, wickedly jagged spine of rock on the top of a mountain ridge, surrounded by sheer drops of hundreds of metres.

You enter on the north side through thickets of boxwood. The heaviest fortifications enclose the lower eastern end of the ridge, with a keep and barbican controlling the main gate. The castle is much larger than the others despite its precarious hold on the earth, with extensive buildings inside the outer wall, culminating in a keep and tower shutting off the highest point of the ridge, where such a pit of air opens at your feet that no artificial defence is necessary. Surprisingly, the castle was taken by the French without much difficulty in 1240, and most of the existing fortifications were built after that. Whatever you do, don't go up in a thunderstorm; there can be some fierce ones in summer, and the ridge brings down the lightning as surely as a high-tension cable.

If you need to **stay** the night, head for **ROUFFIAC**. The hotel here, the *Auberge de Peyrepertuse* (Ⓣ04.68.45.40.40; ❷; closed late Dec to mid-Jan), also has dormitory accommodation, plus a restaurant (from €18). There are **bus** services on Wednesday and Saturday to St-Paul-de-Fenouillet on the main Perpignan D117 road, returning at 11am. Walkers can also call on the services of Balade Cathare (Ⓣ04.68.45.05.10), based in Rouffiac, which runs a mini-bus shuttling people and bags around the area; it helps if you can give them as much notice as possible.

Moving on from Peyrepertuse, by car or by the GR36, you can return to St-Paul-de-Fenouillet through the narrow **Gorges de Galamus**, and in many places you can get down to the river for a swim. On the way you pass the eagle's-nest **Hermitage St-Antoine**, built into the side of the ravine. Alternatively, the drive eastwards offers more castles, including Padern and the especially fine **Aguilar**, near Tuchan, which overlooks the hills and vales of the Côtes de Roussillon-Villages wine area, with magnificent views from the twisty climbing roads. From here you have the possibility of heading either north towards Narbonne or south through Tautavel to Perpignan.

Roussillon

The area that makes up the eastern fringe of the Pyrenees and the flatter stretch of land down to the Mediterranean coast is known as **Roussillon**, or **French Catalonia**. Catalan power first came into its own in the tenth century under the independent counts of Barcelona, who then became kings of Aragon as well in 1162. They attempted to create a joint power base with Occitan France under the counts of Toulouse, but that came to an unhappy end with the death of Pedro II at the battle of Muret in 1213, when he came to the aid of Raymond VI of Toulouse against Simon de Montfort during the anti-Cathar crusade. The height of Catalan power was reached in the thirteenth and fourteenth centuries, when the Franco-Catalan frontier was fixed along the base of the Corbières hills north of Perpignan. But Jaime I made the mistake of dividing his kingdom between his two sons at his death. What is now the French part became the kingdom of Majorca with its capital at Perpignan, but, coveted by the rival brother, the king of Aragon, it sought alliance with the kings of France, who saw this as a splendid opportunity to straighten out their southern border, thus ensuring continuous squabbling that was only finally ended by the Treaty of the Pyrenees, negotiated by Louis XIV in 1659.

After the treaty, the French began a ruthless process of Frenchification, which was successful in Perpignan where the bourgeoisie tended to identify their commercial interest with a central power; the mountain hinterland, however, was left largely untouched until modern times, when the collapse of traditional agriculture, the introduction of compulsory education and the devastation of the vineyards by phylloxera combined to drive the people off the land – a process which still continues today, albeit at a slower rate.

Although there's no real separatist impetus among French Catalans today, their sense of identity is still strong: the language is very much alive, and the national colours of yellow and red are much in evidence wherever you go. The **Pic du Canigou**, which completely dominates Roussillon, seems much larger in presence than its actual 2784m, and it remains a powerful symbol of Catalan nationalism, attracting hordes of Catalans from Barcelona to celebrate the summer solstice. And in the little town of **Prades**, which, as the place of exile from Franquista Spain of the cellist Pau Casals, became a symbol of Catalan resistance.

Most of the region's attractions are easily reached from the region's one major town, **Perpignan**. The coast and immediate hinterland above the Spanish frontier is beautiful, though predictably crowded, and the finest spots are in the **Tech** and **Têt valleys** which cut back west into the Pyrenees, where you can view the Romanesque monasteries of **Serrabonne**, **St-Michel-de-Cuxa** and **St-Martin-du-Canigou**, Vauban's fortress town of **Villefranche-de-Conflent**, the museum at **Céret** with its unique series of Picasso ceramics and **Mont Canigou** itself and its foothill orchards of peaches and cherries.

Perpignan

This far south, climate and geography alone would ensure a palpable Spanish influence. But more than this, a good part of **PERPIGNAN**'s population is of Spanish origin – refugees from the Civil War and their descendants. The southern influence is further augmented by a substantial admixture of North Africans, including both Arabs and white French settlers repatriated after Algerian independence in 1962.

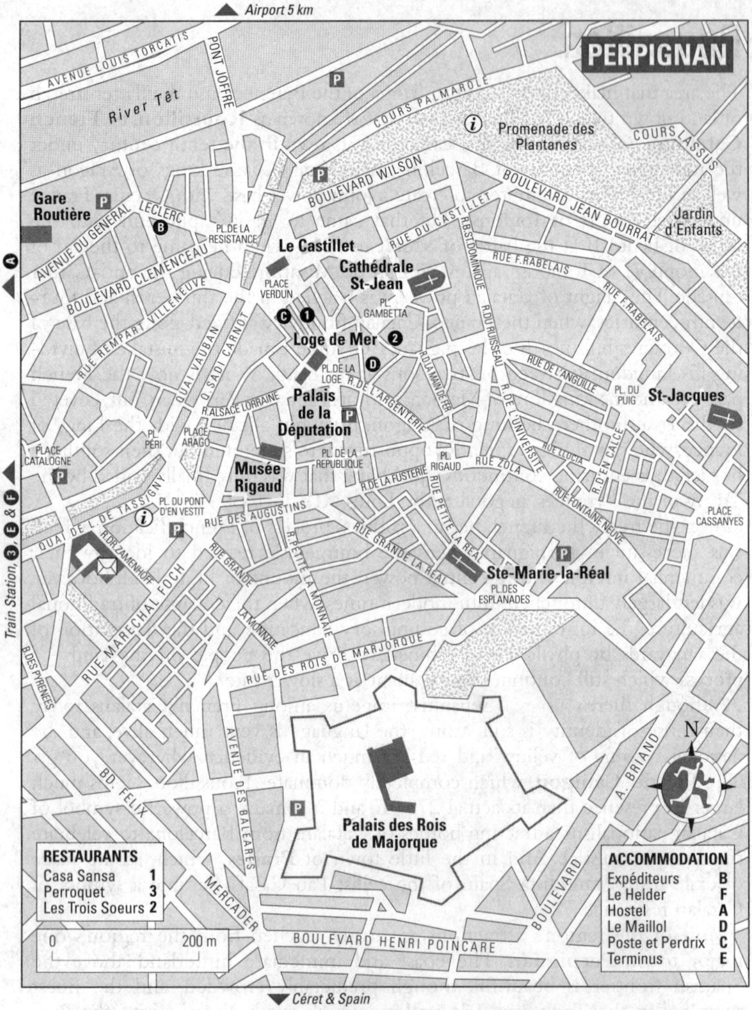

PERPIGNAN

RESTAURANTS	
Casa Sansa	1
Perroquet	3
Les Trois Soeurs	2

ACCOMMODATION	
Expéditeurs	B
Le Helder	F
Hostel	A
Le Maillol	D
Poste et Perdrix	C
Terminus	E

While there are a few memorable monuments to visit, Perpignan is an enjoyable city with a lively street life. Its heyday was in the thirteenth and fourteenth centuries, when the kings of Majorca held their court here, and it is from this period that most of its historical interest derives. Well placed on the main Mediterranean coast international lines of communication, it is much the best base for exploring the eastern end of the Pyrenees, and the Cathar castles of the Corbières to the northwest.

Arrival, information and accommodation

The **gare SNCF** is on avenue Général-de-Gaulle, while long-distance **buses** pull in beside Pont Arago, on avenue Général-Leclerc. Both stations are a fifteen- to twenty-minute walk from the **municipal tourist office** in the Palais des Congrès at the end of boulevard Wilson (mid-June to mid-Sept

Mon–Sat 9am–7pm, Sun 10am–4pm; rest of year Mon–Sat 9am–6pm, Sun 9am–noon; Ⓣ04.68.66.30.30, Ⓦwww.perpignantourisme.com). For information and tickets for city buses, visit Kiosque CTP (Mon–Sat 9am–noon & 1.45–6.15pm) on place Péri, near the regional tourist office.

There are some cheap **hotels** near the station, the best of which are *Le Helder*, 4 av Général-de-Gaulle (Ⓣ04.68.34.38.05, Ⓕ04.68.34.31.09; ❷), and the *Terminus*, 2 av Général-de-Gaulle (Ⓣ04.68.34.32.54, Ⓕ04.68.35.48.16; ❷), right opposite the station. Another very cheap possibility, and convenient for the *gare routière*, is the *Expéditeurs*, on the rather desolate avenue Leclerc (Ⓣ04.68.35.15.80; ❶), with a good cheap restaurant. More comfortable are the *Hôtel Poste et Perdrix*, 6 rue Fabriques-Nabot (Ⓣ04.68.34.42.53, Ⓕ04.68.34.58.20; ❸), and *Le Maillol*, tucked away down impasse des Cardeurs off rue St-Jean (Ⓣ04.68.51.10.20, Ⓔhotellemaillol@worldonline.fr; ❷). In addition, there is a welcoming, if somewhat noisy, **HI hostel** (Ⓣ04.68.34.63.32), behind the public gardens of La Pépinière by Pont Arago (entrance around the back of the police HQ on avenue de Grande-Bretagne), and two **campsites**: *La Garrigole* (Ⓣ04.68.54.66.10), on rue Maurice-Lévy (take bus #19), and the bigger *Roussillon Camping Catalan*, on route de Bompas (Ⓣ04.68.62.16.92) 8km north of the city (no bus).

The City

The best place to begin your exploration of Perpignan is at **Le Castillet**, built as a gateway in the fourteenth century and now home to the **Casa Pairal** (Wed–Mon: May–Sept 10am–7pm, Oct–April 11am–5.30pm; €4), an interesting museum of Roussillon's Catalan folk culture, featuring religious art, agricultural and pastoral exposés, and all sorts of local crafts. From the roof there is a great view of the dominant pile of Canigou, while to the northwest you may be able to pick out the Château de Quéribus (see p.849), standing clear of its ridge. A short distance down rue Louis-Blanc you come to the **place de la Loge**, focus of the renovated and pedestrianized heart of the old town. Dominating the cafés and brasseries of the narrow square is Perpignan's most interesting building, the Gothic **Loge de Mer**. Designed to hold the city's stock exchange and maritime court, and decorated with gargoyles and lacy balustrades, its ground floor has been taken over by an incongruous fast-food joint. Side by side next door are the **Hôtel de Ville**, with its magnificent wrought-iron gates and Maillol's statue of La Méditerranée in the courtyard, and the fifteenth-century **Palais de la Députation**, once the parliament of Roussillon.

From place de la Loge, rue St-Jean runs down to the fourteenth-century **Cathédrale St-Jean** on place Gambetta (Mon & Wed–Sat 10am–noon & 2–5pm, Tues & Sun 2–5pm; free), its external walls built of bands of river stones sandwiched by brick. The interior is most interesting for its elaborate Catalan altarpieces, shadowy in the gloom of the dimly lit nave, and for the tortured wooden crucifix, known as the *Dévôt Christ*, in a side chapel to the south. Dating from around 1400, it's of Rhenish origin and was probably brought back from the Low Countries by a travelling merchant. Past the chapel, on the left is the entrance to the **Campo Santo**, one of France's oldest cemeteries, dating back some 600 years (same hours as cathedral, but closed in summer).

South of the cathedral, rue de la Révolution-Française and rue de l'Anguille lead into the close, dilapidated maze of the **Maghrebian and Romany quarter**, where women congregate on the secluded inner lanes but are seldom seen on the more public thoroughfares. Here you'll find North African shops and cafés, especially on rue Llucia, and a daily market on place Cassanyes. At the heart of the quarter, the wide and grimy place du Puig is overlooked by a Vauban barracks converted into public housing. Just past it, at the top of a shady uphill street, is the elegant Catalan church of **St-Jacques**, dating from around 1200, on the edge of **La Miranda gardens** (daily: July & Aug 3–7pm; Sept–June 2.30–5.30pm), laid out on a section of the old city walls. It's from this church that the Procession de la Sanch (see below) sets out on Maundy (Holy) Thursday.

A twenty-minute walk away through place des Esplanades, crowning the hill that dominates the southern part of the old town, is the **Palais des Rois de Majorque** (daily: June–Sept 10am–6pm; Oct–May 9am–5pm; €3). Although Vauban's walls surround it now, the two-storey palace and its great arcaded courtyard date originally from the late thirteenth century. Thanks to the Spanish influence, there's a sophistication and finesse about the architecture and detailing – for instance in the beautiful marble porch to the lower of the two chapels – that you don't often find in the heavier styles of the north.

Finally, back north at 16 rue de l'Ange near place Arago, you'll find Perpignan's museum of art, the **Musée Rigaud** (Wed–Mon: May–Sept noon–7pm, Oct–April 11am–5.30pm; €4), dedicated to the work of the locally born portraitist Hyacinthe Rigaud, who became official painter to the court of Versailles in the early eighteenth century. The collection also includes works by Dufy, Maillol, Picasso, Tapiès, Appel and others.

Eating, drinking and entertainment

For **eating**, there's nothing to beat the popular *Perroquet*, near the station at 1 av de Gaulle, which has a good selection of very reasonably priced Catalan dishes (closed Wed Sept–April; dinner menus from €20), with the *Expéditeurs* hotel-restaurant (see p.853; closed Mon, Sat eve & Sun; menus from €12) running a close second. For something smarter, head for the more elegant *Casa Sansa*, 2 rue Fabriques-Nadal (☎04.68.34.21.84), founded in 1846 and serving Catalan cuisine (menus from €24–38), or try *Les Trois Soeurs*, 2 rue Fontfroide (☎04.68.51.22.33; menus from €15), for elaborate seafood creations and a Saturday night dinner theatre (Oct–June 7.30pm).

There are plenty of places for a leisurely **drink** in Perpignan. The *Bodega du Castillet*, in the rue Fabriques-Couvertes, is a favourite bar with the locals (and also serves good-value tapas), and there are several decent cafés on place Arago. On place Verdun, under the plane trees in front of Le Castillet, the *Grand Café de la Poste* is a great place to watch the world go by, and it's here, too, that on summer evenings you see the Catalan dance, the *sardana*, being performed by kids, grandparents – anyone whom the spirit moves. There's also **live street theatre and music** in the city centre every Thursday night during July and August (ask at the tourist office for details).

In midsummer, you can witness more music and general Catalan merrymaking at the festival of **Les Feux de St-Jean**, though Perpignan is better known for **La Procession de la Sanch**, the Maundy Thursday procession of penitents that goes from the church of St-Jacques to the cathedral between 3pm and 5pm.

Around Perpignan

CANET-PLAGE is the best place near Perpignan to test the waters of the Mediterranean, although there is nothing to recommend the place, except that its beach is wide and sandy and the sea is wet; take a 25-minute bus ride east from place Catalogne in Perpignan (CTP bus #1; hourly). The same goes for the other resorts around here: Port Leucate, Port Bacarès (complete with weathered Greek ferry beached to make a casino and nightclub) and St-Cyprien.

Perhaps more interesting, 15km north and served by several trains a day, is the **Château de Salses** (daily: Jun–Sept 9.30am–6pm, Oct–May 10am–12.15pm & 2–5pm; €5.50). Built by the Catalans in the early fifteenth century, it was one of the first forts to be designed with a ground-hugging profile to protect it from artillery fire, and its superior design apparently put Vauban's nose so out of joint that he wanted it demolished, a task that proved impossible. Halfway between Perpignan and Salses is the town of **Rivesaltes**, where you can catch the seasonal Train du Pays Cathare et du Fenouillèdes (see p.849) – an ideal way to access the hilly Cathar country.

Another place, with not so much to see but interesting from an anthropological point of view, is the vine-girt village of **TAUTAVEL**, 25km northwest off the St-Paul-de-Fenouillet road. In 1971 the remains of the oldest known European human being – dated to around 450,000 BC – were discovered near the village, and a reconstruction of the skull is on display in the village's **Musée de la Préhistoire** (Jan & Dec Mon, Sun & hols 1.30–5.30pm; Feb–March & Oct–Nov daily 1.30–5.30pm; April–June & Sept daily 10am–12.30pm & 1.30–7pm; July & Aug daily 10am–8pm; €7). Also on show are various finds from the cave where he was unearthed, the **Caune d'Arago**, a few kilometres north, which can itself be visited in July and August (daily 10am–noon & 12.30–5.30pm) or by arrangement with the museum. The local wines are good, too, along with those of Estagel and Rivesaltes, and can be sampled at the numerous *domaines* in the area.

Thirteen kilometres to the south of Perpignan, on the way to the resorts of the Côte Vermeille (see below) and served by the same buses and trains, lies the town of **ELNE**. This small place once had the honour of seeing Hannibal camp at its walls en route to Rome, and used to be the capital of Roussillon. It was only overtaken by Perpignan when the latter became the seat of the kings of Majorca. Today, it's worth a stop for its fortified, partially Romanesque **cathedral** and extremely beautiful **cloister** (daily: April & May 9.30am–6pm, June–Sept 9.30am–7pm, Oct 9.30am–12.30pm & 2–6pm, Nov–March 9.30am–12.30pm & 2–5pm; €5). Though only one side of the cloister is strictly Romanesque, immaculately carved with motifs such as foliage, lions, goats and biblical figures, the three fourteenth-century Gothic ones have been made to harmonize perfectly. It's the best introduction to Roussillon Romanesque you could want, especially if you're planning to visit places like Serrabonne and St-Michel-de-Cuxa further west. Below the cathedral there are still a few streets of the old town left, twisting back down to the drab and unremarkable modern development.

The Côte Vermeille

Known as the **Côte Vermeille**, the last few kilometres of shore before Spain, where the Pyrenees sweep down to the sea, once held a handful of attractive seaside villages. Tourism has put paid to that, though this does mean that all are well served by buses and trains from Perpignan. Travelling south, **Argèles** is the first resort you come to, but you're best off passing straight through and on to the fishing towns of **Collioure**, **Port-Vendres** and **Banyuls**.

Argelès and Collioure

ARGELÈS, the first of the resorts, with the last of the wide sandy beaches, on this stretch of coast, is lively and friendly but packed out with foreign tourists.

The **Musée Casa de les Albères** in rue de l'Égalité (June–Sept Mon–Fri 9am–noon & 3–6pm, Sat 9am–noon; €2) has some interesting exhibits of local arts and traditions.

A few kilometres south, **COLLIOURE**, set in its bay and once the prettiest of these places, inspired Matisse and Derain in 1905 to embark on their explosive Fauvist colour experiments; it's now overly quaint, to the point where you can follow the *Chemin de Fauvisme*, with reproductions of their works fixed to walls around the town. Palm trees line the curving beach, while behind the town, slopes of vines and olives rise to ridges crowned with ruined forts and watchtowers. The town is dominated by the **Château-Royal** (daily: June–Sept 10am–6pm; Oct–May 9am–5pm; €4), which was founded by the Templars in the twelfth century and which has undergone numerous alterations, especially at the hands of the kings of Majorca and Aragon in the fourteenth century and again after the Treaty of the Pyrenees gave Collioure to France. Today, it's largely given over to summertime exhibitions. Collioure's other landmark is the distinctive round belfry of the seventeenth-century **church of Notre-Dame-des-Anges** (daily 9am–noon & 2–6pm), formerly the harbour lighthouse; inside the nave are some exuberant Baroque altarpieces. Behind it two small **beaches** are divided by a causeway leading to the **chapel of St-Vincent**, built on what used to be a rocky islet, while to the left a concrete path follows the rocky shore to the bay of **Le Racou** back towards Argelès.

Behind the château lies the **old harbour**, where half a dozen brightly painted lateen-rigged fishing boats are often beached, all that remains of Collioure's traditional fleet. The attractive surrounding streets of pink- and beige-washed houses are the centre of tourist activity. The **tourist office** is here on place de 18-Juin (July & Aug daily 9am–8pm; Sept–June Mon–Sat 9am–noon & 2–6.30pm; ⓣ04.68.82.15.47, ⓦwww.collioure.com). Two pleasant and comfortable places to **stay** are the atmospheric *Hostellerie des Templiers* (ⓣ04.68.98.31.10, ⓦwww.hotel-templiers.com; ❸) at 12 quai de l'Amirauté, and the sea-view *Triton*, 1 rue Jean-Bart (ⓣ04.68.98.39.39, ⓔhoteltriton@wanadoo.fr; ❸). The best **campsite** is the seaside *La Girelle* (ⓣ04.68.81.25.56, ⓕ04.68.81.87.02; closed Oct–March), but there are numerous others in the area, should it be full. Rue Camille-Pelletan, leading out to the harbour, has some cafés and **restaurants**. Off the main strip, try *El Capillo*, 22 rue St-Vincent (from €18; closed Nov to mid-March) for the local girlled fish, or the smarter *La Marinade*, on place 18-Juin (lunch menus from €10, diner from €23; closed Dec–Feb), serving Catalan dishes.

Port-Vendres and Banyuls

PORT-VENDRES, 3km further down the coast, is a functional sort of place. Although the harbour has never been as busy as it was in the nineteenth century, with colonial trade and ferries from North Africa, it still lands more fish than any other place on this stretch of coast. The boats come in between about 4.30pm and 6pm every day except Sunday; you can watch them unload and auction the catch on the dock at the far end of the harbour. Otherwise, there's little to see here.

South towards **BANYULS**, 7km further on, where the **GR10** finally comes down to the sea, the road winds through attractive scenery, with the Albères hills rising steeply on the right. The town itself, built round a broad sweep of pebble beach, is pleasant but lacks the charm of Collioure and the energy of more popular resorts. There are, however, several things to see and do there. One is the seafront **aquarium** of the Laboratoire Arago (daily: July & Aug 9am–noon & 2–10pm; Sept–June 9am–noon & 2–6.30pm; €4), run by the Sorbonne's marine biology department, whose tanks contain a comprehensive collection of the region's fish and submarine life. Also worth a look are the works of the sculptor **Aristide Maillol**, who was born in Banyuls; they can be seen in front of the *mairie* and on the port, as well as at the **museum** at Mas Maillol, 4km outside the town, where he is buried (daily: May–Sept 10am–noon & 4–7pm; Oct–April 10am–noon & 2–5pm; Ⓦwww.museemaillol.com; €3). You could also sample the dark, full-bodied Banyuls **wine**, an *appellation* which, apart from Banyuls itself, applies only to the vineyards of Collioure, Port-Vendres and Cerbère. The best place to do this is the Cellier des Templiers, on route du Mas-Reig, just under the rail line at the foot of the steep brown-stone terraces of Banyuls' own vineyards (April–Oct daily 9am–7pm; rest of year Mon–Sat 9am–noon & 2–6pm).

For further information consult the **tourist office** opposite the Hôtel de Ville on the seafront (July & Aug daily 9.30am–12.30pm & 2.30–7pm; Sept–June Tues–Sat 9.30am–12.30pm & 2–6.30pm; Ⓣ04.68.88.31.58, Ⓦwww.banyuls-sur-mer.com). Of the cheaper **hotels**, the best is *Le Manoir*, 20 rue de Maréchal-Joffre (Ⓣ04.68.88.32.98; ❷), and there's a municipal **campsite** on avenue Guy Malé (Ⓣ04.68.88.32.13; closed mid-Oct to March). For somewhere to **eat**, try *Chez Rosa*, at 22 rue St-Pierre, which serves hearty fare at reasonable prices (lunch from €10, dinner from €16; closed eve in winter); alternatively, head for the more upmarket *La Pergola* (from €25) and *Al Fanal* (from €20), both on the seafront avenue du Fontaulé.

A magnificent winding drive snakes up from Banyuls through the vineyards to the **Tour Madeloc**, a watchtower built by Jaime I of Majorca at the end of the thirteenth century on the crest of a ridge at about 650m. On a clear day, you can see down into Spain, along the coast, across to Montpellier and over the Corbières, with the castles of Quéribus and Peyrepertuse easily visible.

Céret and the valley of the Tech

The first stop on the D115, the main road which follows the **Tech valley** inland all the way up to the Spanish border just past Prats-de-Mollo, is **CÉRET**, capital of the Vallespir region, and served like the rest of the valley by regular buses from Perpignan's *gare routière*. It's a delightful place, friendly and bustling, with a wonderfully shady old town overhung by huge plane trees. The streets are typically narrow and winding, opening onto small squares like the **place des Neuf-Jets**, so called because of its trickling fountain. There's a large and varied Saturday **market**, which spills out of place Pablo-Picasso into the main street, avenue d'Espagne, where two remnants of the medieval walls, the **Porte de France** and **Porte d'Espagne**, are visible. In summer, Céret is also a big centre for *corridas* (bullfights); the arena is on the other side of town from the market, out towards the Amélie-les-Bains road. Annual high points include the Easter Sunday procession of the Resurrected Christ, at the time of year when Céret's famous cherry harvest is also getting under way. And there's an international *sardana* jamboree on the penultimate Sunday in August.

Céret's main sight, however, is the remarkable **Musée d'Art Moderne** (mid-June to mid-Sept daily: 10am–7pm; rest of year daily except Tues 10am–6pm; Ⓦwww.musee-ceret.com; €5.50), just off boulevard Maréchal-Joffre. In the early years of this century, Céret's charms, coupled with the presence here of the Catalan artist and sculptor Manolo, drew a number of avant-garde artists to the town, including Matisse and Picasso, who personally dedicated a number of pictures to the museum; it also contains work by Chagall, Dalí and Dufy, among others. The Picassos include a marvellous series of ceramic bowls illustrating bullfighting scenes and a sketch of a *sardana*.

You can get more information on the *corridas* and other aspects of the town from the **tourist office** on avenue Clemenceau (July & Aug Mon–Sat 9am–12.30pm & 2–7pm; Sept–May Mon–Fri 10am–noon & 2–5pm, Sat 10am–noon; ⓣ04.68.87.00.53, ⓦwww.ot-ceret.fr). If you wish to **stay**, try the very attractive and reasonably priced *Hôtel Vidal* in the place du 4-Septembre (ⓣ04.68.87.00.85, ⓦwww.hotelvidalceret.com; ❷; restaurant from €15). For campers, there's a municipal **campsite** just out of town on the Maureillas road. **Eating** options include a good, cheap restaurant-crêperie, *Le Pied dans le Plat*, on place des Neuf-Jets, while gourmets with money to spare can try the best food for miles around at *Les Feuillants* (ⓣ04.68.87.37.88; closed Sun eve & Mon; from €30), serving utterly delicious Catalan cuisine.

Amélie-les-Bains and Arles-sur-Tech

West of Céret, past the leaping single span of its fourteenth-century **Pont du Diable**, the view opens north towards the towering imminence of the Canigou Massif. **AMÉLIE-LES-BAINS**, the next place you come to, is a rather stodgy health spa for the elderly and rheumatic, and is hardly worth a stop. If an **overnight stay** is necessary, however, you're best off heading for the attractive *Hôtel La Chaumière* at 2 av du Vallespir (ⓣ04.68.39.05.35; ❶), right on the river in the middle of town.

ARLES-SUR-TECH, 4km up the valley, is a more interesting proposition. It has a beautiful Romanesque **Abbey** (Mon–Sat 9am–noon & 2–6pm; €3.40), whose Carolingian origins in the ninth century are thought to account for its back-to-front alignment of altar at the west end and the entrance at the east. The massive interior is impressive, but the abbey's most renowned feature is the **cloister**, whose pointed white marble arches and twin columns prefigure the Gothic, showing its relative lateness compared to other examples of Romanesque in the region, like Serrabonne. Twin towers flank the church, while against the wall outside the east front – whose plainness is beautifully relieved, as the sun turns, by the shadow of blind arcading – stands a very ancient (fourth- or fifth-century) sarcophagus, known as the **Ste Tombe**, which has the mysterious and scientifically inexplicable habit of slowly filling with very pure water. Every year, on 30 July, when Arles celebrates its fête dedicated to SS Abdon and Sennen, the water is siphoned out and distributed after Mass to the pilgrims who have come to worship. The town's other points of interest include the probably prehistoric **Fête de l'Ours**, a festival designed to exorcize human fear of the bear, traditionally held at the end of February when the bears woke from their winter hibernation. There's also a torchlight **Procession de la Sanch** at Easter. The **GR10** passes through Arles, climbing north towards the Cortalets refuge on Canigou and south towards the Roc de France.

The **tourist office** (Mon–Sat 9am–noon & 2–6pm; ⓣ04.68.39.11.99, ⓦwww.villes-arles-sur-tech.fr) is in rue Barjau. Your best **accommodation** option is the attractive Hôtel les Glycines on rue du Jeu-de-Paume (ⓣ04.68.39.10.09, ⓔhotelglycines@wanadoo.fr; ❸), with a good restaurant (from €18) and wisteria-shaded terrace. There's a **campsite** on the west side of town.

A couple of kilometres out of Arles, on the road to Prats-de-Mollo, is the entrance to the **Gorges de la Fou**, some 2km in length, very narrow and up to 250m deep (ⓣ04.68.39.16.21; Apr–Nov daily 10am–6pm weather permitting; €5). It's spectacular, but unfortunately something of a tourist trap, with a car park, admission charge, snacks and a metal catwalk all along the bottom of the gorge.

Prats-de-Mollo and the Spanish frontier

After the gorge, the road climbs on towards the border, between valley sides thick with walnut, oak and sweet chestnut, to **PRATS-DE-MOLLO**. Prats is the last French town before the border with Spain, and has a very Spanish atmosphere. Most of the population seems to sit around or play pétanque in **El Firal**, the main square. It's surprisingly unspoiled for a border town, and its **ville haute** makes for a wonderful wander, with steep cobbled streets and a weather-worn grey church with marvellous ironwork on the door under the porch. The encircling walls were rebuilt in the seventeenth century after the suppression of a local revolt against the taxation newly imposed by Louis XIV after the Treaty of the Pyrenees brought these lands under his sway. The **Fort Lagarde** (daily: April–June 2–6pm; July & Aug 10am–6pm; Sept–March 2–5pm; €3.50), on the heights above the town, also dates from this period, built to keep the local population in check as much as keeping the Spanish out. For **accommodation**, try the *Bellevue* (ⓣ04.68.39.72.48, ⓦwww.logis-de-france.fr; ❸; closed Nov–March), overlooking El Firal. If you're **camping**, head for the municipal site 1km along the road towards La Preste.

From Prats-de-Mollo it's only 13km to the border on the **Col d'Ares**. The next place of any size on the other side of the border is Camprodon, a village about 18km away. Alternatively, if you're feeling energetic, you can bus or hitch the 8km north to the spa town of La Preste, and then walk over the **Col Prégon**. It's about an hour's steep climb to the top, followed by another hour's more gentle descent down to the small village of Espinavell – leave the road at the first turning on the right before you get into La Preste, and then take the path from La Forge.

From the Tech to the Têt

The only practical route between the **valleys of the Tech and the Têt**, especially if you're hitching, is the D618 across the eastern spurs of Canigou from Amélie-les-Bains to Bouleternère. It's 43 slow kilometres of mountain road, twisting and climbing through magnificent woods of holm oak, cork oak, regular oak, chestnut, ash and cherry, with explosions of yellow broom and tangles of wild honeysuckle, past isolated half-derelict farms or mas, some still tenanted by survivors of the post-1968 migration that repopulated the abandoned countryside with utopian-seeking urbanites. About halfway along, the three-house hamlet of **Belpuig** stands on the road. One of its buildings is the **Chapelle de la Trinité**, a tiny, dark Romanesque church in grey and yellow stone with elaborate doors and a particularly fine crucifix from the twelfth century. Past the cemetery and up the hill beside a pine plantation, a path climbs to the ruined **Château de Belpuig**, some fifteen minutes' walk from the road with long-range views over the surrounding country.

From here the road descends into the valley bottom, through the pretty hamlet of **Boule d'Amont**, before climbing again to the remarkable **Prieuré de Serrabonne** (mid-Jan to Oct daily except public holidays 10am–6pm; €3), some 4km up an asphalt lane above the road, one of the finest examples – perhaps the finest – of Roussillon Romanesque, and offering spectacular views over the rocky Boulès valley and into the valley of the Têt. The interior of the church (consecrated in 1151) is breathtakingly simple, making the beautiful carvings on the capitals of the pillars in the tribune even more striking: the carvings vividly depict lions, centaurs, griffins and human figures with oriental faces and haircuts – motifs brought back from the Crusades – all in the local pink marble. The altar is made of the same stone, as are the pillars and equally elaborate capitals of the cloister, which is set to one side of the church on a high terrace. Despite the rigours of monastic life here – all abandoned now – the settlement was well developed, and the remains of terraced cultivation and irrigation systems are still visible.

The valley of the Têt and the Pic du Canigou

The upper part of the **Têt valley**, known as the **Pays de Conflent**, is utterly dominated by the **Pic du Canigou**. The valley bottoms are lush with peach and apple orchards – with the possibility of work as a picker from June onwards – but the mountain presides over all, vast and uncompromising.

Prades

The valley capital is **PRADES**, easily accessible by train and bus on the Perpignan–Villefranche–La Tour-de-Carol route, and the obvious starting point for all excursions in the Canigou region. It's an attractive place, although there are no great sights beyond the **church of St-Pierre** in the town centre, and it enjoys a standing way out of proportion to its size or economic power. This is largely thanks to the Catalan cellist Pau (Pablo) Casals, who set up home here as an exile and fierce opponent of the Franco regime in Spain. In 1950 he instituted the internationally renowned **music festival** now held every year in the abbey of St-Michel-de-Cuxa (see below) from late July to the middle of August. Today he is commemorated in a small **museum** (July & Aug Mon–Fri 9am–noon & 2–6pm, rest of year Mon–Fri 9am–noon & 2–5pm; free). Prades is also a centre of ardent Catalan feeling, hosting a Catalan university in August and boasting the first Catalan-language primary school in France.

The **tourist office** at 4 rue Victor-Hugo (July & Aug Mon–Sat 9am–12.30pm & 2–7pm, Sun 9am–noon; Sept–June Mon–Fri 9am–noon & 2–5pm; Ⓣ04.68.05.41.02, Ⓦwww.prades-tourisme.com) is a mine of information about the area and can sort out advance bookings for the music festival. For **accommodation**, try the *Hostalrich* (Ⓣ04.68.96.05.38, Ⓕ04.68.96.00.73; ❶), or the friendly and spotlessly clean *Les Glycines* (Ⓣ04.68.96.51.65, Ⓦwww.glycines.com; ❷), both on avenue de-Gaulle, at the south end of rue Victor-Hugo. If you have a car, you could try the delightful *Hôtel St Joseph*, across the river in Molitg-les-Bains (Ⓣ04.68.05.02.11, Ⓕ04.68.05.05.23; ❸; closed Nov–March) which has an excellent restaurant (from €12). The municipal **campsite** (Ⓣ04.68.96.29.83; closed Oct–March) is by the river on the road to Molitg.

Three kilometres south of Prades is one of the loveliest abbeys in the country, **St-Michel-de-Cuxa** ("Cuixà" in Catalan) (May–Sept Mon–Sat 9.30–11.50am & 2–6pm, Sun 2–6pm; Oct–April Mon–Sat 9.30–11.50am & 2–5pm, Sun 2–5pm; €4), dating from around 1000 AD. Although it was mutilated after the Revolution it is still beautiful, with its crenellated tower silhouetted against the wooded slopes of Canigou. The bare stone crypt and church – the altar slab was rediscovered doing duty as a balcony on a house in the village of Vinça – are impressive enough, but the glory of the place is the **cloister**. Although some of the capitals were shipped off to the Cloisters Museum in New York early in the twentieth century, those that remain are a feast for the eyes. Carved in the twelfth century in rose-pink marble from Villefranche, they are decorated with exact and highly stylized human, animal and vegetable motifs. The monastery is still inhabited by a small community of Benedictines from Monserrat in Spain.

Vernet-les-Bains and around

A quiet and not unpleasant little spa, **VERNET-LES-BAINS**, 15km along the D27 from Cuxa, can make a useful base for picking up provisions and information to climb the Pic du Canigou. It has a **tourist office** in place de la Mairie (Mon–Fri 9am–noon & 2–6pm; ⓣ04.68.05.55.35, ⓦwww.ot-vernet-les-bains.fr) and plenty of eating and drinking possibilities in the main square, place de la République. The town's two-star **hotels** offer a range of amenities and all are good value: two of the best are *Eden*, 2 promenade du Cady (ⓣ04.68.05.54.09, ⓦwww.logis-de-france.fr; ❷), and the *Princess*, rue de Lavandiers (ⓣ04.68.05.56.22, ⓦwww.hotel-princess,com; ❸). There are several **campsites** around Vernet and a **gîte d'étape** (ⓣ04.68.05.51.30) just up the road in Casteil. For a meal, try the popular *Le Pommier* in placette du Cady, just off the main square (summer only; from €12).

Just 2km from Vernet-les-Bains, or a half-hour walk above the hamlet of Casteil, is the stunning abbey of **St-Martin-du-Canigou**. Resurrected from its ruins at the turn of the century, the monastery occupies a narrow promontory of rock at over 1000m altitude. Quiet and serene, it's surrounded by the deep shade of chestnut and oak woods, and above it rise the precipitous slopes and eroded pinnacles of Canigou. Below, the ground drops sheer into the ravine of the Cady stream that rushes down from the Col de Jou. The buildings are visitable in French-only tours (hourly departures: Feb to Easter Mon & Wed–Sat 10am, noon & 2.30–4.30pm, Sun 10am, 12.30pm & 2.30–4.30pm; Easter to mid-June & late-Sept Mon–Sat 10am, noon & 2.30–4.30pm, Sun 10am, 12.30pm & 2.30–4.30pm; mid-June to mid-Sept Mon–Sat 10am, noon & 2–5pm, Sun 10am, 12.30pm & 2–5pm; €3.85). What you see is a beautiful little garden and cloister overlooking the ravine, a low dark atmospheric chapel beneath the church and the church itself. Founded in the tenth century, St-Martin was the inspiration for the Romanesque architecture of the region. The graves of the founder, Count Guifred of Cerdagne, and his wife lie in the rock by the church door.

From the reception building, a **path** leads up to a rocky viewpoint from which you can look down on the monastery and away across the valley to the surrounding mountains. As you go up, you pass a signpost to Moura on a path which leads first to the Col de Segalès on the GR10, then, on the HRP, to the *Cabane Arago* and finally to the summit of Canigou (see below). For a different route back to Casteil, a path drops down into the Cady ravine just at the start of the monastery buildings.

The Pic du Canigou

You can get at least part of the way up the **Pic du Canigou** by car or you can follow the trail heading up the river valley from Vernet on foot. Although given the roughness of the road you may not want to risk driving your own vehicle, **cars** can get as far as the Chalet des Cortalets refuge either by the track from Villerach or the even steeper and rougher mining road that begins by the *Al Pouncy* **campsite** near Fillols and passes the Refuge de Balatg and the now vandalized *Cabane des Cortalets*, where herds of cows and horses graze untended (they are the best barometer of mountain weather, descending to lower altitudes when bad weather is imminent). Both routes take about an hour. Alternatively, you could **rent a jeep** and driver from Ria (Ⓣ04.68.05.27.08) or Corbières Grand Riad (Ⓣ04.68.05.24.24) in Prades or Garage Villaceque (Ⓣ04.68.05.66.58) in Vernet-les-Bains. For **walkers**, the standard ascent is from Vernet on a path that begins about 1km along the road to Fillols, joining up with the **GR10** at the Refuge de Bonaigua (about 3hr) which you leave (about 90min) below the **Pic Joffre** to follow the HRP up the ridge to the summit (about 1hr). It's not for faint hearts, because the final ascent up a chimney is rather exposed. There's a five-hour alternative, starting from Casteil, passing the *Refuge Marialles* (Ⓣ04.68.96.22.90; open June–Oct; food served) on the GR10, then following the HRP for the last stretch via the *Refuge Arago*.

From the *Chalet des Cortalets* (Ⓣ04.68.96.36.19; ❷; May–Oct; other times emergency shelter only), which has a restaurant, it's an easy ninety-minute walk to the top. Strike west through the last trees, past a little lake, with a magnificent view into the cirque below the summit, round the back of the Pic Joffre, and up the long stony ridge to the cross and Catalan flag that crown the summit.

Although the **ascent** by this route is straightforward in good weather, you should be properly shod and clothed and have good large-scale maps. If you're not experienced and encounter frozen snow, turn back: a German couple slid to their deaths on the slopes between Pic Joffre and the summit in 1991. Midsummer is a great time to do the climb. On the night of June 23, Catalans for kilometres around, including half the population of Barcelona, gather on the top to light the bonfire from which a flame is carried to kindle all the *feux de St-Jean* of the Catalan villages, though the scene around the refuge can be pretty horrendous, with tents, ghetto blasters and litter galore.

Villefranche-de-Conflent and the Petit Train Jaune

A medieval garrison town suffering from arrested development, **VILLE-FRANCHE-DE-CONFLENT**, 6km up the Têt from Prades, is a tourist classic and lives off it, but is nevertheless an interesting place. Founded around 1100 by the counts of Cerdagne to bar the road to Moorish invaders, remodelled by Vauban in the seventeenth century after rebelling against annexation by France, its streets and fortifications have remained untouched by subsequent development. Worth a look is the **church of St-Jacques**, with a primitively carved thirteenth-century baptismal font just inside the door, and you can walk the **walls** for a fee (daily: Feb–May & Oct–Dec 10am–12.30pm & 2–6pm; June & Sept 10am–7pm; July & Aug 10am–8pm; €3.50). If you do so, you'll see why Vauban constructed the **Libéria fortress** on the heights overlooking the town to protect it from "aerial" bombardment. Getting up to the Libéria (daily: June–Sept 9am–8pm; Oct–May 10am–6pm; €5.50) involves taking the free minibus leaving from near the town's main gate. You can return to town by descending a stairway of a thousand steps which ends just across the old bridge and rail line at the end of rue St-Pierre.

The **tourist office** (Feb–Dec daily 10am–12.30pm & 2–5.30pm; Ⓣ04.68.96.22.96, Ⓕ04.68.96.23.93) is in place d'Église. There is no accommodation in town, but magnificent old *Auberge du Cédre* (Ⓣ04.68.96.05.05; ❷; closed Nov–April; meals from €11.50) is situated just east of the old walls and next to it the welcoming *chambre d'hôtes* Mireille Pena (Ⓣ04.68.96.52.35, Ⓔmpebafain@aol.com; ❹).

Villefranche is the terminus for trains from Perpignan. From here up to **La Tour-de-Carol** on the Spanish frontier, transport is by SNCF bus, or, far nicer, the narrow-gauge **Petit Train Jaune**, which climbs to the valley head at a pace that allows you a walker's or cyclist's proximity to the scenery, especially in summer when some of the carriages are open-air (late May to Sept 4–6 daily; Ⓣ04.68.96.56.62, Ⓦwww.ter-sncf.com/trains_touristiques/train_jaune.htm; €32 return). Best of all the frequency of the trains makes it practical to hop off and on, allowing you to explore the areas around the smaller, isolated stations.

On up the Têt

Just beyond Thuès-Entre-Valls, southwest of Villefranche on the south side of the main N116, the wild wooded canyon of the **Gorges de la Carança** cuts south into the mountains towards Spain. A path follows the gorge to a junction with the GR10 at the refuge of the *Ras de la Carança* (3–4hr), while a further path continues on to meet the HRP on the frontier in another four hours.

At Fontpédrouse, 5km beyond Thuès, a road branches south across the river and up a grassy spur above the River Aigues towards the village of Prat-Balaguer. From the top of the rise directly opposite Fontpédrouse, a path leads down to the Aigues where water from **hot springs** forms three separate pools at different temperatures, and you can skinny-dip for free.

Another 10km up the main road brings you onto the wide **plateau of the Cerdagne**, whose once powerful counts controlled lands from Barcelona to Roussillon and endowed the monasteries of St-Michel-de-Cuxa, St-Martin-du-Canigou and Ripoll, now well inside Spain. It's an area that has never been sure whether it is Spanish or French. After the French annexation of Roussillon, it was partitioned, with Spain retaining – as it does today – the enclave of Lliva.

The first place you come to is the little garrison town of **Mont-Louis**, built by Vauban in 1679 and still used as a base for paratroops and marines. There isn't much to see, but it is a far pleasanter place to stay than the monstrous ski resort of **Font-Romeu** just down the road. The main ski station has 40 pistes descending from 2400 to 1800m, while most of the neighbouring towns have their own mini-station. There's a **tourist office** (July & Aug daily 9.30am–noon & 2–7pm; Sept–June Tues–Sat 10am–noon & 2–6pm; Ⓣ04.68.04.21.97, Ⓦwww.mont-louis.net) and the best deal for **accommodation** is *La Volute* (Ⓣ & Ⓕ04.68.04.27.21; ❸), a B&B set in the seventeenth-century former governor's mansion. **Campers** should head for the site at *Pla de Barres*, 3km away on the road to the Lac des Bouillousses (Ⓣ04.68.04.21.18; closed mid-Sept to mid-June), or there's a **gîte d'étape** at La Cassagne farm (Ⓣ04.68.04.21.40; ❶), half an hour back down the main road. For **food**, *Lou Roubaillou*, near the barracks in rue des Écoles Laïques, serves up excellent mountain produce (menus in the €20–30 range).

Of things to do round about, there's a good four-hour walk from the pretty mountain village of **EYNE** up a valley renowned for its flowers and medicinal plants to the Col d'Eyne, and numerous walks in the **Carlit Massif** around the **Lac des Bouillousses** – where there's a CAF refuge (Ⓣ04.68.04.20.76), though the lake itself and parts accessible by car get very crowded in season. The region's curiosity is the **four solaire**, or solar power station (1hr guided tours daily: mid-June to mid-Sept daily 10am–12.30pm & 2–7pm, rest of year Mon–Sat 10am–12.30pm & 2–6.30pm; €5), at **ODEILLO** just below Font-Romeu, although the most impressive part of this, a screen composed of thousands of mirrors, can in fact be seen from the road.

Travel details

Trains

Bayonne to: Biarritz (18–22 daily; 10–15min); Bordeaux (18–22 daily; 1hr 45min–3hr 30min); Boussens (4 daily; 3hr); Cambo-les-Bains (3 daily; 25min); Hendaye (16–20 daily; 35min); Lourdes (5–8 daily; 1hr 45min–3hr 20min); Orthez (5–6 daily; 45min–1hr 15min); Pau (5–7 daily; 1hr 15min–2hr); St-Gaudens (3 daily; 2hr 45min–3hr 45min); St-Jean-de-Luz (16–20 daily; 25min); St-Jean-Pied-de-Port (3 daily; 1hr); Tarbes (5 daily; 2hr–3hr 30min); Toulouse (18–22 daily; 2hr 25min–3hr 45min).
Foix to: Ax-les-Thermes (6 daily; 50min); Barcelona (4 daily; 5hr 15min–6hr); Latour-de-Carol (6 daily; 2hr); Tarascon-sur-Ariège (13 daily; 15–25min); Toulouse (13 daily; 45min to 1hr 15min).
Luchon to: Toulouse (12 daily; 2hr–3hr).
Pau to: Bordeaux (5–7 daily; 1hr 15min–2hr); Oloron-Ste-Marie (10 daily; 45min); Orthez (5–6 daily; 20min).
Perpignan to Argelès (26 daily; 20min); Banyuls-sur-Mer (26 daily; 30min); Barcelona (2–3 daily; 2hr 15min–5hr); Cerbère (26 daily; 40min); Collioure (24 daily; 25min); Elne (24 daily; 10min); Narbonne (24 daily; 36–45min); Port-Bou (7–8 daily; 50min); Prades (9 daily; 45min); Salses (12daily; 15min); Toulouse (15 daily; 2hr 30min–3hr 45min); Villefranche-de-Conflent (12 daily; 50min).
Quillan to: Carcassonne (2–3 daily; 1hr); Limoux (2–3 daily; 30min).
Tarbes to: Bordeaux (6–9 daily; 3hr 15min); Dax (6–9 daily; 1hr 50min); Lourdes (8–9 daily; 20min); Orthez (3–5; 1hr 10min).
Villefranche-de-Conflent to Latour-de-Carol (5 daily; 2hr 45min).

Buses

Bayonne to: Biarritz (local transport; 15–20min); Cambo-les-Bains (several daily; 30–40min); Capbreton (hourly; 30min); Hendaye (3–7 daily; 30min); Orthez (3 daily; 50min); Pau (2–3 daily; 1hr 10min) San Sebastian (1 daily Mon–Sat; 1hr 45min); St-Etienne-de-Baigorry (4–6; 2hr); St-Jean-de-Luz (6–14 daily; 40min).
Biarritz to: Hendaye (5–7 daily; 30min); Orthez (2–3 daily; 1hr 45min); Pau (2–3 daily; 2hr 30min); St-Etienne-de-Baigorry (2 daily; 2hr 10min); St-Jean-de-Luz (11–16 daily; 25min); St-Jean-Pied-de-Port (2–6 daily; 1hr 10–45min); Salies-de-Béarn (2 daily; 1hr 20min).
Foix to: Ax-les-Thermes (2 daily; 1hr); Lavelanet (2–3 daily; 35min); Mirepoix (2–3 daily; 1hr 30min); Niaux (2 Fri; 35min); Pamiers (8 daily; 30min); Quillan (1 daily; 2hr); Tarascon (2–5 daily; 20min); Toulouse (1 daily; 1hr, 45min).
Lannemazan to: St-Lary (4–5 daily; 1hr).
Laruns to: Fabrèges (2 daily Mon–Fri year-round, 1 daily Sat & Sun July & Aug; 55min); Gabas (2 daily Mon–Fri year-round, 1 daily Sat & Sun July & Aug; 25min).
Lourdes to: Bagnères-de-Bigorre (2–4 daily; 45min–1hr); Barèges (5–9 daily; 1hr 5min); Cauterets, changing at Pierrefitte-Nestalas (2–6 daily; 1hr); Gavarnie, changing at Luz (June to mid-Sept 2 daily; 1hr 15min); Luz-St-Sauveur (5–7 daily; 45min); Pau (4–8 daily; 1hr 15min).
Oloron-Ste-Marie to: Bedous (4–8 daily; 30min); Urdos (4–8 daily; 50min).
Pamiers to: Foix (8 daily; 30min).
Pau to: Agen (1–2 daily; 3hr); Bayonne (3–4 daily; 2hr 15min); Biarritz (2–3 daily; 2hr 30min); Eaux-Bonnes (3 daily on; 1hr 25min); La Gourette (3 daily ; 1hr 45min); Laruns (3 daily; 1hr 15min); Mauléon (1 daily; 1hr 50min); Oloron-Ste-Marie (6–9 daily; 45min); Orthez (2–3 daily; 45min); Salies-de-Béarn (3 daily; 1hr 10min).
Perpignan to: Amélie-les-Bains (7 daily; 1hr); Argelès (3 daily; 30min); Arles-sur-Tech (7 daily; 1hr 15min); Axat (2 daily, 1hr 40min); Banyuls-sur-Mer (3 daily; 1hr 10min); Céret (14 daily; 55min); Collioure (3 daily; 45min); Font-Romeu (2–3 daily; 2hr 30min); Latour-de-Carol (2–3 daily; 3hr); Mont-Louis (4 daily; 2hr 15min); Port-Vendres (3 daily; 55min); Prades (7 daily; 1hr); Prats-de-Molló (7 daily; 1hr 40min); La Preste (3 daily; 2hr 5min); Villefranche-le-Conflent (7 daily; 1hr 15min).
Quillan to: Axat (2 daily; 20min); Carcassonne (2 daily; 1hr 20min); Comus (1–2 daily; 1hr 5min); Perpignan (2 daily; 1hr 30min); Quérigut (3 weekly in summer; 1hr 30min).
St-Girons to: Aulus-les-Bains (1–2 daily; 1hr 15min); Boussens (6–8 daily; 40min); Foix (1–4 daily; 1hr); Toulouse (2–3 daily; 2hr).
St-Jean-de-Luz to: Cambo-les-Bains (2–4 daily; 45min); Espelette (2 daily; 35min); Hendaye (9–16 daily; 30min); Sare (2–3 daily; 30min).
Tarascon to: Auzat (2 daily; 30min).
Tarbes to: Auch (2–6 daily; 1hr 40min); Bagnères-de-Bigorre (4–6 daily; 30–45min); Lourdes (hourly; 30min); Pau (6 daily; 1hr).

11

Languedoc

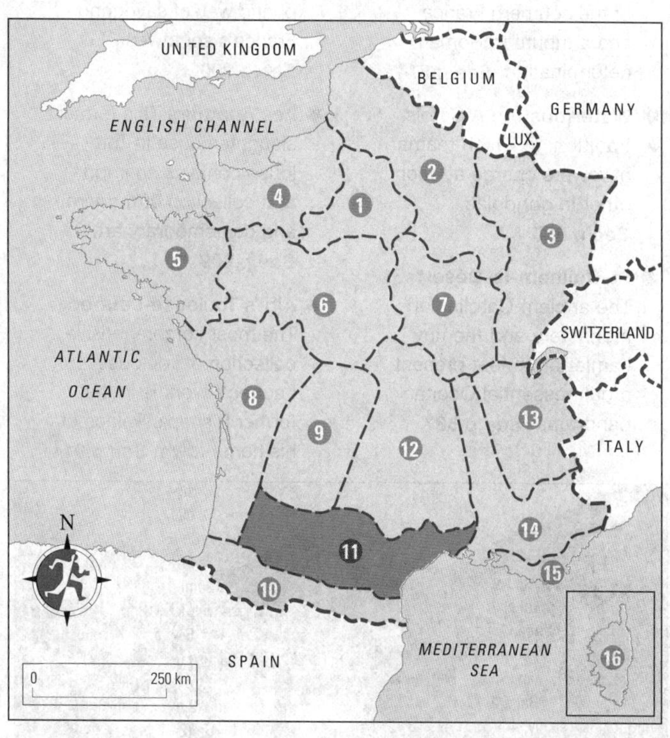

CHAPTER 11

Highlights

* **Bulls** Whether in the ring or on your plate as a succulent *boeuf à la gardienne*, the *taureaux* of the plains of Languedoc are famous. **See p.871**

* **Pont du Gard** This graceful aqueduct is an emblem of the southern France and a tribute to Roman determination. **See p.874**

* **Waterjousting** A Setois tradition, in which teams of rowers charge at each other in gondolas. **See p.883**

* **St-Guilhem-le-Désert** The ancient Carolingian monastery and the tiny hamlet at its feet present a quintessential Occitan panorama. **See p.887**

* **Carcassonne** The Middle Ages come alive in this walled fortress town. **See p.898**

* **The Canal du Midi** Cycling, walking or drifting along this tree-shaded canal is the most atmospheric way of savouring France's southwest. **See p.900**

* **Les Abattoirs** This former slaughterhouse in Toulouse contains an important collection of modern and contemporary art. **See p.909**

* **Albi's Toulouse-Lautrec** The most comprehensive collection of Toulouse Lautrec's work is in the former Bishop's Palace of his home-town. **See p.914**

△ St-Guilhem-le-Désert

Languedoc

Languedoc is more an idea than a geographical entity. The modern *région* covers only a fraction of the lands where Occitan or the *langue d'oc* – the language of *oc*, the southern Gallo-Latin word for *oui* – once dominated. These stretched south from Bordeaux and Lyon into Spain and northwest Italy.

The heartland today is the Bas Languedoc – the coastal plain and dry, stony, vine-growing hills between Carcassonne and Nîmes. It's here that the Occitan movement has its power base, demanding recognition of its linguistic and cultural distinctiveness. A good part of its appeal derives from resentment of political domination by remote and alien Paris, aggravated by the area's traditional poverty. In recent times this has been focused on Parisian determination to drag the province into the modern world, with massive tourist development on the coast and the drastic transformation of the cheap wine industry. But it is also mixed up in a vague collective folk memory with the brutal repression of the Protestant Huguenots around 1700, the thirteenth-century massacres of the Cathars and the subsequent obliteration of the brilliant *langue d'oc* troubadour tradition. It is a hostility that has made an essentially rural and conservative population vote traditionally for the Left – at least until the elections of 2002, which saw wide support for Le Pen's resurgent Front National. Although a sense of Occitan identity remains strong in the region, it has very little currency as a spoken or literary language, despite the popularity of university-level language courses and the foundation of Occitan-speaking elementary schools.

Toulouse, the cultural capital, though included in this chapter, lies outside the modern *région* but is a deserved high spot among numerous and various other attractions. There are great stretches of dramatic landscape and river gorges, from the **Cévennes** foothills in the east to the **Montagne Noire** and **Corbières** hills in the west. There's superb ecclesiastical architecture in **Albi** and **St-Guilhem-le-Désert**, and medieval towns at **Cordes** and **Carcassonne**, which also provides access to the unforgettably romantic Cathar castles to the south. **Nîmes** has extensive Roman remains, and there are great swathes of **beach** where – away from the major resorts – you can still find a kilometre or two to yourself.

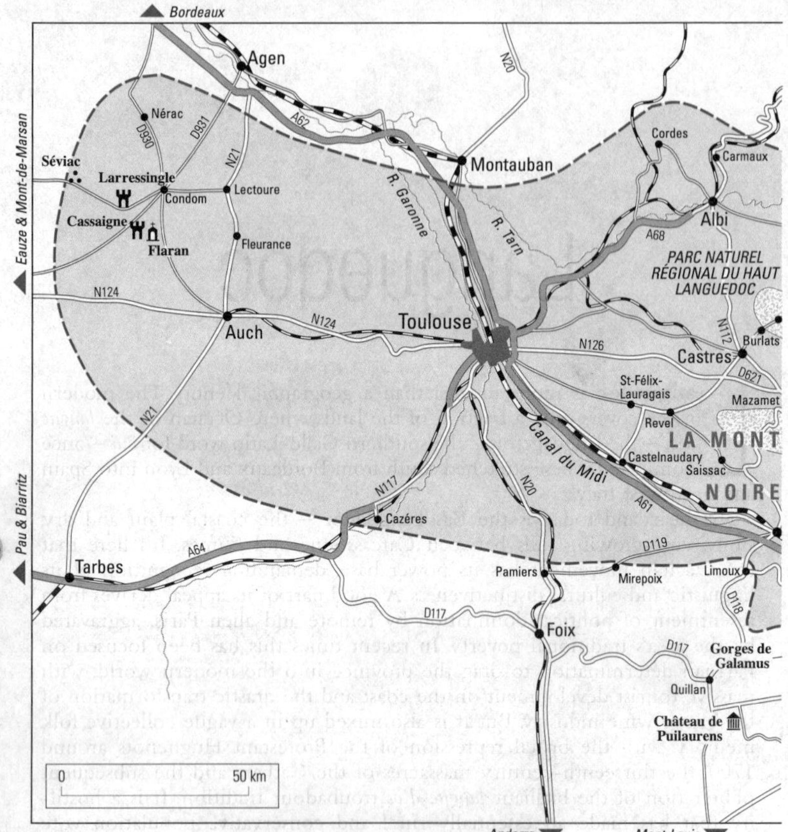

Eastern Languedoc

Heading south from Paris via Lyon and the Rhône valley, you can go one of two ways: east to Provence and the Côte d'Azur – which is what most people do – or west to **Nîmes**, **Montpellier** and the comparatively untouched northern Languedoc coast. Nîmes itself, while not officially part of the modern administrative *région*, makes for a good introduction to the area, a hectic modern town impressive both for its Roman past and for some scattered attractions – the **Pont du Gard** for one – nearby. Montpellier, also, is worth a day or two, not so much for any historical attractions as for a heady vibrancy and ease of access to the ancient villages, churches and fine scenery of the upper **Hérault valley**. This was the part of Languedoc most affected by the spread of Protestantism in the sixteenth century, an experience that has marked the region's character more than any other. The Protestants, with their attachment to rationality and self-improvement, espoused the cause of French over Occitan, supported the Revolution and the Republic, fought Napoléon III's coup against the 1848

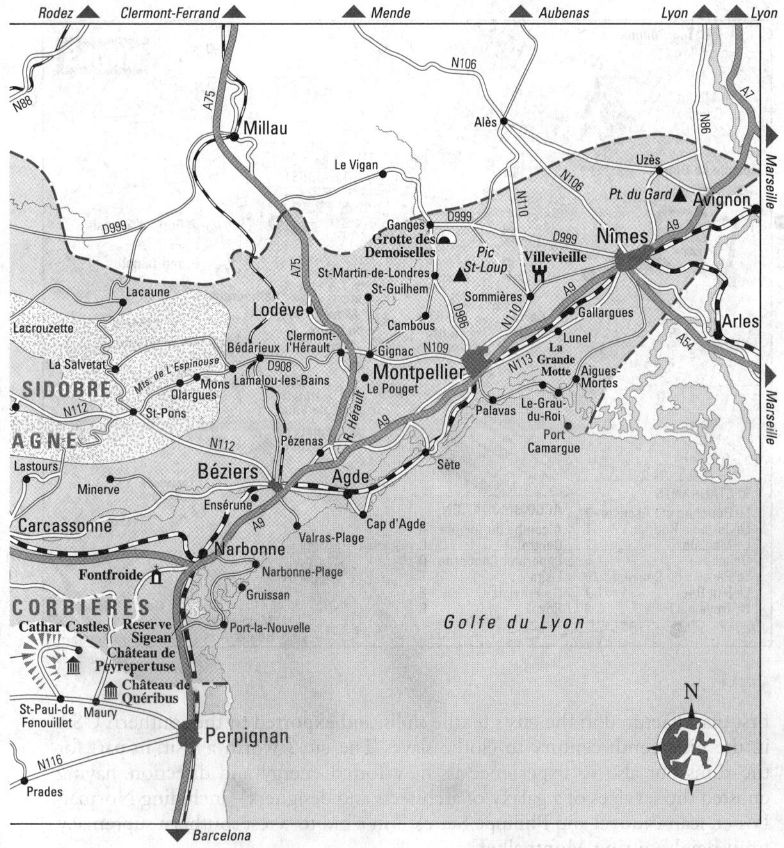

Revolution and adhered to the anticlerical and socialist movement under the Third Republic. They dominated the local textile industry in the nineteenth century and were extremely active in the Resistance to the Nazis.

They also suffered a great deal for their cause, as did the whole region. After the Revocation of the Edict of Nantes in 1685 – the treaty which had granted religious toleration at the end of the sixteenth century – persecution drove their most committed supporters, especially in the Cévennes to the north, to form clandestine *assemblées du Désert*, and finally, in 1702, to take up arms in the first guerrilla war of modern times, La Guerre des Camisards, conflicts which still resonate in the minds of both Huguenot and Catholic families.

Nîmes and around

On the border between Provence and Languedoc, the name of **NÎMES** is inescapably linked to two things – denim and Rome. The latter's influence is highly visible in some of the most extensive Roman remains in Europe, while the former (*de Nîmes*), equally visible on the backsides of the populace, was

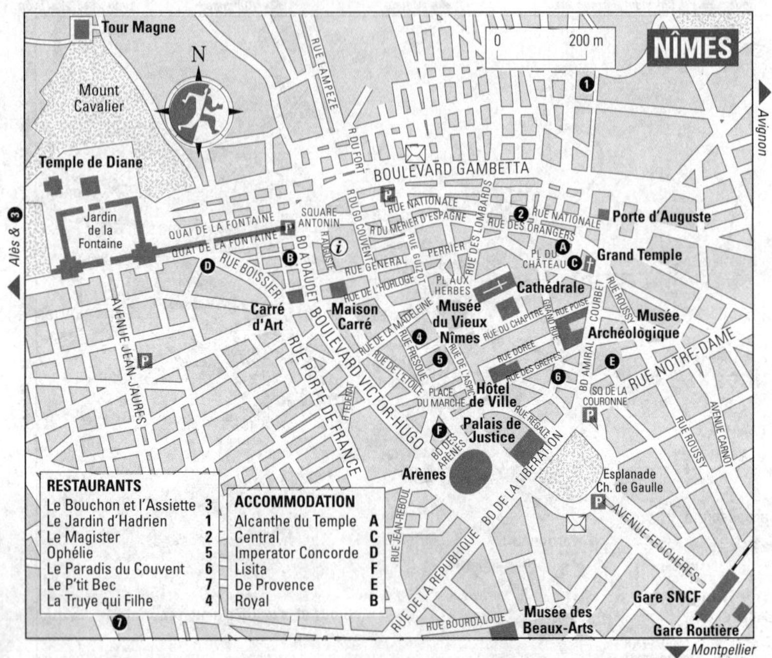

first manufactured in the city's textile mills, and exported to the southern USA in the nineteenth century to clothe slaves. The city's worth a visit, in part for the ruins but also to experience its new-found energy and direction, having enlisted the services of a galaxy of architects and designers – including Norman Foster, Jean Nouvel and Philippe Starck – in a bid to wrest southern supremacy from neighbouring Montpellier.

Arrival, information and accommodation

The Camargue **airport**, which Nîmes and Arles share, lies 20km south-east of the city. A shuttle service links it to the town centre (2–4 daily; ⓣ04.66.29.27.29; "Gambetta" or "Imperator" stop; €5) as do taxis (around €23). The **gare SNCF** is ten minutes' walk southeast of the city centre at the end of avenue Feuchères, which leads down from Esplanade Charles -de-Gaulle, with the **gare routière** (ⓣ04.66.29.52.00) just behind in rue Ste-Félicité (access through the train station). The main **tourist office** is at 6 rue Auguste, by the Maison Carrée (Easter–June & Sept Mon–Fri 8am–7pm, Sat 9am–7pm, Sun 10am–6pm; July & Aug Mon–Fri 8am–8pm, Sat 9am–7pm, Sun 10am–6pm; Oct–Easter Mon–Fri 8.30am–7pm, Sat 9am–7pm, Sun 10am–5pm; ⓣ04.66.58.38.00, ⓦwww.ot-nimes.fr).

There are several decent **hotels** in the city. The clean and economical *Alcanthe du Temple*, 1 rue Charles Babout (ⓣ04.66.67.54.61, ⓦwww.hotel-du-temple .com; closed Jan; ❸), is one of the old town's best bargains. Friendly, well-kept and set in an eighteenth-century house, *De Provence*, 5/7 square de la Couronne (ⓣ04.66.76.04.92, ⓦwww.hoteldeprovence.com; ❷), has excellent amenities, such as cable TV, for its price. The old-fashioned but rather delightful *Hôtel Lisita*,

2bis bd des Arènes (Ⓣ04.66.67.66.20, Ⓕ04.66.76.22.30; ❷), is popular with visiting bullfighters, and another attractive alternative is the *Central*, 2 place du Château, close to the Protestant church (Ⓣ04.66.67.27.75, Ⓕ04.66.21.77.79; ❸). For a more upmarket option, opt for either the atmospheric *Royal*, near the Maison Carrée at 3 bd Alphonse-Daudet (Ⓣ04.66.67.32.89; ❸), or the city's finest choice – and a favourite of Hemingway's – the *Imperator Concorde*, on quai de la Fontaine (Ⓣ04.66.21.90.30, Ⓔhotel.imperatorconcorde@wanadoo.fr; ❻).

There's an attractive **HI hostel** with tent space on chemin de la Cigale, 2km northwest of the centre (Ⓣ04.66.23.25.04, Ⓦwww.fuaj.org/aj/nimes; July & Aug membership required; Sept–June no curfew); take bus #2 direction "Alès /Villeverte" from the gare SNCF to stop "Stade" – the last bus goes at 8pm. The municipal **campsite** (Ⓣ04.66.38.09.21) is on rte de Générac, 5km south of the city centre, beyond the modern Stade Costières and the autoroute.

The City

Most of what you'll want to see is contained within the boulevards de la Libération, Amiral-Courbet, Gambetta and Victor-Hugo, and there's much pleasure to be had from just wandering the narrow lanes that they enclose, discovering unexpected squares with their fountains and cafés.

Les Arènes

The focal point of the city, the first-century Roman arena, known as **Les Arènes** (daily: July & Aug 9am–7pm; Sept–June 10am–5pm; closed during special events; €4.55, combined ticket with Tour Magne, €5.55), lies at the junction of boulevards de la Libération and Victor-Hugo. One of the best-preserved Roman arenas anywhere, its arcaded two-storey facade conceals massive interior vaulting, riddled with corridors and supporting raked tiers of seats with a capacity of more than 20,000 spectators, whose staple fare was the blood and guts of gladiatorial combat. When Rome's sway was broken by the barbarian invasions, the arena became a fortress and eventually a slum, home to an incredible 2000 people when it was cleared in the early 1800s. Today it has recovered something of its former role, with the passionate summer crowds still turning out for some real-life blood-letting – Nîmes is the premier European bullfighting scene outside Spain.

The bullfight

Nîmes' great passion is **bullfighting**, and its *ferias* are acknowledged and well attended by both aficionados and fighters at the highest level. The wildest and most famous is the Feria de Pentecôte, which lasts five days over the Whitsun weekend. A couple of million people crowd into the town (hotel rooms need to be booked a year in advance), and seemingly every city native opens a bodega at the bottom of the garden for dispensing booze. There are *corridas*, which end with the killing of the bull, *courses* where *cocards* are snatched from the bulls head, and semi-amateur *courses libres* when a small posse of bulls is run through the streets and the daring try to snatch the *cocards* from their heads. In 1996, Nîmes witnessed the acclamation of the first-ever woman matador, Cristina Sanchez, though she took an early retirement in 1999, blaming the machismo of the profession. Two other *ferias* take place: one at carnival time in February, when the inflatable roof of the Arènes is pulled over for protection from the weather; the other in the third week of September at grape-harvest time, the Feria des Vendanges. The **tourist office** can supply full details and advise you about accommodation if you want to visit at *feria* time.

The Maison Carrée and Porte d'Auguste

Behind the arena, through the beautiful little place du Marché, rue Fresque leads towards the city's other famous landmark, the **Maison Carrée** (Tues–Sun: 9am–7pm; free), a neat, jewel-like temple, celebrated for its integrity and harmony of proportion. Built in 5 AD, it's dedicated to the adopted sons of Emperor Augustus – all part of the business of blowing up the imperial personality cult. No surprise, then, that Napoléon, with his love of flummery and ennobling his cronies to boost his own legitimacy, should have taken it as the model for the church of the Madeleine in Paris. The temple stands in its own small square opposite rue Auguste, where the Roman forum used to be, with pieces of Roman masonry scattered around. On the north side of place de la Maison Carrée, there's a gleaming example of French architectural boldness, the **Carrée d'Art**, by British architect Norman Foster. In spite of its size, this box of glass, aluminium and concrete sits modestly among the ancient roofs of Nîmes, its slender portico echoing that of the Roman temple opposite. Light pours in through walls and roof, giving it a grace and weightlessness that makes it not in the least incongruous. Housed within the Carrée d'Art is the excellent **Musée d'Art Contemporain** (Tues–Sun 10am–6pm; €4.55), containing an impressive collection of French and Western European art of the last four decades. There's a roof-terrace café at the top, overlooking the Maison Carrée.

Though already a prosperous city on the Via Domitia, the main Roman road from Italy to Spain, Nîmes did especially well under Augustus. He gave the city its walls, remnants of which surface here and there, and its gates, as the inscription on the surviving **Porte d'Auguste** at the end of rue Nationale – the Roman main street – records. The emperor is also responsible for the chained crocodile, which figures on Nîmes' coat of arms. The device was copied from an Augustan coin struck to commemorate his defeat of Antony and Cleopatra after he settled veterans of that campaign on the surrounding land.

The Cathédrale Notre-Dame-et-St-Castor and around

Running back east into the old quarter from the Maison Carrée, **rue de l'Horloge** leads to the delightful **place aux Herbes**, with two or three cafés and bars and a fine twelfth-century house on the corner of rue de la Madeleine. In the former bishop's palace, the **Musée du Vieux Nîmes** (Tues–Sun 10am–6pm; €4.55) has displays of Renaissance furnishings and decor and documents to do with local history. Opposite, the **Cathédrale Notre-Dame-et-St-Castor** sports a handsome sculpted frieze on the west front, illustrating the story of Adam and Eve, and a pediment inspired by the Maison Carrée. It's practically the only existing medieval building in town, as most were destroyed in the turmoil that followed the Michelade, the St Michael's Day massacre of Catholic clergy and notables by Protestants in 1567. Despite brutal repression in the wake of the Camisard insurrection of 1702, Nîmes was, and remains, a doggedly Protestant stronghold. Apart from that, the cathedral is of little interest, having been seriously mutilated in the Wars of Religion and significantly altered in the nineteenth century. The author Alphonse Daudet was born in its shadow, as was Jean Nicot – a doctor, no less – who introduced tobacco into France from Portugal in 1560 and gave his name to the world's most popular drug.

Banned from public office, the Protestants put their energy into making money. The results of their efforts can be seen in the seventeenth- and eighteenth-century *hôtels* they built in the streets around the cathedral – rues de l'Aspic, Chapitre, Dorée and Grande-Rue, among others. Their church is the serious-looking **Grand Temple** on boulevard Amiral-Courbet, a short walk south of Porte d'Auguste. On the same street, the **Musée Archéologique** and **Muséum d'Histoire Naturelle** (Tues–Sun 10am–6pm; €4.55 for both museums), housed in a seventeenth-century Jesuit chapel at no. 13, are full of Roman bits and bobs and stuffed animals. There's another museum, the **Musée des Beaux-Arts**, south of the Arènes in rue de la Cité-Foulc (Tues–Sun 10am–6pm; €4.55), which prides itself on a huge Gallo-Roman mosaic showing the Marriage of Admetus, but is otherwise pretty ordinary. If you're planning on making the rounds of the museums, opt for the three-day *forfait* museum pass (available at the tourist office; €9.80) which gives one-time access to the four sites (including the Musée d'Art Contemporain) listed above.

The interior of the **Hôtel de Ville**, between rue Dorée and rue des Greffes, has been redesigned by the architect Jean-Michel Wilmotte to combine high-tech with classical stone. Most of the other major examples of revolutionary building are out on the southern edge of town: Jean Nouvel's pseudo-Mississippi-steamboat housing project off the Arles road behind the *gare SNCF*, named **Nemausus** after the deity of the local spring that gave Nîmes its name; and the magnificent sports stadium, the **Stades des Costières**, by Vittorio Gregotti, close to the *autoroute* along the continuation of avenue Jean-Jaurès.

Jardin de la Fontaine

Perhaps the most refreshing thing you can do while in Nîmes is head northwest of the centre to the **Jardin de la Fontaine**, France's first public garden, created in 1750. Behind the formal entrance, where fountains, nymphs and formal trees enclose the so-called **Temple de Diana**, steps climb the steep wooded slope, adorned with grottoes and nooks and artful streams, to the **Tour Magne** (Tues–Sun: July & Aug 9am–7pm; Sept–June 10am–5pm; €2.45). The 32-metre tower, taken from Augustus' city walls, gives terrific views out over the surrounding country – as far, it is claimed, as the Pic du Canigou on the edge of the Pyrenees. At the foot of the slope flows the gloriously green and shady **Canal de la Fontaine**, built to supplement the rather unsteady supply of water from the *fontaine*, the Nemausus spring, whose presence in a dry, limestone landscape gave Nîmes its existence.

Eating and drinking

The best places to hang out for **coffees and drinks** are the numerous little squares scattered through the old town: place de la Maison-Carrée, place du Marché, place aux Herbes (breakfast here early at the *Café des Beaux-Arts* to watch the sun creep up behind the cathedral tower). Three classic Nîmes cafés are the *Napoléon*, in boulevard Victor-Hugo, and the *Grande* and *Petite Bourse*, side by side at the back of the Arènes on the corner of boulevard Victor-Hugo. Later in the evening, consider the very pretty *Carrée d'Art* piano bar on rue Gaston-Bossier, near the canal and the postmodern place d'Assas.

For **eating**, boulevard de la Libération and boulevard Amiral-Courbet harbour a stock of reasonably priced brasseries and pizzerias, and the squares too are full of possibilities. *La Truye qui Filhe*, 9 rue Fresque (lunchtimes only, closed Sun & Aug), is an attractive self-service, where you can eat for around €8.50, while the *Le Paradis du Couvent* (Ⓣ04.66.76.26.30; closed Mon out of season), 21 rue du Grand Couvent, in a former convent, dishes out typical herb-infused Provençal and Nîmoise cuisine (from €14.30). Other recommended options include the *Le P'tit Bec* (Ⓣ04.66.38.05.83; closed Sun eve & Mon), on 87bis rue de la République and the best mid-range place for typical Gardoise cuisine (from €16), such as *boeuf à la gardienne*, as well as the welcoming *Ophélie*

(☎04.61.21.00.19; closed Sun & Mon, part Feb & Aug), 35 rue Fresque, home to good-value *terroir* dishes served in a romantic seventeenth-century locale (menu at €22). *Le Jardin d'Hadrien*, 111 rue Enclos-Rey (☎04.66.21.86.65), dishes out inventive southeastern Gard cuisine with both fish and beef-based *plats* at reasonable prices (menus at €17–26), while *Le Bouchon et l'Assiette* (☎04.66.62.02.93; closed Tues & Wed), 5bis rue de Sauve, serves up elaborate *gastronomique* variations on traditional *tarniase* themes (menus from €15–39). Lastly, *Le Magister* (☎04.66.76.11.00; closed Sat noon & Sun) at 5 rue Nationale is an affordable, daringly *gastronomique* restaurant (€30 menu/).

The Pont du Gard and Uzès

Some twenty kilometres northeast from Nîmes, the **Pont du Gard** is the greatest surviving stretch of a fifty-kilometre-long Roman aqueduct built in the middle of the first century to supply fresh water to the city. With just a seventeen-metre difference in altitude between start and finish, the aqueduct was quite an achievement, running as it does over hill and dale, through a tunnel, along the top of a wall, cut into trenches, and over rivers; the Pont du Gard carries it over the River Gard. Today the bridge is something of a tourist trap, but nonetheless a supreme piece of engineering, a brilliant combination of function and aesthetics; indeed, it made the impressionable Rousseau wish he'd been born Roman.

Three tiers of **arches** span the river, with the covered water conduit on the top, rendered with a special plaster waterproofed with a paint apparently based on fig juice. A visit here used to be a must for French journeymen masons on their traditional tour of the country, and many of them have left their names and home towns carved on the stonework. Markings made by the original builders are still visible on individual stones in the arches, such as "FR S III – frons sinistra", front side left no. 3. The Pont du Gard has recently undergone a massive restoration programme and now features an extensive multi-media complex, the **Site de Pont du Gard**, which includes a state-of-the-art musuem (daily: May–Sept 9.30am–7pm; Oct–April 9.30am–5pm; €6), botanical gardens (April to mid-Oct daily 9.30am–6pm; €4), and a range of regular activities aimed at children. With the swimmable waters of the Gardon and ample picnic possibilities available as well, you could easily spend an entire day here.

Uzès

Seventeen kilometres further on, near the start of the aqueduct and served by daily buses from Nîmes, **UZÈS** is a lovely old town perched on a hill above the River Alzon. Half a dozen medieval towers – the most fetching is the windowed Pisa-like **Tour Fenestrelle**, tacked onto the much later cathedral – rise above its tiled roofs and narrow lanes of Renaissance and Neoclassical houses. The latter were the residences of the seventeenth- and eighteenth-century local bourgeoisie, who had grown rich like their Protestant co-religionists in Nîmes on textiles. From the mansion of Le Portalet, with its view out over the valley, walk past the Renaissance church of **St-Étienne** and into the medieval place aux Herbes, where there's a Saturday morning market, and up the arcaded rue de la République. The Gide family used to live off the square, the young André spending summer vacations with his granny there. To the right of rue de la République is the **castle of Le Duché** (90-minute guided tours daily: mid-June to mid-Sept 10am–6.30pm; mid-Sept to mid-June 10am–noon & 2–6pm; €11), still inhabited by the same family a thousand years on, and dominated by

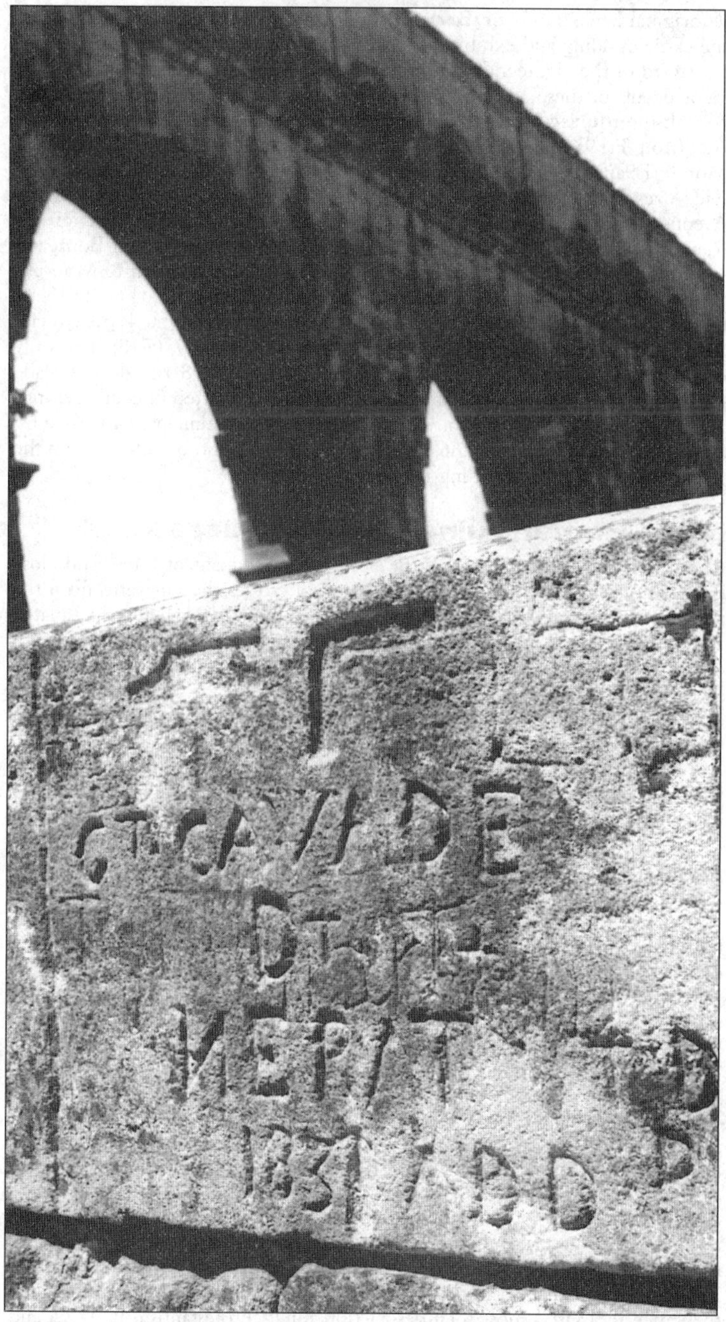

△ Pont du Gard

its original keep, the **Tour Bermonde**. Today, there are guided tours around the castle building and exhibits of local history and vintage cars. Opposite, the courtyard of the eighteenth-century **Hôtel de Ville** holds summer concerts.

For details of these and other summer events, including more bull-running, consult the **tourist office** in place Albert 1er on boulevard Gambetta (July & Aug Mon–Fri 9am–6pm, Sat 10am–noon & 2–5pm, Sun 10am–5pm; Sept–June Mon–Fri 9am–noon & 1.30–6pm, Sat 10am–1pm; ⓣ04.66.22.68.88, ⓦwww.ville-uzes.fr). The **gare routière** (ⓣ04.66.22.00.58) is further west on Avenue de la Libération. Should you need **accommodation**, head for the friendly *Hostellerie Provençal* in two old row houses at 1 rue Grand Bourgade, south of the church of St-Étienne (ⓣ04.66.22.11.06; closed Sun & Mon eve Sept–June & Feb; ❷), or the attractively renovated *La Taverne* (ⓣ04.66.22.13.10, ⓔlataverne.uzes@wanadoo.fr; 4), behind the tourist office at 4 rue Xavier Sigalon, with a good *terroir* restaurant up the road at no. 7 (€18). The only other option in town is the deluxe *General d'Entraigues*, 8 rue de la Calade (ⓣ04.66.22.32.68, ⓦwww.lcm.fr/savry; ❹–❾), in a converted fifteenth-century mansion opposite the cathedral. Alternatively, there's a municipal **campsite** off avenue Maxime-Pascal (ⓣ04.66.22.11.79; closed mid-Sept to mid-June), on the Bagnols-sur-Cèze road running northeast of town.

More Roman ruins and Sommières

About 25km west of Nîmes, off the Sommières road out of Lunel and close to the A9 *autoroute*, the Roman **Via Domitia** crosses the vineyards from the village of Gallargues to the bank of the River Vidourle, where one isolated arch of the original **Roman bridge** remains. On the west bank, a fine stretch of the old **cobbled way** is visible climbing the slopes of the former Roman settlement of **Ambrussum**, a fortified staging post on the road. From the top of the hill you can look down on the modern international traffic still passing the same way, on the *autoroute* and parallel rail line.

About 10km to the north, 28km from Nîmes and still on the Vidourle, the little medieval town of **SOMMIÈRES**, with a much-modified Roman bridge, is where Lawrence Durrell spent the last years of his life. The town itself boasts no major sights, though it's well preserved and atmospheric. However, a visit to the **castle of Villevieille** (May & June daily 2–7pm; July–Sept daily 2–8pm; Oct–April school hols only 2–7pm; €6), on the hillside 3km above Sommières, should not be missed. Owned by the same family for nearly eight hundred years, the castle is full of exquisite antique furniture. There are daily **buses** to Sommières from Nîmes; for **accommodation**, try the *Relais de L'Estelou* (ⓣ04.66.77.71.08, ⓦwww.relaisdelestelou.com; ❹), an arty hotel set in the town's old *gare*, or Colette Labbe's *chambres d'hôtes* in 8 avenue Emile Jamais (ⓣ& ⓕ04.66.77.78.69; ❸). There's also a municipal **campsite** on rue Eugène-Rouch.

Montpellier

A thousand years of trade and intellectual activity have made **MONTPELLIER** a teeming, energetic city. Benjamin of Tudela, the tireless twelfth-century Jewish traveller, reported its streets crowded with traders from every corner of Egypt, Greece, Gaul, Spain, Genoa and Pisa. A few hiccups – like being sold to France in 1349, almost total destruction for its Protestantism in 1622, and depression in the wine trade in the early years of the last century – have done

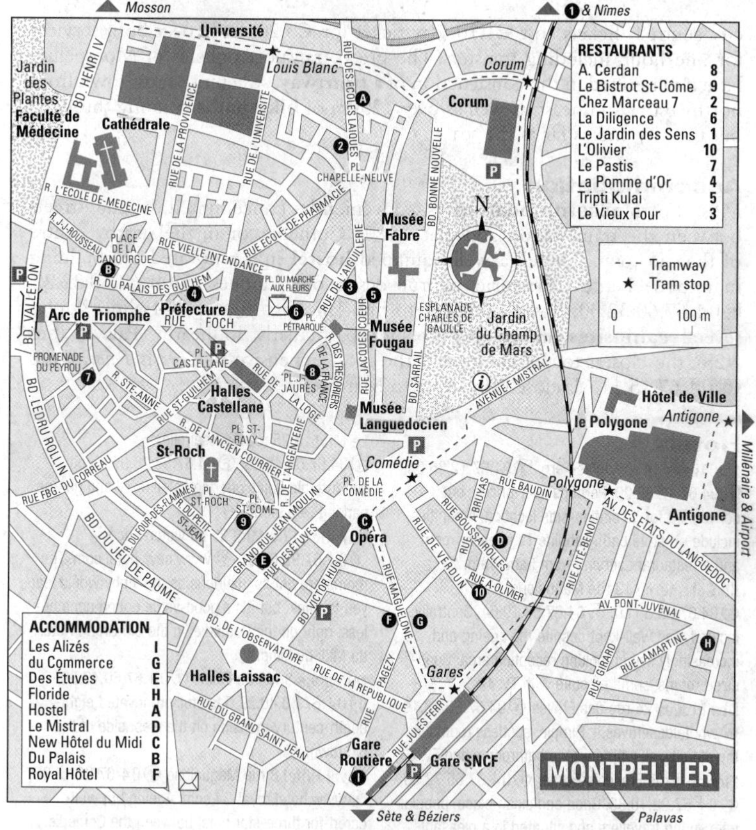

little to dent this progress. Today it vies with Toulouse for the title of most dynamic city in the south. The reputation of its university especially, founded in the thirteenth century and most famous for its medical school, is a long-standing one: more than 60,000 students still set the intellectual and cultural tone of the city – the average age of whose residents is said to be just 25.

Arrival and information

The **gare SNCF** and **gare routière** (Ⓣ04.67.92.01.43) are next to each other at the opposite end of rue Maguelone from the central place de la Comédie. The **airport**, Montpellier-Méditerranée (Ⓣ04.67.20.85.00), is 8km to the southeast beside the Étang de Mauguio; buses run every half-hour from the *gare routière* (hourly; 15min €4.60) and a taxi will cost you €18–25. Much of the city centre is pedestrianized, so you'll have to look further out for places to park: the best areas are Antigone, to the east, and boulevard des Arceaux, to the west.

The **tourist office** (Mon–Fri 9am–6.30pm; July & Aug also Sat 9am–6pm), which has money exchange facilities, lies at the east end of place de la Comédie, opposite the Polygone shopping centre. TAM **city buses** ply between the stations and outer districts (as far as coastal Palavas), while the Petibus traverses the city centre – tickets cost €1.10 (day ticket for €3.20) and cover both services for one hour, including transfers. The green transport policies of Montpellier have also resulted in the construction of a **tramway**, sweeping across town from northwest to southeast, as well as over 120km of **bike paths** running throughout the city and as far as the sea.

Accommodation

Most hotel **accommodation** is conveniently concentrated in the streets between the train station and place de la Comédie, or in the nearby centre of the old town. There's a well-equipped **hostel** in a renovated old building in impasse Petite Corraterie, off rue des Écoles Laïques (Ⓣ04.67.60.32.22, Ⓕ04.67.60.32.30; closed mid-Dec to mid-Jan; bus #6, stop "Ursalines"), plus several **campsites** around Montpellier, particularly in nearby Palavas (bus #28); the closest to the centre and the most expensive is *L'Oasis Palavasienne* (Ⓣ04.67.15.11.61; closed mid-Oct to March).

Hotels

Les Alizés 14 rue Jules-Ferry Ⓣ04.67.12.85.35, Ⓕ04.67.12.85.20. Perhaps over-priced, but convenient for its station-side location. Amenities include en-suite bath, satellite TV in every room, and a restaurant serving from 5am–1am. ❹

du Commerce 13 rue Maguelone Ⓣ04.67.58.36.80, Ⓕ04.67.58.10.64. Centrally located, and well-kept despite the ageing and increasingly seedy-looking reception area. Good-sized rooms, some en suite with TV. ❷

Des Étuves 24 rue des Étuves Ⓣ04.67.60.78.19, Ⓦwhoteldesetuves.fr. Simple, spotless rooms in the old city, all with en-suite bathrooms and TV. ❷

Floride 1 rue François-Perrier Ⓣ04.67.65.73.30, Ⓕ04.67.22.10.83. Good and clean place, popular with young travellers and situated in a pleasant neighbourhood. Some rooms are en suite and all come with TV. ❷

Le Mistral 25 rue Boussairolles Ⓣ04.67.58.45.25, Ⓕ04.67.58.23.95. Good, comfortable hotel, offering satellite TV and garage parking (€5 extra). ❷

New Hôtel du Midi 22 bd Victor-Hugo Ⓣ04.67.92.69.61, Ⓦwww.new-hotel.com. The rooms are not as luxurious as the lobby would lead you to think, but it's a good-value option nonetheless, right on the Comédie, in the old Grand Hôtel du Midi building. ❼

Du Palais 3 rue du Palais Ⓣ04.67.60.47.38, Ⓕ04.67.60.40.23. Tastefully renovated eighteenth-century mansion on the west side of the old town. ❺

Royal Hôtel 8 rue Maguelone Ⓣ04.67.92.13.36, Ⓦwww.hotel.royal-34.com. Ageing but well-cared-for three-star hotel between the Comédie and the gare SNCF. ❸

The City

Montpellier's city centre – the **old town** – is small, compact, architecturally homogeneous, full of charm and teeming with life, except in July and August when the students are on holiday and everyone else is at the beach. And the place is almost entirely pedestrianized, so you can walk the narrow streets without looking anxiously over your shoulder.

Place de la Comédie and the old town

At the hub of the city's life, joining the old part to its newer additions, is **place de la Comédie**, or "L'Oeuf" to the initiated. This colossal, oblong square, paved with cream-coloured marble, has a fountain at its centre and cafés either side. One end is closed by the **Opéra**, an ornate nineteenth-century theatre; the other opens onto the **Esplanade**, a beautiful tree-lined promenade that snakes it's way to the Corum **concert hall**, dug into the hillside and topped off in pink granite, with splendid views from the roof. South of the Corum, the city's most trumpeted museum, the **Musée Fabre**, has closed for major renovation. Visitors may have to wait until 2006 to view its large and historically important collection of seventeenth- to nineteenth-century European painting, including works by Delacroix, Raphael, Jan van Steen and Veronese.

From the north side of L'Oeuf, **rue de la Loge** and **rue Foch**, opened in the 1880s in Montpellier's own Haussmann-izing spree, slice through the heart of the old city. Either side of them, a maze of narrow lanes slopes away to the encircling modern boulevards. Few buildings survive from before the 1622 siege, but the city's busy bourgeoisie quickly made up for the loss, proclaiming their financial power in lots of austere seventeenth- and eighteenth-century mansions. Known as "Lou Clapas" (rubble), the area is rapidly being restored and gentrified. It's a pleasure to wander through and come upon the secretive little squares like place St-Roch, place St-Ravy and place de la Canourgue.

First left off rue de la Loge is **Grande-Rue Jean-Moulin**, where Moulin, hero of the Resistance, lived at no. 21. To the left, at no. 32, the present-day Chamber of Commerce is located in one of the finest eighteenth-century *hôtels*, the Hôtel St-Côme, originally built as a demonstration operating theatre for medical students. On the opposite corner, rue de l'Argenterie forks up to **place Jean-Jaurès**. This square is a nodal point in the city's student life: on fine evenings between 6pm and 7pm you get the impression that the half of the population not in place de la Comédie is sitting here and in the adjacent place du Marché-aux-Fleurs. Through the Gothic doorway of no. 10 of place Jean-Jaurès, is the so-called palace of the kings of Aragon, who ruled Montpellier for a stretch in the thirteenth century. Close by is the **Halles Castellane**, a graceful, iron-framed market hall.

A short walk from place Jean-Jaurès, the Hôtel de Varenne, on place Pétrarque, houses two local history museums of somewhat specialized interest; the **Musée de l'Histoire de Montpellier** (Tues–Sat 9.30am–noon & 1.30–5pm; €1.50) concentrates on the city's history, and the more interesting, private **Musée Fougau** on the top floor (Wed & Thurs 3–6pm; free), deals with the folk history of Languedoc and things Occitan. Off to the right, the lively little rue des Trésoriers-de-France has one of the best seventeenth-century houses in the city, the **Hôtel Lunaret**, at no. 5, while round the block on rue Jacques Coeur you'll find the **Musée Languedocien** (Mon–Sat 2–5pm; €5), which houses a very mixed collection of Greek, Egyptian and other antiquities.

Jardin des Plantes and around

On the hill at the end of rue Foch, from which the royal artillery bombarded the Protestants in 1622, the formal gardens of the **Promenade du Peyrou** look out across the city and away to the Pic St-Loup, which dominates the hinterland behind Montpellier, with the distant smudge of the Cévennes beyond. At the farther end a swagged and pillared water tower marks the end of an eighteenth-century aqueduct modelled on the Pont du Gard. Beneath the grand sweep of its double tier of arches is a daily fruit and veg market and a huge Saturday **flea market**. At the city end of the promenade, a vainglorious **triumphal arch** shows Louis XIV-Hercules stomping on the Austrian eagle and the English lion, tactlessly reminding the locals of his victory over their Protestant "heresy".

Lower down the hill, on boulevard Henri-IV, the lovely but slightly run-down **Jardin des Plantes** (July & Aug daily noon–8pm; Sept–June 2–5pm; free), with avenues of exotic trees, was founded in 1593 and is France's oldest botanical garden. Across the road is the long-suffering **cathedral**, with its massive porch, sporting a patchwork of styles from the fourteenth to the nineteenth centuries. Inside is a memorial to the bishop of Montpellier who sided with the half-million destitute vine-growers who came to demonstrate against their plight in 1907 and were fired on by government troops for their pains. Above the cathedral, in the university's prestigious medical school on rue de l'École-de-Médecine, the **Musée Atger** (Mon, Wed & Thurs 1.30–5.45pm; free) has a distinguished academic collection of French and Italian drawings, while the macabre **Musée d'Anatomie** (daily 2.30–5pm; free) displays all sorts of revolting things in bottles. Close by is the pretty little place de la Canourgue, and, beyond, down rue d'Aigrefeuille, the old university quarter, with some good bookshops on rue de l'Université.

Antigone

South of place de la Comédie stretches the controversial quarter of **Antigone**, a chain of postmodern squares and open spaces designed to provide a mix of fair-rent housing and offices, aligned along a monumental axis from the place du Nombre-d'Or, through place du Millénaire, to the glassed-in arch of the Hôtel de la Région. It's more interesting in scale and design than most attempts at urban renewal, but it has failed to attract the crowds away from the place de la Comédie and is often deserted. The enclosed spaces in particular work well, with their theatrical references to classical architecture, like oversized cornices and columns supporting only sky. The more open spaces are, however, disturbing, with something totalitarian and inhuman about their scale and blandness.

Eating, drinking and entertainment

Montpellier's year-round vitality supports a variety of **restaurants** and **bars** to suit all budgets and tastes. **Cafés** line every square while some of the more expensive restaurants use the city's ancient interiors to stunning effect. And Montpellier's youthful population ensures an energetic bar and nightclub scene right through to the early hours.

There's always plenty of **drinking** activity in the place de la Comédie, place du Marché-aux-Fleurs and place Jean-Jaurès, and two good options are *O'Carolans* Irish pub, south of rue Foch at 5 rue du Petit-Scel, and *Antidote*, a snappy bar on place de la Canourgue, which attracts the arty set. The *Café de la Mer*, at 5 place de Marché-aux-Fleurs, is a popular, gay-friendly establishment with a busy terrace. Still the old perennial for late-night dancing and live gigs is the *Rockstore* near the station at 20 rue de Verdun (Ⓣ04.67.58.70.10), while *Le Crypt*, on place Jean-Jaurès, and *Cargo*, on place St-Denis, offer techno and blues respectively. In addition to clubs and bars, Montpellier has a very lively **theatre** and **music scene**, as well as a tradition of engaging *café-littéraires* on a variety of themes; *Le César* at 17 place Nombre d'Or (Ⓣ04.67.20.27.02) hosts two such cafés, the *café des femmes* and the *café des arts*, held 6.30–8.30pm on the first and third Monday of each month, respectively. For what's on at the various venues, look for posters around town or check the free weekly listings magazines, *Le Sortir* and *Olé*.

Restaurants and cafés

A. Cerdan 8 rue Collot Ⓣ04.67.60.86.96. High-quality cuisine combining Norman and Algerian specialties, just off of the place de la Comedie. Lunch from €8 and dinners from €13–25. Closed Sun and noon Mon

Le Bistrot St-Côme 2 pl St-Côme. The best of a phalanx of open-air eateries dominating the south side of pl St-Côme. Non-stop service from noon–11.30pm and a range of menus and formules of standard but dependable French fare, ranging €12–22.

Chez Marceau 7 pl de la Chapelle Neuve Ⓣ04.67.66.08.09. Excellent-value Languedocian cuisine (both inland and coastal varieties) with a wonderful shaded terrace. The *pâtés du canard* are particularly notable. Menus from €10–20. Closed Sun lunch in summer, otherwise Sun & Wed.

La Diligence 2 place Pétrarque ⓣ04.67.66.12.21. *La Diligence* boasts an atmospheric, vaulted medieval setting perfect for a good-value dip into the finest French cuisine. Menus from €18–58. Closed Sat lunch, Sun & Mon lunch.

Le Jardin des Sens 11 av St-Lazaire t ⓣ04.67.79.63.38. Located just north of Le Corum, this is one of the highest-rated restaurants in Languedoc. Excellent *terroir*-based creations in elegant surroundings. Menus €46–130. Closed Sun, Mon & Wed lunch.

L'Olivier 12 rue Aristide-Olivier ⓣ04.67.92.86.28. Pretty little restaurant north of the station offering excellent-value traditional French cuisine. Menus at €26–43. Closed Sun, Mon and Aug.

Le Pastis 3 rue Terral (ⓣ04.67.02.78.59). Great southern French cooking in a fine old mansion. Lunch menu at €14, dinner from €23. Closed lunch Mon & Sat and all day Sun.

La Pomme d'Or 23 rue du Palais des Guilhem ⓣ04.67.52.82.62. Arty restaurant-bar with a predominantly gay clientele. Featuring inventive menus from €16. Closed Mon.

Salmon Shop 5 rue de la Petite-Loge. An airy establishment, located just off place Jean-Jaurès, with a novel "mountain cabin" interior, and offering oak-smoked salmon main courses in half a dozen guises at around €18. Closed Sun lunch.

Tripti Kulai 20 rue Jacques-Coeur. Quirky vegetarian restaurant, serving dishes with flair, including a good choice of salads. Prices from €7 at lunch, €18 for dinner. Closed Sun.

Le Vieux Four 59 rue de l'Aiguillerie ⓣ04.67.60.55.95. Meat-eaters should head for this cosy, candlelit place specializing in *grillades au feu de bois*. Menus from €19.50–25. Eves only; closed Sun in summer.

Listings

Bike rental Bikes can be rented at Vill'a Vélo at the *gare routière* (ⓣ04.67.92.92.67), or direct from TAM (€6 per day).

Books English books at: As You Like It, 8 rue du Bras de Fer; Book Shop, 4 rue de l'Université. Travel books at: Les Cinq Continents, 20 rue Jacques-Coeur.

Festivals Montpellier is renowned for its cultural life, and hosts a number of annual festivals. Le Printemps des Comédiens (mid-June to mid-July) is a theatre festival; Montpellier Danse (end June to mid-July) is a festival of dance. There's also the music festival, Le Festival de Radio-France et de Montpellier, held in the second half of July, and the Festival du Cinéma Méditerranéen, in the second half of October. The tourist office will provide information about programmes and booking.

Internet There are lots of cybercafés around town; try *Cybersurf*, 22 pl du Millénaire in Antigone (Mon–Fri 8am–9pm, Sat & Sun 10am–6pm).

Markets The best central food markets are Halles Castellane, on rue de la Loge, and Laissac, place A. Laissace (daily 7.30am–1pm). There's also a Sunday morning car boot fair at La Paillade on the city's western outskirts.

Medical emergency ⓣ04.67.22.81.67 or ⓣ15; Centre Hospitallier de Montpellier, 555 rte de Ganges (ⓣ04.67.33.93.02) – take bus #16 from the gare to "Route de ganges" or the tram to "Hôpital Lapeyronie" and walk.

Post office The main office is on place Rondelet, 34000 Montpellier (Mon–Fri 9am–7pm, Sat 9am–noon).

Shopping The most convenient place is the Polygone mall, which contains a FNAC and Galeries Lafayette.

Swimming The nearest beaches for a dip are at Palavas (tram direction "Odysseum" to Port Marianne, then bus #28), but the best are slightly to the west of the town.

The coast: Aigues-Mortes to Agde

On the face of it the **Languedoc coast** isn't particularly enticing, lined with bleak beaches and treeless strands, often irritatingly windswept and cut off from their hinterland by marshy *étangs* (lagoons). But the area does have long hours of sunshine, 200km of sand still only sporadically populated and relatively unpolluted water. Resort towns – mostly geared towards families who settle in for a few weeks at a time – have sprung up, sometimes engulfing once quiet fishing towns, but there's still enough unexploited territory to make this coast a good getaway from the crowds, and many of the old towns have managed to sustain their character and traditions despite the summer onslaught.

La Grande-Motte, Le Grau-du-Roi and Aigues-Mortes

First-built of the new resorts, on the fringes of the Camargue, **LA GRANDE-MOTTE** is a 1960s vintage beach-side Antigone – a "futuristic" planned community which has aged as gracefully as the bean bag and eight-track tape. In summer, its seaside and streets are crowded with semi-naked bodies; in winter, it's a depressing, wind-battered place with few permanent residents. If you plan on **staying**, both *Camping Louis Pibols* (Ⓣ04.67.56.50.08; closed Nov–March) and *Camping le Garden* (Ⓣ04.67.56.50.09; closed Nov–Feb) offer excellent facilities and are just a couple of minutes' walk from the beach.

A little way east are Port-Camargue, with a sprawling, modern marina, and **LE GRAU-DU-ROI**, which manages to retain something of its character as a working fishing port. Tourist traffic still has to give way every afternoon at 4.30pm when the swing bridge opens and lets in the trawlers to unload the day's catch onto the quayside, from where it's whisked off to auction – *la criée* – conducted today largely by electronic means rather than the harsh-voiced shouting of former times. For a reasonable place to **stay**, try the *Hôtel Quai d'Azur*, on rue du Vidourle, near the harbour entrance (Ⓣ04.66.51.41.94, Ⓕ04.66.53.41.94; ❷; closed mid-Nov to April), or the huge *Camping L'Eden* (Ⓣ04.66.51.49.81; closed Nov–Feb), just east of town.

Eight kilometres inland lies the appealingly named town of **AIGUES-MORTES** ("dead waters"), built as a fortress port by Louis IX in the thirteenth century for his departure on the Seventh Crusade. Its massive walls and towers remain virtually intact. Outside the ramparts, amid drab modern development, flat salt pans lend a certain otherworldly appeal, but inside all is geared to the tourist. If you visit, consider a climb up the **Tour de Constance** on the northwest corner of the town walls (daily: May–Aug 10am–6pm; Sept–April 10am–1pm & 2–4.30pm; €6), where Camisard women were imprisoned (Marie Durand was incarcerated for 38 years), and a walk along the wall, where you can gaze out over the weird mist-shrouded flats of the Camargue.

Palavas and Maguelone

A dozen kilometres south of the city by road, **PALAVAS** is the bathing station for the citizens of Montpellier – a concrete sprawl with little to recommend it apart from the presence of the sea, though there's plenty of summertime activity in the discos and the rip-off quayside bars and restaurants. The best place to swim and sunbathe is a little way to the west off the long flat strand that borders the marsh, where some of Europe's few flamingos feed, and herons, egrets and other sea birds squabble and dive. Here also is the **Cathédrale de Maguelone** (daily 9am–7pm), dating mainly from the twelfth century, pale and grey and fortress-like on an island of vines and pines in the middle of the marsh. In the Middle Ages there was a thriving town here, and its cathedral was declared by Urban II to be "second only to that of Rome". However, the cathedral is all that remains of the settlement, which was largely destroyed by Louis XIII because of its Protestant leanings. Cavernous and cool, the strong, simple church interior serves as the venue for a music festival in the second half of June.

Sète

Some 28km southeast of Montpellier, twenty minutes away by train, **SÈTE** has been an important port for three hundred years. The upper part of the town straddles the slopes of the Mont St-Clair, which overlooks the vast Bassin de Thau, breeding ground of mussels and oysters, while the lower part is intersected by waterways lined with tall terraces and seafood restaurants. It has a lively workaday bustle in addition to its tourist activity, at its height during the summer *joutes nautiques* (see box below).

The crowded and vibrant pedestrian streets are scattered with café tables. A short climb up from the harbour is the **cimetière marin**, the sailors' cemetery, where poet Paul Valéry is buried. A native of the town, he called Sète his "singular island", and the **Musée Paul Valéry**, in rue Denoyer (Wed–Sun 10am–noon & 2–6pm; €3.05), opposite the cemetery, has a room devoted to him, as well as a small but strong collection of modern French paintings. If you're feeling energetic, you should keep going up the hill, through the pines to the top, for a view that's fabulous when it's not engulfed in sea mist. Below the sailors' cemetery, and neatly poised above the water, is Vauban's **Fort St-Pierre**, now home to an open-air theatre. Over on the west side of the hill, George Brassens, associate of Sartre and the radical voice of a whole French generation, is buried in the Cimetière le Py, in spite of his song *Plea to be Buried on the Beach at Sète*. In **Éspace Brassens** (Tues–Sun: July & Aug 10am–noon & 2–7pm; June & Sept 10am–noon & 2–6pm; €5 – French-only voice-recorded commentary), overlooking the cemetery, the locally born singer-songwriter lives again through his words and music, narrating his life-story in French on the museum's headsets. Closer to the centre of town you'll find the quirky new **Musée International des Arts Modestes** (Wed–Mon 10–noon & 2–6pm; €5) at 23 quai Maréchal-Lattre, containing a collection of art made from cast-off goods and spinning on popular culture themes.

Practicalities

The **gare routière** is awkwardly placed on quai de la République, and the **gare SNCF** further out still on quai Maréchal-Joffre – though it is on the main bus route, which circles Mont St-Clair (last bus about 7pm). **Ferries** for Morocco (1–2 weekly) and Mallorca (1–3 weekly) depart from the gare maritime at 4 quai d'Alger (Ⓣ04.67.46.68.00). Be warned that **hitching** out of Sète is horribly difficult; you're better off taking a train or bus to the nearest town and trying from there. The **tourist office**, at 60 Grand'Rue Mario-Roustan (July & Aug Mon–Sat 10am–1pm & 3–8pm, Sun 10am–1pm; Sept Mon–Fri 9.30am–noon & 2.30–6pm, Sat 9.30am–noon; Oct–June Mon, Wed & Fri 9.30am–noon & 2.30–6pm, Sat 9.30am–noon; Ⓣ04.67.74.71.71, Ⓦwww.ville-sete.fr), has a good array of English-language information.

Joutes nautiques

Water-jousting is a venerable coastal tradition which pits boat-borne jousting teams against each other in an effort to unseat their opponents. The sport consists of two sleek boats, each manned by eight oarsmen and bearing a lance-carrying jouster, charging at each other on a near head-on course. As the boats approach, the jousters attempt to strike their adversary from his mount. There are about a dozen *sociétés des joutes* in Sète itself, and you can see them in action all through the summer.

For **accommodation**, try the decaying but funky *Grand Hôtel de Paris* (Ⓣ04.67.74.98.10; closed Oct–April; ❸) at 2 rue Frédéric-Mistral. For somewhere more comfortable, there's the Belle Époque splendour of the *Grand Hôtel,* 17 quai de Lattre-de-Tassigny (Ⓣ04.67.74.71.77, Ⓦwww.sete-hotel.com; ❺), and *L'Orque Bleu* at 10 quai Aspirant-Herber (Ⓣ04.67.74.72.13, Ⓔlorque-bleue@wanadoo.fr; ❸). The **HI hostel** (March–Nov; Ⓣ04.67.53.46.68, Ⓕ04.67.51.34.01) is high up in the town on rue Général-Revest. Campers should ask the tourist office for details of the numerous campsites in the area.

There's a barrage of **restaurants** along quai Général-Duran, from the Pont de la Savonnerie right down to the fish market at the mouth of the pleasure port, all offering seafood in the €12–28 bracket. *Le Toit de Calou*, just south of the tourist office at 82 Grand'rue (closed Sun; Ⓣ04.67.74.04.24), offers some respite – a dark and cosy place with à la carte selections from €15 and a good cellar of regional wine. For a more upscale seafood meal, try *La Galinette*, 26 place des Mouettes (Ⓣ04.67.51.16.77; closed Sun eve, Fri lunch & Sat lunch out of season; menus from €35), on the north side of town.

Agde and around

Midway between Sète and Béziers, at the western end of the Bassin de Thau, **AGDE** is historically the most interesting of the coastal towns. Originally Phoenician, and maintained by the Romans, it thrived for centuries on trade with the Levant. Outrun as a seaport by Sète, it later degenerated into a sleepy fishing harbour.

Today, it's a major tourist centre with a good deal of charm, notably in the narrow back lanes between rue de l'Amour and the riverside, where fishing boats tie up. The town's most distinctive and surprising feature is its colour – black – from the volcanic stone of the Mont St-Loup quarries. There are few sights apart from the impressively fortified **cathedral**, though the **waterfront** is attractive, and by the bridge you can watch the Canal du Midi slip quietly and modestly into the River Hérault on the very last leg of its journey from Toulouse to the Bassin de Thau and Sète.

The **tourist office** is in place Molière near the bridge (July & Aug daily 9am–7pm; Sept–June Mon–Sat 9am–noon & 2–6pm; Ⓣ04.67.94.29.68, Ⓔot-agde@wanadoo.fr). Of the town's **hotels** *La Galoite* (Ⓣ04.67.94.45.58, Ⓦwww.lagaliote.fr; ❷–❺), located in the old bishop's palace on place J.-Jaurès, is the best, while *Le Donjon* (Ⓣ04.67.94.12.32, Ⓦwww.hotelledonjon.com; ❸) in another atmospheric old building next door comes a close second. For cheaper but still comfortable rooms, try *Hôtel des Arcades* (Ⓣ04.67.94.21.64; ❷), in an old convent at 16 rue Louis-Bages. Aside from the numerous places to **eat** around La Promenade, a good bet is *La Fine Fourchetté* (Ⓣ04.67.94.49.56) at 2 rue du Mont-Saint-Loup, featuring a delightfully intriguing *carte* (menus from €10). The area's finest restaurant is *La Tramissière* (Ⓣ04.67.94.20.87; bus #275 from the main road through town; closed Nov–March & frequently Sun & Mon), a *gastronomique* halfway between Agde and Grau on the far bank of the Hérault (€27.50 and up; rooms here ❹–❾)

An hourly **bus service** operates between the town and the sea at **Cap d'Agde** (see below); you can pick it up at the *gare SNCF* at the end of avenue Victor-Hugo, at the bridge and on La Promenade. Should you want to explore the Canal du Midi, boat trips are organized by Bateaux du Soleil, 6 rue Chassefières (Ⓣ04.67.94.08.79).

Cap d'Agde

CAP D'AGDE lies to the south of Mont St-Loup, 7km from Agde. The largest (and by far the most successful) of the newer resorts, it sprawls laterally from the volcanic mound of St-Loup in an excess of pseudo-traditional modern buildings that offer every type of facility and entertainment – all expensive. It is perhaps best known for its colossal **quartier naturiste**, one of the largest in France, with the best of the beaches, space for 20,000 visitors, and its own restaurants, banks, post offices and shops. Access is possible, though expensive, if you're not actually staying there (€9 per car, €2.80 on foot; both until 8pm only).

If you have time to fill, head for the **Musée de l'Éphèbe** (July & Aug daily 9am–12.30pm & 2.30–6.30pm; Sept–June Wed–Sat 9am–noon & 2–6pm, Sun 2–6pm; €3.80), which displays antiquities discovered locally, many of them from beneath the sea. Alternatively, the **Fort de Brescou** (mid-June to Aug; €2.50), which dates back to 1680, lies on a rocky, seagull-infested island just off shore; it can be reached by ferries departing from the centre port at Cap d'Agde or from Grau d'Agde (Mon, Tues & Thurs–Sun 10.30am, 2.30pm & 6.30pm; €7).

Inland from Montpellier

For getting out into the country of the Bas Languedoc, there are two good routes from Montpellier, both served by regular buses: the D986 to **Ganges** and the N109 to **Lodève**.

The Ganges route

The Ganges road weaves north across the Plateau des Garrigues, a landscape of scrubby trees, thorns and fragrant herbs cut by torrent beds. The plateau is dominated by the high limestone ridge of the **Pic St-Loup** until you reach the first worthwhile stopping place, **ST-MARTIN-DE-LONDRES**, 25km on, whose name derives from the old Celtic word for "swamp". It's a lovely little town of arcaded houses and cobbled passageways set around the roadside place de la Fontaine. Pride of the place is an exceptionally handsome early Romanesque **church**, reached through a vaulted passage just uphill from the square. The honey-coloured stone is simply decorated with Lombard arcading, the plain rounded porch with a worn relief of St Martin on horseback, while the interior has an unusual clover-shaped ground plan. There's no hotel, only a **gîte**, *La Bergerie du Bayle* (Ⓣ & Ⓕ04.67.55.72.16, ❶), which also serves good-value meals. The **campsite**, *Pic de Loup* (Ⓣ04.67.55.00.53; closed Oct–March), sits just east of town on the main road.

About 6km south, off the Gignac road near Viols-le-Fort (on the bus route) and the Château de Cambous, there's a marvellous **prehistoric village** (April –June & Sept Sat & Sun 2–6pm: July & Aug Tues, Wed & Fri–Sun 2–7pm; Oct–March Sun 2–6pm; €2.50), dating from 2500 BC and only discovered in 1967. The site consists of a group of cabins, each about 20m long, their outlines clearly delineated, with the holes for the roof supports and the door slabs still in place. A reconstruction shows them to have been much like the sheep stalls in the old *bergeries* that dot the plateau.

Further north, through dramatic river gorges almost as far as Ganges, you reach the **Grotte des Demoiselles** (daily: July & Aug 9am–7pm; April–June & Sept 9am–noon & 2–6pm; Oct–March 9.30am–noon & 2–5pm; Ⓦwww.Demoiselles.com; €7.50), the most spectacular of the region's many caves: a

The Camisards

By issuing the Revocation of the Edict of Nantes in 1685, Louis XIV ended religious freedom in France, outlawing the Calvanist Protestantism of the Hugenots. Some five hundred thousand chose to flee the country, including many merchants and textile workers, while those who remained were subjected to **oppression**; some feigned conversion, some were deported to the colonies, and others fled to the "desert" – the wild and isolated hills of the Cèvennes. It was here that they staged the **Camisard** revolt, so-called for the shirts they wore as a sign of recognition (from "chemise," French for "shirt").

In July 1702, the parish priest of Chayla arrested a small group of fugitive Protestants, and was killed in the ensuing struggle. Knowing that retribution would be swift and cruel, Protestants across the Cèvennes began a guerrilla war which pitted their forces, numbering between three and five thousand, against some thirty thousand royal troops. Unable to conclude the struggle militarily against the rebel guerrillas, the French army succeeded in bribing one of the leaders to change sides, precipitating the defeat of the movement in 1704.

set of vast cathedral-like caverns hung with stalactites descending with millennial slowness to meet the limpid waters of eerily still pools. Located deep inside the mountain, it's reached by funicular (hourly departures).

Ganges

GANGES itself, 46km from Montpellier and also connected by regular buses (which continue to Le Vigan on the southern edge of the Cévennes), is a rather nondescript but busy market town (Friday's the day), whose old quarter is notable for its vaulted alleys designed for defence in the Wars of Religion. This, too, was a Protestant town, peopled by refugees from the plains, who made it famous for its silk stockings. It was here that the last-ditch revolt of the Camisards (see box, above) earned its name; the rebels sacked and pillaged a shirt factory and went off wearing the shirts (*chemises/camises*). Heading north from Ganges on your own steam will lead you deeper into Protestant territory, to the Huguenot villages around Le Vigan (see p.970).

The **tourist office** (Mon–Fri 10am–noon & 2–6pm, Sat 10am–noon; Ⓣ04.67.73.00.56, Ⓦwww.otcevennesmediterranee.com) is on plan de l'Ormeau. On the same square you'll find the basic *De la Poste* (closed Jan; Ⓣ04.67.73.85.88, Ⓔhotel.dela.poste@wanadoo.fr; ❷), the best overnight choice in town. Just outside the town, on the road towards Navacelles, is the beautifully sited *Hotel des Gorges de Vis* (Ⓣ04.67.73.85.05; ❷), a good option if you have transport. The **campsite** *Auberge du Montolieu* lies on the route de Vigan on the edge of town. For somewhere to **eat**, try *Le Josyln' Melodie* (Ⓣ04.67.73.66.02; closed Wed; menus €7.35 at lunch, €12.50 at dinner), a homely little Lyonnais place at 4 place Fabre d'Olivet.

The Lodève route

The second inland route runs due west from Montpellier, passing **Gignac** – the turn-off for the spectacular **Gorges de l'Hérault** and **St-Guilhem-le-Désert** – before reaching **Clermont-l'Hérault**, a transport hub from where you can access the Haut Languedoc to the west or the old cathedral town of **Lodève** further north.

Gignac and Aniane

The small town of **GIGNAC** lies amid vineyards 30km west of Montpellier, and boasts a fine eighteenth-century bridge spanning the Hérault. There's just one **hotel**, the modern *Motel Vieux Moulin* (Ⓣ04.67.57.57.95, Ⓕ04.67.57.69.19; ❸) beside the river next door to *Camping du Pont* (Ⓣ04.67.57.52.40). For more upmarket accommodation, head 5km north to the town of **ANIANE**, home to the imposing classical church of St-Sauveur and the *Hostellerie St-Benoît* (Ⓣ04.67.57.71.63, Ⓔhostellerie.st-benoit@wanadoo.fr; ❸; closed late Dec to mid-Feb), which has a pool and a good restaurant (€16). Three kilometres further on is the eleventh-century **Pont du Diable**, supposedly the earliest medieval bridge in the country. The narrowest part of the Hérault gorge begins here.

St-Guilhem-le-Désert and around

The glorious abbey and village of **ST-GUILHEM-LE-DÉSERT** lies in a side ravine, 6km further north from the Pont du Diable. A ruined castle spikes the ridge above, and the ancient tiled houses of the village ramble down the banks of the rushing Verdus, which is everywhere channelled into carefully tended gardens. The grand focus is the tenth- to twelfth-century **abbey church**, founded at the beginning of the ninth century by St Guilhem, comrade-in-arms of Charlemagne. The church is a beautiful and atmospheric building, though architecturally impoverished by the dismantling and sale of its cloister – now in New York – in the nineteenth century. It stands on place de la Liberté, surrounded by honey-coloured houses and arcades with traces of Romanesque and Renaissance domestic styles in some of the windows. The interior of the church is plain and somewhat severe compared to the warm colours of the exterior, best seen from rue Cor-de-Nostra-Dama/Font-du-Portal, where you get the classic view of the perfect apse.

There are a couple of easy and worthwhile **walks** you can make from here – up the valley of the Verdus into the red-stained walls of the **Cirque du Bout-du-Monde** (from place de la Liberté, take rue du Bout-du-Monde out of the village and continue for about 30min), or up the zigzagging path of the GR74, through the sweet-scented shrubs and flowers towards the castle ridge (also about 30min). From the crest of the ridge the view down onto the village is magnificent. The path divides here: one branch leads back right to the ruins of the castle, while the other continues along the GR74 to the Ermitage Notre-Dame-de-Belle-Grâce (90min), and on to join the GR7 at St-Maurice-Navacelles on the Causse de Larzac.

In season the village is on every tour operator's route, making early mornings and late afternoons the best times for visiting. A number of **gîtes** in and around St-Guilhem can put you up for the night, including the English-speaking *Gîte de la Tour* (Ⓣ & Ⓕ04.67.57.34.00), located in a medieval tower in the village, and the CAF *gîte* (Ⓣ04.67.52.72.11), also in town. The nearest **campsite** is *Le Moulin de Siau* (Ⓣ04.67.57.51.08; closed mid-Sept to mid-June), near Aniane on the road back down to Gignac. Nearby, cave enthusiasts will enjoy the **Grotte de Clamouse** (daily: July & Aug 10am–7pm; June & Sept 10am–6pm; Feb–May & Oct 10am–5pm; Nov–Jan noon–5pm; €6.80). This extensive and beautiful stalactite cave is entered along a subterranean river and opens up into three expansive grottos.

Clermont-l'Hérault

Eight kilometres west of Gignac, the market town of **CLERMONT-L'HÉRAULT** – accessible by bus from Montpellier – is a rather dull little cantonal capital, whose only recommendation is that it is a good jumping-off point for visiting the area around **Lac Salagou** to the west, an attractive man-made reservoir sited amidst striking iron-rich terrain. The sole interesting site in town is a thirteenth-century **church**, fortified in the fourteenth century to defend it against the English.

The **tourist office** (Mon–Sat 9am–noon & 2–6pm, Sun 10am–noon; ⓣ04.67.96.23.86, ⓦwww.clermont-herault.fr) is at 9 rue René-Gosse, close to the cathedral. By far the best place to stay is *Le Terminus*, on allées Roger-Salengro, near the old station (ⓣ04.67.88.45.00, ⓔleterminus@wanadoo.fr; ❷). If you're camping, head for the year-round site *Le Salagou* (ⓣ04.67.96.13.13), northwest of Clermont near the lake. Reasonable **meals** can be had at Clermont-Ferrand at *L'Arlequin*, tucked under the south wall of the church on place St-Paul (closed Sun & Mon; menus from €14).

Around Clermont-l'Hérault

Three kilometres west from Clermont-l'Hérault, along the main road to Bédarieux, lies **VILLENEUVETTE**, a model factory and workers' settlement created in the seventeenth century for the production of high-quality wool for sale in the Mediterranean. Initially successful, the factory eventually closed down in 1954, but the settlement still boasts 85 inhabitants. There's a very nice, if somewhat pricey, **hotel** tacked on to the village walls – *La Source* (ⓣ04.67.96.05.07, ⓦwww.hotellasource.com; ❸; closed Jan to mid-Feb & late Nov), with a good restaurant (from €17–28), pool and garden. Eight kilometres further west just off the Bédarieux road, in the picturesque little village of **MOURÈZE**, you'll find an alternative hotel, *Les Hauts de Mourez* (ⓣ04.67.94.04.84, ⓕ04.67.96.25.85; ❹; closed Nov–March). Further accommodation options are available in **SALASC**, at the *Auberge Campagnard* (ⓣ & ⓕ04.67.96.15.62; 3 with breakfast), and at **OCTON** in the comfortable old hotel *La Calade* (ⓣ & ⓕ04.67.96.19.21; ❸; closed mid-Dec to April) in the village centre (closed Tues & Wed out of season; menus from €15).

Three other interesting and little-visited places wast of Clermont are only feasible if you have a car. The first is a very fine **dolmen** on the end of a low ridge overlooking the D32 – best reached from the village of **LE POUGET**, where it is signposted. Continuing along the D139, you come within sight of the pale grey ruins of the keep and chapel of the **Château d'Aumelas**, romantically silhouetted on the edge of the *causse* (limestone plateau). To reach it by road – considerably further – you need to bear right onto the D114 and then take a dirt track opposite a farm. It's a beautiful and silent place, and the chapel is in near-perfect condition. Two kilometres further along the D114, down an unsigned and bumpy track leading right onto the *causse*, there is a marvellous and remote silvery chapel, **St-Martin-de-Cardonnet**, built in the twelfth century – all that remains of an ancient priory.

On to Lodève

Heading north from Clermont to **LODÈVE**, 19km away, the swift A75 *autoroute* brings heavy traffic down from Clermont-Ferrand. It passes through countryside further scarred by uranium mining – the area around the village of St-Martin-du-Bosc has some of the highest soil concentration of radioactivity in the world.

Lodève, entirely enclosed by vine-terraced hills at the confluence of the Lergues and Soulondres rivers, is almost in the shadow of the **Causse de Larzac**. There are no real sights here, but it's a pleasant, old-fashioned place to pause on your way up to Le Caylar or La Couvertoirade on the *causse*. The

cathedral – a stop on the pilgrim route to Santiago de Compostela – is worth a look, as is the unusual World War I **Monument aux Morts**, in the adjacent park, by local sculptor Paul Dardé; more of his work is on display at the town **museum** in the Hôtel Fleury (Tues–Sun 9.30am–12.30pm & 2–6pm; €6) and the **Halle Dardé** (daily 9am–7pm; free) in the place du Marché. With a bit of organizing it's also possible to visit the **Atelier National de Tissage de Tapis** (Tues–Thurs 2–6pm; €3.20; call ahead ⓣ04.67.96.40.40), on the outskirts of Lodève, where priceless Gobelins tapestries are woven.

The **tourist office** is at 7 place de la République (Mon–Fri 9am–noon & 2–6pm, Sat 9am–5pm & July & Aug only also Sun 9.30am–1.30pm; ⓣ04.67.88.86.44, ⓦwww.lodeve.com), next door to the **gare routière**, where you can catch buses to Montpellier, Béziers, Millau, Rodez and St-Afrique. The best place to **stay** in town is the *Hôtel du Nord* (ⓣ & ⓕ04.67.44.10.08, ⓦwww.hotellodeve.com; ❷) at 18 bd de la Liberté, or the family-run *Hôtel de la Paix* (ⓣ04.67.44.07.46, ⓔhotel-de-la-paix@wanadoo.fr; ❸; closed Feb to mid-March;) on 11 bd Montalangue. There's a big **market** on Saturdays, and three times a week in summer local farmers bring in their produce.

Southern Languedoc

Southern Languedoc presents an exciting and varied landscape, its coastal flats stretching south from the mouth of the Aude towards Perpignan, interrupted by occasional low, rocky hills. Just inland sits **Béziers**, its imposing cathedral set high above the languid River Orb, girded on the north by the amazingly preserved Renaissance town of **Pézenas** and on the south by the ancient pre-Roman settlement of the **Ensérune**. It's also a gateway to the spectacular uplands of the **Monts de l'Espinouse** and the **Parc Naturel Régional du Haut Languedoc**, a haven for ramblers. Just south of Béziers, the ancient Roman capital of **Narbonne** guards the mouth of the Aude. Following the course of this river, which is shadowed by the historic **Canal du Midi**, you arrive at the quintessential medieval citadel, the famous fortress-town of **Carcassonne**. Once a shelter for renegade Cathar heretics, Carcassonne is also a fine departure point for the Cathar castles – a string of romantically ruined castles covered on pp.848–850.

Béziers and around

Though no longer the rich city of its nineteenth-century heyday, **BÉZIERS** has risen out of its recent dreariness with admirable panâche. The town is the capital of the Languedoc wine country and a focus for the Occitan movement, as well as being the birthplace of Resistance hero Jean Moulin. The fortunes of the movement and the vine have long been closely linked; Occitan activists have helped to organize the militant local vine-growers, and there were ugly events during the mid-1970s, when blood was shed in violent confrontations with the authorities over the importation of cheap foreign wines and the low prices paid for the essentially poor-grade local product. Things are calmer now, as the conservatism of Languedoc farmers has given way to more modern attitudes in the face of public demand for something better than the traditional table wine. As a result, some of the steam has also gone out of the movement; interest today is more in the culture than in anti-Paris separatist feelings. The town is also home to two great Languedocian adopted traditions: English **rugby** and the Spanish **corrida**, both of which are followed with a passion. The best time to visit is during the mid-August **feria**, a raucous four-day party that can be enjoyed even if bullfighting isn't to your taste.

The City

The finest view of the old town is from the west, as you come in from Carcassonne: crossing the willow-lined River Orb by the Pont-Neuf, you can look upstream at the sturdy arches of the **Pont-Vieux**, above which rises a steep-banked hill crowned by the **Cathédrale St-Nazaire**, resembling a castle more than a church with its crenellated towers. The best approach to the cathedral is up the medieval lanes at the end of Pont-Vieux, rue Canterelles and passage Canterellettes. Its architecture is mainly Gothic, the original building having been burnt in 1209 during the sacking of Béziers, when Armand Amaury's crusaders massacred some seven thousand people at the church of the Madeleine for refusing to hand over about twenty Cathars. "Kill them all," the pious abbot is said to have ordered, "God will recognize his own!"

From the top of the cathedral **tower**, there's a superb view out across the vine-dominated surrounding landscape. Next door, you can wander through the ancient **cloister** (daily: May–Sept 10am–7pm; Oct–April 10am–noon & 2–5pm; free) and out into the shady **bishop's garden** overlooking the river. In the adjacent **place de la Révolution**, a monument commemorates the people who died resisting Napoléon III's *coup d'état* in 1851 and their leader, Mayor Casimir Péret, who was shipped off to Cayenne where he drowned in a Papillon-style escape attempt. Also on the square, the Hôtel Fabrégat houses a **Musée des Beaux-Arts** (Tues–Fri 9am–noon & 2–6pm; €2.35), which, apart from an interesting collection of Greek Cycladic vases, won't keep you long. Nearby, **Hôtel Fayet**, at 9 rue Capus (same hours and ticket), has been pressed into service as an annexe to the museum, though it's as much of interest for its period interiors as its collection of nineteenth- and early twentieth-century art and works by local sculptor, Jean-Antoine Injalbert.

The city's other museum, the **Musée du Biterrois**, in the old St-Jacques barracks on avenue de la Marne near the train station (Tues–Sun: July & Aug 9am–7pm; Sept–June 9am–noon & 2–6pm; €3.10), displays a variety of entertaining exhibits, ranging from Greek amphorae and nineteenth-century door knockers to distilling manuals, clogs and winepresses. You might also take a look at the remains of the modest **Roman amphitheatre** two streets to the north of the museum off of rue St-Jacques, which at the time of writing was being developed as an open-air museum. Once having a capacity of over 13,000 spectators, its stones were used to construct the medieval walls. Away from the medieval streets round the cathedral, the centre of life in Béziers is the **allées Paul-Riquet**, a broad, leafy esplanade lined with cafés, crêpes stalls, restaurants, banks and shops; it's named after the seventeenth-century tax collector who lost health and fortune in his obsession with building the Canal du Midi to join the Atlantic and the Mediterranean. Laid out in the last century, the *allées* runs from an elaborate nineteenth-century theatre on place de la Victoire to the gorgeous little park of the **Plateau des Poètes**, whose ponds, palms and lime trees were laid out in the so-called English manner by the man who created the Bois de Boulogne in Paris.

Practicalities

From the **gare SNCF** on boulevard Verdun, the best way into town is through the landscaped gardens of the Plateau des Poètes opposite the station entrance and up the allées Paul-Riquet. The **gare routière** is in place de Gaulle, at the northern end of the allées, while the **tourist office** is in the new Palais des Congrès at 29 avenue Saint-Saëns (July & Aug Mon–Sat 9am–7pm, Sun 9.30am–12.30pm; Sept–June Mon–Sat 9am–noon & 2–6pm; ⓣ04.67.76.47.00, ⓦwww.ville-beziers.fr).

For a central place to **stay**, the cheapest option is the clean but run-down *Angleterre*, 22 place Jean-Jaurès (ⓣ04.67.28.48.42, ⓔhotelangleterre@voila.fr; ❶). Good alternatives include the *Hôtel des Poètes*, 80 allées Paul-Riquet (ⓣ04.67.76.38.66, ⓕ04.67.76.25.88; ❷), at the southern end of the boulevard overlooking the gardens, the smarter *Hôtel du Théâtre*, 13 rue Coquille (ⓣ04.67.49.13.43, ⓕ04.67.49.31.58; ❷), right beside the municipal theatre, and the new *France* (ⓣ04.67.28.44.72, ⓦwww.hotel2france.com; ❷) at 36 rue Boiëdieu. The town's deluxe option, *Hôtel Imperator* (ⓣ04.67.49.02.25, ⓦwww.hotel-Imperator.com; ❸), stands at 28 allées Paul-Riquet. There's no **campsite** in town, but you'll find one at nearby Villeneuve-lez-Béziers (ⓣ04.67.39.36.09; closed Nov–Feb).

A string of **restaurants** with patios are lined along the west side of Allées Paul Riquet serving the usual steak-frîtes type menus for about €12. Better fare can be found in the old quarter, especially on rue Viennet; the best choice may be *Le Petit Table* at no. 12, where you can enjoy an excellent home-cooked meal for €11, including wine; the elegant *Le Cep d'Or*, at no. 7, is a bit pricier and serves mostly seafood (closed Sun eve & Mon; menus from €15–20). *L'Ambassade* (ⓣ04.67.76.06.24; closed Sun & Mon), at 22 boulevard de Verdun is one of the town's best places (menus from €25), while *Le Bistrot des Halles*, further north on place de la Madeleine behind the market square, is popular for its varied, well-priced menus (closed Sun & Mon; from €15).

Béziers has one of the star **rugby** clubs in France, A.S.B.H., based at the Stade de la Méditerranée in the eastern suburbs (ⓣ04.67.11.03.76). If you fancy pottering along the Canal du Midi, you can rent **bikes** at La Maison du Canal (ⓣ04.67.62.18.18) beside the Port Neuf, south of the gare SNCF.

Pézenas

PÉZENAS lies 18km east of Béziers on the old N9. Market centre of the coastal plain, it looks across to rice fields and shallow lagoons, hazy in the heat and dotted with pink flamingos. The town was catapulted to glory when it became the seat of the parliament of Languedoc and the residence of its governors in 1465, and it reached its zenith in the late seventeenth century when the prince Armand de Bourbon made it a "second Versailles". The legacy of this illustrious past can be seen in the town's exquisite array of fourteenth- to seventeenth-century mansions.

The town also plays up its association with **Molière**, who visited several times with his troupe in the mid-seventeenth century, when he enjoyed the patronage of Prince Armand. He put on his own plays at the **Hôtel d'Alfonce** on rue Conti, including the first performance of *Le Médecin Volant*, according to local tradition. The building is now privately owned, but in summer you can visit the courtyard that served as Molière's theatre (June–Sept Mon–Sat

10am–noon & 3–7pm; €2). When in town, he lodged at the Maison du Barbier-Gély in the unspoiled **place Gambetta**, today occupied by the **tourist office** (July & Aug Mon–Tues, Thurs & Sat 9am–7pm, Wed & Fri 9am–10pm, Sun 10am–7pm; Sept–June Mon–Sat 9am–noon & 2–6pm & Sun 10am–noon & 2–5pm; ⓣ04.67.98.36.40, ⓦwww.paysdepezenas.net). Although Molière features in the eclectic **Musée Vulliod St-Germain** (Mon–Sat 10am–noon & 2–5pm, Sun 2–5pm; €2), housed in a sixteenth-century palace just off the square, it's the grand salon, with its Aubusson tapestries and collection of seventeenth- and eighteenth-century furniture, that steals the show.

Practicalities

The tourist office distributes a guide to all the town's eminent houses, taking in the former **Jewish ghetto** on rue des Litanies and rue Juiverie, but you can just as easily follow the explanatory plaques posted all over the centre, starting at the east end of rue François-Outrin where it leaves the town's main square, place du 14-Juillet. The **gare routière** is on the opposite side of the square on the river bank, with buses to Montpellier, Béziers and Agde, while an enormous **market** takes place each Saturday on cours Jean-Jaurès, a five-minute walk away.

There are two **hotels** in Pézenas: *Genieys*, at 9 rue Aristide-Briand (ⓣ04.67.98.13.99, ⓦwww.logis-de-france.fr; ❷), and the splendid *Molière*, 18 place du 14-Juillet (ⓣ04.67.98.14.00, ⓕ04.67.98.98.28; ❸). There are plenty of **restaurants** to choose from and most have menus for under €18. *Le Pomme d'Amour* (closed Jan & Feb, out of season also Mon eve & Tues), on rue Albert-Paul-Alliés, with good duck dishes, and *Le Conti*, 27 rue Conti (closed Sun & out of season Mon), is a popular pizzeria. The best spot, however, is *Les Palmiers* in 50 rue de Mercière (ⓣ04.67.09.42.56; June–Sept only), a beautiful and welcoming establishment featuring inventive Mediterranean-style cuisine from about €25. For those with a sweet tooth, there are two local delicacies to sample: flavoured sugar-drops called *berlingots*, and *petits pâtés* – bobbin-shaped pastries related to mince pies, reputedly introduced by the Indian cook in the household of Clive of India who stayed in Pézenas in 1770.

Narbonne and around

On the Toulouse–Nice main train line, 25km west of Béziers, is **NARBONNE**, once the capital of Rome's first colony in Gaul, Gallia Narbonensis, and a thriving port and communications centre in classical times and again in the Middle Ages. Plague, war with the English and the silting-up of its harbour finished it off in the fourteenth century, though a tentative prosperity returned in the late nineteenth century with the birth of the modern wine industry. Today, despite the ominous presence of the Malvesi nuclear power plant just 5km out of town, it's a pleasant provincial city with a small but well-kept old town, dominated by the great truncated choir of its cathedral and bisected by a grassy esplanade on the banks of the Canal de la Robine.

In the summer of 1991 Narbonne acquired notoriety as a flash point in France's continuing problems with its ethnic minorities, as the Harkis – Algerians who had enlisted in the French forces and fought with them against their own people in the Algerian war of independence in the late 1950s – began angrily to protest official neglect of their community. The discontent has rumbled on, and the Harkis have organized a political group, the Mouvement Harki, to counter the city's far-right municipal administration.

The Town

One of the few Roman remnants in Narbonne is the **Horreum**, at the north end of rue Rouget-de-l'Isle (April–Sept daily 9.30am–12.15pm & 2–6pm; Oct–March Tues–Sun 10am–noon & 2–5pm; €5, valid for three days and includes entry to the town's other museums), an unusual underground grain store divided into a series of small chambers leading off a rectangular passageway. At the opposite end of the same street, close to the attractive tree-lined banks of the **Canal de la Robine**, is Narbonne's other principal attraction, the enormous Gothic **Cathédrale St-Just-et-St-Pasteur**. With the Palais des Archévêques and its forty-metre keep, it forms a massive pile of masonry that completely dominates the restored lanes of the old town, and – like the cathedral of Béziers – can be seen for kilometres around. In spite of its size, it's actually only the choir of a much more ambitious church, whose construction was halted to avoid wrecking the city walls. The immensely tall interior has some beautiful fourteenth-century stained glass in the chapels on the northeast side of the apse and imposing Aubusson tapestries – one of the most valuable tapestries is kept in the **Salle du Trésor** (April–Sept 9.30am–12.15pm & 2–6pm; Oct–March 10am–noon & 2–5pm; €3), along with a small collection of ecclesiastical treasures. In summer the high north **tower** is open for a panoramic view of the surrounding vineyards (June–Sept daily 10am–5pm; Oct–May by appointment only; ⓣ04.68.33.70.18; €2).

The adjacent **place de l'Hôtel-de-Ville** is dominated by the great towers of St-Martial, the Madeleine and Bishop Aycelin's keep. From there the passage de l'Ancre leads through to the **Palais des Archévêques** (Archbishops' Palace), housing a fairly ordinary **museum of art** and a good **archeology museum** (both museums have the same hours and ticket as the Horreum), whose interesting Roman remains include a massive 3.5-metre wood and lead ship's rudder, and a huge mosaic. Across into the southern part of the town, beyond the bisecting Canal de la Robine and the built-over Pont des Marchands, the small early Christian crypt of the church of **St-Paul**, off rue de l'Hôtel-Dieu (Mon–Sat 9am–noon & 2–6pm; free), is worth a quick look, as is the deconsecrated church of **Notre-Dame-de-Lamourguié** which now houses a collection of Roman sculptures and epigraphy (same hours and cost as the Horreum).

Practicalities

The **gare routière** and the **gare SNCF** are next door to each other on avenue Carnot on the northwest side of town. The **tourist office** is on place Salengro, next to the cathedral (April–Sept daily 9.30am–12.15pm & 2–6pm; Oct–March Tues–Sun 10am–noon & 2–5pm; ⓣ04.68.65.15.60, ⓦwww.Mairie-Narbonne.fr).

The best budget **accommodation** is the modern and friendly *MJC Centre International de Séjour*, in place Salengro (ⓣ04.68.32.01.00, ⓕ04.68.65.80.20; ❶). Two more reasonable hotels are *Will's Hotel*, 23 av Pierre-Sémard (ⓣ04.68.90.44.50, ⓕ04.68.32.26.28; ❷), a homely backpackers' favourite near the station, and the spruce *Hôtel de France*, 6 rue Rossini (ⓣ04.68.32.09.75, ⓦwww.hotelnarbonne.com ❷), beside the attractive market hall. A fancier option is the plush *La Résidence*, 6 rue du 1er-Mai (ⓣ04.68.32.19.41, ⓕ04.68.65.18.48; ❻), in a nineteenth-century renovated house, but best is *La Dorade*, 44 rue Jean-Jaurès, (ⓣ04.68.32.65.95, ⓕ04.68.65.81.62; ❸), facing the canal and set in a spectacular building built in 1648. The nearest **campsite** is *Les Roches Grises*, on the route de Perpignan to the southwest of town; take bus #2 from the Hôtel-de-Ville.

As for **food**, the best choice in Narbonne is *L'Alsace*, 2 av Pierre-Sémard (ⓣ04.68.65.10.24; closed Tues; menus from €16), with great decor and mammoth servings of good, simple *terroir* and northeastern French dishes. Alternatively you'll find a string of alfresco snack bars and brasseries along the terraces bordering the Canal de la Robine in the town centre, while *L'Estagnol* (ⓣ04.68.65.09.27; closed Sun & Mon eve; menus €16–20), across the canal on Cours Mirabeau, attracts the crowds with its good-value, simple fare. For something a little fancier, try *Aux Trois Caves*, at 4 rue Benjamin-Crémieux (menus €18–36), with *terroir* dining in a medieval cellar (€16–28), or the elegant *La Petite Cour*, north of the canal at 22 bd Gambetta (ⓣ04.68.90.48.03), in a high-ceilinged room decked with seascape murals; seafood is the order of the day, with a good choice of menus around €14 at lunchtime, and €45 in the evening.

Fontfroide and the Étang de Bages

For a side trip from Narbonne – only 15km southwest, but nigh impossible without transport of your own – the lovely **abbey** of **FONTFROIDE** enjoys a beautiful location, tucked into a fold in the dry cypress-clad hillsides. The extant buildings go back to the twelfth century, with some elegant seventeenth-century additions in the entrance and courtyards, and were in use from their foundation until 1900, first by Benedictines, then Cistercians. It was one of the Cistercian monks, Pierre de Castelnau, whose murder as papal legate set off the Albigensian Crusade against the Cathars in 1208.

Visits to the restored abbey are only possible on a guided tour (daily: most-Jan by appointment only; Feb–March & Nov to early-Jan 10am–noon & 2–4pm; April to early-July & Sept–Oct 10am–12.15pm & 1.45–5.30pm; most-July to Aug 9.30am–6pm; €6.25), and star features include the cloister, with its marble pillars and giant wisteria, the church itself, some fine ironwork and the rose garden. The stained glass in the windows of the lay brothers' dormitory consists of fragments from churches in north and eastern France damaged in World War I.

Just south of Narbonne, the **Étang de Bages et de Sigean** forms a large lagoon frequently visited by flamingos. A scenic drive leads out over the étang to the village of **BAGES**. It's a notably arty community with some houses featuring unusually decorous ceramic drainpipes. From Bages the road continues south along the edge of the *étang* to **PEYRIAC-DE-MER**, and the **Réserve Africaine Sigean** (daily: mid-April to early-Sept 9am–6.30pm, otherwise 9am–4pm; €9), a better-than-average wildlife park with over 150 species from Africa and the rest of the world.

The coast: Valras to Gruissan

The coast close to Béziers and Narbonne enjoys the same attributes – and problems – as the rest of the Languedoc shoreline: fantastic sand but not a stitch of shade, and endless tacky development buffeted by a wind that would flay the shell off a tortoise.

For a quick escape from Béziers, you can take a thirty-minute bus ride across the flat vine-covered coastal plain to **VALRAS**, at the mouth of the River Orb, whose old-fashioned family resort status is still just discernible. Further south, St-Pierre and Narbonne-Plage (reachable by bus from Narbonne) are uninspiring, modern resorts, and the only redeeming feature of this stretch of coast is the mini-landscape of the **Montagne de la Clape**, a former island, pine-covered and craggy, and not more than 200m above sea level, despite its name. At its far end the fishing village of **GRUISSAN**, 13km from Narbonne (there are buses), built in concentric rings around the hub of the Tour Barberousse, is the only real place of character left, and it, too, is under assault by the developers. Out along the beach, *plages des chalets*, is a section of houses originally built on stilts to keep them clear of the sea, but since the danger of flooding has receded many have now added ground floors.

The one really worthwhile thing to visit near Gruissan is the **Chapelle Notre-Dame-des-Auzils**. It's about 4km up a winding lane into the Montagne and stands in a quiet and highly atmospheric spot in the pine woods. All along the road leading to it are moving **memorials** to the people of Gruissan lost at sea in merchant ships, trawlers and warships, from Haiti to the Greek island of Skiros. If the chapel's open, take a peek inside at the *ex votos* offered by grateful seamen and their families, many of them now painted onto the walls, the originals having been stolen in the 1960s.

Parc Naturel Régional du Haut Languedoc

Embracing Mont Caroux in the east and the Montagne Noire in the west, the **Parc Naturel Régional du Haut Languedoc** is the southernmost extension of the Massif Central. The west, above Castres and Mazamet, is Atlantic in feel and climate, with deciduous forests and lush valleys, while the east is dry, craggy and calcareous. Except in high summer you can have it almost to yourself. Buses serve the **Orb valley** and cross the centre of the park to **La Salvetat** and **Lacaune**, but you really need transport of your own to make the most of it.

Bédarieux to St-Pons: the valleys of the Orb and Jaur

Some 34km north of Béziers, the pleasant if unremarkable town of **BÉDARIEUX** lies on the edge of the park. Served by buses from both Béziers and Montpellier, and by train from Béziers, it makes a good base for entering the park, especially as the bus service continues along the Orb and Jaur valleys to St-Pons beneath the southern slopes of the Monts de l'Espinouse.

The best part of town is to the east of the river, where the tall and crumbly old houses are redolent of a rural France long since vanished in more prosperous areas. You'll find the **tourist office** on place aux Herbes (Mon, Tues, Thurs & Fri 9am–12.30pm & 2–7.30pm, Sat 9am–12.30pm; ⓣ04.67.95.08.79, ⓦwww.bedarieux.fr). The town's only **hotel**, *Le Delta* (ⓣ04.67.23.21.19; ❷), is on rue de Clairacm and there's also a municipal **campsite** on boulevard Jean-Moulin (ⓣ04.67.23.30.19; closed Oct to mid-June). The best **restaurant** deal can be had at *Le Rapier*, by the Hôtel de Ville on rue de la République, where a four-course meal including dessert, coffee and wine runs around €14.

The Orb valley and Mons

Continuing west, the D908 is an easy hitch (if you don't want to wait for the bus) through spectacular scenery, with the peaks of the Monts de l'Espinouse rising up to 1000m on your right. The spa town of **LAMALOU-LES-BAINS**, 8km on, is notably livelier than neighbouring settlements, boasting the attraction of recuperative springs where the likes of André Gide, Dumas **fils** and crowned heads of Spain and Morocco soothed their aches and pains. At the west end of the town by the main road, the **cemetery** is an untypically grand necropolis crowned with ornate mausoleums, while the ancient **church** on the north side of town contains carvings left by Mozarab refugees from Spain.

At the village of Colombières, 5km to the west, a path leaves the road to take you up into the **Gorges de Madale**. Here it joins the GR7, which crosses the southern part of the park to Labastide-Rouairoux beyond St-Pons.

Seven or eight kilometres further along the D908 is **MONS**, which features a *gîte d'étape* (ⓣ04.67.97.80.43) next to the church, and a comfortable new B&B, *Manoir le Trivalle* (ⓣ04.67.97.85.56, ⓦwww.monslatrivalle.com; ❺). Some 2km away on the D14, there's a municipal **campsite** (ⓣ04.67.97.72.64). From Mons a road climbs 5km up the dramatic Gorges d'Héric to the hamlet of Héric, with the Gorges de l'Orb winding their way southwards back to Béziers along the D14.

Olargues and St-Pons-de-Thomières

Five kilometres after Mons, you reach the medieval village of **OLARGUES**, scrambling up the south bank of the Jaur above its thirteenth-century single-span bridge. The steep twisting streets, presumably almost unchanged since the bridge was built, lead up to a thousand-year-old belfry crowning the top of the hill. With the river and gardens below, the ancient and earth-brown farms on the infant slopes of Mont Caroux beyond, and swifts swirling round the tower in summer, you get a powerful sense of age and history. There's a tiny **tourist office** on rue de la Place near the church (July & Aug daily 10.30am–12.30pm & 4.30–8pm; ⓣ04.67.97.71.26, ⓔmairie.olargues@libertysurf.fr), as well as an old train station now served only by SNCF **buses**. The *Laissac*, just outside town in the Domaine de Rieumégé (ⓣ04.67.97.73.99; ⓦwww.tbsfrance/com/rieumege; ❺), is a decent-enough hotel, but a better deal is Pauline Giles' homely *Les Quatr' Farceurs* in rue de la Comporte (in rue de la Comporte (ⓣ & ⓕ04.67.97.81.33, ⓦwww.olargues.co.uk; ❸), which also serves huge meals with free-flowing wine for €18. **Campers** should head for *Camping Le Baous*, down by the river (ⓣ04.67.97.71.50; closed mid-Sept to mid-April).

ST-PONS-DE-THOMIÈRES, 18km further west, is a little larger and noisier: it's on the Béziers–Castres and Béziers–La Salvetat bus routes, as well as the Bédarieux–Mazamet route. This is the "capital" of the park, with the **Maison du Parc** at 13 rue du Cloître (Mon–Fri 8am–noon & 1.30–6pm; ⓣ04.67.97.38.22, ⓦwww.parc-haut-languedoc.fr) by the **cathedral** – the latter a strange mix of Romanesque and classical. The town also boasts a small and reasonably interesting **museum of prehistory** (mid-June to Oct daily 10am–noon & 2.30–6pm; Nov to mid-June Wed, Sat & Sun 10am–noon & 2–5pm; €3.50), across the river from the **tourist office** on place du Forail (July & Aug daily 9am–7.30pm; Sept–June Mon–Fri 10am–noon & 2.30–6pm, Sat 10am–noon; ⓣ04.67.97.06.65, ⓦwww.saint-pons-tourisme.com).

If you need to **stay**, try the basic *Le Somail*, near the tourist office (ⓣ04.67.97.00.12, ⓕ04.67.97.05.84; ❶), or the much smarter *Les Bergeries de Ponderach*, a seventeenth-century château 1km out of town on the Narbonne road (ⓣ04.67.97.02.57, ⓦwww.bergeries-ponderach.com; ❹–❻), with a good restaurant. The municipal **campsite** (ⓣ04.67.97.34.85) is on the main road east to Bédarieux. There's also a good camping *à la ferme*, *La Borio de Roque* (ⓣ04.67.97.10.97; closed Oct to mid-June), 4km north of St-Pons on the D907, and *chambres d'hôte* 2km further on at *La Ferme* *de Tailhos* (Ⓣ04.67.97.27.62; ❸). Continue along this road and you reach the Col du Cabaretou, with the stunningly situated *Auberge du Cabaretou* (Ⓣ04.67.95.31.62, Ⓕ04.67.97.32.74; ❷; closed mid-Jan to mid-Feb), with a *terroir* restaurant serving a mini-menu for €18, and others starting at €30. North of here the D907 leads to La Salvetat in the heart of the park.

The uplands of the park

The uplands of the park are a wild and little travelled area, dominated by the towering peak of **Mont Caroux** and stretching west along the ridge of the **Monts de l'Espinouse**. This is prime hiking territory, where thick forest of stunted oak alternates with broad mountain meadows, opening up on impressive vistas. Civilization appears again to the west in the upper Agout valley, where **Fraisse** and **La Salvetat** have become thriving bases for outdoor recreation, and to the north, at the medieval spa town of **Lacaune**. There's no transport crossing the uplands, but the prettiest route through the park to Mont Caroux and L'Espinouse is the D180 from **Le Poujol-sur-Orb**, 2km west of Lamalou-les-Bains.

Combes, Douch and Héric

From Le Poujol, the D180 winds up through cherry orchards to the village of **COMBES**, where the *Auberge de Combes* (Ⓣ04.67.95.66.55, Ⓕ04.67.95.63.49; ❷; Oct–May weekends only; restaurant from €20) offers both *gîte d'étape* and *chambres d'hôte* **accommodation**, and on through the **Forêt des Écrivains-Combattants**, named after the French writers who died in World War I. Just above the hamlet of Rosis, the road levels out in a small mountain valley, whose slopes are brilliant yellow with broom in June.

A left fork leads to the hamlet of **DOUCH**, beneath the summit of Le Caroux – a place where time truly seems to have stood still. Half-a-dozen rough stone houses, inhabited by a handful of elderly residents, cluster tightly together for protection against the elements. For accommodation, there is a *gîte d'étape* (Ⓣ04.67.95.65.76) and a *chambres d'hôte* (Ⓣ04.67.95.79.81). In the meadows below nestles a picturesque church with an ancient cemetery full of graves like iron cots.

The University of Toulouse maintains a research unit here to survey the largest *mouflon* population in France. If you go out early in the morning or just before dark in the evening, you'll have a good chance of seeing these short-fleeced sheep, and wild boar, too, as they come out to feed. The road provides some good vantage points a little further north round the **Col de l'Ourtigas** and the Pas de la Lauze.

The best short **walk** to do from Douch is down the GR7 to the hamlet of **HÉRIC** in the gorge of the same name. The path starts on the left at the end of the road in Douch and follows the telephone line. Once over the col and into the head of the gorge it becomes a beautiful paved mule track looping down through beech and chestnut woods. In the past people lived off the chestnuts, selling them, eating them and making flour from them. It takes about forty minutes to reach the two or three brownstone houses of Héric, inhabited for several generations by the Clavel family, and 90 minutes to climb back up. They run a *gîte d'étape* and can provide **meals**, too, on reservation (Ⓣ04.67.97.77.29). A good longer walk from Douch is the popular three-kilometre ascent of **Le Caroux** (1040m), south of the village with fine views from the summit along L'Espinouse (see overleaf), south to Béziers, the sea and even the Pyrenees, on a clear day.

Into the Agout valley

Continuing north from Douch, the D180 climbs another 12km above deep ravines, offering spectacular views to the summit of **L'Espinouse**. The Col de l'Ourtigas is a good place to stretch your legs and take in the grandeur surrounding you. Here the landscape changes from Mediterranean cragginess to marshy moor-like meadow and big conifer plantations, and the road begins to descend west into the valley of the River Agout. It runs through tiny Salvergues, with plain workers' cottages and a striking fortress-church; Cambon, where the natural woods begin; postcard-pretty **FRAISSE-SUR-AGOUT** – where you can stay at the municipal *gîte* (ⓣ04.67.97.61.14, ⓦwww.gites-de-france-herault.asso.fr); and thence to **LA SALVETAT-SUR-AGOUT**. Situated between the artificial lakes of La Raviège and Laouzas, the latter is another attractive mountain town built on a hill above the river, with car-wide streets and houses clad in huge slate tiles. It's usually half asleep except at holiday time, when it becomes a busy outdoor activities centre. With several **campsites** and the friendly, English-owned *La Pergola* hotel (ⓣ04.67.97.55.48, ⓕ04.67.97.56.76; ❶), it's a convenient stopover for the centre of the park. The municipal **campsite** (ⓣ04.67.97.62.45; closed Sept–April) is by the sports ground off the D907, and there's a **tourist office** in place des Archers at the top of the hill (Mon–Fri 9am–noon & 2–6pm, Sat & Sun 10am–noon & 2–5pm, Sept–June closed Sun; ⓣ & ⓕ04.67.97.64.44, ⓦwww.lasalvetatot.com).

Lacaune

Twenty kilometres further north, **LACAUNE** makes another agreeable stop if you're heading for Castres. Surrounded by rounded wooded heights around the 1000m mark, it's very much a mountain town, one of the centres of Protestant Camisard resistance at the end of the seventeenth century, when its inaccessibility made the region ideal for clandestine worship. There are **bus** connections most days – not at very convenient times, usually afternoon or very early morning – to Castres, Albi and Bédarieux.

The air is fresh, and the town, though somewhat grey in appearance because of the slates and greyish stucco common throughout the region, is cheerful enough. For a place to **stay**, try *Fusiés*, an erstwhile coaching inn opposite the church on rue de la République (ⓣ05.63.37.02.03, ⓔespoutis@infonie.fr; ❸; closed most Jan), offering an old-fashioned classiness, or the simpler *Hôtel Calas*, a little way up the hill (ⓣ05.63.37.03.28, ⓔhotelcalas@wanadoo.fr; ❷; closed mid-Dec to mid-Jan), which has a highly rated restaurant (menus €14–29).

From here to Castres the most agreeable route is along the wooded **Gijou valley**, following the now defunct train track, past minuscule Gijounet and **LACAZE**, where a nearly derelict **château** strikes a picturesque pose in a bend of the river.

Carcassonne and around

Right on the main Toulouse–Montpellier train link, **CARCASSONNE** couldn't be easier to reach; and for anyone travelling through this region it is a must – one of the most dramatic, if also most-visited, towns in the whole of Languedoc. Carcassonne owes its division into two separate "towns" – the **Cité** and the **Ville Basse** – to the wars against the Cathars. Following Simon de Montfort senior's capture of the town in 1209, its people tried in 1240 to restore their traditional ruling family, the Trencavels. In reprisal King Louis IX expelled them, only permitting their return on condition they built on the low ground by the River Aude.

Arrival and information

Arriving by **train**, you'll find yourself in the *ville basse* on the north bank of the Canal du Midi at the northern limits of the town. To reach the **centre** from the train station, cross the canal bridge by an oval lock, pass the Jardin Chénier and follow rue Clémenceau, which will take you through the central **place Carnot** and out to the exterior boulevard on the southern side of town (a fifteen-minute walk). The **gare routière** is on boulevard de Varsovie on the northwest side of town, south of the canal, while the **airport** (Ⓣ04.68.71.96.46) lies just west of the city. An hourly service (15min; €5) leaves from outside the terminal and stops in town at the **gare SNCF**, place Gambetta and the cité; a taxi to the center will cost €8–15). If you are planning on visiting other medieval sites in the vicinity of Carcassonne (including the Cathar castles), you might purchase the Intersite Card, which gives you a discounted admission price to many castles and monuments (see p.848 for details).

The **tourist office** is at 15 bd Camille-Pelletan (July & Aug daily 9am–7pm; Sept–June Mon–Sat 9am–6pm; Ⓣ04.68.10.24.30, Ⓦwww.carcassonne-tourisme.com), at the end of square Gambetta, where the main road from Montpellier enters the town across the Pont-Neuf and the River Aude. There's also an annexe (daily: July & Aug 9am–7pm; Sept–June 9am–5pm) just inside the main gate to the medieval Cité, Porte Narbonnaise. For information on the **Cathars**, consult the Centre National d'Études Cathares, 53 rue de Verdun (Ⓣ04.68.47.24.66), while local bookshops offer plenty of Cathar literature and souvenir picture books, some in English.

Accommodation

With the exception of the modern, clean, but frequently booked-up **HI hostel** on rue Trencavel (Ⓣ04.68.25.23.16, Ⓔcarcassonne@fuaj.org), the price of staying in the Cité can be high. If you don't mind paying, the *de la Cité* (Ⓣ04.68.71.98.71, Ⓦwww.hoteldelacite.orient-express.com; ❾; closed Dec to mid-Jan) offers opulent surroundings. *Le Donjon*, 2 rue Comte-Roger (Ⓣ04.68.11.23.00, Ⓦwww.hotel-donjon.fr; ❻), is more economical, but still luxurious. *Hôtel Espace Cité*, just outside the main gate at 132 rue Trivalle (Ⓣ04.68.25.24.24, Ⓦwww.hotel.espacecite.fr; ❷), has all mod cons and efficient service at reasonable prices.

There are, however, some very reasonably priced hotels in the *ville basse*. Pride of place goes to the *Grand Hôtel Terminus*, at 2 av de Maréchal Joffre (Ⓣ04.68.25.25.00, Ⓕ04.68.75.53.09; ❺; closed Dec–Feb), a station-side hotel of decaying steam-age luxury, with a splendid *fin-de-siècle* facade. The *Montségur*, 27 allée d'Iéna (Ⓣ04.68.25.31.41, Ⓔinfo@hotelmontsegur.com; ❹), is a comfortable nineteenth-century town house, with ample-size rooms, but is not very close to the Cité. A good economy option is the surprisingly well-equipped *St-Joseph*, at 81 rue de la Liberté (Ⓣ04.68.71.96.89, Ⓕ04.68.71.36.28; ❶).

There's a **campsite**, *Camping de la Cité*, on route St-Hilaire (Ⓣ04.68.25.11.17, Ⓕ04.68.47.33.13), with good shady sites, a shop and some bungalows. Tucked off among parkland to the south of town it can be reached by local bus (line 8) or by foot (about 20min) from the Cité.

The Cité

The attractions of the well-preserved and lively *ville basse* notwithstanding, what everybody comes for is the **Cité**, the double-walled and turreted fortress that crowns the hill above the River Aude. From a distance it's the epitome of the fairy-tale medieval town. Viollet-le-Duc rescued it from ruin in 1844, and his "too-perfect" restoration has been furiously debated ever since. It is, as you would expect, a real tourist trap. Yet, in spite of the chintzy cafés, arty-crafty shops and the crowds, you'd have to be a very stiff-necked purist not to be moved at all.

To reach the Cité from the *ville basse*, take bus #2 from outside the station, or a *navette* from square Gambetta. Alternatively, you can walk it in under thirty minutes, crossing the Pont-Vieux and climbing rue Barbacane, past the church of St-Gimer to the sturdy bastion of the **Porte d'Aude**. This is effectively the back entrance – the main gate is **Porte Narbonnaise**, round on the east side.

There is no charge for admission to the streets or the grassy *lices* – "lists" – between the walls, though cars are banned from 10am to 6pm. However,

Canal du Midi

The **Canal du Midi** runs for 240km from the River Garonne at Toulouse via Carcassonne to the Mediterranean at Agde. It was the brainchild of Pierre-Paul Riquet, a minor noble and tax collector, who succeeded in convincing Louis XIV (and more importantly, his first minister, Colbert) of the merits of linking the Atlantic and the Mediterranean via the Garonne.

The work, begun in 1667, took fourteen years to complete, using tens of thousands of workers. The crux of the problem from the engineering point of view was how to feed the canal with water, when its high point at Naurouze, west of Carcassonne, was 190m above sea level and 58m above the Garonne at Toulouse. Riquet responded by building a system of reservoirs in the Montagne Noire, channelling run-off from the heights down to Naurouze. He spent the whole of his fortune on the canal and, sadly, died just six months before its inauguration in 1681.

The canal was a success and sparked a wave of prosperity along its course, with traffic increasing steadily until 1857, when the Sète-Bordeaux railway was inaugurated, reducing trade on the canal to all but nothing. Today, the canal remains a marvel of engineering and beauty, incorporating no fewer than 99 locks (*écluses*) and 130 bridges, almost all of which date back to the first era of construction. A double file of trees lines most of its length, giving it a distinctive "Midi" look and impeding loss of water through evaporation, while the greenery is enhanced in spring by the bloom of yellow irises and wild gladioli. With all of this and the occasional glimpses afforded of a world beyond – a distant smudge of hills and the towers of Carcassonne – the canal is a pleasure to travel. You can follow it by road, and many sections have foot or bicycle paths, but the best way to travel it, of course, is by boat.

Outfits in all the major ports rent houseboats and barges, and there are many cruise options to choose from as well. For **boat rental and cruises**, contact Crown Blue Line, Le Grand Bassin, BP1201, 11492 Castelnaudary (Ⓣ04.68.94.52.72, Ⓔboathols@crown-blueline.com), or Locaboat, Le Grand Bassin (Ⓣ03.86.91.72.72, Ⓦwww.locaboat.com), both of which have a number of branches in Languedoc and the Midi; or Nautic in Carcassonne (Ⓣ04.68.71.88.95, Ⓕ04.67.94.05.91). Canal **information** can be found at the port offices of Voies Navigables de France, at 2 Port St-Étienne in Toulouse (Ⓣ05.61.36.24.24, Ⓦwww.vnf.fr), who also have English-speaking offices at the major canal ports. For a quicker taste of the locks, the cruise barge Lou Gabaret does ninety-minute and longer excursions; contact Allan Millian, 27 rue des 3 Couronnes, Carcassonne (Ⓣ04.68.71.61.26).

to see the inner fortress of the **Château Comtal** and to walk the walls, you'll have to join a guided tour (daily: April–Sept 9.30am–6.30pm; Oct–March 9.30am–5pm; guided tour only; €6.10). The thirty- to forty-minute tours – several per day in English from June to September – assume some knowledge of French history, and point out the various phases in the construction of the fortifications, from Roman and Visigothic to Romanesque and the post-Cathar adaptations of the French kings.

In addition to wandering the narrow streets, don't miss the beautiful **church of St-Nazaire** (mid-June to mid-Sept Mon–Fri 9–11.45am & 1.45–6pm & Sun 9–10.45am & 2–4.30pm; rest of year closes at 5pm), towards the southern corner of the Cité at the end of rue St-Louis. It's a serene combination of Romanesque nave with carved capitals and Gothic transepts and choir adorned with some of the loveliest stained glass in Languedoc. In the south transept is a tombstone believed to belong to Simon de Montfort senior. You can also climb the **tower** (same hours; €1.50), for spectacular views over the Cité.

Eating, drinking and entertainment

With over fifty **restaurants** within its walls, the Cité is a good place to look for somewhere to eat, though it tends to be on the expensive side. First choice is the *Auberge de Dame Carcas*, 3 place du Château (Ⓣ04.68.71.23.23; closed Sun eve, Mon lunch & Feb; menu at €13.50), a traditional bistro, offering cassoulet and other regional dishes. Otherwise try the *Jardin de la Tour*, 11 rue Porte d'Aude (closed Sun eve & Nov–March), with outside tables, or the smart *Brasserie du Donjon*, in the hotel of the same name; both serve *terroir* menus from €18.

There's a much greater variety of affordable places in the *ville basse*: among these *Le Petit Couvert*, at 18 rue de l'Aigle d'Or, has good cheap menus (closed Sun & Mon & March; from €10.60) and a small street-side terrace, while *La Brochetterie les Saveurs*, 2 rue Denisse, is a friendly restaurant featuring Moroccan fare (closed Sun & Mon; €12 menu). Nearby, at 29 bd Jean-Jaurès, the *Divine Comédie* serves a varied menu of pasta, pizzas and regional dishes in generous portions (closed Sun; from €12). For something more sophisticated, try *l'Écurie* (Ⓣ04.68.72.04.04) at 43 bd Barbès, offering local cuisine with adventurous touches, such as roast lamb with thyme and garlic (menus €21–32; closed Sun). For picnic provisions, head for the market on place Carnot (Tues, Thurs & Sat mornings).

Carcassonne hosts two major festivals: the month-long **Festival de la Cité** in July, with dance, theatre and music, the highpoint of which is the mammoth fireworks display on Bastille Day (July 14); and the elaborate medieval pageant, **Les Médiévales**, held in the first fortnight of August.

Castelnaudary

Thirty-six kilometres west of Carcassonne, on the main road from Toulouse, **CASTELNAUDARY** is one of those innumerable French country towns that boast no particular sights but are nonetheless a real pleasure to spend a couple of hours in, having coffee or shopping for a picnic in the market. Today it serves as an important commercial centre for the rolling Lauragais farming country hereabouts, as it once was for the traffic on the Canal du Midi. In fact, the most flattering view of the town is still that from the canal's **Grand Bassin**, which makes it look remarkably like a Greek island town, with its ancient houses climbing the hillside from the water's edge.

In town you'll find some fine old **mansions**, a restored **windmill** and an eighteenth-century **semaphore** tower. However, Castelnaudary's chief claim to fame is as the world capital of **cassoulet**, which, according to tradition, must be made in an earthenware pot from Issel (a *cassolo*) with beans grown in Pamiers or Lavelanet, and cooked in a baker's oven fired with rushes from the Montagne Noire. To try it, go to the **Grand-Hôtel Fourcade**, 14 rue des Carmes (ⓣ04.68.23.02.08, ⓔhotelfourcade@ataraxie.fr; ❶–❸; closed Jan), where you can gorge yourself for €15, then sleep off the after-effects by taking a room upstairs. More attractive alternatives for spending the night are the modern *Hôtel du Canal*, 2 av Arnaut-Vidal (ⓣ04.68.94.05.05, ⓦwww.hotelducanal.com; ❸), in a shady position beside the canal just west of the Grand Bassin, and the *Hôtel du Centre et du Lauragais* (ⓣ04.68.23.25.95, ⓕ04.68.94.01.66; ❸; closed Jan to mid-Feb), a converted nineteenth-century house that's centrally located at 31 cours de la République, close to the post office. The **tourist office** is in Castelnaudary's central Halle aux Grains (mid-July to mid-Sept daily 9am–1pm & 2–7pm; mid-Sept to mid-July Mon–Sat 9.30am–12.30pm & 2–6.30pm; ⓣ04.68.23.05.73, ⓔotsi.castelnaudary@wanadoo.fr).

Minerve

The village of **MINERVE** lies a dozen kilometres north of the Canal du Midi, and halfway between Carcassonne and Béziers in the middle of the Minervois wine country. Its location is extraordinary, isolated on an island of rock between the gorges of the Briant and Cesse rivers, the latter of which has cut its course through two enormous tunnels in the rock known as the Ponts Naturels.

The village turned Cathar at the beginning of the thirteenth century, which made it a target for Simon de Montfort's crusade. On July 22, 1210, after a seven-week siege, he took the castle and promptly burnt 180 *parfaits* (or "purified souls"). Nothing remains of the castle save for the ruins of a wall, but there's a memorial to the *parfaits* by the **church** – and, inside, one of the most ancient altars in Gaul, dated 456.

If looking to stay, there's free **camping** in the valley bottom by the cemetery along with the *Relais Chantovent* (ⓣ04.68.91.14.18, ⓕ04.68.91.81.99; ❸), which is also one of the better places in town to get a meal (menus from €15). The **tourist office** (July & Aug daily 10am–noon & 2–6pm; ⓣ04.68.91.81.43) has information about other accommodation possibilities in the area.

The Montagne Noire

There are two good routes from Carcassonne north into the **Montagne Noire**, which forms the western extremity of the Parc Naturel Régional du Haut Languedoc: Carcassonne–Revel and Carcassonne–Mazamet by the valley of the Orbiel. Neither is served by public transport, but both offer superlative scenery.

The Revel route

The **Revel route** follows the N113 out of Carcassonne, then the D629 through Montolieu (17km) and Saissac. **MONTOLIEU**, semi-fortified and built on the edge of a ravine, has set itself the target of becoming France's secondhand book capital (a conscious imitation of Wales's Hay-on-Wye), with shops overflowing with dog-eared and antiquarian tomes. Drop in at the Librairie Booth, by the bridge over the ravine for English titles.

SAISSAC, 8km further on, is much more an upland village. Conifers and beech wood, interspersed with patches of rough pasture, surround it, and gardens are terraced down its steep slopes. Remains of towers and fortifications poke out among the ancient houses, and on a spur below the village stand the romantic ruins of its castle and the church of St-Michel.

If you wish to **stay** in the area, try the rather aged *Hôtel de la Montagne Noire* (ⓣ04.68.24.46.36, ⓕ04.68.24.46.20; ❷) on the road through Saissac. To eat, head to *Au Beau Site* (ⓣ04.68.24.40.37; closed Sat & Sun Sept–June) in the town below, which has good views and menus from €20. More idyllic accommodation is available north of town at *Domaine du Lampy-Neuf* (ⓣ04.68.24.46.07, ⓕ04.68.24.44.81; ❷), a *chambres d'hôte* by the banks of the Bassin du Lampy, which also functions as a *gîte*. If you have your own transport, the best **campground** hereabouts, and an experience in itself, is the *Camping du Bout du Monde* (ⓣ04.68.94.20.92; all year round), at a beautiful tumble-down farm near Verdun-en-Lauragais, 5km west of Saissac. You camp among the broom at the edge of the woods.

Some 14km west of Saissac on the D103 (or just a few kilometres southwest of the *Bout du Monde* campsite), the ancient village of **ST-PAPOUL**, with its walls and Benedictine **abbey**, makes for a gentle side trip. The abbey is best known for the sculpted corbels on the exterior of the nave, executed by the "Master of Cabestany". These can be viewed at any time without charge, although the interior of the church and its pretty fourteenth-century cloister (daily: April–June & Sept–Oct 10am–noon & 2–6pm; July & Aug 10am–7pm; Nov–March Sat, Sun & hols 10am–noon & 2–5pm; €3.50) are also worth a peek.

Back on the "main" D629, the road winds down through the forest, past the Bassin de St-Férréol, constructed by Riquet to supply water to the Canal du Midi, and on to **REVEL**. Revel is a *bastide* dating from 1342, featuring an attractive arcaded central square with a superb wooden-pillared medieval *halle* in the middle. Now a prosperous market town (market day is Saturday), it makes an agreeably provincial stopover. The *Auberge du Midi* at 34 bd Gambetta (ⓣ05.61.83.50.50, ⓦwww.logis-de-france.com; ❸; closed mid-Nov to early-Dec) is set in a refined old nineteenth-century mansion, and also has the town's best restaurant (menus from €29–43). Close by at 7 rue de Taur, you'll find the *Commanderie Hôtel* (ⓣ05.63.46.61.24; ❸; closed part Feb, part June, part Sept), a good second choice, with an old timber-frame facade and a remodelled interior.

Lastours and the valley of the Orbiel

The alternative route from Carcassonne into the Montagne Noire takes you through the region known as the **Cabardès**. Cut by the deep ravines of the Orbiel and its tributary streams, it's covered with Mediterranean scrub lower down and forests of chestnut and pine higher up. The area is extremely poor and depopulated, with rough stone villages and hamlets crouching in the valleys. Until relatively recently, its people lived off beans and chestnut flour and the meat from their pigs, and worked from very ancient times in the region's copper, iron, lead, silver and gold mines. Nothing now remains of that tradition save for the gold mine at Salsigne, a huge and unsightly open pit atop a bleak windswept plateau.

The most memorable site in the **Orbiel valley** is the **Châteaux de Lastours** (Feb–March & Nov–Dec Sat, Sun & hols 10am–5pm; April–June & Sept daily 10am–6pm; July & Aug daily 9am–8pm; Oct 10am–5pm; €4), the most northerly of the Cathar castles (see p.848), 16km north of Carcassonne. As the name suggests, there is more than one castle – four in fact, their ruined keeps jutting superbly from a sharp ridge of scrub and cypress that plunges to rivers on both sides. The two oldest castles, Cabaret (mid-eleventh century) and Surdespine (1153), fell into de Montfort's hands in 1211, after their lords had given shelter to the Cathars. The other two, Tour Régine and Quertinheux, were added after 1240, when the site became royal property, and a garrison was maintained here as late as the Revolution. Today, despite their ruined state, they look as impregnable and beautiful as ever. A path winds up from the roadside, bright in early summer with iris, cistus, broom and numerous other flowers.

About 7km upriver from Lastours, the road and river divide. The left fork leads to the village of **MAS-CABARDÈS**, hunkered down defensively in the river bottom. The right goes to **ROQUEFÈRE**, whose ancient château hosts summertime theatre. From here a steep, serpentine road winds up through magnificent scenery to the tiny hamlet of **CUPSERVIES**, balanced on the edge of a sudden and deep ravine where the Rieutort stream drops some 90m into the bottom. A couple of kilometres further, by the crossroads at **CANINAC**, there's a tenth-century chapel, **St-Sernin**, in the middle of the woods. To get here without transport, there's a marked footpath from Roquefère, which then returns via Labastide-Esparbairenque (a 4hr 30min round trip).

Toulouse and western Languedoc

With its own sunny, cosmopolitan charms, **Toulouse** is a very accessible kick-off point for any destination in the southwest of France. Of the immediately surrounding places, **Albi** is the number-one priority, with its highly original cathedral and comprehensive collection of Toulouse-Lautrec paintings. Once you've made it that far, it's worth the extra hop to the well-preserved medieval town of **Cordes**. West of Toulouse the land opens up into the broad plains of the **Gers**, a sleepy and rather dull expanse of wheatfields and rolling hills. Those in search of a solitary little-visited France will enjoy its uncrowded monuments, especially lovers of rich *terrines* and Armagnac.

Toulouse

TOULOUSE, with its beautiful historic centre, is one of the most vibrant and metropolitan provincial cities in France. This is a transformation that has come about since World War II, under the guidance of the French state which has poured in money to make Toulouse the think-tank of high-tech industry and a sort of premier trans-national Euroville. Always an **aviation** centre

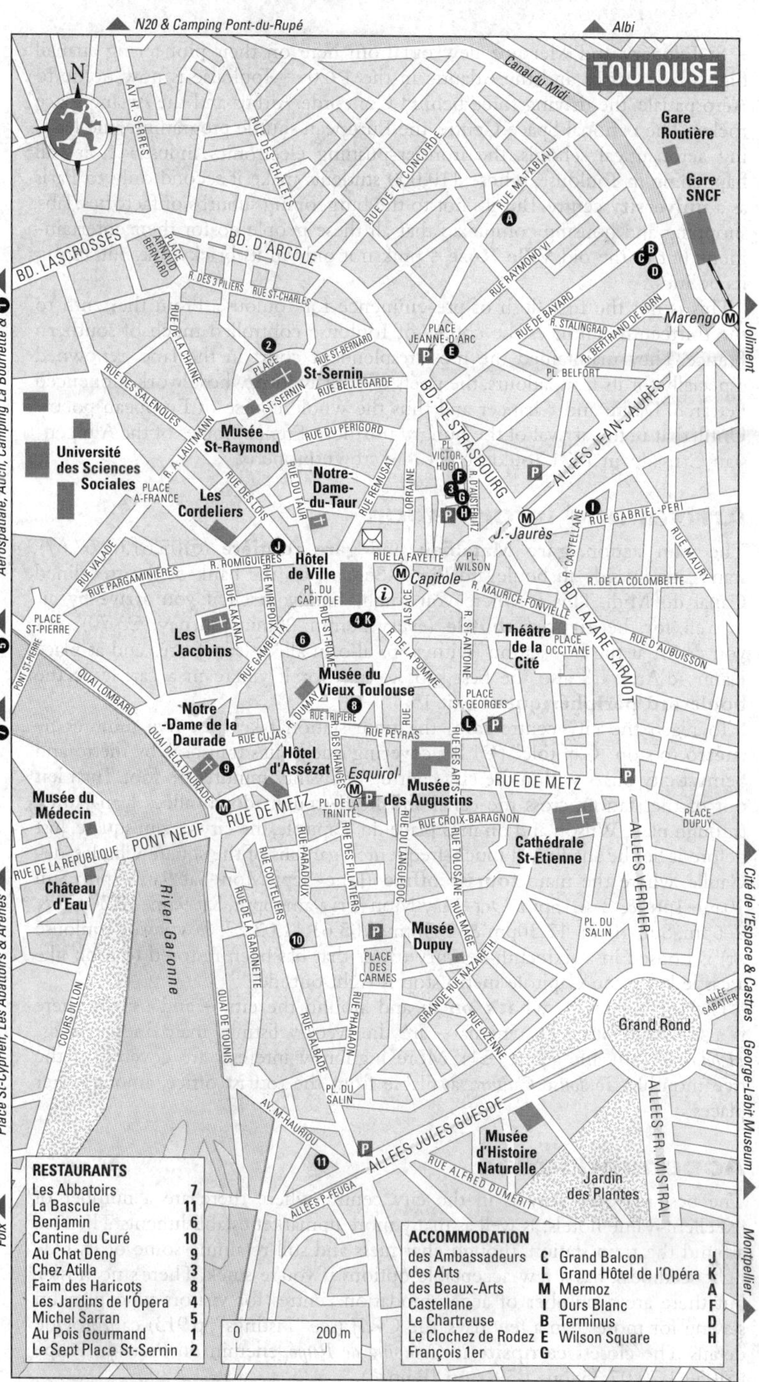
N20 & Camping Pont-du-Rupé
Albi
TOULOUSE
Canal du Midi
Gare Routière
Gare SNCF
N
Aerospatiale, Auch, Camping La Bouriette & 1
5
7
Place St-Cyprien, Les Abattoirs & Arènes
Foix
Joliment
Cité de l'Espace & Castres
George-Labit Museum
Montpellier
AV H. SERRES
RUE DES CHALETS
RUE DE LA CONCORDE
RUE MATABIAU
RUE RAYMOND VI
BD. LASCROSSES
PLACE ARNAUD BERNARD
BD. D'ARCOLE
R. DES 3 PILIERS
RUE ST-CHARLES
RUE DE BAYARD
R. STALINGRAD
R. BERTRAND DE BORN
Marengo
PLACE JEANNE-D'ARC
RUE ST-BERNARD
PLACE ST-SERNIN
St-Sernin
RUE BELLEGARDE
PL. BELFORT
RUE DE LA CHAINE
RUE DES SALENQUES
R. A. LAUTMANN
Musée St-Raymond
RUE DU PERIGORD
BD. DE STRASBOURG
ALLEES JEAN-JAURÈS
Université des Sciences Sociales
PLACE A-FRANCE
Les Cordeliers
RUE DES LOIS
RUE DU TAUR
Notre-Dame-du-Taur
RUE REMUSAT
LORRAINE
PL. VICTOR-HUGO
R. D'AUSTERLITZ
R. CASTELLANE
RUE GABRIEL-PERI
RUE MAURY
J.-Jaurès
RUE VALADE
RUE PARGAMINIERES
R. ROMIGUIERES
Hôtel de Ville
PL. DU CAPITOLE
RUE LA FAYETTE
PL. WILSON
Capitole
R. DE LA COLOMBETTE
R. MAURICE-FONVIELLE
BD. LAZARE CARNOT
PLACE ST-PIERRE
PONT ST-PIERRE
RUE LAKANAL
RUE MIREPOIX
Les Jacobins
RUE GAMBETTA
RUE ST-ROME
R. DE LA POMME
ALSACE
R. ST-ANTOINE
Théâtre de la Cité
PLACE OCCITANE
RUE D'AUBUISSON
QUAI LOMBARD
Musée du Vieux Toulouse
PLACE ST-GEORGES
RUE DUMAY
RUE TRIPIERE
Notre-Dame de la Daurade
RUE CUJAS
R. DES CHANGES
RUE PEYRAS
RUE DES ARTS
QUAI DE LA DAURADE
Hôtel d'Assézat
Esquirol
Musée des Augustins
RUE DE METZ
Musée du Médecin
PL. DE LA TRINITÉ
RUE CROIX-BARAGNON
PLACE DUPUY
PONT NEUF
Cathédrale St-Etienne
RUE DE LA REPUBLIQUE
RUE PARADOUX
RUE DES FILATIERS
RUE DU LANGUEDOC
RUE TOLOSANE
ALLEES VERDIER
Château d'Eau
River Garonne
RUE COUTELIERS
RUE DE LA GARONETTE
Musée Dupuy
RUE MAGE
PL. DU SALIN
PLACE DES CARMES
GRANDE RUE NAZARETH
COURS DILLON
QUAI DE TOUNIS
RUE PHARAON
RUE DALBADE
RUE OZENNE
ALLEE SABATIER
Grand Rond
PL. DU SALIN
AV. M-HAURIOU
ALLEES JULES GUESDE
Musée d'Histoire Naturelle
RUE ALFRED DUMERIT
Jardin des Plantes
ALLEES FR. MISTRAL
ALLEES P-FEUGA
RESTAURANTS
Les Abbatoirs 7
La Bascule 11
Benjamin 6
Cantine du Curé 10
Au Chat Deng 9
Chez Atilla 3
Faim des Haricots 8
Les Jardins de l'Ópera 4
Michel Sarran 5
Au Pois Gourmand 1
Le Sept Place St-Sernin 2
0 200 m
ACCOMMODATION
des Ambassadeurs C
des Arts L
des Beaux-Arts M
Castellane I
Le Chartreuse B
Le Clochez de Rodez E
François 1er G
Grand Balcon J
Grand Hôtel de l'Opéra K
Mermoz A
Ours Blanc F
Terminus D
Wilson Square H

– St-Exupéry and Mermoz flew out from here on their pioneering airmail flights over Africa and the Atlantic in the 1920s – Toulouse is now home to Aérospatiale, the driving force behind Concorde, Airbus and the Ariane space rocket. The national Space Centre, the European shuttle programme, the leading aeronautical schools, the frontier-pushing electronics industry… it's all happening in Toulouse, whose 110,000 students make it second only to Paris as a **university** centre. But it's not to the burgeoning suburbs of factories, labs, shopping and housing complexes that all these people go for their entertainment, but to the old **Ville Rose** – pink not only in its brickwork, but also in its politics.

This is not the first flush of pre-eminence for Toulouse. From the tenth to the thirteenth centuries the counts of Toulouse controlled much of southern France. They maintained the most resplendent court in the land, renowned especially for its troubadours, the poets of courtly love, whose work influenced Petrarch, Dante and Chaucer and thus the whole course of European poetry. Until, that is, the arrival of the hungry northern French nobles of the Albigensian Crusade; in 1271 Toulouse became crown property.

Arrival and information

The train station, **gare Matabiau**, and **gare routière** (Ⓣ05.61.61.67.67), stand side by side in boulevard Pierre-Sémard on the bank of the tree-lined Canal du Midi. This is where you might find yourself if you arrive by air as well, for the **airport shuttle** (every 20min; 20min journey; €3.70) puts you down at the bus station (with stops also in allées Jean-Jaurès and at place Jeanne-d'Arc). It's also the best spot to aim for if you're in a car: leave the **boulevard périphérique** at exit 15.

To reach the city centre from the train station takes just five minutes by **métro** to stop "Capitole" (€1.20, covering one hour's transport by métro and Semvat city buses within the city centre), or twenty minutes on foot. Turn left out of the station, cross the canal and head straight down allées Jean-Jaurès, through place Wilson and on into place du Capitole, the city's main square. Just before it lie the shady and much-frequented gardens of the square Charles-de-Gaulle, where the main **tourist office** (June–Sept Mon–Sat 9am–7pm, Sun 10am–1pm & 2–6.15pm; Oct–May Mon–Fri 9am–6pm, Sat 9am–12.30pm & 2–6pm, Sun 10am–12.30pm & 2–5pm; Ⓣ05.61.11.02.22, Ⓦwww.ot-toulouse.fr) is housed in a sixteenth-century tower that has been restored to look like a castle keep; the Capitole métro stop is right outside.

The top guides to **what's on** in and around the city – and usually there is a lot, from opera to cinema – are the weekly listings magazines *Toulouse Hebdo* (€0.50) and *Flash* (€1). More highbrow interests are covered in the free monthly *Toulouse Culture*, available from the tourist office, among other places.

Accommodation

The best place to **stay** is in the city centre, where there are a number of excellent-value hotels, as well as many more upmarket establishments. The area around the train station, though charmless and still retaining some of its red-light seediness, has a few acceptable options if you're stuck. There's no hostel, but there are a number of accommodation centres for visitors who plan on staying for more than a few days: the CRIJ (see "Listings", p.913) can provide details. The closest **campsite** is *Camping de Rupé*, chemin du Pont du Rupé (Ⓣ05.61.70.07.35; bus #59, stop "Rupé").

Hotels

des Ambassadeurs 68 rue Bayard ⓣ05.61.62.65.84, ⓕ05.61.62.97.38. Very friendly, little hotel run by a young couple, just down from the station. All rooms have TV, en-suite bath and phone – a surprisingly good deal given the price. ❶
des Arts 1bis rue Cantegril ⓣ05.61.23.36.21, ⓕ05.61.12.22.37. On a corner diagonally opposite the Augustins museum, this is a top choice in the lower price range, with large, quirky rooms (some with a fireplace) in a superb old building. ❶
des Beaux-Arts 1 pl du pont-Neuf ⓣ05.34.45.42.42, ⓦwww.hoteldesbeauxarts.com. Located in a 150-year-old building, this hotel's contemporary but refined interior contrasts well with its ageing facade, making for solid, old-world elegance. Each room is individually decorated and some have views of the Garonne. ❺
Castellane 17 rue Castellane ⓣ05.61.62.18.82, ⓦwww.castellanehotel.com. A cheerful hotel with a wide selection of room types and sizes – most of which are bright and quiet. One of the few wheelchair-accessible hotels in this price range. ❸
Le Chartreuse 4bis bd Bonrepos ⓣ05.61.62.93.39, ⓔla.chartreuse@wanadoo.fr. Efficiently modern if soulless choice, right by the station. Great value, considering the amenities: each room has a private shower, toilet and TV. ❶
Le Clochez de Rodez 14 pl de Jeanne-d'Arc ⓣ05.61.62.42.92, ⓦwww.couleursud.com. Comfortable and central, with secure parking and all mod-cons. Despite its size, it exudes a very personal hospitality. ❺
François 1er 4 rue d'Austerlitz ⓣ05.61.21.54.52, ⓕ05.61.22.88.25. Small but basic hotel near the main market. Clean and very friendly, but rather desperately in need of remodelling – a good fall-back in if the neighbouring hotels are full. Rooms have TV. Closed part Aug. ❷
Grand Balcon 8 rue Romiguières ⓣ05.61.21.48.08, ⓕ05.61.21.59.98. Just off place du Capitole, this ageing classic was frequented by the aviation pioneers, such as St-Exupéry, who first established Toulouse as a capital of manned flight. It's now rather run-down, but definitely a good bargain, and smack in the centre of things. Closed most of Aug. ❷
Grand Hôtel de l'Opéra 1 pl du Capitole ⓣ05.61.21.82.66, ⓦwww.grand-hotel-opera.com. The grand dame of Toulouse's hotels presides over the place du Capitole in the guise of a seventeenth-century convent. The rich decor, peppered with antiques and artwork, underlines the atmosphere of sophistication. Also has a fitness centre for working off that second helping of foie gras. ❾
Mermoz 50 rue de Matabiau ⓣ05.61.63.04.04, ⓦwww.hotel-mermoz.com. Immaculate, comfortable rooms in a 1930s Art Deco-style hotel close to the station. Also has wheelchair access and a parking garage. ❻
Ours Blanc 25 pl de Victor-Hugo ⓣ05.61.21.62.40, ⓦwww.hotel-ours-blanc.fr. Right by the covered market and steps from the Capitole, this welcoming hotel is one of the city's better bargains. The entire building has recently been renovated and each room has TV, air conditioning and telephone, as well as a private bath. ❸
Terminus 13 bd Bonrepos ⓣ05.61.62.44.78, ⓦwww.terminus31.com. This old three-star station-side hotel has large, renovated rooms that make it worth the price, and there are special room prices for off-season weekends. Parking and buffet breakfast (€7) available, the only drawback being that the hotel is rather far from the sights. ❸
Wilson Square12 rue d'Austerlitz ⓣ05.61.21.67.57, ⓦwww.hotel-wilson.com. Clean and well-kept place at the top end of Austerlitz, with TV, AC and a lift. Also has a great pâtisserie on street level. ❷

The City

The part of the city you'll want to see forms a rough hexagon clamped round a bend in the wide, brown River Garonne and contained within a ring of nineteenth-century boulevards – Strasbourg, Carnot, Jules-Guesde and others. An outer ring enclosing these is formed by the Canal du Midi, which here joins the Garonne on its way from the Mediterranean to the Atlantic.

Old Toulouse is effectively quartered by two nineteenth-century streets: the long shopping street, **rue d'Alsace-Lorraine/rue du Languedoc**, which runs north–south; and **rue de Metz**, which runs east–west onto the Pont-Neuf and across the Garonne. It's all very compact and easily walkable, and the city's **métro** is of little use for getting to sites of interest.

In addition to the general pleasure of wandering the streets, there are three very good museums and some real architectural treasures in the churches of St-Sernin and Les Jacobins and in the magnificent Renaissance town houses – *hôtels particuliers* – of the merchants who grew rich on the woad-dye trade. This formed the basis of the city's economy from the mid-fifteenth to the mid-sixteenth century, when the arrival of indigo from the Indian colonies wiped it out.

Place du Capitole is the centre of gravity for the city's social life. Its smart cafés throng with people at lunchtime and in the early evening when the dying sun flushes the pink facade of the big town hall opposite. This is the scene of a mammoth Wednesday **market** for food, clothes and junk, and of a smaller organic food market on Tuesday and Saturday mornings. From place du Capitole, a labyrinth of narrow medieval streets radiates out to the town's several other squares, such as place Wilson, the more intimate place St-Georges, the delightful triangular place de la Trinité and place St-Étienne in front of the cathedral.

For green space, you have to head for the sunny banks of the Garonne or the lovely formal gardens of the **Grand-Rond** and **Jardin des Plantes** in the southeast corner of the centre. A less obvious but attractive alternative is the towpath of the Canal du Midi; the best place to join it is a short walk southeast of the Jardin des Plantes, by the neo-Moorish pavilion of the **Georges-Labit museum**, which houses a good collection of Egyptian and Oriental art.

The Capitole and the hôtels particuliers

Occupying the whole of the eastern side of the eponymous square, the **Capitole** has been the seat of Toulouse's city government since the twelfth century. In medieval times it housed the *capitouls*, who made up the oligarchic and independent city council, from which its name derives. This institution, under the name of *consulat*, was common to other Languedoc towns and may have been the inspiration for England's first parliamentary essays, often attributed to Simon de Montfort, son of the general who became familiar with these parts in the course of his merciless campaigns against the Cathar heretics in the early 1200s. Today, these medieval origins are disguised by an elaborate pink and white classical facade (1750) of columns and pilasters, from which the flags of Languedoc, the Republic and the European Union are proudly flown. If there are no official functions taking place, you can have a peek inside (Mon–Fri 9am–5pm, Sat 9am–1pm; free) at the Salle des Illustres and a couple of other rooms covered in flowery, late nineteenth-century murals and some more subdued Impressionist works by Henri Martin.

Many of the old *capitouls* built their **hôtels** in the dense web of now mainly pedestrianized streets round about. The material they used was almost exclusively the flat Toulousain brick, whose rosy colour gives the city its nickname of *Ville Rose*. It is an attractive material, lending a small-scale, detailed finish to otherwise plain facades, and setting off admirably any wood- or stonework. Although many of the *hôtels* survive, they are rarely open to the public, so you have to do a lot of nonchalant sauntering into courtyards to get a look at them. The best known, open to visitors thanks to its very handsome Bremberg collection of paintings, is the **Hôtel Assézat**, at the river end of rue de Metz (Tues–Sun 10am–6pm, Thurs until 9pm; ⓦ www.fondation-bemberg.com; €4.60, plus €3 for temporary exhibits). Started in 1555 under the direction of Nicolas Bachelier, Toulouse's most renowned Renaissance architect, and never finished, it is a sumptuous palace of brick and stone, sporting columns of the three classical orders of Doric, Ionic and Corinthian, plus a lofty staircase tower surmounted by an octagonal lantern. The paintings within include works by Cranach the Elder, Tintoretto and Canaletto as well as moderns like Pissarro, Monet, Gauguin, Vlaminck, Dufy and a roomful of Bonnards. From April to October there's also a *salon de thé* in the covered entrance gallery.

Other fine houses exist just to the south: on rue Pharaon, in place des Carmes, on rue du Languedoc and on rue Dalbade, where the Hôtel Clary (also known as de Pierre), at no. 25, is unusual for being built of stone. To the north, it's worth wandering along rue St-Rome, rue des Changes, rue de la Bourse and rue du May, where the Hôtel du May at no. 7 houses the **Musée du Vieux-Toulouse** (mid-May to mid-Oct Mon–Sat 2–6pm; €2.20), a rather uninspiring museum of the city's history.

The Musée des Augustins, the cathedral and the riverside

Right at the junction of rue de Metz and rue d'Alsace-Lorraine stands the **Musée des Augustins** (Mon & Thurs–Sun 10am–6pm, Wed 10am–9pm; Ⓦwww.augustins.org; €2.20). Outwardly unattractive, the nineteenth-century building incorporates two surviving cloisters of an Augustinian priory (one now restored as a monastery garden) and contains outstanding collections of Romanesque and medieval sculpture, much of it saved from the now-vanished churches of Toulouse's golden age. Many of the pieces form a fascinating, highly naturalistic display of contemporary manners and fashions: merchants with forked beards touching one another's arms in a gesture of familiarity, and the Virgin represented as a pretty, bored young mother looking away from the Child who strains to escape her hold.

To the south of the museum, just past the Chambre de Commerce, the pretty **rue Croix-Baragnon**, full of smart shops and galleries, opens at its eastern end onto the equally attractive **place St-Étienne**, which boasts the city's oldest fountain, the Griffoul (1546). Behind it stands the lopsided **cathedral of St-Étienne**, whose construction was spread over so many centuries that it makes no architectural sense at all. But there's ample compensation in the quiet and elegant streets of the quarter immediately to the south, and in the **Musée Paul-Dupuy**, a few minutes' walk away along rue Tolosane and rue Mage at 13 rue de la Pléau (Mon–Sat: mid-May to mid-Oct 10am–6pm; rest of year 10am–5pm; €2.20), which has a beautifully displayed and surprisingly interesting collection of clocks, watches, clothes, pottery and furniture from the Middle Ages to the present day, as well as a good display of religious art.

If you follow the rue de Metz westward from the Musée des Augustins, you come to the **Pont-Neuf** – begun in 1544, despite its name – where you can cross over to the **St-Cyprien quarter** on the left bank of the Garonne. At the end of the bridge on the left, an old water tower, erected in 1822 to supply clean water to the city's drinking fountains, now houses the **Galerie Municipale du Château d'Eau** (Mon & Wed–Sun 2–7pm; Ⓦwww.galeriechateaudeau.com; €2.20), an influential photography exhibition space and information centre, with frequent changes of exhibition. Next door in the old hospital buildings, there's a small **medical museum** (Mon–Fri 5–7pm, Sat & Sun 1–7pm; free), housing a selection of surgical instruments and pharmaceutical equipment.

But the star of the left bank is undoubtedly Toulouse's new contemporary art gallery, **Les Abattoirs**, at 76 allées Charles-de-Fitte (Tues–Sun noon–8pm; Ⓦwww.lesabattoirs.org; €6.10). This splendid venue opened in 2000 and is not only one of France's best contemporary art museums, but an inspiring example of urban regeneration, constructed in a vast brick abattoir complex dating from 1828. The space itself is massive, with huge chambers perfectly suited to display even the largest canvases. The collection comprises over 2000 works (painting, sculpture, mixed- and multimedia) by artists from 44 countries, but the most striking piece is undoubtedly Picasso's massive 14m by 20m theatre backdrop, *La dépouille du Minotaure en costume d'Arlequin*, painted in 1936 for Romain Rolland's *Le 14 Juillet*, which towers over the lower gallery.

The churches of Les Jacobins and St-Sernin

A short distance west of place du Capitole, on rue Lakanal, you can't miss the **church of the Jacobins**. Constructed in 1230 by the Order of Preachers (Dominicans) which St Dominic had founded here in 1216 to preach against Cathar heretics, the church is a huge fortress-like rectangle of unadorned brick, buttressed – like Albi cathedral – by plain brick piles, quite unlike what you'd normally associate with Gothic architecture. The interior is a single space divided by a central row of ultra-slim pillars from whose minimal capitals spring an elegant splay of vaulting ribs – 22 from the last in line – like palm fronds. Beneath the altar lie the bones of the philosopher St Thomas Aquinas. On the north side, you step out into the calming hush of a **cloister** with a formal array of box trees and cypress in the middle, and its adjacent art **exhibition hall** (daily 10am–7pm; €5, cloister only €2.50). Nearby, at the corner of rue Gambetta and rue Lakanal, poke your nose into the stone-galleried courtyard of the **Hôtel de Bernuy**, one of the city's most elaborate Renaissance houses.

From the north side of place du Capitole, **rue du Taur** leads past the belfry wall of **Notre-Dame-du-Taur**, whose diamond-pointed arches and decorative motifs represent the acme of Toulousain bricklaying skills, to place St-Sernin. Here you're confronted with the largest Romanesque church in France, the **basilica of St-Sernin**, begun in 1080 to accommodate the passing hordes of Santiago pilgrims, and one of the loveliest examples of its genre. Its most striking external features are the octagonal brick belfry with rounded and pointed arches, diamond lozenges, colonnettes and mouldings picked out in stone, and the apse with nine radiating chapels. Entering from the south, you pass under the Porte Miégeville, whose twelfth-century carvings launched the influential Toulouse school of sculpture. Inside, the great high nave rests on brick piers, flanked by double aisles of diminishing height, surmounted by a gallery running right around the building. The small fee for the **ambulatory** (daily 10am–6pm; €2) is well worth it for the exceptional eleventh-century marble reliefs on the end wall of the choir and for the extraordinary wealth of reliquaries which repose in the spacious **crypt**.

Right outside St-Sernin is the city's archeological museum, **Musée St-Raymond** (daily: June–Aug 10am–7pm; Sept–May 10am–6pm; €2.20), housed in what remains of the block built for poor students of the medieval university and containing a large collection of objects ranging from prehistoric to Roman, as well as an excavated necropolis in the basement. On Sunday mornings the whole of place St-Sernin turns into a marvellous, teeming **flea market**.

The suburbs

To see something of the modern face of Toulouse, it's necessary to venture out into the suburbs, where you can visit a high-tech amusement park and a very specialized but surprisingly interesting aircraft assembly plant. The first of these is the **Cité de l'Espace** (daily: July & Aug 9.30am–7pm; Sept–June 9.30am–6pm; Ⓦ www.cite-espace.com; €14, children over 6 €10.50), beside exit 17 of the A612 *périphérique* on the road to Castres, or take bus #19 from place Marengo (school hols only). The theme is space and space exploration, including satellite communications, space probes and, best of all, the opportunity to walk inside a mock-up of the Mir space station – fascinating, but absolutely chilling. Many of the exhibits are interactive and, though it's a bit on the pricey side, you could easily spend a half-day here, especially if you've got children in tow.

In 1970 Toulouse became home to **Aérospatiale**, which, along with the aerospace industries of Germany, Britain and Spain, now manufactures Airbus passenger jets. The planes are assembled, painted and tested in a vast hangar, L'Usine Clément Ader, before taking their maiden flights from next-door Blagnac airport. Members of the public are allowed inside the plant on a highly informative guided tour (July & Aug contact the tourist office, Sept–June ring Ⓣ05.61.18.06.01, Ⓦwww.taxiway.fr; €9; normally in French), but you need to apply at least two weeks before with your passport details, or a few days before for citizens of EU-member countries. After a brief bus tour round the site and a short PR film, you climb high above the eerily quiet assembly bays where just one hundred people churn out five planes a week, ably assisted by scores of computerized robots. Look out for the latest Airbus, the A380, a two-storey superliner which dwarfs even the Jumbo.

Eating, drinking and entertainment

Regular daytime **café-lounging** can be pursued around the popular student-arty hangout of place Arnaud-Bernard, while place du Capitole is the early evening meeting place. Place St-Georges remains popular, though its clientele is no longer convincingly bohemian, and place Wilson also has its enthusiasts.

There are several good areas to look for a place to **eat**. One of the most attractive and fashionable, with a wide choice, is the rue de la Colombette, in the St-Aubin district just across boulevard Carnot. Another is place Arnaud-Bernard and the tiny adjacent place des Tiercerettes, just north of St-Sernin. Rue du Taur has a number of Vietnamese places and sandwich bars, and the narrow rue du May has a crêperie, pasta place and restaurant. For lunch, however, there is no surpassing the row of five or six small restaurants jammed in line on the mezzanine floor above the gorgeous **food market** in place Victor-Hugo, off boulevard de Strasbourg. They only function at lunchtime, are all closed on Monday, and cost as little as €12. Both food and atmosphere are perfect.

Cafés

Bibent 5 place du Capitole. On the south side of the square, this is Toulouse's most distinguished café, with exuberant plasterwork, marble tables and cascading chandeliers.

Le Café des Artistes place de la Daurade. Lively young café overlooking the Garonne. A perfect spot to watch the sun set on warm summer evenings, as floodlights pick out the brick buildings along the *quais*.

Le Florida 12 place du Capitole. Relaxed café with a retro air. One of the most pleasant places to hang out on the central square.

Jour de Fête 43 rue de Taur. Trendy tea room and brasserie with a small street-side patio. Friendly service and a young university-set crowd.

Au Trait d'Union 12 rue des Gestes. Funky tea-house and art gallery down a small street just off the place du Capitole. Closed Sun & Mon.

Restaurants

Les Abbatoirs 97 allée Charles-de-Fitte Ⓣ05.61.42.04.95. Family-run for two generations, this is one of the last of the traditional slaughterhouse-side meat emporia, with a reputation for top-of-the-line intestinal delicacies, such as calves brains and pig's feet. Menus from €16. Closed Sun, Mon & Aug.

La Bascule 14 av Maurice-Hauriou Ⓣ05.61.52.09.51. A Toulouse institution. Its chromy interior is pure Art Deco and the food well preprared and presented. The menu includes regional dishes like cassoulet, *foie de canard* and oysters from the Bay of Arcachon. Menus from €20. Closed Sun.

Benjamin 7 rue des Gestes Ⓣ05.61.22.92.66. A long-standing institution for economical *terroir* food; service is pleasant and professional, although the atmosphere is somewhat anonymous. A wide selection of duck-based lunch and dinner menus from €11–19. Open daily.

Cantine du Curé 2 rue H.-de-Grosse. Cosy *terroir* restaurant, housed in a small but atmospheric old building, complete with wooden beams, by the entrance to the Dalbade church. One of the two tiny dining areas has a fireplace. Evening menu from €27.

Au Chat Deng 40 rue Peyrolières. Small, hip bistro with cool blue decor across from the Petit Voisin bar. The selection is not overly imaginative, with a sold southern French base and occasional Italian incursions (usually in the form of pasta). Menus from €18–24, but considerably more à la carte. Closed Sun.

Chez Atilla in the market at pl Victor-Hugo. The best of the market restaurants, this no-nonsense lunch-time establishment is also one of Toulouse's best options for seafood – their Spanish *zarzuela* stew is a fish-lover's dream. Menus from €10. Closed Mon & part Aug.

Faim des Haricots 3 rue de Puits Vert Ⓣ05.61.22.49.25. Toulouse's newest vegetarian option, with generous all-you-can-eat salad and dessert buffets (both €8), "bottomless" bowls of soup and a plat du jour. Open Mon–Sat lunch &Thurs–Sat dinner; closed first half Aug.

Les Jardins de l'Ópera 1 pl du Capitole Ⓣ05.61.21.05.56. The *Grand Hôtel*'s restaurant is Toulouse's best and most luxurious. If you fancy a splurge this is the place to do it – the food is outstanding – but you will pay for it: a basic menu starts at €40. Closed Sun & part Aug.

Michel Sarran 21 bd Armand-Duportal Ⓣ05.61.12.32.32. Justifiably renowned *gastronomique* restaurant, a fifteen-minute walk from the place du Capitole (follow rue des Lois and rue des Salenques to the end, and turn left). Imaginative dishes with a strong Mediterranean streak are served with style and warmth. Menus from €40–95. Closed part Aug.

Au Pois Gourmand 3 rue Émile Heybrard Ⓣ05.61.31.95.95 Great location in a riverside nineteenth-century house with a beautiful patio. The quality French cuisine does not come cheap here (menus from €22–60), but is of a predictably high standard, and the *carte* presents a pleasant departure from purely regional dishes. Bus #66 or #14 from metro St-Cyprien-République. Closed Sat lunch & Sun.

Le Sept Place St-Sernin 7 pl St-Sernin Ⓣ05.62.30.05.30. A small house behind the basilica conceals a lively and cheerful restaurant serving inventive and original cuisine with a constantly changing *carte*, followed by dazzling desserts. Menus from €23–45. Closed Sat lunch & Sun.

Bars and clubs

L'Ambassade 22 bd de la Gare. Downbeat club where funk and soul rule. Live jazz on Sunday nights. Mon–Fri 7pm–2am, Sat & Sun 7pm–5am.

Bagdam Café 4 rue de la Croix Ⓣ05.61.99.03.62. Bohemian place, catering for women only, with readings, music and drama as well as coffee, drinks and food. Tues–Sat from 7pm. Closed mid-Aug to mid-Sept.

Bar du Matin 16 place des Carmes. Great old street-corner bar in the finest beer, peanuts and pastis tradition. A friendly and deservedly popular place. Mon–Sat 8am–11pm.

Bodega-Bodega 1 rue Gabriel-Péri. The old Telegraph newspaper building makes a superb venue for this bar-restaurant, with its hugely popular disco after 10pm. Daily 7pm–2am, till 4am on Sat.

Le Chat d'Oc 7 rue de Metz. Hip bar near the Garonne, attracting a mixed crowd which gets younger as the night progresses. Nightly animations include DJs and occasional live acts. Mon–Fri 7am–2am, Sat 9am–5am.

Erich Coffie 9 rue Joseph-Vié Ⓣ05.61.42.04.27. Just west of the river in the quartier St-Cyprien, this is one of the city's liveliest and most enjoyable music bars (food available), with an eclectic music policy. Live bands most evenings. Open Tues–Sat from 10pm.

Le Fair Play 4 allées Paul-Feuga. A great bar for sports fans, which fills up whenever there's a football or rugby match or jai alai to watch. Happy hour Thurs 6–8pm.

The Frog & Rosbif 14 rue de l'Industrie. Stop by this friendly British pub, just off boulevard Lazare-Carnot, for a pint of Darktagnan stout, or one of their other excellent home-brews. Quiz nights, football and fish and chips draw a surprisingly international crowd. Mon–Fri & Sun 5.30pm–2am, Sat 2pm–4am. Closed part Aug.

Hey Joe place Héraclès. Popular disco with theme nights on Thursdays. Men pay €8, women get in free; happy hour midnight–1am. Open daily 11pm–5am.

Le Petit Voisin 37 rue Peyrolières. A neighbourhood place, just like the name says, laid-back during the day, and with DJs at night. Open Mon–Fri 7.30am–2am, Sat 8am–4am. Closed mid-Aug.

Tanygasy 41 rue Paradoux. Bohemian tea room featuring art exhibits, and occasional happenings. Open Tues–Sat noon–8pm & Sun 4–8pm; closed much of July & August.

L'Ubu 16 rue St-Rome ⓣ05.61.23.26.75. Long-standing pillar of the city's dance scene, which remains as popular as ever. Mon–Sat 11pm till dawn.

Film, theatre and live music

Drinking and dancing aside, there's plenty to do at night in Toulouse. Several **cinemas** regularly show v.o. films, including: ABC, 13 rue St-Bernard (ⓣ05.61.29.81.00); Cinémathèque, 68 rue de Taur (ⓣ05.62.30.30.10); Cratere, 95 Grande rue St-Michel (ⓣ05.61.52.50.53); and Utopia, 24 rue Montardy (ⓣ05.61.23.66.20). There's also an extremely vibrant **theatre** culture here. The tourist office can give you a full list of venues, which range from the official Théâtre de la Cité, 1 rue Pierre-Baudis (ⓣ05.34.45.05.05, ⓦwww.tnt-cite.com), to the workshop Nouveau Théâtre Jules-Julien, 6 av des Écoles-Jules-Juliens (Mon–Fri 9am–noon & 2–5pm; ⓣ05.61.25.79.92). The larger venues, such as Odyssud, 4 av du Parc Blagnac (ⓣ05.61.71.75.15; bus #66), feature both theatre and **opera**, while the Orchestre National du Capitole has its base in the Halle aux Grains on place Dupuy (ⓣ05.61.99.78.00, ⓦwww.onct.mairie-toulouse.fr). The city's biggest **concert venue** (9000 seats), specializing in rock, is Zénith at 11 av Raymond Badiou (ⓣ05.62.74.49.49; metro Arènes, Patte d'Oie; bus # 14, 46, 63–67), while Cave-Poesie at 71 rue de Taur (ⓣ05.61.23.62.00) is home to literary workshops and gatherings of a decidedly bohemian spirit.

Listings

Airport Aéroport Toulouse-Blagnac ⓣ05.61.42.44.00 and 05.24.61.80.00, ⓦwww.toulouse.aeroport.fr; for shuttle bus information ⓣ05.34.60.64.00.

Bicycle rental Bikes and scooters available at Rev'moto, 14 bd de la Gare (ⓣ05.62.47.07.08). Serious cyclists planning a longer trip may want to contact the Association Vélo, 2 rue de la Daurade, 31000 Toulouse (ⓣ05.61.11.87.09, ⓦwww.multimania.com/velotlse).

Books For English-language books, Books and Mermaides, 3 rue Mirepoix, specializes in second-hand tomes and will exchange, while The Bookshop, 17 rue Lakanal, stocks new titles. There are book markets on Thursday mornings in place Arnaud-Bernard, and all day Saturday in place St-Etienne.

Car rental A2L, 81 bd Déodat-de-Séverac ⓣ05.61.59.33.99; Avis, gare SNCF ⓣ05.61.63.71.71; Budget, 49 rue Bayard ⓣ05.61.63.18.18; Europcar, 15 bd Bonrepos ⓣ05.61.62.52.89; Hertz, gare SNCF ⓣ05.61.62.94.12.

Consulates Britain, Immueble Victoria Center, 20 chemin de Laporte ⓣ05.61.15.02.02; Canada, 10 rue Jules de Resseguier ⓣ05.61.52.19.06; USA, 25 allées Jean-Jaurés ⓣ05.34.31.36.50.

Gay and lesbian For information contact the gay and lesbian students' group Jules et Julies (Comité des Étudiants, Université du Mirail, 5 Allée Machado, 31058) or Gais et Lesbiennes en Marche (ⓣ06.11.87.38.81, ⓔgelem@altern.org).

Internet Cyber Media-Net, 19 rue de Lois (Mon–Fri 9am–11.30pm, Sat 10am–midnight), or @fterbug, 12 pl St-Sernin (Mon–Fri noon–2am, Sat noon–5am, Sun 2.30–10.30pm).

Pharmacy The Pharmacie de Nuit, 70–76 allées Jean-Jaurès (entry on rue Arnaud Vidal) is open 8pm–8am.

Police 23 bd de l'Embouchure ⓣ05.61.12.77.77.

Taxi ⓣ05.62.16.26.16 ("taxi touristique" tariff: €31 for a one-hour circuit of the town starting from the Capitole or €46 for two hours; extra surcharge for hotel pick up).

Youth information CRIJ, 17 rue de Metz (Mon–Sat 10am–1pm & 2–7pm; ⓣ05.61.21.20.20).

Albi and around

ALBI, 77km and an hour's train ride northeast of Toulouse, is a small industrial town with two unique sights: a museum containing the most comprehensive collection of Toulouse-Lautrec's work (Albi was his birthplace); and one of the most remarkable Gothic cathedrals you'll ever see. Its other claim to fame comes from its association with Catharism; though not itself an important centre, it gave its name – Albigensian – to both the heresy and the crusade to suppress it.

The town hosts three good **festivals** over the course of the year: jazz in May, theatre at the end of June/beginning of July, and classical music at the end of July/beginning of August. During July and August there are also free organ recitals in the cathedral (Wed 5pm & Sun 4pm).

The Town

The **Cathédrale Ste-Cécile** (June–Sept daily 8.30am–7pm; Oct–May Mon–Sat 9am–noon & 2.30–6.30pm, Sun 8.30am–7pm; free; entry to choir €1, to treasury €3), begun about 1280, is visible from miles around, dwarfing the town like some vast bulk carrier run aground, the belfry its massive superstructure. If the comparison sounds unflattering, perhaps it is not amiss, for this is not a conventionally beautiful building; it's all about size and boldness of conception. The sheer plainness of the exterior is impressive on this scale, and it's not without interest: arcading, buttressing, the contrast of stone against brick – every differentiation of detail becomes significant. Entrance is through the south portal, by contrast the most extravagant piece of Flamboyant sixteenth-century frippery. The interior, a hall-like nave of colossal proportions, is dominated by a huge mural of the *Last Judgement*, believed to be the work of Flemish artists in the late fifteenth century. Above, the vault is covered in richly colourful paintings of sixteenth-century Italian workmanship, while a rood screen, delicate as lace, shuts off the choir: Adam makes a show of covering himself, Eve strikes a flaunting model's pose beside the central doorway, and the rest of the screen is adorned with countless statuary.

Next to the cathedral, a powerful red-brick castle, the thirteenth-century **Palais de la Berbie**, houses the **Musée Toulouse-Lautrec** (Mar & Oct Wed–Mon 10am–noon & 2–5.30pm; April & May daily 10am–noon & 2–6pm; June & Sept daily 9am–noon & 2–6pm; July & Aug daily 9am–6pm; Nov–Feb Wed–Mon 10am–noon & 2–5pm; €4.50), containing paintings, drawings, lithographs and posters from the earliest work to the very last – an absolute must for anyone interested in Belle Époque seediness and, given the predominant Impressionism of the time, the rather offbeat painting style of its subject. However, perhaps the most impressive thing about this museum is the building itself, its parapets, gardens and walkways giving stunning views over the river and its bridges.

Opposite the east end of the cathedral, rue Mariés leads into the shopping streets of the old town, most of it impeccably renovated and restored. The little square and covered passages by the **church of St-Salvy** are worth a look as you go by. Eventually you come to the broad **Lices Pompidou**, the main thoroughfare of modern Albi, which leads down to the river and the road to Cordes. Less touristy, this is the best place to look for somewhere to eat and drink.

Practicalities

From the **gare SNCF** on place Stalingrad it's a ten-minute walk into town along avenues Maréchal-Joffre and de-Gaulle; you'll see the **gare routière** on your right in place Jean-Jaurès as you reach the limits of the old town. The tourist office is in one corner of the Palais de la Berbie (July & Aug Mon–Sat 9am–7pm, Sun 10am–12.30pm & 2.30–5pm; Sept–June Mon–Sat 9am–12.30pm & 2–6pm, Sun 10am–12.30pm & 2.30–5pm; ⓣ05.63.49.48.80, ⓦwww.tourisme.fr/albi); ask for a copy of their English-language leaflet describing three walking tours round Albi.

There are two attractive **hotels** near the station on avenue Maréchal-Joffre: *La Régence*, at no. 27 (ⓣ05.63.54.01.42, ⓦwww.hotellaregence.com; ❷), and the slightly more expensive *Georges V*, at no. 29 (ⓣ05.63.54.24.16, ⓔhote.georgev@ilink.fr; ❷). On the opposite side of the town, on the north bank of the river, you'll find the luxurious *Mercure les Bastides* (ⓣ05.63.47.66.66, ⓔmercure.albi@wanadoo.fr; ❺) at 41 rue Porta. In the heart of old Albi near the cathedral, both the *Hotel St-Clair*, 8 rue St-Clair (ⓣ05.63.54.25.66, ⓔmichelandrieu@hotmail.com; ❷), and *Le Vieil Alby*, 25 rue Toulouse-Lautrec (ⓣ05.63.54.15.69, ⓕ05.63.54.96.75; ❸), are agreeable places to stay. Otherwise, there's a municipal **campsite** (ⓣ05.63.60.37.06; closed mid-Oct to March) in the Parc de Caussels, about 2km east on the D999 Millau road.

Albi's **cuisine** is predominantly *terroir* – local cooking notable only for *lou tastou*, the local version of tapas. The best *terroir* restaurant is *Moulin de Mothe*, on rue de Lamothe (ⓣ05.63.60.38.15; closed Wed & Sun eve except July & Aug; menus €25–28), on the north bank west from the pont vieux. Also serving *terroir*, *La Tête de l'Art*, 7 rue de la Piale (ⓣ05.63.38.44.75; closed Tues eve & all Wed; from €13.50), is set apart by unrestrained atmosphere and wacky decor, while *L'Esprit du Vin*, 11 quai Choiseul (ⓣ05.63.54.60.44; closed Sun eve, all Mon & Feb; from €42–60), has imaginative *gastronomique* cuisine. For something different *La Casa Loca*, rue Puech Bérenguier (ⓣ05.63.47.26.00; closed Sun), features genuine Spanish food and tapas (menus from €9). *Tournesol*, off place du Vigan (ⓣ05.63.38.44.60; closed Sun & Mon, lunch only except Fri), is Albi's vegetarian option (from €12.).

Cagnac-les-Mines and Cordes

The country between Albi and Carmaux, 16km to the north, has long been a coal-mining and industrial area, associated in particular with the political activity of Jean Jaurès, father figure of French socialism. Elected deputy for Albi in 1893, after defending the striking miners of Carmaux, he then championed the glassworkers in 1896 in a strike that led to the setting up of a pioneering workers' co-operative, La Verrerie Ouvrière, which still functions today. The tourist office in Albi can provide a list of interesting industrial sites in the area, including the pit at **CAGNAC-LES-MINES**, just north of Albi, where the Musée Mine de Cagnac (Mon–Sat 10.30–11.30am & 2.30–5.30pm & Sun 10.30–11.30am & 3–5pm; €7), presents a vivid recreation of the world of the coal mine, and is undoubtedly the region's most original museum.

Of more conventional tourist interest is the town of **CORDES**, perched on a conical hill 24km northwest of Albi, from which it's a brief trip by train (as far as Cordes-Vindrac, 5km away, with bike rental from the station) or bus (daily except Sun), or an easy hitch. Founded in 1222 by Raymond VII, Count of Toulouse, Cordes was a Cathar stronghold, and the ground beneath the town is riddled with tunnels for storage and refuge in time of trouble. As one of the southwest's oldest and best-preserved *bastides*, complete with thirteenth- and fourteenth-century houses climbing steep cobbled lanes, Cordes is inevitably a major tourist attraction: medieval banners flutter in the streets and artisans practise their crafts. The **Musée Charles-Portal** (April & May Sun 3–6pm; June & Sept Sat & Sun same times; July & Aug daily 11am–12.30pm & 3.30–6.30pm; €3) depicts the history of the town. Lovers of the bizarre should take a look at the **Musée de l'Art du Sucre** (daily: Feb–March & Sept–Dec 10am–noon & 2–6.30pm; April–June 10am–12.30pm & 2–7pm; July & Aug 9am–7pm; €3), containing outrageous sugar-sculptures created by famous local *pâtissier*, Yves Thuriès, and his underlings. The nicest **hotel** in town is the *Grand Écuyer* (Ⓣ05.63.53.79.50, Ⓔgrand.ecuyer@thuries.fr; ❺; closed mid-Oct to Easter) in the former palace of Raymond VII. Across from the Charles-Porte museum, *Hôtel de la Cité*, is a lower-priced alternative (Ⓣ05.63.56.03.53, Ⓔcite@thuries.fr; ❹; closed Nov–April), housed in a medieval building. There's also a **campsite** (Ⓣ & Ⓕ05.63.56.11.10; closed Oct–March) 1km southeast down the Gaillac road.

Castres and around

In spite of its industrial activities, **CASTRES**, 40km south of Albi and 55km east of Toulouse, has kept a lot of its charm, in the streets on the right bank of the Agout and, in particular, the riverside quarter where the old tanners' and weavers' houses overhang the water. The centre is a bustling, businesslike sort of place, with a big morning **market** on Saturdays on place Jean-Jaurès. By the rather unremarkable old cathedral, the former bishop's palace holds the Hôtel de Ville and Castres' **Musée Goya** (July & Aug daily 9am–noon & 2–6pm; Sept–June Tues–Sun same times; July–Aug €3, otherwise €2.29), home to the biggest collection of Spanish paintings in France outside the Louvre. Goya is represented by some lighter political paintings and a large collection of engravings, and there are also works by other famous Iberian artists, like Murillo and Velázquez.

Castres' other specialist museum is the **Musée Jean-Jaurès** (July & Aug daily 9am–noon & 2–6pm; Sept–June Tues–Sun 9am–noon & 2–5/6pm; €1.50), dedicated to its famous native son. It's located in place Pélisson, and getting to it takes you through the streets of the old town, past the splendid seventeenth-century **Hôtel Nayrac**, on rue Frédéric-Thomas. The museum was opened in 1988 by President Mitterrand – appropriately enough, because Mitterrand's Socialist Party is the direct descendant of Jaurès' SFIO, founded in 1905, which split at the Congress of Tours in 1920, when the "Bolshevik" element left to form the French Communist Party. The museum, though slightly hagiographic as you might expect, nonetheless pays well-deserved tribute to one of France's boldest and best political writers, thinkers and activists of modern times. Jaurès supported Dreyfus, founded the newspaper *L'Humanité*, campaigned against the death penalty and colonialism, and was murdered for his courageous pacifist stance at the outbreak of World War I – oddly enough by a man called Villain. There could be no better epitaph than his own last article in *L'Humanité*, in which he wrote: "The most important thing is that we should continue to act and to keep our minds perpetually fresh and alive … That is the real safeguard, the guarantee of our future."

Practicalities

Arriving from Toulouse by train, you'll find the **gare SNCF** a kilometre southwest of the town centre on avenue Albert-1er. The **gare routière** is on place Soult, with bus services to Mazamet and Lacaune. The **tourist office** stands beside the Pont Vieux at 3 rue Milhau-Ducommun (April–Oct Mon–Sat 8.30am–7pm, Sun 10am–noon & 2–6pm; Nov–March Mon–Sat 8.30am–12.30pm & 1.30–6.30pm, Sun 2–6pm; ⓣ05.63.62.63.62, ⓦwww.ville-castres.fr).

Castres has two marvellous seventeenth-century mansions converted into luxurious but affordable **hotels**; the more deluxe is the *Renaissance* at 17 rue Victor Hugo (ⓣ05.63.59.30.42, ⓕ05.63.72.11.57; ❹), while close behind is the *L'Europe*, just up the same street at no. 5 (ⓣ05.63.59.00.33, ⓕ05.63.59.21.38; ❹). Otherwise, the *Rivière*, 10 quai Tourcaudière (ⓣ05.63.59.04.53, ⓕ05.63.59.61.97; ❷), has pleasant views over the Agout and helpful staff, and the very friendly and clean *Le Périgord*, 22 rue Zola (ⓣ05.63.59.04.74; ❶), is a bargain. The municipal **campsite** (ⓣ05.63.59.72.30; closed Oct–March) is in a riverside park 2km northeast of town on the road to Roquecourbe, which you can also reach by river-taxi (round trip €4).

For simple, inexpensive **meals**, you can't beat the upstairs dining room in the *Brasserie des Jacobins*, on place Jean-Jaurès. Alternatively, *Le Médiéval* (ⓣ05.63.51.13.78; closed Sun & Mon), at 44 rue Milhau-Ducommun, has an eleventh-century dining room poised above the Agout, and offers reasonable *terroir* and *gastronomique* menus from €18.

Le Sidobre

Just east of Castres rises the westernmost extremity of the Parc Naturel Régional du Haut Languedoc, cut by deep river valleys and covered with marvellous woods. This is **Le Sidobre**, an area renowned for its granite: huge boulders litter the woods, often carved by the millennia into zoomorphic or other shapes – Les Trois Fromages and l'Oie, for example – that give them commercial value in the eyes of the tourist industry. Exploration is best done on foot: the **GR36** footpath passes this way.

LACROUZETTE, 15km from Castres, is the main town and capital of the granite industry. The demand for tombstones being impervious to recession, the town continues to prosper, though it's not the most beautiful place. However, if you're on your way up the Agout and Gijou valleys to Lacaze and Lacaune, the *Au Relais du Sidobre*, 8 rte de Vabre (ⓣ05.63.50.60.06, ⓦwww.logis-de-france.com; ❷), makes a convenient and pleasant stopover. For something more unique, head for the *chambres d'hôtes* of the luxurious fourteenth- to sixteenth-century castle in **BURLATS**, 10km northeast of Castres (ⓣ05.63.35.29.20, ⓔle.castel.de-burlats@wanadoo.fr; ❹).

The Gers

West of Toulouse, the *département* of **Gers** lies at the heart of the historic region of Gascony. In the long struggle for supremacy between the English and the French in the Middle Ages it had the misfortune to form the frontier zone between the English base at Bordeaux and the French at Toulouse – hence the large number of fortified villages, or *bastides*, dominating the hilltops. The attractive if unspectacular rolling agricultural land is dotted with ancient, honey-stoned farms. Settlement is sparse and – with the exception of **Auch**, the capital – major monuments are largely lacking, which keeps it well off the beaten tourist trails, although the gently varied topography and tranquillity make it an ideal region for biking and hiking.

The region's traditional sources of renown are its stout-hearted mercenary warriors – of whom Alexandre Dumas' d'Artagnan and Edmond Rostand's Cyrano de Bergerac are the supreme literary exemplars – its rich cuisine and its Armagnac. The food and brandy still flourish: Gers is the biggest producer of foie gras in the country. Other traditional dishes are *magret de canard*, Henri IV's *poulet au pot* (the chicken that he promised to provide for every peasant's Sunday dinner), confit of duck and goose, thick *garbure* soup and *daube de por*. Then there's *croustade*, a tart of apple and Armagnac, the speciality of Gascon *pâtissiers*. And to wash it all down the red wines of Madiran, Buzet and St-Mont, and the whites of Pacherenc du Vic-Bilh.

Auch

The sleepy provincial capital of Gers, **AUCH**, is most easily accessible by rail from Toulouse, 78km to the east. The old town, which is the only part worth exploring, stands on a bluff overlooking the tree-lined River Gers, with the cathedral towering dramatically over the town.

It is this building – the **Cathédrale Ste-Marie** – which makes a trip to Auch worthwhile. Although not finished until the latter part of the seventeenth century, it is built in basically late Gothic style, with a classical facade. Of particular interest are the choir stalls (daily: April–June & Sept 8.30am–noon & 2–6pm; July & Aug 83.0am–6.30pm; Oct–March 8.30am–noon & 2–5pm; €1.50) and the stained glass; both were begun in the early 1500s, though the windows are of clearly Renaissance inspiration, while the choir remains Gothic. The stalls are thought to have been carved by the same craftsmen who executed those at St-Bertrand-de-Comminges, and show the same extraordinary virtuosity and detail. The eighteen windows, unusual in being a complete set, parallel the scenes and personages depicted in the stalls. They are the work of a Gascon painter, Arnaud de Moles, and are equally rich in detail.

Immediately south of the cathedral, in the tree-filled place Salinis, is the forty-metre-high **Tour d'Armagnac**, which served as an ecclesiastical court and prison in the fourteenth century. Descending from here to the river is a **monumental stairway** of 234 steps, with a statue of d'Artagnan gracing one of the terraces. From place de la République, in front of the cathedral's main west door, rue d'Espagne connects with rue de la Convention and what is left of the narrow medieval stairways known as the **pousterles**, which give access to the lower town. On the north side of place de la République, the tourist office inhabits a splendid half-timbered fifteenth-century house on the corner with rue Dessoles, a pedestrianized street boasting an array of fine buildings. Just down the steps to the east of rue Dessoles, on place Louis-Blanc, the former convent, now the **Musée des Jacobins** (May–Sept daily 10am–noon & 2–6pm; rest of year Tues–Sun 10am–noon & 2–5pm; €3) houses one of the best collections of pre-Columbian and later South American art in France, left to the town by an adventurous son, M. Pujos, who had lived in Chile in the last years of the nineteenth century. Also of interest is its small collection of traditional Gascon furniture, religious artefacts and Gallo-Roman remains.

Practicalities

The **tourist office** (mid-July to mid-Aug Mon–Sat 9.30am–6.30pm & Sun 10am–12.15pm & 3–6.15pm; rest of year Mon–Sat 9,15am–noon & 2–6/6.30pm; ⓣ05.62.05.22.89, ⓦwww.mairie-auch.fr) stands at the corner of place de la République and rue Dessoles. West of here, place de la Libération leads to the allées d'Étigny, with the **gare routière** off to the right.

Ironically the sleepy capital of the Gers has almost no where for visitors to bed down. The only choice in the centre is the relatively luxurious *Hotel de France* at 2 place de la Libération (ⓣ05.62.61.71.71; ④), right by the *mairie* and only a few minutes' walk west of the cathedral. The only other alternative is the more economical *Hôtel de Paris*, 38 av de la Marne (ⓣ05.62.63.26.22, f05.62.60.04.27; ②; closed Nov). To get there from the *gare SNCF*, turn right on avenue de la Gare, follow it to the end, then turn left. Otherwise, the municipal **campsite** (ⓣ05.62.05.00.22; closed mid-Nov to mid-April) is beside the river on the south side of town, and there's a GR653 *gîte d'étape* 4km east at the Château St-Cricq (ⓣ05.62.63.10.17).

Avenue d'Alsace, in the lower town, is the best place to look for inexpensive places to **eat**. Alternatively, up by the cathedral, place de la République and place de la Libération boast a fair selection of cafés and brasseries; try *Café Daroles* by the fountain (menus from €16 or €11.50 at lunch). For something traditional, *La Table d'Hôtes*, off rue Dessoles at 7 rue Lamartine, offers good Gascon fare from €15 (closed Sun eve & Wed). The well-reputed restaurant of the *de France* has menus from €25, although à la carte will set you back considerably more.

Around Auch

Outside Auch is a handful of quiet country towns – **Fleurance**, **Lectoure** and **Condom** – with no great sights, but which, along with the surrounding

Armagnac

Armagnac is a dry, golden brandy distilled in the district extending into the Landes and Lot and Garonne *départements*, divided into three distinct areas: Haut-Armagnac (around Auch), Ténarèze (Condom) and Bas-Armagnac (Éauze), in ascending order of output and quality. Growers of the grape like to compare brandy with whisky, equating malts with the individualistic, earthy Armagnac distilled by small producers, and blended whiskies with the more consistent, standardized output of the large-scale houses. Armagnac grapes are grown on sandy soils and, importantly, the wine is distilled only once, giving the spirit a lower alcohol content but more flavour. Aged in local black oak, Armagnac matures quickly, so young Armagnacs are relatively smoother than corresponding Cognacs.

Distilled originally for medicinal reasons, Armagnac has many claims made for its efficacy. Perhaps the most optimistic are those of the priest of Éauze de St-Mont, who held that the eau-de-vie cured gout and hepatitis. More reasonably, he also wrote that it "stimulates the spirit if taken in moderation, recalls the past, gives many joy above all else, conserves youth. If one retains it in the mouth, it unties the tongue and gives courage to the timid."

Many of the producers welcome visitors and offer tastings, whether you go to one of the bigger *chais* of Condom or Éauze, or follow a faded sign at the bottom of a farm track. For more **information**, contact the Bureau National Interprofessionnel de l'Armagnac, place de la Liberté, 32800 Éauze (ⓣ05.62.08.11.00, ⓦwww.cognacnet.com/armagnac).

countryside, make for a lazy taste of French provincial life. They are all connected by bus from Auch, but away from the main roads – the N21 for Fleurance and Lectoure, and the D930 for Condom – you'll be stuck without your own transport.

Fleurance and Lectoure

FLEURANCE, 24km north of Auch, a *bastide* which was named – in the best spirit of optimism – after Italy's Florence, a namesake which it has utterly failed to live up to. This dull little town's only passing merit is its nineteenth-century stone **market hall**, set in an arcaded square and home to an imaginatively built town hall. Two rare fourteenth-century cannons are fixed to one of the exterior walls. While here, you might peek in the church, marked by its octagonal Toulouse-style belfry and notable for three stained-glass windows executed by Arnaud de Moles, the artist of Auch cathedral. The **tourist office** is on place de la République (July & Aug Mon–Sat 9am–6.30pm, Sun 9am–12.30pm; Sept–June Mon–Sat 9am–1pm & 3.30–6pm; ⓣ05.62.06.27.80, ⓦwww.tourismefleurance.free.fr). If you wish to stay, the only **hotels** are the central two-star *Le Relais* (ⓣ05.62.06.05.08, ⓕ05.62.06.03.84; ❸) and, just out of town on the route d'Agen, the modern *Le Fleurance* (ⓣ05.62.06.14.85, ⓔle.fleurance.hotel@wanadoo.fr; ❸) set in parkland.

Eleven kilometres further north sits **LECTOURE**, the smallest and prettiest of the three towns, built along a narrow escarpment looking out over the surrounding farmland. Capital of the colony of Novempopulania in Roman times and of the counts of Armagnac until their demise at the hands of Louis XI in 1473, it's now renowned for its melons. In the middle of the main street, the **Cathédrale de St-Gervais-et-de-St-Protais** raises its enormous tower above the town, while down the rue Fontelié, behind the tourist office, among scarcely altered medieval houses, you come to the unremarkable thirteenth-century vaulted Gothic **Fontaine de Diane**. The real reason for stopping here is the **Musée Archéologique** (Mon & Wed–Fri 10am–noon & 2–6pm; €2), in basement of the *mairie* (the former wine cellar of the bishops' palace). Here you'll find some impressive rarities including a collection of "taurine" Roman funerary stones, testament to the once popular local oracular cult, and various Merovingian-era decroated clothing clasps.

The **tourist office**, on place de la Cathédrale (July & Aug Mon–Sat 9.30am–12.30pm & 2–7pm, Sun 9am–noon & 2–4pm; otherwise Mon–Sat 9.30am–12.30pm & 2.30–6.30pm; ⓣ05.62.68.76.98, ⓦwww.lectoure.fr), runs the GR65 **gîte d'étape** on nearby rue St-Gervais (same phone number). Just around the corner from the *gîte* is the superb but unfortunately named *Hôtel de Bastard* in rue Lagrange (ⓣ05.62.68.82.44, ⓦwww.hotel-de-bastard.com; ❸; closed late-Dec to Jan; menus from €56), while the *Auberge des Bouviers* at 8 rue Montebello near the central market hall, makes for an atmospheric place to eat (from €19.50). Heading on to Condom with your own transport, stop in at La Romieu, half-way between the two towns, where the badly weathered **collegiate church**, once a stop on the Santiago trail, contains a sacristy with worn but notable fourteenth-century murals. (May–Sept Mon–Sat 10am–7pm & Sun 2–7pm; Oct–May Mon–Sat 10am–noon & 2–6pm & Sun 2–6pm; €4).

Condom

Some 43km north of Auch and 21km west of Lectoure lies the town of **CONDOM**. Contrary to what one might assume, there's no connection between the place and the device. Unremarkable in every other sphere, Condom is nonetheless good for a quick visit or an overnight stop, and makes an ideal base for exploring several interesting sights in the neighborhood. The old town retains some atmosphere with its uniformly honey-brown houses, but the sixteenth-century cathedral, completed just in time to be ravaged by the Wars of Religion is badly damaged and unremarkable. Armagnac drinkers will be interested in the **Musée de l'Armagnac**, 2 rue Jules-Ferry (daily except Tues: April–Sept 10am–noon & 3–6pm; Oct–March 2–5pm; €2.20), and the **Chais Ryst-Duperon**, where the liquor is aged (July & Aug daily 10am–noon & 2–6pm; Sept–June Wed–Sun 10am–noon & 2–5pm; free). For other places to taste and buy Armagnac, ask the **tourist office** in place Bossuet (July & Aug Mon–Sat 9am–12.30pm & 2–7pm, Sun 9am–12.30pm; Sept–Oct Mon–Sat 9am–noon & 2–6pm; ⓣ05.62.28.00.80, ⓦwww.condom.org).

The cheapest place to **stay** is the *Relais de la Ténaréze*, at 20 av d'Aquitaine (ⓣ05.62.28.02.54, f05.62.28.46.96; ❷). Two more appealing options, both with pools, are the *Hôtel Le Logis des Cordeliers*, in rue de la Paix (ⓣ05.62.28.03.68, ⓦwww.logisdescordeliers.com; ❸; closed Jan), and, for a splurge, the *Hôtel des Trois Lys* (ⓣ05.62.28.33.33, ⓦwww.lestroislys.com; ❺; closed Feb; restaurant from €20). There's a GR65 *gîte d'étape* at the Centre Salvandy (ⓣ05.62.28.23.80), and a municipal **campsite** (ⓣ05.62.28.17.32; closed Nov–March) near the river on the road to Éauze. For a straightforward place to **eat**, try *Pizzéria l'Origan*, at 4 rue Cadéot in the town centre (closed Sun & Mon), or *Café des Sports*, on rue Charron by the cathedral, which also does pizzas, as well as a reasonable menu at €16. A more upmarket alternative is *Le Moulin du Petit Gascon* (ⓣ05.62.28.28.42; closed Dec–Feb, also Sun eve & Mon; menus from €18), out of town by the campsite, and attractively sited beside a canal lock.

Around Condom

The sights around Condom can be visited in a morning by car, but are equally accessible (time permitting) by bicycle or hiking trail. Just 5km west of Condom, the tiny twelfth-century village of **LARRESSINGLE** was once home to Condom's bishops who lived in fortified splendour away from the hoi polloi. The compact village is girded by a moat and walls and contains the bishop's keep and stout church. It is best visited in low and shoulder seasons and preferable before 10am or after 7pm; now an obligatory stop on local tours, only one busload is more than enough to dissipate its considerable charms. Those going by car may head a further 13km west to **Séviac** (March–Nov daily 10am–6pm; €4) an important Gallo-Roman villa dating from the fourth and fifth centuries AD, and where impressive mosaics have been uncovered.

Otherwise, follow the signs for the **Chateau de Cassaigne** (daily Mon–Sat 9am-noon & 2–6pm, closed Mon mid-Sept to mid-June; free). This renaissance palace-estate set among spacious gardens was built as the new home for Condom's bishops after they abandoned Larressingle in the eighteenth century. After the tour you can enjoy a *dégustation* of the local vintage. A further 4km will take you back to the main road to Condom, and just before the junction you wil arrive at the abbey of **FLARAN** (daily: Feb–June & Sept to early Jan 10am–12.30pm & 2–6pm; July & Aug 9.30am–7pm; €4). This Cistercian monastery dates back to 1151, and although compact maintains the key elements of the monastic house: the weighty and austere Romaneesque church, a cloister, a beautiful chapter house, luxurious pre-Revolution monks' apartments and a refectory. All the more remarkable is the tale of its reconstruction after a member of the family who owned Flaran set fire to the monastery as part of insurance scam in 1972. Justice was served, the culprit was imprisoned and the local authorities impounded the site and converted it into public patrimony.

Travel details

Trains

Béziers to: Agde (18 daily; 45min); Arles (10–14 daily; 2hr 10min); Avignon (4–10 daily; 2hr); Bédarieux (4–8 daily; 40min); Carcassonne (22 daily; 15min); Clermont-Ferrand (3 daily; 6–7hr); Marseille (8 daily; 3hr 10min); Millau (4–6 daily; 2hr); Montpellier (26 daily; 45min); Nîmes (20 daily; 1hr 15min); Narbonne (18 daily; 14min); Paris (30 daily; 4.5–12hr); Perpignan (18 daily; 40min–1hr); Sète (23 daily; 25min).

Carcassonne to: Arles (4–8 daily; 2hr 40min–3hr 30min); Béziers (22 daily; 45min); Bordeaux (18–22 daily; 3hr 20min–4hr 30min); Limoux (16 daily; 25min); Marseille (12–18 daily; 3hr 20min–5hr 30min); Montpellier (18 daily; 1hr 30min—4hr); Narbonne (22 daily; 35min); Nîmes (26 daily; 2hr 5min–3hr 10min); Quillan (6 daily; 1hr 15min); Toulouse (22 daily; 45min–1hr).

Montpellier to: Arles (10–14 daily; 1hr 20min); Avignon (22 daily; 1hr 15min–2hr); Béziers (18 daily; 40min); Carcassonne (22 daily; 1hr 15min); Lyon (18 daily; 1hr 40min–3hr 30min); Marseille (18–22 daily; 2hr 20min); Mende (18 daily; 3hr 40min–4hr 30min); Narbonne (26 daily; 45min–1hr 15min); Paris (16 daily; 3hr 15min—6hr); Perpignan (12 daily; 2hr 15min); Sète (22 daily; 15–20min); Toulouse (18 daily; 2hr 15min–2hr 55min).

Narbonne to: Arles (18–22 daily; 2hr); Avignon (4–8 daily; 2hr 10min); Béziers (18 daily; 14min); Bordeaux (18–22 daily; 3hr 45min–6hr); Carcassonne (22 daily; 35min); Cerbère (12–16 daily; 1hr–1hr 30min); Marseille (20 daily; 2hr 40min–3hr 30min); Montpellier (26 daily; 45min–1hr 15min); Nîmes (20 daily; 1hr 45min); Perpignan (24 daily; 36–45min); Port-Bou (1 daily; 50min); Sète (23 daily; 45min); Toulouse (18 daily; 1hr 30min).

Nîmes to: Arles (22 daily; 30–40min); Avignon (14–18 daily; 30min); La Bastide-St-Laurent (6–8 daily; 1hr 45min–2hr 40min); Béziers (36 daily; 1hr 15min); Carcassonne (26 daily; 2hr 5min–3hr 10min); Clermont-Ferrand (12–16 daily; 5–6hr); Génolhac (16–20 daily; 1hr 15min–2hr); Marseille (20 daily; 40min–1hr 15min); Montpellier (26 daily; 30min); Narbonne (20 daily; 1hr 45min); Paris (23 daily; 3hr–9hr 30min); Perpignan (12 daily; 2hr 45min); Sète (22 daily; 48min); Villefort (12–16 daily; 1hr 30min–2hr 30min).

Toulouse to: Albi (17 daily; 1hr); Auch (18–20 daily; 1hr 15min–2hr 30min); Ax-les-Thermes (6 daily; 1hr 55min); Barcelona (4 daily; 5hr–6hr 30min); Bayonne (18–22 daily; 2hr 25min–3hr 45min); Bordeaux (18–22 daily; 2hr 30min); Brive (14–18 daily; 2hr 20min–4hr); Castres (11 daily; 1hr 5min); Foix (13 daily; 47min–1hr 15min); Lourdes (8–16 daily; 1hr 40min); Lyon (14–18 daily; 4–6hr); Marseille (22 daily; 3hr 30min–6hr); Mazamet (11 daily; 1hr 30min–1hr 55min); Pamiers (13 daily; 50min to 1hr 10min); Paris (13 daily; 5hr 20min–6hr 45min); Pau (6–10 daily; 2hr–2hr 30min); Tarascon-sur-Ariège (13 daily; 1hr 20min); Tarbes (6–13 daily; 1hr 45min); La-Tour-de-Carol (6 daily; 2hr 30min).

Buses

Albi to: Cordes-sur-Ciel (2 daily; 35min).

Auch to: Agen (6–12 daily; 1hr 30min); Bordeaux (1 daily; 3hr 40min); Condom (1–2 daily; 40min); Fleurance (4–11 daily; 20min); Lannemezan (1 daily; 1hr 45min); Lectoure (4–11 daily; 40min); Montauban (Mon–Sat 1–3 daily; 2hr); Tarbes (3–4 daily; 2hr); Toulouse (1–4 daily; 1hr 30min).

Bédarieux to: Olargues (1–2 daily; 40min); Pont-de-Tarassac (1–2 daily; 30min); St-Pons-de-Thomières (3 daily; 1hr 20min).

Béziers to: Agde (2 daily & 5 in summer; 25min); Castres (2 daily; 2hr 50min); Mazamet (2 daily; 2hr); Montpellier (11 daily; 1hr 30min); Narbonne (2 daily; 1hr); Pézenas (10 daily; 32min); St-Pons-de-Thomières (4 daily; 1hr 20min); La Salvetat (1–2 daily; 2hr 10min).

Carcassonne to: Castelnaudary (5 daily; 45min); Quillan (2 daily; 1hr 20min); Toulouse (1 daily; 2hr 20min).

Montpellier to: Aigues-Mortes (2–4 daily; 1hr); Bédarieux (3–4 daily; 1hr 35min); La Cavalerie (daily; 1hr 50min); Clermont-l'Hérault (3–4 daily; 1hr); Ganges (4–5 daily; 1hr 15min); Gignac (for St-Guilhem: 6–8 daily; 40min); La Grande-Motte (8–12 daily; 1hr 5min; in summer hourly); Grau-du-Roi (8–12 daily; 1hr 10min); Lodève (4 daily; 1hr 15min); Millau (2–8 daily; 2hr 20min); Nîmes (2 daily; 50min); Palavas (local service); Rodez (1–3 daily; 3hr 55min); St-Martin-de-Londres (6 daily; 50min); Sète (10 daily; 1hr 10min); Le Vigan (3–5 daily; 1hr 40min); Viols-le-Fort (2–9 daily; 40min).

Narbonne to: Béziers (2 daily; 1hr); Carcassonne (1–4 daily; 1hr 30min); Gruissan (3–6 daily; 45min); Narbonne-Plage (2–8 daily; 45min); Perpignan (1 daily; 2hr).

Nîmes to: Aigues-Mortes (17 daily; 55min); Avignon (4 daily; 1hr 30min); Ganges (2–3 daily; 1hr 30min); La Grand Motte (9 daily; 1hr 30min); Le Grau-du-Roi (17 daily; 1hr 15min); Montpellier (2 daily; 50min); Pont du Gard (8 daily; 45min);

Sommières (8 daily; 45min); Uzès (12–13 daily; 30min–1hr); Le Vigan (3–5 daily; 1hr 50min).
Sète to: Montpellier (10 daily; 1hr 10min).
Toulouse to: Albi 6 daily; 1hr 40min); Auch (1–3 daily; 1hr 30min); Ax-les-Thermes (2–3 daily; 2hr 30min–3hr); Castres (1 2–4 daily; 1hr 40min–2hr); Foix (1 daily; 1hr 45min); Pamiers (2–3 daily; 1hr 30min); St-Girons (3 daily; 2hr 30min); Tarascon (2–3 daily; 2hr 20min).

12

The Massif Central

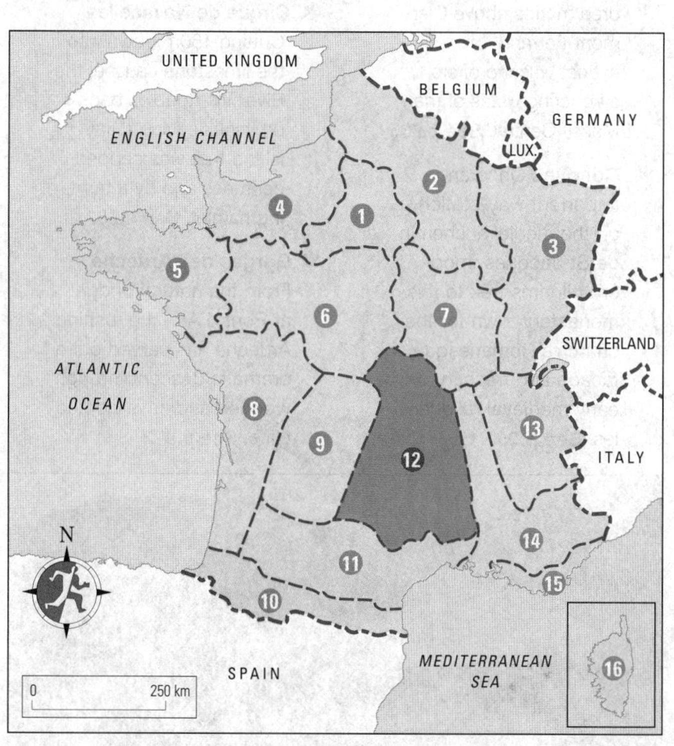

CHAPTER 12 **Highlights**

✱ **Cheese** The pasture lands of France's central region produce some of it's best cheeses: Roquefort, Laguiole and St. Nectaire. **See p.927**

✱ **Puy de Dôme** four hundred metres above Clermont-Ferrand, this long-extinct volcano offers staggering vistas of the Massif Central. **See p.935**

✱ **Conques** Once an important way-station on the medieval chemin de St-Jacques, modern pilgrims trek to this monastery town for the church's Romanesque facade and treasury of early medieval reliquaries. **See p.956**

✱ **Canoeing** The river gorges of the Tarn, Lot and Ardèche provide near limitless opportunities for kayaking and canoeing. **See pp.963 & 973**

✱ **Cirque de Navacelles** Cutting 150m down into the limestone causse, the River Vis doubles back on itself, leaving a tiny island that was capped centuries ago by a farming hamlet. **See p.969**

✱ **Gorges de l'Ardèche** From the natural bridge at Pont d'Arc, the rushing Ardèche has carved out a dramatic descent through wooded and cave-riddled cliffs. **See p.973**

△ Donkeys, Massif Central

12

The Massif Central

One of the loveliest spots on earth . . . a country without roads, without guides, without any facilities for locomotion, where every discovery must be conquered at the price of danger or fatigue . . . a soil cut up with deep ravines, crossed in every way by lofty walls of lava, and furrowed by numerous torrents.

Thus one of George Sand's characters described the Haute-Loire, the central *département* of **the Massif Central**, and it's a description that could still be applied to some of the region. Thickly forested and sliced by numerous rivers and lakes, these once volcanic uplands are geologically the oldest part of France and culturally one of the most firmly rooted in the past. Industry and tourism have made few inroads here, and the people remain rural and taciturn, with an enduring sense of regional identity. They also have a largely unfounded reputation for unfriendliness.

The Massif Central takes up a huge portion of the centre of France, but only a handful of towns have gained a foothold in its rugged terrain: **Le Puy**, spiked

The food of the Massif Central

Don't expect anything very refined from the **cuisine of the Auvergne and Massif Central**: it's solid peasant fare as befits a poor and rugged region. The best-known dish is **potée auvergnate**, basically a kind of cabbage soup. It's easy to make and very nourishing. The ingredients – potatoes, pork or bacon, cabbage, beans, turnips – though added at different intervals, are all boiled up together. Another popular cabbage dish is **chou farci**, cabbage stuffed with pork and beef and cooked with bacon.

Two potato dishes are very common – **la truffade** and **l'aligot**. For truffade, the potatoes are sliced and fried in lard, then fresh Cantal cheese is added; for an aligot, the potatoes are puréed and mixed with cheese. Less palatable for the squeamish, there's **tripoux**, usually a stuffing of either sheep's feet or calf's innards, cooked in a casing of stomach lining. **Fricandeau**, a kind of pork pâté, is also wrapped in sheep's stomach.

By way of dessert, **clafoutis** is a popular fruit tart in which the fruit is baked with a batter of flour and egg simply poured over it. The classical fruit ingredient is black cherries, though pears, blackcurrants or apples can also be used.

The Auvergne and the Ardèche in the east produce some wines, though these are not of any great renown. **Cheese**, however, is a different story. In addition to the four great cow's milk cheeses – St-Nectaire (see p.944), Cantal, Fourme d'Ambert and Bleu d'Auvergne – this region also produces the prince of all cheeses, **Roquefort**, made from sheep's milk at the edge of the Causse du Larzac (see p.968).

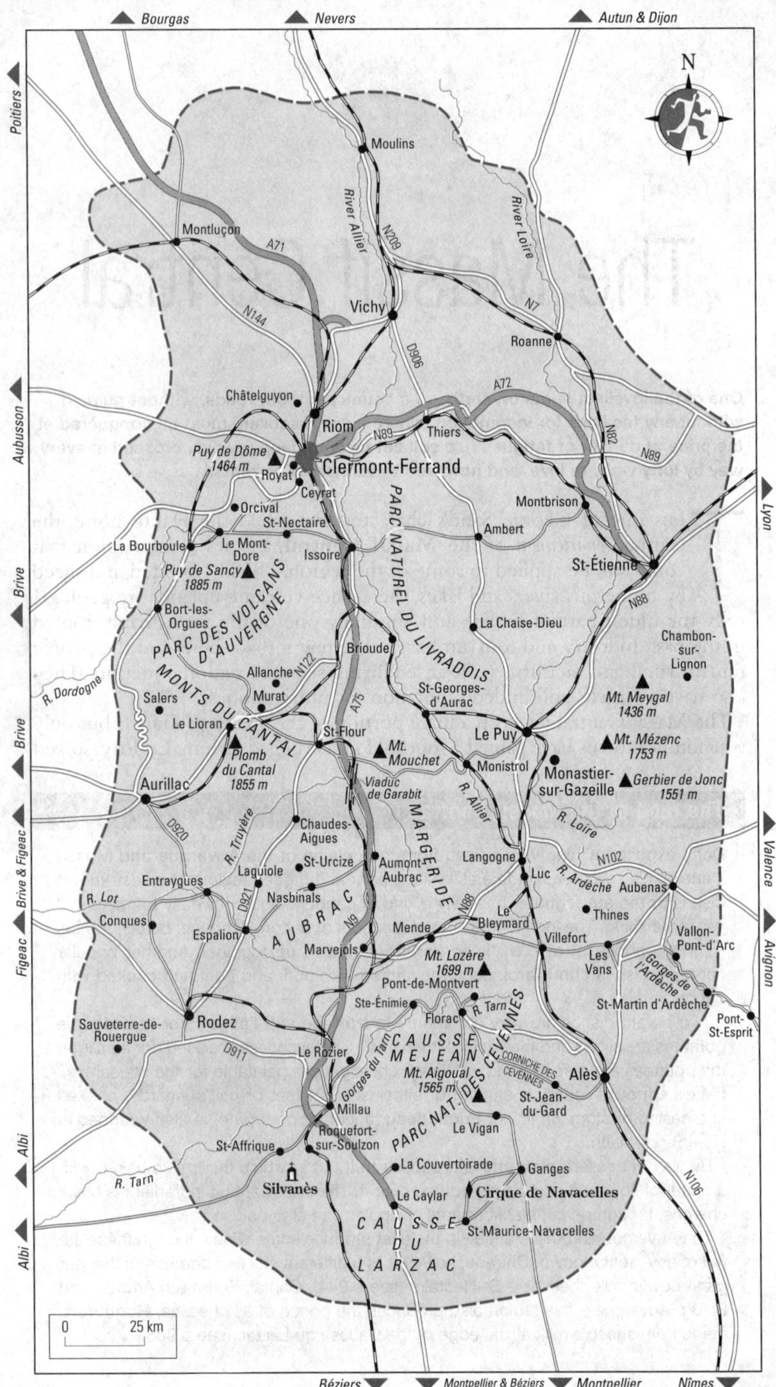
Bourgas
Nevers
Autun & Dijon
N
Poitiers
Aubusson
Brive
Brive
Brive & Figeac
Figeac
Albi
Albi
Lyon
Valence
Avignon
Béziers
Montpellier & Béziers
Montpellier
Nîmes
Moulins
River Allier
N209
River Loire
Montluçon
A71
N144
Vichy
N7
Roanne
D906
A72
Châtelguyon
Riom
N89
Thiers
N82
N89
Puy de Dôme
1464 m
Royat
Clermont-Ferrand
Ceyrat
Montbrison
Orcival
St-Nectaire
Ambert
La Bourboule
Le Mont-Dore
Issoire
St-Étienne
Puy de Sancy
1885 m
PARC DES VOLCANS D'AUVERGNE
PARC NATUREL DU LIVRADOIS
Bort-les-Orgues
La Chaise-Dieu
N88
Chambon-sur-Lignon
Brioude
Allanche
N122
R. Dordogne
MONTS DU CANTAL
Salers
Murat
A75
St-Georges-d'Aurac
Mt. Meygal
1436 m
Le Lioran
St-Flour
Le Puy
Mt. Mézenc
1753 m
Plomb du Cantal
1855 m
Mt. Mouchet
Monistrol
Monastier-sur-Gazeille
Gerbier de Jonc
1551 m
Aurillac
Viaduc de Garabit
R. Allier
D920
R. Truyère
MARGERIDE
R. Loire
Chaudes-Aigues
Langogne
N102
St-Urcize
Aumont-Aubrac
Luc
R. Ardèche
Aubenas
Laguiole
Entraygues
Nasbinals
R. Lot
D921
AUBRAC
N88
Le Bleymard
Thines
Conques
Espalion
N9
Mende
Villefort
Vallon-Pont-d'Arc
Marvejols
Mt. Lozère
1699 m
Les Vans
Gorges de l'Ardèche
Pont-de-Montvert
St-Martin d'Ardèche
Ste-Énimie
Florac
R. Tarn
Pont-St-Esprit
Rodez
Sauveterre-de-Rouergue
CAUSSE MEJEAN
D911
Le Rozier
Gorges du Tarn
PARC NAT. DES CEVENNES
CORNICHE DES CEVENNES
Mt. Aigoual
1565 m
Alès
St-Jean-du-Gard
Millau
Roquefort-sur-Soulzon
Le Vigan
St-Affrique
Silvanès
La Couvertoirade
Ganges
R. Tarn
N106
Le Caylar
Cirque de Navacelles
CAUSSE DU LARZAC
St-Maurice-Navacelles
0
25 km

with theatrical pinnacles of lava, is the most compelling, with its steep streets and majestic cathedral; the spa town of **Vichy** has an antiquated elegance and charm; even heavily industrial **Clermont-Ferrand,** the capital, has a certain cachet in the black volcanic stone of its historic centre and its stunning physical setting beneath the **Puy de Dôme**, a 1464-metre-high volcanic plug. There is pleasure, too, in the unpretentious provinciality of **Aurillac** and in the untouched medieval architecture of smaller places like **Murat**, **Besse**, **Salers**, **Orcival**, **Sauveterre-de-Rouergue**, **La Couvertoirade** and in the hugely influential abbey of **Conques**. But, above all, this is a country where the sights are landscapes rather than towns, churches and museums.

The heart of the region is the **Auvergne**, a wild and unexpected scene of extinct volcanoes (*puys*), stretching from the grassy domes and craters of the **Monts-Dômes** to the eroded skylines of the **Monts-Dore**, and deeply ravined **Cantal mountains** to the rash of darkly wooded pimples surrounding Le Puy. It's one of the poorest regions in France and has long remained outside the main national lines of communication: much of it is above 1000m in height and snowbound in winter. However, the Clermont-Montpellier *autoroute* is now near completion, providing a convenient means of travel from the capital to the gorges of the Tarn and Ardêche. There's little arable land in the region, just thousands of acres of upland pasture, traditionally grazed by sheep brought up from the southern lowlands for the summer. Nowadays, cows far outnumber the sheep, some raised for beef and some still for the production of Auvergne's four great cheeses (see box, p.927). The **population** has emigrated for generations, especially to Paris, where the café and restaurant trade has long been in the hands of Auvergnats. The same flight of population has affected the equally infertile but beautiful and more Mediterranean southern part of the region: the hills and valleys of the **Cévennes**, where Robert Louis Stevenson and his donkey made one of the more famous literary hikes in 1878.

Many of France's greatest rivers rise in the Massif Central: the **Dordogne** in the Monts-Dore, the **Loire** on the slopes of the Gerbier de Jonc in the east, and in the Cévennes the **Lot** and the **Tarn**. It is these last two rivers which create the distinctive character of the southern parts of the Massif Central, dividing and defining the special landscapes of the *causses*, or limestone plateaux, with their stupendous gorges. This is territory tailor-made for walkers and lovers of the **outdoors**, and everywhere you go tourist offices will supply ideas and routes for walks and bike rides.

The Parc des Volcans d'Auvergne

The **Parc Naturel Régional des Volcans d'Auvergne** encompasses the whole of the western edge of the Massif Central, from **Vichy** in the north to **Aurillac** in the south. It consists of three groups of extinct volcanoes – the

Monts-Dômes, the **Monts-Dore** and the **Monts du Cantal** – linked by the high plateaux of Artense and the Cézallier. It's big, wide-open country, sparsely populated and with largely treeless pasture grazed by the cows whose milk produces Cantal and St-Nectaire cheese.

The park organization, whose headquarters are at the **Maison du Parc**, Château de Montlosier, 20km southwest of Clermont-Ferrand just off the Mont-Dore road (May–Oct Mon–Fri 8.30am–12.30pm & 1–5pm; ⓣ04.73.65.64.00), oversees various subsidiary *maisons du parc*, each a kind of museum devoted to different themes or activities: fauna and flora, shepherd life, peat bogs and so on.

The best way to understand the park, its landscapes and activities is to walk or bike around it. Four **GR footpaths** cross or make circuits within the park. The **GR40** runs from north to south. The **GR441** makes a circuit round the Monts-Dômes, called the **Tour de la Chaîne des Puys**. The **GR400** encircles the Cantal mountains, and the **GR30** the lakes of the Artense plateau and Cézallier, under the title of the **Tour des Lacs d'Auvergne**. There are also lots of shorter walks; ask at local tourist offices for more information, and for details of mountain bike rental.

If only because of the practicalities of transport, you will likely pass through **Clermont-Ferrand**, the capital of the *départment*. Given its rather dramatic historical associations – it was the site of Pope Urban II's speech which launched the Crusades in 1095 – the city may disappoint, but nonetheless the town is worth an afternoon of rambling. Otherwise, the towns in the area are few and of secondary interest, although **Orcival**, **Murat** and **Salers** are unexpectedly attractive; **St-Nectaire** contains an exceptionally beautiful small church in the distinct Auvergne version of Romanesque; and **St-Flour** and Aurillac have an agreeable provincial insularity.

Clermont-Ferrand and around

CLERMONT-FERRAND lies at the northern tip of the Massif Central. Although its situation is magnificent, almost encircled by the wooded and grassy volcanoes of the **Monts-Dômes**, it has for over a century been a typical smokestack industrial centre, the home base of Michelin tyres, which makes it a rather incongruous capital for the rustic, even backward province of the Auvergne.

Its roots, both as a spa and a communications and trading centre, go back to Roman times. It was just outside the town, on the plateau of Gergovia to the south, that the Gauls under the leadership of **Vercingétorix** won their only, albeit indecisive, victory against Julius Caesar's invading Romans. In the Middle Ages, the two towns of Clermont and Montferrand were divided by commercial and political rivalry and ruled respectively by a bishop and the count of Auvergne. Louis XIII united them administratively in 1630, but it was not until the rapid industrial expansion of the late nineteenth century that the two really became indistinguishable. Indeed, it was Clermont that took the ascendancy, relegating Montferrand to a suburban backwater.

Michelin came into being thanks to the inventions of Charles Mackintosh, the Scotsman of raincoat fame. His niece married Édouard Daubrée, a Clermont sugar manufacturer, and brought with her some ideas about making rubber goods that she had learnt from her uncle. In 1889, the company became Michelin and Co, just in time to catch the development of the automobile and the World War I aircraft industry. The family ruled the town and employed 30,000

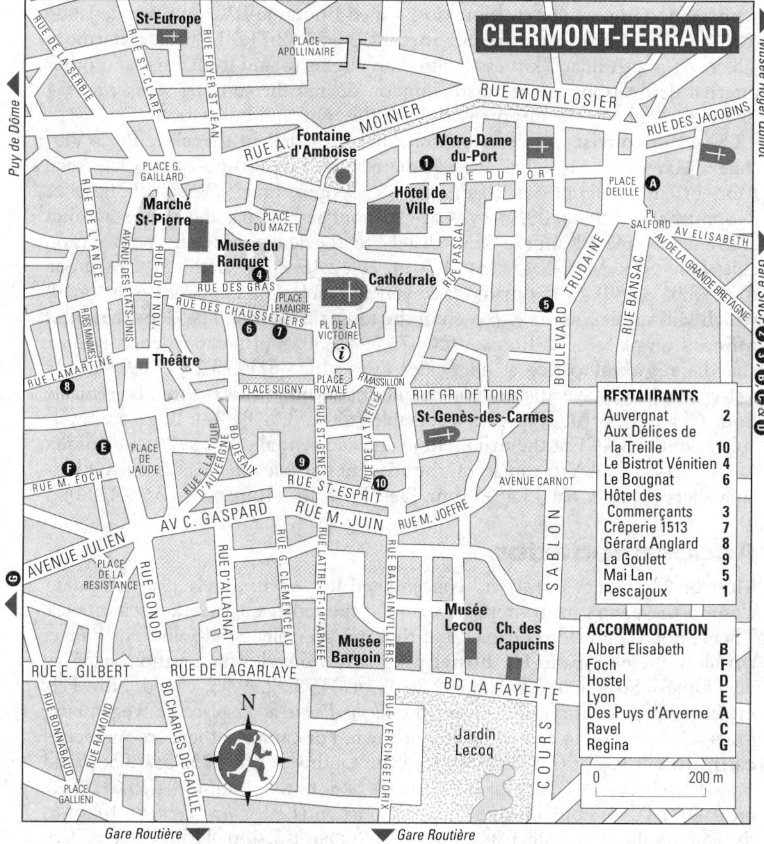

of its citizens until the early 1980s, when the industry went into decline. In the years since, the workforce has been halved, causing rippling unemployment throughout Clermont's economy. Many of those who have lost their jobs are Portuguese immigrants, imported over the last forty years to fill the labour vacuum and well integrated with the local population.

As in many other traditional industrial towns hit by recession and changing global patterns of trade, Clermont has had to struggle to reorientate itself, turning to service industries and the creation of a university of 34,000 students. Nonetheless, many people have moved elsewhere in search of work, reducing the population by nearly a tenth. The town has changed physically, too, as many of the old factories have been demolished. Despite all of this, the old centre has a surprisingly hip and youthful feel, with pavement bars packed out in the evenings as the boutiques and galleries which have sprung up wind down for the day.

Arrival and information

The **gare SNCF** is on avenue de l'Union Soviétique, from where it is a ten-minute bus journey to place de Jaude, at the western edge of the cathedral hill. The **gare routière** (☎04.73.35.05.62) is on boulevard François-Mitterrand, with a city transport information kiosk called Boutique T2C on place de Jaude (Ⓣ04.73.28.56.56). The city **airport** (Ⓣ04.73.62.71.00, Ⓦwww.clermont-fd.cci.fr) is at Aulnat, 7km east, with daily flights to and from Paris and other internal destinations, as well as to London during the summer. A *navette* (€4 one way) connects the airport with both the train and bus station.

The main **tourist office** is opposite the cathedral in the place de la Victoire (May–Sept Mon–Fri 9am–7pm, Sat & Sun 10am–7pm; Oct–April Mon–Fri 10am–6pm, Sat 10am–1pm & 2–6pm, Sun 9.30am–12.30pm & 2–6pm; Ⓣ04.73.98.65.00, Ⓦwww.ot-clermont-ferrand.fr), and there's another conveniently placed annexe immediately to the left outside the train station exit (June–Sept Mon–Sat 9.15–11.30am & 12.15–5pm; Oct–May closed Sat; Ⓣ04.73.91.87.89). At the main office you can pick up a *Passe Decouverte* (€10) which will admit you once to each of the town's museums. The **departmental office** is on place de la Bourse (Ⓣ04.73.42.22.50, Ⓦplanetepuydedome.com), and the **regional office** at 44 av des Etats Unis (Ⓣ04.73.29.49.49, Ⓦwww.crt-auvergne.fr). Specific hiking or mountain-bike information is available from Chamina, 5 rue Pierre-le-Vénérable (Ⓣ04.73.92.81.44). Bikes are available from the SNCF, at the main station and at a central office at 20 pl Remoux (Ⓣ04.73.14.12.36). You can access the **Internet** at *Internet@Café* at 34 rue Ballainvilliers (Mon & Sat 11am–11pm, Tues–Fri 8am–11pm; Ⓣ04.73.92.42.80).

Accommodation

Most of Clermont's **hotels** are concentrated just off the lively place de Jaude, close to the town's main shops, and around the rather characterless station area. There's not a tremendous choice, but they are generally good value. For budget travellers, there's a basic **HI hostel** just across from the train station at 55 av de l'Union Soviétique (Ⓣ04.73.92.26.39, Ⓕ04.73.92.99.96; closed Nov–Feb; membership obligatory), and a foyer, the *Home Dome*, at 12 place de Regensburg (Ⓣ04.73.29.40.70), in the southwest of town. For campers, there are municipal **campsites** at Royat (*L'Oclède*), 4km to the southwest (Ⓣ04.73.35.97.05; closed Nov–March; bus #41), Ceyrat (*Le Chanset*), 5km to the south (Ⓣ04.73.61.30.73; bus #4C & #41, stop "Preguille"), and Cournon (*Le Pré des Laveuses*), 10km to the east, on the River Allier (Ⓣ04.73.84.81.30; bus #3, stop "Plaine de jeux").

Albert Elisabeth 37 av Albert-Elisabeth Ⓣ04.73.92.47.41, Ⓦwww.hotel-albertelisabeth.com. Well-run family hotel, with pastel-decorated rooms; handy for the train station. ❸

Foch 22 rue Maréchal-Foch Ⓣ04.73.93.48.40, Ⓕ04.73.35.47.41. Tucked away down a side street off place de Jaude, this is a good-value budget hotel, with bright, summery rooms. ❷

Lyon 16 pl de Jaude Ⓣ04.73.93.32.55, Ⓔhotel.de.lyon@wanadoo.fr. Tastefully furnished, though the lively bar and brasserie below can get a little noisy at night (*plats* around €8.50). ❸

Des Puys d'Arverne 16 pl Delille Ⓣ04.73.91.92.06, Ⓔclermont@hoteldespuys.com. A modern, top-of-the-range hotel, offering spacious rooms, some with balconies. Its first-rate gourmet restaurant has splendid views of the town and Le Puy de Dôme (menus from €14.50–44). ❺

Ravel 8 rue de Maringues Ⓣ04.73.91.51.33, Ⓕ04.73.92.28.48. Opposite the old Marché St-Joseph, this friendly hotel offers attractive rooms, with sunny, Mediterranean decor. Closed Jan. ❷

Regina 14 rue Bonnabaud Ⓣ04.73.93.44.76, Ⓕ04.73.35.04.63. Looks a little grubby from the outside, but inside, an elegant spiral staircase leads up to fresh, clean rooms. ❸

The City

The most dramatic and flattering approach to Clermont is from the Aubusson road or along the scenic rail line from Le Mont-Dore, both of which cross the chain of the Monts-Dômes just north of the Puy de Dôme. This way you descend through the leafy western suburbs with marvellous views over the town, dominated by the black towers of the cathedral sitting atop the volcanic stump that forms the hub of the old town.

The Cathédrale Notre-Dame and around

Clermont's reputation as a *ville noire* becomes immediately understandable when you enter the appealing medieval quarter, clustered in a characteristic muddle around the cathedral. The colour is due not to industrial pollution but to the black volcanic rock used in the construction of many of its buildings. The **Cathédrale Notre-Dame** stands at the centre and highest point of the old town; Freda White evocatively described its sombre grey-black-stone lava from the quarries at nearby Volvic as "like the darkest shade of a pigeon's wing". Begun in the mid-thirteenth century, it was not finished until the nineteenth, under the direction of Viollet-le-Duc, who was the architect of the west front and those typically Gothic crocketed spires, whose too methodically cut stonework at close range betrays the work of the machine rather than the mason's hand. The interior is swaddled in gloom, illuminated all the more startlingly by the brilliant colours of the rose windows in the transept and the stained-glass windows in the choir, most dating back to the fourteenth century. Remnants of medieval frescoes survive, too: a particularly beautiful Virgin and Child adorns the right wall of the Chapelle Ste-Madeleine and an animated battle scene between the crusaders and Saracens unfolds on the central wall of the Chapelle St-Georges.

If the day is fine, it's worth climbing the **Tour de la Bayette** (Mon–Fri 10am–5.15pm, Sun 3–6pm; €1.50) by the north transept door: you look back over the rue des Gras to the Puy de Dôme looming dramatically over the city, with white morning mist retreating down its sides like seaweed from a rock.

Northeast of the cathedral, down the elegant old rue du Port, stands Clermont's other great church, the Romanesque **Basilique Notre-Dame-du-Port** – a century older than the cathedral and in almost total contrast both in style and substance, built from softer stone in pre-lava-working days and consequently corroding badly from exposure to Clermont's polluted air. For all that, it's a beautiful building in pure Auvergnat Romanesque style, featuring a Madonna and Child over the south door in the strangely stylized local form, both figures stiff and upright, the Child more like a dwarf than an infant. Inside, it exudes the broody mysteriousness so often generated by the Romanesque style. Put a coin in the slot and you can light up the intricately carved ensemble of leaves, knights and biblical figures on the church's pillars and capitals. It was here in all probability that Pope Urban II preached the First Crusade in 1095 to a vast crowd who received his speech with the Occitan cry of *Dios lo volt* (God wills it) – a phrase adopted by the crusaders in justification of all subsequent massacres.

For general animation, shopping, drinking and eating, the streets between the cathedral and place de Jaude are best, with the main morning market taking place in the conspicuously modern **place St-Pierre** just off rue des Gras. **Place de Jaude** remains another monument to planners' deviation in spite of the shops, the cafés well placed to take in the morning sun and an attempt to make it more attractive with trees and a fountain. Smack in the middle of the traffic, a romantic equestrian statue of Vercingétorix lines up with the Puy de Dôme.

Outside the city centre

Away from these central streets, there are a few concrete sights to tempt the pedestrian. Among these are **rue Ballainvilliers**, whose eighteenth-century facades recall the sombre elegance of Edinburgh and lead to the **Musée Bargoin** (Tues–Sun 10am–6pm; €4), with displays of archeological finds from round about. These include lots of fascinating domestic bits: Roman shoes, baskets, bits of dried fruit, glass and pottery, as well as a remarkable burial find from nearby Martres-de-Veyre dating back to the second century AD. Though not of great interest, the **Musée Lecoq**, directly behind the Musée Bargoin (May–Sept Tues–Sat noon & 2–6pm, Sun 2–6pm; Oct–April 10am–noon & 2–5pm; €4), is devoted mainly to natural history – and named after the gentleman who also founded the public garden full of beautiful trees and formal beds just across the street.

Clermont-Ferrand's most impressive musuem, the **Musée d'Art Roger-Quillot** (Tues–Sun 10am–6pm; e4), is situated on place Louis-Deteix in **Monteferrand**, some 2.5km northeast of the centre (bus #1, 9 or 16 from Place de Jaude). Housed in a daringly renovated eighteenth-century Ursuline convent, this museum holds a broad collection of over two thousand works of art from the medieval to the contemporary. Notable pieces include a collection of carved capitals and a stunning enamelled reliquary of Thomas Becket. Montferrand is today little more than a suburb of larger Clermont, standing out on a limb to the north – if you journey out for the museum you should take time to stroll around. Built on the *bastide* plan, its principal streets, rue de la Rodade and rue Jules-Guesde (the latter named after the founder of the French Communist Party, as Montferrand was home to many of the Michelin factory workers), are still lined with the fine town houses of its medieval merchants and magistrates.

Eating and drinking

Staying in the station area, there are a couple of reasonable places to **eat**. The best is the oak-beamed, rustic-looking *Auvergnat*, 27 av de l'Union Soviétique (from €16), whose repertoire includes standard Auvergne dishes like *truffade*. Less expensive and very friendly, with a terrace at the back, is the *Hôtel des Commerçants*, opposite the station (from €9.80).

In the centre of town, the best of the cheaper places is the ever-popular *Crêperie 1513*, 3 rue des Chaussetiers, opposite the cathedral, which occupies a superb Renaissance mansion built in 1513 (lunchtime menu at €9), while in the same street, at no. 29, *Le Bougnat* offers local regional cuisine at affordable prices (closed Sun & Mon eve, Tues lunch; from €12). Close by at 36 rue des Gras, there's good pizza and pasta at *Le Bistrot Vénitien* from €15 (closed Sun). On the other side of the cathedral, you can get first-class Vietnamese cooking for around €20 at the *Mai Lan*, 41 bd Trudaine (closed Sun & Mon lunch), and a lunchtime crêpe-menu from €9 at the *Pescajoux* in the old rue du Port at no. 13. Finally, excellent and cheap North African *briques* can be had for as little as €3.50 at *La Goulette*, 12 rue St-Esprit.

For a more specialized gastronomic experience, there's nothing to beat the refined and inventive cooking of *Gérard Anglard* at 17 rue Lamartine, off place de Jaude, especially the lunchtime menu at €18 (Ⓣ04.73.93.52.25; closed Sun & first two weeks Aug). Also very well-reputed is the quirky *Aux Délices de la Treille* (Ⓣ04.73.91.26.90) at 33 rue de la Treille where you can pack into the tiny and flamboyant dining room or eat in the narrow street (€12 at lunchtime, otherwise €16 plus). And, if you don't mind the drive – barely 5km southeast off the old N9 Issoire road – the *Petit Bonneval* at **Pérignat-lès-Sarliève** makes a delicious stop for dinner on a summer evening (Ⓣ04.73.79.11.11; closed Sun eve; menus from €19).

For a daytime drink, *Le Suffren*, on the corner of place de Jaude, is one of the most popular places to hang out. More unusual is *Les Goûters de Justine*, a *salon de thé*, tucked away in old rue Pascal and furnished with antique chairs, old sofas and oriental carpets. At night one of the most fashionable places is studenty *Le Dérailleur*, 9 av Georges-Clemenceau, while young rockers head for the suburban village of Orcines, beneath the Puy de Dôme, to long-standing *Phidias*, aka *Boudu's*, on route de la Baraque (ⓣ04.73.62.18.34; until 5am; closed Sun & Mon).

The Puy de Dôme

Visiting Clermont without going to the top of the **Puy de Dôme** (1464m) would be like visiting Athens without seeing the Acropolis. And if you choose your moment – early in the morning or late in the evening – you can easily avoid the worst of the crowds.

Clearly signposted from place de Jaude, it's about 15km from the city centre by the D941. The last 6.5km is a private road and costs €4.50; there is also a shuttle bus (10am–6pm: May–June & Sept Sat & Sun; July–Aug daily; €3.50) serving the route when the road is closed to vehicles. If you're driving, make sure to pump your brakes on the descent; otherwise you may find yourself waiting for a long time before driving off, while your brakes cool down. Alternatively, you can leave the car at the **Col de Ceyssat** and climb the Puy on foot in about an hour. The route is reserved for cyclists in summer (May–Sept Wed & Sun 7–8.30am).

The result of a volcanic explosion about 10,000 years ago, the Puy is an abrupt 400m from base to summit. Although the weather station buildings and enormous television mast are pretty ugly close up, the staggering views and sense of airy elevation more than compensate. Even if Mont Blanc itself is not always visible way to the east – it can be if conditions are favourable – you can see huge distances, all down the Massif Central to the Cantal mountains. Above all, you get a bird's-eye view of the other volcanic summits to the north and south, largely forested since the nineteenth century and including the perfect 100-metre-deep grassy crater of the **Puy de Pariou**.

Immediately below the summit are the scant remains of a substantial **Roman temple** dedicated to Mercury (free entry), some of the finds from which are displayed in the Musée Bargoin in Clermont-Ferrand. Beside it is a memorial commemorating the exploits of Eugène Renaux, who landed a plane here in 1911 in response to the offer of a 100,000 franc prize by the Michelin brothers. Today the aviators are hang-gliders and paragliding enthusiasts, drifting like gaudy birds around the stern of a ship.

Riom and around

Just 15km north of Clermont-Ferrand, **RIOM** is sedate and provincial. One-time capital of the entire Auvergne, its Renaissance architecture, fashioned out of the local black volcanic stone, now secures the town's status as a highlight of the northern Massif. In 1942, just before the first trains of Jewish deportees were shipped to Nazi Germany, Léon Blum, Jewish prime minister and architect of the Socialist Popular Front government, was put on trial in Riom by Marshal Pétain, France's collaborationist ruler, in an attempt to blame the country's defeat in 1940 on the Left. Defending himself, Blum turned the trial into an indictment of collaboration and Nazism. Under pressure from Hitler, Pétain called it off, but nonetheless deported Blum to Germany, an experience which he survived, to give evidence against Pétain himself after the war.

You may only want to spend a morning here, but Riom does provide a worthwhile stopover for lunch if you're on the way up to Vichy. It's an aloof, old-world kind of place, still Auvergne's judicial capital, with a nineteenth-century **Palais de Justice** that stands on the site of a grand palace built when the dukes of Berry controlled this region in the fourteenth century. Only the Gothic **Ste-Chapelle** survives of the original palace, with fine stained-glass windows taking up almost the entirety of three of the walls (guided visits only, every 30min: May Wed 3–5pm; June & Sept Mon–Fri 3–5pm; July & Aug Mon–Fri 10am–noon & 2.30–5.30pm; €0.50).

The best way to admire the town's impressive ensemble of basalt-stone houses, with their red-tiled roofs, is to climb up to the viewing platform of the sixteenth-century **clock tower**, at 5 rue de l'Horloge, off the main street, rue du Commerce (May, June & Sept Mon & Sun 2–6pm, Tues–Sat 10am–noon & 2–6pm; July & Aug daily 10am–noon & 2–6pm; €0.50). There's an interesting museum on the region's folk traditions at 10bis rue Delille, the **Musée Régional d'Auvergne** (daily except Tues: June–Sept 10am–noon & 2.30–6pm; Oct–May 10am–noon & 2.30–5.30pm; €4, or €6 joint ticket with the Musée Mandet; free on Wed), with the **Musée Mandet**'s displays of Roman finds and unexciting paintings not far away at 4 rue de l'Hôtel-de-Ville (same hours; €4, free on Wed). At 44 rue du Commerce, the **church of Notre-Dame-du-Marthuret** holds Riom's most valued treasures, two statues of the Virgin and Child – one a Black Madonna, the other, the so-called *Vierge à l'Oiseau*, a touchingly realistic piece of carving that portrays the young Christ with a bird fluttering in his hands. A copy stands in the entrance hall of the church (its original site), where you can see it with the advantage of daylight.

Practicalities

Riom's **tourist office** is at 16 rue du Commerce (July & Aug Mon–Sat 9.30am–12.30pm & 2–6.30pm, Sun 10am–noon & 2.30–4pm; Sept–June Mon–Sat 9.30am–12.30pm & 2–6pm; ⓣ04.73.38.59.45, ⓦwww.riom-auvergne.com). If you decide to stay, the town's basic cheapie is *Hôtel le Square*, 26 bd Desaix (ⓣ & ⓕ04.73.38.46.51; ❷), which runs a decent restaurant (crêpes and omelettes for around €12). *Les Petits Ventres*, across from the market at 6 rue Anne-Dubourg (ⓣ04.73.38.21.65; closed Sun & Mon lunch & Tues & late-Aug) is one of the best places for local cuisine (from €17). As an alternate follow the locals to *Ane Gris* at 13 rue Gomot (closed Mon lunch and Sun), which serves *truffade* (€14) and *aligot* (€12).

Around Riom

From Riom SNCF buses run to **MOZAC**, on the edge of town, with a twelfth-century **abbey church** whose Romanesque sculpture is as beautiful as you'd expect, and continue to the bourgeois spa resort of **CHÂTEL-GUYON** in around twenty minutes. With thirty different **hot springs**, great views over the surrounding countryside and *puys*, and a couple of well-equipped **campsites**, this is as good a place as any if you want to rest up for a night. For an easy stroll from here, you can wander out along the leafy **valleys of the Sardon and Prades**.

The little town of **VOLVIC** is also close by, renowned for its spring water and the quarries that furnished the black rock for Clermont's cathedral, as well as so many other Auvergnat buildings. Its **Maison de la Pierre**, on rue Viallard (guided tours hourly: March, April & Oct to mid-Nov 10am–5pm, May–Sept 10am–6pm; €4), features a surprisingly engaging display about the use of lava

Volvic to Laschamp walk

For a good day's walk and a thorough exploration of the *puys*, take the train from Clermont to Volvic-Gare. Follow the D90 road beside the train line for about 1km until you join up with the **GR441** path, where the road turns right under the track. Keep along your side of the train track for a few minutes longer and follow the GR441 round to the left, almost doubling back southwest along the line of the wooded Puys Nugères, Jumes and Coquille to the northern foot of the Puy de Chopine (2–3hr). Here you join up with the **GR4** and follow the combined GR4–441 across the Orcines–Pontgibaud road to the summit of the Puy de Dôme (about 2hr 30min from the road). From the Puy, descend to the Col de Ceyssat in half an hour (good chance of a lift back to Clermont), or continue to **Laschamp** (50min), where there is a **gîte d'étape** (7–8hr, though a fit walker could do it in 6hr).

You should not set off without either the relevant section of the GR4 Topoguide or, preferably, the IGN 1:25,000 map, the *Chaîne des Puys*, which also marks the GR441 from Volvic-Gare. If you don't feel up to a walk, there's a really beautiful train ride from Clermont to the town of Le Mont-Dore, all round the chain of the puys.

rock, including a historical and geological explanation, as well as a tour of the disused quarries – a warm jacket is advised.

Vichy

VICHY is famous for two things: its World War II puppet government under Marshal Pétain, and its curative sulphurous springs, which attract thousands of ageing and ailing visitors, or *curistes*, every year. There's no mention of Pétain's government in town, but the fact that Vichy is one of France's foremost spa resorts colours everything you see here. The town is almost entirely devoted to catering for its largely elderly, genteel and rich population, which swells several-fold in summer; they come here to drink the water, wallow in it, inhale its steam or be sprayed with it. An attempt is now being made to rejuvenate the image of Vichy by appealing to a younger, more fitness-conscious generation.

The Town

All of this makes Vichy seem unappealing, and yet it has a certain element of charm. There's a real *fin-de-siècle* atmosphere about the place and a curious fascination in its continuing function. The town revolves around the **Parc des Sources**, a stately tree-shaded park that takes up most of the centre. At its north end stands the **Hall des Sources**, an enormous iron-framed greenhouse in which people sit and chat or read newspapers, while from a large tiled stand in the middle the various waters emerge from their spouts, beside the just-visible remains of the Roman establishment. The *curistes* line up to get their prescribed cupful, and for a small fee you can join them. The Célestins is the only one of the springs that is bottled and widely drunk: if you're into a taste experience, try the remaining five. They are progressively more sulphurous and foul, with the Source de l'Hôpital, which has its own circular building at the far end of the park, an almost unbelievably nasty creation. Each of the springs is prescribed for a different ailment and the tradition is that, apart from the Célestins, they must all be drunk on the spot to be efficacious – a dubious but effective way of drawing in the crowds.

Although all the springs technically belong to the nation and treatment is partially funded by the state, they are in fact run privately for profit by the

Compagnie Fermière, first created in the mid-nineteenth century to prepare for a visit by the Emperor Napoléon III, whose interest in the waters brought Vichy to public notice. The Compagnie not only has a monopoly on selling the waters but also runs the casino and numerous hotels – even the chairs conveniently dotted around the Parc des Sources are owned by it.

Directly behind the Hall des Sources, on the leafy **Esplanade Napoléon III**, is the enormous, Byzantine-style **Grand Établissement Thermal**, the former thermal baths, decorated with Moorish arches, gold-and-blue domes and blue ceramic panels of voluptuous mermaids. All that remains inside of the original baths is the grand entrance hall, with its fountain and two beautiful murals, *La Bain* and *La Source*, painted by Osberd in 1903. The arcades leading off either side of the hall, once the site of gyms and treatment rooms, now house expensive boutiques.

To provide distraction for the *curistes*, a grand **casino** and **opera house** were built at the southern end of the Parc des Sources. From May to September the opera house is the venue for regular concerts and opera productions, while lighter music oom-pahs out from the open-air bandstand in the park behind it.

After the waters, Vichy's curiosities are limited. There's a pleasant, wooded riverside in the **Parc de l'Allier**, also created for Napoléon III. And, not far from here, the old town boasts the strange **church of St-Blaise**, actually two churches in one, with a 1930s Baroque structure built onto the original Romanesque one – an effect that sounds hideous but is rather imaginative. Inside, another Auvergne Black Virgin, Notre-Dame-des-Malades, stands surrounded by plaques offered by the grateful healed who stacked their odds with both her and the sulphur.

Practicalities

Vichy's **gare SNCF** is about a ten-minute walk from the centre, on the eastern edge of the city centre at the end of rue de Paris. The **gare routière** sits on the corner of rue Doumier and rue Jardet, by the central place Charles-de-Gaulle, and there's a public transport information line on ⓣ04.70.30.17.30. The building that used to house the wartime Vichy government at 19 rue du Parc is now home to the **tourist office** (April–June & Sept Mon–Sat 9am–12.30pm & 1.30–7pm, Sun 9.30am–12.30pm & 3–7pm; July & Aug 9am–7.30pm, Sun 9.30am–12.30pm & 3–7pm; Oct–March Mon–Fri 9am–noon & 1.30–6pm, Sat 9am–noon & 2–6pm, Sun 2.30–5.30pm; ⓣ04.70.98.71.94, ⓦwww.vichytourisme.com).

There are so many **hotels** that finding a place to stay is not difficult. There are several around the station, but more pleasant are the friendly, grand neo-Baroque *Midland*, 4 rue de l'Intendance, in a quiet street off rue de Paris (ⓣ04.70.97.48.48, ⓔhotelmidlandvichy@wanadoo.fr; ❸; closed mid-Oct to mid-April; good restaurant with menus from €17), and the *Hôtel Londres*, 7 bd de Russie, behind the casino (ⓣ04.70.98.28.27; ❷; closed Nov to Feb), which was the secret meeting place for Jean Moulin and fellow Resistance fighters in 1941. There's a municipal **campsite**, *La Graviere*, at the Centre Omnisports (ⓣ04.70.59.21.00; closed Oct to late-May).

For **eating**, apart from the hotel-restaurants listed above, the simplest solution is to head for the area around the junction of rue Clemenceau and rue de Paris, where there are several brasseries and cafés. To do so, however, would be to miss out on the best that Vichy has to offer – a surprising range of top-notch restaurants. Two of the best include the frenetically eclectic *Jacques Decoret* on 7 av de Gramont (ⓣ04.70.97.65.06; closed Tues & Wed & Aug), which has menus drawing on flavours as jarringly diverse as Oaxaca and Marseille from €32–90, and the more affordable and less daring *La Table d'Antoine* at 8 rue Burnol (ⓣ04.70.98.99.71; closed Sun lunch & Mon; from €19).

The Monts-Dore

The **Monts-Dore** lie about 50km southwest of Clermont. Also volcanic in origin – the main period of activity was around five million years ago – they are much more rugged and more obviously mountainous than their gentler, younger neighbours, the Monts-Dômes. Their centre is the precipitous, plunging valley of the River Dordogne, which rises on the slopes of the **Puy de Sancy**, at 1885m the highest point in the Massif Central, just above the little town of **Le Mont-Dore**.

In spite of their relative ruggedness, there are few crags or rock faces and their upper slopes, albeit steep, are grassy and treeless for miles and miles. They are known as *montagnes à vaches* – mountains for cows – as they traditionally provided summer pasture land for herds of cows, raised above all for their milk and the production of **St-Nectaire** cheese. The herdsmen who milked them and made the cheese set up their primitive summer homes in the dozens of (now mainly ruined) stone huts, or *burons*, that scatter the landscape.

Although these traditional activities still continue, many of the upland herds are now beef cattle being fattened for the autumn sales, often for export to Italy, Germany and Spain. And tourism has become an important part of the local economy, although mostly unobtrusive and low-key, with mainly walkers in summer and cross-country skiers in winter.

Le Mont-Dore and the Puy de Sancy

Squeezed out along the narrow wooded valley of the infant Dordogne, grey-slated **LE MONT-DORE**, 50km southwest of Clermont, is a long-established spa resort, with Roman remnants testifying to just how old it is. Its popularity goes back to the eighteenth century, when metalled roads replaced the old mule paths and made access possible, but reached its apogee with the opening of the rail line around 1900. It is an altogether wholesome and civilized sort of place.

The **Établissement Thermal** – the baths, which give the place its *raison d'être* – are in the middle of town and are certainly worth visiting (30min. guided tours Mon–Sat: mid-May to mid-Oct on the hour; €2). Early every morning, the *curistes* stream into its neo-Byzantine halls – an extravaganza of tiles, striped columns and ornate ironwork – hoping for a remedy in this self-proclaimed "world centre for treatment of asthma". For many Parisians, of all ages and walks of life, this is their annual mecca: whiling away their days sniffing sulphur from bunsen burner tubes, and sitting in thick steam.

Walkers also frequent the town, the principal attraction being the **Puy de Sancy** (1885m), whose jagged skyline blocks the head of the Dordogne valley, 3km away (mid-May to Sept; 4 buses daily from the tourist office; €3.10). Accessible by *téléférique* (€6.50 return) since the 1930s, it's one of the busiest tourist sites in the country. As a result, the path from the *téléférique* station to the summit has had to be railed and paved with baulks of timber to prevent total erosion. Combined with the scars of access tracks for the ski installations, this has done little for its beauty.

However, with a little sweat and effort you can escape to wilder areas of the mountain. The **GR30** passes this way and on down to La Bourboule, giving a good sense of the typical landscape: long views over meadows full of gentians and violets, grazed by sheep and cows. Start out along the summit path and at the first intermediate peak, take a right and go downhill. The GR30 is signposted. It follows the western ridge of the Dordogne valley for about an hour and a half, before turning ninety degrees left, away from the valley. Keep straight ahead at this point, go down a gravelly track, with the rocky dome of **Le Capucin**, above Le Mont-Dore, directly in front of you. The track enters the woods to the left of this bump by a ruined house. Five minutes later, on the right, just past a concrete water-pipe junction, a path drops steeply down through beech trees to Le Capucin *funiculaire* station and down again to Le Mont-Dore (3hr).

Practicalities

Without a car, Le Mont-Dore is most easily accessible by train from Clermont. The **train** and **bus stations** are at the entrance to the town. A ten-minute walk down avenue Michelet takes you to the centre, where the **tourist office** sits in the park on avenue de la Libèration (May–June Mon–Sat 9am–12.30pm & 2–6.30pm; July & Aug Mon–Sat 9am–1pm & 2–7pm, Sun 9am–noon & 2–6pm; ⓣ04.73.65.20.21, ⓦwww.mont-dore.com); the helpful staff will advise about other walking and cycling possibilities (VTT rental), as well as day bus excursions to some otherwise rather inaccessible places round about.

Accommodation is not hard to come by, as the town is brimming with hotels. Close to the baths, at 8 rue Favart, *Hôtel aux Champs d'Auvergne* (ⓣ04.73.65.00.37, ⓦwww.auxchampsdauvergne.com; ❶; closed Nov to mid-Dec; restaurant from €12) is very welcoming and serves copious breakfasts, while the elegant *Hôtel de la Paix*, nearby on rue Rigny (ⓣ04.73.65.00.17, ⓦwww.hotel-de-la-paix.info; ❸), has comfortable, clean rooms and an excellent restaurant (menus €19–49). One of the best deals, with mod cons at a bargain price, is the *Beau Site* at 17 rue des Déportés (ⓣ04.73.65.05.51, ⓕ04.73.65.26.88; ❸; closed mid-Oct to Dec & mid-March to April; restaurant from €13), beside the main baths. There's an efficient modern **hostel** on the Puy de Sancy road, with a stunning view of the mountains (ⓣ04.73.65.03.53, ⓔle-mont-dore@fuaj.org; closed Nov), and two very cheap *gîtes*, *Chalet Melki-Rose* (ⓣ04.73.65.0418, ⓔecir.asptt@wanadoo.fr), at 53 av Clermont, and *Les Hautes Pierres* (ⓣ04.73.65.25.65, ⓦwww.gite-les-hautes-pierres.com; Jan–Oct or by request) on Chemin de Vergnes. The municipal **campsite**, *Les Crouzets* (ⓣ & ⓕ04.73.65.21.60; closed mid-Oct to mid-Dec), is nearby, opposite the station. The other municipal campsite is *L'Esquiladou* (ⓣ04.73.65.23.74; closed Nov–April), off to the right on the road to La Bourboule.

Walking and skiing around La Bourboule

Fit and serious walkers may want to conquer the **Puy de Sancy**, a six-hour hike south of La Bourboule on the GR30–41, passing after about two hours the two fine waterfalls of the **Cascade de la Vernière** and **Plat à Barbe** – themselves a satisfying destination. For the summit of Puy de Sancy, see the account of Le Mont-Dore, p.939. An easier walk out of La Bourboule is to the summit of the **Banne d'Ordanche** (1500m): pick up the GR path to the east of the town where it crosses the D130 road and the train line, then take the signposted GR41 where it diverges from the GR30.

During winter months, both Le Mont-Dore and La Bourboule double as ski resorts – centres of a **ski-de-fond** (cross-country) network of circular pistes, some over 20km long, and there is limited downhill skiing as well, although at a maximum of 1150m this is not a resort for enthusiasts. Skiable paths also connect La Bourboule to other ski centres in the locality – Sancy, Besse, Chastreix and Picherande.

△ Summit of Puy de Sancy

As far as **eating** is concerned, there are large numbers of brasseries and cafés in the centre offering *plats* for €6.50–8. A particularly pleasant place is rustic *Le Bougnat*, 23 av Clemenceau, which serves various Auvergnat traditional dishes, as well as raclette and fondue (ⓣ04.73.65.28.19; closed Mon; menus from €15). A great place for a **drink** is the atmospheric, 1940s-style *Café de Paris*, located on rue Jean Moulin.

La Bourboule

LA BOURBOULE is just 7km down the road from Le Mont-Dore. Known as the sister to Le Mont-Dore, it's another traditional spa – the "capital of allergies" – but with a more open feel and, because of its lower altitude, temperatures a degree or two warmer. The big **casino**, the domed **Grands Thermes baths** and several other Belle Époque buildings which once housed privately run baths are ornate, gilded and wonderfully vulgar, with a faded, permanently off-season look to them – much like the whole town. All in all, it's a cool, tranquil place to unwind: as the tourist office's leaflet says, "You will be able to put your vital node to rest in La Bourboule".

Behind the Hôtel de Ville, the large wooded **Parc Fenestre** has a *téléférique* taking you right up to **Plateau de Charlannes** (1300m), where it's possible to stroll in the woods or ski in winter; the **tourist office** in the Hôtel de Ville on place de la République (April–June & Sept daily 9.30am–noon & 1.30/2–6pm; July & Aug Mon–Sat 9am–7pm & Sun 9am–6pm; Oct–March Mon–Sat 9.30am–noon & 1.30–5.30, Sun 9.30am–12.30pm; ⓣ04.73.65.57.71, ⓦwww.bourboule.com) sells a booklet of local walks.

Hotels here are plentiful, three good bargains being the *Aviation Hôtel*, in rue de Metz (ⓣ04.73.81.32.32, ⓦwww.avaition.fr; ❹; closed Oct–Dec 20; restaurant from €15), with indoor pool; the welcoming, Art Deco-style *Le Pavillon*, 209 av d'Angleterre (ⓣ04.73.65.50.18, ⓔhotel.lepavillon@wanadoo.fr; ❸; closed Oct–March; restaurant from €15); and the more basic *Les Fleurs* on avenue de Mussy (ⓣ04.73.81.09.44, ⓦwww.hotellesfleurs.com; ❷; closed Nov & Dec; vegetarian restaurant from €18–25). There's also a good selection of **campsites**, with the *Camping municipal* on avenue Maréchal Lattre-de-Tas-

Walks around Orcival

Walking possibilities from Orcival include trips to **Lac de Servières** and **Lac de Guéry**. The first takes two and a half hours, the second some five hours. For Lac de Servières, follow the **GR141–30** south through the woods above the valley of the Sioule. The lake is a beauty; it's 1200m up, with gently sloping shores surrounded by pasture and conifers. You can either head southeast to the **gîte d'étape** at Pessade (ⓣ04.73.79.31.07), or continue to the larger Lac de Guéry, lent a slightly eerie air by the black basaltic boulders strewn across the surrounding meadows, where there's a romantically situated lakeside hotel, the *Lac de Guéry* (ⓣ04.73.65.02.76, ⓦwww.auberge-lac-guery.fr; ❸; closed mid-Oct to mid-Jan; restaurant from €16).

If you're driving to Le Mont-Dore, only 9km further on from here, just before the Lac de Guéry, the road takes you round the head of the **Fontsalade valley**, where two prominent rocks composed of banks of basalt organ-pipes rise spectacularly from the woods: the **Roche Tuilière** and the **Roche Sanadoire**. A footpath takes you on a two-hour walk round the valley, starting from the roadside belvedere overlooking Sanadoire. A little higher up, on the bare slopes of the **Puy de l'Aiguiller**, a roadside memorial commemorates some English airmen killed in an accident while making a parachute drop to the *maquis* in March 1944.

signy (Ⓣ04.73.81.10.20), and another at Murat-le-Quaire, 4km away, along the Mont-Dore road (Ⓣ04.73.65.54.81).

Orcival

Twenty-seven kilometres southwest of Clermont and about 20km north of Le Mont-Dore, lush pastures and green hills punctuated by the abrupt eruptions of the *puys* enclose the small village of **ORCIVAL**, the hometown of ex-President Valéry Giscard d'Estaing. A pretty, popular, place, founded by the monks of La Chaise-Dieu in the twelfth century, it makes a suitable base for hiking in the region.

Orcival is dominated by the stunning Romanesque **church of Notre-Dame** (daily 8am–noon & 2–7pm), built of the same dark-grey volcanic stone as the cathedral in Clermont and topped with a spire and fanned with tiny chapels. Once a major parish, it counted no less than 24 priests in the mid-1200s, and the ironwork on the north door, with its curious forged human head motif, dates from that era. Inside, attention focuses on the choir, neatly and harmoniously contained by the semicircle of pillars defining the ambulatory. Mounted on a stone column in the centre is the celebrated **Virgin of Orcival**, a gilded and enamelled twelfth-century statue in typical Romance style; the object of a popular cult since the Middle Ages and still carried through the streets on Ascension Day.

There's no public transport to Orcival itself; the nearest **bus station** is at Rochefort-Montagne, 6km away, served by buses from Clermont-Ferrand. There is, however, a helpful **tourist office** (July & Aug daily 10am–noon & 2–7pm; rest of year holiday periods only Tues–Sat 2–5pm; Ⓣ04.73.65.89.78, Ⓔterresdomes.sancy@wanadoo.fr), just below the church. Modest **accommodation** can be found at the *Hôtel des Touristes* (Ⓣ04.73.65.82.55, Ⓕ04.73.65.91.11; ❷; closed mid-Nov to mid-Feb; restaurant from €12) and the *Hôtel Vieux Logis* (Ⓣ04.73.65.82.03, Ⓦwww.au-vieux-logis.com; ❶; closed Nov to mid-Dec), both near the church. There's a lakeside **campsite**, *Camping de l'Étang de Fléchat* (Ⓣ04.73.65.82.96; closed mid-Sept to April), 2km outside Orcival, but a better bet is the municipal site at St-Bonnet, 5km to the north of the village (Ⓣ04.73.65.83.32; closed Oct–April), set on a hillside with wonderful views of the surrounding mountains.

St-Nectaire and around

ST-NECTAIRE lies some way to the southeast of Orcival, midway between Le Mont-Dore and Issoire. It comprises the tiny spa of **St-Nectaire-le-Bas**, whose main street is lined with grand but fading Belle Époque hotels, which was added on to the old village of **St-Nectaire-le-Haut**, overlooked by a magnificent Romanesque **church** (daily 9am–7pm). Like the church in Orcival and Notre-Dame-du-Port in Clermont, this is one of the most striking examples of the Auvergne's Romanesque architecture. The carved capitals around the apse retain the tantalizing hues of the paint which once covered the whole interior, while the church's treasures are guarded in the north transept and include a magnificent gilded bust of St. Baudime (the third-century missionary of the Auvergne and parish-founder), a polychrome Virgin in Majesty, and two enamelled plaques, all dating from the twelfth century. Among the town's other curiosities are a couple of caverns, the spa (a two-hour basic session from €12), and the Fontaines Pétrifiantes, where decorative castings are lowered into a mineral spring and glazed over by the power of nature (closed at time of writing but slated to re-open in 2005). The surrounding countryside is notable for its menhirs and other pre-historic megaliths; the tourist office has information on how to find them.

St-Nectaire cheese

St-Nectaire is an *appellation contrôlée*, to which only cheeses made from herds grazing in a limited area to the south of the Monts-Dore are entitled. It is made in two stages. First, a white creamy cheese or *tomme* is produced. This is matured for two to three months in a cellar at a constant temperature, resulting in the growth of a mould on the skin of the cheese which produces the characteristic smell, taste and whitish or yellowy-grey colour.

There are two kinds: St-Nectaire **fermier** and St-Nectaire **laitier**. The *fermier* is the strongest and tastiest and some of it is still made entirely on the farm. Increasingly, however, individual farmers make the *tomme* stage, but then sell it on to wholesalers for the refining. The *laitier* is much more an "industrial" product, made from the milk of lots of different herds, sold onto a co-operative or cheese manufacturer for all its stages.

The **tourist office** (July & Aug daily 9.30am–12.15pm & 2–6.45pm; Sept–June Mon–Sat 9.30–11.45am & 2–4.45pm; ⓣ04.73.88.50.86, ⓦwww.ville-saint-nectaire.fr) is located in the "Grandes Thermes" complex on the main road. Also along the narrow valley floor, where the main street runs, two of the old **hotels** have been refurbished and provide a quiet and comfortable place to stay. One, in particular, the friendly *Hôtel Régina* (ⓣ04.73.88.54.55, ⓕ04.73.88.50.56; ❸; closed Dec & Jan), has an excellent restaurant with menus from €15. Greater comfort can be found at the *Mercure*, a converted spa, now renovated as hotel (ⓣ04.73.88.57.00, ⓔH1814@accor-hotels.com; ❺; closed Nov, Dec & part Jan & March), also with a fine restaurant (menu €21). The best-value **campsite** is the *Clé des Champs* (ⓣ04.73.88.52.33, ⓦwww.campingcledeschamps.com), and there's also a *gîte d'étape, Le Clos du Vallon* (ⓣ04.73.88.50.92; irregular opening times), for walkers on the GR30, which heads north from here to Lac Aydat in five hours, or west to the forest-girt **Lac Chambon** in three hours via Murol. There's another *gîte* on the way at Phialeix (ⓣ04.73.79.32.43; closed Nov–March).

For shorter walks out of St-Nectaire, take the D150 past the church through the old village towards the **Puy de Mazeyres** (919m), and turn up a path to the right for the final climb to the summit (1hr), where you get a superb aerial view of the country round about. Alternatively, follow the D966 along the Couze de Chambon valley to **SAILLANT**, where the stream cascades down a high lava rock face in the middle of the village.

Murol

MUROL, 6km west of St-Nectaire by road (July & Aug twice-daily bus to Clermont) or 5.5km by footpath, is an attractive, sleepy little place best known for its powerful medieval **château**, dramatically situated on top of a basalt cone commanding the approaches for kilometres around (April–June & Sept daily 10am–noon & 1.30–6pm; July & Aug daily 10am–7pm; Oct–March Sat, Sun & hols 2–5pm; €4). In summer, a local organization re-enacts the medieval life of the castle in costume (€7.50).

There are several small family-run **hotels** here. Try the *Hôtel des Pins*, on rue de Levat (ⓣ04.73.88.60.50, ⓕ04.73.88.60.29; ❷; closed Oct to May; restaurant from €10), or the *Hôtel de Paris*, on place de l'Hôtel-de-Ville (ⓣ04.73.88.60.09, ⓕ04.73.88.69.62; ❷; closed Nov to Easter). Of the **campsites**, the best value is the *Ribeyre*, a short distance away at **JASSAT** (ⓣ04.73.88.64.29, ⓔlaribeyre.free.fr; closed mid-Sept to April).

Besse

Eleven kilometres due south of Murol, **BESSE** is one of the prettiest and oldest villages in the region. Its fascinating winding streets of noble lava-built houses – some as old as the fifteenth century – sit atop the valley of the Couze de Pavin, with one of the original fortified town **gates** still in place at the upper end of the village.

Its wealth was due to its role as the principal market for the farms on the eastern slopes of the Monts-Dore, and its co-operative is still one of the main producers of St-Nectaire cheese (see box, opposite). The annual **festivals** of the Montée and Dévalade, marking the ascent of the herds to the high pastures in July and their descent in autumn, are still celebrated by the procession of the Black Virgin of Vassivière from the **church of St-André** in Besse to the chapel of **LA VASSIVIÈRE**, west of **Lac Pavin**, and back again in autumn (July 2 & the first Sun after Sept 21).

Lac Pavin lies 5km west of the village, on the way to the purpose-built downhill ski resort of **SUPER-BESSE** (both are connected to Besse by an hourly *navette*). It's a perfect volcanic lake, filling the now wooded crater. The **GR30** goes through, passing by the **Puy de Montchal**, whose summit (1407m) gives you a fine view over several other lakes and the rolling plateau south towards **ÉGLISENEUVE-D'ENTRAIGUES**, 13km by road, where the Parc des Volcans' **Maison du Fromage** gives a detailed account of the making of the different cheeses of Auvergne (daily: mid-May to June & Sept 2–6pm; July & Aug 10am–12.30pm & 2.30–7pm; €3.50).

Besse's **tourist office** is next to the church on place du Dr Pipet (July & Aug daily 9am–noon & 2–6pm; Sept–June daily 10am–noon & 2–6pm ⓣ04.73.79.52.84, ⓦwww.superbesse.com), and will provide information and advice about walking, mountain biking and skiing. Good, simple fare can be had next door at the *Le Sancy*, which has a *plat du jour* for €6.50. For a place to **stay**, there's none better than the attractive old *Hostellerie du Beffroi*, 24 rue Abbé-Blot (ⓣ04.73.79.50.08, ⓕ04.73.79.57.87; ❸–❻), whose good restaurant serves up a range of local specialities from €20.

The Monts du Cantal

The **Cantal Massif** forms the most southerly extension of the Parc des Volcans. Still nearly 80km in diameter and once 3000m in height, it is one of the world's largest (albeit extinct) volcanoes, shaped like a wheel without a rim. The hub is formed by the three great conical peaks that survived the erosion of the original single cone: **Plomb du Cantal** (1855m), **Puy Mary** (1787m) and **Puy de Peyre-Arse** (1686m).

From this centre a series of deep-cut wooded valleys radiates out like spokes. The most notable are the **valley of Mandailles** and the **valleys of the Cère and Alagnon** in the southwest, where the road and rail line run, and in the north the **valleys of Falgoux and the Rhue**. Between the valleys, especially on the north side, are huge expanses of gently sloping grassland, including the **Plateau du Limon**, and it's these which for centuries have been the mainstay of life in the Cantal: summer pasture for the cows whose milk makes the firm yellow Cantal cheese, pressed in the form of great crusty drums. But this traditional activity has long been in serious decline; as elsewhere, many of the herds are now beef cattle. And tourism is on the increase, in particular walking, horse-riding and skiing.

The main walking routes are the fairly arduous **GR400**, which does a circuit of the whole massif, and the **GR4**, which crosses it from the north to the southeast. There are also more than fifty shorter routes, details of which are obtainable through Chamina publications (see p.932). The two main summits, Plomb du Cantal and Puy Mary, are – for better or worse – accessible to all: the former by *téléférique* from Super-Lioran, the latter by a veritable highway of a footpath from the road at Pas de Peyrol. The best section of the GR4–400 for an experienced hiker with limited time is the three-hour stretch between Super-Lioran and the Puy Mary, with the possibility of taking in a couple of extra summits on the way. For motorists, there's the long, sinuous **Route des Crêtes**, which does a rather wider circuit than the GR400. But, be warned, if you hit a period of bad weather, you'll drive a long way seeing no more than white banks of mist illumined by your headlights.

The main centres within the massif lie on the N122 between Murat and Aurillac: **LE LIORAN**, where the road and rail tunnels begin, and **SUPER-LIORAN**, the downhill and cross-country ski centre, with many hotels, including the rustic and comfortable *Rocher de Cerf* (Ⓣ04.71.49.50.14, Ⓕ04.71.49.54.07; ❹; half-pension normally required, otherwise ❷) and several *gîtes d'étape*, as well as a **tourist office** (Mon–Sat: July & Aug 9.30am–12.30pm & 2–6.30pm; Sept–June 8.30am–12.30pm & 1.30–6pm; Ⓣ04.71.49.50.08, Ⓦwww.lelioran.com). **THIEZAC**, 10km south, also has a **tourist office** (July & Aug daily 9.30am–12.30pm & 3.30–7pm; Sept–June Tues–Sat 9.30am–12.30pm & 2–5pm; Ⓣ04.71.47.03.50, Ⓔotthiezac@wanadoo.fr), as well as the *Hôtel La Belle* Vallée (Ⓣ04.71.47.00.22, Ⓦwww.elanceze.com; ❸; closed Nov–Dec 20; restaurant €14–28), three *gîtes d'étape* and a municipal **campsite**, *La Bedisse* (Ⓣ04.71.47.00.41; closed mid-Sept to May). Further south at **VIC-SUR-CÈRE** there's a **tourist office** (July & Aug daily 9.30am–12.30pm & 2.30–7.30pm; June & Sept daily 9.30–noon & 2–6pm; Ⓣ04.71.47.50.68), and accommodation at the *Hôtel des Bains*, 9 av de la Promenade (Ⓣ04.71.47.50.16, Ⓦwww.cantal-logis.com/vicsurcere/hoteldesbains; ❸; closed Oct–April; restaurant from €20), and the riverside municipal **campsite** (Ⓣ04.71.47.54.18; closed mid-Sept to March).

Aurillac

AURILLAC, the provincial capital of the Cantal, lies on the west side of the mountains, 98km east of Brive and 160km from Clermont-Ferrand. In spite of its good main-line train connections and the fact that its population has almost doubled in the last forty years to around 30,000, it remains one of the most out-of-the-way French provincial capitals. It was until recently a major manufacturer of umbrellas, though that seems doomed to eventual extinction, like its older traditional lace-making and tanning industries. It is now mainly an administrative and commercial centre, with important cattle markets in the suburb of Sistrières on Mondays. Although there are no important sights, it makes a pleasant and unpretentious place to stop over on your way into the Massif Central from the west.

The most interesting part of town is the kernel of old streets, now largely pedestrianized and full of good shops, just to the north of the central **place du Square**. **Rue Duclaux** leads through to the attractive **place de l'Hôtel-de-Ville**, where the big Wednesday and Saturday markets are held in the shadow of the handsome grey-stone **Hôtel de Ville**, built in restrained Republican-classical style in 1803. Beyond it, the continuation of **rue des Forgerons** leads to the beautiful little **place St-Géraud**, with a round twelfth-century fountain

Cattle ranching in the Cantal: Allanche

For an insider's view of the farming life of the Massif there's no better place to go than the age-old **cattle sales at Allanche**, little more than a straggling main street of ancient houses surrounded by windswept upland pastures, about 25km northeast of Murat.

The September 7 sale, when the season's calves are sold off before winter, is typical. Activity starts at 1am or 2am with the clanging of cowbells, the cries of drivers and the thrumming of truck engines. By 4am two or three thousand cattle are tethered to the iron stanchions in the floodlit grassy marketplace, inspected and appraised by men in wellies and overalls and pancake-shaped berets. There is a great deal of bucking and bellowing and sudden uncontrollable charging as beasts, some quite sizeable specimens, are unloaded or loaded. For information on other sales call the tourist office in Allanche (Ⓣ & Ⓕ04.71.20.48.43, Ⓦwww.cezallier.org).

If you are tempted to stay to see the spectacle, there's a **campsite** at the south edge of the village (Ⓣ04.71.20.45.87; closed mid-Sept to mid-June), while in the centre of town, by the old bridge you'll find the recenty renovated *Relais de Remparts* (Ⓣ04.71.20.98.00, Ⓕ04.71.20.98.01; ❷; restaurant from €11).

overlooked by a Romanesque house that was probably part of the original abbey guesthouse, and the externally rather unprepossessing **church of St-Géraud**, which nonetheless has a beautifully ribbed late Gothic ceiling.

At the back of the church, past a delightful small garden, **rue de la Fontaine** comes out on the riverbank by the Pont du Buis, with a shady walk back along cours d'Angoulême on the other side to the Pont-Rouge and **place Gerbert**, where there is an ancient *lavoir*, or washing place. On a steep bluff overlooking this end of town towers the eleventh-century keep of the Château St-Étienne, containing the town's only worthwhile museum, the **Muséum des Volcans** (Jan to mid-June & mid-Sept to Dec Tues–Sat 10am–6.30pm & Sun 2–6.30pm; mid-Sept to mid-June Tues–Sat 2–6pm; €4), with a good section on volcanoes and a splendid view over the mountains to the east.

Southeast of the town towards Aubrac, the road leads through **Carlat**, once an important feudal fiefdom, as well as the particularly attractive villages of **Mur-de-Barrez**, **Brommat** and **Albinhac**, with some lovely old houses and curious churches in the latter two villages.

Practicalities

The **gare SNCF** and **gare routière** are together on place Sémard, a ten-minute walk from the central place du Square along avenue de la République and rue de la Gare. The **tourist office** occupies a small kiosk on the downhill side of place du Square (April–June & Sept Mon–Sat 9am–noon & 2–6.30pm, Sun 10am–noon & 2–5pm; July & Aug daily 9am–7pm; Oct–March Mon–Sat 9am–noon & 2–6.30pm; Ⓣ04.71.48.46.58, Ⓦwww.iaurillac.com), with a number of guidebooks and maps on sale, as well as a money-changing facility when the banks are closed. There's **Internet** access at the *Faisan Doré* cyber café, 8 place d'Aurigues.

For a **place to stay** in the centre of town, try the smart and comfortable *Le Square*, 15 place du Square (Ⓣ04.71.48.24.72, Ⓦwww.cantal-hotel.com; ❸), with a restaurant whose stuffed cabbage has won several prizes (from €15). Rather more deluxe accommodation can be found at the *Grand Hotel de Bordeaux* at 2 av République (Ⓣ04.71.48.01.84, Ⓦwww.hotel-de-bordeaux.fr; ❹), set in a nineteenth century mansion.

There are a number of **restaurants** where you can sample Auvergnat specialities. Two of the most popular are the atmospheric *Le Terroir du Cantal*, 5 rue du Buis (closed Sun & out of season Mon; from €15), with its rough-stone walls and wooden benches, and *Poivre et Sel*, 4 rue du 14-Juillet (closed Sun & Mon; menus from €11), featuring classic dishes such as *magret de canard*. The pretty, riverside *Birdland*, by the Pont-Rouge, done out in the French version of pub style, serves pizzas for around €8.50 and menus for €17 (closed Sun); if you're looking for **nightlife**, the *L'Aventure* disco is part of the same establishment (Thurs–Sun 11pm–4/5am; €10). Finally, Aurillac's most unexpected event is an annual international **street theatre festival** (Ⓦwww.aurillac.net) during the last full week in August, which attracts performers from all over Europe and fills the town with rather more exotic characters than are normally to be seen in these provincial parts.

Salers

SALERS lies 42km north of Aurillac, at the foot of the northwest slopes of the Cantal and within sight of the Puy Violent. Scarcely altered in size or aspect since its sixteenth-century heyday, it remains an extraordinarily homogeneous example of the architecture of that time. If things appears rather grand for a place so small, it's because the town became the administrative centre for the highlands of the Auvergne in 1564 and home of its magistrates. Exploiting this past is really all it has left, but Salers still makes a very worthwhile visit.

If you arrive by the Puy Mary road, you'll enter town by the **church**, which is worth a look for the super-naturalistic statuary of the *Entombment of Christ* (1496), hidden in a side chapel near the entrance. In front of you, the cobbled **rue du Beffroi** leads uphill, under the massive clock tower, and into the central **place Tyssandier-d'Escous**. It is a glorious little square, surrounded by the fifteenth-century mansions of the provincial aristocracy with pepper-pot turrets, mullioned windows and carved lintels, among them the sturdy **Maison du Bailliage**, and, nearby, the **Maison des Templiers**, housing the small Musée de Salers (mid-April to Sept daily 10.30am–noon & 2–7.30pm, closed Tues except July & Aug; €3). Though the museum itself is rather dull, with exhibitions on the Salers cattle breed, traditional costumes and the local cheese-making industry, it's worth having a look at the vaulted ceiling of the entrance passageway, with its carved lions and heads of saints, such as St John the Baptist, framed by wild flowing hair. Before you're done, be sure to make your way to the **Promenade de Barrouze** for the view out across the surrounding green hills and the Puy Violent.

The **tourist office** is in place Tyssandier-d'Escous (Feb–May, Oct–Nov 11 Mon–Sat 10am–noon & 2.30–7pm, Sun 2.30–5.30pm; June–Sept Mon–Sat 10am–noon & 2.30–7pm, Sun 10am–noon & 3–7pm (Ⓣ04.71.40.70.68, Ⓦwww.pays-de-salers.com). If you want to **stay**, try the *Hôtel des Remparts*, near the Promenade de Barrouze (Ⓣ04.71.40.70.33, Ⓦwww.salers-hotel-remparts.com ❸; closed mid-Oct to mid-Dec), whose restaurant specializes in Auvergnat cuisine (from €13), or the more luxurious *Le Gerfaut* in rte du Puy-Mary (t.04.71.40.75.75, Ⓦwww.salers-hotel-gerfaut.com; ❸; closed Nov–Easter). There's a municipal **campsite** on the Puy Mary road (Ⓣ04.71.40.73.09; closed mid-Oct to mid-May).

Murat

MURAT, on the eastern edge of the Cantal, is the closest town to the high peaks and a busy little place, its cafés and shops bustling uncharacteristically for the region. It is also the easiest to access, lying on the N122 road and main train line, about 12km northeast of Le Lioran. Rather than any particular sight, it's the ensemble of greystone houses that attracts, many dating from the fifteenth and sixteenth centuries. Crowded together on their medieval lanes, they make a magnificent sight, especially as you approach from the St-Flour road, with the backdrop of the steep basalt cliffs of the **Rocher Bonnevie**, once the site of the local castle and now surmounted by a huge white statue of the Virgin Mary. Facing the town, perched on the distinctive mound of the **Rocher Bredons**, on your left as you approach, there's the lovely Romanesque **Église de Bredons** (July & Aug daily 10am–noon & 2.30–6.30pm; free), containing some fine eighteenth-century altarpieces. One of the finest of the old houses is now open to the public as the **Maison de la Faune** (July & Aug Mon–Sat 10am–noon & 3–7pm, Sun 3–7pm; Sept–June Mon–Sat 10am–noon & 2–6pm, Sun 3–5pm; €4), full of stuffed animals and birds illustrating the wildlife of the Parc des Volcans.

The **monument** to deportees on place de l'Hôtel-de-Ville and the name of the **avenue des 12-et-24-Juin-1944**, opposite the tourist office, both commemorate one of the blackest days in Murat's recent history. On June 12, 1944, a local Resistance group interrupted a German raid on the town and killed a senior SS officer. In reprisal, the Germans burnt several houses down on June 24 and arrested 120 people, 80 of whom died in deportation. Near the river, below the Rocher Bredons, a stone with an inscription marks the spot where the villagers were assembled before being deported.

Practicalities

The **tourist office** is at 2 rue du faubourg Notre-Dame (July & Aug Mon–Sat 9.30am–noon & 1.30–7pm, Sun 9.30am–1pm & 2.30–6.30pm; Sept–June Mon–Sat 10am–noon & 2–6pm; ⓣ04.71.20.09.47, ⓦwww.ville-de-murat.com), and you can rent **mountain bikes** from La Godille, opposite, or from Bernard Escure, in place Gandilhon-Gens-d'Armes. The **gare SNCF** is on the main road, avenue du Dr-Mallet, where there are also some good places to **stay**. The most comfortable is the *Hôtel des Breuils*, a handsome, ivy-covered bourgeois house at no. 34 (ⓣ04.71.20.01.25, ⓔhostellerie.les.breuils@wanadoo.fr; ❸; closed Nov–Christmas & April), with a heated outdoor pool, while at no. 22, there is the equally friendly and simple *Les Globe-Trotters* (ⓣ04.71.20.07.22, ⓕ04.71.20.16.88; ❶; closed mid-Oct to mid-Nov). A few doors down at no. 18, *Les Messageries* (ⓣ04.71.20.04.04, ⓕ04.71.20.02.81; ❸) has somewhat clinical rooms, but the restaurant (from €12–25) serves up good hearty cooking, including home-made terrines and fruit tarts. The town's **campsite**, *Les Stalapos*, is southwest of the centre in rue du Stade (ⓣ04.71.20.01.83, ⓔville-de-murat@wanadoo.fr; closed Oct–April).

St-Flour and the Margeride

Seat of a fourteenth-century bishopric, **ST-FLOUR** stands dramatically on a cliff-girt basalt promontory above the River Ander, 92km west of Le Puy and 92km south of Clermont-Ferrand. Prosperous in the Middle Ages because of its strategic position on the main road from northern France to Languedoc and the proximity of the grasslands of the Cantal whose herds provided the raw materials for its tanning and leather industries, it fell into somnolent decline in modern times, only partially reversed in the last thirty-odd years.

While the lower town that has grown up around the station is of little interest, the wedge of old streets that occupies the point of the promontory surrounding the cathedral has considerable charm. The best time to come is on a Saturday morning when the old town is filled with market stalls selling sausages, cheese and other local produce. If you're in a car, leave it in the car park in the chestnut-shaded square, **Les Promenades**. One end of the square is dominated by the **memorial** to Dr Mallet, his two sons and other hostages and assorted citizens executed in reprisals by the Germans during World War II.

The narrow streets of the old town lead off from here and converge on the **place d'Armes**, where the fourteenth-century **Cathédrale St-Pierre** stands, backing onto the edge of the cliff, with a terrace giving good views out over the countryside. From the outside, the plain grey volcanic rock of the cathedral makes for a rather severe and uninspiring appearance; it's an impression that is partly mitigated inside by the fine vaulting of the ceiling and the presence of a number of works of art, most notably a carved, black-painted walnut figure of Christ with a strikingly serene expression, dating from the thirteenth century.

Facing the cathedral on the place d'Armes are some attractive old buildings, housing a couple of cafés under their arcades, while at the north and south extremities of the square stand the town's two museums. At the north end, the fine fourteenth-century building that was once the headquarters of the town's consuls contains the **Musée Alfred Douët**'s somewhat ragbag collections of furniture, tapestries and paintings (mid-April to mid-Oct daily 9am–noon & 2–6pm; mid-Oct to mid-April closed Sun; €3.30, joint ticket with Haute-Auvergne museum €3.40); the view from the cliffs behind the museum gives a sense of the impregnable position of the town. At the south end of the square, the current Hôtel de Ville, formerly the bishop's palace built in 1610, houses the more interesting **Musée de la Haute-Auvergne** (mid-April to mid-Oct daily 10am–noon & 2–6pm; mid-Oct to mid-April closed Sun; same prices as above), whose collections include some beautifully carved Auvergnat furniture and exquisitely made traditional musical instruments, such as the *cabrette*, a kind of accordion peculiar to the Auvergne.

Practicalities

The **gare SNCF** is on avenue Charles de Gaulle in the lower town. A few trains from Clermont-Ferrand and Aurillac stop here, but most journeys involve changing at Neussargues onto a SNCF bus, which can drop you off on the Promenades in the old town, saving you the walk up. The **tourist office** is on the Promenades, opposite the memorial (July & Aug Mon–Sat 9am–8pm, Sun 10am–12.30pm & 3–7pm; Apr–June & Sept–Oct Mon–Sat 9am–6pm, Sun 3.30–5.30pm; Nov–March Mon–Sat 9am–6pm; Ⓣ04.71.60.22.50, Ⓦwww.st-flour.com).

The best deal for **accommodation** in the atmospheric upper town is the magnificent, old-style *La Maison des Planchettes* at 7 rue des Planchettes (Ⓣ04.71.60.10.08, Ⓦwww.maison-des-planchettes.com; ❶) which has half-pensions for as low as €30 band a *terroir* restaurant with menus from €12. Another great option is the *Hotel de France*, 28 rue de Lacs (Ⓣ04.71.60.04.75, Ⓦwww.saint-flour-hoteldefrance.com; ❶), a welcoming, family-run establishment. The best place for both local cuisine and *gastronomique* is *Le Nautilus* on 23 av Charles-de-Gaulle (Ⓣ04.71.60.11.36; closed Oct–Easter) with menus from €15–55. The town's municipal **campsite**, *Les Orgues*, is off avenue des Orgues in the old town (Ⓣ04.71.60.44.01; closed mid-Sept to mid-May).

The Margeride

South and east of St-Flour stretch the wild, rolling, sparsely populated wooded hills of the **Margeride**, one of the strongholds of the wartime Resistance groups. If you have your own transport, the D4 makes a slow but spectacular route east (92km) to Le Puy, crossing the forested heights of **Mont Mouchet**, at 1465m the highest point of the Margeride. A side turning, the D48 (signposted), takes you to the national Resistance **monument** by the woodman's hut that served as HQ to the local Resistance commander during the June 1944 battle to delay German reinforcements moving north to strengthen resistance to the D-day landings in Normandy. There's an **eco-museum** here (May to mid-Sept daily 9.30am–noon & 2–7pm; mid-Sept to mid-Oct Mon–Fri 9.30am–noon & 2–7pm, Sat & Sun 10am–noon & 2–6pm; €4), sketching the progression of the Resistance movement in the area. The views back west from these heights to the Cantal are superb.

Further south, the modern *autoroute* crosses the gorge of the River Truyère beside the delicate steel tracery of the **Viaduc de Garabit**, built by Gustave Eiffel (of Tower fame) in 1884 to carry the newly constructed rail line; experience he put to important use in the Tower. Not far away, about 20km south of St-Flour and perched above the waters of the lake created by the damming of the Truyère for hydroelectric power, are the romantic ruins of the keep of the **Château d'Alleuze**, stronghold in the 1380s of one Bernard de Garlan, a notorious leader of lawless mercenaries employed by the English in the Hundred Years War to sow panic and destruction in French-held parts of the country.

The southwest: Aubrac and Rouergue

In the southwest corner of the Massif Central, the landscapes start to change and the mean altitude begins to drop. The wild, desolate moorland of the **Aubrac** is cut and contained by the savage gorges of **the Lot and Truyère rivers**. To the south of them, the arid but more southern-feeling plateaux of the *causses* form a sort of intermediate step to the lower hills and coastal plains of Languedoc. And they in turn are cut by the dramatic trenches formed by the **gorges of the Tarn**, **Jonte** and **Dourbie**, along with the spectacular caves of the **Aven Armand** and **Dargilan**. These are places best avoided at the height of the holiday season, when they turn into overcrowded outdoor playgrounds for amateur canoeists, parties of schoolchildren, motorists and campers.

The bigger towns, like **Rodez** and **Millau** in the old province of the **Rouergue**, also have much more of a southern feel. Both are worth a visit, although their attractions need not keep you for more than half a day. Rodez has a fine cathedral and Millau is worth considering as a base for exploring the causses and river gorges of the Tarn and Jonte.

The two great architectural draws of the area are **Conques**, with its medieval village and magnificent abbey, which owes its existence to the Santiago pilgrim route (now the GR65), and the perfect little *bastide* town of **Sauveterre-de-Rouergue**.

The mountains of Aubrac

The **Aubrac** lies to the south of St-Flour, east of the valley of the River Truyère and north of the valley of the Lot. It's a region of bleak, windswept uplands with long views and huge skies, dotted with glacial lakes and granite villages hunkered down out of the weather. The highest points are between 1200m and 1400m, and there are more cows up here than people; you see them grazing the boggy, peaty pastures, divided by dry-stone walls and turf-brown streams. There are few trees: a scatter of willow and ash and the occasional stand of hardy beeches on the tops, and only abandoned shepherds' huts testify to more populous times. It's an area that's invisible in bad weather, but which, in good conditions, has a bleak beauty, little disturbed by tourism or modernization.

Once this was sheep country, where shepherds from the dry summer lowlands of Quercy and Languedoc brought their flocks for the season. They were displaced in the nineteenth century by cows, raised for their more commercially exploitable production of milk and cheese, destined for the growing towns. And these in turn, as available labour shrank with the depopulation of the villages, ceded the pastures to beef cattle, as in the Cantal further north.

Aumont-Aubrac and Aubrac

The waymarked **Tour d'Aubrac** footpath does a complete circuit of the area in around ten days, starting from the town of **AUMONT-AUBRAC**, where you'll find *Chez Camillou* at 10 rue Languedoc (Ⓣ04.66.42.80.22, Ⓔcamillou@club-internet.fr; ❸; restaurant from €16; periodic closings mid-Nov to mid-Feb), the *Relais de Peyre*, across the street at no. 9 (Ⓣ04.66.42.85.88, Ⓕ04.66.42.90.08; ❷; closed Jan; restaurant from €14.50–23.50), and a municipal **campsite** (Ⓣ04.66.42.80.02). There is also a daily train connection on the Millau–St-Flour line.

The marathon **GR65** from Le Puy to Santiago de Compostela in Spain also crosses the area from northeast to southwest en route to Conques. In fact, the tiny village of **AUBRAC**, which gave its name to the region, owes its existence to this Santiago pilgrim route; around 1120, a way-station was opened here for the express purpose of providing shelter for the pilgrims on these inhospitable heights. Little remains of it today, beyond the windy **Tour des Anglais**, into which is incorporated the friendly *Hôtel de la Dômerie* (Ⓣ05.65.44.28.42, Ⓕ05.65.44.21.47; ❸; closed mid-Nov to April; restaurant from €18–37).

St-Urcize and Nasbinals

This is the wildest and most starkly beautiful part of the Aubrac. The close-huddled village of **ST-URCIZE**, 13km north of the town of Aubrac, hangs off the side of the valley of the River Lhère, with a lovely Romanesque church at its centre and a World War I **memorial**, with so many names on it you wouldn't have thought it possible such a small place could furnish so much cannon fodder. The village is ghostly out of season, with most of the unspoiled granite houses owned by people who live elsewhere. Should you wish to **stay**, there's a campsite and the welcoming *Hôtel Remise* (Ⓣ04.71.23.20.02, Ⓕ04.71.23.20.02; ❷; excellent food for around €15; closed Jan). On the other hand, if you can afford it, it would be a shame to pass up *Guy Prouhèze*, in 2 rte de Languedoc (Ⓣ04.66.42.80.07, Ⓦwww.prouheze.com; closed Nov–March; ❺), a hotel featuring a famed *gastronomique* restaurant (menus €31–89; closed

Sun noon & Mon). Those on a budget can enjoy a gourmet experience at *L'Ousta Bas* (Ⓣ04.66.42.87.44; closed off-season Tues & Wed and weekdays Nov–March), which has *terroir* menus from €14.50.

NASBINALS, 8km to the southeast, is rather bigger and livelier, and something of a cross-country ski resort in winter. It, too, has a beautiful small-scale **church** of the twelfth century, joined onto the adjacent house with a round fortified tower incorporated in the transept wall by the entrance. Just above the building, the *Hôtel de La Route d'Argent* (Ⓣ04.66.32.50.03, Ⓕ04.66.32.56.77; ❷) provides comfortable accommodation and good food (from €18). The village **tourist office** is on the other side of the road (July & Aug Mon–Sat 9.30am–noon & 2.30–6pm, Sun 10am–noon; Sept–June Mon & Wed–Sat 10am–noon & 2–5pm; Ⓣ04.66.32.55.73, Ⓦot.nasbinals.free.fr) and can rent out mountain bikes. A **campsite** (Ⓣ04.66.32.50.17) and **gîte d'étape** (Ⓣ04.66.32.50.65; meals available) are located on the St-Urcize road.

Laguiole

Seventeen kilometres west of St-Urcize and 24km north of Espalion, **LAGUIOLE** passes for a substantial town in these parts. Derived from the Occitan word for "little church", it's a name which now stands for knives and cheese. The **knives**, which draw hordes of French to the town's many shops, are characterized by a long, pointed blade and bone handle that fits the palm; the genuine article should bear the effigy of a bee stamped on the clasp that holds the blade open. It's an industry that started in the nineteenth century, then moved to industrial Thiers, outside Clermont-Ferrand, before returning to Laguiole in 1987, when the Société Laguiole (the only outlet for the genuine article) opened a factory designed by Philippe Starck on the St-Urcize road, with a giant knife projecting from the roof of the windowless all-aluminium building. They have a shop on the main through-road, on the corner of the central marketplace close to the **tourist office** in the Place du Forail (Mon–Sat 9am–12.30pm & 3–7pm, Sun 10.30am–noon & 2–7pm; Ⓣ05.65.44.35.94, Ⓦwww.laguiole-online.com). Laguiole's **cheese-making** tradition dates back to the twelfth century; unpasteurized cow's milk is formed into massive cylindrical cheeses, and aged up to eighteen months. The hard, tangy result is a world apart from neighbouring Roquefort; to sample or buy, the factory outlet on the north edge of town is the best bargain.

There's nothing of great significance to see in the village, though the **Musée du Haut-Rouergue** (irregular hours; free), with its collection of objects illustrative of the pastoral life, might be of interest. Nonetheless, it is a relatively metropolitan base for exploring round about. This is made particularly enticing by the fact that *Michel Bras*, a highly rated **hotel** (Ⓣ05.65.51.18.20, Ⓦwww.michel-bras.com; ❾) with one of the country's finest restaurants (menus €49–143) is located just outside of town on the Route d'aubrac. For the more budget conscious there are several hotels on the main street. Try the *Aubrac* opposite the marketplace (Ⓣ05.65.44.32.13, Ⓔhotel-aubrac@wanadoo.fr; ❷; restaurant from €9.70), or the *Grand Hôtel Auguy* (Ⓣ05.65.44.31.11, Ⓔgrand-hotel.auguy@wanadoo.fr; ❹), 2 allée de l'Amicale, with a good restaurant from €28–72.

Alternatively, there's a sort of *chambre d'hôte* at Le Combaïre, in a quiet rural setting 3km west on the D42 (Ⓣ05.65.44.33.26, Ⓕ05.65.44.37.38; ❷); *gîtes d'étape* at Le Vayssaire (Ⓣ05.65.48.44.69) and Soulages-Bonneval (Ⓣ05.65.44.42.18, Ⓕ05.65.44.42.80; meals available), 5km away on the D54; and a municipal **campsite** (Ⓣ05.65.44.39.72; closed mid-Sept to mid-May) on the St-Urcize road. Communications, however, are not good, and if you don't have a car your only chance of getting in or out is the daily bus to Rodez.

Marvejols

MARVEJOLS lies at the southeast extremity of the Aubrac, on the main N9 road and the Paris–Béziers train line. The country changes drastically as you approach. The bare, granite-strewn plateau opens into a wide deep basin, wooded with pines and punctuated by the erosion-formed table-topped pinnacles known hereabouts as *trucs*. It's a small, undeveloped and unpretentious country town, whose ancient streets are contained within surviving medieval gates, and there's little to do beyond savouring the atmosphere.

The **tourist office** is in the main gateway on the main road (June–Sept Mon–Sat 9am–noon & 2–7pm, Sun 10am–noon; Oct–May Mon–Sat 9am–noon & 2–6pm; Ⓣ04.66.32.02.14, Ⓦwww.ville-marvejols.fr). Should you need to **stay**, the pleasant *Hôtel les Rochers* (Ⓣ04.66.32.10.58, Ⓔhotel.rocher@worldonline.fr; ❷; good restaurant from €14–30), is opposite the gare SNCF, which is 800m uphill to the right off the N9 in the direction of Chirac. The *Domaine de Carrière* (Ⓣ04.66.32.28.14, Ⓕ04.66.32.49.60) an eighteenth-century mansion on the edge of town also offers rooms (❸), as well as excellent dining (from €22). There's a municipal **campsite** beside a tributary stream on the other side of the River Colagne from the town.

Rodez and the upper valley of the Lot

A particularly beautiful and out-of-the-way stretch of country lies on the southwestern periphery of the Massif Central, bordered roughly by the valley of the **River Lot** in the north and the **Viaur** in the south. The upland areas are open and wide, with views east to the mountains of the Cévennes and south to the Monts de Lacaune and the Monts de l'Espinouse. **Rodez**, capital of the

Wolves and the Béte du Gévaudan

In Marvejols, at the junction of the bridge across the Colagne and the N9, there stands a hideous, flattened-out bronze statue of a semi-wolf, which represents the terrible legendary **Bête du Gévaudan**, supposedly the culprit of a series of horrific attacks in the eighteenth century. Between 1764 and 1767, the whole area between here and Le Puy was terrorized, and 25 women, 68 children and 6 men were slain. The king sent his dragoons, then his best huntsman, who eventually found and killed an enormous wolf, but the mysterious deaths continued until one Jean Chastel shot another wolf near Saugues.

It has never been established if a wolf was really guilty of these deaths – a wolf that attacked women and children almost exclusively, that moved about so rapidly, that never touched a sheep – and the question remains whether it was perhaps a human psychopath.

If you would like reassurance about the temperament of real wolves, visit the **Parc Zoologique du Gévaudan** in the hamlet of Ste-Lucie just off the N9, 9km north of Marvejols, where more than a hundred wolves live in semi-liberty (guided visits roughly every one and a half hours: Feb–Dec daily 10am–6pm; €6.50), the first to do so in France since the beginning of the last century.

Rouergue, with a fine cathedral, is the only place of any size, accessible on the main train and bus routes. But the most dramatic places are in the river valleys, in particular the great abbey of **Conques** and the small towns of **Entraygues** and **Estaing**.

Rodez

Until the 1960s, **RODEZ** and the Rouergue were synonymous with back-country poverty and underdevelopment. Today it's an active and prosperous provincial town with a charming, renovated centre, even though the approach, through spreading commercial districts, is uninspiring.

Built on high ground above the River Aveyron, the **old town**, dominated by the massive red-sandstone **Cathédrale Notre-Dame**, is visible for kilometres around. No matter from what direction you approach, you'll find yourself in the **place d'Armes**, where the cathedral's plain, fortress-like west front and the seventeenth-century bishop's palace sit side by side – both buildings were incorporated into the town's defences. The Gothic cathedral, its plain facade relieved only by an elaborately flowery rose window, was begun in 1277 and took three hundred years to complete. Towering over the square is the cathedral's 87-metre **belfry**, decorated with pinnacles, balustrades and statuary almost as fantastical as that of Strasbourg cathedral. The impressively spacious interior, architecturally as plain as the facade, is adorned with a magnificently extravagant seventeenth-century walnut organ loft and choir stalls that were crafted by André Sulpice in 1468.

Leaving by the splendid south porch, you find yourself in the tiny place Rozier in front of the fifteenth-century **Maison Cannoniale**, whose courtyard is guarded by jutting turrets. From the back of the cathedral to the north and the south, a network of well-restored medieval streets connects place de-Gaulle, place de la Préfecture and the attractive place du Bourg, with its fine sixteenth-century houses. In place Foch, just south of the cathedral, the Baroque chapel of the old **lycée** is worth a look for its amazing painted ceiling, while in place Raynaldy, the modern **Hôtel de Ville** and the **médiathèque** are interesting examples of attempts to graft modern styles onto old buildings.

Practicalities

The **tourist office** is situated on place Foch, just off boulevard Gambetta and the place d'Armes, near the cathedral (June & Sept Mon–Sat 9am–12.30pm & 1.30–6.30pm, July & Aug Mon–Sat 9am–12.30pm & 1.30–6.30pm & Sun 10am–noon; Oct–May Mon 2.30–5.30pm, Tues–Fri 9am–12.30pm & 1.30–5.30pm, Sat 9.30am–12.30pm & 2.30–5.30pm; Ⓣ05.65.68.02.27, Ⓦwww.ot-rodez.fr). The **gare routière** is on avenue V.-Hugo (Ⓣ05.65.68.11.13), and the **gare SNCF** on boulevard Joffre, on the northern edge of town.

For reasonable, if somewhat charmless, hotel **accommodation**, try the *Hôtel des Voyageurs* at 22 av Maréchal-Joffre (Ⓣ05.65.42.08.41; Ⓕ05.65.78.90.23; ❶), or the better *Hôtel du Clocher*, off the east end of the cathedral at 4 rue Séguy (Ⓣ05.65.71.22.11, Ⓕ05.65.68.64.27; ❷). More upmarket is *La Tour Maje*, on boulevard Gally behind the tourist office (Ⓣ05.65.68.34.68, Ⓦwww.hotel-tour-maje.fr; ❸), a modern building tacked onto a medieval tower. Budget accommodation is available at the **HI hostel** in **ONET-LE-CHÂTEAU**, 3km to the north, at 26 bd des Capucines, Quatre-Saisons (Ⓣ05.65.77.51.05, Ⓔfjt-aj-rodez@wanadoo.fr; bus #1 or #3, direction "Quatre Saisons", stop "Marché d'Oc/Les Rosiers/Capucine"), with a good canteen serving local specialities for around €7. Rodez' municipal **campsite** (Ⓣ05.65.67.09.52; closed Oct–May) is on the riverbank in the quartier Layoule, about 1km from the centre.

As for **eating**, one of the best places to sample local cuisine is *La Taverne*, 23 rue de l'Embergue (closed Sun; menus from €10.50), with an attractive terrace at the back, while the place to go for more gourmet food is the classy *Goûts et Couleurs*, 38 rue Bonald (closed Sun & Mon), where menus range from €26 to €60. *Le Bistroquet*, 17 rue du Bal, off place d'Olmet (closed Sun & Mon), does good salads and grills for around €11. For a **drink**, head for the *Café de la Paix*, on place Jean-Jaurès, or *au Bureau*, in the Tour Maje.

Sauveterre-de-Rouergue and the gorges of the Viaur

Forty kilometres southwest of Rodez and 6.5km northwest of Naucelle, **SAUVETERRE-DE-ROUERGUE** makes the most rewarding side trip in this part of the Rouergue. It is a perfect, otherworldly *bastide*, founded in 1281, with a large, wide central square, part cobbled, part gravelled, and surrounded by stone and half-timbered houses built over arcaded ground floors. Narrow streets lead off to the outer road, lined with stone-built houses the colour of rusty iron. On summer evenings, pétanque players come out to roll their bowls beneath chestnut and plane trees, while swallows and swifts swoop and dive overhead.

In summer, a **bus** runs once a weekday here in the late afternoon from Rodez. The **tourist office** is in the main square (June–Sept Mon 2.30–6pm, Tues–Fri 10am–12.30pm & 2.30–6pm, Sat 10am–12.30pm; Ⓣ05.65.72.02.52, Ⓕ05.65.72.55.58). There are several agreeable **hotels**, including the cheap and charming *Hôtel La Grappe d'Or*, on the outer road (Ⓣ05.65.72.00.62; ❷), whose restaurant (closed Oct–April) offers an excellent menu at €13.50, with dishes like *gésiers chauds*, *tripoux*, cheese, ice cream and *fouace* (a kind of sweet cake). More upmarket is the *Sénéchal*, at the entrance to the village (Ⓣ05.65.71.29.00, Ⓦwww.senechal.net; ❼; closed Jan to late-March), with an indoor pool and an excellent restaurant (closed Mon plus Tues lunch; from €24–99). There's also a **campsite**, just off the D997 (Ⓣ05.65.47.05.32).

The country round about, known as the **Ségala**, is high (around 500m) and wide, cut by sudden and deep river valleys full of lush greenery. The most spectacular of these is the valley of the **River Viaur** to the south and west of Sauveterre, where a car is essential. If you're heading west towards Najac, there's a marvellous backcountry route through La Salvetat, crossing the Viaur at Bellecombe and again at Moulin-de-Bar, where there's a riverside **campsite**, *Le Gomvassou*. The wartime Resistance was very active hereabouts and there are numerous memorials to the Resistance fighters who lost their lives in the aftermath of the D-day landings. There is a particularly interesting one beside the tiny church in **JOUQUEVIEL**, further downstream, dedicated to a unit of Polish volunteers and 161 escaped Soviet POWs.

Conques

CONQUES, 37km north of Rodez, is one of the great villages of southwest France. It occupies a spectacular position on the flanks of the steep, densely wooded gorge of the little **River Dourdou**, a tributary of the Lot. For all its glory, Conques is not easy to get to. The only public transport to the village is a seasonal bus that runs up the Tarn valley from Entreaygues via Vieillevie and as far as St. Geniez d'Olt. The shuttle makes one run in each direction (June & Sept Mon; July–Aug Tues, Thurs & Sat; confirm departure times with the tourist office at Conques), allowing you to visit Conques and return the same day.

It's the abbey which brought the village into existence. Its origins go back to a hermit called Dadon who settled here around 800 AD and founded a community of Benedictine monks, one of whom pilfered the relics of the martyred girl, Ste Foy, from the monastery at Agen. Known for her ability to cure blindness and liberate captives, Ste Foy's presence brought the pilgrims flocking to Conques in ever-increasing numbers, which earned the abbey a prime place on the pilgrimage route to Compostela.

The abbey church

At the village's centre, dominating the landscape, stands the renowned Romanesque **church of Ste-Foy**, whose giant pointed towers are echoed in those of the medieval houses that cluster tightly about it. Begun in the eleventh century, its plain fortress-like facade rises on a small cobbled square beside the tourist office and pilgrims' fountain, the slightly shiny silver-grey schist prettily offset by the greenery and flowers of the terraced gardens.

In startling contrast to this plainness, the elaborately sculpted *Last Judgement* in the **tympanum** above the door admonishes all who see it to espouse virtue and eschew vice. Christ sits in judgement in the centre, with the chosen on his right hand, among them Dadon the hermit and the emperor Charlemagne, while his left hand directs the damned to Hell, as usual so much more graphically and interestingly portrayed with all its gory tortures than the boring bliss of Paradise, depicted in the bottom left panel.

The **inside** of the church was designed to accommodate the large numbers of pilgrims and channel them down the aisles and round the ambulatory. From here they could contemplate Ste Foy's relics displayed in the choir, encircled by a lovely wrought-iron screen, still in place. There is some fine carving on the capitals, especially in the triforium arches, too high up to see from the nave: you need to climb to the organ loft, which gives you a superb perspective on the whole interior. This is also a good place to admire the windows, designed by the Abstract artist Pierre Soulages, which consist of plain plates of glass that subtly change colour with the light outside.

The unrivalled asset of this church is the survival of its medieval treasure of extraordinarily rich, bejewelled **reliquaries**, including a gilded statue of Ste Foy, bits of which are as old as the fifth century, and one known as the *A of Charlemagne*, because it is thought to have been the first in a series given as presents by the emperor to monasteries he founded. Writing in 1010, a cleric named Bernard d'Angers gave an idea of the effect of these wonders on the medieval pilgrim: "The crowd of people prostrating themselves on the ground was so dense it was impossible to kneel down. … When they saw it for the first time [Ste Foy], all in gold and sparkling with precious stones and looking like a human face, the majority of the peasants thought that the statue was really looking at them and answering their prayers with her eyes." The treasure is kept in a room adjoining the now ruined cloister (daily: April–Sept 9.30am–12.30pm & 2–6.30pm; Oct–March 9.30am–12.30pm & 2–6pm; €5.50); the second part of the Conques museum, displayed on three floors of a house on the cathedral square, consists of a miscellany of sixteenth-century and later tapestries, furnishings and assorted bits of medieval masonry.

The village

The **village** of Conques is very small, largely depopulated and mainly contained within the medieval **walls**, parts of which still survive, along with three of its **gates**. The houses date mainly from the late Middle Ages. The whole ensemble of cobbled lanes and stairways is a pleasure to stroll through. There are two main streets, the old **rue Haute**, or "upper street", which was the route for the pilgrims coming from Estaing and Le Puy and passing onto Figeac and Cahors through the **Porte de la Vinzelle**; and the lane, now **rue Charlemagne**, which leads steeply downhill through the **Porte de Barry** to the river and the ancient **Pont Romain**, with the little **chapel of St-Roch** off to the left, from where you get a fine view of the village and church. Better still: climb the road on the far side of the valley. The rather grandiose-sounding **European centre for medieval art and civilization**, hidden in a bunker right at the top of the hill (9am–noon & 2–6pm), sometimes has exhibitions and displays. Throughout August, the village hosts a prestigious **classical music festival**, most of the concerts taking place at the abbey church; contact the tourist office for more information.

Walkers can use sections of the **GR65** and **GR62**, both of which pass through the village; the tourist office will provide information about shorter local walks.

Practicalities

The **tourist office** is on the square beside the church (daily: April–Sept 9.30am–12.30pm & 2–6.30pm; Oct–March 10am–noon & 2–6pm; ⓣ08.20.82.08.03, ⓦwww.conques.fr). For somewhere central to **stay**, the *Auberge St-Jacques* (ⓣ05.65.72.86.36, ⓦwww.aubergestjacques.fr; ❸), near the church, provides good-value, old-fashioned accommodation and also has a popular restaurant, with menus from €15 and *plats du jour* at €8–11. A good alternative is the *Auberge du Pont Romain*, on the main road below the hill on which Conques stands (ⓣ05.65.69.84.07, ⓕ05.65.69.85.12; ❷; closed first two weeks Nov; menus from €13) – it's a twenty-minute walk from here to the church. A little way upstream, the attractive *Moulin de Cambelong* (ⓣ05.65.72.84.77, ⓦwww.moulindecambelong.com; ❼) offers more comfort – some rooms have spacious wooden balconies with great views of the river – and a first-rate restaurant, specializing in duck dishes (a la carte from €45).

There's **hostel**-type accommodation at the *Résidence Dadon* (❶) directly above the abbey in rue Emile Roudié, and a *gîte d'étape* neaby (both booked through the tourist office). There are several **campsites** in Conques: try *Beau Rivage* (ⓣ05.65.69.82.23; closed Oct–March), on the banks of the Dourdou, just below the village, *St-Cyprien-sur-Dourdou* (ⓣ05.65.72.80.52), 7km to the south, or *Le Moulin* (ⓣ05.65.72.87.28; closed Nov–March), at Grand-Vabre, 5km downstream.

The upper valley: Grand-Vabre to Entraygues

The most beautiful stretch of the **Lot valley** is the 21.5km between the bridge of Coursavy, below **Grand-Vabre**, just north of Conques, and **Entraygues**: deep, narrow and wild, with the river running full and strong, as yet unaffected by the dams higher up, with scattered farms and houses high on the hillsides among long-abandoned terracing. The shady, tree-tunnelled road is level and not heavily used, making it ideal for cycling.

There are two hotels 6.5km east in **VIEILLEVIE**, where canoe rental is also available: the *Hôtel de la Terrasse* (Ⓣ04.71.49.94.00, Ⓔhotel-de-la-terrasse@wanadoo.fr; ❸; closed mid-Nov to April; restaurant €16–32) and the ramshackle but homely *Le Cantou* (Ⓣ04.71.49.98.82; ❶; restaurant from €13.50). A further possibility is the delightful *Auberge du Fel*, some 10km further on, high on the north slopes of the valley in the hamlet of **LE FEL** (Ⓣ05.65.44.52.30, Ⓦwww.auberge-du-fel.com; ❸; closed mid-Nov to March; excellent restaurant with menus from €18–36), which by an unexpected quirk of climate produces a little local wine. There is also a beautifully sited municipal **campsite** high on the hillside (Ⓣ05.65.44.51.86; closed Oct–May).

Entraygues and around

ENTRAYGUES, with its riverside streets and attractive grey houses, has an airy, open feel that belies its mountain sleepiness. It lies right in the angle of the junction of the Lot with the equally beautiful River Truyère. The brown towers of a thirteenth-century **château** overlook the meeting of the waters, and a magnificent four-arched **bridge** of the same date crosses the Truyère a little way upstream, alongside the ancient tanners' houses.

The **tourist office** is on the main street (July & August Mon–Sat 9.30am–12.30pm & 3–7pm, Sun 10am–12.30pm; Sept–June Mon 2–6pm, Tues–Fri 9.30–12.15pm & 2–6pm, Sat 9.30am–12.15pm & 2–5pm; Ⓣ05.65.44.56.10, Ⓔot-pays-entraygues@wanadoo.fr). It frequently remains open outside of its official hours and will provide information about walking, mountain biking and canoeing in the area. Reasonable **places to stay** include the *Hôtel Le Centre*, on the main street (Ⓣ05.65.44.51.19, Ⓕ05.65.48.63.09; ❷; restaurant from €11–29), and the *Lion d'Or*, on the corner of the main street and the bank of the Lot (Ⓣ05.65.44.50.01, Ⓕ05.65.44.55.43; ❸), with an outdoor swimming pool and garden and attached restaurant (from €15). There's also a **campsite**, *Le Val-de-Saures* (Ⓣ05.65.44.56.92; closed Oct–April), and two *gîtes d'étape* – Mme Galan (Ⓣ05.65.44.50.73) and *Le Battedou* (Ⓣ05.65.48.61.62) – on the GR65 at **GOLINHAC**, about 7km south of Entraygues on the other side of the Lot. There is one **bus** per weekday to Aurillac in the north and Rodez to the south.

There are further accommodation options at **ESTAING**, another beautiful village huddled round a rocky bluff and castle in a bend of the Lot about 10km beyond Golinhac. The *Hôtel aux Armes d'Estaing*, named after the family who occupied the castle for five hundred years, offers attractive rooms and very good food in the centre of the village (Ⓣ05.65.44.70.02, Ⓔremi.catusse@wanadoo.fr; ❷; closed mid-Nov to mid-March; restaurant from €14–35). There's also a municipal **campsite** (Ⓣ05.65.44.72.77; closed Oct–April) and **gîte d'étape** on the GR65 (Ⓣ05.65.44.71.74). A date to watch out for, however, is the first Sunday in July when the place fills up with people, many in medieval dress, who come to honour the relics of **St Fleuret**, bishop of Clermont, who died here in 621 AD and is buried in the fifteenth-century church by the castle.

Espalion

The substantial little town of **ESPALION** lies in a mild, fertile opening in the valley of the Lot, 10km from Estaing and 32km northeast of Rodez. It was the "first smile of the south" to the muleteers, pilgrims and other travellers coming down from the rude heights of the Massif Central and places north. Home town of Benoît Rouquayrol and Auguste Denayrouze, inventors of diving suits, Espalion is best known in France for its exiles, in particular its countless sons and daughters who set up in the café business in Paris from the 1850s onwards.

The only interesting part of town is the **riverside quarter**, with its galleried and balconied old houses, once used as tanneries, hanging over the water. The finest view of the area is from the Pont Neuf, where the main road to Rodez crosses the Lot, as just upstream there's a lovely red sandstone packhorse **bridge** with a domed and turreted **château** dating from 1572 right behind it.

Surprisingly, there's an interesting museum dedicated principally to the life of the region: **Musée Joseph Vaylet**, in an old medieval church, on the main road, boulevard Poulenc (daily July–Sept 10am–noon & 2–7pm; Oct–June Wed–Sat & Sun 2–6pm; €4), contains mainly furniture and domestic objects, plus an exhibition of diving gear (thanks to the two Espalionnais mentioned above).

Don't miss the glorious little twelfth-century Romanesque **church of St-Hilarion de Perse**, built on the spot, so the story goes, where, in the reign of Charlemagne, the Saracens lopped off the head of St Hilarion. It sits on the edge of the cemetery, about fifteen minutes' walk to the left of the bridge on the château side of the river, past the campsite. Built in red sandstone, with a wall belfry and wide porch with sculpted tympanum and dozens of figures adorning the corbel ends of the apse, it's a delight.

Also well worth a visit is the **Château de Calmont d'Olt** (July & Aug daily 9am–noon & 2–7pm; €6.75), for its unbeatable views of the town and the country beyond. It's a rough and atmospheric old fortress dating from the eleventh century, on the very peak of an abrupt bluff, 535m high and a stiff 1km climb above the town on the south bank. Particularly good for children is a regular programme of activities throughout the day (afternoon only out of season), including demonstrations of medieval siege engines and artillery.

Practicalities

The **tourist office** is just across the Pont Vieux in rue St-Antoine (June & Sept Mon–Fri 9am–noon & 2–6pm & Sat 10am–noon & 2.30–5.30pm; July & Aug Mon–Fri 10am–1pm & 2–7pm, Sat 10am–1pm & 2–6pm, Sun 10am–12.30pm; Oct–May Tues–Fri 9am–noon & 2–6pm, Sat 10am–noon & 2.30–5.30pm; ⓣ05.65.44.10.63, ⓦwww.ot-espalion.fr). For **accommodation**, there's no better place to stay than the *Hôtel Moderne* on the crossroads in the middle of town at 27 bd de Guizard (ⓣ05.65.44.05.11, ⓦwww.hotelmoderne12.com; ❷; closed mid-Nov to mid-Dec). The rooms are comfortable, but, more importantly, its restaurant is first-rate, especially for river fish (menus from €12–45). There's also a municipal **gîte** (ⓣ06.77.58.53.08) at 5 rue St. Joseph. A riverside **campsite**, Roc de l'Arche, sits behind the château (ⓣ05.65.44.06.79; closed Sept to mid-April), but better, if you have the time and the means, is the prettier, simpler and cheaper riverside *Belle Rive* (ⓣ05.65.44.05.85; closed Oct to mid-May) in the attractive village of **ST-CÔME D'OLT**, another 4km upstream, where there's also a **gîte d'étape** in a beautiful old house (ⓣ05.65.44.07.24; closed Nov–Feb) lying on the GR65, GR6 and GR620.

Espalion has a second superb **restaurant**, *Méjane*, by the old bridge (ⓣ05.65.48.22.37; closed Sun eve, & Mon lunch & Wed in July & Aug; menus €21–49.50), specializing in regional cuisine with a post-nouvelle influence, while for uncomplicated eating, there are several brasseries on the main through-street.

Millau, Roquefort and the Gorges du Tarn

MILLAU, subprefecture of the Aveyron *département* and second town after Rodez in the old province of Rouergue, occupies a beautiful site in a bend of the River Tarn at its junction with the Dourbie. It's enclosed on all sides by impressive white cliffs, formed where the rivers have worn away the edges of the *causses*, especially on the north side, where the spectacular table-top hill of the **Puech d'Andan** stands sentinel over the town. From medieval until modern times, thanks to its proximity to the sheep pastures of the *causses*, the town was a major manufacturer of leather goods, especially gloves. Although outclassed by cheaper producers in the mass market and suffering serious unemployment as a result, Millau still leads in top-of-the-range goods. In recent years the town hit the headlines with the construction of the astonishing Grand Viaduc du Millau in 2004, a 2.5-kilometre bridge supported by seven enormous pillars that, at times, puncture through the cloud level (the tallest is 326m high). Designed by British architects Foster and Partners (of Sir Norman Foster fame), French engineer Michel Virbgeux (whose previous credits include the wonderful Pont de Normandie) and Eiffage, a construction firm that traces its heritage back to Gustav Eiffel, it is as much a work of art as it is a way of getting traffic to the Côte d'Azur from Paris faster than of old.

Arrival, information and accommodation

From the **bus and train stations** it's about a ten-minute walk down rue Alfred Merle to the main square, place du Mandarous. The **tourist office** is on place du Beffroi in the centre of the old town (Easter–June & Sept–Oct Mon–Fri 9am–12.30pm & 2–6.30pm, Sat 9am–6.30pm, Sun 9.30am–4pm; July & Aug Mon–Sat 9am–7pm, Sun 10am–12.30pm & 2–6.30pm; Oct–Easter Mon–Fri 9am–12.30pm & 2–6.30pm, Sat 9am–6.30pm; Ⓣ05.65.60.02.42, Ⓦwww.ot-millau.fr). **Bikes and outdoor equipment** can be rented from Roc et Canyon, 55 av Jean-Jaurès.

For an overnight **stay**, try the good-value *Hôtel du Commerce*, 8 place du Mandarous (Ⓣ05.65.60.00.56, Ⓕ05.65.47.66.01; ❶), with clean, well-furnished rooms; those at the back are best to avoid any noise from the square. A bit more expensive, but with more character, is *Des Causses*, in an attractive building on the N9 at 56 av Jean-Jaurès (Ⓣ05.65.70.23.00, Ⓔles-causses-aveyron@wanadoo.fr; ❶–❹), which has a reasonable restaurant (from €30). Even more evocative is the *Emma Calvé* at 28 rue Jean-Jarués (Ⓣ05.65.60.13.49, Ⓦemmacalve.ifrance.com; ❺), once home of the popular nineteenth-century singer of that name and with decor and furnishings evocative of the old bourgeousie. There's a good **hostel** about 1km down Avenue Jean-Jaurès at 26 rue Lucien-Costes (Ⓣ05.65.61.27.74) as well as several **gites**, and scattered round about are several **campsites**: one of the best is *Cureplat* (Ⓣ05.65.60.15.75; closed Oct–March) at 121 av de Millau Plage, on the left bank of the Tarn, north of the confluence with the Dourbie – take the bridge at the end of Avenue Gambetta.

The Town

Millau is a very pleasant, lively provincial town whose clean and well-preserved old streets have a summery, southern charm. It owes its original prosperity to its position on the ford where the Roman road from Languedoc to the north crossed the Tarn, marked today by the truncated remains of a medieval **bridge** surmounted by a watermill jutting out into the river beside the modern bridge.

Whether you arrive from north or south, you'll find yourself sooner or later in **place du Mandarous**, the main square, where avenue de la République, the road to Rodez, begins. South of here, the **old town** is built a little way back from the river to avoid floods and contained within an almost circular ring of shady boulevards. The rue Droite cuts through the centre, linking the three squares: place Emma-Calvé, place des Halles and place Foch. The prettiest by far is **place Foch**, with its cafés, shaded by two big plane trees and bordered by houses supported on stone pillars; some are as old as the twelfth century. In one corner, the **church of Notre-Dame** is worth a look for its octagonal Toulouse-style belfry, originally Romanesque. In the other, there's the very interesting **Musée de Millau** (May–Sept daily 10am–noon & 2–6pm; Oct–March closed Sun; €5), housed in a stately eighteenth-century mansion. Its collections revolve around the bizarre combination of archeology and gloves, and include the magnificent red pottery of the Graufesenque works (see below), as well as a complete 180-million-year-old plesiosaurus. Millau's other two squares have been the subject of some rather questionable attempts at reconciling old stones and Richard Rogers-inspired contemporary urban design. Off one of these squares, place Emma-Calvé, the **clock tower** (June & Sept Mon–Sat 10–11.30am & 3–5.30pm; July & Aug daily 10am–noon & 3.30–6pm; €3.50) is worth a climb for the great all-round view. Take a look also in the streets off the square – rue du Voultre, rue de la Peyrollerie and their tributaries – for a sense of the old working-class and bourgeois districts.

Clear evidence of the town's importance in Roman times is to be seen in the **Graufesenque pottery works**, just upstream on the south bank (daily: May–Sept 9am–noon & 2–6.30pm; Oct–April 9am–noon & 2–6pm; €4), whose renowned red terracotta ware (*terra sigillata*) was distributed throughout the Roman world. It was a huge production centre in the first century AD, involving some six hundred pottery shops; today, there's an archeology museum with a permanent exhibition of the bowls, vases and cups that were produced.

Eating and drinking

If you're just looking for a quick **meal**, you'll find numerous brasseries and cafés on place du Mandarous. For something more traditional, dine in the maginificent surroundings of *La Mustardière* at 34 av de la République (Ⓣ05.65.60.20.63; closed Dec–Feb; €33–50) which serves excellent *gastronomique* and *terroir* specialities, or the less upmarket *La Braconne*, on place Foch (Ⓣ05.65.60.30.93; closed Sun eve & Mon; from €16), offering high-calorie fare such as stuffed goose and pork with juniper berries. Alternatively, head for boulevard de la Capelle on the northeast side of the old town, where two good establishments spread their tables under the trees: *La Mangeoire*, at no. 8 (closed Mon; menu from €14–45), which serves grilled fish, meat and game dishes; and next door, *La Marmite du Pêcheur*, featuring menus from €18, including *aligot*. A popular place for a **drink** is *La Locomotive*, at 33 av Gambetta (till 2am), which has live music evenings in summer.

Roquefort-sur-Soulzon and the Abbey of Silvanès

Twenty-one kilometres south of Millau, the little village of **ROQUEFORT-SUR-SOULZON** has nothing to say for itself except cheese, and almost every building is devoted to the cheese-making process.

What gives the cheese its special flavour is the fungus, *penicillium roqueforti*, that grows exclusively in the fissures in the rocks created by the collapse of the sides of the valley on which Roquefort now stands. Legend has it that once upon a time a local shepherd one day forgot his lunch of bread and cheese, and found it some months later, covered with mould. He bit tentatively and discovered to his surprise that instead of ruining the cheese, the mould had much improved its taste.

While the sheep's milk used in the making of the cheese comes from different flocks and dairies as far afield as the Pyrenees, the crucial fungus is grown here, on bread. Just 2g of powdered fungus are enough for 4000 litres of milk, which in turn makes 330 Roquefort cheeses; they are matured in Roquefort's many-layered cellars, first unwrapped for three weeks and then wrapped up again. It takes three to six months for the full flavour to develop.

Two of the cheese manufacturers have organized **visits**: Société (daily: July & Aug 9.30am–6.30pm; Sept–June 10am–noon & 1.30–5pm; €3) and Papillon (April–June & Sept daily 9.30–11.30am & 1.30–5.30pm; July & Aug daily 9.30am–6.30pm, rest of year Mon–Fri 9–11.30am & 1.30–4.30pm; free). Each visit consists of a short film, followed by a tour of the cellars and tasting – not, in fact, very interesting.

Some 25km further south, deep in the isolation of the *causes*, squats the twelfth-century **Cistercian Abbey of Silvanès** (daily 9am–12.30pm & 2–6pm; €2), founded in 1137 and the first Cistercian house in the region. Having largely survived the depradations of war and revolution, the abbey serves today as an important religious and cultural centre. Although you'll have to manage your own transport, it's worth visiting not only for the evocative setting, but also for the excellently preserved thirteenth-century church as well as the surviving monastic buildings, including a refectory and scriptorium dating back to the 1100s. There are a couple of **hotels** in the village by the abbey, but only 4km from the monastery you can stay at the magnificent sixteenth-century *Château de Gissac* (ⓣ05.65.98.14.60, ⓦwww.sylvanes.com; ❻) which also offers half and full pensions.

The Gorges du Tarn

Jampacked with tourists in July and August, but absolutely spectacular nonetheless, the **Gorges du Tarn** cuts through the limestone plateaux of the Causse de Sauveterre and the Causse Méjean in a precipitous trench 400–500m deep and 1000–1500m wide. Its sides, cloaked with woods of feathery pine and spiked with pinnacles of eroded rock, are often sheer and always very steep, creating within them a microclimate in sharp distinction to the inhospitable plateaux above. The permanent population is tiny, though there's plenty of evidence of more populous times in abandoned houses and once-cultivated terraces. Because of the press of people and the subsequent overpricing of **accommodation**, the best bet, if you want to stay along the gorge, is to head up onto the Causse Méjean, where there are several small family-run hotels and *chambres d'hôte*, among which is the attractively sited *Auberge de la Cascade* in St-Chély-du-Tarn (ⓣ04.66.48.52.82, ⓕ04.66.48.52.45; ❷; closed Nov–March; restaurant from €14).

The most attractive section of the gorge runs northeast for 53km from the pretty village of **LE ROZIER**, 21km northeast of Millau, to **ISPAGNAC**. If you want to stay in Le Rozier, good accommodation can be found at the *Grand Hôtel Voyageurs* (ⓣ05.65.62.60.09, ⓦwww.hotelvoyageurs.com; ❷; menu from €18; closed Nov–Easter) and there's a municipal **campsite** (ⓣ05.65.62.63.98, ⓕ05.65.62.60.83; closed Oct–April). A better bet, however, is *Le Vallon* (ⓣ04.66.44.21.24, ⓦwww.hotel-vallon.com; ❶) in Ispagnac, a small hotel with an excellent *terroir* restaurant (from €16) and which has family-size rooms and good-value half-pensions.

A narrow and very twisty road follows the right bank of the river from Le Rozier, but it's not the best way to see the scenery. For the car-borne, the best views are from the road to St-Rome-de-Dolan above Les Vignes, and from the roads out of La Malène and the attractive **STE-ÉNIMIE**, where you'll find a well-informed **tourist office** (Easter-June & Sept–Oct Mon–Fri 9.30am–12.30pm & 1.30–5.30pm, Sat 9am–12.30pm & 2–5.30pm; July & Aug Mon–Sat 9am–7pm & Sun 9am–12.30pm; Nov–Easter Mon–Fri 9.30am–12.30pm & 1.30–5.30pm; Ⓣ04.66.48.53.44, Ⓔotsi-gorgesdutarn@wanadoo.fr). La Malène has a municipal **campsite** (Ⓣ04.66.48.58.55; closed mid-Oct to March) and *La Blanquière* site (Ⓣ04.66.48.54.93, Ⓔcamping.blaquière@wanadoo.fr; closed mid-Sept to May), which is beautifully sited on the main road towards Les Vignes some 6km from town.

But it's best to walk if possible, or follow the river's course by boat or canoe – there are dozens of places to rent canoes (€15 per person for 2–3 hours, plus pick-up). For walkers, the **GR6a**, a variant of the GR6 which crosses the *causses*, climbs steeply out of Le Rozier between the junction of the Tarn with the equally spectacular gorges of the River Jonte onto the Causse Méjean, then follows the rim of the Tarn gorge for a while before descending to rejoin the GR6 at Les Vignes (4–5hr).

Also eminently worth seeing are two beautiful **caves** about 25km up the Jonte from Le Rozier. **Aven Armand** (daily: March–May & Sept to early-Nov 10am–noon & 1.30–5.45pm; June–Aug 9.30am–6pm, €8), on the edge of the Causse Méjean, which is fitted with a funicular, claims the world's tallest stalagmite towering 30m above the cave floor. The **Grotte de Dargilan** (daily: April–June & Sept 10am–noon & 2–5.30pm; July & Aug 10am–6.30pm; Oct 10am–noon & 2–4.30pm; €8), on the south side of the river on the edge of the Causse Noir, known as the "pink cave" from the colour of its rock, is known as one of the country's most beuatiful stalactite caverns. **HYELZAS**, near the Aven Armand cave, has a *gîte d'étape* (M. Pratlong; Ⓣ04.66.45.66.56).

The Cévennes and Ardèche

The **Cévennes** mountains and River **Ardèche** form the southeastern defences of the Massif Central, overlooking the Rhône valley to the east and the Mediterranean littoral to the south. The bare upland landscapes of the inner or western edges are those of the central Massif. The outer edges, Mont Aigoual and its radiating valleys and the tributary valleys of the Ardèche, are distinctly Mediterranean: deep, dry, close and clothed in forests of sweet chestnut, oak and pine.

Remote and inaccessible country until well into the twentieth century, the region has bred rugged and independent inhabitants. For centuries it was the most resolute stronghold of Protestantism in France, and it was in these valleys that the persecuted Protestants put up their fiercest resistance to the tyranny of Louis XIV and Louis XV. In World War II, it was heavily committed to the

Resistance, while in the aftermath of 1968, it became the promised land of the hippies – *zippies*, as the locals called them; they moved into the countless abandoned farms and hamlets, whose native inhabitants had been driven away by hardship and poverty. The odd hippy has stuck it out, true to the last to the alternative life. In more recent times, it has been colonized by Dutch and Germans.

The author Robert Louis Stevenson crossed it in 1878 with Modestine, a donkey he bought in miserable Le Monastier-sur-Gazeille near the astounding town of **Le Puy** and sold at journey's end in the former Protestant stronghold of **St-Jean-du-Gard**, a now-famous route described in *Travels with a Donkey* (see p.1338).

The Parc National des Cévennes

The **Parc National des Cévennes** was created in 1970 to protect and preserve the life, landscape, flora, fauna and architectural heritage of the Cévennes. North to south, it stretches from **Mende** on the Lot to **Le Vigan** and includes both **Mont Lozère** and **Mont Aigoual**. Access, to the periphery at least, is surprisingly easy, thanks to the Paris–Clermont–Alès–Nîmes train line and the Montpellier–Mende link.

Numerous walking routes crisscross the area: **GRs 6**, **7** and **60** cross all or part of the range, and other paths complete various circuits. The **GR66** does the tour of Mont Aigoual in 78.5km, the **GR68** of Mont Lozère in 110km. Another good route is the 130-kilometre **Tour des Cévennes** on the GR67. If you do go off hiking, remember that these are proper mountains for all their southerly latitude. You need good hiking boots, warm and weatherproof clothing, emergency shelter, adequate food, maps and guidebooks. The current weather situation is obtainable on: ⓣ07.08.36.68.02 (Ardèche); ⓣ08.36.68.02.30 (Gard); ⓣ08.36.68.02.48 (Lozère).

The **main information office** for the park is at Florac (see p.967). It publishes numerous leaflets on the flora, fauna and traditions of the park, plus activities and routes for walkers, cyclists, canoeists and horse riders. It also provides a list of **gîtes d'étape** in the park and can provide information for those following Stevenson's route, including where to hire a donkey. In July and August, it's wise to book ahead for accommodation; otherwise you could find yourself sleeping out.

Mende and Mont Lozère

Capital of the Lozère *département*, **MENDE** lies well down in the deep valley of the Lot at the northern tip of the Parc des Cévennes, 28km east of Marvejols and 40km north of Florac, with train and bus links to the Paris–Nîmes and Clermont–Millau lines. It's a very attractive, unspoilt southern town, and a nice place to make an overnight stay.

Standing against the haze of the mountain background, the town's main landmark, the **Cathedral**, owes its construction to Pope Urban V, who was born locally and wished to give something back to his native soil. Although work began in 1369, progress was hampered by war and natural disasters and the building wasn't completed until the end of the nineteenth century. The most obvious signs of its patchy construction are the two unequal towers that frame the front entrance, from where there's a fine view back along the pine-clad Lot valley. Inside is a handsome choir, and, suspended from the clerestory, eight great

Aubusson tapestries, depicting the life of the Virgin. She's also present in one of the side chapels of the choir in the form of a statue made from olive wood, thought to have been brought back from the Middle East during the crusades.

Aside from the cathedral, most pleasure resides in a quiet wander in the town's minuscule squares and narrow medieval streets, with their houses bulging outwards, as though buckling under the weight of the upper stories. In **rue Notre-Dame**, which separated the Christian from Jewish quarters in medieval times, the thirteenth-century house at no. 17 was once a synagogue. If you carry on down to the river, you'll see the medieval packhorse bridge, the **Pont Notre-Dame**, with its worn cobbles.

Practicalities

The **tourist office** is at 14 bd Henri-Bourrillon, to the right as you reach the centre of town from the N88 (July & Aug Mon–Sat 9am–12.30pm & 2–7.15pm, Sun 9am–noon & 2.30–6pm; Sept–June Mon–Fri 9am–12.30pm & 2–6pm, Sat 9am–noon; ⓣ04.66.94.00.23, ⓦwww.ot-mende.fr). The departmental tourist office is in the same building, with all the information you could want on the Lozère. The **gare SNCF** (ⓣ04.66.49.00.39) lies across the river, north of the centre. **Buses** depart from either the station or place du Foirail, at the southern end of boulevard Henri-Bourrillon.

For a place to **stay**, best choice is the *Lion d'Or* at 12–14 bd Britexte (ⓣ04.66.49.16.46, ⓦwww.liondor-mende.com; ❸) set in a beautiful, renovated old building and featuring an excellent *terroir* restaurant (from €20). Another good choice is the pretty *Hôtel de France* on boulevard Lucien-Arnault, the northern part of the inner ring road (ⓣ04.66.65.00.04, ⓦwww.hoteldefrance-mende.com; ❸; closed Dec & Jan; menu from €13.75). Slightly further out of town, on the river at 2 av du 11 Novembre, the classy *Hôtel Pont-Roupt* (ⓣ04.66.65.01.43, ⓦwww.hotel-pont-roupt.com; ❷) offers such luxuries as an indoor pool, terrace and good restaurant: dishes include *truite au lard* and *salade au Roquefort* (from €21–46). The best **restaurant** in town is *La Safranière* in Chabrits (ⓣ04.46.69.31.54; Sun lunch, Mn & Mar), which daringly blends *terrior* and *gastronimique* styles (menus €17–42). Another good choice is *Le Mazel* (closed Mon eve & Tues; from €13), though the setting – in the only modern square in the old town – is a little disappointing. More atmospheric, *Les Voutes*, in a renovated medieval building at 13 rue d'Aigues-Passes, specializes in pizzas and *plats du jour* (from €7).

Mont Lozère

Mont Lozère is a windswept and desolate barrier of granite and yellow grassland, rising to 1699m at the summit of **Finiels**, still grazed by herds of cows, but in nothing like the numbers of bygone years when half the cattle in Languedoc came up here for their summer feed. Snowbound in winter and wild and dangerous in bad weather, it has claimed many a victim among lost travellers. In some of the squat granite hamlets on the northern slopes, like Servies, Auriac and Les Sagnes, you can still hear the bells, known as *clochers de tourmente*, that tolled in the wind to give travellers some sense of direction when the cloud was low.

If you're travelling by car from Mende, the way to the summit is via the village of **LE BLEYMARD**, about 30km to the east on the bank of the infant River Lot, with accommodation in the form of the comfortably rustic *Hôtel La Remise* (ⓣ04.66.48.65.80, ⓦwww.hotel-laremise.com; ❷; *terroir* restaurant from €16). From here, the D20 winds 7km up through the conifers to another country-style hotel/*gîte* and restaurant, the *Chalet-Hotel du Mont Lozère*

(Ⓣ04.68.48.62.84, Ⓦwww.chalet-mt-lozere.fr; ❷), where it's joined by the GR7, which has taken a more direct route from Le Bleymard. This is the route that Stevenson took, waymarked as the "Tracé Historique de Stevenson". Road and footpath run together as far as the **Col de Finiels**, where the GR7 strikes off on its own to the southeast. The source of the River Tarn is about 3km east of the col, the summit of Lozère 2km to the west. From the col, the road and Stevenson's route drop down in tandem, through the lonely hamlet of **FINIELS** to the pretty but touristy village of **LE PONT-DE-MONTVERT**.

At Le Pont, a seventeenth-century **bridge** crosses the Tarn by a stone tower that once served as a tollhouse. In this building in 1702, the Abbé du Chayla, a priest appointed by the Crown to reconvert the rebellious Protestants enraged by the revocation of the Edict of Nantes, set up a torture chamber to coerce the recalcitrant. Incensed by his brutality, a group of them under the leadership of one Esprit Séguier attacked and killed him on July 23. Reprisals were extreme; nearly 12,000 were executed, thus precipitating the Camisards' guerrilla war against the state (see p.886).

At the edge of the village, there's also an *écomusée* on the life and character of the region, the **Maison du Mont Lozère** (May–Sept daily 10.30am–12.30pm & 2.30–6.30pm; €3.50). If you're tempted to **stay**, there's the small and atmospheric *Auberge des Cévennes* (Ⓣ04.66.45.80.01; ❶; closed mid-Nov to March; restaurant from €15), overlooking the bridge. There's also a *gîte d'étape* in the Maison du Mont Lozère (Ⓣ04.66.45.80.10 or 04.66.45.80.73; closed Jan & Feb; reservations obligatory).

Florac and Mont Aigoual

Situated 39km south of Mende, **FLORAC** lies in the bottom of the trench-like valley of the Tarnon just short of its junction with the Tarn. Behind the village rises the steep wall that marks the edge of the Causse Méjean. When you get here, you will have already passed the frontier between the northern and Mediterranean landscapes; the dividing line seems to be the **Col de Montmirat** at the western end of Mont Lozère. Once you begin the descent, the scrub and steep gullies and the tiny abandoned hamlets, with their eyeless houses oriented towards the sun, speak clearly of the south.

The village, with some 2000 inhabitants, is strung out along the left bank of the Tarnon and the main street, **avenue Jean-Monestier**. There's little to see, though the close lanes of the village up towards the valley side have their charms, especially the plane-shaded **place du Souvenir**. A red-schist castle stands above the village, housing the **Centre d'Information du Parc National des Cévennes** (Easter–Oct daily 9.30am–12.30pm & 2–6pm; Oct–Easer Mon–Fri 9.30am–12.30pm & 2–6pm; Ⓣ04.66.49.53.01, Ⓔpnc@bsi.fr). The helpful **tourist office** is on avenue Jean-Monestier (Mon–Sat 9am–12.30pm & 2–6pm; Ⓣ04.66.45.01.14, Ⓦwww.florac-tourisme.com). **Mountain bike rental** is available from Cévennes Evasion, in place Boyer (Ⓣ04.66.45.18.31).

The **accommodation** on offer is not fantastic. The best place is the *Grand Hôtel du Parc* on avenue Jean-Monestier (Ⓣ04.66.45.03.05, Ⓦwww.grand-hotelduparc.fr; ❸; closed Dec to March; restaurant €15–30), with pleasant gardens and a pool. Two other solid options are the homey *Archibald Hôtel*, on avenue Maurice Tour, which has a lovely terrace over the stream, though the rooms are a bit dowdy (Ⓣ04.66.45.00.01, Ⓦwww.archibaldhotel.com; ❷; closed Jan & Feb; restaurant €15–25) and the more comfortable *Les Gorges du Tarn* at 48 rue de Pecheur (Ⓣ04.66.45.00.63, Ⓔgorges-du-tarn

.adonis@wanadoo.fr; ④). Local **gîtes d'etape** include *Le Presbytère*, 18 rue du Pêcher (Ⓣ04.66.45.24.54, Ⓦwww.causses-cevennes.com/Lagrave.htm; closed mid-Nov to Jan) and the *gîte détape communal*, 1 rue du Four (Mme. Rives: Ⓣ04.66.45.14.93, Ⓔmairie@ville-florac.fr; closed Dec);). The best-value **campsite** is the municipal one at Le Pont-du-Tarn out on the road towards Ispagnac (Ⓣ04.66.45.18.26; closed mid-Oct to March).

Florac's Esplanade is a good place to look for somewhere to **eat**, otherwise the *Adonis* restaurant in the *Les Gorges* hotel serves high-quality local cuisine (menus €17–35; closed Sun lunch), while another good choice is the river-side *La Source du Pêcher* at 1 rue de Rémuret in the old town (Ⓣ04.66.45.03.01; menus from €15–30; closed Nov–Easter).

Mont Aigoual

It's 24km by road up the beautiful valley of the Tarnon to the **Col de Perjuret**, where a right turn will take you on to the **Causse Méjean** and to the strange rock formations of **Nîmes-le-Vieux**, and a left turn along a rising ridge a further 15km to the 1565-metre summit of **Mont Aigoual** (GR6, GR7, GR66). From the latter, it is said that you can see a third of France, from the Alps to the Pyrenees, with the Mediterranean coast from Marseille to Sète at your feet. It's not a craggy summit, although the ground drops away pretty steeply into the valley of the River Hérault on the south side, but the view and the sense of exposure to the elements is dramatic enough. At the summit is an **observatory** which has been in use for over a century. A small but interesting **exhibition** (May–Sept daily 10am–6pm; free) shows modern weather-forecasting techniques alongside displays of old barometers and weather vanes. The observatory also harbours a CAF refuge and gîte d'étape (Ⓣ04.67.82.62.78; closed Oct–April).

The descent to Le Vigan by the valley of the Hérault is superb; a magnificent twisty road follows the deepening ravine through dense beech and chestnut woods, to come out at the bottom in rather Italianate scenery, with tall, close-built villages and vineyards beside the stream. The closest accommodation to the summit is the *Hôtel du Touring* (Ⓣ04.67.82.60.04, Ⓕ04.67.82.65.09; ②; restaurant menus from €11–18.50; closed April & Nov to mid-Dec) at **L'ESPÉROU**, a rather soulless mountain resort just below the summit. Better to go down to the charming village of **VALLERAUGUE**, with its brown-grey schist houses and leafy riverside setting. There are a number of hotels here, including the welcoming *Petit Luxembourg* (Ⓣ04.67.82.20.44, Ⓕ04.67.82.24.66; ②; menus €15–30).

The Causse du Larzac

In the 1970s, the **Causse du Larzac** was continually in the headlines over sustained political resistance to the high-profile presence of the French military. Originally there was a small military camp outside the village of **LA CAVALERIE** on the N9, long tolerated for the cash its soldiers brought in. But in the early 1970s the army decided to expand the place and use it as a permanent strategic base, expropriating a hundred or so farms. The result was explosive. A federation was formed – Paysans du Larzac – which attracted the support of numerous ecological, left-wing and Occitan groups in a protracted campaign of resistance under the slogan "Gardarem lo Larzac" ("Let's protect Larzac"). Successful acts of sabotage were committed, and three huge peace festivals were held here, in 1973, 1974 and 1977. The army's plans were scotched by Mitterrand when he came to power in 1981, but you still find Larzac graffiti from here to Lyon, shorthand for opposition to the army, the state and the Parisian central government, and in favour of self-determination and independence for the south.

The best way to immerse yourself in the empty, sometimes eerie atmosphere of Larzac is to walk: **GRs 7**, **71** and **74** cross the plateau, though you shouldn't attempt them without a *Topoguide*. If you have no time for anything else, the area between La Couvertoirade, Le Caylar and Ganges in the foothills of the Cévennes will give you a real sense of life on the *causse*.

LA COUVERTOIRADE lies 5km off the main road (parking €3). Billed as a perfect "Templar" village, its present remains postdate the dissolution of that Order in the late thirteenth century. Anomalies aside, it is a striking site, still completely enclosed by its towers and walls and almost untouched by renovation. Its forty remaining inhabitants live by tourism, and you have to pay to walk around the **ramparts** (daily: mid-March to June & Sept to mid-Nov 10am–noon & 2–5pm; July & Aug 10am–7pm; €5 including a video presentation; English audio-guide available). Just outside the walls on the south side is a *lavogne*, a paved water hole of a kind seen all over the *causse* for watering the flocks, whose milk is used for Roquefort cheese. If you want to stay, there's the municipal **gîte d'étape** (Ⓣ05.65.59.12.22, Ⓔcontact@conservatoire-Larzac.fr) in the far corner from the entrance, serving the GR71 and GR71C. A bus from Millau (Mon, Wed & Fri) serves the village during July & August. Half-a-dozen kilometres south, the closest point served by regular public transport, the village of **LE CAYLAR** clusters in similar fashion at the foot of a rocky outcrop, the top of which has been fashioned into a fortress – worth clambering up for the aerial view of the surrounding *causse*, where mean little patches of cultivated ground have been stolen from among the merciless upthrusts of rock.

St-Maurice-Navacelles and the Cirque de Navacelles

If you've got your own transport and a good map, the back road from here, via St-Michel to **ST-MAURICE-NAVACELLES**, is strongly recommended. Wild box grows along the lanes, often meticulously clipped into hedges. Here and there among the scrubby oak and thorn or driving along the road at milking time, you pass flocks of sheep. Occasional farmhouses materialize, like *Les Besses* – one of the few still in use – huge, self-contained and fortress-like, with the living quarters upstairs and the sheep stalls down below. St-Maurice-Navacelles, on the GR7 and GR74, is a small and sleepy hamlet with a fine World War I memorial by Paul Dardé at its centre. Its services include a summer-only shop and a *gite* (04.76.44.62.55) which also does meals. There's no official **campsite**, but if you ask they'll direct you to a grassy place by the cemetery, where a traditional *glacière* – a stone-lined pit for storing snow for use as ice before the days of refrigerators – has been restored. Its chief advantage is as a base for visiting the **Cirque de Navacelles**, 10km north on the D130 past the beautiful ruined seventeenth-century sheep farm of *La Prunarède*. The cirque is a widening in the 150-metre deep trench of the Vis gorges, formed by a now dry loop in the river that has left a neat pyramid of rock sticking up in the middle like a wheel hub. An ancient and scarcely inhabited hamlet survives in the bottom – a bizarre phenomenon in an extraordinary location, and you get literally a bird's-eye view of it from the edge of the cliff above. Both road and GR7 go through. Continuing to Le Vigan or Ganges via Montdardier, you pass a prehistoric **stone circle** on the left of the road, a silent and evocative place, especially in a close *causse* mist.

Le Vigan and the Huguenot strongholds

Only 64km from Montpellier and 18km from Ganges, **LE VIGAN** makes a good starting point for exploring the southern part of the Cévennes. It's a leafy, cool and thoroughly agreeable place, at its liveliest during the **Fête d'Isis** at the beginning of August and the colossal fair that takes over the Parc des Châtaigniers on September 9 and 22.

The prettiest part of the town is around the central **place du Quai**, shaded by lime trees and bordered by cafés and brasseries. From here it's only a two-minute walk south, down rue Pierre-Gorlier, to reach the gracefully arched **Pont Vieux**. Beside it stands the **Musée Cévenol** (April–Oct daily except Tues 10am–noon & 2–6pm; Nov–March Wed only 10am–noon & 2–6pm; €4.50), a well-presented look at traditional rural occupations in the area, including the woodcutter, butcher, shepherd and wolf-hunter. There's also a room devoted to the area's best-known twentieth-century writer, André Chamson, noted for his novels steeped in the traditions and countryside of the Cévennes. Interestingly, Coco Chanel also features in the museum: she had local family connections and it seems found inspiration for her designs in the *cévenol* silks.

The **tourist office** occupies a modern block in the centre of the place du Marché, at the opposite end of the place du Quai from the church (July & Aug Mon–Sat 8.30am–12.30pm & 1.30–7pm, Sun 10am–12.30pm; Sept–June Mon–Fri 8.30am–12.30pm & 2–6pm, Sat 9am–12.30pm & 2–5pm; ⓣ04.67.81.01.72, ⓔot.le-vigan@wanadoo.fr). For somewhere to **stay**, try the simple but attractive *Hôtel du Commerce*, with its wisteria-covered balcony and little garden, at 26 rue des Barris (ⓣ04.67.81.03.28, ⓕ04.67.81.43.20; ❶; closed mid-Oct to mid-Nov). The best alternative is a couple of kilometres out of town, south towards Montdardier on the D48: the handsome old *Auberge Cocagne* in the village of **AVÈZE** (ⓣ04.67.81.02.70, ⓕ04.67.81.07.67; ❶; closed mid-Nov to mid-Feb; restaurant from €13). There are also **campsites** in Avèze (ⓣ04.67.81.95.01; closed mid-Sept to mid-June), or 2km upriver from Le Vigan, on the opposite bank, is the well-shaded riverside Val de l'Arre (ⓣ04.67.81.02.77, ⓦwww.campingfrance.com/valdelarre; closed Oct–March). There's a **gîte d'étape** at 1 rue de la Carrierrasse (ⓣ04.67.81.01.71). One of the best places to eat in Le Vigan is *Jardin des Cévennes* (closed Mon), in place du Terral, just off the main square; menus start at €16 and feature French classics with a local twist, such as *filet mignon* with a chestnut sauce. A good alternative is *Le Chandelier* (closed Mon), housed in a converted cellar on rue du Pouzadou; the €13 menu includes *confit de canard* and a choice of delicious desserts.

From Le Vigan, or more particularly from the Pont de l'Hérault bridge, a beautiful lane (D153) slowly winds around 45km northeast through typical south Cévennes landscape – deep valleys thick with sweet chestnut and thinly peopled with isolated farms half-buried in greenery – from Sumène to St-Jean-du-Gard. **SUMÈNE** is a run-down but lovely old place, the entrance to its close, narrow streets still blocked by medieval **gates**. It was once a centre for silk spinning, which for a couple of centuries until the 1900s was the mainstay of economic life in the Cévennes – that and the cultivation of the sweet chestnut, which provided the staple diet for the entire population.

There's a **gîte d'étape** at **COLOGNAC** (ⓣ04.66.85.28.84) and another in the valley bottom outside the rather nondescript village of **LASALLE** (ⓣ04.66.85.27.29), where options also include the hotel *L'Enclos* (ⓣ04.66.85.44.30; closed Dec–Feb; ❷) and the campsite *La Salendrinque* (ⓣ04.66.85.24.57; open April–Oct).

St-Jean-du-Gard and around

Thirty-two kilometres west of Alès, **ST-JEAN-DU-GARD** was the centre of Protestant resistance during the Camisard war in 1702–04 (see below). It straggles along the bank of the River Gardon, crossed by a graceful, arched eighteenth-century bridge, with a number of picturesque old houses still surviving in the main street, **Grande-Rue**. One of them contains the splendid **Musée des Vallées Cévenoles** (Apr–Oct daily 10am–12.30pm & 2–7pm; Nov–Mar Tues–Sat 9am–noon & 2–6pm, Sun 2–6pm; €4), a museum of local life with displays of tools, trades, furniture, clothes, domestic articles and a fascinating collection of pieces related to the silk industry. The work of spinning the silk was done by women in factories and lists of regulations and rules on display give some idea of the tough conditions in which they had to work.

The **tourist office** is just off the main street by the post office (July & Aug Mon & Wed–Fri 9am–1pm & 3–6pm, Tues & Sat 9am–7pm, Sun 10am–noon; Sept–June Mon–Fri 9am–12.30pm & 1.30–5pm, Sat 10am–12.30pm; ⓣ04.66.85.32.11, ⓦotsi.st.jeandugard.free.fr). They can advise you about the times of the **steam train** that operates between St-Jean and Anduze (April–Aug daily; Sept & Oct Tues–Sun; €10.50 return). There's a big **market** all along Grande-Rue on Tuesday mornings.

The best bet for **accommodation** is *Auberge du Peras* on route de Nîmes (ⓣ04.66.85.35.94, ⓔaubergeduperas@aol.com; ❸; good restaurant from €13). There's a *gîte d'étape* 3km north on the D907 at **LE MOULINET**; contact Mme Laurtay on ⓣ04.66.85.10.98.

The Musée du Désert

Signposts at St-Jean direct you to the museum at **MAS SOUBEYRAN**, a minuscule hamlet of beautiful rough-stone houses in a gully above the village of Mialet, about 12km east. The **Musée du Désert** (daily: March–June & Sept–Nov 9.30am–noon & 2–6pm; July & Aug 9.30am–7pm; €4) is in the house that once belonged to Rolland, one of the Camisards' self-taught but most successful military leaders, and it remains much the same as it would have been in 1704, the year of his death. It catalogues the appalling sufferings and sheer dogged heroism of the Protestant Huguenots in defence of their freedom of conscience; and the "desert" they had to traverse between the Revocation of the Edict of Nantes in 1685 and the promulgation of the Edict of Tolerance in 1787, which restored their original rights (full emancipation came with the Declaration of the Rights of Man in the first heady months of the Revolution in 1789). During this period, they had no civil rights, unless they abjured their faith. They could not bury their dead, baptize their children or marry. Their priests were forced into exile on pain of death. The recalcitrant were subjected to the infamous *dragonnades*, which involved the forcible billeting of troops on private homes at the expense of the occupants. As if this were not enough, the soldiers would beat their drums continuously for days and nights in people's bedrooms in order to deprive them of sleep. Protestants were also put to death or sent to the galleys for life and their houses were destroyed.

Not surprisingly, such brutality led to armed rebellion, inspired by the prophesying of the lay preachers who had replaced the banished priests, calling for a holy war. The rebels were hopelessly outnumbered and the revolt was ruthlessly put down in 1704 (see box, p.886). On display are documents, private letters and lists of those who died for their beliefs, including the names of five thousand who died as galley slaves (*galériens pour la foi*) and the women who were immured in the Tour de Constance prison in Aigues-Mortes. Also on show are also the chains and rough uniform of a *galérien.*

Prafrance and the Mine Témoin

Twelve kilometres southeast of St-Jean in the direction of Anduze, **PRAFRANCE** in noteworthy for **La Bambouseraie** (March to mid-Nov daily 9.30am–6pm; €6.50), an extraordinary and appealing garden consisting exclusively of bamboos of all shapes and sizes. An easy way to get here is to take the steam train (see p.971) from St-Jean-du-Gard; it takes just ten minutes.

If you want to leave the area by main-line train, the place to head for is **ALÈS** on the Nîmes–Paris line. This was a major coal-mining centre, though 25,000 jobs have been lost and all but two opencast pits closed in the last four decades. Today, it has a superb museum on the history and techniques of coal-mining, known as the **Mine Témoin**, in the underground workings of a disused mine on chemin de la Cité Ste-Marie in the Rochebelle district (French-only guided tours daily: June 9am–6.30pm; July & Aug 9am–7.30pm; Sept–May 9am–12.30pm & 2–5.30pm; €6.70; last visit 1hr 30min before closing).

Aubenas and the northern Cévennes

A small but prosperous and surprisingly industrial town of around 12,000, **AUBENAS** sits in the middle of the southern part of the Ardèche *département*, high up on a hill overlooking the middle valley of the River Ardèche. Located 91km southeast of Le Puy and 42km west of Montélimar, the town, with a character and non-tourist-dependent economy of its own, makes a much better base than overly crowded places further downstream around Vallon-Pont-d'Arc.

The central knot of streets with their cobbles and bridges, occupying the highest point of town around **place de l'Hôtel-de-Ville**, have great charm, particularly towards place de la Grenette and place 14-Juillet. Place de l'Hôtel-de-Ville is dominated by the eleventh-century **château**, from which the local *seigneurs* ruled the area right up until the Revolution (90 min. guided tours: April–June & Sept Tues & Thurs–Sat tour at 10.30am & 2pm; July & Aug daily 11am & 2–5pm; Oct & Dec–March Tues, Thurs & Sat tour at 2pm; closed on hols; €3.50). Other sights include the heavily restored thirteenth-century **St-Laurent church**, which has an elaborate fifteenth-century chapel (July & Aug Mon–Fri 5pm; €3.50), and the curious seventeenth-century hexagonal **Dôme Bênoit chapel** (July & Aug Mon–Fri 5pm; €3.50). There's a magnificent view of the Ardèche snaking up the valley from under an arch beside the castle, as there is from the end of bd Gambetta 200m downhill, where the **tourist office** is located on the (July & Aug Mon–Sat 9am–12.30pm & 1.30–7pm; Sept–June Mon–Sat 9am–noon & 2–6pm; ⓣ04.75.89.02.03, ⓦwww.aubenas-tourisme.com).

For somewhere to **stay**, the budget choice is the old-fashioned *Hôtel des Négociants*, right next to the château on place de l'Hôtel-de-Ville (ⓣ04.75.35.18.74; ❶; closed Oct), which does nourishing meals from €9. At the top end of the scale the 5-room *La Bastide du Soleil* (ⓣ04.75.36.91.66 ⓦwww.chateauxhotels.com/bastidesoleil; ❻–❽; closed Dec–Jan) offers a splendid blend of antique charm and modern convenience (restaurant fromm €30). There's a municipal **campsite** on Route de Lazuel (ⓣ04.75.35.18.15). Cafés and brasseries line boulevard de Vernon on the south side of town; the best place for both food and atmosphere is *Le Fournil*, 34 rue du 4-Septembre, set in a fifteenth-century house at the end of Béranger-de-la-Tour, in the heart of the old town (closed Sun eve & Mon; from €18–33), or *Le Chat Qui Pêche*, nearby on place de la Grenette (closed Tues & Wed except in July & Aug; from €16–32).

The Gorges de l'Ardèche

The **Gorges de l'Ardèche** begin at the **Pont d'Arc**, a very beautiful arch that the river has cut for itself through the limestone, just downstream from **VALLON**, itself 39km south of Aubenas. They continue for about 35km to **ST-MARTIN-D'ARDÈCHE** in the valley of the Rhône.

The fantastic gorges wind back and forth, much of the time dropping 300m straight down in the almost dead-flat scrubby Plateau des Gras. Unfortunately they are also an appalling tourist trap; the road following the rim, with spectacular viewpoints marked out at regular intervals, is jammed with traffic in summer. The river, down in the bottom, which is where you really want to be to appreciate the grandeur of the canyon, is likewise packed with canoes in high season. It is walkable, depending on the water level, but you would need to bivouac midway at either Gaud or Gournier. Generally speaking, if you can't go out of season, you're better off giving it a miss.

The plateau itself is riddled with caves. **Aven Marzal**, a stalactite cavern north of the gorge (daily 11am–5.30pm; €7, joint ticket with zoo €12), has a prehistoric **zoo**, which consists of reconstructions of dinosaurs and friends (Feb, Mar, Oct & Nov Sun & school hols 10.30am–6pm; April–Sept daily 11.30am–5pm; €7.20), but the frequency of visits to the cave depends on the number of visitors waiting – they are approximately every twenty minutes in July and August, falling to four per day in other months. Best of the area's caves is the **Aven Orgnac**, to the south of the gorge (90 min. tour daily: Feb, Mar, Nov and Dec hols 10.30am–4.45pm, April, Jun & Sept 9.30am–5.30pm, July–Aug 9.30am–6.30pm, Oct 9.30am–5.15pm; €9.20), one of France's most spectacular and colourful stalactite formations. In addition to the normal tours, you can also opt for the "visites spéléologiques" hard-core caving tours; they last 3 and 8 hours respectively and it's best to reserve two weeks ahead (ⓣ04.75.38.65.10). There's also a very good prehistory **museum** (daily: March–June & Sept to mid-Nov 10am–noon & 2–6pm; July & Aug 10am–6pm; €5, joint ticket €9.20).

Further upstream near Vallon-Pont-d'arc, a complex series of cave paintings was discovered in December 1994, after being left untouched for 30,000 years, making the **Chauvet-Pont d'Arc** cave the oldest-known decorated cave in the world. The cave system is currently being investigated by archeologists and causing a major rethink about the history of art. The paintings depict woolly rhinos, bison, lions and bears, and display a remarkable mastery of perspective. It's unlikely that Chauvet-Pont d'Arc will ever be open to the public. However, there is a small but rewarding **exhibition** on the cave complex at Vallon, behind the *mairie*. The highlight is a video taken inside the caves, showing many of the paintings close up (Tues–Sun: mid-March to May & Sept to mid-Nov 10am–noon & 2–5.30pm; Jun–Aug 10am–1pm & 3–8pm; €4).

Practicalities

Accommodation in the area can be a problem during the high season. A good option is the *Hôtel du Tourisme*, on rue du Miarou in Vallon (ⓣ04.75.88.02.12, ⓦwww.hotel-tourisme-pont-darc.com; closed Dec–Feb; ❹), but by far the best is *Le Manoir du Raveyron*, rue Henri-Barbusse (ⓣ04.75.88.03.59,

Ⓔle.manoir.du.raveyron@wanadoo.fr; ❹; closed Oct to mid-March), with a good restaurant from €20. The river is lined with **campsites**, the cheapest being the municipal one (Ⓣ04.75.88.04.73; closed Oct–March). There's a **gîte d'étape** on place de la Mairie (Ⓣ04.75.88.07.87), and a **tourist office** on the south side of town (May–June & Sept Mon–Sat 9am–noon & 2–5pm; July & Aug Mon–Sat 9am–1pm & 3–7pm, Sun 9am–noon; Oct–April Mon–Sat 9am–noon & 2–4pm Ⓣ04.75.88.04.01, Ⓦwww.vallon-pont-darc.com). Eight kilometres upstream is a well-priced municipal **campsite** at **RUOMS** (Ⓣ04.75.93.99.16; closed Oct to mid-May).

The valley of the Chassezac and the Corniche du Vivarais

Between Aubenas and Les Vans, 27km to the southwest, several wild mountain streams flow out of the northern part of the Cévennes to join the Ardèche. One of the most beautiful is the **Chassezac**, which rises north of Villefort and carves a dry, twisting ravine covered with pine, bracken and sweet chestnut down to **LES VANS**.

The centre of the town is occupied by the wide and cheerful **place Léopold-Ollier**. Nearby you'll find the comfortable *Viverais* (Ⓣ04.75.37.22.73, Ⓦwww.le-vivarais-hotel.com; ❷; closed mid-Sept to Apr), which has a *terroir* restaurant (menus €13) and offers full-pensions. Worth seeking out, however, is the beuatifully renovated former convent, *Le Carmel*, at 7 montée Carmel (Ⓣ04.75.94.99.60, Ⓦwww.le-carmel.com; ❹; closed mid-Dec to Feb), home to one of the area's best restauants (€25). You must book either place well in advance in high season. Other attractions are the remains of the old town and, just outside, the bizarre rock formations of the **Bois de Paiolive**. There's a **gîte d'étape** across the river at Chambonas (Ⓣ04.75.37.24.99).

Thines to the Col de Meyrand

THINES is a dozen twisting kilometres up the Chassezac from Les Vans, past isolated farms, abandoned terracing and numerous tumbling streams, then a further 5km or so up a side valley. The lane that leads to it is no wider than a car, and nature encroaches on either side. Traces remain of the old mule road, and in the torrent bed stand the stumps of packhorse bridges long since carried away. The village itself is at the end of the road high on a spur, looking back down the valley: just a handful of squat, grey-stone houses tightly grouped around a very lovely twelfth-century **church**, decorated with bands of red and white stone, the faces of its sculptures smashed during the Wars of Religion. At the top of the village, where the **GR4** and the local **GRP** enter from the scrubby heights behind, there is a strange **rock-cut relief** commemorating Resistance people killed here in August 1943. There's also a **gîte**, *L'Encas Chez Nathalie* (Ⓣ04.75.36.97.72; closed Oct–March), offering meals, and a *ferme auberge* (Mme Archambault; Ⓣ04.75.36.94.47; closed mid-Nov to Easter).

If your car is reasonably robust, you can get up onto the D4 on the 1000m ridge above Thines by a track that starts just above the bridge over the stream below the village. This is the so-called **Corniche du Vivarais Cévenol**, which you would otherwise have to make a long detour to reach. **SABLIÈRES**, another desolate Cévennes village, lies in the valley of the Drobie down to your right.

The landscape changes completely up here. The Mediterranean influence is left behind; it's windswept moorland, with natural beechwoods and mountain ash around the few bleak farms and plantations of conifers on the tops. The land rises steadily to over 1400m above the **Col de Meyrand**, itself at 1370m, from where it's possible to head back down to the main road and train line at **LUC**, 18km to the west.

Le Puy-en-Velay and the northeast

Right in the middle of the Massif Central, 78km from St-Étienne and 132km from Clermont, **LE PUY-EN-VELAY**, often shortened to Le Puy, is one of the most remarkable towns in the whole of France, with a landscape and architecture that are totally theatrical. Slung between the higher mountains to east and west, the countryside erupts in a chaos of volcanic acne: everywhere is a confusion of abrupt conical hills, scarred with dark outcrops of rock and topknotted with woods. Even in the centre of the town, these volcanic thrusts burst through.

In the past, Le Puy enjoyed influence and prosperity because of its ecclesiastical institutions, which were supported in part by the production of the town's famous green lentils. It was – and in a limited way, still is – a centre for pilgrims embarking on the 1600-kilometre trek to Santiago de Compostela. The specific starting point is place du Plot (also the scene of a lively Saturday market) and rue St-Jacques. History has it that Le Puy's Bishop Godescalk, in the tenth century, was the first pilgrim to make the journey. During the Wars of Religion the town managed to resist the Protestant fervour of much of the Massif Central. Recently, however, it has fallen somewhat on hard times, and its traditional industries – tanning and lace – have essentially gone bust. Even today Le Puy is somewhat inaccessible for the capital of a *département*: the three main roads out all cross passes more than 1000m high, which causes problems in winter.

Arrival, information and accommodation

If you arrive at the **gare SNCF** or **gare routière** (Ⓣ04.71.09.25.60), facing each other in place Maréchal-Leclerc, you'll find yourself barely a ten-minute walk from the central place du Clauzel and the **tourist office** (Easter–June & Sept–Oct Mon–Sat 8.30–noon & 1.30–6.15pm, Sun 9am–noon & 2–6pm; July & Aug daily 8.30am–7.30pm; Nov–Easter Mon–Sat 8.30am–noon & 1.30–6.15pm, Sun 10am–noon; Ⓣ04.71.09.38.41, Ⓦwww.ot-lepuyenvelay.fr). The town hall at 1 place Monsiegneur de Galard is home to the **Comité Départemental du Tourisme** (June–Aug Mon–Sat 8.30am–7.30pm, Sun 9am–noon & 2–6pm; Sept–May Mon–Sat 8.30am–noon & 2–6pm; Ⓣ04.71.07.41.54, Ⓦwww.mididelauvergne.com). Here you'll find information useful for venturing into the countryside.

Le Puy doesn't have a superabundance of **hotels**, so it's wise to book ahead in peak season. The budget options include the clean and pleasant *Dyke Hôtel*, at no. 37 (Ⓣ04.71.09.05.03, Ⓕ04.71.02.58.66; ❷), and the basic *Régional*, at no. 36 (Ⓣ04.71.09.37.74; ❶), both on boulevard Maréchal-Fayolle, the main boulevard connecting the station and place du Clauzel. On the same street but more luxurious is the renovated old mansion, at no. 34 (Ⓣ04.71.09.14.71, Ⓦwww.hotelrestregina.com; ❸–❻; restaurant €15–35). Best of all is *Le Bristol*, 7 av Foch (Ⓣ04.71.09.13.38, Ⓦwww.hotelbristol-lepuy.com; ❸), set in one of the area's oldest buildings, a former pilgrim's hostel, with a restaurant offering an excellent regional set menu from €10. For those on a tight budget, there's a good **HI hostel** at the attractive Centre Pierre-Cardinal, 9 rue Jules-Vallès

(Ⓣ04.71.05.52.40, Ⓔauberge.jeunesse@mairie-le-puy-en-velay.fr; closed weekends Oct–March), just off rue Lafayette, in the heart of the old town. **Campers** should head for the municipal *Camping d'Audinet*, near the River Loire in the northeast corner of town.

The Town

It would be hard to lose your bearings in Le Puy, for wherever you go there's no losing sight of the colossal, brick-red statue of the Virgin and Child that towers above the town on the **Rocher Corneille**, 755m above sea level and 130 abrupt metres above the lower town. The Virgin is cast from 213 guns captured at Sebastopol and painted red to match the tiled roofs below. You can climb up to the statue's base and, irreverent though it may seem, even up inside it (daily: 9/10am–5/7.30pm; €3). From here you get stunning views of the city, the church of St-Michel atop its needle-pointed pinnacle a few hundred metres northwest, and the surrounding volcanic countryside.

In the maze of steep cobbled streets and steps that terrace the Rocher, lace-makers – a traditional, though now commercialized, industry – do a fine trade, with doilies and lace shawls hanging enticingly outside souvenir shops. The main focus here, in the **old town**, is the Byzantine-looking **Cathédrale Notre-Dame-de-France**, begun in the eleventh century and decorated with parti-coloured layers of stone and mosaic patterns and roofed with a line of six domes. It's best approached up the rue des Tables, where you get the full theatrical force of its five-storeyed west front towering above you. In the rather exotic eastern gloom of the interior, a black-faced Virgin in spreading lace and golden robes stands upon the main altar, the copy of a revered original destroyed during the Revolution; the copy is still paraded through the town every August 15. Other lesser treasures are displayed at the back of the church in the sacristy, beyond which is the entrance to the exceptionally beautiful eleventh- and twelfth-century **cloister** (daily: June & Sept 9am–12.30pm & 2–6.30pm; July–Aug 9am–6.30pm; Oct–March 9.30am–noon & 2–5pm; €4.60), with its carved capitals, cornices and magnificent views of the cathedral and the towering Virgin and Child overhead. The passageway to the cloisters takes you past the so-called **Fever Stone**, whose origins may have been as a prehistoric dolmen and which was reputed to have the power of curing fevers. The surrounding ecclesiastical buildings and the **place du For**, on the south side of the cathedral, all date from the same period and form a remarkable ensemble.

It's a ten-minute walk from the cathedral to the **church of St-Michel** (signposts lead the way), perched atop the 82-metre needle-pointed lava pinnacle of the **Rocher d'Aiguilhe**. The little Romanesque church, built on Bishop Godescalk's return from his pilgrimage and consecrated in 962, is a beauty in its own right, and its improbable situation atop this ridiculous needle of rock is quite extraordinary – it's a long haul up 265 steps to the entrance (daily: Feb to mid-March 2–5pm; mid-March to April & Oct to mid-Nov 9.30am–noon & 2–5.30pm; May–Sept 9am–6pm; €2.50).

The new town and Pagès Verveine distillery

In the new part of town, beyond the squat **Tour Pannessac**, which is all that remains of the city walls, **place de Breuil** joins **place Michelet** and forms a social hub backed by the spacious Henri Vinay public gardens, where the **Musée Crozatier** (May–Sept daily 10am–noon & 2–6pm, but closed Tues mid-June to mid-Sept; Oct–April Mon & Wed–Sat 10am–noon & 2–4pm, Sun 2–6pm; €3) is best known for its collections relating to the region's traditional lace-making activities. Busy boulevard Maréchal-Fayolle converges with place Cadelade, where there's another of Le Puy's crazier aspects: the extraordinary bulbous tower of what used to be the **Pagès Verveine distillery**. The verveine (verbena) plant is normally used to make *tisane* (herb tea), but in this region provides a vivid green, powerful digestive liqueur instead. Production has now moved to a distillery 5km outside Le Puy, which is open for guided tours and tasting (Mon–Fri 10am–noon & 1.30–6.30pm: June–Sept Mon–Sat, Oct–May Mon–Fri; €5.30). To get there take the N88 and exit at the *zone industrielle* Blavozy.

Eating and drinking

For a city its size, Le Puy has an impressive array of fine yet economical **restaurants**, so there is little need to resort to the row of anonymous brasseries on the main street opposite the tourist office. The best of the eateries is the creative cuisine of the *François Gagnaire Restaurant* at 4 av Charbonnier (ⓣ04.71.02.75.55; closed Sun eve, Mon and Tues lunch; from €27); try the *Saint-Jacques* with green lentils. Other good choices include *Tournayre Eric*, set in a seventeenth-century building at 12 rue Chènebouterie (ⓣ04.71.09.58.94; closed Sun & Wed eve, Mon & Jan), specializing in the regional fare (menus €19–65), and the *gastronomique Lapierre* at 6 rue Capucins (ⓣ04.71.09.08.44; closed Dec & Jan, Sun out of season & Sat) with menus from €22. Two cheaper establishments, both on rue Raphaël beginning at the bottom of rue des Tables, are the *Nom de la Rose*, at no. 48 (closed Sun & Sept–May: Mon), offering Mexican food, with menus from €13.90, and *La Felouque*, at no. 49 (closed Feb & Sept–May: Tues; from €8–25), which serves Middle Eastern dishes and excellent grilled salmon.

For a **drink** or light snack, the terrace of *Le Petit Gourmande*, at the bottom of rue des Tables, makes a pleasant stop in summer (closed Jan; galettes for €5, a la carte from €13). A good place for an evening drink is *Harry's Bar*, on rue Raphaël, near the corner with rue des Tables.

North of Le Puy

North of Le Puy, the D906 crosses a vast and terminally depopulated area of pine-clad uplands – now the Parc Naturel Régional Livradois-Forez – and continues all the way to Vichy, via the historic town of **La Chaise-Dieu** and the old industrial centres of **Ambert** and **Thiers**.

La Chaise-Dieu

After 42km you come to the little town of **LA CHAISE-DIEU**, renowned for the **abbey church of St-Robert** (daily: June–Sept 9am–noon & 2–7pm; Oct–May 10am–noon & 2–5pm; €3), whose square towers dominate the town. Founded in 1044 and restored in the fourteenth century at the expense of Pope Clement VI, who had served as a monk here, the church was destroyed by the Huguenots in 1562, burnt down in 1692, and remained unfinished when the Revolution brought a wave of anticlericalism. It was only really finished in the twentieth century. Its interior contains the tomb of Clement VI, some magnificent Flemish tapestries of Old and New Testament scenes hanging in the choir, which also boasts some fine Gothic stalls, and a celebrated fresco of the **Danse Macabre**, depicting Death plucking at the coarse plump bodies of 23 living figures, representing the different classes of society (open May–Oct; €3.70 or €1.60 for treasury only). "It is yourself", says the fifteenth-century text below, as indeed it might easily have been in an age when plague and war were rife.

Nearby on the place de l'Echo, the **Salle de l'Echo** (same times except closed Sun am; free) is another product of the risk of contagion – if not from plague, then from leprosy. For in this room, once used for hearing confession from the sick and dying, two people can turn their backs on each other, stand in opposite corners and still have a perfectly audible conversation just by whispering.

A **classical music festival** takes place here in late August and early September, details of which are available from the **tourist office**, on place de la Mairie (Easter–June & Sept Tues–Sun 10am–noon & 2–6pm; July & Aug daily 9am–12.30pm & 1.30–7pm; Oct–March Tues–Sat 10am–noon & 2–6pm; ⓣ04.71.00.01.16, ⓦwww.tourisme.fr/lachaisedieu). The *Hôtel Monastère et Terminus*, on avenue de la Gare (ⓣ04.71.00.00.73, ⓦwww.hotel-monastere-terminus.com; ❷; closed Nov–March; restaurant from €6–22), and *De La Casadei in Place l'Abbaye* (ⓣ04.71.00.01.85, ⓔcasadei@es-conseil.com; ❷; restaurant from €14), offer reasonable comfort for a night's stay. There's also a municipal **campsite** on the Vichy side of the D906 (ⓣ04.71.00.07.88; closed Oct–May).

Ambert

Twenty-five kilometres north of La Chaise-Dieu, the little town of **AMBERT** was, from the fourteenth to eighteenth centuries, the centre of papermaking in France. It especially supplied the printers of Lyon, a connection that brought the region into contact with new ideas, in particular the revolutionary teachings of the Reformed Church. Although those small-scale operations have long since been sidelined, there is still a **paper mill** in operation at Richard-de-Bas just east of the town, with its **Musée Historique du Papier** (daily: July & Aug 9am–7pm; Sept–June 9–11am & 2–5pm; €5), featuring exhibits and explanations from papyrus to handmade samples from medieval days. In the town itself, there's a small **museum** (July & Aug daily 10am–noon & 2–5pm; Sept–June closed Mon; €4) devoted to the manufacture of the soft blue Fourme d'Ambert cheese, the region's speciality.

Thiers

THIERS, another 49km to the north, has an illustrious industrial history as the country's greatest manufacturer of knives. In spite of serious decline, especially since decolonization and the loss of such huge captive markets, it still accounts for some seventy percent of French production. It's an interesting little town, built over the steep slopes of the valley of the Durolle, whose water power drove the forges and blade-makers' wheels for centuries. There's the **Maison des Couteliers**, devoted to local knife-crafting, at 58 rue de la Coutellerie in the centre (Feb–June & Sept–Oct Tues–Sun 10am–noon & 2–6pm; July & Aug daily 10am–6pm; Nov & Dec Wed–Sun 10am–noon & 2–6pm; €4.75), while all along the deep valley bottom you can see where the old workshops were. You probably wouldn't want to stay overnight – there are frequent trains from Clermont Ferrand (30min).

East of Le Puy

East of Le Puy lies the barrier of the mountains of the Vivarais, rounded and wooded with beech, pine and fir, interspersed with open cow pastures. The highest points are the **Gerbier de Jonc** (1551m) and **Mont Mézenc** (1753m), with long views west across the whole of the Massif Central.

The Gerbier is a curious wooded mound rising out of the otherwise flattish surrounding uplands, about 50km southeast of Le Puy, with the River Loire rising on its upper slopes – home to a bucolic and still-isolated countryside. To get out there, take the D535 through **MONASTIER-SUR-GAZEILLE**, where R. L. Stevenson bought his donkey and started his famous journey. Although the village is pretty, with a particularly lovely church, there's something forlorn and unfriendly about it. The rather bleak *Hôtel Le Provence* above the village would do for a night's stay (ⓣ04.71.03.82.37, ⓔinfo @le-provence.fr; ❷; restaurant €11-21). The riverside municipal **campsite** (ⓣ04.71.03.82.24; closed Oct–May) and **gîte d'étape** (ⓣ04.71.03.82.24) are more welcoming. From here 30km of winding lanes lead to the summit itself.

Fifty kilometres further north, and about 40km east of Le Puy, behind the gentle bulk of **Mont Meygal** (1436m), lies the area known as the *Montagne Protestante*, because its people converted very early and have remained staunch Protestants ever since, albeit with some fairly strange tendencies among them. Black-stone farmhouses stand in isolation among the pastures strewn with autumn crocuses and the dark woods of fir. At the centre of the region lies **CHAMBON-SUR-LIGNON**, a rambling, rather unattractive village with a somewhat faded air, made famous, however, for its extraordinary wartime record as a haven for several thousand Jewish children. Everyone knew of their presence and was involved in protecting them, and no one ever betrayed them, bound together in their obdurate resolve by their strong Protestant beliefs. Their story is told in *Les Armes de l'Esprit*, a documentary film made by one of the surviving children who emigrated to the US, available from the *mairie*. Albert Camus also stayed nearby in 1942 and wrote part of *La Peste* here. The **tourist office** is on the central square (July & Aug Mon–Sat 9am–noon & 2.30–6.30pm, Sun 10.30am–12.30pm; Sept–June Mon–Sat 9am–noon & 2.30–6pm; ⓣ04.71.59.71.56, ⓦwww.ot-lechambonsurlignon.fr). More local information can be had from the tourist office in **TENCE**, a rather more attractive village, 8km down the road (July–Aug Mon–Sat 9am–noon & 2–6pm & Sun 10.30am–12.30pm; May–June & Sept Tues–Sat 9am–noon & 2–6pm, Oct–April Tues–Sat 9am–noon & 2–5pm; ⓣ04.71.59.81.99, ⓦwww .ot-tence.fr). That said, hearty local fare can be enjoyed in Chambon at *La Trifola*, 4 rte de Tence (ⓣ04.71.59.77.20; around €22; clsoed Mon eve & Tues).

St-Étienne

ST-ÉTIENNE, 78km northeast of Le Puy, was until recently a particularly bland town. Almost unrelievedly industrial, it was a major armaments manufacturer, enclosed for kilometres around by mineworkings, warehouses and factory chimneys. Like so many other industrial centres, it fell on hard times, and the demolition gangs have moved in to raze its archaic industrial past. Only in recent yers has an equilibrium been re-achieved thanks to a concerted program to revitalize the devayed town.

The centre is now quite cheerful, bouyed by a collection of small new musuems, the best of which is the **Musée d'Art Moderne** at La Terrasse, in the north of the city (daily except Tues 10am–6pm; €4.40). This justifies a detour for anyone with an interest in twentieth-century art – a quite unexpected treasure house of contemporary work, both pre- and post-World War II, with a good modern American section, in which Andy Warhol and Frank Stella figure prominently, along with work by Rodin, Matisse, Léger and Ernst, and rooms filled entirely with French art, imaginatively laid out to exciting effect. La Terrasse station is served by frequent trains from St-Étienne's central station, Châteaucreux. The **Musée d'Art et d'Industrie**, 2 place Louis-Comte, is also good on St-Étienne's industrial background, including the development of the revolutionary Jacquard loom, and an impressive exhibition of arms and armour (daily except Tues 10am–6pm, €4.40).

There are flights (with RyanAir from the London-Stansted for example) to St-Étienne's small **airport** (ⓣ04.77.55.71.71), and a *navette* service into the town centre. The **tourist office** on 16 av de la Liberation (April–Sept Mon–Sat 9am–7pm & Sun 9am–noon; Oct–March Mon–Sat 9am–6pm & Sun 10am–noon; ⓣ04.77.49.39.00, ⓦwww.tourisme-st-etienne.com) is around ten minutes' walk from Châteaucreux train station along avenue D.-Rochereau. If you have to stay, try *Hôtel de la Tour*, 1 rue Mercière (ⓣ04.77.32.28.48, ⓕ04.77.21.27.90; ❶), *Le Cheval Noir*, 11 rue François-Gillet (ⓣ04.77.33.41.72, ⓕ04.77.37.79.19; ❸), or *Hôtel Terminus du Forez*, 29 av D.-Rochereau (ⓣ04.77.32.48.47, ⓔhotel.forez@wanadoo.fr; ❹). If you've come for the night or only for a day of art, treat yourself to a fine meal at *La Bouche Pleine* at 2 pl Chavanelle (ⓣ04.77.33.92.47; closed Sat & Sun in Aug; menus from €20).

Travel details

Trains

Alès to: Nîmes (6–9 daily; 35min); Villefort (6–8 daily; 1hr).
Aurillac to: Brive (4 daily; 1hr 40min); Le Lioran (3–5 daily; 40min); Murat (3–5 daily; 50min); Neussargues (3–5 daily; 1hr); Toulouse (3–7; 2hr 40in); Vic-sur-Cère (3–5 daily; 15min).
Clermont-Ferrand to: Aurillac (4–6 daily; 2hr 30min–5hr); Béziers (3 daily; 6–7hr); La Bourboule (4 daily; 1hr 20min); Brive (3 daily; 3hr 40min); Limoges (4 daily; 3hr 30min–4hr); Le Lioran (3–4 daily; 2–4hr); Lyon (12–18 daily; 2hr 45min–3hr 30min); Marvejols (4 daily; 2hr 15min–3hrs); Millau (1 daily; 4hr 15min); Le Mont-Dore (4 daily; 1hr 30min); Murat (5–7 daily; 1hr 40min); Neussargues (12–14 daily; 1hr 30min–3hr 30min); Nîmes (12–16 daily; 5–6hr); Paris (5–10 daily; 2–5hr); Riom (12–14 daily; 10min); St-Étienne (2–3 daily; 2hr 10min) St-Flour (4 daily; 1hr 20min–2hr); Thiers (6 daily; 35min); Vic-sur-Cère (5–7 daily; 2hr 15min); Vichy (12–14 daily; 40min); Volvic (5 daily; 24min).
Le Puy to: St-Étienne (8 daily; 1hr 20min).
Mende to: La Bastide-Puylaurent (2–3 daily; 50min); Marvejols (3–5 daily; 40min); Montpellier (16–20 daily; 3hr–4hr 30min); Nîmes (16–20 daily daily; 2hr 30min–4hr); St-Flour (1–2 daily; 1hr 40min).
Millau to: Aumont-Aubrac (4 daily; 1hr 30min); Béziers (3 daily; 2hr); Marvejols (5 daily; 1hr 10min); Paris (2 daily direct; 8hr–9hr 30min).
Rodez to: Millau (7 daily; 1hr 10min–2hr 30min).
St-Étienne to: Clermont-Ferrand (3–6 daily; 2hr 40min); Lyon (3 daily; 45min); Paris (3 daily; 2hr 50min); St-Germain-des-Fosses (2 daily; 3hr).
St-Flour to: Neussargues (2–3 daily; 25min).
Vichy to: Clermont-Ferrand (12–14 dialy; 40min); Nîmes (12–16 daily; 7–9hr); Paris (4 daily; 3hr 30min).

Buses

Ambert to: St-Étienne (1 daily; 2hr).
Aubenas to: Alès (2–3 daily; 2hr 10min); Entraygues (1–4 daily; 1hr); Valence (7 daily; 2hr); Vallon-Pont-d'Arc (1–2 daily; 45min); Les Vans (4 daily; 1hr 10min).
Aurillac to: Brommat, changing at Mur-de-Barrez (3 weekly; 2hr); Carlat (3–4 daily; 30min); Entraygues (1 daily; 1hr 30min); Mandailles (1 daily; 1hr 20min); Murat (1 daily; 1hr 40min); St-Flour (1 daily; 2hr 10min); Super-Lioran (1 daily; 1hr 20min); Vic-sur-Cère (2–3 daily; 40min).
Clermont-Ferrand to: Ambert (1–2 daily: 1hr 40min); Aydat (1–2 daily; 40min); Besse (July & Aug 2 daily; 1hr 35min); La Chaise-Dieu (1 Mon; 2hr); Lyon (daily; 4hr); Mauriac (1–2 daily; 2hr 45min); Moulins (4 daily; 2hr 30min); Murol (July & Aug 2 daily; 1hr 10min); Le Puy (1 daily; 2hr 15min); Riom (2 daily; 40min); St-Flour (2 weekly; 2hr); St-Nectaire (July & Aug 2 daily; 1hr); Superbesse (July & Aug 2 daily; 1hr 45min); Thiers (several daily; 1hr); Vichy (5 daily; 1hr 45min).
Conques to: Entraygues (June & Sept Tues; July & Aug Tues, Thurs & Sat 1 daily; 35min); Espalion (June & Sept Tues; July & Aug Tues, Thurs & Sat 1 daily; 1hr 20min); Najac (June & Sept Tues; July & Aug Tues & Fri 1 daily; 2hr 30min); St-Geniez-d'Olt (June & Sept Tues; July & Aug Tues, Thurs & Sat 1 daily; 2hr 15min).

La Bourboule to: Le Mont-Dore (3–5 daily; 10min); Le Sancy (3–5 daily; 35min).
Le Puy to: Aubenas (2 weekly; 3hr 15min); La Chaise-Dieu (2 daily; 1hr); Clermont-Ferrand (1 daily; 3hr); St-Étienne (4 daily; 2hr 10min).
Le Vigan to: Ganges (1–6 daily; 25min); Montpellier (3 daily; 2hr); Nîmes (3–5 daily; 1hr 50min); Valleraugue (July & Aug 1 daily; 30min).
Mende to: Marvejols (3 daily; 50min); Le Puy (2 daily; 2hr); St-Chély (1 daily; 1hr 10min); St-Étienne (1 daily; 3hr).
Millau to: Aven Armand (July & Aug daily; 1hr 45min); Le Caylar (2–6 daily; 40min); Le Rozier (1–4 daily; 40min); Montpellier (3–8 daily; 2hr 20min); Rodez (4 daily; 1hr 30min); Roquefort (July & Aug 3 weekly; 30min); St-Affrique (3–6 daily; 45min); Ste-Énimie (July & Aug daily; 2hr 25min); Toulouse (2 daily; 4hr).
Neussargues to: Allanche (2–3 daily; 20min); Condat (2–3 daily; 30min); Riom-ès-Montagnes (2–3 daily; 1hr 15min); St-Flour (2 daily; 30min).
Riom to: Volvic (4–8 daily; 25min).
Rodez to: Albi (3 daily; 2hr); Conques (1 daily; 1hr); Entraygues (1–2 daily; 2hr); Espalion (3–4 daily; 45min); Laguiole (1 daily; 1hr 45min); Le Caylar (1–4 daily; 2hr 40min); Mende (1 daily; 3hr 30min); Millau (3–8 daily; 1hr 40min); Montauban (1 daily; 3hr 15min); Montpellier (1–4 daily; 3hr 55min); Mur-de-Barrez (1 daily; 2hr 45min); Sauveterre-de-Rouergue (5 weekly; 55min); Séverac-le-Château (several daily; 45min); Toulouse (2–4 daily; 3hr 30min); Villefranche-de-Rouergue (1–2 daily; 1hr 30min).
St-Chély-d'Aubrac to: Espalion (1 daily; 30min).
St-Flour to: Laguiole (Tues, Thurs & Sat 1 daily; 3hr).
St-Martin-d'Ardèche to: Avignon (1 daily; 1hr 40min); Pont St-Esprit (2 daily; 15min); Vallon-Pont-d'Arc (2 daily; 1hr 10min).
Vichy to: Ambert (4 daily; 2hr 10min); La Chaise-Dieu (daily; 2hr 45min); Thiers (several daily; 40min).
Villefranche-de-Rouergue to: Conques (July & Aug Tues & Fri 1 daily; 2hr); Najac (July & Aug Tues & Fri 1 daily; 30min).

13

The Alps

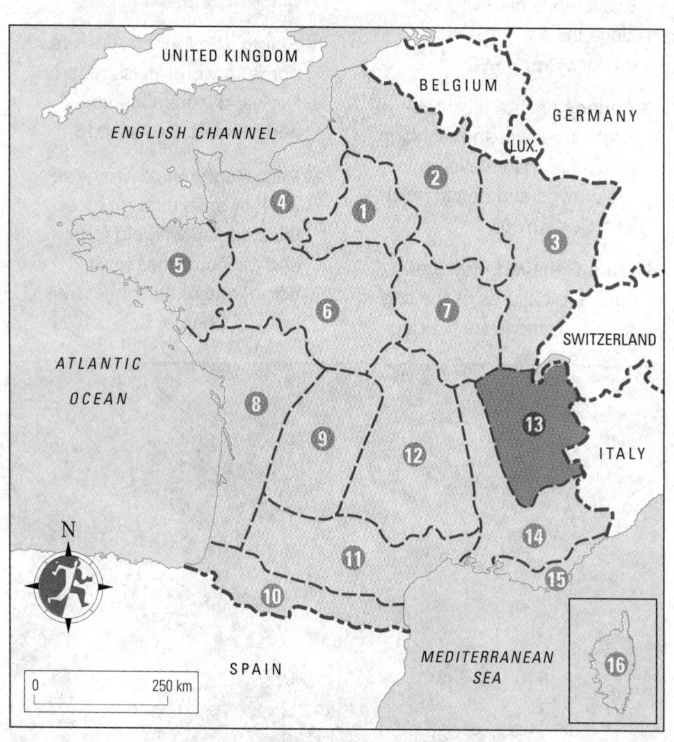
UNITED KINGDOM
BELGIUM
GERMANY
LUX.
ENGLISH CHANNEL
SWITZERLAND
ATLANTIC
OCEAN
ITALY
N
SPAIN
MEDITERRANEAN
SEA
0
250 km
1
2
3
4
5
6
7
8
9
10
11
12
13
14
15
16

CHAPTER 13

Highlights

✱ **Grenoble** The "Capital of the Alps" is a modern, thriving city, offering lively nightlife and fine museums. **See p.987**

✱ **Chartreuse** Carthusian monks have been making this famous green liqueur since the seventeenth century. **See p.996**

✱ **Annecy** Annecy's picture-postcard views and stunning lake more than make up for the crowds and commercialism. **See p.1001**

✱ **Lake Geneva** Enjoy the sedate pleasures of the spa towns on the French side of this huge lake, or hop on one of the frequent ferries to Switzerland. **See p.1005**

✱ **Aiguille du Midi** Brave one of the world's highest cable-car ascents for a truly spectacular view of Mont Blanc. **See p.1011**

✱ **Skiing** The French Alps are home to world-class resorts like Val d'Isère, Chamonix and Méribel. **See p.1016**

✱ **Parc Régional du Queyras** Walk or drive through mountains riddled with old forts and ruined castles to St-Véran, one of the highest villages in Europe. **See p.1027**

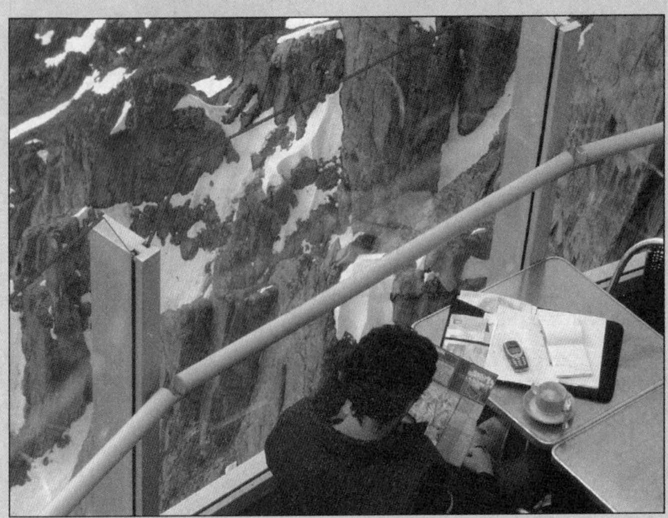

△ Reading at Brevant

13

The Alps

"I need torrents, rocks, firs, dark woods, mountains, steep roads to climb or descend, abysses beside me to make me afraid"; so wrote Rousseau in his Confessions, and he certainly found what he was looking for in the Alps. Formed by the collision of two continental plates two hundred million years ago, the range contains some of France's most dramatic landscapes, with roads, rail lines and population confined to the deep valley floors. To get the best out of this region you have to walk – or in winter, ski (the box on p.1016 has a short roundup of the resorts). There are six **national** or **regional parks** in the area covered by this chapter – Vanoise, Chartreuse, Bauges, Écrins, Queyras and Vercors – all with round-the-park trails, requiring one to two weeks' walking. **The Tour of Mont Blanc** path is of similar length. Then there are two transalpine routes: **the Route des Grandes Alpes**, which crosses all the major massifs from Thonon-les-Bains on Lake Geneva to Menton, and **Le Balcon des Alpes**, a gentler, village-to-village itinerary through the western foothills.

All these routes are clearly marked, equipped with refuge huts and *gîtes d'étape*, and described in Topoguides (see Basics, p.83). The **Bureau Info Montagne** office in Grenoble will provide information on all GR paths. In addition, local tourist offices often produce detailed maps of walks in their own areas. The Alps are also an ideal place for rock climbing, since many of the best faces are already bolted. You shouldn't undertake any high-level **long-distance hikes**, however, unless you're an experienced hill-walker; if you aren't, but nonetheless like the sound of some of these trails, read a specialized hiking book before making any plans, or simply limit your sights to more local targets. You can find plenty of day walks from bases in or close to the parks; and there are some spectacular road routes, too. The **Vercors**, **Chartreuse**, **Aravis**, **Faucigny** and **Chablais** areas are the gentlest and quietest introductions.

As for accommodation, you can **camp** freely on the fringes of the parks, but once inside you're supposed to pitch only in an emergency and move on after one night. **Hotels** are often seasonal (closed in late spring and late autumn), overbooked and overpriced – if you're on a budget but don't want to carry camping equipment, using **gîtes** and **refuges** is a better solution. The Alps are almost as crowded in midsummer as they are in winter (the **Chamonix-Mont Blanc** area is the worst black spot), but you're more or less obliged to go in high season if you want to walk: unreliable weather aside, anywhere above 2000m will be snowbound until the beginning of July. Drivers should remember that some high passes such as the **Col du Galibier** and the **Col de l'Iseran** in the east of the region can remain closed well into June, requiring long detours or excursions into Italy via expensive Alpine tunnels.

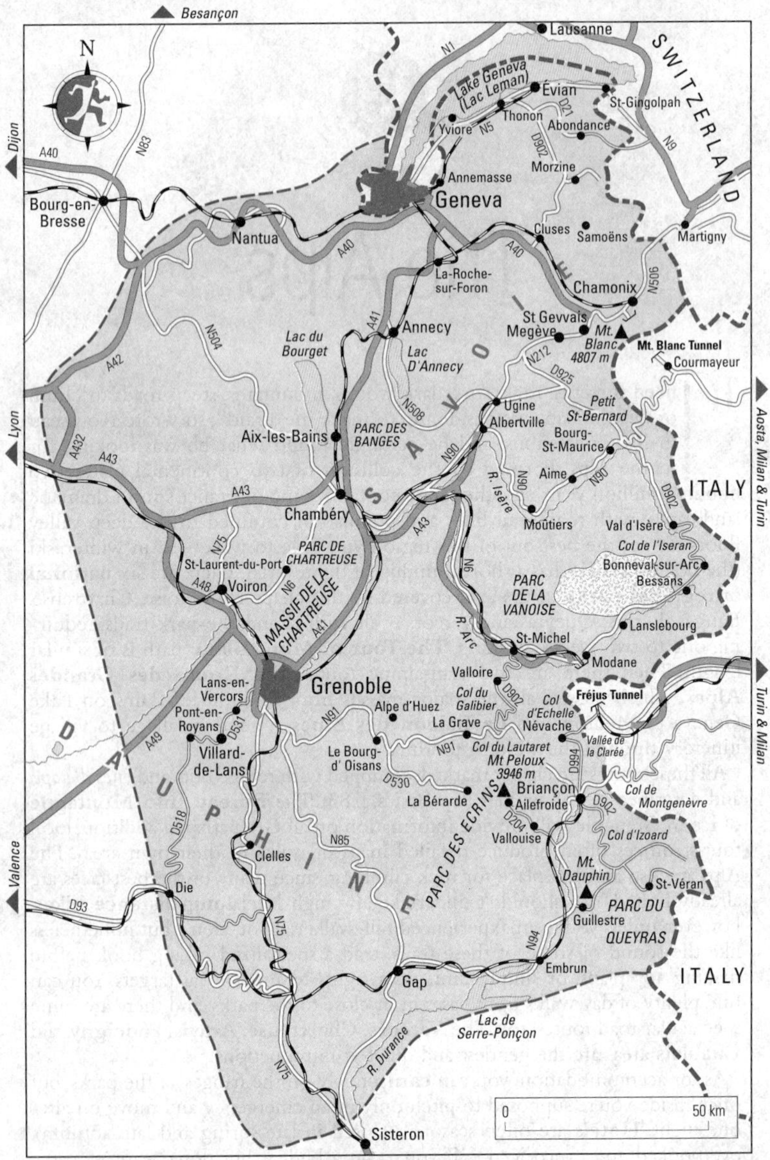

The towns in the Alps offer good facilities for campers and hikers, and often provide attractions of their own. **Grenoble** is the economic and intellectual capital of the region, and has a lively cultural scene; **Chambéry** and picturesque **Annecy** are good bases for expeditions into the Parc des Bauges and Massif de Chartreuse, and the countryside around the **Lac d'Annecy** respectively; and **Briançon**, the highest town in Europe, is close to the Écrins and

Queyras parks. The websites Ⓦwww.rhonealpes-tourisme.com and Ⓦwww.alpes-guide.com are useful introductions to the region.

Grenoble

Beautifully situated on the Drac and Isère rivers, and surrounded by mountains, **GRENOBLE**, the self-styled "capital of the Alps", is a lively, modern city, home to several universities, with more than 50,000 students. In the Middle Ages, the Princes of Dauphiné held court here, until the province was annexed by France in the fourteenth century, and the city is also famous for the Journée des Tuiles, a local uprising in 1788 which is held to be the first act of the French Revolution. Grenoble's prosperity was originally founded on glove-making, but in the nineteenth century its economy diversified to include mining, cement, paper mills, hydroelectric power and metallurgy. Its international profile was boosted in 1968, when it hosted the Winter Olympics, and today it's a centre of chemical and electronics industries and nuclear

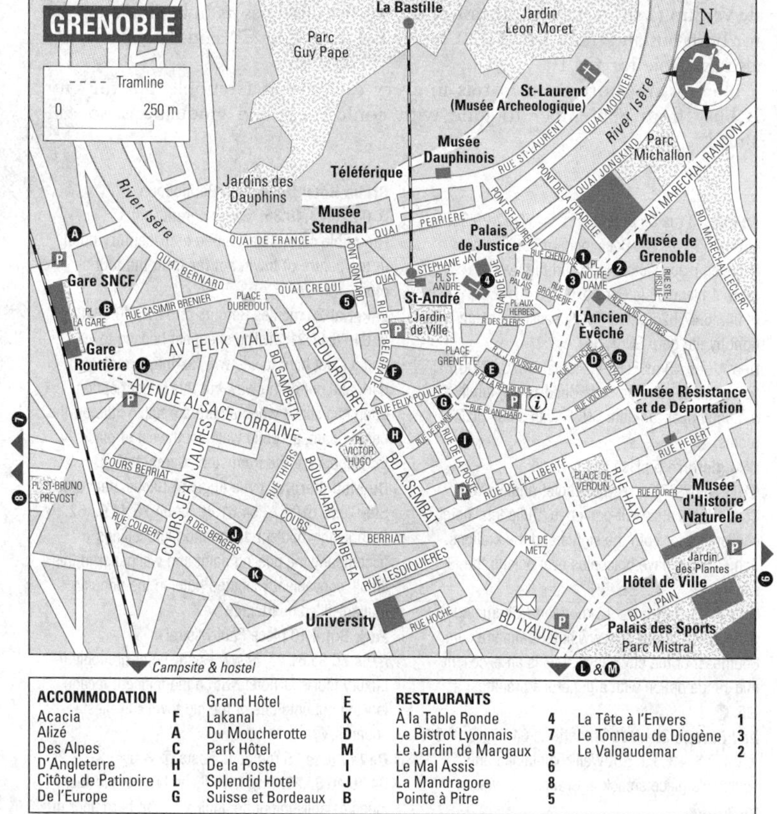

research, with the big, new laboratories of the Atomic Energy Commission on the banks of the Drac.

Arrival, information and accommodation

The **gare SNCF** and the **gare routière** are next door to each other at the western end of avenue Félix Viallet, just ten minutes' walk from the most interesting sections of the city, which are mainly on the left bank of the Isère. Not far from central place Grenette, at 14 rue de la République, is the **tourist office** (daily: July–Aug 9am–6.30pm; Sept–June Mon–Sat 9am–6.30pm, Sun 10am–1pm & 2–5pm; ⓣ04.76.42.41.41, ⓦwww.grenoble-isere.info), where you'll also find the local SNCF and public transport information offices. Walkers and climbers should check out the former CIMES office, now known as the **Bureau Info Montagne** (Mon–Fri 9am–noon & 2–6pm, Sat 10am–noon & 2–5pm; ⓣ04.76.42.45.90, ⓦwww.grenoble-montagne.com), in the Maison de la Montagne, 3 rue Raoul Blanchard, across the street from the back of the tourist office, or the **Club Alpin Français** at 32 av Félix Viallet (Tues–Wed 2–6pm, Thurs–Fri 2–8pm, Sat 9am–noon; ⓣ04.76.87.03.73) for hiking suggestions and detailed information on refuges.

The **transport** network, combining bus and tram routes, has the bleak place de Verdun (a short walk southeast of the tourist office) as its hub. Single tickets for both bus and tram cost €1.20, ten-ticket strips cost €9, and daily passes are also available for €3.10.

There is no shortage of **hotels** in every category in Grenoble, but the city is busy from September to June with conferences and graduations, so call ahead.

Hotels

Acacia 13 rue de Belgrade ⓣ04.76.87.29.90, ⓕ04.76.47.21.25. Cosy modern hotel halfway between place Victor Hugo and the river. ❸

Alizé 1 place de la Gare ⓣ04.76.43.12.91, ⓕ04.76.47.62.79. Extremely basic but clean hotel right by the gare SNCF. ❶

Des Alpes 45 av Félix-Viallet ⓣ04.76.87.00.71, ⓦwww.hotel-des-alpes.fr. Good-value, family-run hotel near the gare SNCF, with small plain rooms. ❸

D'Angleterre 5 place Victor-Hugo ⓣ04.76.87.37.21, ⓦwww.hotel-angleterre.fr. Comfortable and well-equipped "Tulip Inn" hotel, convenient for both the sights and the stations. Some rooms have balconies overlooking the square. ❼

Citôtel de Patinoire 12 rue Marie-Chamoux ⓣ04.76.44.43.65, ⓦwww.hotel-patinoire.com. Southeast of the city centre, this is an excellent mid-range option with a generous breakfast at €5. ❸

De l'Europe 22 place Grenette ⓣ04.76.46.16.94, ⓕ04.76.43.13.65. Well-maintained and hospitable place smack in Grenoble's liveliest square. ❷

Grand Hôtel 5 rue de la République ⓣ04.76.44.49.36, ⓦwww.grand-hotel-grenoble.com. Smart nineteenth-century hotel in the centre of town, not far from the tourist office. ❺–❻

Lakanal 26 rue des Bergers ⓣ04.76.46.03.42, ⓕ04.76.17.21.24. The cheapest beds in town, and it's not hard to see why, as they are dingy, dark and out of the way, but this budget option often has space when others are full. A little off the beaten path, a 10min walk southwest of place Victor-Hugo, near the tram stop "Gambetta". ❶

Du Moucherotte 1 rue Auguste-Gaché, near place Ste-Claire ⓣ04.76.54.61.40, ⓕ04.76.44.62.52. Surprisingly opulent decor and high ceilings accompany the peeling paint and wallpaper in this small, conveniently located hotel in the popular student-filled quarter. ❶

Park Hôtel 10 place Paul-Mistral ⓣ04.76.85.81.23, ⓦwww.park-hotel-grenoble.fr. Luxury four-star hotel, with a magnificent facade looking out onto one of the old town's liveliest squares. ❾

De la Poste 25 rue de la Poste ⓣ & ⓕ 04.76.46.67.25. Tiny, friendly and rather old-fashioned establishment beginning on the third floor of an apartment building and located on a pedestrian street, off place Vaucanson. ❷

Splendid Hotel 22 rue Thiers ⓣ04.76.46.33.12, ⓦwww.splendid-hotel.com. The walls are all painted with different pastel-style murals in this all *en-suite* two-star. It's a quiet, mid-range hotel, a 10min walk from the commercial centre. ❹

Suisse et Bordeaux 6 place de la Gare ⓣ04.76.47.55.87 ⓦwww.hotel-sb-grenoble.com. Friendly and clean hotel across from the train station. ❸

Hostel and campsite

Hostel 10 av de Gresivaudan, ⓣ04.76.09.33.52 ⓔgrenoble@fuaj.org. Modern and recently renovated hostel just south of the city in Echirolles. Take bus #1 to "Quinzaine," or tram A to "La Rampe." €13.25 including breakfast, non-members €2.90 extra.

Camping des Trois Pucelles 58 rue des Allobroges, in Seyssins on the left bank of the Drac, 4km west of town ⓣ04.76.96.45.73, ⓦwww.camping-trois-pucelles.com. Take tram A to "Albert 1er", and change to bus #5 for "Mas des Iles," or take bus #23.

The City

The best way to start your stay is to take the **téléférique** (March–May & Oct Mon 11am–7.25pm, Tues–Sat 9.30am–11.45pm, Sun 9.15am–7.25pm; June & Sept Mon 11am–11.45pm, Tues–Sat 9.15am–11.45pm, Sun 9.15am–7.25pm; July & Aug Mon 11am–1.15am, Tues–Sun 9.15am–1.15am; Nov–Feb Mon 11am–6.30pm, Tues–Sun 10.45am–6.30pm; €5.50 return) from the riverside quai Stéphane-Jay to **Fort de la Bastille** on the steep slopes above the north bank of the Isère. The ride is hair-raising, as you're whisked steeply and swiftly into the air in a sort of transparent egg, which allows you to see very clearly how far you would fall in the event of an accident. If you don't like the sound of the cable car, you can climb the steep but pleasant footpath from the St-Laurent church or from the Musée Dauphinois (both covered overleaf).

Although the fort is of little interest, the **view** is fantastic. At your feet the Isère flows under the old bridges which join the St-Laurent quarter, colonized by Italian immigrants in the nineteenth century, to the nucleus of the medieval town, whose red roofs cluster tightly around the church of St-André. To the east, snowfields gleam in the gullies of the Belledonne massif (2978m). Southeast is Taillefer and south-southeast the dip where the Route Napoléon passes over the mountains to Sisteron and the Mediterranean – this is the road Napoleon took after his escape from Elba in March 1815 on his way to rally his forces for the campaign that led to his final defeat at Waterloo. To the west are the steep white cliffs of the Vercors massif; the highest peak, dominating the city, is Moucherotte (1901m). The jagged summits at your back are the outworks of the Chartreuse massif. Northeast on a clear day you can see the white peaks of Mont Blanc up the deep glacial valley of the Isère, known as La Grésivaudan. It was in this valley that the first French hydroelectric project went into action in 1869. For heading back into town, a path down through the public gardens offers an alternative to the cable car.

City passes

Many of the city museums have changed from charging admission to being **free**, but it still may be worth it to buy a **city pass** from the tourist office to cover public transport, a guided tour of the old town, admission to one of the museums that is not free (like the Musée de Grenoble), a return trip on the téléférique and a €2 parking voucher (one-day pass €16). The much more expensive Multipass Plus (€26) is not great value, offering a discounted movie ticket and reductions in some stores in addition to the previous offers.

Upstream from the téléférique station is the sixteenth-century **Palais de Justice** (open to the public), with place St-André and the **church of St-André** behind. Built in the thirteenth century, the church once served as the palace chapel of the princes of Dauphiné, though it has been heavily restored since, and today is of little architectural interest. Meanwhile, the narrow streets leading towards places Grenette, Vaucanson and Verdun pass through the liveliest and most colourful quarter of the city. Life focuses on a chain of little squares – aux Herbes, Claveyson, de Gordes, Grenette and Notre-Dame – where people congregate at the numerous cafés and restaurants. The small produce **market** (Tues–Sun 6am–1pm) on place aux Herbes is a great place to stock up on inexpensive local produce.

Close to place St-André, in the former town hall at 1 rue Hector-Berlioz, in the corner of the Jardin de Ville gardens, is the **Musée Stendhal** (mid-July to mid-Sept Tues–Sat 9am–noon & 2–6pm; mid-Sept to mid-July Tues–Sat 2–6pm, closed all hols; free), with a couple of rooms containing family portraits and manuscripts associated with the much-revered author, who was born in Grenoble as Marie-Henri Beyle. You can also visit his grandfather's house, **La Maison Stendhal**, where he spent his childhood, at 20 Grande-Rue, just off place Grenette (same hours as the Musée in summer, in winter Tues–Sat 10am–noon; free).

Near the bustling place Notre-Dame, on the riverbank at 5 place de Lavalette, is the **Musée de Grenoble** (July–Sept Mon & Thus–Sun 10am–6pm, Wed 10am–9pm; Oct–June Mon & Thus–Sun 11am–7pm, Wed 11am–10pm; €5), an enormous modern complex housing a gallery of mainly contemporary art. The building itself is impressive, but the collection is uneven, though many major schools of painting are represented, including a few works by Rubens and Canaletto. The best rooms are those of nineteenth- and twentieth-century artists including Gauguin, Chagall and Matisse. Directly on the east side of place Notre-Dame is **L'Ancien Évêché** (Mon & Wed–Sat 9am–6pm, Sun 10am–7pm; free). Housed in the old bishop's palace, the museum offers a brisk tour through Grenoble's history from the Stone Age to the twentieth century. The remains of the Roman town walls and a fifth-century **baptistry** are on show in the basement, while among the prized exhibits upstairs are Neolithic jade jewellery, Bronze Age weapons and a wealth of Roman artefacts, including a colourful mosaic floor panel, decorated with a pair of parrots.

On the opposite bank of the Isère, the **Musée Archéologique Église St-Laurent**, on place St-Laurent (Mon & daily except Tues 9am–6pm; €3.20; free entry Wed afternoon), gives a fascinating insight into the history of the city, as you descend through various stages of excavations in this former church, passing through an early Christian necropolis, an eighth-century crypt and a high medieval cloister. A few minutes to the west, lying up a steep cobbled path opposite the St-Laurent footbridge, the **Musée Dauphinois**, 30 rue Maurice-Gignoux (May–Oct daily except Tues 10am–7pm; Nov–April 10am–6pm; free), housed in the former convent of Ste-Marie-d'en-Haut, is largely devoted to the history, arts and crafts of the province of Dauphiné. There are exhibits on the lives of the rugged and self-sufficient mountain people, including mock-ups of the modest rustic homes that they shared with their animals during the seven-month long winters. There's also an exhibition illustrating the **history of skiing**, and, in the basement, a splendid Baroque chapel, with grey and gold wall paintings depicting episodes from the New Testament and scenes from the life of St-François-de-Sales, who founded the convent in the seventeenth century.

Wedged between the park and the old town at 14 rue Hébert is the **Musée de la Résistance et de la Déportation de l'Isère** (July & Aug daily except Tues 10am–7pm; Sept–June daily except Tues 9am–6pm; free), with a touching and high-tech exhibition of photographs, video footage and memorabilia from the brutal Nazi occupation of the Dauphiné, with all captions translated into English. Two blocks south, standing among the fine trees of the Jardin des Plantes at 1 rue Dolomieu is the **Muséum d'Histoire Naturelle** (Mon–Fri 9.30am–noon & 1.30–5.30pm, Sat–Sun & hols 2–6pm; €3.80). It has a marvellous collection, ranking second after the Paris museum for sheer depth and breadth – it includes all the Alpine birds of prey and an aquarium.

Eating, drinking and nightlife

Eating in Grenoble is a pleasure; it's less expensive than Paris but just as creative. There are a wide variety of restaurants catering to all budgets and tastes – a call ahead is recommended for most of the places noted below, especially in the evenings. For those with a knowledge of French, it's useful to pick up a copy of the *Guide Dahu* in local *tabacs* – a restaurant and nightlife guide compiled by local students (€2).

Interesting, atmospheric places to **drink** are also easy to find, with places Grenette, St-André and Notre-Dame full of café-bars, though the more interesting ones are usually on the streets between those squares. On Place Notre-Dame, try *Bar 1900* or *Le Shaman Café*, which also has good food, while on place St-André, *Le Bagatel* and *Le Perroquet* are particularly popular. If you're looking for a local bohemian hangout, try the *Café des Arts* over the bridge at 36 rue St-Laurent or *Le Cybernet Café* at 3 rue Bayard, which despite its name has no Internet access, while on place Claveyson you could also drop into *Styx*, an atmospheric little cocktail bar in a nineteenth-century wine cellar. The popular **gay** establishment, *Rutli*, is west of the old town at 9 rue Étienne Marcel (daily 6pm–1am). Grenoble's student population keeps the **nightlife** hopping, with clubs like *L'Arkange*, 50 rue St-Laurent (Thurs–Sat 10pm–5am; closed

Food in the Alps

Alpine cuisine overall is heavy, its obvious intent being to line the stomach in cold weather, while the drink is light and often disappointing. One of the best regional items is the rock-hard cured **sausage**, or *saucisson*, which is exported from here to butcher shops all over the country, and can be found in large quantities in the weekly morning markets held in every town. At restaurants in the **Savoie** and **Haute Savoie** *départements* serve fish from the local lakes, as well as lots of cheese, from the familiar **fondue** to the lesser-known **raclette** and **tartiflette**, both cheese-based dishes with ham and potatoes. As early as lunch you'll start to see the ever-present *pastis*, and the regional rosé, in addition to red wine that is so magenta that it resembles rosé. These wines are light and fruity, and most are without much complexity, but Belgian beer is plentiful, as are reds from the Côtes du Rhône. You may not see many people drinking the **génépy**, a local mountain liqueur, but you may be able to taste it as a sauce in your dessert or as a *parfum* in a local ice cream. In Savoie the main cheeses are **Roblochon** (for the *tartiflette*), **Emmental**, **Chèvre** (often in a form that's good for melting), **Comte** and **Beaufort**—in the fromagerie make sure to ask for the Beaufort d'Été, which is more flavourful since it's made when the cows have better access to grass and flowers.

In the **Haute Alpes** near Briançon, food takes a more Provençal turn - expect desserts to be accompanied by honey, and *saucisson* to be surrounded by or filled with flavourful herbs. For more interesting and creative food head to **Grenoble**, where chefs are more likely to take the local ingredients and turn them into something new.

Sept), and *Le Vertigo*, 18 Grande-Rue (Wed–Sat 10.30pm–5.30am), among the liveliest venues. *Dotty Night*, 56 rte de Lyon (daily except Mon 11pm–5.30am), caters for a slightly older crowd.

Restaurants

À la Table Ronde 7 place St-André ⓣ04.76.44.51.41. While not famous for its food – local fare which never quite rises above average quality – this is an atmospheric place, notable for being the second oldest restaurant in France (1739), numbering among its clients Rousseau and Léon Blum. Menus from €11 lunch and €23 evening.

Le Bistrot Lyonnais 168 cours Berriat ⓣ04.76.21.95.33. It's worth the walk behind the train station to try the food from this charming restaurant's truffle-infused menu. Menus from €17 for lunch, €21 dinner. Closed Sat & Sun and three weeks in Aug.

Le Jardin de Margaux 10 rue de Pont Carpin ⓣ04.76.54.83.34. Located on the far side of Parc Mistral, you'll need to take a cab, but once you arrive this understated gastronomic restaurant welcomes you with inexpensive and imaginative fare. Menus from €16. Closed Mon, Wed, Sat lunch & Sun eve.

Le Mal Assis 9 rue Bayard ⓣ04.76.54.75.93. A small and elegant traditional family-run restaurant, serving dishes with a Provençal flavour and an excellent wine *carte*. Menus from €23. Closed Sun & Mon and mid-July to Aug.

La Mandragore 11 rue Marx-Dormoy ⓣ04.76.96.18.95. Probably one of the best organic, vegetarian restaurants in the country, serving extraordinarily creative and tasty green cuisine. The menu changes daily, and even meat-eaters will leave satisfied. Vegan meals can be supplied upon request. Lunch €11.50, dinner menus from €18. Near the St Bruno stop (one stop west of the train station on tram lines A or B). Closed Sat eve, Sun, Mon & Aug.

Pointe à Pitre 2 rue Marius-Gontard ⓣ04.76.47.26.10. Extremely friendly restaurant serving up specialities from the French Caribbean at reasonable prices, though it's à la carte only, with *plats* from €10. Daily 7pm–1am, lunch upon request.

La Tête à l'Envers 10 rue Chenoise ⓣ04.76.51.13.42. It's a one-man show in this tiny restaurant. What it lacks in size it makes up in sheer creativity – a new menu every other day includes a plate of four appetizers (€9), entrees served with eight different vegetables (from €11), and a plate of six desserts (€8) – guess the flavourings of five of the six and win a free coffee or *digestif*. Closed Sun, Mon & Aug.

Le Tonneau de Diogène place Notre-Dame ⓣ04.16.42.38.40. A cheap standby, with uninspiring steak-*frites*-type cuisine, but incredibly popular with tourists and a good place to meet fellow travellers. Meals from under €7. Closed Sun eve & Mon lunch.

Le Valgaudemar 2 rue St-Hugues ⓣ04.76.51.38.85. Referred to affectionately by students as Le Valgo, this cosy, rustic-styled haven in the heart of Grenoble serves traditional specialities of the Hautes-Alpes. Lunch from €11 and dinner from €17. Closed Sun & Mon, Tues & Wed eve, and Aug.

Listings

Bike rental Cycle des Arts 14, rue des Arts ⓣ04.76.47.18.83; Veloparc Gare, 1 place de la Gare ⓣ04.76.85.08.94; Metrovelo Gare, 1 place de la Gare ⓣ08.20.22.38.38.

Bookshop Arthand, 23 Grande-Rue, sells some English-language books.

Car rental ADA, 1 place de la Gare ⓣ04.76.43.00.36; Avis, gare SNCF ⓣ04.76.47.11.33 and 22 cours Jean-Jaurès ⓣ04.76.86.62.50; Budget, 30 rue Emile Gueymard ⓣ04.76.46.66.90; Europcar, gare SNCF ⓣ04.76.86.27.81; Hertz, gare SNCF ⓣ04.76.86.55.80; Self Car, 24 rue Émile Gueymard ⓣ04.76.50.96.96.

Internet Neptune, 2 rue de la Paix (Mon–Sat 9am–10pm, Sun 1–8pm); Pl@net On-Line, 1 place Vaucanson (ⓣ04.76.47.44.74; Mon–Sat 10am–1am, Sun 1–10pm).

Medical emergencies Centre Hospitalier Universitaire ⓣ04.76.76.75.75; ambulance Alp'Azur ⓣ04.76.21.11.11.

Pharmacy Pharmacie Bethalet, 8 place Victor-Hugo; Pharmacie du Château d'Eau, 6 place Grenette; late-night and holidays call ⓣ04.76.63.42.55 for the "pharmacie de garde".

Police 36 bd Maréchal Leclerc ⓣ04.76.60.40.40.

Taxi ⓣ04.76.54.42.54.

The Vercors and Chartreuse massifs

The **Vercors Massif** and **Chartreuse Massif** are very close to Grenoble, particularly the Vercors, which stretches out to the southwest of the city, parallel to the River Drac on the west side of the N75. Chartreuse is north of the city, running up the west bank of the River Isère towards Chambéry.

Both ranges are relatively gentle, making them ideal practice for less experienced walkers. The Grenoble **Bureau Info Montagne** office (see p.988) publishes route descriptions. Neither massif is heavily populated, and the lack of

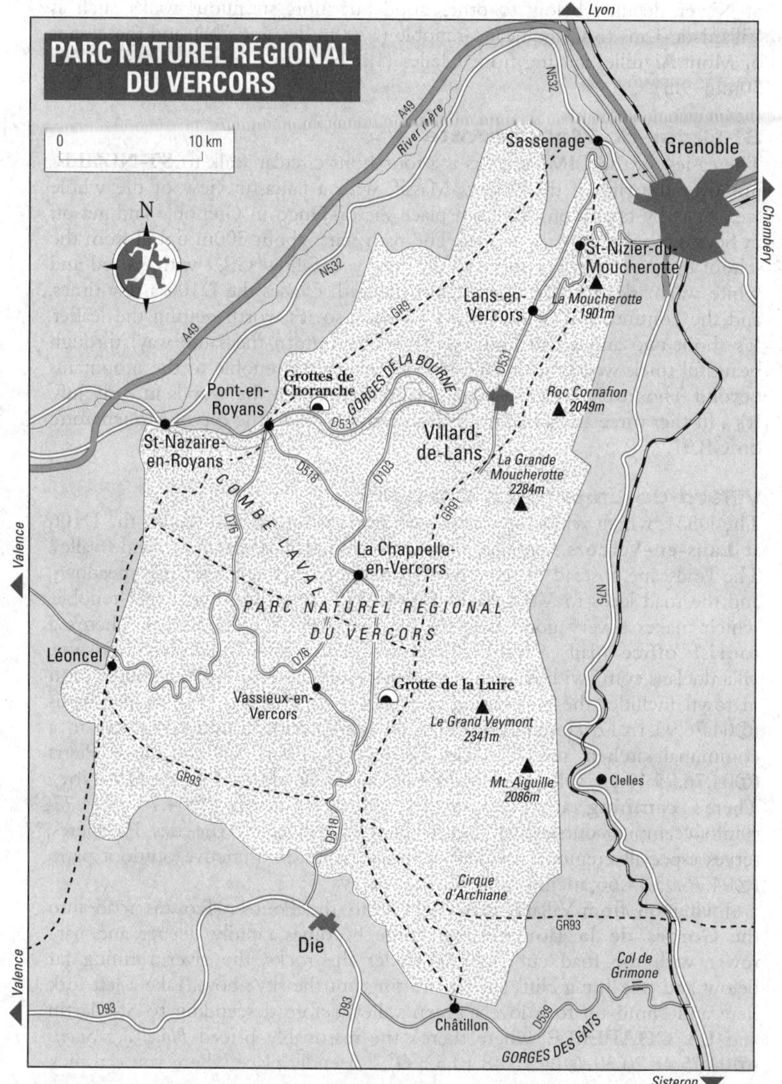

industry makes them authentic and unspoilt Alpine destinations, popular with all types of energetic outdoor enthusiasts from cavers to mountain bikers.

The Vercors Massif

The **Vercors Massif**, a limestone plateau featuring ridges, valleys and a variety of wildlife, is very pretty and undeveloped, but its proximity to Grenoble means that prices are slightly higher and there is sometimes congestion on the little mountain roads. The 5100 **bus** leaves from the *gare routière* in Grenoble for the park's larger towns several times a day. BIM leaflets detail a number of walks of varying difficulty around the area from the simplest and most accessible to St-Nizier, detailed below, to other good but more strenuous walks, such as Villard-de-Lans to Claix, near Grenoble (1700m descent; 7hr), and the circuit of Mont Aiguille, starting from Clelles (1hr by train south of Grenoble; 6hr 30min–9hr).

St-Nizier-du-Moucherotte

The easiest of the CIMES walks is a four-hour circular walk to **ST-NIZIER**, just over the rim of the Vercors Massif, with a fantastic view of the whole area. Start by taking bus #5 from place Victor-Hugo in Grenoble and get off in Seyssinet village by the school. The path starts about 200m uphill from the school on the right. For most of the way you follow GR9 with its red and white waymarks. It's not difficult, but the path crosses the D106 a few times, and the continuation is not always obvious, so it's worth getting the leaflet. It's about two and a half hours to St-Nizier (return the same way) through beautiful thick woods with long views back over Grenoble to the mountains beyond. The lovely purplish martagon lily blooms in the woods in early July. It's a further three and a half hours (there and back) to the top of Moucherotte on GR91.

Villard-de-Lans to La Chapelle

The D531, which winds up to the park from Sassenage and crosses the D106 at **Lans-en-Vercors**, emerges onto a plateau that resembles a wide valley. The landscape, instead of seeming mountainous, is filled with hay meadows, and the road leads to **VILLARD-DE-LANS**, 24km southwest of Grenoble, which makes a very good base for exploring the Vercors further. There's a **tourist office** (daily 9am–12.30pm & 2–7pm; Ⓣ04.76.95.10.38, Ⓦwww.villarddelans.com) with information about walks and skiing. Accommodation in town includes the welcoming and neat *Villa Primerose*, 147 av des Bains (Ⓣ04.76.95.13.17, closed Nov; ❷), with self-catering facilities available in a communal kitchen; and the smart *Hôtel Le Pré Fleuri*, 509 rue Albert Piétri (Ⓣ04.76.95.10.96, Ⓔle-pre-fleuri@wanadoo.fr; ❹; closed May & Oct–Nov). There's **camping** at *L'Oursiere*, just north of town (Ⓣ04.76.95.14.77, Ⓔinfo@camping-oursiere.fr). For food, *Côte Jardin*, 80 rue des Pionneres, serves especially regional specialities inside or on an attractive outdoor patio (Ⓣ04.76.95.14.66; menus from €15).

Moving on from Villard, turn right onto the Pont-en-Royans road into the **Gorges de la Bourne**. The gorge becomes rapidly deeper and narrower with the road cut right in under the rocks, the river running far below, and tree-hung cliffs almost shutting out the sky above. Take a left fork here and climb up to a lovely green valley before descending to St-Martin and **LA CHAPELLE**, where there's the reasonably priced *Hôtel des Sports* (Ⓣ04.75.48.20.39, Ⓕ04.75.48.10.52; ❷), a friendly place where you can pick up tips on local cycling routes. From La Chapelle the road climbs again to the wide dry plateau of Vassieux, bordered to the east by a rocky ridge rising from thick pine forest and to the west by low hills covered with scrubby vegetation. Underground is interesting too: stay on the road to Pont-en-Royans and you come to the **Grottes de Choranche**, renowned for the beauty of its gigantic stalactites. Part of the complex, the Grotte de Coufin, can be visited by guided tour (April & Oct every 30min, 10am–noon & 1.30–6pm; May, June & Sept every 30min, 9.30am–noon & 1.30–6pm; July & Aug every 20min, 9.30am–6.30pm; Nov–March hourly 10.30am–4.30pm; €7.70).

Vassieux-en-Vercors

It was around the village of **VASSIEUX-EN-VERCORS**, 10km south of La Chapelle, that the fighters of the Vercors maquis suffered a bloody and bitter defeat at the hands of the SS in July 1944. During 1942–43 they had been gradually turning the Vercors into a Resistance stronghold, to the annoyance of the Germans and the French militia. The Germans finally, in June 1944, decided to wipe them out. They encircled and attacked the maquisards with vastly superior forces and parachuted an SS division into Vassieux. The French appealed in vain for Allied support and were very bitter about the lack of response. The Germans took vicious reprisals and, despite their attempts to disperse into the woods, 700 maquisards and civilians were killed and several villages razed. The Germans' most ferocious act was to murder the wounded, along with their nurses and doctors, in the **Grotte de la Luire**, a cave off the La Chapelle–Col de Rousset road (April–Oct).

Vassieux itself, a dull little village now rebuilt, has a memorial cemetery and small museum, the **Memorial de la Résistance du Vercors** (April–Sept daily 10am–6pm; Oct–March 10am–5pm; €4.50), with documents, photos and other memorabilia to do with the maquis and the battle. In the field outside are the remains of two gliders used by the German paratroops. Also near the town, the **Musée de la Préhistoire** (same times and price) is built over the site of a 4000-year-old flint mine and axe works, and contains various tools and relics that have been found there. If you want to stay, try the comfortable *Auberge du Tétras Lyre* in rue Abbé Gagnol (Ⓣ04.75.48.28.04, Ⓦwww.tetraslyre.com; ❷; restaurant with menus from €14.50).

Die to Grimone

From Vassieux, the **Col de Rousset** road winds south through 8km of woods of pine and fir before taking the final steep twisting descent of 10km to **DIE**, with terrific views of the white crags and pinnacles of the southeast end of the massif. Although it's an attractive little place, Die is worth no more than a brief stop to sample the local *crémant* (sparkling white wine), Clairette de Die, which can be tasted and bought in the caves surrounding the town. One good place to taste is the **Jaillance** cave on avenue de la Clairette, which offers a free tour and tasting (Ⓣ04.75.22.30.15; daily 9am–12.30pm & 2–6.30pm, July–Aug 9am–7pm). There's a **tourist office** in place St-Pierre (May–Sept daily 9am–12.30pm & 2.30–7pm; Oct–April Mon–Sat 9am–noon & 2–6pm, Sun 9.30am–12.30pm; Ⓣ04.75.22.03.03, Ⓦwww.diois-tourisme.com). If you plan to **stay** the night here, there are five **campsites**, the cheapest being the *Camping de Justin* in the quartier du Pont Rompu (Ⓣ & Ⓕ04.75.22.14.77; closed Oct–Dec) on the edge of town. For **hotels** try the modest but more comfortable *Hôtel St-Dominigue*, 44 rue Camille Buffardel (Ⓣ04.75.22.03.08, Ⓕ04.75.22.24.48; ❸). *La Dolce Vita* restaurant on place de l'Horloge serves menus from €10.

Six kilometres south along the River Drôme at the Pont de Quart the road forks left for **CHÂTILLON**, 6km away – not a bad place to take a break on a hot day, as you can swim in the river below the bridge. Châtillon village is lovely, lying in a narrowing valley bottom surrounded by apple and peach orchards, vineyards, walnut trees and fields of lavender; it also has a couple of good hotels and three campsites.

From here, the road enters the sunless trench of the Gorges des Gats, winding up between sheer rock walls to **GRIMONE**, a mountain hamlet on the flanks of a grassy valley with fir trees darkening the higher slopes. The Col de Grimone is visible above the village. A path cuts across the valley directly to the col from where it's about 7km down to the main Grenoble road, a tarmac trudge alleviated by the view eastwards to the mountains.

The Chartreuse Massif and Grande Chartreuse monastery

The Chartreuse Massif, designated in 1995 as the **Parc Naturel Régional de Chartreuse** (Ⓦwww.parc-chartreuse.net), stretches north from Grenoble towards Chambéry and, like Vercors, is not easy to visit without your own vehicle. The landscape, however, is spectacular and very different to that of the Vercors: precipitous limestone peaks, mountain pastures and thick forest.

The main local landmark is the **Grande Chartreuse monastery**, situated up the narrow Gorges des Guiers Morts, southeast of St-Laurent-du-Pont, and some 35km from Grenoble, one of nineteen Carthusian monasteries still functioning worldwide. The Carthusian Order, dating from the eleventh century, was the last great monastic reform movement, and was founded in answer to the degeneration of the Cistercian Order. Practising a strictly hermit-like existence, its members live in cells and meet only for Mass and a weekly communal meal, eaten in silence. Since 1605, however, the Carthusians have been better known as the producers of **Chartreuses** – powerfully alcoholic herbal elixirs, ranging from the better-known green and yellow variants to a number of gentler fruit liqueurs. The monastery is not open to the public, but near the village of **ST-PIERRE-DE-CHARTREUSE**, 5km back on the Grenoble road, you can visit the **Musée de la Grande Chartreuse**, formerly La Correrie monastery, which illustrates the life of the Carthusian Order (daily: April & Oct 10am–noon & 2–6pm; May–June & Sept 9.30am–noon & 2–6.30pm; July–Aug 9.30am–6.30pm; €3). St-Pierre is also known for its annual festival devoted to Belgian-born singer Jacques Brel, which takes place in July; ask at the **tourist office** on Place de la Mairie (Ⓣ04.76.88.62.08, Ⓦwww.st-pierre-chartreuse.com) for more details. If you're looking for a hotel, St-Pierre has several options, the best of which is *Beau Site* (Ⓣ04.76.88.61.34, Ⓦwww.hotelbeausite.com; ❹; closed mid-Oct to Dec).

For those less interested in religious austerity and more interested in that mysterious green liqueur, a visit to **VOIRON**, 30km west of the park and on the train line from Grenoble to Lyon, is in order. The **Caves de la Chartreuse** on boulevard Edgar-Kofler (April–June & Sept–Oct daily 9–11.30am & 2–6.30pm; July & Aug daily 9am–6.30pm; Nov–March Mon–Fri 9–11.30am & 2–5.30pm; free), are where the "elixir of life" is now bottled. The tour is good fun – it takes visitors through the world's largest liqueur cellars and includes a rather corny 3-D film on the history of the monastery, and a tasting of one of the monks' alcoholic beverages. The town's **tourist office** is at 58 cours Becquart-Castelbon (Mon–Sat 9am–noon & 2–6pm; Ⓣ04.76.05.00.38. There's not much else to see in Voiron, which is best known as the home of the Rossignol ski factory, but if you're looking for a **hotel**, try the small but comfortable *La Chaumière* (Ⓣ04.76.05.16.24, Ⓕ04.76.05.13.27; ❸).

Chambéry and around

CHAMBÉRY, 55km north of Grenoble, lies just south of the Lac du Bourget in a valley separating the Chartreuse Massif from the Bauges mountains, historically an important strategic position commanding the entrance to the big Alpine valleys leading to the passes into Italy. The town grew up around the château built by Count Thomas of Savoie in 1232, and became the Savoyard capital, enjoying a Golden Age in the fourteenth and fifteenth centuries. Although superseded as capital by Turin in 1562, it remained an important commercial and cultural centre. The philosopher Rousseau spent some of his happiest years in the town during the 1730s, proclaiming: "If there is in the world a little town where one tastes the sweetness of life in pleasant and certain commerce, it is Chambéry." Only incorporated into France in 1860, modern Chambéry is a bustling provincial town with a wealth of grand Italianate architecture and a strong sense of its regional identity – look out for the "Savoie Libre" bumper stickers throughout this and the "Haute Savoie" *départements*. The town also makes a good starting point for a tour of the Parc des Bauges, a sparsely populated and little visited area of varied Alpine landscapes and abundant wildlife, spreading north and east of the town. Around 13km north of Chambéry, meanwhile, is the spa resort **Aix-les-Bains**, with its famous thermal baths and the stunning **Lac du Bourget**.

The Town

Halfway down the broad, leafy boulevard de la Colonne is Chambéry's most famous monument, the splendidly extravagant and somewhat off-scale **Fontaine des Éléphants**, erected in homage to the Comte de Boigne, a native son who amassed a fortune working as a mercenary in India in the eighteenth century, and who used much of his vast wealth to fund major urban developments in his home town. Just south of this on square de Lannoy-de-Bissy is the **Musée Savoisien** (Mon & Wed–Sun 10am–noon & 2–6pm; €3.10), which chronicles the history of Savoie from the Bronze Age onwards. On the first floor are some very lovely paintings, including a finely executed fifteenth-century work showing the Annunciation, and painted wooden statues from various churches in the region; on the second floor, there's a collection of tools, carts, hay-sledges, and some fine furniture from a house in Bessans, with a fascinating kitchen range made of wood and lined with lauzes (slabs of schist). Of most interest, though, are the extremely rare thirteenth-century wall paintings from Cruet, housed in their own temperature-regulated room, which, unusually, depict secular scenes; in this case, frenzied battles and images of elegant court life.

Next to the museum, in the enclosed little place Métropole, the **cathedral** has a handsome, though much restored, Flamboyant facade. The inside is painted in elaborate nineteenth-century trompe l'oeil, imitating the twisting shapes and whorls of the high Gothic style. The cathedral's treasury (Sat only 3–6pm, or ask and someone may open it for you; free) is worth a look for its twelfth-century ivory diptych and thirteenth-century *pyxis* (a case for holding the Eucharist).

A passage leads from the square to **rue de la Croix-d'Or**, with numerous restaurants and the Italianate **Théâtre Charles Dullin**, named after the avant-garde director who was born in the region. To the right, there's the long, rectangular **place St-Léger**, with a fountain and more cafés, where street musicians perform on summer evenings. Rousseau and Mme de Warens lived here in 1735, and also had a country cottage, **Les Charmettes**, just 2km south of the town on the rustic chemin des Charmettes. It's now the **Musée Jean-Jacques Rousseau** (April–Sept daily except Tues 10am–noon & 2–6pm; Oct–March daily except Tues 10am–noon & 2–4.30pm; €3.10), furnished in the style of the famous philosopher's day, with a lovely garden and apple orchard alongside.

Towards the northern end of the square, the town's smartest street, **rue de Boigne**, to the right, leads back to the Fontaine des Éléphants, but if you turn left the road leads to the **Château des Ducs de Savoie** (interiors & Sainte-Chapelle only accessible by guided tours, which begin from the office across the street: May, June & Sept daily 2.30pm; July & Aug Mon–Sat 10.30am, 2.30, 3.30 & 4.30pm, afternoons only on Sun; €4). A massive and imposing structure, it was once the main home of the dukes of Savoie, and is now occupied by the préfecture. Next to the château is the elegant **Sainte-Chapelle**, whose lancet windows and star vaulting are in the same late Gothic style as the cathedral. It was built to house the Holy Shroud, that much-venerated and today highly controversial piece of linen reputed to bear the image of the dead Christ. It was badly damaged in a sixteenth-century fire, and when the dukes later transferred their capital to Turin, the Shroud went with them, but a full-size nineteenth-century photograph remains on display here. The chapel contains the biggest carillon in Europe, a seventy-bell monster that you can hear in action on Saturdays at 10.30am and 5.30pm.

A short walk north from the exit of the castle along promenade Veyrat is the **Musée des Beaux Arts** (Mon & Wed–Sat 10am–noon & 2–6pm; €3.10), which is largely devoted to works by lesser-known sixteenth- to eighteenth-century Italian artists, though the pride of the collection is Uccello's *Portrait of a Young Man*, and there are also a few minor Titian cartoons. Meanwhile, for weekend visitors the church of **St-Pierre-de-Lemenc**, off boulevard de Lemenc, is worth the twenty-minute walk north of the centre, for its small but intriguing **crypt**, housing a Romanesque baptistry, rare fourteenth-century wall paintings and a fifteenth-century stone sculpture group. Upstairs lies the tomb of St-Concord, a twelfth-century Archbishop of Armagh, who died here en route to Rome (Sat 5–6pm, Sun 9.30–10.30am).

Practicalities

The **gare SNCF** is on rue Sommeiller, 500m north of the old town, with the **gare routière** just outside in place de la Gare. Five minutes' walk away at no. 24 boulevard de la Colonne, where all the **city buses** stop, is the **tourist office** (Mon–Sat 9am–noon & 1.30–6pm, Sun 9.30am–noon; July & Aug open until 7pm Mon–Sat and untill 12.30pm Sun; Ⓣ04.79.33.42.47, Ⓦwww.chambery-tourisme.com). If you're planning on exploring the Vanoise, the Maison du Parc at 135 rue Docteur-Juilland (Ⓣ04.79.62.30.54) to the west of town can help with maps and information.

There's plenty of inexpensive **accommodation** scattered about the centre of Chambéry. One budget option is *Le Savoyard*, 35 place Monge (Ⓣ04.79.33.36.55, Ⓔsavoyard@noos.fr; ❸), conveniently located southeast of the cathedral, while for larger, more creatively decorated and central rooms try *Hôtel des Princes* at 4 rue de Boigne (Ⓣ04.79.33.45.36, Ⓕ04.79.70.31.47; ❹).

But for rural peace and a lovely view, head for *Hôtel aux Pervenches*, 600 chemin des Charmettes (Ⓣ04.79.33.34.26, Ⓦwww.pervenches.net; ❻), with a good restaurant serving menus from €14.50, in the village of **LES CHARMETTES**, Rousseau's summertime home, 2km south of the centre. The nearest **campsite** is *Le Nivolet* (Ⓣ04.79.85.47.79) at **BASSENS**, reached on bus #4, direction "St. Albans", from the square in front of the tourist office.

Good **food** at decent prices is not hard to come by. Mid-range Savoyard restaurants abound – many specializing in lake and river fish – the best of these being *La Chaumière*, 14–16 rue Denfert-Rochereau, with menus starting at €12.50 (Ⓣ04.79.33.16.26; closed Sun unless you reserve), or try *Le Savoyard* in the hotel of the same name. For a lighter, vegetarian option *Le Bar @ Thym*, 22 Place Monge, serves new dishes daily in the afternoon and early evening (Ⓣ04.79.70.96.40, closed Sun & Mon). If you fancy a splurge, however, truly exceptional cuisine can be found at *Le St-Real*, in a converted seventeenth-century church at 86 rue St-Real (Ⓣ04.79.70.09.33; closed Sun), one of the best restaurants in the *département*, but pricey at €30–73.20. *Le Tonneau* at 2 rue St-Antoine (Ⓣ04.79.33.78.26) is a good alternative, with a similar cuisine, but at half the price.

The Parc des Bauges

Created in 1995, the **Parc des Bauges** (Ⓦwww.parcdesbauges.com) encompasses a vast and largely unspoiled area of rolling green hills, mountains, forests, open grasslands and valleys, sparsely dotted with tiny villages, and stretching from Chambéry in the west to Albertville in the east and Lac d'Annecy in the north. It makes for pleasant and, for the most part, undemanding walking country, though otherwise you'll need your own transport to get about.

The **Maison du Parc** (Ⓣ04.79.54.86.40) is located in the otherwise unremarkable village of **Le Châtelard**, just below Mt Julioz (1675m) in the centre of the Bauges Massif – take the D912 north from Chambéry to Lescheraines, then follow the D911 to the southeast after **Le Pont**. They can advise on walking and cycling routes, and also help arrange accommodation in the local area. Just beyond Le Châtelard is the tiny, peaceful village of **École**, with the **Maison Faune-Flore** (July to mid-Sept daily 10am–7pm; mid-Sept to June Sat & Sun 1.30–7pm & by reservation; Ⓣ04.79.52.22.56; €2), which has a small display on the local wildlife, mainly aimed at children, and a good stock of books and brochures. Heading further south, you come to **St-Pierre-d'Albigny**, which, with around 3000 inhabitants, is one of the larger villages in the park. The main attraction here is the imposing **Château de Miolans** (April Sat & Sun 1.30–7pm; May–June & Sept daily except Sun 10am–noon & 1.30–7pm; Jul–Aug daily 10am–7pm; €5.50), a grim eleventh-century fortress which looms over the village on the hill above. It was used as a notorious prison in the eighteenth-century, briefly welcoming the Marquis de Sade as an inmate, and the damp and dingy dungeons are a stark contrast to the breathtaking views over the lush vineyards in the valley below. If you want to **stay**, there's a small **hotel** in the village, the *Central* (Ⓣ04.79.28.50.05; ❸). Another option closer to Chambéry in the charming medieval village of **Montmélian** you'll find the friendly *George* (Ⓣ04.79.84.05.87, Ⓦwww.hotelgeorge.fr; ❷).

Aix-Les-Bains

AIX-LES-BAINS train station is on the western edge of town, just off boulevard Président Wilson, from where it's a brief stroll up avenue Charles de

Gaulle into the centre. The town has been one of France's premier spa resorts since the eighteenth century, with a wealth of elegant architecture, recalling Aix-les-Bains' Belle Époque heyday, when high society from across Europe dropped by to relax and take the waters – Queen Victoria, calling herself the "Countess of Balmoral", made several incognito visits, and her **statue** remains as a reminder on the left side of avenue Charles de Gaulle as you walk up the hill. These days, Aix-les-Bains is a sedate and genteel place, populated mostly by French pensioners, who descend on the town en masse throughout the year for state-funded thermal treatments. Unless you're after a mud-bath or a glass of sulphurous water, the main draw today is the magnificent **Lac du Bourget**, 3km from the centre of town and the largest natural lake in France. Rising above Aix is Mt Revard (1550m), a vast plateau, made up of gentle meadows and forests, offering a range of trails for ramblers and cyclists – it is also one of France's finest cross-country skiing areas.

The town centres on place **Maurice Mollard**, where you'll find the monstrous Art-Deco *Thermes Nationaux*, accessible only with a French doctor's note. Enter to the right of the front doors for the **tourist office** (daily: June–Aug 9am–6.30pm; Sept–May 9am–noon & 2–6pm; Ⓣ04.79.88.68.00, Ⓦwww.aixlesbains.com). Buses leave every 7 minutes for the brand new **Thermes Chevalley**, which are open to everyone, for a fee (Mon, Fri & Sat 2–8pm, Tues–Thurs 2–6pm, Sun 10am–8pm, Ⓦwww.thermaix.com, €15 per day). Just across from the baths is the *mairie*, which is built right into a Roman temple. In front is another grand Roman remnant, the **Arc de Campanus**, a rare funerary monument from the first century BC.

Also in the town centre, you'll find the petite **Parc Thermal**, laid out with flowerbeds, ancient trees and a fountain, as well as a 300-seat outdoor theatre, which hosts a variety of events during the summer months. The compact warren of pedestrianized streets that makes up the old town lies on the far side of the *mairie*, while north of place Mollard at 10 bd Côtes is the charming **Musée Faure** (Mon & Wed–Sun 10am–noon & 1.30–6pm; €4), an elegant house where a small but impressive collection of nineteenth-century art is on display, including a room of Rodins, paintings from the best known Impressionists, and some lovely Degas pastels.

Around 3km west of the town centre, along avenue du Grand Port, lies the **Lac du Bourget**, a place of great beauty, connected to the River Rhône by the Canal de Savières, a protected wildlife reserve and home to the now scarce European beaver. "Nowhere could one find such perfect concord between water, mountains, earth and sky", enthused the French writer Balzac, and it's clear what attracted him, and so many other poets and artists to this place. The Côte Sauvage rises precipitously above the sparkling blue water on the lake's west bank, dominated at its southern end by the looming presence of the Dent du Chat (1390m), while in the nearby town of St-Pierre de Curtille is the picturesque **Abbaye d'Hautecombe**, the final resting place of many members of the royal house of Savoie, including the last King and Queen of Italy (accessible by boat or off the D18 on the opposite side of the lake; open year round for free audio-guide tours daily 10–11.15am & 2–5pm). There are daily sightseeing cruises on the lake between March and November (€10.50–17) as well as more expensive lunch, dinner and evening cruises. For details and tickets, contact the Bateaux du Lac du Bourget office at the port (Ⓣ04.79.88.92.09, Ⓦwww.gwel.com).

Aix-les-Bains has almost a hundred **hotels**, though as they're bustling year round with pensioners advance bookings are advisable. For a taste of real *fin-de-siècle* elegance, try the *Astoria*, 7 place des Thermes (ⓣ04.79.35.12.28, ⓦwww.hotelastoria.fr; ❺), while a cheaper but equally comfortable option is the more modern *Agora*, rue de Chambéry (ⓣ04.79.34.20.20, ⓦwww.hotel-agora.com; ❹). The basic *Beaulieu*, 29 av Charles de Gaulle (ⓣ04.79.35.01.02, ⓕ04.79.34.04.82; ❷), is handy for the train station, while if you want to be nearer the lake, the friendly *Davat*, 21 chemin des Bateliers (ⓣ04.79.63.40.40, ⓦwww.davat.fr; ❸), is a good choice. There are four **campsites** near the lake, the best of which is *International du Sierroz* on boulevard Barrier (ⓔcampingsierroz@aixlesbains.com). There's an equally broad range of **restaurants**; one of the best is *Le Manoir*, 37 rue Georges 1er (ⓣ04.79.61.44.00), with excellent gourmet menus starting at around €25. The restaurants that line rue des Bains are more central and less expensive; try the pizzeria *Le Passe* at 6 rue du Dauphin, just off rue des Bains, with menus starting at €11. One of the most relaxing places to enjoy a coffee or an apéritif is *La Rotonde*, a very pleasant outdoor café in the Parc Thermal. Several **Internet** cafes line rue de Chambéry, the road that descends diagonally from the park.

Annecy and around

At the edge of the turquoise Lac d'Annecy, bounded to the east by the turreted peaks of La Tournette and to the west by the long wooded ridge of Le Semnoz, **ANNECY** is one of the most beautiful and popular resort towns of the French Alps, though the tourist traffic can get a bit wearing in high season. Historically, it enjoyed a brief flurry of importance in the early sixteenth century, when Geneva opted for the Reformation and the fugitive Catholic bishop decamped here with a train of ecclesiastics and a prosperous, cultivated elite. The main attractions, however, are not historic, but scenic; surrounded by picturesque mountains Annecy resembles a fairy-tale city, and is replete with a castle on a hill and an island prison.

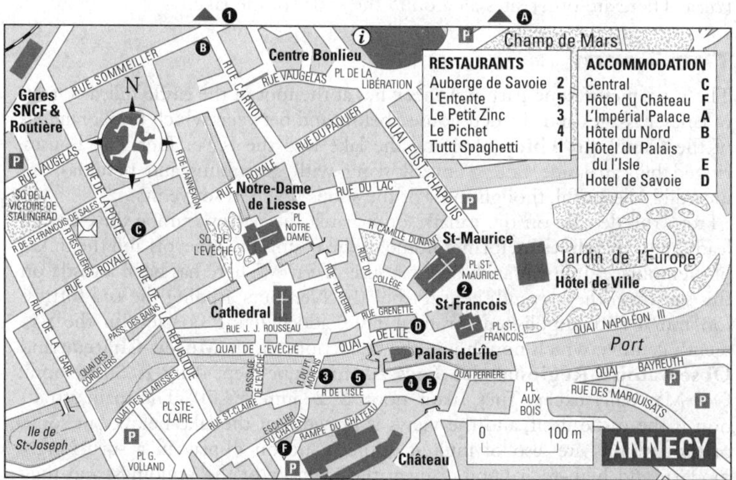

Arrival, information and accommodation

The **gare SNCF** and **gare routière** complex is northwest of the centre, five minutes' walk north of the rue Royale. The road's continuation is the arcaded **rue Pâquier**, which contains the modern shopping precinct of **Centre Bonlieu**, housing the **tourist office** (April to mid-June & last two weeks Sept Mon–Sat 9am–12.30pm & 1.45–6pm, Sun 10am–3pm; mid-June to mid-Sept Mon–Sat 9am–6.30pm, Sun 9am–noon & 1.45–6.30pm; Oct–March Mon–Sat 9am–12.30pm & 1.45–6pm; ⓣ04.50.45.00.33, ⓦwww.annecytourisme.com). There are a number of **Internet cafés** in Annecy – in the old town try *L'Emailerie*, Faubourg des Annonciades (June–Aug daily 10am–8pm; Sept–May Mon–Sat 10.30am–12.30pm & 2.30–7.30pm;). There's **bike rental** from Roul' ma poule at 2 rue des Marquisats (ⓣ04.50.27.86.83).

Annecy has a number of good **hotels**. Reserve well in advance in high season, or you can chance it on one of the quirky no-star hotels on the far side of the train station. One of the cheapest in the centre of town is the small and serviceable *Central*, 6 rue Royale (ⓣ04.50.45.05.37, ⓔStefanPicollet@hotmail.com, ❷), while more comfortable options include the *Hôtel du Nord*, near the train station at 24 rue Sommeiller (ⓣ04.50.45.08.78, ⓦwww.annecy-hotel-du-nord.com; ❸), and the *Hotel de Savoie*, 1 place St-François (ⓣ04.50.45.15.45, ⓦwww.hoteldesavoie.fr; ❹), on the canal in the pedestrian area. Just uphill from the madding crowds is the homely *Hôtel du Château*, 16 rampe du Château (ⓣ04.50.45.27.66, ⓕ04.50.52.75.26; ❸), with a terrace overlooking the town. Upmarket options include the charming *Hôtel du Palais de l'Isle*, 13 rue Perrière, in the heart of the medieval town (ⓣ04.50.45.86.87, ⓦwww.hoteldupalaisdelisle.com; ❺), and the luxurious four-star *L'Impérial Palace*, 32 av d'Albigny (ⓣ04.50.09.30.00, ⓦwww.hotel-imperial-palace.com; ❾), in a beautiful mansion on the northeast bank of the lake beside the casino.

There's a modern **hostel** a short distance from the centre, just uphill past the Centre Hospitalier at 4 rte du Semnoz, overlooking the lake (ⓣ04.50.45.33.19, ⓔannecy@fuaj.org; closed Dec to mid-Jan); in the summer take summer bus marked "ligne d'été", or follow the signs to Semnoz. The municipal **campsite**, *Le Belvedere* (ⓣ04.50.45.48.30), is situated off boulevard de la Corniche – turn right up the lane opposite chemin du Tillier; it's on the left past the *Hôtel Belvédère*. There are other sites all around the shore of the lake.

The Town

The most picturesque part of Annecy lies at the foot of the castle hill, a warren of lanes, passages and arcaded houses, below and between which flow branches of the **Canal du Thiou**, draining the lake into the River Fier. The houses, ringed by canal-side railings overflowing with geraniums and petunias, are incredibly beautiful, though most of the shops now sell souvenirs.

From rue de l'Île on the canal's south bank, the narrow rampe du Château leads up to the **château**, former home of the counts of Genevois and the dukes of Nemours, a junior branch of the house of Savoy. There has been a castle on this site from the eleventh century but the Nemours, finding the old fortress too rough and unpolished for their taste, added living quarters in the sixteenth century, which now house the collections of the **Musée-Château** and **Observatoire Régional des Lacs Alpins** (June–Sept daily 10.30am–6pm; Oct–May daily except Tues 10am–noon & 2–5pm; €4.70). The main attraction is the castle itself, and the views it provides of the lake below, but some of the exhibits are also of interest. Objects are on display in a surprisingly modern and high-tech fashion given the exterior of the buildings, and they range from archeological finds from around the lake, to Savoyard popular art and woodwork, to an aquarium with lake fish and an informative exhibition on the geography of the Alps.

At the base of the château is **rue Ste-Claire**, the main street of the old town, with arcaded shops and houses. At no. 18 is the **Hôtel Favre**, where in 1606 Antoine Favre, an eminent lawyer, and Bishop de Sales founded the literary-intellectual Académie Florimontane "because the Muses thrive in the mountains of Savoie". At the west end of the street is its original medieval gateway. Parallel to rue Ste-Claire, on the far side of the canal, rue J-J. Rousseau passes the seventeenth-century former **bishop's palace** and the unremarkable **cathedral**, where Rousseau once sang as a chorister.

Nearby on the canal you'll find the picture-perfect **Palais de l'Île**, a tiny twelfth-century fort which served in turn as palace, mint, court and prison (the latter as late as World War II), which has changed recently from a history museum to the far more modern **Centre for Urban Interpretation** (June–Sept daily 10.30am–6pm; Oct–May daily except Tues 10am–noon & 2–5pm; €3.10). One room on the ground floor explains the building's history, while the rest are full of French audio-visual presentations on urban environments in the region.

A few steps to the north, the fifteenth-century **church of St-Maurice** conceals some excellent fifteenth- and sixteenth-century religious art. Across the square to the east of the church, the **Hôtel de Ville** backs onto shady public gardens, from where a bridge crosses a canal to the lakeside lawns of the extensive **Champ de Mars**.

From the Hôtel de Ville a stroll south along the lake past the **marina** leads to the free grassy **Plage de Marquisats**, while a slightly longer walk in the other direction around the lake past the casino reaches the **Plage d'Albigny**. In recent years when the lake is warm there have been duck fleas (*puces de canard*), making the lake risky for swimming in very hot weather. Ask around if cases have been noted, and make sure to shower after swimming.

Eating and drinking

Annecy's **restaurants** churn out rather unimaginative fare to feed the tourist crowds. You'll find a string of inexpensive restaurants overlooking the canal along quai Perrière, and rue Ste-Claire, among which *Le Pichet*, 13 rue Perrière (Ⓣ04.50.45.32.41; menus from €13), is dependable. *Le Petit Zinc* (Ⓣ04.50.51.12.93), nearby at 11 rue Pont-Morens, manages best to rise above the surrounding mediocrity, serving hearty Savoyard fare in a warm interior (lunch from €14, dinner from €16 and €26). One of the best venues is the *Auberge de Savoie* (Ⓣ04.50.45.03.05; closed Wed; menus €23–45) on the far side of the canal at place St-François, serving Savoyard specialities. Cheaper options include *L'Entente*, 5 rue de l'Île (Ⓣ04.50.51.03.73; lunch from €8.25, dinner from €14), which offers tasty North African cuisine, and *Tutti Spaghetti*, 84 rue Carnot, that serves a wide choice of pasta dishes from €7.

Rue Ste-Claire, which leads to rue de l'Isle, has some of the town's liveliest **nightlife** in the music-bars *Pub Médiévale* and *Red Zed*. And for a quiet coffee, the bohemian-flavoured *Café Cort*, by the old town gate overlooking place Ste Claire, will fit the bill.

Around Annecy

While Annecy's high-season crowds may be bearable for only a day or two, the town's environs offer a number of agreeable excursions. As well as **boat tours**,

cycling is an enjoyable means of appreciating Lac Annecy. The forty-kilometre road circuit of the lake is a very popular Sunday morning activity among sporty Annéciens and a traffic-free cycle route follows the west shore of the lake. The surrounding hills offer walking and mountain-biking excursions (as well as more specialized pursuits) to suit all. Experienced walkers should enjoy the relatively undemanding ascent of **La Tournette** (2351m) on the eastern side of the lake, while gentler walks and cycle routes are to be found in the forested **Semnoz mountains** on the lake's west side.

Ten kilometres west of Annecy, the **Gorges du Fier** and nearby Château Montrottier combine both natural and historical spectacle within a short distance of each other; and, if you're leaving Annecy to the north, the **Ponts de la Caille** also deserve a look.

Around the lake

Although a very busy road rings Lake Annecy, a far more tranquil way of appreciating the lakeside is aboard one of the frequent **boats** that depart from Annecy's canalside port, with the possibility of stopovers or returning later in the day. Trips stopping off at various points on the lake are offered by Compagnie de Navigation on place aux Bois, beside Quai Bayreuth – a full circuit costs €12.30.

On the east shore of the lake, signposted out of the village of **MENTHON-ST-BERNARD**, is the grand, turreted **Château de Menthon** (May, June & Sept Fri–Sun & hols 2–6pm; July & Aug daily noon–6pm; €6, €7 for weekend medieval costume shows). Inhabited since the twelfth century and birthplace of St Bernard, the patron saint of mountaineers, the fortress was extensively renovated in the nineteenth century in the romantic Gothic revival style and possesses a fine collection of period furniture and views across the lake back to Annecy. You can **eat** here at the lakeside *Buvette du Port*, which offers *plats du jour* for around €8, while for a place to **stay**, *try Le Saint-Bernard* in the centre of the village (Ⓣ04.50.60.01.55, Ⓦwww.hotelstbernard.com; ❸), which also has a good restaurant. A few kilometres down the road is the lovely lakeside village of **TALLOIRES**, whose eleventh-century Benedictine abbey has been converted into the luxurious *Hôtel de l'Abbaye de Talloires* on chemin des Moines (Ⓣ04.50.60.77.33, Ⓦwww.abbaye-talloires.com; ❾; closed Nov to mid-April).

On the west side of the lake, the village of **DUINGT** occupies a peninsula where there are two more thousand-year-old **châteaux**, one in ruins and the other partly rebuilt. Like Menthon-St-Bernard and Talloires, it has a small beach, with the opportunity to rent pleasure craft. The village has a few good-value **hotels**, among them the *Auberge du Roselet* (Ⓣ04.50.68.67.19, Ⓦwww.hotel-restaurant-leroselet.com; ❹). For a more tranquil overnight stay, head 7km south to the village of **DOUSSARD**, where the *Hôtel Arcalod* at Grand Parc (Ⓣ04.50.44.30.22, Ⓦwww.hotelarcalod.com; closed Oct–Feb; ❹) offers lakeside accommodation and a swimming pool.

La Tournette and the Semnoz mountains

Experienced hill-walkers wanting a stiff but straightforward mountain ascent could tackle **La Tournette** (2351m), which dominates the east side of the lake with its patchy snowfields and crenellated summits. A road just north of Talloires crosses the **Col de la Forclaz**, doubles back to the left before the hamlet of **MONTMIN**, and ends in a steep but drivable track up to the **Col de l'Aulp**, less than 1000m from the summit. From the col, the climb is immediate, steep and clear, leading to a **refuge**, where snow and increasing exposure demand extra care. Some scrambling (with fixed chains and handrails) is required to take you up to a broad, exposed shoulder on the way to the summit. To the east, the **Chaîne des Aravis** stretches before the snowbound massif of Mont Blanc on the horizon, just 50km away, while in the other direction the turquoise lake and Annecy itself lie at your feet.

Facing La Tournette on the lake's opposite shore, the wooded ridges of the **Semnoz mountains** offer less radical hiking. From the village of Duingt, a four-hour walk leads southwards up the Taillefer ridge, involving just over 300m of ascent to the 765-metre summit of **Taillefer** itself. From the town church follow the signs for **Grotte de Notre Dame du Lac**, a steep walk up the ridge, and follow the red and yellow markers thereafter. Towards the summit of Taillefer, there's some scrambling, but nothing too difficult, and 1500m after the peak the path turns round and returns north via the hamlet of **LES MAISONS**.

The highest peak in the Semnoz is the **Crêt de Châtillon**, 16km directly south of Annecy along the D41. At 1699m it offers panoramic views, most impressively east past La Tournette towards Mont Blanc. A twenty-minute walk across meadows from the road's highest point leads to the cross on the summit and an orientation table pointing out the surrounding features.

The Gorges du Fier and Pont de la Caille

West of Annecy, the River Fier, which trickles out of the lake through Annecy's picturesque canals, has cut a narrow crevice through the limestone rock at the **Gorges du Fier** (daily: mid-March to mid-June & mid-Sept to mid-Oct 9am–noon & 2–6pm; mid-June to mid-Sept 9am–7pm; €4.50). Signposted off the D14 at Lovagny, a footpath leads down into the 300-metre-long gorge, which is traversed along an impressive high-level walkway pinned to the gorge side. On the way to the gorges you'll catch glimpses of the **Château de Montrottier** (mid-March to May & Sept daily except Tues 9am–1pm & 2–6pm; June–Aug daily 9am–1pm & 2–7pm; Oct daily 2–5pm; €5.50), which can be reached by continuing along the road for another 3km. The castle, which dates from the thirteenth century, possesses an eclectic collection of furniture, earthenware and lace as well as exotic objects from former French colonies in West Africa and the Far East, amassed during the nineteenth century by one Léon Mares.

Sixteen kilometres north of Annecy, just after the N201 Geneva road parts from the autoroute, the highway spectacularly bridges the gorge of the River Usses, 140m below. It is one of the two impressive **Ponts de la Caille**. Next to the highway bridge stands the older bridge, the **Pont Charles-Albert**, which was built in 1838. It was built under the orders of the King of Sardinia, Charles Albert, and its crenellated towers, supported by two dozen cables, are an impressive example of bold mid-nineteenth-century engineering. The "new" bridge, Pont Moderne, was built in 1925, at which time it possessed one of the longest single spans in Europe.

Lake Geneva

Some 40km north of Annecy lies the dolphin-shaped expanse of **Lake Geneva** ("Lac Léman" to the French), forming a natural border with Switzerland. Over 70km long, 14km wide and an amazing 310m deep, the lake is fed and drained by the Rhône. It's a real inland sea, subject to violent storms, as Byron and Shelley discovered to their discomfort in 1816. On a calm day, though, sailing slowly across its silky-smooth surface is a serene experience.

Thonon-les-Bains and Yvoire

The largest town on the French side is **THONON-LES-BAINS**. Far less touristy than its surrounding neighbours Évian and Yvoire, it makes a good base for exploring the lakeside and the surrounding Chablais region, and is also the starting point of the 700-kilometre-long Route des Grandes Alpes, a popular, signposted tourist route which winds its way through the mountains to Menton, on the Mediterranean coast. Though of only minor interest itself, the town's position overlooking the lake is stunning. The waterfront, connected to the upper town by **funicular railway** (daily every 2–4min: April–June & Sept 8am–9pm; July–Aug 8am–11pm; €1.80 round trip), is a pleasant place to while away a summer afternoon, with its tiny fishermen's cottages, cafés, restaurants and snack kiosks. Running northwards, the flower-decked lake-front promenade, the Quai de Ripaille, leads past the marina and the fantastic public **swimming pools** (daily May–Sept 9am–7pm; €3.50) to the **Château de Ripaille** (guided tours daily: Feb–March & Oct–Nov 3pm; April–June & Sept 11am, 2.30pm & 4pm; July–Aug 11am & on the half hour 2.30–5pm; €6). Built in the fifteenth century by Amédée VIII, the colourful first Duke of Savoie – who later served ten years as anti-pope, before retiring to become Bishop of Geneva – the château looks more like a lovely country manor with turrets than a castle, due in part to major restoration in the late nineteenth century, which left a rich legacy of Art-Nouveau interiors. The vineyard attached to the property produces one of the region's best-regarded wines, which are available to taste and buy at the château on weekdays.

The **tourist office** is on place du Marché (June–Sept daily 8.30am–noon & 1.30–7pm; Oct–May Mon–Fri 9am–noon & 2–6.30pm, Sat 10am–noon & 2–6.30pm; Ⓣ04.50.71.55.55, Ⓦwww.thononlesbains.com), while there's also a summertime tourist office kiosk at the harbour (July–Aug daily 10.30am–12.30pm & 2–7pm; Ⓣ04.50.26.19.94). As Thonon is not a gargantuan lakeside resort, its **hotels** are modest but pleasant two-star affairs. Try the lakeside *Le Port*, 1 quai de Ripaille (Ⓣ & Ⓕ04.50.71.37.05; ❹), or the basic but comfortable *Le Comte Rouge*, 10 bd du Canal (Ⓣ04.50.71.06.04, Ⓕ04.50.81.93.49; ❷), near the train station and the town centre. There's a **campsite**, *Le Saint-Disdille* (April–Sept Ⓣ04.50.71.14.11) on the eastern edge of town just off the avenue de St-Disdille. One of Thonon's best **restaurants** is *Le Scampi*, 1 avenue du Léman, which specializes in fresh fish from the lake, with menus starting at €18 (Ⓣ04.50.71.10.04). The best bet for a fancy meal is the €27 lunch at the *Le Jardin du Château* in the grounds of the Chateau de Ripaille (July & Aug 11am–6pm; Ⓣ04.50.26.64.44). Less expensive options in town include the Chinese *Royal Thonon*, 3 rue des Ursules (Ⓣ04.05.71.92.03), and the tiny *Au Petit Bouchon Lyonnais*, 5 rue Michaud (Ⓣ04.50.26.33.15).

Some 16km to the west lies the pretty medieval village of **YVOIRE**, famous for its extravagant flower displays, which seem to drip in profusion from every building in summer, when the narrow cobbled lanes are frequently choked with hordes of day-trippers. The main attraction is the lovely **Labyrinthe-Jardin des Cinq Sens** off rue du Lac (April to mid-May daily 11am–6pm; mid-May to mid-Sept 10am–7pm; mid-Sept to Oct 1–5pm; €8), a spread of immaculate formal gardens laid out with a huge variety of plants, designed to appeal to each of the five senses. The tourist office is on place de la Mairie (April–Oct daily 10am–12.30pm & 1.30–5pm; Nov–March closed Sat & Sun; ⓣ04.50.72.80.21, ⓦwww.presquile-leman.com). Finding a room in the village can be difficult, especially in high season, though you could try *Hôtel le Pré de la Cure* on place de la Mairie (ⓣ04.50.72.83.58, ⓕ04.50.72.91.15, closed mid-Nov to March; ❹). Finding somewhere to eat is rather easier, with several harbour-side restaurants serving up fresh fish dishes to the tourist crowds.

Évian

Moving eastwards, **ÉVIAN**, or Évian-les-Bains as it is known officially, is a pleasant and peaceful spa resort, though there isn't a great deal to see or do other than simply enjoy the serenity of the waterfront, or take leisurely trips on the lake. The mineral water for which the town is famous is now bottled at Amphion, 3km along the lakeside (reserve at the tourist office for one of the four daily tours, ⓣ04.50.26.93.23, €1.70), but the **Source Cachat** on Avenue des Sources still gushes away behind the Évian company's Art-Nouveau offices in rue Nationale, providing unlimited free and delicious water round the clock. There's a funicular that begins from just above the **casino**; though the views are underwhelming, it has the advantage of being free (mid-May to mid-Sept 10am–7pm; every 20min).

The waterfront is elegantly laid out with squares of billiard-table grass, brilliant flowerbeds and exotic trees, mini-golf, water slides and other peaceful ways of amusing oneself. There are **ferries** to explore other towns around the lake, including Lausanne (12 daily; €18.20 return) and Geneva (2 daily; €35 return) in Switzerland and Yvoire (3 daily; €26 return) and Thonon-les-Bains on the French side (4 daily; €16 return). CGN Ferries also runs a number of sightseeing **cruises** (ⓦwww.cgn.ch), which do circuits of the lake, stopping at picturesque spots; enquire at the **tourist office** on place d'Allinges (May–Sept Mon–Fri 8.30am–noon & 2–7pm, Sat 9am–noon & 3–7pm, Sun 10am–noon & 3–6pm; Oct–April Mon–Fri 8.30am–noon & 2–7pm; ⓣ04.50.75.04.26, ⓦwww.eviantourism.com) for details. The tourist office also reserves spaces on a boat that goes to **Les Pré-Curieux** water gardens, picturesque lakeside gardens, each organized around a water-based ecosystem. The tour also includes a visit to a colonial house that contains educational exhibitions on the wetlands (open May–Sept, visit by reservation at tourist office, or email ⓔinfo@precurieux.com).

Évian has a few top-notch four-star **hotels** if you're after some full-on luxury, but there are many more affordable options available too, the best of which is the *Hôtel Continental*, 65 rue Nationale (ⓣ04.50.75.37.54, ⓦwww.continental-evian.com; ❹), in the centre of town, with rooms on the top floor that have a view of the lake. The nearby *Bourgogne*, place Charles Cottet (ⓣ04.50.75.01.05, ⓔbourgogne@wanadoo.fr; ❻), offers large rooms and a higher standard of comfort, while the *Terminus*, at 32 av le Gare (ⓣ04.50.75.15.07, ⓕ04.50.74.63.23; ❸), is a basic option directly across from the train station. On the waterfront, the *Savoy*, 17 quai Besson (ⓣ04.50.83.15.00, ⓕ04.50.75.68.07; ❻), provides three-star amenities without breaking the bank. There's also a **hostel** on avenue de Neuvecelle (ⓣ04.50.75.35.87) – the D21 towards Abondance – and a **campsite**, the *Grande Rive*, off avenue de Grande-Rive (ⓣ04.50.75.42.19; closed Oct–April), less than 1km from the town centre. There are plenty of places to eat: at the cheaper end, try *Le Siam*, 5 rue Clermont, with good Thai food starting at €8, or some of the pizzerias on the east end of rue Nationale. The restaurants at the *Bourgogne* and the *Savoy* Hotels offer more upmarket menus, with prices starting at €15.

Northern pre-Alps: Samoëns and around

The **Northern pre-Alps**, climbing back from the shore of Lake Geneva, are softer, greener and a lot less crowded than the mighty ranges further south. A fine place to absorb the region's atmosphere is the gentle and attractive village of **SAMOËNS**, 21km from Cluses on the main Geneva–Chamonix road, lying at the foot of the Aiguille de Criou, with the tall peak of Le Buet in the distance. Its principal architectural claim to fame is its sixteenth-century Gothic church on a Romanesque base, with a doorway with crouching lions like those in the Queyras (see p.1027).

The village is chiefly known, however, for its stonemasons and for Marie-Louise Cognacq-Jay, who left to seek her fortune in Paris at the age of 15 in 1853, and found it – as the founder of the famous French department store, La Samaritaine. There's a beautiful **botanical garden** (daily: summer 8am–noon & 1–7pm; winter 8am–noon & 1.30–5.30pm; free) on the slope above the old village centre, created by Madame Jay and planted with specimens of mountain flora from all over the world. Hers was an exceptional success, but migration was part of the pattern of local life. Up to World War I the men of the village would set out every spring with their tools on their backs to seek work in the cities of France and Switzerland. Their guild, *les frahans*, evolved its own peculiar dialect, *le mourne*, so they could communicate secretly among themselves.

For a **hotel**, try *Les Drugères* (Ⓣ04.50.34.43.84, Ⓦhotel.lesdrugeres.com; ❹; closed May & Nov) or *Les Glaciers* (Ⓣ04.50.34.40.06, Ⓦwww.hotel-les-glaciers.com; closed spring & autumn ❺). Both hotels have restaurants and good-sized, comfortable rooms; the latter also has an indoor and outdoor pool. The cheapest option in town is *Le Tuet* (Ⓣ04.50.34.40.60, Ⓕ04.50.34.91.56; ❷, full board ❸), while there's a municipal campsite, *Le Giffre* (Ⓣ04.50.34.41.92. Ⓔcamping@samoens.com) by the River Giffre, which meanders around the town, and a *gîte d'étape*, *Les Moulins*, 1km away on the road up to Les Allamands (Ⓣ04.50.34.95.69).

Sixt and the Cirque du Fer-à-Cheval

East of Samoëns, the valley narrows into the Gorge des Tines before opening out again at **SIXT**, 7km away, another pretty village on the confluence of two branches of the Giffre: the Giffre-Haut, which comes down from Salvagny; and the Giffre-Bas, which rises in the Cirque du Fer-à-Cheval.

The cirque begins about 6km from Sixt – there's a footpath along the left bank of the Giffre-Bas. It's a vast semicircle of rock walls, up to 700m in height and 4–5km long, blue with haze on a summer's day and striated with the long chains of white water from the waterfalls. The left-hand end of the cirque is dominated by a huge spike of rock known as La Corne du Chamois (The Goat's Horn). At its foot the valley of the Giffre bends sharply north to its source in the glaciers above the Fond de la Combe. The bowl of the cirque is thickly wooded except for a circular meadow in the middle where the road ends.

There's a **tourist office** and a park office in Sixt in the town centre (both Mon–Sat 9am–noon & 2–7pm; Ⓣ04.50.34.49.36, Ⓦwww.sixtferacheval.com). The park office produces a useful and well-illustrated folder of walks in the region. Sixt also has three *gîtes d'étape* and a hotel, *Le Petit Tetras* (Ⓣ04.50.34.42.51, Ⓦwww.le-petit-tetras.fr; ❹; closed mid-Sept to Dec), a modern chalet with an outdoor pool.

Mont Blanc

Due east from Annecy, and 60km south of Évian on the Swiss and Italian borders, looms **Mont Blanc** (4807m), Western Europe's highest peak, right on the Italian border. First climbed in 1786, this mountain is the biggest tourist draw in the Alps, but its grandeur is undiminished by the hordes of visitors, and if you're walking in the area, you can soon get away from the crowds. The closest airport is in Geneva, but if you're coming from France then Annecy is the easiest city from which to approach the mountain, and, of the two road routes, the one east via the old ski resort of Megève is more interesting. The two main approach roads to Mont Blanc come together at Le Fayet, a village just outside **St-Gervais**, where the **tramway du Mont Blanc** begins its 75-minute haul to the **Nid d'Aigle**, a vantage point on the northwest slope (€22 return). From here it's an easy one-hour round-trip walk to the Glacier de Bionnassay. The remainder of Mont Blanc activities are based from around **Chamonix-Mont Blanc**, the French base camp for all Mont Blanc activities, just 20km from St-Gervais.

Chamonix-Mont Blanc

Bustling, cosmopolitan **CHAMONIX**, with its rash of restaurants and flashy boutiques, may have long since had its village identity submerged in a sprawl of tourist development, but the stunning backdrop of glaring snowfields, eerie green glaciers and ridges of shark-toothed aiguilles surrounding Mont Blanc

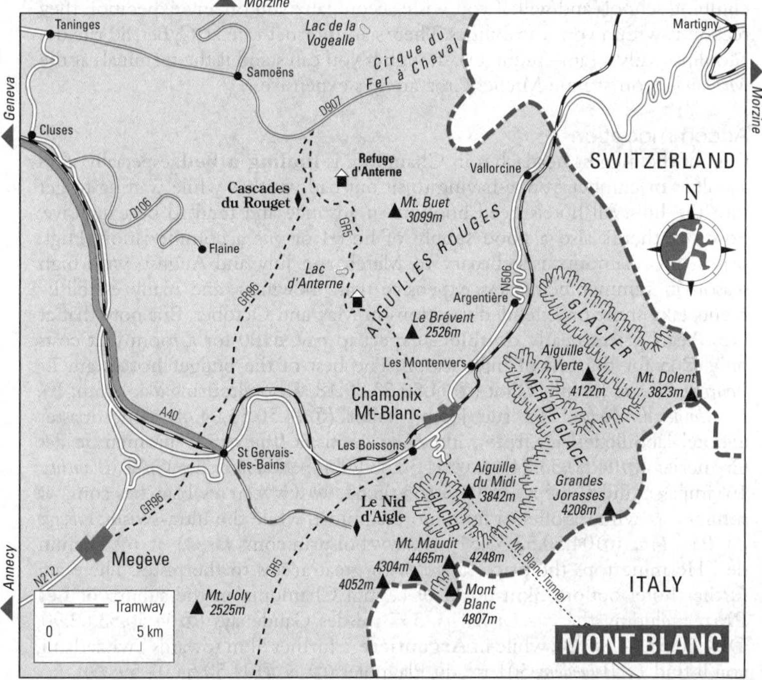

are more than ample compensation. The websites Ⓦwww.chamonix.net and Ⓦwww.chamonixexperience.com are good sources of information on the town.

The mountains provide the town's main sights and activities, but on days when the bad weather sets in, there are a few things to do in town. The **Musée Alpin**, off avenue Michel-Croz in the town centre (daily: June to mid-Oct 2–7pm; mid-Dec to June 3–7pm; €4), will interest mountaineers, but its collection of equipment and documents is a bit disappointing. The star exhibit is Jacques Balmat's account of his first ascent of Mont Blanc in 1786. The **Richard Bozon Sports Centre** on avenue de la Plage has ice skating, a pool, sauna and hamam, climbing wall and tennis courts (hours vary, Ⓣ04.50.53.09.07). Across the street is the **library**, which contains a good selection of English-language books (Mon, Tues & Thurs–Sat 2.30–6.30pm, Wed 10am–noon).

Practicalities

The **tourist office**, at 85 place du Triangle-de-l'Amitié (daily: July & Aug 8.30am–7.30pm; Sept–June 8.30am–12.30pm & 2–7pm; Ⓣ04.50.53.00.24, Ⓦwww.chamonix.com), offers up-to-the minute **walking and climbing information**. The nearby Maison de la Montagne houses the Compagnie des Guides (daily: 8.30am–noon & 3.30–7.30pm; Ⓣ04.50.53.00.88, Ⓦwww.chamonix-guides.com) for those who don't want to ski off-piste or hike unaccompanied, the Office de Haute Montagne (daily: July to mid-Aug 9am–noon & 3–6pm; Ⓣ04.50.53.22.08, Ⓦwww.ohm-chamonix.com) and a meteorological service (Ⓣ04.50.53.22.08). The tourist office also publishes a map of summer walks in the area (€4), while the guides run rock- and ice-climbing schools and will, if you wish, accompany you on any expedition they reckon is within your capabilities. There's an Internet café at *CyBar*, 80 rue des Moulins (daily 11am–midnight), though if you can stand it the terminals at the *McDonald's* on avenue Michel Croz are less expensive.

Accommodation

One of the biggest headaches in Chamonix is **finding a bed**, especially if, as a walker or climber, you're having to sit out bad weather while waiting to get into the hills. All hotels need booking in advance and tend to be expensive; however, there's also a good supply of hostel or *gîte* accommodation. High season in Chamonix is February to March and July and August, with high season in summer being less expensive than in winter, and many establishments take short or extended vacations in May and October. But note that at New Years prices nearly **double** – expect to pay €100 for a room that costs only €65 for the rest of high season. The best of the budget **hotels** are *Le Touring*, 95 rue Joseph-Vallot (Ⓣ04.50.53.59.18, Ⓔhoteltouring@aol.com; ❹), *La Boule de Neige*, 362 rue Joseph-Vallot (Ⓣ04.50.53.04.48, Ⓔpostmaster@hotel-labouledeneige.fr; ❸), and *Hôtel Crémerie Balmat*, 749 promenade des Crémeries (Ⓣ04.50.53.24.44, Ⓕ04.50.53.29.42; ❸). *Hotel Les Crêtes Blanches*, 16 impasse du Génépy (Ⓣ04.50.53.05.62, Ⓦwww.cretes-blanches.com; ❹ summer, ❼ winter), offers a little more comfort, while the ultra-swish *Auberge du Bois Prin* (Ⓣ04.50.53.33.51, Ⓦwww.boisprin.com; ❽–❾) at 69 chemin de l´Hermine tops the price range, with great access to the pistes. There are further hotel options 3km north of central Chamonix in the suburb of **Les Praz**, including the *gîte La Bagna,* 337 rte des Gaudenays (Ⓣ04.50.53.62.90, Ⓕ04.50.53.64.88; ❸), while in **Argentière**, a further 5km towards Switzerland, you'll find *Le Belvédère*, 501 rte du Plagnolet (Ⓣ & Ⓕ04.50.54.02.59; ❷).

Gîte accommodation can be found not far from the centre, at *La Tapia*, 152 rte de la Frasse (ⓣ04.50.53.18.19, ⓕ04.50.53.67.01; ❸), which has wonderful views. For cheaper and more basic rooms, there's a *gîte d'étape*, the *Ski Station*, close to the Brévent cable-car station at 6 rte des Moussoux (ⓣ04.50.53.20.25). And for a chalet near the centre of town that runs itself like a *gîte* try the extraordinarily friendly and good-value *Red Mountain Lodge*, 435 rue Joseph Vallot, a completely English-speaking establishment (ⓣ04.50.53.94.79; ⓔredmountainlodge@yahoo.com; open May–Oct). The modern, comfortable **hostel** is at 127 Montée Jacques-Balmat, in the western part of town called Les-Pèlerins-en-Haut (ⓣ04.50.53.14.52, ⓕ04.50.55.92.34; closed one week in mid-May & Nov to mid-Dec); take the bus towards Les Houches and get off at "Pèlerins École" – the hostel is signposted from there.

Campsites are numerous, though in high season there may only be room for a small mountain tent. Two convenient sites are *Camping de la Mer de Glace*, less than 2km north of town, close to Les Praz (ⓣ04.50.53.44.03; closed mid-Sept to May), and *Les Rosières* off the route des Praz (ⓣ04.50.53.10.42; year round).

Eating, drinking and nightlife

For high-quality **dining**, head for *Atmosphère*, 123 place Balmat (ⓣ04.50.55.97.97), offering elaborate dishes in a cosy setting from €19, or the ultra-hip *Munchies*, offering French-Japanese-Thai fusion with mains starting at €16 (ⓣ04.50.53.45.41). *Chez Nous*, 78 rue de Lyret, specializes in reasonably priced fondue starting at €11.50 (ⓣ04.50.53.91.29). There's an abundance of cheaper restaurants around town, including a number of pizzerias, such as *Valentino* on place Balmat (ⓣ04.50.53.67.72). Other lower-end options include *La Poêle*, 79 av de l'Aiguille-du-Midi, which specializes in omelettes (ⓣ04.50.55.96.13; €4.60–12), and *El Dorado*, right next door, for Tex-Mex and Internet (ⓣ04.50.53.31.23). Rue Joseph-Vallot has plenty of gourmet food shops with local cheeses and other Alpine delicacies, and there are several well-stocked supermarkets in town for making a picnic.

If you're after a **drink**, rue des Moulins is packed from end to end with English-speaking bars and clubs, but it's worth venturing a little bit out of town to the *MBC* (Micro Brasserie de Chamonix), 350 route du Bouchet, serving homemade microbrews in a laid back atmosphere. And for coffee or a *pastis* with a view of the river or late-night music, try *La Terrace*, 43 Place Balmat. For après-ski clubbing, it's worth taking a look at *Arbate*, on chemin du Sapi, and *Cantina*, on impasse des Rhododendrons, both of which have live bands and **dancing** some nights.

Around Chamonix – lifts and télérifiques

There are a number of exhilarating excursions around Chamonix which are worth experiencing – it may be worth getting a **multipass** that covers all the lifts in the area (starting at €50 for 36 hours or €65 for two non-consecutive days).

The most famous excursion is the very expensive, and often very crammed, **téléférique** (summer daily from 7am; return €34, advance reservations €2, call ⓣ08.92.68.00.67) to the **Aiguille du Midi** (3842m), one of the longest cable-car ascents in the world, rising no less than 3000m above the valley floor in two impossibly steep stages. Penny-pinching by buying a ticket only as far as the Plan du Midi, which is used principally by climbers heading up to the routes on the Aiguilles du Chamonix, is a waste of money: go all the way or not at all. If you do go up, make the effort to go before 9am, as the summits tend to cloud over towards midday, and huge crowds may force you to wait for hours if you go up later. Take warm clothes – even on a summer's day it'll be below zero on the top – and suntan lotion is also advisable to protect against the glare off the snow. You need a steady head, too: the drop beneath the little bubble of steel and glass is terrifying.

The Aiguille is an exposed granite pinnacle on which a restaurant and the téléférique dock are precariously balanced, and from where the view is incredible. At your feet is the snowy plateau of the **Col du Midi**, with the glaciers of the Vallée Blanche and Géant crawling off left at their millennial pace. To the right a steep snowfield leads to the easy ridge route to the summit of Mont Blanc with its cap of ice. Away to the front, rank upon rank of snow-and-ice-capped monsters recede into the distance. Most impressive of all, closing the horizon to your left, from the east to south, is a mind-blowing cirque of needle-sharp peaks and precipitous cliffs: the Aiguille Verte, Triollet and the Jorasses, with the Matterhorn and Monte Rosa visible in the far distance across a glorious landscape of rock, snow and cloud-filled valleys – the lethal testing ground of all climbers. From the Aiguille you can continue to **Pont Helbronner** on a ski lift above the Glacier du Géant, and from there descend to **Italy**, from where a bus will take you back through the Mont Blanc tunnel to Chamonix (€50 including the Aiguille du Midi ascent, not included on the flexipass).

Alternatively, descending all the way from the Aiguille, it's a moderate but short hike from the midway station **Plan de l'Aiguille** to Lac Bleu (1hr round trip), or a two-and-a-half hour hike along the Plan de l'Aiguille-Montvers traverse to the top of the **rack railway**. Another option for ascending the north face is to take the rack railway from the Gare du Montenvers through the pine woods up to the vast glacier known as the Mer de Glace (May–Sept 8.30am–5.30pm; Oct to mid-Nov & mid-Dec to April 10am–4pm; €14 return). Once you get there you have the option of taking a short cable-car ride down into the **ice cave** carved out of the Mer de Glace every summer (an additional €6).

A third – cheaper – alternative is to take the lift up to the **Glacier des Bossons** (daily: July & Aug 8am–6pm; €8), where you can see the biggest precipice in Europe (a drop of 3500m), as well as the Alps' lowest ice face. A nature trail at the top, along with the spectacular views, makes for a good half-day outing.

Chamonix Valley: some hikes

Opposite Mont Blanc, the north side of Chamonix valley is enclosed by the lower but nonetheless impressive **Aiguilles Rouges**, with another *téléférique* to **Le Brévent** (15 min; €15.50 return), the 2526-metre peak directly above the town. Classic walks this side of the valley include the **Lac Blanc**, starting from Les Praz and the Flégère *téléférique* (20min; €15.50 return), or walking to the top of the Flégère lift via the lovely lunch stop *La Floria* on the trail of the same name. The **Grand** and **Petit Balcon Sud** trails traverse the Aiguilles Rouges (from the top of Flégère to the top of Planpraz is a relatively easy two hours), and at points the trails open up to spectacular views of Mont Blanc. A highly recommended two-day hike is the **GR5** stage north from Le Brévent to the village of Sixt via **Lac d'Anterne**, with a night at the Refuge d'Anterne. The classic long-distance route is the two-week **Tour du Mont Blanc** (TMB), described in a *Topoguide*, Andrew Harvey's *Tour of Mont Blanc and Chamonix-Mont Blanc: A Walker's Guide*.

The Vanoise

The **Vanoise**, the rugged massif rising up to the southeast of **Albertville**, and over to the Italian border is a superb area for skiing and hiking. The dramatic range, whose highest peaks rise to altitudes in excess of 3500 metres, is roughly diamond-shaped, hemmed in by the valley of the **Isère** to the northeast, where **Bourg-St-Maurice** is the best base for exploration, and the **Arc Valley** in the southwest. The glacier-capped southeast quadrant of the Vanoise, where both of these great rivers have their source, has been incorporated in the **Parc National de la Vanoise**, across which lonely and spectacular GR trails offer unparalleled opportunities for seasoned hikers. Easiest road access to the region is from Chambéry or Grenoble, although driving the winding and precipitous old highways from Annecy or Chamonix is an adventure in itself.

The Isère valley and around

The scenic route south from Chamonix and Mégeve is on the tiny D2188 over the **Col des Saisies** through **Les Saisies**, a small but friendly resort town, and through **Beaufort** along the D902 to **Bourg-St-Maurice**. There's no public

△ Tour de France, Les Deux Alps to La Plange

transportation here, but it's a good place to drive – Les Saisies has few tourists and offers excellent **views** of Mont Blanc from the South. The town has some hotels and a **campsite**, *Le Grand Tetras* (Ⓣ04.79.38.85.17), but the best place to **stay** or eat is down the hill in **HAUTELUCE** at *La Ferme du Chozal*, a renovated farmhouse with boutique-hotel style (Ⓣ04.79.38.18.18, Ⓦwww.lafermeduchozal.com; ❻). The nearby **church** has an opulent interior, with a chandelier taking up much of the air space above the pews.

The less harrowing route is through **ALBERTVILLE**, 8km south of where the N508 from Annecy joins the N212 from Chamonix. From here, the N90 climbs southeast along the bends of the Isère River for 50km to **MOÛTIERS**, the turn-off for the massive Les Trois Vallées ski region. Here the river course swings northeast, passing **AIME**, whose main Grande-Rue presents a pretty and little-spoilt succession of buildings. Six kilometres later, you reach Bourg-St-Maurice, the midpoint of the upper Isère valley, which is known as the Tarentaise. The town is of little interest itself, but can be a useful place to stop. The big purpose-built ski resorts of **LA PLAGNE** and **LES ARCS** are nearby and the classic pass into the Italian Val d'Aosta, the **Col du Petit St-Bernard**, is right behind. It's a rather spooky crossing, reaching a height of 2188m, with a couple of barrack-like buildings and a row of statues of St Bernard, who built a hostel for mountain travellers here in the twelfth century. It's at its most dramatic when you're coming over from the Italian side in the early evening, right into the eye of the setting sun. With its Swiss twin, the Grand St-Bernard, it was the only route around the Mont Blanc massif until the Mont Blanc tunnel was opened in 1965.

There are a few reasonable places to **stay** in Bourg-St-Maurice, the best being *L'Autantic*, a modern chalet in a wonderful forested setting at 69 rte Hauteville (Ⓣ04.79.07.01.70, Ⓦwww.hotel-autentic.com; ❸). A more central and extremely cheap option is *Hôtel La Colonne*, 90 rue Jean Moulin (Ⓣ04.79.07.05.49; ❶). There's also a **HI hostel**, *La Verdache*, just beyond Seez (Ⓣ04.79.41.01.93, Ⓔseez-les-arcs@fuaj.org; closed Oct to mid-Dec and two weeks in May), 4km away on the dreary main road, avenue Leclerc. The **train** and bus stations are in the centre of town; the **tourist office** is almost opposite the train station (Mon–Fri 9am–noon & 2–7pm, Sat 8.30am–7pm, Sun 9am–12.30pm & 3.30–7pm; Ⓣ04.79.07.04.92). *Camping le Versoyen* lies on route des Arcs (Ⓣ04.79.07.03.45, Ⓦwww.leversoyen.com), on the right past the sports ground on the Val d'Isère road.

Around 5km beyond Bourg-St-Maurice, a road turns right into the valley bottom to **LA SAVINAZ** and **LA GURRAZ**, whose creamy **church tower** is a landmark for miles around. High above, though looking ominously close, the green ice cliffs that terminate the Glacier de la Gurraz hang off the edge of **Mont Pourri** (3779m). From the turn, the lane veers steeply down through trees and meadows past ruined houses to the river. The climb up the opposite bank is hard going, past impossibly steep fields, before taking a right fork for La Gurraz across a rickety plank bridge in the jaws of a defile. It's about an hour's walk, for seasoned hikers, once you're on the lane.

The village is tiny and untouched by tourism. Its dozen old houses have wide eaves and weathered balconies spread with sweet drying hay, and firewood stacked outside. The houses are all sited in the lee of a knoll for protection against the avalanches that come thundering off the glacier above, thousands of tonnes of snow and rock, almost sheer down into a cirque behind. If you are unlucky enough to be out of doors when an avalanche occurs, the blast knocks you off your feet and can even suffocate you. There are no provisions available, so bring your own. Other hamlets on the opposite flank of the val-

Skiing in the Alps

It was the **Winter Olympics** of 1992, based around Albertville, which brought the French Alps into the international skiing spotlight. High altitudes (ensuring good and lasting snow cover), long and varied runs, extensive lift-networks, excellent facilities, superb vistas and relatively mild weather make for some of the most enjoyable skiing in Europe. At any of the resorts you can simply turn up, buy a pass (€18–45 a day, €75–325 a week) and rent equipment by the day, though if you're planning on coming just to ski, your best bet is to arrange an accommodation/lift-ticket package from home; the price will be better and you won't have to look for accommodation, which can be hard to come by. **High season** covers the Christmas and New Year period and February to mid-April, and should be avoided both for high prices and for crowds. Finally, make sure your insurance covers you for ski-related mishaps. Detailed ski information can be obtained from local ski clubs and organizations, or online at ⓦwww.skifrance.fr.

The resorts

Most **French resorts** are ugly purpose-built affairs, but their layout is such that you can often ski straight out of your front door in the morning, and the lift systems are quick and efficient. There's also an emphasis on family skiing in France, with most resorts offering day-care facilities.

The best resorts lie along the Franco-Italian and Franco-Swiss borders. Of these **Val d'Isère** (ⓦwww.valdisere.com) is a deserving favourite, and, combined with Tignes, covers a massive area serviced by over 100 lifts, with a variety of runs, some as high as 3200m. It has many hotels and a lively après-ski scene, but it's a long and treacherous drive to the town, with nowhere really to go once you're there. Its partner resort, **Tignes** (ⓦwww.tignes.net), also features excellent skiing for all levels, but is more family-oriented. Despite its fame, **Chamonix** (ⓦwww.chamonix.com), further north, is not the most user friendly of resorts, and access to the slopes is dependent on shuttle buses or a car. That said, for advanced skiers, it's probably the best choice for its impressive range of challenging pistes. As a large and popular resort, it also has an impressive array of activities for non-skiers, with an extensive Anglo-friendly nightlife.

ley are just as interesting, the prettiest being **LE MONAL**, in the mouth of a small hanging valley, also accessible by car from **LA THUILE**, further along the Bourg-St-Maurice road.

From La Gurraz, a signposted path climbs to Refuge de la Martin in an hour and a half. It zigzags up the slope behind the village of La Savinaz, onto a spur by a ruined chalet, where a right-hand path goes up the rocks overhead to the edge of the glacier. The refuge path continues left along the side of a deep gully, crosses a ferocious torrent by a plank bridge and follows a mule track up to the mountain pastures by the refuge, where cows and sheep graze. The Mont Pourri glaciers are directly above. Opposite is the big Glacier de la Sassière and up to your right Val d'Isère, with the Col de l'Iseran behind.

Tignes and Val d'Isère

Continuing south, climbing 10km further up the Isère valley from La Gurraz, you come to **TIGNES**, an unattractive, purpose-built resort near the artificial Lac de Chevril, which has little to offer aside from foot access to the Parc National de la Vanoise (see box, p.1019) via the GR5, which passes through town, and a hostel, *Les Clarines* (ⓣ04.79.41.01.93, ⓔtignes@fuaj.org; closed

Further west from the Italian border, with good access to Chambéry and Albertville by road, Courchevel, Méribel and Val Thorens/Les Menuires make up **Les Trois Vallées**, the world's largest ski area. Its ingenious lift-network makes skiing from village to village easy, and near endless off-piste possibilities await the intrepid. Of the component resorts, **Courchevel** (ⓦwww.courchevel.com) exudes expensive luxury, while **Méribel** (ⓦwww.meribel.net) is traditionally British-dominated, with a good range of cheaper hotels and lots of après-ski action. Ugly **Les Menuires** (ⓦwww.lesmenuires.com) is family-oriented, with a number of cheap hotels, while younger crowds head for **Val Thorens** (ⓦwww.valthorens.com), a lively resort popular with the snowboard set. North of the Trois Vallées, **Les Arcs** (ⓦwww.lesarcs.com) has excellent snow, and terrain for all levels. It's high on the list for snowboarders, and is easily accessible from Britain by rail, but has a decidedly mellow après-ski.

On top of the famous centres, there are several less-known but decent resorts. **Flaine**, north of St-Gervais (ⓦwww.flaine.com), is very good for both beginner and quite advanced skiers, and has some newly renovated lifts above the extremely quiet and unattractive town. **La Plagne** (ⓦwww.la-plagne.com), southwest of Bourg-St-Maurice in the Isère, is a huge ski-station, with a wide range of pistes, though accommodation is dominated by apartments, and nightlife is minimal. For traditional Alpine atmosphere, La Clusaz and Megève, both of which are on the mountain route between St-Gervais and Annecy, are good choices. Although the pistes and snow conditions are not the best due to its relatively low altitude, **La Clusaz** (ⓦwww.laclusaz.com) retains a village feel, and has moderately priced accommodation. **Megève** (ⓦwww.megeve.com) is the most beautiful French resort, with "olde worlde charm" and a jet-set feel. Mediocre conditions are bolstered by extensive snow-making, but advanced skiers will be disappointed.

Finally, most resorts also offer some **cross-country** trails, but some mountains specialize in it. **Les Saisies** (ⓦwww.lessaisies.com), with 80km of trails, is well known for having hosted many of the cross country events in the 1992 Olympics, though it offers some downhill as well. The rolling hills of the **Semnoz** around Annecy also have some good trails.

May & first three weeks in June). Linked to Tignes by ski-lifts, the resort of **VAL D'ISÈRE** sits in the shadow of the Col de l'Iseran on its north side, 12km further up river and best reached by bus from Bourg-St-Maurice. Once a tiny mountain village, Val d'Isère is now a hideous agglomeration of cafés, supermarkets, apartments and chalets – but with some of the finest skiing in Europe. Because it is so hard to get to, the resort really does close down in the off-season, with only one hotel of the many in town open in May. In the summer it makes a convenient centre for walking or for year-round skiing on the glacier – details from the **tourist office** (daily 8.30am–7.30pm; ⓣ04.79.06.06.60, ⓦwww.valdisere.com) – but **staying** here will certainly lighten your wallet. One of the cheapest options is *Séracs* (ⓣ04.79.06.03.61, ⓦwww.seracs.net; ❸), or try *Sakura* (ⓣ04.79.06.04.08, ⓦwww.sakura7.com; summer ❹, winter ❼), while there's a **campsite** nearby on the edge of the resort at Le Laisinant.

The Col de l'Iseran

From Val d'Isère, both the **D902** and the **GR5** veer south from the river, climbing towards the **Col de l'Iseran**. Despite the dangers of weather and the arduous climb, the pass has been used for centuries, being by far the quickest route between the remote upper valleys of the Isère and Arc. The volume of traffic was too small to disturb the nature of the tiny communities that eked out an existence on the approaches, but twentieth-century roads and the development of winter sports have changed all that. Small mountain communities have metamorphosed into monster modern developments, catering to an upmarket ski crowd. From October to June, the pass is blocked by snow, but in summer, being the highest pass in the Alps (2770m), it's a must-see sight for tourists with cars.

The GR5 reaches its zenith at the **Pointe des Lessières**, where on a clear day you have views of the Italian side of Mont Blanc and the whole of the frontier chain of peaks. Whether you head back or continue on to Bonneval, the walk is a solid two-and-a-half hours. If you continue south, a clear day will afford splendid views of the glaciers at the head of the Arc. As you descend along the Lenta stream through masses of anemones blooming in the stony ground, the riverbed winds through a desolate cirque, before dropping through a narrow defile towards the town.

The Arc valley

The **Arc valley** is wide and light below the col, though the treeless landscape can be more foreboding than joyous, especially under a stormy sky. Bare crags hang above the steep meadows on the north flanks; glaciers threaten to the south and east. Descending through meadows and patches of cultivation in the valley bottom with the lighter foliage of larches gracing the mountainsides you pass through humble hamlets of squat rough grey-stone houses – the homes of people who have had to struggle to wring a living from harsh weather and unyielding soil. It's surprising at first to find such a wealth of exuberant **Baroque art** in the outwardly simple **churches** in small villages like Avrieux, Bramans, Termignon, Lanslevillard and Bessans. But probably it's precisely because of the harshness and poverty of their lives that the mountain people sought to express their piety with such colourful vitality. Schools of local artists flourished, particularly in the seventeenth and eighteenth centuries, inspired and influenced by itinerant Italian artists who came and went across the adjacent frontier.

The first settlement of any size as you descend into the valley is **BONNEVAL-SUR-ARC**, 1835m above sea level, at the foot of the Col de l'Iseran, which looks out on the huge glaciers of the Sources de l'Arc to the east. Better preserved and more obviously picturesque than other towns of the valley, Bonneval stops a lot of tourists on their way to and from the col. It's in danger of becoming twee, with its houses clustered tightly around the church, and only the narrowest of lanes between them. You sense how very isolated these places were until only a few years ago, cut off for months by heavy snow, forced in upon their own resources. Several graves in the churchyard record deaths by avalanche.

From here the valley descends to **BESSANS**, which retains its village character better than most. Its squat dwellings are built of rough stone with tiny windows, and roofed with heavy slabs to withstand the long hard winters. Most have south-facing balconies to make the most of the sun and galleries under deep eaves for drying *grebons*, the bricks of cow dung and straw used locally for fuel. The **church** has a collection of seventeenth-century painted wooden statues and a retable, signed by Jean Clappier, a member of a local family who produced several generations of artists. On the other side of the small cemetery, the **chapel of St-Antoine** has exterior murals of the Virtues and

Deadly Sins and inside, some fine sixteenth-century frescoes. Two kilometres beyond Bessans you pass the chapel of Notre-Dame-des-Grâces on the left, with another *ex voto* by Clappier. There's a small **tourist office** in the centre of Bessans (Ⓣ04.79.05.96.52, Ⓦwww.bessans.com), and some **accommodation**, including the *Hôtel Le Mont-Iseran* (Ⓣ04.79.05.95.97, Ⓦwww.montiseran.com; ❸; closed mid-April to mid-June & Oct–Jan) and the *Hôtel La Vanoise* (Ⓣ04.79.05.96.79, Ⓦwww.hotel-vanoise.com; ❸).

In **LANSLEBOURG**, some 25km downstream from Bonneval, Haute Maurienne Information, in the town's old church (daily except Sat 3–7pm; Ⓣ04.79.05.91.57, Ⓦwww.hautemaurienne.com), organizes tours of village churches along the Arc valley. Lanslebourg is also the start of the climb to the **Mont Cenis pass** over to Susa in Italy, another ancient transalpine route. Last stop before the perils of the trek, it was once a prosperous and thriving town. Relief at finishing the climb from the French side was tempered by an alarming descent *en ramasse*, a sort of crude sledge, which shot downhill at breakneck speed, much to the alarm of travellers. "So fast you lose all sense and understanding", a terrified merchant from Douai recounted in 1518. Lanslebourg has a municipal **campsite** (Ⓣ04.79.05.82.83) and a **HI hostel** with a fantastic view and good rooms (Ⓣ04.79.05.90.96, Ⓔval-cenis@fuaj.org; closed April–May & mid-Sept to mid-Oct); alternatively, try the comfortable, rustic *Hôtel de la Vieille Poste* (Ⓣ04.79.05.93.47, Ⓦwww.lavieilleposte.com ❸; closed Nov–June).

MODANE, 20km downstream from Lanslebourg, is where the Arc valley starts to cut down dramatically through the high plateau, leading off towards Chambéry. It's a dreary little place, destroyed by Allied bombing in 1943 and now little more than a rail junction. Nonetheless, it's a good kicking-off point for walkers on the south side of the **Vanoise Massif**, the area contained between the upper valleys of the Isère and Arc rivers. It's easily accessible by train from Chambéry and has a **tourist office**, in place Sommeiller (Mon–Sat 9am–noon & 2–6pm; Ⓣ04.79.05.28.58, Ⓦwww.canton-de-modane.com), which will give advice on walks in the surrounding area. If you want to **stay**, try the simple but clean *Hôtel Le Commerce*, 20 place Sommeiller (Ⓣ04.79.05.00.78; ❷), or the well-sited grassy municipal **campsite**, *Les Combes* (Ⓣ04.79.05.00.23), just up the road to the Fréjus tunnel (which leads to Bardonecchia in Italy).

The Parc National de la Vanoise

The **Parc National de la Vanoise** (Ⓦwww.vanoise.com) occupies the eastern end of the Vanoise Massif. It's extremely popular, with over 500km of marked paths, including the **GR5**, **GR55** and **GTA** (Grande Traversée des Alpes), with numerous refuges along the trails. For information on the spot, the tourist offices in Modane, Val d'Isère and Bourg-St-Maurice are helpful. The Maison du Parc in Chambéry (see p.997) also gives advice and sells maps.

To cross the park, take the **GR5** from the northern edge of the transpontine section of Modane. When the trail splits, continue north on the **GR55**. From here the path leads to Pralognan, over the **Col de la Vanoise** and right across the park to the Lac de Tignes – a tremendous walk. An alternative is to stick with the GR5 (past the *Refuge de l'Orgère* from where a path north similarly joins up with the **GR55** and the previous route), which keeps east of La Dent Parrachée mountain, and follows a great loop up towards the **Refuge d'Entre-Deux-Eaux** before turning south and continuing up the north flank of the Arc valley and over the Col de l'Iseran to Val d'Isère.

North of the Écrins: Grenoble to Briançon

Connecting Grenoble to Briançon, the **N91** twists through the precipitous valley of the Romanche and over the **Col du Lautaret** (2058m), which is kept open all year round and served regularly by the Grenoble–Briançon bus. As well as being an exciting foretaste of the high mountain scenery to come, this route offers the opportunity for some worthwhile detours, including the climb across the Col du Galibier to Valloire and hikes along the Valley of Guisane. Although it's not the biggest village along the route, **Le Bourg-d'Oisans** is an attractive town which is the traditional capital of the region. Sprawling **Les Deux-Alpes** is bigger, but has been wholly subsumed by the skiing industry.

Le Bourg-d'Oisans

The first major settlement on the route, **LE BOURG-D'OISANS**, 20km southeast of Grenoble, is of no great interest in itself, but it's a good place to catch your breath. You can pick up information from the **tourist office**, on quai Girard, by the river in the middle of town (July & Aug 9am–7pm; Sept–June Mon–Sat 9am–noon & 2–7pm; ⓣ04.76.80.03.25, ⓦwww.oisans.com), and the **park information centre** on rue Gambetta (July & Aug 8am–noon & 3–7pm; Sept–June Mon–Fri 8am–noon & 2–5.30pm; ⓣ04.76.80.00.51). There are some good-value **hotels** here, among them *L'Oberland*, on avenue du Gare (ⓣ04.76.80.24.24, ⓔoberland.hotel@wanadoo.fr; ❸), and the *Hôtel Le Florentin* on rue Thiers 8 (ⓣ04.76.80.01.61, ⓔhotel.florentin@wanadoo.fr; ❹; restaurant from €15). There's also a municipal **campsite** on rue Humbert near the town centre and a concentration of sites across the river on the Alpe d'Huez road. If you like the idea of cycling in vigorous mountain air, **bikes** can be rented from Cycles d'Oisans on rue Viennois – not such a crazy undertaking as you might think if you keep to the valley bottoms where the gradients aren't too fearsome.

L'Alpe d'Huez

One place you're unlikely to be cycling to is the ski resort of **L'ALPE D'HUEZ**, signposted just outside Le Bourg. It's situated more than a vertical kilometre above the valley floor, and the eleven-kilometre road, which crawls up the valley side, is often used as a stage in the Tour de France. As you ascend through the 21 hairpins, there's a fine view of the acutely crumpled strata of rock exposed by passing glaciers on the south side of the Romanche valley. Undoubtedly a skier's paradise in winter, the purpose-built resort itself has little character in July and August, when it's only partially open. The extensive network of *télécabines*, extending as far as the 3327-metre **Pic du Lac Blanc**, at the bottom of the Chaîne des Rousses ridge north of the resort, does support some summertime skiing, but they can also be used to undertake some superb **high mountain walks**. Two recommended ones (details from the tourist office – see below), are the eight-kilometre Lac Blanc and Refuge de la Fare walk, which winds through the bleak wilderness past the lakes encircling the Dôme des Petites Rousses to the east of the glacier-clad *chaîne*, or the less exposed ten-kilometre hike to the gorges of the Sarennes valley, to the east of the resort along the **GR54**. In addition to the locally published map, walkers might find the more detailed IGN 3335E 1:50,000 map useful. A narrow and impressively scenic road through the Sarennes valley also offers an alternative descent back to the Romanche valley floor when the Col de Sarennes is free of snow. The **tourist office** in the Maison de l'Alpe, in place Paganon (May–Nov daily 9am–12.30pm & 2.30–6pm, Dec–April daily 9am–7pm; Ⓣ04.76.11.44.44, Ⓦwww.alpedhuez.com), gives information about accommodation and walks.

La Bérarde

To reach the tiny hamlet and mountaineering centre of **LA BÉRARDE**, right in the midst of the mightiest peaks of the **Parc National des Écrins** (see p.1024 for more on the park, and for the towns to the east of La Meije) at the end of the Vénéon valley, leave the road from Grenoble some 6km after Le Bourg-d'Oisans and follow the narrow D530 for 38km up to the village. There you'll find a CAF refuge (Ⓣ04.76.79.53.83; closed Oct–March), a mountain rescue base and the small *Hôtel Tairraz* (Ⓣ04.76.79.53.46; ❸; closed Oct–March; restaurant from €14), which has adequate double rooms as well as dormitories. There are plenty of accessible valley walks without the need to risk your neck, including the approach to the back of the magnificent, near-4000-metre bulk of La Meije, with its dazzling glacier, the Glacier Carré.

La Grave and the Col du Lautaret

A few kilometres out of Le Bourg, southeast on the N91, the ascent into the **Gorges de l'Infernet** commences as the slate-black valley walls close around you, broadening out again as you cross the Barrage du Lac du Chambon, where roads diverge to the resort of **LES DEUX-ALPES** and the Col de Sarennes to the north. Continuing towards La Grave you'll pass two waterfalls issuing from the north side of the valley: early summer run-off enhances the slender, 300-metre plume of the **Cascade de la Pisse**, while, 6km further on, the near-vertical fall of churning white water called the **Saut de la Pucelle** ("the virgin's leap") is a breathtaking sight.

LA GRAVE, 26km from Le Bourg at the foot of the Col du Lautaret, faces the majestic glaciers of the north side of **La Meije**. It's a good base for walking: the **GR54** climbs up to Le Chazelet on the slopes northwest of the village and continues to the **Plateau de Paris** and the **Lac Noir**, which affords breathtaking views of La Meije. A similar and less energetic appreciation of these stunning vistas can be made by taking the **cable car** close to the 3200-metre summit of Le Rateau, just west of La Meije (mid-June to early Sept & late Dec to early May; €18 return), a 35-minute ride that's very good value for money when you consider that the view of the barely accessible interior of the Écrins is normally seen by only the most intrepid mountain-walkers. Make sure you buy the slightly more expensive ticket that goes all the way to the top.

From La Grave it's only 11km to the top of the **Col du Lautaret**, a pass that's been in use for centuries. The Roman road from Milan to Vienne crossed it, and its name comes from the small temple (*altaretum*) the Romans built to placate the deity of the mountains. Around the col is a huge expanse of meadow long known to botanists for its glorious variety of Alpine flowers, seen at their best in mid-July. You'll also find a botanic garden here – **Le Jardin Botanique Alpin du Lautaret** – which was founded at this high but accessible spot in 1899 and is maintained by the University of Grenoble (June–Sept daily 10am–6pm; €4, free at the beginning & end of the season); it displays plants from mountain ranges throughout the world.

The Galibier and Valloire

Turn north at Lautaret and you're on your way to the even higher **Col du Galibier** (no public transport), which is closed by snow from mid-October to mid-June – sometimes the snow lingers longer, making life for riders in the Tour de France yet more hellish. The road to the pass is a tremendous haul up to 2556m, utterly bare and wild, with the huge red-veined peak of the Grand Galibier rearing up on the right and a fearsome spiny ridge blocking the horizon beyond. The pass used to mark the frontier between France and Savoie, and you can see fine views of Mont Blanc to the north. A monument on the south side of the col commemorates Henri Desgranges, founder of the Tour de France. Crossing the col is one of the most gruelling stages in the race, with a long, brutal ascent and terrifying descent at breakneck speed. The road loops down in hairpin after hairpin, through **VALLOIRE**, a sizeable ski resort, whose church is one of the most richly decorated in Savoie, then over the **Col du Télégraphe** at 1570m and down into the deep wooded valley of the Arc, known as **La Maurienne**, with the Massif de la Vanoise rising abruptly behind. Valloire has pleasant, reasonably priced **hotels** in *Le Tatami* (ⓣ04.79.59.06.08, ⓦletatami.free.fr; ❸, half-pension) and the *Christiania Hôtel* (ⓣ04.79.59.00.57, ⓦwww.christiania-hote.com; ❹; restaurant from €15).

Le Casset

LE CASSET, back on the Briançon road about 12km beyond the Col du Lautaret, is a hamlet of dilapidated old houses clustered around a church with a bulbous dome. There's nothing to see in the town but the site is superb, with the Glacier du Casset dazzling above the green of the larches. Parking here makes it easy to access the **GR54**; a good day's walk is to follow the path out of the village as far as the **Col d'Arsine** (about 3hr), from which point you can either turn back or go on down to La Grave on the north side of the park, making an overnight stop at the *CAF Refuge del' Alpe/Villar d'Arène* (ⓣ04.76.79.94.66), below the col.

The path from Le Casset crosses the Guisane and follows a track through dark woods, first on the left and later on the right bank of the Petit Tabuc stream. From the end of the track you cross some grassy clearings before entering the trees again and climbing up to a milky looking mini-lake, the **Lac de la Douche**, at the foot of the Glacier du Casset. From here a clear path zigzags up a very steep slope, coming out in a long valley and eventually leading to the Col d'Arsine. About halfway up are some tumbledown huts, the **Chalets d'Arsine**, by a series of blue-grey tarns. Up on the left from the chalets are a whole series of glaciers. The biggest is the **Glacier d'Arsine**, hanging from the walls of the long jagged ridge suspended between the Montagne des Agneaux and the Pic de Neige Cordier to the west.

There's a café and grocery store in the village of Le Casset, while for somewhere to stay, there's a **campsite** and **gîte d'étape**, *Le Casset* (ⓣ04.92.24.45.74), near the church. Other budget accommodation nearby includes a *gîte d'étape*, *Fourou* (ⓣ04.92.24.41.13; closed Sept–Dec), in Monetier-les-Bains, and a **HI hostel** at Le Bez in the ski resort of Serre-Chevalier (see opposite).

Briançon and the Écrins region

Located 26km south of Modane and nearly 100km east of Grenoble on the N91, **BRIANÇON** is the capital of the Écrins. An imposing citadel set on a rocky height above the valleys of the Durance and Guisane only 10km from the Italian border, the town guards the road to the desolate and windswept **Col de Montgenèvre**, one of the oldest and most important passes into Italy.

Originally a Gallic settlement, the town was fortified by the Romans to guard their Mons Matrona road from Milan to Vienne. During the Middle Ages, it was the capital of the République des Escartons, a federation of mountain communities grouped together for mutual defence and the preservation of their liberties and privileges.

It's well worth taking an hour to hike around the **old town** and fortified walls of Briançon, and the town is also a good base for exploring the **Parc National des Écrins** and the villages to the north. If you come by car the best thing is to stop at the **Champ de Mars** at the top of the hill and look around from there. The old town is well fortified – it has been a fortified city since the fourteenth century, but it is Sébastian Leprestre de Vauban's late seventeenth-century stout walls that remain today. The French city needed protection from the Savoie towns to the north, and from the Protestant communities in the area that had been forced to flee into the nearby mountains. Enter the town through the **Porte Pignerol**, from where the narrow main street – known as the *grande gargouille* because of the "gurgling" stream running down the middle – tips steeply downhill, bordered by mostly eighteenth-century houses. To the right is the sturdy plain **collegiate church**, designed under the supervision of Vauban, again with an eye to defence. Beyond it, there's a fantastic **view** from the walls, especially on a clear starry night, when the snows on the surrounding barrier of mountains give off a silvery glow.

Vauban's **citadel** above the Porte Pignerol, the highest point of the fortifications, can be visited for free in July and August, and by guided tour the rest of the year, usually starting at 3pm from just inside the northern gate (€3.80). From rue Aspirant Jan, which winds up below the fortress, there is a wonderful view of the gorges of the Durance River below, and of the Asfeld Bridge, completed in 1731. As you walk around, look out for the magnificent **sundials** that decorate many of the houses. Each one has a little maxim in French, and they can be seen all over the Haute Alpes *département*.

Practicalities

Briançon's **tourist office** is in the place du Temple close to the Porte Pignerol gateway (Mon–Sat 8.30am–noon & 1.30–6.30pm, Sun 10am–12.30pm & 2.30–6pm; ⓣ04.92.21.08.50, ⓦwww.briancon.com). The mountain guides' office is in Parc Chancel (summer daily 9.30am–noon & 3–7pm; ⓣ04.92.20.15.73), and the Maison du Parc National des Écrins is in place Médecin-Général-Blanchard (ⓣ04.92.21.42.15, ⓦwww.les-ecrins-parc-national.fr.com). There are a number of inexpensive **hotels** in Briançon. One of the least expensive is *Pension des Remparts*, in the citadel itself at 14 av de Vauban (ⓣ & ⓕ04.92.21.08.73; ❷; closed Nov), or try the slightly nicer *Auberge de la Paix* (ⓣ04.92.21.37.43, ⓦwww.auberge-de-la-paix.com; ❸). A more comfortable option is *L'Alpe Hôtel Club du Soleil* on avenue du Dauphiné (ⓣ04.92.20.02.00, ⓦwww.alpe-hotel.com; ❹), a large modern place in the centre of town, with a sauna and swimming pool. There's also a very nice **hostel** at Le Bez, near **Serre-Chevalier** (ⓣ04.92.24.74.54, ⓔserre-chevalier@fuaj.org), 8km north on the main Grenoble road and served by local buses. The nearest **campsite** is *Camping des Cinq Vallées* at St-Blaise (ⓣ04.92.21.06.27, ⓦwww.camping5valees.com, open June–Sept), 2km from town. There are a number of **gîtes d'étape**, including the cosy *Le Petit Phoque*, 2km along the Montgenèvre road at Le Fontenil (ⓣ & ⓕ04.92.20.07.27; closed first two weeks in Nov).

As for **eating**, the old town has a number of options. It's full of wonderful Italian cafés, with delicious cakes and pizzas, and there are plenty of reasonably priced restaurants such as *Les Templiers* and *Le Petit Bouchon*, both of which have patios on the place du Temple (beside the tourist office), and solid, cheap menus for €10–12. To escape the *tartiflette* there's reasonable Indian food from €13 at *Palais de Jaipur*, 8 place General Eberle (Ⓣ04.92.21.09.18).

The Clarée valley

For a beautiful day excursion from Briançon, head for the valley of the **River Clarée**. Without your own transport, you'll have to walk through the valley, which is made simple and possible by the **GR5**, which passes through the main villages through the valley.

Leave Briançon by the Montgenèvre road (N94) and take the left fork after 2km. A lane follows the wooded riverbank along the bottom of a narrow ravine parallel to the Italian frontier. If you want to spend a night up here, the depopulated and half-ruined hamlet of **PLAMPINET**, 11km from the beginning of the valley road, has both hotel and hostel-type **accommodation** in a vast renovated farm, *La Cleida* (Ⓣ04.92.21.32.48; ❶; open mid-June to mid-Sept, and Christmas & Feb school hols), with comfortable beds, as well as better-equipped rooms at the *Auberge de la Clarée* by the bridge (Ⓣ04.92.21.37.71; ❷). Alternatively, head for **NÉVACHE**, 6km past Plampinet, where the valley widens; it has already seen a good deal of holiday development, though the village's old nucleus of wide-roofed houses still huddles protectively around the church. This is worth a look for its carving, Baroque altarpiece and a few items in the treasury, including some eleventh-century doors. There are plenty of **gîtes** here, including *Le Creux des Souches* (Ⓣ04.92.21.16.34).

Beyond Névache, towards the head of the valley, the scenery becomes even finer – in May the meadows are carpeted with crocuses and run with snow melt, and fat marmots whistle from the rocks. Six kilometres past the village are more **refuges**, including two by the first bridge – *Fontcouverte* and *La Fruitière* – and another at the end of the road, as well as the CAF *Refuge des Drayères* on the slopes of Mont Thabor (Ⓣ04.92.21.36.01), none of which are open for much longer than the summer season. A full list of refuges and *gîtes* with a map of their locations is available from the tourist office at Briançon.

The Parc National des Écrins

The **Parc National des Écrins** (Ⓦwww.les-ecrins-parc-national.fr) covers 230,000 acres of Alpine terrain, some 50km southeast of Grenoble and 20km west of Briançon, its highest peaks rising to 4102m in the **Massif de Pelvoux** in the north of the park. The Écrins is the second most popular place for climbing in the country (Mont Blanc being the first), and with its sunny weather, mazy rivers, and impressive wildflowers it's hard not to regard the park as a big playground. Not only are many of the massifs bolted for sport climbing, but plenty have actually been turned into ropes courses, or *Via Ferrata* – the wires and ladders are already built in so that inexperienced climbers can strap on a harness and spend a day climbing (pick up the *Via Ferrata en Grand Briançonnais* brochure at any of the tourist offices). The small towns in the park are of little interest in themselves, especially in comparison with the architecture and culture of the Queyras and the nightlife in Chamonix, but the Écrins is worth a trip for the sheer variety of sports that it offers in a much less crowded setting than Mont Blanc.

The easiest route into the park is from **Argentières**, an unattractive former mining town 16km south of Briançon (for tours of the town's silver mines call Ⓣ04.92.23.02.94 in advance). From here a small road cuts west into the valley towards **Vallouise**, with the ice-capped monster of Mont Pelvoux itself (3946m) rearing in front of you all the way. For information on **La Bérarde** on the far side of the park, closer to Grenoble, see p.1021.

La Bâtie and Les Vigneaux

The first place you come to on the road into the park from Argentières is **LA BÂTIE**, where there are remains of the so-called **Mur des Vaudois**. The origins of the wall are uncertain: it was probably built either to keep out companies of marauding soldiers-turned-bandits, or to control the spread of plague in the fourteenth century. Despite its name, the wall actually has nothing to do with the Valdois, a sect prominent in this part of the country (see box, p.1026).

A couple of kilometres beyond La Bâtie on the right is the lovely village of **LES VIGNEAUX**, surrounded by apple orchards and backed by the fierce crags of Montbrison. The village **church** has a fine old door and lock under a vaulted porch. Beside it on the exterior wall of the church are two bands of paintings depicting the Seven Deadly Sins. A man carrying a leg of mutton and drinking wine from a flask represents Gluttony, while a woman with rouged cheeks, green stockings and an enticing expanse of thigh on display represents Lust. In the lower band they are all getting their comeuppance, writhing in the agonies of hellfire.

Vallouise

VALLOUISE lies under a steep wooded spur at the junction of two rivers, the Gyrond (which combines the Gyr and the Onde, smaller rivers north of town) and the Gérendoine, about 10km from Argentière. The great glaciered peaks visible up the latter valley are Les Bans; up in front is Mont Pelvoux. The nucleus of the old village – narrow lanes between sombre stone chalets – is again its **church**, fifteenth-century with a sixteenth-century porch on pink marble pillars. A fresco of the Adoration of the Magi adorns the tympanum above the door, itself a magnificent object, with carved Gothic panels along the top and an ancient lock-and-bolt with a chimera's head. Inside are some more frescoes, and a collection of naive wooden statues.

The **GR54**, which does the circuit of the Écrins park, passes through Vallouise: the stage on from here to Le Monetier via Lac de l'Eychauda is one of the best. Another good walk is to the hamlet of **PUY AILLAUD**, high on the west flank of the Gyr valley. The path starts just to the right of the church and zigzags up the steep slope behind it with almost aerial views of the valley beneath.

Vallouise has a **campsite**, some **gîtes** and a handful of **hotels**: the *Edelweiss* is the least expensive (ⓣ04.92.23.38.58, ⓕ04.92.23.33.46; ❸; closed mid-April to mid-June & mid-Sept to mid-Dec), or for apartment accommodation try *Alpbase*, a series of chalets rented out by a British couple for short periods (ⓣ04.92.23.45.69, ⓦwww.alpbase.com;), but all rooms in the village are likely to be full in July and August. The Vallouise Maison du Parc des Écrins provides hiking information (ⓣ04.92.23.32.31) and there's a **tourist office** in place de l'Église (May–Sept daily 9am–noon & 3–7pm; Oct–April daily 9am–noon & 2.30–6.30pm ⓣ04.92.23.36.12, ⓦwww.lavallouise.com), and a Bureau des Guides hut in the main car park (ⓣ04.92.23.32.29, ⓦwww.guides-ecrins.com). There's a minibus service as far as Ailefroide in summer, starting from the bar next to the *Edelweiss* hotel; to walk takes two hours or so. For **food** try the microbrewery *L&L AlpHand* on place du Village (ⓣ04.92.23.20.00; closed May to mid-June).

The Valdois

The **Valdois** ("Waldensians" in English) were a heretical sect founded in the late twelfth century by Pierre Valdo, a merchant from Lyon, who preached against worldly wealth and the corruption of the clergy and, practising as he preached, gave his wealth to the poor. Excommunicated in 1186, the Valdois came more and more to deny the authority of the Church, and sought refuge from persecution in the remote mountain valleys of Pelvoux, especially in the area around Vallouise and Argentières.

There was a crop of executions for sorcery in the early fifteenth century, and many of the victims were probably Valdois, burnt to death in wooden cabins built for this purpose. In 1488, Charles VIII launched a full-scale crusade against them. There's a spot west of Ailefroide known as Baume Chapelue where they were smoked out by the military and butchered. In 1562 they joined the growing Huguenot cause, but after the Revocation of the Edict of Nantes, they were finally exterminated in the eighteenth century, when 8000 troops went on the rampage, creating total desolation and "leaving neither people nor animals".

Ailefroide

The road that continues another 6km up to **AILEFROIDE** is absolutely spectacular, as is the site of Ailefroide itself, overwhelmed by the daunting ridges, peaks and glaciers of Pelvoux and the Barre des Écrins, at 4102m the highest summit in the massif. The village is really no more than a huge campsite (ⓣ04.92.23.46.43, ⓦwww.lavallouise.com) with a couple of shops and a climbing centre: not quite wilderness (it can get quite crowded in August) but a long drive from the nearest city. Beyond Ailefroide, however, towards the end of the road at the Pré du Madame Carle and the old Refuge Cézanne, you'll be rewarded with some magnificent scenery.

The classic walk to do is the steep climb to the CAF *Refuge du Glacier Blanc* (ⓣ04.92.23.50.24), right beside the beetling glacier, but it can be a real circus on a summer's day. Quieter, and a good deal longer, is the approach to the CAF *Refuge du Sélé* (ⓣ04.92.23.39.49) and the Pointe du Sélé, due west of Ailefroide, but bear in mind that this is a difficult trek for experienced hikers, not an afternoon stroll.

Briançon to Queyras

The direct route from Briançon to Queyras, crossing the 2360m **Col d'Izoard**, is a beautiful trip, but, with no buses covering the distance, you need a car to do it. Leaving Briançon, the D902 begins to climb the steep Cerveyrette valley, the seemingly endless series of switchbacks entering an ever denser forest until it arrives at **LE LAUS**, a cluster of old stone houses with long, sloping, wooden roofs set in meadows beside the stream. Soon you reach the tree line and cross the **Col d'Izouard** to the **Casse Déserte**, a wild, desolate region with huge screes running down off the peaks and weirdly eroded orangey rocks. From the top the view extends over many kilometres of mountain landscape, and it's from here that the vertiginous descent commences, entering another river valley, which is lined by a succession of tiny hamlets, **BRUNISSARD**, **LA CHALP** and, finally, larger **ARVIEUX**, lying in a high valley surrounded by fields and meadows, just 6km from Château-Queyras. A splendidly ornate Baroque church, dedicated to St-Thomas-Becket, stands guard at the entrance to the village. The **GR5** passes through, running a parallel route from Briançon; if you started out late and can't reach Arvieux by nightfall, there is also a **gîte**, *Les Bons Enfants*

(Ⓣ04.92.46.73.85, Ⓔlesbonsenfants@free.fr) in Brunissard higher up in the valley. Or, once in Arivieux, you can try *La Casse Déserte* (Ⓣ04.92.46.72.91; ❷).

Mont-Dauphin and Embrun

If the Col d'Izoard is closed, or if you don't like slow, winding, high roads, then the Queyras can be reached from the north or the south on the N94. From Briançon, the river Durance meanders leisurely through a wide valley, following the N94, until some 27km later it passes **MONT-DAUPHIN**, a formidably **bastioned village**, and one of the many Alpine fortifications designed by Vauban in the seventeenth century, commanding the entrance to the valley of the Guil. There's a **tourist office** (Mon–Sat 9am–noon & 3–6pm; Ⓣ & Ⓕ04.92.45.17.80), a **gîte**, *Le Glacier Bleu* (Ⓣ04.92.45.18.47, Ⓦwww.leglacierbleu.fr), and several restaurants inside the walled perimeter.

Twenty kilometres further along its course the river reaches **EMBRUN**, south of Briançon and the Queyras on the way to Gap, a beautiful little town of narrow streets on a rocky bluff above the Durance on the edge of both the Parc du Queyras and the Parc des Écrins. It has been a fortress town for centuries. Hadrian made it the capital of the Maritime Alps, and from the third century to the Revolution it was the seat of an important archbishopric. The chief sight is its twelfth-century cathedral (concerts in summertime), with a porch in alternating courses of black and white marble in the Italian Lombard style, its roof supported on columns of pink marble resting on lions' backs – an arrangement that inspired numerous imitators throughout the region. The **tourist office**, in a former chapel of the Cordeliers on place Général-Dosse (July & Aug Mon–Sat 9am–7.30pm, Sun 9.30am–noon & 4–7pm; Sept–June Mon–Sat 9am–noon & 2–6.30pm; Ⓣ04.92.43.72.72, Ⓦwww.ot-embrun.fr), is next door to the bureau for **mountain guides**, which organizes a daily programme of walks in the surrounding mountains. There's an **Internet** café, *Omnis Cyberspace*, 30 rue de la Liberté, just down the street. The park zones and the area south of Embrun have extensive facilities for outdoor activities ranging from rafting to sailing and climbing (enquire at the tourist office).

There are two very agreeable **hotels** by the central place de la Mairie: the simple, but delightful *Hôtel du Commerce*, just off the square in rue St-Pierre (Ⓣ04.92.43.54.54, Ⓕ04.92.43.81.89; ❷), with an excellent restaurant serving menus from €14; and the flower-decked *Hôtel de la Mairie* on the square itself (Ⓣ04.92.43.20.65, Ⓦwww.hoteldelamairie.com; ❸; closed Oct–Nov), also with good restaurant (closed Mon & Sun eve in winter; from €15) serving tasty local specialities. There are several campsites as well: two reasonably priced ones are *Le Moulin* (Ⓣ04.92.43.00.41; closed mid-Sept to Jan), on the left after the bridge on the Gap road (N94), and *La Tour*, on route de la Madeleine close to the Durance off the D994 (Ⓣ04.92.43.17.66; closed Sept to late June).

Just a few kilometres past Embrun is **Lac de Serre-Ponçon**, the largest man-made lake in Europe, created in the 1950s by damming and taming the wild Durance. A **hostel** overlooks the lake 10km from Embrun at **SAVINES-LE-LAC** (Ⓣ04.92.44.20.16, Ⓕ04.92.44.24.54; closed mid-Sept to April), a town that was moved from what is now the bottom of the lake to its current location.

Parc Régional du Queyras

The **Parc Régional du Queyras** (Ⓦwww.queyras.com), spreading southeast of Briançon to the Italian border, is much more Mediterranean in appearance

than the mountains to the north, with low scrub covering the mountainsides, poor shallow soil, white friable rock and a huge variety of flora. The open land along the park's rolling roads makes it particularly enjoyable to spend a few hours driving along them up to **St-Véran**, an Alpine village near the Italian border. The park has some good walking opportunities, with the **GR58** path making a circuit of the park, running through St-Véran and **L'Échalp**, and the **GR5** crossing through Ceillac and Arvieux on its way from Briançon towards Embrun.

Guillestre

The road into the Queyras park follows the River Guil from Mont-Dauphin. First stop is **GUILLESTRE**, a pretty mountain village that only really comes to life in summer. Its houses, in typical Queyras style, have open granaries on the upper floors and its church has a lion-porch in emulation of the cathedral at Embrun. Head for the **tourist office** on the modern square at the top of the main street for information about the surrounding area (mid-June to Aug Mon–Sat 9am–7pm, Sun 9am–noon & 3–7pm; Sept to mid-June Mon–Sat 9am–noon & 2–6pm; ⓣ04.92.45.04.37).

The village lies at the foot of the long climb southwards to the **Col de Vars** (2111m), which gives access to the remote and beautiful walking country of the upper Ubaye valley; it's six hours, via Lac Miroir, Lac Ste-Anne and the Col Girardin, to the CAF *Refuge de Maljasset* (ⓣ04.92.84.34.04; closed Jan & mid-May to mid-June).

If you want to stay in Guillestre, there's a primitive **hostel**, *Les Quatre Vents* (ⓣ & ⓕ04.92.45.04.32; closed Oct & Nov), in the same grounds as the municipal campsite. For more comfortable accommodation, try the *Hôtel Martinet* (ⓣ04.92.45.00.28, ⓔinfo@hotel-le-martinet.com; ❸; restaurant from €12) or the well-appointed *Hôtel Barnières* (ⓣ04.92.45.05.07, ⓕ04.92.45.28.74; ❹; closed Oct–May; restaurant from €17), 300m above the town.

Château-Ville-Vieille and around

The road route into the park from Guillestre strikes northeast through the narrow gorge of the **Combe du Queyras**, scarcely more than a claustrophobic crack between walls up to 400m high. Far below the road, the clear stream boils down over red and green rocks. It was only in the twentieth century that road-building techniques became sufficiently sophisticated to cope with these narrows – previously they had to be circumvented by a detour over the adjacent heights.

At the upper end of the Combe, the valley broadens briefly, and ahead you see the ruinous fort of **Château-Queyras** barring the way so completely that there's scarcely room for the road to squeeze around its base – Vauban at work again, though the original fortress was medieval. There is an exhibit on the geological conditions that created the Alps in the crypt of the castle's chapel (daily: May & Sept 10am–6pm; June–Aug 9am–7pm; €3.50). Just beyond is **CHÂTEAU-VILLE-VIEILLE**, where the road for St-Véran branches right over the Guil and up the ravine of the Aigue Blanche torrent. A smaller place than Guillestre, it has only a few old houses still intact and a **church** with its square tower and octagonal steeple flanked by four short triangular pinnacles – a style characteristic of this corner of the Alps.

Straight on, the road follows the Guil through the villages of Aiguilles, Abriès and L'Échalp (all with *gîtes d'étape*), to the **Belvédère du Viso**, close to the Italian border, and **Monte Viso**, at 3841m the highest peak in the area.

East of L'Échalp, a variant of the **GR58**, which does the circuit of the park, climbs up to the **Col de la Croix**, used in former times by Italian peasants bringing their produce to market in Abriès. South of the village, the path climbs to the pastures of **Alpe de Médille**, where you can see across to Monte Viso, then on past the lakes of **Egourgéou**, **Bariche** and **Foréant** to **Col Vieux** and west to the *Refuge Agnel*; from here you can continue on to St-Véran.

St-Véran

At 2042m, **ST-VÉRAN** claims to be the highest permanently inhabited village in Europe. It lies on the east side of the valley of the Aigue Blanche, backed by steep lush mountain pasture, 7km south ofVille-Vieille. Opposite, rock walls and slopes of scree rise to snowy ridges. In the valley bottom and on any treeless patch of ground, no matter how steep, you can see the remains of abandoned terraces. They were in use up until World War II, though, as with most high Alpine villages, traditional farming has now practically died out. Today the principal economic activity is entertaining tourists. The very accommodating **tourist office** is halfway down the main high street (Ⓣ04.92.45.82.21, Ⓦwww.saintveran.com; Mon–Sat 9am–12.30pm & 2–6.30pm, Sun in high season).

St-Véran's houses are part stone and part timber, and there are several refurbished old drinking fountains, made entirely of wood. The stone **church** stands prettily on the higher of the two "streets", its white tower silhouetted against the bare crags across the valley. The columns of its porch rest on crudely carved lions, one holding a man in its paws. The interior is surprisingly rich, with Baroque altars and retables.

Just south of the village, there is a triple **cross** adorned with the instruments of Christ's Passion and an inscription urging the passer-by to choose between the devout or rebellious life ("l'homme révolté qui n'est jamais content"); the **GR58**, waymarked and easy to follow, turns right down to the river, beside which there are some good spots for **camping sauvage**. The path continues up the left bank through woods of pine and larch as far as the chapel of Notre-Dame-de-Clausis. There, above the treeline, it crosses to the right bank of the stream and winds up damp grassy slopes to the **Col de Chamoussière**, about three-and-a-half hours from St-Véran. The ridge to the right of the col marks the frontier with Italy. In the valley below, you can see the **Refuge Agnel**, about an hour away, with the **Pain de Sucre** (3208m) behind it. From there you can continue to L'Échalp (see p.1028). In early July, there are glorious flowers – violets, Black Vanilla orchids, pinks and gentians – in the meadows leading up to the col.

It's hard to get good-value **accommodation** around St-Véran. One good deal is the *Auberge Monchu* (Ⓣ04.92.45.83.96, Ⓦwww.lemonchu.fr; ❷ half-board per person; closed mid-April to mid-June & mid-Sept to Christmas), which also provides *gîte d'étape* facilities and is a few kilometres south of St-Véran proper. There are also a few **hotels**, including the *Beauregard* (Ⓣ04.92.45.86.86, Ⓦwww.hotelbeauregard.fr; ❸), just below the village with a lovely swimming pool. And in the road along at the top of St-Véran you'll find *Le Grand Tétras* (Ⓣ04.92.45.82.42, Ⓕ04.92.45.85.98; ❹ demi-pension; closed Oct–April) and *Les Gabelous* **gîte d'étape** (Ⓣ04.92.45.81.39, Ⓕ04.92.45.81.39).

Travel details

Trains

Annecy to: Aix-les-Bains (frequent; 30–40min); Chambéry (frequent; 45min); Grenoble (several daily; 2hr); Lyon (several daily; 2hr); Paris (frequent; 4hr 30min); St-Gervais (9-10 daily; 1hr 35min–2hr).
Annemasse to: Annecy, changing at La-Roche-sur-Foron (4–5 daily; 1hr 30min); Évian (frequent; 35min); Paris (1 daily; 8hr).
Briançon to: Marseille (3 daily; 4hr 30min); Grenoble (4 daily; 4hr).
Chambéry to: Aix-les-Bains (frequent; 10min); Annecy (frequent; 45min); Bourg-St-Maurice (5 daily; 2hr); Geneva (several daily; 1hr 30min); Grenoble (several daily; 1hr); Lyon (frequent; 1hr 30min–2hr 30min); Modane (frequent; 1hr 20min); Paris (frequent; 5hr 30min).
Evian to: Geneva (7 daily; 1hr); Thonon-les-Bains (frequent; 15min).
Grenoble to: Annecy (several daily; 2hr); Briançon, changing at Veynes-Dévoluy (1–2 daily; 4hr); Chambéry (several daily; 1hr); Gap (1–2 daily; 2hr 30min); Lyon (frequent; 1hr 30min–1hr 45min); Paris-Lyon (several daily; 3hr 10min–7hr 15min).
St-Gervais to: Chamonix (5–7 daily; 45min).

Buses

Annecy to: Albertville (4 daily; 50min); Évian (4 daily; 1hr 30min); Lyon (2 daily; 2hr 30min); Talloires (6 daily; 50min).
Bourg-St-Maurice to: Aosta (1 daily July & Aug; 2hr 30min); Val d'Isère (1–2 daily; 50min–1hr 20min).
Briançon to: Mont-Dauphin (3–5 daily; 1hr 15min).
Chambéry to: Aix-les-Bains (several daily; 20min); Annecy (several daily; 1hr); Grenoble (several daily; 1hr).
Chamonix to: Annecy, via La-Roche-sur-Foron (3 daily; 3hr); Annecy, via Megève (1 daily; 3hr); Geneva (1 daily; 2hr 30min); Grenoble (1 daily; 3hr 30min).
Cluses to: Samoëns (1–3 daily; 35min); Sixt (1–3 daily; 45min).
Grenoble to: L'Alpe d'Huez (2 daily; 45min); Bourg-d'Oisans (4–6 daily; 1hr 20min); Briançon (several daily; 2hr); Chambéry (several daily; 1hr); Col du Lau-taret (1 daily; 2hr); Gap (1 daily; 2hr 45min); La Grave (1 daily; 1hr 40min); Monetier-les-Bains (1 daily; 2hr 25min); St-Pierre-de-Chartreuse (at least 1 daily; 1hr); Villard-de-Lans and other towns in the Vercors (at least 1 daily; 45min).
Mont-Dauphin to (summer only): Ceillac (2 daily; 35min); Guillestre (2–3 daily; 5min); St-Véran (2–3 daily; 1hr 30min); Vars (2 daily; 50min); Ville-Vieille (2–3 daily; 1hr 5min).
Thonon-les-Bains to: Évian (frequent; 25min); Yvoire (3–4 daily; 20min).
Valloire to (summer only): St-Michel-de-Maurienne (2 daily; 45min).

The Rhône valley and Provence

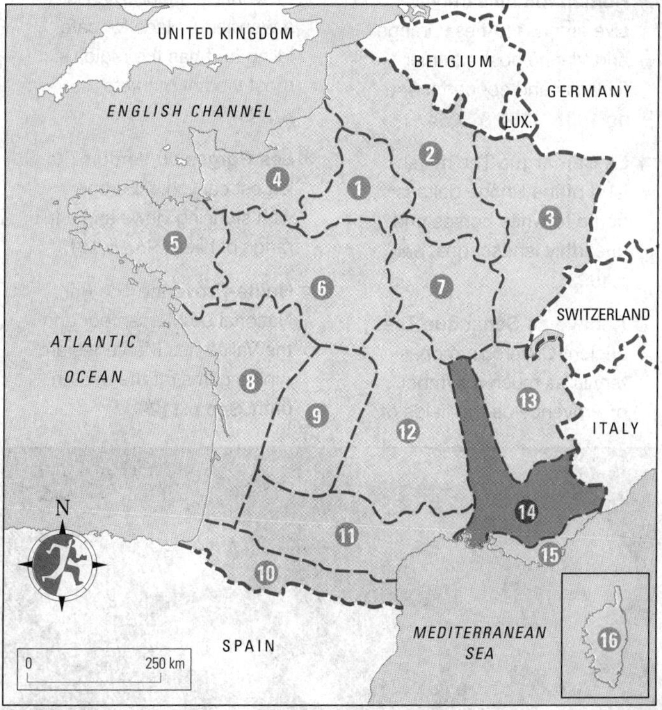

CHAPTER 14 **Highlights**

* **Lyon** *Traboulez* through the Renaissance quarter and savour the culinary genius of some of France's top chefs. See p.1039

* **Avignon** The former city of popes has spectacular monuments and museums to go along with the annual Festival d'Avignon. See p.1070

* **Roman remains** Impressive arenas in Arles, Orange and Vienne host summer festivals and concerts. See pp.1087, 1061 & 1054

* **La Camargue** The marshland of the Rhône delta is home to white horses and unearthly landscapes. See p.1093

* **Abbaye de Sénanque** The ancient Cistercian monastery is as much a symbol of Provence as the fields of lavender surrounding it. See p.110

* **Medieval hilltop villages** Gordes and Les Baux are the most famous, but Saignon and Entrecasteaux are equally picturesque, and much less frequented. See pp.110, 1085, 1103 & 1112

* **Aix** The most beautiful of Provence's major cities is a wonderful place for café idling and has the region's most vibrant markets. See p.1104

* **Les Gorges du Verdon** The largest canyon in Europe, with stunning views and a full range of hikes. See p.1113

* **Haute-Provence** The Parc National du Mercantour and the Vallée des Merveilles are Alpine gems off the beaten path. See p.1120

△ Pétanque balls, Roussillon

14

The Rhône valley and Provence

Of all the areas of France, **Provence** is the most irresistible. Geographically it ranges from the snow-capped mountains of the **southern Alps** to the delta plains of the **Camargue** and has the greatest European canyon, the **Gorges du Verdon**. Fortified towns guard its old borders; countless villages perch defensively on hilltops; and its great cities – **Aix-en-Provence** and **Avignon** – are full of cultural glories. The sensual inducements of Provence include warmth, food and wine, and the perfumes of Mediterranean vegetation. Along with its coast – which is covered in the following chapter – it has attracted the rich and famous, the artistic and reclusive, and countless arrivals who have found themselves unable to conceive of life elsewhere.

In appearance, despite the throngs of foreigners and French from other regions, **inland Provence** remains remarkably unscathed. The history of its earliest known natives, of the Greeks, then Romans, raiding Saracens, schismatic popes, and shifting allegiances to different counts and princes, is still in evidence. Provence's complete integration into France dates only from the nineteenth century and, though the Provençal language is only spoken by a small minority, the accent is distinctive even to a foreign ear. In the east the rhythms of speech become clearly Italian.

Unless you're intending to stay for months, the main problem with Provence is choosing where to go. In the west, along the **Rhône valley**, are the Roman cities of **Orange**, **Vaison-la-Romaine**, **Carpentras** and **Arles**, and the papal city of **Avignon**, with its fantastic summer festival. **Aix-en-Provence** is the mini-Paris of the region and was home to Cézanne, for whom the **Mont Ste-Victoire** was an enduring subject; Van Gogh's links are with **St-Rémy** and Arles. The Gorges du Verdon, **the Parc National du Mercantour** along the Italian border, **Mont Ventoux** northeast of Carpentras, and the flamingo-filled lagoons of the **Camargue** are just a selection of the diverse and stunning landscapes of this region.

Before you reach Provence from the north there are the **vineyards of the Rhône valley** and, before them, the French centre of gastronomy and second largest city of the country, **Lyon**. With its choice of restaurants, clubs, culture and all the accoutrements of an affluent and vital Western city, it stands in opulent contrast to the medieval hilltop villages of Provence.

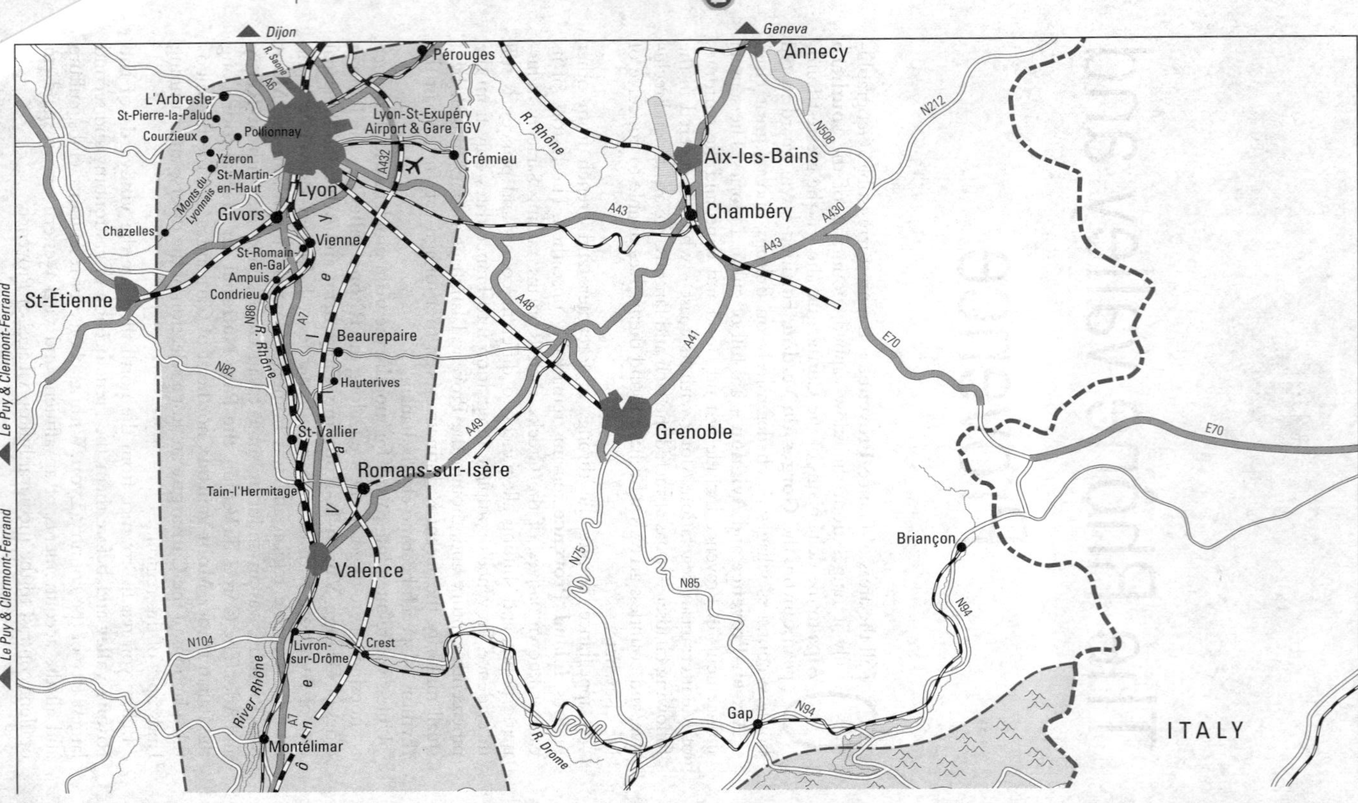

Dijon
Geneva
Turin
Le Puy & Clermont-Ferrand
Le Puy & Clermont-Ferrand
Annecy
Aix-les-Bains
Chambéry
Grenoble
Pérouges
Crémieu
Lyon-St-Exupéry Airport & Gare TGV
L'Arbresle
St-Pierre-la-Palud
Pollionnay
Courzieux
Yzeron
St-Martin-en-Haut
Monts du Lyonnais
Lyon
Givors
Chazelles
Vienne
St-Romain-en-Gal
Ampuis
Condrieu
St-Étienne
Beaurepaire
Hauterives
St-Vallier
Romans-sur-Isère
Tain-l'Hermitage
Valence
Livron-sur-Drôme
Crest
Montélimar
Briançon
Gap
ITALY
R. Saône
R. Rhône
River Rhône
R. Drome
A6
A7
A41
A43
A48
A49
A430
A432
E70
N212
N508
N86
N82
N104
N75
N85
N94

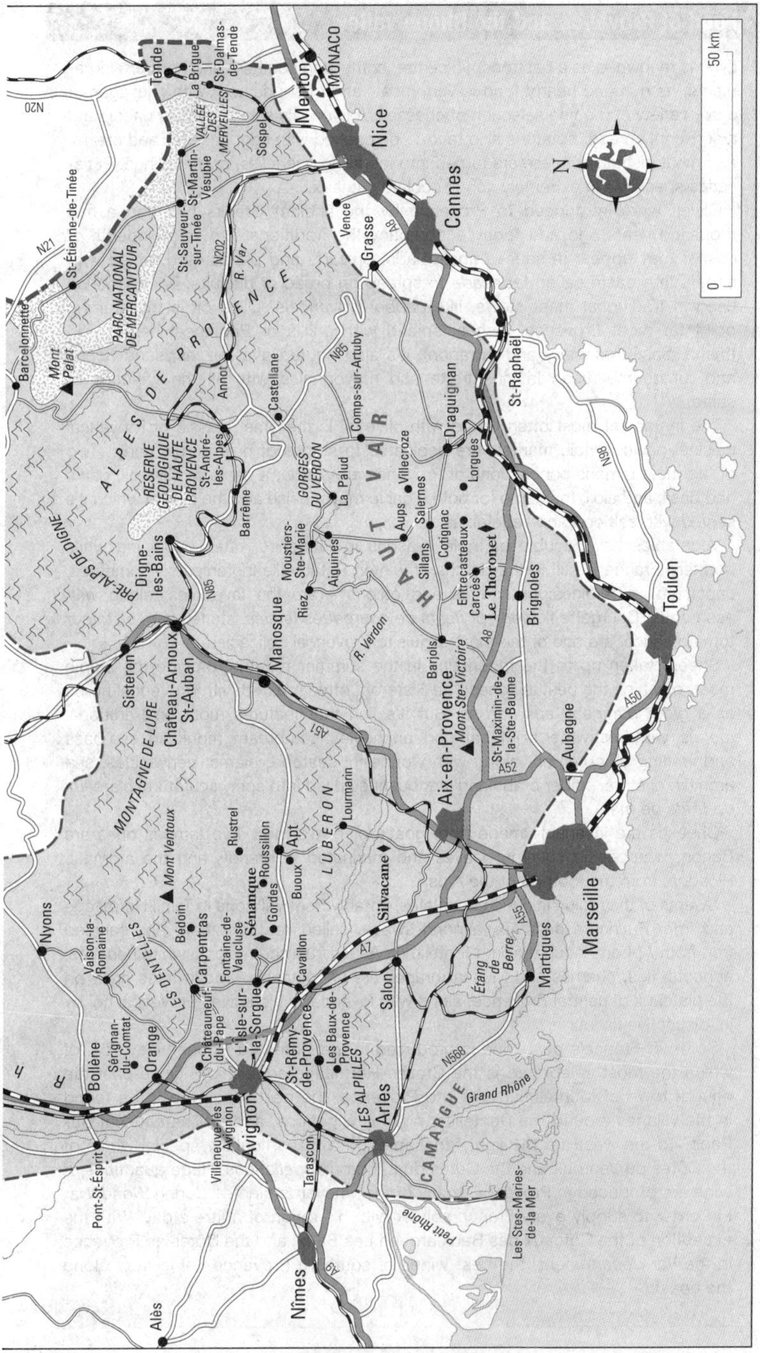

Nyons
Bollène
Pont-St-Ésprit
Vaison-la-Romaine
Sérignan-du-Comtat
Alès
Orange
LES DENTELLES
MONTAGNE DE LURE
Mont Ventoux
Bédoin
Châteauneuf-du-Pape
Carpentras
Villeneuve-lès-Avignon
Avignon
Fontaine-de-Vaucluse
L'Isle-sur-la-Sorgue
Sénanque
Rustrel
Gordes
Roussillon
Nîmes
Tarascon
St-Rémy-de-Provence
Cavaillon
Buoux
Apt
Les Baux-de-Provence
LUBERON
Lourmarin
LES ALPILLES
Arles
Salon
Silvacane
A9
A7
A51
CAMARGUE
Petit Rhône
Grand Rhône
N568
Étang de Berre
A55
Les Stes-Maries-de-la Mer
Martigues
Marseille
Aix-en-Provence
Mont Ste-Victoire
Aubagne
A50
Toulon
Sisteron
Château-Arnoux
St-Auban
N85
Manosque
PRE-ALPS DE DIGNE
Digne-les-Bains
RESERVE GEOLOGIQUE DE HAUTE PROVENCE
St-André-les-Alpes
Barrême
ALPES DE PROVENCE
Barcelonnette
Mont Pelat
St-Étienne-de-Tinée
N21
N20
PARC NATIONAL DE MERCANTOUR
Tende
La Brigue
St-Dalmas-de-Tende
St-Sauveur-sur-Tinée
St-Martin-Vésubie
VALLÉE DES MERVEILLES
Annot
N202
R. Var
Castellane
Sospel
Menton
MONACO
Moustiers-Ste-Marie
Riez
GORGES DU VERDON
Aiguines
La Palud
Comps-sur-Artuby
R. Verdon
HAUT VAR
Aups
Villecroze
Sillans
Salernes
Barjols
Cotignac
Entrecasteaux
Carcès
Lorgues
Draguignan
Le Thoronet
A8
St-Maximin-de-la-Ste-Baume
A52
Brignoles
St-Raphaël
N98
Vence
Grasse
Nice
Cannes
N
0
50 km

Food of Provence and the Rhône valley

Lyon is renowned as a gastronomic centre, combining southern and northern ingredients. Its rich and hearty food is very meat- and offal-oriented, with sausages of every variety and a fine selection of cheeses. A Lyonnais salad includes bacon and a soft-cooked egg; potatoes also tend to be cooked with egg, cheeses and cream; and meat, fish and cheese are turned into fat, filling *quenelles*, or dumplings. Patisseries specialize in extremely rich chocolate gâteaux.

Olives were introduced to Provence by the ancient Greeks two and a half thousand years ago and today accompany the traditional Provençal apéritif of *pastis*; they appear in sauces and salads, on tarts and pizzas, and mixed with capers in a paste called *tapenade* to spread on bread or biscuits. They are also used in traditional meat stews, like *daube Provençale*. Olive oil is the starting point for most Provençal dishes; spiced with chillis or Provençal herbs (wild thyme, basil, rosemary and tarragon), it's also poured over pizzas, sandwiches and, of course, used in vinaigrette and mayonnaise with all the varieties of salad.

The ingredient most often mixed with olive oil is the other classic of Provençal cuisine: garlic. Whole markets are dedicated to strings of pale purple garlic. Two of the most famous concoctions of Provence are *pistou*, a paste of olive oil, garlic and basil, and aïoli, the name for both a garlic mayonnaise and the dish in which it's served with salt cod and vegetables.

Vegetables have double or triple seasons in Provence, often beginning while northern France is still in the depths of winter. Ratatouille ingredients – tomatoes, capsicum, aubergines, courgettes and onions – are the favourites, along with asparagus. Courgette flowers, or *fleurs de courgettes farcies*, stuffed with *pistou* or tomato sauce, are one of the most exquisite Provençal delicacies.

Sheep, taken up to the mountains in the summer months, provide the staple meat, of which the best is *agneau de Sisteron*, often roasted with Provençal herbs as *a gigot d'agneau aux herbes*. But it's fish that features most on traditional *menus*, with freshwater trout, salt cod, anchovies, sea bream, monkfish, sea bass and whiting all common, along with wonderful seafood: clams, periwinkles, sea urchins, oysters, spider crabs and langoustines piled into spiky sculptural *plateaux de fruits de mer*.

Cheeses are invariably made from goat's or ewe's milk. Two famous ones are Banon, wrapped in chestnut leaves and marinated in brandy, and the aromatic Picadon, from the foothills of the Alps.

Sweets of the region include chocolates, notably from Valrhona in Tain l'Hermitage and from Puyricard near Aix, almond sweets called *calissons* from Aix, candied fruit from Apt and nougat from Montélimar. As for fruit, the melons, white peaches, apricots, figs, cherries and Muscat grapes are unbeatable. Almond trees grow on the plateaux of central Provence, along with lavender, which gives Provençal honey its distinctive flavour.

Some of France's best wine is produced in the Côtes du Rhône vineyards, of which the most celebrated is the Crozes-Hermitage *appellation*. Once past the nougat town of Montélimar and into Provence, the best wines are to be found in the villages around the Dentelles, notably Gigondas, and at Châteauneuf-du-Pape. To the west are the light, drinkable, but not particularly special wines of the Côtes du Ventoux and the Côtes du Lubéron *appellations*. Huge quantities of wine are produced in Provence, many of the vineyards planted during World War I in order to supply every French soldier with his ration of a litre a day. With the exception of the Côteaux des Baux around Les Baux, and the Côtes de Provence in the Var *département*, the best wines of southern Provence come from along the coast.

The Rhône valley

The **Rhône valley**, the north–south route of ancient armies, medieval traders and modern rail and road, is now as industrialized as the least attractive parts of the north. Though the river is still a means of transport, its waters now also cool the reactors of the Marcoule and Tricastin nuclear power station between **Montélimar** and Avignon and act as a dumping ground for the heavy industries along its banks. Following the River Rhône holds few attractions, with the exceptions of the scenic stretch of **vineyards** and fruit orchards between the Roman city of **Vienne** and the distinctly southern city of **Valence**. But the big magnet is, of course, the gastronomic paradise of **Lyon**, with hundreds of sophisticated bars and restaurants.

Lyon and around

LYON is physically the second biggest city in France, a result of its uncontrolled urban sprawl. Viewed at high speed from the Autoroute du Soleil, the impression it gives is of a major confluence of rivers and roads, around which only petrochemical industries thrive. In fact, from the sixteenth century right up until the postwar dominance of metalworks and chemicals, silk was the city's main industry, generating the wealth which left behind a multitude of Renaissance buildings. But what has stamped its character most on Lyon is the commerce and banking that grew up with its industrial expansion. It is this that gives the city its affluent, self-confident air.

The city is now busy forging a role for itself within a new Europe, with international schools and colleges, the new HQ for Interpol, a recently inaugurated eco-friendly tram system, a second TGV station with links to the north that bypass Paris, and high-tech industrial parks for international companies, making it a modern city *par excellence*. More so than any other French city, it has embraced the monetarist vision of the European Union and is acting, with some success, as a postmodern city-state within it.

Most French people would find themselves in Lyon for business rather than for recreation: it's a get-up-and-go place, not a lie-back-and-rest one, with an almost Swiss sense of cleanliness, order and efficiency. But as a wonderfully manageable slice of urban France, Lyon certainly has its charms. Foremost among these is **gastronomy**; there are more restaurants per Gothic and Renaissance square metre of the old town than anywhere else on earth, and the city could form a football team with its superstars of the international chef circuit. While the **textile museum** is the second famous reason for stopping here, Lyon's nightlife, cinema and theatre (including the famous Lyonnais puppets), its antique markets, music and other cultural festivities might tempt you to stay at least a few days. As if that weren't enough, Lyon's distinctive older quarters and its winding, secret *traboules* are an urban explorer's paradise.

Lyon is organized into arrondissements, of which there are nine. A visit to Lyon will necessarily take you into the Presqu'île (1er and 2^e^ arrondissements), the area between the Rivers Saône and Rhône, and you're likely to spend some time in Vieux Lyon (5^e^) on the west bank of the Saône, as well as the east bank of the Rhône (3e), including the modern development known as La Part-Dieu.

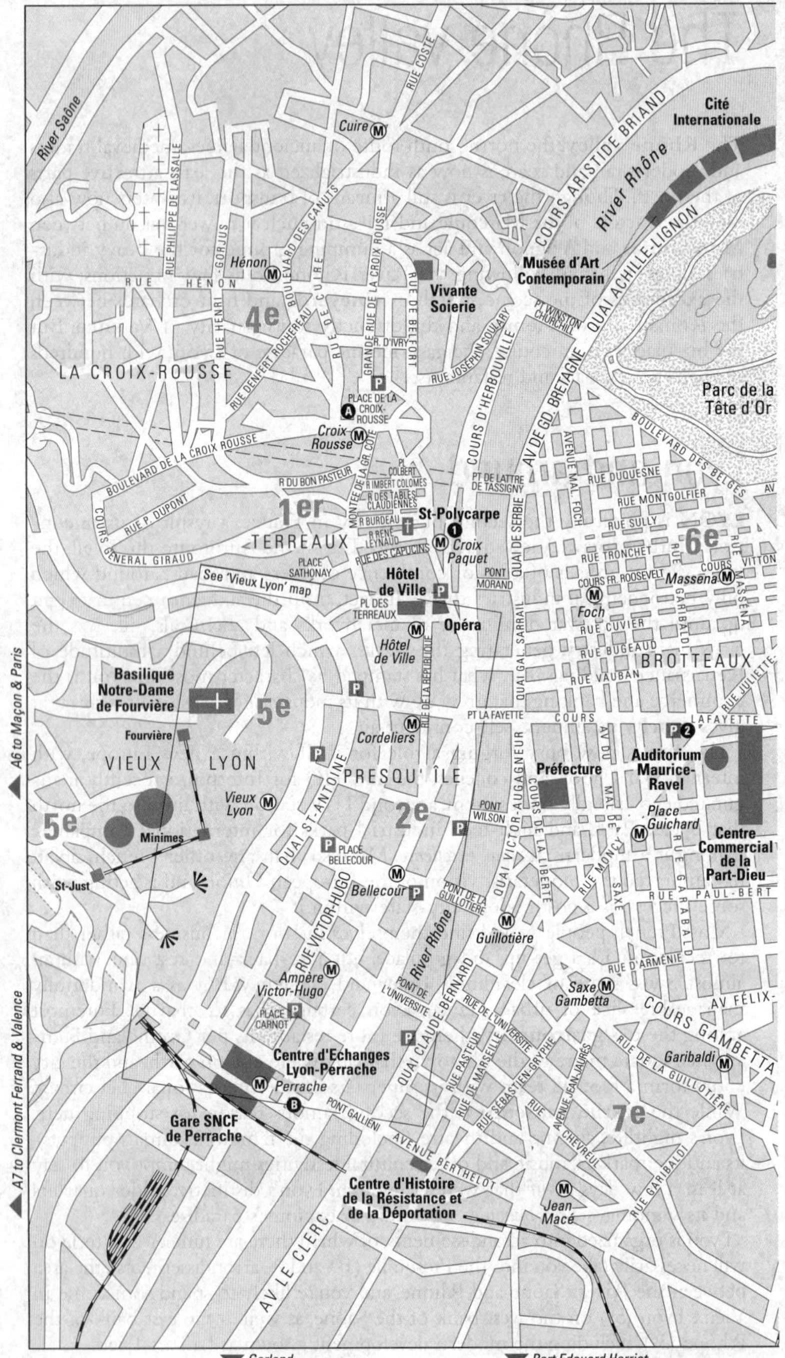
River Saône
Cuire
RUE COSTE
Cité Internationale
COURS ARISTIDE BRIAND
River Rhône
QUAI ACHILLE-LIGNON
Musée d'Art Contemporain
RUE PHILIPPE DE LASSALLE
RUE HENRI-GORJUS
BOULEVARD DES CANUTS
Hénon
RUE HÉNON
4e
RUE DE CUIRE
GRANDE RUE DE LA CROIX ROUSSE
RUE DE BELFORT
Vivante Soierie
R. D'IVRY
RUE JOSÉPHIN SOULARY
PT WINSTON CHURCHILL
COURS D'HERBOUVILLE
AV DE GD BRETAGNE
LA CROIX-ROUSSE
RUE DENFERT ROCHEREAU
PLACE DE LA CROIX-ROUSSE
A
Croix Rousse
Parc de la Tête d'Or
BOULEVARD DES BELGES
BOULEVARD DE LA CROIX ROUSSE
MONTÉE DE LA GR. CÔTE
R DU BON PASTEUR
PL COLBERT
R IMBERT COLOMES
R DES TABLES CLAUDIENNES
R BURDEAU
R RENÉ LEYNAUD
PT DE LATTRE DE TASSIGNY
AVENUE MAL. FOCH
RUE DUQUESNE
RUE MONTGOLFIER
RUE SULLY
COURS GENERAL GIRAUD
RUE P. DUPONT
1er
TERREAUX
St-Polycarpe
1
Croix Paquet
RUE DES CAPUCINS
QUAI DE SERBIE
6e
RUE TRONCHET
COURS VITTON
PLACE SATHONAY
See 'Vieux Lyon' map
Hôtel de Ville
PONT MORAND
COURS FR. ROOSEVELT
Massena
COURS MASSENA
PL DES TERREAUX
Opéra
Foch
RUE CUVIER
RUE GARIBALDI
QUAI GAL. SARRAIL
Hôtel de Ville
RUE BUGEAUD
BROTTEAUX
RUE VAUBAN
RUE JULIETTE
Basilique Notre-Dame de Fourvière
5e
RUE DE LA RÉPUBLIQUE
PT LA FAYETTE
COURS LAFAYETTE
2
Fourvière
Cordeliers
Auditorium Maurice-Ravel
VIEUX LYON
PRESQU'ÎLE
Préfecture
QUAI VICTOR-AUGAGNEUR
AV DU MAL DE SAXE
QUAI ST-ANTOINE
Vieux Lyon
PONT WILSON
Place Guichard
5e
Minimes
2e
COURS DE LA LIBERTÉ
Centre Commercial de la Part-Dieu
PLACE BELLECOUR
RUE MONCEY
St-Just
Bellecour
PONT DE LA GUILLOTIÈRE
RUE PAUL-BERT
River Rhône
Guillotière
RUE VICTOR-HUGO
RUE D'ARMÉNIE
Ampère Victor-Hugo
PONT DE L'UNIVERSITÉ
QUAI CLAUDE-BERNARD
RUE DE L'UNIVERSITÉ
Saxe Gambetta
AV FÉLIX-
COURS GAMBETTA
PLACE CARNOT
RUE PASTEUR
RUE DE MARSEILLE
RUE SÉBASTIEN-GRYPHE
AVENUE JEAN-JAURÈS
Centre d'Echanges Lyon-Perrache
Garibaldi
RUE DE LA GUILLOTIÈRE
Perrache
B
PONT GALLIENI
RUE CHEVREUL
7e
Gare SNCF de Perrache
AVENUE BERTHELOT
RUE GARIBALDI
Centre d'Histoire de la Résistance et de la Déportation
Jean Macé
AV LE CLERC
A6 to Maçon & Paris
A7 to Clermont Ferrand & Valence
Gerland
Port Edouard Herriot

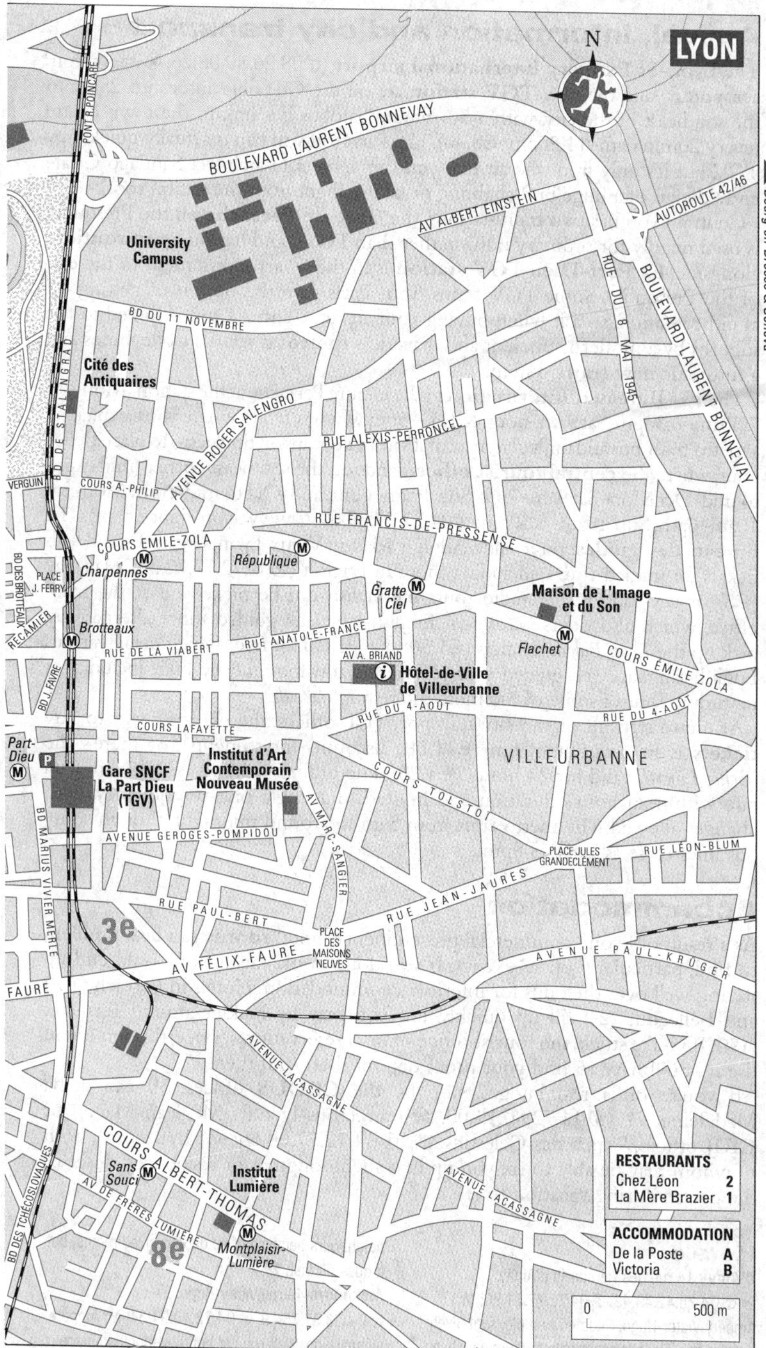
LYON
N
BOULEVARD LAURENT BONNEVAY
PONT R.POINCARE
AV ALBERT EINSTEIN
AUTOROUTE 42/46
Bourg-en-Bresse & Geneva
University Campus
RUE DU 8 MAI 1945
BOULEVARD LAURENT BONNEVAY
BD DU 11 NOVEMBRE
BD DE STALINGRAD
Cité des Antiquaires
AVENUE ROGER SALENGRO
RUE ALEXIS-PERRONCEL
VERGUIN
COURS A.-PHILIP
RUE FRANCIS-DE-PRESSENSÉ
COURS EMILE-ZOLA
République
Charpennes
BD DES BROTTEAUX
PLACE J. FERRY
Gratte Ciel
Maison de L'Image et du Son
RÉCAMIER
Brotteaux
Flachet
RUE DE LA VIABERT
RUE ANATOLE-FRANCE
AV A. BRIAND
COURS ÉMILE ZOLA
BD J. FAVRE
Hôtel-de-Ville de Villeurbanne
RUE DU 4-AOÛT
RUE DU 4-AOÛT
COURS LAFAYETTE
Part-Dieu
Gare SNCF La Part Dieu (TGV)
Institut d'Art Contemporain Nouveau Musée
VILLEURBANNE
COURS TOLSTOI
AV MARC-SANGIER
AVENUE GEROGES-POMPIDOU
BD MARIUS VIVIER MERLE
PLACE JULES GRANDCLÉMENT
RUE LÉON-BLUM
RUE PAUL-BERT
RUE JEAN-JAURES
3e
PLACE DES MAISONS NEUVES
AV FÉLIX-FAURE
AVENUE PAUL-KRÜGER
FAURE
AVENUE LACASSAGNE
COURS ALBERT-THOMAS
BD DES TCHÉCOSLOVAQUES
Sans Souci
AV DE FRÈRES LUMIÈRE
Institut Lumière
AVENUE LACASSAGNE
8e
Montplaisir-Lumière
RESTAURANTS
Chez Léon 2
La Mère Brazier 1
ACCOMMODATION
De la Poste A
Victoria B
0
500 m
Venissieux, HI hostel & Centre International de Séjour
St Exupéry Airport & TGV Station & Grenoble

Arrival, information and city transport

The **Lyon-St Exupéry international airport** (Ⓣ08.26.80.08.26, Ⓦwww.lyon.aeroport.fr) and the new **TGV station** are off the Grenoble autoroute, 25km to the southeast of the city, with a 50-minute Satobus bus link to the town centre (every 20min 6am–11.20pm; €8.40). The Paris to Lyon trip is actually quicker by TGV, but it's only from the air that you can appreciate architect Santiago Calatrava's design of a huge bird alighting or taking flight from the station roof.

Central Lyon has two train stations: the **Gare de Perrache** on the Presqu'île is used mainly for ordinary trains rather than TGVs, and has the **gare routière** alongside; **La Part-Dieu TGV station** is in the 3e arrondissement to the east of the Presqu'île. Some TGV trains from Paris give the option of getting off at either station, so ask when buying your ticket. Central Lyon is linked to the suburbs by a modern, efficient and driverless **métro**, as well as trolleybuses and a futuristic new **tram** system.

There's a **Bureau d'Information** in the Centre Perrache at the station (Mon–Fri 7.30am–6.30pm, Sat 9am–noon & 1.30–5pm; Ⓦwww.tcl.fr), where you can pick up a métro, tram, bus and funicular map; or it's just two stops on the métro to place Bellecour, where the **central tourist office** stands on the southeast corner (mid-April to mid-Oct Mon–Sat 9am–7pm, Sun 10am–6pm; mid-Oct to mid-April Mon–Sat 10am–6pm, Sun 10am–5.30pm; Ⓣ04.72.77.69.69, Ⓦwww.lyon-france.com). The **bureau des guides**, on avenue Adolph Max in Vieux Lyon, organizes and sells tickets for guided **tours**, including those in English (Ⓣ04.72.77.72.33). Half-day (€8) or day-long (€12) audio tours in English can be picked up at the main office, which also offers occasional English-language guided tours; alternatively, pick up the *Lyon Balades* leaflets (€1.50 each or €6 for five) which detail various English-language self-guided tours of the city on foot and by bike, including a rewarding tour of some of the more interesting *traboules*.

At métro stations or the city transport TCL offices, the cheapest way to buy **tickets** is in a carnet of ten (€11.50, discounts for students), or there's the *Ticket Liberté*, valid for 24 hours (€4.20). The ordinary tickets (€1.40) are flat-rate within an hour's duration and limited to a single one-way journey, with changes allowed. The métro runs from 5am to around midnight, though some bus lines close as early as 8pm.

Accommodation

As a result of Lyon's commercial pre-eminence, hotel **rooms** can be a problem to find, particularly on weekdays. If you don't book ahead, you could end up paying well over the odds for inferior accommodation. Hotels in Perrache (2e) and Bellecour (2e) fill up quickly, but you may be luckier around Terreaux (1er). If you're stuck, the tourist office offers a reservation service, though if you use it you'll have to find your room deposit there and then.

If you're on a real budget, stop by the **CROUS** offices, 59 rue de la Madeleine, 7e (Ⓣ04.72.80.13.00, Ⓦwww.crous-lyon.fr; M° Jean-Macé), or **CRIJ** offices, 9 quai des Celestins, 2e (Ⓣ04.72.77.00.66; M° Bellecour), both of whom may be able to fix you up in student lodgings or residences closer to the centre during vacation time.

Hotels

D'Ainay 14 rue des Remparts d'Ainay, 2e Ⓣ04.78.42.43.42, Ⓕ04.72.77.51.90; M° Ampère Victor-Hugo. Situated in a pleasant, lively quarter, this place is preferable to its many cheap neighbours because of its decent-sized rooms, but it does fill fast. ❷

Alexandra 49 rue Victor-Hugo, 2e Ⓣ04.78.37.75.79, Ⓕ04.72.40.94.34; M° Ampère Victor-Hugo. Well-run old hotel overlooking place

Ampère, a lively pedestrian zone. Parking available. ❷

College 5 place St-Paul, 5e Ⓣ04.72.10.05.05, Ⓦwww.college-hotel.com; M° Vieux-Lyon. Stylish three-star boutique hotel in a great Vieux Lyon location. ❼

Cour des Loges 2–8 rue du Boeuf, 5e Ⓣ04.72.77.44.44, Ⓦwww.courdesloges.com; M° Vieux-Lyon. Lyon's finest hotel, set in a seventeenth-century former Jesuit college, with a stunning dining area in the glazed atrium. ❾

Globe et Cécil 21 rue Gasparin, 2e Ⓣ04.78.42.58.95, Ⓦwww.globeetcecilhotel.com; M° Bellecour. Attractive, central and upmarket place with good service and a touch of originality in the decor. ❽

De la Marne 78 rue de la Charité, 2e Ⓣ04.78.37.07.46, Ⓕ04.72.41.70.64; M° Perrache. Convenient and pleasant, with cheerful, newly refurbished rooms and smart marble bathrooms. ❸

De la Poste 1 rue Victor-Fort, 4e Ⓣ & Ⓕ04.78.28.62.67; M° Croix-Rousse. A clean, acceptable old-fashioned cheapie near place Croix-Rousse. ❶

St-Pierre-des-Terreaux 8 rue Paul-Chenavard, 1er Ⓣ04.78.28.24.61, Ⓕ04.72.00.21.07; M° Hôtel-de-Ville. A convenient if rather charmless establishment in a good location. ❸

St-Vincent 9 rue Pareille, 1er Ⓣ04.78.27.22.56, Ⓦwww.hotel-saintvincent.com; M° Hôtel-de-Ville. Atmospheric old hotel near the Saône and the St-Vincent footbridge. Some rooms have exposed beams, stone walls and marble fireplaces. ❷

Du Théâtre 10 rue de Savoie, 2e Ⓣ04.78.42.33.32, Ⓕ04.72.40.00.61; M° Bellecour. A comfortable hotel with some character, well run by a pleasant young couple. ❹

Vaubecour 28 rue Vaubecour, 2e Ⓣ04.78.37.44.91, Ⓕ04.78.42.90.17; M° Ampère Victor-Hugo. One block from the Saône, on the second floor of a grand nineteenth-century building. A bit shabby, but friendly and comfortable for the price. ❷

Victoria 3 rue Delandine, 2e Ⓣ04.78.37.57.61, Ⓦwww.hotelvictorialyon.com; M° Perrache. A reasonable two-star near the Perrache station. ❷

Hostels and campsite

HI hostel (Vieux Lyon) 41–45 Montée du Chemin Neuf, 5e Ⓣ04.78.15.05.50, Ⓔlyon@fuaj.org; M° Vieux-Lyon/Minimes. Modern hostel, with great views over Lyon and access to the Internet. Set in a steep part of the old town, the nearest métro station is Vieux-Lyon, but if you want to avoid the climb, get the funicular to Minimes and walk down the Montée du Chemin Neuf. Beds are €13.25.

HI hostel 51 rue Roger-Salengro, Vénissieux Ⓣ04.78.76.39.23, Ⓔlyon-sud@fuaj.org; M° Gare de Vénissieux. Excellent hostel 4km southeast of the centre, with a full range of facilities. Beds in both doubles and dorms are €9.30. Take bus #36 from the métro, stop "J Curie – Auberge de Jeunesse".

Centre International de Séjour de Lyon 103 bd Etats-Unis, 8e Ⓣ04.37.90.42.42, Ⓦwww.cis-lyon.com. Not far from the Vénissieux hostel, but a bit more expensive; the advantage is that it's out of earshot of the main ring road. €14.90 for a dorm bed, doubles also available. Take bus #32 from Perrache or #36 from Part-Dieu, stop "États-Unis-Beauvisage". Check in from 2.30pm. Open 24hr. ❶

Camping Porte de Lyon Dardilly Ⓣ04.78.35.64.55, Ⓦwww.camping-lyon.com. East along the A6 from Lyon or by bus #89 (stop "Camping International") from the gare de Vaise. Alternatively #3 from Hôtel de Ville. Pleasant though expensive, with a tourist information bureau. €13.70 for a tent and two people.

The City

The centre of Lyon is the **Presqu'île**, or "peninsula", the tongue of land between the rivers Saône and Rhône, just north of their confluence. Most of it lies within the 2e arrondissement, but it's known by its *quartiers*, which include **Bellecour**, around the central square, and **Perrache**, around the station. At the top end of the Presqu'île, as the Saône veers west, is the 1er arrondissement, known as **Terreaux**, centred on place des Terreaux and the Hôtel de Ville. On the west bank of the Saône is the old town, or **Vieux Lyon**, at the foot of Fourvière, on which the Romans built their capital of Gaul, Lugdunum. Vieux Lyon is made up of three villages: St-Paul, St-Jean and St-Georges, and forms the eastern end of the 5e arrondissement. The 9e lies to its north.

Lyon City Card and Discovery Weekend

The **Lyon City Card** (€18, €28 or €38 for one, two or three days) grants unlimited access to the métro, bus and tramway, nineteen museums (including the Roman ruins in St-Romain-en-Gal), guided city tours and several short boat trips. The card is available from the tourist office and the major TCL (public transit) offices. More limited in scope is the €6 one day ticket allowing access to the municipal museums only.

The **Discover Weekend** (from €120 per person) includes two nights in a two-, three- or four-star hotel, the City Card, and lunch at a local *bouchon*. The package is available online through the tourist office website.

To the north of the Presqu'île is the old silk-weavers' district of **La Croix-Rousse**, the 4e arrondissement. **Modern Lyon** lies east of the Rhône, with the 7e and 8e arrondissements to the south, the 3e arrondissement in the middle, with **La Part-Dieu TGV station** amidst an assertive cultural and commercial centre, and the 6e arrondissement, known as **Brotteaux**, to the north. North of Brotteaux is Lyon's main open space, the **Parc de la Tête d'Or**. The district of **Villeurbanne**, home to the university and the Théâtre National Populaire, lies east of the 6e and the park.

The Presqu'île

The pink gravelly acres of **place Bellecour** were first laid out in 1617, and today form a focus on the peninsula, with views up to the looming bulk of Notre-Dame-de-Fourvière. The square is vast, dwarfing even the central statue of Louis XIV in the guise of a Roman emperor. Running south, **rue Auguste-Comte** is full of antique shops selling heavily framed eighteenth-century art works, and **rue Victor-Hugo** is a pedestrian precinct that continues north of place Bellecour on rue de la République all the way up to the back of the Hôtel de Ville below the area of La Croix-Rousse.

South of place Bellecour on rue de la Charité is Lyon's best museum, the **Musée des Tissus** (Tues–Sun 10am–5.30pm; €5), housed in the eighteenth-century former town palace of the Duke of Villeroy. It doesn't quite live up to its claim to cover the history of decorative cloth through the ages, but it does have brilliant collections from certain periods, notably third-century Greek-influenced and sixth-century Coptic tapestries, woven silk and painted linen from Egypt. The fragment of woven wool *aux poissons* ("with fish"; second to third century AD) has an artistry unmatched in European work until at least the eighteenth century. There are silks from Baghdad and carpets from Iran, Turkey, India and China. The stuff produced in Lyon itself reflects the luxurious nature of the silk trade: seventeenth- to nineteenth-century hangings and chair covers, including hangings from Marie-Antoinette's bedroom at Versailles, from Empress Josephine's room at Fontainebleau and from the palaces of Catherine the Great of Russia. Sadly, there's almost nothing from the period of the Revolution, but there are some lovely twentieth-century pieces – including Sonia Delaunay's *Tissus Simultanés* – and couture creations from Worth to Mariano Fortuny, Paco Rabanne and Christian Lacroix. The **Musée des Arts Décoratifs** next door (Tues–Sun 10am–noon & 2–5.30pm; same ticket as Musée des Tissus) displays faïence, porcelain, furniture and a couple of eighteenth-century rooms removed from old houses in the Presqu'ile, plus a room-sized nineteenth-century panorama of Lyon and a collection of superb modern silverware by noted architects, including Richard Meier and Zaha Hadid.

To the south, the station area around Perrache is of little interest, but over the Rhône, across the adjacent pont Gallieni, at 14 av Berthelot, is the **Centre d'Histoire de la Résistance et de la Déportation** (Wed–Sun 9am–5.30pm; €3.80; M° Perrache/Jean-Macé). In addition to a library of books, videos, memoirs and other documents recording experiences of resistance, occupation and deportation to the camps, there's an exhibition space housed over the very cellars and cells in which Klaus Barbie, the Gestapo boss of Lyon, tortured and murdered his victims. Barbie was brought back from Bolivia and tried in Lyon in 1987 for crimes against humanity; the principal "exhibit" is a moving and unsettling 45-minute video (five shows daily; French only) of the trial in which some of his victims recount their terrible ordeal.

To the north of place Bellecour at the top of quai St-Antoine is the **quartier Mercière**, the old commercial centre of the town, with sixteenth- and seventeenth-century houses lining rue Mercière, and the **church of St-Nizier**, whose bells used to announce the nightly closing of the city's gates. In the silk-weavers' uprising of 1831 (see box, overleaf), workers fleeing the soldiers took refuge in the church, only to be massacred. Today, traces of this working-class life are almost gone, edged out by bars, restaurants and designer shops, the latter along rue du Président Edouard Herriot and the long pedestrian rue de la République in particular. Close to St-Nizier, at 13 rue de la Poulaillerie, is the **Musée de l'Imprimerie et de la Banque** (Wed–Sun 9.30am–noon & 2–6pm; €3.80); unfortunately, its collection is unattractively displayed, which is a pity, for Lyon was both a leading publishing and banking centre in Renaissance times.

Further north, the monumental nineteenth-century **fountain** in front of the even more monumental **Hôtel de Ville** on place des Terreaux symbolizes rivers straining to reach the ocean. It was designed by Bartholdi, of Statue of Liberty fame, although the rows of watery leaks that sprout up unexpectedly across the rest of the square are a modern addition. Opposite is the large bulk of the **Musée des Beaux-Arts** (Mon–Thurs, Sat & Sun 10am–6pm; Fri 10.30am–6pm; €6), housed in a former Benedictine abbey and whose collections are second in France only to those in the Louvre. The museum is organized roughly by genre, with nineteenth- and twentieth-century sculpture, represented by Canova, Barye and Rodin's *Temptation of St Anthony* in the ex-chapel on the ground floor. There's a fine collection of medieval French, Dutch, German and Italian woodcarving on the first floor along with antiquities, coins and *objets d'art*. The representation of twentieth-century painting was strengthened in 1998 by the donation of Lyon-born actress Jaqueline Delubac's collection, including works by Picasso and Matisse. There are also Braques, a brace of typically domestic Bonnards and a gory Francis Bacon. The nineteenth century is represented by the Impressionists and their forerunners, Corot and Courbet; there are works by the Lyonnais artists Antoine Berjon and Fleury Richard, and from there you can work your way back through Rubens, Zurbarán, El Greco, Tintoretto and a hundred others.

Behind the Hôtel de Ville, on the edge of several linked squares, stands Lyon's **opera house** (tours Sat at 1pm; €9, book through the tourist office on place Bellecour). Radically redesigned in 1993 by the architect Jean Nouvel, its original Neoclassical elevations are now topped by a huge glass Swiss roll of a roof, and the interior is now entirely black with silver stairways climbing into the darkness.

La Croix-Rousse

La Croix-Rousse is the old silk-weavers' district and spreads up the steep slopes of the hill above the northern end of the Presqu'île. It's still a

The silk strike of 1831

Though the introduction of the Jacquard loom of 1804 made it possible for one person to produce 25cm of silk in a day instead of taking four people four days, **silk workers**, or *canuts* – whether masters and apprentices, or especially women and child workers – were badly paid whatever their output. Over the three decades following the introduction of the Jacquard, the price paid for a length of silk fell by over fifty percent. Attempts to regulate the price were ignored by the dealers, even though hundreds of skilled workers were languishing in debtors' jails. On November 21, 1831, the *canuts* called an all-out **strike**. As they processed down the Montée de la Grande Côte with their black flags and the slogan "Live working or die fighting", they were shot at and three people died. After a rapid retreat uphill they built barricades, assisted by half the National Guard, who refused to fire cannon at their "comrades of Croix-Rousse". For three days the battle raged on all four banks, the silk workers using sticks, stones and knives to defend themselves, and the bourgeoisie running scared, with only the area between the rivers, place des Terreaux and just north of St-Nizier still under their control. Unfortunately for the *canuts*, their employers were able to call on outside aid, and 30,000 extra troops arrived to quash the rebellion. Some 600 people were killed or wounded, and in the end the silk industrialists were free to pay whatever pitiful fee they chose, but the uprising was one of the first instances of organized labour taking to the streets during the most revolutionary fifty years of French history.

working-class area, but barely a couple of dozen people operate the modern high-speed computerized looms that are kept in business by the restoration and maintenance of France's palaces and châteaux. You can see an authentic silkworker's atelier at the **Soierie Vivante**, 21 rue Richan (Tues 2–6.30pm, Wed–Sat 9am–noon & 2–6.30pm, M° Croix Rousse; €3), while at **Passage Thiaffait** on rue René Leynaud one of the original **traboules** – alleyways and tunnelled passages originally built to provide shelter from the weather for the silk-weavers as they moved their delicate pieces of work from one part of the manufacturing process to another – has been refurbished to provide premises for young couturiers.

The streets running down from **boulevard de la Croix-Rousse**, as well as many across the river in Vieux Lyon, are intersected by these *traboules*. Normally hidden by plain doors, they are impossible to distinguish from normal entryways; hence they proved an indispensable escape network for prewar gangsters, wartime Resistance fighters and, more recently, for political activists, who used them to thwart police efforts to prevent protests during the official visit of the Chinese ambassador in 2000. Try going up past the right of St-Polycarpe on **rue Réné-Leynaud** above place Terreaux, then take rue Pouteau. Turn right into **rue des Tables Claudiennes**, and enter no. 55 emerging opposite 29 rue Imbert-Colomes. Climb the stairs into 14bis, cross three more courtyards, including the spectacular Cour des Voraces, and you finally emerge at **place Colbert**.

Officially the *traboules* of La Croix-Rousse and Vieux-Lyon are public thoroughfares during daylight hours – one of the tourist office's *Lyon Balades* guides explores them – but you may find some closed today for security reasons, especially as the area is gradually being gentrified. The long climb up the part-pedestrianized **Montée de la Grande Côte**, however, still gives an idea of what the *quartier* was like in the sixteenth century, when the *traboules* were first built. Take a look at the pretty **place Sathonay** at the bottom, where a

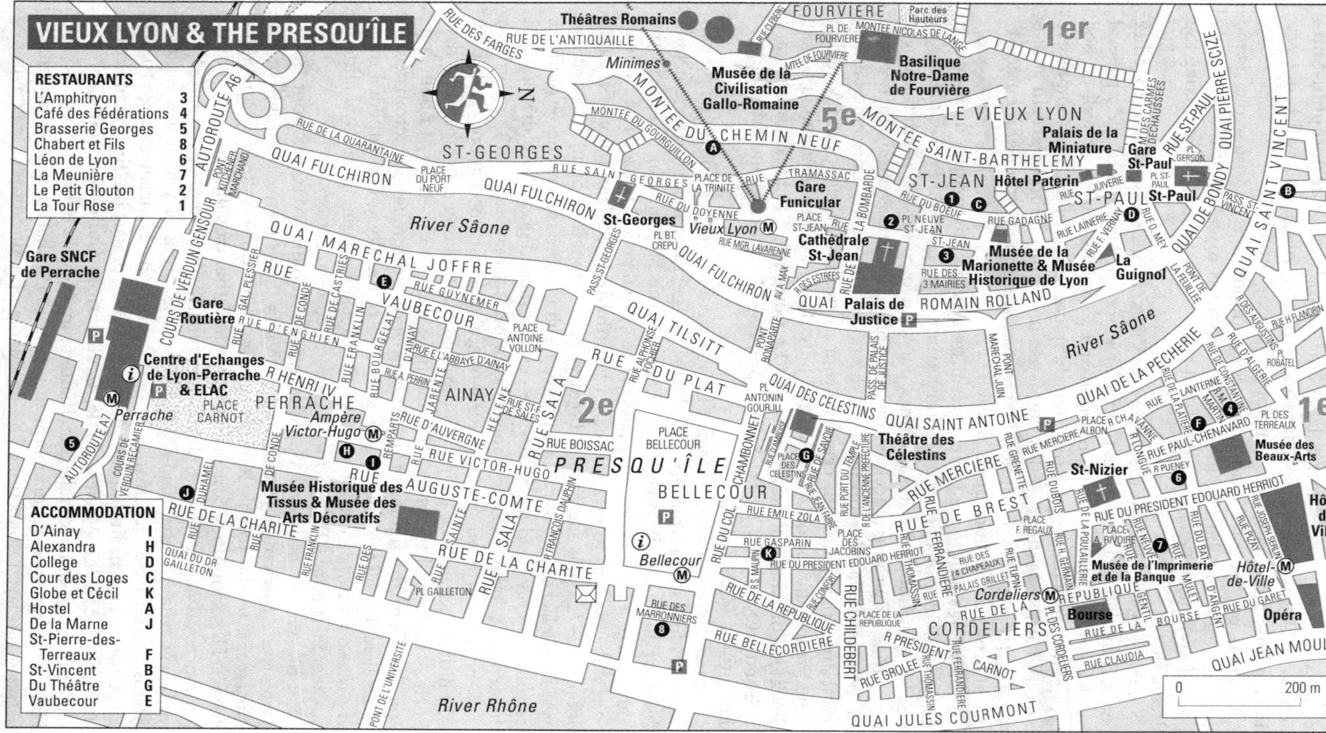
VIEUX LYON & THE PRESQU'ÎLE
RESTAURANTS
L'Amphitryon 3
Café des Fédérations 4
Brasserie Georges 5
Chabert et Fils 8
Léon de Lyon 6
La Meunière 7
Le Petit Glouton 2
La Tour Rose 1
ACCOMMODATION
D'Ainay I
Alexandra H
College D
Cour des Loges C
Globe et Cécil K
Hostel A
De la Marne J
St-Pierre-des-Terreaux F
St-Vincent B
Du Théâtre G
Vaubecour E
Théâtres Romains
Minimes
Musée de la Civilisation Gallo-Romaine
Basilique Notre-Dame de Fourvière
FOURVIERE
LE VIEUX LYON
Palais de la Miniature
Gare St-Paul
St-Paul
ST-JEAN
Hôtel Paterin
ST-PAUL
ST-GEORGES
St-Georges
Vieux Lyon
Gare Funicular
Cathédrale St-Jean
Musée de la Marionette & Musée Historique de Lyon
La Guignol
Palais de Justice
River Saône
Gare SNCF de Perrache
Gare Routière
Centre d'Echanges de Lyon-Perrache & ELAC
Perrache
PLACE CARNOT
PERRACHE
AINAY
Ampère Victor-Hugo
Musée Historique des Tissus & Musée des Arts Décoratifs
2e
PRESQU'ÎLE
PLACE BELLECOUR
BELLECOUR
Bellecour
Théâtre des Célestins
St-Nizier
Musée des Beaux-Arts
Hôtel de Ville
Hôtel-de-Ville
Musée de l'Imprimerie et de la Banque
Cordeliers
Bourse
Opéra
CORDELIERS
1er
5e
River Rhône
QUAI FULCHIRON
QUAI MARECHAL JOFFRE
QUAI TILSITT
QUAI ROMAIN ROLLAND
QUAI DES CELESTINS
QUAI SAINT ANTOINE
QUAI DE LA PECHERIE
QUAI SAINT VINCENT
QUAI PIERRE SCIZE
QUAI DE BONDY
QUAI JEAN MOULIN
QUAI JULES COURMONT
MONTEE DU CHEMIN NEUF
MONTEE SAINT-BARTHELEMY
RUE DE LA REPUBLIQUE
RUE DU PRESIDENT EDOUARD HERRIOT
RUE VICTOR-HUGO
RUE AUGUSTE-COMTE
RUE DE LA CHARITE
RUE MERCIERE
RUE DE BREST
La Croix-Rousse
Cours Gambetta
Cours Lafayette & La Part Dieu
0 200 m

public garden and a lively local café are overlooked by Croix-Rousse Mairie, and, if you have enough energy left, come down by the **rue Joséphin-Soulary**, which looks more like a lane in a country village and will bring you down a long flight of steps to the pont Winston-Churchill.

Reached by one of the three *passerelles* (footbridges) crossing the Saône from Terreaux and the Presqu'île, **Vieux Lyon** is made up of the three villages of St-Jean, St-Georges and St-Paul at the base of the hill overlooking the Presqu'île.

South of place St-Paul, the streets of Vieux Lyon, pressed close together beneath the hill of **Fourvière**, form a backdrop of Renaissance and medieval facades, bright night-time illumination and a swelling chorus of well-dressed Lyonnais in search of supper or a midday splurge. One of the most impressive buildings at the northern end is the sixteenth-century **Hôtel Paterin** at 4–6 rue Juiverie, a galleried mansion best viewed from the bottom of montée St-Barthélémy, just up from place St-Paul.

A short way south of the Hôtel Paterin, the **Musée Historique de Lyon**, on the ground floor of a fifteenth-century mansion on place du Petit-Collège, has a good collection of Nevers ceramics, but was closed for major refurbishment at the time of writing (check with tourist office for information). In any case, the **Musée de la Marionnette**, on the first floor, is a lot more entertaining, and features the eighteenth-century Lyonnais creations, Guignol and Madelon – the French equivalents of Punch and Judy. If you want to see them in action, check out the times of performances at **Le Guignol**, 2 rue Garrand, by quai de Bondy (Oct–May Wed, Sat & Sun 3pm; €8–13; for tickets and other puppet shows ⓣ04.78.28.92.57).

If you're *traboule*-hunting in Vieux Lyon, two of the best can be found on two streets leading south from place du Petit-Collège: the winding passage behind the door at 27 rue de Boeuf, and that at 28 rue St-Jean, which leads to the courtyard of a fifteenth-century palace. The central pedestrianized **rue St-Jean** ends at the twelfth- to fifteenth-century **Cathédrale St-Jean** (Mon–Fri 8am–noon & 2–7.30pm; Sat, Sun & holidays 8am–noon & 2–5pm). Though the west facade lacks most of its statuary as a result of various wars and revolutions, it's still impressive, and the thirteenth-century stained glass above the altar and in the rose windows of the transepts is in perfect condition. In the northern transept is a fourteenth-century astronomical clock, its mechanism cloaked by a beautiful Renaissance casing: it's capable of computing moveable feast days (such as Easter) till the year 2019, and most days on the strike of noon, 2pm, 3pm and 4pm, the figures of the Annunciation go through an automated set piece, heralded by the lone bugler at the top of the clock. The cathedral treasury is also worth a look for its religious artefacts, ranging from Byzantine to nineteenth-century (Wed–Sun 10am–noon & 2–6pm; free).

Just beyond the cathedral, opposite avenue Adolphe-Max and pont Bonaparte, is the **funicular station** and the Vieux Lyon métro, from where you can ascend to the town's Roman remains (direction "St-Just", stop "Minimes"). The antiquities consist of two ruined **theatres** dug into the hillside (entrance at 6 rue de l'Antiquaille; mid-April to mid-Sept 9am–9pm; mid-Sept to mid-April 9am–7pm; free) – the larger of which was built by Augustus and extended in the second century by Hadrian to seat 10,000 spectators – and an underground museum of Lyonnais life from prehistoric times to 7 AD, the **Musée de la Civilisation Gallo-Romaine**, 17 rue Cléberg (Tues–Sun: March–Oct 10am–6pm; Nov–Feb 10am–5pm; €3.80). Here, a unique pre-Roman bronze processional chariot heralds an imaginatively displayed collection. The fragments of a fine bronze engraving of a speech by the Lyon-born Emperor Claudius, as well as the sheer number and splendour of the mosaics here, serve to underline Roman Lyon's importance. Nowadays, the ancient theatres are the focal point for the **Nuits de Fourvière** music and film festival that takes place annually in June and July (Ⓣ04.72.32.00.00, Ⓦwww.nuitsdefourviere.fr).

From the museum, it's just a moment's walk to the **Basilique Notre-Dame de Fourvière**, a fussily-ornamented wedding cake of a church built, like the Sacré-Coeur in Paris, in the aftermath of the 1871 Commune to emphasize the defeat of the godless socialists. And like the Sacré-Coeur, its hilltop position has become an almost defining element in the city's skyline. What makes a visit worthwhile is the magnificent view of the city, best appreciated from the top of the **Tour de l'Observatoire** (Wed–Sun 10.30am–noon & 2–6.30pm; €2), from which you can distinguish the different quarters and see how they have grown and been shaped by the Saône and Rhône over the centuries. The Basilique is also accessible direct from the Vieux-Lyon funicular station: if you arrive by this route, it's worth walking down along the **montée St-Barthélemy** footpath, which winds back to Vieux Lyon through the hanging gardens below the church.

Modern Lyon

On the skyline from Fourvière, you can't miss the gleaming pencil-like skyscraper that belongs to Lyon's homegrown Crédit Lyonnais bank. This is the centrepiece of **La Part-Dieu**, a business-culture-commerce conglomerate which includes one of the biggest public libraries outside Paris, a mammoth concert hall and a busy shopping centre (M° Part-Dieu). The elegant tower aside, it's all rather lumpen and unfriendly to look at. Penetrate the forbidding exterior of the main market at 102 cours Lafayette, however, and you'll discover a gastronomic wonderland within, with superb seafood, poultry, cheese and charcuterie stalls (Mon–Thurs 7.30am–noon & 3–7pm; Fri & Sat 7.30am–7pm; Sun 7.30am–noon).

For a break from city buildings head north to the **Parc de la Tête d'Or** (M° to Masséna, then walk up rue Masséna), where there are ponds and rose gardens, botanical gardens, a small zoo and lots of amusements for kids. It's overlooked by the bristling antennae of the international headquarters of Interpol, part of a new **Cité Internationale**, which also includes luxury apartments and a new **Musée d'Art Contemporain**, at 81 quai Charles-de-Gaulle (Wed–Sun noon–7pm; Ⓦwww.moca-lyon.org; €3.80; Line B to M° Saxe Gambetta or M° Place Guichard then bus #4, stop "Musée d'Art Contemporain"). The museum owns the largest public collection of installation art in the world, hosts excellent temporary exhibitions and is also the one of the homes of the Lyon art biennial. Designed by Renzo Piano, it's a curious-looking structure with a 1930s Neoclassical facade on the park side and a pink concrete cinema tacked onto the riverside. The colour echoes the adjacent **Palais des Congrès** conference centre, whose front is masked by a glass screen curving up over the roof, reminiscent of Jean Nouvel's Institut du Monde Arabe in Paris. There are some screens, catwalks and companionways: the features that have become part of the currency of architectural language since the Pompidou Centre first shocked the world. But it looks good, if a little artificial and immaculate behind its security barriers. To the east, dividing the park and the university, is boulevard de Stalingrad, where antique-fanciers can browse in the **Cité des Antiquaires** arcades at no. 117 (Thurs, Sat & Sun 9.30am–12.30pm & 2.30–7pm; closed Sun afternoon in summer).

In Villeurbanne, not far to the east of Part-Dieu, is the **Institut d'Art**

Contemporain, 11 rue Dr-Dolard (June–Sept Wed 1–8pm, Thurs–Sun 1–7pm; Oct–May Wed–Sun 1–6pm; Ⓦwww.i-art-c.org; €4; bus #1, stop "Cité/Nouveau Musée"), where thought-provoking and engaging exhibitions by contemporary artists question the function of art and architecture and their relation to society. It's also worth looking out for exhibitions at Villeurbanne's **Maison du Livre de l'Image et du Son**, to the east on avenue Émile-Zola (Mon 2–7pm, Tues–Fri 11am–7pm, Sat 10am–6pm; M° Flachet), which might feature anything from medieval illuminations to CD-ROMs.

Further south, on the edge of the 8e arrondissement, is the **Institut Lumière**, 25 rue du Premier-Film (Tues–Sun 11am–6.30pm; Ⓦwww.institut-lumiere.org; €6; M° Monplaisir-Lumière). The building was the home of Antoine Lumière, father of Auguste and Louis, who made the first films, and the exhibits feature early magic lanterns and the cameras used by the brothers, along with various art photographs. The Institut also shows several different films nightly; check their website for the schedule.

Right down in the south of the city, in the **Gerland quartier** (7e), is a newly developed area with a marina and a park on the Rhône's east bank, which provides an illusion of nature around the mirrored Institut Pasteur and the thrusting wings and arches of the École Normale Supérieure. Across the bridge from the southern tip of the Presqu'île, just off place Antonin Perrin, squats the massive **Tony Garnier Hall** (M° Debourg), a former abbatoir, whose 17,000 cubic metres is completely free of roof-supporting columns. Its walls graced with contemporary murals, it is now the main host to Lyon's art biennial – a major European show of new art convened here every other year (Sept–Jan in odd-numbered years).

Eating, drinking and entertainment

You'll find **restaurants** offering dishes from every region of France and overseas in Lyon. Vieux Lyon is the area with the greatest concentration of eateries, though you'll find cheaper and less busy ones between place des Jacobins and place Sathonay at the top of the Presqu'île, with a particularly dense and atmospheric concentration in rue Mercière. The possibilities are endless, but on weekends booking ahead is always a good idea.

The **bouchon**, the traditional Lyonnais eating establishment, is the best place to eat *quenelles*, sausages, tripe and the like. Its name derives either from *bouchon* (cork), or *bouchonner* (to rub down). One popular theory has it that wine bottles were lined up as the evening progressed, and at the end of the night the bill was determined by measuring from the first cork to the last. Another explanation, however, is that inns serving wine would attach small bundles of straw to their signs, indicating that horses could be cared for (*bouchonnés*) while the coachmen went inside to have a drink.

Lyon is almost as good a place for **nightlife** and **entertainment** as it is for eating, with a good range of clubs, cinema, opera, jazz, classical music concerts and theatre. The best places to wander if you are looking for a **bar** are rue Mercière, the area around place des Terreaux and the Opéra (where most of Lyon's **lesbian and gay** scene is also found) and, most particularly, the streets of Vieux Lyon. Make a point of crossing the river by the *passerelles*; the whole district looks magnificent at night.

For listings, pick up a free copy of the weekly newspaper, *Le Petit Bulletin*, or the free monthly *...491* from tourist offices and outlets citywide. Alternatively buy a copy of the weekly *Lyon Poche*, available from newsagents (every Wed; €1), or look online at Ⓦwww.lyonpoche.com.

Restaurants

L'Amphitryon 33 rue St-Jean, 5e ⓣ04.78.37.23.68; Mº Vieux Lyon. Usually packed restaurant serving Lyonnais specialities; menus from €12. Service till midnight.

Café des Fédérations 8 rue du Major-Martin, 1er ⓣ04.78.28.26.00; Mº Hôtel-de-Ville. Typical *bouchon* serving the earthiest of Lyonnais specialities (marinated tripe, black pudding and fish *quenelles*) in an atmosphere to match: there's even sawdust on the floor. Menu at €23 for dinner. Closed Sat, Sun & Aug.

Brasserie Georges 30 cours de Verdun, 2e ⓣ04.72.56.54.54; Mº Perrache. Vast Art-Deco brasserie originally founded in 1836; *choucroutes* are the speciality. Menus at €19, €21.50 & €24.50.

Chabert et Fils 11 rue des Marronniers, 2e ⓣ04.78.37.01.94; Mº Bellecour. *Bouchon* offering the ubiquitous *quenelle* and *andouillette* (offal sausage) specialities, along with other first-rate dishes. Menus €16.50–33.

Chez Léon Halles de la Part-Dieu, 102 cours Lafayette, 3e ⓣ04.78.62.30.28; Mº Part-Dieu. Tiny, bustling oyster bar in the market halls. Around €19 for lunch. Closed outside the oyster season, which usually means May–Aug.

Léon de Lyon 1 rue Pléney, 1er ⓣ04.72.10.11.12; Mº Hôtel-de-Ville. Sophisticated and delicious food, with original culinary creations as well as traditional Lyonnais recipes in this upmarket brasserie. Menus from €105, but there's a lunch menu for €57. Closed first three weeks in Aug.

La Mère Brazier 12 rue Royale, 1er ⓣ04.78.28.15.49; Mº Croix-Paquet. A beautiful setting complements the excellent food at this restaurant, still run by Mme Brazier, the granddaughter of the couple who founded it in 1921. Menus at €45 and €55, but you can easily spend more. Closed Sat lunch, Sun, Tues & Aug.

La Meunière 11 rue Neuve, 1er ⓣ04.78.28.62.91; Mº Hôtel-de-Ville. Booking is essential in this excellent *bouchon*, but it's worth it, with menus of Lyonnais specialities from €15 to €27. Closed Sun, Mon & mid-July to mid-Aug.

Paul Bocuse 40 rue de la Plage, Collonges-au-Mont-d'Or ⓣ04.72.42.90.90. Lyon's most famous restaurant, named after its celebrity chef-owner, is 9km north of the city, on the west bank of the Saône. Traditional French gastronomy is the bill of fare, with bass *en croûte* or soup with black truffle. From €60 upwards.

Le Petit Glouton 56 rue St-Jean, 5e ⓣ04.78.37.30.10; Mº Vieux Lyon. A small but airy and unpretentious bistro in the heart of Vieux Lyon. You can dine inside or on the small street-side terrace from €12.

La Tour Rose 22 rue du Boeuf, 5e ⓣ04.78.92.69.10; Mº Vieux Lyon. Gastronomic palace with concoctions like asparagus with an oyster mousse or salad of lobster and spinach with a creamed truffle sauce. From €53. Closed Sun. Worth peeking at is the actual Tour Rose (the tower of a small Renaissance house) in the courtyard next door at nearby no.16.

Bars and clubs

Albion Public House 12 rue Ste-Catherine, 1er; Mº Hôtel-de-Ville. Oldest English-style pub in Lyon with draught beer and a good selection of whiskies. You can play darts, watch Premiership football or surf the Net. Regular live music and theme nights. Daily 5pm–3am; closed end July to early Aug.

Café 203 9 rue du Garet, 1er; Mº Hôtel-de-Ville. Lively bar taking its name from the classic Peugeots parked out front. Cheap *plats du jour* at all hours. Daily 7am–1am, closed Sun lunch.

Café Comptoir Chez Mimi 68 rue St-Jean, 5e; Mº Vieux Lyon. Tiny, convivial bistro which looks like it was decorated from a flea market, offering drinks, salads, and omelettes. Simple but good if you can get a seat. Wed–Sat noon–1am & 6.30-11.30pm; Sun noon–9pm.

Eden Rock Café 68 rue Mercière, 2e; Mº Cordeliers. Massive bar, decorated with memorabilia and modern art from the States, with cheap beer and food served until 1am. Live music Wed–Sat with an accent on rock. Tues & Wed noon–1am, Thurs noon–2am, Fri & Sat noon–3am; closed part of Aug.

L'Éspace Gerson 1 place Gerson, 5e; Mº Vieux Lyon. Cool modern bar with frequent jazz and performance art, plus billiards. €7–15 entry normally. Mon–Sat 8pm–midnight.

Fish opposite 21 quai Augagneur, 3e; Mº Guillotière. One of Lyon's hippest nightclubs, specializing in house. Admission €7–15, prices higher after midnight. Tues–Fri 10pm–5am, in summer from 7pm; Tues student night, Fri theme night.

Hot Club 26 rue du Lanterne, 1er ⓦwww.hotclubjazz.com; Mº Hôtel-de-Ville. Jazz jam sessions and concerts of all varieties in a vaulted cellar. Tues–Sat 9pm–1am; closed Aug.

La Marquise opposite 20 quai Augagneur, 3e; Mº Guillotière. Old barge with dance club below deck. DJs spin jungle, salsa and house. There is usually no cover unless it's a special guest DJ, in which case you'll pay €6–8. Wed–Sat from anytime between 8 & 11pm onwards.

La Mi Graine 11 place St-Paul, 5e; Mº Vieux Lyon. Welcoming small café with live music and/or DJs Thurs–Sat. Also serves meals. Open daily 11.30am–3am.

Ninkasi 267 rue Marcel Mérieux, 7e; M° Gerland. Lyon's own microbrewery, with salads and burgers upstairs, bar, DJs and live music downstairs. Outdoor film screenings Wed in summer. Mon–Thurs 10–1am; Fri & Sat 10–3am; Sun 4pm–midnight.
Paradiso Club 24 rue Pizay, 1er; M° Hôtel-de-Ville. Over-25s disco with regular Chippendales and singles' nights. €13 cover. Daily 10.30pm–dawn.

Lesbian and gay bars and clubs

Cap'Opera 2 place Louis Pradel, 1er; M° Hôtel-de-Ville. Trendy, officially "mixed" (but really mostly gay) DJ bar close to the opera house. Mon–Sat 2pm–3am.
Forum Bar 15 rue des Quatre Chapeaux, 2e; M° Cordeliers. Convivial men's bar with bearish decor and clientele, tucked in an alley just north of the places des Jacobins and de la République. Mon–Thurs & Sun 5pm–2am, Fri & Sat 5pm–3am.
Lax Bar 2 rue Coysevox, 1er; M° Hôtel-de-Ville. As much a youth club as a bar, with Internet access, pool table and giant video screen. Mixed, but it tends to be gayer later. Open 4pm–3am.
T'chom Kaffé 26 rue Hippolyte Flandrin, 1er; M° Hôtel-de-Ville. Relaxed café/bar popular with gay men and lesbians. Regular exhibitions of work by young artists. Tues–Sat 5pm–1am.

Theatre, music and film

Look out for **stage productions** by the Théâtre National Populaire (TNP), 8 place Lazare-Goujon (ⓣ04.78.03.30.00; M° Gratte Ciel), based across the street from Villeurbanne's town hall. Less radical stuff is shown at the city's gilded Théâtre des Célestins, in place des Célestins, 2e (ⓣ04.72.77.40.00, ⓦwww.celestins-lyon.org; M° Bellecour). The **opera house**, one of the best in France, is on place de la Comédie, 1er (ⓣ04.72.00.45.45, ⓦwww.opera-lyon.org; M° Hôtel-de-Ville), with cheap tickets sold just before performances begin. For avant-garde, classic and obscure **films**, usually in their original language, check the listings for the cinemas CNP Terreaux, Bellecour, Fourmi Lafayette, Opéra and Ambiance, as well as the Institut Lumière. Also, look out for the Lyon dance biennial, which brings in hundreds of artists and troupes from around the world (last three weeks of Sept in even-numbered years; ⓦwww.biennale-de-lyon.org).

Listings

Bike Rental Holiday Bikes, 199 rue Vendome, 3e ⓣ04.78.60.11.10, ⓦwww.holiday-bikes.com.
Boat trips Société Naviginter, 13bis quai Rambaud, 2e ⓣ04.78.42.96.81. Leaving from quai des Célestins, boats run up the Saône or down to the confluence with the Rhône at the Île Barbe (April–June & Sept–Oct Tues–Sun, July & Aug daily; €7). The same company offers lunch and dinner cruises from €37.
Car rental Europcar, 40 rue de la Villette, 3e ⓣ08.25.00.25.22; Hertz, 40 rue Villette, 3e ⓣ04.72.33.89.89; Avis, Gare Part-Dieu, 3e ⓣ04.72.33.37.19. All the above also have offices at the airport and at the Perrache centre.
Consulates Canada, 21 rue Bourgelat, 2e ⓣ04.72.77.64.07; UK, 24 rue Childebert, 2e ⓣ04.72.77.81.70; USA, 16 rue République, 2e ⓣ04.78.38.36.88.
Disabled travellers For information on facilities for the disabled contact Délégation Départmentale APF, 73ter, rue Francis de Pressensé, Villeurbanne ⓣ04.72.43.01.01, ⓕ04.78.93.61.99.
Emergencies Samu – emergency medical attention ⓣ15; Police ⓣ17; SOS Médecins ⓣ04.78.83.51.51. Hospitals: Croix Rousse, (ⓣ04.72.07.10.46); Hôpital Édouard-Herriot, place d'Arsonval, 3e (ⓣ04.72.11.69.53). For house calls contact the medical referral centres (ⓣ04.72.33.00.33).
Internet *Espace Connectik*, 19 quai St-Antoine, 2e (Mon–Sat 11am–7pm), has plenty of terminals but is rather expensive; *Raconte Moi de la Terre*, 38 rue Thomassin, 2e (Mon–Sat 10am–7.30pm), is cheaper and also serves snacks.
Lesbian and gay info ARIS (Accueil Rencontres Informations Services), 16 rue Polycarpe ⓣ04.78.27.10.10. Gay and lesbian centre organizing various activities and producing a useful scene guide. État d'Esprit, 19 rue Royale ⓣ04.78.27.76.53, is a gay and lesbian bookstore that also holds cultural events. Forum Gai et Lesbien, 17 rue Romarin ⓣ04.78.39.97.72, ⓦwww.fgllyon.org. Lyon celebrates lesbian and gay pride in mid-June.

Money exchange AOC, 20 rue Gasparin (Mon–Sat 9.30am–6.30pm); AOC Opéra, 3 rue de la République (Mon–Fri 9am–6pm).
Pharmacy Blanchet, 5 place des Cordeliers, 2e ⓣ04.78.42.12.42. Daily till midnight.

Police The main commissariat is on rue de la Charité, 2e ⓣ04.78.42.26.56.
Post office PTT, place Antonin-Poncet, Lyon 69002.
Taxis ⓣ04.78.28.23.23 or ⓣ04.78.27.31.31.

Around Lyon

Within easy reach of the city, the **Monts du Lyonnais** to the south and west of Lyon may not reach spectacular heights, but they offer quiet and solitude among steep, forested hills and unassuming villages surrounded by cherry orchards, the region's main source of income. Tourism is low-key, but food and accommodation in the hostels of the mountain villages are rarely a problem for visitors to the area's parks and museums. **Bus** services from the main *gare routière* and the western *gare de Gorge du Loup* (M° Gorge du Loup; 9e) to the larger villages are reasonably frequent, and to the east of Lyon, the medieval town of **Pérouges** can easily be reached by train from both stations. The mountains can be visited every Sunday from June until the middle of September by steam train, leaving from **L'Arbresle**, just west of Lyon (frequent trains from Lyon-Perrache; €9 return); it's a scenic service but not very useful for getting anywhere.

St-Pierre-la-Palud and St-Martin-en-Haut

Fifteen kilometres west of Lyon, the **Musée de la Mine** at **ST-PIERRE-LA-PALUD** (March–Nov Sat, Sun & hols 2–6pm; €4.60) is guaranteed to instil admiration for the endurance of the miners who put up with working conditions like those simulated in the reconstructed mine shaft which forms the main exhibit. Going down into the copper sulphate mine shaft while an ex-miner explains its workings in meticulous detail (2hr; in French) is not recommended if you're claustrophobic. Back on the surface, you move on to an exhibition about the former mining village and pit.

Although most of the villages in the Lyonnais mountains have a restaurant or two, finding a place to stay is somewhat more challenging. In **ST-MARTIN-EN-HAUT**, an hour's bus ride from the *gare de Gorge du Loup* in Lyon, is the hotel *Le Relais des Bergers* (ⓣ04.78.48.51.22; ❸), probably the best bet for the area. There's also a **tourist office** (Tues–Sat 9am–noon & 2–6pm, Sun 10am–noon & 2–6pm; ⓣ04.78.48.64.32), and a municipal **campsite** just outside the village on the D122 (ⓣ04.78.48.62.16; all year).

Pérouges and Crémieu

Twenty-nine kilometres northeast of Lyon on the N84, **PÉROUGES** is a beautiful village of cobbled alleyways and ancient houses, some of them pleasing ruins. Its charm has not gone unnoticed by the French film industry – historical dramas like *The Three Musketeers* and *Monsieur Vincent* were filmed within its fortifications – nor by some of the residents, who have fought long and hard for preservation orders on its most interesting buildings. The result is an immaculate, if perhaps rather stifling, work of conservation.

Local traditional life is also thriving in the hands of a hundred or so workers who still weave locally grown hemp. No particular monument stands out, but the central square, the **place du Halle**, and its main street, the **rue du Prince**, have some of the best-preserved French medieval remains. The **lime tree** on place du Halle is a symbol of liberty, planted in 1792. The place both to **stay** and eat in Pérouges, if you can afford it, is the *Ostellerie du Vieux Pérouges* (ⓣ04.74.61.00.88, ⓦwww.ostellerie.com; ❼), in a medieval town house fronting the square; its **restaurant** serves traditional mountain dishes of rabbit and carp, with menus from €32.

CRÉMIEU, to the south on the D517, is less immediately compelling, despite its local sausages (*sabodet*), monumental architecture and eight hundred years of history. The town was once an important commercial centre, as signified by the fifteenth-century **market buildings** on rue du Lt-Col-Bel, the ruined château of the kingdom of Dauphiné and the site of the former mint. With whole streets of handsome fifteenth-, sixteenth- and seventeenth-century houses, it deserves further exploration. Several of the imposing medieval city gates also survive. The artisan boulanger in a fifteenth-century house opposite the Hôtel de Ville makes a useful stop for picnic provisions.

Vienne and around

Heading south from Lyon on the A7, a twenty-kilometre stretch of oil refineries, steel, chemical and paper works, cement, fertilizer and textile factories, all spewing plumes of grey and orange pollution into the air, may well tempt you to make a bee-line for the lavender fields of Provence. However, a short detour off the autoroute brings you to **VIENNE**, which, along with **St-Romain-en-Gal**, across the river, makes for the most interesting stop on the Rhône before Orange.

With their riverside positions, Vienne and St-Romain prospered as Rome's major wine port and *entrepôt* on the Rhône, and many Roman monuments survive to attest to this past glory. Several important churches recall Vienne's medieval heyday as well: it was a bishop's seat from the fifth century and the hometown of twelfth-century Pope Calixtus II. Today, the compact old quarter is crisscrossed with pedestrian precincts which make for enjoyable menu-browsing around **rue des Clercs** and **place Charles-de-Gaulle**. And there's a feeling that despite the distant rumble of the autoroute calling you to sunnier climes, the town has maintained its character and sense of purpose.

The Town

Roman monuments are scattered liberally around the streets of Vienne, and it requires little effort to take in the magnificently restored **Temple d'Auguste et de Livie** on place du Palais, a perfect, scaled-down version of Nîmes' Maison Carrée, or the bulky remains of the **Théâtre de Cybèle**, off place de Miremont. The **Théâtre Antique**, off rue du Cirque at the base of Mont Pipet to the north (April–Aug daily 9.30am–1pm & 2–6pm; Sept–Oct Tues–Sun 9.30am–1pm & 2–6pm; Nov–March Tues–Sat 9.30am–12.30pm & 2–5pm, Sun 1.30–5.30pm; €2, or €6 combined ticket), is more of a haul but it's worth making the trip for the view of the town and river from the very top seats. The theatre is the venue of an **international jazz festival** for the first two weeks of July, when it pulls in some of the biggest names on the jazz and rock circuit.

Vienne museum pass

The Théâtre Antique, Église and Cloître de St-André-le-Bas, Musée des Beaux-Arts et d'Archéologie and Église-Musée St-Pierre can be visited on a single ticket (€6), which can be picked up at any of the sites.

The **Église-Musée St-Pierre** (April–Oct Tues–Sun 9.30am–1pm & 2–6pm; Nov–March Tues–Fri 9.30am–12.30pm & 2–5pm, Sat & Sun 2–6pm; €2 or €6 combined ticket with other museums) stands on the site of one of France's first cathedrals. Since its origins in the fifth century, the building has suffered much reconstruction and abuse, including a stint as a factory in the nineteenth century, though the monumental portico of the former church is still striking. Today it has something of the atmosphere of an architectural salvage yard, housing substantial but broken chunks of Roman columns, capitals and cornice. Close by is the most prominent – and vaunted – of Vienne's monuments, the **Cathédrale St-Maurice** (daily 8am–6pm; free), whose unwieldy facade, a combination of Romanesque and Gothic, appears as if its upper half has been dumped on top of a completely alien building. The interior, with its ninety-metre-long vaulted nave, is impressive though, spare and elegant, with some modern stained-glass windows and traces of fifteenth-century frescoes.

The **Église** (visits by arrangement; enquire at the cloister) and **Cloître de St-André-le-Bas** (same hours and ticket as St-Pierre) on place du Jeu de Paume, a few streets north of the cathedral, date from the ninth and twelfth centuries. The back tower of the church, on rue de la Table Ronde, is a remarkable monument, studded with tiny carved stone faces, while the cloister, entered through a space where temporary exhibits are held, is a beautiful little Romanesque affair, whose walls are decorated with local tombstones, some dating from the fifth century.

The major museum in Vienne is the **Musée des Beaux-Arts et d'Archéologie** on place de Miremont (same hours and ticket as St-Pierre), with a preponderance of eighteenth-century French pottery, but also some attractive pieces of third-century Roman silverware. More enlightening is the small textile museum, the **Musée de la Draperie** (mid-April to mid-Sept Wed–Sun 2–6pm; €2), in the Espace St-Germain to the south of the centre off rue Vimaine, which, with the aid of videos, working looms and weavers, illustrates the complete process of cloth-making as it was practised in the city for over two hundred years.

Practicalities

The cours Brillier runs at right angles to the river, with the **tourist office** at no. 3, near quai Jean-Jaurès (Mon–Sat 9am–noon & 2–6pm; Sun 10am–noon & 2–5pm; ⓣ04.74.53.80.30, ⓦwww.vienne-tourisme.com), and the **gare SNCF** at the other end. Halfway up the cours, rue Boson leads up to the west front of the cathedral.

If you plan to **stay**, try the *Poste*, 47 cours Romestang (ⓣ04.74.85.02.04, ⓕ04.74.85.16.17; ❸), between the station and place de Miremont, which has good rooms overlooking the *cours*. One of the few other budget options is the *Ibis*, by the *gare routière* in place Camille-Jouffray (ⓣ04.74.78.41.11, ⓦwww.ibishotel.com; ❹), just down from the tourist office. The *Hotel Central* is well located, as the name implies, decent enough but rather gloomy (ⓣ04.74.85.18.38, ⓔhotel-central-vienne@wanadoo.fr; ❹). If you have your own transport, however, you should stay at the *Château des Sept Fontaines*, 5km northwest on the N7 at **Seyssuel** (ⓣ04.74.85.25.70, ⓦwww.hotel7fontaines.com; ❹; closed Dec–April), with a large garden and comfortable rooms. There's also an **HI hostel** on the other side of the park from the tourist office at 11 quai Riondet (ⓣ04.74.53.21.97, ⓕ04.74.31.98.93; reserve ahead Fri–Sun mid-Sept to mid-May; €8–8.90 per person).

The old town has a number of promising **places to eat**, including a good selection of cheapies in rue de la Table Ronde (near St-André-le-Bas), among them *L'Estancot* at no. 4 (☎04.74.85.12.09; closed Mon & Sun; €16) and *Au Petit Chez Soi* at no. 6 (☎04.74.85.19.77; closed Sun evening & Mon), serving *moules-frites* for €11.50. Alternatively, classy and welcoming *Le Bec Fin*, 7 place St-Maurice (☎04.74.85.76.72; closed Sun & Wed evening & Mon), offers filling menus of Lyonnais dishes from €27. However, if you fancy a splurge, head for the superlative restaurant in the hôtel *La Pyramide*, 14 bd Fernand-Point (☎04.74.53.01.96; closed Sun & Mon), with menus from €88 to €130; going à la carte will cost you at least €78. For **drinking**, there are a number of bars in town, including *Les 12 Mesures* in rue des Clercs, *The Celtic House* in rue Allmer, and the gay-friendly *West Saloon*, with live blues at weekends, on rue de la Table Ronde. For Internet access, go to *Surf en Ville*, at 16 rue des Clercs (Mon–Fri 11am–8pm, Sat 2pm–midnight).

St-Romain-en-Gal

Facing Vienne across the Rhône, several hectares of Roman ruins constitute the site of **ST-ROMAIN-EN-GAL**, also the name of the modern town surrounding it. The excavations (still ongoing), just across the road bridge from Vienne, attest to a significant community dating from the first century BC to the third AD, and give a vivid picture of the daily life and domestic architecture of Roman France. You enter through the excellent modern **Musée Archéologique de St-Romain-en-Gal** (site & museum March–Oct daily except Mon 10am–6pm; Nov–Feb daily except Mon 10am–5pm; €3.80), which displays frescoes, superb mosaics and other objects recovered from the site, along with explanatory models. The ruins themselves are clearly laid out, with illuminating reconstructions and informative but not overly technical explanatory plaques in English – ideal for adults and children alike. Be sure to check out the Romans' lavishly decorated marble public toilets, by the entry ramp to the dig.

Between Vienne and Valence

Between Vienne and Valence are some of the oldest, most celebrated **vineyards** in France: the renowned Côte Rotie, Hermitage and Crozes-Hermitage *appellations*. If you've got any spare luggage space, it's well worth stopping to pick up a bottle from the local co-op; even their *vin ordinaire* is superlative and unbelievably cheap, considering its quality. Just south of Ampuis on the west bank, 8km south of Vienne, is the tiny area producing one of the most exquisite French white wines, Condrieu, and close by one of the most exclusive – Château-Grillet – an *appellation* covering just this single château (by appointment; ☎04.74.59.51.56).

Between **St-Vallier** and **Tain l'Hermitage**, the Rhône becomes quite scenic, and after Tain you can see the Alps. In spring you're more likely to be conscious of orchards everywhere rather than vines. Cherries, pears, apples, peaches and apricots, as well as bilberries and strawberries, are cultivated in abundance.

Tain-l'Hermitage and around

TAIN-L'HERMITAGE, accessible from both the N7 and the A7, is unpretentious and uneventful. The only reason to stay here is to drink wine and eat chocolate. You can sample a good selection of the renowned Hermitage and Crozes-Hermitage **wines** within walking distance of the *gare SNCF* at the vast Cave de Tain-l'Hermitage, 22 rte de Larnage (daily: 9am–noon & 2–6pm; July & Aug 9am–12.30pm & 1.30–7pm; ☎04.75.08.91.86), and if your visit happens to fall on the last weekend in February you can try out wines from 78 vineyards in the Foire aux Vins des Côtes du Rhône Septentrionales. The celebrated **chocolates** in question are made by Valrhona and available at their shop (Mon–Fri 9am–7pm, Sat 9am–6pm) on avenue du Président-Roosevelt (the RN7), past the junction with the RN95 as you're heading south.

The **tourist office**, at 70 av Jean-Jaurès (Mon–Sat 9am–noon & 2–6pm; ⓣ04.75.08.06.81, ⓦwww.tain-tourisme.com), on the RN7 further north, can provide you with lists of vineyard addresses. If you need to **stay**, try the inexpensive but rather tired *Hôtel de la Gare* at 19 av du Dr Paul Durand, (ⓣ06.13.48.37.47, ⓕ04.75.07.11.71; ❷), or the smarter *Les 2 Côteaux*, 18 rue Joseph-Péala, directly across Jean-Jaurès from place Taurobole next to the rather splendid pedestrian suspension bridge (ⓣ04.75.08.33.01, ⓕ04.75.08.44.20; ❷). For a cheap **meal** in Tain try the crêperie *La Récré*, 8 place Taurobole (€5 upwards), as an alternative to the stuffier establishments on avenue Jean-Jaurès. The town's best restaurant, *Jean-Marc Reynaud*, 82 av du Président-Roosevelt (ⓣ04.75.07.22.10; Sun evening & Mon à la carte only, closed one week Aug & two weeks Jan), has an excellent value €30 menu, with à la carte upwards of €50.

On the third weekend of September, the different wine-producing villages celebrate their cellars in the **Fête des Vendanges**. But at any time of the year you can go bottle-hunting along the N86 for some 30km north of Tain along the right bank, following the *dégustation* signs and then crossing back over between Serrières and Chanas.

Hauterives

HAUTERIVES, 25km northeast of Tain, is a small village with a remarkable creation – a manic, surreal **Palais Idéal** (daily: Jan & Dec 9.30am–12.30pm & 1.30–4.30pm; Feb, March, Oct & Nov 9.30am–12.30pm & 1.30–5.30pm; April–June & Sept 9am–12.30pm & 1.30–6.30pm; July & Aug 9am–12.30pm & 1.30–7.30pm; ⓦwww.facteurcheval.com; €5) built by a local postman by the name of Ferdinand Cheval (1836–1912). The house is truly bizarre, a bubbling frenzy reminiscent of the *modernista* architecture of Spain, with features that recall Thai or Indian temples. The eccentric building took thirty years to carve, and Cheval designed an equally bizarre tombstone which can also be seen. Various Surrealists have paid homage to the building and psychoanalysts have given it much thought, but it defies all classification. The *palais* is a tourist magnet, reached along a lane cluttered with shops hawking assorted gewgaws. The rest of the village, however, is relatively unspoilt. If you want to **stay** here, you have the choice of the *Camping du Château* on the edge of town on the N538 (ⓣ04.75.68.80.19, ⓕ04.75.68.90.94; closed Oct–March) and a **hotel**, *Le Relais* (ⓣ04.75.68.81.12, ⓕ04.75.68.92.42; ❶; closed mid-Jan to Feb), opposite the village church.

Romans-sur-Isère

South of Hauterives and 15km east of the Rhône at Tain is **ROMANS-SUR-ISÈRE**. It's not the most exciting of towns but it does have a fascinating museum of shoemaking – the industry that has kept Romans going for the last five centuries. The extensive **Musée Internationale de la Chaussure** is in the former Convent of the Visitation at 2 rue Ste-Marthe (May, June & Sept Tues–Sat 10am–6pm, Sun 2.30–6pm; July & Aug Mon–Sat 10am–6pm, Sun 2.30–6pm; Oct–April Tues–Sat 10am–5pm & Sun 2.30–6pm; €4.10, or joint ticket with Palais Idéal, see above, €6) and also includes a permanent exhibition on the Resistance. Your toes will curl in horror at the extent to which women have been immobilized by their footwear from ancient times to the present on every continent, while at the same time you can't help but admire the craziness of some of the creations. Romans is also a good place to buy shoes, with several factory shops in the town including Charles Jourdan, and a smart outlet centre to the east along avenue Gambetta.

The rather neglected old town has plenty of beautiful old corners to explore, and the region has two gastronomic specialities: a ringed spongy bread flavoured with orange water, known as a *pogne*, and *ravioles*, cornflour-based ravioli with an eggy, cheesy, buttery filling. You can sample these at *La Cassolette*, at 16 rue Rebatte in a beautiful old stone house off place Jacquemart (ⓣ04.75.02.55.71; closed Sun, Mon & three weeks from last week in July; menus from €12.50).

There's a **tourist office** on place Jean-Jaurès (April–Oct Mon–Fri 9am–7pm, Sat 9am–6pm, Sun 9.30am–12.30pm; Nov–March Mon–Sat 9am–6pm, Sun 9.30am–12.30pm; ⓣ04.75.02.28.72), and several **hotels**, including *Des Balmes*, northwest of the town centre in the *quartier* of the same name (ⓣ04.75.02.29.52, ⓦwww.hoteldesbalmes.com; ❸), with an excellent and inexpensive restaurant (closed Sun evening out of season). Cheaper options include the *Magdeleine*, 31 av Pierre-Sémard (ⓣ04.75.02.33.53; ❷; closed Sun evening out of season), and the *Cendrillon*, 9 place Carnot, across from the train station (ⓣ04.75.02.83.77, ❷). The municipal **campsite**, *Les Chasses* (ⓣ04.75.72.35.27; closed Oct–April), is 1km off the N92 northeast of the city, next to the aerodrome.

Valence

At an indefinable point along the Rhône, there's an invisible sensual border, and by the time you reach **VALENCE**, you know you've crossed it. The quality of light is different and the temperature higher, bringing with it the scent of eucalyptus and pine, and the colours and contours suddenly seem worlds apart from the cold lands of Lyon and the north. Valence is the obvious place to celebrate your arrival in the **Midi** (as the French call the south), with plenty of good bars and restaurants in the old town, though little else.

Arrival, information and accommodation

If you come in on the autoroute, running along the Rhône's left bank, you exit onto avenue Gambetta, with the old town, its ramparts replaced by boulevards, on your left. To the southeast of the old town are the **gare routière**, the

TGV Méditerranée

Opened to the public in June 2001, the TGV Méditerranée line has cut the travelling time between Paris and Marseille to a mere three hours. Twelve years in the making, with a budget of more than €3.5 billion, the project included 250km of new track laid between Valence and Marseille, and the construction of three ultra-modern stations on the outskirts of Valence, Avignon and Aix-en-Provence. Most travellers heading to these cities will alight at one of the new stations, from where there are shuttles into the centre of town. Likewise, those departing by TGV from Valence, Avignon or Aix will need to first take the shuttle out to the station in order to board their train. The new line also links Lyon, Valence, Avignon, Aix and Marseille directly with the Charles de Gaulle airport outside of Paris.

gare SNCF and the **tourist office** on parvis de la Gare (May–Aug Mon–Sat 9am–7pm, Sun 9am–noon; Sept–April Mon–Fri 9am–6.30pm & Sat 9am–5pm; ⓣ08.92.70.70.99, ⓦwww.tourisme-valence.com). The new **TGV** station is 10km northeast, along the autoroute to Romans. There are regular shuttles and trains (daily 6.30am–10.50pm; €2) which connect the *gare TGV* with the *gare SNCF*.

For mid-range hotel **rooms**, try the *Europe*, 15 av Félix-Faure (ⓣ04.75.82.62.65, ⓕ04.75.82.62.66; ❸), with satellite TV and en-suite showers. If you want to splash out, *Yan's* has spacious rooms in a stylish modern building with park and pool southeast of the city on the route de Montéléger (ⓣ04.75.55.52.52, ⓦwww.yanshotel.com; ❻). Among the many cheaper options are the *De Lyon*, 23 av Pierre Semard, a decent two star with Internet access (ⓣ04.75.41.44.66; ❷), and its smarter neighbour *Les Négociants*, 27 av Pierre Semard (ⓣ04.75.44.01.86; ⓦwww.hotelvision.com/valence.negociants; ❷).

The Town

The focus of Vieux Valence, the **Cathédrale St-Apollinaire** (Mon 8am–6.30pm, Tues–Sat 8am–7pm, Sun 11.30am–6.30pm), was consecrated in 1095 by Pope Urban II (who proclaimed the First Crusade), and largely reconstructed in the seventeenth century after a local baron went on the rampage, avenging the execution of three Protestants during the Wars of Religion. More work was carried out later, including the horribly mismatched nineteenth-century tower, but the interior still preserves its original Romanesque grace – especially the columns around the ambulatory.

Between the cathedral and **Église de St-Jean** at the northern end of Grande Rue, which has preserved its Romanesque tower and porch capitals, are some of the oldest and narrowest streets of Vieux Valence. They are known as **côtes**: côte St-Estève just northwest of the cathedral; côte St-Martin off rue du Petit-Paradis; and côte Sylvante off rue du Petit-Paradis' continuation, rue A.-Paré. Diverse characters who would have walked these steep and crooked streets include Rabelais, a student at the university founded here in 1452 and suppressed during the Revolution, and the teenage Napoleon Bonaparte, who began his military training as a cadet at the artillery school.

Though Valence lacks the cohesion of the medieval towns and villages further south, it does have several vestiges of the sixteenth-century city, most notably the Renaissance **Maison des Têtes** at 57 Grande Rue. Be sure if you can to look at the ceiling in the passageway here (office hours only), where sculpted roses transform into the cherub-like heads after which the palace is named. Also worth a look is the **Maison Dupré-Latour**, on rue Pérollerie, which has a superbly sculptured porch and spiral staircase. By contrast the **Musée de Valence**, near the cathedral on place des Ormeaux (mid-June to Sept Tues–Sat 10am–noon & 2–6.45pm, Sun 2–6.45pm; Oct to mid-June 2–5.45pm; €3), contains a mishmash of unremarkable local art and archeological finds, and frankly is not worth the price of admission.

A good place if you need to fill in time is the **Parc Jouvet** overlooking the river (and the motorway) south of avenue Gambetta. At sunset, or even better at dawn, this is definitely the best place to be in the city – a tranquil oasis away from the town's bustle – with a bottle of Cornas or sparkling St-Peray from the vineyards across the water.

Eating and drinking

For **restaurants**, *L'Épicerie*, 18 place Belat (ⓣ04.75.42.74.46; closed Sat lunch, Sun & Aug), is one of the most congenial places to eat, with art exhibitions on the fifteenth-century walls, jazz some nights and imaginative food on menus from €22 to €39. Another good option is the friendly *Père Joseph*, 9 place des Clercs (Ⓣ04.75.42.57.80), which serves excellent traditional food, with a menu at €23, but if you want to eat very well and are prepared to pay €115 for the pleasure (or €59 for a lunch weekday menu), *Restaurant Pic*, 285 av Victor-Hugo (Ⓣ04.75.44.15.32; closed Sun evening & Mon, plus Tues Nov–March & three weeks in Jan), is the city's top-notch eating house: Quercy lamb with vegetable confit and tempura of dates, or roast veal with parsley gnocchi, lemon and anchovies are among the delights. Valence also has several good old-fashioned brasseries with a wide range of dishes and prices, including *Café Victor-Hugo*, 30 av Victor-Hugo, and *Le Bistrot des Clercs*, 48 Grande Rue; plus an excellent *salon de thé*, *One Two Tea*, at 37 Grande Rue. If you missed sampling some *pogne* in Romans, head for the bakery Maurin Fils, at 17 av Pierre Semard.

Montélimar

In **MONTÉLIMAR**, 40km south of Valence, every street proclaims the glory of the nougat that has been made here for centuries and is the town's chief *raison d'être*. It's a lively enough place with a pleasant *vieille ville* and a fascinating museum dedicated to miniaturization.

The main street of the old town, **rue Pierre-Julien**, runs from the one remaining medieval **gateway** on the nineteenth-century ring of boulevards at place St-Martin, south past the **church of Sainte-Croix** with its well-populated square, and onto place Marx-Dormoy. At no. 19, opposite the post office, is the **Musée de la Miniature** (July & Aug daily 10am–6pm; Sept–June Wed–Sun 2–6pm; €4.90), whose tiny exhibits, some so small you have to use a microscope, have been created by leading contemporary artists. There's a grain of rice bearing a portrait of Pushkin and one of his poems, and a table laid with a chess game is no bigger than a five cent coin.

Leading off rue Pierre-Julien are many medieval lanes with sixteenth- and seventeenth-century town houses, though the facades and old arcades of **place du Marché** serve chiefly nowadays as a backdrop to parked cars. Above the old town to the east is the impressive **Château des Adhémars** on rue du Château (April–June & Sept–Oct daily 9.30–11.30am & 2–5.30pm; July & Aug daily 9.30–11.30am & 2–6pm; Nov–March daily except Tues 9.30–11.30am & 2–5.30pm; €3.50). Originally belonging to the family after whom the town ("Mount of the Adhémars") was named, the castle is mostly fourteenth-century, but also boasts a fine eleventh-century chapel and twelfth-century living-quarters. If you wish to find out more about the town's famous **nougat** (the word is a contraction of a phrase meaning "you spoil us"), you can visit the Nougats Gerbe d'Or factory in **the Parc d'Activité Fortuneau**, south of the centre (daily 8.30am–noon & 2–6pm), where you will be shown around the plant and have a chance to sample (and buy) the end product.

Practicalities

The **gare SNCF** is a short way west of the old town across the Jardin Public, with the **tourist office** close by on the corner of allée Champs-de-Mars and boulevard Maitre Desmarais (July & Aug Mon–Sat 9am–7pm, Sun 10am–1pm & 3–5pm; Sept–June Mon–Sat 9am–12.15pm and 2–6.30pm, Sun 10am–1pm & 3–5pm; Ⓣ04.75.01.00.20, Ⓦwww.montelimar-tourisme.com). There are plenty of **hotels** around the boulevards, including the very pleasant *Sphinx*, in a seventeenth-century town house at 19 bd Marre-Desmarais (Ⓣ04.75.01.86.64, Ⓦwww.sphinx-hotel.fr; ❸; closed mid-Dec to mid-Jan), and *Du Printemps*, north of the old town at 8 chemin de la Manche (Ⓣ04.75.46.03.14, Ⓦwww.hotel-du-printemps.com; ❹), with a pool and garden. In the old town the *Pierre*, 7 place des Clercs (Ⓣ04.75.01.33.16; ❸), is, despite the unpromising exterior, comfortable and very peaceful, apart from the nearby bell of Sainte-Croix tolling the hours. The **campsite**, *L'Ile Blanc* (Ⓣ04.75.51.20.05; Ⓦwww.camping-montelimar.com; closed Oct–March), is at Montélimar-Ancône, 5km northwest of the town. For good traditional **food**, head for the *Relais de l'Empereur*, 1 place Max-Dormoy (Ⓣ04.75.01.29.00; closed mid-Nov to mid-Dec; menus from €20). Montélimar's prime (and very pleasant) spot for **café** lounging is outside the old town on the stretch of boulevard between the tourist office and the Théâtre Municipal.

Western Provence

The richest area of Provence, the Côte d'Azur apart, is the **west**. Most of the large-scale production of fruit, vegetables and wine is based here in the low-lying plains beside the Rhône and the Durance rivers. The only heights are the rocky outbreaks of the **Dentelles** and the **Alpilles**, and the narrow east–west ridges of **Mont Ventoux**, the **Luberon** and the **Mont Ste-Victoire**. The two dominant cities of inland Provence, **Avignon** and **Aix**, both have rich histories and contemporary fame in their festivals of art; **Arles**, **Orange** and **Vaison-la-Romaine** have impressive Roman remains. Around the Rhône delta, the **Camargue** is a unique self-contained region, as different from the rest of Provence as it is from anywhere else in France.

Orange and around

ORANGE was the former seat of the counts of Orange, a title created by Charlemagne in the eighth century and passed to the Dutch crown in the sixteenth century. The family's most famous member was Prince William, who ascended the English throne with his consort Mary in the 1688 "Glorious Revolution". Today the town is best known for its spectacular **Roman theatre**, which hosts the important summer Chorégies **music festival**. While the rest of Orange is certainly attractive, there's not a lot to detain you once you've visited the theatre and adjacent museum and taken a quick look at the Roman triumphal arch at the northern approach to the town centre. Unfortunately, the victory of Le Pen's Front National in the municipal elections of 1995, and again in 2001, has forced the May strip-cartoon festival, which brought in all kinds of weird and wonderful entertainment, to be abandoned.

Arrival, information and accommodation

The **gare SNCF** is about 1.5km east of the centre, at the end of avenue Frédéric-Mistral. The nearest bus stop is at the bottom of rue Jean-Reboul, the

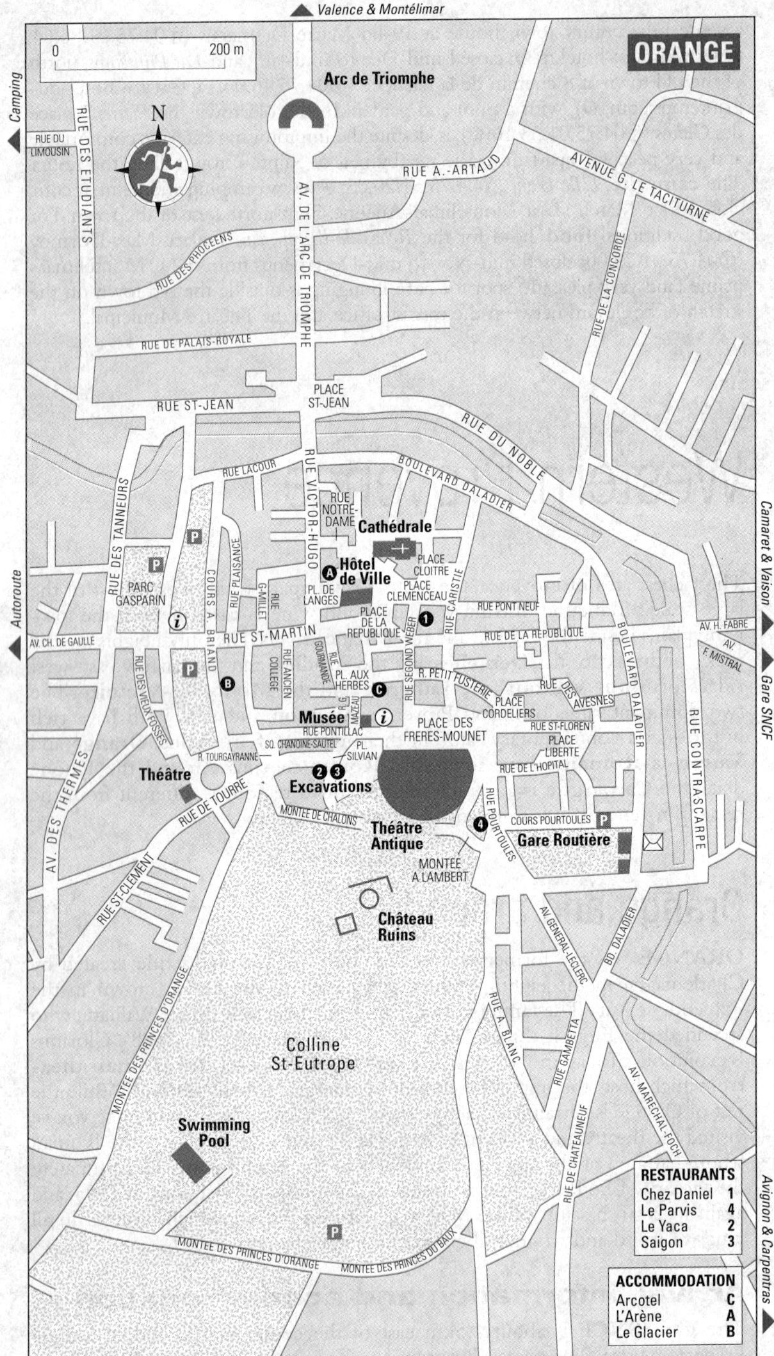
ORANGE
0
200 m
Valence & Montélimar
Camping
Autoroute
Camaret & Vaison
Gare SNCF
Avignon & Carpentras
Arc de Triomphe
Cathédrale
Hôtel de Ville
Musée
Théâtre
Excavations
Théâtre Antique
Gare Routière
Château Ruins
Colline St-Eutrope
Swimming Pool
PARC GASPARIN
RESTAURANTS
Chez Daniel 1
Le Parvis 4
Le Yaca 2
Saigon 3
ACCOMMODATION
Arcotel C
L'Arène A
Le Glacier B

first left as you walk away from the station. Bus #1, direction "Aygues", takes you to the Théâtre Antique, opposite which there's a **seasonal tourist office** (April–June & Sept Mon–Sat 10am–1pm & 2.15–6pm, Sun 10am–12.30pm & 2.30–6pm; July & Aug daily 10am–1pm & 2.15–7pm), from which it's a short distance on foot to the main **tourist office** on cours Aristide-Briand (April–June & Sept Mon–Sat 9.30am–7pm; July & Aug Mon–Sat 9.30am–7pm, Sun 10am–6pm; Oct–March Mon–Sat 10am–1pm & 2–5pm; ⓣ04.90.34.70.88, ⓦwww.provence-orange.com). The **gare routière** is close to the centre on boulevard Edouard Daladier.

Of the **hotels**, good options include small, appealing and good-value *Arcotel*, 8 place aux Herbes (ⓣ04.90.34.09.23, ⓔjor8525@aol.com; ❶); *L'Arène*, on pretty place de Langes (ⓣ04.90.11.40.40, ⓕ04.90.11.40.45; ❹), with spacious rooms and all mod cons; and the very comfortable *Le Glacier*, 46 cours Aristide-Briand (ⓣ04.90.34.02.01, ⓦwww.le-glacier.com; ❸). Orange's **campsite**, *Le Jonquier*, rue Alexis-Carrel (ⓣ04.90.34.49.48, ⓕ04.90.51.16.97; closed Oct–March), to the northwest, is equipped with tennis courts and a pool. The price for two people and a tent is €21.

The Town

Days off in Orange circa 55 AD were most entertainingly spent from dawn to dusk watching farce, clownish improvisations, song and dance, and occasionally, for the sake of a visiting dignitary, a bit of Greek tragedy in Latin at the huge Roman **theatre** (daily: March & Oct 9am–6pm; April, May & Sept 9am–7pm; June–Aug 9am–8pm; Nov–Feb 9am–5pm; €7.50, including audioguide and combined ticket with museum), built into the hill which squats on the south side of the old town. The theatre was as much a way of disseminating Roman culture in the conquered provinces as a place of entertainment, and despite its impressive dimensions was by no means exceptional for a city of Orange's size. Its acoustics allowed a full audience of 9000 to hear every word. The hill of St-Eutrope, into which the seats were built, plus a vast awning strung from the top of the stage wall, protected the spectators from the weather. It is one of the best-preserved examples in existence, with its stage wall still standing 103m across and 36m high, and completely plain like some monstrous prison wall when you see it from outside. The interior, although missing much of its original decoration, has its central, larger-than-life-size statue of Augustus, and niches for lesser statues. Despite Augustus' overbearing swagger, the statue's creators prudently allowed for the head to be changed should the emperor's rule prove less enduring than his marble likeness.

The best view of the theatre in its entirety is from St-Eutrope hill. You can follow a path up the hill either from the top of cours Aristide-Briand (montée P. de Chalons) or from cours Pourtoules (montée Albert Lambert) until you are looking directly down onto the stage. The ruins around your feet are those of the short-lived seventeenth-century castle of the princes of Orange. Louis XIV had it destroyed in 1673 and the principality of Orange was officially annexed to France forty years later.

The **municipal museum**, across the road from the theatre entrance (same hours and ticket as theatre), has documents concerning the Orange dynasty, including a suitably austere portrait of the founder of the Netherlands, William "the Silent". It also has Roman bits and pieces from the theatre and a collection rotated on a yearly basis containing diverse items such as the contents of a seventeenth-century pharmacy and an unlikely selection of works by Frank Brangwyn (1867–1956), the largely forgotten Bruges-born British Arts and

Crafts painter whose figurative works adorn the House of Lords in London and the Rockefeller Center in New York.

If you've arrived by road from the north you'll have passed the town's second major Roman monument, the **Arc de Triomphe**, whose intricate frieze and relief celebrate imperial victories against the Gauls. It was built around 20 BC outside the town walls to recall the victories of the Roman Second Legion.

Orange's old town is very small, hemmed in between the theatre and the River Meyne, featuring some pretty fountain-adorned squares and houses with ancient porticoes and courtyards.

Eating, drinking and entertainment

For **food**, cheap pizzas, pasta and more expensive seafood platters can be had at *Chez Daniel*, rue Segond Weber (daily; evenings only Fri–Sun; pizzas from €8), while *Le Yaca*, 24 place Silvain (Ⓣ04.90.34.70.03; closed Tues evening & Wed off season & Nov), gives a generous choice of dishes for €20 in an old vaulted chamber. Kitchens close rather early in Orange, especially on Sundays, but one place that stays open late is the very acceptable Vietnamese-Chinese *Saïgon*, next to the theatre at 20 place Sylvain (Ⓣ04.90.34.18.19, menus from around €12). However, the best food you're likely to get in the city is at *Le Parvis*, 3 cours des Pourtoules (Ⓣ04.90.34.82.00; closed Sun evening & Mon), with a weekday lunch menu from €16.50. For **drinking**, head for place Clemenceau in the centre, where there's *Le Négo* and the less expensive *Café de l'Univers*, painted in Provençal yellow. On the other side of cours Aristide-Briand, the *Café des Thermes*, 29 rue des Vieux-Fossés, has pool, a good selection of beers and a youngish clientele.

Orange's main festival is the **Chorégies**, a programme of opera, oratorios and orchestral concerts in July – details and tickets from the Bureau des Chorégies, 18 place Silvain (Ⓣ04.90.34.24.24, Ⓦwww.choregies.asso.fr). The theatre is also used throughout the year for jazz, film, folk and rock concerts. Prices range from €3 to €180; details from the Service Culturel de la Ville, 14 place Silvain (Ⓣ04.90.51.57.57). Tickets for all events can be bought from FNAC shops in all big French cities, and at the theatre box office in Orange.

Sérignan-du-Comtat

The village of **SÉRIGNAN-DU-COMTAT**, 8km northeast of Orange (three buses daily from Orange and Avignon), was the final home of **Jean-Henri Fabre**, a remarkable self-taught scientist, famous for his insect studies, who also composed poetry, wrote songs and painted his specimens with artistic brilliance as well as scientific accuracy. In the 1860s he had to resign from his teaching post at Avignon because parents and priests thought his lectures on the fertilization of flowering plants were licentious, if not downright pornographic. His **house** – on the N976 towards Orange – which he named the *Harmas* – contains a jungle-like garden, his study – with his complete classification of the herbs of France – and, on the ground floor, a selection from his extraordinary watercolour series of the fungi of the Vaucluse. Despite a decision to prioritize renovation of the house and garden in 1999, however, it remains closed to the public at the time of writing. At the crossroads in the centre of the town there's a **statue** of Fabre in front of the red-shuttered buildings of the church and *mairie*.

Châteauneuf-du-Pape

If you're heading down to Avignon, the slower route through **CHÂTEAUNEUF-DU-PAPE** (1–2 buses daily from Orange) exerts a strong pull. The village takes its name from the summer palace of the Avignon popes, but neither the views down the Rhône valley towards Avignon from the ruins of the fourteenth-century **château** (freely accessible) nor the medieval streets around **place du Portail** – the hub of the village – give Châteauneuf its special appeal. Rather it's the wines produced by the local vineyards, warmed at night by the large pebbles that cover the ground and soak up the sun's heat during the day, that are its real attraction. The rich ruby red is one of France's most renowned, but the white, too, is exquisite.

The *appellation* Châteauneuf-du-Pape does not, alas, come cheap. For the uninitiated, the best place to taste a good selection from the scores of domains before making an investment is at the boutique **La Maison des Vins**, at 8 rue du Maréchal Foch (July & Aug daily 10am–7pm; Sept–June daily 10am–12.30pm & 2–6.30pm). For a more casual introduction, the Cave Père-Anselme on avenue Bienheureux-Pierre-de-Luxembourg has a **Musée du Vin** (daily July & Aug 9am–1pm & 2–7pm; Sept–June 9am–noon & 2–6pm; free), plus free tastings of its wines. Otherwise, the **tourist office** on place du Portail (July & Aug Mon–Sat 9.30am–7pm, Sun 10am–1pm & 2–6pm; Sept–June Mon–Sat 9.30am–12.30pm & 2–6pm; ⓣ04.90.83.71.08, ⓕ04.90.83.50.34), or the Fédération des Syndicats de Producteurs, 12 av Louis-Pasteur (ⓣ04.90.83.72.21), can provide a complete list of producers, or you can visit an Association de Vignerons, such as Prestige et Tradition at 3 rue de la République (Aug & Sept Mon–Fri 7.30am–noon & 1.30–4pm), who bottle the wine of ten producers.

If your visit coincides with the first weekend of August you'll find free *dégustation* stalls throughout the village as well as parades, dances, equestrian contests, medieval entertainment and so forth, all to celebrate the reddening of the grapes in the **Fête de la Véraison**. As well as wine, a good deal of grape liqueur – *marc* – gets consumed.

Accommodation is confined to four very pleasant but small **hotels**: *La Garbure*, 3 rue Joseph-Ducos (ⓣ04.90.83.75.08, ⓦwww.la-garbure.com; ❹); the four-star *Hostellerie du Château des Fines Roches*, on route d'Avignon (ⓣ04.90.83.70.23, ⓦwww.chateaufinesroches.com; ❾); *La Mère Germaine*, on avenue Cdt-Lemaitre (ⓣ04.90.83.54.37, ⓦwww.lameregermaine.com; ❸); and *La Sommellerie*, 3km from the village on route de Roquemaure (ⓣ04.90.83.50.00, ⓦwww.hotel-la-sommellerie.com; ❻, closed Jan to mid-Feb).

You can **eat** well for around €15 at the brasserie *La Mule du Pape*, 2 rue de la République (restaurant closed Sun & evenings out of season), or pay a bit more at *La Mère Germaine* (see above), with its well-crafted Provençal dishes, and much more at *La Sommellerie* (see above; closed Sun evening & Mon out of season; menus €29–80), where the cook is one of France's master chefs. Everything here is made on the premises, from the bread to the fine desserts, and meat is cooked on an outdoor wood fire.

Vaison-la-Romaine and around

VAISON-LA-ROMAINE lies 27km northeast of Orange and hit the headlines in 1992 when the River Ouvèze, which divides the medieval and eighteenth-century towns, burst its banks, destroying riverside houses, the modern road bridge and an entire industrial quarter. Though the town has recovered remarkably, its character has changed – it seems much more commercialized and less friendly.

It still, however, has the strong attractions of its immaculate medieval **haute ville**, with a ruined clifftop castle, a **Roman bridge** that held out against the floods, a cloistered former cathedral and the exceptional excavated remains of two **Roman districts**. Just south of Vaison there are sculptures in natural settings to be discovered at the **Crestet Centre d'Art**.

Arrival, information and accommodation

Buses to and from Carpentras, Orange and Avignon stop at the **gare routière** on avenue des Choralies near the junction with avenue Victor-Hugo, east of the town centre on the north side of the river. The **tourist office** is on place du Chanoine-Sautel (July & Aug Mon–Sat 9am–noon & 2–6pm, Sun 9am–noon; Sept–June Mon–Sat 9am–noon & 2–5.45pm; Ⓣ04.90.36.02.11, Ⓦwww.vaison-la-romaine.com), between the two archeological sites in the north of the modern town.

There's not a great choice of **hotels** in Vaison, and few bargains. The town's best hotel and restaurant is *Le Beffroi*, a sixteenth-century residence on rue de l'Évêché in the *haute ville* (Ⓣ04.90.36.04.71, Ⓔbeffroi@wanadoo.fr; ❻; closed mid-Jan to March); a little further up the same street there's an exquisite B&B, *L'Évêché* (Ⓣ04.90.36.13.46, Ⓦwww.eveche.free.fr, ❺, where you breakfast on a terrace with wonderful views over the river and beyond. *Fête en Provence*, a restaurant in the *haute ville* also rents out rooms (Ⓣ04.90.36.36.43, Ⓦwww.la-fete-en-provence.com; ❹). For **campers**, there's the central *Camping du Théâtre Romain* on chemin du Brusquet, off avenue des Choralies, Quartier des Arts (Ⓣ04.90.28.78.66, Ⓦwww.camping-theatre.com; closed mid-Nov to mid-March, €18.50 for two people and a tent).

The Town

The **haute ville** lies on the south side of the river, with **rue du Pont** climbing up towards place des Poids and the fourteenth-century **gateway** to the town. More steep zigzags take you past the Gothic gate and overhanging portcullis of the **belfry** and into the heart of this sedately quiet, uncommercialized and rich *quartier*.

On the north bank from the **Pont Romain**, a Roman bridge that has been patched up over the years, Grande-Rue leads up to the central streets of rue de la République and cours Henri-Fabre, after which it becomes avenue Général-de-Gaulle. The two excavated **Roman residential districts** lie to either side of this avenue: **Puymin** to the east (April & May 9.30am–6pm; June & Sept 9.30am–6pm; July & Aug 9.30am–6.45pm; Oct–March 10am–noon & 2–5pm) and **La Villasse** to the west (April & May Mon & Wed–Sun 10am–noon & 2.30–6pm; Tues 2.30–6pm; June & Sept 9.30am–12.30pm & 2–6pm; July & Aug 9.30am–12.30pm & 2–6.45pm; Oct–March 10am–noon & 2–5pm); ticket for both plus Puymin museum and cathedral cloisters €7).

The Puymin excavations contain the theatre, several mansions and houses, a colonnade known as the *portique de Pompée* and the museum for all the items discovered. The excavations of La Villasse reveal a street with pavements and gutters with the layout of a row of arcaded shops running parallel, more patrician houses (some with mosaics still intact), a basilica and the baths. The houses require a certain amount of imagination, but the street plan of La Villasse, the colonnade with its statues in every niche, and the theatre, which still seats 7000 people during the July festival, make it easy to visualize a comfortable, well-serviced Roman town.

Most of the detail and decoration of the buildings are displayed in the **museum** in the Puymin district (same hours as Puymin archeological site).

Tiny fragments of painted plaster have been jigsawed together with convincing reconstructions of how whole painted walls would have looked. There are mirrors of silvered bronze, lead water pipes, taps shaped as griffins' feet, dolphin door knobs, weights and measures, plus impressive busts and statues.

Tickets can be bought at the Puymin entrance just by the tourist office or in the cloisters of the former **Cathédrale Notre-Dame**, west down chemin Couradou, which runs along the south side of La Villasse. The apse of the cathedral is a confusing overlay of sixth-, tenth- and thirteenth-century construction, using pieces quarried from the Roman ruins. The **cloisters** are fairly typical of early medieval workmanship – pretty enough but not wildly exciting. The only surprising feature is the large inscription visible on the north wall of the cathedral, a convoluted precept for the monks.

Eating and drinking

The **restaurant** to head for is *Le Bateleur*, 1 place Théodore-Aubanel, downstream from the Pont Romain on the north bank (Ⓣ04.90.36.28.04; closed Mon, Thurs evening, Sat lunch out of season; closed Mon & Sat lunch July–Oct; menus €25 & €35, *plats* around €20); the lamb stuffed with almonds and the *rascasse* (scorpion fish) soufflé are highly recommended. Alternatively, *La Fontaine* at *Le Beffroi* on rue de l'Evêché in the medieval village (Ⓣ04.90.36.04.71; closed Nov–March) offers Provençal dishes in menus from €26–42. You can get crêpes and pizzas in the old town and brasserie fare on place de Montfort, the obvious **drinking** place to gravitate towards. For a more local atmosphere, try *Vasio Bar* on cours Taulignan.

Le Crestet and Mont Ventoux

South of Vaison, 3.5km down the Malaucène road, a turning to the right leads to the tiny hilltop village of **LE CRESTET** from where signs direct you the short distance to the Crestet Centre d'Art (free access), where modern sculptures have been placed, almost hidden, in an expanse of oak and pine woods. Though the Centre itself is now closed, there's a map in the lay-by above it, indicating the position of various artworks it is still possible to view dotted among the woods. Some of the sculptures are formed from the trees themselves, others are startling metal structures such as a mobile and a Meccano cage.

MONT VENTOUX, whose outline repeatedly appears upon the horizon from the Rhône and Durance valleys, rises some 20km east of Vaison. White with snow, black with storm-cloud shadow or reflecting myriad shades of blue, the barren pebbles of the uppermost 300m are like a weathervane for all of western Provence. Winds can accelerate to 250km per hour around the meteorological, TV and military masts and dishes on the summit, but if you can stand still for a moment the view in all directions is unbelievable. A road, the D974, climbs all the way to the top, though no buses go there. The road up the northern face from Malaucène is wider, straighter, and better surfaced than the southern ascent.

If you want to make the ascent on foot, the best path is from Les Colombets or Les Fébriers, two hamlets off the D974, east of **BEDOIN**, whose **tourist office** on the espace M.-L.-Gravier (mid-June to Sept Mon–Sat 9am–12.30pm & 2–6pm; Oct to mid-June Mon–Fri 9am–12.30pm & 2–6pm, Sat 9.30am–12.30pm; Ⓣ04.90.65.63.95) can give details of routes (including a once a week night-time ascent in July & Aug), plus addresses of campsites and *gîtes ruraux*. It also sells a guide to eleven walks on Mont Ventoux for €5.

Mont Ventoux is one of the challenges of the Tour de France, hence its appeal in summer for committed cyclists. Within sight of the stony summit is a memorial to the British cyclist Tommy Simpson, who died here from heart failure on one of the hottest days ever recorded in the race; according to race folklore his last words were "Put me back on the bloody bike."

The Dentelles and around

The **Dentelles**, a row of jagged limestone pinnacles, run across an arid, windswept and near-deserted upland area, the **Massif Montmirail-St-Amand**, just south of Vaison-la-Romaine. Their name refers to lace – the limestone protrusions were thought to resemble the contorted pins on a lace-making board – though the word's alternative connection with teeth (dents means "teeth") is equally appropriate.

The area is best known for its wines. On the western and southern slopes lie the wine-producing villages of **Gigondas**, **Beaumes-de-Venise**, **Sablet**, **Séguret**, **Vacqueyras** and, across the River Ouvèze, **Rasteau**. Each one carries the distinction of having its own individual *appellation contrôlée* within the Côtes du Rhône or Côtes du Rhône Villages areas: in other words, their wines are exceptional. In addition, some of the villages are alluringly picturesque, with Séguret super-conscious of its Provençal beauty.

The most reputed red **wine** in the Dentelles is made at Gigondas – it's strong with an aftertaste of spice and nuts. You can taste the produce from forty different *domaines* at the **Caveau du Gigondas** on place de la Mairie in the village (daily 10am–noon & 2–6.30pm). The most distinctive wine, and elixir for those who like it sweet, is the pale amber-coloured Beaumes-de-Venise muscat which you can buy from the Cave des Vignerons (Mon–Sat 8.30am–noon & 2–6pm, Sun 9am–12.30pm & 2–6pm) on the D7 just outside Beaumes.

Besides *dégustation* and bottle-buying, you can go for long walks in the Dentelles, stumbling upon mysterious ruins or photogenic panoramas of Mont Ventoux and the Rhône valley. The pinnacles are favourite scaling faces for apprentice rock-climbers – though their wind-eroded patterns can be appreciated just as well without risking your neck on an ascent. Information on walking and climbing is available from the *gîte* (see below), as well as Gigondas' **tourist office** on place du Portail (April–June, Sept & Oct Mon–Sat 10am–noon & 2–6pm; July & Aug daily 9.30am–12.30pm & 2.30–7.30pm; Nov–March Mon–Sat 10am–noon & 2–5pm; Ⓣ04.90.65.85.46, Ⓔot-gigondas@axit.fr), which also sells a local footpath map for €2.50.

Although it's possible to get to the villages by public transport from Vaison or Carpentras, your own vehicle is definitely an advantage. **Hotel** possibilities include, in Beaumes, the old-fashioned and quiet *Auberge St-Roch*, on avenue Jules-Ferry (Ⓣ04.90.65.08.21, *demi-pension*; ❺; restaurant closed Wed out of season), and *Le Relais des Dentelles*, past the old village and over the river (Ⓣ04.90.62.95.27; ❷; restaurant closed Sun evening, Mon & Jan). Gigondas has *Les Florets*, 2km from the village along the route des Dentelles (Ⓣ04.90.65.85.01, Ⓕ04.90.65.83.80; ❾, half-board obligatory in season), and the more upmarket *Hôtel Montmirail*, which you reach via Vacqueyras (Ⓣ04.90.65.84.01, Ⓦwww.hotelmontmirail.com; ❹; closed mid-Oct to mid-March). There are also **campsites** in Sablet (Ⓣ04.90.46.82.55), Beaumes (Ⓣ04.90.62.95.07) and Vacqueyras (Ⓣ04.90.65.84.24, Ⓕ04.90.65.83.28), and a *gîte d'étape* at the entrance to Gigondas (Ⓣ04.90.65.80.85,

Ⓦwww.provence-trekking.com; ❶, closed Jan & Feb), with double rooms and dormitory accommodation (€12).

Besides the restaurants of the hotels mentioned above, places to stop to **eat** or drink are few and far between once you leave the villages. In Séguret *Le Bastide Bleue*, route de Sablet (Ⓣ04.90.46.83.43; closed Tues & Wed out of season, plus Jan & Feb; menus €20–24), is renowned for its use of fresh local ingredients. In Gigondas, *L'Oustalet*, place Gabriel Andéol (Ⓣ04.90.65.85.30; closed Jan to mid-Feb plus Mon out of season; menus €45), has a pleasant shaded terrace and serves hearty home-style food; cheaper eats can be had at the *Café de la Poste* on rue Principale.

Carpentras

With a population of around 30,000, **CARPENTRAS** is a substantial city for this part of the world. It's also a very old one, its known history commencing in 5 BC as the capital of a Celtic tribe. The Greeks who founded Marseille came to Carpentras to buy honey, wheat, goats and skins, and the Romans had a base here. For a brief period in the fourteenth century, it became the papal headquarters and gave protection to Jews expelled from France.

Carpentras is currently in the throes of gradual refurbishment, so that immaculately restored squares and fountains alternate with gently decayed streets of seventeenth- and eighteenth-century houses, some forming arcades over the pavement. The local history museum – the **Musée Comtadin** on boulevard Albin-Durand (daily except Tues: April–Oct 10am–noon & 2–6pm; Nov–March 10am–noon & 2–4pm; €1) – is dark and dour. The erotic fantasies of a seventeenth-century cardinal frescoed by Nicolas Mignard in the **Palais de Justice**, formerly the episcopal palace, were effaced by a later incumbent. The *palais* is attached to the dull **Cathédrale St-Siffrein**, behind which, almost hidden in the corner, stands a **Roman arch** inscribed with scenes of prisoners in chains. Fifteen hundred years after its erection, Jews – coerced, bribed or otherwise persuaded – entered the cathedral in chains to be unshackled as converted Christians. The door they passed through, the **Porte Juif**, is on the southern side and bears strange symbolism of rats encircling and devouring a globe. The **synagogue** (Mon–Thurs 10am–noon & 3–5pm, Fri 10am–noon & 3–4pm; closed Jewish feast days; free), near the Hôtel de Ville, is a seventeenth-century construction on fourteenth-century foundations, making it the oldest surviving place of Jewish worship in France.

Carpentras cheers up every Friday for the **market**, which from the end of November to early March specializes in truffles, and during **festival** time in the second half of July. It also makes a useful base for excursions into the Dentelles, Mont Ventoux and the towns and villages south towards Apt.

Buses (trains are freight only) arrive either on avenue Victor-Hugo or place Terradou, a short walk away from place Aristide-Briand, where the **tourist office** is located (mid-June to mid-Sept Mon–Sat 9am–7pm, Sun 9.30am–1pm; mid-Sept to mid-June Mon–Sat 9.30am–12.30pm & 2–6pm; Ⓣ04.90.63.00.78, Ⓦwww.tourisme.fr/carpentras). If you want to **stay**, central options include the very pleasant, soundproofed and air-conditioned *Le Théâtre*, 7 bd Albin-Durand (Ⓣ04.90.63.02.90; ❹; closed Jan), and the more basic but adequate *Univers*, 110 place A.-Briand (Ⓣ04.90.63.00.05, Ⓕ04.90.63.71.20; ❷). For something grander with greater character, try *Le Fiacre*, 153 rue Vigne (Ⓣ04.90.63.03.15, Ⓦwww.hotel-du-fiacre.com; ❹), an eighteenth-century town house with lovely architectural features in many of the rooms, and a garden. A little way out of town, the *Safari Hotel*, 1 av J.-H.-Fabre

(Ⓣ04.90.63.35.35, Ⓦwww.nid-provencal.com; ⑤), is a bit characterless but has a pool and Internet connection. The local **campsite**, *Lou Comtadou*, is closed from November to March (Ⓣ04.90.67.03.16).

As far as **eating** goes, *Le Marijo* at 73 rue Raspail (Ⓣ04.90.60.42.65; closed Sun) is excellent, with menus from €20, while *Le Vert Galant*, 12 rue Clapies (Ⓣ04.90.67.15.50; closed Mon lunch year-round, Sun all day May–Sept, Sun eve Oct–April), serves more sophisticated fare, with menus from €28. Once the sun goes down in Carpentras, the best place for café or **bar** crawling is place Aristide Briand, where *Le Club* at no. 106 and the nearby *Pub Peter Polo* maintain a semblance of nightlife.

Avignon

AVIGNON, great city of the popes, and for centuries one of the major artistic centres of France, can be dauntingly crowded in summer and stiflingly hot. Away from the main tourist drag the old town is often remarkably unkempt, with a laissez-faire approach to rubbish collection at odds with its UNESCO World Heritage status and an intrusive graffiti problem that leaves even the prettiest facades disfigured. But it's worth braving for its spectacular

The Festival of Avignon

Unlike most provincial festivals of international renown, the **Festival d'Avignon** is dominated by theatre rather than classical music, though there's also plenty of that, as well as lectures, exhibitions and dance. It uses the city's great buildings as backdrops to performances, and takes place every year for three weeks from the second week in July. During festival time everything stays open late and everything gets booked up; there can be up to 200,000 visitors, and getting around or doing anything normal becomes virtually impossible.

Originally created in 1947 by actor-director **Jean Vilar**, over the years programmes have included theatrical interpretations as diverse as Molière, Euripides and Chekhov, performed by companies from across Europe. While big-name directors (Jacques Lasalle, Alain Françon) draw the largest crowds to the main venue, the Cour d'Honneur in the Palais des Papes, there's more than enough variety in all the smaller productions, dance performances and lectures to keep everyone sufficiently entertained. In addition to the introduction of new works staged by lesser-known directors and theatre troupes, each year the festival also spotlights a different culture, which in the past have ranged from showings of the Hindi epic *Ramayana* to the debut of THEOREM (Theatres from the East and from the West), a European cultural venture designed to bring together the two halves of Europe on the stage.

The main **festival programme**, with details of how to book, is available from the second week in May from the Bureau du Festival d'Avignon, 20 rue du portail Boquier, 84000 Avignon (Ⓦwww.festival-avignon.com), or from the tourist office. Ticket prices are reasonable (€5–33) and go on sale from the second week in June. As well as phone sales (11am–7pm; Ⓣ04.90.14.14.14), they can be bought from FNAC shops in all major French cities and via the FNAC website. During the festival, tickets are available until three hours before the performance. The Festival Off programme is available from mid-May from Avignon Public Off BP5, 75521 Paris Cedex 11 (Ⓣ01.48.05.01.19, Ⓦwww.avignon-off.org). During the festival, the office is in the Conservatoire de Musique on place du Palais. Tickets prices range from €9 to €17 and a *Carte Public Adhérent* for €13 gives you thirty percent off all shows.

monuments and museums, countless impressively decorated buildings, ancient churches, chapels and convents. During the **Festival d'Avignon** in July and the beginning of August, it is *the* place to be.

Central Avignon is still enclosed by its medieval walls, built in 1403 by the antipope Benedict XIII, the last of nine **popes** who based themselves here throughout most of the fourteenth century. The first pope to come to Avignon was Clement V in 1309, who was invited over by the astute King Philippe le Bel ("the Good"), ostensibly to protect Clement from impending anarchy in Rome. In reality, Philip saw a chance to extend his power over the Church by keeping the pope in the safety of Provence, during what came to be known as the Church's "Babylonian captivity". Clement's successors were a varied group, from the villainous John XXII (of Umberto Eco's *Name of the Rose* fame), to the dedicated Urban V, and later Gregory XI, who managed to re-establish the papacy in Rome in 1378. However, this was not the end of the papacy here – after Gregory's death in Rome, dissident local cardinals elected their own pope in Avignon, provoking the Western Schism: a ruthless struggle for the control of the Church's wealth, which lasted until the pious Benedict fled Avignon for self-exile near Valencia in 1409.

As home to one of the richest courts in Europe, fourteenth-century Avignon attracted hordes of princes, dignitaries, poets and raiders, who arrived to beg from, rob, extort money from and entertain the popes. According to Petrarch, the overcrowded, plague-ridden papal entourage was "a sewer where all the filth of the universe has gathered". Burgeoning from within its low battlements, the town must have been a colourful, frenetic sight.

Arrival, information and accommodation

Both the **gare SNCF** on boulevard St-Roch and the adjacent **gare routière** (Ⓣ04.90.82.07.35) are close to Porte de la République, on the south side of the old city. In addition to the main *gare*, there's a new **TGV** station, which has cut travel to Paris down to two and a half hours, near the hospital 2km south of the city centre. Regular shuttles connect the TGV station with Avignon Centre (daily 6.14am–11.11pm; €1.05); passengers are picked up or dropped off next to the post office, a short walk from the main tourist office. The city's main **local bus** information centre can be found at 1 av de Lattre de Tassigny (stops "Poste", "Cité Administrative", "Gare Routière" and "Gare" are all within a five-minute walk). From Cité Administrative all buses go to place de l'Horloge. Tickets may be bought from drivers and at TCRA (Transports en Commun de la Région d'Avignon; Ⓦwww.tcra.fr) kiosks throughout town (€1.05 each; €8 for a book of 10). If you're driving, the best **parking** option is the free, guarded car park on the Île de Piot, between Avignon and Villeneuve; a free shuttle runs every 10min (July 1–Aug 7 daily 7am–2am, Aug 8–15 daily 7am–8pm; Aug 15–June 30 Mon–Fri 7am–8pm & Sat 1–8pm) between the car park and Porte de l'Oulle.

Cours Jean-Jaurès runs into the old city from the Porte de la République, with the main **tourist office** a little way up on the right at no. 41 (April–Oct Mon–Sat 9am–6pm, till 7pm in July, Sun 10am–5pm; Nov–March Mon–Fri 9am–6pm, Sat 9am–5pm, Sun 10am–noon; Ⓣ04.32.74.32.74, Ⓦwww.avignon-tourisme.com).

Even outside festival time, finding a **room** in Avignon can be a problem: cheap hotels fill fast and it's never a bad idea to book in advance. It's worth remembering too that Villeneuve-lès-Avignon is only just across the river and may have rooms when its larger neighbour is full. Between the two, the Île de la Barthelasse is an idyllic spot for **camping**, and you may find the odd farmhouse advertising rooms.

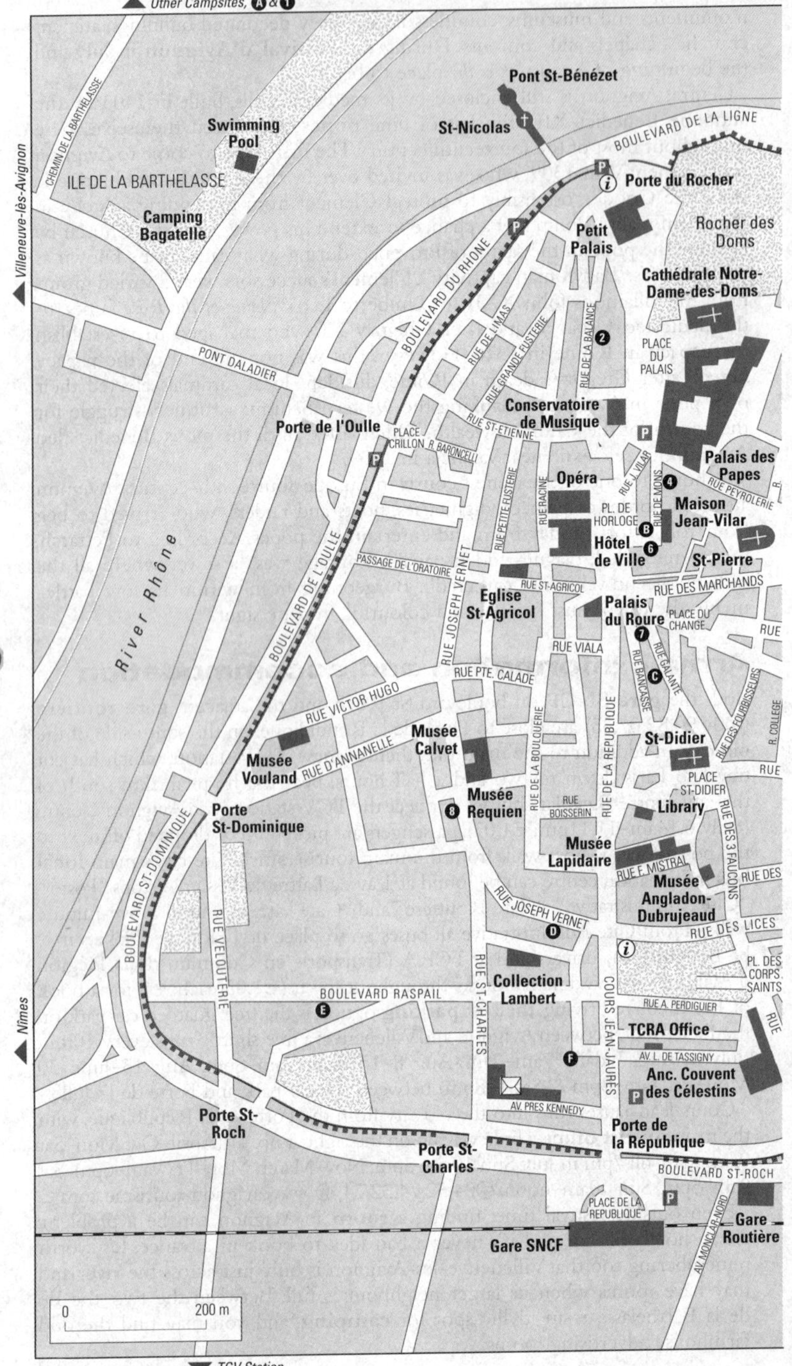

Other Campsites, A & 1
Pont St-Bénézet
St-Nicolas
Swimming Pool
CHEMIN DE LA BARTHELASSE
ILE DE LA BARTHELASSE
Camping Bagatelle
Villeneuve-lès-Avignon
BOULEVARD DE LA LIGNE
Porte du Rocher
Petit Palais
Rocher des Doms
Cathédrale Notre-Dame-des-Doms
BOULEVARD DU RHONE
RUE DE LIMAS
RUE GRANDE FUSTERIE
RUE DE LA BALANCE
PLACE DU PALAIS
PONT DALADIER
Conservatoire de Musique
RUE ST-ETIENNE
Porte de l'Oulle
PLACE CRILLON
R. BARONCELLI
Palais des Papes
RUE J. VILAR
RUE DE MONS
RUE PEYROLERIE
Opéra
RUE RACINE
PL. DE HORLOGE
Maison Jean-Vilar
Hôtel de Ville
St-Pierre
RUE PETITE FUSTERIE
PASSAGE DE L'ORATOIRE
RUE ST-AGRICOL
RUE DES MARCHANDS
River Rhône
BOULEVARD DE L'OULLE
RUE JOSEPH VERNET
Eglise St-Agricol
Palais du Roure
PLACE DU CHANGE
RUE VIALA
RUE BANCASSE
RUE GALANTE
RUE PTE. CALADE
RUE DES FOURBISSEURS
RUE VICTOR HUGO
Musée Calvet
St-Didier
R. COLLEGE
Musée Vouland
RUE D'ANNANELLE
RUE DE LA BOULQUERIE
RUE DE LA REPUBLIQUE
PLACE ST-DIDIER
Musée Requien
RUE BOISSERIN
Library
RUE DES 3 FAUCONS
Porte St-Dominique
Musée Lapidaire
RUE F. MISTRAL
Musée Angladon-Dubrujeaud
BOULEVARD ST-DOMINIQUE
RUE VELOUTERIE
RUE JOSEPH VERNET
RUE DES LICES
PL. DES CORPS. SAINTS
Collection Lambert
RUE ST-CHARLES
COURS JEAN-JAURES
BOULEVARD RASPAIL
RUE A. PERDIGUIER
TCRA Office
Nîmes
AV. L. DE TASSIGNY
Anc. Couvent des Célestins
AV. PRES KENNEDY
Porte St-Roch
Porte de la République
Porte St-Charles
BOULEVARD ST-ROCH
PLACE DE LA REPUBLIQUE
AV. MONCLAR-NORD
Gare Routière
Gare SNCF
0
200 m
TGV Station

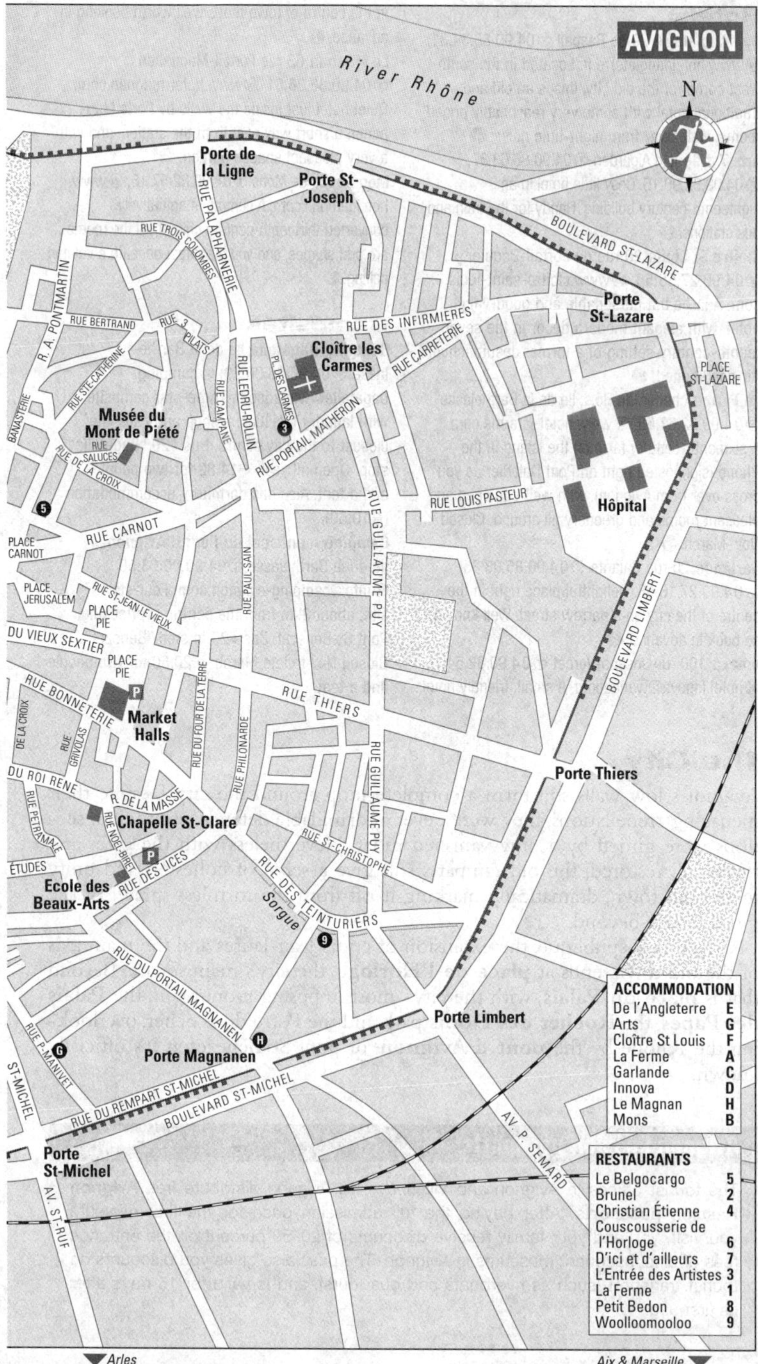
AVIGNON
River Rhône
N
Orange & Carpentras
APT
Arles
Aix & Marseille
Porte de la Ligne
Porte St-Joseph
Porte St-Lazare
Boulevard St-Lazare
Place St-Lazare
Cloître les Carmes
Musée du Mont de Piété
Hôpital
Market Halls
Chapelle St-Clare
Ecole des Beaux-Arts
Porte Thiers
Porte Limbert
Porte Magnanen
Porte St-Michel
Rue Trois Colombes
Rue Palapharnerie
R. A. Pontmartin
Rue Bertrand
Rue 3 Pilats
Rue Ste-Catherine
Banasterie
Rue Ledru-Rollin
Rue Campane
Pl. des Carmes
Rue des Infirmieres
Rue Carreterie
Rue Portail Matheron
Rue Saluces
Rue de la Croix
Rue Carnot
Place Carnot
Place Jerusalem
Rue St-Jean le Vieux
Place Pie
Du Vieux Sextier
Rue Paul-Sain
Rue Guillaume Puy
Rue Louis Pasteur
Boulevard Limbert
Rue Bonneterie
De la Croix
Rue Grivolas
Rue du Four de la Terre
Rue Philonarde
Rue Thiers
Du Roi Rene
R. de la Masse
Rue Petramale
Rue Noel-Biret
Rue St-Christophe
Rue des Lices
Études
Rue des Teinturiers
Sorgue
Rue du Portail Magnanen
Rue P.-Manivet
St-Michel
Rue du Rempart St-Michel
Boulevard St-Michel
Av. P. Semard
Av. St-Ruf
ACCOMMODATION
De l'Angleterre E
Arts G
Cloître St Louis F
La Ferme A
Garlande C
Innova D
Le Magnan H
Mons B
RESTAURANTS
Le Belgocargo 5
Brunel 2
Christian Étienne 4
Couscousserie de l'Horloge 6
D'ici et d'ailleurs 7
L'Entrée des Artistes 3
La Ferme 1
Petit Bedon 8
Woolloomooloo 9

Hotels

De l'Angleterre 29 bd Raspail ⓣ04.90.86.34.31, ⓦwww.hoteldangleterre.fr. Located in the south-west corner of the old city, this is an old and traditional hotel with some very reasonably priced rooms, well away from night-time noise. ❹

Arts 7 & 9 rue d'Aigarden ⓣ04.90.86.63.87, ⓕ04.90.82.90.15. Cosy little hotel in an eighteenth-century building. Handy for the train and bus stations. ❷

Cloître St Louis 20 rue de Portail-Boquier ⓣ04.90.27.55.55, ⓦwww.cloitre-saint-louis.com. A large but personable and good-value hotel, with elegant modern decor in the seventeenth-century setting of a former Jesuit school. Air-conditioned. ❽

La Ferme chemin du Bois, Île de la Barthelasse ⓣ04.90.82.57.53, ⓦwww.hotel-laferme.com. A sixteenth-century farm on the island in the Rhône (signposted right off Pont Daladier as you cross over from Avignon), with well-equipped and pleasant rooms and greenery all around. Closed Nov–March. ❺

Garlande 20 rue Galante ⓣ04.90.85.08.85, ⓕ04.90.27.16.58. Delightful place right in the centre of the city on a narrow street. Well known, so book in advance. ❹

Innova 100 rue Joseph-Vernet ⓣ04.90.82.54.10, ⓔhotel.innova@wanadoo.fr. A small, friendly hotel in the centre of town that's well worth booking in advance. ❷

Le Magnan 63 rue Portail-Magnanen ⓣ04.90.86.36.51, ⓦwww.hotel-magnan.com. Quiet hotel just inside the walls by Porte Magnanen a short way east from the station, and with a very pleasant shaded garden. ❹

Mons 5 rue de Mons ⓣ04.90.82.57.16, ⓦwww.hoteldemons.com. A central, imaginatively converted thirteenth-century chapel. All the rooms are odd shapes, and you breakfast beneath a vaulted ceiling. ❸

Campsites

Camping Bagatelle Île de la Barthelasse ⓣ04.90.86.30.39, ⓔcamping.bagatelle@wanadoo.fr. Three-star campsite, with laundry facilities, a shop and café; the closest to the city centre. Bus #20 "Bagatelle" stop. Open all year. €14.82 for two people and a tent. Also has dormitory accommodation (€10.50).

Camping municipal du Pont d'Avignon Île de la Barthelasse ⓣ04.90.80.63.50, ⓔinfo@camping-avignon.com. Four-star site, about 3km from the centre, overlooking Pont St-Bénézet. Bus #20 to stop "Bénézet". Closed Nov to late March. €20.50 for two people and a tent.

The City

Avignon's low walls still form a complete loop around the city. Despite their menacing crenellations, they were never a formidable defence, even when sections were girded by a now-vanished moat. Nevertheless with the gates and towers all restored, the old ramparts still give a sense of cohesion and unity to the old town, dramatically marking it off from the formless sprawl of the modern city beyond.

Rue de la République, the extension of cours Jean-Jaurès and the main axis of the old town, ends at **place de l'Horloge**, the city's main square. Beyond that is **place du Palais**, with the city's most imposing monument, the **Palais des Papes**, the **Rocher des Doms** park and the Porte du Rocher, overlooking the Rhône by the **pont d'Avignon**, or pont St-Bénézet as it's officially known.

Avignon Passion passports

The tourist offices in Avignon and Villeneuve-lès-Avignon distribute free **Avignon Passion passports**. After paying the full admission price for the first museum you visit, you and your family receive discounts of 20–50 percent on the entrance fees of all subsequent museums in Avignon. The pass also gives you discounts on tourist transport (such as riverboats and bus tours), and is valid for 15 days after its first use.

The Palais des Papes and around

Rising high above the east side of place du Palais is the **Palais des Papes** (daily: mid-March to Oct 9am–7pm; Nov to mid-March 9.30am–5.45pm; last ticket 1hr before closing; mid-March to Oct €9.50, or €11.50 for palace and the Pont; Nov to mid-March €7.50, ticket includes an audio-guide; guided tours on request). With its massive stone vaults, battlements and sluices for pouring hot oil on attackers, the palace was built primarily as a fortress, though the two pointed towers which hover above its gate are incongruously graceful. Close up it is simply too monstrous to take in all at once; cross to the northwestern side of the place du Palais as far as you can go to take in the wide-angle view, or follow rue Peyrollerie, rue Banasterie and the Escaliers Ste Anne around the less familiar south and east sides for tantalizing, dramatic close-ups of the massive walls, the humble dimensions of the surrounding houses only adding to the impression of vastness. Inside the palace, so little remains of the original decoration and furnishings that you can be deceived into thinking that all the popes and their retinues were as pious and austere as the last official occupant, Benedict XIII. The denuded interior leaves hardly a whiff of the corruption and decadence of fat, feuding cardinals and their mistresses, the thronging purveyors of jewels, velvet and furs, musicians, chefs and painters competing for patronage, the riotous banquets and corridor schemings.

The visit begins in the **Pope's Tower**, otherwise known as the Tower of Angels. You enter the **Treasury** where the serious business of the church's deeds and finances went on. Four large holes found in the floor (covered over) of the smaller downstairs room served as safes. The same cunning storage device was used for the chamberlain who lived upstairs in the **Chambre du Camérier** (just off the Jesus Hall), where the safes have been revealed. As he was the Pope's right-hand man, the quarters would have been lavishly decorated, but successive occupants have left their mark, most recently military whitewash, and what is now visible is a confusion of layers. The other door in this room leads into the **Papal Vestiary**, where the Pope would dress before sessions in the consistory. He also had a small library here and could look out onto the gardens below.

A door on the north side of the Jesus Hall leads to the **Consistoire** of the **Vieux Palais**, where sovereigns and ambassadors were received and the canonizations examined and proclaimed. The room was damaged by fire in 1413, and the only decoration that remains are fragments of frescoes moved from the cathedral, and a nineteenth-century line-up of the popes, in which all nine look remarkably similar thanks to the artist using the same model for each portrait. Some medieval artistry is in evidence, however, in the **Chapelle St-Jean**, off the Consistoire, and more particularly in the **Chapelle St-Martial** on the floor above, currently closed for restoration. Both were decorated by a Sienese artist, Matteo Giovanetti, and commissioned by Clement VI, who demanded for the Chapelle St-Martial the maximum amount of blue – the most expensive pigment, derived from lapis lazuli. The **kitchen** on this floor also gives a hint of the scale of papal gluttony with its square walls becoming an octagonal chimneypiece for a vast central cooking fire. As you cross from the Vieux Palais to the **Palais Neuf**, Clement VI's bedroom and the Chambre du Cerf – his study – are further evidence of this pope's secular concerns, the walls in the former adorned with wonderful entwined oak and vine leaf motifs, the latter with superb hunting and fishing scenes. But austerity resumes in the cathedral-like proportions of the **Grande Chapelle**, or Chapelle Clementine, and in the **Grande Audience**, its twin in terms of volume on the floor below.

When you've completed the circuit, which includes a heady walk along the roof terraces, you can watch a glossy but informative film on the history of the palace (French only, but English version available from the palace shop, €15). There are also concerts: programmes are available from the ticket office.

Next to the Palais des Papes, the **Cathédrale Notre-Dame-des-Doms** might once have been a luminous Romanesque structure, but the interior has had a bad attack of Baroque, and the result is an incoherent mess. In addition, nineteenth-century maniacs mounted an enormous gilded Virgin on the belfry, which would look silly enough anywhere, but when dwarfed by the fifty-metre towers of the popes' palace is absurd. There's greater reward behind, in the **Rocher des Doms** park. As well as ducks and swans and views over the river to Villeneuve and beyond, it has a sundial in which your own shadow tells the time.

The **Petit Palais** (daily except Tues: June–Sept 10am–1pm & 2–6pm; Oct–May 9.30am–1pm & 2–5.30pm; €6), not far from the park's main entrance, contains a daunting collection of first-rate thirteenth- to fifteenth-century painting and sculpture, most of it by masters from northern Italian cities. As you progress through the collection, you can watch as the masters wrestle with and finally conquer the representation of perspective – a revolution from medieval art, where the size of figures depended on their importance rather than position. Highlight of the collection, in room XVI, Botticelli's sublime *Virgin and Child* depicts a tender Mary, playfully coddling a smiling infant.

Behind the Petit Palais, and well signposted, is the half-span of Pont St-Bénézet, or the **Pont d'Avignon** of the famous song (same hours as Palais des Papes; €4, €11.50 combined ticket with Palais des Papes, audio guide in English included). One theory has it that the lyrics say "*Sous le pont*" (under the bridge) rather than "*Sur le pont*" (on the bridge), and refer to the thief and trickster clientele of a tavern on the Île de la Barthelasse (which the bridge once crossed on its way to Villeneuve) dancing with glee at the arrival of more potential victims. Keeping the bridge in repair from the ravages of the Rhône was finally abandoned in 1660, three and a half centuries after it was built, and only four of the original 22 arches remain. Despite its limited transportational use, the bridge remained a focus of river boatmen, who constructed a chapel to their patroness on the first of the bridge's bulwarks. And the bridge's failure over the centuries to withstand the rigours of its function didn't stop its builder, Bénézet, from becoming the patron saint of architects.

Around place de l'Horloge

The café-lined **place de l'Horloge**, frenetically busy most of the time, is the site of the city's imposing **Hôtel de Ville** and **clock tower**, and the **Opéra**. Around the square, on rues de Mons, Molière and Corneille, famous faces appear in windows painted on the buildings. Many of these figures from the past were visitors to Avignon, and of those who recorded their impressions of the city it was the sound of over a hundred bells ringing that stirred them most. On a Sunday morning, traffic lulls permitting, you can still hear myriad different peals from churches, convents and chapels in close proximity. The fourteenth-century **church of St-Agricol**, just behind the Hôtel de Ville (closed for restoration at the time of writing), is one of Avignon's best Gothic edifices.

To the south, just behind rue St-Agricol on rue Collège du Roure, is the beautiful fifteenth-century **Palais du Roure**, a centre of Provençal culture. The gateway and the courtyard are definitely worth a look; there may well be temporary art exhibitions, and if you want a rambling tour through the attics to see Provençal costumes, publications and presses, photographs of the Camargue in the 1900s and an old stagecoach, you need to turn up at 3pm on Tuesday (€4.60).

To the west of place de l'Horloge are the most desirable Avignon addresses – both now and three hundred years ago – and it's below the mellow stone facades along **rue Joseph-Vernet** and **rue Petite-Fusterie** that you'll find Avignon's most luxurious shops.

The Banasterie and Carmes quartiers

The **quartier de la Banasterie**, lying immediately east of the Palais des Papes, is almost solid seventeenth- and eighteenth-century, and the heavy wooden doors, with their highly sculptured lintels, today bear the nameplates of lawyers, psychiatrists and doctors. Here, tourist-oriented commercialism is kept in check, and at night in particular this is an atmospheric and beautiful part of the city.

Between Banasterie and **place des Carmes** are a tangle of tiny streets guaranteed to get you lost. Pedestrians have priority over cars on many of them, and there are plenty of tempting café or restaurant stops. At 6 rue Saluces, you'll find the peculiar **Musée du Mont de Piété**, an ex-pawnbroker's shop and now home to the town's archives (Mon 10am–noon & 1.30–5pm, Tues–Fri 8.30–noon & 1.30–5pm; free). It has a small display of papal bulls and painted silk desiccators for determining the dry weight of what was the city's chief commodity.

Rue de la République to place Pie

Between the chainstore blandness of rue de la République and the hideous modern **market hall** on **place Pie** (mornings Tues–Sun) is the main pedestrian precinct, centring on **place de la Principale**. **Rue des Marchands** and **rue du Vieux-Sextier** have their complement of chapels and late medieval mansions, in particular the **Hôtel des Rascas** on the corner of rue des Marchands and rue Fourbisseurs, and the **Hôtel de Belli** on the corner of rue Fourbisseurs and rue du Vieux-Sextier. The Renaissance **church of St-Pierre** on place St-Pierre has superb doors sculpted in 1551, and a retable dating from the same period. More Renaissance art is on show in the fourteenth-century **church of St-Didier** (daily 8am–6.30pm), chiefly *The Carrying of the Cross* by Francesco Laurana, commissioned by King René of Provence in 1478. There are also fourteenth-century frescoes in the left-hand chapel.

Musée Calvet and around

The excellent **Musée Calvet**, 65 rue Joseph-Vernet (daily except Tues 10am–1pm & 2–6pm; €6), and the impressive eighteenth-century palace housing it, have been undergoing gradual restoration and transformation for the past few years. Although several rooms on the ground floor remain closed to the public, the majority of the collection is now on display in five rooms, beginning with the **Galerie des Sculptures**. A better introduction to a museum couldn't be wished for, with a handful of languorous nineteenth-century marble sculptures, including Bosio's *Young Indian*, perfectly suited to this elegant space. The end of the gallery houses the Puech collection with a large selection of silverware, Italian and Dutch paintings and, more unusually, a Flemish curiosities cabinet, painted with scenes from the story of Daniel. Upstairs is a fine set of seasons by Nicolas Mignard, whilst Joseph Vernet sticks to representing the different times of the day. Further down, Horace Vernet donated the subtle *Death of Young Barra* by Jacques-Louis David as well as Géricault's *Battle of Nazareth*. On the way out don't miss the Victor Martin collection, including Vlaminck's *At the Bar*, Bonnard's *Winter Day* and the haunting *Downfall* by Chaïm Soutine.

Avignon's remaining museums are considerably less compelling. Next door to the Musée Calvet is the **Musée Requien** (Tues–Sat 9am–noon & 2–6pm; free); its subject is natural history and its sole advantage is in being free and having clean toilets. With little more to recommend it is the **Musée Lapidaire**, a museum of Roman and Gallo-Roman stones housed in the Baroque chapel at 27 rue de la République (daily except Tues 10am–1pm & 2–6pm; €2). Finally, at the **Musée Vouland**, at the end of rue Victor-Hugo near Porte St-Dominique (Tues–Sat: May–Oct 10am–noon & 2–6pm, Sun 2–6pm; Nov–April 2–6pm; €4), you can feast your eyes on the fittings, fixtures and furnishings that French aristocrats enjoyed both before and after the Revolution. There's also some brilliant Moustiers faïence, exquisite marquetry and Louis XV inkpots with silver rats holding the lids. Just west of the tourist office, down rue Violette, is the **Collection Lambert** (Tues–Sun: July & Aug 11am–7pm; Sept–June 11am–6pm; €5.50), Avignon's first attempt at a contemporary art gallery, which leans heavily towards conceptual, installation and video art. Though it's not especially high powered, the permanent collection includes a few Nan Goldin photographs and works by Anselm Kiefer and Cy Twombly, and there are occasionally interesting temporary exhibitions.

Southeast: to rue des Teinturiers

Between rue de la République and place St-Didier, on rue Labourer, is the **Musée Angladon** (Wed–Sun 1–6pm, plus Tues in high season; €6), displaying the remains of the private collection of Jacques Doucet. Although the collection, which once contained works like Picasso's *Demoiselles d'Avignon* and Douanier Rousseau's *The Snakecharmer* (now in the Musée d'Orsay), has seen better days, it is still very much worth a look. The visit begins with a series of rooms furnished and decorated as coherent units, the first Renaissance and the remainder eighteenth-century (including an orientalist room). The paintings which remain are alone worth the admission price, and include Foujita's *Portrait of Mme Foujita* and a *Self-Portrait*, Modigliani's *The Pink Blouse*, various Picassos and Van Gogh's *The Railroad Cars*, the only painting from Van Gogh's stay in Provence to be on permanent display in the region.

Through the park by the tourist office (where there's an old British red phone box) you come to **place des Corps-Saints**, a lively area of cafés and restaurants whose tables fill the square. Just to the north, rue des Lices runs eastwards, past the École des Beaux-Arts, to **rue des Teinturiers**, the city's most atmospheric street. Its name refers to the eighteenth- and nineteenth-century business of calico printing. The cloth was washed in the Sorgue canal which still runs alongside the street, turning the wheels of long-gone mills, and, although the water is fairly murky and sometimes smelly, this is still a great street for evening strolls, with a large number of cheap restaurants.

Eating and drinking

Reasonably priced midday **meals** are easy to come by in Avignon and eating well in the evening needn't break the bank. The large terraced café-brasseries on place de l'Horloge and rue de la République all serve quick, if not necessarily memorable, meals. Rue des Teinturiers is good if you're on a budget, and the streets between place Crillon and place du Palais are full of temptation if you're not.

Restaurants and cafés

Le Belgocargo 10 place des Châtaignes ☎04.90.85.72.99. Belgian restaurant, specializing in *moules-frites* and beer; lunch menu with drink for €7.50. Closed Sun out of season.

Brunel 46 rue Balance ☎04.90.85.24.83. Superb regional dishes, with evening menus from €28. Closed Sun & Mon, and first half of Aug.

Christian Étienne 10 rue de Mons ☎04.90.86.16.50. One of Avignon's best restaurants, housed in a fourteenth-century mansion and offering exotic combinations such as fennel sorbet with a saffron sauce plus some great seafood dishes. Menus from €30–85. Closed Sun & Mon.

Couscousserie de l'Horloge 2 rue de Mons ☎04.90.85.84.86. Popular Algerian-run restaurant with a jovial atmosphere and excellent North African food. Try the delicious €12 *tagine aux prunes* and wash it down with an Algerian *coteaux Mascara* red. Menu at €23.

D'ici et d'ailleurs 4 rue Galante ☎04.90.14.63.65. Tasteful modern surroundings, Provençal dishes from "here", international flavours from "there"; good and not expensive. Menus €15.50 and €19. Service until 11pm; closed Sun.

L'Entrée des Artistes 1 place des Carmes ☎04.90.82.46.90. Small, friendly bistro serving traditional French dishes; €17 weekday menu. Closed Sat, Sun & early Aug to early Sept.

La Ferme chemin du Bois, Île de la Barthelasse ☎04.90.82.57.53. A traditional farmhouse, serving well-prepared simple dishes, from €22. Closed Mon & Wed, plus Nov to mid-March.

Petit Bedon 70 rue Joseph-Vernet ☎04.90.82.33.98. The "Potbelly" is a well-regarded and smart Provençal restaurant, though not quite the bargain it was. Menus €28 & €32. Closed Sun & Mon.

Shakespeare 155 rue Carreterie. English bookshop and *salon de thé*. Closed Sun, Mon & evenings.

Utopia Bar 4 rue Escaliers Ste-Anne. In the shadow of the Palais des Papes, this elegant but slightly snooty café has changing exhibitions adorning the walls, live jazz some nights, and is just next door to a good cinema.

Woolloomooloo 16 bis rue des Teinturiers ☎04.90.85.28.44. An old printshop with all the presses still in place. The cuisine is from just about everywhere, as are the teas. Menus at €11 & €15 (lunch) or €17. Occasional theme nights. Closed Mon.

Bars and clubs

Le Cid 11 place de l'Horloge ☎04.90.82.30.38 Trendy mixed gay/straight bar and terrace which stays open long after the rest of place de l'Horloge has closed for the night.

L'Esclave 12 rue du Limas ☎04.90.85.14.91. Avignon's liveliest gay and lesbian bar, with regular DJs, drag shows and karaoke nights. Tues–Sun from 11pm.

Le Lounge 83 rue Joseph Vernet. Swanky modern cocktail bar with DJ Thurs–Sat. Open 6pm–1.30am.

Pub Z cnr rue Bonneterie & rue Artaud, close to Les Halles. Rock bar with black and white decor and DJs Fri and Sat. Open till 1.30am; closed Sun & last two weeks of Aug.

The Red Lion 21–23 rue St Jean le Vieux ☎04.91.72.71.80. English-style pub with live music twice a week and regular theme evenings.

Le Red Zone 25 rue Carnot ☎04.90.27.02.44. Bar with DJs and weekly concerts. Daily 9pm–3am.

Tapalocas 15 rue Galante ☎04.90.82.56.84. Tapas at €2.20 a dish, happy hour on aperitifs between 6–7.30pm and Spanish music, sometimes live. Daily noon–1am.

Theatre, music and film

There's a fair amount of nightlife and cultural events in Avignon: the **Opéra**, on place de l'Horloge (☎04.90.82.81.40), mounts a good range of productions; Le Chêne Noir, 8bis rue Ste-Catherine (☎04.90.86.58.11), is a theatre company worth seeing, with mime, musicals or Molière on offer; and plenty of **classical concerts** are performed in churches, usually for free. The *Cinéma Utopia*, at La Manutention, rue Escalier Ste-Anne (☎04.90.82.65.36), shows films in *version originale* (ie undubbed); the same complex houses the *AJMI Jazz Club* (☎04.90.86.08.61), which hosts live jazz every Thursday night and features major acts and some adventurous new groups. The café *La Tache d'Encre*, rue Tarasque (☎04.90.85.97.13; closed Sun), presents local theatre performances. To find out what's on, get hold of the tourist office's free bimonthly calendar *Rendez-Vous*. They may also have the weekly arts, events and music magazine *César* (also free), which is otherwise found in arts centres.

Listings

Bike rental CM 84 Cycles et Motorisés, 80 rue Guillaume Puy ⓣ04.90.86.32.49; Holiday Bikes, 20 bd St-Roch ⓣ04.32.76.25.88; Provence Bike, 52 bd St-Roch ⓣ04.90.27.92.61 (also scooters and motorbikes).

Boat trips Grands Bateaux de Provence, allée de l'Oulle ⓣ04.90.85.62.25, ⓔbateaugbp@aol.com, offering year-round trips upstream towards Châteauneuf-du-Pape and downstream to Arles; two-week advance booking recommended; tickets from €24.70 without meal or €45–57 if meal included.

Car rental National/Citer, *gare TGV* ⓣ04.90.27.30.07, *gare SNCF* bd St Roch ⓣ04.90.85.96.47; Rent a Car, 130 av Pierre Sémard ⓣ04.90.88.08.02; Sixt, 3 bd St-Ruf ⓣ04.90.86.06.61.

Emergencies Doctor/ambulance ⓣ15; hospital, Centre Hospitalier H.-Duffaut, 305 rue Raoul-Follereau ⓣ04.32.75.33.33; night chemist, call police ⓣ04.90.80.50.00 for addresses.

Internet Cyber Highway, 30 rue des Infirmières; Webzone 3 rue St Jean le Vieux/place Pie.

Laundry 9 rue du Chapeau Rouge; 27 rue Portail-Magnanen; 113 av St-Ruf.

Money exchange Cie Avignonnaise de la Change, 19 rue de la République ⓣ04.90.16.04.04; Mondial Change, 34 rue de la Balance; post office, cours Kennedy.

Police 13ter quai St Lazare ⓣ08.00.00.84.00 simply ⓣ17

Post office Poste, cours Président-Kennedy, Avignon 84000.

Swimming pool Piscine Olympique on the Île de la Barthelasse (mid-May to Aug 10am–7pm).

Taxis place Pie ⓣ04.90.82.20.20.

Villeneuve-lès-Avignon

VILLENEUVE-LÈS-AVIGNON rises up a rocky escarpment above the west bank of the Rhône, looking down upon its older neighbour from behind far more convincing fortifications. Historically, Villeneuve operated largely as a suburb of Avignon, with palatial residences constructed by the cardinals and a great monastery founded by Pope Innocent VI.

To this day, Villeneuve is technically a part of Languedoc and not Provence, and would score better in the hierarchy of towns to visit were it further from Avignon, whose monuments it can almost match for colossal scale and impressiveness. Despite the closeness of its relationship with Avignon it is, however, a very different – and really rather sleepy – kind of place, and as such retains a repose and a sense of timelessness that bustling Avignon inevitably lacks. In summer it provides venues for the Avignon Festival as well as alternatives for accommodation overspill, and it's certainly worth a day, whatever time of year you visit.

Arrival, information and accommodation

From Avignon's post office on cours Président Kennedy, across the way from the *gare SNCF*, the half-hourly #11 bus (take care not to go in the direction "Les Angles–Villeneuve") runs direct to place Charles-David ("Office du Tourisme" stop) taking less than ten minutes, or five if you catch it from Porte d'Oulle. After 7.30pm you'll have to take a taxi or walk – it's only 3km. Place Charles-David is where you'll find both the **tourist office** (July & Aug daily 10am–7pm; Sept–June Mon–Sat 9am–12.30pm & 2–6pm; ⓣ04.90.25.61.33, ⓦwww.villeneuve-lez-avignon.fr/tourisme), and a food **market** on Thursday morning and bric-a-brac on Saturday morning. A little south of the square rue Farigoule runs west to rue de la République, the main street, which runs due north past place Jean Jaurès. It's here you'll find what limited restaurant and bar life there is.

If money is no object, the first choice for **accommodation** has to be *Le Prieuré*, 7 place du Chapitre (ⓣ04.90.15.90.15, ⓦwww.leprieure.fr; ❾), both for the rooms and for its restaurant. For half the price or less, you could stay in equally ancient surroundings at *L'Atelier*, 5 rue de la Foire (ⓣ04.90.25.01.84, ⓦwww.hoteldelatelier.com; ❸–❻), a sixteenth-century house with huge open fireplaces and a walled garden, or at a Louis XIV mansion, *Les Cèdres*, 39 av Pasteur (ⓣ04.90.25.43.92, ⓔlescedres.hotel@lemel.fr; ❸–❻), with pool and restaurant. There is also the bed and breakfast, *Jardin de la Livrée*, 4bis rue Camp de Bataille (ⓣ04.90.26.05.05; ❸), with comfortable rooms and a good-value restaurant. For a cheaper option, try the **YMCA hostel**, 7bis chemin de la Justice (ⓣ04.90.25.46.20, ⓦwww.ymca-avignon.com; ❶), beautifully situated overlooking the river by Pont du Royaume, with balconied rooms for one to four people (€18 for dorm bed) and an open-air swimming pool (stop "Pont d'Avignon" on Avignon–Villeneuve bus or "Gabriel Péri" on the Villeneuve-Avignon bus). For **campers**, the three-star *Camping Municipal de la Laune* is in chemin St-Honoré (ⓣ04.90.27.49.40; ⓕ04.90.25.88.03; closed mid-Oct to March), off the D980, near the sports stadium and swimming pools.

The Town

For a good overview of Villeneuve – and Avignon – make your way to the **Tour Philippe-le-Bel** at the bottom of montée de la Tour (bus stop "Philippe-le-Bel"). This tower was built to guard the French end of Avignon's Pont St-Bénézet (or Pont d'Avignon), and a climb to the top (March–Nov Tues–Sun 10am–12.30pm & 2–6.30pm; €1.60) will be rewarded with stunning views.

Even more indicative of French distrust of its neighbours is the enormous **Fort St-André** (daily: April–Sept 10am–1pm & 2–6pm; Oct–March 10am–1pm & 2–5pm; €4.60), whose bulbous double-towered gateway and vast white walls loom over the town. Inside, refreshingly, there's not a hint of a postcard stall or souvenir shop – just tumbledown houses and the former **abbey**, with its gardens of olive trees, ruined chapels, lily ponds and dovecotes (Tues–Sun: July & Aug 10am–12.30pm & 2–6pm; Sept–June 10am–noon & 2–5pm; €4). Its cliff-face terrace is the classic spot for artists to aim their brushes, or photographers their cameras, over Avignon. You can reach the approach to the fortress, montée du Fort, from place Jean-Jaurès on rue de la République, or by the "rapid slope" of **rue Pente-Rapide**, a cobbled street of tiny houses leading off rue des Recollets on the north side of place Charles-David.

Almost at the top of rue de la République, on the right, allée des Muriers leads from place des Chartreux to the entrance of **La Chartreuse du Val de Bénédiction** (daily: April–Sept 9am–6.30pm; Oct–March 9.30am–5.30pm; €6.10). This Carthusian monastery, one of the largest in France, was founded by the sixth of the Avignon popes, Innocent VI (pope 1352–62), whose sharp profile is outlined on his tomb in the church. The buildings, which were sold off after the Revolution and gradually restored last century, are totally unembellished. With the exception of the Giovanetti frescoes in the chapel beside the refectory, all the paintings and treasures of the monastery have been dispersed, leaving you with a strong impression of the austerity of the Carthusian order. You're free to wander around unguided, through the three cloisters, the church, chapels, cells and communal spaces, which have little to see but plenty of atmosphere to absorb. It's one of the best venues in the Festival of Avignon.

Another festival venue is the fourteenth-century **Église Collègiale Notre-Dame** and its cloister on place St-Marc close to the *mairie* (April–Sept 10am–12.30pm & 2–6.30pm; Oct–March daily 10am–noon & 2–5pm; free). Notre-Dame's most important treasure is a rare fourteenth-century smiling Madonna and Child made from a single tusk of ivory, now housed, along with many of the paintings from the Chartreuse, in the **Musée Pierre-de-Luxembourg**, just to the north along rue de la République (same hours as Église Collègiale Notre-Dame; €3). The spacious layout includes a single room, with comfortable sofas and ample documentation, given over to the most stunning painting in the collection – *The Coronation of the Virgin*, painted in 1453 by Enguerrand Quarton as the altarpiece for the church in the Chartreuse.

Eating and drinking

There's a modest choice of **eating** places in the sleepy town centre. Try *La Banaste*, 28 rue de la République (Ⓣ04.90.25.64.20; closed Thurs; menus from €21.50), which serves plentiful *terroir* meals. For a blowout, head for posh *La Magnanerie*, 37 rue Camp de Bataille (Ⓣ04.90.25.11.11), off rue de la République, with a menu for €33 (à la carte over €50), or the luxurious restaurant of *Le Prieuré*, where subtly blended Mediterranean flavours dominate (lunch menus from €36, à la carte €70–85). Alternatively, *Aubertin*, 1 rue de l'Hôpital (Ⓣ04.90.25.94.84; closed Sun & Mon), serves a €36 menu in the shade of the old arcades by the Collègiale Notre-Dame. A little further out of town, at 3 av Pasteur, is the popular *Mon Mari Etait Pâtissier* (Ⓣ04.90.25.52.79; closed Sun evening & Mon; menus from €30), where the chef has moved on from pastries to swordfish.

St-Rémy-de-Provence and the Alpilles

The watery and intensely cultivated scenery of the Petite Crau plain south of Avignon changes abruptly with the eruption of the **Chaîne des Alpilles**, whose peaks look like the surf of a wave about to engulf the plain. At their northern foot nestles **ST-RÉMY-DE-PROVENCE**, a dreamy place approached along long avenues of plane trees and whose busy boulevards contain an old town no more than half a kilometre in diameter. Outside this ring, the modern town is sparingly laid out, so for once you don't have to plough your way through dense developments to reach the centre. It's a beautiful place, as unspoilt as the villages around it.

Arrival, information and accommodation

There's no train station in St-Rémy; **buses** from Avignon, Aix and Arles drop you in place de la République, the main square abutting the old town on the east. The **tourist office**, which at the time of writing was temporarily located north of the boulevards at avenue Maréchal Juin, is scheduled to return from 2005 to place Jean-Jaurès (Easter–Oct Mon–Sat 9am–12.30pm & 2–7pm, Sun 10am–noon & 3–6pm; Nov–Easter Mon–Sat 9am–noon & 2–6pm; Ⓣ04.90.92.05.22, Ⓦwww.saintremy-de-provence.com), just south of the centre, reached by following avenue Durand-Maillane off the boulevards; they have excellent free guides to **cycling and walking routes** in and around the Alpilles and can provide addresses for renting **horses**. If you want to rent a **bike**, try Telecycles (Ⓣ04.90.92.83.15). Without a car, it's difficult to get to Glanum or Les Baux except by foot or taxi (taxis ⓣ06.07.02.25.64 or ⓣ06.09.31.50.38).

St-Rémy has a fairly wide choice of **accommodation**, though bargains are hard to come by. In the old town, *Ville Verte*, on the corner of place de la République and avenue Fauconnet (ⓣ04.90.92.06.14, ⓦwww.hotel-villeverte.com; closed Jan; ❸), has a garden and a pool, and some rooms on the ground floor with kitchenettes. Outside the old town, try *Hostellerie du Chalet Fleuri*, 15 av Frédéric Mistral (ⓣ04.90.92.03.62, ⓕ04.90.92.60.28; ❸), to the north, with parking, a restaurant and garden, or *Le Castellet des Alpilles*, 6 place Mireille (ⓣ04.90.92.07.21, ⓦwww.castelet.alpilles.com; ❹; closed Nov–March), to the south past the tourist office, which is small and friendly, and has some rooms with great views.

There are three functional and busy **campsites** near St-Rémy: the municipal *Le Mas de Nicolas*, 800m from the centre on a turning off the route de Mollèges (ⓣ04.90.92.27.05; €13; closed mid-Oct to mid-March); *Monplaisir*, 1km from the centre on chemin de Monplaisir (ⓣ04.90.92.22.70, ⓦwww.camping-monplaisir.fr; €11.50; closed mid-Nov to Feb); and *Pegomas*, on avenue Jean Moulin to the east of the boulevards (ⓣ04.90.92.01.21, ⓦwww.campingpegomas.com; €13; closed Nov–Feb).

The Town

To reach the old town from place de la République, take avenue de la Résistance, which runs alongside the town's imposing main church, the **Collégiale St-Martin** (organ recitals July–Sept Sat 5.30pm), and start wandering up the alleyways into immaculate, leafy squares. For an introduction to the region, a good first visit would be to the **Musée des Alpilles** on place Favier, housed in the Hôtel Mistral de Mondragon (daily: April–Sept 10am–6pm; Oct–March 10am–5pm; €3). The museum features interesting displays on folklore, festivities and traditional crafts, plus some intriguing local landscapes, creepy portraits by Marshal Pétain's first wife and souvenirs of local boy Nostradamus.

The neighbouring **Musée Archéologique** in the Hôtel de Sade (daily: April–Aug 11am–6pm; Sept–March 11am–5pm; €2.50, €6.50 including entry

Nostradamus

Michel de Nostredame was born in St-Rémy in 1503, and, educated as a physician, he first received recognition for his innovative treatment of plague victims. It wasn't until the latter part of his life that his interest in astrology and the occult would lead to the publication of *The Prophecies of Michel Nostradamus*, a collection of 942 prophetic quatrains. Already well known in his own day, Nostradamus used a deliberately obscure and cryptic writing style for fear that he would be persecuted by the authorities were they to understand completely his **predictions**. The end result was some extremely ambiguous French verse, which has since been the subject of numerous forgeries, urban legends and some very liberal interpretations. Today he is most often given credit for predicting the rise of Napoleon and Hitler, and major catastrophes such as the Great Fire of London in 1666. While Nostradamus may or may not have been able to accurately foresee the future, his success as a writer remains undisputed: his collection of prophecies, now known as *Centuries*, has been kept in print continuously since its first publication in 1551. The tourist office in St-Rémy publishes an excellent leaflet, *Provence in the days of Nostradamus*, with **itineraries** leading from St-Rémy to Salon and back again, though the Nostradamus link is often tenuous.

to Glanum), displays finds from the archeological digs at the Greco-Roman town of Glanum. The hour or so which it takes to wander through the museum may be a bit much for the non-committed, but there are some stunning pieces, in particular the temple decorations.

In addition to the two fifteenth- to sixteenth-century hôtels that house the museums, you'll find more ancient stately residences as you wander through the old town, particularly along **rue Parage**. On rue Hoche is the birthplace of **Nostradamus**, though only the facade is contemporary with the savant, and the house is not open for visits. The Hôtel d'Estrine, 8 rue Estrine, houses the **Centre d'Art Présence Van Gogh** (April–Dec Tues–Sun 10.30am–12.30pm & 2.30–6.30pm; €3.20), which hosts contemporary art exhibitions and has a permanent exhibition of Van Gogh reproductions and extracts from letters, as well as audiovisual presentations on the painter.

Eating, drinking and festivals

You'll find plenty of **brasseries** and **restaurants** in and around old St-Rémy. There are a few good options on rue Carnot (leading from boulevard Victor-Hugo east through the old town to boulevard Marceau), including the Provençal *La Gousée d'Ail* at no. 25 (Ⓣ04.90.92.16.87; closed Thurs & Sat lunch, plus Feb), with a lunch menu at €15 and dinner at €30 and live jazz the last Thursday of the month, and *La Maison Jaune* at no. 15 (Ⓣ04.90.92.56.14; closed Mon & Tues lunch in summer, Mon & Sun evening in winter, plus Jan & Feb), with a €30 weekday lunch menu and a fabulous menu *dégustation Provençal* for €47. Alternatively, *Le Jardin de Frédéric*, 8 bd Gambetta (Ⓣ04.90.92.27.76; closed Sun & Mon lunch), with a €16 lunch menu, usually has some interesting dishes on offer, and *Xa*, 24 bd Mirabeau (Ⓣ04.90.92.41.23; closed Wed & Nov–March; €24 menu), is a new modish restaurant with excellent food. For a scenic spot to dine on crêpes, try *Lou Planet*, 7 place Favier, by the Musée des Alpilles, and for brasserie fare head for *Le Bistrot des Alpilles*, 15 bd Mirabeau (open till midnight). For chic café-lounging, head for the rather elegant *Café des Arts*, 30 bd Victor-Hugo (menu €30).

The best time to visit St-Rémy is during the **Fête de Transhumance** on Whit Monday, when a 2000-strong flock of sheep, accompanied by goats and donkeys, does a tour of the town before being packed off to the Alps for the summer. Another good time to come is for the **Carreto Ramado**, on August 15, a harvest thanksgiving procession in which the religious or secular symbolism of the floats reveals the political colour of the various village councils, while a pagan rather than workers' **May Day** is celebrated with donkey-drawn floral floats on which people play fifes and tambourines.

South of St-Rémy: Les Antiques, St-Paul-de-Mausole and Glanum

About 1.5km south of the old town, following avenue Pasteur, which becomes avenue Vincent-Van-Gogh, you'll come to **Les Antiques** (free access), a triumphal arch supposedly celebrating the Roman conquest of Marseille, and a mausoleum thought to commemorate two grandsons of Augustus. Save for a certain amount of weather erosion, the mausoleum is perfectly intact, while on the arch you can still make out the sculptures of fruits and leaves representing the fertility of "the Roman Province" (hence "Provence"), and the figures of chained captives, symbolizing Roman might.

The arch would have been a familiar sight to **Vincent Van Gogh**, who in 1889 requested that he be put under medical care for several months. He was living in Arles at the time, and the hospital chosen by his friends was in the old monastery **St-Paul-de-Mausole**, a hundred metres or so east of Les Antiques; it remains a psychiatric clinic today. Although the regime was more prison than hospital, Van Gogh was allowed to wander out around the Alpilles and painted prolifically during his twelve-month stay. *The Oliviers' Fields*, *The Reaper*, *The Enclosed Field* and *The Evening Stroll* are among the 150 canvases of this period. The **church** and **cloisters** can be visited (daily: April–Oct 9.30am–7pm; Nov–March 10.15am–4.45pm; €3.20): take avenue Edgar-Leroy or allée St-Paul from avenue Vincent-Van-Gogh, go past the main entrance of the clinic and into the gateway on the left at the end of the wall.

Not very far beyond the hospital is a signposted farm called **Mas de la Pyramide** (daily: July & Aug 9am–noon & 2–7pm; Sept–June 9am–noon & 2–5pm; €4). It's an old troglodyte farm in the Roman quarries for Glanum with a lavender and cherry orchard surrounded by cavernous openings into the rock filled with ancient farm equipment and rusting bicycles. The farmhouse is part medieval and part Gallo-Roman, with pictures of the owner's family who have lived there for generations.

One of the most impressive ancient settlements in France, **Glanum**, 500m south of Les Antiques (daily: April–Sept 9am–7pm; Oct–March 10.30am–5pm; €6.10), was dug out from alluvial deposits at the very foot of the Alpilles. The site was originally a Neolithic homestead; then, between the second and first centuries BC, the Gallo-Greeks, probably from Massalia (Marseille), built a city here, on which the Gallo-Romans, from the end of the first century BC to the third century AD, constructed yet another town.

Though Glanum is one of the most important archeological sites in France, it can be very difficult to get to grips with. Not only were the later buildings moulded onto the earlier, but the fashion at the time of Christ was for a Hellenistic style. You can distinguish the Greek levels from the Roman most easily by the stones: the earlier civilization used massive hewn rocks while the Romans preferred smaller and more accurately shaped stones. The leaflet at the admission desk is helpful, as are the attendants if your French is good enough.

The site is bisected by a road running from north to south, with several **Hellenic houses** to the northwest. East of here are the **Thermes**, a complex of furnaces, bathing chambers and pools, and beyond this the **Maison du Capricorne** with some fine mosaics. A **forum** dating from Roman times is south of here, near a restored **theatre** and the superb sculptures on the Roman **Temples Geminées** (Twin Temples). The temples also have fragments of mosaics, fountains of both Greek and Roman periods and first-storey walls and columns. As the site narrows in the ravine at the southern end, you'll find a Grecian edifice around a **sacred spring** – the feature that made this location so desirable. Steps lead down to a pool, with a slab above for the libations of those too disabled to descend. An inscription records that Agrippa was responsible for restoring it in 27 BC and dedicating it to Valetudo, the Roman goddess of health.

Les Baux and the Val d'Enfer

At the top of the Alpilles ridge, 7km southwest of St-Rémy, lies the distinctly unreal fortified village of **LES BAUX-DE-PROVENCE**, where the ruined eleventh-century citadel is hard to distinguish from the edge of the plateau, whose rock is both foundation and part of the structure.

Once Les Baux lived off the power and widespread possessions in Provence of its medieval lords, who owed allegiance to no one. When the dynasty died out at the end of the fourteenth century, however, the town, which had once numbered 6000 inhabitants, passed to the counts of Provence and then to the kings of France. In 1632, Richelieu razed the feudal citadel to the ground and fined the population into penury for their disobedience. From that date until the nineteenth century, both citadel and village were inhabited almost exclusively by bats and crows. The discovery in the neighbouring hills of the mineral bauxite (whose name derives from "Les Baux") brought back some life to the village, and tourism has more recently transformed the place. Today the population stays steady at around 400, while the number of visitors exceeds 1.5 million each year. Day-tripping crowds thin rapidly in Les Baux after around 5pm so, depending on the season, it can be worthwhile turning up rather late and enjoying the splendid castle in relative peace.

The lived-in village has many very beautiful buildings. There are half a dozen museums, one of the best being the **Musée Yves Brayer** in the Hôtel des Porcelets (mid-Feb to March & Oct–Dec daily except Tues 10am–12.30pm & 2–5.30pm; April–Sept daily 10am–12.30pm & 2–6.30pm; €4), showing the paintings of the twentieth-century figurative artist whose work also adorns the seventeenth-century **Chapelle des Pénitents Blancs**. Changing exhibitions of contemporary Provençal artists' works are displayed in the **Hôtel de Manville** (10am–6pm; free). The museum of the **Fondation Louis Jou** in the fifteenth-century Hôtel Jean de Brion contains the presses, wood lettering blocks and hand-printed books of a master typographer (April–Dec Mon & Thurs–Sun 11am–1pm & 2–6pm; Jan–March visits by reservation only, free entry first Sun of month Oct–April ; ⓣ04.90.54.34.17; €3), while the **Musée des Santons** in the old Hôtel de Ville (daily 8am–7pm; free) displays traditional Provençal Nativity figures.

Following the signs to the Château will bring you to the entrance to the now-abandoned **Citadelle de la Ville Morte**, the main reason for coming to Les Baux (daily: March–June 9am–7pm, July & Aug 9am–8.30pm; Sept & Oct 9am–6.30pm; Nov 9.30am–6pm Dec–Feb 9am–5pm; €7), and where you can find ruins and several more museums. The **Musée d'Histoire des Baux** in the vaulted space of Tour de Brau has a collection of archeological remains and models to illustrate the history from medieval splendour to bauxite works. The most impressive ruins are those of the feudal castle demolished on Richelieu's orders; there's also the partially restored **Chapelle Castrale** and the **Tour Sarrasine**, the cemetery, ruined houses half carved out of the rocky escarpment and some spectacular views, the best of which is out across the Grande Crau from beside the statue of Provençal poet Charloun Riev at the southern edge of the plateau.

The **tourist office** is at the beginning of Grand-Rue (daily: July & Aug 9am–7pm; Sept–June 9am–6pm; ⓣ04.90.54.34.39, ⓦwww.lesbauxdeprovence.com). You have to park – and pay – before entering the village. Nothing in Les Baux comes cheap, least of all **accommodation**. There's just one moderate option, the *Hostellerie de la Reine Jeanne*, by the entrance to the village (ⓣ04.90.54.32.06, ⓦwww.la-reinejeanne.com, ❸; closed mid-Nov to mid-Feb), with a good restaurant (menus from €21). If you're feeling rich and want to treat yourself, head for the luxurious hotel-restaurant *Oustau de Baumanière*, just below Les Baux to the west on the road leading down to the Val d'Enfer (ⓣ04.90.54.33.07, ⓦwww.oustaudebaumaniere.com; ❾).

The Val d'Enfer

Within walking distance of Les Baux, along the D27 leading northwards, is the valley of quarried and eroded rocks named the **Val d'Enfer** – the Valley of Hell. One quarry has been turned into an audiovisual experience under the title of the **Cathédrale des Images** (mid-Feb to March & Oct to early Jan 10am–6pm; April–Sept daily 10am–7pm; €7), signposted to the right downhill from Les Baux's car park. The projection is continuous, so you don't have to wait to go in. You're surrounded by images projected all over the floor, ceilings and walls of these vast rectangular caverns, and by music that resonates strangely in the captured space. The content of the show, which changes yearly, doesn't really matter (recent ones include the Egyptian city of Alexandria); it's an extraordinary sensation, wandering on and through the shapes and colours. As an erstwhile work site put to good use, it couldn't be bettered.

Arles

ARLES is a major town on the tourist circuit, its fame sealed by the extraordinarily well-preserved Roman arena, **Les Arènes**, at the city's heart, and backed by an impressive variety of other stones and monuments, both Roman and medieval. It was the key city of the region in Roman times, then, with Aix, main base of the counts of Provence before unification with France. For centuries it was Marseille's only rival, profiting from the inland trade route up the Rhône whenever the enemies of France were blocking Marseille's port. Arles declined when the railway put an end to this advantage, and it was an inward-looking depressed town that **Van Gogh** came to in the late nineteenth century. Today it's a staid and conservative place with an unmistakable small-town feel, but comes to life for the **Saturday market**, which brings in throngs of farmers from the surrounding countryside, and during the various **festivals** of *tauromachie* between Easter and All Saints, when the town's frenzy for bulls rivals that of neighbouring Nîmes.

Arrival, information and accommodation

Arriving by train eases you gently into the city, with the **gare SNCF** conveniently located a few blocks to the north of the Arènes. Most buses also arrive here at the unstaffed adjacent **gare routière**, though some, including all local buses, stop on the north side of boulevard Georges-Clemenceau just east of rue Gambetta. Rue Jean-Jaurès, with its continuation rue Hôtel-de-Ville, is the main axis of old Arles. At the southern end it meets boulevard Georges-Clemenceau and boulevard des Lices, with the **tourist office** directly opposite (April–Sept daily 9am–6.45pm; Oct–Nov plus Christmas and New Year Mon–Sat 9am–5.45pm, Sun 10.30am–2.15pm; Dec–March Mon–Sat 9am–4.45pm, Sun 10.30am–2.15pm; Ⓣ04.90.18.41.20, Ⓦwww.tourisme.ville-arles.fr); there's also an annexe in the *gare SNCF* (Mon–Sat 9am–1pm). You can rent **bikes** from Peugeot, 15 rue du Pont, or Europbike, 1 rue Philippe Lebon, and **cars** from Europcar (Ⓣ04.90.93.23.24), Eurorent (Ⓣ04.90.93.50.14) or Hertz (Ⓣ04.90.96.75.23), all on avenue Victor-Hugo. To connect to the **Internet**, head for *Hexaworld*, on rue 4 Septembre, near place Voltaire.

Museum passes

The **Pass Monuments** (€13.50) grants free admission to all of Arles' museums and monuments except the Fondation Vincent Van Gogh, and is available either from the tourist office or at the sites themselves.

There's little shortage of **hotel** rooms at either end of the scale. The best place to look for cheap rooms is in the area around Porte de la Cavalerie near the station. If you get stuck, the tourist office will find you accommodation for a €1 fee.

Hotels

De l'Amphithéatre 5–7 rue Diderot ⓣ04.90.96.10.30, ⓦwww.hotelamphitheatre.fr. Situated close to Les Arènes, this place has plenty of warm colours, tiles and wrought ironwork. ❸

D'Arlatan 26 rue du Sauvage ⓣ04.90.93.56.66, ⓦwww.hotel-arlatan.fr. This may not be Arles' most expensive hotel, but it is probably the most luxurious, set in a beautiful old fifteenth-century mansion and decorated with antiques. Closed Jan. ❻

Calendal 5 rue Porte de Laure ⓣ04.90.96.11.89, ⓦwww.lecalendal.com. Pleasant, welcoming hotel with generous, air-conditioned rooms overlooking a garden. Closed Jan. ❹

Le Cloître 16 rue du Cloître ⓣ04.90.96.29.50, ⓕ04.90.96.02.88. A cosy hotel with some rooms giving views of St-Trophime. Closed Nov to mid-March. ❹

Constantin 59 bd de Craponne, off bd Clemenceau ⓣ04.90.96.04.05, ⓔhotelconstantin@wanadoo.fr. Pleasant, well-kept and comfortable hotel, with prices kept down by the proximity of the Nîmes highway (some traffic noise) and its location a little way from the centre. ❸

Du Forum 10 place Forum ⓣ04.90.93.48.95, ⓦwww.hotelduforum.com. Spacious rooms in an old house in the ancient heart of the city, with a swimming pool in the garden. A bit noisy but very welcoming. Closed Nov–Feb. ❸

Gauguin 5 place Voltaire ⓣ04.90.96.14.35, ⓕ04.90.18.98.87. Comfortable, cheap and well run. Advisable to book. ❷

Musée 11 rue du Grand-Prieuré ⓣ04.90.93.88.88, ⓦwww.hoteldumusee.com.fr. Small, good value family-run place in a quiet location opposite Musée Réattu, with a pretty, flower-filled terrace and air-conditioned rooms. ❸

Hostel and campsites

Auberge de Jeunesse 20 av Foch ⓣ04.90.96.18.25, ⓔarles@fuaj.org. Old-style hostel with dormitory accommodation only. Bus no. 4 from town, direction "Fourchon"; alight at stop "Fournier". €13.70 per bed Closed Jan.

La Bienheureuse 7km out on the N453 at Raphèles-les-Arles ⓣ04.90.98.48.06, ⓕ04.90.98.06.64. Best of Arles' half-dozen campsites; the restaurant here is furnished with pieces similar to those displayed in the Musée Arlaten and full of pictures of popular Arlesian traditions. Regular buses from Arles. €9.90 for two people and a tent. Open all year.

Camping City 67 rte de Crau ⓣ04.90.93.08.86, ⓦwww.camping-city.com. The closest campsite to town on the Crau bus route. €17 for two people and a tent. Closed Oct–March.

The City

The centre of Arles fits into a neat triangle between boulevard E.-Combes to the east, boulevards Clemenceau and des Lices to the south, and the Rhône to the west. The **Musée de l'Arles Antique** is southwest of the expressway by the river, not far from the end of boulevard Clemenceau; **Les Alyscamps** is down across the train lines to the southeast. But these apart, all the **Roman and medieval monuments** are within easy walking distance in this very compact city centre.

Roman Arles

Roman Arles provided grain for most of the western empire and was one of the major ports for trade and shipbuilding. Under Constantine it became the capital of Gaul and reached its height as a world trading centre in the fifth century. Once the empire crumbled, however, Arles found itself isolated between the Rhône, the Alpilles and the marshlands of the Camargue – an isolation that allowed its Roman heritage to be preserved.

A good place to start any tour of Roman Arles is the **Musée de l'Arles Antique** (daily: March–Oct 9am–7pm; Nov–Feb 10am–5pm; €5.50), southwest of the town centre on the spit of land between the Rhône and the Canal

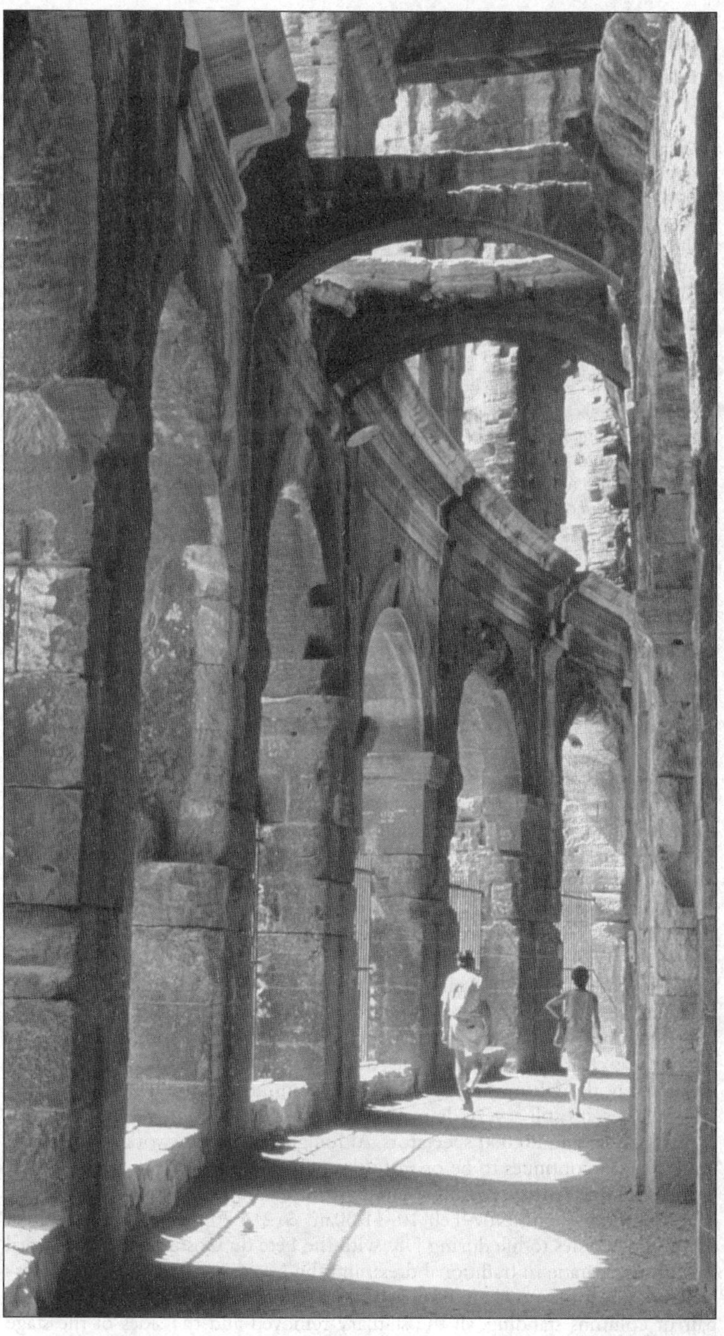

△ Les Arènes, Arles

The bullfight

Bullfighting, or more properly *tauromachie* (roughly, "the art of the bull"), comes in two styles in Arles and the Camargue. In the local **courses camarguaises**, which are held at fêtes from late spring to early autumn (the most prestigious of which is Arles' Cocarde d'Or in early July), *razeteurs* run at the bulls in an effort to pluck ribbons and cockades tied to the bulls' horns, cutting them free with special barbed gloves. The drama and grace of the spectacle is in the stylish way the men leap over the barrier away from the bull, and in the competition for prize money between the *razeteurs*. In this gentler bullfight, people are rarely injured and the bulls are not killed.

More popular, however, are the brutal Spanish-style **corridas** (late April, early July & September, at Arles), consisting of a strict ritual leading up to the all-but-inevitable death of the bull. After its entry into the ring, the bull is subjected to the *bandilleros* who stick decorated barbs in its back, the *picadors*, who lance it from horseback, and finally, the *torero*, who endeavours to lead the bull through as graceful a series of movements as possible before killing it with a single sword stroke to the heart. In one *corrida* six bulls are killed by three *toreros*, for whom injuries (sometimes fatal) are not uncommon. Whether you approve or not, *tauromachie*, which has a history of some centuries here, is your best way of taking part in local life and of experiencing the Roman arena in Arles (€6 per seat). The tourist office, local papers and publicity around the arena will give you the details, or call the Bureau des Arènes ⓣ04.90.96.03.70.

de Rhône. It's housed in a resolutely contemporary building positioned on the axis of the second-century **Cirque Romaine**, an enormous chariot racetrack (the excavation of which has been temporarily halted due to lack of funding) that stretches 450m from the museum to the town side of the expressway. The museum is a treat – open-plan, flooded with natural light and immensely spacious. It covers the prehistory of the area, then takes you through the five centuries of Roman rule, from Julius Caesar's legionary base through Christianization to the period when spices and gems from Africa and Arabia were being traded here. Fabulous mosaics are laid out with walkways above; and there are numerous sarcophagi with intricate sculpting depicting everything from music and lovers to gladiators and Christian miracles.

Back in the centre of Arles, the most impressive Roman monument is the amphitheatre, known as **Les Arènes** (daily: March, April & Oct 9am–5.30pm, May–Sept 9am–6pm; Nov–Feb 10am–4.30pm; €4, or covered by *Pass Monuments* – see box, p.1087), dating from the end of the first century. To give an idea of its size, it used to shelter over two hundred dwellings and three churches built into the two tiers of arches that form its oval surround. This medieval quarter was cleared in 1830 and the Arènes was once more used for entertainment. Today, though missing its third storey and most of the internal stairways and galleries, it's still a very dramatic structure and a stunning venue for performances, seating 20,000 spectators. Although restoration work is scheduled until 2006, it continues to be open to the public.

The **Théâtre Antique** (daily: March, April & Oct 9–11.30am & 2–5.30pm; May–Sept 9am–6pm; Nov–Feb 10–11.30am & 2–4.30pm; €3), just south of the Arènes, comes to life during July, with the Fête du Costume in which local folk groups parade in traditional dress, and the Mosaïque Gitane Romany festival. The theatre is nowhere near as well preserved as the arena, with only one pair of columns standing, all the statuary removed and the sides of the stage littered with broken bits of stone.

At the river end of rue Hôtel-de-Ville, the **Thermes de Constantin** (daily: March, April & Oct 9–11.20am & 2–5.30pm; May–Sept 9am–noon & 2–6pm; Nov–Feb 10–11.30am & 2–4.30pm; €3), which may well have been the biggest Roman baths in Provence, are all that remain of the emperor's palace that extended along the waterfront. The Roman forum was up the hill on the site of **place du Forum**, still the centre of life in Arles. You can see the pillars of an ancient temple embedded in the corner of the *Nord-Pinus* hotel.

The Romans had their burial ground southeast of the centre, and it was used by well-to-do Arlesians well into the Middle Ages. Now only one alleyway, foreshortened by a train line, is preserved. To reach **Les Alyscamps** (daily: March–April & Oct 9–11.30am & 2–5.30pm; May–Sept 9am–6pm; Nov–Feb 10–11.30am & 2–4.30pm; €3.50), follow avenue des Alyscamps from the east end of boulevard des Lices. Sarcophagi still line the shaded walk, whose tree trunks are azure blue in Van Gogh's rendering. There are numerous tragedy masks, too, though any with special decoration have long since been moved to serve as municipal gifts, as happened often in the seventeenth century, or to reside in the museums. But there is still magic to this walk, which ends at the twelfth-century Romanesque St Honorat's church, wonderfully simple and cool on a hot day.

The cathedral, museums and medieval Arles

The doorway of the **Cathédrale St-Trophime** on Arles' **central place de la République** is one of the most famous examples of twelfth-century Provençal stonecarving in existence. It depicts the Last Judgement, trumpeted by angels playing with the enthusiasm of jazz musicians while the damned are led naked in chains down to hell and the blessed, all draped in long robes, process upwards. The cathedral itself was started in the ninth century on the spot where, in 597 AD, St Augustine was consecrated as the first bishop of the English, and it was largely completed by the twelfth century. A font in the north aisle and an altar illustrating the crossing of the Red Sea in the north transept were both originally Gallo-Roman sarcophagi. The nave is decorated with d'Aubusson tapestries, while there is superlative Romanesque and Gothic stonecarving in the extraordinarily beautiful **cloisters**, accessible from place de la République to the right of the cathedral (daily: March–April & Oct 9am–5.30pm; May–Sept 9am–6pm; Nov–Feb 10am–4.30pm; €3.50).

Across place de la République from the cathedral stands the palatial seventeenth-century **Hôtel de Ville**, inspired by Versailles. You can walk through its vast entrance hall, with its flattened vaulted roof designed to avoid putting extra stress on the **Cryptoporticus du Forum** below. This is a huge, dark, dank and wonderfully spooky three-sided underground gallery, built by the Romans, possibly as a food store, possibly as a barracks for public slaves, but certainly to provide sturdy foundations for the forum above. Access is from rue Balze (daily: March–April & Oct 9–11.30am & 2–5.30pm; May–Sept 9am–noon & 2–6pm; Nov–Feb 10–11.30am & 2–4.30pm; €3.50).

In case you feel that life stopped in Arles, if not after the Romans, then at least after the Middle Ages, head for the **Musée Arlaten** on rue de la République (daily: April, May & Sept 9.30am–12.30pm & 2–6pm; June–Aug 9.30am–1pm & 2–6.30pm; Oct–March 9.30am–12.30pm & 2–5pm; €4). The museum was set up in 1896 by Frédéric Mistral, the Nobel Prize-winning novelist who was responsible for the turn-of-the-twentieth-century revival of interest in all things Provençal, and whose statue stands in place du Forum. The collections of costumes, documents, tools, pictures and paraphernalia of Provençal life are alternately tedious and intriguing. The evolution of Arlesian dress is charted in great detail for all social classes from the eighteenth century to World War I and there's a mouthwatering life-size scene of a bourgeois Christmas dinner.

Another must-see in Arles is the main collection of the **Musée Réattu** (daily: March, April & Oct 10am–noon & 2–5pm; May–Sept 10am–noon & 2–6.30pm; Nov–Feb 1–5pm; €4), housed in a beautiful fifteenth-century priory opposite the Roman baths. Much of it comprises tedious and rigid eighteenth-century works by the museum's founder and his contemporaries, but dotted round this are some good modern works: Zadkine's study in bronze for the two Van Gogh brothers, Mario Prassinos' monochrome studies of the Alpilles, César's *Compression 1973* and, best of all, Picasso's *Woman with Violin* sculpture and 57 ink-and-crayon sketches made in Arles between December 1970 and February 1971. Amongst the split faces and clowns is a beautifully simple portrait of his mother.

Van Gogh in Arles

At the back of the Réattu museum, lanterns line the river wall where **Van Gogh** used to wander, wearing candles on his hat, watching the night-time light: *The Starry Night* is the Rhône at Arles. Much of the riverfront and its bars and bistros were destroyed during World War II. Another casualty of the bombing was the "Yellow House" on place Lamartine, where the artist lived before entering the hospital at St-Rémy. However, the café painted in *Café de Nuit* still stands in place du Forum, and the distinctive Pont Langlois drawbridge painted by the artist in March 1888 can be seen on the southern edge of the town (poorly signposted off the D35). Van Gogh had arrived by train in February 1888 to be greeted by snow and a bitter mistral wind. But he started painting straight away, and in this period produced such celebrated canvases as *The Sunflowers*, *Van Gogh's Chair*, *The Red Vines* and *The Sower*. Van Gogh found few kindred souls in Arles and finally managed to persuade Gauguin to join him in mid-autumn. Although the two were to influence each other substantially in the following weeks, their relationship quickly soured as the increasingly bad November weather forced them to spend more time together indoors. According to Gauguin, Van Gogh, feeling threatened by his friend's possible departure, finally succumbed to a fit of psychosis and attacked first Gauguin and then himself. He was packed off to the Hôtel-Dieu hospital on rue du Président-Wilson down from the Musée Arlaten, now the **Espace Van Gogh**, an academic and cultural centre with arty shops in its arcades and courtyard flowerbeds re-created according to Van Gogh's painting and descriptions of the hospital garden.

Arles has none of the artist's works but the **Fondation Vincent Van Gogh** (April–Oct daily 10.30am–8pm; Nov–March Tues–Sun 11am–5pm; €7), facing the Arènes at 26 Rond-Point des Arènes, exhibits works by contemporary artists inspired by Van Gogh, including Francis Bacon, Jasper Johns, Hockney and Lichtenstein, and sunflower-drenched photographs by the likes of Cartier-Bresson and Doisneau.

Eating and drinking

Arles has a good number of excellent-quality and cheap **restaurants**, and if you're looking for quick meals, or just want to watch the world go by, there's a wide choice of brasseries on the main boulevards. Place du Forum is the centre of **café** life; here you'll find *Le Café La Nuit*, immaculately re-created à la Van Gogh and open late, and the young and noisy *Bistrot Arlésien*. Nevertheless, don't be surprised to discover that most of Arles packs up for the night around 10.30pm.

L'Entrevue place Nina Berberova ⓣ04.90.93.37.28. Hip Moroccan/Provençal café with an attached *hamam*. Menu €25.

Le Galoubet 18 rue du Dr-Fanton ⓣ04.90.93.18.11. Pleasant, vine-covered terrace and elegant dining room in which to taste the modern Provençal cuisine on a good-value €25 menu. Closed Sun and Mon lunch.

La Gueule du Loup 39 rue des Arènes ⓣ04.90.96.96.69. Cosy restaurant serving traditional dishes, with menus from €25. Closed Mon lunch.

Le Jardin du Manon 14 av des Alyscamps ⓣ04.90.93.38.68. Hospitable Provençal restaurant serving elaborate regional dishes and delicious desserts, which you can enjoy in a small patio garden. €14–36. Closed Wed.

Lou Marquès Hôtel Jules-César, bd des Lices ⓣ04.90.52.52.52. The top gourmet palace in the top grand hotel. The specialities, which include *baudroie* (monkfish), langoustine salad and Camargue rice cake, are all served with the utmost pomposity. Menus from €27. The other restaurant in the hotel, *Le Cloître*, has a lunch menu at around €20. *Lou Marquès* closed Sat & Mon lunch, *Le Cloître* Wed & Sun evening, both closed Nov & Dec.

La Paillote 28 rue Dr-Fanton ⓣ04.90.96.33.15. Very friendly place with a good €15 menu. Closed Wed.

Toast Vin & Cie 2 rue Dr-Fanton ⓣ04.90.96.22.26. Hearty open sandwiches served with different salads, from €12–15. Lunch menu €12.50. Closed Sun.

The Camargue

The boundaries of the **CAMARGUE** are not apparent until you come upon them. Its shimmering horizons are infinite because land, lagoon and sea share the same horizontal plain. Both wild and human life have traits peculiar to this drained, ditched and now protected delta land. Today, the whole of the Camargue is a Parc Naturel Régional, with great efforts made to keep an equilibrium between tourism, agriculture, industry and hunting on the one hand, and the indigenous ecosystems on the other.

The Camargue is home to the **bulls** and to the **white horses** that the region's *gardiens*, or herdsmen, ride. Neither beast is truly wild, though both run in semi-liberty. The Camargue horse, whose origin is unknown, remains a distinct breed, born dark brown or black and turning white around its fourth year. It is never stabled, surviving the humid heat of summer and the wind-racked winter cold outdoors. The *gardiens* likewise are a hardy community. Their traditional homes, or *cabanes*, are thatched and windowless one-storey structures, with bulls' horns over the door to ward off evil spirits. They still conform, to some extent, to the popular cowboy myth, and play a major role in guarding Camarguais traditions. Throughout the summer they're kept busy in every village arena with spectacles involving bulls and horses, and the work carries local glamour. Winter is a good deal harder, and fewer and fewer Camarguais property owners can afford the extravagant use of land that bull-rearing requires.

The Camargue bulls and horses are just one element in the area's exceptionally rich **wildlife**, which includes flamingos, marsh and sea birds, waterfowl and birds of prey; wild boars, beavers and badgers; tree frogs, water snakes and pond turtles; and a rich flora of reeds, wild irises, tamarisk, wild rosemary and juniper trees. These last, which grow to a height of 6m, form the **Bois des Rièges** on the islands between the **Étang du Vaccarès** and the sea, part of the central national reserve to which access is restricted to those with professional credentials.

After World War II, the northern marshes were drained and re-irrigated with fresh water. The main crop planted was rice, and so successful was it that by the 1960s the Camargue was providing three-quarters of all French

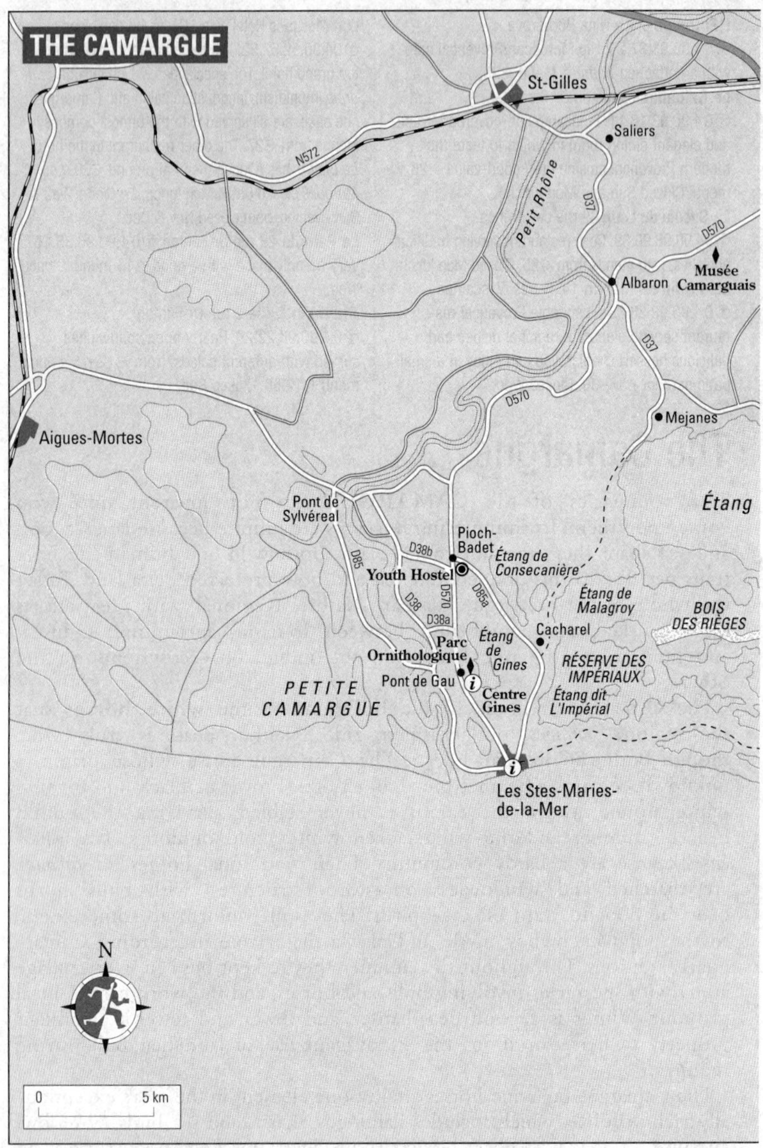

consumption of the grain. Vines were also reintroduced – in the nineteenth century they had survived the disease that devastated every other wine-producing region because their stems were under water. There are other crops – wheat, rapeseed and fruit orchards – as well as trees in isolated clumps. To the east, along the last stretch of the Grand Rhône, the chief business is the production of salt, which was first organized in the Camargue by the

The legend of Sarah

Sarah was the servant of Mary Jacobé, Jesus' aunt, and Mary Salomé, mother of two of the apostles, who, along with Mary Magdalene and various other New Testament characters, are said to have been driven out of Palestine by the Jews and put on a boat without sails or oars.

The boat apparently drifted to an island in the mouth of the Rhône, where the Egyptian god Ra was worshipped. Here Mary Jacobé, Mary Salomé and Sarah, who was herself Egyptian, settled to carry out conversion work, while the others headed off for other parts of Provence. In 1448 their relics were "discovered" in the fortress church of Stes-Maries on the erstwhile island, around the time that the Romanies were migrating to western Europe from the Balkans and from Spain.

Romanies have been making their **pilgrimage** to Stes-Maries since at least the sixteenth century. It's a time for weddings and baptisms, as well as music, dancing and fervent religious observance. After Mass on May 24, the shrines of the saints are lowered from the high chapel to an altar where the faithful stretch out their arms to touch them. Then the statue of Black Sarah is carried by the Romanies to the sea. On the following day the statues of Mary Jacobé and Mary Salomé, sitting in a wooden boat, follow the same route, accompanied by the mounted *gardiens* in full Camargue cowboy dress, Arlesians in traditional costume, and spectators. The sea, the Camargue, the pilgrims and the Romanies are blessed by the bishop from a fishing boat, before the procession returns to the church with much bell-ringing, guitar-playing, tambourines and singing. Another ceremony in the afternoon sees the shrines lifted back up to their chapel.

Oct–March daily except Tues 10.15am–4.45pm; €4.60), halfway between Gimeaux and Albaron, which documents the traditions and livelihoods of the Camarguais people through the centuries, in the old sheep barn of a working farm. At Pont de Gau, just 4km short of Stes-Maries, the **Maison du Parc** (April–Sept daily 10am–6pm; Oct–March daily except Fri 9.30am–5pm; ⓣ04.90.97.86.32; free) has exhibitions on the local environment and is the place to go for detailed maps of paths and dykes. Just down the road is the engrossing **Parc Ornithologique** (daily: April–Sept 9am–sunset; Oct–March 10am–sunset; €6.50), with some of the less easily spotted birds kept in aviaries, plus trails across a twelve-hectare marsh and a longer walk with vantage points, all with ample signs and information.

Arrival, information and accommodation

There's good, secure parking on the seafront in Stes-Maries at the Police Municipale, close to the **tourist office** on avenue Van-Gogh, which will happily weigh you down with information detailing all the town's festivals and events (daily: Jan, Feb, Nov & Dec 9am–5pm; March & Oct 9am–6pm; April–June & Sept 9am–7pm; July & Aug 9am–8pm; ⓣ04.90.97.82.55, ⓦwww.saintesmaries.com).

From April to October **rooms** in Stes-Maries should be booked in advance, and for the Romany festival, several months before. Prices go up considerably during the summer and at any time of the year are more expensive than at Arles. Outlying *mas* (farmhouses) renting out rooms tend to be quite expensive. **Camping** on the beach is not officially tolerated, but even at Stes-Maries people sleeping beneath the stars rarely get told to move on. The fifteen-kilometre seaside plage de Piemanson, also known as the plage d'Arles, south of Salin-de-Giraud, 10km east of Stes-Maries, is a favoured venue for *camping sauvage* in summer.

Hotels

Camille 13 av de la Plage ⓣ04.90.97.80.26, ⓦwww.hotel-camille.camargue.fr Fairly plain but decent modern cheapie with a sea view; some rooms have balconies. Closed mid-Nov to mid-March. ❷

Le Fangassier rte de Cacharel ⓣ04.90.97.85.02, ⓦwww.fangassier.camargue.fr. Pleasant hotel fairly close to the centre of town, with friendly staff. ❷

Hostellerie du Pont du Gau rte d'Arles Pont de Gau, 4km north of Stes-Maries, between the Maison du Parc and the Parc Ornithologique ⓣ04.90.97.81.53, ⓕ04.90.97.98.54. Old-fashioned Camarguais decor, pleasant rooms and a good restaurant. Closed Jan to mid-Feb. ❸

Mangio Fango rte d'Arles ⓣ04.90.97.80.56, ⓔmangio.fango@wanadoo.fr. Situated 600m from Stes-Maries, overlooking the Étang des Launes, with pool and patios. Closed Nov & Dec. ❹

Hotel des Rièges rte de Cacharel ⓣ04.90.97.85.07 ⓦwww.hoteldesrieges.com. An upmarket hotel in an old farmhouse, with swimming pool and garden. Down a track signed off the D85a at the edge of Stes-Maries. Closed mid-Nov to mid-Dec & Jan. ❹

Les Vagues 12 av T.-Aubunal ⓣ & ⓕ04.90.97.84.40. A low-priced modern option above a smart restaurant, overlooking the marina on the rte d'Aigues-Mortes. ❷

Hostel and campsites

Hostel on the Arles–Stes-Maries bus route, 10km north of Stes-Maries in the hamlet of Pioch-Badet ⓣ04.90.97.51.72, ⓕ04.90.97.54.88. Bike rental, horse rides and other excursions. Open all year, but must make reservations. €24.40 (half-board only).

Camping La Brise rue Marcel-Carrière ⓣ04.90.97.84.67, ⓕ04.90.97.72.01. A three-star site, with a pool and laundry facilities, and tents, mobile homes or bungalows for rent. On the Arles–Stes-Maries bus route, on the east side of the village (stop "La Brise"). Open all year. €18 for two people and a tent.

Camping Le Clos du Rhône at the mouth of the Petit Rhône, 2km west of the village on the rte d'Aigues-Mortes ⓣ04.90.97.85.99, ⓕ04.90.97.78.85. A busy four-star site with a pool, laundry and shop. Only two of the Arles–Stes-Maries buses continue to here (stop "Clos du Rhône"). Closed Oct–March. €21.40 for two people and a tent.

The Town

Stes-Maries is a neat and pleasant, if excessively commercialized town, in size scarcely more than a large village. Its open streets of plain, low white houses are quite unlike the Provençal norm, and the grey-gold Romanesque church, with its strange outline of battlements and watchtower, is really the only distinctive monument. It exploits its monopoly as the only Camargue resort and every leisure activity is catered for, to excess. There are kilometres of **beach**; a pleasure port with boat trips to the lagoons; horses or bikes to ride; watersports; the *arènes* for bullfights, cavalcades and other entertainment (events are posted on a board outside); and flamenco guitarists playing on the restaurant and café terraces – it can all be very good fun.

As for sights, the fortified **church of Stes-Maries** allows a look at Sarah's tinselled and sequinned statue, which is carried into the sea each year (see box, p.1097). It's at the back of the crypt on the right, and always surrounded by candles and abandoned crutches and callipers from the miraculously cured. The church itself has beautifully pure lines and fabulous acoustics. During the time of the Saracen raids it provided shelter for all the villagers and even has its own freshwater well. The church **tower** (March–June & Sept–Oct 10am–12.30pm & 2–6.30pm, Sun 10am–7pm; July–Aug daily 10am–8pm; Nov–Feb Wed, Sat & Sun 10am–noon & 2–5pm; €2) affords the best possible view over the Camargue; it's the tallest thing for miles.

A few steps south of the church on rue Victor-Hugo, the **Musée Baroncelli** (opening hours vary, check with tourist office; €1.50) is named after the man who, in 1935, was responsible for initiating the Romanies' procession down to the sea with Sarah. This was motivated by a desire to give a special place in the pilgrimage to the Romanies. The museum covers this event, other Camarguais traditions and the region's fauna and flora.

Eating and drinking

Few of the **restaurants** in Stes-Maries are bargains, though there are plenty to choose from, and out of season the quality improves and prices come down. Right by the marina the restaurant at *Les Vagues* on rue T.-Aubanel (Ⓣ04.90.97.84.40) serves pleasant fish dishes on a range of menus from €16–31.50. Or try the tapas and bargain wine at *Kahlua Bodéga Pub*, 1 rue Jean Roche (Ⓣ04.90.97.98.41; closed Jan, Tues out of season; tapas €3.50 each). The best places to try local fish specialities, however, are at the beach hut restaurants *Chez Juju* and *Chez Marc et Mireille* in **BEAUDUC**, over the dykes on the spit of sand on the opposite side of the bay from Stes-Maries. They're not easy to get to, but if you're hiking or cycling in the area, it's worth the extra mile. By car it's a good thirty minutes from Salin-de-Giraud.

From Avignon to Gordes

If you're heading east from Avignon towards Apt and the Luberon, two worthwhile stops are romantic **Fontaine-de-Vaucluse** and the picturesque **Gordes**, close to the **Abbaye de Sénanque**. Between Gordes and Apt are the old ochre-quarrying villages of **Roussillon** and **Rustrel**. Visiting all these places without your own transport is not that easy; Fontaine is accessible by bus from Avignon or from L'Isle-sur-la-Sorgue's *gare SNCF* 6km away, Gordes from Cavaillon, 24km southwest of Avignon, and Roussillon only infrequently from Apt.

Fontaine-de-Vaucluse

The source of the Sorgue, the stream that runs alongside rue des Teinturiers in Avignon, is at **FONTAINE-DE-VAUCLUSE**, 29km southeast of Avignon, and is one of the most powerful natural springs in the world. At the top of the gorge above the village is a mysterious tapering fissure deeper than the sheer 230-metre cliffs that barricade its opening. This is where the waters of the Sorgue appear, sometimes in spectacular fashion, bursting down the gorge (in March and April normally), at other times – when you might wonder what the fuss is about – seeping stealthily through subterranean channels to meet the river bed further down. The best time to admire it is in the early morning before the crowds arrive.

Fontaine-de-Vaucluse was once a rustic backwater where the fourteenth-century poet Petrarch pined for his Laura. It remains a somewhat romantic place despite its hordes of visitors and the attendant tourist clutter. If you're intrigued by the source of the river, visit the **L'Ecomusée du Gouffre** (hourly 45-minute tours in French: Feb–May & Oct–Nov 9.30am–noon & 2–6pm; June–Sept 9.30am–7.30pm; closed Dec & Jan; €5) at the *rond point* at the start of the chemin de la Fontaine, the path to the source. Nearby you'll find the rather dull **Musée du Santon** (April–June & Sept 10am–7pm; July & Aug 10am–8pm; Oct–March 10am–6pm; €4), displaying an unremarkable collection of Provençal Nativity figures. A short way up the path on the riverside you'll find the Vallis Clausa paper mill, whose products are geared to the fine art market.

Further up the path there's also the impressive **Musée d'Histoire 1939–1945** (daily except Tues: March–May 10am–noon & 2–6pm, June–Sept 10am–6pm, October 10am–noon & 2–5pm; Nov–Feb Sat & Sun 10am–noon & 2–5pm; €3.50), portraying life under the Vichy regime and commemorating the Resistance. Across the river, through an alleyway just past the bridge, is the much more interesting **Musée de Pétrarque** (daily except Tues: March–May 10am–noon & 2–6pm; June–Sept 9.30am–noon & 2–6.30pm; first two weeks Oct 10am–noon & 2–6.30pm; mid-Oct to Dec 10am–noon & 2–5pm; €3.50), with beautiful books dating back to the fifteenth century and pictures of Petrarch, his beloved Laura and of Fontaine, where he passed sixteen years of his unrequited passion.

The **tourist office** is on chemin de la Fontaine (Tues–Sat 10am–1pm & 2–6pm; ⓣ04.90.20.32.22, ⓔofficetourisme.vaucluse@wanadoo.fr). The most characterful hotel in the village itself is the *Hôtel les Sources* (ⓣ04.90.20.31.84, ⓕ04.90.20.39.09; ❺), with a whole variety of *vieille France* rooms. On the road out towards Saumane de Vaucluse, 3km from the village, is a budget hotel worth trying, *Font de Lauro* (ⓣ & ⓕ04.90.20.31.49; ❶). There's also a **hostel** on chemin de la Vignasse, 1km south on the road to Lagnes (ⓣ04.90.20.31.65, ⓔfontaine@fuaj.org; closed mid-Nov to Jan; €8.90 per bed), and a **campsite**, *Les Prés* (ⓣ04.90.20.32.38; all year), 500m downstream from the village, with tennis courts and swimming pool. For **food**, you have a choice of several reasonably priced restaurants in town, including *Château* (ⓣ04.90.20.31.54; menus €22 and up) and *Lou Fanau* (ⓣ04.90.20.31.90; closed Wed; menu €17.50), both of which serve solid regional food.

Gordes and around

GORDES, just 5km east of Fontaine as the crow flies, but 18km by road, is a picturesque Provençal village much favoured by Parisian media personalities, film directors, artists and the like. This might prompt you to give it a miss – and it is an expensive place – but there are good reasons for its popularity with the rich and famous, for it's a spectacular sight. You climb winding roads past buildings of ancient stone before arriving at the summit, where a church and houses surround a mighty twelfth- to sixteenth-century **château**, housing the contemporary paintings of the Flemish artist Pol Mara (daily 10am–noon & 2–6pm; €4).

The **tourist office** is in the château (Mon–Sat 9am–noon & 2–6pm, Sun 10am–noon & 2–6pm; ⓣ04.90.72.02.75, ⓦwww.gordes-village.com). If you're looking for somewhere to **stay**, the most reasonably priced hotel within the village is Le Provençal (ⓣ04.90.72.10.01, ⓕ04.90.72.04.20; ❹), while *Les Romarins* (ⓣ04.90.72.12.13, ⓦwww.hoteldesromarins.com; ❻), overlooking the village on the route de Sénanque, is an old country house with comfortable, traditionally styled rooms. The best **eating** place in town is the *Comptoir des Arts* on place du Château (ⓣ04.90.72.01.31; closed Fri & Sat lunch), always full of Parisians in summer, and serving menus from €32.50. *Le Teston* (ⓣ04.90.72.02.54; closed Sun evening & Wed) on place Genty Pantaly is a bit less expensive, and offers good Provençal standards, with lunchtime *plats* around €11.

Four kilometres north of Gordes, set amidst lavender fields in a deep cleft in the hills, stands the twelfth-century Cistercian **Abbaye de Sénanque** (visits by 1hr guided tour only; ⓣ04.90.72.05.72 or enquire at abbey shop; €6). It's still in use as a monastery and you can visit the church, cloisters and all the main rooms of this substantial and austere building; a shop sells the monks' produce, including a liqueur, as well as honey and lavender essence.

The other historical site of note near Gordes is the **Village des Bories** (daily 9am–sunset; €5.50), 3.5km east off the D2 to Cavaillon, a strange collection of dry-stone dwellings with peculiar geometric shapes that suggest prehistoric

△ Abbaye de Sénanque

14

pedigree. In fact most were built in the eighteenth century and inhabited up until a hundred years ago.

The best and most surreal detour in the vicinity is to the old **ochre mines** between Gordes and Apt. The houses in the village of **ROUSSILLON**, 5km east of Gordes, radiate all the different shades of the seventeen ochre tints once quarried here; a well-signed footpath leads from the car park on place de la Poste to the old workings. More dramatic quarries, known as the **Colorado Provençal**, are signed off the D22 towards Gignac, just before you reach **RUSTREL**, about 10km northeast of Apt. Various paths lead you to an amphitheatre of coffee, vanilla and strawberry ice cream whipped into pinnacles and curving walls.

The Luberon

After its descent from the Alps, the River Durance makes a wide curve to the west before joining the Rhône, skirting the massive rock-fold known as the **Luberon** that runs for 50km between Cavaillon and Manosque. The Luberon has long been escape country for well-heeled Parisians, Dutch and British, but has also attracted a good number of artists; the main attraction is the countryside itself and the tiny, immaculately preserved villages.

The Luberon's northern face is damper, more alpine in character than the southern face, extremely cold in winter, and dotted with tiny villages clinging stubbornly to the foothills. The southern slopes, by contrast, are Mediterranean in scent and feel. It's almost all wooded, except for the summer sheep pastures at the top, and there's just one main route across it, through the Combe de Lourmarin.

Apt

The sole town base for exploring the Luberon is **APT**, though in itself it's not much of a town for sightseeing, nor is it renowned for the charm and friendliness of its people. Its large confectionery factory spews mucky froth into the concrete-channelled River Coulon and, as late as early spring, when mimosa is blossoming down on the coast, the temperature around Apt can drop to well below freezing. It cheers up, however, every Saturday for the weekly market when cars are barred from the town centre to allow artisans and cultivators from all the surrounding countryside to set up stalls. As well as featuring every imaginable Provençal edible, the **market** is accompanied by barrel organs, jazz musicians, stand-up comics, aged hippies and assorted freaks.

Arriving by bus – Apt's *gare SNCF* is freight-only – you'll be dropped at **place de la Bouquerie**, the main square lined with cafés and restaurants, or at the **gare routière** on avenue de la Libération at the eastern end of the town on avenue Saignon (Ⓣ04.90.74.20.21). The **tourist office** is at 20 av Philippe-de-Girard (May–Sept Mon–Sat 9am–noon & 2–6pm, Sun 9.30am–12.30pm; Oct–April Mon–Sat 9am–noon & 2–6pm; Ⓣ04.90.74.03.18, Ⓦwww.ot-apt.fr), just up to the left from place de la Bouquerie as you face the river. There's a good choice of **accommodation** in Apt, unlike the more scenic hilltop villages, where all rooms are reserved months before the summer season. On the southeastern edge of the town centre is the friendly *L'Aptois*, 289 cours Lauze de Perret (Ⓣ04.90.74.02.02, Ⓦwww.aptois.fr.st; ❷); while the more basic *Le Palais*, 24 place Gabriel-Péri (Ⓣ04.90.04.89.32, Ⓔhotel-le-palais@wanadoo.fr; ❷; closed mid-Nov to March), is right in the centre; and there are very pleasant rooms across the river at the *Auberge du Luberon*, 8 place du Faubourg du Ballet (ⓣ04.90.74.12.50, ⓦwww.auberge-luberon-peuzin.com; ❹). **Campers**, for once, are treated to a municipal ground within easy walking distance of the town: *Les Cèdres* on avenue de Viton (ⓣ & ⓕ04.90.74.14.61; closed Dec to mid-Feb), across the bridge from place St-Pierre, €12.40 for two people and a tent.

Outside Apt, you could try the *Auberge du Presbytère* on place de la Fontaine in the village of **SAIGNON**, perched on a hillside 4km southeast of Apt (ⓣ04.90.74.11.50, ⓦwww.provence-luberon.com; ❹); the rustic *Auberge des Seguins*, tucked away in a spectacular canyon near **BUOUX**, a village 10km south of Apt (ⓣ04.90.74.16.37, ⓕ04.90.74.03.26; ❸), which also has a restaurant; or the welcoming *Relais de Roquefure* (closed during 2004 but scheduled to reopen in 2005; ⓣ04.90.04.88.88❹) in **LE CHÊNE**, 6km from Apt on the N100 towards Avignon. At Rustrel, the *Bastide St Joseph*, rte de Banon (ⓣ04.90.04.97.80; ⓦwww.guideweb.com/provence/bb/sant-joseph; ❼), is a tastefully renovated eighteenth-century *bastide* with a pool.

If you haven't stuffed yourself with chocolates and candied fruit (Apt's speciality), you can get cheap and decent **meals** at the *Grand Café Grégoire* on place Bouquerie (open till 10pm; menu €15). Further out on the Avignon road, at Le Chêne, there's real gourmandise to be had at *Bernard Mathys* (ⓣ04.90.04.84.64; closed Tues & Wed; menus from €40).

The Parc Naturel Régional du Luberon

A large area of the Luberon has been designated **the Parc Naturel Régional du Luberon** (ⓦwww.parcduluberon.com), with the aim of conserving the natural fauna and flora and limiting development. The park is administered by the **Maison du Parc**, 60 place Jean-Jaurès in Apt (April–Sept Mon–Sat 8.30am–noon & 1.30–7pm; Oct–March Mon–Fri 8.30am–noon & 1.30–6pm; ⓣ04.90.04.42.00), which is the place to go for information about every aspect of the Luberon. The centre also houses a small **Musée de la Paléontologie** (€1.50), which is specifically designed to amuse children and is fun. A submarine-type "time capsule" door leads down to push-button displays that include magnified views of insect fossils and their modern descendants.

Given the region's general dearth of public transport, the only practical and pleasurable way to explore the park without a car is by hiking or cycling. The organization **Vélo Loisir en Luberon** (ⓣ04.92.79.05.82; ⓦwww.veloloisirluberon.com) is a consortium of hotels, campsites and cycle hire and repair shops which promotes cycle tourism throughout the region and can provide transfers to airports or rail stations, guided cycle tours, forward transport of luggage, suggested itineraries and technical assistance and repairs. In Apt, bikes can be hired from Guy Agnel, 86 quai Général-Leclerc, or Cycles Ricaud, a few doors down.

The Abbaye de Silvacane

If you're heading for Aix-en-Provence from Apt, you'll pass close to another ancient Cistercian abbey contemporary with Sénanque, 29km south of Apt, just across the Durance. After a long history of abandonment and evictions, the **Abbaye de Silvacane** (June–Sept daily 10am–6pm; Oct–May daily except Tues 10am–1pm & 2–5pm; €6.10) is once again a monastic institution. Isolated from the surrounding villages on the bank of the Durance, its architecture has hardly changed over the last 700 years; you can visit the stark, pale-stoned splendour of the church, its cloisters and surrounding buildings.

Aix-en-Provence

AIX-EN-PROVENCE would be the dominant city of central Provence were it not for the great metropolis of Marseille, just 25km away. Historically, culturally and socially, the two cities are moons apart and the tendency is to love one and hate the other. Aix is complacently conservative and a stunningly beautiful place, its riches based on landowning and the liberal professions. The youth of Aix are immaculately dressed; hundreds of foreign students, particularly Americans, come to study here; and there's a certain snobbishness, almost of Parisian proportions.

From the twelfth century until the Revolution, Aix was the capital of Provence. In its days as an independent county, its most mythically beloved ruler, "Good" King René of Anjou (1409–80), held a brilliant court renowned for its popular festivities and patronage of the arts. René was an archetypal Renaissance man, a speaker of many languages (including Greek and Hebrew), a scientist, poet and economist; he also introduced the muscat grape to the region – today he stands in stone in picture-book medieval fashion, a bunch of grapes in his left hand, looking down the majestic seventeenth-century cours Mirabeau.

Arrival, information and accommodation

Cours Mirabeau, which replaced the town's old southern fortifications, is the main thoroughfare of Aix, with the multi-fountained place Général-de-Gaulle, or La Rotonde, at its west end, the main point of arrival. The **gare SNCF** is on rue Gustavo-Desplace at the end of avenue Victor-Hugo, the avenue leading south from the square; the **gare routière** is on avenue de l'Europe, at the end of avenue des Belges (Ⓣ04.42.91.26.80). The new **TGV** station is 10km to the southwest of Aix; regular shuttles connect the station with the *gare routière* (every 30 min: daily 4.45am–10.30pm; €3.70). **Driving** into Aix can be confusing: the entire ring of boulevards encircling the old town is essentially one giant roundabout, circulating anti-clockwise; hotels are signposted off this ring in yellow. Parking in Aix isn't easy; the ring is probably the best bet for on-street parking as the old town is pretty nightmarish; there are also some good, modern underground car parks, notably at the Centre de Congrès. The **tourist office** is located on the *rond point* at the western end of cours Mirabeau at 2 place Général-de-Gaulle (June & Sept daily 8.30am–8pm; July & Aug 8.30am–9pm; Sept–May Mon–Sat 8.30am–7pm, Sun 10am–1pm & 2–6pm; Ⓣ04.42.16.11.61, Ⓦwww.aixenprovencetourism.com), between avenue des Belges and avenue Victor-Hugo.

From mid-June to the end of July (festival time) your chances of getting a **hotel** room are pretty slim unless you've reserved a couple of months in advance at least. Outside this time, there is a decent range of accommodation to choose from.

Visa pass

The **Visa Pour Aix et le Pays D'Aix** grants a 20–50 percent discount on selected museums in and around Aix, in addition to a reduced rate at concerts and on local buses and half-price guided tours. It can be purchased at the tourist office or museums for €2.

Hotels

Des Arts 69 bd Carnot Ⓣ04.42.38.11.77 Ⓕ04.42.26.77.31. Very welcoming, though slightly noisy hotel, with the cheapest rooms to be found in the centre of Aix. You can't book, so turn up early. Quieter, more expensive rooms are at the back. ❷

La Caravelle 29 bd Roi-René Ⓣ04.42.21.53.05, Ⓕ04.42.96.55.46. By the boulevards to the south-east of the city. The more expensive (renovated) rooms overlook courtyard gardens. ❸–❹

Cardinal 22–24 rue Cardinale Ⓣ04.42.38.32.30, Ⓔhotel-cardinal@wanadoo.fr. Clean, peaceful and welcoming establishment; great value. ❹

De France 63 rue Espariat Ⓣ04.42.27.90.15, Ⓔhoteldefrance-aix@wanadoo.fr. Right in the centre and with very comfortable rooms. ❸

Le Manoir 8 rue d'Entrecasteaux Ⓣ04.42.26.27.20, Ⓦwww.hotelmanoir.com. Comfortable and characterful old hotel in a central but discreet location with parking. Breakfast is taken in the sixteenth-century cloister. ❸

Number One 10 cours des Minimes Ⓣ04.42.64.45.01, Ⓕ04.42.64.45.01. Fairly basic and it's on a busy road, but this is one of the cheapest options in Aix. ❷

Paul 10 av Pasteur Ⓣ04.42.23.23.89, Ⓔhotel.paul@wanadoo.fr. Good value for Aix, with a garden. Rooms have private shower and phone and there are also some for three and four people. ❷

Des Quatre-Dauphins 54 rue Roux-Alphéran Ⓣ04.42.38.16.39, Ⓕ04.42.38.60.19. Old-world charm in the *quartier* Mazarin. ❹

St-Christophe 2 av Victor-Hugo Ⓣ04.42.26.01.24, Ⓦwww.hotel-saintchristophe.com. Comfortable air-conditioned two-star hotel above a popular brasserie, close to both the station and cours Mirabeau. ❺

Hostels and campsites

HI hostel 3 av Marcel-Pagnol Ⓣ04.42.20.15.99, Ⓕ04.42.59.36.12. Located 2km west of the centre, this hostel has small dorm rooms (€13.25) and no cooking facilities but it does have a restaurant, laundry, baggage deposit, tennis and volleyball courts, and was completely renovated in 2002. Take bus #4, direction "La Mayanelle", stop "Vasarely". Closed Christmas–Feb. ❶

CROUS Cité Universitaire des Gazelles, 38 av Jules-Ferry Ⓣ04.42.93.47.70. This student organization can sometimes find cheap rooms on one of Aix's two main campuses during July & Aug. Take bus #5, direction "Moulin de Testas", stop "Moulin de Testas". ❶

Airotel Camping Chanteclerc rte de Nice, Val St-André Ⓣ04.42.26.12.98, Ⓕ04.42.27.33.53. Also 3km from the centre on bus #3 or #10, this site is equally expensive, with excellent facilities. Open all year.

Camping Arc-en-Ciel rte de Nice, Pont des Trois Sautets Ⓣ04.42.26.14.28. Located 3km south-east of town on bus #3, this is not a particularly cheap site but has very good facilities. Closed Oct–March.

The City

The whole of the **old city of Aix**, clearly defined by its ring of boulevards and the majestic cours Mirabeau, is the great monument here, far more compelling than any one single building or museum within it. With so many streets alive with people, so many tempting restaurants, cafés and shops, plus the best markets in Provence, it's easy to pass several days wandering around without the need for any itinerary or destination. As a preliminary introduction to Aixois life, a café-stopping stroll beneath the gigantic plane trees that shade the cours Mirabeau is mandatory.

Vieil Aix

To explore the network of jumbled little lanes and narrow roads that make up the heart of Aix, wander north from leafy **cours Mirabeau** to anywhere within the ring of *cours* and boulevards. The layout of **Vieil Aix** is not designed to assist your sense of direction, but it hardly matters when there's a fountained square to rest at every 50m and a continuous architectural backdrop of treats from the sixteenth and seventeenth centuries. On Saturdays, and to a lesser extent on Tuesdays and Thursdays, the centre is taken up with **markets**: fruit and veg on place Richelme and place de la Madeleine; produce of all kinds on place des Prêcheurs, from fresh fruit and vegetables to cheeses, dried wild mushrooms and olive oil; flowers on place de l'Hôtel-de-Ville; clothes on rues

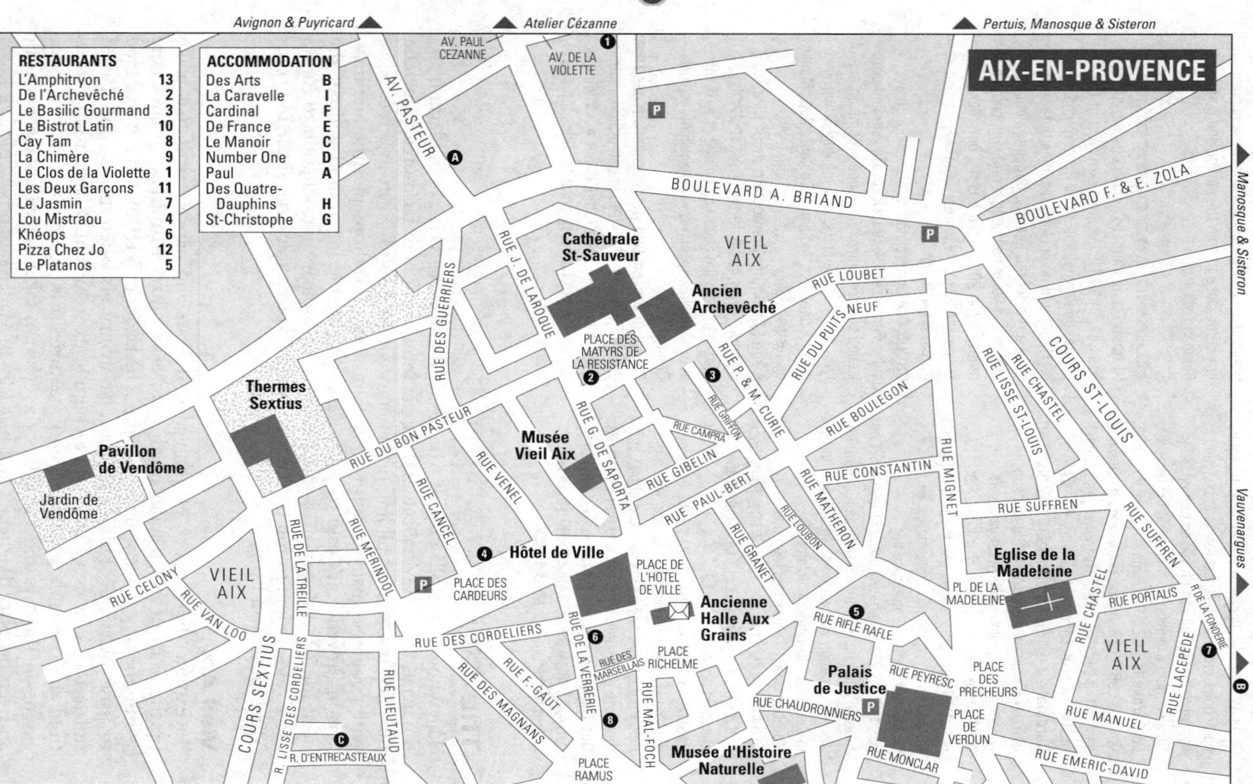
AIX-EN-PROVENCE
Avignon & Puyricard
Atelier Cézanne
Pertuis, Manosque & Sisteron
Manosque & Sisteron
Vauvenargues
Avignon
RESTAURANTS
L'Amphitryon 13
De l'Archevêché 2
Le Basilic Gourmand 3
Le Bistrot Latin 10
Cay Tam 8
La Chimère 9
Le Clos de la Violette 1
Les Deux Garçons 11
Le Jasmin 7
Lou Mistraou 4
Khéops 6
Pizza Chez Jo 12
Le Platanos 5
ACCOMMODATION
Des Arts B
La Caravelle I
Cardinal F
De France E
Le Manoir C
Number One D
Paul A
Des Quatre-Dauphins H
St-Christophe G
AV. PAUL CEZANNE
AV. DE LA VIOLETTE
AV. PASTEUR
BOULEVARD A. BRIAND
BOULEVARD F. & E. ZOLA
VIEIL AIX
Cathédrale St-Sauveur
Ancien Archevêché
RUE J. DE LAROQUE
RUE DES GUERRIERS
PLACE DES MATYRS DE LA RESISTANCE
RUE LOUBET
RUE DU PUITS NEUF
RUE P. & M. CURIE
RUE GRIFFON
RUE CAMPRA
RUE BOULEGON
RUE LISSE ST-LOUIS
RUE CHASTEL
COURS ST-LOUIS
Thermes Sextius
RUE DU BON PASTEUR
Musée Vieil Aix
RUE G. DE SAPORTA
RUE GIBELIN
RUE PAUL-BERT
RUE CONSTANTIN
RUE MIGNET
RUE SUFFREN
Pavillon de Vendôme
Jardin de Vendôme
RUE VENEL
RUE CANCEL
RUE MATHERON
RUE LOUBON
RUE GRANET
Hôtel de Ville
PLACE DE L'HOTEL DE VILLE
Eglise de la Madeleine
PL. DE LA MADELEINE
RUE PORTALIS
R DE LA FONDERIE
RUE CELONY
RUE VAN LOO
RUE DE LA TREILLE
RUE MERINDOL
PLACE DES CARDEURS
Ancienne Halle Aux Grains
RUE RIFLE RAFLE
RUE DES CORDELIERS
RUE DE LA VERRERIE
RUE DES MARSEILLAIS
PLACE RICHELME
Palais de Justice
RUE PEYRESC
PLACE DES PRECHEURS
RUE LACEPEDE
COURS SEXTIUS
R. LISSE DES CORDELIERS
RUE LIEUTAUD
RUE DES MAGNANS
RUE F.-GAUT
RUE MAL-FOCH
RUE CHAUDRONNIERS
PLACE DE VERDUN
RUE MANUEL
R. D'ENTRECASTEAUX
PLACE RAMUS
Musée d'Histoire Naturelle
RUE MONCLAR
RUE EMERIC-DAVID

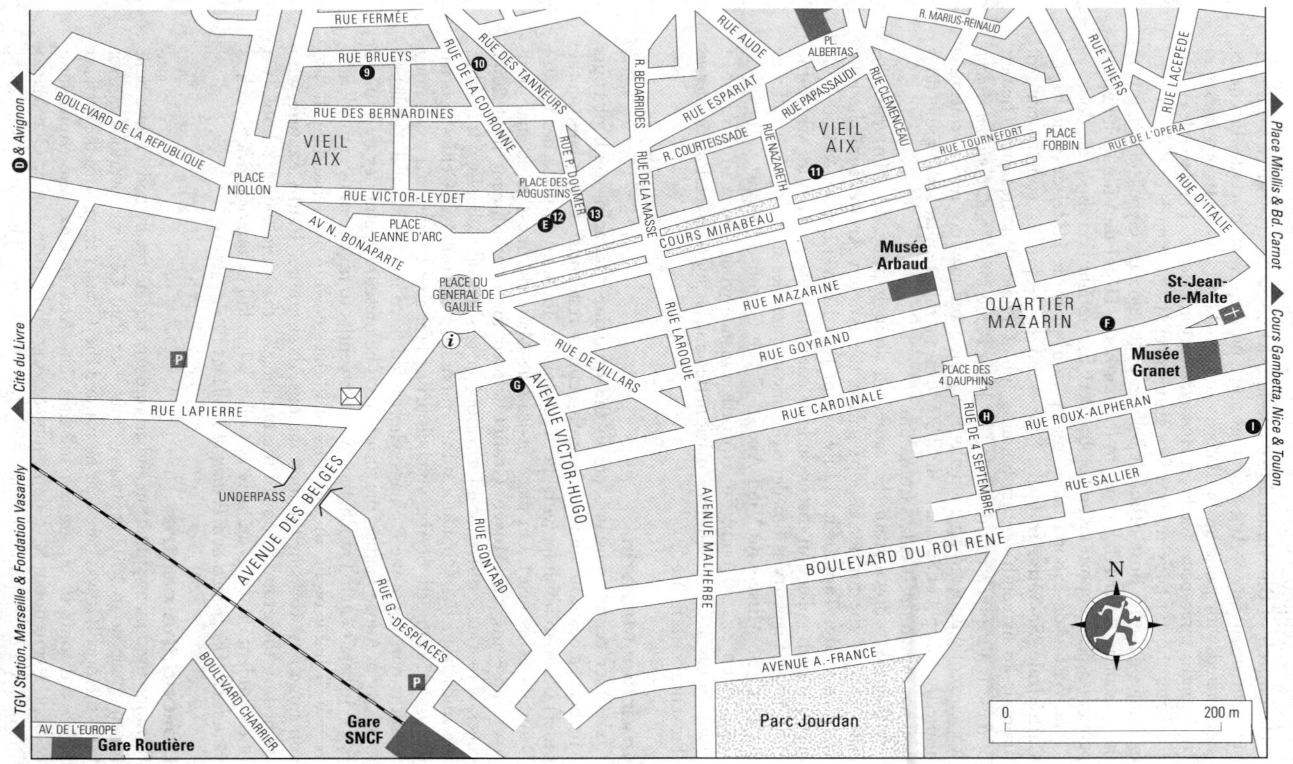
D & Avignon
Cité du Livre
TGV Station, Marseille & Fondation Vasarely
Place Miollis & Bd. Carnot
Cours Gambetta, Nice & Toulon
RUE FERMÉE
RUE BRUEYS
RUE DES TANNEURS
RUE DE LA COURONNE
R. BEDARRIDES
RUE AUDE
PL. ALBERTAS
R. MARIUS-REINAUD
RUE THIERS
RUE LACEPEDE
BOULEVARD DE LA REPUBLIQUE
RUE DES BERNARDINES
VIEIL AIX
RUE ESPARIAT
RUE PAPASSAUDI
RUE CLEMENCEAU
VIEIL AIX
RUE TOURNEFORT
PLACE FORBIN
RUE DE L'OPERA
RUE D'ITALIE
PLACE NIOLLON
RUE VICTOR-LEYDET
PLACE DES AUGUSTINS
RUE P. DOUMER
RUE DE LA MASSE
R. COURTEISSADE
RUE NAZARETH
COURS MIRABEAU
PLACE JEANNE D'ARC
AV N. BONAPARTE
PLACE DU GENERAL DE GAULLE
Musée Arbaud
RUE MAZARINE
RUE LAROQUE
QUARTIER MAZARIN
St-Jean-de-Malte
Musée Granet
RUE GOYRAND
RUE DE VILLARS
AVENUE VICTOR-HUGO
PLACE DES 4 DAUPHINS
RUE CARDINALE
RUE DE 4 SEPTEMBRE
RUE ROUX-ALPHERAN
RUE LAPIERRE
UNDERPASS
AVENUE DES BELGES
RUE GONTARD
AVENUE MALHERBE
RUE SALLIER
BOULEVARD DU ROI RENE
N
RUE G.-DESPLACES
AVENUE A.-FRANCE
BOULEVARD CHARRIER
Gare SNCF
Parc Jourdan
0
200 m
AV. DE L'EUROPE
Gare Routière

Peyresc, Rifle-Rafle, Bouteilles, Chaudronniers and Monclar; and a flea market on place de Verdun.

The **church of the Madeleine** (Sept–June Mon–Sat 8–11.30am & 3–5.30pm; Sun 8am–noon; July & Aug mornings only), on the central place des Prêcheurs, is decorated with paintings by Rubens and Van Loo (who was born in Aix in 1684), and a three-panel medieval *Annunciation*. On place de l'Hôtel – de –Ville, a delicate though fairly massive foot hangs over the architrave of the old corn exchange, now the **post office**. It belongs to the goddess Cybele, dallying with the masculine River Rhône. Just to the north, the **Hôtel de Ville** itself displays perfect classical proportions and embroidery in wrought iron above the door.

Rue Gaston-de-Saporta takes you up from place de Hôtel-de-Ville to the **Cathédrale St-Sauveur** (daily: 8am–noon & 2–6pm), a conglomerate of fifteenth- to sixteenth-century building, full of medieval art treasures. The best of these is a triptych commissioned by King René in 1475, *Le Buisson Ardent*. It is currently undergoing a lengthy restoration and may not return to its new home, the Chapel of St Lazare, until 2006; meanwhile regular DVD projections of it are shown on Tuesdays from 3pm.

A short way down from the cathedral, through place des Martyrs-de-la-Résistance, is the former bishop's palace, the **Ancien Archevêché**, housing the **Musée des Tapisseries** (daily except Tues 10am–12.30pm & 1.30–5pm; €2), a superb collection that includes a contemporary section, for which the definition of tapestry is broadened to include textiles made of rope, raffia or feathers. The **Musée du Vieil Aix** at 17 rue Gaston-de-Saporta (Tues–Sun: 10am–noon & 2.30–6pm; €4) is worth a glance while you're in this part of town. It has a set of religious marionettes and a huge collection of *santons* (Provençal crib figures).

Quartier Mazarin

Aix's other central museums are in the **quartier Mazarin**, south of cours Mirabeau, a beautiful mid-seventeenth-century residential district built on the orders of an archbishop, with the four-dolphin fountain of place des Quatre Dauphins at its heart. On place St-Jean-de-Malte the most substantial of all Aix's museums, the **Musée Granet** (closed for refurbishment until 2006; check with tourist office for information), covers art and archeology. It exhibits the finds from the Oppidum d'Entremont (see opposite), a Celtic-Ligurian township 3km north of Aix, which flourished for about a hundred years, along with the remains of the Romans who routed them in 124 BC and established their city of Aquae Sextiae, the future Aix. The museum's paintings are a mixed bag – Italian, Dutch, French, mostly seventeenth- to nineteenth-century – not very well hung or lit, though this may change with the rebuilding. It also contains a few works by the most famous Aixois painter, **Paul Cézanne**, who studied on the ground floor of the building, at that time the art school. Two of his student drawings are here as well as a handful of minor canvases such as *Bathsheba*, *The Bathers* and *Portrait of Madame*.

Beyond the centre

Cézanne used many studios in and around Aix but he finally had a house built for the purpose in 1902 at what is now 9 av Paul-Cézanne, overlooking Aix from the north. It was here that he painted the *Grandes Baigneuses*, the *Jardinier Vallier* and some of his greatest still lifes. The **Atelier Cézanne** (April–June & Sept 10am–noon & 2–6pm; July & Aug daily 10am–6pm; Oct–March 10am–noon & 2–5pm; €5.5; bus #20, stop "P. Cézanne") is exactly as it was at the time of his death in 1906; coat, hat, wineglass and easel, the objects he liked to paint, his pipe, a few letters and drawings … everything save the pictures he was working on.

Collective cultural life is the basis of the **Cité du Livre** in the old match-making factory at 8–10 rue des Allumettes, a short way southwest from the tourist office (Tues, Thurs & Fri noon–6pm, Wed & Sat 10am–6pm; free). Entered by doorways in the form of giant books leaning together as if on a shelf, it includes libraries, a cinema, theatre space, a *videothèque d'art lyrique* (where you can watch just about any French opera performance) and all manner of exhibitions. Since 1996 the complex has been the home base for the internationally renowned modernist dance company, Ballet Preljocaj.

For a totally different experience, both visually and conceptually, you can escape the sometimes cloying grandeur of seventeenth-century Aix by visiting the **Fondation Vasarely** on avenue Marcel-Pagnol in Jas-de-Bouffan, 4km west of the city centre (Mon–Sat: July & Aug 11am–1pm & 2–7pm, Sept–June 10am–1pm & 2–6pm; €7; bus #4, stop "V. Vasarely"). There are innumerable sliding showcases, showing images related to all the themes of architect/artist Vasarely's work, including his "plastic alphabet" and designs for apartment buildings. But the seven hexagonal spaces on the ground floor, each hung with six huge designs, is where you'll get the immediate impact of this extraordinary man's work.

And finally, 3km north of the city, the **Oppidum d'Entremont** (daily except Tues 9am–noon & 2–6pm; free; take bus #20 from Cours Sextius) is the excavated site of the Gallic settlement which preceded the foundation of the town, predating the Roman conquest by more than 200 years. You'll find the remains of a fortified enclosure, spectacularly sited, as well as excavations of the residential and commercial quarters of the town.

Eating, drinking and entertainment

Aix is stuffed full of **restaurants** of every price and ethnic origin. Place des Cardeurs, just northwest of the Hôtel de Ville, is nothing but restaurant, brasserie and café tables, while rue de la Verrerie running south from Hôtel de Ville and place Ramus have an immense variety of Indian, Chinese and North African restaurants. Rue des Tanneurs is a good street for low budgets. The café-brasseries on cours Mirabeau are also tempting, and in between them you'll find cheaper snackeries. More expensive are Aix's soft biscuits, the elliptical candied-fruit and almond-flavoured *calissons*. They're very good with a strong dark espresso. Local gourmet *chocolatier* Puyricard has a shop at 7 rue Rifle-Rafle.

Cafés and restaurants

L'Amphitryon 2–4 rue Paul Doumer ⓣ04.42.26.54.10. Eclectic cuisine with market-fresh ingredients, served on a flower-drenched terrace in historical old Aix. An excellent restaurant which won't break the bank. Menu from €18. Closed Sun, Mon & second half Aug.

De l'Archevêché place des Martyrs-de-la-Résistance ⓣ04.42.21.43.57. Smart lunch spot with good midday pasta, tapas, tagines and salads from around €10.

Le Basilic Gourmand 6 rue du Griffon ⓣ04.42.96.08.58. Classic Provençal food on a €12.50 lunch menu, evenings à la carte only. Amiable staff, bric-a-brac decor and occasional live music. Closed Sun & Mon.

Le Bistrot Latin 18 rue Couronne ⓣ04.42.38.22.88. Superbly presented scallop and tapenade profiteroles and honey and garlic rabbit are two of the top dishes here. Lunch menu €15, evening from €22. Closed Sat, Sun & Mon lunch out of season.

Cay Tam 29 rue Verrerie ⓣ04.42.27.28.11. The best East Asian cooking in Aix. Vietnamese dishes are the main feature, but dim sum is also available. Menus from €14.50. Closed Mon & Tues, lunch Wed & Fri.

La Chimère 15 rue Brueys ⓣ04.42.38.30.00. New spin on French standards, with dishes like salad of octopus with provençal herbs or roast sea bream with lemon, tian of vegetables and *sauce vierge*. Menu €22.50. Closed Sun.

Le Clos de la Violette 10 av de la Violette ⓣ04.42.23.30.71. Aix's most renowned restaurant serves dishes that might not sound very seductive, like stuffed lamb's feet, but are in fact gastronomic delights. More obviously alluring are the puddings: a *clafoutis* of greengages and pistachios with peach sauce and a tart of melting dark chocolate. Lunch menu €54, otherwise menus start at €120 and if you're going à la carte the *plats* alone start around €40. Closed Sun, Mon & Wed lunch & middle 2 weeks Aug.

Les Deux Garçons 53 cours Mirabeau. The erstwhile haunt of Camus is done up in faded 1900s style and still attracts a motley assortment of literati. Good brasserie food, but not cheap (from €20.10). Service daily till midnight.

Le Jasmin 6 rue de la Fonderie ⓣ04.42.38.05.89. Tasty and distinctive Persian food for around €16.50. For dessert try the traditional Iranian *choleh zard*, a rice dish with saffron, spices and nuts. Closed Sun.

Lou Mistraou 38 place des Cardeurs ⓣ04.42.96.98.69. Provençal restaurant with a €20 veggie menu, though watch out for the anchovies. Closed Sun & Mon in winter, plus Jan.

Khéops 28 rue de la Verrerie ⓣ04.42.96.59.05. Egyptian cuisine featuring falafel, stuffed pigeon and gorgeous milk-based desserts. Menu €14. Closed Wed lunch.

Pizza Chez Jo/Bar des Augustins place des Augustins ⓣ04.42.26.12.47. This place is usually packed for its cheap pizzas and traditional *plats du jour*. From €9. Closed Sun.

Le Platanos 13 rue Rifle-Rafle ⓣ04.42.21.33.19. Very cheap and popular Greek place with €10 lunch menu. Closed Sun & Mon.

Nightlife and festivals

For **jazz**, the best club is *Hot Brass*, chemin d'Éguilles-Célony (ⓣ04.42.96.06.23), or there's *Le Scat*, 11 rue Verrerie, with jazz, rock and funk. If you'd rather a more mainstream **disco**, head for *Le Cox*, 24 rue de la Verrerie (from 9pm). For **pubs** with live music or DJs, try *Le Manoir* and *The Red Clover* at 25 and 30 rue Verrerie, respectively, or *Pub Solferino*, place d'Armenie. Aix's **gay** bar is *Mediterranean Boy*, 6 rue de la Paix, with video screens and a pool table.

During the annual **music festivals**, Aix en Musique (world music, jazz, experimental and classical; June; ⓣ04.42.21.69.69) and the Festival International d'Art Lyrique (opera and classical concerts; last two weeks of July; ⓣ04.42.17.34.34), the alternative scene – of street theatre, rock concerts and impromptu gatherings – turns the whole of Vieil Aix into one long party. Tickets for events range from €12 to €185 and can be obtained, along with programmes, from La Boutique du Festival at Espace Forbin, 11, rue Gaston de Saporta (ⓣ04.42.17.34.34, ⓦwww.festival-aix.com). Details of the Danse à Aix international dance festival (two weeks in mid-July) are available from 1 place Rewald off cours Gambetta (ⓣ04.42.96.05.01).

Listings

Bike rental Cycles Zammit, 27 rue Mignet ⓣ04.42.23.19.53.

Books Paradox Bookstore, 15 rue du 4-Septembre, or Book in Bar, 1bis rue Cabassol, for English books; Vents du Sud, 7 rue Maréchal Foch, is the best French bookshop.

Car rental ADA Location, 1 av Henri Mouret ⓣ04.42.52.36.36; Avis, 11 bd Gambetta ⓣ04.42.21.64.16; Europcar, 55 bd de la République ⓣ04.42.27.83.00; Rent a Car, 35 rue de la Molle ⓣ04.42.38.58.29.

Cinema The Cézanne, rue Marcel Guillaume, sometimes screens English or American films in *version originale*, ie with the original soundtrack.

Emergencies Centre Hospitalier, av des Tamaris ⓣ04.42.33.90.28; SOS Médecins ⓣ04.42.26.24.00; for a late-night pharmacy, ring the gendarmerie on ⓣ04.42.26.31.96.

Internet *Le Hublot*, 15/17 rue Paul Bert; *Pl@net Web*, 20 rue Victor Leydet.

Laundry 15 rue Jacques de la Roque; 5 rue de la Fontaine; 60 rue Boulegon; 36 cours Sextius.

Money exchange L'Agence, 15 cours Mirabeau; Change Nazareth, 7 rue Nazareth; La Poste, 2 rue Lapierre.

Police place Niollon ⓣ04.42.91.91.11.

Post office 2 rue Lapierre, 13100 Aix.

Taxis ⓣ04.42.21.61.61; ⓣ04.42.27.71.11 (24hr).

Mont Ste-Victoire

Mont Ste-Victoire, a rough pyramid whose apex has been pulled off-centre, lies 10km east of Aix. Ringed at its base by the dark green and orange-brown of pine woods and cultivated soil, the limestone rock reflects light, turning blue, grey, pink or orange. In the last years of his life **Cézanne** painted and drew Ste-Victoire more than fifty times, and, as part of his childhood landscape, it came to embody the incarnation of life within nature.

You may, however, be more interested in climbing Mont Ste-Victoire and in the view from it, though hiking on the Mont, and many other summits in the area, is forbidden from July to mid-September. The southern face has a sheer 500-metre drop, but from the north the two-hour walk requires nothing more than determination. The **GR9**, also called the Chemin des Venturiers, leaves from a small car park on the D10 just before **VAUVENARGUES**, 14km east of Aix. Having reached the 945-metre ridge, marked by a monumental nineteenth-century cross that doesn't figure in any of Cézanne's pictures, you can follow the path east along the ridge to the summit of the massif and then descend south to **PUYLOUBIER** (about 15km from the cross; reckon on four and a half hours). Bring plenty of water and protection against the fierce sun if walking in hot weather. Much of the walk was badly affected by forest fires in 1989 and consequently, to guard against erosion, you're urged to stick to the path.

At Vauvenargues (several buses daily from the Aix *gare routière*), a perfect weather-beaten, red-shuttered fourteenth-century **château** (definitely not open to the public) stands just outside the village, with nothing between it and the slopes of Ste-Victoire. **Picasso** bought the château in 1958, lived there until his death and now lies buried in the gardens, his grave adorned with his sculpture *Woman with a Vase*. There is a friendly, good-value hotel in the village, *Au Moulin de Provence*, 33 rue de Maquisards (Ⓣ04.42.66.02.22; ❸), whose owners speak English.

Eastern Provence

In **eastern Provence**, it's the landscapes not the towns that dominate. The gentle hills and villages of the **Haut-Var**, the northern half of the Var *département*, make for happy exploration by car or bike, before the foothills of the Alps gradually close in, eventually reaching heights of over 3000m in the far north-eastern corner, around **Barcelonnette**. Winter visitors are almost exclusively skiers, while the summer brings a variety of dedicated hikers, bird-watchers, botanists and climbers. The **Parc National du Mercantour** is a conservation area in this mountainous terrain, but the most exceptional geographical feature is the **Gorges du Verdon** – Europe's answer to the Grand Canyon – in the heart of Provence.

Between Valence and Montélimar, the River Drôme joins the Rhône at **Livron-sur-Drôme**. Following the Drôme upstream by train towards Sisteron, or by road towards **Sisteron** or Barcelonnette, is one of the most dramatic ways of entering eastern Provence.

Haut-Var villages and Aups

Between **ST-MAXIMIN-DE-LA-STE-BAUME**, 35km east of Aix and famous for its supposed possession of the relics of Mary Magdalene, and **DRAGUIGNAN**, an unremarkable military town except for the wonderful *Les Milles Colonnes* restaurant in place aux Herbes, a network of small roads wind through farmland, vineyards and woods and alongside streams and lakes, linking a dozen villages, all of which are ideal for Provençal-style loafing. The only problem is the general scarcity of accommodation.

East of the **Lac de Carcès**, between Cabasse and Carcès, off the D19, lies the last of the three great Cistercian monasteries of Provence. Even more so than Silvacane and Sénanque, the **Abbaye du Thoronet** (April–Sept Mon–Sat 10am–6.30pm, Sun 10am–noon & 2–6.30pm; Oct–March Mon–Sat 10am–1pm & 2–5pm, Sun 10am–noon & 2–5pm; €6.10) has been unscathed by the vicissitudes of time, and during the Revolution was kept intact as a remarkable monument of history and art; today it is occasionally used for concerts. It was first restored in the 1850s, while a more recent campaign has brought it to clear-cut perfection. As with the other two abbeys, its interior spaces, delineated by walls of pale rose-coloured stone, are inspiring.

LORGUES, further east, has a serious gourmet stop in the **restaurant** *Chez Bruno* on route de Vidauban (ⓣ04.94.85.93.93; closed Mon & Sun evening out of season; seasonal truffle menu at €105, à la carte around €54), where the truffle reigns supreme, appearing in myriad forms, even in desserts. There's a Terre des Truffes shop in an annexe to the main building, and space to land your helicopter. Heading 13km northwest, **ENTRECASTEAUX** has an ancient stone **laundry** by the river that's still used, and a very beautiful **château** (guided tours daily except Sat at 4pm; ⓣ04.94.04.43.95; €6).

COTIGNAC, 9km west of Entrecasteaux, is the Haut-Var village *par excellence*, with a shaded main square for pétanque and passages and stairways bursting with begonias, jasmine and geraniums leading through a cluster of medieval houses. More gardens sprawl at the foot of the bubbly rock cliff that forms the back wall of the village, threaded with troglodyte walkways.

North of Cotignac, **SILLANS-LA-CASCADE** has a beautiful walk, signposted off the main road, to an immense waterfall and aquamarine pool (about 20min). **SALERNES**, 6km east of Sillans, makes tiles and pottery and has the old-fashioned *Relais de la Belle Epoque* **hotel** and restaurant on route de Sillans (ⓣ04.94.70.60.30, ⓕ04.94.70.78.84; menus €19; ❹). **VILLECROZE** and **TOURTOUR** to the northeast are both suitably picturesque. The *Auberge des Lavandes*, on place du Général-de-Gaulle in Villecroze (ⓣ04.94.70.76.00, ⓕ04.94.70.56.45; ❸), is one of the best-value hotels in the region, while in Tourtour, on route de Flayosc, you can shelter in total luxury at *La Bastide de Tourtour* (ⓣ04.98.10.54.20, ⓦwww.verdon.net; ❾). A second option in Tourtour, which won't break the bank, is *La Petite Auberge* (ⓣ04.98.10.26.16, ⓔpiju2@wanadoo.fr; ❼). Between the two villages is a highly reputed **restaurant**, *Les Chênes Verts* (ⓣ04.94.70.55.06; closed Tues evening & Wed), with a menu *dégustation* at €48.

Aups

As a base for visiting the villages of Haut-Var or the Gorges du Verdon, the small town of **AUPS** is ideal, as long as you have your own transport. It has a lot of charm and still depends to a large extent on agriculture rather than tourism. Scarcely more than a village itself, its speciality is truffles and, if you're here on a Thursday between November and mid-March, you can witness the **truffle market**.

On **place Martin-Bidauré**, which, along with **place Frédéric-Mistral** (Wed & Sat market), makes up the leafy open space before the start of the old town, a rare monument commemorates the town's citizens who died in 1851 defending the republic and its laws. The year was that of Louis Napoléon's coup d'état and establishment of the Second Empire. Peasant and artisan resistance was strongest in Provence, and the defeat of the insurgents was followed by a bloody massacre of men and women. This might explain the enormous *République Française, Liberté, Egalité, Fraternité* sign on the **church of St-Pancrace**, proclaiming it as state property. The church was designed by an English architect 400 years ago, and has recently had its doors restored by two local British carpenters.

Surprisingly for such a small place, Aups has a museum of modern art, the **Musée Simon Segal** in the former chapel of a convent on avenue Albert-1er (July & Aug daily 10am–noon & 4–7pm; €2.30). The best works are those by the Russian-born painter Simon Segal, but there are interesting local scenes in the other paintings, such as the Roman bridge at Aiguines, now drowned beneath the artificial lake of Sainte-Croix. Just outside Aups, 3.5km along the Tourtour road, is a sculpture park by local artist Maria de Faykod (daily except Tues: June 2–7pm; July & Aug 10am–noon & 3–7pm; Sept–Oct & Dec–May 2–6pm; closed Nov; €6), with dramatic human forms in marble.

Practicalities

The **tourist office** is part of the *mairie* on place Frédéric-Mistral (June Mon–Sat 9am–12.30pm & 2.30–6pm; July & Aug daily 9am–1pm & 3.30–7.30pm; Sept–May Mon–Sat 9am–12.30pm & 2–5.30pm; ⓣ04.94.84.00.69, ⓦmembres.lycos.fr/otsiaups). All the hotels are good value: *Le Provençal* on place Martin-Bidauré (ⓣ04.94.70.00.24, ⓕ04.94.84.06.25; ❸) and the *Grand Hôtel* on place Duchâtel (ⓣ04.94.70.10.82; ❷; ⓕ04.94.70.94.74; closed March; ❷) are both good inexpensive options. There are two **campsites** close to town: the two-star *Camping Les Prés*, to the right off allée Charles-Boyer towards Tourtour (ⓣ04.94.70.00.93, ⓕ04.94.70.14.41; open all year; €11), with bikes to rent nearby, and the three-star *Saint Lazare* 2km along the Moissac road (ⓣ04.94.70.12.86, ⓕ04.94.70.01.55; closed Oct–March; €11.60), which has a pool.

For **meals**, your first choice should be the hotel-restaurant *St-Marc* (ⓣ04.94.70.06.08, ⓔhotel-restaurant-le-st-marc@wanadoo.fr; ❸; closed three weeks in November). Serving local dishes, truffles and boar in season, it offers a very cheap lunch menu and evening menus from €23 (Sept–June closed Tues & Wed). For snacks, try the boulangerie-patisserie À la Claire Fontaine on place Général Giraud or the Boulanger Arpsoise at 12 rue M. Foch.

The Gorges du Verdon and around

From Aups, the road north leads to the western end of the **Gorges du Verdon**. A more dramatic approach crosses the vast military terrain of the Camp de Canjuers from Comps-sur-Artuby. The road runs west through 16km of deserted heath and hills, with each successive horizon higher than the last. When you reach the canyon, it's as if a silent earthquake had taken place during your journey.

This vantage point, known as the **Balcons de la Mescla**, is a memorable *coup de théâtre*, with the view withheld until you are almost upon it. You look down 250m to the base of the V-shaped, 21km-long gorge incised by the River Verdon through piled strata of limestone. Ever changing in its volume and energy, the river falls from Rougon at the top of the gorge, disappearing into tunnels, decelerating for shallow, languid moments and finally exiting in full, steady flow at the **Pont de Galetas**. The huge artificial **Lac de Sainte-Croix**, filled by the Verdon as it leaves the gorge, is great for swimming when the water levels are high; otherwise the beach becomes a bit sludgy. West from the Balcons runs the **Corniche sublime**, the D71, built expressly to give the most breathtaking and hair-raising views crossing the 182-metre Pont de l'Artuby. On the north side, the **Route des Crêtes**, the D952 is even more dramatic – not least because on some of the highest stretches there's nothing to stop you driving straight off into the abyss – but it's not so consistently scenic, even though at some points you look down a sheer 800m drop to the sliver of water below. The mid-section of the Route des Crêtes is one way (westbound only), so if you want to do it all you'll have to start from the more scenic eastern end. It closes each winter from November 15 to March 15.

The entire circuit around the gorge is 130km long and it's cycling country solely for the preternaturally fit. Even for drivers it's hard work, as the hidden bends and hairpins in the road are perilous and, in July and August, so is the traffic.

Public transport around the canyon is less than comprehensive. There's just one bus in each direction between Aix, Moustiers, La Palud, Rougon and Castellane on Monday, Wednesday and Saturday from July to mid-September and just once a week on a Saturday during the rest of the year.

The north side of the gorge: La Palud-sur-Verdon and Rougon

The loop of the Route des Crêtes joins at **LA PALUD-SUR-VERDON**, a tiny village on the northern face of the gorge and the best base from which to explore it. Life in the village revolves around the *Lou Cafetie* bar-restaurant. There are one or two other places to eat and a local produce market on Sunday.

The **tourist office** and the **Maison de l'Environnement** – a newly opened ecological centre – are off the main road in the château of La Palud (daily except Tues mid-March to mid-June & mid-Sept to mid-Nov 10am–noon & 4–6pm, mid-June to mid-Sept 10am–1pm & 4–7pm; Ⓣ & Ⓕ04.92.77.32.02, Ⓦwww.lapaludsurverdon.com; exhibition €4), with a **Bureau des Guides** (July–Aug Mon–Sat 10am–12.30pm & 4–7pm; other month hours erratic – call for information on Ⓣ04.92.77.30.50) on the main road nearby, where you can find out about guided walks, climbing, canyoning, rafting and other activities. UCPA (Union National de Centres Sportifs de Plein Air) in Le Vignal (Ⓣ04.92.77.31.66, Ⓦwww.ucpa.com) has information on all Verdon activities, and is another contact point for guides, as is the climbing shop and restaurant *Le Perroquet Vert* (Ⓣ04.92.77.33.39; menu €18). If you want to **stay**, there's *Le Provence* on the route de la Maline (Ⓣ04.92.77.38.88, Ⓕ04.92.77.31.05; closed Nov–Easter; ❸) and the slightly more expensive *Auberge des Crêtes*, 1km east towards Castellane (Ⓣ04.92.77.38.47, Ⓕ04.92.77.30.40; closed Nov–Easter; ❸). The *Auberge du Point Sublime*, 8km to the east in **ROUGON** (Ⓣ04.92.83.60.35, Ⓕ04.92.83.74.31; ❸), is stunningly situated and not wildly expensive. There's a municipal **campsite**, *Le Grand Canyon*, 800m from the village on the route de Castellane (Ⓣ04.92.77.38.13; Ⓕ04.92.77.30.87). If these are full, there are no fewer than five other campsites around the town. Two **gîtes** to try are *L'Étable*, on route des Crêtes in Palud (Ⓣ04.92.77.30.63), and *Le Wapiti*, just outside the village on the Moustiers road (Ⓣ04.92.77.30.02; closed Nov to Easter), both offering accommodation for around €30. The *Chalet de la Maline*, on route des Crêtes 8km to the south of La Palud (Ⓣ04.92.77.38.05, Ⓔla.maline@wanadoo.fr; closed mid-Nov to Easter; €12), is a mountain refuge run by the Club Alpin Français, and is also a good trailhead from which to start descents into the gorge. La Palud's **youth hostel** (Ⓣ04.92.77.38.72) was closed for renovation during 2004 but scheduled to reopen in 2005.

The south side of the gorge: Aiguines and the Falaise des Cavaliers

AIGUINES, perched high above the **Lac de Sainte-Croix** on its eastern side, has a turreted château (not open to the public) and a history of woodturning – the boules for pétanque made from ancient boxwood roots used to be its speciality. There's some very expensive and beautiful woodwork, as well as pottery and faïence, to be viewed at the small commercial art gallery opposite the **tourist office** (Mon–Fri 9am–noon & 2–5.30pm; Ⓣ04.94.70.21.64, Ⓦwww.aiguines.com).

For **rooms**, there's the hotel-restaurant *Le Vieux Château* (Ⓣ04.94.70.22.95, Ⓕ04.94.84.22.36; ❼, half-board compulsory; closed Nov–March), or the rather characterless *Altitude 823* (Ⓣ04.98.10.22.17, Ⓕ04.98.10.22.16; ❻, half-board compulsory; closed Nov–March). Of the seven **campsites** in the vicinity, *Le Galetas* (Ⓣ04.94.70.20.48; closed mid-Oct to March; €9.60) is almost within diving distance of the lake, a long way down from the village. However, the best place to stay on the south side – as long as you don't suffer from vertigo – is the *Hôtel du Grand Canyon du Verdon* by the dramatic precipice of the Falaise des Cavaliers (Ⓣ04.94.76.91.31, Ⓕ04.94.76.92.29; ❸; closed Nov to Easter), on the Corniche Sublime, a good 20km from Aiguines, with stunning views. The restaurant serves reasonable food.

West of the gorge: Moustiers-Ste-Marie, Riez and Quinson

The complex traffic management and long lines of parked cars on the approach to **MOUSTIERS-STE-MARIE** tell you all you need to know about the summer popularity of the place: once you reach the village, it's little more than a picturesque setting for a shopping expedition, since almost every house seems to be selling the pastel, pretty Moustiers faïence. But it is *very* picturesque, almost absurdly so: the backdrop of sheer cliffs and the single star suspended high above the village being the sort of view that launched a thousand calendars. You can best escape the shoppers by making the steep ascent to the appropriately named **church of Notre Dame de Beauvoir**, and it's all rather more appealing out of season. Just below the village is celebrity chef Alain Ducasse's luxurious **hotel-restaurant** *La Bastide de Moustiers* (Ⓣ04.92.70.47.47, Ⓦwww.bastide-moustiers.com; ❾), set in a seventeenth-century country house, with weekday menus from €42. It's idyllic, except perhaps when the helicopter pad is in use.

A more unspoilt village is low-key **RIEZ**, 15km west of Moustiers, where the main business is derived from the lavender fields that cover this corner of

Provence. Just over the river on the road south is a lavender distillery making essence for the perfume industry. At the other end of the town, 1km along the road to Digne, is the **Maison de l'Abeille** (House of the Bee), a research and visitors' centre (June–Sept daily 10am–12.30pm & 2.30–7.30pm; Oct–May Tues–Sat 2–6pm; free). Visitors can buy various honeys (including the local speciality, lavender honey) and hydromel – the honey alcohol of antiquity made from nectar – and, if you show interest, you'll get an enthusiastic tour.

In size, Riez is more village than town, but it soon becomes clear that it was once more influential than it is now. Some of the houses on **Grande-Rue** and **rue du Marché** – the two streets above the main allées Louis-Gardiol – have rich Renaissance facades, and the **Hôtel de Ville** on place Quinquonces is a former episcopal palace. The scant remains of the sixth-century **cathedral** (freely visited), which was abandoned 400 years ago, have been excavated just across the river from allées Louis-Gardiol. Much more impressive is the **baptistry** across the road (mid-June to mid-Sept Mon, Tues, Fri & Sat 3–7pm; €2), restored in the nineteenth century but originally constructed, like the cathedral, around 600 AD. If you recross the river and follow it downstream, you'll find the even older and much more startling relics of four **Roman columns** standing in a field.

A rather more strenuous walk, heading first for the clock tower above Grande-Rue and then taking the path past the cemetery and on uphill (leaving the cemetery to your left), brings you to a cedar-shaded platform on the hilltop where the pre-Roman Riezians lived. The only building now occupying the site is the eighteenth-century Chapelle Ste-Maxime, with a gaudily patterned interior.

The **tourist office** is at 4 cours allées Louis-Gardiol (July & Aug Mon–Sat 9am–1pm & 3–7pm, Sun 9am–1pm; Sept–June Mon–Fri 8.30am–12.30pm & 1.30–6pm; ⓣ04.92.77.99.09, ⓕ04.92.77.99.07). For **accommodation**, there's an executive-style hotel on the other side of the river, the *Hôtel Carina* (ⓣ04.92.77.85.43, ⓕ04.92.77.85.44; ❹; closed Nov–Easter), with views and comfort to make up for its lack of character. Alternatively head out of town on the route de Valensole, where 1km off the main road you'll find the excellent-value *Château de Pontfrac* (ⓣ04.92.77.78.77, ⓦwww.chateaudepontfrac.com; ❺), offering a swimming pool and access to facilities such as riding stables (bring your own horse). If you want to **eat** in the village and aren't in a rush, try *Le Rempart* on 17 rue du Marché, next to the bell tower (ⓣ04.92.77.89.54); the Provençal and Italian dishes are superb, and a two to three hour meal for most diners seems to be the norm. Lunch menus start at €12, dinners from €17.

Some 21km south of Riez along the D11, the village of **QUINSON** marks the start of the Basses Gorges du Verdon, which if you haven't seen the upper gorge will probably strike you as dramatically scenic. The chief attraction here, however, is the **Musée du Préhistoire des Gorges du Verdon**, route de Montmeyan (Feb, March & Oct–Dec daily except Tues 10am–6pm; April–June & Sept daily except Tues 10am–7pm; July & Aug daily 10am–8pm; €7), designed by the British architect Sir Norman Foster in a clean and sympathetic modern style, so that despite its immense size it does not dominate the village. It's the largest museum of human prehistory in Europe, using the latest audio-visual techniques to chart one million years of human habitation in Provence. In addition to the museum itself, there's a themed path leading past reconstructed prehistoric homes to the **cave of Baume Bonne** (guided visits by arrangement), the most important of the sixty or so archeological sites around Quinson. Excavations here have traced human habitation back 400,000 years.

Castellane

Few towns can have as dramatic a setting as **CASTELLANE**, east of the gorge, 12km upstream from La Palud on the Route Napoléon (see below), and sitting at the foot of an immense rock face topped by a chapel, **Notre Dame du Roc**. Billed as the "gateway" to the Gorges du Verdon, Castellane's chief business is the servicing of activity-based tourism. Houses in the old part of town huddle together as if seeking protection from the sheer violence of the landscape, with some lanes barely shoulder-wide. There's not a lot to see, so you might as well climb up to the chapel – thirty minutes from behind the modern church. The gorge itself is out of sight, but the view is still worth the trouble.

The **tourist office**, at the top of rue Nationale (July & Aug Mon–Sat 9am–12.30pm & 2–7pm, Sun 10am–12.30pm; Sept–June Mon–Fri 9am–noon & 2–6pm; Ⓣ04.92.83.61.14, Ⓦwww.castellane.org), can provide a full list of the many **hotels** and campsites in the village and its environs. The *Auberge Bon Accueil* on place Marcel-Sauvaire (Ⓣ04.92.83.62.01; Ⓦwww.auberge-du-bon-accueil.com; ❷; closed mid-Oct to mid-March) is one of the cheapest, while the three-star *Hôtel du Commerce* on place de l'Église (Ⓣ04.92.83.61.00, Ⓦwww.hotel-fradet.com; ❹; closed Nov–Feb) is the swanky option, and has an amazing **restaurant** serving Provençal menus from €21 up. The closest **campsite** to town, a mere hundred metres off place Marcel-Sauvaire on boulevard Frédéric Mistral, is *Le Frédéric Mistral* (Ⓣ04.92.83.62.27, closed mid-Nov to Feb). Castellane is full of adventure activity specialists offering everything from **canyoning** to **canoeing** on the Lac de Castellane and the Gorges du Verdon. For information, go to Aqua Verdon at 8 rue Nationale (Ⓣ04.92.83.72.75, Ⓦwww.aquaverdon.com) or try Aboard Rafting (Ⓣ04.92.83.76.11) on place de l'Église, or Aqua Viva Est (Ⓣ04.92.83.75.74) on boulevard de la République, both of which also rent out mountain **bikes**.

The Route Napoléon to Sisteron

North of Castellane, the **Route Napoléon** passes through the barren scrubby rocklands of some of the most obscure and empty parts of Provence. The road was built in the 1930s to commemorate the great leader's journey north through Haute Provence on return from exile on Elba in 1815, in the most audacious and vain recapture of power in French history. Using mule paths still deep with winter snow, Napoleon and his 700 soldiers forged ahead towards **Digne-les-Bains** and **Sisteron** on their way to Grenoble – a total of 350km – in just six days. One hundred days later, he lost the battle of Waterloo and was permanently incarcerated on the island of St Helena.

At Barrème, the road is joined by the narrow-gauge **Chemins de Fer de la Provence** (see box, p.1187), also known as the Train des Pignes, which runs between Nice and Digne-les-Bains. Other stations on the line are Annot and St-André-les-Alpes; though neither has bus connections with Castellane, the town is connected to both Nice and Marseille by bus. Local tourist offices will have timetables.

Digne-les-Bains

DIGNE-LES-BAINS is the chief town of the Alpes-de-Haute-Provence *département*, and lies in a superb position between the Durance valley and the start of the real mountains. Bustling by day but rather lifeless in the evening, it has particular attractions for geologists and admirers of Tibet. Covering over 150,000 hectares to the north and east of Dignes, the **Réserve Naturelle Géologique de Haute Provence** is the largest geological reserve in Europe, with fossils dating back 300 million years. The starting point is the **Musée-Promenade** (Ⓣ04.92.36.70.70; April–Oct daily 9am–noon & 2–5.30pm, closes Fri 4.30pm; Nov–March Mon–Fri 9am–noon & 2–5.30pm; €4.60) just north of the city, down to the left after the bridge across the Bléone on the Barles road, with extremely good videos, workshops and exhibitions on the reserve, and a new gallery of fossilized insects. Themed walks fan out from the museum. A couple of kilometres further along the Barles road you can see, on a bank to your left, a wall of ammonites.

The town's connection with Tibet is through the explorer Alexandra David-Neel, who managed to spend two months in the forbidden city of Lhasa disguised as a beggar in 1924. She spent the last years of her long life in Digne, dying there at the age of 101, and her house, Samten Dzong, at 27 av du Maréchal-Juin, is now home to the **Musée Alexandra David-Neel** (guided visits only; July–Sept at 10am, 2pm, 3.30pm & 4.30pm; Oct–June at 10am, 2pm & 4pm; free), devoted to her memory. The Dalai Lama himself has visited the place twice. Also a cut above the normal is the town's recently renovated municipal museum, the **Musée Gassendi** at 64 bd Gassendi (daily except Tues: April–Sept 11am–7pm; Oct–March 1.30–5.30pm; €4), with some great sixteenth- to nineteenth-century paintings and homages to local seventeenth-century mathematician and savant Pierre Gassendi.

The **tourist office** is on the Rond-Point du 11–Novembre-1918 (summer Mon–Sat 8.45am–12.30pm & 2–6.30pm, Sun 10am–noon; winter Mon–Sat 8.45am–noon & 2–6pm; Ⓣ04.92.36.62.62, Ⓦwww.ot-dignelesbains.fr), with the **gare routière** adjacent. The **gare Chemins de Fer de la Provence** is to the west over the river on avenue Pierre-Sémard; there are no longer any passenger trains from the adjacent *gare SNCF*. A very cheap **hotel** option is the *Origan*, 6 rue Pied-de-Ville (Ⓣ & Ⓕ04.92.31.62.13, Ⓦwww.origan.fr; ❶), with an excellent **restaurant** which has menus starting at €18 (closed Mon). *Le Grand Paris*, 19 bd Thiers (Ⓣ04.92.31.11.15, Ⓦwww.hotel-grand-paris.com; ❺; closed Dec–Feb), is considerably more luxurious and also has a good, though expensive, restaurant (closed midday Mon & Tues out of season; €25 lunchtime menu Mon–Sat, otherwise from €41).

Sisteron

The Route Napoléon leads eventually to **SISTERON**, 25km northwest of Digne as the crow flies, and the most important mountain gateway to Provence. The site has been fortified since time immemorial and even now, half destroyed by the Anglo-American bombardment of 1944, its citadel stands as a fearsome sentinel over the city and the solitary bridge across the River Durance.

A visit to the **citadel** (April–Nov daily 9am–6.30pm; €4.80) is highly rewarding, with 360° views from the upper rampart, while far below a superbly atmospheric subterranean passage leads down 280 steps to another vantage point, though the door at the bottom is frequently locked. There is a leaflet in English but no guides, just recordings in French attempting to re-create historic moments, such as Napoleon's march, of course, and the imprisonment in 1639 of Jan Kazimierz, the future king of Poland. Most of the extant defences were constructed after the Wars of Religion, and added to a century later by Vauban when Sisteron was a front-line fort against neighbouring Savoy. The eleventh-century castle was destroyed in the mid-thirteenth century during a pogrom against the local Jewish population.

In July and August, the festival known as Nuits de la Citadelle has open-air performances of music, drama and dance in the citadel grounds. There is also a small **historical museum** with a room dedicated to Napoleon, and temporary art exhibitions in the vertiginous late medieval chapel, **Notre-Dame-du-Château**, restored to its Gothic glory and given very beautiful subdued stained-glass windows in the 1970s.

Back in Sisteron's old town, you'll see three huge **towers**, which belonged to the ramparts built in 1370. Beside them is the **Cathédrale Notre-Dame-des-Pommiers** (daily 3–6pm), a well-proportioned twelfth-century church whose entryway is flanked by marble columns, but whose interior contains nothing of interest. From the cathedral, rue Deleuze leads to **place de l'Horloge**, where the Wednesday and Saturday **market** is held and which, on the second Saturday of every month, hosts a fair.

Arriving by train at Sisteron, turn right out of the **gare SNCF** along avenue de la Libération until you reach place de la République, where you'll find the **tourist office** (July & Aug Mon–Sat 9am–7pm, Sun 10am–noon & 2–5pm; Sept–June Mon–Sat 9am–noon & 2–6pm; ⓣ04.92.61.12.03, ⓦwww.sisteron.com) and the **gare routière**. The genteel and old-fashioned *Grand Hôtel du Cours* on allée de Verdon (ⓣ04.92.61.04.51, ⓔhotelducours@wanadoo.fr; ❹; closed mid-Nov to mid-March) is the best **hotel** in town. For cheaper rooms, head for *La Citadelle* (see below). Sisteron's four-star **campsite** is across the river and 3km along the D951 (ⓣ04.92.61.19.69; closed Nov–Feb; €13 for two people and a tent).

The food in Sisteron's **restaurants** is nothing special, though the view down the valley from the terrace of the *Hôtel-Restaurant de la Citadelle*, 126 rue Saunerie, certainly is (ⓣ06.82.67.80.76, ⓕ04.92.61.06.39; ❶; menus from €13.50). *Le Cours*, on the allée de Verdon (ⓣ04.92.61.00.50), serves copious meals, with the renowned *gigot d'agneau de Sisteron* included on a €20 menu, and you'll find plenty of eating places along rue Saunerie and on the squares around the clock tower. *Le Mondial* bar, on the left at the top of rue Droite, stays open late, as does *L'Horloge* on place de l'Horloge. Finally, if you fancy a **swim**, there's a large artificial lake between the allée de Verdon and the river.

Northeast Provence

Depending on the season, the **northeastern corner of Provence** is two different worlds. In winter, the sheep and shepherds find warmer pastures, leaving the snowy heights to horned mouflons, chamois and the perfectly camouflaged ermine. The villages where shepherds came to summer markets are battened down for the long, cold haul, while modern conglomerations of Swiss-style chalet houses, sports shops and discotheques come to life around the ski lifts. From November to May many of the mountain road passes are closed, cutting off the dreamy northern town of **Barcelonnette** from its lower neighbours.

In spring, the fruit trees in the narrow valley orchards blossom, and melting waters swell the Vésubie, the Tinée and the Roya, sometimes flooding villages and carrying whole streets away. In summer and early autumn you move from the valleys to the snow-capped peaks through groves of chestnut and olive

The Parc National du Mercantour

The **Parc National du Mercantour** is a long, narrow band of mountainland running for 75km close to the Italian border, from south of the town of Barcelonnette almost as far as Sospel, 16km north of the Mediterranean. The area is a haven for wildlife, with colonies of chamois, mouflon, ibex and marmots, breeding pairs of golden eagles and other rare birds of prey, great spotted woodpeckers and hoopoes, blackcocks and ptarmigan. The flora too is very special, with many unique species of lilies, orchids and Alpine plants, including the rare multi-flowering saxifrage.

It's crossed by numerous paths, including the GR5 and GR52, with refuge huts providing basic food and bedding for hikers. For more detailed information, contact the **Maisons du Parc** in Barcelonnette, St-Étienne-de-Tinée or St-Martin-Vésubie, which provide maps and accommodation details as well as advice on footpaths and weather conditions. Camping, lighting fires, picking flowers, playing radios or doing anything that might disturb the delicate environment is strictly outlawed.

trees, then pine forests edged with wild raspberries and bilberries, up to moors and grassy slopes covered with Alpine flowers.

An uninhabited area of 68,500 hectares along the Italian border has been designated the **Parc National du Mercantour** (see box, above). It can be explored from the small towns of **St-Étienne-de-Tinée**, **St-Martin-Vésubie, St-Sauveur-sur-Tinée** and from the **upper Roya valley**, but all the countryside in this mountainous region is breathtaking. To the south, the Italianate town of Sospel is a real delight.

Transport other than by foot or vehicle is a problem. Apart from the Turin–Nice train line down the Roya valley, there are regular bus connections going out from Barcelonnette or from Sospel but they don't meet, and there are only infrequent buses between villages on market days.

Barcelonnette

BARCELONNETTE is a place of immaculate charm, with snow-capped mountains visible at every turn. It's not very big, and a more ideal spot for doing nothing would be hard to find. The central square, **place Manuel**, has café tables from which to gaze at the blue sky or at the white clock tower commemorating the centenary of the 1848 Revolution. It's close to several ski resorts and to the northern edge of the Parc du Mercantour.

The **Maison du Parc** for the Mercantour (summer only: June 15–30 & Sept 1–15 daily 3–6pm; July & Aug 10am–noon & 3–7pm; ⓣ04.92.81.21.31, ⓦwww.parc-mercantour.com) shares premises at 10 av de la Libération with the **Musée de la Vallée** (June & Sept Tues–Sat 3–7pm; July 1–10 2.30–6pm; July 12–end Aug 10am–noon & 2.30–7pm; Oct–May groups by arrangement; €3.20), which details the popular emigration to Mexico during the nineteenth century. Barcelonnette is full of Mexican connections (many came back with fortunes); during the August Mexican festival, the **Maison du Mexique**, opposite the Musée de la Vallée, puts on films and exhibitions.

Barcelonnette's **tourist office** is on place Frédéric-Mistral (July & Aug daily 9am–8pm; Sept–June Mon–Sat 9am–noon & 2–6pm; ⓣ04.92.81.04.71, ⓦwww.barcelonnette.com). The best place to **stay** is the Mexican-style *Azteca* on rue François-Arnaud (ⓣ04.92.81.46.36, ⓦwww.hotel-azteca.fr.st; 4), closely followed by the *Grande Épervière*, 18 rue des Trois-Frères-Arnaud (ⓣ04.92.81.00.70, ⓦwww.hotel-grande-eperviere.com; ❸). The *Grand Hôtel*, overlooking place Manuel (ⓣ04.92.81.03.14, ⓦwww.grandhotelbarcelonnette.fr.fm; ❸), is one of the cheaper options. There are three local **campsites**, the

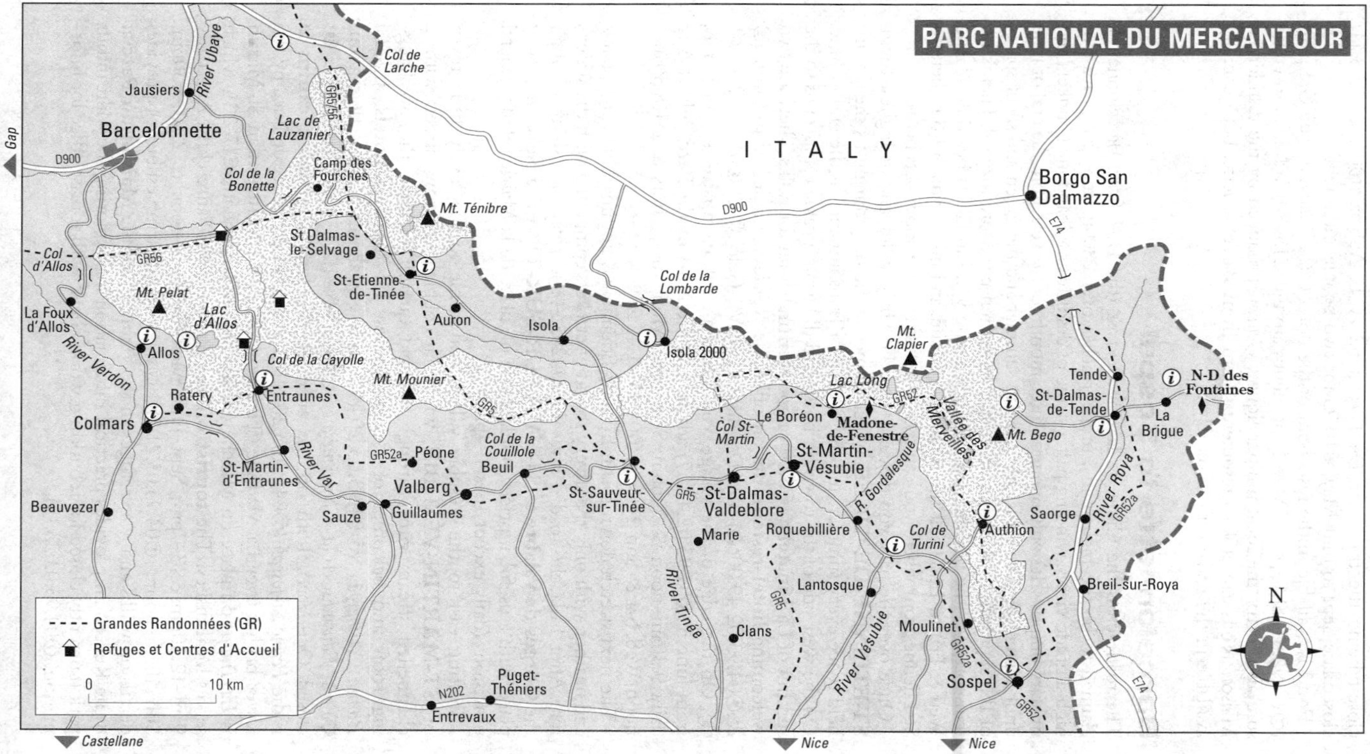

PARC NATIONAL DU MERCANTOUR

- - - Grandes Randonnées (GR)

Refuges et Centres d'Accueil

0 10 km

closest being the three-star *Du Plan* at 52 av E.-Aubert (Ⓣ04.92.81.08.11; closed late Sept to mid-May; €10.95 for two people and a tent).

Food is available in the restaurant of the hotel *Cheval Blanc*, on rue Grenette (Ⓣ04.92.81.00.19; open May–Sept menus around €15–20). While in town be sure also to try the local juniper liquor, *Genepy*, produced by the distiller La Maison Rousseau at La Fresquiere, 10km from Barcelonnette, but generally available in the town on market days.

Barcelonnette to Sospel

The road across the Cime de la Bonette pass (the D64 from Barcelonnette), claimed to be the highest in Europe, reaches over 2800m and gives a feast of high-altitude views, winding past a string of desolate and abandoned bunkers and military outposts. It's only open for three months of the year, from the end of June until September. The air is cold even in summer and the green and silent spaces of the approach to the summit, circled by barren peaks, are magical. There's no transport over the pass, but from Barcelonnette you can take a bus (July & Aug Wed & Fri) to Jausiers at the route's north end, and hike or hitch from there to St-Étienne, from where you can then connect to Nice and points between.

Once over the pass, you descend into the Tinée valley and its highest town, **ST-ÉTIENNE-DE-TINÉE**, which comes to life only during its sheep fairs, held twice every summer, and the Fête de la Transhumance at the end of June. On the west side of the town off boulevard d'Auron, a cable car ascends to the summit of **La Pinatelle** (€5.50), a good starting point for walks. There are two welcoming **hotel-restaurants** on offer: the *Regalivou*, boulevard d'Auron (Ⓣ & Ⓕ04.93.02.49.00; ❸), and *Des Amis*, 1 rue Val-Gélé (Ⓣ & Ⓕ04.93.02.40.30; ❹). On the edge of the village, you'll find a small **campsite** (summer only, from June 5; Ⓣ04.93.02.41.57) adjacent to the **Maison du Parc** (July & Aug daily 9.30am–noon & 2–6pm; Sept–June Mon, Tues, Thurs & Fri 8.30am–noon, Wed, Sat & Sun 2–6pm; Ⓣ04.93.01.42.27).

The next stretch downstream from St-Étienne has nothing but white quartz and heather, with only the silvery sound of crickets competing with the water's roar. After Isola, the road – now the D2205 – and river turn south through the **Gorges de Valabre** to **ST-SAUVEUR-SUR-TINÉE**, a pleasantly sleepy place, with a useful, if pricey, boulangerie on place de la Mairie selling general provisions (daily except Tues 1–4pm).

Shifting east to the Vésubie valley, you come to the lovely little town of **ST-MARTIN-VÉSUBIE** where a cobbled, narrow street with a channelled stream runs through the old quarter beneath the overhanging roofs and balconies of Gothic houses. Of the four **hotels**, try *La Bonne Auberge* (Ⓣ04.93.03.20.49, Ⓦwww.labonneauberge.06.fr.com; ❷) or *Edward's et la Châtaigneraie* (Ⓣ04.93.03.21.22, Ⓕ04.93.03.33.99; ❸; closed Oct–May), both on the allées de Verdon. The closest **campsite** is the *Ferme St-Joseph* (Ⓣ04.93.03.20.14; all year), on the route de Nice by the lower bridge over La Madone. The most pleasant **restaurant** in St-Martin is *La Trappa* on place du Marché (closed Dec & Jan; menus €17–22), which serves local dishes. The **tourist office** on place Félix-Faure (July–Aug daily 9am–12.30pm & 3–7pm; Sept–June Mon–Sat 9am–noon & 2.30–5.30pm, Sun 10am–noon; Ⓣ04.93.03.21.28; Ⓦwww.saintmartinvesubie.fr) provides details on walks and *gîtes*/refuges in the vicinity, and the **Maison du Parc** at 8 rue Kellerman provides practical information for exploring the Mercantour park (currently closed for rebuilding work; check with tourist office for information; Ⓣ04.93.03.23.15).

Sospel and the Roya valley

The D2566 from the Vésubie valley crosses the dramatic col de Turini to join the **Roya valley** at **SOSPEL**, a dreamy Italianate town spanning the gentle River Bévéra. You may find it over-tranquil after the excitements of the high mountains or the flashy speed of the Côte d'Azur, but it can make a pleasant break.

The main street, **avenue Jean-Médecin**, follows the river on its southern bank. The central bridge, the **Vieux Pont**, was built in the eleventh century to link the town centre on the south bank with its suburb across the river. The best approach to the old town is from the eastern place St-Pierre, along the gloomy, deeply shadowed rue St-Pierre. Suddenly it opens up into **place St-Michel**, one of the most beautiful series of peaches-and-cream Baroque facades in all Provence, made up of the **Église St-Michel**, two chapels and several arcaded houses. The road behind the church, rue de l'Abbaye, reached by steps between the chapels, leads up to an ivy-covered **castle** ruin, from which you get a good view of the town. An even better view can be had from the **Fort St-Roch**, part of the ignominious interwar Maginot Line, along chemin de St-Roch, which houses the **Musée de la Résistance**, illustrating the courageous local Resistance movement during World War II (April–June & Oct Sat & Sun 2–6pm; July–Sept Tues–Sun 2–6pm; €5).

The **gare SNCF** is southeast of the town on avenue A.-Borriglione, which becomes avenue des Martyrs-de-la-Résistance, before leading down to the park on place des Platanes opposite place St-Pierre. The **tourist office** is housed in the Vieux Pont (daily: April–Sept 9.30am–noon & 2–6pm; Oct–March 9.30am–noon & 2–5pm; Ⓣ04.93.04.15.80, Ⓕ04.93.04.19.96). If you want to **stay**, the *Hôtel de France*, 9 bd de Verdun (Ⓣ04.93.04.00.01, Ⓕ04.93.04.20.46; ❸), and the *Auberge Provençale*, on route du Col de Castillon, 1500m uphill from the town (Ⓣ04.93.04.00.31, Ⓔaubpro@aol.com; ❹), offer comparable quality, the latter with a pleasant garden and terrace from which to admire the town. There are three **campsites** around Sospel, the closest of which is *Le Mas Fleuri* in quartier La Vasta (Ⓣ04.93.04.03.48, Ⓦwww.camping-mas-fleuri.com; all year; €14.50 for two people and a tent), with its own pool, 2km along the D2566 to Moulinet, following the river upstream.

There are various **eating** places along avenue Jean-Médecin. Alternatively, try *L'Escargot d'Or*, 3 bd de Verdun (Ⓣ04.93.04.00.43; closed Thurs & Nov), just across the eastern bridge, where you can eat for between €12.50 and €29.50 on a terrace above the river.

The upper Roya valley

One of the strangest sights in the Provençal Alps is best approached from **ST-DALMAS-DE-TENDE** in the upper Roya valley, three stops on the train from Sospel. The first person to stumble upon the lakes and tumbled rocks of the **Vallée des Merveilles**, on the western flank of Mount Bego, was a fifteenth-century traveller who had lost his way. He described it as "an infernal place with figures of the devil and thousands of demons scratched on the rocks": a pretty accurate description, except that some of the carvings are of animals, tools, people working and mysterious symbols, dated to some time in the second millennium BC.

The easiest route into the valley is the ten-kilometre hike (5–7hr there and back) that starts at *Les Mesches Refuge*, about 8km west of St-Dalmas-de-Tende, on the D91. The engravings are beyond the *Refuge des Merveilles*. Note that certain areas are out of bounds unless accompanied by an official guide – and remember that blue skies and sun can quickly turn into violent hailstorms and lightning, so go prepared, properly shod and clothed, and take your own food and water. **Guided walks** depart from the refuge and last between 2hr 30min and 3hr 30min (June, Sept & Oct weekends only, 8am & 1pm; July–Aug daily 8am, 11am, 1pm, 3pm; €8; contact Maison du Parc in Tende Ⓣ04.93.04.67.00 or local tourist offices; one guide speaks English).

St-Dalmas is the nearest town to the Vallée des Merveilles and has a reasonably priced **hotel** on rue des Martyrs-de-la-Résistance, the Terminus (Ⓣ04.93.04.96.96, Ⓕ04.93.04.96.97; ❷).

LA BRIGUE, one stop up the line from St-Dalmas-de-Tende, is a good base for the Vallée des Merveilles, with some good-value hotels. While you're here, make the trip 4km east of town to the sanctuary of **Notre-Dame-des-Fontaines**, whose frescoes were executed by one Jean Canavéso at around the same time as the anonymous fifteenth-century traveller was freaking out about the demons of the Vallée des Merveilles. The frescoes, which cover the entire building, are akin to an arcade of video nasties. The goriest detail is a devil extracting Judas's soul from his disembowelled innards. The chapel is open in the summer (June–Sept daily except Tues 10am–noon & 2–5.30pm; closed Thurs afternoon; €1.50), and in the winter you can visit it with a guide from the **tourist office** on place St-Martin (summer daily 9am–12.30pm & 1.30–5pm; winter Tues–Sat 9.30am–12.30pm & 1.30–4.30pm; Ⓣ04.93.04.60.04, Ⓦwww.labrigue-tourisme.org; closed mid-Jan to mid-Feb). The three **hotels** in La Brigue are: *Le Mirval*, rue Vincent-Ferrier (Ⓣ04.93.04.63.71, Ⓕ04.93.04.79.81; ❸); and, on place St-Martin, the *Auberge St-Martin* (Ⓣ04.93.04.62.17, Ⓕ04.93.04.89.66; closed mid-Nov–Feb; ❷) and the *Fleurs des Alpes* (Ⓣ04.93.04.61.05, Ⓕ04.93.04.59.68; ❷).

One more stop north on the train line brings you to **TENDE**, where the French spoken has a distinctly Italian accent. If you've missed the Vallée des Merveilles engravings you can see them reproduced outside the beautifully designed **Musée des Merveilles** on avenue du 16-Septembre-1947 (May to mid-Oct daily 10am–6.30pm; mid-Oct to April daily except Tues 10am–5pm; €4.57), a very contemporary museum covering the wildlife, prehistory and geology of the region. That apart, the old town is fun to wander through, looking at the symbols of old trades on the door lintels, the overhanging roofs and multiple balconies. The **tourist office** is on avenue du 16-Septembre-1947 (May–Sept Mon–Sat 9am–12.30pm & 2–6pm; Oct–April Mon–Sat 9am–12.30pm & 2–5.30pm; Ⓣ04.93.04.73.71, Ⓕ04.93.04.35.09). To **stay**, there's the basic *Du Centre* on place de la République (Ⓣ04.93.04.62.19; ❶). Tende has plenty of shops and restaurants, though nothing very special on the gourmet front.

Travel details

Trains

Aix-en-Provence to: Briançon (2–3 daily; 3hr 40min); Marseille (every 30min; 30–45min); Sisteron (3–4 daily; 1hr 20min).
Aix-en-Provence TGV to: Avignon TGV (17 daily; 25min); Lyon (10 daily; 1hr 35min); Marseille (10 daily; 15 min); Paris (10 daily; 3 hr); Paris CDG Airport (4 daily; 3hr 20 min); Valence TGV (6 daily; 1hr).
Arles to: Avignon (11–16 daily; 20min); Avignon TGV (4 daily; 40 min); Lyon (10 daily; 2hr 45min); Marseille (frequent; 45min–1hr).
Avignon to: Arles (hourly; 20–45min); Cavaillon (9–14 daily; 30min); Lyon (8–11 daily; 2hr 20min); Marseille (4–13 daily; 1hr 20min); Orange (every 15min-1hr; 15–25min); Valence (half hourly at peak times; 1hr 25min); Vienne (11 daily; 2hr).

Avignon TGV to: Aix-en-Provence TGV (9 daily; 25min); Lyon (13 daily; 1hr 30min); Marseille (12 daily; 30 min); Paris (8 daily; 2hr 40min); Paris CDG Airport (6 daily; 3hr 30min); Valence TGV (9 daily; 30–40min).
Digne to: Nice (4 daily; 3hr 20min).
Lyon (La Part-Dieu or Perrache) to: Annecy (8 daily; 2hr 15min); Arles (9 daily; 2hr 45min); Avignon (11 daily; 2hr 20min); Avignon TGV (16 daily; 1hr 15min); Bourg-en-Bresse (8–14 daily; 50min–1hr 15min; Clermont-Ferrand (5–8 daily; 3hr); Dijon (13–18 daily; 2hr); Grenoble (16–21 daily; 1hr 30min–2hr); Lille-Europe (9 daily; 3hr 10min); Marseille (every 2hr; 2hr 10min–3hr 45min); Montélimar (9 daily; 1hr 35min); Orange (8 daily; 2hr 5min); Paris (hourly; 2hr); Paris CDG Airport (10 daily; 2hr 10min); Roanne (hourly; 1hr 30min); St-Étienne (hourly, more frequent at peak times; 45min–1hr); Tain l'Hermitage (hourly; 1hr); Valence (hourly; 1hr 5min); Valence TGV (11 daily; 35–40min); Vienne (frequent; 20min).
Lyon St-Exupéry TGV to: Marseille (1 daily; 1hr 30min); Paris (9–10 daily; 1hr 50min).
Sospel to: La Brigue (1 daily; 40min); Nice (5–6 daily; 50min); St-Dalmas-de-Tende (3 daily; 40min); Tende (3 daily; 50min).
Valence to: Briançon (3 daily; 3hr 45min); Die (3–5 daily; 1hr 10min); Gap (3–5 daily; 2hr 30min); Grenoble (18–20 daily; 1hr 15min–1hr 40min); Montélimar (frequent: approx hrly at peak times; 30min), Tain l'Hermitage (frequent; 12min).
Valence TGV to: Aix-en-Provence TGV (6 daily; 1hr); Avignon TGV (13 daily; 35min); Marseille (14 daily; 1hr 10min); Paris (9 daily; 2hr 10min); Paris CDG Airport (7 daily; 2hr 50min).
Vienne to: Avignon (9 daily; 2hr); Lyon (frequent; 20–30min); Valence (frequent; 50min).

Buses

Aix-en-Provence to: Apt (2 daily; 1hr 55min); Arles (6 daily; 1hr 30min); Avignon (1–6 daily; 1hr 15min); Barcelonnette (1 daily; 3hr 5min); Les Baux (1 daily; 1hr 10min); Carpentras (2 daily; 1hr 40min); Cavaillon (2 daily; 1hr); Draguignan (2 daily; 2hr 55min); Marseille (frequent; 30–50min); Sisteron (2–4 daily; 2hr); Vauvenargues (2–7 daily; 30min).
Arles to: Aix (5 daily; 1hr 15min); Avignon (5 daily; 50min); Avignon TGV (5 daily; 35–40min); Cavaillon (3 daily; 1hr 15min); Stes-Maries-de-la-Mer (6 daily; 50min); St-Rémy (3 daily; 25–30min).
Aups to: Aiguines (1 daily; 35min); Cotignac (2 daily; 20–25min); Draguignan (2–6 daily; 40min–1hr); Sillans (2 daily; 10min); Tourtour (2–4 daily; 10–20min).
Avignon to: Aix (1–6 daily; 1hr 15min); Apt (6 daily; 1hr 10min–1hr 30min); Arles (5 daily; 50min); Les Baux (4 daily; 45min); Carpentras (frequent; 35–45min); Cavaillon (frequent; 35min); Châteauneuf-du-Pape (1–2 daily; 30–45min); Digne (1–2 daily; 3hr 10min); Fontaine-de-Vaucluse (7 daily; 55min); L'Isle-sur-la-Sorgue (19 daily; 40min); Orange (Mon–Fri every 30–45min; Sun 5 trains; 45min); St-Rémy (4 daily; 40min); Vaison (2–8 daily; 1hr 25min).
Barcelonnette to: Digne (1 daily; 1hr 45min); Gap (2 daily; 1hr 20min); Marseille (1 daily; 3hr 50min).
Carpentras to: Aix (2–3 daily; 1hr 25min–1hr 50min); Avignon (frequent; 35–45min); Beaumes (1–2 daily; 20min); Cavaillon (2–4 daily; 45min); Gigondas (1–3 daily; 30min); L'Isle-sur-la-Sorgue (2–3 daily; 20min); Marseille (2–4 daily; 1hr 15min–2hr 5min); Orange (4–5 daily; 40–45min); Sablet (1–3 daily; 35min); Vacqueyras (1–3 daily; 30min); Vaison (1–3 daily; 45min).
Cavaillon to: Gordes (3–4 daily; 25–30 min).
Digne to: Aix (3 daily; 2hr); Aups (2 daily; 30–40min); Avignon (1–2 daily; 3hr 15min); Barcelonnette (1 daily; 1hr 30min); Castellane (1 daily; 1hr 10min); Grenoble (1 daily; 4hr 50min); Marseille (4 daily; 2hr–2hr 30min); Moustiers-Ste-Marie (1daily; 1hr 20min); Nice (2 daily; 3hr–3hr 15 min); Sisteron (2 daily; 45–50min).
Draguignan to: Aups (1–2 daily; 1hr 10min); Moustiers-Ste-Marie (1–2 daily; 2hr); Nice airport (2 daily; 1hr).
Gordes to: Cavaillon (3–4 daily; 30–35min).
Lyon to: St-Martin-en-Haut (2–9 daily; 55min); Vienne (2 daily; 40min–1hr 20min).
Orange to: Avignon (Mon–Sat hourly; Sun 5 trains; 50min); Carpentras (4–5 daily; 40–45min); Châteauneuf-du-Pape (1–5 daily; 25min); Sablet (1–3 daily; 35min); Seguret (3 daily; 40min); Sérignan (3 daily; 20min); Vaison (2–11 daily; 40–50min).
St Rémy to: Les Baux (4 daily; 15–20min).
Sospel to: Menton (2–5 daily; 40–45min).

15

The Côte d'Azur

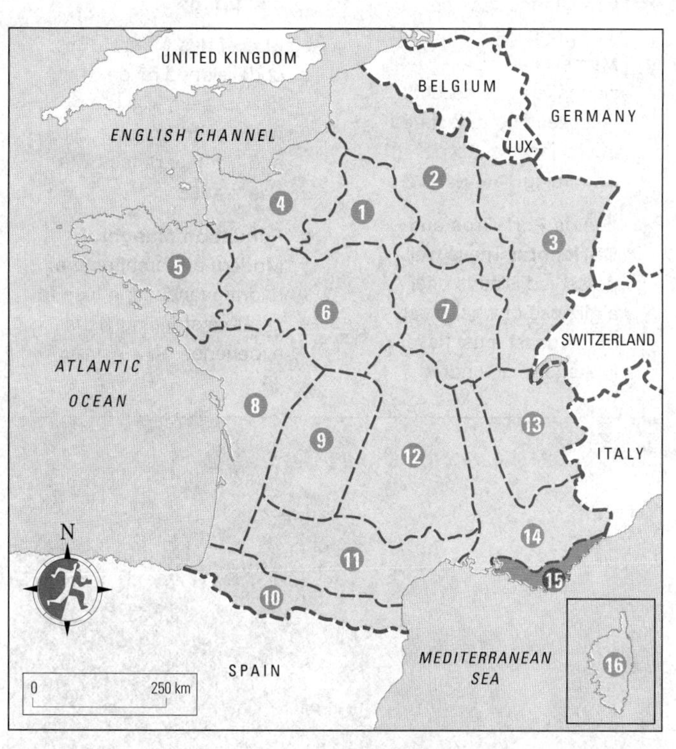

15 THE CÔTE D'AZUR

CHAPTER 15 **Highlights**

* **Vieux Port, Marseille** The gritty port, with its bars, cafés and restaurants, attracts the most colourful characters in southern France. See p.1136

* **Les Calanques** The limestone cliffs between Marseille and Cassis make for excellent hikes leading to isolated coves in which to go swimming. See p.1146

* **Îles de Port-Cros and St-Honorat** These well-preserved islands offer a glimpse of what much of the coast must have looked like a hundred years ago. See pp.1155 & 1177

* **Nice** The Riviera's capital of street life is laid back, surprisingly cultured and easy to enjoy, whatever your budget. See p.1186

* **Massif des Maures** This undeveloped range of hazy coastal hills is a world apart from the glitz and glamour of the Côte. See p.1158

* **Fondation Maeght** Modern art, architecture and the landscape fuse to create a stunning visual experience. See p.1184

△ Sunset, Cannes

15

The Côte d'Azur

The **Côte d'Azur** polarizes opinions like few other places in France. For some, it is the quintessential Mediterranean playground – the glamour queen of the coast – for others, it has become almost a parody of its image, an overdeveloped expensive victim of its own hype.

But in the gaps between the uncontrolled and often eclectic developments, and on the offshore islands, the remarkable beauty of the hills and land's edge, the scent of the plant life, the mimosa blossom in February and the impossibly

Food and wine of the Côte d'Azur

The **Côte d'Azur**, as part of Provence, shares its culinary fundamentals of olive oil, garlic and the herbs that flourish in dry soil, its gorgeous vegetables and fruits, plus Menton's lemons, the goat's cheeses and, of course, the predominance of fish.

The fish soups of **bouillabaisse**, famous in Marseille, and **bourride**, served with a garlic and chilli-flavoured mayonnaise known as *rouille*, are served all along the coast, as are **fish** covered with Provençal herbs and grilled over an open flame. **Seafood** – from spider crabs to clams, sea urchins to crayfish, crabs, lobster, mussels and oysters – are piled onto huge *plateaux de mer*, which don't necessarily represent Mediterranean harvest, more the luxury associated with this coast.

The **Italian influence** is even stronger on the coast than it is inland, particularly in Nice, with delicate ravioli stuffed with asparagus, prawns, wild mushrooms or *pestou*, pizzas with wafer-thin bases and every sort of pasta as a vehicle for anchovies, olives, garlic and tomatoes. **Nice** has its own specialities, such as *socca*, a chickpea flour pancake, *pissaladière*, a tart of fried onions with anchovies and black olives, *salade niçoise* and *pan bagnat*, which combines egg, olives, salad, tuna and olive oil, and *mesclum*, a salad of bitter leaves including dandelion: consequently, Nice is about as good a spot to enjoy cheap street food as you'll find. *Petits farcies* – stuffed aubergines, peppers or tomatoes – are a standard feature on Côte d'Azur menus, as well as in inland Provence.

The Italian **dessert** tiramisu, made of mascarpone cheese, chocolate and cream, appears in Nice, while St-Tropez has its own sweet speciality in the sickly *tarte Tropezienne*. The sweet chestnuts that grow in the Massif des Maures are candied or turned into purée. Outlets for ice cream and sorbets are ubiquitous.

As for **wine**, the rosés of Provence might not have great status in the viniculture hierarchy, but for baking summer days they are hard to beat. The best of the Côte wines come from Bandol: Cassis too has its own *appellation*, and around Nice the Bellet wines are worth discovering. Fancy cocktails are a Côte speciality, and *pastis* is the preferred thirst quencher at any time of the day.

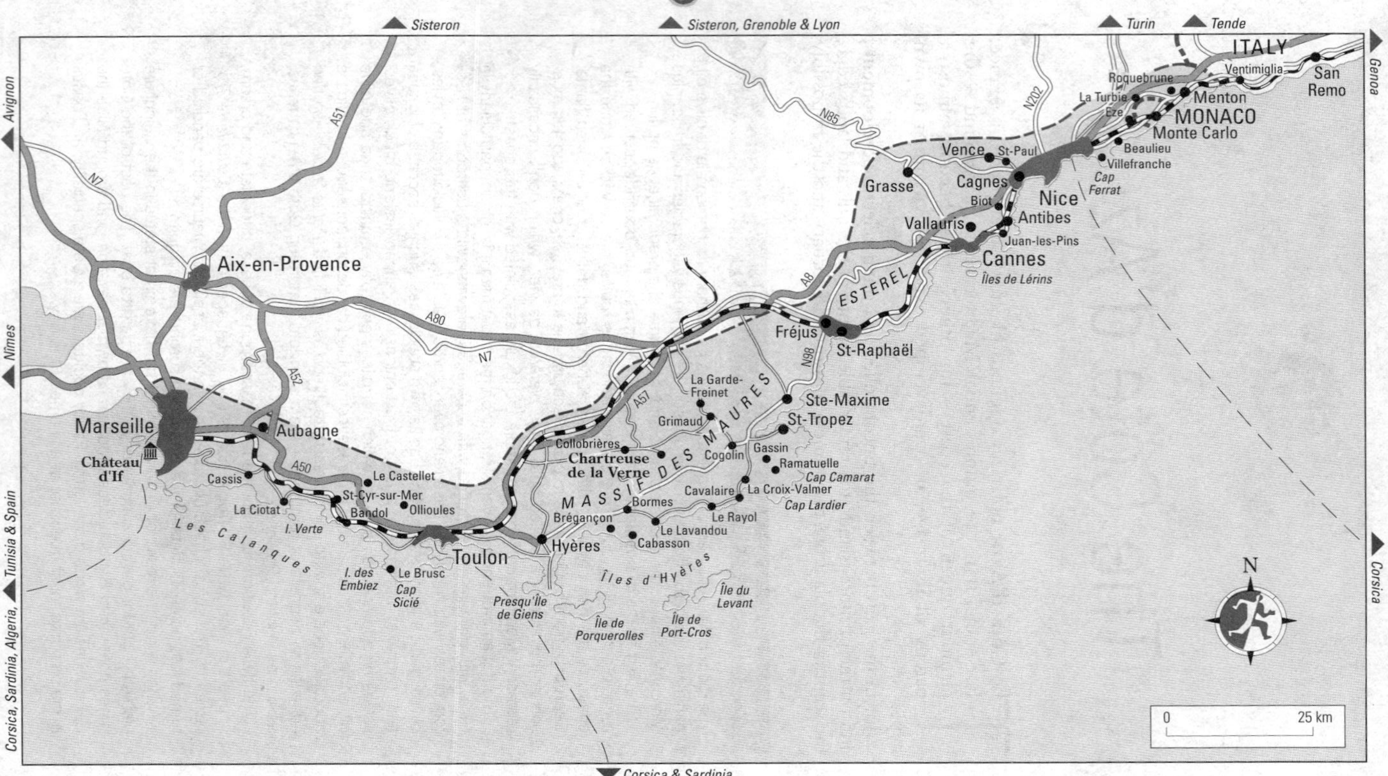
Sisteron
Sisteron, Grenoble & Lyon
Turin
Tende
Genoa
Avignon
Nîmes
Corsica, Sardinia, Algeria, Tunisia & Spain
Corsica & Sardinia
Corsica
ITALY
Ventimiglia
San Remo
Roquebrune
La Turbie
Eze
Menton
MONACO
Monte Carlo
Beaulieu
Villefranche
Cap Ferrat
N202
N85
Vence
St-Paul
Grasse
Cagnes
Biot
Nice
Antibes
Vallauris
Juan-les-Pins
Cannes
Îles de Lérins
A51
N7
Aix-en-Provence
A80
A8
ESTEREL
Fréjus
St-Raphaël
N98
A52
A57
La Garde-Freinet
Ste-Maxime
Grimaud
St-Tropez
MASSIF DES MAURES
Marseille
Aubagne
Collobrières
Chartreuse de la Verne
Cogolin
Gassin
Ramatuelle
Cap Camarat
Château d'If
Cassis
A50
Le Castellet
Cavalaire
La Croix-Valmer
Cap Lardier
St-Cyr-sur-Mer
Bormes
La Ciotat
Bandol
Ollioules
Brégançon
Le Rayol
I. Verte
Le Lavandou
Les Calanques
Cabasson
Hyères
Toulon
I. des Embiez
Le Brusc
Cap Sicié
Îles d'Hyères
Île du Levant
Presqu'île de Giens
Île de Porquerolles
Île de Port-Cros
N
0
25 km

blue water after which the coast is named, the Côte d'Azur remains undeniably captivating. The chance to see the works of innumerable artists seduced by the land and light also justifies the trip: Cocteau in **Menton** and **Villefranche**, Matisse and Chagall in **Nice** and **Vence**, Léger in **Biot**, Picasso in **Antibes** and Vallauris, and collections of Fauvists and Impressionists at St-Tropez and Hauts-de-Cagnes. And it must be said that **Monaco** and **Cannes**, places you either love or hate, certainly have an entertainment value, while the two great cities of **Marseille** and Nice have their own special magnetism.

The months to try to avoid are July and August, when hotels are booked up, overflowing campsites become health hazards, the locals get short-tempered, and the vegetation is at its most barren, and November, when many museums, hotels and restaurants close and the weather is wet.

From Marseille to Toulon

From the vast and wonderful scruffiness of **Marseille** to the utilitarian naval base of **Toulon**, this stretch of the Mediterranean is definitely not what most people think of as the Côte d'Azur. There is no continuous corniche, few villas in the grand style, and work is geared to an annual rather than summer cycle. **Cassis** is the exception, but the overriding attraction here is Marseille – a city that couldn't be confused with any other.

Marseille

The most renowned and populated city in France after Paris, **MARSEILLE** has – like the capital – prospered and been ransacked over the centuries. It has lost its privileges to sundry French kings and foreign armies, recovered its fortunes, suffered plagues, religious bigotry, republican and royalist Terror and had its own Commune and Bastille-storming. It was the presence of so many Marseillaise Revolutionaries marching from the Rhine to Paris in 1792 which gave the *Hymn of the Army of the Rhine* its name of *La Marseillaise*, later to become the national anthem.

In recent years Marseille has undergone something of a renaissance, shaking off much of its old reputation for sleaze and danger – the crime rate is actually lower than in Nice – to attract a wider range of visitors. The new TGV link has made it more accessible to weekending northerners, who can be seen picking up their hire cars at the *gare St-Charles* on Friday nights. Slowly, the splendid facades along La Canebière are getting scrubbed up, and the shops in the streets to the south are increasingly trendy or elegant. But the forward march of progress is not relentless: all too often last year's prestige civic project becomes this year's broken and bottle-strewn fountain. A detachment of the city's plentiful prostitutes and vagrants has gradually recolonized the intersection of rue St-Saëns and rue Glandevès, a few paces from the elegant opera house and the touristy restaurants of the Vieux Port. But that's Marseille. If

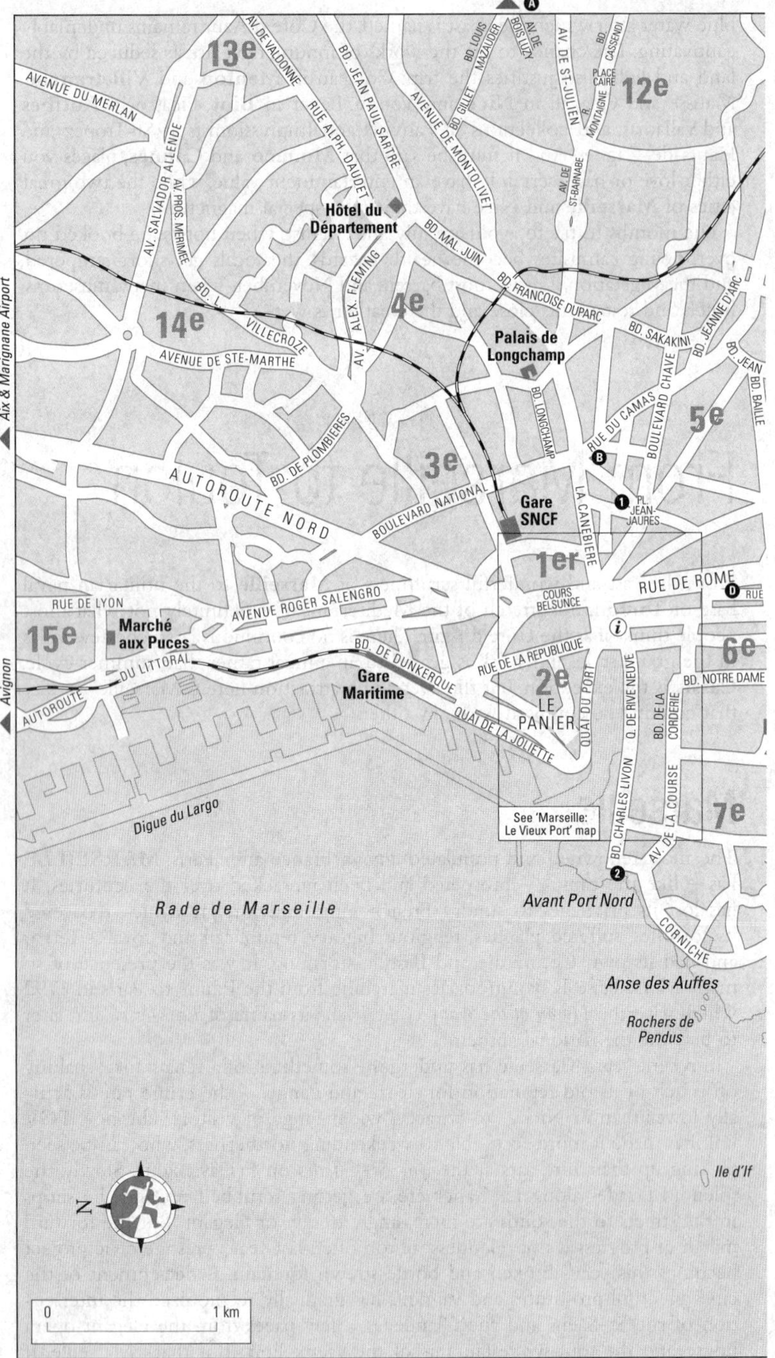
13e
12e
14e
4e
3e
5e
1er
2e
6e
7e
15e
AVENUE DU MERLAN
AV. DE VALDONNE
BD. JEAN PAUL SARTRE
BD. LOUIS MAZAUDIER
AV. DE BOIS LUZY
AV. DE ST-JULIEN
BD. CASSENDI
PLACE CAIRE
R. MONTAIGNE
AVENUE DE MONTOLIVET
BD. GILLET
RUE ALPH. DAUDET
AV. SALVADOR ALLENDE
AV. PROS. MERIMEE
AV. DE ST-BARNABE
Hôtel du Département
BD. MAL. JUIN
AV. ALEX. FLEMING
BD. FRANCOISE DUPARC
BD. JEANNE D'ARC
BD. SAKAKINI
BD. L. VILLECROZE
AVENUE DE STE-MARTHE
Palais de Longchamp
BD. JEAN
BD. BAILLE
BD. LONGCHAMP
BOULEVARD CHAVE
RUE DU CAMAS
BD. DE PLOMBIERES
AUTOROUTE NORD
BOULEVARD NATIONAL
Gare SNCF
LA CANEBIERE
PL. JEAN-JAURES
RUE DE ROME
RUE
COURS BELSUNCE
RUE DE LYON
AVENUE ROGER SALENGRO
Marché aux Puces
BD. DE DUNKERQUE
RUE DE LA REPUBLIQUE
Gare Maritime
DU LITTORAL
AUTOROUTE
QUAI DU PORT
Q. DE RIVE NEUVE
BD. DE LA CORDERIE
BD. NOTRE DAME
LE PANIER
QUAI DE LA JOLIETTE
BD. CHARLES LIVON
AV. DE LA COURSE
Digue du Largo
See 'Marseille: Le Vieux Port' map
Rade de Marseille
Avant Port Nord
CORNICHE
Anse des Auffes
Rochers de Pendus
Ile d'If
Aix & Marignane Airport
Avignon
N
0
1 km

15
THE CÔTE D'AZUR

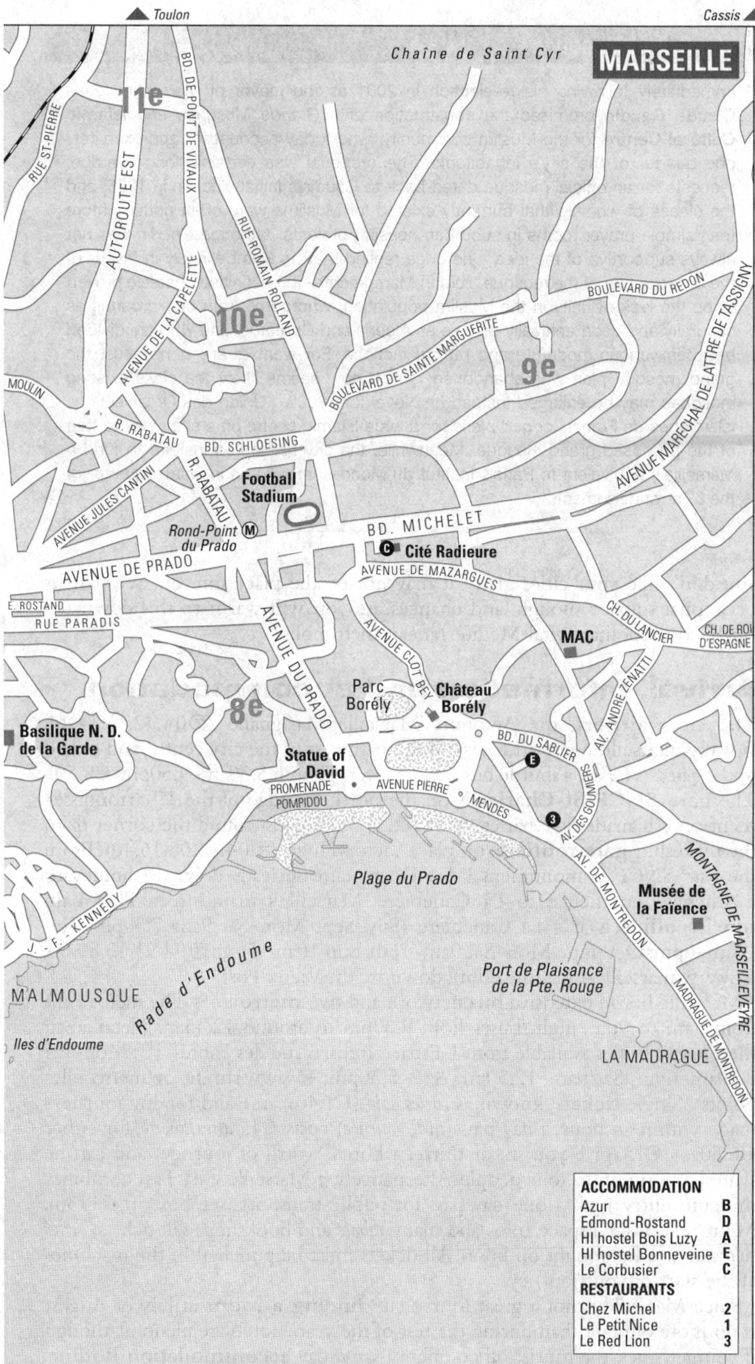
Toulon
Cassis
MARSEILLE
Chaîne de Saint Cyr
11e
10e
9e
8e
RUE ST-PIERRE
AUTOROUTE EST
BD. DE PONT DE VIVAUX
RUE ROMAIN ROLLAND
AVENUE DE LA CAPELETTE
BOULEVARD DU REDON
BOULEVARD DE SAINTE MARGUERITE
AVENUE MARECHAL DE LATTRE DE TASSIGNY
MOULIN
R. RABATAU
BD. SCHLOESING
AVENUE JULES CANTINI
Football Stadium
Rond-Point du Prado
BD. MICHELET
Cité Radieure
AVENUE DE PRADO
AVENUE DE MAZARGUES
E. ROSTAND
RUE PARADIS
AVENUE DU PRADO
AVENUE CLOT BEY
CH. DU LANCIER
CH. DE ROI D'ESPAGNE
MAC
AV. ANDRE ZENATTI
Parc Borély
Château Borély
Basilique N. D. de la Garde
BD. DU SABLIER
Statue of David
PROMENADE POMPIDOU
AVENUE PIERRE MENDES
AV. DES GOUMIERS
AV. DE MONTREDON
MONTAGNE DE MARSEILLEVEYRE
Plage du Prado
Musée de la Faïence
J. - F. - KENNEDY
Rade d'Endoume
MALMOUSQUE
Port de Plaisance de la Pte. Rouge
MADRAGUE DE MONTREDON
Iles d'Endoume
LA MADRAGUE
ACCOMMODATION
Azur B
Edmond-Rostand D
HI hostel Bois Luzy A
HI hostel Bonneveine E
Le Corbusier C
RESTAURANTS
Chez Michel 2
Le Petit Nice 1
Le Red Lion 3

The Grand Mosque

Immediately following his re-election in 2001 as the mayor of Marseille, **Jean-Claude Gaudin** promised the construction of a *Grande Mosquée* and **Islamic Cultural Centre** for the Muslim community, who today account for approximately one quarter of the city's inhabitants. The proposal was certainly long overdue; requests for an official mosque dated back to Gaudin's initial election in 1995, and the places of worship that currently existed for Muslims were often nothing more than simple prayer rooms in suburban housing projects. Although Gaudin was not always supportive of the idea – he once replied that he was definitely in favour of the construction of the mosque, "but in Marrakech" – the definitive obstacle proved to be the lack of unity in the Muslim population, who come from backgrounds as culturally and geographically diverse as Algeria and Comoros, and who are divided between various moderate and radical factions. For want of any consensus, the grand mosque plan was abandoned, and it now seems likely the city's existing mosques may be enlarged instead. In November 2003, l'Union des Organisations Islamiques de France lodged plans for a large Islamic centre on a site close to that of the proposed grand mosque. Meanwhile, the city has opted instead to fund a Marseillais equivalent to Paris's Institut du Monde Arabe in an industrial quarter of the 3e arrondissement.

you don't like your cities gritty, it may not be the place for you. See past its occasional squalor though, and chances are you will warm to this down-to-earth, cosmopolitan, vital Mediterranean metropolis.

Arrival, information and accommodation

The city's **airport**, the Aéroport Marseille/Marignane (ⓣ04.42.14.14.14, ⓦwww.marseille.aeroport.fr), is 20km northwest of the city centre, and linked to the *gare SNCF* by a shuttle bus service (every 20min 5.30am–9.50pm; €8.50). The **gare SNCF St-Charles** is on the northern edge of the 1er arrondissement on esplanade St-Charles (ⓣ08.92.35.35.35), just round the corner from the makeshift **gare routière**, on place Victor-Hugo (ⓣ04.91.08.16.40). From the *gare SNCF*, a monumental Art Deco staircase leads down to boulevard d'Athènes and thence to La Canebière, Marseille's main street. The main **tourist office** is at 4 La Canebière (July–Sept Mon–Sat 9am–7.30pm, Sun 10am–6pm; Oct–June Mon–Sat 9am–7pm, Sun 10am–5pm; ⓣ04.91.13.89.00, ⓦwww.marseille-tourisme.com), down by the Vieux Port.

Marseille has an extensive **bus** network and two **métro** lines. The métro runs from 5am to 9pm, night buses from 9.30pm to around 12.45am (detailed in the *Fluobus* leaflet available from L'Espace Infos, 6 rue des Fabres, 1er; Mon–Fri 8.30am–6pm, Sat 9am–12.30pm & 2–5.30pm; ⓦwww.rtm.fr; or métro sales points). Single **tickets**, known as *cartes solo* (€1.40), are valid for any journeys made within an hour; a day pass (*carte journée*) costs €4; *cartes liberté*, for either €6.50 or €13, give you six or thirteen hours' worth of journeys and can be shared among up to four people. Alternatively, a Marseille City Pass combines museum entry with a one-day pass for public transport (see box on p.1136). Métro stations, L'Espace Infos and many *tabacs* and bookshops sell tickets; *cartes solo* can also be bought on buses. All tickets must be punched in the machines at the start of your journey.

Since Marseille is not a great tourist city, **finding a room** in July or August is no more difficult than during the rest of the year. Hotels are plentiful, though if you get stuck the tourist office offers a same day **accommodation hotline**,

Allotel (ⓣ08.26.88.68.26; premium rates apply). The most inexpensive options are the city's **hostels**, both quite a way from the centre. Finally, if you're coming to town on a Friday (Nov–March only), look out for the "Bonne Weekend en Ville" scheme, a two-nights-for-the-price-of-one package offered by many hotels in Marseille (check with the tourist office).

Hotels

Alizé 35 quai des Belges, 1er ⓣ04.91.33.66.97, ⓦwww.alize-hotel.com. Comfortable, soundproofed rooms that are nicer than the slightly gloomy public areas suggest. The more expensive look over the Vieux Port. ❹

Azur 24 cours Franklin Roosevelt, 1er ⓣ04.91.42.74.38, ⓦwww.azur-hotel.fr. Quiet, friendly place with cosy rooms; not far from the restaurants and nightlife on cours Julien and place Jean-Jaurès. ❸

Le Béarn 63 rue Sylvabelle, 6e ⓣ04.91.37.75.83, ⓕ04.91.81.54.98. Rather shabby but comfortable cheapie, in a quiet location close to the centre. ❶

Belle-Vue 34 quai du Port, 2e ⓣ04.96.17.05.40, ⓦwww.hotel-bellevue.fr. Smart, great-value modern boutique hotel above a famous portside cabaret. The only downside is there's no lift. ❹

Le Corbusier Immeuble Le Corbusier, 280 bd Michelet, 8^{e} ⓣ04.91.16.78.00, ⓦwww.hotellecorbusier.com. Simple rooms with great views on the third floor of the architect's iconic prototype tower block; book well in advance. ❸

Edmond-Rostand 31 rue Dragon, 6^{e} ⓣ04.91.37.74.95, ⓦwww.hoteledmondrostand.com. Helpful management and good atmosphere; rooms come with TV and there's parking available. ❸

Etap Vieux Port 46 rue Sainte, 1er ⓣ04.9154.73.73, ⓦwww.accorhotels.com. Chain hotel in an unbeatable location, with exposed beams and stonework in the older part of the building. An excellent budget choice. ❸

Lutétia 38 allée Léon-Gambetta, 1er ⓣ04.91.50.81.78, ⓕ04.91.50.23.52. Very central hotel, with pleasant rooms. ❸

Pavillon 27 rue Pavillon, 1er ⓣ04.91.33.76.90, ⓕ04.91.33.87.56. Basic but decent backpacker haunt; in a lively, central street, and very friendly. ❶

St Ferréol's Hôtel 19 rue Pisançon, cnr rue St-Ferréol, 1er ⓣ04.91.33.12.21, ⓦwww.hotel-stferreol.com. Pretty decor, marble baths with jacuzzis, in a central pedestrianized area. ❹

Tonic Hotel 43 quai des Belges, 1er ⓣ04.91.55.67.46, ⓦwww.tonichotelmarseille.com. Smart and modern, with a great portside location. ❺

Hostels

HI hostel Bois Luzy 76 allée des Primevères, 12e ⓣ & ⓕ04.91.49.06.18. Slightly run-down hostel housed in former château a long way out from the centre. Dorms (€8.90) and double rooms available. The distance and 10.30pm curfew are quite restricting, the one positive aspect being the peace and quiet. Bus #8 from La Canebière, direction "St-Julien", stop "Bois Luzy". ❶

HI hostel Bonneveine 47 av J.-Vidal, 8e ⓣ04.91.17.63.30, ⓦwww.fuaj.org. The 9–20 person dorms (€9.30) are crowded, but this place is close to the beach, has laundry facilities, a cafeteria, bar, and 1am curfew. Currently undergoing renovation. M^{o} Rond-Point-du-Prado, then bus #44 direction "Floralia Rimet", stop "Place Bonnefon". Closed mid-Dec to mid-Jan.

The City

Marseille is divided into fifteen arrondissements which spiral out from the focal point of the city, the **Vieux Port**. Due north lies the old town, **Le Panier**, site of the original Greek settlement of Massalia. The wide boulevard leading from the head of the Vieux Port, La Canebière is the central east–west axis of the town. The **Centre Bourse** and the little streets of **quartier Belsunce** border it to the north, while the main shopping streets lie to the south. The main north–south axis is **rue d'Aix**, becoming cours Belsunce then rue de Rome, avenue du Prado and finally boulevard Michelet. The lively, youngish quarter around place Jean-Jaurès and the trendy cours Julien lies to the east of rue de Rome. From the headland west of the Vieux Port, the **corniche** heads south past the city's most favoured residential districts towards the **beaches** and promenade nightlife of the **Plage du Prado**.

City Pass and museum hours and prices

A **City Pass** (€16 for one day, €23 for two days) grants free entry to all fourteen of Marseille's museums, the botanical garden at Parc Borély, the Château d'If and the ferry ride to the island, and includes a pass for public transport. The card is available from the tourist office. Note that municipal museums are free on Sundays.

The Vieux Port

The cafés around the east end of the **Vieux Port** indulge the sedentary pleasures of observing street life, despite the fumes of exhausts and of fish sold straight off the boats on quai des Belges. Prime afternoon café lounging spot is the north (Le Panier) side, where the terraces are sunnier and the streets are cleaner. The rows of seafood restaurants on the pedestrianized streets between the southern quay and cours d'Estienne-d'Orves ensure that the Vieux Port remains the centre of city life in the evening, too.

Two **fortresses** guard the harbour entrance. **St-Jean**, on the north side, dates from the Middle Ages when Marseille was an independent republic, and is now only open when hosting exhibitions. Its enlargement in 1660 and the construction of **St-Nicolas**, on the south side of the port, represent the city's final defeat as a separate entity. Louis XIV ordered the new fort to keep an eye on the city after he had sent in an army, suppressed the city's council, fined it, arrested all opposition and – in an early example of rate-capping – set ludicrously low limits on Marseille's subsequent expenditure and borrowing. The best view of the Vieux Port is from the **Palais du Pharo**, on the headland beyond Fort St-Nicolas, or, for a wider angle, from **Notre-Dame-de-la-Garde** (daily: mid-June to mid-Aug 7am–10pm; mid-Aug to mid-June 7am–6pm); bus #60 or tourist train from Vieux Port), the city's Second Empire landmark atop the hill south of the harbour. Crowned by a monumental gold Virgin that gleams to ships far out at sea, it's the most distinctive of all Marseille landmarks, and immaculate after recent, extensive restoration. Inside, model ships hang from the rafters while the paintings and drawings displayed are by turns kitsch, unintentionally comic or deeply moving, as they depict the shipwrecks, house fires and car crashes from which the virgin has supposedly rescued grateful believers. A World War I soldier's helmet, pierced by a bullet hole, is a prominent exhibit.

A short way inland from the Fort St-Nicolas, above the Bassin de Carénage, is Marseille's oldest church, the **Basilique St-Victor** (daily 9am–7pm; €2 entry for crypt). Originally part of a monastery founded in the fifth century on the burial site of various martyrs, the church was built, enlarged and fortified – a vital requirement given its position outside the city walls – over a period of 200 years from the middle of the tenth century. It looks and feels like a fortress, with some of the walls almost 3m thick, and it's no conventional ecclesiastical beauty, though the interior has an austere power and the **crypt** is a fascinating, crumbling warren of rounded and propped-up arches, small side chapels and secretive passageways. Its proportions are more impressive than the church above, and it contains a number of sarcophagi, including one with the remains of St Maurice.

Le Panier

To the north of the Vieux Port is the oldest part of Marseille, **Le Panier**, where, up until the last war, tiny streets, steep steps and houses of every era formed a *vieille ville* typical of the Côte. In 1943, however, with Marseille

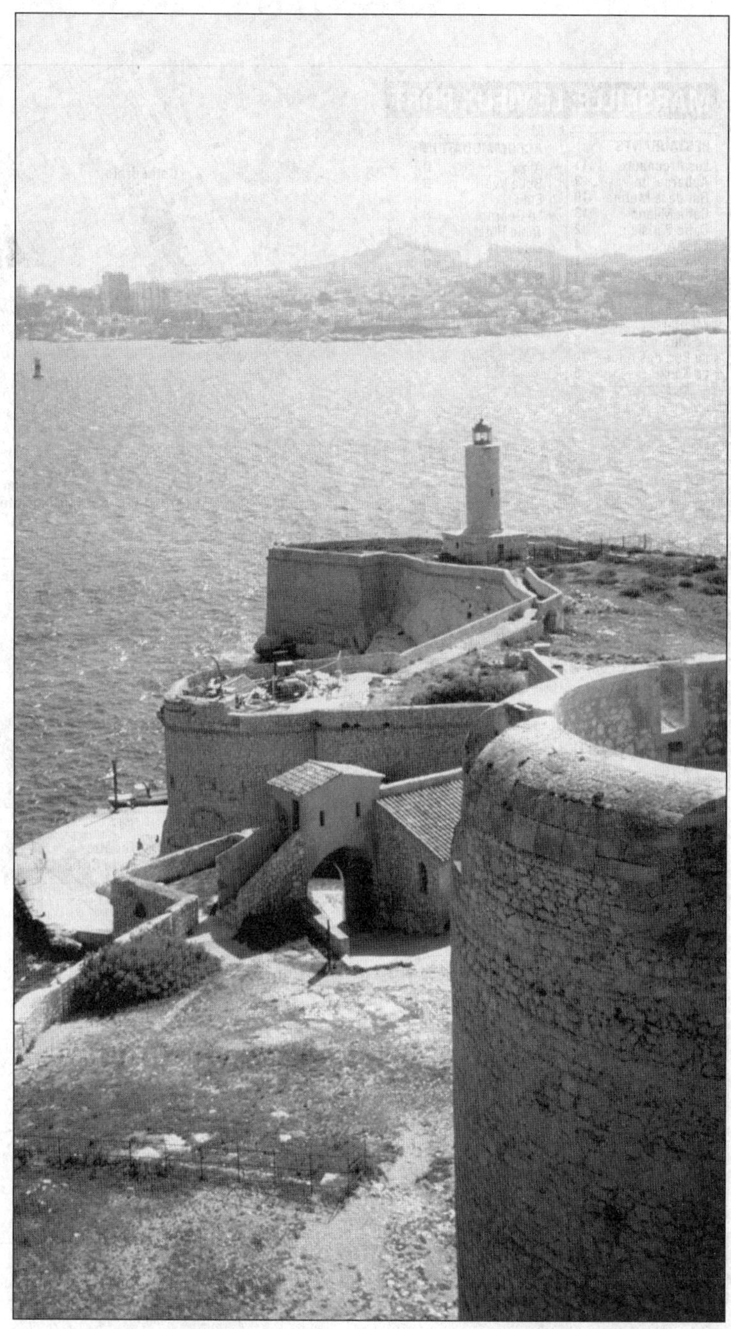

△ Maseille from the Château d'If

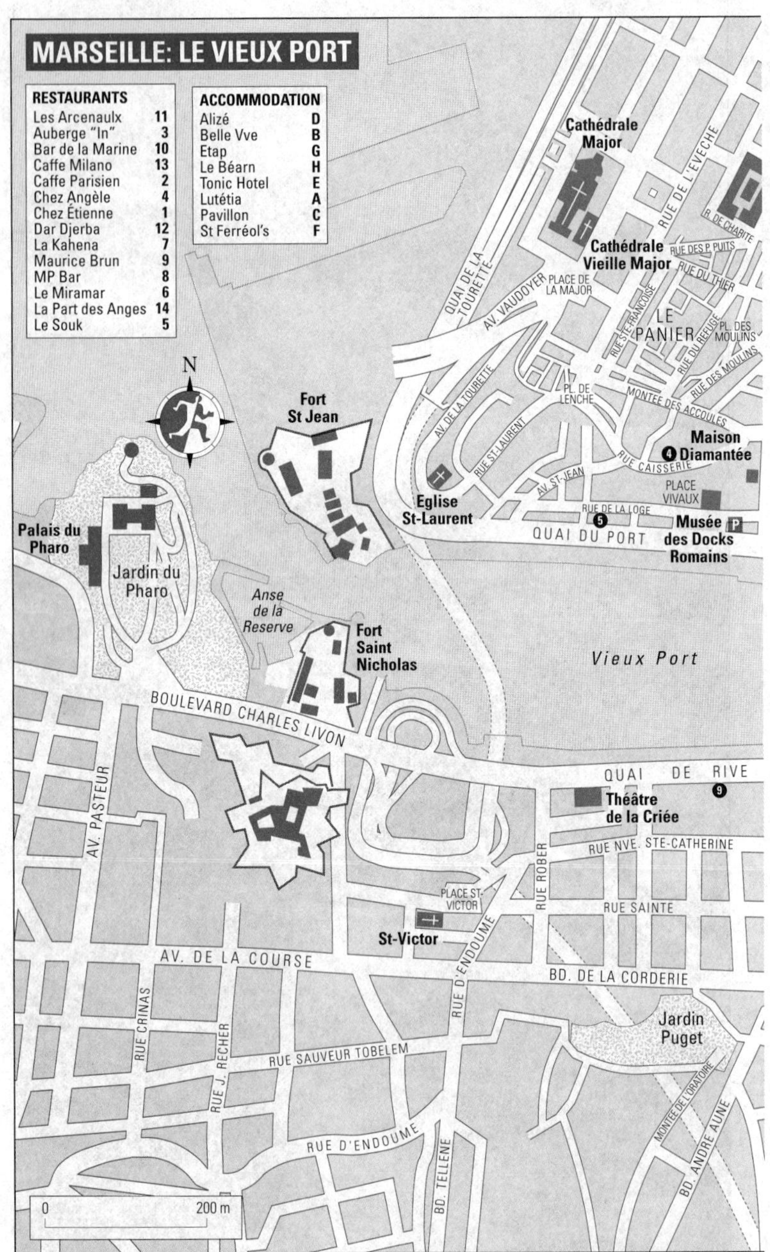

MARSEILLE: LE VIEUX PORT
RESTAURANTS
Les Arcenaulx 11
Auberge "In" 3
Bar de la Marine 10
Caffe Milano 13
Caffe Parisien 2
Chez Angèle 4
Chez Étienne 1
Dar Djerba 12
La Kahena 7
Maurice Brun 9
MP Bar 8
Le Miramar 6
La Part des Anges 14
Le Souk 5
ACCOMMODATION
Alizé D
Belle Vve B
Etap G
Le Béarn H
Tonic Hotel E
Lutétia A
Pavillon C
St Ferréol's F
N
Cathédrale Major
Cathédrale Vieille Major
RUE DE L'EVECHE
R. DE CHARITE
RUE DES P. PUITS
RUE DU THIER
QUAI DE LA TOURETTE
AV. VAUDOYER
PLACE DE LA MAJOR
LE PANIER
RUE STE-FRANÇOISE
RUE DU REFUGE
PL. DES MOULINS
RUE DES MOULINS
PL. DE LENCHE
MONTEE DES ACCOULES
AV. DE LA TOURETTE
RUE ST-LAURENT
Maison Diamantée
RUE CAISSERIE
AV. ST-JEAN
PLACE VIVAUX
Fort St Jean
Eglise St-Laurent
RUE DE LA LOGE
QUAI DU PORT
Musée des Docks Romains
Palais du Pharo
Jardin du Pharo
Anse de la Reserve
Fort Saint Nicholas
Vieux Port
BOULEVARD CHARLES LIVON
QUAI DE RIVE
Théâtre de la Criée
AV. PASTEUR
RUE NVE. STE-CATHERINE
RUE ROBER
PLACE ST-VICTOR
RUE SAINTE
St-Victor
AV. DE LA COURSE
RUE D'ENDOUME
BD. DE LA CORDERIE
Jardin Puget
RUE CRINAS
RUE J. RECHER
RUE SAUVEUR TOBELEM
MONTEE DE L'ORATOIRE
BD. ANDRE AUNE
BD. TELLENE
0
200 m

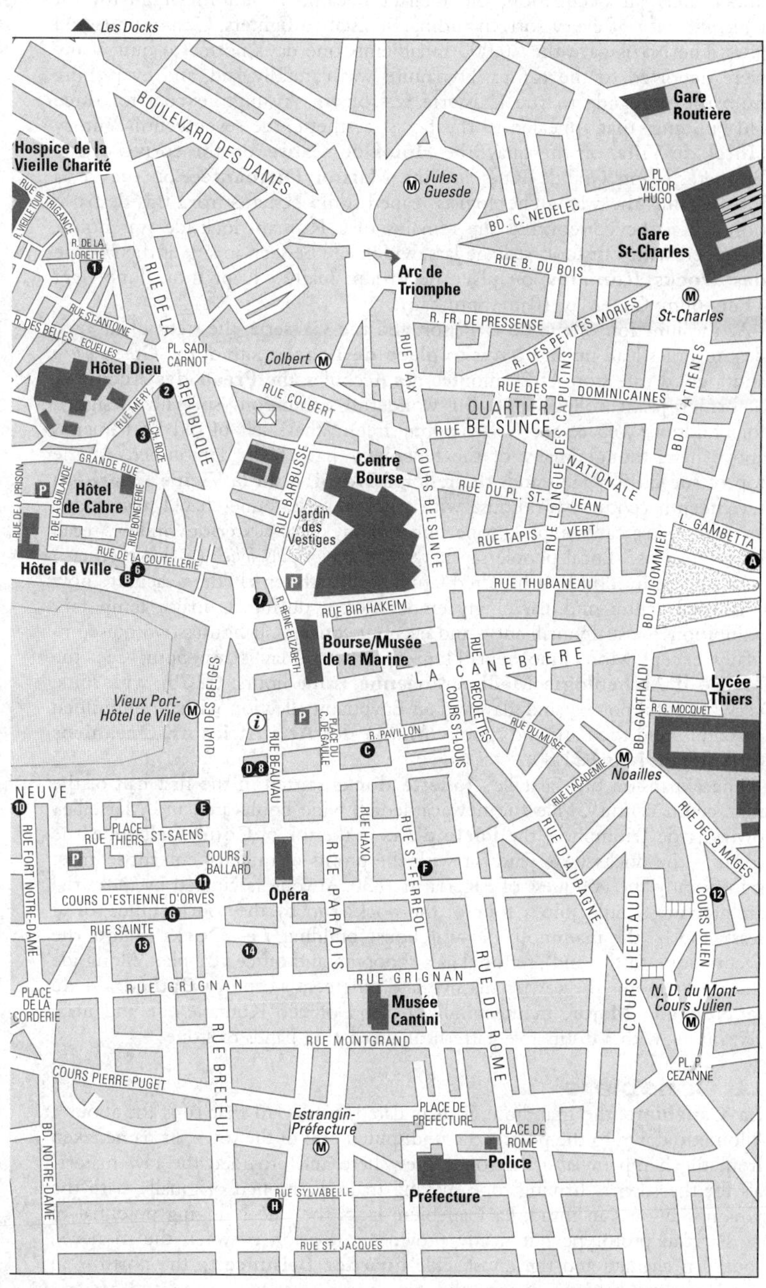

15 THE CÔTE D'AZUR

under German occupation, the quarter became an unofficial ghetto for *Untermenschen* of every sort, including Resistance fighters, Communists and Jews. The Nazis gave the 20,000 inhabitants one day's notice to quit; many were deported to the camps. Dynamite was carefully laid, and everything from the waterside to rue Caisserie was blown sky-high, except for three old buildings that appealed to the fascist aesthetic: the seventeenth-century **Hôtel de Ville**, on the quay; the **Hôtel de Cabre**, on the corner of rue Bonneterie and Grande-Rue; and the **Maison Diamantée**, on rue de la Prison. After the war, archeologists reaped some benefits from this destruction when they discovered the remains of a Roman dockside warehouse, equipped with vast food-storage jars, which can be seen in situ at the **Musée des Docks Romains**, on place de Vivaux (daily except mon: June–Sept 11am–6pm; Oct–May 10am–5pm; €3).

At the junction of rue de la Prison and rue Caisserie, the steps of montée des Accoules lead up and across to **place de Lenche**, site of the Greek *agora* and a good café stop. At 29 montée des Accoules, the **Préau des Accoules**, a former Jesuit college, puts on wonderful exhibitions specially designed for children (Wed & Sat 1.30–5.30pm; free). What's left of old Le Panier is above here, though many of the tenements have been demolished. At the top of rue du Réfuge stands the restored **Hospice de la Vieille Charité**, a seventeenth-century workhouse with a gorgeous Baroque chapel surrounded by columned arcades in pink stone; only the tiny grilled exterior windows recall its original use. Local people say it was "*beaucoup plus jolie*" ("a lot prettier") when it was lived in by a hundred families, all with ten children each. It's now a cultural centre, and alarmingly empty except during its major temporary exhibitions – usually brilliant – and evening concerts. It houses two museums (daily except Mon: June–Sept 11am–6pm; Oct–May 10am–5pm; €3); the **Musée d'Archéologie Méditerranéenne** (same hours; €2.70), with some very beautiful pottery and glass and an Egyptian collection with a mummified crocodile, and the dark and spooky **Musée des Arts Africains, Océaniens et Amérindiens** (€1.80).

The expansion of Marseille's **Joliette docks** started in the first half of the nineteenth century. Like the new cathedral, wide boulevards and Marseille's own Arc de Triomphe – the **Porte d'Aix** at the top of **Cours Belsunce**/rue d'Aix – the docks were paid for with the profits of military enterprise, most significantly the conquest of Algeria in 1830. Anyone fascinated by industrial architecture should join a tour of the docks run by the tourist office, or at least stop by the mammoth old warehouse building, **Les Docks** (follow rue République to the end), restored as a shopping and office complex. Alongside the docks looms the town's massive late nineteenth-century **Cathédrale de la Nouvelle Major**, architecturally a blend of neo-Romanesque and neo-Byzantine, with a distinctive pattern of alternating bands of stone.

La Canebière

La Canebière, the grandiose, if dilapidated, boulevard that runs for about a kilometre down to the port, is the undisputed hub of the town, its name taken from the hemp (*canabé*) that once grew here and provided the raw materials for the town's thriving rope-making trade. Fashioned originally with the Champs-Élysées in mind, La Canebière lacks the café-lounging potential of its Parisian prototype but neatly provides a division between the moneyed southern *quartiers* and the ramshackle **quartier Belsunce** to the north – an extraordinary, dynamic, mainly Arab area and a great trading ground. Stereos, suits and jeans from France and Germany are traded alongside spices, cloth and metalware from across the Mediterranean on flattened cardboard boxes in the streets – and not a French middleman in sight.

One block west, the **Centre Bourse** provides a stark contrast in a fiendish giant hypermall of noise, air conditioning and overlighting – useful, nevertheless, for mainstream shopping. Behind it is the **Jardin des Vestiges**, where the ancient port extended, curving northwards from the present quai des Belges. Excavations have revealed a stretch of the Greek port and bits of the **city wall** with the bases of three square towers and a gateway, dated to the second or third century BC. In the Centre Bourse complex, the **Musée d'Histoire de Marseille** (Mon–Sat noon–7pm; €2) presents the rest of the finds, including a third-century wreck of a Roman trading vessel. Back at the Vieux Port end of La Canebière is the **Musée de la Marine** (Wed–Sun 10am–6pm; €2), housed on the ground floor of the grandiose, Neoclassical stock exchange and with a superb collection of shipbuilders' models, including the legendary 1930s liner *Normandie* and Marseille's own prewar queen of the seas, the *Providence*.

The Palais Longchamp and the Hôtel du Département

The **Palais Longchamp**, 2km east of the port at the end of boulevard Longchamp (bus #8, or M° Longchamp-Cinq-Avenues), forms the grandiose conclusion of an aqueduct that brought water from the Durance to the city. Although the aqueduct is no longer in use, water is still pumped into the centre of the colonnade connecting the two palatial wings. Below, an enormous statue looks as if it honours some great feminist victory – three muscular women above four bulls wallowing passively in a pool from which a cascade drops four or five storeys to ground level.

The palace's north wing is the city's **Musée des Beaux-Arts** (daily except Mon June–Sept 11am–6pm; Oct–May 10am–5pm; €2; scheduled to close for refurbishment at the time of writing), a hot and slightly stuffy place, but with a fair share of delights, including works by Rubens, Jordaens, Corot and Signac. Most unusual are three paintings by Françoise Duparc (1726–76), whose first name has consistently found itself masculinized to François in catalogues both French and English. The nineteenth-century satirist from Marseille, Honoré Daumier, has a whole room for his cartoons. Plans for the city, sculptures and the famous profile of Louis XIV by Marseille-born Pierre Puget are on display along with graphic contemporary canvases of the plague that decimated the city in 1720.

Northwest of the Palais Longchamp, at the end of boulevard Mal-Juin, stands the new **Hôtel du Département** (M° St-Just). Deliberately set away from the centre of town in the run-down St-Just–Chartreux *quartier*, the seat of local government for the Bouches-du-Rhône *département* was the biggest public building to be erected in the French provinces in the twentieth century. It was designed by the English architect Will Alsop, who used his hallmark ovoid glass tube shapes above and alongside vast rectangular blocks of blue steel and glass. The Hôtel's great glass foyer is not always accessible even during working hours, but the tourist office arranges architectural tours (€6.50).

South of La Canebière

The prime shopping district of Marseille is encompassed by three streets running **south from La Canebière**: rue Paradis, rue St-Ferréol and **rue de Rome**. Some of the smaller, intervening streets close to La Canebière are pretty seedy, with prostitutes on every corner day and night, but the atmosphere is usually friendly. Between rues St-Ferréol and Rome, on rue Grignan, is the city's most important art museum, the **Musée Cantini** (daily except Mon: June–Sept 11am–6pm; Oct–May 10am–5pm; €3), with Fauvists and Surrealists well represented, plus works by Matisse, Léger, Picasso, Ernst, Le Corbusier, Miró and Giacometti.

A few blocks east of rue de Rome is one of the most pleasant places to idle in the city, **cours Julien** (M° N-D-du-Mont Cours Julien), with pools, fountains, pavement restaurant tables and enticing boutiques, populated by Marseille's arty and bohemian crowd and its diverse immigrant community, all of it buried under copious quantities of graffiti. Streets full of bars and music shops lead east to **place Jean-Jaurès**, locally known as "la Pleine", where the daily market is a treat, particularly on Saturdays.

The corniche, beaches and Parc Borély

The most popular stretch of sand close to the city centre is the **plage des Catalans**, a few blocks south of the Palais du Pharo. This marks the beginning of Marseille's **corniche**, avenue J.-F.-Kennedy, which follows the cliffs past the dramatic statue and arch that frames the setting sun of the **Monument aux Morts des Orients**. South of the monument, steps lead down to an inlet, **Anse des Auffes**, which is the nearest Marseille gets to being picturesque. Small fishing boats are beached on the rocks, the dominant sound is the sea, and narrow stairways and lanes lead nowhere. The corniche then turns inland, bypassing the **Malmousque peninsula**, whose coastal path gives access to tiny bays and beaches – perfect for swimming when the mistral wind is not inciting the waves. You can see along the coast as far as Cap Croisette and, out to sea, the abandoned monastery on the Îles d'Endoume and the Château d'If (see below).

The corniche ends at the **Plage du Prado**, the city's main sand beach, where the water is remarkably clean, though the beach itself is gritty. A short way up **avenue du Prado**, avenue du Park-Borély leads into the city's best green space, the **Parc Borély**, with a boating lake, rose gardens, palm trees and a botanical garden (May–Sept Mon–Fri 2–6pm, Sat & Sun 3–6.45pm; Oct–April Mon–Fri 1–4.45pm, Sat & Sun 2–4.45pm; hours subject to change, check with tourist office; €3). The quickest way to the park and the beaches is by bus #19 or #83 from M° Rd-Pt-du-Prado; for the corniche, take bus #83 from the Vieux Port.

The Château d'If

The **Château d'If** (daily except Mon: April–Sept 9am–7pm; Oct–March 9am–5.30pm; €4.60), on the tiny island of If, is best known as the penal setting for Alexandre Dumas' *The Count of Monte Cristo*. Having made his watery escape after fourteen years of incarceration as the innocent victim of treachery, the hero of the piece, Edmond Dantès, describes the island thus: "Blacker than the sea, blacker than the sky, rose like a phantom the giant of granite, whose projecting crags seemed like arms extended to seize their prey". The reality, for most prisoners, was worse: they went insane or died (and sometimes both) before reaching the end of their sentences. Only the nobles living in the less fetid upper-storey cells had much chance of survival, like de Niozelles, who was given six years for failing to take his hat off in the presence of Louis XIV, and Mirabeau, who was doing time for debt. The sixteenth-century castle and its cells are horribly well preserved, and the views back towards Marseille are fantastic. **Boats** for If leave regularly from the quai des Belges on the Vieux Port (hourly 9am–5pm, last return at 6.30pm; journey time 15–20min; €10).

The Musée de la Faïence, the MAC and the Cité Radieuse

From the plage du Prado the promenade continues, with a glittering array of restaurants, clubs and cafés, all the way to the suburb of **Montredon** where the nineteenth-century Château Pastré, set in a huge park, contains the **Musée de la Faïence** (daily except Mon: June–Sept 11am–6pm; Oct–May 10am–5pm; €3). The eighteenth- and nineteenth-century ceramics, most produced in Marseille, are of an extremely high quality, and a small collection of novel modern and contemporary pieces is housed on the top floor. The entrance to the park (free) is at 157 avenue de Montredon (bus #19 from M° Rd-Pt-du-Prado, stop "Montredon-Chancel"). Along the coast from here are easily accessible *calanques* (rocky inlets), ideal for evening swims and supper picnics as the sun sets.

Between Montredon and **boulevard Michelet**, the main road out of the city, is the contemporary art museum, **MAC** (daily except Mon: June–Sept 11am–6pm; Oct–May 10am–5pm; €3), at 69 av d'Haïfa (bus #23 or #45 from M° Rd-Pt-du-Prado, stop "Haïfa" or "Marie-Louise"). The permanent collection, in perfect pure-white surrounds, includes works from the 1960s to the present day by Buren, Christo, Klein, Niki de Saint-Phalle, Tinguely and Warhol, as well as Marseillais artists César and Ben. There's also a cinema, the **Cinémac** (Ⓣ04.91.25.01.07), showing feature films, shorts and videos on different themes each month.

Set back just west of boulevard Michelet stands a building that broke the mould, Le Corbusier's seventeen-storey block of flats, the **Unité d'Habitation**, designed in 1946 and completed in 1952. The Cité only fails to amaze now because so many architects the world over have tried to imitate Le Corbusier's revolutionary model, but up close the difference in quality between this and what followed is apparent. The layout is very complex, and larger apartments are split across two floors with balconies on both sides. At ground level the building is decorated with Le Corbusier's famous human figure, the Modulor; on the third floor there is a hotel (see p.1135) and café with wonderful sea views. The iconic rooftop recreation area cannot be visited, though you can ride the lift to the top and peek out at it. To reach the Unité, take bus #21 from M° Rd-Pt-du-Prado to "Le Corbusier".

Eating and drinking

The Marseillais eat just as well, if not better, than the ageing aristos and skin-stretched celebrities of the Riviera. Fish and **seafood** are the main ingredients, and the superstar of dishes is the city's own expensive invention, **bouillabaisse**, a saffron- and garlic-flavoured soup with bits of fish, croutons and *rouille* thrown in; theories conflict as to which fish should be included and where and how they must be caught, but one essential is the *rascasse* or scorpion fish. The other city speciality is the less exotic *pieds et paquets* – mutton or lamb belly and trotters.

Good **restaurant** hunting grounds to head for include cours Julien or place Jean-Jaurès (international options), the Vieux Port quays and the pedestrian precinct behind the southern side of the port (a bit more upmarket and fishy), the plage du Prado (glitzy and pricey) or Le Panier (snacks and old-time bistros). Gourmet palaces lurk close to the corniche, while stalls on cours Belsunce sell chips and sandwiches with meaty fillings for under €4. Note that on Sunday pickings are slim, and many Marseille restaurants also take long summer breaks.

Cafés and bars

Bar de la Marine 15 quai Rive Neuve, 7e. A favourite bar for Vieux Port lounging and the inspiration for Pagnol's celebrated Marseille trilogy of *Marius* (1929), *Fanny* (1931) and *César* (1936). Open 7pm–2am.

Café Parisien 1 place Sadi-Carnot, 2e. Very beautiful, distinctly elegant café that's a successful blend of old and new. Lunchtime *plats* from €6.40.

Le MP Bar 10 rue Beauvau, 1er. Gay and lesbian bar near the Opera. The one-way windows add a paranoid touch but the crowd is lively, young and fun. Daily 5.30pm–dawn.

Le Petit Nice 26 place Jean-Jaurès, 1er. Cosy, local bar overlooking the market. Mon–Sat 6.30pm–1am.

Le Red Lion 231 av Pierre Mendès-France, 8e. Popular spot when the weather's nice, along Plage Borély. Thurs–Sat until 4am, other days until 2am.

Restaurants

Les Arcenaulx 25 cours d'Éstienne-d'Orves, 1er ⓣ04.91.59.80.30. Superb food with menus from €25 in an intellectual haunt which is also a bookshop. Mixed gay and straight crowd. Closed Sun.

Auberge "In" 25 rue du Chevalier-Roze, 2e ⓣ04.91.90.51.59. Health-food shop on the edge of Le Panier, with a vegetarian *menu fixe* served lunchtimes and early evenings (menu €13; hot *plats* from €8). Closed Sun.

Caffe Milano 43 rue Sainte, 1er ⓣ04.91.33.14.33. Tastefully refurbished old café serving pasta and gnocchi plus novel *plats* from around €10. Closed Sat lunch & Sun.

Chez Angèle 50 rue Caisserie, 2e ⓣ04.91.90.63.35. Packed, recently smartened-up Le Panier local, with an excellent *menu fixe*.

Chez Étienne 43 rue Lorette, 2e. Old-fashioned Le Panier bistro; hectic, cramped and crowded. Robust *plats* such as *pavé de boeuf* from €15 as well as cheaper pizzas. No bookings, no telephone. Closed Sun.

Chez Michel 6 rue des Catalans, 7e ⓣ04.91.52.64.22. There's no debate about the *bouillabaisse* ingredients here. A basket of five fishes, including the elusive and most expensive one, the *rascasse*, is presented to the customer before the soup is made. Quite simply the place to eat this dish. Expect to pay €47 for the *bouillabaisse* alone.

Dar Djerba 15 cours Julien, 6e ⓣ04.91.48.55.36. Excellent Tunisian restaurant with beautiful tiling and generous portions of couscous. Around €22.90. Closed Sun.

La Kahena 2 rue de la République, 1er ⓣ04.91.90.61.93. North African restaurant close to the Vieux Port with merguez sausages at €10 and couscous from €8. Open daily.

Les Mets de Provence Chez Maurice Brun 18 quai Rive-Neuve, 7e ⓣ04.91.33.35.38. A Marseille institution serving authentic Provençal food; lunch menu €36 including wine, evening €52. Closed Sat lunch, Sun & Mon.

Le Miramar 12 quai du Port, 2e ⓣ04.91.91.10.40. This local favourite is not cheap, but with its portside location and gregarious owner it's well worth the price (à la carte from €53). Best bet is the *bouillabaisse*. Closed Sun & Mon.

La Part des Anges 33 rue Sainte, 1e ⓣ04.91.33.55.70. Superb *bar à vins* with knowledgeable staff. Warm salad of *andouilles* and other delicacies accompany a quality selection of local wines; à la carte from around €20.

Le Souk 98 quai du Port, 2e ⓣ04.91.91.29.29. Top-notch North African restaurant with excellent quality food and smart service. Count on spending €30. Closed Mon.

Nightlife

Marseille's **nightlife** has something for everyone, with plenty of live rock and jazz, as well as the more choice pastimes of theatre-, opera- and concert-going. Virgin Megastore, at 75 rue St-Ferréol (Mon–Sat 9.30am–9pm, Sun 2.30–8pm), and the ticket bureau in the tourist office are the best places to go for **tickets and information** on gigs, concerts, theatre, free films and whatever cultural events are going on. Virgin also stocks a small selection of English books and runs a café on the top floor. Other places with info are the book and record shop FNAC, on the top floor of the Centre Bourse (Mon–Sat 10am–7pm), the café, travel agency and comic shop La Passerelle, 26 rue des Trois-Mages (noon–midnight), and the New Age music shop Tripsichord, further down at nos.18–20. At any of these places, you can pick up a copy of *Ventilo*, Marseille's independent free weekly listings paper, which comes out on a Wednesday. Alternatively, look for the monthly listings booklet *paf*, available for free at the tourist office or the Espace Culture, 42 La Canebière.

The most animated nightlife is to be found around place Jean Jaurès, with plenty of **bars** to choose from and live music to listen to. The **clubs** around cours d'Estienne-d'Orves – mainly jazz, some Caribbean – are for trendy kids from the upper-crust arrondissements, with prices to match.

Live music and clubs

Le Bazar 90 bd Rabatau, 8e ⓣ04.91.79.08.88. Marseille's largest and most popular disco, mixed gay and straight crowd; DJs spin house music. Free entry, cheap drinks and dress code. Thurs–Sun 11pm–dawn.

Café Julien 39 cours Julien, 6e ⓣ04.91.24.34.14. Lively bar with mixed clientele, part of the Espace Julien. Nightly DJs and weekend live rock and reggae music. Closed Mon.

La Caravelle 34 quai du Port, 2e. Prewar cabaret on the first floor of the *Hotel Bellevue* with portside views; free plates of tapas 6–9.30pm, live jazz weekends. Daily till 2am.

Casting Café 148 av Pierre Mendès-France, 8e ⓣ04.91.71.24.12. Marseille's "fashion" café, with weekly shows by local designers. Drinks, tapas, as well as full-blown meals (€13–20) till 11.30pm. Daily 9am–midnight.

Exodus 9 rue des Trois-Mages, 1er ⓣ04.91.42.02.39. World music concerts (from India to Latin America); Mondays improv theatre. Otherwise Wed–Sun from 9pm.

L'Intermédiare 63 place Jean Jaurès, 6e ⓣ04.91.47.01.25. Crowded, two-floor bar with a variety of bands downstairs. Daily from 8.30pm; free.

Machine à Coudre 6 rue Jean Roque, 1er ⓣ04.91.55.62.65. Small venue hosting alternative rock and reggae shows; €6 cover. Open weekends 10pm–2am.

New Cancan 3 rue Sénac, 1er ⓣ04.91.48.59.76. Cheesy, dated, expensive, but busy gay and lesbian club with dance floor and large cruising space. Mon & Thurs–Sun 11pm–6am.

Pelle Mêle 8 place aux Huiles, 1er ⓣ04.91.54.85.26. Jazz bistro near the Vieux Port. Tues–Sat 5pm–2am.

Le Poste à Galène 103 rue Ferrari, 5e ⓣ04.91.47.57.99. Nightly DJs, theme nights and occasional concerts in a former hangar. €6 cover. Mon–Sat from 9.30pm.

Film, theatre and concerts

Ballet National de Marseille 20 bd Gabès, 8e ⓣ04.91.32.72.72, ⓦwww.ballet-de-marseille.com. The home base of Roland Petit's famous dance company.

César 4 place Castellane, 6e ⓣ04.91.37.12.80. One of around half a dozen cinemas in Marseille regularly showing *v.o.* films.

Chocolat Théâtre 59 cours Julien, 6e ⓣ04.91.42.19.29, ⓦwww.chocolattheatre.com. Theatre-restaurant-exhibition space with shows ranging from male striptease to avant-garde improvisations.

Théâtre National de Marseille "La Criée", 30 quai Rive Neuve, 7e ⓣ04.91.54.70.54, ⓦwww.theatre-lacriee.com. The top theatre in town, hosting a varied programme from French classics to modern experimental works.

Les Variétés 37 rue Vincent Scotto, 1er ⓣ08.36.68.20.15. Downtown cinema offering *v.o.* films.

Listings

Airlines Air France ⓣ0820.820.820; British Airways ⓣ0825.825.040.

Bike rental Holiday Bikes, 129 Cours Lieutaud ⓣ04.91.92.76.04; ⓦwww.holiday-bikes.com.

Bookstore Ad Hoc Books, 8 rue Pisançon, 1er ⓣ04.91.33.51.92; Mon–Sat 10am–7pm.

Car rental Avis, Gare St Charles, ⓣ04.91.64.71.00; Citer, 20 bd Schloesing, 8e ⓣ04.91.83.05.05; Europcar, 59 Allée Léon Gambetta, 1er ⓣ04.91.10.74.90.

Consulates UK, 24 av du Prado, 6e ⓣ04.91.15.72.10; USA, place Varian Fry, 6e ⓣ04.91.54.92.00.

Disabled visitors Office Municipal pour Handicapés (128 av du Prado, 8e ⓣ04.91.81.58.80) gives information on disabled access and facilities in Marseille. For transport, call ⓣ04.91.11.41.00.

Emergencies Ambulance ⓣ15; Doctor ⓣ15, or SOS Médecins ⓣ04.91.52.91.52; 24hr casualty: La Conception, 144 rue St-Pierre, 5e ⓣ04.91.38.36.52.

Ferries SNCM (61 bd des Dames ⓣ08.91.70.18.01, ⓦwww.sncm.fr) runs ferries to Corsica and Tunisia.

Internet *Escaliq*, rue Coutellerie, corner rue de la République; Mon–Fri 9.30am–7pm, Sat 3–7pm; *Info Café*, 1 quai Rive Neuve; Mon–Sat 9am–10pm, Sun 2.30–7.30pm.
Laundry 38 rue Papety, place des Catalans ☎06.03.74.96.82; Isidore Razon, 73 av Joseph Vidal, 8e; Chantal Peyrot, rue St Savournin, nr place Jean Jaurès, 1er; ☎04.91.42.37.70.
Lost property 10 rue de la Cathédrale, 2e ☎04.91.90.99.37.
Money exchange Change du Port, 8 La Canebière; ☎04.91.55.61.30; Comptoir Marseillais de Bourse, 22 La Canebière; ☎04.91.54.93.94; daily 9am–6pm.
Pharmacy Pharmacie du Vieux Port, 4 quai du Port, ☎04.91.90.00.57; until 8pm.
Police Commissariat Centrale, 2 rue Antoine Becker, 2e ☎04.91.39.80.00.
Post office 1 place de l'Hôtel-des-Postes, 13001 Marseille.
Taxis ☎04.91.02.20.20, ☎04.9151.50.00, English-speaking ☎04.91.97.12.12.
Youth information Centre d'Information Jeunesse, 96 La Canebière, 1er ☎04.91.24.33.50, provides information on youth activities and programmes.

Cassis, La Ciotat and Bandol

Hard as it is to picture now, chic little **Cassis** once had a busy industrial harbour, while at **La Ciotat** ships were built right up until 1989. La Ciotat is probably the friendliest of all the resorts between Marseille and Toulon, and has the distinction of being at the origin of film-making. Tucked in a cove between La Ciotat and Toulon, **Bandol** is a rarity on the Côte d'Azur, a family resort which has managed to maintain something of an unhurried air.

Cassis

A lot of people rate **CASSIS** the best resort this side of St-Tropez – its inhabitants most of all. Hemmed in by high white cliffs, its modern development has been limited to a model toytown on the steep inclines above the harbour. Portside posing and drinking aside, there's not much to do except sunbathe and look up at the ruins of the town's medieval **castle**, built in 1381 and refurbished by Monsieur Michelin, the authoritarian boss of the family tyres and guides firm.

The favoured lazy pastime, though, is to take a boat trip to the **calanques** – long, narrow, deep fjord-like inlets that have cut into the limestone cliffs. Several companies operate from the port, but check if they let you off or just tour in and out, and be prepared for rough seas. If you're feeling energetic, you can take the well-marked footpath from the route des Calanques behind the western beach; it's about ninety minutes' walk to the furthest and best *calanque*, **En Vau**, where you can climb down rocks to the shore. Intrepid pine trees

The Cosquer Cave

In 1991, diver **Henri Cosquer** found paintings and engravings of animals, painted handprints and finger tracings in a cave between Marseille and Cassis, whose sole entrance has been underwater since the end of the last ice age. Carbon dating has shown that the oldest work of art here was created around 27,000 years ago. Over a hundred animals have been identified, including seals, auks, horses, ibex, bison, chamois, red deer and a giant deer only known from fossils. Fish are also featured, along with sea creatures that might be jellyfish. Most of the finger tracings are done in charcoal and have fingertips missing, possibly a sign language. Since the entrance is 37m below sea level and several divers have died exploring it, it's unlikely that the cave will ever be accessible to the public.

find root-holds, and sunbathers find ledges on the chaotic white cliffs. The water is deep blue and swimming between the vertical cliffs is an experience not to be missed.

Les Sports Loisirs Nautiques (ⓣ04.42.01.80.01) rents out windsurfing and watersports equipment by the beach next to the port. The spectacular clifftop **Route des Crêtes** links Cassis with La Ciotat, and is a highly popular route with bikers, drivers and photographers hereabouts. Regular belvederes allow you to stop and take the perfect shot of distant headlands receding into the sunset – vertigo permitting.

Practicalities

Buses from Marseille arrive at rond-point du Gendarmerie from where it's a couple of minutes' walk down to the port and the beach. The **gare SNCF** is 3km out of town, with nine bus connections (route #2) daily. The **tourist office** is at quai des Moulins in the port (March–May & Oct Mon–Fri 9.30am–12.30pm & 2–6pm, Sat 10am–noon & 2–5pm, Sun 10am–noon; June & Sept Mon–Fri 9am–12.30pm & 2–6.30pm, Sat 9.30am–12.30pm & 3–6pm; July & Aug Mon–Fri 9am–7pm, Sat & Sun 9.30am–12.30pm & 3–6pm; Nov–Feb Mon–Fri 9.30am–12.30pm & 2–5pm, Sat 10am–noon & 2–5pm, Sun 10am–noon; ⓣ04.42.01.71.17, ⓦwww.cassis.fr).

Cassis is a small place, so demand for cheaper **rooms** in high season is intense. The least expensive are at *Le Commerce*, 1 rue St-Clair (ⓣ04.42.01.09.10, ⓕ04.42.01.14.17; ❷, closed mid-Nov to mid-Jan), and *Le Provençal*, 7 av Victor-Hugo (ⓣ04.42.01.72.13, ⓕ04.42.01.39.58; ❸), close to the port. For a little more money, and a view over the port, try *Le Golfe*, on quai Barthélémy (ⓣ04.42.01.00.21, ⓕ04.42.01.92.08; ❹; closed Nov–March). Further out, there's also *Le Joli Bois*, route de la Gineste (ⓣ04.42.01.02.68; ❷), just off the main road to Marseille, 3km from Cassis and with few amenities. Far more isolated is the gorgeously scenic but rather inaccessible **hostel** *La Fontasse*, in the hills above the *calanques* west of Cassis (ⓣ04.42.01.02.72; mid-March to Dec); from the D559 (stop "Les Calanques"), a road leads down towards the Col de la Gardiole, and when it becomes a track, take the left fork – after another 2km you'll find the hostel. Rainwater, beds (€8.90) and electricity are the only mod cons, but if you want to explore this wild uninhabited stretch of limestone heights, the people running it are happy to give advice. To get to Cassis you can descend to the *calanques* and walk along the coast (about 1hr). If you're **camping**, don't bother going into town – the campsite, *Les Cigales* (ⓣ04.42.01.07.34; closed mid-Nov to mid-March; €14.60 for car, tent and two people), is just off the D559 from Marseille before avenue de la Marne turns down into Cassis, a gruelling one-kilometre walk uphill from the port.

Restaurant tables are in abundance along the portside quai des Baux and quai Calendal; prices vary greatly, but if you can afford it your best bet has to be to follow your nose, and seek out the most enticing fish smells. The authentic Provençal ratatouille and freshly caught fish at *Chez Gilbert*, 19 quai Baux (ⓣ04.42.01.71.36; closed Tues eve, Wed & Jan; menu €21), are hard to beat. *El Sol*, at no. 23 (ⓣ04.42.01.76.10; closed Tues eve & Wed), with less elaborate *terroir* fare, costs a bit less. In the backstreets, *Le Clos des Arômes* at 10 rue Abbé Mouton (ⓣ04.42.01.71.84, closed Mon, Tues & Wed lunch; menu €23) is well regarded locally and has a pretty garden.

La Ciotat

Shipbuilding cranes still loom incongruously over the little port of **LA CIOTAT**, where 300,000–tonne oil and gas tankers were once built. Today, the town's economy relies on property development, tourism and providing facilities for yachts, yet it remains a pleasantly unpretentious place. La Ciotat is not a town for museum or monument seeing. It's a relaxing place with excellent beaches to loaf on and a lively waterfront with plenty of places to eat and drink.

In 1895, **August and Louis Lumière** filmed the first ever moving pictures here, including the arrival of a train at the *gare SNCF*, which had Parisians jumping out of their seats in fright when it was premiered there. The world's oldest movie house, the **Eden Cinema**, still stands on the corner of boulevard A.-France and boulevard Jean-Jaurès, though it awaits restoration, and the main venue for the annual film festival in June is the modern Cinéma Lumière on place Evariste Gras. The brothers are commemorated by a solid 1950s monument on plage Lumière – named after them – and in a mural on the covered market halls that house the modern cinema, visible as you walk up rue Reynier from boulevard Guérin north of the port.

The streets of the old town, apart from rue Poilus, are uneventful and a bit run-down. If you feel the need to do something constructive you can take a boat trip out to the tiny offshore **Île Verte** from the quai de Gaulle (May, June & Sept departures every hour; July & Aug every 30min; journey time 15min; ⓣ04.42.83.11.44; €7), and to a number of nearby *calanques* from quai Ganteaume (ⓣ06.09.35.25.68). Alternatively, take a walk through the **Parc du Mugel** (daily: April–Sept 8am–8pm; Oct–May 9am–6pm; free; bus #30 to "La Garde", stop "Mugel"), with its strange cluster of rock formations on the promontory beyond the shipyards. A path leads up through overgrown vegetation to a narrow terrace overlooking the sea. If you continue on bus #30 to Figuerolles you can reach the **Anse de Figuerolles** calanque down the avenue of the same name, and its neighbour, the **Gameau**.

Practicalities

The **gare SNCF** is 5km from the Vieux Port, but from Monday to Saturday a bus meets every train; the service is less frequent on Sundays. The old town and port look out across the Baie de la Ciotat, whose inner curve provides the beaches and resort lifestyle of La Ciotat's modern extension, **La Ciotat Plage**. The **gare routière** is at the end of boulevard Anatole-France by the Vieux Port right beside the **tourist office** (mid-June to Sept Mon–Sat 9am–8pm, Sun 10am–1pm; Oct to mid-June Mon–Sat 9am–noon & 2–6pm; ⓣ04.42.08.61.32, ⓦwww.laciotatourisme.com).

For **hotels**, the best cheapies are *La Marine*, 1 av Fernand Gassion (ⓣ & ⓕ04.42.08.35.11; ❷), and *La Rotonde*, 44 bd de la République (ⓣ04.42.08.67.50, ⓦwww.hotellarotonde-laciotat.com; ❸), both on the fringes of the old town. In La Ciotat Plage, *Miramar*, 3 bd Beaurivage (ⓣ04.42.83.33.79; ⓦwww.miramarlaciotat.com; ❻), is right on the palm-fringed seafront, while across the bay, on Corniche du Liouquet, you can stay in little villas in a park at *Ciotel Le Cap* (April–Oct; ⓣ04.42.83.90.30, ⓦwww.leciotel.com; ❽). La Ciotat has seven campsites, three of them by the sea, of which *St-Jean*, 30 av St-Jean (ⓣ04.42.83.13.01, ⓦwww.asther.com/stjean; from €17 for two people & a tent; closed Oct–March), is the closest to the centre (bus #40, stop "St-Jean Village").

La Ciotat's best **restaurant** is *La Fresque*, 18 rue des Combattants (ⓣ04.42.08.00.60; closed Sun eve & Mon), with exquisite seafood dishes and menus for €21–32. Otherwise, *Coquillages Franquin*, 13 bd Anatole-France (ⓣ04.42.83.59.50; closed Sun eve & Mon), serves perfectly respectable fish dishes and has a €19.50 menu, and there are plenty of cafés and brasseries around the Vieux Port and along boulevard Beaurivage in La Ciotat Plage.

Bandol and around

Across La Ciotat bay are the fine sand and shingle beaches and unremarkable family resort of **LES LECQUES**, an offshoot of the old inland town of **ST-CYR-SUR-MER**, to which it is fused by an expanding strip of modern suburbia. The **train station** is in St-Cyr, but the tourist office (July & Aug Mon–Sat 9am–7pm, Sun 10am–1pm & 4–7pm; Sept–June Mon–Fri 9am–6pm, Sat 9am–noon & 2–6pm; Ⓣ04.94.26.73.73, Ⓦwww.saintcyrsurmer.com) is on the place de l'Appel du 18 Juin, on the seafront in Les Lecques. St-Cyr has the cheapest **accommodation**, such as the rather basic but serviceable *Auberge Le Clos Fleurie* (Ⓣ04.94.26.27.46; ❷), near the station on avenue Général-de-Gaulle, but there's a greater choice in Les Lecques. A ten-kilometre **coastal path** (signposted in yellow) runs from the east end of Les Lecques' beach through a rare villa-free stretch of secluded beaches and *calanques* to the unpretentious resort of **BANDOL**, while inland are **vineyards** producing some of the best wines on the Côte, the *appellation* Bandol. The *appellation* covers a large area stretching from St-Cyr to Le Castellet up in the hills to the edge of Ollioules, just east of Toulon; you'll see *dégustation* signs along the route. The reds are the most reputed, maturing for over ten years on a good harvest, with bouquets sliding between pepper, cinnamon, vanilla and black cherries.

In Bandol there are a number of reasonable **hotel** options near the centre, including *Hôtel Florida*, 26 impasse de Nice (Ⓣ04.94.29.41.72; ❸; half board (❻) obligatory in high season), and *La Cigale Bleue* on av de la Gare (Ⓣ04.94.29.41.40; ❸) alternatively, the *Golf Hotel* (Ⓣ04.94.29.45.83; Ⓦwww.golfhotel.fr; open Feb–Nov & Christmas; ❸) is very pleasant and right on Rénecros beach, a short distance west of the town centre. The **tourist office**, on allée Vivien by the quayside (July & Aug daily 9am–7pm; late June & early Sept 9am–noon & 2–6pm; Sept–June Mon–Fri 9am–noon & 2–6pm, Sat 9am–noon; Ⓣ04.94.29.41.35, Ⓦwww.bandol.fr), will help if you're stuck during the busy high season.

The other stretch of **coastal path** this side of Toulon is along the southern edge of the **Sicié peninsula** from Le Brusc. The path climbs up to the sturdy clifftop chapel of Notre-Dame-du-Mai, once a primitive lighthouse, which affords fantastic views of the coast and hinterland. The chapel itself is only open in May and on certain special dates (Easter Monday, August 15, and for the pilgrimage on September 14).

Toulon

Never the loveliest of French cities, **TOULON** was half destroyed in the last war and brutally rebuilt. It's still dominated by the military and associated industries. The arsenal that Louis XIV created is today one of the major employers of southeast France, and the port is home to the French Navy's Mediterranean fleet. The shipbuilding yards of La Seyne have, however, been axed, closing the book on a centuries-old and at times notorious industry. Up until the eighteenth century, slaves and convicts were still powering the king's galleys, and following the Revolution, convicts were sent to Toulon with iron collars round their necks for sentences of hard labour. After 1854 convicts were deported to the colonies in whose conquest ships from Toulon played a major part.

Today, heavy traffic crawls through the centre, the old town is fringed by forbidding 1960s architecture, and the damage done to Toulon's reputation by a period of overtly racist National Front control – which thankfully ended in 2001 – will take decades to repair. And yet the city is fighting back hard. The splendid municipal theatre has been refurbished, the new Hôtel des Arts in the former Conseil Général building on boulevord Maréchal Leclerc pulls in touring exhibitions of modern art from Paris and elsewhere, and everywhere there's an orgy of repaving, replanting and general beautification. A certain seediness lingers despite all the fountains and flowerbeds, but given the high standards and low prices of some of Toulon's accommodation it makes a logical enough stopover if you're passing this way.

The **gare SNCF**, on place de l'Europe, and **gare routière**, on place Albert-1er, lie northeast of the town centre; a new *gare routière* adjacent to the *gare SNCF* was scheduled for completion as this book went to press. There's a **tourist office** (June–Sept Mon & Wed–Sat 9am–6pm, Tues 10am–6pm; Sun 10am–noon; Oct–May Mon & Wed–Sat 9.30am–5.30pm, Tues 10am–5.30pm, Sun 10am–noon; ⓣ04.94.18.53.00, ⓦwww.toulontourisme.com) on place Raimu, in the **old town**: head down rue Vauban, turn left at place d'Armes, follow the busy avenue that runs parallel to the coast, and turn left into rue Letuaire. Around place Victor-Hugo you'll find any number of cheap shops and places to eat, and a market (Tues–Sun).

If you do stop over here, there's plenty of budget **accommodation**: the basic but cheap *Hôtel des Allées*, 18 allées Amiral-Courbet (ⓣ04.94.91.10.02; ❶); the modern and comfortable *3 Dauphins*, 9 place des 3 Dauphins (ⓣ04.94.92.65.79; ⓕ04.94.09.09.17; ❷); or the bright and more upmarket *Little Palace*, opposite the *3 Dauphins* at 6–8 rue Berthelot (ⓣ04.94.92.26.62, ⓦwww.hotel-littlepalace.com; ❸) – all very central.

The central resorts and islands

Out of season, the stretch of coastline between **Hyères** and the **St-Raphaël–Fréjus** conurbation and its backdrop of wooded hills hold their own against the cynicism engendered by tourist brochure overkill. The magic lies in the scented Mediterranean vegetation, silver beaches glimpsed between purple cliffs, secluded islands and medieval hilltop villages.

Hyères, which preserves a certain air of gentility, flashy St-Raphaël and historic Fréjus are the only significant towns, though the urban sprawl around the erstwhile fishing villages of **Le Lavandou**, **Cavalaire-sur-Mer** and **Ste-Maxime** keeps any sense of wilderness at bay. But there are moments when it's almost possible to imagine the coastline of old: near the **Cap de Bregançon** south of **Bormes**, between **Le Rayol** and Cavalaire, in the **Domaine de Rayol gardens**, and around the southern tip of the **St-Tropez**

peninsula. And out to sea, on the **Îles d'Hyères** (often called the Îles d'Or) you can experience unspoilt landscapes with some of the best fauna and flora in Provence. **La Croix-Valmer** is probably the most pleasant of the resorts, and **St-Tropez** is a must – for a day's visit at least. Inland, amidst the dense wooded hills of the **Massif des Maures**, are the gorgeous ancient villages of **Collobrières** and **La Garde Freinet**.

Sheer expense aside, **transport** is the one big problem. There is a regular bus service along the coast, but there are no trains, traffic is extremely slow in high season, and cycling doesn't get you very far unless you're Tour de France material.

Hyères

HYÈRES is the oldest resort on the Côte, listing Queen Victoria and Tolstoy among its early admirers, but the lack of a central seafront meant the town lost out when the foreign rich switched from winter convalescents to quayside strollers. It is, nevertheless, a very popular resort, but has the rare distinction, for this part of the world, of not being totally dependent on the summer influx. The town exports cut flowers and exotic plants, the most important being the date palm, which graces every street in the city – and numerous desert palaces in Arabia. The orchards, nursery gardens and vineyards, taking up land which elsewhere would have become a rash of holiday shelving units, are crucial to its economy. Hyères is consequently rather appealing.

Arrival, information and accommodation

The **gare SNCF** is on place de l'Europe, 1500m south of the town centre, with frequent buses (#14) to **place Clemenceau**, at the entrance to the old town, and to the **gare routière** on place Mal-Joffret, two blocks south (ⓣ04.94.12.55.00, ⓦwww.sodetrav.fr). The modern Hyères–Toulon **airport** is between Hyères and Hyères-Plage, 3km from the centre (ⓣ04.94.00.83.83), to which it's connected by an infrequent shuttle bus. The **tourist office** is at the Forum du Casino, 3 av Ambroise Thomas (July & Aug daily 8.30am–7.30pm; Sept–June Mon–Fri 9am–6pm, Sat 10am–4pm; ⓣ04.94.01.84.50, ⓦwww.ot-hyeres.fr); there is a subsidiary office close to Rond-Point Henri Petit at the western entrance to the town for car-borne visitors. **Bikes** and **mopeds** can be rented from Holiday Bikes, at 10 rue Jean d'Agrève, near port Saint-Pierre (ⓣ04.94.38.79.45, ⓦwww.holiday-bikes.com).

Hotels in the old town include the *Hôtel le Soleil*, on rue du Rempart (ⓣ04.94.65.16.26, ⓦwww.citotel.com; ❺), in a renovated house at the foot of the parc St-Bernard, and the smaller *Hôtel du Portalet*, 4 rue de Limans (ⓣ04.94.65.39.40, ⓔhotelduportalet@aol.com; ❸). Overlooking the port at Ayguade is *La Reine Jane* (ⓣ04.94.66.32.64, ⓦwww.reine-jane.com; ❷; closed Jan).

There are any number of **campsites** on the coast. Two smaller ones are *Camping-Bernard*, a two-star in Le Ceinturon (ⓣ04.94.66.30.54, ⓕ04.94.66.48.30; closed Oct–Easter), and *Clair de Lune*, avenue du Clair de Lune (ⓣ04.94.58.20.19, ⓦwww.campingclairedelune.com; closed mid-Nov to Jan), a three-star one on the Presqu'Île de Giens.

The Town

Walled and medieval **old Hyères** perches on the slopes of Casteou hill, 5km from the sea; below it lies the **modern town**, with avenue Gambetta the main north–south axis. At the coast, the **Presqu'Île de Giens** is leashed to the mainland by an isthmus, known as **La Capte**, and a parallel sand bar enclosing the salt marshes and a lake. Le Ceinturon, Ayguade and Les Salins d'Hyères are the villages-cum-resorts along the coast northeast from Hyères-Plages; L'Almanarre is to the west where the sand bar starts.

From place Clemenceau, a medieval gatehouse, the **Porte Massillon**, opens onto rue Massillon and the **old town**. At **place Massillon**, you encounter a perfect Provençal square, with terraced cafés overlooking the twelfth-century Tour St-Blaise (also known as the Tour des Templiers), the remnant of a Knights Templar fort now elegantly converted into exhibition space for contemporary art (April–Oct Mon & Wed–Sat 10am–noon & 4–7pm; Nov–March Wed–Sun 10am–noon & 2–5pm; free). Behind the tower, rue Ste Catherine leads uphill to **place St-Paul**, from which you have a panoramic view over a section of medieval town wall to Costabelle hill and the Golfe de Giens.

Wide steps fan out from the Renaissance door of the former collegiate **church of St-Paul** (April–Sept Mon & Wed–Sun 10am–noon & 4–7pm; Oct–March Wed–Sun 10am–noon & 2–5.30pm), whose distinctive belfry is pure Romanesque, as is the choir, though the simplicity of the design is masked by the collection of votive offerings hung inside. The decoration also includes some splendid wrought-iron candelabra, and a Christmas crib with over-life-size *santons* (traditional crib figures). Today, the church is only used for special services – the main place of worship is the mid-thirteenth-century former monastery **church of St-Louis**, on place de la République.

To the right of St-Paul, a Renaissance house bridges rue St-Paul, its turret supported by a pillar rising beside the steps. Through this arch you can head up rue Ste-Claire to the entrance of **parc Ste-Claire** (daily 8am–dusk; free), the exotic gardens around **Castel Ste-Claire**, once home to the American writer and interior designer Edith Wharton and now the offices of the Parc National de Port-Cros. Cobbled paths lead up the hill towards the **parc St-Bernard** (daily 8am–dusk; free), full of almost every Mediterranean flower known. At the top of the park, above montée des Noailles (which by car you reach from cours Strasbourg and avenue Long), is the **Villa Noailles**, a Cubist mansion enclosed within part of the old citadel walls, designed by Mallet-Stevens in the 1920s and a home to all the luminaries of Dada and Surrealism. Though it seems to be undergoing a never-ending programme of restoration, you can look round its gardens and the interior of the house, which is used as an exhibition space for contemporary art showings (summer Mon & Wed–Sun 10am–noon & 4–7pm; winter Wed–Sun 10am–noon & 2–5pm; free). To the west of the park and further up the hill are the remains of the **castle**, whose keep and ivy-clad towers outreach the oak and lotus trees and give stunning views out to the Îles d'Hyères and east to the Massif des Maures. Access to parts of the hilltop complex continues to be restricted by restoration work.

The switch from medieval to eighteenth- and nineteenth-century Hyères at **avenue des Îles-d'Or** and its continuation, **avenue Général-de-Gaulle**, is as abrupt as it is radical, with wide boulevards and open spaces, opulent villas and waving palm fronds creating a spa town atmosphere. If you're keen on the ancient history of this coast, the **Site Archéologique d'Olbia** in Almanarre (April–Sept: Tues, Thurs & Fri 9.30am–12.30pm & 3–6pm, Sat 3–6pm; €4.50) is worth a visit: the remains of the original fortified Greek trading post of Olbia are supplemented by later Roman and medieval remains, including those of the abbey of Saint-Pierre de l'Almanarre. An alternative pastime is to wander around the spectacular array of cacti and palms in the **Jardins Olbius-Riquier**, just to the southeast of the bottom of avenue Gambetta (daily 7.30am–dusk; free). The park also has a small zoo and miniature train to keep kids happy.

Eating and drinking

For **eating and drinking**, there are terraced café-brasseries in place Massillon and, all around this corner of the old town, a good choice of crêperies, pizzerias and bistros serving *plats du jour* for around €12. *Le Bistrot de Marius*, 1 place Massillon (☎04.94.35.88.38; closed Mon & Tues outside school holidays), is a little more elegant than most, with plenty of fish on its €16–30 menus. On the edge of the new town, *Les Jardins de Bacchus*, 32 av Gambetta (☎04.94.65.77.63; menus from €28.80; closed Sat lunch, Sun dinner, Mon), serves novel concoctions with panache, while a little way out of town, at 15 av du Toulon, *La Crèche Provençale* (☎04.94.65.30.28; closed Sat lunch & Mon; menus from €27) is excellent value for sophisticated food.

Around Hyères

Hyères's coastal suburbs have plenty of beaches for you to choose from, but can be subject to mosquito plagues in spring and summer. **L'Almanarre**, about 5km south of town, hosts French sailing championships at the end of April and has a narrow crescent of sand from which you can swim. **La Capte** is rather built-up, but offers warmer, shallow water and a long sandy beach. Alternatively, take the route du Sel (closed mid-Nov to mid-April) to the **Presqu'Île de Giens** for a glimpse of the saltworks and the flamingos on the adjoining lake. Besides the peculiarity of its attachment to the mainland (last broken by storms in 1811), **Giens** is a fairly nondescript and overpopulated resort. There are, however, some fine cliffs facing the sea, and in rough weather you can understand why so many wrecks have been discovered here. **La Tour Fondue**, a Richelieu construction on the eastern side of Giens, overlooks the small port that serves the Îles d'Hyères.

Traffic fumes and the proximity to the airport make the beaches between Hyères-Plage and Le Ceinturon/Ayguade rather undesirable despite the pines and ubiquitous palms. Best to head further up the coast to the little fishing port of **Les Salins d'Hyères**. East of Les Salins, where the coastal road finally turns inland, you can follow a path between abandoned salt-flats and the sea to a naturist beach.

The Îles d'Hyères

A haven from tempests in ancient times, then the peaceful home of monks and farmers, the **Îles d'Hyères** became, from the Middle Ages onwards, the target of piracy and coastal attacks by an endless succession of assorted aggressors. The three main islands, **Porquerolles**, **Port-Cros** and **Levant**, are covered in half-destroyed, rebuilt or abandoned forts, dating from the sixteenth century, when François I started a trend of under-funded fort building, up to the twentieth century, when the German gun positions on Port-Cros and Levant were put out of action by the Americans. Porquerolles and Levant are not yet

Ferries to the Îles d'Hyères

Departures from:

La Tour Fondue Presqu'Île de Giens (Ⓣ04.94.58.21.81, Ⓦwww.tlv-tvm.com). The closest port to Porquerolles; summer services to all three islands, all year round to Porquerolles.

Le Lavandou Gare Maritime (Ⓣ04.94.71.01.02, Ⓦwww.vedettesilesdor.fr). The closest port to Port-Cros and Levant; year-round daily services to Levant and Port-Cros; thrice-weekly service to Porquerolles (daily July & Aug). The same line runs services from Cavalaire to Port Cros and Porquerolles from April to Sept and from La Croix Valmer in July & Aug.

Port d'Hyères Hyères-Plage (Ⓣ04.94.57.44.07, Ⓦwww.tlv-tvm.com). Services to Port-Cros and Levant all year and to all three islands in July & Aug.

St-Raphaël Vieux Port (Ⓣ04.94.95.17.46, Ⓦwww.tmr-saintraphael.com). Services to Port-Cros Fri only July & Aug.

Toulon Batelier de la Rade (Ⓣ04.94.46.24.65). Crossings to Porquerolles April–Oct only.

free of garrisons, thanks to the knack of the French armed forces for securing prime beauty sites for their bases. Their presence has, however, prevented the otherwise inevitable Côte build-up and, in the non-military areas, the islands' very fragile environment is protected by the Parc National de Port-Cros and the Conservatoire Botanique de Porquerolles. Sheer pressure of visitor numbers has created problems even in this pristine environment, however, and so to further protect the islands' delicate ecosystems from damage caused by large numbers of walkers, in 2004 the authorities announced plans to limit visitor numbers to 5000 daily on Porquerolles and 1500 daily on Port-Cros. Ferry operators have been instructed to turn away further bookings once the daily total has been reached.

The islands' wild, scented greenery and fine sand beaches constitute the essence of what makes this part of the planet so desirable – and are a reminder of what so much of the mainland coast was like forty years ago. To **stay** on them, the only reasonable option is Levant, as long as you book months in advance. Accommodation on Porquerolles is limited, expensive and again needs reserving in advance; on Port-Cros it's almost non-existent. All visitors should take note of the signs forbidding smoking (away from the ports), flower-picking and littering.

Île de Porquerolles

The most easily accessible of the Îles d'Hyères is **Porquerolles**, whose permanent village, also called **PORQUEROLLES**, has a few hotels and restaurants, plenty of cafés, a market and interminable games of boules. It dates from a nineteenth-century military settlement, and the village still focuses around the central **place d'Armes**, the erstwhile military exercise ground. In summer its population explodes to over 10,000, but there is some activity all year round. This is the only cultivated island of the three and there are three Côtes de Provence domains that can be visited.

Porquerolles is big enough to find yourself alone amid its stunning landscapes. The **lighthouse** due south of the village and the **calanques** to its east make good destinations for an hour's walk, though don't even think of swimming on this side of the island, unless you fancy cliff diving. The southern shoreline is all cliffs, with scary paths meandering close to the edge through heather and exuberant maquis scrub. The longest beach is the **plage de Notre-Dame**, 3km northeast of the village just before the *terrain militaire* on the northern tip. The nearest beach to the village is the **plage d'Argent**, 1km away (continue west from the port past the Arche de Noë and take the first, well-signed right). This 500-metre strip of white sand fringes a curving bay backed by pine forests, and has a pleasant **restaurant**, *La Plage d'Argent* (Ⓣ04.94.58.32.48; closed mid-Sept to March; midday *plat du jour* €14–25).

Practicalities

There's a small **information centre** by the harbour (daily: April–Sept 9am–5.30pm; Oct–March 9am–12.30pm; Ⓣ04.94.58.33.76, Ⓦwww.porquerolles.com) where you can get basic maps of the island. You can rent **bikes** from several outlets in the village; La Bécane (Ⓣ04.94.58.37.94) and L'Indien (Ⓣ04.94.58.35.65) are both on the central place d'Armes. Expect to pay upwards of €100 a night for **hotel** accommodation in Porquerolles in season; marginally cheaper is the *Relais de la Poste*, place d'Armes (Ⓣ04.98.04.62.62, Ⓦwww.lerelaisdelaposte.com; ❺; closed Oct–Easter). Otherwise, you might try *Les Mèdes*, rue de la Douane (Ⓣ04.94.12.41.24, Ⓦwww.hotel-les-medes.fr; ❽; closed Jan–March), or *Sainte-Anne*, on place d'Armes (Ⓣ04.98.04.63.00, Ⓦwww.sainteanne.com; ❼; closed Jan, Nov & Dec), which has the most character. There's no campsite on Porquerolles and *camping sauvage* is strictly forbidden, so don't miss the last ferry to the mainland. Most of the cafés and **restaurants** in the village are pure tourist fodder, with the exception of the *Auberge des Glycines*, on place d'Armes (Ⓣ04.94.58.30.36; menu €21.90), which also has attractive but pricey rooms (❾), but if you arrive in the morning you'll be able to buy picnic provisions.

Île de Port-Cros

The dense vegetation and mini-mountains of **Port-Cros** (Ⓦwww.portcrosparcnational.fr) make its exploration much tougher than Porquerolles, even though it's less than half the size. Aside from ruined forts and the handful of buildings around the port, the only intervention on the island's wildlife are the classification labels on some of the plants and the extensive network of paths; you're not supposed to stray from these signposted routes and it would be very difficult to do so given the thickness of the undergrowth. The entire island is a protected zone, and has the richest fauna and flora of all the islands. Kestrels, eagles and sparrowhawks nest here; there are shrubs that flower and bear fruit at the same time, and more common species like broom, lavender, rosemary and heather flourish in abundance. One kilometre from the port (and a 45-minute walk) is the nearest beach, **plage de la Palud**; a similar time to reach Mont Vinaigre, the island's highest point, via the **Vallon de la Solitude**. From here there are views over the island's south coast and the islet of Gabinière. In total there are some 30km of paths on Port Cros, though all except those to the beaches are liable to closure during times of high fire risk.

The only **hotel**, *Le Manoir d'Hélène* (Ⓣ04.94.05.90.52, Ⓕ04.94.05.90.89; ❾ half-board; closed mid-Oct to mid-April; menus from €40), has few vacancies; there are five half-board rooms at the restaurant, *Hostellerie Provençale* (Ⓣ04.94.05.90.43; closed mid-Oct to Easter; ❾). Almost as expensive is dining in the few **restaurants** around the port, though you can get a sandwich or a slice of pizza. Once you leave the village, however, there's nothing; at the very least, walkers should be sure they have enough water with them. Again, camping is forbidden.

Île du Levant

The **Île du Levant** – ninety percent military reserve – is almost always humid and sunny. Cultivated plant life goes wild, with the result that giant geraniums and nasturtiums climb three-metre hedges, overhung by gigantic eucalyptus trees and yucca plants. The tiny bit of the island spared by the military is a **nudist colony**, set up in the village of **HELIOPOLIS** in the early 1930s. About sixty people live here all the year round, joined by thousands who come just for the summer, and by tens of thousands of day-trippers.

Visitors who come to the colony for just a couple of hours tend to be treated as voyeurs, but if you **stay**, even for one night, you'll generally receive a much friendlier reception. The most reasonable **hotels** on the island are *Les Arbousiers* (Ⓣ04.94.05.90.73, Ⓔarbousiers83@wanadoo.fr; ❸; closed mid-Oct to March) and *Gaëtan* (Ⓣ04.94.05.91.78, Ⓕ04.94.36.77.17; ❷; closed Oct–March). There are two **campsites**: *Le Colombero* (Ⓣ04.94.05.90.29; closed Oct–Easter) and *La Pinède* (Ⓣ04.94.05.92.81, Ⓦwww.campingdulevant.free.fr).

Levant has a better choice of **restaurants** than the other islands, though price and quality still don't match, even taking into account the cost of transporting supplies. The restaurant of the hotel *La Source* is reasonable, with a €17 menu.

The Corniche des Maures

The Côte really gets going with the resorts of the **Corniche des Maures**, as multi-million-dollar residences lurk increasingly in the hills, even more luxurious yachts moor in the bays, and seafront prices become alarming. This is the place where the rich and famous go to seed: Douglas Fairbanks Jr, the late Grand Duke of Luxembourg and a host of sundry titled names have pushed this coastline into legend.

The Corniche des Maures has beaches that shine silver (from the mica crystals in the sand), tall dark pines, oaks and eucalyptus to shade them, glittering rocks of purple, green and reddish hue and chestnut-forested hills keeping winds away.

Bormes-les-Mimosas and around

Seventeen kilometres east of Hyères, tasteful, chic **BORMES-LES-MIMOSAS**, like all good Provençal villages, is indisputably medieval in flavour, with a ruined but restored **castle** at the summit of its hill, protected by spiralling lines of pantiled houses backing onto immaculately restored flights of steps. You can almost smell the money as you ascend to the village from the coast. The mimosas here, and all along the Côte d'Azur, are no more indigenous than the people passing in their Porsches: the tree was introduced from Mexico in the 1860s, but the town still has some of the most luscious climbing flowers of any Côte town.

To the southwest of Bormes is one of those rare unbuilt-up stretches of coast around **BREGANÇON** and **CABASSON**, good wine-growing terrain, harbouring a presidential residence in the castle at **Cap de Bregançon**. Unfortunately, access to the sea is heavily controlled, with three **beaches** charging hefty parking fees (and in one instance a small charge for cyclists). The beach by the castle past Cabasson is the best.

Practicalities

Two reasonable **hotels** in old Bormes are *La Terrasse*, 19 place Gambetta (Ⓣ04.94.71.15.22; ❷; closed Dec & Jan), with simple rooms; and the rather plain and old-fashioned *Bellevue*, on place Gambetta (Ⓣ04.94.71.15.15, Ⓦbellevuebormes.fr.st; ❷; closed mid-Nov–Jan). In Cabasson, there's also the very attractive and peaceful *Les Palmiers*, 240 chemin du Petit-Fort (Ⓣ04.94.64.81.94, Ⓦwww.hotellespalmiers.com; ❾; closed mid-Nov to Jan; half-board compulsory in summer), with its own path to the beach. All **campsites** are just below the main road or in La Favière by the mindlessly ugly pleasure port, closer to Le Lavandou than to Bormes. One of the best options is the four-star *Clos-Mar-Jo* at 895 chemin de Bênat (Ⓣ04.94.71.53.39; €17.50 for two people; closed Oct–March). For more information, the **tourist office** in Bormes is on place Gambetta (April–Sept daily 9am–12.30pm & 2.30–6.30pm; Oct–March Mon–Sat 9am–12.30pm & 2–5.30pm; Ⓣ04.94.01.38.38, Ⓦwww.bormeslesmimosas.com).

Good **restaurants** include *La Tonnelle* on place Gambetta (Ⓣ04.94.71.34.84; closed Wed & Thurs lunch, dinner only July & Aug; lunch menus from €25), specializing in local recipes including *daube de boeuf*; the elegant *L'Escoundudo*, 2 ruelle du Moulin (Ⓣ04.94.71.15.53; closed Tues & Wed out of season; menus from €52), whose *carte* varies between traditional Provençal and gastronomique; and *Pâtes … et Pâtes*, on place du Bazar (Ⓣ04.94.64.85.75; closed Tues eve & all day Wed), which serves the best pasta in town from around €9. More ordinary dinners can be had at the less expensive hotels listed above.

Le Lavandou to La Croix-Valmer

One of many Mediterranean fishing villages turned pleasure port, **LE LAVANDOU**, a few kilometres east of Bormes, has nothing wildly special to recommend it, apart from its decent sandy beaches and the seduction of its name (which comes from *lavoir* or "wash-house" rather than "lavender"), some tempting shops and a general Azur atmosphere. From the central promenade of quai Gabriel-Péri the sea is all but invisible thanks to the pleasure boats moored at the three harbours, and it's only upmarket restaurant demand that keeps the dozen or so fishing vessels, from a fleet that once numbered fifty, still in business. If you want to indulge in watersports or nightlife, the **tourist office** on quai Gabriel-Péri (April–May & Oct daily 9am–noon & 3–6.30pm; June–Sept 9am–12.30pm & 3–7pm; Nov–March Mon–Sat 9am–noon & 3–6pm; Ⓣ04.94.00.40.50, Ⓦwww.lelavandou.com) will happily advise. If you want to stay, try the *Hôtel L'Oustaou*, 20 av Général de Gaulle, (Ⓣ04.94.71.12.18; ❸), a clean, family-run place in the town centre, not far from the beach.

The town beach at Le Lavandou is quite broad and sandy, but if you're after the fabled silver beaches you need to head out of town and east along the classic Côte d'Azur corniche lined with pink oleander bushes and purple bougainvillea, to **Cavalière**, **Pramousquier**, **Le Canadel** and **Le Rayol**. It's hardly countryside, but you can explore the Pointe du Layet headland just east of Cavalière, follow the sinuous D27 up to the **Col du Canadel** for breathtaking views and beautiful cork-oak woodland, and, in **Le Rayol**, visit a superb garden, the **Domaine de Rayol** (Tues–Sun: April–Sept 9.30am–12.30pm & 2.30–6.30pm; Feb–March & Oct–Nov 9.30am–12.30pm & 2–5.30pm; closed Dec–Jan; €6.50) with plants from differing parts of the world that share the Mediterranean climate.

Beyond Le Rayol the corniche climbs away from the coast through 3km of open countryside, scarred almost every year by fires. As abruptly as this wilderness commences, it ends with the sprawling, rather bland family resort of **Cavalaire-sur-Mer**. From here another exceptional stretch of coastline, dressed only in its natural covering of rock and woodlands, is visible across the Baie de Cavalaire. This is the **Domaine de Cap Lardier**, a wonderful coastal conservation area around the southern tip of the St-Tropez peninsula, easily accessible from **LA CROIX-VALMER**. The resort's centre is 2.5km from the sea, but this only adds to its charm, since some of the land in between is taken up by vineyards producing a very decent Côte de Provence.

La Croix-Valmer's **tourist office** is at Esplanade de la Gare (mid-June to mid-Sept Mon–Sat 9.15am–12.30pm & 2.30–7pm, Sun 9.15am–1pm; mid-Sept to mid-June Mon–Fri 9.15am–noon & 2–6pm, Sat & Sun 9.15am–noon; ⓣ04.94.55.12.12, ⓦwww.lacroixvalmer.fr) just up from the junction of the D559 and D93. A good-value **hotel** for this part of the world is *La Bienvenue* on rue L.-Martin (ⓣ04.94.17.08.08, ⓦwww.hotel-la-bienvenue.com; ❷; closed Nov–March) in the village centre. One of the least expensive options near the beach is the family-run *Hostellerie La Ricarde*, quartier de la Plage (ⓣ04.94.79.64.07, ⓕ04.94.54.30.14; ❷; closed Oct–March), whilst at the other end of the scale is *Le Château de Valmer*, on route de Gigaro (ⓣ04.94.55.15.15, ⓦwww.chateau-valmer.com; ❾; closed mid-Oct to April), a seriously luxurious old Provençal manor house within walking distance of the sea. You can **camp** at the four-star *Sélection*, on boulevard de la Mer (ⓣ04.94.55.10.30, ⓦwww.selectioncamping.com; from €21 per tent; closed mid-Oct to mid-March; booking advisable), 400m from the sea and with excellent facilities. Good, inexpensive pizzas are guaranteed (€9 up) at *L'Italien* (ⓣ04.94.79.67.16) on plage de Gigaro, at almost the last commercial outlet before the conservation area. Two other good but expensive **restaurants** on this beach are *La Brigantine* and *Souleïas*.

The Massif des Maures

The secret of the Côte d'Azur is that however grossly vulgar the conglomeration of the coast, Provence is still just behind – old, sparsely populated, village-oriented and dependent on the land for produce, not real estate. Between Marseille and Menton, the most bewitching hinterland is the **Massif des Maures**, stretching from Hyères to Fréjus. The highest point of these hills stops short of 800m, but the quick succession of ridges, the sudden drops and views and then closure again, and the curling, looping roads, are pervasively mountainous. Where the lie of the land gives a wide bowl of sunlit slopes, vines are grown. Elsewhere the hills are thickly forested, with Aleppo and umbrella pines, holly, cork oaks and sweet chestnut trees. In spring, the sombre forest is enlivened by millions of wild flowers at the roadside, and the narrow, tortuous upland roads are highly popular with cyclists; in winter, this is the haunt of hunters with rifles. Amidst the brush lope the last of the Hermann's tortoises which once could be found along the whole of the northern Mediterranean coast – the few which escape predators and collectors can live to almost 100 years.

Much of the Massif is inaccessible even to walkers. However, the **GR9 footpath** follows the highest and most northerly ridge from Pignans on the N97 past Notre-Dame-des-Anges, La Sauvette, **La Garde-Freinet** and down to the head of the Golfe de St-Tropez. If you're **cycling**, the D14 that runs for

The forest fires of 2003

The summer of 2003 was not a happy one for Provence. A terrorist bomb in Nice was quickly forgotten in the face of the worst **forest fires** for a generation on the Côte d'Azur. A dry spring was followed by a long heatwave coupled with high mistral winds, which conspired to create tinderbox conditions, leading to fires in much of the region, from Salon de Provence to the Riviera. Worst affected was the densely forested Massif des Maures, where fires came closer to the coastal resorts than many could ever remember and 20,000 residents and holidaymakers were evacuated. People too frightened to return to their homes took to the beach for safety at Les Issambres, near Ste Maxime, while two holidaymakers died trying to flee flames in the wooded country between Grimaud and La Garde Freinet. Campsites on the fringes of Fréjus were engulfed by flames, and 700 firefighters struggled to control a vast fire at La Motte, near Draguignan. The authorities introduced stop and search procedures as it became clear at least some of the fires had been started deliberately, following the discovery of Molotov cocktails. But most of the fires probably started naturally or through carelessness, which sparked a wider debate among environmentalists about the wisdom of planting so many non-native pine trees. The scars, which are highly visible on the hillsides between Grimaud and La Garde Freinet and around Les Issambres, will take some years to heal.

42km through the middle, parallel to the coast, from Pierrefeu-du-Var, north of Hyères, to **Cogolin** near St-Tropez, is manageable and stunning, climbing from 150m to 411m above sea level.

Collobrières and La Chartreuse de la Verne

At the heart of the Massif is the ancient village of **COLLOBRIÈRES**, reputed to have been the first place in France to learn from the Spanish that a certain tree plugged into bottles allows a wine industry to grow. From the Middle Ages until very recent times, cork production has been the major business of the village and Collobrières is still the best place in the region to buy items roughly fashioned from raw cork. However, the sweet chestnut tree is the mainstay of the local economy nowadays. The church, the *mairie* and the houses don't seem to have been modernized for a century, but the **Confiserie Azurienne** on boulevard Koenig (9.30am–12.30pm & 2–7pm) exudes efficiency and modern business skill in the manufacture of all things chestnut: ice cream, jam, nougat, purée and *marrons glacés*.

Collobrières' **tourist office** on boulevard Charles-Caminat (July & Aug Mon 2–6pm, Tues–Sat 10am–12.30pm & 3–6.30pm; Sept–June Tues–Sat 10am–noon & 2–6pm; Ⓣ04.94.48.08.00, Ⓦwww.collotour.com; not always opened during its published opening hours) can supply details of walks in the fantastic surrounding hills for €2. If you're too overdosed on sticky chestnut to move, there are two **hotels**: *Notre-Dame*, 15 av de la Libération (Ⓣ04.94.48.07.13, Ⓕ04.94.48.05.95; ❶; closed mid-Dec to Jan), and the excellent-value *Auberge des Maures*, 19 bd Lazare Carnot (Ⓣ04.94.48.07.10, Ⓕ04.94.48.02.73; ❶, and ❷ per person full board). There are also two great **chambres d'hôtes**: *L'Atelier*, Colette Brésis' ceramic studio at Le Vallon des Fées, 2km west of the village along the D14 (Ⓣ04.94.48.05.92; ❸; closed Nov–March); and Loïc & Andrée de Saleneuve's *La Bastide de La Cabrière*, 6km in the direction of Gonfaron on the D39 (Ⓣ04.94.48.04.31, Ⓕ04.94.48.09.90; ❺, breakfast included). A municipal **campsite**, the St-Roch, south of the village near place Charles-de-Gaulle, is open mid-June to mid-September (bookings through the tourist office). *Camping sauvage* is forbidden; one stray spark and you could be responsible for a thousand acres of burnt forest.

For food other than chestnuts, the **restaurant** *La Petite Fontaine*, 6 place de la République (ⓣ04.94.48.00.12; closed Sun evening & Mon), is congenial and affordable, with menus from €23, but books up fast. If you want to buy some local **wines**, visit the Cave Cooperative close to the *Hôtel Notre-Dame* at the western entrance to the village. Local **market** days are Thursday and Sunday.

Hidden in the forest, 12km from Collobrières on a progressively more awful and rutted track off the D14 towards Grimaud, is a huge and now largely restored twelfth-century monastery, **La Chartreuse de la Verne** (daily except Tues: Feb–May, Oct–Dec 11am–5pm; June–Sept 11am–6pm; €5), abandoned at the time of the Revolution. If anything, the ongoing restoration work has left it looking a little too pristine, and the huge tower crane spoils any lost-in-time effect, though there's no denying the wonder of its setting.

Grimaud

GRIMAUD, 25km east of Collobrières along the twisting D14 and more easily reached from St Tropez or La Croix Valmer, is a film set of a *village perché*. The cone of houses enclosing the eleventh-century church and culminating in the ruins of a medieval castle appears as a single, perfectly unified entity, decorated by its trees and flowers. The most vaunted street in this ensemble is the arcaded **rue des Templiers**, which leads up to the pure Romanesque **Église de St-Michel** and a house of the Knights Templar, while the view from the **castle** ruins is superb. There's a small **tourist office** at 1 bd des Aliziers just off the main road passing the village (daily: July & Aug 9am–12.30pm & 3–7pm; Sept–June 9am–12.30pm & 2.30–6.15pm; ⓣ04.94.55.43.83, ⓦwww.grimaud-provence.com). If you're stopping to **eat**, great-value menus from €30 are offered at *Le Coteau Fleuri*, place des Pénitents (ⓣ04.94.43.20.17, ⓔcoteaufleuri@wanadoo.fr; closed Tues all day, Mon & Fri lunch, plus Nov, early Dec & ten days early Jan), which also has a few **rooms** (❻).

Cogolin

COGOLIN, the town just south of Grimaud, is remarkable for its combination of tourism with traditional craft manufacturing – reeds for wind instruments, pipes for smoking, wrought-iron furniture, silk yarn and knotted wool carpets. These are all serious businesses for the one-off, made-to-order, high-quality and high-cost Côte d'Azur market. As a consequence Cogolin is fairly animated all year round – a fact reflected in its fiendish traffic problem and even more fiendish traffic control measures.

Visits to some of the **craft factories** can be arranged and are free. The helpful **tourist office** on place de la République (July & Aug Mon–Fri 9am–1pm & 2–7pm, Sat 9am–1pm & 3–7pm, Sun 9.30am–12.30pm; Sept–June Mon–Fri 9am–12.30pm & 2–6.30pm, Sat 9am–12.30pm; ⓣ04.94.55.01.10, ⓦwww.cogolin-provence.com) will provide you with a complete list of addresses and times, and help with making appointments. Or you can just wander down **avenue Georges-Clemenceau** and pop into the retail outlets. Pipes made from briar wood are on show in Courrieu, at no. 58 (daily 9am–noon & 2–6pm); the Manufacture de Tapis, just off the avenue on boulevard Louis-Blanc, re-creates designs by famous artists such as Léger and Mondrian (exhibition room open Mon–Thurs 8am–noon & 2–6pm, Fri until 5pm). World-famous musicians get their reeds from Rigotti, on rue Barbusse; visits are restricted however to musicians only.

From place Bellevue, at the top of the town away from the bustling centre, you can see across the St-Tropez peninsula, to Gassin, Ramatuelle and St-Tropez itself. Having taken in that view and seen enough of Cogolin's manufacturing businesses, the one thing left to do is try the local **wines**: the Cave des Vignerons is on rue Marceau, just before the junction with the N98 heading westwards (closed Sun). There are a couple of reasonably inexpensive **hotels** in Cogolin that make viable bases for trips into congested St-Tropez: the amiable, comfortable *Coq Hôtel*, place de la Mairie (Ⓣ04.94.54.13.71, Ⓕ04.94.54.03.06; ❺); and the *Clemenceau*, next door (Ⓣ04.94.54.15.17, Ⓕ04.94.54.42.78; ❷). Both, however, are in somewhat noisy, central locations.

La Garde-Freinet

The attractive village of **LA GARDE-FREINET**, 10km northwest of Grimaud, was founded in the late twelfth century by people from the nearby villages of Saint Clément and Miremer. The original fortified settlement sat further up the hillside, and the foundations of the fortress are still visible above the village beside the ruins of a fifteenth-century castle (take the path from La Planette car park at the western end of the village). Today the occupiers of the village include Oxbridge professors and other leisured Brits, but it still feels that it belongs to the locals (thanks in part to the regeneration of forestry business around cork and chestnut). It also has medieval charm; easy walks to stunning panoramas; markets twice a week (Wed & Sun); a chestnut cooperative on the northern approach to the village; tempting food shops like La Voute, selling organic produce and good local wines; and very reasonable accommodation possibilities. The enthusiastic and helpful **tourist office** operates from the Chapelle St Jean, on place de la Mairie (Easter–Oct Mon–Sat 10am–12.30pm & 3–6pm, Sun 10am–12.30pm; Nov–Easter Mon–Sat 10am–12.30pm & 3–6pm; Ⓣ04.94.43.67.41, Ⓦwww.lagardefreinet-tourisme.com), and will provide details for all of the Maures region, including suggesting **walks** and hikes such as the spectacular 21-kilometre GR9 route des Crêtes to the west of the village.

For **rooms**, *La Claire Fontaine* on place Vieille (Ⓣ04.94.43.63.76; Ⓕ04.94.55.23.54, ❸) and *Le Fraxinois* on place Neuve (Ⓣ04.94.43.62.84, Ⓕ04.94.43.69.65; ❸) are incredibly good value for this part of the world. The two three-star campsites are the municipal *St-Eloi*, opposite the municipal pool (Ⓣ04.94.43.62.40; €10 for a tent, two people and car; closed Oct–April), and *La Ferme de Bérard*, 5km along the D558 towards Grimaud (Ⓣ04.94.43.21.23, Ⓕ04.94.43.32.33; €11.60 for two adults, car and tent; closed Nov–Feb).

The place to be of an evening is *Le Lézard* bar, art gallery and restaurant, on the exquisite place du Marché (Ⓣ04.94.43.62.73; menu from €19.50; occasional live music). *La Colombe Joyeuse*, on place Vieille (Ⓣ04.94.43.65.24; closed Tues in winter; €15 menu), has pigeon as its à la carte speciality, whilst *La Faucado*, on the main road to the south (Ⓣ04.94.43.60.41; closed Tues in winter; €32 midday menu, otherwise à la carte from €35), is overpriced, but serves some beautiful dishes from local produce.

St-Tropez and its peninsula

The origins of **ST-TROPEZ** are unremarkable: a little fishing village that grew up around a port founded by the Greeks of Marseille, which was destroyed by the Saracens in 739 and finally fortified in the late Middle Ages.

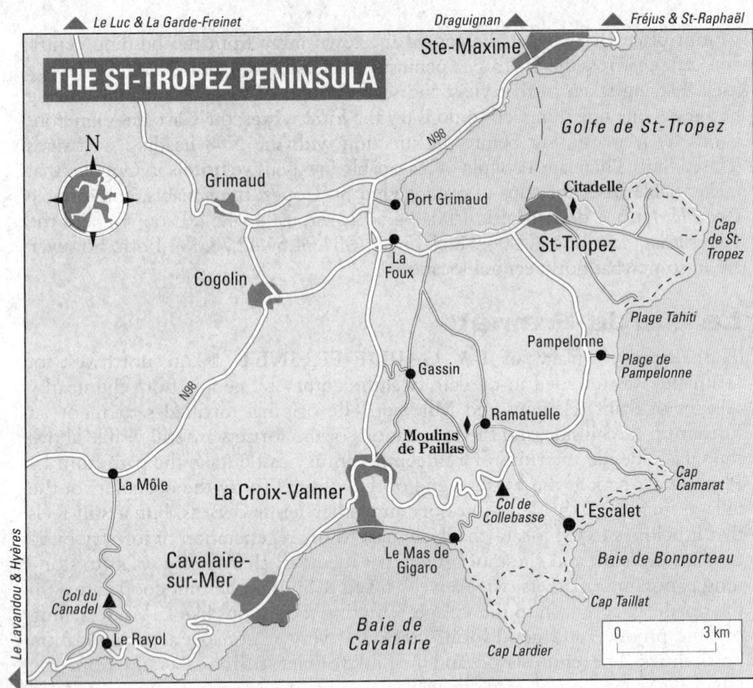

Its sole distinction from the myriad other fishing villages along this coast was its inaccessibility. Stuck out on the southern shores of the Golfe de St-Tropez, away from the main coastal routes on a wide peninsula that never warranted real roads, St-Tropez could only easily be reached by boat. This held true as late as the 1880s, when the novelist Guy de Maupassant sailed his yacht into the port during his final high-living binge before the onset of syphilitic insanity.

Soon after de Maupassant's fleeting visit, the painter and leader of the neo-Impressionists, Paul Signac, was sailing down the coast when bad weather forced him to moor in St-Tropez. He instantly decided to build a house there, to which he invited his friends. Matisse was one of the first to accept, with Bonnard, Marquet, Dufy, Dérain, Vlaminck, Seurat and Van Dongen following suit, and by the eve of World War I St-Tropez was pretty well established as a hangout for bohemians. The 1930s saw a new influx of artists, this time of writers as much as painters: Cocteau, Colette and Anaïs Nin, whose journal records "girls riding bare-breasted in the back of open cars". In 1956 Roger Vadim arrived to film Brigitte Bardot in *Et Dieu Créa la Femme*. The international cult of Tropezian sun, sex and celebrities took off – even the 1960s hippies who flocked to the revamped Mediterranean Mecca of liberation managed to look glamorous – and the resort has been big-money mainstream ever since.

Arrival, information and accommodation

Buses run between the main coast road at **La Foux** and St-Tropez, 5.5km away, every two hours or so, dropping you at the **gare routière** on avenue Général-de-Gaulle. From here it's a short walk, along avenue du 8-Mai-1945, to the **Vieux Port**, where you'll find the **tourist office** opposite, on quai Jean-Jaurès (daily: April–June, Sept & Oct 9.30am–12.30pm & 2–7pm; July & Aug 9.30am–8pm; Nov–March 9.30am–12.30pm & 2–6pm; ⓣ04.94.97.45.21, ⓦwww.saint-tropez.st). **Bikes** and **motorbikes** can be rented at Holiday Bikes at 14 av G. Leclerc (ⓣ04.94.97.09.39, ⓦwww.holiday-bikes.com).

With more and more people wanting to pay homage to St-Tropez, **accommodation** is a problem; indeed, between April and September you won't find a room unless you've booked months in advance or are prepared to pay exorbitant prices. The tourist office can help with reservations, but, transport permitting, you might be better off staying in La Croix-Valmer or La Garde-Freinet. Out of season you may be luckier, though in winter many hotels close. One of the best-value places in town is *Lou Troupelen* (ⓣ04.94.97.44.88, ⓦwww.nova.fr/lou-troupelen; ❺; closed Oct – April), a short walk from the centre, which has clean, comfortable rooms. If they're booked up, try the *Lou Cagnard*, 18 av Paul Roussel (ⓣ04.94.97.04.24, ⓕ04.94.97.09.44; ❸; closed Nov & Dec), which looks dreary from the outside but has a decent garden. If you're prepared to pay a bit more, *Baron Lodge*, 23 rue de l'Aïoli (ⓣ04.94.97.06.57, ⓦwww.hotel-le-baron.com; ❹), overlooking the citadel, is a bit quieter than those in the centre and is open all year round. *Le Sube*, 15 quai Suffren (ⓣ04.94.97.30.04, ⓦwww.hotel-sube.com; ❽), offers unique views over the port and yacht-like decor, or there's the luxurious *La Ponche*, on place du Révelin (ⓣ04.94.97.02.53, ⓦwww.laponche.com; ❾; closed Nov to mid-Feb), an old block of fishermen's houses with a host of famous arty names in its guest book.

Camping near St-Tropez is also a problem. The nearest sites are the two on the plage du Pampelonne, which charge extortionate rates and are massively crowded in high summer. Otherwise, 6km away on the N559 near Gassin is the three-star *Camping Parc Montana* (ⓣ04.94.55.20.20, ⓕ04.94.56.34.77; closed Oct–March). Within a three-kilometre radius of Ramatuelle are *Les Tournels* on route de Camarat (ⓣ04.94.55.90.90, ⓦwww.tournels.com; closed mid-Jan to end Feb) and *La Croix du Sud* on route des Plages (ⓣ04.94.55.51.23, ⓕ04.94.79.89.21; closed Oct–March).

The Town

Beware of coming to St-Tropez in high summer, unless by helicopter or yacht (or by hydrofoil from Ste Maxime) and with limitless credit. The road from La Foux is a mess of superstores and fast food restaurants and the traffic jams are nightmarish; the pedestrian jams to the port are not much better; the hotels and restaurants are full and very expensive; overnighting in vehicles is prohibited; and the beaches are not the cleanest. Save your visit, if you can, for a spring or autumn day, and you'll perhaps understand why this place has had such history and such hype.

The **Vieux Port**, with the old town rising above the eastern quay, is where you'll get the classic St-Tropez experience: the quayside café clientele *face-à-face* with the yacht-deck martini sippers and the latest fashions parading in between, defining the French word *frimer*, which means to stroll ostentatiously in places like St-Tropez. Ostentatious it certainly is: the motor yachts are so vast you can't see the harbour properly, and in the area around the port strolling visitors are menaced by outsize limousines that can barely squeeze through the narrow lanes. You'll either love it or hate it.

Up from the port, at the end of quai Jean-Jaurès, you enter place de l'Hôtel-de-Ville, with the **Château Suffren**, originally built in 980 by Count Guillaume 1er of Provence (occasionally hosting art exhibitions), and the very pretty *mairie*. A street to the left leads down to the rocky **baie de la Glaye**; while, straight ahead, rue de la Ponche passes through an ancient gateway to place du Revelin above the exceptionally pretty **fishing port** and its tiny beach. Turning inland and upwards, struggling past continuous shopfronts, stalls and café tables, you finally reach the open space around the sixteenth-century **citadel**. It houses a local history **museum** (daily except Tues: April–Oct 10am–12.30pm & 1–6.30pm; Nov–March 10am–12.30pm & 1.30–5.30pm; €4) which occasionally hosts art exhibitions. The walk round the ramparts (currently closed for restoration) has the best views of the gulf and the back of the town – views that have not changed since their translations in oil onto canvas before the war.

Some of these paintings you can see at the marvellous **Musée de l'Annonciade**, in the deconsecrated sixteenth-century chapel on place Georges-Grammont, right on the port (daily except Tues: Jan–May, Oct & Dec 10am–noon & 2–6pm; June–Sept 10am–1pm & 3–11pm; €5.50). It was originally Signac's idea to have a permanent exhibition space for the neo-Impressionists and Fauvists who painted here, though it was not until 1955 that the collections of various individuals were put together. The Annonciade features works by Signac, Matisse and most of the other artists who worked here: grey, grim, northern views of Paris, Boulogne and Westminster, and then local, brilliantly sunlit scenes by the same brush – a real delight and unrivalled outside Paris for the 1890–1940 period of French art.

The other pole of St-Tropez's life, south of the Vieux Port, is **place des Lices**. The café-brasseries have become a bit too Champs-Elysées in style, and a new commercial block has been added near the northern corner, but you can still sit on benches in the shade of decayed but surviving plane trees and watch the boules games.

The beaches

The beach within easiest walking distance is **Les Graniers**, below the citadel just beyond the port des Pêcheurs along rue Cavaillon. From there, a path follows the coast around the **baie des Canebiers**, with its small beach, to Cap St-Pierre, Cap St-Tropez, the very crowded **Les Salins** beach and right round to Tahiti-Plage, about 11km away.

Tahiti-Plage is the start of the almost straight, five-kilometre north–south **Pampelonne** beach, famous bronzing belt of St-Tropez and world initiator of the topless bathing cult. The water is shallow for 50m or so, and the beach is exposed to the wind, and sometimes scourged by dried sea vegetation, not to mention more distasteful garbage. But spotless glitter comes from the unending line of beach bars and restaurants, all with patios and sofas, serving cocktails and gluttonous ice creams (as well as full-blown meals). Though you'll stumble across people in the nude on all stretches of the beach, only some of the bars welcome people carrying wallets and nothing else.

Transport from St-Tropez to the beaches is provided by a frequent **minibus** service from place des Lices to Salins, or an infrequent bus service to Ramatuelle which runs along the route de Pampelonne. If you're driving, you'll be forced to pay high parking charges at all the beaches, or to leave your car or motorbike some distance from the sea and easy prey to thieves.

Eating and drinking

There are **restaurants** to cover every budget in St-Tropez, as well as plenty of snack bars and takeaway outfits, particularly on rue Georges-Clemenceau and place des Lices.

Le Bistrot 3 place des Lices ⓣ04.94.97.11.33. Updated *fin-de-siècle* decor for traditional preening and excellent but expensive eats; midday *plat du jour* €18, otherwise from €33. Closed Wed in winter.

Café des Arts place des Lices ⓣ04.94.97.02.25. The number-one brasserie on the square. Old-timers still gather in the bar at the back; salads from €12, à la carte minimum €30.

Café Sénéquier 90 quai Jean Jaurès. The top quayside café; horribly expensive, but sells sensational nougat (also on sale from the shop at the back).

Gandhi 3 quai de l'Epi ⓣ04.94.97.71.71. Curries and tandoori, with a good selection of fish and shellfish on the menu. Lunch menu from €15.50 and dinner from €25. Closed Wed.

Le Gorille 1 quai Suffren. Straightforward quayside fare for around €15. July & Aug open 24hr.

Joseph 1 place de l'Hôtel de Ville ⓣ04.94.97.01.66. Brunch buffet (€18), seafood, and great desserts; à la carte around €60.

Le Petit Charron 6 rue des Charrons ⓣ04.94.97.73.78. Tiny terrace and dining room serving beautifully cooked Provençal specialities. Menus from €36. Closed Sun out of season.

Le Petit Joseph 6 rue Sibille ⓣ04.94.97.03.90. Upmarket Asian fusion cuisine; à la carte €45. Open evenings only.

Regis et Lolo 19 montée de la Citadelle ⓣ04.94.97.15.53. Small, friendly bistro, usually full of exuberant youth; around €20–30.

La Tarte Tropezienne 36 rue G.-Clemenceau. Pâtisserie claiming to have invented the rather sickly sponge and cream custard cake, though you no longer have to come to St Tropez to sample it – the company has evolved into quite a large chain with branches the length of the Côte d'Azur.

Nightlife

In season St-Tropez stays up late, as you'd expect. You can spend the evening trying on fancy clothes in the amazing array of couturier shops; the boules games on place des Lices continue until well after dusk; and the portside spectacle doesn't falter till the early hours. If you're mad enough to want to pay to see – and be seen with – the **nightlife** creatures of St-Tropez, clubs include *Les Caves du Roy*, in the flashy *Hôtel Byblos* on rue Paul-Signac (the most expensive and exclusive); *L'Esquinade*, on rue du Four, which has been going strong since Bardot was young and is now a **gay** club that stays open in winter; and the *VIP Room* on the Nouveau Port.

Gassin and Ramatuelle

Though the coast of the **St-Tropez peninsula** sprouts second residences like a cabbage patch gone to seed, the interior is almost uninhabited, thanks to government intervention, complex ownerships and the value of some local wines. The best view of this richly green and flowering countryside is from the hilltop village of Gassin, its lower neighbour Ramatuelle, or the tiny road between them, the dramatic route des Moulins de Paillas, where three ruined windmills could once catch every wind.

GASSIN is the shape and size of a small ship perched on a summit; once an eighth-century Muslim stronghold, it is now, of course, highly chic, best known today as the birthplace of soccer idol David Ginola and as the place where Mick Jagger married Bianca. It's an excellent place for a blowout dinner, sitting outside by the village wall with a spectacular panorama east over the peninsula. Of the handful of **restaurants**, *Bello Visto*, 9 place des Barrys (ⓣ04.94.56.17.30, ⓕ04.94.43.45.36; closed Tues lunch), has very acceptable Provençal specialities on a €25 menu, plus nine rooms at excellent prices for this brilliant setting (❹).

RAMATUELLE is bigger than its neighbour, though just as old, and is surrounded by some of the best Côte de Provence vineyards. The twisting, arcaded streets are full of arts and crafts of dubious talent, but it's all very pleasant nonetheless. The most beautiful French actor ever to have appeared on screen, Gérard

Philippe (1922–59), is buried in Ramatuelle's **cemetery**. His ivy-covered tomb, shaded by a rose bush, is set against the wall on the right as you look down. Hotels worth trying are the fairly basic *Le Giulia*, 31 rue Clemenceau (ⓣ04.94.79.20.46; ❸), and *L'Écurie du Castellas*, route des Moulins (ⓣ04.98.10.81.07, ⓕ04.94.79.20.67; ❺; closed Nov). For **food**, great pasta dishes are to be had at *Au Fil à la Pâte*, 7 rue Victor-Léon (ⓣ04.94.79.16.40; closed Nov–Feb), with good *plats du jour* at €11.

Port Grimaud

At the head of the Golfe de St-Tropez, just north of La Foux on the main coast road, the ultimate Côte d'Azur property development half stands and half floats. **PORT GRIMAUD** was created in the 1960s as a private lagoon pleasure city, with waterways for roads and yachts parked at the bottom of every garden. It's very well done, with all the houses in exquisitely tasteful old Provençal style. Their owners – Joan Collins for example – are more than just a little well-heeled. It's surprising that the whole enclave isn't wired off and patrolled by fiercesome dogs.

The main visitors' entrance is 800m up the well-signed road off the N98. You don't have to pay to get in, but you can't explore all the islands without hiring a boat or joining a crowded boat tour (around €3.50). Even access to the church tower for views is controlled by an automatic paying barrier (€1.50). However, if you want to **eat and drink**, there are rows upon rows of brasseries, restaurants and cafés, clearly designed for the visiting public rather than the residents, and not particularly good value (though affordable enough).

Ste-Maxime and around

Facing St-Tropez across its gulf, **STE-MAXIME** is the perfect Côte stereotype: palmed corniche and enormous pleasure-boat harbour, beaches crowded with confident bronzed windsurfers and waterskiers, and an outnumbering of estate agents to any other businesses by something like ten to one. It sprawls a little too much – merging with its northern neighbours to create a continuous suburban strip all the way to Fréjus – but the magnetic appeal of the water's edge is hard to deny, and though it's hardly as colourful as St-Tropez, it's a good deal less pretentious and the beaches are cleaner.

If your budget denies you the pleasures of waterskiing, wet-biking and windsurfing, you might find Ste-Maxime a little lacking in diversions. You can, at least, eat at reasonable cost, since there are plenty of crêperies, glaciers and snack places along the central avenue Charles de Gaulle.

For the spenders, the east-facing plage de la Nartelle, 2km west from the centre towards Les Issambres, is the strip of sand to head for. Here, at **Cherry Beach** and its six neighbours, you'll pay for shaded cushioned comfort, you can enter the water on a variety of different vehicles, eat grilled fish, have drinks brought to your mattress and listen to a piano player as dusk falls. A kilometre or so further on, **plage des Éléphants** has much the same facilities. Its name recalls the town's link to Jean de Brunhoff, creator of Babar the elephant, who had a holiday home in Ste-Maxime.

Ste-Maxime's *vieille ville* has several good **markets**: a covered flower and food market on rue Fernand-Bessy (June–Sept daily 7am–1pm & 4–8pm; Oct–May every morning except Tues); a Thursday morning food market on and around place du Marché; bric-a-brac every Friday morning on place

Jean-Mermoz; and arts and crafts in the pedestrian streets (mid-June to mid-Sept daily 10am–11pm).

High up in the Massif des Maures on the road to Le Muy, some 10km north of Ste-Maxime, the marvellous **Musée du Phonographe et de la Musique Mécanique**, in the parc St-Donat (Easter to Sept Wed–Sun 10am–noon & 4–6.30pm; €3), is the result of one amazing woman's forty-year obsession with collecting audio equipment. She has amassed a wide selection of automata, musical boxes and pianolas, as well as various outstanding pieces: one of Thomas Edison's "talking machines" of 1878, the first recording machines of the 1890s and an amplified lyre (1903). Almost half the exhibits still work. If you get a tour from Madame herself, you'll find it hard to resist her enthusiasm for the history of this branch of technology.

Practicalities

Buses into town stop outside the **tourist office** on the promenade Simon-Lorière (June & Sept Mon–Sat 9am–12.30pm & 2–7pm; July & Aug Mon–Sat 9am–8pm, Sun 10am–noon & 4–7pm; Oct–May Mon–Sat 9am–noon & 2–6pm; ⓣ04.94.55.75.55, ⓦwww.sainte-maxime.com), which can give you information on trips and advice on hotel vacancies – once again, rare in summer. If you're heading for St-Tropez from Ste-Maxime, an alternative to the bus, at not much greater cost, is to go by **boat**; the twenty-minute service from Ste-Maxime's *gare maritime* on the port (€10.40 return) runs all year round except in January, with more frequent crossings in July and August. Bikes can be rented at **Holiday Bikes**, 10, route du Plan de la Tour (ⓣ04.94.43.90.19, ⓦwww.holiday-bikes.com).

As you would expect in such a popular Riviera destination, finding accommodation in Ste-Maxime can be a nightmare in high season: if you're coming in July or August, call as far ahead as possible to make a reservation. The best of the cheaper **hotels** is the good-value and welcoming *Auberge Provençale*, 49 rue Aristide Briand (ⓣ04.94.55.76.90, ⓕ04.94.55.76.91; ❸), with its own restaurant; or there's the small *Castellamar*, 21 av G.-Pompidou (ⓣ04.94.96.19.97; ❸; closed Oct–March), on the west side of the river but still close to the centre and the sea. For more comfortable surroundings, try the central *Hôtellerie de la Poste*, 11 bd Frédéric-Mistral (ⓣ04.94.96.18.33, ⓕ04.94.55.58.63; ❼), a modern but attractive hotel with very nice rooms; or the small and unobtrusive *Marie-Louise*, 2km west in the Hameau de Guerre-Vieille (ⓣ04.94.96.06.05, ⓦwww.hotel-marielouise.com; ❹), tucked away in greenery but in sight of the sea. For camping, *Les Cigalons*, in quartier de la Nartelle, is the two-star seaside option (ⓣ04.94.96.05.51, ⓦwww.campingcigalon.com; closed mid-Oct to March). It also rents holiday bungalows.

For non-beach **eating**, the *Hostellerie de la Belle Aurore*, 5 bd Jean-Moulin (ⓣ04.94.96.02.45; closed Wed outside high season & mid-Oct to May; weekday menu €35), offers gourmet food on a sea-view terrace; or, less expensively, there's classic French cuisine at *La Table des Gémeaux*, 33 rue des Maures (ⓣ04.94.49.16.54; menus starting at €15).

Fréjus and St-Raphaël

The major conurbation of **St-Raphaël** on the coast and Fréjus, 3km inland, has a history dating back to the Romans. Fréjus was established as a naval base under Julius Caesar and Augustus, St-Raphaël as a resort for its veterans. The ancient port at Fréjus, or Forum Julii, had 2km of quays and was connected by a walled canal to the sea, which was considerably closer then. After the battle of Actium in 31 BC, the ships of Antony and Cleopatra's defeated fleet were brought here.

The area between Fréjus and the sea is now the suburb of **Fréjus-Plage** with a vast 1980s marina, **Port-Fréjus**. Both Fréjus and Fréjus-Plage merge with St-Raphaël, which in turn merges with **Boulouris** to the east.

Despite the obsession with facilities for the seaborne rich – there were already two pleasure ports at St-Raphaël before Port-Fréjus was built – this is no bad place for a stopover. There's a wide price range of hotels and restaurants in St-Raphaël, reasonable sandy beaches, good transport links and some interesting sightseeing to be done in Fréjus.

Fréjus

The population of **FRÉJUS**, remarkably, was greater in the first century BC than it is today if you just count the residents of the town centre, which lies well within the Roman perimeter. But very little remains of the original Roman walls that once circled the city; and the harbour that made Fréjus an important Mediterranean port silted up early on and was finally filled in after the Revolution. It's the **medieval centre**, as much as the classical remnants, that evokes the antiquity of this ancient town.

Arrival, information and accommodation

Up to fourteen trains a day in each direction stop at Fréjus' **gare SNCF**, just five to eight minutes away from St-Raphaël. Trains to St-Raphaël itself are much more common, and it's usually easiest to alight there and then take the #6, #7, #10 or #13 Agglobus, which run frequently between the two towns; the #10 reasonably fast and direct. The **gare routière** is on the east side of the town centre on place Paul-Vernet (Ⓣ04.94.53.78.46), opposite which is the **tourist office**, at 325 rue Jean-Jaurès (June & Sept Mon–Sat 10am–noon & 2.30–6.30pm; July & Aug Mon–Sat 9am–noon & 2.30–6.30pm, Sun 10am–noon & 3–6pm; Oct–May Mon–Sat 9am–noon & 2–6pm; Ⓣ04.94.51.83.83, Ⓦwww.ville-frejus.fr). Cycles Patrick Béraud at 337 rue de Triberg (Ⓣ04.94.51.20.20), and Holiday Bikes, 595 avenue de la Corniche d'Azur in Saint-Aygulf (Ⓣ04.94.81.35.94, Ⓦwww.holiday-bikes.com), have **bikes** for rent. To connect to the **Internet**, head for Espace Bureaucratique, 58 rue de Grisolle (Ⓣ04.94.17.15.70).

If you're looking to stay the night in Fréjus, three central **hotels** worth trying are the plush *Aréna*, 145 rue de Général-de-Gaulle (Ⓣ04.94.17.09.40, Ⓦwww.arena-hotel.com; ❻), with pretty, if rather small rooms and a pool; *La Bellevue*, place Paul-Vernet (Ⓣ04.94.17.21.58; ❷), in a convenient though not particularly quiet location; and *La Riviera*, 90 rue Grisolle (Ⓣ04.94.51.31.46, Ⓕ04.94.17.18.34; ❶), very small and not very modern, but clean and perfectly acceptable. There's an **HI hostel** 2km northeast from the centre of Fréjus at 675 chemin du Counillier (Ⓣ04.94.53.18.75, Ⓕ04.94.53.25.86); bus #7 leaves quai 7 of the St-Raphaël *gare routière* on the hour until 7pm (6pm Sun), or take bus #10 or #13 from St-Raphaël or Fréjus, direction "L'Hôpital" to stop "Les Chênes" and walk up avenue du Gal-d'Armée Jean-Calliès – the chemin du Counillier is the first left. Beds are €9.30. There are many **campsites** in the Fréjus area, mostly to the west of the town, some of them extremely large. One of the more moderate-sized sites is *Les Acacias*, 370 rue Henri-Giraud (Ⓣ04.94.53.21.22, Ⓔcampingacacias@ifrance.com; April–Oct), 2.5km from the centre.

The Roman town

A tour of the Roman remains will give you a good idea of the extent of Forum Julii, but they are scattered throughout and beyond the town centre and take a full day to get around. Turning right out of the *gare SNCF* and then right down boulevard Severin-Decuers brings you to the **Butte St-Antoine**, against whose east wall the waters of the port would have lapped, and which once was capped by a fort. It was one of the port's defences, and one of the ruined **towers** may have been a lighthouse. A path around the southern wall follows the quayside (some stretches are visible) to the medieval **Lanterne d'Auguste**, built on the Roman foundations of a structure marking the entrance of the canal into the ancient harbour.

In the other direction from the station, past the Roman **Porte des Gaules** and along rue Henri-Vadon, you come to the **amphitheatre** (April–Oct Mon & Wed–Sat 10am–1pm & 2.30–6.30pm; Nov–March Mon & Wed–Fri 10am–noon & 1.30–5.30pm, Sat 9.30am–12.30pm & 1.30–5.30pm; free), smaller than those at Arles and Nîmes, but still able to seat around 10,000. Today it's used for bullfights and concerts. Its upper tiers have been reconstructed in the same greenish local stone used by the Romans, but the vaulted galleries on the ground floor are largely original. The Roman **theatre** (April–Oct Mon & Wed–Sat 10am–1pm & 2.30–6.30pm; Nov–March Mon & Wed–Fri 10am–noon & 1.30–5.30pm; free) is north of the town, along avenue du Théâtre-Romain, its original seats long gone, though again it's still used for shows in summer. Northeast of it, in the parc Aurelienne at the far end of avenue du XVème-Corps-d'Armée, six arches are visible of the forty-kilometre **aqueduct**, once as high as the ramparts. Closer to the centre, on rue des Moulins, are the arcades of the **Porte d'Orée**, positioned on the former harbour's edge alongside what was probably a **bath complex**.

The medieval town

The **Cité Episcopale**, or cathedral close, takes up two sides of **place Formigé**, the marketplace and heart of both contemporary and medieval Fréjus. It comprises the cathedral flanked by the fourteenth-century bishop's palace, now the Hôtel de Ville, the baptistry, chapterhouse, cloisters and archeological museum. Visits to the cloisters and baptistry are guided (June–Sept daily 9am–6.30pm; Oct–May Tues–Sun 9am–noon & 2–5pm; €4.60); access to the main body of the cathedral is free (9am–noon & 2.30–6.30pm).

The oldest part of the complex is the **baptistry**, built in the fourth or fifth century and so contemporary with the decline of the city's Roman founders. Its two doorways are of different heights, signifying the enlarged spiritual stature of the baptized. Bits of the early Gothic **cathedral** may belong to a tenth-century church, but its best features, apart from the bright diamond-shaped tiles on the spire, are Renaissance: the choir stalls, a wooden crucifix on the left of the entrance and the intricately carved doors with scenes of a Saracen massacre, protected by a wooden cover and only opened for the guided tours. Far the most beautiful and engaging component of the whole ensemble, however, are the **cloisters**. In a small garden of scented bushes around a well, slender marble columns, carved in the twelfth century, support a fourteenth-century ceiling of wooden panels painted with apocalyptic creatures. Out of the original 1200 pictures, 400 remain, and subjects include multi-headed monsters, mermaids, satyrs and scenes of bacchanalian debauchery. The treasures of the **Musée Archéologique** on the upper storey of the cloisters (April–Oct Mon–Sat 10am–1pm & 2.30–6.30pm; Nov–March Mon & Wed–Fri 10am–noon & 1.30–5.30pm, Sat 9.30am–12.30pm & 1.20–5.30pm;

free) include a complete Roman mosaic of a leopard and a copy of a double-headed bust of Hermes.

Eating, drinking and entertainment

One of the best **restaurants** in the old town is the tiny *Les Potiers*, 135 rue des Potiers (☎04.94.51.33.74), with menus of fresh seasonal ingredients from €22.50. The rather more expensive restaurant at *L'Aréna* hotel is excellent for fish and seafood, with menus at €45 and up. Cheaper eats can be found on place Agricola, place de la Liberté and the main shopping streets. *Cadet Rousselle*, at the top of place Agricola (☎04.94.53.36.92), is a crêperie that for once offers a decent-sized lunch – the €12 menu includes three crêpes. At Fréjus-Plage there's a string of eating options, though menus are monotonously alike, with more upmarket *plateau des fruits de mer* outlets at Port-Fréjus. The *Bar du Marché*, on the place de la Liberté, is a good establishment for a bit of café lounging. The main **market days** are Wednesday and Saturday. If you happen to be in town on July 14 and 15, you can take in a Spanish-style **bullfight**; there's also a bullfighting festival during August.

Around Fréjus

Unlikely remnants of the more recent past come in the shape of a Vietnamese pagoda, and an abandoned mosque, both built by French colonial troops. The **Mosquée Missiri de Djenné** is on the left off the D4 to Bagnols, in the middle of an army camp 2km from the RN7 junction. A strange, guava-coloured, fort-like building, it's a replica of a Sudanese mosque in Mali, decorated inside with fading murals of desert journeys gracefully sketched in white on the dark-pink walls. Sadly it's fenced off, though much of the interior is visible from outside. The **pagoda** (daily 9am–noon & 2–7pm; €1.50), still maintained as a Buddhist temple, is on the crossroads of the RN7 to Cannes and the D100, about 2km out of Fréjus. Alongside the pagoda is the massive, and rather moving, memorial to the dead of the Indo-Chinese wars of the 1940s and 1950s (Mon & Wed–Sun 10am–5.30pm). Much in the manner of the US Vietnam memorial, it is inscribed with the name of every fallen Frenchman; the sheer length of the lists suggesting the years 1950–54 were the most bloody.

If **mountain biking** tempts you, there are a number of trails which start in the Base Nature, just west of Port-Fréjus along the coast, and head up into the forested hills of the **Massif de l'Esterel** to the northeast of the town. The trails range from a flat, five-kilometre ride around a marsh to more serious 35-kilometre rides in the massif. The tourist office sells trail maps for €8.50, or call the Point Accueil VTT for more information (☎04.94.51.91.10).

For children, there's a **zoo** in Le Capitou, close to exit 38 on the D4 heading north (daily: March–May & Sept–Oct 10am–5pm; June–Aug 10am–6pm; Nov–Feb 10am–4pm; €12, children aged 3–10 €8; bus #2), and a water amusement park, **Aquatica** (daily: June & Sept 10am–6pm; July & Aug 10am–7pm; €22, children €18; bus #9), off the RN98 to St-Aygulf. Toboggans and pedal boats, chutes into an enchanted river, lakes, a huge swimming pool with artificial waves, a beach for the less energetic and a Black Hole are some of its main attractions.

St-Raphaël

A large resort and now one of the richest towns on the Côte, **ST-RAPHAËL** became fashionable at the turn of the twentieth century. Its seafront Belle

Époque mansions and hotels, flattened by bombardments in World War II, have mostly been rebuilt, while the **old town** beyond place Carnot on the other side of the railway line is pleasantly low-key, no longer the main commercial focus of the town but one of the better places to stroll and browse. On rue des Templiers a crumbling fortified Romanesque church has fragments of the Roman aqueduct that brought water from Fréjus in its courtyard along with a local history and underwater archeology **museum** (daily: July & Aug Wed–Sun 11am–5pm; Sept–June Wed 9am–noon & 2–5pm, Thurs 9am–noon Sat 2–5pm; entry to church and museum free).

The **beaches** stretch between the old port in the centre and the newer **Port Santa Lucia**, with opportunities for every kind of watersport. You can also take boat trips to St-Tropez, the Îles d'Hyères and the much closer *calanques* of the Esterel coast from the *gare maritime* on the south side of the Vieux Port. When you're tired of sea and sand you can lose whatever money you have left on slot machines or blackjack at the **Grand Casino** on Square de Gand overlooking the Vieux Port (daily 10am–dawn), or there are plenty of snooty discotheques.

Practicalities

St-Raphaël's **gare SNCF**, in the centre of town, is the main station for the Marseille–Ventigmilia line; the **gare routière** is on square du Dr Régis, across the rail line behind the *gare SNCF*. Information on the surrounding region is available from the **tourist office**, opposite the *gare SNCF* on rue Waldeck-Rousseau (daily: July & Aug 9am–7pm; Sept–June 9am–12.30pm & 2–6.30pm; Ⓣ04.94.19.52.52, Ⓦwww.saint-raphael.com), close to all the major car hire outlets. **Bikes** can be rented from Patrick Moto, 280 av Général-Leclerc (Ⓣ04.94.53.65.99).

Seafront **accommodation** in St-Raphaël is available on promenade René-Coty at the *Beau Séjour* (Ⓣ04.94.95.03.75, Ⓦwww.hotelbeausejour.fr; ❹; closed Nov–March), one of the cheaper hotels along here, with a pleasant terrace; or at the elegant old *Excelsior* (Ⓣ04.94.95.02.42, Ⓦwww.excelsior-hotel.com; ❽), whose rooms are luxurious and well equipped. *Bellevue*, 22 bd Félix-Martin (Ⓣ04.94.19.90.10, Ⓕ04.94.19.90.11; ❷), is good value for its central location; and *La Bonne Auberge*, 54 rue de la Garonne (Ⓣ04.94.95.69.72; ❷; closed mid-Nov to mid-March), is a cheapie close to the old port. East of the centre, the *Hôtel du Soleil*, 47 bd du Domaine de Soleil, off boulevard Christian-Lafon (Ⓣ04.94.83.10.00, Ⓦperso.wanadoo.fr/hotel.du.soleil; ❹), is a small, pretty villa with its own garden. There's **hostel** accommodation (€20) and double rooms in Boulouris, 5km east of St-Raphaël, at the *Centre International Le Manoir*, chemin de l'Escale (Ⓣ04.94.95.20.58, Ⓦwww.cei-manoir.com; ❷; open 20 June–Aug 15). The *Centre* has friendly, helpful staff and is close to the beach right by the Boulouris *gare SNCF* (10 trains daily from St-Raphaël; 7–11 buses daily). A two-star **campsite** close to the beach, *Camping de L'Ile d'Or*, on the N98 in Boulouris (Ⓣ & Ⓕ04.94.95.52.13), is open from late March until the end of September.

Food markets are held every day on place Victor-Hugo and place de la République. You'll find reasonably priced cafés and brasseries around these, and plenty of pizzerias, crêperies and restaurants of varying quality around the Vieux Port, Port Santa Lucia and along the promenades. Of the more expensive establishments, one of the best is *Le Sirocco*, 35 quai Albert-1er (Ⓣ04.94.95.39.99), a smart restaurant specializing in fish, with menus around €17.50–38.50 plus a view of the port; alternatively, try the very likeable *La Sarriette* at 45 rue de la République in the old town (Ⓣ04.94.19.28.13;

closed Sun eve & Mon), with Provençal menus from €15.50 and a wonderful lavender-scented crème brulée.

For **drinking**, try the selection of beers at the *Blue Bar* on promenade René Coty, plage du Veillat (open till 4am in summer); *Aux Ambassadeurs*, a brasserie in the Casino complex that attracts a young crowd (till 1am); the *Coco-Club* at Port Santa Lucia (till 4am) for more expensive cocktails; or one of the beachfront discos like *La Réserve* on promenade René Coty or *L'Odysée* or *La Playa* in Fréjus-Plage. If you're staying outside the centre though, note that late-night taxis are almost impossible to come by in this part of the world. St Raphael has the only gay bar in the area, *Pipeline*, at 16 rue Charabois behind the town hall.

The Riviera

The **Riviera**, the seventy-odd kilometres of coast between **Cannes** and **Menton** by the Italian border, was once an inhospitable shore with few natural harbours, its tiny local communities preferring to cluster round feudal castles high above the sea. It wasn't until the nineteenth century that the first foreign aristocrats began to choose to winter in the region's mild climate. But the real transformation came with the onslaught of 1950s mass tourism, as films like Alfred Hitchcock's *To Catch a Thief* and Roger Vadim's *...et Dieu Créa la Femme* generated an image of elegance and excitement. Nowadays, it's an almost uninterrupted promenade, lined by palms and megabuck hotels, with speeding sports cars on the corniche roads and yachts like ocean liners moored at each resort.

Attractions, however, still remain, most notably in the legacies of the artists who stayed here: Picasso, Léger, Matisse, Renoir and Chagall. **Nice**, too, has real substance as a major city.

Cannes and around

If you've got it, **CANNES** is as good a place as any in the South of France to flaunt it. Superficial it may be, but in many ways it's the definitive Riviera resort of popular fantasy, with its immaculate seafront hotels and exclusive beach concessions, glamorous yachts and designer boutiques. It's a place where appearances count, especially during the film festival in May, when the orgy of self-promotion reaches its annual peak. The vast seafront Palais des Festivals is the heart of the film festival but also hosts conferences, tournaments and trade shows throughout the year. Other year-round attractions include people-watching and window-shopping, about the only things hereabouts that don't cost a fortune. Yet despite its glittery reputation Cannes works surprisingly well as a big seaside resort, since there are good, sandy public beaches away from the famed Plage de la Croisette, and if it all gets too much the **Îles de Lérins**, a short boat ride offshore, offer a sublime contrast. As an alternative, visitors can

Museums passport

The **Carte Musées Côte d'Azur** gives free entry to over sixty of the region's most important art and history museums, monuments and gardens. The pass costs €10 for one day, €17 for three days (consecutive), and €27 for seven days (non-consecutive, but with a fifteen-day limit), and is available from participating museums, major tourist offices (excepting Cannes), branches of Thomas Cook exchange and several FNAC department stores.

escape the glitz of present day Cannes by exploring the nineteenth-century glitz of La Californie, the aristocratic suburb once populated by Russian and British royals.

The old town, known as **Le Suquet** after the hill on which it stands, provides a great panorama of the twelve-kilometre beach, and has, on its summit, the remains of the fortified priory lived in by Cannes' eleventh-century monks and the beautiful twelfth-century Chapelle Ste-Anne. These house the **Musée de la Castre** (Tues–Sun: April–May & Sept 10am–1pm & 2–6pm; June–Aug 10am–1pm & 3–7pm; Oct–March 10am–1pm & 2–5pm; €3), which has an extraordinary collection of musical instruments from all over the world, along with pictures and prints of old Cannes and an ethnology and archeology section.

You'll find the non-paying **beaches** to the west of Le Suquet, along the plages du Midi, though there's also a tiny public section of beach on **La Croisette**, just east of the Palais des Festivals. La Croisette is certainly the sight to see, with its palace hotels on one side and private beaches on the other. It's possible to find your way down to the beach without paying, but not easy (you can of course walk along it below the rows of sun beds). The beaches, owned by the deluxe *palais-hôtels* – the *Martinez*, *Carlton* and *Noga Hilton* – are where you're most likely to spot a face familiar in celluloid or a topless hopeful, especially during the film festival, though you'll be lucky to see further than the sweating backs of the paparazzi. Alternative entertainment can be had buying your own food in the **Forville covered market** two blocks behind the *mairie*, or by wandering through the day's flower shipments on the allées de la Liberté, just back from the Vieux Port.

Strolling on and off the main streets of Cannes – **rue d'Antibes**, **rue Meynardier** and the **promenade de la Croisette** – is like wading through a hundred current issues ofVogue. If you thought the people on the beach were wearing next to nothing, now you can see where they bought the sunglasses and swimming suits, the moisturizers and creams, the watch, the perfume, and the collar and leash for little Fou-Fou.

Practicalities

The **gare SNCF** is on rue Jean-Jaurès, five blocks north of the orange, concrete **Palais des Festivals** on the seafront There are **tourist offices** at the train station (Mon–Fri 9am–7pm; ⓣ04.93.99.19.77) and in the Palais des Festivals (daily: July & Aug 9am–8pm, Sept–June 9am–7pm; ⓣ04.92.99.84.22, ⓦwww.cannes.fr), and two **gares routières**: one on place B.-Cornut-Gentille between the *mairie* and Le Suquet, serving coastal destinations; and the other next to the *gare SNCF* for buses inland to places such as Grasse. The Bus Azur runs twenty-one lines, serving all of Cannes and the surrounding area (ⓣ0825.825.599; €1.30 single ticket).

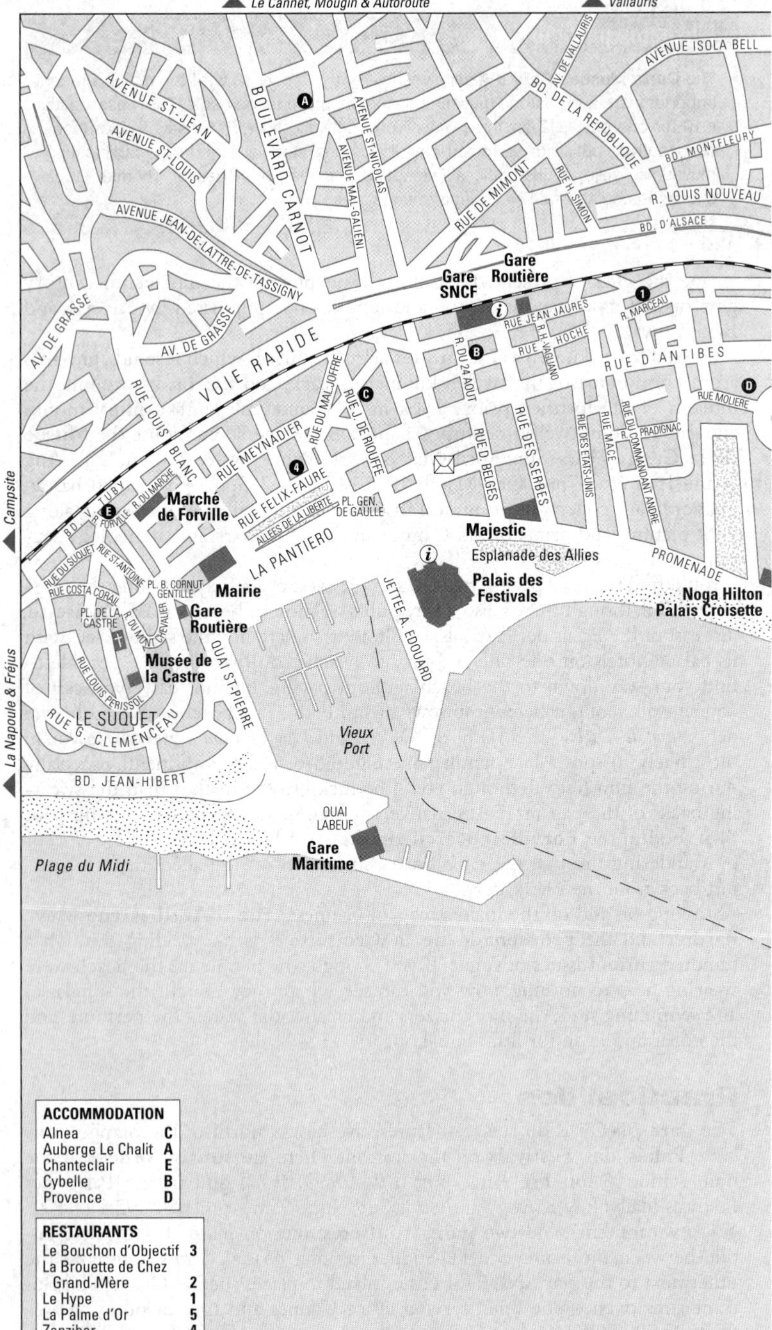
Le Cannet, Mougin & Autoroute
Vallauris
Campsite
La Napoule & Fréjus
AVENUE ST-JEAN
AVENUE ST-LOUIS
AVENUE JEAN-DE-LATTRE-DE-TASSIGNY
BOULEVARD CARNOT
AVENUE ST-NICOLAS
AVENUE MAL-GALIÉNI
AV. DE VALLAURIS
AVENUE ISOLA BELL
BD. DE LA REPUBLIQUE
BD. MONTFLEURY
R. LOUIS NOUVEAU
BD. D'ALSACE
RUE DE MIMONT
RUE H. SIMON
AV. DE GRASSE
VOIE RAPIDE
RUE LOUIS BLANC
Gare SNCF
Gare Routière
RUE JEAN JAURES
R. MARCEAU
R. DU 24 AOUT
R. H. VAGLIANO
RUE HOCHE
RUE D'ANTIBES
RUE MOLIERE
RUE DU MAL JOFFRE
RUE J. DE RIOUFFE
RUE MEYNADIER
RUE FELIX-FAURE
ALLEES DE LA LIBERTE
PL. GEN. DE GAULLE
RUE D. BELGES
RUE DES SERBES
RUE DES ETATS-UNIS
RUE MACE
RUE DU COMMANDANT ANDRE
R. PRADIGNAC
BD. V. TUBY
R. DU MARCHE
R. FORVILLE
Marché de Forville
LA PANTIERO
Majestic
Esplanade des Allies
PROMENADE
Palais des Festivals
Noga Hilton Palais Croisette
RUE DU SUQUET
RUE ST-ANTOINE
RUE COSTA CORAIL
PL. B. CORNUT GENTILLE
Mairie
Gare Routière
PL. DE LA CASTRE
R. DU MONT CHEVALIER
Musée de la Castre
RUE LOUIS PERISSOL
QUAI ST-PIERRE
JETTEE A. EDOUARD
LE SUQUET
RUE G. CLEMENCEAU
BD. JEAN-HIBERT
Vieux Port
QUAI LABEUF
Gare Maritime
Plage du Midi
ACCOMMODATION
Alnea C
Auberge Le Chalit A
Chanteclair E
Cybelle B
Provence D
RESTAURANTS
Le Bouchon d'Objectif 3
La Brouette de Chez Grand-Mère 2
Le Hype 1
La Palme d'Or 5
Zanzibar 4

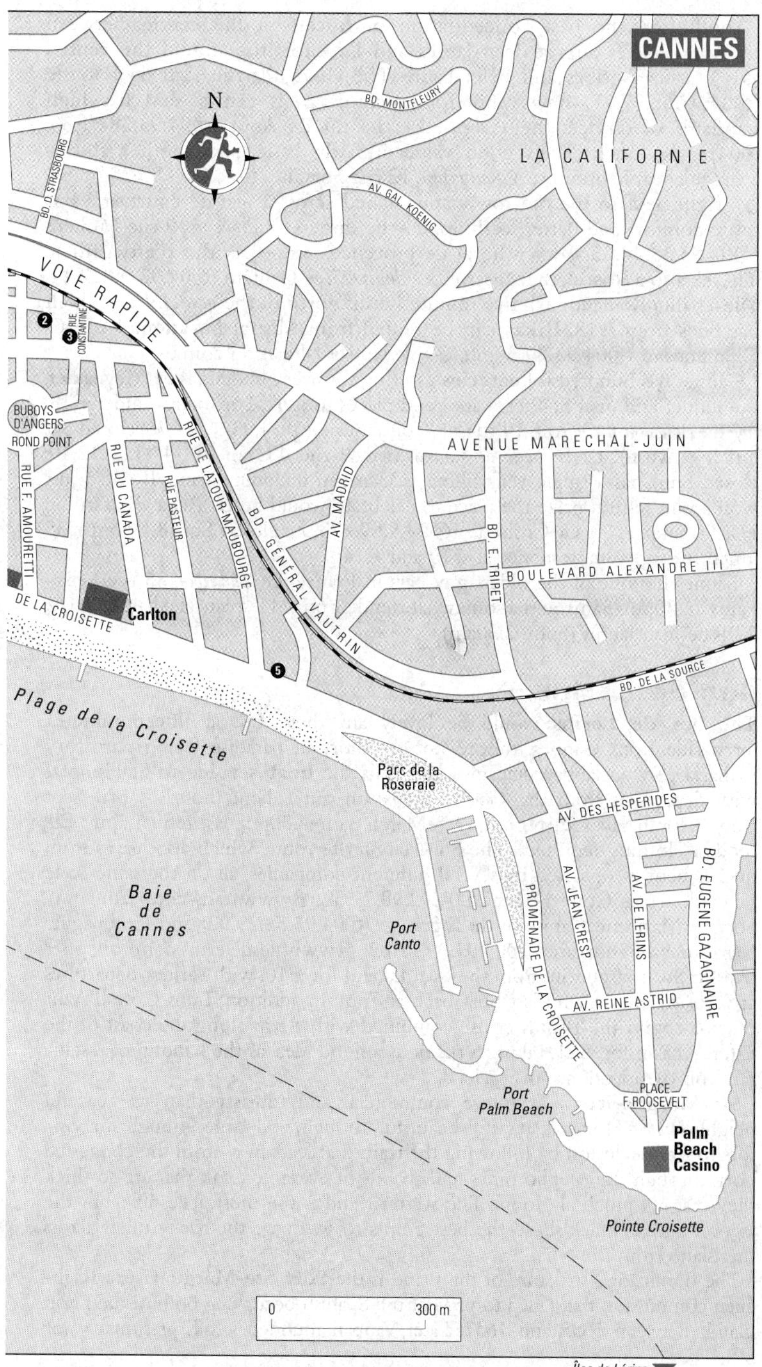
CANNES
N
BD. MONTFLEURY
LA CALIFORNIE
AV. GAL. KOENIG
BD. D. STRASBOURG
VOIE RAPIDE
RUE CONSTANTINE
BUBOYS D'ANGERS
ROND POINT
RUE F. AMOURETTI
RUE DU CANADA
RUE PASTEUR
RUE DE LATOUR-MAUBOURGE
BD. GÉNÉRAL VAUTRIN
AV. MADRID
AVENUE MARECHAL-JUIN
Antibes & Nice
BD. E. TRIPET
BOULEVARD ALEXANDRE III
DE LA CROISETTE
Carlton
BD. DE LA SOURCE
Plage de la Croisette
Parc de la Roseraie
AV. DES HESPERIDES
BD. EUGENE GAZAGNAIRE
AV. JEAN CRESP
AV. DE LERINS
PROMENADE DE LA CROISETTE
Baie de Cannes
Port Canto
AV. REINE ASTRID
Port Palm Beach
PLACE F. ROOSEVELT
Palm Beach Casino
Pointe Croisette
0
300 m
Îles de Lérins

You'll find the best concentration of **hotels** in the centre, between the *gare SNCF* on rue Jean-Jaurès and La Croisette, around the central axis of rues Antibes and Félix-Faure. The *Alnea*, 20 rue Jean de Riouffe (Ⓣ04.93.68.77.77, Ⓦwww.hotel-alnea.com; ❺), is central and has high standards of service; the *Cybelle*, 14 rue du 24 Août (Ⓣ04.93.38.31.33, Ⓕ04.93.38.43.47; ❷), is good value, if fairly basic, and another above-average cheapie option is *Chanteclair*, 12 rue Forville (Ⓣ & Ⓕ04.93.39.68.88; ❸), right next to the old town, approached across a private courtyard. For more comfort and better facilities, try the three-star *Provence*, 9 rue Molière (Ⓣ04.93.38.44.35, Ⓦwww.hotel-de-provence.com; ❻), with a pretty garden. There's also a **hostel**, the *Auberge Le Chalit*, 27 av Galliéni (Ⓣ04.93.99.22.11, Ⓔle-chalit@wanadoo.fr), five minutes' walk north of the *gare SNCF*, which has beds from €18. **Bikes** can be rented from Mistral Location, 4 rue G. Clemenceau (Ⓣ04.93.39.30.60, Ⓦwww.mistral-location.com).

Cannes has hundreds of **eateries** catering for every budget. Rue Meynadier, Le Suquet and quai St-Pierre are good places to look. For menus under €18, try Le *Bouchon d'Objectif*, 10 rue de Constantine (Ⓣ04.93.99.21.76; closed Sat lunch & Mon). *La Brouette de Grand-Mère*, 9 rue d'Oran (Ⓣ04.93.39.12.10; closed Sun) has a single very filling €33 menu including wine. If you'd just won a film festival prize the place to celebrate would be *La Palme d'Or* in the *Hôtel Martinez*, 73 La Croisette (Ⓣ04.92.98.73.00; closed Sun & Mon; €55 lunch menu; evening menus at €70 and €140).

Cannes has one of the oldest **gay** bars in France, *Le Zanzibar*, 85 rue Félix-Faure (6.30pm–5am), and a somewhat trendier mixed lesbian-gay bar, *Le Hype*, 52 Rue Jean Jaurès (5pm–2.30am).

Îles de Lérins

The **Îles de Lérins** would be lovely anywhere, but at fifteen minutes' ferry ride from Cannes, they're not far short of paradise facing purgatory. Planaria (Ⓦwww.abbayedelerins.com) runs the **boat service** to St-Honorat with departures from the *Gare Maritime* on qui Labeuf (hourly: April–Sept 8am–5.30pm, last return 6pm; Oct–March 8am–4.30pm, last return 5pm; €9; modest clothing required). The Ste-Marguerite route, which also leaves from quai Labeuf, is operated by several different companies, all on the same basic schedule. Trans Côte d'Azur (Ⓣ04.92.98.71.30; Ⓦwww.trans-cote-azur.com), Société Maritime Cannoise de Tourisme (Ⓣ04.93.38.29.92) and Compagnie Maritime de Tourisme (Ⓣ04.93.39.11.82; Ⓦwww.ilesdelerins.com) all offer trips to Ste-Marguerite from the quai Labeuf for €10, with earliest departures at 7.30 in summer and last boat back at 7pm. In addition, Trans Côte d'Azur offers a round-the-islands cruise combined with a trip along the coast of the Esterel massif for €21. Taking a picnic is a good idea, as the handful of restaurants on the islands are overpriced.

Ste-Marguerite is far more commercial and touristy than its peaceful neighbour, St-Honorat. It's still beautiful, though, and large enough for visitors to find seclusion by following the trails that lead away from the congested port, through the Aleppo pines and woods of evergreen oak that are so thick they cast a sepulchral gloom. The western end is the most accessible, but the lagoon here is brackish, so the best points to swim are the rocky inlets across the island from the port.

The dominating structure of the island is the **Fort Ste-Marguerite**, a Richelieu commission that failed to prevent the Spanish occupying both of the Lérin islands between 1635 and 1637. Later, Vauban rounded it off, presumably for

Louis XIV's gloire – since the strategic value of greatly enlarging a fort facing your own mainland without upgrading the one facing the sea is pretty minimal. There are cells to see, including the one in which Dumas' *Man in the Iron Mask* is supposed to have been held, and the **Musée de la Mer** (April–Sept Tues–Sun 10.30am–1.30pm & 2.15–5.45pm;Oct–March 10.30am–1.30pm 22.15–4.45pm; €3), containing mostly Roman local finds but also remnants of a tenth-century Arab ship. Access is free to the grassy ramparts of this vast construction.

Owned by monks almost continuously since its namesake and patron founded a monastery here in 410 AD, **St-Honorat**, the smaller southern island, was home to a famous bishops' seminary, where St Patrick trained before setting out for Ireland. The present **abbey** buildings (summer guided visits only: July–Sept Mon–Sat 10am–12.30pm & 2.30–4.45pm, Sun 2.30–4.45pm; Oct–June free access 10.30am–4pm) date mostly from the nineteenth century, though some vestiges of the medieval and earlier constructions remain in the austere church (free to visit) and the cloisters. A shop sells the benevolent white wine, spirits and honey produced by the 28 Cistercian brothers of the monastic community. Behind the cloisters on the sea's edge stands the eleventh-century fortified monastery. Of all the forts along the coast, this is the only one that looks as if it would still serve its original function.

Apart from one small restaurant near the landing stage, there are no bars, hotels or cars: just vines, lavender, herbs and olive trees mingled with wild poppies and daisies, and pine and eucalyptus trees shading the paths beside the white rock shore mixing with the scents of rosemary, thyme and wild honeysuckle.

Vallauris

Picasso spent ten years just northeast of Cannes in **VALLAURIS**, set in the hills above the Golfe Juan. It was here that he first began to use clay, thereby reviving one of the traditional crafts of this little town. Today the main street, **avenue Georges-Clemenceau**, sells nothing but pottery, much of it the garishly glazed bowls and figurines that could feature in souvenir shops anywhere. Picasso used to work in the **Madoura workshop**, on avenue des Ancien-Combattants-d'AFN, to the right as you come down avenue Georges-Clemenceau; it still has sole rights on reproducing Picasso's designs, which it sells, at a price, in the shop (Mon–Fri only).

The bronze statue of **Man with a Sheep**, Picasso's gift to the town, stands in the main square and marketplace, place de la Libération, beside the church and castle. The local authorities also suggested he should decorate the early medieval deconsecrated **chapel** in the castle courtyard (daily except Tues: mid-June to mid-Sept 10am–12.15pm & 2–6pm; rest of year closes at 5pm; €3.10), which he finally did in 1952: his subject was war and peace. The space is tiny, with the architectural simplicity of an air-raid shelter, and at first glance it's easy to be unimpressed by the painted panels covering the vault – as many critics still are – since the work looks mucky and slapdash, with paint-runs on the plywood panel surface. But stay a while and the passion of this violently drawn pacifism slowly emerges. On the "War" panel, a music score is trampled by hooves and about to be engulfed in flames; a fighter's lance tenuously holds the scales of justice and a shield that bears the outline of a dove. "Peace" is represented by Pegasus, the winged horse of Greek myth; people dancing and suckling babies; trees bearing fruit; owls; books; and the freedom of the spirit to mix up images and concepts with well-intentioned mischief. The ticket for the chapel also gives admission to the **Musée de Céramique** in the castle (same hours and ticket), which exhibits Picasso's and other ceramics.

There are regular buses from Cannes and from Golfe-Juan SNCF to the top of bd M Rouvier immediately behind the chateau. The **tourist office** is at the bottom of avenue Georges-Clemenceau on square du 8–Mai-1945 (July & Aug daily 9am–7pm; Sept–June Mon–Sat 9am–noon & 2–6pm; ⓣ04.93.63.82.58).

Grasse

GRASSE, 16km inland from Cannes and with some stunning views over the Côte, is the world capital of *parfumiers* and has been for almost 300 years. These days it likes to flaunt itself, promoting its perfumed image as a chic eighteenth-century village with a medieval heart surrounded by hectares of scented flowers. Making perfumes is presented as a mysterious process, an alchemy, turning the soul of the flower into a liquid of luxury and desire, and the industry is at pains to keep quiet about modern innovations and techniques.

Grasse is the official starting point of the Route Napoléon but is equally easy to visit as a day-trip from the coast.

The Town

Vieux Grasse, despite a window dressing of touristy shops and restaurants, is a surprisingly run-down place, a working-class enclave where lines of washing festoon the dark, narrow streets – rates of pay for the pickers of raw ingredients for perfume essences are notoriously low and parts of the town are shuttered and seedy. Inhabitants say it's like a village where everyone knows each other; out of season it can be quiet to the point of being eerie.

Place aux Aires, at the top of the old town, is the main meeting point for all and sundry and the venue for the daily flower and vegetable **market**. It's ringed by arcades of different heights and the elegant wrought-iron balcony of the *Hôtel Isnard* at no. 33, and at one time was the exclusive preserve of the tanning industry. At the opposite end of Vieux Grasse lie the **cathedral** – containing various paintings, including three by Rubens and a wondrous triptych by the sixteenth-century Niçois painter Louis Bréa – and the **bishop's palace**, now the Hôtel de Ville, both built in the twelfth century.

A museum you might like to take a quick flit through is the **Musée d'Art et d'Histoire de Provence**, 2 rue Mirabeau (June–Sept 10am–6.30pm; Oct & Dec–May daily except Tues 10am–12.30pm & 2–5.30pm; €3, or €4 for temporary exhibitions), housed in a luxurious town house commissioned by Mirabeau's sister for her social entertainment duties. As well as all the gorgeous fittings and the original eighteenth-century kitchen, the historical collection adds a nice eclectic touch. It includes wonderful eighteenth- to nineteenth-century faïence from Apt and Le Castellet, Mirabeau's death mask, a tin bidet and six prehistoric bronze leg bracelets. The fascinating **Musée International de la Parfumerie**, 8 place du Cours (same hours and prices as Musée d'Histoire) displays perfume bottles from the ancient Greeks via Marie-Antoinette to the present and has a reconstruction of a perfume factory with a little test you can do on identifying fragrances. The one-hour guided tours are highly recommended.

The perfume factories

There are thirty major **parfumeries** in and around Grasse, most of them making not perfume but essences-plus-formulas which are then sold to Dior,

Lancôme, Estée Lauder and the like, who make up their own brand-name perfumes. One litre of pure rose essence can cost as much as €19,000; perfume contains twenty percent essence (eau de toilette and eau de Cologne considerably less). The major cost in this multi-billion-dollar business is marketing. The grand Parisian couturiers, whose clothes, on strictly cost-accounting grounds, serve simply to promote the perfume, go to inordinate lengths to sell their latest fragrance, spending millions of euros a year on advertising alone.

The ingredients that the "nose" – as the creator of the perfume's formula is known – has to play with include resins, roots, moss, beans, bark, civet (extract of cat genitals), ambergris (intestinal goo from whales), bits of beaver and musk from Tibetan goats. If that hasn't put you off, you can visit the various **showrooms**, with overpoweringly fragrant shops and free guided tours, in English, of the traditional perfume factory set-up (the actual working industrial complexes are strictly out of bounds). These visits are free and usually open daily without interruption in summer; a few to choose from are **Fragonard**, 20 bd Fragonard (Ⓦwww.fragonard.com); **Galimard**, 73 rte de Cannes (Ⓦwww.galimard.com); and **Molinard** at 60 bd Victor-Hugo (Ⓦwww.molinard.com).

Practicalities

Grasse's **gare routière** is to the north of the old town at the Parking Notre-Dame-des-Fleurs. Head downhill on avenue Thiers becoming boulevard du Jeu de Ballon (where there's an annexe of the tourist office) and you'll find the museums fronting Place du Cours, with the main **tourist office** on cours Honoré-Cresp (July–Sept Mon–Sat 9am–7pm, Sun 9am–1pm & 6pm; Oct–June Mon–Sat 9am–12.30pm & 1.30–6pm; Ⓣ04.93.36.66.66, Ⓦwww.ville-grasse.fr).

Two possible **hotels** at the cheaper end of the market are: *Napoléon*, 6 av Thiers (Ⓣ04.93.36.05.87, Ⓕ04.93.36.41.09; ❷), right next to the *gare routière*, and *Les Palmiers*, 17 av Y.-Baudoin (Ⓣ & Ⓕ04.93.36.07.24; ❷), with a pleasant garden and good views, if not particularly friendly. More expensive, the *Panorama*, on place du Cours (Ⓣ04.93.36.80.80, Ⓦwww.hotelpanorama-grasse.com; ❹), offers rooms with views and all mod cons.

Compared with the coastal towns Grasse isn't terribly well endowed with **restaurants**. The best in town is *La Bastide Saint Antoine*, 48 rue Henri Dunant (Ⓣ04.93.70.94.94), which serves *cuisine gourmande* with a Provençal twist (lunch menus €53; otherwise menus from €130) in a bright sophisticated decor. For drinks, the bars on place aux Aires are friendly; there are a couple of pizzerias in the alleys leading off the square. At *Maison Venturini*, 1 rue Marcel Journet (Ⓣ04.93.36.20.47; closed Sun & Mon), you can buy fabulous sweet *fougassettes* – a local pastry – flavoured with the Grasse speciality of orange blossom, to take away.

Antibes and around

ANTIBES, or rather its promontory the **Cap d'Antibes**, is one of the select places on the Côte d'Azur where the *really* rich and the very, *very* successful still live, or at least have residences. Yet it's not immediately obvious why this area should be so desirable: it's just as built-up as the rest of the Riviera, with no open countryside separating Golfe Juan, **Juan-les-Pins** and Antibes. Long-time resident Graham Greene said it was the only town on the Côte that hadn't lost its soul; perhaps he was right, though he also gave his reason for living there as simply to be with the woman he loved. Be that as it may, Antibes is a pleasing old town, extremely animated, with one of the finest **markets** on the coast and the best **Picasso collection** in its ancient seafront castle; and the southern end of the Cap still has its woods of pine, in which the most exclusive mansions hide. Perhaps the key to its charm is that, unlike Cannes or St-Tropez, it doesn't try too hard.

The sixteenth-century **Château Grimaldi** is a beautifully cool, light space, with hexagonal terracotta floor tiles, windows over the sea and a terrace garden with sculptures by Germaine Richier, Miró, César and others. In 1946, Picasso was offered the dusty building – by then already a museum – as a studio. Several extremely prolific months followed before he moved to Vallauris, leaving all his Antibes output to what is now the **Musée Picasso** (Tues–Sun: mid-June to mid-Sept 10am–6pm; rest of year 10am–noon & 2–6pm; €5). Although Picasso donated other works later on, the bulk of the collection belongs to this one period. There's an uncomplicated exuberance in the numerous still lifes of sea urchins, the goats and fauns in Cubist non-disguise and the wonderful Ulysses and his Sirens – a great round head against a mast around which the ship, sea and sirens swirl. Picasso himself is the subject of works here by other painters and photographers, including Man Ray, Hans Hartung and Bill Brandt; there are several anguished canvases by Nicolas de Staël, who stayed in Antibes for a few months from 1954 to 1955; and works by other contemporaries and more recent artists. Alongside the castle is the **cathedral**, built on the site of an ancient temple. The choir and apse survive from the Romanesque building that served the city in the Middle Ages while the nave and stunning ochre facade are Baroque. Inside, in the south transept, is a sumptuous medieval altarpiece surrounded by immaculate panels of tiny detailed scenes.

One block inland, the morning **covered market** on cours Masséna overflows with Provençal goodies and a profusion of cut **flowers**, the traditional and still-flourishing Antibes business (June–Aug daily 6am–1pm; Sept–May Tues–Sun 6am–1pm). On Thursday, Friday and Saturday (plus Easter–Sept Sun) a craft market takes over in the afternoon. When the stalls are all packed up, café tables take their place.

Cap d'Antibes

Plage de la Salis, the longest Antibes beach, runs along the eastern neck of Cap d'Antibes, with no big hotels owning mattress exploitation rights – an amazing rarity on the Riviera. To the south, at the top of chemin du Calvaire, you can get superb views from the **Chapelle de la Garoupe** (10am–noon & 2.30–7pm), which contains Russian spoils from the Crimean War and hundreds of *ex votos*. To the west, on boulevard du Cap between chemins du Tamisier and G.-Raymond, you can wander around the **Jardin Thuret** (Mon–Fri: July & Aug 8am–6pm; Sept–June 8.30am–5.30pm; free unless part of a group), botanical gardens belonging to a national research institute. Back on the east shore, further south, a second beach, **plage de la Garoupe**, now heavily colonized by sun beds, is linked by a footpath to the peninsula's southern tip. There are more sandy coves and little harbours along the western shore, where you'll also find the **Musée Napoléonien** (Tues–Sat: mid-June to mid-Sept 10am–6pm; mid-Sept to mid-June 10am–4.30pm; €3), at the end of avenue J.-F.-Kennedy. This documents the great return from Elba along with the usual Bonaparte paraphernalia of hats, cockades and signed commands.

Juan-les-Pins

JUAN-LES-PINS, less than 2km from the centre of Antibes, is another of those overloaded Côte d'Azur names: the summer St-Moritz, the night-time playground for the extravagantly outfitted front-page myths who retreat at dawn, like supernatural creatures, to their well-screened cages on Cap d'Antibes. Until this century it was nothing more than a pine grove on the western neck of Cap d'Antibes. A casino was built in 1908 and by the late 1920s Juan-les-Pins had taken off as the original summer resort of the Côte d'Azur. Revealing swimsuits, as opposed to swimming "dresses", were reputedly first worn here in the 1930s. Now, like so much of the Côte, it's a little hard to see what all the fuss is about – or to imagine it as a pine forest. But Juan-les-Pins is at least built to a lower density and with a little more style than some of its neighbours – though the modern Casino on the seafront is a blot on the landscape.

Juan's **international jazz festival** in the middle two weeks of July is the best in the region and takes place in what's left of the pine forest, the **Jardin de La Pinède** (known simply as La Pinède), and **Square Gould** above the beach by the casino. This urban park and the 2km of sheltered sand beach are all that Juan-les-Pins has to offer for free, apart from the dizzying array of architectural styles along its streets.

Practicalities

Antibes' **gare SNCF** lies to the north of the old town at the top of avenue Robert-Soleau. Turn right out of the station and three minutes' walk along avenue R.-Soleau will bring you to place de Gaulle. The **tourist office** is on this square, at no. 11 (July & Aug daily 9am–7pm; Sept–June Mon–Fri 9am–12.30pm & 1.30–6pm, Sat 9am–noon & 2–6pm; ⓣ04.92.90.53.00, ⓦwww.antibes-juanlespins.com). The **gare routière** is off the adjoining place Guynemer (ⓣ04.93.34.37.60), with frequent buses to and from the *gare SNCF* (Mon–Sat); otherwise it's a five-minute walk from the train station. Bus #2A goes to Cap d'Antibes; bus #1A and #3A to Juan-les-Pins, #10A to Biot. Bikes can be rented from three outlets on boulevard Wilson, at nos. 43, 93 and 122. Rue de la République leads into the heart of Vieux Antibes around place Nationale, from where rue Sade leads to cours Masséna, beyond which lie the cathedral, the castle and the sea. For **Internet** access, head to *Xtreme Café*, at 6 rue Aubernon (Tues–Sat 3–11pm, Sun 10am–9pm), or *ASA* at 6, rue du Marc.

The most economical **hotel** in the centre of Antibes, *Le Nouvel Hôtel*, 1 av du 24–Août (ⓣ04.93.34.44.07, ⓕ04.93.34.44.08; ❸), is a stone's throw from the *gare routière*; avenue de l'Estérel in Juan-les-Pins is another good place to try for cheap hotels. For greater comfort, try the *Mas Djoliba*, 29 av de Provence (ⓣ04.93.34.02.48, ⓦwww.hotel-djoliba.com; ❻), between the old town and the beach, or *Le Ponteil*, 11 impasse Jean-Mensier (ⓣ04.93.34.67.92, ⓕ04.93.34.49.47; ❼; half-board obligatory), in a quiet location at the end of a cul-de-sac close to the sea. For something secluded and elegant, it's worth trying *Val des Roses*, an upmarket **chambres d'hôte** on chemin des Lauriers just off the plage de la Salis (ⓣ06.85.06.06.29, ⓦwww.val-des-roses.com; ❼).

There's a **hostel** on Cap d'Antibes, the *Relais International de la Jeunesse* on boulevard de la Garoupe (ⓣ04.93.61.34.40, ⓕ04.93.92.62.85; closed Nov–May; €14.40; buses #1 & #2 stop right outside), which needs booking well in advance. All of Antibes' **campsites** are 3–5km north of the city in the quartier of La Brague (bus #10A or one train stop to Gare de Biot). The three-star *Logis de La Brague* (Ⓣ04.93.33.54.72; Ⓦwww.camping-logisbrague.com; closed Oct–April) is closest to the station, while the two-star *Idéal-Camping* (Ⓣ04.93.74.27.07; closed Oct–April) is south of the station; both are on the route de Nice and close to the sea.

Place Nationale and cours Masséna are lined with **cafés**; rue James Close is nothing but **restaurants** and rue Thuret and its side streets also offer numerous menus to browse. For pizzas, there's *Don Juan*, 17 rue Thuret, and *La Famiglia*, a cheap family-run outfit at 34 av Thiers (closed Wed). *Le Romantic*, 5 rue Rostan (Ⓣ04.93.34.59.39; closed Mon), lives up to its name and offers menus from €26, although in the evening the *terroir*-dominated *carte* will take the bill as high as €46. *Chez Juliette*, 18 rue Sade, serves regional specialities downstairs in the *cave*, which helps diners beat the midday heat (Ⓣ04.93.34.67.37; lunch menu €13).

Juan-les-Pins has one of the **star restaurants** of the Côte, *La Terrasse Christian Morisset*, on avenue Gallice (Ⓣ04.93.61.20.37; closed Tues & Wed out of season; lunch menu €60, otherwise €92 minimum), with original Art–Deco decor, exquisite fish and seafood dishes and mouth-melting desserts. At the other end of the scale you can get brasserie food, crêpes, pizzas and similar snacks from **street stalls** till the early hours, and many shops and bars also keep going in summer till 3am or 4am. Juan-les-Pins is also one of the liveliest places along the coast for nightlife, with a whole host of **nightclubs** and bars for you to spend any surplus euros. Entrance is typically €15 with a "complimentary" drink. You might like to try *Le Village/ Voom Voom* at 1 bd de la Pinède, which attracts a young crowd and goes on till dawn; or *Le Pam-Pam*, 137 bd Président Wilson, with frequent live Brazilian bands.

Finally, if you've run out of reading material, head for Heidi's English Bookshop at 24 rue Aubernon in Antibes (daily 10am–7pm), the cheapest English **bookshop** on the coast.

Biot

Frequent buses connect Antibes with the village of **BIOT**, 8km to the north, where Fernand Léger lived for a few years at the end of his life. A stunning collection of his intensely life-affirming works, created between 1905 and 1955, can be seen at the **Musée Fernand Léger**, built especially to display them (daily except Tues: July–Sept 10.30am–6pm; Oct–June 10am–12.30pm & 2–5.30pm; €4, reduced price on Sun). The museum was closed for rebuilding work during 2004 and early 2005 that aimed to improve circulation. It is just east of the village on the chemin du Val de Pome, stop "Fernand Léger" on the Antibes bus, or a thirty-minute walk from Biot's *gare SNCF*.

The village itself is extremely beautiful (if rather self-consciously so) and oozes with art in every form – architectural, sculpted, ceramic, jewelled, painted and culinary. The **tourist office**, at 46 rue Saint Sebastien, at the western entrance to the village (July & Aug Mon–Fri 10am–7pm, Sat & Sun 2.30–7pm; Sept–June Mon–Fri 9am–noon & 2–6pm, Sat & Sun 2–6pm; Ⓣ04.93.65.78.00, Ⓦwww.biot-coteazur.com), can provide copious lists of art galleries and glassworks – the traditional industry that brought Léger here, and which produces the famous hand-blown **bubble glass**. If you book well in advance you could stay at the very reasonable *Hôtel des Arcades*, 16 place des Arcades (Ⓣ04.93.65.01.04, Ⓕ04.93.65.01.05; ❸), full of old-fashioned charm and with huge rooms in the medieval centre of the village. Its **café-restaurant**, which also doubles as an art gallery, serves delicious traditional Provençal food (closed Sun evening & Mon; €32 menu), or try the delightful *salon de thé Le Mas Des Orangers* at 3 Rue des Roses.

Above the Baie des Anges

Between Antibes and Nice, the **Baie des Anges** laps at a long stretch of fairly undistinguished twentieth-century resorts. At Villeneuve-Loubet-Plage the vast concrete sails of the Marina Baie des Anges – an unmissable landmark along the entire length of this coast – give the landscape a controversial and defiantly modernist stamp. Harder to forgive is the strip-mall squalor of drive-in restaurants, furniture stores and car dealerships that represents what passes for a townscape in the surrounding area.

The old towns and softer visual stimulation lie inland. **Cagnes** is another artists' town – associated in particular with Renoir – as is **St-Paul-de-Vence**, which houses the wonderful modern art collection of the Fondation Maeght. Vence has a small chapel decorated by Matisse, and is a relaxing place to stay, if quiet in the evenings.

Cagnes

CAGNES is a confusing, formless agglomeration, made up of a nondescript seaside district known as Cros-de-Cagnes, the immaculate medieval village of Haut-de-Cagnes overlooking the town from the northwest heights, and Cagnes-sur-Mer, the rather unappealing, traffic-choked town centre wedged between the two. The three busy coastal roads slicing through the town don't add to its appeal.

At the top of place de Gaulle, the main square in **Cagnes-sur-Mer**, avenue Auguste-Renoir runs right and crosses the road to La Gaude. A short way further on, chemin des Collettes leads off to the left up to **Les Collettes**, the house that Renoir had built in 1908 and where he spent the last twelve years of his life. It's now a **memorial museum** (daily except Tues: Jan–June, Sept, Oct & Dec 10am–noon & 2–5pm; July & Aug 10am–noon & 2–6pm; €3; free entry to garden), and you can wander around the house and through the olive and rare orange groves that surround it. One of the two studios in the house – north-facing to catch the late afternoon light – is arranged as if Renoir had just popped out. Albert André's painting, *A Renoir Painting*, shows the ageing artist hunched over his canvas; plus there's a bust of him by Aristide Maillol, and a crayon sketch by Richard Guido. Bonnard and Dufy were also visitors to Les Collettes; Dufy's *Hommage à Renoir*, transposing a detail of Moulin de la Galette, hangs here. Renoir's own work is represented by several sculptures, including *La Maternité* and a medallion of his son Coco, some beautiful watercolours and ten paintings from his Cagnes period.

Haut-de-Cagnes is a favourite haunt of successes in the contemporary art world, as well as those of decades past, and it lives up to everything dreamed of in a Riviera *village perché*. The ancient village backs up to a crenellated feudal **château** (Jan–June, Sept, Oct & Dec Mon & Wed–Sun 10am–noon & 2–5pm; July & Aug Tues–Sun 10am–noon & 2–6pm; €3; free shuttle bus from bus station, or by foot, the steep ascent along rue Général-Bérenger and montée de la Bourgade), with a stunning Renaissance interior, housing museums of local history, olive cultivation, the **donation Solidor** – a diverse collection of paintings of the famous cabaret artist Suzy Solidor – and the Musée Méditerranéan d'Art Moderne.

Practicalities

The **gare SNCF** Cagnes-sur-Mer (one stop from the *gare SNCF* Cros-de-Cagnes) is southwest of the centre alongside the autoroute; turn right on the northern side of the autoroute along avenue de la Gare to head into town. If you want to rent a **bike**, take the second right, rue Pasqualini, where you'll find Cycles Marcel at no. 5 (Ⓣ04.93.20.64.07). The sixth turning on your right, rue des Palmiers, leads to the **tourist office** at 6 bd Maréchal-Juin (June & Sept Mon–Sat 9am–noon & 2–7pm; July & Aug Mon–Sat 9am–7pm; Sun 9am–noon & 3–7pm; Oct–May Mon–Sat 9am–noon & 2–6pm; Ⓣ04.93.20.61.64, Ⓦwww.cagnes-tourisme.com). Bus #2 runs from the *gare SNCF* to the **gare routière** on square Bourdet.

Cros de Cagnes has the largest choice of **hotels**, but also plenty of traffic: you might try *Beaurivage*, 39 bd de la Plage on the seafront (Ⓣ04.93.20.16.09, Ⓦwww.beaurivage.org; ④), which has very pleasant rooms with views of the sea, or there's *Chez Nous*, 96 bd de la Plage (Ⓣ04.93.07.02.56, Ⓕ04.92.27.06.63) which is set back a little from the road. If you're feeling extremely flush, you could try *Le Cagnard*, rue Sous Barri (Ⓣ04.93.20.73.21, Ⓦwww.le-cagnard.com; ⑨; restaurant closed mid-Nov to mid-Dec; menus €46–81), a top-notch hotel with a restaurant in the ancient guard room of the château. **Campsites** are not marvellous, though there are plenty of them, mostly in the district of Val Fleuri east of the town. The three-star *Le Todos*, 4.5km north of Cros-de-Cagnes' seafront at 159bis Vallon des Vaux (Ⓣ04.93.31.20.05, Ⓦwww.letodos.fr; closed Oct–March; €17.60 for two people, car and tent), has its own swimming pool, restaurant, bar and shop.

The best places to **eat** are in Haut-de-Cagnes, and for café lounging, place du Château or place Grimaldi, to either side of the castle, are the obvious spots. *Le Manoir* at 81 montée de la Bourgade, (Ⓣ04.93.20.89.51) serves good Italian dishes with menus at €16 and €22. *Le Clap*, despite the unfortunate name, at 4 rue Hippolyte-Guis, off montée de la Bourgade (Ⓣ04.93.73.92.80), has reasonable menus starting from €20.

In summer there are free **jazz concerts** on place du Château and, at the end of August, a bizarre **square boules** competition takes place down montée de la Bourgade.

St-Paul-de-Vence: the Fondation Maeght

Further into the hills, the fortified village of **ST-PAUL-DE-VENCE** is home to yet another artistic treat, and one of the best in the whole region: the remarkable **Fondation Maeght** created in the 1950s by Aimé and Marguerite Maeght, art collectors and dealers who knew all the great artists who worked in Provence (daily: July–Sept 10am–7pm; Oct–June 10am–12.30pm & 2–6pm; €11; Ⓦwww.maeght.com). The Nice–Vence **bus** has two stops in St-Paul: the Fondation is signposted from the second, and is approximately 1km from the old town, a few hundred metres up a steep hill from the main D7 road through the village. By **car** or **bike**, follow the signs just before you reach the village, off the D7 from La-Colle-sur-Loup or the D2 from Villeneuve.

Once through the gates, any idea of dutifully seeing the catalogue of priceless museum pieces crumbles; this, instead, is a sublime fusion of art, modern architecture and landscape. Alberto Giacometti's *Cat* is sometimes stalking along the edge of the grass; Miró's *Egg* smiles above a pond and his totemed Fork is outlined against the sky. It's hard not to be bewitched by the Calder mobile swinging over watery tiles, by Léger's *Flowers, Birds and a Bench* on a sunlit rough stone wall, or by the clanking tubular fountain by Pol Bury. The building itself is a superb piece of architecture: multi-levelled and flooded with daylight, and the collection it houses of works by Braque, Miró, Chagall, Léger and Matisse, along with more recent artists and the young up-and-comings, is fabulous. Not all the works are exhibited at any one time, and during the summer, when the main annual exhibition is mounted, none are on show, apart from those that make up the decoration of the building.

The other famous sight in this extremely busy tourist village is the hotel-restaurant **La Colombe d'Or** on place du Général-de-Gaulle (ⓣ04.93.32.80.02, ⓦwww.la-colombe-dor.com; ⑨; closed Oct 25–Dec 20), where if you're prepared to splash out €61 for a mediocre meal or more than €200 for a room, you can enjoy the Braques, Picassos, Matisses and Bonnards that hang from the walls, most of which were acquired by the establishment in the lean post-World War I years in lieu of the artists' unpaid bills.

Vence

A few kilometres north, with abundant water and the sheltering pre-Alps behind, **VENCE** has always been a significant city. The old town is blessed with numerous ancient houses, gateways, fountains, chapels and a **cathedral** (daily 9am–6pm) containing Roman funeral inscriptions and a Chagall mosaic. In the 1920s it became yet another haven for painters and writers: André Gide, Raoul Dufy, D.H. Lawrence (who died here in 1930 whilst being treated for tuberculosis contracted in England) and Marc Chagall were all long-term visitors, along with **Matisse** whose work is the reason most people come.

Towards the end of World War II, Matisse moved to Vence to escape the Allied bombing of the coast, and his legacy is the town's most famous and exciting building, the **Chapelle du Rosaire**, at 466 av Henri-Matisse, off the road to St-Jeannet which leaves the town from carrefour Jean-Moulin at the top of avenue des Poilus (Mon, Wed & Sat 2–5.30pm; Tues & Thurs 10–11.30am & 2–5.30pm, Sun for Mass from 10am; €2.50; closed mid-Nov to mid-Dec). The chapel was his last work – consciously so – and not, as some have tried to explain, a religious conversion. "My only religion is the love of the work to be created, the love of creation, and great sincerity", he said in 1952 when the five-year project was completed.

The drawings on the chapel walls – black outline figures on white tiles – were executed by Matisse with a paintbrush fixed to a two-metre long bamboo stick specifically to remove his own stylistic signature from the lines. He succeeded in this to the extent that many people are bitterly disappointed, not finding the "Matisse" they expect. The only source of colour in the chapel comes from the light diffused through green, blue and yellow stained-glass windows, which changes according to the time of day. Yet it is a total work – every part of the chapel is Matisse's design – and one that the artist was content with. There's also a small collection of photos and sketches by the artist in an adjoining building.

Vieux Vence has all the chic boutiques and arty restaurants worthy of an *haut-lieu* of the Côte aristocracy, but it also has an everyday feel about it, with ordinary people and run-of-the-mill cafés. On place du Frêne, by the western gateway, the fifteenth-century **Château de Villeneuve Fondation Emile Hugues** (Tues–Sun: July–Oct 10am–6pm; Nov–June 10am–12.30pm & 2–6pm; €5) provides a beautiful temporary exhibition space for the works of artists such as Matisse, Dufy, Dubuffet and Chagall.

Practicalities

Arriving by bus, you'll be dropped near place du Frêne at the **gare routière** on place du Grand-Jardin, where you'll find the **tourist office** (July–August Mon–Sat 9am–7pm; Sept–June Mon–Sat 9am–6pm; ⓣ04.93.58.06.38,

ⓦwww.ville-vence.fr) and **bike rental** at Vence Motos on av Henri Isnard, just behind the tourist office.

Vence is a real town, with affordable **places to stay**. If you're on a tight budget, your best bet is the noisy but central *La Victoire*, on place du Grand Jardin (ⓣ04.93.58.61.30, ⓕ04.93.58.74.68; ❷); otherwise try the welcoming and peaceful *La Closerie des Genêts*, 4 impasse Maurel, off avenue M.-Maurel to the south of the old town (ⓣ04.93.58.33.25, ⓕ04.93.58.97.01; ❸), and *Le Provence*, 9 av M.-Maurel (ⓣ04.93.58.04.21, ⓕ04.93.58.35.62; ❸), with a pleasant garden. A little more luxury, including a pool, is available at *La Villa Roseraie*, 51 av Henri-Giraud (ⓣ04.93.58.02.20, ⓔrvilla5536@aol.com; ❼). There's a **campsite**, *Domaine de la Bergerie* (€23 for two people and a tent), 3km west off the road to Tourettes-sur-Loup (ⓣ04.93.58.09.36; closed mid-Oct to mid-March).

For a special, excellent-value **meal**, try *La Farigoule*, 15 av Henri-Isnard (ⓣ04.93.58.01.27; closed Tues & Wed; menus from €22). The fabled chef Jacques Maximin has opened a gourmet palace in Vence: imaginatively titled the *Maximin Restaurant*, 689 chemin de la Gaude (ⓣ04.93.58.90.75; closed Mon & Tues), it prepares exquisite fare, with the cheapest menu starting at €40 and rising rapidly in price and indulgence. For more run-of-the-mill fare, try the astounding choice of pizzas from €10 at *Le Pêcheur du Soleil*, 1 place Godeau. You'll find plenty of cafés in the squares of Vieux Vence. *Le Clemenceau*, on place Clemenceau, is the big café-brasserie-glacier, but you might find *Henry's Bar*, on place de Peyra, more congenial. *La Régence*, on place du Grand-Jardin, serves excellent coffee to sip beneath its stylish parasols.

Nice

The capital of the Riviera and fifth largest city in France, **NICE** scarcely deserves its glittering reputation. Living off inflated property values and fat business accounts, its ruling class has hardly evolved from the eighteenth-century Russian and English aristocrats who first built their mansions here; today it's the *rentiers* and retired people of various nationalities whose dividends and pensions give the city its startlingly high ratio of per capita income to economic activity.

Their votes ensured the monopoly of municipal power held for decades by the right-wing dynasty, whose corruption was finally exposed in 1990 when mayor Jacques Médecin fled to Uruguay. He was finally extradited and jailed. Despite the disappearance of 400 million francs of taxpayers' money, public opinion remained in his favour. From his Grenoble prison cell, Médecin, who had twinned Nice with Cape Town at the height of South Africa's apartheid regime, backed the former National Front member and close friend of Jean-Marie Le Pen, Jacques Peyrat, in the 1995 local elections. Peyrat won with ease, and, re-elected in 2001, he has lately made no secret of his desire to have the new public prosecutor, Eric de Montgolfier – who made his reputation fighting white-collar crime and political corruption – removed from his post, before his investigations into the Riviera underworld put yet another city magistrate into prison.

Politics apart, Nice has other reasons to qualify it as one of the more dubious destinations on the Riviera: it's a pickpocket's paradise; the traffic is a nightmare; miniature poodles (and their deposits) appear to be mandatory; there's graffiti everywhere; and the beach isn't even sand. And yet Nice still manages somehow to be delightful. The sun and the sea and the laid-back, affable

Chemins de Fer de la Provence

The **Chemins de Fer de la Provence** runs one of France's most scenic and fun rail routes from the *gare de Provence* on Nice's rue Alfred Binet, ten minutes' walk north of the *gare SNCF*, or take bus #4 from av Jean Médecin, the main avenue to the left of you as you emerge from the *gare SNCF*. The line runs up the valley of the Var between **Nice** and **Digne-les-Bains**, climbing through some spectacular scenery as it goes. Four trains run daily, year-round, and the whole journey takes 3hr 15min, and costs €35.30 (for more information call ⓣ04.97.03.80.80 or check online at ⓦwww.trainprovence.com).

Niçois cover a multitude of sins. The medieval rabbit warren of the old town, the Italianate facades of modern Nice and the rich, exuberant, *fin-de-siècle* residences that made the city one of Europe's most fashionable winter retreats have all survived intact. It has retained mementos from its ancient past, when the Romans ruled the region from here, and earlier still, when the Greeks founded the city; its modern cultural offerings – which include some of the best art in the south of France – are considerable. Nice seems to be enjoying a modest upswing after a few years of mixed fortunes, and is slowly looking a bit smarter. In addition, its bus and train connections make Nice by far the best base for visiting the rest of the Riviera.

Arrival, information and accommodation

Arriving by **air**, you can get different buses into town: bus #23 to the *gare SNCF* (€1.30); speedy *navettes* – #99 to the *gare SNCF* (taking around 15min; €3.50); or the #98 (same price) to the hideously ugly **gare routière** – which is at least very central – close to the old town, beneath the promenade du Paillon on boulevard Jean-Jaurès (ⓣ04.93.85.61.81). Both the bus and train stations have left-luggage counters.

You'll find the main **tourist office** beside the *gare SNCF* on avenue Thiers (daily: June–Sept 8am–8pm; Oct–May 8am–7pm, Sun 8am–6pm; ⓣ08.92.70.74.07, ⓦwww.nicetourism.com). It's one of the most useful, helpful and generous of Côte tourist offices and has **annexes** at 5 promenade des Anglais (June–Sept Mon–Sat 8am–8pm, Sun 9am–6pm; Oct–May Mon–Sat 9am–6pm; same ⓣ as main office) and at Terminal one of the airport (daily 8am–10pm). Any of these offices can supply you with a free listings magazine, *Côte d'Azur en Fêtes*.

Buses operate frequent services around the city, with most routes stopping after 9pm. Three night bus lines run until 1.10am, with one, the #N4, running later than that. Fares are flat-rate and you can buy a single ticket (€1.30), a one day Sunpass (€4) or a Sunmaxi carnet of 14 tickets (€16) on the bus. There are also five-day (€12.96) or weekly passes (€16.77), all of which can be bought at *tabacs*, kiosks, newsagents or from Sunbus, the transport office at 10 av Félix-Faure, where you can also pick up a free route map. **Bicycles**, **rollerblades** and **motorbikes** can be rented from Nicea Location Rent at 12 rue de Belgique (ⓣ04.93.82.42.71, ⓔnicealocation@wanadoo.fr) just by the *gare SNCF*. Bus routes are liable to disruption while Nice builds its hotly anticipated new tramway, the work for which is currently tearing up both the city centre and parts of the **gare routière**.

Before you start hunting around for **accommodation**, it's well worth taking advantage of the **reservation service** offered by the tourist office at the train

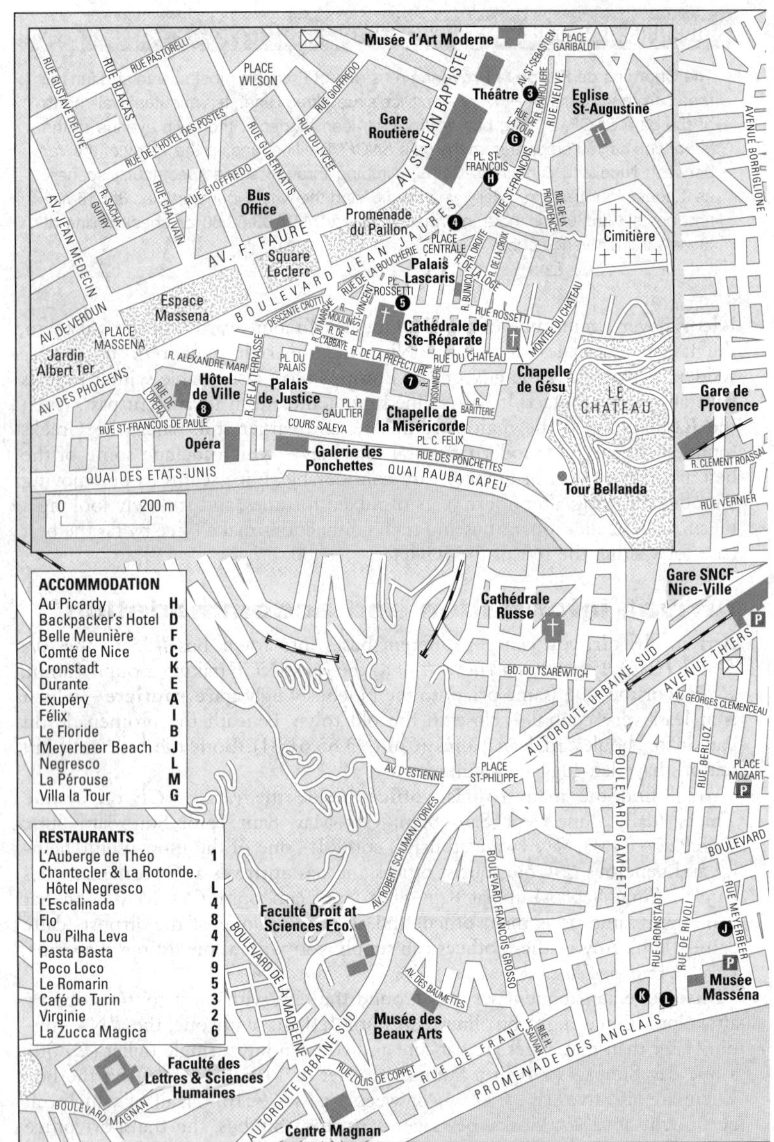

station. The area around the station teems with cheap hotels, some of them seedy, though there are a few gems. There are one or two cheap hotels right in the heart of Vieux Nice, too. Sleeping on the beach, which used to be common though always illegal, is now difficult since it's brightly illuminated the whole length of the promenade des Anglais.

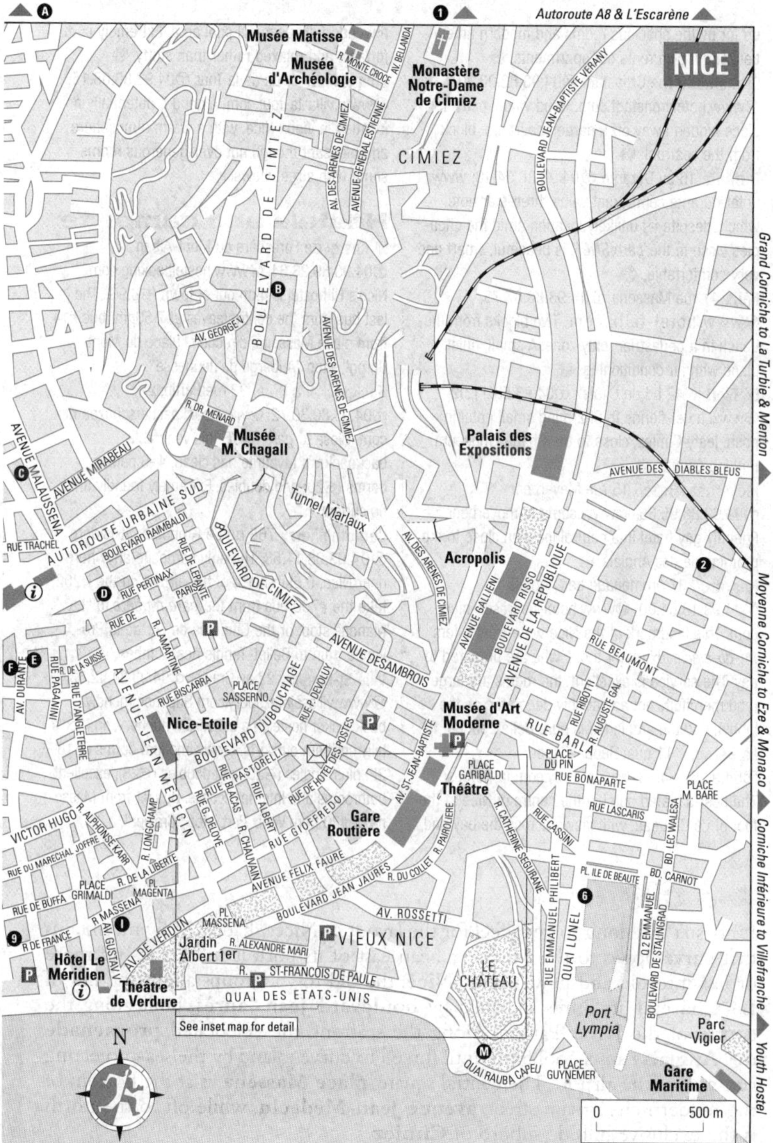

Hotels

Au Picardy 10 bd Jean-Jaurès ⓣ04.93.85.75.51. Convenient, no-frills, cheapie in Vieux Nice, across from the *gare routière*. ❷

Belle Meunière 21 av Durante ⓣ04.93.88.66.15, ⓕ04.93.82.51.76. Small but efficiently run backpacker place in an elegantly wasted Belle Époque villa close to the *gare SNCF*. Dorms from €15. ❸

Comté de Nice 29 rue de Dijon ⓣ04.93.88.94.56, ⓦwww.hotelcomtedenice.com. In a quiet neighbourhood five minutes' walk north of the *gare SNCF*. What it lacks in charm is made up for by the spacious rooms and modern amenities, and it also rents out apartments. ④

Cronstadt 3 rue Cronstadt ⓣ04.93.82.00.30, ⓦwww.hotelcronstadt.com. Good value, peaceful place hidden away off a garden court one block from the seafront. ④

Durante 16 av Durante ⓣ04.93.88.84.40; www.hotel-durante.com. Great value three-star hotel which, despite its unlikely location amid the cheapies close to the *gare SNCF*, is peaceful, smart and very comfortable. ④

Félix 41 rue Masséna ⓣ04.93.88.67.73, ⓦwww.hotel-felix.com. Two blocks from the beach in a pedestrian-only zone. A small, quiet place with air conditioning. ③

Le Floride 42 bd de Cimiez ⓣ04.93.53.11.02, ⓦwww.hotel-floride.fr. Charming small hotel in posh, leafy Cimiez, close to the Chagall museum. Parking on site. ④

Meyerbeer Beach 15 rue Meyerbeer ⓣ04.93.88.95.65, ⓦwww.come.to/meyerbeer. Friendly gay hotel in a central location close to the promenade des Anglais. ④

Negresco 37 promenade des Anglais ⓣ04.93.16.64.00, ⓦwww.hotel-negresco-nice.com. This landmark of the Nice waterfront offers *fin-de-siècle* luxury for those who are prepared to pay. The service is excellent, the rooms are large (and mercifully not as garishly decorated as the lobby), and the ambience is pure Belle Époque. ⑨

La Pérouse 11 quai Rauba-Capeu ⓣ04.93.62.34.63, ⓦwww.hroy.com/la-perouse. The best-situated hotel in the centre of Nice at the foot of Le Château, with views across the bay and a wonderfully peaceful pool area. Extremely comfortable and relaxed rather than stuffy. ⑨

Villa la Tour 4 rue de la Tour ⓣ04.93.80.08.15, ⓦwww.villa-la-tour.com. A good if potentially noisy location in Vieux Nice, with a warm atmosphere and pleasant though not over-generous rooms, some with street views. ③

Hostels and campsite

HI hostel rte Forestière du Mont-Alban ⓣ04.93.89.23.64, ⓦwww.hostelbooking.com. Nice's HI hostel is 4km out of town (€8.90). The last bus from the centre leaves at 7.50pm; bus #14 from place Masséna, direction "Place du Mont-Boron", stop "Auberge de Jeunesse".

Backpacker's Hotel 32 rue Pertinax ⓣ04.93.80.30.72, ⓦwww.backpackerschezpatrick.com. Close to *gare SNCF*, this venerable backpacker's favourite has clean, 4–6 person dorms (€20) and doubles. Extremely friendly and no curfew.

Camping Terry 768 rte de Grenoble, St-Isidore ⓣ04.93.08.11.58. The only campsite anywhere near Nice, 6.5km north of the airport on the N202; take the #700 bus from the *gare routière* to "La Manda" stop, or the Chemins de Fer de la Provence train to Bellet-Tennis des Combes.

Villa St-Exuprry 22 av Gravier ⓣ04.93.84.42.83, ⓦwww.villasaintexupery.com Superior, friendly backpacker hostel in a converted nunnery, on Nice's hilly northern outskirts. Smart, modern dorms (€18–22) plus singles (€30) and doubles (€28), excellent bathrooms and Internet access. Bus #1 from Masséna or #20 from Vieux Port, stop "Gravier".

The City

It doesn't take long to get a feel for the layout of Nice. Shadowed by mountains that curve down to the Mediterranean east of its port, it still breaks up more or less into old and new. **Vieux Nice**, the old town, groups about the hill of **Le Château**, its limits signalled by **boulevard Jean-Jaurès**, built along the course of the River Paillon. Along the seafront, the celebrated **promenade des Anglais** runs a cool 5km until forced to curve inland by the sea-projecting runways of the airport. The central square, **place Masséna**, is at the bottom of the modern city's main street, **avenue Jean-Médecin**, while off to the north is the exclusive hillside suburb of **Cimiez**.

The château and Vieux Nice

For initial orientation, with fantastic sea and city views, fresh air and the scent of Mediterranean vegetation, the best place to make for is the **Château park** (daily: April, May & Sept 9am–7pm; June–Aug 9am–8pm; Oct–March 10am–5.30pm). It's where Nice began as the ancient Greek city of Nikea, hence the mosaics and stone vases in mock Grecian style. There's no château as such, but the real pleasure lies in looking down on the scrambled rooftops and gleaming mosaic tiles ofVieux Nice and along the sweep of the promenade des Anglais.

Museum passes

Entrance is free to all Nice's municipal **museums** on the first and third Sunday of each month; otherwise a single adult pays €4 (except where stated otherwise). A seven-day pass allowing a single entrance to all museums except the Chagall and Asian Art Museums costs €6. A museum pass, valid for fifteen visits of your choice within one year, is available from all the museums, price €18.30 (concessions €9.15). For information on the Carte Musées Côte d'Azur which gives you access to most museums and monuments (65 in total) in the region, see p.1173.

To reach the park, you can either take the lift by the Tour Bellanda, at the eastern end of quai des États-Unis, or climb the steps from rue de la Providence or montée du Château in the old town.

Vieux Nice has been greatly gentrified over the last decade, but the expensive shops, smart restaurants and art galleries still coexist with little hardware stores selling brooms and bottled gas, tiny cafés full of men in blue overalls, and washing strung between the tenements. It certainly doesn't feel sanitized: its dark and mysterious alleys are resistant to over-prettification and away from the showpiece squares a certain shabbiness lingers. What is undeniable is the extent to which Vieux Nice is now dominated by tourism: throbbing with life day and night in August, much of it seems deserted in November. The streets are too narrow for buses and are best explored on foot.

The central square is **place Rossetti**, where the soft-coloured Baroque **Cathédrale de Ste-Réparate** (daily 8am–7pm) just manages to be visible in the concatenation of eight narrow streets. There are two cafés to relax in, with the choice of sun or shade, and a magical ice-cream parlour, Fenocchio, with an extraordinary choice of flavours. The real magnet of the old town, though, is **cours Saleya** and the adjacent place Pierre-Gautier and place Charles-Félix. These are wide-open, sunlit spaces alongside grandiloquent municipal buildings and Italianate chapels and the site of the city's main **market**. Every day except Monday from 6am to 1.30pm there are gorgeous displays of fruit, vegetables, cheeses and sausages, plus cut flowers and potted roses, mimosa and other scented plants displayed till 5.30pm (except Sunday afternoons); on Monday the stalls sell bric-a-brac and secondhand clothes (7.30am–6pm). Café and restaurant tables fill the *cours* on summer nights.

To feast your eyes on Baroque splendour, pop into the **chapels** and **churches** of Vieux Nice: La Chapelle de la Miséricorde, on cours Saleya (closed for refurbishment at the time of writing); L'Église du Gesu, on rue Droite (9am–6pm); or L'Église St-Augustin, on place St-Augustin (open Tues–Sat 9am–noon & 2–5pm; Sun 9am–noon) which also contains a fine *Pietà* by Louis Bréa. For contemporary graphic and photographic art, some of the best **art galleries** in Vieux Nice include Galerie Espace Ste-Réparate, 4 rue Ste-Réparate; Galerie Municipale Renoir, 8 rue de la Loge; and Galerie du Château, 14 rue Droite.

Also on rue Droite is the **Palais Lascaris** (daily except 10am–6pm; free; closed Nov), a seventeenth-century palace built by the Duke of Savoy's Field-Marshal, Jean-Paul Lascaris, whose family arms, engraved on the ceiling of the entrance hall, bear the motto "Not even lightning strikes us". It's all very sumptuous, with frescoes, tapestries and chandeliers, along with a collection of porcelain vases from an eighteenth-century pharmacy.

Place Masséna and around

The stately **place Masséna** is the hub of the new town, built in 1835 across the path of the River Paillon, with good views north past fountains and palm trees to the mountains. A balustraded terrace and steps on the south of the square lead to Vieux Nice; the new town lies to the north. It's a pretty and spacious expanse, without being very significant – in fact the only things of interest here are the sundry ice-cream vendors who shelter their goods under the arcades during summer. A short walk to the west lie the **Jardins Albert 1er**, on the promenade des Anglais, where the Théâtre de Verdure occasionally hosts concerts.

The covered course of the Paillon to the north of place Masséna has provided the sites for the city's more recent municipal prestige projects. At their worst, up beyond traverse Barla, they take the form of giant packing crates for high-tech goods, in the multimedia, megabuck conference centre grotesquely called the **Acropolis**. Though theoretically a public building, with exhibition space, a cinema and bowling alley (11am–2am), international business often limits casual entry. The fountains outside, however, are fairly spectacular.

Downstream from the Acropolis is the vast marble **Musée d'Art Moderne et d'Art Contemporain**, or MAMAC (Tues–Sun 10am–6pm; Ⓦwww.mamac-nice.org), with rotating exhibitions of avant-garde French and American movements from the 1960s to the present. New Realism (smashing, burning, squashing and wrapping the detritus or mundane objects of everyday life) and Pop Art feature strongly with works by, among others, Warhol, Klein, Lichtenstein, César, Arman and Christo. It's good fun, and the huge, light galleries are a delight to walk around.

Running north from place Masséna, **avenue Jean-Médecin** is the city's main shopping street, with nothing much to distinguish it from any other big French city high street. You'll find all the mainstream clothes and household accessory chains, plus FNAC for books and records, at the Nice-Étoile **shopping complex** between rue Biscarra and boulevard Dubouchage. **Couturier** shops are to be found west of place Masséna on rue du Paradis and rue Alphonse Karr. Both these streets intersect with the pedestrianized **rue Masséna** and the end of **rue de France** – all hotels, bars, restaurants, ice-cream and fast-food outlets, with no regard for quality or style.

Skirting this, the chief interest in western Nice is in the older architecture: eighteenth- and nineteenth-century Italian Baroque and Neoclassical, florid Belle Époque and unclassifiable exotic aristo-fantasy. The trophy for the most gilded, exotic and elaborate edifice goes to the **Russian Orthodox Cathedral**, off boulevard Tsaréwitch at the end of avenue Nicolas-II (daily: April, May, Sept & Oct 9.15am–noon & 2.30–5.30pm; July & Aug 9am–noon & 2.30–6pm; Nov–March 9.30am–noon & 2.30–5pm; closed during services; €2.50; bus #14, #17 or #71, stop "Tsaréwitch").

The promenade des Anglais and the beaches

The point where the Paillon flows into the sea marks the beginning of the world-famous palm-fringed **promenade des Anglais**, created by nineteenth-century English residents for their afternoon's sea-breeze stroll along the Mediterranean sea coast. Today it's more or less a permanent traffic jam, but still bordered by some of the most fanciful turn-of-the-twentieth-century architecture on the Côte d'Azur. At nos. 13–15, the Palais de la Méditerranée is once again a luxurious casino, though the splendid Art-Deco facade is all that remains of the legendary 1930s original: the new casino behind it also incorporates a four star hotel. The new casino's decor, at least, is 1930s in inspiration.

Most celebrated of all is the opulent **Negresco Hotel** at no. 37, built in 1906, and filling up the block between rues de Rivoli and Cronstadt. Though they will try to stop you if you are not deemed to be wearing *tenue correcte* (especially in the evenings), you can try wandering in to take a look at the Salon Louis XIV and the Salon Royale. The first, on the left of the foyer, has a seventeenth-century painted oak ceiling and mammoth fireplace, plus royal portraits, all from various French châteaux. The Salon Royale, in the centre of the hotel, is a vast domed oval room, decorated with 24-carat gold leaf and the biggest carpet ever to have come out of the Savonnerie workshops. The chandelier is one of a pair commissioned from Baccarat by Tsar Nicholas II – the other hangs in the Kremlin.

Just before the *Negresco*, with its entrance at 65 rue de France, stands the **Musée Masséna**, the city's art and history museum. Closed indefinitely for major renovations, only its unexceptional but shady gardens are open to the public (daily 9am–5pm).

A kilometre or so down the promenade and a couple of blocks inland at 33 avenue des Baumettes is the **Musée des Beaux-Arts** (Tues–Sun 10am–6pm; bus #38, stop "Chéret"), where the chief glory is the collection of 28 works by Raoul Dufy, who like no other artist is intimately connected with the visual image of Nice. It has too many whimsical canvases by Jules Chéret, who died in Nice in 1932, a great many Belle Époque paintings to go with the building, a room dedicated to the Van Loos, plus modern works that come as unexpected delights: a Rodin bust of Victor Hugo and some very amusing Van Dongens, such as *The Archangel's Tango*. Monet, Sisley – one of his famous poplar alleys – and Degas also grace the walls. Continuing southwest along the promenade des Anglais towards the airport, you'll find the **Musée International d'Art Naïf Anatole Jakovsky** (daily except Tues 10am–6pm), home to a refreshingly different, and surprisingly good, collection of over six hundred pieces of amateur art from around the world.

The **beach** below the promenade des Anglais is all pebbles and mostly public, with showers provided. It's not particularly clean and you need to watch out for broken glass. There are fifteen private beaches, clustering at the more scenic, eastern end of the bay close to Vieux Nice, but nothing like to the extent of Cannes. If you don't mind rocks, you might want to try the string of coves beyond the port that starts with the **plage de la Réserve** opposite parc Vigier (bus #20 or #30). From the water you can look up at the nineteenth-century fantasy palaces built onto the steep slopes of the **Cap du Nice**. Further up, past **Coco Beach** (bus #30 only, stop "Villa La Côte"), rather smelly steps lead down to a coastal path which continues around the headland. Towards dusk this becomes a gay pick-up place.

On the far side of the castle sits the **old port**, flanked by gorgeous red to ochre eighteenth-century buildings and headed by the Neoclassical Notre-Dame du Port; it's full of bulbous yachts but has little quayside life despite the restaurants along quai Lunel. On the hill to the east, prehistoric life in the region has been reconstructed on the site of an excavated fossil beach in the well-designed **Musée de Terra Amata**, 25 bd Carnot (Tues–Sun 10am–6pm).

Cimiez

The northern suburb of **Cimiez** has always been posh. The approach up boulevard de Cimiez is punctuated by vast Belle Époque piles: at the foot of the hill stands the gargantuan *Majestic*, while the summit is dominated by the equally vast *Hotel Régina*, built for a visit by Queen Victoria. The heights of

Cimiez were the social centre of the local elite some 1700 years ago, when the town was capital of the Roman province of Alpes-Maritimae. Part of a small amphitheatre still stands, and excavations of the **Roman baths** have revealed enough detail to distinguish the sumptuous and elaborate facilities for the top tax official and his cronies, the plainer public baths and a separate complex for women. All the finds, plus an illustration of the town's history up to the Middle Ages, are displayed in the impressive, modern **Musée d'Archéologie**, rue Monte-Croce (daily except Tues 10am—6pm; bus #15, #17, #20 or #22, stop "Arènes").

The seventeenth-century villa between the excavations and the arena is the **Musée Matisse** (daily except Tues 10am–6pm; Ⓦwww.musee-matisse-nice.org). Matisse spent his winters in Nice from 1916 onwards, staying in hotels on the promenade – from where *A Storm at Nice* was painted – and then from 1921 to 1938 renting an apartment overlooking place Charles-Félix. It was here that he painted his most sensual, colour-flooded canvases of odalisques posed against exotic draperies. As well as the Mediterranean light, Matisse loved the cosmopolitan aspect of Nice, the Rococo salons of the hotels and the presence of fellow artists Renoir, Bonnard and Picasso in neighbouring towns. He died in Cimiez in November 1954, aged 85. Almost all his last works in Nice were cut-out compositions, with an artistry of line showing how he could wield a pair of scissors with just as much strength and delicacy as a paintbrush.

The Roman remains and the Musée Matisse back onto an old olive grove, one of the best open spaces in Nice and venue for the July **jazz festival**. At its eastern end are the sixteenth-century buildings and exquisite gardens of the **Monastère Notre-Dame de Cimiez** (Mon–Sat 10am–noon & 3–6pm; free); the oratory has brilliant murals illustrating alchemy, while the church houses three masterpieces of medieval painting by Louis and Antoine Bréa. Adjoining the monastery is the Musée Franciscain.

At the foot of Cimiez hill, just off boulevard Cimiez on avenue du Docteur-Menard, **Chagall's Biblical Message** is housed in a museum built specially for the work and opened by the artist in 1972 (daily except Tues: July–Sept 10am–6pm; Oct–June 10am–5pm; €5.50, or €6.70 for temporary exhibitions; bus #15, stop "Musée Chagall"). The rooms are light, white and cool, with windows allowing you to see the greenery of the garden beyond the indescribable shades between pink and red of the *Song of Songs* canvases. The seventeen paintings are all based on the Old Testament and complemented with etchings and engravings. To the building itself, Chagall contributed a mosaic and stained-glass window.

The Phoenix Parc Floral de Nice

Right out by the airport is a vast tourist attraction, the **Phoenix Parc Floral de Nice**, 405 promenade des Anglais (daily: April–Sept 9am–8pm; Oct–March 9am–5pm; €2; exit St-Augustin from the motorway or bus #9, #10, or #23 from Nice). It's a cross between botanical gardens, a bird and insect zoo and a tacky theme park: automated dinosaurs and mock Mayan temples along with alpine streams, ginkgo trees, butterflies and cockatoos.

The best reason to make the trip out to the park is Nice's newest museum, the **Musée Départemental des Arts Asiatiques** (daily except Tues: May to mid-Oct 10am–6pm; mid-Oct to April 10am–5pm; €6; Ⓦwww.arts-asiatiques.com), housed in a beautiful building designed by Japanese architect Kenzo Tange. It houses a collection of ethnographic artefacts, including silk goods and pottery, as well as traditional and contemporary art. The highlight is a pavilion designed to convey the peaceful philosophy of Zen.

Eating, nightlife and festivals

Nice is a great place for **food** indulgence, whether you're picnicking on market fare, snacking on Niçois specialities or dining in the palace hotels. The Italian influence is strong in all restaurants, with pasta on every menu; seafood is also a staple. For **snacks**, many of the cafés sell sandwiches with typically Provençal fillings such as fresh basil, olive oil, goat's cheese and *mesclum*, the unique green salad mix of the region. If you want to buy the best bread or croissants in town, seek out Espuno, 22 rue Vernier, in the old town.

Despite the usual fast-food chains and tourist traps dotted around, most areas of Nice have plenty of reasonable restaurants. Vieux Nice has a dozen on every street catering for a wide variety of budgets; the port quaysides have very good, but pricey, fish restaurants. In summer it's wise to book tables or turn up before 8pm, especially in Vieux Nice.

Vieux Nice is also the centre of Nice's lively **pub** and **club** scene. A good place to set out is along rue Central in the old town, where many pubs have early evening happy hours. Many Vieux Nice bars boast huge selections of beers and spirits and many offer regular live music. As for Niçois nightclubs, bouncers judging your wallet or exclusive membership lists are the rule.

Nice's **lesbian and gay** nightlife scene is surprisingly active given the city's reactionary politics, and for lesbian and gay visitors the city has a relaxed feel. In 2004, after many years with no public Pride celebration, Nice held its first Pink Parade.

Cafés and bars

Bar des Oiseaux 9 rue St-Vincent. Named after the birds that fly down from their nests in the loft and the pet parrot and screeching myna bird that perch by the door. Serves delicious and copious baguette sandwiches, and salads from €9. Open from 9pm. Also occasional theatre performances in the evenings (€5 door charge).

Cave de la Tour 3 rue de la Tour ⓣ04.93.80.03.31. Local *bar à vins* that serves wine from the bottle, or for the more daring, straight from huge vats.

Nocy-be 2 rue Jules-Gilley. This New-Agey tea house has a cushioned interior which evokes a bedouin tent. Countless varieties of teas and infusions. Open Tues–Sun 5pm–12.30am.

O'Hara's Tavern 22 rue Droite ⓣ04.93.80.43.22. Tiny Irish bar on the corner of rue Rossetti serving the creamiest, priciest Guinness this side of the Irish Sea. TV sports. Daily 7pm–2.30am.

Trois Diables 2 cours Saleya. One of the few bars on the cours Saleya offering reasonably priced drinks. Regular DJs; karaoke night. Open till 2.30am.

Restaurants

L'Auberge de Théo 52 av Cap-de-Croix ⓣ04.93.81.26.19. Pleasant Italian food up in Cimiez. €20 menu (except Sat & Sun evening). Closed Mon, Sun eve out of season & third week Aug to second week Sept.

Chantecler & La Rotonde Hôtel Negresco 37 promenade des Anglais ⓣ04.93.16.64.00. *Chantecler* is the best restaurant in Nice with menus starting at €90 for dinner, but chef Bruno Turbot provides a lunchtime menu for €45, which will give you a good idea of how sublime Niçois food at its best can be. At *La Rotonde* you can taste less fancy but still mouthwatering *plats* from €19 up. Closed Jan.

L'Escalinada 22 rue Pairolière ⓣ04.93.62.11.71. Tucked away among the bustle of Old Nice's market street, this is the place for down-home Niçois cooking in a relaxed and unpretentious atmosphere. *Daube de boeuf* €12; also stuffed courgette flowers.

Flo 4 rue Sacha Guitry ⓣ04.93.13.38.38. Wonderful Art – Deco brasserie in the grand, Parisian manner, housed in a former theatre where Mistinguett and Piaf once performed. Open until midnight, menu €29.90.

Lou Pilha Leva place Central and rue du Collet ⓣ04 93 13 99 08. The place to go for a light meal or late-night snack. *Socca, beignets d'aubergines*, and stuffed courgette are some of the delectable and inexpensive choices. Open daily till midnight in July & Aug; 10pm in the off-season.

Pasta Basta 18 rue de la Préfecture ⓣ04.93.80.03.57. Excellent home-made pasta and gnocchi with a huge choice of sauces makes up for the slightly offhand service in this small Vieux Nice restaurant. From around €6.80.

Poco Loco 2 rue Dalpozzo ⓣ04.93.88.85.83, ⓦwww.poco-loco.com. Lively place with authentic Mexican food (€12 for tacos, €10–12 for *plats*). Just off the promenade des Anglais.

Le Romarin Place Rossetti ⓣ04.93.85.65.20. Nicois specialities and pizzas, with plenty of outdoor seating, tucked into a corner of Place Rossetti. The *menu Nissart* at €18 is a good introduction to the local cuisine.

Café de Turin 5 place Garibaldi ⓣ04.93.62.29.52. Punters queue around the block for the spectacular seafood at this restaurant on the edge of Vieux Nice. *Panaché de fruits de mer* from €17.

Virginie 2 place A.-Blanqui ⓣ04.93.55.10.07. Excellent *plateau des fruits de mer* in a truly local setting. Salads and *plats* from around €8.

La Zucca Magica 4bis quai Papacino ⓣ04.93.56.25.27. The Italian chefs here serve up some of the most sophisticated vegetarian fare on the Côte; reservations several days in advance are essential. Menus at €17 & €27. Closed Sun & Mon.

Clubs

Blue Whales 1 rue Mascoïnat ⓣ04.93.62.90.94. Intimate venue with friendly atmosphere, and live music after 10.30pm ranging from Latin to rock. Open till 4.30am; half price 5.30–9pm.

Dizzy Club 26 quai Lunel ⓣ04.93.26.54.79. Portside disco and cocktail bar with entrance fee. Midnight–5am.

L'Iguane 5 quai des Deux-Emmanuel ⓣ04.93.56.83.83. Very stylish night bar with dance floor for the *poseurs*. Daily till 6am.

Subway 19 rue Droite. Reggae, soul and rock; reasonably priced. Fri & Sat from 11.30pm.

Wayne's 15 rue de la Préfecture ⓣ04.93.13.46.99. Popular bar on the edge of the old town run by an expat who shares the French penchant for good old rock'n'roll. Live bands – of greatly varying quality. Daily 2.30pm–1am.

Lesbian and gay clubs and bars

Castro Street 18bis, rue Emmanuel Philibert. Raunchy men's cruise bar just up from the Vieux Port. 10pm–2.30pm.

Cherry's Café 35 quai des Etats-Unis ⓣ04.93.13.85.45. Relaxed seafront café bar close to cours Saleya.

Le Klub 6 rue Halevy. Nice's biggest and best gay disco, with a spacious bar overlooking the long dance floor. It attracts a fashionable, good-looking crowd, including some straights. Open from 11.30pm.

Sapho Bar 2 rue Colonna d'Istria ⓣ04.93.62.58.42. In Vieux Nice, a lesbian bar with a cosy and amicable atmosphere and various themed party nights. Open Wed–Sun.

Le Six 6 rue de la Terrasse. Smart, air-conditioned bar in Vieux Nice. Regular cabaret. Open 10pm–3.30am.

Festivals

Details of Nice's lively **festival** calendar are available from the publication *Cotê d'Azur en Fêtes*, or the main tourist office. The **Mardi Gras Carnival** opens the year's events in February (ⓦwww.nicecarnival.com), with the last week of July taken up by the **Nice Jazz Festival** in the Parc de Cimiez (ⓣ08.92.70.75.07, ⓦwww.nicejazzfest.com for info; or contact the main tourist office in May/June).

Listings

Airlines Air France ⓣ0820.820.820; British Airways ⓣ0825.825.040; British Midland ⓣ01.41.91.87.04; Delta ⓣ0800.354.080; easyJet ⓣ0825.082.508; Virgin Express ⓣ08.21.23.02.02.

Airport information ⓣ0820.423.333, ⓦwww.nice.aeroport.fr.

Books The Cat's Whiskers, 30 rue Lamartine, sells English-language books.

Car rental Major firms are represented at the airport. Otherwise try: Avis, *gare SNCF* ⓣ04.93.87.90.11; Budget, 23 rue Belgique ⓣ04.93.16.24.16; Europcar, 3 av Gustave V ⓣ04.92.14.44.50; Hertz, 1 promenade des Anglais ⓣ04.93.87.11.87.

Cinema Rialto, 4 rue de Rivoli ⓣ04.93.88.08.41; the Cinémathèque de Nice, 3 esplanade Kennedy ⓣ04.93.24.06.66; and Le Mercury, 16 place Garibaldi ⓣ08.36.68.81.06; all show *v.o.* films.

Consulates Canada, 10 rue Lamartine ⓣ04.93.92.93.22; USA, 7 av Gustave V ⓣ04.93.88.89.55.

Disabled access Transport for people with reduced mobility ⓣ04.93.96.09.99; Centre Communal d'Actions Sociales ⓣ04.93.13.51.00.

Emergencies Doctor: SOS Médecins

☎08.10.85.01.01; Casualty: Hôpital St-Roch, 5 rue Pierre-Dévoluy ☎04.92.03.33.75; Ambulance: ☎15; police ☎17.
Ferries to Corsica SNCM ☎04.93.13.66.66, ⓦwww.sncm.fr, or Corsica Ferries ☎08.25.09.50.95, ⓦwww.corsicaferries.com, both in the gare maritime, quai du Commerce.
Internet *CyberArt Café*, 20 rue Pertinax Tues–Sat 10.30am–8pm; ☎04.93.80.57.78; *Technosoft*, 16 rue Paganini, daily 9am–10pm; ☎04.93.16.89.81, by the *gare*.
Laundry Laverie Automatique Assalit, 29 rue Assalit; Laverie du Mono, 8 rue Belgique.
Lost property 1 rue de la Terrasse ☎04.97.13.44.10.
Money exchange Change Gambetta, 2 bd Gambetta Mon–Sat 9am–6pm; Thomas Cook, 12 av Thiers ☎04.93.82.13.00 daily 7am–10pm.
Pharmacy 7 rue Masséna daily 7.30pm–8.30am; ☎04.93.87.78.94; 66 av J.-Médecin ☎04.93.62.54.44.
Police Commissariat Central de Police, 1 av Maréchal Foch ☎04.92.17.22.22.
Post office 21 av Thiers, 06000 Nice Mon–Fri 8am–7pm, Sat 8am–noon.
Taxis ☎04.93.13.78.78 or ☎08.99.70.08.78.
Trains Information and reservations ☎08.92.35.35.35. For the scenic line to Digne: Chemins de Fer de la Provence, 4 bis rue Alfred Binet ☎04.97.03.80.80.
Youth information Centre Information Jeunesse, 19 rue Gioffredo ☎04.93.80.93.93.

The Corniches

Three **corniche roads** run east from Nice to the independent principality of Monaco and to Menton, the last town of the French Riviera. Napoleon built the **Grande Corniche** on the route of the Romans' Via Julia Augusta, and the **Moyenne Corniche** dates from the first quarter of the twentieth century, when aristocratic tourism on the Riviera was already causing congestion on the lower, coastal road, the **Corniche Inférieure**. The upper two are the classic location for executive car commercials, and for fatal car crashes in films. Real deaths occur too – most notoriously Princess Grace of Monaco, who died on the Moyenne Corniche – a bitter irony, since the corniches had been the backdrop to one of her greatest film successes, *To Catch a Thief*.

Buses take all three routes; the **train** follows the lower corniche, and all three are superb means of seeing the most mountainous stretch of the Côte d'Azur. Staying in a **hotel** anywhere between Nice and Menton is expensive; it makes more sense to base yourself in Nice and treat these routes as pleasure rides.

The Corniche Inférieure

The characteristic Côte d'Azur mansions that represent the stylistically incompatible fantasies of their original owners parade along the **Corniche Inférieure**. Or they lurk screened from view on the promontories of **Cap Ferrat**, their gardens infested with killer cacti and piranha ponds if the "Défense d'entrer – Danger de Mort" signs are anything to go by.

VILLEFRANCHE-SUR-MER is just over the other side of Mont Alban from Nice, and marks the beginning of one of the most picturesque and unspoiled sections of the Riviera, though the cruise liners attracted by the deep-water anchorage in Villefranche's beautiful bay ensure a steady stream of tour buses climbing the hill from the port. But as long as your visit doesn't coincide with shore excursions, the old town on the waterfront, with its active fleet of fishing boats, sixteenth-century citadel and its covered medieval rue Obscure running beneath the houses, is a tranquil and charming place to while away an afternoon.

The tiny fishing harbour is overlooked by the medieval **Chapelle de St-Pierre** (spring 9.30am–noon & 3–7pm; summer 10am–noon & 4–8.30pm; autumn 9.30am–noon & 2–6pm; winter 9.30am–noon & 2–5pm; €2),

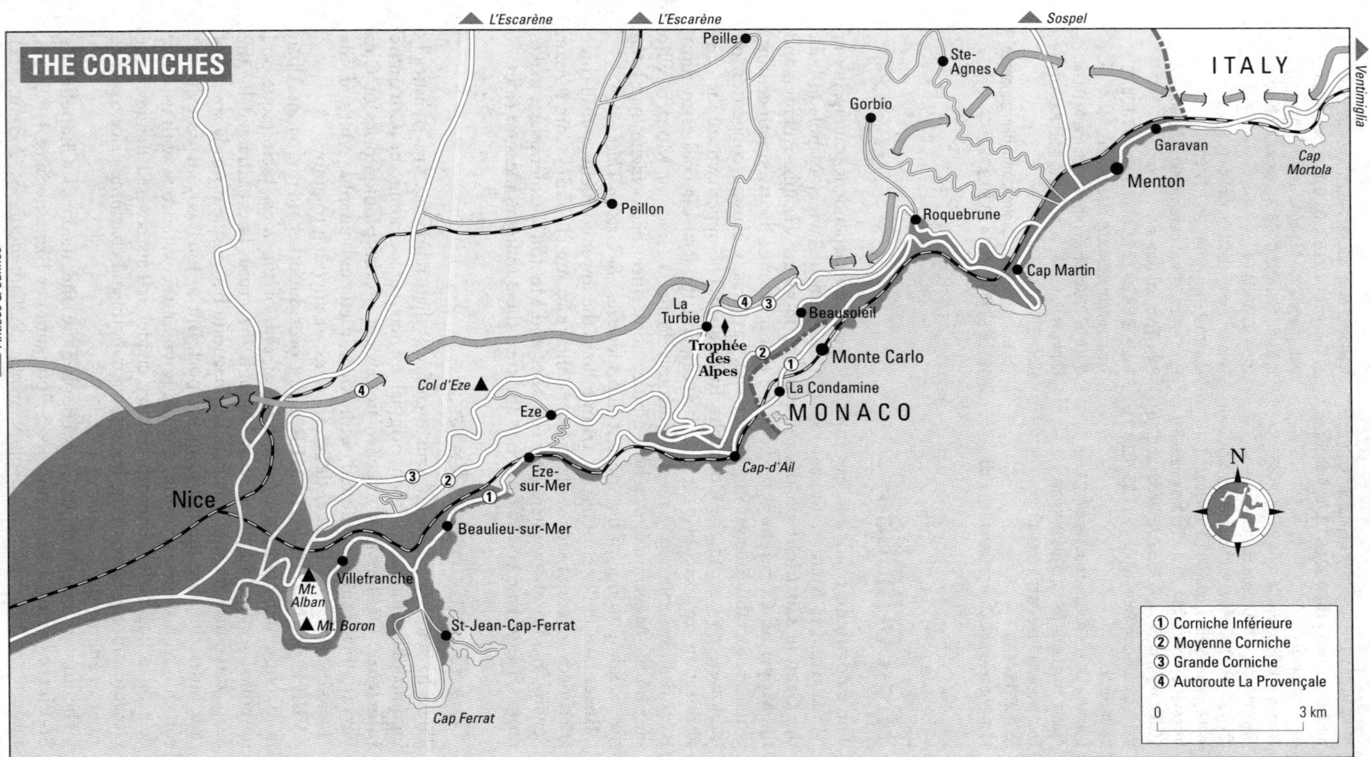
THE CORNICHES
L'Escarène
L'Escarène
Sospel
Ventimiglia
Antibes & Cannes
ITALY
Peille
Ste-Agnes
Gorbio
Peillon
Garavan
Menton
Cap Mortola
Roquebrune
Cap Martin
La Turbie
Trophée des Alpes
Beausoleil
Monte Carlo
La Condamine
MONACO
Col d'Eze
Eze
Cap-d'Ail
Eze-sur-Mer
Nice
Beaulieu-sur-Mer
Villefranche
Mt. Alban
Mt. Boron
St-Jean-Cap-Ferrat
Cap Ferrat
N
① Corniche Inférieure
② Moyenne Corniche
③ Grande Corniche
④ Autoroute La Provençale
0
3 km

decorated by Jean Cocteau in 1957 in shades he described as "ghosts of colours". The drawings portray scenes from the life of St Peter and homages to the women of Villefranche and to the gypsies. The chapel is used just once a year, on June 29, when local fishermen celebrate the feast day of St Peter and St Paul with a Mass.

On the main road along the neck of the **Cap Ferrat peninsula**, between Villefranche and Beaulieu, stands the **Villa Éphrussi** (mid-Feb to june & Sept–Oct 10am–6pm; Nov to mid-Feb Mon–Fri limited visit 2–6pm, Sat & Sun 10am–6pm July & Aug 10am–7pm; €8.50). Built in 1912 for a Rothschild heiress, it overflows with decorative art, paintings, sculpture and artefacts ranging from the fourteenth to the nineteenth centuries, and from European to Far Eastern origins. In addition, the villa is surrounded by huge, elaborate gardens.

Attractive, Belle Époque **BEAULIEU** overlooks the pretty Baie des Fourmis and is sheltered by a ring of hills that ensure some of the highest temperatures on the Côte. Its main point of interest is the **Villa Kérylos** (March–June & Sept & Oct 10am–6pm; July–Aug 10am–7pm; Nov–Feb Mon–Fri 2–6pm, Sat–Sun 10am–6pm; €7.50), a near-perfect reproduction of an ancient Greek villa, just east of the casino on avenue Gustav-Eiffel. Théodore Reinach, the archeologist who had it built in 1900, lived here for twenty years, eating, dressing and acting like an Athenian citizen, taking baths with his male friends and assigning separate suites to women. However perverse the concept, it's a visual knockout, with faithfully reproduced mosaics and vases and lavish use of marble and alabaster. The villa is only five minutes' walk from the **gare SNCF**. For those tempted to **stay** overnight, two economical options are the family-run *Hôtel Riviera*, at 6 rue Paul Doumer, right in the centre near the sea (Ⓣ04.93.01.04.92, Ⓕ04.93.01.19.31; ❸), and the *Select*, 1 place Général-de-Gaulle (Ⓣ04.93.01.05.42, Ⓕ04.93.01.34.30; ❸), which is basic but clean, comfortable and excellent value for this part of the world.

The Moyenne Corniche

Of the three roads, the **Moyenne Corniche** is the most photogenic, a real cliff-hanging, car-chase highway. Eleven kilometres from Nice, the medieval village of **EZE** winds round its conical rock just below the corniche. No other *village perché* is more infested with antique dealers, pseudo-artisans and other caterers to the touristic rich, and it requires a major mental feat to recall that the labyrinth of tiny vaulted passages and stairways was designed not for charm but from fear of attack. At the summit, a cactus garden, the **Jardin Exotique** (daily: 9am–nightfull; €3), covers the site of the former castle.

From place du Centenaire, just outside the old village, you can reach the shore through open countryside via the **sentier Frédéric-Nietzsche**. The philosopher is said to have conceived part of *Thus Spoke Zarathustra*, his shaggy dog story against believing answers to ultimate questions, on this path – which isn't quite as hard going as the book. You arrive at the Corniche Inférieure at the eastern limit of Eze-sur-Mer (coming upwards, it's signposted to La Village).

The Grande Corniche

At every other turn on the **Grande Corniche**, you're invited to park your car and enjoy a belvédère. At certain points, such as **Col d'Eze**, you can turn off upwards for even higher views. Eighteen stunning kilometres from Nice, you reach the village of **LA TURBIE** and its **Trophée des Alpes**, a huge monument raised in 6 BC to celebrate the subjugation of the tribes of Gaul. Originally a statue of Augustus Caesar stood on the 45-metre plinth, which was pillaged, ransacked for building materials and blown up over the centuries. Painstakingly restored in the 1930s, it now stands statueless, 35m high, and, viewed from a distance, still looks imperious. If you want a closer inspection, you'll have to buy a ticket (mid-May to Sept 20 9.30am–1pm & 2.30–6.30pm; Sept 21 to mid-May 10am–1pm & 2.30–5pm; €4.60). Several buses a day run from here to Monaco and Nice, from Monday to Saturday.

As the corniche descends towards Cap Martin, it passes the eleventh-century castle of **ROQUEBRUNE**, its village nestling round the base of the rock. The **castle** (daily: Jan, Nov & Dec 10am–12.30pm & 2–5pm; Feb–March & Oct 10am–12.30pm & 2–6pm; April–June & Sept 10am–12.30pm & 2–6.30pm; July–Aug 10am–12.30pm & 3–7.30pm; €3.50) has been kitted out enthusiastically in medieval fashion, while the tiny vaulted passages and stairways of the village are almost too good to be true. One thing that hasn't been restored is the vast millennial **olive tree** that lies just to the east of the village on the chemin de Menton. To get to the *vieux village* from the **gare SNCF**, turn east and then right up avenue de la Côte d'Azur, then first left up escalier Corinthille, across the Grande Corniche and up escalier Chanoine-J.-B.-Grana. The best **hotel** in the old village is *Les Deux Frères*, place des Deux-Frères (ⓣ04.93.28.99.00, ⓦwww.lesdeuxfreres.com; ❼), which is worth booking in advance to try to get one of the rooms with the awesome view.

Southeast of the old town and the station is the peninsula of **Cap Martin**, with a **coastal path**, giving you access to a wonderful shoreline of white rocks and wind-bent pines. The path is named after **Le Corbusier**, who spent several summers in Roquebrune and died by drowning off Cap Martin in 1965. His grave – designed by himself – is in the **cemetery** (square J near the flagpole), high above the old village on promenade 1er-DFL.

A gourmet treat here is the panoramic **restaurant** *Le Vistaero*, on the Grande Corniche (ⓣ04.92.10.40.00; closed Feb), with menus at €60 and €95.

Monaco

Monstrosities are common on the Côte d'Azur, but nowhere – not even Cannes – can outdo **MONACO**. This tiny independent principality, no bigger than London's Hyde Park, has lived off gambling and catering for the desires of the idle international rich for the last hundred years. Rampant property development in the postwar era elbowed aside much of its former Italianate prettiness, and today there's no mistaking its thick forest of 1960s and 70s tower blocks for anywhere else on the Riviera.

The principality has been in the hands of the ruling Grimaldi family since the thirteenth century, and legally Monaco would once again become part of France were the royal line to die out. The current ruler, Prince Rainier, is the one constitutionally autocratic ruler left in Europe, under whose nose every French law is passed for approval prior to being applied to Monaco. There is a parliament, but with limited functions and elected only by Monegasque nationals – about sixteen percent of the population. But there is no opposition to the ruling family. The citizens and non-French residents pay no income tax and their riches are protected by rigorous security forces: Monaco has more police per square metre than any other country in the world. They didn't prevent the bizarre murder in 1999 of billionaire banker Edmond Safra, however, nor the subsequent escape of his murderer from the principality's prison – two embarrassingly interlinked events which gave Monaco's ultra-safe reputation something of a knock.

One time to avoid Monaco – unless you're a motor-racing enthusiast – is the last week in May, when racing cars burn around the port and casino for the Formula 1 **Monaco Grand Prix**. Every space in sight of the circuit is inaccessible without a ticket, making casual sightseeing out of the question.

The Principality

The oldest part of the two-kilometre-long state is **Monaco-Ville**, around the palace on the high rocky promontory, with the new suburb and marina of **Fontvieille** in its western shadow. **La Condamine** is the old port quarter on the other side of the promontory; **Larvotto**, the bathing resort with artificial beaches of imported sand, reaches to the eastern border; and **Monte-Carlo** is in the middle.

Monte-Carlo

Monte-Carlo is the area of Monaco where the real money is flung about, and its famous **casino** (Ⓦ www.casino-monte-carlo.com; bus #1, #2 or #6) demands to be seen. Entrance is restricted to over-18s and you may have to show your passport; dress code is rigid, with shorts and T-shirts frowned upon, though it's notable that most visitors are scarcely the last word in tourist chic. Skirts, jackets and ties are obligatory for the more interesting sections. Bags and large coats are checked at the door.

Day-trippers and gambling dilettantes usually don't enter the casino proper, but head for the small room (free) of one-armed bandits and poker machines by the main entrance. Without further commitment you can also wander around the impressive entry hall, use the luxurious toilets and check out the small theatre (containing temporary exhibitions). The first gambling hall of the inner sanctum is the **Salons Européens** (open from noon; €10), where further slot machines surround the American roulette, craps and blackjack tables, the managers are Vegas-trained, the lights low and the air oppressively smoky. Above this slice of Nevada, however, the decor is *fin-de-siècle* Rococo extravagance, while the ceilings in the adjoining Pink Salon Bar are adorned with female nudes smoking cigarettes. The heart of the place is the **Salons Privés** (from 4pm), through the Salles Touzet. To get in, you have to look like a gambler, not a tourist (no cameras), and dispense with €20 at the door. Much larger and more richly decorated than the European Rooms, its early-afternoon or out-of-season atmosphere is that of a cathedral. No clinking coins, just sliding chips and softly spoken croupiers. Elderly gamblers pace silently, fingering hefty banknotes (the maximum unnegotiated stake here is €76,000), closed-circuit TV cameras above the chandeliers watch the gamblers watching the tables, and no one drinks. On midsummer evenings the place is packed out and the vice loses its sacred and exclusive touch. At the time of writing, parts of the Casino are closed for refurbishment.

Phoning Monaco

Monaco phone numbers have only eight digits and no -04 French area code. If you are phoning from France you must dial Monaco's international code 00377–, then the number (leaving out the first 0).

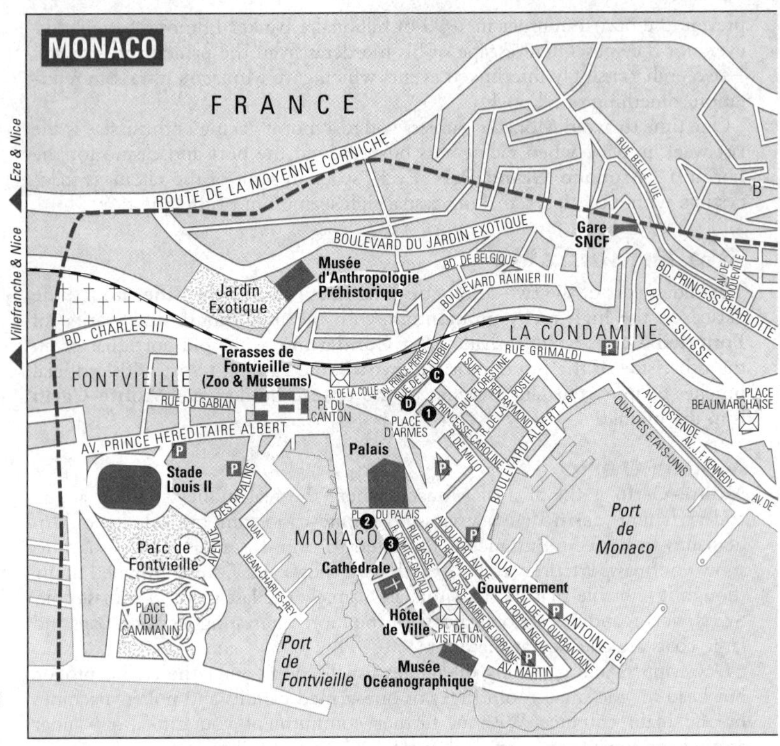

Adjoining the casino is the gaudy **opera house**, and around the palm-tree-lined place du Casino are more casinos plus the city's palace-hotels and *grands cafés*. The American Bar of the **Hôtel de Paris** is, according to its publicity, the place where "the world's most elite society" meets. As long as you dress up and are prepared to be challenged if you haven't ordered a €30 drink, you can entertain yourself free of charge against the background of Belle Époque decadence by watching humans whose bank accounts are possibly the most interesting thing about them.

Monaco-Ville, Fontvieille and Larvotto

After the casino, the amusements of **Monaco-Ville** (bus #1 or #2), where every other shop sells Prince Rainier mugs and assorted junk, are less rewarding, though the glacé-iced old town is the one part of the principality to have been spared the developer's worst. You can trail gasping round the lavish state apartments of the **Palace** (daily: June–Sept 9.30am–6pm; Oct 10am–5pm; €6); look at waxwork princes in **L'Historial des Princes de Monaco**, 27 rue Basse (daily: March–Sept 9.30am–6pm; Oct–Feb 11am–5pm; €3.80); watch a dreadful slide show on different aspects of the place in the **Monte Carlo Story** (daily: Jan–June, Sept & Oct hourly from 2–5pm; July & Aug 2–6pm; Nov & Dec closed; €6.50) underground across from the Musée Océanographique; or traipse around the tombs of the former princes and Princess Grace in the neo-Romanesque-Byzantine **cathedral**, whose right-hand transept features a reredos by Louis Bréa.

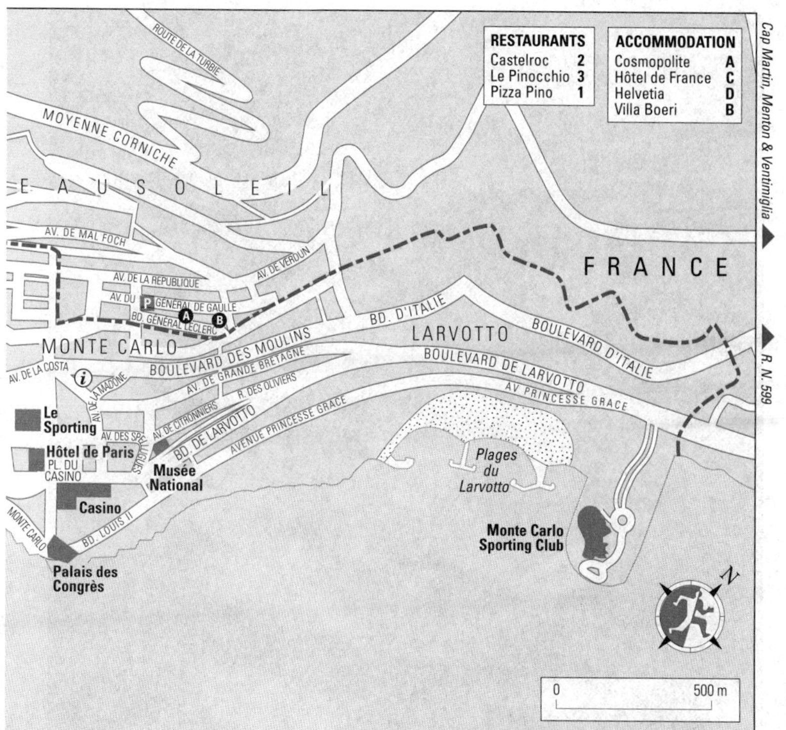

One point of real interest in the old town, however, is to be found on the place de la Visitation: the **Musée de la Chapelle de la Visitation** (Tues–Sun 10am–4pm; €3), displaying a part of the collection of religious art of Barbara Piasecka Johnson. This small but exquisite collection includes works by Zurbarán, Rivera, Rubens, and even an extremely rare, early religious work by Vermeer.

Perhaps the best site to visit in the whole of Monaco is the **aquarium** in the basement of the imposing **Musée Océanographique** (daily: April–June & Sept 9am–7pm; July–Aug 9.30am–7.30pm; Oct–March 10am–6pm; €11), where the fishy beings outdo the weirdest Kandinsky or Hieronymus Bosch creations. Less exceptional, but still peculiar, cactus equivalents can be viewed in the **Jardin Exotique**, on boulevard du Jardin Exotique high above Fontvieille (daily: mid-May to mid-Sept 9am–7pm; mid-Sept to mid-May 9am–6pm or nightfall; €6.70; bus #2). Admission also includes entry to the Musée d'Anthropologie Préhistorique, tracing the history of the human race from Neanderthal man to Grimaldi prince, and the Grotte de l'Observatoire, prehistoric caves with illuminated stalagmites and stalactites.

There are yet more museums in **Fontvieille**, the part of town just south of the palace, including collections of His Serene Highness's cars (daily 10am–6pm; €6), his coins and stamps (daily 10am–6pm; €3) and his model ships (daily 10am–6pm; €4), plus a zoo of his rare wild animals (daily: March–May 10am–noon & 2–6pm; June–Sept 9am–noon & 2–7pm; Oct–Feb 10am–noon & 2–5pm; €4), at the **Terrasses de Fontvieille** (bus #6) by the port.

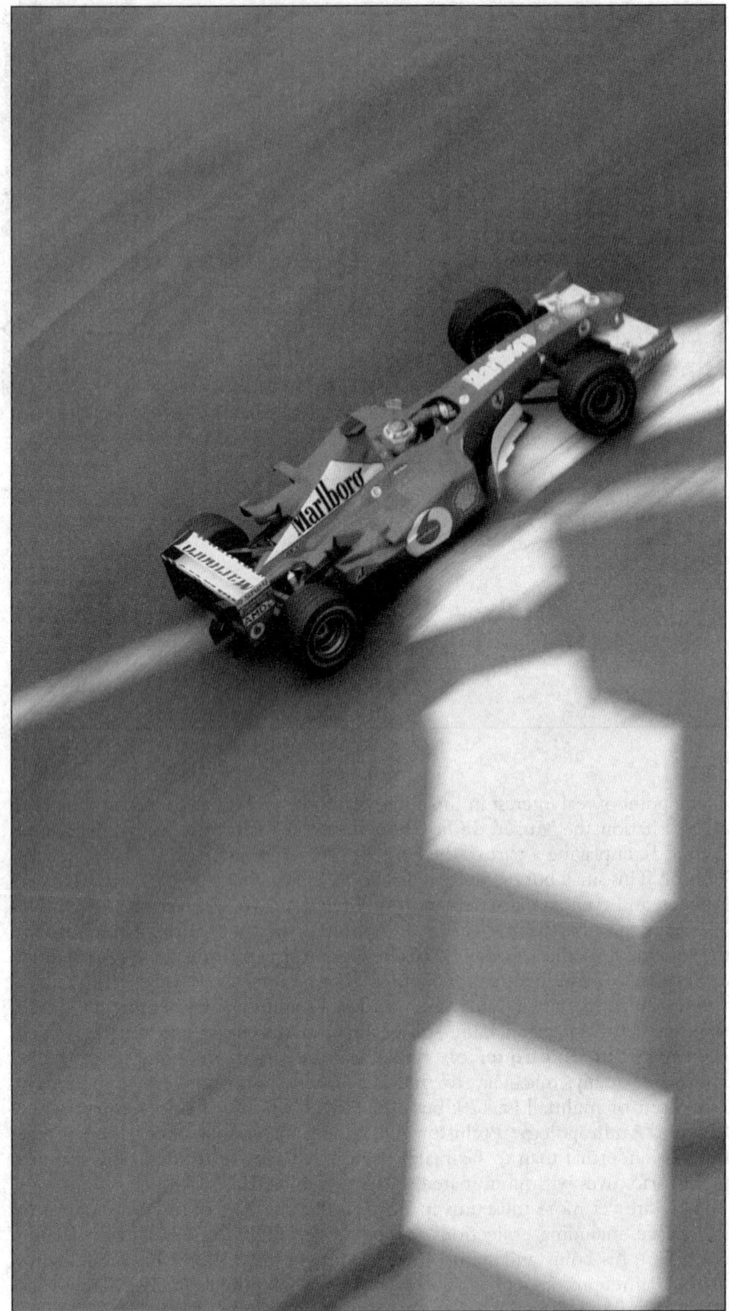

△ Monaco Grand Prix

Near the Larvotto beach, the **Musée National**, 17 av Princesse Grace (daily: Easter–Sept 10am–6.30pm; Sept–Easter 10am–12.15pm & 2.30–6.30pm; €6), is dedicated to the history of **dolls and automata**, and is better than you would think: some of the dolls' house scenes and the creepy automata are quite surreal and fun.

Practicalities

The **gare SNCF** is at the top of boulevard Rainier III, with four separate exits: signs for Le Rocher-Fontvieille will deposit you at the end of avenue Prince Pierre above place d'Armes; directions for Monte-Carlo will lead you to place Sainte Dévote. The two remaining exits lead to boulevard de Belgique and a pedestrian walkway in front of the station. Municipal buses ply the length of the principality from 7am to 9pm (€1.40 single; four-trip card €3.40). Buses following the lower corniche stop at place d'Armes; other routes have a variety of stations; all stop in Monte Carlo. Local bus #4 from the *gare routière*, and buses #1 & #2 run to the "Tourisme-Casino" stop, close to the **tourist office** at 2a bd des Moulins (Mon–Sat 9am–7pm, Sun 10am–noon; Ⓣ92.16.61.66, Ⓦwww.monaco-tourisme.com). The tourist office also has a conveniently located annex in the *gare SNCF*, for those arriving by train (Tues–Sat: July–Sept 8am–7.30pm; rest of year 9am–4.30pm). One very useful public service is the incredibly clean and efficient **free lift** linking the lower and higher streets (marked on the tourist office map). **Bicycles** can be rented from Auto-Moto-Garage, 7 rue de Millo, off place d'Armes (Ⓣ93.50.10.80).

The best areas for **hotels** is Beausoleil, just across the northern boundary in France, where you'll find the pleasant *Villa Boeri*, at 29 bd du Général-Leclerc (Ⓣ04.93.78.38.10, Ⓕ04.93.41.90.95; ④), only a couple of minutes' walk from Monte Carlo centre. Close by, the *Hotel Cosmopolite* at no. 19 (Ⓣ04.93.78.36.00, Ⓕ04.93.41.84.22; ④) is unexceptional but comfortable, soundproofed and air conditioned. In Monaco-Ville itself you could try the *Hôtel de France*, at 6 rue de la Turbie (Ⓣ93.30.24.64, Ⓦwww.monte-carlo.mc/france; ④). Another reasonable option is *Helvetia*, 1bis rue Grimaldi (Ⓣ93.30.21.71, Ⓔhotel-helvetia@monte-carlo.mc; ③), a small and comfortable old hotel, recently refurbished and with most rooms en-suite. Monaco has no campsite, and caravans are illegal in the state – as are bathing costumes, bare feet and bare chests once you step off the beach. Camper vans have to be parked at the Parking des Écoles, in Fontvieille, and then only between 8am and 8pm.

La Condamine and the old town are replete with **restaurants**, but good food and reasonable prices don't exactly match. Menu prices in the vicinity of the casino can reach absurd levels, and not just in the palace hotels. The best-value cuisine is Italian, notably *Le Pinocchio*, at 30 rue Comte-F.-Gastaldi (Ⓣ93.30.96.20; closed Dec), with €10–14 *plats du jour*, and *Pizza Pino*, 7 place d'Armes (Ⓣ93.50.22.54), which has filling pasta dishes starting at €10. Alternatively, try *Castelroc*, in the old town on place du Palais (Ⓣ93.30.36.68; closed Sat & Dec–Jan), which has a generous €20 menu. It's really not worth going upmarket in Monaco unless you're prepared to hit €150-a-head bills, in which case head for the Belle Époque glory of the *Louis XV* (closed Tues, Wed, Dec & early March) in the *Hôtel de Paris*.

Your best bet for non-casino **nightlife** is the large *Stars 'N' Bars* on the quai Antoine 1er, packed out on Fridays and Saturdays, with a lively club upstairs where drinks will cost you €9.

Menton

Of all the Côte d'Azur resorts, **MENTON** – the warmest and most Italianate, being within a couple of kilometres of the border – is the one that retains an atmosphere of aristocratic tourism, being even more of a rich retirement haven than Nice. It doesn't go in for the ostentatious wealth of Monaco nor the creativity cachet of Cannes and some hilltop towns, but glories chiefly in its climate and year-round lemon crops. It's ringed by protective mountains, so hardly a whisper of wind disturbs this suntrap of a city; you'll notice the difference in winter, when you'll need a change of clothes between here and the exposed central resorts.

Arrival, information and accommodation

Roquebrune and Cap Martin merge into Menton along the three-kilometre shore of the **Baie du Soleil**. The modern town is arranged around three main streets parallel to the promenade du Soleil. The **gare SNCF** is on the top one, boulevard Albert-1er, from which a short walk to the left as you come out brings you to the north–south avenue de Verdun and avenue Boyer divided by the Jardins Biovès – central location for citrus sculptures during February's **Fête du Citron**. The **tourist office** is at 8 av Boyer (July & Aug Mon–Sat 9am–7pm, Sun 9am–1pm; Sept–June Mon–Fri 8.30am–12.30pm & 2–6pm, Sat 9am–noon & 2–6pm; ⓣ04.92.41.76.76, ⓦwww.villedementon.com), in the Palais de l'Europe; the building was once a casino, but now hosts various cultural activities and contemporary art exhibitions. They will sell you a Menton Riviera Gardens pass for €20, or a museum pass for €10.

The **gare routière** and the **urban bus station** are between the continuation of the two avenues north of the train line on the avenue de Sospel. All the local bus lines (€1.15) pass through the *gare routière*. The district of **Garavan**, further east again, is the most exclusive residential area and overlooks the modern marina.

Accommodation is, as ever, a problem. Menton is no less popular than the other major resorts, so in summer you should definitely book ahead. The tourist office won't make reservations for you, though they will tell you where there are rooms free.

Hotels

L'Aiglon 7 av de la Madonne ⓣ04.93.57.55.55, ⓦwww.hotelaiglon.net. Spacious rooms in a nineteenth-century residence surrounded by a large garden. ❼

Beauregard 10 rue Albert-1er ⓣ04.93.28.63.63, ⓦwww.hotelmenton.com/hotel.beauregard. Classically furnished comfortable cheapie. Bed and breakfast, full or half board. ❷

Belgique 1 av de la Gare ⓣ04.93.35.72.66, ⓔhotel.belgique@wanadoo.fr. More mundane option than the above, but no less clean, and conveniently close to the station. Closed mid-Nov to mid-Dec. ❸

M. Paul Gazzano 151 rte de Castellar ⓣ04.93.57.39.73. *Chambres d'hôte* 2km from Menton; a delightful house with a terrace looking down over the wooded slopes to the sea. ❹

Napoléon 29 porte de France, Garavan ⓣ04.93.35.89.50, ⓦnapoleon-menton.com. Traditionally furnished but modern seafront hotel with sea or mountain views from the rooms. ❼

Hostels and campsite

HI hostel plateau St-Michel ⓣ04.93.35.93.14, ⓔmenton@fuaj.org. This well-run hostel is up a gruelling flight of steps signposted "Camping St-Michel", from the north side of the rail tracks. If you're carrying bags take bus #6 from the *gare routière* (3 daily), direction "Ciappes de Castellar", stop "Camping St-Michel". Beds €8.90.

Maison des Loisirs promenade de la Mer ⓣ04.93.35.77.05, ⓔot@villedementon.com. Hostel run by the municipality offering accommodation for groups only. There's also a good restaurant.

Camping St-Michel plateau St-Michel ⓣ & ⓕ04.93.35.81.23; open April–Sept. Reasonably priced campsite (€5 per person) on a hilly site adjacent to the youth hostel, with plenty of shade and good views out to sea.

The Town

The **promenade du Soleil** runs along the pebbly beachfront of Menton's aptly named Baie du Soleil, stretching from the quai Napoléon-III past the casino towards Roquebrune. The most diverting building on the front is a seventeenth-century fort by the quai Napoléon-III south of the old port, now the **Musée Jean Cocteau** (Wed–Mon 10am–noon & 2–6pm; €3), set up by the artist himself. It contains pictures of his Mentonaise lovers in the *Inamorati* series, a collection of delightful *Fantastic Animals* and the powerful tapestry of *Judith and Holofernes* simultaneously telling the sequence of seduction, assassination and escape. There are also photographs, poems, ceramics and a portrait by his friend Picasso.

As the quai bends around the western end of the Baie de Garavan from the Cocteau museum, a long flight of black-and-white pebbled steps leads up into the **vieille ville** to the **Parvis St-Michel**, an attractive Italianate square hosting concerts during the summer and giving a good view out over the bay. The frontage of the **Église St-Michel** proclaims its Baroque supremacy in perfect pink and yellow proportions, and a few more steps up to another square will reward you with the beautiful facade of the **chapel of the Pénitents-Noirs** in apricot-and-white marble, with pastel campaniles and disappearing stairways between long-lived houses. The **cemetery**, at the very top of the old town on the site once occupied by the town's château, is low on gloom and high on panoramic views, and is a good place to find yourself at sunset.

In the middle of the modern town, the **Salles des Mariages** (Mon–Fri 8.30am–12.30pm & 2–5pm; €1.50), or registry office, forms part of the **Hôtel de Ville** on place Ardoiono and was decorated in inimitable style by Jean Cocteau in 1957. It can be visited without matrimonial intentions by asking the receptionist at the main door.

On avenue de la Madone, at the other end of the modern town, an impressive collection of paintings from the Middle Ages to the twentieth century can be seen in the **Palais Carnolès** (daily except Tues 10am–noon & 2–6pm; free; bus #3), the old summer residence of the princes of Monaco. Of the early works, the *Madonna and Child with St Francis* by Louis Bréa is exceptional. The most recent include canvases by Graham Sutherland, who spent some of his last years in Menton.

If it's cool enough to be walking outside, the public parks up in the hills and the gardens of **Garavan**'s once elegant villas make a change from shingle beaches. The best of all the Garavan gardens is **Les Colombières**, just north of boulevard de Garavan, but it's a private garden (check for information on guided visits with the tourist office). Designed by the artist Ferdinand Bac between 1918 and 1927, there are staircases screened by cypresses, balustrades to lean against for the soaring views through pines and olive trees out to sea, fountains, statues and a frescoed swimming pool. Alternatively, there are the public **Parc du Pian**, shaded by olive trees, nearer to the *vieille ville* on the #3 bus route (stop Stade), and the **Jardin Exotique Val Rameh** (daily except Tues: April–Sept 10am–12.30pm & 3–6pm; Oct–March 10am–12.30pm & 2–5pm; €4; guided visits €6.50; bus #3 stop "Stade"), both below boulevard de Garavan.

Eating and drinking

Menton's **restaurants** tend towards the informal and touristy rather than the gourmet. If you're not bothered about what you eat as long as it's cheap, the pedestrianized rue St-Michel is promising ground. For a proper restaurant meal in elegant if rather stiff surroundings, there's *Le Café Fiori* in *Hôtel Les Ambassadeurs*, 3 rue Partenoux (☎04.93.28.75.75; open summer evenings and winter daily lunch & dinner), with an evening bistro menu for €35 and an €20 lunch menu. Down on the port at 15, quai Bonaparte, *La Lyre* (☎04.93.35.38.16) serves excellent calamares and other Italian dishes at round €13. Menton also has two excellent Moroccan restaurants, both around the €20 mark: *Le Darkoum*, 23 rue St-Michel (☎04.93.35.44.88), and *La Mamounia*, 51 porte de France, Garavan (☎04.93.57.95.39).

Travel details

Trains

Cannes to: Antibes (every 12–40min; 11–16min); Biot (every 15min–1hr 30min; 18min); Cagnes-sur-Mer (every 15min–1hr 30min; 20–35min); Juan-les-Pins (every 15min–1hr 30min; 10min); Marseille (14–20 daily; 2hr); Monaco (every 20min–1hr 10min; 1hr 10min); Menton (every 20min–1hr 10min; 1hr 25min); Nice (every 10min–1hr 10min; 22–40min); Paris (8 daily; 5hr 17min); Paris CDG Airport (5 daily; 5hr 42min–6hr 25min); St-Raphaël (every 10–45min; 22–40min).

Marseille to: Aix (every 30min–1hr 20min; 40min); Aix TGV (8 daily; 15min); Arles (hourly; 50min); Avignon (12 daily; 1hr 15min); Avignon TGV (hourly; 30min); Briançon (3 daily; 4hr 10min); Cannes (15–23 daily; 2hr 10min); Cassis (10–19 daily; 22min); Fréjus (4–7 daily; 1hr 35min); Hyères (1–5 daily; 1hr 15min); La Ciotat (11–21 daily; 25–30min); Les Arcs-Draguignan (12 daily; 1hr 20min–2hr 5min); Lyon Part-Dieu (15 daily; 1hr 45min); Menton (2–3 daily; 3hr 20min–3hr 35min); Nice (15–23 daily; 2hr 20min–2hr 55min); Paris (hourly; 3hr–3hr 15min); Paris CDG Airport (7 daily; 4hr); St-Raphaël (15 daily; 1hr 45min); Toulon (16 daily; 40min–45min).

Nice to: Beaulieu-sur-Mer (20+ daily; 11–12min); Cagnes-sur-Mer (20+ daily; 15min); Cap d'Ail (16+ daily; 18min); Cap Martin-Roquebrune (16+ daily; 30min); Digne (4 daily; 3hr 15min); Eze-sur-Mer (16+ daily; 22min); Fréjus (3–5 daily; 1hr – 1hr 16min); Marseille (15+ daily; 2hr 20min–3hr 30min); Menton (every 15–40min; 30–40min); Paris (8 daily; 5hr 35min–5hr 45min); Paris CDG Airport (1 daily; 6hr 11min); St-Raphaël (every 30–45min; 50min–1hr 30min); Sospel (6 daily; 50min); Tende (3 daily, otherwise change at Ventimiglia; 1hr 30min); Villefranche-sur-Mer (16+ daily; 8min).

St-Raphaël to: Boulouris (9 daily; 4min); Cannes (every 5–40min; 25–40min); Marseille (14–20 daily; 1hr 40min); Nice (every 5–40min; 45min–1hr 5min).

Toulon to: Hyères (5–9 daily; 20min); Marseille (every 40min–1hr 10min; 55min–1hr 5min); Paris (3 daily; 3hr 50min); Paris CDG Airport (7 daily; 4hr 50min).

Buses

Cannes to: Antibes (every 20min; 33min); Biot (every 20min; 44min); Cagnes-sur-Mer (every 20min; 50–55min); Grasse (every 20–30min; 40–50min); Golfe Juan (every 20min; 15–20min); Nice (every 20min; 55min–1hr 35min); Nice Airport (every 30min–1hr; 50min); St-Raphaël (1–2 daily; 40–45min); Vallauris (every 20min; 30min).

Hyères to: Bormes (approx. hourly; 25min); La Croix-Valmer (8 daily; 1hr 10min); Le Lavandou (hourly; 30min); Le Rayol (9 daily; 50min); St-Tropez (8 daily; 1hr 35min); Toulon (hourly; 35–50min).

Le Lavandou to: Bormes (hourly; 8–12min); Hyères (hourly; 35min); La Croix-Valmer (8 daily; 1hr 15min); Le Rayol (8–9 daily; 20min); St-Tropez (8 daily; 1hr 5min); Toulon (hourly; 1hr–1hr 15min).

Marseille to: Aix (every 5–10min; 30–50min); Arles (4 daily; 2hr 10min–2hr 30min); Aubagne (every 15min–1hr; 20min); Barcelonnette (23 daily; 3hr 30min–4hr 45min); Cassis (13 daily; 35–50min); Digne (4 daily; 2hr–2hr 50min); Grenoble (1 daily; 3hr 55min); La Ciotat (19 daily; 45min); Sisteron (4 daily; 2hr 25min).

Menton to: Monaco (every 15min; 35min); Nice (every 15min; 1hr 20–1hr 30min); Sospel (2–5 daily; 35–55min).

Monaco to: Eze-Village (2–3 daily; 15min); Menton (every 15min; 40–45min); Nice (every 15min; 45–50min); La Turbie (4 daily; 40min).

Nice to: Aix (3–5 daily; 2hr 20min–4hr 10min); Beaulieu (every 15min; 15–20min); Cagnes-sur-Mer (every 20min; 25–45min); Digne (1–2

daily; 3hr–3hr 25min); Draguignan (3 weekly; 1hr 15min); Eze-sur-Mer (every 15min; 20min); Eze-Village (2–3 daily; 20min); Grasse (every 30–40min; 1hr 10min–1hr 25min); La Turbie (4 daily; 40min); Menton (every 15min; 55min–1hr 20min); Monaco (every 15min; 30–40min); Roquebrune (every 15min; 45min–1hr); St-Jean Cap Ferrat (6 daily; 25min); St-Paul de Vence (every 45min–1hr; 45min–1hr); Sisteron (1–2 daily; 3hr 45min–4hr 10min); Toulon (2 daily from place Masséna; 2hr 30min); Vence (every 20–30min; 50min-1hr 5min); Villefranche (every 15min; 10min).
St–Raphaël to: Cannes (1–2 daily; 30–45min) Cogolin (8 daily; 1hr); Draguignan (5–15 daily; 1hr 50min–1hr 25min); La Foux (8 daily; 1hr 10min); Fréjus (every 10–20min; 20–35min); Grimaud (7 daily; 45–55min); Nice Airport (4 daily; 1hr 15min); Ste-Maxime (8 daily; 25–30min); Le Trayas (towards Cannes: 7–11 daily; 35–40min); St-Tropez (8 daily; 1hr 10min–1hr 25min).
St-Tropez to: Bormes (8 daily; 1hr–1hr 15min); Cogolin (10 daily; 15min); Gassin (2 weekly; 25min); Grimaud (10 daily; 20–25min); Hyères (8 daily; 1hr 30min–1hr 40min); La Croix-Valmer (8 daily; 15–20min); La Garde Freinet (1–2 daily; 40–45min); Le Lavandou (8 daily; 55min–1hr 5min); Le Rayol (8 daily; 35–45min); Ramatuelle (4 daily; 25min); Ste-Maxime (10 daily; 35–45min); St-Raphaël (8 daily; 1hr 15min–1hr 30min); Toulon (8 daily; 1hr 55min–2hr 15min).
Toulon to: Aix (5–7 daily; 1hr 15min); Hyères (every 45min–1 hour; 30–45min); La Croix-Valmer (8 daily; 1hr 40min–2hr 5min); Le Lavandou (every 45min–1hr; 1hr–1hr 20min); Nice (2 daily; 2hr 30min); St-Raphaël (4 daily; 2hr); St-Tropez (8 daily; 2hr–2hr 25min).

Flights

Hyères Paris (5 daily; 1hr 25min).
Marseille to: Lyon (2–4 daily; 1hr); Paris (every 30min; 1hr 20min).
Nice to: Lille (2 daily; 1hr 40min); Lyon (3 daily; 55min); Paris (every 30min; 1hr 25min).

Ferries

For Îles d'Hyères and Îles de Lérins services, see box on p.1154 & p.1176.
Marseille to: Corsica (2–6 daily; 8–12hr).
Nice to: Corsica (April–Sept daily; Oct–May 1 daily–1 weekly; 2hr 30min–11hr 30min).
Toulon to: Corsica 7–9 weekly 7–11hr) more in summer.

16

Corsica

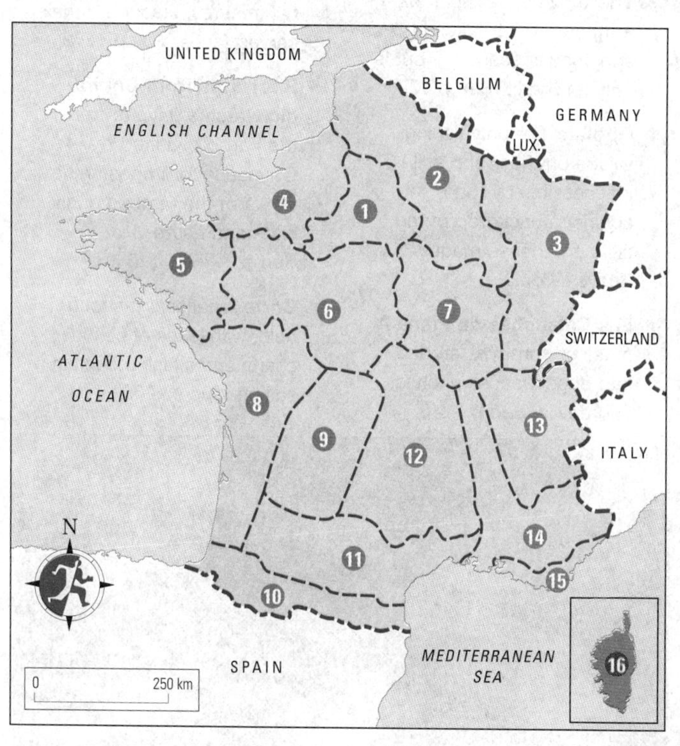

16 CORSICA

CHAPTER 16 Highlights

* **Plage de Saleccia** Soft white shell sand, turquoise water and not a building in sight. See p.1229
* **Calvi** Corsica's hallmark resort, framed by snow peaks and a spectacular blue gulf. See p.1232
* **The GR20** Gruelling 170km footpath, which takes in spectacular scenery – but is only for the fit. See p.1236
* **Girolata** The only fishing village on the island still inaccessible by road, set against a backdrop of red cliffs and dense maquis. See p.1238
* **Les Calanches de Piana** A mass of porphyry, eroded into dogs' heads, witches and devils. See p.1240
* **Apéritif at L'Hôtel Les Roches Rouges** Sublime sea views and a *fin-de-siècle* ambience make this the spot for a *muscat corse*. See p.1241
* **Filitosa menhirs** Among the Western Mediterranean's greatest archeological treaures, unique for their carved faces. See p.1253
* **Boat trips from Bonifacio** Catch a *navette* from the harbour visited by Odysseus for imposing views of the famous chalk cliffs and *haute ville*. See p.1259
* **Corte** A nationalist stronghold, with loads of period charm and a high mountain setting. See p.1268

△ Boat trip from Bonifacio

16

Corsica

Nearly two million people visit **Corsica** each year, drawn by the mild climate and by some of the most diverse landscapes in all Europe. Nowhere in the Mediterranean has beaches finer than the island's perfect half-moon bays of white sand and transparent water, or seascapes more inspiring than the red porphyry Calanches of the west coast. Even though the annual visitor influx now exceeds the island's population seven or eight times over, tourism hasn't spoilt the place: there are a few resorts, but overdevelopment is rare and high-rise blocks are confined to the main towns.

Bastia, capital of the north, was the principal Genoese stronghold, and its fifteenth-century citadelle has survived almost intact. Of the island's two large towns, this is the more purely Corsican, and commerce rather than tourism is its main concern. Also relatively undisturbed, the northern Cap Corse harbours inviting sandy coves and fishing villages such as **Macinaggio** and **Centuri-Port**. Within a short distance of Bastia, the fertile region of the Nebbio contains a scattering of churches built by Pisan stoneworkers, the prime example being the cathedral of Santa Maria Assunta at the appealingly chic little port of **St-Florent**.

To the west of here, **L'Île-Rousse** and **Calvi**, the latter graced with an impressive citadelle and fabulous sandy beach, are major targets for holiday-makers. The spectacular **Scandola nature reserve** can be visited by boat from the tiny resort of **Porto**, from where walkers can also strike into the wild **Gorges de Spelunca**. **Corte**, at the heart of Corsica, is the best base for exploring the mountains and gorges of the interior which form part of the **Parc Naturel Régional** that runs almost the entire length of the island.

Sandy beaches and rocky coves punctuate the west coast all the way down to **Ajaccio**, Napoleon's birthplace and the island's capital, where pavement cafés and palm-lined boulevards are thronged with tourists in summer. Slightly fewer make it to nearby **Filitosa**, greatest of the many prehistoric sites scattered across the south. **Propriano**, the town perhaps most transformed by the tourist boom, lies close to stern **Sartène**, former seat of the wild feudal lords who once ruled this region and still the quintessential Corsican town.

More megalithic sites are to be found south of Sartène on the way to **Bonifacio**, a comb of ancient buildings perched atop furrowed white cliffs at the southern tip of the island. Equally popular **Porto-Vecchio** provides a springboard for excursions to the amazing beaches of the south. The eastern plain has less to boast of, but the Roman site at **Aléria** is worth a visit for its excellent museum.

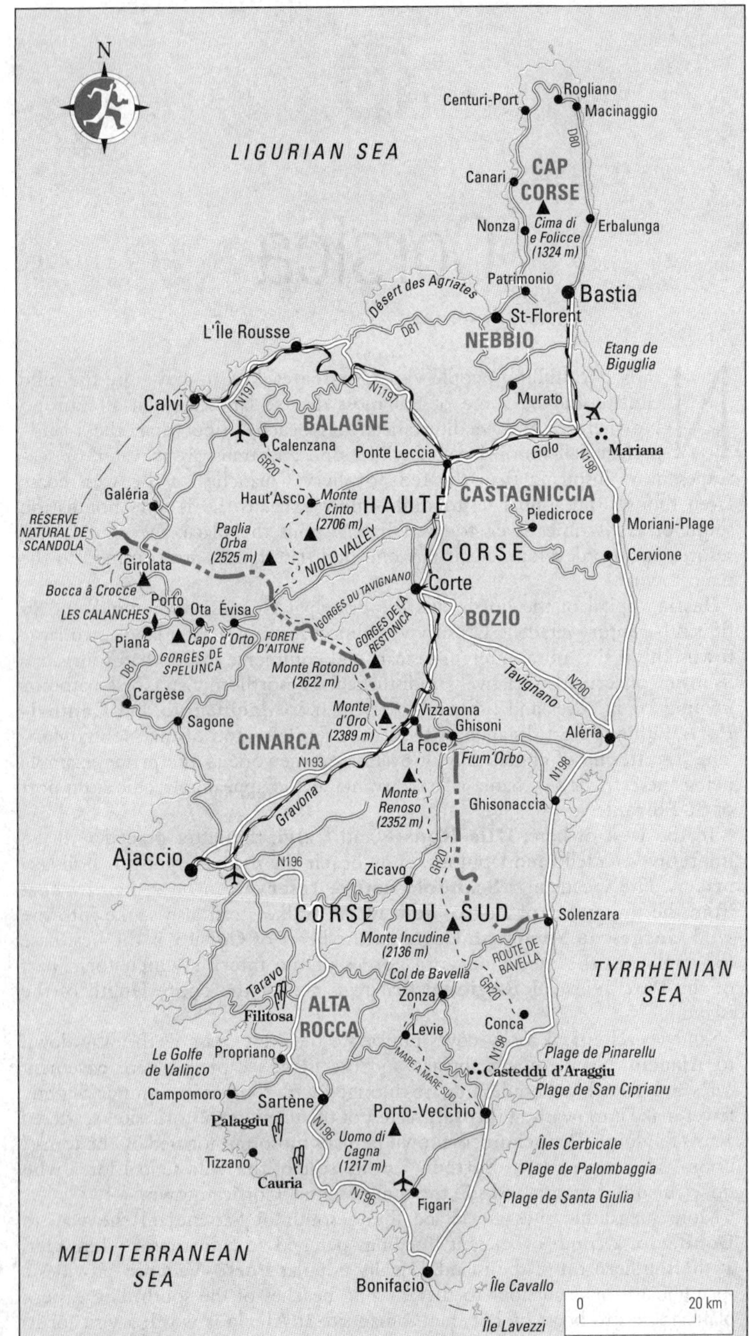
N
LIGURIAN SEA
Centuri-Port
Rogliano
Macinaggio
D80
CAP CORSE
Canari
Cima di e Folicce (1324 m)
Nonza
Erbalunga
Patrimonio
Bastia
Désert des Agriates
St-Florent
D81
NEBBIO
L'Île Rousse
Etang de Biguglia
Calvi
N197
N1197
Murato
BALAGNE
Calenzana
Mariana
Ponte Leccia
Golo
N198
GR20
CASTAGNICCIA
Galéria
Haut'Asco
Monte Cinto (2706 m)
HAUTE
Piedicroce
Moriani-Plage
RÉSERVE NATURAL DE SCANDOLA
Paglia Orba (2525 m)
NIOLO VALLEY
CORSE
Cervione
Girolata
Corte
Bocca â Crocce
GORGES DU TAVIGNANO
GORGES DE LA RESTONICA
Porto
Ota
Évisa
BOZIO
LES CALANCHES
Piana
Capo d'Orto
FORET D'AITONE
GORGES DE SPELUNCA
D81
Monte Rotondo (2622 m)
Tavignano
N200
Cargèse
Monte d'Oro (2389 m)
Vizzavona
Ghisoni
Sagone
CINARCA
La Foce
Aléria
N193
Fium'Orbo
N198
Monte Renoso (2352 m)
Gravona
Ghisonaccia
Ajaccio
N196
Zicavo
GR20
CORSE DU SUD
Solenzara
Monte Incudine (2136 m)
ROUTE DE BAVELLA
TYRRHENIAN SEA
Col de Bavella
Taravo
GR20
Zonza
ALTA ROCCA
Filitosa
Conca
Levie
Le Golfe de Valinco
Propriano
N198
MARE A MARE SUD
Plage de Pinarellu
Casteddu d'Araggiu
Campomoro
Plage de San Ciprianu
Sartène
Porto-Vecchio
Palaggiu
N196
Uomo di Cagna (1217 m)
Îles Cerbicale
Tizzano
Plage de Palombaggia
Cauria
N196
Figari
Plage de Santa Giulia
MEDITERRANEAN SEA
Bonifacio
Île Cavallo
0
20 km
Île Lavezzi

16 CORSICA

The food of Corsica

It's the herbs – thyme, marjoram, basil, fennel and rosemary – of the maquis (the dense, scented scrub that covers lowland Corsica) that lend the island's cuisine its distinctive aromas, especially in the south, where flavours are less subtle than in the north.

You'll find the best **charcuterie** in the hills of the interior, where pork is smoked and cured in the cold cellars of village houses – it's particularly tasty in Castagniccia, where wild pigs feed on the chestnuts which were once the staple diet of the locals. Here you can also taste chestnut fritters (*fritelli a gaju frescu*) and chestnut porridge (*pulenta*) sprinkled with sugar or eau de vie. **Brocciu**, a soft mozzarella-like cheese made with ewe's milk, is found everywhere on the island, forming the basis for many dishes, including omelettes and cannelloni. *Fromage corse* is also very good – a hard **cheese** made in the sheep- and goat-rearing central regions, where *cabrettu a l'istrettu* (kid stew) is a speciality.

Game – mainly stews of hare and wild boar but also roast woodcock, partridge and wood pigeon – features throughout the island's mountain and forested regions. Here blackbirds (*merles*) are made into a fragrant pâté, and eel and trout are fished from the unpolluted rivers. **Sea fish** like red mullet (*rouget*), bream (*loup de mer*) and a great variety of shellfish is eaten along the coast – the best crayfish (*langouste*) comes from around the Golfe de St-Florent, whereas oysters (*huîtres*) and mussels (*moules*) are a speciality of the eastern plain.

Of the local **wine**, try Domaine Fiumicicoli from the Sartène area, which comes in both rosé and red, and Domaine Abbatucci's fragrant white, from the area around Filitosa. The favoured apéritifs are the sweet muscat produced on Cap Corse and the drink known as Cap Corse, a fortified wine flavoured with quinine and herbs. Note that **tap water** is particularly good quality in Corsica, coming from the fresh mountain streams.

Some history

Set on the western Mediterranean trade routes, Corsica has always been of strategic and commercial appeal. Greeks, Carthaginians and Romans came in successive waves, driving native Corsicans into the interior. The Romans were ousted by Vandals, and for the following thirteen centuries the island was attacked, abandoned, settled and sold as a nation-state, with generations of islanders fighting against foreign government. In 1768 France bought Corsica from Genoa, but over two hundred years of French rule have had a limited effect and the island's Baroque churches, Genoese fortresses, fervent Catholic rituals and a Tuscan-influenced indigenous language and cuisine show a more profound affinity with Italy.

Corsica's uneasy relationship with the mainland has worsened in recent decades. Economic neglect and the French government's reluctance to encourage Corsican language and culture spawned a nationalist movement in the early 1970s, whose clandestine armed wing – the FLNC (Fronte di Liberazione Nazionale di a Corsica) – has been engaged ever since in a bloody conflict with the central government. The violence seldom affects tourists but signs of the "troubles" are everywhere, from the graffiti-sprayed roadsigns to the bullet holes plastering public buildings.

Relations between the island's hard-line nationalists and Paris may be perennially fraught, but there's little support among ordinary islanders for the armed struggle, and still less for total independence. Corsica is bankrolled by $480 million of direct subsidies annually, with a further $1.3 billion to bolster its bloated bureaucracy. Another $800 million has poured in from the EU since 1994,

Corsica practicalities

Getting to Corsica

One French company, SNCM – along with its freight subsidiary CMN – dominates **ferry** services to Corsica. In addition, an Italian operator, Corsica Ferries, has superfast services from **Nice** to Calvi and Bastia. Crossings take between seven and twelve hours on a regular ferry, and from two-and-a-half to three-and-a-half hours on the giant hydrofoil ("NGV", or *navire à grande vitesse*). The cost depends on the season, with the lowest between October and May; during July and August fares triple. A one-way crossing costs anything from €21 to €48 per person, plus €42 and €125 per vehicle.

From **Marseille** a maximum of seven ferries a week run to Ajaccio and Bastia, with between one and three weekly services to L'Île-Rousse, and one to five to Propriano. There are up to four ferries a week from **Toulon** to Ajaccio, Bastia and Propriano, and more frequent services from Nice to Ajaccio (up to six weekly) and Bastia (up to twelve weekly). Between two and five a week run from Nice to Calvi or L'Île Rousse. See p.1274 for more details. You can **book** SNCM and CNM tickets via their central reservation desk (ⓣ08.91.70.18.01, ⓦwww.sncm.fr). For Corsica Ferries contact ⓣ04.92.00.42.93, ⓦwww.corsicaferries.fr. Note that reservations are essential for journeys in July and August.

Direct **flights** to Corsica depart from most major French cities with charters cheaper than scheduled services. The largest operator is Air France (ⓣ08.20.82.08.20, ⓦwww.airfrance.fr), whose 14-day advance fares from Paris start at €225 return in July and August, dropping to €125 out of season. Compagnie Corse Méditerranée (ⓣ08.02.80.28.02, ⓦwww.ccm-airlines.com) offers routes from a range of mainland airports. Their fares from the Côte d'Azur vary little: roughly €110 return, or €55 one-way. For information on charter deals – which typically cost around €195 return – call at any Ollandini travel agent in France (ⓣ04.95.23.92.94, ⓦwww.ollandini-voyages.fr), or Nouvelles Frontières (ⓣ08.25.00.08.25, ⓦwww.nouvelles-frontieres.fr).

Getting around

With public transport woefully inadequate, the most convenient way of **getting around** Corsica is by rental car. Hertz (ⓣ04.95.23.57.04, ⓦwww.hertz.fr), Avis (ⓣ04.95.23.56.90, ⓦwww.avis.fr), Europcar (ⓣ04.95.30.09.50, ⓦwww.europcar.com) and Rent-a-Car (ⓣ04.95.51.34.45, ⓦwww.rentacar.fr) all have offices at airports and towns across the island, allowing you to collect and return vehicles in different places. If your budget won't stretch to a week (€200–250), it's worth renting for a couple of days to explore the back roads of the interior. Bus services are fairly frequent between Bastia, Corte and Ajaccio, and along the east coast from Bastia to Porto-Vecchio and Bonifacio. Getting accurate timetable information for bus services can also be difficult – the best way to check information is at a tourist office.

Corsica's diminutive **train**, the *Micheline* or *Trinighellu* (little train), rattles through the mountains from Ajaccio to Bastia via Corte, with a branch line running northwest to Calvi. It's slower than the bus, but goes through some stupendous scenery. A good investment if you intend to use the train a lot is the Carte Zoom, which gives 7 consecutive days of travel, plus free use of the station *consignes* (left luggage rooms), for €47.

Motorcycles and **scooters** can be rented at several towns and resorts, but cost as much as cars. A 125cc machine, for example, will set you back around €60–70 per day (€250–275 per week), plus a deposit of €750 or more. Remember to check your insurance policy to make sure you have adequate cover – Corsican roads are among the most lethal in Europe.

making Corsica the most heavily subsidized region of France. Moreover, Corsicans are exempt from social security contributions and the island as a whole enjoys preferential tax status, while one third of the permanent population is an employee of the state. Increasingly, nationalist violence is seen as biting the hand that feeds it. Opinion, however, remains divided on the best way forward for Corsica. In 2003, an end to the troubles seemed tantalizingly close as Chirac's administration, despite strong opposition from the Gaullist Right, proposed a new package of devolutionary measures and placed them before the island in a referendum. But the initiative was narrowly defeated, a setback many commentators have attributed less to lack of support for greater autonomy than to the PR bungle that followed the arrest of Corsica's most wanted terrorist on the eve of the vote. The triumphalist tone adopted by Paris following the capture of Yvan Colonna, wanted for the murder of the island's former governor, provoked a patriotic backlash that may well have been decisive. Interior Minister Nicholas Sarkozy responded by condemning the result as a "wasted opportunity". The administration's policy on Corsica has been moribund ever since.

Bastia and around

The dominant tone of Corsica's most successful commercial town, **BASTIA**, is one of charismatic dereliction, as the city's industrial zone is spread onto the lowlands to the south, leaving the centre of town with plenty of aged charm. The old quarter, known as the Terra Vecchia, comprises a tightly packed network of haphazard streets, flamboyant Baroque churches and lofty tenements, their crumbling golden-grey walls set against a backdrop of maquis-covered hills. Terra Nova, the historic district on the opposite side of the old port, is a tidier area that's now Bastia's trendy quarter.

The city dates from Roman times, when a base was set up at Biguglia to the south, beside a freshwater lagoon, or *étang*. Little remains of the former colony, but the site merits a day trip for the well-preserved pair of Pisan churches at Marana, rising from the southern fringes of Poretta airport. Bastia began to thrive under the Genoese, when wine was exported to the Italian mainland from Porto Cardo, forerunner of Bastia's Vieux Port, or Terra Vecchia. Despite the fact that in 1811 Napoleon appointed Ajaccio capital of the island, initiating a rivalry between the two towns which exists to this day, Bastia soon established a stronger trading position with mainland France. The Nouveau Port, created in 1862 to cope with the increasing traffic with France and Italy, became the mainstay of the local economy, exporting chiefly agricultural products from Cap Corse, Balagne and the eastern plain.

Arrival, information and accommodation

Bastia's Poretta **airport** (ⓣ04.95.54.54.54, ⓦwww.bastia.aeroport.fr) is 16km south of town, just off the Route Nationale (N193). **Shuttle buses** into the centre coincide with flights, dropping passengers at the north side of the main square, place St-Nicolas, and terminating at the train station for €8 (one way). **Taxis** from the airport cost €35. **Ferries** arrive at the **Nouveau Port**, just a five-minute walk from the centre of town. Bastia doesn't have a proper bus station, which can cause confusion, with services arriving and departing from different locations around the north side of the main square. **Buses** from Ajaccio, Bonifacio, Porto-Vecchio and the east coast stop outside the travel agents opposite the post office (PTT) on avenue Maréchal-Sébastiani, whereas those

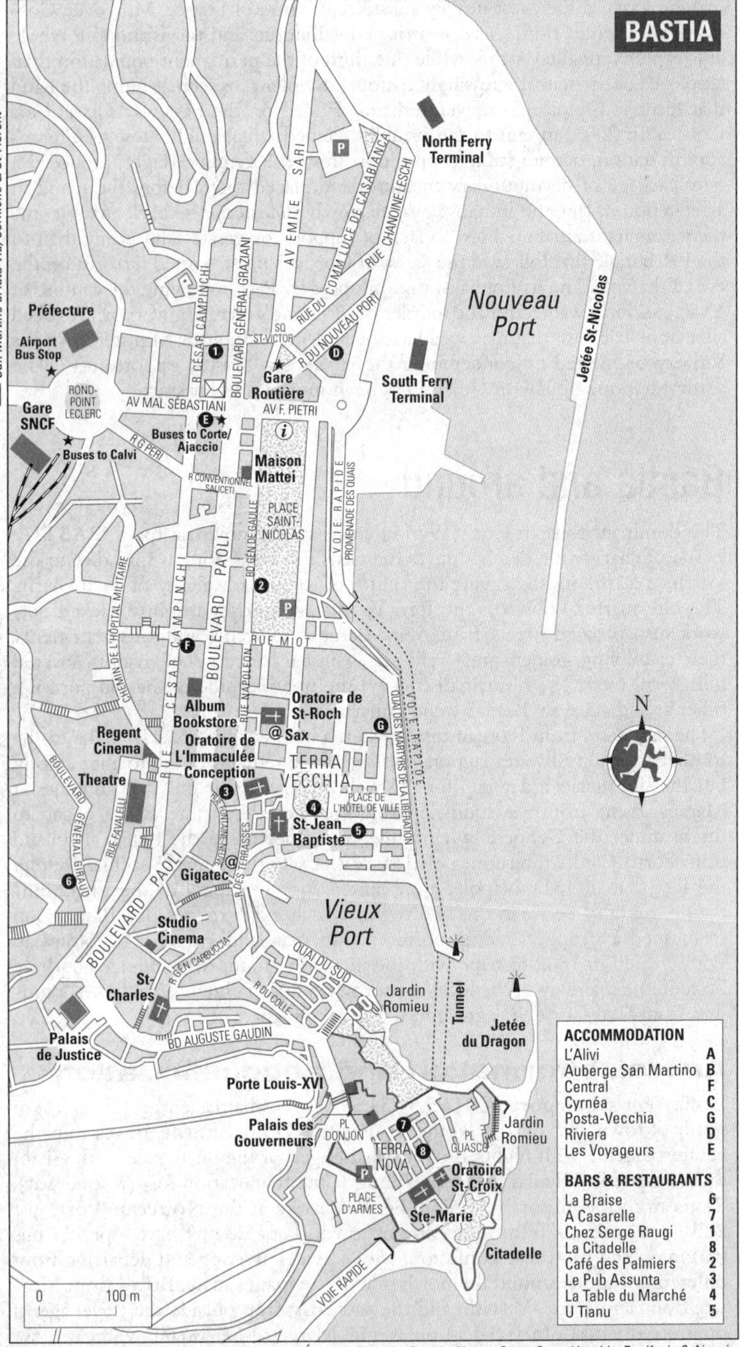
A, B, C, Camping Casanova, Camping Les Orangers & Cap Corse
BASTIA
San Martino di lota Via, Corniche & St-Florent
North Ferry Terminal
Nouveau Port
Jetée St-Nicolas
South Ferry Terminal
Préfecture
Airport Bus Stop
ROND-POINT LECLERC
Gare SNCF
Buses to Calvi
Buses to Corte/Ajaccio
Gare Routière
SQ ST-VICTOR
AV MAL SÉBASTIANI
AV F. PIETRI
Maison Mattei
PLACE SAINT-NICOLAS
Album Bookstore
Oratoire de St-Roch
Sax
Regent Cinema
Theatre
Oratoire de L'Immaculée Conception
TERRA VECCHIA
PLACE DE L'HÔTEL DE VILLE
St-Jean Baptiste
Gigatec
Vieux Port
Studio Cinema
St-Charles
Palais de Justice
Jardin Romieu
Tunnel
Jetée du Dragon
Porte Louis-XVI
Palais des Gouverneurs
PL DONJON
TERRA NOVA
PL GUASCO
Oratoire St-Croix
Ste-Marie
PLACE D'ARMES
Citadelle
0 100 m
ACCOMMODATION
L'Alivi A
Auberge San Martino B
Central F
Cyrnéa C
Posta-Vecchia G
Riviera D
Les Voyageurs E
BARS & RESTAURANTS
La Braise 6
A Casarelle 7
Chez Serge Raugi 1
La Citadelle 8
Café des Palmiers 2
Le Pub Assunta 3
La Table du Marché 4
U Tianu 5
Camping San Damiano, L'Arinella, La Marana, Étang de Biguglia, Poretta Airport, Corte, Porto-Vecchio, Bonifacio & Ajaccio

coming from Calvi pull in further up the same street outside the **train station** (Ⓣ04.95.32.80.61). Local suburban services, and those from St-Florent and Cap Corse, work out of a small square, north of avenue Maréchal-Sébastiani – which, confusingly, is referred to as the *gare routière*, even though it's little more than a roadside stop. A summary of bus times and departure points is available at the tourist office, at the north end of place St-Nicolas (June to mid-Sept daily 8am–8pm; mid-Sept to May Mon–Sat 8am–6pm, Sun 9am–1pm; Ⓣ04.95.54.20.40, Ⓦwww.bastia-tourisme.com).

Although you're usually guaranteed to find somewhere to stay in Bastia, the choice of **hotels** is not great, particularly at the budget end the scale. Most of the classier places line the road to Cap Corse north of the port; the more basic ones are found in the centre of town, within striking distance of place St-Nicolas. Wherever you plan to stay, it's essential to reserve well in advance.

There's also a handful of **campsites** located outside the town. The most convenient if you're relying on public transport are at Miomo, 5km north (buses every 30min Mon–Sat, hourly Sun, until 7.30pm, from the top of place St-Nicolas opposite the tourist office).

Hotels

L'Alivi rte du Cap, Ville Pietrabugno Ⓣ04.95.55.00.00, Ⓦwww.hotel-alivi.com. Large three-star, 3km north of the city, with a pool, car park and private access to the beach. The rooms are light, spacious and sea-facing with glorious views from their terraces. ❼

Auberge San Martino place de l'Église, San Martino di Lota, 11km north of Bastia Ⓣ04.95.32.23.68. Unpretentious, welcoming and typically Corsican place high above the corniche in the middle of a gorgeous old village, offering a handful of simple rooms (all en suite). There's no obligation to go for half board, but given the hospitality most people do (see "Eating and drinking" p.1222). The only drawback is you need your own transport to get here. Advance booking essential. ❷

Central 3 rue Miot Ⓣ04.95.31.82.40, Ⓦwww.centralhotel.fr. Just off the southwest corner of place St-Nicolas. Attractively decorated rooms, a welcoming *patronne* and the smell of fresh bread wafting from the boulangerie next door make this by far the most pleasant and best-value place to stay in the centre. ❸

Cyrnéa Pietranea Ⓣ04.95.31.41.71, Ⓕ04.95.31.72.65. Congenial little two-star, 4km out of town. All rooms are en suite, but only some overlook the water. You also get the run of a little garden strewn with sun loungers, which leads to a secluded pebble beach. ❹

Posta-Vecchia quai-des-Martyrs-de-la-Libération Ⓣ04.95.32.32.38, Ⓦwww.hotel-postavecchia.com. The only hotel in the Vieux Port, and good value, with views across the sea from its (pricier) rooms at the front. Smaller, cheaper options are in the old block across the lane. ❸

Riviera 1bis rue du Nouveau-Port Ⓣ04.95.31.07.16, Ⓕ04.95.34.17.39. Basic, and a bit noisy, but near the harbour. ❹

Les Voyageurs 9 av Maréchal-Sébastiani Ⓣ04.95.34.90.80, Ⓦwww.hotel-lesvoyageurs.com. Swish three-star opposite the post office, done out in pale yellow and with two categories of rooms: the larger, pricier ones have tubs instead of showers. ❺

Campsites

Casanova Miomo, 5km north along the rte du Cap Ⓣ04.95.33.91.42. Larger and greener than its neighbour, but fractionally more expensive, and with a bar. Open April–Oct.

Les Orangers Miomo, 5km north along the rte du Cap Ⓣ04.95.33.24.09. Tiny site crammed onto narrow terraces, just off the main road. The cheaper of the pair in this suburb. Open April–Oct.

San Damiano Pineto, 10km south of Bastia Ⓣ04.95.33.68.02, Ⓦwww.camping.sandamiano.com. Huge, pricey site with top facilities, including a pool and Jacuzzi; take the road to the left across the bridge at Furiani roundabout (5km south on the N193). Open April–Oct.

The Town

Bastia is not especially large, and all its sights can easily be seen in a day without the use of a car. The spacious **place St-Nicolas** is the obvious place to get your bearings: open to the sea and lined with shady trees and cafés, it's the main focus of town life. Running parallel to it on the landward side are boulevard Paoli and rue César-Campinchi, the two main shopping streets, but all Bastia's historic sights lie within **Terra Vecchia**, the old quarter immediately south of place St-Nicolas, and **Terra Nova**, the area surrounding the Citadelle. Tucked away below the imposing, honey-coloured bastion is the much-photographed **Vieux Port**, with its boat-choked marina and crumbling eighteenth-century tenement buildings. By contrast, the **Nouveau Port**, north of the *place*, is bland and modern, with little of note other than restaurants, bars and a self-service laundry.

Terra Vecchia

From place St-Nicolas the main route into Terra Vecchia is **rue Napoléon**, a narrow street with some ancient offbeat shops and a pair of sumptuously decorated chapels on its east side. The first of these, the **Oratoire de St-Roch**, is a Genoese Baroque extravagance, reflecting the wealth of the rising bourgeoisie. Built in 1604, it has walls of finely carved wooden panelling and a magnificent gilt organ.

A little further along stands the **Oratoire de L'Immaculée Conception**, built in 1611 as the showplace of the Genoese in Corsica, who used it for state occasions. Overlooking a pebble mosaic of a sun, the austere facade belies the flamboyant interior, where crimson velvet draperies, a gilt and marble ceiling, frescoes and crystal chandeliers create the ambience of an opera house. The sacristy houses a tiny **museum** (daily 9am–6pm; free) of minor religious works, of which the wooden statue of St Erasmus, a patron saint of fishermen, dating from 1788, is most arresting.

Just behind the oratoire, the place de l'Hôtel-de-Ville is commonly known as **place du Marché** after the lively farmers' market that takes place here each morning, from around 7am until 2pm. Dominating the south end of the square is the **church of St-Jean-Baptiste**, an immense ochre edifice that dominates the Vieux Port. Its twin campaniles are Bastia's distinguishing feature, but the interior is less than impressive. Built in 1636, the church was restored in the eighteenth century in a hideous Rococo overkill of multicoloured marble. Decorating the walls are a few unremarkable Italian paintings from Napoleon's uncle, Cardinal Fesch, an avid collector of Renaissance art.

Around the church extends the oldest part of Bastia, a secretive zone of dark alleys, vaulted passageways and seven-storey houses. By turning right outside and following rue St-Jean you'll come to rue Général-Carbuccia, the heart of Terra Vecchia. Corsican independence leader Pascal Paoli once lived here, at no. 7, and Balzac stayed briefly at no. 23 when his ship got stuck in Corsica on the way to Sardinia. Set in a small square at the end of the road is the **church of St-Charles**, a Jesuit chapel whose wide steps provide an evening meeting place for the locals; opposite stands the **Maison de Caraffa**, an elegant house with a strikingly graceful balcony.

The **Vieux Port** is easily the most photogenic part of town: soaring houses seem to bend inwards towards the water and peeling plaster and boat hulls glint in the sun, while the south side remains in the shadow of the great rock that supports the citadelle. Site of the original Roman settlement of *Porto Cardo*, the Vieux Port later bustled with Genoese traders, but since the building of the ferry terminal and commercial docks to the north it has become a backwater. The most atmospheric time to come here is early evening, when huge flocks of swifts swirl in noisy clouds above the harbour. Things liven up after sunset, with the glow and noise from the waterside bars and restaurants, which continue round the north end of the port along the wide **quai des Martyrs de la Libération**, where live bands clank out pop covers for the tourists in summer.

A small "Cuncolta" sign above a door on the north side of the Vieux Port marks the spot where a car bomb exploded in July 1996, killing a prominent nationalist. Fifteen other people were hurt in the blast, which was the first time a bomb had been planted in a public place, in broad daylight, since the beginning of the troubles in Corsica.

Terra Nova

The military and administrative core of old Bastia, **Terra Nova** (or the citadelle) has a distinct air of affluence, its lofty apartments now colonized by Bastia's yuppies. The area is focused on **place du Donjon**, which gets its name from the squat round tower that formed the nucleus of Bastia's fortifications and was used by the Genoese to incarcerate Corsican patriots – Sampiero Corso (the nationalist hero who mounted an insurrection against the Genoese in 1657) was held in the dungeon for four years in the early sixteenth century. Next to the tower, the *Bar de la Citadelle* commands a magnificent view that extends to Elba on a clear day.

Facing the bar is the impressive fourteenth-century **Palais des Gouverneurs**. With its great round tower, arcaded courtyard and pristine peach-coloured paintwork, this building has a distinctly Moorish feel and was built for the governor and local bishop during the town's Genoese heyday. When the French transferred the capital to Ajaccio it became a prison, then was destroyed during a British attack of 1794 (in which an ambitious young captain named Horatio Nelson played a decisive part). The subsequent rebuilding was not the last, as parts of it were blown up by American B-52s in 1943 – on the day after Corsica's liberation, when thousands of Bastiais were celebrating in the streets. Extensive restoration work – due for completion in 2005 – has regained something of the building's former grandeur. Part of the palace is given over to the **Musée d'Ethnographie** (scheduled to reopen in 2005; daily: June 9am–6.30pm; July & Aug 9am–8pm; Sept–May 9am–noon & 2–6pm; last entry 45min before closing time; admission around €5), which presents the history of Corsica from prehistoric times to the present day. Its vaulted chambers contain some fascinating historical titbits, including a diminutive Roman sarcophagus decorated with hunting scenes, busts of famous Corsicans and an original 1755 Flag of Independence, with its distinctive Moorish emblem.

Back in place du Donjon, if you cross the square and follow rue Notre-Dame you come out at the **Église Ste-Marie**. Built in 1458 and overhauled in the seventeenth century, it was the cathedral of Bastia until 1801, when the bishopric was transferred to Ajaccio. Inside, the church's principal treasure is a small silver statue of the Virgin (housed in a glass case on the right wall as you face the altar), which is carried through Terra Nova and Terra Vecchia on August 15, the Festival of the Assumption. Immediately behind Ste-Maire in rue de l'Évêché stands the **Oratoire Sainte-Croix**, a sixteenth-century chapel decorated in Louis XV style, with lashings of rich blue paint and gilt scrollwork. It houses another holy item, the *Christ des Miracles*, a blackened oak crucifix much venerated by Bastia's fishermen, which in 1428 was discovered floating in the sea surrounded by a luminous haze. A festival celebrating the miracle takes place in Bastia on May 3, when local fishing families carry it around Terra Nova. Beyond the church, the narrow streets open out to the secluded **place Guasco**, where a few benches offer the chance of a rest before descending back into the fray.

The beaches

Crowded with schoolchildren in the summer, the pebbly **town beach** in Bastia is only worth visiting if you're desperate for a swim. To reach it, go left at the flower shop on the main road south out of town, just beyond the citadelle. A more salubrious alternative is the long beach of **L'Arinella** at Montesoro, a further 1km along the same road, the beginning of a sandy shore that extends along the whole east coast. A bus to L'Arinella leaves from outside *Café Riche* on boulevard Paoli every twenty minutes; just get off at the last stop and cross the train line to the sea. There are a couple of sailing and windsurfing clubs here, and a bar.

Eating and drinking

Numerous pizza vans are scattered about town, evidence of a strong Italian influence that's also apparent in the predominance of **pizzerias** and pasta places in the Nouveau Port area. The town also boasts some excellent inexpensive **restaurants** serving Corsican specialities: the posh places on the quai des Martyrs do the best *aziminu*, a Corsican version of *bouillabaisse*. Most of the good restaurants are to be found around the Vieux Port and on the quai des Martyrs, with a sprinkling in the citadelle.

Drinking is a serious business in Bastia, with the Casanis *pastis* factory on the outskirts in Lupino making the town's favourite drink. There are many bars and cafés all over town, varying from the stark and brightly lit bars of Terra Vecchia, which are the haunt of old men, to the elegant, dimly lit cafés on place St-Nicolas, which entertain a younger, more lively clientele. For a more sedate atmosphere, boulevard Paoli and rue Campinchi are lined with chi-chi *salons de thé* offering elaborate creamy confections, local chestnut cake and doughnuts.

Bars and cafés

Chez Serge Raugi 2bis rue Capanelle, off bd Général Graziani. Arguably Corsica's greatest ice-cream maker, with tables on a cramped pavement terrace or upstairs on an even smaller mezzanine floor. In winter, they also do a legendary chickpea tart to take away.

Café des Palmiers place St-Nicolas. One of the few cafés along this stretch, with delicious fresh pastries, attentive service and comfy wicker chairs that catch the sun at breakfast time.

Le Pub Assunta 4 rue Fontaine-Neuve. Large, lively bar with a good selection of draught beers, a snooker table and a terrace opening onto the old quarter. Serves fast food too, and puts on live music with local bands on Thurs.

Restaurants

Auberge San Martino place de l'Église, San Martino-di-Lota, 11km north of Bastia ☎04.95.32.23.68. One of the most convivial and best-value restaurants in the region, and reason enough to venture out along the corniche – a spectacular drive in itself. Exposed beams and old farm tools set the tone. The food's copious, inexpensive and authentically local: anchovies *à la bastiaise*, game stews and wild boar lasagne, with home-made *migliaccoli* (chestnut fritters) or *fiadone* for dessert. Menus €15–20; closed mid-Dec to mid-Jan.

La Braise 7 bd Hyacinte-de-Montrea/bd Général Giraud ☎04.95.31.36.97. Authentic Corsican pizzeria, whose succulent meat dishes and pizzas, cooked over wood grills with maquis herbs, have made its owner – a "Russian-Chuwawa-Indian retired boxer" – a local celebrity. €20 for the works, or €7–10 for pizzas. Closed Sun & Aug.

A Casarelle 6 rue Sainte-Croix ☎04.95.32.02.32. Innovative Corsican-French cuisine served on a terrace on the edge of the citadelle. The chef's specialities are traditional dishes of the Balagne, such as *casgiate* (nuggets of fresh cheese baked in fragrant chestnut leaves) or the rarely prepared *storzapreti* (balls of *brocciu*, spinach and herbs in tomato sauce). €15 per head for lunch, €23 for dinner or €30 à la carte. Closed Sat & Sun lunchtimes.

La Citadelle 6 rue du Dragon ☎04.95.31.44.70. One of the finest places to eat on the island, in the heart of Terra Nova. Sumptuous French cuisine served in a cellar with mellow lighting and an old olive press in the corner. Prices are high (€33 for the three-course *menu fixe*, or around €40 per head à la carte without wine), but you get what you pay for.

La Table du Marché place du Marché ⓣ04.95.31.64.25. Elegant, old-fashioned lunch venue on the atmospheric market square, serving a popular €22 menu of dependable *cuisine du terroir* to a mostly local clientele. Get there around midday for a seat on the terrace.

U Tianu 4 rue Rigo ⓣ04 95 31 36 67. Tiny, unpretentious, family-run restaurant with lots of atmosphere hidden in a narrow backstreet behind the Vieux Port. Their limited but excellent-value menus (€19) change daily but feature typical country dishes.

Listings

Bike rental Locacycles, behind the Palais de Justice ⓣ04.95.32.30.64.
Car rental Avis/Ollandini, 40 bd Paoli ⓣ04.95.31.95.64; Rent-a-Car at the airport ⓣ04.95.54.55.11.
Ferries SNCM has desks in both ferry terminal buildings and at 15 bd de Gaulle ⓣ04.95.54.66.88.
Internet *Gigatec*, 8 rue Fontaine-Neuve, just above the Vieux Port; or nearby *Sax*, 1 rue Neuve-Saint-Roch. Both charge around €3 per hour and have ISDN lines.
Motorbike rental Toga Location, in the marina north of the Nouveau Port ⓣ04.95.34.14.14.
Post office Av Maréchal-Sébastiani. Mon–Fri 8am–7pm, Sat 8am–noon.

La Marana, Mariana and the Étang de Biguglia

Traditionally the summer haunt of prosperous Bastia families, the sixteen-kilometre littoral known as **LA MARANA** lies a few kilometres south of Bastia. The beach here offers shady pine woods, restaurants and bars, though the sea is quite polluted. The whole of this part of the coast is divided into holiday residences or sections of beach attached to bars, the latter freely open to the public.

Fed by the rivers Bevinco and Golo, the **Étang de Biguglia** is the largest lagoon in Corsica, and one of its best sites for rare migrant birds. In summer, reed and Cetti's warblers nest in the reeds, while in winter, Biguglia supports a resident community of grey herons, kingfishers, great-crested grebes, little grebes, water rails and various species of duck.

The Roman town of **MARIANA**, just south of Étang de Biguglia, can be approached by taking the turning for Poretta airport, 16km along the N193, or the more scenic coastal route through **La Marana**. It was founded in 93 BC as a military colony, but today's houses, baths and basilica are too ruined to be of great interest. It's only the square baptistry, with its remarkable mosaic floor decorated with dancing dolphins and fish looped around bearded figures representing the four rivers of paradise, that is worth seeking out.

Adjacent to Mariana stands the **church of Santa Maria Assunta**, known as **La Canonica**. Built in 1119 close to the old capital of Biguglia, it's the finest of around three hundred churches built by the Pisans in their effort to evangelize the island. Modelled on a Roman basilica, the perfectly proportioned edifice is decorated outside with Corinthian capitals plundered from the main Mariana site and with plates of Cap Corse marble, their delicate pink and yellow ochre hues fusing to stunning effect.

Marooned amid muddy fields about 300m to the south of La Canonica is another ancient church, **San Parteo**, built in the eleventh and twelfth centuries over the site of a pagan burial ground. A smaller edifice than La Canonica, it displays some elegant arcading and fine sculpture – on the south side, the door lintel is supported by two writhing beasts reaching to a central tree, a motif of oriental origins.

Cap Corse

Until Napoléon III had a coach road built around **Cap Corse** in the nineteenth century, the promontory was effectively cut off from the rest of the island, relying on Italian maritime traffic for its income – hence its distinctive Tuscan dialect. Many Capicursini later left to seek their fortunes in the colonies of the Caribbean, which explains the distinctly ostentatious mansions, or *palazzi*, built by the successful emigrés (nicknamed "les Américains") on their return. For all the changes brought by the modern world, Cap Corse still feels like a separate country, with wild flowers in profusion, vineyards and quiet, traditional fishing villages.

Forty kilometres long and only fifteen across, the peninsula is divided by a spine of mountains called the Serra, which peaks at Cima di e Folicce, 1324m above sea level. The coast on the east side of this divide is characterized by tiny ports, or *marines*, tucked into gently sloping river-mouths, alongside coves which become sandier as you go further north. The villages of the western coast are sited on rugged cliffs, high above the rough sea and tiny rocky inlets that can be glimpsed from the corniche road.

For those without transport, a circular-tour bus operates daily from Bastia during August, run by Transports Micheli (Mon–Sat 1 daily; ⓣ04.95.35.64.02). There are also municipal buses throughout the year to **Erbalunga**, a placid fishing village on the east of Cap Corse. In addition, sporadic services run from Bastia's *gare routière* to **Macinaggio** (Mon, Wed & Fri; Transports Saladini ⓣ04.95.35.43.88), on the far north tip of the cape, and to **Canari** (Mon & Wed; Transports Saoletti ⓣ04.95.37.84.05), on the western side.

Erbalunga

Built along a rocky promontory 10km north of Bastia, the small port of **ERBALUNGA** is the highlight of the east coast, with aged, pale buildings stacked like crooked boxes behind a small harbour and ruined Genoese watchtower. A little colony of French artists lived here in the 1920s, and the village has drawn a steady stream of admirers ever since. It attracts a fair number of tourists throughout the year, and come summer it's transformed into something of a cultural enclave, with concerts and art events adding a spark to local nightlife. The town is most famous, however, for its Good Friday procession, known as the **Cerca** (Search), which evolved from an ancient fertility rite. Hooded penitents, recruited from the ranks of a local religious brotherhood, form a spiral known as a *Granitola*, or snail, which unwinds as the candlelit procession moves into the village square.

A port since the time of the Phoenicians, Erbalunga was once a more important trading centre than Bastia or Ajaccio. In the eleventh century, with the increasing exportation of wine and olive oil, it became the capital of an independent village-state, ruled by the da Gentile family, who lived in the **palazzu** that dominates place de-Gaulle.

The one **hotel**, the gorgeous *Castel Brando* (ⓣ04.95.30.10.30, ⓦwww.castelbrando.com; April to mid-Oct; ❼), stands at the entrance to the *place*, shaded by a curtain of mature date palms, like the backdrop to a classic Visconti movie. It's an elegant, old, stone-floored *palazzu* with a lovely pool and its own car park. Period furniture and antique Corsican engravings fill the rooms and apartments, which are all air-conditioned; those on the top floor have great views. Pick of the harbourside **restaurants** is the renowned *Le Pirate* (ⓣ04.95.33.24.20; Easter–Oct) for whose *cuisine gastronomique* well-heeled Bastias flock here throughout the year. Seafood delicacies dominate their menu, but vegetarians are well catered for with entrées from the *carte*. The house set menu costs around €30; à la carte courses range from €17–55. A less expensive option is *A Piazzetta* (ⓣ04.95.33.28.69), in the tiny square behind the harbour, which does excellent *moules-frites*, a range of tasty pasta dishes from €12–21, and superb sorbets.

Macinaggio (Macinaghju) and around

A port since Roman times, well-sheltered **MACINAGGIO**, 20km north of Erbalunga, was developed by the Genoese in 1620 for the export of olive oil and wine to the Italian peninsula. The Corsican independence leader, Pascal Paoli, landed here in 1790 after his exile in England, whereupon he kissed the ground and uttered the words "O ma patrie, je t'ai quitté esclave, je te retrouve libre" ("Oh my country, I left you as a slave, I rediscover you a free man") – a plaque commemorating the event adorns the wall above the ship chandlers. There's not much of a historic patina to the place nowadays, but with its boat-jammed **marina** and its line of colourful seafront awnings, Macinaggio has a certain appeal, made all the stronger by its proximity to some of the best beaches on Corsica. Another reason to linger is to sample the superb **Clos Nicrosi** wines, grown in the terraces below Rogliano. Of all Corsica's top AOC labels, it's perhaps the hardest to find, but at their little shop on the north side of the Rogliano road, opposite the *U Ricordu* hotel, you can taste the *domaine*'s famously crisp white and heavily scented muscat.

The least expensive **place to stay** is the recently renovated *Hôtel des Îles*, opposite the marina (ⓣ04.95.35.43.02, ⓕ04.95.35.47.05; open April–Oct; ❸), which also has a serviceable restaurant on its ground floor. All the tiny rooms have showers and toilets; those at the front of the building overlook the port but get noisy at night, being above the most popular bar in the resort, so if you're a light sleeper ask for a room at the back. Otherwise try the more modern *U Libecciu*, down the lane leading from the marina to the Plage de Tamarone (ⓣ04.95.35.43.22, ⓦwww.u-libecciu.com; April–Oct, obligatory half board July & Aug; ❺); it's a modern building with no view to speak of, but the rooms are spacious and particularly good value in shoulder season. The three-star *U Ricordu*, on the south side of the road to Rogliano (ⓣ04.95.35.40.20, ⓦwww.hotel-uricordu.com; March–Sept, with obligatory half board Aug; ❽), is the most luxurious option hereabouts, with a swimming pool, sauna, tennis courts and over-the-top tariffs. Macinaggio's only **campsite**, *U Stazzu*, lies 1km north of the harbour and is signposted from the Rogliano road (ⓣ04.95.35.43.76; May–Oct). The ground is like rock, but it's cheap and there's ample shade and easy access to the nearby beach; particularly good breakfasts are also served in the site's little café.

Besides the hotel **restaurants** above, commendable places to eat in Macinaggio include the *Pizzeria San Columbu*, at the end of the port facing out to sea; for a taste of local seafood, try *Les Îles*, the most dependable of a string of places with tables under awnings on the quayside, with a good-value €16 menu.

North of the town lie some stunning stretches of white sand and clear sea. A marked footpath, known as **Le Sentier des Douaniers** because it used to be patrolled by customs officials, threads its way across the hills and coves along the coast, giving access to an area that cannot by reached by road. The **Baie de Tamarone**, 2km along this path, has deep clear waters, making it a good place for diving and snorkelling. Just behind the beach, the road forks, and if you follow the left-hand track for twenty minutes you'll come to a stunning arc of turquoise sea known as the **rade de Santa Maria**, site of the isolated Romanesque **Chapelle Santa-Maria**. Raised on the foundations of a sixth-century church, the building comprises two chapels, one tenth- the other twelfth-century, merged into one, hence the two discrepant apses. The bay's other principal landmark is the huge **Tour Chiapelle**. Dramatically cleft in half and entirely surrounded by water, the ruined three-storeyed tower was one of three built on the northern tip of the cape by the Genoese in the sixteenth century (the others are at Tollare and Barcaggio) as lookout posts against the increasingly troublesome Moorish pirates. As Macinaggio grew in importance, the *torri* began to be used also by health and customs officers, who controlled the maritime traffic with Genoa. Pascal Paoli established his garrison here in 1761, having been unsuccessful in his attempt to take Macinaggio, and contemplated building a rival port. The **tourist office** in Macinaggio will furnish you with a free **map** and route description of the path. Otherwise get hold of a copy of IGN #4347 OT; which covers the entire route to Centuri-Port (7–8hrs).

Centuri-Port

When Dr Johnson's biographer, James Boswell, arrived here from England in 1765, the former Roman settlement of **CENTURI-PORT** was a tiny fishing village, recommended to him for its peaceful detachment from the dangerous turmoil of the rest of Corsica. Not much has changed since Boswell's time: Centuri-Port exudes tranquillity despite a serious influx of summer residents, many of them artists who come to paint the fishing boats in the slightly prettified harbour, where the grey-stone wall is highlighted by the green serpentine roofs of the encircling cottages, restaurants and bars. The only drawback is that you'll find the small beach disappointingly muddy and not ideal for sunbathing (although it is an excellent spot for snorkelling).

Centuri-Port has more **hotels** than anywhere else on Cap Corse. *Hôtel-Restaurant du Pêcheur* (Ⓣ04.95.35.60.14; Easter to mid-November; ❸), the pink building in the harbour, is among the most pleasant and has a popular restaurant. If it's full, try *Hôtel La Jetée*, to the left on the road as you arrive in Centuri (Ⓣ04.95.35.64.46, Ⓕ04.95.35.64.18; April–Sept; ❸), whose rooms are ordinary and for the most part without sea views, but the cheapest in the village during high season. The *Vieux Moulin* (Ⓣ04.95.35.60.15, Ⓦwww.le-vieux-moulin.net; March–Oct; ❺), opposite, is the most stylish option: a converted *maison d'Americain* with a wonderful terrace and attractively furnished en-suite rooms. For **campers**, choice is limited to the undistinguished *Camping l'Isolettu*, 400m south along the D35 (Ⓣ04.95.35.62.81, Ⓕ04.95.35.63.63; May–Oct).

Nonza

Set high on a black rocky pinnacle that plunges vertically into the sea, the village of **NONZA**, 18km south of Centuri, is one of the highlights of the Cap Corse shoreline. It was formerly the main stronghold of the da Gentile family, and the remains of their **fortress** are still standing on the furthest rocks on the overhanging cliff.

The village is also famous for **St Julia**, patron saint of Corsica, who was martyred here in the fifth century. The story goes that she had been sold into slavery at Carthage and was being taken by ship to Gaul when the slavers docked here. A pagan festival was in progress, and when Julia refused to participate she was crucified; the gruesome legend relates that her breasts were then cut off and thrown onto a stone, from which sprang two springs, now enshrined in a chapel by the beach. To get there, follow the sign on the right-hand side of the road before you enter the square, which points to La **Fontaine de Ste-Julia**, down by the rocks. Reached by a flight of six hundred steps, Nonza's long grey **beach** is discoloured as a result of pollution from the now disused asbestos mine up the coast. This may not inspire confidence, but the locals insist it's safe (they take their own kids there in summer), and from the bottom you do get the best view of the tower, which looks as if it's about to topple into the sea.

The only **accommodation** in the village is the *Auberge Patrizi* (Ⓣ04.95.37.82.16; ❹), attached to the big restaurant below the church. Its rooms occupy an attractively converted stone house, five minutes' walk down a steep flight of steps towards the beach.

The Nebbio (U Nebbiu)

Taking its name from the thick mists that sweep over the region in winter, the **Nebbio** has for centuries been one of the most fertile parts of the island, producing honey, chestnuts and some of the island's finest wine. Tourism, however, has so far made little impact on this depopulated area, which comprises the amphitheatre of rippled hills, vineyards and cultivated valleys that converge on St-Florent, a handful of kilometres due west of Bastia. Aside from EU subsidies, the major money earner here is viticulture: some of the wines produced around the commune of **Patrimonio** rival those of Sartène, and *caves* offering wine tastings are a feature of the whole region.

A bishopric until 1790, **St-Florent** is a chic coastal resort at the base of Cap Corse. It remains the Nebbio's chief town, and is the obvious base for day-trips to the beautifully preserved Pisan church of Santa Maria Assunta, just outside the town, and the **Désert des Agriates**, a wilderness of parched maquis-covered hills whose rugged coastline harbours one of Corsica's least accessible, but most beautiful, beaches.

The principal **public transport** serving the Nebbio is the twice-daily bus from Bastia to St-Florent, operated by Transports Santini (Ⓣ04.95.37.02.98) which leaves the *gare routière* at 10.30am and 5.30pm between June and September, and at 11am and 6pm during the rest of the year (except Oct–May Wed & Sat, when they leave at noon & 5.30pm).

St-Florent and around

Viewed from across the bay, **ST-FLORENT** (San Fiurenzu) appears as a bright line against the black tidal wave of the Tenda hills, the pale stone houses seeming to rise straight out of the sea, overlooked by a squat circular citadelle. It's a relaxing town, with a decent beach and a good number of restaurants, but the key to its success is the **marina**, which is jammed with expensive boats throughout the summer. Neither the tourists, however, nor indeed St-Florent's proximity to Bastia, entirely eclipse the air of isolation conferred on the town by its brooding backdrop of mountains and scrubby desert.

In Roman times, a town called Cersunam – referred to as Nebbium by chroniclers from the ninth century onwards – existed a kilometre east of the present village. Few traces remain of the settlement, and in the fifteenth century it was eclipsed by the port that developed around the new Genoese citadelle. St-Florent, as it became known, prospered as one of Genoa's strongholds, and it was from here that Paoli set off for London in 1796, never to return.

Place des Portes, the centre of town life, has café tables facing the sea in the shade of plane trees, and in the evening fills with strollers and pétanque players. In rue du Centre, which runs west off the square, parallel to the seafront and marina, you'll find some restaurants, a few shops and a couple of wine-tasting places – be sure to sample the sweet, maquis-scented muscat made around here. The fifteenth-century circular **citadelle** can be reached on foot from place Doria at the seafront in the old quarter. Destroyed by Nelson's bombardment in 1794, it has been renovated and affords superb views from its terrace.

Just a kilometre to the east of the town off a small road running off place des Portes, on the original site of Cersanum, the **church of Santa Maria Assunta** – the so-called "cathedral of the Nebbio" – is a fine example of Pisan Romanesque architecture. Built of warm yellow limestone, the building has a distinctly barn-like appearance – albeit a superlatively elegant one. Gracefully symmetrical blind arcades decorate the western facade, and at the entrance twisting serpents and wild animals adorn the pilasters on each side of the door. The interior, too, appears deceptively simple. Carved shells, foliage and animals adorn the capitals of the pillars dividing the nave where, immediately to the right, you'll see a glass case containing the mummified figure of St Flor, a Roman soldier martyred in the third century.

Practicalities

Bus times vary a little from year to year, but can be checked at the **tourist office**, at the top of the village in the same building as the **post office**, 100m north of place des Portes (July & Aug Mon–Fri 8.30am–12.30pm & 2–7pm, Sat & Sun 9am–noon & 3–6pm; Sept–June Mon–Fri 9am–noon & 2–5pm, Sat 9am–noon; Ⓣ & Ⓕ04.95.37.06.04).

St-Florent is a popular resort, and **hotels** fill up quickly, especially at the height of summer when prior booking is essential. The *De l'Europe* in place des Portes (Ⓣ04.95.37.00.33, Ⓕ04.95.37.17.36; ❹) is the most attractive option in town – and the only one open in winter. Otherwise, try *Du Centre*, just up the road from the *Europe* (Ⓣ04.95.37.00.68, Ⓕ04.95.37.41.01; ❹; closed Nov–April), which has tiny rooms but is the cheapest place in town, or the more modern and swisher *Maxime*, just off place des Portes (Ⓣ04.95.37.05.30, Ⓕ04.95.37.13.07; ❺; closed Nov–April). A couple of kilometres northeast on the Bastia road, *Le Maloni* (Ⓣ04.95.37.14.30, Ⓦwww.malonihotel.com; ❸) is a friendly, popular, budget choice close to the beach and offering simple en-suite rooms opening on to a leafy garden.

A fair number of **campsites** are dotted about the coast, but are packed in August and closed out of season. *Camping Kallisté*, route de la Plage (Ⓣ04.95.37.03.08, Ⓕ04.95.37.19.77; closed Oct–May), is the closest to town and most congenial, but it's also a notch pricier than the others; the quickest way to get there on foot is via the bridge in the marina, from where you follow the beach as far as an (unmarked) white gate. To reach the scruffier *Camping U Pezzu* (Ⓣ04.95.37.01.65; closed Oct–May), follow the plage de la Roya road behind the *Kallisté* for 1km; the similarly priced *Aqua Dolce* (Ⓣ04.95.37.08.63, Ⓕ04.95.37.12.82; closed Oct–May) lies a further 500m in the same direction.

St-Florent is renowned for the seafood from its gulf and there's no better location to enjoy it than down on the quayside, where a handful of swish gourmet places stand alongside standard pizzerias and tourist **restaurants**. Charging €40–60 per head for four courses, *La Rascasse* (Ⓣ04.95.37.06.99) has become renowned for its imaginative spins on local seafood: cream of ray's wing, mussel and chestnut fritters, and lobster sautéed in cured ham with tartlets of warm *brocciu*. In a similar price bracket is the nearby *La Gaffe* (Ⓣ04.95.37.00.12;

closed Tues, except in July & Aug), where you can order sumptuous devilfish stew on a bed of tagliatelle, with menus at €28 and €40. As a budget option, *A Marina-'Chez Cesar'* (☎04.95.37.15.33; closed Tues or Weds in low season) is hard to beat, serving delicious wood-fired pizzas, lasagnes and grills.

Patrimonio (Patrimoniu)

Leaving St-Florent by the Bastia road, the first village you come to, after 6km, is **PATRIMONIO**, centre of the first Corsican wine region to gain *appellation contrôlée* status. Apart from the renowned local muscat, which can be sampled in the village or at one of the *caves* along the route from St-Florent, Patrimonio's chief asset is the sixteenth-century **church of St-Martin**, occupying its own little hillock and visible for kilometres around. The colour of burnt sienna, it stands out vividly against the rich green vineyards. In a garden 200m south of the church stands a limestone **statue-menhir** known as U Nativu, a late megalithic piece dating from 900–800 BC. A carved T-shape on its front represents a breastbone, and two eyebrows and a chin can also be made out.

The Désert des Agriates

Extending westwards from the Golfe de St-Florent to the mouth of the Ostriconi River, the **Désert des Agriates** is a vast area of uninhabited land, dotted with clumps of cacti and scrub-covered hills. It may appear inhospitable now, but during the time of the Genoese this rocky moonscape was, as its name implies, a veritable breadbasket (*agriates* means "cultivated fields"). In fact, so much wheat was grown here that the Italian overlords levied a special tax on grain to prevent any build-up of funds that might have financed an insurrection. Fires and soil erosion eventually took their toll, however, and by the 1970s the area had become a total wilderness.

Numerous crackpot schemes to redevelop the Désert have been mooted over the years – from atomic weapon test zones to concrete Club-Med-style resorts – but during the past few decades the government has gradually bought up the land from its various owners (among them the Rothschild family) and designated it as a protected nature reserve. Nevertheless, species such as the Agriates' rare wild boar remain under threat, mainly from trigger-happy hunters and bush fires.

A couple of rough *pistes* wind into the desert, but without some kind of 4WD vehicle the only feasible way to explore the area and its rugged coastline, which includes two of the island's most beautiful **beaches**, is by foot. From St-Florent, a pathway winds northwest to **plage de Perajola**, just off the main Calvi highway (N1197), in three easy stages. The first takes around 5hr 30min, and leads past the famous **Martello tower** and much-photographed **plage de Loto** to **plage de Saleccia**, a huge sweep of soft white sand and turquoise sea that was used as a location for the invasion sequences in the film *The Longest Day*. There's a seasonal **campsite** here, *U Paradisu* (☎04.95.37.82.51; closed Nov–April). From plage de Saleccia, it takes around three hours to reach the second night halt, **plage de Ghignu**, where a simple *gîte d'étape* (☎04.95.37.09.86) provides basic facilities for €10 per night. The last stretch to Perajola can be covered in under six hours.

Note that the only water sources along the route are at Saleccia and Ghignu, so take plenty with you. It's also worth knowing that between May and October, **excursion boats**, leaving throughout the day from the jetty in St-Florent marina (€12 return, or €6 one way), ferry passengers across the gulf to and from plage de Loto. If you time your walk well, you can pick one up for the return leg back to town.

The Balagne (A Balagna)

The **Balagne**, the region stretching west from the Ostriconi valley as far as the red-cliffed wilderness of Scandola, has been renowned since Roman times as "Le Pays de l'Huile et Froment" (Land of Oil and Wheat). Backed by a wall of imposing, pale-grey mountains, the characteristic outcrops of orange granite punctuating its spectacular coastline shelter a string of idyllic beaches, many of them sporting ritzy marinas and holiday complexes. These, along with the region's two honeypot towns, **L'Île Rousse** and **Calvi**, get swamped in summer, but the scenery more than compensates. In any case, Calvi, with its cream-coloured citadelle, breathtaking white-sand bay and mountainous backdrop, should not be missed.

Year-round **transport** in the Balagne is limited to the *Micheline* train, which descends the Ostriconi valley and runs west along the coast as far as Calvi, and a bus connection with Bastia, via Ponte Leccia. In July and August, you can also travel to Calvi from Porto by bus, and between Calvi and L'Île Rousse on hourly tram-trains.

L'Île Rousse

Developed by Pascal Paoli in the 1760s as a "gallows to hang Calvi", the port of **L'ÎLE ROUSSE** (Isula Rossa) simply doesn't convince as a Corsican town, its palm trees, smart shops, neat flower gardens and colossal pink seafront hotel creating an atmosphere that has more in common with the French Riviera. Pascal Paoli had great plans for his new town on the Haute-Balagne coast, which was laid out from scratch in 1758 as a port to export the olive oil produced in the region. A large part of the new port was built on a grid system, featuring lines of straight parallel streets quite at odds with the higgledy-piggledy nature of most Corsican villages and towns. Thanks to the busy trading of wine and oil, it soon began to prosper and, two and a half centuries later, still thrives as a successful port. These days, however, the main traffic consists of holiday-makers, lured here by brochure shots of the nearby beaches. This is officially the hottest corner of the island, and the town is thus deluged by German and Italian sun-worshippers in July and August. Given the proximity of Calvi, and so much unspoilt countryside, it's hard to see why you should want to stop here for more than a couple of hours.

Arrival, information and accommodation

The **train station** (Ⓣ04.95.60.00.50) is on route du Port, 500m south of where the ferries arrive. The Bastia–Calvi **bus** stops just south of place Paoli in the town's main thoroughfare, avenue Piccioni. The **SNCM office** is on avenue J.-Calizi (Ⓣ04.95.60.09.56), and the **tourist office** on the south side of place Paoli (April–June & Sept–Oct Mon–Fri 9am–noon & 2–5pm; July & Aug daily 9am–1pm & 2.30–7.30pm; Ⓣ04.95.60.04.35, Ⓦwww.ot-ile-rousse.fr). For **Internet** access, go to *Cyber One Café*, on the way out of town towards Bastia.

L'Île Rousse fills up early in the year and it can be difficult to find a **hotel** at any time from May to October. Most places are modern buildings, more functional than personable. The town has two main **campsites**: *Les Oliviers*, 1km east (Ⓣ04.95.60.19.92), and *Le Bodri* (Ⓣ04.95.16.19.70), 3km west off the main Calvi road. The latter site, which is slap on the beach, can be reached direct by rail – ask for "l'arrêt Bodri".

Hotels

Le Grillon 10 av Paul-Doumer ⓣ04.95.60.00.49, ⓕ04.95.60.43.69. The best cheap hotel in town, just 1km from the centre on the St-Florent/Bastia road. Nothing special, but quiet and immaculately clean. April–Oct. ❸

Napoléon Bonaparte 3 place Paoli ⓣ04.95.60.06.09, ⓕ04.95.60.11.51. Converted *palazzu*, built in the eighteenth century, renovated in the 1930s, and garishly refurbished (in ice-cream pink) a decade ago. Noel Coward famously holidayed here, and the King of Morocco occupied a whole floor during his exile in the 1950s. Now falling apart at the seams and undeserving of its three stars and high-season tariffs. April–Sept. ❾

De la Puntella rte du Port ⓣ04.95.60.04.34, ⓕ04.95.60.40.87. Smart little "studios" (rooms with four beds, kitchenette and bathroom), which are usually booked on a weekly basis during August; particularly good value for families. Ample parking too. ❹

Santa Maria rte du Port ⓣ04.95.63.05.05, ⓦwww.hotelsantamaria.com. Next to the ferry port, this is one of the larger and best-value three-star places. Their recently refurbished, air-conditioned rooms have small balconies or patios opening on to a garden and pool, and there's exclusive access to a tiny pebble beach. ❼

Splendid 4 bd Valéry-François ⓣ04.95.60.00.24, ⓕ04.95.60.04.57. Well-maintained, 1930s-style building with a small swimming pool and some sea views from upper floors; very reasonable tariffs, given the location. April–Oct. ❺

The town and beaches

All roads in L'Île Rousse lead to **place Paoli**, a shady square that's open to the sea and has as its focal point a fountain surmounted by a bust of "U Babbu di u Patria" (Father of the Nation), one of many local tributes to Pascal Paoli. There's a Frenchified covered **market** at the entrance to the square, which hosts a popular artisan-cum-antiques sale on Saturday mornings, while on the west side rises the grim facade of the **church of the Immaculate Conception**.

To reach the **Île de la Pietra**, the islet that gives the town its name, continue north, passing the station on your left. Once over the causeway connecting the islet to the mainland, you can walk through the crumbling mass of red granite as far as the lighthouse at the far end, from where the view of the town is spectacular, especially at sundown, when you get the full effect of the red glow of the rocks.

Immediately in front of the promenade, the **town beach** is a crowded Côte d'Azur-style strand, blocked by ranks of sun loungers and parasols belonging to the row of lookalike café-restaurants behind it. With your own transport, you're better off heading 3km west up the N197, where a signpost pointing right off the main road (next to the turning for *Camping Bodri*) leads 300m downhill to a fee-charging municipal car park (€5 for the day; no shade) from where you can walk to two of the most beautiful beaches on the north coast. To your right as you face the sea, **Plage de Botri** is the more sheltered, backed by soft white dunes in which is nestled a smart but overpriced *paillote* (beach bar). The sand is clean and the water crystal clear, but from late June onwards this normally isolated cove is swamped by campers from the nearby campsite. A short walk further west around the rocky Punta di Ginebre, **Baie de Giunchetu** is a larger, though less picturesque beach. Note that you can reach both of these by train: just behind Plage de Botri is a little request stop at which you can ask to be dropped by any of the services running between L'Île Rousse and Calvi.

Eating and drinking

Though there's an abundance of mediocre **eating** places in the narrow alleys of the old town, a few restaurants do stand out, some offering classic gourmet menus and others serving superb fresh seafood. The best cafés are found along the southern side of place Paoli.

Le Grillon 10 av Paul-Doumer ⓣ04.95.60.00.49. Hotel dining hall with a limited but consistently good menu of mainly French dishes. Their steak *au roquefort* and cod in spicy Créole sauce are perennially popular, while for vegetarians there's a delicious courgette-and-basil pâté, rounded off with home-made honey-and-almond ice cream. Menus at €13 and €16.

Les Jardins d'Emma col de Fogata, 2km along the Calvi, on the left road just past Super U supermarket, ⓣ04.95.60.49.07. This is the place to head to if you fancy a more sophisticated meal. The cuisine is "*gastro-corse*" on a single four-course €32 menu that changes daily. House specialities include spider crab soup and sea bass stuffed with *brocciu*; and they do stupendous desserts.

L'Ostéria place Santelli ⓣ04.95.60.08.39. On a quiet backstreet in the old quarter, this established Corsican speciality restaurant offers an excellent set menu (€17.50), featuring delicious courgette fritters, *soupe de nos villages*, tarragon-scented *gratin d'aubergines*, stuffed sardines and fresh pan-fried prawns. You can sit in a vaulted room adorned with farm implements or on the shaded terrace.

A Quadrera 6 rue Napoléon ⓣ04.95.60.44.52. Sunny Mediterranean salads, quality charcuterie and imaginative seafood dishes, stylishly served inside an eighteenth-century town house with exposed stone walls. Their €17 menu offers great value for money; count on around €28 à la carte.

Calvi

Seen from the water, **CALVI** is a beautiful spectacle, with its three immense bastions topped by a crest of ochre buildings, sharply defined against a hazy backdrop of mountains. Twenty kilometres west along the coast from L'Île Rousse, the town began as a fishing port on the site of the present-day *ville basse* below the citadelle, and remained just a cluster of houses and fishing shacks until the Pisans conquered the island in the tenth century. Not until the arrival of the Genoese, however, did the town become a stronghold when, in 1268, Giovaninello de Loreto, a Corsican nobleman, built a huge citadelle on the windswept rock overlooking the port and named it Calvi. A fleet commanded by Nelson launched a brutal two-month attack on the town in 1794, when Nelson lost the sight in his eye; he left saying he hoped never to see the place again.

The French concentrated on developing Ajaccio and Bastia during the nineteenth century, and Calvi became primarily a military base, used as a point for smuggling arms to the mainland in World War II. A hangout for European glitterati in the 1950s, the town these days has the ambience of a slightly kitsch Côte d'Azur resort, whose glamorous marina, souvenir shops and fussy boutiques jar with the down-to-earth villages of its rural hinterland. It's also an important base for the French Foreign Legion, and immaculately uniformed legionnaires are a common sight around the bars lining avenue de la République.

Arrival, information and accommodation

Ste-Catherine airport lies 7km south of Calvi (ⓣ04.95.65.08.09, ⓦwww.calvi.aeroport.fr); the only public transport into town is by **taxi**, which shouldn't cost more than €16–18. The **train station** (ⓣ04.95.65.00.61) is on avenue de la République, close to the marina, where you'll find the **tourist office** on quai Landry (mid-June to Sept daily 9am–7pm; Oct to mid-June Mon–Fri 9am–noon & 2–5.30pm, Sat 9am–noon; ⓣ04.95.65.16.67, ⓦwww.tourisme.fr/calvi). **Buses** from Bastia and towns along the north coast stop outside the train station on place de la Porteuse d'Eau, whereas those from Porto pull in behind the marina.

Ferries, including NGV hydrofoils, dock at the Port de Commerce at the foot of the citadelle. Corse Consignation et Représentation, agents for **SNCM**, are on the quai Landry (ⓣ04.95.65.01.38); Corsica Ferries' office is over in the

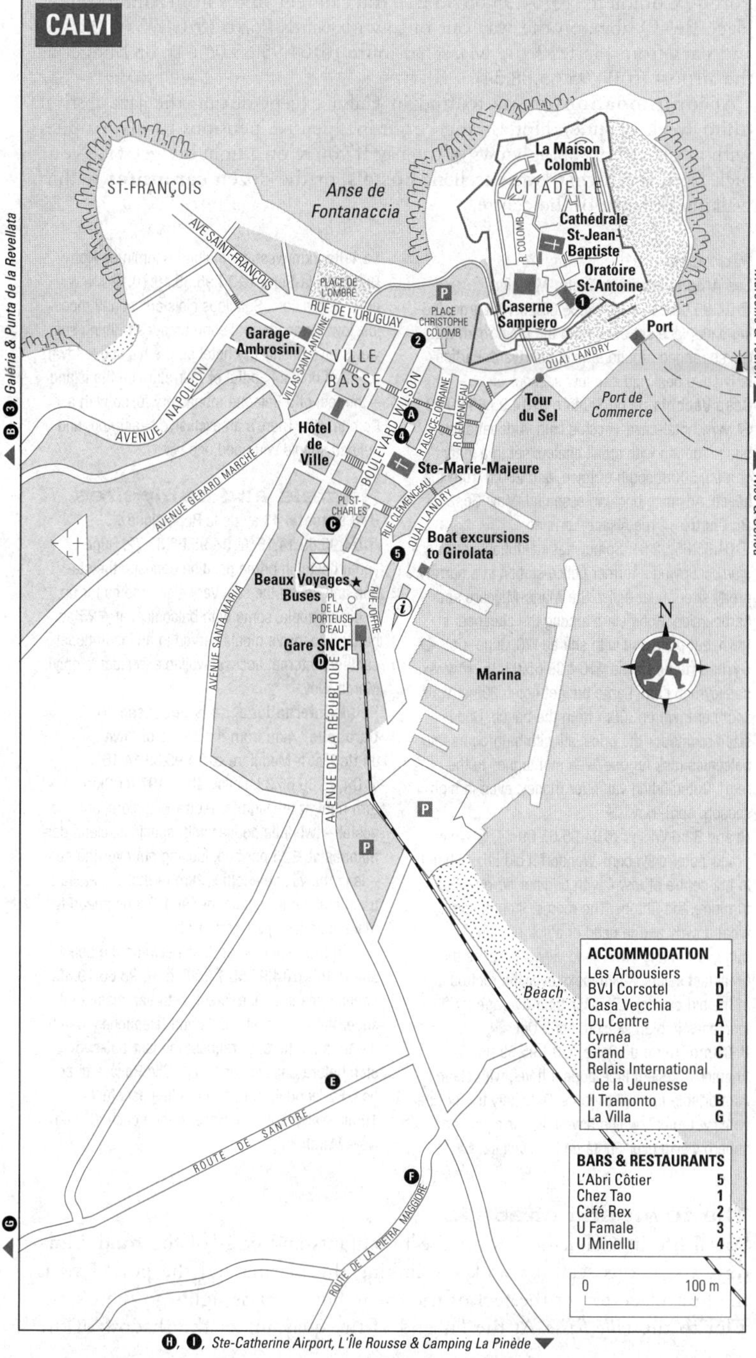
CALVI
ST-FRANÇOIS
Anse de Fontanaccia
AVE SAINT-FRANÇOIS
PLACE DE L'OMBRE
RUE DE L'URUGUAY
PLACE CHRISTOPHE COLOMB
La Maison Colomb
CITADELLE
R. COLOMB
Cathédrale St-Jean-Baptiste
Oratoire St-Antoine
Caserne Sampiero
Port
QUAI LANDRY
Garage Ambrosini
VILLAS SAINT-ANTOINE
VILLE BASSE
AVENUE NAPOLEON
BOULEVARD WILSON
R. ALSACE-LORRAINE
R. CLEMENCEAU
Tour du Sel
Port de Commerce
Hôtel de Ville
Ste-Marie-Majeure
AVENUE GERARD MARCHE
PL ST-CHARLES
RUE CLEMENCEAU
QUAI LANDRY
Boat excursions to Girolata
Beaux Voyages Buses
PL DE LA PORTEUSE D'EAU
RUE JOFFRE
Gare SNCF
AVENUE SANTA MARIA
AVENUE DE LA RÉPUBLIQUE
Marina
N
Beach
ROUTE DE SANTORE
ROUTE DE LA PIETRA MAGGIORE
B, 3, Galéria & Punta de la Revellata
Marseille & Toulon
Nice & Genoa
G
H, I, Ste-Catherine Airport, L'Île Rousse & Camping La Pinède
ACCOMMODATION
Les Arbousiers F
BVJ Corsotel D
Casa Vecchia E
Du Centre A
Cyrnéa H
Grand C
Relais International de la Jeunesse I
Il Tramonto B
La Villa G
BARS & RESTAURANTS
L'Abri Côtier 5
Chez Tao 1
Café Rex 2
U Famale 3
U Minellu 4
0
100 m

Port de Commerce (Ⓣ04.95.65.43.21). You can rent **bikes** from Ambrosini on place Bel-Ombra, on the way out of town towards Porto (Ⓣ04.95.65.02.13), and **cars** from Hertz, 2 rue Maréchal-Joffre (Ⓣ04.95.65.06.64), or Budget at the airport (Ⓣ04.95.65.88.34).

Accommodation is easy to find in Calvi except during the jazz festival (third week of June). Hotels range from inexpensive pensions to luxury piles with pools and sweeping views of the bay. If you're on a tight budget, take your pick from the town's two excellent **hostels**, or the dozen **campsites** within walking distance of the centre.

Hotels

Les Arbousiers rte de Pietra-Maggiore Ⓣ04.95.65.04.47, Ⓕ04.95.65.26.14. Large, fading pink place set back from the main road, with rooms ranged around a quiet courtyard. Particularly good deal mid and low season. ❹

Casa Vecchia rte de Santore Ⓣ04.95.65.09.33, Ⓦwww.hotel-casa-vecchia.com. A dependable budget option with small chalets set in a leafy garden, 500m south of town, and 200m from the beach. Advance booking essential. May–Sept. ❹

Du Centre 14 rue Alsace-Lorraine Ⓣ04.95.65.02.01. Somewhat institutional old *pension* occupying a former police station in a narrow, pretty street near église Ste-Marie-Majeure and harbourside. Rooms are among the cheapest in town, but plain and with shared WC. June–Oct. ❸

Cyrnéa rte de Bastia Ⓣ04.95.65.03.35, Ⓦwww.hotelcyrnea.com. Large budget hotel, 20min walk south of town or 300m from the beach. Good-sized rooms for the price, all with bathrooms and balconies (ask for one "vue montagne" to the rear). Outstanding value for money, even in high season. April–Nov. ❹

Grand 3 bd Wilson Ⓣ04 95 65 09 74, Ⓦwww.grand-hotel-calvi.com. Wonderful old luxury hotel in the centre of town, with original *fin-de-siècle* furniture and fittings. The rooms, though somewhat dowdy and in need of a lick of paint, are huge, and many have good views (as does the breakfast salon, which looks over the rooftops of the old quarter). Smaller-than-average tariff increases in high season. April–Oct. ❼

Il Tramonto rte de Porto Ⓣ04.95.65.04.17. Another excellent little budget hotel, with clean, comfortable and light rooms. Definitely try for one with "vue mer", which have little terraces and superb views over Punta de la Revellata. ❹

La Villa 2km west town along Chemin de Notre-Dame-de-la-Serra Ⓣ04.95.65.10.10, Ⓦwww.hotel-lavilla.com. Spacious cloisters, sunny mosaics, low terracotta roofs and arcades framing sea views give this luxury hotel on the hill above town – one of only a handful of four-stars on the island – the feel of a Balagne monastery fused with a Roman villa. There's an exclusive beach too, and helipad should you need one. ❾

Hostels and campsites

BVJ Corsotel 43 av de la République Ⓣ04.95.65.14.15, Ⓕ04.95.65.33.72. Huge youth hostel in prime position opposite the station and facing the sea. Very clean rooms for up to eight people, some with balconies, at €25 per bed. Inexpensive meals served in an institutional canteen. Internet access available (residents only). March–Nov.

Relais International de la Jeunesse "U Carabellu" 4km from the centre of town on rte Pietra-Maggiore Ⓣ04.95.65.14.16, Ⓕ04.95.80.65.33. Follow the N197 for 2km, turn right at the sign for Pietra-Maggiore, and the hostel – two little houses with spacious, clean dormitories at €25 per bed, looking out over the gulf – is in the village another 2km further on (along a track that's impassable for cars). Phone ahead to make sure it's open. May–Oct.

La Pinède 2km east of Calvi between the beach and N197 Ⓣ04.95.65.17.00, Ⓕ05.96.65.19.60. Popular site in a pine forest, with bar, restaurant, supermarket, tennis courts and telephones. Catch the train out here, or request the last-but-two stop before Calvi coming from L'Île Rousse direction. Far enough from town to be peaceful (a 10min walk), but very close to the beach. Closed Nov–March.

The town and citadelle

Social life in Calvi focuses on the restaurants and cafés of the **quai Landry**, a spacious seafront walkway linking the marina and the port. This is the best place to get the feel of the town, but as far as sights go there's not a lot to the *ville basse*. At the far end of the quay, under the shadow of the citadelle, stands the sturdy **Tour du Sel**, a medieval lookout post once used to store imported salt. If you head up through the narrow passageways off quai Landry, you'll come to rue Clemenceau, where restaurants and souvenir shops are packed into every available space. In a small square giving onto the street stands the pink-painted **Église Ste-Marie-Majeure**, built in 1774, whose spindly bell tower rises elegantly above the cafés on the quay but whose interior contains nothing of interest. From the church's flank, a flight of steps connects with boulevard Wilson, a wide modern high street which rises to place Christophe-Colomb, point of entry for the *haute ville*, or **citadelle**.

Beyond the ancient gateway to the citadelle, with its inscription of the town's motto ("Civitas Calvis Semper Fidelis" – always faithful), you come immediately to the enormous **Caserne Sampiero**, formerly the governor's palace. Built in the thirteenth century, when the great round tower was used as a dungeon, the castle is currently used for military purposes, and therefore closed to the public. The best way of seeing the rest of the citadelle is to follow the ramparts, which connect the three immense bastions. From each bastion the views across the sea, the Balagne and the Cinto Massif are magnificent.

Within the walls the houses are tightly packed along tortuous stairways and narrow passages that converge on the diminutive place d'Armes. Dominating the square is the **Cathédrale St-Jean-Baptiste**, set at the highest point of the promontory and sitting uncomfortably amid the ramshackle buildings. This chunky ochre edifice was founded in the thirteenth century, but was partly destroyed during the Turkish siege of 1553 and then suffered extensive damage twelve years later, when the powder magazine in the governor's palace exploded. It was rebuilt in the form of a Greek cross. The church's great treasure is the **Christ des Miracles**, housed in the chapel on the right of the choir; this crucifix was brandished at marauding Turks during the 1553 siege, an act which reputedly saved the day.

To the north of place d'Armes in rue de Fil stands **La Maison Colomb**, the shell of a building which Calvi believes – as the plaque on the wall states – was Christopher Columbus's birthplace, though the claim rests on pretty tenuous, circumstantial evidence. The house itself was destroyed by Nelson's troops during the siege of 1794, but as recompense a statue was erected in 1992, the 500th anniversary of Columbus's "discovery" of America; the date of this historic landfall, October 12, is now a public holiday in Calvi.

Calvi's outstanding **beach** sweeps right round the bay from the end of quai Landry, but most of the first kilometre or so is owned by bars which rent out sun loungers for a hefty price. To avoid these, follow the track behind the sand which will bring you to the start of a more secluded stretch. The sea might not be as sparklingly clear as at many other Corsican beaches, but it's warm, shallow and free of rocks. You can also sunbathe, and swim off the rocks, at the foot of the citadelle, which has the added attraction of fine views across the bay.

Eating and drinking

Eating is a major pastime in Calvi, and you'll find a wide selection of restaurants and snack bars catering for all tastes. Fish restaurants predominate in the marina, where – at a price – you can eat excellent seafood fresh from the bay. It's cheaper to eat in the inland streets of the *ville basse* whose stairways and cramped forecourts hide a host of buzzing pizzerias and Corsican restaurants.

The GR20

Winding some 170km from Calenzana (12km from Calvi) to Conca (22km from Porto-Vecchio), the **GR20** is Corsica's most demanding long-distance footpath. Only one-third of the estimated 17,000 hikers who start it each season complete all sixteen stages (*étapes*), which can be covered in ten to twelve days if you're in good physical shape – if you're not, don't even think about attempting this route. Marked with red-and-white splashes of paint, it comprises a series of harsh ascents and descents, sections of which exceed 2000m and become more of a climb than a walk, with stanchions, cables and ladders driven into the rock as essential aids. The going is made tougher by the necessity of carrying a sleeping bag, all-weather kit and two or three days' food with you. That said, the rewards more than compensate. The GR20 takes in the most spectacular mountain terrain in Corsica and along the way you can spot the elusive mouflon (mountain sheep), glimpse lammergeier (a rare vulture) wheeling around the crags, and swim in ice-cold torrents and waterfalls.

The first thing you need to do before setting off is get hold of the Parc Régional's indispensable **Topoguide**, published by the Fédération Française de la Randonnée Pédestre, which gives a detailed description of the route, along with relevant sections of IGN contour maps, lists of refuges and other essential information. Most good bookshops in Corsica stock them, or call at the park office in Ajaccio (see p.1247). More detailed coverage of the route (in English) is featured in David Abram's *Trekking in Corsica* book (see p.1345).

The route can be undertaken in either **direction**, but most hikers start in the north at Calenzana, tackling the most demanding *étapes* early on. The hardship is alleviated by extraordinary mountainscapes as you round the Cinto massif, skirt the Asco, Niolo, Tavignano and Restonica valleys, and scale the sides of Monte d'Oro and Rotondo. At Vizzavona on the main Bastia–Corte–Ajaccio road, roughly the halfway mark, you can call it a day and catch a bus or train back to the coast, or press on south across two more ranges to the needle peaks of Bavella. With much of the for-

Cafés, complete with raffia parasols, line the marina, becoming more expensive the nearer they are to the Tour du Sel.

Cafés and bars

Café Rex top of bd Wilson, on the corner of place Christophe-Colomb. The most down-to-earth and animated bar in central Calvi, with a small but sunny terrace and a mixed clientele. A good breakfast venue for crowd-watching.

Chez Tao rue St-Antoine, in the citadelle ⓣ04.95.65.00.73. Legendary nightclub, opened in the wake of the Bolshevik Revolution by a Muslim White Russian, and long the haunt of the Riviera's glitterati. Now turned into pricey piano bar serving fussy nouvelle cuisine and local fish dishes, costing around €30 à la carte. June–Sept 7pm–midnight.

Restaurants

L'Abri Côtier On quai Landry, but entrance on rue Joffre ⓣ04.95.65.12.76. Mostly seafood dishes (such as sea bass with fennel) and pizzas (from €9.50), served on a lovely terrace looking out to sea. Their set menus (€12–27) and *suggestions du jour* are invariably the best deals; for vegetarians, there's a copious veggie platter.

U Famale rte de Porto, just outside the centre of town on the way to Punta de la Revellata ⓣ04.95.65.18.82. Worth the walk out here for their delicious, beautifully presented Corsican specialities – mussels or lamb simmered in ewe's cheese and white wine, a fine *soupe Corse*, and melt-in-the-mouth *fiadone* (traditional flan). Menus at €17 & €24 plus a full à la carte choice, and pizzas from €9. And there are great views over the bay from their *salle panoramique* to Punta de la Revellata.

U Minellu Off bd Wilson, nr Ste-Marie-Majeure. Wholesome Corsican specialities served in a narrow stepped alley, or on a shady terrace with pretty mosaic tables. Their menu features baked lamb, *cannelloni al brocciu*, spider crab dressed "à la Calvaise", and a cheese platter – great value at €18.

est east of here blackened by fire, hikers in recent years have been leaving the GR20 at Zonza, below the Col de Bavella (served by daily buses to Ajaccio and Porto-Vecchio), and walking to the coast along the less arduous Mare a Mare Sud trail.

Accommodation along the route is provided by **refuges**, where, for around €9, you can take a hot shower, use an equipped kitchen and bunk down on mattresses. Usually converted *bergeries*, these places are staffed by wardens during the peak period (June–Sept). Advance reservation is not possible; beds are allocated on a first-come-first-served basis, so be prepared to bivouac if you arrive late. Another reason to be on the trail soon after dawn is that it allows you to break the back of the *étape* before 2pm, when clouds tend to bubble over the mountains and obscure the views.

The **weather** in the high mountains is notoriously fickle. A sunny morning doesn't necessarily mean a sunny day, and during July and August violent storms can rip across the route without warning. It's therefore essential to take good wet-weather gear with you, as well as a hat, sunblock and shades. In addition, make sure you set off on each stage with adequate **food** and **water**. At the height of the season, many refuges sell basic supplies (*alimentation*), but you shouldn't rely on this service; ask hikers coming from the opposite direction where their last supply stop was and plan accordingly (basic provisions are always available at the main passes of Col de Vergio, Col de Vizzavona, Col de Bavella and Col de Verde). The refuge wardens (*gardiens*) will be able to advise you on how much water to carry at each stage.

Finally a word of **warning**: each year, injured hikers have to be air-lifted to safety off remote sections of the GR20, normally because they strayed from the marked route and got lost. Occasionally, fatal accidents also occur for the same reason, so always keep the paint splashes in sight, especially if the weather closes in – don't rely purely on the many cairns that punctuate the route, as these sometimes mark more hazardous paths to high peaks.

The Réserve Naturel de Scandola and Girolata

The **Réserve Naturel de Scandola** takes up the promontory dividing the Balagne from the Golfe de Porto, its name derived from the wooden tiles (*scandules*) that cover many of the island's mountain houses. But the area's roof-like rock formations are only part of its amazing geological repertoire: its stacked slabs, towering pinnacles and gnarled claw-like outcrops were formed by Monte Cinto's volcanic eruptions 250 million years ago, and subsequent erosion has fashioned shadowy caves, grottoes and gashes in the rock. Scandola's colours are as remarkable as the shapes, the hues varying from the charcoal grey of granite to the incandescent rusty purple of porphyry.

The headland and its surrounding water were declared a nature reserve in 1975 and now support significant colonies of seabirds, dolphins and seals, as well as 450 types of seaweed and some remarkable fish such as the grouper, a species more commonly found in the Caribbean. In addition, nests belonging to the rare Audouin's gull are visible on the cliffs, and you might see the odd osprey – there used to be only seven pairs here, but careful conservation has increased this number to 24.

Scandola is off-limits to hikers and can be viewed only by **boat** (Colombo Lines ⓣ04.95.62.32.10, ⓦwww.colombo-line.com), which means taking one of the daily excursions from Calvi or Porto. These leave from Calvi at 9.15am and 2pm, and from Porto at various intervals throughout the daytime and early evening (April–Oct), the first two stopping for two hours at Girolata (see below) and returning in the late afternoon. It's a fascinating journey and well worth the €40 fare, although it's a good idea to take a picnic, as the restaurants in Girolata are very pricey and not particularly good.

Girolata

Connected by a mere mule track to the rest of the island (90min on foot from the nearest road), the tiny fishing haven of **GIROLATA**, immediately east of Scandola, has a dreamlike quality that's highlighted by the vivid red of the surrounding rocks. A short stretch of stony beach and a few houses are dominated by a stately watchtower, built by the Genoese later in the seventeenth century in the form of a small castle on a bluff overlooking the cove. For most of the year, this is one of the most idyllic spots on the island, with only the odd yacht and party of hikers to threaten the settlement's tranquillity. From June through September, though, daily boat trips from Porto and Calvi ensure the village is packed during the middle of the day, so if you want to make the most of the scenery and peace and quiet, walk here and stay a night in one of the *gîtes*.

The head of the Girolata trail is at **Bocca â Crocce** (Col de la Croix), on the Calvi–Porto road, from where a clear path plunges downhill through dense maquis and forest to a flotsam-covered cove known as **Cala di Tuara** (30min). The more rewarding of the two tracks that wind onwards to Girolata is the more gentle one running left around the headland, but if you feel like stretching your legs, follow the second, more direct route uphill to a pass.

In Girolata, *La Cabane du Berger* (ⓣ04.95.20.16.98; May–Oct; €30 per person for dorm bed half board) offers a choice of **accommodation** in dorms or small wood cabins in the garden behind (these accommodate two people); you can also put your tent up here. Meals are served in their quirky wood-carved bar, but the food isn't up to much. The same is true of the other *gîte*, *Le Cormorant*, among the houses at the north end of the cove (ⓣ04.95.20.15.55; July & Aug; €30; half board obligatory), which has eighteen dorm spaces and a small restaurant overlooking the boat jetty. Unless you're staying at one of the *gîtes*, you'll be better off paying a little extra to eat at one of the two restaurants just up the steps. With a terrace overlooking the beach, *Le Bel Ombra* is the pricier of the pair, offering local seafood specialities, including fresh Scandola lobster. *Le Bon Espoir*, next door, is marginally cheaper, with menus from €19 to €27.50. Note that neither restaurant accepts credit cards.

Porto (Portu) and around

The overwhelming proximity of the mountains, combined with the pervasive eucalyptus and spicy scent of the maquis, give **PORTO**, 30km south of Calvi, a uniquely intense atmosphere that makes it one of the most interesting places to stay on the west coast. Except for a watchtower built here by the Genoese in the second half of the sixteenth century, the site was only built upon with the onset of tourism since the 1950s; today the village is still so small that it can become claustrophobic in July and August, when overcrowding is no joke.

Off season, the place becomes eerily deserted, so you'd do well to choose your times carefully; the best months are May, June and September.

The crowds and traffic jams tend to be most oppressive passing the famous **Calanches**, a huge mass of weirdly eroded pink rock just southwest of Porto, but you can easily sidestep the tourist deluge in picturesque **Piana**, which overlooks the gulf from its southern shore, or by heading inland from Porto through the **Gorges de Spelunca**. Forming a ravine running from the sea to the watershed of the island, this spectacular gorge gives access to the equally grandiose **Forêt d'Aïtone**, site of Corsica's most ancient Laricio pine trees and a deservedly popular hiking area. Throughout the forest, the river and its tributaries are punctuated by strings of *piscines naturelles* (natural swimming pools) – a refreshing, tranquil alternative to the beaches hereabouts, which tend to be crammed in peak season. If you're travelling between Porto and Ajaccio, a worthwhile place to break the journey is the clifftop village of **Cargèse** where the two main attractions are the Greek church and spectacular beach.

Arrival and information

Buses from Calvi, via Galéria, and from Ajaccio, via Cargèse, pull into the junction at the end of route de la Marine, opposite the Banco supermarket, en route to the marina. Timetables are posted at the stops themselves, and at the **tourist office**, down in the marina (May, June & Sept daily 9am–noon & 3–7pm; July & Aug daily 9am–7pm; Oct–April Mon–Thurs 2–6pm; ⓣ04.95.26.10.55, ⓦwww.porto-tourisme.com), where you can buy *Topoguides* and brochures for hikes in the area. Timetable information and tickets for the **boat excursions** to Scandola, the Calanches and Girolata are available in advance from the operators at their counters in the marina.

Accommodation

Competition between **hotels** is more cut-throat in Porto than in any other resort on the island. During slack periods towards the beginning and end of the season, most places engage in a full-on price war, pasting up cheaper tariffs than their neighbours – all of which is great for punters. In late July and August, however, the normal sky-high rates prevail. Photos of all the hotels listed below are posted on the local tourist office website (see Arrival and information, below).

Hotels

Le Belvédère Porto marina ⓣ04.95.26.12.01, ⓕ04.95.26.11.97. This three-star is the smartest of the hotels overlooking the marina, with great views from its comfortable rooms and terraces of Capo d'Orto. Reasonable rates given the location. ❺

Brise de Mer On the left of rte de la Marine as you approach tower from the village, opposite the telephone booths ⓣ04.95.26.10.28, ⓦwww.brise-de-mer.com. A large, old-fashioned place with very friendly service and a congenial terrace restaurant. Rooms at the back have the best views. April to mid-Oct. ❸

Le Colombo At the top of the village opposite the turning for Ota ⓣ04.95.26.10.14. An informal, sixteen-room hotel overlooking the valley, imaginatively decorated in sea-blue colours with driftwood and flotsam sculpture. ❼

Le Golfe At the base of the rock in the marina ⓣ04.95.26.13.33. Small, cosy and unpretentious; every room has a balcony with a sea view. Among the cheapest at this end of the village. May–Oct. ❸

Le Maquis At the top of the village just beyond the Ota turning ⓣ04.95.26.12.19, ⓦwww.hotel-du-maquis.com. A perennially popular, well-maintained budget hotel; rooms are basic, but comfortable enough, and they give good off-season discounts. Advance booking recommended; half board obligatory July and Aug. ❸

Panorama rte de la Marine ⓣ04.95.26.11.05. The cheapest hotel in Porto, with only five rooms (shared toilets) backing on to the marina. April–Oct. ❷

Campsites

Camping Le Porto On the right as you approach Porto from Piana ☎04.95.26.13.67. Further out of the village than the other site, but smaller, and with plenty of shade. Mid-June to Sept.

Camping Sol e Vista At the main road junction near the supermarkets ☎04.95.26.15.71. A superb location on shady terraces ascending a steep hillside with a small café at the top. Great views of Capo d'Orto cliffs opposite, and immaculate toilet blocks. April–Nov.

The Town

Eucalyptus-bordered **route de la Marine** links the two parts of the resort. The village proper, known as **Vaïta**, comprises a strip of supermarkets, shops and hotels 1km from the sea, but the main focus of activity is the small **marina**, located at the avenue's end. Overlooking the entrance to the harbour is the much-photographed **Genoese Tower** (May–Sept daily 9am–8.45pm; €2.50, or €6.50 for combined entry with the aquarium, see below), a square chimney-shaped structure that was cracked by an explosion in the seventeenth century, when it was used as an arsenal. An awe-inspiring view of the crashing sea and maquis-shrouded mountains makes it worth the short climb. Occupying a converted powder house down in the square opposite the base of the tower is the newly established **Aquarium de la Poudrière** (June–Aug daily 10am–10pm, Sept–May Mon–Sat 10am–7pm; €5.50, or €6.50 for combined ticket with the tower), where you can view the various species of sealife that inhabit the gulf, including grouper, moray eels and sea horses.

The **beach** consists of a pebbly cove south beyond the shoulder of the massive rock supporting the tower. To reach it from the marina, follow the little road that skirts the rock, cross the wooden bridge which spans the River Porto on your left, then walk through the car park under the trees. Although it's rather rocky and exposed, and the sea very deep, the great crags overshadowing the shore give the place a vivid edge.

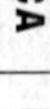

Eating and drinking

The overall standard of restaurants in Porto is pitiably poor, with overpriced food and indifferent service the norm, particularly during high season. There are, however, a handful of exceptions.

Le Maquis In the hotel of the same name. Honest, affordable home cooking served either in a warm bar or on a tiny terrace that hangs over the valley. Their good value €20 menu includes delicious scorpion fish in mussel sauce.

La Mer Opposite the tower ☎04.95.26.11.27. One of the finest seafood restaurants in the area, with fish fresh from the gulf, imaginatively prepared and served in an ideal setting. Menus from €27.

Le Sud Along the walkway leading from the square to the marina ☎04.95.26.14.11. Arguably the best restaurant in Porto, thanks to their strict policy of serving nothing except the freshest local food. Simple and delicious cooking from around the Mediterranean ("*cuisine de tous les suds*") served on a stylish terrace overlooking the marina. Menu at €25, or roughly €35 à la carte.

The Calanches

The UNESCO-protected site of the **Calanches**, 5km southwest of Porto, takes its name from *calanca*, the Corsican word for creek or inlet, but the outstanding characteristics here are the vivid orange and pink rock masses and pinnacles which crumble into the dark blue sea. Liable to unusual patterns of erosion, these tormented rock formations and porphyry needles, some of which soar

300m above the waves, have long been associated with different animals and figures, of which the most famous is the Tête de Chien (Dog's Head) at the north end of the stretch of cliffs. Other figures and creatures conjured up include a Moor's head, a monocled bishop, a bear and a tortoise.

One way to see the fantastic cliffs of the Calanches is by boat from Porto; excursions leave daily in summer, cost €22 and last about an hour. Alternatively, you could drive along the corniche road which weaves through the granite archways on its way to Piana. Eight kilometres along the road from Porto, the *Roches Bleues* café is a convenient landmark for walkers.

Piana

Picturesque **PIANA** occupies a prime location overlooking the Calanches, but for some reason does not suffer the deluge of tourists that Porto endures. Retaining a sleepy feel, the village comprises a cluster of pink houses ranged around an eighteenth-century church and square, from the edge of which the panoramic views over the Golfe de Porto are sublime.

If you want to **stay**, head straight for the *Les Roches Rouges* (Ⓣ04.95.27.81.81, Ⓦwww.lesrochesrouges.com; April–Oct; ❺), an elegant old *grand hôtel* rising from the eucalyptus canopy on the outskirts. Having lain empty for two decades, the turn-of-the-century building was restored with most of its original fittings and furniture intact, and possesses loads of *fin-de-siècle* style. The rooms are huge and light, with large shuttered windows, but make sure you get one facing the water. Non-residents are welcome to drop in for a sundowner on the magnificent terrace, or for a meal in the fresco-covered restaurant, whose *menus gastronomiques* (€25–50), dominated by local seafood delicacies, are as sophisticated as the ambience. A cheaper alternative is the *Continental*, an old house with high wooden ceilings and a leafy garden, on the right as you leave Piana for Porto (Ⓣ04.95.27.89.00; ❷). On the west edge of the village there's also an excellent *gîte d'étape* (Ⓣ04.95.27.84.03), offering dormitory bunk beds (€17 per person) and simple double rooms (❷) in addition to ample **camping** space on a grassy terrace overlooking the gulf.

The Gorges de Spelunca

Spanning the 2km between the villages of Ota and Évisa, a few kilometres inland from Porto, the **Gorges de Spelunca** are a formidable sight, with bare orange granite walls, 1km deep in places, plunging into the foaming green torrent created by the confluence of the rivers Porto, Tavulella, Onca, Campi and Aïtone. The sunlight, ricocheting across the rock walls, creates a sinister effect that's heightened by the dark jagged needles of the encircling peaks. The most dramatic part of the gorge can be seen from the road, which hugs the edge for much of its length.

ÉVISA's bright orange roofs emerge against a lush background of chestnut forests about 10km from Ota, on the eastern edge of the gorge, and the village makes the best base for hiking in the area. Situated 830m above sea level, it caters well for hikers and makes a pleasant stop for a taste of mountain life – the air is invariably crisp and clear, and the food particularly good.

The best **place to stay** is the rambling *La Châtaigneraie*, on the west edge of the village on the Porto road (Ⓣ04.95.26.24.47, Ⓦwww.hotel-la-chataigneraie.com; April–Oct; ❸). Set amid chestnut trees, this traditional schist and granite building has a dozen smart, cosy rooms (with and without toilets) in an annexe around the back of the main building. On the front side, a pleasant little restaurant serves mountain cooking such as wild boar stew with *pulenta* made from local chestnuts.

Calanches walks

The rock formations visible from the road are not a patch on what you can see from the waymarked **trails** winding through the Calanches, which vary from easy ambles to strenuous stepped ascents. An excellent leaflet highlighting the pick of the routes is available free from tourist offices. Whichever one you choose, leave early in the morning or late in the afternoon to avoid the heat in summer, and take plenty of water.

The most popular walk is the one to the **Château Fort** (1hr), which begins at a sharp hairpin in the D81, 700m north of the *Café Roches Rouges* (look for the car park and signboard at the roadside). Passing the famous **Tête de Chien**, it snakes along a ridge lined by dramatic porphyry forms to a huge square chunk of granite resembling a ruined castle. Just before reaching it there's an open platform from where the views of the gulf and Paglia Orba, Corsica's third highest mountain, are superb – one of the best sunset spots on the island – but bring a torch to help find the path back.

For a more challenging extension to the above walk, begin instead at the **Roches Rouges café**. On the opposite side of the road, two paths strike up the hill: follow the one on your left nearest the stream (as you face away from the café), which zig-zags steeply up the rocks, over a pass and down the other side to rejoin the D81 in around 1hr 15min. A hundred and fifty metres west of the spot where you meet the road is the trailhead for the Château Fort walk, with more superb views.

A small Oratory niche in the cliff by the roadside, 500m south of *Café Roches Rouges*, contains a Madonna statue, Santa Maria, from where the wonderful **sentier muletier** (1hr) climbs into the rocks above. Before the road was blasted through the Calanches in 1850, this old paved path, an extraordinary feat of workmanship supported in places by dry-stone banks and walls, formed the main artery between the villages of Piana and Ota. After a very steep start, the route contours through the rocks and pine woods above the restored mill at Pont de Gavallaghiu, emerging after one hour back on the D81, roughly 1.5km south of the starting point. Return by the same path.

Capo d'Orto

From Porto, you have to crane your neck to see the tooth-shaped escarpments of **Capo d'Orto** (1294m), Corsica's most imposing coastal peak, which looms

The young *patronne* is American, so English is spoken. The *Du Centre*, opposite the statue in the centre (Ⓣ04.95.26.20.92; no credit cards; closed mid-Oct to Jan; ❸), is a pleasant fall-back, with small rooms but an excellent Corsican speciality restaurant on its ground floor; the €26 menu features the chef's renowned *sanglier* (wild boar) steak in chocolate sauce, and a melt-in-the-mouth chestnut *parfait*. Half board (€100 for two) is obligatory from June through September; if you plan just to eat, be sure to reserve a table before 5pm. At the other end of the village, *L'Aïtone* (Ⓣ04.95.26.20.04, Ⓕ04.95.26.24.18; ❺) is a large country hotel with a wide range of differently priced rooms, a swimming pool and relaxing bar-restaurant that enjoys a reputation both for gastronomic prowess and for its fine views. For **campers**, the *Camping Acciola* (Ⓣ04.95.26.23.01), a small site with a café-bar and great views of the mountains, lies roughly 3km out of Evisa: take the D84 for 2km, and turn right at the T-junction towards Cristinacce; the site lies another 400m on your left.

Forêt d'Aïtone

Thousands of soaring Laricio pines, some of them as much as 50m tall, make up the **Forêt d'Aïtone**, just a few kilometres east of Évisa. The most beautiful forest in Corsica, it extends over ten square kilometres between Évisa and above the head of the Spelunca Valley. Its north and west faces, and those of the massif's subsidiary summits – Capo Vittellu and the Tre Signore – still harbour unexplored rock walls up which new climbing routes are opened every year. But the approach from the more gently shelving western side is a popular forest walk via an old paved mule track, with a final section following cairns over exposed rock. The main incentive to do it are the vast panoramic views from the summit, which even by Corsican standards are extraordinary, taking in the entire gulf and central watershed.

The route is covered on the tourist office's free map; otherwise try to get hold of IGN #4150 OT. Don't rely on the **water** sources marked on either, which can dry up in summer; and bring at least three litres per person in warm weather. Highly exposed and largely treeless, the summit of Capo d'Orto is no place to be in a storm; even a light rainfall can render the easy scramble to the top tricky in places. In dry conditions, however, the route offers no technical obstacles.

The round trip from **Piana** takes about five hours. You can save yourself a dull thirty-minute plod at the start by driving or hitching 1.5km east along the D81: just after the sharp bend at the Pont de Mezzanu, look for a stony piste cutting off the road to the right, where you can park. Following the track along, you'll then arrive at a **football pitch**; walk diagonally across it to a little **footbridge**, on the far side of which you should turn right, as shown by a signpost. From here a well-worn *sentier muletier* presses east up the right bank of a stream under a dense cover of pine trees. After 45 minutes, it starts to zigzag more steeply northeast up a side valley, reaching a low saddle pass, **Bocca di Piazza Monica** (910m), where you meet another path (from the *Roches Rouges* café in the Calanches). Head right at this first junction and keep following the orange waymarks east around the line of the hill until you arrive at another signpost pointing the route left, over bare rock, towards the summit, visible shortly after. From the hollow on the far side of the pass, a long sequence of **cairns** threads a steepening route through the rocks to the top, reached after 3hr 15min from the car park. Allow 1hr 30min–2hr for the descent by the same route.

the Col de Verghio (1477m), the highest point in Corsica traversable by road. Well-worn tourist paths cross the forest at various points, but local wildlife still thrives here.

Some of the oldest pines in the forest are approaching five hundred years old. Fine-grained, strong and very resistant to weathering, the Laricio was highly valued by the Genoese for ships' masts and furniture, and it was they who first built a road down the valley to the coast, later upgraded by the French using convict labour. Throughout the nineteenth century, forests all over Corsica were regularly decimated, as the island has the very best specimens of this species, which only grows in forests higher than 1000m. When the British artist and poet Edward Lear came here in the 1860s, he noted with regret "the ravages of [the] hatchets: here and there on the hillside are pale patches of cleared ground, with piles of cut and barked pines … everywhere giant trees lie prostrate".

One of the most popular short **walks** goes to the **Belvédère**, a great natural balcony giving magnificent views across the copper-tinted rocks of the Spelunca gorge. To reach it, look for the wide lay-by on the left-hand side of the road, 5km northeast of Evisa. A signpost pointing left indicates the well-trodden route through the forest. Following the unsurfaced forest track that peels left a little further up the main road, you can also drop down to the **piscine naturelle d'Aïtone**, one of the more accessible bathing spots in the forest, where the river crashes through a series of idyllic pools and falls.

Cargèse (Carghjese)

Sitting high above a deep blue bay on a cliff scattered with olive trees, **CARGÈSE**, 20km southwest of Porto, exudes a lazy charm that attracts hundreds of well-heeled summer residents to its pretty white houses and hotels. The full-time locals, half of whom are descendants of Greek refugees who fled the Turkish occupation of the Peloponnese in the seventeenth century, seem to accept with nonchalance this inundation – and the proximity of a large Club Med complex – but the best times to visit are May and late September, when Cargèse is all but empty.

Two churches stand on separate hummocks at the heart of the village, a reminder of the old antagonism between the two cultures (resentful Corsican patriots ransacked the Greeks' original settlement in 1715 because of the newcomers' refusal to take up arms against their Genoese benefactors). The **Roman Catholic church** was built for the minority Corsican families in 1828 and is one of the latest examples of Baroque with a trompe l'oeil ceiling, though this can't really compete with the view from the terrace outside. The **Greek church**, however, is the more interesting of the two: a large granite neo-Gothic edifice built in 1852 to replace a building that had become too small for its congregation. Inside, the outstanding feature is an unusual iconostasis, a gift from a monastery in Rome, decorated with uncannily modern-looking portraits. Behind it hang icons brought over from Greece with the original settlers – the graceful Virgin and Child, to the right-hand side of the altar, is thought to date as far back as the twelfth century.

The best beach in the area, **plage de Pero**, is 2km north of the village – head up to the junction with the Piana road and take the left fork down to the sea. Overlooked by a Genoese tower, this white stretch of sand has a couple of bars and easily absorbs the crowds that descend on it in August. **Plage du Chiuni**, a further 2km along the same road, is much busier thanks to its windsurfing facilities and the presence of Club Med. A more secluded spot is **plage du Monachi**, 1km south of the village; this small, sandy cove is reached by climbing down the track at the side of the road past the little chapel on the cliffside.

Practicalities

There's a **tourist office** on rue Dr-Dragacci (daily: July–Sept 9am–noon & 4–7pm; Oct–June 3–5pm; ⓣ04.95.26.41.31, ⓦwww.corsica.net/cargese), which can help find accommodation and sells tickets for summer boat trips to the Calanches, costing about €40. **Buses** for Ajaccio and Porto stop outside the post office, set back from the road in the main square.

The least expensive of the **hotels** in Cargèse is the *De France*, on rue Colonel Fieschi (ⓣ04.95.26.41.07; ❷), whose rooms are a bit dark and noisy (the front rooms open on to the main road), but unbelievably cheap, even in August. Overlooking the crossroads at the top of the village, two comfortable midscale options are *Le Continental* (ⓣ04.95.26.42.24; ❹) and *St Jean* (ⓣ04.95.26.46.68, ⓦwww.lesaintjean.com; ❺). Better still, head down the lane dropping from opposite these last two places to the wonderful Plage de Pero beach, where you'll find the *Thalassa* (ⓣ04.95.26.40.08, ⓕ04.95.26.41.66; ❺), among the oldest-established hotels on the west coast, and the nearby

Les Lentisques (Ⓣ04.95.26.42.34, Ⓦwww.leslentisques.com; ⑤), a congenial, family-run three-star with a large, breezy breakfast hall and ten simple rooms (fully en suite and sea-facing). The nearest **campsite**, *Camping Torraccia* (Ⓣ04.95.26.42.39), is 4km north of Cargèse on the main road.

A fair number of **restaurants** are scattered about the village, as well as the standard crop of basic pizzerias, but the most tempting places to eat are down in the harbour. On a raised deck overlooking the jetty, *Le Cabanon de Charlotte* serves local seafood in a wooden cabin, with menus from €15 to €20, or you can go for their fresh fish of the day. Starters include locally made charcuterie and Cargèse's only Greek salad. For a **drink**, go no further than the main square, where you can watch all the action from *Bar Chantilly*.

Ajaccio (Aiacciu)

Edward Lear claimed that on a wet day it would be hard to find so dull a place as **AJACCIO**, a harsh judgement with an element of justice. The town has none of Bastia's sense of purpose and can seem to lack a definitive identity of its own, but it is a relaxed and good-looking place, with an exceptionally mild climate, and a wealth of cafés, restaurants and shops.

Although it's an attractive idea that Ajax, hero of the Trojan War, once stopped here, the name of Ajaccio actually derives from the Roman *Adjaccium* (place of rest), a winter stop-off point for shepherds descending from the mountains to stock up on goods and sell their produce. This first settlement, to the north of the present town in the area called Castelvecchio, was destroyed by the Saracens in the tenth century, and modern Ajaccio grew up around the citadelle that was founded in 1492. **Napoleon** gave the town international fame, but though the self-designated *Cité Impériale* is littered with statues and street names related to the Bonaparte family, you'll find the Napoleonic cult has a less dedicated following in his home town than you might imagine. The emperor is still considered by many Ajacciens as a self-serving Frenchman rather than as a Corsican, and his impact on the townscape of his birthplace isn't enormous.

Since the early 1980s, the town has gained an unwelcome reputation for nationalist violence. The most infamous terrorist atrocity of recent years was the murder, in February 1998, of the French government's most senior official on the island, Claude Erignac, who was gunned down as he left the opera. However, separatist violence rarely (if ever) affects tourists, and for visitors Ajaccio remains memorable for the things that have long made it attractive – its battered old town, relaxing cafés and the encompassing view of its glorious bay.

Arrival, information and accommodation

Ajaccio's Campo dell'Oro **airport** (Ⓣ04.95.23.56.56; Ⓦwww.ajaccio.aeroport.fr) is 6km south of town; shuttle buses (three per hour 6.30am–10.45pm; Ⓣ04.95.23.29.41) provide an inexpensive link with the centre, stopping on cours Napoléon, the main street – tickets cost €4, and the journey takes around twenty minutes. Heading in the other direction, the best place to pick up buses to the airport is the parking lot adjacent to the main **bus station** (*terminal routière*), a five-minute walk north of the centre (Ⓣ04.95.21.28.01). Ferries also dock nearby, and the SNCM office is directly opposite at quai l'Herminier (Ⓣ04.95.29.66.99). The **gare SNCF** lies almost a kilometre north along boulevard Sampiero (Ⓣ04.95.23.11.03), a continuation

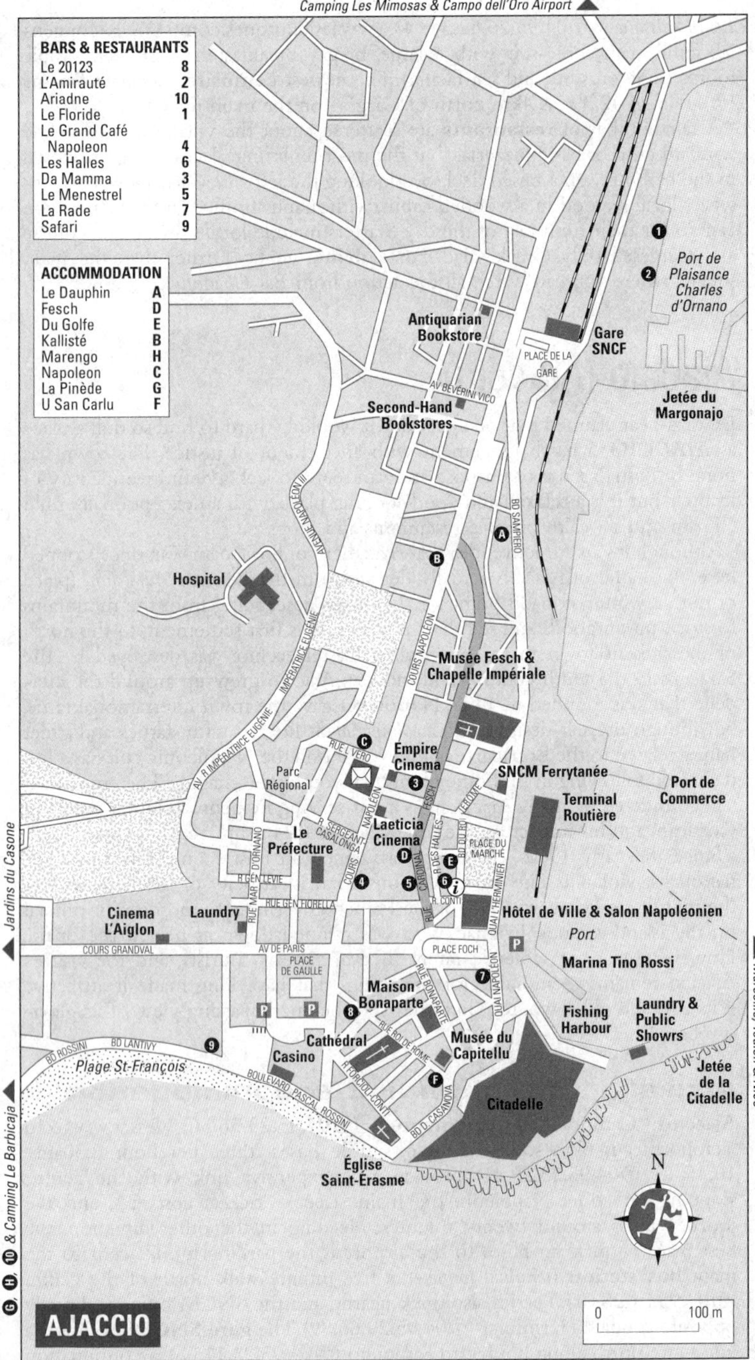
Camping Les Mimosas & Campo dell'Oro Airport
BARS & RESTAURANTS
Le 20123 8
L'Amirauté 2
Ariadne 10
Le Floride 1
Le Grand Café Napoleon 4
Les Halles 6
Da Mamma 3
Le Menestrel 5
La Rade 7
Safari 9
ACCOMMODATION
Le Dauphin A
Fesch D
Du Golfe E
Kallisté B
Marengo H
Napoleon C
La Pinède G
U San Carlu F
Port de Plaisance Charles d'Ornano
Antiquarian Bookstore
Gare SNCF
PLACE DE LA GARE
AV BEVERINI VICO
Jetée du Margonajo
Second-Hand Bookstores
AVENUE NAPOLEON III
BD SAMPIERO
Hospital
COURS NAPOLEON
Musée Fesch & Chapelle Impériale
IMPÉRATRICE EUGÉNIE
AV. R IMPÉRATRICE EUGÉNIE
RUE L VERO
Empire Cinema
SNCM Ferrytanée
Port de Commerce
Parc Régional
Terminal Routière
R. SERGEANT CASALONGA
Laeticia Cinema
Le Préfecture
RUE MAR D'ORNANO
R DES HALLES
BD DU ROI JEROME
PLACE DU MARCHÉ
COURS NAPOLEON
R GÉN LEVIE
RUE CARDINAL FESCH
QUAI L'HERMINIER
R. CONTI
RUE GEN FIORELLA
Hôtel de Ville & Salon Napoléonien
Laundry
Cinema L'Aiglon
Jardins du Casone
Port
COURS GRANDVAL
AV DE PARIS
PLACE FOCH
Marina Tino Rossi
PLACE DE GAULLE
RUE BONAPARTE
QUAI NAPOLEON
Maison Bonaparte
Fishing Harbour
Laundry & Public Showrs
Marseille, Toulon & Nice
RUE ROI DE ROME
Musée du Capitellu
BD ROSSINI
BD LANTIVY
Cathédral
Casino
Plage St-François
R FORCIOLI-CONTI
Jetée de la Citadelle
BOULEVARD PASCAL ROSSINI
BD D. CASANOVA
Citadelle
Église Saint-Érasme
N
G, H, 10 & Camping Le Barbicaja
0
100 m
AJACCIO

of the quai l'Herminier. The **tourist office** on boulevard du Roi Jérôme (April–June & Sept Mon–Sat 8am–7pm, Sun 9am–1pm; July & Aug Mon–Sat 8am–8.30pm, Sun 9am–1pm & 4–7pm; Oct–March Mon–Fri 8.30am–6pm, Sat 8.30am–noon; ⓣ04.95.51.53.03, ⓦwww.tourisme.fr/ajaccio) hands out large free glossy maps and posts transport timetables for checking departure times. Anyone planning a long-distance hike should head for the office of the national parks association, the **Parc Naturel Régional de Corse**, 2 rue Sergeant-Casalonga, around the corner from the Préfecture on cours Napoléon (Mon–Fri 8am–noon & 2–6pm; ⓦwww.parc-naturel-corse.com; ⓣ04.95.51.79.00), where you can buy *Topoguides*, maps, guidebooks and leaflets. Cars can be rented from Rent-a-Car, at the *Hôtel Kallisté*, 51 cours Napoléon (ⓣ04.95.51.34.45), and the airport (ⓣ04.95.23.56.36); Aloha, at the airport only (ⓣ04.95.23.57.19); Avis-Ollandini, 1 route d'Alata (ⓣ04.95.23.92.50) and the airport (ⓣ04.95.21.28.01); and Hertz-Locasud, 8 cours Grandval (ⓣ04.95.21.70.94) and the airport (ⓣ04.95.22.14.84).

Ajaccio suffers from a dearth of inexpensive **accommodation**, but there are a fair number of mid- and upscale places. Whatever your budget, it's essential to **book ahead**, especially for weekends between late May and September, when beds are virtually impossible to come by at short notice.

Hotels

Le Dauphin 11 bd Sampiero ⓣ04.95.21.12.94, ⓕ04.95.21.88.69. No-frills place above a bar, opposite the port de Commerce. Some rooms are on the grotty side for the price, but their budget options in an adjacent building (with shared showers and toilets) are among the cheapest beds in town. Includes breakfast. ❹

Fesch 7 rue Cardinal-Fesch ⓣ04.95.51.62.62, ⓦwww.hotel-fesch.com. One of the oldest-established hotels in Ajaccio, and famous as the site of a (bloodless) armed siege in 1980, when it was occupied by fugitive nationalist guerrillas and their French secret service hostages. Following a recent refit, all rooms are bright and modern with a/c and TVs; balconies cost extra. ❺

Du Golfe 5 bd du Roi Jérôme ⓣ04.95.21.47.64, ⓦwww.hoteldugolfe.com. Large, well-appointed three-star whose slightly pricier (soundproofed) front rooms overlook the market square and bay. Reasonable value given the location, and handy for ferry port, bus and train stations. ❺

Kallisté 51 cours Napoléon ⓣ04.95.51.34.45, ⓦwww.hotel-kalliste-ajaccio.com. Recently revamped three-storey hotel right in the centre, with plenty of parking space. Soundproofed rooms for up to four people, all with cable TVs and bathrooms. Internet facilities in lobby, and the staff speak English. The best choice in this category. ❹

Marengo 12 bd Mme-Mère ⓣ04.95.21.43.66, ⓕ04.95.21.51.26. A ten-minute walk west of the centre, up a quiet side-street off bd Mme-Mère. Slightly boxed in by tower blocks, but a secluded, quiet and pleasant small hotel (with only 16 rooms) away from the city bustle. Open mid-March to mid-Nov. ❸

Napoleon 4 rue Lorenzo-Vero ⓣ04.95.51.54.00, ⓦwww.hotel-napoleon-ajaccio.com. Dependable midscale hotel slap in the centre of town, up a side road off cours Napoléon, in a recently revamped Second Empire style. Comfortable, very welcoming and good value for the location. ❻

La Pinède rte des Sanguinaires ⓣ04.95.52.00.44, ⓦwww.la-pinede.com. Most secluded and peaceful of the swish hotels, 4km west of the town centre. It's 300m from the beach (up a narrow lane signposted right off the main road as you head out of town), but with great views of the gulf, a large pool and tennis court. ❽

U San Carlu 8 bd Danielle-Casanova ⓣ04.95.21.13.84, ⓕ04.95.21.09.99. Sited opposite the citadelle and close to the beach, this three-star hotel is the poshest option in the old town. Well-appointed rooms, own parking facilities, and a special room for disabled guests in the basement. ❻

Campsites

Le Barbicaja 4.5km west along the rte des Sanguinaires ⓣ04.95.52.01.17. Crowded site, but close to the beach and easier to reach by bus (#5 from place de Gaulle) than *Les Mimosas*. Open April–Oct.

Les Mimosas 3km northwest of town ⓣ04.95.20.99.85, ⓕ04.95.10.01.77. A shady and well-organized site with clean toilet blocks, friendly management and fair rates. It's a long trudge if you're loaded with luggage so take a taxi (around €15). Open May–Oct.

The Town

The core of the **old town** holds the most interest in Ajaccio: a cluster of ancient streets spreading north and south of **place Foch**, which opens out to the seafront by the port and the marina. Nearby, to the west, **place de Gaulle** forms the town centre and is the source of the main thoroughfare, **cours Napoléon**, which extends parallel to the sea almost 2km to the northeast. West of place de Gaulle stretches the modern part of town fronted by the **beach**, overlooked at its eastern end by the citadelle.

Around place de Gaulle and the new town

Place de Gaulle (otherwise known as place du Diamant, after the Diamanti family who once owned much of the property in Ajaccio) is the most useful point of orientation, even if it's not much to look at – just a windy concrete

Napoleon and Corsica

Napoleon Bonaparte was born in Ajaccio in 1769, a year after the French took over the island from the Genoese. They made a thorough job of it, crushing the Corsican leader Paoli's troops at Ponte Nuovo and driving him into exile. Napoleon's father Carlo, a close associate of Paoli, fled the scene of the battle with his pregnant wife in order to escape the victorious French army. But Carlo's subsequent behaviour was quite different from that of his former leader – he came to terms with the French, becoming a representative of the newly styled Corsican nobility in the National Assembly, and using his contacts with the French governor to get a free education for his children.

At the age of nine, Napoleon was awarded a scholarship to the **Brienne military academy**, an institution specially founded to teach the sons of the French nobility the responsibilities of their status, and the young son of a Corsican Italian-speaking household used his time well, leaving Brienne to enter the exclusive **École Militaire** in Paris. At the age of sixteen he was commissioned into the artillery. When he was twenty the Revolution broke out in Paris and the scene was set for a remarkable career.

Always an ambitious opportunist, he obtained leave from his regiment, returned to Ajaccio, joined the local Jacobin club and – with his eye on a colonelship in the Corsican militia – promoted enthusiastically the interests of the Revolution. However, things did not quite work out as he had planned, for Pascal Paoli had also returned to Corsica.

Carlo Bonaparte had died some years before, and Napoleon was head of a family that had formerly given Paoli strong support. Having spent the last twenty years in London, **Paoli** was pro-English and had developed a profound distaste for revolutionary excesses. Napoleon's French allegiance and his Jacobin views antagonized the older man, and his military conduct didn't enhance his standing at all. Elected second-in-command of the volunteer militia, Napoleon was involved in an unsuccessful attempt to wrest control of the citadelle from royalist sympathizers. He thus took much of the blame when, in reprisal for the killing of one of the militiamen, several people were gunned down in Ajaccio, an incident which engendered eight days of civil war. In June 1793, Napoleon and his family were chased back to the mainland by the Paolists.

Napoleon promptly renounced any special allegiance he had ever felt for Corsica. He Gallicized the spelling of his name, preferring Napoléon to his baptismal Napoleone. And, although he was later to speak with nostalgia about the scents of the Corsican countryside, he put the city of his birth fourth on the list of places he would like to be buried.

platform surrounded by a shopping complex. The only noteworthy thing on the square is the huge, bronze equestrian statue, a pompous lump commissioned by Napoléon III in 1865 showing the first Napoleon in Roman attire, surrounded by his four brothers.

Devotees of Napoleon should take a stroll 1km up **cours Grandval**, the wide street rising west of place de Gaulle and ending in a square, the **Jardins du Casone**, where gaudily spectacular son et lumière shows and costumed re-enactments take place throughout the tourist season. An impressive monument to Napoleon dominates the square, standing atop an appropriately huge, proto-Fascist pedestal inscribed with the names of his battles. Behind the monument lies a graffiti-bedaubed cave where Napoleon is supposed to have frolicked as a child.

Place Foch

Once the site of the town's medieval gate, **place Foch** lies at the heart of old Ajaccio. A delightfully shady square sloping down to the sea and lined with cafés and restaurants, it gets its local name – place des Palmiers – from the row of palms bordering the central strip. Dominating the top end, a fountain of four marble lions provides a mount for the inevitable statue of Napoleon, this one by Ajaccien sculptor Maglioli. A humbler effigy occupies a niche high on the nearest wall – a figurine of Ajaccio's patron saint, **La Madonnuccia**, dating from 1656, a year in which Ajaccio's local council, fearful of infection from plague-struck Genoa, placed the town under the guardianship of the Madonna in a ceremony conducted on this spot.

At the northern end of place Foch is the **Hôtel de Ville** of 1826, with its prison-like wooden doors. The first-floor **Salon Napoléonien** (mid-June to mid-Sept Mon–Sat 9–11.45am & 2–5.45pm; mid-Sept to mid-June Mon–Fri 9–11.45am & 2–4.45pm; €2.30) contains a replica of the ex-emperor's death mask in pride of place, along with a solemn array of Bonaparte family portraits and busts. A smaller medal room has a fragment from Napoleon's coffin and part of his dressing case, plus a model of the ship that brought his body back from St Helena, and a picture of the house where he died.

South of place Foch

The south side of place Foch, standing on the former dividing line between the poor district around the port and the bourgeoisie's territory, gives access to **rue Bonaparte**, the main route through the latter quarter. Built on the promontory rising to the citadelle, the secluded streets in this part of town – with their dusty buildings and hole-in-the-wall restaurants lit by flashes of sea or sky at the end of the alleys – retain more of a sense of the old Ajaccio than anywhere else.

Napoleon was born in what's now the colossal **Maison Bonaparte**, on place Letizia (May–Sept Mon 2–6pm, Tues–Fri 9am–noon & 2–6pm, Sat 9–11.45am & 2–6pm, Sun 9am–noon; Oct–April Mon 2–6pm, Tues–Sat 10am–noon & 2–5pm, Sun 10am–noon; €4), off the west side of rue Napoléon. The house passed to Napoleon's father in the 1760s and here he lived, with his wife and family, until his death. But in May 1793, the Bonapartes were driven from the house by Paoli's partisans, who stripped the place down to the floorboards. Requisitioned by the English in 1794, Maison Bonaparte became an arsenal and a lodging house for English officers until Napoleon's mother Letizia herself funded its restoration. Owned by the state since 1923, the house now bears few traces of the Bonaparte family's existence.

One of the few original pieces of furniture left in the house is the wooden sedan chair in the hallway – the pregnant Letizia was carried back from church in it when her contractions started. Upstairs, there's an endless display of portraits, miniatures, weapons, letters and documents. Amongst the highlights of the first room are a few maps of Corsica dating from the eighteenth century, some deadly "vendetta" daggers and two handsome pairs of pistols belonging to Napoleon's father. The next-door Alcove Room was, according to tradition, occupied by Napoleon in 1799 when he stayed here for the last time, while in the third room you can see the sofa upon which the future emperor first saw the light of day on August 15, 1769. Adjoining the heavily restored long gallery is a tiny room known as the Trapdoor Room, whence Letizia and her children made their getaway from the marauding Paolists.

Napoleon was baptized in 1771 in the **Cathedral** (Mon–Sat 8am–1.30pm & 2.30–6pm; no tourist visits on Sun), around the corner in rue Forcioli-Conti. Modelled on St Peter's in Rome, it was built in 1587–93 on a much smaller scale than intended, owing to lack of funds – an apology for its diminutive size is inscribed in a plaque inside, on the wall to the left as you enter. Inside, to the right of the door, stands the font where he was dipped at the age of 23 months; his sister, Elisa Baciochi, donated the great marble altar in 1811. Before you go, take a look in the chapel to the left of the altar, which houses a gloomy Delacroix painting of the Virgin.

A left turn at the eastern end of rue Forcioli-Conti brings you onto boulevard Danielle-Casanova. Here, opposite the citadelle, an elaborately carved capital marks the entrance to the **Musée du Capitellu** (May–Oct Mon–Wed 10am–noon & 2–6pm; €4), a tiny museum mainly given over to offering a picture of domestic life in nineteenth-century Ajaccio. The house belonged to a wealthy Ajaccien family, the Baciochi, who were related to Napoleon through his sister's marriage. Amid the watercolour landscapes and marble busts, the glass display cases hold the most fascinating exhibits, including a rare edition of the first history of Corsica, written by Agostino Giustiniani, a bishop of the Nebbio who drowned in 1536, and the 1769 Code Corse, a list of laws set out by Louis XV for the newly acquired Corsica.

Opposite the museum, the restored **citadelle**, a hexagonal fortress and tower stuck out on a wide promontory into the sea, is occupied by the military and usually closed to the public. Founded in the 1490s, the fort wasn't completed until the occupation of Ajaccio by Sampiero Corso and the powerful Marshal Thermes in 1553–58. The building overlooks the town **beach**, plage St-François, a short curve of yellow sand which faces the expansive mountain-ringed bay. Several flights of steps lead down to the beach from boulevard Danielle-Casanova.

North of place Foch

The dark narrow streets backing onto the port to the north of place Foch are Ajaccio's traditional trading ground. Each weekday and Saturday morning (and on Sundays during the summer), the square directly behind the Hôtel de Ville hosts a small **fresh produce market** – a rarity in Corsica – where you can browse and buy top-quality fresh produce from around the island, including myrtle liqueur, wild-boar sauces, ewe's cheese from the Niolo valley and a spread of fresh vegetables, fruit and flowers.

Behind here, the principal road leading north is **rue Cardinal-Fesch**, a delightful meandering street lined with boutiques, cafés and restaurants. Halfway along the street, set back from the road behind iron gates, stands Ajaccio's best gallery, the **Musée Fesch** (July & Aug Mon 1.30–6pm, Tues–Thurs 9am–6.30pm, Fri & Sat 10.30am–12.15pm, Sun 10.30am–6pm; Sept–June Mon 1–5.15pm, Tues–Sun 9.15am–12.15pm & 2.15–5.15pm; €5.30). Cardinal Joseph Fesch was

Napoleon's step-uncle and bishop of Lyon, and he used his lucrative position to invest in large numbers of paintings, many of them looted by the French armies in Holland, Italy and Germany. His bequest to the town includes seventeenth-century French and Spanish masters, but it's the Italian paintings that are the chief attraction: Raphael, Titian, Bellini, Veronese and Botticelli all have a place here.

You'll need a separate ticket for the **Chapelle Impériale** (same hours; €1.50), which stands across the courtyard from the museum. With its gloomy monochrome interior the chapel itself is unremarkable, and its interest lies in the crypt, where various members of the Bonaparte family are buried. It was the cardinal's dying wish that all the Bonaparte family be brought together under one roof, so the chapel was built in 1857 and the bodies – all except Napoleon's – subsequently ferried in.

Eating, drinking and nightlife

At mealtimes, the alleyways and little squares of Ajaccio's old town become one large, interconnecting **restaurant** terrace lit by rows of candles. All too often, however, the breezy locations and views of the gulf mask indifferent cooking and inflated prices. With the majority of visitors spending merely a night or two here in transit, only those places catering for a local clientele attempt to provide real value for money. **Bars** and **cafés** jostle for pavement space along cours Napoléon, generally lined with people checking out the promenaders, and on place de Gaulle, where old-fashioned cafés and *salons de thé* offer a still more sedate scene. If you fancy a view of the bay, try one of the flashy cocktail bars that line the seafront on boulevard Lantivy, which, along with the casino, a few cinemas and a handful of overpriced clubs, comprise the sum total of Ajaccio's **nightlife**.

Bars and cafés

Le Grand Café Napoleon 10 cours Napoléon, opposite the *préfecture*. Allegedly the oldest café in town, with Second Empire decor and a *troisième âge* clientele. The bar inside was the scene of a famous shootout during World War II, when a cell of key Resistance members was disturbed by the Italian caribinieri and forced to flee, guns blazing. The €16 lunch menu ranks among the best midday meal deals in town.

Le Menestrel 5 rue Cardinal-Fesch. Dubbed "*le rendez-vous des artistes*" because local musicians play here most evenings after 7pm; café jazz, traditional mandolin and guitar tunes, with the odd chanson singalong number. Popular with bus parties of pensioners.

La Rade 1 place Foch. The most congenial of the cafés fronting the Marina Tino Rossi, and an ideal spot for crowd-watching over a chilled *pastis*.

Safari 18 bd Lantivy. One of a row of lookalike cocktail bars next to the casino, overlooking the promenade. Good for a breezy coffee, and for watching Ajaccio's *beau monde* strut their stuff on Saturday nights.

Restaurants

Le 20123 2 rue Roi-de-Rome ⓣ04.95.21.50.05. Decked out like a small hill village, complete with *fontaine* and parked Vespa, the decor here's a lot more frivolous than the food: serious Corsican gastronomy featured on a single €26 menu. Top-notch cooking, and organic AOC wine. Closed Mon, except in July & Aug.

L'Amirauté Port de Plaisance Charles-d'Ornano ⓣ04.95.22.48.22. Right on the quayside, looking across a clutter of yachts and cruise liners to the mountains. Both the food (salads, grilled fish, Corsican speciality *plats du jour*) and atmosphere are quintessential Ajaccio, and for once the prices are restrained. Count on €18–23 à la carte. Closed Sun & Mon eve.

Ariadne rte des Sanguinaires, near *Barbicaja* campsite ⓣ04.95.52.09.63. The oldest and most cheerful of Ajaccio's many beachside *paillotes*, with a terrace opening straight on to the sand. World cuisine dominates the menu and there's usually live music from 8.30pm. Most main courses €12–17. Open Easter–Oct Tues–Sun. You can get there from place de Gaulle on bus #5.

Le Floride Port de Plaisance Charles-d'Ornano ⓣ04.95.22.67.48. Sublime local seafood, stylishly prepared and served in an airy dining hall overlooking the marina. Weekday lunchtimes are dominated by business clients, but the suits and mobile phones peter out in the evenings. If your budget can stretch to it, go for their €34 *menu poisson frais*. Closed Sat & Sun lunchtimes.

Les Halles rue des Halles ☎04.95.21.42.68. Open since 1933, and the favourite lunch venue for market stallholders and local office workers. They do a cheap and cheerful €14 menu with wild boar or fresh fish of the day, and a choice of omelettes and fresh pasta.

Da Mamma passage Guinghetta ☎04.95.21.39.44. Tucked away down a narrow passageway connecting cours Napoléon and rue Cardinal-Fesch. Authentic but affordable Corsican cuisine – such as *cannelloni al brocciu*, roast kid and seafood – on set menus from €12 to €25, served either in a stone-walled dining room or under a rubber tree in a tiny courtyard. Snappy service, convivial atmosphere, and the house wine's not bad; their budget menus are less than exciting however.

Le Golfe de Valinco

From Ajaccio, the vista of whitewashed villas and sandy beaches lining the opposite side of the gulf may tempt you out of town when you first arrive. On closer inspection, however, **Porticcio** turns out to be a faceless string of leisure settlements for Ajaccio's smart set, complete with tennis courts, malls and flotillas of jet-skis. Better to skip this stretch and press on south along the route nationale (RN194) which, after scaling the **Col de Celaccia**, winds down to the stunning **Golfe de Valinco**. A vast blue inlet bounded by rolling, scrub-covered hills, the gulf presents the first dramatic scenery along the coastal highway. It also marks the start of militant and Mafia-ridden south Corsica, more closely associated with vendetta, banditry and separatism than any other part of the island. Many of the mountain villages glimpsed from the roads hereabouts are riven with age-old divisions, exacerbated in recent years by the spread of organized crime and nationalist violence. But the island's seamier side is rarely discernible to the hundreds of thousands of visitors who pass through each summer, most of whom stay around the small port of **Propriano**, at the eastern end of the gulf. In addition to offering most of the area's tourist amenities, this busy resort town lies within easy reach of the menhirs at **Filitosa**, one of the western Mediterranean's most important prehistoric sites, and the secluded fishing village of **Campomoro**, on the opposite shore of the gulf, from where you can strike out south on foot to explore one of Corsica's wildest stretches of coast.

The Golfe de Valinco region is reasonably well served by public **transport**, with buses running four times per day between Ajaccio and Bonifacio, via Propriano and Sartène. Note, however, that outside July and August there are no services along this route on Sundays.

Propriano (Pruprià)

Tucked into the narrowest part of the Golfe de Valinco, the small port of **PROPRIANO**, 57km southeast of Ajaccio, centres on a fine natural harbour that was exploited by the ancient Greeks, Carthaginians and Romans, but became a prime target for Saracen pirate raids in the eighteenth century, when it was largely destroyed. Redeveloped in the 1900s, it now boasts a thriving marina, and handles ferries to Toulon, Marseille and Sardinia. The town around the port has also grown in importance, largely under the direction of a powerful coalition of nationalist-backed politicians and shady mafia figures, which has held at bay the kind of power struggles that have undermined other resorts of comparable size.

Propriano's underworld connections, however, in no way deter the tourists, who come here in droves for the area's **beaches**. The nearest of these, **plage de Lido**, lies 1km west, just beyond the Port de Commerce; it's patrolled by lifeguards during the summer and is much safer and more appealing than the grubby **plage de Baracci**, 1km north of town, where the undertow is precariously strong. Just 3km beyond the Baracci beach, the D157 branches off to the left and continues along the coast, which is built up with hotels and package-tour holiday blocks until **Olmeto plage**, 10km west, where an abundance of campsites are on offer (see below). You can reach Olmeto on the three daily buses from Propriano to Porto.

Practicalities

Ferries from the mainland and Sardinia dock in the Port de Commerce, ten minutes' walk from where the **buses** stop at the top of rue du Général-de-Gaulle, the town's main street. The SNCM office is on quai Commandant-L'Herminier (Ⓣ04.95.76.04.36), while the **tourist office** is down in the harbour master's office in the marina (June & Sept Mon–Sat 9am–noon & 3–7pm; July & Aug daily 8am–8pm; Oct–May Mon–Fri 9am–noon & 2–6pm; Ⓣ04.95.76.01.49, Ⓦwww.propriano.net).

There's a reasonable choice of **hotels** in the centre of town, including the high-tech *Loft*, 3 rue Camille-Pietri (Ⓣ04.95.76.17.48, Ⓕ04.95.76.22.04; ④), directly behind the port; and the *Bellevue* on avenue Napoléon (Ⓣ04.95.76.01.86, Ⓕ04.95.76.38.94; ④), overlooking the marina and with the cheapest central rooms. If you have a car, two other places worth trying are the *Arcu di Sole*, 3km northeast on the route de Baracci (Ⓣ04.95.76.05.10, Ⓕ04.95.76.13.36; ⑤), which has a pool and gourmet restaurant, or the more modest *Ferme Équestre Baracci* (Ⓣ & Ⓕ04.95.76.19.48; ④), an excellent little *gîte d'étape* and riding centre just down the road from the Arcu di Sole, with half-a-dozen twin-bedded doubles (with or without toilets) and a dining room offering good-value evening meals (€16; order in advance by 5pm).

Campers are well provided for, although the best sites are well out of town: for the best facilities go to *Camping Colomba* (Ⓣ04.95.76.06.42), 3km north along route de Baracci, which has a swimming pool. At Olmeta plage, the most appealing site is *U Libecciu* (Ⓣ04.95.74.01.28), the first place on the beach coming from Propriano, or you could try *Chez Antoine* (Ⓣ04.95.76.06.06) in Marina d'Olmeto, north of the beach.

Cafés and **restaurants** are concentrated along the marina's avenue Napoléon, where *Resto Nicoli* is just about the cheapest place to eat, with excellent omelettes and Italian specialities. For fresh seafood, though, you can't beat *L'Hippocampe* (Ⓣ04.95.76.11.01), tucked away behind the port on rue Pandolphi, where the good value €16 and €30 menus are served indoors or on a flower-filled pavement terrace. On the opposite side of town, behind the marina, *Le Tout Va Bien* (Ⓣ04.95.76.12.14) is another dependable option, housed in a converted stone fisherman's cottage, where you can enjoy fine gastronomic cuisine at affordable prices (menus €21–28) on a terrace overlooking the harbour.

Filitosa

Set deep in the countryside of the fertile Vallée du Taravo, the extraordinary **Station Préhistorique de Filitosa** (Easter–Oct 9am–sunset; out of season by arrangement only; Ⓣ04.95.74.00.91; €5), 17km north of Propriano, comprises a wonderful array of statue-menhirs and prehistoric structures encapsulat-

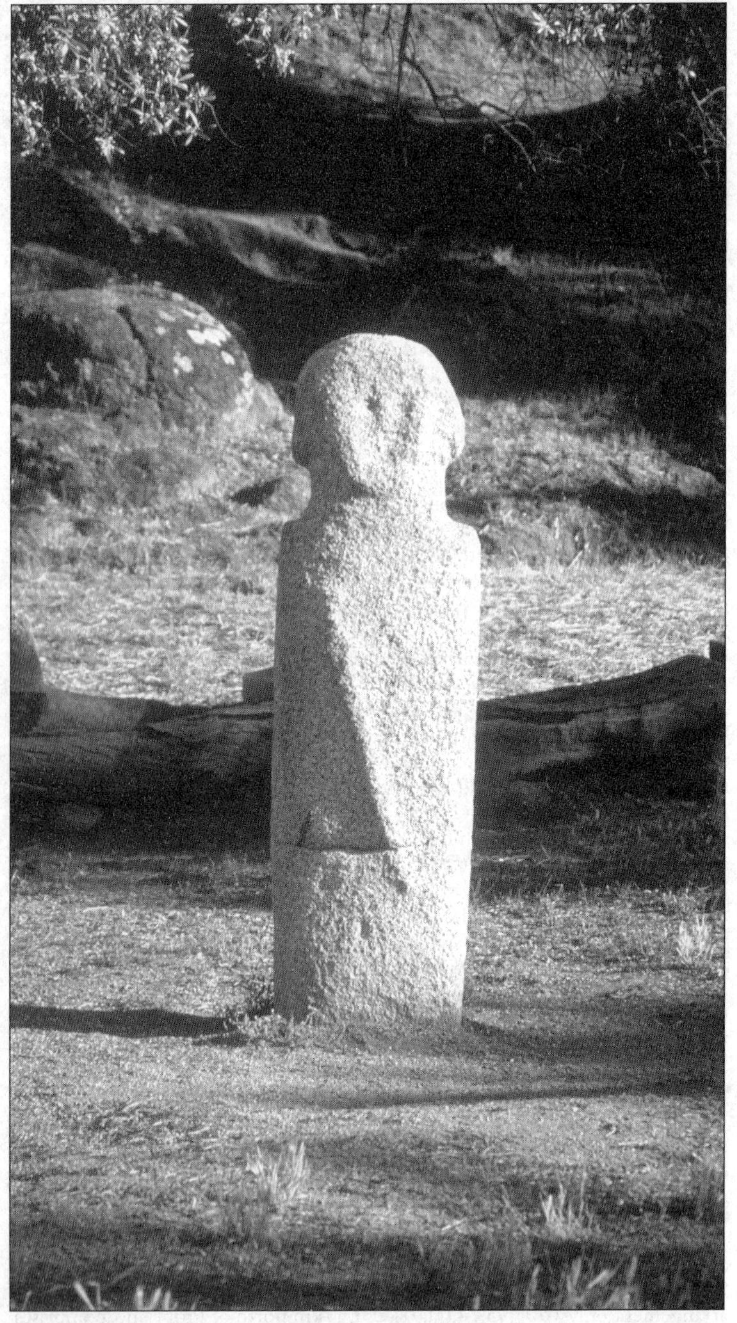

△ Prehistoric menhir at Filitosa

ing some eight thousand years of history. Vehicles can be left in the small car park in the hamlet of Filitosa, where you pay the entrance fee; from here it's a fifteen-minute walk to the entrance, where you'll find a café, a small museum and a workshop producing reproduction prehistoric ceramics. There's no public transport to the site.

Filitosa was settled by Neolithic farming people who lived here in rock shelters until the arrival of navigators from the east in about 3500 BC. These invaders were the creators of the menhirs, the earliest of which were possibly phallic symbols worshipped by an ancient fertility cult. When the seafaring people known as the Torréens (after the towers they built on Corsica) conquered Filitosa around 1300 BC, they destroyed most of the menhirs, incorporating the broken stones into the area of dry-stone walling surrounding the site's two *torri*, or towers, examples of which can be found all over the south of Corsica. The site remained undiscovered until a farmer stumbled across the ruins on his land in the late 1940s.

Filitosa V looms up on the right shortly after the main entrance to the site. The largest statue-menhir on the island, it's an imposing sight, with clearly defined facial features and a sword and dagger outlined on the body. Beyond a sharp left turn lies the oppidum or central monument, its entrance marked by the **eastern platform**, thought to have been a lookout post. The cave-like structure sculpted out of the rock is the only evidence of Neolithic occupation and is generally agreed to have been a burial mound. Straight ahead, the Torréen **central monument** comprises a scattered group of menhirs on a circular walled mound, surmounted by a dome and entered by a corridor of stone slabs and lintels. Nobody is sure of its exact function.

Nearby **Filitosa XIII** and **Filitosa IX**, implacable lumps of granite with long noses and round chins, are the most impressive of the menhirs. Filitosa XIII is typical of the figures made just before the Torréen invasion, with its vertical dagger carved in relief – **Filitosa VII** also has a clearly sculpted sword and shield. **Filitosa VI**, from the same period, is remarkable for its facial detail. On the eastern side of the central monument stand some vestigial Torréen houses, where fragments of ceramics dating from 5500 BC were discovered; they represent the most ancient finds on the site, and some of them are displayed in the museum.

The **western monument**, a two-roomed structure built underneath another walled mound, is thought to have been some form of Torréen religious building. A flight of steps leads to the foot of this mound, where a footbridge opens onto a meadow that's dominated by five statue-menhirs arranged in a semicircle beneath a thousand-year-old olive tree. A bank separates them from the quarry from which the megalithic sculptors hewed the stone for the menhirs – a granite block is marked ready for cutting.

The **museum** is a shoddy affair, with poorly labelled exhibits and very little contextual information, but the artefacts themselves are fascinating. The major item here is the formidable **Scalsa Murta**, a huge menhir dating from around 1400 BC and discovered at Olmeto. Like other statue-menhirs of this period, this one has two indents in the back of its head, which are thought to indicate that these figures would have been adorned with headdresses. Other notable exhibits are **Filitosa XII**, which has a hand and a foot carved into the stone, and **Trappa II**, a strikingly archaic face.

Campomoro

Isolated at the mouth of the Golfe de Valinco, **CAMPOMORO**, 17km southwest of Propriano, ranks among the most congenial seaside villages on the island. The main attraction here is a two-kilometre-long **beach**, overlooked by an immense and well-preserved Genoese watchtower. In late July and August, it's swamped by Italian families from the adjacent campsites, but for the rest of the year Campomoro remains a tranquil enough place, with barely enough permanent residents to support a post office.

Another incentive to venture out here is the wild and windswept stretch of coast south of Campomoro, which is punctuated by outlandish rock formations and a string of empty pebble beaches. The absence of a road into the area, recently designated a **regional nature reserve**, means the only way to explore it is by boat or on foot, via the waymarked coastal path that begins below Campomoro's watchtower. From here, the path is easy to follow for the first eighty minutes or so as it threads through a series of dramatic granite outcrops, eroded into phantasmagorical shapes. But once you hit the **anse d'Eccia**, a sandy bottle-necked cove, the going gets tougher. Determined, well-equipped hikers can walk all the way to **Tizzano**, 20km down the coast, via the much-photographed Senetosa Tower, but to do so it's essential to take along a detailed map, plenty of fresh water and camping equipment in case you get lost. For additional route advice, contact the owner of Big Blue boat trips at his caravan near the tourist office in Propriano (ⓣ04.95.76.04.26). He takes customers to anse d'Eccia by catamaran, and provides photographs to help you follow the trail back to Campomoro; the cost of this half-day trip is around €25.

Practicalities

There are no bus services to Campomoro, but hitching is fairly reliable once you've turned off the main Propriano–Bonifacio road. The village possesses a couple of campsites and two **hotels**: *Le Ressac*, about 100m behind the chapel (ⓣ04.95.74.22.25, ⓕ04.95.74.23.43; April–Oct; ❺), a friendly family-run place with excellent views across the bay, is generally a better option than the more expensive, more formal *Le Campomoro*, overlooking the beach at the tower end of the village (ⓣ04.95.74.20.89, ⓕ04.95.74.20.89; ❺). Of the two **campsites**, *Camping Peretto Les Roseaux*, 300m from the post office towards the tower (ⓣ04.95.74.20.52; May–Oct), is the more peaceful. For **food**, try the popular *La Mouette* café opposite the church (ⓣ04.95.74.22.26), which serves a selection of filling salads for around €8–10 on its beachside terrace. More sophisticated Corsican cooking is served at *Le Ressac*'s restaurant, which offers two menus: one at €19, offering Corsican standards such as *cannelloni al brocciu*, squid, and lamb stew; and a pricier €28 *menu poisson*, which features the best of the day's catch from the local boats.

Sartène (Sartè) and around

Prosper Mérimée famously dubbed **SARTÈNE** "*la plus corse des villes corses*" (the most Corsican of Corsican towns), but the nineteenth-century German chronicler Gregorovius put a less complimentary spin on it when he described it as a "town peopled by demons". Sartène hasn't shaken off its hostile image, due in large part to a heavy presence of wealthy-looking godfather types. On the other hand it's a smart, clean place, noticeably better groomed than many small Corsican towns, its principal income coming from Sartène wine, the best on the island. The main square doesn't offer many diversions once you've explored the enclosed old town and prehistory museum, and the only time of year Sartène teems with tourists is at Easter for **U Catenacciu**, a Good Friday procession that packs the main square with onlookers.

Close to Sartène are some of the island's best-known **prehistoric sites**, most notably Filitosa, the megaliths of **Cauria** and the **Alignement de Palaggiu** – Corsica's largest array of prehistoric standing stones.

The Town

Place Porta – its official name, place de la Libération, has never caught on – forms Sartène's nucleus. Once the arena for bloody vendettas, it's now a well-kept square opening onto a wide terrace that overlooks the rippling green valley of the Rizzanese. Flanking the south side of place Porta is the **church of Ste-Marie**, built in the 1760s but completely restored to a smooth granitic appearance. Inside the church, the most notable feature is the weighty wooden cross and chair carried through the town by hooded penitents during the Easter **Catenacciu** procession.

A flight of steps to the left of the **Hôtel de Ville**, formerly the governor's palace, leads past the post office to a ruined **lookout tower**, which is all that remains of the town's twelfth-century ramparts. This apart, the best of the old town is to be found behind the Hôtel de Ville in the **Santa Anna** district, a labyrinth of constricted passageways and ancient fortress-like houses that rarely give any signs of life. Featuring few windows and often linked to their neighbours by balconies, these houses are entered by first-floor doors which would have been approached by ladders – dilapidated staircases have replaced these necessary measures against unwelcome intruders. To the left of rue des Frères-Bartoli are the strangest of all the vaulted passageways, where outcrops of rock block the paths between the ancient buildings. Just to the west of the Hôtel de Ville, signposted off the tiny place Maggiore, you'll find the **impasse Carababa**, a remarkable architectural puzzle of a passageway cut through the awkwardly stacked houses.

Sartène's only other cultural attraction is **Musée de la Préhistoire Corse** (closed at time of writing, pending a move to new premises across town; check with tourist office), Corsica's centre for archeological research. The museum contains a rather dry collection of mostly Neolithic and Torréen pottery fragments, with some bracelets from the Iron Age and painted ceramics from the thirteenth to sixteenth centuries.

Practicalities

Arriving in Sartène by **bus**, you'll be dropped either at the top of avenue Gabriel-Péri or at the end of cours Général-de-Gaulle. The **tourist office**, on rue Borgu (summer only Mon–Fri 9am–noon & 2.30–6pm; ⓣ04.95.77.15.40), can help find accommodation in the area if the hotels listed below are full.

The only **hotel** in Sartène itself is *Les Roches* on rue Jean-Jaurès, a large family-run place just below the old town (ⓣ04.95.77.07.61, ⓕ04.95.77.19.93; ❹); it commands panoramic views of the Vallée du Rizzanese and has a restaurant that serves hearty Corsican food. Otherwise try the *Villa Piana*, 1km out of town on the Propriano road (ⓣ04.95.77.07.04, ⓦwww.lavillapiana.com; ❻), an upmarket place, with a pool and tennis court, overlooking the Golfe de Valinco – or simply stay in Propriano, which has a wider choice of accommodation. The nearest **campsite**, *Camping Olva* (*Les Eucalyptus*), lies 5km along the D69 to Castagna (ⓣ04.95.77.11.58; closed Nov–April) – it offers a free bus service to and from Sartène.

As for **restaurants**, a dependable choice is *Zia Paulina*, tucked away at the end of an atmospheric alleyway, rue des Frères-Bartoli, in the *vieille ville*: Sartenais specialities dominate both their good-value €17 and €23 menus, and there's a generous selection of local wines to choose from. **Cafés** cluster around place Porta, and are great places for crowd-watching. With your own vehicle, you might also consider venturing 5km northwest along the Propriano road to the *Ferme-Auberge A Tinedda* (Ⓣ04.95.77.09.31), which serves definitive *cuisine du terroir* such as *tripettes sartenaises*, *cannelloni au brocciu* and *riz fermier*, washed down with quality local AOC wines. You can eat in their intimate dining room or outside on a rear terrace facing the garden, where most of the chef's ingredients come from. The single *menu du jour* costs €28; advance reservation is essential.

The megalithic sites

Sparsely populated today, the rolling hills of the southwestern corner of Corsica are rich in prehistoric sites. The megaliths of **Cauria**, standing in ghostly isolation 10km southwest from Sartène, comprise the Dolmen de Fontanaccia, the best-preserved monument of its kind on Corsica, while the nearby alignments of **Stantari** and **Renaggiu** have an impressive congregation of statue-menhirs.

More than 250 menhirs can be seen northwest of Cauria at **Palaggiu**, another rewardingly remote site. Equally wild is the coast hereabouts, with deep clefts and coves providing some excellent spots for diving and secluded swimming.

The only public transport in this region is the twice-daily Ajaccio–Bonifacio bus.

Cauria

To reach the **Cauria megalithic site**, you need to turn off the N196 about 2km outside Sartène, at the Col de l'Albitrina (291m), taking the D48 towards Tizzano. Four kilometres along this road a left turning brings you onto a winding road through maquis, until eventually the **Dolmen de Fontanaccia** comes into view on the horizon, crowning the crest of a low hill amidst a sea of maquis. A blue sign at the parking space indicates the track to the dolmen, a fifteen-minute walk away.

Known to the locals as the **Stazzona del Diavolu** (Devil's Forge), a name that does justice to its enigmatic power, the Dolmen de Fontanaccia is in fact a burial chamber from around 2000 BC. This period was marked by a change in burial customs – whereas bodies had previously been buried in stone coffins in the ground, they were now placed above, in a mound of earth enclosed in a stone chamber. What you see today is a great stone table, comprising six huge granite blocks nearly 2m high, topped by a stone slab that remained after the earth eroded away.

The twenty "standing men" of the **Alignement de Stantari**, 200m to the east of the dolmen, date from the same period. All are featureless, except two which have roughly sculpted eyes and noses, with diagonal swords on their fronts and sockets in their heads where horns would probably have been attached.

Across a couple of fields to the south is the **Alignement de Renaggiu**, a gathering of forty menhirs standing in rows amid a small shadowy copse, set against the enormous granite outcrop of Punta di Cauria. Some of the menhirs have fallen, but all face north to south, a fact that seems to rule out any connection with a sun-related cult.

Palaggiu

To reach the **Alignement de Palaggiu**, the largest concentration of menhirs in Corsica, regain the D48 and head southwards past the Domaine la Mosconi vineyard (on your right, 3km after the Cauria turn-off), 1500m beyond which a green metal gate on the right side of the road marks the turning. From here a badly rutted dirt track leads another 1200m to the stones, lost in the maquis, with vineyards spread over the hills in the half-distance. Stretching in straight lines across the countryside like a battleground of soldiers, the 258 menhirs include three statue-menhirs with carved weapons and facial features – they are amidst the first line you come to. Dating from around 1800 BC, the statues give few clues as to their function, but it's a reasonable supposition that proximity to the sea was important – the famous Corsican archeologist Roger Grosjean's theory is that the statues were some sort of magical deterrent to invaders.

Bonifacio (Bonifaziu)

BONIFACIO enjoys a superbly isolated location at Corsica's southernmost point, a narrow peninsula of dazzling white limestone creating a town site unlike any other. The much-photographed **haute ville**, a maze of narrow streets flanked by tall Genoese tenements, rises seamlessly out of sheer cliffs that have been hollowed and striated by the wind and waves, while on the landward side the deep cleft between the peninsula and the mainland forms a perfect natural harbour. A haven for boats for centuries, this inlet is nowadays a chic marina that attracts yachts from around the Med. Separated from the rest of the island by a swathe of dense maquis, Bonifacio has maintained a certain temperamental detachment from the rest of Corsica, and is distinctly more Italian than French in atmosphere. The town retains Renaissance features found only here, and its inhabitants have their own dialect based on Ligurian, a legacy of the days when this was practically an independent Genoese colony.

Such a place has its inevitable drawbacks: exorbitant prices, overwhelming crowds in August and a commercial cynicism that's atypical of Corsica as a whole. However, the old town forms one of the most arresting spectacles in the Mediterranean, easily transcending all the tourist frippery that surrounds it, and warrants at least a day-trip. If you plan to come in peak season, try to get here early in the day before the bus parties arrive at around 10am.

Arrival, information and accommodation

Figari **airport**, 17km north of Bonifacio (ⓣ04.95.71.10.10), handles flights from mainland France and a few charters from the UK. There's a seasonal **bus** service operated by Transports Rossi (ⓣ04.95.71.00.11) that in theory should meet incoming flights, stopping at Bonifacio en route to Porto-Vecchio; otherwise, your only option is to take a taxi into town – around €45. If you're coming by bus from other parts of the island you'll be dropped at the car park by the marina, close to most of the hotels. The **tourist office** is up in the *haute ville*, in the Fort San Nicro at the bottom of rue F. Scamaroni (July–Sept daily 9am–8pm; Oct–June Mon–Fri 9am–12.30pm & 2–5.15pm; ⓣ04.95.73.11.88, ⓦwww.bonifacio.fr); they can check for you which hotels have vacancies. **Cars** can be rented from Avis, quai Banda del Ferro ⓣ04.95.73.01.28; Citer, quai Noel-Beretti ⓣ04.95.73.13.16; Hertz, quai Banda del Ferro ⓣ04.95.73.06.41. All of the above also have branches at the airport. If you need to change money, note that Bonifacio's only **ATM**, at the

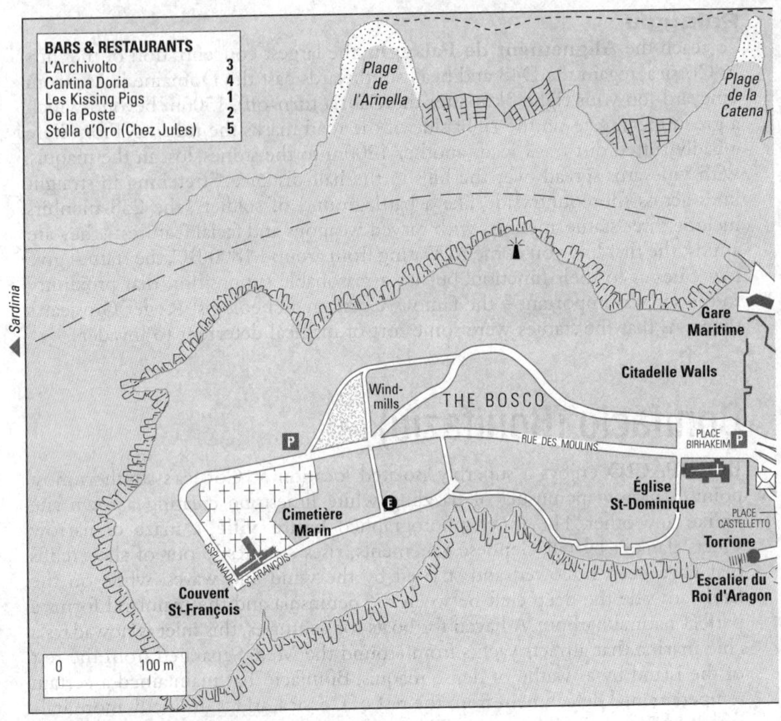

Société Générale on the quai J. Comparetti, frequently runs out of cash, so get there early in the day or you'll be at the mercy of the rip-off bureaux de change dotted around the town. *Bomiboom.com*, also on quai Comparetti, offers pricey **Internet** access (€0.15/min).

Finding a **place to stay** can be a chore, as Bonifacio's hotels are quickly booked up in high season; for a room near the centre, reserve well in advance. Better still, save yourself the trouble, and a considerable amount of money, by finding a room somewhere else and travelling here for the day; tariffs in this town are the highest on the island. The same applies to the large campsites dotted along the road to Porto-Vecchio, which can get very crowded.

Hotels

La Caravelle 35 quai J. Comparetti Ⓣ04.95.73.00.03, Ⓦwww.hotel-caravelle-corse.com. Long-established place in prime location on the quayside, whose standard rooms are on the small side for the price. ❼

Centre Nautique on the marina Ⓣ04.95.73.02.11, Ⓦwww.centre-nautique.com. Chic but relaxed hotel on the waterfront, fitted out with mellow wood and nautical charts. All rooms are tastefully furnished and consist of two storeys connected with a spiral staircase. The best upmarket option in town. ❽

Des Étrangers 4 av Sylvère-Bohn Ⓣ04.95.73.01.09, Ⓕ04.95.73.16.97. Simple rooms (the costlier ones have TV and a/c) facing the main road, just up from the port. Nothing special, but pretty good value for Bonifacio. April–Oct. ❺

Le Roi d'Aragon 13 quai J. Comparetti Ⓣ04.95.73.03.99, Ⓕ04.95.73.07.94. A recently revamped three-star overlooking the marina, with better than average off-season discounts. Some of the rooms are small, but the pricier ones have sunny interconnecting terraces looking across the port. ❻

Ⓐ, Camping Campo di Liccia, Camping Pian del Fosse, Porto-Vecchio, Bastia, ▲ Figari Airport, Sartène & Ajaccio

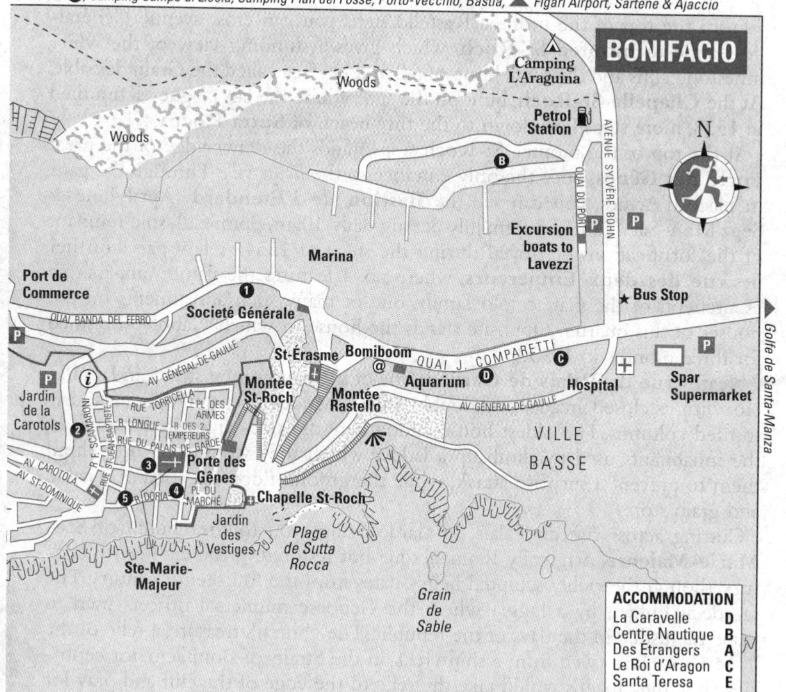

Santa Teresa quartier Saint-François ☎04.95.73.11.32, Ⓕ04.95.73.15.99. Large three-star on the clifftop overlooking Cimetière Marin, worth a mention for its stupendous views across the straits to Sardinia. Not all the rooms are sea-facing though, so ask for "*vue mer avec balcon*" when you book. ⑧

Campsites

L'Araguina av Sylvère-Bohn ☎04.95.73.02.96. Closest place to town, but unwelcoming, horrendously cramped and with inadequate washing and toilet facilities. Avoid unless desperate. April–Sept.

Campo di Liccia 3km north towards Porto-Vecchio, ☎04.95.73.03.09. Well shaded and large, so you're guaranteed a place. April–Oct.

Pian del Fosse 4km out of town on the rte de Santa Manza ☎04.95.73.16.34. Big three-star site that recently had a makeover. Very peaceful and quiet in June and September, and well placed for the beaches. April to mid-Oct.

The Town

Apart from the cafés, hotels and restaurants of **quai Comparetti**, the only attraction in the **ville basse** is the marina's **aquarium** (daily: May, June, Sept & Oct 10am–8pm, July & Aug 10am–midnight; €3.80), where a solitary blue lobster is the star attraction. At the far end lies the **port** where ferries leave for Sardinia and, in between, a cluster of restaurants and shops lies at the foot of **montée Rastello**, the steps up to the **haute ville**. In the *haute ville* many of the houses are bordered by enormous battlements which, like the houses themselves, have been rebuilt many times – the most significant modifications were made by the French during their brief period of occupation following the 1554 siege, after they had reduced the town walls to rubble.

From the top of the montée Rastello steps you can cross avenue Général-de-Gaulle to **montée St-Roch**, which gives a stunning view of the white limestone cliffs and the huge lump of fallen rock-face called the Grain de Sable. At the **Chapelle St-Roch**, built on the spot where the last plague victim died in 1528, more steps lead down to the tiny beach of **Sutta Rocca**.

At the top of the montée St-Roch steps stands the drawbridge of the great **Porte des Gênes**, once the only entrance to the *haute ville*. Through the gate, in place d'Armes, you can see the **Bastion de l'Étendard** (April–June & Sept Mon–Sat 11am–5.30pm; July & Aug daily 10am–9pm; €2), sole remnant of the fortifications destroyed during the siege of 1554. A few paces further lies **rue des deux Empereurs**, where no. 4 features the flamboyant marble escutcheon of the Cattacciolo family, one of many such adornments on the houses of this quarter. Opposite stands the house in which Napoleon resided for three months in 1793.

Nearby **rue du Palais de Garde** is one of the handsomest streets in Bonifacio, with its closed arcades and double-arched windows separated by curiously stunted columns. The oldest houses along here did not originally have doors; the inhabitants used to climb up a ladder which they would pull up behind them to prevent a surprise attack, while the ground floor was used as a stable and grain store.

Cutting across rue du Palais de Garde brings you to the church of **Ste-Marie-Majeure**, originally Romanesque but restored in the eighteenth century, though the richly sculpted belfry dates from the fourteenth century. The facade is hidden by a loggia where the Genoese municipal officers used to dispense justice in the days of the republic. The church's treasure, a relic of the True Cross, was saved from a shipwreck in the Straits of Bonifacio; for centuries after, the citizens would take the relic to the edge of the cliff and pray for calm seas whenever storms raged. The relic is kept in the sacristy, along with an ivory cask containing relics of St Boniface, and you'll only be able to get a glimpse if you can find someone to open the room for you.

South of here, rue Doria leads towards the Bosco (see below); at the end of this road a left down rue des Pachas will bring you to the **Torrione**, a 35-metre-high lookout post built in 1195 on the site of Count Bonifacio's castle. Descending the cliff from here, the **Escalier du Roi d'Aragon**'s 187 steps (June–Sept daily 11am–5.30pm; €2) were said to have been built in one night by the Aragonese in an attempt to gain the town in 1420, but in fact they had already been in existence for some time and were used by the people to fetch water from a well.

The Bosco

To the west of the tower lies the **Bosco**, a quarter named after the wood that used to stand here in the tenth century. In those days a community of hermits dwelt here, but nowadays the limestone plateau is open and desolate. The only sign of life comes from the military training camp where young Corsicans sweat out their national service. The entrance to the Bosco is marked by the **church of St-Dominique**, a rare example of Corsican Gothic architecture – it was built in 1270, most probably by the Templars, and later handed over to the Dominicans.

Beyond the church, rue des Moulins leads on to the ruins of three **mills** dating from 1283, two of them decrepit, the third restored. Behind them stands a memorial to the 750 people who died when a troopship named *Sémillante* ran aground here in 1855, on its way to the Crimea, one of the many disasters wreaked by the notoriously windy straits.

The tip of the plateau is occupied by the **Cimetière Marin**, its white crosses standing out sharply against the deep blue of the sea. Open until sundown, the cemetery is a fascinating place to explore, with its flamboyant mausoleums displaying a jumble of architectural ornamentations: stuccoed facades, Gothic arches and classical columns. Next to the cemetery stands the **Couvent St-François**, allegedly founded after St Francis sought shelter in a nearby cave – the story goes that the convent was the town's apology to the holy man, over whom a local maid had nearly poured a bucket of slops. Immediately to the south, the **Esplanade St-François** commands fine views across the bay to Sardinia.

Eating, drinking and nightlife

Eating possibilities in Bonifacio might seem unlimited, but it's best to avoid the chintzy restaurants in the marina, few of which merit their exorbitant prices – the places in the *haute ville* are less pretentious. For a snack, try the boulangerie-patisserie Faby, 4 rue St-Jean-Baptiste in the *haute ville*, a tiny local bakery serving Bonifacien treats such as *pain des morts* (sweet buns with walnuts and raisins), *fugazzi* (*galettes* flavoured with eau de vie, orange, lemon and aniseed) and *migliacis*, buns made with fresh ewe's cheese, in addition to the usual range of spinach and *brocciu bastelles*, baked here in the traditional way – on stone.

The **bars** and **cafés** on quai Comparetti are the social focus for the town and what little nightlife there is revolves around the terraces here. Bonifacio's only nightclub was blown up by nationalist bombers a couple of years back, so for a real *nuit blanche* you'll have to head for Porto Vecchio.

Restaurants

L'Archivolto rue de l'Archivolto ⓣ04.95.73.17.48. With its candlelit, antique- and junk-filled interior, this would be the most commendable place to eat in the *haute ville* were the cooking a little less patchy and the prices fairer. But it still gets packed out – advance reservation is recommended. Lunch menus around €15; evening à la carte only, around €25–28 for three courses. Open Easter–Oct.

Cantina Doria 27 rue Doria ⓣ04.95.73.50.49. Down-to-earth Corsican specialities at down-to-earth prices. Their popular three-course €14 menu – which includes the house speciality, aubergines *à la bonifacienne* – offers unbeatable value for the *haute ville*, though you'll soon bump up your bill if you succumb to the temptations of the excellent wine selection.

Centre Nautique In the hotel of the same name, this is Bonifacio's most chic breakfast venue: coffee, hot croissants, baguettes and freshly squeezed orange juice on a deck, with views of the bastion across the marina. Well worth splashing out €11 for, but get here early for the best tables.

Les Kissing Pigs 16 quai Banda del Ferro ⓣ04.95.73.56.09. One of the liveliest addresses in Bonifacio, run by a Scottish-Corsican couple. Island charcuterie and cheeses are its speciality, but they also do good-value *menus fixes* from €14 to €20. As you'd expect, the decor is dominated by kissing pig photos and other snout-themed ephemera.

De la Poste 6 rue F. Scamaroni. A cheap and cheerful pizza place serving oven-baked lasagne, spaghetti *al brocciu*, stuffed mussels and delicious pizzas (€7–10).

Stella d'Oro (Chez Jules) 7 rue Doria, near église St-Jean-Baptiste. À la carte place with stone walls and wood beams, whose top-notch Corsican dishes include the definitive *merrizzane* (stuffed aubergine) – *the* local speciality. They also do a famous spaghetti in lobster sauce and ravioli *brocciu*. Midday menu at €22; count on €35 à la carte.

Around Bonifacio

There are impressive views of the citadelle from the **cliffs** at the head of the montée Rastello (reached via the pathway running left from the top of the steps), but they're not a patch on the spectacular panorama to be had from the sea. Throughout the day, a flotilla of excursion **boats** ferries visitors out to the best vantage points, taking in a string of caves and other landmarks only accessible by water en route, including the **Îles Lavezzi**, the scattering of small islets where the troop ship *Sémillante* was shipwrecked in 1855, now designated as a nature reserve. The whole experience of bobbing around to an amplified running commentary is about as touristy as Bonifacio gets, but it's well worth enduring just to round the mouth of the harbour and see the *vieille ville*, perched atop the famous chalk cliffs. The boats leave from the east side of the marina: tickets cost €10–12 for trips to the caves, and around €27 for the longer excursions to Lavezzi.

The **beaches** along this part of the coast are generally smaller and less appealing than most in southern Corsica, although those fringing the **Golfe de Santa Manza**, to the north, are set amid some fine scenery. On the southernmost tip of the island, reached via a narrow but easily motorable road, a trio of small coves are the most popular beaches within easy reach of town. The first, **plage de Pianterella**, 7km east of Bonifacio, is also the dullest, backed by an unsavoury swamp. Walk south around the headland for fifteen minutes and you'll reach the more pleasant **plage de Sperone**, a pearl-white cove with calm, shallow water that's ideal for kids. However, this beach gets jam-packed in the summer and you may want to venture further along the coast to **Calalonga**, where you stand a better chance of escaping the crowds. To get there, head east of town on the D58, and take the first turning right, after around 3km.

By far the most photogenic beach in this area is **Rondinara**, a perfect shell-shaped cove of turquoise water enclosed by dunes and a pair of twin headlands. Thankfully, it's well off the beaten track, although the recent appearance of a surfaced road all the way to the beach could well change that. To see it at its emptiest, get here early in the morning. The turning for Rondinara is sign-posted 10km north along the N198.

Porto-Vecchio and around

Set on a hillock overlooking a beautiful deep blue bay, **PORTO-VECCHIO**, 25km north of Bonifacio, was rated by James Boswell as one of "the most distinguished harbours in Europe". It was founded in 1539 as a second Genoese stronghold on the east coast, Bastia being well established in the north. The site was perfect: close to the unexploited and fertile plain, it benefited from secure high land and a sheltered harbour, although the mosquito population spread malaria and wiped out the first Ligurian settlers within months. Things began to take off mainly thanks to the cork industry, which still thrived well into the twentieth century. Today a third of Corsica's wine is exported from Porto-Vecchio, but most revenue comes from tourists, the vast majority of them well-heeled Italians who flock here for the fine outlying **beaches**: spectacular stretches of shoreline lie to the south, with Palombaggia the most popular and Golfe de Santa Giulia coming a close second, while to the north, the deep inlet of the Golfe de Porto-Vecchio boasts some fine pine-backed strands. To the northwest, the little town of **Zonza** makes a good base for exploring the dramatic forestry that surrounds the **route de Bavella**.

Around the centre of town there's not much to see, apart from the well-preserved **fortress** and the small grid of **ancient streets** backing onto the main place de la République. East of the square you can't miss the **Porte Génoise**, which frames a delightful expanse of sea and salt pans and through which you'll find the quickest route down to the modern marina, lined with cafés and hotels.

Practicalities

Porto-Vecchio doesn't have a **bus** station; instead, the various companies who come here stop and depart outside their agents' offices on the edge of the old town. Coming from Bastia or the eastern plain (eg Solenzara or Aléria) you'll be dropped at the Corsicatours office on 7 rue Jean-Jaurès; services to and from Ajaccio via Bonifacio, Sartène and Propriano stop outside the Trinitours office on rue Pasteur, just north of the citadelle; finally, the minibus connecting Porto-Vecchio with Ajaccio, via the chief villages of Bavella and Alta Rocca, pulls in at Île de Beauté Voyages, at 13 rue Générale de Gaulle, near the post office. From here it's a five-minute walk to the main square, place de l'Hôtel-de-Ville, site of the efficient **tourist office** (June & Sept Mon–Sat 9am–1pm & 3–6pm; July & Aug Mon–Sat 9am–8pm, Sun 9am–1pm; Oct–May Mon–Fri 9am–noon & 2–6pm, Sat 9am–noon; ⓣ04.95.70.09.58, ⓦwww.accueil-portovecchio.com), where you can consult timetables for local buses.

Accommodation is easy to come by except in high summer. One of the least expensive places is the central *Le Moderne*, 10 cours Napoléon (ⓣ04.95.70.06.36; ❹; closed Oct–April), followed by the basic *Panorama*, 12 rue Jean-Nicoli, just above the old town (ⓣ04.95.70.07.96, ⓕ04.95.70.46.78; ❸), which isn't all that well maintained but offers the cheapest beds in town. If you can afford it, it's worth spending a bit extra to stay down by the marina, where pick of the bunch is the very pleasant *Goéland*, port de Plaisance (ⓣ04.95.70.14.15, ⓔhotel-goeland@wanadoo.fr; ❼). Of the many **campsites** in the area, *Matonara* (ⓣ04.95.70.37.05), just north of the centre at the Quatre-Chemins intersection, is the most easily accessible – it's large, with lots of cork trees for shade. Otherwise, try the well-equipped *Arutoli* on route de l'Ospédale, 2km northwest of town along the D368 (ⓣ04.95.70.12.73, ⓦwww.arutoli.com), which has an enormous pool.

For **eating**, a safe choice is *Le Tourisme*, opposite the church (ⓣ04.95.70.06.45), which serves fragrant Porto-Vecchien specialities – such as mussels in fennel and *pastis* served on a bed of tagliatelle; they offer a €24 menu, and there's a range of various good-value *formules* at lunchtime from €14. *Chez Anna*, a classy little pasta place on rue Camille De Rocca Serra (ⓣ04.95.70.19.97), is a little more tucked away but worth hunting out for its delicious stuffed aubergines and fresh gnocchi with mussels. Top-quality Corsican charcuterie, cheese, wine and other local delicacies can be sampled at *A Cantina di l'Oriu*, 5 cours Napoléon: get there for "Happy Hour" (6–7pm) when they offer taster plates with a glass of wine for €7.50. At other times, count on €12 and upwards for assorted meats and olives.

Nightlife in Porto-Vecchio centres on the main square in the old town where, in the summer, hordes of Italians strut their stuff. A lively bar to head for is *Pub de Bastion*, at the northeastern end of the old town, which claims to serve three hundred varieties of beer and stages live music (ghastly rock cover bands) most Friday and Saturday nights. The only bona fide club in the area, however, is *Via Notte* (ⓣ04.95.72.02.12, ⓦwww.vianotte.com), a trashy Italian-oriented place that stages top Euro DJs in July and August (when admission charges and drink prices go through the roof).

Golfe de Porto-Vecchio

Much of the coast of the **Golfe de Porto-Vecchio** and its environs is characterized by ugly development and hectares of swampland, yet some of the clearest, bluest sea and whitest beaches on Corsica are also found around here. The most frequented of these, Palombaggia and Santa Giulia, can be reached by **bus** from the town in summer, timetables for which are posted in the tourist office (see p.1265); at other times you'll need your own transport. The same applies to the **Casteddu d'Araggiu**, one of the island's best-preserved Bronze Age sites, which stands on a ledge overlooking the gulf to the north of town.

Heading south of Porto-Vecchio along the main N198, take the turning signposted for **Palombaggia**, a golden semicircle of sand edged by short twisted umbrella pines that are punctuated by fantastically shaped red rocks. This might be the most beautiful beach on the island were it not for the crowds, which pour on to it in such numbers that a wattle fence has had to be erected to protect the dunes. A few kilometres further along the same road takes you to **Santa Giulia**, a sweeping sandy bay backed by a lagoon. Despite the presence of several holiday villages and facilities for windsurfing and other, noisier watersports, crowds are less of a problem here, and the shallow bay is an extraordinary turquoise colour.

North of Porto-Vecchio, the first beach worth a visit is **San Ciprianu**, a half-moon bay of white sand, reached by turning left off the main road at the Elf petrol station. Carry on for another 7km, and you'll come to the even more picturesque beach at **Pinarellu**, an uncrowded, long sweep of soft white sand with a Genoese watchtower and, like the less inspiring beaches immediately north of here, benefiting from the spectacular backdrop of the Massif de l'Ospédale.

The coast between Porto-Vecchio and Solenzara is also strewn with **prehistoric monuments**. The most impressive of these, **Casteddu d'Araggiu**, lies 12km north along the D759. From the site's car park (signposted off the main road), it's a twenty-minute stiff climb through maquis and scrubby woodland to the ruins. Built in 2000 BC and inhabited by a community that lived by farming and hunting, the *casteddu* consists of a complex of chambers built into a massive circular wall of pink granite, splashed with vivid green patches of lichen, from the top of which the views over the gulf are superb.

The route de Bavella

Starting from the picture-postcard-pretty mountain village of **ZONZA**, 40km northwest of Porto-Vecchio, and running northeast towards the coast, the D268 – known locally as the **route de Bavella** – is perhaps the most dramatic road in all Corsica. Well served by buses, it also affords one of the simplest approaches to the spectacular landscapes of the interior. The road penetrates a dense expanse of old pine and chestnut trees as it rises steadily to the **Col de Bavella** (1218m), where a towering statue of **Notre-Dame-des-Neiges** marks the windswept pass itself. An amazing panorama of peaks and forests spreads out from the col: to the northwest the serrated granite ridge of the Cirque de Gio Agostino is dwarfed by the pink pinnacles of the Aiguilles de Bavella; behind soars Monte Incudine.

Just below the pass, the seasonal hamlet of **BAVELLA** comprises a handful of congenial cafés, corrugated-iron-roofed chalets and hikers' hostels from where you can follow a series of waymarked **trails** to nearby viewpoints. Deservedly the most popular of these is the two-hour walk to the **Trou de la Bombe**, a circular opening that pierces the Paliri crest of peaks. From the car park behind the *Auberge du Col* (see opposite), follow the red-and-white waymarks of GR20 for 800m, then head right when you see orange splashes. Those with a head for heights should climb right into the hole for the dizzying view down the sheer 500m cliff on the other side. Even more amazing views may be had from the summit of the adjacent peak, **Calanca Murata**, which you can scale after a steep forty-minute haul from the head of the ravine just below Trou de la Bombe. Small stone cairns mark the route. At no stage do you need to climb, but the views, which take in the entire Bavella massif to the west and a huge sweep of the eastern plains, are on a par with those from any of the island's major peaks.

From Bavella, it's a steep descent through what's left of the **Forêt de Bavella**, which was devastated by fire in 1960 but still harbours some huge Laricio pines. The winding road offers numerous breathtaking glimpses of the Aiguilles de Bavella and plenty of places to pull over for a swim in the river.

The best **place to stay** locally is Zonza, which has a cluster of hotels, all with more than decent restaurants, such as *Le Tourisme*, set back on the west side of the Quenza road north of the village (Ⓣ04.95.78.67.72, Ⓦwww.hoteldutourisme.fr; ❹; April–Oct), or *L'Aiglon* in the village centre (Ⓣ04.95.78.67.72, Ⓦwww.aiglonhotel.com; ❹; April–Oct). For hikers, clean and comfortable dormitory accommodation is available at the *Auberge du Col* (Ⓣ04.95.72.09.87, Ⓕ04.95.72.16.48; ❶; April–Oct), the best set-up of the small *gîtes d'étapes* at Bavella. Regular **buses** run to Zonza from Ajaccio, Propriano, Sartène and Porto-Vecchio; for the current timetables ask at a tourist office.

Aléria

Built on the estuary at the mouth of the River Tavignano on the island's east coast, 40km southeast of Corte along the N200, **ALÉRIA** was first settled in 564 BC by a colony of Greek Phoceans as a trading port for the copper and lead they mined and the wheat, olives and grapes they farmed. After an interlude of Carthaginian rule, the Romans arrived in 259 BC, built a naval base and re-established its importance in the Mediterranean. Aléria remained the east coast's principal port right up until the eighteenth century. Little is left of the historic town except Roman ruins and a thirteenth-century Genoese fortress, which stands high against a background of chequered fields and green vineyards. To the south, a strip of modern buildings straddling the main road makes up the modern town, known as **Cateraggio**, but it's the village set on the hilltop just west of here which holds most interest.

The best plan is to begin with the **Musée Jerôme Carcopino** (mid-May to Sept daily 8am–noon & 2–7pm; Oct to mid-May Mon–Sat 8am–noon & 2–5pm; €2), housed in the Fort Matra and crammed with remarkable finds from the **Roman site**, including Hellenic and Punic coins, rings, belt links, elaborate oil lamps decorated with Christian symbols, Attic plates and a second-century marble bust of Jupiter Ammon. Etruscan bronzes fill another room, with jewellery and armour from the fourth to the second century BC.

It's a stone's throw from here to the Roman site (closes 30min before museum; same ticket), where most of the excavation was done as recently as the 1950s, even though the French novelist Prosper Merimée had noticed signs of the Roman settlement during his survey of the island in 1830. Most of the site still lies beneath ground and is undergoing continuous digging, but the balneum (bathhouse), the base of Augustus's triumphal arch, the foundations of the forum and traces of shops have already been unearthed.

First discovered was the arch, which formed the entrance to the governor's residence – the praetorium – on the western edge of the forum. In the adjacent balneum, a network of reservoirs and cisterns, the caldarium bears traces of the underground pipes that would have heated the room, and a patterned mosaic floor is visible inside the neighbouring chamber. To the north of the site lie the foundation walls of a large house, while at the eastern end of the forum the foundations of the temple can be seen. At its northern edge, over a row of column stumps, are the foundations of the apse of an early Christian church.

Some traces of the **Greek settlement**, comprising the remains of an acropolis, have been discovered further to the east. It's believed that the main part of the town would have extended from the present site over to this acropolis and down to the Tavignano estuary. The port was located to the east of the main road, where the remnants of a second-century bathhouse have been found.

Practicalities

Aléria can be reached on any of the daily **buses** running between Bastia and the south of the island via the east coast.

Of the few **hotels** huddled around the crossroads on the highway in the modern centre of the village, *Les Orangers* (Ⓣ04.95.57.00.31, Ⓕ04.95.57.05.55; June–Sept; ❷) is the cheapest. Alternatively, *L'Empereur* (Ⓣ04.95.57.02.13, Ⓕ04.95.57.02.33; Easter to Oct; ❹), a big hotel around the corner just north of the crossroads, is clean and comfortable, with large motel-style rooms opening onto a central garden. Top of the range here is the recently refurbished three-star *L'Atrachjata*, a little further north (Ⓣ04.95.57.03.93, Ⓦwww.hotel-atrachjata.net; ❻), which is plush and fully air-conditioned.

One of the most pleasant **campsites** on the east coast lies 3km east of the Cateraggio crossroads: the *Marina d'Aléria* (Ⓣ04.95.57.01.42, Ⓕ04.95.57.04.29; Easter–Oct) backs onto the beach and is well equipped, with facilities including washing machines and refrigerated lockers.

To sample the famous oysters hauled fresh each day from the nearby lagoon, there's no better place than *Le Pieds Dans L'Eau* **restaurant** (Ⓣ04.95.57.04.55; menu at €27, plus plenty of à la carte options), resting on stilts above the water 2km north of Aléria on the main highway (look for a narrow lane turning east opposite a derelict, graffiti-covered wine warehouse). Their seafood platter – featuring clams, mussels and a terrine made from dried mullet's eggs called *poutargue* – is the kind of food one imagines the Romans must have feasted on when they farmed the *étang* two millennia ago.

Corte (Corti)

Stacked up the side of a wedge-shaped crag, against a spectacular backdrop of granite mountains, **CORTE** epitomizes *l'âme corse*, or "Corsican soul" – a small town marooned amid a grandiose landscape, where a spirit of dogged defiance and patriotism is never far from the surface. Corte has been the home of Corsican nationalism since the first National Constitution was drawn up here in 1731, and was also where **Pascal Paoli**, "U Babbu di u Patria" (Father of the Nation), formed the island's first democratic government later in the eighteenth century. Self-consciously insular and grimly proud, it can seem an inhospitable place at times, although the presence of the island's only university lightens the atmosphere noticeably during term-time, when the bars and cafés lining its long main street fill with students. For the outsider, Corte's charm is concentrated in the tranquil *haute ville*, where the forbidding **citadelle** – site of the island's premier **museum** – presides over a warren of narrow, cobbled streets. Immediately behind it, the Restonica and Tavignano gorges afford easy access to some of the region's most memorable mountain scenery, best enjoyed from the marked trails that wind through them.

Arrival, information and accommodation

Buses from Ajaccio and Bastia stop in the centre of town on avenue Xavier-Luciani; the **gare SNCF** (ⓣ04.95.46.00.97) is at the foot of the hill near the university, a ten-minute walk from the centre and campsites. If you're driving, the best place to **park** is at the top of avenue Jean-Nicoli, the road which leads into town from Ajaccio. Corte's **tourist office** is situated just inside the main gates of the citadelle, near the museum (Jan–May Mon–Fri 9am–noon & 2–6pm, plus Sat in May; June & Sept Mon–Sat 9am–1pm & 2–7pm; July & Aug daily 9am–8pm; ⓣ04.95.46.26.70, ⓦwww.corte-tourisme.com). In the same building is the information office of the **Parc Régional** (same hours and phone number).

Finding a **place to stay** can be a problem from mid-June until early September, when it's advisable to book in advance. With three **campsites** in the town, and a couple a short drive away, tent space is at less of a premium, although the sites across the river get crowded in high season.

Hotels

L'Albadu ancienne rte d'Ajaccio, 2.5km southwest of town ⓣ04.95.46.24.55, ⓕ04.95.46.13.08. Simply furnished rooms with showers (shared toilets) on a working farm-cum-equestrian centre. Warm family atmosphere, beautiful horses, fine views and top Corsican speciality food. Advance reservation essential. ❷

Dominique Colonna Vallée de la Restonica, 2km south of town ⓣ04.95.45.25.65, ⓦwww.dominique-colonna.com. The more modern of this pair of jointly owned luxury *auberges*, set amid pine woods next to the stream. With less character than its neighbour (see *La Restonica* below), but smart and efficient and with all the mod cons you'd expect of a three-star. Closed Nov to mid-March. ❼

HR allée du 9-Septembre ⓣ04.95.45.11.11, ⓕ04.95.61.02.85. This converted concrete-block *gendarmerie*, 200m southwest of the SNCF station, looks grim from the outside, but its 125 rooms are comfortable enough and its rates rock-bottom; bathroom-less options are the best deal. No credit cards. ❸

Du Nord et de l'Europe 22 cours Paoli ⓣ04.95.46.00.33, ⓦwww.hoteldunord-corte.com. Pleasant, clean place right in the centre. Despite recent renovation, the building has oodles of charm and the (variously priced) rooms are large for the tariffs. Reception in the *Café du Cours* next door. ❹

De la Paix 1 av Général-de-Gaulle ⓣ04.95.46.06.72, ⓔsocoget@wanadoo.fr. Large, smart and central, in an elegant part of town. Their pricier rooms have large balconies and TVs. No credit cards. ❹

De la Poste 2 place du Duc-de-Padoue ⓣ04.95.46.01.37. The cheapest rooms in the centre, in a huge old building that opens onto a quiet square just off the main drag. Comfortable enough, but on the gloomy side. ❷

La Restonica Vallée de la Restonica, 2km southwest from town ⓣ04.95.46.09.58, ⓦwww.aubergerestonica.com. Sumptuous comfort in a wood-lined riverside hotel set up by a former French-national footballer, Dominique Colonna, who bought it after winning the lottery. There's a large pool and garden terrace. Half board obligatory in season (€135 for two). ❺

Hostels and campsites

L'Albadu 2.5km southwest of town ⓣ04.95.46.24.55. Perfect little *camping à la ferme*, situated on a hillside above Corte. Basic, but much nicer than any of the town sites, and well worth the walk.

Gîte d'Étape U Tavignanu ("Chez M. Gambini") behind the citadelle ⓣ04.95.46.16.85. Run-of-the-mill hikers' hostel with small dorms and a relaxing garden terrace that looks over the valley. Peaceful, secluded, and the cheapest place to stay after the campsites. Follow the signs for the Tavignano trail (marked with orange spots of paint) around the back of the citadelle. €14 per bed (includes breakfast).

Restonica 500m south of the town centre. Middle-sized site on the riverside, close to town, with low terraces, plenty of shade and its own café-bar.

U Sognu rte de la Restonica ⓣ04.95.46.09.07. At the foot of the valley, a 15min walk from the centre. Has a good view of the citadelle, plenty of poplar trees for shade, and toilets in a converted barn. There's also a small bar and restaurant (in summer).

Tuani Vallée de la Restonica, 7km southeast ⓣ04.95.46.11.62. Too far up the valley without your own car, but the wildest and most atmospheric of the campsites around Corte, overlooking a rushing stream, deep in the woods. Ideally placed for an early start on Monte Rotondo. Basic facilities, although they do have a cheerful little café serving good *bruschettas* and other hot snacks.

The Town

Corte is a very small town whose centre effectively consists of one street, **cours Paoli**, which runs from place Paoli at the southern end, a tourist-friendly zone packed with cafés, restaurants and market stalls, to **place du Duc-de-Padoue**, an elegant square of *fin-de-siècle* buildings.

The old **haute ville** is next to the cours Paoli, reached by climbing one of the cobbled ramps on the west side of the street or by taking the steep rue Scoliscia from place Paoli. **Place Gaffori**, the hub of the *haute ville*, is dominated by a statue of General Gian-Pietru Gaffori pointing vigorously towards the church. On its base a bas-relief depicts the siege of the Gaffori house by the Genoese, who attacked in 1750 when the general was out of town and his wife Faustina was left holding the fort. Their house stands right behind, and you can clearly make out the bullet marks made by the besiegers.

Opposite the house is the **church of the Annunciation**, built in 1450 but restored in the seventeenth century. Inside, there's a delicately carved pulpit and a hideous wax statue of St Theophilus, patron of the town, on his deathbed. The saint's birthplace – behind the church in place Théophile – is marked by the **Oratoire St-Théophile**, a large arcaded building which commands a magnificent view across the gorges of Tavignano and Restonica.

For the best view of the citadelle, follow the signs uphill to the viewing platform, the **Belvédère**, which faces the medieval tower, suspended high above the town on its pinnacle of rock and dwarfed by the immense crags behind. The platform also gives a wonderful view of the converging rivers and encircling forest – a summer bar adds to the attraction.

Just above the place Gaffori, left of the gateway to the citadelle, stands the **Palais National**, a great, solid block of a mansion that's the sole example of Genoese civic architecture in Corte. Having served as the seat of Paoli's government for a while, it became the Università di Corsica in 1765, offering free education to all (Napoleon's father studied here). In the spirit of the Enlightenment, Franciscan monks taught the contemporary social thought of philosophers such as Rousseau and Montesquieu as well as traditional subjects like theology, mathematics and law. The university closed in 1769 when the French took over the island after the Treaty of Versailles, not to be resurrected until 1981. Today several modern buildings have been added, among them the Institut Universitaire d'Études Corses, dedicated to the study of Corsican history and culture.

The Museu di a Corsica and citadelle

The monumental gateway just behind the Palais National leads from place Poilu into Corte's Genoese citadelle, whose lower courtyard is dominated by the modern buildings of **Museu di a Corsica** (April–June 19 & Sept 20–Oct daily except Tues 10am–6pm; June 20–Sept 19 daily 10am–8pm;

Nov–March Tues–Sat 10am–6pm; €5.35), a state-of-the-art museum inaugurated in 1997 to house the collection of ethnographer Révérend Père Louis Doazan, a Catholic priest who spent 27 years amassing a vast array of objects relating to the island's traditional transhumant and peasant past. Gifted to the state in 1972, the three thousand pieces he collected remained in storage for nearly a quarter of a century until a suitable site could be found to exhibit them. The austere building certainly makes the most of its historically significant location at the heart of the island, but ultimately upstages the lacklustre selection of old farm implements, craft tools and peasant dress inside it.

The museum's entrance charge also admits you to Corte's principal landmark, the **citadelle**. The only such fortress in the interior of the island, the Genoese structure served as a base for the Foreign Legion from 1962 until 1984, but now houses a pretty feeble exhibition of nineteenth-century photographs. It's reached by a huge staircase of Restonica marble, which leads to the medieval tower known as the **Nid d'Aigle** (Eagle's Nest). The fortress, of which the tower is the only original part, was built by Vincentello d'Istria in 1420, and the barracks were added during the reign of Louis-Philippe (1830–48). These were later converted into a prison, in use as recently as World War II, when the Italian occupiers incarcerated Corsican Resistance fighters in tiny cells. Adjacent to the cells is a former **watchtower** which at the time of Paoli's government was inhabited by the hangman.

Eating and drinking

Corte has only three **restaurants** worthy of note, plus the usual handful of pizzerias and crêperies. As a rule of thumb, avoid anywhere fronted by gaudy food photographs and multilingual menus; their dishes may be cheap, but they offer poor value for money – for not much more you'll eat a lot better in one of the places listed below.

Cafés and bars

Les Délices du Palais cours Paoli. Frilly little crêperie-cum-*salon-de-thé* whose bakery sells a selection of delicious Corsican patisserie: try their *colzone* (spinach pasties), or *brocciu* baked in flaky chestnut-flour pastry.

L'Escapade place Paoli. Inexpensive crêpes from €4 to €8, but best of all are their home-made ice creams: 24 flavours, including melt-in-the-mouth watermelon (*pastèque*) and pear (*poire*).

De la Place place Paoli. On the shady side of the main square, this is the place to hole up for a spot of crowd-watching over a *barquettes de frites* (a pile of chips) and draught Pietra.

Restaurants

U Museu rampe Ribanelle in the *haute ville* at the foot of the citadelle, 30m down rue Colonel-Feracci ⓣ04.95.61.08.36. Congenial and well-situated place. Try the €15.50 *menu corse*, featuring lasagne in wild boar sauce, trout, and *tripettes* (imaginatively translated as "trips"). Their hot goat's cheese (*chèvre chaud*) salad, filling enough for two, comes on a groaning bed of richly flavoured potatoes. Great value for money, atmospheric terrace and the house wines are local AOC.

Le Paglia Orba 1 av Xavier-Luciani ⓣ04.95.61.07.89. Quality Corsican cooking at very reasonable prices, served on a raised terrace overlooking the street. Most people come for their succulent pizzas (€6–8), but they also offer plenty of choice à la carte, particularly for vegetarians. Pan-fried veal served with *stozapreti* (nuggets of *brocciu* and herbs) is their *plat de résistance*. Menus from €13.

Au Plat d'Or place Paoli ⓣ04.95.46.27.16. The classiest option in Corte: Corsican specialities made from locally produced ingredients, and served under awnings on the shady side of place Paoli. Meat and seafood dishes are their forte, but they also do pizzas, pastas and home-made desserts. Menu for €21 (four courses). Closed Sun.

Central Corsica

Central Corsica is a non-stop parade of stupendous scenery, and the best way to immerse yourself in it is to get onto the region's ever-expanding network of trails and forest tracks. The ridge of granite mountains forming the spine of the island is closely followed by the epic **GR20** footpath, which can be picked up from various villages and is scattered with refuge huts, most of them offering no facilities except shelter. For the less active there also are plenty of roads penetrating deep into the **forests** of Vizzavona, La Restonica and Rospa Sorba, crossing lofty passes that provide exceptional views across the island.

The most popular attractions in the centre, though, are the magnificent **gorges** of La Restonica and Tavignano, both within easy reach of Corte.

Gorges du Tavignano

A deep cleft of ruddy granite beginning 5km to the west of Corte, the **Gorges du Tavignano** offers one of central Corsica's great walks, marked in yellow paint flashes alongside the broad cascading River Tavignano. You can pick up the trail from opposite the Chapelle Sainte-Croix in Corte's *haute ville* and follow it as far as the Lac de Nino, 30km west of the town, where it joins the GR20. There's a refuge, *A Sega*, 15km along the route.

From the trailhead in Corte, the old mule track steadily climbs the steep left bank of the river across a bare hillside scarred with the remains of old farming terraces. Massive rocks border the river below, which you can scramble down to in places for a secluded swim. Some 5km into the walk, the gorge proper begins and the scenery becomes wilder, with rock faces surging up on each side. Passing through patches of dense maquis interspersed with evergreen oak and chestnut trees, you gradually rejoin the river, crossed at the Passarelle de Rossolino footbridge after around two and a half hours. Once on the right bank, the mountainside grows steeper as the path skirts the Ravin de Bruscu, swathed in forest that was severely damaged by fire in 2000, then winds gently above the stream to the refuge, reached after five and a half hours from Corte.

Gorges de la Restonica

The glacier-moulded rocks and deep pools of the **Gorges de la Restonica** make the D936 running southwest from Corte the busiest mountain road in Corsica – if you come in high summer, expect to encounter traffic jams all the way up to the car park at the **Bergeries de Grotelle**, 15km from Corte. **Minibuses** run from Corte to the Bergeries, costing €12; taxis charge around €35, but hitching is usually reliable. The gorges begin after 6km, just beyond where the route penetrates the **Forêt de la Restonica**, a glorious forest of chestnut, Laricio pine and the tough maritime pine endemic to Corte. Not surprisingly, it's a popular place to walk, picnic and bathe in the many pools fed by the cascading torrent of the River Restonica, easily reached by scrambling down the rocky banks.

From the *bergeries*, a well-worn path winds along the valley floor to a pair of beautiful glacial lakes. The first and larger, **Lac de Melo**, is reached after an easy hour's hike through the rocks. One particularly steep part of the path has been fitted with security chains, but the scramble around the side of the passage is perfectly straightforward, and much quicker. Once past Lac de Melo, press on for another forty minutes along the steeper marked trail over a moraine to the second lake, **Lac de Capitello**, the more spectacular of the pair. Hemmed in by vertical cliffs, the deep turquoise-blue pool affords fine views of the Rotondo massif on the far side of the valley, and in clear weather you can spend an hour or two exploring the surrounding crags, the haunt of rock pipits. Beyond here, the trail climbs higher to meet the GR20, and should only be attempted by well-equipped mountain-walkers.

Vizzavona and its forest

Monte d'Oro dominates the route south of Corte to **VIZZAVONA**, about 10km away. Shielded by trees, the village is invisible from the main road, so keep your eyes peeled for a turning on the right signposted for the train station. With its handful of *gîtes d'étape* and restaurants, Vizzavona is an ideal place to spend a few days walking in the forest, although it gets crowded in summer when it fills with hikers taking a break from the GR20, which passes nearby. The glorious **forest** of beech and Laricio pine surrounding the hamlet is among the most popular walking areas in Corsica, thanks to the easy access by main road or train. A lot of people come here to tackle the ascent of 2389-metre-high **Monte d'Oro**, but there are many less demanding trails to follow, among them the busy route to the **Cascade des Anglais**, connected to Vizzavona by the red-and-white waymarks of the GR20.

Among the **accommodation** options here, top of the range is *I Laricci* (Ⓣ04.95.47.21.12, Ⓦwww.ilaricci.com; ❺; closed Nov–March) a recently converted alpine-style hotel with pitched roofs and charming Moroccan carpets decorating the walls of its dining room. In addition to comfortable en-suite rooms, they also have beds in dorms for walkers (€29 half board). A cheaper option is *Resto-Refuge-Bar "De la Gare"* (Ⓣ & Ⓕ04.95.47.22.20; ❷; May–Oct), directly opposite the station. When full, the dormitories here are stuffy and cramped; half board (€34) isn't obligatory, which is just as well as the food isn't up to much, either. For more atmosphere, head 3km further south along the main road to the hamlet of **LA FOCE**, where the venerable old *Monte d'Oro* (Ⓣ04.95.47.21.06, Ⓦwww.monte-oro.com; ❸) occupies a prime spot overlooking the valley – with its period furniture and fittings, *fin-de-siècle* feel and magnificent terrace looking out onto the mountain, it ranks among the most congenial hotels in Corsica. Adjacent to the *Monte d'Oro*, on the main road, is a little *gîte d'étape* (Ⓣ04.95.45.25.27; ❷) that's nowhere near as gloomy as it looks and makes a handy fallback if the places down in the village are fully booked. The nearest bona fide **campsite** is the *Savaggio*, 4km north of Vizzavona (Ⓣ04.95.47.22.14; open year round); note that the train will make a special request stop at the site if you give the conductor plenty of warning.

Travel details

Note that the details apply to June–Sept only; during the winter both train and bus services are considerably scaled down.

Trains

Ajaccio to: Bastia (4 daily; 3hr 15min–3hr 30min); Calvi (2 daily; 4hr 25min–5hr); Corte (4 daily; 1hr 45min–2hr); L'Île Rousse (2 daily; 4hr); Vizzavona (4 daily; 1hr).

Bastia to: Ajaccio (2–4 daily; 3hr 10min–3hr 40min); Biguglia (2–4 daily; 10min); Calvi (2 daily; 3hr); Corte (2–4 daily; 1hr 30min); L'Île Rousse (2 daily; 2hr 30min); Ponte Leccia (2–4 daily; 1hr); Vizzavona (2–4 daily; 2hr 10min).

Calvi to: Ajaccio (2 daily; 4hr); Bastia (2 daily; 2hr 45min); Corte (2 daily; 2hr 15min); L'Île Rousse (2–10 daily; 30min).

Corte to: Ajaccio (4 daily; 1hr 30min); Bastia (4 daily; 1hr 10min); Calvi (2 daily; 2hr 30min); L'Île Rousse (2 daily; 1hr 55min); Vizzavona (4 daily; 40min).

L'Île Rousse to: Ajaccio (2 daily; 3hr 30min); Bastia (2 daily; 1hr 50min); Corte (2 daily; 1hr 45min).

Vizzavona to: Ajaccio (4 daily; 55min); Bastia (4 daily; 2hr); Corte (4 daily; 1hr); Ponte Leccia (4 daily; 1hr 15min).

Buses

Ajaccio to: Bastia (2 daily; 3hr); Bonifacio (3 daily; 4hr); Cargèse (2–3 daily; 1hr 10min); Corte (2 daily; 1hr 45min); Évisa (1–3 daily; 2hr); Porto (1–2 daily; 2hr 10min); Porto-Vecchio (2–5 daily; 3hr 10min–3hr 45min); Propriano (2–6 daily; 1hr 50min); Sartène (2–6 daily; 2hr 15min); Vizzavona (2 daily; 1hr); Zonza (3 daily; 2hr 15min–3hr).

Aléria to: Bastia (2 daily; 1hr 30min); Corte (3 weekly; 1hr 25min); Porto-Vecchio (2 daily; 1hr 20min).

Bastia to: Ajaccio (2 daily; 3hr); Bonifacio (2–4 daily; 3hr 50min); Calvi (2 daily; 2hr 20min); Centuri (3 weekly; 2hr); Corte (2–3 daily; 1hr 15min); Erbalunga (hourly; 30min); L'Île Rousse (2 daily; 1hr 40min); Porto-Vecchio (2 daily; 3hr); St-Florent (2 daily; 1hr).

Bonifacio to: Ajaccio (2 daily; 3hr 30min–4hr); Bastia (2–4 daily; 3hr 35min); Porto-Vecchio (1–4 daily; 30min); Propriano (2–4 daily; 1hr 40min–2hr 10min); Sartène (2 daily; 1hr 25min–2hr).

Calvi to: Bastia (1 daily; 2hr 15min); L'Île Rousse (2 daily; 40min); Porto (1 daily; 2hr 30min); St-Florent (1 daily; 1hr 20min).

Cargèse to: Ajaccio (1–2 daily; 1hr 10min); Porto (2–3 daily; 1hr).

Corte to: Ajaccio (2 daily; 2hr); Bastia (2 daily; 1hr 15min); Évisa (4 daily; 2hr); Porto (4 daily; 2hr 30min).

Évisa to: Ajaccio (1–3 daily; 1hr 45min).

Porto to: Ajaccio (1–2 daily; 2hr); Calvi (1 daily; 3hr); Cargèse (2–3 daily; 1hr 15min).

Porto-Vecchio to: Ajaccio (2–4 daily; 3hr 30min); Bastia (2 daily; 3hr); Bonifacio (1–4 daily; 30min); Propriano (2–4 daily; 2hr 10min); Sartène (2–4 daily; 40min).

Propriano to: Ajaccio (2–4 daily; 1hr 35min–1hr 50min); Bonifacio (2–4 daily; 2hr 15min); Porto-Vecchio (2–4 daily; 2hr 10min); Sartène (2–4 daily; 20min).

Ferries

Marseille to: Ajaccio (3–7 weekly; 11hr overnight, or 4hr 35min NGV); Bastia (1–3 weekly; 10hr); L'Île Rousse (1–3 weekly; 11hr 30min overnight); Porto-Vecchio (1–3 weekly; 14hr 30min overnight); Propriano (1 weekly; 12hr overnight).

Nice to: Ajaccio (1–6 weekly; 12hr overnight); Bastia (1–12 weekly; 6hr, or 2hr 30min NGV); Calvi (2–5 weekly; 2hr 45min NGV); L'Île Rousse (1–3 weekly; 7hr overnight, or 2hr 45min NGV).

Toulon to: Ajaccio (1–4 weekly; 10hr overnight); Bastia (1–3 weekly; 8hr 30min overnight).

Contexts

Contexts

History

As a major European power, France has had a long and colourful history, exerting influence around the world, and what follows is necessarily a brief account of major events in the country's past. For more in-depth coverage see the Rough Guide *History of France* or the choices given in "Books", p.1339.

Early civilizations

Traces of human existence are rare in France until about 50,000 BC. Thereafter, beginning with the "Mousterian civilization", they become ever more numerous, with an especially heavy concentration of sites in the Périgord region of the Dordogne, where, near the village of Les Eyzies, remains were discovered in 1868 of a late Stone Age people, subsequently dubbed "Cro-Magnon". Flourishing from around 25,000 BC, these cave-dwelling hunters seem to have developed quite a sophisticated culture, the evidence of which is preserved in the beautiful paintings and engravings on the walls of the region's caves.

By 10,000 BC human communities had spread out widely across the whole of France. The ice cap receded, the climate became warmer and wetter, and by about 7000 BC **farming and pastoral communities** had begun to develop. By 4500 BC, the first **dolmens** (megalithic stone tombs) showed up in Brittany; around 2000 BC copper made its appearance; and by 1800 BC the **Bronze Age** had arrived in the east and southeast of the country, and trade links had begun with Spain, central Europe and southern Britain.

Significant population shifts occurred, too, at this time. Around 1200 BC the **Urnfield people**, who buried their dead in sunken urns, began to make incursions from the east. By 900 BC, they had been joined by the **Halstatt people** who worked with iron and settled in Burgundy, Alsace and Franche-Comté near the principal ore **deposits**. At some point around 450 BC, the first Celts made an appearance in the region.

Pre-Roman Gaul

There were about fifteen million people living in **Gaul**, as the Romans called what we know as France (and parts of Belgium), when Julius Caesar arrived in 58 BC to complete the Roman conquest.

The southern part of this territory – more or less equivalent to modern **Provence** – had been a colony since 118 BC and exposed to the influences of Italy and Greece for much longer. **Greek colonists** had founded Massalia (Marseille) as far back as 600 BC. But even the inhabitants of the rest of the country, what the Romans called "long-haired Gaul", were far from shaggy barbarians. Though the economy was basically rural, the **Gauls** had established large **hilltop towns** by 100 BC, notably at Bibracte near Autun, where archeologists have identified separate merchants' quarters.

The Gauls also invented the barrel and soap and were skilful manufacturers. By 500 BC they were capable of making metal-wheeled carts, as was proved by the "chariot tomb" of **Vix**, where a young woman was found buried lying on a cart with its wheels removed and propped against the wall. She was wearing rich gold jewellery and next to her were Greek vases and black figure pottery, dating the burial at around 500 BC and revealing the extent of commercial relations. Interestingly, too, the Gauls' money was based on the gold staters minted by Philip of Macedon, father of Alexander the Great.

Romanization

Gallic **tribal rivalries** made the Romans' job much easier, and when at last they were able to unite under **Vercingétorix** in 52 BC, the occasion was their total and final defeat by **Julius Caesar** at the battle of **Alésia**.

This event was one of the major turning points in the history of France. **Roman victory** fixed the frontier between Gaul and the Germanic peoples at the Rhine. It saved Gaul from disintegrating because of internal dissension and made it a Roman province. During the five centuries of peace that followed, the Gauls farmed, manufactured and traded, became urbanized and educated – and learnt Latin. Roman victory at Alésia laid the foundations of modern French culture and established them firmly enough to survive the centuries of chaos and destruction that followed the collapse of Roman power.

Lugdunum (Lyon) was founded as the capital of Roman Gaul as early as 43 BC, but it was the emperors **Augustus** and **Claudius** who really set the process of **Romanization** going. Augustus founded numerous cities – including Autun, Limoges and Bayeux – built roads, settled Roman colonists on the land and reorganized the entire administration. Gauls were incorporated into the Roman army and given citizenship; Claudius made it possible for them to hold high office and become members of the Roman Senate, blurring the distinction and resentment between colonizer and colonized. Vespasian secured the frontiers beyond the Rhine, thus ensuring a couple of hundred years of peace and economic expansion.

Serious **disruptions** of the Pax Romana only began in the third century AD. Oppressive aristocratic rule and an economic crisis turned the destitute peasantry into gangs of marauding brigands – precursors of the medieval *jacquerie*. But most devastating of all, there began a series of incursions across the Rhine frontier by various restless **Germanic tribes**; first came the Alemanni, who pushed down as far as Spain, ravaging farmland and destroying towns.

In the fourth century the reforms of the emperor **Diocletian** secured some decades of respite from both internal and external pressures. Towns were rebuilt and fortified, an interesting development that foreshadowed feudalism and the independent power of the nobles since, due to the uncertainty of the times, big landed estates or *villae* tended to become more and more self-sufficient – economically, administratively and militarily.

By the fifth century, however, the Germanic invaders were back: Alans, **Vandals** and **Suevi**, with **Franks** and **Burgundians** in their wake. While the Roman administration assimilated them as far as possible, granting them land in return for military duties, they gradually achieved independence from the empire. Many Gauls, by now thoroughly Latinized, entered the service of the **Burgundian court of Lyon** or of the **Visigoth kings of Toulouse** as skilled administrators and advisers.

The Franks and Charlemagne

By 500 AD, the **Franks**, who gave their name to modern France, had become the dominant invading power. Their most celebrated king, **Clovis**, consolidated his hold on northern France and drove the Visigoths out of the southwest into Spain. In 507 he made the until-then insignificant little trading town of Paris his capital and became a Christian, which inevitably hastened the **Christianization** of Frankish society.

Under the succeeding **Merovingian** dynasty the kingdom began to disintegrate until in the eighth century the Pepin family, who were the Merovingians' chancellors, began to take effective control. In 732, one of their most dynamic scions, **Charles Martel**, reunited the kingdom and saved western Christendom from the northward expansion of Islam by defeating the Spanish Moors at the **battle of Poitiers**.

In 754 Charles's son, Pepin, had himself crowned king by the pope, thus inaugurating the **Carolingian dynasty** and establishing for the first time the principle of the divine right of kings. His son was **Charlemagne**, who extended Frankish control over the whole of what had been Roman Gaul, and far beyond. On Christmas Day in 800, he was crowned emperor of the **Holy Roman Empire**, though again, following his death, the kingdom fell apart in squabbles over who was to inherit various parts of his empire. At the Treaty of Verdun in 843, his grandsons agreed on a division of territory that corresponded roughly with the extent of modern France and Germany.

Charlemagne's administrative system had involved the royal appointment of counts and bishops to govern the various provinces of the empire. Under the destabilizing attacks of Norsemen/Vikings (who evolved into the Normans) during the ninth century, Carolingian kings were obliged to delegate more power and autonomy to these **provincial governors**, whose lands, like **Aquitaine** and **Burgundy**, already had separate regional identities as a result of earlier invasions – the Visigoths in Aquitaine, the Burgundians in Burgundy.

Gradually the power of these governors overshadowed that of the king, whose lands were confined to the Île-de-France. When the last Carolingian died in 987, it was only natural that they should elect one of their own number to take his place. This was Hugues Capet, founder of a dynasty that lasted until 1328.

The rise of the French kings

The years 1000 to 1500 saw the gradual extension and consolidation of the power of the **French kings**, accompanied by the growth of a centralized administrative system and bureaucracy. These factors also determined their foreign policy, which was chiefly concerned with restricting papal interference in French affairs and checking the English kings' continuing involvement in French territory. While progress towards these goals was remarkably steady and single-minded, there were setbacks, principally in the seesawing fortunes of the conflict with the English.

Surrounded by vassals much stronger than themselves, **Hugues Capet** and his successors remained weak throughout the eleventh century, though they made the most of their feudal rights. As dukes of the French, counts of Paris and anointed kings, they enjoyed a prestige their vassals dared not offend – not least because that would have set a precedent of disobedience for their own lesser vassals.

At the beginning of the twelfth century, having successfully tamed his own vassals in the Île-de-France, Louis VI had a stroke of luck. **Eleanor**, daughter of the powerful duke of Aquitaine, was left in his care on her father's death, so he promptly married her off to his son, the future Louis VII.

Unfortunately, the marriage ended in divorce and immediately, in 1152, Eleanor married Henry of Normandy, shortly to become **Henry II** of England. Thus the **English** crown gained control of a huge chunk of French territory, stretching from the Channel to the Pyrenees. Though their fortunes fluctuated over the ensuing three hundred years, the English rulers remained a perpetual thorn in the side of the French kings, with a dangerous potential for alliance with any rebellious French vassals.

Philippe Auguste (1179–1223) made considerable headway in undermining English rule by exploiting the bitter relations between Henry II and his three sons, one of whom was Richard the Lionheart. But he fell out with Richard when they took part in the **Third Crusade** together. Luckily, Richard died before he was able to claw back Philippe's gains, and by the end of his reign Philippe had recovered all of Normandy and the English possessions north of the Loire.

For the first time, the royal lands were greater than those of any other French lord. The foundations of a systematic administration and civil service had been established in **Paris**, and Philippe had firmly and quietly marked his independence from the papacy by refusing to take any interest in the crusade against the heretic Cathars of Languedoc. When Languedoc and Poitou came under royal control in the reign of his son Louis VIII, France was by far the greatest power in western Europe.

C

The Hundred Years War

In 1328 the Capetian monarchy had its first succession crisis, which led directly to the ruinous **Hundred Years War** with the English. Charles IV, last of the line, had only daughters as heirs, and when it was decided that France could not be ruled by a queen, the English king, **Edward III**, whose mother was Charles's sister, claimed the throne of France for himself.

The French chose **Philippe, Count of Valois**, instead, and Edward acquiesced for a time. But when Philippe began whittling away at his possessions in Aquitaine, Edward renewed his claim and embarked on war. Though, with its population of about twelve million, France was a far richer and more powerful country, its army was no match for the superior organization and tactics of the English. Edward won an outright victory at **Crécy** in 1346 and seized the port of Calais as a permanent bridgehead. Ten years later, his son, the Black Prince, actually took the French king, Jean le Bon, prisoner at the **battle of Poitiers**.

Although by 1375 French military fortunes had improved to the point where the English had been forced back to Calais and the Gascon coast, the strains of war and administrative abuses, as well as the madness of Charles VI, caused other kinds of damage. In 1358 there were **insurrections** among the Picardy peasantry (the *jacquerie*) and among the townspeople of Paris under the leadership of Étienne Marcel. Both were brutally repressed, as were subsequent risings in Paris in 1382 and 1412.

When it became clear that the king was mad, two rival camps began to vie for power: the **Burgundians**, led by the king's cousin and Duke of Burgundy, Jean sans Peur, and the **Armagnacs**, who gathered round the Duke of Orléans, Charles' brother. The situation escalated when Jean sans Peur had Orléans assassinated, and when fighting broke out between the two factions, they both called on the English for help. In 1415 Henry V of England inflicted another crushing defeat on the French army at **Agincourt**. The Burgundians seized Paris, took the royal family prisoner and recognized Henry as heir to the French throne. When Charles VI died in 1422, Henry's brother, the duke of Bedford, took over the government of France north of the Loire, while the young French heir, the Dauphin Charles, ineffectually governed the south from his refugee capital at Bourges.

At this point **Jeanne d'Arc** arrived on the scene. In 1429 she persuaded Charles to launch an aggressive campaign, helped raise the English siege of the crucial town of Orléans and had the Dauphin crowned at Reims as Charles VII. Joan fell into the hands of the Burgundians, who sold her to the English, resulting in her being tried and burnt as a heretic. But her dynamism and martyrdom raised French morale and tipped the scales against the English: except for a toehold at Calais, they were finally driven from France altogether in 1453.

By the end of the century, **Dauphiné**, **Burgundy**, **Franche-Comté** and **Provence** were under royal control, and an effective standing army had been created. The taxation system had been overhauled, and France had emerged from the Middle Ages a rich, powerful state, firmly under the centralized authority of an absolute monarch.

The Wars of Religion

After half a century of self-confident but inconclusive pursuit of military glory in Italy, brought to an end by the **Treaty of Cateau-Cambrésis** in 1559, France was plunged into another period of devastating internal conflict. The **Protestant** ideas of Luther and Calvin had gained widespread adherence among all classes of society, despite sporadic brutal attempts by François I and Henri II to stamp them out.

When **Catherine de Médicis**, acting as regent for Henri III, implemented a more tolerant policy, she provoked violent reaction from the ultra-Catholic faction led by the **Guise** family. Their massacre of a Protestant congregation coming out of church in March 1562 began a civil **War of Religion** that, interspersed with ineffective truces and accords, lasted for the next thirty years.

Well organized and well led by the Prince de Condé and Admiral Coligny, the **Huguenots** – French Protestants – kept their end up very successfully, until Condé was killed at the battle of Jarnac in 1569. Three years later came one of the blackest events in the memory of French Protestants, even today: the m**assacre of St Bartholomew's Day**. Coligny and three thousand Protestants who had gathered in Paris for the wedding of Marguerite, the king's sister, to the Protestant Henri of Navarre were slaughtered at the instigation of the Guises, and the bloodbath was repeated across France, especially in the south and west where the Protestants were strongest.

In 1584 Henri III's son died, leaving his brother-in-law, **Henri of Navarre**, heir to the throne, to the fury of the Guises and their Catholic league, who seized Paris and drove out the king. In retaliation, Henri III murdered the Duc de Guise, and found himself forced into alliance with Henri of Navarre, whom the pope had excommunicated. In 1589 Henri III was himself assassinated, leaving Henri of Navarre to become Henri IV of France. It took another four years of fighting and the abjuration of his faith for the new king to be recognized. "Paris is worth a Mass," he is reputed to have said.

Once on the throne Henri IV set about reconstructing and reconciling the nation. By the **Edict of Nantes** of 1598 the Huguenots were accorded freedom of conscience, freedom of worship in certain places, the right to attend the same schools and hold the same offices as Catholics, their own courts and the possession of a number of fortresses as a guarantee against renewed attack, the most important being La Rochelle and Montpellier.

Kings, cardinals and absolute power

The main themes of the seventeenth century, when France was largely ruled by just two kings, **Louis XIII** (1610–43) and **Louis XIV** (1643–1715), were, on the domestic front, the strengthening of the centralized state embodied in the person of the king; and in external affairs, the securing of frontiers in the Pyrenees, on the Rhine and in the north, coupled with the attempt to prevent the unification of the territories of the Habsburg kings of Spain and Austria. Both kings had the good fortune to be served by capable, hard-working ministers dedicated to these objectives. Louis XIII had **Cardinal Richelieu** and Louis XIV had cardinals **Mazarin** and **Colbert**. Both reigns were disturbed in their early years by the inevitable aristocratic attempts at a coup d'état.

Having crushed revolts by Louis XIII's brother Gaston, Duke of Orléans, **Richelieu**'s commitment to extending royal absolutism brought him into renewed conflict with the Protestants. Believing that their retention of separate fortresses within the kingdom was a threat to security, he attacked and took La Rochelle in 1627. Although he was unable to extirpate their religion altogether, Protestants were never again to present a military threat.

The other important facet of Richelieu's domestic policy was the promotion of economic self-sufficiency – **mercantilism**. To this end, he encouraged the growth of the luxury craft industries, especially textiles, in which France was to excel right up to the Revolution. He built up the navy and granted privileges to companies involved in establishing **colonies** in North America, Africa and the West Indies.

In pursuing his foreign policy objectives, Richelieu adroitly kept France out of actual military involvement by paying substantial sums to the great Swedish king and general, Gustavus Adolphus, helping him to fund wars against the Habsburgs in Germany. When in 1635, the French were finally obliged to commit their own troops, they made significant gains against the Spanish in the Netherlands, Alsace and Lorraine, and won Roussillon for France.

Richelieu died just a few months before Louis XIII in 1642. As Louis XIV was still an infant, his mother, Anne of Austria, acted as regent, served by Richelieu's protégé, **Cardinal Mazarin**, who was hated just as much as his predecessor by the traditional aristocracy and the *parlements*. These unelected bodies, which had the function of high courts and administrative councils, were protective of their privileges and angry that an upstart should receive such preferment. Spurred by these grievances, which were in any case exacerbated by the ruinous cost of the Spanish wars, various groups in French society combined in a series of revolts, known as the **Frondes**.

The first Fronde, in 1648, was led by the *parlement* of Paris, which took up the cause of the hereditary provincial tax-collecting officials – a group that resented the supervisory role of the *intendants*, who had been appointed by the central royal bureaucracy to keep an eye on them. Paris rose in revolt but capitulated at the advance of royal troops. This was quickly followed by an aristocratic Fronde, supported by various peasant risings round the country. These revolts were suppressed easily enough. They were not really revolutionary movements but, rather, the attempts of various groups to preserve their privileges in the face of the growing power of the state.

The economic pressures that contributed to their support were relieved when in 1659 Mazarin successfully brought the Spanish wars to an end with the **Treaty of the Pyrenees**, cemented by the marriage of Louis XIV and the daughter of Philip IV of Spain. On reaching the age of majority in 1661, **Louis XIV** declared that he was going to be his own man and do without a first minister. He proceeded to appoint a number of able ministers, with whose aid he embarked on a long struggle to modernize the administration.

The war ministers, Le Tellier and his son Louvois, provided Louis with a well-equipped and well-trained professional army that could muster some 400,000 men by 1670. But the principal reforms were carried out by **Colbert**, who set about streamlining the state's finances and tackling bureaucratic corruption. Although he was never able to overcome the opposition completely, he did manage to produce a surplus in state revenue. Attempting to compensate for deficiencies in the taxation system by stimulating trade, he set up a free-trade area in northern and central France, continued Richelieu's mercantilist economic policies, established the French East India Company, and built up the navy and merchant fleets with a view to challenging the world commercial supremacy of the Dutch.

These were all policies that the hard-working king was involved in and approved of. But in addition to his love of an extravagant court life at Versailles, which earned him the title of the **Sun King**, he had another obsession, ruinous to the state – the love of a prestigious military victory. There were sound political reasons for the **campaigns** he embarked on, but they did not help balance the budget.

Using his wife's Spanish connection, Louis demanded the cession of certain Spanish provinces in the Low Countries, and then embarked on a war against the Dutch in 1672. Forced to make peace at the **Treaty of Nijmegen** in 1678 by his arch-enemy, the Protestant William of Orange (later king of England), he nonetheless came out of the war with the annexation to French territory of **Franche-Comté**, plus a number of northern towns. In 1681 he simply grabbed Strasbourg, and got away with it.

In 1685, under the influence of his very Catholic mistress, Madame de Maintenon, the king removed all privileges from the **Huguenots** by revoking the Edict of Nantes. This incensed the Protestant powers, who combined under the auspices of the League of Augsburg. Another long and exhausting war followed, ending, most unfavourably for the French, in the **Peace of Rijswik** (1697).

No sooner was this concluded than Louis became embroiled in the question of who was to succeed the moribund Charles II of Spain. Both

Louis and Leopold Habsburg, the Holy Roman Emperor, had married sisters of Charles. The prospect of Leopold acquiring the Spanish Habsburgs' possessions in addition to his own vast lands was not welcome to Louis or any other European power. However, when Charles died and it was discovered that he'd named Louis' grandson, Philippe, as his heir, that was a shift in the balance of power the English, Dutch and Austrians were not prepared to tolerate.

William of Orange, now king of England as well as ruler of the Dutch United Provinces, organized a Grand Alliance against Louis. The so-called **War of the Spanish Succession** broke out and went badly for the French, thanks largely to the brilliant English general, the Duke of Marlborough. A severe winter in 1709 compounded the hardships with famine and riots at home, causing Louis to seek negotiations. The terms were too harsh for him and the war dragged on until 1713, leaving the country totally impoverished. The Sun King went out with scarcely a whimper.

Louis XV and the parlements

While France remained in many ways a prosperous and powerful state, largely because of colonial trade, the tensions between central government and traditional vested interests proved too great to be reconciled.

The parlement of Paris became more and more the focus of opposition to the royal will, eventually bringing the country to a state of virtual ungovernability in the reign of Louis XVI. Meanwhile, the diversity of mutually irreconcilable interests sheltering behind that parliamentary umbrella came more and more to the fore, bringing the country to a climax of tension which would only be resolved in the turmoil of **Revolution**.

The next king, **Louis XV**, was two when his great-grandfather died. During the **Regency**, the traditional aristocracy and the *parlements*, who for different reasons hated Louis XIV's advisers, scrambled – successfully – to recover a lot of their lost power and prestige. An experiment with government by aristocratic councils failed, and attempts to absorb the immense national debt by selling shares in an overseas trading company ended in a huge collapse. When the prudent and reasonable **Cardinal Fleury** came to prominence upon the regent's death in 1726, the nation's lot began to improve. The Atlantic seaboard towns grew rich on trade with the American and Caribbean colonies, though industrial production did not improve much and the disparity in wealth between the countryside and the growing towns continued to increase.

In mid-century there followed more disastrous military ventures, including the **War of Austrian Succession** and the **Seven Years War**, both of which were in effect contests with England for control of the colonial territories in America and India – contests that France lost. The need to finance the wars led to the introduction of a new tax, the Twentieth, which was to be levied on everyone. The *parlement*, which had successfully opposed earlier taxation and fought the Crown over its religious policies, dug its heels in again. This led to renewed conflict over Louis' pro-Jesuit religious policy. The Paris *parlement* staged a strike, was exiled from Paris, then inevitably reinstated. Disputes about its role continued until the *parlement* of Paris was actually abolished in 1771, to the outrage of the privileged groups in society, which considered it the defender of their special interests.

The division between the *parlements* and the king and his ministers continued to sharpen during the reign of **Louis XVI**, which began in 1774. Attempts by the enlightened finance minister Turgot to cooperate with the *parlements* and introduce reforms to alleviate the tax burden on the poor produced only short-term results. The national debt trebled between 1774 and 1787. Ironically, the one radical attempt to introduce an effective and equitable tax system led directly to the Revolution. Calonne, finance minister in 1786, tried to get his proposed tax approved by an **Assembly of Notables**, a device that had not been employed for more than a hundred years. His purpose was to bypass the *parlement*, which could be relied on to oppose any radical proposal. The attempt backfired. He lost his position, and the *parlement* ended up demanding a meeting of the **Estates-General**, representing the nobles, the clergy and the bourgeoisie, as being the only body competent to discuss such matters. The town responded by exiling and then recalling the *parlement* of Paris several times. As law and order began to break down, it gave in and agreed to summon the Estates-General on May 17, 1789.

Revolution

Against a background of deepening economic crisis and general misery, exacerbated by the catastrophic harvest of 1788, controversy focused on how the **Estates-General** should be constituted, and whether they should meet separately as on the last occasion in 1614. This was the solution favoured by the *parlement* of Paris, a measure of its reactionary nature: separate meetings would make it easy for the privileged, namely the clergy and nobility, to outvote the **Third Estate**, the bourgeoisie. The king ruled that they should hold a joint meeting, with the Third Estate represented by as many deputies as the other two Estates combined, but no decisions were made about the order of voting.

On June 17, 1789, the Third Estate seized the initiative and declared itself the National Assembly. Some of the lower clergy and liberal nobility joined them. Louis XVI appeared to accept the situation, and on July 9 the Assembly declared itself the National Constituent Assembly. However, the king then tried to intimidate it by calling in troops, which unleashed the anger of the people of Paris, the *sans-culottes* (literally, "without trousers").

On July 14 the *sans-culottes* stormed the fortress of the **Bastille**, symbol of the oppressive nature of the *ancien régime* (old regime). Similar insurrections occurred throughout the country, accompanied by widespread peasant attacks on landowners' châteaux and the destruction of records of debt and other symbols of their oppression. On the night of August 4, the Assembly abolished the feudal rights and privileges of the nobility – a momentous shift of gear in the Revolutionary process, although in reality it did little to alter the situation. Later that month they adopted the **Declaration of the Rights of Man**. In December church lands were nationalized, and the pope retaliated by declaring the Revolutionary principles impious.

Bourgeois elements in the Assembly tried to bring about a compromise with the nobility, with a view to establishing a constitutional monarchy, but these overtures were rebuffed. Émigré aristocrats were already working to bring about foreign invasion to overthrow the Revolution. In June 1791 the king was arrested trying to escape from Paris. The Assembly, following an initiative of the wealthier bourgeois **Girondin** faction, decided to go to war to protect the Revolution.

On August 10, 1792, the *sans-culottes* set up a **revolutionary Commune** in Paris and imprisoned the king. The Revolution was taking a radical turn. A new National Convention was elected and met on the day the ill-prepared Revolutionary armies finally halted the Prussian invasion at Valmy. A major rift swiftly developed between the more moderate **Girondins** and the **Jacobins** and *sans-culottes* over the abolition of the monarchy. The radicals carried the day. In January 1793, Louis XVI was executed. By June the Girondins had been ousted.

Counter-revolutionary forces were gathering in the provinces and abroad. A Committee of Public Safety was set up as chief organ of the government. Left-wing popular pressure brought laws on general conscription and price controls and a deliberate policy of de-Christianization, and **Robespierre** was pressed onto the Committee as the best man to contain the pressure from the streets.

The **Terror** began. As well as ordering the death of the hated queen, Marie-Antoinette, Robespierre felt strong enough to guillotine his opponents on both Right and Left. But the effect of so many rolling heads was to cool people's faith in the Revolution; by mid-1794, Robespierre himself was arrested and executed, and his fall marked the end of radicalism. More conservative forces gained control of the government, decontrolled the economy, repressed popular risings, limited the suffrage, and established a five-man executive Directory (1795).

The rise of Napoleon

In 1799, **General Napoleon Bonaparte**, who had made a name for himself as commander of the Revolutionary armies in Italy and Egypt, returned to France and took power in a coup d'état. He was appointed First Consul, with power to choose officials and initiate legislation. He redesigned the tax system and created the Bank of France, replaced the power of local institutions by a corps of *préfets* answerable to himself, made judges into state functionaries – in short, laid the foundations of the modern French administrative system.

Though Napoleon upheld the fundamental reforms of the Revolution, the retrograde nature of his regime became more and more apparent with the proscription of the Jacobins, granting of amnesty to the émigrés and restoration of their unsold property, reintroduction of slavery in the colonies, recognition of the Church and so on. Although alarmingly revolutionary in the eyes of the rest of Europe, his Civil Code worked essentially to the advantage of the bourgeoisie. In 1804 he crowned himself **emperor** in the presence of the pope.

Decline, however, came with military failure. After 1808, Spain – under the rule of Napoleon 's brother – rose in revolt, aided by the British. This signalled a turning of the tide in the long series of dazzling military successes. The nation began to grow weary of the burden of unceasing war.

In 1812, Napoleon threw himself into a **Russian campaign**, hoping to complete his European conquests. He reached Moscow, but the long retreat in terrible winter conditions annihilated his veteran Grande Armée. By 1814, he was forced to abdicate by a coalition of European powers, who installed **Louis XVIII**, brother of the decapitated Louis XVI, as monarch. In a last effort to recapture power, Napoleon escaped from exile in Elba and reorganized his armies, only to meet final defeat at **Waterloo** on June 18, 1815. Louis XVIII was restored to power.

The restoration and 1830

The years following Napoleon's downfall were marked by a determined campaign, including the **White Terror**, on the part of those reactionary elements who wanted to wipe out all trace of the Revolution and restore the *ancien régime*. **Louis XVIII** resisted these moves and was able to appoint a moderate royalist minister, Decazes, under whose leadership the liberal faction that wished to preserve the Revolutionary reforms made steady gains. This process, however, was wrecked by the assassination of the Duc de Berry in an attempt to wipe out the Bourbon family. In response to reactionary outrage, the king dismissed Decazes. An attempted liberal insurrection was crushed and the four Sergeants of La Rochelle were shot by firing squad. Censorship became more rigid and education was once more subjected to the authority of the Church.

In 1824, Louis was succeeded by the thoroughly reactionary **Charles X**, who pushed through a law indemnifying émigré aristocrats for property lost during the Revolution. When the opposition won a majority in the elections of 1830, the king dissolved the Chamber and restricted the already narrow suffrage.

Barricades went up in the streets of Paris. Charles X abdicated and parliament was persuaded to accept **Louis-Philippe,** Duc d'Orléans, as king. On the face of it, divine right had been superseded by popular sovereignty as the basis of political legitimacy. The **1814 Charter**, which upheld Revolutionary and Napoleonic reforms, was reaffirmed, censorship abolished, the tricolour restored as the national flag, and suffrage widened.

However, the **Citizen King**, as he was called, had somewhat more absolutist notions about being a monarch. In the 1830s his regime survived repeated challenges from both attempted coups by reactionaries and some serious labour unrest in Lyon and Paris. The 1840s were calmer under the ministry of **Guizot**, the first Protestant to hold high office, and it was at this time that **Algeria** was colonized.

Guizot, however, was not popular. He resisted attempts to extend the vote to enfranchise the middle ranks of the bourgeoisie. In 1846, economic crisis brought bankruptcies, unemployment and food shortages. Conditions were appalling for the growing urban working class, whose hopes of a more just future received a theoretical basis in the **socialist writings** and activities of Blanqui, Fourier, Louis Blanc and Proudhon, among others.

When the government banned an opposition *banquet* – the only permissible form of political meeting – in February 1848, workers and students took to the streets. When the army fired on a demonstration and killed forty people, civil war appeared imminent. The Citizen King fled to England.

The Second Republic

A provisional government was set up and a **republic** proclaimed. The government issued a right-to-work declaration, set up national workshops to relieve unemployment and extended the vote to all adult males – an unprecedented move for its time.

All was not plain sailing, though. By the time elections were held in April, a new tax designed to ameliorate the financial crisis had antagonized the countryside. A massive conservative majority was re-elected, to the dismay of the radicals. Three days of bloody street fighting at the barricades followed, when General Cavaignac, who had distinguished himself in the suppression of Algerian resistance, turned the artillery on the workers. More than 1500 were killed and 12,000 arrested and exiled.

A reasonably democratic constitution was drawn up and elections called to choose a president. To everyone's surprise, Louis-Napoléon, nephew of the emperor, romped home. In spite of his liberal reputation, he restricted the vote again, censored the press and pandered to the Catholic Church. In 1852, following a coup and further street fighting, he had himself proclaimed Emperor Napoléon III.

Napoléon III and the Commune

Through the 1850s, **Napoléon III** ran an authoritarian regime whose most notable achievement was a rapid growth in industrial and economic power. Foreign trade trebled, the rail system grew enormously, and the first investment banks were established. In 1858, in the aftermath of an attempt on his life by an Italian patriot, the emperor suddenly embarked on a policy of **liberalization**, initially of the economy, which alienated much of the business class. Reforms included the right to form trade unions and to strike, an extension of public education, lifting of censorship and the granting of ministerial "responsibility" under a government headed by the liberal opposition.

Disaster, however, was approaching in the shape of the **Franco-Prussian** war. Involved in a conflict with Bismarck and the rising power of Germany, Napoléon III declared war. The French army was quickly defeated and the emperor himself taken prisoner in 1870. The result at home was a universal demand for the proclamation of a **third republic**. The German armistice agreement insisted on the election of a national assembly to negotiate a proper peace treaty. France lost Alsace and Lorraine and was obliged to pay hefty war reparations.

Outraged by the monarchist majority re-elected to the new Assembly and by the attempt of its chief minister, Thiers, to disarm the National Guard, the people of Paris created their own municipal government known as the **Commune**. However, it had barely existed two months before it was savagely crushed. On May 21, the "*semaine sanglante*" began in which government troops fought with the Communards street by street, massacring around 25,000, the last of them lined up against the wall of Père Lachaise cemetery and shot. It was a brutal episode that left a permanent scar on the country's political and psychological landscape.

The Third Republic

In 1889, the collapse of a company set up to build the Panama Canal involved several members of the government in a corruption scandal, which was one factor in the dramatic **socialist gains** in the elections of 1893. More importantly, the urban working class was becoming more class-conscious under the influence of the ideas of Karl Marx. The strength of the movement, however, was undermined by divisions, the chief one being Jules Guesde's Marxian

Party. Among the independent socialists was **Jean Jaurès**, who joined with Guesde in 1905 to found the **Parti Socialiste**. The trade union movement, unified in 1895 as the **Confédération Générale du Travail** (CGT), remained aloof in its anarcho-syndicalist preference for direct action.

In 1894, **Captain Dreyfus**, a Jewish army officer, was convicted by court martial of spying for the Germans and shipped off to the penal colony of Devil's Island for life. It soon became clear that he had been framed – by the army itself – yet they refused to reconsider his case. The affair immediately became an issue between the Catholic Right and the Republican Left, with Jaurès, Émile Zola and Clemenceau coming out in favour of Dreyfus. Charles Maurras, founder of the fascist Action Française – precursor of Europe's Blackshirts – took the part of the army.

Dreyfus was officially rehabilitated in 1904, with his health ruined by penal servitude in the tropics. But in the wake of the affair the more radical element in the Republican movement had begun to dominate the administration, bringing the army under closer civilian control and dissolving most of the religious orders.

The country enjoyed a period of renewed prosperity in the years preceding World War I, yet there remained serious unresolved conflicts in the political fabric of French society. On the Right was Maurras' lunatic fringe with its strong-arm Camelots du Roi, and on the Left, the far bigger constituency of the working class – unrepresented in government. Although most workers now voted for it, the Socialist Party was not permitted to participate in bourgeois governments under the constitution of the Second International, to which it belonged. Several major strikes were brutally suppressed.

World War I

With the outbreak of **World War I** in 1914, France found itself swiftly overrun by Germany and its allies, and defended by its old enemy, Britain. At home, the hitherto anti-militarist trade union and socialist leaders (Jaurès was assassinated in 1914) rallied to the flag and to the forces.

The cost of the war was even greater for France than for the other participants because it was fought largely on French soil. Over a quarter of the eight million men called up were either killed or injured; industrial production fell to sixty percent of the prewar level. This – along with memories of the Franco-Prussian war of 1870 – was the reason that the French were more aggressive than either the British or the Americans in seeking war reparations from the Germans.

In the **postwar struggle for recovery** the interests of the urban working class were again passed over, save for Clemenceau's eight-hour-day legislation in 1919. An attempted general strike in 1920 came to nothing, and the workers' strength was again undermined by the irreversible split in the Socialist Party at the 1920 Congress of Tours. The pro-Lenin majority formed the **French Communist Party**, while the minority faction, under the leadership of Léon Blum, retained the old SFIO (Section Française de l'Internationale Ouvrière) title. The bitterness caused by this split has bedevilled the French Left ever since. Both parties resolutely stayed away from government.

As the **Depression** deepened in the 1930s and Nazi power across the Rhine became more menacing, fascist thuggery and antiparliamentary activity increased in France, culminating in a pitched battle outside the Chamber of Deputies in February 1934. The effect of this fascist activism was to unite the Left, including the Communists led by the Stalinist Maurice Thorez, in the **Front Populaire**. When they won the 1936 elections with a handsome majority in the Chamber, there followed a wave of strikes and factory sit-ins – a spontaneous expression of working-class determination to get their just desserts after a century and a half of frustration.

Frightened by the apparently revolutionary situation, the major employers signed the **Matignon Agreement** with Blum, which provided for wage increases, nationalization of the armaments industry and partial nationalization of the Bank of France, a forty-hour week, paid annual leave and collective bargaining on wages. These **reforms** were pushed through parliament, but when Blum tried to introduce exchange controls to check the flight of capital, the Senate threw the proposal out and he resigned. The Left remained out of power, with the exception of coalition governments, until 1981. Most of the Front Populaire's reforms were promptly undone.

World War II

The agonies of **World War II** were compounded for France by the additional traumas of **occupation**, **collaboration** and **Resistance** – in effect, a civil war.

After the lightning defeat of the Anglo-French forces in May–June 1940, **Maréchal Pétain**, a cautious and conservative veteran of World War I, emerged from retirement to sign an armistice with Hitler and head the collaborationist **Vichy government**, which ostensibly governed the southern part of the country, while the Germans occupied the strategic north and the Atlantic coast. Pétain's prime minister, Laval, believed it was his duty to adapt France to the new authoritarian age heralded by the Nazi conquest of Europe.

There has been endless controversy over who collaborated, how much and how far it was necessary in order to save France from even worse sufferings. One thing at least is clear: Nazi occupation provided a good opportunity for the Maurras breed of out-and-out French fascist to go on the rampage, tracking down Communists, Jews, Resistance fighters, freemasons – indeed all those who, in their demonology, were considered "alien" bodies in French society.

While some Communists were involved in the **Resistance** right from the start, Hitler's attack on the Soviet Union in 1941 freed the remainder from ideological inhibitions and brought them into the movement on a large scale. Resistance numbers were further increased by young men taking to the hills to escape conscription as labour in Nazi industry. Général de Gaulle's radio appeal from London on June 18, 1940 rallied the French opposed to right-wing defeatism and resulted in the Conseil National de la Résistance, unifying the different Resistance groups in May 1943. The man to whom this task had been entrusted was Jean Moulin, shortly to be captured by the Gestapo and tortured to death by Klaus Barbie, who was convicted for his war crimes in 1987.

Although British and American governments found him irksome, **de Gaulle** was able to impose himself as the unchallenged spokesman of the Free French, leader of a government in exile, and to insist that the voice of France be heard as an equal in the Allied councils of war. Even the Communists accepted his leadership, though he was far from representing the kind of political interests with which they could sympathize.

Thanks, however, to his persistence, representatives of his provisional government moved into liberated areas of France behind the Allied advance after D-Day, thereby saving the country from what would certainly have been at least localized outbreaks of civil war. It was also thanks to his insistence that Free French units, notably General Leclerc's Second Armoured Division, were allowed to perform the psychologically vital role of being the first Allied troops to enter Paris, Strasbourg and other emotionally significant towns in France.

The aftermath of war

France emerged from the war demoralized, bankrupt and bomb-wrecked. The only possible provisional government in the circumstances was de Gaulle's **Free French** and the Conseil National de la Résistance, which meant a coalition of Left and Right. As an opening move to deal with the mess, coal mines, air transport and Renault cars were nationalized. But a new constitution was required and **elections**, in which French women voted for the first time, resulted in a large Left majority in the new Constituent Assembly – which, however, soon fell to squabbling over the form of the new constitution. De Gaulle resigned in disgust. If he was hoping for a wave of popular sympathy, he didn't get it.

The constitution finally agreed on, with little enthusiasm in the country, was not much different from the discredited Third Republic. And the new **Fourth Republic** appropriately began its life with a series of short-lived coalitions. In the early days the foundations for welfare were laid, banks nationalized and trade union rights extended. With the exclusion of the Communists from the government in 1947, however, thanks to the Cold War and the carrot of American aid under the Marshall Plan, France found itself once more dominated by the Right.

If the post-Liberation desire for political reform was quickly frustrated, the spirit that inspired it did bear fruit in other spheres. From being a rather backward and largely agricultural economy prewar, France in the 1950s achieved enormous industrial **modernization and expansion**, its growth rate even rivalling that of West Germany at times. In foreign policy France opted to remain in the US fold, but at the same time took the initiative in promoting closer **European integration**, first through the European Coal and Steel Community and then, in 1957, through the creation of the European Economic Community.

Colonial wars

In its **colonial policy**, on the other hand, the Fourth Republic seemed firmly committed to nineteenth-century imperialism, despite the cosmetic reform of renaming the Empire the French Union.

On the surrender of Japan to the Allies in 1945, **Vietnam**, the northern half of the French Indochina colony, came under the control of Ho Chi Minh and his Communist organization Vietminh. Attempts to negotiate were bungled, and there began an eight-year armed struggle which ended with French defeat at Dien Bien Phu and partition of the country at the Geneva Conference in 1954 – at which point the Americans took over in the south, with well-known consequences.

In that year the government decided to create an **independent nuclear arsenal** and got embroiled in the **Algerian war of liberation**. The situation was complicated from the French viewpoint by the legal fiction that Algeria was a *département*, an integral part of France, and by the fact that there were a million or so settlers, or *pieds noirs*, claiming to be French, plus there was oil in the south. But by 1958, half a million troops, most of them conscripts, had been committed to the war, with all the attendant horrors of torture, massacres of civilian populations and so forth.

When it began to seem in 1958 that the government would take a more liberal line towards Algeria, the hard-line Rightists among the settlers and in the army staged a putsch and threatened to declare war on France. Général de Gaulle, waiting in the wings to resume his mission to save France, let it be known that in its hour of need and with certain conditions – ie stronger powers for the president – the country might call upon his help. Thus, on June 1, 1958, the National Assembly voted him full powers for six months and the Fourth Republic came to an end.

De Gaulle's presidency

As prime minister, then president of the **Fifth Republic** – with powers as much strengthened as he had wished – **de Gaulle** wheeled and dealed with the *pieds noirs* and Algerian rebels, while the war continued. In 1961, a General Salan staged a military revolt and set up the OAS (Secret Army Organization) to prevent a settlement. When his coup failed, his organization made several attempts on de Gaulle's life – thereby strengthening the feeling on the mainland that it was time to be done with Algeria.

An episode in the same year – covered up and censored until the 1990s – when between seventy and two hundred French Algerians were killed by the police in Paris, reinforced this feeling. This "secret massacre" began with a peaceful demonstration in protest against police powers to impose a curfew on any place in France frequented by North Africans. The police, it seems, went mad – shooting at crowds, batoning protesters and then throwing their bodies into the Seine. For weeks corpses were recovered, but the French media remained silent.

Eventually in 1962, a referendum gave an overwhelming yes to **Algerian independence**, and *pieds noirs* refugees flooded into France. Most of the rest of the French colonial empire had achieved independence by this time also, and the succeeding years were to see a resurgence of fascist and racist activity, among both the French "returnees" and the usual insular, anti-immigrant sectors. From the mid-1950s to the mid-1970s a French labour shortage led to massive recruitment campaigns for workers in North Africa, Portugal, Spain, Italy and Greece. People were promised housing, free medical care, trips home and well-paid jobs. When they arrived in France, however, these **immigrants** found themselves paid half as much as their French co-workers, accommodated in prison-style hostels and sometimes poorer than they had been at home. They had no vote, no automatic permit renewal, were subject to frequent racial abuse and assault and were forbidden to form their own organizations.

De Gaulle's leadership was haughty and autocratic in style, more concerned with *gloire* and grandeur than the everyday problems of ordinary lives. His quirky strutting on the world stage greatly irritated France's partners. He blocked British entry to the EC, cultivated the friendship of the Germans, rebuked the US for its imperialist policies in Vietnam, withdrew from NATO, refused to sign a nuclear test ban treaty and called for a "free Québec". If this projection of French influence pleased some, the very narrowly won presidential election of 1965 (in which Mitterrand was his opponent) showed that a good half of French voters would not be sorry to see the last of the general.

May 1968

Notwithstanding a certain domestic discontent, the sudden explosion of **May 1968** took everyone by surprise. Beginning with protests against the paternalistic nature of the education system by students at the University of Nanterre, the movement of revolt rapidly spread to the Sorbonne and out into factories and offices.

On the night of May 10, barricades went up in the streets of the Quartier Latin in Paris, and the CRS (riot police) responded by wading into everyone, including bystanders and Red Cross volunteers, with unbelievable ferocity. A **general strike** followed, and within a week more than a million people were out, with many factory occupations and professionals joining in with journalists striking for freedom of expression, doctors setting up new radically organized practices and so forth.

Autogestion – workers' participation – was the dominant slogan, and more than specific demands for reform, there was a general feeling that all French institutions needed overhauling.

De Gaulle seemed to lose his nerve and on May 27 he vanished from the scene. It turned out he had gone to assure himself of the support of the commander of the French army of the Rhine. On his return he appealed to the nation to elect him as the only effective barrier against left-wing dictatorship, and dissolved parliament. The frightened silent majority voted massively in his favour.

Although there were few short-term radical changes (except in education), the shock waves of May 1968 continued to be felt over the next two decades. Women's liberation, ecology groups, a relaxing of the formality of French society, a lessening of authoritarianism – all these can be traced to the heady days of May.

Pompidou and Giscard

Having petulantly staked his presidency on the outcome of yet another referendum (on a couple of constitutional amendments) and lost, de Gaulle once more took himself off to his country estate and retirement. He was succeeded as president by his business-oriented former prime minister, **Georges Pompidou**.

The new regime was devotedly capitalist, and Pompidou hoped to eradicate the memory of 1968 in the creation of wealth, property and competition. His visions, however, had little time to attain reality. Having survived an election in 1972, Pompidou died, suddenly. His successor – and the 1974 presidential election winner by a narrow margin over the socialist François Mitterrand – was the former finance minister **Valéry Giscard d'Estaing**.

Having announced that his aim was to make France "an advanced liberal society", Giscard opened his term of office with some spectacular media coups, inviting Parisian trash collectors to breakfast, visiting prisons in Lyon and addressing the nation on television from his living room every evening.

But, aside from reducing the voting age to 18 and liberalizing divorce laws, the advanced liberal society did not make a lot of progress. In the wake of the 1974 oil crisis the government introduced economic austerity measures. Giscard fell out with his ambitious prime minister, **Jacques Chirac**, who set out to challenge the leadership with his own RPR Gaullist party. And in addition to his superior, monarchical style, Giscard further compromised his popularity by accepting diamonds from the (literally) child-eating emperor of the Central African Republic, Bokassa, and by involvement in various other scandals.

The Left seemed well placed to win the coming 1978 elections, when the fragile union between the Socialists and Communists cracked, the latter fearing their roles as the coalition's junior partners. The result was another right-wing victory, with Giscard able to form a new government, with the grudging support of the RPR. Law and order and immigrant controls were the dominant features of Giscard's second term.

The Mitterrand Era, 1981–95

When François Mitterrand won the presidential elections over Giscard in 1981, inaugurating the first Socialist government for decades, the mood of euphoria was akin to that felt when Tony Blair was elected prime minister of Britain in 1997. Hopes and expectations were high. The government pledged to increase state control over industry, introduce higher taxes for the rich, devolve more power to local government, raise the living standards of the least well-off and pursue European integration. By 1984, however, the flight of capital, inflation and budget deficits had forced a complete turnaround. Prime minister **Laurent Fabius** presided over a cabinet of centrist to conservative "socialist" ministers, clinging desperately to power. The 1986 parliamentary election saw the Right, under Jacques Chirac, winning a clear majority in parliament, so beginning *cohabitation* – the head of state and head of government belonging to opposite sides of the political fence. Chirac embarked on a policy of privatization and monetary control, measures that the Left felt unable to reverse when the parliament eventually swung back the other way, two years later. The 1980s ended with the most absurd blow-out of public funds ever – the **bicentennial celebrations of the French Revolution**. They symbolized a culture industry spinning mindlessly around the vacuum at the centre of the French vision for the future. And they highlighted the contrast between the unemployed and homeless begging on the streets and the limitless cash available for prestige projects.

During this period, Jean-Marie Le Pen, extreme right-winger and leader of the racist Front National, began to attract support for his proposals that immigrants should have second-class citizenship, segregated education and separate social security. In 1991, Mitterrand sacked Socialist prime minister Michel Rocard, and appointed **Édith Cresson** as France's first woman prime minister. Her brand of left-wing nationalist rhetoric combined with centrist pragmatism made her highly unpopular at home and abroad. Furthermore, she jumped on the racism bandwagon and said that special planes should be chartered to deport illegal immigrants.

In 1992, Mitterrand staked his reputation on the important **Maastricht referendum** which was carried by a narrow margin in favour, splitting the Right and widening the gulf between the Socialists and Communists. Only the extreme end of the political spectrum, the Communists and the Front

National remained determinedly anti-Europe. The voters divided along the lines of the poorer rural areas voting "No" and the rich urbanites voting "Yes". The very narrow margin in favour was a considerable disappointment to Mitterrand.

Scandals over cover-ups and corruption that had started under Fabius continued to dog the Socialists, culminating in their rout in the 1993 parliamentary elections, and the mysterious suicide a few months later of their last prime minister, **Pierre Bérégovoy**. Ushering in another period of *cohabitation*, **Edouard Balladur**, a fresh and fatherly face from the Right, was appointed prime minister. His government carried out a new privatization programme but soon lost the respect of its natural supporters after a series of U-turns following demonstrations by Air France workers, teachers, farmers, fishermen and school pupils, and the state's rescue of the Crédit Lyonnais bank after spectacular losses.

Mitterrand tottered on to the end of his presidential term, looking less and less like the nation's favourite uncle. Two months after Bérégovoy's suicide, Réné Bousquet, head of police in the Vichy government and responsible for the rounding up of Jews in 1942, was murdered. A personal friend of Mitterrand's, he was thought to have carried shady secrets about the president to his grave. A biography of Mitterrand, *Le Grand Secret*, stirred up further controversy about the president's war record as an official in the Vichy regime before he joined the Resistance. The book was banned in France but avidly read on the Internet.

Allegations of **corruption** against mayors, members of parliament, ministers and leading figures in industry were becoming an almost weekly occurrence. In 1994 a member of parliament leading a crusade against drugs and corruption on the Côte d'Azur was assassinated. Instead of increasing democracy, decentralization appeared to have licensed fraud and nepotism on an alarming scale. Several mayors ended up in jail, but it seemed as if the Paris establishment was above the law. Meanwhile, the country's profile abroad was also suffering. In 1994, France sent troops into **Rwanda**, whose previous murderous government they had supported and armed. French troops were accused of giving protection to French-speaking Hutus responsible for the genocide, and of acting too late to save any of the English-speaking Tutsis.

By the time Mitterrand finally stepped down, he had been the French head of state for fourteen years, during a period when crime rose and increasing numbers of people found themselves excluded from society by racism, poverty and homelessness. Corruption scandals touched the president, politicians of all parties and business chiefs and, as faith in old left-wing certainties foundered, support for extreme Right policies propelled the Front National from a minority faction to a serious electoral force. Despite this, when he died in January 1996, Mitterrand was genuinely mourned as a man of culture and vision, a supreme political operator, and for his unwavering commitment to the vision of a united Europe.

Mitterand's reputation has been badly tarnished in the last few years however, with a number of scandals surfacing. These include the arrest in 2000 of his son Jean-Christophe on suspicion of selling arms to Angola, and the jailing of his ex-foreign minister and close friend Roland Dumas for his part in a huge corruption scandal involving the Elf oil company. One of the most damaging accusations to come to light is that Mitterand ordered his anti-terrorist unit, formed in 1982, to secretly tap the phones of anyone he considered a potential threat to his public image.

Chirac's presidency

Elected as president in 1995 and winning a second mandate in 2002, Chirac has shown himself every bit as astute a politician as Mitterand, and no less prone to scandal and controversy. One of the first decisions he took on election in 1995 was to delay signing the Nuclear Non-Proliferation Treaty until France had carried out a new series of **nuclear tests** in the South Pacific. This provoked almost universal condemnation, but Chirac and most of the French press gloried in Gallic isolation, with no qualms at the French navy capturing Greenpeace's *Rainbow Warrior II*, almost ten years to the day after the bombing of *Rainbow Warrior I* in Auckland harbour by French secret service agents.

On the home front, Chirac's **austerity measures**, designed to prepare France for European monetary union, provoked a series of damaging strikes in 1995 and 1996, and led to growing popular disenchantment with the idea of closer European integration. The **Front National** played up their image of standing up for the small man against the corrupt political establishment, and at municipal elections in June 1995 gained control of three towns, including the major port of Toulon. The **Algerian bomb attacks**, which rocked Paris in the mid-1990s, further played into the hands of the far Right and diminished public confidence in the government as guardians of law and order. The interior minister, **Charles Pasqua**, tapped into the general feelings of insecurity and stepped up anti-immigration measures. As a result, around 250,000 people living and working in France had their legal status removed. In March 1996 three hundred Malian immigrants, many of them failed asylum-seekers, sought refuge in a Paris church, only to be forcibly evicted by riot police.

Feeling increasingly beleaguered and unable to deliver on the economy, Chirac called a snap parliamentary election in May 1997. His gamble failed spectacularly as he saw the Right trounced by the Socialists. Chirac was forced into a weak *cohabitation* with the Socialists, headed by **Lionel Jospin**, who promptly introduced the 35-hour working week, a 50:50 gender quota for representatives of political parties and, in 1999, the **Pacs** or Pacte Civile de Solidarité, a contract giving cohabiting couples, particularly gay couples, almost the same rights as married people. Jospin's government was soon hit by a series of scandals, however, including the resignation of internationally respected finance minister Dominique Strauss-Kahn over his alleged involvement in a party-funding scandal, though he was later acquitted. In 1999, Mitterrand-era cabinet ministers went on trial for involvement in the **tainted blood** scandal of the mid-1980s, in which four thousand transfusion recipients contracted AIDS. The court doled out acquittals and suspended sentences for the three main defendants, prompting outrage from the victims and their families, and ever-growing public cynicism.

Skeletons in the mayoral cupboard

The most persistent **corruption scandals**, however, have dogged the Right, rather than the Left, focusing on the finances of the Paris town hall dating back to the 1980s. In 1995 it was revealed that Prime Minister **Alain Juppé** had rented a luxury flat in Paris for his son at below-market rates, and in 1998 the conservative Paris mayor **Jean Tiberi** was implicated in a scandal involving subsidized real-estate and fake town-hall jobs – with real salaries – for party activists and relatives. The prosecutors seemed to be edging ever closer to Chirac himself. In 2001 the president was accused of using some three million francs in cash from illegal sources to pay for luxury holidays, and in 2003 it was revealed that in eight years in office as mayor of Paris he and his wife had run up grocery bills of 2.2 million euros – over half of which had been reimbursed in cash, often against dodgy receipts. When investigating magistrates tried to question Chirac he claimed presidential immunity, a position that was upheld by France's highest court, though only as long as he remained in office. The prospect of having to stand trial if he failed to win a second mandate may well have had a galvanizing effect on Chirac's campaign for president in 2002.

The courts seemed to have toughened up by November 2003, when a vast corruption case against the formerly state-owned oil corporation Elf finally concluded with jail sentences for three top executives. Between 1989 and 1993, 350 million euros had been creamed off by senior management, much of the money used to buy political favours at home and in Africa, and to fund grotesque luxury lifestyles. For Chirac, an ominous note was sounded in 2004 when **Alain Juppé**, then mayor of Bordeaux, leader of the UMP and the president's right-hand man, was convicted of involvement in the town hall fake jobs scam. Seemingly unabashed, Chirac denounced those pursuing what he described as politically motivated campaigns that had deprived France of the services of a great man – Juppé was banned from office for ten years. In reaction to Chirac's arrogance and apparent untouchability, the left-leaning newspaper *Libération* announced the "Berlusconization" of French politics.

The election earthquake

The far-right vote was damagingly split in 1996 when Bruno Mégret, Front National leader **Jean-Marie Le Pen**'s ambitious lieutenant, formed a breakaway party. In April 1998, Le Pen was temporarily stripped of his civic rights, including the right to run as a candidate in any election, for punching a woman Socialist candidate. Many voters, previously attracted by Le Pen's undoubted charisma, fell away, and commentators declared that the far Right was finished. They were proved far wrong in the **presidential elections in the spring of 2002**.

In the early stages of the campaign it seemed that the Socialist candidate, Lionel Jospin, had a real chance of winning. He'd performed well on the economy and his hopes of victory had been bolstered by the election of Socialist **Bertrand Delanoë** as Mayor of Paris in March 2001 – the first time that the socialists had won control of the capital since the bloody uprising of the Paris Commune in 1871. In the run-up to the elections, however, Jospin's lead over Chirac dwindled. The economy began to falter, unemployment was once more on the rise and fears over crime were widespread. Jospin was also hampered by his image – he was described by one journalist as having all the charisma of a retired Swedish professor of religious studies. The backslapping, high-living Chirac, on the other hand, despite his scandal-mired background and non-existent record of achievement over the previous five years, had lost none of his ability to charm.

That they would both emerge as winners of the **first round** seemed a foregone conclusion. It was with utter shock, therefore, that the country heard the announcement on the evening of April 21 that Jospin had failed to make it through, beaten into third place by the extremist Jean-Marie Le Pen – leaving Chirac and Le Pen to stand against each other in the final run-off in May. Le Pen had won just over 17 percent, Jospin 16 and Chirac 19.67. The result, widely referred to as an "earthquake", sent shockwaves throughout the country and abroad. The left-wing *Libération* declared that France had become the "shame of democracy".

Much media space was devoted to analysing what had led to such an unexpected result. Widespread **voter apathy** and disillusionment were cited as the main culprits. Many voters had abstained or voted for marginal candidates as a way of protesting against the mainstream parties. The Left were criticized for putting up too many candidates – the Trotskyist Arlette Laguiller, for example, scored an unprecedented 5.7 percent. It was also felt that Chirac unwittingly helped Le Pen by campaigning on immigration and law and order, thus giving credibility to the very issues which formed the core of Le Pen's manifesto. Le Pen himself had fought a canny campaign, toning down his racist rhetoric and making capital out of the mainstream parties' sleaze and remoteness from ordinary people.

It was a wake-up call to the nation. On May 1, 800,000 people packed the boulevards of Paris to protest against Le Pen and his anti-immigration policies, in the biggest **demonstration** the capital had seen since the student protests of 1968. Chirac's victory in the next round was assured, with the Socialists calling on their supporters to vote for Chirac in order to keep Le Pen out. Two weeks later in the run-off, Chirac duly swept the board, winning by an unprecedented 82 percent, though the result could hardly be seen as a ringing endorsement of the incumbent. With the **parliamentary elections** still to come, Chirac's supporters rallied round to create an umbrella grouping of right-wing parties, called the **Union for a Presidential Majority**, to try and win for Chirac the majority in parliament that he'd failed to secure in 1997. The Socialists, severely shaken by Jospin's earlier defeat, were no match and the Right won, sweeping to power with 369 of the 577 seats in the National Assembly. In an attempt to address widespread concerns about lack of representation and government accountability, one of Chirac's first measures was a **devolution** bill, giving more power to 26 regional assemblies and ending centuries of central government steadily accruing power to itself.

The Iraq war

In 2003, a reinvigorated Chirac thrust himself into the international spotlight by adopting a remarkably intransigent stance over the **Iraq war**. As self-appointed spokesman for the no-sayers, notwithstanding Russia's more tersely presented opposition, Chirac declared in early March that he would wield France's Security Council veto if the US tried to table a resolution that contained an ultimatum leading to war. It was a bravura performance to an approving domestic crowd, the nationalist Right admiring Chirac's Gaullist flexing of France's international muscles and the Left reluctantly applauding his jaw-jutting opposition to American imperialism. The literary-minded foreign minister, Dominique de Villepin, commented "we find it paradoxical and contradictory to resort to force while we are making progress on disarmament". Internationally, some interpreted France's stance as a principled defence of the UN and the due process of international law, others as cynical political posturing aimed at protecting France's own interests in the region and gaining cheap domestic political support. Chirac was also playing a sophisticated game by testing the European Union's diplomatic clout and its ability to act as a balance to the trans-Atlantic superpower. With the EU soon to be enlarged to 25 – and most of the new members wedded to liberal economic policies and diplomatic subservience to the US – the old Franco-German bloc risked losing its dominant position in Europe.

Whether blamed on US bullishness or French pig-headedness, the result was an almighty farmyard scrap that left the US-led "coalition of the willing" exposed in Iraq without the diplomatic cover of definitive UN sanction. On either side of the Atlantic, the cherished Franco-American relationship suffered what was possibly its worst spat ever, with French fries renamed freedom fries in a number of US states, American tourist numbers plummeting, and all of France suffused in a kneejerk anti-American fury (though it didn't affect sales of hamburgers). The French tourist board even drafted Woody Allen in an attempt to stem the holiday haemorrhage, launching a US campaign that had the comedian saying "I don't want to have to freedom-kiss my wife when what I really want to do is French-kiss her".

One thing France's tough stance wasn't based on was any particularly pro-Arab or pro-Islamic bias, despite the presence of 5 million **Muslims** in France – the largest community in Europe. During 2003, Chirac presided over a government setting expulsion targets for illegal immigrants and enacting a hugely controversial bill – though it was backed by almost two thirds of the population and passed in parliament by 494 votes to 36 – banning "ostensibly religious" signs, notably Islamic headscarves, from schools and hospitals. Proposing the measure in December 2003, Chirac avowed that "Secularity is one of the republic's great achievements…We must not allow it to be weakened." Ironically, this principle of *laïcité* did indeed date back to the Republic's defence of religious tolerance, as well as the backlash against anti-Semitism that followed the Dreyfus affair of the 1890s (see p.1289). In early 2004, Muslim feelings were hardly mollified when the government set about deporting a number of radical imams.

Political reform and climate change

Faced with an ageing population, stubbornly high unemployment (at just under ten percent) and a budget deficit persistently exceeding the eurozone's three-percent ceiling, the newly confident Right decided it would take on France's most sacred cow: the public sector. For once, the problem wasn't so much milking it as trying to impose a milk ration on everyone else. Dubbed Agenda 2006, the **reform programme**'s targets were loathed by economic liberalizers and loved by most of the French public, and indeed the world's Left, in equal measure. First to go under the knife would be the state's generous pensions and unemployment benefits, then worker-friendly hiring and firing rights, and finally the world-leading health service. Raffarin's government insisted that there simply wasn't enough money in the pot, and that because life expectancy had increased, would-be pensioners would have to work for longer to preserve their pension at the expected level. But most of France saw the programme less as prudent milk-rationing and more as getting their sacred cow ready to be sent off to slaughter. In the spring of 2003 the country suffered wave after wave of public-sector strikes and marches rolled through the streets. The traditional Labour Day parades trebled in size to number over 300,000 marchers; two weeks later, on May 13, two million workers went out on strike; and on May 26 half a million protested in the streets of Paris. And this was only in defence of pensions, never mind the health service.

The government's assault on ingrained Gallic ways wasn't restricted to grand-scale economics. The tax on cigarettes was raised three times in 2003, making a packet cost half as much again as it had the previous year, while **speed traps** were installed on the autoroutes and Paris policemen cracked down on driving offences. The death toll on the roads dropped within a few months of the measures being introduced, but smoking-related deaths and the budget deficit are likely to prove harder to solve. By 2004, the government had curbed its ambitions, while still insisting that reform was essential. The new finance minister **Nicolas Sarkozy** – widely tipped as Chirac's successor – set out a programme of privatizations and public-sector parsimony. The health-care budget would be trimmed, but so would the defence budget, and the electorate would be further mollified by consumer-focused tax breaks. The public response was unequivocal. François Hollande, the secretary-general of the Parti Socialiste, vowed to be the first to the barricades to defend against any further assaults on the welfare state, and in the regional elections of March 2004 just one of the 22 mainland regional councils remained in the control of the centre-right. Overnight, the electoral map had turned a furious pink.

In 2003 **climate change** also bludgeoned its way onto the headlines, by indirectly causing the deaths of some 15,000 people over the norm. In Paris, temperatures in the first half of August were the hottest ever recorded, regularly topping 40°C (104°F) – more than ten degrees above the average maximum for the time of year. The authorities blamed lack of air-conditioning and the duration of the heatwave; the opposition blamed an ill-prepared health ministry. In December, flash floods once again tore through southeastern France, though it was claimed that these were the result of urban sprawl and intensive agriculture rather than abnormal rainfall. Whatever the cause, no government authority seemed willing to take responsibility for doing anything about it. As summer 2004 began to heat up, rumours spread that the health service planned to issue all those over 70 with a refreshing Evian facial spray.

Art

Since the Middle Ages, France has held – with occasional gaps – a leading position in the history of European painting, with Paris, above all, attracting artists from the whole continent. The story of French painting is one of richness and complexity, partly due to this influx of foreign painters and partly due to the capital's stability as an artistic centre.

Beginnings

In the late Middle Ages, the itinerant life of the nobles led them to prefer small and transportable works of art; splendidly **illuminated manuscripts** were much praised and the best painters, usually trained in Paris, continued to work on a small scale until the fifteenth century. In spite of the small size of the illuminated image, painters made startling steps towards a realistic interpretation of the world and in the exploration of new subject matters.

Many of these illuminators were also panel painters, foremost of whom was **Jean Fouquet** (c.1420–1481), born in Tours in the Loire valley and the central artistic personality of fifteenth-century France. Court painter to Charles VIII, Fouquet drew from both Flemish and Italian sources, utilizing the new fluid oil technique that had been perfected in Flanders, and concerning himself with the problem of representing space convincingly, much like his Italian contemporaries. Through this he moulded a distinct personal style, combining richness of surface with broad, generalized forms and, in his feeling for volume and ordered geometric shapes, laying down principles that became intrinsic to French art for centuries to come, from Poussin to Seurat and Cézanne.

Two other fifteenth-century French artists are worthy of brief mention, principally for the broad range of artistic expression they embody. **Enguerrand Quarton** (c.1410–c.1466) was the most famous Provençal painter of the time; his art, profoundly religious in subject as well as feeling, already shows the impact of the Mediterranean sun in the strong light that pervades his paintings. His *Pietà* in the Louvre is both stark and intensely poignant, while the *Coronation of the Virgin* that hangs at Villeneuve-lès-Avignon is a vast panoramic vision not only of heaven but also of a very real earth, in what ranks as one of the first city/landscapes in the history of French painting: Avignon itself is faithfully depicted and the Mont Ste-Victoire, later to be made famous by Cézanne, is recognizable in the distance.

The **Master of Moulins**, active in the 1480s and 1490s, was noticeably more northern in temperament, painting both religious altarpieces and portraits commissioned by members of the royal family or the fast-increasing bourgeoisie.

Mannerism and Italian influence

At the end of the fifteenth and the beginning of the sixteenth centuries, the French invasion of Italy brought both artists and patrons into closer contact with the Italian Renaissance.

The most famous of the artists who were lured to France was **Leonardo da Vinci**, spending the last three years of his life (1516–19) at the court of François Ier. From the Loire valley, which until then had been his favourite residence, the French king moved nearer to Paris, where he had several palaces decorated. Italian artists were once again called upon, and two of them, **Rosso** and **Primaticcio**, who arrived in France in 1530 and 1532 respectively, were to shape the artistic scene in France for the rest of the sixteenth century.

Both artists introduced to France the latest Italian style, **Mannerism**, a sometimes anarchic derivation of the High Renaissance of Michelangelo and Raphael. Mannerism, with its emphasis on the fantastic, the luxurious and the large-scale decorative, was eminently compatible with the taste of the court, and it was first put to the test in the revamping of the old Château de Fontainebleau.

There, a horde of French painters headed by the two Italians came to form what was subsequently called the **School of Fontainebleau**. Most French artists worked at Fontainebleau at some point in their career, or were influenced by its homogeneous style, but none stands out as a personality of any stature, and for the most part the painting of the time was dull and fanciful in the extreme.

Antoine Caron (c.1520–c.1600), who often worked for Catherine de Médicis, the widow of Henri II, contrived complicated allegorical paintings in which elongated figures are arranged within wide, theatre-like scenery packed with ancient monuments and Roman statues. Even the Wars of Religion, raging in the 1550s and 1560s, failed to rouse French artists' sense of drama, and representations of the many massacres then going on were detached and fussy in tone.

Portraiture tended to be more inventive. The portraits of **Jean Clouet** (c.1485–1541) and his son **François** (c.1510–72), both official painters to François Ier, combined sensitivity in the rendering of the sitter's features with a keen sense of abstract design in the arrangement of the figure, conveying with great clarity social status and giving clues to the sitter's profession. Though influenced by sixteenth-century Italian and Flemish portraits, their work remains, nonetheless, very French in its general sobriety.

The seventeenth century

In the **seventeenth century**, Italy continued to be a source of inspiration for French artists, most of whom were drawn to Rome – at that time the most exciting artistic centre in Europe, dominated by Italian painters such as Michelangelo Merisi da Caravaggio and Annibale Carracci.

Some French painters like **Moise Valentin** (c.1594–1632) worked in Rome and were directly influenced by Caravaggio; others, such as the great painter from Lorraine, **Georges de la Tour** (1593–1652), benefited from his innovations at one remove, gaining inspiration from the Utrecht Caravaggisti who were active at the time in Holland. Starting with a descriptive realism in which naturalistic detail made for a varied painted surface, La Tour gradually simplified both forms and surfaces, producing deeply felt religious paintings in which figures appear to be carved out of the surrounding gloom by the magical light of a candle. Sadly, his output was very small – just some forty or so works in all.

Lowlife subjects and attention to naturalistic detail were also important aspects of the work of the **Le Nain brothers**, especially **Louis** (1593–1648), who depicted with great sympathy, but never with sentimentality, the condition of the peasantry. He chose moments of inactivity or repose within the lives of the peasants, and his paintings achieve timelessness and monumentality by their very stillness.

The other Italian artist of influence, the Bolognese **Annibale Carracci** (d. 1609), impressed French painters not only with his skill as a decorator but, more tellingly, with his ordered, balanced landscapes, which were to prove of prime importance for the development of the classical landscape in general, and in particular for those painted by **Claude Lorrain** (1604/5–82).

Claude, who started work as a pastry cook, was born in Lorraine, near Nancy. He left France for Italy to practise his trade, and worked in the household of a landscape painter in Rome, somehow persuading his master, who painted landscapes in the classical manner of Carracci, to let him abandon pastry for painting. Later he travelled to Naples, where the beauty of the harbour and bay made a lasting impression on him, the golden light of the southern port, and of Rome and its surrounding countryside, providing him with endless subjects of study which he drew, sketched and painted for the rest of his life. Claude's landscapes are airy compositions in which religious or mythological figures are lost within an idealized, Arcadian nature, bathed in a luminous, transparent light which, golden or silvery, lends a tranquil mood.

Landscapes, harsher and even more ordered, but also recalling the Arcadian mood of antiquity, were painted by the other French painter who elected to make Rome his home, **Nicolas Poussin** (1594–1665). Like Claude, Poussin selected his themes from the rich sources of Greek, Roman and Christian myths and stories; unlike Claude, however, his figures are not subdued by nature but rather dominate it, in the tradition of the masters of the High Renaissance, such as Raphael and Titian, whom he greatly admired. During the working out of a painting Poussin would make small models, arrange them on an improvised stage and then sketch the puppet scene – which may explain why his figures often have a still, frozen quality. Poussin only briefly returned to Paris, called by the king, Louis XIII, to undertake some large decorative works quite unsuited to his style or character. Back in Rome he refined a style that became increasingly classical and severe.

Many other artists visited Italy, but most returned to France, the luckiest to be employed at the court to boost the royal images of Louis XIII and XIV and the egos of their respective ministers, Richelieu and Colbert. **Simon Vouet** (1590–1649), **Charles Le Brun** (1619–90) and **Pierre Mignard** (1612–95) all performed that task with skill, often using ancient history and mythology to suggest flattering comparisons with the reigning monarch.

The official aspect of their works was paralleled by the creation of the new **Academy of Painting and Sculpture** in 1648, an institution that dominated the arts in France for the next few hundred years, if only by the way artists reacted against it. **Philippe de Champaigne** (1602–74), a painter of Flemish origin, alone stands out at the time as remotely different, removed from the intrigues and pleasures of the court and instead strongly influenced by the teaching and moral code of Jansenism, a purist and severe form of the Catholic faith. The apparent simplicity and starkness of his portraits hides an unusually perceptive understanding of his sitters' personalities. But it was the more courtly, fun-loving portraits and paintings by such artists as Mignard that were to influence most of the art of the following century.

The early eighteenth century

The semi-official art encouraged by the foundation of the Academy became more frivolous and light-hearted in the **eighteenth century**. The court at Versailles lost its attractions, and many patrons now were to be found among the hedonistic bourgeoisie and aristocracy living in Paris. History painting, as opposed to genre scenes or portraiture, retained its position of prestige, but at the same time the various categories began to merge and many artists tried their hands at landscape, genre, history or decorative works, bringing aspects of one type into another. **Salons**, at which painters exhibited their works, were held with increasing frequency and bred a new phenomenon in the art world – the art critic. The philosopher **Diderot** was one of the first of these arbiters of taste, doers and undoers of reputations.

Possibly the most complex personality of the eighteenth century was **Jean-Antoine Watteau** (1684–1721). Primarily a superb draughtsman, Watteau's use of soft and yet rich, light colours reveals how much he was struck by the great seventeenth-century Flemish painter Rubens. The open-air scenes of flirtatious love painted by Rubens and by the fifteenth/sixteenth-century Venetian Giorgione provided Watteau with precedents for his own subtle depictions of dreamy couples (sometimes depictions of characters from the Italian Commedia dell'Arte) strolling in delicate, mythical landscapes. In some of these *Fêtes Galantes* and in pictures of solitary musicians or actors (*Gilles*), Watteau conveyed a mood of melancholy, loneliness and poignancy that was largely lacking in the works of his many imitators and followers (Nicolas Lancret, J.-B. Pater).

The work of **François Boucher** (1703–70) was probably more representative of the eighteenth century: the pleasure-seeking court of Louis XV found the lightness of morals and colours in his paintings immensely congenial. Boucher's virtuosity is seen at its best in his paintings of women, always rosy, young and fantasy-erotic.

Jean-Honoré Fragonard (1732–1806) continued this exploration of licentious themes but with an exuberance, a richness of colour and a vitality (*The Swing*) that was a feast for the eyes and raised the subject to a glorification of love. Far more restrained were the paintings of **Jean-Baptiste-Siméon Chardin** (1699–1779), who specialized in homely genre scenes and still lifes, painted with a simplicity that belied his complex use of colours, shapes and space to promote a mood of stillness and tranquillity. **Jean-Baptiste Greuze** (1725–1805) chose stories that anticipated reaction against the laxity of the times; the moral, at times sentimental, character of his paintings was all-pervasive, reinforced by a stage-like composition well suited to cautionary tales.

Neoclassicism

This new seriousness became more severe with the rise of **Neoclassicism**, a movement for which purity and simplicity were essential components of the systematic depiction of edifying stories from the classical authors. Roman history and legends were the most popular subjects, and though **Jacques-Louis David** (1748–1825), a pupil of an earlier exponent of Neoclassicism, J.M. Vien, conformed to that to a certain extent, he was different in that he was also keenly sensitive to the changing mood and philosophies of his time and to the reaction against frivolity and self-indulgence. Many of his paintings are reflections of republican ideals and of contemporary history, from the *Death of Marat* to events from the life of Napoleon, who was his patron. For the emperor and his family, David painted some of his most successful portraits – *Madame Recamier* is not only an exquisite example of David's controlled use of shapes and space and his debt to antique Rome, but can also be seen as a paradigm of Neoclassicism.

Two painters, **Jean-Antoine Gros** (1771–1835) and **Baron Gérard** (1770–1837), followed David closely in style and in themes (portraits, Napoleonic history and legend), but often with a touch of softness and heroic poetry that pointed the way to Romanticism.

Jean-Auguste-Dominique Ingres (1780–1867) was a pupil of David; he also studied in Rome before coming back to Paris to develop the purity of line that was the essential and characteristic element of his art. His effective use of it to build up forms and bind compositions can be admired in conjunction with his recurrent theme of female nudes bathing, or in his magnificent and stately portraits that depict the nuances of social status.

Romanticism

Completely opposed to the stress on drawing advocated by Ingres, two artists created, through their emphasis on colour, form and composition, pictures that look forward to the later part of the nineteenth century and the Impressionists. **Théodore Géricault** (1791–1824), whose short life was still dominated by the heroic vision of the Napoleonic era, explored dramatic themes of human suffering in such paintings as *The Raft of the Medusa*, while his close contemporary, **Eugène Delacroix** (1798–1863), epitomized the **Romantic movement** – its search for emotions and its love of nature, power and change.

Delacroix was deeply aware of tradition, and his art was influenced, visually and conceptually, by the great masters of the Renaissance and the seventeenth and eighteenth centuries. In many ways he may be regarded as the last great religious and decorative French painter, but through his technical virtuosity, freedom of brushwork and richness of colours, he can also be seen as the essential forerunner of the Impressionists. For Delacroix there was no conflict between colour and design: David and Ingres saw these elements as separate aspects of creation, but Delacroix used colours as the basis and structure of his designs. His technical freedom was partly due to his admiration for two English painters, John Constable and his close friend, Richard Parkes Bonington, with whom he shared a studio for a few months. Bonington especially had a freshness of approach to colour and a free handling of paint, both of which had a strong impact on Delacroix. His numerous themes ranged from intimate female nudes, often with mysterious and erotic Middle Eastern overtones, to studies of animals and hunting scenes. Ancient and contemporary history supplied him with some of his most harrowing and dramatic paintings: *The Massacre at Chios* was based on an event that took place during the Greek War of Independence against the Turks, and *Liberty Guiding the People* was painted to commemorate the Revolution of 1830. Both paintings were his personal response to contemporary events and the human tragedies they entailed.

Other painters working in the Romantic tradition were still haunted by the Napoleonic legends, as well as by North Africa (Algeria) and the Middle East, which had become better known to artists and patrons alike during the Napoleonic wars. These were the subjects of paintings by **Horace Vernet** (1789–1863), **Jean-Louis-Ernest Meissonier** (1815–91) and **Théodore Chassériau** (1819–56).

Among their contemporaries was **Honoré Daumier** (1808–79): very much an isolated figure, influenced by the boldness of approach of caricaturists, he was content to depict everyday subjects such as a laundress or a third-class rail car – caustic commentaries on professions and politics that work as brilliant observations of the times.

Landscape painting and realism

Some painters of the first part of the **nineteenth century** were fascinated by other themes. Nature, in its true state, unadorned by conventions, became a subject for study, and running parallel to this was the realization that painting could be the visual externalization of the artist's own emotions and feelings. These two aspects, which until this time had only been very tentatively touched upon, were now more fully explored and led directly to the innovations of the Impressionists and later painters.

Jean-Baptiste-Camille Corot (1796–1875) started to paint landscapes that were fresh, direct and influenced as much by the unpretentious and realistic country scenes of seventeenth-century Holland as by the balanced compositions of Claude. His loving and attentive studies of nature were much admired by later artists, including Monet.

At the same time a whole group of painters developed similar attitudes to landscape and nature, helped greatly by the practical improvement of being able to buy oil paint in tubes rather than as unmixed pigments. Known as the **Barbizon School** after the village on the outskirts of Paris around which they painted, they soon discovered the joy and excitement of *plein-air* (open-air) painting.

Théodore Rousseau (1812–67) was their nominal leader, his paintings of forest undergrowth and forest clearings displaying an intimacy that came from the immediacy of the image. **Charles-François Daubigny** (1817–78), like Rousseau, often infused a sense of drama into his landscapes.

Jean-François Millet (1814–75) is perhaps the best-known associate of the Barbizon group, though he was more interested in the human figure than simple nature. Landscapes, however, were essential settings for his figures; indeed, his most famous pictures are those exploring the place of people in nature and their struggle to survive. *The Sower*, for instance, was a typical Millet theme, suggesting the heroic working life of the peasant. As is so often the case for painters touching on new themes or on ideas that are uncomfortable to the rich and powerful, Millet enjoyed little success during his lifetime, and his art was only widely recognized after his death.

The moralistic and romantic undertone in Millet's work was something that **Gustave Courbet** (1819–77) strove to avoid. Courbet was a socialist and his frank, outspoken attitude led to his being accused of taking part in the destruction of the column in Paris's place Vendôme after the outbreak of the Commune and, eventually, to his exile. After an initial resounding success in the Salon exhibition of 1849, he endured constant criticism from the academic world and patrons alike: scenes of ordinary life, such as the *Funeral at Orléans*, which he often chose to depict, were regarded as unsavoury and deliberately ugly.

But Courbet had a deep admiration for the old masters, especially for Rembrandt and the Spanish painters of the seventeenth and eighteenth centuries. This link with tradition was probably one of the underlying themes of his large masterpiece, *The Studio*, which was emphatically rejected by the jury of the 1855 Exposition Universelle, and in which Courbet portrayed himself, surrounded by his model, his friends, colleagues and admirers, among them the poet Baudelaire. Courbet subsequently decided to hold a private exhibition of some forty of his works, writing at the same time a manifesto explaining his intentions of being true to his vision of the world and of creating "living art". Writing the word **Realism** in large letters on the door leading to the exhibition, he stated his intentions and gave a label to his art.

Impressionism

Like Courbet, **Edouard Manet** (1832–83) was strongly influenced by Spanish painters, whose works had become more easily accessible to artists when a large collection belonging to the Orléans family was confiscated by the state in 1848. Unlike Courbet, though, he never saw himself as a socialist or indeed as a rebel or avant-garde painter, yet his technique and interpretation of themes was quite new and shocked as many people as it inspired. Manet used bold contrasts of light and very dark colours, giving his paintings a forcefulness that critics often took for a lack of sophistication. And his detractors saw much to decry in his reworking of an old subject originally treated by the sixteenth-century Venetian painter, Giorgione, *Le Déjeuner sur l'Herbe*. Manet's version was shocking because he placed naked and dressed figures together, and because the men were dressed in the costume of the day, implying a pleasure party too specifically contemporary to be "respectable".

Manet was not interested in painting moral lessons, however, and some of his most successful pictures are reflections of ordinary life in bars and public places, where respectability, as understood by the late nineteenth-century bourgeoisie, was certainly lacking. To Manet, painting was to be enjoyed for its own sake and not as a tool for moral instruction – in itself an outlook on the role of art that was quite new, not to say revolutionary, and marked a definite break with the paintings of the past. With Manet, the basis of our present expectations and understanding of modern art was established.

From the 1870s, Manet began to adopt the **Impressionist** techniques of painting out-of-doors, and his work became lighter and freer. Although it is doubtful whether Manet either wanted or expected to assume the role of leader, he found himself a much-admired member of that group of painters, one of whom was **Claude Monet** (1840–1926). Born in Le Havre, Monet came into contact with **Eugène Boudin** (1824–98), whose colourful beach scenes anticipated the way the Impressionists approached colour. He then went to Paris to study under Charles Gleyre, a respected teacher in whose studio he met many of the people with whom he formulated his ideas. Monet soon discovered that, for him, light and the way in which it builds up forms and creates an infinity of colours was the element that governed all representations.

Under the impact of Manet's bright hues and his unconventional attitude ("art for art's sake"), Monet soon began using pure colours side by side, blended together to create areas of brightness and shade.

In 1874, a group of thirty artists exhibited together for the first time. Among them were some of the best-known names of this period of French art: Degas, Monet, Renoir, Pissarro. One of Monet's paintings was entitled *Impression: Sun Rising*, a title that was singled out by the critics to ridicule the colourful, loose and unacademic style of these young artists. Overnight they became, derisively, the "**Impressionists**".

Camille Pissarro (1830–1903) was slightly older than most of them and seems to have played the part of an encouraging father-figure, always keenly aware of any new development or new talent. Not a great innovator himself, Pissarro was a very gifted artist whose use of Impressionist technique was supplemented by a lyrical feeling for nature and its seasonal changes. But it was really with **Monet** that Impressionist theory ran its full course: he studied endlessly the impact of light on objects and the way in which it reveals colours. To understand this phenomenon better, Monet painted the same motif again and again under different conditions of light, at different times of the day, and in different seasons, producing whole series of paintings such as *Grain Stacks*, *Poplars* and, much later, his *Waterlilies*. In the late 1870s and the early 1880s many other artists helped formulate the new style, though few remained true to its principles for very long.

Auguste Renoir (1841–1919), who started life as a painter of porcelain, was swept up by Monet's ideas for a while, but soon felt the need to look again at the old masters and to emphasize the importance of drawing to the detriment of colour. Renoir regarded the representation of the female nude as the most taxing and rewarding subject that an artist could tackle. Like Boucher in the eighteenth century, Renoir's nudes are luscious, but rarely, if ever, erotic. They have a healthy, uncomplicated quality that was, in his later paintings, to become cloyingly, almost overpoweringly, sickly and sweet. Better were his portraits of women fully clothed, both for their obvious and innate sympathy and for their keen sense of design.

Edgar Degas (1834–1917) was yet another artist who, although he exhibited with the Impresssionists, did not follow their precepts very closely. The son of a rich banker, he was trained in the tradition of Ingres: design and drawing were an integral part of his art, and, whereas Monet was fascinated mainly by light, Degas wanted to express movement in all its forms. His pictures are vivid expressions of the body in action, usually straining under fairly exacting circumstances – dancers and circus artistes were among his favourite subjects, as well as more mundane depictions of laundresses and other working women.

Like so many artists of the day, Degas had his imagination fired by the discovery of **Japanese prints**, which could for the first time be seen in quantity. These provided him with new ideas of composition, not least in their asymmetry of design and the use of large areas of unbroken colour. **Photography**, too, had an impact, if only because it finally liberated artists from the task of producing accurate, exacting descriptions of the world.

Degas' extraordinary gift as a draughtsman was matched only by that of the Provençal aristocrat **Henri de Toulouse-Lautrec** (1864–1901). Toulouse-Lautrec, who had broken both his legs as a child, was unusually small, a physical deformity that made him particularly sensitive to free and vivacious movements. A great admirer of Degas, he chose similar themes: people in cafés and theatres, working women and variety dancers all figured large in his work. But, unlike Degas, Toulouse-Lautrec looked beyond the body, and his work is scattered with social comment, sometimes sardonic and bitter. In his portrayal of Paris prostitutes, there is sympathy and kindness; to study them better he lived in a brothel, revealing in his paintings the weariness and sometimes gentleness of these women.

Post-Impressionism

Though a rather vague term, as it's difficult to date exactly when the backlash against Impressionism took place, **Post-Impressionism** represents in many ways a return to more formal concepts of painting – in composition, in attitudes to subject and in drawing.

Paul Cézanne (1839–1906), for one, associated only very briefly with the Impressionists and spent most of his working life in relative isolation, obsessed with rendering, as objectively as possible, the essence of form. He saw objects as basic shapes – cylinders, cones, and so on – and tried to give the painting a unity of texture that would force the spectator to view it not so much as a representation of the world but rather as an entity in its own right, as an object as real and dense as the objects surrounding it. It was this striving for pictorial unity that led him to cover the entire surface of the picture with small, equal brush strokes which made no distinction between the textures of a tree, a house or the sky.

The detached, unemotional way in which Cézanne painted was not unlike that of the seventeenth-century artist Poussin, and he found a contemporary parallel in the work of **Georges Seurat** (1859–91). Seurat was fascinated by current theories of light and colour, and he attempted to apply them in a systematic way, creating different shades and tones by placing tiny spots of pure colour side by side, which the eye could in turn fuse together to see the colours mixed out of their various components. This **pointillist** technique also had the effect of giving monumentality to everyday scenes of contemporary life.

While Cézanne, Seurat and, for that matter, the Impressionists sought to represent the outside world objectively, several other artists – the **Symbolists** – were seeking a different kind of truth, through the subjective experience of fantasy and dreams. **Gustave Moreau** (1840–98) represented, in complex paintings, the intricate worlds of the romantic fairy tale, his visions expressed in a wealth of naturalistic details. The style of **Puvis de Chavannes** (1824–98) was more restrained and more obviously concerned with design and the decorative. And a third artist, **Odilon Redon** (1840–1916), produced some weird and visionary graphic work that especially intrigued Symbolist writers; his less frequent works in colour belong to the later part of his life.

The subjectivity of the Symbolists was of great importance to the art of **Paul Gauguin** (1848–1903). He started life as a stockbroker who collected Impressionist paintings, a Sunday artist who gave up his job in 1883 to dedicate himself to painting.

During his stay in Pont-Aven in Brittany, Gauguin worked with a number of artists who called themselves the **Nabis**, among them **Paul Sérusier** and **Émile Bernard**. He began exploring ways of expressing concepts and emotions by means of large areas of colour and powerful forms, and developed a unique style that was heavily indebted to his knowledge of Japanese prints and of the tapestries and stained glass of medieval art. His search for the primitive expression of primitive emotions took him eventually to the South Sea islands and Tahiti, where he found some of his most inspiring subjects and painted some of his best-known canvases.

A similar derivation from Symbolist art and a wish to exteriorize emotions and ideas by means of strong colours, lines and shapes underlies the work of **Vincent Van Gogh** (1853–90), a Dutch painter who came to live in France. Like Gauguin, with whom he had an admiring but stormy friendship, Van Gogh started painting relatively late in life, lightening his palette in Paris under the influence of the Impressionists, and then heading south to Arles where, struck by the harshness of the Mediterranean light, he turned out such frantic expressionistic pieces as *The Reaper* and *Wheatfield with Crows*. In all his later pictures the paint is thickly laid on in increasingly abstract patterns that follow the shapes and tortuous paths of his deep inner melancholy.

Both Gauguin and Van Gogh saw objects and colours as means of representing ideas and subjective feelings. **Édouard Vuillard** (1868–1940) and **Pierre Bonnard** (1867–1947) combined this with Cézanne's insistence on unifying the surface and texture of the picture. The result was, in both cases, paintings of often intimate scenes in which figures and objects are blended together in a series of complicated patterns. In some of Vuillard's works, people dressed in checked material, for example, merge into the flowered wallpaper behind them, and in the paintings of Bonnard, the glowing design of the canvas itself is as important as what it's trying to represent.

The twentieth century and contemporary art

The **twentieth century** kicked off to a colourful start with the **Fauvist** exhibition of 1905, an appropriately anarchic beginning to a century which, in France above all, was to see radical changes in attitudes towards painting. The painters who took part in the exhibition included, most influentially, **Henri Matisse** (1869–1954), **André Derain** (1880–1954), **Georges Rouault** (1871–1958) and **Albert Marquet** (1875–1947), and they were quickly nicknamed the Fauves (Wild Beasts) for their use of bright, wild colours that often bore no relation whatsoever to the reality of the object depicted. Skies were just as likely to be green as blue since, for the Fauves, colour was a way of composing, of structuring a picture, and not necessarily a reflection of real life. Raoul Dufy (1877–1953) used Fauvist colours in combination with theories of abstraction to paint an effervescent industrial age.

Fauvism was just the beginning: the first decades of the twentieth century were times of intense excitement and artistic activity in Paris, and painters and sculptors from all over Europe flocked to the capital to take part in the liberation from conventional art that individuals and groups were gradually instigating. **Pablo Picasso** (1881–1973) was one of the first, arriving in Paris in 1900 from Spain and soon thereafter starting work on his first Blue Period paintings, which describe the sad and squalid life of itinerant actors in tones of blue. Later, while Matisse was experimenting with colours and their decorative potential, Picasso came under the sway of Cézanne and his organization of forms into geometrical shapes. He also learned from "primitive", and especially African, sculpture, and out of these studies came a painting that heralded a definite new direction, not only for Picasso's own style but for the whole of modern art – *Les Demoiselles d'Avignon*. Executed in 1907, this painting combined Cézanne's analysis of forms with the visual impact of African masks.

It was from this semi-abstract picture that Picasso went on to develop the theory of **Cubism**, inspiring artists such as **Georges Braque** (1882–1963) and **Juan Gris** (1887–1927), another Spaniard, and formulating a whole new movement. The Cubists' aim was to depict objects not so much as they saw them but rather as they knew them to be: a bottle and a guitar were shown from the front, from the side and from the back as if the eye could take in all at once every facet and plane of the object. Braque and Picasso first analysed forms into these facets (analytical Cubism), then gradually reduced them to series of colours and shapes (synthetic Cubism), among which a few recognizable symbols such as letters, fragments of newspaper and numbers appeared. The complexity of different planes overlapping one another made the deciphering of Cubist paintings sometimes difficult, and the very last phase of Cubism tended increasingly towards abstraction.

Spin-offs of Cubism were many: such movements as **Orphism**, headed by **Robert Delaunay** (1885–1941) and **Francis Picabia** (1879-1953), who experimented not with objects but with the colours of the spectrum, and **Futurism**, which evolved first in Italy, then in Paris, and explored movement and the bright new technology of the industrial age. **Fernand Léger** (1881–1955), one of the main exponents of the so-called School of Paris, had also become acquainted with modern machinery during **World War I**, and he exploited his fascination with its smoothness and power to create geometric and monumental compositions of technical imagery that were indebted to both Cézanne and Cubism.

The war, meanwhile, had affected many artists: in Switzerland, **Dada** was born out of the scorn artists felt for the petty bourgeois and nationalistic values that had led to the bloodshed, a nihilistic movement that sought to knock down all traditionally accepted ideas. It was best exemplified in the work of the Frenchman **Marcel Duchamp** (1887–1968), who selected everyday objects ("ready-mades") and elevated them, without modification, to the rank of works of art simply by taking them out of their ordinary context and putting them on display – his most notorious piece was a urinal which he called *Fontaine* and exhibited in New York in 1917. His conviction that art could be made out of anything was to have a huge influence on later twentieth-century artists, especially conceptual artists, for whom "art as idea" was key.

Dada was a literary as well as an artistic movement, and through one of its main poets, André Breton, it led to the inception of **Surrealism**. It was the unconscious and its dark unchartered territories that interested the Surrealists: they derived much of their imagery from Freud and even experimented in words and images with free-association techniques. Strangely enough, most of the "French" Surrealists were foreigners, primarily the German **Max Ernst** (1891–1976) and the Spaniard **Salvador Dalí** (1904–89), though Frenchman **Yves Tanguy** (1900–55) also achieved international recognition. Mournful landscapes of weird, often terrifying images evoked the landscape of nightmares in often very precise details and with an anguish that went on to influence artists for years to come. **Picasso**, for instance, shocked by the massacre at the Spanish town of Guernica in 1936, drew greatly from Surrealism to produce the disquieting figures of his painting of the same name.

World War II interrupted Paris's position as the artistic melting pot of Europe. Artists had rushed there at the beginning of the twentieth century and after World War I, contributing by their individuality, originality and different nationalities to the richness and constant renewal of artistic endeavour.

Although at the outbreak of World War II many artists emigrated to the US, where the economic climate was more favourable, Paris remained full of vibrant new work. Sculptors like the Romanian **Brancusi** (1876–1957) and the Swiss **Giacometti** (1886–1966) lived most of their lives in Paris, for example.

The last coherent French art movement of the century, largely of the 1950s and 1960s, was **Nouveau Réalisme**, similar to Pop Art, which concentrated on the distortion of the objects and signs of contemporary culture, and loosely encompassed artists and sculptors such as Dubuffet, Arman, César, Jean Tinguely and Niki de Saint-Phalle.

Jean Dubuffet (1901–85) pioneered the depreciation of traditional artistic materials and methods, fashioning junk, tar, sand and glass into the shape of human beings. His work (which provoked much outrage) influenced both the French-born American, **Arman** (b.1928), and **César** (b.1921), both of whom made use of scrap metals – their output ranging from presentations of household debris to towers of crushed cars. Even more controversially, the Swiss **Daniel Spoerri** (b.1930) used the remnants – including the crockery – of his dinners and glued them onto a canvas.

Nouveau Réaliste sculpture is best represented by the works of another Swiss, **Jean Tinguely** (1925–91), whose work was concerned mainly with movement and the machine, satirizing technological civilization. His most famous work, executed in collaboration with **Niki de Saint-Phalle** (b.1926), is the exuberant fountain outside the Pompidou Centre, featuring fantastical birds and beasts shooting water in all directions.

Loosely associated with the Nouveaux Réalistes, though resisting all classification, **Yves Klein** (1928–1962) laid the foundations for several currents in contemporary art. He is seen as a precursor of Minimalism thanks to his exhibition "Le Vide" in 1958, in which he redefined the void and the immaterial as having a pure energy. He was fascinated by the colour blue, which he considered to possess a spiritual quality. He even patented his own colour, International Klein Blue, a deep and luminous blue which he used to execute a series of monochromes. He also used the colour in a series of "body prints", in which he covered female models with paint and got them to leave their imprints on paper, prefiguring body and performance art.

A number of artists keen to experiment with **conceptual art** banded together in the 1960s and became known as the **BMPT**, from the surnames of Daniel Buren, Olivier Mosset, Michel Parmentier and Niele Toroni. They rejected the prevailing notion that painting was dead, though were against personal expression and traditional methods, focusing instead on colour and the reconfiguring of the canvas to create three-dimensional structures. The best-known of the four, **Daniel Buren**, caused a furore in 1986 with his installation in the courtyard of the Palais Royal consisting of numerous black-and-white, vertically striped columns of differing heights. His work was widely criticized and vilified by the press. Now, however, in his sixties, the one-time *enfant terrible* of the art world has become one of France's most respected living artists – a status confirmed by a one-man show at the Pompidou Centre in 2002.

Other movements that have emerged in the last few decades have been smaller and less coherent. The two most significant are **Supports-Surfaces** and the graffiti-inspired **Figuration Libre**. The geometrically abstract Supports-Surfaces emerged in Nice in 1969, founded by the likes of **Claude Villat** (b.1936), and represented in sculpture by **Jean-Pierre Pincemin** (b.1944). The Nantes artist **Jean-Charles Blais** (b.1956) is one of the leaders of Figuration Libre (which began in 1981), and is known for high-relief abstracts which combine traditional painting techniques with the montage of found objects.

A recent trend has been towards massive *mise-en-scène* works, such as **Christian Boltanski**'s (b.1944) large, auto-referential installations, or the work of the Bulgarian **Christo** (b.1935) and his wife and collaborator **Jeanne-Claude** (b.1935), who cover buildings using different materials, and wrapped Paris's Pont-Neuf in woven polyamide fabric in 1985, in order to focus attention on the structure itself rather than its function. **Jean-Marc Bustamante** (b.1952) constructs *in situ* installations, using building materials in his art, while **Jean-Luc Vilmout** (b.1952) often co-opts the buildings themselves, resulting in a blurring of the aesthetic and the functional. **Annette Messager**'s (b.1943) large-scale installations use everyday objects to create unsettling works, often challenging perceptions of women. Another artist whose work explores feminist themes is **Louise Bourgeois** (b.1911), now in her nineties, but still prolific, producing oddly erotic and remarkable combinations of wrought iron, old clothes and other material.

Younger artists rapidly making a name for themselves include **Pierre Huyghe** (b.1962), who uses video to explore the relationships between reality and fiction, history and memory, often taking film clips as his source material. **Fabrice Hybert** (b.1961) also works with video, as well as other media. His work taps into what he describes as the "enormous reservoir of the possible". At the Venice Biennale in 1997 he set up a working television studio, broadcasting alongside the national channels, with which the public could freely interact. **Marie Ange Guilleminot** (b.1960) challenges the role of the observer, involving them in the act of creation. In one of her recent projects inspired by a visit to the Hiroshima peace memorial, children were invited to come and make origami birds, eventually to form part of a monument to be sent to Japan, commemorating the loss of children's lives as a result of war. Finally, in painting, the Lyonnais **Marc Desgrandchamps** (b.1960) is a name to look out for, although he may be hard to spot given that his work runs a gamut of styles from abstract to photorealism.

Architecture

France's architectural legacy is rich and important, reflecting the power and personality of successive kings, the Church and the state, vying to outdo their peers with bold, lavish statements in brick and stone. Many architectural trends filtered into France from Italy – Romanesque, Renaissance and Baroque – but they have been refined and developed by the French. Rococo grew from Baroque, Neoclassicism came from the Renaissance, and Art Nouveau was a brilliant, confused jumble of Baroque features combined with the newly developed cast-iron industry. Architecture in the twentieth century produced two great names – Auguste Perret and Le Corbusier – but France's contemporary scene is still thriving, with a host of new developments throughout the country.

The Romans

The south of France was colonized by the **Romans** by around 120 BC in order to expand their trading operations, and they set up substantial settlements at Marseille, Narbonne, Orange, Arles, Fréjus, Glanum near St-Rémy, and Nice, with a network of roads linking them.

The Romans were fine town-planners, linking complexes of buildings with straight roads punctuated by decorative fountains, arches and colonnades. They built essentially in the Greek style, and their large, functional buildings were concerned more with strength and solidity than aesthetic. A number of substantial Roman building works survive: in **Nîmes** you can see the Maison Carrée, the best-preserved Roman temple still standing, and the Temple of Diana, one of just four vaulted Roman temples in Europe. Gateways remain at **Autun**, **Orange**, **Saintes** and **Reims**, and largely intact amphitheatres can be seen at Nîmes and **Arles**. The **Pont du Gard** aqueduct outside Nîmes is still a magnificent and ageless monument of civil engineering, built to carry the town's fresh water over the gorge, and Orange has its massive theatre, with Europe's only intact Roman facade. There are excavated archeological sites at **Glanum** near St-Rémy, **Vienne**, **Vaison-la-Romaine** and **Lyon**.

Carolingian and Romanesque

The **Carolingian dynasty** of Charlemagne attempted a revival of the symbols of civilized authority by recourse to Roman or "**Romanesque**" (ninth to twelfth centuries) models. Of this era, practically nothing remains visible, though the motifs of arch and vault are carried on in their simplest forms, and the semicircular apse and the basilican plan of nave and aisles persist as the basis of the succeeding phases of Christian architecture. An interesting anomaly is the plan of the **church of St-Front** at Périgueux, a copy of St Mark's in Venice, brought by trading influence west along the Garonne in the early twelfth century.

Elsewhere development may be divided roughly north–south of the Loire. Southern Romanesque is naturally more Roman, with stone barrel vaults, aisleless naves and domes. **St-Trophime** at Arles (1150) has a porch directly derived from Roman models and, with the church at St-Gilles nearby, exhibits a delight in carved ornament peculiar to the south at this time. The cathedral at **Angoulême** typifies the use of all these elements.

The south, too, was the readiest route for the introduction of new cultural developments, and it's here that the pointed arch and vault first appear – from Spanish Muslim sources – in churches such as **Notre-Dame** at Avignon, the cathedral at **Autun** and **Ste-Madeleine** at Vézelay (1089–1206), which contains the earliest pointed cross vault in France.

In the north of the country, the nave with aisles is more usual, together with the development of twin western towers to mask the end of the aisles. The **Abbaye aux Hommes** at Caen (1066–77) is typical. It contains the elements later developed as "Gothic", in piers, pillars, buttresses, arcades, ribbed vaults and spires. The best examples are found in Normandy, and it's from here, with the introduction of the pointed arch from the south, that the Gothic style developed.

Gothic

The reasons behind the development of the **Gothic style** (twelfth to sixteenth centuries) lie in the pursuit of the sublime; to achieve great height without apparent great weight would seem to imitate religious ambition. Its development in the north is partly due to the availability of good building stone and soft stone for carving, but perhaps more to the growth of royal aspiration and power based in the Île de France, which, allied with the papacy, stimulated the building of the great **cathedrals** of Paris, Bourges, Chartres, Laon, Le Mans, Reims and Amiens in the twelfth and thirteenth centuries.

The Gothic phase began with the building of the choir of the **abbey of St-Denis** near Paris in 1140, and ran through to the end of the fifteenth century. Architecturally, it encompasses the development of wider, traceried windows of coloured glass, filling the wall spaces liberated by the refinement of vertical structure; the "rose" or wheel is an early and especially French feature in window tracery. The glass at Chartres shows better than anywhere the concerted architectural effect of these developments. Another distinctive element is the flying buttress outside the walls to resist the outward push of the vaulting.

In the south, as at Albi and Angers, the great churches are generally broader and simpler in plan and external appearance, with aisles often almost as high as the nave. Many secular buildings survive – some of the most notable in their present form being the work of Viollet-le-Duc, the pre-eminent nineteenth-century restorer – and even whole towns, for example **Carcassonne** and **Aigues Mortes**; **Avignon** has the bridge and the papal palace.

Castles, of necessity, lent themselves less to the disappearing walls of the Gothic style. The **Château de Pierrefonds**, as restored by Viollet, may be taken as typical. The walls of many others disappeared by force, not whim, as gunpowder made them obsolete and a more settled and subjugated order led to the development of château-palaces, such as **Châteaudun** and **Blois**. The **Château de Josselin** in Brittany is a marvellous example of the smaller fortresses that became common towards the end of the Gothic period. In addition, a series of colonial settlements, the **bastides**, or fortified towns, of the English occupation, remain in the Dordogne region and are a refreshing antidote to triumphal French bombast.

Renaissance

French military adventures in Italy in the early sixteenth century hastened the arrival of a new style borrowing heavily from the Italian **Renaissance**. Coupled with the persistence of Gothic traditions and the necessity of steep roofs and tall chimneys in the French climate, it appears immediately "Frenchified" rather than in its pure imported form. The châteaux of kings and courtiers in the area round Paris and in the Loire valley, such as **Blois**, **Chambord** and **Chenonceau**, exemplify this style, with their wholly un-Italian concentration of interest on the skyline and an elaboration of detail in the facades at the expense of the clear modelling of form. The wing of the **Château de Blois** containing the famous staircase designed for François Ier in 1515 shows a characteristic new emphasis on horizontal lines, but the many Italian motifs are still overlaid on a basically Gothic form. With the passing of time, however, the dominant style in France became more purely classical; an adjacent wing at Blois, designed by **Mansart** in 1635, is still distinctively French, but much more true to classical principles. Above all, the **Louvre** embodies the whole history of the classical style in France, having been worked over by all the grand names of French architecture from Lescot in the early sixteenth century, via François Mansart and Claude Perrault in the seventeenth, to the later years of the nineteenth century.

It's unfortunate that the Renaissance style in France is chiefly seen in giant structures such as the Louvre and Versailles, which because of their scale can scarcely be experienced as buildings. That this is the case is largely due to the developing despotism and concentration of power under Louis XIII and Louis XIV. But there was a lighter side. François Mansart, at Blois and **Maisons Lafitte** (1640), shows a certain suavity and elegance, attitudes that appear again in the eighteenth century in the town houses of the Rococo period. On the other hand, **Claude Perrault** (1613–88), who designed the great colonnaded east front of the Louvre, gives an austere face to the official architecture of despotism, magnificent but far too imperial to be much enjoyed by common mortals. The high-pitched roofs, which had been almost universal until then, are replaced here by the classical balustrade and pediment, the style grand but cold and supremely secular. Art and architecture were at the time organized by boards and academies, including the Académie Royale d'Architecture, and style and employment were strictly controlled by royal direction. Between 1643 and 1774 France was governed by two monarchs who both ruled by the same maxim – absolute power. With such a limitation of ideas at the source of patronage, it's hardly surprising that there was a certain dullness to the era.

Baroque

In a similar way to the preceding century, the churches of the **seventeenth and eighteenth centuries** have a coldness quite different from the German, Flemish and Italian **Baroque**. When the Renaissance style first appeared in the early sixteenth century, there was no great need for new church building, the country being so well endowed from the Gothic centuries. **St-Étienne-du-Mont** (1517–1620) and **St-Eustache** (1532–89), both in Paris, show how old forms persisted with only an overlay of the new style.

It was with the Jesuits in the seventeenth century that the Church embraced the new style to combat the forces of rational disbelief. In Paris the churches of the **Sorbonne** (1653) and **Val-de-Grâce** (1645) exemplify this, as do a good number of other grandiose churches in the **Baroque** style, through **Les Invalides** at the end of the seventeenth century to the **Panthéon** of the late eighteenth century. Here is the Church triumphant, rather than the state, but no more beguiling.

The architect of Les Invalides was **Jules Hardouin Mansart**, a product of the Académie Royale d'Architecture, which harked back to the ancient, classical tradition. Mansart also greatly extended the palace of **Versailles** and so created the Cinemascope view of France with that seemingly endless horizon of royalty. As an antidote to this pomposity, the **Petit Trianon** at Versailles is as refreshing now as it was to Louis XV, who had it built in 1762 as a place of escape for his mistress. This is even more true of that other pearl formed of the grit of boredom in the enclosed world of Versailles – **La Petite Ferme**, where Marie-Antoinette played at being a milkmaid, which epitomizes the Arcadian and "picturesque" fantasy of the painters Boucher and Fragonard.

The lightness and charm that was undermining official grandeur with Arcadian fancies and **Rococo** decoration was, however, snuffed out by the Revolution. There's no real Revolutionary architecture, as the necessity of order and authority soon asserted itself and an autocracy every bit as absolute returned with Napoleon, drawing on the old grand manner but with a stronger trace of the stern old Roman. One architect, **Claude Ledoux**, was highly original and influential, both in England and Germany. And the visionary millennialist **Boullée** could also be said to be a child of Revolutionary times, though it's likely that such men were inspired as much by the rediscovered plainness of the Greek Doric order as by radical politics.

In Paris it was not the democratic Doric but the imperial Corinthian order that re-emerged triumphant in the church of the **Madeleine** (1806) and, with the **Arc de Triomphe** like some colossal paperweight, reimposed the authority of academic architecture in contrast to the fancy-dress structures of contemporary Regency England.

The nineteenth century

The restoration of legitimate monarchy after the **fall of Napoleon** stimulated a revival of interest in older Gothic and early Renaissance styles, which offered a symbol of dynastic reassurance not only to the state but also to the newly rich. So in the private and commercial architecture of the nineteenth century these earlier styles predominate – in mine-owners' villas and bankers' headquarters.

This traditional style was also favoured by **Baron Haussmann** (1809–1891), the architect who transformed Paris over a period of twenty years. He got rid of the city's narrow streets and cramped medieval buildings, and replaced them with wide boulevards, large squares and imposing edifices, largely creating the modern city we see today.

By the mid-nineteenth century, a neo-Baroque strain had established itself, a style exemplified by Charles Garnier's Opéra in Paris (1861–74), which, under the heading of Second Empire and with its associations of voluptuous good living, seductive painting and general "ooh-la-la", provides probably the most persistent image of France among the non-French.

In addition to the correct, official Classicism and the robust, exuberant and commercial Baroque, there is a third strand running through the nineteenth century that was ultimately more fruitful. The rational engineering approach, embodied in the official **School of Roads and Bridges** and invigorated by the teaching of Viollet-le-Duc, who reinterpreted Gothic style as pure structure, led to the development of new techniques out of which "modern" architectural style was born. Iron was the first significant new material, often used in imitation of Gothic forms and destined to be developed as an individual architectural style in America. In the **Eiffel Tower** (1889), France set up a potent symbol of things to come.

A more significantly French development was in the use of reinforced concrete towards the end of the century, most notably by **Auguste Perret**, whose 1903 apartment house at 25 rue Franklin in Paris turns the concrete structure into a visible virtue and breaks with conventional facades. Changes in the patterns of work and travel were making the need for new urban planning very acute in such cities as Paris. Perret and other **modernists** were all for the high-rise buildings that were going to better the haphazard layouts in America by a rational integration to new street systems. Some of their designs for gigantic skyscraper avenues and suburban rings now look like totalitarian horror-movie sets. But it was tradition, not charity, that blocked their projects at the time.

The twentieth century and beyond

The greatest proponent of the super New York scale, who also had genuine if mistaken concern for how people lived, was **Le Corbusier**, the most famous **twentieth-century** French architect. His stature may now appear diminished by the ascendancy of a blander style in concrete boxing, as well as by the significant technical and social failures of his buildings and his total disregard for historic streets and monuments.

But while his manifesto, *Vers une architecture moderne*, sounds like a call to arms for a new and revolutionary movement, Le Corbusier should perhaps be more fairly assessed as the original, inimitable and highly individual artist he undoubtedly was. You should try to see some of his work – there's the Cité **Radieuse** in Marseille and plenty of examples in Paris – to make up your own mind about the man largely responsible for changing the face and form of buildings throughout the world.

One respect in which Paris at the turn of the century lagged behind London, Glasgow, Chicago and New York was in **underground transport**. First proposed in the 1870s, it took twenty years of furious debate before the Paris métro was finally realized in 1900. The design of the entrances was as controversial as every other aspect of the system, but the first commission went to **Hector Guimard**, renowned for his variations on the then-current fashion in style. The whirling metal railings, Art Nouveau lettering and bizarre antennae-like orange lamps were his creation. Conservatives were less amused when it came to sites such as the Opéra. **Charles Garnier**, architect of that edifice, demanded classical marble and bronze porticoes for every station, and his line was followed, on a less grandiose scale, wherever the métro steps surfaced by a major monument, and putting Guimard out of a job. Some of the early ones remain (**Place des Abbesses** is one), as do some of the white-tiled interiors, replaced after World War II in central stations by bright paint with matching seats and display cases.

Art Nouveau designs also found their way onto buildings – the early department stores in Paris, such as Printemps and La Samaritaine, are the best examples – but the new materials and simple geometry of the modern or International Style favoured the **Art Deco** look; again, you're most likely to come across them in the capital.

The miserable 1950s and 1960s buildings found all over the country are probably best skipped over. From the 1970s onwards, however, France again established itself as one of the most exciting patrons of international **contemporary architecture**. The **Pompidou Centre**, by **Renzo Piano** and **Richard Rogers**, derided, adored and visited by millions, maximizes space by putting the service elements usually concealed in walls and floors on the outside. The visible ducts, cables and pipes are painted in accordance with the colour code of architectural plans. You might think the whole thing is a professional in-joke, but the Pompidou Centre is one of the great contemporary buildings in western Europe – for its originality, popularity and practicality.

Paris was the focus of more innovative and exciting architecture in the 1980s with President Mitterand's *grands projets* ("grand projects"). One of his most ambitious projects was to extend the grand axis from the Louvre to the Arc de Triomphe westwards with the **Grande Arche de la Défense**, symbol of the new La Défense business district. Designed by Von Spreckelsen, the Grande Arche isn't really an arch but a huge hollow cube aligned with the Arc de Triomphe and conceived as an open gateway or window to the world. Mitterand also left his stamp at the other end of the grand axis with Ieoh Ming Pei's glass **pyramid** in the Cour Napoléon, the main entrance to the Louvre. Hugely controversial at first, it's now widely accepted and admired. The pyramid was just one part of a bigger project, the "Grand Louvre", designed to free up more exhibition space. As part of the reorganization, the **Ministry of Finance** moved out of their coveted offices, thus clearing the Richelieu wing of the Louvre for museum use. The Ministry decamped to a new building in **Bercy** designed by Paul Chemetov and nicknamed the "steamboat" because of its titanic length and its anchoring in the Seine. It's just one of many new buildings that have recently gone up in Bercy, formerly full of wine warehouses and now extensively redeveloped. The district's centrepiece is the Parc de Bercy, lined with neo-Haussmanian buildings and containing Frank Gehry's (architect of Bilbao's Guggenheim Museum) free-form, exuberant American Centre.

One of Mitterand's pet projects was the **Opéra Bastille**, intended as a "modern and popular" alternative to the Opéra Garnier. It was built by the young Uruguayan Carlos Ott, who was selected because his design seemed to make best use of the quirkily shaped site. The resulting building, divided into simple volumes, the most visible of which is the cylindrical extension housing the 2700-seat auditorium, met with mixed responses however, and was thought by many to be too large for the space. The building hasn't weathered particularly well either: bits of the facade's sheathing have started coming away and are being temporarily held in place with unsightly netting. The auditorium does have good acoustics however, nearly all the seats have frontal views of the stage and it's packed most nights.

Rather more successful is the **Cité de la Musique**, commissioned from acclaimed architect Christian de Portzamparc. The complex, which includes a grand concert hall, music conservatoire and museum, is designed, metaphorically, like a symphony, made up of many instruments and sounds to create a harmonious ensemble. The Cité is the finishing touch to the **Parc**

de la Villette complex which was built under Giscard d'Estaing on the site of an old abattoir, and which also houses the Cité des Sciences and Bernard Tschumi's 21 "*folies*" of urban life. Perhaps the most outstanding of Mitterand's grands travaux is the **Institut du Monde Arabe** by **Jean Nouvel**, France's most eminent contemporary architect, with a design which ingeniously marries high-tech architecture and motifs from traditional Arabic culture. In a reference to the decorative wooden sunscreens used in Islamic countries, the facade is patterned with geometric metal screens punctured with apertures that are supposed to work a bit like a camera lens, opening and closing in response to the amount of sunlight received (though in fact the computer-operating system is unreliable).

Mitterand's last project was the **Bibliothèque Nationale**. Designed by Dominique Perrault, it's made up of four L-shaped tower blocks, resembling four open books, set around an inaccessible sunken garden. This apparently facile design is made up for by the complexity (and expense) of the detail. The aluminium shutters are covered in rare *oukoumé* reddish wood, which contrasts with the grey *ipé* and yellow *doussié* wood, to give the impression from a distance that the towers are bookshelves containing different bound volumes. Two-thirds of the library's 11 million books are stored in the basement; indeed, Perrault has likened his design to an iceberg, with much of its volume invisible beneath the towers. The Bibliothèque forms a central part of the **Paris Rive Gauche** project, an ongoing development of the 13e arrondissement. The scheme, which includes a new university, as well as housing and office space, has proceeded in a rather piecemeal fashion, widely criticized as a series of botches and corrections, with no overall vision or coherent plan.

Outside Paris, the latest state-funded projects confirm French seriousness about innovative design. In Marseille there's Will Alsop's mammoth seat of regional government, while the first cathedral to be built in France since the nineteenth century, the **Cathédrale d'Évry**, masterminded by Swiss Mario Botta and finished in 1995, is a huge cylindrical red-brick tower which, besides being a place of worship, houses an art centre, concert hall and cinema screen. Its roof is slanted at 45 degrees to receive more light, and is crowned by 24 trees emulating the laurel wreaths of Roman emperors Hadrian and Augustus. Its stained-glass window is at the foot of the building and symbolizes the roots of a tree. The new **European Parliament** building in Strasbourg, designed by the Architecture Studio group, was finished in 1997, and is a huge boomerang-shaped structure with a glass dome and metal tower. It sits across the river from the eccentric, high-tech Richard Rogers-designed **European Court of Human Rights**.

Museums continue to attract innovative architects. In Nîmes, Norman Foster's **Carré d'Art** modern art museum (1993), is characterized by its simple transparent design, while his **Musée de Préhistoire des Gorges du Verdon** (2001) in Provence uses local materials – part of the museum is folded into the landscape and blends on one side into an existing stone wall, while the entrance hall resembles the very caves the museum celebrates. **Jean Nouvel's Quai Branly** museum, on the banks of the Seine beside the Eiffel Tower, is due to open in 2005. Housing the arts of Asia, Africa and Oceania, the museum will resemble a long walkway and will be set in a lush garden designed by Gilles Clément, who landscaped the Parc André Citroën.

In **housing**, new styles and forms are to be seen in city suburbs and vacation resorts, many of them disastrous and visually unappealing, but interesting to look at when you don't have to live there. One of the largest projects of recent years is the **Antigone** development in Montpellier, laid out by the Catalan architect **Ricardo Bofill**. It's a whole new district, with shops, schools and leisure facilities with the buildings all in Neoclassical style, a welcome change from the usual featureless tower blocks, though some find it unsettlingly reminiscent of fascist architecture of the 1930s.

The country's ever-advancing transport network has provided sites for some of the most high-tech office buildings with state-of-the-art engineering in Europe, as in **Roissy**, around the Charles-de-Gaulle airport and especially at **Euralille**, the large urban complex around Lille's TGV/Eurostar station, masterminded by Dutch architect Rem Koolhaas.

The French are also very good at preserving the past – too good, some would say. A passion for restoring "*la patrimoine*" results in many fine old buildings being practically rebuilt – the dominant restoration theory in France is to restore to perfection rather than halt decay. More often than not, restoration is carried out by the **Maisons de Compagnonage**, the old craft guilds, which have maintained traditional building skills, handing them down as of old from master to apprentice (and never to women), while also taking on new industrial skills.

Cinema

The first (satisfied) cinema audience in the world was French. Screened to patrons of the Grand Café, on Paris's boulevard des Capucines, in December 1895, Louis **Lumière**'s single-reelers may have been jerky documentaries, but they were light-years ahead of anything that had come before. Soon after, Georges Méliès' magical-fantastical features were proving a big hit with theatre audiences, and the twin cinematic poles of Realism and Surrealism had been established. France took to cinema with characteristic enthusiasm and seriousness. Ciné-clubs were formed all over the country, journals were published, critics made films and film-makers became critics. The avant-garde wing of French cinema acquired the moniker of **French Impressionism**, a genre characterized by experimental directors such as Louis Delluc, Jean Epstein and Abel Gance, who used experimental, highly visual techniques to express altered states of consciousness. It was only a short step from here to the all-out **Surrealism** of the artist-polymath Jean Cocteau, and the Spanish director Luis Buñuel.

Towards the end of the 1920s, histrionic adaptations of novels, epic historical dramas and broad comedies attracted mass audiences, but the silent heyday ended abruptly with the advent of sound in 1929. Most silent stars faded into obscurity, but a number of directors successfully made the transition, notably Jean Renoir, the son of the painter, René Clair, Julien Duvivier, Jean Gremillon and Abel Gance. Among the newcomers were Jean Vigo, who died young in 1934, and Marcel Carné, who worked with the powerful scripts of the poet Jacques Prévert. The film-makers of the 1930s developed a bold new style, dubbed **Poetic Realism** for its pessimism, powerful visual aesthetic – high-contrast, often nocturnal – and devotion to "realistic", usually working-class, settings.

In 1936 the collector Henri Langlois set up the **Cinémathèque Française**, devoted to the preservation and screening of old and art films – an indication of the speed with which the "*septième art*" had found its niche within the pantheon of French culture. Langlois played an important role in saving thousands of films from destruction during the war, but the Occupation had surprisingly little effect on the industry. Renoir and Clair sought temporary sanctuary in Hollywood, and domestic production dipped, but hundreds of films continued to be made in Vichy France at a time when audiences sought the solace and comfort of the cinema in record numbers.

Post-war and pre-television, the late 1940s and early 1950s was another boom time for French cinema. Poetic Realism morphed into **film noir**, whose emphasis on darkness and corruption gave birth in turn to the thriller, a genre exemplified by the films of Henri-Georges Clouzot and Jean-Pierre Melville. During this period the mainstream cinema industry became highly organized and technically slick, older directors such as Clair, Renoir and Jacques Becker making superbly controlled masterpieces spanning genres as diverse as thrillers, comedies and costume dramas.

The first shot of the coming revolution – a warning shot only – was fired by the acerbic young critic François Truffaut, writing in the legendary film magazine, **Les Cahiers du cinéma**, in the mid-1950s. In opposition to what he and fellow critics dubbed *la tradition de qualité*, Truffaut envisaged a new kind of cinema based on the independent vision of a writer-director, an *auteur* (author), who would make films in a purer and and more responsive manner. Directors such as Melville and Louis Malle – who made his first film with the diver Jacques Cousteau – were beginning to make moves in this direction, but Truffaut's vision was only fully realized towards the end of the decade, when the **Nouvelle Vague** ("New Wave") came rolling in. Claude Chabrol's *Les Cousins*, Truffaut's own *Les Quatre-cents coups*, Eric Rohmer's *Le Signe du lion*, Alain Resnais' *Hiroshima mon amour* and Jean-Luc Godard's *À bout de souffle* were all released in 1959. The trademark freedom of these *auteur*-directors' films – loosely scripted, highly individualistic and typically shot on location – ushered in the modern era.

The 1960s was the heyday of the *auteur*. Truffaut established his pre-eminent status by creating an extraordinary oeuvre encompassing science fiction, thriller, autobiography and film noir, all his films characteristically elegant and excitingly shot. But the "new wave" hadn't carried all before it: René Clément, Henri-Georges Clouzot and even Jean Renoir were still working throughout the decade, Jean-Pierre Melville continued shooting his characteristically noir **films policiers** (crime-thrillers), and the Catholic director Robert Bresson carried on making films on his favourite theme of salvation. And Jacques Tati, the maverick genius behind the legendary comic character M. Hulot, made two of his greatest and most radical quasi-silent films, *Playtime* and *Trafic*, at either end of the 1960s.

The 1970s is probably the least impressive decade in terms of output, but a shot in the arm was delivered in the 1980s by the **Cinéma du Look**, a genre epitomized in the films of Jean-Jacques Beineix, Luc Besson and Leos Carax. Stylish, image-conscious and postmodern, films such as *Diva* or *Betty Blue* owed much to the look of American pulp cinema and contemporary advertising. Meanwhile, throughout the 1980s and into the 1990s, high-gloss costume dramas – historical or adaptations of novels – were the focus of much attention. Often called **Heritage Cinema**, the best films of this genre are the superbly crafted creations of Claude Berri, though Jean-Pierre Rappeneau's *Cyrano de Bergerac* is probably the internationally recognized standard-bearer. At the other end of the scale lies **cinéma beur**: naturalistic, socially responsible and low-budget films made by French-born film-makers of North African origin – *les beurs* in French slang. The newest trends in contemporary art cinema follow a related path of social realism. In recent years, a number of younger directors, notably Mathieu Kassovitz, have made films set in the deprived suburbs (*la banlieue*), creating a number of sub-genres that have been acclaimed variously as **New Realism**, **cinéma de banlieue** and **le jeune cinéma** ("young cinema").

Today, France remains the second-largest exporter of films in the world. The industry's continued health is largely due to the intransigence of the French state, which continues to protect and promote domestic cinema as part of its policy of **l'exception culturelle** – despite the complaints of the free-marketeers who would have the French market "liberalized". Half of the costs of making a feature film in France are paid for by state subsidies, levied on television stations, box-office receipts and video sales. Currently, American-made films capture around 50 percent of the French market, while home-grown productions make up around 40 percent. But the future looks promising: recent years have seen the number of films made in France rise to almost two hundred a year, most of them domestically funded.

Note that the **films reviewed below** are only intended to give an overview of the landmarks of French cinema; we can't review every Godard film or every much-loved classic, nor cover every significant director. Alternative English titles are given for those films renamed for the main foreign release. Films marked ★ are highly recommended.

The classic era

Silent films

Lumière and Méliès Early Lumière films such as *L'Arrivé d'un train en gare* (1895) don't have the same impact now as when they made audiences jump with fright, but *L'Arroseur arrosé* (1896) works around a tight narrative that is still entertaining – a boy plays a prank on a gardener doing the watering and is chased and punished. By contrast with Lumière's documentary approach, Méliès's early short films, such as *Le Voyage dans la lune* (1902), used studio sets to create groundbreaking magical-surreal effects.

Paris qui dort/The Crazy Ray René Clair, 1924. Clair's first feature was heavily indebted to Surrealism. An inventor activates a ray that suspends time across the entire city of Paris – giving Clair plenty of opportunities to try out trick photography. Only a few Parisians are unaffected, including the watchman on top of the Eiffel Tower. Liberated from their inhibitions, they go on a criminal rampage.

Nana Jean Renoir, 1926. Second son of the painter Auguste Renoir, the greatest of France's early directors began his career making silent movies, of which the best is this ambitious and complex adaptation of Zola's novel, *Nana*. Fans of Renoir's later work may find the film's style surprisingly mannered, especially the performance of his wife Catherine Hessling, which owes a lot to Expressionist cinema.

★ **Un Chapeau de paille d'Italie** René Clair, 1927. As the film opens, the hero's horse eats the straw hat (*chapeau de paille*) of a young woman in the Bois de Boulogne, thus setting in motion a fast-paced and farcical chain of events as he attempts to find a replacement hat while simultaneously trying to get to his own wedding.

Napoléon vu par Abel Gance/Napoleon Abel Gance, 1927. This five-hour masterpiece is often called the greatest silent flick ever made, and not just because of its length. A histrionic thread of nationalism runs throughout, but the epic scale and use of experimental techniques such as split screen, superimposition and horseback-mounted camerawork – for chase scenes – make this one of the most ambitious films ever made.

La Passion de Jeanne d'Arc Carl Dreyer, 1927. Restricting himself to the events of Jeanne's trial and execution, Danish director Dreyer focuses on both the saint's physical and spiritual anguish at the hands of the intractable church authorities. Amidst bleached-out interiors, the slow tracking shots and unflinching close-ups – in particular of Renée Falconetti's extraordinarily expressive face – create an atmosphere of almost unbearable intensity.

★ **Un Chien andalou/An Andalusian Dog** Luis Buñuel, 1929. Made in collaboration with Salvador Dali, this short opens with a woman's eye being cut into with a razorblade. While it doesn't get any less weird or shocking for the rest of its twenty-minute length, it's surprisingly watchable – when it came out, it was a big hit at Paris's Studio des Ursulines cinema. Buñuel further developed his Surrealist techniques in the feature-length talkie *L'Age d'or* (1930), which was banned shortly after its first screening at Montmartre's Studio 38.

Le Sang d'un poète/Blood of a Poet Jean Cocteau, 1930. A response to Buñuel's *L'Age d'or*, this early, dreamy short by the poet-director mixes autobiographical events and documentary footage with mind-grabbing Surrealist images, leaving the viewer as unsure as the hero about what is real and what is fantasy. Indelibly stamped with Cocteau's hallmark camp morbidness.

Poetic Realism

Le Million René Clair, 1931. In 1930 Clair had made the first great French talkie, *Sous les toits de Paris*, using a montage of songs, sounds and images, but it wasn't until *Le Million* that the true musical film was born – there's more singing than dialogue. A hunt for a lost winning lottery ticket provides plenty of opportunity for madcap comedy, suspense and romance. Not exactly a Poetic Realist film, but essential 1930s viewing anyway.

★ **L'Atalante** Jean Vigo, 1934. Aboard a barge, a newly married couple struggle to reconcile themselves to their new situation. Eventually, the wife, Juliette, tries to flee, but is brought back by the unconventional deck-hand, Père Jules, superbly portrayed by the great Michel Simon. This sensual and naturalistic portrait of a relationship was made just before Vigo died, and is his only feature film.

La Belle équipe/They Were Five Julien Duvivier, 1936. A group of unemployed workers wins the lottery and sets up a cooperative restaurant. The result depends on which version you see – the one with an upbeat conclusion that was such a hit with contemporary audiences, or the darker ending preferred by Duvivier himself. Jean Gabin stars as the defeated hero, as in Duvivier's other greats, *La Bandéra* (1935) and the cult classic, *Pépé-le-Moko* (1937).

La Bête humaine Jean Renoir, 1938. This dark adaptation of Zola's powerful story of erotic passion, violence and revenge was scripted by Renoir himself in just two weeks. Jean Gabin is superbly cast in the role of the homicidal engine driver, but the real hero is the steam train itself, which is thrillingly shot, especially in the classic five-minute opening sequence. A classic of the Poetic Realist genre, along with Renoir's *Le Crime de Monsieur Lange* (1936) and *La Grande illusion* (1937).

★ **Le Jour se lève/Daybreak** Marcel Carné, 1939. This brooding classic from the Poetic Realist stable has Jean Gabin, the greatest star of the era, playing another of his iconic working-class hero roles. After shooting his rival, the villainous old music-hall star Valentin, François (Gabin) is holed up in a hotel bedroom. In the course of the night, he recalls the events that led up to the murder. Tragedy comes with the daybreak. Also stars the great female idol of the 1930s, Arletty, and a superb script by the poet Jacques Prévert. Carné's *Hôtel du Nord* (1938) and *Quai des brumes* (1938) are in a similar vein.

★ **La Règle du jeu/The Rules of the Game** Jean Renoir, 1939. Now hailed as the foremost masterpiece of the prewar era, this was a complete commercial failure when it was released. The Marquis de la Chesnaye invites his wife, mistress and a pilot friend to spend a weekend hunting and partying in the countryside. Matching the four are a group of four servants with similarly interweaved love lives. Renoir himself plays Octave, who moves between the two groups. A complex, almost farcical plot based around misunderstanding and accusations of infidelity moves inexorably towards disaster.

Le Ciel est à vous/The Woman Who Dared Jean Grémillon, 1944. Praised for its positive outlook by Pétain and the Resistance alike, "The Sky is Yours" is an inspiring and moving portrait of a heroically determined but otherwise ordinary woman, played by Madeleine Renaud, who discovers a passion for flight. Grémillon's career peaked with this film, and his post-war work is relatively disappointing.

★ **Les Enfants du Paradis** Marcel Carné, 1945. Probably the greatest of the collaborations between Carné and the poet-scriptwriter, Jacques Prévert, this film is set in the low-life world of the popular theatre of 1840s Paris. Beautiful and worldly actress Garance (the great Arletty) is loved by arch-criminal Lacenaire, ambitious actor Lemaître, and brilliant, troubled mime Baptiste – unforgettably played by the top mime of the 1940s, Jean-Louis Barrault. The outstanding character portrayals and romantic, humane ethos are reminiscent of a great nineteenth-century novel.

Post-war cinema

La Belle et la bête/Beauty and the Beast Jean Cocteau, 1946. Cocteau's theatrical rendition of the "Beauty and the Beast" tale teeters on the edge of the surreal. The sets are laden with self-referential symbols – clocks, mirrors, magical lamps – and the acting highly stylized, but the pace is as compelling as any thriller. *Orphée* (1950) is more widely considered to be Cocteau's masterpiece, a surreal retelling of the Orpheus tale in a setting strongly redolent of wartime France.

★ **Les Vacances de Monsieur Hulot/Mr Hulot's Holiday** Jacques Tati, 1951. The slapstick comic mime Jacques Tati created his most memorable character in Hulot, the unwitting creator of chaos and nonchalant hero of this gut-wrenchingly funny film. So full of brilliantly conceived and impeccably timed sight gags that you hardly notice the innovative absence of much dialogue or plot. Groundbreaking cinema, and superlative entertainment. The later *Mon oncle* (1958) has an edgier feel, adopting a distinctly critical attitude to modern life.

Casque d'or/Golden Marie Jacques Becker, 1952. Becker's first great film depicts an overwhelming and ultimately tragic romance between a gang-member, Manda, and the beautiful, golden-haired prostitute Marie, nicknamed Casque d'or ("golden helmet") – portrayed with legendary seductiveness by Simone Signoret. Underneath the love story, however, lies the murkiness and moral corruption of a brilliantly re-created turn-of-the-century Paris. Becker went on to make the seminal crime thriller, *Touchez pas au grisbi/Honour Among Thieves* (1953).

Les Jeux interdits René Clément, 1952. A small Parisian girl loses her parents and her dog in a Stuka attack on a column of refugees, and is rescued and befriended by a peasant boy. Together, they seek solace from the war by building an animal cemetery in an abandoned barn. This moving meditation on childhood and death extracted two remarkable performances from the child actors.

Le Salaire de la peur/The Wages of Fear Henri-Georges Clouzot, 1953. This is the tensest, most suspense-driven of all the films made by the "French Hitchcock", focusing on four men driving an explosive-laden lorry hundreds of miles to a burning, third-world oil field. Tight and shatteringly sustained right up to the magnificent finale.

Un Condamné à mort s'est échappé/A Man Escaped Robert Bresson, 1956. A prisoner, Fontaine (François Leterrier), calmly plans his escape from prison, working with a painstaking slowness that is brilliantly matched by the intensely absorbed, magnificent camerawork – a hymn to the close up. The sparing, precisely realistic sound creates an incredibly intense mood, even before there's any real action. Working with real locations and amateur actors, Bresson echoed the work of the Italian Neo-realists, and foreshadowed the work of the Nouvelle Vague directors. Sometimes entitled *Le Vent souffle où il veut*.

Et ... Dieu créa la femme/And God Created Woman Roger Vadim, 1956. This film should be called "And Roger Vadim created Brigitte Bardot", as its chief interest is not its harmless plot – love and adultery in St-Tropez – but its scantily clad main actress, who spends most of the time sunbathing and dancing in front of fascinated males. Deemed "obscene" by the moralizing authorities of the time, it helped liberate the way the body was represented in film.

Ascenseur pour l'échafaud/Elevator to the Gallows/Frantic Louis Malle, 1957. This thriller is Louis Malle's remarkable debut. Two lovers (Jeanne Moreau and Maurice Ronet) murder the woman's husband but get trapped by a series of unlucky coincidences. Beautifully shot – especially when Jeanne Moreau wanders through the streets of Paris, accompanied by Miles Davis' superb original score – and as breathtaking as any Hitchcock film.

The modern era

The Nouvelle Vague

Les Cousins/The Cousins Claude Chabrol, 1959. The Balzac-inspired plot centres around Charles (Gérard Blain), an earnest provincial student, who comes to live in Neuilly with his glamorous cousin Paul (Jean-Claude Brialy). Despite its disappointing ending, the film is highly watchable as a near-caricature of the Nouvelle Vague - idle students in the Quartier Latin, extravagant parties, convertible cars and exciting music.

Les Quatre-Cents coups/The 400 Blows François Truffaut, 1959. A young *cinéphile* and critic turned filmmaker, François Truffaut triumphed at the 1959 Cannes film festival with this semi-autobiographical film, showing a Parisian adolescent (Jean-Pierre Léaud) trying to escape his lonely, loveless existence, and slowly drifting towards juvenile delinquency. Léaud's poignant performance, and Truffaut's sensitive, sympathetic observation, make this one of the most lovable films of the Nouvelle Vague.

★ **A bout de souffle/Breathless** Jean-Luc Godard, 1959. This is the film that came nearest to defining the Nouvelle Vague: insolent charm, cool music and sexy actors. Jean-Paul Belmondo is a petty criminal, Michel, while Jean Seberg plays Patricia, his American girlfriend. The film's revolutionary style, with its jerky, unconventional narrative, abrupt cuts and rough camerawork, proved one of the most influential of the twentieth century.

★ **Hiroshima, mon amour** Alain Resnais, 1959. On her last days of shooting a film in Hiroshima, a French actress (Emmanuelle Riva) falls in love with a Japanese architect (Eiji Okada). Gradually, she reveals the story of her affair with a German soldier during the Occupation, and her subsequent disgrace. Based on an original script by Marguerite Duras, Resnais' first film masterfully weaves together past and present in a haunting story of love and memory.

Jules et Jim François Truffaut, 1962. Jules (Oskar Werner) and Jim (Henri Serre) love the same woman, the fascinating Katherine (Jeanne Moreau), who proves unable to choose between them. This tragic story of impossible love spanning over twenty years contains some beautiful moments of pure *joie de vivre*, expressing Truffaut's yearning for a lost paradise of innocence and harmony.

Cléo de Cinq à Sept/Cleo from 5 to 7 Agnès Varda, 1962. In real time – the camera only leaves her twice – this visually impressive film documents ninety minutes in the life of a young and beautiful pop singer. While waiting for a hospital report, Cléo (Corinne Marchand) goes on a journey through the streets of Paris, where she encounters various friends and meets a conscript bound for the Algerian war. A subtle portrait of a woman moving from vanity and self-obsession to love, by the only female filmmaker of the Nouvelle Vague.

★ **Ma nuit chez Maude/My Night at Maud's** Eric Rohmer, 1969. Rohmer's career-long obsessions with sexuality, conversation, existential choices and the love triangle are given free rein in this moody, lingering portrait of a flirtation. Jean-Louis Trintignant plays a handsome egotist who, during the course of one long night, is drawn into a strange and inconclusive relationship with his friend's friend, the hypnotically attractive Maude (Françoise Fabian).

Comedies

Belle de jour Luis Buñuel, 1966. At first sight, this is a far cry from Buñuel's prewar collaborations with Dalí though as the action progresses, the film moves away from the initial acerbic comedy towards a bizarre surrealism where fantasy and reality merge. The subject matter is perfectly apt: Catherine Deneuve plays Séverine, who lives out her sexual fantasies and obsessions in a brothel – thus (almost) fulfilling the fantasy of half the male cinemagoing population.

★ **Playtime** Jacques Tati, 1967. Tati once more plays Hulot, cinema's most radical slapstick creation, but with a newly profound sense of purpose. From a simple premise – he is showing a group of tourists round a futuristic Paris – he creates an intimately observed and perfectly controlled farce. Just as the city has somehow been transformed into a refined and faceless world of glass and steel. Tati's comedy has become infinitely subtle and reflective.

Zazie dans le métro/Zazie Louis Malle, 1960. In one of his few comedies, Malle successfully rendered novelist Raymond Queneau's verbal experiments by using cartoon-like visual devices. Twelve-year-old Catherine Demongeot is perfect as the delightfully rude little girl driving everybody mad; and the film offers some great shots of Paris, climaxing in a spectacular scene at the top of the Eiffel Tower.

La Grande Vadrouille Gérard Oury, 1966. Head and shoulders the biggest blockbuster in French cinema history, "The Big Jaunt" stars Bourvil and Louis de Funès as a conductor and a decorator. Set in wartime Paris, the comic plot sees three Allied soldiers parachuting down on the hapless pair. In their desperation to be rid of the parachutists, they end up leading them to the free zone.

La Cage aux folles/Birds of a Feather Edouard Molinaro, 1978. Renato runs a cabaret nightclub at which his boyfriend, Albin, is the headlining drag act. When Renato's son, Laurent, decides to get married, the couple are drawn into an escalating farce as they try to present themselves as a conventional mother-and-son couple to Laurent's conservative in-laws. A supremely camp international hit.

Trois Hommes et un couffin Coline Serreau, 1985. "Three Men and a Cradle" was a giant box-office success even before it was trashily remade in Hollywood as *Three Men and a Baby*. In Serreau's film, the three friends live together in Paris when a bombshell arrives in the shape of the baby daughter of one of their ex-girlfriends. Cue lots of gender gags, along with a farcical sub-plot involving a nappy-hidden cache of heroin.

Les Visiteurs/The Visitors Jean-Marie Poiré, 1993. A medieval knight and his squire are transported to present-day France, where they discover their castle has been turned into a country hotel by their descendants. The earthily comic encounters between time-travellers and modern middle-classes make for an extremely funny comedy of manners. French audiences so loved being sent up that this became the third most successful film in French history.

Gazon maudit/French Twist Josiane Balasko, 1995. "Cursed Lawn" – as the title translates literally – is a lesbian sex-comedy turned massive mainstream hit. It successfully milks the comic potential of butch urban lesbian Marijo's explosive entry into a *ménage à trois* with a hitherto straight, provincial couple. The resulting confusion of gender and sexual roles is a very watchable blend of slapstick and gentler social comedy.

Le Dîner de cons/The Dinner Game Francis Veber, 1998. In this light-hearted, straight-up farce, a group of friends compete as to who can invite the most ridiculous person to dinner. Inevitably, and hilariously, the tables are turned. Bravura performances from Thierry Lhermitte as the smug publisher whose life falls apart in front of Jacques Villeret, his buffoon-like guest.

Le Fabuleux Destin d'Amélie Poulain/Amélie Jean-Pierre Jeunet, 2001. Known as plain *Amélie* outside France, this sentimental, feel-good portrait of a youthful ingenue wandering around a romanticized Montmartre was a worldwide hit. Amélie (Audrey Tatou) is on a mission to help the world find happiness; her own is harder to fix up. Filmed on location, though it looks edible enough to be an idealized set.

Thrillers/films policiers

Pierrot-le-fou Jean-Luc Godard, 1965. Godard's fascination with American pulp fiction is most brilliantly exploited in this highly charged and deeply sophisticated thriller. Accidentally caught up in a murderous gangland killing, Ferdinand (Jean-Paul Belmondo) flees with his babysitter (Godard's then-wife, Anna Karina) to the apparent safety of a Mediterranean island. The bizarre and tragic denouement is one of the great scenes of French cinema.

Le Samouraï/The Samurai Jean-Pierre Melville, 1967. The main attraction of this modern-day film noir is Alain Delon, who gives a brilliantly impassive yet stylish performance as Jef Costello, an ice-cold hit man on the run. Hunted by both the police and his own employers, he responds with brilliant ingenuity and violence. One of the all-time great *films policiers*.

L'Armée des ombres/The Army in the Shadows Jean-Pierre Melville, 1969. A small group of Resistance fighters, played by Yves Montand, Simone Signoret and Jean-Pierre Meurisse, are betrayed, questioned and then released, free to enact their revenges and to continue their subversive activities. This is one of the most remarkable depictions of the Resistance in French cinema: the tight, minimalist style creates a suffocating tension that culminates in the unforgettable conclusion.

Le Boucher/The Butcher Claude Chabrol, 1969. A young schoolteacher in a tiny southwest village lives in an apartment above her school. Her loneliness is eased by a surprising fledgling romance with the local butcher – a kindly yet sinister figure – until a sequence of schoolgirl murders sows doubt in her mind. This would be gripping as a portrayal of village life even without the underlying tension and lurking violence.

z/The Anatomy of a Political Assassination Costa-Gavras, 1969. In this stunningly filmed offering from Greek director Costas-Gavras, Yves Montand, an activist in a fascist-run country (Greece, though it's unnamed) is assassinated after giving an inflammatory speech. The great Jean-Louis Trintignant plays the rigorous investigating judge unravelling a complex police conspiracy. Won an Oscar for Best Foreign Film and single-handedly created a new genre, the political thriller.

Coup de Torchon/Clean Slate Bertrand Tavernier, 1981. The setting is colonial West Africa, 1938. Ineffective, humiliated police chief Cordier (Philippe Noiret) decides to take murderous revenge on his wife, her lover, his mistress's husband and the locals he views as uniformly corrupt. As much an extremely black comedy as a true thriller.

Monsieur Hire Patrice Leconte, 1989. A slow-moving, unsettlingly erotic psychological thriller based on a novel by Georges Simenon. Michel Blanc plays the spookily impassive Monsieur Hire, a voyeur who always watches his neighbour, Alice, undressing. One day he sees her boyfriend commit a murder. He becomes the prime suspect in the police's investigation, and is slowly drawn into Alice's world, with tragic consequences.

Films d'amour

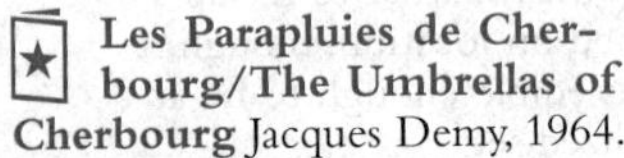

Les Parapluies de Cherbourg/The Umbrellas of Cherbourg Jacques Demy, 1964. Demy's most successful film also gave Catherine Deneuve one of her first great roles. It is an extraordinarily stylized musical, shot in bright, artificial-looking colours, and entirely sung rather than spoken. Demy disturbingly twists the traditional cheerfulness of the musical genre to give a dark, bitter ending to this story of love and abandonment, set during the Algerian war.

Un Homme et une femme/ A Man and a Woman Claude Lelouch, 1966. An actress-widow (Anouk Aimée) and a racing-driver-widower (Jean-Louis Trintignant) meet by chance while visiting their children at a boarding school. Slowly and uncertainly at first, their relationship develops past the initial misunderstandings and things not said. A bittersweet but lyrical film about falling in love a second time, with a rapturous score.

★ **Baisers Volés** François Truffaut, 1968. The third of Truffaut's five-part semi-autobiographical sequence, which began with *Les Quatre-cents coups*, is probably the simplest and most delightful. Returning from military service, idealistic young Antoine Doinel (Jean-Pierre Léaud), mooches about Paris while working variously as a hotel worker, private detective and TV repairman. Through various amorous and bizarre adventures he slowly finds his way back towards the girl he loved and left behind.

La Maman et la putain/The Mother and the Whore Jean Eustache, 1972. Years after the revolutionary "events" of May 1968, Alexandre (Jean-Pierre Léaud) is still living the left-wing café life in St-Germain. He has an older girlfriend, but soon takes up with a young, unstable nurse, who also moves in. The tensions – sexual, emotional, political – between the three of them are explored at an excruciating pace and pitch. Eustache's penultimate feature reprises many of the themes of the original "new wave".

★ **Le Dernier métro** François Truffaut, 1980. This huge commercial success stars Catherine Deneuve and Gérard Depardieu as two actors who fall in love while rehearsing a play during the German Occupation. Wartime Paris is evoked through lavish photography and a growing feeling of imprisonment inside the confined space of the theatre. Swept the Césars that year, for Best Film, Director, Actor and Actress.

Loulou Maurice Pialat, 1980. In this tale of an "inappropriate" love affair Isabelle Huppert plays Nelly, a woman who abandons her husband and middle-class life to shack up with Loulou, a pleasure-loving slob played with great relish by Gérard Depardieu. Add the apparently improvised dialogue, and Pialat seems to have stumbled into Eric Rohmer territory, but this is a much less gentle world with an edge of violence and sexual obsessiveness that is never far from the surface.

L'Ami de mon amie/Boyfriends and Girlfriends Eric Rohmer, 1987. This is Rohmer at his most beguiling and apparently superficial, featuring a strangely symmetrical plot and a script that loads a seemingly inconsequential dialogue with emotional nuance. Two glossy young women in a flashy newtown outside Paris – Cergy-Pontoise – become friends. Whle Blanche is away, Léa falls in love with Blanche's boyfriend Alexandre; when Blanche comes back, she in turn falls in love with Léa's boyfriend, Fabien. Behind the light comedy lurks a profound film about love and free will.

Le Mari de la coiffeuse/The Hairdresser's Husband Patrice Leconte, 1990. Leconte's film about a man who grows up obsessed with hairdressers, and ends up marrying one, epitomizes the best in French romantic film-making. A quirky, subtle and engagingly twisted portrait of an obsessive relationship.

La Belle Noiseuse Jacques Rivette, 1991. Based loosely on a Balzac short story, "the beautiful troublemaker" originally stretched to four hours, though the more commonly screened "Divertimento" cut is half that length. A washed-out painter (the splendidly stuttering Michel Piccoli) lives in the deep south with his wife (Jane Birkin). An admiring younger painter offers his beautiful girlfriend (Emmanuelle Béart) as a nude model. Her fraught sittings become the catalyst for all the latent tensions in the two relationships to slowly, quietly explode.

Un Cœur en hiver/A Heart in Winter/A Heart of Stone Claude Sautet, 1992. In this thoughtful, fresh *ménage à trois* scenario, violinist Camille (Emmanuelle Béart) is paired first with Maxime (André Dussolier), a violin shop owner, and then with loner Stéphane (Daniel Auteuil), the chief craftsman. As the title "A Heart in Winter" suggests, this is a moody but ultimately sentimental film about love, and the fear of love.

Trois Couleurs: Rouge Krzysztof Kieslowski, 1994. The final part of Polish-born director's Kieslowski's "tricolore" trilogy is perhaps the most satisfying, though to get the most out of the powerful denouement, in which all the strands are pulled together through a series of chances and accidents, you really need to have watched *Bleu* and *Blanc* as well. A young model, Valentine (Irène Jacob), runs over a dog and traces its owner, a reclusive retired judge (Jean-Louis Trintignant) who assuages his loneliness by tapping his neighbours' phone calls. The film's "colour" is expressed through presiding red-brown tones and the theme of *fraternité*, the third principle of the French Republic.

Heritage cinema

Jean de Florette Claude Berri, 1986. This masterful adaptation of Marcel Pagnol's novel began a new trend in French cinema, that of the rose-tinted *cinema du patrimoine*. It drew on an idealized heritage – in this case, the gorgeous, rugged setting of inland, prewar Provence. Gérard Depardieu plays Jean, a bookish and deformed refugee from the city who is struggling to create a self-sufficient rural utopia. He is opposed by the shrewd peasant Papet (Yves Montand), who wants to create a lucrative orchard, and the simpleton Ugolin (Daniel Auteuil), who dreams of giant fields of carnations. The excellent sequel, *Manon des Sources* (1987), launched the stellar career of the improbably pouting Emmanuelle Béart.

Au Revoir les enfants/Goodbye, Children Louis Malle, 1987. Malle's autobiographical tale is one of the finest film portraits of the war, and of school life in general. It is minutely observed, and desperately moving without being unduly sentimental. Three Jewish boys are hidden among the pupils at a Catholic boys' boarding school. Eventually, the Gestapo discover the ruse.

La Vie et rien d'autre/Life and Nothing But Bertrand Tavernier, 1989. The master of high-gloss heritage cinema here turns his hand to a grim film set in the aftermath of World War I. Philippe Noiret plays an army major charged with finding the right candidate for the memorial to the Unknown Soldier, under the Arc de Triomphe. During his search, he meets a rich Parisian woman who is trying to find her husband. They find consuming love amid the ashes.

★ **Cyrano de Bergerac** Jean-Paul Rappeneau, 1990. It's hard to know what's finest about this extravagantly romantic film: Rostand's original story, set in seventeenth-century France, or Gérard Depardieu's landmark performance as the large-nosed swashbuckler-poet, Cyrano, who hopelessly loves the brilliant and beautiful Roxanne. The film's panache is made all the more magnificent by the ease with which the cast deliver the verse dialogue – brilliantly rendered into English subtitles by Anthony Burgess. Hilarious, exciting and, ultimately, sublimely weepy.

Indochine Régis Warnier, 1991. This sweeping colonial melodrama stars the mature Catherine Deneuve as a ruthlessly independent and sexually emancipated rubber baroness in prewar French Indochina (Vietnam). As the colony begins to crumble, so does her relationship with her adopted daughter, a scion of the Indochinese royal family.

Cinéma du Look

Diva Jean-Jacques Beineix, 1980. *Diva*'s glossy yet quirky feel established the presiding tone of the *cinéma du look*. Like many conventional crime thrillers, the story is set in motion by an accident: moped-riding postman Jules mixes up two tapes – a bootleg recording of an opera singer and a message from a prostitute linking a detective with a vice ring. But the film is much more about style than suspense, its beguiling depiction of a sexy, bohemian and youthful Paris contrasting with the operatic soundtrack.

Subway Luc Besson, 1985. The favoured urban-nocturnal setting of the *cinéma du look* is given its coolest expression in *Subway*. Like Diva, the action focuses on one man in possession of something he shouldn't have – in this case it's shock-headed Christophe Lambert, with a cache of documents. Hunted by police and criminals alike, he hides out in the Paris métro where he manages to form a rock band with a crowd of various low-lifes – before being found by Isabelle Adjani. Film noir meets MTV.

★ **37°2 le matin/Betty Blue** Jean-Jacques Beineix, 1986. Pouty Béatrice Dalle puts on a compellingly erotic performance as Betty, a free-thinking girl who lives in a beach house with struggling writer Zorg. The film opens in romantic mood with a sustained and passionate sex scene but rapidly spirals towards its disturbing ending. The film's intense and sometimes weird stylishness, along with its memorable score, made it an international hit.

Nikita Luc Besson, 1990. More of a hit abroad than at home, *Nikita* is a sci-fi thriller buzzing with edgy cool. After killing a policeman in a gang shoot-out, the eponymous heroine is remanded to the Kafkaesque "Centre" where she is trained as a government assassin and sent on missions of dubious morality. Glossy on the surface, but underpinned by themes of anarchy versus fascism, and the tension between female star and male director/spectator. *Leon* (1994) finds a similar vein.

★ **Delicatessen** Jean-Pierre Jeunet/Marc Caro, 1991. Set in a crumbling apartment block in a dystopian fantasy city – Occupation Paris meets comic book – a grotesque local butcher murders his assistants and sells them as human meat, until his daughter falls in love with the latest butcher boy and the subterranean vegetarian terrorists find out. Hilarious and bizarre in equal measure, with superb cameos from the neighbours.

Les Amants du Pont-Neuf Léos Carax, 1991. Homeless painter Michèle (Juliette Binoche) is losing her sight. One day, on Paris's Pont-Neuf, she meets an indigent, fire-eating acrobat (Denis Lavant), and they tumble together into a consuming love, madly played out against the background of their life on the streets. An intense and beautiful film.

New Realism: Beur, Banlieue and Jeune

Le Thé à la menthe Abdelkrim Bahloul, 1984. In this funny and ultimately touching film, an Algerian immigrant living in the Barbès quarter of northern Paris writes home to his mother to let her know how successful he has become in his new life. In fact, he struggles to get by on minor scams and chancey ventures. When his mother makes a surprise visit, he foolishly tries to carry on the pretence – to great comic effect.

Le Thé au harem d'Archimède Mehdi Charef, 1985. A concrete housing wasteland is the harsh setting for this somewhat meandering story of a friendship between two young *zonards* from the Paris banlieue. Despite their different ethnicity – Madjid is a *beur* (French-born, of North African origin), Pat is white French – the two friends share much: delinquent habits, poverty and futile but potent dreams. Slow as buddy flicks go, but fascinating.

★ **Hexagone** Malik Chibane, 1991. Shooting in just 24 days, and using amateur actors, Chibane somehow pulled off exactly what he planned: to raise the profile of the new generation of *beurs*. The story is a simple enough rite-of-passage tale focused on five young friends who get in trouble, but the recurring motif of the sacrifice of Abraham gives it a thoughtful twist. The street-slang peppered script and cinematography – strong on handheld shots of the inner city landscape – are superb.

Bye-Bye Karim Dridi, 1995. Two North African brothers living in France are told by their father that they must return to the family home in the Maghreb. Mouloud refuses, and drifts into delinquency, while Ismaël gets a job in a Marseille shipyard, where he has an affair with a white workmate's girlfriend. Ultimately, the brothers decide to leave France anyway. Sympathetic characterization leavens the down-beat subject matter, and the raï and French hip-hop soundtrack is superb.

★ **La Haine/Hate** Mathieu Kassovitz, 1995. The flagship film of the *cinéma de banlieue*, films of the tough suburbs, centres on three friends: Hubert, of black African origin; Saïd, a *beur* (from North Africa); and Vinz, who has white Jewish roots – and a gun. They spend a troubled night wandering Paris before heading back to the *banlieue* and a violent homecoming. Brilliantly treads the line between gritty realism and street cool – the fact that it's shot in black-and-white helps, as does the soundtrack from French rapper MC Solaar, among others.

Y aura-t-il de la neige à Noël? Sandrine Veysset, 1996. This moving, sometimes painful depiction of a rural childhood comes in three separate sections – summer, autumn and winter. Veysset depicts the lives of seven children who work on a southern farm owned by their menacing, exploitative father. The unwaveringly realistic tone is a great antidote to the old cinematic clichés of the rural idyll, but fairy-tale moments of childish joy break through.

La Ville est tranquille Robert Guédiguian, 2000. Notwithstanding its title, this harrowing film describes the dysfunctional society of a far-from-quiet city – Marseille – focusing on the hardships of Michèle (Ariane Ascaride), a 40-year-old woman working in a fish factory while fighting to save her heroin-addict daughter. After a series of light, happy tales, Robert Guédiguian magnificently turns here to a more realistic and political tone.

James McConnachie and Eva Lœchner

Books

Publishers are detailed below in the form of British publisher/American publisher, where both exist. Where books are published in one country only, UK or US follows the publisher's name. Books marked ★ are highly recommended. Abbreviations: o/p (out of print); UP (University Press).

France in literature

Listed below is a highly selective recommendation of works – mostly novels – that are rooted in the various French regions, and which would make good holiday reading.

Paris and around

Honoré de Balzac *Old Goriot*
Steven Barclay (ed) *A Place in the World Called Paris*
Charles Baudelaire *Baudelaire's Paris*, trans Laurence Kitchen
André Breton *Nadja*
Blaise Cendrars *To the End of the World*
Didier Daeninckx *Murder in Memoriam*
Charles Dickens *A Tale of Two Cities*
Gustave Flaubert *A Sentimental Education*
André Gide *The Counterfeiters*
Ernest Hemingway *A Moveable Feast*
Victor Hugo *Les Misérables*
Jack Kerouac *Satori in Paris*
Henry Miller *Quiet Days in Clichy, Tropic of Cancer, Tropic of Capricorn*
Anaïs Nin *Journals 1917–1974*
George Orwell *Down and Out in Paris and London*
Georges Perec *Life: A User's Manual*
Marcel Proust *Remembrance of Things Past*
Raymond Queneau *Zazie dans le Métro*
Paul Rambali *French Blues*
Jean Rhys *Quartet, Good Morning Midnight*
Jean-Paul Sartre *Roads to Freedom trilogy*
Georges Simenon *Any Maigret thriller*
Michel Tournier *The Golden Droplet*
Émile Zola *Nana, L'Assommoir, La Bête Humaine, La Curée, Le Ventre de Paris*

Calais to Champagne

Sebastian Faulks *Birdsong*
Julien Gracq *A Balcony in the Forest, The Opposing Shore*
Émile Zola *Germinal, La Débâcle*

Alsace, Franche-Comté and Jura

John Berger *Pig Earth*
Bernard Clavel *The Spaniard*
Colette *My Mother's House*
Pierre Gascar *Women and the Sun*
Stendhal *Scarlet and Black*

Travel

Julian Barnes *Something to Declare* (Picador/Macmillan). This journalistically highbrow collection of essays on French culture – films, music, the Tour de France, and of course Flaubert – wears its French-style intellectualism on its sleeve, but succeeds in getting under the skin anyway.

 **Walter Benjamin** *The Arcades Project* (Belknap/Harvard). An all-encompassing portrait of Paris

Normandy and Brittany

Honoré de Balzac *Les Chouans*

Colette *Ripening Seed*

Gustave Flaubert *Madame Bovary*

André Gide *Strait is the Gate*

Pierre Loti *Pêcheur d'Islande*

Guy de Maupassant *Selected Short Stories*

Jean Rouard *Fields of Glory, Of Illustrious Men*

Jean-Paul Sartre *La Nausée*

The Loire

Alain Fournier *Le Grand Meaulnes*

Honoré de Balzac *Eugénie Grandet*

Rabelais *Gargantua and Pantagruel*

George Sand *The Devil's Pool*

Émile Zola *The Earth*

Burgundy

Gabriel Chevallier *Clochemerle, Atlantic Coast*

François Mauriac *Thérèse*

The Pyrenees

Pierre Loti *Ramuntcho*

Languedoc

Hannah Closs *High Are the Mountains*

Rhône Valley and Provence

Lawrence Durrell *The Avignon Quintet*

Jean Giono *The Horseman on the Roof, The Man Who Planted Trees, Joy of Man's Desiring*

Marcel Pagnol *Jean de Florette, Manon des Sources*

Émile Zola *Fortune of the Rougons*

Côte d'Azur

Colette *Collected Stories*

Alexandre Dumas *The Count of Monte Cristo*

F. Scott Fitzgerald *Tender is the Night*

Graham Greene *Loser Takes All, May We Borrow Your Husband?*

Katherine Mansfield *Selected Short Stories*

Françoise Sagan *Bonjour Tristesse*

from 1830 to 1870, in which the passages are used as a lens through which to view Parisian society. Never completed, Benjamin's magnum opus is a kaleidoscopic assemblage of essays, notes and quotations, gathered under such headings as "Baudelaire", "Prostitution", "Mirrors" and "Idleness".

James Boswell *An Account of Corsica*, current edition published as *The Journal of a Tour to Corsica* (In Print Publishing, UK). Typically robust and witty account of encounters with the Corsican people. Excerpts published in *Journals of James Boswell* (Mandarin/Yale UP).

★ **Dorothy Carrington** *Granite Island* (Penguin, UK, o/p). By far the best study of Corsica ever written in English. A fascinating and immensely comprehensive book, combining the writer's personal experiences with an evocative portrayal of historical figures and events.

Julien Green *Paris* (Marion Boyars). A collection of very personal sketches and impressions of the city, by an American who has lived all his life in Paris, writes in French, and is considered one of the great French writers of the century. Bilingual text.

Richard Holmes *Fatal Avenue* (Pimlico/Trafalgar Square). The phrase is de Gaulle's, used to describe France's northeast frontier whose notorious topographical vulnerability has made it the natural route for invaders since time began. An exciting and informative read.

Richard Holmes *Footsteps* (Flamingo/Vintage). A marvellous mix of objective history and personal account, such as the tale of the author's own excitement at the events of May 1968 in Paris, which led him to investigate and reconstruct the experiences of the British in Paris during the 1789 Revolution.

Michael de Larrabeiti *French Leave* (Hale). In the summer of 1949, aged just 15, Michael de Larrabeiti set off on his own by bicycle to Paris from the UK. This book provides a wonderfully evocative testimony to his love of France as he looks back over fifty years working and travelling throughout the country.

Laurence Sterne *A Sentimental Journey Through France and Italy* (Penguin/Viking). Rambling tale by the eccentric eighteenth-century author of *Tristram Shandy* who, despite the title, never gets further than Versailles.

Robert Louis Stevenson *Travels with a Donkey* (OUP/Koneman). Mile-by-mile account of Stevenson's twelve-day trek in the Haute Loire and Cévennes uplands with the donkey Modestine. Devotees of Stevenson's footpaths – and there are a surprising number in France – might be interested in his first book, *Inland Voyage*, on the waterways of the north.

Freda White *Three Rivers of France* (Pavilion/Faber, o/p), *West of the Rhone* (Faber, US, o/p), *Ways of Aquitaine* (Faber, o/p). Freda White spent a great deal of time in France in the 1950s before tourism came along to the backwater communities that were her interest. These are all evocative books, slipping in the history and culture painlessly, if not always too accurately.

History

General

★ **Alfred Cobban** *A History of Modern France* (3 vols: 1715–99, 1799–1871 and 1871–1962; Penguin; Viking). Complete and very readable account of the main political, social and economic strands in French history, from the death of Louis XIV to mid-de Gaulle.

★ **Alistair Horne** *Seven Ages of Paris* (Pan). Compelling and thoroughly readable account of the city's history, focusing on seven key ages, from the twelfth century to de Gaulle.

Colin Jones *The Cambridge Illustrated History of France* (CUP, UK, o/p). A political and social history of France from prehistoric times to the mid-1990s, concentrating on issues of regionalism, gender, race and class. Good illustrations and a friendly, non-academic writing style.

Ian Littlewood *History of France* (Rough Guides). This pocket-sized guide offers a handy chronology plus background snippets on cultural movements and key historical figures.

Theodore Zeldin *A History of French Passions: 1848–1945* (OUP, UK). Brilliant and original set of books tackling French history by theme. Vol 1 covers Ambition and Love, Vol 2 Intellect and Pride, and so on. Highly readable and unusually stimulating.

The Middle Ages

★ **Natalie Zemon Davis** *The Return of Martin Guerre* (Harvard UP, US). A vivid account of peasant life in the sixteenth century and a perplexing and titillating hoax in the Pyrenean village of Artigat.

★ **J. H. Huizinga** *The Waning of the Middle* Ages (Penguin/Dover). Primarily a study of the culture of the Burgundian and French courts – but a masterpiece that goes far beyond this, building up meticulous detail to re-create the whole life and mentality of the fourteenth and fifteenth centuries.

R. J. Knecht *Renaissance Warrior and Patron: The Reign of Francis I* (Cambridge University Press, UK). Fascinating account of one of the great Renaissance kings by a leading academic.

Emmanuel Le Roy Ladurie *Montaillou* (Penguin/Random House). Village gossip on who's sleeping with whom, tales of trips to Spain and details of work, all extracted by the Inquisition from Cathar peasants of the eastern Pyrenees in the fourteenth century, and stored away until recently in the Vatican archives. Though academic and heavy going in places, most of this book reads like a novel.

Nancy Mitford *Madame de Pompadour* (Penguin/New York Review of Books Classics). Mitford's unashamedly biased admiration for Pompadour – Louis XV's mistress and France's greatest art patron – makes this a fascinating read.

Stephen O'Shea *The Perfect Heresy* (Walker & Co, US). Lively but partisan non-academic account of the history of the Cathars and their faith and the Catholic campaign mounted to wipe them out.

Saint-Simon *Saint-Simon at Versailles* (Hamish Hamilton/Random House, o/p). A courtier under Louis XIV, and an addictively prolific diarist, the Duc de Saint-Simon had a sharp eye and a gift for anecdotes that brings alive the extraordinary world of Versailles. This edition admirably condensed in three volumes by Lucy Norton.

Barbara Tuchman *A Distant Mirror* (Papermac; Ballantine). The history of the fourteenth century – plagues, wars, peasant uprisings and crusades – told through the life of a sympathetic French nobleman whose career takes him through England, Italy and Byzantium and finally ends in a Turkish prison.

Marina Warner *Joan of Arc* (Vintage). The most illuminating and erudite of all the books on Joan, placing her within a historical, spiritual and intellectual tradition and attempting to tease out the nuances of her historical context.

Eighteenth and nineteenth centuries

Dorothy Carrington *Napoleon and his Parents on the Threshold of History* (NAL-Dutton, US, o/p). Lucid study of Napoleon's early years.

Rupert Christiansen *Tales of the New Babylon, Paris 1869–1875* (Minerva/published in US as *Paris Babylon* by Penguin). The compulsive and irresistible story of Paris in the last years of the Second Empire and the physical and social upheavals of the Prussian siege and the Commune. It combines a serious historical overview with tabloid-style detail.

Richard Cobb & Colin Jones (eds) *The French Revolution* (Simon & Schuster, o/p). One of the best 1989 offerings on 1789 with lots of pictures, texts of the time and clear explanations by a host of historians.

Vincent Cronin *Napoleon* (Fontana/HarperCollins). Enthusiastic and accessible biography.

Norman Hampson *A Social History of the French Revolution* (Routledge/Kegan & Paul). An analysis that concentrates on the personalities involved. Its particular interest lies in the attention it gives to the *sans-culottes*, the ordinary poor of Paris.

Christopher Hibbert *The French Revolution* (Penguin). Well-paced and entertaining narrative treatment by a master historian.

Alistair Horne *The Fall of Paris* (Papermac/Penguin). A very readable and humane account of the extraordinary period of the Prussian siege of Paris in 1870 and the ensuing struggles of the Commune.

Lissagaray *History of the Paris Commune* (New Park, UK, o/p). A highly personal and partisan account of the politics and fighting by a participant. Although Lissagaray is reticent about it, history has it that the last solitary Communard on the last barricade – in rue Ramponneau in Belleville – was in fact himself.

Philip Mansel *Paris Between Empires* (John Murray/St Martin's Press). Passionate and meticulous account of Parisian politics and society in the fragile, revolution-bedevilled period between the end of Napoleon's empire and the beginning of Napoléon III's.

Karl Marx *On the Paris Commune* (Lawrence & Wishart in the collected works; Pathfinder). Rousing prose from Karl, along with a history of the Commune by Engels.

Peter McPhee *A Social History of France 1780–1880* (Routledge, o/p). A scholarly work arguing that historians have underestimated the fundamental differences between how people lived and thought in 1880 compared with the time of the 1789 Revolution. He goes into such subjects as relations between men and women, the loss of diversity in rural France of languages and culture, and changes in the physical environment.

Thomas Paine *The Rights of Man* (Penguin). Written in 1791 in response to English conservatives' views on the situation in France, this reasoned and passionate tract expresses the ideas of both the American and French revolutions. It was immediately banned on publication, and its author charged with treason, but enough copies had crossed the Channel and been translated for Paine to be elected to the Convention by the people of Calais.

Simon Schama *Citizens* (Penguin /Random House). Bestselling and highly tendentious revisionist history of the Revolution, which pretty well takes the line that the ideologues of the Revolution were a gang of fanatics who simply failed to see how good the *ancien régime* was. It reveals as much about the intellectual climate of conservative America in the 1980s as it does about 1789, but it's a well-written, racy and provocative book.

Chantal Thomas *The Wicked Queen: The Origins of the Myth of Marie-Antionette* (Zone Books). Scholarly but lively review of the muckraking of France's most infamous queen, orginally published in French in 1989. Draws in a host of colourful characters of aristocratic and revolutionary Paris, and contains translations of the sensationalist pamphlets which were written against the queen.

J. M. Thompson *The French Revolution* (Blackwell). A detailed and passionate account, first published in 1943, but still a classic.

Twentieth century

Marc Bloch *Strange Defeat* (Norton). Moving personal study of the reasons for France's defeat and subsequent caving-in to fascism. Found among the papers of this Sorbonne historian after his death at the hands of the Gestapo in 1942.

★ **Geoff Dyer** *The Missing of the Somme* (Penguin, UK, o/p). Structured round the author's visits to the war graves of northern France, this is a highly moving meditation on the trauma of World War I and the way its memory has been perpetuated.

Robert Gildea *France Since 1945* (Oxford University Press, UK). Pithy but serious contemporary history, with a particular interest in France's national self-image.

Julian Jackson *The Fall of France: The Nazi Invasion of 1940* (Oxford University Press, UK). Fascinating and balanced account of May and June 1940, skilfully unpicking the cultural, political and military reasons behind France's speedy defeat.

H. R. Kedward *In Search of the Maquis: Rural Resistance in South France 1942–44* (OUP, UK, o/p). Slightly dry style, but full of fascinating detail about the brave and often mortal struggle of the countless ordinary people across France who fought to drive the Germans from their country.

★ **François Maspero** *Cat's Grin* (New Amsterdam Books, US). Semi-autobiographical novel about a young teenager in Paris during the war with his brother in the Resistance, his parents taken to concentration camps as Paris is liberated, and everyone else busily collaborating. An intensely moving and revealing account of the war period.

★ **Barbara Tuchman** *The Proud Tower* (Papermac/Ballantine). A portrait of England, France, the US, Germany and Russia in the years 1890–1914. Written in Tuchman's inimitable and readable style, it includes a superb chapter on the extraordinary passions and enmities of the Dreyfus Affair which rocked French society between 1894 and 1899 and on the different currents in the rising socialist movement in the run-up to World War I, centring on the life of Jean Jaurès.

Paul Webster *Pétain's Crime: The Full Story of French Collaboration in the Holocaust* (Papermac/IR Dee). The fascinating and alarming story of the Vichy regime's more than willing collaboration with the Holocaust and the bravery of those, especially the Communist resistance in occupied France, who attempted to prevent it.

Alexander Worth *France 1940–55* (Beacon Press, US, o/p). Extremely good and emotionally engaged portrayal of the taboo Occupation period in French history, followed by the Cold War and colonial struggle years in which the same political tensions and heart-searchings were at play.

Society and politics

N. A. Addinall (ed) *French Political Parties: A Documentary Guide* (U of Wales Press, UK). Clear and concise textbook introduction to the constitution and political parties of the Fifth Republic; quotations and source materials are not translated but this need not deter non-French speakers.

John Ardagh *France in the New Century: Portrait of a Changing Society* (Penguin). Long-time writer on France gets to grips with the last twenty years. Attempts to be a comprehensive survey, but gets rather too drawn into party politics and statistics.

Roland Barthes *Mythologies* (Vintage; Noonday) and *The Eiffel Tower* (California UP, US). *Mythologies* is an immensely readable structuralist critique on the socio-historical importance of myth and its signs in France today, accompanied by a series of quirky examples. The short text, *The Eiffel Tower*, demystifies the Eiffel tower as synecdoche of Paris – Barthes accepts Maupassant's solution of eliminating it from the vista by going to have dinner in the Eiffel Tower restaurant.

Jean Baudrillard *Selected Writings* (Stanford UP, US). Essential reading to get an overview of the most interesting contemporary French philosopher and artist. His notion of the simulacrum (the image of the essence of an object) and the role of the object as sign within the consumer system is complex but revelatory.

Simone de Beauvoir *The Second Sex* (Vintage, UK). One of the prime texts of Western feminism, written in 1949, covering women's inferior status in history, literature, mythology, psychoanalysis, philosophy and everyday life. The style is dry and intellectual, but the subject matter easily compensates.

Denis Belloc *Slow Death in Paris* (Quartet, UK). A harrowing account of a heroin addict in Paris. Not recommended holiday reading but, if you want to know about the seedy underbelly of the city, this is the book.

Mary Blume *A French Affair: The Paris Beat 1965–1998* (Plume, US). Incisive and witty observations on contemporary French life by the *International Herald Tribune* reporter who was stationed there for three decades.

Émilie Carles *Wild Herb Soup* (Indigo, UK). A moving and inspiring autobiography of a girl born and raised in a remote Alpine valley in the early twentieth century.

Claire Duchen *Feminism in France: From May '68 to Mitterrand* (Routledge, UK). Charts the evolution of the women's movement through to its mid-1980s crisis, clarifying the divergent political stances and feminist theory that informs the various groups and placing them in the wider French political context.

★ **Jonathan Fenby** *On the Brink* (Warner/Arcade Publishing). While France isn't perhaps quite as endangered as the title suggests, this provocative book takes a long, hard look at the problems facing contemporary France.

Mark Girouard *Life in the French Country House* (Cassell). Girouard meticulously re-creates the social and domestic life that went on between the walls of French châteaux, starting with the great halls of early castles and ending with the commercial marriage venues of the twentieth century.

Gisèle Halimi *Milk for the Orange Tree* (Quartet, UK). A gutsy autobiographical story of a woman who was born in Tunisia, the daughter of an Orthodox Jewish family, and who ran away to Paris to become a lawyer, and defender of women's rights, Algerian FLN fighters and all unpopular causes.

★ **Bernard Henri-Lévy** *Adventures on the Freedom Road: The French Intellectuals in the 20th Century* (Harvill, UK & US). Huge, clever and complex essays by contemporary philosopher-celebrity, mercilessly analysing the response of all the great French thinkers, of Left and Right, to the key events of the century. Easy to dip into, surprisingly readable and very provocative.

David Thomson *Democracy in France Since 1870* (Cassell, UK, o/p). An enquiry into why a country with such a strong socialist tradition should have had so many reactionary governments.

Gillian Tindall *Célestine: Voices from a French Village* (Minerva/Holt). Intrigued by some nineteenth century love letters left behind in the house she has bought in Chassignolles, Berry, Tindall researches the history of the village back to the 1840s. She produces a meticulous, thoughtful and moving portrait of rural French life and its slow but dramatic transformation. A brilliant piece of social history.

Eugen Weber *My France* (Harvard UP, US). A collection of essays, fascinating and offbeat, about numerous aspects of French culture and politics. Some prior knowledge of mainstream French history is needed to make the most of them.

★ **Theodore Zeldin** *The French* (Harvill/Kodansha). A wise and original book that attempts to describe a country through the prism of the author's intensely personal conversations with a fascinating range of French people. Chapter titles include "How to be chic" and "How to appreciate a grandmother".

Art and poetry

John Berger *The Success and Failure of Picasso* (Penguin, o/p/Vintage). The success is self-explanatory; the failure (and the tragedy) lies in Picasso's poverty of subject matter – or so Berger argues in this brief and highly persuasive book. Perhaps the best one-volume study of Picasso in English.

★ **Brassaï** *The Secret Paris of the Thirties* (Thames & Hudson, UK, o/p). Extraordinary photos of the capital's nightlife in the 1930s – brothels, music halls, street-cleaners, transvestites and the underworld – each one a work of art and a familiar world (now long since gone) to Brassaï and his mate, Henry Miller, who accompanied him on his nocturnal expeditions.

David J. Brown *Bridges Across Time* (Mitchell Beazley, UK, o/p). A very beautiful book about both the technical and aesthetic aspects of bridge-building; not exclusively about France, but includes many French bridges from the Roman Pont du Gard to the Pont d'Avignon, Eiffel's constructions and the state-of-the-art Pont de Normandie across the Seine estuary.

★ **André Chastel** *French Art* (Flammarion, France). Authoritative, three-volume study by one of France's leading art historians. Discusses individual works of art in some detail in an attempt – from architecture to tapestry, as well as painting – to locate the Frenchness of French art. With glossy photographs and serious-minded but readable text.

Kenneth J. Comant *Carolingian and Romanesque Architecture, 800–1200* (Yale UP, US). Good European study with a focus on Cluny and the Santiago pilgrim route.

Norma Evenson *Paris: A Century of Change, 1878–1978* (Yale UP, US). A large, illustrated volume that makes the development of urban planning and the fabric of Paris an enthralling subject – mainly because the author's ultimate concern is always with people, not panoramas.

Edward Lucie-Smith *A Concise History of French Painting* (Thames & Hudson, US, o/p). If you're after an art reference book, this will do as well as any, though there are of course hundreds of books on particular French art movements.

★ **John Richardson** *The Life of Picasso: Vol 1 1881–1906* (Pimlico/Random House) and *Vol 2 1907–17* (Cape/Random House). No twentieth-century artist has ever been subjected to as much scrutiny as Picasso receives in Richardson's exhaustive and brilliantly illustrated biography. The author has taken many years to complete the first two volumes, and there's a risk he'll never reach the end, but the mould-breaking years have now been covered. Volumes 3 and 4 are in the pipeline.

★ **Stephen Romer** (editor) *20th-Century French Poetry* (Faber and Faber, UK). A collection of around 150 French poems spanning the whole of the century. Although there's no French text, many of the translations are works of art in themselves, consummately rendered by the likes of Samuel Beckett, T.S. Eliot and Paul Auster. An equally enjoyable read for the novice and those already familiar with modern French poetry.

Vivian Russell *Monet's Garden* (Frances Lincoln/Stewart Tabori & Chang). Sumptuous colour photographs by the author, old photographs of the artist and reproductions of his paintings. Superb opening chapter on Monet as "poet of nature" and a detailed description of the garden's evolution, seasonal cycle and its current maintenance which will delight serious gardeners.

Jean-Jacques Sempé *The World According To Sempé* (Harvill UK & US). The cartoonist Jean-Jacques Sempé has long been known in France for his lovingly drawn cartoons and gently satirical take on the passions and follies of ordinary people. This collection translated into English brings together a selection of his best work from across his career.

Gertrude Stein *The Autobiography of Alice B Toklas* (Penguin/Vintage). The goings-on at Stein's famous salon in Paris. The most accessible of her works, written from the point of view of Stein's long-time lover, gives an amusing account of the Paris art and literary scene of the 1910s and 1920s.

Guides

100 Walks in the French Alps (Hodder & Stoughton). A very good guide to hiking in the Alps, detailing which walks are appropriate for different abilities.

★ **David Abram** *Trekking in Corsica* (Trailblazer, UK). Trailblazer's guide to the island's long-distance footpaths covers the GR20, Mare a Mare Nord & Sud and Mare e Monti Nord routes, as well as the Campomorro–Roccapina coast path. Even allowing for our inevitable bias (it's written by the author of our Corsica chapter) this is the most comprehensive book of its kind in English, with lively route descriptions and background features, plus 67 hand-drawn trekking maps. You also get a handy full-colour field guide to common Corsican flora.

James Bromwich *The Roman Remains of Southern France* (Routledge, UK). The only comprehensive guide to the subject – detailed, well illustrated and approachable. In addition to accounts of the famous sites, it will lead you off the map to little-known discoveries.

Glynn Christian *Edible France* (Grub Street/Interlink). A guide to food rather than restaurants: regional produce, local specialities, markets and best shops for buying goodies to bring back home.

Cicerone Walking Guides (Cicerone, UK). Neat, durable guides, with detailed route descriptions. Titles include *Tour of Mont Blanc*; *Chamonix-Mont Blanc*; *Tour of the Oisans* (GR54); *French Alps* (GR5); *The Way of Saint James* (GR65); *Tour of the Queyras*; *The Pyrenean Trail* (GR10); *Walks and Climbs in the Pyrenees*.

Robin G. Collomb *Corsica Mountains* (West Col, UK). Covers all the principal mountain peaks, with information on different approaches and ascents backed up with diagrams.

★ **Elizabeth David** *French Provincial Cooking* (Penguin, UK). A classic cookery book, written in 1960 by the English expert on French food. The recipes are in fine prose rather than manual speak, with excellent detail and warnings about tricky processes or the need for particular skills; and they work, even with non-French ingredients.

Mary Davis *The Green Guide to France* (Green Print, UK). Definitely not the Michelin, this is a resource guide to French national parks and wildlife reserves, veggie restaurants, communes and the like.

Emplois d'Été en France (published in France, distributed by Vacation Work, UK). Annual listings (in French) of thousands of summer jobs available in France.

Footpaths of Europe Series (16 titles/Robertson McCarta, UK). Route guides to most areas of France including Corsica, covering the system of GR footpaths, illustrated with 1:50,000 colour survey maps. These are English versions of the *Topoguides des Sentiers de Grande Randonnée* (CNSGR, Paris), which are widely available in France and not hard to follow with a working knowledge of French.

Victoria Pybus *Live and Work in France* (Vacation Work, UK, o/p). An invaluable guide for anyone considering residence or work in France; packed with ideas and advice on job hunting, bureaucracy, tax, health and so on.

Haute-Savoie & Mont Blanc (Two Wheels, UK, o/p). The only English-language guide to mountain-biking, detailing fifty off-road routes of varying difficulty in that region.

Louisa Jones *Gardens of the French Riviera* (Flammarion, France). The history and traditions of Riviera gardens accompanied by gorgeous photographs.

W. Lippert *Fleurs des Montagnes, Alpages et Forêts* (Miniguide Nathan Tout Terrain, Paris). Best palm-sized colour guide if you want something to pack away with your gear in the mountains.

Carol Pineau & Maureen Kelly *Working in France* (AL Books, US, o/p). A practical guide, aimed at American readers, on how to get jobs in France, highlighting the cultural differences that affect job interviews and business practice generally.

Kev Reynolds *Walks and Climbs in the Pyrenees* (Cicerone Press, UK). The classic English guide for walking in the Pyrenees.

Georges Véron *Haute Randonnée Pyrénées* (Randonnées Pyrénéennes, Paris/Gastons-West Col, o/p). East-to-west description of the High Level route across the Pyrenees.

Patricia Wells *The Paris Cookbook* (Kyle Cathie, UK). American journalist and long-time resident of the capital, Patricia Wells takes her inspiration for these sophisticated recipes from her favourite Parisian restaurants, shops and markets.

Language

Language

French

French can be a deceptively familiar language because of the number of words and structures it shares with English. Despite this, it's far from easy, though the bare essentials are not difficult to master and can make all the difference. Even just saying "Bonjour Madame/Monsieur" and then gesticulating will usually get you a smile and helpful service. People working in tourist offices, hotels and so on, almost always speak English and tend to use it when you're struggling to speak French – be grateful, not insulted.

Phrasebooks and courses

Rough Guide French Phrasebook (Rough Guides). Mini dictionary-style phrasebook with both English–French and French–English sections, along with cultural tips for tricky situations and a menu reader.

Mini French Dictionary (Harrap/Prentice Hall). French–English and English–French, plus a brief grammar and pronunciation guide.

Breakthrough French (Pan; book and two cassettes). Excellent teach-yourself course.

French and English Slang Dictionary (Harrap/Prentice Hall); **Dictionary of Modern Colloquial French** (Routledge). Both volumes are a bit large to carry, but they are the key to all you ever wanted to understand about the French vernacular.

Verbaid (Verbaid, Hawk House, Heath Lane, Farnham, Surrey GU9 0PR). CD-size laminated paper "verb wheel" giving you the tense endings for the regular verbs.

A Vous La France; France Extra; Franc-Parler (BBC Publications/EMC Publishing; each consists of a book and two cassettes). BBC courses, running from beginners' level to fairly advanced. Ⓦ www.bbc.co.uk/education/languages/french has a number of online courses ranging from beginner level to more advanced.

Pronunciation

One easy rule to remember is that **consonants** at the ends of words are usually silent. *Pas plus tard* (not later) is thus pronounced "pa-plu-tarr". But when the following word begins with a vowel, you run the two together: *pas après* (not after) becomes "pazaprey".

Vowels are the hardest sounds to get right. Roughly:

a as in hat
e as in get
é between get and gate
è between get and gut
eu like the **u** in hurt
i as in machine
o as in hot
o, au as in over
ou as in food
u as in a pursed-lip version of use

More awkward are the **combinations in/im, en/em, an/am, on/om, un/um** at the ends of words, or followed by consonants other than **n** or **m**. Again, roughly:

in/im like the **an** in **an** xious

an/am, en/em like the **on** in **Don**caster when said with a nasal accent

on/om like the **on** in **Don**caster said by someone with a heavy cold

un/um like the **u** in **u**nderstand

Consonants are much as in English, except that: **ch** is always "sh", **c** is "s", **h** is silent, **th** is the same as "t", **ll** is like the "y" in yes, **w** is "v", and **r** is growled (or rolled).

Basic words and phrases

French nouns are divided into masculine and feminine. This causes difficulties with adjectives, whose endings have to change to suit the gender of the nouns they qualify. If you know some grammar, you will know what to do. If not, stick to the masculine form, which is the simplest – it's what we have done in this glossary.

today	**aujourd'hui**	that one	**celà**
yesterday	**hier**	open	**ouvert**
tomorrow	**demain**	closed	**fermé**
in the morning	**le matin**	big	**grand**
in the afternoon	**l'après-midi**	small	**petit**
in the evening	**le soir**	more	**plus**
now	**maintenant**	less	**moins**
later	**plus tard**	a little	**un peu**
at one o'clock	**à une heure**	a lot	**beaucoup**
at three o'clock	**à trois heures**	cheap	**bon marché**
at ten-thirty	**à dix heures et demie**	expensive	**cher**
at midday	**à midi**	good	**bon**
man	**un homme**	bad	**mauvais**
woman	**une femme**	hot	**chaud**
here	**ici**	cold	**froid**
there	**là**	with	**avec**
this one	**ceci**	without	**sans**

Numbers

1	**un**	7	**sept**
2	**deux**	8	**huit**
3	**trois**	9	**neuf**
4	**quatre**	10	**dix**
5	**cinq**	11	**onze**
6	**six**	12	**douze**

13	**treize**	70	**soixante-dix**
14	**quatorze**	75	**soixante-quinze**
15	**quinze**	80	**quatre-vingts**
16	**seize**	90	**quatre-vingt-dix**
17	**dix-sept**	95	**quatre-vingt-quinze**
18	**dix-huit**	100	**cent**
19	**dix-neuf**	101	**cent-et-un**
20	**vingt**	200	**deux cents**
21	**vingt-et-un**	300	**trois cents**
22	**vingt-deux**	500	**cinq cents**
30	**trente**	1000	**mille**
40	**quarante**	2000	**deux milles**
50	**cinquante**	5000	**cinq milles**
60	**soixante**	1,000,000	**un million**

Days and dates

January	**janvier**	Sunday	**dimanche**
February	**février**	Monday	**lundi**
March	**mars**	Tuesday	**mardi**
April	**avril**	Wednesday	**mercredi**
May	**mai**	Thursday	**jeudi**
June	**juin**	Friday	**vendredi**
July	**juillet**	Saturday	**samedi**
August	**août**	August 1	**le premier août**
September	**septembre**	March 2	**le deux mars**
October	**octobre**	July 14	**le quatorze juillet**
November	**novembre**	November 23	**le vingt-trois novembre**
December	**décembre**	2006	**deux mille six**

Talking to people

When addressing people a simple *bonjour* is not enough; you should always use *Monsieur* for a man, *Madame* for a woman, *Mademoiselle* for a young woman or girl. This isn't as formal as it seems, and it has its uses when you've forgotten someone's name or want to attract someone's attention.

Excuse me	**Pardon**	...English	**...anglais[e]**
Do you speak English?	**Parlez-vous anglais?**	...Irish	**...irlandais[e]**
How do you say it in French?	**Comment ça se dit en français?**	...Scottish	**...écossais[e]**
What's your name?	**Comment vous appelez-vous?**	...Welsh	**...gallois[e]**
My name is...	**Je m'appelle...**	...American	**...américain[e]**
I'm...	**Je suis...**	...Australian	**...australien[ne]**
		...Canadian	**...canadien[ne]**
		...a New Zealander	**...néo-zélandais[e]**

yes	**oui**
no	**non**
I understand	**Je comprends**
I don't understand	**Je ne comprends pas**
Can you speak slower?	**S'il vous plaît, parlez moins vite**
OK/agreed	**d'accord**
please	**s'il vous plaît**
thank you	**merci**
hello	**bonjour**
goodbye	**au revoir**
good morning /afternoon	**bonjour**
good evening	**bonsoir**
good night	**bonne nuit**
How are you?	**Comment allez-vous?/Ça va?**
Fine, thanks	**Très bien, merci**
I don't know	**Je ne sais pas**
Let's go	**Allons-y**
See you tomorrow	**À demain**
See you soon	**À bientôt**
Sorry	**Pardon/Je m'excuse**
Leave me alone (aggressive)	**Fichez-moi la paix!**
Please help me	**Aidez-moi, s'il vous plaît**

Finding the way

bus	**autobus/bus/car**
bus station	**gare routière**
bus stop	**arrêt**
car	**voiture**
train/taxi/ferry	**train/taxi/ferry**
boat	**bâteau**
plane	**avion**
shuttle	**navette**
train station	**gare (SNCF)**
platform	**quai**
What time does it leave?	**Il part à quelle heure?**
What time does it arrive?	**Il arrive à quelle heure?**
a ticket to…	**un billet pour…**
single ticket	**aller simple**
return ticket	**aller retour**
validate your ticket	**compostez votre billet**
valid for	**valable pour**
ticket office	**vente de billets**
how many kilometres?	**combien de kilomètres?**
how many hours?	**combien d'heures?**
hitchhiking	**autostop**
on foot	**à pied**
Where are you going?	**Vous allez où?**
I'm going to…	**Je vais à …**
I want to get off at…	**Je voudrais descendre à …**
the road to…	**la route pour…**
near	**près/pas loin**
far	**loin**
left	**à gauche**
right	**à droite**
straight on	**tout droit**
on the other side of	**à l'autre côté de**
on the corner of	**à l'angle de**
next to	**à côté de**
behind	**derrière**
in front of	**devant**
before	**avant**
after	**après**
under	**sous**
to cross	**traverser**
bridge	**pont**
upper town	**ville haute/haute ville**
lower town	**ville basse/basse ville**
old town	**vieille ville**

Questions and requests

The simplest way of asking a question is to start with *s'il vous plaît* (please), then name the thing you want in an interrogative tone of voice. For example:

Where is there a bakery?	**S'il vous plaît, la boulangerie?**
Which way is it to the Eiffel Tower?	**S'il vous plaît, la route pour la tour Eiffel?**

Similarly with requests:

Can we have a room for two? **S'il vous plaît, une chambre pour deux?**

Can I have a kilo of oranges? **S'il vous plaît, un kilo d'oranges?**

Question words

where?	**où?**
how?	**comment?**
how many/how much?	**combien?**
when?	**quand?**
why?	**pourquoi?**
at what time?	**à quelle heure?**
what is/which is?	**quel est?**

Accommodation

a room for one/two persons	**une chambre pour une/deux personne(s)**
a double bed	**un lit double**
a room with a shower	**une chambre avec douche**
a room with a bath	**une chambre avec salle de bain**
for one/two/three nights	**pour une/deux/trios nuits**
Can I see it?	**Je peux la voir?**
a room on the courtyard	**une chambre sur la cour**
a room over the street	**une chambre sur la rue**
first floor	**premier étage**
second floor	**deuxième étage**
with a view	**avec vue**
key	**clef**
to iron	**repasser**
do laundry	**faire la lessive**
sheets	**draps**
blankets	**couvertures**
quiet	**calme**
noisy	**bruyant**
hot water	**eau chaude**
cold water	**eau froide**
Is breakfast included?	**Est-ce que le petit déjeuner est compris?**
I would like breakfast	**Je voudrais prendre le petit déjeuner**
I don't want breakfast	**Je ne veux pas de petit déjeuner**
bed and breakfast	**chambre d'hôte**
Can we camp here?	**On peut camper ici?**
campsite	**un camping/terrain de camping**
tent	**une tente**
tent space	**un emplacement**
hostel	**foyer**
youth hostel	**auberge de jeunesse**

Cars

service station	**garage**
service	**service**
to park the car	**garer la voiture**
car park	**un parking**
no parking	**défense de stationner /stationnement interdit**
gas station	**poste d'essence**
fuel	**essence**
(to) fill it up	**faire le plein**
oil	**huile**
air line	**ligne à air**
put air in the tyres	**gonfler les pneus**
battery	**batterie**

the battery is dead	**la batterie est morte**	insurance	**assurance**
plugs	**bougies**	green card	**carte verte**
to break down	**tomber en panne**	traffic lights	**feux**
gas can	**bidon**	red light	**feu rouge**
		green light	**feu vert**

Health matters

doctor	**médecin**	stomach ache	**mal à l'estomac**
I don't feel well	**Je ne me sens pas bien**	period	**règles**
medicines	**médicaments**	pain	**douleur**
prescription	**ordonnance**	it hurts	**ça fait mal**
I feel sick	**Je suis malade**	chemist	**pharmacie**
I have a headache	**J'ai mal à la tête**	hospital	**hôpital**

Other needs

bakery	**boulangerie**	tobacconist	**tabac**
food shop	**alimentation**	stamps	**timbres**
delicatessen	**charcuterie, traiteur**	bank	**banque**
cake shop	**pâtisserie**	money	**argent**
cheese shop	**fromagerie**	toilets	**toilettes**
supermarket	**supermarché**	police	**police**
to eat	**manger**	telephone	**téléphone**
to drink	**boire**	cinema	**cinéma**
tasting, eg wine tasting	**dégustation**	theatre	**théâtre**
camping gas	**camping gaz**	to reserve/book	**réserver**

Food and dishes

Basic terms

l'addition	bill/check	**à emporter**	takeaway
beurre	butter	**formule**	lunchtime set menu
bio or biologique	organic	**fourchette**	fork
bouteille	bottle	**fumé**	smoked
chauffé	heated	**huile**	oil
couteau	knife	**lait**	milk
cru	raw	**moutarde**	mustard
cuillère	spoon	**œuf**	egg
cuit	cooked	**offert**	free
emballé	wrapped	**pain**	bread

pimenté	spicy
plat	main course
poivre	pepper
salé	salted/savoury
sel	salt
sucre	sugar
sucré	sweet
table	table
verre	glass
vinaigre	vinegar

Snacks

un sandwich/une baguette	a sandwich
au jambon	with ham
au fromage	with cheese
au saucisson	with sausage
à l'ail	with garlic
au poivre	with pepper
au pâté (de campagne)	with pâté (country-style)
croque-monsieur	grilled cheese and ham sandwich
croque-madame	grilled cheese and bacon, sausage, chicken or egg sandwich
pain bagnat	bread roll with egg, olives, salad, tuna, anchovies and olive oil
panini	toasted Italian sandwich
tartine	buttered bread or open sandwich
œufs	eggs
au plat	fried
à la coque	boiled
durs	hard-boiled
brouillés	scrambled
omelette	omelette
nature	plain
aux fines herbes	with herbs
au fromage	with cheese

Pasta (pâtes), pancakes (crêpes) and flans (tartes)

nouilles	noodles
pâtes fraîches	fresh pasta
raviolis	pasta parcels of meat or chard à Provençal, not Italian invention
crêpe au sucre /aux œufs	pancake with sugar /eggs
galette	buckwheat pancake
socca	thin chickpea flour pancake
panisse	thick chickpea flour pancake
pissaladière	tart of fried onions with anchovies and black olives
tarte flambée	thin pizza-like pastry topped with onion, cream and bacon or other combinations

Soups (soupes)

baudroie	fish soup with vegetables, garlic and herbs
bisque	shellfish soup
bouillabaisse	soup with five fish
bouillon	broth or stock
bourride	thick fish soup
consommé	clear soup
garbure	potato, cabbage and meat soup

pistou	parmesan, basil and garlic paste added to soup
potage	thick vegetable soup
potée auvergnate	cabbage and meat soup
rouille	red pepper, garlic and saffron mayonnaise served with fish soup
soupe à l'oignon	onion soup with rich cheese topping
velouté	thick soup, usually fish or poultry

Starters (hors d'œuvres)

assiette anglaise	plate of cold meats
assiette composée	mixed salad plate, usually cold meat and vegetables
crudités	raw vegetables with dressings
hors d'œuvres	combination of the above plus smoked or marinated fish

Fish (poisson), seafood (fruits de mer) and shellfish (crustaces or coquillages)

aiglefin	small haddock or fresh cod
anchois	anchovies
anguilles	eels
barbue	brill
baudroie	monkfish or anglerfish
bigourneau	periwinkle
brème	bream
bulot	whelk
cabillaud	cod
calmar	squid
carrelet	plaice
claire	type of oyster
colin	hake
congre	conger eel
coques	cockles
coquilles	scallops St-Jacques
crabe	crab
crevettes grises	shrimp
crevettes roses	prawns
daurade	sea bream
éperlan	smelt or whitebait
escargots	snails
favou(ille)	tiny crab
flétan	halibut
friture	assorted fried fish
gambas	king prawns
hareng	herring
homard	lobster
huîtres	oysters
langouste	spiny lobster
langoustines	saltwater crayfish (scampi)
limande	lemon sole
lotte de mer	monkfish
loup de mer	sea bass
maquereau	mackerel
merlan	whiting
moules (marinière)	mussels (with shallots in white wine sauce)
oursin	sea urchin
palourdes	clams
poissons de roche	fish from shoreline rocks
praires	small clams
raie	skate
rouget	red mullet
saumon	salmon
sole	sole
thon	tuna
truite	trout
turbot	turbot
violet	sea squirt

Fish dishes and terms

aïoli	garlic mayonnaise served with salt cod and other fish	**grillé**	grilled
anchoïade	anchovy paste or sauce	**hollandaise**	butter and vinegar sauce
arête	fish bone	**à la meunière**	in a butter, lemon and parsley sauce
assiette de pêcheur	assorted fish	**mousse/mousseline**	mousse
beignet	fritter	**pané**	breaded
darne	fillet or steak	**poutargue**	mullet roe paste
la douzaine	a dozen	**raïto**	red wine, olive, caper, garlic and shallot sauce
frit	fried	**quenelles**	light dumplings
friture	deep-fried small fish	**thermidor**	lobster grilled in its shell with cream sauce
fumé	smoked		
fumet	fish stock		
gigot de mer	large fish baked whole		

Meat (viande) and poultry (volaille)

agneau (de pré-salé)	lamb (grazed on salt marshes)	**hâchis**	chopped meat or mince hamburger
andouille /andouillette	tripe sausage	**langue**	tongue
bavette	French cut of beef equivalent to flank	**lapin/lapereau**	rabbit/young rabbit
bifteck	steak	**lard/lardons**	bacon/diced bacon
bœuf	beef	**lièvre**	hare
boudin blanc	sausage of white meats	**merguez**	spicy, red sausage
boudin noir	black pudding	**mouton**	mutton
caille	quail	**museau de veau**	calf's muzzle
canard	duck	**oie**	goose
caneton	duckling	**onglet**	French cut of beef steak that makes a prime steak
contrefilet	sirloin roast	**os**	bone
coquelet	cockerel	**poitrine**	breast
dinde/dindon	turkey	**porc**	pork
entrecôte	rib steak	**poulet**	chicken
faux filet	sirloin steak	**poussin**	baby chicken
foie	liver	**ris**	sweetbreads
foie gras	(duck/goose) liver	**rognons**	kidneys
gibier	game	**rognons blancs**	testicles
gigot (d'agneau)	leg (of lamb)	**sanglier**	wild boar
grenouilles (cuisses de)	frogs (legs)	**steak**	steak
grillade	grilled meat	**tête de veau**	calf's head (in jelly)
		tournedos	thick slices of fillet
		tripes	tripe

tripoux	mutton tripe
veau	veal
venaison	venison
volailles	poultry

Meat and poultry dishes and terms

aïado	roast shoulder of lamb stuffed with garlic and other ingredients
aile	wing
au feu de bois	cooked over wood fire
au four	baked
baeckoffe	Alsatian hotpot of pork, mutton and beef baked with potato layers
blanquette, daube, estouffade, hochepôt, navarin, ragoût	types of stew
blanquette de veau	veal in cream and mushroom sauce
bœuf bourguignon	beef stew with Burgundy, onions and mushrooms
canard à l'orange	roast duck with an orange and wine sauce
canard pâté de périgourdin foie gras	roast duck with prunes and truffles
carré	best end of neck, chop or cutlet
cassoulet	casserole of beans, sausages and duck /goose
choucroute	pickled cabbage with peppercorns, sausages, bacon and salami
civet	game stew
confit	meat preserve
côte	chop, cutlet or rib
cou	neck
coq au vin	chicken slow-cooked with wine, onions and mushrooms
cuisse	thigh or leg
épaule	shoulder
en croûte	in pastry
farci	stuffed
garni	with vegetables
gésier	gizzard
grillade	grilled meat
grillé	grilled
hâchis	chopped meat or mince hamburger
magret de canard	duck breast
marmite	casserole
médaillon	round piece
mijoté	stewed
pavé	thick slice
pieds et paques	mutton or pork tripe and trotters
poêlé	pan-fried
poulet de Bresse	chicken from Bresse the best
râble	saddle
rôti	roast
sauté	lightly fried in butter
steak au poivre (vert/rouge)	steak in a black (green/red) peppercorn sauce
steak tartare	raw chopped beef, topped with a raw egg yolk
tagine	North African casse-role
tournedos rossini	beef fillet with foie gras and truffles
viennoise	fried in egg and breadcrumbs

Terms for steaks

bleu	almost raw
saignant	rare
à point	medium rare
bien cuit	well done
très bien cuit	very well done
brochette	kebab

Garnishes and sauces

américaine	white wine, cognac and tomato
arlésienne au porto	with tomatoes, onions, aubergines, potatoes and rice in port
auvergnat	with cabbage, sausage and bacon
béarnaise	sauce of egg yolks, white wine, shallots and vinegar
beurre blanc	sauce of white wine and shallots, with butter
bonne femme	with mushroom, bacon, potato and onions
bordelaise	in a red wine, shallot and bone-marrow sauce
boulangère	baked with potatoes and onions
bourgeoise	with carrots, onions, bacon, celery and braised lettuce
chasseur	white wine, mushrooms and shallots
châtelaine	with artichoke hearts and chestnut purée
diable	strong mustard seasoning
forestière	with bacon and mushroom
fricassée	rich, creamy sauce
mornay	cheese sauce
pays d'auge	cream and cider
périgourdine	with foie gras and possibly truffles
piquante	gherkins or capers, vinegar and shallots
provençale	tomatoes, garlic, olive oil and herbs
savoyarde	with gruyère cheese
véronique	grapes, wine and cream

Vegetables (légumes), herbs (herbes) and spices (épices)

ail	garlic
anis	aniseed
artichaut	artichoke
asperge	asparagus
avocat	avocado
basilic	basil
betterave	beetroot
blette/bette	Swiss chard
cannelle	cinnamon
capre	caper
cardon	cardoon, a beet related to artichoke
carotte	carrot
céleri	celery
champignons, cèpes, ceps, girolles, chanterelles, pleurotes	mushrooms
chou (rouge)	(red) cabbage
choufleur	cauliflower
concombre	cucumber

cornichon	gherkin	**panais**	parsnip
échalotes	shallots	**pélandron**	type of string bean
endive	chicory	**pâte**	pasta or pastry
épinard	spinach	**persil**	parsley
estragon	tarragon	**petits pois**	peas
fenouil	fennel	**piment rouge/vert**	red/green chilli pepper
férigoule	thyme (in Provençal)	**pois chiche**	chickpeas
fèves	broad beans	**pois mange-tout**	snow peas
flageolets	flageolet beans	**pignons**	pine nuts
gingembre	ginger	**poireau**	leek
haricots	haricot beans	**poivron (vert, rouge)**	sweet pepper (green, red)
verts	string beans	**pommes de terre**	potatoes
rouges	kidney beans	**primeurs**	spring vegetables
beurres	yellow snap beans	**radis**	radish
laurier	bay leaf	**riz**	rice
lentilles	lentils	**safran**	saffron
maïs	maize (corn)	**salade verte**	green salad
menthe	mint	**sarrasin**	buckwheat
moutarde	mustard	**tomate**	tomato
oignon	onion	**truffes**	truffles

Vegetable dishes and terms

alicot	puréed potato with cheese	**mousseline**	mashed potato with cream and eggs
allumettes	very thin chips	**à la parisienne**	sautéed potatoes, with white wine and shallot sauce
à l'anglaise	boiled	**parmentier**	with potatoes
beignet	fritter	**petits farcis**	stuffed tomatoes, aubergines, courgettes and peppers
duxelles	fried mushrooms and shallots with cream	**râpée**	grated or shredded
farci	stuffed	**sauté**	lightly fried in butter
feuille	leaf	**à la vapeur**	steamed
fines herbes	mixture of tarragon, parsley and chives	**en verdure**	garnished with green vegetables
gratiné	browned with cheese or butter		
à la grecque	cooked in oil and lemon		
jardinière	with mixed diced vegetables		

Fruit (fruit) and nuts (noix)

abricot	apricot	**mangue**	mango
acajou	cashew nut	**marron**	chestnut
amande	almond	**melon**	melon
ananas	pineapple	**mirabelle**	small yellow plum
banane	banana	**myrtille**	bilberry
brugnon, nectarine	nectarine	**noisette**	hazelnut
cacahouète	peanut	**noix**	walnuts; nuts
cassis	blackcurrant	**orange**	orange
cérise	cherry	**pamplemousse**	grapefruit
citron	lemon	**pastèque**	watermelon
citron vert	lime	**pêche**	peach
datte	date	**pistache**	pistachio
figue	fig	**poire**	pear
fraise (de bois)	strawberry (wild)	**pomme**	apple
framboise	raspberry	**prune**	plum
fruit de la passion	passion fruit	**pruneau**	prune
grenade	pomegranate	**raisin**	grape
groseille	redcurrant	**reine-claude**	greengage

Fruit dishes and terms

agrumes	citrus fruits	**fougasse**	bread flavoured with orange-flower water or almonds (can be savoury)
beignet	fritter	**frappé**	iced
compôte	stewed fruit		
coulis	sauce of puréed fruit		
crème de marrons	chestnut purée		
flambé	set aflame in alcohol		

Desserts (desserts or entremets) and pastries (pâtisserie)

bombe	moulded ice-cream dessert	**clafoutis**	heavy custard and fruit tart
brioche	sweet, high yeast breakfast roll	**crème Chantilly**	vanilla-flavoured and sweetened whipped cream
calisson	almond sweet	**crème fraîche**	sour cream
charlotte	custard and fruit in lining of almond fingers	**crème pâtissière**	thick, eggy pastry -filling
chichi	doughnut shaped in a stick	**crêpe suzette**	thin pancake with orange juice and liqueur

fromage blanc	cream cheese
gaufre	waffle
glace	ice cream
Île flottante /œufs à la neige	whipped egg-white floating on custard
macaron	macaroon
madeleine	small sponge cake
marrons Mont Blanc	chestnut purée and cream on a rum-soaked sponge cake
mousse au chocolat	chocolate mousse
omelette norvégienne	baked alaska
palmier	caramelized puff pastry
parfait	frozen mousse, sometimes ice cream
petit-suisse	a smooth mixture of cream and curds
petits fours	bite-sized cakes/ pastries
poires belle hélène	pears and ice cream in chocolate sauce
tarte tatin	upside-down apple tart
tarte tropezienne	sponge cake filled with custard cream topped with nuts
tiramisu	mascarpone cheese, chocolate and cream
yaourt/yogourt	yoghurt

LANGUAGE | Food and dishes

Glossary

alimentation food

appellation mostly used in compounds, most common of which is **appellation contrôlée** government certification guaranteeing the quality of a French wine

arrondissement city borough

autoroute motorway/freeway

bastide fortified town

boulangerie baker's

boulevard ring road **périphérique**

causse limestone plateau

centre ville town centre

chais warehouses

chambre d'hôte B&B accommodation in someone's house

charcuterie butcher's

confiserie shop selling sweets, chocolate and sometimes ice cream

département administrative division of France, roughly equivalent to an English county

dégustation tasting, as in wine tasting

église church

formule lunchtime set menu

foyer residential hostel for young workers and students

fromagerie cheese shop

gare station

gîte d'étape hostel-type accommodation aimed at walkers and bikers

grands projets series of large-scale architectural projects initiated by Mitterand in the 1980s

halles market

hôtel particulier mansion or town house

Hôtel de Ville town hall

mairie town hall

Maquis French World War II Resistance movement, taking its name from the thick shrub found in coastal areas of the Mediterranean which provided cover for members

navette shuttle service

pâtisserie cakeshop

plage beach

plats du jour daily specials

pont bridge

puy mountain formed from a volcano

quartier district in a town or city

rue street

tabac tobacconist's, also selling bus/métro tickets and phone cards

table d'hôte a communal dining table in a restaurant

traiteur delicatessen

Architectural terms

These are either terms you'll come across in the Guide, or come up against while travelling around.

abbaye abbey

ambulatory passage round the outer edge of the choir of a church

apse semicircular termination at the east end of a church

Baroque High Renaissance period of art and architecture, distinguished by extreme ornateness

basse vill lower town

bastide walled town

Carolingian dynasty (and art, sculpture, etc) named after Charlemagne; mid-eighth to early tenth centuries

château mansion, country house, castle

château fort castle

chevet east end of a church

Classical architectural style incorporating Greek and Roman elements: pillars, domes, colonnades, etc, at its height in France in the seventeenth century and revived, as Neoclassical, in the nineteenth century

clerestory upper storey of a church, incorporating the windows

donjon castle keep

église church

flamboyant florid form of Gothic

haute ville upper town

hôtel particulier mansion or town house

Merovingian dynasty (and art, etc), ruling France andparts of Germany from sixth to mid-eighth centuries

narthex entrance hall of church

nave main body of a church

porte gateway

Renaissance art/architectural style developed in fifteenth-century Italy and imported to France in the sixteenth century by François Ier

retable altarpiece

Roman Romanesque (easily confused with Romain-Roman)

Romanesque early medieval architecture distinguished by squat, rounded forms and naive sculpture, called Norman in Britain

stucco plaster used to embellish ceilings, etc

tour tower

transept transverse arms of a church

tympanum sculpted panel above a church door

voussoir sculpted rings in arch over church door

Rough Guides

advertiser

Rough Guides travel...

UK & Ireland
Britain
Devon & Cornwall
Dublin
Edinburgh
England
Ireland
Lake District
London
London DIRECTIONS
London Mini Guide
Scotland
Scottish Highlands & Islands
Wales

Europe
Algarve
Amsterdam
Amsterdam DIRECTIONS
Andalucía
Athens DIRECTIONS
Austria
Baltic States
Barcelona
Belgium & Luxembourg
Berlin
Brittany & Normandy
Bruges & Ghent
Brussels
Budapest
Bulgaria
Copenhagen
Corfu
Corsica
Costa Brava
Crete
Croatia
Cyprus
Czech & Slovak Republics
Dodecanese & East Aegean
Dordogne & The Lot
Europe
Florence
France
Germany
Greece
Greek Islands
Hungary
Ibiza & Formentera
Iceland
Ionian Islands
Italy
Languedoc & Roussillon
Lisbon
Lisbon DIRECTIONS
The Loire
Madeira
Madrid
Mallorca
Malta & Gozo
Menorca
Moscow
Netherlands
Norway
Paris
Paris DIRECTIONS
Paris Mini Guide
Poland
Portugal
Prague
Provence & the Côte d'Azur
Pyrenees
Romania
Rome
Sardinia
Scandinavia
Sicily
Slovenia
Spain
St Petersburg
Sweden
Switzerland
Tenerife & La Gomera
Tenerife DIRECTIONS
Turkey
Tuscany & Umbria
Venice & The Veneto
Venice DIRECTIONS
Vienna

Asia
Bali & Lombok
Bangkok
Beijing
Cambodia
China
Goa
Hong Kong & Macau
India
Indonesia
Japan
Laos
Malaysia, Singapore & Brunei
Nepal
Philippines
Singapore
South India
Southeast Asia
Sri Lanka
Thailand
Thailand's Beaches & Islands
Tokyo
Vietnam

Australasia
Australia
Melbourne
New Zealand
Sydney

North America
Alaska
Big Island of Hawaii
Boston
California
Canada
Chicago
Florida
Grand Canyon
Hawaii
Honolulu
Las Vegas
Los Angeles
Maui
Miami & the Florida Keys
Montréal
New England
New Orleans
New York City
New York City DIRECTIONS
New York City Mini Guide
Pacific Northwest
Rocky Mountains
San Francisco
San Francisco DIRECTIONS
Seattle
Southwest USA
Toronto
USA
Vancouver
Washington DC
Yosemite

Caribbean & Latin America
Antigua & Barbuda
Antigua DIRECTIONS
Argentina
Bahamas
Barbados
Barbados DIRECTIONS
Belize
Bolivia
Brazil
Caribbean
Central America
Chile
Costa Rica
Cuba
Dominican Republic
Ecuador
Guatemala
Jamaica
Maya World
Mexico
Peru
St Lucia
South America

Rough Guides are available from good bookstores worldwide. New titles are published every month. Check www.roughguides.com for the latest news.

...music & reference

Trinidad & Tobago

Africa & Middle East
Cape Town
Egypt
The Gambia
Jordan
Kenya
Marrakesh DIRECTIONS
Morocco
South Africa, Lesotho & Swaziland
Syria
Tanzania
Tunisia
West Africa
Zanzibar
Zimbabwe

Travel Theme guides
First-Time Around the World
First-Time Asia
First-Time Europe
First-Time Latin America
Skiing & Snowboarding in North America
Travel Online
Travel Health
Walks in London & SE England
Women Travel

Restaurant guides
French Hotels & Restaurants
London
New York
San Francisco

Maps
Algarve
Amsterdam
Andalucia & Costa del Sol
Argentina
Athens
Australia
Baja California
Barcelona
Berlin
Boston
Brittany
Brussels
Chicago
Crete
Croatia
Cuba
Cyprus
Czech Republic
Dominican Republic
Dubai & UAE
Dublin
Egypt
Florence & Siena
Frankfurt
Greece
Guatemala & Belize
Iceland
Ireland
Kenya
Lisbon
London
Los Angeles
Madrid
Mexico
Miami & Key West
Morocco
New York City
New Zealand
Northern Spain
Paris
Peru
Portugal
Prague
Rome
San Francisco
Sicily
South Africa
South India
Sri Lanka
Tenerife
Thailand
Toronto
Trinidad & Tobago
Tuscany
Venice
Washington DC
Yucatán Peninsula

Dictionary Phrasebooks
Czech
Dutch
Egyptian Arabic
EuropeanLanguages (Czech, French, German, Greek, Italian, Portuguese, Spanish)
French
German
Greek
Hindi & Urdu
Hungarian
Indonesian
Italian
Japanese
Mandarin Chinese
Mexican Spanish
Polish
Portuguese
Russian
Spanish
Swahili
Thai
Turkish
Vietnamese

Music Guides
The Beatles
Bob Dylan
Cult Pop
Classical Music
Country Music
Elvis
Hip Hop
House
Irish Music
Jazz
Music USA
Opera
Reggae
Rock
Techno
World Music (2 vols)

History Guides
China
Egypt
England
France
India
Islam
Italy
Spain
USA

Reference Guides
Books for Teenagers
Children's Books, 0–5
Children's Books, 5–11
Cult Fiction
Cult Football
Cult Movies
Cult TV
Ethical Shopping
Formula 1
The iPod, iTunes & Music Online
The Internet
Internet Radio
James Bond
Kids' Movies
Lord of the Rings
Muhammed Ali
Man Utd
Personal Computers
Pregnancy & Birth
Shakespeare
Superheroes
Unexplained Phenomena
The Universe
Videogaming
Weather
Website Directory

Also! More than 120 Rough Guide music CDs are available from all good book and record stores. Listen in at www.worldmusic.net

Rough Guide Maps

Rough Guide Maps, printed on waterproof and rip-proof Yupo™ paper, offer an unbeatable combination of practicality, clarity of design and amazing value.

CITY MAPS

Amsterdam · Barcelona · Berlin · Boston · Brussels · Dublin
Florence & Siena · Frankfurt · London · Los Angeles
Miami · New York · Paris · Prague · Rome
San Francisco · Venice · Washington DC and more...

COUNTRY & REGIONAL MAPS

Andalucía · Argentina · Australia · Baja California · Cuba
Cyprus · Dominican Republic · Egypt · Greece
Guatemala & Belize · Ireland · Mexico · Morocco
New Zealand · South Africa · Sri Lanka · Tenerife · Thailand
Trinidad & Tobago Yucatán Peninsula · and more...

US$9.99 Can$13.99 £5.99

Visit us online
roughguides.com

Information on over 25,000 destinations around the world

- **Read** Rough Guides' trusted travel info
- **Share** journals, photos and travel advice with other readers
- Get exclusive Rough Guide **discounts** and travel **deals**
- Earn membership points every time you contribute to the Rough Guide **community** and get **free** books, flights and trips
- Browse thousands of CD reviews and artists in our **music** area

DIRECTIONS

PUBLISHED MAY 2004

1843533146

1843533154

1843533162

1843533170

1843533189

1843533537

PUBLISHED AUGUST 2004

1843533065

1843533197

1843533200

1843533219

1843533227

1843533225

US$10.99 · Can$15.99 · £6.99

ROUGH GUIDES SOFTWARE

Share your adventures on the move

Rough Guides have launched **intouch**, a new all in one software package for planning your trip and staying in touch with people back home before, during and after your travels.

Create an itinerary and budget using on-screen information and maps, and take advantage of the diary to keep family and friends informed of your whereabouts.

The diary can be linked to your mobile phone so that you can send a text message, **intouch** will automatically send an email or cheap SMS to those listed on your account.

You can also post photos and diary entries online and then download them to make a journal on your return.

Rough Guides **intouch** is easy to install and you don't need to take anything with you - just hit the synchronize button and then use it from any internet café in the world.

Rough Guides **intouch** includes:
Planning tools
Free email address
Free personal website
Digital photo storage And much more......

£5 OFF your purchase of Rough Guides **intouch** if you buy online at www.roughguidesintouch.com reference code: Rough Guide Books

Recommended retail price £24.99 available through leading retailers e.g. WH Smith, Waterstones and PC World

WHSmith

NOTES

NOTES

NORTH SOUTH TRAVEL

North South Travel is a small travel agent offering excellent personal service. Like other air ticket retailers, we offer discount fares worldwide. But unlike others, all available profits contribute to grassroots projects in the South through the NST Development Trust Registered Charity No. 1040656.

Great difference

For **quotes** or queries, contact Brenda Skinner or her helpful staff. Recent **donations** made from the NST Development Trust include support to Djoliba Trust, providing micro-credit to onion growers in the Dogon country in Mali; assistance to displaced people and rural communities in eastern Congo; a grant to Wells For India, which works for clean water in Rajasthan;support to the charity Children of the Andes, working for poverty relief in Colombia; and a grant to the Omari Project which works with drug-dependent young people in Watamu, Kenya.

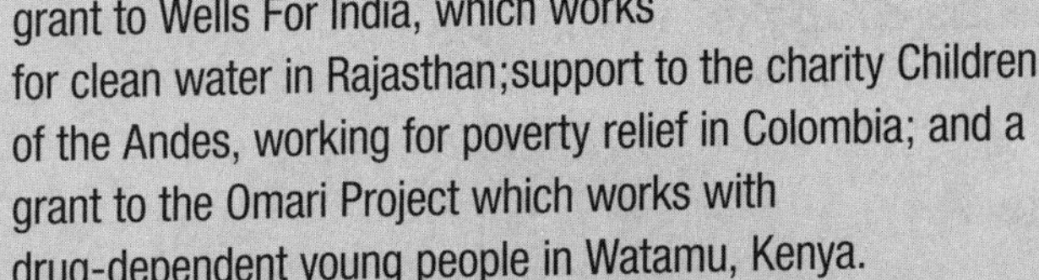

Tel/Fax 01245 608 291.
Email brenda@northsouthtravel.co.uk
Website www.northsouthtravel.co.uk

North South Travel,
Moulsham Mill,
Parkway,
Chelmsford,
Essex CM2 7PX,
UK

The world's finest map and travel bookshops

Explore Discover Inspire

Maps
Travel Guides
Illustrated Books
Travel Literature
World Atlases
Globes
World Wall Maps
Climbing Maps & Books
Maritime Maps & Books
Historical Maps
Instruments
Children's

Stanfords Flagship Store
12-14 Long Acre
Covent Garden
London
WC2 9LP
(T) 020 7836 1321

39 Spring Gardens
Manchester
M2 2BG
(T) 0161 831 0250

29 Corn Street
Bristol
BS1 1HT
(T) 0117 929 9966

International Mail Order Department
+44 (0)20 7836 1321

www.stanfords.co.uk

Inspiring exploration and discovery for 150 year

450 BRANCHES WORLDWIDE

SPECIALISTS IN TRAVEL FOR STUDENTS & YOUNG PEOPLE

LOW COST FLIGHTS > OVERLAND & ADVENTURE TOURS
ACCOMMODATION > TRAVEL INSURANCE > CAR HIRE
CITY & CLUBBING BREAKS > ROUND THE WORLD > GAP YEAR
SKI & SNOWBOARD > TRAVEL HELP > WELL TRAVELLED STAFF

STA TRAVEL LTD

0870 160 6070
www.statravel.co.uk

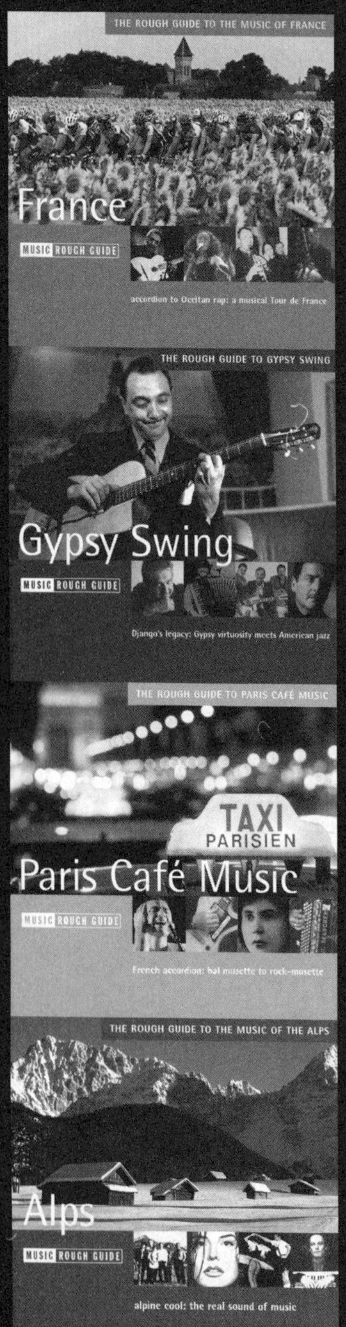

MUSIC ROUGH GUIDE

Rough Guides To A World Of Music

'stick to the reliable Rough Guide series'
The Guardian (UK)

'Over the past few years the Rough Guide CDs, with their stylish covers, have distinguished themselves as approachable and well-chosen introductions to the music of the countries concerned. They have been consistently well-reviewed and, like the guidebooks themselves, stand out as an obvious first choice for journeys in world music'
Simon Broughton, Editor Songlines

Hear sound samples at WWW.WORLDMUSIC.NET

Rough Guides Radio

Now you can visit **www.worldmusic.net/listen/radio.html** to tune into the exciting Rough Guide Radio Show, with a new show each month presenting new releases, interviews, features and competitions.

Available from book and record shops worldwide or order direct from

World Music Network , 6 Abbeville Mews
88 Clapham Park Road , London SW4 7BX, UK

T. 020 7498 5252 F. 020 7498 5353
E. post@worldmusic.net

low cost
hotels
with all the
frills...
...in france!
paris
from
£22
nice
from
£22
prices are per person per night sharing a twin/double with breakfast & taxes inc.
bordeaux
from
£38
up to
50% off
hotels' standard rates
no booking fee!
up to 50% off hotels' standard rates
2 star to deluxe properties in 150 destinations
high-level service from friendly & knowledgeable staff
easy booking through our call centre or online
book now on:
0845 230 8888
www.hotelconnect.co.uk
ABTA ASSURED
hotelconnect
the hotel specialist

Don't bury your head in the sand!

Take cover!

with Rough Guide Travel Insurance

Worldwide cover, for Rough Guide readers worldwide

UK Freefone **0800 015 09 06**
Worldwide **(+44) 1392 314 665**
Check the web at
www.roughguides.com/insurance

Insurance organized by Torribles Insurance Brokers Ltd, 21 Prince Street, Bristol, BS1 4PH, England

small print and

Index

A Rough Guide to Rough Guides

In the summer of 1981, Mark Ellingham, a recent graduate from Bristol University, was travelling round Greece and couldn't find a guidebook that really met his needs. On the one hand there were the student guides, insistent on saving every last cent, and on the other the heavyweight cultural tomes whose authors seemed to have spent more time in a research library than lounging away the afternoon at a taverna or on the beach.

In a bid to avoid getting a job, Mark and a small group of writers set about creating their own guidebook. It was a guide to Greece that aimed to combine a journalistic approach to description with a thoroughly practical approach to travellers' needs – a guide that would incorporate culture, history and contemporary insights with a critical edge, together with up-to-date, value-for-money listings. Back in London, Mark and the team finished their Rough Guide, as they called it, and talked Routledge into publishing the book.

That first *Rough Guide to Greece*, published in 1982, was a student scheme that became a publishing phenomenon. The immediate success of the book – with numerous reprints and a Thomas Cook prize shortlisting – spawned a series that rapidly covered dozens of destinations. Rough Guides had a ready market among low-budget backpackers, but soon also acquired a much broader and older readership that relished Rough Guides' wit and inquisitiveness as much as their enthusiastic, critical approach. Everyone wants value for money, but not at any price.

Rough Guides soon began supplementing the "rougher" information about hostels and low-budget listings with the kind of detail on restaurants and quality hotels that independent-minded visitors on any budget might expect, whether on business in New York or trekking in Thailand.

These days the guides – distributed worldwide by the Penguin group – offer recommendations from shoestring to luxury and cover more than 200 destinations around the globe, including almost every country in the Americas and Europe, more than half of Africa and most of Asia and Australasia. Our ever-growing team of authors and photographers is spread all over the world, particularly in Europe, the USA and Australia.

In 1994, we published the *Rough Guide to World Music* and *Rough Guide to Classical Music*; and a year later, the *Rough Guide to the Internet*. All three books have become benchmark titles in their fields – which encouraged us to expand into other areas of publishing, mainly around popular culture. Rough Guides now publish:

- Travel guides to more than 200 worldwide destinations
- Dictionary phrasebooks to 22 major languages
- History guides ranging from Ireland to Islam
- Maps printed on rip-proof and waterproof Polyart™ paper
- Music guides running the gamut from Opera to Elvis
- Restaurant guides to London, New York and San Francisco
- Reference books on topics as diverse as the Weather and Shakespeare
- Sports guides from Formula 1 to Man Utd
- Pop culture books from *Lord of the Rings* to Cult TV
- World Music CDs in association with World Music Network

Visit **www.roughguides.com** to see our latest publications.

Rough Guide credits

Text editor: Edward Aves, Helena Smith, Stephen Timblin
Layout: Ajay Verma
Cartography: Ashutosh Bharti
Picture research: Jj Luck
Proofreader: Madhu Mohapatra, Ken Bell, Rima Zaheer
Editorial: **London** Martin Dunford, Kate Berens, Claire Saunders, Geoff Howard, Ruth Blackmore, Gavin Thomas, Polly Thomas, Richard Lim, Clifton Wilkinson, Alison Murchie, Sally Schafer, Karoline Densley, Andy Turner, Keith Drew, Ella O'Donnell, Edward Aves, Andrew Lockett, Joe Staines, Duncan Clark, Peter Buckley, Matthew Milton, Daniel Crewe, Nikki Birrell; **New York** Andrew Rosenberg, Richard Koss, Chris Barsanti, Steven Horak, AnneLise Sorensen, Amy Hegarty
Design & Pictures: London Simon Bracken, Dan May, Diana Jarvis, Mark Thomas, Jj Luck, Harriet Mills, Chloë Roberts; **Delhi** Madhulita Mohapatra, Umesh Aggarwal, Ajay Verma, Jessica Subramanian, Amit Verma
Production: Julia Bovis, Sophie Hewat, Katherine Owers
Cartography: **London** Maxine Repath, Ed Wright, Katie Lloyd-Jones; **Delhi** Manish Chandra, Rajesh Chhibber, Jai Prakash Mishra, Ashutosh Bharti, Rajesh Mishra, Animesh Pathak, Jasbir Sandhu, Karobi Gogoi
Online: **New York** Jennifer Gold, Cree Lawson, Suzanne Welles, Benjamin Ross; **Delhi** Manik Chauhan, Narender Kumar, Manish Shekhar Jha, Rakesh Kumar, Lalit K. Sharma
Marketing & Publicity: **London** Richard Trillo, Niki Hanmer, David Wearn, Demelza Dallow, Kristina Pentland; **New York** Geoff Colquitt, Megan Kennedy, Milena Perez; **Delhi** Reem Khokhar
Custom publishing and foreign rights: Philippa Hopkins
Finance: Gary Singh
Manager India: Punita Singh
Series editor: Mark Ellingham
PA to Managing Director: Megan McIntyre
Managing Director: Kevin Fitzgerald

Publishing information

This ninth edition published April 2005 by
Rough Guides Ltd,
80 Strand, London WC2R 0RL
345 Hudson St, 4th Floor,
New York, NY 10014, USA
Distributed by the Penguin Group
Penguin Books Ltd,
80 Strand, London WC2R 0RL
Penguin Putnam, Inc.
375 Hudson Street, NY 10014, USA
Penguin Group (Australia)
250 Camberwell Road, Camberwell
Victoria 3124, Australia
Penguin Books Canada Ltd,
10 Alcorn Avenue, Toronto, Ontario,
Canada M4V 1E4
Penguin Group (New Zealand)
Cnr Rosedale and Airborne Roads
Albany, Auckland, New Zealand
Typeset in Bembo and Helvetica to an original design by Henry Iles.

Printed in Italy by LegoPrint S.p.A

© Rough Guides 2005. Kate Baillie and Tim Salmon wrote original material for this book.

No part of this book may be reproduced in any form without permission from the publisher except for the quotation of brief passages in reviews.

1400pp includes index
A catalogue record for this book is available from the British Library

ISBN 1-84353-413-4

The publishers and authors have done their best to ensure the accuracy and currency of all the information in **The Rough Guide to France**; however, they can accept no responsibility for any loss, injury, or inconvenience sustained by any traveller as a result of information or advice contained in the guide.

3 5 7 9 8 6 4

Help us update

We've gone to a lot of effort to ensure that the third edition of **The Rough Guide to France** is accurate and up-to-date. However, things change – places get "discovered", opening hours are notoriously fickle, restaurants and rooms raise prices or lower standards. If you feel we've got it wrong or left something out, we'd like to know, and if you can remember the address, the price, the time, the phone number, so much the better.

We'll credit all contributions, and send a copy of the next edition (or any other Rough Guide if you prefer) for the best letters. Everyone who writes to us and isn't already a subscriber will receive a copy of our full-colour thrice-yearly newsletter. Please mark letters: "**Rough Guide France Update**" and send to: Rough Guides, 80 Strand, London WC2R 0RL, or Rough Guides, 4th Floor, 345 Hudson St, New York, NY 10014. Or send an email to **mail@roughguides.com**

Have your questions answered and tell others about your trip at **www.roughguides.atinfopop.com**

Acknowledgements

Andrew Benson wishes to thank Renaud Lallement (Nancy), Thierry Herselin (Rouen), Claire Pedotti (Strasbourg and Mulhouse), Pierre Léglise-Costa and Ana Côrte-Real (Paris), and Hélène and Bernard Guegan (Caen and Brittany), for all their assistance, company and hospitality, along with staff at too many tourist offices to mention, but especially the one at Cherbourg; and thanks to all at Rough Guides, especially Helena Smith, Edward Aves and Stephen Timblin for their thorough but fair editing.

Ruth Blackmore thanks Ursula Williams; the Steiner family, especially Jakob and Emanuelle; Dr P.L. Tawn; and Dylan Reisenberger.

Brian Catlos thanks Núria Silleras Fernández, Francis Castan (CDT Aveyron), Marie-Yvonne Holley (CRT Aquitaine), Christian Riviere (CDT Tarn), Martine Bouchet (CDT Lot), Virginie Sanfelieu (Club de Sites Gard), François Caussarieu (CDT Béarn), Hélène Aznar and Ross Velton.

Jan Dodd would like to thank James McConnachie for generously sharing his musical insights among other things, Roger Norum for the low-down on hip-hop, Arielle Berdy for updating me on French theatre, and Neville Walker.

S.E. Kramer would like to thank the staff at the Red Mountain Lodge for a memorable time in Chamonix, Duodecim and the staff at the Saisies tourism office, and of course *La Famille Chetaille* and David Mayet for their hospitality and companionship in France. In the London office thanks to Helena, Karoline, Joe and the reference guys. And finally, thanks to Robbie, my partner, for everything.

Roger Norum thanks Kate for bringing me on and Helena for editorial guidance and moral support. Thank you also to Janice and Michele for memorable Bordeaux Bordeaux drinking in the wee hours and to Delphine for not correcting my past subjunctives and reminding me why I love France. Also, a special shoutout to the ever-helpful Dijon tourist office and to the lovely Basque police for impounding my car.

Neville Walker would like to thank the *Hotel Floride* in Nice for being so nice, and Geoff Hinchley for being my bag carrier.

SMALL PRINT

Readers' letters

Thanks to all the readers who took the trouble to write in or email us with their comments on the eight edition. They include:

Bob Amatt, Lionel Athey, Iain Baker, David Beadle, Colin Birtwistle, Chris Burin, Roger Burton, Rita Calderwood, Maria Campbell, Gemma Carroll, John Cheshire, Thomas Christiansen, Mireille Clavel, Pam Cohen, Jeffrey Coleman & Carol Tye, Dr M.J. Collins, Alan & Jackie Corbishley, Gwenn Dafydd, Scott Darby, Gary Dixon, Philippa Dolphin, Josephine & Alan Dougall, Carol & Donald Eagle, Kylia Eastwell, Barbara Fairman, A.F. Ford, Chris Frean, Alan Grahame, Mrs H.E. Griffiths, Clive Grimshaw, Ken Hawkins, V. Hope, Bob Houston, Barry Keeton, Rhian King, Michael Krom, Mike Krumboltz, K. Leduck, Linda Lovejoy, David Lypnyj, Alistair MacDougall, Stephen McCombie, Sally A. Madgwick, Elsbeth Mendesda, Doug Miles, Chris Miller, Steven Miller, Jean & Dave Morgan, Annette Muller, C laire Nicholl, David Osbourne, Chris Pauwels, Charlie Pearman, John Purrington, E.A. Ratzer, C. Trelawney Ross, Veronica Schmitt, C.A. Smith, Peter Stephenson, Holger Stoelben, Thelma Stones, Mrs. P. Sweetlove, Kim Tipple, Jennifer Tite, Dr. J.G. Weir, Suzanne Wells, Tom White, Tony Williams, Elaine Wilson, Sandra Winterbotham, Les Woodland, Wade Wright.

Photo credits

Cover credits

Main picture © Imagestate
Small front top picture Paris métro © Mark Thomas
Small front lower picture Lautrec, near Castres © Richard Gibson
Back top picture Provence © Robert Harding
Back lower picture Sénanque © Alamy

Introduction

Lavender fields, Valensole, Provence © Chris Coe/Axiom
Azay Le Rideau, Loire valley © Ellen Rooney/Axiom
Statues of the Eiffel Tower, Paris © Ian Cumming/Axiom
The Louvre at night © Chris Coe/Axiom
Market, Charolle © William Shaw/Axiom
2CV outside farmhouse, Corsica © Axiom
Window display of a Boulangerie in the Midi-Pyrenees © M. Busselle
Monet's house and gardens, Giverny © Tom Ives/Corbis
Le Corbusier's Chapelle de Notre-Dame-du-Haut, Ronchamp Archivo Iconografico, S.A./Corbis
Statue, Versailles © Yann Arthus-Bertrand/Corbis *Liberty Leading the People* by Eugene
Delacroix © Archivo Iconografico, S.A./Corbis © Catherine Karnow/Corbis
Montmarte art stall © Mark Thomas

Things not to miss

Canal du Midi © Forestier Yves/Corbis Sygma
Carnac © J. Degrange/Greg Evans International
Cheese © James McConnachie
Bastille Day © Peter Turnley/Corbis
Tour de France © PDA/Empics
The Louvre © Robert Holmes/Corbis
Les Calanques © Michael Jenner
Wiine © Neil Setchfield
Prehistoric cave art © J.P. Bouchard/Robert Harding
Mont St-Michel © Ruth Tomlinson/Robert Harding
Les Gorges du Verdon © Nik Wheeler/Robert Harding
Winter Sports in the Alps © Chris Martin/Axiom
Avignon © John Miller/Robert Harding
Bayeux Tapestry © Chris Coe/Axiom
The GR20 © Jean Françoiz Vibert
Bastide towns © Robert Harding
Gorges de L'Ardèche © Roger Antrobus/Corbis
Champagne tasting at Epernay © Neil Setchfield
The Iseenheim altarpiece © 1997, Photo Scala, Florence
Amiens cathedral © R. Ashworth/Robert Harding
Chateaux of the Loire © Chris Coe/Axiom
Bordeaux © Michael Jenner
Strasbourg cathedral © Geoff Renner/Robert Harding
Beaches © David Abram
Medieval Provençal villages © Nik Wheeler/Robert Harding
Fontenay Abbey © Robert Harding
Cafés © James McConnachie
Carcassonne © D. Hastilow/Trip
Le Canigou © Francesc Muntada/Corbis
War memorials © Brain Harris/Axiom
Jardin du Luxembourg © James McConnachie
Annecy © John Miller/Robert Harding
Outdoor activities © Ian Cumming/Axiom

Black and white

Paris Metro sign © Mark Thomas
Eiffel tower © Mark Thomas
Café scene © James McConnachie
Wall of Names at Thiepval Memorial © Michael St. Maur Sheil/Corbis
Troyes house © S.E. Kramer
Hunawihr © Guy Thouvenin/Robert Harding
The European Parliament, Strasbourg © C. Bowman/Robert Harding
The Bayeux Tapestry, Normandy © Robert Harding
Statue of St. Peter, Rouen Cathedral © Jeremy Horner/Corbis
Cancale oysters © Guy Thouvenin/Robert Harding
Côte de Granit Rose, Brittany © David Hughes/Robert Harding
Chenonceau © James McConnachie
Garden of Love, Villandry © James McConnachie
Tonnerre tomb © James McConnachie
Faience workshop © James McConnachie
Pointe de la Coubre near Royan © David Hughes/Robert Harding
Vieux port, La Rochelle © David Hughes/Robert Harding
Cave paintings, Lascaux © Robert Harding
The Dordogne, Beynac © Michael Busselle
The Ariége valley © Michael Busselle/Robert Harding
Lourdes © Charles Bowman
St-Guilhem-le-Dèsert © B.Seach/Trip
Pont du Gard © Helena Smith
Donkeys, Massif Central © Brian Catlos
Summit of Puy de Sancy © David Hughes/Robert Harding
Reading at Brevant © S. E. Kramer
Tour de France, Les Deux Alps to La Plange © Gero Breloer/Empics
Petanque balls, Roussillon © Guy Thouvenin/Robert Harding
Les Arènes © Robert Harding/Exporer
Abbaye de Senanque © Bruno Morandi/Robert Harding
Sunset, cannes © Richard Watkins
Marseille from the Chateau d'If © Richard Watkins
Monaco Grand Prix © Jed Leicester/Empics
Boat trip from Bonifacio © David Abram
Prehistoric menhir at Filitosa © David Abram

Index

Map entries are in colour.

A

B

C

D

E

F

I

J

K

L

M

INDEX

N

O

P

INDEX

INDEX

Q

R

S